W9-BML-475

THE
HOLY BIBLE

containing the
Old and New Testaments

New Revised Standard Version: Catholic Edition

CATHOLIC BIBLE PRESS
a division of
℟ THOMAS NELSON PUBLISHERS

Text of the New Revised Standard Version: Catholic Edition

NAMES AND ORDER OF
THE BOOKS OF THE BIBLE

THE OLD TESTAMENT

THE NEW TESTAMENT

ABBREVIATIONS

The following abbreviations are used for the books of the Bible:

Old Testament

Gen	Genesis	Tob	Tobit	Bar	Baruch
Ex	Exodus	Jdt	Judith	Ezek	Ezekiel
Lev	Leviticus	Esth	Esther	Dan	Daniel
Num	Numbers	1 Macc	1 Maccabees	Hos	Hosea
Deut	Deuteronomy	2 Macc	2 Maccabees	Joel	Joel
Josh	Joshua	Job	Job	Am	Amos
Judg	Judges	Ps	Psalms	Ob	Obadiah
Ruth	Ruth	Prov	Proverbs	Jon	Jonah
1 Sam	1 Samuel	Eccl	Ecclesiastes	Mic	Micah
2 Sam	2 Samuel	Song	Song of Solomon	Nah	Nahum
1 Kings	1 Kings	Wis	Wisdom of Solomon	Hab	Habakkuk
2 Kings	2 Kings	Sir	Sirach	Zeph	Zephaniah
1 Chr	1 Chronicles		(Ecclesiasticus)	Hag	Haggai
2 Chr	2 Chronicles	Isa	Isaiah	Zech	Zechariah
Ezra	Ezra	Jer	Jeremiah	Mal	Malachi
Neh	Nehemiah	Lam	Lamentations		

New Testament

Mt	Matthew	Gal	Galatians	Philem	Philemon
Mk	Mark	Eph	Ephesians	Heb	Hebrews
Lk	Luke	Phil	Philippians	Jas	James
Jn	John	Col	Colossians	1 Pet	1 Peter
Acts	Acts of the	1 Thess	1 Thessalonians	2 Pet	2 Peter
	Apostles	2 Thess	2 Thessalonians	1 Jn	1 John
Rom	Romans	1 Tim	1 Timothy	2 Jn	2 John
1 Cor	1 Corinthians	2 Tim	2 Timothy	3 Jn	3 John
2 Cor	2 Corinthians	Titus	Titus	Jude	Jude
				Rev	Revelation

In the notes to the books of the Old Testament the following abbreviations are used:

Ant.	Josephus, *Antiquities of the Jews*
Aram	Aramaic
Ch, chs	Chapter, chapters
Cn	Correction; made where the text has suffered in transmission and the versions provide no satisfactory restoration but where the Standard Bible Committee agrees with the judgment of competent scholars as to the most probable reconstruction of the original text
Gk	Septuagint, Greek version of the Old Testament
Heb	Hebrew of the consonantal Masoretic Text of the Old Testament
Josephus	Flavius Josephus (Jewish historian, about A.D. 37 to about 95)
Macc.	The book(s) of the Maccabees
Ms(s)	Manuscript(s)
MT	The Hebrew of the pointed Masoretic Text of the Old Testament
OL	Old Latin
Q Ms(s)	Manuscript(s) found at Qumran by the Dead Sea
Sam	Samaritan Hebrew text of the Old Testament
Syr	Syriac Version of the Old Testament
Syr H	Syriac Version of Origen's Hexapla
Tg	Targum
Vg	Vulgate, Latin Version of the Old Testament

Guide to Pronunciation
of Proper Names

This edition of the New Revised Standard Version includes a simplified self-pronunciation system for proper names. The system is designed to provide assistance to the reader without filling the text with a complicated variety of symbols, many of which provide unneeded pronunciation clues.

Well-known proper names such as Moses, Nazareth, and Timothy are printed without pronunciation marks of any kind. Such names are a familiar part of our cultural heritage, and they are instantly recognizable to most readers.

More difficult proper names (as well as certain transliterated non-English words) are shown in the text with simplified pronunciation markings. (Two notes of caution: The anglicized pronunciation of a name differs at times from that of the ancient language. Also, there are differences of opinion among speakers of English concerning the most desirable pronunciation of certain names.)

Three kinds of marks are used:

    ′   The acute accent mark: shows which syllable of a name is to be stressed. A compound name—with parts separated by a hyphen—has an accent mark in each part having more than one syllable.

    ·   The centered dot: shows where an unaccented syllable ends and another syllable begins.

    —   The macron: printed over a vowel that has a "long" sound. The macron is shown over the following vowels when they are sounded as indicated:

> *a* as in gate
> *e* as in key
> *i* as in ice
> *o* as in hope
> *u* as in use or rule
> *y* as in type

The macron also indicates the pronunciation of certain diphthongs, or vowel combinations:

> over the *a* in *ai* as in pail
> over the *i* in *ai* as in aisle

A vowel that does not have a "long" sound is printed with no pronunciation mark. In most cases the sound of such a vowel can be determined closely enough by observing how the name is spelled, divided into syllables, and accented.

PREFACE

This Catholic edition of the New Revised Standard Version of the Bible has been authorized by the National Conference of Catholic Bishops in the U.S.A. and by the National Council of the Churches of Christ in the U.S.A. It has received the ecclesiastical approval of the Catholic Bishops of both the United States and Canada. The undersigned, who prepared this edition, is a member of the Revised Standard Version Bible Translation Committee as well as an active member and past president of the Catholic Biblical Association of America.

Roman Catholics are already familiar with the accuracy and elegance of the New Revised Standard Version, first published in 1990. It has previously appeared in two major types of edition: an edition of the Old and New Testaments alone, the Bible of most Protestants; and an edition of the Old and New Testaments with the Apocryphal/Deuterocanonical Books placed between the two Testaments. The text of the latter edition received the Imprimatur (official approbation) of the United States and Canadian Catholic Bishops. The New Revised Standard Version is truly an ecumenical translation, for it was produced by Roman Catholic, Eastern Orthodox, Protestant, and Jewish scholars. Because of this Catholic presence no change in the translation was requested for this edition. The only exceptions are the Book of Esther, which exists in two different forms that are explained below, and the Book of Daniel, which includes the deuterocanonical portions that are listed below.

Regarding the number of the books of the Old Testament canon and their arrangement, however, Protestants and Jews on the one hand, and Roman Catholics and Orthodox Christians on the other, hold different beliefs. From the time of the Reformation in the sixteenth century, Protestants have adopted the Jewish canon of the Old Testament, which was established by the rabbis at the end of the first century of the Common Era. This canon includes only those books that were written in Hebrew and Aramaic. In addition to these books, however, Roman Catholics, following the ancient tradition of the Christian church, also hold the Deuterocanonical Books of the Old Testament to be sacred and inspired, and therefore canonical. Protestants and Jews call these books Apocrypha, a word that means "hidden or concealed," an inappropriate title for works that were part of the Greek Old Testament (the Septuagint) from pre-Christian times. The Roman Catholic canon, which was fixed by the time of the Council of Hippo in 393 and reaffirmed by the two Councils of Carthage in 397 and 419, was formally defined by the Council of Trent in 1546. This canon contains seven Deuterocanonical Books: Tobit, Judith, the Wisdom of Solomon, Sirach (the Wisdom of Ben Sira, also known as Ecclesiasticus), Baruch including the Letter of Jeremiah as chapter 6, and 1 and 2 Maccabees; and extra portions of two other books: the Additions to Esther; and the Prayer of Azariah and the Song of the Three Jews inserted between verses 23 and 24 of Daniel 3, Susanna as Daniel 13, and Bel and the Dragon as Daniel 14. Over and above these books and extra portions, the Bible of Greek and Slavonic Orthodox Christians includes 1 Esdras, the Prayer of Manasseh, Psalm 151, and 3 Maccabees. The Slavonic Bible also contains 2 Esdras, and an appendix to the Greek Bible includes 4 Maccabees.

Several of the Deuterocanonical Books were written originally in Hebrew or Aramaic, the rest in Greek. More than two-thirds of the Book of Sirach is now extant in Hebrew, and four fragments of the Book of Tobit in Hebrew and Aramaic were recovered from Qumran Cave IV. It seems certain that Judith and the additions to Daniel were also written originally in Hebrew. Hebrew is the original language of the prose parts of Baruch; the poetic parts were composed in Greek. The Wisdom of Solomon was written completely in Greek. The original language of 1 Maccabees was Hebrew while 2 Maccabees was composed in Greek.

The Book of Esther has two different forms: the short Hebrew original; and the longer Greek version that contains one hundred and seven additional verses comprising six distinct portions, A through F. It is the translation of the entire

Greek version that appears in the Deuterocanonical section of the New Revised Standard Version. In this Catholic edition, however, the translation of the Greek portions has been inserted at the appropriate places of the translation of the Hebrew form of the book. Some of the Greek portions apparently had a Hebrew origin; the others were written in Greek.

What is distinctive about this Catholic edition—as well as every other edition published by Roman Catholics—is that the Deuterocanonical Books and portions are placed in their proper order among the other books of the Old Testament. Thus, Tobit, Judith, the long form of Esther, and 1 and 2 Maccabees are found among the so-called historical books directly after Nehemiah. The Wisdom of Solomon and the Book of Sirach follow after the Song of Solomon among the wisdom books. Because Baruch, the well-known secretary of Jeremiah, is said to be the author of the work that bears his name, the book is placed after Jeremiah and Lamentations. This order of books comes from the Latin Vulgate translated by St. Jerome in the late fourth and early fifth centuries. It is essentially the same order as that found in the fourth-century Codex Vaticanus, one of the oldest extant manuscripts of the Septuagint.

Roman Catholics will welcome this edition of the New Revised Standard Version of the Bible for personal reading and study as well as liturgical usage. Based on the latest manuscript discoveries and critical editions, it offers the fruits of the best biblical scholarship in the idiom of today while being sensitive to the contemporary concern for inclusive language when referring to human beings.

ALEXANDER A. DI LELLA, O.F.M.
Andrews-Kelly-Ryan Distinguished Professor of Biblical Studies
The Catholic University of America

September 30, 1992
Feast of St. Jerome

TO THE READER

This preface is addressed to you by the Committee of translators, who wish to explain, as briefly as possible, the origin and character of our work. The publication of our revision is yet another step in the long, continual process of making the Bible available in the form of the English language that is most widely current in our day. To summarize in a single sentence: the New Revised Standard Version of the Bible is an authorized revision of the Revised Standard Version, published in 1952, which was a revision of the American Standard Version, published in 1901, which, in turn, embodied earlier revisions of the King James Version, published in 1611.

In the course of time, the King James Version came to be regarded as "the Authorized Version." With good reason it has been termed "the noblest monument of English prose," and it has entered, as no other book has, into the making of the personal character and the public institutions of the English-speaking peoples. We owe to it an incalculable debt.

Yet the King James Version has serious defects. By the middle of the nineteenth century, the development of biblical studies and the discovery of many biblical manuscripts more ancient than those on which the King James Version was based made it apparent that these defects were so many as to call for revision. The task was begun, by authority of the Church of England, in 1870. The (British) Revised Version of the Bible was published in 1881-1885; and the American Standard Version, its variant embodying the preferences of the American scholars associated with the work, was published, as was mentioned above, in 1901. In 1928 the copyright of the latter was acquired by the International Council of Religious Education and thus passed into the ownership of the churches of the United States and Canada that were associated in this Council through their boards of education and publication.

The Council appointed a committee of scholars to have charge of the text of the American Standard Version and to undertake inquiry concerning the need for further revision. After studying the questions whether or not revision should be undertaken, and if so, what its nature and extent should be, in 1937 the Council authorized a revision. The scholars who served as members of the Committee worked in two sections, one dealing with the Old Testament and one with the New Testament. In 1946 the Revised Standard Version of the New Testament was published. The publication of the Revised Standard Version of the Bible, containing the Old and New Testaments, took place on September 30, 1952. A translation of the Apocryphal/Deuterocanonical Books of the Old Testament followed in 1957. In 1977 this collection was issued in an expanded edition, containing three additional texts received by Eastern Orthodox communions (3 and 4 Maccabees and Psalm 151). Thereafter the Revised Standard Version gained the distinction of being officially authorized for use by all major Christian churches: Protestant, Anglican, Roman Catholic, and Eastern Orthodox.

The Revised Standard Version Bible Committee is a continuing body, comprising about thirty members, both men and women. Ecumenical in representation, it includes scholars affiliated with various Protestant denominations, as well as several Roman Catholic members, an Eastern Orthodox member, and a Jewish member who serves in the Old Testament section. For a period of time the Committee included several members from Canada and from England.

Because no translation of the Bible is perfect or is acceptable to all groups of readers, and because discoveries of older manuscripts and further investigation of linguistic features of the text continue to become available, renderings of the Bible have proliferated. During the years following the publication of the Revised Standard Version, twenty-six other English translations and revisions of the Bible were produced by committees and by individual scholars—not to mention twenty-five other translations and revisions of the New Testament alone. One of the latter was the second edition of the RSV New Testament, issued in 1971, twenty-five years after its initial publication.

Following the publication of the RSV Old Testament in 1952, significant advances were made in the discovery and interpretation of documents in Semitic languages related to Hebrew. In addition to the information that had become available in the late 1940s from the Dead Sea texts of Isaiah and Habakkuk, subsequent acquisitions from the same area brought to light many other early copies of all the books of the Hebrew Scriptures (except Esther), though most of these copies are fragmentary. During the same period early Greek manuscript copies of books of the New Testament also became available.

In order to take these discoveries into account, along with recent studies of documents in Semitic languages related to Hebrew, in 1974 the Policies Committee of the Revised Standard Version, which is a standing committee of the National Council of the Churches of Christ in the U.S.A., authorized the preparation of a revision of the entire RSV Bible.

For the Old Testament the Committee has made use of the *Biblia Hebraica Stuttgartensia* (1977; ed. sec. emendata, 1983). This is an edition of the Hebrew and Aramaic text as current early in the Christian era and fixed by Jewish scholars (the "Masoretes") of the sixth to the ninth centuries. The vowel signs, which were added by the Masoretes, are accepted in the main, but where a more probable and convincing reading can be obtained by assuming different vowels, this has been done. No notes are given in such cases, because the vowel points are less ancient and reliable than the consonants. When an alternative reading given by the Masoretes is translated in a footnote, this is identified by the words "Another reading is."

Departures from the consonantal text of the best manuscripts have been made only where it seems clear that errors in copying had been made before the text was standardized. Most of the corrections adopted are based on the ancient versions (translations into Greek, Aramaic, Syriac, and Latin), which were made prior to the time of the work of the Masoretes and which therefore may reflect earlier forms of the Hebrew text. In such instances a footnote specifies the version or versions from which the correction has been derived and also gives a translation of the Masoretic Text. Where it was deemed appropriate to do so, information is supplied in footnotes from subsidiary Jewish traditions concerning other textual readings (the *Tiqqune Sopherim*, "emendations of the scribes"). These are identified in the footnotes as "Ancient Heb tradition."

Occasionally it is evident that the text has suffered in transmission and that none of the versions provides a satisfactory restoration. Here we can only follow the best judgment of competent scholars as to the most probable reconstruction of the original text. Such reconstructions are indicated in footnotes by the abbreviation Cn ("Correction"), and a translation of the Masoretic Text is added.

For the Apocryphal/Deuterocanonical Books of the Old Testament the Committee has made use of a number of texts. For most of these books the basic Greek text from which the present translation was made is the edition of the Septuagint prepared by Alfred Rahlfs and published by the Württemberg Bible Society (Stuttgart, 1935). For several of the books the more recently published individual volumes of the Göttingen Septuagint project were utilized. For the Book of Tobit it was decided to follow the form of the Greek text found in codex Sinaiticus (supported as it is by evidence from Qumran); where this text is defective, it was supplemented and corrected by other Greek manuscripts. For the three Additions to Daniel (namely, Susanna, the Prayer of Azariah and the Song of the Three Jews, and Bel and the Dragon) the Committee continued to use the Greek version attributed to Theodotion (the so-called "Theodotion-Daniel"). In translating Ecclesiasticus (Sirach), while constant reference was made to the Hebrew fragments of a large portion of this book (those discovered at Qumran and Masada as well as those recovered from the Cairo Geniza), the Committee generally followed the Greek text (including verse numbers) published by Joseph Ziegler in the Göttingen Septuagint (1965). But in many places the Committee has translated the Hebrew text when this provides a reading that is clearly superior to the Greek; the Syriac and Latin versions were also consulted throughout and occasionally adopted. Finally, in the Book of Esther we have placed the deuterocanonical portions, translated from Robert Hanhart's Göttingen edition of the Greek (1983), in their original context within the translation of the Hebrew text.

For the New Testament the Committee has based its work on the most recent edition of *The Greek New Testament*, prepared by an interconfessional and international committee and published by the United Bible Societies (1966; 3rd ed. corrected, 1983; information concerning changes to be introduced into the critical apparatus of the forthcoming 4th edition was available to the Committee). As in that edition, double brackets are used to enclose a few passages that are generally regarded to be later additions to the text, but which we have retained because of their evident antiquity and their importance in the textual tradition. Only in very rare instances have we replaced the text or the punctuation of the Bible Societies' edition by an alternative that seemed to us to be superior. Here and there in the footnotes the phrase, "Other ancient authorities read," identifies alternative readings preserved by Greek manuscripts and early versions. In both Testaments, alternative renderings of the text are indicated by the word "Or."

As for the style of English adopted for the present revision, among the mandates given to the Committee in 1980 by the Division of Education and Ministry of the National Council of the Churches of Christ (which now holds the copyright of the RSV Bible) was the directive to continue in the tradition of the King James Bible, but to introduce such changes as are warranted on the basis of accuracy, clarity, euphony, and current English usage. Within the constraints set by the original texts and by the mandates of the Division, the Committee has followed the maxim, "As literal as possible, as free as necessary." As a consequence, the New Revised Standard Version (NRSV) remains essentially a literal translation. Paraphrastic renderings have been adopted only sparingly, and then chiefly to compensate for a deficiency in the English language—the lack of a common gender third person singular pronoun.

During the almost half a century since the publication of the RSV, many in the churches have become sensitive to the danger of linguistic sexism arising from the inherent bias of the English language towards the masculine gender, a bias that in the case of the Bible has often restricted or obscured the meaning of the original text. The mandates from the Division specified that, in references to men and women, masculine-oriented language should be eliminated as far as this can be done without altering passages that reflect the historical situation of ancient patriarchal culture. As can be appreciated, more than once the Committee found that the several mandates stood in tension and even in conflict. The various concerns had to be balanced case by case in order to provide a faithful and acceptable rendering without using contrived English. Only very occasionally has the pronoun "he" or "him" been retained in passages where the reference may have been to a woman as well as to a man; for example, in several legal texts in Leviticus and Deuteronomy. In such instances of formal, legal language, the options of either putting the passage in the plural or of introducing additional nouns to avoid masculine pronouns in English seemed to the Committee to obscure the historic structure and literary character of the original. In the vast majority of cases, however, inclusiveness has been attained by simple rephrasing or by introducing plural forms when this does not distort the meaning of the passage. Of course, in narrative and in parable no attempt was made to generalize the sex of individual persons.

Another aspect of style will be detected by readers who compare the more stately English rendering of the Old Testament with the less formal rendering adopted for the New Testament. For example, the traditional distinction between *shall* and *will* in English has been retained in the Old Testament as appropriate in rendering a document that embodies what may be termed the classic form of Hebrew, while in the New Testament the abandonment of such distinctions in the usage of the future tense in English reflects the more colloquial nature of the koine Greek used by most New Testament authors except when they are quoting the Old Testament.

Careful readers will notice that here and there in the Old Testament the word LORD (or in certain cases GOD) is printed in capital letters. This represents the traditional manner in English versions of rendering the Divine Name, the "Tetragrammaton" (see the notes on Exodus 3.14, 15), following the precedent of the ancient Greek and Latin translators and the long established practice in the reading of the Hebrew Scriptures in the synagogue. While it is almost if not quite certain that the Name was originally pronounced "Yahweh," this pronunciation was not indicated when the Masoretes added vowel sounds to the consonantal Hebrew text. To the four consonants YHWH of the Name, which had come to be regarded as too sacred to be pronounced, they attached vowel signs indicating that in its place should be read the Hebrew word *Adonai* meaning "Lord" (or *Elohim* meaning "God"). Ancient Greek translators employed the word *Kyrios* ("Lord") for the Name. The Vulgate likewise used the Latin word *Dominus* ("Lord"). The form "Jehovah" is of late medieval origin; it is a combination of the consonants of the Divine Name and the vowels attached to it by the Masoretes but belonging to an entirely different word. Although the American Standard Version (1901) had used "Jehovah" to render the Tetragrammaton (the sound of Y being represented by J and the sound of W by V, as in Latin), for two reasons the Committees that produced the RSV and the NRSV returned to the more familiar usage of the King James Version. (1) The word "Jehovah" does not accurately represent any form of the Name ever used in Hebrew. (2) The use of any proper name for the one and only God, as though there were other gods from whom the true God had to be distinguished, began to be discontinued in Judaism before the Christian era and is inappropriate for the universal faith of the Christian Church.

It will be seen that in the Psalms and in other prayers addressed to God the archaic second person singular pronouns (*thee, thou, thine*) and verb forms (*art, hast, hadst*) are no longer used. Although some readers may regret this change, it should be pointed out that in the original languages neither the Old Testament nor the New makes any linguistic distinction between addressing a human being and addressing the Deity. Furthermore, in the tradition of the King James Version one will not expect to find the use of capital letters for pronouns that refer to the Deity — such capitalization is an unnecessary innovation that has only recently been introduced into a few English translations of the Bible. Finally, we have left to the discretion of the licensed publishers such matters as section headings, cross-references, and clues to the pronunciation of proper names.

This new version seeks to preserve all that is best in the English Bible as it has been known and used through the years. It is intended for use in public reading and congregational worship, as well as in private study, instruction, and meditation. We have resisted the temptation to introduce terms and phrases that merely reflect current moods, and have tried to put the message of the Scriptures in simple, enduring words and expressions that are worthy to stand in the great tradition of the King James Bible and its predecessors.

In traditional Judaism and Christianity, the Bible has been more than a historical document to be preserved or a classic of literature to be cherished and admired; it is recognized as the unique record of God's dealings with people over the ages. The Old Testament sets forth the call of a special people to enter into covenant relation with the God of justice and steadfast love and to bring God's law to the nations. The New Testament records the life and work of Jesus Christ, the one in whom "the Word became flesh," as well as describes the rise and spread of the early Christian Church. The Bible carries its full message, not to those who regard it simply as a noble literary heritage of the past or who wish to use it to enhance political purposes and advance otherwise desirable goals, but to all persons and communities who read it so that they may discern and understand what God is saying to them. That message must not be disguised in phrases that are no longer clear, or hidden under words that have changed or lost their meaning; it must be presented in language that is direct and plain and meaningful to people today. It is the hope and prayer of the translators that this version of the Bible may continue to hold a large place in congregational life and to speak to all readers, young and old alike, helping them to understand and believe and respond to its message.

For the Committee,

Bruce M. Metzger

The Pentateuch

The Pentateuch is the first five books of the Bible, called "Torah" in the Hebrew Scriptures. Though we often call these books "The Law," Torah does not mean "law," but "teaching". Basic to the Torah is the idea of the covenant. A covenant is an agreement. In the Bible covenants are special, because God is one of the parties to the covenant. Biblical covenants have three parts: (1) a statement about God's saving act (what God brings to the agreement); (2) a statement about what God expects from humanity in response; (3) a sign or symbol as a reminder of the covenant. The Torah is, in part, a record of God's covenant and the implications of the covenant for human life in society.

Genesis begins with the creation, setting the covenant in the context of God's rule over the entire universe. The first covenant is with Adam and Eve, representatives of all humanity, and includes the understanding that human beings will be responsible stewards of all of creation. The second covenant is with Noah, the promise that the world will never again be destroyed by flood. Then the biblical account focuses on one particular person, Abraham, who enters into covenant with God and is given the promise that he and his descendants will become a blessing to all humanity. Through the narratives dealing with Abraham and Sarah, Isaac and Rebekah, Jacob and Leah and Rachel, and Joseph the questions of faithfulness to the covenant and hope for the fulfillment of God's promises take concrete form.

Exodus centers on the escape of God's people from Egypt under the leadership of Moses and the making of the great covenant at Mt. Sinai. The parts of the covenant are clear: God's gracious saving act is seen in Passover and Exodus; the expectation of human response is summarized in the Ten Commandments; and the Feast of the Passover is the great sign and reminder. Moses, Aaron, and Miriam are both the leaders of God's people and the models of struggle and faith.

Leviticus takes its name from the Latin word for "book of the Levites." The major concern of the book is the holiness of the community of Israel. Holiness means to be set apart by God for a special purpose. Holiness is expressed in proper forms of worship and living out the love of God in the routine of daily life. The "Holiness Code" (chs. 17 — 27) is a good example of how worship and justice mingle together in the life of Israel.

Numbers is named for the census that begins the book. The narrative part of the book is the wilderness journey from Kadesh-barnea to the Promised Land. Included are the great accounts of the spies entering Canaan, the 40 years of wandering, and the miracles of Moses. Finally come the conquests of the Kingdoms of Sihon and Og in the Transjordan, and the story of Balaam. The book ends with Israel prepared to enter the Promised Land under the leadership of Joshua.

Deuteronomy is written as Moses' farewell speech before the tribes enter the Land. It reviews God's acts of salvation and the implications of salvation for life. The book itself was apparently found in the temple in the reign of Josiah (621 B.C.). The discovery sparked a great religious reform. One of the real concerns of Deuteronomy is how to make old traditions relevant for a new time. The most important statement of belief is the "Shema", found in 6:4-5.

THE ANCIENT NEAR EAST

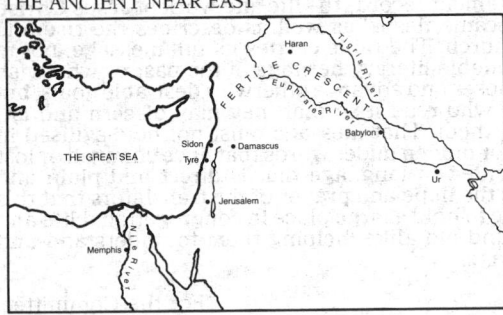

GENESIS

Six Days of Creation and the Sabbath
(Gen 2.4b–9; Job 38.4–11; Jn 1.1–5)

1 In the beginning when God created*a* the heavens and the earth, ²the earth was a formless void and darkness covered the face of the deep, while a wind from God*b* swept over the face of the waters. ³Then God said, "Let there be light"; and there was light. ⁴And God saw that the light was good; and God separated the light from the darkness. ⁵God called the light Day, and the darkness he called Night. And there was evening and there was morning, the first day.

6 And God said, "Let there be a dome in the midst of the waters, and let it separate the waters from the waters." ⁷So God made the dome and separated the waters that were under the dome from the waters that were above the dome. And it was so. ⁸God called the dome Sky. And there was evening and there was morning, the second day.

9 And God said, "Let the waters under the sky be gathered together into one place, and let the dry land appear." And it was so. ¹⁰God called the dry land Earth, and the waters that were gathered together he called Seas. And God saw that it was good. ¹¹Then God said, "Let the earth put forth vegetation: plants yielding seed, and fruit trees of every kind on earth that bear fruit with the seed in it." And it was so. ¹²The earth brought forth vegetation: plants yielding seed of every kind, and trees of every kind bearing fruit with the seed in it. And God saw that it was good. ¹³And there was evening and there was morning, the third day.

14 And God said, "Let there be lights in the dome of the sky to separate the day from the night; and let them be for signs and for seasons and for days and years, ¹⁵and let them be lights in the dome of the sky to give light upon the earth." And it was so.

¹⁶God made the two great lights—the greater light to rule the day and the lesser light to rule the night—and the stars. ¹⁷God set them in the dome of the sky to give light upon the earth, ¹⁸to rule over the day and over the night, and to separate the light from the darkness. And God saw that it was good. ¹⁹And there was evening and there was morning, the fourth day.

20 And God said, "Let the waters bring forth swarms of living creatures, and let birds fly above the earth across the dome of the sky." ²¹So God created the great sea monsters and every living creature that moves, of every kind, with which the waters swarm, and every winged bird of every kind. And God saw that it was good. ²²God blessed them, saying, "Be fruitful and multiply and fill the waters in the seas, and let birds multiply on the earth." ²³And there was evening and there was morning, the fifth day.

24 And God said, "Let the earth bring forth living creatures of every kind: cattle and creeping things and wild animals of the earth of every kind." And it was so. ²⁵God made the wild animals of the earth of every kind, and the cattle of every kind, and everything that creeps upon the ground of every kind. And God saw that it was good.

26 Then God said, "Let us make humankind*c* in our image, according to our likeness; and let them have dominion over the fish of the sea, and over the birds of the air, and over the cattle, and over all the wild animals of the earth,*d* and over every creeping thing that creeps upon the earth."

27 So God created humankind*c* in
   his image,

*a*Or *when God began to create* or *In the beginning God created*   *b*Or *while the spirit of God* or *while a mighty wind*   *c*Heb *adam*   *d*Syr: Heb *and over all the earth*

in the image of God he created
them;[e]
male and female he created
them.

28 God blessed them, and God said to them, "Be fruitful and multiply, and fill the earth and subdue it; and have dominion over the fish of the sea and over the birds of the air and over every living thing that moves upon the earth." 29 God said, "See, I have given you every plant yielding seed that is upon the face of all the earth, and every tree with seed in its fruit; you shall have them for food. 30 And to every beast of the earth, and to every bird of the air, and to everything that creeps on the earth, everything that has the breath of life, I have given every green plant for food." And it was so. 31 God saw everything that he had made, and indeed, it was very good. And there was evening and there was morning, the sixth day.

2 Thus the heavens and the earth were finished, and all their multitude. 2 And on the seventh day God finished the work that he had done, and he rested on the seventh day from all the work that he had done. 3 So God blessed the seventh day and hallowed it, because on it God rested from all the work that he had done in creation.

4 These are the generations of the heavens and the earth when they were created.

Another Account of the Creation
(Gen 1.26–30)

In the day that the LORD God made the earth and the heavens, 5 when no plant of the field was yet in the earth and no herb of the field had yet sprung up—for the LORD God had not caused it to rain upon the earth, and there was no one to till the ground; 6 but a stream would rise from the earth, and water the whole face of the ground— 7 then the LORD God formed man from the dust of the ground,[f] and breathed into his nostrils the breath of life; and the man became a living being. 8 And the LORD God planted a garden in Eden, in the east; and there he put the man whom he had formed. 9 Out of the ground the LORD God made to grow every tree that is pleasant to the sight and good for food, the tree of life also in the midst of the garden, and the tree of the knowledge of good and evil.

10 A river flows out of Eden to water the garden, and from there it divides and becomes four branches. 11 The name of the first is Pī'shon; it is the one that flows around the whole land of Hav'i·lah, where there is gold; 12 and the gold of that land is good; bdellium and onyx stone are there. 13 The name of the second river is Gī'hon; it is the one that flows around the whole land of Cush. 14 The name of the third river is Tigris, which flows east of Assyria. And the fourth river is the Euphrates.

15 The LORD God took the man and put him in the garden of Eden to till it and keep it. 16 And the LORD God commanded the man, "You may freely eat of every tree of the garden; 17 but of the tree of the knowledge of good and evil you shall not eat, for in the day that you eat of it you shall die."

18 Then the LORD God said, "It is not good that the man should be alone; I will make him a helper as his partner." 19 So out of the ground the LORD God formed every animal of the field and every bird of the air, and brought them to the man to see what he would call them; and whatever the man called every living creature, that was its name. 20 The man gave names to all cattle, and to the birds of the air, and to every animal of the field; but for the man[g] there was not found a helper as his partner. 21 So the LORD God caused a deep sleep to fall upon the man, and he slept; then he took one of his ribs and closed up its place with flesh. 22 And the rib that the LORD God had taken from the man he made into a woman and brought her to the man. 23 Then the man said,

"This at last is bone of my bones
and flesh of my flesh;
this one shall be called
Woman,[h]
for out of Man[i] this one was
taken."

24 Therefore a man leaves his father and his mother and clings to his wife, and they become one flesh. 25 And the man and his wife were both naked, and were not ashamed.

The First Sin and Its Punishment
(Rom 5.12–21)

3 Now the serpent was more crafty than any other wild animal that

---

e Heb *him*   f Or *formed a man* (Heb
adam) *of dust from the ground* (Heb
adamah)   g Or *for Adam*
h Heb *ishshah*   i Heb *ish*

the LORD God had made. He said to the woman, "Did God say, 'You shall not eat from any tree in the garden'?" [2] The woman said to the serpent, "We may eat of the fruit of the trees in the garden; [3] but God said, 'You shall not eat of the fruit of the tree that is in the middle of the garden, nor shall you touch it, or you shall die.' " [4] But the serpent said to the woman, "You will not die; [5] for God knows that when you eat of it your eyes will be opened, and you will be like God,[j] knowing good and evil." [6] So when the woman saw that the tree was good for food, and that it was a delight to the eyes, and that the tree was to be desired to make one wise, she took of its fruit and ate; and she also gave some to her husband, who was with her, and he ate. [7] Then the eyes of both were opened, and they knew that they were naked; and they sewed fig leaves together and made loincloths for themselves.

8 They heard the sound of the LORD God walking in the garden at the time of the evening breeze, and the man and his wife hid themselves from the presence of the LORD God among the trees of the garden. [9] But the LORD God called to the man, and said to him, "Where are you?" [10] He said, "I heard the sound of you in the garden, and I was afraid, because I was naked; and I hid myself." [11] He said, "Who told you that you were naked? Have you eaten from the tree of which I commanded you not to eat?" [12] The man said, "The woman whom you gave to be with me, she gave me fruit from the tree, and I ate." [13] Then the LORD God said to the woman, "What is this that you have done?" The woman said, "The serpent tricked me, and I ate." [14] The LORD God said to the serpent,

"Because you have done this,
    cursed are you among all
        animals
    and among all wild creatures;
upon your belly you shall go,
    and dust you shall eat
    all the days of your life.
[15] I will put enmity between you
        and the woman,
    and between your offspring
        and hers;
he will strike your head,
    and you will strike his heel."
[16] To the woman he said,
"I will greatly increase your
        pangs in childbearing;

    in pain you shall bring forth
        children,
yet your desire shall be for your
        husband,
    and he shall rule over you."
[17] And to the man[k] he said,
"Because you have listened to
        the voice of your wife,
    and have eaten of the tree
about which I commanded you,
    'You shall not eat of it,'
cursed is the ground because of
        you;
    in toil you shall eat of it all the
        days of your life;
[18]   thorns and thistles it shall bring
        forth for you;
    and you shall eat the plants of
        the field.
[19]   By the sweat of your face
        you shall eat bread
until you return to the ground,
    for out of it you were taken;
you are dust,
    and to dust you shall return."
20 The man named his wife Eve,[l] because she was the mother of all living. [21] And the LORD God made garments of skins for the man[m] and for his wife, and clothed them.
22 Then the LORD God said, "See, the man has become like one of us, knowing good and evil; and now, he might reach out his hand and take also from the tree of life, and eat, and live forever"— [23] therefore the LORD God sent him forth from the garden of Eden, to till the ground from which he was taken. [24] He drove out the man; and at the east of the garden of Eden he placed the cherubim, and a sword flaming and turning to guard the way to the tree of life.

Cain Murders Abel
(Lk 11.51; Heb 11.4; 12.24)

4 Now the man knew his wife Eve, and she conceived and bore Cain, saying, "I have produced[n] a man with the help of the LORD." [2] Next she bore his brother Abel. Now Abel was a keeper of sheep, and Cain a tiller of the ground. [3] In the course of time Cain brought to the LORD an offering of the fruit of the ground, [4] and Abel for his part brought of the firstlings of his flock, their fat portions. And the LORD

[j] Or *gods*   [k] Or *to Adam*   [l] In Heb *Eve* resembles the word for *living*   [m] Or *for Adam*   [n] The verb in Heb resembles the word for *Cain*

had regard for Abel and his offering, [5]but for Cain and his offering he had no regard. So Cain was very angry, and his countenance fell. [6]The LORD said to Cain, "Why are you angry, and why has your countenance fallen? [7]If you do well, will you not be accepted? And if you do not do well, sin is lurking at the door; its desire is for you, but you must master it."

8 Cain said to his brother Abel, "Let us go out to the field."[o] And when they were in the field, Cain rose up against his brother Abel, and killed him. [9]Then the LORD said to Cain, "Where is your brother Abel?" He said, "I do not know; am I my brother's keeper?" [10]And the LORD said, "What have you done? Listen; your brother's blood is crying out to me from the ground! [11]And now you are cursed from the ground, which has opened its mouth to receive your brother's blood from your hand. [12]When you till the ground, it will no longer yield to you its strength; you will be a fugitive and a wanderer on the earth." [13]Cain said to the LORD, "My punishment is greater than I can bear! [14]Today you have driven me away from the soil, and I shall be hidden from your face; I shall be a fugitive and a wanderer on the earth, and anyone who meets me may kill me." [15]Then the LORD said to him, "Not so![p] Whoever kills Cain will suffer a sevenfold vengeance." And the LORD put a mark on Cain, so that no one who came upon him would kill him. [16]Then Cain went away from the presence of the LORD, and settled in the land of Nod,[q] east of Eden.

Beginnings of Civilization

17 Cain knew his wife, and she conceived and bore Ē'noch; and he built a city, and named it Ē'noch after his son Ē'noch. [18]To Ē'noch was born I'rad; and I'rad was the father of Me·hū'ja·el, and Me·hū'ja·el the father of Me·thū'sha·el, and Me·thū'sha·el the father of Lā'mech. [19]Lā'mech took two wives; the name of the one was Ā'dah, and the name of the other Zil'lah. [20]Ā'dah bore Ja'bal; he was the ancestor of those who live in tents and have livestock. [21]His brother's name was Jū'bal; he was the ancestor of all those who play the lyre and pipe. [22]Zil'lah bore Tū'-bal-cāin, who made all kinds of bronze and iron tools. The sister of Tū'bal-cāin was Nā'a·mah.

23 Lā'mech said to his wives:

"Ā'dah and Zil'lah, hear my
    voice;
you wives of Lā'mech, listen to
    what I say:
I have killed a man for
    wounding me,
    a young man for striking me.
24 If Cain is avenged sevenfold,
    truly Lā'mech
        seventy-sevenfold."

25 Adam knew his wife again, and she bore a son and named him Seth, for she said, "God has appointed[r] for me another child instead of Abel, because Cain killed him." [26]To Seth also a son was born, and he named him Ē'nosh. At that time people began to invoke the name of the LORD.

Adam's Descendants to Noah and His Sons
(1 Chr 1.1–4; Lk 3.36–38)

5 This is the list of the descendants of Adam. When God created humankind,[s] he made them[t] in the likeness of God. [2]Male and female he created them, and he blessed them and named them "Humankind"[s] when they were created.

3 When Adam had lived one hundred thirty years, he became the father of a son in his likeness, according to his image, and named him Seth. [4]The days of Adam after he became the father of Seth were eight hundred years; and he had other sons and daughters. [5]Thus all the days that Adam lived were nine hundred thirty years; and he died.

6 When Seth had lived one hundred five years, he became the father of Ē'nosh. [7]Seth lived after the birth of Ē'nosh eight hundred seven years, and had other sons and daughters. [8]Thus all the days of Seth were nine hundred twelve years; and he died.

9 When Ē'nosh had lived ninety years, he became the father of Kē'nan. [10]Ē'nosh lived after the birth of Kē'nan eight hundred fifteen years, and had other sons and daughters. [11]Thus all the days of Ē'nosh were nine hundred five years; and he died.

12 When Kē'nan had lived seventy years, he became the father of Ma·hal'-a·lel. [13]Kē'nan lived after the birth of

o Sam Gk Syr Compare Vg: MT lacks
Let us go out to the field   p Gk Syr Vg:
Heb *Therefore*   q That is *Wandering*
r The verb in Heb resembles the word for
Seth   s Heb *adam*   t Heb *him*

Ma·hal′a·lel eight hundred and forty years, and had other sons and daughters. [14]Thus all the days of Ke′nan were nine hundred and ten years; and he died.

15 When Ma·hal′a·lel had lived sixty-five years, he became the father of Jar′ed. [16]Ma·hal′a·lel lived after the birth of Jar′ed eight hundred thirty years, and had other sons and daughters. [17]Thus all the days of Ma·hal′a·lel were eight hundred ninety-five years; and he died.

18 When Jar′ed had lived one hundred sixty-two years he became the father of E′noch. [19]Jar′ed lived after the birth of E′noch eight hundred years, and had other sons and daughters. [20]Thus all the days of Jar′ed were nine hundred sixty-two years; and he died.

21 When E′noch had lived sixty-five years, he became the father of Me·thu′se·lah. [22]E′noch walked with God after the birth of Me·thu′se·lah three hundred years, and had other sons and daughters. [23]Thus all the days of E′noch were three hundred sixty-five years. [24]E′noch walked with God; then he was no more, because God took him.

25 When Me·thu′se·lah had lived one hundred eighty-seven years, he became the father of La′mech. [26]Me·thu′se·lah lived after the birth of La′mech seven hundred eighty-two years, and had other sons and daughters. [27]Thus all the days of Me·thu′se·lah were nine hundred sixty-nine years; and he died.

28 When La′mech had lived one hundred eighty-two years, he became the father of a son; [29]he named him Noah, saying, "Out of the ground that the LORD has cursed this one shall bring us relief from our work and from the toil of our hands." [30]La′mech lived after the birth of Noah five hundred ninety-five years, and had other sons and daughters. [31]Thus all the days of La′mech were seven hundred seventy-seven years; and he died.

32 After Noah was five hundred years old, Noah became the father of Shem, Ham, and Ja′pheth.

The Wickedness of Humankind

6 When people began to multiply on the face of the ground, and daughters were born to them, [2]the sons of God saw that they were fair; and they took wives for themselves of all that they chose. [3]Then the LORD said, "My spirit shall not abide[u] in mortals forever, for they are flesh; their days shall be one hundred twenty years." [4]The Neph′i·lim were on the earth in those days—and also afterward—when the sons of God went in to the daughters of humans, who bore children to them. These were the heroes that were of old, warriors of renown.

5 The LORD saw that the wickedness of humankind was great in the earth, and that every inclination of the thoughts of their hearts was only evil continually. [6]And the LORD was sorry that he had made humankind on the earth, and it grieved him to his heart. [7]So the LORD said, "I will blot out from the earth the human beings I have created—people together with animals and creeping things and birds of the air, for I am sorry that I have made them." [8]But Noah found favor in the sight of the LORD.

Noah Pleases God
(Heb 11.7; 1 Pet 3.20)

9 These are the descendants of Noah. Noah was a righteous man, blameless in his generation; Noah walked with God. [10]And Noah had three sons, Shem, Ham, and Ja′pheth.

11 Now the earth was corrupt in God's sight, and the earth was filled with violence. [12]And God saw that the earth was corrupt; for all flesh had corrupted its ways upon the earth. [13]And God said to Noah, "I have determined to make an end of all flesh, for the earth is filled with violence because of them; now I am going to destroy them along with the earth. [14]Make yourself an ark of cypress[u] wood; make rooms in the ark, and cover it inside and out with pitch. [15]This is how you are to make it: the length of the ark three hundred cubits, its width fifty cubits, and its height thirty cubits. [16]Make a roof[v] for the ark, and finish it to a cubit above; and put the door of the ark in its side; make it with lower, second, and third decks. [17]For my part, I am going to bring a flood of waters on the earth, to destroy from under heaven all flesh in which is the breath of life; everything that is on the earth shall die. [18]But I will establish my covenant with you; and you shall come into the ark, you, your sons, your wife, and your sons' wives with you. [19]And of every

[u]Meaning of Heb uncertain
[v]Or *window*

living thing, of all flesh, you shall bring two of every kind into the ark, to keep them alive with you; they shall be male and female. 20 Of the birds according to their kinds, and of the animals according to their kinds, of every creeping thing of the ground according to its kind, two of every kind shall come in to you, to keep them alive. 21 Also take with you every kind of food that is eaten, and store it up; and it shall serve as food for you and for them." 22 Noah did this; he did all that God commanded him.

The Great Flood
(Lk 17.26–27)

7 Then the LORD said to Noah, "Go into the ark, you and all your household, for I have seen that you alone are righteous before me in this generation. 2 Take with you seven pairs of all clean animals, the male and its mate; and a pair of the animals that are not clean, the male and its mate; 3 and seven pairs of the birds of the air also, male and female, to keep their kind alive on the face of all the earth. 4 For in seven days I will send rain on the earth for forty days and forty nights; and every living thing that I have made I will blot out from the face of the ground." 5 And Noah did all that the LORD had commanded him.

6 Noah was six hundred years old when the flood of waters came on the earth. 7 And Noah with his sons and his wife and his sons' wives went into the ark to escape the waters of the flood. 8 Of clean animals, and of animals that are not clean, and of birds, and of everything that creeps on the ground, 9 two and two, male and female, went into the ark with Noah, as God had commanded Noah. 10 And after seven days the waters of the flood came on the earth.

11 In the six hundredth year of Noah's life, in the second month, on the seventeenth day of the month, on that day all the fountains of the great deep burst forth, and the windows of the heavens were opened. 12 The rain fell on the earth forty days and forty nights. 13 On the very same day Noah with his sons, Shem and Ham and Ja'-pheth, and Noah's wife and the three wives of his sons entered the ark, 14 they, and every wild animal of every kind, and all domestic animals of every kind, and every creeping thing that creeps on the earth, and every bird of

every kind—every bird, every winged creature. 15 They went into the ark with Noah, two and two of all flesh in which there was the breath of life. 16 And those that entered, male and female of all flesh, went in as God had commanded him; and the LORD shut him in.

17 The flood continued forty days on the earth; and the waters increased, and bore up the ark, and it rose high above the earth. 18 The waters swelled and increased greatly on the earth; and the ark floated on the face of the waters. 19 The waters swelled so mightily on the earth that all the high mountains under the whole heaven were covered; 20 the waters swelled above the mountains, covering them fifteen cubits deep. 21 And all flesh died that moved on the earth, birds, domestic animals, wild animals, all swarming creatures that swarm on the earth, and all human beings; 22 everything on dry land in whose nostrils was the breath of life died. 23 He blotted out every living thing that was on the face of the ground, human beings and animals and creeping things and birds of the air; they were blotted out from the earth. Only Noah was left, and those that were with him in the ark. 24 And the waters swelled on the earth for one hundred fifty days.

The Flood Subsides

8 But God remembered Noah and all the wild animals and all the domestic animals that were with him in the ark. And God made a wind blow over the earth, and the waters subsided; 2 the fountains of the deep and the windows of the heavens were closed, the rain from the heavens was restrained, 3 and the waters gradually receded from the earth. At the end of one hundred fifty days the waters had abated; 4 and in the seventh month, on the seventeenth day of the month, the ark came to rest on the mountains of Ar'a·rat. 5 The waters continued to abate until the tenth month; in the tenth month, on the first day of the month, the tops of the mountains appeared.

6 At the end of forty days Noah opened the window of the ark that he had made 7 and sent out the raven; and it went to and fro until the waters were dried up from the earth. 8 Then he sent out the dove from him, to see if the waters had subsided from the face of

the ground; ⁹but the dove found no place to set its foot, and it returned to him to the ark, for the waters were still on the face of the whole earth. So he put out his hand and took it and brought it into the ark with him. ¹⁰He waited another seven days, and again he sent out the dove from the ark; ¹¹and the dove came back to him in the evening, and there in its beak was a freshly plucked olive leaf; so Noah knew that the waters had subsided from the earth. ¹²Then he waited another seven days, and sent out the dove; and it did not return to him any more.

13 In the six hundred first year, in the first month, the first day of the month, the waters were dried up from the earth; and Noah removed the covering of the ark, and looked, and saw that the face of the ground was drying. ¹⁴In the second month, on the twenty-seventh day of the month, the earth was dry. ¹⁵Then God said to Noah, ¹⁶"Go out of the ark, you and your wife, and your sons and your sons' wives with you. ¹⁷Bring out with you every living thing that is with you of all flesh—birds and animals and every creeping thing that creeps on the earth—so that they may abound on the earth, and be fruitful and multiply on the earth." ¹⁸So Noah went out with his sons and his wife and his sons' wives. ¹⁹And every animal, every creeping thing, and every bird, everything that moves on the earth, went out of the ark by families.

God's Promise to Noah

20 Then Noah built an altar to the LORD, and took of every clean animal and of every clean bird, and offered burnt offerings on the altar. ²¹And when the LORD smelled the pleasing odor, the LORD said in his heart, "I will never again curse the ground because of humankind, for the inclination of the human heart is evil from youth; nor will I ever again destroy every living creature as I have done.

²² As long as the earth endures,
    seedtime and harvest, cold and
      heat,
    summer and winter, day and
      night,
    shall not cease."

The Covenant with Noah

9 God blessed Noah and his sons, and said to them, "Be fruitful and multiply, and fill the earth. ²The fear and dread of you shall rest on every animal of the earth, and on every bird of the air, on everything that creeps on the ground, and on all the fish of the sea; into your hand they are delivered. ³Every moving thing that lives shall be food for you; and just as I gave you the green plants, I give you everything. ⁴Only, you shall not eat flesh with its life, that is, its blood. ⁵For your own lifeblood I will surely require a reckoning: from every animal I will require it and from human beings, each one for the blood of another, I will require a reckoning for human life.

6   Whoever sheds the blood of a
      human,
    by a human shall that person's
      blood be shed;
    for in his own image
      God made humankind.

⁷And you, be fruitful and multiply, abound on the earth and multiply in it."

8 Then God said to Noah and to his sons with him, ⁹"As for me, I am establishing my covenant with you and your descendants after you, ¹⁰and with every living creature that is with you, the birds, the domestic animals, and every animal of the earth with you, as many as came out of the ark.ʷ ¹¹I establish my covenant with you, that never again shall all flesh be cut off by the waters of a flood, and never again shall there be a flood to destroy the earth." ¹²God said, "This is the sign of the covenant that I make between me and you and every living creature that is with you, for all future generations: ¹³I have set my bow in the clouds, and it shall be a sign of the covenant between me and the earth. ¹⁴When I bring clouds over the earth and the bow is seen in the clouds, ¹⁵I will remember my covenant that is between me and you and every living creature of all flesh; and the waters shall never again become a flood to destroy all flesh. ¹⁶When the bow is in the clouds, I will see it and remember the everlasting covenant between God and every living creature of all flesh that is on the earth." ¹⁷God said to Noah, "This is the sign of the covenant that I have established between me and all flesh that is on the earth."

ʷ Gk: Heb adds *every animal of the earth*

Noah and His Sons

18 The sons of Noah who went out of the ark were Shem, Ham, and Jā'pheth. Ham was the father of Cā'naan. 19 These three were the sons of Noah; and from these the whole earth was peopled.

20 Noah, a man of the soil, was the first to plant a vineyard. 21 He drank some of the wine and became drunk, and he lay uncovered in his tent. 22 And Ham, the father of Cā'naan, saw the nakedness of his father, and told his two brothers outside. 23 Then Shem and Jā'pheth took a garment, laid it on both their shoulders, and walked backward and covered the nakedness of their father; their faces were turned away, and they did not see their father's nakedness. 24 When Noah awoke from his wine and knew what his youngest son had done to him, 25 he said,

"Cursed be Cā'naan;
    lowest of slaves shall he be to
        his brothers."
26 He also said,

"Blessed by the LORD my God be
    Shem;
and let Cā'naan be his slave.
27 May God make space for x
    Jā'pheth,
and let him live in the tents of
    Shem;
and let Cā'naan be his slave."

28 After the flood Noah lived three hundred fifty years. 29 All the days of Noah were nine hundred fifty years; and he died.

Nations Descended from Noah
(1 Chr 1.5–27)

10 These are the descendants of Noah's sons, Shem, Ham, and Jā'pheth; children were born to them after the flood.

2 The descendants of Jā'pheth: Gō'mer, Mā'gog, Mā'daī, Jā'van, Tū'bal, Mē'shech, and Tī'ras. 3 The descendants of Gō'mer: Ash'ke·naz, Rī'phath, and Tō·gar'mah. 4 The descendants of Jā'van: E·lī'shah, Tar'shish, Kit'tim, and Rod'a·nim. y 5 From these the coastland peoples spread. These are the descendants of Jā'pheth z in their lands, with their own language, by their families, in their nations.

6 The descendants of Ham: Cush, Egypt, Put, and Cā'naan. 7 The descendants of Cush: Sē'ba, Hav'i·lah, Sab'-tah, Rā'a·mah, and Sab'te·ca. The descendants of Rā'a·mah: Shē'ba and Dē'dan. 8 Cush became the father of Nim'rod; he was the first on earth to become a mighty warrior. 9 He was a mighty hunter before the LORD; therefore it is said, "Like Nim'rod a mighty hunter before the LORD." 10 The beginning of his kingdom was Bā'bel, Ē'rech, and Ac'cad, all of them in the land of Shī'nar. 11 From that land he went into Assyria, and built Nin'e·veh, Re·hō'both-ir, Cā'lah, and 12 Rē'sen between Nin'e·veh and Cā'lah; that is the great city. 13 Egypt became the father of Lū'dim, An'a·mim, Le·hā'bim, Naph'tū·him, 14 Path·rū'sim, Cas·lū'-him, and Caph'to·rim, from which the Phi·lis'tines come. a

15 Cā'naan became the father of Sī'don his firstborn, and Heth, 16 and the Jeb'ū·sītes, the Am'o·rītes, the Gir'ga·shītes, 17 the Hī'vītes, the Ar'-kītes, the Sī'nītes, 18 the Ar'vad·ītes, the Zem'a·rītes, and the Hā'math·ītes. Afterward the families of the Cā'-naan·ītes spread abroad. 19 And the territory of the Cā'naan·ītes extended from Sī'don, in the direction of Ge'rar, as far as Gā'za, and in the direction of Sod'om, Go·mor'rah, Ad'mah, and Ze·boi'im, as far as Lā'sha. 20 These are the descendants of Ham, by their families, their languages, their lands, and their nations.

21 To Shem also, the father of all the children of Ē'ber, the elder brother of Jā'pheth, children were born. 22 The descendants of Shem: Ē'lam, As'shur, Ar·pach'shad, Lud, and Ar'am. 23 The descendants of Ar'am: Uz, Hul, Ge'-ther, and Mash. 24 Ar·pach'shad became the father of Shē'lah; and Shē'-lah became the father of Ē'ber. 25 To Ē'ber were born two sons: the name of the one was Pē'leg, b for in his days the earth was divided, and his brother's name was Jok'tan. 26 Jok'tan became the father of Al·mō'dad, Shē'leph, Hā·zar·mā'veth, Jē'rah, 27 Ha·dor'am, Ū'zal, Dik'lah, 28 Ō'bal, A·bim'a·el, Shē'ba, 29 O'phir, Hav'i·lah, and Jō'-bab; all these were the descendants of Jok'tan. 30 The territory in which they

---

x Heb yapht, a play on Japheth
y Heb Mss Sam Gk See 1 Chr 1.7: MT Dodanim   z Compare verses 20, 31.
Heb lacks These are the descendants of Japheth   a Cn: Heb Casluhim, from which the Philistines come, and Caphtorim   b That is Division

lived extended from Mē'sha in the direction of Sē'phar, the hill country of the east. 31 These are the descendants of Shem, by their families, their languages, their lands, and their nations.

32 These are the families of Noah's sons, according to their genealogies, in their nations; and from these the nations spread abroad on the earth after the flood.

The Tower of Babel

11 Now the whole earth had one language and the same words. 2 And as they migrated from the east,c they came upon a plain in the land of Shī'nar and settled there. 3 And they said to one another, "Come, let us make bricks, and burn them thoroughly." And they had brick for stone, and bitumen for mortar. 4 Then they said, "Come, let us build ourselves a city, and a tower with its top in the heavens, and let us make a name for ourselves; otherwise we shall be scattered abroad upon the face of the whole earth." 5 The LORD came down to see the city and the tower, which mortals had built. 6 And the LORD said, "Look, they are one people, and they have all one language; and this is only the beginning of what they will do; nothing that they propose to do will now be impossible for them. 7 Come, let us go down, and confuse their language there, so that they will not understand one another's speech." 8 So the LORD scattered them abroad from there over the face of all the earth, and they left off building the city. 9 Therefore it was called Bā'bel, because there the LORD confusedd the language of all the earth; and from there the LORD scattered them abroad over the face of all the earth.

Descendants of Shem
(1 Chr 1.17–27; Lk 3.34–36)

10 These are the descendants of Shem. When Shem was one hundred years old, he became the father of Ar·pach'shad two years after the flood; 11 and Shem lived after the birth of Ar·pach'shad five hundred years, and had other sons and daughters.

12 When Ar·pach'shad had lived thirty-five years, he became the father of Shē'lah; 13 and Ar·pach'shad lived after the birth of Shē'lah four hundred three years, and had other sons and daughters.

14 When Shē'lah had lived thirty years, he became the father of Ē'ber; 15 and Shē'lah lived after the birth of Ē'ber four hundred three years, and had other sons and daughters.

16 When Ē'ber had lived thirty-four years, he became the father of Pē'leg; 17 and Ē'ber lived after the birth of Pē'leg four hundred thirty years, and had other sons and daughters.

18 When Pē'leg had lived thirty years, he became the father of Rē'ū; 19 and Pē'leg lived after the birth of Rē'ū two hundred nine years, and had other sons and daughters.

20 When Rē'ū had lived thirty-two years, he became the father of Sē'rug; 21 and Rē'ū lived after the birth of Sē'rug two hundred seven years, and had other sons and daughters.

22 When Sē'rug had lived thirty years, he became the father of Nā'hor; 23 and Sē'rug lived after the birth of Nā'hor two hundred years, and had other sons and daughters.

24 When Nā'hor had lived twenty-nine years, he became the father of Tē'rah; 25 and Nā'hor lived after the birth of Tē'rah one hundred nineteen years, and had other sons and daughters.

26 When Tē'rah had lived seventy years, he became the father of Abram, Nā'hor, and Har'an.

Descendants of Terah

27 Now these are the descendants of Tē'rah. Tē'rah was the father of Abram, Nā'hor, and Har'an; and Har'an was the father of Lot. 28 Har'an died before his father Tē'rah in the land of his birth, in Ūr of the Chal·dē'ans. 29 Abram and Nā'hor took wives; the name of Abram's wife was Sar'aī, and the name of Nā'hor's wife was Mil'cah. She was the daughter of Har'an the father of Mil'cah and Is'cah. 30 Now Sar'aī was barren; she had no child.

31 Tē'rah took his son Abram and his grandson Lot son of Har'an, and his daughter-in-law Sar'aī, his son Abram's wife, and they went out together from Ūr of the Chal·dē'ans to go into the land of Cā'naan; but when they came to Har'an, they settled there. 32 The days of Tē'rah were two hundred five years; and Tē'rah died in Har'an.

---

c Or *migrated eastward*   d Heb *balal*, meaning *to confuse*

The Call of Abram
(Acts 7.2–5)

12 Now the LORD said to Abram, "Go from your country and your kindred and your father's house to the land that I will show you. ² I will make of you a great nation, and I will bless you, and make your name great, so that you will be a blessing. ³ I will bless those who bless you, and the one who curses you I will curse; and in you all the families of the earth shall be blessed."*e*

4 So Abram went, as the LORD had told him; and Lot went with him. Abram was seventy-five years old when he departed from Har'an. ⁵ Abram took his wife Sar'aī and his brother's son Lot, and all the possessions that they had gathered, and the persons whom they had acquired in Har'an; and they set forth to go to the land of Cā'naan. When they had come to the land of Cā'naan, ⁶ Abram passed through the land to the place at Shē'chem, to the oak*f* of Mō'reh. At that time the Cā'naan-ītes were in the land. ⁷ Then the LORD appeared to Abram, and said, "To your offspring*g* I will give this land." So he built there an altar to the LORD, who had appeared to him. ⁸ From there he moved on to the hill country on the east of Beth'el, and pitched his tent, with Beth'el on the west and Aī on the east; and there he built an altar to the LORD and invoked the name of the LORD. ⁹ And Abram journeyed on by stages toward the Neg'eb.

Abram and Sarai in Egypt

10 Now there was a famine in the land. So Abram went down to Egypt to reside there as an alien, for the famine was severe in the land. ¹¹ When he was about to enter Egypt, he said to his wife Sar'aī, "I know well that you are a woman beautiful in appearance; ¹² and when the Egyptians see you, they will say, 'This is his wife'; then they will kill me, but they will let you live. ¹³ Say you are my sister, so that it may go well with me because of you, and that my life may be spared on your account." ¹⁴ When Abram entered Egypt the Egyptians saw that the woman was very beautiful. ¹⁵ When the officials of Pharaoh saw her, they praised her to Pharaoh. And the woman was taken into Pharaoh's house. ¹⁶ And for her sake he dealt well with Abram; and he had sheep, oxen, male donkeys, male and female slaves, female donkeys, and camels. ¹⁷ But the LORD afflicted Pharaoh and his house with great plagues because of Sar'aī, Abram's wife. ¹⁸ So Pharaoh called Abram, and said, "What is this you have done to me? Why did you not tell me that she was your wife? ¹⁹ Why did you say, 'She is my sister,' so that I took her for my wife? Now then, here is your wife, take her, and be gone." ²⁰ And Pharaoh gave his men orders concerning him; and they set him on the way, with his wife and all that he had.

Abram and Lot Separate

13 So Abram went up from Egypt, he and his wife, and all that he had, and Lot with him, into the Neg'eb. 2 Now Abram was very rich in livestock, in silver, and in gold. ³ He journeyed on by stages from the Neg'eb as far as Beth'el, to the place where his tent had been at the beginning, between Beth'el and Aī, ⁴ to the place where he had made an altar at the first; and there Abram called on the name of the LORD. ⁵ Now Lot, who went with Abram, also had flocks and herds and tents, ⁶ so that the land could not support both of them living together; for their possessions were so great that they could not live together, ⁷ and there was strife between the herders of Abram's livestock and the herders of Lot's livestock. At that time the Cā'naan-ītes and the Per'iz-zītes lived in the land.

8 Then Abram said to Lot, "Let there be no strife between you and me, and between your herders and my herders; for we are kindred. ⁹ Is not the whole land before you? Separate yourself from me. If you take the left hand, then I will go to the right; or if you take the right hand, then I will go to the left." ¹⁰ Lot looked about him, and saw that the plain of the Jordan was well watered everywhere like the garden of the LORD, like the land of Egypt, in the direction of Zō'ar; this was before the LORD had destroyed Sod'om and Go-mor'rah. ¹¹ So Lot chose for himself all the plain of the Jordan, and Lot journeyed eastward; thus they separated from each other. ¹² Abram settled

---

e Or *by you all the families of the earth shall bless themselves*   *f* Or *terebinth*
g Heb *seed*

in the land of Cā'naan, while Lot settled among the cities of the Plain and moved his tent as far as Sod'om. ¹³Now the people of Sod'om were wicked, great sinners against the LORD.

14 The LORD said to Abram, after Lot had separated from him, "Raise your eyes now, and look from the place where you are, northward and southward and eastward and westward; ¹⁵for all the land that you see I will give to you and to your offspring ʰ forever. ¹⁶I will make your offspring like the dust of the earth; so that if one can count the dust of the earth, your offspring also can be counted. ¹⁷Rise up, walk through the length and the breadth of the land, for I will give it to you." ¹⁸So Abram moved his tent, and came and settled by the oaksⁱ of Mam're, which are at Hē'bron; and there he built an altar to the LORD.

Lot's Captivity and Rescue

14 In the days of King Am'ra·phel of Shī'nar, King Ar'i·och of El·lā'sar, King Ched·or·la·ō'mer of Ē'lam, and King Tī'dal of Goi'im, ²these kings made war with King Bē'ra of Sod'om, King Bir'sha of Go·mor'rah, King Shī'nab of Ad'mah, King Shem·ē'ber of Ze·boi'im, and the king of Bē'la (that is, Zō'ar). ³All these joined forces in the Valley of Sid'dim (that is, the Dead Sea).ʲ ⁴Twelve years they had served Ched·or·la·ō'mer, but in the thirteenth year they rebelled. ⁵In the fourteenth year Ched·or·la·ō'mer and the kings who were with him came and subdued the Reph'a·im in Ash'-te·roth-kar-nā'im, the Zū'zim in Ham, the Ē'mim in Shā'veh-kir·i·a·thā'im, ⁶and the Hor'ites in the hill country of Sē'ir as far as El-par'an on the edge of the wilderness; ⁷then they turned back and came to En-mish'pat (that is, Kā'-desh), and subdued all the country of the A·mal'e·kītes, and also the Am'-o·rītes who lived in Haz'a·zon-tā'mar. ⁸Then the king of Sod'om, the king of Go·mor'rah, the king of Ad'mah, the king of Ze·boi'im, and the king of Bē'la (that is, Zō'ar) went out, and they joined battle in the Valley of Sid'dim ⁹with King Ched·or·la·ō'mer of Ē'lam, King Tī'dal of Goi'im, King Am'ra·phel of Shī'nar, and King Ar'i·och of El·lā'sar, four kings against five. ¹⁰Now the Valley of Sid'dim was full of bitumen pits; and as the kings of Sod'om and Go·mor'rah fled, some fell into them, and the rest fled to the hill country. ¹¹So the enemy took all the goods of Sod'om and Go·mor'rah, and all their provisions, and went their way; ¹²they also took Lot, the son of Abram's brother, who lived in Sod'om, and his goods, and departed.

13 Then one who had escaped came and told Abram the Hebrew, who was living by the oaksⁱ of Mam're the Am'o·rīte, brother of Esh'col and of Ā'ner; these were allies of Abram. ¹⁴When Abram heard that his nephew had been taken captive, he led forth his trained men, born in his house, three hundred eighteen of them, and went in pursuit as far as Dan. ¹⁵He divided his forces against them by night, he and his servants, and routed them and pursued them to Hō'bah, north of Damascus. ¹⁶Then he brought back all the goods, and also brought back his nephew Lot with his goods, and the women and the people.

Abram Blessed by Melchizedek
(Heb 7.1–2)

17 After his return from the defeat of Ched·or·la·ō'mer and the kings who were with him, the king of Sod'om went out to meet him at the Valley of Shā'veh (that is, the King's Valley). ¹⁸And King Mel·chiz'e·dek of Salem brought out bread and wine; he was priest of God Most High.ᵏ ¹⁹He blessed him and said,

"Blessed be Abram by God Most High,ᵏ

maker of heaven and earth;

20 and blessed be God Most High,ᵏ

who has delivered your

enemies into your hand!"

And Abram gave him one tenth of everything. ²¹Then the king of Sod'om said to Abram, "Give me the persons, but take the goods for yourself." ²²But Abram said to the king of Sod'om, "I have sworn to the LORD, God Most High,ᵏ maker of heaven and earth, ²³that I would not take a thread or a sandal-thong or anything that is yours, so that you might not say, 'I have made Abram rich.' ²⁴I will take nothing but what the young men have eaten, and the share of the men who went with me—Ā'ner, Esh'col, and Mam're. Let them take their share."

ʰHeb seed   ⁱOr terebinths   ʲHeb Salt Sea   ᵏHeb El Elyon

G
E
N
E
S
I
S

God's Covenant with Abram
(Heb 11.8–10)

15 After these things the word of the LORD came to Abram in a vision, "Do not be afraid, Abram, I am your shield; your reward shall be very great." ² But Abram said, "O Lord GOD, what will you give me, for I continue childless, and the heir of my house is El·i·e'zer of Damascus?"¹ ³ And Abram said, "You have given me no offspring, and so a slave born in my house is to be my heir." ⁴ But the word of the LORD came to him, "This man shall not be your heir; no one but your very own issue shall be your heir." ⁵ He brought him outside and said, "Look toward heaven and count the stars, if you are able to count them." Then he said to him, "So shall your descendants be." ⁶ And he believed the LORD; and the LORDᵐ reckoned it to him as righteousness.

7 Then he said to him, "I am the LORD who brought you from Ur of the Chal·de'ans, to give you this land to possess." ⁸ But he said, "O Lord GOD, how am I to know that I shall possess it?" ⁹ He said to him, "Bring me a heifer three years old, a female goat three years old, a ram three years old, a turtledove, and a young pigeon." ¹⁰ He brought him all these and cut them in two, laying each half over against the other; but he did not cut the birds in two. ¹¹ And when birds of prey came down on the carcasses, Abram drove them away.

12 As the sun was going down, a deep sleep fell upon Abram, and a deep and terrifying darkness descended upon him. ¹³ Then the LORDᵐ said to Abram, "Know this for certain, that your offspring shall be aliens in a land that is not theirs, and shall be slaves there, and they shall be oppressed for four hundred years; ¹⁴ but I will bring judgment on the nation that they serve, and afterward they shall come out with great possessions. ¹⁵ As for yourself, you shall go to your ancestors in peace; you shall be buried in a good old age. ¹⁶ And they shall come back here in the fourth generation; for the iniquity of the Am'o·rītes is not yet complete."

17 When the sun had gone down and it was dark, a smoking fire pot and a flaming torch passed between these pieces. ¹⁸ On that day the LORD made a covenant with Abram, saying, "To your descendants I give this land, from the river of Egypt to the great river, the river Euphrates, ¹⁹ the land of the Ken'ītes, the Ken'iz·zītes, the Kad'mon·ītes, ²⁰ the Hit'tītes, the Per'iz·zītes, the Reph'a·im, ²¹ the Am'o·rītes, the Ca'naan·ītes, the Gir'ga·shītes, and the Jeb'ū·sītes."

The Birth of Ishmael

16 Now Sar'aī, Abram's wife, bore him no children. She had an Egyptian slave-girl whose name was Ha'gar, ² and Sar'aī said to Abram, "You see that the LORD has prevented me from bearing children; go in to my slave-girl; it may be that I shall obtain children by her." And Abram listened to the voice of Sar'aī. ³ So, after Abram had lived ten years in the land of Ca'naan, Sar'aī, Abram's wife, took Ha'gar the Egyptian, her slave-girl, and gave her to her husband Abram as a wife. ⁴ He went in to Ha'gar, and she conceived; and when she saw that she had conceived, she looked with contempt on her mistress. ⁵ Then Sar'aī said to Abram, "May the wrong done to me be on you! I gave my slave-girl to your embrace, and when she saw that she had conceived, she looked on me with contempt. May the LORD judge between you and me!" ⁶ But Abram said to Sar'aī, "Your slave-girl is in your power; do to her as you please." Then Sar'aī dealt harshly with her, and she ran away from her.

7 The angel of the LORD found her by a spring of water in the wilderness, the spring on the way to Shur. ⁸ And he said, "Ha'gar, slave-girl of Sar'aī, where have you come from and where are you going?" She said, "I am running away from my mistress Sar'aī." ⁹ The angel of the LORD said to her, "Return to your mistress, and submit to her." ¹⁰ The angel of the LORD also said to her, "I will so greatly multiply your offspring that they cannot be counted for multitude." ¹¹ And the angel of the LORD said to her,

"Now you have conceived and
    shall bear a son;
you shall call him Ish'ma·el,ⁿ
    for the LORD has given heed to
    your affliction.
12 He shall be a wild ass of a man,
    with his hand against everyone,

---

¹Meaning of Heb uncertain   ᵐHeb he   ⁿThat is *God hears*

and everyone's hand against
   him;
and he shall live at odds with all
   his kin."

13 So she named the LORD who spoke to
her, "You are El-roi";^o for she said,
"Have I really seen God and remained
alive after seeing him?"^p 14 Therefore
the well was called Bĕ′er-la′haĭ-roi;^q it
lies between Kā′desh and Bĕ′red.

15 Hā′gar bore Abram a son; and
Abram named his son, whom Hā′gar
bore, Ish′ma·el. 16 Abram was eighty-
six years old when Hā′gar bore him^r
Ish′ma·el.

The Sign of the Covenant
(Ex 12.43—13.2)

17 When Abram was ninety-nine
years old, the LORD appeared to
Abram, and said to him, "I am God
Almighty;^s walk before me, and be
blameless. 2 And I will make my covenant between me and you, and will
make you exceedingly numerous."
3 Then Abram fell on his face; and God
said to him, 4 "As for me, this is my
covenant with you: You shall be the
ancestor of a multitude of nations. 5 No
longer shall your name be Abram,^t
but your name shall be Abraham;^u for
I have made you the ancestor of a multitude of nations. 6 I will make you exceedingly fruitful; and I will make nations of you, and kings shall come
from you. 7 I will establish my covenant between me and you, and your
offspring after you throughout their
generations, for an everlasting covenant, to be God to you and to your off-
spring^v after you. 8 And I will give to
you, and to your offspring after you,
the land where you are now an alien,
all the land of Cā′naan, for a perpetual
holding; and I will be their God."

9 God said to Abraham, "As for you,
you shall keep my covenant, you and
your offspring after you throughout
their generations. 10 This is my covenant, which you shall keep, between
me and you and your offspring after
you: Every male among you shall be
circumcised. 11 You shall circumcise
the flesh of your foreskins, and it shall
be a sign of the covenant between me
and you. 12 Throughout your generations every male among you shall be
circumcised when he is eight days old,
including the slave born in your house
and the one bought with your money
from any foreigner who is not of your
offspring. 13 Both the slave born in

your house and the one bought with
your money must be circumcised. So
shall my covenant be in your flesh an
everlasting covenant. 14 Any uncircumcised male who is not circumcised
in the flesh of his foreskin shall be cut
off from his people; he has broken my
covenant."

15 God said to Abraham, "As for
Sar′aĭ your wife, you shall not call her
Sar′aĭ, but Sarah shall be her name. 16 I
will bless her, and moreover I will give
you a son by her. I will bless her, and
she shall give rise to nations; kings of
peoples shall come from her." 17 Then
Abraham fell on his face and laughed,
and said to himself, "Can a child be
born to a man who is a hundred years
old? Can Sarah, who is ninety years
old, bear a child?" 18 And Abraham
said to God, "O that Ish′ma·el might
live in your sight!" 19 God said, "No, but
your wife Sarah shall bear you a son,
and you shall name him Isaac.^w I will
establish my covenant with him as an
everlasting covenant for his offspring
after him. 20 As for Ish′ma·el, I have
heard you; I will bless him and make
him fruitful and exceedingly numerous; he shall be the father of twelve
princes, and I will make him a great
nation. 21 But my covenant I will establish with Isaac, whom Sarah shall bear
to you at this season next year." 22 And
when he had finished talking with him,
God went up from Abraham.

23 Then Abraham took his son Ish′-
ma·el and all the slaves born in his
house or bought with his money, every
male among the men of Abraham's
house, and he circumcised the flesh of
their foreskins that very day, as God
had said to him. 24 Abraham was
ninety-nine years old when he was circumcised in the flesh of his foreskin.
25 And his son Ish′ma·el was thirteen
years old when he was circumcised in
the flesh of his foreskin. 26 That very
day Abraham and his son Ish′ma·el
were circumcised; 27 and all the men of
his house, slaves born in the house and
those bought with money from a foreigner, were circumcised with him.

^o Perhaps *God of seeing* or *God who sees*
^p Meaning of Heb uncertain   ^q That is
the Well of the Living One who sees me
^r Heb *Abram*   ^s Traditional rendering of
Heb *El Shaddai*   ^t That is *exalted
ancestor*   ^u Here taken to mean
ancestor of a multitude   ^v Heb *seed*
^w That is *he laughs*

G
E
N
E
S
I
S

A Son Promised to Abraham and Sarah
(Heb 13.2)

18 The LORD appeared to Abraham^x by the oaks^y of Mam're, as he sat at the entrance of his tent in the heat of the day. ²He looked up and saw three men standing near him. When he saw them, he ran from the tent entrance to meet them, and bowed down to the ground. ³He said, "My lord, if I find favor with you, do not pass by your servant. ⁴Let a little water be brought, and wash your feet, and rest yourselves under the tree. ⁵Let me bring a little bread, that you may refresh yourselves, and after that you may pass on—since you have come to your servant." So they said, "Do as you have said." ⁶And Abraham hastened into the tent to Sarah, and said, "Make ready quickly three measures^z of choice flour, knead it, and make cakes." ⁷Abraham ran to the herd, and took a calf, tender and good, and gave it to the servant, who hastened to prepare it. ⁸Then he took curds and milk and the calf that he had prepared, and set it before them; and he stood by them under the tree while they ate.

⁹ They said to him, "Where is your wife Sarah?" And he said, "There, in the tent." ¹⁰Then one said, "I will surely return to you in due season, and your wife Sarah shall have a son." And Sarah was listening at the tent entrance behind him. ¹¹Now Abraham and Sarah were old, advanced in age; it had ceased to be with Sarah after the manner of women. ¹²So Sarah laughed to herself, saying, "After I have grown old, and my husband is old, shall I have pleasure?" ¹³The LORD said to Abraham, "Why did Sarah laugh, and say, 'Shall I indeed bear a child, now that I am old?' ¹⁴Is anything too wonderful for the LORD? At the set time I will return to you, in due season, and Sarah shall have a son." ¹⁵But Sarah denied, saying, "I did not laugh"; for she was afraid. He said, "Oh yes, you did laugh."

Judgment Pronounced on Sodom

¹⁶ Then the men set out from there, and they looked toward Sod'om; and Abraham went with them to set them on their way. ¹⁷The LORD said, "Shall I hide from Abraham what I am about to do, ¹⁸seeing that Abraham shall become a great and mighty nation, and all the nations of the earth shall be blessed in him?^a ¹⁹No, for I have chosen^b him, that he may charge his children and his household after him to keep the way of the LORD by doing righteousness and justice; so that the LORD may bring about for Abraham what he has promised him." ²⁰Then the LORD said, "How great is the outcry against Sod'om and Go·mor'rah and how very grave their sin! ²¹I must go down and see whether they have done altogether according to the outcry that has come to me; and if not, I will know."

²² So the men turned from there, and went toward Sod'om, while Abraham remained standing before the LORD.^c ²³Then Abraham came near and said, "Will you indeed sweep away the righteous with the wicked? ²⁴Suppose there are fifty righteous within the city; will you then sweep away the place and not forgive it for the fifty righteous who are in it? ²⁵Far be it from you to do such a thing, to slay the righteous with the wicked, so that the righteous fare as the wicked! Far be that from you! Shall not the Judge of all the earth do what is just?" ²⁶And the LORD said, "If I find at Sod'om fifty righteous in the city, I will forgive the whole place for their sake." ²⁷Abraham answered, "Let me take it upon myself to speak to the Lord, I who am but dust and ashes. ²⁸Suppose five of the fifty righteous are lacking? Will you destroy the whole city for lack of five?" And he said, "I will not destroy it if I find forty-five there." ²⁹Again he spoke to him, "Suppose forty are found there." He answered, "For the sake of forty I will not do it." ³⁰Then he said, "Oh do not let the Lord be angry if I speak. Suppose thirty are found there." He answered, "I will not do it, if I find thirty there." ³¹He said, "Let me take it upon myself to speak to the Lord. Suppose twenty are found there." He answered, "For the sake of twenty I will not destroy it." ³²Then he said, "Oh do not let the Lord be angry if I speak just once more. Suppose ten are found there." He answered, "For

---

^x Heb *him*   ^y Or *terebinths*
^z Heb *seahs*   ^a Or *and all the nations of the earth shall bless themselves by him*
^b Heb *known*   ^c Another ancient tradition reads *while the LORD remained standing before Abraham*

the sake of ten I will not destroy it." ³³And the LORD went his way, when he had finished speaking to Abraham; and Abraham returned to his place.

The Depravity of Sodom

19 The two angels came to Sod'om in the evening, and Lot was sitting in the gateway of Sod'om. When Lot saw them, he rose to meet them, and bowed down with his face to the ground. ²He said, "Please, my lords, turn aside to your servant's house and spend the night, and wash your feet; then you can rise early and go on your way." They said, "No; we will spend the night in the square." ³But he urged them strongly; so they turned aside to him and entered his house; and he made them a feast, and baked unleavened bread, and they ate. ⁴But before they lay down, the men of the city, the men of Sod'om, both young and old, all the people to the last man, surrounded the house; ⁵and they called to Lot, "Where are the men who came to you tonight? Bring them out to us, so that we may know them." ⁶Lot went out of the door to the men, shut the door after him, ⁷and said, "I beg you, my brothers, do not act so wickedly. ⁸Look, I have two daughters who have not known a man; let me bring them out to you, and do to them as you please; only do nothing to these men, for they have come under the shelter of my roof." ⁹But they replied, "Stand back!" And they said, "This fellow came here as an alien, and he would play the judge! Now we will deal worse with you than with them." Then they pressed hard against the man Lot, and came near the door to break it down. ¹⁰But the men inside reached out their hands and brought Lot into the house with them, and shut the door. ¹¹And they struck with blindness the men who were at the door of the house, both small and great, so that they were unable to find the door.

Sodom and Gomorrah Destroyed
(Mt 11.23–24; Lk 17.28–32)

¹²Then the men said to Lot, "Have you anyone else here? Sons-in-law, sons, daughters, or anyone you have in the city—bring them out of the place. ¹³For we are about to destroy this place, because the outcry against its people has become great before the LORD, and the LORD has sent us to destroy it." ¹⁴So Lot went out and said to his sons-in-law, who were to marry his daughters, "Up, get out of this place; for the LORD is about to destroy the city." But he seemed to his sons-in-law to be jesting.

15 When morning dawned, the angels urged Lot, saying, "Get up, take your wife and your two daughters who are here, or else you will be consumed in the punishment of the city." ¹⁶But he lingered; so the men seized him and his wife and his two daughters by the hand, the LORD being merciful to him, and they brought him out and left him outside the city. ¹⁷When they had brought them outside, they[d] said, "Flee for your life; do not look back or stop anywhere in the Plain; flee to the hills, or else you will be consumed." ¹⁸And Lot said to them, "Oh, no, my lords; ¹⁹your servant has found favor with you, and you have shown me great kindness in saving my life; but I cannot flee to the hills, for fear the disaster will overtake me and I die. ²⁰Look, that city is near enough to flee to, and it is a little one. Let me escape there—is it not a little one?—and my life will be saved!" ²¹He said to him, "Very well, I grant you this favor too, and will not overthrow the city of which you have spoken. ²²Hurry, escape there, for I can do nothing until you arrive there." Therefore the city was called Zō'ar.[e] ²³The sun had risen on the earth when Lot came to Zō'ar.

24 Then the LORD rained on Sod'om and Go·mor'rah sulfur and fire from the LORD out of heaven; ²⁵and he overthrew those cities, and all the Plain, and all the inhabitants of the cities, and what grew on the ground. ²⁶But Lot's wife, behind him, looked back, and she became a pillar of salt.

27 Abraham went early in the morning to the place where he had stood before the LORD; ²⁸and he looked down toward Sod'om and Go·mor'rah and toward all the land of the Plain and saw the smoke of the land going up like the smoke of a furnace. 29 So it was that, when God destroyed the cities of the Plain, God remembered Abraham, and sent Lot out of the midst of the overthrow, when he overthrew the cities in which Lot had settled.

d Gk Syr Vg: Heb he   e That is Little

G
E
N
E
S
I
S

The Shameful Origin of Moab and Ammon

30 Now Lot went up out of Zō'ar and settled in the hills with his two daughters, for he was afraid to stay in Zō'ar; so he lived in a cave with his two daughters. ³¹And the firstborn said to the younger, "Our father is old, and there is not a man on earth to come in to us after the manner of all the world. ³²Come, let us make our father drink wine, and we will lie with him, so that we may preserve offspring through our father." ³³So they made their father drink wine that night; and the firstborn went in, and lay with her father; he did not know when she lay down or when she rose. ³⁴On the next day, the firstborn said to the younger, "Look, I lay last night with my father; let us make him drink wine tonight also; then you go in and lie with him, so that we may preserve offspring through our father." ³⁵So they made their father drink wine that night also; and the younger rose, and lay with him; and he did not know when she lay down or when she rose. ³⁶Thus both the daughters of Lot became pregnant by their father. ³⁷The firstborn bore a son, and named him Mō'ab; he is the ancestor of the Mō'ab·ītes to this day. ³⁸The younger also bore a son and named him Ben-am'mī; he is the ancestor of the Am'mon·ītes to this day.

Abraham and Sarah at Gerar

20 From there Abraham journeyed toward the region of the Neg'eb, and settled between Kā'desh and Shur. While residing in Gē'rar as an alien, ²Abraham said of his wife Sarah, "She is my sister." And King A·bim'e·lech of Gē'rar sent and took Sarah. ³But God came to A·bim'e·lech in a dream by night, and said to him, "You are about to die because of the woman whom you have taken; for she is a married woman." ⁴Now A·bim'e·lech had not approached her; so he said, "Lord, will you destroy an innocent people? ⁵Did he not himself say to me, 'She is my sister'? And she herself said, 'He is my brother.' I did this in the integrity of my heart and the innocence of my hands." ⁶Then God said to him in the dream, "Yes, I know that you did this in the integrity of your heart; furthermore it was I who kept you from sinning against me. Therefore I did not let you touch her. ⁷Now

then, return the man's wife; for he is a prophet, and he will pray for you and you shall live. But if you do not restore her, know that you shall surely die, you and all that are yours."

8 So A·bim'e·lech rose early in the morning, and called all his servants and told them all these things; and the men were very much afraid. ⁹Then A·bim'e·lech called Abraham, and said to him, "What have you done to us? How have I sinned against you, that you have brought such great guilt on me and my kingdom? You have done things to me that ought not to be done." ¹⁰And A·bim'e·lech said to Abraham, "What were you thinking of, that you did this thing?" ¹¹Abraham said, "I did it because I thought, There is no fear of God at all in this place, and they will kill me because of my wife. ¹²Besides, she is indeed my sister, the daughter of my father but not the daughter of my mother; and she became my wife. ¹³And when God caused me to wander from my father's house, I said to her, 'This is the kindness you must do me: at every place to which we come, say of me, He is my brother.' " ¹⁴Then A·bim'e·lech took sheep and oxen, and male and female slaves, and gave them to Abraham, and restored his wife Sarah to him. ¹⁵A·bim'e·lech said, "My land is before you; settle where it pleases you." ¹⁶To Sarah he said, "Look, I have given your brother a thousand pieces of silver; it is your exoneration before all who are with you; you are completely vindicated." ¹⁷Then Abraham prayed to God; and God healed A·bim'e·lech, and also healed his wife and female slaves so that they bore children. ¹⁸For the LORD had closed fast all the wombs of the house of A·bim'e·lech because of Sarah, Abraham's wife.

The Birth of Isaac
(Heb 11.11)

21 The LORD dealt with Sarah as he had said, and the LORD did for Sarah as he had promised. ²Sarah conceived and bore Abraham a son in his old age, at the time of which God had spoken to him. ³Abraham gave the name Isaac to his son whom Sarah bore him. ⁴And Abraham circumcised his son Isaac when he was eight days old, as God had commanded him. ⁵Abraham was a hundred years old when his son Isaac was born to him. ⁶Now Sarah said, "God has brought

laughter for me; everyone who hears will laugh with me." ⁷And she said, "Who would ever have said to Abraham that Sarah would nurse children? Yet I have borne him a son in his old age."

Hagar and Ishmael Sent Away
(Gal 4.21–30)

8 The child grew, and was weaned; and Abraham made a great feast on the day that Isaac was weaned. ⁹But Sarah saw the son of Hā′gar the Egyptian, whom she had borne to Abraham, playing with her son Isaac.ᶠ ¹⁰So she said to Abraham, "Cast out this slave woman with her son; for the son of this slave woman shall not inherit along with my son Isaac." ¹¹The matter was very distressing to Abraham on account of his son. ¹²But God said to Abraham, "Do not be distressed because of the boy and because of your slave woman; whatever Sarah says to you, do as she tells you, for it is through Isaac that offspring shall be named for you. ¹³As for the son of the slave woman, I will make a nation of him also, because he is your offspring." ¹⁴So Abraham rose early in the morning, and took bread and a skin of water, and gave it to Hā′gar, putting it on her shoulder, along with the child, and sent her away. And she departed, and wandered about in the wilderness of Bē′er-shē′ba.

15 When the water in the skin was gone, she cast the child under one of the bushes. ¹⁶Then she went and sat down opposite him a good way off, about the distance of a bowshot; for she said, "Do not let me look on the death of the child." And as she sat opposite him, she lifted up her voice and wept. ¹⁷And God heard the voice of the boy; and the angel of God called to Hā′gar from heaven, and said to her, "What troubles you, Hā′gar? Do not be afraid; for God has heard the voice of the boy where he is. ¹⁸Come, lift up the boy and hold him fast with your hand, for I will make a great nation of him." ¹⁹Then God opened her eyes and she saw a well of water. She went, and filled the skin with water, and gave the boy a drink.

20 God was with the boy, and he grew up; he lived in the wilderness, and became an expert with the bow. ²¹He lived in the wilderness of Par′an; and his mother got a wife for him from the land of Egypt.

Abraham and Abimelech Make a Covenant

22 At that time A·bim′e·lech, with Phi′col the commander of his army, said to Abraham, "God is with you in all that you do; ²³now therefore swear to me here by God that you will not deal falsely with me or with my offspring or with my posterity, but as I have dealt loyally with you, you will deal with me and with the land where you have resided as an alien." ²⁴And Abraham said, "I swear it."

25 When Abraham complained to A·bim′e·lech about a well of water that A·bim′e·lech's servants had seized, ²⁶A·bim′e·lech said, "I do not know who has done this; you did not tell me, and I have not heard of it until today." ²⁷So Abraham took sheep and oxen and gave them to A·bim′e·lech, and the two men made a covenant. ²⁸Abraham set apart seven ewe lambs of the flock. ²⁹And A·bim′e·lech said to Abraham, "What is the meaning of these seven ewe lambs that you have set apart?" ³⁰He said, "These seven ewe lambs you shall accept from my hand, in order that you may be a witness for me that I dug this well." ³¹Therefore that place was called Bē′-er-shē′ba;ᵍ because there both of them swore an oath. ³²When they had made a covenant at Bē′er-shē′ba, A·bim′e·lech, with Phi′col the commander of his army, left and returned to the land of the Phi·lis′tines. ³³Abraham ʰ planted a tamarisk tree in Bē′er-shē′ba, and called there on the name of the LORD, the Everlasting God.ⁱ ³⁴And Abraham resided as an alien many days in the land of the Phi·lis′tines.

The Command to Sacrifice Isaac
(Heb 11.17–19)

22 After these things God tested Abraham. He said to him, "Abraham!" And he said, "Here I am." ²He said, "Take your son, your only son Isaac, whom you love, and go to the land of Mō·rī′ah, and offer him there as a burnt offering on one of the mountains that I shall show you." ³So Abraham rose early in the morning, saddled his donkey, and took two of his young men with him, and his son Isaac; he cut the wood for the burnt

ᶠGk Vg: Heb lacks *with her son Isaac* ᵍThat is *Well of seven* or *Well of the oath*   ʰHeb He   ⁱOr *the* LORD, *El Olam*

G
E
N
E
S
I
S

offering, and set out and went to the place in the distance that God had shown him. 4 On the third day Abraham looked up and saw the place far away. 5 Then Abraham said to his young men, "Stay here with the donkey; the boy and I will go over there; we will worship, and then we will come back to you." 6 Abraham took the wood of the burnt offering and laid it on his son Isaac, and he himself carried the fire and the knife. So the two of them walked on together. 7 Isaac said to his father Abraham, "Father!" And he said, "Here I am, my son." He said, "The fire and the wood are here, but where is the lamb for a burnt offering?" 8 Abraham said, "God himself will provide the lamb for a burnt offering, my son." So the two of them walked on together.

9 When they came to the place that God had shown him, Abraham built an altar there and laid the wood in order. He bound his son Isaac, and laid him on the altar, on top of the wood. 10 Then Abraham reached out his hand and took the knife to kill*j* his son. 11 But the angel of the LORD called to him from heaven, and said, "Abraham, Abraham!" And he said, "Here I am." 12 He said, "Do not lay your hand on the boy or do anything to him; for now I know that you fear God, since you have not withheld your son, your only son, from me." 13 And Abraham looked up and saw a ram, caught in a thicket by its horns. Abraham went and took the ram and offered it up as a burnt offering instead of his son. 14 So Abraham called that place "The LORD will provide;"*k* as it is said to this day, "On the mount of the LORD it shall be provided."*l*

15 The angel of the LORD called to Abraham a second time from heaven, 16 and said, "By myself I have sworn, says the LORD: Because you have done this, and have not withheld your son, your only son, 17 I will indeed bless you, and I will make your offspring as numerous as the stars of heaven and as the sand that is on the seashore. And your offspring shall possess the gate of their enemies, 18 and by your offspring shall all the nations of the earth gain blessing for themselves, because you have obeyed my voice." 19 So Abraham returned to his young men, and they arose and went together to Bē′er-shē′ba; and Abraham lived at Bē′er-shē′ba.

The Children of Nahor

20 Now after these things it was told Abraham, "Mil′cah also has borne children, to your brother Nā′hor: 21 Uz the firstborn, Buz his brother, Ke·mū′el the father of Ar′am, 22 Chē′-sed, Hā′zō, Pil′dash, Jid′laph, and Be·thū′el." 23 Be·thū′el became the father of Rebekah. These eight Mil′cah bore to Nā′hor, Abraham's brother. 24 Moreover, his concubine, whose name was Re·ū′mah, bore Tē′bah, Ga′ham, Ta′hash, and Mā′a·cah.

Sarah's Death and Burial

23 Sarah lived one hundred twenty-seven years; this was the length of Sarah's life. 2 And Sarah died at Kir′i·ath-ar′ba (that is, Hē′-bron) in the land of Cā′naan; and Abraham went in to mourn for Sarah and to weep for her. 3 Abraham rose up from beside his dead, and said to the Hit′tites, 4 "I am a stranger and an alien residing among you; give me property among you for a burying place, so that I may bury my dead out of my sight." 5 The Hit′tites answered Abraham, 6 "Hear us, my lord; you are a mighty prince among us. Bury your dead in the choicest of our burial places; none of us will withhold from you any burial ground for burying your dead." 7 Abraham rose and bowed to the Hit′tites, the people of the land. 8 He said to them, "If you are willing that I should bury my dead out of my sight, hear me, and entreat for me Ē′phron son of Zō′-har, 9 so that he may give me the cave of Mach·pē′lah, which he owns; it is at the end of his field. For the full price let him give it to me in your presence as a possession for a burying place." 10 Now Ē′phron was sitting among the Hit′tites; and Ē′phron the Hit′tite answered Abraham in the hearing of the Hit′tites, of all who went in at the gate of his city, 11 "No, my lord, hear me; I give you the field, and I give you the cave that is in it; in the presence of my people I give it to you; bury your dead." 12 Then Abraham bowed down before the people of the land. 13 He said to Ē′phron in the hearing of the people of the land, "If you only will listen to me! I will give the price of the field; accept it from me, so that I may bury my dead

j Or to slaughter   k Or will see; Heb traditionally transliterated Jehovah Jireh
l Or he shall be seen

there." [14] Ē'phron answered Abraham, [15] "My lord, listen to me; a piece of land worth four hundred shekels of silver—what is that between you and me? Bury your dead." [16] Abraham agreed with Ē'phron; and Abraham weighed out for Ē'phron the silver that he had named in the hearing of the Hit'tītes, four hundred shekels of silver, according to the weights current among the merchants.

17 So the field of Ē'phron in Mach·pē'lah, which was to the east of Mam're, the field with the cave that was in it and all the trees that were in the field, throughout its whole area, passed [18] to Abraham as a possession in the presence of the Hit'tītes, in the presence of all who went in at the gate of his city. [19] After this, Abraham buried Sarah his wife in the cave of the field of Mach·pē'lah facing Mam're (that is, Hē'bron) in the land of Cā'naan. [20] The field and the cave that is in it passed from the Hit'tītes into Abraham's possession as a burying place.

The Marriage of Isaac and Rebekah

24 Now Abraham was old, well advanced in years; and the LORD had blessed Abraham in all things. [2] Abraham said to his servant, the oldest of his house, who had charge of all that he had, "Put your hand under my thigh [3] and I will make you swear by the LORD, the God of heaven and earth, that you will not get a wife for my son from the daughters of the Cā'naan·ites, among whom I live, [4] but will go to my country and to my kindred and get a wife for my son Isaac." [5] The servant said to him, "Perhaps the woman may not be willing to follow me to this land; must I then take your son back to the land from which you came?" [6] Abraham said to him, "See to it that you do not take my son back there. [7] The LORD, the God of heaven, who took me from my father's house and from the land of my birth, and who spoke to me and swore to me, 'To your offspring I will give this land,' he will send his angel before you, and you shall take a wife for my son from there. [8] But if the woman is not willing to follow you, then you will be free from this oath of mine; only you must not take my son back there." [9] So the servant put his hand under the thigh of Abraham his master and swore to him concerning this matter.

10 Then the servant took ten of his master's camels and departed, taking all kinds of choice gifts from his master; and he set out and went to Ar'am-nā·ha·rā'im, to the city of Nā'hor. [11] He made the camels kneel down outside the city by the well of water; it was toward evening, the time when women go out to draw water. [12] And he said, "O LORD, God of my master Abraham, please grant me success today and show steadfast love to my master Abraham. [13] I am standing here by the spring of water, and the daughters of the townspeople are coming out to draw water. [14] Let the girl to whom I shall say, 'Please offer your jar that I may drink,' and who shall say, 'Drink, and I will water your camels'—let her be the one whom you have appointed for your servant Isaac. By this I shall know that you have shown steadfast love to my master."

15 Before he had finished speaking, there was Rebekah, who was born to Be·thū'el son of Mil'cah, the wife of Nā'hor, Abraham's brother, coming out with her water jar on her shoulder. [16] The girl was very fair to look upon, a virgin, whom no man had known. She went down to the spring, filled her jar, and came up. [17] Then the servant ran to meet her and said, "Please let me sip a little water from your jar." [18] "Drink, my lord," she said, and quickly lowered her jar upon her hand and gave him a drink. [19] When she had finished giving him a drink, she said, "I will draw for your camels also, until they have finished drinking." [20] So she quickly emptied her jar into the trough and ran again to the well to draw, and she drew for all his camels. [21] The man gazed at her in silence to learn whether or not the LORD had made his journey successful.

22 When the camels had finished drinking, the man took a gold nose-ring weighing a half shekel, and two bracelets for her arms weighing ten gold shekels, [23] and said, "Tell me whose daughter you are. Is there room in your father's house for us to spend the night?" [24] She said to him, "I am the daughter of Be·thū'el son of Mil'cah, whom she bore to Nā'hor." [25] She added, "We have plenty of straw and fodder and a place to spend the night." [26] The man bowed his head and worshiped the LORD [27] and said, "Blessed be the LORD, the God of my master Abraham, who has not forsaken his steadfast love and his faithfulness to-

ward my master. As for me, the LORD has led me on the way to the house of my master's kin."

28 Then the girl ran and told her mother's household about these things. 29 Rebekah had a brother whose name was Lāʹban; and Lāʹban ran out to the man, to the spring. 30 As soon as he had seen the nose-ring, and the bracelets on his sister's arms, and when he heard the words of his sister Rebekah, "Thus the man spoke to me," he went to the man; and there he was, standing by the camels at the spring. 31 He said, "Come in, O blessed of the LORD. Why do you stand outside when I have prepared the house and a place for the camels?" 32 So the man came into the house; and Lāʹban unloaded the camels, and gave him straw and fodder for the camels, and water to wash his feet and the feet of the men who were with him. 33 Then food was set before him to eat; but he said, "I will not eat until I have told my errand." He said, "Speak on."

34 So he said, "I am Abraham's servant. 35 The LORD has greatly blessed my master, and he has become wealthy; he has given him flocks and herds, silver and gold, male and female slaves, camels and donkeys. 36 And Sarah my master's wife bore a son to my master when she was old; and he has given him all that he has. 37 My master made me swear, saying, 'You shall not take a wife for my son from the daughters of the Cāʹ-naan-ites, in whose land I live; 38 but you shall go to my father's house, to my kindred, and get a wife for my son.' 39 I said to my master, 'Perhaps the woman will not follow me.' 40 But he said to me, 'The LORD, before whom I walk, will send his angel with you and make your way successful. You shall get a wife for my son from my kindred, from my father's house. 41 Then you will be free from my oath, when you come to my kindred; even if they will not give her to you, you will be free from my oath.'

42 "I came today to the spring, and said, 'O LORD, the God of my master Abraham, if now you will only make successful the way I am going! 43 I am standing here by the spring of water; let the young woman who comes out to draw, to whom I shall say, "Please give me a little water from your jar to drink," 44 and who will say to me, "Drink, and I will draw for your camels

also"—let her be the woman whom the LORD has appointed for my master's son.'

45 "Before I had finished speaking in my heart, there was Rebekah coming out with her water jar on her shoulder; and she went down to the spring, and drew. I said to her, 'Please let me drink.' 46 She quickly let down her jar from her shoulder, and said, 'Drink, and I will also water your camels.' So I drank, and she also watered the camels. 47 Then I asked her, 'Whose daughter are you?' She said, 'The daughter of Be·thūʹel, Nāʹhor's son, whom Milʹcah bore to him.' So I put the ring on her nose, and the bracelets on her arms. 48 Then I bowed my head and worshiped the LORD, and blessed the LORD, the God of my master Abraham, who had led me by the right way to obtain the daughter of my master's kinsman for his son. 49 Now then, if you will deal loyally and truly with my master, tell me; and if not, tell me, so that I may turn either to the right hand or to the left."

50 Then Lāʹban and Be·thūʹel answered, "The thing comes from the LORD; we cannot speak to you anything bad or good. 51 Look, Rebekah is before you, take her and go, and let her be the wife of your master's son, as the LORD has spoken."

52 When Abraham's servant heard their words, he bowed himself to the ground before the LORD. 53 And the servant brought out jewelry of silver and of gold, and garments, and gave them to Rebekah; he also gave to her brother and to her mother costly ornaments. 54 Then he and the men who were with him ate and drank, and they spent the night there. When they rose in the morning, he said, "Send me back to my master." 55 Her brother and her mother said, "Let the girl remain with us a while, at least ten days; after that she may go." 56 But he said to them, "Do not delay me, since the LORD has made my journey successful; let me go that I may go to my master." 57 They said, "We will call the girl, and ask her." 58 And they called Rebekah, and said to her, "Will you go with this man?" She said, "I will." 59 So they sent away their sister Rebekah and her nurse along with Abraham's servant and his men. 60 And they blessed Rebekah and said to her,

"May you, our sister, become
    thousands of myriads;

may your offspring gain
 possession
 of the gates of their foes."
⁶¹Then Rebekah and her maids rose up, mounted the camels, and followed the man; thus the servant took Rebekah, and went his way.

62 Now Isaac had come from *m* Bĕʹ-er-la-ʹhaī-roi, and was settled in the Negʹeb. ⁶³Isaac went out in the evening to walk *n* in the field; and looking up, he saw camels coming. ⁶⁴And Rebekah looked up, and when she saw Isaac, she slipped quickly from the camel, ⁶⁵and said to the servant, "Who is the man over there, walking in the field to meet us?" The servant said, "It is my master." So she took her veil and covered herself. ⁶⁶And the servant told Isaac all the things that he had done. ⁶⁷Then Isaac brought her into his mother Sarah's tent. He took Rebekah, and she became his wife; and he loved her. So Isaac was comforted after his mother's death.

Abraham Marries Keturah
(1 Chr 1.32–33)

25 Abraham took another wife, whose name was Ke-tūʹrah. ²She bore him Zimʹran, Jokʹshan, Mĕʹdan, Midʹi-an, Ishʹbak, and Shūʹah. ³Jokʹshan was the father of Shĕʹba and Dĕʹdan. The sons of Dĕʹ-dan were As-shūʹrim, Le-tūʹshim, and Le-umʹmim. ⁴The sons of Midʹi-an were Ĕʹphah, Ĕʹpher, Hăʹnoch, A-bīʹda, and El-dāʹah. All these were the children of Ke-tūʹrah. ⁵Abraham gave all he had to Isaac. ⁶But to the sons of his concubines Abraham gave gifts, while he was still living, and he sent them away from his son Isaac, eastward to the east country.

The Death of Abraham

7 This is the length of Abraham's life, one hundred seventy-five years. ⁸Abraham breathed his last and died in a good old age, an old man and full of years, and was gathered to his people. ⁹His sons Isaac and Ishʹma-el buried him in the cave of Mach-pēʹlah, in the field of Ĕʹphron son of Zōʹhar the Hitʹtīte, east of Mamʹre, ¹⁰the field that Abraham purchased from the Hitʹtītes. There Abraham was buried, with his wife Sarah. ¹¹After the death of Abraham God blessed his son Isaac. And Isaac settled at Bĕʹer-la-ʹhaī-roi.

Ishmael's Descendants
(1 Chr 1.29–31)

12 These are the descendants of Ishʹma-el, Abraham's son, whom Hăʹ-gar the Egyptian, Sarah's slave-girl, bore to Abraham. ¹³These are the names of the sons of Ishʹma-el, named in the order of their birth: Ne-bāʹi-oth, the firstborn of Ishʹma-el; and Kĕʹdar, Adʹbĕ-el, Mibʹsam, ¹⁴Mishʹma, Dū-ʹmah, Masʹsa, ¹⁵Hăʹdad, Tĕʹma, Jĕʹtur, Năʹphish, and Kedʹe-mah. ¹⁶These are the sons of Ishʹma-el and these are their names, by their villages and by their encampments, twelve princes according to their tribes. ¹⁷(This is the length of the life of Ishʹma-el, one hundred thirty-seven years; he breathed his last and died, and was gathered to his people.) ¹⁸They settled from Havʹ-i-lah to Shur, which is opposite Egypt in the direction of Assyria; he settled down *o* alongside of *p* all his people.

The Birth and Youth
of Esau and Jacob
(Rom 9.10–12)

19 These are the descendants of Isaac, Abraham's son: Abraham was the father of Isaac, ²⁰and Isaac was forty years old when he married Rebekah, daughter of Be-thūʹel the Ar-a-mĕʹan of Padʹdan-arʹam, sister of Lāʹban the Ar-a-mĕʹan. ²¹Isaac prayed to the LORD for his wife, because she was barren; and the LORD granted his prayer, and his wife Rebekah conceived. ²²The children struggled together within her; and she said, "If it is to be this way, why do I live?" *q* So she went to inquire of the LORD. ²³And the LORD said to her,

"Two nations are in your womb,
   and two peoples born of you
      shall be divided;
the one shall be stronger than
      the other,
   the elder shall serve the
      younger."
²⁴When her time to give birth was at hand, there were twins in her womb. ²⁵The first came out red, all his body like a hairy mantle; so they named him Esau. ²⁶Afterward his brother came out, with his hand gripping Esau's

m Syr Tg: Heb *from coming to*
n Meaning of Heb word is uncertain
o Heb *he fell*   *p* Or *down in opposition*
to   *q* Syr: Meaning of Heb uncertain

G
E
N
E
S
I
S

heel; so he was named Jacob.[r] Isaac was sixty years old when she bore them.

27 When the boys grew up, Esau was a skillful hunter, a man of the field, while Jacob was a quiet man, living in tents. [28]Isaac loved Esau, because he was fond of game; but Rebekah loved Jacob.

Esau Sells His Birthright
(Heb 12.16)

29 Once when Jacob was cooking a stew, Esau came in from the field, and he was famished. [30]Esau said to Jacob, "Let me eat some of that red stuff, for I am famished!" (Therefore he was called E'dom.[s]) [31]Jacob said, "First sell me your birthright." [32]Esau said, "I am about to die; of what use is a birthright to me?" [33]Jacob said, "Swear to me first."[t] So he swore to him, and sold his birthright to Jacob. [34]Then Jacob gave Esau bread and lentil stew, and he ate and drank, and rose and went his way. Thus Esau despised his birthright.

Isaac and Abimelech

26 Now there was a famine in the land, besides the former famine that had occurred in the days of Abraham. And Isaac went to Gē'rar, to King A·bim'e·lech of the Phi·lis'tines. [2]The LORD appeared to Isaac[u] and said, "Do not go down to Egypt; settle in the land that I shall show you. [3]Reside in this land as an alien, and I will be with you, and will bless you; for to you and to your descendants I will give all these lands, and I will fulfill the oath that I swore to your father Abraham. [4]I will make your offspring as numerous as the stars of heaven, and will give to your offspring all these lands; and all the nations of the earth shall gain blessing for themselves through your offspring, [5]because Abraham obeyed my voice and kept my charge, my commandments, my statutes, and my laws."

6 So Isaac settled in Gē'rar. [7]When the men of the place asked him about his wife, he said, "She is my sister"; for he was afraid to say, "My wife," thinking, "or else the men of the place might kill me for the sake of Rebekah, because she is attractive in appearance." [8]When Isaac had been there a long time, King A·bim'e·lech of the Phi·lis'tines looked out of a window and saw him fondling his wife Rebekah. [9]So

A·bim'e·lech called for Isaac, and said, "So she is your wife! Why then did you say, 'She is my sister'?" Isaac said to him, "Because I thought I might die because of her." [10]A·bim'e·lech said, "What is this you have done to us? One of the people might easily have lain with your wife, and you would have brought guilt upon us." [11]So A·bim'e·lech warned all the people, saying, "Whoever touches this man or his wife shall be put to death."

12 Isaac sowed seed in that land, and in the same year reaped a hundredfold. The LORD blessed him, [13]and the man became rich; he prospered more and more until he became very wealthy. [14]He had possessions of flocks and herds, and a great household, so that the Phi·lis'tines envied him. [15](Now the Phi·lis'tines had stopped up and filled with earth all the wells that his father's servants had dug in the days of his father Abraham.) [16]And A·bim'e·lech said to Isaac, "Go away from us; you have become too powerful for us."

17 So Isaac departed from there and camped in the valley of Gē'rar and settled there. [18]Isaac dug again the wells of water that had been dug in the days of his father Abraham; for the Phi·lis'tines had stopped them up after the death of Abraham; and he gave them the names that his father had given them. [19]But when Isaac's servants dug in the valley and found there a well of spring water, [20]the herders of Gē'rar quarreled with Isaac's herders, saying, "The water is ours." So he called the well E'sek,[v] because they contended with him. [21]Then they dug another well, and they quarreled over that one also; so he called it Sit'nah.[w] [22]He moved from there and dug another well, and they did not quarrel over it; so he called it Re·ho'both,[x] saying, "Now the LORD has made room for us, and we shall be fruitful in the land."

23 From there he went up to Bē'er-shē'ba. [24]And that very night the LORD appeared to him and said, "I am the God of your father Abraham; do not be afraid, for I am with you and will bless you and make your offspring numer-

---

[r]That is *He takes by the heel* or *He supplants* [s]That is *Red* [t]Heb *today* [u]Heb *him* [v]That is *Contention* [w]That is *Enmity* [x]That is *Broad places* or *Room*

G
E
N
E
S
I
S

ous for my servant Abraham's sake." 25 So he built an altar there, called on the name of the LORD, and pitched his tent there. And there Isaac's servants dug a well.

26 Then A·bim′e·lech went to him from Ge′rar, with A·huz′zath his adviser and Phi′col the commander of his army. 27 Isaac said to them, "Why have you come to me, seeing that you hate me and have sent me away from you?" 28 They said, "We see plainly that the LORD has been with you; so we say, let there be an oath between you and us, and let us make a covenant with you 29 so that you will do us no harm, just as we have not touched you and have done to you nothing but good and have sent you away in peace. You are now the blessed of the LORD." 30 So he made them a feast, and they ate and drank. 31 In the morning they rose early and exchanged oaths; and Isaac set them on their way, and they departed from him in peace. 32 That same day Isaac's servants came and told him about the well that they had dug, and said to him, "We have found water!" 33 He called it Shi′bah; y therefore the name of the city is Be′er-she′ba z to this day.

Esau's Hittite Wives

34 When Esau was forty years old, he married Judith daughter of Be·e′ri the Hit′tite, and Bas′e·math daughter of E′lon the Hit′tite; 35 and they made life bitter for Isaac and Rebekah.

Isaac Blesses Jacob

27 When Isaac was old and his eyes were dim so that he could not see, he called his elder son Esau and said to him, "My son"; and he answered, "Here I am." 2 He said, "See, I am old; I do not know the day of my death. 3 Now then, take your weapons, your quiver and your bow, and go out to the field, and hunt game for me. 4 Then prepare for me savory food, such as I like, and bring it to me to eat, so that I may bless you before I die."

5 Now Rebekah was listening when Isaac spoke to his son Esau. So when Esau went to the field to hunt for game and bring it, 6 Rebekah said to her son Jacob, "I heard your father say to your brother Esau, 7 'Bring me game, and prepare for me savory food to eat, that I may bless you before the LORD before I die.' 8 Now therefore, my son, obey my word as I command you. 9 Go to the flock, and get me two choice kids, so

that I may prepare from them savory food for your father, such as he likes; 10 and you shall take it to your father to eat, so that he may bless you before he dies." 11 But Jacob said to his mother Rebekah, "Look, my brother Esau is a hairy man, and I am a man of smooth skin. 12 Perhaps my father will feel me, and I shall seem to be mocking him, and bring a curse on myself and not a blessing." 13 His mother said to him, "Let your curse be on me, my son; only obey my word, and go, get them for me." 14 So he went and got them and brought them to his mother; and his mother prepared savory food, such as his father loved. 15 Then Rebekah took the best garments of her elder son Esau, which were with her in the house, and put them on her younger son Jacob; 16 and she put the skins of the kids on his hands and on the smooth part of his neck. 17 Then she handed the savory food, and the bread that she had prepared, to her son Jacob.

18 So he went in to his father, and said, "My father"; and he said, "Here I am; who are you, my son?" 19 Jacob said to his father, "I am Esau your firstborn. I have done as you told me; now sit up and eat of my game, so that you may bless me." 20 But Isaac said to his son, "How is it that you have found it so quickly, my son?" He answered, "Because the LORD your God granted me success." 21 Then Isaac said to Jacob, "Come near, that I may feel you, my son, to know whether you are really my son Esau or not." 22 So Jacob went up to his father Isaac, who felt him and said, "The voice is Jacob's voice, but the hands are the hands of Esau." 23 He did not recognize him, because his hands were hairy like his brother Esau's hands; so he blessed him. 24 He said, "Are you really my son Esau?" He answered, "I am." 25 Then he said, "Bring it to me, that I may eat of my son's game and bless you." So he brought it to him, and he ate; and he brought him wine, and he drank. 26 Then his father Isaac said to him, "Come near and kiss me, my son." 27 So he came near and kissed him; and he smelled the smell of his garments, and blessed him, and said,

"Ah, the smell of my son

y A word resembling the word for *oath*
z That is *Well of the oath* or *Well of seven*

is like the smell of a field that
the LORD has blessed.

28 May God give you of the dew of
heaven,
and of the fatness of the earth,
and plenty of grain and wine.

29 Let peoples serve you,
and nations bow down to you.
Be lord over your brothers,
and may your mother's sons
bow down to you.
Cursed be everyone who curses
you,
and blessed be everyone who
blesses you!"

Esau's Lost Blessing
(Heb 12.17)

30 As soon as Isaac had finished
blessing Jacob, when Jacob had
scarcely gone out from the presence of
his father Isaac, his brother Esau came
in from his hunting. 31 He also prepared savory food, and brought it to
his father. And he said to his father,
"Let my father sit up and eat of his
son's game, so that you may bless me."
32 His father Isaac said to him, "Who
are you?" He answered, "I am your
firstborn son, Esau." 33 Then Isaac
trembled violently, and said, "Who
was it then that hunted game and
brought it to me, and I ate it all[a] before
you came, and I have blessed him?—
yes, and blessed he shall be!" 34 When
Esau heard his father's words, he cried
out with an exceedingly great and bitter cry, and said to his father, "Bless
me, me also, father!" 35 But he said,
"Your brother came deceitfully, and he
has taken away your blessing." 36 Esau
said, "Is he not rightly named Jacob?[b]
For he has supplanted me these two
times. He took away my birthright;
and look, now he has taken away my
blessing." Then he said, "Have you not
reserved a blessing for me?" 37 Isaac
answered Esau, "I have already made
him your lord, and I have given him all
his brothers as servants, and with
grain and wine I have sustained him.
What then can I do for you, my son?"
38 Esau said to his father, "Have you
only one blessing, father? Bless me,
me also, father!" And Esau lifted up his
voice and wept.

39 Then his father Isaac answered
him:

"See, away from[c] the fatness of
the earth shall your home
be,

and away from[d] the dew of
heaven on high.

40 By your sword you shall live,
and you shall serve your
brother;
but when you break loose,[e]
you shall break his yoke from
your neck."

Jacob Escapes Esau's Fury

41 Now Esau hated Jacob because
of the blessing with which his father
had blessed him, and Esau said to himself, "The days of mourning for my father are approaching; then I will kill
my brother Jacob." 42 But the words of
her elder son Esau were told to Rebekah; so she sent and called her
younger son Jacob and said to him,
"Your brother Esau is consoling himself by planning to kill you. 43 Now
therefore, my son, obey my voice; flee
at once to my brother La'ban in
Har'an, 44 and stay with him a while,
until your brother's fury turns away—
45 until your brother's anger against
you turns away, and he forgets what
you have done to him; then I will send,
and bring you back from there. Why
should I lose both of you in one day?"

46 Then Rebekah said to Isaac, "I
am weary of my life because of the
Hit'tite women. If Jacob marries one of
the Hit'tite women such as these, one
of the women of the land, what good
will my life be to me?"

28 Then Isaac called Jacob and
blessed him, and charged him,
"You shall not marry one of the Ca'-
naan·ite women. 2 Go at once to Pad'-
dan-ar'am to the house of Be·thu'el,
your mother's father; and take as wife
from there one of the daughters of La'-
ban, your mother's brother. 3 May God
Almighty[f] bless you and make you
fruitful and numerous, that you may
become a company of peoples. 4 May
he give to you the blessing of Abraham, to you and to your offspring with
you, so that you may take possession
of the land where you now live as an
alien—land that God gave to Abraham." 5 Thus Isaac sent Jacob away;
and he went to Pad'dan-ar'am, to La'-
ban son of Be·thu'el the Ar·a·me'an,

---

[a] Cn: Heb *of all*   [b] That is *He supplants*
or *He takes by the heel*   [c] Or *See, of*
[d] Or *and of*   [e] Meaning of Heb
uncertain   [f] Traditional rendering of
Heb *El Shaddai*

the brother of Rebekah, Jacob's and Esau's mother.

Esau Marries Ishmael's Daughter

6 Now Esau saw that Isaac had blessed Jacob and sent him away to Pad'dan-ar'am to take a wife from there, and that as he blessed him he charged him, "You shall not marry one of the Cā'naan·ite women," 7 and that Jacob had obeyed his father and his mother and gone to Pad'dan-ar'am. 8 So when Esau saw that the Cā'naan·ite women did not please his father Isaac, 9 Esau went to Ish'ma·el and took Mā'ha·lath daughter of Abraham's son Ish'ma·el, and sister of Ne·bā'i·oth, to be his wife in addition to the wives he had.

Jacob's Dream at Bethel

10 Jacob left Bē'er-shē'ba and went toward Har'an. 11 He came to a certain place and stayed there for the night, because the sun had set. Taking one of the stones of the place, he put it under his head and lay down in that place. 12 And he dreamed that there was a ladder g set up on the earth, the top of it reaching to heaven; and the angels of God were ascending and descending on it. 13 And the LORD stood beside him h and said, "I am the LORD, the God of Abraham your father and the God of Isaac; the land on which you lie I will give to you and to your offspring; 14 and your offspring shall be like the dust of the earth, and you shall spread abroad to the west and to the east and to the north and to the south; and all the families of the earth shall be blessed i in you and in your offspring. 15 Know that I am with you and will keep you wherever you go, and will bring you back to this land; for I will not leave you until I have done what I have promised you." 16 Then Jacob woke from his sleep and said, "Surely the LORD is in this place—and I did not know it!" 17 And he was afraid, and said, "How awesome is this place! This is none other than the house of God, and this is the gate of heaven."

18 So Jacob rose early in the morning, and he took the stone that he had put under his head and set it up for a pillar and poured oil on the top of it. 19 He called that place Beth'el; j but the name of the city was Luz at the first. 20 Then Jacob made a vow, saying, "If God will be with me, and will keep me in this way that I go, and will give me bread to eat and clothing to wear, 21 so that I come again to my father's house in peace, then the LORD shall be my God, 22 and this stone, which I have set up for a pillar, shall be God's house; and of all that you give me I will surely give one tenth to you."

Jacob Meets Rachel

29 Then Jacob went on his journey, and came to the land of the people of the east. 2 As he looked, he saw a well in the field and three flocks of sheep lying there beside it; for out of that well the flocks were watered. The stone on the well's mouth was large, 3 and when all the flocks were gathered there, the shepherds would roll the stone from the mouth of the well, and water the sheep, and put the stone back in its place on the mouth of the well.

4 Jacob said to them, "My brothers, where do you come from?" They said, "We are from Har'an." 5 He said to them, "Do you know Lā'ban son of Na'hor?" They said, "We do." 6 He said to them, "Is it well with him?" "Yes," they replied, "and here is his daughter Rachel, coming with the sheep." 7 He said, "Look, it is still broad daylight; it is not time for the animals to be gathered together. Water the sheep, and go, pasture them." 8 But they said, "We cannot until all the flocks are gathered together, and the stone is rolled from the mouth of the well; then we water the sheep."

9 While he was still speaking with them, Rachel came with her father's sheep; for she kept them. 10 Now when Jacob saw Rachel, the daughter of his mother's brother Lā'ban, and the sheep of his mother's brother Lā'ban, Jacob went up and rolled the stone from the well's mouth, and watered the flock of his mother's brother Lā'ban. 11 Then Jacob kissed Rachel, and wept aloud. 12 And Jacob told Rachel that he was her father's kinsman, and that he was Rebekah's son; and she ran and told her father.

13 When Lā'ban heard the news about his sister's son Jacob, he ran to meet him; he embraced him and kissed him, and brought him to his house. Jacob k told Lā'ban all these things, 14 and Lā'ban said to him, "Surely you

g Or stairway or ramp h Or stood above it i Or shall bless themselves j That is House of God k Heb He are my bone and my flesh!" And he stayed with him a month.

Jacob Marries Laban's Daughters

15 Then Lā′ban said to Jacob, "Because you are my kinsman, should you therefore serve me for nothing? Tell me, what shall your wages be?" 16 Now Lā′ban had two daughters; the name of the elder was Leah, and the name of the younger was Rachel. 17 Leah's eyes were lovely,[l] and Rachel was graceful and beautiful. 18 Jacob loved Rachel; so he said, "I will serve you seven years for your younger daughter Rachel." 19 Lā′ban said, "It is better that I give her to you than that I should give her to any other man; stay with me." 20 So Jacob served seven years for Rachel, and they seemed to him but a few days because of the love he had for her.

21 Then Jacob said to Lā′ban, "Give me my wife that I may go in to her, for my time is completed." 22 So Lā′ban gathered together all the people of the place, and made a feast. 23 But in the evening he took his daughter Leah and brought her to Jacob; and he went in to her. 24 (Lā′ban gave his maid Zil′pah to his daughter Leah to be her maid.) 25 When morning came, it was Leah! And Jacob said to Lā′ban, "What is this you have done to me? Did I not serve with you for Rachel? Why then have you deceived me?" 26 Lā′ban said, "This is not done in our country— giving the younger before the first-born. 27 Complete the week of this one, and we will give you the other also in return for serving me another seven years." 28 Jacob did so, and completed her week; then Lā′ban gave him his daughter Rachel as a wife. 29 (Lā′ban gave his maid Bil′hah to his daughter Rachel to be her maid.) 30 So Jacob went in to Rachel also, and he loved Rachel more than Leah. He served Lā′-ban[m] for another seven years.

31 When the LORD saw that Leah was unloved, he opened her womb; but Rachel was barren. 32 Leah conceived and bore a son, and she named him Reuben;[n] for she said, "Because the LORD has looked on my affliction; surely now my husband will love me." 33 She conceived again and bore a son, and said, "Because the LORD has heard[o] that I am hated, he has given me this son also"; and she named him Sim′e·on. 34 Again she conceived and bore a son, and said, "Now this time my husband will be joined[p] to me, be-

cause I have borne him three sons"; therefore he was named Levi. 35 She conceived again and bore a son, and said, "This time I will praise[q] the LORD"; therefore she named him Judah; then she ceased bearing.

30 When Rachel saw that she bore Jacob no children, she envied her sister; and she said to Jacob, "Give me children, or I shall die!" 2 Jacob became very angry with Rachel and said, "Am I in the place of God, who has withheld from you the fruit of the womb?" 3 Then she said, "Here is my maid Bil′hah; go in to her, that she may bear upon my knees and that I too may have children through her." 4 So she gave him her maid Bil′hah as a wife; and Jacob went in to her. 5 And Bil′hah conceived and bore Jacob a son. 6 Then Rachel said, "God has judged me, and has also heard my voice and given me a son"; therefore she named him Dan.[r] 7 Rachel's maid Bil′hah conceived again and bore Jacob a second son. 8 Then Rachel said, "With mighty wrestlings I have wrestled[s] with my sister, and have prevailed"; so she named him Naph′ta·li.

9 When Leah saw that she had ceased bearing children, she took her maid Zil′pah and gave her to Jacob as a wife. 10 Then Leah's maid Zil′pah bore Jacob a son. 11 And Leah said, "Good fortune!" so she named him Gad.[t] 12 Leah's maid Zil′pah bore Jacob a second son. 13 And Leah said, "Happy am I! For the women will call me happy"; so she named him Ash′er.[u]

14 In the days of wheat harvest Reuben went and found mandrakes in the field, and brought them to his mother Leah. Then Rachel said to Leah, "Please give me some of your son's mandrakes." 15 But she said to her, "Is it a small matter that you have taken away my husband? Would you take away my son's mandrakes also?" Rachel said, "Then he may lie with you tonight for your son's mandrakes." 16 When Jacob came from the field in the evening, Leah went out to meet him, and said, "You must come in to me; for I have hired you with my son's mandrakes." So he lay with her that

---

l Meaning of Heb uncertain   *m* Heb *him*
n That is *See, a son*   *o* Heb *shama*
p Heb *lawah*   *q* Heb *hodah*   *r* That is
He judged   *s* Heb *niphtal*   *t* That is
Fortune   *u* That is *Happy*

night. 17 And God heeded Leah, and she conceived and bore Jacob a fifth son. 18 Leah said, "God has given me my hire v because I gave my maid to my husband"; so she named him Is'-sa·char. 19 And Leah conceived again, and she bore Jacob a sixth son. 20 Then Leah said, "God has endowed me with a good dowry; now my husband will honor w me, because I have borne him six sons"; so she named him Zeb'ū·lun. 21 Afterwards she bore a daughter, and named her Dī'nah.

22 Then God remembered Rachel, and God heeded her and opened her womb. 23 She conceived and bore a son, and said, "God has taken away my reproach"; 24 and she named him Joseph, x saying, "May the LORD add to me another son!"

Jacob Prospers at Laban's Expense

25 When Rachel had borne Joseph, Jacob said to Lā'ban, "Send me away, that I may go to my own home and country. 26 Give me my wives and my children for whom I have served you, and let me go; for you know very well the service I have given you." 27 But Lā'ban said to him, "If you will allow me to say so, I have learned by divination that the LORD has blessed me because of you; 28 name your wages, and I will give it." 29 Jacob said to him, "You yourself know how I have served you, and how your cattle have fared with me. 30 For you had little before I came, and it has increased abundantly; and the LORD has blessed you wherever I turned. But now when shall I provide for my own household also?" 31 He said, "What shall I give you?" Jacob said, "You shall not give me anything; if you will do this for me, I will again feed your flock and keep it: 32 let me pass through all your flock today, removing from it every speckled and spotted sheep and every black lamb, and the spotted and speckled among the goats; and such shall be my wages. 33 So my honesty will answer for me later, when you come to look into my wages with you. Every one that is not speckled and spotted among the goats and black among the lambs, if found with me, shall be counted stolen." 34 Lā'ban said, "Good! Let it be as you have said." 35 But that day Lā'ban removed the male goats that were striped and spotted, and all the female goats that were speckled and spotted, every one that had white on it, and ev-

ery lamb that was black, and put them in charge of his sons; 36 and he set a distance of three days' journey between himself and Jacob, while Jacob was pasturing the rest of Lā'ban's flock.

37 Then Jacob took fresh rods of poplar and almond and plane, and peeled white streaks in them, exposing the white of the rods. 38 He set the rods that he had peeled in front of the flocks in the troughs, that is, the watering places, where the flocks came to drink. And since they bred when they came to drink, 39 the flocks bred in front of the rods, and so the flocks produced young that were striped, speckled, and spotted. 40 Jacob separated the lambs, and set the faces of the flocks toward the striped and the completely black animals in the flock of Lā'ban; and he put his own droves apart, and did not put them with Lā'ban's flock. 41 Whenever the stronger of the flock were breeding, Jacob laid the rods in the troughs before the eyes of the flock, that they might breed among the rods, 42 but for the feebler of the flock he did not lay them there; so the feebler were Lā'ban's, and the stronger Jacob's. 43 Thus the man grew exceedingly rich, and had large flocks, and male and female slaves, and camels and donkeys.

Jacob Flees with Family and Flocks

31 Now Jacob heard that the sons of Lā'ban were saying, "Jacob has taken all that was our father's; he has gained all this wealth from what belonged to our father." 2 And Jacob saw that Lā'ban did not regard him as favorably as he did before. 3 Then the LORD said to Jacob, "Return to the land of your ancestors and to your kindred, and I will be with you." 4 So Jacob sent and called Rachel and Leah into the field where his flock was, 5 and said to them, "I see that your father does not regard me as favorably as he did before. But the God of my father has been with me. 6 You know that I have served your father with all my strength; 7 yet your father has cheated me and changed my wages ten times, but God did not permit him to harm me. 8 If he said, 'The speckled shall be your wages,' then all the flock bore speckled; and if he said, 'The striped shall be your wages,' then all the flock bore

v Heb sakar   w Heb zabal   x That is He adds

striped. 9 Thus God has taken away the livestock of your father, and given them to me.

10 During the mating of the flock I once had a dream in which I looked up and saw that the male goats that leaped upon the flock were striped, speckled, and mottled. 11 Then the angel of God said to me in the dream, 'Jacob,' and I said, 'Here I am!' 12 And he said, 'Look up and see that all the goats that leap on the flock are striped, speckled, and mottled; for I have seen all that Lā′ban is doing to you. 13 I am the God of Beth′el, y where you anointed a pillar and made a vow to me. Now leave this land at once and return to the land of your birth.' " 14 Then Rachel and Leah answered him, "Is there any portion or inheritance left to us in our father's house? 15 Are we not regarded by him as foreigners? For he has sold us, and he has been using up the money given for us. 16 All the property that God has taken away from our father belongs to us and to our children; now then, do whatever God has said to you."

17 So Jacob arose, and set his children and his wives on camels; 18 and he drove away all his livestock, all the property that he had gained, the livestock in his possession that he had acquired in Pad′dan-ar′am, to go to his father Isaac in the land of Cā′naan.

19 Now Lā′ban had gone to shear his sheep, and Rachel stole her father's household gods. 20 And Jacob deceived Lā′ban the Ar·a·mē′an, in that he did not tell him that he intended to flee. 21 So he fled with all that he had; starting out he crossed the Euphrates, z and set his face toward the hill country of Gil′e·ad.

Laban Overtakes Jacob

22 On the third day Lā′ban was told that Jacob had fled. 23 So he took his kinsfolk with him and pursued him for seven days until he caught up with him in the hill country of Gil′e·ad. 24 But God came to Lā′ban the Ar·a·mē′an in a dream by night, and said to him, "Take heed that you say not a word to Jacob, either good or bad."

25 Lā′ban overtook Jacob. Now Jacob had pitched his tent in the hill country, and Lā′ban with his kinsfolk camped in the hill country of Gil′e·ad. 26 Lā′ban said to Jacob, "What have you done? You have deceived me, and carried away my daughters like cap-

tives of the sword. 27 Why did you flee secretly and deceive me and not tell me? I would have sent you away with mirth and songs, with tambourine and lyre. 28 And why did you not permit me to kiss my sons and my daughters farewell? What you have done is foolish. 29 It is in my power to do you harm; but the God of your father spoke to me last night, saying, 'Take heed that you speak to Jacob neither good nor bad.' 30 Even though you had to go because you longed greatly for your father's house, why did you steal my gods?"

31 Jacob answered Lā′ban, "Because I was afraid, for I thought that you would take your daughters from me by force. 32 But anyone with whom you find your gods shall not live. In the presence of our kinsfolk, point out what I have that is yours, and take it." Now Jacob did not know that Rachel had stolen the gods. a

33 So Lā′ban went into Jacob's tent, and into Leah's tent, and into the tent of the two maids, but he did not find them. And he went out of Leah's tent, and entered Rachel's. 34 Now Rachel had taken the household gods and put them in the camel's saddle, and sat on them. Lā′ban felt all about in the tent, but did not find them. 35 And she said to her father, "Let not my lord be angry that I cannot rise before you, for the way of women is upon me." So he searched, but did not find the household gods.

36 Then Jacob became angry, and upbraided Lā′ban. Jacob said to Lā′ban, "What is my offense? What is my sin, that you have hotly pursued me? 37 Although you have felt about through all my goods, what have you found of all your household goods? Set it here before my kinsfolk and your kinsfolk, so that they may decide between us two. 38 These twenty years I have been with you; your ewes and your female goats have not miscarried, and I have not eaten the rams of your flocks. 39 That which was torn by wild beasts I did not bring to you; I bore the loss of it myself; of my hand you required it, whether stolen by day or stolen by night. 40 It was like this with me: by day the heat consumed me, and the cold by night, and my sleep fled from my eyes. 41 These twenty years I have been in your house; I served you four-

y Cn: Meaning of Heb uncertain
z Heb the river   a Heb them

teen years for your two daughters, and six years for your flock, and you have changed my wages ten times. ⁴²If the God of my father, the God of Abraham and the Fear*b* of Isaac, had not been on my side, surely now you would have sent me away empty-handed. God saw my affliction and the labor of my hands, and rebuked you last night."

Laban and Jacob Make a Covenant

43 Then La'ban answered and said to Jacob, "The daughters are my daughters, the children are my children, the flocks are my flocks, and all that you see is mine. But what can I do today about these daughters of mine, or about their children whom they have borne? ⁴⁴Come now, let us make a covenant, you and I; and let it be a witness between you and me." ⁴⁵So Jacob took a stone, and set it up as a pillar. ⁴⁶And Jacob said to his kinsfolk, "Gather stones," and they took stones, and made a heap; and they ate there by the heap. ⁴⁷La'ban called it Je'gar-sa·ha·du'tha;*c* but Jacob called it Gal'e·ed.*d* ⁴⁸La'ban said, "This heap is a witness between you and me to-day." Therefore he called it Gal'e·ed, ⁴⁹and the pillar*e* Miz'pah,*f* for he said, "The LORD watch between you and me, when we are absent one from the other. ⁵⁰If you ill-treat my daughters, or if you take wives in addition to my daughters, though no one else is with us, remember that God is witness between you and me."

51 Then La'ban said to Jacob, "See this heap and see the pillar, which I have set between you and me. ⁵²This heap is a witness, and the pillar is a witness, that I will not pass beyond this heap to you, and you will not pass beyond this heap and this pillar to me, for harm. ⁵³May the God of Abraham and the God of Na'hor"—the God of their father—"judge between us." So Jacob swore by the Fear*b* of his father Isaac, ⁵⁴and Jacob offered a sacrifice on the height and called his kinsfolk to eat bread; and they ate bread and tarried all night in the hill country.

55*g* Early in the morning La'ban rose up, and kissed his grandchildren and his daughters and blessed them; then he departed and returned home.

32 Jacob went on his way and the angels of God met him; ²and when Jacob saw them he said, "This is

God's camp!" So he called that place Ma·ha·na'im.*h*

Jacob Sends Presents to Appease Esau

3 Jacob sent messengers before him to his brother Esau in the land of Se'ir, the country of E'dom, ⁴instructing them, "Thus you shall say to my lord Esau: Thus says your servant Jacob, 'I have lived with La'ban as an alien, and stayed until now; ⁵and I have oxen, donkeys, flocks, male and female slaves; and I have sent to tell my lord, in order that I may find favor in your sight.' "

6 The messengers returned to Jacob, saying, "We came to your brother Esau, and he is coming to meet you, and four hundred men are with him." ⁷Then Jacob was greatly afraid and distressed; and he divided the people that were with him, and the flocks and herds and camels, into two companies, ⁸thinking, "If Esau comes to the one company and destroys it, then the company that is left will escape."

9 And Jacob said, "O God of my father Abraham and God of my father Isaac, O LORD who said to me, 'Return to your country and to your kindred, and I will do you good,' ¹⁰I am not worthy of the least of all the steadfast love and all the faithfulness that you have shown to your servant, for with only my staff I crossed this Jordan; and now I have become two companies. ¹¹Deliver me, please, from the hand of my brother, from the hand of Esau, for I am afraid of him; he may come and kill us all, the mothers with the children. ¹²Yet you have said, 'I will surely do you good, and make your offspring as the sand of the sea, which cannot be counted because of their number.' "

13 So he spent that night there, and from what he had with him he took a present for his brother Esau, ¹⁴two hundred female goats and twenty male goats, two hundred ewes and twenty rams, ¹⁵thirty milch camels and their colts, forty cows and ten bulls, twenty female donkeys and ten male donkeys. ¹⁶These he delivered into the hand of his servants, every drove by itself, and said to his servants, "Pass on ahead of

---

b Meaning of Heb uncertain
c In Aramaic *The heap of witness*
d In Hebrew *The heap of witness*
e Compare Sam: MT lacks *the pillar*
f That is *Watchpost*   *g* Ch 32.1 in Heb
h Here taken to mean *Two camps*

G
E
N
E
S
I
S

me, and put a space between drove and drove." [17]He instructed the foremost, "When Esau my brother meets you, and asks you, 'To whom do you belong? Where are you going? And whose are these ahead of you?' [18]then you shall say, 'They belong to your servant Jacob; they are a present sent to my lord Esau; and moreover he is behind us.' " [19]He likewise instructed the second and the third and all who followed the droves, "You shall say the same thing to Esau when you meet him, [20]and you shall say, 'Moreover your servant Jacob is behind us.' " For he thought, "I may appease him with the present that goes ahead of me, and afterwards I shall see his face; perhaps he will accept me." [21]So the present passed on ahead of him; and he himself spent that night in the camp.

Jacob Wrestles at Peniel

22 The same night he got up and took his two wives, his two maids, and his eleven children, and crossed the ford of the Jab′bok. [23]He took them and sent them across the stream, and likewise everything that he had. [24]Jacob was left alone; and a man wrestled with him until daybreak. [25]When the man saw that he did not prevail against Jacob, he struck him on the hip socket; and Jacob's hip was put out of joint as he wrestled with him. [26]Then he said, "Let me go, for the day is breaking." But Jacob said, "I will not let you go, unless you bless me." [27]So he said to him, "What is your name?" And he said, "Jacob." [28]Then the man[l] said, "You shall no longer be called Jacob, but Israel,[j] for you have striven with God and with humans,[k] and have prevailed." [29]Then Jacob asked him, "Please tell me your name." But he said, "Why is it that you ask my name?" And there he blessed him. [30]So Jacob called the place Pe·ni′el,[l] saying, "For I have seen God face to face, and yet my life is preserved." [31]The sun rose upon him as he passed Pe·nu′el, limping because of his hip. [32]Therefore to this day the Israelites do not eat the thigh muscle that is on the hip socket, because he struck Jacob on the hip socket at the thigh muscle.

Jacob and Esau Meet

33 Now Jacob looked up and saw Esau coming, and four hundred men with him. So he divided the chil-

dren among Leah and Rachel and the two maids. [2]He put the maids with their children in front, then Leah with her children, and Rachel and Joseph last of all. [3]He himself went on ahead of them, bowing himself to the ground seven times, until he came near his brother.

4 But Esau ran to meet him, and embraced him, and fell on his neck and kissed him, and they wept. [5]When Esau looked up and saw the women and children, he said, "Who are these with you?" Jacob said, "The children whom God has graciously given your servant." [6]Then the maids drew near, they and their children, and bowed down; [7]Leah likewise and her children drew near and bowed down; and finally Joseph and Rachel drew near, and they bowed down. [8]Esau said, "What do you mean by all this company that I met?" Jacob answered, "To find favor with my lord." [9]But Esau said, "I have enough, my brother; keep what you have for yourself." [10]Jacob said, "No, please; if I find favor with you, then accept my present from my hand; for truly to see your face is like seeing the face of God—since you have received me with such favor. [11]Please accept my gift that is brought to you, because God has dealt graciously with me, and because I have everything I want." So he urged him, and he took it.

12 Then Esau said, "Let us journey on our way, and I will go alongside you." [13]But Jacob said to him, "My lord knows that the children are frail and that the flocks and herds, which are nursing, are a care to me; and if they are overdriven one day, all the flocks will die. [14]Let my lord pass on ahead of his servant, and I will lead on slowly, according to the pace of the cattle that are before me and according to the pace of the children, until I come to my lord in Se′ir."

15 So Esau said, "Let me leave with you some of the people who are with me." But he said, "Why should my lord be so kind to me?" [16]So Esau returned that day on his way to Se′ir. [17]But Jacob journeyed to Suc′coth,[m] and built himself a house, and made booths for

---

[l]Heb he   [j]That is *The one who strives with God* or *God strives*   [k]Or *with divine and human beings*   [l]That is *The face of God*   [m]That is *Booths*

his cattle; therefore the place is called Suc'coth.

Jacob Reaches Shechem

18 Jacob came safely to the city of She'chem, which is in the land of Cā'naan, on his way from Pad'dan-ar'am; and he camped before the city. 19 And from the sons of Hā'mor, She'chem's father, he bought for one hundred pieces of money[n] the plot of land on which he had pitched his tent. 20 There he erected an altar and called it El-Ē·lō'he-Is'rā·el. [o]

The Rape of Dinah

34 Now Dī'nah the daughter of Leah, whom she had borne to Jacob, went out to visit the women of the region. 2 When She'chem son of Hā'mor the Hī'vīte, prince of the region, saw her, he seized her and lay with her by force. 3 And his soul was drawn to Dī'nah daughter of Jacob; he loved the girl, and spoke tenderly to her. 4 So She'chem spoke to his father Hā'mor, saying, "Get me this girl to be my wife."

5 Now Jacob heard that She'chem[p] had defiled his daughter Dī'nah; but his sons were with his cattle in the field, so Jacob held his peace until they came. 6 And Hā'mor the father of She'chem went out to Jacob to speak with him, 7 just as the sons of Jacob came in from the field. When they heard of it, the men were indignant and very angry, because he had committed an outrage in Israel by lying with Jacob's daughter, for such a thing ought not to be done.

8 But Hā'mor spoke with them, saying, "The heart of my son She'chem longs for your daughter; please give her to him in marriage. 9 Make marriages with us; give your daughters to us, and take our daughters for yourselves. 10 You shall live with us; and the land shall be open to you; live and trade in it, and get property in it." 11 She'chem also said to her father and to her brothers, "Let me find favor with you, and whatever you say to me I will give. 12 Put the marriage present and gift as high as you like, and I will give whatever you ask me; only give me the girl to be my wife."

13 The sons of Jacob answered She'chem and his father Hā'mor deceitfully, because he had defiled their sister Dī'nah. 14 They said to them, "We cannot do this thing, to give our sister to one who is uncircumcised, for that would be a disgrace to us. 15 Only on this condition will we consent to you: that you will become as we are and every male among you be circumcised. 16 Then we will give our daughters to you, and we will take your daughters for ourselves, and we will live among you and become one people. 17 But if you will not listen to us and be circumcised, then we will take our daughter and be gone."

18 Their words pleased Hā'mor and Hā'mor's son She'chem. 19 And the young man did not delay to do the thing, because he was delighted with Jacob's daughter. Now he was the most honored of all his family. 20 So Hā'mor and his son She'chem came to the gate of their city and spoke to the men of their city, saying, 21 "These people are friendly with us; let them live in the land and trade in it, for the land is large enough for them; let us take their daughters in marriage, and let us give them our daughters. 22 Only on this condition will they agree to live among us, to become one people: that every male among us be circumcised as they are circumcised. 23 Will not their livestock, their property, and all their animals be ours? Only let us agree with them, and they will live among us." 24 And all who went out of the city gate heeded Hā'mor and his son She'chem; and every male was circumcised, all who went out of the gate of his city.

Dinah's Brothers Avenge Their Sister

25 On the third day, when they were still in pain, two of the sons of Jacob, Sim'e·on and Levi, Dī'nah's brothers, took their swords and came against the city unawares, and killed all the males. 26 They killed Hā'mor and his son She'chem with the sword, and took Dī'nah out of She'chem's house, and went away. 27 And the other sons of Jacob came upon the slain, and plundered the city, because their sister had been defiled. 28 They took their flocks and their herds, their donkeys, and whatever was in the city and in the field. 29 All their wealth, all their little ones and their wives, all that was in the houses, they captured and made their prey. 30 Then Jacob said to Sim'e·on and Levi, "You have brought trouble on me by making me odious to the in-

---

[n]Heb *one hundred qesitah*   [o]That is *God, the God of Israel*   [p]Heb *he*

habitants of the land, the Cā'naan·ites and the Per'iz·zites; my numbers are few, and if they gather themselves against me and attack me, I shall be destroyed, both I and my household." ³¹ But they said, "Should our sister be treated like a whore?"

Jacob Returns to Bethel

35 God said to Jacob, "Arise, go up to Beth'el, and settle there. Make an altar there to the God who appeared to you when you fled from your brother Esau." ² So Jacob said to his household and to all who were with him, "Put away the foreign gods that are among you, and purify yourselves, and change your clothes; ³ then come, let us go up to Beth'el, that I may make an altar there to the God who answered me in the day of my distress and has been with me wherever I have gone." ⁴ So they gave to Jacob all the foreign gods that they had, and the rings that were in their ears; and Jacob hid them under the oak that was near She'chem.

5 As they journeyed, a terror from God fell upon the cities all around them, so that no one pursued them. ⁶ Jacob came to Luz (that is, Beth'el), which is in the land of Ca'naan, he and all the people who were with him, ⁷ and there he built an altar and called the place El-beth'el, q because it was there that God had revealed himself to him when he fled from his brother. ⁸ And Deb'or·ah, Rebekah's nurse, died, and she was buried under an oak below Beth'el. So it was called Al'lon-bac'-uth. r

9 God appeared to Jacob again when he came from Pad'dan-ar'am, and he blessed him. ¹⁰ God said to him, "Your name is Jacob; no longer shall you be called Jacob, but Israel shall be your name." So he was called Israel. ¹¹ God said to him, "I am God Almighty: s be fruitful and multiply; a nation and a company of nations shall come from you, and kings shall spring from you. ¹² The land that I gave to Abraham and Isaac I will give to you, and I will give the land to your offspring after you." ¹³ Then God went up from him at the place where he had spoken with him. ¹⁴ Jacob set up a pillar in the place where he had spoken with him, a pillar of stone; and he poured out a drink offering on it, and poured oil on it. ¹⁵ So Jacob called the place where God had spoken with him Beth'el.

The Birth of Benjamin and the Death of Rachel

16 Then they journeyed from Beth'el; and when they were still some distance from Eph'rath, Rachel was in childbirth, and she had hard labor. ¹⁷ When she was in her hard labor, the midwife said to her, "Do not be afraid; for now you will have another son." ¹⁸ As her soul was departing (for she died), she named him Ben-ō'ni; t but his father called him Benjamin. u ¹⁹ So Rachel died, and she was buried on the way to Eph'rath (that is, Bethlehem), ²⁰ and Jacob set up a pillar at her grave; it is the pillar of Rachel's tomb, which is there to this day. ²¹ Israel journeyed on, and pitched his tent beyond the tower of E'der.

22 While Israel lived in that land, Reuben went and lay with Bil'hah his father's concubine; and Israel heard of it.

Now the sons of Jacob were twelve. ²³ The sons of Leah: Reuben (Jacob's firstborn), Sim'e·on, Levi, Judah, Is'-sa·char, and Zeb'ū·lun. ²⁴ The sons of Rachel: Joseph and Benjamin. ²⁵ The sons of Bil'hah, Rachel's maid: Dan and Naph'ta·lī. ²⁶ The sons of Zil'pah, Leah's maid: Gad and Ash'er. These were the sons of Jacob who were born to him in Pad'dan-ar'am.

The Death of Isaac

27 Jacob came to his father Isaac at Mam're, or Kir'i·ath-ar'ba (that is, Hē'bron), where Abraham and Isaac had resided as aliens. ²⁸ Now the days of Isaac were one hundred eighty years. ²⁹ And Isaac breathed his last; he died and was gathered to his people, old and full of days; and his sons Esau and Jacob buried him.

Esau's Descendants
(1 Chr 1.35–42)

36 These are the descendants of Esau (that is, E'dom). ² Esau took his wives from the Cā'naan·ites: Ā'dah daughter of E'lon the Hit'tīte, Ō·hol·i·bā'mah daughter of An'ah

q That is God of Bethel   r That is Oak of weeping   s Traditional rendering of Heb El Shaddai   t That is Son of my sorrow   u That is Son of the right hand or Son of the South son[v] of Zib′e·on the Hi′vite, [3] and Bas′e·math, Ish′ma·el's daughter, sister of Ne·ba′i·oth. [4] A′dah bore E·li′phaz to Esau; Bas′e·math bore Reu′el; [5] and O·hol·i·ba′mah bore Je′ush, Ja′lam, and Ko′rah. These are the sons of Esau who were born to him in the land of Ca′naan.

6 Then Esau took his wives, his sons, his daughters, and all the members of his household, his cattle, all his livestock, and all the property he had acquired in the land of Ca′naan; and he moved to a land some distance from his brother Jacob. [7] For their possessions were too great for them to live together; the land where they were staying could not support them because of their livestock. [8] So Esau settled in the hill country of Se′ir; Esau is E′dom.

9 These are the descendants of Esau, ancestor of the E′dom·ites, in the hill country of Se′ir. [10] These are the names of Esau's sons: E·li′phaz son of A′dah the wife of Esau; Reu′el, the son of Esau's wife Bas′e·math. [11] The sons of E·li′phaz were Te′man, O′mar, Ze′pho, Ga′tam, and Ke′naz. [12] (Tim′na was a concubine of E·li′phaz, Esau's son; she bore Am′a·lek to E·li′phaz.) These were the sons of A′dah, Esau's wife. [13] These were the sons of Reu′el: Na′hath, Ze′rah, Sham′mah, and Miz′zah. These were the sons of Esau's wife, Bas′e·math. [14] These were the sons of Esau's wife O·hol·i·ba′mah, daughter of An′ah son[w] of Zib′e·on: she bore to Esau Je′ush, Ja′lam, and Ko′rah.

Clans and Kings of Edom

15 These are the clans[x] of the sons of Esau. The sons of E·li′phaz the firstborn of Esau: the clans[x] Te′man, O′mar, Ze′pho, Ke′naz, [16] Ko′rah, Ga′tam, and Am′a·lek; these are the clans[x] of E·li′phaz in the land of E′dom; they are the sons of A′dah. [17] These are the sons of Esau's son Reu′el: the clans[x] Na′hath, Ze′rah, Sham′mah, and Miz′zah; these are the clans[x] of Reu′el in the land of E′dom; they are the sons of Esau's wife Bas′e·math. [18] These are the sons of Esau's wife O·hol·i·ba′mah: the clans[x] Je′ush, Ja′lam, and Ko′rah; these are the clans[x] born of Esau's wife O·hol·i·ba′mah, the daughter of An′ah. [19] These are the sons of Esau (that is, E′dom), and these are their clans.[x]

20 These are the sons of Se′ir the Hor′ite, the inhabitants of the land: Lo′tan, Sho′bal, Zib′e·on, An′ah, [21] Di′shon, E′zer, and Di′shan; these are the clans[x] of the Hor′ites, the sons of Se′ir in the land of E′dom. [22] The sons of Lo′tan were Ho′ri and He′man; and Lo′tan's sister was Tim′na. [23] These are the sons of Sho′bal: Al′van, Man′a·hath, E′bal, She′pho, and O′nam. [24] These are the sons of Zib′e·on: A′i·ah and An′ah; he is the An′ah who found the springs[y] in the wilderness, as he pastured the donkeys of his father Zib′e·on. [25] These are the children of An′ah: Di′shon and O·hol·i·ba′mah daughter of An′ah. [26] These are the sons of Di′shon: Hem′dan, Esh′ban, Ith′ran, and Che′ran. [27] These are the sons of E′zer: Bil′han, Za′a·van, and A′kan. [28] These are the sons of Di′shan: Uz and Ar′an. [29] These are the clans[x] of the Hor′ites: the clans[x] Lo′tan, Sho′bal, Zib′e·on, An′ah, [30] Di′shon, E′zer, and Di′shan; these are the clans[x] of the Hor′ites, clan by clan[z] in the land of Se′ir.

31 These are the kings who reigned in the land of E′dom, before any king reigned over the Israelites. [32] Be′la son of Be′or reigned in E′dom, the name of his city being Din′ha·bah. [33] Be′la died, and Jo′bab son of Ze′rah of Boz′rah succeeded him as king. [34] Jo′bab died, and Hu′sham of the land of the Te′man·ites succeeded him as king. [35] Hu′sham died, and Ha′dad son of Be′dad, who defeated Mid′i·an in the country of Mo′ab, succeeded him as king, the name of his city being A′vith. [36] Ha′dad died, and Sam′lah of Mas·re′kah succeeded him as king. [37] Sam′lah died, and Sha′ul of Re·ho′both on the Euphrates succeeded him as king. [38] Sha′ul died, and Ba′al-ha′nan of Ach′bor succeeded him as king. [39] Ba′al-ha′nan son of Ach′bor died, and Ha′dar succeeded him as king, the name of his city being Pa′u; his wife's name was Me·het′a·bel, the daughter of Ma′tred, daughter of Me·za·hab′.

40 These are the names of the clans[x] of Esau, according to their families and their localities by their names: the clans[x] Tim′na, Al′vah, Je′theth, [41] O·hol·i·ba′mah, E′lah, Pi′non, [42] Ke′naz, Te′man, Mib′zar, [43] Mag′di·el, and I′ram; these are the clans[x] of

E'dom (that is, Esau, the father of E'dom), according to their settlements in the land that they held.

Joseph Dreams of Greatness

37 Jacob settled in the land where his father had lived as an alien, the land of Ca'naan. ²This is the story of the family of Jacob.

Joseph, being seventeen years old, was shepherding the flock with his brothers; he was a helper to the sons of Bil'hah and Zil'pah, his father's wives; and Joseph brought a bad report of them to their father. ³Now Israel loved Joseph more than any other of his children, because he was the son of his old age; and he had made him a long robe with sleeves.ᵃ ⁴But when his brothers saw that their father loved him more than all his brothers, they hated him, and could not speak peaceably to him.

5 Once Joseph had a dream, and when he told it to his brothers, they hated him even more. ⁶He said to them, "Listen to this dream that I dreamed. ⁷There we were, binding sheaves in the field. Suddenly my sheaf rose and stood upright; then your sheaves gathered around it, and bowed down to my sheaf." ⁸His brothers said to him, "Are you indeed to reign over us? Are you indeed to have dominion over us?" So they hated him even more because of his dreams and his words.

9 He had another dream, and told it to his brothers, saying, "Look, I have had another dream: the sun, the moon, and eleven stars were bowing down to me." ¹⁰But when he told it to his father and to his brothers, his father rebuked him, and said to him, "What kind of dream is this that you have had? Shall we indeed come, I and your mother and your brothers, and bow to the ground before you?" ¹¹So his brothers were jealous of him, but his father kept the matter in mind.

Joseph Is Sold by His Brothers

12 Now his brothers went to pasture their father's flock near She'-chem. ¹³And Israel said to Joseph, "Are not your brothers pasturing the flock at She'chem? Come, I will send you to them." He answered, "Here I am." ¹⁴So he said to him, "Go now, see if it is well with your brothers and with the flock; and bring word back to me." So he sent him from the valley of He'-bron.

He came to She'chem, ¹⁵and a man found him wandering in the fields; the man asked him, "What are you seeking?" ¹⁶"I am seeking my brothers," he said; "tell me, please, where they are pasturing the flock." ¹⁷The man said, "They have gone away, for I heard them say, 'Let us go to Do'than.'" So Joseph went after his brothers, and found them at Do'than. ¹⁸They saw him from a distance, and before he came near to them, they conspired to kill him. ¹⁹They said to one another, "Here comes this dreamer. ²⁰Come now, let us kill him and throw him into one of the pits; then we shall say that a wild animal has devoured him, and we shall see what will become of his dreams." ²¹But when Reuben heard it, he delivered him out of their hands, saying, "Let us not take his life." ²²Reuben said to them, "Shed no blood; throw him into this pit here in the wilderness, but lay no hand on him"—that he might rescue him out of their hand and restore him to his father. ²³So when Joseph came to his brothers, they stripped him of his robe, the long robe with sleevesᵇ that he wore; ²⁴and they took him and threw him into a pit. The pit was empty; there was no water in it.

25 Then they sat down to eat; and looking up they saw a caravan of Ish'-ma-el-ites coming from Gil'e-ad, with their camels carrying gum, balm, and resin, on their way to carry it down to Egypt. ²⁶Then Judah said to his brothers, "What profit is it if we kill our brother and conceal his blood? ²⁷Come, let us sell him to the Ish'-ma-el-ites, and not lay our hands on him, for he is our brother, our own flesh." And his brothers agreed. ²⁸When some Mid'i-an-ite traders passed by, they drew Joseph up, lifting him out of the pit, and sold him to the Ish'ma-el-ites for twenty pieces of silver. And they took Joseph to Egypt.

29 When Reuben returned to the pit and saw that Joseph was not in the pit, he tore his clothes. ³⁰He returned to his brothers, and said, "The boy is gone; and I, where can I turn?" ³¹Then they took Joseph's robe, slaughtered a goat, and dipped the robe in the blood. ³²They had the long robe with sleevesᵇ taken to their father, and they

ᵃTraditional rendering (compare Gk): *a coat of many colors*; Meaning of Heb uncertain   ᵇSee note on 37.3

said, "This we have found; see now whether it is your son's robe or not." ³³He recognized it, and said, "It is my son's robe! A wild animal has devoured him; Joseph is without doubt torn to pieces." ³⁴Then Jacob tore his garments, and put sackcloth on his loins, and mourned for his son many days. ³⁵All his sons and all his daughters sought to comfort him; but he refused to be comforted, and said, "No, I shall go down to She′ol to my son, mourning." Thus his father bewailed him. ³⁶Meanwhile the Mid′i·an·ites had sold him in Egypt to Pot′i·phar, one of Pharaoh's officials, the captain of the guard.

Judah and Tamar

38 It happened at that time that Judah went down from his brothers and settled near a certain A·dul′lam·ite whose name was Hi′rah. ²There Judah saw the daughter of a certain Ca′naan·ite whose name was Shu′a; he married her and went in to her. ³She conceived and bore a son; and he named him Er. ⁴Again she conceived and bore a son whom she named O′nan. ⁵Yet again she bore a son, and she named him She′lah. She ᶜ was in Che′zib when she bore him. ⁶Judah took a wife for Er his firstborn; her name was Ta′mar. ⁷But Er, Judah's firstborn, was wicked in the sight of the LORD, and the LORD put him to death. ⁸Then Judah said to O′nan, "Go in to your brother's wife and perform the duty of a brother-in-law to her; raise up offspring for your brother." ⁹But since O′nan knew that the offspring would not be his, he spilled his semen on the ground whenever he went in to his brother's wife, so that he would not give offspring to his brother. ¹⁰What he did was displeasing in the sight of the LORD, and he put him to death also. ¹¹Then Judah said to his daughter-in-law Ta′mar, "Remain a widow in your father's house until my son She′lah grows up"—for he feared that he too would die, like his brothers. So Ta′mar went to live in her father's house.

12 In course of time the wife of Judah, Shu′a's daughter, died; when Judah's time of mourning was over,ᵈ he went up to Tim′nah to his sheepshearers, he and his friend Hi′rah the A·dul′lam·ite. ¹³When Ta′mar was told, "Your father-in-law is going up to Tim′nah to shear his sheep," ¹⁴she put off her widow's garments, put on a veil, wrapped herself up, and sat down at the entrance to E·na′im, which is on the road to Tim′nah. She saw that She′lah was grown up, yet she had not been given to him in marriage. ¹⁵When Judah saw her, he thought her to be a prostitute, for she had covered her face. ¹⁶He went over to her at the road side, and said, "Come, let me come in to you," for he did not know that she was his daughter-in-law. She said, "What will you give me, that you may come in to me?" ¹⁷He answered, "I will send you a kid from the flock." And she said, "Only if you give me a pledge, until you send it." ¹⁸He said, "What pledge shall I give you?" She replied, "Your signet and your cord, and the staff that is in your hand." So he gave them to her, and went in to her, and she conceived by him. ¹⁹Then she got up and went away, and taking off her veil she put on the garments of her widowhood.

20 When Judah sent the kid by his friend the A·dul′lam·ite, to recover the pledge from the woman, he could not find her. ²¹He asked the townspeople, "Where is the temple prostitute who was at E·na′im by the wayside?" But they said, "No prostitute has been here." ²²So he returned to Judah, and said, "I have not found her; moreover the townspeople said, 'No prostitute has been here.' " ²³Judah replied, "Let her keep the things as her own, otherwise we will be laughed at; you see, I sent this kid, and you could not find her."

24 About three months later Judah was told, "Your daughter-in-law Ta′mar has played the whore; moreover she is pregnant as a result of whoredom." And Judah said, "Bring her out, and let her be burned." ²⁵As she was being brought out, she sent word to her father-in-law, "It was the owner of these who made me pregnant." And she said, "Take note, please, whose these are, the signet and the cord and the staff." ²⁶Then Judah acknowledged them and said, "She is more in the right than I, since I did not give her to my son She′lah." And he did not lie with her again.

27 When the time of her delivery came, there were twins in her womb. ²⁸While she was in labor, one put out

---

ᶜGk: Heb *He*   ᵈHeb *when Judah was comforted*

a hand; and the midwife took and bound on his hand a crimson thread, saying, "This one came out first." 29 But just then he drew back his hand, and out came his brother; and she said, "What a breach you have made for yourself!" Therefore he was named Per'ez. e 30 Afterward his brother came out with the crimson thread on his hand; and he was named Zē'rah. f

Joseph and Potiphar's Wife

39 Now Joseph was taken down to Egypt, and Pot'i·phar, an officer of Pharaoh, the captain of the guard, an Egyptian, bought him from the Ish'ma·el·ites who had brought him down there. 2 The LORD was with Joseph, and he became a successful man; he was in the house of his Egyptian master. 3 His master saw that the LORD was with him, and that the LORD caused all that he did to prosper in his hands. 4 So Joseph found favor in his sight and attended him; he made him overseer of his house and put him in charge of all that he had. 5 From the time that he made him overseer in his house and over all that he had, the LORD blessed the Egyptian's house for Joseph's sake; the blessing of the LORD was on all that he had, in house and field. 6 So he left all that he had in Joseph's charge; and, with him there, he had no concern for anything but the food that he ate.

Now Joseph was handsome and good-looking. 7 And after a time his master's wife cast her eyes on Joseph and said, "Lie with me." 8 But he refused and said to his master's wife, "Look, with me here, my master has no concern about anything in the house, and he has put everything that he has in my hand. 9 He is not greater in this house than I am, nor has he kept back anything from me except yourself, because you are his wife. How then could I do this great wickedness, and sin against God?" 10 And although she spoke to Joseph day after day, he would not consent to lie beside her or to be with her. 11 One day, however, when he went into the house to do his work, and while no one else was in the house, 12 she caught hold of his garment, saying, "Lie with me!" But he left his garment in her hand, and fled and ran outside. 13 When she saw that he had left his garment in her hand and had fled outside, 14 she called out to the members of her household and said to

them, "See, my husband g has brought among us a Hebrew to insult us! He came in to me to lie with me, and I cried out with a loud voice; 15 and when he heard me raise my voice and cry out, he left his garment beside me, and fled outside." 16 Then she kept his garment by her until his master came home, 17 and she told him the same story, saying, "The Hebrew servant, whom you have brought among us, came in to me to insult me; 18 but as soon as I raised my voice and cried out, he left his garment beside me, and fled outside."

19 When his master heard the words that his wife spoke to him, saying, "This is the way your servant treated me," he became enraged. 20 And Joseph's master took him and put him into the prison, the place where the king's prisoners were confined; he remained there in prison. 21 But the LORD was with Joseph and showed him steadfast love; he gave him favor in the sight of the chief jailer. 22 The chief jailer committed to Joseph's care all the prisoners who were in the prison, and whatever was done there, he was the one who did it. 23 The chief jailer paid no heed to anything that was in Joseph's care, because the LORD was with him; and whatever he did, the LORD made it prosper.

The Dreams of Two Prisoners

40 Some time after this, the cupbearer of the king of Egypt and his baker offended their lord the king of Egypt. 2 Pharaoh was angry with his two officers, the chief cupbearer and the chief baker, 3 and he put them in custody in the house of the captain of the guard, in the prison where Joseph was confined. 4 The captain of the guard charged Joseph with them, and he waited on them; and they continued for some time in custody. 5 One night they both dreamed—the cupbearer and the baker of the king of Egypt, who were confined in the prison— each with his own dream, and each dream with its own meaning. 6 When Joseph came to them in the morning, he saw that they were troubled. 7 So he asked Pharaoh's officers, who were with him in custody in his master's house, "Why

---

e That is *A breach*   f That is *Brightness*; perhaps alluding to the crimson thread
g Heb *he*

are your faces downcast today?" 8They said to him, "We have had dreams, and there is no one to interpret them." And Joseph said to them, "Do not interpretations belong to God? Please tell them to me."

9 So the chief cupbearer told his dream to Joseph, and said to him, "In my dream there was a vine before me, 10and on the vine there were three branches. As soon as it budded, its blossoms came out and the clusters ripened into grapes. 11Pharaoh's cup was in my hand; and I took the grapes and pressed them into Pharaoh's cup, and placed the cup in Pharaoh's hand." 12Then Joseph said to him, "This is its interpretation: the three branches are three days; 13within three days Pharaoh will lift up your head and restore you to your office; and you shall place Pharaoh's cup in his hand, just as you used to do when you were his cupbearer. 14But remember me when it is well with you; please do me the kindness to make mention of me to Pharaoh, and so get me out of this place. 15For in fact I was stolen out of the land of the Hebrews; and here also I have done nothing that they should have put me into the dungeon."

16 When the chief baker saw that the interpretation was favorable, he said to Joseph, "I also had a dream: there were three cake baskets on my head, 17and in the uppermost basket there were all sorts of baked food for Pharaoh, but the birds were eating it out of the basket on my head." 18And Joseph answered, "This is its interpretation: the three baskets are three days; 19within three days Pharaoh will lift up your head—from you!—and hang you on a pole; and the birds will eat the flesh from you."

20 On the third day, which was Pharaoh's birthday, he made a feast for all his servants, and lifted up the head of the chief cupbearer and the head of the chief baker among his servants. 21He restored the chief cupbearer to his cupbearing, and he placed the cup in Pharaoh's hand; 22but the chief baker he hanged, just as Joseph had interpreted to them. 23Yet the chief cupbearer did not remember Joseph, but forgot him.

Joseph Interprets Pharaoh's Dream

41 After two whole years, Pharaoh dreamed that he was standing by the Nile, 2and there came up out of the Nile seven sleek and fat cows, and they grazed in the reed grass. 3Then seven other cows, ugly and thin, came up out of the Nile after them, and stood by the other cows on the bank of the Nile. 4The ugly and thin cows ate up the seven sleek and fat cows. And Pharaoh awoke. 5Then he fell asleep and dreamed a second time; seven ears of grain, plump and good, were growing on one stalk. 6Then seven ears, thin and blighted by the east wind, sprouted after them. 7The thin ears swallowed up the seven plump and full ears. Pharaoh awoke, and it was a dream. 8In the morning his spirit was troubled; so he sent and called for all the magicians of Egypt and all its wise men. Pharaoh told them his dreams, but there was no one who could interpret them to Pharaoh.

9 Then the chief cupbearer said to Pharaoh, "I remember my faults today. 10Once Pharaoh was angry with his servants, and put me and the chief baker in custody in the house of the captain of the guard. 11We dreamed on the same night, he and I, each having a dream with its own meaning. 12A young Hebrew was there with us, a servant of the captain of the guard. When we told him, he interpreted our dreams to us, giving an interpretation to each according to his dream. 13As he interpreted to us, so it turned out; I was restored to my office, and the baker was hanged."

14 Then Pharaoh sent for Joseph, and he was hurriedly brought out of the dungeon. When he had shaved himself and changed his clothes, he came in before Pharaoh. 15And Pharaoh said to Joseph, "I have had a dream, and there is no one who can interpret it. I have heard it said of you that when you hear a dream you can interpret it." 16Joseph answered Pharaoh, "It is not I; God will give Pharaoh a favorable answer." 17Then Pharaoh said to Joseph, "In my dream I was standing on the banks of the Nile; 18and seven cows, fat and sleek, came up out of the Nile and fed in the reed grass. 19Then seven other cows came up after them, poor, very ugly, and thin. Never had I seen such ugly ones in all the land of Egypt. 20The thin and ugly cows ate up the first seven fat cows, 21but when they had eaten them no one would have known that they had done so, for they were still as ugly as before. Then I awoke. 22I fell asleep

G
E
N
E
S
I
S

a second time[h] and I saw in my dream seven ears of grain, full and good, growing on one stalk, 23 and seven ears, withered, thin, and blighted by the east wind, sprouting after them; 24 and the thin ears swallowed up the seven good ears. But when I told it to the magicians, there was no one who could explain it to me."

25 Then Joseph said to Pharaoh, "Pharaoh's dreams are one and the same; God has revealed to Pharaoh what he is about to do. 26 The seven good cows are seven years, and the seven good ears are seven years; the dreams are one. 27 The seven lean and ugly cows that came up after them are seven years, as are the seven empty ears blighted by the east wind. They are seven years of famine. 28 It is as I told Pharaoh; God has shown to Pharaoh what he is about to do. 29 There will come seven years of great plenty throughout all the land of Egypt. 30 After them there will arise seven years of famine, and all the plenty will be forgotten in the land of Egypt; the famine will consume the land. 31 The plenty will no longer be known in the land because of the famine that will follow, for it will be very grievous. 32 And the doubling of Pharaoh's dream means that the thing is fixed by God, and God will shortly bring it about. 33 Now therefore let Pharaoh select a man who is discerning and wise, and set him over the land of Egypt. 34 Let Pharaoh proceed to appoint overseers over the land, and take one-fifth of the produce of the land of Egypt during the seven plenteous years. 35 Let them gather all the food of these good years that are coming, and lay up grain under the authority of Pharaoh for food in the cities, and let them keep it. 36 That food shall be a reserve for the land against the seven years of famine that are to befall the land of Egypt, so that the land may not perish through the famine."

Joseph's Rise to Power

37 The proposal pleased Pharaoh and all his servants. 38 Pharaoh said to his servants, "Can we find anyone else like this—one in whom is the spirit of God?" 39 So Pharaoh said to Joseph, "Since God has shown you all this, there is no one so discerning and wise as you. 40 You shall be over my house, and all my people shall order themselves as you command; only with re-

gard to the throne will I be greater than you." 41 And Pharaoh said to Joseph, "See, I have set you over all the land of Egypt." 42 Removing his signet ring from his hand, Pharaoh put it on Joseph's hand; he arrayed him in garments of fine linen, and put a gold chain around his neck. 43 He had him ride in the chariot of his second-in-command; and they cried out in front of him, "Bow the knee!"[i] Thus he set him over all the land of Egypt. 44 Moreover Pharaoh said to Joseph, "I am Pharaoh, and without your consent no one shall lift up hand or foot in all the land of Egypt." 45 Pharaoh gave Joseph the name Zaph'e·nath-pa·nē'ah; and he gave him As'e·nath daughter of Pō·ti'phe·ra, priest of On, as his wife. Thus Joseph gained authority over the land of Egypt.

46 Joseph was thirty years old when he entered the service of Pharaoh king of Egypt. And Joseph went out from the presence of Pharaoh, and went through all the land of Egypt. 47 During the seven plenteous years the earth produced abundantly. 48 He gathered up all the food of the seven years when there was plenty[j] in the land of Egypt, and stored up food in the cities; he stored up in every city the food from the fields around it. 49 So Joseph stored up grain in such abundance—like the sand of the sea— that he stopped measuring it; it was beyond measure.

50 Before the years of famine came, Joseph had two sons, whom As'e·nath daughter of Pō·ti'phe·ra, priest of On, bore to him. 51 Joseph named the firstborn Ma·nas'seh,[k] "For," he said, "God has made me forget all my hardship and all my father's house." 52 The second he named E'phra·im,[l] "For God has made me fruitful in the land of my misfortunes."

53 The seven years of plenty that prevailed in the land of Egypt came to an end; 54 and the seven years of famine began to come, just as Joseph had said. There was famine in every country, but throughout the land of Egypt there was bread. 55 When all the land

[h] Gk Syr Vg: Heb lacks I fell asleep a second time   [i] Abrek, apparently an Egyptian word similar in sound to the Hebrew word meaning to kneel   [j] Sam Gk: MT the seven years that were   [k] That is Making to forget   [l] From a Hebrew word meaning to be fruitful

of Egypt was famished, the people cried to Pharaoh for bread. Pharaoh said to all the Egyptians, "Go to Joseph; what he says to you, do." 56 And since the famine had spread over all the land, Joseph opened all the storehouses,*m* and sold to the Egyptians, for the famine was severe in the land of Egypt. 57 Moreover, all the world came to Joseph in Egypt to buy grain, because the famine became severe throughout the world.

Joseph's Brothers Go to Egypt

42 When Jacob learned that there was grain in Egypt, he said to his sons, "Why do you keep looking at one another? 2 I have heard," he said, "that there is grain in Egypt; go down and buy grain for us there, that we may live and not die." 3 So ten of Joseph's brothers went down to buy grain in Egypt. 4 But Jacob did not send Joseph's brother Benjamin with his brothers, for he feared that harm might come to him. 5 Thus the sons of Israel were among the other people who came to buy grain, for the famine had reached the land of Ca'naan.

6 Now Joseph was governor over the land; it was he who sold to all the people of the land. And Joseph's brothers came and bowed themselves before him with their faces to the ground. 7 When Joseph saw his brothers, he recognized them, but he treated them like strangers and spoke harshly to them. "Where do you come from?" he said. They said, "From the land of Ca'naan, to buy food." 8 Although Joseph had recognized his brothers, they did not recognize him. 9 Joseph also remembered the dreams that he had dreamed about them. He said to them, "You are spies; you have come to see the nakedness of the land!" 10 They said to him, "No, my lord; your servants have come to buy food. 11 We are all sons of one man; we are honest men; your servants have never been spies." 12 But he said to them, "No, you have come to see the nakedness of the land!" 13 They said, "We, your servants, are twelve brothers, the sons of a certain man in the land of Ca'naan; the youngest, however, is now with our father, and one is no more." 14 But Joseph said to them, "It is just as I have said to you; you are spies! 15 Here is how you shall be tested: as Pharaoh lives, you shall not leave this place unless your youngest brother comes

here! 16 Let one of you go and bring your brother, while the rest of you remain in prison, in order that your words may be tested, whether there is truth in you; or else, as Pharaoh lives, surely you are spies." 17 And he put them all together in prison for three days.

18 On the third day Joseph said to them, "Do this and you will live, for I fear God: 19 if you are honest men, let one of your brothers stay here where you are imprisoned. The rest of you shall go and carry grain for the famine of your households, 20 and bring your youngest brother to me. Thus your words will be verified, and you shall not die." And they agreed to do so. 21 They said to one another, "Alas, we are paying the penalty for what we did to our brother; we saw his anguish when he pleaded with us, but we would not listen. That is why this anguish has come upon us." 22 Then Reuben answered them, "Did I not tell you not to wrong the boy? But you would not listen. So now there comes a reckoning for his blood." 23 They did not know that Joseph understood them, since he spoke with them through an interpreter. 24 He turned away from them and wept; then he returned and spoke to them. And he picked out Sim'e·on and had him bound before their eyes. 25 Joseph then gave orders to fill their bags with grain, to return every man's money to his sack, and to give them provisions for their journey. This was done for them.

Joseph's Brothers Return to Canaan

26 They loaded their donkeys with their grain, and departed. 27 When one of them opened his sack to give his donkey fodder at the lodging place, he saw his money at the top of the sack. 28 He said to his brothers, "My money has been put back; here it is in my sack!" At this they lost heart and turned trembling to one another, saying, "What is this that God has done to us?"

29 When they came to their father Jacob in the land of Ca'naan, they told him all that had happened to them, saying, 30 "The man, the lord of the land, spoke harshly to us, and charged us with spying on the land. 31 But we said to him, 'We are honest men, we

---

m Gk Vg Compare Syr: Heb *opened all that was in* (or, *among*) *them* are not spies. [32] We are twelve brothers, sons of our father; one is no more, and the youngest is now with our father in the land of Ca′naan.' [33] Then the man, the lord of the land, said to us, 'By this I shall know that you are honest men: leave one of your brothers with me, take grain for the famine of your households, and go your way. [34] Bring your youngest brother to me, and I shall know that you are not spies but honest men. Then I will release your brother to you, and you may trade in the land.' "

35 As they were emptying their sacks, there in each one's sack was his bag of money. When they and their father saw their bundles of money, they were dismayed. [36] And their father Jacob said to them, "I am the one you have bereaved of children: Joseph is no more, and Sim′e·on is no more, and now you would take Benjamin. All this has happened to me!" [37] Then Reuben said to his father, "You may kill my two sons if I do not bring him back to you. Put him in my hands, and I will bring him back to you." [38] But he said, "My son shall not go down with you, for his brother is dead, and he alone is left. If harm should come to him on the journey that you are to make, you would bring down my gray hairs with sorrow to She′ol."

The Brothers Come Again, Bringing Benjamin

43 Now the famine was severe in the land. [2] And when they had eaten up the grain that they had brought from Egypt, their father said to them, "Go again, buy us a little more food." [3] But Judah said to him, "The man solemnly warned us, saying, 'You shall not see my face unless your brother is with you.' [4] If you will send our brother with us, we will go down and buy you food; [5] but if you will not send him, we will not go down, for the man said to us, 'You shall not see my face, unless your brother is with you.' " [6] Israel said, "Why did you treat me so badly as to tell the man that you had another brother?" [7] They replied, "The man questioned us carefully about ourselves and our kindred, saying, 'Is your father still alive? Have you another brother?' What we told him was in answer to these questions. Could we in any way know that he would say, 'Bring your brother down'?" [8] Then Judah said to his father Israel, "Send the boy with me, and let us be on our way, so that we may live and not die—you and we and also our little ones. [9] I myself will be surety for him; you can hold me accountable for him. If I do not bring him back to you and set him before you, then let me bear the blame forever. [10] If we had not delayed, we would now have returned twice."

11 Then their father Israel said to them, "If it must be so, then do this: take some of the choice fruits of the land in your bags, and carry them down as a present to the man—a little balm and a little honey, gum, resin, pistachio nuts, and almonds. [12] Take double the money with you. Carry back with you the money that was returned in the top of your sacks; perhaps it was an oversight. [13] Take your brother also, and be on your way again to the man; [14] may God Almighty[n] grant you mercy before the man, so that he may send back your other brother and Benjamin. As for me, if I am bereaved of my children, I am bereaved." [15] So the men took the present, and they took double the money with them, as well as Benjamin. Then they went on their way down to Egypt, and stood before Joseph.

16 When Joseph saw Benjamin with them, he said to the steward of his house, "Bring the men into the house, and slaughter an animal and make ready, for the men are to dine with me at noon." [17] The man did as Joseph said, and brought the men to Joseph's house. [18] Now the men were afraid because they were brought to Joseph's house, and they said, "It is because of the money, replaced in our sacks the first time, that we have been brought in, so that he may have an opportunity to fall upon us, to make slaves of us and take our donkeys." [19] So they went up to the steward of Joseph's house and spoke with him at the entrance to the house. [20] They said, "Oh, my lord, we came down the first time to buy food; [21] and when we came to the lodging place we opened our sacks, and there was each one's money in the top of his sack, our money in full weight. So we have brought it back with us. [22] Moreover we have brought down with us additional money to buy food. We do not know who put our money in

---

[n] Traditional rendering of Heb El Shaddai

our sacks." ²³He replied, "Rest assured, do not be afraid; your God and the God of your father must have put treasure in your sacks for you; I received your money." Then he brought Sim′e·on out to them. ²⁴When the steward^o had brought the men into Joseph's house, and given them water, and they had washed their feet, and when he had given their donkeys fodder, ²⁵they made the present ready for Joseph's coming at noon, for they had heard that they would dine there.

26 When Joseph came home, they brought him the present that they had carried into the house, and bowed to the ground before him. ²⁷He inquired about their welfare, and said, "Is your father well, the old man of whom you spoke? Is he still alive?" ²⁸They said, "Your servant our father is well; he is still alive." And they bowed their heads and did obeisance. ²⁹Then he looked up and saw his brother Benjamin, his mother's son, and said, "Is this your youngest brother, of whom you spoke to me? God be gracious to you, my son!" ³⁰With that, Joseph hurried out, because he was overcome with affection for his brother, and he was about to weep. So he went into a private room and wept there. ³¹Then he washed his face and came out; and controlling himself he said, "Serve the meal." ³²They served him by himself, and them by themselves, and the Egyptians who ate with him by themselves, because the Egyptians could not eat with the Hebrews, for that is an abomination to the Egyptians. ³³When they were seated before him, the firstborn according to his birthright and the youngest according to his youth, the men looked at one another in amazement. ³⁴Portions were taken to them from Joseph's table, but Benjamin's portion was five times as much as any of theirs. So they drank and were merry with him.

Joseph Detains Benjamin

44 Then he commanded the steward of his house, "Fill the men's sacks with food, as much as they can carry, and put each man's money in the top of his sack. ²Put my cup, the silver cup, in the top of the sack of the youngest, with his money for the grain." And he did as Joseph told him. ³As soon as the morning was light, the men were sent away with their donkeys. ⁴When they had gone only a short distance from the city, Joseph said to his steward, "Go, follow after the men; and when you overtake them, say to them, 'Why have you returned evil for good? Why have you stolen my silver cup?^p ⁵Is it not from this that my lord drinks? Does he not indeed use it for divination? You have done wrong in doing this.' "

6 When he overtook them, he repeated these words to them. ⁷They said to him, "Why does my lord speak such words as these? Far be it from your servants that they should do such a thing! ⁸Look, the money that we found at the top of our sacks, we brought back to you from the land of Ca′naan; why then would we steal silver or gold from your lord's house? ⁹Should it be found with any one of your servants, let him die; moreover the rest of us will become my lord's slaves." ¹⁰He said, "Even so; in accordance with your words, let it be: he with whom it is found shall become my slave, but the rest of you shall go free." ¹¹Then each one quickly lowered his sack to the ground, and each opened his sack. ¹²He searched, beginning with the eldest and ending with the youngest; and the cup was found in Benjamin's sack. ¹³At this they tore their clothes. Then each one loaded his donkey, and they returned to the city.

14 Judah and his brothers came to Joseph's house while he was still there; and they fell to the ground before him. ¹⁵Joseph said to them, "What deed is this that you have done? Do you not know that one such as I can practice divination?" ¹⁶And Judah said, "What can we say to my lord? What can we speak? How can we clear ourselves? God has found out the guilt of your servants; here we are then, my lord's slaves, both we and also the one in whose possession the cup has been found." ¹⁷But he said, "Far be it from me that I should do so! Only the one in whose possession the cup was found shall be my slave; but as for you, go up in peace to your father."

Judah Pleads for Benjamin's Release

18 Then Judah stepped up to him and said, "O my lord, let your servant please speak a word in my lord's ears, and do not be angry with your servant;

^oHeb *the man* ^pGk Compare Vg: Heb lacks *Why have you stolen my silver cup?*

for you are like Pharaoh himself. [19] My lord asked his servants, saying, 'Have you a father or a brother?' [20] And we said to my lord, 'We have a father, an old man, and a young brother, the child of his old age. His brother is dead; he alone is left of his mother's children, and his father loves him.' [21] Then you said to your servants, 'Bring him down to me, so that I may set my eyes on him.' [22] We said to my lord, 'The boy cannot leave his father, for if he should leave his father, his father would die.' [23] Then you said to your servants, 'Unless your youngest brother comes down with you, you shall see my face no more.' [24] When we went back to your servant my father we told him the words of my lord. [25] And when our father said, 'Go again, buy us a little food,' [26] we said, 'We cannot go down. Only if our youngest brother goes with us, will we go down; for we cannot see the man's face unless our youngest brother is with us.' [27] Then your servant my father said to us, 'You know that my wife bore me two sons; [28] one left me, and I said, Surely he has been torn to pieces; and I have never seen him since. [29] If you take this one also from me, and harm comes to him, you will bring down my gray hairs in sorrow to She′ol.' [30] Now therefore, when I come to your servant my father and the boy is not with us, then, as his life is bound up in the boy's life, [31] when he sees that the boy is not with us, he will die; and your servants will bring down the gray hairs of your servant our father with sorrow to She′ol. [32] For your servant became surety for the boy to my father, saying, 'If I do not bring him back to you, then I will bear the blame in the sight of my father all my life.' [33] Now therefore, please let your servant remain as a slave to my lord in place of the boy; and let the boy go back with his brothers. [34] For how can I go back to my father if the boy is not with me? I fear to see the suffering that would come upon my father."

Joseph Reveals Himself to His Brothers

45 Then Joseph could no longer control himself before all those who stood by him, and he cried out, "Send everyone away from me." So no one stayed with him when Joseph made himself known to his brothers. [2] And he wept so loudly that the Egyptians heard it, and the household of

Pharaoh heard it. [3] Joseph said to his brothers, "I am Joseph. Is my father still alive?" But his brothers could not answer him, so dismayed were they at his presence.

4 Then Joseph said to his brothers, "Come closer to me." And they came closer. He said, "I am your brother, Joseph, whom you sold into Egypt. [5] And now do not be distressed, or angry with yourselves, because you sold me here; for God sent me before you to preserve life. [6] For the famine has been in the land these two years; and there are five more years in which there will be neither plowing nor harvest. [7] God sent me before you to preserve for you a remnant on earth, and to keep alive for you many survivors. [8] So it was not you who sent me here, but God; he has made me a father to Pharaoh, and lord of all his house and ruler over all the land of Egypt. [9] Hurry and go up to my father and say to him, 'Thus says your son Joseph, God has made me lord of all Egypt; come down to me, do not delay. [10] You shall settle in the land of Go′shen, and you shall be near me, you and your children and your children's children, as well as your flocks, your herds, and all that you have. [11] I will provide for you there—since there are five more years of famine to come—so that you and your household, and all that you have, will not come to poverty.' [12] And now your eyes and the eyes of my brother Benjamin see that it is my own mouth that speaks to you. [13] You must tell my father how greatly I am honored in Egypt, and all that you have seen. Hurry and bring my father down here." [14] Then he fell upon his brother Benjamin's neck and wept, while Benjamin wept upon his neck. [15] And he kissed all his brothers and wept upon them; and after that his brothers talked with him.

16 When the report was heard in Pharaoh's house, "Joseph's brothers have come," Pharaoh and his servants were pleased. [17] Pharaoh said to Joseph, "Say to your brothers, 'Do this: load your animals and go back to the land of Ca′naan. [18] Take your father and your households and come to me, so that I may give you the best of the land of Egypt, and you may enjoy the fat of the land.' [19] You are further charged to say, 'Do this: take wagons from the land of Egypt for your little ones and for your wives, and bring your father, and come. [20] Give no

thought to your possessions, for the best of all the land of Egypt is yours.' "

21 The sons of Israel did so. Joseph gave them wagons according to the instruction of Pharaoh, and he gave them provisions for the journey. 22 To each one of them he gave a set of garments; but to Benjamin he gave three hundred pieces of silver and five sets of garments. 23 To his father he sent the following: ten donkeys loaded with the good things of Egypt, and ten female donkeys loaded with grain, bread, and provision for his father on the journey. 24 Then he sent his brothers on their way, and as they were leaving he said to them, "Do not quarrel q along the way."

25 So they went up out of Egypt and came to their father Jacob in the land of Cā'naan. 26 And they told him, "Joseph is still alive! He is even ruler over all the land of Egypt." He was stunned; he could not believe them. 27 But when they told him all the words of Joseph that he had said to them, and when he saw the wagons that Joseph had sent to carry him, the spirit of their father Jacob revived. 28 Israel said, "Enough! My son Joseph is still alive. I must go and see him before I die."

Jacob Brings His Whole Family to Egypt
(Ex 6.14–25)

46 When Israel set out on his journey with all that he had and came to Bē'er-shē'ba, he offered sacrifices to the God of his father Isaac. 2 God spoke to Israel in visions of the night, and said, "Jacob, Jacob." And he said, "Here I am." 3 Then he said, "I am God,r the God of your father; do not be afraid to go down to Egypt, for I will make of you a great nation there. 4 I myself will go down with you to Egypt, and I will also bring you up again; and Joseph's own hand shall close your eyes."

5 Then Jacob set out from Bē'er-shē'ba; and the sons of Israel carried their father Jacob, their little ones, and their wives, in the wagons that Pharaoh had sent to carry him. 6 They also took their livestock and the goods that they had acquired in the land of Cā'-naan, and they came into Egypt, Jacob and all his offspring with him, 7 his sons, and his sons' sons with him, his daughters, and his sons' daughters; all his offspring he brought with him into Egypt.

8 Now these are the names of the Israelites, Jacob and his offspring, who came to Egypt. Reuben, Jacob's firstborn, 9 and the children of Reuben: Ha'noch, Pal'lū, Hez'ron, and Car'mī. 10 The children of Sim'e-on: Je-mū'el, Jā'min, O'had, Jā'chin, Zō'har, and Shā'ūl,s the son of a Cā'naan-īte woman. 11 The children of Levi: Ger'-shon, Kō'hath, and Me-rar'ī. 12 The children of Judah: Er, O'nan, Shē'lah, Per'ez, and Zē'rah (but Er and O'nan died in the land of Cā'naan); and the children of Per'ez were Hez'ron and Hā'mul. 13 The children of Is'sa-char: Tō'la, Pū'vah, Jash'ub,t and Shim'-ron. 14 The children of Żeb'ū-lun: Sē'-red, Ē'lon, and Jah'lē-el 15 (these are the sons of Leah, whom she bore to Jacob in Pad'dan-ar'am, together with his daughter Dī'nah; in all his sons and his daughters numbered thirty-three). 16 The children of Gad: Ziph'i-on, Hag'gī, Shū'nī, Ez'bon, Ē'rī, A-rō'dī, and A-rē'lī. 17 The children of Ash'er: Im'nah, Ish'vah, Ish'vī, Bē-rī'ah, and their sister Sē'rah. The children of Be-rī'ah: Hē'ber and Mal'chi-el 18 (these are the children of Zil'pah, whom Lā'ban gave to his daughter Leah; and these she bore to Jacob—sixteen persons). 19 The children of Jacob's wife Rachel: Joseph and Benjamin. 20 To Joseph in the land of Egypt were born Ma-nas'seh and Ē'phra-im, whom As'e-nath daughter of Pō-ti'-phe-ra, priest of On, bore to him. 21 The children of Benjamin: Bē'la, Bē'cher, Ash'bel, Gē'ra, Nā'a-man, Ē'hī, Rosh, Mup'pim, Hup'pim, and Ard 22 (these are the children of Rachel, who were born to Jacob—fourteen persons in all). 23 The children of Dan: Hā'shum. u 24 The children of Naph'ta-lī: Jah'zē-el, Gū'nī, Jē'zer, and Shil'lem 25 (these are the children of Bil'hah, whom Lā'ban gave to his daughter Rachel, and these she bore to Jacob—seven persons in all). 26 All the persons belonging to Jacob who came into Egypt, who were his own offspring, not including the wives of his sons, were sixty-six persons in all. 27 The children of Joseph, who were born to him in Egypt, were two; all the persons of the house of Jacob who came into Egypt were seventy.

---

q Or *be agitated*   r Heb *the God*
s Or *Saul*   t Compare Sam Gk Num 26.24 1 Chr 7.1: MT *Iob*   u Gk: Heb *Hushim*

Jacob Settles in Goshen

28 Israel[v] sent Judah ahead to Joseph to lead the way before him into Gō′shen. When they came to the land of Gō′shen, 29 Joseph made ready his chariot and went up to meet his father Israel in Gō′shen. He presented himself to him, fell on his neck, and wept on his neck a good while. 30 Israel said to Joseph, "I can die now, having seen for myself that you are still alive." 31 Joseph said to his brothers and to his father's household, "I will go up and tell Pharaoh, and will say to him, 'My brothers and my father's household, who were in the land of Cā′naan, have come to me. 32 The men are shepherds, for they have been keepers of livestock; and they have brought their flocks, and their herds, and all that they have.' 33 When Pharaoh calls you, and says, 'What is your occupation?' 34 you shall say, 'Your servants have been keepers of livestock from our youth even until now, both we and our ancestors'—in order that you may settle in the land of Gō′shen, because all shepherds are abhorrent to the Egyptians."

47 So Joseph went and told Pharaoh, "My father and my brothers, with their flocks and herds and all that they possess, have come from the land of Cā′naan; they are now in the land of Gō′shen." 2 From among his brothers he took five men and presented them to Pharaoh. 3 Pharaoh said to his brothers, "What is your occupation?" And they said to Pharaoh, "Your servants are shepherds, as our ancestors were." 4 They said to Pharaoh, "We have come to reside as aliens in the land; for there is no pasture for your servants' flocks because the famine is severe in the land of Cā′naan. Now, we ask you, let your servants settle in the land of Gō′shen." 5 Then Pharaoh said to Joseph, "Your father and your brothers have come to you. 6 The land of Egypt is before you; settle your father and your brothers in the best part of the land; let them live in the land of Gō′shen; and if you know that there are capable men among them, put them in charge of my livestock."

7 Then Joseph brought in his father Jacob, and presented him before Pharaoh, and Jacob blessed Pharaoh. 8 Pharaoh said to Jacob, "How many are the years of your life?" 9 Jacob said to Pharaoh, "The years of my earthly sojourn are one hundred thirty; few and hard have been the years of my life. They do not compare with the years of the life of my ancestors during their long sojourn." 10 Then Jacob blessed Pharaoh, and went out from the presence of Pharaoh. 11 Joseph settled his father and his brothers, and granted them a holding in the land of Egypt, in the best part of the land, in the land of Ram′e·ses, as Pharaoh had instructed. 12 And Joseph provided his father, his brothers, and all his father's household with food, according to the number of their dependents.

The Famine in Egypt

13 Now there was no food in all the land, for the famine was very severe. The land of Egypt and the land of Cā′naan languished because of the famine. 14 Joseph collected all the money to be found in the land of Egypt and in the land of Cā′naan, in exchange for the grain that they bought; and Joseph brought the money into Pharaoh's house. 15 When the money from the land of Egypt and from the land of Cā′naan was spent, all the Egyptians came to Joseph, and said, "Give us food! Why should we die before your eyes? For our money is gone." 16 And Joseph answered, "Give me your livestock, and I will give you food in exchange for your livestock, if your money is gone." 17 So they brought their livestock to Joseph; and Joseph gave them food in exchange for the horses, the flocks, the herds, and the donkeys. That year he supplied them with food in exchange for all their livestock. 18 When that year was ended, they came to him the following year, and said to him, "We can not hide from my lord that our money is all spent; and the herds of cattle are my lord's. There is nothing left in the sight of my lord but our bodies and our lands. 19 Shall we die before your eyes, both we and our land? Buy us and our land in exchange for food. We with our land will become slaves to Pharaoh; just give us seed, so that we may live and not die, and that the land may not become desolate."

20 So Joseph bought all the land of Egypt for Pharaoh. All the Egyptians sold their fields, because the famine was severe upon them; and the land

[v] Heb *He*

became Pharaoh's. 21 As for the people, he made slaves of them w from one end of Egypt to the other. 22 Only the land of the priests he did not buy; for the priests had a fixed allowance from Pharaoh, and lived on the allowance that Pharaoh gave them; therefore they did not sell their land. 23 Then Joseph said to the people, "Now that I have this day bought you and your land for Pharaoh, here is seed for you; sow the land. 24 And at the harvests you shall give one-fifth to Pharaoh, and four-fifths shall be your own, as seed for the field and as food for yourselves and your households, and as food for your little ones." 25 They said, "You have saved our lives; may it please my lord, we will be slaves to Pharaoh." 26 So Joseph made it a statute concerning the land of Egypt, and it stands to this day, that Pharaoh should have the fifth. The land of the priests alone did not become Pharaoh's.

The Last Days of Jacob

27 Thus Israel settled in the land of Egypt, in the region of Gō'shen; and they gained possessions in it, and were fruitful and multiplied exceedingly. 28 Jacob lived in the land of Egypt seventeen years; so the days of Jacob, the years of his life, were one hundred forty-seven years.

29 When the time of Israel's death drew near, he called his son Joseph and said to him, "If I have found favor with you, put your hand under my thigh and promise to deal loyally and truly with me. Do not bury me in Egypt. 30 When I lie down with my ancestors, carry me out of Egypt and bury me in their burial place." He answered, "I will do as you have said." 31 And he said, "Swear to me"; and he swore to him. Then Israel bowed himself on the head of his bed.

Jacob Blesses Joseph's Sons
(Heb 11.21)

48 After this Joseph was told, "Your father is ill." So he took with him his two sons, Ma·nas'seh and E'phra·im. 2 When Jacob was told, "Your son Joseph has come to you," he x summoned his strength and sat up in bed. 3 And Jacob said to Joseph, "God Almighty y appeared to me at Luz in the land of Cā'naan, and he blessed me, 4 and said to me, 'I am going to make you fruitful and increase your numbers; I will make of you a company of peoples, and will give this land to your offspring after you for a perpetual holding.' 5 Therefore your two sons, who were born to you in the land of Egypt before I came to you in Egypt, are now mine; E'phra·im and Ma·nas'seh shall be mine, just as Reuben and Sim'ē·on are. 6 As for the offspring born to you after them, they shall be yours. They shall be recorded under the names of their brothers with regard to their inheritance. 7 For when I came from Pad'dan, Rachel, alas, died in the land of Cā'naan on the way, while there was still some distance to go to Eph'rath; and I buried her there on the way to Eph'rath" (that is, Bethlehem).

8 When Israel saw Joseph's sons, he said, "Who are these?" 9 Joseph said to his father, "They are my sons, whom God has given me here." And he said, "Bring them to me, please, that I may bless them." 10 Now the eyes of Israel were dim with age, and he could not see well. So Joseph brought them near him; and he kissed them and embraced them. 11 Israel said to Joseph, "I did not expect to see your face; and here God has let me see your children also." 12 Then Joseph removed them from his father's knees, z and he bowed himself with his face to the earth. 13 Joseph took them both, E'phra·im in his right hand toward Israel's left, and Ma·nas'seh in his left hand toward Israel's right, and brought them near him. 14 But Israel stretched out his right hand and laid it on the head of E'phra·im, who was the younger, and his left hand on the head of Ma·nas'seh, crossing his hands, for Ma·nas'seh was the firstborn. 15 He blessed Joseph, and said,

"The God before whom my
     ancestors Abraham and
     Isaac walked,
the God who has been my
     shepherd all my life to this
     day,
16 the angel who has redeemed me
     from all harm, bless the
     boys;
and in them let my name be
     perpetuated, and the name

---

w Sam Gk Compare Vg: MT *He removed
them to the cities*   x Heb *Israel*
y Traditional rendering of Heb *El
Shaddai*   z Heb *from his knees*

of my ancestors Abraham
and Isaac;
and let them grow into a
multitude on the earth."

17 When Joseph saw that his father laid his right hand on the head of E′phra·im, it displeased him; so he took his father's hand, to remove it from E′phra·im's head to Ma·nas′seh's head. 18 Joseph said to his father, "Not so, my father! Since this one is the firstborn, put your right hand on his head." 19 But his father refused, and said, "I know, my son, I know; he also shall become a people, and he also shall be great. Nevertheless his younger brother shall be greater than he, and his offspring shall become a multitude of nations." 20 So he blessed them that day, saying,

"By you[a] Israel will invoke
blessings, saying,
'God make you[a] like E′phra·im
and like Ma·nas′seh.'"

So he put E′phra·im ahead of Ma·nas′-seh. 21 Then Israel said to Joseph, "I am about to die, but God will be with you and will bring you again to the land of your ancestors. 22 I now give to you one portion[b] more than to your brothers, the portion[b] that I took from the hand of the Am′o·rites with my sword and with my bow."

Jacob's Last Words to His Sons

49 Then Jacob called his sons, and said: "Gather around, that I may tell you what will happen to you in days to come.

2 Assemble and hear, O sons of
Jacob;
listen to Israel your father.

3 Reuben, you are my firstborn,
my might and the first fruits of
my vigor,
excelling in rank and excelling
in power.
4 Unstable as water, you shall no
longer excel
because you went up onto
your father's bed;
then you defiled it—you[c] went
up onto my couch!

5 Sim′e·on and Levi are brothers;
weapons of violence are their
swords.
6 May I never come into their
council;
may I not be joined to their
company—

for in their anger they killed
men,
and at their whim they
hamstrung oxen.
7 Cursed be their anger, for it is
fierce,
and their wrath, for it is cruel!
I will divide them in Jacob,
and scatter them in Israel.

8 Judah, your brothers shall praise
you;
your hand shall be on the neck
of your enemies;
your father's sons shall bow
down before you.
9 Judah is a lion's whelp;
from the prey, my son, you
have gone up.
He crouches down, he stretches
out like a lion,
like a lioness—who dares
rouse him up?
10 The scepter shall not depart
from Judah,
nor the ruler's staff from
between his feet,
until tribute comes to him;[d]
and the obedience of the
peoples is his.
11 Binding his foal to the vine
and his donkey's colt to the
choice vine,
he washes his garments in wine
and his robe in the blood of
grapes;
12 his eyes are darker than wine,
and his teeth whiter than milk.

13 Zeb′u·lun shall settle at the
shore of the sea;
he shall be a haven for ships,
and his border shall be at
Si′don.

14 Is′sa·char is a strong donkey,
lying down between the
sheepfolds;
15 he saw that a resting place was
good,
and that the land was
pleasant;
so he bowed his shoulder to the
burden,

---

[a]you here is singular in Heb
[b]Or *mountain slope* (Heb *shekem*, a play on the name of the town and district of Shechem)   [c]Gk Syr Tg: Heb *he*
[d]Or *until Shiloh comes* or *until he comes to Shiloh* or (with Syr) *until he comes to whom it belongs*

and became a slave at forced
labor.

16 Dan shall judge his people
as one of the tribes of Israel.

17 Dan shall be a snake by the
roadside,
a viper along the path,
that bites the horse's heels
so that its rider falls
backward.

18 I wait for your salvation,
O LORD.

19 Gad shall be raided by raiders,
but he shall raid at their heels.

20 Ash'er's*e* food shall be rich,
and he shall provide royal
delicacies.

21 Naph'ta·li is a doe let loose
that bears lovely fawns.*f*

22 Joseph is a fruitful bough,
a fruitful bough by a spring;
his branches run over the
wall.*g*

23 The archers fiercely attacked
him;
they shot at him and pressed
him hard.

24 Yet his bow remained taut,
and his arms*h* were made
agile
by the hands of the Mighty One
of Jacob,
by the name of the Shepherd,
the Rock of Israel,

25 by the God of your father, who
will help you,
by the Almighty*i* who will
bless you
with blessings of heaven
above,
blessings of the deep that lies
beneath,
blessings of the breasts and of
the womb.

26 The blessings of your father
are stronger than the blessings
of the eternal mountains,
the bounties*j* of the
everlasting hills;
may they be on the head of
Joseph,
on the brow of him who was
set apart from his brothers.

27 Benjamin is a ravenous wolf,

in the morning devouring the
prey,
and at evening dividing the
spoil."

28 All these are the twelve tribes of
Israel, and this is what their father said
to them when he blessed them, blessing each one of them with a suitable
blessing.

Jacob's Death and Burial

29 Then he charged them, saying to
them, "I am about to be gathered to my
people. Bury me with my ancestors—
in the cave in the field of E'phron the
Hit'tite, 30 in the cave in the field at
Mach·pe'lah, near Mam're, in the land
of Ca'naan, in the field that Abraham
bought from E'phron the Hit'tite as a
burial site. 31 There Abraham and his
wife Sarah were buried; there Isaac
and his wife Rebekah were buried; and
there I buried Leah— 32 the field and
the cave that is in it were purchased
from the Hit'tites." 33 When Jacob
ended his charge to his sons, he drew
up his feet into the bed, breathed his
last, and was gathered to his people.

50 Then Joseph threw himself on
his father's face and wept over
him and kissed him. 2 Joseph commanded the physicians in his service
to embalm his father. So the physicians embalmed Israel; 3 they spent
forty days in doing this, for that is the
time required for embalming. And the
Egyptians wept for him seventy days.

4 When the days of weeping for him
were past, Joseph addressed the
household of Pharaoh, "If now I have
found favor with you, please speak to
Pharaoh as follows: 5 My father made
me swear an oath; he said, 'I am about
to die. In the tomb that I hewed out for
myself in the land of Ca'naan, there
you shall bury me.' Now therefore let
me go up, so that I may bury my father;
then I will return." 6 Pharaoh answered, "Go up, and bury your father,
as he made you swear to do."

7 So Joseph went up to bury his father. With him went up all the servants
of Pharaoh, the elders of his household, and all the elders of the land of

e Gk Vg Syr: Heb *From Asher*   *f* Or *that
gives beautiful words*   *g* Meaning of
Heb uncertain   *h* Heb *the arms of his
hands*   *i* Traditional rendering of Heb
Shaddai   *j* Cn Compare Gk: Heb *of my
progenitors to the boundaries*

Egypt, [8] as well as all the household of Joseph, his brothers, and his father's household. Only their children, their flocks, and their herds were left in the land of Gō'shen. [9] Both chariots and charioteers went up with him. It was a very great company. [10] When they came to the threshing floor of Ā'tad, which is beyond the Jordan, they held there a very great and sorrowful lamentation; and he observed a time of mourning for his father seven days. [11] When the Cā'naan·ite inhabitants of the land saw the mourning on the threshing floor of Ā'tad, they said, "This is a grievous mourning on the part of the Egyptians." Therefore the place was named Ā'bel-miz'ra·im; [k] it is beyond the Jordan. [12] Thus his sons did for him as he had instructed them. [13] They carried him to the land of Cā'-naan and buried him in the cave of the field at Mach·pē'lah, the field near Mam're, which Abraham bought as a burial site from Ē'phron the Hit'tite. [14] After he had buried his father, Joseph returned to Egypt with his brothers and all who had gone up with him to bury his father.

Joseph Forgives His Brothers

15 Realizing that their father was dead, Joseph's brothers said, "What if Joseph still bears a grudge against us and pays us back in full for all the wrong that we did to him?" [16] So they approached[l] Joseph, saying, "Your father gave this instruction before he died, [17] 'Say to Joseph: I beg you, forgive the crime of your brothers and the wrong they did in harming you.' Now therefore please forgive the crime of the servants of the God of your father." Joseph wept when they spoke to him. [18] Then his brothers also wept,[m] fell down before him, and said, "We are here as your slaves." [19] But Joseph said to them, "Do not be afraid! Am I in the place of God? [20] Even though you intended to do harm to me, God intended it for good, in order to preserve a numerous people, as he is doing today. [21] So have no fear; I myself will provide for you and your little ones." In this way he reassured them, speaking kindly to them.

Joseph's Last Days and Death
(Heb 11.22)

22 So Joseph remained in Egypt, he and his father's household; and Joseph lived one hundred ten years. [23] Joseph saw Ē'phra·im's children of the third generation; the children of Mā'chir son of Ma·nas'seh were also born on Joseph's knees.

24 Then Joseph said to his brothers, "I am about to die; but God will surely come to you, and bring you up out of this land to the land that he swore to Abraham, to Isaac, and to Jacob." [25] So Joseph made the Israelites swear, saying, "When God comes to you, you shall carry up my bones from here." [26] And Joseph died, being one hundred ten years old; he was embalmed and placed in a coffin in Egypt.

[k] That is *mourning* (or *meadow*) *of Egypt*
[l] Gk Syr: Heb *they commanded*
[m] Cn: Heb *also came*

EXODUS

1 These are the names of the sons of Israel who came to Egypt with Jacob, each with his household: [2] Reuben, Sim'e·on, Levi, and Judah, [3] Is'-sa·char, Zeb'u·lun, and Benjamin, [4] Dan and Naph'ta·lī, Gad and Ash'er. [5] The total number of people born to Jacob was seventy. Joseph was already in Egypt. [6] Then Joseph died, and all his brothers, and that whole generation. [7] But the Israelites were fruitful and prolific; they multiplied and grew exceedingly strong, so that the land was filled with them.

The Israelites Are Oppressed

8 Now a new king arose over Egypt, who did not know Joseph. [9] He said to his people, "Look, the Israelite people are more numerous and more powerful than we. [10] Come, let us deal shrewdly with them, or they will increase and, in the event of war, join our enemies and fight against us and escape from the land." [11] Therefore they set taskmasters over them to oppress them with forced labor. They built supply cities, Pi'thom and Ram'e·ses, for Pharaoh. [12] But the more they were oppressed, the more they multiplied and spread, so that the Egyptians came to dread the Israelites. [13] The Egyptians became ruthless in imposing tasks on the Israelites, [14] and made their lives bitter with hard service in mortar and brick and in every kind of field labor. They were ruthless in all the tasks that they imposed on them.

15 The king of Egypt said to the Hebrew midwives, one of whom was named Shiph'rah and the other Pu'ah, [16] "When you act as midwives to the Hebrew women, and see them on the birthstool, if it is a boy, kill him; but if it is a girl, she shall live." [17] But the midwives feared God; they did not do as the king of Egypt commanded them, but they let the boys live. [18] So the king of Egypt summoned the midwives and said to them, "Why have you done this, and allowed the boys to live?" [19] The midwives said to Pharaoh, "Because the Hebrew women are not like the Egyptian women; for they are vigorous and give birth before the midwife comes to them." [20] So God dealt well with the midwives; and the people multiplied and became very strong. [21] And because the midwives feared God, he gave them families. [22] Then Pharaoh commanded all his people, "Every boy that is born to the Hebrews[a] you shall throw into the Nile, but you shall let every girl live."

Birth and Youth of Moses
(Heb 11.23)

2 Now a man from the house of Levi went and married a Le'vite woman. [2] The woman conceived and bore a son; and when she saw that he was a fine baby, she hid him three months. [3] When she could hide him no longer she got a papyrus basket for him, and plastered it with bitumen and pitch; she put the child in it and placed

it among the reeds on the bank of the river. [4] His sister stood at a distance, to see what would happen to him.

5 The daughter of Pharaoh came down to bathe at the river, while her attendants walked beside the river. She saw the basket among the reeds and sent her maid to bring it. [6] When she opened it, she saw the child. He was crying, and she took pity on him, "This must be one of the Hebrews' children," she said. [7] Then his sister said to Pharaoh's daughter, "Shall I go and get you a nurse from the Hebrew women to nurse the child for you?" [8] Pharaoh's daughter said to her, "Yes." So the girl went and called the child's mother. [9] Pharaoh's daughter said to her, "Take this child and nurse it for me, and I will give you your wages." So the woman took the child and nursed it. [10] When the child grew up, she brought him to Pharaoh's daughter, and she took him as her son. She named him Moses,[b] "because," she said, "I drew him out[c] of the water."

Moses Flees to Midian
(Heb 11.24–25)

11 One day, after Moses had grown up, he went out to his people and saw their forced labor. He saw an Egyptian beating a Hebrew, one of his kinsfolk. [12] He looked this way and that, and seeing no one he killed the Egyptian and hid him in the sand. [13] When he went out the next day, he saw two Hebrews fighting; and he said to the one who was in the wrong, "Why do you strike your fellow Hebrew?" [14] He answered, "Who made you a ruler and judge over us? Do you mean to kill me as you killed the Egyptian?" Then Moses was afraid and thought, "Surely the thing is known." [15] When Pharaoh heard of it, he sought to kill Moses.

But Moses fled from Pharaoh. He settled in the land of Mid'i·an, and sat down by a well. [16] The priest of Mid'i·an had seven daughters. They came to draw water, and filled the troughs to water their father's flock. [17] But some shepherds came and drove them away. Moses got up and came to their defense and watered their flock. [18] When they returned to their father Reu'el, he said, "How is it that you have come back so soon today?" [19] They said, "An

---

[a] Sam Gk Tg: Heb lacks *to the Hebrews*
[b] Heb *Mosheh*   [c] Heb *mashah*

Egyptian helped us against the shepherds; he even drew water for us and watered the flock." ²⁰He said to his daughters, "Where is he? Why did you leave the man? Invite him to break bread." ²¹Moses agreed to stay with the man, and he gave Moses his daughter Zip·po'rah in marriage. ²²She bore a son, and he named him Ger'shom; for he said, "I have been an alien^d residing in a foreign land."

23 After a long time the king of Egypt died. The Israelites groaned under their slavery, and cried out. Out of the slavery their cry for help rose up to God. ²⁴God heard their groaning, and God remembered his covenant with Abraham, Isaac, and Jacob. ²⁵God looked upon the Israelites, and God took notice of them.

Moses at the Burning Bush
(Ex 6.2—7.7; 11.1–4; 12.35–36)

3 Moses was keeping the flock of his father-in-law Jeth'ro, the priest of Mid'i·an; he led his flock beyond the wilderness, and came to Ho'reb, the mountain of God. ²There the angel of the LORD appeared to him in a flame of fire out of a bush; he looked, and the bush was blazing, yet it was not consumed. ³Then Moses said, "I must turn aside and look at this great sight, and see why the bush is not burned up." ⁴When the LORD saw that he had turned aside to see, God called to him out of the bush, "Moses, Moses!" And he said, "Here I am." ⁵Then he said, "Come no closer! Remove the sandals from your feet, for the place on which you are standing is holy ground." ⁶He said further, "I am the God of your father, the God of Abraham, the God of Isaac, and the God of Jacob." And Moses hid his face, for he was afraid to look at God.

7 Then the LORD said, "I have observed the misery of my people who are in Egypt; I have heard their cry on account of their taskmasters. Indeed, I know their sufferings, ⁸and I have come down to deliver them from the Egyptians, and to bring them up out of that land to a good and broad land, a land flowing with milk and honey, to the country of the Ca'naan·ites, the Hit'tites, the Am'o·rites, the Per'iz·zites, the Hi'vites, and the Jeb'u·sites. ⁹The cry of the Israelites has now come to me; I have also seen how the Egyptians oppress them. ¹⁰So come, I will send you to Pharaoh to

bring my people, the Israelites, out of Egypt." ¹¹But Moses said to God, "Who am I that I should go to Pharaoh, and bring the Israelites out of Egypt?" ¹²He said, "I will be with you; and this shall be the sign for you that it is I who sent you: when you have brought the people out of Egypt, you shall worship God on this mountain."

The Divine Name Revealed

13 But Moses said to God, "If I come to the Israelites and say to them, 'The God of your ancestors has sent me to you,' and they ask me, 'What is his name?' what shall I say to them?" ¹⁴God said to Moses, "I AM WHO I AM."^e He said further, "Thus you shall say to the Israelites, 'I AM has sent me to you.'" ¹⁵God also said to Moses, "Thus you shall say to the Israelites, 'The LORD,^f the God of your ancestors, the God of Abraham, the God of Isaac, and the God of Jacob, has sent me to you':

This is my name forever,
　and this my title for all
　　generations.

¹⁶Go and assemble the elders of Israel, and say to them, 'The LORD, the God of your ancestors, the God of Abraham, of Isaac, and of Jacob, has appeared to me, saying: I have given heed to you and to what has been done to you in Egypt. ¹⁷I declare that I will bring you up out of the misery of Egypt, to the land of the Ca'naan·ites, the Hit'tites, the Am'o·rites, the Per'iz·zites, the Hi'vites, and the Jeb'u·sites, a land flowing with milk and honey.' ¹⁸They will listen to your voice; and you and the elders of Israel shall go to the king of Egypt and say to him, 'The LORD, the God of the Hebrews, has met with us; let us now go a three days' journey into the wilderness, so that we may sacrifice to the LORD our God.' ¹⁹I know, however, that the king of Egypt will not let you go unless compelled by a mighty hand.^g ²⁰So I will stretch out my hand and strike Egypt with all my wonders that I will perform in it; after that he will let you go. ²¹I will bring this people into such favor with the Egyptians that, when you go, you will

---

^dHeb ger　　^eOr I AM WHAT I AM or I WILL BE WHAT I WILL BE　　^fThe word "LORD" when spelled with capital letters stands for the divine name, YHWH, which is here connected with the verb hayah, "to be"　　^gGk Vg: Heb no, not by a mighty hand

ot go empty-handed; 22 each woman shall ask her neighbor and any woman living in the neighbor's house for jewelry of silver and of gold, and clothing, and you shall put them on your sons and on your daughters; and so you shall plunder the Egyptians.'"

Moses' Miraculous Power

4 Then Moses answered, "But suppose they do not believe me or listen to me, but say, 'The LORD did not appear to you.'" 2 The LORD said to him, "What is that in your hand?" He said, "A staff." 3 And he said, "Throw it on the ground." So he threw the staff on the ground, and it became a snake; and Moses drew back from it. 4 Then the LORD said to Moses, "Reach out your hand, and seize it by the tail"—so he reached out his hand and grasped it, and it became a staff in his hand— 5 "so that they may believe that the LORD, the God of their ancestors, the God of Abraham, the God of Isaac, and the God of Jacob, has appeared to you."

6 Again, the LORD said to him, "Put your hand inside your cloak." He put his hand into his cloak; and when he took it out, his hand was leprous,[h] as white as snow. 7 Then God said, "Put your hand back into your cloak"—so he put his hand back into his cloak, and when he took it out, it was restored like the rest of his body— 8 "If they will not believe you or heed the first sign, they may believe the second sign. 9 If they will not believe even these two signs or heed you, you shall take some water from the Nile and pour it on the dry ground; and the water that you shall take from the Nile will become blood on the dry ground."

10 But Moses said to the LORD, "O my Lord, I have never been eloquent, neither in the past nor even now that you have spoken to your servant; but I am slow of speech and slow of tongue." 11 Then the LORD said to him, "Who gives speech to mortals? Who makes them mute or deaf, seeing or blind? Is it not I, the LORD? 12 Now go, and I will be with your mouth and teach you what you are to speak." 13 But he said, "O my Lord, please send someone else." 14 Then the anger of the LORD was kindled against Moses and he said, "What of your brother Aaron, the Le'vite? I know that he can speak fluently; even now he is coming out to meet you, and when he sees you his heart will be glad. 15 You shall speak to

him and put the words in his mouth; and I will be with your mouth and with his mouth, and will teach you what you shall do. 16 He indeed shall speak for you to the people; he shall serve as a mouth for you, and you shall serve as God for him. 17 Take in your hand this staff, with which you shall perform the signs."

Moses Returns to Egypt

18 Moses went back to his father-in-law Jeth'rō and said to him, "Please let me go back to my kindred in Egypt and see whether they are still living." And Jeth'rō said to Moses, "Go in peace." 19 The LORD said to Moses in Mid'i·an, "Go back to Egypt; for all those who were seeking your life are dead." 20 So Moses took his wife and his sons, put them on a donkey and went back to the land of Egypt; and Moses carried the staff of God in his hand.

21 And the LORD said to Moses, "When you go back to Egypt, see that you perform before Pharaoh all the wonders that I have put in your power; but I will harden his heart, so that he will not let the people go. 22 Then you shall say to Pharaoh, 'Thus says the LORD: Israel is my firstborn son. 23 I said to you, "Let my son go that he may worship me." But you refused to let him go; now I will kill your firstborn son.'"

24 On the way, at a place where they spent the night, the LORD met him and tried to kill him. 25 But Zip·pō'rah took a flint and cut off her son's foreskin, and touched Moses'[i] feet with it, and said, "Truly you are a bridegroom of blood to me!" 26 So he let him alone. It was then she said, "A bridegroom of blood by circumcision."

27 The LORD said to Aaron, "Go into the wilderness to meet Moses." So he went; and he met him at the mountain of God and kissed him. 28 Moses told Aaron all the words of the LORD with which he had sent him, and all the signs with which he had charged him. 29 Then Moses and Aaron went and assembled all the elders of the Israelites. 30 Aaron spoke all the words that the LORD had spoken to Moses, and performed the signs in the sight of the people. 31 The people believed; and when they heard that the LORD had

h A term for several skin diseases; precise meaning uncertain   i Heb his given heed to the Israelites and that he had seen their misery, they bowed down and worshiped.

Bricks without Straw

5 Afterward Moses and Aaron went to Pharaoh and said, "Thus says the LORD, the God of Israel, 'Let my people go, so that they may celebrate a festival to me in the wilderness.'" 2 But Pharaoh said, "Who is the LORD, that I should heed him and let Israel go? I do not know the LORD, and I will not let Israel go." 3 Then they said, "The God of the Hebrews has revealed himself to us; let us go a three days' journey into the wilderness to sacrifice to the LORD our God, or he will fall upon us with pestilence or sword." 4 But the king of Egypt said to them, "Moses and Aaron, why are you taking the people away from their work? Get to your labors!" 5 Pharaoh continued, "Now they are more numerous than the people of the land⟨j⟩ and yet you want them to stop working!" 6 That same day Pharaoh commanded the taskmasters of the people, as well as their supervisors, 7 "You shall no longer give the people straw to make bricks, as before; let them go and gather straw for themselves. 8 But you shall require of them the same quantity of bricks as they have made previously; do not diminish it, for they are lazy; that is why they cry, 'Let us go and offer sacrifice to our God.' 9 Let heavier work be laid on them; then they will labor at it and pay no attention to deceptive words."

10 So the taskmasters and the supervisors of the people went out and said to the people, "Thus says Pharaoh, 'I will not give you straw. 11 Go and get straw yourselves, wherever you can find it; but your work will not be lessened in the least.'" 12 So the people scattered throughout the land of Egypt, to gather stubble for straw. 13 The taskmasters were urgent, saying, "Complete your work, the same daily assignment as when you were given straw." 14 And the supervisors of the Israelites, whom Pharaoh's taskmasters had set over them, were beaten, and were asked, "Why did you not finish the required quantity of bricks yesterday and today, as you did before?"

15 Then the Israelite supervisors came to Pharaoh and cried, "Why do you treat your servants like this? 16 No straw is given to your servants, ye⟨t⟩ they say to us, 'Make bricks!' Loo⟨k⟩ how your servants are beaten! You ar⟨e⟩ unjust to your own people."⟨k⟩ 17 H⟨e⟩ said, "You are lazy, lazy; that is wh⟨y⟩ you say, 'Let us go and sacrifice to th⟨e⟩ LORD.' 18 Go now, and work; for n⟨o⟩ straw shall be given you, but you sha⟨ll⟩ still deliver the same number o⟨f⟩ bricks." 19 The Israelite supervisor⟨s⟩ saw that they were in trouble whe⟨n⟩ they were told, "You shall not lesse⟨n⟩ your daily number of bricks." 20 A⟨s⟩ they left Pharaoh, they came upon Mo⟨-⟩ ses and Aaron who were waiting t⟨o⟩ meet them. 21 They said to them, "Th⟨e⟩ LORD look upon you and judge! Yo⟨u⟩ have brought us into bad odor wit⟨h⟩ Pharaoh and his officials, and have pu⟨t⟩ a sword in their hand to kill us."

22 Then Moses turned again to th⟨e⟩ LORD and said, "O LORD, why have yo⟨u⟩ mistreated this people? Why did yo⟨u⟩ ever send me? 23 Since I first came t⟨o⟩ Pharaoh to speak in your name, he ha⟨s⟩ mistreated this people, and you hav⟨e⟩ done nothing at all to deliver your peo⟨-⟩ ple."

Israel's Deliverance Assured
(Ex 3.1—4.17)

6 Then the LORD said to Moses⟨,⟩ "Now you shall see what I will d⟨o⟩ to Pharaoh: Indeed, by a mighty han⟨d⟩ he will let them go; by a mighty han⟨d⟩ he will drive them out of his land."

2 God also spoke to Moses and sai⟨d⟩ to him: "I am the LORD. 3 I appeared t⟨o⟩ Abraham, Isaac, and Jacob as God Al⟨-⟩ mighty,⟨l⟩ but by my name 'The LORD'⟨m⟩ I did not make myself known to them⟨.⟩ 4 I also established my covenant with them, to give them the land of Ca⟨-⟩ naan, the land in which they resided a⟨s⟩ aliens. 5 I have also heard the groanin⟨g⟩ of the Israelites whom the Egyptian⟨s⟩ are holding as slaves, and I have re⟨-⟩ membered my covenant. 6 Say there⟨-⟩ fore to the Israelites, 'I am the LORD⟨,⟩ and I will free you from the burdens o⟨f⟩ the Egyptians and deliver you fro⟨m⟩ slavery to them. I will redeem you wit⟨h⟩ an outstretched arm and with might⟨y⟩ acts of judgment. 7 I will take you a⟨s⟩ my people, and I will be your God. Yo⟨u⟩ shall know that I am the LORD you⟨r⟩

⟨j⟩Sam: Heb *The people of the land are now many* ⟨k⟩Gk Compare Syr Vg: Heb *beaten, and the sin of your people* ⟨l⟩Traditional rendering of Heb *El Shaddai* ⟨m⟩Heb *YHWH*; see note at 3.15

God, who has freed you from the burdens of the Egyptians. [8] I will bring you into the land that I swore to give to Abraham, Isaac, and Jacob; I will give it to you for a possession. I am the LORD.' " [9] Moses told this to the Israelites; but they would not listen to Moses, because of their broken spirit and their cruel slavery.

10 Then the LORD spoke to Moses, [11] "Go and tell Pharaoh king of Egypt to let the Israelites go out of his land." [12] But Moses spoke to the LORD, "The Israelites have not listened to me; how then shall Pharaoh listen to me, poor speaker that I am?"[n] [13] Thus the LORD spoke to Moses and Aaron, and gave them orders regarding the Israelites and Pharaoh king of Egypt, charging them to free the Israelites from the land of Egypt.

The Genealogy of Moses and Aaron
(Gen 46.8–27)

14 The following are the heads of their ancestral houses: the sons of Reuben, the firstborn of Israel: Hă′noch, Pal′lū, Hez′ron, and Car′mī; these are the families of Reuben. [15] The sons of Sim′ē·on: Je·mū′el, Jā′min, Ō′had, Jā′chin, Zō′har, and Shā′ūl,[o] the son of a Cā′naan·īte woman; these are the families of Sim′ē·on. [16] The following are the names of the sons of Levi according to their genealogies: Ger′shon,[p] Kō′hath, and Me·rar′ī, and the length of Levi's life was one hundred thirty-seven years. [17] The sons of Ger′shon:[p] Lib′nī and Shim′ē·ī, by their families. [18] The sons of Kō′hath: Am′ram, Iz′har, Hĕ′bron, and Uz′zi·el, and the length of Kō′hath's life was one hundred thirty-three years. [19] The sons of Me·rar′ī: Mah′lī and Mū′shī. These are the families of the Lē′vītes according to their genealogies. [20] Am′ram married Joch′e·bed his father's sister and she bore him Aaron and Moses, and the length of Am′ram's life was one hundred thirty-seven years. [21] The sons of Iz′har: Kō′rah, Nĕ′pheg, and Zich′rī. [22] The sons of Uz′zi·el: Mish′a·el, El′za·phan, and Sith′rī. [23] Aaron married E·lish′e·ba, daughter of Am·min′a·dab and sister of Nah′shon, and she bore him Nā′dab, A·bī′hū, El·ē·ā′zar, and Ith′a·mar. [24] The sons of Kō′rah: As′sir, El·kā′nah, and A·bī′a·saph; these are the families of the Kō′ra·hītes. [25] Aaron's son El·ē·ā′zar married one of the daughters of Pū′ti·el, and she bore him

Phin′e·has. These are the heads of the ancestral houses of the Lē′vītes by their families.

26 It was this same Aaron and Moses to whom the LORD said, "Bring the Israelites out of the land of Egypt, company by company." [27] It was they who spoke to Pharaoh king of Egypt to bring the Israelites out of Egypt, the same Moses and Aaron.

Moses and Aaron Obey God's Commands

28 On the day when the LORD spoke to Moses in the land of Egypt, [29] he said to him, "I am the LORD; tell Pharaoh king of Egypt all that I am speaking to you." [30] But Moses said in the LORD's presence, "Since I am a poor speaker,[q] why would Pharaoh listen to me?"

7 The LORD said to Moses, "See, I have made you like God to Pharaoh, and your brother Aaron shall be your prophet. [2] You shall speak all that I command you, and your brother Aaron shall tell Pharaoh to let the Israelites go out of his land. [3] But I will harden Pharaoh's heart, and I will multiply my signs and wonders in the land of Egypt. [4] When Pharaoh does not listen to you, I will lay my hand upon Egypt and bring my people the Israelites, company by company, out of the land of Egypt by great acts of judgment. [5] The Egyptians shall know that I am the LORD, when I stretch out my hand against Egypt and bring the Israelites out from among them." [6] Moses and Aaron did so; they did just as the LORD commanded them. [7] Moses was eighty years old and Aaron eighty-three when they spoke to Pharaoh.

Aaron's Miraculous Rod
(Ex 4.1–5)

8 The LORD said to Moses and Aaron, [9] "When Pharaoh says to you, 'Perform a wonder,' then you shall say to Aaron, 'Take your staff and throw it down before Pharaoh, and it will become a snake.' " [10] So Moses and Aaron went to Pharaoh and did as the LORD had commanded; Aaron threw down his staff before Pharaoh and his officials, and it became a snake. [11] Then Pharaoh summoned the wise men and the sorcerers; and they also,

---

[n] Heb *me? I am uncircumcised of lips*
[o] Or *Saul*   [p] Also spelled *Gershom*; see 2.22   [q] Heb *am uncircumcised of lips*; see 6.12

the magicians of Egypt, did the same by their secret arts. [12] Each one threw down his staff, and they became snakes; but Aaron's staff swallowed up theirs. [13] Still Pharaoh's heart was hardened, and he would not listen to them, as the LORD had said.

The First Plague: Water Turned to Blood

14 Then the LORD said to Moses, "Pharaoh's heart is hardened; he refuses to let the people go. [15] Go to Pharaoh in the morning, as he is going out to the water; stand by at the river bank to meet him, and take in your hand the staff that was turned into a snake. [16] Say to him, 'The LORD, the God of the Hebrews, sent me to you to say, "Let my people go, so that they may worship me in the wilderness." But until now you have not listened.' [17] Thus says the LORD, "By this you shall know that I am the LORD." See, with the staff that is in my hand I will strike the water that is in the Nile, and it shall be turned to blood. [18] The fish in the river shall die, the river itself shall stink, and the Egyptians shall be unable to drink water from the Nile.' " [19] The LORD said to Moses, "Say to Aaron, 'Take your staff and stretch out your hand over the waters of Egypt—over its rivers, its canals, and its ponds, and all its pools of water—so that they may become blood; and there shall be blood throughout the whole land of Egypt, even in vessels of wood and in vessels of stone.' "

20 Moses and Aaron did just as the LORD commanded. In the sight of Pharaoh and of his officials he lifted up the staff and struck the water in the river, and all the water in the river was turned into blood, [21] and the fish in the river died. The river stank so that the Egyptians could not drink its water, and there was blood throughout the whole land of Egypt. [22] But the magicians of Egypt did the same by their secret arts; so Pharaoh's heart remained hardened, and he would not listen to them; as the LORD had said. [23] Pharaoh turned and went into his house, and he did not take even this to heart. [24] And all the Egyptians had to dig along the Nile for water to drink, for they could not drink the water of the river.

25 Seven days passed after the LORD had struck the Nile.

The Second Plague: Frogs

8 [r] Then the LORD said to Moses, "Go to Pharaoh and say to him, 'Thus says the LORD: Let my people go, so that they may worship me. [2] If you refuse to let them go, I will plague your whole country with frogs. [3] The river shall swarm with frogs; they shall come up into your palace, into your bedchamber and your bed, and into the houses of your officials and of your people, [s] and into your ovens and your kneading bowls. [4] The frogs shall come up on you and on your people and on all your officials.' " [5] [t] And the LORD said to Moses, "Say to Aaron, 'Stretch out your hand with your staff over the rivers, the canals, and the pools, and make frogs come up on the land of Egypt.' " [6] So Aaron stretched out his hand over the waters of Egypt; and the frogs came up and covered the land of Egypt. [7] But the magicians did the same by their secret arts, and brought frogs up on the land of Egypt.

8 Then Pharaoh called Moses and Aaron, and said, "Pray to the LORD to take away the frogs from me and my people, and I will let the people go to sacrifice to the LORD." [9] Moses said to Pharaoh, "Kindly tell me when I am to pray for you and for your officials and for your people, that the frogs may be removed from you and your houses and be left only in the Nile." [10] And he said, "Tomorrow." Moses said, "As you say! So that you may know that there is no one like the LORD our God, [11] the frogs shall leave you and your houses and your officials and your people; they shall be left only in the Nile." [12] Then Moses and Aaron went out from Pharaoh; and Moses cried out to the LORD concerning the frogs that he had brought upon Pharaoh. [u] [13] And the LORD did as Moses requested: the frogs died in the houses, the courtyards, and the fields. [14] And they gathered them together in heaps, and the land stank. [15] But when Pharaoh saw that there was a respite, he hardened his heart, and would not listen to them, just as the LORD had said.

The Third Plague: Gnats

16 Then the LORD said to Moses, "Say to Aaron, 'Stretch out your staff

---

[r] Ch 7.26 in Heb　　[s] Gk: Heb *upon your people*　　[t] Ch 8.1 in Heb　　[u] Or *frogs, as he had agreed with Pharaoh*

nd strike the dust of the earth, so that
t may become gnats throughout the
whole land of Egypt.' " 17 And they did
so; Aaron stretched out his hand with
his staff and struck the dust of the
earth, and gnats came on humans and
animals alike; all the dust of the earth
turned into gnats throughout the
whole land of Egypt. 18 The magicians
tried to produce gnats by their secret
arts, but they could not. There were
gnats on both humans and animals.
19 And the magicians said to Pharaoh,
"This is the finger of God!" But Pharaoh's heart was hardened, and he
would not listen to them, just as the
LORD had said.

The Fourth Plague: Flies

20 Then the LORD said to Moses,
'Rise early in the morning and present
yourself before Pharaoh, as he goes
out to the water, and say to him, 'Thus
says the LORD: Let my people go, so
that they may worship me. 21 For if you
will not let my people go, I will send
swarms of flies on you, your officials,
and your people, and into your houses;
and the houses of the Egyptians shall
be filled with swarms of flies; so also
the land where they live. 22 But on that
day I will set apart the land of Gō'shen,
where my people live, so that no
swarms of flies shall be there, that you
may know that I the LORD am in this
land. 23 Thus I will make a distinction ᵛ
between my people and your people.
This sign shall appear tomorrow.' "
24 The LORD did so, and great swarms
of flies came into the house of Pharaoh
and into his officials' houses; in all of
Egypt the land was ruined because of
the flies.

25 Then Pharaoh summoned Moses
and Aaron, and said, "Go, sacrifice to
your God within the land." 26 But Moses said, "It would not be right to do so;
for the sacrifices that we offer to the
LORD our God are offensive to the
Egyptians. If we offer in the sight of
the Egyptians sacrifices that are offensive to them, will they not stone us?
27 We must go a three days' journey
into the wilderness and sacrifice to the
LORD our God as he commands us."
28 So Pharaoh said, "I will let you go to
sacrifice to the LORD your God in the
wilderness, provided you do not go
very far away. Pray for me." 29 Then
Moses said, "As soon as I leave you, I
will pray to the LORD that the swarms
of flies may depart tomorrow from
Pharaoh, from his officials, and from
his people; only do not let Pharaoh
again deal falsely by not letting the
people go to sacrifice to the LORD."

30 So Moses went out from Pharaoh and prayed to the LORD. 31 And the
LORD did as Moses asked: he removed
the swarms of flies from Pharaoh,
from his officials, and from his people;
not one remained. 32 But Pharaoh
hardened his heart this time also, and
would not let the people go.

The Fifth Plague: Livestock Diseased

9 Then the LORD said to Moses, "Go
to Pharaoh, and say to him, 'Thus
says the LORD, the God of the Hebrews: Let my people go, so that they
may worship me. 2 For if you refuse to
let them go and still hold them, 3 the
hand of the LORD will strike with a
deadly pestilence your livestock in the
field: the horses, the donkeys, the camels, the herds, and the flocks. 4 But the
LORD will make a distinction between
the livestock of Israel and the livestock
of Egypt, so that nothing shall die of all
that belongs to the Israelites.' " 5 The
LORD set a time, saying, "Tomorrow
the LORD will do this thing in the land."
6 And on the next day the LORD did so;
all the livestock of the Egyptians died,
but of the livestock of the Israelites not
one died. 7 Pharaoh inquired and
found that not one of the livestock of
the Israelites was dead. But the heart
of Pharaoh was hardened, and he
would not let the people go.

The Sixth Plague: Boils
(Deut 28.27)

8 Then the LORD said to Moses and
Aaron, "Take handfuls of soot from
the kiln, and let Moses throw it in the
air in the sight of Pharaoh. 9 It shall
become fine dust all over the land of
Egypt, and shall cause festering boils
on humans and animals throughout
the whole land of Egypt." 10 So they
took soot from the kiln, and stood before Pharaoh, and Moses threw it in
the air, and it caused festering boils on
humans and animals. 11 The magicians
could not stand before Moses because
of the boils, for the boils afflicted the
magicians as well as all the Egyptians.
12 But the LORD hardened the heart of
Pharaoh, and he would not listen to
them, just as the LORD had spoken to
Moses.

ᵛ Gk Vg: Heb *will set redemption*

The Seventh Plague: Thunder and Hail

13 Then the LORD said to Moses, "Rise up early in the morning and present yourself before Pharaoh, and say to him, 'Thus says the LORD, the God of the Hebrews: Let my people go, so that they may worship me. 14 For this time I will send all my plagues upon you yourself, and upon your officials, and upon your people, so that you may know that there is no one like me in all the earth. 15 For by now I could have stretched out my hand and struck you and your people with pestilence, and you would have been cut off from the earth. 16 But this is why I have let you live: to show you my power, and to make my name resound through all the earth. 17 You are still exalting yourself against my people, and will not let them go. 18 Tomorrow at this time I will cause the heaviest hail to fall that has ever fallen in Egypt from the day it was founded until now. 19 Send, therefore, and have your livestock and everything that you have in the open field brought to a secure place; every human or animal that is in the open field and is not brought under shelter will die when the hail comes down upon them.' " 20 Those officials of Pharaoh who feared the word of the LORD hurried their slaves and livestock off to a secure place. 21 Those who did not regard the word of the LORD left their slaves and livestock in the open field.

22 The LORD said to Moses, "Stretch out your hand toward heaven so that hail may fall on the whole land of Egypt, on humans and animals and all the plants of the field in the land of Egypt." 23 Then Moses stretched out his staff toward heaven, and the LORD sent thunder and hail, and fire came down on the earth. And the LORD rained hail on the land of Egypt; 24 there was hail with fire flashing continually in the midst of it, such heavy hail as had never fallen in all the land of Egypt since it became a nation. 25 The hail struck down everything that was in the open field throughout all the land of Egypt, both human and animal; the hail also struck down all the plants of the field, and shattered every tree in the field. 26 Only in the land of Gō'shen, where the Israelites were, there was no hail.

27 Then Pharaoh summoned Moses and Aaron, and said to them, "This time I have sinned; the LORD is in the right, and I and my people are in the wrong. 28 Pray to the LORD! Enough of God's thunder and hail! I will let you go; you need stay no longer." 29 Moses said to him, "As soon as I have gone out of the city, I will stretch out my hands to the LORD; the thunder will cease, and there will be no more hail, so that you may know that the earth is the LORD's. 30 But as for you and your officials, I know that you do not yet fear the LORD God." 31 (Now the flax and the barley were ruined, for the barley was in the ear and the flax was in bud. 32 But the wheat and the spelt were not ruined, for they are late in coming up.) 33 So Moses left Pharaoh, went out of the city, and stretched out his hands to the LORD; then the thunder and the hail ceased, and the rain no longer poured down on the earth. 34 But when Pharaoh saw that the rain and the hail and the thunder had ceased, he sinned once more and hardened his heart, he and his officials. 35 So the heart of Pharaoh was hardened, and he would not let the Israelites go, just as the LORD had spoken through Moses.

The Eighth Plague: Locusts
(Joel 1.2–4)

10 Then the LORD said to Moses, "Go to Pharaoh; for I have hardened his heart and the heart of his officials, in order that I may show these signs of mine among them, 2 and that you may tell your children and grandchildren how I have made fools of the Egyptians and what signs I have done among them—so that you may know that I am the LORD."

3 So Moses and Aaron went to Pharaoh, and said to him, "Thus says the LORD, the God of the Hebrews, 'How long will you refuse to humble yourself before me? Let my people go, so that they may worship me. 4 For if you refuse to let my people go, tomorrow I will bring locusts into your country. 5 They shall cover the surface of the land, so that no one will be able to see the land. They shall devour the last remnant left you after the hail, and they shall devour every tree of yours that grows in the field. 6 They shall fill your houses, and the houses of all your officials and of all the Egyptians—something that neither your parents nor your grandparents have seen, from the day they came on earth to this

day.'" Then he turned and went out from Pharaoh.

7 Pharaoh's officials said to him, "How long shall this fellow be a snare to us? Let the people go, so that they may worship the Lord their God; do you not yet understand that Egypt is ruined?" 8 So Moses and Aaron were brought back to Pharaoh, and he said to them, "Go, worship the Lord your God! But which ones are to go?" 9 Moses said, "We will go with our young and our old; we will go with our sons and daughters and with our flocks and herds, because we have the Lord's festival to celebrate." 10 He said to them, "The Lord indeed will be with you, if ever I let your little ones go with you! Plainly, you have some evil purpose in mind. 11 No, never! Your men may go and worship the Lord, for that is what you are asking." And they were driven out from Pharaoh's presence.

12 Then the Lord said to Moses, "Stretch out your hand over the land of Egypt, so that the locusts may come upon it and eat every plant in the land, all that the hail has left." 13 So Moses stretched out his staff over the land of Egypt, and the Lord brought an east wind upon the land all that day and all that night; when morning came, the east wind had brought the locusts. 14 The locusts came upon all the land of Egypt and settled on the whole country of Egypt, such a dense swarm of locusts as had never been before, nor ever shall be again. 15 They covered the surface of the whole land, so that the land was black; and they ate all the plants in the land and all the fruit of the trees that the hail had left; nothing green was left, no tree, no plant in the field, in all the land of Egypt. 16 Pharaoh hurriedly summoned Moses and Aaron and said, "I have sinned against the Lord your God, and against you. 17 Do forgive my sin just this once, and pray to the Lord your God that at the least he remove this deadly thing from me." 18 So he went out from Pharaoh and prayed to the Lord. 19 The Lord changed the wind into a very strong west wind, which lifted the locusts and drove them into the Red Sea; *w* not a single locust was left in all the country of Egypt. 20 But the Lord hardened Pharaoh's heart, and he would not let the Israelites go.

The Ninth Plague: Darkness

21 Then the Lord said to Moses,

"Stretch out your hand toward heaven so that there may be darkness over the land of Egypt, a darkness that can be felt." 22 So Moses stretched out his hand toward heaven, and there was dense darkness in all the land of Egypt for three days. 23 People could not see one another, and for three days they could not move from where they were; but all the Israelites had light where they lived. 24 Then Pharaoh summoned Moses, and said, "Go, worship the Lord. Only your flocks and your herds shall remain behind. Even your children may go with you." 25 But Moses said, "You must also let us have sacrifices and burnt offerings to sacrifice to the Lord our God. 26 Our livestock also must go with us; not a hoof shall be left behind, for we must choose some of them for the worship of the Lord our God, and we will not know what to use to worship the Lord until we arrive there." 27 But the Lord hardened Pharaoh's heart, and he was unwilling to let them go. 28 Then Pharaoh said to him, "Get away from me! Take care that you do not see my face again, for on the day you see my face you shall die." 29 Moses said, "Just as you say! I will never see your face again."

Warning of the Final Plague
(Ex 3.21–22; 12.35–36)

11 The Lord said to Moses, "I will bring one more plague upon Pharaoh and upon Egypt; afterwards he will let you go from here; indeed, when he lets you go, he will drive you away. 2 Tell the people that every man is to ask his neighbor and every woman is to ask her neighbor for objects of silver and gold." 3 The Lord gave the people favor in the sight of the Egyptians. Moreover, Moses himself was a man of great importance in the land of Egypt, in the sight of Pharaoh's officials and in the sight of the people.

4 Moses said, "Thus says the Lord: About midnight I will go out through Egypt. 5 Every firstborn in the land of Egypt shall die, from the firstborn of Pharaoh who sits on his throne to the firstborn of the female slave who is behind the handmill, and all the firstborn of the livestock. 6 Then there will be a loud cry throughout the whole land of Egypt, such as has never been or will ever be again. 7 But not a dog shall growl at any of the Israelites—not at

w Or Sea of Reeds

people, not at animals—so that you may know that the LORD makes a distinction between Egypt and Israel. [8]Then all these officials of yours shall come down to me, and bow low to me, saying, 'Leave us, you and all the people who follow you.' After that I will leave." And in hot anger he left Pharaoh.

9 The LORD said to Moses, "Pharaoh will not listen to you, in order that my wonders may be multiplied in the land of Egypt." [10]Moses and Aaron performed all these wonders before Pharaoh; but the LORD hardened Pharaoh's heart, and he did not let the people of Israel go out of his land.

The First Passover Instituted
(Num 9.1–14; Deut 16.1–8; Ezek 45.21–25)

12 The LORD said to Moses and Aaron in the land of Egypt: [2]This month shall mark for you the beginning of months; it shall be the first month of the year for you. [3]Tell the whole congregation of Israel that on the tenth of this month they are to take a lamb for each family, a lamb for each household. [4]If a household is too small for a whole lamb, it shall join its closest neighbor in obtaining one; the lamb shall be divided in proportion to the number of people who eat of it. [5]Your lamb shall be without blemish, a year-old male; you may take it from the sheep or from the goats. [6]You shall keep it until the fourteenth day of this month; then the whole assembled congregation of Israel shall slaughter it at twilight. [7]They shall take some of the blood and put it on the two doorposts and the lintel of the houses in which they eat it. [8]They shall eat the lamb that same night; they shall eat it roasted over the fire with unleavened bread and bitter herbs. [9]Do not eat any of it raw or boiled in water, but roasted over the fire, with its head, legs, and inner organs. [10]You shall let none of it remain until the morning; anything that remains until the morning you shall burn. [11]This is how you shall eat it: your loins girded, your sandals on your feet, and your staff in your hand; and you shall eat it hurriedly. It is the passover of the LORD. [12]For I will pass through the land of Egypt that night, and I will strike down every firstborn in the land of Egypt, both human beings and animals; on all the gods of Egypt I will execute judgments: I am the LORD. [13]The blood shall be a sign

for you on the houses where you live: when I see the blood, I will pass over you, and no plague shall destroy you when I strike the land of Egypt.

14 This day shall be a day of remembrance for you. You shall celebrate it as a festival to the LORD; throughout your generations you shall observe it as a perpetual ordinance. [15]Seven days you shall eat unleavened bread; on the first day you shall remove leaven from your houses, for whoever eats leavened bread from the first day until the seventh day shall be cut off from Israel. [16]On the first day you shall hold a solemn assembly, and on the seventh day a solemn assembly; no work shall be done on those days; only what everyone must eat, that alone may be prepared by you. [17]You shall observe the festival of unleavened bread, for on this very day I brought your companies out of the land of Egypt: you shall observe this day throughout your generations as a perpetual ordinance. [18]In the first month, from the evening of the fourteenth day until the evening of the twenty-first day, you shall eat unleavened bread. [19]For seven days no leaven shall be found in your houses; for whoever eats what is leavened shall be cut off from the congregation of Israel, whether an alien or a native of the land. [20]You shall eat nothing leavened; in all your settlements you shall eat unleavened bread.

21 Then Moses called all the elders of Israel and said to them, "Go, select lambs for your families, and slaughter the passover lamb. [22]Take a bunch of hyssop, dip it in the blood that is in the basin, and touch the lintel and the two doorposts with the blood in the basin. None of you shall go outside the door of your house until morning. [23]For the LORD will pass through to strike down the Egyptians; when he sees the blood on the lintel and on the two doorposts, the LORD will pass over that door and will not allow the destroyer to enter your houses to strike you down. [24]You shall observe this rite as a perpetual ordinance for you and your children. [25]When you come to the land that the LORD will give you, as he has promised, you shall keep this observance. [26]And when your children ask you, 'What do you mean by this observance?' [27]you shall say, 'It is the passover sacrifice to the LORD, for he passed over the houses of the Israelites

in Egypt, when he struck down the Egyptians but spared our houses.' " And the people bowed down and worshiped.

28 The Israelites went and did just as the LORD had commanded Moses and Aaron.

The Tenth Plague:
Death of the Firstborn
(Ex 11.1–10)

29 At midnight the LORD struck down all the firstborn in the land of Egypt, from the firstborn of Pharaoh who sat on his throne to the firstborn of the prisoner who was in the dungeon, and all the firstborn of the livestock. 30 Pharaoh arose in the night, he and all his officials and all the Egyptians; and there was a loud cry in Egypt, for there was not a house without someone dead. 31 Then he summoned Moses and Aaron in the night, and said, "Rise up, go away from my people, both you and the Israelites! Go, worship the LORD, as you said. 32 Take your flocks and your herds, as you said, and be gone. And bring a blessing on me too!"

The Exodus: From Rameses to Succoth

33 The Egyptians urged the people to hasten their departure from the land, for they said, "We shall all be dead." 34 So the people took their dough before it was leavened, with their kneading bowls wrapped up in their cloaks on their shoulders. 35 The Israelites had done as Moses told them; they had asked the Egyptians for jewelry of silver and gold, and for clothing, 36 and the LORD had given the people favor in the sight of the Egyptians, so that they let them have what they asked. And so they plundered the Egyptians.

37 The Israelites journeyed from Ram′e·ses to Suc′coth, about six hundred thousand men on foot, besides children. 38 A mixed crowd also went up with them, and livestock in great numbers, both flocks and herds. 39 They baked unleavened cakes of the dough that they had brought out of Egypt; it was not leavened, because they were driven out of Egypt and could not wait, nor had they prepared any provisions for themselves.

40 The time that the Israelites had lived in Egypt was four hundred thirty years. 41 At the end of four hundred thirty years, on that very day, all the companies of the LORD went out from the land of Egypt. 42 That was for the LORD a night of vigil, to bring them out of the land of Egypt. That same night is a vigil to be kept for the LORD by all the Israelites throughout their generations.

Directions for the Passover
(Gen 17.9–14; Ex 12.1–13)

43 The LORD said to Moses and Aaron: This is the ordinance for the passover: no foreigner shall eat of it, 44 but any slave who has been purchased may eat of it after he has been circumcised; 45 no bound or hired servant may eat of it. 46 It shall be eaten in one house; you shall not take any of the animal outside the house, and you shall not break any of its bones. 47 The whole congregation of Israel shall celebrate it. 48 If an alien who resides with you wants to celebrate the passover to the LORD, all his males shall be circumcised; then he may draw near to celebrate it; he shall be regarded as a native of the land. But no uncircumcised person shall eat of it; 49 there shall be one law for the native and for the alien who resides among you.

50 All the Israelites did just as the LORD had commanded Moses and Aaron. 51 That very day the LORD brought the Israelites out of the land of Egypt, company by company.

13 The LORD said to Moses: 2 Consecrate to me all the firstborn; whatever is the first to open the womb among the Israelites, of human beings and animals, is mine.

The Festival of Unleavened Bread
(Ex 12.14–20)

3 Moses said to the people, "Remember this day on which you came out of Egypt, out of the house of slavery, because the LORD brought you out from there by strength of hand; no leavened bread shall be eaten. 4 Today, in the month of A′bib, you are going out. 5 When the LORD brings you into the land of the Ca′naan·ites, the Hit′-tites, the Am′o·rites, the Hi′vites, and the Jeb′u·sites, which he swore to your ancestors to give you, a land flowing with milk and honey, you shall keep this observance in this month. 6 Seven days you shall eat unleavened bread, and on the seventh day there shall be a festival to the LORD. 7 Unleavened bread shall be eaten for seven days; no leavened bread shall be seen in your

EXODUS

possession, and no leaven shall be seen among you in all your territory. 8 You shall tell your child on that day, 'It is because of what the LORD did for me when I came out of Egypt.' 9 It shall serve for you as a sign on your hand and as a reminder on your forehead, so that the teaching of the LORD may be on your lips; for with a strong hand the LORD brought you out of Egypt. 10 You shall keep this ordinance at its proper time from year to year.

The Consecration of the Firstborn

11 "When the LORD has brought you into the land of the Cā′naan-ites, as he swore to you and your ancestors, and has given it to you, 12 you shall set apart to the LORD all that first opens the womb. All the firstborn of your livestock that are males shall be the LORD's. 13 But every firstborn donkey you shall redeem with a sheep; if you do not redeem it, you must break its neck. Every firstborn male among your children you shall redeem. 14 When in the future your child asks you, 'What does this mean?' you shall answer, 'By strength of hand the LORD brought us out of Egypt, from the house of slavery. 15 When Pharaoh stubbornly refused to let us go, the LORD killed all the firstborn in the land of Egypt, from human firstborn to the firstborn of animals. Therefore I sacrifice to the LORD every male that first opens the womb, but every firstborn of my sons I redeem.' 16 It shall serve as a sign on your hand and as an emblem x on your forehead that by strength of hand the LORD brought us out of Egypt."

The Pillars of Cloud and Fire
(Ex 40.34–38; Num 9.15–23; 1 Kings 8.10–11)

17 When Pharaoh let the people go, God did not lead them by way of the land of the Phi·lis′tines, although that was nearer; for God thought, "If the people face war, they may change their minds and return to Egypt." 18 So God led the people by the roundabout way of the wilderness toward the Red Sea. y The Israelites went up out of the land of Egypt prepared for battle. 19 And Moses took with him the bones of Joseph who had required a solemn oath of the Israelites, saying, "God will surely take notice of you, and then you must carry my bones with you from here." 20 They set out from Suc′coth,

and camped at É′tham, on the edge of the wilderness. 21 The LORD went in front of them in a pillar of cloud by day, to lead them along the way, and in a pillar of fire by night, to give them light, so that they might travel by day and by night. 22 Neither the pillar of cloud by day nor the pillar of fire by night left its place in front of the people.

Crossing the Red Sea

14 Then the LORD said to Moses: 2 Tell the Israelites to turn back and camp in front of Pī-ha·hī′roth, between Mig′dōl and the sea, in front of Bā′al-zē′phon; you shall camp opposite it, by the sea. 3 Pharaoh will say of the Israelites, 'They are wandering aimlessly in the land; the wilderness has closed in on them.' 4 I will harden Pharaoh's heart, and he will pursue them, so that I will gain glory for myself over Pharaoh and all his army; and the Egyptians shall know that I am the LORD. And they did so.

5 When the king of Egypt was told that the people had fled, the minds of Pharaoh and his officials were changed toward the people, and they said, "What have we done, letting Israel leave our service?" 6 So he had his chariot made ready, and took his army with him; 7 he took six hundred picked chariots and all the other chariots of Egypt with officers over all of them. 8 The LORD hardened the heart of Pharaoh king of Egypt and he pursued the Israelites, who were going out boldly. 9 The Egyptians pursued them, all Pharaoh's horses and chariots, his chariot drivers and his army; they overtook them camped by the sea, by Pī-ha·hī′roth, in front of Bā′al-zē′-phon.

10 As Pharaoh drew near, the Israelites looked back, and there were the Egyptians advancing on them. In great fear the Israelites cried out to the LORD. 11 They said to Moses, "Was it because there were no graves in Egypt that you have taken us away to die in the wilderness? What have you done to us, bringing us out of Egypt? 12 Is this not the very thing we told you in Egypt, 'Let us alone and let us serve the Egyptians'? For it would have been better for us to serve the Egyptians than to die in the wilderness." 13 But

---

x Or *as a frontlet*; Meaning of Heb uncertain　　y Or *Sea of Reeds*

Moses said to the people, "Do not be afraid, stand firm, and see the deliverance that the LORD will accomplish for you today; for the Egyptians whom you see today you shall never see again. ¹⁴The LORD will fight for you, and you have only to keep still."

15 Then the LORD said to Moses, "Why do you cry out to me? Tell the Israelites to go forward. ¹⁶But you lift up your staff, and stretch out your hand over the sea and divide it, that the Israelites may go into the sea on dry ground. ¹⁷Then I will harden the hearts of the Egyptians so that they will go in after them; and so I will gain glory for myself over Pharaoh and all his army, his chariots, and his chariot drivers. ¹⁸And the Egyptians shall know that I am the LORD, when I have gained glory for myself over Pharaoh, his chariots, and his chariot drivers."

19 The angel of God who was going before the Israelite army moved and went behind them; and the pillar of cloud moved from in front of them and took its place behind them. ²⁰It came between the army of Egypt and the army of Israel. And so the cloud was there with the darkness, and it lit up the night; one did not come near the other all night.

21 Then Moses stretched out his hand over the sea. The LORD drove the sea back by a strong east wind all night, and turned the sea into dry land; and the waters were divided. ²²The Israelites went into the sea on dry ground, the waters forming a wall for them on their right and on their left. ²³The Egyptians pursued, and went into the sea after them, all of Pharaoh's horses, chariots, and chariot drivers. ²⁴At the morning watch the LORD in the pillar of fire and cloud looked down upon the Egyptian army, and threw the Egyptian army into panic. ²⁵He clogged*z* their chariot wheels so that they turned with difficulty. The Egyptians said, "Let us flee from the Israelites, for the LORD is fighting for them against Egypt."

The Pursuers Drowned

26 Then the LORD said to Moses, "Stretch out your hand over the sea, so that the water may come back upon the Egyptians, upon their chariots and chariot drivers." ²⁷So Moses stretched out his hand over the sea, and at dawn the sea returned to its normal depth. As the Egyptians fled before it, the LORD tossed the Egyptians into the sea. ²⁸The waters returned and covered the chariots and the chariot drivers, the entire army of Pharaoh that had followed them into the sea; not one of them remained. ²⁹But the Israelites walked on dry ground through the sea, the waters forming a wall for them on their right and on their left.

30 Thus the LORD saved Israel that day from the Egyptians; and Israel saw the Egyptians dead on the seashore. ³¹Israel saw the great work that the LORD did against the Egyptians. So the people feared the LORD and believed in the LORD and in his servant Moses.

The Song of Moses
(Ex 14.13–14: Ps 78.12–14)

15   Then Moses and the Israelites sang this song to the LORD:

"I will sing to the LORD, for he
    has triumphed gloriously;
    horse and rider he has thrown
      into the sea.
2 The LORD is my strength and my
    might,*a*
    and he has become my
      salvation;
    this is my God, and I will praise
      him,
    my father's God, and I will
      exalt him.
3 The LORD is a warrior;
    the LORD is his name.

4 "Pharaoh's chariots and his
      army he cast into the sea;
    his picked officers were sunk
      in the Red Sea.*b*
5 The floods covered them;
    they went down into the
      depths like a stone.
6 Your right hand, O LORD,
    glorious in power—
    your right hand, O LORD,
      shattered the enemy.
7 In the greatness of your majesty
    you overthrew your
      adversaries;
    you sent out your fury, it
      consumed them like
      stubble.
8 At the blast of your nostrils the
      waters piled up,
    the floods stood up in a heap;
    the deeps congealed in the
      heart of the sea.

z Sam Gk Syr: MT *removed*   *a* Or *song*
b Or *Sea of Reeds*

E
X
O
D
U
S

9 The enemy said, 'I will pursue, I
   will overtake,
I will divide the spoil, my
   desire shall have its fill of
   them.
I will draw my sword, my
   hand shall destroy them.'
10 You blew with your wind, the
    sea covered them;
they sank like lead in the
   mighty waters.

11 "Who is like you, O LORD,
    among the gods?
Who is like you, majestic in
   holiness,
awesome in splendor, doing
   wonders?
12 You stretched out your right
    hand,
the earth swallowed them.

13 "In your steadfast love you led
    the people whom you
    redeemed;
you guided them by your
   strength to your holy
   abode.
14 The peoples heard, they
    trembled;
pangs seized the inhabitants of
   Phi·lis'ti·a.
15 Then the chiefs of E'dom were
    dismayed;
trembling seized the leaders of
   Mō'ab;
all the inhabitants of Cā'naan
   melted away.
16 Terror and dread fell upon them;
by the might of your arm, they
   became still as a stone
until your people, O LORD,
   passed by,
until the people whom you
   acquired passed by.
17 You brought them in and
    planted them on the
    mountain of your own
    possession,
the place, O LORD, that you
   made your abode,
the sanctuary, O LORD, that
   your hands have
   established.
18 The LORD will reign forever and
    ever."

19 When the horses of Pharaoh
with his chariots and his chariot drivers went into the sea, the LORD brought
back the waters of the sea upon them;
but the Israelites walked through the
sea on dry ground.

The Song of Miriam
(Num 26.59)

20 Then the prophet Miriam, Aaron's sister, took a tambourine in her
hand; and all the women went out after
her with tambourines and with dancing. 21 And Miriam sang to them:
"Sing to the LORD, for he has
   triumphed gloriously;
horse and rider he has thrown
   into the sea."

Bitter Water Made Sweet

22 Then Moses ordered Israel to set
out from the Red Sea,c and they went
into the wilderness of Shur. They went
three days in the wilderness and found
no water. 23 When they came to
Mar'ah, they could not drink the water
of Mar'ah because it was bitter. That is
why it was called Mar'ah. d 24 And the
people complained against Moses,
saying, "What shall we drink?" 25 He
cried out to the LORD; and the LORD
showed him a piece of wood;e he
threw it into the water, and the water
became sweet.
There the LORDf made for them a
statute and an ordinance and there he
put them to the test. 26 He said, "If you
will listen carefully to the voice of the
LORD your God, and do what is right in
his sight, and give heed to his commandments and keep all his statutes, I
will not bring upon you any of the diseases that I brought upon the Egyptians; for I am the LORD who heals
you."
27 Then they came to E'lim, where
there were twelve springs of water and
seventy palm trees; and they camped
there by the water.

Bread from Heaven

16 The whole congregation of the
   Israelites set out from E'lim;
and Israel came to the wilderness of
Sin, which is between E'lim and Sinai,
on the fifteenth day of the second
month after they had departed from
the land of Egypt. 2 The whole congregation of the Israelites complained
against Moses and Aaron in the wilderness. 3 The Israelites said to them,
"If only we had died by the hand of the
LORD in the land of Egypt, when we sat
by the fleshpots and ate our fill of
bread; for you have brought us out into

cOr Sea of Reeds   dThat is Bitterness
eOr a tree   fHeb he

this wilderness to kill this whole assembly with hunger."

4 Then the LORD said to Moses, "I am going to rain bread from heaven for you, and each day the people shall go out and gather enough for that day. In that way I will test them, whether they will follow my instruction or not. ⁵On the sixth day, when they prepare what they bring in, it will be twice as much as they gather on other days." ⁶So Moses and Aaron said to all the Israelites, "In the evening you shall know that it was the LORD who brought you out of the land of Egypt, ⁷and in the morning you shall see the glory of the LORD, because he has heard your complaining against the LORD. For what are we, that you complain against us?" ⁸And Moses said, "When the LORD gives you meat to eat in the evening and your fill of bread in the morning, because the LORD has heard the complaining that you utter against him—what are we? Your complaining is not against us but against the LORD."

9 Then Moses said to Aaron, "Say to the whole congregation of the Israelites, 'Draw near to the LORD, for he has heard your complaining.'" ¹⁰And as Aaron spoke to the whole congregation of the Israelites, they looked toward the wilderness, and the glory of the LORD appeared in the cloud. ¹¹The LORD spoke to Moses and said, ¹²"I have heard the complaining of the Israelites; say to them, 'At twilight you shall eat meat, and in the morning you shall have your fill of bread; then you shall know that I am the LORD your God.'"

13 In the evening quails came up and covered the camp; and in the morning there was a layer of dew around the camp. ¹⁴When the layer of dew lifted, there on the surface of the wilderness was a fine flaky substance, as fine as frost on the ground. ¹⁵When the Israelites saw it, they said to one another, "What is it?"ᵍ For they did not know what it was. Moses said to them, "It is the bread that the LORD has given you to eat. ¹⁶This is what the LORD has commanded: 'Gather as much of it as each of you needs, an omer to a person according to the number of persons, all providing for those in their own tents.'" ¹⁷The Israelites did so, some gathering more, some less. ¹⁸But when they measured it with an omer, those who gathered

much had nothing over, and those who gathered little had no shortage; they gathered as much as each of them needed. ¹⁹And Moses said to them, "Let no one leave any of it over until morning." ²⁰But they did not listen to Moses; some left part of it until morning, and it bred worms and became foul. And Moses was angry with them. ²¹Morning by morning they gathered it, as much as each needed; but when the sun grew hot, it melted.

22 On the sixth day they gathered twice as much food, two omers apiece. When all the leaders of the congregation came and told Moses, ²³he said to them, "This is what the LORD has commanded: 'Tomorrow is a day of solemn rest, a holy sabbath to the LORD; bake what you want to bake and boil what you want to boil, and all that is left over put aside to be kept until morning.'" ²⁴So they put it aside until morning, as Moses commanded them; and it did not become foul, and there were no worms in it. ²⁵Moses said, "Eat it today, for today is a sabbath to the LORD; today you will not find it in the field. ²⁶Six days you shall gather it; but on the seventh day, which is a sabbath, there will be none."

27 On the seventh day some of the people went out to gather, and they found none. ²⁸The LORD said to Moses, "How long will you refuse to keep my commandments and instructions? ²⁹See! The LORD has given you the sabbath, therefore on the sixth day he gives you food for two days; each of you stay where you are; do not leave your place on the seventh day." ³⁰So the people rested on the seventh day.

31 The house of Israel called it manna; it was like coriander seed, white, and the taste of it was like wafers made with honey. ³²Moses said, "This is what the LORD has commanded: 'Let an omer of it be kept throughout your generations, in order that they may see the food with which I fed you in the wilderness, when I brought you out of the land of Egypt.'" ³³And Moses said to Aaron, "Take a jar, and put an omer of manna in it, and place it before the LORD, to be kept throughout your generations." ³⁴As the LORD commanded Moses, so Aaron placed it before the covenant,ʰ

ᵍOr "It is manna" (Heb *man hu*, see verse 31)   ʰOr *treaty* or *testimony*; Heb *eduth*

EXODUS

for safekeeping. 35 The Israelites ate manna forty years, until they came to a habitable land; they ate manna, until they came to the border of the land of Cā'naan. 36 An omer is a tenth of an ephah.

Water from the Rock
(Num 20.1–13)

17 From the wilderness of Sin the whole congregation of the Israelites journeyed by stages, as the LORD commanded. They camped at Reph'-i-dim, but there was no water for the people to drink. 2 The people quarreled with Moses, and said, "Give us water to drink." Moses said to them, "Why do you quarrel with me? Why do you test the LORD?" 3 But the people thirsted there for water; and the people complained against Moses and said, "Why did you bring us out of Egypt, to kill us and our children and livestock with thirst?" 4 So Moses cried out to the LORD, "What shall I do with this people? They are almost ready to stone me." 5 The LORD said to Moses, "Go on ahead of the people, and take some of the elders of Israel with you; take in your hand the staff with which you struck the Nile, and go. 6 I will be standing there in front of you on the rock at Hō'reb. Strike the rock, and water will come out of it, so that the people may drink." Moses did so, in the sight of the elders of Israel. 7 He called the place Mas'sah[i] and Mer'-i-bah,[j] because the Israelites quarreled and tested the LORD, saying, "Is the LORD among us or not?"

Amalek Attacks Israel and Is Defeated
(Gen 14.7; Num 13.29; 14.25)

8 Then Am'a-lek came and fought with Israel at Reph'i-dim. 9 Moses said to Joshua, "Choose some men for us and go out, fight with Am'a-lek. Tomorrow I will stand on the top of the hill with the staff of God in my hand." 10 So Joshua did as Moses told him, and fought with Am'a-lek, while Moses, Aaron, and Hur went up to the top of the hill. 11 Whenever Moses held up his hand, Israel prevailed; and whenever he lowered his hand, Am'a-lek prevailed. 12 But Moses' hands grew weary; so they took a stone and put it under him, and he sat on it. Aaron and Hur held up his hands, one on one side, and the other on the other side; so his hands were steady until the sun set. 13 And Joshua defeated Am'a-lek and his people with the sword.

14 Then the LORD said to Moses, "Write this as a reminder in a book and recite it in the hearing of Joshua: I will utterly blot out the remembrance of Am'a-lek from under heaven." 15 And Moses built an altar and called it, The LORD is my banner. 16 He said, "A hand upon the banner of the LORD![k] The LORD will have war with Am'a-lek from generation to generation."

Jethro's Advice
(Deut 1.9–18)

18 Jeth'rō, the priest of Mid'i-an, Moses' father-in-law, heard of all that God had done for Moses and for his people Israel, how the LORD had brought Israel out of Egypt. 2 After Moses had sent away his wife Zip-pō'rah, his father-in-law Jeth'rō took her back, 3 along with her two sons. The name of the one was Ger'shom (for he said, "I have been an alien[l] in a foreign land"), 4 and the name of the other, El-i-ē'zer[m] (for he said, "The God of my father was my help, and delivered me from the sword of Pharaoh"). 5 Jeth'rō, Moses' father-in-law, came into the wilderness where Moses was encamped at the mountain of God, bringing Moses' sons and wife to him. 6 He sent word to Moses, "I, your father-in-law Jeth'rō, am coming to you, with your wife and her two sons." 7 Moses went out to meet his father-in-law; he bowed down and kissed him; each asked after the other's welfare, and they went into the tent. 8 Then Moses told his father-in-law all that the LORD had done to Pharaoh and to the Egyptians for Israel's sake, all the hardship that had beset them on the way, and how the LORD had delivered them. 9 Jeth'rō rejoiced for all the good that the LORD had done to Israel, in delivering them from the Egyptians.

10 Jeth'rō said, "Blessed be the LORD, who has delivered you from the Egyptians and from Pharaoh. 11 Now I know that the LORD is greater than all gods, because he delivered the people from the Egyptians,[n] when they dealt

---

[i] That is *Test*   [j] That is *Quarrel*
[k] Cn: Meaning of Heb uncertain
[l] Heb *ger*   [m] Heb *Eli*, my God; *ezer*, help
[n] The clause *because . . . Egyptians* has been transposed from verse 10

arrogantly with them." 12 And Jeth'rō, Moses' father-in-law, brought a burnt offering and sacrifices to God; and Aaron came with all the elders of Israel to eat bread with Moses' father-in-law in the presence of God.

13 The next day Moses sat as judge for the people, while the people stood around him from morning until evening. 14 When Moses' father-in-law saw all that he was doing for the people, he said, "What is this that you are doing for the people? Why do you sit alone, while all the people stand around you from morning until evening?" 15 Moses said to his father-in-law, "Because the people come to me to inquire of God. 16 When they have a dispute, they come to me and I decide between one person and another, and I make known to them the statutes and instructions of God." 17 Moses' father-in-law said to him, "What you are doing is not good. 18 You will surely wear yourself out, both you and these people with you. For the task is too heavy for you; you cannot do it alone. 19 Now listen to me. I will give you counsel, and God be with you! You should represent the people before God, and you should bring their cases before God; 20 teach them the statutes and instructions and make known to them the way they are to go and the things they are to do. 21 You should also look for able men among all the people, men who fear God, are trustworthy, and hate dishonest gain; set such men over them as officers over thousands, hundreds, fifties and tens. 22 Let them sit as judges for the people at all times; let them bring every important case to you, but decide every minor case themselves. So it will be easier for you, and they will bear the burden with you. 23 If you do this, and God so commands you, then you will be able to endure, and all these people will go to their home in peace."

24 So Moses listened to his father-in-law and did all that he had said. 25 Moses chose able men from all Israel and appointed them as heads over the people, as officers over thousands, hundreds, fifties, and tens. 26 And they judged the people at all times; hard cases they brought to Moses, but any minor case they decided themselves. 27 Then Moses let his father-in-law depart, and he went off to his own country.

The Israelites Reach Mount Sinai

19 On the third new moon after the Israelites had gone out of the land of Egypt, on that very day, they came into the wilderness of Sinai. 2 They had journeyed from Reph'i·dim, entered the wilderness of Sinai, and camped in the wilderness; Israel camped there in front of the mountain. 3 Then Moses went up to God; the LORD called to him from the mountain, saying, "Thus you shall say to the house of Jacob, and tell the Israelites: 4 You have seen what I did to the Egyptians, and how I bore you on eagles' wings and brought you to myself. 5 Now therefore, if you obey my voice and keep my covenant, you shall be my treasured possession out of all the peoples. Indeed, the whole earth is mine, 6 but you shall be for me a priestly kingdom and a holy nation. These are the words that you shall speak to the Israelites."

7 So Moses came, summoned the elders of the people, and set before them all these words that the LORD had commanded him. 8 The people all answered as one: "Everything that the LORD has spoken we will do." Moses reported the words of the people to the LORD. 9 Then the LORD said to Moses, "I am going to come to you in a dense cloud, in order that the people may hear when I speak with you and so trust you ever after."

The People Consecrated

When Moses had told the words of the people to the LORD, 10 the LORD said to Moses: "Go to the people and consecrate them today and tomorrow. Have them wash their clothes 11 and prepare for the third day, because on the third day the LORD will come down upon Mount Sinai in the sight of all the people. 12 You shall set limits for the people all around, saying, 'Be careful not to go up the mountain or to touch the edge of it. Any who touch the mountain shall be put to death. 13 No hand shall touch them, but they shall be stoned or shot with arrows; o whether animal or human being, they shall not live.' When the trumpet sounds a long blast, they may go up on the mountain." 14 So Moses went down from the mountain to the people. He consecrated the people, and they washed

o Heb lacks *with arrows*

EXODUS

their clothes. ¹⁵And he said to the people, "Prepare for the third day; do not go near a woman."

16 On the morning of the third day there was thunder and lightning, as well as a thick cloud on the mountain, and a blast of a trumpet so loud that all the people who were in the camp trembled. ¹⁷Moses brought the people out of the camp to meet God. They took their stand at the foot of the mountain. ¹⁸Now Mount Sinai was wrapped in smoke, because the LORD had descended upon it in fire; the smoke went up like the smoke of a kiln, while the whole mountain shook violently. ¹⁹As the blast of the trumpet grew louder and louder, Moses would speak and God would answer him in thunder. ²⁰When the LORD descended upon Mount Sinai, to the top of the mountain, the LORD summoned Moses to the top of the mountain, and Moses went up. ²¹Then the LORD said to Moses, "Go down and warn the people not to break through to the LORD to look; otherwise many of them will perish. ²²Even the priests who approach the LORD must consecrate themselves or the LORD will break out against them." ²³Moses said to the LORD, "The people are not permitted to come up to Mount Sinai; for you yourself warned us, saying, 'Set limits around the mountain and keep it holy.'" ²⁴The LORD said to him, "Go down, and come up bringing Aaron with you; but do not let either the priests or the people break through to come up to the LORD; otherwise he will break out against them." ²⁵So Moses went down to the people and told them.

The Ten Commandments
(Deut 5.1–22)

20 Then God spoke all these words:

2 I am the LORD your God, who brought you out of the land of Egypt, out of the house of slavery; ³you shall have no other gods before ᵖ me.

4 You shall not make for yourself an idol, whether in the form of anything that is in heaven above, or that is on the earth beneath, or that is in the water under the earth. ⁵You shall not bow down to them or worship them; for I the LORD your God am a jealous God, punishing children for the iniquity of parents, to the third and the fourth generation of those who reject me, ⁶but showing steadfast love to the

thousandth generation �q of those who love me and keep my commandments.

7 You shall not make wrongful use of the name of the LORD your God, for the LORD will not acquit anyone who misuses his name.

8 Remember the sabbath day, and keep it holy. ⁹Six days you shall labor and do all your work. ¹⁰But the seventh day is a sabbath to the LORD your God; you shall not do any work—you, your son or your daughter, your male or female slave, your livestock, or the alien resident in your towns. ¹¹For in six days the LORD made heaven and earth, the sea, and all that is in them, but rested the seventh day; therefore the LORD blessed the sabbath day and consecrated it.

12 Honor your father and your mother, so that your days may be long in the land that the LORD your God is giving you.

13 You shall not murder. ʳ

14 You shall not commit adultery.

15 You shall not steal.

16 You shall not bear false witness against your neighbor.

17 You shall not covet your neighbor's house; you shall not covet your neighbor's wife, or male or female slave, or ox, or donkey, or anything that belongs to your neighbor.

18 When all the people witnessed the thunder and lightning, the sound of the trumpet, and the mountain smoking, they were afraid ˢ and trembled and stood at a distance, ¹⁹and said to Moses, "You speak to us, and we will listen; but do not let God speak to us, or we will die." ²⁰Moses said to the people, "Do not be afraid; for God has come only to test you and to put the fear of him upon you so that you do not sin." ²¹Then the people stood at a distance, while Moses drew near to the thick darkness where God was.

The Law concerning the Altar

22 The LORD said to Moses: Thus you shall say to the Israelites: "You have seen for yourselves that I spoke with you from heaven. ²³You shall not make gods of silver alongside me, nor shall you make for yourselves gods of gold. ²⁴You need make for me only an altar of earth and sacrifice on it your burnt offerings and your offerings of

ᵖ Or besides   q Or to thousands
ʳ Or kill   ˢ Sam Gk Syr Vg: MT they saw

well-being, your sheep and your oxen; in every place where I cause my name to be remembered I will come to you and bless you. 25 But if you make for me an altar of stone, do not build it of hewn stones; for if you use a chisel upon it you may profane it. 26 You shall not go up by steps to my altar, so that your nakedness may not be exposed on it."

The Law concerning Slaves
(Deut 15.12–18)

21 These are the ordinances that you shall set before them:

2 When you buy a male Hebrew slave, he shall serve six years, but in the seventh he shall go out a free person, without debt. 3 If he comes in single, he shall go out single; if he comes in married, then his wife shall go out with him. 4 If his master gives him a wife and she bears him sons or daughters, the wife and her children shall be her master's and he shall go out alone. 5 But if the slave declares, "I love my master, my wife, and my children; I will not go out a free person," 6 then his master shall bring him before God.t He shall be brought to the door or the doorpost; and his master shall pierce his ear with an awl; and he shall serve him for life.

7 When a man sells his daughter as a slave, she shall not go out as the male slaves do. 8 If she does not please her master, who designated her for himself, then he shall let her be redeemed; he shall have no right to sell her to a foreign people, since he has dealt unfairly with her. 9 If he designates her for his son, he shall deal with her as with a daughter. 10 If he takes another wife to himself, he shall not diminish the food, clothing, or marital rights of the first wife.u 11 And if he does not do these three things for her, she shall go out without debt, without payment of money.

The Law concerning Violence

12 Whoever strikes a person mortally shall be put to death. 13 If it was not premeditated, but came about by an act of God, then I will appoint for you a place to which the killer may flee. 14 But if someone willfully attacks and kills another by treachery, you shall take the killer from my altar for execution.

15 Whoever strikes father or mother shall be put to death.

16 Whoever kidnaps a person, whether that person has been sold or is still held in possession, shall be put to death.

17 Whoever curses father or mother shall be put to death.

18 When individuals quarrel and one strikes the other with a stone or fist so that the injured party, though not dead, is confined to bed, 19 but recovers and walks around outside with the help of a staff, then the assailant shall be free of liability, except to pay for the loss of time, and to arrange for full recovery.

20 When a slaveowner strikes a male or female slave with a rod and the slave dies immediately, the owner shall be punished. 21 But if the slave survives a day or two, there is no punishment; for the slave is the owner's property.

22 When people who are fighting injure a pregnant woman so that there is a miscarriage, and yet no further harm follows, the one responsible shall be fined what the woman's husband demands, paying as much as the judges determine. 23 If any harm follows, then you shall give life for life, 24 eye for eye, tooth for tooth, hand for hand, foot for foot, 25 burn for burn, wound for wound, stripe for stripe.

26 When a slaveowner strikes the eye of a male or female slave, destroying it, the owner shall let the slave go, a free person, to compensate for the eye. 27 If the owner knocks out a tooth of a male or female slave, the slave shall be let go, a free person, to compensate for the tooth.

Laws concerning Property

28 When an ox gores a man or a woman to death, the ox shall be stoned, and its flesh shall not be eaten; but the owner of the ox shall not be liable. 29 If the ox has been accustomed to gore in the past, and its owner has been warned but has not restrained it, and it kills a man or a woman, the ox shall be stoned, and its owner also shall be put to death. 30 If a ransom is imposed on the owner, then the owner shall pay whatever is imposed for the redemption of the victim's life. 31 If it gores a boy or a girl, the owner shall be dealt with according to this same rule. 32 If the ox gores a male or female slave, the owner shall pay to the slave-

t Or to the judges　u Heb of her

owner thirty shekels of silver, and the ox shall be stoned.

33 If someone leaves a pit open, or digs a pit and does not cover it, and an ox or a donkey falls into it, 34 the owner of the pit shall make restitution, giving money to its owner, but keeping the dead animal.

35 If someone's ox hurts the ox of another, so that it dies, then they shall sell the live ox and divide the price of it; and the dead animal they shall also divide. 36 But if it was known that the ox was accustomed to gore in the past, and its owner has not restrained it, the owner shall restore ox for ox, but keep the dead animal.

Laws of Restitution

22 ᵛ When someone steals an ox or a sheep, and slaughters it or sells it, the thief shall pay five oxen for an ox, and four sheep for a sheep. ʷ The thief shall make restitution, but if unable to do so, shall be sold for the theft. 4 When the animal, whether ox or donkey or sheep, is found alive in the thief's possession, the thief shall pay double.

2 ˣ If a thief is found breaking in, and is beaten to death, no bloodguilt is incurred; 3 but if it happens after sunrise, bloodguilt is incurred.

5 When someone causes a field or vineyard to be grazed over, or lets livestock loose to graze in someone else's field, restitution shall be made from the best in the owner's field or vineyard.

6 When fire breaks out and catches in thorns so that the stacked grain or the standing grain or the field is consumed, the one who started the fire shall make full restitution.

7 When someone delivers to a neighbor money or goods for safekeeping, and they are stolen from the neighbor's house, then the thief, if caught, shall pay double. 8 If the thief is not caught, the owner of the house shall be brought before God, ʸ to determine whether or not the owner had laid hands on the neighbor's goods.

9 In any case of disputed ownership involving ox, donkey, sheep, clothing, or any other loss, of which one party says, "This is mine," the case of both parties shall come before God; ʸ the one whom God condemns ᶻ shall pay double to the other.

10 When someone delivers to another a donkey, ox, sheep, or any other animal for safekeeping, and it dies or is injured or is carried off, without anyone seeing it, 11 an oath before the LORD shall decide between the two of them that the one has not laid hands on the property of the other; the owner shall accept the oath, and no restitution shall be made. 12 But if it was stolen, restitution shall be made to its owner. 13 If it was mangled by beasts, let it be brought as evidence; restitution shall not be made for the mangled remains.

14 When someone borrows an animal from another and it is injured or dies, the owner not being present, full restitution shall be made. 15 If the owner was present, there shall be no restitution; if it was hired, only the hiring fee is due.

Social and Religious Laws

16 When a man seduces a virgin who is not engaged to be married, and lies with her, he shall give the bride-price for her and make her his wife. 17 But if her father refuses to give her to him, he shall pay an amount equal to the bride-price for virgins.

18 You shall not permit a female sorcerer to live.

19 Whoever lies with an animal shall be put to death.

20 Whoever sacrifices to any god, other than the LORD alone, shall be devoted to destruction.

21 You shall not wrong or oppress a resident alien, for you were aliens in the land of Egypt. 22 You shall not abuse any widow or orphan. 23 If you do abuse them, when they cry out to me, I will surely heed their cry; 24 my wrath will burn, and I will kill you with the sword, and your wives shall become widows and your children orphans.

25 If you lend money to my people, to the poor among you, you shall not deal with them as a creditor; you shall not exact interest from them. 26 If you take your neighbor's cloak in pawn, you shall restore it before the sun goes down; 27 for it may be your neighbor's only clothing to use as cover; in what else shall that person sleep? And if your neighbor cries out to me, I will listen, for I am compassionate.

ᵛ Ch 21.37 in Heb   ʷ Verses 2, 3, and 4 rearranged thus: 3b, 4, 2, 3a   ˣ Ch 22.1 in Heb   ʸ Or *before the judges*   ᶻ Or *the judges condemn*

28 You shall not revile God, or curse a leader of your people.

29 You shall not delay to make offerings from the fullness of your harvest and from the outflow of your presses.*a*

The firstborn of your sons you shall give to me. 30 You shall do the same with your oxen and with your sheep: seven days it shall remain with its mother; on the eighth day you shall give it to me.

31 You shall be people consecrated to me; therefore you shall not eat any meat that is mangled by beasts in the field; you shall throw it to the dogs.

Justice for All

23 You shall not spread a false report. You shall not join hands with the wicked to act as a malicious witness. 2 You shall not follow a majority in wrongdoing; when you bear witness in a lawsuit, you shall not side with the majority so as to pervert justice; 3 nor shall you be partial to the poor in a lawsuit.

4 When you come upon your enemy's ox or donkey going astray, you shall bring it back.

5 When you see the donkey of one who hates you lying under its burden and you would hold back from setting it free, you must help to set it free.*a*

6 You shall not pervert the justice due to your poor in their lawsuits. 7 Keep far from a false charge, and do not kill the innocent and those in the right, for I will not acquit the guilty. 8 You shall take no bribe, for a bribe blinds the officials, and subverts the cause of those who are in the right.

9 You shall not oppress a resident alien; you know the heart of an alien, for you were aliens in the land of Egypt.

Sabbatical Year and Sabbath

10 For six years you shall sow your land and gather in its yield; 11 but the seventh year you shall let it rest and lie fallow, so that the poor of your people may eat; and what they leave the wild animals may eat. You shall do the same with your vineyard, and with your olive orchard.

12 Six days you shall do your work, but on the seventh day you shall rest, so that your ox and your donkey may have relief, and your homeborn slave and the resident alien may be refreshed. 13 Be attentive to all that I have

said to you. Do not invoke the names of other gods; do not let them be heard on your lips.

The Annual Festivals
(Ex 34.18–26; Deut 16.1–17)

14 Three times in the year you shall hold a festival for me. 15 You shall observe the festival of unleavened bread; as I commanded you, you shall eat unleavened bread for seven days at the appointed time in the month of Ā′bib, for in it you came out of Egypt.

No one shall appear before me empty-handed.

16 You shall observe the festival of harvest, of the first fruits of your labor, of what you sow in the field. You shall observe the festival of ingathering at the end of the year, when you gather in from the field the fruit of your labor. 17 Three times in the year all your males shall appear before the Lord God.

18 You shall not offer the blood of my sacrifice with anything leavened, or let the fat of my festival remain until the morning.

19 The choicest of the first fruits of your ground you shall bring into the house of the Lord your God.

You shall not boil a kid in its mother's milk.

The Conquest of Canaan Promised

20 I am going to send an angel in front of you, to guard you on the way and to bring you to the place that I have prepared. 21 Be attentive to him and listen to his voice; do not rebel against him, for he will not pardon your transgression; for my name is in him.

22 But if you listen attentively to his voice and do all that I say, then I will be an enemy to your enemies and a foe to your foes.

23 When my angel goes in front of you, and brings you to the Am′o·rītes, the Hit′tītes, the Per′iz·zītes, the Cā′naan·ītes, the Hī′vītes, and the Jeb′ū·sītes, and I blot them out, 24 you shall not bow down to their gods, or worship them, or follow their practices, but you shall utterly demolish them and break their pillars in pieces. 25 You shall worship the Lord your God, and I *b* will bless your bread and your water; and I will take sickness away from among

a Meaning of Heb uncertain   *b* Gk Vg: Heb *he*

you. [26] No one shall miscarry or be barren in your land; I will fulfill the number of your days. [27] I will send my terror in front of you, and will throw into confusion all the people against whom you shall come, and I will make all your enemies turn their backs to you. [28] And I will send the pestilence[c] in front of you, which shall drive out the Hi′vites, the Ca′naan·ites, and the Hit′-tites from before you. [29] I will not drive them out from before you in one year, or the land would become desolate and the wild animals would multiply against you. [30] Little by little I will drive them out from before you, until you have increased and possess the land. [31] I will set your borders from the Red Sea[d] to the sea of the Phi·lis′tines, and from the wilderness to the Euphrates; for I will hand over to you the inhabitants of the land, and you shall drive them out before you. [32] You shall make no covenant with them and their gods. [33] They shall not live in your land, or they will make you sin against me; for if you worship their gods, it will surely be a snare to you.

The Blood of the Covenant

24 Then he said to Moses, "Come up to the LORD, you and Aaron, Na′dab, and A·bi′hu, and seventy of the elders of Israel, and worship at a distance. [2] Moses alone shall come near the LORD; but the others shall not come near, and the people shall not come up with him."

[3] Moses came and told the people all the words of the LORD and all the ordinances; and all the people answered with one voice, and said, "All the words that the LORD has spoken we will do." [4] And Moses wrote down all the words of the LORD. He rose early in the morning, and built an altar at the foot of the mountain, and set up twelve pillars, corresponding to the twelve tribes of Israel. [5] He sent young men of the people of Israel, who offered burnt offerings and sacrificed oxen as offerings of well-being to the LORD. [6] Moses took half of the blood and put it in basins, and half of the blood he dashed against the altar. [7] Then he took the book of the covenant, and read it in the hearing of the people; and they said, "All that the LORD has spoken we will do, and we will be obedient." [8] Moses took the blood and dashed it on the people, and said, "See the blood of the covenant that the LORD has made with

you in accordance with all these words."

On the Mountain with God

[9] Then Moses and Aaron, Na′dab, and A·bi′hu, and seventy of the elders of Israel went up, [10] and they saw the God of Israel. Under his feet there was something like a pavement of sapphire stone, like the very heaven for clearness. [11] God[e] did not lay his hand on the chief men of the people of Israel; also they beheld God, and they ate and drank.

[12] The LORD said to Moses, "Come up to me on the mountain, and wait there; and I will give you the tablets of stone, with the law and the commandment, which I have written for their instruction." [13] So Moses set out with his assistant Joshua, and Moses went up into the mountain of God. [14] To the elders he had said, "Wait here for us, until we come to you again; for Aaron and Hur are with you; whoever has a dispute may go to them."

[15] Then Moses went up on the mountain, and the cloud covered the mountain. [16] The glory of the LORD settled on Mount Sinai, and the cloud covered it for six days; on the seventh day he called to Moses out of the cloud. [17] Now the appearance of the glory of the LORD was like a devouring fire on the top of the mountain in the sight of the people of Israel. [18] Moses entered the cloud, and went up on the mountain. Moses was on the mountain for forty days and forty nights.

Offerings for the Tabernacle
(Ex 35.4–9)

25 The LORD said to Moses: [2] Tell the Israelites to take for me an offering; from all whose hearts prompt them to give you shall receive the offering for me. [3] This is the offering that you shall receive from them: gold, silver, and bronze, [4] blue, purple, and crimson yarns and fine linen, goats' hair, [5] tanned rams' skins, fine leather,[f] acacia wood, [6] oil for the lamps, spices for the anointing oil and for the fragrant incense, [7] onyx stones and gems to be set in the ephod and for the breastpiece. [8] And have them make me a sanctuary, so that I may dwell among them. [9] In accordance with all

[c] Or *hornets*: Meaning of Heb uncertain
[d] Or *Sea of Reeds* [e] Heb *He*
[f] Meaning of Heb uncertain

that I show you concerning the pattern of the tabernacle and of all its furniture, so you shall make it.

The Ark of the Covenant
(Ex 37.1–9)

10 They shall make an ark of acacia wood; it shall be two and a half cubits long, a cubit and a half wide, and a cubit and a half high. [11] You shall overlay it with pure gold, inside and outside you shall overlay it, and you shall make a molding of gold upon it all around. [12] You shall cast four rings of gold for it and put them on its four feet, two rings on the one side of it, and two rings on the other side. [13] You shall make poles of acacia wood, and overlay them with gold. [14] And you shall put the poles into the rings on the sides of the ark, by which to carry the ark. [15] The poles shall remain in the rings of the ark; they shall not be taken from it. [16] You shall put into the ark the covenant[g] that I shall give you.

17 Then you shall make a mercy seat[h] of pure gold; two cubits and a half shall be its length, and a cubit and a half its width. [18] You shall make two cherubim of gold; you shall make them of hammered work, at the two ends of the mercy seat.[i] [19] Make one cherub at the one end, and one cherub at the other; of one piece with the mercy seat[i] you shall make the cherubim at its two ends. [20] The cherubim shall spread out their wings above, overshadowing the mercy seat[i] with their wings. They shall face one to another; the faces of the cherubim shall be turned toward the mercy seat.[i] [21] You shall put the mercy seat[i] on the top of the ark; and in the ark you shall put the covenant[g] that I shall give you. [22] There I will meet with you, and from above the mercy seat,[i] from between the two cherubim that are on the ark of the covenant,[g] I will deliver to you all my commands for the Israelites.

The Table for the Bread of the Presence
(Ex 37.10–16)

23 You shall make a table of acacia wood, two cubits long, one cubit wide, and a cubit and a half high. [24] You shall overlay it with pure gold, and make a molding of gold around it. [25] You shall make around it a rim a handbreadth wide, and a molding of gold around the rim. [26] You shall make for it four rings of gold, and fasten the rings to the four corners at its four legs. [27] The rings that hold the poles used for carrying the table shall be close to the rim. [28] You shall make the poles of acacia wood, and overlay them with gold, and the table shall be carried with these. [29] You shall make its plates and dishes for incense, and its flagons and bowls with which to pour drink offerings; you shall make them of pure gold. [30] And you shall set the bread of the Presence on the table before me always.

The Lampstand
(Ex 37.17–24)

31 You shall make a lampstand of pure gold. The base and the shaft of the lampstand shall be made of hammered work; its cups, its calyxes, and its petals shall be of one piece with it; [32] and there shall be six branches going out of its sides, three branches of the lampstand out of one side of it and three branches of the lampstand out of the other side of it; [33] three cups shaped like almond blossoms, each with calyx and petals, on one branch, and three cups shaped like almond blossoms, each with calyx and petals, on the other branch—so for the six branches going out of the lampstand. [34] On the lampstand itself there shall be four cups shaped like almond blossoms, each with its calyxes and petals. [35] There shall be a calyx of one piece with it under the first pair of branches, a calyx of one piece with it under the next pair of branches, and a calyx of one piece with it under the last pair of branches—so for the six branches that go out of the lampstand. [36] Their calyxes and their branches shall be of one piece with it, the whole of it one hammered piece of pure gold. [37] You shall make the seven lamps for it; and the lamps shall be set up so as to give light on the space in front of it. [38] Its snuffers and trays shall be of pure gold. [39] It, and all these utensils, shall be made from a talent of pure gold. [40] And see that you make them according to the pattern for them, which is being shown you on the mountain.

The Tabernacle
(Ex 36.8–38)

26 Moreover you shall make the tabernacle with ten curtains of

g Or *treaty*, or *testimony*; Heb *eduth*
h Or *a cover*   i Or *the cover*

fine twisted linen, and blue, purple, and crimson yarns; you shall make them with cherubim skillfully worked into them. ² The length of each curtain shall be twenty-eight cubits, and the width of each curtain four cubits; all the curtains shall be of the same size. ³ Five curtains shall be joined to one another; and the other five curtains shall be joined to one another. ⁴ You shall make loops of blue on the edge of the outermost curtain in the first set; and likewise you shall make loops on the edge of the outermost curtain in the second set. ⁵ You shall make fifty loops on the one curtain, and you shall make fifty loops on the edge of the curtain that is in the second set; the loops shall be opposite one another. ⁶ You shall make fifty clasps of gold, and join the curtains to one another with the clasps, so that the tabernacle may be one whole.

7 You shall also make curtains of goats' hair for a tent over the tabernacle; you shall make eleven curtains. ⁸ The length of each curtain shall be thirty cubits, and the width of each curtain four cubits; the eleven curtains shall be of the same size. ⁹ You shall join five curtains by themselves, and six curtains by themselves, and the sixth curtain you shall double over at the front of the tent. ¹⁰ You shall make fifty loops on the edge of the curtain that is outermost in one set, and fifty loops on the edge of the curtain that is outermost in the second set.

11 You shall make fifty clasps of bronze, and put the clasps into the loops, and join the tent together, so that it may be one whole. ¹² The part that remains of the curtains of the tent, the half curtain that remains, shall hang over the back of the tabernacle. ¹³ The cubit on the one side, and the cubit on the other side, of what remains in the length of the curtains of the tent, shall hang over the sides of the tabernacle, on this side and that side, to cover it. ¹⁴ You shall make for the tent a covering of tanned rams' skins and an outer covering of fine leather.ʲ

The Framework

15 You shall make upright frames of acacia wood for the tabernacle. ¹⁶ Ten cubits shall be the length of a frame, and a cubit and a half the width of each frame. ¹⁷ There shall be two pegs in each frame to fit the frames together; you shall make these for all the frames of the tabernacle. ¹⁸ You shall make the frames for the tabernacle: twenty frames for the south side; ¹⁹ and you shall make forty bases of silver under the twenty frames, two bases under the first frame for its two pegs, and two bases under the next frame for its two pegs; ²⁰ and for the second side of the tabernacle, on the north side twenty frames, ²¹ and their forty bases of silver, two bases under the first frame, and two bases under the next frame; ²² and for the rear of the tabernacle westward you shall make six frames. ²³ You shall make two frames for corners of the tabernacle in the rear; ²⁴ they shall be separate beneath, but joined at the top, at the first ring; it shall be the same with both of them; they shall form the two corners. ²⁵ And so there shall be eight frames, with their bases of silver, sixteen bases; two bases under the first frame, and two bases under the next frame.

26 You shall make bars of acacia wood, five for the frames of the one side of the tabernacle, ²⁷ and five bars for the frames of the other side of the tabernacle, and five bars for the frames of the side of the tabernacle at the rear westward. ²⁸ The middle bar, halfway up the frames, shall pass through from end to end. ²⁹ You shall overlay the frames with gold, and shall make their rings of gold to hold the bars; and you shall overlay the bars with gold. ³⁰ Then you shall erect the tabernacle according to the plan for it that you were shown on the mountain.

The Curtain

31 You shall make a curtain of blue, purple, and crimson yarns, and of fine twisted linen; it shall be made with cherubim skillfully worked into it. ³² You shall hang it on four pillars of acacia overlaid with gold, which have hooks of gold and rest on four bases of silver. ³³ You shall hang the curtain under the clasps, and bring the ark of the covenantᵏ in there, within the curtain; and the curtain shall separate for you the holy place from the most holy. ³⁴ You shall put the mercy seatˡ on the ark of the covenantᵏ in the most holy place. ³⁵ You shall set the table outside

ʲ Meaning of Heb uncertain
ᵏ Or *treaty*, or *testimony*; Heb *eduth*
ˡ Or *the cover*

the curtain, and the lampstand on the south side of the tabernacle opposite the table; and you shall put the table on the north side.

36 You shall make a screen for the entrance of the tent, of blue, purple, and crimson yarns, and of fine twisted linen, embroidered with needlework. 37You shall make for the screen five pillars of acacia, and overlay them with gold; their hooks shall be of gold, and you shall cast five bases of bronze for them.

The Altar of Burnt Offering
(Ex 38.1–7)

27 You shall make the altar of acacia wood, five cubits long and five cubits wide; the altar shall be square, and it shall be three cubits high. 2You shall make horns for it at its four corners; its horns shall be of one piece with it, and you shall overlay it with bronze. 3You shall make pots for it to receive its ashes, and shovels and basins and forks and firepans; you shall make all its utensils of bronze. 4You shall also make for it a grating, a network of bronze; and on the net you shall make four bronze rings at its four corners. 5You shall set it under the ledge of the altar so that the net shall extend halfway down the altar. 6You shall make poles for the altar, poles of acacia wood, and overlay them with bronze; 7the poles shall be put through the rings, so that the poles shall be on the two sides of the altar when it is carried. 8You shall make it hollow, with boards. They shall be made just as you were shown on the mountain.

The Court and Its Hangings
(Ex 38.9–20)

9 You shall make the court of the tabernacle. On the south side the court shall have hangings of fine twisted linen one hundred cubits long for that side; 10its twenty pillars and their twenty bases shall be of bronze, but the hooks of the pillars and their bands shall be of silver. 11Likewise for its length on the north side there shall be hangings one hundred cubits long, their pillars twenty and their bases twenty, of bronze, but the hooks of the pillars and their bands shall be of silver. 12For the width of the court on the west side there shall be fifty cubits of hangings, with ten pillars and ten bases. 13The width of the court on the front to the east shall be fifty cubits.

14There shall be fifteen cubits of hangings on the one side, with three pillars and three bases. 15There shall be fifteen cubits of hangings on the other side, with three pillars and three bases. 16For the gate of the court there shall be a screen twenty cubits long, of blue, purple, and crimson yarns, and of fine twisted linen, embroidered with needlework; it shall have four pillars and with them four bases. 17All the pillars around the court shall be banded with silver; their hooks shall be of silver, and their bases of bronze. 18The length of the court shall be one hundred cubits, the width fifty, and the height five cubits, with hangings of fine twisted linen and bases of bronze. 19All the utensils of the tabernacle for every use, and all its pegs and all the pegs of the court, shall be of bronze.

The Oil for the Lamp
(Lev 24.1–4)

20 You shall further command the Israelites to bring you pure oil of beaten olives for the light, so that a lamp may be set up to burn regularly. 21In the tent of meeting, outside the curtain that is before the covenant,m Aaron and his sons shall tend it from evening to morning before the LORD. It shall be a perpetual ordinance to be observed throughout their generations by the Israelites.

Vestments for the Priesthood
(Ex 39.1–7)

28 Then bring near to you your brother Aaron, and his sons with him, from among the Israelites, to serve me as priests—Aaron and Aaron's sons, Na′dab and A·bi′hū, El·e·a′zar and Ith′a·mar. 2You shall make sacred vestments for the glorious adornment of your brother Aaron. 3And you shall speak to all who have ability, whom I have endowed with skill, that they make Aaron's vestments to consecrate him for my priesthood. 4These are the vestments that they shall make: a breastpiece, an ephod, a robe, a checkered tunic, a turban, and a sash. When they make these sacred vestments for your brother Aaron and his sons to serve me as priests, 5they shall use gold, blue, purple, and crimson yarns, and fine linen.

mOr *treaty,* or *testimony;* Heb *eduth*

The Ephod

6 They shall make the ephod of gold, of blue, purple, and crimson yarns, and of fine twisted linen, skillfully worked. [7] It shall have two shoulder-pieces attached to its two edges, so that it may be joined together. [8] The decorated band on it shall be of the same workmanship and materials, of gold, of blue, purple, and crimson yarns, and of fine twisted linen. [9] You shall take two onyx stones, and engrave on them the names of the sons of Israel, [10] six of their names on the one stone, and the names of the remaining six on the other stone, in the order of their birth. [11] As a gem-cutter engraves signets, so you shall engrave the two stones with the names of the sons of Israel; you shall mount them in settings of gold filigree. [12] You shall set the two stones on the shoulder-pieces of the ephod, as stones of remembrance for the sons of Israel; and Aaron shall bear their names before the LORD on his two shoulders for remembrance. [13] You shall make settings of gold filigree, [14] and two chains of pure gold, twisted like cords; and you shall attach the corded chains to the settings.

The Breastplate
(Ex 39.8–21)

15 You shall make a breastpiece of judgment, in skilled work; you shall make it in the style of the ephod; of gold, of blue and purple and crimson yarns, and of fine twisted linen you shall make it. [16] It shall be square and doubled, a span in length and a span in width. [17] You shall set in it four rows of stones. A row of carnelian,[n] chrysolite, and emerald shall be the first row; [18] and the second row a turquoise, a sapphire[o] and a moonstone; [19] and the third row a jacinth, an agate, and an amethyst; [20] and the fourth row a beryl, an onyx, and a jasper; they shall be set in gold filigree. [21] There shall be twelve stones with names corresponding to the names of the sons of Israel; they shall be like signets, each engraved with its name, for the twelve tribes. [22] You shall make for the breastpiece chains of pure gold, twisted like cords; [23] and you shall make for the breastpiece two rings of gold, and put the two rings on the two edges of the breastpiece. [24] You shall put the two cords of gold in the two rings at the edges of the breastpiece; [25] the two ends of the two cords you shall attach to the two settings, and so attach it in front to the shoulder-pieces of the ephod. [26] You shall make two rings of gold, and put them at the two ends of the breastpiece, on its inside edge next to the ephod. [27] You shall make two rings of gold, and attach them in front to the lower part of the two shoulder-pieces of the ephod, at its joining above the decorated band of the ephod. [28] The breastpiece shall be bound by its rings to the rings of the ephod with a blue cord, so that it may lie on the decorated band of the ephod, and so that the breastpiece shall not come loose from the ephod. [29] So Aaron shall bear the names of the sons of Israel in the breastpiece of judgment on his heart when he goes into the holy place, for a continual remembrance before the LORD. [30] In the breastpiece of judgment you shall put the U'rim and the Thum'mim, and they shall be on Aaron's heart when he goes in before the LORD; thus Aaron shall bear the judgment of the Israelites on his heart before the LORD continually.

Other Priestly Vestments
(Ex 39.22–31)

31 You shall make the robe of the ephod all of blue. [32] It shall have an opening for the head in the middle of it, with a woven binding around the opening, like the opening in a coat of mail,[p] so that it may not be torn. [33] On its lower hem you shall make pomegranates of blue, purple, and crimson yarns, all around the lower hem, with bells of gold between them all around—[34] a golden bell and a pomegranate alternating all around the lower hem of the robe. [35] Aaron shall wear it when he ministers, and its sound shall be heard when he goes into the holy place before the LORD, and when he comes out, so that he may not die.

36 You shall make a rosette of pure gold, and engrave on it, like the engraving of a signet, "Holy to the LORD." [37] You shall fasten it on the turban with a blue cord; it shall be on the front of the turban. [38] It shall be on Aaron's forehead, and Aaron shall take on himself any guilt incurred in the holy

[n] The identity of several of these stones is uncertain   [o] Or *lapis lazuli*
[p] Meaning of Heb uncertain

offering that the Israelites consecrate as their sacred donations; it shall always be on his forehead, in order that they may find favor before the LORD.

39 You shall make the checkered tunic of fine linen, and you shall make a turban of fine linen, and you shall make a sash embroidered with needlework.

40 For Aaron's sons you shall make tunics and sashes and headdresses; you shall make them for their glorious adornment. 41 You shall put them on your brother Aaron, and on his sons with him, and shall anoint them and ordain them and consecrate them, so that they may serve me as priests. 42 You shall make for them linen undergarments to cover their naked flesh; they shall reach from the hips to the thighs; 43 Aaron and his sons shall wear them when they go into the tent of meeting, or when they come near the altar to minister in the holy place; or they will bring guilt on themselves and die. This shall be a perpetual ordinance for him and for his descendants after him.

The Ordination of the Priests
(Lev 8.1–36)

29 Now this is what you shall do to them to consecrate them, so that they may serve me as priests. Take one young bull and two rams without blemish, 2 and unleavened bread, unleavened cakes mixed with oil, and unleavened wafers spread with oil. You shall make them of choice wheat flour. 3 You shall put them in one basket and bring them in the basket, and bring the bull and the two rams. 4 You shall bring Aaron and his sons to the entrance of the tent of meeting, and wash them with water. 5 Then you shall take the vestments, and put on Aaron the tunic and the robe of the ephod, and the ephod, and the breastpiece, and gird him with the decorated band of the ephod; 6 and you shall set the turban on his head, and put the holy diadem on the turban. 7 You shall take the anointing oil, and pour it on his head and anoint him. 8 Then you shall bring his sons, and put tunics on them, 9 and you shall gird them with sashes q and tie headdresses on them; and the priesthood shall be theirs by a perpetual ordinance. You shall then ordain Aaron and his sons.

10 You shall bring the bull in front

of the tent of meeting. Aaron and his sons shall lay their hands on the head of the bull, 11 and you shall slaughter the bull before the LORD, at the entrance of the tent of meeting, 12 and shall take some of the blood of the bull and put it on the horns of the altar with your finger, and all the rest of the blood you shall pour out at the base of the altar. 13 You shall take all the fat that covers the entrails, and the appendage of the liver, and the two kidneys with the fat that is on them, and turn them into smoke on the altar. 14 But the flesh of the bull, and its skin, and its dung, you shall burn with fire outside the camp; it is a sin offering.

15 Then you shall take one of the rams, and Aaron and his sons shall lay their hands on the head of the ram, 16 and you shall slaughter the ram, and shall take its blood and dash it against all sides of the altar. 17 Then you shall cut the ram into its parts, and wash its entrails and its legs, and put them with its parts and its head, 18 and turn the whole ram into smoke on the altar; it is a burnt offering to the LORD; it is a pleasing odor, an offering by fire to the LORD.

19 You shall take the other ram; and Aaron and his sons shall lay their hands on the head of the ram, 20 and you shall slaughter the ram, and take some of its blood and put it on the lobe of Aaron's right ear and on the lobes of the right ears of his sons, and on the thumbs of their right hands, and on the big toes of their right feet, and dash the rest of the blood against all sides of the altar. 21 Then you shall take some of the blood that is on the altar, and some of the anointing oil, and sprinkle it on Aaron and his vestments and on his sons and his sons' vestments with him; then he and his vestments shall be holy, as well as his sons and his sons' vestments.

22 You shall also take the fat of the ram, the fat tail, the fat that covers the entrails, the appendage of the liver, the two kidneys with the fat that is on them, and the right thigh (for it is a ram of ordination), 23 and one loaf of bread, one cake of bread made with oil, and one wafer, out of the basket of unleavened bread that is before the LORD; 24 and you shall place all these on the palms of Aaron and on the palms of his sons, and raise them as an elevation

q Gk: Heb sashes, Aaron and his sons

offering before the LORD. 25 Then you shall take them from their hands, and turn them into smoke on the altar on top of the burnt offering of pleasing odor before the LORD; it is an offering by fire to the LORD.

26 You shall take the breast of the ram of Aaron's ordination and raise it as an elevation offering before the LORD; and it shall be your portion. 27 You shall consecrate the breast that was raised as an elevation offering and the thigh that was raised as an elevation offering from the ram of ordination, from that which belonged to Aaron and his sons. 28 These things shall be a perpetual ordinance for Aaron and his sons from the Israelites, for this is an offering; and it shall be an offering by the Israelites from their sacrifice of offerings of well-being, their offering to the LORD.

29 The sacred vestments of Aaron shall be passed on to his sons after him; they shall be anointed in them and ordained in them. 30 The son who is priest in his place shall wear them seven days, when he comes into the tent of meeting to minister in the holy place.

31 You shall take the ram of ordination, and boil its flesh in a holy place; 32 and Aaron and his sons shall eat the flesh of the ram and the bread that is in the basket, at the entrance of the tent of meeting. 33 They themselves shall eat the food by which atonement is made, to ordain and consecrate them, but no one else shall eat of them, because they are holy. 34 If any of the flesh for the ordination, or of the bread, remains until the morning, then you shall burn the remainder with fire; it shall not be eaten, because it is holy.

35 Thus you shall do to Aaron and to his sons, just as I have commanded you; through seven days you shall ordain them. 36 Also every day you shall offer a bull as a sin offering for atonement. Also you shall offer a sin offering for the altar, when you make atonement for it, and shall anoint it, to consecrate it. 37 Seven days you shall make atonement for the altar, and consecrate it, and the altar shall be most holy; whatever touches the altar shall become holy.

The Daily Offerings
(Num 28.1–8)

38 Now this is what you shall offer on the altar: two lambs a year old regularly each day. 39 One lamb you shall offer in the morning, and the other lamb you shall offer in the evening; 40 and with the first lamb one-tenth of a measure of choice flour mixed with one-fourth of a hin of beaten oil, and one-fourth of a hin of wine for a drink offering. 41 And the other lamb you shall offer in the evening, and shall offer with it a grain offering and its drink offering, as in the morning, for a pleasing odor, an offering by fire to the LORD. 42 It shall be a regular burnt offering throughout your generations at the entrance of the tent of meeting before the LORD, where I will meet with you, to speak to you there. 43 I will meet with the Israelites there, and it shall be sanctified by my glory; 44 I will consecrate the tent of meeting and the altar; Aaron also and his sons I will consecrate, to serve me as priests. 45 I will dwell among the Israelites, and I will be their God. 46 And they shall know that I am the LORD their God, who brought them out of the land of Egypt that I might dwell among them; I am the LORD their God.

The Altar of Incense
(Ex 37.25–28)

30 You shall make an altar on which to offer incense; you shall make it of acacia wood. 2 It shall be one cubit long, and one cubit wide; it shall be square, and shall be two cubits high; its horns shall be of one piece with it. 3 You shall overlay it with pure gold, its top, and its sides all around and its horns; and you shall make for it a molding of gold all around. 4 And you shall make two golden rings for it; under its molding on two opposite sides of it you shall make them, and they shall hold the poles with which to carry it. 5 You shall make the poles of acacia wood, and overlay them with gold. 6 You shall place it in front of the curtain that is above the ark of the covenant,r in front of the mercy seats that is over the covenant,r where I will meet with you. 7 Aaron shall offer fragrant incense on it; every morning when he dresses the lamps he shall offer it, 8 and when Aaron sets up the lamps in the evening, he shall offer it, a regular incense offering before the LORD throughout your generations. 9 You shall not offer unholy incense on

r Or treaty, or testimony; Heb eduth
s Or the cover

it, or a burnt offering, or a grain offering; and you shall not pour a drink offering on it. [10]Once a year Aaron shall perform the rite of atonement on its horns. Throughout your generations he shall perform the atonement for it once a year with the blood of the atoning sin offering. It is most holy to the LORD.

The Half Shekel for the Sanctuary

[11] The LORD spoke to Moses: [12]When you take a census of the Israelites to register them, at registration all of them shall give a ransom for their lives to the LORD, so that no plague may come upon them for being registered. [13]This is what each one who is registered shall give: half a shekel according to the shekel of the sanctuary (the shekel is twenty gerahs), half a shekel as an offering to the LORD. [14]Each one who is registered, from twenty years old and upward, shall give the LORD's offering. [15]The rich shall not give more, and the poor shall not give less, than the half shekel, when you bring this offering to the LORD to make atonement for your lives. [16]You shall take the atonement money from the Israelites and shall designate it for the service of the tent of meeting; before the LORD it will be a reminder to the Israelites of the ransom given for your lives.

The Bronze Basin

[17] The LORD spoke to Moses: [18]You shall make a bronze basin with a bronze stand for washing. You shall put it between the tent of meeting and the altar, and you shall put water in it; [19]with the water[t] Aaron and his sons shall wash their hands and their feet. [20]When they go into the tent of meeting, or when they come near the altar to minister, to make an offering by fire to the LORD, they shall wash with water, so that they may not die. [21]They shall wash their hands and their feet, so that they may not die: it shall be a perpetual ordinance for them, for him and for his descendants throughout their generations.

The Anointing Oil and Incense
(Ex 37.29)

[22] The LORD spoke to Moses: [23]Take the finest spices: of liquid myrrh five hundred shekels, and of sweet-smelling cinnamon half as much, that is, two hundred fifty, and

two hundred fifty of aromatic cane, [24]and five hundred of cassia—measured by the sanctuary shekel—and a hin of olive oil; [25]and you shall make of these a sacred anointing oil blended as by the perfumer; it shall be a holy anointing oil. [26]With it you shall anoint the tent of meeting and the ark of the covenant,[u] [27]and the table and all its utensils, and the lampstand and its utensils, and the altar of incense, [28]and the altar of burnt offering with all its utensils, and the basin with its stand; [29]you shall consecrate them, so that they may be most holy; whatever touches them will become holy. [30]You shall anoint Aaron and his sons, and consecrate them, in order that they may serve me as priests. [31]You shall say to the Israelites, "This shall be my holy anointing oil throughout your generations. [32]It shall not be used in any ordinary anointing of the body, and you shall make no other like it in composition; it is holy, and it shall be holy to you. [33]Whoever compounds any like it or whoever puts any of it on an unqualified person shall be cut off from the people."

[34] The LORD said to Moses: Take sweet spices, stacte, and onycha, and galbanum, sweet spices with pure frankincense (an equal part of each), [35]and make an incense blended as by the perfumer, seasoned with salt, pure and holy; [36]and you shall beat some of it into powder, and put part of it before the covenant[u] in the tent of meeting where I shall meet with you; it shall be for you most holy. [37]When you make incense according to this composition, you shall not make it for yourselves; it shall be regarded by you as holy to the LORD. [38]Whoever makes any like it to use as perfume shall be cut off from the people.

Bezalel and Oholiab
(Ex 35.30—36.1)

31
The LORD spoke to Moses: [2]See, I have called by name Bez'a·lel son of U'ri son of Hur, of the tribe of Judah: [3]and I have filled him with divine spirit,[v] with ability, intelligence, and knowledge in every kind of craft, [4]to devise artistic designs, to work in gold, silver, and bronze, [5]in cutting stones for setting, and in carving wood, in every kind of craft.

[t]Heb *it*　[u]Or *treaty*, or *testimony*; Heb *eduth*　[v]Or *with the spirit of God*

6Moreover, I have appointed with him Ō·hō'li·ab son of A·his'a·mach, of the tribe of Dan; and I have given skill to all the skillful, so that they may make all that I have commanded you: 7the tent of meeting, and the ark of the covenant,w and the mercy seatx that is on it, and all the furnishings of the tent, 8the table and its utensils, and the pure lampstand with all its utensils, and the altar of incense, 9and the altar of burnt offering with all its utensils, and the basin with its stand, 10and the finely worked vestments, the holy vestments for the priest Aaron and the vestments of his sons, for their service as priests, 11and the anointing oil and the fragrant incense for the holy place. They shall do just as I have commanded you.

The Sabbath Law

12 The LORD said to Moses: 13You yourself are to speak to the Israelites: "You shall keep my sabbaths, for this is a sign between me and you throughout your generations, given in order that you may know that I, the LORD, sanctify you. 14You shall keep the sabbath, because it is holy for you; everyone who profanes it shall be put to death; whoever does any work on it shall be cut off from among the people. 15Six days shall work be done, but the seventh day is a sabbath of solemn rest, holy to the LORD; whoever does any work on the sabbath day shall be put to death. 16Therefore the Israelites shall keep the sabbath, observing the sabbath throughout their generations, as a perpetual covenant. 17It is a sign forever between me and the people of Israel that in six days the LORD made heaven and earth, and on the seventh day he rested, and was refreshed."

The Two Tablets of the Covenant

18 When Gody finished speaking with Moses on Mount Sinai, he gave him the two tablets of the covenant,w tablets of stone, written with the finger of God.

The Golden Calf
(Deut 9.6–29)

32 When the people saw that Moses delayed to come down from the mountain, the people gathered around Aaron, and said to him, "Come, make gods for us, who shall go before us; as for this Moses, the man who brought us up out of the land of Egypt, we do not know what has become of him." 2Aaron said to them, "Take off the gold rings that are on the ears of your wives, your sons, and your daughters, and bring them to me." 3So all the people took off the gold rings from their ears, and brought them to Aaron. 4He took the gold from them, formed it in a mold,z and cast an image of a calf; and they said, "These are your gods, O Israel, who brought you up out of the land of Egypt!" 5When Aaron saw this, he built an altar before it; and Aaron made proclamation and said, "Tomorrow shall be a festival to the LORD." 6They rose early the next day, and offered burnt offerings and brought sacrifices of well-being; and the people sat down to eat and drink, and rose up to revel.

7 The LORD said to Moses, "Go down at once! Your people, whom you brought up out of the land of Egypt, have acted perversely; 8they have been quick to turn aside from the way that I commanded them; they have cast for themselves an image of a calf, and have worshiped it and sacrificed to it, and said, 'These are your gods, O Israel, who brought you up out of the land of Egypt!' " 9The LORD said to Moses, "I have seen this people, how stiff-necked they are. 10Now let me alone, so that my wrath may burn hot against them and I may consume them; and of you I will make a great nation."

11 But Moses implored the LORD his God, and said, "O LORD, why does your wrath burn hot against your people, whom you brought out of the land of Egypt with great power and with a mighty hand? 12Why should the Egyptians say, 'It was with evil intent that he brought them out to kill them in the mountains, and to consume them from the face of the earth'? Turn from your fierce wrath; change your mind and do not bring disaster on your people. 13Remember Abraham, Isaac, and Israel, your servants, how you swore to them by your own self, saying to them, 'I will multiply your descendants like the stars of heaven, and all this land that I have promised I will give to your descendants, and they shall inherit it forever.' " 14And the LORD changed his

---

wOr treaty, or testimony; Heb eduth
xOr the cover   yHeb he
zOr fashioned it with a graving tool;
Meaning of Heb uncertain

mind about the disaster that he planned to bring on his people.

15 Then Moses turned and went down from the mountain, carrying the two tablets of the covenant[a] in his hands, tablets that were written on both sides, written on the front and on the back. [16] The tablets were the work of God, and the writing was the writing of God, engraved upon the tablets. [17] When Joshua heard the noise of the people as they shouted, he said to Moses, "There is a noise of war in the camp." [18] But he said,

"It is not the sound made by
        victors,

or the sound made by losers;

it is the sound of revelers that I
        hear."

[19] As soon as he came near the camp and saw the calf and the dancing, Moses' anger burned hot, and he threw the tablets from his hands and broke them at the foot of the mountain. [20] He took the calf that they had made, burned it with fire, ground it to powder, scattered it on the water, and made the Israelites drink it.

21 Moses said to Aaron, "What did this people do to you that you have brought so great a sin upon them?" [22] And Aaron said, "Do not let the anger of my lord burn hot; you know the people, that they are bent on evil. [23] They said to me, 'Make us gods, who shall go before us; as for this Moses, the man who brought us up out of the land of Egypt, we do not know what has become of him.' [24] So I said to them, 'Whoever has gold, take it off'; so they gave it to me, and I threw it into the fire, and out came this calf!"

25 When Moses saw that the people were running wild (for Aaron had let them run wild, to the derision of their enemies), [26] then Moses stood in the gate of the camp, and said, "Who is on the LORD's side? Come to me!" And all the sons of Levi gathered around him. [27] He said to them, "Thus says the LORD, the God of Israel, 'Put your sword on your side, each of you! Go back and forth from gate to gate throughout the camp, and each of you kill your brother, your friend, and your neighbor.' " [28] The sons of Levi did as Moses commanded, and about three thousand of the people fell on that day. [29] Moses said, "Today you have ordained yourselves[b] for the service of the LORD, each one at the cost of a son

or a brother, and so have brought a blessing on yourselves this day."

30 On the next day Moses said to the people, "You have sinned a great sin. But now I will go up to the LORD; perhaps I can make atonement for your sin." [31] So Moses returned to the LORD and said, "Alas, this people has sinned a great sin; they have made for themselves gods of gold. [32] But now, if you will only forgive their sin—but if not, blot me out of the book that you have written." [33] But the LORD said to Moses, "Whoever has sinned against me I will blot out of my book. [34] But now go, lead the people to the place about which I have spoken to you; see, my angel shall go in front of you. Nevertheless, when the day comes for punishment, I will punish them for their sin."

35 Then the LORD sent a plague on the people, because they made the calf—the one that Aaron made.

The Command to Leave Sinai

33 The LORD said to Moses, "Go, leave this place, you and the people whom you have brought up out of the land of Egypt, and go to the land of which I swore to Abraham, Isaac, and Jacob, saying, 'To your descendants I will give it.' [2] I will send an angel before you, and I will drive out the Ca'naan·ites, the Am'o·rites, the Hit'tites, the Per'iz·zites, the Hi'vites, and the Jeb'u·sites. [3] Go up to a land flowing with milk and honey; but I will not go up among you, or I would consume you on the way, for you are a stiff-necked people."

4 When the people heard these harsh words, they mourned, and no one put on ornaments. [5] For the LORD had said to Moses, "Say to the Israelites, 'You are a stiff-necked people; if for a single moment I should go up among you, I would consume you. So now take off your ornaments, and I will decide what to do to you.' " [6] Therefore the Israelites stripped themselves of their ornaments, from Mount Ho'reb onward.

The Tent outside the Camp

7 Now Moses used to take the tent and pitch it outside the camp, far off from the camp; he called it the tent of

---

[a] Or treaty, or testimony; Heb eduth
[b] Gk Vg Compare Tg: Heb Today ordain yourselves

E
X
O
D
U
S

meeting. And everyone who sought the LORD would go out to the tent of meeting, which was outside the camp. [8] Whenever Moses went out to the tent, all the people would rise and stand, each of them, at the entrance of their tents and watch Moses until he had gone into the tent. [9] When Moses entered the tent, the pillar of cloud would descend and stand at the entrance of the tent, and the LORD would speak with Moses. [10] When all the people saw the pillar of cloud standing at the entrance of the tent, all the people would rise and bow down, all of them, at the entrance of their tent. [11] Thus the LORD used to speak to Moses face to face, as one speaks to a friend. Then he would return to the camp; but his young assistant, Joshua son of Nun, would not leave the tent.

Moses' Intercession

12 Moses said to the LORD, "See, you have said to me, 'Bring up this people'; but you have not let me know whom you will send with me. Yet you have said, 'I know you by name, and you have also found favor in my sight.' [13] Now if I have found favor in your sight, show me your ways, so that I may know you and find favor in your sight. Consider too that this nation is your people." [14] He said, "My presence will go with you, and I will give you rest." [15] And he said to him, "If your presence will not go, do not carry us up from here. [16] For how shall it be known that I have found favor in your sight, I and your people, unless you go with us? In this way, we shall be distinct, I and your people, from every people on the face of the earth."

17 The LORD said to Moses, "I will do the very thing that you have asked; for you have found favor in my sight, and I know you by name." [18] Moses said, "Show me your glory, I pray." [19] And he said, "I will make all my goodness pass before you, and will proclaim before you the name, 'The LORD'; [c] and I will be gracious to whom I will be gracious, and will show mercy on whom I will show mercy. [20] But," he said, "you cannot see my face; for no one shall see me and live." [21] And the LORD continued, "See, there is a place by me where you shall stand on the rock; [22] and while my glory passes by I will put you in a cleft of the rock, and I will cover you with my hand until I have passed by; [23] then I will take away

my hand, and you shall see my back; but my face shall not be seen."

Moses Makes New Tablets
(Deut 10.1–5)

34 The LORD said to Moses, "Cut two tablets of stone like the former ones, and I will write on the tablets the words that were on the former tablets, which you broke. [2] Be ready in the morning, and come up in the morning to Mount Sinai and present yourself there to me, on the top of the mountain. [3] No one shall come up with you, and do not let anyone be seen throughout all the mountain; and do not let flocks or herds graze in front of that mountain." [4] So Moses cut two tablets of stone like the former ones; and he rose early in the morning and went up on Mount Sinai, as the LORD had commanded him, and took in his hand the two tablets of stone. [5] The LORD descended in the cloud and stood with him there, and proclaimed the name, "The LORD." [c] [6] The LORD passed before him, and proclaimed,

"The LORD, the LORD,
a God merciful and gracious,
slow to anger,
and abounding in steadfast love
      and faithfulness,
7 keeping steadfast love for the
      thousandth generation, [d]
forgiving iniquity and
      transgression and sin,
yet by no means clearing the
      guilty,
but visiting the iniquity of the
      parents
upon the children
and the children's children,
to the third and the fourth
      generation."

[8] And Moses quickly bowed his head toward the earth, and worshiped. [9] He said, "If now I have found favor in your sight, O Lord, I pray, let the Lord go with us. Although this is a stiff-necked people, pardon our iniquity and our sin, and take us for your inheritance."

The Covenant Renewed
(Ex 23.14–19; Deut 7.1–6; 16.1–17)

10 He said: I hereby make a covenant. Before all your people I will perform marvels, such as have not been performed in all the earth or in any nation; and all the people among

---

[c] Heb YHWH; see note at 3.15   [d] Or for thousands

whom you live shall see the work of the LORD; for it is an awesome thing that I will do with you.

11 Observe what I command you today. See, I will drive out before you the Am'o·rites, the Ca'naan·ites, the Hit'-tites, the Per'iz·zites, the Hi'vites, and the Jeb'u·sites. [12] Take care not to make a covenant with the inhabitants of the land to which you are going, or it will become a snare among you. [13] You shall tear down their altars, break their pillars, and cut down their sacred poles[e] [14] (for you shall worship no other god, because the LORD, whose name is Jealous, is a jealous God). [15] You shall not make a covenant with the inhabitants of the land, for when they prostitute themselves to their gods and sacrifice to their gods, someone among them will invite you, and you will eat of the sacrifice. [16] And you will take wives from among their daughters for your sons, and their daughters who prostitute themselves to their gods will make your sons also prostitute themselves to their gods.

17 You shall not make cast idols.

18 You shall keep the festival of unleavened bread. Seven days you shall eat unleavened bread, as I commanded you, at the time appointed in the month of A'bib; for in the month of A'bib you came out from Egypt.

19 All that first opens the womb is mine, all your male[f] livestock, the firstborn of cow and sheep. [20] The firstborn of a donkey you shall redeem with a lamb, or if you will not redeem it you shall break its neck. All the firstborn of your sons you shall redeem.

No one shall appear before me empty-handed.

21 Six days you shall work, but on the seventh day you shall rest; even in plowing time and in harvest time you shall rest. [22] You shall observe the festival of weeks, the first fruits of wheat harvest, and the festival of ingathering at the turn of the year. [23] Three times in the year all your males shall appear before the LORD God, the God of Israel. [24] For I will cast out nations before you, and enlarge your borders; no one shall covet your land when you go up to appear before the LORD your God three times in the year.

25 You shall not offer the blood of my sacrifice with leaven, and the sacrifice of the festival of the passover shall not be left until the morning.

26 The best of the first fruits of your ground you shall bring to the house of the LORD your God.

You shall not boil a kid in its mother's milk.

27 The LORD said to Moses: Write these words; in accordance with these words I have made a covenant with you and with Israel. [28] He was there with the LORD forty days and forty nights; he neither ate bread nor drank water. And he wrote on the tablets the words of the covenant, the ten commandments.[g]

The Shining Face of Moses

29 Moses came down from Mount Sinai. As he came down from the mountain with the two tablets of the covenant[h] in his hand, Moses did not know that the skin of his face shone because he had been talking with God. [30] When Aaron and all the Israelites saw Moses, the skin of his face was shining, and they were afraid to come near him. [31] But Moses called to them; and Aaron and all the leaders of the congregation returned to him, and Moses spoke with them. [32] Afterward all the Israelites came near, and he gave them in commandment all that the LORD had spoken with him on Mount Sinai. [33] When Moses had finished speaking with them, he put a veil on his face; [34] but whenever Moses went in before the LORD to speak with him, he would take the veil off, until he came out; and when he came out, and told the Israelites what he had been commanded, [35] the Israelites would see the face of Moses, that the skin of his face was shining; and Moses would put the veil on his face again, until he went in to speak with him.

Sabbath Regulations

35 Moses assembled all the congregation of the Israelites and said to them: These are the things that the LORD has commanded you to do: 2 Six days shall work be done, but on the seventh day you shall have a holy sabbath of solemn rest to the LORD; whoever does any work on it shall be put to death. [3] You shall kindle no fire in all your dwellings on the sabbath day.

---

[e] Heb *Asherim*   [f] Gk Theodotion Vg Tg: Meaning of Heb uncertain
[g] Heb *words*   [h] Or *treaty*, or *testimony*; Heb *eduth*

EXODUS

Preparations for Making
the Tabernacle
(Ex 25.1–9; 39.32–43)

4 Moses said to all the congregation of the Israelites: This is the thing that the LORD has commanded: ⁵Take from among you an offering to the LORD; let whoever is of a generous heart bring the LORD's offering: gold, silver, and bronze; ⁶blue, purple, and crimson yarns, and fine linen; goats' hair, ⁷tanned rams' skins, and fine leather;ⁱ acacia wood, ⁸oil for the light, spices for the anointing oil and for the fragrant incense, ⁹and onyx stones and gems to be set in the ephod and the breastpiece.

10 All who are skillful among you shall come and make all that the LORD has commanded: the tabernacle, ¹¹its tent and its covering, its clasps and its frames, its bars, its pillars, and its bases; ¹²the ark with its poles, the mercy seat,ʲ and the curtain for the screen; ¹³the table with its poles and all its utensils, and the bread of the Presence; ¹⁴the lampstand also for the light, with its utensils and its lamps, and the oil for the light; ¹⁵and the altar of incense, with its poles, and the anointing oil and the fragrant incense, and the screen for the entrance, the entrance of the tabernacle; ¹⁶the altar of burnt offering, with its grating of bronze, its poles, and all its utensils, the basin with its stand; ¹⁷the hangings of the court, its pillars and its bases, and the screen for the gate of the court; ¹⁸the pegs of the tabernacle and the pegs of the court, and their cords; ¹⁹the finely worked vestments for ministering in the holy place, the holy vestments for the priest Aaron, and the vestments of his sons, for their service as priests.

Offerings for the Tabernacle

20 Then all the congregation of the Israelites withdrew from the presence of Moses. ²¹And they came, everyone whose heart was stirred, and everyone whose spirit was willing, and brought the LORD's offering to be used for the tent of meeting, and for all its service, and for the sacred vestments. ²²So they came, both men and women; all who were of a willing heart brought brooches and earrings and signet rings and pendants, all sorts of gold objects, everyone bringing an offering of gold to the LORD. ²³And everyone who pos-

sessed blue or purple or crimson yarn or fine linen or goats' hair or tanned rams' skins or fine leather,ⁱ brought them. ²⁴Everyone who could make an offering of silver or bronze brought it as the LORD's offering; and everyone who possessed acacia wood of any use in the work, brought it. ²⁵All the skillful women spun with their hands, and brought what they had spun in blue and purple and crimson yarns and fine linen; ²⁶all the women whose hearts moved them to use their skill spun the goats' hair. ²⁷And the leaders brought onyx stones and gems to be set in the ephod and the breastpiece, ²⁸and spices and oil for the light, and for the anointing oil, and for the fragrant incense. ²⁹All the Israelite men and women whose hearts made them willing to bring anything for the work that the LORD had commanded by Moses to be done, brought it as a freewill offering to the LORD.

Bezalel and Oholiab
(Ex 31.1–11)

30 Then Moses said to the Israelites: See, the LORD has called by name Bez'a·lel son of U'rī son of Hur, of the tribe of Judah; ³¹he has filled him with divine spirit,ᵏ with skill, intelligence, and knowledge in every kind of craft, ³²to devise artistic designs, to work in gold, silver, and bronze, ³³in cutting stones for setting, and in carving wood, in every kind of craft. ³⁴And he has inspired him to teach, both him and O·hō'li·ab son of A·his'a·mach, of the tribe of Dan. ³⁵He has filled them with skill to do every kind of work done by an artisan or by a designer or by an embroiderer in blue, purple, and crimson yarns, and in fine linen, or by a weaver—by any sort of artisan or skilled designer.

36 Bez'a·lel and O·hō'li·ab and every skillful one to whom the LORD has given skill and understanding to know how to do any work in the construction of the sanctuary shall work in accordance with all that the LORD has commanded.

2 Moses then called Bez'a·lel and O·hō'li·ab and every skillful one to whom the the LORD had given skill, everyone whose heart was stirred to come to do the work; ³and they received from Moses all the freewill of-

ⁱMeaning of Heb uncertain   ʲOr the cover   ᵏOr the spirit of God ferings that the Israelites had brought for doing the work on the sanctuary. They still kept bringing him freewill offerings every morning, 4 so that all the artisans who were doing every sort of task on the sanctuary came, each from the task being performed, 5 and said to Moses, "The people are bringing much more than enough for doing the work that the LORD has commanded us to do." 6 So Moses gave command, and word was proclaimed throughout the camp: "No man or woman is to make anything else as an offering for the sanctuary." So the people were restrained from bringing; 7 for what they had already brought was more than enough to do all the work.

Construction of the Tabernacle
(Ex 26.1–37)

8 All those with skill among the workers made the tabernacle with ten curtains; they were made of fine twisted linen, and blue, purple, and crimson yarns, with cherubim skillfully worked into them. 9 The length of each curtain was twenty-eight cubits, and the width of each curtain four cubits; all the curtains were of the same size.

10 He joined five curtains to one another, and the other five curtains he joined to one another. 11 He made loops of blue on the edge of the outermost curtain of the first set; likewise he made them on the edge of the outermost curtain of the second set; 12 he made fifty loops on the one curtain, and he made fifty loops on the edge of the curtain that was in the second set; the loops were opposite one another. 13 And he made fifty clasps of gold, and joined the curtains one to the other with clasps; so the tabernacle was one whole.

14 He also made curtains of goats' hair for a tent over the tabernacle; he made eleven curtains. 15 The length of each curtain was thirty cubits, and the width of each curtain four cubits; the eleven curtains were of the same size. 16 He joined five curtains by themselves, and six curtains by themselves. 17 He made fifty loops on the edge of the outermost curtain of the one set, and fifty loops on the edge of the other connecting curtain. 18 He made fifty clasps of bronze to join the tent together so that it might be one whole.

19 And he made for the tent a covering of tanned rams' skins and an outer covering of fine leather.[l]

20 Then he made the upright frames for the tabernacle of acacia wood. 21 Ten cubits was the length of a frame, and a cubit and a half the width of each frame. 22 Each frame had two pegs for fitting together; he did this for all the frames of the tabernacle. 23 The frames for the tabernacle he made in this way: twenty frames for the south side; 24 and he made forty bases of silver under the twenty frames, two bases under the first frame for its two pegs, and two bases under the next frame for its two pegs. 25 For the second side of the tabernacle, on the north side, he made twenty frames 26 and their forty bases of silver, two bases under the first frame and two bases under the next frame. 27 For the rear of the tabernacle westward he made six frames. 28 He made two frames for corners of the tabernacle in the rear. 29 They were separate beneath, but joined at the top, at the first ring; he made two of them in this way, for the two corners. 30 There were eight frames with their bases of silver: sixteen bases, under every frame two bases.

31 He made bars of acacia wood, five for the frames of the one side of the tabernacle, 32 and five bars for the frames of the other side of the tabernacle, and five bars for the frames of the tabernacle at the rear westward. 33 He made the middle bar to pass through from end to end halfway up the frames. 34 And he overlaid the frames with gold, and made rings of gold for them to hold the bars, and overlaid the bars with gold.

35 He made the curtain of blue, purple, and crimson yarns, and fine twisted linen, with cherubim skillfully worked into it. 36 For it he made four pillars of acacia, and overlaid them with gold; their hooks were of gold, and he cast for them four bases of silver. 37 He also made a screen for the entrance to the tent, of blue, purple, and crimson yarns, and fine twisted linen, embroidered with needlework; 38 and its five pillars with their hooks. He overlaid their capitals and their bases with gold, but their five bases were of bronze.

[l] Meaning of Heb uncertain

Making the Ark of the Covenant
(Ex 25.10–22)

37 Bez′a·lel made the ark of acacia wood; it was two and a half cubits long, a cubit and a half wide, and a cubit and a half high. [2] He overlaid it with pure gold inside and outside, and made a molding of gold around it. [3] He cast for it four rings of gold for its four feet, two rings on its one side and two rings on its other side. [4] He made poles of acacia wood, and overlaid them with gold, [5] and put the poles into the rings on the sides of the ark, to carry the ark. [6] He made a mercy seat [m] of pure gold; two cubits and a half was its length, and a cubit and a half its width. [7] He made two cherubim of hammered gold; at the two ends of the mercy seat [n] he made them, [8] one cherub at the one end, and one cherub at the other end; of one piece with the mercy seat [n] he made the cherubim at its two ends. [9] The cherubim spread out their wings above, overshadowing the mercy seat [n] with their wings. They faced one another; the faces of the cherubim were turned toward the mercy seat. [n]

Making the Table for the Bread of the Presence
(Ex 25.23–30)

[10] He also made the table of acacia wood, two cubits long, one cubit wide, and a cubit and a half high. [11] He overlaid it with pure gold, and made a molding of gold around it. [12] He made around it a rim a handbreadth wide, and made a molding of gold around the rim. [13] He cast for it four rings of gold, and fastened the rings to the four corners at its four legs. [14] The rings that held the poles used for carrying the table were close to the rim. [15] He made the poles of acacia wood to carry the table, and overlaid them with gold. [16] And he made the vessels of pure gold that were to be on the table, its plates and dishes for incense, and its bowls and flagons with which to pour drink offerings.

Making the Lampstand
(Ex 25.31–40)

[17] He also made the lampstand of pure gold. The base and the shaft of the lampstand were made of hammered work; its cups, its calyxes, and its petals were of one piece with it. [18] There were six branches going out of its sides, three branches of the lampstand out of one side of it and three branches of the lampstand out of the other side of it; [19] three cups shaped like almond blossoms, each with calyx and petals, on one branch, and three cups shaped like almond blossoms, each with calyx and petals, on the other branch—so for the six branches going out of the lampstand. [20] On the lampstand itself there were four cups shaped like almond blossoms, each with its calyxes and petals. [21] There was a calyx of one piece with it under the first pair of branches, a calyx of one piece with it under the next pair of branches, and a calyx of one piece with it under the last pair of branches. [22] Their calyxes and their branches were of one piece with it, the whole of it one hammered piece of pure gold. [23] He made its seven lamps and its snuffers and its trays of pure gold. [24] He made it and all its utensils of a talent of pure gold.

Making the Altar of Incense
(Ex 30.1–5)

[25] He made the altar of incense of acacia wood, one cubit long, and one cubit wide; it was square, and was two cubits high; its horns were of one piece with it. [26] He overlaid it with pure gold, its top, and its sides all around, and its horns; and he made for it a molding of gold all around, [27] and made two golden rings for it under its molding, on two opposite sides of it, to hold the poles with which to carry it. [28] And he made the poles of acacia wood, and overlaid them with gold.

Making the Anointing Oil and the Incense
(Ex 30.22–38)

[29] He made the holy anointing oil also, and the pure fragrant incense, blended as by the perfumer.

Making the Altar of Burnt Offering
(Ex 27.1–8)

38 He made the altar of burnt offering also of acacia wood; it was five cubits long, and five cubits wide; it was square, and three cubits high. [2] He made horns for it on its four corners; its horns were of one piece with it, and he overlaid it with bronze. [3] He made all the utensils of the altar, the pots, the shovels, the basins, the forks, and the firepans: all its utensils

[m] Or *a cover*   [n] Or *the cover*

he made of bronze. ⁴He made for the altar a grating, a network of bronze, under its ledge, extending halfway down. ⁵He cast four rings on the four corners of the bronze grating to hold the poles; ⁶he made the poles of acacia wood, and overlaid them with bronze. ⁷And he put the poles through the rings on the sides of the altar, to carry it with them; he made it hollow, with boards.

8 He made the basin of bronze with its stand of bronze, from the mirrors of the women who served at the entrance to the tent of meeting.

Making the Court of the Tabernacle
(Ex 27.9–19)

9 He made the court; for the south side the hangings of the court were of fine twisted linen, one hundred cubits long; ¹⁰its twenty pillars and their twenty bases were of bronze, but the hooks of the pillars and their bands were of silver. ¹¹For the north side there were hangings one hundred cubits long; its twenty pillars and their twenty bases were of bronze, but the hooks of the pillars and their bands were of silver. ¹²For the west side there were hangings fifty cubits long, with ten pillars and ten bases; the hooks of the pillars and their bands were of silver. ¹³And for the front to the east, fifty cubits. ¹⁴The hangings for one side of the gate were fifteen cubits, with three pillars and three bases. ¹⁵And so for the other side; on each side of the gate of the court were hangings of fifteen cubits, with three pillars and three bases. ¹⁶All the hangings around the court were of fine twisted linen. ¹⁷The bases for the pillars were of bronze, but the hooks of the pillars and their bands were of silver; the overlaying of their capitals was also of silver, and all the pillars of the court were banded with silver. ¹⁸The screen for the entrance to the court was embroidered with needlework in blue, purple, and crimson yarns and fine twisted linen. It was twenty cubits long and, along the width of it, five cubits high, corresponding to the hangings of the court. ¹⁹There were four pillars; their four bases were of bronze, their hooks of silver, and the overlaying of their capitals and their bands of silver. ²⁰All the pegs for the tabernacle and for the court all around were of bronze.

Materials of the Tabernacle

21 These are the records of the tabernacle, the tabernacle of the covenant,ᵒ which were drawn up at the commandment of Moses, the work of the Lē′vītes being under the direction of Ith′a·mar son of the priest Aaron. ²²Bez′a·lel son of U′rī son of Hur, of the tribe of Judah, made all that the Lord commanded Moses; ²³and with him was Ō·hō′li·ab son of A·his′a·mach, of the tribe of Dan, engraver, designer, and embroiderer in blue, purple, and crimson yarns, and in fine linen.

24 All the gold that was used for the work, in all the construction of the sanctuary, the gold from the offering, was twenty-nine talents and seven hundred thirty shekels, measured by the sanctuary shekel. ²⁵The silver from those of the congregation who were counted was one hundred talents and one thousand seven hundred seventy-five shekels, measured by the sanctuary shekel; ²⁶a beka a head (that is, half a shekel, measured by the sanctuary shekel), for everyone who was counted in the census, from twenty years old and upward, for six hundred three thousand, five hundred fifty men. ²⁷The hundred talents of silver were for casting the bases of the sanctuary, and the bases of the curtain; one hundred bases for the hundred talents, a talent for a base. ²⁸Of the thousand seven hundred seventy-five shekels he made hooks for the pillars, and overlaid their capitals and made bands for them. ²⁹The bronze that was contributed was seventy talents, and two thousand four hundred shekels; ³⁰with it he made the bases for the entrance of the tent of meeting, the bronze altar and the bronze grating for it and all the utensils of the altar, ³¹the bases all around the court, and the bases of the gate of the court, all the pegs of the tabernacle, and all the pegs around the court.

Making the Vestments for
the Priesthood
(Ex 28.1–43)

39 Of the blue, purple, and crimson yarns they made finely worked vestments, for ministering in the holy place; they made the sacred

ᵒOr *treaty*, or *testimony*; Heb *eduth*

vestments for Aaron; as the LORD had commanded Moses.

2 He made the ephod of gold, of blue, purple, and crimson yarns, and of fine twisted linen. 3 Gold leaf was hammered out and cut into threads to work into the blue, purple, and crimson yarns and into the fine twisted linen, in skilled design. 4 They made for the ephod shoulder-pieces, joined to it at its two edges. 5 The decorated band on it was of the same materials and workmanship, of gold, of blue, purple, and crimson yarns, and of fine twisted linen; as the LORD had commanded Moses.

6 The onyx stones were prepared, enclosed in settings of gold filigree and engraved like the engravings of a signet, according to the names of the sons of Israel. 7 He set them on the shoulder-pieces of the ephod, to be stones of remembrance for the sons of Israel; as the LORD had commanded Moses.

8 He made the breastpiece, in skilled work, like the work of the ephod, of gold, of blue, purple, and crimson yarns, and of fine twisted linen. 9 It was square; the breastpiece was made double, a span in length and a span in width when doubled. 10 They set in it four rows of stones. A row of carnelian,p chrysolite, and emerald was the first row; 11 and the second row, a turquoise, a sapphire,q and a moonstone; 12 and the third row, a jacinth, an agate, and an amethyst; 13 and the fourth row, a beryl, an onyx, and a jasper; they were enclosed in settings of gold filigree. 14 There were twelve stones with names corresponding to the names of the sons of Israel; they were like signets, each engraved with its name, for the twelve tribes. 15 They made on the breastpiece chains of pure gold, twisted like cords; 16 and they made two settings of gold filigree and two gold rings, and put the two rings on the two edges of the breastpiece; 17 and they put the two cords of gold in the two rings at the edges of the breastpiece. 18 Two ends of the two cords they had attached to the two settings of filigree; in this way they attached it in front to the shoulder-pieces of the ephod. 19 Then they made two rings of gold, and put them at the two ends of the breastpiece, on its inside edge next to the ephod. 20 They made two rings of gold, and attached them in front to the lower part of the two shoulder-pieces of the ephod, at its

joining above the decorated band of the ephod. 21 They bound the breastpiece by its rings to the rings of the ephod with a blue cord, so that it should lie on the decorated band of the ephod, and that the breastpiece should not come loose from the ephod; as the LORD had commanded Moses.

22 He also made the robe of the ephod woven all of blue yarn; 23 and the opening of the robe in the middle of it was like the opening in a coat of mail,r with a binding around the opening, so that it might not be torn. 24 On the lower hem of the robe they made pomegranates of blue, purple, and crimson yarns, and of fine twisted linen. 25 They also made bells of pure gold, and put the bells between the pomegranates on the lower hem of the robe all around, between the pomegranates; 26 a bell and a pomegranate, a bell and a pomegranate all around on the lower hem of the robe for ministering; as the LORD had commanded Moses.

27 They also made the tunics, woven of fine linen, for Aaron and his sons, 28 and the turban of fine linen, and the headdresses of fine linen, and the linen undergarments of fine twisted linen, 29 and the sash of fine twisted linen, and of blue, purple, and crimson yarns, embroidered with needlework; as the LORD had commanded Moses.

30 They made the rosette of the holy diadem of pure gold, and wrote on it an inscription, like the engraving of a signet, "Holy to the LORD." 31 They tied to it a blue cord, to fasten it on the turban above; as the LORD had commanded Moses.

The Work Completed
(Ex 35.10–19)

32 In this way all the work of the tabernacle of the tent of meeting was finished; the Israelites had done everything just as the LORD had commanded Moses. 33 Then they brought the tabernacle to Moses, the tent and all its utensils, its hooks, its frames, its bars, its pillars, and its bases; 34 and the covering of tanned rams' skins and the covering of fine leather,r and the curtain for the screen; 35 the ark of the covenants

---

p The identification of several of these stones is uncertain   q Or *lapis lazuli*
r Meaning of Heb uncertain
s Or *treaty*, or *testimony*; Heb *eduth*

with its poles and the mercy seat;[t] [36]the table with all its utensils, and the bread of the Presence; [37]the pure lampstand with its lamps set on it and all its utensils, and the oil for the light; [38]the golden altar, the anointing oil and the fragrant incense, and the screen for the entrance of the tent; [39]the bronze altar, and its grating of bronze, its poles, and all its utensils; the basin with its stand; [40]the hangings of the court, its pillars, and its bases, and the screen for the gate of the court, its cords, and its pegs; and all the utensils for the service of the tabernacle, for the tent of meeting; [41]the finely worked vestments for ministering in the holy place, the sacred vestments for the priest Aaron, and the vestments of his sons to serve as priests. [42]The Israelites had done all the work just as the LORD had commanded Moses. [43]When Moses saw that they had done all the work just as the LORD had commanded, he blessed them.

The Tabernacle Erected and Its Equipment Installed

40 The LORD spoke to Moses: [2]On the first day of the first month you shall set up the tabernacle of the tent of meeting. [3]You shall put in it the ark of the covenant,[u] and you shall screen the ark with the curtain. [4]You shall bring in the table, and arrange its setting; and you shall bring in the lampstand, and set up its lamps. [5]You shall put the golden altar for incense before the ark of the covenant,[u] and set up the screen for the entrance of the tabernacle. [6]You shall set the altar of burnt offering before the entrance of the tabernacle of the tent of meeting, [7]and place the basin between the tent of meeting and the altar, and put water in it. [8]You shall set up the court all around, and hang up the screen for the gate of the court. [9]Then you shall take the anointing oil, and anoint the tabernacle and all that is in it, and consecrate it and all its furniture, so that it shall become holy. [10]You shall also anoint the altar of burnt offering and all its utensils, and consecrate the altar, so that the altar shall be most holy. [11]You shall also anoint the basin with its stand, and consecrate it. [12]Then you shall bring Aaron and his sons to the entrance of the tent of meeting, and shall wash them with water, [13]and put on Aaron the sacred vestments, and

you shall anoint him and consecrate him, so that he may serve me as priest. [14]You shall bring his sons also and put tunics on them, [15]and anoint them, as you anointed their father, that they may serve me as priests: and their anointing shall admit them to a perpetual priesthood throughout all generations to come.

16   Moses did everything just as the LORD had commanded him. [17]In the first month in the second year, on the first day of the month, the tabernacle was set up. [18]Moses set up the tabernacle; he laid its bases, and set up its frames, and put in its poles, and raised up its pillars; [19]and he spread the tent over the tabernacle, and put the covering of the tent over it; as the LORD had commanded Moses. [20]He took the covenant[u] and put it into the ark, and put the poles on the ark, and set the mercy seat[t] above the ark; [21]and he brought the ark into the tabernacle, and set up the curtain for screening, and screened the ark of the covenant;[u] as the LORD had commanded Moses. [22]He put the table in the tent of meeting, on the north side of the tabernacle, outside the curtain, [23]and set the bread in order on it before the LORD; as the LORD had commanded Moses. [24]He put the lampstand in the tent of meeting, opposite the table on the south side of the tabernacle, [25]and set up the lamps before the LORD; as the LORD had commanded Moses. [26]He put the golden altar in the tent of meeting before the curtain, [27]and offered fragrant incense on it; as the LORD had commanded Moses. [28]He also put in place the screen for the entrance of the tabernacle. [29]He set the altar of burnt offering at the entrance of the tabernacle of the tent of meeting, and offered on it the burnt offering and the grain offering as the LORD had commanded Moses. [30]He set the basin between the tent of meeting and the altar, and put water in it for washing, [31]with which Moses and Aaron and his sons washed their hands and their feet. [32]When they went into the tent of meeting, and when they approached the altar, they washed; as the LORD had commanded Moses. [33]He set up the court around the tabernacle and the altar, and put up the screen at the gate of the court. So Moses finished the work.

[t]Or *the cover*   [u]Or *treaty,* or *testimony;* Heb *eduth*

The Cloud and the Glory
(Ex 13.21–22; Num 9.15–23)

34 Then the cloud covered the tent of meeting, and the glory of the LORD filled the tabernacle. 35 Moses was not able to enter the tent of meeting because the cloud settled upon it, and the glory of the LORD filled the tabernacle. 36 Whenever the cloud was taken up from the tabernacle, the Israelites would set out on each stage of their journey; 37 but if the cloud was not taken up, then they did not set out until the day that it was taken up. 38 For the cloud of the LORD was on the tabernacle by day, and fire was in the cloud*v* by night, before the eyes of all the house of Israel at each stage of their journey.

v Heb *it*

LEVITICUS

The Burnt Offering

1 The LORD summoned Moses and spoke to him from the tent of meeting, saying: 2 Speak to the people of Israel and say to them: When any of you bring an offering of livestock to the LORD, you shall bring your offering from the herd or from the flock.

3 If the offering is a burnt offering from the herd, you shall offer a male without blemish; you shall bring it to the entrance of the tent of meeting, for acceptance in your behalf before the LORD. 4 You shall lay your hand on the head of the burnt offering, and it shall be acceptable in your behalf as atonement for you. 5 The bull shall be slaughtered before the LORD; and Aaron's sons the priests shall offer the blood, dashing the blood against all sides of the altar that is at the entrance of the tent of meeting. 6 The burnt offering shall be flayed and cut up into its parts. 7 The sons of the priest Aaron shall put fire on the altar and arrange wood on the fire. 8 Aaron's sons the priests shall arrange the parts, with the head and the suet, on the wood that is on the fire on the altar; 9 but its entrails and its legs shall be washed with water. Then the priest shall turn the whole into smoke on the altar as a burnt offering, an offering by fire of pleasing odor to the LORD.

10 If your gift for a burnt offering is from the flock, from the sheep or goats, your offering shall be a male without blemish. 11 It shall be slaughtered on the north side of the altar before the LORD, and Aaron's sons the priests shall dash its blood against all sides of the altar. 12 It shall be cut up into its parts, with its head and its suet, and the priest shall arrange them on the wood that is on the fire on the altar; 13 but the entrails and the legs shall be washed with water. Then the priest shall offer the whole and turn it into smoke on the altar; it is a burnt offering, an offering by fire of pleasing odor to the LORD.

14 If your offering to the LORD is a burnt offering of birds, you shall choose your offering from turtledoves or pigeons. 15 The priest shall bring it to the altar and wring off its head, and turn it into smoke on the altar; and its blood shall be drained out against the side of the altar. 16 He shall remove its crop with its contents*a* and throw it at the east side of the altar, in the place for ashes. 17 He shall tear it open by its wings without severing it. Then the priest shall turn it into smoke on the altar, on the wood that is on the fire; it is a burnt offering, an offering by fire of pleasing odor to the LORD.

Grain Offerings

2 When anyone presents a grain offering to the LORD, the offering shall be of choice flour; the worshiper shall pour oil on it, and put frankin-

a Meaning of Heb uncertain

cense on it, [2] and bring it to Aaron's sons the priests. After taking from it a handful of the choice flour and oil, with all its frankincense, the priest shall turn this token portion into smoke on the altar, an offering by fire of pleasing odor to the LORD. [3] And what is left of the grain offering shall be for Aaron and his sons, a most holy part of the offerings by fire to the LORD.

4 When you present a grain offering baked in the oven, it shall be of choice flour: unleavened cakes mixed with oil, or unleavened wafers spread with oil. [5] If your offering is grain prepared on a griddle, it shall be of choice flour mixed with oil, unleavened; [6] break it in pieces, and pour oil on it; it is a grain offering. [7] If your offering is grain prepared in a pan, it shall be made of choice flour in oil. [8] You shall bring to the LORD the grain offering that is prepared in any of these ways; and when it is presented to the priest, he shall take it to the altar. [9] The priest shall remove from the grain offering its token portion and turn this into smoke on the altar, an offering by fire of pleasing odor to the LORD. [10] And what is left of the grain offering shall be for Aaron and his sons; it is a most holy part of the offerings by fire to the LORD.

11 No grain offering that you bring to the LORD shall be made with leaven, for you must not turn any leaven or honey into smoke as an offering by fire to the LORD. [12] You may bring them to the LORD as an offering of choice products, but they shall not be offered on the altar for a pleasing odor. [13] You shall not omit from your grain offerings the salt of the covenant with your God; with all your offerings you shall offer salt.

14 If you bring a grain offering of first fruits to the LORD, you shall bring as the grain offering of your first fruits coarse new grain from fresh ears, parched with fire. [15] You shall add oil to it and lay frankincense on it; it is a grain offering. [16] And the priest shall turn a token portion of it into smoke— some of the coarse grain and oil with all its frankincense; it is an offering by fire to the LORD.

Offerings of Well-Being

3 If the offering is a sacrifice of well-being, if you offer an animal of the herd, whether male or female, you shall offer one without blemish before the LORD. [2] You shall lay your hand on the head of the offering and slaughter it at the entrance of the tent of meeting; and Aaron's sons the priests shall dash the blood against all sides of the altar. [3] You shall offer from the sacrifice of well-being, as an offering by fire to the LORD, the fat that covers the entrails and all the fat that is around the entrails; [4] the two kidneys with the fat that is on them at the loins, and the appendage of the liver, which he shall remove with the kidneys. [5] Then Aaron's sons shall turn these into smoke on the altar, with the burnt offering that is on the wood on the fire, as an offering by fire of pleasing odor to the LORD.

6 If your offering for a sacrifice of well-being to the LORD is from the flock, male or female, you shall offer one without blemish. [7] If you present a sheep as your offering, you shall bring it before the LORD [8] and lay your hand on the head of the offering. It shall be slaughtered before the tent of meeting, and Aaron's sons shall dash its blood against all sides of the altar. [9] You shall present its fat from the sacrifice of well-being, as an offering by fire to the LORD: the whole broad tail, which shall be removed close to the backbone, the fat that covers the entrails, and all the fat that is around the entrails; [10] the two kidneys with the fat that is on them at the loins, and the appendage of the liver, which you shall remove with the kidneys. [11] Then the priest shall turn these into smoke on the altar as a food offering by fire to the LORD.

12 If your offering is a goat, you shall bring it before the LORD [13] and lay your hand on its head; it shall be slaughtered before the tent of meeting; and the sons of Aaron shall dash its blood against all sides of the altar. [14] You shall present as your offering from it, as an offering by fire to the LORD, the fat that covers the entrails, and all the fat that is around the entrails; [15] the two kidneys with the fat that is on them at the loins, and the appendage of the liver, which you shall remove with the kidneys. [16] Then the priest shall turn these into smoke on the altar as a food offering by fire for a pleasing odor.

All fat is the LORD's. [17] It shall be a perpetual statute throughout your generations, in all your settlements: you must not eat any fat or any blood.

L
E
V
I
T
I
C
U
S

Sin Offerings

4 The LORD spoke to Moses, saying, 2 Speak to the people of Israel, saying: When anyone sins unintentionally in any of the LORD's commandments about things not to be done, and does any one of them:

3 If it is the anointed priest who sins, thus bringing guilt on the people, he shall offer for the sin that he has committed a bull of the herd without blemish as a sin offering to the LORD. 4 He shall bring the bull to the entrance of the tent of meeting before the LORD and lay his hand on the head of the bull; the bull shall be slaughtered before the LORD. 5 The anointed priest shall take some of the blood of the bull and bring it into the tent of meeting. 6 The priest shall dip his finger in the blood and sprinkle some of the blood seven times before the LORD in front of the curtain of the sanctuary. 7 The priest shall put some of the blood on the horns of the altar of fragrant incense that is in the tent of meeting before the LORD; and the rest of the blood of the bull he shall pour out at the base of the altar of burnt offering, which is at the entrance of the tent of meeting. 8 He shall remove all the fat from the bull of sin offering: the fat that covers the entrails and all the fat that is around the entrails; 9 the two kidneys with the fat that is on them at the loins; and the appendage of the liver, which he shall remove with the kidneys, 10 just as these are removed from the ox of the sacrifice of well-being. The priest shall turn them into smoke upon the altar of burnt offering. 11 But the skin of the bull and all its flesh, as well as its head, its legs, its entrails, and its dung— 12 all the rest of the bull—he shall carry out to a clean place outside the camp, to the ash heap, and shall burn it on a wood fire; at the ash heap it shall be burned.

13 If the whole congregation of Israel errs unintentionally and the matter escapes the notice of the assembly, and they do any one of the things that by the LORD's commandments ought not to be done and incur guilt; 14 when the sin that they have committed becomes known, the assembly shall offer a bull of the herd for a sin offering and bring it before the tent of meeting. 15 The elders of the congregation shall lay their hands on the head of the bull before the LORD, and the bull shall be slaughtered before the LORD. 16 The anointed priest shall bring some of the blood of the bull into the tent of meeting, 17 and the priest shall dip his finger in the blood and sprinkle it seven times before the LORD, in front of the curtain. 18 He shall put some of the blood on the horns of the altar that is before the LORD in the tent of meeting; and the rest of the blood he shall pour out at the base of the altar of burnt offering that is at the entrance of the tent of meeting. 19 He shall remove all its fat and turn it into smoke on the altar. 20 He shall do with the bull just as is done with the bull of sin offering; he shall do the same with this. The priest shall make atonement for them, and they shall be forgiven. 21 He shall carry the bull outside the camp, and burn it as he burned the first bull; it is the sin offering for the assembly.

22 When a ruler sins, doing unintentionally any one of all the things that by commandments of the LORD his God ought not to be done and incurs guilt, 23 once the sin that he has committed is made known to him, he shall bring as his offering a male goat without blemish. 24 He shall lay his hand on the head of the goat; it shall be slaughtered at the spot where the burnt offering is slaughtered before the LORD; it is a sin offering. 25 The priest shall take some of the blood of the sin offering with his finger and put it on the horns of the altar of burnt offering, and pour out the rest of its blood at the base of the altar of burnt offering. 26 All its fat he shall turn into smoke on the altar, like the fat of the sacrifice of well-being. Thus the priest shall make atonement on his behalf for his sin, and he shall be forgiven.

27 If anyone of the ordinary people among you sins unintentionally in doing any one of the things that by the LORD's commandments ought not to be done and incurs guilt, 28 when the sin that you have committed is made known to you, you shall bring a female goat without blemish as your offering, for the sin that you have committed. 29 You shall lay your hand on the head of the sin offering; and the sin offering shall be slaughtered at the place of the burnt offering. 30 The priest shall take some of its blood with his finger and put it on the horns of the altar of burnt offering, and he shall pour out the rest of its blood at the base of the altar. 31 He shall remove all its fat, as the fat

is removed from the offering of well-being, and the priest shall turn it into smoke on the altar for a pleasing odor to the LORD. Thus the priest shall make atonement on your behalf, and you shall be forgiven.

32　If the offering you bring as a sin offering is a sheep, you shall bring a female without blemish. 33 You shall lay your hand on the head of the sin offering; and it shall be slaughtered as a sin offering at the spot where the burnt offering is slaughtered. 34 The priest shall take some of the blood of the sin offering with his finger and put it on the horns of the altar of burnt offering, and pour out the rest of its blood at the base of the altar. 35 You shall remove all its fat, as the fat of the sheep is removed from the sacrifice of well-being, and the priest shall turn it into smoke on the altar, with the offerings by fire to the LORD. Thus the priest shall make atonement on your behalf for the sin that you have committed, and you shall be forgiven.

5 When any of you sin in that you have heard a public adjuration to testify and—though able to testify as one who has seen or learned of the matter—does not speak up, you are subject to punishment. 2 Or when any of you touch any unclean thing—whether the carcass of an unclean beast or the carcass of unclean livestock or the carcass of an unclean swarming thing—and are unaware of it, you have become unclean, and are guilty. 3 Or when you touch human uncleanness—any uncleanness by which one can become unclean—and are unaware of it, when you come to know it, you shall be guilty. 4 Or when any of you utter aloud a rash oath for a bad or a good purpose, whatever people utter in an oath, and are unaware of it, when you come to know it, you shall in any of these be guilty. 5 When you realize your guilt in any of these, you shall confess the sin that you have committed. 6 And you shall bring to the LORD, as your penalty for the sin that you have committed, a female from the flock, a sheep or a goat, as a sin offering; and the priest shall make atonement on your behalf for your sin.

7　But if you cannot afford a sheep, you shall bring to the LORD, as your penalty for the sin that you have committed, two turtledoves or two pigeons, one for a sin offering and the other for a burnt offering. 8 You shall bring them to the priest, who shall offer first the one for the sin offering, wringing its head at the nape without severing it. 9 He shall sprinkle some of the blood of the sin offering on the side of the altar, while the rest of the blood shall be drained out at the base of the altar; it is a sin offering. 10 And the second he shall offer for a burnt offering according to the regulation. Thus the priest shall make atonement on your behalf for the sin that you have committed, and you shall be forgiven.

11　But if you cannot afford two turtledoves or two pigeons, you shall bring as your offering for the sin that you have committed one-tenth of an ephah of choice flour for a sin offering; you shall not put oil on it or lay frankincense on it, for it is a sin offering. 12 You shall bring it to the priest, and the priest shall scoop up a handful of it as its memorial portion, and turn this into smoke on the altar, with the offerings by fire to the LORD; it is a sin offering. 13 Thus the priest shall make atonement on your behalf for whichever of these sins you have committed, and you shall be forgiven. Like the grain offering, the rest shall be for the priest.

Offerings with Restitution

14　The LORD spoke to Moses, saying: 15 When any of you commit a trespass and sins unintentionally in any of the holy things of the LORD, you shall bring, as your guilt offering to the LORD, a ram without blemish from the flock, convertible into silver by the sanctuary shekel; it is a guilt offering. 16 And you shall make restitution for the holy thing in which you were remiss, and shall add one-fifth to it and give it to the priest. The priest shall make atonement on your behalf with the ram of the guilt offering, and you shall be forgiven.

17　If any of you sin without knowing it, doing any of the things that by the LORD's commandments ought not to be done, you have incurred guilt, and are subject to punishment. 18 You shall bring to the priest a ram without blemish from the flock, or the equivalent, as a guilt offering; and the priest shall make atonement on your behalf for the error that you committed unintentionally, and you shall be forgiven. 19 It is a guilt offering; you have incurred guilt before the LORD.

6 [b] The LORD spoke to Moses, saying: [2] When any of you sin and commit a trespass against the LORD by deceiving a neighbor in a matter of a deposit or a pledge, or by robbery, or if you have defrauded a neighbor, [3] or have found something lost and lied about it—if you swear falsely regarding any of the various things that one may do and sin thereby— [4] when you have sinned and realize your guilt, and would restore what you took by robbery or by fraud or the deposit that was committed to you, or the lost thing that you found, [5] or anything else about which you have sworn falsely, you shall repay the principal amount and shall add one-fifth to it. You shall pay it to its owner when you realize your guilt. [6] And you shall bring to the priest, as your guilt offering to the LORD, a ram without blemish from the flock, or its equivalent, for a guilt offering. [7] The priest shall make atonement on your behalf before the LORD, and you shall be forgiven for any of the things that one may do and incur guilt thereby.

Instructions concerning Sacrifices

[8] [c] The LORD spoke to Moses, saying: [9] Command Aaron and his sons, saying: This is the ritual of the burnt offering. The burnt offering itself shall remain on the hearth upon the altar all night until the morning, while the fire on the altar shall be kept burning. [10] The priest shall put on his linen vestments after putting on his linen undergarments next to his body; and he shall take up the ashes to which the fire has reduced the burnt offering on the altar, and place them beside the altar. [11] Then he shall take off his vestments and put on other garments, and carry the ashes out to a clean place outside the camp. [12] The fire on the altar shall be kept burning; it shall not go out. Every morning the priest shall add wood to it, lay out the burnt offering on it, and turn into smoke the fat pieces of the offerings of well-being. [13] A perpetual fire shall be kept burning on the altar; it shall not go out.

[14] This is the ritual of the grain offering: The sons of Aaron shall offer it before the LORD, in front of the altar. [15] They shall take from it a handful of the choice flour and oil of the grain offering, with all the frankincense that is on the offering, and they shall turn its memorial portion into smoke on the altar as a pleasing odor to the LORD. [16] Aaron and his sons shall eat what is left of it; it shall be eaten as unleavened cakes in a holy place; in the court of the tent of meeting they shall eat it. [17] It shall not be baked with leaven. I have given it as their portion of my offerings by fire; it is most holy, like the sin offering and the guilt offering. [18] Every male among the descendants of Aaron shall eat of it, as their perpetual due throughout your generations, from the LORD's offerings by fire; anything that touches them shall become holy.

[19] The LORD spoke to Moses, saying: [20] This is the offering that Aaron and his sons shall offer to the LORD on the day when he is anointed: one-tenth of an ephah of choice flour as a regular offering, half of it in the morning and half in the evening. [21] It shall be made with oil on a griddle; you shall bring it well soaked, as a grain offering of baked [d] pieces, and you shall present it as a pleasing odor to the LORD. [22] And so the priest, anointed from among Aaron's descendants as a successor, shall prepare it; it is the LORD's—a perpetual due—to be turned entirely into smoke. [23] Every grain offering of a priest shall be wholly burned; it shall not be eaten.

[24] The LORD spoke to Moses, saying: [25] Speak to Aaron and his sons, saying: This is the ritual of the sin offering. The sin offering shall be slaughtered before the LORD at the spot where the burnt offering is slaughtered; it is most holy. [26] The priest who offers it as a sin offering shall eat of it; it shall be eaten in a holy place, in the court of the tent of meeting. [27] Whatever touches its flesh shall become holy; and when any of its blood is spattered on a garment, you shall wash the bespattered part in a holy place. [28] An earthen vessel in which it was boiled shall be broken; but if it is boiled in a bronze vessel, that shall be scoured and rinsed in water. [29] Every male among the priests shall eat of it; it is most holy. [30] But no sin offering shall be eaten from which any blood is brought into the tent of meeting for atonement in the holy place; it shall be burned with fire.

7 This is the ritual of the guilt offering. It is most holy; [2] at the spot

[b] Ch 5.20 in Heb   [c] Ch 6.1 in Heb
[d] Meaning of Heb uncertain

where the burnt offering is slaughtered, they shall slaughter the guilt offering, and its blood shall be dashed against all sides of the altar. ³All its fat shall be offered: the broad tail, the fat that covers the entrails, ⁴the two kidneys with the fat that is on them at the loins, and the appendage of the liver, which shall be removed with the kidneys. ⁵The priest shall turn them into smoke on the altar as an offering by fire to the LORD; it is a guilt offering. ⁶Every male among the priests shall eat of it; it shall be eaten in a holy place; it is most holy.

7 The guilt offering is like the sin offering, there is the same ritual for them; the priest who makes atonement with it shall have it. ⁸So, too, the priest who offers anyone's burnt offering shall keep the skin of the burnt offering that he has offered. ⁹And every grain offering baked in the oven, and all that is prepared in a pan or on a griddle, shall belong to the priest who offers it. ¹⁰But every other grain offering, mixed with oil or dry, shall belong to all the sons of Aaron equally.

Further Instructions

11 This is the ritual of the sacrifice of the offering of well-being that one may offer to the LORD. ¹²If you offer it for thanksgiving, you shall offer with the thank offering unleavened cakes mixed with oil, unleavened wafers spread with oil, and cakes of choice flour well soaked in oil. ¹³With your thanksgiving sacrifice of well-being you shall bring your offering with cakes of leavened bread. ¹⁴From this you shall offer one cake from each offering, as a gift to the LORD; it shall belong to the priest who dashes the blood of the offering of well-being. ¹⁵And the flesh of your thanksgiving sacrifice of well-being shall be eaten on the day it is offered; you shall not leave any of it until morning. ¹⁶But if the sacrifice you offer is a votive offering or a freewill offering, it shall be eaten on the day that you offer your sacrifice, and what is left of it shall be eaten the next day; ¹⁷but what is left of the flesh of the sacrifice shall be burned up on the third day. ¹⁸If any of the flesh of your sacrifice of well-being is eaten on the third day, it shall not be acceptable, nor shall it be credited to the one who offers it; it shall be an abomination, and the one who eats of it shall incur guilt.

19 Flesh that touches any unclean thing shall not be eaten; it shall be burned up. As for other flesh, all who are clean may eat such flesh. ²⁰But those who eat flesh from the LORD's sacrifice of well-being while in a state of uncleanness shall be cut off from their kin. ²¹When any one of you touches any unclean thing—human uncleanness or an unclean animal or any unclean creature—and then eats flesh from the LORD's sacrifice of well-being, you shall be cut off from your kin.

22 The LORD spoke to Moses, saying: ²³Speak to the people of Israel, saying: You shall eat no fat of ox or sheep or goat. ²⁴The fat of an animal that died or was torn by wild animals may be put to any use, but you must not eat it. ²⁵If any one of you eats the fat from an animal of which an offering by fire may be made to the LORD, you who eat it shall be cut off from your kin. ²⁶You must not eat any blood whatever, either of bird or of animal, in any of your settlements. ²⁷Any one of you who eats any blood shall be cut off from your kin.

28 The LORD spoke to Moses, saying: ²⁹Speak to the people of Israel, saying: Any one of you who would offer to the LORD your sacrifice of well-being must yourself bring to the LORD your offering from your sacrifice of well-being. ³⁰Your own hands shall bring the LORD's offering by fire; you shall bring the fat with the breast, so that the breast may be raised as an elevation offering before the LORD. ³¹The priest shall turn the fat into smoke on the altar, but the breast shall belong to Aaron and his sons. ³²And the right thigh from your sacrifices of well-being you shall give to the priest as an offering; ³³the one among the sons of Aaron who offers the blood and fat of the offering of well-being shall have the right thigh for a portion. ³⁴For I have taken the breast of the elevation offering, and the thigh that is offered, from the people of Israel, from their sacrifices of well-being, and have given them to Aaron the priest and to his sons, as a perpetual due from the people of Israel. ³⁵This is the portion allotted to Aaron and to his sons from the offerings made by fire to the LORD, once they have been brought forward to serve the LORD as priests; ³⁶these the LORD commanded to be given them, when he anointed them, as a

LEVITICUS

perpetual due from the people of Israel throughout their generations.

37 This is the ritual of the burnt offering, the grain offering, the sin offering, the guilt offering, the offering of ordination, and the sacrifice of wellbeing, 38 which the LORD commanded Moses on Mount Sinai, when he commanded the people of Israel to bring their offerings to the LORD, in the wilderness of Sinai.

The Rites of Ordination
(Ex 29.1–37)

8 The LORD spoke to Moses, saying: 2 Take Aaron and his sons with him, the vestments, the anointing oil, the bull of sin offering, the two rams, and the basket of unleavened bread; 3 and assemble the whole congregation at the entrance of the tent of meeting. 4 And Moses did as the LORD commanded him. When the congregation was assembled at the entrance of the tent of meeting, 5 Moses said to the congregation, "This is what the LORD has commanded to be done."

6 Then Moses brought Aaron and his sons forward, and washed them with water. 7 He put the tunic on him, fastened the sash around him, clothed him with the robe, and put the ephod on him. He then put the decorated band of the ephod around him, tying the ephod to him with it. 8 He placed the breastpiece on him, and in the breastpiece he put the U'rim and the Thum'mim. 9 And he set the turban on his head, and on the turban, in front, he set the golden ornament, the holy crown, as the LORD commanded Moses.

10 Then Moses took the anointing oil and anointed the tabernacle and all that was in it, and consecrated them. 11 He sprinkled some of it on the altar seven times, and anointed the altar and all its utensils, and the basin and its base, to consecrate them. 12 He poured some of the anointing oil on Aaron's head and anointed him, to consecrate him. 13 And Moses brought forward Aaron's sons, and clothed them with tunics, and fastened sashes around them, and tied headdresses on them, as the LORD commanded Moses.

14 He led forward the bull of sin offering; and Aaron and his sons laid their hands upon the head of the bull of sin offering, 15 and it was slaughtered. Moses took the blood and with his fin-

ger put some on each of the horns of the altar, purifying the altar; then he poured out the blood at the base of the altar. Thus he consecrated it, to make atonement for it. 16 Moses took all the fat that was around the entrails, and the appendage of the liver, and the two kidneys with their fat, and turned them into smoke on the altar. 17 But the bull itself, its skin and flesh and its dung, he burned with fire outside the camp, as the LORD commanded Moses.

18 Then he brought forward the ram of burnt offering. Aaron and his sons laid their hands on the head of the ram, 19 and it was slaughtered. Moses dashed the blood against all sides of the altar. 20 The ram was cut into its parts, and Moses turned into smoke the head and the parts and the suet. 21 And after the entrails and the legs were washed with water, Moses turned into smoke the whole ram on the altar; it was a burnt offering for a pleasing odor, an offering by fire to the LORD, as the LORD commanded Moses.

22 Then he brought forward the second ram, the ram of ordination. Aaron and his sons laid their hands on the head of the ram, 23 and it was slaughtered. Moses took some of its blood and put it on the lobe of Aaron's right ear and on the thumb of his right hand and on the big toe of his right foot. 24 After Aaron's sons were brought forward, Moses put some of the blood on the lobes of their right ears and on the thumbs of their right hands and on the big toes of their right feet; and Moses dashed the rest of the blood against all sides of the altar. 25 He took the fat—the broad tail, all the fat that was around the entrails, the appendage of the liver, and the two kidneys with their fat—and the right thigh. 26 From the basket of unleavened bread that was before the LORD, he took one cake of unleavened bread, one cake of bread with oil, and one wafer, and placed them on the fat and on the right thigh. 27 He placed all these on the palms of Aaron and on the palms of his sons, and raised them as an elevation offering before the LORD. 28 Then Moses took them from their hands and turned them into smoke on the altar with the burnt offering. This was an ordination offering for a pleasing odor, an offering by fire to the LORD. 29 Moses took the breast and raised it as an elevation offering before the LORD; it was Moses' portion of

the ram of ordination, as the LORD commanded Moses.

30 Then Moses took some of the anointing oil and some of the blood that was on the altar and sprinkled them on Aaron and his vestments, and also on his sons and their vestments. Thus he consecrated Aaron and his vestments, and also his sons and their vestments.

31 And Moses said to Aaron and his sons, "Boil the flesh at the entrance of the tent of meeting, and eat it there with the bread that is in the basket of ordination offerings, as I was commanded, 'Aaron and his sons shall eat it'; 32 and what remains of the flesh and the bread you shall burn with fire. 33 You shall not go outside the entrance of the tent of meeting for seven days, until the day when your period of ordination is completed. For it will take seven days to ordain you; 34 as has been done today, the LORD has commanded to be done to make atonement for you. 35 You shall remain at the entrance of the tent of meeting day and night for seven days, keeping the LORD's charge so that you do not die; for so I am commanded." 36 Aaron and his sons did all the things that the LORD commanded through Moses.

Aaron's Priesthood Inaugurated

9 On the eighth day Moses summoned Aaron and his sons and the elders of Israel. 2 He said to Aaron, "Take a bull calf for a sin offering and a ram for a burnt offering, without blemish, and offer them before the LORD. 3 And say to the people of Israel, 'Take a male goat for a sin offering; a calf and a lamb, yearlings without blemish, for a burnt offering; 4 and an ox and a ram for an offering of well-being to sacrifice before the LORD; and a grain offering mixed with oil. For today the LORD will appear to you.'" 5 They brought what Moses commanded to the front of the tent of meeting; and the whole congregation drew near and stood before the LORD. 6 And Moses said, "This is the thing that the LORD commanded you to do, so that the glory of the LORD may appear to you." 7 Then Moses said to Aaron, "Draw near to the altar and sacrifice your sin offering and your burnt offering, and make atonement for yourself and for the people; and sacrifice the offering of the people, and make

atonement for them; as the LORD has commanded."

8 Aaron drew near to the altar, and slaughtered the calf of the sin offering, which was for himself. 9 The sons of Aaron presented the blood to him, and he dipped his finger in the blood and put it on the horns of the altar; and the rest of the blood he poured out at the base of the altar. 10 But the fat, the kidneys, and the appendage of the liver from the sin offering he turned into smoke on the altar, as the LORD commanded Moses; 11 and the flesh and the skin he burned with fire outside the camp.

12 Then he slaughtered the burnt offering. Aaron's sons brought him the blood, and he dashed it against all sides of the altar. 13 And they brought him the burnt offering piece by piece, and the head, and he turned into smoke on the altar. 14 He washed the entrails and the legs and, with the burnt offering, turned them into smoke on the altar.

15 Next he presented the people's offering. He took the goat of the sin offering that was for the people, and slaughtered it, and presented it as a sin offering like the first one. 16 He presented the burnt offering, and sacrificed it according to regulation. 17 He presented the grain offering, and, taking a handful of it, he turned it into smoke on the altar, in addition to the burnt offering of the morning.

18 He slaughtered the ox and the ram as a sacrifice of well-being for the people. Aaron's sons brought him the blood, which he dashed against all sides of the altar, 19 and the fat of the ox and of the ram—the broad tail, the fat that covers the entrails, the two kidneys and the fat on them, *e* and the appendage of the liver. 20 They first laid the fat on the breasts, and the fat was turned into smoke on the altar; 21 and the breasts and the right thigh Aaron raised as an elevation offering before the LORD, as Moses had commanded.

22 Aaron lifted his hands toward the people and blessed them; and he came down after sacrificing the sin offering, the burnt offering, and the offering of well-being. 23 Moses and Aaron entered the tent of meeting, and then came out and blessed the people;

e Gk: Heb *the broad tail, and that which covers, and the kidneys* and the glory of the LORD appeared to all the people. 24 Fire came out from the LORD and consumed the burnt offering and the fat on the altar; and when all the people saw it, they shouted and fell on their faces.

Nadab and Abihu

10 Now Aaron's sons, Na'dab and A·bi'hu, each took his censer, put fire in it, and laid incense on it; and they offered unholy fire before the LORD, such as he had not commanded them. 2 And fire came out from the presence of the LORD and consumed them, and they died before the LORD. 3 Then Moses said to Aaron, "This is what the LORD meant when he said,

'Through those who are near me
  I will show myself holy,
and before all the people
  I will be glorified.'"

And Aaron was silent.

4 Moses summoned Mish'a·el and El'za·phan, sons of Uz'zi·el the uncle of Aaron, and said to them, "Come forward, and carry your kinsmen away from the front of the sanctuary to a place outside the camp." 5 They came forward and carried them by their tunics out of the camp, as Moses had ordered. 6 And Moses said to Aaron and to his sons El·e·a'zar and Ith'a·mar, "Do not dishevel your hair, and do not tear your vestments, or you will die and wrath will strike all the congregation; but your kindred, the whole house of Israel, may mourn the burning that the LORD has sent. 7 You shall not go outside the entrance of the tent of meeting, or you will die; for the anointing oil of the LORD is on you." And they did as Moses had ordered.

8 And the LORD spoke to Aaron: 9 Drink no wine or strong drink, neither you nor your sons, when you enter the tent of meeting, that you may not die; it is a statute forever throughout your generations. 10 You are to distinguish between the holy and the common, and between the unclean and the clean; 11 and you are to teach the people of Israel all the statutes that the LORD has spoken to them through Moses.

12 Moses spoke to Aaron and to his remaining sons, El·e·a'zar and Ith'-a·mar: Take the grain offering that is left from the LORD's offerings by fire, and eat it unleavened beside the altar, for it is most holy; 13 you shall eat it in a holy place, because it is your due and

your sons' due, from the offerings by fire to the LORD; for so I am commanded. 14 But the breast that is elevated and the thigh that is raised, you and your sons and daughters as well may eat in any clean place; for they have been assigned to you and your children from the sacrifices of the offerings of well-being of the people of Israel. 15 The thigh that is raised and the breast that is elevated they shall bring, together with the offerings by fire of the fat, to raise for an elevation offering before the LORD; they are to be your due and that of your children forever, as the LORD has commanded.

16 Then Moses made inquiry about the goat of the sin offering, and—it had already been burned! He was angry with El·e·a'zar and Ith'a·mar, Aaron's remaining sons, and said, 17 "Why did you not eat the sin offering in the sacred area? For it is most holy, and God*f* has given it to you that you may remove the guilt of the congregation, to make atonement on their behalf before the LORD. 18 Its blood was not brought into the inner part of the sanctuary. You should certainly have eaten it in the sanctuary, as I commanded." 19 And Aaron spoke to Moses, "See, today they offered their sin offering and their burnt offering before the LORD; and yet such things as these have befallen me! If I had eaten the sin offering today, would it have been agreeable to the LORD?" 20 And when Moses heard that, he agreed.

Clean and Unclean Foods
(Deut 14.3–21)

11 The LORD spoke to Moses and Aaron, saying to them: 2 Speak to the people of Israel, saying:

From among all the land animals, these are the creatures that you may eat. 3 Any animal that has divided hoofs and is cleft-footed and chews the cud—such you may eat. 4 But among those that chew the cud or have divided hoofs, you shall not eat the following: the camel, for even though it chews the cud, it does not have divided hoofs; it is unclean for you. 5 The rock badger, for even though it chews the cud, it does not have divided hoofs; it is unclean for you. 6 The hare, for even though it chews the cud, it does not have divided hoofs; it is unclean for you. 7 The pig, for even though it has

f Heb he

divided hoofs and is cleft-footed, it does not chew the cud; it is unclean for you. 8 Of their flesh you shall not eat, and their carcasses you shall not touch; they are unclean for you.

9 These you may eat, of all that are in the waters. Everything in the waters that has fins and scales, whether in the seas or in the streams—such you may eat. 10 But anything in the seas or the streams that does not have fins and scales, of the swarming creatures in the waters and among all the other living creatures that are in the waters—they are detestable to you 11 and detestable they shall remain. Of their flesh you shall not eat, and their carcasses you shall regard as detestable. 12 Everything in the waters that does not have fins and scales is detestable to you.

13 These you shall regard as detestable among the birds. They shall not be eaten; they are an abomination: the eagle, the vulture, the osprey, 14 the buzzard, the kite of any kind; 15 every raven of any kind; 16 the ostrich, the nighthawk, the sea gull, the hawk of any kind; 17 the little owl, the cormorant, the great owl, 18 the water hen, the desert owl,g the carrion vulture, 19 the stork, the heron of any kind, the hoopoe, and the bat.h

20 All winged insects that walk upon all fours are detestable to you. 21 But among the winged insects that walk on all fours you may eat those that have jointed legs above their feet, with which to leap on the ground. 22 Of them you may eat: the locust according to its kind, the bald locust according to its kind, the cricket according to its kind, and the grasshopper according to its kind. 23 But all other winged insects that have four feet are detestable to you.

Unclean Animals

24 By these you shall become unclean; whoever touches the carcass of any of them shall be unclean until the evening, 25 and whoever carries any part of the carcass of any of them shall wash his clothes and be unclean until the evening. 26 Every animal that has divided hoofs but is not cleft-footed or does not chew the cud is unclean for you; everyone who touches one of them shall be unclean. 27 All that walk on their paws, among the animals that walk on all fours, are unclean for you; whoever touches the carcass of any of

them shall be unclean until the evening, 28 and the one who carries the carcass shall wash his clothes and be unclean until the evening; they are unclean for you.

29 These are unclean for you among the creatures that swarm upon the earth: the weasel, the mouse, the great lizard according to its kind, 30 the gecko, the land crocodile, the lizard, the sand lizard, and the chameleon. 31 These are unclean for you among all that swarm; whoever touches one of them when they are dead shall be unclean until the evening. 32 And anything upon which any of them falls when they are dead shall be unclean, whether an article of wood or cloth or skin or sacking, any article that is used for any purpose; it shall be dipped into water, and it shall be unclean until the evening, and then it shall be clean. 33 And if any of them falls into any earthen vessel, all that is in it shall be unclean, and you shall break the vessel. 34 Any food that could be eaten shall be unclean if water from any such vessel comes upon it; and any liquid that could be drunk shall be unclean if it was in any such vessel. 35 Everything on which any part of the carcass falls shall be unclean; whether an oven or stove, it shall be broken in pieces; they are unclean, and shall remain unclean for you. 36 But a spring or a cistern holding water shall be clean, while whatever touches the carcass in it shall be unclean. 37 If any part of their carcass falls upon any seed set aside for sowing, it is clean; 38 but if water is put on the seed and any part of their carcass falls on it, it is unclean for you.

39 If an animal of which you may eat dies, anyone who touches its carcass shall be unclean until the evening. 40 Those who eat of its carcass shall wash their clothes and be unclean until the evening; and those who carry the carcass shall wash their clothes and be unclean until the evening.

41 All creatures that swarm upon the earth are detestable; they shall not be eaten. 42 Whatever moves on its belly, and whatever moves on all fours, or whatever has many feet, all the creatures that swarm upon the earth, you shall not eat; for they are detestable. 43 You shall not make your-

gOr *pelican*   hIdentification of several of the birds in verses 13-19 is uncertain selves detestable with any creature that swarms; you shall not defile yourselves with them, and so become unclean. 44 For I am the LORD your God; sanctify yourselves therefore, and be holy, for I am holy. You shall not defile yourselves with any swarming creature that moves on the earth. 45 For I am the LORD who brought you up from the land of Egypt, to be your God; you shall be holy, for I am holy.

46 This is the law pertaining to land animal and bird and every living creature that moves through the waters and every creature that swarms upon the earth, 47 to make a distinction between the unclean and the clean, and between the living creature that may be eaten and the living creature that may not be eaten.

Purification of Women after Childbirth
(Cp Lk 2.22–24)

12 The LORD spoke to Moses, saying: 2 Speak to the people of Israel, saying:

If a woman conceives and bears a male child, she shall be ceremonially unclean seven days; as at the time of her menstruation, she shall be unclean. 3 On the eighth day the flesh of his foreskin shall be circumcised. 4 Her time of blood purification shall be thirty-three days; she shall not touch any holy thing, or come into the sanctuary, until the days of her purification are completed. 5 If she bears a female child, she shall be unclean two weeks, as in her menstruation; her time of blood purification shall be sixty-six days.

6 When the days of her purification are completed, whether for a son or for a daughter, she shall bring to the priest at the entrance of the tent of meeting a lamb in its first year for a burnt offering, and a pigeon or a turtledove for a sin offering. 7 He shall offer it before the LORD, and make atonement on her behalf; then she shall be clean from her flow of blood. This is the law for her who bears a child, male or female. 8 If she cannot afford a sheep, she shall take two turtledoves or two pigeons, one for a burnt offering and the other for a sin offering; and the priest shall make atonement on her behalf, and she shall be clean.

Leprosy, Varieties and Symptoms

13 The LORD spoke to Moses and Aaron, saying:

2 When a person has on the skin of his body a swelling or an eruption or a spot, and it turns into a leprous[i] disease on the skin of his body, he shall be brought to Aaron the priest or to one of his sons the priests. 3 The priest shall examine the disease on the skin of his body, and if the hair in the diseased area has turned white and the disease appears to be deeper than the skin of his body, it is a leprous[i] disease; after the priest has examined him he shall pronounce him ceremonially unclean. 4 But if the spot is white in the skin of his body, and appears no deeper than the skin, and the hair in it has not turned white, the priest shall confine the diseased person for seven days. 5 The priest shall examine him on the seventh day, and if he sees that the disease is checked and the disease has not spread in the skin, then the priest shall confine him seven days more. 6 The priest shall examine him again on the seventh day, and if the disease has abated and the disease has not spread in the skin, the priest shall pronounce him clean; it is only an eruption; and he shall wash his clothes, and be clean. 7 But if the eruption spreads in the skin after he has shown himself to the priest for his cleansing, he shall appear again before the priest. 8 The priest shall make an examination, and if the eruption has spread in the skin, the priest shall pronounce him unclean; it is a leprous[i] disease.

9 When a person contracts a leprous[i] disease, he shall be brought to the priest. 10 The priest shall make an examination, and if there is a white swelling in the skin that has turned the hair white, and there is quick raw flesh in the swelling, 11 it is a chronic leprous[i] disease in the skin of his body. The priest shall pronounce him unclean; he shall not confine him, for he is unclean. 12 But if the disease breaks out in the skin, so that it covers all the skin of the diseased person from head to foot, so far as the priest can see, 13 then the priest shall make an examination, and if the disease has covered all his body, he shall pronounce him clean of the disease; since it has all turned white, he is clean. 14 But if raw flesh ever appears on him, he shall be unclean; 15 the priest shall examine the raw flesh and pronounce him unclean.

[i] A term for several skin diseases; precise meaning uncertain

Raw flesh is unclean, for it is a leprous[j] disease. 16 But if the raw flesh again turns white, he shall come to the priest; 17 the priest shall examine him, and if the disease has turned white, the priest shall pronounce the diseased person clean. He is clean.

18 When there is on the skin of one's body a boil that has healed, 19 and in the place of the boil there appears a white swelling or a reddish-white spot, it shall be shown to the priest. 20 The priest shall make an examination, and if it appears deeper than the skin and its hair has turned white, the priest shall pronounce him unclean; this is a leprous[j] disease, broken out in the boil. 21 But if the priest examines it and the hair on it is not white, nor is it deeper than the skin but has abated, the priest shall confine him seven days. 22 If it spreads in the skin, the priest shall pronounce him unclean; it is diseased. 23 But if the spot remains in one place and does not spread, it is the scar of the boil; the priest shall pronounce him clean.

24 Or, when the body has a burn on the skin and the raw flesh of the burn becomes a spot, reddish-white or white, 25 the priest shall examine it. If the hair in the spot has turned white and it appears deeper than the skin, it is a leprous[j] disease; it has broken out in the burn, and the priest shall pronounce him unclean. This is a leprous[j] disease. 26 But if the priest examines it and the hair in the spot is not white, and it is no deeper than the skin but has abated, the priest shall confine him seven days. 27 The priest shall examine him the seventh day; if it is spreading in the skin, the priest shall pronounce him unclean. This is a leprous[j] disease. 28 But if the spot remains in one place and does not spread in the skin but has abated, it is a swelling from the burn, and the priest shall pronounce him clean; for it is the scar of the burn.

29 When a man or woman has a disease on the head or in the beard, 30 the priest shall examine the disease. If it appears deeper than the skin and the hair in it is yellow and thin, the priest shall pronounce him unclean; it is an itch, a leprous[j] disease of the head or the beard. 31 If the priest examines the itching disease, and it appears no deeper than the skin and there is no black hair in it, the priest shall confine the person with the itching disease for seven days. 32 On the seventh day the priest shall examine the itch; if the itch has not spread, and there is no yellow hair in it, and the itch appears to be no deeper than the skin, 33 he shall shave, but the itch he shall not shave. The priest shall confine the person with the itch for seven days more. 34 On the seventh day the priest shall examine the itch; if the itch has not spread in the skin and it appears to be no deeper than the skin, the priest shall pronounce him clean. He shall wash his clothes and be clean. 35 But if the itch spreads in the skin after he was pronounced clean, 36 the priest shall examine him. If the itch has spread in the skin, the priest need not seek for the yellow hair; he is unclean. 37 But if in his eyes the itch is checked, and black hair has grown in it, the itch is healed, he is clean; and the priest shall pronounce him clean.

38 When a man or a woman has spots on the skin of the body, white spots, 39 the priest shall make an examination, and if the spots on the skin of the body are of a dull white, it is a rash that has broken out on the skin; he is clean.

40 If anyone loses the hair from his head, he is bald but he is clean. 41 If he loses the hair from his forehead and temples, he has baldness of the forehead but he is clean. 42 But if there is on the bald head or the bald forehead a reddish-white diseased spot, it is a leprous[j] disease breaking out on his bald head or his bald forehead. 43 The priest shall examine him; if the diseased swelling is reddish-white on his bald head or on his bald forehead, which resembles a leprous[j] disease in the skin of the body, 44 he is leprous,[j] he is unclean. The priest shall pronounce him unclean; the disease is on his head.

45 The person who has the leprous[j] disease shall wear torn clothes and let the hair of his head be disheveled; and he shall cover his upper lip and cry out, "Unclean, unclean." 46 He shall remain unclean as long as he has the disease; he is unclean. He shall live alone; his dwelling shall be outside the camp.

47 Concerning clothing: when a leprous[j] disease appears in it, in woolen or linen cloth, 48 in warp or

[j] A term for several skin diseases; precise meaning uncertain

woof of linen or wool, or in a skin or in anything made of skin, [49]if the disease shows greenish or reddish in the garment, whether in warp or woof or in skin or in anything made of skin, it is a leprous[k] disease and shall be shown to the priest. [50]The priest shall examine the disease, and put the diseased article aside for seven days. [51]He shall examine the disease on the seventh day. If the disease has spread in the cloth, in warp or woof, or in the skin, whatever be the use of the skin, this is a spreading leprous[k] disease; it is unclean. [52]He shall burn the clothing, whether diseased in warp or woof, woolen or linen, or anything of skin, for it is a spreading leprous[k] disease; it shall be burned in fire.

[53] If the priest makes an examination, and the disease has not spread in the clothing, in warp or woof or in anything of skin, [54]the priest shall command them to wash the article in which the disease appears, and he shall put it aside seven days more. [55]The priest shall examine the diseased article after it has been washed. If the diseased spot has not changed color, though the disease has not spread, it is unclean; you shall burn it in fire, whether the leprous[k] spot is on the inside or on the outside.

[56] If the priest makes an examination, and the disease has abated after it is washed, he shall tear the spot out of the cloth, in warp or woof, or out of skin. [57]If it appears again in the garment, in warp or woof, or in anything of skin, it is spreading; you shall burn with fire that in which the disease appears. [58]But the cloth, warp or woof, or anything of skin from which the disease disappears when you have washed it, shall then be washed a second time, and it shall be clean.

[59] This is the ritual for a leprous[k] disease in a cloth of wool or linen, either in warp or woof, or in anything of skin, to decide whether it is clean or unclean.

Purification of Lepers and Leprous Houses
(Cp Mt 8.1–4; Lk 5.12–14)

14 The LORD spoke to Moses, saying: [2]This shall be the ritual for the leprous[k] person at the time of his cleansing:

He shall be brought to the priest; [3]the priest shall go out of the camp, and the priest shall make an examination. If the disease is healed in the leprous[k] person, [4]the priest shall command that two living clean birds and cedarwood and crimson yarn and hyssop be brought for the one who is to be cleansed. [5]The priest shall command that one of the birds be slaughtered over fresh water in an earthen vessel. [6]He shall take the living bird with the cedarwood and the crimson yarn and the hyssop, and dip them and the living bird in the blood of the bird that was slaughtered over the fresh water. [7]He shall sprinkle it seven times upon the one who is to be cleansed of the leprous[k] disease; then he shall pronounce him clean, and he shall let the living bird go into the open field. [8]The one who is to be cleansed shall wash his clothes, and shave off all his hair, and bathe himself in water, and he shall be clean. After that he shall come into the camp, but shall live outside his tent seven days. [9]On the seventh day he shall shave all his hair: of head, beard, eyebrows; he shall shave all his hair. Then he shall wash his clothes, and bathe his body in water, and he shall be clean.

[10] On the eighth day he shall take two male lambs without blemish, and one ewe lamb in its first year without blemish, and a grain offering of three-tenths of an ephah of choice flour mixed with oil, and one log[l] of oil. [11]The priest who cleanses shall set the person to be cleansed, along with these things, before the LORD, at the entrance of the tent of meeting. [12]The priest shall take one of the lambs, and offer it as a guilt offering, along with the log[l] of oil, and raise them as an elevation offering before the LORD. [13]He shall slaughter the lamb in the place where the sin offering and the burnt offering are slaughtered in the holy place; for the guilt offering, like the sin offering, belongs to the priest: it is most holy. [14]The priest shall take some of the blood of the guilt offering and put it on the lobe of the right ear of the one to be cleansed, and on the thumb of the right hand, and on the big toe of the right foot. [15]The priest shall take some of the log[l] of oil and pour it into the palm of his own left hand, [16]and dip his right finger in the oil that is in his left hand and sprinkle

---

[k] A term for several skin diseases; precise meaning uncertain   [l] A liquid measure

some oil with his finger seven times before the LORD. [17] Some of the oil that remains in his hand the priest shall put on the lobe of the right ear of the one to be cleansed, and on the thumb of the right hand, and on the big toe of the right foot, on top of the blood of the guilt offering. [18] The rest of the oil that is in the priest's hand he shall put on the head of the one to be cleansed. Then the priest shall make atonement on his behalf before the LORD: [19] the priest shall offer the sin offering, to make atonement for the one to be cleansed from his uncleanness. Afterward he shall slaughter the burnt offering; [20] and the priest shall offer the burnt offering and the grain offering on the altar. Thus the priest shall make atonement on his behalf and he shall be clean.

[21] But if he is poor and cannot afford so much, he shall take one male lamb for a guilt offering to be elevated, to make atonement on his behalf, and one-tenth of an ephah of choice flour mixed with oil for a grain offering and a log[m] of oil; [22] also two turtledoves or two pigeons, such as he can afford, one for a sin offering and the other for a burnt offering. [23] On the eighth day he shall bring them for his cleansing to the priest, to the entrance of the tent of meeting, before the LORD; [24] and the priest shall take the lamb of the guilt offering and the log[m] of oil, and the priest shall raise them as an elevation offering before the LORD. [25] The priest shall slaughter the lamb of the guilt offering and shall take some of the blood of the guilt offering, and put it on the lobe of the right ear of the one to be cleansed, and on the thumb of the right hand, and on the big toe of the right foot. [26] The priest shall pour some of the oil into the palm of his own left hand, [27] and shall sprinkle with his right finger some of the oil that is in his left hand seven times before the LORD. [28] The priest shall put some of the oil that is in his hand on the lobe of the right ear of the one to be cleansed, and on the thumb of the right hand, and the big toe of the right foot, where the blood of the guilt offering was placed. [29] The rest of the oil that is in the priest's hand he shall put on the head of the one to be cleansed, to make atonement on his behalf before the LORD. [30] And he shall offer, of the turtledoves or pigeons such as he can afford, [31] one[n] for a sin offering and the

other for a burnt offering, along with a grain offering; and the priest shall make atonement before the LORD on behalf of the one being cleansed. [32] This is the ritual for the one who has a leprous[o] disease, who cannot afford the offerings for his cleansing.

[33] The LORD spoke to Moses and Aaron, saying:

[34] When you come into the land of Ca′naan, which I give you for a possession, and I put a leprous[o] disease in a house in the land of your possession, [35] the owner of the house shall come and tell the priest, saying, "There seems to me to be some sort of disease in my house." [36] The priest shall command that they empty the house before the priest goes to examine the disease, or all that is in the house will become unclean; and afterward the priest shall go in to inspect the house. [37] He shall examine the disease; if the disease is in the walls of the house with greenish or reddish spots, and if it appears to be deeper than the surface, [38] the priest shall go outside to the door of the house and shut up the house seven days. [39] The priest shall come again on the seventh day and make an inspection; if the disease has spread in the walls of the house, [40] the priest shall command that the stones in which the disease appears be taken out and thrown into an unclean place outside the city. [41] He shall have the inside of the house scraped thoroughly, and the plaster that is scraped off shall be dumped in an unclean place outside the city. [42] They shall take other stones and put them in the place of those stones, and take other plaster and plaster the house.

[43] If the disease breaks out again in the house, after he has taken out the stones and scraped the house and plastered it, [44] the priest shall go and make inspection; if the disease has spread in the house, it is a spreading leprous[o] disease in the house; it is unclean. [45] He shall have the house torn down, its stones and timber and all the plaster of the house, and taken outside the city to an unclean place. [46] All who enter the house while it is shut up shall be unclean until the evening; [47] and all who sleep in the house shall wash their

---

[m] A liquid measure [n] Gk Syr: Heb *afford,* [31] *such as he can afford, one* [o] A term for several skin diseases; precise meaning uncertain

clothes; and all who eat in the house shall wash their clothes.

48 If the priest comes and makes an inspection, and the disease has not spread in the house after the house was plastered, the priest shall pronounce the house clean; the disease is healed. 49 For the cleansing of the house he shall take two birds, with cedarwood and crimson yarn and hyssop, 50 and shall slaughter one of the birds over fresh water in an earthen vessel, 51 and shall take the cedarwood and the hyssop and the crimson yarn, along with the living bird, and dip them in the blood of the slaughtered bird and the fresh water, and sprinkle the house seven times. 52 Thus he shall cleanse the house with the blood of the bird, and with the fresh water, and with the living bird, and with the cedarwood and hyssop and crimson yarn; 53 and he shall let the living bird go out of the city into the open field; so he shall make atonement for the house, and it shall be clean.

54 This is the ritual for any leprous*p* disease: for an itch, 55 for leprous*p* diseases in clothing and houses, 56 and for a swelling or an eruption or a spot, 57 to determine when it is unclean and when it is clean. This is the ritual for leprous*p* diseases.

Concerning Bodily Discharges

15 The LORD spoke to Moses and Aaron, saying: 2 Speak to the people of Israel and say to them:

When any man has a discharge from his member,*q* his discharge makes him ceremonially unclean. 3 The uncleanness of his discharge is this: whether his member*q* flows with his discharge, or his member*q* is stopped from discharging, it is uncleanness for him. 4 Every bed on which the one with the discharge lies shall be unclean; and everything on which he sits shall be unclean. 5 Anyone who touches his bed shall wash his clothes, and bathe in water, and be unclean until the evening. 6 All who sit on anything on which the one with the discharge has sat shall wash their clothes, and bathe in water, and be unclean until the evening. 7 All who touch the body of the one with the discharge shall wash their clothes, and bathe in water, and be unclean until the evening. 8 If the one with the discharge spits on persons who are clean, then they shall wash their clothes, and bathe in water,

and be unclean until the evening. 9 Any saddle on which the one with the discharge rides shall be unclean. 10 All who touch anything that was under him shall be unclean until the evening, and all who carry such a thing shall wash their clothes, and bathe in water, and be unclean until the evening. 11 All those whom the one with the discharge touches without his having rinsed his hands in water shall wash their clothes, and bathe in water, and be unclean until the evening. 12 Any earthen vessel that the one with the discharge touches shall be broken; and every vessel of wood shall be rinsed in water.

13 When the one with a discharge is cleansed of his discharge, he shall count seven days for his cleansing; he shall wash his clothes and bathe his body in fresh water, and he shall be clean. 14 On the eighth day he shall take two turtledoves or two pigeons and come before the LORD to the entrance of the tent of meeting and give them to the priest. 15 The priest shall offer them, one for a sin offering and the other for a burnt offering; and the priest shall make atonement on his behalf before the LORD for his discharge.

16 If a man has an emission of semen, he shall bathe his whole body in water, and be unclean until the evening. 17 Everything made of cloth or of skin on which the semen falls shall be washed with water, and be unclean until the evening. 18 If a man lies with a woman and has an emission of semen, both of them shall bathe in water, and be unclean until the evening.

19 When a woman has a discharge of blood that is her regular discharge from her body, she shall be in her impurity for seven days, and whoever touches her shall be unclean until the evening. 20 Everything upon which she lies during her impurity shall be unclean; everything also upon which she sits shall be unclean. 21 Whoever touches her bed shall wash his clothes, and bathe in water, and be unclean until the evening. 22 Whoever touches anything upon which she sits shall wash his clothes, and bathe in water, and be unclean until the evening; 23 whether it is the bed or anything upon which she sits, when he touches it he shall be unclean until the evening. 24 If any man lies with her, and her im-

---

p A term for several skin diseases; precise meaning uncertain   *q* Heb *flesh* purity falls on him, he shall be unclean seven days; and every bed on which he lies shall be unclean.

25 If a woman has a discharge of blood for many days, not at the time of her impurity, or if she has a discharge beyond the time of her impurity, all the days of the discharge she shall continue in uncleanness; as in the days of her impurity, she shall be unclean. 26 Every bed on which she lies during all the days of her discharge shall be treated as the bed of her impurity; and everything on which she sits shall be unclean, as in the uncleanness of her impurity. 27 Whoever touches these things shall be unclean, and shall wash his clothes, and bathe in water, and be unclean until the evening. 28 If she is cleansed of her discharge, she shall count seven days, and after that she shall be clean. 29 On the eighth day she shall take two turtledoves or two pigeons and bring them to the priest to the entrance of the tent of meeting. 30 The priest shall offer one for a sin offering and the other for a burnt offering; and the priest shall make atonement on her behalf before the LORD for her unclean discharge.

31 Thus you shall keep the people of Israel separate from their uncleanness, so that they do not die in their uncleanness by defiling my tabernacle that is in their midst.

32 This is the ritual for those who have a discharge: for him who has an emission of semen, becoming unclean thereby, 33 for her who is in the infirmity of her period, for anyone, male or female, who has a discharge, and for the man who lies with a woman who is unclean.

The Day of Atonement

16 The LORD spoke to Moses after the death of the two sons of Aaron, when they drew near before the LORD and died. 2 The LORD said to Moses:

Tell your brother Aaron not to come just at any time into the sanctuary inside the curtain before the mercy seat[r] that is upon the ark, or he will die; for I appear in the cloud upon the mercy seat.[r] 3 Thus shall Aaron come into the holy place: with a young bull for a sin offering and a ram for a burnt offering. 4 He shall put on the holy linen tunic, and shall have the linen undergarments next to his body, fasten the linen sash, and wear the linen turban; these are the holy vestments. He shall bathe his body in water, and then put them on. 5 He shall take from the congregation of the people of Israel two male goats for a sin offering, and one ram for a burnt offering.

6 Aaron shall offer the bull as a sin offering for himself, and shall make atonement for himself and for his house. 7 He shall take the two goats and set them before the LORD at the entrance of the tent of meeting; 8 and Aaron shall cast lots on the two goats, one lot for the LORD and the other lot for Az′a·zel.[s] 9 Aaron shall present the goat on which the lot fell for the LORD, and offer it as a sin offering; 10 but the goat on which the lot fell for Az′a·zel[s] shall be presented alive before the LORD to make atonement over it, that it may be sent away into the wilderness to Az′a·zel.[s]

11 Aaron shall present the bull as a sin offering for himself, and shall make atonement for himself and for his house; he shall slaughter the bull as a sin offering for himself. 12 He shall take a censer full of coals of fire from the altar before the LORD, and two handfuls of crushed sweet incense, and he shall bring it inside the curtain 13 and put the incense on the fire before the LORD, that the cloud of the incense may cover the mercy seat[r] that is upon the covenant,[t] or he will die. 14 He shall take some of the blood of the bull, and sprinkle it with his finger on the front of the mercy seat,[r] and before the mercy seat[r] he shall sprinkle the blood with his finger seven times.

15 He shall slaughter the goat of the sin offering that is for the people and bring its blood inside the curtain, and do with its blood as he did with the blood of the bull, sprinkling it upon the mercy seat[r] and before the mercy seat.[r] 16 Thus he shall make atonement for the sanctuary, because of the uncleannesses of the people of Israel, and because of their transgressions, all their sins; and so he shall do for the tent of meeting, which remains with them in the midst of their uncleannesses. 17 No one shall be in the tent of meeting from the time he enters to make atonement in the sanctuary until he comes out and has made atonement

---

[r] Or *the cover*   [s] Traditionally rendered *a scapegoat*   [t] Or *treaty*, or *testament*; Heb *eduth*

for himself and for his house and for all the assembly of Israel. ¹⁸Then he shall go out to the altar that is before the LORD and make atonement on its behalf, and shall take some of the blood of the bull and of the blood of the goat, and put it on each of the horns of the altar. ¹⁹He shall sprinkle some of the blood on it with his finger seven times, and cleanse it and hallow it from the uncleannesses of the people of Israel.

20 When he has finished atoning for the holy place and the tent of meeting and the altar, he shall present the live goat. ²¹Then Aaron shall lay both his hands on the head of the live goat, and confess over it all the iniquities of the people of Israel, and all their transgressions, all their sins, putting them on the head of the goat, and sending it away into the wilderness by means of someone designated for the task. ^u ²²The goat shall bear on itself all their iniquities to a barren region; and the goat shall be set free in the wilderness.

23 Then Aaron shall enter the tent of meeting, and shall take off the linen vestments that he put on when he went into the holy place, and shall leave them there. ²⁴He shall bathe his body in water in a holy place, and put on his vestments; then he shall come out and offer his burnt offering and the burnt offering of the people, making atonement for himself and for the people. ²⁵The fat of the sin offering he shall turn into smoke on the altar. ²⁶The one who sets the goat free for Az′a·zel ^v shall wash his clothes and bathe his body in water, and afterward may come into the camp. ²⁷The bull of the sin offering and the goat of the sin offering, whose blood was brought in to make atonement in the holy place, shall be taken outside the camp; their skin and their flesh and their dung shall be consumed in fire. ²⁸The one who burns them shall wash his clothes and bathe his body in water, and afterward may come into the camp.

29 This shall be a statute to you forever: In the seventh month, on the tenth day of the month, you shall deny yourselves, ^w and shall do no work, neither the citizen nor the alien who resides among you. ³⁰For on this day atonement shall be made for you, to cleanse you; from all your sins you shall be clean before the LORD. ³¹It is a sabbath of complete rest to you, and you shall deny yourselves; ^w it is a

statute forever. ³²The priest who is anointed and consecrated as priest in his father's place shall make atonement, wearing the linen vestments, the holy vestments. ³³He shall make atonement for the sanctuary, and he shall make atonement for the tent of meeting and for the altar, and he shall make atonement for the priests and for all the people of the assembly. ³⁴This shall be an everlasting statute for you, to make atonement for the people of Israel once in the year for all their sins. And Moses did as the LORD had commanded him.

The Slaughtering of Animals

17 The LORD spoke to Moses: 2 Speak to Aaron and his sons and to all the people of Israel and say to them: This is what the LORD has commanded. ³If anyone of the house of Israel slaughters an ox or a lamb or a goat in the camp, or slaughters it outside the camp, ⁴and does not bring it to the entrance of the tent of meeting, to present it as an offering to the LORD before the tabernacle of the LORD, he shall be held guilty of bloodshed; he has shed blood, and he shall be cut off from the people. ⁵This is in order that the people of Israel may bring their sacrifices that they offer in the open field, that they may bring them to the LORD, to the priest at the entrance of the tent of meeting, and offer them as sacrifices of well-being to the LORD. ⁶The priest shall dash the blood against the altar of the LORD at the entrance of the tent of meeting, and turn the fat into smoke as a pleasing odor to the LORD, ⁷so that they may no longer offer their sacrifices for goat-demons, to whom they prostitute themselves. This shall be a statute forever to them throughout their generations.

8 And say to them further: Anyone of the house of Israel or of the aliens who reside among them who offers a burnt offering or sacrifice, ⁹and does not bring it to the entrance of the tent of meeting, to sacrifice it to the LORD, shall be cut off from the people.

Eating Blood Prohibited

10 If anyone of the house of Israel or of the aliens who reside among them eats any blood, I will set my face

---

^uMeaning of Heb uncertain
^vTraditionally rendered *a scapegoat*
^wOr *shall fast*

against that person who eats blood, and will cut that person off from the people. [11] For the life of the flesh is in the blood; and I have given it to you for making atonement for your lives on the altar; for, as life, it is the blood that makes atonement. [12] Therefore I have said to the people of Israel: No person among you shall eat blood, nor shall any alien who resides among you eat blood. [13] And anyone of the people of Israel, or of the aliens who reside among them, who hunts down an animal or bird that may be eaten shall pour out its blood and cover it with earth.

14 For the life of every creature—its blood is its life; therefore I have said to the people of Israel: You shall not eat the blood of any creature, for the life of every creature is its blood; whoever eats it shall be cut off. [15] All persons, citizens or aliens, who eat what dies of itself or what has been torn by wild animals, shall wash their clothes, and bathe themselves in water, and be unclean until the evening; then they shall be clean. [16] But if they do not wash themselves or bathe their body, they shall bear their guilt.

Sexual Relations

18 The LORD spoke to Moses, saying:
2 Speak to the people of Israel and say to them: I am the LORD your God. [3] You shall not do as they do in the land of Egypt, where you lived, and you shall not do as they do in the land of Ca′naan, to which I am bringing you. You shall not follow their statutes. [4] My ordinances you shall observe and my statutes you shall keep, following them: I am the LORD your God. [5] You shall keep my statutes and my ordinances; by doing so one shall live: I am the LORD.

6 None of you shall approach anyone near of kin to uncover nakedness: I am the LORD. [7] You shall not uncover the nakedness of your father, which is the nakedness of your mother; she is your mother, you shall not uncover her nakedness. [8] You shall not uncover the nakedness of your father's wife; it is the nakedness of your father. [9] You shall not uncover the nakedness of your sister, your father's daughter or your mother's daughter, whether born at home or born abroad. [10] You shall not uncover the nakedness of your son's daughter or of your daughter's

daughter, for their nakedness is your own nakedness. [11] You shall not uncover the nakedness of your father's wife's daughter, begotten by your father, since she is your sister. [12] You shall not uncover the nakedness of your father's sister; she is your father's flesh. [13] You shall not uncover the nakedness of your mother's sister, for she is your mother's flesh. [14] You shall not uncover the nakedness of your father's brother, that is, you shall not approach his wife; she is your aunt. [15] You shall not uncover the nakedness of your daughter-in-law: she is your son's wife; you shall not uncover her nakedness. [16] You shall not uncover the nakedness of your brother's wife; it is your brother's nakedness. [17] You shall not uncover the nakedness of a woman and her daughter, and you shall not take[x] her son's daughter or her daughter's daughter to uncover her nakedness; they are your[y] flesh; it is depravity. [18] And you shall not take[x] a woman as a rival to her sister, uncovering her nakedness while her sister is still alive.

19 You shall not approach a woman to uncover her nakedness while she is in her menstrual uncleanness. [20] You shall not have sexual relations with your kinsman's wife, and defile yourself with her. [21] You shall not give any of your offspring to sacrifice them[z] to Mo′lech, and so profane the name of your God: I am the LORD. [22] You shall not lie with a male as with a woman; it is an abomination. [23] You shall not have sexual relations with any animal and defile yourself with it, nor shall any woman give herself to an animal to have sexual relations with it: it is perversion.

24 Do not defile yourselves in any of these ways, for by all these practices the nations I am casting out before you have defiled themselves. [25] Thus the land became defiled; and I punished it for its iniquity, and the land vomited out its inhabitants. [26] But you shall keep my statutes and my ordinances and commit none of these abominations, either the citizen or the alien who resides among you [27] (for the inhabitants of the land, who were before you, committed all of these abominations, and the land became defiled); [28] otherwise the land will vomit you out

---

x Or *marry*   y Gk: Heb lacks *your*
z Heb *to pass them over*

for defiling it, as it vomited out the nation that was before you. 29 For whoever commits any of these abominations shall be cut off from their people. 30 So keep my charge not to commit any of these abominations that were done before you, and not to defile yourselves by them: I am the LORD your God.

Ritual and Moral Holiness

19 The LORD spoke to Moses, saying: 2 Speak to all the congregation of the people of Israel and say to them: You shall be holy, for I the LORD your God am holy. 3 You shall each revere your mother and father, and you shall keep my sabbaths: I am the LORD your God. 4 Do not turn to idols or make cast images for yourselves: I am the LORD your God.

5 When you offer a sacrifice of well-being to the LORD, offer it in such a way that it is acceptable on your behalf. 6 It shall be eaten on the same day you offer it, or on the next day; and anything left over until the third day shall be consumed in fire. 7 If it is eaten at all on the third day, it is an abomination; it will not be acceptable. 8 All who eat it shall be subject to punishment, because they have profaned what is holy to the LORD; and any such person shall be cut off from the people.

9 When you reap the harvest of your land, you shall not reap to the very edges of your field, or gather the gleanings of your harvest. 10 You shall not strip your vineyard bare, or gather the fallen grapes of your vineyard; you shall leave them for the poor and the alien: I am the LORD your God.

11 You shall not steal; you shall not deal falsely; and you shall not lie to one another. 12 And you shall not swear falsely by my name, profaning the name of your God: I am the LORD.

13 You shall not defraud your neighbor; you shall not steal; and you shall not keep for yourself the wages of a laborer until morning. 14 You shall not revile the deaf or put a stumbling block before the blind; you shall fear your God: I am the LORD.

15 You shall not render an unjust judgment; you shall not be partial to the poor or defer to the great: with justice you shall judge your neighbor. 16 You shall not go around as a slanderer a among your people, and you

shall not profit by the blood b of your neighbor: I am the LORD.

17 You shall not hate in your heart anyone of your kin; you shall reprove your neighbor, or you will incur guilt yourself. 18 You shall not take vengeance or bear a grudge against any of your people, but you shall love your neighbor as yourself: I am the LORD.

19 You shall keep my statutes. You shall not let your animals breed with a different kind; you shall not sow your field with two kinds of seed; nor shall you put on a garment made of two different materials.

20 If a man has sexual relations with a woman who is a slave, designated for another man but not ransomed or given her freedom, an inquiry shall be held. They shall not be put to death, since she has not been freed; 21 but he shall bring a guilt offering for himself to the LORD, at the entrance of the tent of meeting, a ram as guilt offering. 22 And the priest shall make atonement for him with the ram of guilt offering before the LORD for his sin that he committed; and the sin he committed shall be forgiven him.

23 When you come into the land and plant all kinds of trees for food, then you shall regard their fruit as forbidden; c three years it shall be forbidden d to you, it must not be eaten. 24 In the fourth year all their fruit shall be set apart for rejoicing in the LORD. 25 But in the fifth year you may eat of their fruit, that their yield may be increased for you: I am the LORD your God.

26 You shall not eat anything with its blood. You shall not practice augury or witchcraft. 27 You shall not round off the hair on your temples or mar the edges of your beard. 28 You shall not make any gashes in your flesh for the dead or tattoo any marks upon you: I am the LORD.

29 Do not profane your daughter by making her a prostitute, that the land not become prostituted and full of depravity. 30 You shall keep my sabbaths and reverence my sanctuary: I am the LORD.

31 Do not turn to mediums or wizards; do not seek them out, to be defiled by them: I am the LORD your God.

a Meaning of Heb uncertain
b Heb *stand against the blood*   c Heb *as their uncircumcision*
d Heb *uncircumcision*

32 You shall rise before the aged, and defer to the old; and you shall fear your God: I am the LORD.

33 When an alien resides with you in your land, you shall not oppress the alien. ³⁴ The alien who resides with you shall be to you as the citizen among you; you shall love the alien as yourself, for you were aliens in the land of Egypt: I am the LORD your God.

35 You shall not cheat in measuring length, weight, or quantity. ³⁶ You shall have honest balances, honest weights, an honest ephah, and an honest hin: I am the LORD your God, who brought you out of the land of Egypt. ³⁷ You shall keep all my statutes and all my ordinances, and observe them: I am the LORD.

Penalties for Violations of Holiness

20 The LORD spoke to Moses, saying: ² Say further to the people of Israel:

Any of the people of Israel, or of the aliens who reside in Israel, who give any of their offspring to Mŏ′lech shall be put to death; the people of the land shall stone them to death. ³ I myself will set my face against them, and will cut them off from the people, because they have given of their offspring to Mŏ′lech, defiling my sanctuary and profaning my holy name. ⁴ And if the people of the land should ever close their eyes to them, when they give of their offspring to Mŏ′lech, and do not put them to death, ⁵ I myself will set my face against them and against their family, and will cut them off from among their people, them and all who follow them in prostituting themselves to Mŏ′lech.

6 If any turn to mediums and wizards, prostituting themselves to them, I will set my face against them, and will cut them off from the people. ⁷ Consecrate yourselves therefore, and be holy; for I am the LORD your God. ⁸ Keep my statutes, and observe them; I am the LORD; I sanctify you. ⁹ All who curse father or mother shall be put to death; having cursed father or mother, their blood is upon them.

10 If a man commits adultery with the wife of ᵉ his neighbor, both the adulterer and the adulteress shall be put to death. ¹¹ The man who lies with his father's wife has uncovered his father's nakedness; both of them shall be put to death; their blood is upon them. ¹² If a man lies with his daughter-in-

law, both of them shall be put to death; they have committed perversion, their blood is upon them. ¹³ If a man lies with a male as with a woman, both of them have committed an abomination; they shall be put to death; their blood is upon them. ¹⁴ If a man takes a wife and her mother also, it is depravity; they shall be burned to death, both he and they, that there may be no depravity among you. ¹⁵ If a man has sexual relations with an animal, he shall be put to death; and you shall kill the animal. ¹⁶ If a woman approaches any animal and has sexual relations with it, you shall kill the woman and the animal; they shall be put to death, their blood is upon them.

17 If a man takes his sister, a daughter of his father or a daughter of his mother, and sees her nakedness, and she sees his nakedness, it is a disgrace, and they shall be cut off in the sight of their people; he has uncovered his sister's nakedness, he shall be subject to punishment. ¹⁸ If a man lies with a woman having her sickness and uncovers her nakedness, he has laid bare her flow and she has laid bare her flow of blood; both of them shall be cut off from their people. ¹⁹ You shall not uncover the nakedness of your mother's sister or of your father's sister, for that is to lay bare one's own flesh; they shall be subject to punishment. ²⁰ If a man lies with his uncle's wife, he has uncovered his uncle's nakedness; they shall be subject to punishment; they shall die childless. ²¹ If a man takes his brother's wife, it is impurity; he has uncovered his brother's nakedness; they shall be childless.

22 You shall keep all my statutes and all my ordinances, and observe them, so that the land to which I bring you to settle in may not vomit you out. ²³ You shall not follow the practices of the nation that I am driving out before you. Because they did all these things, I abhorred them. ²⁴ But I have said to you: You shall inherit their land, and I will give it to you to possess, a land flowing with milk and honey. I am the LORD your God; I have separated you from the peoples. ²⁵ You shall therefore make a distinction between the clean animal and the unclean, and between the unclean bird and the clean; you shall not bring abomination on

ᵉ Heb repeats *if a man commits adultery with the wife of*

yourselves by animal or by bird or by anything with which the ground teems, which I have set apart for you to hold unclean. ²⁶You shall be holy to me; for I the LORD am holy, and I have separated you from the other peoples to be mine.

27 A man or a woman who is a medium or a wizard shall be put to death; they shall be stoned to death, their blood is upon them.

The Holiness of Priests
(Cp Ezek 44.15–31)

21 The LORD said to Moses: Speak to the priests, the sons of Aaron, and say to them:

No one shall defile himself for a dead person among his relatives, ²except for his nearest kin: his mother, his father, his son, his daughter, his brother; ³likewise, for a virgin sister, close to him because she has had no husband, he may defile himself for her. ⁴But he shall not defile himself as a husband among his people and so profane himself. ⁵They shall not make bald spots upon their heads, or shave off the edges of their beards, or make any gashes in their flesh. ⁶They shall be holy to their God, and not profane the name of their God; for they offer the LORD's offerings by fire, the food of their God; therefore they shall be holy. ⁷They shall not marry a prostitute or a woman who has been defiled; neither shall they marry a woman divorced from her husband. For they are holy to their God, ⁸and you shall treat them as holy, since they offer the food of your God; they shall be holy to you, for I the LORD, I who sanctify you, am holy. ⁹When the daughter of a priest profanes herself through prostitution, she profanes her father; she shall be burned to death.

10 The priest who is exalted above his fellows, on whose head the anointing oil has been poured and who has been consecrated to wear the vestments, shall not dishevel his hair, nor tear his vestments. ¹¹He shall not go where there is a dead body; he shall not defile himself even for his father or mother. ¹²He shall not go outside the sanctuary and thus profane the sanctuary of his God; for the consecration of the anointing oil of his God is upon him: I am the LORD. ¹³He shall marry only a woman who is a virgin. ¹⁴A widow, or a divorced woman, or a woman who has been defiled, a prosti-

tute, these he shall not marry. He shall marry a virgin of his own kin, ¹⁵that he may not profane his offspring among his kin; for I am the LORD; I sanctify him.

16 The LORD spoke to Moses, saying: ¹⁷Speak to Aaron and say: No one of your offspring throughout their generations who has a blemish may approach to offer the food of his God. ¹⁸For no one who has a blemish shall draw near, one who is blind or lame, or one who has a mutilated face or a limb too long, ¹⁹or one who has a broken foot or a broken hand, ²⁰or a hunchback, or a dwarf, or a man with a blemish in his eyes or an itching disease or scabs or crushed testicles. ²¹No descendant of Aaron the priest who has a blemish shall come near to offer the LORD's offerings by fire; since he has a blemish, he shall not come near to offer the food of his God. ²²He may eat the food of his God, of the most holy as well as of the holy. ²³But he shall not come near the curtain or approach the altar, because he has a blemish, that he may not profane my sanctuaries; for I am the LORD; I sanctify them. ²⁴Thus Moses spoke to Aaron and to his sons and to all the people of Israel.

The Use of Holy Offerings

22 The LORD spoke to Moses, saying: ²Direct Aaron and his sons to deal carefully with the sacred donations of the people of Israel, which they dedicate to me, so that they may not profane my holy name; I am the LORD. ³Say to them: If anyone among all your offspring throughout your generations comes near the sacred donations, which the people of Israel dedicate to the LORD, while he is in a state of uncleanness, that person shall be cut off from my presence: I am the LORD. ⁴No one of Aaron's offspring who has a leprousᶠ disease or suffers a discharge may eat of the sacred donations until he is clean. Whoever touches anything made unclean by a corpse or a man who has had an emission of semen, ⁵and whoever touches any swarming thing by which he may be made unclean or any human being by whom he may be made unclean— whatever his uncleanness may be— ⁶the person who touches any such shall be unclean until evening and

ᶠA term for several skin diseases; precise meaning uncertain shall not eat of the sacred donations unless he has washed his body in water. 7 When the sun sets he shall be clean; and afterward he may eat of the sacred donations, for they are his food. 8 That which died or was torn by wild animals he shall not eat, becoming unclean by it: I am the LORD. 9 They shall keep my charge, so that they may not incur guilt and die in the sanctuary*g* for having profaned it: I am the LORD; I sanctify them.

10 No lay person shall eat of the sacred donations. No bound or hired servant of the priest shall eat of the sacred donations; 11 but if a priest acquires anyone by purchase, the person may eat of them; and those that are born in his house may eat of his food. 12 If a priest's daughter marries a layman, she shall not eat of the offering of the sacred donations; 13 but if a priest's daughter is widowed or divorced, without offspring, and returns to her father's house, as in her youth, she may eat of her father's food. No lay person shall eat of it. 14 If a man eats of the sacred donation unintentionally, he shall add one-fifth of its value to it, and give the sacred donation to the priest. 15 No one shall profane the sacred donations of the people of Israel, which they offer to the LORD, 16 causing them to bear guilt requiring a guilt offering, by eating their sacred donations: for I am the LORD; I sanctify them.

Acceptable Offerings

17 The LORD spoke to Moses, saying: 18 Speak to Aaron and his sons and all the people of Israel and say to them: When anyone of the house of Israel or of the aliens residing in Israel presents an offering, whether in payment of a vow or as a freewill offering that is offered to the LORD as a burnt offering, 19 to be acceptable in your behalf it shall be a male without blemish, of the cattle or the sheep or the goats. 20 You shall not offer anything that has a blemish, for it will not be acceptable in your behalf.

21 When anyone offers a sacrifice of well-being to the LORD, in fulfillment of a vow or as a freewill offering, from the herd or from the flock, to be acceptable it must be perfect; there shall be no blemish in it. 22 Anything blind, or injured, or maimed, or having a discharge or an itch or scabs—these you shall not offer to the LORD or put any of them on the altar as offerings by fire to the LORD. 23 An ox or a lamb that has a limb too long or too short you may present for a freewill offering; but it will not be accepted for a vow. 24 Any animal that has its testicles bruised or crushed or torn or cut, you shall not offer to the LORD; such you shall not do within your land, 25 nor shall you accept any such animals from a foreigner to offer as food to your God; since they are mutilated, with a blemish in them, they shall not be accepted in your behalf.

26 The LORD spoke to Moses, saying: 27 When an ox or a sheep or a goat is born, it shall remain seven days with its mother, and from the eighth day on it shall be acceptable as the LORD's offering by fire. 28 But you shall not slaughter, from the herd or the flock, an animal with its young on the same day. 29 When you sacrifice a thanksgiving offering to the LORD, you shall sacrifice it so that it may be acceptable in your behalf. 30 It shall be eaten on the same day; you shall not leave any of it until morning: I am the LORD.

31 Thus you shall keep my commandments and observe them: I am the LORD. 32 You shall not profane my holy name, that I may be sanctified among the people of Israel: I am the LORD; I sanctify you, 33 I who brought you out of the land of Egypt to be your God: I am the LORD.

Appointed Festivals

23 The LORD spoke to Moses, saying: 2 Speak to the people of Israel and say to them: These are the appointed festivals of the LORD that you shall proclaim as holy convocations, my appointed festivals.

The Sabbath, Passover, and Unleavened Bread
(Num 28.16–25)

3 Six days shall work be done; but the seventh day is a sabbath of complete rest, a holy convocation; you shall do no work: it is a sabbath to the LORD throughout your settlements.

4 These are the appointed festivals of the LORD, the holy convocations, which you shall celebrate at the time appointed for them. 5 In the first month, on the fourteenth day of the month, at twilight,*h* there shall be a

g Vg: Heb *incur guilt for it and die in it*
h Heb *between the two evenings*

passover offering to the LORD, [6] and on the fifteenth day of the same month is the festival of unleavened bread to the LORD; seven days you shall eat unleavened bread. [7] On the first day you shall have a holy convocation; you shall not work at your occupations. [8] For seven days you shall present the LORD's offerings by fire; on the seventh day there shall be a holy convocation: you shall not work at your occupations.

The Offering of First Fruits

9 The LORD spoke to Moses: [10] Speak to the people of Israel and say to them: When you enter the land that I am giving you and you reap its harvest, you shall bring the sheaf of the first fruits of your harvest to the priest. [11] He shall raise the sheaf before the LORD, that you may find acceptance; on the day after the sabbath the priest shall raise it. [12] On the day when you raise the sheaf, you shall offer a lamb a year old, without blemish, as a burnt offering to the LORD. [13] And the grain offering with it shall be two-tenths of an ephah of choice flour mixed with oil, an offering by fire of pleasing odor to the LORD; and the drink offering with it shall be of wine, one-fourth of a hin. [14] You shall eat no bread or parched grain or fresh ears until that very day, until you have brought the offering of your God: it is a statute forever throughout your generations in all your settlements.

The Festival of Weeks
(Ex 34.22; Num 28.26–31; Deut 16.9–10)

15 And from the day after the sabbath, from the day on which you bring the sheaf of the elevation offering, you shall count off seven weeks; they shall be complete. [16] You shall count until the day after the seventh sabbath, fifty days; then you shall present an offering of new grain to the LORD. [17] You shall bring from your settlements two loaves of bread as an elevation offering, each made of two-tenths of an ephah; they shall be of choice flour, baked with leaven, as first fruits to the LORD. [18] You shall present with the bread seven lambs a year old without blemish, one young bull, and two rams; they shall be a burnt offering to the LORD, along with their grain offering and their drink offerings, an offering by fire of pleasing odor to the LORD. [19] You shall also offer one male goat for a sin offering, and two male lambs a year old as a sacrifice of well-being. [20] The priest shall raise them with the bread of the first fruits as an elevation offering before the LORD, together with the two lambs; they shall be holy to the LORD for the priest. [21] On that same day you shall make proclamation; you shall hold a holy convocation; you shall not work at your occupations. This is a statute forever in all your settlements throughout your generations.

22 When you reap the harvest of your land, you shall not reap to the very edges of your field, or gather the gleanings of your harvest; you shall leave them for the poor and for the alien: I am the LORD your God.

The Festival of Trumpets
(Num 29.1–6)

23 The LORD spoke to Moses, saying: [24] Speak to the people of Israel, saying: In the seventh month, on the first day of the month, you shall observe a day of complete rest, a holy convocation commemorated with trumpet blasts. [25] You shall not work at your occupations; and you shall present the LORD's offering by fire.

The Day of Atonement
(Num 29.7–11)

26 The LORD spoke to Moses, saying: [27] Now, the tenth day of this seventh month is the day of atonement; it shall be a holy convocation for you: you shall deny yourselves[i] and present the LORD's offering by fire; [28] and you shall do no work during that entire day; for it is a day of atonement, to make atonement on your behalf before the LORD your God. [29] For anyone who does not practice self-denial[j] during that entire day shall be cut off from the people. [30] And anyone who does any work during that entire day, such a one I will destroy from the midst of the people. [31] You shall do no work: it is a statute forever throughout your generations in all your settlements. [32] It shall be to you a sabbath of complete rest, and you shall deny yourselves;[i] on the ninth day of the month at evening, from evening to evening you shall keep your sabbath.

The Festival of Booths
(Num 29.12–40; Deut 16.13–17)

33 The LORD spoke to Moses, say-

[i] Or *shall fast* [j] Or *does not fast*

ing: ³⁴Speak to the people of Israel, saying: On the fifteenth day of this seventh month, and lasting seven days, there shall be the festival of booths^k to the LORD. ³⁵The first day shall be a holy convocation; you shall not work at your occupations. ³⁶Seven days you shall present the LORD's offerings by fire; on the eighth day you shall observe a holy convocation and present the LORD's offerings by fire; it is a solemn assembly; you shall not work at your occupations.

37   These are the appointed festivals of the LORD, which you shall celebrate as times of holy convocation, for presenting to the LORD offerings by fire— burnt offerings and grain offerings, sacrifices and drink offerings, each on its proper day— ³⁸apart from the sabbaths of the LORD, and apart from your gifts, and apart from all your votive offerings, and apart from all your freewill offerings, which you give to the LORD.

39   Now, the fifteenth day of the seventh month, when you have gathered in the produce of the land, you shall keep the festival of the LORD, lasting seven days; a complete rest on the first day, and a complete rest on the eighth day. ⁴⁰On the first day you shall take the fruit of majestic^l trees, branches of palm trees, boughs of leafy trees, and willows of the brook; and you shall rejoice before the LORD your God for seven days. ⁴¹You shall keep it as a festival to the LORD seven days in the year; you shall keep it in the seventh month as a statute forever throughout your generations. ⁴²You shall live in booths for seven days; all that are citizens in Israel shall live in booths, ⁴³so that your generations may know that I made the people of Israel live in booths when I brought them out of the land of Egypt: I am the LORD your God.

44   Thus Moses declared to the people of Israel the appointed festivals of the LORD.

The Lamp
(Ex 27.20–21)

24 The LORD spoke to Moses, saying: ²Command the people of Israel to bring you pure oil of beaten olives for the lamp, that a light may be kept burning regularly. ³Aaron shall set it up in the tent of meeting, outside the curtain of the covenant,^m to burn from evening to morning before the LORD regularly; it shall be a statute for-

ever throughout your generations. ⁴He shall set up the lamps on the lampstand of pure goldⁿ before the LORD regularly.

The Bread for the Tabernacle

5   You shall take choice flour, and bake twelve loaves of it; two-tenths of an ephah shall be in each loaf. ⁶You shall place them in two rows, six in a row, on the table of pure gold. ^o ⁷You shall put pure frankincense with each row, to be a token offering for the bread, as an offering by fire to the LORD. ⁸Every sabbath day Aaron shall set them in order before the LORD regularly as a commitment of the people of Israel, as a covenant forever. ⁹They shall be for Aaron and his descendants, who shall eat them in a holy place, for they are most holy portions for him from the offerings by fire to the LORD, a perpetual due.

Blasphemy and Its Punishment

10   A man whose mother was an Israelite and whose father was an Egyptian came out among the people of Israel; and the Israelite woman's son and a certain Israelite began fighting in the camp. ¹¹The Israelite woman's son blasphemed the Name in a curse. And they brought him to Moses—now his mother's name was She-lo'mith, daughter of Dib'ri, of the tribe of Dan— ¹²and they put him in custody, until the decision of the LORD should be made clear to them.

13   The LORD said to Moses, saying: ¹⁴Take the blasphemer outside the camp; and let all who were within hearing lay their hands on his head, and let the whole congregation stone him. ¹⁵And speak to the people of Israel, saying: Anyone who curses God shall bear the sin. ¹⁶One who blasphemes the name of the LORD shall be put to death; the whole congregation shall stone the blasphemer. Aliens as well as citizens, when they blaspheme the Name, shall be put to death. ¹⁷Anyone who kills a human being shall be put to death. ¹⁸Anyone who kills an animal shall make restitution for it, life for life. ¹⁹Anyone who maims another shall suffer the same injury in return: ²⁰fracture for fracture, eye for eye,

---

^kOr *tabernacles*: Heb *succoth*
^lMeaning of Heb uncertain
^mOr *treaty*, or *testament*; Heb *eduth*
ⁿHeb *pure lampstand*   ^oHeb *pure table*

tooth for tooth; the injury inflicted is the injury to be suffered. 21 One who kills an animal shall make restitution for it; but one who kills a human being shall be put to death. 22 You shall have one law for the alien and for the citizen: for I am the LORD your God. 23 Moses spoke thus to the people of Israel; and they took the blasphemer outside the camp, and stoned him to death. The people of Israel did as the LORD had commanded Moses.

The Sabbatical Year
(Deut 15.1–11)

25 The LORD spoke to Moses on Mount Sinai, saying: 2 Speak to the people of Israel and say to them: When you enter the land that I am giving you, the land shall observe a sabbath for the LORD. 3 Six years you shall sow your field, and six years you shall prune your vineyard, and gather in their yield; 4 but in the seventh year there shall be a sabbath of complete rest for the land, a sabbath for the LORD: you shall not sow your field or prune your vineyard. 5 You shall not reap the aftergrowth of your harvest or gather the grapes of your unpruned vine: it shall be a year of complete rest for the land. 6 You may eat what the land yields during its sabbath—you, your male and female slaves, your hired and your bound laborers who live with you; 7 for your livestock also, and for the wild animals in your land all its yield shall be for food.

The Year of Jubilee

8 You shall count off seven weeks[p] of years, seven times seven years, so that the period of seven weeks of years gives forty-nine years. 9 Then you shall have the trumpet sounded loud; on the tenth day of the seventh month—on the day of atonement—you shall have the trumpet sounded throughout all your land. 10 And you shall hallow the fiftieth year and you shall proclaim liberty throughout the land to all its inhabitants. It shall be a jubilee for you: you shall return, every one of you, to your property and every one of you to your family. 11 That fiftieth year shall be a jubilee for you: you shall not sow, or reap the aftergrowth, or harvest the unpruned vines. 12 For it is a jubilee; it shall be holy to you: you shall eat only what the field itself produces.

13 In this year of jubilee you shall return, every one of you, to your prop-

erty. 14 When you make a sale to your neighbor or buy from your neighbor, you shall not cheat one another. 15 When you buy from your neighbor, you shall pay only for the number of years since the jubilee; the seller shall charge you only for the remaining crop years. 16 If the years are more, you shall increase the price, and if the years are fewer, you shall diminish the price; for it is a certain number of harvests that are being sold to you. 17 You shall not cheat one another, but you shall fear your God; for I am the LORD your God.

18 You shall observe my statutes and faithfully keep my ordinances, so that you may live on the land securely. 19 The land will yield its fruit, and you will eat your fill and live on it securely. 20 Should you ask, What shall we eat in the seventh year, if we may not sow or gather in our crop? 21 I will order my blessing for you in the sixth year, so that it will yield a crop for three years. 22 When you sow in the eighth year, you will be eating from the old crop; until the ninth year, when its produce comes in, you shall eat the old. 23 The land shall not be sold in perpetuity; for the land is mine; with me you are but aliens and tenants. 24 Throughout the land that you hold, you shall provide for the redemption of the land.

25 If anyone of your kin falls into difficulty and sells a piece of property, then the next of kin shall come and redeem what the relative has sold. 26 If the person has no one to redeem it, but then prospers and finds sufficient means to do so, 27 the years since its sale shall be computed and the difference shall be refunded to the person to whom it was sold, and the property shall be returned. 28 But if there is not sufficient means to recover it, what was sold shall remain with the purchaser until the year of jubilee; in the jubilee it shall be released, and the property shall be returned.

29 If anyone sells a dwelling house in a walled city, it may be redeemed until a year has elapsed since its sale; the right of redemption shall be one year. 30 If it is not redeemed before a full year has elapsed, a house that is in a walled city shall pass in perpetuity to the purchaser, throughout the generations; it shall not be released in the jubilee. 31 But houses in villages that

p Or sabbaths

have no walls around them shall be classed as open country; they may be redeemed, and they shall be released in the jubilee. ³²As for the cities of the Lěʹvītes, the Lěʹvītes shall forever have the right of redemption of the houses in the cities belonging to them. ³³Such property as may be redeemed from the Lěʹvītes—houses sold in a city belonging to them—shall be released in the jubilee; because the houses in the cities of the Lěʹvītes are their possession among the people of Israel. ³⁴But the open land around their cities may not be sold; for that is their possession for all time.

35 If any of your kin fall into difficulty and become dependent on you, �q you shall support them; they shall live with you as though resident aliens. ³⁶Do not take interest in advance or otherwise make a profit from them, but fear your God; let them live with you. ³⁷You shall not lend them your money at interest taken in advance, or provide them food at a profit. ³⁸I am the LORD your God, who brought you out of the land of Egypt, to give you the land of Caʹnaan, to be your God.

39 If any who are dependent on you become so impoverished that they sell themselves to you, you shall not make them serve as slaves. ⁴⁰They shall remain with you as hired or bound laborers. They shall serve with you until the year of the jubilee. ⁴¹Then they and their children with them shall be free from your authority; they shall go back to their own family and return to their ancestral property. ⁴²For they are my servants, whom I brought out of the land of Egypt; they shall not be sold as slaves are sold. ⁴³You shall not rule over them with harshness, but shall fear your God. ⁴⁴As for the male and female slaves whom you may have, it is from the nations around you that you may acquire male and female slaves. ⁴⁵You may also acquire them from among the aliens residing with you, and from their families that are with you, who have been born in your land; and they may be your property. ⁴⁶You may keep them as a possession for your children after you, for them to inherit as property. These you may treat as slaves, but as for your fellow Israelites, no one shall rule over the other with harshness.

47 If resident aliens among you prosper, and if any of your kin fall into difficulty with one of them and sell themselves to an alien, or to a branch of the alien's family, ⁴⁸after they have sold themselves they shall have the right of redemption; one of their brothers may redeem them, ⁴⁹or their uncle or their uncle's son may redeem them, or anyone of their family who is of their own flesh may redeem them; or if they prosper they may redeem themselves. ⁵⁰They shall compute with the purchaser the total from the year when they sold themselves to the alien until the jubilee year; the price of the sale shall be applied to the number of years: the time they were with the owner shall be rated as the time of a hired laborer. ⁵¹If many years remain, they shall pay for their redemption in proportion to the purchase price; ⁵²and if few years remain until the jubilee year, they shall compute thus: according to the years involved they shall make payment for their redemption. ⁵³As a laborer hired by the year they shall be under the alien's authority, who shall not, however, rule with harshness over them in your sight. ⁵⁴And if they have not been redeemed in any of these ways, they and their children shall go free in the jubilee year. ⁵⁵For to me the people of Israel are servants; they are my servants whom I brought out from the land of Egypt: I am the LORD your God.

Rewards for Obedience
(Deut 7.12–24; 28.1–14)

26 You shall make for yourselves no idols and erect no carved images or pillars, and you shall not place figured stones in your land, to worship at them; for I am the LORD your God. ²You shall keep my sabbaths and reverence my sanctuary: I am the LORD.

3 If you follow my statutes and keep my commandments and observe them faithfully, ⁴I will give you your rains in their season, and the land shall yield its produce, and the trees of the field shall yield their fruit. ⁵Your threshing shall overtake the vintage, and the vintage shall overtake the sowing; you shall eat your bread to the full, and live securely in your land. ⁶And I will grant peace in the land, and you shall lie down, and no one shall make you afraid; I will remove dangerous animals from the land, and no sword shall go through your land. ⁷You shall give chase to your enemies, and they shall

�q Meaning of Heb uncertain

fall before you by the sword. ⁸Five of you shall give chase to a hundred, and a hundred of you shall give chase to ten thousand; your enemies shall fall before you by the sword. ⁹I will look with favor upon you and make you fruitful and multiply you; and I will maintain my covenant with you. ¹⁰You shall eat old grain long stored, and you shall have to clear out the old to make way for the new. ¹¹I will place my dwelling in your midst, and I shall not abhor you. ¹²And I will walk among you, and will be your God, and you shall be my people. ¹³I am the LORD your God who brought you out of the land of Egypt, to be their slaves no more; I have broken the bars of your yoke and made you walk erect.

Penalties for Disobedience
(Deut 28.15–68)

14 But if you will not obey me, and do not observe all these commandments, ¹⁵if you spurn my statutes, and abhor my ordinances, so that you will not observe all my commandments, and you break my covenant, ¹⁶I in turn will do this to you: I will bring terror on you; consumption and fever that waste the eyes and cause life to pine away. You shall sow your seed in vain, for your enemies shall eat it. ¹⁷I will set my face against you, and you shall be struck down by your enemies; your foes shall rule over you, and you shall flee though no one pursues you. ¹⁸And if in spite of this you will not obey me, I will continue to punish you sevenfold for your sins. ¹⁹I will break your proud glory, and I will make your sky like iron and your earth like copper. ²⁰Your strength shall be spent to no purpose: your land shall not yield its produce, and the trees of the land shall not yield their fruit.

21 If you continue hostile to me, and will not obey me, I will continue to plague you sevenfold for your sins. ²²I will let loose wild animals against you, and they shall bereave you of your children and destroy your livestock; they shall make you few in number, and your roads shall be deserted.

23 If in spite of these punishments you have not turned back to me, but continue hostile to me, ²⁴then I too will continue hostile to you: I myself will strike you sevenfold for your sins. ²⁵I will bring the sword against you, executing vengeance for the covenant; and if you withdraw within your cities,

I will send pestilence among you, and you shall be delivered into enemy hands. ²⁶When I break your staff of bread, ten women shall bake your bread in a single oven, and they shall dole out your bread by weight; and though you eat, you shall not be satisfied.

27 But if, despite this, you disobey me, and continue hostile to me, ²⁸I will continue hostile to you in fury; I in turn will punish you myself sevenfold for your sins. ²⁹You shall eat the flesh of your sons, and you shall eat the flesh of your daughters. ³⁰I will destroy your high places and cut down your incense altars; I will heap your carcasses on the carcasses of your idols. I will abhor you. ³¹I will lay your cities waste, will make your sanctuaries desolate, and I will not smell your pleasing odors. ³²I will devastate the land, so that your enemies who come to settle in it shall be appalled at it. ³³And you I will scatter among the nations, and I will unsheathe the sword against you; your land shall be a desolation, and your cities a waste.

34 Then the land shall enjoyʳ its sabbath years as long as it lies desolate, while you are in the land of your enemies; then the land shall rest, and enjoyʳ its sabbath years. ³⁵As long as it lies desolate, it shall have the rest it did not have on your sabbaths when you were living on it. ³⁶And as for those of you who survive, I will send faintness into their hearts in the lands of their enemies; the sound of a driven leaf shall put them to flight, and they shall flee as one flees from the sword, and they shall fall though no one pursues. ³⁷They shall stumble over one another, as if to escape a sword, though no one pursues; and you shall have no power to stand against your enemies. ³⁸You shall perish among the nations, and the land of your enemies shall devour you. ³⁹And those of you who survive shall languish in the land of your enemies because of their iniquities; also they shall languish because of the iniquities of their ancestors.

40 But if they confess their iniquity and the iniquity of their ancestors, in that they committed treachery against me and, moreover, that they continued hostile to me— ⁴¹so that I, in turn, continued hostile to them and brought them into the land of their enemies; if

ʳOr *make up for*

then their uncircumcised heart is humbled and they make amends for their iniquity, 42 then will I remember my covenant with Jacob; I will remember also my covenant with Isaac and also my covenant with Abraham, and I will remember the land. 43 For the land shall be deserted by them, and enjoys its sabbath years by lying desolate without them, while they shall make amends for their iniquity, because they dared to spurn my ordinances, and they abhorred my statutes. 44 Yet for all that, when they are in the land of their enemies, I will not spurn them, or abhor them so as to destroy them utterly and break my covenant with them; for I am the LORD their God; 45 but I will remember in their favor the covenant with their ancestors whom I brought out of the land of Egypt in the sight of the nations, to be their God: I am the LORD.

46 These are the statutes and ordinances and laws that the LORD established between himself and the people of Israel on Mount Sinai through Moses.

Votive Offerings

27 The LORD spoke to Moses, saying: 2 Speak to the people of Israel and say to them: When a person makes an explicit vow to the LORD concerning the equivalent for a human being, 3 the equivalent for a male shall be: from twenty to sixty years of age the equivalent shall be fifty shekels of silver by the sanctuary shekel. 4 If the person is a female, the equivalent is thirty shekels. 5 If the age is from five to twenty years of age, the equivalent is twenty shekels for a male and ten shekels for a female. 6 If the age is from one month to five years, the equivalent for a male is five shekels of silver, and for a female the equivalent is three shekels of silver. 7 And if the person is sixty years old or over, then the equivalent for a male is fifteen shekels, and for a female ten shekels. 8 If any cannot afford the equivalent, they shall be brought before the priest and the priest shall assess them; the priest shall assess them according to what each one making a vow can afford.

9 If it concerns an animal that may be brought as an offering to the LORD, any such that may be given to the LORD shall be holy. 10 Another shall not be exchanged or substituted for it, either good for bad or bad for good; and if one animal is substituted for another, both that one and its substitute shall be holy. 11 If it concerns any unclean animal that may not be brought as an offering to the LORD, the animal shall be presented before the priest. 12 The priest shall assess it: whether good or bad, according to the assessment of the priest, so it shall be. 13 But if it is to be redeemed, one-fifth must be added to the assessment.

14 If a person consecrates a house to the LORD, the priest shall assess it: whether good or bad, as the priest assesses it, so it shall stand. 15 And if the one who consecrates the house wishes to redeem it, one-fifth shall be added to its assessed value, and it shall revert to the original owner.

16 If a person consecrates to the LORD any inherited landholding, its assessment shall be in accordance with its seed requirements: fifty shekels of silver to a homer of barley seed. 17 If the person consecrates the field as of the year of jubilee, that assessment shall stand; 18 but if the field is consecrated after the jubilee, the priest shall compute the price for it according to the years that remain until the year of jubilee, and the assessment shall be reduced. 19 And if the one who consecrates the field wishes to redeem it, then one-fifth shall be added to its assessed value, and it shall revert to the original owner; 20 but if the field is not redeemed, or if it has been sold to someone else, it shall no longer be redeemable. 21 But when the field is released in the jubilee, it shall be holy to the LORD as a devoted field; it becomes the priest's holding. 22 If someone consecrates to the LORD a field that has been purchased, which is not a part of the inherited landholding, 23 the priest shall compute for it the proportionate assessment up to the year of jubilee, and the assessment shall be paid as of that day, a sacred donation to the LORD. 24 In the year of jubilee the field shall return to the one from whom it was bought, whose holding the land is. 25 All assessments shall be by the sanctuary shekel: twenty gerahs shall make a shekel.

26 A firstling of animals, however, which as a firstling belongs to the LORD, cannot be consecrated by anyone; whether ox or sheep, it is the LORD's. 27 If it is an unclean animal, it

s Or *make up for*

shall be ransomed at its assessment, with one-fifth added; if it is not redeemed, it shall be sold at its assessment.

28 Nothing that a person owns that has been devoted to destruction for the LORD, be it human or animal, or inherited landholding, may be sold or redeemed; every devoted thing is most holy to the LORD. 29 No human beings who have been devoted to destruction can be ransomed; they shall be put to death.

30 All tithes from the land, whether the seed from the ground or the fruit from the tree, are the LORD's; they are holy to the LORD. 31 If persons wish to redeem any of their tithes, they must add one-fifth to them. 32 All tithes of herd and flock, every tenth one that passes under the shepherd's staff, shall be holy to the LORD. 33 Let no one inquire whether it is good or bad, or make substitution for it; if one makes substitution for it, then both it and the substitute shall be holy and cannot be redeemed.

34 These are the commandments that the LORD gave to Moses for the people of Israel on Mount Sinai.

NUMBERS

The First Census of Israel
(Cp 2 Sam 24.1–9; 1 Chr 21.1–6)

1 The LORD spoke to Moses in the wilderness of Sinai, in the tent of meeting, on the first day of the second month, in the second year after they had come out of the land of Egypt, saying: 2 Take a census of the whole congregation of Israelites, in their clans, by ancestral houses, according to the number of names, every male individually; 3 from twenty years old and upward, everyone in Israel able to go to war. You and Aaron shall enroll them, company by company. 4 A man from each tribe shall be with you, each man the head of his ancestral house. 5 These are the names of the men who shall assist you:

From Reuben, E·li′zur son of Shed′e·ur.
6 From Sim′e·on, She·lu′mi·el son of Zu·ri·shad′dai.
7 From Judah, Nah′shon son of Am·min′a·dab.
8 From Is′sa·char, Ne·than′el son of Zu′ar.
9 From Zeb′u·lun, E·li′ab son of He′lon.
10 From the sons of Joseph:
from E′phra·im, E·lish′a·ma son of Am·mi′hud;
from Ma·nas′seh, Ga·ma′li·el son of Pe·dah′zur.
11 From Benjamin, A·bi′dan son of Gid·e·o′ni.
12 From Dan, A·hi·e′zer son of Am·mi·shad′dai.
13 From Ash′er, Pa′gi·el son of Och′ran.
14 From Gad, E·li′a·saph son of Deu′el.
15 From Naph′ta·li, A·hi′ra son of E′nan.

16 These were the ones chosen from the congregation, the leaders of their ancestral tribes, the heads of the divisions of Israel.

17 Moses and Aaron took these men who had been designated by name, 18 and on the first day of the second month they assembled the whole congregation together. They registered themselves in their clans, by their ancestral houses, according to the number of names from twenty years old and upward, individually, 19 as the LORD commanded Moses. So he enrolled them in the wilderness of Sinai.

20 The descendants of Reuben, Israel's firstborn, their lineage, in their clans, by their ancestral houses, according to the number of names, individually, every male from twenty years old and upward, everyone able to go to war: 21 those enrolled of the tribe of Reuben were forty-six thousand five hundred.

22 The descendants of Sim'e·on, their lineage, in their clans, by their ancestral houses, those of them that were numbered, according to the number of names, individually, every male from twenty years old and upward, everyone able to go to war: 23those enrolled of the tribe of Sim'e·on were fifty-nine thousand three hundred.

24 The descendants of Gad, their lineage, in their clans, by their ancestral houses, according to the number of the names, from twenty years old and upward, everyone able to go to war: 25those enrolled of the tribe of Gad were forty-five thousand six hundred fifty.

26 The descendants of Judah, their lineage, in their clans, by their ancestral houses, according to the number of names, from twenty years old and upward, everyone able to go to war: 27those enrolled of the tribe of Judah were seventy-four thousand six hundred.

28 The descendants of Is'sa·char, their lineage, in their clans, by their ancestral houses, according to the number of names, from twenty years old and upward, everyone able to go to war: 29those enrolled of the tribe of Is'sa·char were fifty-four thousand four hundred.

30 The descendants of Zeb'u·lun, their lineage, in their clans, by their ancestral houses, according to the number of names, from twenty years old and upward, everyone able to go to war: 31those enrolled of the tribe of Zeb'u·lun were fifty-seven thousand four hundred.

32 The descendants of Joseph, namely, the descendants of E'phra·im, their lineage, in their clans, by their ancestral houses, according to the number of names, from twenty years old and upward, everyone able to go to war: 33those enrolled of the tribe of E'phra·im were forty thousand five hundred.

34 The descendants of Ma·nas'seh, their lineage, in their clans, by their ancestral houses, according to the number of names, from twenty years old and upward, everyone able to go to war: 35those enrolled of the tribe of Ma·nas'seh were thirty-two thousand two hundred.

36 The descendants of Benjamin, their lineage, in their clans, by their ancestral houses, according to the number of names, from twenty years

old and upward, everyone able to go to war: 37those enrolled of the tribe of Benjamin were thirty-five thousand four hundred.

38 The descendants of Dan, their lineage, in their clans, by their ancestral houses, according to the number of names, from twenty years old and upward, everyone able to go to war: 39those enrolled of the tribe of Dan were sixty-two thousand seven hundred.

40 The descendants of Ash'er, their lineage, in their clans, by their ancestral houses, according to the number of names, from twenty years old and upward, everyone able to go to war: 41those enrolled of the tribe of Ash'er were forty-one thousand five hundred.

42 The descendants of Naph'ta·li, their lineage, in their clans, by their ancestral houses, according to the number of names, from twenty years old and upward, everyone able to go to war: 43those enrolled of the tribe of Naph'ta·li were fifty-three thousand four hundred.

44 These are those who were enrolled, whom Moses and Aaron enrolled with the help of the leaders of Israel, twelve men, each representing his ancestral house. 45So the whole number of the Israelites, by their ancestral houses, from twenty years old and upward, everyone able to go to war in Israel— 46their whole number was six hundred three thousand five hundred fifty. 47The Le'vites, however, were not numbered by their ancestral tribe along with them.

48 The LORD had said to Moses: 49Only the tribe of Levi you shall not enroll, and you shall not take a census of them with the other Israelites. 50Rather you shall appoint the Le'vites over the tabernacle of the covenant,a and over all its equipment, and over all that belongs to it; they are to carry the tabernacle and all its equipment, and they shall tend it, and shall camp around the tabernacle. 51When the tabernacle is to set out, the Le'vites shall take it down; and when the tabernacle is to be pitched, the Le'vites shall set it up. And any outsider who comes near shall be put to death. 52The other Israelites shall camp in their respective regimental camps, by companies; 53but the Le'vites shall camp around the tabernacle of the covenant,a that

aOr treaty, or testimony; Heb eduth

there may be no wrath on the congregation of the Israelites; and the Lē′vītes shall perform the guard duty of the tabernacle of the covenant.*b* 54 The Israelites did so; they did just as the LORD commanded Moses.

The Order of Encampment and Marching

2 The LORD spoke to Moses and Aaron, saying: 2 The Israelites shall camp each in their respective regiments, under ensigns by their ancestral houses; they shall camp facing the tent of meeting on every side. 3 Those to camp on the east side toward the sunrise shall be of the regimental encampment of Judah by companies. The leader of the people of Judah shall be Nah′shon son of Am·min′a·dab, 4 with a company as enrolled of seventy-four thousand six hundred. 5 Those to camp next to him shall be the tribe of Is′sa·char. The leader of the Is′sa·char·ītes shall be Ne·than′el son of Zū′ar, 6 with a company as enrolled of fifty-four thousand four hundred. 7 Then the tribe of Zeb′ū·lun: The leader of the Zeb′ū·lun·ītes shall be E·lī′ab son of Hē′lon, 8 with a company as enrolled of fifty-seven thousand four hundred. 9 The total enrollment of the camp of Judah, by companies, is one hundred eighty-six thousand four hundred. They shall set out first on the march.

10 On the south side shall be the regimental encampment of Reuben by companies. The leader of the Reū′ben·ītes shall be E·lī′zur son of Shed′ē·ur, 11 with a company as enrolled of forty-six thousand five hundred. 12 And those to camp next to him shall be the tribe of Sim′ē·on. The leader of the Sim′ē·on·ītes shall be She·lū′mi·el son of Zū·ri·shad′daī, 13 with a company as enrolled of fifty-nine thousand three hundred. 14 Then the tribe of Gad: The leader of the Gad′ītes shall be E·lī′a·saph son of Reū′el, 15 with a company as enrolled of forty-five thousand six hundred fifty. 16 The total enrollment of the camp of Reuben, by companies, is one hundred fifty-one thousand four hundred fifty. They shall set out second.

17 The tent of meeting, with the camp of the Lē′vītes, shall set out in the center of the camps; they shall set out just as they camp, each in position, by their regiments.

18 On the west side shall be the reg-imental encampment of Ē′phra·im by companies. The leader of the people of Ē′phra·im shall be E·lish′a·ma son of Am·mī′hud, 19 with a company as enrolled of forty thousand five hundred. 20 Next to him shall be the tribe of Ma·nas′seh. The leader of the people of Ma·nas′seh shall be Ga·mā′li·el son of Pe·dah′zur, 21 with a company as enrolled of thirty-two thousand two hundred. 22 Then the tribe of Benjamin: The leader of the Ben′ja·min·ītes shall be A·bī′dan son of Gid·ē·ō′ni, 23 with a company as enrolled of thirty-five thousand four hundred. 24 The total enrollment of the camp of Ē′phra·im, by companies, is one hundred eight thousand one hundred. They shall set out third on the march.

25 On the north side shall be the regimental encampment of Dan by companies. The leader of the Dan′-ītes shall be A·hi·ē′zer son of Am·mi·shad′daī, 26 with a company as enrolled of sixty-two thousand seven hundred. 27 Those to camp next to him shall be the tribe of Ash′er. The leader of the Ash′er·ītes shall be Pā′gi·el son of Och′ran, 28 with a company as enrolled of forty-one thousand five hundred. 29 Then the tribe of Naph′ta·lī: The leader of the Naph′ta·lītes shall be A·hi′ra son of Ē′nan, 30 with a company as enrolled of fifty-three thousand four hundred. 31 The total enrollment of the camp of Dan is one hundred fifty-seven thousand six hundred. They shall set out last, by companies.*c*

32 This was the enrollment of the Israelites by their ancestral houses; the total enrollment in the camps by their companies was six hundred three thousand five hundred fifty. 33 Just as the LORD had commanded Moses, the Lē′vītes were not enrolled among the other Israelites.

34 The Israelites did just as the LORD had commanded Moses: They camped by regiments, and they set out the same way, everyone by clans, according to ancestral houses.

The Sons of Aaron
(Lev 10.1–7)

3 This is the lineage of Aaron and Moses at the time when the LORD spoke with Moses on Mount Sinai. 2 These are the names of the sons

b Or *treaty*, or *testimony*; Heb *eduth*
c Compare verses 9, 16, 24: Heb *by their regiments*

of Aaron: Nă'dab the firstborn, and A·bī'hū, El·e·a'zar, and Ith'a·mar; 3these are the names of the sons of Aaron, the anointed priests, whom he ordained to minister as priests. 4Nă'dab and A·bī'hū died before the LORD when they offered illicit fire before the LORD in the wilderness of Sinai, and they had no children. El·e·a'zar and Ith'a·mar served as priests in the lifetime of their father Aaron.

The Duties of the Levites

5 Then the LORD spoke to Moses, saying: 6Bring the tribe of Levi near, and set them before Aaron the priest, so that they may assist him. 7They shall perform duties for him and for the whole congregation in front of the tent of meeting, doing service at the tabernacle; 8they shall be in charge of all the furnishings of the tent of meeting, and attend to the duties for the Israelites as they do service at the tabernacle. 9You shall give the Le'vites to Aaron and his descendants; they are unreservedly given to him from among the Israelites. 10But you shall make a register of Aaron and his descendants; it is they who shall attend to the priesthood, and any outsider who comes near shall be put to death.

11 Then the LORD spoke to Moses, saying: 12I hereby accept the Le'vites from among the Israelites as substitutes for all the firstborn that open the womb among the Israelites. The Le'vites shall be mine, 13for all the firstborn are mine; when I killed all the firstborn in the land of Egypt, I consecrated for my own all the firstborn in Israel, both human and animal; they shall be mine. I am the LORD.

A Census of the Levites
(Cp Num 1.47–54)

14 Then the LORD spoke to Moses in the wilderness of Sinai, saying: 15Enroll the Le'vites by ancestral houses and by clans. You shall enroll every male from a month old and upward. 16So Moses enrolled them according to the word of the LORD, as he was commanded. 17The following were the sons of Levi, by their names: Ger'shon, Kō'hath, and Me·rar'ī. 18These are the names of the sons of Ger'shon by their clans: Lib'nī and Shim'e·ī. 19The sons of Kō'hath by their clans: Am'ram, Iz'-har, Hē'bron, and Uz'zi·el. 20The sons of Me·rar'ī by their clans: Mah'lī and

Mū'shī. These are the clans of the Le'-vites, by their ancestral houses.

21 To Ger'shon belonged the clan of the Lib'nītes and the clan of the Shim'e·ītes; these were the clans of the Ger'shon·ītes. 22Their enrollment, counting all the males from a month old and upward, was seven thousand five hundred. 23The clans of the Ger'-shon·ītes were to camp behind the tabernacle on the west, 24with E·lī'a·saph son of Lā'el as head of the ancestral house of the Ger'shon·ītes. 25The responsibility of the sons of Ger'shon in the tent of meeting was to be the tabernacle, the tent with its covering, the screen for the entrance of the tent of meeting, 26the hangings of the court, the screen for the entrance of the court that is around the tabernacle and the altar, and its cords—all the service pertaining to these.

27 To Kō'hath belonged the clan of the Am'ram·ītes, the clan of the Iz'-har·ītes, the clan of the Hē'bron·ītes, and the clan of the Uz'zi·el·ītes; these are the clans of the Kō'hath·ītes. 28Counting all the males, from a month old and upward, there were eight thousand six hundred, attending to the duties of the sanctuary. 29The clans of the Kō'hath·ītes were to camp on the south side of the tabernacle, 30with E·lī·zā'phan son of Uz'zi·el as head of the ancestral house of the clans of the Kō'hath·ītes. 31Their responsibility was to be the ark, the table, the lampstand, the altars, the vessels of the sanctuary with which the priests minister, and the screen—all the service pertaining to these. 32El·e·a'zar son of Aaron the priest was to be chief over the leaders of the Le'vites, and to have oversight of those who had charge of the sanctuary.

33 To Me·rar'ī belonged the clan of the Mah'lītes and the clan of the Mū'-shītes: these are the clans of Me·rar'ī. 34Their enrollment, counting all the males from a month old and upward, was six thousand two hundred. 35The head of the ancestral house of the clans of Me·rar'ī was Zū'ri·el son of Ab·i·hā'il; they were to camp on the north side of the tabernacle. 36The responsibility assigned to the sons of Me·rar'ī was to be the frames of the tabernacle, the bars, the pillars, the bases, and all their accessories—all the service pertaining to these; 37also the pillars of the court all around, with their bases and pegs and cords.

38 Those who were to camp in front of the tabernacle on the east—in front of the tent of meeting toward the east—were Moses and Aaron and Aaron's sons, having charge of the rites within the sanctuary, whatever had to be done for the Israelites; and any outsider who came near was to be put to death. 39 The total enrollment of the Le'vītes whom Moses and Aaron enrolled at the commandment of the LORD, by their clans, all the males from a month old and upward, was twenty-two thousand.

The Redemption of the Firstborn

40 Then the LORD said to Moses: Enroll all the firstborn males of the Israelites, from a month old and upward, and count their names. 41 But you shall accept the Le'vītes for me—I am the LORD—as substitutes for all the firstborn among the Israelites, and the livestock of the Le'vītes as substitutes for all the firstborn among the livestock of the Israelites. 42 So Moses enrolled all the firstborn among the Israelites, as the LORD commanded him. 43 The total enrollment, all the firstborn males from a month old and upward, counting the number of names, was twenty-two thousand two hundred seventy-three.

44 Then the LORD spoke to Moses, saying: 45 Accept the Le'vītes as substitutes for all the firstborn among the Israelites, and the livestock of the Le'-vītes as substitutes for their livestock; and the Le'vītes shall be mine. I am the LORD. 46 As the price of redemption of the two hundred seventy-three of the firstborn of the Israelites, over and above the number of the Le'vītes, 47 you shall accept five shekels apiece, reckoning by the shekel of the sanctuary, a shekel of twenty gerahs. 48 Give to Aaron and his sons the money by which the excess number of them is redeemed. 49 So Moses took the redemption money from those who were over and above those redeemed by the Le'vītes; 50 from the firstborn of the Israelites he took the money, one thousand three hundred sixty-five shekels, reckoned by the shekel of the sanctuary; 51 and Moses gave the redemption money to Aaron and his sons, according to the word of the LORD, as the LORD had commanded Moses.

The Kohathites

4 The LORD spoke to Moses and Aaron, saying: 2 Take a census of the Kō'hath·ites separate from the other Le'vītes, by their clans and their ancestral houses, 3 from thirty years old up to fifty years old, all who qualify to do work relating to the tent of meeting. 4 The service of the Kō'hath·ites relating to the tent of meeting concerns the most holy things.

5 When the camp is to set out, Aaron and his sons shall go in and take down the screening curtain, and cover the ark of the covenant d with it; 6 then they shall put on it a covering of fine leather, e and spread over that a cloth all of blue, and shall put its poles in place. 7 Over the table of the bread of the Presence they shall spread a blue cloth, and put on it the plates, the dishes for incense, the bowls, and the flagons for the drink offering; the regular bread also shall be on it; 8 then they shall spread over them a crimson cloth, and cover it with a covering of fine leather, e and shall put its poles in place. 9 They shall take a blue cloth, and cover the lampstand for the light, with its lamps, its snuffers, its trays, and all the vessels for oil with which it is supplied; 10 and they shall put it with all its utensils in a covering of fine leather, e and put it on the carrying frame. 11 Over the golden altar they shall spread a blue cloth, and cover it with a covering of fine leather, e and shall put its poles in place; 12 and they shall take all the utensils of the service that are used in the sanctuary, and put them in a blue cloth, and cover them with a covering of fine leather, e and put them on the carrying frame. 13 They shall take away the ashes from the altar, and spread a purple cloth over it; 14 and they shall put on it all the utensils of the altar, which are used for the service there, the firepans, the forks, the shovels, and the basins, all the utensils of the altar; and they shall spread on it a covering of fine leather, e and shall put its poles in place. 15 When Aaron and his sons have finished covering the sanctuary and all the furnishings of the sanctuary, as the camp sets out, after that the Kō'hath·ites shall come to carry these, but they must not touch the holy

---

d Or *treaty*, or *testimony*; Heb *eduth*
e Meaning of Heb uncertain

things, or they will die. These are the things of the tent of meeting that the Kŏ′hath·ites are to carry.

16 El·e·a′zar son of Aaron the priest shall have charge of the oil for the light, the fragrant incense, the regular grain offering, and the anointing oil, the oversight of all the tabernacle and all that is in it, in the sanctuary and in its utensils.

17 Then the LORD spoke to Moses and Aaron, saying: 18 You must not let the tribe of the clans of the Kŏ′-hath·ites be destroyed from among the Lĕ′vites. 19 This is how you must deal with them in order that they may live and not die when they come near to the most holy things: Aaron and his sons shall go in and assign each to a particular task or burden. 20 But the Kŏ′-hath·ites*f* must not go in to look on the holy things even for a moment; otherwise they will die.

The Gershonites and Merarites

21 Then the LORD spoke to Moses, saying: 22 Take a census of the Ger′-shon·ites also, by their ancestral houses and by their clans; 23 from thirty years old up to fifty years old you shall enroll them, all who qualify to do work in the tent of meeting. 24 This is the service of the clans of the Ger′shon·ites, in serving and bearing burdens: 25 They shall carry the curtains of the tabernacle, and the tent of meeting with its covering, and the outer covering of fine leather*g* that is on top of it, and the screen for the entrance of the tent of meeting, 26 and the hangings of the court, and the screen for the entrance of the gate of the court that is around the tabernacle and the altar, and their cords, and all the equipment for their service; and they shall do all that needs to be done with regard to them. 27 All the service of the Ger′shon·ites shall be at the command of Aaron and his sons, in all that they are to carry, and in all that they have to do; and you shall assign to their charge all that they are to carry. 28 This is the service of the clans of the Ger′-shon·ites relating to the tent of meeting, and their responsibilities are to be under the oversight of Ith′a·mar son of Aaron the priest.

29 As for the Me·rar′ites, you shall enroll them by their clans and their ancestral houses; 30 from thirty years old up to fifty years old you shall enroll them, everyone who qualifies to do the work of the tent of meeting. 31 This is what they are charged to carry, as the whole of their service in the tent of meeting: the frames of the tabernacle, with its bars, pillars, and bases, 32 and the pillars of the court all around with their bases, pegs, and cords, with all their equipment and all their related service; and you shall assign by name the objects that they are required to carry. 33 This is the service of the clans of the Me·rar′ites, the whole of their service relating to the tent of meeting, under the hand of Ith′a·mar son of Aaron the priest.

Census of the Levites

34 So Moses and Aaron and the leaders of the congregation enrolled the Kŏ′hath·ites, by their clans and their ancestral houses, 35 from thirty years old up to fifty years old, everyone who qualified for work relating to the tent of meeting; 36 and their enrollment by clans was two thousand seven hundred fifty. 37 This was the enrollment of the clans of the Kŏ′hath·ites, all who served at the tent of meeting, whom Moses and Aaron enrolled according to the commandment of the LORD by Moses.

38 The enrollment of the Ger′-shon·ites, by their clans and their ancestral houses, 39 from thirty years old up to fifty years old, everyone who qualified for work relating to the tent of meeting— 40 their enrollment by their clans and their ancestral houses was two thousand six hundred thirty. 41 This was the enrollment of the clans of the Ger′shon·ites, all who served at the tent of meeting, whom Moses and Aaron enrolled according to the commandment of the LORD.

42 The enrollment of the clans of the Me·rar′ites, by their clans and their ancestral houses, 43 from thirty years old up to fifty years old, everyone who qualified for work relating to the tent of meeting— 44 their enrollment by their clans was three thousand two hundred. 45 This is the enrollment of the clans of the Me·rar′ites, whom Moses and Aaron enrolled according to the commandment of the LORD by Moses.

46 All those who were enrolled of the Lĕ′vites, whom Moses and Aaron and the leaders of Israel enrolled, by their clans and their ancestral houses,

f Heb *they*   *g* Meaning of Heb uncertain

47 from thirty years old up to fifty years old, everyone who qualified to do the work of service and the work of bearing burdens relating to the tent of meeting, 48 their enrollment was eight thousand five hundred eighty. 49 According to the commandment of the LORD through Moses they were appointed to their several tasks of serving or carrying; thus they were enrolled by him, as the LORD commanded Moses.

Unclean Persons
(Cp Lev 15.1–33)

5 The LORD spoke to Moses, saying: 2 Command the Israelites to put out of the camp everyone who is leprous,*h* or has a discharge, and everyone who is unclean through contact with a corpse; 3 you shall put out both male and female, putting them outside the camp; they must not defile their camp, where I dwell among them. 4 The Israelites did so, putting them outside the camp; as the LORD had spoken to Moses, so the Israelites did.

Confession and Restitution
(Lev 6.1–7)

5 The LORD spoke to Moses, saying: 6 Speak to the Israelites: When a man or a woman wrongs another, breaking faith with the LORD, that person incurs guilt 7 and shall confess the sin that has been committed. The person shall make full restitution for the wrong, adding one fifth to it, and giving it to the one who was wronged. 8 If the injured party has no next of kin to whom restitution may be made for the wrong, the restitution for wrong shall go to the LORD for the priest, in addition to the ram of atonement with which atonement is made for the guilty party. 9 Among all the sacred donations of the Israelites, every gift that they bring to the priest shall be his. 10 The sacred donations of all are their own; whatever anyone gives to the priest shall be his.

Concerning an Unfaithful Wife

11 The LORD spoke to Moses, saying: 12 Speak to the Israelites and say to them: If any man's wife goes astray and is unfaithful to him, 13 if a man has had intercourse with her but it is hidden from her husband, so that she is undetected though she has defiled herself, and there is no witness against her since she was not caught in the act; 14 if a spirit of jealousy comes on him, and he is jealous of his wife who has defiled herself; or if a spirit of jealousy comes on him, and he is jealous of his wife, though she has not defiled herself; 15 then the man shall bring his wife to the priest. And he shall bring the offering required for her, one-tenth of an ephah of barley flour. He shall pour no oil on it and put no frankincense on it, for it is a grain offering of jealousy, a grain offering of remembrance, bringing iniquity to remembrance.

16 Then the priest shall bring her near, and set her before the LORD; 17 the priest shall take holy water in an earthen vessel, and take some of the dust that is on the floor of the tabernacle and put it into the water. 18 The priest shall set the woman before the LORD, dishevel the woman's hair, and place in her hands the grain offering of remembrance, which is the grain offering of jealousy. In his own hand the priest shall have the water of bitterness that brings the curse. 19 Then the priest shall make her take an oath, saying, "If no man has lain with you, if you have not turned aside to uncleanness while under your husband's authority, be immune to this water of bitterness that brings the curse. 20 But if you have gone astray while under your husband's authority, if you have defiled yourself and some man other than your husband has had intercourse with you," 21 —let the priest make the woman take the oath of the curse and say to the woman—"the LORD make you an execration and an oath among your people, when the LORD makes your uterus drop, your womb discharge; 22 now may this water that brings the curse enter your bowels and make your womb discharge, your uterus drop!" And the woman shall say, "Amen. Amen."

23 Then the priest shall put these curses in writing, and wash them off into the water of bitterness. 24 He shall make the woman drink the water of bitterness that brings the curse, and the water that brings the curse shall enter her and cause bitter pain. 25 The priest shall take the grain offering of jealousy out of the woman's hand, and shall elevate the grain offering before the LORD and bring it to the altar; 26 and the priest shall take a handful of

h A term for several skin diseases; precise meaning uncertain the grain offering, as its memorial portion, and turn it into smoke on the altar, and afterward shall make the woman drink the water. 27 When he has made her drink the water, then, if she has defiled herself and has been unfaithful to her husband, the water that brings the curse shall enter into her and cause bitter pain, and her womb shall discharge, her uterus drop, and the woman shall become an execration among her people. 28 But if the woman has not defiled herself and is clean, then she shall be immune and be able to conceive children.

29 This is the law in cases of jealousy, when a wife, while under her husband's authority, goes astray and defiles herself, 30 or when a spirit of jealousy comes on a man and he is jealous of his wife; then he shall set the woman before the LORD, and the priest shall apply this entire law to her. 31 The man shall be free from iniquity, but the woman shall bear her iniquity.

The Nazirites

6 The LORD spoke to Moses, saying: 2 Speak to the Israelites and say to them: When either men or women make a special vow, the vow of a nazirite, [i] to separate themselves to the LORD, 3 they shall separate themselves from wine and strong drink; they shall drink no wine vinegar or other vinegar, and shall not drink any grape juice or eat grapes, fresh or dried. 4 All their days as nazirites [j] they shall eat nothing that is produced by the grapevine, not even the seeds or the skins.

5 All the days of their nazirite vow no razor shall come upon the head; until the time is completed for which they separate themselves to the LORD, they shall be holy; they shall let the locks of the head grow long.

6 All the days that they separate themselves to the LORD they shall not go near a corpse. 7 Even if their father or mother, brother or sister, should die, they may not defile themselves; because their consecration to God is upon the head. 8 All their days as nazirites [j] they are holy to the LORD.

9 If someone dies very suddenly nearby, defiling the consecrated head, then they shall shave the head on the day of their cleansing; on the seventh day they shall shave it. 10 On the eighth day they shall bring two turtledoves or two young pigeons to the priest at the entrance of the tent of meeting, 11 and

the priest shall offer one as a sin offering and the other as a burnt offering, and make atonement for them, because they incurred guilt by reason of the corpse. They shall sanctify the head that same day, 12 and separate themselves to the LORD for their days as nazirites, [j] and bring a male lamb a year old as a guilt offering. The former time shall be void, because the consecrated head was defiled.

13 This is the law for the nazirites [j] when the time of their consecration has been completed: they shall be brought to the entrance of the tent of meeting, 14 and they shall offer their gift to the LORD, one male lamb a year old without blemish as a burnt offering, one ewe lamb a year old without blemish as a sin offering, one ram without blemish as an offering of well-being, 15 and a basket of unleavened bread, cakes of choice flour mixed with oil and unleavened wafers spread with oil, with their grain offering and their drink offerings. 16 The priest shall present them before the LORD and offer their sin offering and burnt offering, 17 and shall offer the ram as a sacrifice of well-being to the LORD, with the basket of unleavened bread; the priest also shall make the accompanying grain offering and drink offering. 18 Then the nazirites [j] shall shave the consecrated head at the entrance of the tent of meeting, and shall take the hair from the consecrated head and put it on the fire under the sacrifice of well-being. 19 The priest shall take the shoulder of the ram, when it is boiled, and one unleavened cake out of the basket, and one unleavened wafer, and shall put them in the palms of the nazirites, [j] after they have shaved the consecrated head. 20 Then the priest shall elevate them as an elevation offering before the LORD; they are a holy portion for the priest, together with the breast that is elevated and the thigh that is offered. After that the nazirites [j] may drink wine.

21 This is the law for the nazirites [j] who take a vow. Their offering to the LORD must be in accordance with the nazirite [i] vow, apart from what else they can afford. In accordance with whatever vow they take, so they shall

---

[i] That is one separated or one consecrated   [j] That is those separated or those consecrated

do, following the law for their consecration.

The Priestly Benediction

22 The LORD spoke to Moses, saying: 23 Speak to Aaron and his sons, saying, Thus you shall bless the Israelites: You shall say to them,

24 The LORD bless you and keep you;
25 the LORD make his face to shine upon you, and be gracious to you;
26 the LORD lift up his countenance upon you, and give you peace.

27 So they shall put my name on the Israelites, and I will bless them.

Offerings of the Leaders

7 On the day when Moses had finished setting up the tabernacle, and had anointed and consecrated it with all its furnishings, and had anointed and consecrated the altar with all its utensils, 2 the leaders of Israel, heads of their ancestral houses, the leaders of the tribes, who were over those who were enrolled, made offerings. 3 They brought their offerings before the LORD, six covered wagons and twelve oxen, a wagon for every two of the leaders, and for each one an ox; they presented them before the tabernacle. 4 Then the LORD said to Moses: 5 Accept these from them, that they may be used in doing the service of the tent of meeting, and give them to the Lē'vītes, to each according to his service. 6 So Moses took the wagons and the oxen, and gave them to the Lē'vītes. 7 Two wagons and four oxen he gave to the Ger'shon·ites, according to their service; 8 and four wagons and eight oxen he gave to the Me·rar'-ites, according to their service, under the direction of Ith'a·mar son of Aaron the priest. 9 But to the Kō'hath·ites he gave none, because they were charged with the care of the holy things that had to be carried on the shoulders.

10 The leaders also presented offerings for the dedication of the altar at the time when it was anointed; the leaders presented their offering before the altar. 11 The LORD said to Moses: They shall present their offerings, one leader each day, for the dedication of the altar.

12 The one who presented his offering the first day was Nah'shon son of Am·min'a·dab, of the tribe of Judah;

13 his offering was one silver plate weighing one hundred thirty shekels, one silver basin weighing seventy shekels, according to the shekel of the sanctuary, both of them full of choice flour mixed with oil for a grain offering; 14 one golden dish weighing ten shekels, full of incense; 15 one young bull, one ram, one male lamb a year old, for a burnt offering; 16 one male goat for a sin offering; 17 and for the sacrifice of well-being, two oxen, five rams, five male goats, and five male lambs a year old. This was the offering of Nah'shon son of Am·min'a·dab.

18 On the second day Ne·than'el son of Zū'ar, the leader of Is'sa·char, presented an offering; 19 he presented for his offering one silver plate weighing one hundred thirty shekels, one silver basin weighing seventy shekels, according to the shekel of the sanctuary, both of them full of choice flour mixed with oil for a grain offering; 20 one golden dish weighing ten shekels, full of incense; 21 one young bull, one ram, one male lamb a year old, as a burnt offering; 22 one male goat as a sin offering; 23 and for the sacrifice of well-being, two oxen, five rams, five male goats, and five male lambs a year old. This was the offering of Ne·than'el son of Zū'ar.

24 On the third day E·lī'ab son of Hē'lon, the leader of the Zeb'ū-lun·ites: 25 his offering was one silver plate weighing one hundred thirty shekels, one silver basin weighing seventy shekels, according to the shekel of the sanctuary, both of them full of choice flour mixed with oil for a grain offering; 26 one golden dish weighing ten shekels, full of incense; 27 one young bull, one ram, one male lamb a year old, for a burnt offering; 28 one male goat for a sin offering; 29 and for the sacrifice of well-being, two oxen, five rams, five male goats, and five male lambs a year old. This was the offering of E·lī'ab son of Hē'lon.

30 On the fourth day E·lī'zur son of Shed'ē·ur, the leader of the Reū'-ben·ites: 31 his offering was one silver plate weighing one hundred thirty shekels, one silver basin weighing seventy shekels, according to the shekel of the sanctuary, both of them full of choice flour mixed with oil for a grain offering; 32 one golden dish weighing ten shekels, full of incense; 33 one young bull, one ram, one male lamb a year old, for a burnt offering; 34 one

male goat for a sin offering; [35] and for the sacrifice of well-being, two oxen, five rams, five male goats, and five male lambs a year old. This was the offering of E·li′zur son of Shed′e·ur.

36 On the fifth day She·lū′mi·el son of Zū·ri·shad′daī, the leader of the Sim′e·on·ites: [37] his offering was one silver plate weighing one hundred thirty shekels, one silver basin weighing seventy shekels, according to the shekel of the sanctuary, both of them full of choice flour mixed with oil for a grain offering; [38] one golden dish weighing ten shekels, full of incense; [39] one young bull, one ram, one male lamb a year old, for a burnt offering; [40] one male goat for a sin offering; [41] and for the sacrifice of well-being, two oxen, five rams, five male goats, and five male lambs a year old. This was the offering of She·lū′mi·el son of Zū·ri·shad′daī.

42 On the sixth day E·li′a·saph son of Deū′el, the leader of the Gad′ites: [43] his offering was one silver plate weighing one hundred thirty shekels, one silver basin weighing seventy shekels, according to the shekel of the sanctuary, both of them full of choice flour mixed with oil for a grain offering; [44] one golden dish weighing ten shekels, full of incense; [45] one young bull, one ram, one male lamb a year old, for a burnt offering; [46] one male goat for a sin offering; [47] and for the sacrifice of well-being, two oxen, five rams, five male goats, and five male lambs a year old. This was the offering of E·li′a·saph son of Deū′el.

48 On the seventh day E·lish′a·ma son of Am·mi′hud, the leader of the E′phra·im·ites: [49] his offering was one silver plate weighing one hundred thirty shekels, one silver basin weighing seventy shekels, according to the shekel of the sanctuary, both of them full of choice flour mixed with oil for a grain offering; [50] one golden dish weighing ten shekels, full of incense; [51] one young bull, one ram, one male lamb a year old, for a burnt offering; [52] one male goat for a sin offering; [53] and for the sacrifice of well-being, two oxen, five rams, five male goats, and five male lambs a year old. This was the offering of E·lish′a·ma son of Am·mi′hud.

54 On the eighth day Ga·ma′li·el son of Pe·dah′zur, the leader of the Ma·nas′sites: [55] his offering was one silver plate weighing one hundred

thirty shekels, one silver basin weighing seventy shekels, according to the shekel of the sanctuary, both of them full of choice flour mixed with oil for a grain offering; [56] one golden dish weighing ten shekels, full of incense; [57] one young bull, one ram, one male lamb a year old, for a burnt offering; [58] one male goat for a sin offering; [59] and for the sacrifice of well-being, two oxen, five rams, five male goats, and five male lambs a year old. This was the offering of Ga·ma′li·el son of Pe·dah′zur.

60 On the ninth day A·bi′dan son of Gid·e·o′ni, the leader of the Ben′-ja·min·ites: [61] his offering was one silver plate weighing one hundred thirty shekels, one silver basin weighing seventy shekels, according to the shekel of the sanctuary, both of them full of choice flour mixed with oil for a grain offering; [62] one golden dish weighing ten shekels, full of incense; [63] one young bull, one ram, one male lamb a year old, for a burnt offering; [64] one male goat for a sin offering; [65] and for the sacrifice of well-being, two oxen, five rams, five male goats, and five male lambs a year old. This was the offering of A·bi′dan son of Gid·e·o′ni.

66 On the tenth day A·hi·e′zer son of Am·mi·shad′daī, the leader of the Dan′ites: [67] his offering was one silver plate weighing one hundred thirty shekels, one silver basin weighing seventy shekels, according to the shekel of the sanctuary, both of them full of choice flour mixed with oil for a grain offering; [68] one golden dish weighing ten shekels, full of incense; [69] one young bull, one ram, one male lamb a year old, for a burnt offering; [70] one male goat for a sin offering; [71] and for the sacrifice of well-being, two oxen, five rams, five male goats, and five male lambs a year old. This was the offering of A·hi·e′zer son of Am·mi·shad′daī.

72 On the eleventh day Pa′gi·el son of Och′ran, the leader of the Ash′-er·ites: [73] his offering was one silver plate weighing one hundred thirty shekels, one silver basin weighing seventy shekels, according to the shekel of the sanctuary, both of them full of choice flour mixed with oil for a grain offering; [74] one golden dish weighing ten shekels, full of incense; [75] one young bull, one ram, one male lamb a year old, for a burnt offering; [76] one male goat for a sin offering; [77] and for

the sacrifice of well-being, two oxen, five rams, five male goats, and five male lambs a year old. This was the offering of Pā′gi·el son of Och′ran.

78 On the twelfth day A·hī′ra son of E′nan, the leader of the Naph′ta·lites: 79his offering was one silver plate weighing one hundred thirty shekels, one silver basin weighing seventy shekels, according to the shekel of the sanctuary, both of them full of choice flour mixed with oil for a grain offering; 80one golden dish weighing ten shekels, full of incense; 81one young bull, one ram, one male lamb a year old, for a burnt offering; 82one male goat for a sin offering; 83and for the sacrifice of well-being, two oxen, five rams, five male goats, and five male lambs a year old. This was the offering of A·hī′ra son of E′nan.

84 This was the dedication offering for the altar, at the time when it was anointed, from the leaders of Israel: twelve silver plates, twelve silver basins, twelve golden dishes, 85each silver plate weighing one hundred thirty shekels and each basin seventy, all the silver of the vessels two thousand four hundred shekels according to the shekel of the sanctuary, 86the twelve golden dishes, full of incense, weighing ten shekels apiece according to the shekel of the sanctuary, all the gold of the dishes being one hundred twenty shekels; 87all the livestock for the burnt offering twelve bulls, twelve rams, twelve male lambs a year old, with their grain offering; and twelve male goats for a sin offering; 88and all the livestock for the sacrifice of well-being twenty-four bulls, the rams sixty, the male goats sixty, the male lambs a year old sixty. This was the dedication offering for the altar, after it was anointed.

89 When Moses went into the tent of meeting to speak with the LORD, *k* he would hear the voice speaking to him from above the mercy seat *l* that was on the ark of the covenant *m* from between the two cherubim; thus it spoke to him.

The Seven Lamps
(Ex 25.31–40)

8 The LORD spoke to Moses, saying: 2Speak to Aaron and say to him: When you set up the lamps, the seven lamps shall give light in front of the lampstand. 3Aaron did so; he set up its lamps to give light in front of the lamp-

stand, as the LORD had commanded Moses. 4Now this was how the lampstand was made, out of hammered work of gold. From its base to its flowers, it was hammered work; according to the pattern that the LORD had shown Moses, so he made the lampstand.

Consecration and Service
of the Levites

5 The LORD spoke to Moses, saying: 6Take the Le′vites from among the Israelites and cleanse them. 7Thus you shall do to them, to cleanse them: sprinkle the water of purification on them, have them shave their whole body with a razor and wash their clothes, and so cleanse themselves. 8Then let them take a young bull and its grain offering of choice flour mixed with oil, and you shall take another young bull for a sin offering. 9You shall bring the Le′vites before the tent of meeting, and assemble the whole congregation of the Israelites. 10When you bring the Le′vites before the LORD, the Israelites shall lay their hands on the Le′vites, 11and Aaron shall present the Le′vites before the LORD as an elevation offering from the Israelites, that they may do the service of the LORD. 12The Le′vites shall lay their hands on the heads of the bulls, and he shall offer the one for a sin offering and the other for a burnt offering to the LORD, to make atonement for the Le′vites. 13Then you shall have the Le′vites stand before Aaron and his sons, and you shall present them as an elevation offering to the LORD.

14 Thus you shall separate the Le′vites from among the other Israelites, and the Le′vites shall be mine. 15Thereafter the Le′vites may go in to do service at the tent of meeting, once you have cleansed them and presented them as an elevation offering. 16For they are unreservedly given to me from among the Israelites; I have taken them for myself, in place of all that open the womb, the firstborn of all the Israelites. 17For all the firstborn among the Israelites are mine, both human and animal. On the day that I struck down all the firstborn in the land of Egypt I consecrated them for myself, 18but I have taken the Le′vites in place of all the firstborn among the Israelites. 19Moreover, I have given the

---

k Heb *him*   *l* Or *the cover*   *m* Or *treaty,* or *testimony;* Heb *eduth*

Lē'vītes as a gift to Aaron and his sons from among the Israelites, to do the service for the Israelites at the tent of meeting, and to make atonement for the Israelites, in order that there may be no plague among the Israelites for coming too close to the sanctuary.

20 Moses and Aaron and the whole congregation of the Israelites did with the Lē'vītes accordingly; the Israelites did with the Lē'vītes just as the LORD had commanded Moses concerning them. 21 The Lē'vītes purified themselves from sin and washed their clothes; then Aaron presented them as an elevation offering before the LORD, and Aaron made atonement for them to cleanse them. 22 Thereafter the Lē'-vītes went in to do their service in the tent of meeting in attendance on Aaron and his sons. As the LORD had commanded Moses concerning the Lē'vītes, so they did with them.

23 The LORD spoke to Moses, saying: 24 This applies to the Lē'vītes: from twenty-five years old and upward they shall begin to do duty in the service of the tent of meeting; 25 and from the age of fifty years they shall retire from the duty of the service and serve no more. 26 They may assist their brothers in the tent of meeting in carrying out their duties, but they shall perform no service. Thus you shall do with the Lē'-vītes in assigning their duties.

The Passover at Sinai
(Ex 12.1–20)

9 The LORD spoke to Moses in the wilderness of Sinai, in the first month of the second year after they had come out of the land of Egypt, saying: 2 Let the Israelites keep the passover at its appointed time. 3 On the fourteenth day of this month, at twilight, n you shall keep it at its appointed time; according to all its statutes and all its regulations you shall keep it. 4 So Moses told the Israelites that they should keep the passover. 5 They kept the passover in the first month, on the fourteenth day of the month, at twilight, n in the wilderness of Sinai. Just as the LORD had commanded Moses, so the Israelites did. 6 Now there were certain people who were unclean through touching a corpse, so that they could not keep the passover on that day. They came before Moses and Aaron on that day, 7 and said to him, "Although we are unclean through touching a corpse, why

must we be kept from presenting the LORD's offering at its appointed time among the Israelites?" 8 Moses spoke to them, "Wait, so that I may hear what the LORD will command concerning you."

9 The LORD spoke to Moses, saying: 10 Speak to the Israelites, saying: Anyone of you or your descendants who is unclean through touching a corpse, or is away on a journey, shall still keep the passover to the LORD. 11 In the second month on the fourteenth day, at twilight, n they shall keep it; they shall eat it with unleavened bread and bitter herbs. 12 They shall leave none of it until morning, nor break a bone of it; according to all the statute for the passover they shall keep it. 13 But anyone who is clean and is not on a journey, and yet refrains from keeping the passover, shall be cut off from the people for not presenting the LORD's offering at its appointed time; such a one shall bear the consequences for the sin. 14 Any alien residing among you who wishes to keep the passover to the LORD shall do so according to the statute of the passover and according to its regulation; you shall have one statute for both the resident alien and the native.

The Cloud and the Fire
(Ex 13.21–22; 40.34–38)

15 On the day the tabernacle was set up, the cloud covered the tabernacle, the tent of the covenant; o and from evening until morning it was over the tabernacle, having the appearance of fire. 16 It was always so: the cloud covered it by day p and the appearance of fire by night. 17 Whenever the cloud lifted from over the tent, then the Israelites would set out; and in the place where the cloud settled down, there the Israelites would camp. 18 At the command of the LORD the Israelites would set out, and at the command of the LORD they would camp. As long as the cloud rested over the tabernacle, they would remain in camp. 19 Even when the cloud continued over the tabernacle many days, the Israelites would keep the charge of the LORD, and would not set out. 20 Sometimes the cloud would remain a few days over the tabernacle, and according to

n Heb between the two evenings
o Or treaty, or testimony; Heb eduth
p Gk Syr Vg: Heb lacks by day

the command of the LORD they would remain in camp; then according to the command of the LORD they would set out. 21 Sometimes the cloud would remain from evening until morning; and when the cloud lifted in the morning, they would set out, or if it continued for a day and a night, when the cloud lifted they would set out. 22 Whether it was two days, or a month, or a longer time, that the cloud continued over the tabernacle, resting upon it, the Israelites would remain in camp and would not set out; but when it lifted they would set out. 23 At the command of the LORD they would camp, and at the command of the LORD they would set out. They kept the charge of the LORD, at the command of the LORD by Moses.

The Silver Trumpets

10 The LORD spoke to Moses, saying: 2 Make two silver trumpets; you shall make them of hammered work; and you shall use them for summoning the congregation, and for breaking camp. 3 When both are blown, the whole congregation shall assemble before you at the entrance of the tent of meeting. 4 But if only one is blown, then the leaders, the heads of the tribes of Israel, shall assemble before you. 5 When you blow an alarm, the camps on the east side shall set out; 6 when you blow a second alarm, the camps on the south side shall set out. An alarm is to be blown whenever they are to set out. 7 But when the assembly is to be gathered, you shall blow, but you shall not sound an alarm. 8 The sons of Aaron, the priests, shall blow the trumpets; this shall be a perpetual institution for you throughout your generations. 9 When you go to war in your land against the adversary who oppresses you, you shall sound an alarm with the trumpets, so that you may be remembered before the LORD your God and be saved from your enemies. 10 Also on your days of rejoicing, at your appointed festivals, and at the beginnings of your months, you shall blow the trumpets over your burnt offerings and over your sacrifices of well-being; they shall serve as a reminder on your behalf before the LORD your God: I am the LORD your God.

Departure from Sinai

11 In the second year, in the second month, on the twentieth day of the month, the cloud lifted from over the tabernacle of the covenant. q 12 Then the Israelites set out by stages from the wilderness of Sinai, and the cloud settled down in the wilderness of Par'an. 13 They set out for the first time at the command of the LORD by Moses. 14 The standard of the camp of Judah set out first, company by company, and over the whole company was Nah'shon son of Am·min'a·dab. 15 Over the company of the tribe of Is'sa·char was Nethan'el son of Zū'ar; 6 and over the company of the tribe of Zeb'ū·lun was E·lī'ab son of Hē'lon.

17 Then the tabernacle was taken down, and the Ger'shon·ites and the Me·rar'ites, who carried the tabernacle, set out. 18 Next the standard of the camp of Reuben set out, company by company; and over the whole company was E·lī'zur son of Shed'ē·ur. 19 Over the company of the tribe of Sim'ē·on was She·lū'mi·el son of Zū·ri·shad'dai, 20 and over the company of the tribe of Gad was E·lī'a·saph son of Deū'el.

21 Then the Kō'hath·ites, who carried the holy things, set out; and the tabernacle was set up before their arrival. 22 Next the standard of the E'phra·im·ite camp set out, company by company, and over the whole company was E·lish'a·ma son of Am·mī'hud. 23 Over the company of the tribe of Ma·nas'seh was Ga·mā'li·el son of Pe·dah'zur, 24 and over the company of the tribe of Benjamin was A·bī'dan son of Gid·e·ō'ni.

25 Then the standard of the camp of Dan, acting as the rear guard of all the camps, set out, company by company, and over the whole company was A·hī·ē'zer son of Am·mi·shad'dai. 26 Over the company of the tribe of Ash'er was Pā'gi·el son of Och'ran, 27 and over the company of the tribe of Naph'ta·lī was A·hī'ra son of Ē'nan. 28 This was the order of march of the Israelites, company by company, when they set out.

29 Moses said to Hō'bab son of Reū'el the Mid'i·an·ite, Moses' father-in-law, "We are setting out for the place of which the LORD said, 'I will give it to you'; come with us, and we will treat you well; for the LORD has promised good to Israel." 30 But he said to him, "I will not go, but I will go back to my own land and to my kindred." 31 He said, "Do not leave us, for you

q Or treaty, or *testimony;* Heb *eduth*

know where we should camp in the wilderness, and you will serve as eyes for us. [32] Moreover, if you go with us, whatever good the LORD does for us, the same we will do for you."

33 So they set out from the mount of the LORD three days' journey with the ark of the covenant of the LORD going before them three days' journey, to seek out a resting place for them, [34] the cloud of the LORD being over them by day when they set out from the camp.

35 Whenever the ark set out, Moses would say,

"Arise, O LORD, let your enemies
    be scattered,
and your foes flee before you."

[36] And whenever it came to rest, he would say,

"Return, O LORD of the ten
    thousand thousands of
    Israel."[r]

Complaining in the Desert

11 Now when the people complained in the hearing of the LORD about their misfortunes, the LORD heard it and his anger was kindled. Then the fire of the LORD burned against them, and consumed some outlying parts of the camp. [2] But the people cried out to Moses; and Moses prayed to the LORD, and the fire abated. [3] So that place was called Tab'-e·rah,[s] because the fire of the LORD burned against them.

4 The rabble among them had a strong craving; and the Israelites also wept again, and said, "If only we had meat to eat! [5] We remember the fish we used to eat in Egypt for nothing, the cucumbers, the melons, the leeks, the onions, and the garlic; [6] but now our strength is dried up, and there is nothing at all but this manna to look at."

7 Now the manna was like coriander seed, and its color was like the color of gum resin. [8] The people went around and gathered it, ground it in mills or beat it in mortars, then boiled it in pots and made cakes of it; and the taste of it was like the taste of cakes baked with oil. [9] When the dew fell on the camp in the night, the manna would fall with it.

10 Moses heard the people weeping throughout their families, all at the entrances of their tents. Then the LORD became very angry, and Moses was displeased. [11] So Moses said to the LORD, "Why have you treated your servant so badly? Why have I not found favor in your sight, that you lay the burden of all this people on me? [12] Did I conceive all this people? Did I give birth to them, that you should say to me, 'Carry them in your bosom, as a nurse carries a sucking child,' to the land that you promised on oath to their ancestors? [13] Where am I to get meat to give to all this people? For they come weeping to me and say, 'Give us meat to eat!' [14] I am not able to carry all this people alone, for they are too heavy for me. [15] If this is the way you are going to treat me, put me to death at once—if I have found favor in your sight—and do not let me see my misery."

The Seventy Elders

16 So the LORD said to Moses, "Gather for me seventy of the elders of Israel, whom you know to be the elders of the people and officers over them; bring them to the tent of meeting, and have them take their place there with you. [17] I will come down and talk with you there; and I will take some of the spirit that is on you and put it on them; and they shall bear the burden of the people along with you so that you will not bear it all by yourself. [18] And say to the people: Consecrate yourselves for tomorrow, and you shall eat meat; for you have wailed in the hearing of the LORD, saying, 'If only we had meat to eat! Surely it was better for us in Egypt.' Therefore the LORD will give you meat, and you shall eat. [19] You shall eat not only one day, or two days, or five days, or ten days, or twenty days, [20] but for a whole month—until it comes out of your nostrils and becomes loathsome to you—because you have rejected the LORD who is among you, and have wailed before him, saying, 'Why did we ever leave Egypt?' " [21] But Moses said, "The people I am with number six hundred thousand on foot; and you say, 'I will give them meat, that they may eat for a whole month'! [22] Are there enough flocks and herds to slaughter for them? Are there enough fish in the sea to catch for them?" [23] The LORD said to Moses, "Is the LORD's power limited?[t] Now you shall see whether my word will come true for you or not."

24 So Moses went out and told the people the words of the LORD; and he gathered seventy elders of the people,

[r] Meaning of Heb uncertain   [s] That is *Burning*   [t] Heb *LORD's hand too short?*

and placed them all around the tent. 25 Then the LORD came down in the cloud and spoke to him, and took some of the spirit that was on him and put it on the seventy elders; and when the spirit rested upon them, they prophesied. But they did not do so again.

26 Two men remained in the camp, one named El′dad, and the other named Mē′dad, and the spirit rested on them; they were among those registered, but they had not gone out to the tent, and so they prophesied in the camp. 27 And a young man ran and told Moses, "El′dad and Mē′dad are prophesying in the camp." 28 And Joshua son of Nun, the assistant of Moses, one of his chosen men, *u* said, "My lord Moses, stop them!" 29 But Moses said to him, "Are you jealous for my sake? Would that all the LORD's people were prophets, and that the LORD would put his spirit on them!" 30 And Moses and the elders of Israel returned to the camp.

The Quails

31 Then a wind went out from the LORD, and it brought quails from the sea and let them fall beside the camp, about a day's journey on this side and a day's journey on the other side, all around the camp, about two cubits deep on the ground. 32 So the people worked all that day and night and all the next day, gathering the quails; the least anyone gathered was ten homers; and they spread them out for themselves all around the camp. 33 But while the meat was still between their teeth, before it was consumed, the anger of the LORD was kindled against the people, and the LORD struck the people with a very great plague. 34 So that place was called Kib′roth-hat·ta′a·vah, *v* because there they buried the people who had the craving. 35 From Kib′roth-hat·ta′a·vah the people journeyed to Ha·zē′roth.

Aaron and Miriam Jealous of Moses

12 While they were at Ha·zē′roth, Miriam and Aaron spoke against Moses because of the Cū′shite woman whom he had married (for he had indeed married a Cū′shite woman); 2 and they said, "Has the LORD spoken only through Moses? Has he not spoken through us also?" And the LORD heard it. 3 Now the man Moses was very humble, *w* more so than anyone else on the face of the

earth. 4 Suddenly the LORD said to Moses, Aaron, and Miriam, "Come out, you three, to the tent of meeting." So the three of them came out. 5 Then the LORD came down in a pillar of cloud, and stood at the entrance of the tent, and called Aaron and Miriam; and they both came forward. 6 And he said, "Hear my words:

> When there are prophets among
> you,
> I the LORD make myself
> known to them in visions;
> I speak to them in dreams.
> 7 Not so with my servant Moses;
> he is entrusted with all my
> house.
> 8 With him I speak face to face—
> clearly, not in riddles;
> and he beholds the form of the
> LORD.

Why then were you not afraid to speak against my servant Moses?" 9 And the anger of the LORD was kindled against them, and he departed.

10 When the cloud went away from over the tent, Miriam had become leprous, *x* as white as snow. And Aaron turned towards Miriam and saw that she was leprous. 11 Then Aaron said to Moses, "Oh, my lord, do not punish us *y* for a sin that we have so foolishly committed. 12 Do not let her be like one stillborn, whose flesh is half consumed when it comes out of its mother's womb." 13 And Moses cried to the LORD, "O God, please heal her." 14 But the LORD said to Moses, "If her father had but spit in her face, would she not bear her shame for seven days? Let her be shut out of the camp for seven days, and after that she may be brought in again." 15 So Miriam was shut out of the camp for seven days; and the people did not set out on the march until Miriam had been brought in again. 16 After that the people set out from Ha·zē′roth, and camped in the wilderness of Par′an.

Spies Sent into Canaan
(Deut 1.19–33)

13 The LORD said to Moses, 2 "Send men to spy out the land of Cā′naan, which I am giving to the Israelites; from each of their ancestral

---

u Or *of Moses from his youth*   *v* That is *Graves of craving*   *w* Or *devout*   *x* A term for several skin diseases; precise meaning uncertain   *y* Heb *do not lay sin upon us* tribes you shall send a man, every one a leader among them." 3 So Moses sent them from the wilderness of Par'an, according to the command of the LORD, all of them leading men among the Israelites. 4 These were their names: From the tribe of Reuben, Sham'mū·a son of Zac'cur; 5 from the tribe of Sim'ē·on, Shā'phat son of Hō'rī; 6 from the tribe of Judah, Caleb son of Je·phūn'neh; 7 from the tribe of Is'sa·char, I'gal son of Joseph; 8 from the tribe of E'phra·im, Hō·shē'a son of Nun; 9 from the tribe of Benjamin, Pal'tī son of Rā'phū; 10 from the tribe of Zeb'ū·lun, Gad'di·el son of Sō'dī; 11 from the tribe of Joseph (that is, from the tribe of Ma·nas'seh), Gad'dī son of Sū'sī; 12 from the tribe of Dan, Am'mi·el son of Ge·mal'lī; 13 from the tribe of Ash'er, Seth'ur son of Michael; 14 from the tribe of Naph'ta·lī, Nah'bī son of Voph'sī; 15 from the tribe of Gad, Ge·ū'el son of Mā'chī. 16 These were the names of the men whom Moses sent to spy out the land. And Moses changed the name of Hō·shē'a son of Nun to Joshua.

17 Moses sent them to spy out the land of Cā'naan, and said to them, "Go up there into the Neg'eb, and go up into the hill country, 18 and see what the land is like, and whether the people who live in it are strong or weak, whether they are few or many, 19 and whether the land they live in is good or bad, and whether the towns that they live in are unwalled or fortified, 20 and whether the land is rich or poor, and whether there are trees in it or not. Be bold, and bring some of the fruit of the land." Now it was the season of the first ripe grapes.

21 So they went up and spied out the land from the wilderness of Zin to Rē'hob, near Lē'bō-hā'math. 22 They went up into the Neg'eb, and came to Hē'bron; and A·hī'man, Shē'shaī, and Tal'maī, the An'a·kītes, were there. (Hē'bron was built seven years before Zō'an in Egypt.) 23 And they came to the Wadi Esh'col, and cut down from there a branch with a single cluster of grapes, and they carried it on a pole between two of them. They also brought some pomegranates and figs. 24 That place was called the Wadi Esh'col,ᶻ because of the cluster that the Israelites cut down from there.

The Report of the Spies

25 At the end of forty days they re-turned from spying out the land. 26 And they came to Moses and Aaron and to all the congregation of the Israelites in the wilderness of Par'an, at Kā'desh; they brought back word to them and to all the congregation of the land, and showed them the fruit of the land. 27 And they told him, "We came to the land to which you sent us; it flows with milk and honey, and this is its fruit. 28 Yet the people who live in the land are strong, and the towns are fortified and very large; and besides, we saw the descendants of Ā'nak there. 29 The A·mal'-e·kītes live in the land of the Neg'eb; the Hit'tītes, the Jeb'ū·sītes, and the Am'o·rītes live in the hill country; and the Cā'naan·ītes live by the sea, and along the Jordan."

30 But Caleb quieted the people be-fore Moses, and said, "Let us go up at once and occupy it, for we are well able to overcome it." 31 Then the men who had gone up with him said, "We are not able to go up against this peo-ple, for they are stronger than we." 32 So they brought to the Israelites an unfavorable report of the land that they had spied out, saying, "The land that we have gone through as spies is a land that devours its inhabitants; and all the people that we saw in it are of great size. 33 There we saw the Neph'-i·lim (the An'a·kītes come from the Neph'i·lim); and to ourselves we seemed like grasshoppers, and so we seemed to them."

The People Rebel

14 Then all the congregation raised a loud cry, and the peo-ple wept that night. 2 And all the Israel-ites complained against Moses and Aaron; the whole congregation said to them, "Would that we had died in the land of Egypt! Or would that we had died in this wilderness! 3 Why is the LORD bringing us into this land to fall by the sword? Our wives and our little ones will become booty; would it not be better for us to go back to Egypt?" 4 So they said to one another, "Let us choose a captain, and go back to Egypt."

5 Then Moses and Aaron fell on their faces before all the assembly of the congregation of the Israelites. 6 And Joshua son of Nun and Caleb son of Je·phūn'neh, who were among those who had spied out the land, tore

ᶻ That is *Cluster*

their clothes [7] and said to all the congregation of the Israelites, "The land that we went through as spies is an exceedingly good land. [8] If the LORD is pleased with us, he will bring us into this land and give it to us, a land that flows with milk and honey. [9] Only, do not rebel against the LORD; and do not fear the people of the land, for they are no more than bread for us; their protection is removed from them, and the LORD is with us; do not fear them." [10] But the whole congregation threatened to stone them.

Then the glory of the LORD appeared at the tent of meeting to all the Israelites. [11] And the LORD said to Moses, "How long will this people despise me? And how long will they refuse to believe in me, in spite of all the signs that I have done among them? [12] I will strike them with pestilence and disinherit them, and I will make of you a nation greater and mightier than they."

Moses Intercedes for the People

[13] But Moses said to the LORD, "Then the Egyptians will hear of it, for in your might you brought up this people from among them, [14] and they will tell the inhabitants of this land. They have heard that you, O LORD, are in the midst of this people; for you, O LORD, are seen face to face, and your cloud stands over them and you go in front of them, in a pillar of cloud by day and in a pillar of fire by night. [15] Now if you kill this people all at one time, then the nations who have heard about you will say, [16] 'It is because the LORD was not able to bring this people into the land he swore to give them that he has slaughtered them in the wilderness.' [17] And now, therefore, let the power of the LORD be great in the way that you promised when you spoke, saying,

[18] 'The LORD is slow to anger,
　and abounding in steadfast love,
　forgiving iniquity and
　　transgression,
but by no means clearing the
　　guilty,
visiting the iniquity of the
　　parents
upon the children
to the third and the fourth
　　generation.'

[19] Forgive the iniquity of this people according to the greatness of your steadfast love, just as you have pardoned this people, from Egypt even until now."

[20] Then the LORD said, "I do forgive, just as you have asked; [21] nevertheless—as I live, and as all the earth shall be filled with the glory of the LORD— [22] none of the people who have seen my glory and the signs that I did in Egypt and in the wilderness, and yet have tested me these ten times and have not obeyed my voice, [23] shall see the land that I swore to give to their ancestors; none of those who despised me shall see it. [24] But my servant Caleb, because he has a different spirit and has followed me wholeheartedly, I will bring into the land into which he went, and his descendants shall possess it. [25] Now, since the A·mal′e·kites and the Ca′naan·ites live in the valleys, turn tomorrow and set out for the wilderness by the way to the Red Sea."[a]

An Attempted Invasion is Repulsed
(Deut 1.41–45)

[26] And the LORD spoke to Moses and to Aaron, saying: [27] How long shall this wicked congregation complain against me? I have heard the complaints of the Israelites, which they complain against me. [28] Say to them, "As I live," says the LORD, "I will do to you the very things I heard you say: [29] your dead bodies shall fall in this very wilderness; and of all your number, included in the census, from twenty years old and upward, who have complained against me, [30] not one of you shall come into the land in which I swore to settle you, except Caleb son of Je·phun′neh and Joshua son of Nun. [31] But your little ones, who you said would become booty, I will bring in, and they shall know the land that you have despised. [32] But as for you, your dead bodies shall fall in this wilderness. [33] And your children shall be shepherds in the wilderness for forty years, and shall suffer for your faithlessness, until the last of your dead bodies lies in the wilderness. [34] According to the number of the days in which you spied out the land, forty days, for every day a year, you shall bear your iniquity, forty years, and you shall know my displeasure." [35] I the LORD have spoken; surely I will do thus to all this wicked congregation gathered together against me: in this

[a] Or Sea of Reeds

wilderness they shall come to a full end, and there they shall die.

36 And the men whom Moses sent to spy out the land, who returned and made all the congregation complain against him by bringing a bad report about the land— 37the men who brought an unfavorable report about the land died by a plague before the LORD. 38But Joshua son of Nun and Caleb son of Je·phun'neh alone remained alive, of those men who went to spy out the land.

39 When Moses told these words to all the Israelites, the people mourned greatly. 40They rose early in the morning and went up to the heights of the hill country, saying, "Here we are. We will go up to the place that the LORD has promised, for we have sinned." 41But Moses said, "Why do you continue to transgress the command of the LORD? That will not succeed. 42Do not go up, for the LORD is not with you; do not let yourselves be struck down before your enemies. 43For the A·mal'-e·kites and the Ca'naan·ites will confront you there, and you shall fall by the sword; because you have turned back from following the LORD, the LORD will not be with you." 44But they presumed to go up to the heights of the hill country, even though the ark of the covenant of the LORD, and Moses, had not left the camp. 45Then the A·mal'-e·kites and the Ca'naan·ites who lived in that hill country came down and defeated them, pursuing them as far as Hor'mah.

Various Offerings

15 The LORD spoke to Moses, saying: 2Speak to the Israelites and say to them: When you come into the land you are to inhabit, which I am giving you, 3and you make an offering by fire to the LORD from the herd or from the flock—whether a burnt offering or a sacrifice, to fulfill a vow or as a freewill offering or at your appointed festivals—to make a pleasing odor for the LORD, 4then whoever presents such an offering to the LORD shall present also a grain offering, one-tenth of an ephah of choice flour, mixed with one-fourth of a hin of oil. 5Moreover, you shall offer one-fourth of a hin of wine as a drink offering with the burnt offering or the sacrifice, for each lamb. 6For a ram, you shall offer a grain offering, two-tenths of an ephah of choice flour mixed with one-third of a

hin of oil; 7and as a drink offering you shall offer one-third of a hin of wine, a pleasing odor to the LORD. 8When you offer a bull as a burnt offering or a sacrifice, to fulfill a vow or as an offering of well-being to the LORD, 9then you shall present with the bull a grain offering, three-tenths of an ephah of choice flour, mixed with half a hin of oil, 10and you shall present as a drink offering half a hin of wine, as an offering by fire, a pleasing odor to the LORD.

11 Thus it shall be done for each ox or ram, or for each of the male lambs or the kids. 12According to the number that you offer, so you shall do with each and every one. 13Every native Israelite shall do these things in this way, in presenting an offering by fire, a pleasing odor to the LORD. 14An alien who lives with you, or who takes up permanent residence among you, and wishes to offer an offering by fire, a pleasing odor to the LORD, shall do as you do. 15As for the assembly, there shall be for both you and the resident alien a single statute, a perpetual statute throughout your generations; you and the alien shall be alike before the LORD. 16You and the alien who resides with you shall have the same law and the same ordinance.

17 The LORD spoke to Moses, saying: 18Speak to the Israelites and say to them: After you come into the land to which I am bringing you, 19whenever you eat of the bread of the land, you shall present a donation to the LORD. 20From your first batch of dough you shall present a loaf as a donation; you shall present it just as you present a donation from the threshing floor. 21Throughout your generations you shall give to the LORD a donation from the first of your batch of dough.

22 But if you unintentionally fail to observe all these commandments that the LORD has spoken to Moses— 23everything that the LORD has commanded you by Moses, from the day the LORD gave commandment and thereafter, throughout your generations— 24then if it was done unintentionally without the knowledge of the congregation, the whole congregation shall offer one young bull for a burnt offering, a pleasing odor to the LORD, together with its grain offering and its drink offering, according to the ordinance, and one male goat for a sin offering. 25The priest shall make atonement for all the congregation of

the Israelites, and they shall be forgiven; it was unintentional, and they have brought their offering, an offering by fire to the LORD, and their sin offering before the LORD, for their error. 26 All the congregation of the Israelites shall be forgiven, as well as the aliens residing among them, because the whole people was involved in the error.

27 An individual who sins unintentionally shall present a female goat a year old for a sin offering. 28 And the priest shall make atonement before the LORD for the one who commits an error, when it is unintentional, to make atonement for the person, who then shall be forgiven. 29 For both the native among the Israelites and the alien residing among them—you shall have the same law for anyone who acts in error. 30 But whoever acts highhandedly, whether a native or an alien, affronts the LORD, and shall be cut off from among the people. 31 Because of having despised the word of the LORD and broken his commandment, such a person shall be utterly cut off and bear the guilt.

Penalty for Violating the Sabbath
(Ex 31.12–17)

32 When the Israelites were in the wilderness, they found a man gathering sticks on the sabbath day. 33 Those who found him gathering sticks brought him to Moses, Aaron, and to the whole congregation. 34 They put him in custody, because it was not clear what should be done to him. 35 Then the LORD said to Moses, "The man shall be put to death; all the congregation shall stone him outside the camp." 36 The whole congregation brought him outside the camp and stoned him to death, just as the LORD had commanded Moses.

Fringes on Garments

37 The LORD said to Moses: 38 Speak to the Israelites, and tell them to make fringes on the corners of their garments throughout their generations and to put a blue cord on the fringe at each corner. 39 You have the fringe so that, when you see it, you will remember all the commandments of the LORD and do them, and not follow the lust of your own heart and your own eyes. 40 So you shall remember and do all my commandments, and you shall be holy to your God. 41 I am the LORD your God, who brought you out of the land of Egypt, to be your God: I am the LORD your God.

Revolt of Korah, Dathan, and Abiram

16 Now Kō′rah son of Iz′har son of Kō′hath son of Levi, along with Dā′than and A·bī′ram sons of E·lī′ab, and On son of Pe′leth—descendants of Reuben—took 2 two hundred fifty Israelite men, leaders of the congregation, chosen from the assembly, well-known men,[b] and they confronted Moses. 3 They assembled against Moses and against Aaron, and said to them, "You have gone too far! All the congregation are holy, everyone of them, and the LORD is among them. So why then do you exalt yourselves above the assembly of the LORD?" 4 When Moses heard it, he fell on his face. 5 Then he said to Kō′rah and all his company, "In the morning the LORD will make known who is his, and who is holy, and who will be allowed to approach him; the one whom he will choose he will allow to approach him. 6 Do this: take censers, Kō′rah and all your[c] company, 7 and tomorrow put fire in them, and lay incense on them before the LORD; and the man whom the LORD chooses shall be the holy one. You Lē′vites have gone too far!" 8 Then Moses said to Kō′rah, "Hear now, you Lē′vites! 9 Is it too little for you that the God of Israel has separated you from the congregation of Israel, to allow you to approach him in order to perform the duties of the LORD's tabernacle, and to stand before the congregation and serve them? 10 He has allowed you to approach him, and all your brother Lē′vites with you; yet you seek the priesthood as well! 11 Therefore you and all your company have gathered together against the LORD. What is Aaron that you rail against him?"

12 Moses sent for Dā′than and A·bī′ram sons of E·lī′ab; but they said, "We will not come! 13 Is it too little that you have brought us up out of a land flowing with milk and honey to kill us in the wilderness, that you must also lord it over us? 14 It is clear you have not brought us into a land flowing with milk and honey, or given us an inheritance of fields and vineyards. Would

b Cn: Heb *and they confronted Moses, and two hundred fifty men . . . well-known men*   *c* Heb *his* you put out the eyes of these men? We will not come!"

15 Moses was very angry and said to the LORD, "Pay no attention to their offering. I have not taken one donkey from them, and I have not harmed any one of them." 16 And Moses said to Kō´rah, "As for you and all your company, be present tomorrow before the LORD, you and they and Aaron; 17 and let each one of you take his censer, and put incense on it, and each one of you present his censer before the LORD, two hundred fifty censers; you also, and Aaron, each his censer." 18 So each man took his censer, and they put fire in the censers and laid incense on them, and they stood at the entrance of the tent of meeting with Moses and Aaron. 19 Then Kō´rah assembled the whole congregation against them at the entrance of the tent of meeting. And the glory of the LORD appeared to the whole congregation.

20 Then the LORD spoke to Moses and to Aaron, saying: 21 Separate yourselves from this congregation, so that I may consume them in a moment. 22 They fell on their faces, and said, "O God, the God of the spirits of all flesh, shall one person sin and you become angry with the whole congregation?"

23 And the LORD spoke to Moses, saying: 24 Say to the congregation: Get away from the dwellings of Kō´rah, Dā´than, and A·bī´ram. 25 So Moses got up and went to Dā´than and A·bī´ram; the elders of Israel followed him. 26 He said to the congregation, "Turn away from the tents of these wicked men, and touch nothing of theirs, or you will be swept away for all their sins." 27 So they got away from the dwellings of Kō´rah, Dā´than, and A·bī´ram; and Dā´than and A·bī´ram came out and stood at the entrance of their tents, together with their wives, their children, and their little ones. 28 And Moses said, "This is how you shall know that the LORD has sent me to do all these works; it has not been of my own accord: 29 If these people die a natural death, or if a natural fate comes on them, then the LORD has not sent me. 30 But if the LORD creates something new, and the ground opens its mouth and swallows them up, with all that belongs to them, and they go down alive into Shē´ōl, then you shall know that these men have despised the LORD."

31 As soon as he finished speaking all these words, the ground under them was split apart. 32 The earth opened its mouth and swallowed them up, along with their households— everyone who belonged to Kō´rah and all their goods. 33 So they with all that belonged to them went down alive into Shē´ōl; the earth closed over them, and they perished from the midst of the assembly. 34 All Israel around them fled at their outcry, for they said, "The earth will swallow us too!" 35 And fire came out from the LORD and consumed the two hundred fifty men offering the incense.

36 d Then the LORD spoke to Moses, saying: 37 Tell El·e·ā´zar son of Aaron the priest to take the censers out of the blaze; then scatter the fire far and wide. 38 For the censers of these sinners have become holy at the cost of their lives. Make them into hammered plates as a covering for the altar, for they presented them before the LORD and they became holy. Thus they shall be a sign to the Israelites. 39 So El·e·ā´zar the priest took the bronze censers that had been presented by those who were burned; and they were hammered out as a covering for the altar— 40 a reminder to the Israelites that no outsider, who is not of the descendants of Aaron, shall approach to offer incense before the LORD, so as not to become like Kō´rah and his company—just as the LORD had said to him through Moses.

41 On the next day, however, the whole congregation of the Israelites rebelled against Moses and against Aaron, saying, "You have killed the people of the LORD." 42 And when the congregation had assembled against them, Moses and Aaron turned toward the tent of meeting; the cloud had covered it and the glory of the LORD appeared. 43 Then Moses and Aaron came to the front of the tent of meeting, 44 and the LORD spoke to Moses, saying, 45 "Get away from this congregation, so that I may consume them in a moment." And they fell on their faces. 46 Moses said to Aaron, "Take your censer, put fire on it from the altar and lay incense on it, and carry it quickly to the congregation and make atonement for them. For wrath has gone out from the LORD; the plague has begun." 47 So Aaron took it as Moses

d Ch 17.1 in Heb

N
U
M
B
E
R
S

had ordered, and ran into the middle of the assembly, where the plague had already begun among the people. He put on the incense, and made atonement for the people. [48] He stood between the dead and the living; and the plague was stopped. [49] Those who died by the plague were fourteen thousand seven hundred, besides those who died in the affair of Kōʹrah. [50] When the plague was stopped, Aaron returned to Moses at the entrance of the tent of meeting.

The Budding of Aaron's Rod

17 [e] The LORD spoke to Moses, saying: [2] Speak to the Israelites, and get twelve staffs from them, one for each ancestral house, from all the leaders of their ancestral houses. Write each man's name on his staff, [3] and write Aaron's name on the staff of Levi. For there shall be one staff for the head of each ancestral house. [4] Place them in the tent of meeting before the covenant,[f] where I meet with you. [5] And the staff of the man whom I choose shall sprout; thus I will put a stop to the complaints of the Israelites that they continually make against you. [6] Moses spoke to the Israelites; and all their leaders gave him staffs, one for each leader, according to their ancestral houses, twelve staffs; and the staff of Aaron was among theirs. [7] So Moses placed the staffs before the LORD in the tent of the covenant.[f]

[8] When Moses went into the tent of the covenant[f] on the next day, the staff of Aaron for the house of Levi had sprouted. It put forth buds, produced blossoms, and bore ripe almonds. [9] Then Moses brought out all the staffs from before the LORD to all the Israelites; and they looked, and each man took his staff. [10] And the LORD said to Moses, "Put back the staff of Aaron before the covenant,[f] to be kept as a warning to rebels, so that you may make an end of their complaints against me, or else they will die." [11] Moses did so; just as the LORD commanded him, so he did.

[12] The Israelites said to Moses, "We are perishing; we are lost, all of us are lost! [13] Everyone who approaches the tabernacle of the LORD will die. Are we all to perish?"

Responsibility of Priests and Levites

18 The LORD said to Aaron: You and your sons and your ancestral house with you shall bear responsibility for offenses connected with the sanctuary, while you and your sons alone shall bear responsibility for offenses connected with the priesthood. [2] So bring with you also your brothers of the tribe of Levi, your ancestral tribe, in order that they may be joined to you, and serve you while you and your sons with you are in front of the tent of the covenant.[f] [3] They shall perform duties for you and for the whole tent. But they must not approach either the utensils of the sanctuary or the altar, otherwise both they and you will die. [4] They are attached to you in order to perform the duties of the tent of meeting, for all the service of the tent; no outsider shall approach you. [5] You yourselves shall perform the duties of the sanctuary and the duties of the altar, so that wrath may never again come upon the Israelites. [6] It is I who now take your brother Leʹvites from among the Israelites; they are now yours as a gift, dedicated to the LORD, to perform the service of the tent of meeting. [7] But you and your sons with you shall diligently perform your priestly duties in all that concerns the altar and the area behind the curtain. I give your priesthood as a gift;[g] any outsider who approaches shall be put to death.

The Priests' Portion

[8] The LORD spoke to Aaron: I have given you charge of the offerings made to me, all the holy gifts of the Israelites; I have given them to you and your sons as a priestly portion due you in perpetuity. [9] This shall be yours from the most holy things, reserved from the fire: every offering of theirs that they render to me as a most holy thing, whether grain offering, sin offering, or guilt offering, shall belong to you and your sons. [10] As a most holy thing you shall eat it; every male may eat it; it shall be holy to you. [11] This also is yours: I have given to you, together with your sons and daughters, as a perpetual due, whatever is set aside from the gifts of all the elevation offerings of the Israelites; everyone who is clean in your house may eat them. [12] All the best of the oil and all the best of the wine and of the grain, the choice

[e]Ch 17.16 in Heb [f]Or *treaty*, or *testimony*; Heb *eduth* [g]Heb *as a service of gift*

produce that they give to the LORD, I have given to you. [13] The first fruits of all that is in their land, which they bring to the LORD, shall be yours; everyone who is clean in your house may eat of it. [14] Every devoted thing in Israel shall be yours. [15] The first issue of the womb of all creatures, human and animal, which is offered to the LORD, shall be yours; but the firstborn of human beings you shall redeem, and the firstborn of unclean animals you shall redeem. [16] Their redemption price, reckoned from one month of age, you shall fix at five shekels of silver, according to the shekel of the sanctuary (that is, twenty gerahs). [17] But the firstborn of a cow, or the firstborn of a sheep, or the firstborn of a goat, you shall not redeem; they are holy. You shall dash their blood on the altar, and shall turn their fat into smoke as an offering by fire for a pleasing odor to the LORD; [18] but their flesh shall be yours, just as the breast that is elevated and as the right thigh are yours. [19] All the holy offerings that the Israelites present to the LORD I have given to you, together with your sons and daughters, as a perpetual due; it is a covenant of salt forever before the LORD for you and your descendants as well. [20] Then the LORD said to Aaron: You shall have no allotment in their land, nor shall you have any share among them; I am your share and your possession among the Israelites.

21 To the Lē′vītes I have given every tithe in Israel for a possession in return for the service that they perform, the service in the tent of meeting. [22] From now on the Israelites shall no longer approach the tent of meeting, or else they will incur guilt and die. [23] But the Lē′vītes shall perform the service of the tent of meeting, and they shall bear responsibility for their own offenses; it shall be a perpetual statute throughout your generations. But among the Israelites they shall have no allotment, [24] because I have given to the Lē′vītes as their portion the tithe of the Israelites, which they set apart as an offering to the LORD. Therefore I have said of them that they shall have no allotment among the Israelites.

25 Then the LORD spoke to Moses, saying: [26] You shall speak to the Lē′vītes, saying: When you receive from the Israelites the tithe that I have given you from them for your portion, you shall set apart an offering from it to the LORD, a tithe of the tithe. [27] It shall be reckoned to you as your gift, the same as the grain of the threshing floor and the fullness of the wine press. [28] Thus you also shall set apart an offering to the LORD from all the tithes that you receive from the Israelites; and from them you shall give the LORD's offering to the priest Aaron. [29] Out of all the gifts to you, you shall set apart every offering due to the LORD; the best of all of them is the part to be consecrated. [30] Say also to them: When you have set apart the best of it, then the rest shall be reckoned to the Lē′vītes as produce of the threshing floor, and as produce of the wine press. [31] You may eat it in any place, you and your households; for it is your payment for your service in the tent of meeting. [32] You shall incur no guilt by reason of it, when you have offered the best of it. But you shall not profane the holy gifts of the Israelites, on pain of death.

Ceremony of the Red Heifer

19 The LORD spoke to Moses and Aaron, saying: [2] This is a statute of the law that the LORD has commanded: Tell the Israelites to bring you a red heifer without defect, in which there is no blemish and on which no yoke has been laid. [3] You shall give it to the priest El·e·a′zar, and it shall be taken outside the camp and slaughtered in his presence. [4] The priest El·e·a′zar shall take some of its blood with his finger and sprinkle it seven times towards the front of the tent of meeting. [5] Then the heifer shall be burned in his sight; its skin, its flesh, and its blood, with its dung, shall be burned. [6] The priest shall take cedarwood, hyssop, and crimson material, and throw them into the fire in which the heifer is burning. [7] Then the priest shall wash his clothes and bathe his body in water, and afterwards he may come into the camp; but the priest shall remain unclean until evening. [8] The one who burns the heifer[h] shall wash his clothes in water and bathe his body in water; he shall remain unclean until evening. [9] Then someone who is clean shall gather up the ashes of the heifer, and deposit them outside the camp in a clean place; and they shall be kept for the congregation of the Israelites for the water for cleansing. It is a purification offering. [10] The one who

[h] Heb *it*

gathers the ashes of the heifer shall wash his clothes and be unclean until evening.

This shall be a perpetual statute for the Israelites and for the alien residing among them. ¹¹ Those who touch the dead body of any human being shall be unclean seven days. ¹² They shall purify themselves with the water on the third day and on the seventh day, and so be clean; but if they do not purify themselves on the third day and on the seventh day, they will not become clean. ¹³ All who touch a corpse, the body of a human being who has died, and do not purify themselves, defile the tabernacle of the LORD; such persons shall be cut off from Israel. Since water for cleansing was not dashed on them, they remain unclean; their uncleanness is still on them.

14 This is the law when someone dies in a tent: everyone who comes into the tent, and everyone who is in the tent, shall be unclean seven days. ¹⁵ And every open vessel with no cover fastened on it is unclean. ¹⁶ Whoever in the open field touches one who has been killed by a sword, or who has died naturally,ⁱ or a human bone, or a grave, shall be unclean seven days. ¹⁷ For the unclean they shall take some ashes of the burnt purification offering, and running water shall be added in a vessel; ¹⁸ then a clean person shall take hyssop, dip it in the water, and sprinkle it on the tent, on all the furnishings, on the persons who were there, and on whoever touched the bone, the slain, the corpse, or the grave. ¹⁹ The clean person shall sprinkle the unclean ones on the third day and on the seventh day, thus purifying them on the seventh day. Then they shall wash their clothes and bathe themselves in water, and at evening they shall be clean. ²⁰ Any who are unclean but do not purify themselves, those persons shall be cut off from the assembly, for they have defiled the sanctuary of the LORD. Since the water for cleansing has not been dashed on them, they are unclean.

21 It shall be a perpetual statute for them. The one who sprinkles the water for cleansing shall wash his clothes, and whoever touches the water for cleansing shall be unclean until evening. ²² Whatever the unclean person touches shall be unclean, and anyone who touches it shall be unclean until evening.

The Waters of Meribah
(Ex 17.1–7)

20 The Israelites, the whole congregation, came into the wilderness of Zin in the first month, and the people stayed in Kaʹdesh. Miriam died there, and was buried there.

2 Now there was no water for the congregation; so they gathered together against Moses and against Aaron. ³ The people quarreled with Moses and said, "Would that we had died when our kindred died before the LORD! ⁴ Why have you brought the assembly of the LORD into this wilderness for us and our livestock to die here? ⁵ Why have you brought us up out of Egypt, to bring us to this wretched place? It is no place for grain, or figs, or vines, or pomegranates; and there is no water to drink." ⁶ Then Moses and Aaron went away from the assembly to the entrance of the tent of meeting; they fell on their faces, and the glory of the LORD appeared to them. ⁷ The LORD spoke to Moses, saying: ⁸ Take the staff, and assemble the congregation, you and your brother Aaron, and command the rock before their eyes to yield its water. Thus you shall bring water out of the rock for them; thus you shall provide drink for the congregation and their livestock.

9 So Moses took the staff from before the LORD, as he had commanded him. ¹⁰ Moses and Aaron gathered the assembly together before the rock, and he said to them, "Listen, you rebels, shall we bring water for you out of this rock?" ¹¹ Then Moses lifted up his hand and struck the rock twice with his staff; water came out abundantly, and the congregation and their livestock drank. ¹² But the LORD said to Moses and Aaron, "Because you did not trust in me, to show my holiness before the eyes of the Israelites, therefore you shall not bring this assembly into the land that I have given them." ¹³ These are the waters of Merʹi·bah,ʲ where the people of Israel quarreled with the LORD, and by which he showed his holiness.

Passage through Edom Refused

14 Moses sent messengers from Kaʹdesh to the king of Eʹdom, "Thus says your brother Israel: You know all the adversity that has befallen us:

ⁱ Heb lacks *naturally*   ʲ That is *Quarrel*

[15]how our ancestors went down to Egypt, and we lived in Egypt a long time; and the Egyptians oppressed us and our ancestors; [16]and when we cried to the LORD, he heard our voice, and sent an angel and brought us out of Egypt; and here we are in Kā′desh, a town on the edge of your territory. [17]Now let us pass through your land. We will not pass through field or vineyard, or drink water from any well; we will go along the King's Highway, not turning aside to the right hand or to the left until we have passed through your territory."

[18] But E′dom said to him, "You shall not pass through, or we will come out with the sword against you." [19]The Israelites said to him, "We will stay on the highway; and if we drink of your water, we and our livestock, then we will pay for it. It is only a small matter; just let us pass through on foot." [20]But he said, "You shall not pass through." And E′dom came out against them with a large force, heavily armed. [21]Thus E′dom refused to give Israel passage through their territory; so Israel turned away from them.

The Death of Aaron

[22] They set out from Kā′desh, and the Israelites, the whole congregation, came to Mount Hor. [23]Then the LORD said to Moses and Aaron at Mount Hor, on the border of the land of E′dom, [24]"Let Aaron be gathered to his people. For he shall not enter the land that I have given to the Israelites, because you rebelled against my command at the waters of Mer′i·bah. [25]Take Aaron and his son El·e·a′zar, and bring them up Mount Hor; [26]strip Aaron of his vestments, and put them on his son El·e·a′zar. But Aaron shall be gathered to his people,[k] and shall die there." [27]Moses did as the LORD had commanded; they went up Mount Hor in the sight of the whole congregation. [28]Moses stripped Aaron of his vestments, and put them on his son El·e·a′zar; and Aaron died there on the top of the mountain. Moses and El·e·a′zar came down from the mountain. [29]When all the congregation saw that Aaron had died, all the house of Israel mourned for Aaron thirty days.

The Bronze Serpent

21 When the Cā′naan·ite, the king of Ar′ad, who lived in the Neg′eb, heard that Israel was coming by the way of Ath′a·rim, he fought against Israel and took some of them captive. [2]Then Israel made a vow to the LORD and said, "If you will indeed give this people into our hands, then we will utterly destroy their towns." [3]The LORD listened to the voice of Israel, and handed over the Cā′-naan·ites; and they utterly destroyed them and their towns; so the place was called Hor′mah.[l]

[4] From Mount Hor they set out by the way to the Red Sea,[m] to go around the land of E′dom; but the people became impatient on the way. [5]The people spoke against God and against Moses, "Why have you brought us up out of Egypt to die in the wilderness? For there is no food and no water, and we detest this miserable food." [6]The LORD sent poisonous[n] serpents among the people, and they bit the people, so that many Israelites died. [7]The people came to Moses and said, "We have sinned by speaking against the LORD and against you; pray to the LORD to take away the serpents from us." So Moses prayed for the people. [8]And the LORD said to Moses, "Make a poisonous[o] serpent, and set it on a pole; and everyone who is bitten shall look at it and live." [9]So Moses made a serpent of bronze, and put it upon a pole; and whenever a serpent bit someone, that person would look at the serpent of bronze and live.

The Journey to Moab

[10] The Israelites set out, and camped in O′both. [11]They set out from O′both, and camped at I′ye-ab′a·rim, in the wilderness bordering Mō′ab toward the sunrise. [12]From there they set out, and camped in the Wadi Zē′red. [13]From there they set out, and camped on the other side of the Ar′non, in[p] the wilderness that extends from the boundary of the Am′o·rītes; for the Ar′non is the boundary of Mō′ab, between Mō′ab and the Am′o·rītes. [14]Wherefore it is said in the Book of the Wars of the LORD,

"Wa′heb in Sū′phah and the wadis.
The Ar′non [15]and the slopes of the wadis
that extend to the seat of Ar,

[k]Heb lacks *to his people*
[l]Heb *Destruction*   [m]Or *Sea of Reeds*
[n]Or *fiery*; Heb *seraphim*   [o]Or *fiery*;
Heb *seraph*   [p]Gk: Heb *which is in*

and lie along the border of
Mō′ab.″^q

16 From there they continued to
Bē′er;^r that is the well of which the
LORD said to Moses, "Gather the people together, and I will give them water." ¹⁷Then Israel sang this song:

"Spring up, O well!—Sing to
it!—
¹⁸ the well that the leaders sank,
that the nobles of the people
dug,
with the scepter, with the staff."

From the wilderness to Mat′ta·nah,
¹⁹from Mat′ta·nah to Na·hal′i·el, from
Na·hal′i·el to Bā′moth, ²⁰and from
Bā′moth to the valley lying in the region of Mō′ab by the top of Pis′gah
that overlooks the wasteland.^s

King Sihon Defeated
(Deut 2.26–37)

21 Then Israel sent messengers to
King Sī′hon of the Am′o·rītes, saying,
²²"Let me pass through your land; we
will not turn aside into field or vineyard; we will not drink the water of
any well; we will go by the King's
Highway until we have passed
through your territory." ²³But Sī′hon
would not allow Israel to pass through
his territory. Sī′hon gathered all his
people together, and went out against
Israel to the wilderness; he came to
Jā′haz, and fought against Israel. ²⁴Israel put him to the sword, and took
possession of his land from the Ar′non
to the Jab′bok, as far as to the Am′mon·ites; for the boundary of the Am′mon·ites was strong. ²⁵Israel took all
these towns, and Israel settled in all
the towns of the Am′o·rītes, in Hesh′-
bon, and in all its villages. ²⁶For Hesh′-
bon was the city of King Sī′hon of the
Am′o·rītes, who had fought against
the former king of Mō′ab and captured
all his land as far as the Ar′non.
²⁷Therefore the ballad singers say,

"Come to Hesh′bon, let it be
built;
let the city of Sī′hon be
established.
²⁸ For fire came out from
Hesh′bon,
flame from the city of Sī′hon.
It devoured Ar of Mō′ab,
and swallowed up^t the heights
of the Ar′non.
²⁹ Woe to you, O Mō′ab!
You are undone, O people of
Chē′mosh!
He has made his sons fugitives,

and his daughters captives,
to an Am′o·rīte king, Sī′hon.
³⁰ So their posterity perished
from Hesh′bon^u to Dī′bon,
and we laid waste until fire
spread to Med′e·ba."^v

31 Thus Israel settled in the land of
the Am′o·rītes. ³²Moses sent to spy out
Jā′zer; and they captured its villages,
and dispossessed the Am′o·rītes who
were there.

King Og Defeated
(Deut 3.1–22)

33 Then they turned and went up
the road to Bā′shan; and King Og of
Bā′shan came out against them, he
and all his people, to battle at Ed′rē·i.
³⁴But the LORD said to Moses, "Do not
be afraid of him; for I have given him
into your hand, with all his people, and
all his land. You shall do to him as you
did to King Sī′hon of the Am′o·rītes,
who ruled in Hesh′bon." ³⁵So they
killed him, his sons, and all his people,
until there was no survivor left; and
they took possession of his land.

Balak Summons Balaam
to Curse Israel

22 The Israelites set out, and
camped in the plains of Mō′ab
across the Jordan from Jericho. ²Now
Bā′lak son of Zip′por saw all that Israel had done to the Am′o·rītes.
³Mō′ab was in great dread of the people, because they were so numerous;
Mō′ab was overcome with fear of the
people of Israel. ⁴And Mō′ab said to
the elders of Mid′i·an, "This horde will
now lick up all that is around us, as an
ox licks up the grass of the field." Now
Bā′lak son of Zip′por was king of
Mō′ab at that time. ⁵He sent messengers to Bā′laam son of Bē′or at Pē′-
thor, which is on the Euphrates, in the
land of A′maw,^w to summon him, saying, "A people has come out of Egypt;
they have spread over the face of the
earth, and they have settled next to me.
⁶Come now, curse this people for me,
since they are stronger than I; perhaps
I shall be able to defeat them and drive
them from the land; for I know that

---

^qMeaning of Heb uncertain   ^rThat is
Well   ^sOr Jeshimon   ^tGk: Heb and
the lords of   ^uGk: Heb we have shot at
them; Heshbon has perished
^vCompare Sam Gk: Meaning of MT
uncertain   ^wOr land of his kinsfolk

whomever you bless is blessed, and whomever you curse is cursed."

7 So the elders of Mō'ab and the elders of Mid'i·an departed with the fees for divination in their hand; and they came to Bā'laam, and gave him Balak's message. [8] He said to them, "Stay here tonight, and I will bring back word to you, just as the LORD speaks to me"; so the officials of Mō'ab stayed with Bā'laam. [9] God came to Bā'laam and said, "Who are these men with you?" [10] Bā'laam said to God, "King Bā'lak son of Zip'por of Mō'ab, has sent me this message: [11] 'A people has come out of Egypt and has spread over the face of the earth; now come, curse them for me; perhaps I shall be able to fight against them and drive them out.' " [12] God said to Bā'laam, "You shall not go with them; you shall not curse the people, for they are blessed." [13] So Bā'laam rose in the morning, and said to the officials of Bā'lak, "Go to your own land, for the LORD has refused to let me go with you." [14] So the officials of Mō'ab rose and went to Bā'lak, and said, "Bā'laam refuses to come with us."

15 Once again Bā'lak sent officials, more numerous and more distinguished than these. [16] They came to Bā'laam and said to him, "Thus says Bā'lak son of Zip'por: 'Do not let anything hinder you from coming to me; [17] for I will surely do you great honor, and whatever you say to me I will do; come, curse this people for me.' " [18] But Bā'laam replied to the servants of Bā'-lak, "Although Bā'lak were to give me his house full of silver and gold, I could not go beyond the command of the LORD my God, to do less or more. [19] You remain here, as the others did, so that I may learn what more the LORD may say to me." [20] That night God came to Bā'laam and said to him, "If the men have come to summon you, get up and go with them; but do only what I tell you to do." [21] So Bā'laam got up in the morning, saddled his donkey, and went with the officials of Mō'ab.

Balaam, the Donkey, and the Angel

22 God's anger was kindled because he was going, and the angel of the LORD took his stand in the road as his adversary. Now he was riding on the donkey, and his two servants were with him. [23] The donkey saw the angel of the LORD standing in the road, with a drawn sword in his hand; so the don-key turned off the road, and went into the field; and Bā'laam struck the donkey, to turn it back onto the road. [24] Then the angel of the LORD stood in a narrow path between the vineyards, with a wall on either side. [25] When the donkey saw the angel of the LORD, it scraped against the wall, and scraped Bā'laam's foot against the wall; so he struck it again. [26] Then the angel of the LORD went ahead, and stood in a narrow place, where there was no way to turn either to the right or to the left. [27] When the donkey saw the angel of the LORD, it lay down under Bā'laam; and Bā'laam's anger was kindled, and he struck the donkey with his staff. [28] Then the LORD opened the mouth of the donkey, and it said to Bā'laam, "What have I done to you, that you have struck me these three times?" [29] Bā'laam said to the donkey, "Because you have made a fool of me! I wish I had a sword in my hand! I would kill you right now!" [30] But the donkey said to Bā'laam, "Am I not your donkey, which you have ridden all your life to this day? Have I been in the habit of treating you this way?" And he said, "No."

31 Then the LORD opened the eyes of Bā'laam, and he saw the angel of the LORD standing in the road, with his drawn sword in his hand; and he bowed down, falling on his face. [32] The angel of the LORD said to him, "Why have you struck your donkey these three times? I have come out as an adversary,[x] because your way is perverse[x] before me. [33] The donkey saw me, and turned away from me these three times. If it had not turned away from me, surely just now I would have killed you and let it live." [34] Then Bā'-laam said to the angel of the LORD, "I have sinned, for I did not know that you were standing in the road to oppose me. Now therefore, if it is displeasing to you, I will return home." [35] The angel of the LORD said to Bā'-laam, "Go with the men; but speak only what I tell you to speak." So Bā'laam went on with the officials of Bā'lak.

36 When Bā'lak heard that Bā'laam had come, he went out to meet him at Ir-mō'ab, on the boundary formed by the Ar'non, at the farthest point of the boundary. [37] Bā'lak said to Bā'laam, "Did I not send to summon you? Why

---

x Meaning of Heb uncertain

did you not come to me? Am I not able to honor you?" ³⁸Bă′laam said to Bă′lak, "I have come to you now, but do I have power to say just anything? The word God puts in my mouth, that is what I must say." ³⁹Then Bă′laam went with Bă′lak, and they came to Kir′i·ath-hū′zoth. ⁴⁰Bă′lak sacrificed oxen and sheep, and sent them to Bă′-laam and to the officials who were with him.

Balaam's First Oracle

41 On the next day Bă′lak took Bă′-laam and brought him up to Bă′moth-bă′al; and from there he could see part
23 of the people of Israel.^y ¹Then Bă′laam said to Bă′lak, "Build me seven altars here, and prepare seven bulls and seven rams for me." ²Bă′lak did as Bă′laam had said; and Bă′lak and Bă′laam offered a bull and a ram on each altar. ³Then Bă′laam said to Bă′lak, "Stay here beside your burnt offerings while I go aside. Perhaps the LORD will come to meet me. Whatever he shows me I will tell you." And he went to a bare height.

4 Then God met Bă′laam; and Bă′-laam said to him, "I have arranged the seven altars, and have offered a bull and a ram on each altar." ⁵The LORD put a word in Bă′laam's mouth, and said, "Return to Bă′lak, and this is what you must say." ⁶So he returned to Bă′lak,^z who was standing beside his burnt offerings with all the officials of Mō′ab. ⁷Then Bă′laam^a uttered his oracle, saying:

"Bă′lak has brought me from Ar′am,
  the king of Mō′ab from the eastern mountains:
'Come, curse Jacob for me;
  Come, denounce Israel!'
⁸ How can I curse whom God has not cursed?
  How can I denounce those whom the LORD has not denounced?
⁹ For from the top of the crags I see him,
  from the hills I behold him;
Here is a people living alone,
  and not reckoning itself among the nations!
¹⁰ Who can count the dust of Jacob,
  or number the dust-cloud^b of Israel?
Let me die the death of the upright,

and let my end be like his!"

11 Then Bă′lak said to Bă′laam, "What have you done to me? I brought you to curse my enemies, but now you have done nothing but bless them." ¹²He answered, "Must I not take care to say what the LORD puts into my mouth?"

Balaam's Second Oracle

13 So Bă′lak said to him, "Come with me to another place from which you may see them; you shall see only part of them, and shall not see them all; then curse them for me from there." ¹⁴So he took him to the field of Zō′phim, to the top of Pis′gah. He built seven altars, and offered a bull and a ram on each altar. ¹⁵Bă′laam said to Bă′lak, "Stand here beside your burnt offerings, while I meet the LORD over there. ¹⁶The LORD met Bă′laam, put a word into his mouth, and said, "Return to Bă′lak, and this is what you shall say." ¹⁷When he came to him, he was standing beside his burnt offerings with the officials of Mō′ab. Bă′lak said to him, "What has the LORD said?" ¹⁸Then Bă′laam uttered his oracle, saying:

"Rise, Bă′lak, and hear;
  listen to me, O son of Zip′por:
¹⁹ God is not a human being, that he should lie,
  or a mortal, that he should change his mind.
Has he promised, and will he not do it?
  Has he spoken, and will he not fulfill it?
²⁰ See, I received a command to bless;
  he has blessed, and I cannot revoke it.
²¹ He has not beheld misfortune in Jacob;
  nor has he seen trouble in Israel.
The LORD their God is with them,
  acclaimed as a king among them.
²² God, who brings them out of Egypt,
  is like the horns of a wild ox for them.
²³ Surely there is no enchantment against Jacob,
  no divination against Israel;

now it shall be said of Jacob and
    Israel,
  'See what God has done!'
24 Look, a people rising up like a
    lioness,
    and rousing itself like a lion!
It does not lie down until it has
    eaten the prey
    and drunk the blood of the
     slain."

25 Then Bā′lak said to Bā′laam,
"Do not curse them at all, and do not
bless them at all." 26 But Bā′laam an-
swered Bā′lak, "Did I not tell you,
'Whatever the LORD says, that is what
I must do'?"

27 So Bā′lak said to Bā′laam,
"Come now, I will take you to another
place; perhaps it will please God that
you may curse them for me from
there." 28 So Bā′lak took Bā′laam to the
top of Pē′or, which overlooks the
wasteland.c 29 Bā′laam said to Bā′lak,
"Build me seven altars here, and prepare seven bulls and seven rams for
me." 30 So Bā′lak did as Bā′laam had
said, and offered a bull and a ram on
each altar.

Balaam's Third Oracle

24 Now Bā′laam saw that it
pleased the LORD to bless Is-
rael, so he did not go, as at other times,
to look for omens, but set his face toward the wilderness. 2 Bā′laam looked
up and saw Israel camping tribe by
tribe. Then the spirit of God came upon
him, 3 and he uttered his oracle, saying:

"The oracle of Bā′laam son of
    Bē′or,
  the oracle of the man whose
    eye is clear,d
4 the oracle of one who hears the
    words of God,
  who sees the vision of the
    Almighty,e
  who falls down, but with eyes
    uncovered:
5 how fair are your tents, O Jacob,
    your encampments, O Israel!
6 Like palm groves that stretch far
    away,
  like gardens beside a river,
  like aloes that the LORD has
    planted,
  like cedar trees beside the
    waters.
7 Water shall flow from his
    buckets,
  and his seed shall have
    abundant water,

his king shall be higher than
    A′gag,
  and his kingdom shall be
    exalted.
8 God who brings him out of
    Egypt,
  is like the horns of a wild ox
    for him;
he shall devour the nations that
    are his foes
  and break their bones.
He shall strike with his
    arrows.f
9 He crouched, he lay down like a
    lion,
  and like a lioness; who will
    rouse him up?
Blessed is everyone who blesses
    you,
  and cursed is everyone who
    curses you."

10 Then Bā′lak's anger was kindled
against Bā′laam, and he struck his
hands together. Bā′lak said to Bā′-
laam, "I summoned you to curse my
enemies, but instead you have blessed
them these three times. 11 Now be off
with you! Go home! I said, 'I will reward you richly,' but the LORD has denied you any reward." 12 And Bā′laam
said to Bā′lak, "Did I not tell your messengers whom you sent to me, 13 'If
Bā′lak should give me his house full of
silver and gold, I would not be able to
go beyond the word of the LORD, to do
either good or bad of my own will;
what the LORD says, that is what I will
say'? 14 So now, I am going to my people; let me advise you what this people
will do to your people in days to come."

Balaam's Fourth Oracle

15 So he uttered his oracle, saying:
"The oracle of Bā′laam son of
    Bē′or,
  the oracle of the man whose
    eye is clear,d
16 the oracle of one who hears the
    words of God,
  and knows the knowledge of
    the Most High,g
  who sees the vision of the
    Almighty,e
  who falls down, but with his
    eyes uncovered:
17 I see him, but not now;
  I behold him, but not near—

---

c Or *overlooks Jeshimon*　d Or *closed* or
open　e Traditional rendering of Heb
Shaddai　f Meaning of Heb uncertain
g Or *of Elyon*

a star shall come out of Jacob,
and a scepter shall rise out of
Israel;
it shall crush the borderlands[h]
of Mō'ab,
and the territory[i] of all the
Sheth'ītes.
18 Ē'dom will become a possession,
Sē'ir a possession of its
enemies,[j]
while Israel does valiantly.
19 One out of Jacob shall rule,
and destroy the survivors of
Ir."
20 Then he looked on Am'a·lek,
and uttered his oracle, saying:
"First among the nations was
Am'a·lek,
but its end is to perish forever."
21 Then he looked on the Ken'īte,
and uttered his oracle, saying:
"Enduring is your dwelling
place,
and your nest is set in the
rock;
22 yet Kāin is destined for burning.
How long shall As'shur take
you away captive?"
23 Again he uttered his oracle, saying:
"Alas, who shall live when God
does this?
24 But ships shall come from
Kit'tim
and shall afflict As'shur and
Ē'ber;
and he also shall perish
forever."
25 Then Bā'laam got up and went
back to his place, and Bā'lak also went
his way.

Worship of Baal of Peor

25 While Israel was staying at
Shit'tim, the people began to
have sexual relations with the women
of Mō'ab. 2 These invited the people to
the sacrifices of their gods, and the
people ate and bowed down to their
gods. 3 Thus Israel yoked itself to the
Bā'al of Pē'or, and the LORD's anger
was kindled against Israel. 4 The LORD
said to Moses, "Take all the chiefs of
the people, and impale them in the sun
before the LORD, in order that the
fierce anger of the LORD may turn
away from Israel." 5 And Moses said to
the judges of Israel, "Each of you shall
kill any of your people who have
yoked themselves to the Bā'al of
Pē'or."
6 Just then one of the Israelites

came and brought a Mid'i·an·īte
woman into his family, in the sight of
Moses and in the sight of the whole
congregation of the Israelites, while
they were weeping at the entrance of
the tent of meeting. 7 When Phin'e·has
son of El·ē·ā'zar, son of Aaron the
priest, saw it, he got up and left the
congregation. Taking a spear in his
hand, 8 he went after the Israelite man
into the tent, and pierced the two of
them, the Israelite and the woman,
through the belly. So the plague was
stopped among the people of Israel.
9 Nevertheless those that died by the
plague were twenty-four thousand.
10 The LORD spoke to Moses, saying: 11 "Phin'e·has son of El·ē·ā'zar,
son of Aaron the priest, has turned
back my wrath from the Israelites by
manifesting such zeal among them on
my behalf that in my jealousy I did not
consume the Israelites. 12 Therefore
say, 'I hereby grant him my covenant
of peace. 13 It shall be for him and for
his descendants after him a covenant
of perpetual priesthood, because he
was zealous for his God, and made
atonement for the Israelites.' "
14 The name of the slain Israelite
man, who was killed with the Mid'-
i·an·īte woman, was Zim'rī son of
Sa'lū, head of an ancestral house belonging to the Sim'ē·on·ītes. 15 The
name of the Mid'i·an·īte woman who
was killed was Cōz'bī daughter of Zur,
who was the head of a clan, an ancestral house in Mid'i·an.
16 The LORD said to Moses, 17 "Harass the Mid'i·an·ītes, and defeat them;
18 for they have harassed you by the
trickery with which they deceived you
in the affair of Pē'or, and in the affair
of Cōz'bī, the daughter of a leader of
Mid'i·an, their sister; she was killed on
the day of the plague that resulted
from Pē'or."

A Census of the New Generation

26 After the plague the LORD said
to Moses and to El·ē·ā'zar son
of Aaron the priest, 2 "Take a census of
the whole congregation of the Israelites, from twenty years old and upward, by their ancestral houses, everyone in Israel able to go to war." 3 Moses
and El·ē·ā'zar the priest spoke with
them in the plains of Mō'ab by the Jordan opposite Jericho, saying, 4 "Take a

---

hOr forehead   iSome Mss read skull
jHeb Seir, its enemies, a possession

census of the people,^{k} from twenty years old and upward," as the LORD commanded Moses.

The Israelites, who came out of the land of Egypt, were:

5 Reuben, the firstborn of Israel. The descendants of Reuben: of Hă'-noch, the clan of the Hă'noch·ītes; of Pal'lū, the clan of the Pal'lū·ītes; ^{6}of Hez'ron, the clan of the Hez'ron·ītes; of Car'mī, the clan of the Car'mītes. ^{7}These are the clans of the Reū'-ben·ītes; the number of those enrolled was forty-three thousand seven hundred thirty. ^{8}And the descendants of Pal'lū: E·lī'ab. ^{9}The descendants of E·lī'ab: Nem'ū·el, Dā'than, and A·bī'-ram. These are the same Dā'than and A·bī'ram, chosen from the congregation, who rebelled against Moses and Aaron in the company of Kō'rah, when they rebelled against the LORD, ^{10}and the earth opened its mouth and swallowed them up along with Kō'rah, when that company died, when the fire devoured two hundred fifty men; and they became a warning. ^{11}Notwithstanding, the sons of Kō'rah did not die.

12 The descendants of Sim'e·on by their clans: of Nem'ū·el, the clan of the Nem'ū·el·ītes; of Jā'min, the clan of the Jā'min·ītes; of Jā'chin, the clan of the Jā'chin·ītes; ^{13}of Zē'rah, the clan of the Zē'ra·hītes; of Shā'ūl, the clan of the Shā'u·lītes.^{l} ^{14}These are the clans of the Sim'e·on·ītes, twenty-two thousand two hundred.

15 The children of Gad by their clans: of Zē'phon, the clan of the Zē'-phon·ītes; of Hag'gī, the clan of the Hag'gītes; of Shū'nī, the clan of the Shū'nītes; ^{16}of Oz'nī, the clan of the Oz'nītes; of Ē'rī, the clan of the Ē'rītes; ^{17}of Ar'od, the clan of the Ar'o·dītes; of A·rē'lī, the clan of the A·rē'lītes. ^{18}These are the clans of the Gad'ītes: the number of those enrolled was forty thousand five hundred.

19 The sons of Judah: Er and O'nan; Er and O'nan died in the land of Cā'-naan. ^{20}The descendants of Judah by their clans were: of Shē'lah, the clan of the Shē'la·nītes; of Per'ez, the clan of the Per'e·zītes; of Zē'rah, the clan of the Zē'ra·hītes. ^{21}The descendants of Per'ez were: of Hez'ron, the clan of the Hez'ron·ītes; of Hā'mul, the clan of the Hā'mul·ītes. ^{22}These are the clans of Judah: the number of those enrolled was seventy-six thousand five hundred.

23 The descendants of Is'sa·char by their clans: of Tō'la, the clan of the Tō'la·ītes; of Pū'vah, the clan of the Pū'nītes; ^{24}of Jash'ub, the clan of the Jash'ub·ītes; of Shim'ron, the clan of the Shim'ron·ītes. ^{25}These are the clans of Is'sa·char: sixty-four thousand three hundred enrolled.

26 The descendants of Zeb'ū·lun by their clans: of Sē'red, the clan of the Sē'red·ītes; of Ē'lon, the clan of the Ē'lon·ītes; of Jah'lē·el, the clan of the Jah'lē·el·ītes. ^{27}These are the clans of the Zeb'ū·lun·ītes; the number of those enrolled was sixty thousand five hundred.

28 The sons of Joseph by their clans: Ma·nas'seh and Ē'phra·im. ^{29}The descendants of Ma·nas'seh: of Mā'chir, the clan of the Mā'chir·ītes; and Mā'chir was the father of Gil'e·ad; of Gil'e·ad, the clan of the Gil'e·ad·ītes. ^{30}These are the descendants of Gil'-e·ad: of Ī·ē'zer, the clan of the Ī·ē'zer·ītes; of Hē'lek, the clan of the Hē'lek·ītes; ^{31}and of As'ri·el, the clan of the As'ri·el·ītes; and of Shē'chem, the clan of the Shē'chem·ītes; ^{32}and of She·mī'da, the clan of the She·mī'da·ītes; and of Hē'pher, the clan of the Hē'pher·ītes. ^{33}Now Ze·loph'e·had son of Hē'pher had no sons, but daughters: and the names of the daughters of Ze·loph'e·had were Mah'lah, Noah, Hog'lah, Mil'cah, and Tir'zah. ^{34}These are the clans of Ma·nas'seh; the number of those enrolled was fifty-two thousand seven hundred.

35 These are the descendants of Ē'phra·im according to their clans: of Shū·thē'lah, the clan of the Shū·the·lā'hītes; of Bē'cher, the clan of the Bē'cher·ītes; of Tā'han, the clan of the Tā'ha·nītes. ^{36}And these are the descendants of Shū·thē'lah: of Ē'ran, the clan of the Ē'ran·ītes. ^{37}These are the clans of the Ē'phra·im·ītes: the number of those enrolled was thirty-two thousand five hundred. These are the descendants of Joseph by their clans.

38 The descendants of Benjamin by their clans: of Bē'la, the clan of the Bē'la·ītes; of Ash'bel, the clan of the Ash'bel·ītes; of A·hī'ram, the clan of the A·hī'ram·ītes; ^{39}of She·phū'pham, the clan of the Shū'pham·ītes; of Hū'-pham, the clan of the Hū'pham·ītes.

^{k}Heb lacks *take a census of the people*: Compare verse 2 ^{l}Or *Saul . . . Saulites*

NUMBERS

40 And the sons of Bē'la were Ard and
Nā'a·man: of Ard, the clan of the Ard'-
ites; of Nā'a·man, the clan of the Nā'-
a·mites. 41 These are the descendants
of Benjamin by their clans; the number
of those enrolled was forty-five thousand six hundred.

42 These are the descendants of
Dan by their clans: of Shū'ham, the
clan of the Shū'ham·ites. These are the
clans of Dan by their clans. 43 All the
clans of the Shū'ham·ites: sixty-four
thousand four hundred enrolled.

44 The descendants of Ash'er by
their families: of Im'nah, the clan of
the Im'nites; of Ish'vī, the clan of the
Ish'vites; of Bē·rī'ah, the clan of the
Bē·rī'ites. 45 Of the descendants of
Bē·rī'ah: of Hē'ber, the clan of the Hē'-
ber·ites; of Mal'chi·el, the clan of the
Mal'chi·el·ites. 46 And the name of the
daughter of Ash'er was Sē'rah.
47 These are the clans of the Ash'-
er·ites: the number of those enrolled
was fifty-three thousand four hundred.

48 The descendants of Naph'ta·lī by
their clans: of Jah'zē·el, the clan of the
Jah'zē·el·ites; of Gū'nī, the clan of
the Gū'nites; 49 of Jē'zer, the clan of
the Jē'zer·ites; of Shil'lem, the clan
of the Shil'lem·ites. 50 These are the
Naph'ta·lites m by their clans: the number of those enrolled was forty-five
thousand four hundred.

51 This was the number of the Israelites enrolled: six hundred and one
thousand seven hundred thirty.

52 The LORD spoke to Moses, saying: 53 To these the land shall be apportioned for inheritance according to the
number of names. 54 To a large tribe
you shall give a large inheritance, and
to a small tribe you shall give a small
inheritance; every tribe shall be given
its inheritance according to its enrollment. 55 But the land shall be apportioned by lot; according to the names
of their ancestral tribes they shall inherit. 56 Their inheritance shall be apportioned according to lot between the
larger and the smaller.

57 This is the enrollment of the Lē'-
vites by their clans: of Ger'shon, the
clan of the Ger'shon·ites; of Kō'hath,
the clan of the Kō'hath·ites; of
Me·rar'ī, the clan of the Me·rar'ites.
58 These are the clans of Levi: the clan
of the Lib'nites, the clan of the Hē'-
bron·ites, the clan of the Mah'lites, the
clan of the Mū'shites, the clan of the
Kō'ra·hites. Now Kō'hath was the father of Am'ram. 59 The name of

Am'ram's wife was Joch'e·bed daughter of Levi, who was born to Levi in
Egypt; and she bore to Am'ram:
Aaron, Moses, and their sister Miriam.
60 To Aaron were born Nā'dab,
A·bī'hū, El·ē·ā'zar, and Ith'a·mar.
61 But Nā'dab and A·bī'hū died when
they offered illicit fire before the LORD.
62 The number of those enrolled was
twenty-three thousand, every male
one month old and up; for they were
not enrolled among the Israelites because there was no allotment given to
them among the Israelites.

63 These were those enrolled by
Moses and El·ē·ā'zar the priest, who
enrolled the Israelites in the plains of
Mō'ab by the Jordan opposite Jericho.
64 Among these there was not one of
those enrolled by Moses and Aaron the
priest, who had enrolled the Israelites
in the wilderness of Sinai. 65 For the
LORD had said of them, "They shall die
in the wilderness." Not one of them
was left, except Caleb son of Je·phūn'-
neh and Joshua son of Nun.

The Daughters of Zelophehad

27 Then the daughters of Ze·loph'-
e·had came forward. Ze·loph'-
e·had was son of Hē'pher son of Gil'-
e·ad son of Mā'chir son of Ma·nas'seh
son of Joseph, a member of the
Ma·nas'site clans. The names of his
daughters were: Mah'lah, Noah, Hog'-
lah, Mil'cah, and Tir'zah. 2 They stood
before Moses, El·ē·ā'zar the priest, the
leaders, and all the congregation, at
the entrance of the tent of meeting, and
they said, 3 "Our father died in the wilderness; he was not among the company of those who gathered themselves together against the LORD in the
company of Kō'rah, but died for his
own sin; and he had no sons. 4 Why
should the name of our father be taken
away from his clan because he had no
son? Give to us a possession among
our father's brothers."

5 Moses brought their case before
the LORD. 6 And the LORD spoke to Moses, saying: 7 The daughters of
Ze·loph'e·had are right in what they
are saying; you shall indeed let them
possess an inheritance among their father's brothers and pass the inheritance of their father on to them. 8 You
shall also say to the Israelites, "If a
man dies, and has no son, then you
shall pass his inheritance on to his

m Heb *clans of Naphtali*

daughter. 9 If he has no daughter, then you shall give his inheritance to his brothers. 10 If he has no brothers, then you shall give his inheritance to his father's brothers. 11 And if his father has no brothers, then you shall give his inheritance to the nearest kinsman of his clan, and he shall possess it. It shall be for the Israelites a statute and ordinance, as the LORD commanded Moses."

Joshua Appointed Moses' Successor
(Deut 31.1–8)

12 The LORD said to Moses, "Go up this mountain of the Ab′a·rim range, and see the land that I have given to the Israelites. 13 When you have seen it, you also shall be gathered to your people, as your brother Aaron was, 14 because you rebelled against my word in the wilderness of Zin when the congregation quarreled with me. n You did not show my holiness before their eyes at the waters." (These are the waters of Mer′i·bath-kā′desh in the wilderness of Zin.) 15 Moses spoke to the LORD, saying, 16 "Let the LORD, the God of the spirits of all flesh, appoint someone over the congregation 17 who shall go out before them and come in before them, who shall lead them out and bring them in, so that the congregation of the LORD may not be like sheep without a shepherd." 18 So the LORD said to Moses, "Take Joshua son of Nun, a man in whom is the spirit, and lay your hand upon him; 19 have him stand before El·ē·a′zar the priest and all the congregation, and commission him in their sight. 20 You shall give him some of your authority, so that all the congregation of the Israelites may obey. 21 But he shall stand before El·ē·a′zar the priest, who shall inquire for him by the decision of the U′rim before the LORD; at his word they shall go out, and at his word they shall come in, both he and all the Israelites with him, the whole congregation." 22 So Moses did as the LORD commanded him. He took Joshua and had him stand before El·ē·a′zar the priest and the whole congregation; 23 he laid his hands on him and commissioned him—as the LORD had directed through Moses.

Daily Offerings
(Ex 29.38–46)

28 The LORD spoke to Moses, saying: 2 Command the Israelites,

and say to them: My offering, the food for my offerings by fire, my pleasing odor, you shall take care to offer to me at its appointed time. 3 And you shall say to them, This is the offering by fire that you shall offer to the LORD: two male lambs a year old without blemish, daily, as a regular offering. 4 One lamb you shall offer in the morning, and the other lamb you shall offer at twilight o 5 also one-tenth of an ephah of choice flour for a grain offering, mixed with one-fourth of a hin of beaten oil. 6 It is a regular burnt offering, ordained at Mount Sinai for a pleasing odor, an offering by fire to the LORD. 7 Its drink offering shall be one-fourth of a hin for each lamb; in the sanctuary you shall pour out a drink offering of strong drink to the LORD. 8 The other lamb you shall offer at twilight o with a grain offering and a drink offering like the one in the morning; you shall offer it as an offering by fire, a pleasing odor to the LORD.

Sabbath Offerings

9 On the sabbath day: two male lambs a year old without blemish, and two-tenths of an ephah of choice flour for a grain offering, mixed with oil, and its drink offering— 10 this is the burnt offering for every sabbath, in addition to the regular burnt offering and its drink offering.

Monthly Offerings

11 At the beginnings of your months you shall offer a burnt offering to the LORD: two young bulls, one ram, seven male lambs a year old without blemish; 12 also three-tenths of an ephah of choice flour for a grain offering, mixed with oil, for each bull; and two-tenths of choice flour for a grain offering, mixed with oil, for the one ram; 13 and one-tenth of choice flour mixed with oil as a grain offering for every lamb—a burnt offering of pleasing odor, an offering by fire to the LORD. 14 Their drink offerings shall be half a hin of wine for a bull, one-third of a hin for a ram, and one-fourth of a hin for a lamb. This is the burnt offering of every month throughout the months of the year. 15 And there shall be one male goat for a sin offering to the LORD; it shall be offered in addition

n Heb lacks with me   o Heb between the two evenings

to the regular burnt offering and its drink offering.

Offerings at Passover
(Lev 23.5–14)

16 On the fourteenth day of the first month there shall be a passover offering to the LORD. 17 And on the fifteenth day of this month is a festival; seven days shall unleavened bread be eaten. 18 On the first day there shall be a holy convocation. You shall not work at your occupations. 19 You shall offer an offering by fire, a burnt offering to the LORD: two young bulls, one ram, and seven male lambs a year old; see that they are without blemish. 20 Their grain offering shall be of choice flour mixed with oil: three-tenths of an ephah shall you offer for a bull, and two-tenths for a ram; 21 one-tenth shall you offer for each of the seven lambs; 22 also one male goat for a sin offering, to make atonement for you. 23 You shall offer these in addition to the burnt offering of the morning, which belongs to the regular burnt offering. 24 In the same way you shall offer daily, for seven days, the food of an offering by fire, a pleasing odor to the LORD; it shall be offered in addition to the regular burnt offering and its drink offering. 25 And on the seventh day you shall have a holy convocation; you shall not work at your occupations.

Offerings at the Festival of Weeks
(Lev 23.15–22)

26 On the day of the first fruits, when you offer a grain offering of new grain to the LORD at your festival of weeks, you shall have a holy convocation; you shall not work at your occupations. 27 You shall offer a burnt offering, a pleasing odor to the LORD: two young bulls, one ram, seven male lambs a year old. 28 Their grain offering shall be of choice flour mixed with oil, three-tenths of an ephah for each bull, two-tenths for one ram, 29 one-tenth for each of the seven lambs; 30 with one male goat, to make atonement for you. 31 In addition to the regular burnt offering with its grain offering, you shall offer them and their drink offering. They shall be without blemish.

Offerings at the Festival of Trumpets
(Lev 23.23–25)

29 On the first day of the seventh month you shall have a holy convocation; you shall not work at your occupations. It is a day for you to blow the trumpets, 2 and you shall offer a burnt offering, a pleasing odor to the LORD: one young bull, one ram, seven male lambs a year old without blemish. 3 Their grain offering shall be of choice flour mixed with oil, three-tenths of one ephah for the bull, two-tenths for the ram, 4 and one-tenth for each of the seven lambs; 5 with one male goat for a sin offering, to make atonement for you. 6 These are in addition to the burnt offering of the new moon and its grain offering, and the regular burnt offering and its grain offering, and their drink offerings, according to the ordinance for them, a pleasing odor, an offering by fire to the LORD.

Offerings on the Day of Atonement
(Lev 23.26–32)

7 On the tenth day of this seventh month you shall have a holy convocation, and deny yourselves; p you shall do no work. 8 You shall offer a burnt offering to the LORD, a pleasing odor: one young bull, one ram, seven male lambs a year old. They shall be without blemish. 9 Their grain offering shall be of choice flour mixed with oil, three-tenths of an ephah for the bull, two-tenths for the one ram, 10 one-tenth for each of the seven lambs; 11 with one male goat for a sin offering, in addition to the sin offering of atonement, and the regular burnt offering and its grain offering, and their drink offerings.

Offerings at the Festival of Booths
(Lev 23.33–44)

12 On the fifteenth day of the seventh month you shall have a holy convocation; you shall not work at your occupations. You shall celebrate a festival to the LORD seven days. 13 You shall offer a burnt offering, an offering by fire, a pleasing odor to the LORD: thirteen young bulls, two rams, fourteen male lambs a year old. They shall be without blemish. 14 Their grain offering shall be of choice flour mixed with oil, three-tenths of an ephah for each of the thirteen bulls, two-tenths for each of the two rams, 15 and one-tenth for each of the fourteen lambs; 16 also one male goat for a sin offering, in addition to the regular burnt offer-

p Or and fast

ing, its grain offering and its drink offering.

17 On the second day: twelve young bulls, two rams, fourteen male lambs a year old without blemish, 18 with the grain offering and the drink offerings for the bulls, for the rams, and for the lambs, as prescribed in accordance with their number; 19 also one male goat for a sin offering, in addition to the regular burnt offering and its grain offering, and their drink offerings.

20 On the third day: eleven bulls, two rams, fourteen male lambs a year old without blemish, 21 with the grain offering and the drink offerings for the bulls, for the rams, and for the lambs, as prescribed in accordance with their number; 22 also one male goat for a sin offering, in addition to the regular burnt offering and its grain offering and its drink offering.

23 On the fourth day: ten bulls, two rams, fourteen male lambs a year old without blemish, 24 with the grain offering and the drink offerings for the bulls, for the rams, and for the lambs, as prescribed in accordance with their number; 25 also one male goat for a sin offering, in addition to the regular burnt offering, its grain offering and its drink offering.

26 On the fifth day: nine bulls, two rams, fourteen male lambs a year old without blemish, 27 with the grain offering and the drink offerings for the bulls, for the rams, and for the lambs, as prescribed in accordance with their number; 28 also one male goat for a sin offering, in addition to the regular burnt offering and its grain offering and its drink offering.

29 On the sixth day: eight bulls, two rams, fourteen male lambs a year old without blemish, 30 with the grain offering and the drink offerings for the bulls, for the rams, and for the lambs, as prescribed in accordance with their number; 31 also one male goat for a sin offering, in addition to the regular burnt offering, its grain offering, and its drink offerings.

32 On the seventh day: seven bulls, two rams, fourteen male lambs a year old without blemish, 33 with the grain offering and the drink offerings for the bulls, for the rams, and for the lambs, as prescribed in accordance with their number; 34 also one male goat for a sin offering, besides the regular burnt offering, its grain offering, and its drink offering.

35 On the eighth day you shall have a solemn assembly; you shall not work at your occupations. 36 You shall offer a burnt offering, an offering by fire, a pleasing odor to the LORD: one bull, one ram, seven male lambs a year old without blemish, 37 and the grain offering and the drink offerings for the bull, for the ram, and for the lambs, as prescribed in accordance with their number; 38 also one male goat for a sin offering, in addition to the regular burnt offering and its grain offering and its drink offering.

39 These you shall offer to the LORD at your appointed festivals, in addition to your votive offerings and your freewill offerings, as your burnt offerings, your grain offerings, your drink offerings, and your offerings of well-being.

40 q So Moses told the Israelites everything just as the LORD had commanded Moses.

Vows Made by Women

30 Then Moses said to the heads of the tribes of the Israelites: This is what the LORD has commanded. 2 When a man makes a vow to the LORD, or swears an oath to bind himself by a pledge, he shall not break his word; he shall do according to all that proceeds out of his mouth.

3 When a woman makes a vow to the LORD, or binds herself by a pledge, while within her father's house, in her youth, 4 and her father hears of her vow or her pledge by which she has bound herself, and says nothing to her; then all her vows shall stand, and any pledge by which she has bound herself shall stand. 5 But if her father expresses disapproval to her at the time that he hears of it, no vow of hers, and no pledge by which she has bound herself, shall stand; and the LORD will forgive her, because her father had expressed to her his disapproval.

6 If she marries, while obligated by her vows or any thoughtless utterance of her lips by which she has bound herself, 7 and her husband hears of it and says nothing to her at the time that he hears, then her vows shall stand, and her pledges by which she has bound herself shall stand. 8 But if, at the time that her husband hears of it, he expresses disapproval to her, then he shall nullify the vow by which she was obligated, or the thoughtless utterance

q Ch 30.1 in Heb

of her lips, by which she bound herself; and the LORD will forgive her. 9(But every vow of a widow or of a divorced woman, by which she has bound herself, shall be binding upon her.) 10And if she made a vow in her husband's house, or bound herself by a pledge with an oath, 11and her husband heard it and said nothing to her, and did not express disapproval to her, then all her vows shall stand, and any pledge by which she bound herself shall stand. 12But if her husband nullifies them at the time that he hears them, then whatever proceeds out of her lips concerning her vows, or concerning her pledge of herself, shall not stand. Her husband has nullified them, and the LORD will forgive her. 13Any vow or any binding oath to deny herself,r her husband may allow to stand, or her husband may nullify. 14But if her husband says nothing to her from day to day,s then he validates all her vows, or all her pledges, by which she is obligated; he has validated them, because he said nothing to her at the time that he heard of them. 15But if he nullifies them some time after he has heard of them, then he shall bear her guilt.

16 These are the statutes that the LORD commanded Moses concerning a husband and his wife, and a father and his daughter while she is still young and in her father's house.

War against Midian

31 The LORD spoke to Moses, saying, 2"Avenge the Israelites on the Mid'i·an·ites; afterward you shall be gathered to your people." 3So Moses said to the people, "Arm some of your number for the war, so that they may go against Mid'i·an, to execute the LORD's vengeance on Mid'i·an. 4You shall send a thousand from each of the tribes of Israel to the war." 5So out of the thousands of Israel, a thousand from each tribe were conscripted, twelve thousand armed for battle. 6Moses sent them to the war, a thousand from each tribe, along with Phin'-e·has son of El·e·a'zar the priest,t with the vessels of the sanctuary and the trumpets for sounding the alarm in his hand. 7They did battle against Mid'-i·an, as the LORD had commanded Moses, and killed every male. 8They killed the kings of Mid'i·an: E'vi, Rē'-kem, Zur, Hur, and Rē'ba, the five kings of Mid'i·an, in addition to others who were slain by them; and they also killed Ba'laam son of Bē'or with the sword. 9The Israelites took the women of Mid'i·an and their little ones captive; and they took all their cattle, their flocks, and all their goods as booty. 10All their towns where they had settled, and all their encampments, they burned, 11but they took all the spoil and all the booty, both people and animals. 12Then they brought the captives and the booty and the spoil to Moses, to El·e·a'zar the priest, and to the congregation of the Israelites, at the camp on the plains of Mō'ab by the Jordan at Jericho.

Return from the War

13 Moses, El·e·a'zar the priest, and all the leaders of the congregation went to meet them outside the camp. 14Moses became angry with the officers of the army, the commanders of thousands and the commanders of hundreds, who had come from service in the war. 15Moses said to them, "Have you allowed all the women to live? 16These women here, on Ba'-laam's advice, made the Israelites act treacherously against the LORD in the affair of Pē'or, so that the plague came among the congregation of the LORD. 17Now therefore, kill every male among the little ones, and kill every woman who has known a man by sleeping with him. 18But all the young girls who have not known a man by sleeping with him, keep alive for yourselves. 19Camp outside the camp seven days; whoever of you has killed any person or touched a corpse, purify yourselves and your captives on the third and on the seventh day. 20You shall purify every garment, every article of skin, everything made of goats' hair, and every article of wood."

21 El·e·a'zar the priest said to the troops who had gone to battle: "This is the statute of the law that the LORD has commanded Moses: 22gold, silver, bronze, iron, tin, and lead— 23everything that can withstand fire, shall be passed through fire, and it shall be clean. Nevertheless it shall also be purified with the water for purification; and whatever cannot withstand fire, shall be passed through the water. 24You must wash your clothes on the seventh day, and you shall be clean;

---

rOr to fast   sOr from that day to the next   tGk: Heb adds to the war afterward you may come into the camp."

Disposition of Captives and Booty

25 The LORD spoke to Moses, saying, 26"You and El·e·a'zar the priest and the heads of the ancestral houses of the congregation make an inventory of the booty captured, both human and animal. 27Divide the booty into two parts, between the warriors who went out to battle and all the congregation. 28From the share of the warriors who went out to battle, set aside as tribute for the LORD, one item out of every five hundred, whether persons, oxen, donkeys, sheep, or goats. 29Take it from their half and give it to El·e·a'zar the priest as an offering to the LORD. 30But from the Israelites' half you shall take one out of every fifty, whether persons, oxen, donkeys, sheep, or goats—all the animals—and give them to the Le'vites who have charge of the tabernacle of the LORD."

31 Then Moses and El·e·a'zar the priest did as the LORD had commanded Moses:

32 The booty remaining from the spoil that the troops had taken totaled six hundred seventy-five thousand sheep, 33seventy-two thousand oxen, 34sixty-one thousand donkeys, 35and thirty-two thousand persons in all, women who had not known a man by sleeping with him.

36 The half-share, the portion of those who had gone out to war, was in number three hundred thirty-seven thousand five hundred sheep and goats, 37and the LORD's tribute of sheep and goats was six hundred seventy-five. 38The oxen were thirty-six thousand, of which the LORD's tribute was seventy-two. 39The donkeys were thirty thousand five hundred, of which the LORD's tribute was sixty-one. 40The persons were sixteen thousand, of which the LORD's tribute was thirty-two persons. 41Moses gave the tribute, the offering for the LORD, to El·e·a'zar the priest, as the LORD had commanded Moses.

42 As for the Israelites' half, which Moses separated from that of the troops, 43the congregation's half was three hundred thirty-seven thousand five hundred sheep and goats, 44thirty-six thousand oxen, 45thirty thousand five hundred donkeys, 46and sixteen thousand persons. 47From the Israelites' half Moses took one of every fifty,

both of persons and of animals, and gave them to the Le'vites who had charge of the tabernacle of the LORD; as the LORD had commanded Moses.

48 Then the officers who were over the thousands of the army, the commanders of thousands and the commanders of hundreds, approached Moses, 49and said to Moses, "Your servants have counted the warriors who are under our command, and not one of us is missing. 50And we have brought the LORD's offering, what each of us found, articles of gold, armlets and bracelets, signet rings, earrings, and pendants, to make atonement for ourselves before the LORD." 51Moses and El·e·a'zar the priest received the gold from them, all in the form of crafted articles. 52And all the gold of the offering that they offered to the LORD, from the commanders of thousands and the commanders of hundreds, was sixteen thousand seven hundred fifty shekels. 53(The troops had all taken plunder for themselves.) 54So Moses and El·e·a'zar the priest received the gold from the commanders of thousands and of hundreds, and brought it into the tent of meeting as a memorial for the Israelites before the LORD.

Conquest and Division of Transjordan
(Deut 3.12–22)

32 Now the Reu'ben·ites and the Gad'ites owned a very great number of cattle. When they saw that the land of Ja'zer and the land of Gil'e·ad was a good place for cattle, 2the Gad'ites and the Reu'ben·ites came and spoke to Moses, to El·e·a'zar the priest, and to the leaders of the congregation, saying, 3"At'a·roth, Di'bon, Ja'zer, Nim'rah, Hesh'bon, E·le·a'leh, Se'bam, Ne'bo, and Be'on— 4the land that the LORD subdued before the congregation of Israel—is a land for cattle; and your servants have cattle." 5They continued, "If we have found favor in your sight, let this land be given to your servants for a possession; do not make us cross the Jordan."

6 But Moses said to the Gad'ites and to the Reu'ben·ites, "Shall your brothers go to war while you sit here? 7Why will you discourage the hearts of the Israelites from going over into the land that the LORD has given them? 8Your fathers did this, when I sent them from Ka'desh-bar'ne·a to see the land.

N U M B E R S

⁹When they went up to the Wadi Esh'-col and saw the land, they discouraged the hearts of the Israelites from going into the land that the LORD had given them. ¹⁰The LORD's anger was kindled on that day and he swore, saying, ¹¹'Surely none of the people who came up out of Egypt, from twenty years old and upward, shall see the land that I swore to give to Abraham, to Isaac, and to Jacob, because they have not unreservedly followed me— ¹²none except Caleb son of Je·phŭn'neh the Ken'iz·zīte and Joshua son of Nun, for they have unreservedly followed the LORD.' ¹³And the LORD's anger was kindled against Israel, and he made them wander in the wilderness for forty years, until all the generation that had done evil in the sight of the LORD had disappeared. ¹⁴And now you, a brood of sinners, have risen in place of your fathers, to increase the LORD's fierce anger against Israel! ¹⁵If you turn away from following him, he will again abandon them in the wilderness; and you will destroy all this people."

16 Then they came up to him and said, "We will build sheepfolds here for our flocks, and towns for our little ones, ¹⁷but we will take up arms as a vanguard*ᵘ* before the Israelites, until we have brought them to their place. Meanwhile our little ones will stay in the fortified towns because of the inhabitants of the land. ¹⁸We will not return to our homes until all the Israelites have obtained their inheritance. ¹⁹We will not inherit with them on the other side of the Jordan and beyond, because our inheritance has come to us on this side of the Jordan to the east."

20 So Moses said to them, "If you do this—if you take up arms to go before the LORD for the war, ²¹and all those of you who bear arms cross the Jordan before the LORD, until he has driven out his enemies from before him ²²and the land is subdued before the LORD— then after that you may return and be free of obligation to the LORD and to Israel, and this land shall be your possession before the LORD. ²³But if you do not do this, you have sinned against the LORD; and be sure your sin will find you out. ²⁴Build towns for your little ones, and folds for your flocks; but do what you have promised."

25 Then the Gad'ītes and the Reū'-ben·ītes said to Moses, "Your servants will do as my lord commands. ²⁶Our little ones, our wives, our flocks, and all our livestock shall remain there in the towns of Gil'e·ad; ²⁷but your servants will cross over, everyone armed for war, to do battle before the LORD, just as my lord orders."

28 So Moses gave command concerning them to El·e·ā'zar the priest, to Joshua son of Nun, and to the heads of the ancestral houses of the Israelite tribes. ²⁹And Moses said to them, "If the Gad'ītes and the Reū'ben·ītes, everyone armed for battle before the LORD, will cross over the Jordan with you and the land shall be subdued before you, then you shall give them the land of Gil'e·ad for a possession; ³⁰but if they will not cross over with you armed, they shall have possessions among you in the land of Cā'naan." ³¹The Gad'ītes and the Reū'ben·ītes answered, "As the LORD has spoken to your servants, so we will do. ³²We will cross over armed before the LORD into the land of Cā'naan, but the possession of our inheritance shall remain with us on this side of*ᵛ* the Jordan."

33 Moses gave to them—to the Gad'ītes and to the Reū'ben·ītes and to the half-tribe of Ma·nas'seh son of Joseph—the kingdom of King Sī'hon of the Am'o·rītes and the kingdom of King Og of Bā'shan, the land and its towns, with the territories of the surrounding towns. ³⁴And the Gad'ītes rebuilt Dī'bon, At'a·roth, A·rō'er, ³⁵At'roth-shō'phan, Jā'zer, Jog'be·hah, ³⁶Beth-nim'rah, and Beth-har'-an, fortified cities, and folds for sheep. ³⁷And the Reū'ben·ītes rebuilt Hesh'bon, E·le·ā'leh, Kir·i·a·thā'im, ³⁸Ne'bō, and Bā'al-me'on (some names being changed), and Sib'mah; and they gave names to the towns that they rebuilt. ³⁹The descendants of Mā'chir son of Ma·nas'seh went to Gil'e·ad, captured it, and dispossessed the Am'o·rītes who were there; ⁴⁰so Moses gave Gil'e·ad to Mā'chir son of Ma·nas'seh, and he settled there. ⁴¹Jā'ir son of Ma·nas'seh went and captured their villages, and renamed them Hav'voth-jā'ir.*ʷ* ⁴²And Nō'bah went and captured Ke'nath and its villages, and renamed it Nō'bah after himself.

*ᵘ*Cn: Heb *hurrying*   *ᵛ*Heb *beyond*
*ʷ*That is *the villages of Jair*

*The Stages of Israel's Journey
from Egypt*

33 These are the stages by which the Israelites went out of the land of Egypt in military formation under the leadership of Moses and Aaron. 2 Moses wrote down their starting points, stage by stage, by command of the LORD; and these are their stages according to their starting places. 3 They set out from Ram'e·ses in the first month, on the fifteenth day of the first month; on the day after the passover the Israelites went out boldly in the sight of all the Egyptians, 4 while the Egyptians were burying all their firstborn, whom the LORD had struck down among them. The LORD executed judgments even against their gods.

5 So the Israelites set out from Ram'e·ses, and camped at Suc'coth. 6 They set out from Suc'coth, and camped at E'tham, which is on the edge of the wilderness. 7 They set out from E'tham, and turned back to Pī-ha·hī'roth, which faces Bā'al-ze'phon; and they camped before Mig'dol. 8 They set out from Pī-ha·hī'roth, passed through the sea into the wilderness, went a three days' journey in the wilderness of E'tham, and camped at Mar'ah. 9 They set out from Mar'ah and came to E'lim; at E'lim there were twelve springs of water and seventy palm trees, and they camped there. 10 They set out from E'lim and camped by the Red Sea.x 11 They set out from the Red Seax and camped in the wilderness of Sin. 12 They set out from the wilderness of Sin and camped at Doph'kah. 13 They set out from Doph'kah and camped at A'lush. 14 They set out from A'lush and camped at Reph'i·dim, where there was no water for the people to drink. 15 They set out from Reph'i·dim and camped in the wilderness of Sinai. 16 They set out from the wilderness of Sinai and camped at Kib'roth-hat·ta'a·vah. 17 They set out from Kib'roth-hat·ta'a·vah and camped at Ha·ze'roth. 18 They set out from Ha·ze'roth and camped at Rith'mah. 19 They set out from Rith'mah and camped at Rim'mon-per'ez. 20 They set out from Rim'mon-per'ez and camped at Lib'nah. 21 They set out from Lib'nah and camped at Ris'sah. 22 They set out from Ris'sah and camped at Ke·he·la'thah. 23 They set out from Ke·he·la'thah and camped at Mount She'pher. 24 They set out from Mount She'pher and camped at Ha·ra'dah. 25 They set out from Ha·ra'dah and camped at Mak·he'loth. 26 They set out from Mak·he'loth and camped at Ta'hath. 27 They set out from Ta'hath and camped at Te'rah. 28 They set out from Te'rah and camped at Mith'kah. 29 They set out from Mith'kah and camped at Hash·mo'nah. 30 They set out from Hash·mo'nah and camped at Mo·se'roth. 31 They set out from Mo·se'roth and camped at Ben'e-ja'a·kan. 32 They set out from Ben'e-ja'a·kan and camped at Hor-hag·gid'gad. 33 They set out from Hor-hag·gid'gad and camped at Jot'ba·thah. 34 They set out from Jot'ba·thah and camped at A·bro'nah. 35 They set out from A·bro'nah and camped at E'zi·on-ge'ber. 36 They set out from E'zi·on-ge'ber and camped in the wilderness of Zin (that is, Ka'desh). 37 They set out from Ka'desh and camped at Mount Hor, on the edge of the land of E'dom.

38 Aaron the priest went up Mount Hor at the command of the LORD and died there in the fortieth year after the Israelites had come out of the land of Egypt, on the first day of the fifth month. 39 Aaron was one hundred twenty-three years old when he died on Mount Hor.

40 The Ca'naan·ite, the king of Ar'ad, who lived in the Neg'eb in the land of Ca'naan, heard of the coming of the Israelites.

41 They set out from Mount Hor and camped at Zal·mo'nah. 42 They set out from Zal·mo'nah and camped at Pu'non. 43 They set out from Pu'non and camped at O'both. 44 They set out from O'both and camped at I'ye-ab'a·rim, in the territory of Mo'ab. 45 They set out from I'yim and camped at Di'bon-gad. 46 They set out from Di'bon-gad and camped at Al'mon-dib·la·tha'im. 47 They set out from Al'mon-dib·la·tha'im and camped in the mountains of Ab'a·rim, before Ne'bo. 48 They set out from the mountains of Ab'a·rim and camped in the plains of Mo'ab by the Jordan at Jericho; 49 they camped by the Jordan from Beth-jesh'i·moth as far as A'bel-shit'tim in the plains of Mo'ab.

Directions for the Conquest of Canaan

50 In the plains of Mo'ab by the Jordan at Jericho, the LORD spoke to Mo-

x Or *Sea of Reeds*

N
U
M
B
E
R
S

ses, saying: 51 Speak to the Israelites, and say to them: When you cross over the Jordan into the land of Ca′naan, 52 you shall drive out all the inhabitants of the land from before you, destroy all their figured stones, destroy all their cast images, and demolish all their high places. 53 You shall take possession of the land and settle in it, for I have given you the land to possess. 54 You shall apportion the land by lot according to your clans; to a large one you shall give a large inheritance, and to a small one you shall give a small inheritance; the inheritance shall belong to the person on whom the lot falls; according to your ancestral tribes you shall inherit. 55 But if you do not drive out the inhabitants of the land from before you, then those whom you let remain shall be as barbs in your eyes and thorns in your sides; they shall trouble you in the land where you are settling. 56 And I will do to you as I thought to do to them.

The Boundaries of the Land

34 The LORD spoke to Moses, saying: 2 Command the Israelites, and say to them: When you enter the land of Ca′naan (this is the land that shall fall to you for an inheritance, the land of Ca′naan, defined by its boundaries), 3 your south sector shall extend from the wilderness of Zin along the side of E′dom. Your southern boundary shall begin from the end of the Dead Sea y on the east; 4 your boundary shall turn south of the ascent of Ak·rab′bim, and cross to Zin, and its outer limit shall be south of Ka′desh-bar′ne·a; then it shall go on to Ha′zar-ad′dar, and cross to Az′mon; 5 the boundary shall turn from Az′mon to the Wadi of Egypt, and its termination shall be at the Sea.

6 For the western boundary, you shall have the Great Sea and its z coast; this shall be your western boundary.

7 This shall be your northern boundary: from the Great Sea you shall mark out your line to Mount Hor; 8 from Mount Hor you shall mark it out to Le′bo-ha′math, and the outer limit of the boundary shall be at Ze′dad; 9 then the boundary shall extend to Ziph′ron, and its end shall be at Ha′-zar-e′nan; this shall be your northern boundary.

10 You shall mark out your eastern boundary from Ha′zar-e′nan to She′-

pham; 11 and the boundary shall continue down from She′pham to Rib′lah on the east side of A′in; and the boundary shall go down, and reach the eastern slope of the sea of Chin′ne·reth; 12 and the boundary shall go down to the Jordan, and its end shall be at the Dead Sea. y This shall be your land with its boundaries all around.

13 Moses commanded the Israelites, saying: This is the land that you shall inherit by lot, which the LORD has commanded to give to the nine tribes and to the half-tribe; 14 for the tribe of the Reu′ben·ites by their ancestral houses and the tribe of the Gad′ites by their ancestral houses have taken their inheritance, and also the half-tribe of Ma·nas′seh; 15 the two tribes and the half-tribe have taken their inheritance beyond the Jordan at Jericho eastward, toward the sunrise.

Tribal Leaders

16 The LORD spoke to Moses, saying: 17 These are the names of the men who shall apportion the land to you for inheritance: the priest El·e·a′zar and Joshua son of Nun. 18 You shall take one leader of every tribe to apportion the land for inheritance. 19 These are the names of the men: Of the tribe of Judah, Caleb son of Je·phun′neh. 20 Of the tribe of the Sim′e·on·ites, She-mu′el son of Am·mi′hud. 21 Of the tribe of Benjamin, E·li′dad son of Chis′lon. 22 Of the tribe of the Dan′ites a leader, Buk′ki son of Jog′li. 23 Of the Jo′seph·ites: of the tribe of the Ma·nas′sites a leader, Han′ni·el son of E′phod, 24 and of the tribe of the E′phra·im·ites a leader, Ke·mu′el son of Shiph′tan. 25 Of the tribe of the Zeb′-u·lun·ites a leader, E·li·za′phan son of Par′nach. 26 Of the tribe of the Is′-sa·char·ites a leader, Pal′ti·el son of Az′zan. 27 And of the tribe of the Ash′-er·ites a leader, A·hi′hud son of She·lo′mi. 28 Of the tribe of the Naph′-ta·lites a leader, Pe·dah′el son of Am·mi′hud. 29 These were the ones whom the LORD commanded to apportion the inheritance for the Israelites in the land of Ca′naan.

Cities for the Levites

35 In the plains of Mo′ab by the Jordan at Jericho, the LORD spoke to Moses, saying: 2 Command the Israelites to give, from the inheri-

y Heb *Salt Sea*   z Syr: Heb lacks *its*

tance that they possess, towns for the Lē'vītes to live in; you shall also give to the Lē'vītes pasture lands surrounding the towns. ³The towns shall be theirs to live in, and their pasture lands shall be for their cattle, for their livestock, and for all their animals. ⁴The pasture lands of the towns, which you shall give to the Lē'vītes, shall reach from the wall of the town outward a thousand cubits all around. ⁵You shall measure, outside the town, for the east side two thousand cubits, for the south side two thousand cubits, for the west side two thousand cubits, and for the north side two thousand cubits, with the town in the middle; this shall belong to them as pasture land for their towns.

6 The towns that you give to the Lē'vītes shall include the six cities of refuge, where you shall permit a slayer to flee, and in addition to them you shall give forty-two towns. ⁷The towns that you give to the Lē'vītes shall total forty-eight, with their pasture lands. ⁸And as for the towns that you shall give from the possession of the Israelites, from the larger tribes you shall take many, and from the smaller tribes you shall take few; each, in proportion to the inheritance that it obtains, shall give of its towns to the Lē'vītes.

Cities of Refuge
(Deut 19.1–13; Josh 20.1–9)

9 The LORD spoke to Moses, saying: ¹⁰Speak to the Israelites, and say to them: When you cross the Jordan into the land of Cā'naan, ¹¹then you shall select cities to be cities of refuge for you, so that a slayer who kills a person without intent may flee there. ¹²The cities shall be for you a refuge from the avenger, so that the slayer may not die until there is a trial before the congregation.

13 The cities that you designate shall be six cities of refuge for you: ¹⁴you shall designate three cities beyond the Jordan, and three cities in the land of Cā'naan, to be cities of refuge. ¹⁵These six cities shall serve as refuge for the Israelites, for the resident or transient alien among them, so that anyone who kills a person without intent may flee there.

Concerning Murder and Blood Revenge

16 But anyone who strikes another with an iron object, and death ensues, is a murderer; the murderer shall be put to death. ¹⁷Or anyone who strikes another with a stone in hand that could cause death, and death ensues, is a murderer; the murderer shall be put to death. ¹⁸Or anyone who strikes another with a weapon of wood in hand that could cause death, and death ensues, is a murderer; the murderer shall be put to death. ¹⁹The avenger of blood is the one who shall put the murderer to death; when they meet, the avenger of blood shall execute the sentence. ²⁰Likewise, if someone pushes another from hatred, or hurls something at another, lying in wait, and death ensues, ²¹or in enmity strikes another with the hand, and death ensues, then the one who struck the blow shall be put to death; that person is a murderer; the avenger of blood shall put the murderer to death, when they meet.

22 But if someone pushes another suddenly without enmity, or hurls any object without lying in wait, ²³or, while handling any stone that could cause death, unintentionally[a] drops it on another and death ensues, though they were not enemies, and no harm was intended, ²⁴then the congregation shall judge between the slayer and the avenger of blood, in accordance with these ordinances; ²⁵and the congregation shall rescue the slayer from the avenger of blood. Then the congregation shall send the slayer back to the original city of refuge. The slayer shall live in it until the death of the high priest who was anointed with the holy oil. ²⁶But if the slayer shall at any time go outside the bounds of the original city of refuge, ²⁷and is found by the avenger of blood outside the bounds of the city of refuge, and is killed by the avenger, no bloodguilt shall be incurred. ²⁸For the slayer must remain in the city of refuge until the death of the high priest; but after the death of the high priest the slayer may return home.

29 These things shall be a statute and ordinance for you throughout your generations wherever you live.

30 If anyone kills another, the murderer shall be put to death on the evidence of witnesses; but no one shall be put to death on the testimony of a single witness. ³¹Moreover you shall accept no ransom for the life of a murderer who is subject to the death penalty; a murderer must be put to

_____
ᵃHeb *without seeing*

death. 32 Nor shall you accept ransom for one who has fled to a city of refuge, enabling the fugitive to return to live in the land before the death of the high priest. 33 You shall not pollute the land in which you live; for blood pollutes the land, and no expiation can be made for the land, for the blood that is shed in it, except by the blood of the one who shed it. 34 You shall not defile the land in which you live, in which I also dwell; for I the LORD dwell among the Israelites.

Marriage of Female Heirs

36 The heads of the ancestral houses of the clans of the descendants of Gil′e·ad son of Mā′chir son of Ma·nas′seh, of the Jō′seph·īte clans, came forward and spoke in the presence of Moses and the leaders, the heads of the ancestral houses of the Israelites; 2 they said, "The LORD commanded my lord to give the land for inheritance by lot to the Israelites; and my lord was commanded by the LORD to give the inheritance of our brother Ze′loph′e·had to his daughters. 3 But if they are married into another Israelite tribe, then their inheritance will be taken from the inheritance of our ancestors and added to the inheritance of the tribe into which they marry; so it will be taken away from the allotted portion of our inheritance. 4 And when the jubilee of the Israelites comes, then their inheritance will be added to the inheritance of the tribe into which they have married; and their inheritance will be taken from the inheritance of our ancestral tribe."

5 Then Moses commanded the Israelites according to the word of the LORD, saying, "The descendants of the tribe of Joseph are right in what they are saying. 6 This is what the LORD commands concerning the daughters of Ze·loph′e·had, 'Let them marry whom they think best; only it must be into a clan of their father's tribe that they are married, 7 so that no inheritance of the Israelites shall be transferred from one tribe to another; for all Israelites shall retain the inheritance of their ancestral tribes. 8 Every daughter who possesses an inheritance in any tribe of the Israelites shall marry one from the clan of her father's tribe, so that all Israelites may continue to possess their ancestral inheritance. 9 No inheritance shall be transferred from one tribe to another; for each of the tribes of the Israelites shall retain its own inheritance.' "

10 The daughters of Ze·loph′e·had did as the LORD had commanded Moses. 11 Mah′lah, Tir′zah, Hog′lah, Mil′cah, and Noah, the daughters of Ze·loph′e·had, married sons of their father's brothers. 12 They were married into the clans of the descendants of Ma·nas′seh son of Joseph, and their inheritance remained in the tribe of their father's clan.

13 These are the commandments and the ordinances that the LORD commanded through Moses to the Israelites in the plains of Mō′ab by the Jordan at Jericho.

DEUTERONOMY

Events at Horeb Recalled

1 These are the words that Moses spoke to all Israel beyond the Jordan—in the wilderness, on the plain opposite Sūph, between Par′an and Tō′phel, Lā′ban, Ha·zē′roth, and Di·za·hab′. 2 (By the way of Mount Sē′ir it takes eleven days to reach Kā′-desh-bar′ne·a from Hō′reb.) 3 In the fortieth year, on the first day of the eleventh month, Moses spoke to the Israelites just as the LORD had commanded him to speak to them. 4 This was after he had defeated King Sī′hon of the Am′o·rītes, who reigned in Hesh′bon, and King Og of Bā′shan,

who reigned in Ash'ta·roth and*a* in Ed're·i. [5] Beyond the Jordan in the land of Mo'ab, Moses undertook to expound this law as follows:

6 The LORD our God spoke to us at Ho'reb, saying, "You have stayed long enough at this mountain. [7] Resume your journey, and go into the hill country of the Am'o·rites as well as into the neighboring regions—the Ar'a·bah, the hill country, the She·phe'lah, the Neg'eb, and the seacoast—the land of the Ca'naan·ites and the Lebanon, as far as the great river, the river Euphrates. [8] See, I have set the land before you; go in and take possession of the land that I*b* swore to your ancestors, to Abraham, to Isaac, and to Jacob, to give to them and to their descendants after them."

Appointment of Tribal Leaders
(Ex 18.13–27)

9 At that time I said to you, "I am unable by myself to bear you. [10] The LORD your God has multiplied you, so that today you are as numerous as the stars of heaven. [11] May the LORD, the God of your ancestors, increase you a thousand times more and bless you, as he has promised you! [12] But how can I bear the heavy burden of your disputes all by myself? [13] Choose for each of your tribes individuals who are wise, discerning, and reputable to be your leaders." [14] You answered me, "The plan you have proposed is a good one." [15] So I took the leaders of your tribes, wise and reputable individuals, and installed them as leaders over you, commanders of thousands, commanders of hundreds, commanders of fifties, commanders of tens, and officials, throughout your tribes. [16] I charged your judges at that time: "Give the members of your community a fair hearing, and judge rightly between one person and another, whether citizen or resident alien. [17] You must not be partial in judging; hear out the small and the great alike; you shall not be intimidated by anyone, for the judgment is God's. Any case that is too hard for you, bring to me, and I will hear it." [18] So I charged you at that time with all the things that you should do.

Israel's Refusal to Enter the Land
(Num 13.1–33)

19 Then, just as the LORD our God had ordered us, we set out from Ho'reb and went through all that great and terrible wilderness that you saw, on the way to the hill country of the Am'o·rites, until we reached Ka'desh-bar'ne·a. [20] I said to you, "You have reached the hill country of the Am'o·rites, which the LORD our God is giving us. [21] See, the LORD your God has given the land to you; go up, take possession, as the LORD, the God of your ancestors, has promised you; do not fear or be dismayed."

22 All of you came to me and said, "Let us send men ahead of us to explore the land for us and bring back a report to us regarding the route by which we should go up and the cities we will come to." [23] The plan seemed good to me, and I selected twelve of you, one from each tribe. [24] They set out and went up into the hill country, and when they reached the Valley of Esh'col they spied it out [25] and gathered some of the land's produce, which they brought down to us. They brought back a report to us, and said, "It is a good land that the LORD our God is giving us."

26 But you were unwilling to go up. You rebelled against the command of the LORD your God; [27] you grumbled in your tents and said, "It is because the LORD hates us that he has brought us out of the land of Egypt, to hand us over to the Am'o·rites to destroy us. [28] Where are we headed? Our kindred have made our hearts melt by reporting, 'The people are stronger and taller than we; the cities are large and fortified up to heaven! We actually saw there the offspring of the An'a·kim!' " [29] I said to you, "Have no dread or fear of them. [30] The LORD your God, who goes before you, is the one who will fight for you, just as he did for you in Egypt before your very eyes, [31] and in the wilderness, where you saw how the LORD your God carried you, just as one carries a child, all the way that you traveled until you reached this place. [32] But in spite of this, you have no trust in the LORD your God, [33] who goes before you on the way to seek out a place for you to camp, in fire by night, and in the cloud by day, to show you the route you should take."

The Penalty for Israel's Rebellion
(Num 14.20–45)

34 When the LORD heard your

a Gk Syr Vg Compare Josh 12.4: Heb lacks *and*   *b* Sam Gk: MT *the* LORD

DEUTERONOMY

words, he was wrathful and swore: [35] "Not one of these—not one of this evil generation—shall see the good land that I swore to give to your ancestors, [36] except Caleb son of Je·phun'neh. He shall see it, and to him and to his descendants I will give the land on which he set foot, because of his complete fidelity to the LORD." [37] Even with me the LORD was angry on your account, saying, "You also shall not enter there. [38] Joshua son of Nun, your assistant, shall enter there; encourage him, for he is the one who will secure Israel's possession of it. [39] And as for your little ones, who you thought would become booty, your children, who today do not yet know right from wrong, they shall enter there; to them I will give it, and they shall take possession of it. [40] But as for you, journey back into the wilderness, in the direction of the Red Sea." [c]

41 You answered me, "We have sinned against the LORD! We are ready to go up and fight, just as the LORD our God commanded us." So all of you strapped on your battle gear, and thought it easy to go up into the hill country. [42] The LORD said to me, "Say to them, 'Do not go up and do not fight, for I am not in the midst of you; otherwise you will be defeated by your enemies.'" [43] Although I told you, you would not listen. You rebelled against the command of the LORD and presumptuously went up into the hill country. [44] The Am'o·rites who lived in that hill country then came out against you and chased you as bees do. They beat you down in Se'ir as far as Hor'mah. [45] When you returned and wept before the LORD, the LORD would neither heed your voice nor pay you any attention.

The Desert Years

46 After you had stayed at Ka'desh as many days as you did, [1] we journeyed back into the wilderness, in the direction of the Red Sea, [c] as the LORD had told me and skirted Mount Se'ir for many days. [2] Then the LORD said to me: [3] "You have been skirting this hill country long enough. Head north, [4] and charge the people as follows: You are about to pass through the territory of your kindred, the descendants of Esau, who live in Se'ir. They will be afraid of you, so, be very careful [5] not to engage in battle with them, for I will not give you even so

much as a foot's length of their land, since I have given Mount Se'ir to Esau as a possession. [6] You shall purchase food from them for money, so that you may eat; and you shall also buy water from them for money, so that you may drink. [7] Surely the LORD your God has blessed you in all your undertakings; he knows your going through this great wilderness. These forty years the LORD your God has been with you; you have lacked nothing." [8] So we passed by our kin, the descendants of Esau who live in Se'ir, leaving behind the route of the Ar'a·bah, and leaving behind E'lath and E'zi·on·ge'ber.

When we had headed out along the route of the wilderness of Mo'ab, [9] the LORD said to me: "Do not harass Mo'ab or engage them in battle, for I will not give you any of its land as a possession, since I have given Ar as a possession to the descendants of Lot." [10] (The E'mim—a large and numerous people, as tall as the An'a·kim—had formerly inhabited it. [11] Like the An'a·kim, they are usually reckoned as Reph'a·im, though the Mo'ab·ites call them E'mim. [12] Moreover, the Ho'rim had formerly inhabited Se'ir, but the descendants of Esau dispossessed them, destroying them and settling in their place, as Israel has done in the land that the LORD gave them as a possession.) [13] "Now then, proceed to cross over the Wadi Ze'red."

So we crossed over the Wadi Ze'red. [14] And the length of time we had traveled from Ka'desh-bar'ne·a until we crossed the Wadi Ze'red was thirty-eight years, until the entire generation of warriors had perished from the camp, as the LORD had sworn concerning them. [15] Indeed, the LORD's own hand was against them, to root them out from the camp, until all had perished.

16 Just as soon as all the warriors had died off from among the people, [17] the LORD spoke to me, saying, [18] "Today you are going to cross the boundary of Mo'ab at Ar. [19] When you approach the frontier of the Am'mon·ites, do not harass them or engage them in battle, for I will not give the land of the Am'mon·ites to you as a possession, because I have given it to the descendants of Lot." [20] (It also is usually reckoned as a land of Reph'a·im. Reph'a·im formerly inhab-

[c] Or *Sea of Reeds*

ited it, though the Am'mon·ites call them Zam·zum'mim, ²¹a strong and numerous people, as tall as the An'-a·kim. But the LORD destroyed them from before the Am'mon·ites so that they could dispossess them and settle in their place. ²²He did the same for the descendants of Esau, who live in Se'ir, by destroying the Ho'rim before them so that they could dispossess them and settle in their place even to this day. ²³As for the Av'vim, who had lived in settlements in the vicinity of Ga'za, the Caph'to·rim, who came from Caph'-tor, destroyed them and settled in their place.) ²⁴"Proceed on your journey and cross the Wadi Ar'non. See, I have handed over to you King Si'hon the Am'o·rite of Hesh'bon, and his land. Begin to take possession by engaging him in battle. ²⁵This day I will begin to put the dread and fear of you upon the peoples everywhere under heaven; when they hear report of you, they will tremble and be in anguish because of you."

Defeat of King Sihon
(Num 21.21–32)

26 So I sent messengers from the wilderness of Ked'e·moth to King Si'hon of Hesh'bon with the following terms of peace: ²⁷"If you let me pass through your land, I will travel only along the road; I will turn aside neither to the right nor to the left. ²⁸You shall sell me food for money, so that I may eat, and supply me water for money, so that I may drink. Only allow me to pass through on foot— ²⁹just as the descendants of Esau who live in Se'ir have done for me and likewise the Mo'-ab·ites who live in Ar—until I cross the Jordan into the land that the LORD our God is giving us." ³⁰But King Si'hon of Hesh'bon was not willing to let us pass through, for the LORD your God had hardened his spirit and made his heart defiant in order to hand him over to you, as he has now done.

31 The LORD said to me, "See, I have begun to give Si'hon and his land over to you. Begin now to take possession of his land." ³²So when Si'hon came out against us, he and all his people for battle at Ja'haz, ³³the LORD our God gave him over to us; and we struck him down, along with his offspring and all his people. ³⁴At that time we captured all his towns, and in each town we utterly destroyed men, women, and children. We left not a single survivor.

³⁵Only the livestock we kept as spoil for ourselves, as well as the plunder of the towns that we had captured. ³⁶From A·ro'er on the edge of the Wadi Ar'non (including the town that is in the wadi itself) as far as Gil'e·ad, there was no citadel too high for us. The LORD our God gave everything to us. ³⁷You did not encroach, however, on the land of the Am'mon·ites, avoiding the whole upper region of the Wadi Jab'bok as well as the towns of the hill country, just as ᵈ the LORD our God had charged.

Defeat of King Og
(Num 21.33–35)

3 When we headed up the road to Ba'shan, King Og of Ba'shan came out against us, he and all his people, for battle at Ed're·i. ²The LORD said to me, "Do not fear him, for I have handed him over to you, along with his people and his land. Do to him as you did to King Si'hon of the Am'o·rites, who reigned in Hesh'bon." ³So the LORD our God also handed over to us King Og of Ba'shan and all his people. We struck him down until not a single survivor was left. ⁴At that time we captured all his towns; there was no citadel that we did not take from them— sixty towns, the whole region of Ar'gob, the kingdom of Og in Ba'shan. ⁵All these were fortress towns with high walls, double gates, and bars, besides a great many villages. ⁶And we utterly destroyed them, as we had done to King Si'hon of Hesh'bon, in each city utterly destroying men, women, and children. ⁷But all the livestock and the plunder of the towns we kept as spoil for ourselves.

8 So at that time we took from the two kings of the Am'o·rites the land beyond the Jordan, from the Wadi Ar'non to Mount Hermon ⁹(the Si·do'ni·ans call Hermon Sir'i·on, while the Am'o·rites call it Se'nir), ¹⁰all the towns of the tableland, the whole of Gil'e·ad, and all of Ba'shan, as far as Sal'e·cah and Ed're·i, towns of Og's kingdom in Ba'shan. ¹¹(Now only King Og of Ba'shan was left of the remnant of the Reph'a·im. In fact his bed, an iron bed, can still be seen in Rab'bah of the Am'mon·ites. By the common cubit it is nine cubits long and four cubits wide.) ¹²As for the land that we took possession of at that time, I

ᵈGk Tg: Heb *and all*

gave to the Reu′ben·ites and Gad′ites the territory north of A·ro′er,e that is on the edge of the Wadi Ar′non, as well as half the hill country of Gil′e·ad with its towns, 13 and I gave to the half-tribe of Ma·nas′seh the rest of Gil′e·ad and all of Ba′shan, Og's kingdom. (The whole region of Ar′gob: all that portion of Ba′shan used to be called a land of Reph′a·im; 14 Ja′ir the Ma·nas′site acquired the whole region of Ar′gob as far as the border of the Gesh′u·rites and the Ma′a·ca·thites, and he named them—that is, Ba′shan—after himself, Hav′voth-ja′ir,f as it is to this day.) 15 To Ma′chir I gave Gil′e·ad. 16 And to the Reu′ben·ites and the Gad′ites I gave the territory from Gil′e·ad as far as the Wadi Ar′non, with the middle of the wadi as a boundary, and up to the Jab′bok, the wadi being boundary of the Am′mon·ites; 17 the Ar′a·bah also, with the Jordan and its banks, from Chin′ne·reth down to the sea of the Ar′a·bah, the Dead Sea,g with the lower slopes of Pis′gah on the east.

18 At that time, I charged you as follows: "Although the LORD your God has given you this land to occupy, all your troops shall cross over armed as the vanguard of your Israelite kin. 19 Only your wives, your children, and your livestock—I know that you have much livestock—shall stay behind in the towns that I have given to you. 20 When the LORD gives rest to your kindred, as to you, and they too have occupied the land that the LORD your God is giving them beyond the Jordan, then each of you may return to the property that I have given to you." 21 And I charged Joshua as well at that time, saying: "Your own eyes have seen everything that the LORD your God has done to these two kings; so the LORD will do to all the kingdoms into which you are about to cross. 22 Do not fear them, for it is the LORD your God who fights for you."

Moses Views Canaan from Pisgah

23 At that time, too, I entreated the LORD, saying: 24 "O Lord GOD, you have only begun to show your servant your greatness and your might; what god in heaven or on earth can perform deeds and mighty acts like yours! 25 Let me cross over to see the good land beyond the Jordan, that good hill country and the Lebanon." 26 But the LORD was angry with me on your account and would not heed me. The LORD said to me, "Enough from you! Never speak to me of this matter again! 27 Go up to the top of Pis′gah and look around you to the west, to the north, to the south, and to the east. Look well, for you shall not cross over this Jordan. 28 But charge Joshua, and encourage and strengthen him, because it is he who shall cross over at the head of this people and who shall secure their possession of the land that you will see." 29 So we remained in the valley opposite Beth-pe′or.

Moses Commands Obedience

4 So now, Israel, give heed to the statutes and ordinances that I am teaching you to observe, so that you may live to enter and occupy the land that the LORD, the God of your ancestors, is giving you. 2 You must neither add anything to what I command you nor take away anything from it, but keep the commandments of the LORD your God with which I am charging you. 3 You have seen for yourselves what the LORD did with regard to the Ba′al of Pe′or—how the LORD your God destroyed from among you everyone who followed the Ba′al of Pe′or, 4 while those of you who held fast to the LORD your God are all alive today.

5 See, just as the LORD my God has charged me, I now teach you statutes and ordinances for you to observe in the land that you are about to enter and occupy. 6 You must observe them diligently, for this will show your wisdom and discernment to the peoples, who, when they hear all these statutes, will say, "Surely this great nation is a wise and discerning people!" 7 For what other great nation has a god so near to it as the LORD our God is whenever we call to him? 8 And what other great nation has statutes and ordinances as just as this entire law that I am setting before you today?

9 But take care and watch yourselves closely, so as neither to forget the things that your eyes have seen nor to let them slip from your mind all the days of your life; make them known to your children and your children's children— 10 how you once stood before the LORD your God at Ho′reb, when the LORD said to me, "Assemble the people for me, and I will let them hear my words, so that they may learn

---

e Heb territory from Aroer   f That is
Settlement of Jair   g Heb Salt Sea

to fear me as long as they live on the earth, and may teach their children so"; [11] you approached and stood at the foot of the mountain while the mountain was blazing up to the very heavens, shrouded in dark clouds. [12] Then the LORD spoke to you out of the fire. You heard the sound of words but saw no form; there was only a voice. [13] He declared to you his covenant, which he charged you to observe, that is, the ten commandments;[h] and he wrote them on two stone tablets. [14] And the LORD charged me at that time to teach you statutes and ordinances for you to observe in the land that you are about to cross into and occupy.

15 Since you saw no form when the LORD spoke to you at Hō′reb out of the fire, take care and watch yourselves closely, [16] so that you do not act corruptly by making an idol for yourselves, in the form of any figure—the likeness of male or female, [17] the likeness of any animal that is on the earth, the likeness of any winged bird that flies in the air, [18] the likeness of anything that creeps on the ground, the likeness of any fish that is in the water under the earth. [19] And when you look up to the heavens and see the sun, the moon, and the stars, all the host of heaven, do not be led astray and bow down to them and serve them, things that the LORD your God has allotted to all the peoples everywhere under heaven. [20] But the LORD has taken you and brought you out of the iron-smelter, out of Egypt, to become a people of his very own possession, as you are now.

21 The LORD was angry with me because of you, and he vowed that I should not cross the Jordan and that I should not enter the good land that the LORD your God is giving for your possession. [22] For I am going to die in this land without crossing over the Jordan, but you are going to cross over to take possession of that good land. [23] So be careful not to forget the covenant that the LORD your God made with you, and not to make for yourselves an idol in the form of anything that the LORD your God has forbidden you. [24] For the LORD your God is a devouring fire, a jealous God.

25 When you have had children and children's children, and become complacent in the land, if you act corruptly by making an idol in the form of anything, thus doing what is evil in the sight of the LORD your God, and provoking him to anger, [26] I call heaven and earth to witness against you today that you will soon utterly perish from the land that you are crossing the Jordan to occupy; you will not live long on it, but will be utterly destroyed. [27] The LORD will scatter you among the peoples; only a few of you will be left among the nations where the LORD will lead you. [28] There you will serve other gods made by human hands, objects of wood and stone that neither see, nor hear, nor eat, nor smell. [29] From there you will seek the LORD your God, and you will find him if you search after him with all your heart and soul. [30] In your distress, when all these things have happened to you in time to come, you will return to the LORD your God and heed him. [31] Because the LORD your God is a merciful God, he will neither abandon you nor destroy you; he will not forget the covenant with your ancestors that he swore to them.

32 For ask now about former ages, long before your own, ever since the day that God created human beings on the earth; ask from one end of heaven to the other: has anything so great as this ever happened or has its like ever been heard of? [33] Has any people ever heard the voice of a god speaking out of a fire, as you have heard, and lived? [34] Or has any god ever attempted to go and take a nation for himself from the midst of another nation, by trials, by signs and wonders, by war, by a mighty hand and an outstretched arm, and by terrifying displays of power, as the LORD your God did for you in Egypt before your very eyes? [35] To you it was shown so that you would acknowledge that the LORD is God; there is no other besides him. [36] From heaven he made you hear his voice to discipline you. On earth he showed you his great fire, while you heard his words coming out of the fire. [37] And because he loved your ancestors, he chose their descendants after them. He brought you out of Egypt with his own presence, by his great power, [38] driving out before you nations greater and mightier than yourselves, to bring you in, giving you their land for a possession, as it is still today. [39] So acknowledge today and take to heart that the LORD is God in heaven above and on the earth be-

h Heb the ten words

neath; there is no other. 40 Keep his statutes and his commandments, which I am commanding you today for your own well-being and that of your descendants after you, so that you may long remain in the land that the LORD your God is giving you for all time.

Cities of Refuge East of the Jordan

41 Then Moses set apart on the east side of the Jordan three cities 42 to which a homicide could flee, someone who unintentionally kills another person, the two not having been at enmity before; the homicide could flee to one of these cities and live: 43 Bē'zer in the wilderness on the tableland belonging to the Reū'ben-ites, Rā'moth in Gil'-e·ad belonging to the Gad'ites, and Gō'lan in Bā'shan belonging to the Ma·nas'sītes.

Transition to the Second Address

44 This is the law that Moses set before the Israelites. 45 These are the decrees and the statutes and ordinances that Moses spoke to the Israelites when they had come out of Egypt, 46 beyond the Jordan in the valley opposite Beth-pē'or, in the land of King Sī'hon of the Am'o·rītes, who reigned at Hesh'bon, whom Moses and the Israelites defeated when they came out of Egypt. 47 They occupied his land and the land of King Og of Bā'shan, the two kings of the Am'o·rītes on the eastern side of the Jordan: 48 from A·rō'er, which is on the edge of the Wadi Ar'-non, as far as Mount Sir'i·on[i] (that is, Hermon), 49 together with all the Ar'-a·bah on the east side of the Jordan as far as the Sea of the Ar'a·bah, under the slopes of Pis'gah.

The Ten Commandments
(Ex 20.1–17)

5 Moses convened all Israel, and said to them:
Hear, O Israel, the statutes and ordinances that I am addressing to you today; you shall learn them and observe them diligently. 2 The LORD our God made a covenant with us at Hō'reb. 3 Not with our ancestors did the LORD make this covenant, but with us, who are all of us here alive today. 4 The LORD spoke with you face to face at the mountain, out of the fire. 5 (At that time I was standing between the LORD and you to declare to you the words[j] of the LORD; for you were afraid because of

the fire and did not go up the mountain.) And he said:

6 I am the LORD your God, who brought you out of the land of Egypt, out of the house of slavery; 7 you shall have no other gods before[k] me.

8 You shall not make for yourself an idol, whether in the form of anything that is in heaven above, or that is on the earth beneath, or that is in the water under the earth. 9 You shall not bow down to them or worship them; for I the LORD your God am a jealous God, punishing children for the iniquity of parents, to the third and fourth generation of those who reject me, 10 but showing steadfast love to the thousandth generation[l] of those who love me and keep my commandments.

11 You shall not make wrongful use of the name of the LORD your God, for the LORD will not acquit anyone who misuses his name.

12 Observe the sabbath day and keep it holy, as the LORD your God commanded you. 13 Six days you shall labor and do all your work. 14 But the seventh day is a sabbath to the LORD your God; you shall not do any work—you, or your son or your daughter, or your male or female slave, or your ox or your donkey, or any of your livestock, or the resident alien in your towns, so that your male and female slave may rest as well as you. 15 Remember that you were a slave in the land of Egypt, and the LORD your God brought you out from there with a mighty hand and an outstretched arm; therefore the LORD your God commanded you to keep the sabbath day.

16 Honor your father and your mother, as the LORD your God commanded you, so that your days may be long and that it may go well with you in the land that the LORD your God is giving you.

17 You shall not murder.[m]

18 Neither shall you commit adultery.

19 Neither shall you steal.

20 Neither shall you bear false witness against your neighbor.

21 Neither shall you covet your neighbor's wife.

Neither shall you desire your neighbor's house, or field, or male or female

---

[i] Syr: Heb *Sion*   [j] Q Mss Sam Gk Syr Vg Tg: MT *word*   [k] Or *besides*   [l] Or *to thousands*   [m] Or *kill*

slave, or ox, or donkey, or anything that belongs to your neighbor.

Moses the Mediator of God's Will
(Ex 20.18–21)

22 These words the LORD spoke with a loud voice to your whole assembly at the mountain, out of the fire, the cloud, and the thick darkness, and he added no more. He wrote them on two stone tablets, and gave them to me. 23 When you heard the voice out of the darkness, while the mountain was burning with fire, you approached me, all the heads of your tribes and your elders; 24 and you said, "Look, the LORD our God has shown us his glory and greatness, and we have heard his voice out of the fire. Today we have seen that God may speak to someone and the person may still live. 25 So now why should we die? For this great fire will consume us; if we hear the voice of the LORD our God any longer, we shall die. 26 For who is there of all flesh that has heard the voice of the living God speaking out of fire, as we have, and remained alive? 27 Go near, you yourself, and hear all that the LORD our God will say. Then tell us everything that the LORD our God tells you, and we will listen and do it."

28 The LORD heard your words when you spoke to me, and the LORD said to me: "I have heard the words of this people, which they have spoken to you; they are right in all that they have spoken. 29 If only they had such a mind as this, to fear me and to keep all my commandments always, so that it might go well with them and with their children forever! 30 Go say to them, 'Return to your tents.' 31 But you, stand here by me, and I will tell you all the commandments, the statutes and the ordinances, that you shall teach them, so that they may do them in the land that I am giving them to possess." 32 You must therefore be careful to do as the LORD your God has commanded you; you shall not turn to the right or to the left. 33 You must follow exactly the path that the LORD your God has commanded you, so that you may live, and that it may go well with you, and that you may live long in the land that you are to possess.

The Great Commandment

6 Now this is the commandment—the statutes and the ordinances—that the LORD your God charged me to teach you to observe in the land that you are about to cross into and occupy, 2 so that you and your children and your children's children may fear the LORD your God all the days of your life, and keep all his decrees and his commandments that I am commanding you, so that your days may be long. 3 Hear therefore, O Israel, and observe them diligently, so that it may go well with you, and so that you may multiply greatly in a land flowing with milk and honey, as the LORD, the God of your ancestors, has promised you.

4 Hear, O Israel: The LORD is our God, the LORD alone.[n] 5 You shall love the LORD your God with all your heart, and with all your soul, and with all your might. 6 Keep these words that I am commanding you today in your heart. 7 Recite them to your children and talk about them when you are at home and when you are away, when you lie down and when you rise. 8 Bind them as a sign on your hand, fix them as an emblem[o] on your forehead, 9 and write them on the doorposts of your house and on your gates.

Caution against Disobedience

10 When the LORD your God has brought you into the land that he swore to your ancestors, to Abraham, to Isaac, and to Jacob, to give you—a land with fine, large cities that you did not build, 11 houses filled with all sorts of goods that you did not fill, hewn cisterns that you did not hew, vineyards and olive groves that you did not plant—and when you have eaten your fill, 12 take care that you do not forget the LORD, who brought you out of the land of Egypt, out of the house of slavery. 13 The LORD your God you shall fear; him you shall serve, and by his name alone you shall swear. 14 Do not follow other gods, any of the gods of the peoples who are all around you, 15 because the LORD your God, who is present with you, is a jealous God. The anger of the LORD your God would be kindled against you and he would destroy you from the face of the earth.

16 Do not put the LORD your God to the test, as you tested him at Mas′sah. 17 You must diligently keep the commandments of the LORD your God, and

---

[n] Or *The* LORD *our God is one* LORD, or *The* LORD *our God, the* LORD *is one,* or *The* LORD *is our God, the* LORD *is one*
[o] Or *as a frontlet*

his decrees, and his statutes that he has commanded you. 18 Do what is right and good in the sight of the LORD, so that it may go well with you, and so that you may go in and occupy the good land that the LORD swore to your ancestors to give you, 19 thrusting out all your enemies from before you, as the LORD has promised.

20 When your children ask you in time to come, "What is the meaning of the decrees and the statutes and the ordinances that the LORD our God has commanded you?" 21 then you shall say to your children, "We were Pharaoh's slaves in Egypt, but the LORD brought us out of Egypt with a mighty hand. 22 The LORD displayed before our eyes great and awesome signs and wonders against Egypt, against Pharaoh and all his household. 23 He brought us out from there in order to bring us in, to give us the land that he promised on oath to our ancestors. 24 Then the LORD commanded us to observe all these statutes, to fear the LORD our God, for our lasting good, so as to keep us alive, as is now the case. 25 If we diligently observe this entire commandment before the LORD our God, as he has commanded us, we will be in the right."

A Chosen People
(Ex 34.10–16)

7 When the LORD your God brings you into the land that you are about to enter and occupy, and he clears away many nations before you—the Hit'tites, the Gir'ga·shites, the Am'o·rites, the Ca'naan·ites, the Per'iz·zites, the Hi'vites, and the Jeb'ū·sites, seven nations mightier and more numerous than you—2 and when the LORD your God gives them over to you and you defeat them, then you must utterly destroy them. Make no covenant with them and show them no mercy. 3 Do not intermarry with them, giving your daughters to their sons or taking their daughters for your sons, 4 for that would turn away your children from following me, to serve other gods. Then the anger of the LORD would be kindled against you, and he would destroy you quickly. 5 But this is how you must deal with them: break down their altars, smash their pillars, hew down their sacred poles,p and burn their idols with fire. 6 For you are a people holy to the LORD your God; the LORD your God has chosen you out

of all the peoples on earth to be his people, his treasured possession.

7 It was not because you were more numerous than any other people that the LORD set his heart on you and chose you—for you were the fewest of all peoples. 8 It was because the LORD loved you and kept the oath that he swore to your ancestors, that the LORD has brought you out with a mighty hand, and redeemed you from the house of slavery, from the hand of Pharaoh king of Egypt. 9 Know therefore that the LORD your God is God, the faithful God who maintains covenant loyalty with those who love him and keep his commandments, to a thousand generations, 10 and who repays in their own person those who reject him. He does not delay but repays in their own person those who reject him. 11 Therefore, observe diligently the commandment—the statutes, and the ordinances—that I am commanding you today.

Blessings for Obedience
(Lev 26.1–13; Deut 28.1–14)

12 If you heed these ordinances, by diligently observing them, the LORD your God will maintain with you the covenant loyalty that he swore to your ancestors; 13 he will love you, bless you, and multiply you; he will bless the fruit of your womb and the fruit of your ground, your grain and your wine and your oil, the increase of your cattle and the issue of your flock, in the land that he swore to your ancestors to give you. 14 You shall be the most blessed of peoples, with neither sterility nor barrenness among you or your livestock. 15 The LORD will turn away from you every illness; all the dread diseases of Egypt that you experienced, he will not inflict on you, but he will lay them on all who hate you. 16 You shall devour all the peoples that the LORD your God is giving over to you, showing them no pity; you shall not serve their gods, for that would be a snare to you.

17 If you say to yourself, "These nations are more numerous than I; how can I dispossess them?" 18 do not be afraid of them. Just remember what the LORD your God did to Pharaoh and to all Egypt, 19 the great trials that your eyes saw, the signs and wonders, the mighty hand and the outstretched arm by which the LORD your God brought

p Heb *Asherim*

you out. The LORD your God will do the same to all the peoples of whom you are afraid. 20 Moreover, the LORD your God will send the pestilence q against them, until even the survivors and the fugitives are destroyed. 21 Have no dread of them, for the LORD your God, who is present with you, is a great and awesome God. 22 The LORD your God will clear away these nations before you little by little; you will not be able to make a quick end of them, otherwise the wild animals would become too numerous for you. 23 But the LORD your God will give them over to you, and throw them into great panic, until they are destroyed. 24 He will hand their kings over to you and you shall blot out their name from under heaven; no one will be able to stand against you, until you have destroyed them. 25 The images of their gods you shall burn with fire. Do not covet the silver or the gold that is on them and take it for yourself, because you could be ensnared by it; for it is abhorrent to the LORD your God. 26 Do not bring an abhorrent thing into your house, or you will be set apart for destruction like it. You must utterly detest and abhor it, for it is set apart for destruction.

A Warning Not to Forget God in Prosperity

8 This entire commandment that I command you today you must diligently observe, so that you may live and increase, and go in and occupy the land that the LORD promised on oath to your ancestors. 2 Remember the long way that the LORD your God has led you these forty years in the wilderness, in order to humble you, testing you to know what was in your heart, whether or not you would keep his commandments. 3 He humbled you by letting you hunger, then by feeding you with manna, with which neither you nor your ancestors were acquainted, in order to make you understand that one does not live by bread alone, but by every word that comes from the mouth of the LORD. r 4 The clothes on your back did not wear out and your feet did not swell these forty years. 5 Know then in your heart that as a parent disciplines a child so the LORD your God disciplines you. 6 Therefore keep the commandments of the LORD your God, by walking in his ways and by fearing him. 7 For the LORD your God is bringing you into

a good land, a land with flowing streams, with springs and underground waters welling up in valleys and hills, 8 a land of wheat and barley, of vines and fig trees and pomegranates, a land of olive trees and honey, 9 a land where you may eat bread without scarcity, where you will lack nothing, a land whose stones are iron and from whose hills you may mine copper. 10 You shall eat your fill and bless the LORD your God for the good land that he has given you.

11 Take care that you do not forget the LORD your God, by failing to keep his commandments, his ordinances, and his statutes, which I am commanding you today. 12 When you have eaten your fill and have built fine houses and live in them, 13 and when your herds and flocks have multiplied, and your silver and gold is multiplied, and all that you have is multiplied, 14 then do not exalt yourself, forgetting the LORD your God, who brought you out of the land of Egypt, out of the house of slavery, 15 who led you through the great and terrible wilderness, an arid wasteland with poisonous s snakes and scorpions. He made water flow for you from flint rock, 16 and fed you in the wilderness with manna that your ancestors did not know, to humble you and to test you, and in the end to do you good. 17 Do not say to yourself, "My power and the might of my own hand have gotten me this wealth." 18 But remember the LORD your God, for it is he who gives you power to get wealth, so that he may confirm his covenant that he swore to your ancestors, as he is doing today. 19 If you do forget the LORD your God and follow other gods to serve and worship them, I solemnly warn you today that you shall surely perish. 20 Like the nations that the LORD is destroying before you, so shall you perish, because you would not obey the voice of the LORD your God.

The Consequences of Rebelling against God (Ex 32.1–35)

9 Hear, O Israel! You are about to cross the Jordan today, to go in and dispossess nations larger and mightier than you, great cities, forti-

---

q Or hornets: Meaning of Heb uncertain
r Or by anything that the LORD decrees
s Or fiery; Heb seraph

fied to the heavens, 2 a strong and tall people, the offspring of the An'a·kim, whom you know. You have heard it said of them, "Who can stand up to the An'a·kim?" 3 Know then today that the LORD your God is the one who crosses over before you as a devouring fire; he will defeat them and subdue them before you, so that you may dispossess and destroy them quickly, as the LORD has promised you.

4 When the LORD your God thrusts them out before you, do not say to yourself, "It is because of my righteousness that the LORD has brought me in to occupy this land"; it is rather because of the wickedness of these nations that the LORD is dispossessing them before you. 5 It is not because of your righteousness or the uprightness of your heart that you are going in to occupy their land; but because of the wickedness of these nations the LORD your God is dispossessing them before you, in order to fulfill the promise that the LORD made on oath to your ancestors, to Abraham, to Isaac, and to Jacob.

6 Know, then, that the LORD your God is not giving you this good land to occupy because of your righteousness; for you are a stubborn people. 7 Remember and do not forget how you provoked the LORD your God to wrath in the wilderness; you have been rebellious against the LORD from the day you came out of the land of Egypt until you came to this place.

8 Even at Ho'reb you provoked the LORD to wrath, and the LORD was so angry with you that he was ready to destroy you. 9 When I went up the mountain to receive the stone tablets, the tablets of the covenant that the LORD made with you, I remained on the mountain forty days and forty nights; I neither ate bread nor drank water. 10 And the LORD gave me the two stone tablets written with the finger of God; on them were all the words that the LORD had spoken to you at the mountain out of the fire on the day of the assembly. 11 At the end of forty days and forty nights the LORD gave me the two stone tablets, the tablets of the covenant. 12 Then the LORD said to me, "Get up, go down quickly from here, for your people whom you have brought from Egypt have acted corruptly. They have been quick to turn from the way that I commanded them; they have cast an image for themselves." 13 Furthermore the LORD said to me, "I have seen that this people is indeed a stubborn people. 14 Let me alone that I may destroy them and blot out their name from under heaven; and I will make of you a nation mightier and more numerous than they."

15 So I turned and went down from the mountain, while the mountain was ablaze; the two tablets of the covenant were in my two hands. 16 Then I saw that you had indeed sinned against the LORD your God, by casting for yourselves an image of a calf; you had been quick to turn from the way that the LORD had commanded you. 17 So I took hold of the two tablets and flung them from my two hands, smashing them before your eyes. 18 Then I lay prostrate before the LORD as before, forty days and forty nights; I neither ate bread nor drank water, because of all the sin you had committed, provoking the LORD by doing what was evil in his sight. 19 For I was afraid that the anger that the LORD bore against you was so fierce that he would destroy you. But the LORD listened to me that time also. 20 The LORD was so angry with Aaron that he was ready to destroy him, but I interceded also on behalf of Aaron at that same time. 21 Then I took the sinful thing you had made, the calf, and burned it with fire and crushed it, grinding it thoroughly, until it was reduced to dust; and I threw the dust of it into the stream that runs down the mountain.

22 At Tab'e·rah also, and at Mas'sah, and at Kib'roth-hat·ta'a·vah, you provoked the LORD to wrath. 23 And when the LORD sent you from Ka'desh-bar'nē·a, saying, "Go up and occupy the land that I have given you," you rebelled against the command of the LORD your God, neither trusting him nor obeying him. 24 You have been rebellious against the LORD as long as he has [t] known you.

25 Throughout the forty days and forty nights that I lay prostrate before the LORD when the LORD intended to destroy you, 26 I prayed to the LORD and said, "Lord GOD, do not destroy the people who are your very own possession, whom you redeemed in your greatness, whom you brought out of Egypt with a mighty hand. 27 Remember your servants, Abraham, Isaac, and Jacob; pay no attention to the

---

t Sam Gk: MT *I have*

stubbornness of this people, their wickedness and their sin, [28]otherwise the land from which you have brought us might say, 'Because the LORD was not able to bring them into the land that he promised them, and because he hated them, he has brought them out to let them die in the wilderness.' [29]For they are the people of your very own possession, whom you brought out by your great power and by your outstretched arm."

The Second Pair of Tablets
(Ex 34.1–9)

10 At that time the LORD said to me, "Carve out two tablets of stone like the former ones, and come up to me on the mountain, and make an ark of wood. [2]I will write on the tablets the words that were on the former tablets, which you smashed, and you shall put them in the ark." [3]So I made an ark of acacia wood, cut two tablets of stone like the former ones, and went up the mountain with the two tablets in my hand. [4]Then he wrote on the tablets the same words as before, the ten commandments[u] that the LORD had spoken to you on the mountain out of the fire on the day of the assembly; and the LORD gave them to me. [5]So I turned and came down from the mountain, and put the tablets in the ark that I had made; and there they are, as the LORD commanded me.

[6] (The Israelites journeyed from Be·er'oth-ben'ē-jā'a·kan[v] to Mō·sē'-rah. There Aaron died, and there he was buried; his son El·e·ā'zar succeeded him as priest. [7]From there they journeyed to Gud'gō·dah, and from Gud'gō·dah to Jot'ba·thah, a land with flowing streams. [8]At that time the LORD set apart the tribe of Levi to carry the ark of the covenant of the LORD, to stand before the LORD to minister to him, and to bless in his name, to this day. [9]Therefore Levi has no allotment or inheritance with his kindred; the LORD is his inheritance, as the LORD your God promised him.)

[10] I stayed on the mountain forty days and forty nights, as I had done the first time. And once again the LORD listened to me. The LORD was unwilling to destroy you. [11]The LORD said to me, "Get up, go on your journey at the head of the people, that they may go in and occupy the land that I swore to their ancestors to give them."

The Essence of the Law

[12] So now, O Israel, what does the LORD your God require of you? Only to fear the LORD your God, to walk in all his ways, to love him, to serve the LORD your God with all your heart and with all your soul, [13]and to keep the commandments of the LORD your God[w] and his decrees that I am commanding you today, for your own well-being. [14]Although heaven and the heaven of heavens belong to the LORD your God, the earth with all that is in it, [15]yet the LORD set his heart in love on your ancestors alone and chose you, their descendants after them, out of all the peoples, as it is today. [16]Circumcise, then, the foreskin of your heart, and do not be stubborn any longer. [17]For the LORD your God is God of gods and Lord of lords, the great God, mighty and awesome, who is not partial and takes no bribe, [18]who executes justice for the orphan and the widow, and who loves the strangers, providing them food and clothing. [19]You shall also love the stranger, for you were strangers in the land of Egypt. [20]You shall fear the LORD your God; him alone you shall worship; to him you shall hold fast, and by his name you shall swear. [21]He is your praise; he is your God, who has done for you these great and awesome things that your own eyes have seen. [22]Your ancestors went down to Egypt seventy persons; and now the LORD your God has made you as numerous as the stars in heaven.

Rewards for Obedience

11 You shall love the LORD your God, therefore, and keep his charge, his decrees, his ordinances, and his commandments always. [2]Remember today that it was not your children (who have not known or seen the discipline of the LORD your God), but it is you who must acknowledge his greatness, his mighty hand and his outstretched arm, [3]his signs and his deeds that he did in Egypt to Pharaoh, the king of Egypt, and to all his land; [4]what he did to the Egyptian army, to their horses and chariots, how he made the water of the Red Sea[x] flow over them as they pursued you, so that

---

[u]Heb *the ten words*   [v]Or *the wells of the Bene-jaakan*   [w]Q Ms Gk Syr: MT lacks *your God*   [x]Or *Sea of Reeds*

the LORD has destroyed them to this day; [5] what he did to you in the wilderness, until you came to this place; [6] and what he did to Da'than and A·bi'ram, sons of E·li'ab son of Reuben, how in the midst of all Israel the earth opened its mouth and swallowed them up, along with their households, their tents, and every living being in their company; [7] for it is your own eyes that have seen every great deed that the LORD did.

8 Keep, then, this entire commandment that I am commanding you today, so that you may have strength to go in and occupy the land that you are crossing over to occupy, [9] and so that you may live long in the land that the LORD swore to your ancestors to give them and to their descendants, a land flowing with milk and honey. [10] For the land that you are about to enter to occupy is not like the land of Egypt, from which you have come, where you sow your seed and irrigate by foot like a vegetable garden. [11] But the land that you are crossing over to occupy is a land of hills and valleys, watered by rain from the sky, [12] a land that the LORD your God looks after. The eyes of the LORD your God are always on it, from the beginning of the year to the end of the year.

13 If you will only heed his every commandment[y] that I am commanding you today—loving the LORD your God, and serving him with all your heart and with all your soul— [14] then he[z] will give the rain for your land in its season, the early rain and the later rain, and you will gather in your grain, your wine, and your oil; [15] and he[z] will give grass in your fields for your livestock, and you will eat your fill. [16] Take care, or you will be seduced into turning away, serving other gods and worshiping them, [17] for then the anger of the LORD will be kindled against you and he will shut up the heavens, so that there will be no rain and the land will yield no fruit; then you will perish quickly off the good land that the LORD is giving you.

18 You shall put these words of mine in your heart and soul, and you shall bind them as a sign on your hand, and fix them as an emblem[a] on your forehead. [19] Teach them to your children, talking about them when you are at home and when you are away, when you lie down and when you rise. [20] Write them on the doorposts of your house and on your gates, [21] so that your days and the days of your children may be multiplied in the land that the LORD swore to your ancestors to give them, as long as the heavens are above the earth.

22 If you will diligently observe this entire commandment that I am commanding you, loving the LORD your God, walking in all his ways, and holding fast to him, [23] then the LORD will drive out all these nations before you, and you will dispossess nations larger and mightier than yourselves. [24] Every place on which you set foot shall be yours; your territory shall extend from the wilderness to the Lebanon and from the River, the river Euphrates, to the Western Sea. [25] No one will be able to stand against you; the LORD your God will put the fear and dread of you on all the land on which you set foot, as he promised you.

26 See, I am setting before you today a blessing and a curse: [27] the blessing, if you obey the commandments of the LORD your God that I am commanding you today; [28] and the curse, if you do not obey the commandments of the LORD your God, but turn from the way that I am commanding you today, to follow other gods that you have not known.

29 When the LORD your God has brought you into the land that you are entering to occupy, you shall set the blessing on Mount Ger'i·zim and the curse on Mount E'bal. [30] As you know, they are beyond the Jordan, some distance to the west, in the land of the Ca'naan·ites who live in the Ar'a·bah, opposite Gil'gal, beside the oak[b] of Mo'reh.

31 When you cross the Jordan to go in to occupy the land that the LORD your God is giving you, and when you occupy it and live in it, [32] you must diligently observe all the statutes and ordinances that I am setting before you today.

Pagan Shrines to Be Destroyed

12 These are the statutes and ordinances that you must diligently observe in the land that the LORD, the God of your ancestors, has given you

---

[y] Compare Gk: Heb *my commandments*
[z] Sam Gk Vg: MT *I*   [a] Or *as a frontlet*
[b] Gk Syr: Compare Gen 12.6; Heb *oaks* or *terebinths*

to occupy all the days that you live on the earth.

2 You must demolish completely all the places where the nations whom you are about to dispossess served their gods, on the mountain heights, on the hills, and under every leafy tree. 3 Break down their altars, smash their pillars, burn their sacred poles c with fire, and hew down the idols of their gods, and thus blot out their name from their places. 4 You shall not worship the LORD your God in such ways. 5 But you shall seek the place that the LORD your God will choose out of all your tribes as his habitation to put his name there. You shall go there, 6 bringing there your burnt offerings and your sacrifices, your tithes and your donations, your votive gifts, your freewill offerings, and the firstlings of your herds and flocks. 7 And you shall eat there in the presence of the LORD your God, you and your households together, rejoicing in all the undertakings in which the LORD your God has blessed you.

8 You shall not act as we are acting here today, all of us according to our own desires, 9 for you have not yet come into the rest and the possession that the LORD your God is giving you. 10 When you cross over the Jordan and live in the land that the LORD your God is allotting to you, and when he gives you rest from your enemies all around so that you live in safety, 11 then you shall bring everything that I command you to the place that the LORD your God will choose as a dwelling for his name: your burnt offerings and your sacrifices, your tithes and your donations, and all your choice votive gifts that you vow to the LORD. 12 And you shall rejoice before the LORD your God, you together with your sons and your daughters, your male and female slaves, and the Lē'vītes who reside in your towns (since they have no allotment or inheritance with you).

A Prescribed Place of Worship

13 Take care that you do not offer your burnt offerings at any place you happen to see. 14 But only at the place that the LORD will choose in one of your tribes—there you shall offer your burnt offerings and there you shall do everything I command you.

15 Yet whenever you desire you may slaughter and eat meat within any of your towns, according to the bless-

ing that the LORD your God has given you; the unclean and the clean may eat of it, as they would of gazelle or deer. 16 The blood, however, you must not eat; you shall pour it out on the ground like water. 17 Nor may you eat within your towns the tithe of your grain, your wine, and your oil, the firstlings of your herds and your flocks, any of your votive gifts that you vow, your freewill offerings, or your donations; 18 these you shall eat in the presence of the LORD your God at the place that the LORD your God will choose, you together with your son and your daughter, your male and female slaves, and the Lē'vītes resident in your towns, rejoicing in the presence of the LORD your God in all your undertakings. 19 Take care that you do not neglect the Lē'vīte as long as you live in your land.

20 When the LORD your God enlarges your territory, as he has promised you, and you say, "I am going to eat some meat," because you wish to eat meat, you may eat meat whenever you have the desire. 21 If the place where the LORD your God will choose to put his name is too far from you, and you slaughter as I have commanded you any of your herd or flock that the LORD has given you, then you may eat within your towns whenever you desire. 22 Indeed, just as gazelle or deer is eaten, so you may eat it; the unclean and the clean alike may eat it. 23 Only be sure that you do not eat the blood; for the blood is the life, and you shall not eat the life with the meat. 24 Do not eat it; you shall pour it out on the ground like water. 25 Do not eat it, so that all may go well with you and your children after you, because you do what is right in the sight of the LORD. 26 But the sacred donations that are due from you, and your votive gifts, you shall bring to the place that the LORD will choose. 27 You shall present your burnt offerings, both the meat and the blood, on the altar of the LORD your God; the blood of your other sacrifices shall be poured out beside d the altar of the LORD your God, but the meat you may eat.

28 Be careful to obey all these words that I command you today, e so that it may go well with you and with your children after you forever, because you will be doing what is good

c Heb *Asherim*   d Or *on*   e Gk Sam Syr: MT lacks *today* and right in the sight of the LORD your God.

Warning against Idolatry

29 When the LORD your God has cut off before you the nations whom you are about to enter to dispossess them, when you have dispossessed them and live in their land, [30]take care that you are not snared into imitating them, after they have been destroyed before you: do not inquire concerning their gods, saying, "How did these nations worship their gods? I also want to do the same." [31]You must not do the same for the LORD your God, because every abhorrent thing that the LORD hates they have done for their gods. They would even burn their sons and their daughters in the fire to their gods. [32][f]You must diligently observe everything that I command you; do not add to it or take anything from it.

13 [g]If prophets or those who divine by dreams appear among you and promise you omens or portents, [2]and the omens or the portents declared by them take place, and they say, "Let us follow other gods" (whom you have not known) "and let us serve them," [3]you must not heed the words of those prophets or those who divine by dreams; for the LORD your God is testing you, to know whether you indeed love the LORD your God with all your heart and soul. [4]The LORD your God you shall follow, him alone you shall fear, his commandments you shall keep, his voice you shall obey, him you shall serve, and to him you shall hold fast. [5]But those prophets or those who divine by dreams shall be put to death for having spoken treason against the LORD your God—who brought you out of the land of Egypt and redeemed you from the house of slavery—to turn you from the way in which the LORD your God commanded you to walk. So you shall purge the evil from your midst.

6 If anyone secretly entices you— even if it is your brother, your father's son or[h] your mother's son, or your own son or daughter, or the wife you embrace, or your most intimate friend—saying, "Let us go worship other gods," whom neither you nor your ancestors have known, [7]any of the gods of the peoples that are around you, whether near you or far away from you, from one end of the earth to

the other, [8]you must not yield to or heed any such persons. Show them no pity or compassion and do not shield them. [9]But you shall surely kill them; your own hand shall be first against them to execute them, and afterwards the hand of all the people. [10]Stone them to death for trying to turn you away from the LORD your God, who brought you out of the land of Egypt, out of the house of slavery. [11]Then all Israel shall hear and be afraid, and never again do any such wickedness.

12 If you hear it said about one of the towns that the LORD your God is giving you to live in, [13]that scoundrels from among you have gone out and led the inhabitants of the town astray, saying, "Let us go and worship other gods," whom you have not known, [14]then you shall inquire and make a thorough investigation. If the charge is established that such an abhorrent thing has been done among you, [15]you shall put the inhabitants of that town to the sword, utterly destroying it and everything in it—even putting its livestock to the sword. [16]All of its spoil you shall gather into its public square; then burn the town and all its spoil with fire, as a whole burnt offering to the LORD your God. It shall remain a perpetual ruin, never to be rebuilt. [17]Do not let anything devoted to destruction stick to your hand, so that the LORD may turn from his fierce anger and show you compassion, and in his compassion multiply you, as he swore to your ancestors, [18]if you obey the voice of the LORD your God by keeping all his commandments that I am commanding you today, doing what is right in the sight of the LORD your God.

Pagan Practices Forbidden

14 You are children of the LORD your God. You must not lacerate yourselves or shave your forelocks for the dead. [2]For you are a people holy to the LORD your God; it is you the LORD has chosen out of all the peoples on earth to be his people, his treasured possession.

Clean and Unclean Foods
(Lev 11.1–47)

3 You shall not eat any abhorrent thing. [4]These are the animals you may

---

[f]Ch 13.1 in Heb   [g]Ch 13.2 in Heb
[h]Sam Gk Compare Tg: MT lacks *your father's son or*

eat: the ox, the sheep, the goat, [5]the deer, the gazelle, the roebuck, the wild goat, the ibex, the antelope, and the mountain-sheep. [6]Any animal that divides the hoof and has the hoof cleft in two, and chews the cud, among the animals, you may eat. [7]Yet of those that chew the cud or have the hoof cleft you shall not eat these: the camel, the hare, and the rock badger, because they chew the cud but do not divide the hoof; they are unclean for you. [8]And the pig, because it divides the hoof but does not chew the cud, is unclean for you. You shall not eat their meat, and you shall not touch their carcasses.

9 Of all that live in water you may eat these: whatever has fins and scales you may eat. [10]And whatever does not have fins and scales you shall not eat; it is unclean for you.

11 You may eat any clean birds. [12]But these are the ones that you shall not eat: the eagle, the vulture, the osprey, [13]the buzzard, the kite, of any kind; [14]every raven of any kind; [15]the ostrich, the nighthawk, the sea gull, the hawk, of any kind; [16]the little owl and the great owl, the water hen [17]and the desert owl,[i] the carrion vulture and the cormorant, [18]the stork, the heron, of any kind; the hoopoe and the bat.[j] [19]And all winged insects are unclean for you; they shall not be eaten. [20]You may eat any clean winged creature.

21 You shall not eat anything that dies of itself; you may give it to aliens residing in your towns for them to eat, or you may sell it to a foreigner. For you are a people holy to the LORD your God.

You shall not boil a kid in its mother's milk.

Regulations concerning Tithes

22 Set apart a tithe of all the yield of your seed that is brought in yearly from the field. [23]In the presence of the LORD your God, in the place that he will choose as a dwelling for his name, you shall eat the tithe of your grain, your wine, and your oil, as well as the firstlings of your herd and flock, so that you may learn to fear the LORD your God always. [24]But if, when the LORD your God has blessed you, the distance is so great that you are unable to transport it, because the place where the LORD your God will choose to set his name is too far away from you, [25]then you may turn it into

money. With the money secure in hand, go to the place that the LORD your God will choose; [26]spend the money for whatever you wish—oxen, sheep, wine, strong drink, or whatever you desire. And you shall eat there in the presence of the LORD your God, you and your household rejoicing together. [27]As for the Lē′vītes resident in your towns, do not neglect them, because they have no allotment or inheritance with you.

28 Every third year you shall bring out the full tithe of your produce for that year, and store it within your towns; [29]the Lē′vītes, because they have no allotment or inheritance with you, as well as the resident aliens, the orphans, and the widows in your towns, may come and eat their fill so that the LORD your God may bless you in all the work that you undertake.

Laws concerning the Sabbatical Year
(Ex 21.1–11; Lev 25.1–7)

15 Every seventh year you shall grant a remission of debts. [2]And this is the manner of the remission: every creditor shall remit the claim that is held against a neighbor, not exacting it of a neighbor who is a member of the community, because the LORD'S remission has been proclaimed. [3]Of a foreigner you may exact it, but you must remit your claim on whatever any member of your community owes you. [4]There will, however, be no one in need among you, because the LORD is sure to bless you in the land that the LORD your God is giving you as a possession to occupy, [5]if only you will obey the LORD your God by diligently observing this entire commandment that I command you today. [6]When the LORD your God has blessed you, as he promised you, you will lend to many nations, but you will not borrow; you will rule over many nations, but they will not rule over you.

7 If there is among you anyone in need, a member of your community in any of your towns within the land that the LORD your God is giving you, do not be hard-hearted or tight-fisted toward your needy neighbor. [8]You should rather open your hand, willingly lending enough to meet the need, whatever it may be. [9]Be careful that you do not entertain a mean thought,

---

[i]Or *pelican*   [j]Identification of several of the birds in verses 12-18 is uncertain

thinking, "The seventh year, the year of remission, is near," and therefore view your needy neighbor with hostility and give nothing; your neighbor might cry to the LORD against you, and you would incur guilt. [10]Give liberally and be ungrudging when you do so, for on this account the LORD your God will bless you in all your work and in all that you undertake. [11]Since there will never cease to be some in need on the earth, I therefore command you, "Open your hand to the poor and needy neighbor in your land."

12 If a member of your community, whether a Hebrew man or a Hebrew woman, is sold[k] to you and works for you six years, in the seventh year you shall set that person free. [13]And when you send a male slave[l] out from you a free person, you shall not send him out empty-handed. [14]Provide liberally out of your flock, your threshing floor, and your wine press, thus giving to him some of the bounty with which the LORD your God has blessed you. [15]Remember that you were a slave in the land of Egypt, and the LORD your God redeemed you; for this reason I lay this command upon you today. [16]But if he says to you, "I will not go out from you," because he loves you and your household, since he is well off with you, [17]then you shall take an awl and thrust it through his earlobe into the door, and he shall be your slave[m] forever.

You shall do the same with regard to your female slave.[n]

18 Do not consider it a hardship when you send them out from you free persons, because for six years they have given you services worth the wages of hired laborers; and the LORD your God will bless you in all that you do.

The Firstborn of Livestock

19 Every firstling male born of your herd and flock you shall consecrate to the LORD your God; you shall not do work with your firstling ox nor shear the firstling of your flock. [20]You shall eat it, you together with your household, in the presence of the LORD your God year by year at the place that the LORD will choose. [21]But if it has any defect—any serious defect, such as lameness or blindness—you shall not sacrifice it to the LORD your God; [22]within your towns you may eat it, the unclean and the clean alike, as you

would a gazelle or deer. [23]Its blood, however, you must not eat; you shall pour it out on the ground like water.

The Passover Reviewed
(Ex 12.1–20; 23.14–19; 34.18–26)

16 Observe the month[o] of Ā′bib by keeping the passover for the LORD your God, for in the month of Ā′bib the LORD your God brought you out of Egypt by night. [2]You shall offer the passover sacrifice for the LORD your God, from the flock and the herd, at the place that the LORD will choose as a dwelling for his name. [3]You must not eat with it anything leavened. For seven days you shall eat unleavened bread with it—the bread of affliction—because you came out of the land of Egypt in great haste, so that all the days of your life you may remember the day of your departure from the land of Egypt. [4]No leaven shall be seen with you in all your territory for seven days; and none of the meat of what you slaughter on the evening of the first day shall remain until morning. [5]You are not permitted to offer the passover sacrifice within any of your towns that the LORD your God is giving you. [6]But at the place that the LORD your God will choose as a dwelling for his name, only there shall you offer the passover sacrifice, in the evening at sunset, the time of day when you departed from Egypt. [7]You shall cook it and eat it at the place that the LORD your God will choose; the next morning you may go back to your tents. [8]For six days you shall continue to eat unleavened bread, and on the seventh day there shall be a solemn assembly for the LORD your God, when you shall do no work.

The Festival of Weeks Reviewed
(Ex 34.22; Lev 23.15–21; Num 28.26–31)

9 You shall count seven weeks; begin to count the seven weeks from the time the sickle is first put to the standing grain. [10]Then you shall keep the festival of weeks for the LORD your God, contributing a freewill offering in proportion to the blessing that you have received from the LORD your God. [11]Rejoice before the LORD your God—you and your sons and your daughters, your male and female

---

k Or sells himself or herself   *l Heb him*
m Or bondman   *n Or bondwoman*
o Or new moon

slaves, the Lē′vītes resident in your towns, as well as the strangers, the orphans, and the widows who are among you—at the place that the LORD your God will choose as a dwelling for his name. [12] Remember that you were a slave in Egypt, and diligently observe these statutes.

The Festival of Booths Reviewed
(Lev 23.33–43; Num 29.12–40)

13 You shall keep the festival of booths[p] for seven days, when you have gathered in the produce from your threshing floor and your wine press. [14] Rejoice during your festival, you and your sons and your daughters, your male and female slaves, as well as the Lē′vītes, the strangers, the orphans, and the widows resident in your towns. [15] Seven days you shall keep the festival for the LORD your God at the place that the LORD will choose; for the LORD your God will bless you in all your produce and in all your undertakings, and you shall surely celebrate.

16 Three times a year all your males shall appear before the LORD your God at the place that he will choose: at the festival of unleavened bread, at the festival of weeks, and at the festival of booths.[p] They shall not appear before the LORD empty-handed; [17] all shall give as they are able, according to the blessing of the LORD your God that he has given you.

Municipal Judges and Officers

18 You shall appoint judges and officials throughout your tribes, in all your towns that the LORD your God is giving you, and they shall render just decisions for the people. [19] You must not distort justice; you must not show partiality; and you must not accept bribes, for a bribe blinds the eyes of the wise and subverts the cause of those who are in the right. [20] Justice, and only justice, you shall pursue, so that you may live and occupy the land that the LORD your God is giving you.

Forbidden Forms of Worship

21 You shall not plant any tree as a sacred pole[q] beside the altar that you make for the LORD your God; [22] nor shall you set up a stone pillar—things that the LORD your God hates.

17 You must not sacrifice to the LORD your God an ox or a sheep that has a defect, anything seriously wrong; for that is abhorrent to the LORD your God.

2 If there is found among you, in one of your towns that the LORD your God is giving you, a man or woman who does what is evil in the sight of the LORD your God, and transgresses his covenant [3] by going to serve other gods and worshiping them—whether the sun or the moon or any of the host of heaven, which I have forbidden— [4] and if it is reported to you or you hear of it, and you make a thorough inquiry, and the charge is proved true that such an abhorrent thing has occurred in Israel, [5] then you shall bring out to your gates that man or that woman who has committed this crime and you shall stone the man or woman to death. [6] On the evidence of two or three witnesses the death sentence shall be executed; a person must not be put to death on the evidence of only one witness. [7] The hands of the witnesses shall be the first raised against the person to execute the death penalty, and afterward the hands of all the people. So you shall purge the evil from your midst.

Legal Decisions by Priests and Judges

8 If a judicial decision is too difficult for you to make between one kind of bloodshed and another, one kind of legal right and another, or one kind of assault and another—any such matters of dispute in your towns—then you shall immediately go up to the place that the LORD your God will choose, [9] where you shall consult with the levitical priests and the judge who is in office in those days; they shall announce to you the decision in the case. [10] Carry out exactly the decision that they announce to you from the place that the LORD will choose, diligently observing everything they instruct you. [11] You must carry out fully the law that they interpret for you or the ruling that they announce to you; do not turn aside from the decision that they announce to you, either to the right or to the left. [12] As for anyone who presumes to disobey the priest appointed to minister there to the LORD your God, or the judge, that person shall die. So you shall purge the evil from Israel. [13] All the people will hear and be afraid, and will not act presumptuously again.

p Or *tabernacles*; Heb *succoth*
q Heb *Asherah*

Limitations of Royal Authority

14 When you have come into the land that the LORD your God is giving you, and have taken possession of it and settled in it, and you say, "I will set a king over me, like all the nations that are around me," 15 you may indeed set over you a king whom the LORD your God will choose. One of your own community you may set as king over you; you are not permitted to put a foreigner over you, who is not of your own community. 16 Even so, he must not acquire many horses for himself, or return the people to Egypt in order to acquire more horses, since the LORD has said to you, "You must never return that way again." 17 And he must not acquire many wives for himself, or else his heart will turn away; also silver and gold he must not acquire in great quantity for himself. 18 When he has taken the throne of his kingdom, he shall have a copy of this law written for him in the presence of the levitical priests. 19 It shall remain with him and he shall read in it all the days of his life, so that he may learn to fear the LORD his God, diligently observing all the words of this law and these statutes, 20 neither exalting himself above other members of the community nor turning aside from the commandment, either to the right or to the left, so that he and his descendants may reign long over his kingdom in Israel.

Privileges of Priests and Levites

18 The levitical priests, the whole tribe of Levi, shall have no allotment or inheritance within Israel. They may eat the sacrifices that are the LORD's portion[r] 2 but they shall have no inheritance among the other members of the community; the LORD is their inheritance, as he promised them.

3 This shall be the priests' due from the people, from those offering a sacrifice, whether an ox or a sheep: they shall give to the priest the shoulder, the two jowls, and the stomach. 4 The first fruits of your grain, your wine, and your oil, as well as the first of the fleece of your sheep, you shall give him. 5 For the LORD your God has chosen Levi[s] out of all your tribes, to stand and minister in the name of the LORD, him and his sons for all time.

6 If a Le'vite leaves any of your towns, from wherever he has been residing in Israel, and comes to the place that the LORD will choose (and he may come whenever he wishes), 7 then he may minister in the name of the LORD his God, like all his fellow-Le'vites who stand to minister there before the LORD. 8 They shall have equal portions to eat, even though they have income from the sale of family possessions.[r]

Child-Sacrifice, Divination, and Magic Prohibited

9 When you come into the land that the LORD your God is giving you, you must not learn to imitate the abhorrent practices of those nations. 10 No one shall be found among you who makes a son or daughter pass through fire, or who practices divination, or is a soothsayer, or an augur, or a sorcerer, 11 or one who casts spells, or who consults ghosts or spirits, or who seeks oracles from the dead. 12 For whoever does these things is abhorrent to the LORD; it is because of such abhorrent practices that the LORD your God is driving them out before you. 13 You must remain completely loyal to the LORD your God. 14 Although these nations that you are about to dispossess do give heed to soothsayers and diviners, as for you, the LORD your God does not permit you to do so.

A New Prophet Like Moses

15 The LORD your God will raise up for you a prophet[t] like me from among your own people; you shall heed such a prophet.[u] 16 This is what you requested of the LORD your God at Hō'reb on the day of the assembly when you said: "If I hear the voice of the LORD my God any more, or ever again see this great fire, I will die." 17 Then the LORD replied to me: "They are right in what they have said. 18 I will raise up for them a prophet[t] like you from among their own people; I will put my words in the mouth of the prophet,[v] who shall speak to them everything that I command. 19 Anyone who does not heed the words that the prophet[w] shall speak in my name, I myself will hold accountable. 20 But any prophet who speaks in the name of other gods, or who presumes to speak in my name a word that I have not commanded the prophet to speak—

---

[r] Meaning of Heb uncertain   [s] Heb *him*
[t] Or *prophets*   [u] Or *such prophets*
[v] Or *mouths of the prophets*   [w] Heb *he*

that prophet shall die." ²¹ You may say to yourself, "How can we recognize a word that the LORD has not spoken?" ²² If a prophet speaks in the name of the LORD but the thing does not take place or prove true, it is a word that the LORD has not spoken. The prophet has spoken it presumptuously; do not be frightened by it.

Laws concerning the Cities of Refuge
(Num 35.9–28; Josh 20.1–9)

19 When the LORD your God has cut off the nations whose land the LORD your God is giving you, and you have dispossessed them and settled in their towns and in their houses, ² you shall set apart three cities in the land that the LORD your God is giving you to possess. ³ You shall calculate the distances^x and divide into three regions the land that the LORD your God gives you as a possession, so that any homicide can flee to one of them.

4 Now this is the case of a homicide who might flee there and live, that is, someone who has killed another person unintentionally when the two had not been at enmity before: ⁵ Suppose someone goes into the forest with another to cut wood, and when one of them swings the ax to cut down a tree, the head slips from the handle and strikes the other person who then dies; the killer may flee to one of these cities and live. ⁶ But if the distance is too great, the avenger of blood in hot anger might pursue and overtake and put the killer to death, although a death sentence was not deserved, since the two had not been at enmity before. ⁷ Therefore I command you: You shall set apart three cities.

8 If the LORD your God enlarges your territory, as he swore to your ancestors—and he will give you all the land that he promised your ancestors to give you, ⁹ provided you diligently observe this entire commandment that I command you today, by loving the LORD your God and walking always in his ways—then you shall add three more cities to these three, ¹⁰ so that the blood of an innocent person may not be shed in the land that the LORD your God is giving you as an inheritance, thereby bringing bloodguilt upon you.

11 But if someone at enmity with another lies in wait and attacks and takes the life of that person, and flees into one of these cities, ¹² then the elders of the killer's city shall send to have the culprit taken from there and handed over to the avenger of blood to be put to death. ¹³ Show no pity; you shall purge the guilt of innocent blood from Israel, so that it may go well with you.

Property Boundaries

14 You must not move your neighbor's boundary marker, set up by former generations, on the property that will be allotted to you in the land that the LORD your God is giving you to possess.

Law concerning Witnesses

15 A single witness shall not suffice to convict a person of any crime or wrongdoing in connection with any offense that may be committed. Only on the evidence of two or three witnesses shall a charge be sustained. ¹⁶ If a malicious witness comes forward to accuse someone of wrongdoing, ¹⁷ then both parties to the dispute shall appear before the LORD, before the priests and the judges who are in office in those days, ¹⁸ and the judges shall make a thorough inquiry. If the witness is a false witness, having testified falsely against another, ¹⁹ then you shall do to the false witness just as the false witness had meant to do to the other. So you shall purge the evil from your midst. ²⁰ The rest shall hear and be afraid, and a crime such as this shall never again be committed among you. ²¹ Show no pity: life for life, eye for eye, tooth for tooth, hand for hand, foot for foot.

Rules of Warfare

20 When you go out to war against your enemies, and see horses and chariots, an army larger than your own, you shall not be afraid of them; for the LORD your God is with you, who brought you up from the land of Egypt. ² Before you engage in battle, the priest shall come forward and speak to the troops, ³ and shall say to them: "Hear, O Israel! Today you are drawing near to do battle against your enemies. Do not lose heart, or be afraid, or panic, or be in dread of them; ⁴ for it is the LORD your God who goes with you, to fight for you against your enemies, to give you victory." ⁵ Then the officials shall address the troops, saying, "Has anyone built a new house but not dedi-

x Or *prepare roads to them*

cated it? He should go back to his house, or he might die in the battle and another dedicate it. 6Has anyone planted a vineyard but not yet enjoyed its fruit? He should go back to his house, or he might die in the battle and another be first to enjoy its fruit. 7Has anyone become engaged to a woman but not yet married her? He should go back to his house, or he might die in the battle and another marry her." 8The officials shall continue to address the troops, saying, "Is anyone afraid or disheartened? He should go back to his house, or he might cause the heart of his comrades to melt like his own." 9When the officials have finished addressing the troops, then the commanders shall take charge of them.

10 When you draw near to a town to fight against it, offer it terms of peace. 11If it accepts your terms of peace and surrenders to you, then all the people in it shall serve you at forced labor. 12If it does not submit to you peacefully, but makes war against you, then you shall besiege it; 13and when the LORD your God gives it into your hand, you shall put all its males to the sword. 14You may, however, take as your booty the women, the children, livestock, and everything else in the town, all its spoil. You may enjoy the spoil of your enemies, which the LORD your God has given you. 15Thus you shall treat all the towns that are very far from you, which are not towns of the nations here. 16But as for the towns of these peoples that the LORD your God is giving you as an inheritance, you must not let anything that breathes remain alive. 17You shall annihilate them—the Hit'tītes and the Am'-o·rītes, the Cā'naan·ītes and the Per'-iz·zītes, the Hi'vītes and the Jeb'-ū·sītes—just as the LORD your God has commanded—18so that they may not teach you to do all the abhorrent things that they do for their gods, and you thus sin against the LORD your God.

19 If you besiege a town for a long time, making war against it in order to take it, you must not destroy its trees by wielding an ax against them. Although you may take food from them, you must not cut them down. Are trees in the field human beings that they should come under siege from you? 20You may destroy only the trees that you know do not produce food; you may cut them down for use in building

siegeworks against the town that makes war with you, until it falls.

Law concerning Murder by Persons Unknown

21 If, in the land that the LORD your God is giving you to possess, a body is found lying in open country, and it is not known who struck the person down, 2then your elders and your judges shall come out to measure the distances to the towns that are near the body. 3The elders of the town nearest the body shall take a heifer that has never been worked, one that has not pulled in the yoke; 4the elders of that town shall bring the heifer down to a wadi with running water, which is neither plowed nor sown, and shall break the heifer's neck there in the wadi. 5Then the priests, the sons of Levi, shall come forward, for the LORD your God has chosen them to minister to him and to pronounce blessings in the name of the LORD, and by their decision all cases of dispute and assault shall be settled. 6All the elders of that town nearest the body shall wash their hands over the heifer whose neck was broken in the wadi, 7and they shall declare: "Our hands did not shed this blood, nor were we witnesses to it. 8Absolve, O LORD, your people Israel, whom you redeemed; do not let the guilt of innocent blood remain in the midst of your people Israel." Then they will be absolved of bloodguilt. 9So you shall purge the guilt of innocent blood from your midst, because you must do what is right in the sight of the LORD.

Female Captives

10 When you go out to war against your enemies, and the LORD your God hands them over to you and you take them captive, 11suppose you see among the captives a beautiful woman whom you desire and want to marry, 12and so you bring her home to your house: she shall shave her head, pare her nails, 13discard her captive's garb, and shall remain in your house a full month, mourning for her father and mother; after that you may go in to her and be her husband, and she shall be your wife. 14But if you are not satisfied with her, you shall let her go free and not sell her for money. You must not treat her as a slave, since you have dishonored her.

The Right of the Firstborn

15 If a man has two wives, one of them loved and the other disliked, and if both the loved and the disliked have borne him sons, the firstborn being the son of the one who is disliked, ¹⁶then on the day when he wills his possessions to his sons, he is not permitted to treat the son of the loved as the firstborn in preference to the son of the disliked, who is the firstborn. ¹⁷He must acknowledge as firstborn the son of the one who is disliked, giving him a double portion y of all that he has; since he is the first issue of his virility, the right of the firstborn is his.

Rebellious Children

18 If someone has a stubborn and rebellious son who will not obey his father and mother, who does not heed them when they discipline him, ¹⁹then his father and his mother shall take hold of him and bring him out to the elders of his town at the gate of that place. ²⁰They shall say to the elders of his town, "This son of ours is stubborn and rebellious. He will not obey us. He is a glutton and a drunkard." ²¹Then all the men of the town shall stone him to death. So you shall purge the evil from your midst; and all Israel will hear, and be afraid.

Miscellaneous Laws

22 When someone is convicted of a crime punishable by death and is executed, and you hang him on a tree, ²³his corpse must not remain all night upon the tree; you shall bury him that same day, for anyone hung on a tree is under God's curse. You must not defile the land the LORD your God is giving you for possession.

22 You shall not watch your neighbor's ox or sheep straying away and ignore them; you shall take them back to their owner. ²If the owner does not reside near you or you do not know who the owner is, you shall bring it to your own house, and it shall remain with you until the owner claims it; then you shall return it. ³You shall do the same with a neighbor's donkey; you shall do the same with a neighbor's garment; and you shall do the same with anything else that your neighbor loses and you find. You may not withhold your help.

4 You shall not see your neighbor's donkey or ox fallen on the road and ignore it; you shall help to lift it up.

5 A woman shall not wear a man's apparel, nor shall a man put on a woman's garment; for whoever does such things is abhorrent to the LORD your God.

6 If you come on a bird's nest, in any tree or on the ground, with fledglings or eggs, with the mother sitting on the fledglings or on the eggs, you shall not take the mother with the young. ⁷Let the mother go, taking only the young for yourself, in order that it may go well with you and you may live long.

8 When you build a new house, you shall make a parapet for your roof; otherwise you might have bloodguilt on your house, if anyone should fall from it.

9 You shall not sow your vineyard with a second kind of seed, or the whole yield will have to be forfeited, both the crop that you have sown and the yield of the vineyard itself.

10 You shall not plow with an ox and a donkey yoked together.

11 You shall not wear clothes made of wool and linen woven together.

12 You shall make tassels on the four corners of the cloak with which you cover yourself.

Laws concerning Sexual Relations

13 Suppose a man marries a woman, but after going in to her, he dislikes her ¹⁴and makes up charges against her, slandering her by saying, "I married this woman; but when I lay with her, I did not find evidence of her virginity." ¹⁵The father of the young woman and her mother shall then submit the evidence of the young woman's virginity to the elders of the city at the gate. ¹⁶The father of the young woman shall say to the elders: "I gave my daughter in marriage to this man but he dislikes her; ¹⁷now he has made up charges against her, saying, 'I did not find evidence of your daughter's virginity.' But here is the evidence of my daughter's virginity." Then they shall spread out the cloth before the elders of the town. ¹⁸The elders of that town shall take the man and punish him; ¹⁹they shall fine him one hundred shekels of silver (which they shall give to the young woman's father) because he has slandered a virgin of Israel. She shall remain his wife; he shall not be

y Heb *two-thirds*

permitted to divorce her as long as he lives.

20 If, however, this charge is true, that evidence of the young woman's virginity was not found, ²¹then they shall bring the young woman out to the entrance of her father's house and the men of her town shall stone her to death, because she committed a disgraceful act in Israel by prostituting herself in her father's house. So you shall purge the evil from your midst.

22 If a man is caught lying with the wife of another man, both of them shall die, the man who lay with the woman as well as the woman. So you shall purge the evil from Israel.

23 If there is a young woman, a virgin already engaged to be married, and a man meets her in the town and lies with her, ²⁴you shall bring both of them to the gate of that town and stone them to death, the young woman because she did not cry for help in the town and the man because he violated his neighbor's wife. So you shall purge the evil from your midst.

25 But if the man meets the engaged woman in the open country, and the man seizes her and lies with her, then only the man who lay with her shall die. ²⁶You shall do nothing to the young woman; the young woman has not committed an offense punishable by death, because this case is like that of someone who attacks and murders a neighbor. ²⁷Since he found her in the open country, the engaged woman may have cried for help, but there was no one to rescue her.

28 If a man meets a virgin who is not engaged, and seizes her and lies with her, and they are caught in the act, ²⁹the man who lay with her shall give fifty shekels of silver to the young woman's father, and she shall become his wife. Because he violated her he shall not be permitted to divorce her as long as he lives.

30ᶻ A man shall not marry his father's wife, thereby violating his father's rights.ᵃ

Those Excluded from the Assembly

23 No one whose testicles are crushed or whose penis is cut off shall be admitted to the assembly of the LORD.

2 Those born of an illicit union shall not be admitted to the assembly of the LORD. Even to the tenth generation, none of their descendants shall be ad-

mitted to the assembly of the LORD.

3 No Am'mon·ite or Mō'ab·ite shall be admitted to the assembly of the LORD. Even to the tenth generation, none of their descendants shall be admitted to the assembly of the LORD, ⁴because they did not meet you with food and water on your journey out of Egypt, and because they hired against you Ba'laam son of Be'or, from Pe'-thor of Mes·o·po·ta'mi·a, to curse you. ⁵(Yet the LORD your God refused to heed Ba'laam; the LORD your God turned the curse into a blessing for you, because the LORD your God loved you.) ⁶You shall never promote their welfare or their prosperity as long as you live.

7 You shall not abhor any of the E'dom·ites, for they are your kin. You shall not abhor any of the Egyptians, because you were an alien residing in their land. ⁸The children of the third generation that are born to them may be admitted to the assembly of the LORD.

Sanitary, Ritual, and Humanitarian Precepts

9 When you are encamped against your enemies you shall guard against any impropriety.

10 If one of you becomes unclean because of a nocturnal emission, then he shall go outside the camp; he must not come within the camp. ¹¹When evening comes, he shall wash himself with water, and when the sun has set, he may come back into the camp.

12 You shall have a designated area outside the camp to which you shall go. ¹³With your utensils you shall have a trowel; when you relieve yourself outside, you shall dig a hole with it and then cover up your excrement. ¹⁴Because the LORD your God travels along with your camp, to save you and to hand over your enemies to you, therefore your camp must be holy, so that he may not see anything indecent among you and turn away from you.

15 Slaves who have escaped to you from their owners shall not be given back to them. ¹⁶They shall reside with you, in your midst, in any place they choose in any one of your towns, wherever they please; you shall not oppress them.

17 None of the daughters of Israel

ᶻCh 23.1 in Heb   ᵃHeb *uncovering his father's skirt*

shall be a temple prostitute; none of the sons of Israel shall be a temple prostitute. [18]You shall not bring the fee of a prostitute or the wages of a male prostitute[b] into the house of the LORD your God in payment for any vow, for both of these are abhorrent to the LORD your God.

19 You shall not charge interest on loans to another Israelite, interest on money, interest on provisions, interest on anything that is lent. [20]On loans to a foreigner you may charge interest, but on loans to another Israelite you may not charge interest, so that the LORD your God may bless you in all your undertakings in the land that you are about to enter and possess.

21 If you make a vow to the LORD your God, do not postpone fulfilling it; for the LORD your God will surely require it of you, and you would incur guilt. [22]But if you refrain from vowing, you will not incur guilt. [23]Whatever your lips utter you must diligently perform, just as you have freely vowed to the LORD your God with your own mouth.

24 If you go into your neighbor's vineyard, you may eat your fill of grapes, as many as you wish, but you shall not put any in a container.

25 If you go into your neighbor's standing grain, you may pluck the ears with your hand, but you shall not put a sickle to your neighbor's standing grain.

Laws concerning Marriage and Divorce

24 Suppose a man enters into marriage with a woman, but she does not please him because he finds something objectionable about her, and so he writes her a certificate of divorce, puts it in her hand, and sends her out of his house; she then leaves his house [2]and goes off to become another man's wife. [3]Then suppose the second man dislikes her, writes her a bill of divorce, puts it in her hand, and sends her out of his house (or the second man who married her dies); [4]her first husband, who sent her away, is not permitted to take her again to be his wife after she has been defiled; for that would be abhorrent to the LORD, and you shall not bring guilt on the land that the LORD your God is giving you as a possession.

Miscellaneous Laws

5 When a man is newly married, he shall not go out with the army or be charged with any related duty. He shall be free at home one year, to be happy with the wife whom he has married.

6 No one shall take a mill or an upper millstone in pledge, for that would be taking a life in pledge.

7 If someone is caught kidnaping another Israelite, enslaving or selling the Israelite, then that kidnaper shall die. So you shall purge the evil from your midst.

8 Guard against an outbreak of a leprous[c] skin disease by being very careful; you shall carefully observe whatever the levitical priests instruct you, just as I have commanded them. [9]Remember what the LORD your God did to Miriam on your journey out of Egypt.

10 When you make your neighbor a loan of any kind, you shall not go into the house to take the pledge. [11]You shall wait outside, while the person to whom you are making the loan brings the pledge out to you. [12]If the person is poor, you shall not sleep in the garment given you as[d] the pledge. [13]You shall give the pledge back by sunset, so that your neighbor may sleep in the cloak and bless you; and it will be to your credit before the LORD your God.

14 You shall not withhold the wages of poor and needy laborers, whether other Israelites or aliens who reside in your land in one of your towns. [15]You shall pay them their wages daily before sunset, because they are poor and their livelihood depends on them; otherwise they might cry to the LORD against you, and you would incur guilt.

16 Parents shall not be put to death for their children, nor shall children be put to death for their parents; only for their own crimes may persons be put to death.

17 You shall not deprive a resident alien or an orphan of justice; you shall not take a widow's garment in pledge. [18]Remember that you were a slave in Egypt and the LORD your God redeemed you from there; therefore I command you to do this.

19 When you reap your harvest in your field and forget a sheaf in the field, you shall not go back to get it; it

---

[b]Heb *a dog*   [c]A term for several skin diseases; precise meaning uncertain   [d]Heb lacks *the garment given you as*

shall be left for the alien, the orphan, and the widow, so that the LORD your God may bless you in all your undertakings. 20 When you beat your olive trees, do not strip what is left; it shall be for the alien, the orphan, and the widow.

21 When you gather the grapes of your vineyard, do not glean what is left; it shall be for the alien, the orphan, and the widow. 22 Remember that you were a slave in the land of Egypt; therefore I am commanding you to do this.

25 Suppose two persons have a dispute and enter into litigation, and the judges decide between them, declaring one to be in the right and the other to be in the wrong. 2 If the one in the wrong deserves to be flogged, the judge shall make that person lie down and be beaten in his presence with the number of lashes proportionate to the offense. 3 Forty lashes may be given but not more; if more lashes than these are given, your neighbor will be degraded in your sight.

4 You shall not muzzle an ox while it is treading out the grain.

Levirate Marriage

5 When brothers reside together, and one of them dies and has no son, the wife of the deceased shall not be married outside the family to a stranger. Her husband's brother shall go in to her, taking her in marriage, and performing the duty of a husband's brother to her, 6 and the firstborn whom she bears shall succeed to the name of the deceased brother, so that his name may not be blotted out of Israel. 7 But if the man has no desire to marry his brother's widow, then his brother's widow shall go up to the elders at the gate and say, "My husband's brother refuses to perpetuate his brother's name in Israel; he will not perform the duty of a husband's brother to me." 8 Then the elders of his town shall summon him and speak to him. If he persists, saying, "I have no desire to marry her," 9 then his brother's wife shall go up to him in the presence of the elders, pull his sandal off his foot, spit in his face, and declare, "This is what is done to the man who does not build up his brother's house." 10 Throughout Israel his family shall be known as "the house of him whose sandal was pulled off."

Various Commands

11 If men get into a fight with on another, and the wife of one intervene to rescue her husband from the grip o his opponent by reaching out and seiz ing his genitals, 12 you shall cut off he hand; show no pity.

13 You shall not have in your ba two kinds of weights, large and smal. 14 You shall not have in your house tw kinds of measures, large and smal 15 You shall have only a full and hones weight; you shall have only a full an honest measure, so that your days ma be long in the land that the LORD you God is giving you. 16 For all who d such things, all who act dishonestly are abhorrent to the LORD your God

17 Remember what Am'a·lek did t you on your journey out of Egypt 18 how he attacked you on the way when you were faint and weary, an struck down all who lagged behind you; he did not fear God. 19 Therefor when the LORD your God has give you rest from all your enemies on ev ery hand, in the land that the LOR your God is giving you as an inheri tance to possess, you shall blot out th remembrance of Am'a·lek from unde heaven; do not forget.

First Fruits and Tithes

26 When you have come into th land that the LORD your God i giving you as an inheritance to pos sess, and you possess it, and settle in it 2 you shall take some of the first of al the fruit of the ground, which you har vest from the land that the LORD you God is giving you, and you shall put i in a basket and go to the place that th LORD your God will choose as a dwell ing for his name. 3 You shall go to th priest who is in office at that time, an say to him, "Today I declare to th LORD your God that I have come int the land that the LORD swore to ou ancestors to give us." 4 When the pries takes the basket from your hand an sets it down before the altar of the LORD your God, 5 you shall make thi response before the LORD your God "A wandering Ar·a·me'an was my an cestor; he went down into Egypt an lived there as an alien, few in number and there he became a great nation mighty and populous. 6 When th Egyptians treated us harshly and af flicted us, by imposing hard labor o us, 7 we cried to the LORD, the God o

our ancestors; the LORD heard our voice and saw our affliction, our toil, and our oppression. ⁸The LORD brought us out of Egypt with a mighty hand and an outstretched arm, with a terrifying display of power, and with signs and wonders; ⁹and he brought us into this place and gave us this land, a land flowing with milk and honey. ¹⁰So now I bring the first of the fruit of the ground that you, O LORD, have given me." You shall set it down before the LORD your God and bow down before the LORD your God. ¹¹Then you, together with the Lē'vītes and the aliens who reside among you, shall celebrate with all the bounty that the LORD your God has given to you and to your house.

12 When you have finished paying all the tithe of your produce in the third year (which is the year of the tithe), giving it to the Lē'vītes, the aliens, the orphans, and the widows, so that they may eat their fill within your towns, ¹³then you shall say before the LORD your God: "I have removed the sacred portion from the house, and I have given it to the Lē'vītes, the resident aliens, the orphans, and the widows, in accordance with your entire commandment that you commanded me; I have neither transgressed nor forgotten any of your commandments: ¹⁴I have not eaten of it while in mourning; I have not removed any of it while I was unclean; and I have not offered any of it to the dead. I have obeyed the LORD my God, doing just as you commanded me. ¹⁵Look down from your holy habitation, from heaven, and bless your people Israel and the ground that you have given us, as you swore to our ancestors—a land flowing with milk and honey."

Concluding Exhortation

16 This very day the LORD your God is commanding you to observe these statutes and ordinances; so observe them diligently with all your heart and with all your soul. ¹⁷Today you have obtained the LORD's agreement: to be your God; and for you to walk in his ways, to keep his statutes, his commandments, and his ordinances, and to obey him. ¹⁸Today the LORD has obtained your agreement: to be his treasured people, as he promised you, and to keep his commandments; ¹⁹for him to set you high above all nations that he has made, in praise and in fame and

in honor; and for you to be a people holy to the LORD your God, as he promised.

The Inscribed Stones and Altar on Mount Ebal

27 Then Moses and the elders of Israel charged all the people as follows: Keep the entire commandment that I am commanding you today. ²On the day that you cross over the Jordan into the land that the LORD your God is giving you, you shall set up large stones and cover them with plaster. ³You shall write on them all the words of this law when you have crossed over, to enter the land that the LORD your God is giving you, a land flowing with milk and honey, as the LORD, the God of your ancestors, promised you. ⁴So when you have crossed over the Jordan, you shall set up these stones, about which I am commanding you today, on Mount Ē'bal, and you shall cover them with plaster. ⁵And you shall build an altar there to the LORD your God, an altar of stones on which you have not used an iron tool. ⁶You must build the altar of the LORD your God of unhewn*ᵉ* stones. Then offer up burnt offerings on it to the LORD your God, ⁷make sacrifices of well-being, and eat them there, rejoicing before the LORD your God. ⁸You shall write on the stones all the words of this law very clearly.

9 Then Moses and the levitical priests spoke to all Israel, saying: Keep silence and hear, O Israel! This very day you have become the people of the LORD your God. ¹⁰Therefore obey the LORD your God, observing his commandments and his statutes that I am commanding you today.

Twelve Curses

11 The same day Moses charged the people as follows: ¹²When you have crossed over the Jordan, these shall stand on Mount Ger'i·zim for the blessing of the people: Sim'ē·on, Levi, Judah, Is'sa·char, Joseph, and Benjamin. ¹³And these shall stand on Mount Ē'bal for the curse: Reuben, Gad, Ash'er, Zeb'ū·lun, Dan, and Naph'-ta·lī. ¹⁴Then the Lē'vītes shall declare in a loud voice to all the Israelites:

15 "Cursed be anyone who makes an idol or casts an image, anything abhorrent to the LORD, the work of an

ᵉ Heb *whole*

D
E
U
T
E
R
O
N
O
M
Y

artisan, and sets it up in secret." All the people shall respond, saying, "Amen!"

16 "Cursed be anyone who dishonors father or mother." All the people shall say, "Amen!"

17 "Cursed be anyone who moves a neighbor's boundary marker." All the people shall say, "Amen!"

18 "Cursed be anyone who misleads a blind person on the road." All the people shall say, "Amen!"

19 "Cursed be anyone who deprives the alien, the orphan, and the widow of justice." All the people shall say, "Amen!"

20 "Cursed be anyone who lies with his father's wife, because he has violated his father's rights."f All the people shall say, "Amen!"

21 "Cursed be anyone who lies with any animal." All the people shall say, "Amen!"

22 "Cursed be anyone who lies with his sister, whether the daughter of his father or the daughter of his mother." All the people shall say, "Amen!"

23 "Cursed be anyone who lies with his mother-in-law." All the people shall say, "Amen!"

24 "Cursed be anyone who strikes down a neighbor in secret." All the people shall say, "Amen!"

25 "Cursed be anyone who takes a bribe to shed innocent blood." All the people shall say, "Amen!"

26 "Cursed be anyone who does not uphold the words of this law by observing them." All the people shall say, "Amen!"

Blessings for Obedience
(Lev 26.1–13; Deut 7.12–24)

28 If you will only obey the LORD your God, by diligently observing all his commandments that I am commanding you today, the LORD your God will set you high above all the nations of the earth; 2 all these blessings shall come upon you and overtake you, if you obey the LORD your God:

3 Blessed shall you be in the city, and blessed shall you be in the field.

4 Blessed shall be the fruit of your womb, the fruit of your ground, and the fruit of your livestock, both the increase of your cattle and the issue of your flock.

5 Blessed shall be your basket and your kneading bowl.

6 Blessed shall you be when you come in, and blessed shall you be when you go out.

7 The LORD will cause your enemies who rise against you to be defeated before you; they shall come out against you one way, and flee before you seven ways. 8 The LORD will command the blessing upon you in your barns, and in all that you undertake; he will bless you in the land that the LORD your God is giving you. 9 The LORD will establish you as his holy people, as he has sworn to you, if you keep the commandments of the LORD your God and walk in his ways. 10 All the peoples of the earth shall see that you are called by the name of the LORD, and they shall be afraid of you. 11 The LORD will make you abound in prosperity, in the fruit of your womb, in the fruit of your livestock, and in the fruit of your ground in the land that the LORD swore to your ancestors to give you. 12 The LORD will open for you his rich storehouse, the heavens, to give the rain of your land in its season and to bless all your undertakings. You will lend to many nations, but you will not borrow. 13 The LORD will make you the head, and not the tail; you shall be only at the top, and not at the bottom— if you obey the commandments of the LORD your God, which I am commanding you today, by diligently observing them, 14 and if you do not turn aside from any of the words that I am commanding you today, either to the right or to the left, following other gods to serve them.

Warnings against Disobedience
(Ex 9.8–12; Lev 26.14–46)

15 But if you will not obey the LORD your God by diligently observing all his commandments and decrees, which I am commanding you today, then all these curses shall come upon you and overtake you:

16 Cursed shall you be in the city, and cursed shall you be in the field.

17 Cursed shall be your basket and your kneading bowl.

18 Cursed shall be the fruit of your womb, the fruit of your ground, the increase of your cattle and the issue of your flock.

19 Cursed shall you be when you come in, and cursed shall you be when you go out.

20 The LORD will send upon you disaster, panic, and frustration in everything you attempt to do, until you are

---

fHeb *uncovered his father's skirt*

destroyed and perish quickly, on account of the evil of your deeds, because you have forsaken me. ²¹The LORD will make the pestilence cling to you until it has consumed you off the land that you are entering to possess. ²²The LORD will afflict you with consumption, fever, inflammation, with fiery heat and drought, and with blight and mildew; they shall pursue you until you perish. ²³The sky over your head shall be bronze, and the earth under you iron. ²⁴The LORD will change the rain of your land into powder, and only dust shall come down upon you from the sky until you are destroyed.

25 The LORD will cause you to be defeated before your enemies; you shall go out against them one way and flee before them seven ways. You shall become an object of horror to all the kingdoms of the earth. ²⁶Your corpses shall be food for every bird of the air and animal of the earth, and there shall be no one to frighten them away. ²⁷The LORD will afflict you with the boils of Egypt, with ulcers, scurvy, and itch, of which you cannot be healed. ²⁸The LORD will afflict you with madness, blindness, and confusion of mind; ²⁹you shall grope about at noon as blind people grope in darkness, but you shall be unable to find your way; and you shall be continually abused and robbed, without anyone to help. ³⁰You shall become engaged to a woman, but another man shall lie with her. You shall build a house, but not live in it. You shall plant a vineyard, but not enjoy its fruit. ³¹Your ox shall be butchered before your eyes, but you shall not eat of it. Your donkey shall be stolen in front of you, and shall not be restored to you. Your sheep shall be given to your enemies, without anyone to help you. ³²Your sons and daughters shall be given to another people, while you look on; you will strain your eyes looking for them all day but be powerless to do anything. ³³A people whom you do not know shall eat up the fruit of your ground and of all your labors; you shall be continually abused and crushed, ³⁴and driven mad by the sight that your eyes shall see. ³⁵The LORD will strike you on the knees and on the legs with grievous boils of which you cannot be healed, from the sole of your foot to the crown of your head. ³⁶The LORD will bring you, and the king whom you set over you, to a nation that neither you nor your ancestors have known, where you shall serve other gods, of wood and stone. ³⁷You shall become an object of horror, a proverb, and a byword among all the peoples where the LORD will lead you.

38 You shall carry much seed into the field but shall gather little in, for the locust shall consume it. ³⁹You shall plant vineyards and dress them, but you shall neither drink the wine nor gather the grapes, for the worm shall eat them. ⁴⁰You shall have olive trees throughout all your territory, but you shall not anoint yourself with the oil, for your olives shall drop off. ⁴¹You shall have sons and daughters, but they shall not remain yours, for they shall go into captivity. ⁴²All your trees and the fruit of your ground the cicada shall take over. ⁴³Aliens residing among you shall ascend above you higher and higher, while you shall descend lower and lower. ⁴⁴They shall lend to you but you shall not lend to them; they shall be the head and you shall be the tail.

45 All these curses shall come upon you, pursuing and overtaking you until you are destroyed, because you did not obey the LORD your God, by observing the commandments and the decrees that he commanded you. ⁴⁶They shall be among you and your descendants as a sign and a portent forever.

47 Because you did not serve the LORD your God joyfully and with gladness of heart for the abundance of everything, ⁴⁸therefore you shall serve your enemies whom the LORD will send against you, in hunger and thirst, in nakedness and lack of everything. He will put an iron yoke on your neck until he has destroyed you. ⁴⁹The LORD will bring a nation from far away, from the end of the earth, to swoop down on you like an eagle, a nation whose language you do not understand, ⁵⁰a grim-faced nation showing no respect to the old or favor to the young. ⁵¹It shall consume the fruit of your livestock and the fruit of your ground until you are destroyed, leaving you neither grain, wine, and oil, nor the increase of your cattle and the issue of your flock, until it has made you perish. ⁵²It shall besiege you in all your towns until your high and fortified walls, in which you trusted, come down throughout your land; it shall besiege you in all your towns throughout the land that

the LORD your God has given you. [53] In the desperate straits to which the enemy siege reduces you, you will eat the fruit of your womb, the flesh of your own sons and daughters whom the LORD your God has given you. [54] Even the most refined and gentle of men among you will begrudge food to his own brother, to the wife whom he embraces, and to the last of his remaining children, [55] giving to none of them any of the flesh of his children whom he is eating, because nothing else remains to him, in the desperate straits to which the enemy siege will reduce you in all your towns. [56] She who is the most refined and gentle among you, so gentle and refined that she does not venture to set the sole of her foot on the ground, will begrudge food to the husband whom she embraces, to her own son, and to her own daughter, [57] begrudging even the afterbirth that comes out from between her thighs, and the children that she bears, because she is eating them in secret for lack of anything else, in the desperate straits to which the enemy siege will reduce you in your towns.

[58] If you do not diligently observe all the words of this law that are written in this book, fearing this glorious and awesome name, the LORD your God, [59] then the LORD will overwhelm both you and your offspring with severe and lasting afflictions and grievous and lasting maladies. [60] He will bring back upon you all the diseases of Egypt, of which you were in dread, and they shall cling to you. [61] Every other malady and affliction, even though not recorded in the book of this law, the LORD will inflict on you until you are destroyed. [62] Although once you were as numerous as the stars in heaven, you shall be left few in number, because you did not obey the LORD your God. [63] And just as the LORD took delight in making you prosperous and numerous, so the LORD will take delight in bringing you to ruin and destruction; you shall be plucked off the land that you are entering to possess. [64] The LORD will scatter you among all peoples, from one end of the earth to the other; and there you shall serve other gods, of wood and stone, which neither you nor your ancestors have known. [65] Among those nations you shall find no ease, no resting place for the sole of your foot. There the LORD will give you a trembling heart, failing eyes, and a languishing spirit. [66] Your life shall hang in doubt before you; night and day you shall be in dread, with no assurance of your life. [67] In the morning you shall say, "If only it were evening!" and at evening you shall say, "If only it were morning!"—because of the dread that your heart shall feel and the sights that your eyes shall see. [68] The LORD will bring you back in ships to Egypt, by a route that I promised you would never see again; and there you shall offer yourselves for sale to your enemies as male and female slaves, but there will be no buyer.

29 [g] These are the words of the covenant that the LORD commanded Moses to make with the Israelites in the land of Mō'ab, in addition to the covenant that he had made with them at Hō'reb.

The Covenant Renewed in Moab

[2] [h] Moses summoned all Israel and said to them: You have seen all that the LORD did before your eyes in the land of Egypt, to Pharaoh and to all his servants and to all his land, [3] the great trials that your eyes saw, the signs, and those great wonders. [4] But to this day the LORD has not given you a mind to understand, or eyes to see, or ears to hear. [5] I have led you forty years in the wilderness. The clothes on your back have not worn out, and the sandals on your feet have not worn out; [6] you have not eaten bread, and you have not drunk wine or strong drink— so that you may know that I am the LORD your God. [7] When you came to this place, King Sī'hon of Hesh'bon and King Og of Bā'shan came out against us for battle, but we defeated them. [8] We took their land and gave it as an inheritance to the Reū'ben·ites, the Gad'ites, and the half-tribe of Ma·nas'seh. [9] Therefore diligently observe the words of this covenant, in order that you may succeed[i] in everything that you do.

[10] You stand assembled today, all of you, before the LORD your God—the leaders of your tribes,[j] your elders and your officials, all the men of Israel, [11] your children, your women, and the aliens who are in your camp, both those who cut your wood and those who draw your water— [12] to enter into the covenant of the LORD your God,

g Ch 28.69 in Heb   h Ch 29.1 in Heb
i Or deal wisely   j Gk Syr: Heb your leaders, your tribes

sworn by an oath, which the LORD your God is making with you today; [13] in order that he may establish you today as his people, and that he may be your God, as he promised you and as he swore to your ancestors, to Abraham, to Isaac, and to Jacob. [14] I am making this covenant, sworn by an oath, not only with you who stand here with us today before the LORD our God, [15] but also with those who are not here with us today. [16] You know how we lived in the land of Egypt, and how we came through the midst of the nations through which you passed. [17] You have seen their detestable things, the filthy idols of wood and stone, of silver and gold, that were among them. [18] It may be that there is among you a man or woman, or a family or tribe, whose heart is already turning away from the LORD our God to serve the gods of those nations. It may be that there is among you a root sprouting poisonous and bitter growth. [19] All who hear the words of this oath and bless themselves, thinking in their hearts, "We are safe even though we go our own stubborn ways" (thus bringing disaster on moist and dry alike)[k] — [20] the LORD will be unwilling to pardon them, for the LORD's anger and passion will smoke against them. All the curses written in this book will descend on them, and the LORD will blot out their names from under heaven. [21] The LORD will single them out from all the tribes of Israel for calamity, in accordance with all the curses of the covenant written in this book of the law. [22] The next generation, your children who rise up after you, as well as the foreigner who comes from a distant country, will see the devastation of that land and the afflictions with which the LORD has afflicted it— [23] all its soil burned out by sulfur and salt, nothing planted, nothing sprouting, unable to support any vegetation, like the destruction of Sod'om and Go·mor'rah, Ad'mah and Ze·boi'im, which the LORD destroyed in his fierce anger— [24] they and indeed all the nations will wonder, "Why has the LORD done thus to this land? What caused this great display of anger?" [25] They will conclude, "It is because they abandoned the covenant of the LORD, the God of their ancestors, which he made with them when he brought them out of the land of Egypt. [26] They turned and served other gods, worshiping them,

gods whom they had not known and whom he had not allotted to them; [27] so the anger of the LORD was kindled against that land, bringing on it every curse written in this book. [28] The LORD uprooted them from their land in anger, fury, and great wrath, and cast them into another land, as is now the case." [29] The secret things belong to the LORD our God, but the revealed things belong to us and to our children forever, to observe all the words of this law.

God's Fidelity Assured

30 When all these things have happened to you, the blessings and the curses that I have set before you, if you call them to mind among all the nations where the LORD your God has driven you, [2] and return to the LORD your God, and you and your children obey him with all your heart and with all your soul, just as I am commanding you today, [3] then the LORD your God will restore your fortunes and have compassion on you, gathering you again from all the peoples among whom the LORD your God has scattered you. [4] Even if you are exiled to the ends of the world,[l] from there the LORD your God will gather you, and from there he will bring you back. [5] The LORD your God will bring you into the land that your ancestors possessed, and you will possess it; he will make you more prosperous and numerous than your ancestors.

[6] Moreover, the LORD your God will circumcise your heart and the heart of your descendants, so that you will love the LORD your God with all your heart and with all your soul, in order that you may live. [7] The LORD your God will put all these curses on your enemies and on the adversaries who took advantage of you. [8] Then you shall again obey the LORD, observing all his commandments that I am commanding you today, [9] and the LORD your God will make you abundantly prosperous in all your undertakings, in the fruit of your body, in the fruit of your livestock, and in the fruit of your soil. For the LORD will again take delight in prospering you, just as he delighted in prospering your ancestors, [10] when you obey the LORD your God by observing his commandments and de-

---

[k] Meaning of Heb uncertain   [l] Heb of heaven

crees that are written in this book of the law, because you turn to the LORD your God with all your heart and with all your soul.

Exhortation to Choose Life

11 Surely, this commandment that I am commanding you today is not too hard for you, nor is it too far away. 12 It is not in heaven, that you should say, "Who will go up to heaven for us, and get it for us so that we may hear it and observe it?" 13 Neither is it beyond the sea, that you should say, "Who will cross to the other side of the sea for us, and get it for us so that we may hear it and observe it?" 14 No, the word is very near to you; it is in your mouth and in your heart for you to observe.

15 See, I have set before you today life and prosperity, death and adversity. 16 If you obey the commandments of the LORD your God[m] that I am commanding you today, by loving the LORD your God, walking in his ways, and observing his commandments, decrees, and ordinances, then you shall live and become numerous, and the LORD your God will bless you in the land that you are entering to possess. 17 But if your heart turns away and you do not hear, but are led astray to bow down to other gods and serve them, 18 I declare to you today that you shall perish; you shall not live long in the land that you are crossing the Jordan to enter and possess. 19 I call heaven and earth to witness against you today that I have set before you life and death, blessings and curses. Choose life so that you and your descendants may live, 20 loving the LORD your God, obeying him, and holding fast to him; for that means life to you and length of days, so that you may live in the land that the LORD swore to give to your ancestors, to Abraham, to Isaac, and to Jacob.

Joshua Becomes Moses' Successor
(Num 27.12–23)

31 When Moses had finished speaking all[n] these words to all Israel, 2 he said to them: "I am now one hundred twenty years old. I am no longer able to get about, and the LORD has told me, 'You shall not cross over this Jordan.' 3 The LORD your God himself will cross over before you. He will destroy these nations before you, and you shall dispossess them. Joshua also will cross over before you, as the LORD

promised. 4 The LORD will do to them as he did to Si'hon and Og, the kings of the Am'o·rites, and to their land, when he destroyed them. 5 The LORD will give them over to you and you shall deal with them in full accord with the command that I have given to you. 6 Be strong and bold; have no fear or dread of them, because it is the LORD your God who goes with you; he will not fail you or forsake you."

7 Then Moses summoned Joshua and said to him in the sight of all Israel: "Be strong and bold, for you are the one who will go with this people into the land that the LORD has sworn to their ancestors to give them; and you will put them in possession of it. 8 It is the LORD who goes before you. He will be with you; he will not fail you or forsake you. Do not fear or be dismayed."

The Law to Be Read
Every Seventh Year

9 Then Moses wrote down this law, and gave it to the priests, the sons of Levi, who carried the ark of the covenant of the LORD, and to all the elders of Israel. 10 Moses commanded them: "Every seventh year, in the scheduled year of remission, during the festival of booths,[o] 11 when all Israel comes to appear before the LORD your God at the place that he will choose, you shall read this law before all Israel in their hearing. 12 Assemble the people—men, women, and children, as well as the aliens residing in your towns—so that they may hear and learn to fear the LORD your God and to observe diligently all the words of this law, 13 and so that their children, who have not known it, may hear and learn to fear the LORD your God, as long as you live in the land that you are crossing over the Jordan to possess."

Moses and Joshua Receive
God's Charge

14 The LORD said to Moses, "Your time to die is near; call Joshua and present yourselves in the tent of meeting, so that I may commission him." So Moses and Joshua went and presented themselves in the tent of meeting, 15 and the LORD appeared at the tent in

---

m Gk: Heb lacks *If you obey the commandments of the LORD your God*
n Q Ms Gk: MT *Moses went and spoke*
o Or *tabernacles*; Heb *succoth*

a pillar of cloud; the pillar of cloud stood at the entrance to the tent.

16 The LORD said to Moses, "Soon you will lie down with your ancestors. Then this people will begin to prostitute themselves to the foreign gods in their midst, the gods of the land into which they are going; they will forsake me, breaking my covenant that I have made with them. 17 My anger will be kindled against them in that day. I will forsake them and hide my face from them; they will become easy prey, and many terrible troubles will come upon them. In that day they will say, 'Have not these troubles come upon us because our God is not in our midst?' 18 On that day I will surely hide my face on account of all the evil they have done by turning to other gods. 19 Now therefore write this song, and teach it to the Israelites; put it in their mouths, in order that this song may be a witness for me against the Israelites. 20 For when I have brought them into the land flowing with milk and honey, which I promised on oath to their ancestors, and they have eaten their fill and grown fat, they will turn to other gods and serve them, despising me and breaking my covenant. 21 And when many terrible troubles come upon them, this song will confront them as a witness, because it will not be lost from the mouths of their descendants. For I know what they are inclined to do even now, before I have brought them into the land that I promised them on oath." 22 That very day Moses wrote this song and taught it to the Israelites.

23 Then the LORD commissioned Joshua son of Nun and said, "Be strong and bold, for you shall bring the Israelites into the land that I promised them; I will be with you."

24 When Moses had finished writing down in a book the words of this law to the very end, 25 Moses commanded the Lě′vites who carried the ark of the covenant of the LORD, saying, 26 "Take this book of the law and put it beside the ark of the covenant of the LORD your God; let it remain there as a witness against you. 27 For I know well how rebellious and stubborn you are. If you already have been so rebellious toward the LORD while I am still alive among you, how much more after my death! 28 Assemble to me all the elders of your tribes and your officials, so that I may recite these words in their hearing and call heaven and earth to witness against them. 29 For I know that after my death you will surely act corruptly, turning aside from the way that I have commanded you. In time to come trouble will befall you, because you will do what is evil in the sight of the LORD, provoking him to anger through the work of your hands."

The Song of Moses

30 Then Moses recited the words of this song, to the very end, in the hearing of the whole assembly of Israel:

32 Give ear, O heavens, and I will speak;
    let the earth hear the words of my mouth.
2 May my teaching drop like the rain,
    my speech condense like the dew;
    like gentle rain on grass,
    like showers on new growth.
3 For I will proclaim the name of the LORD;
    ascribe greatness to our God!

4 The Rock, his work is perfect,
    and all his ways are just.
A faithful God, without deceit,
    just and upright is he;
5 yet his degenerate children have dealt falsely with him,[p]
    a perverse and crooked generation.
6 Do you thus repay the LORD,
    O foolish and senseless people?
Is not he your father, who created you,
    who made you and established you?

7 Remember the days of old,
    consider the years long past;
ask your father, and he will inform you;
    your elders, and they will tell you.
8 When the Most High[q]
    apportioned the nations,
    when he divided humankind,
he fixed the boundaries of the peoples
    according to the number of the gods;[r]

p Meaning of Heb uncertain
q Traditional rendering of Heb *Elyon*
r Q Ms Compare Gk Tg: MT *the Israelites*

9 the LORD's own portion was his
  people,
    Jacob his allotted share.

10 He sustained[s] him in a desert
   land,
     in a howling wilderness waste;
   he shielded him, cared for him,
     guarded him as the apple of
       his eye.
11 As an eagle stirs up its nest,
     and hovers over its young;
   as it spreads its wings, takes
     them up,
     and bears them aloft on its
       pinions,
12 the LORD alone guided him;
     no foreign god was with him.
13 He set him atop the heights of
   the land,
     and fed him with[t] produce of
       the field;
   he nursed him with honey from
     the crags,
     with oil from flinty rock;
14 curds from the herd, and milk
     from the flock,
     with fat of lambs and rams;
   Ba'shan bulls and goats,
     together with the choicest
       wheat—
     you drank fine wine from the
       blood of grapes.
15 Jacob ate his fill;[u]
   Jesh'ū·run grew fat, and
     kicked.
   You grew fat, bloated, and
     gorged!
   He abandoned God who made
     him,
     and scoffed at the Rock of his
       salvation.
16 They made him jealous with
     strange gods,
     with abhorrent things they
       provoked him.
17 They sacrificed to demons, not
     God,
     to deities they had never
       known,
   to new ones recently arrived,
     whom your ancestors had not
       feared.
18 You were unmindful of the Rock
     that bore you;[v]
   you forgot the God who gave
     you birth.

19 The LORD saw it, and was
     jealous[w]
   he spurned[x] his sons and
     daughters.

20 He said: I will hide my face from
     them,
   I will see what their end will
     be;
   for they are a perverse
     generation,
     children in whom there is no
       faithfulness.
21 They made me jealous with what
     is no god,
     provoked me with their idols.
   So I will make them jealous with
     what is no people,
     provoke them with a foolish
       nation.
22 For a fire is kindled by my
     anger,
     and burns to the depths of
       She'ōl;
   it devours the earth and its
     increase,
     and sets on fire the
       foundations of the
       mountains.
23 I will heap disasters upon them,
     spend my arrows against
       them:
24 wasting hunger,
     burning consumption,
     bitter pestilence.
   The teeth of beasts I will send
     against them,
     with venom of things crawling
       in the dust.
25 In the street the sword shall
     bereave,
     and in the chambers terror,
   for young man and woman alike,
     nursing child and old gray
       head.
26 I thought to scatter them[y]
     and blot out the memory of
       them from humankind;
27 but I feared provocation by the
     enemy,
     for their adversaries might
       misunderstand
   and say, "Our hand is
     triumphant;
     it was not the LORD who did
       all this."

28 They are a nation void of sense;

s Sam Gk Compare Tg: MT *found*
t Sam Gk Syr Tg: MT *he ate*   u Q Mss
Sam Gk: MT lacks *Jacob ate his fill*
v Or *that begot you*   w Q Mss Gk: MT
lacks *was jealous*   x Cn: Heb *he
spurned because of provocation*
y Gk: Meaning of Heb uncertain

there is no understanding in them.

29 If they were wise, they would understand this;
   they would discern what the end would be.
30 How could one have routed a thousand,
   and two put a myriad to flight,
   unless their Rock had sold them,
   the LORD had given them up?
31 Indeed their rock is not like our Rock;
   our enemies are fools. *z*
32 Their vine comes from the vinestock of Sod'om,
   from the vineyards of Go·mor'rah;
   their grapes are grapes of poison,
   their clusters are bitter;
33 their wine is the poison of serpents,
   the cruel venom of asps.

34 Is not this laid up in store with me,
   sealed up in my treasuries?
35 Vengeance is mine, and recompense,
   for the time when their foot shall slip;
   because the day of their calamity is at hand,
   their doom comes swiftly.

36 Indeed the LORD will vindicate his people,
   have compassion on his servants,
   when he sees that their power is gone,
   neither bond nor free remaining.
37 Then he will say: Where are their gods,
   the rock in which they took refuge,
38 who ate the fat of their sacrifices,
   and drank the wine of their libations?
   Let them rise up and help you,
   let them be your protection!

39 See now that I, even I, am he;
   there is no god besides me.
   I kill and I make alive;
   I wound and I heal;
   and no one can deliver from my hand.
40 For I lift up my hand to heaven,

and swear: As I live forever,
41 when I whet my flashing sword,
   and my hand takes hold on judgment;
   I will take vengeance on my adversaries,
   and will repay those who hate me.
42 I will make my arrows drunk with blood,
   and my sword shall devour flesh—
   with the blood of the slain and the captives,
   from the long-haired enemy.

43 Praise, O heavens, *a* his people,
   worship him, all you gods! *b*
   For he will avenge the blood of his children, *c*
   and take vengeance on his adversaries;
   he will repay those who hate him, *b*
   and cleanse the land for his people. *d*

44 Moses came and recited all the words of this song in the hearing of the people, he and Joshua *e* son of Nun. 45 When Moses had finished reciting all these words to all Israel, 46 he said to them: "Take to heart all the words that I am giving in witness against you today; give them as a command to your children, so that they may diligently observe all the words of this law. 47 This is no trifling matter for you, but rather your very life; through it you may live long in the land that you are crossing over the Jordan to possess."

Moses' Death Foretold

48 On that very day the LORD addressed Moses as follows: 49 "Ascend this mountain of the Ab'a·rim, Mount Ne'bo, which is in the land of Mo'ab, across from Jericho, and view the land of Ca'naan, which I am giving to the Israelites for a possession; 50 you shall die there on the mountain that you ascend and shall be gathered to your kin, as your brother Aaron died on Mount Hor and was gathered to his kin; 51 because both of you broke faith with me among the Israelites at the waters of

---

z Gk: Meaning of Heb uncertain   *a* Q Ms Gk: MT *nations*   *b* Q Ms Gk: MT lacks this line   *c* Q Ms Gk: MT *his servants*   *d* Q Ms Sam Gk Vg: MT *his land his people*   *e* Sam Gk Syr Vg: MT *Hoshea*

Mer'i·bath-ka'desh in the wilderness of Zin, by failing to maintain my holiness among the Israelites. [52] Although you may view the land from a distance, you shall not enter it—the land that I am giving to the Israelites."

Moses' Final Blessing on Israel

33 This is the blessing with which Moses, the man of God, blessed the Israelites before his death. [2] He said:
The LORD came from Sinai,
  and dawned from Se'ir upon
    us;[f]
he shone forth from Mount
  Par'an.
With him were myriads of holy
  ones;[g]
at his right, a host of his
  own.[h]
[3] Indeed, O favorite among[i]
  peoples,
all his holy ones were in your
  charge;
they marched at your heels,
  accepted direction from you.
[4] Moses charged us with the law,
  as a possession for the
    assembly of Jacob.
[5] There arose a king in Jesh'ū·run,
  when the leaders of the people
    assembled—
  the united tribes of Israel.

[6] May Reuben live, and not die
  out,
  even though his numbers are
    few.

[7] And this he said of Judah:
O LORD, give heed to Judah,
  and bring him to his people;
strengthen his hands for him,[j]
  and be a help against his
    adversaries.

[8] And of Levi he said:
Give to Levi[k] your Thum'mim,
  and your U'rim to your loyal
    one,
whom you tested at Mas'sah,
  with whom you contended at
    the waters of Mer'i·bah;
[9] who said of his father and
  mother,
  "I regard them not";
he ignored his kin,
  and did not acknowledge his
    children.
For they observed your word,
  and kept your covenant.

[10] They teach Jacob your
  ordinances,
  and Israel your law;
they place incense before you,
  and whole burnt offerings on
    your altar.
[11] Bless, O LORD, his substance,
  and accept the work of his
    hands;
crush the loins of his
  adversaries,
  of those that hate him, so that
    they do not rise again.

[12] Of Benjamin he said:
The beloved of the LORD rests in
  safety—
the High God[l] surrounds him
  all day long—
  the beloved[m] rests between his
    shoulders.

[13] And of Joseph he said:
Blessed by the LORD be his land,
  with the choice gifts of heaven
    above,
  and of the deep that lies
    beneath;
[14] with the choice fruits of the sun,
  and the rich yield of the
    months;
[15] with the finest produce of the
  ancient mountains,
  and the abundance of the
    everlasting hills;
[16] with the choice gifts of the earth
  and its fullness,
  and the favor of the one who
    dwells on Sinai.[n]
Let these come on the head of
  Joseph,
  on the brow of the prince
    among his brothers.
[17] A firstborn[o] bull—majesty is
  his!
  His horns are the horns of a
    wild ox;
with them he gores the peoples,
  driving them to[p] the ends of
    the earth;

[f] Gk Syr Vg Compare Tg: Heb *upon them*   [g] Cn Compare Gk Sam Syr Vg: MT *He came from Ribeboth-kodesh,*   [h] Cn Compare Gk: meaning of Heb uncertain   [i] Or *O lover of the*   [j] Cn: Heb *with his hands he contended*   [k] Q Ms Gk: MT lacks *Give to Levi*   [l] Heb *above him*   [m] Heb *he*   [n] Cn: Heb *in the bush*   [o] Q Ms Gk Syr Vg: MT *His firstborn*   [p] Cn: Heb *the peoples, together*

such are the myriads of
  E'phra·im,
  such the thousands of
  Ma·nas'seh.

18 And of Zeb'ū·lun he said:
  Rejoice, Zeb'ū·lun, in your going
    out;
  and Is'sa·char, in your tents.
19 They call peoples to the
    mountain;
  there they offer the right
    sacrifices;
  for they suck the affluence of the
    seas
  and the hidden treasures of
    the sand.

20 And of Gad he said:
  Blessed be the enlargement of
    Gad!
  Gad lives like a lion;
  he tears at arm and scalp.
21 He chose the best for himself,
  for there a commander's
    allotment was reserved;
  he came at the head of the
    people,
  he executed the justice of the
    LORD,
  and his ordinances for
    Israel.

22 And of Dan he said:
  Dan is a lion's whelp
    that leaps forth from
    Bā'shan.

23 And of Naph'ta·lī he said:
  O Naph'ta·lī, sated with favor,
    full of the blessing of the
    LORD,
  possess the west and the
    south.

24 And of Ash'er he said:
  Most blessed of sons be Ash'er;
  may he be the favorite of his
    brothers,
  and may he dip his foot in oil.
25 Your bars are iron and bronze;
  and as your days, so is your
    strength.

26 There is none like God,
    O Jesh'ū·run,
  who rides through the heavens
    to your help,
  majestic through the skies.
27 He subdues the ancient gods, q
  shatters r the forces of old; s

he drove out the enemy before
    you,
  and said, "Destroy!"
28 So Israel lives in safety,
  untroubled is Jacob's abode t
  in a land of grain and wine,
  where the heavens drop down
    dew.
29 Happy are you, O Israel! Who is
    like you,
  a people saved by the LORD,
  the shield of your help,
  and the sword of your
    triumph!
  Your enemies shall come
    fawning to you,
  and you shall tread on their
    backs.

*Moses Dies and Is Buried in
the Land of Moab*

34 Then Moses went up from the
plains of Mō'ab to Mount
Nē'bō, to the top of Pis'gah, which is
opposite Jericho, and the LORD
showed him the whole land: Gil'e·ad
as far as Dan, 2 all Naph'ta·lī, the land
of E'phra·im and Ma·nas'seh, all the
land of Judah as far as the Western
Sea, 3 the Neg'eb, and the Plain—that
is, the valley of Jericho, the city of
palm trees—as far as Zō'ar. 4 The LORD
said to him, "This is the land of which
I swore to Abraham, to Isaac, and to
Jacob, saying, 'I will give it to your
descendants'; I have let you see it with
your eyes, but you shall not cross over
there." 5 Then Moses, the servant of the
LORD, died there in the land of Mō'ab,
at the LORD's command. 6 He was buried in a valley in the land of Mō'ab,
opposite Beth-pē'or, but no one knows
his burial place to this day. 7 Moses
was one hundred twenty years old
when he died; his sight was unim-
paired and his vigor had not abated.
8 The Israelites wept for Moses in the
plains of Mō'ab thirty days; then the
period of mourning for Moses was
ended.
  9 Joshua son of Nun was full of the
spirit of wisdom, because Moses had
laid his hands on him; and the Israelites obeyed him, doing as the LORD had
commanded Moses.
  10 Never since has there arisen a

q Or *The eternal God is a dwelling place*
r Cn: Heb *from underneath* s Or *the
everlasting arms* t Or *fountain*

prophet in Israel like Moses, whom the LORD knew face to face. 11 He was unequaled for all the signs and wonders that the LORD sent him to perform in the land of Egypt, against Pharaoh and all his servants and his entire land, 12 and for all the mighty deeds and all the terrifying displays of power that Moses performed in the sight of all Israel.

History

The historical books include Joshua, Judges, Ruth, 1 and 2 Samuel, 1 and 2 Kings, 1 and 2 Chronicles, Ezra, Nehemiah, Tobit, Judith, Esther, and 1 and 2 Maccabees. These books are history in the best sense, that is, they do more than present data about past events. They present the data in a form that tries to explain what the events mean and how God was working in them.

Joshua, Judges, 1 and 2 Samuel, and 1 and 2 Kings record the history of the period from the death of Moses to the fall of the southern kingdom of Judah, from somewhere before 1200 B.C. to 586 B.C. This period includes the settlement of Israel in the land, the tribal government under the Judges, the time of seeking a king, the golden age under David and Solomon, the division and downfall of the kingdoms. All through the narrative runs the understanding of God's judgment and redemption in political and social life. 1 and 2 Chronicles cover much of the same history from a different perspective. The books of Ezra and Nehemiah pick up the account of Israel and Israel's God in the period after the Exile, the time of the rebuilding of Jerusalem and the renewing of the covenant in a harsh new time.

Joshua marks the end of the Exodus period. Israel enters the land under a new generation of leaders, conquers the hill country, and enters into a great ceremony of covenant renewal at Shechem.

Judges is a collection of accounts of tribal heroes and heroines from the period between the time of Joshua and the time of Samuel. These are accounts of charismatic leaders who, in times of crisis, were called by God to save a part of the tribes from the oppression of an enemy. They teach an understanding of history in a pattern of faithfulness, unfaithfulness, judgment, and salvation in the political world.

Ruth emphasizes God working through a foreign woman to bring forth King David. It carries a strong warning against excluding anyone from a place among God's people.

1 and 2 Samuel record the end of the period of the judges and the rise of the kingship in Israel, with all the accompanying tensions between old ways and new ways. The narratives include the lives and rules of Samuel, Saul, and David.

1 and 2 Kings are the history of the monarchy from Solomon to the Exile. Solomon's glory, the building of the temple, the division of the kingdom, the destruction of the two kingdoms, and the rise of prophecy (Elijah and Elisha) are important themes in these books. Faithfulness to God is defined in social and political terms as well as religious.

1 and 2 Chronicles were written after the destruction of Jerusalem and try to answer the question "Why did God choose to punish his people in such a way?" The answer is found in history. God's people were unfaithful and what happened in social and political history is an expression of God's judgment on an unfaithful people.

Ezra picks up the themes of Chronicles and argues for national purity and exclusiveness.

Nehemiah is the account of the rebuilding of the walls of Jerusalem and the reestablishment of the covenant. It, too, argues for exclusiveness.

Tobit is about a righteous Jew, Tobit, who is in exile in Nineveh, and Sarah, who is tortured by a demon in Media. God sends the angel Raphael to help both Tobit and Sarah. Tobit's son, Tobias, goes with Raphael to Media, binds the demon, and marries Sarah. The religious value of the book is in the emphasis on both the national and personal faith of Judaism lived out by the central characters.

Judith begins with a war against the Jews led by the Assyrian general Holofernes. Judith, a beautiful and pious widow, leaves her besieged village, goes to Holofernes and promises him victory. She then kills him, goes back to her village, and arranges an attack on the Assyrian camp. The Assyrians are defeated and driven out of the country. Judith ranks with Deborah, Esther, and Miriam as a heroine and instrument of God.

Esther is a delightful account of a Jewish heroine whose faithfulness saved her people from certain death.

1 and 2 Maccabees are histories from the period of revolt against Syria beginning in 168 B.C. and culminating in the cleansing of the temple and the establishment of Judea as an independent kingdom under the Hasmonean (or Maccabee) rulers. First Maccabees is a history of the revolt from the accession of Antiochus IV in 175 to the death of Simon the High Priest in 132. It records the clash between Judaism and Hellenism and is the primary source for the history of the period. Second Maccabees focuses on the responsibility of the Hellenizers for profaning the temple. It dwells on the deaths of martyrs and develops the idea of the resurrection.

JOSHUA

God's Commission to Joshua

1 After the death of Moses the servant of the LORD, the LORD spoke to Joshua son of Nun, Moses' assistant, saying, 2 "My servant Moses is dead. Now proceed to cross the Jordan, you and all this people, into the land that I am giving to them, to the Israelites. 3 Every place that the sole of your foot will tread upon I have given to you, as I promised to Moses. 4 From the wilderness and the Lebanon as far as the great river, the river Euphrates, all the land of the Hit′tites, to the Great Sea in the west shall be your territory. 5 No one shall be able to stand against you all the days of your life. As I was with Moses, so I will be with you; I will not fail you or forsake you. 6 Be strong and courageous; for you shall put this people in possession of the land that I swore to their ancestors to give them. 7 Only be strong and very courageous, being careful to act in accordance with all the law that my servant Moses commanded you; do not turn from it to the right hand or to the left, so that you may be successful wherever you go. 8 This book of the law shall not depart out of your mouth; you shall meditate on it day and night, so that you may be careful to act in accordance with all that is written in it. For then you shall make your way prosperous, and then you shall be successful. 9 I hereby command you: Be strong and courageous; do not be frightened or dismayed, for the LORD your God is with you wherever you go."

Preparations for the Invasion

10 Then Joshua commanded the officers of the people, 11 "Pass through the camp, and command the people: 'Prepare your provisions; for in three days you are to cross over the Jordan, to go in to take possession of the land that the LORD your God gives you to possess.' "

12 To the Reü′ben·ites, the Gad′-ites, and the half-tribe of Ma·nas′seh Joshua said, 13 "Remember the word that Moses the servant of the LORD commanded you, saying, 'The LORD your God is providing you a place of rest, and will give you this land.' 14 Your wives, your little ones, and your livestock shall remain in the land that Moses gave you beyond the Jordan. But all the warriors among you shall cross over armed before your kindred and shall help them, 15 until the LORD gives rest to your kindred as well as to you, and they too take possession of the land that the LORD your God is giving them. Then you shall return to your own land and take possession of it, the land that Moses the servant of the LORD gave you beyond the Jordan to the east."

16 They answered Joshua: "All that you have commanded us we will do, and wherever you send us we will go. 17 Just as we obeyed Moses in all things, so we will obey you. Only may the LORD your God be with you, as he was with Moses! 18 Whoever rebels against your orders and disobeys your words, whatever you command, shall be put to death. Only be strong and courageous."

Spies Sent to Jericho
(Heb 11.31)

2 Then Joshua son of Nun sent two men secretly from Shit′tim as spies, saying, "Go, view the land, especially Jericho." So they went, and entered the house of a prostitute whose name was Rā′hab, and spent the night there. 2 The king of Jericho was told, "Some Israelites have come here tonight to search out the land." 3 Then the king of Jericho sent orders to Rā′-hab, "Bring out the men who have come to you, who entered your house, for they have come only to search out the whole land." 4 But the woman took the two men and hid them. Then she said, "True, the men came to me, but I did not know where they came from. [5] And when it was time to close the gate at dark, the men went out. Where the men went I do not know. Pursue them quickly, for you can overtake them." [6] She had, however, brought them up to the roof and hidden them with the stalks of flax that she had laid out on the roof. [7] So the men pursued them on the way to the Jordan as far as the fords. As soon as the pursuers had gone out, the gate was shut.

8 Before they went to sleep, she came up to them on the roof [9] and said to the men: "I know that the LORD has given you the land, and that dread of you has fallen on us, and that all the inhabitants of the land melt in fear before you. [10] For we have heard how the LORD dried up the water of the Red Sea[a] before you when you came out of Egypt, and what you did to the two kings of the Am'o·rītes that were beyond the Jordan, to Sī'hon and Og, whom you utterly destroyed. [11] As soon as we heard it, our hearts melted, and there was no courage left in any of us because of you. The LORD your God is indeed God in heaven above and on earth below. [12] Now then, since I have dealt kindly with you, swear to me by the LORD that you in turn will deal kindly with my family. Give me a sign of good faith [13] that you will spare my father and mother, my brothers and sisters, and all who belong to them, and deliver our lives from death." [14] The men said to her, "Our life for yours! If you do not tell this business of ours, then we will deal kindly and faithfully with you when the LORD gives us the land."

15 Then she let them down by a rope through the window, for her house was on the outer side of the city wall and she resided within the wall itself. [16] She said to them, "Go toward the hill country, so that the pursuers may not come upon you. Hide yourselves there three days, until the pursuers have returned; then afterward you may go your way." [17] The men said to her, "We will be released from this oath that you have made us swear to you [18] if we invade the land and you do not tie this crimson cord in the window through which you let us down, and you do not gather into your house your father and mother, your brothers, and all your family. [19] If any of you go out of the doors of your house into the

street, they shall be responsible for their own death, and we shall be innocent; but if a hand is laid upon any who are with you in the house, we shall bear the responsibility for their death. [20] But if you tell this business of ours, then we shall be released from this oath that you made us swear to you." [21] She said, "According to your words, so be it." She sent them away and they departed. Then she tied the crimson cord in the window.

22 They departed and went into the hill country and stayed there three days, until the pursuers returned. The pursuers had searched all along the way and found nothing. [23] Then the two men came down again from the hill country. They crossed over, came to Joshua son of Nun, and told him all that had happened to them. [24] They said to Joshua, "Truly the LORD has given all the land into our hands; moreover all the inhabitants of the land melt in fear before us."

Israel Crosses the Jordan

3 Early in the morning Joshua rose and set out from Shit'tim with all the Israelites, and they came to the Jordan. They camped there before crossing over. [2] At the end of three days the officers went through the camp [3] and commanded the people, "When you see the ark of the covenant of the LORD your God being carried by the levitical priests, then you shall set out from your place. Follow it, [4] so that you may know the way you should go, for you have not passed this way before. Yet there shall be a space between you and it, a distance of about two thousand cubits; do not come any nearer to it." [5] Then Joshua said to the people, "Sanctify yourselves; for tomorrow the LORD will do wonders among you." [6] To the priests Joshua said, "Take up the ark of the covenant, and pass on in front of the people." So they took up the ark of the covenant and went in front of the people.

7 The LORD said to Joshua, "This day I will begin to exalt you in the sight of all Israel, so that they may know that I will be with you as I was with Moses. [8] You are the one who shall command the priests who bear the ark of the covenant, 'When you come to the edge of the waters of the Jordan, you shall stand still in the Jordan.'"

[a] Or *Sea of Reeds*

9 Joshua then said to the Israelites, "Draw near and hear the words of the LORD your God." 10 Joshua said, "By this you shall know that among you is the living God who without fail will drive out from before you the Cā'-naan-ites, Hit'tītes, Hī'vītes, Per'-iz-zītes, Gir'ga-shītes, Am'o-rītes, and Jeb'ū-sītes: 11 the ark of the covenant of the Lord of all the earth is going to pass before you into the Jordan. 12 So now select twelve men from the tribes of Israel, one from each tribe. 13 When the soles of the feet of the priests who bear the ark of the LORD, the Lord of all the earth, rest in the waters of the Jordan, the waters of the Jordan flowing from above shall be cut off; they shall stand in a single heap."

14 When the people set out from their tents to cross over the Jordan, the priests bearing the ark of the covenant were in front of the people. 15 Now the Jordan overflows all its banks throughout the time of harvest. So when those who bore the ark had come to the Jordan, and the feet of the priests bearing the ark were dipped in the edge of the water, 16 the waters flowing from above stood still, rising up in a single heap far off at Adam, the city that is beside Zar'e-than, while those flowing toward the sea of the Ar'a-bah, the Dead Sea, b were wholly cut off. Then the people crossed over opposite Jericho. 17 While all Israel were crossing over on dry ground, the priests who bore the ark of the covenant of the LORD stood on dry ground in the middle of the Jordan, until the entire nation finished crossing over the Jordan.

Twelve Stones Set Up at Gilgal

4 When the entire nation had finished crossing over the Jordan, the LORD said to Joshua: 2 "Select twelve men from the people, one from each tribe, 3 and command them, 'Take twelve stones from here out of the middle of the Jordan, from the place where the priests' feet stood, carry them over with you, and lay them down in the place where you camp tonight.'" 4 Then Joshua summoned the twelve men from the Israelites, whom he had appointed, one from each tribe. 5 Joshua said to them, "Pass on before the ark of the LORD your God into the middle of the Jordan, and each of you take up a stone on his shoulder, one for each of the tribes of the Israelites, 6 so

that this may be a sign among you. When your children ask in time to come, 'What do those stones mean to you?' 7 then you shall tell them that the waters of the Jordan were cut off in front of the ark of the covenant of the LORD. When it crossed over the Jordan, the waters of the Jordan were cut off. So these stones shall be to the Israelites a memorial forever."

8 The Israelites did as Joshua commanded. They took up twelve stones out of the middle of the Jordan, according to the number of the tribes of the Israelites, as the LORD told Joshua, carried them over with them to the place where they camped, and laid them down there. 9 (Joshua set up twelve stones in the middle of the Jordan, in the place where the feet of the priests bearing the ark of the covenant had stood; and they are there to this day.)

10 The priests who bore the ark remained standing in the middle of the Jordan, until everything was finished that the LORD commanded Joshua to tell the people, according to all that Moses had commanded Joshua. The people crossed over in haste. 11 As soon as all the people had finished crossing over, the ark of the LORD, and the priests, crossed over in front of the people. 12 The Reū'ben-ites, the Gad'-ites, and the half-tribe of Ma-nas'seh crossed over armed before the Israelites, as Moses had ordered them. 13 About forty thousand armed for war crossed over before the LORD to the plains of Jericho for battle.

14 On that day the LORD exalted Joshua in the sight of all Israel; and they stood in awe of him, as they had stood in awe of Moses, all the days of his life.

15 The LORD said to Joshua, 16 "Command the priests who bear the ark of the covenant, c to come up out of the Jordan." 17 Joshua therefore commanded the priests, "Come up out of the Jordan." 18 When the priests bearing the ark of the covenant of the LORD came up from the middle of the Jordan, and the soles of the priests' feet touched dry ground, the waters of the Jordan returned to their place and overflowed all its banks, as before.

19 The people came up out of the Jordan on the tenth day of the first

b Heb Salt Sea   c Or treaty, or testimony; Heb eduth

month, and they camped in Gil'gal on the east border of Jericho. 20 Those twelve stones, which they had taken out of the Jordan, Joshua set up in Gil'-gal, 21 saying to the Israelites, "When your children ask their parents in time to come, 'What do these stones mean?' 22 then you shall let your children know, 'Israel crossed over the Jordan here on dry ground.' 23 For the LORD your God dried up the waters of the Jordan for you until you crossed over, as the LORD your God did to the Red Sea,d which he dried up for us until we crossed over, 24 so that all the peoples of the earth may know that the hand of the LORD is mighty, and so that you may fear the LORD your God forever."

The New Generation Circumcised

5 When all the kings of the Am'-o·rītes beyond the Jordan to the west, and all the kings of the Cā'-naan·ites by the sea, heard that the LORD had dried up the waters of the Jordan for the Israelites until they had crossed over, their hearts melted, and there was no longer any spirit in them, because of the Israelites.

2 At that time the LORD said to Joshua, "Make flint knives and circumcise the Israelites a second time." 3 So Joshua made flint knives, and circumcised the Israelites at Gib'-e·ath-ha·ar'a·loth. e 4 This is the reason why Joshua circumcised them: all the males of the people who came out of Egypt, all the warriors, had died during the journey through the wilderness after they had come out of Egypt. 5 Although all the people who came out had been circumcised, yet all the people born on the journey through the wilderness after they had come out of Egypt had not been circumcised. 6 For the Israelites traveled forty years in the wilderness, until all the nation, the warriors who came out of Egypt, perished, not having listened to the voice of the LORD. To them the LORD swore that he would not let them see the land that he had sworn to their ancestors to give us, a land flowing with milk and honey. 7 So it was their children, whom he raised up in their place, that Joshua circumcised; for they were uncircumcised, because they had not been circumcised on the way.

8 When the circumcising of all the nation was done, they remained in their places in the camp until they were healed. 9 The LORD said to

Joshua, "Today I have rolled away from you the disgrace of Egypt." And so that place is called Gil'gal f to this day.

The Passover at Gilgal

10 While the Israelites were camped in Gil'gal they kept the passover in the evening on the fourteenth day of the month in the plains of Jericho. 11 On the day after the passover, on that very day, they ate the produce of the land, unleavened cakes and parched grain. 12 The manna ceased on the day they ate the produce of the land, and the Israelites no longer had manna; they ate the crops of the land of Cā'naan that year.

Joshua's Vision

13 Once when Joshua was by Jericho, he looked up and saw a man standing before him with a drawn sword in his hand. Joshua went to him and said to him, "Are you one of us, or one of our adversaries?" 14 He replied, "Neither; but as commander of the army of the LORD I have now come." And Joshua fell on his face to the earth and worshiped, and he said to him, "What do you command your servant, my lord?" 15 The commander of the army of the LORD said to Joshua, "Remove the sandals from your feet, for the place where you stand is holy." And Joshua did so.

Jericho Taken and Destroyed

6 Now Jericho was shut up inside and out because of the Israelites; no one came out and no one went in. 2 The LORD said to Joshua, "See, I have handed Jericho over to you, along with its king and soldiers. 3 You shall march around the city, all the warriors circling the city once. Thus you shall do for six days, 4 with seven priests bearing seven trumpets of rams' horns before the ark. On the seventh day you shall march around the city seven times, the priests blowing the trumpets. 5 When they make a long blast with the ram's horn, as soon as you hear the sound of the trumpet, then all the people shall shout with a great shout; and the wall of the city will fall down flat, and all the people shall charge straight ahead." 6 So Joshua son of Nun summoned the priests and

d Or Sea of Reeds   e That is the Hill of the Foreskins   f Related to Heb galal to roll said to them, "Take up the ark of the covenant, and have seven priests carry seven trumpets of rams' horns in front of the ark of the LORD." 7 To the people he said, "Go forward and march around the city; have the armed men pass on before the ark of the LORD."

8 As Joshua had commanded the people, the seven priests carrying the seven trumpets of rams' horns before the LORD went forward, blowing the trumpets, with the ark of the covenant of the LORD following them. 9 And the armed men went before the priests who blew the trumpets; the rear guard came after the ark, while the trumpets blew continually. 10 To the people Joshua gave this command: "You shall not shout or let your voice be heard, nor shall you utter a word, until the day I tell you to shout. Then you shall shout." 11 So the ark of the LORD went around the city, circling it once; and they came into the camp, and spent the night in the camp.

12 Then Joshua rose early in the morning, and the priests took up the ark of the LORD. 13 The seven priests carrying the seven trumpets of rams' horns before the ark of the LORD passed on, blowing the trumpets continually. The armed men went before them, and the rear guard came after the ark of the LORD, while the trumpets blew continually. 14 On the second day they marched around the city once and then returned to the camp. They did this for six days.

15 On the seventh day they rose early, at dawn, and marched around the city in the same manner seven times. It was only on that day that they marched around the city seven times. 16 And at the seventh time, when the priests had blown the trumpets, Joshua said to the people, "Shout! For the LORD has given you the city. 17 The city and all that is in it shall be devoted to the LORD for destruction. Only Raʹ-hab the prostitute and all who are with her in her house shall live because she hid the messengers we sent. 18 As for you, keep away from the things devoted to destruction, so as not to covet g and take any of the devoted things and make the camp of Israel an object for destruction, bringing trouble upon it. 19 But all silver and gold, and vessels of bronze and iron, are sacred to the LORD; they shall go into the treasury of the LORD." 20 So the people shouted, and the trumpets were blown.

As soon as the people heard the sound of the trumpets, they raised a great shout, and the wall fell down flat; so the people charged straight ahead into the city and captured it. 21 Then they devoted to destruction by the edge of the sword all in the city, both men and women, young and old, oxen, sheep, and donkeys.

22 Joshua said to the two men who had spied out the land, "Go into the prostitute's house, and bring the woman out of it and all who belong to her, as you swore to her." 23 So the young men who had been spies went in and brought Raʹhab out, along with her father, her mother, her brothers, and all who belonged to her—they brought all her kindred out—and set them outside the camp of Israel. 24 They burned down the city, and everything in it; only the silver and gold, and the vessels of bronze and iron, they put into the treasury of the house of the LORD. 25 But Raʹhab the prostitute, with her family and all who belonged to her, Joshua spared. Her family h has lived in Israel ever since. For she hid the messengers whom Joshua sent to spy out Jericho.

26 Joshua then pronounced this oath, saying,

"Cursed before the LORD be
	anyone who tries
	to build this city—this Jericho!
At the cost of his firstborn he
	shall lay its foundation,
	and at the cost of his youngest
	he shall set up its gates!"

27 So the LORD was with Joshua; and his fame was in all the land.

The Sin of Achan and Its Punishment

7 But the Israelites broke faith in regard to the devoted things: Aʹchan son of Carʹmi son of Zabʹdi son of Zeʹrah, of the tribe of Judah, took some of the devoted things; and the anger of the LORD burned against the Israelites.

2 Joshua sent men from Jericho to Ai, which is near Beth-aʹven, east of Bethʹel, and said to them, "Go up and spy out the land." And the men went up and spied out Ai. 3 Then they returned to Joshua and said to him, "Not all the people need go up; about two or three thousand men should go up and attack Ai. Since they are so few, do not make the whole people toil up there." 4 So

g Gk: Heb *devote to destruction*
Compare 7.21   h Heb *She*

about three thousand of the people went up there; and they fled before the men of Ai. 5 The men of Ai killed about thirty-six of them, chasing them from outside the gate as far as Sheb′a·rim and killing them on the slope. The hearts of the people melted and turned to water.

6 Then Joshua tore his clothes, and fell to the ground on his face before the ark of the LORD until the evening, he and the elders of Israel; and they put dust on their heads. 7 Joshua said, "Ah, Lord GOD! Why have you brought this people across the Jordan at all, to hand us over to the Am′o·rites so as to destroy us? Would that we had been content to settle beyond the Jordan! 8 O Lord, what can I say, now that Israel has turned their backs to their enemies! 9 The Ca′naan·ites and all the inhabitants of the land will hear of it, and surround us, and cut off our name from the earth. Then what will you do for your great name?"

10 The LORD said to Joshua, "Stand up! Why have you fallen upon your face? 11 Israel has sinned; they have transgressed my covenant that I imposed on them. They have taken some of the devoted things; they have stolen, they have acted deceitfully, and they have put them among their own belongings. 12 Therefore the Israelites are unable to stand before their enemies; they turn their backs to their enemies, because they have become a thing devoted for destruction themselves. I will be with you no more, unless you destroy the devoted things from among you. 13 Proceed to sanctify the people, and say, 'Sanctify yourselves for tomorrow; for thus says the LORD, the God of Israel, "There are devoted things among you, O Israel; you will be unable to stand before your enemies until you take away the devoted things from among you." 14 In the morning therefore you shall come forward tribe by tribe. The tribe that the LORD takes shall come near by clans, the clan that the LORD takes shall come near by households, and the household that the LORD takes shall come near one by one. 15 And the one who is taken as having the devoted things shall be burned with fire, together with all that he has, for having transgressed the covenant of the LORD, and for having done an outrageous thing in Israel.'"

16 So Joshua rose early in the morning, and brought Israel near tribe by tribe, and the tribe of Judah was taken. 17 He brought near the clans of Judah, and the clan of the Zē′ra·hites was taken; and he brought near the clan of the Zē′ra·hites, family by family,[i] and Zab′dī was taken. 18 And he brought near his household one by one, and Ā′chan son of Car′mī son of Zab′dī son of Zē′rah, of the tribe of Judah, was taken. 19 Then Joshua said to Ā′chan, "My son, give glory to the LORD God of Israel and make confession to him. Tell me now what you have done; do not hide it from me." 20 And Ā′chan answered Joshua, "It is true; I am the one who sinned against the LORD God of Israel. This is what I did: 21 when I saw among the spoil a beautiful mantle from Shī′nar, and two hundred shekels of silver, and a bar of gold weighing fifty shekels, then I coveted them and took them. They now lie hidden in the ground inside my tent, with the silver underneath."

22 So Joshua sent messengers, and they ran to the tent; and there it was, hidden in his tent with the silver underneath. 23 They took them out of the tent and brought them to Joshua and all the Israelites; and they spread them out before the LORD. 24 Then Joshua and all Israel with him took Ā′chan son of Zē′rah, with the silver, the mantle, and the bar of gold, with his sons and daughters, with his oxen, donkeys, and sheep, and his tent and all that he had; and they brought them up to the Valley of Ā′chor. 25 Joshua said, "Why did you bring trouble on us? The LORD is bringing trouble on you today." And all Israel stoned him to death; they burned them with fire, cast stones on them, 26 and raised over him a great heap of stones that remains to this day. Then the LORD turned from his burning anger. Therefore that place to this day is called the Valley of Ā′chor.[j]

Ai Captured by a Stratagem and Destroyed

8 Then the LORD said to Joshua, "Do not fear or be dismayed; take all the fighting men with you, and go up now to Ai. See, I have handed over to you the king of Ai with his people, his city, and his land. 2 You shall do to Ai and its king as you did to Jericho and its king; only its spoil and its livestock

[i] Mss Syr: MT *man by man.*   [j] That is *Trouble*

you may take as booty for yourselves. Set an ambush against the city, behind it."

3 So Joshua and all the fighting men set out to go up against Ai. Joshua chose thirty thousand warriors and sent them out by night 4with the command, "You shall lie in ambush against the city, behind it; do not go very far from the city, but all of you stay alert. 5I and all the people who are with me will approach the city. When they come out against us, as before, we shall flee from them. 6They will come out after us until we have drawn them away from the city; for they will say, 'They are fleeing from us, as before.' While we flee from them, 7you shall rise up from the ambush and seize the city; for the LORD your God will give it into your hand. 8And when you have taken the city, you shall set the city on fire, doing as the LORD has ordered; see, I have commanded you." 9So Joshua sent them out; and they went to the place of ambush, and lay between Beth'el and Ai, to the west of Ai; but Joshua spent that night in the camp. *k*

10 In the morning Joshua rose early and mustered the people, and went up, with the elders of Israel, before the people to Ai. 11All the fighting men who were with him went up, and drew near before the city, and camped on the north side of Ai, with a ravine between them and Ai. 12Taking about five thousand men, he set them in ambush between Beth'el and Ai, to the west of the city. 13So they stationed the forces, the main encampment that was north of the city and its rear guard west of the city. But Joshua spent that night in the valley. 14When the king of Ai saw this, he and all his people, hurried out early in the morning to the meeting place facing the Ar'a·bah to meet Israel in battle; but he did not know that there was an ambush against him behind the city. 15And Joshua and all Israel made a pretense of being beaten before them, and fled in the direction of the wilderness. 16So all the people who were in the city were called together to pursue them, and as they pursued Joshua they were drawn away from the city. 17There was not a man left in Ai or Beth'el who did not go out after Israel; they left the city open, and pursued Israel.

18 Then the LORD said to Joshua, "Stretch out the sword that is in your hand toward Ai; for I will give it into your hand." And Joshua stretched out the sword that was in his hand toward the city. 19As soon as he stretched out his hand, the troops in ambush rose quickly out of their place and rushed forward. They entered the city, took it, and at once set the city on fire. 20So when the men of Ai looked back, the smoke of the city was rising to the sky. They had no power to flee this way or that, for the people who fled to the wilderness turned back against the pursuers. 21When Joshua and all Israel saw that the ambush had taken the city and that the smoke of the city was rising, then they turned back and struck down the men of Ai. 22And the others came out from the city against them; so they were surrounded by Israelites, some on one side, and some on the other; and Israel struck them down until no one was left who survived or escaped. 23But the king of Ai was taken alive and brought to Joshua.

24 When Israel had finished slaughtering all the inhabitants of Ai in the open wilderness where they pursued them, and when all of them to the very last had fallen by the edge of the sword, all Israel returned to Ai, and attacked it with the edge of the sword. 25The total of those who fell that day, both men and women, was twelve thousand—all the people of Ai. 26For Joshua did not draw back his hand, with which he stretched out the sword, until he had utterly destroyed all the inhabitants of Ai. 27Only the livestock and the spoil of that city Israel took as their booty, according to the word of the LORD that he had issued to Joshua. 28So Joshua burned Ai, and made it forever a heap of ruins, as it is to this day. 29And he hanged the king of Ai on a tree until evening; and at sunset Joshua commanded, and they took his body down from the tree, threw it down at the entrance of the gate of the city, and raised over it a great heap of stones, which stands there to this day.

Joshua Renews the Covenant
(Cp Deut 27.4–5)

30 Then Joshua built on Mount E'bal an altar to the LORD, the God of Israel, 31just as Moses the servant of the LORD had commanded the Israelites, as it is written in the book of the law of Moses, "an altar of unhewn *l*

*k*Heb *among the people*   *l*Heb *whole*

stones, on which no iron tool has been used"; and they offered on it burnt offerings to the LORD, and sacrificed offerings of well-being. 32 And there, in the presence of the Israelites, Joshua[m] wrote on the stones a copy of the law of Moses, which he had written. 33 All Israel, alien as well as citizen, with their elders and officers and their judges, stood on opposite sides of the ark in front of the levitical priests who carried the ark of the covenant of the LORD, half of them in front of Mount Ger'i·zim and half of them in front of Mount E'bal, as Moses the servant of the LORD had commanded at the first, that they should bless the people of Israel. 34 And afterward he read all the words of the law, blessings and curses, according to all that is written in the book of the law. 35 There was not a word of all that Moses commanded that Joshua did not read before all the assembly of Israel, and the women, and the little ones, and the aliens who resided among them.

The Gibeonites Save Themselves by Trickery

9 Now when all the kings who were beyond the Jordan in the hill country and in the lowland all along the coast of the Great Sea toward Lebanon—the Hit'tites, the Am'o·rites, the Ca'naan·ites, the Per'iz·zites, the Hi'vites, and the Jeb'u·sites—heard of this, 2 they gathered together with one accord to fight Joshua and Israel.

3 But when the inhabitants of Gib'e·on heard what Joshua had done to Jericho and to Ai, 4 they on their part acted with cunning: they went and prepared provisions,[n] and took worn-out sacks for their donkeys, and wineskins, worn-out and torn and mended, 5 with worn-out, patched sandals on their feet, and worn-out clothes; and all their provisions were dry and moldy. 6 They went to Joshua in the camp at Gil'gal, and said to him and to the Israelites, "We have come from a far country; so now make a treaty with us." 7 But the Israelites said to the Hi'vites, "Perhaps you live among us; then how can we make a treaty with you?" 8 They said to Joshua, "We are your servants." And Joshua said to them, "Who are you? And where do you come from?" 9 They said to him, "Your servants have come from a very far country, because of the name of the

LORD your God; for we have heard a report of him, of all that he did in Egypt, 10 and of all that he did to the two kings of the Am'o·rites who were beyond the Jordan, King Si'hon of Hesh'bon, and King Og of Ba'shan who lived in Ash'ta·roth. 11 So our elders and all the inhabitants of our country said to us, 'Take provisions in your hand for the journey; go to meet them, and say to them, "We are your servants; come now, make a treaty with us." ' 12 Here is our bread; it was still warm when we took it from our houses as our food for the journey, on the day we set out to come to you, but now, see, it is dry and moldy; 13 these wineskins were new when we filled them, and see, they are burst; and these garments and sandals of ours are worn out from the very long journey." 14 So the leaders[o] partook of their provisions, and did not ask direction from the LORD. 15 And Joshua made peace with them, guaranteeing their lives by a treaty; and the leaders of the congregation swore an oath to them.

16 But when three days had passed after they had made a treaty with them, they heard that they were their neighbors and were living among them. 17 So the Israelites set out and reached their cities on the third day. Now their cities were Gib'e·on, Che·phi'rah, Be·er'oth, and Kir'i·ath-je'a·rim. 18 But the Israelites did not attack them, because the leaders of the congregation had sworn to them by the LORD, the God of Israel. Then all the congregation murmured against the leaders. 19 But all the leaders said to all the congregation, "We have sworn to them by the LORD, the God of Israel, and now we must not touch them. 20 This is what we will do to them: We will let them live, so that wrath may not come upon us, because of the oath that we swore to them." 21 The leaders said to them, "Let them live." So they became hewers of wood and drawers of water for all the congregation, as the leaders had decided concerning them.

22 Joshua summoned them, and said to them, "Why did you deceive us, saying, 'We are very far from you,' while in fact you are living among us? 23 Now therefore you are cursed, and some of you shall always be slaves,

---

[m] Heb he   [n] Cn: Meaning of Heb uncertain   [o] Gk: Heb men

hewers of wood and drawers of water for the house of my God." 24 They answered Joshua, "Because it was told to your servants for a certainty that the LORD your God had commanded his servant Moses to give you all the land, and to destroy all the inhabitants of the land before you; so we were in great fear for our lives because of you, and did this thing. 25 And now we are in your hand: do as it seems good and right in your sight to do to us." 26 This is what he did for them: he saved them from the Israelites; and they did not kill them. 27 But on that day Joshua made them hewers of wood and drawers of water for the congregation and for the altar of the LORD, to continue to this day, in the place that he should choose.

The Sun Stands Still

10 When King A·dō'ni-ze'dek of Jerusalem heard how Joshua had taken Aī, and had utterly destroyed it, doing to Aī and its king as he had done to Jericho and its king, and how the inhabitants of Gib'ē·on had made peace with Israel and were among them, 2 he^p became greatly frightened, because Gib'ē·on was a large city, like one of the royal cities, and was larger than Aī, and all its men were warriors. 3 So King A·dō'-ni-ze'dek of Jerusalem sent a message to King Hō'ham of Hē'bron, to King Pi'ram of Jar'muth, to King Ja·phī'a of Lā'chish, and to King Dē'bir of Eg'lon, saying, 4 "Come up and help me, and let us attack Gib'ē·on; for it has made peace with Joshua and with the Israelites." 5 Then the five kings of the Am'-o·rītes—the king of Jerusalem, the king of Hē'bron, the king of Jar'muth, the king of Lā'chish, and the king of Eg'lon—gathered their forces, and went up with all their armies and camped against Gib'ē·on, and made war against it.

6 And the Gib'ē·on·ites sent to Joshua at the camp in Gil'gal, saying, "Do not abandon your servants; come up to us quickly, and save us, and help us; for all the kings of the Am'o·rītes who live in the hill country are gathered against us." 7 So Joshua went up from Gil'gal, he and all the fighting force with him, all the mighty warriors. 8 The LORD said to Joshua, "Do not fear them, for I have handed them over to you; not one of them shall stand before you." 9 So Joshua came

upon them suddenly, having marched up all night from Gil'gal. 10 And the LORD threw them into a panic before Israel, who inflicted a great slaughter on them at Gib'ē·on, chased them by the way of the ascent of Beth-hō'ron, and struck them down as far as A·ze'-kah and Mak·ke'dah. 11 As they fled before Israel, while they were going down the slope of Beth-hō'ron, the LORD threw down huge stones from heaven on them as far as A·ze'kah, and they died; there were more who died because of the hailstones than the Israelites killed with the sword.

12 On the day when the LORD gave the Am'o·rītes over to the Israelites, Joshua spoke to the LORD; and he said in the sight of Israel,

"Sun, stand still at Gib'ē·on,
　　and Moon, in the valley of
　　　Aī'ja·lon."
13 And the sun stood still, and the
　　moon stopped,
　　until the nation took
　　　vengeance on their
　　　　enemies.

Is this not written in the Book of Jash'ar? The sun stopped in midheaven, and did not hurry to set for about a whole day. 14 There has been no day like it before or since, when the LORD heeded a human voice; for the LORD fought for Israel.

15 Then Joshua returned, and all Israel with him, to the camp at Gil'gal.

Five Kings Defeated

16 Meanwhile, these five kings fled and hid themselves in the cave at Mak·ke'dah. 17 And it was told Joshua, "The five kings have been found, hidden in the cave at Mak·ke'dah." 18 Joshua said, "Roll large stones against the mouth of the cave, and set men by it to guard them; 19 but do not stay there yourselves; pursue your enemies, and attack them from the rear. Do not let them enter their towns, for the LORD your God has given them into your hand." 20 When Joshua and the Israelites had finished inflicting a very great slaughter on them, until they were wiped out, and when the survivors had entered into the fortified towns, 21 all the people returned safe to Joshua in the camp at Mak·ke'dah; no one dared to speak^q against any of the Israelites.

22 Then Joshua said, "Open the

_{p Heb they}　　_{q Heb moved his tongue}

mouth of the cave, and bring those five kings out to me from the cave." [23] They did so, and brought the five kings out to him from the cave, the king of Jerusalem, the king of He′bron, the king of Jar′muth, the king of La′chish, and the king of Eg′lon. [24] When they brought the kings out to Joshua, Joshua summoned all the Israelites, and said to the chiefs of the warriors who had gone with him, "Come near, put your feet on the necks of these kings." Then they came near and put their feet on their necks. [25] And Joshua said to them, "Do not be afraid or dismayed; be strong and courageous; for thus the LORD will do to all the enemies against whom you fight." [26] Afterward Joshua struck them down and put them to death, and he hung them on five trees. And they hung on the trees until evening. [27] At sunset Joshua commanded, and they took them down from the trees and threw them into the cave where they had hidden themselves; they set large stones against the mouth of the cave, which remain to this very day.

[28] Joshua took Mak·ke′dah on that day, and struck it and its king with the edge of the sword; he utterly destroyed every person in it; he left no one remaining. And he did to the king of Mak·ke′dah as he had done to the king of Jericho.

[29] Then Joshua passed on from Mak·ke′dah, and all Israel with him, to Lib′nah, and fought against Lib′nah. [30] The LORD gave it also and its king into the hand of Israel; and he struck it with the edge of the sword, and every person in it; he left no one remaining in it; and he did to its king as he had done to the king of Jericho.

[31] Next Joshua passed on from Lib′nah, and all Israel with him, to La′chish, and laid siege to it, and assaulted it. [32] The LORD gave La′chish into the hand of Israel, and he took it on the second day, and struck it with the edge of the sword, and every person in it, as he had done to Lib′nah. [33] Then King Ho′ram of Ge′zer came up to help La′chish; and Joshua struck him and his people, leaving him no survivors.

[34] From La′chish Joshua passed on with all Israel to Eg′lon; and they laid siege to it, and assaulted it; [35] and they took it that day, and struck it with the edge of the sword; and every person in it he utterly destroyed that day, as he had done to La′chish.

[36] Then Joshua went up with all Israel from Eg′lon to He′bron; they assaulted it, [37] and took it, and struck it with the edge of the sword, and its king and its towns, and every person in it; he left no one remaining, just as he had done to Eg′lon, and utterly destroyed it with every person in it.

[38] Then Joshua, with all Israel, turned back to De′bir and assaulted it, [39] and he took it with its king and all its towns; they struck them with the edge of the sword, and utterly destroyed every person in it; he left no one remaining; just as he had done to He′bron, and, as he had done to Lib′nah and its king, so he did to De′bir and its king.

[40] So Joshua defeated the whole land, the hill country and the Neg′eb and the lowland and the slopes, and all their kings; he left no one remaining, but utterly destroyed all that breathed, as the LORD God of Israel commanded. [41] And Joshua defeated them from Ka′desh-bar′ne·a to Ga′za, and all the country of Go′shen, as far as Gib′e·on. [42] Joshua took all these kings and their land at one time, because the LORD God of Israel fought for Israel. [43] Then Joshua returned, and all Israel with him, to the camp at Gil′gal.

The United Kings of Northern Canaan Defeated

11 When King Ja′bin of Ha′zor heard of this, he sent to King Jo′bab of Ma′don, to the king of Shim′ron, to the king of Ach′shaph, [2] and to the kings who were in the northern hill country, and in the Ar′a·bah south of Chin′ne·roth, and in the lowland, and in Na′photh-dor on the west, [3] to the Ca′naan·ites in the east and the west, the Am′o·rites, the Hit′tites, the Per′iz·zites, and the Jeb′u·sites in the hill country, and the Hi′vites under Hermon in the land of Miz′pah. [4] They came out, with all their troops, a great army, in number like the sand on the seashore, with very many horses and chariots. [5] All these kings joined their forces, and came and camped together at the waters of Me′rom, to fight with Israel.

[6] And the LORD said to Joshua, "Do not be afraid of them, for tomorrow at this time I will hand over all of them, slain, to Israel; you shall hamstring their horses, and burn their chariots with fire." [7] So Joshua came suddenly upon them with all his fighting force, by the waters of Me′rom, and fell upon

J
O
S
H
U
A

them. 8 And the LORD handed them over to Israel, who attacked them and chased them as far as Great Si'don and Mis're·photh-ma'im, and eastward as far as the valley of Miz'peh. They struck them down, until they had left no one remaining. 9 And Joshua did to them as the LORD commanded him; he hamstrung their horses, and burned their chariots with fire.

10 Joshua turned back at that time, and took Ha'zor, and struck its king down with the sword. Before that time Ha'zor was the head of all those kingdoms. 11 And they put to the sword all who were in it, utterly destroying them; there was no one left who breathed, and he burned Ha'zor with fire. 12 And all the towns of those kings, and all their kings, Joshua took, and struck them with the edge of the sword, utterly destroying them, as Moses the servant of the LORD had commanded. 13 But Israel burned none of the towns that stood on mounds except Ha'zor, which Joshua did burn. 14 All the spoil of these towns, and the livestock, the Israelites took for their booty; but all the people they struck down with the edge of the sword, until they had destroyed them, and they did not leave any who breathed. 15 As the LORD had commanded his servant Moses, so Moses commanded Joshua, and so Joshua did; he left nothing undone of all that the LORD had commanded Moses.

Summary of Joshua's Conquests

16 So Joshua took all that land: the hill country and all the Neg'eb and all the land of Go'shen and the lowland and the Ar'a·bah and the hill country of Israel and its lowland, 17 from Mount Ha'lak, which rises toward Se'ir, as far as Ba'al-gad in the valley of Lebanon below Mount Hermon. He took all their kings, struck them down, and put them to death. 18 Joshua made war a long time with all those kings. 19 There was not a town that made peace with the Israelites, except the Hi'vites, the inhabitants of Gib'e·on; all were taken in battle. 20 For it was the LORD's doing to harden their hearts so that they would come against Israel in battle, in order that they might be utterly destroyed, and might receive no mercy, but be exterminated, just as the LORD had commanded Moses.

21 At that time Joshua came and wiped out the An'a·kim from the hill country, from He'bron, from De'bir, from A'nab, and from all the hill country of Judah, and from all the hill country of Israel; Joshua utterly destroyed them with their towns. 22 None of the An'a·kim was left in the land of the Israelites; some remained only in Ga'za, in Gath, and in Ash'dod. 23 So Joshua took the whole land, according to all that the LORD had spoken to Moses; and Joshua gave it for an inheritance to Israel according to their tribal allotments. And the land had rest from war.

The Kings Conquered by Moses
(Cp Num 21.21–35)

12 Now these are the kings of the land, whom the Israelites defeated, whose land they occupied beyond the Jordan toward the east, from the Wadi Ar'non to Mount Hermon, with all the Ar'a·bah eastward: 2 King Si'hon of the Am'o·rites who lived at Hesh'bon, and ruled from A·ro'er, which is on the edge of the Wadi Ar'-non, and from the middle of the valley as far as the river Jab'bok, the boundary of the Am'mon·ites, that is, half of Gil'e·ad, 3 and the Ar'a·bah to the Sea of Chin'ne·roth eastward, and in the direction of Beth-jesh'i·moth, to the sea of the Ar'a·bah, the Dead Sea, r southward to the foot of the slopes of Pis'gah; 4 and King Og s of Ba'shan, one of the last of the Reph'a·im, who lived at Ash'ta·roth and at Ed're·i 5 and ruled over Mount Hermon and Sal'-e·cah and all Ba'shan to the boundary of the Gesh'u·rites and the Ma'-a·ca·thites, and over half of Gil'e·ad to the boundary of King Si'hon of Hesh'-bon. 6 Moses, the servant of the LORD, and the Israelites defeated them; and Moses the servant of the LORD gave their land for a possession to the Reu'-ben·ites and the Gad'ites and the half-tribe of Ma·nas'seh.

The Kings Conquered by Joshua

7 The following are the kings of the land whom Joshua and the Israelites defeated on the west side of the Jordan, from Ba'al-gad in the valley of Lebanon to Mount Ha'lak, that rises toward Se'ir (and Joshua gave their land to the tribes of Israel as a possession according to their allotments, 8 in the hill country, in the lowland, in the

r Heb *Salt Sea*   s Gk: Heb *the boundary of King Og*

Ar'a·bah, in the slopes, in the wilderness, and in the Neg'eb, the land of the Hit'tites, Am'o·rites, Cā'naan·ites, Per'iz·zites, Hī'vites, and Jeb'u·sites):

9	the king of Jericho	one
	the king of Aī, which is next to Beth'el	one
10	the king of Jerusalem	one
	the king of Hē'bron	one
11	the king of Jar'muth	one
	the king of Lā'chish	one
12	the king of Eg'lon	one
	the king of Gē'zer	one
13	the king of Dē'bir	one
	the king of Gē'der	one
14	the king of Hor'mah	one
	the king of Ar'ad	one
15	the king of Lib'nah	one
	the king of A·dul'lam	one
16	the king of Mak·kē'dah	one
	the king of Beth'el	one
17	the king of Tap'pū·ah	one
	the king of Hē'pher	one
18	the king of Ā'phek	one
	the king of La·shar'on	one
19	the king of Mā'don	one
	the king of Hā'zor	one
20	the king of Shim'ron-mē'ron	one
	the king of Ach'shaph	one
21	the king of Tā'a·nach	one
	the king of Me·gid'dō	one
22	the king of Kē'desh	one
	the king of Jok'nē·am in Car'mel	one
23	the king of Dor in Nā'phath-dor	
	the king of Goi'im in Galilee, t	one
24	the king of Tir'zah	one

thirty-one kings in all.

The Parts of Canaan Still Unconquered

13 Now Joshua was old and advanced in years; and the LORD said to him, "You are old and advanced in years, and very much of the land still remains to be possessed. 2 This is the land that still remains: all the regions of the Phi·lis'tines, and all those of the Gesh'u·rites 3 (from the Shī'hor, which is east of Egypt, northward to the boundary of Ek'ron, it is reckoned as Cā'naan·ite; there are five rulers of the Phi·lis'tines, those of Gā'za, Ash'-dod, Ash'ke·lon, Gath, and Ek'ron), and those of the Av'vim, 4 in the south, all the land of the Cā'naan·ites, and Mear'ah that belongs to the Sī·dō'ni·ans, to Ā'phek, to the boundary of the Am'o·rites, 5 and the land of the Gē'bal·ites, and all Lebanon, toward the east, from Bā'al-gad below

Mount Hermon to Lē'bō-hā'math, 6 all the inhabitants of the hill country from Lebanon to Mis're·photh-mā'im, even all the Sī·dō'ni·ans. I will myself drive them out from before the Israelites; only allot the land to Israel for an inheritance, as I have commanded you. 7 Now therefore divide this land for an inheritance to the nine tribes and the half-tribe of Ma·nas'seh."

The Territory East of the Jordan

8 With the other half-tribe of Ma·nas'seh u the Reū'ben·ites and the Gad'ites received their inheritance, which Moses gave them, beyond the Jordan eastward, as Moses the servant of the LORD gave them: 9 from A·rō'er, which is on the edge of the Wadi Ar'non, and the town that is in the middle of the valley, and all the tableland from v Med'e·ba as far as Dī'bon; 10 and all the cities of King Sī'hon of the Am'o·rites, who reigned in Hesh'-bon, as far as the boundary of the Am'-mon·ites; 11 and Gil'e·ad, and the region of the Gesh'u·rites and Mā'-a·ca·thites, and all Mount Hermon, and all Bā'shan to Sal'e·cah; 12 all the kingdom of Og in Bā'shan, who reigned in Ash'ta·roth and in Ed're·ī (he alone was left of the survivors of the Reph'a·im); these Moses had defeated and driven out. 13 Yet the Israelites did not drive out the Gesh'u·rites or the Mā'a·ca·thites; but Gē'shur and Mā'a·cath live within Israel to this day.

14 To the tribe of Levi alone Moses gave no inheritance; the offerings by fire to the LORD God of Israel are their inheritance, as he said to them.

The Territory of Reuben

15 Moses gave an inheritance to the tribe of the Reū'ben·ites according to their clans. 16 Their territory was from A·rō'er, which is on the edge of the Wadi Ar'non, and the town that is in the middle of the valley, and all the tableland by Med'e·ba; 17 with Hesh'-bon, and all its towns that are in the tableland; Dī'bon, and Bā'moth-bā'al, and Beth-bā'al-mē'on, 18 and Jā'haz, and Ked'e·moth, and Meph'a·ath, 19 and Kir·i·a·thā'im, and Sib'mah, and Ze'reth-shā'har on the hill of the valley, 20 and Beth-pē'or, and the slopes of Pis'gah, and Beth-jesh'i·moth, 21 that is, all the towns of the tableland, and

t Gk: Heb *Gilgal*   u Cn: Heb *With it*
v Compare Gk: Heb lacks *from*

all the kingdom of King Sī′hon of the Am′o·rītes, who reigned in Hesh′bon, whom Moses defeated with the leaders of Mid′i·an, Ē′vī and Rē′kem and Zur and Hur and Rē′ba, as princes of Sī′hon, who lived in the land. 22 Along with the rest of those they put to death, the Israelites also put to the sword Bā′-laam son of Bē′or, who practiced divination. 23 And the border of the Reū′-ben·ītes was the Jordan and its banks. This was the inheritance of the Reū′-ben·ītes, according to their families with their towns and villages.

The Territory of Gad

24 Moses gave an inheritance also to the tribe of the Gad′ītes, according to their families. 25 Their territory was Jā′zer, and all the towns of Gil′e·ad, and half the land of the Am′mon·ītes, to A·rō′er, which is east of Rab′bah, 26 and from Hesh′bon to Rā′math-miz′peh and Bet′ō·nim, and from Mā·ha·nā′im to the territory of Dē′-bir,w 27 and in the valley Beth-hā′ram, Beth-nim′rah, Suc′coth, and Zā′phon, the rest of the kingdom of King Sī′hon of Hesh′bon, the Jordan and its banks, as far as the lower end of the Sea of Chin′ne·reth, eastward beyond the Jordan. 28 This is the inheritance of the Gad′ītes according to their clans, with their towns and villages.

The Territory of the Half-Tribe of Manasseh (East)

29 Moses gave an inheritance to the half-tribe of Ma·nas′seh; it was allotted to the half-tribe of the Ma·nas′sites according to their families. 30 Their territory extended from Mā·ha·nā′im, through all Bā′shan, the whole kingdom of King Og of Bā′shan, and all the settlements of Jā′ir, which are in Bā′-shan, sixty towns, 31 and half of Gil′-e·ad, and Ash′ta·roth, and Ed′rē·ī, the towns of the kingdom of Og in Bā′-shan; these were allotted to the people of Mā′chir son of Ma·nas′seh according to their clans—for half the Mā′-chir·ites.

32 These are the inheritances that Moses distributed in the plains of Mō′ab, beyond the Jordan east of Jericho. 33 But to the tribe of Levi Moses gave no inheritance; the LORD God of Israel is their inheritance, as he said to them.

The Distribution of Territory West of the Jordan

14 These are the inheritances that the Israelites received in the land of Cā′naan, which the priest El·ē·a′zar, and Joshua son of Nun, and the heads of the families of the tribes of the Israelites distributed to them. 2 Their inheritance was by lot, as the LORD had commanded Moses for the nine and one-half tribes. 3 For Moses had given an inheritance to the two and one-half tribes beyond the Jordan; but to the Lē′vītes he gave no inheritance among them. 4 For the people of Joseph were two tribes, Ma·nas′seh and Ē′phra·im; and no portion was given to the Lē′vītes in the land, but only towns to live in, with their pasture lands for their flocks and herds. 5 The Israelites did as the LORD commanded Moses; they allotted the land.

Hebron Allotted to Caleb

6 Then the people of Judah came to Joshua at Gil′gal; and Caleb son of Je·phūn′neh the Ken′iz·zīte said to him, "You know what the LORD said to Moses the man of God in Kā′desh-bar′nē·a concerning you and me. 7 I was forty years old when Moses the servant of the LORD sent me from Kā′-desh-bar′nē·a to spy out the land; and I brought him an honest report. 8 But my companions who went up with me made the heart of the people melt; yet I wholeheartedly followed the LORD my God. 9 And Moses swore on that day, saying, 'Surely the land on which your foot has trodden shall be an inheritance for you and your children forever, because you have wholeheartedly followed the LORD my God.' 10 And now, as you see, the LORD has kept me alive, as he said, these forty-five years since the time that the LORD spoke this word to Moses, while Israel was journeying through the wilderness; and here I am today, eighty-five years old. 11 I am still as strong today as I was on the day that Moses sent me; my strength now is as my strength was then, for war, and for going and coming. 12 So now give me this hill country of which the LORD spoke on that day; for you heard on that day how the An′-a·kim were there, with great fortified cities; it may be that the LORD will be

w Gk Syr Vg: Heb Lidebir

with me, and I shall drive them out, as the LORD said."

13 Then Joshua blessed him, and gave He'bron to Caleb son of Je·phun'-neh for an inheritance. [14]So He'bron became the inheritance of Caleb son of Je·phun'neh the Ken'iz·zite to this day, because he wholeheartedly followed the LORD, the God of Israel. [15]Now the name of He'bron formerly was Kir'i·ath-ar'ba;[x] this Ar'ba was[y] the greatest man among the An'a·kim. And the land had rest from war.

The Territory of Judah

15 The lot for the tribe of the people of Judah according to their families reached southward to the boundary of E'dom, to the wilderness of Zin at the farthest south. [2]And their south boundary ran from the end of the Dead Sea,[z] from the bay that faces southward; [3]it goes out southward of the ascent of Ak·rab'bim, passes along to Zin, and goes up south of Ka'desh-bar'ne·a, along by Hez'ron, up to Ad'-dar, makes a turn to Kar'ka, [4]passes along to Az'mon, goes out by the Wadi of Egypt, and comes to its end at the sea. This shall be your south boundary. [5]And the east boundary is the Dead Sea,[z] to the mouth of the Jordan. And the boundary on the north side runs from the bay of the sea at the mouth of the Jordan; [6]and the boundary goes up to Beth-hog'lah, and passes along north of Beth-ar'a·bah; and the boundary goes up to the Stone of Bo'han, Reuben's son; [7]and the boundary goes up to De'bir from the Valley of A'chor, and so northward, turning toward Gil'gal, which is opposite the ascent of A·dum'mim, which is on the south side of the valley; and the boundary passes along to the waters of En-she'mesh, and ends at En-ro'gel; [8]then the boundary goes up by the valley of the son of Hin'nom at the southern slope of the Jeb'u·sites (that is, Jerusalem); and the boundary goes up to the top of the mountain that lies over against the valley of Hin'nom, on the west, at the northern end of the valley of Reph'a·im; [9]then the boundary extends from the top of the mountain to the spring of the Waters of Neph·to'ah, and from there to the towns of Mount E'phron; then the boundary bends around to Ba'a·lah (that is, Kir'i·ath-je'a·rim); [10]and the boundary circles west of Ba'a·lah to Mount Se'ir, passes

along to the northern slope of Mount Je'a·rim (that is, Ches'a·lon), and goes down to Beth-she'mesh, and passes along by Tim'nah; [11]the boundary goes out to the slope of the hill north of Ek'ron, then the boundary bends around to Shik'ke·ron, and passes along to Mount Ba'a·lah, and goes out to Jab'ne·el; then the boundary comes to an end at the sea. [12]And the west boundary was the Mediterranean with its coast. This is the boundary surrounding the people of Judah according to their families.

Caleb Occupies His Portion
(Judg 1.11–15)

13 According to the commandment of the LORD to Joshua, he gave to Caleb son of Je·phun'neh a portion among the people of Judah, Kir'i·ath-ar'ba,[x] that is, He'bron (Ar'ba was the father of A'nak). [14]And Caleb drove out from there the three sons of A'nak: She'-shai, A·hi'man, and Tal'mai, the descendants of A'nak. [15]From there he went up against the inhabitants of De'-bir; now the name of De'bir formerly was Kir'i·ath-se'pher. [16]And Caleb said, "Whoever attacks Kir'i·ath-se'-pher and takes it, to him I will give my daughter Ach'sah as wife." [17]Oth'ni·el son of Ke'naz, the brother of Caleb, took it; and he gave him his daughter Ach'sah as wife. [18]When she came to him, she urged him to ask her father for a field. As she dismounted from her donkey, Caleb said to her, "What do you wish?" [19]She said to him, "Give me a present; since you have set me in the land of the Neg'eb, give me springs of water as well." So Caleb gave her the upper springs and the lower springs.

The Towns of Judah

20 This is the inheritance of the tribe of the people of Judah according to their families. [21]The towns belonging to the tribe of the people of Judah in the extreme South, toward the boundary of E'dom, were Kab'ze·el, E'der, Ja'gur, [22]Ki'nah, Di·mo'nah, A·da'dah, [23]Ke'desh, Ha'zor, Ith'nan, [24]Ziph, Te'lem, Be·a'loth, [25]Ha'zor-ha·dat'tah, Ker'i·oth-hez'ron (that is, Ha'zor), [26]A'mam, She'ma, Mo'la·dah, [27]Ha'zar-gad'dah, Hesh'mon, Beth-

---

[x]That is *the city of Arba*   [y]Heb lacks *this Arba was*   [z]Heb *Salt Sea*

pel'et, 28 Hă'zar-shū'al, Bĕ'er-she'ba, Biz·i·o·thī'ah, 29 Bă'a·lah, Ĭ'im, Ē'zem, 30 El·tō'lad, Chĕ'sil, Hor'mah, 31 Zik'-lag, Mad·man'nah, San·san'nah, 32 Le-bă'oth, Shil'him, Ă'in, and Rim'mon: in all, twenty-nine towns, with their villages.

33 And in the Lowland, Esh'tă·ol, Zō'rah, Ash'nah, 34 Za·nō'ah, En-gan'-nim, Tap'pū·ah, Ē'nam, 35 Jar'muth, A·dul'lam, Sō'cōh, A·zē'kah, 36 Shā-a·ră'im, Ad·i·thā'im, Ge·dē'rah, Ged·e-rō·thā'im: fourteen towns with their villages.

37 Zĕ'nan, Ha·dash'ah, Mig'dal-gad, 38 Dil'an, Miz'peh, Jok'thĕ-el, 39 Lă'chish, Boz'kath, Eg'lon, 40 Cab'-bon, Lah'mam, Chit'lish, 41 Ge·dē'roth, Beth-dă'gon, Nă'a·mah, and Mak·kē'-dah: sixteen towns with their villages.

42 Lib'nah, Ē'ther, Ă'shan, 43 Iph'-tah, Ash'nah, Nĕ'zib, 44 Kē·ī'lah, Ach'-zib, and Ma·rē'shah: nine towns with their villages.

45 Ek'ron, with its dependencies and its villages; 46 from Ek'ron to the sea, all that were near Ash'dod, with their villages.

47 Ash'dod, its towns and its villages; Gă'za, its towns and its villages; to the Wadi of Egypt, and the Great Sea with its coast.

48 And in the hill country, Shă'mir, Jat'tir, Sō'cōh, 49 Dan'nah, Kir'i·ath-san'nah (that is, Dē'bir), 50 Ă'nab, Esh'te·mōh, Ă'nim, 51 Gō'shen, Hō'lon, and Gī'lōh: eleven towns with their villages.

52 A'rab, Dū'mah, Ē'shan, 53 Jă'-nim, Beth-tap'pū·ah, A·phē'kah, 54 Hum'tah, Kir'i·ath-ar'ba (that is, Hē'bron), and Zī'or: nine towns with their villages.

55 Mă'on, Car'mel, Ziph, Jut'tah, 56 Jez'rē·el, Jok'dē·am, Za·nō'ah, 57 Kāin, Gib'ē·ah, and Tim'nah: ten towns with their villages.

58 Hal'hul, Beth-zur, Gĕ'dor, 59 Mă'a·rath, Beth-ā'noth, and El'-tĕ·kon: six towns with their villages.

60 Kir'i·ath-bă'al (that is, Kir'i·ath-jē'a·rim), and Rab'bah: two towns with their villages.

61 In the wilderness, Beth-ar'a·bah, Mid'din, Se·că'cah, 62 Nib'shan, the City of Salt, and En-ge'di: six towns with their villages.

63 But the people of Judah could not drive out the Jeb'ū·sites, the inhabitants of Jerusalem; so the Jeb'ū·sites live with the people of Judah in Jerusalem to this day.

The Territory of Ephraim

16 The allotment of the Jō'-seph·ītes went from the Jordan by Jericho, east of the waters of Jericho, into the wilderness, going up from Jericho into the hill country to Beth'el; 2 then going from Beth'el to Luz, it passes along to At'a·roth, the territory of the Ar'chītes; 3 then it goes down westward to the territory of the Japh'-let·ītes, as far as the territory of Lower Beth-hō'ron, then to Gē'zer, and it ends at the sea.

4 The Jō'seph·ītes—Ma·nas'seh and Ē'phra·im—received their inheritance.

5 The territory of the Ē'phra·im·ītes by their families was as follows: the boundary of their inheritance on the east was At'a·roth-ad'dar as far as Upper Beth-hō'ron, 6 and the boundary goes from there to the sea; on the north is Mich·mē'thath; then on the east the boundary makes a turn toward Tă'a·nath-shi'lōh, and passes along beyond it on the east to Ja·nō'ah, 7 then it goes down from Ja·nō'ah to At'-a·roth and to Nă'a·rah, and touches Jericho, ending at the Jordan. 8 From Tap'pū·ah the boundary goes westward to the Wadi Kă'nah, and ends at the sea. Such is the inheritance of the tribe of the Ē'phra·im·ītes by their families, 9 together with the towns that were set apart for the Ē'phra·im·ītes within the inheritance of the Ma·nas'sītes, all those towns with their villages. 10 They did not, however, drive out the Că'naan·ītes who lived in Gē'zer: so the Că'naan·ītes have lived within Ē'phra·im to this day but have been made to do forced labor.

The Other Half-Tribe of Manasseh (West)

17 Then allotment was made to the tribe of Ma·nas'seh, for he was the firstborn of Joseph. To Mă'-chir the firstborn of Ma·nas'seh, the father of Gil'e·ad, were allotted Gil'-e·ad and Bă'shan, because he was a warrior. 2 And allotments were made to the rest of the tribe of Ma·nas'seh, by their families, A·bi·ē'zer, Hē'lek, As'ri·el, Shē'chem, Hē'pher, and She·mī'da; these were the male descendants of Ma·nas'seh son of Joseph, by their families.

3 Now Ze'loph'e·had son of Hē'-pher son of Gil'e·ad son of Mă'chir son of Ma·nas'seh had no sons, but only

daughters; and these are the names of his daughters: Mah′lah, Noah, Hog′-lah, Mil′cah, and Tir′zah. 4 They came before the priest El·ē·ā′zar and Joshua son of Nun and the leaders, and said, "The LORD commanded Moses to give us an inheritance along with our male kin." So according to the commandment of the LORD he gave them an inheritance among the kinsmen of their father. 5 Thus there fell to Ma·nas′seh ten portions, besides the land of Gil′-e·ad and Bā′shan, which is on the other side of the Jordan, 6 because the daughters of Ma·nas′seh received an inheritance along with his sons. The land of Gil′e·ad was allotted to the rest of the Ma·nas′sītes.

7 The territory of Ma·nas′seh reached from Ash′er to Mich·mē′-thath, which is east of Shē′chem; then the boundary goes along southward to the inhabitants of En-tap′pū·ah. 8 The land of Tap′pū·ah belonged to Ma·nas′seh, but the town of Tap′pū·ah on the boundary of Ma·nas′seh belonged to the Ē′phra·im·ītes. 9 Then the boundary went down to the Wadi Kā′-nah. The towns here, to the south of the wadi, among the towns of Ma·nas′-seh, belong to Ē′phra·im. Then the boundary of Ma·nas′seh goes along the north side of the wadi and ends at the sea. 10 The land to the south is Ē′phra·im′s and that to the north is Ma·nas′seh′s, with the sea forming its boundary; on the north Ash′er is reached, and on the east Is′sa·char. 11 Within Is′sa·char and Ash′er, Ma·nas′seh had Beth-shē′an and its villages, Ib′lē·am and its villages, the inhabitants of Dor and its villages, the inhabitants of En-dor and its villages, the inhabitants of Tā′a·nach and its villages, and the inhabitants of Me·gid′dō and its villages (the third is Nā′phath). *a* 12 Yet the Ma·nas′sītes could not take possession of those towns; but the Cā′naan·ītes continued to live in that land. 13 But when the Israelites grew strong, they put the Cā′-naan·ītes to forced labor, but did not utterly drive them out.

The Tribe of Joseph Protests

14 The tribe of Joseph spoke to Joshua, saying, "Why have you given me but one lot and one portion as an inheritance, since we are a numerous people, whom all along the LORD has blessed?" 15 And Joshua said to them, "If you are a numerous people, go up to the forest, and clear ground there for yourselves in the land of the Per′-iz·zītes and the Reph′a·im, since the hill country of Ē′phra·im is too narrow for you." 16 The tribe of Joseph said, "The hill country is not enough for us; yet all the Cā′naan·ītes who live in the plain have chariots of iron, both those in Beth-shē′an and its villages and those in the Valley of Jez′rē·el." 17 Then Joshua said to the house of Joseph, to Ē′phra·im and Ma·nas′seh, "You are indeed a numerous people, and have great power; you shall not have one lot only, 18 but the hill country shall be yours; for though it is a forest, you shall clear it and possess it to its farthest borders; for you shall drive out the Cā′naan·ītes, though they have chariots of iron, and though they are strong."

The Territories of the Remaining Tribes

18 Then the whole congregation of the Israelites assembled at Shī′lōh, and set up the tent of meeting there. The land lay subdued before them.

2 There remained among the Israelites seven tribes whose inheritance had not yet been apportioned. 3 So Joshua said to the Israelites, "How long will you be slack about going in and taking possession of the land that the LORD, the God of your ancestors, has given you? 4 Provide three men from each tribe, and I will send them out that they may begin to go throughout the land, writing a description of it with a view to their inheritances. Then come back to me. 5 They shall divide it into seven portions, Judah continuing in its territory on the south, and the house of Joseph in their territory on the north. 6 You shall describe the land in seven divisions and bring the description here to me; and I will cast lots for you here before the LORD our God. 7 The Lē′vītes have no portion among you, for the priesthood of the LORD is their heritage; and Gad and Reuben and the half-tribe of Ma·nas′seh have received their inheritance beyond the Jordan eastward, which Moses the servant of the LORD gave them."

8 So the men started on their way; and Joshua charged those who went to write the description of the land, saying, "Go throughout the land and write

a Meaning of Heb uncertain

a description of it, and come back to me; and I will cast lots for you here before the LORD in Shī'lōh." 9 So the men went and traversed the land and set down in a book a description of it by towns in seven divisions; then they came back to Joshua in the camp at Shī'lōh, 10 and Joshua cast lots for them in Shī'lōh before the LORD; and there Joshua apportioned the land to the Israelites, to each a portion.

The Territory of Benjamin

11 The lot of the tribe of Benjamin according to its families came up, and the territory allotted to it fell between the tribe of Judah and the tribe of Joseph. 12 On the north side their boundary began at the Jordan; then the boundary goes up to the slope of Jericho on the north, then up through the hill country westward; and it ends at the wilderness of Beth-ā'ven. 13 From there the boundary passes along southward in the direction of Luz, to the slope of Luz (that is, Beth'el), then the boundary goes down to At'a·roth-ad'dar, on the mountain that lies south of Lower Beth-hō'ron. 14 Then the boundary goes in another direction, turning on the western side southward from the mountain that lies to the south, opposite Beth-hō'ron, and it ends at Kir'i·ath-bā'al (that is, Kir'i·ath-jē'a·rim), a town belonging to the tribe of Judah. This forms the western side. 15 The southern side begins at the outskirts of Kir'i·ath-jē'a·rim; and the boundary goes from there to E'phron, b to the spring of the Waters of Neph·tō'ah; 16 then the boundary goes down to the border of the mountain that overlooks the valley of the son of Hin'nom, which is at the north end of the valley of Reph'a·im; and it then goes down the valley of Hin'nom, south of the slope of the Jeb'u·sites, and downward to En-rō'gel; 17 then it bends in a northerly direction going on to En-shē'mesh, and from there goes to Ge·lī'loth, which is opposite the ascent of A·dum'mim; then it goes down to the Stone of Bō'han, Reuben's son; 18 and passing on to the north of the slope of Beth-ar'a·bah c it goes down to the Ar'a·bah; 19 then the boundary passes on to the north of the slope of Beth-hog'lah; and the boundary ends at the northern bay of the Dead Sea, d at the south end of the Jordan: this is the southern border. 20 The Jordan forms its boundary on the eastern side.

This is the inheritance of the tribe of Benjamin, according to its families, boundary by boundary all around.

21 Now the towns of the tribe of Benjamin according to their families were Jericho, Beth-hog'lah, E'mek-kē'ziz, 22 Beth-ar'a·bah, Zem·a·rā'im, Beth'el, 23 Av'vim, Par'ah, Oph'rah, 24 Chē'phar-am'mo·nī, Oph'nī, and Gē'ba—twelve towns with their villages: 25 Gib'ē·on, Rā'mah, Be·er'oth, 26 Miz'peh, Chē·phī'rah, Mō'zah, 27 Rē'kem, Ir'pē·el, Tar'a·lah, 28 Zē'la, Ha·ē'leph, Je'bus e (that is, Jerusalem), Gib'ē·ah f and Kir'i·ath-jē'a·rim g— fourteen towns with their villages. This is the inheritance of the tribe of Benjamin according to its families.

The Territory of Simeon

19 The second lot came out for Sim'ē·on, for the tribe of Sim'ē·on, according to its families; its inheritance lay within the inheritance of the tribe of Judah. 2 It had for its inheritance Bē'er-shē'ba, Shē'ba, Mō'la·dah, 3 Hā'zar-shū'al, Bā'lah, E'zem, 4 El·tō'lad, Bē'thul, Hor'mah, 5 Zik'lag, Beth-mar'ca·both, Hā'zar-sū'sah, 6 Beth-le-bā'oth, and Sha·rū'hen— thirteen towns with their villages; 7 Ā'in, Rim'mon, E'ther, and Ā'shan— four towns with their villages; 8 together with all the villages all around these towns as far as Bā'a·lath-bē'er, Rā'mah of the Neg'eb. This was the inheritance of the tribe of Sim'ē·on according to its families. 9 The inheritance of the tribe of Sim'ē·on formed part of the territory of Judah; because the portion of the tribe of Judah was too large for them, the tribe of Sim'ē·on obtained an inheritance within their inheritance.

The Territory of Zebulun

10 The third lot came up for the tribe of Zeb'u·lun, according to its families. The boundary of its inheritance reached as far as Sā'rid; 11 then its boundary goes up westward, and on to Mar'a·lah, and touches Dab'be·sheth, then the wadi that is east of Jok'nē·am; 12 from Sā'rid it goes in the other direction eastward toward the

b Cn See 15.9. Heb westward   c Gk: Heb to the slope over against the Arabah   d Heb Salt Sea   e Gk Syr Vg: Heb the Jebusite   f Heb Gibeath   g Gk: Heb Kiriath sunrise to the boundary of Chis′loth-tā′bor; from there it goes to Dab′-e·rath, then up to Ja·phī′a; [13] from there it passes along on the east toward the sunrise to Gath-hē′pher, to Eth-kā′zin, and going on to Rim′mon it bends toward Nē′ah; [14] then on the north the boundary makes a turn to Han·na′thon, and it ends at the valley of Iph′tah-el; [15] and Kat′tath, Na·hal′al, Shim′ron, I′da·lah, and Bethlehem—twelve towns with their villages. [16] This is the inheritance of the tribe of Zeb′u·lun, according to its families—these towns with their villages.

The Territory of Issachar

17 The fourth lot came out for Is′-sa·char, for the tribe of Is′sa·char, according to its families. [18] Its territory included Jez′rē·el, Che·sul′loth, Shū′-nem, [19] Haph·a·rā′im, Shī′on, A·nā′-ha·rath, [20] Rab′bith, Kish′i·on, Ē′bez, [21] Rē′meth, En-gan′nim, En-had′dah, Beth-paz′zez; [22] the boundary also touches Tā′bor, Sha·ha·zū′mah, and Beth-shē′mesh, and its boundary ends at the Jordan—sixteen towns with their villages. [23] This is the inheritance of the tribe of Is′sa·char, according to its families—the towns with their villages.

The Territory of Asher

24 The fifth lot came out for the tribe of Ash′er according to its families. [25] Its boundary included Hel′-kath, Hā′lī, Bē′ten, Ach′shaph, [26] Al·lam′me·lech, Ā′mad, and Mī′shal; on the west it touches Car′mel and Shī·hor-lib′nath, [27] then it turns eastward, goes to Beth-dā′gon, and touches Zeb′u·lun and the valley of Iph′tah-el northward to Beth-ē′mek and Nē·ī′el; then it continues in the north to Cā′bul, [28] Ē′bron, Rē′hob, Ham′mon, Kā′nah, as far as Great Sidon; [29] then the boundary turns to Rā′mah, reaching to the fortified city of Tȳre; then the boundary turns to Hō′sah, and it ends at the sea; Ma·ha′-lab,[h] Ach′zib, [30] Um′mah, Ā′phek, and Rē′hob—twenty-two towns with their villages. [31] This is the inheritance of the tribe of Ash′er according to its families—these towns with their villages.

The Territory of Naphtali

32 The sixth lot came out for the tribe of Naph′ta·lī, for the tribe of Naph′ta·lī, according to its families. [33] And its boundary ran from Hē′leph, from the oak in Zā·a·nan′nim, and Ad′a·mī-nek′eb, and Jab′nē·el, as far as Lak′kum; and it ended at the Jordan; [34] then the boundary turns westward to Az′noth-tā′bor, and goes from there to Huk′kok, touching Zeb′u·lun at the south, and Ash′er on the west, and Judah on the east at the Jordan. [35] The fortified towns are Zid′dim, Zer, Ham′math, Rak′kath, Chin′ne·reth, [36] Ad′a·mah, Rā′mah, Ha′zor, [37] Kē′-desh, Ed′rē·ī, En-hā′zor, [38] I′ron, Mig′-dal-el, Hō′rem, Beth-ā′nath, and Beth-shē′mesh—nineteen towns with their villages. [39] This is the inheritance of the tribe of Naph′ta·lī according to its families—the towns with their villages.

The Territory of Dan

40 The seventh lot came out for the tribe of Dan, according to its families. [41] The territory of its inheritance included Zō′rah, Esh′tā·ol, Ir-shē′mesh, [42] Shā·a·lab′bin, Aī′ja·lon, Ith′lah, [43] Ē′lon, Tim′nah, Ek′ron, [44] El′tē·keh, Gib′be·thon, Bā′a·lath, [45] Jē′hud, Ben′-ē-bē′rak, Gath-rim′mon, [46] Me-jar′-kon, and Rak′kon at the border opposite Jop′pa. [47] When the territory of the Dan′ītes was lost to them, the Dan′ītes went up and fought against Lē′shem, and after capturing it and putting it to the sword, they took possession of it and settled in it, calling Lē′shem, Dan, after their ancestor Dan. [48] This is the inheritance of the tribe of Dan, according to their families—these towns with their villages.

Joshua's Inheritance

49 When they had finished distributing the several territories of the land as inheritances, the Israelites gave an inheritance among them to Joshua son of Nun. [50] By command of the LORD they gave him the town that he asked for, Tim′nath-sē′rah in the hill country of Ē′phra·im; he rebuilt the town, and settled in it.

51 These are the inheritances that the priest El·ē·ā′zar and Joshua son of Nun and the heads of the families of the tribes of the Israelites distributed by lot at Shī′loh before the LORD, at the entrance of the tent of meeting. So they finished dividing the land.

[h] Cn Compare Gk: Heb *Mehebel*

The Cities of Refuge
(Num 35.9–28; Deut 19.1–13)

20 Then the LORD spoke to Joshua, saying, ² "Say to the Israelites, 'Appoint the cities of refuge, of which I spoke to you through Moses, ³ so that anyone who kills a person without intent or by mistake may flee there; they shall be for you a refuge from the avenger of blood. ⁴ The slayer shall flee to one of these cities and shall stand at the entrance of the gate of the city, and explain the case to the elders of that city; then the fugitive shall be taken into the city, and given a place, and shall remain with them. ⁵ And if the avenger of blood is in pursuit, they shall not give up the slayer, because the neighbor was killed by mistake, there having been no enmity between them before. ⁶ The slayer shall remain in that city until there is a trial before the congregation, until the death of the one who is high priest at the time: then the slayer may return home, to the town in which the deed was done.'"

7 So they set apart Ke′desh in Galilee in the hill country of Naph′ta·li, and She′chem in the hill country of E′phra·im, and Kir′i·ath-ar′ba (that is, He′bron) in the hill country of Judah. ⁸ And beyond the Jordan east of Jericho, they appointed Be′zer in the wilderness on the tableland, from the tribe of Reuben, and Ra′moth in Gil′e·ad, from the tribe of Gad, and Go′lan in Ba′shan, from the tribe of Ma·nas′seh. ⁹ These were the cities designated for all the Israelites, and for the aliens residing among them, that anyone who killed a person without intent could flee there, so as not to die by the hand of the avenger of blood, until there was a trial before the congregation.

Cities Allotted to the Levites
(1 Chr 6.54–81)

21 Then the heads of the families of the Le′vites came to the priest El·e·a′zar and to Joshua son of Nun and to the heads of the families of the tribes of the Israelites; ² they said to them at Shi′loh in the land of Ca′naan, "The LORD commanded through Moses that we be given towns to live in, along with their pasture lands for our livestock." ³ So by command of the LORD the Israelites gave to the Le′vites the following towns and pasture lands out of their inheritance.

4 The lot came out for the families of the Ko′hath·ites. So those Le′vites who were descendants of Aaron the priest received by lot thirteen towns from the tribes of Judah, Sim′e·on, and Benjamin.

5 The rest of the Ko′hath·ites received by lot ten towns from the families of the tribe of E′phra·im, from the tribe of Dan, and the half-tribe of Ma·nas′seh.

6 The Ger′shon·ites received by lot thirteen towns from the families of the tribe of Is′sa·char, from the tribe of Ash′er, from the tribe of Naph′ta·li, and from the half-tribe of Ma·nas′seh in Ba′shan.

7 The Me·rar′ites according to their families received twelve towns from the tribe of Reuben, the tribe of Gad, and the tribe of Zeb′u·lun.

8 These towns and their pasture lands the Israelites gave by lot to the Le′vites, as the LORD had commanded through Moses.

9 Out of the tribe of Judah and the tribe of Sim′e·on they gave the following towns mentioned by name, ¹⁰ which went to the descendants of Aaron, one of the families of the Ko′hath·ites who belonged to the Le′vites, since the lot fell to them first. ¹¹ They gave them Kir′i·ath-ar′ba (Ar′ba being the father of A′nak), that is He′bron, in the hill country of Judah, along with the pasture lands around it. ¹² But the fields of the town and its villages had been given to Caleb son of Je·phun′neh as his holding.

13 To the descendants of Aaron the priest they gave He′bron, the city of refuge for the slayer, with its pasture lands, Lib′nah with its pasture lands, ¹⁴ Jat′tir with its pasture lands, Esh·te·mo′a with its pasture lands, ¹⁵ Ho′lon with its pasture lands, De′bir with its pasture lands, ¹⁶ A′in with its pasture lands, Jut′tah with its pasture lands, and Beth-she′mesh with its pasture lands—nine towns out of these two tribes. ¹⁷ Out of the tribe of Benjamin: Gib′e·on with its pasture lands, Ge′ba with its pasture lands, ¹⁸ An′a·thoth with its pasture lands, and Al′mon with its pasture lands—four towns. ¹⁹ The towns of the descendants of Aaron—the priests—were thirteen in all, with their pasture lands.

20 As to the rest of the Ko′hath·ites belonging to the Ko′hath·ite families of the Le′vites, the towns allotted to them were out of the tribe of

E'phra·im. ²¹To them were given Shĕ'-chem, the city of refuge for the slayer, with its pasture lands in the hill country of E'phra·im, Gĕ'zer with its pasture lands, ²²Kib'zā·im with its pasture lands, and Beth-hō'ron with its pasture lands—four towns. ²³Out of the tribe of Dan: El'tĕ·ke with its pasture lands, Gib'be·thon with its pasture lands, ²⁴Aī'ja·lon with its pasture lands, Gath-rim'mon with its pasture lands—four towns. ²⁵Out of the half-tribe of Ma·nas'seh: Tā'a·nach with its pasture lands, and Gath-rim'-mon with its pasture lands—two towns. ²⁶The towns of the families of the rest of the Kō'hath·ites were ten in all, with their pasture lands.

27 To the Ger'shon·ites, one of the families of the Lĕ'vites, were given out of the half-tribe of Ma·nas'seh, Gō'lan in Bā'shan with its pasture lands, the city of refuge for the slayer, and Be·esh·tĕ'rah with its pasture lands—two towns. ²⁸Out of the tribe of Is'sa·char: Kish'i·on with its pasture lands, Dab'e·rath with its pasture lands, ²⁹Jar'muth with its pasture lands, En-gan'nim with its pasture lands—four towns; ³⁰Out of the tribe of Ash'er: Mī'shal with its pasture lands, Ab'don with its pasture lands, ³¹Hel'kath with its pasture lands, and Rĕ'hob with its pasture lands—four towns. ³²Out of the tribe of Naph'ta·lī: Kĕ'desh in Galilee with its pasture lands, the city of refuge for the slayer, Ham'moth-dor with its pasture lands, and Kar'tan with its pasture lands—three towns. ³³The towns of the several families of the Ger'shon·ites were in all thirteen, with their pasture lands.

34 To the rest of the Lĕ'vites—the Me·rar'īte families—were given out of the tribe of Zeb'ū·lun: Jok'nĕ·am with its pasture lands, Kar'tah with its pasture lands, ³⁵Dim'nah with its pasture lands, Na·hal'al with its pasture lands—four towns. ³⁶Out of the tribe of Reuben: Bĕ'zer with its pasture lands, Jah'zah with its pasture lands, ³⁷Ked'e·moth with its pasture lands, and Meph'a·ath with its pasture lands—four towns. ³⁸Out of the tribe of Gad: Rā'moth in Gil'e·ad with its pasture lands, the city of refuge for the slayer, Mā·ha·nā'im with its pasture lands, ³⁹Hesh'bon with its pasture lands, Ja'zer with its pasture lands—four towns in all. ⁴⁰As for the towns of the several Me·rar'īte families, that is, the remainder of the families of the

Lĕ'vites, those allotted to them were twelve in all.

41 The towns of the Lĕ'vites within the holdings of the Israelites were in all forty-eight towns with their pasture lands. ⁴²Each of these towns had its pasture lands around it; so it was with all these towns.

43 Thus the LORD gave to Israel all the land that he swore to their ancestors that he would give them; and having taken possession of it, they settled there. ⁴⁴And the LORD gave them rest on every side just as he had sworn to their ancestors; not one of all their enemies had withstood them, for the LORD had given all their enemies into their hands. ⁴⁵Not one of all the good promises that the LORD had made to the house of Israel had failed; all came to pass.

The Eastern Tribes Return to Their Territory

22 Then Joshua summoned the Reū'ben·ites, the Gad'ītes, and the half-tribe of Ma·nas'seh, ²and said to them, "You have observed all that Moses the servant of the LORD commanded you, and have obeyed me in all that I have commanded you; ³you have not forsaken your kindred these many days, down to this day, but have been careful to keep the charge of the LORD your God. ⁴And now the LORD your God has given rest to your kindred, as he promised them; therefore turn and go to your tents in the land where your possession lies, which Moses the servant of the LORD gave you on the other side of the Jordan. ⁵Take good care to observe the commandment and instruction that Moses the servant of the LORD commanded you, to love the LORD your God, to walk in all his ways, to keep his commandments, and to hold fast to him, and to serve him with all your heart and with all your soul." ⁶So Joshua blessed them and sent them away, and they went to their tents.

7 Now to the one half of the tribe of Ma·nas'seh Moses had given a possession in Bā'shan; but to the other half Joshua had given a possession beside their fellow Israelites in the land west of the Jordan. And when Joshua sent them away to their tents and blessed them, ⁸he said to them, "Go back to your tents with much wealth, and with very much livestock, with silver, gold, bronze, and iron, and with a great

quantity of clothing; divide the spoil of your enemies with your kindred." [9] So the Reū′ben·ites and the Gad′ites and the half-tribe of Ma·nas′seh returned home, parting from the Israelites at Shi′loh, which is in the land of Cā′naan, to go to the land of Gil′e·ad, their own land of which they had taken possession by command of the LORD through Moses.

A Memorial Altar East of the Jordan

[10] When they came to the region[i] near the Jordan that lies in the land of Cā′naan, the Reū′ben·ites and the Gad′ites and the half-tribe of Ma·nas′seh built there an altar by the Jordan, an altar of great size. [11] The Israelites heard that the Reū′ben·ites and the Gad′ites and the half-tribe of Ma·nas′seh had built an altar at the frontier of the land of Cā′naan, in the region[j] near the Jordan, on the side that belongs to the Israelites. [12] And when the people of Israel heard of it, the whole assembly of the Israelites gathered at Shi′loh, to make war against them.

[13] Then the Israelites sent the priest Phin′e·has son of El·e·a′zar to the Reū′ben·ites and the Gad′ites and the half-tribe of Ma·nas′seh, in the land of Gil′e·ad, [14] and with him ten chiefs, one from each of the tribal families of Israel, every one of them the head of a family among the clans of Israel. [15] They came to the Reū′ben·ites, the Gad′ites, and the half-tribe of Ma·nas′seh, in the land of Gil′e·ad, and they said to them, [16] "Thus says the whole congregation of the LORD, 'What is this treachery that you have committed against the God of Israel in turning away today from following the LORD, by building yourselves an altar today in rebellion against the LORD? [17] Have we not had enough of the sin at Pe′or from which even yet we have not cleansed ourselves, and for which a plague came upon the congregation of the LORD, [18] that you must turn away today from following the LORD! If you rebel against the LORD today, he will be angry with the whole congregation of Israel tomorrow. [19] But now, if your land is unclean, cross over into the LORD's land where the LORD's tabernacle now stands, and take for yourselves a possession among us; only do not rebel against the LORD, or rebel against us[k] by building yourselves an altar other than the altar of the LORD our God. [20] Did not A′chan son of Zē′-

rah break faith in the matter of the devoted things, and wrath fell upon all the congregation of Israel? And he did not perish alone for his iniquity!' "

[21] Then the Reū′ben·ites, the Gad′ites, and the half-tribe of Ma·nas′seh said in answer to the heads of the families of Israel, [22] "The LORD, God of gods! The LORD, God of gods! He knows; and let Israel itself know! If it was in rebellion or in breach of faith toward the LORD, do not spare us today [23] for building an altar to turn away from following the LORD; or if we did so to offer burnt offerings or grain offerings or offerings of well-being on it, may the LORD himself take vengeance. [24] No! We did it from fear that in time to come your children might say to our children, 'What have you to do with the LORD, the God of Israel? [25] For the LORD has made the Jordan a boundary between us and you, you Reū′ben·ites and Gad′ites; you have no portion in the LORD.' So your children might make our children cease to worship the LORD. [26] Therefore we said, 'Let us now build an altar, not for burnt offering, nor for sacrifice, [27] but to be a witness between us and you, and between the generations after us, that we do perform the service of the LORD in his presence with our burnt offerings and sacrifices and offerings of well-being; so that your children may never say to our children in time to come, "You have no portion in the LORD." ' [28] And we thought, If this should be said to us or to our descendants in time to come, we could say, 'Look at this copy of the altar of the LORD, which our ancestors made, not for burnt offerings, nor for sacrifice, but to be a witness between us and you.' [29] Far be it from us that we should rebel against the LORD, and turn away this day from following the LORD by building an altar for burnt offering, grain offering, or sacrifice, other than the altar of the LORD our God that stands before his tabernacle!"

[30] When the priest Phin′e·has and the chiefs of the congregation, the heads of the families of Israel who were with him, heard the words that the Reū′ben·ites and the Gad′ites and the Ma·nas′sites spoke, they were satisfied. [31] The priest Phin′e·has son of El·e·a′zar said to the Reū′ben·ites and

[i] Or to Geliloth   [j] Or at Geliloth
[k] Or make rebels of us

the Gad′ites and the Ma·nas′sites, "Today we know that the LORD is among us, because you have not committed this treachery against the LORD; now you have saved the Israelites from the hand of the LORD."

32   Then the priest Phin′e·has son of El·e·a′zar and the chiefs returned from the Reü′ben·ites and the Gad′ites in the land of Gil′e·ad to the land of Ca′naan, to the Israelites, and brought back word to them. 33 The report pleased the Israelites; and the Israelites blessed God and spoke no more of making war against them, to destroy the land where the Reü′ben·ites and the Gad′ites were settled. 34 The Reü′ben·ites and the Gad′ites called the altar Witness;[l] "For," said they, "it is a witness between us that the LORD is God."

Joshua Exhorts the People

23   A long time afterward, when the LORD had given rest to Israel from all their enemies all around, and Joshua was old and well advanced in years, 2 Joshua summoned all Israel, their elders and heads, their judges and officers, and said to them, "I am now old and well advanced in years; 3 and you have seen all that the LORD your God has done to all these nations for your sake, for it is the LORD your God who has fought for you. 4 I have allotted to you as an inheritance for your tribes those nations that remain, along with all the nations that I have already cut off, from the Jordan to the Great Sea in the west. 5 The LORD your God will push them back before you, and drive them out of your sight; and you shall possess their land, as the LORD your God promised you. 6 Therefore be very steadfast to observe and do all that is written in the book of the law of Moses, turning aside from it neither to the right nor to the left, 7 so that you may not be mixed with these nations left here among you, or make mention of the names of their gods, or swear by them, or serve them, or bow yourselves down to them, 8 but hold fast to the LORD your God, as you have done to this day. 9 For the LORD has driven out before you great and strong nations; and as for you, no one has been able to withstand you to this day. 10 One of you puts to flight a thousand, since it is the LORD your God who fights for you, as he promised you. 11 Be very careful, therefore, to love the LORD your God. 12 For if you turn back, and join the survivors of these nations left here among you, and intermarry with them, so that you marry their women and they yours, 13 know assuredly that the LORD your God will not continue to drive out these nations before you; but they shall be a snare and a trap for you, a scourge on your sides, and thorns in your eyes, until you perish from this good land that the LORD your God has given you.

14   "And now I am about to go the way of all the earth, and you know in your hearts and souls, all of you, that not one thing has failed of all the good things that the LORD your God promised concerning you; all have come to pass for you, not one of them has failed. 15 But just as all the good things that the LORD your God promised concerning you have been fulfilled for you, so the LORD will bring upon you all the bad things, until he has destroyed you from this good land that the LORD your God has given you. 16 If you transgress the covenant of the LORD your God, which he enjoined on you, and go and serve other gods and bow down to them, then the anger of the LORD will be kindled against you, and you shall perish quickly from the good land that he has given to you."

The Tribes Renew the Covenant
(Cp Ex 24.9–18)

24   Then Joshua gathered all the tribes of Israel to She′chem, and summoned the elders, the heads, the judges, and the officers of Israel; and they presented themselves before God. 2 And Joshua said to all the people, "Thus says the LORD, the God of Israel: Long ago your ancestors—Te′rah and his sons Abraham and Na′hor—lived beyond the Euphrates and served other gods. 3 Then I took your father Abraham from beyond the River and led him through all the land of Ca′naan and made his offspring many. I gave him Isaac; 4 and to Isaac I gave Jacob and Esau. I gave Esau the hill country of Se′ir to possess, but Jacob and his children went down to Egypt. 5 Then I sent Moses and Aaron, and I plagued Egypt with what I did in its midst; and afterwards I brought you out. 6 When I brought your ancestors out of Egypt, you came to the sea; and the Egyptians pursued your ancestors

[l] Cn Compare Syr: Heb lacks *Witness*

with chariots and horsemen to the Red Sea.[m] [7]When they cried out to the LORD, he put darkness between you and the Egyptians, and made the sea come upon them and cover them; and your eyes saw what I did to Egypt. Afterwards you lived in the wilderness a long time. [8]Then I brought you to the land of the Am·o·rites, who lived on the other side of the Jordan; they fought with you, and I handed them over to you, and you took possession of their land, and I destroyed them before you. [9]Then King Ba´lak son of Zip´por of Mo´ab, set out to fight against Israel. He sent and invited Ba´laam son of Be´or to curse you, [10]but I would not listen to Ba´laam; therefore he blessed you; so I rescued you out of his hand. [11]When you went over the Jordan and came to Jericho, the citizens of Jericho fought against you, and also the Am·o·rites, the Per´iz·zites, the Ca´naan·ites, the Hit´tites, the Gir´ga·shites, the Hi´vites, and the Jeb´u·sites; and I handed them over to you. [12]I sent the hornet[n] ahead of you, which drove out before you the two kings of the Am´o·rites; it was not by your sword or by your bow. [13]I gave you a land on which you had not labored, and towns that you had not built, and you live in them; you eat the fruit of vineyards and oliveyards that you did not plant.

[14] "Now therefore revere the LORD, and serve him in sincerity and in faithfulness; put away the gods that your ancestors served beyond the River and in Egypt, and serve the LORD. [15]Now if you are unwilling to serve the LORD, choose this day whom you will serve, whether the gods your ancestors served in the region beyond the River or the gods of the Am´o·rites in whose land you are living; but as for me and my household, we will serve the LORD."

[16] Then the people answered, "Far be it from us that we should forsake the LORD to serve other gods; [17]for it is the LORD our God who brought us and our ancestors up from the land of Egypt, out of the house of slavery, and who did those great signs in our sight. He protected us along all the way that we went, and among all the peoples through whom we passed; [18]and the LORD drove out before us all the peoples, the Am·o·rites who lived in the land. Therefore we also will serve the LORD, for he is our God."

[19] But Joshua said to the people, "You cannot serve the LORD, for he is a holy God. He is a jealous God; he will not forgive your transgressions or your sins. [20]If you forsake the LORD and serve foreign gods, then he will turn and do you harm, and consume you, after having done you good." [21]And the people said to Joshua, "No, we will serve the LORD!" [22]Then Joshua said to the people, "You are witnesses against yourselves that you have chosen the LORD, to serve him." And they said, "We are witnesses." [23]He said, "Then put away the foreign gods that are among you, and incline your hearts to the LORD, the God of Israel." [24]The people said to Joshua, "The LORD our God we will serve, and him we will obey." [25]So Joshua made a covenant with the people that day, and made statutes and ordinances for them at She´chem. [26]Joshua wrote these words in the book of the law of God; and he took a large stone, and set it up there under the oak in the sanctuary of the LORD. [27]Joshua said to all the people, "See, this stone shall be a witness against us; for it has heard all the words of the LORD that he spoke to us; therefore it shall be a witness against you, if you deal falsely with your God." [28]So Joshua sent the people away to their inheritances.

Death of Joshua and Eleazar

[29] After these things Joshua son of Nun, the servant of the LORD, died, being one hundred ten years old. [30]They buried him in his own inheritance at Tim´nath-se´rah, which is in the hill country of E´phra·im, north of Mount Ga´ash.

[31] Israel served the LORD all the days of Joshua, and all the days of the elders who outlived Joshua and had known all the work that the LORD did for Israel.

[32] The bones of Joseph, which the Israelites had brought up from Egypt, were buried at She´chem, in the portion of ground that Jacob had bought from the children of Ha´mor, the father of She´chem, for one hundred pieces of money;[o] it became an inheritance of the descendants of Joseph.

[33] El·e·a´zar son of Aaron died; and

[m] Or *Sea of Reeds*   [n] Meaning of Heb uncertain   [o] Heb *one hundred qesitah*

they buried him at Gib'e·ah, the town of his son Phin'e·has, which had been given him in the hill country of E'phra·im.

JUDGES

Israel's Failure to Complete the Conquest of Canaan
(Josh 15.13–19)

1 After the death of Joshua, the Israelites inquired of the LORD, "Who shall go up first for us against the Ca'naan·ites, to fight against them?" 2 The LORD said, "Judah shall go up. I hereby give the land into his hand." 3 Judah said to his brother Sim'e·on, "Come up with me into the territory allotted to me, that we may fight against the Ca'naan·ites; then I too will go with you into the territory allotted to you." So Sim'e·on went with him. 4 Then Judah went up and the LORD gave the Ca'naan·ites and the Per'iz·zites into their hand; and they defeated ten thousand of them at Be'zek. 5 They came upon A·do'ni-be'zek at Be'zek, and fought against him, and defeated the Ca'naan·ites and the Per'iz·zites. 6 A·do'ni-be'zek fled; but they pursued him, and caught him, and cut off his thumbs and big toes. 7 A·do'ni-be'zek said, "Seventy kings with their thumbs and big toes cut off used to pick up scraps under my table; as I have done, so God has paid me back." They brought him to Jerusalem, and he died there.

8 Then the people of Judah fought against Jerusalem and took it. They put it to the sword and set the city on fire. 9 Afterward the people of Judah went down to fight against the Ca'naan·ites who lived in the hill country, in the Neg'eb, and in the lowland. 10 Judah went against the Ca'naan·ites who lived in He'bron (the name of He'bron was formerly Kir'i·ath-ar'ba); and they defeated She'shai and A·hi'man and Tal'mai.

11 From there they went against the inhabitants of De'bir (the name of De'bir was formerly Kir'i·ath-se'pher). 12 Then Caleb said, "Whoever attacks Kir'i·ath-se'pher and takes it, I will give him my daughter Ach'sah as wife." 13 And Oth'ni·el son of Ke'naz, Caleb's younger brother, took it; and he gave him his daughter Ach'sah as wife. 14 When she came to him, she urged him to ask her father for a field. As she dismounted from her donkey, Caleb said to her, "What do you wish?" 15 She said to him, "Give me a present; since you have set me in the land of the Neg'eb, give me also Gul'loth·may'im."a So Caleb gave her Upper Gul'loth and Lower Gul'loth.

16 The descendants of Ho'babb the Ken'ite, Moses' father-in-law, went up with the people of Judah from the city of palms into the wilderness of Judah, which lies in the Neg'eb near Ar'ad. Then they went and settled with the A·mal'e·kites.c 17 Judah went with his brother Sim'e·on, and they defeated the Ca'naan·ites who inhabited Ze'phath, and devoted it to destruction. So the city was called Hor'mah. 18 Judah took Ga'za with its territory, Ash'ke·lon with its territory, and Ek'ron with its territory. 19 The LORD was with Judah, and he took possession of the hill country, but could not drive out the inhabitants of the plain, because they had chariots of iron. 20 He'bron was given to Caleb, as Moses had said; and he drove out from it the three sons of A'nak. 21 But the Ben'ja·min·ites did not drive out the Jeb'u·sites who lived in Jerusalem; so the Jeb'u·sites have lived in Jerusalem among the Ben'ja·min·ites to this day.

22 The house of Joseph also went up against Beth'el; and the LORD was with them. 23 The house of Joseph sent out spies to Beth'el (the name of the city was formerly Luz). 24 When the spies saw a man coming out of the city,

a That is Basins of Water   b Gk: Heb lacks Hobab   c See 1 Sam 15.6; Heb people they said to him, "Show us the way into the city, and we will deal kindly with you." ²⁵ So he showed them the way into the city; and they put the city to the sword, but they let the man and all his family go. ²⁶ So the man went to the land of the Hit′tites and built a city, and named it Luz; that is its name to this day.

27 Ma·nas′seh did not drive out the inhabitants of Beth-she′an and its villages, or Ta′a·nach and its villages, or the inhabitants of Dor and its villages, or the inhabitants of Ib′le·am and its villages, or the inhabitants of Me·gid′do and its villages; but the Ca′naan·ites continued to live in that land. ²⁸ When Israel grew strong, they put the Ca′naan·ites to forced labor, but did not in fact drive them out.

29 And E′phra·im did not drive out the Ca′naan·ites who lived in Ge′zer; but the Ca′naan·ites lived among them in Ge′zer.

30 Zeb′u·lun did not drive out the inhabitants of Kit′ron, or the inhabitants of Na·hal′ol; but the Ca′naan·ites lived among them, and became subject to forced labor.

31 Ash′er did not drive out the inhabitants of Ac′co, or the inhabitants of Si′don, or of Ah′lab, or of Ach′zib, or of Hel′bah, or of A′phik, or of Re′hob; ³² so the Ash′er·ites lived among the Ca′naan·ites, the inhabitants of the land; for they did not drive them out.

33 Naph′ta·li did not drive out the inhabitants of Beth-she′mesh, or the inhabitants of Beth-a′nath, but lived among the Ca′naan·ites, the inhabitants of the land; nevertheless the inhabitants of Beth-she′mesh and of Beth-a′nath became subject to forced labor for them.

34 The Am′o·rites pressed the Dan′ites back into the hill country; they did not allow them to come down to the plain. ³⁵ The Am′o·rites continued to live in Har-he′res, in Ai′ja·lon, and in Sha·al′bim, but the hand of the house of Joseph rested heavily on them, and they became subject to forced labor. ³⁶ The border of the Am′o·rites ran from the ascent of Ak·rab′bim, from Se′la and upward.

Israel's Disobedience

2 Now the angel of the LORD went up from Gil′gal to Bo′chim, and said, "I brought you up from Egypt, and brought you into the land that I had promised to your ancestors. I said,

'I will never break my covenant with you. ² For your part, do not make a covenant with the inhabitants of this land; tear down their altars.' But you have not obeyed my command. See what you have done! ³ So now I say, I will not drive them out before you; but they shall become adversaries ᵈ to you, and their gods shall be a snare to you." ⁴ When the angel of the LORD spoke these words to all the Israelites, the people lifted up their voices and wept. ⁵ So they named that place Bo′chim,ᵉ and there they sacrificed to the LORD.

Death of Joshua
(Josh 24.29–31)

6 When Joshua dismissed the people, the Israelites all went to their own inheritances to take possession of the land. ⁷ The people worshiped the LORD all the days of Joshua, and all the days of the elders who outlived Joshua, who had seen all the great work that the LORD had done for Israel. ⁸ Joshua son of Nun, the servant of the LORD, died at the age of one hundred ten years. ⁹ So they buried him within the bounds of his inheritance in Tim′nath-he′res, in the hill country of E′phra·im, north of Mount Ga′ash. ¹⁰ Moreover, that whole generation was gathered to their ancestors, and another generation grew up after them, who did not know the LORD or the work that he had done for Israel.

Israel's Unfaithfulness

11 Then the Israelites did what was evil in the sight of the LORD and worshiped the Ba′als; ¹² and they abandoned the LORD, the God of their ancestors, who had brought them out of the land of Egypt; they followed other gods, from among the gods of the peoples who were all around them, and bowed down to them; and they provoked the LORD to anger. ¹³ They abandoned the LORD, and worshiped Ba′al and the As·tar′tes. ¹⁴ So the anger of the LORD was kindled against Israel, and he gave them over to plunderers who plundered them, and he sold them into the power of their enemies all around, so that they could no longer withstand their enemies. ¹⁵ Whenever they marched out, the hand of the LORD was against them to bring misfortune, as the LORD had warned them

ᵈ OL Vg Compare Gk: Heb *sides*   ᵉ That is *Weepers*

and sworn to them; and they were in great distress.

16 Then the LORD raised up judges, who delivered them out of the power of those who plundered them. [17] Yet they did not listen even to their judges; for they lusted after other gods and bowed down to them. They soon turned aside from the way in which their ancestors had walked, who had obeyed the commandments of the LORD; they did not follow their example. [18] Whenever the LORD raised up judges for them, the LORD was with the judge, and he delivered them from the hand of their enemies all the days of the judge; for the LORD would be moved to pity by their groaning because of those who persecuted and oppressed them. [19] But whenever the judge died, they would relapse and behave worse than their ancestors, following other gods, worshiping them and bowing down to them. They would not drop any of their practices or their stubborn ways. [20] So the anger of the LORD was kindled against Israel; and he said, "Because this people have transgressed my covenant that I commanded their ancestors, and have not obeyed my voice, [21] I will no longer drive out before them any of the nations that Joshua left when he died." [22] In order to test Israel, whether or not they would take care to walk in the way of the LORD as their ancestors did, [23] the LORD had left those nations, not driving them out at once, and had not handed them over to Joshua.

Nations Remaining in the Land

3 Now these are the nations that the LORD left to test all those in Israel who had no experience of any war in Cā'naan [2] (it was only that successive generations of Israelites might know war, to teach those who had no experience of it before): [3] the five lords of the Phi·lis'tines, and all the Cā'naan·ites, and the Sī·dō'ni·ans, and the Hī'vites who lived on Mount Lebanon, from Mount Bā'al-her'mon as far as Lē'bō-hā'math. [4] They were for the testing of Israel, to know whether Israel would obey the commandments of the LORD, which he commanded their ancestors by Moses. [5] So the Israelites lived among the Cā'naan·ites, the Hit'tites, the Am'o·rites, the Per'iz·zites, the Hī'vites, and the Jeb'ū·sites; [6] and they took their daughters as wives for themselves, and their own daughters

they gave to their sons; and they worshiped their gods.

Othniel

7 The Israelites did what was evil in the sight of the LORD, forgetting the LORD their God, and worshiping the Bā'als and the A·shē'rahs. [8] Therefore the anger of the LORD was kindled against Israel, and he sold them into the hand of King Cū'shan-rish·a·thā'im of Ar'am-na·ha·rā'im; and the Israelites served Cū'shan-rish·a·thā'im eight years. [9] But when the Israelites cried out to the LORD, the LORD raised up a deliverer for the Israelites, who delivered them, Oth'ni·el son of Ke'naz, Caleb's younger brother. [10] The spirit of the LORD came upon him, and he judged Israel; he went out to war, and the LORD gave King Cū'shan-rish·a·thā'im of Ar'am into his hand; and his hand prevailed over Cū'shan-rish·a·thā'im. [11] So the land had rest forty years. Then Oth'-ni·el son of Ke'naz died.

Ehud

12 The Israelites again did what was evil in the sight of the LORD; and the LORD strengthened King Eg'lon of Mō'ab against Israel, because they had done what was evil in the sight of the LORD. [13] In alliance with the Am'-mon·ites and the A·mal'e·kites, he went and defeated Israel; and they took possession of the city of palms. [14] So the Israelites served King Eg'lon of Mō'ab eighteen years.

15 But when the Israelites cried out to the LORD, the LORD raised up for them a deliverer, E'hud son of Ge'ra, the Ben'ja·min·ite, a left-handed man. The Israelites sent tribute by him to King Eg'lon of Mō'ab. [16] E'hud made for himself a sword with two edges, a cubit in length; and he fastened it on his right thigh under his clothes. [17] Then he presented the tribute to King Eg'lon of Mō'ab. Now Eg'lon was a very fat man. [18] When E'hud had finished presenting the tribute, he sent the people who carried the tribute on their way. [19] But he himself turned back at the sculptured stones near Gil'gal, and said, "I have a secret message for you, O king." So the king said,[f] "Silence!" and all his attendants went out from his presence. [20] E'hud came to him, while he was sitting alone

_f_ Heb _he said._

in his cool roof chamber, and said, "I have a message from God for you." So he rose from his seat. 21 Then Eʹhud reached with his left hand, took the sword from his right thigh, and thrust it into Egʹlon'sᵍ belly; 22 the hilt also went in after the blade, and the fat closed over the blade, for he did not draw the sword out of his belly; and the dirt came out. ʰ 23 Then Eʹhud went out into the vestibule,ⁱ and closed the doors of the roof chamber on him, and locked them.

24 After he had gone, the servants came. When they saw that the doors of the roof chamber were locked, they thought, "He must be relieving himself ʲ in the cool chamber." 25 So they waited until they were embarrassed. When he still did not open the doors of the roof chamber, they took the key and opened them. There was their lord lying dead on the floor.

26 Eʹhud escaped while they delayed, and passed beyond the sculptured stones, and escaped to Seʹiʹrah. 27 When he arrived, he sounded the trumpet in the hill country of Eʹphra·im; and the Israelites went down with him from the hill country, having him at their head. 28 He said to them, "Follow after me; for the LORD has given your enemies the Moʹab·ites into your hand." So they went down after him, and seized the fords of the Jordan against the Moʹab·ites, and allowed no one to cross over. 29 At that time they killed about ten thousand of the Moʹab·ites, all strong, able-bodied men; no one escaped. 30 So Moʹab was subdued that day under the hand of Israel. And the land had rest eighty years.

Shamgar

31 After him came Shamʹgar son of Aʹnath, who killed six hundred of the Phi·lisʹtines with an oxgoad. He too delivered Israel.

Deborah and Barak

4 The Israelites again did what was evil in the sight of the LORD, after Eʹhud died. 2 So the LORD sold them into the hand of King Jaʹbin of Caʹnaan, who reigned in Haʹzor; the commander of his army was Sisʹe·ra, who lived in Ha·roʹsheth-ha-goiʹim. 3 Then the Israelites cried out to the LORD for help; for he had nine hundred chariots of iron, and had oppressed the Israelites cruelly twenty years.

4 At that time Debʹor·ah, a prophetess, wife of Lapʹpi·doth, was judging Israel. 5 She used to sit under the palm of Debʹor·ah between Raʹmah and Bethʹel in the hill country of Eʹphra·im; and the Israelites came up to her for judgment. 6 She sent and summoned Barʹak son of A·binʹo·am from Keʹdesh in Naphʹta·li, and said to him, "The LORD, the God of Israel, commands you, 'Go, take position at Mount Taʹbor, bringing ten thousand from the tribe of Naphʹta·li and the tribe of Zebʹu·lun. 7 I will draw out Sisʹe·ra, the general of Jaʹbin's army, to meet you by the Wadi Kiʹshon with his chariots and his troops; and I will give him into your hand.' " 8 Barʹak said to her, "If you will go with me, I will go; but if you will not go with me, I will not go." 9 And she said, "I will surely go with you; nevertheless, the road on which you are going will not lead to your glory, for the LORD will sell Sisʹe·ra into the hand of a woman." Then Debʹor·ah got up and went with Barʹak to Keʹdesh. 10 Barʹak summoned Zebʹu·lun and Naphʹta·li to Keʹdesh; and ten thousand warriors went up behind him; and Debʹor·ah went up with him.

11 Now Heʹber the Kenʹite had separated from the other Kenʹites,ᵏ that is, the descendants of Hoʹbab the father-in-law of Moses, and had encamped as far away as Eʹlon-be·za·aʹnanʹnim, which is near Keʹdesh.

12 When Sisʹe·ra was told that Barʹak son of A·binʹo·am had gone up to Mount Taʹbor, 13 Sisʹe·ra called out all his chariots, nine hundred chariots of iron, and all the troops who were with him, from Ha·roʹsheth-ha-goiʹim to the Wadi Kiʹshon. 14 Then Debʹor·ah said to Barʹak, "Up! For this is the day on which the LORD has given Sisʹe·ra into your hand. The LORD is indeed going out before you." So Barʹak went down from Mount Taʹbor with ten thousand warriors following him. 15 And the LORD threw Sisʹe·ra and all his chariots and all his army into a panicˡ before Barʹak; Sisʹe·ra got down from his chariot and fled away on foot, 16 while Barʹak pursued the chariots and the army to Ha·roʹsheth-

---

ᵍ Heb *his*   ʰ With Tg Vg: Meaning of Heb uncertain   ⁱ Meaning of Heb uncertain   ʲ Heb *covering his feet*   ᵏ Heb *from the Kain*   ˡ Heb adds *to the sword;* compare verse 16 ha-goi'im. All the army of Sis'e·ra fell by the sword; no one was left.

17 Now Sis'e·ra had fled away on foot to the tent of Ja'el wife of He'ber the Ken'ite; for there was peace between King Ja'bin of Ha'zor and the clan of He'ber the Ken'ite. 18 Ja'el came out to meet Sis'e·ra, and said to him, "Turn aside, my lord, turn aside to me; have no fear." So he turned aside to her into the tent, and she covered him with a rug. 19 Then he said to her, "Please give me a little water to drink; for I am thirsty." So she opened a skin of milk and gave him a drink and covered him. 20 He said to her, "Stand at the entrance of the tent, and if anybody comes and asks you, 'Is anyone here?' say, 'No.'" 21 But Ja'el wife of He'ber took a tent peg, and took a hammer in her hand, and went softly to him and drove the peg into his temple, until it went down into the ground—he was lying fast asleep from weariness—and he died. 22 Then, as Bar'ak came in pursuit of Sis'e·ra, Ja'el went out to meet him, and said to him, "Come, and I will show you the man whom you are seeking." So he went into her tent; and there was Sis'e·ra lying dead, with the tent peg in his temple.

23 So on that day God subdued King Ja'bin of Ca'naan before the Israelites. 24 Then the hand of the Israelites bore harder and harder on King Ja'bin of Ca'naan, until they destroyed King Ja'bin of Ca'naan.

The Song of Deborah

5 Then Deb'or·ah and Bar'ak son of A·bin'o·am sang on that day, saying:
2 "When locks are long in Israel,
when the people offer
themselves willingly—
bless *m* the LORD!

3 "Hear, O kings; give ear,
O princes;
to the LORD I will sing,
I will make melody to the
LORD, the God of Israel.

4 "LORD, when you went out from
Se'ir,
when you marched from the
region of E'dom,
the earth trembled,
and the heavens indeed poured
water.

5 The mountains quaked before
the LORD, the One of Sinai,
before the LORD, the God of
Israel.

6 "In the days of Sham'gar son of
A'nath,
in the days of Ja'el, caravans
ceased
and travelers kept to the
byways.

7 The peasantry prospered in
Israel,
they grew fat on plunder,
because you arose, Deb'or·ah,
arose as a mother in Israel.

8 When new gods were chosen,
then war was in the gates.
Was shield or spear to be seen
among forty thousand in
Israel?

9 My heart goes out to the
commanders of Israel
who offered themselves
willingly among the people.
Bless the LORD.

10 "Tell of it, you who ride on
white donkeys,
you who sit on rich carpets *n*
and you who walk by the way.

11 To the sound of musicians *n* at
the watering places,
there they repeat the triumphs
of the LORD,
the triumphs of his peasantry
in Israel.

"Then down to the gates
marched the people of the
LORD.

12 "Awake, awake, Deb'or·ah!
Awake, awake, utter a song!
Arise, Bar'ak, lead away your
captives,
O son of A·bin'o·am.

13 Then down marched the
remnant of the noble;
the people of the LORD
marched down for him *o*
against the mighty.

14 From E'phra·im they set out *p*
into the valley, *q*
following you, Benjamin, with
your kin;

m Or *You who offer yourselves willingly
among the people, bless*   *n* Meaning of
Heb uncertain   *o* Gk: Heb *me*
p Cn: Heb *From Ephraim their root*
q Gk: Heb *in Amalek*

from Ma'chir marched down the
commanders,
and from Zeb'u·lun those who
bear the marshal's staff;

15 the chiefs of Is'sa·char came
with Deb'or·ah,
and Is'sa·char faithful to
Bar'ak;
into the valley they rushed out
at his heels.
Among the clans of Reuben
there were great searchings of
heart.

16 Why did you tarry among the
sheepfolds,
to hear the piping for the
flocks?
Among the clans of Reuben
there were great searchings of
heart.

17 Gil'e·ad stayed beyond the
Jordan;
and Dan, why did he abide
with the ships?
Ash'er sat still at the coast of the
sea,
settling down by his landings.

18 Zeb'u·lun is a people that
scorned death;
Naph'ta·li too, on the heights
of the field.

19 "The kings came, they fought;
then fought the kings of
Ca'naan,
at Ta'a·nach, by the waters of
Me·gid'do;
they got no spoils of silver.

20 The stars fought from heaven,
from their courses they fought
against Sis'e·ra.

21 The torrent Ki'shon swept them
away,
the onrushing torrent, the
torrent Ki'shon.
March on, my soul, with
might!

22 "Then loud beat the horses'
hoofs
with the galloping, galloping
of his steeds.

23 "Curse Me'roz, says the angel of
the LORD,
curse bitterly its inhabitants,
because they did not come to the
help of the LORD,
to the help of the LORD against
the mighty.

24 "Most blessed of women be
Ja'el,
the wife of He'ber the Ken'ite,
of tent-dwelling women most
blessed.

25 He asked water and she gave
him milk,
she brought him curds in a
lordly bowl.

26 She put her hand to the tent peg
and her right hand to the
workmen's mallet;
she struck Sis'e·ra a blow,
she crushed his head,
she shattered and pierced his
temple.

27 He sank, he fell,
he lay still at her feet;
at her feet he sank, he fell;
where he sank, there he fell
dead.

28 "Out of the window she peered,
the mother of Sis'e·ra gazed[r]
through the lattice:
'Why is his chariot so long in
coming?
Why tarry the hoofbeats of his
chariots?'

29 Her wisest ladies make answer,
indeed, she answers the
question herself:

30 'Are they not finding and
dividing the spoil?—
A girl or two for every man;
spoil of dyed stuffs for Sis'e·ra,
spoil of dyed stuffs
embroidered,
two pieces of dyed work
embroidered for my neck
as spoil?'

31 "So perish all your enemies,
O LORD!
But may your friends be like
the sun as it rises in its
might."

And the land had rest forty years.

The Midianite Oppression

6 The Israelites did what was evil in
the sight of the LORD, and the
LORD gave them into the hand of Mid'-
i·an seven years. 2 The hand of Mid'-
i·an prevailed over Israel; and because
of Mid'i·an the Israelites provided for
themselves hiding places in the mountains, caves and strongholds. 3 For
whenever the Israelites put in seed, the

---

r Gk Compare Tg: Heb exclaimed

Mid'i·an·ites and the A·mal'e·kites and the people of the east would come up against them. 4 They would encamp against them and destroy the produce of the land, as far as the neighborhood of Ga'za, and leave no sustenance in Israel, and no sheep or ox or donkey. 5 For they and their livestock would come up, and they would even bring their tents, as thick as locusts; neither they nor their camels could be counted; so they wasted the land as they came in. 6 Thus Israel was greatly impoverished because of Mid'i·an; and the Israelites cried out to the LORD for help.

7 When the Israelites cried to the LORD on account of the Mid'i·an·ites, 8 the LORD sent a prophet to the Israelites; and he said to them, "Thus says the LORD, the God of Israel: I led you up from Egypt, and brought you out of the house of slavery; 9 and I delivered you from the hand of the Egyptians, and from the hand of all who oppressed you, and drove them out before you, and gave you their land; 10 and I said to you, 'I am the LORD your God; you shall not pay reverence to the gods of the Am'o·rites, in whose land you live.' But you have not given heed to my voice."

The Call of Gideon

11 Now the angel of the LORD came and sat under the oak at Oph'rah, which belonged to Jo'ash the A·bi·ez'rite, as his son Gideon was beating out wheat in the wine press, to hide it from the Mid'i·an·ites. 12 The angel of the LORD appeared to him and said to him, "The LORD is with you, you mighty warrior." 13 Gideon answered him, "But sir, if the LORD is with us, why then has all this happened to us? And where are all his wonderful deeds that our ancestors recounted to us, saying, 'Did not the LORD bring us up from Egypt?' But now the LORD has cast us off, and given us into the hand of Mid'i·an." 14 Then the LORD turned to him and said, "Go in this might of yours and deliver Israel from the hand of Mid'i·an; I hereby commission you." 15 He responded, "But sir, how can I deliver Israel? My clan is the weakest in Ma·nas'seh, and I am the least in my family." 16 The LORD said to him, "But I will be with you, and you shall strike down the Mid'i·an·ites, every one of them." 17 Then he said to him, "If now I have found favor with you, then show

me a sign that it is you who speak with me. 18 Do not depart from here until I come to you, and bring out my present, and set it before you." And he said, "I will stay until you return."

19 So Gideon went into his house and prepared a kid, and unleavened cakes from an ephah of flour; the meat he put in a basket, and the broth he put in a pot, and brought them to him under the oak and presented them. 20 The angel of God said to him, "Take the meat and the unleavened cakes, and put them on this rock, and pour out the broth." And he did so. 21 Then the angel of the LORD reached out the tip of the staff that was in his hand, and touched the meat and the unleavened cakes; and fire sprang up from the rock and consumed the meat and the unleavened cakes; and the angel of the LORD vanished from his sight. 22 Then Gideon perceived that it was the angel of the LORD; and Gideon said, "Help me, Lord GOD! For I have seen the angel of the LORD face to face." 23 But the LORD said to him, "Peace be to you; do not fear, you shall not die." 24 Then Gideon built an altar there to the LORD, and called it, The LORD is peace. To this day it still stands at Oph'rah, which belongs to the A·bi·ez'rites.

25 That night the LORD said to him, "Take your father's bull, the second bull seven years old, and pull down the altar of Ba'al that belongs to your father, and cut down the sacred pole [s] that is beside it; 26 and build an altar to the LORD your God on the top of the stronghold here, in proper order; then take the second bull, and offer it as a burnt offering with the wood of the sacred pole [s] that you shall cut down." 27 So Gideon took ten of his servants, and did as the LORD had told him; but because he was too afraid of his family and the townspeople to do it by day, he did it by night.

Gideon Destroys the Altar of Baal

28 When the townspeople rose early in the morning, the altar of Ba'al was broken down, and the sacred pole [s] beside it was cut down, and the second bull was offered on the altar that had been built. 29 So they said to one another, "Who has done this?" After searching and inquiring, they were told, "Gideon son of Jo'ash did it." 30 Then the townspeople said to Jo'ash,

s Heb Asherah

"Bring out your son, so that he may die, for he has pulled down the altar of Ba′al and cut down the sacred pole[t] beside it." [31] But Jō′ash said to all who were arrayed against him, "Will you contend for Ba′al? Or will you defend his cause? Whoever contends for him shall be put to death by morning. If he is a god, let him contend for himself, because his altar has been pulled down." [32] Therefore on that day Gideon[u] was called Jer·ub·ba′al, that is to say, "Let Ba′al contend against him," because he pulled down his altar.

[33] Then all the Mid′i·an·ites and the A·mal′e·kītes and the people of the east came together, and crossing the Jordan they encamped in the Valley of Jez′rē·el. [34] But the spirit of the LORD took possession of Gideon; and he sounded the trumpet, and the A·bi·ez′rītes were called out to follow him. [35] He sent messengers throughout all Ma·nas′seh, and they too were called out to follow him. He also sent messengers to Ash′er, Zeb′ū·lun, and Naph′ta·lī, and they went up to meet them.

The Sign of the Fleece

[36] Then Gideon said to God, "In order to see whether you will deliver Israel by my hand, as you have said, [37] I am going to lay a fleece of wool on the threshing floor; if there is dew on the fleece alone, and it is dry on all the ground, then I shall know that you will deliver Israel by my hand, as you have said." [38] And it was so. When he rose early next morning and squeezed the fleece, he wrung enough dew from the fleece to fill a bowl with water. [39] Then Gideon said to God, "Do not let your anger burn against me, let me speak one more time; let me, please, make trial with the fleece just once more; let it be dry only on the fleece, and on all the ground let there be dew." [40] And God did so that night. It was dry on the fleece only, and on all the ground there was dew.

Gideon Surprises and Routs the Midianites

7 Then Jer·ub·ba′al (that is, Gideon) and all the troops that were with him rose early and encamped beside the spring of Har′od; and the camp of Mid′i·an was north of them, below[v] the hill of Mō′reh, in the valley. [2] The LORD said to Gideon, "The troops with you are too many for me to give the Mid′i·an·ites into their hand. Israel would only take the credit away from me, saying, 'My own hand has delivered me.' [3] Now therefore proclaim this in the hearing of the troops, 'Whoever is fearful and trembling, let him return home.' " Thus Gideon sifted them out;[w] twenty-two thousand returned, and ten thousand remained.

[4] Then the LORD said to Gideon, "The troops are still too many; take them down to the water and I will sift them out for you there. When I say, 'This one shall go with you,' he shall go with you; and when I say, 'This one shall not go with you,' he shall not go." [5] So he brought the troops down to the water; and the LORD said to Gideon, "All those who lap the water with their tongues, as a dog laps, you shall put to one side; all those who kneel down to drink, putting their hands to their mouths,[x] you shall put to the other side." [6] The number of those that lapped was three hundred; but all the rest of the troops knelt down to drink water. [7] Then the LORD said to Gideon, "With the three hundred that lapped I will deliver you, and give the Mid′i·an·ites into your hand. Let all the others go to their homes." [8] So he took the jars of the troops from their hands,[y] and their trumpets; and he sent all the rest of Israel back to their own tents, but retained the three hundred. The camp of Mid′i·an was below him in the valley.

[9] That same night the LORD said to him, "Get up, attack the camp; for I have given it into your hand. [10] But if you fear to attack, go down to the camp with your servant Pū′rah; [11] and you shall hear what they say, and afterward your hands shall be strengthened to attack the camp." Then he went down with his servant Pū′rah to the outposts of the armed men that were in the camp. [12] The Mid′i·an·ites and the A·mal′e·kītes and all the people of the east lay along the valley as thick as locusts; and their camels were without number, countless as the sand on the seashore. [13] When Gideon arrived, there was a man telling a dream

---

[t] Heb *Asherah*   [u] Heb *he*   [v] Heb *from*
[w] Cn: Heb *home, and depart from Mount Gilead*"   [x] Heb places the words *putting their hands to their mouths* after the word *lapped* in verse 6
[y] Cn: Heb *So the people took provisions in their hands*

to his comrade; and he said, "I had a dream, and in it a cake of barley bread tumbled into the camp of Mid'i·an, and came to the tent, and struck it so that it fell; it turned upside down, and the tent collapsed." 14 And his comrade answered, "This is no other than the sword of Gideon son of Jō'ash, a man of Israel; into his hand God has given Mid'i·an and all the army."

15 When Gideon heard the telling of the dream and its interpretation, he worshiped; and he returned to the camp of Israel and said, "Get up; for the LORD has given the army of Mid'i·an into your hand." 16 After he divided the three hundred men into three companies, and put trumpets into the hands of all of them, and empty jars, with torches inside the jars, 17 he said to them, "Look at me, and do the same; when I come to the outskirts of the camp, do as I do. 18 When I blow the trumpet, I and all who are with me, then you also blow the trumpets around the whole camp, and shout, 'For the LORD and for Gideon!' "

19 So Gideon and the hundred who were with him came to the outskirts of the camp at the beginning of the middle watch, when they had just set the watch; and they blew the trumpets and smashed the jars that were in their hands. 20 So the three companies blew the trumpets and broke the jars, holding in their left hands the torches, and in their right hands the trumpets to blow; and they cried, "A sword for the LORD and for Gideon!" 21 Every man stood in his place all around the camp, and all the men in camp ran; they cried out and fled. 22 When they blew the three hundred trumpets, the LORD set every man's sword against his fellow and against all the army; and the army fled as far as Beth-shit'tah toward Zer'e·rah,z as far as the border of Ā'bel-me·hō'lah, by Tab'bath. 23 And the men of Israel were called out from Naph'ta·lī and from Ash'er and from all Ma·nas'seh, and they pursued after the Mid'i·an·ītes.

24 Then Gideon sent messengers throughout all the hill country of Ē'phra·im, saying, "Come down against the Mid'i·an·ītes and seize the waters against them, as far as Beth-bar'ah, and also the Jordan." So all the men of Ē'phra·im were called out, and they seized the waters as far as Beth-bar'ah, and also the Jordan. 25 They captured the two captains of Mid'i·an,

Or'eb and Zē'eb; they killed Or'eb at the rock of Or'eb, and Zē'eb they killed at the wine press of Zē'eb, as they pursued the Mid'i·an·ites. They brought the heads of Or'eb and Zē'eb to Gideon beyond the Jordan.

Gideon's Triumph and Vengeance

8 Then the Ē'phra·im·ites said to him, "What have you done to us, not to call us when you went to fight against the Mid'i·an·ītes?" And they upbraided him violently. 2 So he said to them, "What have I done now in comparison with you? Is not the gleaning of the grapes of Ē'phra·im better than the vintage of Ā·bi·ē'zer? 3 God has given into your hands the captains of Mid'i·an, Or'eb and Zē'eb; what have I been able to do in comparison with you?" When he said this, their anger against him subsided.

4 Then Gideon came to the Jordan and crossed over, he and the three hundred who were with him, exhausted and famished.a 5 So he said to the people of Suc'coth, "Please give some loaves of bread to my followers, for they are exhausted, and I am pursuing Zē'bah and Zal·mun'na, the kings of Mid'i·an." 6 But the officials of Suc'coth said, "Do you already have in your possession the hands of Zē'bah and Zal·mun'na, that we should give bread to your army?" 7 Gideon replied, "Well then, when the LORD has given Zē'bah and Zal·mun'na into my hand, I will trample your flesh on the thorns of the wilderness and on briers." 8 From there he went up to Pe·nū'el, and made the same request of them; and the people of Pe·nū'el answered him as the people of Suc'coth had answered. 9 So he said to the people of Pe·nū'el, "When I come back victorious, I will break down this tower."

10 Now Zē'bah and Zal·mun'na were in Kar'kor with their army, about fifteen thousand men, all who were left of all the army of the people of the east; for one hundred twenty thousand men bearing arms had fallen. 11 So Gideon went up by the caravan route east of Nō'bah and Jog'be·hah, and attacked the army; for the army was off its guard. 12 Zē'bah and Zal·mun'na fled; and he pursued them and took the two kings of Mid'i·an,

---

z Another reading is Zeredah
a Gk: Heb pursuing

Ze'bah and Zal·mun'na, and threw all the army into a panic.

13 When Gideon son of Jo'ash returned from the battle by the ascent of Heres, 14 he caught a young man, one of the people of Suc'coth, and questioned him; and he listed for him the officials and elders of Suc'coth, seventy-seven people. 15 Then he came to the people of Suc'coth, and said, "Here are Ze'bah and Zal·mun'na, about whom you taunted me, saying, 'Do you already have in your possession the hands of Ze'bah and Zal·mun'na, that we should give bread to your troops who are exhausted?'" 16 So he took the elders of the city and he took thorns of the wilderness and briers and with them he trampled b the people of Suc'coth. 17 He also broke down the tower of Pe·nu'el, and killed the men of the city.

18 Then he said to Ze'bah and Zal·mun'na, "What about the men whom you killed at Ta'bor?" They answered, "As you are, so were they, every one of them; they resembled the sons of a king." 19 And he replied, "They were my brothers, the sons of my mother; as the LORD lives, if you had saved them alive, I would not kill you." 20 So he said to Je'ther his firstborn, "Go kill them!" But the boy did not draw his sword, for he was afraid, because he was still a boy. 21 Then Ze'bah and Zal·mun'na said, "You come and kill us; for as the man is, so is his strength." So Gideon proceeded to kill Ze'bah and Zal·mun'na; and he took the crescents that were on the necks of their camels.

Gideon's Idolatry

22 Then the Israelites said to Gideon, "Rule over us, you and your son and your grandson also; for you have delivered us out of the hand of Mid'i·an." 23 Gideon said to them, "I will not rule over you, and my son will not rule over you; the LORD will rule over you." 24 Then Gideon said to them, "Let me make a request of you; each of you give me an earring he has taken as booty." (For the enemy c had golden earrings, because they were Ish'-ma·el·ites.) 25 "We will willingly give them," they answered. So they spread a garment, and each threw into it an earring he had taken as booty. 26 The weight of the golden earrings that he requested was one thousand seven hundred shekels of gold (apart from

the crescents and the pendants and the purple garments worn by the kings of Mid'i·an, and the collars that were on the necks of their camels). 27 Gideon made an ephod of it and put it in his town, in Oph'rah; and all Israel prostituted themselves to it there, and it became a snare to Gideon and to his family. 28 So Mid'i·an was subdued before the Israelites, and they lifted up their heads no more. So the land had rest forty years in the days of Gideon.

Death of Gideon

29 Jer·ub·ba'al son of Jo'ash went to live in his own house. 30 Now Gideon had seventy sons, his own offspring, for he had many wives. 31 His concubine who was in She'chem also bore him a son, and he named him A·bim'-e·lech. 32 Then Gideon son of Jo'ash died at a good old age, and was buried in the tomb of his father Jo'ash at Oph'rah of the A·bi·ez'rites.

33 As soon as Gideon died, the Israelites relapsed and prostituted themselves with the Ba'als, making Ba'al-be'rith their god. 34 The Israelites did not remember the LORD their God, who had rescued them from the hand of all their enemies on every side; 35 and they did not exhibit loyalty to the house of Jer·ub·ba'al (that is, Gideon) in return for all the good that he had done to Israel.

Abimelech Attempts to Establish a Monarchy

9 Now A·bim'e·lech son of Jer-ub·ba'al went to She'chem to his mother's kinsfolk and said to them and to the whole clan of his mother's family, 2 "Say in the hearing of all the lords of She'chem, 'Which is better for you, that all seventy of the sons of Jer-ub·ba'al rule over you, or that one rule over you?' Remember also that I am your bone and your flesh." 3 So his mother's kinsfolk spoke all these words on his behalf in the hearing of all the lords of She'chem; and their hearts inclined to follow A·bim'e·lech, for they said, "He is our brother." 4 They gave him seventy pieces of silver out of the temple of Ba'al-be'rith with which A·bim'e·lech hired worthless and reckless fellows, who followed him. 5 He went to his father's house at Oph'rah, and killed his broth-

b With verse 7, Compare Gk: Heb *he taught*   c Heb *they*

ers the sons of Jer·ub·ba′al, seventy men, on one stone; but Jo′tham, the youngest son of Jer·ub·ba′al, survived, for he hid himself. 6 Then all the lords of She′chem and all Beth-mil′lo came together, and they went and made A·bim′e·lech king, by the oak of the pillar*d* at She′chem.

The Parable of the Trees

7 When it was told to Jo′tham, he went and stood on the top of Mount Ger′i·zim, and cried aloud and said to them, "Listen to me, you lords of She′-chem, so that God may listen to you.

8   The trees once went out
     to anoint a king over
       themselves.
So they said to the olive tree,
   'Reign over us.'
9   The olive tree answered them,
   'Shall I stop producing my rich
     oil
     by which gods and mortals
       are honored,
     and go to sway over the
       trees?'
10   Then the trees said to the fig
     tree,
   'You come and reign over us.'
11   But the fig tree answered them,
   'Shall I stop producing my
     sweetness
     and my delicious fruit,
     and go to sway over the
       trees?'
12   Then the trees said to the vine,
   'You come and reign over us.'
13   But the vine said to them,
   'Shall I stop producing my
     wine
     that cheers gods and
       mortals,
     and go to sway over the
       trees?'
14   So all the trees said to the
     bramble,
   'You come and reign over us.'
15   And the bramble said to the
     trees,
   'If in good faith you are
     anointing me king over
     you,
     then come and take refuge
       in my shade;
   but if not, let fire come out of
     the bramble
     and devour the cedars of
       Lebanon.'
16 "Now therefore, if you acted in good faith and honor when you made A·bim′e·lech king, and if you have

dealt well with Jer·ub·ba′al and his house, and have done to him as his actions deserved— 17 for my father fought for you, and risked his life, and rescued you from the hand of Mid′i·an; 18 but you have risen up against my father's house this day, and have killed his sons, seventy men on one stone, and have made A·bim′e·lech, the son of his slave woman, king over the lords of She′chem, because he is your kinsman— 19 if, I say, you have acted in good faith and honor with Jer·ub·ba′al and with his house this day, then rejoice in A·bim′e·lech, and let him also rejoice in you; 20 but if not, let fire come out from A·bim′e·lech, and devour the lords of She′chem, and Beth-mil′lo; and let fire come out from the lords of She′chem, and from Beth-mil′lo, and devour A·bim′e·lech." 21 Then Jo′tham ran away and fled, going to Be′er, where he remained for fear of his brother A·bim′e·lech.

The Downfall of Abimelech

22 A·bim′e·lech ruled over Israel three years. 23 But God sent an evil spirit between A·bim′e·lech and the lords of She′chem; and the lords of She′chem dealt treacherously with A·bim′e·lech. 24 This happened so that the violence done to the seventy sons of Jer·ub·ba′al might be avenged*e* and their blood be laid on their brother A·bim′e·lech, who killed them, and on the lords of She′chem, who strengthened his hands to kill his brothers. 25 So, out of hostility to him, the lords of She′chem set ambushes on the mountain tops. They robbed all who passed by them along that way; and it was reported to A·bim′e·lech.

26 When Ga′al son of E′bed moved into She′chem with his kinsfolk, the lords of She′chem put confidence in him. 27 They went out into the field and gathered the grapes from their vineyards, trod them, and celebrated. Then they went into the temple of their god, ate and drank, and ridiculed A·bim′-e·lech. 28 Ga′al son of E′bed said, "Who is A·bim′e·lech, and who are we of She′chem, that we should serve him? Did not the son of Jer·ub·ba′al and Ze′-bul his officer serve the men of Ha′mor father of She′chem? Why then should we serve him? 29 If only this people

---

*d*Cn: Meaning of Heb uncertain
*e*Heb *might come*

were under my command! Then I would remove A·bim′e·lech; I would say[f] to him, 'Increase your army, and come out.' "

30 When Ze′bul the ruler of the city heard the words of Ga′al son of E′bed, his anger was kindled. [31] He sent messengers to A·bim′e·lech at A·ru′mah,[g] saying, "Look, Ga′al son of E′bed and his kinsfolk have come to She′chem, and they are stirring up[h] the city against you. [32] Now therefore, go by night, you and the troops that are with you, and lie in wait in the fields. [33] Then early in the morning, as soon as the sun rises, get up and rush on the city; and when he and the troops that are with him come out against you, you may deal with them as best you can."

34 So A·bim′e·lech and all the troops with him got up by night and lay in wait against She′chem in four companies. [35] When Ga′al son of E′bed went out and stood in the entrance of the gate of the city, A·bim′e·lech and the troops with him rose from the ambush. [36] And when Ga′al saw them, he said to Ze′bul, "Look, people are coming down from the mountain tops!" And Ze′bul said to him, "The shadows on the mountains look like people to you." [37] Ga′al spoke again and said, "Look, people are coming down from Tab·bur′-e′rez, and one company is coming from the direction of E′lon-me·on·e′nim."[i] [38] Then Ze′bul said to him, "Where is your boast[j] now, you who said, 'Who is A·bim′e·lech, that we should serve him?' Are not these the troops you made light of? Go out now and fight with them." [39] So Ga′al went out at the head of the lords of She′chem, and fought with A·bim′e·lech. [40] A·bim′e·lech chased him, and he fled before him. Many fell wounded, up to the entrance of the gate. [41] So A·bim′e·lech resided at A·ru′mah; and Ze′bul drove out Ga′al and his kinsfolk, so that they could not live on at She′chem.

42 On the following day the people went out into the fields. When A·bim′e·lech was told, [43] he took his troops and divided them into three companies, and lay in wait in the fields. When he looked and saw the people coming out of the city, he rose against them and killed them. [44] A·bim′e·lech and the company that was[k] with him rushed forward and stood at the entrance of the gate of the city, while the two companies rushed on all who were in the fields and killed them. [45] A·bim′e·lech fought against the city all that day; he took the city, and killed the people that were in it; and he razed the city and sowed it with salt.

46 When all the lords of the Tower of She′chem heard of it, they entered the stronghold of the temple of El-be′-rith. [47] A·bim′e·lech was told that all the lords of the Tower of She′chem were gathered together. [48] So A·bim′e·lech went up to Mount Zal′mon, he and all the troops that were with him. A·bim′e·lech took an ax in his hand, cut down a bundle of brushwood, and took it up and laid it on his shoulder. Then he said to the troops with him, "What you have seen me do, do quickly, as I have done." [49] So every one of the troops cut down a bundle and following A·bim′e·lech put it against the stronghold, and they set the stronghold on fire over them, so that all the people of the Tower of She′chem also died, about a thousand men and women.

50 Then A·bim′e·lech went to The′-bez, and encamped against The′bez, and took it. [51] But there was a strong tower within the city, and all the men and women and all the lords of the city fled to it and shut themselves in; and they went to the roof of the tower. [52] A·bim′e·lech came to the tower, and fought against it, and came near to the entrance of the tower to burn it with fire. [53] But a certain woman threw an upper millstone on A·bim′e·lech's head, and crushed his skull. [54] Immediately he called to the young man who carried his armor and said to him, "Draw your sword and kill me, so people will not say about me, 'A woman killed him.' " So the young man thrust him through, and he died. [55] When the Israelites saw that A·bim′e·lech was dead, they all went home. [56] Thus God repaid A·bim′e·lech for the crime he committed against his father in killing his seventy brothers; [57] and God also made all the wickedness of the people of She′chem fall back on their heads, and on them came the curse of Jo′tham son of Jer·ub·ba′al.

---

[f] Gk: Heb *and he said*   [g] Cn See 9.41. Heb *Tormah*   [h] Cn: Heb *are besieging*   [i] *That is Diviners' Oak*   [j] Heb *mouth*   [k] Vg and some Gk Mss: Heb *companies that were*

Tola and Jair

10 After A·bim′e·lech, Tō′la son of Pū′ah son of Dō′dŏ, a man of Is′sa·char, who lived at Shā′mir in the hill country of E′phra·im, rose to deliver Israel. ² He judged Israel twenty-three years. Then he died, and was buried at Shā′mir.

3 After him came Jā′ir the Gil′e·ad·īte, who judged Israel twenty-two years. ⁴ He had thirty sons who rode on thirty donkeys; and they had thirty towns, which are in the land of Gil′e·ad, and are called Hav′voth-jā′ir to this day. ⁵ Jā′ir died, and was buried in Ka′mon.

Oppression by the Ammonites

6 The Israelites again did what was evil in the sight of the LORD, worshiping the Bā′als and the As·tar′tēs, the gods of Ar′am, the gods of Sī′don, the gods of Mō′ab, the gods of the Am′mon·ītes, and the gods of the Phi·lis′tines. Thus they abandoned the LORD, and did not worship him. ⁷ So the anger of the LORD was kindled against Israel, and he sold them into the hand of the Phi·lis′tines and into the hand of the Am′mon·ītes, ⁸ and they crushed and oppressed the Israelites that year. For eighteen years they oppressed all the Israelites that were beyond the Jordan in the land of the Am′o·rītes, which is in Gil′e·ad. ⁹ The Am′mon·ītes also crossed the Jordan to fight against Judah and against Benjamin and against the house of E′phra·im; so that Israel was greatly distressed.

10 So the Israelites cried to the LORD, saying, "We have sinned against you, because we have abandoned our God and have worshiped the Bā′als." ¹¹ And the LORD said to the Israelites, "Did I not deliver you[l] from the Egyptians and from the Am′o·rītes, from the Am′mon·ītes and from the Phi·lis′tines? ¹² The Sī·dō′ni·ans also, and the A·mal′e·kītes, and the Mā′on·ītes, oppressed you; and you cried to me, and I delivered you out of their hand. ¹³ Yet you have abandoned me and worshiped other gods; therefore I will deliver you no more. ¹⁴ Go and cry to the gods whom you have chosen; let them deliver you in the time of your distress." ¹⁵ And the Israelites said to the LORD, "We have sinned; do to us whatever seems good to you; but deliver us this day!" ¹⁶ So they put away the foreign gods from among them and wor-

shiped the LORD; and he could no longer bear to see Israel suffer.

17 Then the Am′mon·ītes were called to arms, and they encamped in Gil′e·ad; and the Israelites came together, and they encamped at Miz′pah. ¹⁸ The commanders of the people of Gil′e·ad said to one another, "Who will begin the fight against the Am′mon·ītes? He shall be head over all the inhabitants of Gil′e·ad."

Jephthah

11 Now Jeph′thah the Gil′e·ad·īte, the son of a prostitute, was a mighty warrior. Gil′e·ad was the father of Jeph′thah. ² Gil′e·ad's wife also bore him sons; and when his wife's sons grew up, they drove Jeph′thah away, saying to him, "You shall not inherit anything in our father's house; for you are the son of another woman." ³ Then Jeph′thah fled from his brothers and lived in the land of Tob. Outlaws collected around Jeph′thah and went raiding with him.

4 After a time the Am′mon·ītes made war against Israel. ⁵ And when the Am′mon·ītes made war against Israel, the elders of Gil′e·ad went to bring Jeph′thah from the land of Tob. ⁶ They said to Jeph′thah, "Come and be our commander, so that we may fight with the Am′mon·ītes." ⁷ But Jeph′thah said to the elders of Gil′e·ad, "Are you not the very ones who rejected me and drove me out of my father's house? So why do you come to me now when you are in trouble?" ⁸ The elders of Gil′e·ad said to Jeph′thah, "Nevertheless, we have now turned back to you, so that you may go with us and fight with the Am′mon·ītes, and become head over us, over all the inhabitants of Gil′e·ad." ⁹ Jeph′thah said to the elders of Gil′e·ad, "If you bring me home again to fight with the Am′mon·ītes, and the LORD gives them over to me, I will be your head." ¹⁰ And the elders of Gil′e·ad said to Jeph′thah, "The LORD will be witness between us; we will surely do as you say." ¹¹ So Jeph′thah went with the elders of Gil′e·ad, and the people made him head and commander over them; and Jeph′thah spoke all his words before the LORD at Miz′pah.

12 Then Jeph′thah sent messengers to the king of the Am′mon·ītes and said, "What is there between you and

[l] Heb lacks *Did I not deliver you*

me, that you have come to me to fight against my land?" [13]The king of the Am′mon·ites answered the messengers of Jeph′thah, "Because Israel, on coming from Egypt, took away my land from the Ar′non to the Jab′bok and to the Jordan; now therefore restore it peaceably." [14]Once again Jeph′thah sent messengers to the king of the Am′mon·ites [15]and said to him: "Thus says Jeph′thah: Israel did not take away the land of Mō′ab or the land of the Am′mon·ites, [16]but when they came up from Egypt, Israel went through the wilderness to the Red Sea[m] and came to Kā′desh. [17]Israel then sent messengers to the king of Ē′dom, saying, 'Let us pass through your land'; but the king of Ē′dom would not listen. They also sent to the king of Mō′ab, but he would not consent. So Israel remained at Kā′desh. [18]Then they journeyed through the wilderness, went around the land of Ē′dom and the land of Mō′ab, arrived on the east side of the land of Mō′ab, and camped on the other side of the Ar′non. They did not enter the territory of Mō′ab, for the Ar′non was the boundary of Mō′ab. [19]Israel then sent messengers to King Sī′hon of the Am′o·rītes, king of Hesh′bon; and Israel said to him, 'Let us pass through your land to our country.' [20]But Sī′hon did not trust Israel to pass through his territory; so Sī′hon gathered all his people together, and encamped at Jā′haz, and fought with Israel. [21]Then the LORD, the God of Israel, gave Sī′hon and all his people into the hand of Israel, and they defeated them; so Israel occupied all the land of the Am′o·rītes, who inhabited that country. [22]They occupied all the territory of the Am′o·rītes from the Ar′non to the Jab′bok and from the wilderness to the Jordan. [23]So now the LORD, the God of Israel, has conquered the Am′o·rītes for the benefit of his people Israel. Do you intend to take their place? [24]Should you not possess what your god Chē′mosh gives you to possess? And should we not be the ones to possess everything that the LORD our God has conquered for our benefit? [25]Now are you any better than King Bā′lak son of Zip′por of Mō′ab? Did he ever enter into conflict with Israel, or did he ever go to war with them? [26]While Israel lived in Hesh′bon and its villages, and in A·rō′er and its villages, and in all the towns that are along the Ar′non, three

hundred years, why did you not recover them within that time? [27]It is not I who have sinned against you, but you are the one who does me wrong by making war on me. Let the LORD, who is judge, decide today for the Israelites or for the Am′mon·ites." [28]But the king of the Am′mon·ites did not heed the message that Jeph′thah sent him.

Jephthah's Vow

29 Then the spirit of the LORD came upon Jeph′thah, and he passed through Gil′e·ad and Ma·nas′seh. He passed on to Miz′pah of Gil′e·ad, and from Miz′pah of Gil′e·ad he passed on to the Am′mon·ites. [30]And Jeph′thah made a vow to the LORD, and said, "If you will give the Am′mon·ites into my hand, [31]then whoever comes out of the doors of my house to meet me, when I return victorious from the Am′-mon·ites, shall be the LORD's, to be offered up by me as a burnt offering." [32]So Jeph′thah crossed over to the Am′mon·ites to fight against them; and the LORD gave them into his hand. [33]He inflicted a massive defeat on them from A·rō′er to the neighborhood of Min′nith, twenty towns, and as far as A′bel-ker′a·mim. So the Am′-mon·ites were subdued before the people of Israel.

Jephthah's Daughter

34 Then Jeph′thah came to his home at Miz′pah; and there was his daughter coming out to meet him with timbrels and with dancing. She was his only child; he had no son or daughter except her. [35]When he saw her, he tore his clothes, and said, "Alas, my daughter! You have brought me very low; you have become the cause of great trouble to me. For I have opened my mouth to the LORD, and I cannot take back my vow." [36]She said to him, "My father, if you have opened your mouth to the LORD, do to me according to what has gone out of your mouth, now that the LORD has given you vengeance against your enemies, the Am′-mon·ites." [37]And she said to her father, "Let this thing be done for me: Grant me two months, so that I may go and wander[n] on the mountains, and bewail my virginity, my companions and I." [38]"Go," he said and sent her away for two months. So she departed, she and her companions, and bewailed her

m Or Sea of Reeds   *n Cn: Heb go down*

virginity on the mountains. 39 At the end of two months, she returned to her father, who did with her according to the vow he had made. She had never slept with a man. So there arose an Israelite custom that 40 for four days every year the daughters of Israel would go out to lament the daughter of Jeph'thah the Gil'e·ad·īte.

Intertribal Dissension

12 The men of E'phra·im were called to arms, and they crossed to Za'phon and said to Jeph'-thah, "Why did you cross over to fight against the Am'mon·ites, and did not call us to go with you? We will burn your house down over you!" 2 Jeph'-thah said to them, "My people and I were engaged in conflict with the Am'-mon·ites who oppressed us[o] severely. But when I called you, you did not deliver me from their hand. 3 When I saw that you would not deliver me, I took my life in my hand, and crossed over against the Am'mon·ites, and the LORD gave them into my hand. Why then have you come up to me this day, to fight against me?" 4 Then Jeph'thah gathered all the men of Gil'e·ad and fought with E'phra·im; and the men of Gil'e·ad defeated E'phra·im, because they said, "You are fugitives from E'phra·im, you Gil'e·ad·ites—in the heart of E'phra·im and Ma·nas'seh."[p] 5 Then the Gil'e·ad·ites took the fords of the Jordan against the E'phra·im·ites. Whenever one of the fugitives of E'phra·im said, "Let me go over," the men of Gil'e·ad would say to him, "Are you an E'phra·im·īte?" When he said, "No," 6 they said to him, "Then say Shib'bo·leth," and he said, "Sib'bo·leth," for he could not pronounce it right. Then they seized him and killed him at the fords of the Jordan. Forty-two thousand of the E'phra·im·ites fell at that time.

7 Jeph'thah judged Israel six years. Then Jeph'thah the Gil'e·ad·īte died, and was buried in his town in Gil'-e·ad.[q]

Ibzan, Elon, and Abdon

8 After him Ib'zan of Bethlehem judged Israel. 9 He had thirty sons. He gave his thirty daughters in marriage outside his clan and brought in thirty young women from outside for his sons. He judged Israel seven years.

10 Then Ib'zan died, and was buried at Bethlehem.

11 After him E'lon the Zeb'u·lun·īte judged Israel; and he judged Israel ten years. 12 Then E'lon the Zeb'u·lun·īte died, and was buried at Ai'ja·lon in the land of Zeb'u·lun.

13 After him Ab'don son of Hil'lel the Pir'a·thon·īte judged Israel. 14 He had forty sons and thirty grandsons, who rode on seventy donkeys; he judged Israel eight years. 15 Then Ab'-don son of Hil'lel the Pir'a·thon·īte died, and was buried at Pir'a·thon in the land of E'phra·im, in the hill country of the A·mal'e·kītes.

The Birth of Samson
(Cp Num 6.1–21)

13 The Israelites again did what was evil in the sight of the LORD, and the LORD gave them into the hand of the Phi·lis'tines forty years.

2 There was a certain man of Zo'-rah, of the tribe of the Dan'ites, whose name was Ma·no'ah. His wife was barren, having borne no children. 3 And the angel of the LORD appeared to the woman and said to her, "Although you are barren, having borne no children, you shall conceive and bear a son. 4 Now be careful not to drink wine or strong drink, or to eat anything unclean, 5 for you shall conceive and bear a son. No razor is to come on his head, for the boy shall be a nazirite[r] to God from birth. It is he who shall begin to deliver Israel from the hand of the Phi·lis'tines." 6 Then the woman came and told her husband, "A man of God came to me, and his appearance was like that of an angel[s] of God, most awe-inspiring; I did not ask him where he came from, and he did not tell me his name; 7 but he said to me, 'You shall conceive and bear a son. So then drink no wine or strong drink, and eat nothing unclean, for the boy shall be a nazirite[r] to God from birth to the day of his death.' "

8 Then Ma·no'ah entreated the LORD, and said, "O, LORD, I pray, let the man of God whom you sent come to us again and teach us what we are to do concerning the boy who will be born."

---

[o] Gk OL, Syr H: Heb lacks *who oppressed us*   [p] Meaning of Heb uncertain: Gk omits *because . . . Manasseh*   [q] Gk: Heb *in the towns of Gilead*   [r] That is *one separated* or *one consecrated*   [s] Or *the angel*

9 God listened to Ma·nō'ah, and the angel of God came again to the woman as she sat in the field; but her husband Ma·nō'ah was not with her. 10 So the woman ran quickly and told her husband, "The man who came to me the other day has appeared to me." 11 Ma·nō'ah got up and followed his wife, and came to the man and said to him, "Are you the man who spoke to this woman?" And he said, "I am." 12 Then Ma·nō'ah said, "Now when your words come true, what is to be the boy's rule of life; what is he to do?" 13 The angel of the LORD said to Ma·nō'ah, "Let the woman give heed to all that I said to her. 14 She may not eat of anything that comes from the vine. She is not to drink wine or strong drink, or eat any unclean thing. She is to observe everything that I commanded her."

15 Ma·nō'ah said to the angel of the LORD, "Allow us to detain you, and prepare a kid for you." 16 The angel of the LORD said to Ma·nō'ah, "If you detain me, I will not eat your food; but if you want to prepare a burnt offering, then offer it to the LORD." (For Ma·nō'ah did not know that he was the angel of the LORD.) 17 Then Ma·nō'ah said to the angel of the LORD, "What is your name, so that we may honor you when your words come true?" 18 But the angel of the LORD said to him, "Why do you ask my name? It is too wonderful."

19 So Ma·nō'ah took the kid with the grain offering, and offered it on the rock to the LORD, to him who works[t] wonders.[u] 20 When the flame went up toward heaven from the altar, the angel of the LORD ascended in the flame of the altar while Ma·nō'ah and his wife looked on; and they fell on their faces to the ground. 21 The angel of the LORD did not appear again to Ma·nō'ah and his wife. Then Ma·nō'ah realized that it was the angel of the LORD. 22 And Ma·nō'ah said to his wife, "We shall surely die, for we have seen God." 23 But his wife said to him, "If the LORD had meant to kill us, he would not have accepted a burnt offering and a grain offering at our hands, or shown us all these things, or now announced to us such things as these."

24 The woman bore a son, and named him Samson. The boy grew, and the LORD blessed him. 25 The spirit of the LORD began to stir him in Mā'-ha·neh-dan, between Zō'rah and Esh'-tā·ol.

Samson's Marriage

14 Once Samson went down to Tim'nah, and at Tim'nah he saw a Phi·lis'tine woman. 2 Then he came up, and told his father and mother, "I saw a Phi·lis'tine woman at Tim'nah; now get her for me as my wife." 3 But his father and mother said to him, "Is there not a woman among your kin, or among all our[v] people, that you must go to take a wife from the uncircumcised Phi·lis'tines?" But Samson said to his father, "Get her for me, because she pleases me." 4 His father and mother did not know that this was from the LORD; for he was seeking a pretext to act against the Phi·lis'-tines. At that time the Phi·lis'tines had dominion over Israel.

5 Then Samson went down with his father and mother to Tim'nah. When he came to the vineyards of Tim'nah, suddenly a young lion roared at him. 6 The spirit of the LORD rushed on him, and he tore the lion apart barehanded as one might tear apart a kid. But he did not tell his father or his mother what he had done. 7 Then he went down and talked with the woman, and she pleased Samson. 8 After a while he returned to marry her, and he turned aside to see the carcass of the lion, and there was a swarm of bees in the body of the lion, and honey. 9 He scraped it out into his hands, and went on, eating as he went. When he came to his father and mother, he gave some to them, and they ate it. But he did not tell them that he had taken the honey from the carcass of the lion.

10 His father went down to the woman, and Samson made a feast there as the young men were accustomed to do. 11 When the people saw him, they brought thirty companions to be with him. 12 Samson said to them, "Let me now put a riddle to you. If you can explain it to me within the seven days of the feast, and find it out, then I will give you thirty linen garments and thirty festal garments. 13 But if you cannot explain it to me, then you shall give me thirty linen garments and thirty festal garments." So they said to him, "Ask your riddle; let us hear it." 14 He said to them,

---

[t] Gk Vg: Heb *and working*
[u] Heb *wonders, while Manoah and his wife looked on*   [v] Cn: Heb *my*

"Out of the eater came
      something to eat.
Out of the strong came
      something sweet."
But for three days they could not ex-
plain the riddle.

15 On the fourth[w] day they said to
Samson's wife, "Coax your husband to
explain the riddle to us, or we will burn
you and your father's house with fire.
Have you invited us here to impover-
ish us?" 16 So Samson's wife wept before him, saying, "You hate me; you do
not really love me. You have asked a
riddle of my people, but you have not
explained it to me." He said to her,
"Look, I have not told my father or my
mother. Why should I tell you?" 17 She
wept before him the seven days that
their feast lasted; and because she
nagged him, on the seventh day he told
her. Then she explained the riddle to
her people. 18 The men of the town said
to him on the seventh day before the
sun went down,

"What is sweeter than honey?
What is stronger than a lion?"
And he said to them,

"If you had not plowed with my
      heifer,
you would not have found out
      my riddle."

19 Then the spirit of the LORD rushed on
him, and he went down to Ash·ke·lon.
He killed thirty men of the town, took
their spoil, and gave the festal garments to those who had explained the
riddle. In hot anger he went back to his
father's house. 20 And Samson's wife
was given to his companion, who had
been his best man.

Samson Defeats the Philistines

15 After a while, at the time of the
wheat harvest, Samson went to
visit his wife, bringing along a kid. He
said, "I want to go into my wife's
room." But her father would not allow
him to go in. 2 Her father said, "I was
sure that you had rejected her; so I
gave her to your companion. Is not her
younger sister prettier than she? Why
not take her instead?" 3 Samson said to
them, "This time, when I do mischief to
the Phi·lis'tines, I will be without
blame." 4 So Samson went and caught
three hundred foxes, and took some
torches; and he turned the foxes[x] tail
to tail, and put a torch between each
pair of tails. 5 When he had set fire to
the torches, he let the foxes go into the
standing grain of the Phi·lis'tines, and

burned up the shocks and the standing
grain, as well as the vineyards and[y]
olive groves. 6 Then the Phi·lis'tines
asked, "Who has done this?" And they
said, "Samson, the son-in-law of the
Tim'nite, because he has taken Samson's wife and given her to his companion." So the Phi·lis'tines came up,
and burned her and her father. 7 Samson said to them, "If this is what you
do, I swear I will not stop until I have
taken revenge on you." 8 He struck
them down hip and thigh with great
slaughter; and he went down and
stayed in the cleft of the rock of E'tam.

9 Then the Phi·lis'tines came up
and encamped in Judah, and made a
raid on Le'hi. 10 The men of Judah said,
"Why have you come up against us?"
They said, "We have come up to bind
Samson, to do to him as he did to us."
11 Then three thousand men of Judah
went down to the cleft of the rock of
E'tam, and they said to Samson, "Do
you not know that the Phi·lis'tines are
rulers over us? What then have you
done to us?" He replied, "As they did to
me, so I have done to them." 12 They
said to him, "We have come down to
bind you, so that we may give you into
the hands of the Phi·lis'tines." Samson
answered them, "Swear to me that you
yourselves will not attack me." 13 They
said to him, "No, we will only bind you
and give you into their hands; we will
not kill you." So they bound him with
two new ropes, and brought him up
from the rock.

14 When he came to Le'hi, the
Phi·lis'tines came shouting to meet
him; and the spirit of the LORD rushed
on him, and the ropes that were on his
arms became like flax that has caught
fire, and his bonds melted off his
hands. 15 Then he found a fresh jawbone of a donkey, reached down and
took it, and with it he killed a thousand
men. 16 And Samson said,

"With the jawbone of a donkey,
      heaps upon heaps,
with the jawbone of a donkey
      I have slain a thousand men."

17 When he had finished speaking, he
threw away the jawbone; and that
place was called Ra'math-le'hi.[z]

18 By then he was very thirsty, and
he called on the LORD, saying, "You
have granted this great victory by the

w Gk Syr: Heb seventh   x Heb them
y Gk Tg Vg: Heb lacks and   z That is
The Hill of the Jawbone

hand of your servant. Am I now to die of thirst, and fall into the hands of the uncircumcised?" [19] So God split open the hollow place that is at Lē′hī, and water came from it. When he drank, his spirit returned, and he revived. Therefore it was named En·hak·kor′ē,[a] which is at Lē′hī to this day. [20] And he judged Israel in the days of the Phi·lis′tines twenty years.

Samson and Delilah

16 Once Samson went to Gā′za, where he saw a prostitute and went in to her. [2] The Gā′zites were told,[b] "Samson has come here." So they circled around and lay in wait for him all night at the city gate. They kept quiet all night, thinking, "Let us wait until the light of the morning; then we will kill him." [3] But Samson lay only until midnight. Then at midnight he rose up, took hold of the doors of the city gate and the two posts, pulled them up, bar and all, put them on his shoulders, and carried them to the top of the hill that is in front of Hē′bron.

[4] After this he fell in love with a woman in the valley of Sō′rek, whose name was Dē·lī′lah. [5] The lords of the Phi·lis′tines came to her and said to her, "Coax him, and find out what makes his strength so great, and how we may overpower him, so that we may bind him in order to subdue him; and we will each give you eleven hundred pieces of silver." [6] So Dē·lī′lah said to Samson, "Please tell me what makes your strength so great, and how you could be bound, so that one could subdue you." [7] Samson said to her, "If they bind me with seven fresh bowstrings that are not dried out, then I shall become weak, and be like anyone else." [8] Then the lords of the Phi·lis′tines brought her seven fresh bowstrings that had not dried out, and she bound him with them. [9] While men were lying in wait in an inner chamber, she said to him, "The Phi·lis′tines are upon you, Samson!" But he snapped the bowstrings, as a strand of fiber snaps when it touches the fire. So the secret of his strength was not known.

[10] Then Dē·lī′lah said to Samson, "You have mocked me and told me lies; please tell me how you could be bound." [11] He said to her, "If they bind me with new ropes that have not been used, then I shall become weak, and be like anyone else." [12] So Dē·lī′lah took

new ropes and bound him with them, and said to him, "The Phi·lis′tines are upon you, Samson!" (The men lying in wait were in an inner chamber.) But he snapped the ropes off his arms like a thread.

[13] Then Dē·lī′lah said to Samson, "Until now you have mocked me and told me lies; tell me how you could be bound." He said to her, "If you weave the seven locks of my head with the web and make it tight with the pin, then I shall become weak, and be like anyone else." [14] So while he slept, Dē·lī′lah took the seven locks of his head and wove them into the web,[c] and made them tight with the pin. Then she said to him, "The Phi·lis′tines are upon you, Samson!" But he awoke from his sleep, and pulled away the pin, the loom, and the web.

[15] Then she said to him, "How can you say, 'I love you,' when your heart is not with me? You have mocked me three times now and have not told me what makes your strength so great." [16] Finally, after she had nagged him with her words day after day, and pestered him, he was tired to death. [17] So he told her his whole secret, and said to her, "A razor has never come upon my head; for I have been a nazirite[d] to God from my mother's womb. If my head were shaved, then my strength would leave me; I would become weak, and be like anyone else."

[18] When Dē·lī′lah realized that he had told her his whole secret, she sent and called the lords of the Phi·lis′tines, saying, "This time come up, for he has told his whole secret to me." Then the lords of the Phi·lis′tines came up to her, and brought the money in their hands. [19] She let him fall asleep on her lap; and she called a man, and had him shave off the seven locks of his head. He began to weaken,[e] and his strength left him. [20] Then she said, "The Phi·lis′tines are upon you, Samson!" When he awoke from his sleep, he thought, "I will go out as at other times, and shake myself free." But he did not know that the LORD had left him. [21] So the Phi·lis′tines seized him

[a] That is *The Spring of the One who Called* [b] Gk: Heb lacks *were told* [c] Compare Gk: in verses 13-14, Heb lacks *and make it tight . . . into the web* [d] That is *one separated* or *one consecrated* [e] Gk: Heb *She began to torment him*

and gouged out his eyes. They brought him down to Gā´za and bound him with bronze shackles; and he ground at the mill in the prison. 22 But the hair of his head began to grow again after it had been shaved.

Samson's Death

23 Now the lords of the Phi·lis´tines gathered to offer a great sacrifice to their god Dā´gon, and to rejoice; for they said, "Our god has given Samson our enemy into our hand." 24 When the people saw him, they praised their god; for they said, "Our god has given our enemy into our hand, the ravager of our country, who has killed many of us." 25 And when their hearts were merry, they said, "Call Samson, and let him entertain us." So they called Samson out of the prison, and he performed for them. They made him stand between the pillars; 26 and Samson said to the attendant who held him by the hand, "Let me feel the pillars on which the house rests, so that I may lean against them." 27 Now the house was full of men and women; all the lords of the Phi·lis´tines were there, and on the roof there were about three thousand men and women, who looked on while Samson performed.

28 Then Samson called to the LORD and said, "Lord GOD, remember me and strengthen me only this once, O God, so that with this one act of revenge I may pay back the Phi·lis´tines for my two eyes."f 29 And Samson grasped the two middle pillars on which the house rested, and he leaned his weight against them, his right hand on the one and his left hand on the other. 30 Then Samson said, "Let me die with the Phi·lis´tines." He strained with all his might; and the house fell on the lords and all the people who were in it. So those he killed at his death were more than those he had killed during his life. 31 Then his brothers and all his family came down and took him and brought him up and buried him between Zō´rah and Esh´tā·ol in the tomb of his father Ma·nō´ah. He had judged Israel twenty years.

Micah and the Levite

17 There was a man in the hill country of E´phra·im whose name was Mī´cah. 2 He said to his mother, "The eleven hundred pieces of silver that were taken from you, about which you uttered a curse, and even

spoke it in my hearing,—that silver is in my possession; I took it; but now I will return it to you."g And his mother said, "May my son be blessed by the LORD!" 3 Then he returned the eleven hundred pieces of silver to his mother; and his mother said, "I consecrate the silver to the LORD from my hand for my son, to make an idol of cast metal." 4 So when he returned the money to his mother, his mother took two hundred pieces of silver, and gave it to the silversmith, who made it into an idol of cast metal; and it was in the house of Mī´cah. 5 This man Mī´cah had a shrine, and he made an ephod and teraphim, and installed one of his sons, who became his priest. 6 In those days there was no king in Israel; all the people did what was right in their own eyes.

7 Now there was a young man of Bethlehem in Judah, of the clan of Judah. He was a Lē´vite residing there. 8 This man left the town of Bethlehem in Judah, to live wherever he could find a place. He came to the house of Mī´cah in the hill country of E´phra·im to carry on his work.h 9 Mī´cah said to him, "From where do you come?" He replied, "I am a Lē´vite of Bethlehem in Judah, and I am going to live wherever I can find a place." 10 Then Mī´cah said to him, "Stay with me, and be to me a father and a priest, and I will give you ten pieces of silver a year, a set of clothes, and your living."i 11 The Lē´vite agreed to stay with the man; and the young man became to him like one of his sons. 12 So Mī´cah installed the Lē´vite, and the young man became his priest, and was in the house of Mī´cah. 13 Then Mī´cah said, "Now I know that the LORD will prosper me, because the Lē´vite has become my priest."

The Migration of Dan

18 In those days there was no king in Israel. And in those days the tribe of the Dan´ites was seeking for itself a territory to live in; for until then no territory among the tribes of Israel had been allotted to them. 2 So the Dan´ites sent five valiant men from the

---

fOr so that I may be avenged upon the Philistines for one of my two eyes
gThe words but now I will return it to you are transposed from the end of verse 3 in Heb   hOr Ephraim, continuing his journey   iHeb living, and the Levite went

whole number of their clan, from Zō'-rah and from Esh'tā·ol, to spy out the land and to explore it; and they said to them, "Go, explore the land." When they came to the hill country of Ē'phra·im, to the house of Mī'cah, they stayed there. 3 While they were at Mī'cah's house, they recognized the voice of the young Le'vīte; so they went over and asked him, "Who brought you here? What are you doing in this place? What is your business here?" 4 He said to them, "Mī'cah did such and such for me, and he hired me, and I have become his priest." 5 Then they said to him, "Inquire of God that we may know whether the mission we are undertaking will succeed." 6 The priest replied, "Go in peace. The mission you are on is under the eye of the LORD."

7 The five men went on, and when they came to La'ish, they observed the people who were there living securely, after the manner of the Sī·dō'ni·ans, quiet and unsuspecting, lacking[j] nothing on earth, and possessing wealth.[k] Furthermore, they were far from the Sī·dō'ni·ans and had no dealings with Ar'am.[l] 8 When they came to their kinsfolk at Zō'rah and Esh'-tā·ol, they said to them, "What do you report?" 9 They said, "Come, let us go up against them; for we have seen the land, and it is very good. Will you do nothing? Do not be slow to go, but enter in and possess the land. 10 When you go, you will come to an unsuspecting people. The land is broad—God has indeed given it into your hands—a place where there is no lack of anything on earth."

11 Six hundred men of the Dan'īte clan, armed with weapons of war, set out from Zō'rah and Esh'tā·ol, 12 and went up and encamped at Kir'i·ath-jē'a·rim in Judah. On this account that place is called Mā'ha·neh-dan[m] to this day; it is west of Kir'i·ath-jē'a·rim. 13 From there they passed on to the hill country of Ē'phra·im, and came to the house of Mī'cah.

14 Then the five men who had gone to spy out the land (that is, La'ish) said to their comrades, "Do you know that in these buildings there are an ephod, teraphim, and an idol of cast metal? Now therefore consider what you will do." 15 So they turned in that direction and came to the house of the young Le'vīte, at the home of Mī'cah, and greeted him. 16 While the six hundred

men of the Dan'ītes, armed with their weapons of war, stood by the entrance of the gate, 17 the five men who had gone to spy out the land proceeded to enter and take the idol of cast metal, the ephod, and the teraphim.[n] The priest was standing by the entrance of the gate with the six hundred men armed with weapons of war. 18 When the men went into Mī'cah's house and took the idol of cast metal, the ephod, and the teraphim, the priest said to them, "What are you doing?" 19 They said to him, "Keep quiet! Put your hand over your mouth, and come with us, and be to us a father and a priest. Is it better for you to be priest to the house of one person, or to be priest to a tribe and clan in Israel?" 20 Then the priest accepted the offer. He took the ephod, the teraphim, and the idol, and went along with the people.

21 So they resumed their journey, putting the little ones, the livestock, and the goods in front of them. 22 When they were some distance from the home of Mī'cah, the men who were in the houses near Mī'cah's house were called out, and they overtook the Dan'-ītes. 23 They shouted to the Dan'ītes, who turned around and said to Mī'cah, "What is the matter that you come with such a company?" 24 He replied, "You take my gods that I made, and the priest, and go away, and what have I left? How then can you ask me, 'What is the matter?' " 25 And the Dan'ītes said to him, "You had better not let your voice be heard among us or else hot-tempered fellows will attack you, and you will lose your life and the lives of your household." 26 Then the Dan'-ītes went their way. When Mī'cah saw that they were too strong for him, he turned and went back to his home.

The Danites Settle in Laish

27 The Dan'ītes, having taken what Mī'cah had made, and the priest who belonged to him, came to La'ish, to a people quiet and unsuspecting, put them to the sword, and burned down the city. 28 There was no deliverer, because it was far from Sī'don and they had no dealings with Ar'am.[o] It was in

j Cn Compare 18.10: Meaning of Heb uncertain k Meaning of Heb uncertain l Symmachus: Heb with anyone m That is Camp of Dan n Compare 17.4, 5; 18.14: Heb teraphim and the cast metal o Cn Compare verse 7: Heb with anyone the valley that belongs to Beth-rē'hob. They rebuilt the city, and lived in it. [29] They named the city Dan, after their ancestor Dan, who was born to Israel; but the name of the city was formerly Lā'ish. [30] Then the Dan'ites set up the idol for themselves. Jonathan son of Ger'shom, son of Moses,[p] and his sons were priests to the tribe of the Dan'ites until the time the land went into captivity. [31] So they maintained as their own Mī'cah's idol that he had made, as long as the house of God was at Shī'lōh.

The Levite's Concubine

19 In those days, when there was no king in Israel, a certain Lē'vīte, residing in the remote parts of the hill country of Ē'phra·im, took to himself a concubine from Bethlehem in Judah. [2] But his concubine became angry with[q] him, and she went away from him to her father's house at Bethlehem in Judah, and was there some four months. [3] Then her husband set out after her, to speak tenderly to her and bring her back. He had with him his servant and a couple of donkeys. When he reached[r] her father's house, the girl's father saw him and came with joy to meet him. [4] His father-in-law, the girl's father, made him stay, and he remained with him three days; so they ate and drank, and he[s] stayed there. [5] On the fourth day they got up early in the morning, and he prepared to go; but the girl's father said to his son-in-law, "Fortify yourself with a bit of food, and after that you may go." [6] So the two men sat and ate and drank together; and the girl's father said to the man, "Why not spend the night and enjoy yourself?" [7] When the man got up to go, his father-in-law kept urging him until he spent the night there again. [8] On the fifth day he got up early in the morning to leave; and the girl's father said, "Fortify yourself." So they lingered[t] until the day declined, and the two of them ate and drank.[u] [9] When the man with his concubine and his servant got up to leave, and his father-in-law, the girl's father, said to him, "Look, the day has worn on until it is almost evening. Spend the night. See, the day has drawn to a close. Spend the night here and enjoy yourself. Tomorrow you can get up early in the morning for your journey, and go home."

[10] But the man would not spend the night; he got up and departed, and arrived opposite Jē'bus (that is, Jerusalem). He had with him a couple of saddled donkeys, and his concubine was with him. [11] When they were near Jē'bus, the day was far spent, and the servant said to his master, "Come now, let us turn aside to this city of the Jeb'u·sītes, and spend the night in it." [12] But his master said to him, "We will not turn aside into a city of foreigners, who do not belong to the people of Israel; but we will continue on to Gib'e·ah." [13] Then he said to his servant, "Come, let us try to reach one of these places, and spend the night at Gib'e·ah or at Rā'mah." [14] So they passed on and went their way; and the sun went down on them near Gib'e·ah, which belongs to Benjamin. [15] They turned aside there, to go in and spend the night at Gib'e·ah. He went in and sat down in the open square of the city, but no one took them in to spend the night.

[16] Then at evening there was an old man coming from his work in the field. The man was from the hill country of Ē'phra·im, and he was residing in Gib'e·ah. (The people of the place were Ben'ja·min·ītes.) [17] When the old man looked up and saw the wayfarer in the open square of the city, he said, "Where are you going and where do you come from?" [18] He answered him, "We are passing from Bethlehem in Judah to the remote parts of the hill country of Ē'phra·im, from which I come. I went to Bethlehem in Judah; and I am going to my home.[v] Nobody has offered to take me in. [19] We your servants have straw and fodder for our donkeys, with bread and wine for me and the woman and the young man along with us. We need nothing more." [20] The old man said, "Peace be to you. I will care for all your wants; only do not spend the night in the square." [21] So he brought him into his house, and fed the donkeys; they washed their feet, and ate and drank.

Gibeah's Crime

22 While they were enjoying them-

p Another reading is *son of Manasseh*
q Gk OL: Heb *prostituted herself against*
r Gk: Heb *she brought him*   s Compare
verse 7 and Gk: Heb *they*   t Cn: Heb
Linger   u Gk: Heb lacks *and drank*
v Gk Compare 19.29. Heb *to the house of
the* LORD

selves, the men of the city, a perverse lot, surrounded the house, and started pounding on the door. They said to the old man, the master of the house, "Bring out the man who came into your house, so that we may have intercourse with him." 23 And the man, the master of the house, went out to them and said to them, "No, my brothers, do not act so wickedly. Since this man is my guest, do not do this vile thing. 24 Here are my virgin daughter and his concubine; let me bring them out now. Ravish them and do whatever you want to them; but against this man do not do such a vile thing." 25 But the men would not listen to him. So the man seized his concubine, and put her out to them. They wantonly raped her, and abused her all through the night until the morning. And as the dawn began to break, they let her go. 26 As morning appeared, the woman came and fell down at the door of the man's house where her master was, until it was light.

27 In the morning her master got up, opened the doors of the house, and when he went out to go on his way, there was his concubine lying at the door of the house, with her hands on the threshold. 28 "Get up," he said to her, "we are going." But there was no answer. Then he put her on the donkey; and the man set out for his home. 29 When he had entered his house, he took a knife, and grasping his concubine he cut her into twelve pieces, limb by limb, and sent her throughout all the territory of Israel. 30 Then he commanded the men whom he sent, saying, "Thus shall you say to all the Israelites, 'Has such a thing ever happened*w* since the day that the Israelites came up from the land of Egypt until this day? Consider it, take counsel, and speak out.'"

The Other Tribes Attack Benjamin

20 Then all the Israelites came out, from Dan to Bē'er-shē'ba, including the land of Gil'e·ad, and the congregation assembled in one body before the LORD at Miz'pah. 2 The chiefs of all the people, of all the tribes of Israel, presented themselves in the assembly of the people of God, four hundred thousand foot-soldiers bearing arms. 3 (Now the Ben'ja·min·ites heard that the people of Israel had gone up to Miz'pah.) And the Israelites said, "Tell us, how did this criminal act

come about?" 4 The Lē'vīte, the husband of the woman who was murdered, answered, "I came to Gib'e·ah that belongs to Benjamin, I and my concubine, to spend the night. 5 The lords of Gib'e·ah rose up against me, and surrounded the house at night. They intended to kill me, and they raped my concubine until she died. 6 Then I took my concubine and cut her into pieces, and sent her throughout the whole extent of Israel's territory; for they have committed a vile outrage in Israel. 7 So now, you Israelites, all of you, give your advice and counsel here."

8 All the people got up as one, saying, "We will not any of us go to our tents, nor will any of us return to our houses. 9 But now this is what we will do to Gib'e·ah: we will go up*x* against it by lot. 10 We will take ten men of a hundred throughout all the tribes of Israel, and a hundred of a thousand, and a thousand of ten thousand, to bring provisions for the troops, who are going to repay*y* Gib'e·ah of Benjamin for all the disgrace that they have done in Israel." 11 So all the men of Israel gathered against the city, united as one.

12 The tribes of Israel sent men through all the tribe of Benjamin, saying, "What crime is this that has been committed among you? 13 Now then, hand over those scoundrels in Gib'-ē·ah, so that we may put them to death, and purge the evil from Israel." But the Ben'ja·min·ites would not listen to their kinsfolk, the Israelites. 14 The Ben'ja·min·ites came together out of the towns to Gib'e·ah, to go out to battle against the Israelites. 15 On that day the Ben'ja·min·ites mustered twenty-six thousand armed men from their towns, besides the inhabitants of Gib'-ē·ah. 16 Of all this force, there were seven hundred picked men who were left-handed; every one could sling a stone at a hair, and not miss. 17 And the Israelites, apart from Benjamin, mustered four hundred thousand armed men, all of them warriors.

18 The Israelites proceeded to go up to Beth'el, where they inquired of God, "Which of us shall go up first to battle

---

w Compare Gk: Heb 30 And all who saw it said, "Such a thing has not happened or been seen *x* Gk: Heb lacks we will go up *y* Compare Gk: Meaning of Heb uncertain against the Ben'ja·min·ites?" And the LORD answered, "Judah shall go up first."

19 Then the Israelites got up in the morning, and encamped against Gib'-e·ah. ²⁰The Israelites went out to battle against Benjamin; and the Israelites drew up the battle line against them at Gib'e·ah. ²¹The Ben'ja·min·ites came out of Gib'e·ah, and struck down on that day twenty-two thousand of the Israelites. ²³ᶻThe Israelites went up and wept before the LORD until the evening; and they inquired of the LORD, "Shall we again draw near to battle against our kinsfolk the Ben'ja·min·ites?" And the LORD said, "Go up against them." ²²The Israelites took courage, and again formed the battle line in the same place where they had formed it on the first day.

24 So the Israelites advanced against the Ben'ja·min·ites the second day. ²⁵Benjamin moved out against them from Gib'e·ah the second day, and struck down eighteen thousand of the Israelites, all of them armed men. ²⁶Then all the Israelites, the whole army, went back to Beth'el and wept, sitting there before the LORD; they fasted that day until evening. Then they offered burnt offerings and sacrifices of well-being before the LORD. ²⁷And the Israelites inquired of the LORD (for the ark of the covenant of God was there in those days, ²⁸and Phin'e·has son of El·e·a'zar, son of Aaron, ministered before it in those days), saying, "Shall we go out once more to battle against our kinsfolk the Ben'ja·min·ites, or shall we desist?" The LORD answered, "Go up, for tomorrow I will give them into your hand."

29 So Israel stationed men in ambush around Gib'e·ah. ³⁰Then the Israelites went up against the Ben'-ja·min·ites on the third day, and set themselves in array against Gib'e·ah, as before. ³¹When the Ben'ja·min·ites went out against the army, they were drawn away from the city. As before they began to inflict casualties on the troops, along the main roads, one of which goes up to Beth'el and the other to Gib'e·ah, as well as in the open country, killing about thirty men of Israel. ³²The Ben'ja·min·ites thought, 'They are being routed before us, as previously." But the Israelites said, 'Let us retreat and draw them away from the city toward the roads." ³³The

main body of the Israelites drew back its battle line to Ba'al-ta'mar, while those Israelites who were in ambush rushed out of their place westᵃ of Ge'ba. ³⁴There came against Gib'e·ah ten thousand picked men out of all Israel, and the battle was fierce. But the Ben'ja·min·ites did not realize that disaster was close upon them.

35 The LORD defeated Benjamin before Israel; and the Israelites destroyed twenty-five thousand one hundred men of Benjamin that day, all of them armed.

36 Then the Ben'ja·min·ites saw that they were defeated.ᵇ

The Israelites gave ground to Benjamin, because they trusted to the troops in ambush that they had stationed against Gib'e·ah. ³⁷The troops in ambush rushed quickly upon Gib'e·ah. Then they put the whole city to the sword. ³⁸Now the agreement between the main body of Israel and the men in ambush was that when they sent up a cloud of smoke out of the city ³⁹the main body of Israel should turn in battle. But Benjamin had begun to inflict casualties on the Israelites, killing about thirty of them; so they thought, "Surely they are defeated before us, as in the first battle." ⁴⁰But when the cloud, a column of smoke, began to rise out of the city, the Ben'ja·min·ites looked behind them—and there was the whole city going up in smoke toward the sky! ⁴¹Then the main body of Israel turned, and the Ben'ja·min·ites were dismayed, for they saw that disaster was close upon them. ⁴²Therefore they turned away from the Israelites in the direction of the wilderness; but the battle overtook them, and those who came out of the cityᶜ were slaughtering them in between.ᵈ ⁴³Cutting downᵉ the Ben'ja·min·ites, they pursued them from No'hahᶠ and trod them down as far as a place east of Gib'e·ah. ⁴⁴Eighteen thousand Ben'-ja·min·ites fell, all of them courageous fighters. ⁴⁵When they turned and fled toward the wilderness to the rock of Rim'mon, five thousand of them were

---

ᶻ Verses 22 and 23 are transposed
ᵃ Gk Vg: Heb *in the plain*   ᵇ This
sentence is continued by verse 45.
ᶜ Compare Vg and some Gk Mss: Heb
cities   ᵈ Compare Syr: Meaning of Heb
uncertain   ᵉ Gk: Heb *Surrounding*
ᶠ Gk: Heb *pursued them at their resting
place*

cut down on the main roads, and they were pursued as far as Gi'dom, and two thousand of them were slain. ⁴⁶So all who fell that day of Benjamin were twenty-five thousand arms-bearing men, all of them courageous fighters. ⁴⁷But six hundred turned and fled toward the wilderness to the rock of Rim'mon, and remained at the rock of Rim'mon for four months. ⁴⁸Meanwhile, the Israelites turned back against the Ben'ja·min·ites, and put them to the sword—the city, the people, the animals, and all that remained. Also the remaining towns they set on fire.

The Benjaminites Saved from Extinction

21 Now the Israelites had sworn at Miz'pah, "No one of us shall give his daughter in marriage to Benjamin." ² And the people came to Beth'el, and sat there until evening before God, and they lifted up their voices and wept bitterly. ³ They said, "O LORD, the God of Israel, why has it come to pass that today there should be one tribe lacking in Israel?" ⁴ On the next day, the people got up early, and built an altar there, and offered burnt offerings and sacrifices of well-being. ⁵ Then the Israelites said, "Which of all the tribes of Israel did not come up in the assembly to the LORD?" For a solemn oath had been taken concerning whoever did not come up to the LORD to Miz'pah, saying, "That one shall be put to death." ⁶ But the Israelites had compassion for Benjamin their kin, and said, "One tribe is cut off from Israel this day. ⁷ What shall we do for wives for those who are left, since we have sworn by the LORD that we will not give them any of our daughters as wives?"

⁸ Then they said, "Is there anyone from the tribes of Israel who did not come up to the LORD to Miz'pah?" It turned out that no one from Ja'besh-gil'e·ad had come to the camp, to the assembly. ⁹ For when the roll was called among the people, not one of the inhabitants of Ja'besh-gil'e·ad was there. ¹⁰ So the congregation sent twelve thousand soldiers there and commanded them, "Go, put the inhabitants of Ja'besh-gil'e·ad to the sword, including the women and the little ones. ¹¹ This is what you shall do; every male and every woman that has lain

with a male you shall devote to de struction." ¹²And they found amon the inhabitants of Ja'besh-gil'e·ad fou hundred young virgins who had neve slept with a man and brought them t the camp at Shi'lōh, which is in th land of Ca'naan.

13 Then the whole congregatio sent word to the Ben'ja·min·ites wh were at the rock of Rim'mon, and prc claimed peace to them. ¹⁴Benjamin re turned at that time; and they gav them the women whom they had save alive of the women of Ja'besh-gil'e·ac but they did not suffice for them.

15 The people had compassion o Benjamin because the LORD had mac a breach in the tribes of Israel. ¹⁶So th elders of the congregation said, "Wha shall we do for wives for those who ar left, since there are no women left i Benjamin?" ¹⁷And they said, "Ther must be heirs for the survivors of Ben jamin, in order that a tribe may not b blotted out from Israel. ¹⁸Yet we can not give any of our daughters to them as wives." For the Israelites had sworr "Cursed be anyone who gives a wife t Benjamin." ¹⁹So they said, "Look, th yearly festival of the LORD is takin place at Shi'lōh, which is north c Beth'el, on the east of the highway tha goes up from Beth'el to She'chem, an south of Le·bō'nah." ²⁰And they in structed the Ben'ja·min·ites, saying "Go and lie in wait in the vineyards ²¹and watch; when the young wome of Shi'lōh come out to dance in th dances, then come out of the vineyard and each of you carry off a wife fo himself from the young women of Shi' lōh, and go to the land of Benjamin ²²Then if their fathers or their brother come to complain to us, we will say t them, 'Be generous and allow us t have them; because we did not captur in battle a wife for each man. But nei ther did you incur guilt by giving you daughters to them.' " ²³The Ben' ja·min·ites did so; they took wives fo each of them from the dancers whon they abducted. Then they went and re turned to their territory, and rebui the towns, and lived in them. ²⁴So th Israelites departed from there at tha time by tribes and families, and the went out from there to their own terri tories.

25 In those days there was no kin in Israel; all the people did what wa right in their own eyes.

RUTH

Elimelech's Family Goes to Moab

1 In the days when the judges ruled, there was a famine in the land, and a certain man of Bethlehem in Judah went to live in the country of Mŏ'ab, he and his wife and two sons. The name of the man was Ē·lim'e·lech and the name of his wife Nā'o·mī, and the names of his two sons were Mah'lon and Chil'i·on; they were Eph'-a·thītes from Bethlehem in Judah. They went into the country of Mŏ'ab and remained there. ³ But Ē·lim'e·lech, the husband of Nā'o·mī, died, and she was left with her two sons. ⁴ These took Mŏ'ab·īte wives; the name of the one was Or'pah and the name of the other Ruth. When they had lived there about ten years, ⁵ both Mah'lon and Chil'i·on also died, so that the woman was left without her two sons and her husband.

Naomi and Her Moabite Daughters-in-Law

6 Then she started to return with her daughters-in-law from the country of Mŏ'ab, for she had heard in the country of Mŏ'ab that the LORD had considered his people and given them food. ⁷ So she set out from the place where she had been living, she and her two daughters-in-law, and they went on their way to go back to the land of Judah. ⁸ But Nā'o·mī said to her two daughters-in-law, "Go back each of you to your mother's house. May the LORD deal kindly with you, as you have dealt with the dead and with me. ⁹ The LORD grant that you may find security, each of you in the house of your husband." Then she kissed them, and they wept aloud. ¹⁰ They said to her, "No, we will return with you to your people." ¹¹ But Nā'o·mī said, "Turn back, my daughters, why will you go with me? Do I still have sons in my womb that they may become your husbands? ¹² Turn back, my daughters, go your way, for I am too old to have a hus-

band. Even if I thought there was hope for me, even if I should have a husband tonight and bear sons, ¹³ would you then wait until they were grown? Would you then refrain from marrying? No, my daughters, it has been far more bitter for me than for you, because the hand of the LORD has turned against me." ¹⁴ Then they wept aloud again. Or'pah kissed her mother-in-law, but Ruth clung to her.

15 So she said, "See, your sister-in-law has gone back to her people and to her gods; return after your sister-in-law." ¹⁶ But Ruth said,
"Do not press me to leave you
    or to turn back from following you!
Where you go, I will go;
    Where you lodge, I will lodge;
your people shall be my people,
    and your God my God.
17 Where you die, I will die—
    there will I be buried.
May the LORD do thus and so to me,
    and more as well,
if even death parts me from you!"
¹⁸ When Nā'o·mī saw that she was determined to go with her, she said no more to her.

19 So the two of them went on until they came to Bethlehem. When they came to Bethlehem, the whole town was stirred because of them; and the women said, "Is this Nā'o·mī?" ²⁰ She said to them,
"Call me no longer Nā'o·mī,ᵃ
    call me Mar'a,ᵇ
    for the Almightyᶜ has dealt
    bitterly with me.
21 I went away full,
    but the LORD has brought me back empty;
    why call me Nā'o·mī

ᵃ That is *Pleasant*   ᵇ That is *Bitter*
ᶜ Traditional rendering of Heb *Shaddai*

when the LORD has dealt
   harshly with[d] me,
and the Almighty[e] has
   brought calamity upon
   me?"

22 So Nā′o·mī returned together with Ruth the Mō′ab·īte, her daughter-in-law, who came back with her from the country of Mō′ab. They came to Bethlehem at the beginning of the barley harvest.

Ruth Meets Boaz

2 Now Nā′o·mī had a kinsman on her husband's side, a prominent rich man, of the family of E·lim′e·lech, whose name was Bō′az. ² And Ruth the Mō′ab·īte said to Nā′o·mī, "Let me go to the field and glean among the ears of grain, behind someone in whose sight I may find favor." She said to her, "Go, my daughter." ³ So she went. She came and gleaned in the field behind the reapers. As it happened, she came to the part of the field belonging to Bō′az, who was of the family of E·lim′e·lech. ⁴ Just then Bō′az came from Bethlehem. He said to the reapers, "The LORD be with you." They answered, "The LORD bless you." ⁵ Then Bō′az said to his servant who was in charge of the reapers, "To whom does this young woman belong?" ⁶ The servant who was in charge of the reapers answered, "She is the Mō′ab·īte who came back with Nā′o·mī from the country of Mō′ab. ⁷ She said, 'Please, let me glean and gather among the sheaves behind the reapers.' So she came, and she has been on her feet from early this morning until now, without resting even for a moment."[f]

8 Then Bō′az said to Ruth, "Now listen, my daughter, do not go to glean in another field or leave this one, but keep close to my young women. ⁹ Keep your eyes on the field that is being reaped, and follow behind them. I have ordered the young men not to bother you. If you get thirsty, go to the vessels and drink from what the young men have drawn." ¹⁰ Then she fell prostrate, with her face to the ground, and said to him, "Why have I found favor in your sight, that you should take notice of me, when I am a foreigner?" ¹¹ But Bō′az answered her, "All that you have done for your mother-in-law since the death of your husband has been fully told me, and how you left your father and mother and your native land and came to a people that you did not know

before. ¹² May the LORD reward you for your deeds, and may you have a full reward from the LORD, the God of Israel, under whose wings you have come for refuge!" ¹³ Then she said, "May I continue to find favor in your sight, my lord, for you have comforted me and spoken kindly to your servant, even though I am not one of your servants."

14 At mealtime Bō′az said to her, "Come here, and eat some of this bread, and dip your morsel in the sour wine." So she sat beside the reapers, and he heaped up for her some parched grain. She ate until she was satisfied, and she had some left over. ¹⁵ When she got up to glean, Bō′az instructed his young men, "Let her glean even among the standing sheaves, and do not reproach her. ¹⁶ You must also pull out some handfuls for her from the bundles, and leave them for her to glean, and do not rebuke her."

17 So she gleaned in the field until evening. Then she beat out what she had gleaned, and it was about an ephah of barley. ¹⁸ She picked it up and came into the town, and her mother-in-law saw how much she had gleaned. Then she took out and gave her what was left over after she herself had been satisfied. ¹⁹ Her mother-in-law said to her, "Where did you glean today? And where have you worked? Blessed be the man who took notice of you." So she told her mother-in-law with whom she had worked, and said, "The name of the man with whom I worked today is Bō′az." ²⁰ Then Nā′o·mī said to her daughter-in-law, "Blessed be he by the LORD, whose kindness has not forsaken the living or the dead!" Nā′o·mī also said to her, "The man is a relative of ours, one of our nearest kin."[g] ²¹ Then Ruth the Mō′ab·īte said, "He even said to me, 'Stay close by my servants, until they have finished all my harvest.'" ²² Nā′o·mī said to Ruth, her daughter-in-law, "It is better, my daughter, that you go out with his young women, otherwise you might be bothered in another field." ²³ So she stayed close to the young women of Bō′az, gleaning until the end of the barley and wheat harvests; and she lived with her mother-in-law.

---

[d]Or has testified against   [e]Traditional rendering of Heb Shaddai   [f]Compare Gk Vg: Meaning of Heb uncertain   [g]Or one with the right to redeem

Ruth and Boaz at the Threshing Floor

3 Nā′o·mī her mother-in-law said to her, "My daughter, I need to seek some security for you, so that it may be well with you. ²Now here is our kinsman Bō′az, with whose young women you have been working. See, he is winnowing barley tonight at the threshing floor. ³Now wash and anoint yourself, and put on your best clothes and go down to the threshing floor; but do not make yourself known to the man until he has finished eating and drinking. ⁴When he lies down, observe the place where he lies; then, go and uncover his feet and lie down; and he will tell you what to do." ⁵She said to her, "All that you tell me I will do."

⁶ So she went down to the threshing floor and did just as her mother-in-law had instructed her. ⁷When Bō′az had eaten and drunk, and he was in a contented mood, he went to lie down at the end of the heap of grain. Then she came stealthily and uncovered his feet, and lay down. ⁸At midnight the man was startled, and turned over, and there, lying at his feet, was a woman! ⁹He said, "Who are you?" And she answered, "I am Ruth, your servant; spread your cloak over your servant, for you are next-of-kin."[h] ¹⁰He said, "May you be blessed by the LORD, my daughter; this last instance of your loyalty is better than the first; you have not gone after young men, whether poor or rich. ¹¹And now, my daughter, do not be afraid, I will do for you all that you ask, for all the assembly of my people know that you are a worthy woman. ¹²But now, though it is true that I am a near kinsman, there is another kinsman more closely related than I. ¹³Remain this night, and in the morning, if he will act as next-of-kin[h] for you, good; let him do it. If he is not willing to act as next-of-kin[h] for you, then, as the LORD lives, I will act as next-of-kin[h] for you. Lie down until the morning."

¹⁴ So she lay at his feet until morning, but got up before one person could recognize another; for he said, "It must not be known that the woman came to the threshing floor." ¹⁵Then he said, "Bring the cloak you are wearing and hold it out." So she held it, and he measured out six measures of barley, and put it on her back; then he went into the city. ¹⁶She came to her mother-in-law, who said, "How did things go with you,[i] my daughter?" Then she told her all that the man had done for her, ¹⁷saying, "He gave me these six measures of barley, for he said, 'Do not go back to your mother-in-law empty-handed.'" ¹⁸She replied, "Wait, my daughter, until you learn how the matter turns out, for the man will not rest, but will settle the matter today."

The Marriage of Boaz and Ruth

4 No sooner had Bō′az gone up to the gate and sat down there than the next-of-kin,[h] of whom Bō′az had spoken, came passing by. So Bō′az said, "Come over, friend; sit down here." And he went over and sat down. ²Then Bō′az took ten men of the elders of the city, and said, "Sit down here"; so they sat down. ³He then said to the next-of-kin,[h] "Nā′o·mī, who has come back from the country of Mō′ab, is selling the parcel of land that belonged to our kinsman E·lim′e·lech. ⁴So I thought I would tell you of it, and say: Buy it in the presence of those sitting here, and in the presence of the elders of my people. If you will redeem it, redeem it; but if you will not, tell me, so that I may know; for there is no one prior to you to redeem it, and I come after you." So he said, "I will redeem it." ⁵Then Bō′az said, "The day you acquire the field from the hand of Nā′o·mī, you are also acquiring Ruth[j] the Mō′ab·īte, the widow of the dead man, to maintain the dead man's name on his inheritance." ⁶At this, the next-of-kin[h] said, "I cannot redeem it for myself without damaging my own inheritance. Take my right of redemption yourself, for I cannot redeem it."

⁷ Now this was the custom in former times in Israel concerning redeeming and exchanging: to confirm a transaction, the one took off a sandal and gave it to the other; this was the manner of attesting in Israel. ⁸So when the next-of-kin[h] said to Bō′az, "Acquire it for yourself," he took off his sandal. ⁹Then Bō′az said to the elders and all the people, "Today you are witnesses that I have acquired from the hand of Nā′o·mī all that belonged to E·lim′e·lech and all that belonged to Chil′i·on and Mah′lon. ¹⁰I have also acquired Ruth the Mō′ab·īte, the wife of Mah′lon, to be my wife, to maintain

h Or one with the right to redeem
i Or "Who are you,   *j OL Vg: Heb from the hand of Naomi and from Ruth*

the dead man's name on his inheritance, in order that the name of the dead may not be cut off from his kindred and from the gate of his native place; today you are witnesses." [11] Then all the people who were at the gate, along with the elders, said, "We are witnesses. May the LORD make the woman who is coming into your house like Rachel and Leah, who together built up the house of Israel. May you produce children in Eph′ra·thah and bestow a name in Bethlehem; [12] and, through the children that the LORD will give you by this young woman, may your house be like the house of Per′ez, whom Tā′mar bore to Judah."

The Genealogy of David
(Matt 1.2–6)

13 So Bō′az took Ruth and she became his wife. When they came together, the LORD made her conceive, and she bore a son. [14] Then the women said to Nā′o·mī, "Blessed be the LORD, who has not left you this day without next-of-kin;[k] and may his name be renowned in Israel! [15] He shall be to you a restorer of life and a nourisher of your old age; for your daughter-in-law who loves you, who is more to you than seven sons, has borne him." [16] Then Nā′o·mī took the child and laid him in her bosom, and became his nurse. [17] The women of the neighborhood gave him a name, saying, "A son has been born to Nā′o·mī." They named him Ō′bed; he became the father of Jesse, the father of David.

18 Now these are the descendants of Per′ez: Per′ez became the father of Hez′ron, [19] Hez′ron of Ram, Ram of Am·min′a·dab, [20] Am·min′a·dab of Nah′shon, Nah′shon of Sal′mon, [21] Sal′mon of Bō′az, Bō′az of Ō′bed, [22] Ō′bed of Jesse, and Jesse of David.

[k] Or *one with the right to redeem*

1 SAMUEL

Samuel's Birth and Dedication

1 There was a certain man of Rā·ma·thā′im, a Zuph′īte[a] from the hill country of E′phra·im, whose name was El·kā′nah son of Je·rō′ham son of E·lī′hū son of Tō′hū son of Zuph, an E′phra·im·īte. [2] He had two wives; the name of the one was Hannah, and the name of the other Pe·nin′nah. Pe·nin′nah had children, but Hannah had no children.

3 Now this man used to go up year by year from his town to worship and to sacrifice to the LORD of hosts at Shī′loh, where the two sons of E′lī, Hoph′nī and Phin′e·has, were priests of the LORD. [4] On the day when El·kā′nah sacrificed, he would give portions to his wife Pe·nin′nah and to all her sons and daughters; [5] but to Hannah he gave a double portion,[b] because he loved her, though the LORD had closed her womb. [6] Her rival used to provoke her severely, to irritate her, because the LORD had closed her womb. [7] So it went on year by year; as often as she went up to the house of the LORD, she used to provoke her. Therefore Hannah wept and would not eat. [8] Her husband El·kā′nah said to her, "Hannah, why do you weep? Why do you not eat? Why is your heart sad? Am I not more to you than ten sons?"

9 After they had eaten and drunk at Shī′loh, Hannah rose and presented herself before the LORD.[c] Now E′lī the priest was sitting on the seat beside the doorpost of the temple of the LORD. [10] She was deeply distressed and prayed to the LORD, and wept bitterly. [11] She made this vow: "O LORD of hosts, if only you will look on the misery of your servant, and remember me, and not forget your servant, but will

[a] Compare Gk and 1 Chr 6.35-36: Heb *Ramathaim-zophim*   [b] Syr: Meaning of Heb uncertain   [c] Gk: Heb lacks *and presented herself before the LORD*

give to your servant a male child, then I will set him before you as a nazirite[d] until the day of his death. He shall drink neither wine nor intoxicants,[e] and no razor shall touch his head."

12 As she continued praying before the LORD, Ē′lī observed her mouth. [13]Hannah was praying silently; only her lips moved, but her voice was not heard; therefore Ē′lī thought she was drunk. [14]So Ē′lī said to her, "How long will you make a drunken spectacle of yourself? Put away your wine." [15]But Hannah answered, "No, my lord, I am a woman deeply troubled; I have drunk neither wine nor strong drink, but I have been pouring out my soul before the LORD. [16]Do not regard your servant as a worthless woman, for I have been speaking out of my great anxiety and vexation all this time." [17]Then Ē′lī answered, "Go in peace; the God of Israel grant the petition you have made to him." [18]And she said, "Let your servant find favor in your sight." Then the woman went to her quarters,[f] ate and drank with her husband,[g] and her countenance was sad no longer.[h]

19 They rose early in the morning and worshiped before the LORD; then they went back to their house at Rā′mah. El·kā′nah knew his wife Hannah, and the LORD remembered her. [20]In due time Hannah conceived and bore a son. She named him Samuel, for she said, "I have asked him of the LORD."

21 The man El·kā′nah and all his household went up to offer to the LORD the yearly sacrifice, and to pay his vow. [22]But Hannah did not go up, for she said to her husband, "As soon as the child is weaned, I will bring him, that he may appear in the presence of the LORD, and remain there forever; I will offer him as a nazirite[d] for all time."[i] [23]Her husband El·kā′nah said to her, "Do what seems best to you, wait until you have weaned him; only—may the LORD establish his word."[j] So the woman remained and nursed her son, until she weaned him. [24]When she had weaned him, she took him up with her, along with a three-year-old bull,[k] an ephah of flour, and a skin of wine. She brought him to the house of the LORD at Shī′lōh; and the child was young. [25]Then they slaughtered the bull, and they brought the child to Ē′lī. [26]And she said, "Oh, my lord! As you live, my lord, I am the woman who was standing here in your presence, praying to the LORD. [27]For this child I prayed; and the LORD has granted me the petition that I made to him. [28]Therefore I have lent him to the LORD; as long as he lives, he is given to the LORD."

She left him there for[i] the LORD.

Hannah's Prayer
(Cp Lk 1.46–55)

2 Hannah prayed and said,
    "My heart exults in the LORD;
        my strength is exalted in my God.[m]
    My mouth derides my enemies,
        because I rejoice in my[n] victory.

2 "There is no Holy One like the LORD,
        no one besides you;
    there is no Rock like our God.
3 Talk no more so very proudly,
        let not arrogance come from your mouth;
    for the LORD is a God of knowledge,
        and by him actions are weighed.
4 The bows of the mighty are broken,
        but the feeble gird on strength.
5 Those who were full have hired themselves out for bread,
        but those who were hungry are fat with spoil.
    The barren has borne seven,
        but she who has many children is forlorn.
6 The LORD kills and brings to life;
        he brings down to Shē′ōl and raises up.
7 The LORD makes poor and makes rich;
        he brings low, he also exalts.
8 He raises up the poor from the dust;

[d]That is one separated or one consecrated   [e]Cn Compare Gk Q Ms 1.22: MT then I will give him to the LORD all the days of his life   [f]Gk: Heb went her way   [g]Gk: Heb lacks and drank with her husband   [h]Gk: Meaning of Heb uncertain   [i]Cn Compare Q Ms: MT lacks I will offer him as a nazirite for all time   [j]MT: Q Ms Gk Compare Syr that which goes out of your mouth   [k]Q Ms Gk Syr: MT three bulls   [l]Gk (Compare Q Ms) and Gk at 2.11: MT And he (that is, Elkanah) worshiped there before   [m]Gk: Heb the LORD   [n]Q Ms: MT your

he lifts the needy from the ash
    heap,
to make them sit with princes
    and inherit a seat of honor.[o]
For the pillars of the earth are
    the LORD's,
    and on them he has set the
    world.

9 "He will guard the feet of his
    faithful ones,
but the wicked shall be cut off
    in darkness;
for not by might does one
    prevail.
10 The LORD! His adversaries shall
    be shattered;
the Most High[p] will thunder in
    heaven.
The LORD will judge the ends of
    the earth;
he will give strength to his
    king,
and exalt the power of his
    anointed."

Eli's Wicked Sons

11 Then El·ka'nah went home to
Ra'mah, while the boy remained to
minister to the LORD, in the presence of
the priest E'li.
12 Now the sons of E'li were scoundrels; they had no regard for the LORD
13 or for the duties of the priests to the
people. When anyone offered sacrifice, the priest's servant would come,
while the meat was boiling, with a
three-pronged fork in his hand, 14 and
he would thrust it into the pan, or kettle, or caldron, or pot; all that the fork
brought up the priest would take for
himself.[q] This is what they did at Shi'-
loh to all the Israelites who came there.
15 Moreover, before the fat was burned,
the priest's servant would come and
say to the one who was sacrificing,
"Give meat for the priest to roast; for
he will not accept boiled meat from
you, but only raw." 16 And if the man
said to him, "Let them burn the fat
first, and then take whatever you
wish," he would say, "No, you must
give it now; if not, I will take it by
force." 17 Thus the sin of the young men
was very great in the sight of the LORD;
for they treated the offerings of the
LORD with contempt.

The Child Samuel at Shiloh

18 Samuel was ministering before
the LORD, a boy wearing a linen ephod.
19 His mother used to make for him a

little robe and take it to him each year,
when she went up with her husband to
offer the yearly sacrifice. 20 Then E'li
would bless El·ka'nah and his wife,
and say, "May the LORD repay[r] you
with children by this woman for the
gift that she made to[s] the LORD"; and
then they would return to their home.
21 And[t] the LORD took note of Hannah; she conceived and bore three
sons and two daughters. And the boy
Samuel grew up in the presence of the
LORD.

Prophecy against Eli's Household

22 Now E'li was very old. He heard
all that his sons were doing to all Israel, and how they lay with the women
who served at the entrance to the tent
of meeting. 23 He said to them, "Why do
you do such things? For I hear of your
evil dealings from all these people.
24 No, my sons; it is not a good report
that I hear the people of the LORD
spreading abroad. 25 If one person sins
against another, someone can intercede for the sinner with the LORD;[u] but
if someone sins against the LORD, who
can make intercession?" But they
would not listen to the voice of their
father; for it was the will of the LORD to
kill them.
26 Now the boy Samuel continued
to grow both in stature and in favor
with the LORD and with the people.
27 A man of God came to E'li and
said to him, "Thus the LORD has said,
'I revealed[v] myself to the family of
your ancestor in Egypt when they
were slaves[w] to the house of Pharaoh.
28 I chose him out of all the tribes of
Israel to be my priest, to go up to my
altar, to offer incense, to wear an
ephod before me; and I gave to the
family of your ancestor all my offerings by fire from the people of Israel.
29 Why then look with greedy eye[x] at
my sacrifices and my offerings that I
commanded, and honor your sons
more than me by fattening yourselves

[o] Gk (Compare Q Ms) adds *He grants the
vow of the one who vows, and blesses
the years of the just*   [p] Cn Heb *against
him he*   [q] Gk Syr Vg: Heb *with it*
[r] Q Ms Gk: MT *give*   [s] Q Ms Gk: MT *for
the petition that she asked of*   [t] Q Ms
Gk: MT *When*   [u] Gk Compare Q Ms:
MT *another, God will mediate for him*
[v] Gk Tg Syr: Heb *Did I reveal*   [w] Q Ms
Gk: MT lacks *slaves*   [x] Q Ms Gk: MT
then kick

on the choicest parts of every offering of my people Israel?' [30]Therefore the LORD the God of Israel declares: 'I promised that your family and the family of your ancestor should go in and out before me forever'; but now the LORD declares: 'Far be it from me; for those who honor me I will honor, and those who despise me shall be treated with contempt. [31]See, a time is coming when I will cut off your strength and the strength of your ancestor's family, so that no one in your family will live to old age. [32]Then in distress you will look with greedy eye[y] on all the prosperity that shall be bestowed upon Israel; and no one in your family shall ever live to old age. [33]The only one of you whom I shall not cut off from my altar shall be spared to weep out his[z] eyes and grieve his[a] heart; all the members of your household shall die by the sword.[b] [34]The fate of your two sons, Hoph'nī and Phin'e·has, shall be the sign to you—both of them shall die on the same day. [35]I will raise up for myself a faithful priest, who shall do according to what is in my heart and in my mind. I will build him a sure house, and he shall go in and out before my anointed one forever. [36]Everyone who is left in your family shall come to implore him for a piece of silver or a loaf of bread, and shall say, Please put me in one of the priest's places, that I may eat a morsel of bread.' "

Samuel's Calling and Prophetic Activity

3 Now the boy Samuel was ministering to the LORD under E'lī. The word of the LORD was rare in those days; visions were not widespread. [2]At that time E'lī, whose eyesight had begun to grow dim so that he could not see, was lying down in his room; [3]the lamp of God had not yet gone out, and Samuel was lying down in the temple of the LORD, where the ark of God was. [4]Then the LORD called, "Samuel! Samuel!"[c] and he said, "Here I am!"[5]and ran to E'lī, and said, "Here I am, for you called me." But he said, "I did not call; lie down again." So he went and lay down. [6]The LORD called again, "Samuel!" Samuel got up and went to E'lī, and said, "Here I am, for you called me." But he said, "I did not call, my son; lie down again." [7]Now Samuel did not yet know the LORD, and the word of the LORD had

not yet been revealed to him. [8]The LORD called Samuel again, a third time. And he got up and went to E'lī, and said, "Here I am, for you called me." Then E'lī perceived that the LORD was calling the boy. [9]Therefore E'lī said to Samuel, "Go, lie down; and if he calls you, you shall say, 'Speak, LORD, for your servant is listening.' " So Samuel went and lay down in his place.

[10] Now the LORD came and stood there, calling as before, "Samuel! Samuel!" And Samuel said, "Speak, for your servant is listening." [11]Then the LORD said to Samuel, "See, I am about to do something in Israel that will make both ears of anyone who hears of it tingle. [12]On that day I will fulfill against E'lī all that I have spoken concerning his house, from beginning to end. [13]For I have told him that I am about to punish his house forever, for the iniquity that he knew, because his sons were blaspheming God,[d] and he did not restrain them. [14]Therefore I swear to the house of E'lī that the iniquity of Eli's house shall not be expiated by sacrifice or offering forever."

[15] Samuel lay there until morning; then he opened the doors of the house of the LORD. Samuel was afraid to tell the vision to E'lī. [16]But E'lī called Samuel and said, "Samuel, my son." He said, "Here I am." [17]E'lī said, "What was it that he told you? Do not hide it from me. May God do so to you and more also, if you hide anything from me of all that he told you." [18]So Samuel told him everything and hid nothing from him. Then he said, "It is the LORD; let him do what seems good to him."

[19] As Samuel grew up, the LORD was with him and let none of his words fall to the ground. [20]And all Israel from Dan to Be'er-she'ba knew that Samuel was a trustworthy prophet of the LORD. [21]The LORD continued to appear at Shī'lōh, for the LORD revealed himself to Samuel at Shī'lōh by the word

4 of the LORD. [1]And the word of Samuel came to all Israel.

The Ark of God Captured

In those days the Phi·lis'tines mus-

---

y Q Ms Gk: MT *will kick*   z Q Ms Gk:
MT *your*   a Q Ms Gk: Heb *your*
b Q Ms See Gk: MT *die like mortals*
c Q Ms Gk See 3.10: MT *the LORD called
Samuel*   d Another reading is *for
themselves*

tered for war against Israel,*e* and Israel went out to battle against them;*f* they encamped at Eb·e·ne'zer, and the Phi·lis'tines encamped at A'phek. ²The Phi·lis'tines drew up in line against Israel, and when the battle was joined,*g* Israel was defeated by the Phi·lis'tines, who killed about four thousand men on the field of battle. ³When the troops came to the camp, the elders of Israel said, "Why has the LORD put us to rout today before the Phi·lis'tines? Let us bring the ark of the covenant of the LORD here from Shi'loh, so that he may come among us and save us from the power of our enemies." ⁴So the people sent to Shi'loh, and brought from there the ark of the covenant of the LORD of hosts, who is enthroned on the cherubim. The two sons of E'li, Hoph'ni and Phin'e·has, were there with the ark of the covenant of God.

5 When the ark of the covenant of the LORD came into the camp, all Israel gave a mighty shout, so that the earth resounded. ⁶When the Phi·lis'tines heard the noise of the shouting, they said, "What does this great shouting in the camp of the Hebrews mean?" When they learned that the ark of the LORD had come to the camp, ⁷the Phi·lis'tines were afraid; for they said, "Gods have*h* come into the camp." They also said, "Woe to us! For nothing like this has happened before. ⁸Woe to us! Who can deliver us from the power of these mighty gods? These are the gods who struck the Egyptians with every sort of plague in the wilderness. ⁹Take courage, and be men, O Phi·lis'tines, in order not to become slaves to the Hebrews as they have been to you; be men and fight."

10 So the Phi·lis'tines fought; Israel was defeated, and they fled, everyone to his home. There was a very great slaughter, for there fell of Israel thirty thousand foot soldiers. ¹¹The ark of God was captured; and the two sons of E'li, Hoph'ni and Phin'e·has, died.

Death of Eli

12 A man of Benjamin ran from the battle line, and came to Shi'loh the same day, with his clothes torn and with earth upon his head. ¹³When he arrived, E'li was sitting upon his seat by the road watching, for his heart trembled for the ark of God. When the man came into the city and told the news, all the city cried out. ¹⁴When E'li

heard the sound of the outcry, he said, "What is this uproar?" Then the man came quickly and told E'li. ¹⁵Now E'li was ninety-eight years old and his eyes were set, so that he could not see. ¹⁶The man said to E'li, "I have just come from the battle; I fled from the battle today." He said, "How did it go, my son?" ¹⁷The messenger replied, "Israel has fled before the Phi·lis'tines, and there has also been a great slaughter among the troops; your two sons also, Hoph'ni and Phin'e·has, are dead, and the ark of God has been captured." ¹⁸When he mentioned the ark of God, E'li*i* fell over backward from his seat by the side of the gate; and his neck was broken and he died, for he was an old man, and heavy. He had judged Israel forty years.

19 Now his daughter-in-law, the wife of Phin'e·has, was pregnant, about to give birth. When she heard the news that the ark of God was captured, and that her father-in-law and her husband were dead, she bowed and gave birth; for her labor pains overwhelmed her. ²⁰As she was about to die, the women attending her said to her, "Do not be afraid, for you have borne a son." But she did not answer or give heed. ²¹She named the child Ich'-a·bod, meaning, "The glory has departed from Israel," because the ark of God had been captured and because of her father-in-law and her husband. ²²She said, "The glory has departed from Israel, for the ark of God has been captured."

The Philistines and the Ark

5 When the Phi·lis'tines captured the ark of God, they brought it from Eb·e·ne'zer to Ash'dod; ²then the Phi·lis'tines took the ark of God and brought it into the house of Da'gon and placed it beside Da'gon. ³When the people of Ash'dod rose early the next day, there was Da'gon, fallen on his face to the ground before the ark of the LORD. So they took Da'gon and put him back in his place. ⁴But when they rose early on the next morning, Da'-gon had fallen on his face to the ground before the ark of the LORD, and the head of Da'gon and both his hands

*e*Gk: Heb lacks *In those days the Philistines mustered for war against Israel*   *f*Gk: Heb *against the Philistines*   *g*Meaning of Heb uncertain   *h*Or *A god has*   *i*Heb *he* were lying cut off upon the threshold; only the trunk of[j] Dā'gon was left to him. [5]This is why the priests of Dā'gon and all who enter the house of Dā'-gon do not step on the threshold of Dā'gon in Ash'dod to this day.

6 The hand of the LORD was heavy upon the people of Ash'dod, and he terrified and struck them with tumors, both in Ash'dod and in its territory. [7]And when the inhabitants of Ash'dod saw how things were, they said, "The ark of the God of Israel must not remain with us; for his hand is heavy on us and on our god Dā'gon." [8]So they sent and gathered together all the lords of the Phi·lis'tines, and said, "What shall we do with the ark of the God of Israel?" The inhabitants of Gath replied, "Let the ark of God be moved on to us."[k] So they moved the ark of the God of Israel to Gath.[l] [9]But after they had brought it to Gath,[m] the hand of the LORD was against the city, causing a very great panic; he struck the inhabitants of the city, both young and old, so that tumors broke out on them. [10]So they sent the ark of the God of Israel[n] to Ek'ron. But when the ark of God came to Ek'ron, the people of Ek'ron cried out, "Why[o] have they brought around to us[p] the ark of the God of Israel to kill us[p] and our[q] people?" [11]They sent therefore and gathered together all the lords of the Phi·lis'tines, and said, "Send away the ark of the God of Israel, and let it return to its own place, that it may not kill us and our people." For there was a deathly panic[r] throughout the whole city. The hand of God was very heavy there; [12]those who did not die were stricken with tumors, and the cry of the city went up to heaven.

The Ark Returned to Israel

6 The ark of the LORD was in the country of the Phi·lis'tines seven months. [2]Then the Phi·lis'tines called for the priests and the diviners and said, "What shall we do with the ark of the LORD? Tell us what we should send with it to its place." [3]They said, "If you send away the ark of the God of Israel, do not send it empty, but by all means return him a guilt offering. Then you will be healed and will be ransomed;[s] will not his hand then turn from you?" [4]And they said, "What is the guilt offering that we shall return to him?" They answered, "Five gold tumors and five gold mice, according to the num-

ber of the lords of the Phi·lis'tines; for the same plague was upon all of you and upon your lords. [5]So you must make images of your tumors and images of your mice that ravage the land, and give glory to the God of Israel; perhaps he will lighten his hand on you and your gods and your land. [6]Why should you harden your hearts as the Egyptians and Pharaoh hardened their hearts? After he had made fools of them, did they not let the people go, and they departed? [7]Now then, get ready a new cart and two milch cows that have never borne a yoke, and yoke the cows to the cart, but take their calves home, away from them. [8]Take the ark of the LORD and place it on the cart, and put in a box at its side the figures of gold, which you are returning to him as a guilt offering. Then send it off, and let it go its way. [9]And watch; if it goes up on the way to its own land, to Beth-she'mesh, then it is he who has done us this great harm; but if not, then we shall know that it is not his hand that struck us; it happened to us by chance."

10 The men did so; they took two milch cows and yoked them to the cart, and shut up their calves at home. [11]They put the ark of the LORD on the cart, and the box with the gold mice and the images of their tumors. [12]The cows went straight in the direction of Beth-she'mesh along one highway, lowing as they went; they turned neither to the right nor to the left, and the lords of the Phi·lis'tines went after them as far as the border of Beth-she'-mesh.

13 Now the people of Beth-she'-mesh were reaping their wheat harvest in the valley. When they looked up and saw the ark, they went with rejoicing to meet it.[t] [14]The cart came into the field of Joshua of Beth-she'-mesh, and stopped there. A large stone was there; so they split up the wood of the cart and offered the cows as a burnt offering to the LORD. [15]The Le'-

1 S A M U E L

---

[j]Heb lacks *the trunk of*   [k]Gk Compare Q Ms: MT *They answered, "Let the ark of the God of Israel be brought around to Gath."*   [l]Gk: Heb lacks *to Gath*   [m]Q Ms: MT lacks *to Gath*   [n]Q Ms Gk: MT lacks *of Israel*   [o]Q Ms Gk: MT lacks *Why*   [p]Heb *me*   [q]Heb *my*   [r]Q Ms reads *a panic from the LORD*   [s]Q Ms Gk: MT *and it will be known to you*   [t]Gk: Heb *rejoiced to see it*

vītes took down the ark of the LORD and the box that was beside it, in which were the gold objects, and set them upon the large stone. Then the people of Beth-shē'mesh offered burnt offerings and presented sacrifices on that day to the LORD. ¹⁶When the five lords of the Phi·lis'tines saw it, they returned that day to Ek'ron.

17 These are the gold tumors, which the Phi·lis'tines returned as a guilt offering to the LORD: one for Ash'dod, one for Gä'za, one for Ash'-ke·lon, one for Gath, one for Ek'ron; ¹⁸also the gold mice, according to the number of all the cities of the Phi·lis'-tines belonging to the five lords, both fortified cities and unwalled villages. The great stone, beside which they set down the ark of the LORD, is a witness to this day in the field of Joshua of Beth-shē'mesh.

The Ark at Kiriath-jearim

19 The descendants of Jec·o·nī'ah did not rejoice with the people of Beth-shē'mesh when they greeted ᵘ the ark of the LORD; and he killed seventy men of them. ᵛ The people mourned because the LORD had made a great slaughter among the people. ²⁰Then the people of Beth-shē'mesh said, "Who is able to stand before the LORD, this holy God? To whom shall he go so that we may be rid of him?" ²¹So they sent messengers to the inhabitants of Kir'i·ath-jē'a·rim, saying, "The Phi-lis'tines have returned the ark of the LORD. Come down and take it up to you." ¹And the people of Kir'i·ath-jē'a·rim came and took up the ark of the LORD, and brought it to the house of A·bin'a·dab on the hill. They consecrated his son, El·e·ā'zar, to have charge of the ark of the LORD.

2 From the day that the ark was lodged at Kir'i·ath-jē'a·rim, a long time passed, some twenty years, and all the house of Israel lamented ʷ after the LORD.

Samuel as Judge

3 Then Samuel said to all the house of Israel, "If you are returning to the LORD with all your heart, then put away the foreign gods and the As·tar'-tēs from among you. Direct your heart to the LORD, and serve him only, and he will deliver you out of the hand of the Phi·lis'tines." ⁴So Israel put away the Bā'als and the As·tar'tēs, and they served the LORD only.

5 Then Samuel said, "Gather all Israel at Miz'pah, and I will pray to the LORD for you." ⁶So they gathered at Miz'pah, and drew water and poured it out before the LORD. They fasted that day, and said, "We have sinned against the LORD." And Samuel judged the people of Israel at Miz'pah.

7 When the Phi·lis'tines heard that the people of Israel had gathered at Miz'pah, the lords of the Phi·lis'tines went up against Israel. And when the people of Israel heard of it they were afraid of the Phi·lis'tines. ⁸The people of Israel said to Samuel, "Do not cease to cry out to the LORD our God for us, and pray that he may save us from the hand of the Phi·lis'tines." ⁹So Samuel took a sucking lamb and offered it as a whole burnt offering to the LORD; Samuel cried out to the LORD for Israel, and the LORD answered him. ¹⁰As Samuel was offering up the burnt offering, the Phi·lis'tines drew near to attack Israel; but the LORD thundered with a mighty voice that day against the Phi·lis'tines and threw them into confusion; and they were routed before Israel. ¹¹And the men of Israel went out of Miz'pah and pursued the Phi·lis'tines, and struck them down as far as beyond Beth-car.

12 Then Samuel took a stone and set it up between Miz'pah and Je·shā'-nah, ˣ and named it Eb·e·nē'zer; ʸ for he said, "Thus far the LORD has helped us." ¹³So the Phi·lis'tines were subdued and did not again enter the territory of Israel; the hand of the LORD was against the Phi·lis'tines all the days of Samuel. ¹⁴The towns that the Phi·lis'-tines had taken from Israel were restored to Israel, from Ek'ron to Gath; and Israel recovered their territory from the hand of the Phi·lis'tines. There was peace also between Israel and the Am'o·rites.

15 Samuel judged Israel all the days of his life. ¹⁶He went on a circuit year by year to Beth'el, Gil'gal, and Miz'-pah; and he judged Israel in all these places. ¹⁷Then he would come back to Rā'mah, for his home was there; he administered justice there to Israel, and built there an altar to the LORD.

ᵘGk: Heb And he killed some of the people of Beth-shemesh, because they looked into   ᵛHeb killed seventy men, fifty thousand men   ʷMeaning of Heb uncertain   ˣGk Syr: Heb Shen   ʸThat is Stone of Help

Israel Demands a King

8 When Samuel became old, he made his sons judges over Israel. ²The name of his firstborn son was Jo'el, and the name of his second, A·bi'jah; they were judges in Be'er-she'ba. ³Yet his sons did not follow in his ways, but turned aside after gain; they took bribes and perverted justice.

4 Then all the elders of Israel gathered together and came to Samuel at Ra'mah, ⁵and said to him, "You are old and your sons do not follow in your ways; appoint for us, then, a king to govern us, like other nations." ⁶But the thing displeased Samuel when they said, "Give us a king to govern us." Samuel prayed to the LORD, ⁷and the LORD said to Samuel, "Listen to the voice of the people in all that they say to you; for they have not rejected you, but they have rejected me from being king over them. ⁸Just as they have done to me,ᶻ from the day I brought them up out of Egypt to this day, forsaking me and serving other gods, so also they are doing to you. ⁹Now then, listen to their voice; only—you shall solemnly warn them, and show them the ways of the king who shall reign over them."

10 So Samuel reported all the words of the LORD to the people who were asking him for a king. ¹¹He said, "These will be the ways of the king who will reign over you: he will take your sons and appoint them to his chariots and to be his horsemen, and to run before his chariots; ¹²and he will appoint for himself commanders of thousands and commanders of fifties, and some to plow his ground and to reap his harvest, and to make his implements of war and the equipment of his chariots. ¹³He will take your daughters to be perfumers and cooks and bakers. ¹⁴He will take the best of your fields and vineyards and olive orchards and give them to his courtiers. ¹⁵He will take one-tenth of your grain and of your vineyards and give it to his officers and his courtiers. ¹⁶He will take your male and female slaves, and the best of your cattleᵃ and donkeys, and put them to his work. ¹⁷He will take one-tenth of your flocks, and you shall be his slaves. ¹⁸And in that day you will cry out because of your king, whom you have chosen for yourselves; but the LORD will not answer you in that day."

Israel's Request for a King Granted

19 But the people refused to listen to the voice of Samuel; they said, "No! but we are determined to have a king over us, ²⁰so that we also may be like other nations, and that our king may govern us and go out before us and fight our battles." ²¹When Samuel had heard all the words of the people, he repeated them in the ears of the LORD. ²²The LORD said to Samuel, "Listen to their voice and set a king over them." Samuel then said to the people of Israel, "Each of you return home."

Saul Chosen to Be King

9 There was a man of Benjamin whose name was Kish son of A·bi'el son of Ze'ror son of Be·co'rath son of A·phi'ah, a Ben'ja·min·ite, a man of wealth. ²He had a son whose name was Saul, a handsome young man. There was not a man among the people of Israel more handsome than he; he stood head and shoulders above everyone else.

3 Now the donkeys of Kish, Saul's father, had strayed. So Kish said to his son Saul, "Take one of the boys with you; go and look for the donkeys." ⁴He passed through the hill country of E'phra·im and passed through the land of Shal'i·shah, but they did not find them. And they passed through the land of Sha'a·lim, but they were not there. Then he passed through the land of Benjamin, but they did not find them.

5 When they came to the land of Zuph, Saul said to the boy who was with him, "Let us turn back, or my father will stop worrying about the donkeys and worry about us." ⁶But he said to him, "There is a man of God in this town; he is a man held in honor. Whatever he says always comes true. Let us go there now; perhaps he will tell us about the journey on which we have set out." ⁷Then Saul replied to the boy, "But if we go, what can we bring the man? For the bread in our sacks is gone, and there is no present to bring to the man of God. What have we?" ⁸The boy answered Saul again, "Here, I have with me a quarter shekel of silver; I will give it to the man of God, to tell us our way." ⁹(Formerly in Israel, anyone who went to inquire of God

ᶻGk: Heb lacks *to me*   ᵃGk: Heb *young men*

would say, "Come, let us go to the seer"; for the one who is now called a prophet was formerly called a seer.) [10] Saul said to the boy, "Good; come, let us go." So they went to the town where the man of God was.

11 As they went up the hill to the town, they met some girls coming out to draw water, and said to them, "Is the seer here?" [12] They answered, "Yes, there he is just ahead of you. Hurry; he has come just now to the town, because the people have a sacrifice today at the shrine. [13] As soon as you enter the town, you will find him, before he goes up to the shrine to eat. For the people will not eat until he comes, since he must bless the sacrifice; afterward those eat who are invited. Now go up, for you will meet him immediately." [14] So they went up to the town. As they were entering the town, they saw Samuel coming out toward them on his way up to the shrine.

15 Now the day before Saul came, the Lord had revealed to Samuel: [16] "Tomorrow about this time I will send to you a man from the land of Benjamin, and you shall anoint him to be ruler over my people Israel. He shall save my people from the hand of the Phi·lis′tines; for I have seen the suffering of[b] my people, because their outcry has come to me." [17] When Samuel saw Saul, the Lord told him, "Here is the man of whom I spoke to you. He it is who shall rule over my people." [18] Then Saul approached Samuel inside the gate, and said, "Tell me, please, where is the house of the seer?" [19] Samuel answered Saul, "I am the seer; go up before me to the shrine, for today you shall eat with me, and in the morning I will let you go and will tell you all that is on your mind. [20] As for your donkeys that were lost three days ago, give no further thought to them, for they have been found. And on whom is all Israel's desire fixed, if not on you and on all your ancestral house?" [21] Saul answered, "I am only a Ben·ja·min·ite, from the least of the tribes of Israel, and my family is the humblest of all the families of the tribe of Benjamin. Why then have you spoken to me in this way?"

22 Then Samuel took Saul and his servant-boy and brought them into the hall, and gave them a place at the head of those who had been invited, of whom there were about thirty. [23] And Samuel said to the cook, "Bring the portion I gave you, the one I asked you to put aside." [24] The cook took up the thigh and what went with it[c] and set them before Saul. Samuel said, "See, what was kept is set before you. Eat; for it is set[d] before you at the appointed time, so that you might eat with the guests."[e]

So Saul ate with Samuel that day. [25] When they came down from the shrine into the town, a bed was spread for Saul[f] on the roof, and he lay down to sleep.[g] [26] Then at the break of dawn[h] Samuel called to Saul upon the roof, "Get up, so that I may send you on your way." Saul got up, and both he and Samuel went out into the street.

Samuel Anoints Saul

27 As they were going down to the outskirts of the town, Samuel said to Saul, "Tell the boy to go on before us, and when he has passed on, stop here yourself for a while, that I may make known to you the word of God."

10 [1] Samuel took a vial of oil and poured it on his head, and kissed him; he said, "The Lord has anointed you ruler over his people Israel. You shall reign over the people of the Lord and you will save them from the hand of their enemies all around. Now this shall be the sign to you that the Lord has anointed you ruler[i] over his heritage: [2] When you depart from me today you will meet two men by Rachel's tomb in the territory of Benjamin at Zel′zah; they will say to you, 'The donkeys that you went to seek are found, and now your father has stopped worrying about them and is worrying about you, saying: What shall I do about my son?' [3] Then you shall go on from there further and come to the oak of Ta′bor; three men going up to God at Beth′el will meet you there, one carrying three kids, another carrying three loaves of bread, and another carrying a skin of wine. [4] They will greet you and give you two loaves of bread, which you shall ac-

---

b Gk: Heb lacks *the suffering of*
c Meaning of Heb uncertain　　d Q Ms Gk: MT *it was kept*　　e Cn: Heb *it was kept for you, saying, I have invited the people*　　f Gk: Heb *and he spoke with Saul*　　g Gk: Heb lacks *and he lay down to sleep*　　h Gk: Heb *and they arose early and at break of dawn*　　i Gk: Heb lacks *over his people Israel. You shall ... anointed you ruler*

cept from them. [5] After that you shall come to Gib′e·ath-e·lo′him,[j] at the place where the Phi·lis′tine garrison is; there, as you come to the town, you will meet a band of prophets coming down from the shrine with harp, tambourine, flute, and lyre playing in front of them; they will be in a prophetic frenzy. [6] Then the spirit of the LORD will possess you, and you will be in a prophetic frenzy along with them and be turned into a different person. [7] Now when these signs meet you, do whatever you see fit to do, for God is with you. [8] And you shall go down to Gil′gal ahead of me; then I will come down to you to present burnt offerings and offer sacrifices of well-being. Seven days you shall wait, until I come to you and show you what you shall do."

Saul Prophesies

9 As he turned away to leave Samuel, God gave him another heart; and all these signs were fulfilled that day. [10] When they were going from there[k] to Gib′e·ah,[l] a band of prophets met him; and the spirit of God possessed him, and he fell into a prophetic frenzy along with them. [11] When all who knew him before saw how he prophesied with the prophets, the people said to one another, "What has come over the son of Kish? Is Saul also among the prophets?" [12] A man of the place answered, "And who is their father?" Therefore it became a proverb, "Is Saul also among the prophets?" [13] When his prophetic frenzy had ended, he went home.[m]

14 Saul's uncle said to him and to the boy, "Where did you go?" And he replied, "To seek the donkeys; and when we saw they were not to be found, we went to Samuel." [15] Saul's uncle said, "Tell me what Samuel said to you." [16] Saul said to his uncle, "He told us that the donkeys had been found." But about the matter of the kingship, of which Samuel had spoken, he did not tell him anything.

Saul Proclaimed King

17 Samuel summoned the people to the LORD at Miz′pah [18] and said to them,[n] "Thus says the LORD, the God of Israel, 'I brought up Israel out of Egypt, and I rescued you from the hand of the Egyptians and from the hand of all the kingdoms that were oppressing you.' [19] But today you have

rejected your God, who saves you from all your calamities and your distresses; and you have said, 'No! but set a king over us.' Now therefore present yourselves before the LORD by your tribes and by your clans."

20 Then Samuel brought all the tribes of Israel near, and the tribe of Benjamin was taken by lot. [21] He brought the tribe of Benjamin near by its families, and the family of the Ma′-trites was taken by lot. Finally he brought the family of the Ma′trites near man by man,[o] and Saul the son of Kish was taken by lot. But when they sought him, he could not be found. [22] So they inquired again of the LORD, "Did the man come here?"[p] and the LORD said, "See, he has hidden himself among the baggage." [23] Then they ran and brought him from there. When he took his stand among the people, he was head and shoulders taller than any of them. [24] Samuel said to all the people, "Do you see the one whom the LORD has chosen? There is no one like him among all the people." And all the people shouted, "Long live the king!"

25 Samuel told the people the rights and duties of the kingship; and he wrote them in a book and laid it up before the LORD. Then Samuel sent all the people back to their homes. [26] Saul also went to his home at Gib′e·ah, and with him went warriors whose hearts God had touched. [27] But some worthless fellows said, "How can this man save us?" They despised him and brought him no present. But he held his peace.

Now Na′hash, king of the Am′mon·ites, had been grievously oppressing the Gad′ites and the Reu′ben·ites. He would gouge out the right eye of each of them and would not grant Israel a deliverer. No one was left of the Israelites across the Jordan whose right eye Na′hash, king of the Am′mon·ites, had not gouged out. But there were seven thousand men who had escaped from the Am′mon·ites and had entered Ja′besh-gil′e·ad.[q]

1 SAMUEL

Saul Defeats the Ammonites

11 About a month later,[r] Na´hash the Am´mon·ite went up and besieged Ja´besh-gil´e·ad; and all the men of Ja´besh said to Na´hash, "Make a treaty with us, and we will serve you." [2] But Na´hash the Am´mon·ite said to them, "On this condition I will make a treaty with you, namely that I gouge out everyone's right eye, and thus put disgrace upon all Israel." [3] The elders of Ja´besh said to him, "Give us seven days' respite that we may send messengers through all the territory of Israel. Then, if there is no one to save us, we will give ourselves up to you." [4] When the messengers came to Gib´-e·ah of Saul, they reported the matter in the hearing of the people; and all the people wept aloud.

5 Now Saul was coming from the field behind the oxen; and Saul said, "What is the matter with the people, that they are weeping?" So they told him the message from the inhabitants of Ja´besh. [6] And the spirit of God came upon Saul in power when he heard these words, and his anger was greatly kindled. [7] He took a yoke of oxen, and cut them in pieces and sent them throughout all the territory of Israel by messengers, saying, "Whoever does not come out after Saul and Samuel, so shall it be done to his oxen!" Then the dread of the LORD fell upon the people, and they came out as one. [8] When he mustered them at Be´zek, those from Israel were three hundred thousand, and those from Judah seventy[s] thousand. [9] They said to the messengers who had come, "Thus shall you say to the inhabitants of Ja´-besh-gil´e·ad: 'Tomorrow, by the time the sun is hot, you shall have deliverance.'" When the messengers came and told the inhabitants of Ja´besh, they rejoiced. [10] So the inhabitants of Ja´besh said, "Tomorrow we will give ourselves up to you, and you may do to us whatever seems good to you." [11] The next day Saul put the people in three companies. At the morning watch they came into the camp and cut down the Am´mon·ites until the heat of the day; and those who survived were scattered, so that no two of them were left together.

12 The people said to Samuel, "Who is it that said, 'Shall Saul reign over us?' Give them to us so that we may put them to death." [13] But Saul said, "No one shall be put to death this day, for today the LORD has brought deliverance to Israel."

14 Samuel said to the people, "Come, let us go to Gil´gal and there renew the kingship." [15] So all the people went to Gil´gal, and there they made Saul king before the LORD in Gil´gal. There they sacrificed offerings of well-being before the LORD, and there Saul and all the Israelites rejoiced greatly.

Samuel's Farewell Address

12 Samuel said to all Israel, "I have listened to you in all that you have said to me, and have set a king over you. [2] See, it is the king who leads you now; I am old and gray, but my sons are with you. I have led you from my youth until this day. [3] Here I am; testify against me before the LORD and before his anointed. Whose ox have I taken? Or whose donkey have I taken? Or whom have I defrauded? Whom have I oppressed? Or from whose hand have I taken a bribe to blind my eyes with it? Testify against me[t] and I will restore it to you." [4] They said, "You have not defrauded us or oppressed us or taken anything from the hand of anyone." [5] He said to them, "The LORD is witness against you, and his anointed is witness this day, that you have not found anything in my hand." And they said, "He is witness."

6 Samuel said to the people, "The LORD is witness, who[u] appointed Moses and Aaron and brought your ancestors up out of the land of Egypt. [7] Now therefore take your stand, so that I may enter into judgment with you before the LORD, and I will declare to you[v] all the saving deeds of the LORD that he performed for you and for your ancestors. [8] When Jacob went into Egypt and the Egyptians oppressed them,[w] then your ancestors cried to the LORD and the LORD sent Moses and Aaron, who brought forth your ancestors out of Egypt, and settled them in this place. [9] But they forgot the LORD their God; and he sold them into the hand of Sis´e·ra, com-

---

r Q Ms Gk: MT lacks *About a month later*   s Q Ms Gk: MT *thirty*
t Gk: Heb lacks *Testify against me*
u Gk: Heb lacks *is witness, who*
v Gk: Heb lacks *and I will declare to you*
w Gk: Heb lacks *and the Egyptians oppressed them*

mander of the army of King Jā'bin of[x] Hā'zor, and into the hand of the Phi·lis'tines, and into the hand of the king of Mō'ab; and they fought against them. [10] Then they cried to the LORD, and said, 'We have sinned, because we have forsaken the LORD, and have served the Bā'als and the As·tar'tēs; but now rescue us out of the hand of our enemies, and we will serve you.' [11] And the LORD sent Jer·ub·bā'al and Bar'ak,[y] and Jeph'thah, and Samson,[z] and rescued you out of the hand of your enemies on every side; and you lived in safety. [12] But when you saw that King Nā'hash of the Am'mon·ites came against you, you said to me, 'No, but a king shall reign over us,' though the LORD your God was your king. [13] See, here is the king whom you have chosen, for whom you have asked; see, the LORD has set a king over you. [14] If you will fear the LORD and serve him and heed his voice and not rebel against the commandment of the LORD, and if both you and the king who reigns over you will follow the LORD your God, it will be well; [15] but if you will not heed the voice of the LORD, but rebel against the commandment of the LORD, then the hand of the LORD will be against you and your king.[a] [16] Now therefore take your stand and see this great thing that the LORD will do before your eyes. [17] Is it not the wheat harvest today? I will call upon the LORD, that he may send thunder and rai..; and you shall know and see that the wickedness that you have done in the sight of the LORD is great in demanding a king for yourselves." [18] So Samuel called upon the LORD, and the LORD sent thunder and rain that day; and all the people greatly feared the LORD and Samuel.

19 All the people said to Samuel, "Pray to the LORD your God for your servants, so that we may not die; for we have added to all our sins the evil of demanding a king for ourselves." [20] And Samuel said to the people, "Do not be afraid; you have done all this evil, yet do not turn aside from following the LORD, but serve the LORD with all your heart; [21] and do not turn aside after useless things that cannot profit or save, for they are useless. [22] For the LORD will not cast away his people, for his great name's sake, because it has pleased the LORD to make you a people for himself. [23] Moreover as for me, far be it from me that I should sin against

the LORD by ceasing to pray for you; and I will instruct you in the good and the right way. [24] Only fear the LORD, and serve him faithfully with all your heart; for consider what great things he has done for you. [25] But if you still do wickedly, you shall be swept away, both you and your king."

Saul's Unlawful Sacrifice

13 Saul was . . .[b] years old when he began to reign; and he reigned . . . and two[c] years over Israel.

2 Saul chose three thousand out of Israel; two thousand were with Saul in Mich'mash and the hill country of Beth'el, and a thousand were with Jonathan in Gib'ē·ah of Benjamin; the rest of the people he sent home to their tents. [3] Jonathan defeated the garrison of the Phi·lis'tines that was at Ge'ba; and the Phi·lis'tines heard of it. And Saul blew the trumpet throughout all the land, saying, "Let the Hebrews hear!" [4] When all Israel heard that Saul had defeated the garrison of the Phi·lis'tines, and also that Israel had become odious to the Phi·lis'tines, the people were called out to join Saul at Gil'gal.

5 The Phi·lis'tines mustered to fight with Israel, thirty thousand chariots, and six thousand horsemen, and troops like the sand on the seashore in multitude; they came up and encamped at Mich'mash, to the east of Beth-ā'ven. [6] When the Israelites saw that they were in distress (for the troops were hard pressed), the people hid themselves in caves and in holes and in rocks and in tombs and in cisterns. [7] Some Hebrews crossed the Jordan to the land of Gad and Gil'e·ad. Saul was still at Gil'gal, and all the people followed him trembling.

8 He waited seven days, the time appointed by Samuel; but Samuel did not come to Gil'gal, and the people began to slip away from Saul.[d] [9] So Saul said, "Bring the burnt offering here to me, and the offerings of well-being." And he offered the burnt offering. [10] As soon as he had finished offering the burnt offering, Samuel arrived; and

x Gk: Heb lacks *Jabin king of*   y Gk Syr: Heb *Bedan*   z Gk: Heb *Samuel*
a Gk: Heb *and your ancestors*
b The number is lacking in the Heb text (the verse is lacking in the Septuagint).
c *Two* is not the entire number; something has dropped out.   d Heb *him*

Saul went out to meet him and salute him. [11] Samuel said, "What have you done?" Saul replied, "When I saw that the people were slipping away from me, and that you did not come within the days appointed, and that the Phi·lis'tines were mustering at Mich'-mash, [12] I said, 'Now the Phi·lis'tines will come down upon me at Gil'gal, and I have not entreated the favor of the LORD'; so I forced myself, and offered the burnt offering." [13] Samuel said to Saul, "You have done foolishly; you have not kept the commandment of the LORD your God, which he commanded you. The LORD would have established your kingdom over Israel forever, [14] but now your kingdom will not continue; the LORD has sought out a man after his own heart; and the LORD has appointed him to be ruler over his people, because you have not kept what the LORD commanded you." [15] And Samuel left and went on his way from Gil'gal.[e] The rest of the people followed Saul to join the army; they went up from Gil'gal toward Gib'e·ah of Benjamin.[f]

Preparations for Battle

Saul counted the people who were present with him, about six hundred men. [16] Saul, his son Jonathan, and the people who were present with them stayed in Ge'ba of Benjamin; but the Phi·lis'tines encamped at Mich'mash. [17] And raiders came out of the camp of the Phi·lis'tines in three companies; one company turned toward Oph'rah, to the land of Shu'al, another company turned toward Beth-ho'ron, and another company turned toward the mountain[g] that looks down upon the valley of Ze·bo'im toward the wilderness.

19 Now there was no smith to be found throughout all the land of Israel; for the Phi·lis'tines said, "The Hebrews must not make swords or spears for themselves"; [20] so all the Israelites went down to the Phi·lis'tines to sharpen their plowshare, mattocks, axes, or sickles;[h] [21] The charge was two-thirds of a shekel[i] for the plowshares and for the mattocks, and one-third of a shekel for sharpening the axes and for setting the goads.[j] [22] So on the day of the battle neither sword nor spear was to be found in the possession of any of the people with Saul and Jonathan; but Saul and his son Jonathan had them.

Jonathan Surprises and Routs the Philistines

23 Now a garrison of the Phi·lis'-tines had gone out to the pass of Mich'-mash. **14** [1] One day Jonathan son of Saul said to the young man who carried his armor, "Come, let us go over to the Phi·lis'tine garrison on the other side." But he did not tell his father. [2] Saul was staying in the outskirts of Gib'e·ah under the pomegranate tree that is at Mig'ron; the troops that were with him were about six hundred men, [3] along with A·hi'jah son of A·hi'tub, Ich'a·bod's brother, son of Phin'e·has son of E'li, the priest of the LORD in Shi'loh, carrying an ephod. Now the people did not know that Jonathan had gone. [4] In the pass,[k] by which Jonathan tried to go over to the Phi·lis'tine garrison, there was a rocky crag on one side and a rocky crag on the other; the name of the one was Bo'-zez, and the name of the other Se'neh. [5] One crag rose on the north in front of Mich'mash, and the other on the south in front of Ge'ba.

6 Jonathan said to the young man who carried his armor, "Come, let us go over to the garrison of these uncircumcised; it may be that the LORD will act for us; for nothing can hinder the LORD from saving by many or by few." [7] His armor-bearer said to him, "Do all that your mind inclines to.[l] I am with you; as your mind is, so is mine."[m] [8] Then Jonathan said, "Now we will cross over to those men and will show ourselves to them. [9] If they say to us, 'Wait until we come to you,' then we will stand still in our place, and we will not go up to them. [10] But if they say, 'Come up to us,' then we will go up; for the LORD has given them into our hand. That will be the sign for us." [11] So both of them showed themselves to the garrison of the Phi·lis'tines; and the Phi·lis'tines said, "Look, Hebrews are coming out of the holes where they have hidden themselves." [12] The men of the garrison hailed Jonathan and his armor-bearer, saying, "Come up to

---

[e] Gk: Heb *went up from Gilgal to Gibeah of Benjamin*   [f] Gk: Heb lacks *The rest ... of Benjamin*   [g] Cn Compare Gk: Heb *toward the border*   [h] Gk: Heb *plowshare*   [i] Heb *was a pim*   [j] Cn: Meaning of Heb uncertain   [k] Heb *Between the passes*   [l] Gk: Heb *Do all that is in your mind. Turn*   [m] Gk: Heb lacks *so is mine*

us, and we will show you something."
Jonathan said to his armor-bearer,
"Come up after me; for the LORD has
given them into the hand of Israel."
[13] Then Jonathan climbed up on his
hands and feet, with his armor-bearer
following after him. The Phi·lis'tines[n]
fell before Jonathan, and his armor-
bearer, coming after him, killed them.
[14] In that first slaughter Jonathan and
his armor-bearer killed about twenty
men within an area about half a furrow
long in an acre[o] of land. [15] There was
a panic in the camp, in the field, and
among all the people; the garrison and
even the raiders trembled; the earth
quaked; and it became a very great
panic.

[16] Saul's lookouts in Gib'e·ah of
Benjamin were watching as the multitude was surging back and forth.[p]
[17] Then Saul said to the troops that
were with him, "Call the roll and see
who has gone from us." When they
had called the roll, Jonathan and his
armor-bearer were not there. [18] Saul
said to A·hi'jah, "Bring the ark[q] of
God here." For at that time the ark[q] of
God went with the Israelites. [19] While
Saul was talking to the priest, the tumult in the camp of the Phi·lis'tines
increased more and more; and Saul
said to the priest, "Withdraw your
hand." [20] Then Saul and all the people
who were with him rallied and went
into the battle; and every sword was
against the other, so that there was
very great confusion. [21] Now the Hebrews who previously had been with
the Phi·lis'tines and had gone up with
them into the camp turned and joined
the Israelites who were with Saul and
Jonathan. [22] Likewise, when all the Israelites who had gone into hiding in
the hill country of E'phra·im heard
that the Phi·lis'tines were fleeing, they
too followed closely after them in the
battle. [23] So the LORD gave Israel the
victory that day.

The battle passed beyond Beth-a'-
ven, and the troops with Saul numbered altogether about ten thousand
men. The battle spread out over the hill
country of E'phra·im.

Saul's Rash Oath

[24] Now Saul committed a very rash
act on that day.[r] He had laid an oath
on the troops, saying, "Cursed be anyone who eats food before it is evening
and I have been avenged on my enemies." So none of the troops tasted

food. [25] All the troops[s] came upon a
honeycomb; and there was honey on
the ground. [26] When the troops came
upon the honeycomb, the honey was
dripping out; but they did not put their
hands to their mouths, for they feared
the oath. [27] But Jonathan had not heard
his father charge the troops with the
oath; so he extended the staff that was
in his hand, and dipped the tip of it in
the honeycomb, and put his hand to his
mouth; and his eyes brightened.
[28] Then one of the soldiers said, "Your
father strictly charged the troops with
an oath, saying, 'Cursed be anyone
who eats food this day.' And so the
troops are faint." [29] Then Jonathan
said, "My father has troubled the land;
see how my eyes have brightened because I tasted a little of this honey.
[30] How much better if today the troops
had eaten freely of the spoil taken
from their enemies; for now the
slaughter among the Phi·lis'tines has
not been great."

[31] After they had struck down the
Phi·lis'tines that day from Mich'mash
to Ai'ja·lon, the troops were very faint;
[32] so the troops flew upon the spoil, and
took sheep and oxen and calves,
and slaughtered them on the ground;
and the troops ate them with the blood.
[33] Then it was reported to Saul, "Look,
the troops are sinning against the
LORD by eating with the blood." And he
said, "You have dealt treacherously;
roll a large stone before me here."[t]
[34] Saul said, "Disperse yourselves
among the troops, and say to them,
'Let all bring their oxen or their sheep,
and slaughter them here, and eat; and
do not sin against the LORD by eating
with the blood.' " So all of the troops
brought their oxen with them that
night, and slaughtered them there.
[35] And Saul built an altar to the LORD;
it was the first altar that he built to the
LORD.

Jonathan in Danger of Death

[36] Then Saul said, "Let us go down
after the Phi·lis'tines by night and despoil them until the morning light; let
us not leave one of them." They said,
"Do whatever seems good to you." But
the priest said, "Let us draw near to

n Heb *They*   o Heb *yoke*   p Gk: Heb
they went and there   q Gk *the ephod*
r Gk: Heb *The Israelites were distressed
that day*   s Heb *land*   t Gk: Heb *me
this day*

God here." 37 So Saul inquired of God, "Shall I go down after the Phi·lis'tines? Will you give them into the hand of Israel?" But he did not answer him that day. 38 Saul said, "Come here, all you leaders of the people; and let us find out how this sin has arisen today. 39 For as the LORD lives who saves Israel, even if it is in my son Jonathan, he shall surely die!" But there was no one among all the people who answered him. 40 He said to all Israel, "You shall be on one side, and I and my son Jonathan will be on the other side." The people said to Saul, "Do what seems good to you." 41 Then Saul said, "O LORD God of Israel, why have you not answered your servant today? If this guilt is in me or in my son Jonathan, O LORD God of Israel, give U'rim; but if this guilt is in your people Israel, u give Thum'mim." And Jonathan and Saul were indicated by the lot, but the people were cleared. 42 Then Saul said, "Cast the lot between me and my son Jonathan." And Jonathan was taken.

43 Then Saul said to Jonathan, "Tell me what you have done." Jonathan told him, "I tasted a little honey with the tip of the staff that was in my hand; here I am, I will die." 44 Saul said, "God do so to me and more also; you shall surely die, Jonathan!" 45 Then the people said to Saul, "Shall Jonathan die, who has accomplished this great victory in Israel? Far from it! As the LORD lives, not one hair of his head shall fall to the ground; for he has worked with God today." So the people ransomed Jonathan, and he did not die. 46 Then Saul withdrew from pursuing the Phi·lis'tines; and the Phi·lis'tines went to their own place.

Saul's Continuing Wars

47 When Saul had taken the kingship over Israel, he fought against all his enemies on every side—against Mō'ab, against the Am'mon·ites, against E'dom, against the kings of Zō'bah, and against the Phi·lis'tines; wherever he turned he routed them. 48 He did valiantly, and struck down the A·mal'e·kītes, and rescued Israel out of the hands of those who plundered them.

49 Now the sons of Saul were Jonathan, Ish'vī, and Mal·chī·shū'a; and the names of his two daughters were these: the name of the firstborn was Mē'rab, and the name of the younger, Mī'chal. 50 The name of Saul's wife was A·hin'ō·am daughter of A·him'a·az. And the name of the commander of his army was Abner son of Ner, Saul's uncle; 51 Kish was the father of Saul, and Ner the father of Abner was the son of A·bī'el.

52 There was hard fighting against the Phi·lis'tines all the days of Saul; and when Saul saw any strong or valiant warrior, he took him into his service.

Saul Defeats the Amalekites but Spares Their King

15 Samuel said to Saul, "The LORD sent me to anoint you king over his people Israel; now therefore listen to the words of the LORD. 2 Thus says the LORD of hosts, 'I will punish the A·mal'e·kītes for what they did in opposing the Israelites when they came up out of Egypt. 3 Now go and attack Am'a·lek, and utterly destroy all that they have; do not spare them, but kill both man and woman, child and infant, ox and sheep, camel and donkey.' "

4 So Saul summoned the people, and numbered them in Te·lā'im, two hundred thousand foot soldiers, and ten thousand soldiers of Judah. 5 Saul came to the city of the A·mal'e·kītes and lay in wait in the valley. 6 Saul said to the Ken'ites, "Go! Leave! Withdraw from among the A·mal'e·kītes, or I will destroy you with them; for you showed kindness to all the people of Israel when they came up out of Egypt." So the Ken'ites withdrew from the A·mal'e·kītes. 7 Saul defeated the A·mal'e·kītes, from Hav'i·lah as far as Shur, which is east of Egypt. 8 He took King A'gag of the A·mal'e·kītes alive, but utterly destroyed all the people with the edge of the sword. 9 Saul and the people spared A'gag, and the best of the sheep and of the cattle and of the fatlings, and the lambs, and all that was valuable, and would not utterly destroy them; all that was despised and worthless they utterly destroyed.

Saul Rejected as King

10 The word of the LORD came to Samuel: 11 "I regret that I made Saul king, for he has turned back from following me, and has not carried out my commands." Samuel was angry; and

---

u Vg Compare Gk: Heb 41 Saul said to the LORD, the God of Israel he cried out to the LORD all night. [12] Samuel rose early in the morning to meet Saul, and Samuel was told, "Saul went to Car'mel, where he set up a monument for himself, and on returning he passed on down to Gil'gal." [13] When Samuel came to Saul, Saul said to him, "May you be blessed by the LORD; I have carried out the command of the LORD." [14] But Samuel said, "What then is this bleating of sheep in my ears, and the lowing of cattle that I hear?" [15] Saul said, "They have brought them from the A·mal'e·kītes; for the people spared the best of the sheep and the cattle, to sacrifice to the LORD your God; but the rest we have utterly destroyed." [16] Then Samuel said to Saul, "Stop! I will tell you what the LORD said to me last night." He replied, "Speak."

17 Samuel said, "Though you are little in your own eyes, are you not the head of the tribes of Israel? The LORD anointed you king over Israel. [18] And the LORD sent you on a mission, and said, 'Go, utterly destroy the sinners, the A·mal'e·kītes, and fight against them until they are consumed.' [19] Why then did you not obey the voice of the LORD? Why did you swoop down on the spoil, and do what was evil in the sight of the LORD?" [20] Saul said to Samuel, "I have obeyed the voice of the LORD, I have gone on the mission on which the LORD sent me, I have brought A'gag the king of Am'a·lek, and I have utterly destroyed the A·mal'e·kītes. [21] But from the spoil the people took sheep and cattle, the best of the things devoted to destruction, to sacrifice to the LORD your God in Gil'gal." [22] And Samuel said,

"Has the LORD as great delight in
     burnt offerings and
     sacrifices,
as in obeying the voice of the
     LORD?
Surely, to obey is better than
     sacrifice,
and to heed than the fat of
     rams.
[23] For rebellion is no less a sin
     than divination,
and stubbornness is like
     iniquity and idolatry.
Because you have rejected the
     word of the LORD,
he has also rejected you from
     being king."

24 Saul said to Samuel, "I have sinned; for I have transgressed the commandment of the LORD and your words, because I feared the people and obeyed their voice. [25] Now therefore, I pray, pardon my sin, and return with me, so that I may worship the LORD." [26] Samuel said to Saul, "I will not return with you; for you have rejected the word of the LORD, and the LORD has rejected you from being king over Israel." [27] As Samuel turned to go away, Saul caught hold of the hem of his robe, and it tore. [28] And Samuel said to him, "The LORD has torn the kingdom of Israel from you this very day, and has given it to a neighbor of yours, who is better than you. [29] Moreover the Glory of Israel will not recant[v] or change his mind; for he is not a mortal, that he should change his mind." [30] Then Saul[w] said, "I have sinned; yet honor me now before the elders of my people and before Israel, and return with me, so that I may worship the LORD your God." [31] So Samuel turned back after Saul; and Saul worshiped the LORD.

32 Then Samuel said, "Bring A'gag king of the A·mal'e·kītes here to me." And A'gag came to him haltingly.[x] A'gag said, "Surely this is the bitterness of death."[y] [33] But Samuel said,

"As your sword has made
          women childless,
     so your mother shall be
          childless among women."

And Samuel hewed A'gag in pieces before the LORD in Gil'gal.

34 Then Samuel went to Ra'mah; and Saul went up to his house in Gib'-ē·ah of Saul. [35] Samuel did not see Saul again until the day of his death, but Samuel grieved over Saul. And the LORD was sorry that he had made Saul king over Israel.

David Anointed as King

16 The LORD said to Samuel, "How long will you grieve over Saul? I have rejected him from being king over Israel. Fill your horn with oil and set out; I will send you to Jesse the Beth'le·hem·ite, for I have provided for myself a king among his sons." [2] Samuel said, "How can I go? If Saul hears of it, he will kill me." And the LORD said, "Take a heifer with you, and say, 'I have come to sacrifice to the LORD.'

v Q Ms Gk: MT *deceive* w Heb *he*
x Cn Compare Gk: Meaning of Heb uncertain   y Q Ms Gk: MT *Surely the bitterness of death is past*

³ Invite Jesse to the sacrifice, and I will show you what you shall do; and you shall anoint for me the one whom I name to you." ⁴ Samuel did what the LORD commanded, and came to Bethlehem. The elders of the city came to meet him trembling, and said, "Do you come peaceably?" ⁵ He said, "Peaceably; I have come to sacrifice to the LORD; sanctify yourselves and come with me to the sacrifice." And he sanctified Jesse and his sons and invited them to the sacrifice.

6 When they came, he looked on E·lī′ab and thought, "Surely the LORD's anointed is now before the LORD." ᶻ ⁷ But the LORD said to Samuel, "Do not look on his appearance or on the height of his stature, because I have rejected him; for the LORD does not see as mortals see; they look on the outward appearance, but the LORD looks on the heart." ⁸ Then Jesse called A·bin′a·dab, and made him pass before Samuel. He said, "Neither has the LORD chosen this one." ⁹ Then Jesse made Sham′mah pass by. And he said, "Neither has the LORD chosen this one." ¹⁰ Jesse made seven of his sons pass before Samuel, and Samuel said to Jesse, "The LORD has not chosen any of these." ¹¹ Samuel said to Jesse, "Are all your sons here?" And he said, "There remains yet the youngest, but he is keeping the sheep." And Samuel said to Jesse, "Send and bring him; for we will not sit down until he comes here." ¹² He sent and brought him in. Now he was ruddy, and had beautiful eyes, and was handsome. The LORD said, "Rise and anoint him; for this is the one." ¹³ Then Samuel took the horn of oil, and anointed him in the presence of his brothers; and the spirit of the LORD came mightily upon David from that day forward. Samuel then set out and went to Rā′mah.

David Plays the Lyre for Saul

14 Now the spirit of the LORD departed from Saul, and an evil spirit from the LORD tormented him. ¹⁵ And Saul's servants said to him, "See now, an evil spirit from God is tormenting you. ¹⁶ Let our lord now command the servants who attend you to look for someone who is skillful in playing the lyre; and when the evil spirit from God is upon you, he will play it, and you will feel better." ¹⁷ So Saul said to his servants, "Provide for me someone who can play well, and bring him to me." ¹⁸ One of the young men answered, "I have seen a son of Jesse the Beth′le·hem·ite who is skillful in playing, a man of valor, a warrior, prudent in speech, and a man of good presence; and the LORD is with him." ¹⁹ So Saul sent messengers to Jesse, and said, "Send me your son David who is with the sheep." ²⁰ Jesse took a donkey loaded with bread, a skin of wine, and a kid, and sent them by his son David to Saul. ²¹ And David came to Saul, and entered his service. Saul loved him greatly, and he became his armor-bearer. ²² Saul sent to Jesse, saying, "Let David remain in my service, for he has found favor in my sight." ²³ And whenever the evil spirit from God came upon Saul, David took the lyre and played it with his hand, and Saul would be relieved and feel better, and the evil spirit would depart from him.

David and Goliath

17 Now the Phi·lis′tines gathered their armies for battle; they were gathered at Sō′coh, which belongs to Judah, and encamped between Sō′coh and A·ze′kah, in E′phes-dam′mim. ² Saul and the Israelites gathered and encamped in the valley of E′lah, and formed ranks against the Phi·lis′tines. ³ The Phi·lis′tines stood on the mountain on the one side, and Israel stood on the mountain on the other side, with a valley between them. ⁴ And there came out from the camp of the Phi·lis′tines a champion named Goliath, of Gath, whose height was six ᵃ cubits and a span. ⁵ He had a helmet of bronze on his head, and he was armed with a coat of mail; the weight of the coat was five thousand shekels of bronze. ⁶ He had greaves of bronze on his legs and a javelin of bronze slung between his shoulders. ⁷ The shaft of his spear was like a weaver's beam, and his spear's head weighed six hundred shekels of iron; and his shield-bearer went before him. ⁸ He stood and shouted to the ranks of Israel, "Why have you come out to draw up for battle? Am I not a Phi·lis′tine, and are you not servants of Saul? Choose a man for yourselves, and let him come down to me. ⁹ If he is able to fight with me and kill me, then we will be your servants; but if I prevail against him and kill him, then you shall be our servants and serve us."

ᶻ Heb *him*   ᵃ MT: Q Ms Gk *four*

¹⁰And the Phi·lis′tine said, "Today I defy the ranks of Israel! Give me a man, that we may fight together." ¹¹When Saul and all Israel heard these words of the Phi·lis′tine, they were dismayed and greatly afraid.

12 Now David was the son of an Eph′ra·thite of Bethlehem in Judah, named Jesse, who had eight sons. In the days of Saul the man was already old and advanced in years.ᵇ ¹³The three eldest sons of Jesse had followed Saul to the battle; the names of his three sons who went to the battle were E·li′ab the firstborn, and next to him A·bin′a·dab, and the third Sham′mah. ¹⁴David was the youngest; the three eldest followed Saul, ¹⁵but David went back and forth from Saul to feed his father's sheep at Bethlehem. ¹⁶For forty days the Phi·lis′tine came forward and took his stand, morning and evening.

17 Jesse said to his son David, "Take for your brothers an ephah of this parched grain and these ten loaves, and carry them quickly to the camp to your brothers; ¹⁸also take these ten cheeses to the commander of their thousand. See how your brothers fare, and bring some token from them."

19 Now Saul, and they, and all the men of Israel, were in the valley of E′lah, fighting with the Phi·lis′tines. ²⁰David rose early in the morning, left the sheep with a keeper, took the provisions, and went as Jesse had commanded him. He came to the encampment as the army was going forth to the battle line, shouting the war cry. ²¹Israel and the Phi·lis′tines drew up for battle, army against army. ²²David left the things in charge of the keeper of the baggage, ran to the ranks, and went and greeted his brothers. ²³As he talked with them, the champion, the Phi·lis′tine of Gath, Goliath by name, came up out of the ranks of the Phi·lis′-tines, and spoke the same words as before. And David heard him.

24 All the Israelites, when they saw the man, fled from him and were very much afraid. ²⁵The Israelites said, "Have you seen this man who has come up? Surely he has come up to defy Israel. The king will greatly enrich the man who kills him, and will give him his daughter and make his family free in Israel." ²⁶David said to the men who stood by him, "What shall be done for the man who kills this

Phi·lis′tine, and takes away the reproach from Israel? For who is this uncircumcised Phi·lis′tine that he should defy the armies of the living God?" ²⁷The people answered him in the same way, "So shall it be done for the man who kills him."

28 His eldest brother E·li′ab heard him talking to the men; and Eliab's anger was kindled against David. He said, "Why have you come down? With whom have you left those few sheep in the wilderness? I know your presumption and the evil of your heart; for you have come down just to see the battle." ²⁹David said, "What have I done now? It was only a question." ³⁰He turned away from him toward another and spoke in the same way; and the people answered him again as before.

31 When the words that David spoke were heard, they repeated them before Saul; and he sent for him. ³²David said to Saul, "Let no one's heart fail because of him; your servant will go and fight with this Phi·lis′tine." ³³Saul said to David, "You are not able to go against this Phi·lis′tine to fight with him; for you are just a boy, and he has been a warrior from his youth." ³⁴But David said to Saul, "Your servant used to keep sheep for his father; and whenever a lion or a bear came, and took a lamb from the flock, ³⁵I went after it and struck it down, rescuing the lamb from its mouth; and if it turned against me, I would catch it by the jaw, strike it down, and kill it. ³⁶Your servant has killed both lions and bears; and this uncircumcised Phi·lis′tine shall be like one of them, since he has defied the armies of the living God." ³⁷David said, "The LORD, who saved me from the paw of the lion and from the paw of the bear, will save me from the hand of this Phi·lis′tine." So Saul said to David, "Go, and may the LORD be with you!"

38 Saul clothed David with his armor; he put a bronze helmet on his head and clothed him with a coat of mail. ³⁹David strapped Saul's sword over the armor, and he tried in vain to walk, for he was not used to them. Then David said to Saul, "I cannot walk with these; for I am not used to them." So David removed them. ⁴⁰Then he took his staff in his hand, and chose five smooth stones from the

ᵇ Gk Syr: Heb *among men*

wadi, and put them in his shepherd's bag, in the pouch; his sling was in his hand, and he drew near to the Phi·lis'-tine.

41 The Phi·lis'tine came on and drew near to David, with his shield-bearer in front of him. 42 When the Phi·lis'tine looked and saw David, he disdained him, for he was only a youth, ruddy and handsome in appearance. 43 The Phi·lis'tine said to David, "Am I a dog, that you come to me with sticks?" And the Phi·lis'tine cursed David by his gods. 44 The Phi·lis'tine said to David, "Come to me, and I will give your flesh to the birds of the air and to the wild animals of the field." 45 But David said to the Phi·lis'tine, "You come to me with sword and spear and javelin; but I come to you in the name of the LORD of hosts, the God of the armies of Israel, whom you have defied. 46 This very day the LORD will deliver you into my hand, and I will strike you down and cut off your head; and I will give the dead bodies of the Phi·lis'tine army this very day to the birds of the air and to the wild animals of the earth, so that all the earth may know that there is a God in Israel, 47 and that all this assembly may know that the LORD does not save by sword and spear; for the battle is the LORD's and he will give you into our hand."

48 When the Phi·lis'tine drew nearer to meet David, David ran quickly toward the battle line to meet the Phi·lis'tine. 49 David put his hand in his bag, took out a stone, slung it, and struck the Phi·lis'tine on his forehead; the stone sank into his forehead, and he fell face down on the ground.

50 So David prevailed over the Phi·lis'tine with a sling and a stone, striking down the Phi·lis'tine and killing him; there was no sword in David's hand. 51 Then David ran and stood over the Phi·lis'tine; he grasped his sword, drew it out of its sheath, and killed him; then he cut off his head with it.

When the Phi·lis'tines saw that their champion was dead, they fled. 52 The troops of Israel and Judah rose up with a shout and pursued the Phi·lis'tines as far as Gath c and the gates of Ek'ron, so that the wounded Phi·lis'tines fell on the way from Shā·a·rā'im as far as Gath and Ek'ron. 53 The Israelites came back from chasing the Phi·lis'-tines, and they plundered their camp. 54 David took the head of the Phi·lis'-tine and brought it to Jerusalem; but he put his armor in his tent.

55 When Saul saw David go out against the Phi·lis'tine, he said to Abner, the commander of the army, "Abner, whose son is this young man?" Abner said, "As your soul lives, O king, I do not know." 56 The king said, "Inquire whose son the stripling is." 57 On David's return from killing the Phi·lis'tine, Abner took him and brought him before Saul, with the head of the Phi·lis'tine in his hand. 58 Saul said to him, "Whose son are you, young man?" And David answered, "I am the son of your servant Jesse the Beth'le·hem·ite."

Jonathan's Covenant with David

18 When David d had finished speaking to Saul, the soul of Jonathan was bound to the soul of David, and Jonathan loved him as his own soul. 2 Saul took him that day and would not let him return to his father's house. 3 Then Jonathan made a covenant with David, because he loved him as his own soul. 4 Jonathan stripped himself of the robe that he was wearing, and gave it to David, and his armor, and even his sword and his bow and his belt. 5 David went out and was successful wherever Saul sent him; as a result, Saul set him over the army. And all the people, even the servants of Saul, approved.

6 As they were coming home, when David returned from killing the Phi·lis'tine, the women came out of all the towns of Israel, singing and dancing, to meet King Saul, with tambourines, with songs of joy, and with musical instruments. e 7 And the women sang to one another as they made merry,

"Saul has killed his thousands,
and David his ten thousands."

8 Saul was very angry, for this saying displeased him. He said, "They have ascribed to David ten thousands, and to me they have ascribed thousands; what more can he have but the kingdom?" 9 So Saul eyed David from that day on.

Saul Tries to Kill David

10 The next day an evil spirit from God rushed upon Saul, and he raved

c Gk Syr: Heb Gai   d Heb he
e Or triangles, or three-stringed instruments

within his house, while David was playing the lyre, as he did day by day. Saul had his spear in his hand; [11] and Saul threw the spear, for he thought, "I will pin David to the wall." But David eluded him twice.

12 Saul was afraid of David, because the LORD was with him but had departed from Saul. [13] So Saul removed him from his presence, and made him a commander of a thousand; and David marched out and came in, leading the army. [14] David had success in all his undertakings; for the LORD was with him. [15] When Saul saw that he had great success, he stood in awe of him. [16] But all Israel and Judah loved David; for it was he who marched out and came in leading them.

David Marries Michal

17 Then Saul said to David, "Here is my elder daughter Mĕ′rab; I will give her to you as a wife; only be valiant for me and fight the LORD's battles." For Saul thought, "I will not raise a hand against him; let the Phi·lis′tines deal with him." [18] David said to Saul, "Who am I and who are my kinsfolk, my father's family in Israel, that I should be son-in-law to the king?" [19] But at the time when Saul's daughter Mĕ′rab should have been given to David, she was given to A′dri·el the Me·hō′la·thīte as a wife.

20 Now Saul's daughter Mĭ′chal loved David. Saul was told, and the thing pleased him. [21] Saul thought, "Let me give her to him that she may be a snare for him and that the hand of the Phi·lis′tines may be against him." Therefore Saul said to David a second time,[f] "You shall now be my son-in-law." [22] Saul commanded his servants, "Speak to David in private and say, 'See, the king is delighted with you, and all his servants love you; now then, become the king's son-in-law.'" [23] So Saul's servants reported these words to David in private. And David said, "Does it seem to you a little thing to become the king's son-in-law, seeing that I am a poor man and of no repute?" [24] The servants of Saul told him, "This is what David said." [25] Then Saul said, "Thus shall you say to David, 'The king desires no marriage present except a hundred foreskins of the Phi·lis′tines, that he may be avenged on the king's enemies.'" Now Saul planned to make David fall by the hand of the Phi·lis′tines. [26] When his servants told David these words, David was well pleased to be the king's son-in-law. Before the time had expired, [27] David rose and went, along with his men, and killed one hundred[g] of the Phi·lis′tines; and David brought their foreskins, which were given in full number to the king, that he might become the king's son-in-law. Saul gave him his daughter Mĭ′chal as a wife. [28] But when Saul realized that the LORD was with David, and that Saul's daughter Mĭ′chal loved him, [29] Saul was still more afraid of David. So Saul was David's enemy from that time forward.

30 Then the commanders of the Phi·lis′tines came out to battle; and as often as they came out, David had more success than all the servants of Saul, so that his fame became very great.

Jonathan Intercedes for David

19 Saul spoke with his son Jonathan and with all his servants about killing David. But Saul's son Jonathan took great delight in David. [2] Jonathan told David, "My father Saul is trying to kill you; therefore be on guard tomorrow morning; stay in a secret place and hide yourself. [3] I will go out and stand beside my father in the field where you are, and I will speak to my father about you; if I learn anything I will tell you." [4] Jonathan spoke well of David to his father Saul, saying to him, "The king should not sin against his servant David, because he has not sinned against you, and because his deeds have been of good service to you; [5] for he took his life in his hand when he attacked the Phi·lis′tine, and the LORD brought about a great victory for all Israel. You saw it, and rejoiced; why then will you sin against an innocent person by killing David without cause?" [6] Saul heeded the voice of Jonathan; Saul swore, "As the LORD lives, he shall not be put to death." [7] So Jonathan called David and related all these things to him. Jonathan then brought David to Saul, and he was in his presence as before.

Michal Helps David Escape from Saul

8 Again there was war, and David went out to fight the Phi·lis′tines. He launched a heavy attack on them, so

---

[f] Heb *by two*   [g] Gk Compare 2 Sam 3.14: Heb *two hundred*

that they fled before him. ⁹ Then an evil spirit from the LORD came upon Saul, as he sat in his house with his spear in his hand, while David was playing music. ¹⁰ Saul sought to pin David to the wall with the spear; but he eluded Saul, so that he struck the spear into the wall. David fled and escaped that night.

11 Saul sent messengers to David's house to keep watch over him, planning to kill him in the morning. David's wife Mī′chal told him, "If you do not save your life tonight, tomorrow you will be killed." ¹² So Mī′chal let David down through the window; he fled away and escaped. ¹³ Mī′chal took an idol ʰ and laid it on the bed; she put a net ⁱ of goats' hair on its head, and covered it with the clothes. ¹⁴ When Saul sent messengers to take David, she said, "He is sick." ¹⁵ Then Saul sent the messengers to see David for themselves. He said, "Bring him up to me in the bed, that I may kill him." ¹⁶ When the messengers came in, the idol ʲ was in the bed, with the covering ⁱ of goats' hair on its head. ¹⁷ Saul said to Mī′chal, "Why have you deceived me like this, and let my enemy go, so that he has escaped?" Mī′chal answered Saul, "He said to me, 'Let me go; why should I kill you?' "

David Joins Samuel in Ramah

18 Now David fled and escaped; he came to Samuel at Rā′mah, and told him all that Saul had done to him. He and Samuel went and settled at Naī′-ōth. ¹⁹ Saul was told, "David is at Naī′-ōth in Rā′mah." ²⁰ Then Saul sent messengers to take David. When they saw the company of the prophets in a frenzy, with Samuel standing in charge of ⁱ them, the spirit of God came upon the messengers of Saul, and they also fell into a prophetic frenzy. ²¹ When Saul was told, he sent other messengers, and they also fell into a frenzy. Saul sent messengers again the third time, and they also fell into a frenzy. ²² Then he himself went to Rā′mah. He came to the great well that is in Sē′cū; ᵏ he asked, "Where are Samuel and David?" And someone said, "They are at Naī′ōth in Rā′mah." ²³ He went there, toward Naī′ōth in Rā′mah; and the spirit of God came upon him. As he was going, he fell into a prophetic frenzy, until he came to Naī′ōth in Rā′mah. ²⁴ He too stripped off his clothes, and he too fell into a

frenzy before Samuel. He lay naked all that day and all that night. Therefore it is said, "Is Saul also among the prophets?"

The Friendship of David and Jonathan

20 David fled from Naī′ōth in Rā′-mah. He came before Jonathan and said, "What have I done? What is my guilt? And what is my sin against your father that he is trying to take my life?" ² He said to him, "Far from it! You shall not die. My father does nothing either great or small without disclosing it to me; and why should my father hide this from me? Never!" ³ But David also swore, "Your father knows well that you like me; and he thinks, 'Do not let Jonathan know this, or he will be grieved.' But truly, as the LORD lives and as you yourself live, there is but a step between me and death." ⁴ Then Jonathan said to David, "Whatever you say, I will do for you." ⁵ David said to Jonathan, "Tomorrow is the new moon, and I should not fail to sit with the king at the meal; but let me go, so that I may hide in the field until the third evening. ⁶ If your father misses me at all, then say, 'David earnestly asked leave of me to run to Bethlehem his city; for there is a yearly sacrifice there for all the family.' ⁷ If he says, 'Good!' it will be well with your servant; but if he is angry, then know that evil has been determined by him. ⁸ Therefore deal kindly with your servant, for you have brought your servant into a sacred covenant ⁱ with you. But if there is guilt in me, kill me yourself; why should you bring me to your father?" ⁹ Jonathan said, "Far be it from you! If I knew that it was decided by my father that evil should come upon you, would I not tell you?" ¹⁰ Then David said to Jonathan, "Who will tell me if your father answers you harshly?" ¹¹ Jonathan replied to David, "Come, let us go out into the field." So they both went out into the field.

12 Jonathan said to David, "By the LORD, the God of Israel! When I have sounded out my father, about this time tomorrow, or on the third day, if he is well disposed toward David, shall I not

---

ʰ Heb *took the teraphim*   ⁱ Meaning of Heb uncertain   ʲ Heb *the teraphim*   ᵏ Gk reads *to the well of the threshing floor on the bare height*   ˡ Heb *a covenant of the LORD* then send and disclose it to you? ¹³But if my father intends to do you harm, the LORD do so to Jonathan, and more also, if I do not disclose it to you, and send you away, so that you may go in safety. May the LORD be with you, as he has been with my father. ¹⁴If I am still alive, show me the faithful love of the LORD; but if I die,ᵐ ¹⁵never cut off your faithful love from my house, even if the LORD were to cut off every one of the enemies of David from the face of the earth." ¹⁶Thus Jonathan made a covenant with the house of David, saying, "May the LORD seek out the enemies of David." ¹⁷Jonathan made David swear again by his love for him; for he loved him as he loved his own life.

18 Jonathan said to him, "Tomorrow is the new moon; you will be missed, because your place will be empty. ¹⁹On the day after tomorrow, you shall go a long way down; go to the place where you hid yourself earlier, and remain beside the stone there.ᵐ ²⁰I will shoot three arrows to the side of it, as though I shot at a mark. ²¹Then I will send the boy, saying, 'Go, find the arrows.' If I say to the boy, 'Look, the arrows are on this side of you, collect them,' then you are to come, for, as the LORD lives, it is safe for you and there is no danger. ²²But if I say to the young man, 'Look, the arrows are beyond you,' then go; for the LORD has sent you away. ²³As for the matter about which you and I have spoken, the LORD is witnessⁿ between you and me forever."

24 So David hid himself in the field. When the new moon came, the king sat at the feast to eat. ²⁵The king sat upon his seat, as at other times, upon the seat by the wall. Jonathan stood, while Abner sat by Saul's side; but David's place was empty.

26 Saul did not say anything that day; for he thought, "Something has befallen him; he is not clean, surely he is not clean." ²⁷But on the second day, the day after the new moon, David's place was empty. And Saul said to his son Jonathan, "Why has the son of Jesse not come to the feast, either yesterday or today?" ²⁸Jonathan answered Saul, "David earnestly asked leave of me to go to Bethlehem; ²⁹he said, 'Let me go; for our family is holding a sacrifice in the city, and my brother has commanded me to be there. So now, if I have found favor in

your sight, let me get away, and see my brothers.' For this reason he has not come to the king's table."

30 Then Saul's anger was kindled against Jonathan. He said to him, "You son of a perverse, rebellious woman! Do I not know that you have chosen the son of Jesse to your own shame, and to the shame of your mother's nakedness? ³¹For as long as the son of Jesse lives upon the earth, neither you nor your kingdom shall be established. Now send and bring him to me, for he shall surely die." ³²Then Jonathan answered his father Saul, "Why should he be put to death? What has he done?" ³³But Saul threw his spear at him to strike him; so Jonathan knew that it was the decision of his father to put David to death. ³⁴Jonathan rose from the table in fierce anger and ate no food on the second day of the month, for he was grieved for David, and because his father had disgraced him.

35 In the morning Jonathan went out into the field to the appointment with David, and with him was a little boy. ³⁶He said to the boy, "Run and find the arrows that I shoot." As the boy ran, he shot an arrow beyond him. ³⁷When the boy came to the place where Jonathan's arrow had fallen, Jonathan called after the boy and said, "Is the arrow not beyond you?" ³⁸Jonathan called after the boy, "Hurry, be quick, do not linger." So Jonathan's boy gathered up the arrows and came to his master. ³⁹But the boy knew nothing; only Jonathan and David knew the arrangement. ⁴⁰Jonathan gave his weapons to the boy and said to him, "Go and carry them to the city." ⁴¹As soon as the boy had gone, David rose from beside the stone heapᵒ and prostrated himself with his face to the ground. He bowed three times, and they kissed each other, and wept with each other; David wept the more.ᵖ ⁴²Then Jonathan said to David, "Go in peace, since both of us have sworn in the name of the LORD, saying, 'The LORD shall be between me and you, and between my descendants and your descendants, forever.'" He got up and left; and Jonathan went into the city.�q

---

ᵐMeaning of Heb uncertain   ⁿGk: Heb lacks *witness*   ᵒGk: Heb *from beside the south*   ᵖVg: Meaning of Heb uncertain   qThis sentence is 21.1 in Heb

David and the Holy Bread

21 [r] David came to Nob to the priest A·him′e·lech. A·him′e·lech came trembling to meet David, and said to him, "Why are you alone, and no one with you?" 2 David said to the priest A·him′e·lech, "The king has charged me with a matter, and said to me, 'No one must know anything of the matter about which I send you, and with which I have charged you.' I have made an appointment[s] with the young men for such and such a place. 3 Now then, what have you at hand? Give me five loaves of bread, or whatever is here." 4 The priest answered David, "I have no ordinary bread at hand, only holy bread—provided that the young men have kept themselves from women." 5 David answered the priest, "Indeed women have been kept from us as always when I go on an expedition; the vessels of the young men are holy even when it is a common journey; how much more today will their vessels be holy?" 6 So the priest gave him the holy bread; for there was no bread there except the bread of the Presence, which is removed from before the LORD, to be replaced by hot bread on the day it is taken away.

7 Now a certain man of the servants of Saul was there that day, detained before the LORD; his name was Dō′eg the Ē′dom·ite, the chief of Saul's shepherds.

8 David said to A·him′e·lech, "Is there no spear or sword here with you? I did not bring my sword or my weapons with me, because the king's business required haste." 9 The priest said, "The sword of Goliath the Phi·lis′tine, whom you killed in the valley of Ē′lah, is here wrapped in a cloth behind the ephod; if you will take that, take it, for there is none here except that one." David said, "There is none like it; give it to me."

David Flees to Gath

10 David rose and fled that day from Saul; he went to King A′chish of Gath. 11 The servants of A′chish said to him, "Is this not David the king of the land? Did they not sing to one another of him in dances,

'Saul has killed his thousands,
    and David his ten thousands'?"
12 David took these words to heart and was very much afraid of King A′chish of Gath. 13 So he changed his behavior

before them; he pretended to be mad when in their presence. [t] He scratched marks on the doors of the gate, and let his spittle run down his beard. 14 A′chish said to his servants, "Look, you see the man is mad; why then have you brought him to me? 15 Do I lack madmen, that you have brought this fellow to play the madman in my presence? Shall this fellow come into my house?"

David and His Followers at Adullam

22 David left there and escaped to the cave of A·dul′lam; when his brothers and all his father's house heard of it, they went down there to him. 2 Everyone who was in distress, and everyone who was in debt, and everyone who was discontented gathered to him; and he became captain over them. Those who were with him numbered about four hundred.

3 David went from there to Miz′peh of Mō′ab. He said to the king of Mō′ab, "Please let my father and mother come[u] to you, until I know what God will do for me." 4 He left them with the king of Mō′ab, and they stayed with him all the time that David was in the stronghold. 5 Then the prophet Gad said to David, "Do not remain in the stronghold; leave, and go into the land of Judah." So David left, and went into the forest of Hē′reth.

Saul Slaughters the Priests at Nob

6 Saul heard that David and those who were with him had been located. Saul was sitting at Gib′e·ah, under the tamarisk tree on the height, with his spear in his hand, and all his servants were standing around him. 7 Saul said to his servants who stood around him, "Hear now, you Ben′ja·min·ites; will the son of Jesse give every one of you fields and vineyards, will he make you all commanders of thousands and commanders of hundreds? 8 Is that why all of you have conspired against me? No one discloses to me when my son makes a league with the son of Jesse, none of you is sorry for me or discloses to me that my son has stirred up my servant against me, to lie in wait, as he is doing today." 9 Dō′eg the Ē′dom·ite, who was in charge of Saul's

r Ch 21.2 in Heb   *s* Q Ms Vg Compare Gk: Meaning of MT uncertain   *t* Heb *in their hands*   *u* Syr Vg: Heb *come out* servants, answered, "I saw the son of Jesse coming to Nob, to A·him′e·lech son of A·hi′tub; 10 he inquired of the LORD for him, gave him provisions, and gave him the sword of Goliath the Phi·lis′tine."

11 The king sent for the priest A·him′e·lech son of A·hi′tub and for all his father's house, the priests who were at Nob; and all of them came to the king. 12 Saul said, "Listen now, son of A·hi′tub." He answered, "Here I am, my lord." 13 Saul said to him, "Why have you conspired against me, you and the son of Jesse, by giving him bread and a sword, and by inquiring of God for him, so that he has risen against me, to lie in wait, as he is doing today?"

14 Then A·him′e·lech answered the king, "Who among all your servants is so faithful as David? He is the king's son-in-law, and is quick v to do your bidding, and is honored in your house. 15 Is today the first time that I have inquired of God for him? By no means! Do not let the king impute anything to his servant or to any member of my father's house; for your servant has known nothing of all this, much or little." 16 The king said, "You shall surely die, A·him′e·lech, you and all your father's house." 17 The king said to the guard who stood around him, "Turn and kill the priests of the LORD, because their hand also is with David; they knew that he fled, and did not disclose it to me." But the servants of the king would not raise their hand to attack the priests of the LORD. 18 Then the king said to Dō′eg, "You, Dō′eg, turn and attack the priests." Dō′eg the E′dom·ite turned and attacked the priests; on that day he killed eighty-five who wore the linen ephod. 19 Nob, the city of the priests, he put to the sword; men and women, children and infants, oxen, donkeys, and sheep, he put to the sword.

20 But one of the sons of A·him′e·lech son of A·hi′tub, named A·bi′a·thar, escaped and fled after David. 21 A·bi′a·thar told David that Saul had killed the priests of the LORD. 22 David said to A·bi′a·thar, "I knew on that day, when Dō′eg the E′dom·ite was there, that he would surely tell Saul. I am responsible w for the lives of all your father's house. 23 Stay with me, and do not be afraid; for the one who seeks my life seeks your life; you will be safe with me."

David Saves the City of Keilah

23 Now they told David, "The Phi·lis′tines are fighting against Kē·i′lah, and are robbing the threshing floors." 2 David inquired of the LORD, "Shall I go and attack these Phi·lis′tines?" The LORD said to David, "Go and attack the Phi·lis′tines and save Kē·i′lah." 3 But David's men said to him, "Look, we are afraid here in Judah; how much more then if we go to Kē·i′lah against the armies of the Phi·lis′tines?" 4 Then David inquired of the LORD again. The LORD answered him, "Yes, go down to Kē·i′lah; for I will give the Phi·lis′tines into your hand." 5 So David and his men went to Kē·i′lah, fought with the Phi·lis′tines, brought away their livestock, and dealt them a heavy defeat. Thus David rescued the inhabitants of Kē·i′lah.

6 When A·bi′a·thar son of A·him′e·lech fled to David at Kē·i′lah, he came down with an ephod in his hand. 7 Now it was told Saul that David had come to Kē·i′lah. And Saul said, "God has given x him into my hand; for he has shut himself in by entering a town that has gates and bars." 8 Saul summoned all the people to war, to go down to Kē·i′lah, to besiege David and his men. 9 When David learned that Saul was plotting evil against him, he said to the priest A·bi′a·thar, "Bring the ephod here." 10 David said, "O LORD, the God of Israel, your servant has heard that Saul seeks to come to Kē·i′lah, to destroy the city on my account. 11 And now, will y Saul come down as your servant has heard? O LORD, the God of Israel, I beseech you, tell your servant." The LORD said, "He will come down." 12 Then David said, "Will the men of Kē·i′lah surrender me and my men into the hand of Saul?" The LORD said, "They will surrender you." 13 Then David and his men, who were about six hundred, set out and left Kē·i′lah; they wandered wherever they could go. When Saul was told that David had escaped from Kē·i′lah, he gave up the expedition. 14 David remained in the strongholds in the wilderness, in the hill country of the Wilderness of Ziph. Saul sought

1 S A M U E L

---

v Heb *and turns aside*   w Gk Vg:
Meaning of Heb uncertain   x Gk Tg:
Heb *made a stranger of*   y Q Ms
Compare Gk: MT *Will the men of Keilah surrender me into his hand? Will*

him every day, but the LORD[z] did not give him into his hand.

David Eludes Saul in the Wilderness

15 David was in the Wilderness of Ziph at Hōʹresh when he learned that[a] Saul had come out to seek his life. [16]Saul's son Jonathan set out and came to David at Hōʹresh; there he strengthened his hand through the LORD.[b] [17]He said to him, "Do not be afraid; for the hand of my father Saul shall not find you; you shall be king over Israel, and I shall be second to you; my father Saul also knows that this is so." [18]Then the two of them made a covenant before the LORD; David remained at Hōʹresh, and Jonathan went home.

19 Then some Ziphʹites went up to Saul at Gibʹe·ah and said, "David is hiding among us in the strongholds of Hōʹresh, on the hill of Ha·chiʹlah, which is south of Jē·shiʹmon. [20]Now, O king, whenever you wish to come down, do so; and our part will be to surrender him into the king's hand." [21]Saul said, "May you be blessed by the LORD for showing me compassion! [22]Go and make sure once more; find out exactly where he is, and who has seen him there; for I am told that he is very cunning. [23]Look around and learn all the hiding places where he lurks, and come back to me with sure information. Then I will go with you; and if he is in the land, I will search him out among all the thousands of Judah." [24]So they set out and went to Ziph ahead of Saul.

David and his men were in the wilderness of Māʹon, in the Arʹa·bah to the south of Jē·shiʹmon. [25]Saul and his men went to search for him. When David was told, he went down to the rock and stayed in the wilderness of Māʹon. When Saul heard that, he pursued David into the wilderness of Māʹon. [26]Saul went on one side of the mountain, and David and his men on the other side of the mountain. David was hurrying to get away from Saul, while Saul and his men were closing in on David and his men to capture them. [27]Then a messenger came to Saul, saying, "Hurry and come; for the Phi·lisʹtines have made a raid on the land." [28]So Saul stopped pursuing David, and went against the Phi·lisʹtines; therefore that place was called the Rock of Escape.[c] [29][d]David then went up

from there, and lived in the strongholds of En-geʹdi.

David Spares Saul's Life

24 When Saul returned from following the Phi·lisʹtines, he was told, "David is in the wilderness of En-geʹdi." [2]Then Saul took three thousand chosen men out of all Israel, and went to look for David and his men in the direction of the Rocks of the Wild Goats. [3]He came to the sheepfolds beside the road, where there was a cave; and Saul went in to relieve himself.[e] Now David and his men were sitting in the innermost parts of the cave. [4]The men of David said to him, "Here is the day of which the LORD said to you, 'I will give your enemy into your hand, and you shall do to him as it seems good to you.' " Then David went and stealthily cut off a corner of Saul's cloak. [5]Afterward David was stricken to the heart because he had cut off a corner of Saul's cloak. [6]He said to his men, "The LORD forbid that I should do this thing to my lord, the LORD's anointed, to raise my hand against him; for he is the LORD's anointed." [7]So David scolded his men severely and did not permit them to attack Saul. Then Saul got up and left the cave, and went on his way.

8 Afterwards David also rose up and went out of the cave and called after Saul, "My lord the king!" When Saul looked behind him, David bowed with his face to the ground, and did obeisance. [9]David said to Saul, "Why do you listen to the words of those who say, 'David seeks to do you harm'? [10]This very day your eyes have seen how the LORD gave you into my hand in the cave; and some urged me to kill you, but I spared[f] you. I said, 'I will not raise my hand against my lord; for he is the LORD's anointed.' [11]See, my father, see the corner of your cloak in my hand; for by the fact that I cut off the corner of your cloak, and did not kill you, you may know for certain that there is no wrong or treason in my hands. I have not sinned against you, though you are hunting me to take my life. [12]May the LORD judge between me

z Q Ms Gk: MT God   a Or saw that
b Compare Q Ms Gk: MT God
c Or Rock of Division; Meaning of Heb uncertain   d Ch 24.1 in Heb   e Heb to cover his feet   f Gk Syr Tg Vg: Heb it (my eye) spared

and you! May the LORD avenge me on you; but my hand shall not be against you. 13 As the ancient proverb says, 'Out of the wicked comes forth wickedness'; but my hand shall not be against you. 14 Against whom has the king of Israel come out? Whom do you pursue? A dead dog? A single flea? 15 May the LORD therefore be judge, and give sentence between me and you. May he see to it, and plead my cause, and vindicate me against you."

16 When David had finished speaking these words to Saul, Saul said, "Is this your voice, my son David?" Saul lifted up his voice and wept. 17 He said to David, "You are more righteous than I; for you have repaid me good, whereas I have repaid you evil. 18 Today you have explained how you have dealt well with me, in that you did not kill me when the LORD put me into your hands. 19 For who has ever found an enemy, and sent the enemy safely away? So may the LORD reward you with good for what you have done to me this day. 20 Now I know that you shall surely be king, and that the kingdom of Israel shall be established in your hand. 21 Swear to me therefore by the LORD that you will not cut off my descendants after me, and that you will not wipe out my name from my father's house." 22 So David swore this to Saul. Then Saul went home; but David and his men went up to the stronghold.

Death of Samuel

25 Now Samuel died; and all Israel assembled and mourned for him. They buried him at his home in Ra'mah.

Then David got up and went down to the wilderness of Par'an.

David and the Wife of Nabal

2 There was a man in Ma'on, whose property was in Car'mel. The man was very rich; he had three thousand sheep and a thousand goats. He was shearing his sheep in Car'mel. 3 Now the name of the man was Na'bal, and the name of his wife Ab'i·gail. The woman was clever and beautiful, but the man was surly and mean; he was a Ca'leb·ite. 4 David heard in the wilderness that Na'bal was shearing his sheep. 5 So David sent ten young men; and David said to the young men, "Go up to Car'mel, and go to Na'bal, and greet him in my name. 6 Thus you shall salute him:

'Peace be to you, and peace be to your house, and peace be to all that you have. 7 I hear that you have shearers; now your shepherds have been with us, and we did them no harm, and they missed nothing, all the time they were in Car'mel. 8 Ask your young men, and they will tell you. Therefore let my young men find favor in your sight; for we have come on a feast day. Please give whatever you have at hand to your servants and to your son David.' "

9 When David's young men came, they said all this to Na'bal in the name of David; and then they waited. 10 But Na'bal answered David's servants, "Who is David? Who is the son of Jesse? There are many servants today who are breaking away from their masters. 11 Shall I take my bread and my water and the meat that I have butchered for my shearers, and give it to men who come from I do not know where?" 12 So David's young men turned away, and came back and told him all this. 13 David said to his men, "Every man strap on his sword!" And every one of them strapped on his sword; David also strapped on his sword; and about four hundred men went up after David, while two hundred remained with the baggage.

14 But one of the young men told Ab'i·gail, Na'bal's wife, "David sent messengers out of the wilderness to salute our master; and he shouted insults at them. 15 Yet the men were very good to us, and we suffered no harm, and we never missed anything when we were in the fields, as long as we were with them; 16 they were a wall to us both by night and by day, all the while we were with them keeping the sheep. 17 Now therefore know this and consider what you should do; for evil has been decided against our master and against all his house; he is so ill-natured that no one can speak to him."

18 Then Ab'i·gail hurried and took two hundred loaves, two skins of wine, five sheep ready dressed, five measures of parched grain, one hundred clusters of raisins, and two hundred cakes of figs. She loaded them on donkeys 19 and said to her young men, "Go on ahead of me; I am coming after you." But she did not tell her husband Na'bal. 20 As she rode on the donkey and came down under cover of the mountain, David and his men came down toward her; and she met them. 21 Now David had said, "Surely it was

in vain that I protected all that this fellow has in the wilderness, so that nothing was missed of all that belonged to him; but he has returned me evil for good. ²² God do so to David^g and more also, if by morning I leave so much as one male of all who belong to him."

23 When Ab'i·gail saw David, she hurried and alighted from the donkey, fell before David on her face, bowing to the ground. ²⁴ She fell at his feet and said, "Upon me alone, my lord, be the guilt; please let your servant speak in your ears, and hear the words of your servant. ²⁵ My lord, do not take seriously this ill-natured fellow, Na'bal; for as his name is, so is he; Na'bal^h is his name, and folly is with him; but I, your servant, did not see the young men of my lord, whom you sent.

26 Now then, my lord, as the LORD lives, and as you yourself live, since the LORD has restrained you from bloodguilt and from taking vengeance with your own hand, now let your enemies and those who seek to do evil to my lord be like Na'bal. ²⁷ And now let this present that your servant has brought to my lord be given to the young men who follow my lord. ²⁸ Please forgive the trespass of your servant; for the LORD will certainly make my lord a sure house, because my lord is fighting the battles of the LORD; and evil shall not be found in you so long as you live. ²⁹ If anyone should rise up to pursue you and to seek your life, the life of my lord shall be bound in the bundle of the living under the care of the LORD your God; but the lives of your enemies he shall sling out as from the hollow of a sling. ³⁰ When the LORD has done to my lord according to all the good that he has spoken concerning you, and has appointed you prince over Israel, ³¹ my lord shall have no cause of grief, or pangs of conscience, for having shed blood without cause or for having saved himself. And when the LORD has dealt well with my lord, then remember your servant."

32 David said to Ab'i·gail, "Blessed be the LORD, the God of Israel, who sent you to meet me today! ³³ Blessed be your good sense, and blessed be you, who have kept me today from bloodguilt and from avenging myself by my own hand! ³⁴ For as surely as the LORD the God of Israel lives, who has restrained me from hurting you, unless you had hurried and come to meet me,

truly by morning there would not have been left to Na'bal so much as one male." ³⁵ Then David received from her hand what she had brought him; he said to her, "Go up to your house in peace; see, I have heeded your voice, and I have granted your petition."

36 Ab'i·gail came to Na'bal; he was holding a feast in his house, like the feast of a king. Na'bal's heart was merry within him, for he was very drunk; so she told him nothing at all until the morning light. ³⁷ In the morning, when the wine had gone out of Na'bal, his wife told him these things, and his heart died within him; he became like a stone. ³⁸ About ten days later the LORD struck Na'bal, and he died.

39 When David heard that Na'bal was dead, he said, "Blessed be the LORD who has judged the case of Na'-bal's insult to me, and has kept back his servant from evil; the LORD has returned the evildoing of Na'bal upon his own head." Then David sent and wooed Ab'i·gail, to make her his wife. ⁴⁰ When David's servants came to Ab'-i·gail at Car'mel, they said to her, "David has sent us to you to take you to him as his wife." ⁴¹ She rose and bowed down, with her face to the ground, and said, "Your servant is a slave to wash the feet of the servants of my lord." ⁴² Ab'i·gail got up hurriedly and rode away on a donkey; her five maids attended her. She went after the messengers of David and became his wife.

43 David also married A·hin'ō·am of Jez're·el; both of them became his wives. ⁴⁴ Saul had given his daughter Mi'chal, David's wife, to Pal'ti son of La'ish, who was from Gal'lim.

David Spares Saul's Life a Second Time

26 Then the Ziph'ites came to Saul at Gib'e·ah, saying, "David is in hiding on the hill of Ha·chi'lah, which is opposite Je·shi'mon."ⁱ ² So Saul rose and went down to the Wilderness of Ziph, with three thousand chosen men of Israel, to seek David in the Wilderness of Ziph. ³ Saul encamped on the hill of Ha·chi'lah, which is opposite Je·shi'monⁱ beside the road. But David remained in the wilderness. When he learned that Saul came after him

^g Gk Compare Syr: Heb *the enemies of David*   ^h That is *Fool*   ⁱ Or *opposite the wasteland*

into the wilderness, ⁴David sent out spies, and learned that Saul had indeed arrived. ⁵Then David set out and came to the place where Saul had encamped; and David saw the place where Saul lay, with Abner son of Ner, the commander of his army. Saul was lying within the encampment, while the army was encamped around him.

6 Then David said to A·him′e·lech the Hit′tīte, and to Jō′ab's brother A·bi′shaī son of Ze·rū′i·ah, "Who will go down with me into the camp to Saul?" A·bi′shaī said, "I will go down with you." ⁷So David and A·bi′shaī went to the army by night; there Saul lay sleeping within the encampment, with his spear stuck in the ground at his head; and Abner and the army lay around him. ⁸A·bi′shaī said to David, "God has given your enemy into your hand today; now therefore let me pin him to the ground with one stroke of the spear; I will not strike him twice." ⁹But David said to A·bi′shaī, "Do not destroy him; for who can raise his hand against the LORD's anointed, and be guiltless?" ¹⁰David said, "As the LORD lives, the LORD will strike him down; or his day will come to die; or he will go down into battle and perish. ¹¹The LORD forbid that I should raise my hand against the LORD's anointed; but now take the spear that is at his head, and the water jar, and let us go." ¹²So David took the spear that was at Saul's head and the water jar, and they went away. No one saw it, or knew it, nor did anyone awake; for they were all asleep, because a deep sleep from the LORD had fallen upon them.

13 Then David went over to the other side, and stood on top of a hill far away, with a great distance between them. ¹⁴David called to the army and to Abner son of Ner, saying, "Abner! Will you not answer?" Then Abner replied, "Who are you that calls to the king?" ¹⁵David said to Abner, "Are you not a man? Who is like you in Israel? Why then have you not kept watch over your lord the king? For one of the people came in to destroy your lord the king. ¹⁶This thing that you have done is not good. As the LORD lives, you deserve to die, because you have not kept watch over your lord, the LORD's anointed. See now, where is the king's spear, or the water jar that was at his head?"

17 Saul recognized David's voice, and said, "Is this your voice, my son David?" David said, "It is my voice, my lord, O king." ¹⁸And he added, "Why does my lord pursue his servant? For what have I done? What guilt is on my hands? ¹⁹Now therefore let my lord the king hear the words of his servant. If it is the LORD who has stirred you up against me, may he accept an offering; but if it is mortals, may they be cursed before the LORD, for they have driven me out today from my share in the heritage of the LORD, saying, 'Go, serve other gods.' ²⁰Now therefore, do not let my blood fall to the ground, away from the presence of the LORD; for the king of Israel has come out to seek a single flea, like one who hunts a partridge in the mountains."

21 Then Saul said, "I have done wrong; come back, my son David, for I will never harm you again, because my life was precious in your sight today; I have been a fool, and have made a great mistake." ²²David replied, "Here is the spear, O king! Let one of the young men come over and get it. ²³The LORD rewards everyone for his righteousness and his faithfulness; for the LORD gave you into my hand today, but I would not raise my hand against the LORD's anointed. ²⁴As your life was precious today in my sight, so may my life be precious in the sight of the LORD, and may he rescue me from all tribulation." ²⁵Then Saul said to David, "Blessed be you, my son David! You will do many things and will succeed in them." So David went his way, and Saul returned to his place.

David Serves King Achish of Gath

27 David said in his heart, "I shall now perish one day by the hand of Saul; there is nothing better for me than to escape to the land of the Phi·lis′tines; then Saul will despair of seeking me any longer within the borders of Israel, and I shall escape out of his hand." ²So David set out and went over, he and the six hundred men who were with him, to King A′chish son of Ma′och of Gath. ³David stayed with A′chish at Gath, he and his troops, every man with his household, and David with his two wives, A·hin′o·am of Jez′re·el, and Ab′i·gail of Car′mel, Na′bal's widow. ⁴When Saul was told that David had fled to Gath, he no longer sought for him.

5 Then David said to A′chish, "If I have found favor in your sight, let a place be given me in one of the country

towns, so that I may live there; for why should your servant live in the royal city with you?" 6So that day Ā'chish gave him Zik'lag; therefore Zik'lag has belonged to the kings of Judah to this day. 7The length of time that David lived in the country of the Phi·lis'-tines was one year and four months.

8 Now David and his men went up and made raids on the Gesh'ū·rītes, the Gir'zītes, and the A·mal'e·kītes; for these were the landed settlements from Te'lam𝒾 on the way to Shur and on to the land of Egypt. 9David struck the land, leaving neither man nor woman alive, but took away the sheep, the oxen, the donkeys, the camels, and the clothing, and came back to Ā'chish. 10When Ā'chish asked, "Against whom𝒌 have you made a raid today?" David would say, "Against the Neg'eb of Judah," or "Against the Neg'eb of the Je·rah'mē·el·ītes," or, "Against the Neg'eb of the Ken'ītes." 11David left neither man nor woman alive to be brought back to Gath, thinking, "They might tell about us, and say, 'David has done so and so.'" Such was his practice all the time he lived in the country of the Phi·lis'tines. 12Ā'chish trusted David, thinking, "He has made himself utterly abhorrent to his people Israel; therefore he shall always be my servant."

28 In those days the Phi·lis'tines gathered their forces for war, to fight against Israel. Ā'chish said to David, "You know, of course, that you and your men are to go out with me in the army." 2David said to Ā'chish, "Very well, then you shall know what your servant can do." Ā'chish said to David, "Very well, I will make you my bodyguard for life."

Saul Consults a Medium
(Cp Deut 18.9–14)

3 Now Samuel had died, and all Israel had mourned for him and buried him in Rā'mah, his own city. Saul had expelled the mediums and the wizards from the land. 4The Phi·lis'tines assembled, and came and encamped at Shū'nem. Saul gathered all Israel, and they encamped at Gil·bō'a. 5When Saul saw the army of the Phi·lis'tines, he was afraid, and his heart trembled greatly. 6When Saul inquired of the LORD, the LORD did not answer him, not by dreams, or by U'rim, or by prophets. 7Then Saul said to his servants, "Seek out for me a woman who

is a medium, so that I may go to her and inquire of her." His servants said to him, "There is a medium at En'dor."

8 So Saul disguised himself and put on other clothes and went there, he and two men with him. They came to the woman by night. And he said, "Consult a spirit for me, and bring up for me the one whom I name to you." 9The woman said to him, "Surely you know what Saul has done, how he has cut off the mediums and the wizards from the land. Why then are you laying a snare for my life to bring about my death?" 10But Saul swore to her by the LORD, "As the LORD lives, no punishment shall come upon you for this thing." 11Then the woman said, "Whom shall I bring up for you?" He answered, "Bring up Samuel for me." 12When the woman saw Samuel, she cried out with a loud voice; and the woman said to Saul, "Why have you deceived me? You are Saul!" 13The king said to her, "Have no fear; what do you see?" The woman said to Saul, "I see a divine being𝒍 coming up out of the ground." 14He said to her, "What is his appearance?" She said, "An old man is coming up; he is wrapped in a robe." So Saul knew that it was Samuel, and he bowed with his face to the ground, and did obeisance.

15 Then Samuel said to Saul, "Why have you disturbed me by bringing me up?" Saul answered, "I am in great distress, for the Phi·lis'tines are warring against me, and God has turned away from me and answers me no more, either by prophets or by dreams; so I have summoned you to tell me what I should do." 16Samuel said, "Why then do you ask me, since the LORD has turned from you and become your enemy? 17The LORD has done to you just as he spoke by me; for the LORD has torn the kingdom out of your hand and given it to your neighbor, David. 18Because you did not obey the voice of the LORD, and did not carry out his fierce wrath against Am'a·lek, therefore the LORD has done this thing to you today. 19Moreover the LORD will give Israel along with you into the hands of the Phi·lis'tines; and tomorrow you and your sons shall be with me; the LORD will also give the army of

𝒾Compare Gk 15.4: Heb *from of old* 𝒌Q Ms Gk Vg: MT lacks *whom* 𝒍Or *a god; or gods*

Israel into the hands of the Phi·lis'-tines."

20 Immediately Saul fell full length on the ground, filled with fear because of the words of Samuel; and there was no strength in him, for he had eaten nothing all day and all night. 21 The woman came to Saul, and when she saw that he was terrified, she said to him, "Your servant has listened to you; I have taken my life in my hand, and have listened to what you have said to me. 22 Now therefore, you also listen to your servant; let me set a morsel of bread before you. Eat, that you may have strength when you go on your way." 23 He refused, and said, "I will not eat." But his servants, together with the woman, urged him; and he listened to their words. So he got up from the ground and sat on the bed. 24 Now the woman had a fatted calf in the house. She quickly slaughtered it, and she took flour, kneaded it, and baked unleavened cakes. 25 She put them before Saul and his servants, and they ate. Then they rose and went away that night.

The Philistines Reject David

29 Now the Phi·lis'tines gathered all their forces at A'phek, while the Israelites were encamped by the fountain that is in Jez're·el. 2 As the lords of the Phi·lis'tines were passing on by hundreds and by thousands, and David and his men were passing on in the rear with A'chish, 3 the commanders of the Phi·lis'tines said, "What are these Hebrews doing here?" A'chish said to the commanders of the Phi·lis'-tines, "Is this not David, the servant of King Saul of Israel, who has been with me now for days and years? Since he deserted to me I have found no fault in him to this day." 4 But the commanders of the Phi·lis'tines were angry with him; and the commanders of the Phi·lis'tines said to him, "Send the man back, so that he may return to the place that you have assigned to him; he shall not go down with us to battle, or else he may become an adversary to us in the battle. For how could this fellow reconcile himself to his lord? Would it not be with the heads of the men here? 5 Is this not David, of whom they sing to one another in dances,

'Saul has killed his thousands,
    and David his ten thousands'?"

6 Then A'chish called David and said to him, "As the LORD lives, you

have been honest, and to me it seems right that you should march out and in with me in the campaign; for I have found nothing wrong in you from the day of your coming to me until today. Nevertheless the lords do not approve of you. 7 So go back now; and go peaceably; do nothing to displease the lords of the Phi·lis'tines." 8 David said to A'chish, "But what have I done? What have you found in your servant from the day I entered your service until now, that I should not go and fight against the enemies of my lord the king?" 9 A'chish replied to David, "I know that you are as blameless in my sight as an angel of God; nevertheless, the commanders of the Phi·lis'tines have said, 'He shall not go up with us to the battle.' 10 Now then rise early in the morning, you and the servants of your lord who came with you, and go to the place that I appointed for you. As for the evil report, do not take it to heart, for you have done well before me. *m* Start early in the morning, and leave as soon as you have light." 11 So David set out with his men early in the morning, to return to the land of the Phi·lis'tines. But the Phi·lis'tines went up to Jez're·el.

David Avenges the Destruction of Ziklag

30 Now when David and his men came to Zik'lag on the third day, the A·mal'e·kites had made a raid on the Neg'eb and on Zik'lag. They had attacked Zik'lag, burned it down, 2 and taken captive the women and all*n* who were in it, both small and great; they killed none of them, but carried them off, and went their way. 3 When David and his men came to the city, they found it burned down, and their wives and sons and daughters taken captive. 4 Then David and the people who were with him raised their voices and wept, until they had no more strength to weep. 5 David's two wives also had been taken captive, A·hin'o·am of Jez're·el, and Ab'i·gail the widow of Na'bal of Car'mel. 6 David was in great danger; for the people spoke of stoning him, because all the people were bitter in spirit for their sons and daughters. But David

---

m Gk: Heb lacks *and go to the place* . . . *done well before me*   *n* Gk: Heb lacks *and all* strengthened himself in the LORD his God.

7 David said to the priest A·bī'-a·thar son of A·him'e·lech, "Bring me the ephod." So A·bī'a·thar brought the ephod to David. ⁸David inquired of the LORD, "Shall I pursue this band? Shall I overtake them?" He answered him, "Pursue; for you shall surely overtake and shall surely rescue." ⁹So David set out, he and the six hundred men who were with him. They came to the Wadi Bē'sor, where those stayed who were left behind. ¹⁰But David went on with the pursuit, he and four hundred men; two hundred stayed behind, too exhausted to cross the Wadi Bē'sor.

11 In the open country they found an Egyptian, and brought him to David. They gave him bread and he ate, they gave him water to drink; ¹²they also gave him a piece of fig cake and two clusters of raisins. When he had eaten, his spirit revived; for he had not eaten bread or drunk water for three days and three nights. ¹³Then David said to him, "To whom do you belong? Where are you from?" He said, "I am a young man of Egypt, servant to an A·mal'e·kīte. My master left me behind because I fell sick three days ago. ¹⁴We had made a raid on the Neg'eb of the Cher'e·thītes and on that which belongs to Judah and on the Neg'eb of Caleb; and we burned Zik'lag down." ¹⁵David said to him, "Will you take me down to this raiding party?" He said, "Swear to me by God that you will not kill me, or hand me over to my master, and I will take you down to them."

16 When he had taken him down, they were spread out all over the ground, eating and drinking and dancing, because of the great amount of spoil they had taken from the land of the Phi·lis'tines and from the land of Judah. ¹⁷David attacked them from twilight until the evening of the next day. Not one of them escaped, except four hundred young men, who mounted camels and fled. ¹⁸David recovered all that the A·mal'e·kītes had taken; and David rescued his two wives. ¹⁹Nothing was missing, whether small or great, sons or daughters, spoil or anything that had been taken; David brought back everything. ²⁰David also captured all the flocks and herds, which were driven ahead of the other cattle; people said, "This is David's spoil."

21 Then David came to the two hundred men who had been too exhausted to follow David, and who had been left at the Wadi Bē'sor. They went out to meet David and to meet the people who were with him. When David drew near to the people he saluted them. ²²Then all the corrupt and worthless fellows among the men who had gone with David said, "Because they did not go with us, we will not give them any of the spoil that we have recovered, except that each man may take his wife and children, and leave." ²³But David said, "You shall not do so, my brothers, with what the LORD has given us; he has preserved us and handed over to us the raiding party that attacked us. ²⁴Who would listen to you in this matter? For the share of the one who goes down into the battle shall be the same as the share of the one who stays by the baggage; they shall share alike." ²⁵From that day forward he made it a statute and an ordinance for Israel; it continues to the present day.

26 When David came to Zik'lag, he sent part of the spoil to his friends, the elders of Judah, saying, "Here is a present for you from the spoil of the enemies of the LORD"; ²⁷it was for those in Beth'el, in Rā'moth of the Neg'eb, in Jat'tir, ²⁸in A·rō'er, in Siph'moth, in Esh·te·mō'a, ²⁹in Rā'cal, in the towns of the Je·rah'mē·el·ītes, in the towns of the Ken'ītes, ³⁰in Hor'-mah, in Bor-ash'an, in A'thach, ³¹in Hē'bron, all the places where David and his men had roamed.

The Death of Saul and His Sons
(1 Chr 10.1–14)

31 Now the Phi·lis'tines fought against Israel; and the men of Israel fled before the Phi·lis'tines, and many fell⁰ on Mount Gil·bō'a. ²The Phi·lis'tines overtook Saul and his sons; and the Phi·lis'tines killed Jonathan and A·bin'a·dab and Mal-chī-shū'a, the sons of Saul. ³The battle pressed hard upon Saul; the archers found him, and he was badly wounded by them. ⁴Then Saul said to his armor-bearer, "Draw your sword and thrust me through with it, so that these uncircumcised may not come and thrust me through, and make sport of me." But his armor-bearer was unwilling; for he was terrified. So Saul

⁰Heb *and they fell slain*

took his own sword and fell upon it. [5] When his armor-bearer saw that Saul was dead, he also fell upon his sword and died with him. [6] So Saul and his three sons and his armor-bearer and all his men died together on the same day. [7] When the men of Israel who were on the other side of the valley and those beyond the Jordan saw that the men of Israel had fled and that Saul and his sons were dead, they forsook their towns and fled; and the Phi·lis'-tines came and occupied them.

[8] The next day, when the Phi·lis'-tines came to strip the dead, they found Saul and his three sons fallen on Mount Gil·bō'a. [9] They cut off his head, stripped off his armor, and sent messengers throughout the land of the Phi·lis'tines to carry the good news to the houses of their idols and to the people. [10] They put his armor in the temple of As·tar'tē;[p] and they fastened his body to the wall of Beth-shan. [11] But when the inhabitants of Jā'besh-gil'ē·ad heard what the Phi·lis'tines had done to Saul, [12] all the valiant men set out, traveled all night long, and took the body of Saul and the bodies of his sons from the wall of Beth-shan. They came to Jā'besh and burned them there. [13] Then they took their bones and buried them under the tamarisk tree in Jā'besh, and fasted seven days.

p Heb plural

2 SAMUEL

David Mourns for Saul and Jonathan

1 After the death of Saul, when David had returned from defeating the A·mal'e·kītes, David remained two days in Zik'lag. [2] On the third day, a man came from Saul's camp, with his clothes torn and dirt on his head. When he came to David, he fell to the ground and did obeisance. [3] David said to him, "Where have you come from?" He said to him, "I have escaped from the camp of Israel." [4] David said to him, "How did things go? Tell me!" He answered, "The army fled from the battle, but also many of the army fell and died; and Saul and his son Jonathan also died." [5] Then David asked the young man who was reporting to him, "How do you know that Saul and his son Jonathan died?" [6] The young man reporting to him said, "I happened to be on Mount Gil·bō'a; and there was Saul leaning on his spear, while the chariots and the horsemen drew close to him. [7] When he looked behind him, he saw me, and called to me. I answered, 'Here sir.' [8] And he said to me, 'Who are you?' I answered him, 'I am an A·mal'e·kīte.' [9] He said to me, 'Come, stand over me and kill me; for convulsions have seized me, and yet my life still lingers.' [10] So I stood over him, and killed him, for I knew that he could not live after he had fallen. I took the crown that was on his head and the armlet that was on his arm, and I have brought them here to my lord."

[11] Then David took hold of his clothes and tore them; and all the men who were with him did the same. [12] They mourned and wept, and fasted until evening for Saul and for his son Jonathan, and for the army of the LORD and for the house of Israel, because they had fallen by the sword. [13] David said to the young man who had reported to him, "Where do you come from?" He answered, "I am the son of a resident alien, an A·mal'-e·kīte." [14] David said to him, "Were you not afraid to lift your hand to destroy the LORD's anointed?" [15] Then David called one of the young men and said, "Come here and strike him down." So he struck him down and he died. [16] David said to him, "Your blood be on your head; for your own mouth has testified against you, saying, 'I have killed the LORD's anointed.' "

17 David intoned this lamentation

over Saul and his son Jonathan. ¹⁸(He ordered that The Song of the Bow*a* be taught to the people of Judah; it is written in the Book of Jash′ar.) He said:

¹⁹ Your glory, O Israel, lies slain
    upon your high places!
  How the mighty have fallen!
²⁰ Tell it not in Gath,
    proclaim it not in the streets of
    Ash′ke·lon;
  or the daughters of the
    Phi·lis′tines will rejoice,
  the daughters of the
    uncircumcised will exult.

²¹ You mountains of Gil·bo′a,
  let there be no dew or rain
    upon you,
  nor bounteous fields!*b*
  For there the shield of the
    mighty was defiled,
  the shield of Saul, anointed
    with oil no more.

²² From the blood of the slain,
    from the fat of the mighty,
  the bow of Jonathan did not turn
    back,
  nor the sword of Saul return
    empty.

²³ Saul and Jonathan, beloved and
    lovely!
  In life and in death they were
    not divided;
  they were swifter than eagles,
    they were stronger than lions.

²⁴ O daughters of Israel, weep over
    Saul,
  who clothed you with crimson,
    in luxury,
  who put ornaments of gold on
    your apparel.

²⁵ How the mighty have fallen
  in the midst of the battle!

  Jonathan lies slain upon your
    high places.
²⁶ I am distressed for you, my
    brother Jonathan;
  greatly beloved were you to me;
  your love to me was
    wonderful,
  passing the love of women.

²⁷ How the mighty have fallen,
  and the weapons of war
    perished!

David Anointed King of Judah

2 After this David inquired of the LORD, "Shall I go up into any of the cities of Judah?" The LORD said to him, "Go up." David said, "To which shall I go up?" He said, "To He′bron." ²So David went up there, along with his two wives, A·hin′o·am of Jez′re·el, and Ab′i·gail the widow of Na′bal of Car′mel. ³David brought up the men who were with him, every one with his household; and they settled in the towns of He′bron. ⁴Then the people of Judah came, and there they anointed David king over the house of Judah.

When they told David, "It was the people of Ja′besh-gil′e·ad who buried Saul," ⁵David sent messengers to the people of Ja′besh-gil′e·ad, and said to them, "May you be blessed by the LORD, because you showed this loyalty to Saul your lord, and buried him! ⁶Now may the LORD show steadfast love and faithfulness to you! And I too will reward you because you have done this thing. ⁷Therefore let your hands be strong, and be valiant; for Saul your lord is dead, and the house of Judah has anointed me king over them."

Ishbaal King of Israel

8 But Abner son of Ner, commander of Saul's army, had taken Ish′-ba·al*c* son of Saul, and brought him over to Ma·ha·na′im. ⁹He made him king over Gil′e·ad, the Ash′ur·ites, Jez′re·el, E′phra·im, Benjamin, and over all Israel. ¹⁰Ish′ba·al,*c* Saul's son, was forty years old when he began to reign over Israel, and he reigned two years. But the house of Judah followed David. ¹¹The time that David was king in He′bron over the house of Judah was seven years and six months.

The Battle of Gibeon

12 Abner son of Ner, and the servants of Ish′ba·al*c* son of Saul, went out from Ma·ha·na′im to Gib′e·on. ¹³Jo′ab son of Ze·ru′i·ah, and the servants of David, went out and met them at the pool of Gib′e·on. One group sat on one side of the pool, while the other sat on the other side of the pool. ¹⁴Abner said to Jo′ab, "Let the young men come forward and have a contest be-

---

*a*Heb *that The Bow*   *b*Meaning of Heb uncertain   *c*Gk Compare 1 Chr 8.33; 9.39: Heb *Ish-bosheth,* "man of shame" fore us." Jō'ab said, "Let them come forward." [15] So they came forward and were counted as they passed by, twelve for Benjamin and Ish'bā·al[d] son of Saul, and twelve of the servants of David. [16] Each grasped his opponent by the head, and thrust his sword in his opponent's side; so they fell down together. Therefore that place was called Hel'kath-haz·zū'rim,[e] which is at Gib'ē·on. [17] The battle was very fierce that day; and Abner and the men of Israel were beaten by the servants of David.

18 The three sons of Ze·rū'i·ah were there, Jō'ab, A·bi'shai, and As'a·hel. Now As'a·hel was as swift of foot as a wild gazelle. [19] As'a·hel pursued Abner, turning neither to the right nor to the left as he followed him. [20] Then Abner looked back and said, "Is it you, As'a·hel?" He answered, "Yes, it is." [21] Abner said to him, "Turn to your right or to your left, and seize one of the young men, and take his spoil." But As'a·hel would not turn away from following him. [22] Abner said again to As'a·hel, "Turn away from following me; why should I strike you to the ground? How then could I show my face to your brother Jō'ab?" [23] But he refused to turn away. So Abner struck him in the stomach with the butt of his spear, so that the spear came out at his back. He fell there, and died where he lay. And all those who came to the place where As'a·hel had fallen and died, stood still.

24 But Jō'ab and A·bi'shai pursued Abner. As the sun was going down they came to the hill of Am'mah, which lies before Gī'ah on the way to the wilderness of Gib'ē·on. [25] The Ben'ja·min·ites rallied around Abner and formed a single band; they took their stand on the top of a hill. [26] Then Abner called to Jō'ab, "Is the sword to keep devouring forever? Do you not know that the end will be bitter? How long will it be before you order your people to turn from the pursuit of their kinsmen?" [27] Jō'ab said, "As God lives, if you had not spoken, the people would have continued to pursue their kinsmen, not stopping until morning." [28] Jō'ab sounded the trumpet and all the people stopped; they no longer pursued Israel or engaged in battle any further.

29 Abner and his men traveled all that night through the Ar'a·bah; they crossed the Jordan, and, marching the whole forenoon,[f] they came to Mā·ha·nā'im. [30] Jō'ab returned from the pursuit of Abner; and when he had gathered all the people together, there were missing of David's servants nineteen men besides As'a·hel. [31] But the servants of David had killed of Benjamin three hundred sixty of Abner's men. [32] They took up As'a·hel and buried him in the tomb of his father, which was at Bethlehem. Jō'ab and his men marched all night, and the day broke upon them at Hē'bron.

Abner Defects to David

3 There was a long war between the house of Saul and the house of David; David grew stronger and stronger, while the house of Saul became weaker and weaker.

2 Sons were born to David at Hē'bron: his firstborn was Am'non, of A·hin'ō·am of Jez're·el; [3] his second, Chil'ē·ab, of Ab'i·gāil the widow of Nā'bal of Car'mel; the third, Ab'sa·lom son of Mā'a·cah, daughter of King Tal'mai of Gē'shur; [4] the fourth, Ad·o·nī'jah son of Hag'gith; the fifth, Sheph·a·tī'ah son of A·bī'tal; [5] and the sixth, Ith're·am, of David's wife Eg'lah. These were born to David in Hē'bron.

6 While there was war between the house of Saul and the house of David, Abner was making himself strong in the house of Saul. [7] Now Saul had a concubine whose name was Riz'pah daughter of Ā'i·ah. And Ish'bā·al[g] said to Abner, "Why have you gone in to my father's concubine?" [8] The words of Ish'bā·al[d] made Abner very angry; he said, "Am I a dog's head for Judah? Today I keep showing loyalty to the house of your father Saul, to his brothers, and to his friends, and have not given you into the hand of David; and yet you charge me now with a crime concerning this woman. [9] So may God do to Abner and so may he add to it! For just what the LORD has sworn to David, that will I accomplish for him, [10] to transfer the kingdom from the house of Saul, and set up the throne of David over Israel and over Judah, from Dan to Bē'er-shē'ba." [11] And Ish'bā·al[g] could not answer Abner another word, because he feared him.

---

[d]Gk Compare 1 Chr 8.33; 9.39: Heb *Ish-bosheth*, "man of shame"   [e]That is *Field of Sword-edges*   [f]Meaning of Heb uncertain   [g]Heb *And he*

12 Abner sent messengers to David at Hē′bron,[h] saying, "To whom does the land belong? Make your covenant with me, and I will give you my support to bring all Israel over to you." [13] He said, "Good; I will make a covenant with you. But one thing I require of you: you shall never appear in my presence unless you bring Saul's daughter Mī′chal when you come to see me." [14] Then David sent messengers to Saul's son Ish′bā·al,[i] saying, "Give me my wife Mī′chal, to whom I became engaged at the price of one hundred foreskins of the Phi·lis′tines." [15] Ish′bā·al[i] sent and took her from her husband Pal′ti·el the son of Lā′ish. [16] But her husband went with her, weeping as he walked behind her all the way to Ba·hū′rim. Then Abner said to him, "Go back home!" So he went back.

17 Abner sent word to the elders of Israel, saying, "For some time past you have been seeking David as king over you. [18] Now then bring it about; for the LORD has promised David: Through my servant David I will save my people Israel from the hand of the Phi·lis′tines, and from all their enemies." [19] Abner also spoke directly to the Ben′ja·min·ites; then Abner went to tell David at Hē′bron all that Israel and the whole house of Benjamin were ready to do. 20 When Abner came with twenty men to David at Hē′bron, David made a feast for Abner and the men who were with him. [21] Abner said to David, "Let me go and rally all Israel to my lord the king, in order that they may make a covenant with you, and that you may reign over all that your heart desires." So David dismissed Abner, and he went away in peace.

Abner Is Killed by Joab

22 Just then the servants of David arrived with Jō′ab from a raid, bringing much spoil with them. But Abner was not with David at Hē′bron, for David[i] had dismissed him, and he had gone away in peace. [23] When Jō′ab and all the army that was with him came, it was told Jō′ab, "Abner son of Ner came to the king, and he has dismissed him, and he has gone away in peace." [24] Then Jō′ab went to the king and said, "What have you done? Abner came to you; why did you dismiss him, so that he got away? [25] You know that Abner son of Ner came to deceive you,

and to learn your comings and goings and to learn all that you are doing."

26 When Jō′ab came out from David's presence, he sent messengers after Abner, and they brought him back from the cistern of Sī′rah; but David did not know about it. [27] When Abner returned to Hē′bron, Jō′ab took him aside in the gateway to speak with him privately, and there he stabbed him in the stomach. So he died for shedding[k] the blood of As′a·hel, Jō′ab's[i] brother. [28] Afterward, when David heard of it, he said, "I and my kingdom are forever guiltless before the LORD for the blood of Abner son of Ner. [29] May the guilt[m] fall on the head of Jō′ab, and on all his father's house; and may the house of Jō′ab never be without one who has a discharge, or who is leprous,[n] or who holds a spindle, or who falls by the sword, or who lacks food!" [30] So Jō′ab and his brother A·bi′shai murdered Abner because he had killed their brother As′a·hel in the battle at Gib′e·on.

31 Then David said to Jō′ab and to all the people who were with him, "Tear your clothes, and put on sackcloth, and mourn over Abner." And King David followed the bier. [32] They buried Abner at Hē′bron. The king lifted up his voice and wept at the grave of Abner, and all the people wept. [33] The king lamented for Abner, saying,

"Should Abner die as a fool
　　　dies?
34　Your hands were not bound,
　　　your feet were not fettered;
　　as one falls before the wicked
　　　you have fallen."

And all the people wept over him again. [35] Then all the people came to persuade David to eat something while it was still day; but David swore, saying, "So may God do to me, and more, if I taste bread or anything else before the sun goes down!" [36] All the people took notice of it, and it pleased them; just as everything the king did pleased all the people. [37] So all the people and all Israel understood that day that the king had no part in the killing of Abner son of Ner. [38] And the king said to his servants, "Do you not know that a

---

[h] Gk: Heb *where he was*
[i] Heb *Ish-bosheth*　　[j] Heb *he*
[k] Heb lacks *shedding*　　[l] Heb *his*
[m] Heb *May it*　　[n] A term for several skin diseases; precise meaning uncertain

prince and a great man has fallen this day in Israel? [39] Today I am powerless, even though anointed king; these men, the sons of Ze·ru'i·ah, are too violent for me. The LORD pay back the one who does wickedly in accordance with his wickedness!"

Ishbaal Assassinated

4 When Saul's son Ish'ba·al[o] heard that Abner had died at He'bron, his courage failed, and all Israel was dismayed. [2] Saul's son had two captains of raiding bands; the name of the one was Ba'a·nah, and the name of the other Re'chab. They were sons of Rim'mon a Ben'ja·min·ite from Be·er'-oth—for Be·er'oth is considered to belong to Benjamin. [3] (Now the people of Be·er'oth had fled to Git'ta·im and are there as resident aliens to this day).

4 Saul's son Jonathan had a son who was crippled in his feet. He was five years old when the news about Saul and Jonathan came from Jez'-re·el. His nurse picked him up and fled; and, in her haste to flee, it happened that he fell and became lame. His name was Me·phib'o·sheth. [p]

5 Now the sons of Rim'mon the Be·er'oth·ite, Re'chab and Ba'a·nah, set out, and about the heat of the day they came to the house of Ish'ba·al,[q] while he was taking his noonday rest. [6] They came inside the house as though to take wheat, and they struck him in the stomach; then Re'chab and his brother Ba'a·nah escaped.[r] [7] Now they had come into the house while he was lying on his couch in his bedchamber; they attacked him, killed him, and beheaded him. Then they took his head and traveled by way of the Ar'-a·bah all night long. [8] They brought the head of Ish'ba·al[q] to David at He'bron and said to the king, "Here is the head of Ish'ba·al,[q] son of Saul, your enemy, who sought your life; the LORD has avenged my lord the king this day on Saul and on his offspring."

9 David answered Re'chab and his brother Ba'a·nah, the sons of Rim'mon the Be·er'oth·ite, "As the LORD lives, who has redeemed my life out of every adversity, [10] when the one who told me, 'See, Saul is dead,' thought he was bringing good news, I seized him and killed him at Zik'lag—this was the reward I gave him for his news. [11] How much more then, when wicked men have killed a righteous man on his bed in his own house! And now shall I not require his blood at your hand, and destroy you from the earth?" [12] So David commanded the young men, and they killed them; they cut off their hands and feet, and hung their bodies beside the pool at He'bron. But the head of Ish'ba·al[q] they took and buried in the tomb of Abner at He'bron.

David Anointed King of All Israel
(1 Chr 11.1–3)

5 Then all the tribes of Israel came to David at He'bron, and said, "Look, we are your bone and flesh. [2] For some time, while Saul was king over us, it was you who led out Israel and brought it in. The LORD said to you: It is you who shall be shepherd of my people Israel, you who shall be ruler over Israel." [3] So all the elders of Israel came to the king at He'bron; and King David made a covenant with them at He'bron before the LORD, and they anointed David king over Israel. [4] David was thirty years old when he began to reign, and he reigned forty years. [5] At He'bron he reigned over Judah seven years and six months; and at Jerusalem he reigned over all Israel and Judah thirty-three years.

Jerusalem Made Capital of the United Kingdom
(1 Chr 11.4–9; 14.1–7)

6 The king and his men marched to Jerusalem against the Jeb'u·sites, the inhabitants of the land, who said to David, "You will not come in here, even the blind and the lame will turn you back"—thinking, "David cannot come in here." [7] Nevertheless David took the stronghold of Zion, which is now the city of David. [8] David had said on that day, "Whoever would strike down the Jeb'u·sites, let him get up the water shaft to attack the lame and the blind, those whom David hates."[s] Therefore it is said, "The blind and the lame shall not come into the house." [9] David occupied the stronghold, and named it the city of David. David built the city all around from the Mil'lo inward. [10] And David became greater and greater, for the LORD, the God of hosts, was with him.

11 King Hiram of Tyre sent messen-

---

[o] Heb lacks *Ishbaal*   [p] In 1 Chr 8.34 and 9.40, *Merib-baal*   [q] Heb *Ish-bosheth*
[r] Meaning of Heb of verse 6 uncertain
[s] Another reading is *those who hate David*

gers to David, along with cedar trees, and carpenters and masons who built David a house. [12] David then perceived that the LORD had established him king over Israel, and that he had exalted his kingdom for the sake of his people Israel.

13 In Jerusalem, after he came from He'bron, David took more concubines and wives; and more sons and daughters were born to David. [14] These are the names of those who were born to him in Jerusalem: Sham'mu·a, Sho'bab, Nathan, Solomon, [15] Ib'har, E·lish'u·a, Ne'pheg, Ja·phi'a, [16] E·lish'a·ma, E·li'a·da, and E·liph'e·let.

Philistine Attack Repulsed
(1 Chr 14.8–17)

17 When the Phi·lis'tines heard that David had been anointed king over Israel, all the Phi·lis'tines went up in search of David; but David heard about it and went down to the stronghold. [18] Now the Phi·lis'tines had come and spread out in the valley of Reph'a·im. [19] David inquired of the LORD, "Shall I go up against the Phi·lis'tines? Will you give them into my hand?" The LORD said to David, "Go up; for I will certainly give the Phi·lis'tines into your hand." [20] So David came to Ba'al-pe·ra'zim, and David defeated them there. He said, "The LORD has burst forth against[t] my enemies before me, like a bursting flood." Therefore that place is called Ba'al-pe·ra'zim.[u] [21] The Phi·lis'tines abandoned their idols there, and David and his men carried them away.

22 Once again the Phi·lis'tines came up, and were spread out in the valley of Reph'a·im. [23] When David inquired of the LORD, he said, "You shall not go up; go around to their rear, and come upon them opposite the balsam trees. [24] When you hear the sound of marching in the tops of the balsam trees, then be on the alert; for then the LORD has gone out before you to strike down the army of the Phi·lis'tines." [25] David did just as the LORD had commanded him; and he struck down the Phi·lis'tines from Ge'ba all the way to Ge'zer.

David Brings the Ark to Jerusalem
(1 Chr 13.1–14; 15.25—16.3)

6 David again gathered all the chosen men of Israel, thirty thousand. [2] David and all the people with him set out and went from Ba'a·le-ju'dah, to bring up from there the ark of God, which is called by the name of the LORD of hosts who is enthroned on the cherubim. [3] They carried the ark of God on a new cart, and brought it out of the house of A·bin'a·dab, which was on the hill. Uz'zah and A·hi'o,[v] the sons of A·bin'a·dab, were driving the new cart [4] with the ark of God;[w] and A·hi'o[v] went in front of the ark. [5] David and all the house of Israel were dancing before the LORD with all their might, with songs[x] and lyres and harps and tambourines and castanets and cymbals.

6 When they came to the threshing floor of Na'con, Uz'zah reached out his hand to the ark of God and took hold of it, for the oxen shook it. [7] The anger of the LORD was kindled against Uz'zah; and God struck him there because he reached out his hand to the ark;[y] and he died there beside the ark of God. [8] David was angry because the LORD had burst forth with an outburst upon Uz'zah; so that place is called Per'ez-uz'zah,[z] to this day. [9] David was afraid of the LORD that day; he said, "How can the ark of the LORD come into my care?" [10] So David was unwilling to take the ark of the LORD into his care in the city of David; instead David took it to the house of O'bed-e'dom the Git'tite. [11] The ark of the LORD remained in the house of O'bed-e'dom the Git'tite three months; and the LORD blessed O'bed-e'dom and all his household.

12 It was told King David, "The LORD has blessed the household of O'bed-e'dom and all that belongs to him, because of the ark of God." So David went and brought up the ark of God from the house of O'bed-e'dom to the city of David with rejoicing; [13] and when those who bore the ark of the LORD had gone six paces, he sacrificed an ox and a fatling. [14] David danced before the LORD with all his might; David was girded with a linen ephod. [15] So David and all the house of Israel

---

[t] Heb paraz   [u] That is Lord of Bursting Forth   [v] Or and his brother
[w] Compare Gk: Heb and brought it out of the house of Abinadab, which was on the hill with the ark of God   [x] Q Ms Gk 1 Chr 13.8: Heb fir-trees   [y] 1 Chr 13.10 Compare Q Ms: Meaning of Heb uncertain   [z] That is Bursting Out Against Uzzah

brought up the ark of the LORD with shouting, and with the sound of the trumpet.

16 As the ark of the LORD came into the city of David, Mi′chal daughter of Saul looked out of the window, and saw King David leaping and dancing before the LORD; and she despised him in her heart.

17 They brought in the ark of the LORD, and set it in its place, inside the tent that David had pitched for it; and David offered burnt offerings and offerings of well-being before the LORD. [18]When David had finished offering the burnt offerings and the offerings of well-being, he blessed the people in the name of the LORD of hosts, [19]and distributed food among all the people, the whole multitude of Israel, both men and women, to each a cake of bread, a portion of meat, [a] and a cake of raisins. Then all the people went back to their homes.

20 David returned to bless his household. But Mi′chal the daughter of Saul came out to meet David, and said, "How the king of Israel honored himself today, uncovering himself today before the eyes of his servants' maids, as any vulgar fellow might shamelessly uncover himself!" [21]David said to Mi′chal, "It was before the LORD, who chose me in place of your father and all his household, to appoint me as prince over Israel, the people of the LORD, that I have danced before the LORD. [22]I will make myself yet more contemptible than this, and I will be abased in my own eyes; but by the maids of whom you have spoken, by them I shall be held in honor." [23]And Mi′chal the daughter of Saul had no child to the day of her death.

God's Covenant with David
(1 Chr 17.1–15)

7 Now when the king was settled in his house, and the LORD had given him rest from all his enemies around him, [2]the king said to the prophet Nathan, "See now, I am living in a house of cedar, but the ark of God stays in a tent." [3]Nathan said to the king, "Go, do all that you have in mind; for the LORD is with you."

4 But that same night the word of the LORD came to Nathan: [5]Go and tell my servant David: Thus says the LORD: Are you the one to build me a house to live in? [6]I have not lived in a house since the day I brought up the people of Israel from Egypt to this day, but I have been moving about in a tent and a tabernacle. [7]Wherever I have moved about among all the people of Israel, did I ever speak a word with any of the tribal leaders [b] of Israel, whom I commanded to shepherd my people Israel, saying, "Why have you not built me a house of cedar?" [8]Now therefore thus you shall say to my servant David: Thus says the LORD of hosts: I took you from the pasture, from following the sheep to be prince over my people Israel; [9]and I have been with you wherever you went, and have cut off all your enemies from before you; and I will make for you a great name, like the name of the great ones of the earth. [10]And I will appoint a place for my people Israel and will plant them, so that they may live in their own place, and be disturbed no more; and evildoers shall afflict them no more, as formerly, [11]from the time that I appointed judges over my people Israel; and I will give you rest from all your enemies. Moreover the LORD declares to you that the LORD will make you a house. [12]When your days are fulfilled and you lie down with your ancestors, I will raise up your offspring after you, who shall come forth from your body, and I will establish his kingdom. [13]He shall build a house for my name, and I will establish the throne of his kingdom forever. [14]I will be a father to him, and he shall be a son to me. When he commits iniquity, I will punish him with a rod such as mortals use, with blows inflicted by human beings. [15]But I will not take [c] my steadfast love from him, as I took it from Saul, whom I put away from before you. [16]Your house and your kingdom shall be made sure forever before me; [d] your throne shall be established forever. [17]In accordance with all these words and with all this vision, Nathan spoke to David.

David's Prayer
(1 Chr 17.16–27)

18 Then King David went in and sat before the LORD, and said, "Who am I, O Lord GOD, and what is my house, that you have brought me thus far? [19]And yet this was a small thing in

---

[a]Vg: Meaning of Heb uncertain
[b]Or *any of the tribes*   [c]Gk Syr Vg
1 Chr 17.13: Heb *shall not depart*
[d]Gk Heb Mss: MT *before you*; Compare 2 Sam 7.26, 29

your eyes, O Lord GOD; you have spoken also of your servant's house for a great while to come. May this be instruction for the people,[e] O Lord GOD! [20] And what more can David say to you? For you know your servant, O Lord GOD! [21] Because of your promise, and according to your own heart, you have wrought all this greatness, so that your servant may know it. [22] Therefore you are great, O LORD God; for there is no one like you, and there is no God besides you, according to all that we have heard with our ears. [23] Who is like your people, like Israel? Is there another[f] nation on earth whose God went to redeem it as a people, and to make a name for himself, doing great and awesome things for them,[g] by driving out[h] before his people nations and their gods?[i] [24] And you established your people Israel for yourself to be your people forever; and you, O LORD, became their God. [25] And now, O LORD God, as for the word that you have spoken concerning your servant and concerning his house, confirm it forever; do as you have promised. [26] Thus your name will be magnified forever in the saying, 'The LORD of hosts is God over Israel'; and the house of your servant David will be established before you. [27] For you, O LORD of hosts, the God of Israel, have made this revelation to your servant, saying, 'I will build you a house'; therefore your servant has found courage to pray this prayer to you. [28] And now, O Lord GOD, you are God, and your words are true, and you have promised this good thing to your servant; [29] now therefore may it please you to bless the house of your servant, so that it may continue forever before you; for you, O Lord GOD, have spoken, and with your blessing shall the house of your servant be blessed forever."

David's Wars
(1 Chr 18.1–13)

8 Some time afterward, David attacked the Phi·lis'tines and subdued them; David took Meth'eg·am'-mah out of the hand of the Phi·lis'tines.

2 He also defeated the Mō'ab·ītes and, making them lie down on the ground, measured them off with a cord; he measured two lengths of cord for those who were to be put to death, and one length[j] for those who were to be spared. And the Mō'ab·ītes became

servants to David and brought tribute.

3 David also struck down King Had·a·dē'zer son of Rē'hob of Zō'bah, as he went to restore his monument[k] at the river Euphrates. [4] David took from him one thousand seven hundred horsemen, and twenty thousand foot soldiers. David hamstrung all the chariot horses, but left enough for a hundred chariots. [5] When the Ar·a·mē'ans of Damascus came to help King Had·a·dē'zer of Zō'bah, David killed twenty-two thousand men of the Ar·a·mē'ans. [6] Then David put garrisons among the Ar·a·mē'ans of Damascus; and the Ar·a·mē'ans became servants to David and brought tribute. The LORD gave victory to David wherever he went. [7] David took the gold shields that were carried by the servants of Had·a·dē'zer, and brought them to Jerusalem. [8] From Bē'tah and from Be·rō'thaī, towns of Had·a·dē'zer, King David took a great amount of bronze.

9 When King Tō'ī of Hā'math heard that David had defeated the whole army of Had·a·dē'zer, [10] Tō'ī sent his son Jō'ram to King David, to greet him and to congratulate him because he had fought against Had·a·dē'zer and defeated him. Now Had·a·dē'zer had often been at war with Tō'ī. Jō'ram brought with him articles of silver, gold, and bronze; [11] these also King David dedicated to the LORD, together with the silver and gold that he dedicated from all the nations he subdued, [12] from Ē'dom, Mō'ab, the Am'mon·ites, the Phi·lis'tines, Am'a·lek, and from the spoil of King Had·a·dē'zer son of Rē'hob of Zō'bah.

13 David won a name for himself. When he returned, he killed eighteen thousand Ē'dom·ites[l] in the Valley of Salt. [14] He put garrisons in Ē'dom; throughout all Ē'dom he put garrisons, and all the Ē'dom·ītes became David's servants. And the LORD gave victory to David wherever he went.

---

e Meaning of Heb uncertain   f Gk: Heb one   g Heb you   h Gk 1 Chr 17.21: Heb for your land   i Cn: Heb before your people, whom you redeemed for yourself from Egypt, nations and its gods   j Heb one full length   k Compare 1 Sam 15.12 and 2 Sam 18.18   l Gk: Heb returned from striking down eighteen thousand Arameans

David's Officers
(1 Chr 18.14–17)

15 So David reigned over all Israel; and David administered justice and equity to all his people. [16] Jō'ab son of Ze·rū'i·ah was over the army; Je·hosh'a·phat son of A·hī'lud was recorder; [17] Zā'dok son of A·hī'tub and A·him'e·lech son of A·bī'a·thar were priests; Se·rāi'ah was secretary; [18] Be·nā'i·ah son of Je·hoi'a·da was over[m] the Cher'e·thites and the Pel'eth·ites; and David's sons were priests.

David's Kindness to Mephibosheth

9 David asked, "Is there still anyone left of the house of Saul to whom I may show kindness for Jonathan's sake?" [2] Now there was a servant of the house of Saul whose name was Zī'ba, and he was summoned to David. The king said to him, "Are you Zī'ba?" And he said, "At your service!" [3] The king said, "Is there anyone remaining of the house of Saul to whom I may show the kindness of God?" Zī'ba said to the king, "There remains a son of Jonathan; he is crippled in his feet." [4] The king said to him, "Where is he?" Zī'ba said to the king, "He is in the house of Mā'chir son of Am'mi·el, at Lō-dē'bar." [5] Then King David sent and brought him from the house of Mā'chir son of Am'mi·el, at Lō-dē'bar. [6] Me·phib'o·sheth[n] son of Jonathan son of Saul came to David, and fell on his face and did obeisance. David said, "Me·phib'o·sheth!" He answered, "I am your servant." [7] David said to him, "Do not be afraid, for I will show you kindness for the sake of your father Jonathan; I will restore to you all the land of your grandfather Saul, and you yourself shall eat at my table always." [8] He did obeisance and said, "What is your servant, that you should look upon a dead dog such as I?"

9 Then the king summoned Saul's servant Zī'ba, and said to him, "All that belonged to Saul and to all his house I have given to your master's grandson. [10] You and your sons and your servants shall till the land for him, and shall bring in the produce, so that your master's grandson may have food to eat; but your master's grandson Me·phib'o·sheth[n] shall always eat at my table." Now Zī'ba had fifteen sons and twenty servants. [11] Then Zī'ba said to the king, "According to all that my lord the king commands his servant, so your servant will do." Me·phib'o·sheth[n] ate at David's[o] table, like one of the king's sons. [12] Me·phib'o·sheth[n] had a young son whose name was Mī'ca. And all who lived in Zī'ba's house became Me·phib'o·sheth's[p] servants. [13] Me·phib'o·sheth[n] lived in Jerusalem, for he always ate at the king's table. Now he was lame in both his feet.

The Ammonites and Arameans Are Defeated
(1 Chr 19.1–19)

10 Some time afterward, the king of the Am'mon·ites died, and his son Hā'nun succeeded him. [2] David said, "I will deal loyally with Hā'nun son of Nā'hash, just as his father dealt loyally with me." So David sent envoys to console him concerning his father. When David's envoys came into the land of the Am'mon·ites, [3] the princes of the Am'mon·ites said to their lord Hā'nun, "Do you really think that David is honoring your father just because he has sent messengers with condolences to you? Has not David sent his envoys to you to search the city, to spy it out, and to overthrow it?" [4] So Hā'nun seized David's envoys, shaved off half the beard of each, cut off their garments in the middle at their hips, and sent them away. [5] When David was told, he sent to meet them, for the men were greatly ashamed. The king said, "Remain at Jericho until your beards have grown, and then return."

6 When the Am'mon·ites saw that they had become odious to David, the Am'mon·ites sent and hired the Ar·a·mē'ans of Beth-rē'hob and the Ar·a·mē'ans of Zō'bah, twenty thousand foot soldiers, as well as the king of Mā'a·cah, one thousand men, and the men of Tob, twelve thousand men. [7] When David heard of it, he sent Jō'ab and all the army with the warriors. [8] The Am'mon·ites came out and drew up in battle array at the entrance of the gate; but the Ar·a·mē'ans of Zō'bah and of Rē'hob, and the men of Tob and Mā'a·cah, were by themselves in the open country.

9 When Jō'ab saw that the battle

---

[m] Syr Tg Vg 20.23; 1 Chr 18.17: Heb lacks *was over* [n] Or *Merib-baal*: See 4.4 note [o] Gk: Heb *my* [p] Or *Merib-baal's*: See 4.4 note

was set against him both in front and in the rear, he chose some of the picked men of Israel, and arrayed them against the Ar·a·mē′ans; [10]the rest of his men he put in the charge of his brother A·bi′shaī, and he arrayed them against the Am′mon·ites. [11]He said, "If the Ar·a·mē′ans are too strong for me, then you shall help me; but if the Am′mon·ites are too strong for you, then I will come and help you. [12]Be strong, and let us be courageous for the sake of our people, and for the cities of our God; and may the LORD do what seems good to him." [13]So Jō′ab and the people who were with him moved forward into battle against the Ar·a·mē′ans; and they fled before him. [14]When the Am′mon·ites saw that the Ar·a·mē′ans fled, they likewise fled before A·bi′shaī, and entered the city. Then Jō′ab returned from fighting against the Am′mon·ites, and came to Jerusalem.

15 But when the Ar·a·mē′ans saw that they had been defeated by Israel, they gathered themselves together. [16]Had·a·dē′zer sent and brought out the Ar·a·mē′ans who were beyond the Euphrates; and they came to Hē′lam, with Shō′bach the commander of the army of Had·a·dē′zer at their head. [17]When it was told David, he gathered all Israel together, and crossed the Jordan, and came to Hē′lam. The Ar·a·mē′ans arrayed themselves against David and fought with him. [18]The Ar·a·mē′ans fled before Israel; and David killed of the Ar·a·mē′ans seven hundred chariot teams, and forty thousand horsemen,[q] and wounded Shō′bach the commander of their army, so that he died there. [19]When all the kings who were servants of Had·a·dē′zer saw that they had been defeated by Israel, they made peace with Israel, and became subject to them. So the Ar·a·mē′ans were afraid to help the Am′mon·ites any more.

David Commits Adultery with Bathsheba

11 In the spring of the year, the time when kings go out to battle, David sent Jō′ab with his officers and all Israel with him; they ravaged the Am′mon·ites, and besieged Rab′-bah. But David remained at Jerusalem.

2 It happened, late one afternoon, when David rose from his couch and was walking about on the roof of the king's house, that he saw from the roof a woman bathing; the woman was very beautiful. [3]David sent someone to inquire about the woman. It was reported, "This is Bath·she′ba daughter of E·lī′am, the wife of U·rī′ah the Hit′tīte." [4]So David sent messengers to get her, and she came to him, and he lay with her. (Now she was purifying herself after her period.) Then she returned to her house. [5]The woman conceived; and she sent and told David, "I am pregnant."

6 So David sent word to Jō′ab, "Send me U·rī′ah the Hit′tīte." And Jō′ab sent U·rī′ah to David. [7]When U·rī′ah came to him, David asked how Jō′ab and the people fared, and how the war was going. [8]Then David said to U·rī′ah, "Go down to your house and wash your feet." U·rī′ah went out of the king's house, and there followed him a present from the king. [9]But U·rī′ah slept at the entrance of the king's house with all the servants of his lord, and did not go down to his house. [10]When they told David, "U·rī′ah did not go down to his house," David said to U·rī′ah, "You have just come from a journey. Why did you not go down to your house?" [11]U·rī′ah said to David, "The ark and Israel and Judah remain in booths;[r] and my lord Jō′ab and the servants of my lord are camping in the open field; shall I then go to my house, to eat and to drink, and to lie with my wife? As you live, and as your soul lives, I will not do such a thing." [12]Then David said to U·rī′ah, "Remain here today also, and tomorrow I will send you back." So U·rī′ah remained in Jerusalem that day. On the next day, [13]David invited him to eat and drink in his presence and made him drunk; and in the evening he went out to lie on his couch with the servants of his lord, but he did not go down to his house.

David Has Uriah Killed

14 In the morning David wrote a letter to Jō′ab, and sent it by the hand of U·rī′ah. [15]In the letter he wrote, "Set U·rī′ah in the forefront of the hardest fighting, and then draw back from him, so that he may be struck down and die." [16]As Jō′ab was besieging the city, he assigned U·rī′ah to the place where he knew there were valiant war-

[q]1 Chr 19.18 and some Gk Mss read *foot soldiers*   [r]Or *at Succoth*

riors. [17]The men of the city came out and fought with Jō′ab; and some of the servants of David among the people fell. Ū·rī′ah the Hit′tīte was killed as well. [18]Then Jō′ab sent and told David all the news about the fighting; [19]and he instructed the messenger, "When you have finished telling the king all the news about the fighting, [20]then, if the king's anger rises, and if he says to you, 'Why did you go so near the city to fight? Did you not know that they would shoot from the wall? [21]Who killed A·bim′e·lech son of Jer·ub·bā′al?[s] Did not a woman throw an upper millstone on him from the wall, so that he died at Thē′bez? Why did you go so near the wall?' then you shall say, 'Your servant Ū·rī′ah the Hit′tīte is dead too.'"

22 So the messenger went, and came and told David all that Jō′ab had sent him to tell. [23]The messenger said to David, "The men gained an advantage over us, and came out against us in the field; but we drove them back to the entrance of the gate. [24]Then the archers shot at your servants from the wall; some of the king's servants are dead; and your servant Ū·rī′ah the Hit′tīte is dead also." [25]David said to the messenger, "Thus you shall say to Jō′ab, 'Do not let this matter trouble you, for the sword devours now one and now another; press your attack on the city, and overthrow it.' And encourage him."

26 When the wife of Ū·rī′ah heard that her husband was dead, she made lamentation for him. [27]When the mourning was over, David sent and brought her to his house, and she became his wife, and bore him a son.

Nathan Condemns David

12 But the thing that David had done displeased the LORD, [1]and the LORD sent Nathan to David. He came to him, and said to him, "There were two men in a certain city, the one rich and the other poor. [2]The rich man had very many flocks and herds; [3]but the poor man had nothing but one little ewe lamb, which he had bought. He brought it up, and it grew up with him and with his children; it used to eat of his meager fare, and drink from his cup, and lie in his bosom, and it was like a daughter to him. [4]Now there came a traveler to the rich man, and he was loath to take one of his own flock or herd to prepare for the wayfarer

who had come to him, but he took the poor man's lamb, and prepared that for the guest who had come to him." [5]Then David's anger was greatly kindled against the man. He said to Nathan, "As the LORD lives, the man who has done this deserves to die; [6]he shall restore the lamb fourfold, because he did this thing, and because he had no pity."

7 Nathan said to David, "You are the man! Thus says the LORD, the God of Israel: I anointed you king over Israel, and I rescued you from the hand of Saul; [8]I gave you your master's house, and your master's wives into your bosom, and gave you the house of Israel and of Judah; and if that had been too little, I would have added as much more. [9]Why have you despised the word of the LORD, to do what is evil in his sight? You have struck down Ū·rī′ah the Hit′tīte with the sword, and have taken his wife to be your wife, and have killed him with the sword of the Am′mon·ites. [10]Now therefore the sword shall never depart from your house, for you have despised me, and have taken the wife of Ū·rī′ah the Hit′-tīte to be your wife. [11]Thus says the LORD: I will raise up trouble against you from within your own house; and I will take your wives before your eyes, and give them to your neighbor, and he shall lie with your wives in the sight of this very sun. [12]For you did it secretly; but I will do this thing before all Israel, and before the sun." [13]David said to Nathan, "I have sinned against the LORD." Nathan said to David, "Now the LORD has put away your sin; you shall not die. [14]Nevertheless, because by this deed you have utterly scorned the LORD,[t] the child that is born to you shall die." [15]Then Nathan went to his house.

Bathsheba's Child Dies

The LORD struck the child that Ū·rī′ah's wife bore to David, and it became very ill. [16]David therefore pleaded with God for the child; David fasted, and went in and lay all night on the ground. [17]The elders of his house stood beside him, urging him to rise from the ground; but he would not, nor did he eat food with them. [18]On the

---

[s] Gk Syr Judg 7.1: Heb *Jerubbesheth*
[t] Ancient scribal tradition: Compare 1 Sam 25.22 note: Heb *scorned the enemies of the LORD*

seventh day the child died. And the servants of David were afraid to tell him that the child was dead; for they said, "While the child was still alive, we spoke to him, and he did not listen to us; how then can we tell him the child is dead? He may do himself some harm." 19 But when David saw that his servants were whispering together, he perceived that the child was dead; and David said to his servants, "Is the child dead?" They said, "He is dead."

20 Then David rose from the ground, washed, anointed himself, and changed his clothes. He went into the house of the LORD, and worshiped; he then went to his own house; and when he asked, they set food before him and he ate. 21 Then his servants said to him, "What is this thing that you have done? You fasted and wept for the child while it was alive; but when the child died, you rose and ate food." 22 He said, "While the child was still alive, I fasted and wept; for I said, 'Who knows? The LORD may be gracious to me, and the child may live.' 23 But now he is dead; why should I fast? Can I bring him back again? I shall go to him, but he will not return to me."

Solomon Is Born

24 Then David consoled his wife Bath·shē′ba, and went to her, and lay with her; and she bore a son, and he named him Solomon. The LORD loved him, 25 and sent a message by the prophet Nathan; so he named him Jed·i·dī′ah,ᵘ because of the LORD.

The Ammonites Crushed
(1 Chr 20.1–3)

26 Now Jō′ab fought against Rab′bah of the Am′mon·ites, and took the royal city. 27 Jō′ab sent messengers to David, and said, "I have fought against Rab′bah; moreover, I have taken the water city. 28 Now, then, gather the rest of the people together, and encamp against the city, and take it; or I myself will take the city, and it will be called by my name." 29 So David gathered all the people together and went to Rab′bah, and fought against it and took it. 30 He took the crown of Mil′comᵛ from his head; the weight of it was a talent of gold, and in it was a precious stone; and it was placed on David's head. He also brought forth the spoil of the city, a very great amount. 31 He brought out the people who were in it, and set them

to work with saws and iron picks a iron axes, or sent them to the bri works. Thus he did to all the cities the Am′mon·ites. Then David and the people returned to Jerusalem.

Amnon and Tamar

13 Some time passed. David's s Ab′sa·lom had a beautiful s ter whose name was Tā′mar; and I vid's son Am′non fell in love with h 2 Am′non was so tormented that made himself ill because of his sis Tā′mar, for she was a virgin and seemed impossible to Am′non to anything to her. 3 But Am′non ha friend whose name was Jon′a·dab, t son of David's brother Shim′ē·ah; a Jon′a·dab was a very crafty man. 4 said to him, "O son of the king, w are you so haggard morning af morning? Will you not tell me?" A non said to him, "I love Tā′mar, brother Ab′sa·lom's sister." 5 Jo a·dab said to him, "Lie down on yc bed, and pretend to be ill; and wh your father comes to see you, say him, 'Let my sister Tā′mar come a give me something to eat, and prepa the food in my sight, so that I may s it and eat it from her hand.' " 6 So Ar non lay down, and pretended to be and when the king came to see hi Am′non said to the king, "Please my sister Tā′mar come and make couple of cakes in my sight, so tha may eat from her hand."

7 Then David sent home to Tā′m saying, "Go to your brother Am′no house, and prepare food for him." 8 Tā′mar went to her brother Amno house, where he was lying down. S took dough, kneaded it, made cakes his sight, and baked the cakes. 9 Th she took the pan and set themʷ (before him, but he refused to eat. Ar non said, "Send out everyone fro me." So everyone went out from hi 10 Then Am′non said to Tā′mar, "Bri the food into the chamber, so tha may eat from your hand." So Tā′m took the cakes she had made, a brought them into the chamber Am′non her brother. 11 But when s brought them near him to eat, he to hold of her, and said to her, "Come, with me, my sister." 12 She answer him, "No, my brother, do not force m

ᵘ That is *Beloved of the LORD*   ᵛ Gk S
l Kings 11.5, 33: Heb *their kings*
ʷ Heb *and poured*

for such a thing is not done in Israel; do not do anything so vile! [13] As for me, where could I carry my shame? And as for you, you would be as one of the scoundrels in Israel. Now therefore, I beg you, speak to the king; for he will not withhold me from you." [14] But he would not listen to her; and being stronger than she, he forced her and lay with her.

15 Then Am′non was seized with a very great loathing for her; indeed, his loathing was even greater than the lust he had felt for her. Am′non said to her, "Get out!" [16] But she said to him, "No, my brother; [x] for this wrong in sending me away is greater than the other that you did to me." But he would not listen to her. [17] He called the young man who served him and said, "Put this woman out of my presence, and bolt the door after her." [18] (Now she was wearing a long robe with sleeves; for this is how the virgin daughters of the king were clothed in earlier times. [y]) So his servant put her out, and bolted the door after her. [19] But Tā′mar put ashes on her head, and tore the long robe that she was wearing; she put her hand on her head, and went away, crying aloud as she went.

20 Her brother Ab′sa·lom said to her, "Has Am′non your brother been with you? Be quiet for now, my sister; he is your brother; do not take this to heart." So Tā′mar remained, a desolate woman, in her brother Ab′sa·lom's house. [21] When King David heard of all these things, he became very angry, but he would not punish his son Am′non, because he loved him, for he was his firstborn. [z] [22] But Ab′sa·lom spoke to Am′non neither good nor bad; for Ab′sa·lom hated Am′non, because he had raped his sister Tā′mar.

Absalom Avenges the Violation of His Sister

23 After two full years Ab′sa·lom had sheepshearers at Bā′al-ha′zor, which is near É′phra·im, and Ab′sa·lom invited all the king's sons. [24] Ab′sa·lom came to the king, and said, "Your servant has sheepshearers; will the king and his servants please go with your servant?" [25] But the king said to Ab′sa·lom, "No, my son, let us not all go, or else we will be burdensome to you." He pressed him, but he would not go but gave him his blessing. [26] Then Ab′sa·lom said, "If

not, please let my brother Am′non go with us." The king said to him, "Why should he go with you?" [27] But Ab′sa·lom pressed him until he let Am′non and all the king's sons go with him. Ab′sa·lom made a feast like a king's feast. [a] [28] Then Ab′sa·lom commanded his servants, "Watch when Am′non's heart is merry with wine, and when I say to you, 'Strike Am′non,' then kill him. Do not be afraid; have I not myself commanded you? Be courageous and valiant." [29] So the servants of Ab′sa·lom did to Am′non as Ab′sa·lom had commanded. Then all the king's sons rose, and each mounted his mule and fled.

30 While they were on the way, the report came to David that Ab′sa·lom had killed all the king's sons, and not one of them was left. [31] The king rose, tore his garments, and lay on the ground; and all his servants who were standing by tore their garments. [32] But Jon′a·dab, the son of David's brother Shim′e·ah, said, "Let not my lord suppose that they have killed all the young men the king's sons; Am′non alone is dead. This has been determined by Ab′sa·lom from the day Am′non [b] raped his sister Tā′mar. [33] Now therefore, do not let my lord the king take it to heart, as if all the king's sons were dead; for Am′non alone is dead."

34 But Ab′sa·lom fled. When the young man who kept watch looked up, he saw many people coming from the Hor·o·nā′im road [c] by the side of the mountain. [35] Jon′a·dab said to the king, "See, the king's sons have come; as your servant said, so it has come about." [36] As soon as he had finished speaking, the king's sons arrived, and raised their voices and wept; and the king and all his servants also wept very bitterly.

37 But Ab′sa·lom fled, and went to Tal′mai son of Am·mi′hud, king of Ge′shur. David mourned for his son day after day. [38] Ab′sa·lom, having fled to Ge′shur, stayed there three years. [39] And the heart of [d] the king went out,

---

[x] Cn Compare Gk Vg: Meaning of Heb uncertain   [y] Cn: Heb were clothed in robes   [z] Q Ms Gk: MT lacks but he would not punish . . . firstborn   [a] Gk Compare Q Ms: MT lacks Absalom made a feast like a king's feast   [b] Heb he   [c] Cn Compare Gk: Heb the road behind him   [d] Q Ms Gk: MT And David

yearning for Ab'sa·lom; for he was now consoled over the death of Am'non.

Absalom Returns to Jerusalem

14 Now Jō'ab son of Ze·rū'i·ah perceived that the king's mind was on Ab'sa·lom. 2 Jō'ab sent to Te·kō'a and brought from there a wise woman. He said to her, "Pretend to be a mourner; put on mourning garments, do not anoint yourself with oil, but behave like a woman who has been mourning many days for the dead. 3 Go to the king and speak to him as follows." And Jō'ab put the words into her mouth.

4 When the woman of Te·kō'a came to the king, she fell on her face to the ground and did obeisance, and said, "Help, O king!" 5 The king asked her, "What is your trouble?" She answered, "Alas, I am a widow; my husband is dead. 6 Your servant had two sons, and they fought with one another in the field; there was no one to part them, and one struck the other and killed him. 7 Now the whole family has risen against your servant. They say, 'Give up the man who struck his brother, so that we may kill him for the life of his brother whom he murdered, even if we destroy the heir as well.' Thus they would quench my one remaining ember, and leave to my husband neither name nor remnant on the face of the earth."

8 Then the king said to the woman, "Go to your house, and I will give orders concerning you." 9 The woman of Te·kō'a said to the king, "On me be the guilt, my lord the king, and on my father's house; let the king and his throne be guiltless." 10 The king said, "If anyone says anything to you, bring him to me, and he shall never touch you again." 11 Then she said, "Please, may the king keep the LORD your God in mind, so that the avenger of blood may kill no more, and my son not be destroyed." He said, "As the LORD lives, not one hair of your son shall fall to the ground."

12 Then the woman said, "Please let your servant speak a word to my lord the king." He said, "Speak." 13 The woman said, "Why then have you planned such a thing against the people of God? For in giving this decision the king convicts himself, inasmuch as the king does not bring his banished one home again. 14 We must all die; we are like water spilled on the ground, which cannot be gathered up. But God will not take away a life; he will devise plans so as not to keep an outcast banished forever from his presence.e 15 Now I have come to say this to my lord the king because the people have made me afraid; your servant thought 'I will speak to the king; it may be that the king will perform the request of his servant. 16 For the king will hear, and deliver his servant from the hand of the man who would cut both me and my son off from the heritage of God. 17 Your servant thought, 'The word of my lord the king will set me at rest'; for my lord the king is like the angel of God, discerning good and evil. The LORD your God be with you!"

18 Then the king answered the woman, "Do not withhold from me anything I ask you." The woman said, "Let my lord the king speak." 19 The king said, "Is the hand of Jō'ab with you in all this?" The woman answered and said, "As surely as you live, my lord the king, one cannot turn right or left from anything that my lord the king has said. For it was your servant Jō'ab who commanded me; it was he who put all these words into the mouth of your servant. 20 In order to change the course of affairs your servant Jō'ab did this. But my lord has wisdom like the wisdom of the angel of God to know all things that are on the earth."

21 Then the king said to Jō'ab, "Very well, I grant this; go, bring back the young man Ab'sa·lom." 22 Jō'ab prostrated himself with his face to the ground and did obeisance, and blessed the king; and Jō'ab said, "Today your servant knows that I have found favor in your sight, my lord the king, in that the king has granted the request of his servant." 23 So Jō'ab set off, went to Gē'shur, and brought Ab'sa·lom to Jerusalem. 24 The king said, "Let him go to his own house; he is not to come into my presence." So Ab'sa·lom went to his own house, and did not come into the king's presence.

David Forgives Absalom

25 Now in all Israel there was no one to be praised so much for his beauty as Ab'sa·lom; from the sole of his foot to the crown of his head there was no blemish in him. 26 When he cut the hair of his head (for at the end

e Meaning of Heb uncertain

every year he used to cut it; when it was heavy on him, he cut it), he weighed the hair of his head, two hundred shekels by the king's weight. [27]There were born to Ab'sa·lom three sons, and one daughter whose name was Ta'mar; she was a beautiful woman.

28 So Ab'sa·lom lived two full years in Jerusalem, without coming into the king's presence. [29]Then Ab'sa·lom sent for Jō'ab to send him to the king; but Jō'ab would not come to him. He sent a second time, but Jō'ab would not come. [30]Then he said to his servants, "Look, Jō'ab's field is next to mine, and he has barley there; go and set it on fire." So Ab'sa·lom's servants set the field on fire. [31]Then Jō'ab rose and went to Ab'sa·lom at his house, and said to him, "Why have your servants set my field on fire?" [32]Ab'sa·lom answered Jō'ab, "Look, I sent word to you: Come here, that I may send you to the king with the question, 'Why have I come from Gē'shur? It would be better for me to be there still.' Now let me go into the king's presence; if there is guilt in me, let him kill me!" [33]Then Jō'ab went to the king and told him; and he summoned Ab'sa·lom. So he came to the king and prostrated himself with his face to the ground before the king; and the king kissed Ab'sa·lom.

Absalom Usurps the Throne

15 After this Ab'sa·lom got himself a chariot and horses, and fifty men to run ahead of him. [2]Ab'sa·lom used to rise early and stand beside the road into the gate; and when anyone brought a suit before the king for judgment, Ab'sa·lom would call out and say, "From what city are you?" When the person said, "Your servant is of such and such a tribe in Israel," [3]Ab'sa·lom would say, "See, your claims are good and right; but there is no one deputed by the king to hear you." [4]Ab'sa·lom said moreover, "If only I were judge in the land! Then all who had a suit or cause might come to me, and I would give them justice." [5]Whenever people came near to do obeisance to him, he would put out his hand and take hold of them, and kiss them. [6]Thus Ab'sa·lom did to every Israelite who came to the king for judgment; so Ab'sa·lom stole the hearts of the people of Israel.

7 At the end of four[f] years Ab'sa·lom said to the king, "Please let me go to Hē'bron and pay the vow that I have made to the LORD. [8]For your servant made a vow while I lived at Gē'shur in Ar'am: If the LORD will indeed bring me back to Jerusalem, then I will worship the LORD in Hē'bron."[g] [9]The king said to him, "Go in peace." So he got up, and went to Hē'bron. [10]But Ab'sa·lom sent secret messengers throughout all the tribes of Israel, saying, "As soon as you hear the sound of the trumpet, then shout: Ab'sa·lom has become king at Hē'bron!" [11]Two hundred men from Jerusalem went with Ab'sa·lom; they were invited guests, and they went in their innocence, knowing nothing of the matter. [12]While Ab'sa·lom was offering the sacrifices, he sent for[h] A·hith'o·phel the Gī'lo·nīte, David's counselor, from his city Gī'lōh. The conspiracy grew in strength, and the people with Ab'sa·lom kept increasing.

David Flees from Jerusalem

13 A messenger came to David, saying, "The hearts of the Israelites have gone after Ab'sa·lom." [14]Then David said to all his officials who were with him at Jerusalem, "Get up! Let us flee, or there will be no escape for us from Ab'sa·lom. Hurry, or he will soon overtake us, and bring disaster down upon us, and attack the city with the edge of the sword." [15]The king's officials said to the king, "Your servants are ready to do whatever our lord the king decides." [16]So the king left, followed by all his household, except ten concubines whom he left behind to look after the house. [17]The king left, followed by all the people; and they stopped at the last house. [18]All his officials passed by him; and all the Cher'e·thītes, and all the Pel'eth·ites, and all the six hundred Git'tītes who had followed him from Gath, passed on before the king.

19 Then the king said to It'tai the Git'tīte, "Why are you also coming with us? Go back, and stay with the king; for you are a foreigner, and also an exile from your home. [20]You came only yesterday, and shall I today make you wander about with us, while I go wherever I can? Go back, and take your kinsfolk with you; and may the

f Gk Syr: Heb *forty*   *g* Gk Mss: Heb lacks *in Hebron*   *h* Or *he sent*

LORD show[i] steadfast love and faithfulness to you." 21 But It'tai answered the king, "As the LORD lives, and as my lord the king lives, wherever my lord the king may be, whether for death or for life, there also your servant will be." 22 David said to It'tai, "Go then, march on." So It'tai the Git'tite marched on, with all his men and all the little ones who were with him. 23 The whole country wept aloud as all the people passed by; the king crossed the Wadi Kid'ron, and all the people moved on toward the wilderness.

24 A·bi'a·thar came up, and Za'dok also, with all the Le'vites, carrying the ark of the covenant of God. They set down the ark of God, until the people had all passed out of the city. 25 Then the king said to Za'dok, "Carry the ark of God back into the city. If I find favor in the eyes of the LORD, he will bring me back and let me see both it and the place where it stays. 26 But if he says, 'I take no pleasure in you,' here I am, let him do to me what seems good to him." 27 The king also said to the priest Za'dok, "Look,[j] go back to the city in peace, you and A·bi'a·thar,[k] with your two sons, A·him'a·az your son, and Jonathan son of A·bi'a·thar. 28 See, I will wait at the fords of the wilderness until word comes from you to inform me." 29 So Za'dok and A·bi'a·thar carried the ark of God back to Jerusalem, and they remained there.

30 But David went up the ascent of the Mount of Olives, weeping as he went, with his head covered and walking barefoot; and all the people who were with him covered their heads and went up, weeping as they went. 31 David was told that A·hith'o·phel was among the conspirators with Ab'salom. And David said, "O LORD, I pray you, turn the counsel of A·hith'o·phel into foolishness."

Hushai Becomes David's Spy

32 When David came to the summit, where God was worshiped, Hu'shai the Ar'chite came to meet him with his coat torn and earth on his head. 33 David said to him, "If you go on with me, you will be a burden to me. 34 But if you return to the city and say to Ab'sa·lom, 'I will be your servant, O king; as I have been your father's servant in time past, so now I will be your servant,' then you will defeat for me the counsel of A·hith'o·phel. 35 The priests Za'dok and A·bi'a·thar will be with you there. So whatever you hear from the king's house, tell it to the priests Za'dok and A·bi'a·thar. 36 Their two sons are with them there, Za'dok's son A·him'a·az and A·bi'a·thar's son Jonathan; and by them you shall report to me everything you hear." 37 So Hu'shai, David's friend, came into the city, just as Ab'sa·lom was entering Jerusalem.

David's Adversaries

16 When David had passed a little beyond the summit, Zi'ba the servant of Me·phib'o·sheth[l] met him with a couple of donkeys saddled, carrying two hundred loaves of bread, one hundred bunches of raisins, one hundred of summer fruits, and one skin of wine. 2 The king said to Zi'ba, "Why have you brought these?" Zi'ba answered, "The donkeys are for the king's household to ride, the bread and summer fruit for the young men to eat, and the wine is for those to drink who faint in the wilderness." 3 The king said, "And where is your master's son?" Zi'ba said to the king, "He remains in Jerusalem; for he said, 'Today the house of Israel will give me back my grandfather's kingdom.'" 4 Then the king said to Zi'ba, "All that belonged to Me·phib'o·sheth[l] is now yours." Zi'ba said, "I do obeisance; let me find favor in your sight, my lord the king."

Shimei Curses David

5 When King David came to Ba·hu'rim, a man of the family of the house of Saul came out whose name was Shim'e·i son of Ge'ra; he came out cursing. 6 He threw stones at David and at all the servants of King David, now all the people and all the warriors were on his right and on his left. 7 Shim'e·i shouted while he cursed, "Out! Out! Murderer! Scoundrel! 8 The LORD has avenged on all of you the blood of the house of Saul, in whose place you have reigned; and the LORD has given the kingdom into the hand of your son Ab'sa·lom. See, disaster has overtaken you; for you are a man of blood."

9 Then A·bi'shai son of Ze·ru'i·a said to the king, "Why should this dead

---

[i]Gk Compare 2.6: Heb lacks *may the LORD show*   [j]Gk: Heb *Are you a seer Do you see?*   [k]Cn: Heb lacks *and Abiathar*   [l]Or *Merib-baal*: See 4.4 note

dog curse my lord the king? Let me go over and take off his head." [10]But the king said, "What have I to do with you, you sons of Ze·ru′i·ah? If he is cursing because the LORD has said to him, 'Curse David,' who then shall say, 'Why have you done so?'" [11]David said to A·bi′shaī and to all his servants, "My own son seeks my life; how much more now may this Ben′ja·min·ite! Let him alone, and let him curse; for the LORD has bidden him. [12]It may be that the LORD will look on my distress,[m] and the LORD will repay me with good for this cursing of me today." [13]So David and his men went on the road, while Shim′e·ī went along on the hillside opposite him and cursed as he went, throwing stones and flinging dust at him. [14]The king and all the people who were with him arrived weary at the Jordan;[n] and there he refreshed himself.

The Counsel of Ahithophel

15 Now Ab′sa·lom and all the Israelites[o] came to Jerusalem; A·hith′-o·phel was with him. [16]When Hu′shaī the Ar′chīte, David's friend, came to Ab′sa·lom, Hu′shaī said to Ab′sa·lom, "Long live the king! Long live the king!" [17]Ab′sa·lom said to Hu′shaī, "Is this your loyalty to your friend? Why did you not go with your friend?" [18]Hu′shaī said to Ab′sa·lom, "No; but the one whom the LORD and this people and all the Israelites have chosen, his I will be, and with him I will remain. [19]Moreover, whom should I serve? Should it not be his son? Just as I have served your father, so I will serve you."

20 Then Ab′sa·lom said to A·hith′-o·phel, "Give us your counsel; what shall we do?" [21]A·hith′o·phel said to Ab′sa·lom, "Go in to your father's concubines, the ones he has left to look after the house; and all Israel will hear that you have made yourself odious to your father, and the hands of all who are with you will be strengthened." [22]So they pitched a tent for Ab′sa·lom upon the roof; and Ab′sa·lom went in to his father's concubines in the sight of all Israel. [23]Now in those days the counsel that A·hith′o·phel gave was as if one consulted the oracle[p] of God; so all the counsel of A·hith′o·phel was esteemed, both by David and by Ab′sa·lom.

17 Moreover A·hith′o·phel said to Ab′sa·lom, "Let me choose twelve thousand men, and I will set out and pursue David tonight. [2]I will come upon him while he is weary and discouraged, and throw him into a panic; and all the people who are with him will flee. I will strike down only the king, [3]and I will bring all the people back to you as a bride comes home to her husband. You seek the life of only one man,[q] and all the people will be at peace." [4]The advice pleased Ab′sa·lom and all the elders of Israel.

The Counsel of Hushai

5 Then Ab′sa·lom said, "Call Hu′-shaī the Ar′chīte also, and let us hear too what he has to say." [6]When Hu′-shaī came to Ab′sa·lom, Ab′sa·lom said to him, "This is what A·hith′o·phel has said; shall we do as he advises? If not, you tell us." [7]Then Hu′shaī said to Ab′sa·lom, "This time the counsel that A·hith′o·phel has given is not good." [8]Hu′shaī continued, "You know that your father and his men are warriors, and that they are enraged, like a bear robbed of her cubs in the field. Besides, your father is expert in war; he will not spend the night with the troops. [9]Even now he has hidden himself in one of the pits, or in some other place. And when some of our troops[r] fall at the first attack, whoever hears it will say, 'There has been a slaughter among the troops who follow Ab′sa·lom.' [10]Then even the valiant warrior, whose heart is like the heart of a lion, will utterly melt with fear; for all Israel knows that your father is a warrior, and that those who are with him are valiant warriors. [11]But my counsel is that all Israel be gathered to you, from Dan to Be′er-she′ba, like the sand by the sea for multitude, and that you go to battle in person. [12]So we shall come upon him in whatever place he may be found, and we shall light on him as the dew falls on the ground; and he will not survive, nor will any of those with him. [13]If he withdraws into a city, then all Israel will bring ropes to that city, and we shall drag it into the valley, until not even a pebble is to be found there." [14]Ab′sa·lom and all the men of Israel said, "The counsel of Hu′shaī the Ar′-

---

[m]Gk Vg: Heb *iniquity*   [n]Gk: Heb lacks *at the Jordan*   [o]Gk: Heb *all the people, the men of Israel*   [p]Heb *word*
[q]Gk: Heb *like the return of the whole (is) the man whom you seek*   [r]Gk Mss: Heb *some of them*

chīte is better than the counsel of A·hith'o·phel." For the LORD had ordained to defeat the good counsel of A·hith'o·phel, so that the LORD might bring ruin on Ab'sa·lom.

Hushai Warns David to Escape

15 Then Hū'shaī said to the priests Za'dok and A·bī'a·thar, "Thus and so did A·hith'o·phel counsel Ab'sa·lom and the elders of Israel; and thus and so I have counseled. 16 Therefore send quickly and tell David, 'Do not lodge tonight at the fords of the wilderness, but by all means cross over; otherwise the king and all the people who are with him will be swallowed up.'" 17 Jonathan and A·him'a·az were waiting at En-rō'gel; a servant-girl used to go and tell them, and they would go and tell King David; for they could not risk being seen entering the city. 18 But a boy saw them, and told Ab'sa·lom; so both of them went away quickly, and came to the house of a man at Ba·hū'-rim, who had a well in his courtyard; and they went down into it. 19 The man's wife took a covering, stretched it over the well's mouth, and spread out grain on it; and nothing was known of it. 20 When Ab'sa·lom's servants came to the woman at the house, they said, "Where are A·him'a·az and Jonathan?" The woman said to them, "They have crossed over the brook s of water." And when they had searched and could not find them, they returned to Jerusalem.

21 After they had gone, the men came up out of the well, and went and told King David. They said to David, "Go and cross the water quickly; for thus and so has A·hith'o·phel counseled against you." 22 So David and all the people who were with him set out and crossed the Jordan; by daybreak not one was left who had not crossed the Jordan.

23 When A·hith'o·phel saw that his counsel was not followed, he saddled his donkey and went off home to his own city. He set his house in order, and hanged himself; he died and was buried in the tomb of his father.

24 Then David came to Mā-ha·nā'im, while Ab'sa·lom crossed the Jordan with all the men of Israel. 25 Now Ab'sa·lom had set A·mā'sa over the army in the place of Jō'ab. A·mā'sa was the son of a man named Ith'ra the Ish'ma·el·īte, t who had married Ab'i·gāl daughter of Nā'hash, sister of Ze·rū'i·ah, Jō'ab's mother. 26 T Israelites and Ab'sa·lom encamped the land of Gil'e·ad.

27 When David came to Mā·h na'im, Shō'bī son of Na'hash fro Rab'bah of the Am'mon·ites, and Mā chir son of Am'mi·el from Lō-dē'ba and Bar·zil'laī the Gil'e·ad·īte fro Rō'ge·lim, 28 brought beds, basins, a earthen vessels, wheat, barley, me parched grain, beans and lentils 29 honey and curds, sheep, and chee from the herd, for David and the pe ple with him to eat; for they said, "T troops are hungry and weary a thirsty in the wilderness."

The Defeat and Death of Absalom

18 Then David mustered the m who were with him, and s over them commanders of thousan and commanders of hundreds. 2 A David divided the army into thr groups: v one third under the co mand of Jō'ab, one third under t command of A·bi'shaī son of Ze·r i·ah, Jō'ab's brother, and one third u der the command of It'taī the Git'tī The king said to them, "I myself w also go out with you." 3 But the m said, "You shall not go out. For if flee, they will not care about us. If ha of us die, they will not care about But you are worth ten thousand of us therefore it is better that you send help from the city." 4 The king said them, "Whatever seems best to yo will do." So the king stood at the si of the gate, while all the army march out by hundreds and by thousand 5 The king ordered Jō'ab and A·bi'sh and It'taī, saying, "Deal gently for n sake with the young man Ab'sa·lon And all the people heard when t king gave orders to all the comman ers concerning Ab'sa·lom.

6 So the army went out into the fie against Israel; and the battle w fought in the forest of E'phra·im. 7 T men of Israel were defeated there the servants of David, and the slaug ter there was great on that day, twen thousand men. 8 The battle spread ov the face of all the country; and the fo

s Meaning of Heb uncertain   t 1 Chr 2.17: Heb Israelite   u Heb and lentils and parched grain   v Gk: Heb sent forth the army   w Gk Vg Symmachus: Heb for now there are ten thousand such as we est claimed more victims that day than the sword.

9 Ab'sa·lom happened to meet the servants of David. Ab'sa·lom was riding on his mule, and the mule went under the thick branches of a great oak. His head caught fast in the oak, and he was left hanging[x] between heaven and earth, while the mule that was under him went on. 10 A man saw it, and told Jō'ab, "I saw Ab'sa·lom hanging in an oak." 11 Jō'ab said to the man who told him, "What, you saw him! Why then did you not strike him there to the ground? I would have been glad to give you ten pieces of silver and a belt." 12 But the man said to Jō'ab, "Even if I felt in my hand the weight of a thousand pieces of silver, I would not raise my hand against the king's son; for in our hearing the king commanded you and A·bi'shaī and It'taī, saying: For my sake protect the young man Ab'sa·lom! 13 On the other hand, if I had dealt treacherously against his life[y] (and there is nothing hidden from the king), then you yourself would have stood aloof." 14 Jō'ab said, "I will not waste time like this with you." He took three spears in his hand, and thrust them into the heart of Ab'sa·lom, while he was still alive in the oak. 15 And ten young men, Jō'ab's armor-bearers, surrounded Ab'sa·lom and struck him, and killed him.

16 Then Jō'ab sounded the trumpet, and the troops came back from pursuing Israel, for Jō'ab restrained the troops. 17 They took Ab'sa·lom, threw him into a great pit in the forest, and raised over him a very great heap of stones. Meanwhile all the Israelites fled to their homes. 18 Now Ab'sa·lom in his lifetime had taken and set up for himself a pillar that is in the King's Valley, for he said, "I have no son to keep my name in remembrance"; he called the pillar by his own name. It is called Ab'sa·lom's Monument to this day.

David Hears of Absalom's Death

19 Then A·him'a·az son of Zā'dok said, "Let me run, and carry tidings to the king that the LORD has delivered him from the power of his enemies." 20 Jō'ab said to him, "You are not to carry tidings today; you may carry tidings another day, but today you shall not do so, because the king's son is dead." 21 Then Jō'ab said to a Cū'shīte,

"Go, tell the king what you have seen." The Cū'shīte bowed before Jō'ab, and ran. 22 Then A·him'a·az son of Zā'dok said again to Jō'ab, "Come what may, let me also run after the Cū'shīte." And Jō'ab said, "Why will you run, my son, seeing that you have no reward[z] for the tidings?" 23 "Come what may," he said, "I will run." So he said to him, "Run." Then A·him'a·az ran by the way of the Plain, and outran the Cū'shīte.

24 Now David was sitting between the two gates. The sentinel went up to the roof of the gate by the wall, and when he looked up, he saw a man running alone. 25 The sentinel shouted and told the king. The king said, "If he is alone, there are tidings in his mouth." He kept coming, and drew near. 26 Then the sentinel saw another man running; and the sentinel called to the gatekeeper and said, "See, another man running alone!" The king said, "He also is bringing tidings." 27 The sentinel said, "I think the running of the first one is like the running of A·him'a·az son of Zā'dok." The king said, "He is a good man, and comes with good tidings."

28 Then A·him'a·az cried out to the king, "All is well!" He prostrated himself before the king with his face to the ground, and said, "Blessed be the LORD your God, who has delivered up the men who raised their hand against my lord the king." 29 The king said, "Is it well with the young man Ab'sa·lom?" A·him'a·az answered, "When Jō'ab sent your servant,[a] I saw a great tumult, but I do not know what it was." 30 The king said, "Turn aside, and stand here." So he turned aside, and stood still.

31 Then the Cū'shīte came; and the Cū'shīte said, "Good tidings for my lord the king! For the LORD has vindicated you this day, delivering you from the power of all who rose up against you." 32 The king said to the Cū'shīte, "Is it well with the young man Ab'sa·lom?" The Cū'shīte answered, "May the enemies of my lord the king, and all who rise up to do you harm, be like that young man."

2
S
A
M
U
E
L

---

x Gk Syr Tg: Heb *was put*   y Another reading is *at the risk of my life*   z Meaning of Heb uncertain   a Heb *the king's servant, your servant*

David Mourns for Absalom

33[b] The king was deeply moved, and went up to the chamber over the gate, and wept; and as he went, he said, "O my son Ab′sa·lom, my son, my son Ab′sa·lom! Would I had died instead of you, O Ab′sa·lom, my son, my son!"

19 It was told Jō′ab, "The king is weeping and mourning for Ab′-sa·lom." 2 So the victory that day was turned into mourning for all the troops; for the troops heard that day, "The king is grieving for his son." 3 The troops stole into the city that day as soldiers steal in who are ashamed when they flee in battle. 4 The king covered his face, and the king cried with a loud voice, "O my son Ab′sa·lom, O Ab′sa·lom, my son, my son!" 5 Then Jō′ab came into the house to the king, and said, "Today you have covered with shame the faces of all your officers who have saved your life today, and the lives of your sons and your daughters, and the lives of your wives and your concubines, 6 for love of those who hate you and for hatred of those who love you. You have made it clear today that commanders and officers are nothing to you; for I perceive that if Ab′sa·lom were alive and all of us were dead today, then you would be pleased. 7 So go out at once and speak kindly to your servants; for I swear by the LORD, if you do not go, not a man will stay with you this night; and this will be worse for you than any disaster that has come upon you from your youth until now." 8 Then the king got up and took his seat in the gate. The troops were all told, "See, the king is sitting in the gate"; and all the troops came before the king.

David Recalled to Jerusalem

Meanwhile, all the Israelites had fled to their homes. 9 All the people were disputing throughout all the tribes of Israel, saying, "The king delivered us from the hand of our enemies, and saved us from the hand of the Phi·lis′-tines; and now he has fled out of the land because of Ab′sa·lom. 10 But Ab′-sa·lom, whom we anointed over us, is dead in battle. Now therefore why do you say nothing about bringing the king back?"

11 King David sent this message to the priests Zā′dok and A·bī′a·thar, "Say to the elders of Judah, 'Why should you be the last to bring the king

back to his house? The talk of all Isra has come to the king.[c] 12 You are m kin, you are my bone and my fles why then should you be the last bring back the king?' 13 And say A·mā′sa, 'Are you not my bone and m flesh? So may God do to me, and mor if you are not the commander of m army from now on, in place of Jō′ab.' 14 A·mā′sa[d] swayed the hearts of a the people of Judah as one, and the sent word to the king, "Return, bo you and all your servants." 15 So th king came back to the Jordan; and Ju dah came to Gil′gal to meet the kir and to bring him over the Jordan.

16 Shim′e·ī son of Gē′ra, the Ben ja·min·īte, from Ba·hū′rim, hurried come down with the people of Judah meet King David; 17 with him were thousand people from Benjamin. An Zī′ba, the servant of the house of Sau with his fifteen sons and his twent servants, rushed down to the Jorda ahead of the king, 18 while the crossin was taking place,[e] to bring over th king's household, and to do his plea sure.

David's Mercy to Shimei

Shim′e·ī son of Gē′ra fell down b fore the king, as he was about to cro the Jordan, 19 and said to the kin "May my lord not hold me guilty remember how your servant di wrong on the day my lord the king le Jerusalem; may the king not bear it mind. 20 For your servant knows that have sinned; therefore, see, I hav come this day, the first of all the hous of Joseph to come down to meet m lord the king." 21 A·bī′shaī son Ze·rū′i·ah answered, "Shall n Shim′e·ī be put to death for this, b cause he cursed the LORD's anointed′: 22 But David said, "What have I to d with you, you sons of Ze·rū′i·ah, tha you should today become an adve sary to me? Shall anyone be put t death in Israel this day? For do I n know that I am this day king over I rael?" 23 The king said to Shim′e "You shall not die." And the king gav him his oath.

David and Mephibosheth Meet

24 Me·phib′o·sheth[f] grandson o

---

[b] Ch 19.1 in Heb   [c] Gk: Heb to the kin to his house   [d] Heb he   [e] Cn: Heb the ford crossed   [f] Or Merib-baal: See 4.4 note

Saul came down to meet the king; he had not taken care of his feet, or trimmed his beard, or washed his clothes, from the day the king left until the day he came back in safety. 25 When he came from Jerusalem to meet the king, the king said to him, "Why did you not go with me, Me·phib′o·sheth?"g 26 He answered, "My lord, O king, my servant deceived me; for your servant said to him, 'Saddle a donkey for me,h so that I may ride on it and go with the king.' For your servant is lame. 27 He has slandered your servant to my lord the king. But my lord the king is like the angel of God; do therefore what seems good to you. 28 For all my father's house were doomed to death before my lord the king; but you set your servant among those who eat at your table. What further right have I, then, to appeal to the king?" 29 The king said to him, "Why speak any more of your affairs? I have decided: you and Zī′ba shall divide the land." 30 Me·phib′o·shethg said to the king, "Let him take it all, since my lord the king has arrived home safely."

David's Kindness to Barzillai

31 Now Bar·zil′laī the Gil′e·ad·īte had come down from Rō′ge·lim; he went on with the king to the Jordan, to escort him over the Jordan. 32 Bar·zil′laī was a very aged man, eighty years old. He had provided the king with food while he stayed at Mā·ha·nā′im, for he was a very wealthy man. 33 The king said to Bar·zil′laī, "Come over with me, and I will provide for you in Jerusalem at my side." 34 But Bar·zil′laī said to the king, "How many years have I still to live, that I should go up with the king to Jerusalem? 35 Today I am eighty years old; can I discern what is pleasant and what is not? Can your servant taste what he eats or what he drinks? Can I still listen to the voice of singing men and singing women? Why then should your servant be an added burden to my lord the king? 36 Your servant will go a little way over the Jordan with the king. Why should the king recompense me with such a reward? 37 Please let your servant return, so that I may die in my own town, near the graves of my father and my mother. But here is your servant Chim′ham; let him go over with my lord the king; and do for him whatever seems good to you."

38 The king answered, "Chim′ham shall go over with me, and I will do for him whatever seems good to you; and all that you desire of me I will do for you." 39 Then all the people crossed over the Jordan, and the king crossed over; the king kissed Bar·zil′laī and blessed him, and he returned to his own home. 40 The king went on to Gil′gal, and Chim′ham went on with him; all the people of Judah, and also half the people of Israel, brought the king on his way.

41 Then all the people of Israel came to the king, and said to him, "Why have our kindred the people of Judah stolen you away, and brought the king and his household over the Jordan, and all David's men with him?" 42 All the people of Judah answered the people of Israel, "Because the king is near of kin to us. Why then are you angry over this matter? Have we eaten at all at the king's expense? Or has he given us any gift?" 43 But the people of Israel answered the people of Judah, "We have ten shares in the king, and in David also we have more than you. Why then did you despise us? Were we not the first to speak of bringing back our king?" But the words of the people of Judah were fiercer than the words of the people of Israel.

The Rebellion of Sheba

20 Now a scoundrel named Shē′ba son of Bich′rī, a Ben′ja·min·īte, happened to be there. He sounded the trumpet and cried out,
"We have no portion in David,
　no share in the son of Jesse!
Everyone to your tents,
　O Israel!"

2 So all the people of Israel withdrew from David and followed Shē′ba son of Bich′rī; but the people of Judah followed their king steadfastly from the Jordan to Jerusalem.

3 David came to his house at Jerusalem; and the king took the ten concubines whom he had left to look after the house, and put them in a house under guard, and provided for them, but did not go in to them. So they were shut up until the day of their death, living as if in widowhood.

4 Then the king said to A·mā′sa,

---

g Or Merib-baal: See 4.4 note　h Gk Syr Vg: Heb said, I will saddle a donkey for myself

"Call the men of Judah together to me within three days, and be here yourself." [5] So A·mā'sa went to summon Judah; but he delayed beyond the set time that had been appointed him. [6] David said to A·bi'shaī, "Now Shē'ba son of Bich'rī will do us more harm than Ab'sa·lom; take your lord's servants and pursue him, or he will find fortified cities for himself, and escape from us." [7] Jō'ab's men went out after him, along with the Cher'e·thītes, the Pel'eth·ītes, and all the warriors; they went out from Jerusalem to pursue Shē'ba son of Bich'rī. [8] When they were at the large stone that is in Gib'-ē·on, A·mā'sa came to meet them. Now Jō'ab was wearing a soldier's garment and over it was a belt with a sword in its sheath fastened at his waist; as he went forward it fell out. [9] Jō'ab said to A·mā'sa, "Is it well with you, my brother?" And Jō'ab took A·mā'sa by the beard with his right hand to kiss him. [10] But A·mā'sa did not notice the sword in Jō'ab's hand; Jō'ab struck him in the belly so that his entrails poured out on the ground, and he died. He did not strike a second blow.

Then Jō'ab and his brother A·bi'shaī pursued Shē'ba son of Bich'rī. [11] And one of Jō'ab's men took his stand by A·mā'sa, and said, "Whoever favors Jō'ab, and whoever is for David, let him follow Jō'ab." [12] A·mā'sa lay wallowing in his blood on the highway, and the man saw that all the people were stopping. Since he saw that all who came by him were stopping, he carried A·mā'sa from the highway into a field, and threw a garment over him. [13] Once he was removed from the highway, all the people went on after Jō'ab to pursue Shē'ba son of Bich'rī.

[14] Shē'ba[i] passed through all the tribes of Israel to Abel of Beth-mā'-a·cah;[j] and all the Bich'rītes[k] assembled, and followed him inside. [15] Jō'-ab's forces[l] came and besieged him in Abel of Beth-mā'a·cah; they threw up a siege ramp against the city, and it stood against the rampart. Jō'ab's forces were battering the wall to break it down. [16] Then a wise woman called from the city, "Listen! Listen! Tell Jō'ab, 'Come here, I want to speak to you.'" [17] He came near her; and the woman said, "Are you Jō'ab?" He answered, "I am." Then she said to him, "Listen to the words of your servant." He answered, "I am listening." [18] Then she said, "They used to say in the old days, 'Let them inquire at Abel'; and so they would settle a matter. [19] I am one of those who are peaceable and faithful in Israel; you seek to destroy a city that is a mother in Israel; why will you swallow up the heritage of the LORD?" [20] Jō'ab answered, "Far be it from me, far be it, that I should swallow up or destroy! [21] That is not the case! But a man of the hill country of E'phra·im, called Shē'ba son of Bich'rī, has lifted up his hand against King David; give him up alone, and I will withdraw from the city." The woman said to Jō'ab, "His head shall be thrown over the wall to you." [22] Then the woman went to all the people with her wise plan. And they cut off the head of Shē'ba son of Bich'rī, and threw it out to Jō'ab. So he blew the trumpet, and they dispersed from the city, and all went to their homes, while Jō'ab returned to Jerusalem to the king.

23 Now Jō'ab was in command of all the army of Israel;[m] Be·nā'i·ah son of Je·hoi'a·da was in command of the Cher'e·thītes and the Pel'eth·ītes; [24] A·dor'am was in charge of the forced labor; Je·hosh'a·phat son of A·hī'lud was the recorder; [25] Shē'va was secretary; Zā'dok and A·bī'a·thar were priests; [26] and Ira the Jā'i·rīte was also David's priest.

David Avenges the Gibeonites

21 Now there was a famine in the days of David for three years, year after year; and David inquired of the LORD. The LORD said, "There is bloodguilt on Saul and on his house, because he put the Gib'ē·on·ites to death." [2] So the king called the Gib'ē·on·ites and spoke to them. (Now the Gib'ē·on·ites were not of the people of Israel, but of the remnant of the Am'o·rītes; although the people of Israel had sworn to spare them, Saul had tried to wipe them out in his zeal for the people of Israel and Judah.) [3] David said to the Gib'ē·on·ites, "What shall I do for you? How shall I make expiation, that you may bless the heritage of the LORD?" [4] The Gib'ē·on·ites said to him, "It is not a matter of silver or gold between us and Saul or his house; neither is it for us to put anyone to death in Israel." He said, "What do you say

[i] Heb He   [j] Compare 20.15: Heb and Beth-maacah   [k] Compare Gk Vg: Heb Berites   [l] Heb They   [m] Cn: Heb Joab to all the army, Israel

that I should do for you?" [5] They said to the king, "The man who consumed us and planned to destroy us, so that we should have no place in all the territory of Israel— [6] let seven of his sons be handed over to us, and we will impale them before the LORD at Gib'e·on on the mountain of the LORD."[n] The king said, "I will hand them over."

7 But the king spared Me·phib'-o·sheth,[o] the son of Saul's son Jonathan, because of the oath of the LORD that was between them, between David and Jonathan son of Saul. [8] The king took the two sons of Riz'pah daughter of Ā'i·ah, whom she bore to Saul, Ar·mō'nī and Me·phib'o·sheth;[o] and the five sons of Mē'rab[p] daughter of Saul, whom she bore to Ā'dri·el son of Bar·zil'lai the Me·hō'la·thīte; [9] he gave them into the hands of the Gib'-e·on·ites, and they impaled them on the mountain before the LORD. The seven of them perished together. They were put to death in the first days of harvest, at the beginning of barley harvest.

10 Then Riz'pah the daughter of Ā'i·ah took sackcloth, and spread it on a rock for herself, from the beginning of harvest until rain fell on them from the heavens; she did not allow the birds of the air to come on the bodies[q] by day, or the wild animals by night. [11] When David was told what Riz'pah daughter of Ā'i·ah, the concubine of Saul, had done, [12] David went and took the bones of Saul and the bones of his son Jonathan from the people of Jā'-besh·gil'e·ad, who had stolen them from the public square of Beth-shan, where the Phi·lis'tines had hung them up, on the day the Phi·lis'tines killed Saul on Gil·bō'a. [13] He brought up from there the bones of Saul and the bones of his son Jonathan; and they gathered the bones of those who had been impaled. [14] They buried the bones of Saul and of his son Jonathan in the land of Benjamin in Zē'la, in the tomb of his father Kish; they did all that the king commanded. After that, God heeded supplications for the land.

Exploits of David's Men
(1 Chr 20.4–8)

15 The Phi·lis'tines went to war again with Israel, and David went down together with his servants. They fought against the Phi·lis'tines, and David grew weary. [16] Ish'bi-bē'nob, one of the descendants of the giants, whose spear weighed three hundred shekels of bronze, and who was fitted out with new weapons,[r] said he would kill David. [17] But A·bi'shai son of Ze·rū'i·ah came to his aid, and attacked the Phi·lis'tine and killed him. Then David's men swore to him, "You shall not go out with us to battle any longer, so that you do not quench the lamp of Israel."

18 After this a battle took place with the Phi·lis'tines, at Gob; then Sib'-be·cai the Hū'sha·thīte killed Saph, who was one of the descendants of the giants. [19] Then there was another battle with the Phi·lis'tines at Gob; and El·hā'nan son of Jā'a·rē·or'e·gim, the Beth'le·hem·īte, killed Goliath the Git'tīte, the shaft of whose spear was like a weaver's beam. [20] There was again war at Gath, where there was a man of great size, who had six fingers on each hand, and six toes on each foot, twenty-four in number; he too was descended from the giants. [21] When he taunted Israel, Jonathan son of David's brother Shim'e·ī, killed him. [22] These four were descended from the giants in Gath; they fell by the hands of David and his servants.

David's Song of Thanksgiving
(Ps 18.1–50)

22 David spoke to the LORD the words of this song on the day when the LORD delivered him from the hand of all his enemies, and from the hand of Saul. [2] He said:

The LORD is my rock, my
　　fortress, and my deliverer,
3　my God, my rock, in whom I
　　take refuge,
my shield and the horn of my
　　salvation,
　my stronghold and my refuge,
　my savior; you save me from
　　violence.
4　I call upon the LORD, who is
　　worthy to be praised,
　and I am saved from my
　　enemies.

5　For the waves of death
　　encompassed me,
　　the torrents of perdition
　　assailed me;

n Cn Compare Gk and 21.9: Heb *at Gibeah of Saul, the chosen of the* LORD
o Or *Merib-baal*: See 4.4 note　　p Two Heb Mss Syr Compare Gk: MT *Michal*
q Heb *them*　　r Heb *was belted anew*

6 the cords of She′ol entangled
    me,
    the snares of death confronted
        me.

7 In my distress I called upon the
    LORD;
    to my God I called.
  From his temple he heard my
    voice,
    and my cry came to his ears.

8 Then the earth reeled and
    rocked;
    the foundations of the heavens
        trembled
    and quaked, because he was
        angry.

9 Smoke went up from his nostrils,
    and devouring fire from his
        mouth;
    glowing coals flamed forth
        from him.

10 He bowed the heavens, and
    came down;
    thick darkness was under his
        feet.

11 He rode on a cherub, and flew;
    he was seen upon the wings of
        the wind.

12 He made darkness around him a
    canopy,
    thick clouds, a gathering of
        water.

13 Out of the brightness before him
    coals of fire flamed forth.

14 The LORD thundered from
    heaven;
    the Most High uttered his
        voice.

15 He sent out arrows, and
    scattered them
    —lightning, and routed them.

16 Then the channels of the sea
    were seen,
    the foundations of the world
        were laid bare
  at the rebuke of the LORD,
    at the blast of the breath of his
        nostrils.

17 He reached from on high, he
    took me,
    he drew me out of mighty
        waters.

18 He delivered me from my strong
    enemy,
    from those who hated me;
    for they were too mighty for
        me.

19 They came upon me in the day
    of my calamity,

but the LORD was my stay.

20 He brought me out into a broad
    place;
    he delivered me, because he
        delighted in me.

21 The LORD rewarded me
    according to my
        righteousness;
    according to the cleanness of
        my hands he recompensed
        me.

22 For I have kept the ways of the
    LORD,
    and have not wickedly
        departed from my God.

23 For all his ordinances were
    before me,
    and from his statutes I did not
        turn aside.

24 I was blameless before him,
    and I kept myself from guilt.

25 Therefore the LORD has
    recompensed me according
        to my righteousness,
    according to my cleanness in
        his sight.

26 With the loyal you show
    yourself loyal;
    with the blameless you show
        yourself blameless;

27 with the pure you show yourself
    pure,
    and with the crooked you
        show yourself perverse.

28 You deliver a humble people,
    but your eyes are upon the
        haughty to bring them
        down.

29 Indeed, you are my lamp,
    O LORD,
    the LORD lightens my
        darkness.

30 By you I can crush a troop,
    and by my God I can leap over
        a wall.

31 This God—his way is perfect;
    the promise of the LORD
        proves true;
    he is a shield for all who take
        refuge in him.

32 For who is God, but the LORD?
    And who is a rock, except our
        God?

33 The God who has girded me
    with strength[s]

[s]Q Ms Gk Syr Vg Compare Ps 18.32: M
God is my strong refuge

has opened wide my path. *t*

34 He made my *u* feet like the feet
of deer,
 and set me secure on the
 heights.

35 He trains my hands for war,
 so that my arms can bend a
 bow of bronze.

36 You have given me the shield of
your salvation,
 and your help *v* has made me
 great.

37 You have made me stride freely,
 and my feet do not slip;

38 I pursued my enemies and
destroyed them,
 and did not turn back until
 they were consumed.

39 I consumed them; I struck them
down, so that they did not
rise;
 they fell under my feet.

40 For you girded me with strength
for the battle;
 you made my assailants sink
 under me.

41 You made my enemies turn their
backs to me,
 those who hated me, and I
 destroyed them.

42 They looked, but there was no
one to save them;
 they cried to the LORD, but he
 did not answer them.

43 I beat them fine like the dust of
the earth,
 I crushed them and stamped
 them down like the mire of
 the streets.

44 You delivered me from strife
with the peoples; *w*
 you kept me as the head of the
 nations;
 people whom I had not known
 served me.

45 Foreigners came cringing to me;
 as soon as they heard of me,
 they obeyed me.

46 Foreigners lost heart,
 and came trembling out of
 their strongholds.

47 The LORD lives! Blessed be my
rock,
 and exalted be my God, the
 rock of my salvation,

48 the God who gave me vengeance
and brought down peoples
under me,

49 who brought me out from my
enemies;

you exalted me above my
adversaries,
 you delivered me from the
 violent.

50 For this I will extol you, O LORD,
among the nations,
 and sing praises to your name.

51 He is a tower of salvation for his
king,
 and shows steadfast love to his
 anointed,
 to David and his descendants
 forever.

The Last Words of David

23 Now these are the last words of
David:
The oracle of David, son of
Jesse,
 the oracle of the man whom
 God exalted, *x*
the anointed of the God of
Jacob,
 the favorite of the Strong One
 of Israel:

2 The spirit of the LORD speaks
through me,
 his word is upon my tongue.

3 The God of Israel has spoken,
 the Rock of Israel has said to
 me:
One who rules over people
justly,
 ruling in the fear of God,

4 is like the light of morning,
like the sun rising on a
cloudless morning,
 gleaming from the rain on the
 grassy land.

5 Is not my house like this with
God?
 For he has made with me an
 everlasting covenant,
ordered in all things and
secure.
Will he not cause to prosper
 all my help and my desire?

6 But the godless are *y* all like
thorns that are thrown
away;
 for they cannot be picked up
 with the hand;

---

t Meaning of Heb uncertain   *u* Another
reading is *his*   *v* Q Ms: MT *your
answering*   *w* Gk: Heb *from strife with
my people*   *x* Q Ms: MT *who was raised
on high*   *y* Heb *But worthlessness*

7 to touch them one uses an iron
bar
or the shaft of a spear.
And they are entirely
consumed in fire on the
spot.ᶻ

David's Mighty Men
(1 Chr 11.10–47)

8 These are the names of the warriors whom David had: Jō′sheb-
bas·she′beth a Tah·che′mo·nīte; he
was chief of the Three;ᵃ he wielded his
spearᵇ against eight hundred whom
he killed at one time.
9 Next to him among the three warriors was El·e·ā′zar son of Dō′dō son
of A·hō′hī. He was with David when
they defied the Phi·lis′tines who were
gathered there for battle. The Israelites withdrew, ¹⁰but he stood his
ground. He struck down the Phi·lis′-
tines until his arm grew weary, though
his hand clung to the sword. The LORD
brought about a great victory that day.
Then the people came back to him—
but only to strip the dead.
11 Next to him was Sham′mah son
of Ā′gee, the Har′a·rīte. The Phi·lis′-
tines gathered together at Le′hī, where
there was a plot of ground full of lentils; and the army fled from the Phi·lis′-
tines. ¹²But he took his stand in the
middle of the plot, defended it, and
killed the Phi·lis′tines; and the LORD
brought about a great victory.
13 Towards the beginning of harvest three of the thirtyᶜ chiefs went
down to join David at the cave of
A·dul′lam, while a band of Phi·lis′tines
was encamped in the valley of Reph′-
a·im. ¹⁴David was then in the stronghold; and the garrison of the Phi·lis′-
tines was then at Bethlehem. ¹⁵David
said longingly, "O that someone
would give me water to drink from the
well of Bethlehem that is by the gate!"
¹⁶Then the three warriors broke
through the camp of the Phi·lis′tines,
drew water from the well of Bethlehem
that was by the gate, and brought it to
David. But he would not drink of it; he
poured it out to the LORD, ¹⁷for he said,
"The LORD forbid that I should do this.
Can I drink the blood of the men who
went at the risk of their lives?" Therefore he would not drink it. The three
warriors did these things.
18 Now A·bi′shai son of Ze·rū′i·ah,
the brother of Jō′ab, was chief of the
Thirty.ᵈ With his spear he fought

against three hundred men and killed
them, and won a name beside the
Three. ¹⁹He was the most renowned of
the Thirty,ᵉ and became their commander; but he did not attain to the
Three.
20 Be·nā′i·ah son of Je·hoi′a·da was
a valiant warriorᶠ from Kab′ze·el, a
doer of great deeds; he struck down
two sons of Ar′i·elᵍ of Mō′ab. He also
went down and killed a lion in a pit on
a day when snow had fallen. ²¹And he
killed an Egyptian, a handsome man.
The Egyptian had a spear in his hand,
but Be·nā′i·ah went against him with a
staff, snatched the spear out of the
Egyptian's hand, and killed him with
his own spear. ²²Such were the things
Be·nā′i·ah son of Je·hoi′a·da did, and
won a name beside the three warriors.
²³He was renowned among the Thirty,
but he did not attain to the Three. And
David put him in charge of his bodyguard.
24 Among the Thirty were As′a·hel
brother of Jō′ab; El·hā′nan son of
Dō′dō of Bethlehem; ²⁵Sham′mah of
Har′od; E·lī′ka of Har′od; ²⁶He′lez the
Pal′tīte; Ira son of Ik′kesh of Te·kō′a;
²⁷A·bi·e′zer of An′a·thoth; Me·bun′na
the Hū′sha·thīte; ²⁸Zal′mon the A·hō′-
hīte; Mā′ha·rai of Ne·toph′ah; ²⁹He′-
leb son of Bā′a·nah of Ne·toph′ah;
It′tai son of Rī′bai of Gib′e·ah of the
Ben′ja·min·ites; ³⁰Be·nā′i·ah of Pir′-
a·thon; Hid′dai of the torrents of Gā′-
ash; ³¹A′bi·al′bon the Ar′ba·thīte; Az′-
ma·veth of Ba·hū′rim; ³²E·lī′ah·ba of
Shā·al′bon; the sons of Jā′shen: Jon′a-
than ³³son ofʰ Sham′mah the Har′-
a·rīte; A·hī′am son of Shar′ar the Har′-
a·rīte; ³⁴E·liph′e·let son of A·has′bai of
Mā′a·cah; E·lī′am son of A·hith′o·phel
the Gī′lo·nīte; ³⁵Hez′roⁱ of Car′mel;
Pā′a·rai the Ar′bīte; ³⁶I′gal son of Na′-
than of Zō′bah; Bā′ni the Gad′ite;
³⁷Ze′lek the Am′mon·ite; Nā′ha·rai
Be·er′oth, the armor-bearer of Jō′ab
son of Ze·rū′i·ah; ³⁸Ira the Ith′rīte;
Gā′reb the Ith′rīte; ³⁹U·rī′ah the Hit-
tīte—thirty-seven in all.

ᶻHeb *in sitting*   ᵃGk Vg Compare 1
Chr 11.11: Meaning of Heb uncertain
ᵇ1 Chr 11.11: Meaning of Heb uncertain
ᶜHeb adds *head*   ᵈTwo Heb Mss Syr:
MT *Three*   ᵉSyr Compare 1 Chr 11.21
Heb *Was he the most renowned of the
Three?*   ᶠAnother reading is *the son of
Ish-hai*   ᵍGk: Heb lacks *sons of*
ʰGk: Heb lacks *son of*   ⁱAnother
reading is *Hezrai*

David's Census of Israel and Judah
(1 Chr 21.1–6)

24 Again the anger of the LORD was kindled against Israel, and he incited David against them, saying, "Go, count the people of Israel and Judah." [2] So the king said to Jō′ab and the commanders of the army,[j] who were with him, "Go through all the tribes of Israel, from Dan to Bē′er-shē′ba, and take a census of the people, so that I may know how many there are." [3] But Jō′ab said to the king, "May the LORD your God increase the number of the people a hundredfold, while the eyes of my lord the king can still see it! But why does my lord the king want to do this?" [4] But the king's word prevailed against Jō′ab and the commanders of the army. So Jō′ab and the commanders of the army went out from the presence of the king to take a census of the people of Israel. [5] They crossed the Jordan, and began from[k] A·rō′er and from the city that is in the middle of the valley, toward Gad and on to Ja′zer. [6] Then they came to Gil′e·ad, and to Ka′desh in the land of the Hit′tites;[l] and they came to Dan, and from Dan[m] they went around to Sī′don, [7] and came to the fortress of Tyre and to all the cities of the Hī′vites and Ca′naan·ites; and they went out to the Neg′eb of Judah at Bē′er-shē′ba. [8] So when they had gone through all the land, they came back to Jerusalem at the end of nine months and twenty days. [9] Jō′ab reported to the king the number of those who had been recorded: in Israel there were eight hundred thousand soldiers able to draw the sword, and those of Judah were five hundred thousand.

Judgment on David's Sin
(1 Chr 21.7–17)

10 But afterward, David was stricken to the heart because he had numbered the people. David said to the LORD, "I have sinned greatly in what I have done. But now, O LORD, I pray you, take away the guilt of your servant; for I have done very foolishly." [11] When David rose in the morning, the word of the LORD came to the prophet Gad, David's seer, saying, [12] "Go and say to David: Thus says the LORD: Three things I offer[n] you; choose one of them, and I will do it to you." [13] So Gad came to David and told him; he asked him, "Shall three[o] years of famine come to you on your land? Or will you flee three months before your foes while they pursue you? Or shall there be three days' pestilence in your land? Now consider, and decide what answer I shall return to the one who sent me." [14] Then David said to Gad, "I am in great distress; let us fall into the hand of the LORD, for his mercy is great; but let me not fall into human hands."

15 So the LORD sent a pestilence on Israel from that morning until the appointed time; and seventy thousand of the people died, from Dan to Bē′er-shē′ba. [16] But when the angel stretched out his hand toward Jerusalem to destroy it, the LORD relented concerning the evil, and said to the angel who was bringing destruction among the people, "It is enough; now stay your hand." The angel of the LORD was then by the threshing floor of A·rau′nah the Jeb′ū·site. [17] When David saw the angel who was destroying the people, he said to the LORD, "I alone have sinned, and I alone have done wickedly; but these sheep, what have they done? Let your hand, I pray, be against me and against my father's house."

David's Altar on the Threshing Floor
(1 Chr 21.18–27)

18 That day Gad came to David and said to him, "Go up and erect an altar to the LORD on the threshing floor of A·rau′nah the Jeb′ū·site." [19] Following Gad's instructions, David went up, as the LORD had commanded. [20] When A·rau′nah looked down, he saw the king and his servants coming toward him; and A·rau′nah went out and prostrated himself before the king with his face to the ground. [21] A·rau′nah said, "Why has my lord the king come to his servant?" David said, "To buy the threshing floor from you in order to build an altar to the LORD, so that the plague may be averted from the people." [22] Then A·rau′nah said to David, "Let my lord the king take and offer up what seems good to him; here are the oxen for the burnt offering, and the

---

j 1 Chr 21.2 Gk: Heb *to Joab the commander of the army*   *k* Gk Mss: Heb *encamped in Aroer south of*   *l* Gk: Heb *to the land of Tahtim-hodshi*   *m* Cn Compare Gk: Heb *they came to Dan-jaan and*   *n* Or *hold over*   *o* 1 Chr 21.12 Gk: Heb *seven* threshing sledges and the yokes of the oxen for the wood. 23 All this, O king, A·rau′nah gives to the king." And A·rau′nah said to the king, "May the LORD your God respond favorably to you."

24 But the king said to A·rau′nah, "No, but I will buy them from you for a price; I will not offer burnt offerings

to the LORD my God that cost me noth ing." So David bought the threshing floor and the oxen for fifty shekels o silver. 25 David built there an altar t the LORD, and offered burnt offering and offerings of well-being. So th LORD answered his supplication fo the land, and the plague was averte from Israel.

1 KINGS

The Struggle for the Succession

1 King David was old and advanced in years; and although they covered him with clothes, he could not get warm. 2 So his servants said to him, "Let a young virgin be sought for my lord the king, and let her wait on the king, and be his attendant; let her lie in your bosom, so that my lord the king may be warm." 3 So they searched for a beautiful girl throughout all the territory of Israel, and found Ab′i·shag the Shū′nam·mīte, and brought her to the king. 4 The girl was very beautiful. She became the king's attendant and served him, but the king did not know her sexually.

5 Now Ad·o·nī′jah son of Hag′gith exalted himself, saying, "I will be king"; he prepared for himself chariots and horsemen, and fifty men to run before him. 6 His father had never at any time displeased him by asking, "Why have you done thus and so?" He was also a very handsome man, and he was born next after Ab′sa·lom. 7 He conferred with Jō′ab son of Ze·rū′i·ah and with the priest A·bī′a·thar, and they supported Ad·o·nī′jah. 8 But the priest Zā′dok, and Be·nā′i·ah son of Je·hoi′a·da, and the prophet Nathan, and Shim′e·ī, and Rē′ī, and David's own warriors did not side with Ad·o·nī′jah.

9 Ad·o·nī′jah sacrificed sheep, oxen, and fatted cattle by the stone Zō′he·leth, which is beside En·rō′gel, and he invited all his brothers, the king's sons, and all the royal officials of Judah, 10 but he did not invite the

prophet Nathan or Be·nā′i·ah or th warriors or his brother Solomon.

11 Then Nathan said to Bath she′ba, Solomon's mother, "Have yo not heard that Ad·o·nī′jah son (Hag′gith has become king an our lord David does not know i 12 Now therefore come, let me give yo advice, so that you may save your ow life and the life of your son Solomo 13 Go in at once to King David, and sa to him, 'Did you not, my lord the kin swear to your servant, saying: You son Solomon shall succeed me as kin and he shall sit on my throne? WI then is Ad·o·nī′jah king?' 14 Then whi you are still there speaking with t king, I will come in after you and co firm your words."

15 So Bath·she′ba went to the kii in his room. The king was very o Ab′i·shag the Shū′nam·mīte was tending the king. 16 Bath·she′ba bow and did obeisance to the king, and tl king said, "What do you wish?" 17 SI said to him, "My lord, you swore your servant by the LORD your Go saying: Your son Solomon shall su ceed me as king, and he shall sit on r throne. 18 But now suddenly Ad·o·n jah has become king, though you, r lord the king, do not know it. 19 He h sacrificed oxen, fatted cattle, a sheep in abundance, and has invit all the children of the king, the pri A·bī′a·thar, and Jō′ab the comman of the army; but your servant Solom he has not invited. 20 But you, my lc the king—the eyes of all Israel are you to tell them who shall sit on t

throne of my lord the king after him. [21] Otherwise it will come to pass, when my lord the king sleeps with his ancestors, that my son Solomon and I will be counted offenders."

22 While she was still speaking with the king, the prophet Nathan came in. [23] The king was told, "Here is the prophet Nathan." When he came in before the king, he did obeisance to the king, with his face to the ground. [24] Nathan said, "My lord the king, have you said, 'Ad·o·nī'jah shall succeed me as king, and he shall sit on my throne'? [25] For today he has gone down and has sacrificed oxen, fatted cattle, and sheep in abundance, and has invited all the king's children, Jō'ab the commander[a] of the army, and the priest A·bī'a·thar, who are now eating and drinking before him, and saying, 'Long live King Ad·o·nī'jah!' [26] But he did not invite me, your servant, and the priest Zā'dok, and Be·nā'i·ah son of Je·hoi'a·da, and your servant Solomon. [27] Has this thing been brought about by my lord the king and you have not let your servants know who should sit on the throne of my lord the king after him?"

The Accession of Solomon
(1 Chr 29.22b–25)

28 King David answered, "Summon Bath·shē'ba to me." So she came into the king's presence, and stood before the king. [29] The king swore, saying, "As the LORD lives, who has saved my life from every adversity, [30] as I swore to you by the LORD, the God of Israel, 'Your son Solomon shall succeed me as king, and he shall sit on my throne in my place,' so will I do this day." [31] Then Bath·shē'ba bowed with her face to the ground, and did obeisance to the king, and said, "May my lord King David live forever!"

32 King David said, "Summon to me the priest Zā'dok, the prophet Nathan, and Be·nā'i·ah son of Je·hoi'a·da." When they came before the king, [33] the king said to them, "Take with you the servants of your lord, and have my son Solomon ride on my own mule, and bring him down to Gī'hon. [34] There let the priest Zā'dok and the prophet Nathan anoint him king over Israel; then blow the trumpet, and say, 'Long live King Solomon!' [35] You shall go up following him. Let him enter and sit on my throne; he shall be king in my place; for I have appointed him to be

ruler over Israel and over Judah." [36] Be·nā'i·ah son of Je·hoi'a·da answered the king, "Amen! May the LORD, the God of my lord the king, so ordain. [37] As the LORD has been with my lord the king, so may he be with Solomon, and make his throne greater than the throne of my lord King David."

38 So the priest Zā'dok, the prophet Nathan, and Be·nā'i·ah son of Je·hoi'a·da, and the Cher'e·thites and the Pel'eth·ites, went down and had Solomon ride on King David's mule, and led him to Gī'hon. [39] There the priest Zā'dok took the horn of oil from the tent and anointed Solomon. Then they blew the trumpet, and all the people said, "Long live King Solomon!" [40] And all the people went up following him, playing on pipes and rejoicing with great joy, so that the earth quaked at their noise.

41 Ad·o·nī'jah and all the guests who were with him heard it as they finished feasting. When Jō'ab heard the sound of the trumpet, he said, "Why is the city in an uproar?" [42] While he was still speaking, Jonathan son of the priest A·bī'a·thar arrived. Ad·o·nī'jah said, "Come in, for you are a worthy man and surely you bring good news." [43] Jonathan answered Ad·o·nī'jah, "No, for our lord King David has made Solomon king; [44] the king has sent with him the priest Zā'dok, the prophet Nathan, and Be·nā'i·ah son of Je·hoi'a·da, and the Cher'e·thites and the Pel'eth·ites; and they had him ride on the king's mule; [45] the priest Zā'dok and the prophet Nathan have anointed him king at Gī'hon; and they have gone up from there rejoicing, so that the city is in an uproar. This is the noise that you heard. [46] Solomon now sits on the royal throne. [47] Moreover the king's servants came to congratulate our lord King David, saying, 'May God make the name of Solomon more famous than yours, and make his throne greater than your throne.' The king bowed in worship on the bed [48] and went on to pray thus, 'Blessed be the LORD, the God of Israel, who today has granted one of my offspring[b] to sit on my throne and permitted me to witness it.' "

49 Then all the guests of Ad·o·nī'jah got up trembling and went their own

[a] Gk: Heb the commanders　　[b] Gk: Heb one

1 KINGS

ways. [50]Ad·o·ni′jah, fearing Solomon, got up and went to grasp the horns of the altar. [51]Solomon was informed, "Ad·o·ni′jah is afraid of King Solomon; see, he has laid hold of the horns of the altar, saying, 'Let King Solomon swear to me first that he will not kill his servant with the sword.' " [52]So Solomon responded, "If he proves to be a worthy man, not one of his hairs shall fall to the ground; but if wickedness is found in him, he shall die." [53]Then King Solomon sent to have him brought down from the altar. He came to do obeisance to King Solomon; and Solomon said to him, "Go home."

David's Instruction to Solomon

2 When David's time to die drew near, he charged his son Solomon, saying: [2]"I am about to go the way of all the earth. Be strong, be courageous, [3]and keep the charge of the LORD your God, walking in his ways and keeping his statutes, his commandments, his ordinances, and his testimonies, as it is written in the law of Moses, so that you may prosper in all that you do and wherever you turn. [4]Then the LORD will establish his word that he spoke concerning me: 'If your heirs take heed to their way, to walk before me in faithfulness with all their heart and with all their soul, there shall not fail you a successor on the throne of Israel.'

[5]"Moreover you know also what Jo′ab son of Ze·ru′i·ah did to me, how he dealt with the two commanders of the armies of Israel, Abner son of Ner, and A·ma′sa son of Je′ther, whom he murdered, retaliating in time of peace for blood that had been shed in war, and putting the blood of war on the belt around his waist, and on the sandals on his feet. [6]Act therefore according to your wisdom, but do not let his gray head go down to She′ol in peace. [7]Deal loyally, however, with the sons of Bar·zil′lai the Gil′e·ad·ite, and let them be among those who eat at your table; for with such loyalty they met me when I fled from your brother Ab′sa·lom. [8]There is also with you Shim′e·i son of Ge′ra, the Ben′ja·min·ite from Ba·hu′rim, who cursed me with a terrible curse on the day when I went to Ma·ha·na′im; but when he came down to meet me at the Jordan, I swore to him by the LORD, 'I will not put you to death with the sword.' [9]Therefore do not hold him guiltless,

for you are a wise man; you will know what you ought to do to him, and you must bring his gray head down with blood to She′ol."

Death of David
(1 Chr 3.4; 29.26–28)

10 Then David slept with his ancestors, and was buried in the city of David. [11]The time that David reigned over Israel was forty years; he reigned seven years in He′bron, and thirty-three years in Jerusalem. [12]So Solomon sat on the throne of his father David; and his kingdom was firmly established.

Solomon Consolidates His Reign

13 Then Ad·o·ni′jah son of Hag′gith came to Bath·she′ba, Solomon's mother. She asked, "Do you come peaceably?" He said, "Peaceably." [14]Then he said, "May I have a word with you?" She said, "Go on." [15]He said, "You know that the kingdom was mine, and that all Israel expected me to reign; however, the kingdom has turned about and become my brother's, for it was his from the LORD. [16]And now I have one request to make of you; do not refuse me." She said to him, "Go on." [17]He said, "Please ask King Solomon—he will not refuse you—to give me Ab′i·shag the Shu′nam·mite as my wife." [18]Bath·she′ba said, "Very well; I will speak to the king on your behalf."

19 So Bath·she′ba went to King Solomon, to speak to him on behalf of Ad·o·ni′jah. The king rose to meet her and bowed down to her; then he sat on his throne, and had a throne brought for the king's mother, and she sat on his right. [20]Then she said, "I have one small request to make of you; do not refuse me." And the king said to her, "Make your request, my mother; for I will not refuse you." [21]She said, "Let Ab′i·shag the Shu′nam·mite be given to your brother Ad·o·ni′jah as his wife." [22]King Solomon answered his mother, "And why do you ask Ab′i·shag the Shu′nam·mite for Ad·o·ni′jah? Ask for him the kingdom as well! For he is my elder brother; ask not only for him but also for the priest A·bi′a·thar and for Jo′ab son of Ze·ru′i·ah!" [23]Then King Solomon swore by the LORD, "So may God do to me, and more also, for Ad·o·ni′jah has devised this scheme at the risk of his life! [24]Now therefore as the LORD lives

who has established me and placed me on the throne of my father David, and who has made me a house as he promised, today Ad·o·nī′jah shall be put to death." 25So King Solomon sent Be·nā′i·ah son of Je·hoi′a·da; he struck him down, and he died.

26 The king said to the priest A·bī′-a·thar, "Go to An′a·thoth, to your estate; for you deserve death. But I will not at this time put you to death, because you carried the ark of the Lord God before my father David, and because you shared in all the hardships my father endured." 27So Solomon banished A·bī′a·thar from being priest to the Lord, thus fulfilling the word of the Lord that he had spoken concerning the house of Ē′lī in Shī′lōh.

28 When the news came to Jō′ab—for Jō′ab had supported Ad·o·nī′jah though he had not supported Ab′sa·lom—Jō′ab fled to the tent of the Lord and grasped the horns of the altar. 29When it was told King Solomon, "Jō′ab has fled to the tent of the Lord and now is beside the altar," Solomon sent Be·nā′i·ah son of Je·hoi′a·da, saying, "Go, strike him down." 30So Be·nā′i·ah came to the tent of the Lord and said to him, "The king commands, 'Come out.'" But he said, "No, I will die here." Then Be·nā′i·ah brought the king word again, saying, "Thus said Jō′ab, and thus he answered me." 31The king replied to him, "Do as he has said, strike him down and bury him; and thus take away from me and from my father's house the guilt for the blood that Jō′ab shed without cause. 32The Lord will bring back his bloody deeds on his own head, because, without the knowledge of my father David, he attacked and killed with the sword two men more righteous and better than himself, Abner son of Ner, commander of the army of Israel, and A·mā′sa son of Jē′ther, commander of the army of Judah. 33So shall their blood come back on the head of Jō′ab and on the head of his descendants forever; but to David, and to his descendants, and to his house, and to his throne, there shall be peace from the Lord forevermore." 34Then Be·nā′i·ah son of Je·hoi′a·da went up and struck him down and killed him; and he was buried at his own house near the wilderness. 35The king put Be·nā′i·ah son of Je·hoi′a·da over the army in his place, and the king put the priest Zā′dok in the place of A·bī′a·thar.

36 Then the king sent and summoned Shim′e·ī, and said to him, "Build yourself a house in Jerusalem, and live there, and do not go out from there to any place whatever. 37For on the day you go out, and cross the Wadi Kid′ron, know for certain that you shall die; your blood shall be on your own head." 38And Shim′e·ī said to the king, "The sentence is fair; as my lord the king has said, so will your servant do." So Shim′e·ī lived in Jerusalem many days.

39 But it happened at the end of three years that two of Shim′e·ī's slaves ran away to King Ā′chish son of Mā′a·cah of Gath. When it was told Shim′e·ī, "Your slaves are in Gath," 40Shim′e·ī arose and saddled a donkey, and went to Ā′chish in Gath, to search for his slaves; Shim′e·ī went and brought his slaves from Gath. 41When Solomon was told that Shim′e·ī had gone from Jerusalem to Gath and returned, 42the king sent and summoned Shim′e·ī, and said to him, "Did I not make you swear by the Lord, and solemnly adjure you, saying, 'Know for certain that on the day you go out and go to any place whatever, you shall die'? And you said to me, 'The sentence is fair; I accept.' 43Why then have you not kept your oath to the Lord and the commandment with which I charged you?" 44The king also said to Shim′e·ī, "You know in your own heart all the evil that you did to my father David; so the Lord will bring back your evil on your own head. 45But King Solomon shall be blessed, and the throne of David shall be established before the Lord forever." 46Then the king commanded Be·nā′i·ah son of Je·hoi′a·da; and he went out and struck him down, and he died.

So the kingdom was established in the hand of Solomon.

Solomon's Prayer for Wisdom
(2 Chr 1.2–13)

3 Solomon made a marriage alliance with Pharaoh king of Egypt; he took Pharaoh's daughter and brought her into the city of David, until he had finished building his own house and the house of the Lord and the wall around Jerusalem. 2The people were sacrificing at the high places, however, because no house had yet been built for the name of the Lord.

3 Solomon loved the Lord, walking

in the statutes of his father David; only, he sacrificed and offered incense at the high places. 4 The king went to Gib′e·on to sacrifice there, for that was the principal high place; Solomon used to offer a thousand burnt offerings on that altar. 5 At Gib′e·on the LORD appeared to Solomon in a dream by night; and God said, "Ask what I should give you." 6 And Solomon said, "You have shown great and steadfast love to your servant my father David, because he walked before you in faithfulness, in righteousness, and in uprightness of heart toward you; and you have kept for him this great and steadfast love, and have given him a son to sit on his throne today. 7 And now, O LORD my God, you have made your servant king in place of my father David, although I am only a little child; I do not know how to go out or come in. 8 And your servant is in the midst of the people whom you have chosen, a great people, so numerous they cannot be numbered or counted. 9 Give your servant therefore an understanding mind to govern your people, able to discern between good and evil; for who can govern this your great people?"

10 It pleased the Lord that Solomon had asked this. 11 God said to him, "Because you have asked this, and have not asked for yourself long life or riches, or for the life of your enemies, but have asked for yourself understanding to discern what is right, 12 I now do according to your word. Indeed I give you a wise and discerning mind; no one like you has been before you and no one like you shall arise after you. 13 I give you also what you have not asked, both riches and honor all your life; no other king shall compare with you. 14 If you will walk in my ways, keeping my statutes and my commandments, as your father David walked, then I will lengthen your life."

15 Then Solomon awoke; it had been a dream. He came to Jerusalem where he stood before the ark of the covenant of the LORD. He offered up burnt offerings and offerings of well-being, and provided a feast for all his servants.

Solomon's Wisdom in Judgment

16 Later, two women who were prostitutes came to the king and stood before him. 17 The one woman said, "Please, my lord, this woman and I live in the same house; and I gave birth while she was in the house. 18 Then on the third day after I gave birth, this woman also gave birth. We were together; there was no one else with us in the house, only the two of us were in the house. 19 Then this woman's son died in the night, because she lay on him. 20 She got up in the middle of the night and took my son from beside me while your servant slept. She laid him at her breast, and laid her dead son at my breast. 21 When I rose in the morning to nurse my son, I saw that he was dead; but when I looked at him closely in the morning, clearly it was not the son I had borne." 22 But the other woman said, "No, the living son is mine, and the dead son is yours." The first said, "No, the dead son is yours, and the living son is mine." So they argued before the king.

23 Then the king said, "The one says, 'This is my son that is alive, and your son is dead'; while the other says, 'Not so! Your son is dead, and my son is the living one.' " 24 So the king said, "Bring me a sword," and they brought a sword before the king. 25 The king said, "Divide the living boy in two; then give half to the one, and half to the other." 26 But the woman whose son was alive said to the king— because compassion for her son burned within her— "Please, my lord, give her the living boy; certainly do not kill him!" The other said, "It shall be neither mine nor yours; divide it." 27 Then the king responded: "Give the first woman the living boy; do not kill him. She is his mother." 28 All Israel heard of the judgment that the king had rendered; and they stood in awe of the king, because they perceived that the wisdom of God was in him, to execute justice.

Solomon's Administrative Officers

4 King Solomon was king over all Israel, 2 and these were his high officials: Az·a·rī′ah son of Za′dok was the priest; 3 El·i·hōr′eph and A·hī′ah sons of Shī′sha were secretaries; Je·hosh′a·phat son of A·hī′lud was recorder; 4 Be·nā′i·ah son of Je·hoi′a·da was in command of the army; Za′dok and A·bī′a·thar were priests; 5 Az·a·rī′ah son of Nathan was over the officials; Za′bud son of Nathan was priest and king's friend; 6 A·hī′shar was in charge of the palace; and Ad·o·nī′ram son of Ab′da was in charge of the forced labor.

7 Solomon had twelve officials over all Israel, who provided food for the king and his household; each one had to make provision for one month in the year. 8 These were their names: Ben-hur, in the hill country of Ḗ′phra·im; 9 Ben-dē′ker, in Mā′kaz, Shā·al′bim, Beth-shē′mesh, and Ḗ′lon-beth-hā′-nan; 10 Ben-hē′sed, in A·rūb′-both (to him belonged Sō′cōh and all the land of Hē′pher); 11 Ben-a·bin′a·dab, in all Nā′phath-dor (he had Tā′phath, Solomon's daughter, as his wife); 12 Bā′a·na son of A·hī′lud, in Tā′a·nach, Me·gid′dō, and all Beth-shē′an, which is beside Zar′e·than below Jez′rē·el, and from Beth-shē′an to Ā′bel-me·hō′lah, as far as the other side of Jok′mē·am; 13 Ben-gē′ber, in Rā′moth-gil′ē·ad (he had the villages of Jā′ir son of Ma·nas′seh, which are in Gil′e·ad, and he had the region of Ar′gob, which is in Bā′shan, sixty great cities with walls and bronze bars); 14 A·hin′a·dab son of Id′dō, in Mā·ha·nā′im; 15 A·him′a·az, in Naph′-ta·lī (he had taken Bas′e·math, Solomon's daughter, as his wife); 16 Bā′a·na son of Hū′shaī, in Ash′er and Be·ā′-loth; 17 Je·hosh′a·phat son of Pa·rū′ah, in Is′sa·char; 18 Shim′ē·ī son of Ē′la, in Benjamin; 19 Gē′ber son of U′rī, in the land of Gil′e·ad, the country of King Sī′hon of the Am′o·rītes and of King Og of Bā′shan. And there was one official in the land of Judah.

Magnificence of Solomon's Rule

20 Judah and Israel were as numerous as the sand by the sea; they ate and drank and were happy. 21 c Solomon was sovereign over all the kingdoms from the Euphrates to the land of the Phi·lis′tines, even to the border of Egypt; they brought tribute and served Solomon all the days of his life. 22 Solomon's provision for one day was thirty cors of choice flour, and sixty cors of meal, 23 ten fat oxen, and twenty pasture-fed cattle, one hundred sheep, besides deer, gazelles, roebucks, and fatted fowl. 24 For he had dominion over all the region west of the Euphrates from Tiph′sah to Gā′za, over all the kings west of the Euphrates; and he had peace on all sides. 25 During Solomon's lifetime Judah and Israel lived in safety, from Dan even to Bē′er-shē′ba, all of them under their vines and fig trees. 26 Solomon also had forty thousand stalls of horses for his chariots, and twelve thousand horsemen. 27 Those officials supplied provisions for King Solomon and for all who came to King Solomon's table, each one in his month; they let nothing be lacking. 28 They also brought to the required place barley and straw for the horses and swift steeds, each according to his charge.

Fame of Solomon's Wisdom

29 God gave Solomon very great wisdom, discernment, and breadth of understanding as vast as the sand on the seashore, 30 so that Solomon's wisdom surpassed the wisdom of all the people of the east, and all the wisdom of Egypt. 31 He was wiser than anyone else, wiser than Ḗ′than the Ez′ra·hīte, and Hē′man, Cal′col, and Dar′da, children of Mā′hol; his fame spread throughout all the surrounding nations. 32 He composed three thousand proverbs, and his songs numbered a thousand and five. 33 He would speak of trees, from the cedar that is in the Lebanon to the hyssop that grows in the wall; he would speak of animals, and birds, and reptiles, and fish. 34 People came from all the nations to hear the wisdom of Solomon; they came from all the kings of the earth who had heard of his wisdom.

Preparations and Materials for the Temple
(2 Chr 2.1–18)

5 d Now King Hiram of Tȳre sent his servants to Solomon, when he heard that they had anointed him king in place of his father; for Hiram had always been a friend to David. 2 Solomon sent word to Hiram, saying, 3 "You know that my father David could not build a house for the name of the LORD his God because of the warfare with which his enemies surrounded him, until the LORD put them under the soles of his feet. e 4 But now the LORD my God has given me rest on every side; there is neither adversary nor misfortune. 5 So I intend to build a house for the name of the LORD my God, as the LORD said to my father David, 'Your son, whom I will set on your throne in your place, shall build the house for my name.' 6 Therefore command that cedars from the Lebanon be cut for me. My servants will join your servants, and I will give you whatever

c Ch 5.1 in Heb   d Ch 5.15 in Heb
e Gk Tg Vg: Heb *my feet* or *his feet*

1 KINGS

wages you set for your servants; for you know that there is no one among us who knows how to cut timber like the Si·do'ni·ans."

7 When Hiram heard the words of Solomon, he rejoiced greatly, and said, "Blessed be the LORD today, who has given to David a wise son to be over this great people." 8 Hiram sent word to Solomon, "I have heard the message that you have sent to me; I will fulfill all your needs in the matter of cedar and cypress timber. 9 My servants shall bring it down to the sea from the Lebanon; I will make it into rafts to go by sea to the place you indicate. I will have them broken up there for you to take away. And you shall meet my needs by providing food for my household." 10 So Hiram supplied Solomon's every need for timber of cedar and cypress. 11 Solomon in turn gave Hiram twenty thousand cors of wheat as food for his household, and twenty cors of fine oil. Solomon gave this to Hiram year by year. 12 So the LORD gave Solomon wisdom, as he promised him. There was peace between Hiram and Solomon; and the two of them made a treaty.

13 King Solomon conscripted forced labor out of all Israel; the levy numbered thirty thousand men. 14 He sent them to the Lebanon, ten thousand a month in shifts; they would be a month in the Lebanon and two months at home; Ad·o·ni'ram was in charge of the forced labor. 15 Solomon also had seventy thousand laborers and eighty thousand stonecutters in the hill country, 16 besides Solomon's three thousand three hundred supervisors who were over the work, having charge of the people who did the work. 17 At the king's command, they quarried out great, costly stones in order to lay the foundation of the house with dressed stones. 18 So Solomon's builders and Hiram's builders and the Ge'-bal·ites did the stonecutting and prepared the timber and the stone to build the house.

Solomon Builds the Temple
(2 Chr 3.1–14)

6 In the four hundred eightieth year after the Israelites came out of the land of Egypt, in the fourth year of Solomon's reign over Israel, in the month of Ziv, which is the second month, he began to build the house of the LORD. 2 The house that King Solomon built

for the LORD was sixty cubits long, twenty cubits wide, and thirty cubits high. 3 The vestibule in front of the nave of the house was twenty cubits wide, across the width of the house. Its depth was ten cubits in front of the house. 4 For the house he made windows with recessed frames.[f] 5 He also built a structure against the wall of the house, running around the walls of the house, both the nave and the inner sanctuary; and he made side chambers all around. 6 The lowest story[g] was five cubits wide, the middle one was six cubits wide, and the third was seven cubits wide; for around the outside of the house he made offsets on the wall in order that the supporting beams should not be inserted into the walls of the house.

7 The house was built with stone finished at the quarry, so that neither hammer nor ax nor any tool of iron was heard in the temple while it was being built.

8 The entrance for the middle story was on the south side of the house: one went up by winding stairs to the middle story, and from the middle story to the third. 9 So he built the house, and finished it; he roofed the house with beams and planks of cedar. 10 He built the structure against the whole house, each story[h] five cubits high, and it was joined to the house with timbers of cedar.

11 Now the word of the LORD came to Solomon, 12 "Concerning this house that you are building, if you will walk in my statutes, obey my ordinances, and keep all my commandments by walking in them, then I will establish my promise with you, which I made to your father David. 13 I will dwell among the children of Israel, and will not forsake my people Israel."

14 So Solomon built the house, and finished it. 15 He lined the walls of the house on the inside with boards of cedar; from the floor of the house to the rafters of the ceiling, he covered them on the inside with wood; and he covered the floor of the house with boards of cypress. 16 He built twenty cubits of the rear of the house with boards of cedar from the floor to the rafters, and he built this within as an inner sanctuary, as the most holy place. 17 The

f Gk: Meaning of Heb uncertain
g Gk: Heb *structure*   h Heb lacks *each story*

house, that is, the nave in front of the inner sanctuary, was forty cubits long. 18 The cedar within the house had carvings of gourds and open flowers; all was cedar, no stone was seen. 19 The inner sanctuary he prepared in the innermost part of the house, to set there the ark of the covenant of the LORD. 20 The interior of the inner sanctuary was twenty cubits long, twenty cubits wide, and twenty cubits high; he overlaid it with pure gold. He also overlaid the altar with cedar. *i* 21 Solomon overlaid the inside of the house with pure gold, then he drew chains of gold across, in front of the inner sanctuary, and overlaid it with gold. 22 Next he overlaid the whole house with gold, in order that the whole house might be perfect; even the whole altar that belonged to the inner sanctuary he overlaid with gold.

The Furnishings of the Temple
(2 Chr 4.1–10, 19–22; 5.1)

23 In the inner sanctuary he made two cherubim of olivewood, each ten cubits high. 24 Five cubits was the length of one wing of the cherub, and five cubits the length of the other wing of the cherub; it was ten cubits from the tip of one wing to the tip of the other. 25 The other cherub also measured ten cubits; both cherubim had the same measure and the same form. 26 The height of one cherub was ten cubits, and so was that of the other cherub. 27 He put the cherubim in the innermost part of the house; the wings of the cherubim were spread out so that a wing of one was touching the one wall, and a wing of the other cherub was touching the other wall; their other wings toward the center of the house were touching wing to wing. 28 He also overlaid the cherubim with gold.

29 He carved the walls of the house all around about with carved engravings of cherubim, palm trees, and open flowers, in the inner and outer rooms. 30 The floor of the house he overlaid with gold, in the inner and outer rooms. 31 For the entrance to the inner sanctuary he made doors of olivewood; the lintel and the doorposts were five-sided. *i* 32 He covered the two doors of olivewood with carvings of cherubim, palm trees, and open flowers; he overlaid them with gold,

and spread gold on the cherubim and on the palm trees.

33 So also he made for the entrance to the nave doorposts of olivewood, four-sided each, 34 and two doors of cypress wood; the two leaves of the one door were folding, and the two leaves of the other door were folding. 35 He carved cherubim, palm trees, and open flowers, overlaying them with gold evenly applied upon the carved work. 36 He built the inner court with three courses of dressed stone to one course of cedar beams.

37 In the fourth year the foundation of the house of the LORD was laid, in the month of Ziv. 38 In the eleventh year, in the month of Bul, which is the eighth month, the house was finished in all its parts, and according to all its specifications. He was seven years in building it.

Solomon's Palace and Other Buildings

7 Solomon was building his own house thirteen years, and he finished his entire house.
2 He built the House of the Forest of the Lebanon one hundred cubits long, fifty cubits wide, and thirty cubits high, built on four rows of cedar pillars, with cedar beams on the pillars. 3 It was roofed with cedar on the forty-five rafters, fifteen in each row, which were on the pillars. 4 There were window frames in the three rows, facing each other in the three rows. 5 All the doorways and doorposts had four-sided frames, opposite, facing each other in the three rows.
6 He made the Hall of Pillars fifty cubits long and thirty cubits wide. There was a porch in front with pillars, and a canopy in front of them.
7 He made the Hall of the Throne where he was to pronounce judgment, the Hall of Justice, covered with cedar from floor to floor.
8 His own house where he would reside, in the other court back of the hall, was of the same construction. Solomon also made a house like this hall for Pharaoh's daughter, whom he had taken in marriage.
9 All these were made of costly stones, cut according to measure, sawed with saws, back and front, from the foundation to the coping, and from outside to the great court. 10 The foundation was of costly stones, huge

i Meaning of Heb uncertain

stones, stones of eight and ten cubits. [11]There were costly stones above, cut to measure, and cedarwood. [12]The great court had three courses of dressed stone to one layer of cedar beams all around; so had the inner court of the house of the LORD, and the vestibule of the house.

Products of Hiram the Bronzeworker
(2 Chr 3.15–17; 4.11–18)

13 Now King Solomon invited and received Hiram from Tȳre. [14]He was the son of a widow of the tribe of Naph'ta·lī, whose father, a man of Tȳre, had been an artisan in bronze; he was full of skill, intelligence, and knowledge in working bronze. He came to King Solomon, and did all his work.

15 He cast two pillars of bronze. Eighteen cubits was the height of the one, and a cord of twelve cubits would encircle it; the second pillar was the same.[j] [16]He also made two capitals of molten bronze, to set on the tops of the pillars; the height of the one capital was five cubits, and the height of the other capital was five cubits. [17]There were nets of checker work with wreaths of chain work for the capitals on the tops of the pillars; seven[k] for the one capital, and seven[k] for the other capital. [18]He made the columns with two rows around each latticework to cover the capitals that were above the pomegranates; he did the same with the other capital. [19]Now the capitals that were on the tops of the pillars in the vestibule were of lily-work, four cubits high. [20]The capitals were on the two pillars and also above the rounded projection that was beside the latticework; there were two hundred pomegranates in rows all around; and so with the other capital. [21]He set up the pillars at the vestibule of the temple; he set up the pillar on the south and called it Jā'chin; and he set up the pillar on the north and called it Bō'az. [22]On the tops of the pillars was lily-work. Thus the work of the pillars was finished.

23 Then he made the molten sea; it was round, ten cubits from brim to brim, and five cubits high. A line of thirty cubits would encircle it completely. [24]Under its brim were panels all around it, each of ten cubits, surrounding the sea; there were two rows of panels, cast when it was cast. [25]It stood on twelve oxen, three facing north, three facing west, three facing south, and three facing east; the sea was set on them. The hindquarters of each were toward the inside. [26]Its thickness was a handbreadth; its brim was made like the brim of a cup, like the flower of a lily; it held two thousand baths.[l]

27 He also made the ten stands of bronze; each stand was four cubits long, four cubits wide, and three cubits high. [28]This was the construction of the stands: they had borders; the borders were within the frames; [29]on the borders that were set in the frames were lions, oxen, and cherubim. On the frames, both above and below the lions and oxen, there were wreaths of beveled work. [30]Each stand had four bronze wheels and axles of bronze; at the four corners were supports for a basin. The supports were cast with wreaths at the side of each. [31]Its opening was within the crown whose height was one cubit; its opening was round, as a pedestal is made; it was a cubit and a half wide. At its opening there were carvings; its borders were four-sided, not round. [32]The four wheels were underneath the borders; the axles of the wheels were in the stands; and the height of a wheel was a cubit and a half. [33]The wheels were made like a chariot wheel; their axles, their rims, their spokes, and their hubs were all cast. [34]There were four supports at the four corners of each stand; the supports were of one piece with the stands. [35]On the top of the stand there was a round band half a cubit high; on the top of the stand, its stays and its borders were of one piece with it. [36]On the surfaces of its stays and on its borders he carved cherubim, lions, and palm trees, where each had space, with wreaths all around. [37]In this way he made the ten stands; all of them were cast alike, with the same size and the same form.

38 He made ten basins of bronze; each basin held forty baths,[l] each basin measured four cubits; there was a basin for each of the ten stands. [39]He set five of the stands on the south side of the house, and five on the north side of the house; he set the sea on the southeast corner of the house.

---

[j]Cn: Heb *and a cord of twelve cubits encircled the second pillar*; Compare Jer 52.21   [k]Heb: Gk *a net*   [l]A Heb measure of volume

40 Hiram also made the pots, the shovels, and the basins. So Hiram finished all the work that he did for King Solomon on the house of the LORD: 41 the two pillars, the two bowls of the capitals that were on the tops of the pillars, the two latticeworks to cover the two bowls of the capitals that were on the tops of the pillars; 42 the four hundred pomegranates for the two latticeworks, two rows of pomegranates for each latticework, to cover the two bowls of the capitals that were on the pillars; 43 the ten stands, the ten basins on the stands; 44 the one sea, and the twelve oxen underneath the sea.

45 The pots, the shovels, and the basins, all these vessels that Hiram made for King Solomon for the house of the LORD were of burnished bronze. 46 In the plain of the Jordan the king cast them, in the clay ground between Suc′-coth and Zar′e·than. 47 Solomon left all the vessels unweighed, because there were so many of them; the weight of the bronze was not determined.

48 So Solomon made all the vessels that were in the house of the LORD: the golden altar, the golden table for the bread of the Presence, 49 the lampstands of pure gold, five on the south side and five on the north, in front of the inner sanctuary; the flowers, the lamps, and the tongs, of gold; 50 the cups, snuffers, basins, dishes for incense, and firepans, of pure gold; the sockets for the doors of the innermost part of the house, the most holy place, and for the doors of the nave of the temple, of gold.

51 Thus all the work that King Solomon did on the house of the LORD was finished. Solomon brought in the things that his father David had dedicated, the silver, the gold, and the vessels, and stored them in the treasuries of the house of the LORD.

Dedication of the Temple
(2 Chr 5.2—6.2)

8 Then Solomon assembled the elders of Israel and all the heads of the tribes, the leaders of the ancestral houses of the Israelites, before King Solomon in Jerusalem, to bring up the ark of the covenant of the LORD out of the city of David, which is Zion. 2 All the people of Israel assembled to King Solomon at the festival in the month Eth′a·nim, which is the seventh month. 3 And all the elders of Israel came, and the priests carried the ark.

4 So they brought up the ark of the LORD, the tent of meeting, and all the holy vessels that were in the tent; the priests and the Le′vites brought them up. 5 King Solomon and all the congregation of Israel, who had assembled before him, were with him before the ark, sacrificing so many sheep and oxen that they could not be counted or numbered. 6 Then the priests brought the ark of the covenant of the LORD to its place, in the inner sanctuary of the house, in the most holy place, underneath the wings of the cherubim. 7 For the cherubim spread out their wings over the place of the ark, so that the cherubim made a covering above the ark and its poles. 8 The poles were so long that the ends of the poles were seen from the holy place in front of the inner sanctuary; but they could not be seen from outside; they are there to this day. 9 There was nothing in the ark except the two tablets of stone that Moses had placed there at Hō′reb, where the LORD made a covenant with the Israelites, when they came out of the land of Egypt. 10 And when the priests came out of the holy place, a cloud filled the house of the LORD, 11 so that the priests could not stand to minister because of the cloud; for the glory of the LORD filled the house of the LORD.

12 Then Solomon said,
"The LORD has said that he
would dwell in thick
darkness.
13 I have built you an exalted
house,
a place for you to dwell in
forever."

Solomon's Speech
(2 Chr 6.3–11)

14 Then the king turned around and blessed all the assembly of Israel, while all the assembly of Israel stood. 15 He said, "Blessed be the LORD, the God of Israel, who with his hand has fulfilled what he promised with his mouth to my father David, saying, 16 'Since the day that I brought my people Israel out of Egypt, I have not chosen a city from any of the tribes of Israel in which to build a house, that my name might be there; but I chose David to be over my people Israel.' 17 My father David had it in mind to build a house for the name of the LORD, the God of Israel. 18 But the LORD said to my father David, 'You did well to con-

1
K
I
N
G
S

sider building a house for my name; [19] nevertheless you shall not build the house, but your son who shall be born to you shall build the house for my name.' [20] Now the LORD has upheld the promise that he made; for I have risen in the place of my father David; I sit on the throne of Israel, as the LORD promised, and have built the house for the name of the LORD, the God of Israel. [21] There I have provided a place for the ark, in which is the covenant of the LORD that he made with our ancestors when he brought them out of the land of Egypt."

Solomon's Prayer of Dedication
(2 Chr 6.12–39)

22 Then Solomon stood before the altar of the LORD in the presence of all the assembly of Israel, and spread out his hands to heaven. [23] He said, "O LORD, God of Israel, there is no God like you in heaven above or on earth beneath, keeping covenant and steadfast love for your servants who walk before you with all their heart, [24] the covenant that you kept for your servant my father David as you declared to him; you promised with your mouth and have this day fulfilled with your hand. [25] Therefore, O LORD, God of Israel, keep for your servant my father David that which you promised him, saying, 'There shall never fail you a successor before me to sit on the throne of Israel, if only your children look to their way, to walk before me as you have walked before me.' [26] Therefore, O God of Israel, let your word be confirmed, which you promised to your servant my father David.

27 "But will God indeed dwell on the earth? Even heaven and the highest heaven cannot contain you, much less this house that I have built! [28] Regard your servant's prayer and his plea, O LORD my God, heeding the cry and the prayer that your servant prays to you today; [29] that your eyes may be open night and day toward this house, the place of which you said, 'My name shall be there,' that you may heed the prayer that your servant prays toward this place. [30] Hear the plea of your servant and of your people Israel when they pray toward this place; O hear in heaven your dwelling place; heed and forgive.

31 "If someone sins against a neighbor and is given an oath to swear, and comes and swears before your altar in this house, [32] then hear in heaven, and act, and judge your servants, condemning the guilty by bringing their conduct on their own head, and vindicating the righteous by rewarding them according to their righteousness.

33 "When your people Israel, having sinned against you, are defeated before an enemy but turn again to you, confess your name, pray and plead with you in this house, [34] then hear in heaven, forgive the sin of your people Israel, and bring them again to the land that you gave to their ancestors.

35 "When heaven is shut up and there is no rain because they have sinned against you, and then they pray toward this place, confess your name, and turn from their sin, because you punish[m] them, [36] then hear in heaven, and forgive the sin of your servants, your people Israel, when you teach them the good way in which they should walk; and grant rain on your land, which you have given to your people as an inheritance.

37 "If there is famine in the land, if there is plague, blight, mildew, locust, or caterpillar; if their enemy besieges them in any[n] of their cities; whatever plague, whatever sickness there is; [38] whatever prayer, whatever plea there is from any individual or from all your people Israel, all knowing the afflictions of their own hearts so that they stretch out their hands toward this house; [39] then hear in heaven your dwelling place, forgive, act, and render to all whose hearts you know—according to all their ways, for only you know what is in every human heart— [40] so that they may fear you all the days that they live in the land that you gave to our ancestors.

41 "Likewise when a foreigner, who is not of your people Israel, comes from a distant land because of your name [42]—for they shall hear of your great name, your mighty hand, and your outstretched arm—when a foreigner comes and prays toward this house, [43] then hear in heaven your dwelling place, and do according to all that the foreigner calls to you, so that all the peoples of the earth may know your name and fear you, as do your people Israel, and so that they may know that your name has been invoked on this house that I have built.

[m] Or *when you answer*   [n] Gk Syr: Heb *in the land*

44 "If your people go out to battle against their enemy, by whatever way you shall send them, and they pray to the LORD toward the city that you have chosen and the house that I have built for your name, 45 then hear in heaven their prayer and their plea, and maintain their cause.

46 "If they sin against you—for there is no one who does not sin—and you are angry with them and give them to an enemy, so that they are carried away captive to the land of the enemy, far off or near; 47 yet if they come to their senses in the land to which they have been taken captive, and repent, and plead with you in the land of their captors, saying, 'We have sinned, and have done wrong; we have acted wickedly'; 48 if they repent with all their heart and soul in the land of their enemies, who took them captive, and pray to you toward their land, which you gave to their ancestors, the city that you have chosen, and the house that I have built for your name; 49 then hear in heaven your dwelling place their prayer and their plea, maintain their cause 50 and forgive your people who have sinned against you, and all their transgressions that they have committed against you; and grant them compassion in the sight of their captors, so that they may have compassion on them 51 (for they are your people and heritage, which you brought out of Egypt, from the midst of the iron-smelter). 52 Let your eyes be open to the plea of your servant, and to the plea of your people Israel, listening to them whenever they call to you. 53 For you have separated them from among all the peoples of the earth, to be your heritage, just as you promised through Moses, your servant, when you brought our ancestors out of Egypt, O Lord GOD."

Solomon Blesses the Assembly
(2 Chr 6.40–42)

54 Now when Solomon finished offering all this prayer and this plea to the LORD, he arose from facing the altar of the LORD, where he had knelt with hands outstretched toward heaven; 55 he stood and blessed all the assembly of Israel with a loud voice:

56 "Blessed be the LORD, who has given rest to his people Israel according to all that he promised; not one word has failed of all his good promise, which he spoke through his servant Moses. 57 The LORD our God be with us, as he was with our ancestors; may he not leave us or abandon us, 58 but incline our hearts to him, to walk in all his ways, and to keep his commandments, his statutes, and his ordinances, which he commanded our ancestors. 59 Let these words of mine, with which I pleaded before the LORD, be near to the LORD our God day and night, and may he maintain the cause of his servant and the cause of his people Israel, as each day requires; 60 so that all the peoples of the earth may know that the LORD is God; there is no other. 61 Therefore devote yourselves completely to the LORD our God, walking in his statutes and keeping his commandments, as at this day."

Solomon Offers Sacrifices
(2 Chr 7.4–11)

62 Then the king, and all Israel with him, offered sacrifice before the LORD. 63 Solomon offered as sacrifices of well-being to the LORD twenty-two thousand oxen and one hundred twenty thousand sheep. So the king and all the people of Israel dedicated the house of the LORD. 64 The same day the king consecrated the middle of the court that was in front of the house of the LORD; for there he offered the burnt offerings and the grain offerings and the fat pieces of the sacrifices of well-being, because the bronze altar that was before the LORD was too small to receive the burnt offerings and the grain offerings and the fat pieces of the sacrifices of well-being.

65 So Solomon held the festival at that time, and all Israel with him—a great assembly, people from Le'bo-ha'math to the Wadi of Egypt—before the LORD our God, seven days. o 66 On the eighth day he sent the people away; and they blessed the king, and went to their tents, joyful and in good spirits because of all the goodness that the LORD had shown to his servant David and to his people Israel.

God Appears Again to Solomon
(2 Chr 7.11–22)

9 When Solomon had finished building the house of the LORD and the king's house and all that Solomon desired to build, 2 the LORD appeared to Solomon a second time, as

---

o Compare Gk: Heb *seven days and seven days, fourteen days* he had appeared to him at Gib'e·on. ³The LORD said to him, "I have heard your prayer and your plea, which you made before me; I have consecrated this house that you have built, and put my name there forever; my eyes and my heart will be there for all time. ⁴As for you, if you will walk before me, as David your father walked, with integrity of heart and uprightness, doing according to all that I have commanded you, and keeping my statutes and my ordinances, ⁵then I will establish your royal throne over Israel forever, as I promised your father David, saying, 'There shall not fail you a successor on the throne of Israel.'

6 "If you turn aside from following me, you or your children, and do not keep my commandments and my statutes that I have set before you, but go and serve other gods and worship them, ⁷then I will cut Israel off from the land that I have given them; and the house that I have consecrated for my name I will cast out of my sight; and Israel will become a proverb and a taunt among all peoples. ⁸This house will become a heap of ruins;ᵖ everyone passing by it will be astonished, and will hiss; and they will say, 'Why has the LORD done such a thing to this land and to this house?' ⁹Then they will say, 'Because they have forsaken the LORD their God, who brought their ancestors out of the land of Egypt, and embraced other gods, worshiping them and serving them; therefore the LORD has brought this disaster upon them.' "

10 At the end of twenty years, in which Solomon had built the two houses, the house of the LORD and the king's house, ¹¹King Hiram of Tyre having supplied Solomon with cedar and cypress timber and gold, as much as he desired, King Solomon gave to Hiram twenty cities in the land of Galilee. ¹²But when Hiram came from Tyre to see the cities that Solomon had given him, they did not please him. ¹³Therefore he said, "What kind of cities are these that you have given me, my brother?" So they are called the land of Ca'bul�q to this day. ¹⁴But Hiram had sent to the king one hundred twenty talents of gold.

Other Acts of Solomon
(2 Chr 8.3–16)

15 This is the account of the forced labor that King Solomon conscripted

to build the house of the LORD and his own house, the Mil'lo and the wall of Jerusalem, Ha'zor, Me·gid'do, Ge'zer ¹⁶(Pharaoh king of Egypt had gone up and captured Ge'zer and burned it down, had killed the Ca'naan·ites who lived in the city, and had given it as dowry to his daughter, Solomon's wife; ¹⁷so Solomon rebuilt Ge'zer), Lower Beth-ho'ron, ¹⁸Ba'a·lath, Ta'mar in the wilderness, within the land, ¹⁹as well as all of Solomon's storage cities, the cities for his chariots, the cities for his cavalry, and whatever Solomon desired to build, in Jerusalem, in Lebanon, and in all the land of his dominion. ²⁰All the people who were left of the Am'o·rites, the Hit'tites, the Per'iz·zites, the Hi'vites, and the Jeb'u·sites, who were not of the people of Israel— ²¹their descendants who were still left in the land, whom the Israelites were unable to destroy completely—these Solomon conscripted for slave labor, and so they are to this day. ²²But of the Israelites Solomon made no slaves; they were the soldiers, they were his officials, his commanders, his captains, and the commanders of his chariotry and cavalry.

23 These were the chief officers who were over Solomon's work: five hundred fifty, who had charge of the people who carried on the work.

24 But Pharaoh's daughter went up from the city of David to her own house that Solomon had built for her; then he built the Mil'lo.

25 Three times a year Solomon used to offer up burnt offerings and sacrifices of well-being on the altar that he built for the LORD, offering incenseʳ before the LORD. So he completed the house.

Solomon's Commercial Activity
(2 Chr 8.17–18)

26 King Solomon built a fleet of ships at E'zi·on-ge'ber, which is near E'loth on the shore of the Red Sea,ˢ in the land of E'dom. ²⁷Hiram sent his servants with the fleet, sailors who were familiar with the sea, together with the servants of Solomon. ²⁸They went to O'phir, and imported from there four hundred twenty talents of

ᵖSyr Old Latin: Heb *will become high*
�q Perhaps meaning *a land good for nothing* ʳGk: Heb *offering incense with it that was* ˢOr *Sea of Reeds*

gold, which they delivered to King Solomon.

Visit of the Queen of Sheba
(2 Chr 9.1–28)

10 When the queen of She′ba heard of the fame of Solomon, (fame due to[t] the name of the LORD), she came to test him with hard questions. 2 She came to Jerusalem with a very great retinue, with camels bearing spices, and very much gold, and precious stones; and when she came to Solomon, she told him all that was on her mind. 3 Solomon answered all her questions; there was nothing hidden from the king that he could not explain to her. 4 When the queen of She′ba had observed all the wisdom of Solomon, the house that he had built, 5 the food of his table, the seating of his officials, and the attendance of his servants, their clothing, his valets, and his burnt offerings that he offered at the house of the LORD, there was no more spirit in her.

6 So she said to the king, "The report was true that I heard in my own land of your accomplishments and of your wisdom, 7 but I did not believe the reports until I came and my own eyes had seen it. Not even half had been told me; your wisdom and prosperity far surpass the report that I had heard. 8 Happy are your wives![u] Happy are these your servants, who continually attend you and hear your wisdom! 9 Blessed be the LORD your God, who has delighted in you and set you on the throne of Israel! Because the LORD loved Israel forever, he has made you king to execute justice and righteousness." 10 Then she gave the king one hundred twenty talents of gold, a great quantity of spices, and precious stones; never again did spices come in such quantity as that which the queen of She′ba gave to King Solomon.

11 Moreover, the fleet of Hiram, which carried gold from O′phir, brought from O′phir a great quantity of almug wood and precious stones. 12 From the almug wood the king made supports for the house of the LORD, and for the king's house, lyres also and harps for the singers; no such almug wood has come or been seen to this day.

13 Meanwhile King Solomon gave to the queen of She′ba every desire that she expressed, as well as what he gave her out of Solomon's royal bounty. Then she returned to her own land, with her servants.

14 The weight of gold that came to Solomon in one year was six hundred sixty-six talents of gold, 15 besides that which came from the traders and from the business of the merchants, and from all the kings of Arabia and the governors of the land. 16 King Solomon made two hundred large shields of beaten gold; six hundred shekels of gold went into each large shield. 17 He made three hundred shields of beaten gold; three minas of gold went into each shield; and the king put them in the House of the Forest of Lebanon. 18 The king also made a great ivory throne, and overlaid it with the finest gold. 19 The throne had six steps. The top of the throne was rounded in the back, and on each side of the seat were arm rests and two lions standing beside the arm rests, 20 while twelve lions were standing, one on each end of a step on the six steps. Nothing like it was ever made in any kingdom. 21 All King Solomon's drinking vessels were of gold, and all the vessels of the House of the Forest of Lebanon were of pure gold; none were of silver—it was not considered as anything in the days of Solomon. 22 For the king had a fleet of ships of Tar′shish at sea with the fleet of Hiram. Once every three years the fleet of ships of Tar′shish used to come bringing gold, silver, ivory, apes, and peacocks.[v]

23 Thus King Solomon excelled all the kings of the earth in riches and in wisdom. 24 The whole earth sought the presence of Solomon to hear his wisdom, which God had put into his mind. 25 Every one of them brought a present, objects of silver and gold, garments, weaponry, spices, horses, and mules, so much year by year.

26 Solomon gathered together chariots and horses; he had fourteen hundred chariots and twelve thousand horses, which he stationed in the chariot cities and with the king in Jerusalem. 27 The king made silver as common in Jerusalem as stones, and made cedars as numerous as the sycamores of the She·phe′lah. 28 Solomon's import of horses was from Egypt and Ku′e, and the king's traders received them from Ku′e at a price. 29 A chariot could be imported from Egypt for six

t Meaning of Heb uncertain   *u* Gk Syr: Heb *men*   *v* Or *baboons* hundred shekels of silver, and a horse for one hundred fifty; so through the king's traders they were exported to all the kings of the Hit′tītes and the kings of Ar′am.

Solomon's Errors

11 King Solomon loved many foreign women along with the daughter of Pharaoh: Mō′ab·īte, Am′mon·īte, E′dom·īte, Sī·dō′ni·an, and Hit′tīte women, ² from the nations concerning which the LORD had said to the Israelites, "You shall not enter into marriage with them, neither shall they with you; for they will surely incline your heart to follow their gods"; Solomon clung to these in love. ³ Among his wives were seven hundred princesses and three hundred concubines; and his wives turned away his heart. ⁴ For when Solomon was old, his wives turned away his heart after other gods; and his heart was not true to the LORD his God, as was the heart of his father David. ⁵ For Solomon followed As·tar′tē the goddess of the Sī·dō′ni·ans, and Mil′com the abomination of the Am′mon·ītes. ⁶ So Solomon did what was evil in the sight of the LORD, and did not completely follow the LORD, as his father David had done. ⁷ Then Solomon built a high place for Che′mosh the abomination of Mō′ab, and for Mō′lech the abomination of the Am′mon·ītes, on the mountain east of Jerusalem. ⁸ He did the same for all his foreign wives, who offered incense and sacrificed to their gods.

9 Then the LORD was angry with Solomon, because his heart had turned away from the LORD, the God of Israel, who had appeared to him twice, ¹⁰ and had commanded him concerning this matter, that he should not follow other gods; but he did not observe what the LORD commanded. ¹¹ Therefore the LORD said to Solomon, "Since this has been your mind and you have not kept my covenant and my statutes that I have commanded you, I will surely tear the kingdom from you and give it to your servant. ¹² Yet for the sake of your father David I will not do it in your lifetime; I will tear it out of the hand of your son. ¹³ I will not, however, tear away the entire kingdom; I will give one tribe to your son, for the sake of my servant David and for the sake of Jerusalem, which I have chosen."

Adversaries of Solomon

14 Then the LORD raised up an adversary against Solomon, Hā′dad the E′dom·īte; he was of the royal house in E′dom. ¹⁵ For when David was in E′dom, and Jō′ab the commander of the army went up to bury the dead, he killed every male in E′dom ¹⁶ (for Jō′ab and all Israel remained there six months, until he had eliminated every male in E′dom); ¹⁷ but Hā′dad fled to Egypt with some E′dom·ītes who were servants of his father. He was a young boy at that time. ¹⁸ They set out from Mid′i·an and came to Par′an; they took people with them from Par′an and came to Egypt, to Pharaoh king of Egypt, who gave him a house, assigned him an allowance of food, and gave him land. ¹⁹ Hā′dad found great favor in the sight of Pharaoh, so that he gave him his sister-in-law for a wife, the sister of Queen Tah′pe·nēs. ²⁰ The sister of Tah′pe·nēs gave birth by him to his son Ge·nū′bath, whom Tah′pe·nēs weaned in Pharaoh's house; Ge·nū′bath was in Pharaoh's house among the children of Pharaoh. ²¹ When Hā′dad heard in Egypt that David slept with his ancestors and that Jō′ab the commander of the army was dead, Hā′dad said to Pharaoh, "Let me depart, that I may go to my own country." ²² But Pharaoh said to him, "What do you lack with me that you now seek to go to your own country?" And he said, "No, do let me go."

23 God raised up another adversary against Solomon, *w* Rē′zon son of E·lī′a·da, who had fled from his master, King Had·a·dē′zer of Zō′bah. ²⁴ He gathered followers around him and became leader of a marauding band, after the slaughter by David; they went to Damascus, settled there, and made him king in Damascus. ²⁵ He was an adversary of Israel all the days of Solomon, making trouble as Hā′dad did; he despised Israel and reigned over Ar′am.

Jeroboam's Rebellion

26 Jer·o·bō′am son of Nē′bat, an E′phra·im·īte of Zer′e·dah, a servant of Solomon, whose mother's name was Ze·rū′ah, a widow, rebelled against the king. ²⁷ The following was the reason he rebelled against the king. Solo-

w Heb *him*

non built the Mil′lo, and closed up the gap in the wall ˣ of the city of his father David. 28 The man Jer·o·bo′am was very able, and when Solomon saw that the young man was industrious he gave him charge over all the forced labor of the house of Joseph. 29 About that time, when Jer·o·bo′am was leaving Jerusalem, the prophet A·hi′jah the Shi′lo·nite found him on the road. A·hi′jah had clothed himself with a new garment. The two of them were alone in the open country 30 when A·hi′jah laid hold of the new garment he was wearing and tore it into twelve pieces. 31 He then said to Jer·o·bo′am: Take for yourself ten pieces; for thus says the LORD, the God of Israel, "See, I am about to tear the kingdom from the hand of Solomon, and will give you ten tribes. 32 One tribe will remain his, for the sake of my servant David and for the sake of Jerusalem, the city that I have chosen out of all the tribes of Israel. 33 This is because he has ʸ forsaken me, worshiped As·tar′te the goddess of the Si·do′ni·ans, Che′mosh the god of Mo′ab, and Mil′com the god of the Am′mon·ites, and has ʸ not walked in my ways, doing what is right in my sight and keeping my statutes and my ordinances, as his father David did. 34 Nevertheless I will not take the whole kingdom away from him but will make him ruler all the days of his life, for the sake of my servant David whom I chose and who did keep my commandments and my statutes; 35 but I will take the kingdom away from his son and give it to you—that is, the ten tribes. 36 Yet to his son I will give one tribe, so that my servant David may always have a lamp before me in Jerusalem, the city where I have chosen to put my name. 37 I will take you, and you shall reign over all that your soul desires; you shall be king over Israel. 38 If you will listen to all that I command you, walk in my ways, and do what is right in my sight by keeping my statutes and my commandments, as David my servant did, I will be with you, and will build you an enduring house, as I built for David, and I will give Israel to you. 39 For this reason I will punish the descendants of David, but not forever." 40 Solomon sought therefore to kill Jer·o·bo′am; but Jer·o·bo′am promptly fled to Egypt, to King Shi′shak of Egypt, and remained in Egypt until the death of Solomon.

Death of Solomon
(2 Chr 9.29–31)

41 Now the rest of the acts of Solomon, all that he did as well as his wisdom, are they not written in the Book of the Acts of Solomon? 42 The time that Solomon reigned in Jerusalem over all Israel was forty years. 43 Solomon slept with his ancestors and was buried in the city of his father David; and his son Re·ho·bo′am succeeded him.

The Northern Tribes Secede
(2 Chr 10.1–19)

12 Re·ho·bo′am went to She′chem, for all Israel had come to She′chem to make him king. 2 When Jer·o·bo′am son of Ne′bat heard of it (for he was still in Egypt, where he had fled from King Solomon), then Jer·o·bo′am returned from ᶻ Egypt. 3 And they sent and called him; and Jer·o·bo′am and all the assembly of Israel came and said to Re·ho·bo′am, 4 "Your father made our yoke heavy. Now therefore lighten the hard service of your father and his heavy yoke that he placed on us, and we will serve you." 5 He said to them, "Go away for three days, then come again to me." So the people went away.

6 Then King Re·ho·bo′am took counsel with the older men who had attended his father Solomon while he was still alive, saying, "How do you advise me to answer this people?" 7 They answered him, "If you will be a servant to this people today and serve them, and speak good words to them when you answer them, then they will be your servants forever." 8 But he disregarded the advice that the older men gave him, and consulted with the young men who had grown up with him and now attended him. 9 He said to them, "What do you advise that we answer this people who have said to me, 'Lighten the yoke that your father put on us'?" 10 The young men who had grown up with him said to him, "Thus you should say to this people who spoke to you, 'Your father made our yoke heavy, but you must lighten it for us'; thus you should say to them, 'My little finger is thicker than my father's loins. 11 Now, whereas my father laid

ˣ Heb lacks *in the wall*   ʸ Gk Syr Vg: Heb *they have*   ᶻ Gk Vg Compare 2 Chr 10.2: Heb *lived in* on you a heavy yoke, I will add to your yoke. My father disciplined you with whips, but I will discipline you with scorpions.' "

12 So Jer·o·bō'am and all the people came to Rē·ho·bō'am the third day, as the king had said, "Come to me again the third day." 13 The king answered the people harshly. He disregarded the advice that the older men had given him 14 and spoke to them according to the advice of the young men, "My father made your yoke heavy, but I will add to your yoke; my father disciplined you with whips, but I will discipline you with scorpions." 15 So the king did not listen to the people, because it was a turn of affairs brought about by the LORD that he might fulfill his word, which the LORD had spoken by A·hī'jah the Shī'lo·nīte to Jer·o·bō'am son of Nē'bat.

16 When all Israel saw that the king would not listen to them, the people answered the king,

"What share do we have in
   David?
We have no inheritance in the
   son of Jesse.
To your tents, O Israel!
Look now to your own house,
   O David."

So Israel went away to their tents. 17 But Rē·ho·bō'am reigned over the Israelites who were living in the towns of Judah. 18 When King Rē·ho·bō'am sent A·dor'am, who was taskmaster over the forced labor, all Israel stoned him to death. King Rē·ho·bō'am then hurriedly mounted his chariot to flee to Jerusalem. 19 So Israel has been in rebellion against the house of David to this day.

First Dynasty: Jeroboam
Reigns over Israel
(2 Chr 11.1–4)

20 When all Israel heard that Jer·o·bō'am had returned, they sent and called him to the assembly and made him king over all Israel. There was no one who followed the house of David, except the tribe of Judah alone.

21 When Rē·ho·bō'am came to Jerusalem, he assembled all the house of Judah and the tribe of Benjamin, one hundred eighty thousand chosen troops to fight against the house of Israel, to restore the kingdom to Rē·ho·bō'am son of Solomon. 22 But the word of God came to She·māi'ah the man of God: 23 Say to King

Rē·ho·bō'am of Judah, son of Solomon, and to all the house of Judah and Benjamin, and to the rest of the people, 24 "Thus says the LORD, You shall not go up or fight against your kindred the people of Israel. Let everyone go home, for this thing is from me." So they heeded the word of the LORD and went home again, according to the word of the LORD.

Jeroboam's Golden Calves

25 Then Jer·o·bō'am built Shē'chem in the hill country of E'phra·im and resided there; he went out from there and built Pe·nū'el. 26 Then Jer·o·bō'am said to himself, "Now the kingdom may well revert to the house of David. 27 If this people continues to go up to offer sacrifices in the house of the LORD at Jerusalem, the heart of this people will turn again to their master King Rē·ho·bō'am of Judah; they will kill me and return to King Rē·ho·bō'am of Judah." 28 So the king took counsel, and made two calves of gold. He said to the people,[a] "You have gone up to Jerusalem long enough. Here are your gods, O Israel, who brought you up out of the land of Egypt." 29 He set one in Beth'el, and the other he put in Dan. 30 And this thing became a sin, for the people went to worship before the one at Beth'el and before the other as far as Dan.[b] 31 He also made houses[c] on high places, and appointed priests from among all the people, who were not Lē'vītes. 32 Jer·o·bō'am appointed a festival on the fifteenth day of the eighth month like the festival that was in Judah, and he offered sacrifices on the altar; so he did in Beth'el, sacrificing to the calves that he had made. And he placed in Beth'el the priests of the high places that he had made. 33 He went up to the altar that he had made in Beth'el on the fifteenth day in the eighth month in the month that he alone had devised; he appointed a festival for the people of Israel, and he went up to the altar to offer incense.

A Man of God from Judah

13 While Jer·o·bō'am was standing by the altar to offer incense, a man of God came out of Judah by the word of the LORD to Beth'el 2 and pro-

---

a Gk: Heb to them   b Compare Gk: Heb went to the one as far as Dan   c Gk Vg Compare 13.32: Heb a house claimed against the altar by the word of the LORD, and said, "O altar, altar, thus says the LORD: 'A son shall be born to the house of David, Jō·sī′ah by name; and he shall sacrifice on you the priests of the high places who offer incense on you, and human bones shall be burned on you.' " ³He gave a sign the same day, saying, "This is the sign that the LORD has spoken: 'The altar shall be torn down, and the ashes that are on it shall be poured out.' " ⁴When he king heard what the man of God cried out against the altar at Beth′el, Jer·o·bō′am stretched out his hand from the altar, saying, "Seize him!" But he hand that he stretched out against him withered so that he could not draw t back to himself. ⁵The altar also was torn down, and the ashes poured out from the altar, according to the sign that the man of God had given by the word of the LORD. ⁶The king said to the man of God, "Entreat now the favor of he LORD your God, and pray for me, so that my hand may be restored to me." So the man of God entreated the LORD; and the king's hand was restored to him, and became as it was before. ⁷Then the king said to the man of God, "Come home with me and dine, and I will give you a gift." ⁸But the man of God said to the king, "If you give me half your kingdom, I will not go in with you; nor will I eat food or drink water in this place. ⁹For thus I was commanded by the word of the LORD: You shall not eat food, or drink water, or return by the way that you came." ¹⁰So he went another way, and did not return by the way that he had come to Beth′el.

11 Now there lived an old prophet in Beth′el. One of his sons came and told him all that the man of God had done that day in Beth′el; the words also that he had spoken to the king, they told to their father. ¹²Their father said to them, "Which way did he go?" And his sons showed him the way that the man of God who came from Judah had gone. ¹³Then he said to his sons, "Saddle a donkey for me." So they saddled a donkey for him, and he mounted it. ¹⁴He went after the man of God, and found him sitting under an oak tree. He said to him, "Are you the man of God who came from Judah?" He answered, "I am." ¹⁵Then he said to him, "Come home with me and eat some food." ¹⁶But he said, "I cannot return with you, or go in with you; nor will I

eat food or drink water with you in this place; ¹⁷for it was said to me by the word of the LORD: You shall not eat food or drink water there, or return by the way that you came." ¹⁸Then the other[d] said to him, "I also am a prophet as you are, and an angel spoke to me by the word of the LORD: Bring him back with you into your house so that he may eat food and drink water." But he was deceiving him. ¹⁹Then the man of God[d] went back with him, and ate food and drank water in his house.

20 As they were sitting at the table, the word of the LORD came to the prophet who had brought him back; ²¹and he proclaimed to the man of God who came from Judah, "Thus says the LORD: Because you have disobeyed the word of the LORD, and have not kept the commandment that the LORD your God commanded you, ²²but have come back and have eaten food and drunk water in the place of which he said to you, 'Eat no food, and drink no water,' your body shall not come to your ancestral tomb." ²³After the man of God[d] had eaten food and had drunk, they saddled for him a donkey belonging to the prophet who had brought him back. ²⁴Then as he went away, a lion met him on the road and killed him. His body was thrown in the road, and the donkey stood beside it; the lion also stood beside the body. ²⁵People passed by and saw the body thrown in the road, with the lion standing by the body. And they came and told it in the town where the old prophet lived.

26 When the prophet who had brought him back from the way heard of it, he said, "It is the man of God who disobeyed the word of the LORD; therefore the LORD has given him to the lion, which has torn him and killed him according to the word that the LORD spoke to him." ²⁷Then he said to his sons, "Saddle a donkey for me." So they saddled one, ²⁸and he went and found the body thrown in the road, with the donkey and the lion standing beside the body. The lion had not eaten the body or attacked the donkey. ²⁹The prophet took up the body of the man of God, laid it on the donkey, and brought it back to the city,[e] to mourn and to bury him. ³⁰He laid the body in his own grave; and they mourned over him, saying, "Alas, my brother!" ³¹Af-

ter he had buried him, he said to his sons, "When I die, bury me in the grave in which the man of God is buried; lay my bones beside his bones. ³²For the saying that he proclaimed by the word of the LORD against the altar in Beth′el, and against all the houses of the high places that are in the cities of Sa·mar′i·a, shall surely come to pass."

33 Even after this event Jer·o·bo′am did not turn from his evil way, but made priests for the high places again from among all the people; any who wanted to be priests he consecrated for the high places. ³⁴This matter became sin to the house of Jer·o·bo′am, so as to cut it off and to destroy it from the face of the earth.

Judgment on the House of Jeroboam

14 At that time A·bi′jah son of Jer·o·bo′am fell sick. ²Jeroboam said to his wife, "Go, disguise yourself, so that it will not be known that you are the wife of Jer·o·bo′am, and go to Shi′loh; for the prophet A·hi′jah is there, who said of me that I should be king over this people. ³Take with you ten loaves, some cakes, and a jar of honey, and go to him; he will tell you what shall happen to the child."

4 Jer·o·bo′am's wife did so; she set out and went to Shi′loh, and came to the house of A·hi′jah. Now A·hi′jah could not see, for his eyes were dim because of his age. ⁵But the LORD said to A·hi′jah, "The wife of Jer·o·bo′am is coming to inquire of you concerning her son; for he is sick. Thus and thus you shall say to her."

When she came, she pretended to be another woman. ⁶But when A·hi′jah heard the sound of her feet, as she came in at the door, he said, "Come in, wife of Jer·o·bo′am; why do you pretend to be another? For I am charged with heavy tidings for you. ⁷Go, tell Jer·o·bo′am, 'Thus says the LORD, the God of Israel: Because I exalted you from among the people, made you leader over my people Israel, ⁸and tore the kingdom away from the house of David to give it to you; yet you have not been like my servant David, who kept my commandments and followed me with all his heart, doing only that which was right in my sight, ⁹but you have done evil above all those who were before you and have gone and made for yourself other gods, and cast images, provoking me to anger, and

have thrust me behind your back ¹⁰therefore, I will bring evil upon the house of Jer·o·bo′am. I will cut off from Jer·o·bo′am every male, both bond and free in Israel, and will consume the house of Jer·o·bo′am, just as one burns up dung until it is all gone. ¹¹Anyone belonging to Jer·o·bo′am who dies in the city, the dogs shall eat; and anyone who dies in the open country, the birds of the air shall eat; for the LORD has spoken.' ¹²Therefore set out, go to your house. When your feet enter the city, the child shall die. ¹³All Israel shall mourn for him and bury him; for he alone of Jer·o·bo′am's family shall come to the grave, because in him there is found something pleasing to the LORD, the God of Israel, in the house of Jer·o·bo′am. ¹⁴Moreover the LORD will raise up for himself a king over Israel, who shall cut off the house of Jer·o·bo′am today, even right now!ᶠ

15 "The LORD will strike Israel, as a reed is shaken in the water; he will root up Israel out of this good land that he gave to their ancestors, and scatter them beyond the Euphrates, because they have made their sacred poles,ᵍ provoking the LORD to anger. ¹⁶He will give Israel up because of the sins of Jer·o·bo′am, which he sinned and which he caused Israel to commit."

17 Then Jer·o·bo′am's wife got up and went away, and she came to Tir′zah. As she came to the threshold of the house, the child died. ¹⁸All Israel buried him and mourned for him, according to the word of the LORD, which he spoke by his servant the prophet A·hi′jah.

Death of Jeroboam

19 Now the rest of the acts of Jer·o·bo′am, how he warred and how he reigned, are written in the Book of the Annals of the Kings of Israel. ²⁰The time that Jer·o·bo′am reigned was twenty-two years; then he slept with his ancestors, and his son Na′dab succeeded him.

Rehoboam Reigns over Judah
(2 Chr 11.5—12.16)

21 Now Re·ho·bo′am son of Solomon reigned in Judah. Re·ho·bo′am was forty-one years old when he began to reign, and he reigned seventeen

ᶠMeaning of Heb uncertain
ᵍHeb Asherim

years in Jerusalem, the city that the LORD had chosen out of all the tribes of Israel, to put his name there. His mother's name was Na'a·mah the Am'mon·īte. 22 Judah did what was evil in the sight of the LORD; they provoked him to jealousy with their sins that they committed, more than all that their ancestors had done. 23 For they also built for themselves high places, pillars, and sacred poles [h] on every high hill and under every green tree; 24 there were also male temple prostitutes in the land. They committed all the abominations of the nations that the LORD drove out before the people of Israel.

25 In the fifth year of King Rē·ho·bō'am, King Shī'shak of Egypt came up against Jerusalem; 26 he took away the treasures of the house of the LORD and the treasures of the king's house; he took everything. He also took away all the shields of gold that Solomon had made; 27 so King Rē·ho·bō'am made shields of bronze instead, and committed them to the hands of the officers of the guard, who kept the door of the king's house. 28 As often as the king went into the house of the LORD, the guard carried them and brought them back to the guardroom. 29 Now the rest of the acts of Rē·ho·bō'am, and all that he did, are they not written in the Book of the Annals of the Kings of Judah? 30 There was war between Rē·ho·bō'am and Jer·o·bō'am continually. 31 Rē·ho·bō'am slept with his ancestors and was buried with his ancestors in the city of David. His mother's name was Na'a·mah the Am'mon·īte. His son A·bī'jam succeeded him.

Abijam Reigns over Judah: Idolatry and War
(2 Chr 13.1—14.1)

15 Now in the eighteenth year of King Jer·o·bō'am son of Ne'·bat, A·bī'jam began to reign over Judah. 2 He reigned for three years in Jerusalem. His mother's name was Ma'a·cah daughter of A·bish'a·lom. 3 He committed all the sins that his father did before him; his heart was not true to the LORD his God, like the heart of his father David. 4 Nevertheless for David's sake the LORD his God gave him a lamp in Jerusalem, setting up his son after him, and establishing Jerusalem; 5 because David did what was right in the sight of the LORD, and did

not turn aside from anything that he commanded him all the days of his life, except in the matter of U·rī'ah the Hit'·tīte. 6 The war begun between Rē·ho·bō'am and Jer·o·bō'am continued all the days of his life. 7 The rest of the acts of A·bī'jam, and all that he did, are they not written in the Book of the Annals of the Kings of Judah? There was war between A·bī'jam and Jer·o·bō'am. 8 A·bī'jam slept with his ancestors, and they buried him in the city of David. Then his son Asa succeeded him.

Asa Reigns over Judah
(2 Chr 14.1—15.19)

9 In the twentieth year of King Jer·o·bō'am of Israel, Asa began to reign over Judah; 10 he reigned forty-one years in Jerusalem. His mother's name was Ma'a·cah daughter of A·bish'a·lom. 11 Asa did what was right in the sight of the LORD, as his father David had done. 12 He put away the male temple prostitutes out of the land, and removed all the idols that his ancestors had made. 13 He also removed his mother Ma'a·cah from being queen mother, because she had made an abominable image for A·she'·rah; Asa cut down her image and burned it at the Wadi Kid'ron. 14 But the high places were not taken away. Nevertheless the heart of Asa was true to the LORD all his days. 15 He brought into the house of the LORD the votive gifts of his father and his own votive gifts—silver, gold, and utensils.

Alliance with Aram against Israel
(2 Chr 16.1—17.1)

16 There was war between Asa and King Ba'a·sha of Israel all their days. 17 King Ba'a·sha of Israel went up against Judah, and built Ra'mah, to prevent anyone from going out or coming in to King Asa of Judah. 18 Then Asa took all the silver and the gold that were left in the treasures of the house of the LORD and the treasures of the king's house, and gave them into the hands of his servants. King Asa sent them to King Ben-ha'·dad son of Tab·rim'mon son of He'·zi·on of Ar'am, who resided in Damascus, saying, 19 "Let there be an alliance between me and you, like that between my father and your father: I am sending you a present of silver and gold; go,

[h] Heb *Asherim*

break your alliance with King Bā'-a·sha of Israel, so that he may withdraw from me." 20 Ben-hā'dad listened to King Asa, and sent the commanders of his armies against the cities of Israel. He conquered I'jon, Dan, A'bel-beth-ma'a·cah, and all Chin'ne·roth, with all the land of Naph'ta·li. 21 When Bā'a·sha heard of it, he stopped building Rā'mah and lived in Tir'zah. 22 Then King Asa made a proclamation to all Judah, none was exempt: they carried away the stones of Rā'mah and its timber, with which Bā'a·sha had been building; with them King Asa built Gē'ba of Benjamin and Miz'pah. 23 Now the rest of all the acts of Asa, all his power, all that he did, and the cities that he built, are they not written in the Book of the Annals of the Kings of Judah? But in his old age he was diseased in his feet. 24 Then Asa slept with his ancestors, and was buried with his ancestors in the city of his father David; his son Je·hosh'a·phat succeeded him.

Nadab Reigns over Israel

25 Nā'dab son of Jer·o·bō'am began to reign over Israel in the second year of King Asa of Judah; he reigned over Israel two years. 26 He did what was evil in the sight of the LORD, walking in the way of his ancestor and in the sin that he caused Israel to commit. 27 Bā'a·sha son of A·hi'jah, of the house of Is'sa·char, conspired against him; and Bā'a·sha struck him down at Gib'be·thon, which belonged to the Phi·lis'tines; for Nā'dab and all Israel were laying siege to Gib'be·thon. 28 So Bā'a·sha killed Nā'dab[i] in the third year of King Asa of Judah, and succeeded him. 29 As soon as he was king, he killed all the house of Jer·o·bō'am; he left to the house of Jer·o·bō'am not one that breathed, until he had destroyed it, according to the word of the LORD that he spoke by his servant A·hi'jah the Shi'lo·nite— 30 because of the sins of Jer·o·bō'am that he committed and that he caused Israel to commit, and because of the anger to which he provoked the LORD, the God of Israel.

31 Now the rest of the acts of Nā'-dab, and all that he did, are they not written in the Book of the Annals of the Kings of Israel? 32 There was war between Asa and King Bā'a·sha of Israel all their days.

Second Dynasty: Baasha Reigns over Israel

33 In the third year of King Asa of Judah, Bā'a·sha son of A·hi'jah began to reign over all Israel at Tir'zah; he reigned twenty-four years. 34 He did what was evil in the sight of the LORD, walking in the way of Jer·o·bō'am and in the sin that he caused Israel to commit.

16 The word of the LORD came to Jē'hu son of Ha·nā'ni against Bā'a·sha, saying, 2 "Since I exalted you out of the dust and made you leader over my people Israel, and you have walked in the way of Jer·o·bō'am, and have caused my people Israel to sin, provoking me to anger with their sins, 3 therefore, I will consume Bā'a·sha and his house, and I will make your house like the house of Jer·o·bō'am son of Nē'bat. 4 Anyone belonging to Bā'a·sha who dies in the city the dogs shall eat; and anyone of his who dies in the field the birds of the air shall eat."

5 Now the rest of the acts of Bā'-a·sha, what he did, and his power, are they not written in the Book of the Annals of the Kings of Israel? 6 Bā'a·sha slept with his ancestors, and was buried at Tir'zah; and his son E'lah succeeded him. 7 Moreover the word of the LORD came by the prophet Jē'hu son of Ha·nā'ni against Bā'a·sha and his house, both because of all the evil that he did in the sight of the LORD, provoking him to anger with the work of his hands, in being like the house of Jer·o·bō'am, and also because he destroyed it.

Elah Reigns over Israel

8 In the twenty-sixth year of King Asa of Judah, E'lah son of Bā'a·sha began to reign over Israel in Tir'zah; he reigned two years. 9 But his servant Zim'ri, commander of half his chariots, conspired against him. When he was at Tir'zah, drinking himself drunk in the house of Ar'za, who was in charge of the palace at Tir'zah, 10 Zim'ri came in and struck him down and killed him, in the twenty-seventh year of King Asa of Judah, and succeeded him.

11 When he began to reign, as soon as he had seated himself on his throne, he killed all the house of Bā'a·sha; he did not leave him a single male of his

[i] Heb *him*

kindred or his friends. 12Thus Zim′ri destroyed all the house of Ba′a·sha, according to the word of the LORD, which he spoke against Ba′a·sha by the prophet Je′hu— 13because of all the sins of Ba′a·sha and the sins of his son E′lah that they committed, and that they caused Israel to commit, provoking the LORD God of Israel to anger with their idols. 14Now the rest of the acts of E′lah, and all that he did, are they not written in the Book of the Annals of the Kings of Israel?

Third Dynasty: Zimri Reigns over Israel

15 In the twenty-seventh year of King Asa of Judah, Zim′ri reigned seven days in Tir′zah. Now the troops were encamped against Gib′be·thon, which belonged to the Phi·lis′tines, 16and the troops who were encamped heard it said, "Zim′ri has conspired, and he has killed the king"; therefore all Israel made Om′ri, the commander of the army, king over Israel that day in the camp. 17So Om′ri went up from Gib′be·thon, and all Israel with him, and they besieged Tir′zah. 18When Zim′ri saw that the city was taken, he went into the citadel of the king's house; he burned down the king's house over himself with fire, and died— 19because of the sins that he committed, doing evil in the sight of the LORD, walking in the way of Jer·o·bo′am, and for the sin that he committed, causing Israel to sin. 20Now the rest of the acts of Zim′ri, and the conspiracy that he made, are they not written in the Book of the Annals of the Kings of Israel?

Fourth Dynasty: Omri Reigns over Israel

21 Then the people of Israel were divided into two parts; half of the people followed Tib′ni son of Gi′nath, to make him king, and half followed Om′ri. 22But the people who followed Om′ri overcame the people who followed Tib′ni son of Gi′nath; so Tib′ni died, and Om′ri became king. 23In the thirty-first year of King Asa of Judah, Om′ri began to reign over Israel; he reigned for twelve years, six of them in Tir′zah.

Samaria the New Capital

24 He bought the hill of Sa·mar′i·a from She′mer for two talents of silver; he fortified the hill, and called the city that he built, Sa·mar′i·a, after the name of She′mer, the owner of the hill.

25 Om′ri did what was evil in the sight of the LORD; he did more evil than all who were before him. 26For he walked in all the way of Jer·o·bo′am son of Ne′bat, and in the sins that he caused Israel to commit, provoking the LORD, the God of Israel, to anger by their idols. 27Now the rest of the acts of Om′ri that he did, and the power that he showed, are they not written in the Book of the Annals of the Kings of Israel? 28Om′ri slept with his ancestors, and was buried in Sa·mar′i·a; his son A′hab succeeded him.

Ahab Reigns over Israel

29 In the thirty-eighth year of King Asa of Judah, A′hab son of Om′ri began to reign over Israel; A′hab son of Om′ri reigned over Israel in Sa·mar′i·a twenty-two years. 30A′hab son of Om′ri did evil in the sight of the LORD more than all who were before him.

Ahab Marries Jezebel and Worships Baal

31 And as if it had been a light thing for him to walk in the sins of Jer·o·bo′am son of Ne′bat, he took as his wife Jez′e·bel daughter of King Eth·ba′al of the Si·do′ni·ans, and went and served Ba′al, and worshiped him. 32He erected an altar for Ba′al in the house of Ba′al, which he built in Sa·mar′i·a. 33A′hab also made a sacred pole.*i* A′hab did more to provoke the anger of the LORD, the God of Israel, than had all the kings of Israel who were before him. 34In his days Hi′el of Beth′el built Jericho; he laid its foundation at the cost of A·bi′ram his firstborn, and set up its gates at the cost of his youngest son Se′gub, according to the word of the LORD, which he spoke by Joshua son of Nun.

Elijah Predicts a Drought

17 Now E·li′jah the Tish′bite, of Tish′be*k* in Gil′e·ad said to A′hab, "As the LORD the God of Israel lives, before whom I stand, there shall be neither dew nor rain these years, except by my word." 2The word of the LORD came to him, saying, 3"Go from here and turn eastward, and hide yourself by the Wadi Che′rith, which is east of the Jordan. 4You shall drink from the wadi, and I have commanded the ravens to feed you there." 5So he went

i Heb Asherah   *k* Gk: Heb of the settlers

and did according to the word of the LORD; he went and lived by the Wadi Che´rith, which is east of the Jordan. 6 The ravens brought him bread and meat in the morning, and bread and meat in the evening; and he drank from the wadi. 7 But after a while the wadi dried up, because there was no rain in the land.

The Widow of Zarephath

8 Then the word of the LORD came to him, saying, 9 "Go now to Zar´e·phath, which belongs to Si´don, and live there; for I have commanded a widow there to feed you." 10 So he set out and went to Zar´e·phath. When he came to the gate of the town, a widow was there gathering sticks; he called to her and said, "Bring me a little water in a vessel, so that I may drink." 11 As she was going to bring it, he called to her and said, "Bring me a morsel of bread in your hand." 12 But she said, "As the LORD your God lives, I have nothing baked, only a handful of meal in a jar, and a little oil in a jug; I am now gathering a couple of sticks, so that I may go home and prepare it for myself and my son, that we may eat it, and die." 13 E·li´jah said to her, "Do not be afraid; go and do as you have said; but first make me a little cake of it and bring it to me, and afterwards make something for yourself and your son. 14 For thus says the LORD the God of Israel: The jar of meal will not be emptied and the jug of oil will not fail until the day that the LORD sends rain on the earth." 15 She went and did as E·li´jah said, so that she as well as he and her household ate for many days. 16 The jar of meal was not emptied, neither did the jug of oil fail, according to the word of the LORD that he spoke by E·li´jah.

Elijah Revives the Widow's Son

17 After this the son of the woman, the mistress of the house, became ill; his illness was so severe that there was no breath left in him. 18 She then said to E·li´jah, "What have you against me, O man of God? You have come to me to bring my sin to remembrance, and to cause the death of my son!" 19 But he said to her, "Give me your son." He took him from her bosom, carried him up into the upper chamber where he was lodging, and laid him on his own bed. 20 He cried out to the LORD, "O LORD my God, have you brought calamity even upon the widow with

whom I am staying, by killing her son?" 21 Then he stretched himself upon the child three times, and cried out to the LORD, "O LORD my God, let this child's life come into him again." 22 The LORD listened to the voice of E·li´jah; the life of the child came into him again, and he revived. 23 E·li´jah took the child, brought him down from the upper chamber into the house, and gave him to his mother; then E·li´jah said, "See, your son is alive." 24 So the woman said to E·li´jah, "Now I know that you are a man of God, and that the word of the LORD in your mouth is truth."

Elijah's Message to Ahab

18 After many days the word of the LORD came to E·li´jah, in the third year of the drought,[1] saying, "Go, present yourself to A´hab; I will send rain on the earth." 2 So E·li´jah went to present himself to A´hab. The famine was severe in Sa·mar´i·a. 3 A´hab summoned O·ba·di´ah, who was in charge of the palace. (Now O·ba·di´ah revered the LORD greatly; 4 when Jez´e·bel was killing off the prophets of the LORD, O·ba·di´ah took a hundred prophets, hid them fifty to a cave, and provided them with bread and water.) 5 Then A´hab said to O·ba·di´ah, "Go through the land to all the springs of water and to all the wadis; perhaps we may find grass to keep the horses and mules alive, and not lose some of the animals." 6 So they divided the land between them to pass through it; A´hab went in one direction by himself, and O·ba·di´ah went in another direction by himself.

7 As O·ba·di´ah was on the way, E·li´jah met him; O·ba·di´ah recognized him, fell on his face, and said, "Is it you, my lord E·li´jah?" 8 He answered him, "It is I. Go, tell your lord that E·li´jah is here." 9 And he said, "How have I sinned, that you would hand your servant over to A´hab, to kill me? 10 As the LORD your God lives, there is no nation or kingdom to which my lord has not sent to seek you; and when they would say, 'He is not here,' he would require an oath of the kingdom or nation, that they had not found you. 11 But now you say, 'Go, tell your lord that E·li´jah is here.' 12 As soon as I have gone from you, the spirit of the LORD will carry

[1] Heb lacks of the drought

you I know not where; so, when I come and tell A'hab and he cannot find you, he will kill me, although I your servant have revered the LORD from my youth. [13] Has it not been told my lord what I did when Jez'e·bel killed the prophets of the LORD, how I hid a hundred of the LORD's prophets fifty to a cave, and provided them with bread and water? [14] Yet now you say, 'Go, tell your lord that E·li'jah is here'; he will surely kill me." [15] E·li'jah said, "As the LORD of hosts lives, before whom I stand, I will surely show myself to him today." [16] So O·ba·di'ah went to meet A'hab, and told him; and A'hab went to meet E·li'jah.

[17] When A'hab saw E·li'jah, A'hab said to him, "Is it you, you troubler of Israel?" [18] He answered, "I have not troubled Israel; but you have, and your father's house, because you have forsaken the commandments of the LORD and followed the Ba'als. [19] Now therefore have all Israel assemble for me at Mount Car'mel, with the four hundred fifty prophets of Ba'al and the four hundred prophets of A·she'rah, who eat at Jez'e·bel's table."

Elijah's Triumph over the Priests of Baal

[20] So A'hab sent to all the Israelites, and assembled the prophets at Mount Car'mel. [21] E·li'jah then came near to all the people, and said, "How long will you go limping with two different opinions? If the LORD is God, follow him; but if Ba'al, then follow him." The people did not answer him a word. [22] Then E·li'jah said to the people, "I, even I only, am left a prophet of the LORD; but Ba'al's prophets number four hundred fifty. [23] Let two bulls be given to us; let them choose one bull for themselves, cut it in pieces, and lay it on the wood, but put no fire to it; I will prepare the other bull and lay it on the wood, but put no fire to it. [24] Then you call on the name of your god and I will call on the name of the LORD; the god who answers by fire is indeed God." All the people answered, "Well spoken!" [25] Then E·li'jah said to the prophets of Ba'al, "Choose for yourselves one bull and prepare it first, for you are many; then call on the name of your god, but put no fire to it." [26] So they took the bull that was given them, prepared it, and called on the name of Ba'al from morning until noon, crying,

"O Ba'al, answer us!" But there was no voice, and no answer. They limped about the altar that they had made. [27] At noon E·li'jah mocked them, saying, "Cry aloud! Surely he is a god; either he is meditating, or he has wandered away, or he is on a journey, or perhaps he is asleep and must be awakened." [28] Then they cried aloud and, as was their custom, they cut themselves with swords and lances until the blood gushed out over them. [29] As midday passed, they raved on until the time of the offering of the oblation, but there was no voice, no answer, and no response.

[30] Then E·li'jah said to all the people, "Come closer to me"; and all the people came closer to him. First he repaired the altar of the LORD that had been thrown down; [31] E·li'jah took twelve stones, according to the number of the tribes of the sons of Jacob, to whom the word of the LORD came, saying, "Israel shall be your name"; [32] with the stones he built an altar in the name of the LORD. Then he made a trench around the altar, large enough to contain two measures of seed. [33] Next he put the wood in order, cut the bull in pieces, and laid it on the wood. He said, "Fill four jars with water and pour it on the burnt offering and on the wood." [34] Then he said, "Do it a second time"; and they did it a second time. Again he said, "Do it a third time"; and they did it a third time, [35] so that the water ran all around the altar, and filled the trench also with water.

[36] At the time of the offering of the oblation, the prophet E·li'jah came near and said, "O LORD, God of Abraham, Isaac, and Israel, let it be known this day that you are God in Israel, that I am your servant, and that I have done all these things at your bidding. [37] Answer me, O LORD, answer me, so that this people may know that you, O LORD, are God, and that you have turned their hearts back." [38] Then the fire of the LORD fell and consumed the burnt offering, the wood, the stones, and the dust, and even licked up the water that was in the trench. [39] When all the people saw it, they fell on their faces and said, "The LORD indeed is God; the LORD indeed is God." [40] E·li'jah said to them, "Seize the prophets of Ba'al; do not let one of them escape." Then they seized them; and E·li'jah brought them down to the Wadi Ki'shon, and killed them there.

The Drought Ends

41 E·lī′jah said to Ā′hab, "Go up, eat and drink; for there is a sound of rushing rain." 42 So Ā′hab went up to eat and to drink. E·lī′jah went up to the top of Car′mel; there he bowed himself down upon the earth and put his face between his knees. 43 He said to his servant, "Go up now, look toward the sea." He went up and looked, and said, "There is nothing." Then he said, "Go again seven times." 44 At the seventh time he said, "Look, a little cloud no bigger than a person's hand is rising out of the sea." Then he said, "Go say to Ā′hab, 'Harness your chariot and go down before the rain stops you.' " 45 In a little while the heavens grew black with clouds and wind; there was a heavy rain. Ā′hab rode off and went to Jez′rē·el. 46 But the hand of the LORD was on E·lī′jah; he girded up his loins and ran in front of Ā′hab to the entrance of Jez′rē·el.

Elijah Flees from Jezebel

19 Ā′hab told Jez′e·bel all that E·lī′jah had done, and how he had killed all the prophets with the sword. 2 Then Jez′e·bel sent a messenger to E·lī′jah, saying, "So may the gods do to me, and more also, if I do not make your life like the life of one of them by this time tomorrow." 3 Then he was afraid; he got up and fled for his life, and came to Bē′er-shē′ba, which belongs to Judah; he left his servant there.

4 But he himself went a day's journey into the wilderness, and came and sat down under a solitary broom tree. He asked that he might die: "It is enough; now, O LORD, take away my life, for I am no better than my ancestors." 5 Then he lay down under the broom tree and fell asleep. Suddenly an angel touched him and said to him, "Get up and eat." 6 He looked, and there at his head was a cake baked on hot stones, and a jar of water. He ate and drank, and lay down again. 7 The angel of the LORD came a second time, touched him, and said, "Get up and eat, otherwise the journey will be too much for you." 8 He got up, and ate and drank; then he went in the strength of that food forty days and forty nights to Hō′reb the mount of God. 9 At that place he came to a cave, and spent the night there.

Then the word of the LORD came to him, saying, "What are you doing here, E·lī′jah?" 10 He answered, "I have been very zealous for the LORD, the God of hosts; for the Israelites have forsaken your covenant, thrown down your altars, and killed your prophets with the sword. I alone am left, and they are seeking my life, to take it away."

Elijah Meets God at Horeb

11 He said, "Go out and stand on the mountain before the LORD, for the LORD is about to pass by." Now there was a great wind, so strong that it was splitting mountains and breaking rocks in pieces before the LORD, but the LORD was not in the wind; and after the wind an earthquake, but the LORD was not in the earthquake; 12 and after the earthquake a fire, but the LORD was not in the fire; and after the fire a sound of sheer silence. 13 When E·lī′jah heard it, he wrapped his face in his mantle and went out and stood at the entrance of the cave. Then there came a voice to him that said, "What are you doing here, E·lī′jah?" 14 He answered, "I have been very zealous for the LORD, the God of hosts; for the Israelites have forsaken your covenant, thrown down your altars, and killed your prophets with the sword. I alone am left, and they are seeking my life, to take it away." 15 Then the LORD said to him, "Go, return on your way to the wilderness of Damascus; when you arrive, you shall anoint Haz′a·el as king over Ar′am. 16 Also you shall anoint Jē′hū son of Nim′shī as king over Israel; and you shall anoint E·lī′sha son of Shā′phat of Ā′bel-me·hō′lah as prophet in your place. 17 Whoever escapes from the sword of Haz′a·el, Jē′hū shall kill; and whoever escapes from the sword of Jē′hū, E·lī′sha shall kill. 18 Yet I will leave seven thousand in Israel, all the knees that have not bowed to Bā′al, and every mouth that has not kissed him."

Elisha Becomes Elijah's Disciple

19 So he set out from there, and found E·lī′sha son of Shā′phat, who was plowing. There were twelve yoke of oxen ahead of him, and he was with the twelfth. E·lī′jah passed by him and threw his mantle over him. 20 He left the oxen, ran after E·lī′jah, and said, "Let me kiss my father and my mother, and then I will follow you." Then E·lī′-

jah[m] said to him, "Go back again; for what have I done to you?" [21] He returned from following him, took the yoke of oxen, and slaughtered them; using the equipment from the oxen, he boiled their flesh, and gave it to the people, and they ate. Then he set out and followed E·li′jah, and became his servant.

Ahab's Wars with the Arameans

20 King Ben-ha′dad of Ar′am gathered all his army together; thirty-two kings were with him, along with horses and chariots. He marched against Sa·mar′i·a, laid siege to it, and attacked it. [2] Then he sent messengers into the city to King A′hab of Israel, and said to him: "Thus says Ben-ha′-dad: [3] Your silver and gold are mine; your fairest wives and children also are mine." [4] The king of Israel answered, "As you say, my lord, O king, I am yours, and all that I have." [5] The messengers came again and said: "Thus says Ben-ha′dad: I sent to you, saying, 'Deliver to me your silver and gold, your wives and children'; [6] nevertheless I will send my servants to you tomorrow about this time, and they shall search your house and the houses of your servants, and lay hands on whatever pleases them,[n] and take it away."

[7] Then the king of Israel called all the elders of the land, and said, "Look now! See how this man is seeking trouble; for he sent to me for my wives, my children, my silver, and my gold; and I did not refuse him." [8] Then all the elders and all the people said to him, "Do not listen or consent." [9] So he said to the messengers of Ben-ha′dad, "Tell my lord the king: All that you first demanded of your servant I will do; but this thing I cannot do." The messengers left and brought him word again. [10] Ben-ha′dad sent to him and said, "The gods do so to me, and more also, if the dust of Sa·mar′i·a will provide a handful for each of the people who follow me." [11] The king of Israel answered, "Tell him: One who puts on armor should not brag like one who takes it off." [12] When Ben-ha′dad heard this message—now he had been drinking with the kings in the booths—he said to his men, "Take your positions!" And they took their positions against the city.

Prophetic Opposition to Ahab

13 Then a certain prophet came up to King A′hab of Israel and said, "Thus says the LORD, Have you seen all this great multitude? Look, I will give it into your hand today; and you shall know that I am the LORD." [14] A′hab said, "By whom?" He said, "Thus says the LORD, By the young men who serve the district governors." Then he said, "Who shall begin the battle?" He answered, "You." [15] Then he mustered the young men who serve the district governors, two hundred thirty-two; after them he mustered all the people of Israel, seven thousand.

16 They went out at noon, while Ben-ha′dad was drinking himself drunk in the booths, he and the thirty-two kings allied with him. [17] The young men who serve the district governors went out first. Ben-ha′dad had sent out scouts,[o] and they reported to him, "Men have come out from Sa·mar′i·a." [18] He said, "If they have come out for peace, take them alive; if they have come out for war, take them alive."

19 But these had already come out of the city: the young men who serve the district governors, and the army that followed them. [20] Each killed his man; the Ar·a·me′ans fled and Israel pursued them, but King Ben-ha′dad of Ar′am escaped on a horse with the cavalry. [21] The king of Israel went out, attacked the horses and chariots, and defeated the Ar·a·me′ans with a great slaughter.

22 Then the prophet approached the king of Israel and said to him, "Come, strengthen yourself, and consider well what you have to do; for in the spring the king of Ar′am will come up against you."

The Arameans Are Defeated

23 The servants of the king of Ar′am said to him, "Their gods are gods of the hills, and so they were stronger than we; but let us fight against them in the plain, and surely we shall be stronger than they. [24] Also do this: remove the kings, each from his post, and put commanders in place of them; [25] and muster an army like the army that you have lost, horse for horse, and chariot for chariot; then we will fight against them in the plain, and

[m] Heb he   [n] Gk Syr Vg: Heb you
[o] Heb lacks scouts

surely we shall be stronger than they." He heeded their voice, and did so.

26 In the spring Ben-haʹdad mustered the Ar·a·meʹans and went up to Aʹphek to fight against Israel. 27 After the Israelites had been mustered and provisioned, they went out to engage them; the people of Israel encamped opposite them like two little flocks of goats, while the Ar·a·meʹans filled the country. 28 A man of God approached and said to the king of Israel, "Thus says the LORD: Because the Ar·a·meʹans have said, 'The LORD is a god of the hills but he is not a god of the valleys,' therefore I will give all this great multitude into your hand, and you shall know that I am the LORD." 29 They encamped opposite one another seven days. Then on the seventh day the battle began; the Israelites killed one hundred thousand Ar·a·meʹan foot soldiers in one day. 30 The rest fled into the city of Aʹphek; and the wall fell on twenty-seven thousand men that were left.

Ben-haʹdad also fled, and entered the city to hide. 31 His servants said to him, "Look, we have heard that the kings of the house of Israel are merciful kings; let us put sackcloth around our waists and ropes on our heads, and go out to the king of Israel; perhaps he will spare your life." 32 So they tied sackcloth around their waists, put ropes on their heads, went to the king of Israel, and said, "Your servant Ben-haʹdad says, 'Please let me live.'" And he said, "Is he still alive? He is my brother." 33 Now the men were watching for an omen; they quickly took it up from him and said, "Yes, Ben-haʹdad is your brother." Then he said, "Go and bring him." So Ben-haʹdad came out to him; and he had him come up into the chariot. 34 Ben-haʹdadᵖ said to him, "I will restore the towns that my father took from your father; and you may establish bazaars for yourself in Damascus, as my father did in Sa·marʹi·a." The king of Israel responded,�q "I will let you go on those terms." So he made a treaty with him and let him go.

A Prophet Condemns Ahab

35 At the command of the LORD a certain member of a company of prophetsʳ said to another, "Strike me!" But the man refused to strike him. 36 Then he said to him, "Because you have not obeyed the voice of the LORD, as soon as you have left me, a lion will kill you." And when he had left him, a lion met him and killed him. 37 Then he found another man and said, "Strike me!" So the man hit him, striking and wounding him. 38 Then the prophet departed, and waited for the king along the road, disguising himself with a bandage over his eyes. 39 As the king passed by, he cried to the king and said, "Your servant went out into the thick of the battle; then a soldier turned and brought a man to me, and said, 'Guard this man; if he is missing, your life shall be given for his life, or else you shall pay a talent of silver.' 40 While your servant was busy here and there, he was gone." The king of Israel said to him, "So shall your judgment be; you yourself have decided it." 41 Then he quickly took the bandage away from his eyes. The king of Israel recognized him as one of the prophets. 42 Then he said to him, "Thus says the LORD, 'Because you have let the man go whom I had devoted to destruction, therefore your life shall be for his life, and your people for his people.'" 43 The king of Israel set out toward home, resentful and sullen, and came to Sa·marʹi·a.

Naboth's Vineyard

21 Later the following events took place: Naʹboth the Jezʹre·el·ite had a vineyard in Jezʹre·el, beside the palace of King Aʹhab of Sa·marʹi·a. 2 And Aʹhab said to Naʹboth, "Give me your vineyard, so that I may have it for a vegetable garden, because it is near my house; I will give you a better vineyard for it; or, if it seems good to you, I will give you its value in money." 3 But Naʹboth said to Aʹhab, "The LORD forbid that I should give you my ancestral inheritance." 4 Aʹhab went home resentful and sullen because of what Naʹboth the Jezʹre·el·ite had said to him; for he had said, "I will not give you my ancestral inheritance." He lay down on his bed, turned away his face, and would not eat.

5 His wife Jezʹe·bel came to him and said, "Why are you so depressed that you will not eat?" 6 He said to her, "Because I spoke to Naʹboth the Jezʹre·el·ite and said to him, 'Give me your vineyard for money; or else, if you pre-

---

ᵖ Heb He responded   q Heb lacks The king of Israel responded   ʳ Heb of the sons of the prophets fer, I will give you another vineyard for it'; but he answered, 'I will not give you my vineyard.'" ⁷His wife Jez'e·bel said to him, "Do you now govern Israel? Get up, eat some food, and be cheerful; I will give you the vineyard of Na'both the Jez're·el·ite."

8 So she wrote letters in A'hab's name and sealed them with his seal; she sent the letters to the elders and the nobles who lived with Na'both in his city. ⁹She wrote in the letters, "Proclaim a fast, and seat Na'both at the head of the assembly; ¹⁰seat two scoundrels opposite him, and have them bring a charge against him, saying, 'You have cursed God and the king.' Then take him out, and stone him to death." ¹¹The men of his city, the elders and the nobles who lived in his city, did as Jez'e·bel had sent word to them. Just as it was written in the letters that she had sent to them, ¹²they proclaimed a fast and seated Na'both at the head of the assembly. ¹³The two scoundrels came in and sat opposite him; and the scoundrels brought a charge against Na'both, in the presence of the people, saying, "Na'both cursed God and the king." So they took him outside the city, and stoned him to death. ¹⁴Then they sent to Jez'e·bel, saying, "Na'both has been stoned; he is dead."

15 As soon as Jez'e·bel heard that Na'both had been stoned and was dead, Jez'e·bel said to A'hab, "Go, take possession of the vineyard of Na'both the Jez're·el·ite, which he refused to give you for money; for Na'both is not alive, but dead." ¹⁶As soon as A'hab heard that Na'both was dead, A'hab set out to go down to the vineyard of Na'both the Jez're·el·ite, to take possession of it.

Elijah Pronounces God's Sentence

17 Then the word of the LORD came to E·li'jah the Tish'bite, saying: ¹⁸Go down to meet King A'hab of Israel, who rules ˢ in Sa·mar'i·a; he is now in the vineyard of Na'both, where he has gone to take possession. ¹⁹You shall say to him, "Thus says the LORD: Have you killed, and also taken possession?" You shall say to him, "Thus says the LORD: In the place where dogs licked up the blood of Na'both, dogs will also lick up your blood."

20 A'hab said to E·li'jah, "Have you found me, O my enemy?" He answered, "I have found you. Because

you have sold yourself to do what is evil in the sight of the LORD, ²¹I will bring disaster on you; I will consume you, and will cut off from A'hab every male, bond or free, in Israel; ²²and I will make your house like the house of Jer·o·bo'am son of Ne'bat, and like the house of Ba'a·sha son of A·hi'jah, because you have provoked me to anger and have caused Israel to sin. ²³Also concerning Jez'e·bel the LORD said, 'The dogs shall eat Jez'e·bel within the bounds of Jez're·el.' ²⁴Anyone belonging to A'hab who dies in the city the dogs shall eat; and anyone of his who dies in the open country the birds of the air shall eat."

25 (Indeed, there was no one like A'hab, who sold himself to do what was evil in the sight of the LORD, urged on by his wife Jez'e·bel. ²⁶He acted most abominably in going after idols, as the Am'o·rites had done, whom the LORD drove out before the Israelites.)

27 When A'hab heard those words, he tore his clothes and put sackcloth over his bare flesh; he fasted, lay in the sackcloth, and went about dejectedly. ²⁸Then the word of the LORD came to E·li'jah the Tish'bite: ²⁹"Have you seen how A'hab has humbled himself before me? Because he has humbled himself before me, I will not bring the disaster in his days; but in his son's days I will bring the disaster on his house."

Joint Campaign with Judah against Aram
(2 Chr 18.1–11)

22 For three years Ar'am and Israel continued without war. ²But in the third year King Je·hosh'a·phat of Judah came down to the king of Israel. ³The king of Israel said to his servants, "Do you know that Ra'moth-gil'e·ad belongs to us, yet we are doing nothing to take it out of the hand of the king of Ar'am?" ⁴He said to Je·hosh'a·phat, "Will you go with me to battle at Ra'moth-gil'e·ad?" Je·hosh'a·phat replied to the king of Israel, "I am as you are; my people are your people, my horses are your horses."

5 But Je·hosh'a·phat also said to the king of Israel, "Inquire first for the word of the LORD." ⁶Then the king of Israel gathered the prophets together, about four hundred of them, and said to them, "Shall I go to battle against

ˢHeb who is

Ra'moth-gil'e·ad, or shall I refrain?" They said, "Go up; for the LORD will give it into the hand of the king." 7 But Je·hosh'a·phat said, "Is there no other prophet of the LORD here of whom we may inquire?" 8 The king of Israel said to Je·hosh'a·phat, "There is still one other by whom we may inquire of the LORD, Mi·cai'ah son of Im'lah; but I hate him, for he never prophesies anything favorable about me, but only disaster." Je·hosh'a·phat said, "Let the king not say such a thing." 9 Then the king of Israel summoned an officer and said, "Bring quickly Mi·cai'ah son of Im'lah." 10 Now the king of Israel and King Je·hosh'a·phat of Judah were sitting on their thrones, arrayed in their robes, at the threshing floor at the entrance of the gate of Sa·mar'i·a; and all the prophets were prophesying before them. 11 Zed·e·ki'ah son of Che·na'a·nah made for himself horns of iron, and he said, "Thus says the LORD: With these you shall gore the Ar·a·me'ans until they are destroyed." 12 All the prophets were prophesying the same and saying, "Go up to Ra'-moth-gil'e·ad and triumph; the LORD will give it into the hand of the king."

Micaiah Predicts Failure
(2 Chr 18.12–27)

13 The messenger who had gone to summon Mi·cai'ah said to him, "Look, the words of the prophets with one accord are favorable to the king; let your word be like the word of one of them, and speak favorably." 14 But Mi·cai'ah said, "As the LORD lives, whatever the LORD says to me, that I will speak." 15 When he had come to the king, the king said to him, "Mi·cai'ah, shall we go to Ra'moth-gil'e·ad to battle, or shall we refrain?" He answered him, "Go up and triumph; the LORD will give it into the hand of the king." 16 But the king said to him, "How many times must I make you swear to tell me nothing but the truth in the name of the LORD?" 17 Then Mi·cai'ah t said, "I saw all Israel scattered on the mountains, like sheep that have no shepherd; and the LORD said, 'These have no master; let each one go home in peace.'" 18 The king of Israel said to Je·hosh'a·phat, "Did I not tell you that he would not prophesy anything favorable about me, but only disaster?" 19 Then Mi·cai'ah t said, "Therefore hear the word of the LORD: I saw the LORD sitting on his throne, with all

the host of heaven standing beside him to the right and to the left of him. 20 And the LORD said, 'Who will entice A'hab, so that he may go up and fall at Ra'moth-gil'e·ad?' Then one said one thing, and another said another, 21 until a spirit came forward and stood before the LORD, saying, 'I will entice him.' 22 'How?' the LORD asked him. He replied, 'I will go out and be a lying spirit in the mouth of all his prophets.' Then the LORD t said, 'You are to entice him, and you shall succeed; go out and do it.' 23 So you see, the LORD has put a lying spirit in the mouth of all these your prophets; the LORD has decreed disaster for you."

24 Then Zed·e·ki'ah son of Che·na'-a·nah came up to Mi·cai'ah, slapped him on the cheek, and said, "Which way did the spirit of the LORD pass from me to speak to you?" 25 Mi·cai'ah replied, "You will find out on that day when you go in to hide in an inner chamber." 26 The king of Israel then ordered, "Take Mi·cai'ah, and return him to A'mon the governor of the city and to Jo'ash the king's son, 27 and say, 'Thus says the king: Put this fellow in prison, and feed him on reduced rations of bread and water until I come in peace.'" 28 Mi·cai'ah said, "If you return in peace, the LORD has not spoken by me." And he said, "Hear, you peoples, all of you!"

Defeat and Death of Ahab
(2 Chr 18.28–34)

29 So the king of Israel and King Je·hosh'a·phat of Judah went up to Ra'moth-gil'e·ad. 30 The king of Israel said to Je·hosh'a·phat, "I will disguise myself and go into battle, but you wear your robes." So the king of Israel disguised himself and went into battle. 31 Now the king of Ar'am had commanded the thirty-two captains of his chariots, "Fight with no one small or great, but only with the king of Israel." 32 When the captains of the chariots saw Je·hosh'a·phat, they said, "It is surely the king of Israel." So they turned to fight against him; and Je·hosh'a·phat cried out. 33 When the captains of the chariots saw that it was not the king of Israel, they turned back from pursuing him. 34 But a certain man drew his bow and unknowingly struck the king of Israel between the scale armor and the breastplate; so he

t Heb *he*

said to the driver of his chariot, "Turn around, and carry me out of the battle, for I am wounded." 35 The battle grew hot that day, and the king was propped up in his chariot facing the Ar·a·mē'-ans, until at evening he died; the blood from the wound had flowed into the bottom of the chariot. 36 Then about sunset a shout went through the army, "Every man to his city, and every man to his country!"

37 So the king died, and was brought to Sa·mār'i·a; they buried the king in Sa·mār'i·a. 38 They washed the chariot by the pool of Sa·mār'i·a; the dogs licked up his blood, and the prostitutes washed themselves in it,*u* according to the word of the LORD that he had spoken. 39 Now the rest of the acts of Ā'hab, and all that he did, and the ivory house that he built, and all the cities that he built, are they not written in the Book of the Annals of the Kings of Israel? 40 So Ā'hab slept with his ancestors; and his son A·ha·zī'ah succeeded him.

Jehoshaphat Reigns over Judah
(2 Chr 20.31—21.1)

41 Je·hosh'a·phat son of Asa began to reign over Judah in the fourth year of King Ā'hab of Israel. 42 Je·hosh'a·phat was thirty-five years old when he began to reign, and he reigned twenty-five years in Jerusalem. His mother's name was A·zū'bah daughter of Shil'hī. 43 He walked in all the way of his father Asa; he did not turn aside from it, doing what was right in the sight of the LORD; yet the high places were not taken away, and

the people still sacrificed and offered incense on the high places. 44 Je·hosh'a·phat also made peace with the king of Israel.

45 Now the rest of the acts of Je·hosh'a·phat, and his power that he showed, and how he waged war, are they not written in the Book of the Annals of the Kings of Judah? 46 The remnant of the male temple prostitutes who were still in the land in the days of his father Asa, he exterminated.

47 There was no king in Ē'dom; a deputy was king. 48 Je·hosh'a·phat made ships of the Tar'shish type to go to Ō'phir for gold; but they did not go, for the ships were wrecked at Ē'zi·on·gē'ber. 49 Then A·ha·zī'ah son of Ā'hab said to Je·hosh'a·phat, "Let my servants go with your servants in the ships," but Je·hosh'a·phat was not willing. 50 Je·hosh'a·phat slept with his ancestors and was buried with his ancestors in the city of his father David; his son Je·hō'ram succeeded him.

Ahaziah Reigns over Israel

51 A·ha·zī'ah son of Ā'hab began to reign over Israel in Sa·mār'i·a in the seventeenth year of King Je·hosh'-a·phat of Judah; he reigned two years over Israel. 52 He did what was evil in the sight of the LORD, and walked in the way of his father and mother, and in the way of Jer·o·bō'am son of Nē'-bat, who caused Israel to sin. 53 He served Bā'al and worshiped him; he provoked the LORD, the God of Israel, to anger, just as his father had done.

u Heb lacks *in it*

2 KINGS

Elijah Denounces Ahaziah

1 After the death of Ā'hab, Mō'ab rebelled against Israel.

2 A·ha·zī'ah had fallen through the lattice in his upper chamber in Sa·mār'i·a, and lay injured; so he sent messengers, telling them, "Go, inquire

of Bā'al·zē'bub, the god of Ek'ron, whether I shall recover from this injury." 3 But the angel of the LORD said to E·lī'jah the Tish'bīte, "Get up, go to meet the messengers of the king of Sa·mār'i·a, and say to them, 'Is it because there is no God in Israel that you are going to inquire of Bā'al·zē'bub, the god of Ek'ron?' ⁴Now therefore thus says the LORD, 'You shall not leave the bed to which you have gone, but you shall surely die.' " So E·li'jah went.

5 The messengers returned to the king, who said to them, "Why have you returned?" ⁶They answered him, "There came a man to meet us, who said to us, 'Go back to the king who sent you, and say to him: Thus says the LORD: Is it because there is no God in Israel that you are sending to inquire of Ba'al-ze'bub, the god of Ek'ron? Therefore you shall not leave the bed to which you have gone, but shall surely die.' " ⁷He said to them, "What sort of man was he who came to meet you and told you these things?" ⁸They answered him, "A hairy man, with a leather belt around his waist." He said, "It is E·li'jah the Tish'bite."

9 Then the king sent to him a captain of fifty with his fifty men. He went up to E·li'jah, who was sitting on the top of a hill, and said to him, "O man of God, the king says, 'Come down.' " ¹⁰But E·li'jah answered the captain of fifty, "If I am a man of God, let fire come down from heaven and consume you and your fifty." Then fire came down from heaven, and consumed him and his fifty.

11 Again the king sent to him another captain of fifty with his fifty. He went up*ᵃ* and said to him, "O man of God, this is the king's order: Come down quickly!" ¹²But E·li'jah answered them, "If I am a man of God, let fire come down from heaven and consume you and your fifty." Then the fire of God came down from heaven and consumed him and his fifty.

13 Again the king sent the captain of a third fifty with his fifty. So the third captain of fifty went up, and came and fell on his knees before E·li'jah, and entreated him, "O man of God, please let my life, and the life of these fifty servants of yours, be precious in your sight. ¹⁴Look, fire came down from heaven and consumed the two former captains of fifty men with their fifties; but now let my life be precious in your sight." ¹⁵Then the angel of the LORD said to E·li'jah, "Go down with him; do not be afraid of him." So he set out and went down with him to the king, ¹⁶and said to him, "Thus says the LORD: Because you have sent messengers to inquire of Ba'al-ze'bub, the god of Ek'ron,—is it because there is

no God in Israel to inquire of hi*
word?—therefore you shall not leav*
the bed to which you have gone, b*
you shall surely die."

Death of Ahaziah

17 So he died according to the wor*
of the LORD that E·li'jah had spoke*
His brother,*ᵇ* Je·ho'ram succeede*
him as king in the second year of Kin*
Je·ho'ram son of Je·hosh'a·phat of Ju*
dah, because A·ha·zi'ah had no so*
¹⁸Now the rest of the acts of A·ha·zi'a*
that he did, are they not written in th*
Book of the Annals of the Kings of I*
rael?

Elijah Ascends to Heaven

2 Now when the LORD was about t*
take E·li'jah up to heaven by*
whirlwind, E·li'jah and E·li'sha wer*
on their way from Gil'gal. ²E·li'ja*
said to E·li'sha, "Stay here; for th*
LORD has sent me as far as Beth'el*
But E·li'sha said, "As the LORD live*
and as you yourself live, I will n*
leave you." So they went down t*
Beth'el. ³The company of prophets*
who were in Beth'el came out to E·li*
sha, and said to him, "Do you kno*
that today the LORD will take you*
master away from you?" And he sai*
"Yes, I know; keep silent."

4 E·li'jah said to him, "E·li'sha, sta*
here; for the LORD has sent me to Jer*
cho." But he said, "As the LORD live*
and as you yourself live, I will n*
leave you." So they came to Jerich*
⁵The company of prophets*ᶜ* who wer*
at Jericho drew near to E·li'sha, an*
said to him, "Do you know that toda*
the LORD will take your master awa*
from you?" And he answered, "Yes,*
know; be silent."

6 Then E·li'jah said to him, "Sta*
here; for the LORD has sent me to th*
Jordan." But he said, "As the LOR*
lives, and as you yourself live, I will n*
leave you." So the two of them wer*
on. ⁷Fifty men of the company *
prophets*ᶜ* also went, and stood *
some distance from them, as they bot*
were standing by the Jordan. ⁸The*
E·li'jah took his mantle and rolled *
up, and struck the water; the wate*
was parted to the one side and to th*
other, until the two of them crossed o*
dry ground.

ᵃGk Compare verses 9, 13: Heb *He
answered* ᵇGk Syr: Heb lacks *His
brother* ᶜHeb *sons of the prophets*

9 When they had crossed, E·lī'jah said to E·lī'sha, "Tell me what I may do for you, before I am taken from you." E·lī'sha said, "Please let me inherit a double share of your spirit." 10 He responded, "You have asked a hard thing; yet, if you see me as I am being taken from you, it will be granted you; if not, it will not." 11 As they continued walking and talking, a chariot of fire and horses of fire separated the two of them, and E·lī'jah ascended in a whirlwind into heaven. 12 E·lī'sha kept watching and crying out, "Father, father! The chariots of Israel and its horsemen!" But when he could no longer see him, he grasped his own clothes and tore them in two pieces.

Elisha Succeeds Elijah

13 He picked up the mantle of E·lī'jah that had fallen from him, and went back and stood on the bank of the Jordan. 14 He took the mantle of E·lī'jah that had fallen from him, and struck the water, saying, "Where is the LORD, the God of E·lī'jah?" When he had struck the water, the water was parted to the one side and to the other, and E·lī'sha went over.

15 When the company of prophets[d] who were at Jericho saw him at a distance, they declared, "The spirit of E·lī'jah rests on E·lī'sha." They came to meet him and bowed to the ground before him. 16 They said to him, "See now, we have fifty strong men among your servants; please let them go and seek your master; it may be that the spirit of the LORD has caught him up and thrown him down on some mountain or into some valley." He responded, "No, do not send them." 17 But when they urged him until he was ashamed, he said, "Send them." So they sent fifty men who searched for three days but did not find him. 18 When they came back to him (he had remained at Jericho), he said to them, "Did I not say to you, Do not go?"

Elisha Performs Miracles

19 Now the people of the city said to E·lī'sha, "The location of this city is good, as my lord sees; but the water is bad, and the land is unfruitful." 20 He said, "Bring me a new bowl, and put salt in it." So they brought it to him. 21 Then he went to the spring of water and threw the salt into it, and said, Thus says the LORD, I have made this water wholesome; from now on nei-

ther death nor miscarriage shall come from it." 22 So the water has been wholesome to this day, according to the word that E·lī'sha spoke.

23 He went up from there to Beth'el; and while he was going up on the way, some small boys came out of the city and jeered at him, saying, "Go away, baldhead! Go away, baldhead!" 24 When he turned around and saw them, he cursed them in the name of the LORD. Then two she-bears came out of the woods and mauled forty-two of the boys. 25 From there he went on to Mount Car'mel, and then returned to Sa·mār'i·a.

Jehoram Reigns over Israel

3 In the eighteenth year of King Je·hosh'a·phat of Judah, Je·hō'ram son of Ā'hab became king over Israel in Sa·mār'i·a; he reigned twelve years. 2 He did what was evil in the sight of the LORD, though not like his father and mother, for he removed the pillar of Bā'al that his father had made. 3 Nevertheless he clung to the sin of Jer·o·bō'am son of Nē'bat, which he caused Israel to commit; he did not depart from it.

War with Moab

4 Now King Mē'sha of Mō'ab was a sheep breeder, who used to deliver to the king of Israel one hundred thousand lambs, and the wool of one hundred thousand rams. 5 But when Ā'hab died, the king of Mō'ab rebelled against the king of Israel. 6 So King Je·hō'ram marched out of Sa·mār'i·a at that time and mustered all Israel. 7 As he went he sent word to King Je·hosh'a·phat of Judah, "The king of Mō'ab has rebelled against me; will you go with me to battle against Mō'ab?" He answered, "I will; I am with you, my people are your people, my horses are your horses." 8 Then he asked, "By which way shall we march?" Je·hō'ram answered, "By the way of the wilderness of E'dom."

9 So the king of Israel, the king of Judah, and the king of E'dom set out; and when they had made a roundabout march of seven days, there was no water for the army or for the animals that were with them. 10 Then the king of Israel said, "Alas! The LORD has summoned us, three kings, only to be handed over to Mō'ab." 11 But

[d] Heb *sons of the prophets*

Je·hosh'a·phat said, "Is there no prophet of the LORD here, through whom we may inquire of the LORD?" Then one of the servants of the king of Israel answered, "E·li'sha son of Shā'-phat, who used to pour water on the hands of E·li'jah, is here." 12 Je·hosh'a·phat said, "The word of the LORD is with him." So the king of Israel and Je·hosh'a·phat and the king of E'dom went down to him.

13 E·li'sha said to the king of Israel, "What have I to do with you? Go to your father's prophets or to your mother's." But the king of Israel said to him, "No; it is the LORD who has summoned us, three kings, only to be handed over to Mō'ab." 14 E·li'sha said, "As the LORD of hosts lives, whom I serve, were it not that I have regard for King Je·hosh'a·phat of Judah, I would give you neither a look nor a glance. 15 But get me a musician." And then, while the musician was playing, the power of the LORD came on him. 16 And he said, "Thus says the LORD, 'I will make this wadi full of pools.' 17 For thus says the LORD, 'You shall see neither wind nor rain, but the wadi shall be filled with water, so that you shall drink, you, your cattle, and your animals.' 18 This is only a trifle in the sight of the LORD, for he will also hand Mō'ab over to you. 19 You shall conquer every fortified city and every choice city; every good tree you shall fell, all springs of water you shall stop up, and every good piece of land you shall ruin with stones." 20 The next day, about the time of the morning offering, suddenly water began to flow from the direction of E'dom, until the country was filled with water.

21 When all the Mō'ab·ites heard that the kings had come up to fight against them, all who were able to put on armor, from the youngest to the oldest, were called out and were drawn up at the frontier. 22 When they rose early in the morning, and the sun shone upon the water, the Mō'ab·ites saw the water opposite them as red as blood. 23 They said, "This is blood; the kings must have fought together, and killed one another. Now then, Mō'ab, to the spoil!" 24 But when they came to the camp of Israel, the Israelites rose up and attacked the Mō'ab·ites, who fled before them; as they entered Mō'ab they continued the attack. e 25 The cities they overturned, and on every good piece of land everyone threw a stone,

until it was covered; every spring ⸱ water they stopped up, and every goc tree they felled. Only at Kir-har'e·set did the stone walls remain, until th slingers surrounded and attacked ⸱ 26 When the king of Mō'ab saw that th battle was going against him, he too with him seven hundred swordsmen ⸱ break through, opposite the king ⸱ E'dom; but they could not. 27 Then h took his firstborn son who was to su ceed him, and offered him as a burr offering on the wall. And great wrat came upon Israel, so they withdre from him and returned to their ow land.

Elisha and the Widow's Oil
(Cp 1 Kings 17.14–16)

4 Now the wife of a member of th company of prophets f cried ⸱ E·li'sha, "Your servant my husband dead; and you know that your servaı feared the LORD, but a creditor hɑ come to take my two children ɑ slaves." 2 E·li'sha said to her, "Whɑ shall I do for you? Tell me, what do yc have in the house?" She answerec "Your servant has nothing in th house, except a jar of oil." 3 He saiı "Go outside, borrow vessels from a your neighbors, empty vessels and nc just a few. 4 Then go in, and shut th door behind you and your childreı and start pouring into all these vessel when each is full, set it aside." 5 So sh left him and shut the door behind he and her children; they kept bringiı vessels to her, and she kept pourinc 6 When the vessels were full, she saiı to her son, "Bring me another vessel But he said to her, "There are r more." Then the oil stopped flowinç 7 She came and told the man of Goı and he said, "Go sell the oil and pa your debts, and you and your childre can live on the rest."

Elisha Raises the Shunammite's Son
(Cp 1 Kings 17.17–24)

8 One day E·li'sha was passiı through Shū'nem, where a wealth woman lived, who urged him to have meal. So whenever he passed thɑ way, he would stop there for a mea 9 She said to her husband, "Look, I ɑ sure that this man who reguları passes our way is a holy man of Goı

e Compare Gk Syr: Meaning of Heb uncertain   f Heb *the sons of the prophets*

Let us make a small roof chamber with walls, and put there for him a bed, table, a chair, and a lamp, so that he can stay there whenever he comes to us."

11 One day when he came there, he went up to the chamber and lay down there. 12 He said to his servant Ge·ha′zī, "Call the Shū′nam·mīte woman." When he had called her, she stood before him. 13 He said to him, "Say to her, Since you have taken all this trouble for us, what may be done for you? Would you have a word spoken on your behalf to the king or to the commander of the army?" She answered, "I live among my own people." 14 He said, "What then may be done for her?" Ge·ha′zī answered, "Well, she has no son, and her husband is old." 15 He said, "Call her." When he had called her, she stood at the door. 16 He said, "At this season, in due time, you shall embrace a son." She replied, "No, my lord, O man of God; do not deceive your servant."

17 The woman conceived and bore a son at that season, in due time, as E·lī′sha had declared to her.

18 When the child was older, he went out one day to his father among the reapers. 19 He complained to his father, "Oh, my head, my head!" The father said to his servant, "Carry him to his mother." 20 He carried him and brought him to his mother; the child sat on her lap until noon, and he died. 21 She went up and laid him on the bed of the man of God, closed the door on him, and left. 22 Then she called to her husband, and said, "Send me one of the servants and one of the donkeys, so that I may quickly go to the man of God and come back again." 23 He said, "Why go to him today? It is neither new moon nor sabbath." She said, "It will be all right." 24 Then she saddled the donkey and said to her servant, "Urge the animal on; do not hold back for me unless I tell you." 25 So she set out, and came to the man of God at Mount Car′mel.

When the man of God saw her coming, he said to Ge·ha′zī his servant, "Look, there is the Shū′nam·mīte woman; 26 run at once to meet her, and say to her, Are you all right? Is your husband all right? Is the child all right?" She answered, "It is all right." 27 When she came to the man of God at the mountain, she caught hold of his feet. Ge·ha′zī approached to push her away. But the man of God said, "Let her alone, for she is in bitter distress; the LORD has hidden it from me and has not told me." 28 Then she said, "Did I ask my lord for a son? Did I not say, Do not mislead me?" 29 He said to Ge·ha′zī, "Gird up your loins, and take my staff in your hand, and go. If you meet anyone, give no greeting, and if anyone greets you, do not answer; and lay my staff on the face of the child." 30 Then the mother of the child said, "As the LORD lives, and as you yourself live, I will not leave without you." So he rose up and followed her. 31 Ge·ha′zī went on ahead and laid the staff on the face of the child, but there was no sound or sign of life. He came back to meet him and told him, "The child has not awakened."

32 When E·lī′sha came into the house, he saw the child lying dead on his bed. 33 So he went in and closed the door on the two of them, and prayed to the LORD. 34 Then he got up on the bed [g] and lay upon the child, putting his mouth upon his mouth, his eyes upon his eyes, and his hands upon his hands; and while he lay bent over him, the flesh of the child became warm. 35 He got down, walked once to and fro in the room, then got up again and bent over him; the child sneezed seven times, and the child opened his eyes. 36 E·lī′sha [h] summoned Ge·ha′zī and said, "Call the Shū′nam·mīte woman." So he called her. When she came to him, he said, "Take your son." 37 She came and fell at his feet, bowing to the ground; then she took her son and left.

Elisha Purifies the Pot of Stew

38 When E·lī′sha returned to Gil′gal, there was a famine in the land. As the company of prophets was [i] sitting before him, he said to his servant, "Put the large pot on, and make some stew for the company of prophets." [j] 39 One of them went out into the field to gather herbs; he found a wild vine and gathered from it a lapful of wild gourds, and came and cut them up into the pot of stew, not knowing what they were. 40 They served some for the men to eat. But while they were eating the stew, they cried out, "O man of God, there is death in the pot!" They could not eat it. 41 He said, "Then bring some

g Heb lacks *on the bed*　　h Heb he
i Heb *sons of the prophets were*
j Heb *sons of the prophets*

flour." He threw it into the pot, and said, "Serve the people and let them eat." And there was nothing harmful in the pot.

Elisha Feeds One Hundred Men
(Cp Mt 14.13–21; 15.32–39)

42 A man came from Bā′al-shal′-i·shah, bringing food from the first fruits to the man of God: twenty loaves of barley and fresh ears of grain in his sack. E·lī′sha said, "Give it to the people and let them eat." 43 But his servant said, "How can I set this before a hundred people?" So he repeated, "Give it to the people and let them eat, for thus says the LORD, 'They shall eat and have some left.' " 44 He set it before them, they ate, and had some left, according to the word of the LORD.

The Healing of Naaman

5 Nā′a·man, commander of the army of the king of Ar′am, was a great man and in high favor with his master, because by him the LORD had given victory to Ar′am. The man, though a mighty warrior, suffered from leprosy.[k] 2 Now the Ar·a·mē′ans on one of their raids had taken a young girl captive from the land of Israel, and she served Nā′a·man's wife. 3 She said to her mistress, "If only my lord were with the prophet who is in Sa·mār′i·a! He would cure him of his leprosy."[k] 4 So Nā′a·man[l] went in and told his lord just what the girl from the land of Israel had said. 5 And the king of Ar′am said, "Go then, and I will send along a letter to the king of Israel."

He went, taking with him ten talents of silver, six thousand shekels of gold, and ten sets of garments. 6 He brought the letter to the king of Israel, which read, "When this letter reaches you, know that I have sent to you my servant Nā′a·man, that you may cure him of his leprosy."[k] 7 When the king of Israel read the letter, he tore his clothes and said, "Am I God, to give death or life, that this man sends word to me to cure a man of his leprosy?[k] Just look and see how he is trying to pick a quarrel with me."

8 But when E·lī′sha the man of God heard that the king of Israel had torn his clothes, he sent a message to the king, "Why have you torn your clothes? Let him come to me, that he may learn that there is a prophet in Israel." 9 So Nā′a·man came with his horses and chariots, and halted at the entrance of E·lī′sha's house. 10 E·lī′sha sent a messenger to him, saying, "Go, wash in the Jordan seven times, and your flesh shall be restored and you shall be clean." 11 But Nā′a·man became angry and went away, saying, "I thought that for me he would surely come out, and stand and call on the name of the LORD his God, and would wave his hand over the spot, and cure the leprosy![k] 12 Are not A·bā′na[m] and Phar′par, the rivers of Damascus, better than all the waters of Israel? Could I not wash in them, and be clean?" He turned and went away in a rage. 13 But his servants approached and said to him, "Father, if the prophet had commanded you to do something difficult, would you not have done it? How much more, when all he said to you was, 'Wash, and be clean'?" 14 So he went down and immersed himself seven times in the Jordan, according to the word of the man of God; his flesh was restored like the flesh of a young boy, and he was clean.

15 Then he returned to the man of God, he and all his company; he came and stood before him and said, "Now I know that there is no God in all the earth except in Israel; please accept a present from your servant." 16 But he said, "As the LORD lives, whom I serve, I will accept nothing!" He urged him to accept, but he refused. 17 Then Nā′a·man said, "If not, please let two mule-loads of earth be given to your servant; for your servant will no longer offer burnt offering or sacrifice to any god except the LORD. 18 But may the LORD pardon your servant on one count: when my master goes into the house of Rim′mon to worship there, leaning on my arm, and I bow down in the house of Rim′mon, when I do bow down in the house of Rim′mon, may the LORD pardon your servant on this one count." 19 He said to him, "Go in peace."

Gehazi's Greed

But when Nā′a·man had gone from him a short distance, 20 Ge·hā′zī, the servant of E·lī′sha the man of God, thought, "My master has let this Ar·a·mē′an Nā′a·man off too lightly by not accepting from him what he offered. As the LORD lives, I will run after

---

[k] A term for several skin diseases; precise meaning uncertain   [l] Heb *he*
[m] Another reading is *Amana*

him and get something out of him."
21 So Ge·ha′zī went after Nā′a·man.
When Nā′a·man saw someone running after him, he jumped down from
the chariot to meet him and said, "Is
everything all right?" 22 He replied,
"Yes, but my master has sent me to
say, 'Two members of a company of
prophets[n] have just come to me from
the hill country of E′phra·im; please
give them a talent of silver and two
changes of clothing.' " 23 Nā′a·man
said, "Please accept two talents." He
urged him, and tied up two talents of
silver in two bags, with two changes of
clothing, and gave them to two of his
servants, who carried them in front of
Ge·ha′zī. [o] 24 When he came to the citadel, he took the bags[p] from them, and
stored them inside; he dismissed the
men, and they left.

25 He went in and stood before his
master; and E·lī′sha said to him,
"Where have you been, Ge·ha′zī?" He
answered, "Your servant has not gone
anywhere at all." 26 But he said to him,
"Did I not go with you in spirit when
someone left his chariot to meet you?
Is this a time to accept money and to
accept clothing, olive orchards and
vineyards, sheep and oxen, and male
and female slaves? 27 Therefore the
leprosy[q] of Nā′a·man shall cling to
you, and to your descendants forever."
So he left his presence leprous,[q] as
white as snow.

The Miracle of the Ax Head

6 Now the company of prophets[n]
said to E·lī′sha, "As you see, the
place where we live under your charge
is too small for us. 2 Let us go to the
Jordan, and let us collect logs there,
one for each of us, and build a place
there for us to live." He answered, "Do
so." 3 Then one of them said, "Please
come with your servants." And he answered, "I will." 4 So he went with
them. When they came to the Jordan,
they cut down trees. 5 But as one was
felling a log, his ax head fell into the
water; he cried out, "Alas, master! It
was borrowed." 6 Then the man of God
said, "Where did it fall?" When he
showed him the place, he cut off a
stick, and threw it in there, and made
the iron float. 7 He said, "Pick it up." So
he reached out his hand and took it.

The Aramean Attack Is Thwarted

8 Once when the king of Ar′am was
at war with Israel, he took counsel

with his officers. He said, "At such and
such a place shall be my camp." 9 But
the man of God sent word to the king
of Israel, "Take care not to pass this
place, because the Ar·a·mē′ans are going down there." 10 The king of Israel
sent word to the place of which the
man of God spoke. More than once or
twice he warned such a place[r] so that
it was on the alert.

11 The mind of the king of Ar′am
was greatly perturbed because of this;
he called his officers and said to them,
"Now tell me who among us sides with
the king of Israel?" 12 Then one of his
officers said, "No one, my lord king. It
is E·lī′sha, the prophet in Israel, who
tells the king of Israel the words that
you speak in your bedchamber." 13 He
said, "Go and find where he is; I will
send and seize him." He was told, "He
is in Dō′than." 14 So he sent horses and
chariots there and a great army; they
came by night, and surrounded the
city.

15 When an attendant of the man of
God rose early in the morning and
went out, an army with horses and
chariots was all around the city. His
servant said, "Alas, master! What shall
we do?" 16 He replied, "Do not be
afraid, for there are more with us than
there are with them." 17 Then E·lī′sha
prayed: "O LORD, please open his eyes
that he may see." So the LORD opened
the eyes of the servant, and he saw; the
mountain was full of horses and chariots of fire all around E·lī′sha. 18 When
the Ar·a·mē′ans[s] came down against
him, E·lī′sha prayed to the LORD, and
said, "Strike this people, please, with
blindness." So he struck them with
blindness as E·lī′sha had asked.
19 E·lī′sha said to them, "This is not the
way, and this is not the city; follow me,
and I will bring you to the man whom
you seek." And he led them to
Sa·mār′i·a.

20 As soon as they entered
Sa·mār′i·a, E·lī′sha said, "O LORD,
open the eyes of these men so that they
may see." The LORD opened their eyes,
and they saw that they were inside
Sa·mār′i·a. 21 When the king of Israel
saw them he said to E·lī′sha, "Father,
shall I kill them? Shall I kill them?"
22 He answered, "No! Did you capture

[n] Heb *sons of the prophets*   [o] Heb *him*
[p] Heb lacks *the bags*   [q] A term for
several skin diseases; precise meaning
uncertain   [r] Heb *warned it*   [s] Heb *they*

with your sword and your bow those whom you want to kill? Set food and water before them so that they may eat and drink; and let them go to their master." ²³ So he prepared for them a great feast; after they ate and drank, he sent them on their way, and they went to their master. And the Ar·a·me′ans no longer came raiding into the land of Israel.

Ben-hadad's Siege of Samaria

24 Some time later King Ben-ha′-dad of Ar′am mustered his entire army; he marched against Sa·mar′i·a and laid siege to it. ²⁵ As the siege continued, famine in Sa·mar′i·a became so great that a donkey's head was sold for eighty shekels of silver, and one-fourth of a kab of dove's dung for five shekels of silver. ²⁶ Now as the king of Israel was walking on the city wall, a woman cried out to him, "Help, my lord king!" ²⁷ He said, "No! Let the LORD help you. How can I help you? From the threshing floor or from the wine press?" ²⁸ But then the king asked her, "What is your complaint?" She answered, "This woman said to me, 'Give up your son; we will eat him today, and we will eat my son tomorrow.' ²⁹ So we cooked my son and ate him. The next day I said to her, 'Give up your son and we will eat him.' But she has hidden her son." ³⁰ When the king heard the words of the woman he tore his clothes—now since he was walking on the city wall, the people could see that he had sackcloth on his body underneath— ³¹ and he said, "So may God do to me, and more, if the head of E·li′sha son of Sha′phat stays on his shoulders today." ³² So he dispatched a man from his presence.

Now E·li′sha was sitting in his house, and the elders were sitting with him. Before the messenger arrived, E·li′sha said to the elders, "Are you aware that this murderer has sent someone to take off my head? When the messenger comes, see that you shut the door and hold it closed against him. Is not the sound of his master's feet behind him?" ³³ While he was still speaking with them, the king[t] came down to him and said, "This trouble is from the LORD! Why should I hope in the LORD any longer?" ¹ But E·li′-sha said, "Hear the word of the LORD, Tomorrow about this time a measure of choice meal shall be sold for a shekel, and two

measures of barley for a shekel, at the gate of Sa·mar′i·a." ² Then the captain on whose hand the king leaned said to the man of God, "Even if the LORD were to make windows in the sky, could such a thing happen?" But he said, "You shall see it with your own eyes, but you shall not eat from it."

The Arameans Flee

3 Now there were four leprous[u] men outside the city gate, who said to one another, "Why should we sit here until we die? ⁴ If we say, 'Let us enter the city,' the famine is in the city, and we shall die there; but if we sit here, we shall also die. Therefore, let us desert to the Ar·a·me′an camp; if they spare our lives, we shall live; and if they kill us, we shall but die." ⁵ So they arose at twilight to go to the Ar·a·me′an camp; but when they came to the edge of the Ar·a·me′an camp, there was no one there at all. ⁶ For the Lord had caused the Ar·a·me′an army to hear the sound of chariots, and of horses, the sound of a great army, so that they said to one another, "The king of Israel has hired the kings of the Hit′tites and the kings of Egypt to fight against us." ⁷ So they fled away in the twilight and abandoned their tents, their horses, and their donkeys leaving the camp just as it was, and fled for their lives. ⁸ When these leprous[u] men had come to the edge of the camp, they went into a tent, ate and drank, carried off silver, gold, and clothing, and went and hid them. Then they came back, entered another tent, carried off things from it, and went and hid them.

9 Then they said to one another, "What we are doing is wrong. This is a day of good news; if we are silent and wait until the morning light, we will be found guilty; therefore let us go and tell the king's household." ¹⁰ So they came and called to the gatekeepers of the city, and told them, "We went to the Ar·a·me′an camp, but there was no one to be seen or heard there, nothing but the horses tied, the donkeys tied, and the tents as they were." ¹¹ Then the gatekeepers called out and proclaimed it to the king's household. ¹² The king got up in the night, and said to his servants, "I will tell you what the Ar·a·me′ans have prepared against us

---

t See 7.2: Heb messenger   u A term for several skin diseases; precise meaning uncertain they know that we are starving; so they have left the camp to hide themselves in the open country, thinking, 'When they come out of the city, we shall take them alive and get into the city.' " [13] One of his servants said, "Let some men take five of the remaining horses, since those left here will suffer the fate of the whole multitude of Israel that have perished already; [v] let us send and find out." [14] So they took two mounted men, and the king sent them after the Ar·a·mē′an army, saying, "Go and find out." [15] So they went after them as far as the Jordan; the whole way was littered with garments and equipment that the Ar·a·mē′ans had thrown away in their haste. So the messengers returned, and told the king.

[16] Then the people went out, and plundered the camp of the Ar·a·mē′ans. So a measure of choice meal was sold for a shekel, and two measures of barley for a shekel, according to the word of the LORD. [17] Now the king had appointed the captain on whose hand he leaned to have charge of the gate; the people trampled him to death in the gate, just as the man of God had said when the king came down to him. [18] For when the man of God had said to the king, "Two measures of barley shall be sold for a shekel, and a measure of choice meal for a shekel, about this time tomorrow in the gate of Sa·mār′i·a," [19] the captain had answered the man of God, "Even if the LORD were to make windows in the sky, could such a thing happen?" And he had answered, "You shall see it with your own eyes, but you shall not eat from it." [20] It did indeed happen to him; the people trampled him to death in the gate.

The Shunammite Woman's Land Restored

8 Now E·lī′sha had said to the woman whose son he had restored to life, "Get up and go with your household, and settle wherever you can; for the LORD has called for a famine, and it will come on the land for seven years." [2] So the woman got up and did according to the word of the man of God; she went with her household and settled in the land of the Phi·lis′tines seven years. [3] At the end of the seven years, when the woman returned from the land of the Phi·lis′tines, she set out to appeal to the king for her house and her land. [4] Now the king was talking with Ge·hā′zī the servant of the man of God, saying, "Tell me all the great things that E·lī′sha has done." [5] While he was telling the king how E·lī′sha had restored a dead person to life, the woman whose son he had restored to life appealed to the king for her house and her land. Ge·hā′zī said, "My lord king, here is the woman, and here is her son whom E·lī′sha restored to life." [6] When the king questioned the woman, she told him. So the king appointed an official for her, saying, "Restore all that was hers, together with all the revenue of the fields from the day that she left the land until now."

Death of Ben-hadad

[7] E·lī′sha went to Damascus while King Ben-hā′dad of Ar′am was ill. When it was told him, "The man of God has come here," [8] the king said to Haz′a·el, "Take a present with you and go to meet the man of God. Inquire of the LORD through him, whether I shall recover from this illness." [9] So Haz′a·el went to meet him, taking a present with him, all kinds of goods of Damascus, forty camel loads. When he entered and stood before him, he said, "Your son King Ben-hā′dad of Ar′am has sent me to you, saying, 'Shall I recover from this illness?' " [10] E·lī′sha said to him, "Go, say to him, 'You shall certainly recover'; but the LORD has shown me that he shall certainly die." [11] He fixed his gaze and stared at him, until he was ashamed. Then the man of God wept. [12] Haz′a·el asked, "Why does my lord weep?" He answered, "Because I know the evil that you will do to the people of Israel; you will set their fortresses on fire, you will kill their young men with the sword, dash in pieces their little ones, and rip up their pregnant women." [13] Haz′a·el said, "What is your servant, who is a mere dog, that he should do this great thing?" E·lī′sha answered, "The LORD has shown me that you are to be king over Ar′am." [14] Then he left E·lī′sha, and went to his master Ben-hā′dad, [w] who said to him, "What did E·lī′sha say to you?" And he answered, "He told me that you would certainly recover." [15] But the next day he took the bed-cover and dipped it in water and

[v] Compare Gk Syr Vg: Meaning of Heb uncertain   [w] Heb lacks Ben-hadad

spread it over the king's face, until he died. And Haz'a·el succeeded him.

Jehoram Reigns over Judah
(2 Chr 21.1–20)

16 In the fifth year of King Jō'ram son of Ā'hab of Israel,ˣ Je·hō'ram son of King Je·hosh'a·phat of Judah began to reign. ¹⁷ He was thirty-two years old when he became king, and he reigned eight years in Jerusalem. ¹⁸ He walked in the way of the kings of Israel, as the house of Ā'hab had done, for the daughter of Ā'hab was his wife. He did what was evil in the sight of the LORD. ¹⁹ Yet the LORD would not destroy Judah, for the sake of his servant David, since he had promised to give a lamp to him and to his descendants forever.

20 In his days Ē'dom revolted against the rule of Judah, and set up a king of their own. ²¹ Then Jō'ram crossed over to Zā'ir with all his chariots. He set out by night and attacked the Ē'dom·ites and their chariot commanders who had surrounded him;ʸ but his army fled home. ²² So Ē'dom has been in revolt against the rule of Judah to this day. Lib'nah also revolted at the same time. ²³ Now the rest of the acts of Jō'ram, and all that he did, are they not written in the Book of the Annals of the Kings of Judah? ²⁴ So Jō'ram slept with his ancestors, and was buried with them in the city of David; his son A·ha·zī'ah succeeded him.

Ahaziah Reigns over Judah
(2 Chr 22.1–6)

25 In the twelfth year of King Jō'ram son of Ā'hab of Israel, A·ha·zī'ah son of King Je·hō'ram of Judah began to reign. ²⁶ A·ha·zī'ah was twenty-two years old when he began to reign; he reigned one year in Jerusalem. His mother's name was Ath·a·lī'ah, a granddaughter of King Om'rī of Israel. ²⁷ He also walked in the way of the house of Ā'hab, doing what was evil in the sight of the LORD, as the house of Ā'hab had done, for he was son-in-law to the house of Ā'hab.

28 He went with Jō'ram son of Ā'hab to wage war against King Haz'a·el of Ar'am at Rā'moth-gil'e·ad, where the Ar·a·mē'ans wounded Jō'ram. ²⁹ King Jō'ram returned to be healed in Jez're·el of the wounds that the Ar·a·mē'ans had inflicted on him at Rā'mah, when he fought against King Haz'a·el of Ar'am. King A·ha·zī'ah son of Je·hō'ram of Judah

went down to see Jō'ram son of Ā'hab in Jez're·el, because he was wounded.

Anointing of Jehu

9 Then the prophet E·lī'sha called a member of the company of prophetsᶻ and said to him, "Gird up your loins; take this flask of oil in your hand, and go to Rā'moth-gil'e·ad. ² When you arrive, look there for Jē'hū son of Je·hosh'a·phat, son of Nim'shī; go in and get him to leave his companions, and take him into an inner chamber. ³ Then take the flask of oil, pour it on his head, and say, 'Thus says the LORD: I anoint you king over Israel.' Then open the door and flee; do not linger."

4 So the young man, the young prophet, went to Rā'moth-gil'e·ad. ⁵ He arrived while the commanders of the army were in council, and he announced, "I have a message for you, commander." "For which one of us?" asked Jē'hū. "For you, commander." ⁶ So Jē'hū ᵃ got up and went inside; the young man poured the oil on his head, saying to him, "Thus says the LORD the God of Israel: I anoint you king over the people of the LORD, over Israel. ⁷ You shall strike down the house of your master Ā'hab, so that I may avenge on Jez'e·bel the blood of my servants the prophets, and the blood of all the servants of the LORD. ⁸ For the whole house of Ā'hab shall perish; I will cut off from Ā'hab every male, bond or free, in Israel. ⁹ I will make the house of Ā'hab like the house of Jer·o·bō'am son of Nē'bat, and like the house of Bā'a·sha son of A·hī'jah. ¹⁰ The dogs shall eat Jez'e·bel in the territory of Jez're·el, and no one shall bury her." Then he opened the door and fled.

11 When Jē'hū came back to his master's officers, they said to him, "Is everything all right? Why did this madman come to you?" He answered them, "You know the sort and how they babble." ¹² They said, "Liar! Come on, tell us!" So he said, "This is just what he said to me: 'Thus says the LORD, I anoint you king over Israel.'" ¹³ Then hurriedly they all took their cloaks and spread them for him on the bareʸ steps; and they blew the trum-

---

ˣ Gk Syr: Heb adds *Jehoshaphat being king of Judah,* ʸ Meaning of Heb uncertain ᶻ Heb *sons of the prophets* ᵃ Heb *he* pet, and proclaimed, "Jē′hū is king."

Joram of Israel Killed

14 Thus Jē′hū son of Je·hosh′a·phat son of Nim′shī conspired against Jō′-ram. Jō′ram with all Israel had been on guard at Rā′moth-gil′e·ad against King Haz′a·el of Ar′am; [15] but King Jō′ram had returned to be healed in Jez′rē·el of the wounds that the Ar·a·mē′ans had inflicted on him, when he fought against King Haz′a·el of Ar′am. So Jē′hū said, "If this is your wish, then let no one slip out of the city to go and tell the news in Jez′rē·el." [16] Then Jē′hū mounted his chariot and went to Jez′rē·el, where Jō′ram was lying ill. King A·ha·zī′ah of Judah had come down to visit Jō′ram.

17 In Jez′rē·el, the sentinel standing on the tower spied the company of Jē′hū arriving, and said, "I see a company." Jō′ram said, "Take a horseman; send him to meet them, and let him say, 'Is it peace?' " [18] So the horseman went to meet him; he said, "Thus says the king, 'Is it peace?' " Jē′hū responded, "What have you to do with peace? Fall in behind me." The sentinel reported, saying, "The messenger reached them, but he is not coming back." [19] Then he sent out a second horseman, who came to them and said, "Thus says the king, 'Is it peace?' " Jē′hū answered, "What have you to do with peace? Fall in behind me." [20] Again the sentinel reported, "He reached them, but he is not coming back. It looks like the driving of Jē′hū son of Nim′shī; for he drives like a maniac."

21 Jō′ram said, "Get ready." And they got his chariot ready. Then King Jō′ram of Israel and King A·ha·zī′ah of Judah set out, each in his chariot, and went to meet Jē′hū; they met him at the property of Nā′both the Jez′rē·el·ite. [22] When Jō′ram saw Jē′hū, he said, "Is it peace, Jē′hū?" He answered, "What peace can there be, so long as the many whoredoms and sorceries of your mother Jez′e·bel continue?" [23] Then Jō′ram reined about and fled, saying to A·ha·zī′ah, "Treason, A·ha·zī′ah!" [24] Jē′hū drew his bow with all his strength, and shot Jō′ram between the shoulders, so that the arrow pierced his heart; and he sank in his chariot. [25] Jē′hū said to his aide Bid′-kar, "Lift him out, and throw him on the plot of ground belonging to Nā′-both the Jez′rē·el·ite; for remember,

when you and I rode side by side behind his father A′hab how the LORD uttered this oracle against him: [26] 'For the blood of Nā′both and for the blood of his children that I saw yesterday, says the LORD, I swear I will repay you on this very plot of ground.' Now therefore lift him out and throw him on the plot of ground, in accordance with the word of the LORD."

Ahaziah of Judah Killed
(2 Chr 22.7–9)

27 When King A·ha·zī′ah of Judah saw this, he fled in the direction of Beth-hag′gan. Jē′hū pursued him, saying, "Shoot him also!" And they shot him[b] in the chariot at the ascent to Gur, which is by Ib′le·am. Then he fled to Me·gid′dō, and died there. [28] His officers carried him in a chariot to Jerusalem, and buried him in his tomb with his ancestors in the city of David.

29 In the eleventh year of Jō′ram son of A′hab, A·ha·zī′ah began to reign over Judah.

Jezebel's Violent Death

30 When Jē′hū came to Jez′rē·el, Jez′e·bel heard of it; she painted her eyes, and adorned her head, and looked out of the window. [31] As Jē′hū entered the gate, she said, "Is it peace, Zim′rī, murderer of your master?" [32] He looked up to the window and said, "Who is on my side? Who?" Two or three eunuchs looked out at him. [33] He said, "Throw her down." So they threw her down; some of her blood spattered on the wall and on the horses, which trampled on her. [34] Then he went in and ate and drank; he said, "See to that cursed woman and bury her; for she is a king's daughter." [35] But when they went to bury her, they found no more of her than the skull and the feet and the palms of her hands. [36] When they came back and told him, he said, "This is the word of the LORD, which he spoke by his servant E·lī′jah the Tish′bīte, 'In the territory of Jez′rē·el the dogs shall eat the flesh of Jez′e·bel; [37] the corpse of Jez′-e·bel shall be like dung on the field in the territory of Jez′rē·el, so that no one can say, This is Jez′e·bel.' "

b Syr Vg Compare Gk: Heb lacks and they shot him

2 K I N G S

Massacre of Ahab's Descendants

10 Now Ā'hab had seventy sons in Sa·mār'i·a. So Jē'hū wrote letters and sent them to Sa·mār'i·a, to the rulers of Jez're·el,c to the elders, and to the guardians of the sons ofd Ā'hab, saying, 2 "Since your master's sons are with you and you have at your disposal chariots and horses, a fortified city, and weapons, 3 select the son of your master who is the best qualified, set him on his father's throne, and fight for your master's house." 4 But they were utterly terrified and said, "Look, two kings could not withstand him; how then can we stand?" 5 So the steward of the palace, and the governor of the city, along with the elders and the guardians, sent word to Jē'hū: "We are your servants; we will do anything you say. We will not make anyone king; do whatever you think right." 6 Then he wrote them a second letter, saying, "If you are on my side, and if you are ready to obey me, take the heads of your master's sons and come to me at Jez're·el tomorrow at this time." Now the king's sons, seventy persons, were with the leaders of the city, who were charged with their upbringing. 7 When the letter reached them, they took the king's sons and killed them, seventy persons; they put their heads in baskets and sent them to him at Jez're·el. 8 When the messenger came and told him, "They have brought the heads of the king's sons," he said, "Lay them in two heaps at the entrance of the gate until the morning." 9 Then in the morning when he went out, he stood and said to all the people, "You are innocent. It was I who conspired against my master and killed him; but who struck down all these? 10 Know then that there shall fall to the earth nothing of the word of the LORD, which the LORD spoke concerning the house of Ā'hab; for the LORD has done what he said through his servant E·lī'jah." 11 So Jē'hū killed all who were left of the house of Ā'hab in Jez're·el, all his leaders, close friends, and priests, until he left him no survivor.

12 Then he set out and went to Sa·mār'i·a. On the way, when he was at Beth-ek'ed of the Shepherds, 13 Jē'hū met relatives of King A·ha·zī'ah of Judah and said, "Who are you?" They answered, "We are kin of A·ha·zī'ah; we have come down to visit the royal princes and the sons of the queen mother." 14 He said, "Take them alive." They took them alive, and slaughtered them at the pit of Beth-ek'ed, forty-two in all; he spared none of them.

15 When he left there, he met Je·hon'a·dab son of Rē'chab coming to meet him; he greeted him, and said to him, "Is your heart as true to mine as mine is to yours?"e Je·hon'a·dab answered, "It is." Jē'hū said,f "If it is, give me your hand." So he gave him his hand. Jē'hū took him up with him into the chariot. 16 He said, "Come with me, and see my zeal for the LORD." So heg had him ride in his chariot. 17 When he came to Sa·mār'i·a, he killed all who were left to Ā'hab in Sa·mār'i·a, until he had wiped them out, according to the word of the LORD that he spoke to E·lī'jah.

Slaughter of Worshipers of Baal

18 Then Jē'hū assembled all the people and said to them, "Ā'hab offered Bā'al small service; but Jē'hū will offer much more. 19 Now therefore summon to me all the prophets of Bā'al, all his worshipers, and all his priests; let none be missing, for I have a great sacrifice to offer to Bā'al; whoever is missing shall not live." But Jē'hū was acting with cunning in order to destroy the worshipers of Bā'al. 20 Jē'hū decreed, "Sanctify a solemn assembly for Bā'al." So they proclaimed it. 21 Jē'hū sent word throughout all Israel; all the worshipers of Bā'al came, so that there was no one left who did not come. They entered the temple of Bā'al, until the temple of Bā'al was filled from wall to wall. 22 He said to the keeper of the wardrobe, "Bring out the vestments for all the worshipers of Bā'al." So he brought out the vestments for them. 23 Then Jē'hū entered the temple of Bā'al with Je·hon'a·dab son of Rē'chab; and he said to the worshipers of Bā'al, "Search and see that there is no worshiper of the LORD here among you, but only worshipers of Bā'al." 24 Then they proceeded to offer sacrifices and burnt offerings.

Now Jē'hū had stationed eighty men outside, saying, "Whoever allows any

c Or *of the city*; Vg Compare Gk
d Gk: Heb *lacks of the sons of*
e Gk: Heb *Is it right with your heart, as my heart is with your heart?* f Gk: Heb *lacks Jehu said* g Gk Syr Tg: Heb *they*

of those to escape whom I deliver into your hands shall forfeit his life." [25] As soon as he had finished presenting the burnt offering, Je'hū said to the guards and to the officers, "Come in and kill them; let no one escape." So they put them to the sword. The guards and the officers threw them out, and then went into the citadel of the temple of Bā'al. [26] They brought out the pillar[h] that was in the temple of Bā'al, and burned it. [27] Then they demolished the pillar of Bā'al, and destroyed the temple of Bā'al, and made it a latrine to this day. [28] Thus Je'hū wiped out Bā'al from Israel. [29] But Je'hū did not turn aside from the sins of Jer·o·bō'am son of Ne'bat, which he caused Israel to commit—the golden calves that were in Beth'el and in Dan. [30] The LORD said to Je'hū, "Because you have done well in carrying out what I consider right, and in accordance with all that was in my heart have dealt with the house of Ā'hab, your sons of the fourth generation shall sit on the throne of Israel." [31] But Je'hū was not careful to follow the law of the LORD the God of Israel with all his heart; he did not turn from the sins of Jer·o·bō'am, which he caused Israel to commit.

Death of Jehu

[32] In those days the LORD began to trim off parts of Israel. Haz'a·el defeated them throughout the territory of Israel: [33] from the Jordan eastward, all the land of Gil'e·ad, the Gad'ites, the Reū'ben·ites, and the Ma·nas'sites, from A·rō'er, which is by the Wadi Ar'non, that is, Gil'e·ad and Bā'shan. [34] Now the rest of the acts of Je'hū, all that he did, and all his power, are they not written in the Book of the Annals of the Kings of Israel? [35] So Je'hū slept with his ancestors, and they buried him in Sa·mār'i·a. His son Je·hō'a·haz succeeded him. [36] The time that Je'hū reigned over Israel in Sa·mār'i·a was twenty-eight years.

Athaliah Reigns over Judah
(2 Chr 22.10–12)

11 Now when Ath·a·lī'ah, A·ha·zī'ah's mother, saw that her son was dead, she set about to destroy all the royal family. [2] But Je·hosh'e·ba, King Jō'ram's daughter, A·ha·zī'ah's sister, took Jō'ash son of A·ha·zī'ah, and stole him away from among the king's children who were about to be killed; she put[i] him and

his nurse in a bedroom. Thus she[j] hid him from Ath·a·lī'ah, so that he was not killed; [3] he remained with her six years, hidden in the house of the LORD, while Ath·a·lī'ah reigned over the land.

Jehoiada Anoints the Child Joash
(2 Chr 23.1–11)

[4] But in the seventh year Je·hoi'·a·da summoned the captains of the Car'ites and of the guards and had them come to him in the house of the LORD. He made a covenant with them and put them under oath in the house of the LORD; then he showed them the king's son. [5] He commanded them, "This is what you are to do: one-third of you, those who go off duty on the sabbath and guard the king's house [6] (another third being at the gate Sur and a third at the gate behind the guards), shall guard the palace; [7] and your two divisions that come on duty in force on the sabbath and guard the house of the LORD[k] [8] shall surround the king, each with weapons in hand; and whoever approaches the ranks is to be killed. Be with the king in his comings and goings."

[9] The captains did according to all that the priest Je·hoi'a·da commanded; each brought his men who were to go off duty on the sabbath, with those who were to come on duty on the sabbath, and came to the priest Je·hoi'a·da. [10] The priest delivered to the captains the spears and shields that had been King David's, which were in the house of the LORD; [11] the guards stood, every man with his weapons in his hand, from the south side of the house to the north side of the house, around the altar and the house, to guard the king on every side. [12] Then he brought out the king's son, put the crown on him, and gave him the covenant;[l] they proclaimed him king, and anointed him; they clapped their hands and shouted, "Long live the king!"

Death of Athaliah
(2 Chr 23.12—24.1)

[13] When Ath·a·lī'ah heard the noise of the guard and of the people,

[h] Gk Vg Syr Tg: Heb *pillars*   [i] With 2 Chr 22.11: Heb lacks *she put*
[j] Gk Syr Vg Compare 2 Chr 22.11: Heb *they*   [k] Heb *the* LORD *to the king*
[l] Or *treaty* or *testimony;* Heb *eduth*

she went into the house of the LORD to the people; [14] when she looked, there was the king standing by the pillar, according to custom, with the captains and the trumpeters beside the king, and all the people of the land rejoicing and blowing trumpets. Ath·a·lī′ah tore her clothes and cried, "Treason! Treason!" [15] Then the priest Je·hoi′a·da commanded the captains who were set over the army, "Bring her out between the ranks, and kill with the sword anyone who follows her." For the priest said, "Let her not be killed in the house of the LORD." [16] So they laid hands on her; she went through the horses' entrance to the king's house, and there she was put to death.

[17] Je·hoi′a·da made a covenant between the LORD and the king and people, that they should be the LORD's people; also between the king and the people. [18] Then all the people of the land went to the house of Bā′al, and tore it down; his altars and his images they broke in pieces, and they killed Mat′tan, the priest of Bā′al, before the altars. The priest posted guards over the house of the LORD. [19] He took the captains, the Cār′ītes, the guards, and all the people of the land; then they brought the king down from the house of the LORD, marching through the gate of the guards to the king's house. He took his seat on the throne of the kings. [20] So all the people of the land rejoiced; and the city was quiet after Ath·a·lī′ah had been killed with the sword at the king's house.

[21] [m]Je·hō′ash[n] was seven years old when he began to reign.

The Temple Repaired
(2 Chr 24.1–14)

12 In the seventh year of Jē′hū, Je·hō′ash began to reign; he reigned forty years in Jerusalem. His mother's name was Zib′i·ah of Bē′er-shē′ba. [2] Je·hō′ash did what was right in the sight of the LORD all his days, because the priest Je·hoi′a·da instructed him. [3] Nevertheless the high places were not taken away; the people continued to sacrifice and make offerings on the high places.

[4] Je·hō′ash said to the priests, "All the money offered as sacred donations that is brought into the house of the LORD, the money for which each person is assessed—the money from the assessment of persons—and the money from the voluntary offerings brought into the house of the LORD, [5] let the priests receive from each of the donors; and let them repair the house wherever any need of repairs is discovered." [6] But by the twenty-third year of King Je·hō′ash the priests had made no repairs on the house. [7] Therefore King Je·hō′ash summoned the priest Je·hoi′a·da with the other priests and said to them, "Why are you not repairing the house? Now therefore do not accept any more money from your donors but hand it over for the repair of the house." [8] So the priests agreed that they would neither accept more money from the people nor repair the house.

[9] Then the priest Je·hoi′a·da took a chest, made a hole in its lid, and set it beside the altar on the right side as one entered the house of the LORD; the priests who guarded the threshold put in it all the money that was brought into the house of the LORD. [10] Whenever they saw that there was a great deal of money in the chest, the king's secretary and the high priest went up, counted the money that was found in the house of the LORD, and tied it up in bags. [11] They would give the money that was weighed out into the hands of the workers who had the oversight of the house of the LORD; then they paid it out to the carpenters and the builders who worked on the house of the LORD, [12] to the masons and the stonecutters, as well as to buy timber and quarried stone for making repairs on the house of the LORD, as well as for any outlay for repairs of the house. [13] But for the house of the LORD no basins of silver, snuffers, bowls, trumpets, or any vessels of gold, or of silver, were made from the money that was brought into the house of the LORD, [14] for that was given to the workers who were repairing the house of the LORD with it. [15] They did not ask an accounting from those into whose hand they delivered the money to pay out to the workers, for they dealt honestly. [16] The money from the guilt offerings and the money from the sin offerings was not brought into the house of the LORD; it belonged to the priests.

Hazael Threatens Jerusalem

[17] At that time King Haz′a·el of Ar′am went up, fought against Gath,

---

[m]Ch 12.1 in Heb   [n]Another spelling is Joash; see verse 19

and took it. But when Haz′a·el set his face to go up against Jerusalem, [18] King Je·hō′ash of Judah took all the votive gifts that Je·hosh′a·phat, Je·hō′-ram, and A·ha·zī′ah, his ancestors, the kings of Judah, had dedicated, as well as his own votive gifts, all the gold that was found in the treasuries of the house of the LORD and of the king's house, and sent these to King Haz′a·el of Ar′am. Then Haz′a·el withdrew from Jerusalem.

Death of Joash
(2 Chr 24.23–27)

19 Now the rest of the acts of Jō′-ash, and all that he did, are they not written in the Book of the Annals of the Kings of Judah? [20] His servants arose, devised a conspiracy, and killed Jō′ash in the house of Mil′lō, on the way that goes down to Sil′la. [21] It was Jō′za·car son of Shim′ē·ath and Je·hō′za·bad son of Shō′mer, his servants, who struck him down, so that he died. He was buried with his ancestors in the city of David; then his son Am·a·zī′ah succeeded him.

Jehoahaz Reigns over Israel

13 In the twenty-third year of King Jō′ash son of A·ha·zī′ah of Judah, Je·hō′a·haz son of Jē′hū began to reign over Israel in Sa·mār′i·a; he reigned seventeen years. [2] He did what was evil in the sight of the LORD, and followed the sins of Jer·o·bō′am son of Nē′bat, which he caused Israel to sin; he did not depart from them. [3] The anger of the LORD was kindled against Israel, so that he gave them repeatedly into the hand of King Haz′a·el of Ar′am, then into the hand of Ben-ha′-dad son of Haz′a·el. [4] But Je·hō′a·haz entreated the LORD, and the LORD heeded him; for he saw the oppression of Israel, how the king of Ar′am oppressed them. [5] Therefore the LORD gave Israel a savior, so that they escaped from the hand of the Ar·a·mē′-ans; and the people of Israel lived in their homes as formerly. [6] Nevertheless they did not depart from the sins of the house of Jer·o·bō′am, which he caused Israel to sin, but walked° in them; the sacred pole ᵖ also remained in Sa·mār′i·a. [7] So Je·hō′a·haz was left with an army of not more than fifty horsemen, ten chariots and ten thousand footmen; for the king of Ar′am had destroyed them and made them like the dust at threshing. [8] Now the

rest of the acts of Je·hō′a·haz and all that he did, including his might, are they not written in the Book of the Annals of the Kings of Israel? [9] So Je·hō′-a·haz slept with his ancestors, and they buried him in Sa·mār′i·a; then his son Jō′ash succeeded him.

Jehoash Reigns over Israel

10 In the thirty-seventh year of King Jō′ash of Judah, Je·hō′ash son of Je·hō′a·haz began to reign over Israel in Sa·mār′i·a; he reigned sixteen years. [11] He also did what was evil in the sight of the LORD; he did not depart from all the sins of Jer·o·bō′am son of Nē′bat, which he caused Israel to sin, but he walked in them. [12] Now the rest of the acts of Jō′ash, and all that he did, as well as the might with which he fought against King Am·a·zī′ah of Judah, are they not written in the Book of the Annals of the Kings of Israel? [13] So Jō′ash slept with his ancestors, and Jer·o·bō′am sat upon his throne; Jō′-ash was buried in Sa·mār′i·a with the kings of Israel.

Death of Elisha

14 Now when E·lī′sha had fallen sick with the illness of which he was to die, King Jō′ash of Israel went down to him, and wept before him, crying, "My father, my father! The chariots of Israel and its horsemen!" [15] E·lī′sha said to him, "Take a bow and arrows"; so he took a bow and arrows. [16] Then he said to the king of Israel, "Draw the bow"; and he drew it. E·lī′sha laid his hands on the king's hands. [17] Then he said, "Open the window eastward"; and he opened it. E·lī′sha said, "Shoot"; and he shot. Then he said, "The LORD's arrow of victory, the arrow of victory over Ar′am! For you shall fight the Ar·a·mē′ans in A′phek until you have made an end of them." [18] He continued, "Take the arrows"; and he took them. He said to the king of Israel, "Strike the ground with them"; he struck three times, and stopped. [19] Then the man of God was angry with him, and said, "You should have struck five or six times; then you would have struck down Ar′am until you had made an end of it, but now you will strike down Ar′am only three times."

20 So E·lī′sha died, and they buried him. Now bands of Mō′ab·ites used to

invade the land in the spring of the year. 21 As a man was being buried, a marauding band was seen and the man was thrown into the grave of E·lī′-sha; as soon as the man touched the bones of E·lī′sha, he came to life and stood on his feet.

Israel Recaptures Cities from Aram

22 Now King Haz′a·el of Ar′am oppressed Israel all the days of Je·hō′-a·haz. 23 But the LORD was gracious to them and had compassion on them; he turned toward them, because of his covenant with Abraham, Isaac, and Jacob, and would not destroy them; nor has he banished them from his presence until now.

24 When King Haz′a·el of Ar′am died, his son Ben-hā′dad succeeded him. 25 Then Je·hō′ash son of Je·hō′-a·haz took again from Ben-hā′dad son of Haz′a·el the towns that he had taken from his father Je·hō′a·haz in war. Three times Jō′ash defeated him and recovered the towns of Israel.

Amaziah Reigns over Judah
(2 Chr 25.1—26.2)

14 In the second year of King Jō′-ash son of Jō′a·haz of Israel, King Am·a·zī′ah son of Jō′ash of Judah, began to reign. 2 He was twenty-five years old when he began to reign, and he reigned twenty-nine years in Jerusalem. His mother's name was Jē·hō·ad′din of Jerusalem. 3 He did what was right in the sight of the LORD, yet not like his ancestor David; in all things he did as his father Jō′ash had done. 4 But the high places were not removed; the people still sacrificed and made offerings on the high places. 5 As soon as the royal power was firmly in his hand he killed his servants who had murdered his father the king. 6 But he did not put to death the children of the murderers; according to what is written in the book of the law of Moses, where the LORD commanded, "The parents shall not be put to death for the children, or the children be put to death for the parents; but all shall be put to death for their own sins."

7 He killed ten thousand Ē′dom·ites in the Valley of Salt and took Sē′la by storm; he called it Jok′thē-el, which is its name to this day.

8 Then Am·a·zī′ah sent messengers to King Je·hō′ash son of Je·hō′a·haz, son of Jē′hū, of Israel, saying, "Come, let us look one another in the face."

9 King Je·hō′ash of Israel sent word to King Am·a·zī′ah of Judah, "A thorn-bush on Lebanon sent to a cedar on Lebanon, saying, 'Give your daughter to my son for a wife'; but a wild animal of Lebanon passed by and trampled down the thorn-bush. 10 You have indeed defeated Ē′dom, and your heart has lifted you up. Be content with your glory, and stay at home; for why should you provoke trouble so that you fall, you and Judah with you?"

11 But Am·a·zī′ah would not listen. So King Je·hō′ash of Israel went up; he and King Am·a·zī′ah of Judah faced one another in battle at Beth-shē′-mesh, which belongs to Judah. 12 Judah was defeated by Israel; everyone fled home. 13 King Je·hō′ash of Israel captured King Am·a·zī′ah of Judah son of Je·hō′ash, son of A·ha·zī′ah, at Beth-shē′mesh; he came to Jerusalem, and broke down the wall of Jerusalem from the Ē′phra·im Gate to the Corner Gate, a distance of four hundred cubits. 14 He seized all the gold and silver, and all the vessels that were found in the house of the LORD and in the treasuries of the king's house, as well as hostages; then he returned to Sa·mār′i·a.

15 Now the rest of the acts that Je·hō′ash did, his might, and how he fought with King Am·a·zī′ah of Judah, are they not written in the Book of the Annals of the Kings of Israel? 16 Je·hō′-ash slept with his ancestors, and was buried in Sa·mār′i·a with the kings of Israel; then his son Jer·o·bō′am succeeded him.

17 King Am·a·zī′ah son of Jō′ash of Judah lived fifteen years after the death of King Je·hō′ash son of Je·hō′-a·haz of Israel. 18 Now the rest of the deeds of Am·a·zī′ah, are they not written in the Book of the Annals of the Kings of Judah? 19 They made a conspiracy against him in Jerusalem, and he fled to Lā′chish. But they sent after him to Lā′chish, and killed him there. 20 They brought him on horses; he was buried in Jerusalem with his ancestors in the city of David. 21 All the people of Judah took Az·a·rī′ah, who was sixteen years old, and made him king to succeed his father Am·a·zī′ah. 22 He rebuilt Ē′lath and restored it to Judah, after King Am·a·zī′ah q slept with his ancestors.

q Heb the king

Jeroboam II Reigns over Israel

23 In the fifteenth year of King
Am·a·zī'ah son of Jō'ash of Judah,
King Jer·o·bō'am son of Jō'ash of Israel began to reign in Sa·mār'i·a; he
reigned forty-one years. 24 He did what
was evil in the sight of the LORD; he did
not depart from all the sins of
Jer·o·bō'am son of Ne'bat, which he
caused Israel to sin. 25 He restored the
border of Israel from Le'bo-hā'math
as far as the Sea of the Ar'a·bah, according to the word of the LORD, the
God of Israel, which he spoke by his
servant Jonah son of A·mit'taī, the
prophet, who was from Gath-he'pher.
26 For the LORD saw that the distress of
Israel was very bitter; there was no
one left, bond or free, and no one to
help Israel. 27 But the LORD had not
said that he would blot out the name of
Israel from under heaven, so he saved
them by the hand of Jer·o·bō'am son of
Jō'ash.

28 Now the rest of the acts of
Jer·o·bō'am, and all that he did, and
his might, how he fought, and how he
recovered for Israel Damascus and
Hā'math, which had belonged to Judah, are they not written in the Book of
the Annals of the Kings of Israel?
29 Jer·o·bō'am slept with his ancestors,
the kings of Israel; his son Zech·a·rī'ah
succeeded him.

Azariah Reigns over Judah
(2 Chr 26.3–23)

15 In the twenty-seventh year of
King Jer·o·bō'am of Israel King
Az·a·rī'ah son of Am·a·zī'ah of Judah
began to reign. 2 He was sixteen years
old when he began to reign, and he
reigned fifty-two years in Jerusalem.
His mother's name was Jec·o·lī'ah of
Jerusalem. 3 He did what was right in
the sight of the LORD, just as his father
Am·a·zī'ah had done. 4 Nevertheless
the high places were not taken away;
the people still sacrificed and made offerings on the high places. 5 The LORD
struck the king, so that he was leprous*r* to the day of his death, and lived
in a separate house. Jō'tham the king's
son was in charge of the palace, governing the people of the land. 6 Now
the rest of the acts of Az·a·rī'ah, and all
that he did, are they not written in the
Book of the Annals of the Kings of Judah? 7 Az·a·rī'ah slept with his ancestors; they buried him with his ances-

tors in the city of David; his son
Jō'tham succeeded him.

Zechariah Reigns over Israel

8 In the thirty-eighth year of King
Az·a·rī'ah of Judah, Zech·a·rī'ah son
of Jer·o·bō'am reigned over Israel in
Sa·mār'i·a six months. 9 He did what
was evil in the sight of the LORD, as his
ancestors had done. He did not depart
from the sins of Jer·o·bō'am son of
Ne'bat, which he caused Israel to sin.
10 Shal'lum son of Jā'besh conspired
against him, and struck him down in
public and killed him, and reigned in
place of him. 11 Now the rest of the
deeds of Zech·a·rī'ah are written in the
Book of the Annals of the Kings of Israel. 12 This was the promise of the
LORD that he gave to Je'hū, "Your sons
shall sit on the throne of Israel to the
fourth generation." And so it happened.

Shallum Reigns over Israel

13 Shal'lum son of Jā'besh began to
reign in the thirty-ninth year of King
Uz·zī'ah of Judah; he reigned one
month in Sa·mār'i·a. 14 Then Men'-
a·hem son of Gā'dī came up from Tir'-
zah and came to Sa·mār'i·a; he struck
down Shal'lum son of Jā'besh in
Sa·mār'i·a and killed him; he reigned
in place of him. 15 Now the rest of the
deeds of Shal'lum, including the conspiracy that he made, are written in the
Book of the Annals of the Kings of Israel. 16 At that time Men'a·hem sacked
Tiph'sah, all who were in it and its territory from Tir'zah on; because they
did not open it to him, he sacked it. He
ripped open all the pregnant women in
it.

Menahem Reigns over Israel

17 In the thirty-ninth year of King
Az·a·rī'ah of Judah, Men'a·hem son of
Gā'dī began to reign over Israel; he
reigned ten years in Sa·mār'i·a. 18 He
did what was evil in the sight of the
LORD; he did not depart all his days
from any of the sins of Jer·o·bō'am
son of Ne'bat, which he caused Israel to sin. 19 King Pūl of Assyria came
against the land; Men'a·hem gave Pūl
a thousand talents of silver, so that he
might help him confirm his hold on the
royal power. 20 Men'a·hem exacted the
money from Israel, that is, from all the

---

r A term for several skin diseases;
precise meaning uncertain

wealthy, fifty shekels of silver from each one, to give to the king of Assyria. So the king of Assyria turned back, and did not stay there in the land. 21 Now the rest of the deeds of Men'-a·hem, and all that he did, are they not written in the Book of the Annals of the Kings of Israel? 22 Men'a·hem slept with his ancestors, and his son Pek·a·hī'ah succeeded him.

Pekahiah Reigns over Israel

23 In the fiftieth year of King Az·a·rī'ah of Judah, Pek·a·hī'ah son of Men'a·hem began to reign over Israel in Sa·mār'i·a; he reigned two years. 24 He did what was evil in the sight of the LORD; he did not turn away from the sins of Jer·o·bō'am son of Ne'bat, which he caused Israel to sin. 25 Pe'kah son of Rem·a·lī'ah, his captain, conspired against him with fifty of the Gil'e·ad·ites, and attacked him in Sa·mār'i·a, in the citadel of the palace along with Ar'gob and A·ri'eh; he killed him, and reigned in place of him. 26 Now the rest of the deeds of Pek·a·hī'ah, and all that he did, are written in the Book of the Annals of the Kings of Israel.

Pekah Reigns over Israel

27 In the fifty-second year of King Az·a·rī'ah of Judah, Pe'kah son of Rem·a·lī'ah began to reign over Israel in Sa·mār'i·a; he reigned twenty years. 28 He did what was evil in the sight of the LORD; he did not depart from the sins of Jer·o·bō'am son of Ne'bat, which he caused Israel to sin. 29 In the days of King Pe'kah of Israel, King Tig'lath-pī·lē'ser of Assyria came and captured I'jon, A'bel-beth-mā'a·cah, Ja·nō'ah, Kē'desh, Hā'zor, Gil'e·ad, and Galilee, all the land of Naph'ta·lī; and he carried the people captive to Assyria. 30 Then Hō·shē'a son of E'lah made a conspiracy against Pe'kah son of Rem·a·lī'ah, attacked him, and killed him; he reigned in place of him, in the twentieth year of Jō'tham son of Uz·zī'ah. 31 Now the rest of the acts of Pe'kah, and all that he did, are written in the Book of the Annals of the Kings of Israel.

Jotham Reigns over Judah
(2 Chr 27.1–9)

32 In the second year of King Pe'-kah son of Rem·a·lī'ah of Israel, King Jō'tham son of Uz·zī'ah of Judah be-

gan to reign. 33 He was twenty-five years old when he began to reign and reigned sixteen years in Jerusalem. His mother's name was Je·rū'sha daughter of Zā'dok. 34 He did what was right in the sight of the LORD, just as his father Uz·zī'ah had done. 35 Nevertheless the high places were not removed; the people still sacrificed and made offerings on the high places. He built the upper gate of the house of the LORD. 36 Now the rest of the acts of Jō'-tham, and all that he did, are they not written in the Book of the Annals of the Kings of Judah? 37 In those days the LORD began to send King Rē'zin of Ar'am and Pe'kah son of Rem·a·lī'ah against Judah. 38 Jō'tham slept with his ancestors, and was buried with his ancestors in the city of David, his ancestor; his son A'haz succeeded him.

Ahaz Reigns over Judah
(2 Chr 28.1–27)

16 In the seventeenth year of Pe'-kah son of Rem·a·lī'ah, King A'haz son of Jō'tham of Judah began to reign. 2 A'haz was twenty years old when he began to reign; he reigned sixteen years in Jerusalem. He did not do what was right in the sight of the LORD his God, as his ancestor David had done, 3 but he walked in the way of the kings of Israel. He even made his son pass through fire, according to the abominable practices of the nations whom the LORD drove out before the people of Israel. 4 He sacrificed and made offerings on the high places, on the hills, and under every green tree.

5 Then King Rē'zin of Ar'am and King Pe'kah son of Rem·a·lī'ah of Israel came up to wage war on Jerusalem; they besieged A'haz but could not conquer him. 6 At that time the king of E'dom[s] recovered E'lath for E'dom, and drove the Judeans from E'lath; and the E'dom·ites came to E'lath, where they live to this day. 7 A'haz sent messengers to King Tig'lath-pī·lē'ser of Assyria, saying, "I am your servant and your son. Come up, and rescue me from the hand of the king of Ar'am and from the hand of the king of Israel, who are attacking me." 8 A'haz also took the silver and gold found in the house of the LORD and in the treasures of the king's house, and sent a present to the king of Assyria. 9 The king of

s Cn: Heb *King Rezin of Aram*
t Cn: Heb *Aram*

Assyria listened to him; the king of Assyria marched up against Damascus, and took it, carrying its people captive to Kir; then he killed Re′zin.

10 When King A′haz went to Damascus to meet King Tig′lath-pi-le′ser of Assyria, he saw the altar that was at Damascus. King A′haz sent to the priest U-ri′ah a model of the altar, and its pattern, exact in all its details. 11 The priest U-ri′ah built the altar; in accordance with all that King A′haz had sent from Damascus, just so did the priest U-ri′ah build it, before King A′haz arrived from Damascus. 12 When the king came from Damascus, the king viewed the altar. Then the king drew near to the altar, went up on it, 13 and offered his burnt offering and his grain offering, poured his drink offering, and dashed the blood of his offerings of well-being against the altar. 14 The bronze altar that was before the LORD he removed from the front of the house, from the place between his altar and the house of the LORD, and put it on the north side of his altar. 15 King A′haz commanded the priest U-ri′ah, saying, "Upon the great altar offer the morning burnt offering, and the evening grain offering, and the king's burnt offering, and his grain offering, with the burnt offering of all the people of the land, their grain offering, and their drink offering; then dash against it all the blood of the burnt offering, and all the blood of the sacrifice; but the bronze altar shall be for me to inquire by." 16 The priest U-ri′ah did everything that King A′haz commanded.

17 Then King A′haz cut off the frames of the stands, and removed the laver from them; he removed the sea from the bronze oxen that were under it, and put it on a pediment of stone. 18 The covered portal for use on the sabbath that had been built inside the palace, and the outer entrance for the king he removed from [u] the house of the LORD. He did this because of the king of Assyria. 19 Now the rest of the acts of A′haz that he did, are they not written in the Book of the Annals of the Kings of Judah? 20 A′haz slept with his ancestors, and was buried with his ancestors in the city of David; his son Hez·e·ki′ah succeeded him.

Hoshea Reigns over Israel

17 In the twelfth year of King A′haz of Judah, Hō·shē′a son of E′lah began to reign in Sa·mār′i·a over Israel; he reigned nine years. 2 He did what was evil in the sight of the LORD, yet not like the kings of Israel who were before him. 3 King Shalmanē′ser of Assyria came up against him; Hō·shē′a became his vassal, and paid him tribute. 4 But the king of Assyria found treachery in Hō·shē′a; for he had sent messengers to King So of Egypt, and offered no tribute to the king of Assyria, as he had done year by year; therefore the king of Assyria confined him and imprisoned him.

Israel Carried Captive to Assyria

5 Then the king of Assyria invaded all the land and came to Sa·mār′i·a; for three years he besieged it. 6 In the ninth year of Hō·shē′a the king of Assyria captured Sa·mār′i·a; he carried the Israelites away to Assyria. He placed them in Hā′lah, on the Hā′bor, the river of Gō′zan, and in the cities of the Medes.

7 This occurred because the people of Israel had sinned against the LORD their God, who had brought them up out of the land of Egypt from under the hand of Pharaoh king of Egypt. They had worshiped other gods 8 and walked in the customs of the nations whom the LORD drove out before the people of Israel, and in the customs that the kings of Israel had introduced. [v] 9 The people of Israel secretly did things that were not right against the LORD their God. They built for themselves high places at all their towns, from watchtower to fortified city; 10 they set up for themselves pillars and sacred poles [w] on every high hill and under every green tree; 11 there they made offerings on all the high places, as the nations did whom the LORD carried away before them. They did wicked things, provoking the LORD to anger; 12 they served idols, of which the LORD had said to them, "You shall not do this." 13 Yet the LORD warned Israel and Judah by every prophet and every seer, saying, "Turn from your evil ways and keep my commandments and my statutes, in accordance with all the law that I commanded your ancestors and that I sent to you by my servants the prophets." 14 They would not listen but were stubborn, as their ancestors had been, who did not be-

2 KINGS

[u] Cn: Heb lacks *from*　[v] Meaning of Heb uncertain　[w] Heb *Asherim*

lieve in the LORD their God. 15 They despised his statutes, and his covenant that he made with their ancestors, and the warnings that he gave them. They went after false idols and became false; they followed the nations that were around them, concerning whom the LORD had commanded them that they should not do as they did. 16 They rejected all the commandments of the LORD their God and made for themselves cast images of two calves; they made a sacred pole,ˣ worshiped all the host of heaven, and served Baʹal. 17 They made their sons and their daughters pass through fire; they used divination and augury; and they sold themselves to do evil in the sight of the LORD, provoking him to anger. 18 Therefore the LORD was very angry with Israel and removed them out of his sight; none was left but the tribe of Judah alone.

19 Judah also did not keep the commandments of the LORD their God but walked in the customs that Israel had introduced. 20 The LORD rejected all the descendants of Israel; he punished them and gave them into the hand of plunderers, until he had banished them from his presence.

21 When he had torn Israel from the house of David, they made Jer·o·boʹam son of Neʹbat king. Jer·o·boʹam drove Israel from following the LORD and made them commit great sin. 22 The people of Israel continued in all the sins that Jer·o·boʹam committed; they did not depart from them 23 until the LORD removed Israel out of his sight, as he had foretold through all his servants the prophets. So Israel was exiled from their own land to Assyria until this day.

Assyria Resettles Samaria

24 The king of Assyria brought people from Babylon, Cuʹthah, Avʹva, Haʹmath, and Seph·ar·vaʹim, and placed them in the cities of Sa·marʹi·a in place of the people of Israel; they took possession of Sa·marʹi·a, and settled in its cities. 25 When they first settled there, they did not worship the LORD; therefore the LORD sent lions among them, which killed some of them. 26 So the king of Assyria was told, "The nations that you have carried away and placed in the cities of Sa·marʹi·a do not know the law of the god of the land; therefore he has sent lions among them; they are killing

them, because they do not know the law of the god of the land." 27 Then the king of Assyria commanded, "Send there one of the priests whom you carried away from there; let himʸ go and live there, and teach them the law of the god of the land." 28 So one of the priests whom they had carried away from Sa·marʹi·a came and lived in Bethʹel; he taught them how they should worship the LORD.

29 But every nation still made gods of its own and put them in the shrines of the high places that the people of Sa·marʹi·a had made, every nation in the cities in which they lived; 30 the people of Babylon made Sucʹcoth-beʹnoth, the people of Cuth made Nerʹgal, the people of Haʹmath made A·shiʹma; 31 the Avʹvites made Nibʹhaz and Tarʹtak; the Se·pharʹvites burned their children in the fire to A·dramʹme·lech and A·namʹme·lech, the gods of Seph·ar·vaʹim. 32 They also worshiped the LORD and appointed from among themselves all sorts of people as priests of the high places, who sacrificed for them in the shrines of the high places. 33 So they worshiped the LORD but also served their own gods, after the manner of the nations from among whom they had been carried away. 34 To this day they continue to practice their former customs.

They do not worship the LORD and they do not follow the statutes or the ordinances or the law or the commandment that the LORD commanded the children of Jacob, whom he named Israel. 35 The LORD had made a covenant with them and commanded them, "You shall not worship other gods or bow yourselves to them or serve them or sacrifice to them, 36 but you shall worship the LORD, who brought you out of the land of Egypt with great power and with an outstretched arm; you shall bow yourselves to him, and to him you shall sacrifice. 37 The statutes and the ordinances and the law and the commandment that he wrote for you, you shall always be careful to observe. You shall not worship other gods; 38 you shall not forget the covenant that I have made with you. You shall not worship other gods, 39 but you shall worship the LORD your God; he will deliver you out of the hand of all your enemies." 40 They would not lis-

---

ˣ Heb *Asherah*   ʸ Syr Vg: Heb *them*

ten, however, but they continued to practice their former custom.

41 So these nations worshiped the LORD, but also served their carved images; to this day their children and their children's children continue to do as their ancestors did.

Hezekiah's Reign over Judah
(2 Chr 29.1–2; 31.1)

18 In the third year of King Hō·shē′a son of Ē′lah of Israel, Hez·e·kī′ah son of King Ā′haz of Judah began to reign. 2 He was twenty-five years old when he began to reign; he reigned twenty-nine years in Jerusalem. His mother's name was Ā′bī daughter of Zech·a·rī′ah. 3 He did what was right in the sight of the LORD just as his ancestor David had done. 4 He removed the high places, broke down the pillars, and cut down the sacred pole.z He broke in pieces the bronze serpent that Moses had made, for until those days the people of Israel had made offerings to it; it was called Ne·hush′tan. 5 He trusted in the LORD the God of Israel; so that there was no one like him among all the kings of Judah after him, or among those who were before him. 6 For he held fast to the LORD; he did not depart from following him but kept the commandments that the LORD commanded Moses. 7 The LORD was with him; wherever he went, he prospered. He rebelled against the king of Assyria and would not serve him. 8 He attacked the Phi·lis′tines as far as Gā′za and its territory, from watchtower to fortified city.

9 In the fourth year of King Hez·e·kī′ah, which was the seventh year of King Hō·shē′a son of Ē′lah of Israel, King Shal·man·ē′ser of Assyria came up against Sa·mār′i·a, besieged it, 10 and at the end of three years, took it. In the sixth year of Hez·e·kī′ah, which was the ninth year of King Hō·shē′a of Israel, Sa·mār′i·a was taken. 11 The king of Assyria carried the Israelites away to Assyria, settled them in Hā′lah, on the Hā′bor, the river of Gō′zan, and in the cities of the Medes, 12 because they did not obey the voice of the LORD their God but transgressed his covenant—all that Moses the servant of the LORD had commanded; they neither listened nor obeyed.

Sennacherib Invades Judah
(Isa 36.1–22; 2 Chr 32.1–19)

13 In the fourteenth year of King Hez·e·kī′ah, King Sen·nach′e·rib of Assyria came up against all the fortified cities of Judah and captured them. 14 King Hez·e·kī′ah of Judah sent to the king of Assyria at Lā′chish, saying, "I have done wrong; withdraw from me; whatever you impose on me I will bear." The king of Assyria demanded of King Hez·e·kī′ah of Judah three hundred talents of silver and thirty talents of gold. 15 Hez·e·kī′ah gave him all the silver that was found in the house of the LORD and in the treasuries of the king's house. 16 At that time Hez·e·kī′ah stripped the gold from the doors of the temple of the LORD, and from the doorposts that King Hez·e·kī′ah of Judah had overlaid and gave it to the king of Assyria. 17 The king of Assyria sent the Tar′tan, the Rab-sar′is, and the Rab′sha·keh with a great army from Lā′chish to King Hez·e·kī′ah at Jerusalem. They went up and came to Jerusalem. When they arrived, they came and stood by the conduit of the upper pool, which is on the highway to the Fuller's Field. 18 When they called for the king, there came out to them E·lī′a·kim son of Hil·kī′ah, who was in charge of the palace, and Sheb′nah the secretary, and Jō′ah son of Ā′saph, the recorder.

19 The Rab′sha·keh said to them, "Say to Hez·e·kī′ah: Thus says the great king, the king of Assyria: On what do you base this confidence of yours? 20 Do you think that mere words are strategy and power for war? On whom do you now rely, that you have rebelled against me? 21 See, you are relying now on Egypt, that broken reed of a staff, which will pierce the hand of anyone who leans on it. Such is Pharaoh king of Egypt to all who rely on him. 22 But if you say to me, 'We rely on the LORD our God,' is it not he whose high places and altars Hez·e·kī′ah has removed, saying to Judah and to Jerusalem, 'You shall worship before this altar in Jerusalem'? 23 Come now, make a wager with my master the king of Assyria: I will give you two thousand horses, if you are able on your part to set riders on them. 24 How then can you repulse a single captain among the least of my master's ser-

z Heb Asherah

2 KINGS

vants, when you rely on Egypt for chariots and for horsemen? 25 Moreover, is it without the LORD that I have come up against this place to destroy it? The LORD said to me, Go up against this land, and destroy it."

26 Then E·li′a·kim son of Hil·ki′ah, and Sheb′nah, and Jo′ah said to the Rab′sha·keh, "Please speak to your servants in the Ar·a·ma′ic language, for we understand it; do not speak to us in the language of Judah within the hearing of the people who are on the wall." 27 But the Rab′sha·keh said to them, "Has my master sent me to speak these words to your master and to you, and not to the people sitting on the wall, who are doomed with you to eat their own dung and to drink their own urine?"

28 Then the Rab′sha·keh stood and called out in a loud voice in the language of Judah, "Hear the word of the great king, the king of Assyria! 29 Thus says the king: 'Do not let Hez·e·ki′ah deceive you, for he will not be able to deliver you out of my hand. 30 Do not let Hez·e·ki′ah make you rely on the LORD by saying, The LORD will surely deliver us, and this city will not be given into the hand of the king of Assyria.' 31 Do not listen to Hez·e·ki′ah; for thus says the king of Assyria: 'Make your peace with me and come out to me; then every one of you will eat from your own vine and your own fig tree, and drink water from your own cistern, 32 until I come and take you away to a land like your own land, a land of grain and wine, a land of bread and vineyards, a land of olive oil and honey, that you may live and not die. Do not listen to Hez·e·ki′ah when he misleads you by saying, The LORD will deliver us. 33 Has any of the gods of the nations ever delivered its land out of the hand of the king of Assyria? 34 Where are the gods of Ha′math and Ar′pad? Where are the gods of Seph·ar·va′im, He′na, and Iv′vah? Have they delivered Sa·mar′i·a out of my hand? 35 Who among all the gods of the countries have delivered their countries out of my hand, that the LORD should deliver Jerusalem out of my hand?'"

36 But the people were silent and answered him not a word, for the king's command was, "Do not answer him." 37 Then E·li′a·kim son of Hil·ki′ah, who was in charge of the palace, and Sheb′na the secretary, and

Jo′ah son of A′saph, the recorder, came to Hez·e·ki′ah with their clothes torn and told him the words of the Rab′sha·keh.

Hezekiah Consults Isaiah
(Isa 37.1–7)

19 When King Hez·e·ki′ah heard it, he tore his clothes, covered himself with sackcloth, and went into the house of the LORD. 2 And he sent E·li′a·kim, who was in charge of the palace, and Sheb′na the secretary, and the senior priests, covered with sackcloth, to the prophet I·sai′ah son of A′moz. 3 They said to him, "Thus says Hez·e·ki′ah, This day is a day of distress, of rebuke, and of disgrace; children have come to the birth, and there is no strength to bring them forth. 4 It may be that the LORD your God heard all the words of the Rab′sha·keh, whom his master the king of Assyria has sent to mock the living God, and will rebuke the words that the LORD your God has heard; therefore lift up your prayer for the remnant that is left." 5 When the servants of King Hez·e·ki′ah came to I·sai′ah, 6 I·sai′ah said to them, "Say to your master, 'Thus says the LORD: Do not be afraid because of the words that you have heard, with which the servants of the king of Assyria have reviled me. 7 I myself will put a spirit in him, so that he shall hear a rumor and return to his own land; I will cause him to fall by the sword in his own land.'"

Sennacherib's Threat
(Isa 37.8–13)

8 The Rab′sha·keh returned, and found the king of Assyria fighting against Lib′nah; for he had heard that the king had left La′chish. 9 When the king*a* heard concerning King Tir·ha′-kah of Ethiopia,*b* "See, he has set out to fight against you," he sent messengers again to Hez·e·ki′ah, saying, 10 "Thus shall you speak to King Hez·e·ki′ah of Judah: Do not let your God on whom you rely deceive you by promising that Jerusalem will not be given into the hand of the king of Assyria. 11 See, you have heard what the kings of Assyria have done to all lands, destroying them utterly. Shall you be delivered? 12 Have the gods of the nations delivered them, the nations that my predecessors destroyed, Go′zan,

a Heb *he*   *b* Or *Nubia*; Heb *Cush*

Har'an, Re'zeph, and the people of Eden who were in Te·las'sar? ¹³ Where is the king of Ha'math, the king of Ar'pad, the king of the city of Seph·ar·va'im, the king of He'na, or the king of Iv'vah?"

Hezekiah's Prayer
(Isa 37.14–35)

14 Hez·e·ki'ah received the letter from the hand of the messengers and read it; then Hez·e·ki'ah went up to the house of the LORD and spread it before the LORD. ¹⁵ And Hez·e·ki'ah prayed before the LORD, and said: "O LORD the God of Israel, who are enthroned above the cherubim, you are God, you alone, of all the kingdoms of the earth; you have made heaven and earth. ¹⁶ Incline your ear, O LORD, and hear; open your eyes, O LORD, and see; hear the words of Sen·nach'e·rib, which he has sent to mock the living God. ¹⁷ Truly, O LORD, the kings of Assyria have laid waste the nations and their lands, ¹⁸ and have hurled their gods into the fire, though they were no gods but the work of human hands—wood and stone—and so they were destroyed. ¹⁹ So now, O LORD our God, save us, I pray you, from his hand, so that all the kingdoms of the earth may know that you, O LORD, are God alone."

20 Then I·sai'ah son of A'moz sent to Hez·e·ki'ah, saying, "Thus says the LORD, the God of Israel: I have heard your prayer to me about King Sen·nach'e·rib of Assyria. ²¹ This is the word that the LORD has spoken concerning him:

She despises you, she scorns you—
    virgin daughter Zion;
she tosses her head—behind your back,
    daughter Jerusalem.

22 Whom have you mocked and reviled?
    Against whom have you raised your voice
and haughtily lifted your eyes?
    Against the Holy One of Israel!
23 By your messengers you have mocked the Lord,
    and you have said, 'With my many chariots
I have gone up the heights of the mountains,
    to the far recesses of Lebanon;
I felled its tallest cedars,

    its choicest cypresses;
I entered its farthest retreat,
    its densest forest.
24 I dug wells
    and drank foreign waters,
I dried up with the sole of my foot
    all the streams of Egypt.'

25 Have you not heard
    that I determined it long ago?
I planned from days of old
    what now I bring to pass,
that you should make fortified cities
    crash into heaps of ruins,
26 while their inhabitants, shorn of strength,
    are dismayed and confounded;
they have become like plants of the field
    and like tender grass,
like grass on the housetops,
    blighted before it is grown.

27 "But I know your rising[c] and your sitting,
    your going out and coming in,
    and your raging against me.
28 Because you have raged against me
    and your arrogance has come to my ears,
I will put my hook in your nose
    and my bit in your mouth;
I will turn you back on the way
    by which you came.

29 "And this shall be the sign for you: This year you shall eat what grows of itself, and in the second year what springs from that; then in the third year sow, reap, plant vineyards, and eat their fruit. ³⁰ The surviving remnant of the house of Judah shall again take root downward, and bear fruit upward; ³¹ for from Jerusalem a remnant shall go out, and from Mount Zion a band of survivors. The zeal of the LORD of hosts will do this.

32 "Therefore thus says the LORD concerning the king of Assyria: He shall not come into this city, shoot an arrow there, come before it with a shield, or cast up a siege ramp against it. ³³ By the way that he came, by the same he shall return; he shall not come into this city, says the LORD. ³⁴ For I will defend this city to save it, for my

c Gk Compare Isa 37.27 Q Ms: MT lacks *rising*

2
K
I
N
G
S

own sake and for the sake of my servant David."

Sennacherib's Defeat and Death
(Isa 37.36–38; 2 Chr 32.20–23)

35 That very night the angel of the LORD set out and struck down one hundred eighty-five thousand in the camp of the Assyrians; when morning dawned, they were all dead bodies. 36Then King Sen·nach′e·rib of Assyria left, went home, and lived at Nin′e·veh. 37As he was worshiping in the house of his god Nis′roch, his sons A·dram′me·lech and Sha·rē′zer killed him with the sword, and they escaped into the land of Ar′a·rat. His son Ē′sar-had′don succeeded him.

Hezekiah's Illness
(2 Chr 32.24–26; Isa 38.1–8)

20 In those days Hez·e·kī′ah became sick and was at the point of death. The prophet I·sāi′ah son of A′moz came to him, and said to him, "Thus says the LORD: Set your house in order, for you shall die; you shall not recover." 2Then Hez·e·kī′ah turned his face to the wall and prayed to the LORD: 3 "Remember now, O LORD, I implore you, how I have walked before you in faithfulness with a whole heart, and have done what is good in your sight." Hez·e·kī′ah wept bitterly. 4Before I·sāi′ah had gone out of the middle court, the word of the LORD came to him: 5 "Turn back, and say to Hez·e·kī′ah prince of my people, Thus says the LORD, the God of your ancestor David: I have heard your prayer, I have seen your tears; indeed, I will heal you; on the third day you shall go up to the house of the LORD. 6I will add fifteen years to your life. I will deliver you and this city out of the hand of the king of Assyria; I will defend this city for my own sake and for my servant David's sake." 7Then I·sāi′ah said, "Bring a lump of figs. Let them take it and apply it to the boil, so that he may recover."

8 Hez·e·kī′ah said to I·sāi′ah, "What shall be the sign that the LORD will heal me, and that I shall go up to the house of the LORD on the third day?" 9I·sāi′ah said, "This is the sign to you from the LORD, that the LORD will do the thing that he has promised: the shadow has now advanced ten intervals; shall it retreat ten intervals?" 10Hez·e·kī′ah answered, "It is normal for the shadow to lengthen ten intervals; rather let the shadow retreat ten intervals." 11The prophet I·sāi′ah cried to the LORD; and he brought the shadow back the ten intervals, by which the sund had declined on the dial of A′haz.

Envoys from Babylon
(Isa 39.1–8)

12 At that time King Mer′o·dach-bal′a·dan son of Bal′a·dan of Babylon sent envoys with letters and a present to Hez·e·kī′ah, for he had heard that Hez·e·kī′ah had been sick. 13Hez·e·kī′ah welcomed them;e he showed them all his treasure house, the silver, the gold, the spices, the precious oil, his armory, all that was found in his storehouses; there was nothing in his house or in all his realm that Hez·e·kī′ah did not show them. 14Then the prophet I·sāi′ah came to King Hez·e·kī′ah, and said to him, "What did these men say? From where did they come to you?" Hez·e·kī′ah answered, "They have come from a far country, from Babylon." 15He said, "What have they seen in your house?" Hez·e·kī′ah answered, "They have seen all that is in my house; there is nothing in my storehouses that I did not show them."

16 Then I·sāi′ah said to Hez·e·kī′ah, "Hear the word of the LORD: 17Days are coming when all that is in your house, and that which your ancestors have stored up until this day, shall be carried to Babylon; nothing shall be left, says the LORD. 18Some of your own sons who are born to you shall be taken away; they shall be eunuchs in the palace of the king of Babylon." 19Then Hez·e·kī′ah said to I·sāi′ah, "The word of the LORD that you have spoken is good." For he thought, "Why not, if there will be peace and security in my days?"

Death of Hezekiah
(2 Chr 32.32–33)

20 The rest of the deeds of Hez·e·kī′ah, all his power, how he made the pool and the conduit and brought water into the city, are they not written in the Book of the Annals of the Kings of Judah? 21Hez·e·kī′ah slept with his ancestors; and his son Ma·nas′seh succeeded him.

dSyr See Isa 38.8 and Tg: Heb it
eGk Vg Syr: Heb When Hezekiah heard about them

Manasseh Reigns over Judah
(2 Chr 33.1–20)

21 Ma·nas′seh was twelve years old when he began to reign; he reigned fifty-five years in Jerusalem. His mother's name was Heph′zi·bah. ²He did what was evil in the sight of the LORD, following the abominable practices of the nations that the LORD drove out before the people of Israel. ³For he rebuilt the high places that his father Hez·e·ki′ah had destroyed; he erected altars for Ba′al, made a sacred pole,ᶠ as King A′hab of Israel had done, worshiped all the host of heaven, and served them. ⁴He built altars in the house of the LORD, of which the LORD had said, "In Jerusalem I will put my name." ⁵He built altars for all the host of heaven in the two courts of the house of the LORD. ⁶He made his son pass through fire; he practiced soothsaying and augury, and dealt with mediums and with wizards. He did much evil in the sight of the LORD, provoking him to anger. ⁷The carved image of A·she′rah that he had made he set in the house of which the LORD said to David and to his son Solomon, "In this house, and in Jerusalem, which I have chosen out of all the tribes of Israel, I will put my name forever; ⁸I will not cause the feet of Israel to wander any more out of the land that I gave to their ancestors, if only they will be careful to do according to all that I have commanded them, and according to all the law that my servant Moses commanded them." ⁹But they did not listen; Ma·nas′seh misled them to do more evil than the nations had done that the LORD destroyed before the people of Israel.

10 The LORD said by his servants the prophets, ¹¹"Because King Ma·nas′seh of Judah has committed these abominations, has done things more wicked than all that the Am′o·rites did, who were before him, and has caused Judah also to sin with his idols; ¹²therefore thus says the LORD, the God of Israel, I am bringing upon Jerusalem and Judah such evil that the ears of everyone who hears of it will tingle. ¹³I will stretch over Jerusalem the measuring line for Sa·mar′i·a, and the plummet for the house of A′hab; I will wipe Jerusalem as one wipes a dish, wiping it and turning it upside down. ¹⁴I will cast off the remnant of my heritage, and give them into the hand of their enemies; they shall become a prey and a spoil to all their enemies, ¹⁵because they have done what is evil in my sight and have provoked me to anger, since the day their ancestors came out of Egypt, even to this day."

16 Moreover Ma·nas′seh shed very much innocent blood, until he had filled Jerusalem from one end to another, besides the sin that he caused Judah to sin so that they did what was evil in the sight of the LORD.

17 Now the rest of the acts of Ma·nas′seh, all that he did, and the sin that he committed, are they not written in the Book of the Annals of the Kings of Judah? ¹⁸Ma·nas′seh slept with his ancestors, and was buried in the garden of his house, in the garden of Uz′za. His son A′mon succeeded him.

Amon Reigns over Judah
(2 Chr 33.21–25)

19 A′mon was twenty-two years old when he began to reign; he reigned two years in Jerusalem. His mother's name was Me·shul′le·meth daughter of Ha′ruz of Jot′bah. ²⁰He did what was evil in the sight of the LORD, as his father Ma·nas′seh had done. ²¹He walked in all the way in which his father walked, served the idols that his father served, and worshiped them; ²²he abandoned the LORD, the God of his ancestors, and did not walk in the way of the LORD. ²³The servants of A′mon conspired against him, and killed the king in his house. ²⁴But the people of the land killed all those who had conspired against King A′mon, and the people of the land made his son Jo·si′ah king in place of him. ²⁵Now the rest of the acts of A′mon that he did, are they not written in the Book of the Annals of the Kings of Judah? ²⁶He was buried in his tomb in the garden of Uz′za; then his son Jo·si′ah succeeded him.

Josiah Reigns over Judah
(2 Chr 34.1–2)

22 Jo·si′ah was eight years old when he began to reign; he reigned thirty-one years in Jerusalem. His mother's name was Je·di′dah daughter of A·dai′ah of Boz′kath. ²He did what was right in the sight of the LORD, and walked in all the way of his

ᶠ Heb Asherah

2 KINGS

father David; he did not turn aside to the right or to the left.

Hilkiah Finds the Book of the Law
(2 Chr 34.8–28)

3 In the eighteenth year of King Jō·sī′ah, the king sent Shā′phan son of Az·a·lī′ah, son of Me·shul′lam, the secretary, to the house of the LORD, saying, ⁴"Go up to the high priest Hil·kī′ah, and have him count the entire sum of the money that has been brought into the house of the LORD, which the keepers of the threshold have collected from the people; ⁵let it be given into the hand of the workers who have the oversight of the house of the LORD; let them give it to the workers who are at the house of the LORD, repairing the house, ⁶that is, to the carpenters, to the builders, to the masons; and let them use it to buy timber and quarried stone to repair the house. ⁷But no accounting shall be asked from them for the money that is delivered into their hand, for they deal honestly."

8 The high priest Hil·kī′ah said to Shā′phan the secretary, "I have found the book of the law in the house of the LORD." When Hil·kī′ah gave the book to Shā′phan, he read it. ⁹Then Shā′phan the secretary came to the king, and reported to the king, "Your servants have emptied out the money that was found in the house, and have delivered it into the hand of the workers who have oversight of the house of the LORD." ¹⁰Shā′phan the secretary informed the king, "The priest Hil·kī′ah has given me a book." Shā′phan then read it aloud to the king.

11 When the king heard the words of the book of the law, he tore his clothes. ¹²Then the king commanded the priest Hil·kī′ah, A·hī′kam son of Shā′phan, Ach′bor son of Mī·cāi′ah, Shā′phan the secretary, and the king's servant A·sāi′ah, saying, ¹³"Go, inquire of the LORD for me, for the people, and for all Judah, concerning the words of this book that has been found; for great is the wrath of the LORD that is kindled against us, because our ancestors did not obey the words of this book, to do according to all that is written concerning us."

14 So the priest Hil·kī′ah, A·hī′kam, Ach′bor, Shā′phan, and A·sāi′ah went to the prophetess Hul′dah the wife of Shal′lum son of Tik′vah, son of Har′has, keeper of the wardrobe; she resided in Jerusalem in the Second Quarter, where they consulted her. ¹⁵She declared to them, "Thus says the LORD, the God of Israel: Tell the man who sent you to me, ¹⁶Thus says the LORD, I will indeed bring disaster on this place and on its inhabitants—all the words of the book that the king of Judah has read. ¹⁷Because they have abandoned me and have made offerings to other gods, so that they have provoked me to anger with all the work of their hands, therefore my wrath will be kindled against this place, and it will not be quenched. ¹⁸But as to the king of Judah, who sent you to inquire of the LORD, thus shall you say to him, Thus says the LORD, the God of Israel: Regarding the words that you have heard, ¹⁹because your heart was penitent, and you humbled yourself before the LORD, when you heard how I spoke against this place, and against its inhabitants, that they should become a desolation and a curse, and because you have torn your clothes and wept before me, I also have heard you, says the LORD. ²⁰Therefore, I will gather you to your ancestors, and you shall be gathered to your grave in peace; your eyes shall not see all the disaster that I will bring on this place." They took the message back to the king.

Josiah's Reformation
(2 Chr 34.29–33)

23 Then the king directed that all the elders of Judah and Jerusalem should be gathered to him. ²The king went up to the house of the LORD, and with him went all the people of Judah, all the inhabitants of Jerusalem, the priests, the prophets, and all the people, both small and great; he read in their hearing all the words of the book of the covenant that had been found in the house of the LORD. ³The king stood by the pillar and made a covenant before the LORD, to follow the LORD, keeping his commandments, his decrees, and his statutes, with all his heart and all his soul, to perform the words of this covenant that were written in this book. All the people joined in the covenant.

4 The king commanded the high priest Hil·kī′ah, the priests of the second order, and the guardians of the threshold, to bring out of the temple of the LORD all the vessels made for Bā′al, for A·shē′rah, and for all the host of

heaven; he burned them outside Jerusalem in the fields of the Kid′ron, and carried their ashes to Beth′el. 5 He deposed the idolatrous priests whom the kings of Judah had ordained to make offerings in the high places at the cities of Judah and around Jerusalem; those also who made offerings to Ba′al, to the sun, the moon, the constellations, and all the host of the heavens. 6 He brought out the image of g A·she′rah from the house of the LORD, outside Jerusalem, to the Wadi Kid′ron, burned it at the Wadi Kid′ron, beat it to dust and threw the dust of it upon the graves of the common people. 7 He broke down the houses of the male temple prostitutes that were in the house of the LORD, where the women did weaving for A·she′rah. 8 He brought all the priests out of the towns of Judah, and defiled the high places where the priests had made offerings, from Ge′ba to Be′er-she′ba; he broke down the high places of the gates that were at the entrance of the gate of Joshua the governor of the city, which were on the left at the gate of the city. 9 The priests of the high places, however, did not come up to the altar of the LORD in Jerusalem, but ate unleavened bread among their kindred. 10 He defiled To′pheth, which is in the valley of Ben-hin′nom, so that no one would make a son or a daughter pass through fire as an offering to Mo′lech. 11 He removed the horses that the kings of Judah had dedicated to the sun, at the entrance to the house of the LORD, by the chamber of the eunuch Na′than-me′lech, which was in the precincts; h then he burned the chariots of the sun with fire. 12 The altars on the roof of the upper chamber of A′haz, which the kings of Judah had made, and the altars that Ma·nas′seh had made in the two courts of the house of the LORD, he pulled down from there and broke in pieces, and threw the rubble into the Wadi Kid′ron. 13 The king defiled the high places that were east of Jerusalem, to the south of the Mount of Destruction, which King Solomon of Israel had built for As′tar′te the abomination of the Si·do′ni·ans, for Che′mosh the abomination of Mo′ab, and for Mil′com the abomination of the Am′mon-ites. 14 He broke the pillars in pieces, cut down the sacred poles, i and covered the sites with human bones.

15 Moreover, the altar at Beth′el,

the high place erected by Jer·o·bo′am son of Ne′bat, who caused Israel to sin— he pulled down that altar along with the high place. He burned the high place, crushing it to dust; he also burned the sacred pole. j 16 As Jo·si′ah turned, he saw the tombs there on the mount; and he sent and took the bones out of the tombs, and burned them on the altar, and defiled it, according to the word of the LORD that the man of God proclaimed, k when Jer·o·bo′am stood by the altar at the festival; he turned and looked up at the tomb of the man of God who had predicted these things. 17 Then he said, "What is that monument that I see?" The people of the city told him, "It is the tomb of the man of God who came from Judah and predicted these things that you have done against the altar at Beth′el." 18 He said, "Let him rest; let no one move his bones." So they let his bones alone, with the bones of the prophet who came out of Sa·mar′i·a. 19 Moreover, Jo·si′ah removed all the shrines of the high places that were in the towns of Sa·mar′i·a, which kings of Israel had made, provoking the LORD to anger; he did to them just as he had done at Beth′el. 20 He slaughtered on the altars all the priests of the high places who were there, and burned human bones on them. Then he returned to Jerusalem.

The Passover Celebrated
(2 Chr 35.1–19)

21 The king commanded all the people, "Keep the passover to the LORD your God as prescribed in this book of the covenant." 22 No such passover had been kept since the days of the judges who judged Israel, or during all the days of the kings of Israel or of the kings of Judah; 23 but in the eighteenth year of King Jo·si′ah this passover was kept to the LORD in Jerusalem.

24 Moreover Jo·si′ah put away the mediums, wizards, teraphim, l idols, and all the abominations that were seen in the land of Judah and in Jerusalem, so that he established the words of the law that were written in the book that the priest Hil·ki′ah had found in the house of the LORD. 25 Before him

g Heb lacks image of   h Meaning of Heb uncertain   i Heb Asherim
j Heb Asherah   k Gk: Heb proclaimed, who had predicted these things
l Or household gods

there was no king like him, who turned to the LORD with all his heart, with all his soul, and with all his might, according to all the law of Moses; nor did any like him arise after him.

26 Still the LORD did not turn from the fierceness of his great wrath, by which his anger was kindled against Judah, because of all the provocations with which Ma·nas'seh had provoked him. 27 The LORD said, "I will remove Judah also out of my sight, as I have removed Israel; and I will reject this city that I have chosen, Jerusalem, and the house of which I said, My name shall be there."

Josiah Dies in Battle
(2 Chr 35.20—36.1)

28 Now the rest of the acts of Jō·sī'ah, and all that he did, are they not written in the Book of the Annals of the Kings of Judah? 29 In his days Pharaoh Ne'cō king of Egypt went up to the king of Assyria to the river Euphrates. King Jō·sī'ah went to meet him; but when Pharaoh Ne'cō met him at Me·gid'dō, he killed him. 30 His servants carried him dead in a chariot from Me·gid'dō, brought him to Jerusalem, and buried him in his own tomb. The people of the land took Je·hō'a·haz son of Jō·sī'ah, anointed him, and made him king in place of his father.

Reign and Captivity of Jehoahaz
(2 Chr 36.1–4)

31 Je·hō'a·haz was twenty-three years old when he began to reign; he reigned three months in Jerusalem. His mother's name was Ha·mū'tal daughter of Jer·e·mī'ah of Lib'nah. 32 He did what was evil in the sight of the LORD, just as his ancestors had done. 33 Pharaoh Ne'cō confined him at Rib'lah in the land of Hā'math, so that he might not reign in Jerusalem, and imposed tribute on the land of one hundred talents of silver and a talent of gold. 34 Pharaoh Ne'cō made E·lī'a·kim son of Jō·sī'ah king in place of his father Jō·sī'ah, and changed his name to Je·hoi'a·kim. But he took Je·hō'a·haz away; he came to Egypt, and died there. 35 Je·hoi'a·kim gave the silver and the gold to Pharaoh, but he taxed the land in order to meet Pharaoh's demand for money. He exacted the silver and the gold from the people of the land, from all according to their assessment, to give it to Pharaoh Ne'cō.

Jehoiakim Reigns over Judah
(2 Chr 36.5–8)

36 Je·hoi'a·kim was twenty-five years old when he began to reign; he reigned eleven years in Jerusalem. His mother's name was Ze·bī'dah daughter of Pe·dāi'ah of Rū'mah. 37 He did what was evil in the sight of the LORD, just as all his ancestors had done.

Judah Overrun by Enemies

24 In his days King Ne·bū·chad·nez'zar of Babylon came up; Je·hoi'a·kim became his servant for three years; then he turned and rebelled against him. 2 The LORD sent against him bands of the Chal·de'ans, bands of the Ar·a·me'ans, bands of the Mō'ab·ites, and bands of the Am'mon·ites; he sent them against Judah to destroy it, according to the word of the LORD that he spoke by his servants the prophets. 3 Surely this came upon Judah at the command of the LORD, to remove them out of his sight, for the sins of Ma·nas'seh, for all that he had committed, 4 and also for the innocent blood that he had shed; for he filled Jerusalem with innocent blood, and the LORD was not willing to pardon. 5 Now the rest of the deeds of Je·hoi'a·kim, and all that he did, are they not written in the Book of the Annals of the Kings of Judah? 6 So Je·hoi'a·kim slept with his ancestors; then his son Je·hoi'a·chin succeeded him. 7 The king of Egypt did not come again out of his land, for the king of Babylon had taken over all that belonged to the king of Egypt from the Wadi of Egypt to the River Euphrates.

Reign and Captivity of Jehoiachin
(2 Chr 36.9–10)

8 Je·hoi'a·chin was eighteen years old when he began to reign; he reigned three months in Jerusalem. His mother's name was Ne·hush'ta daughter of El·nā'than of Jerusalem. 9 He did what was evil in the sight of the LORD, just as his father had done.

10 At that time the servants of King Ne·bū·chad·nez'zar of Babylon came up to Jerusalem, and the city was besieged. 11 King Ne·bū·chad·nez'zar of Babylon came to the city, while his servants were besieging it; 12 King Je·hoi'a·chin of Judah gave himself up to the king of Babylon, himself, his mother, his servants, his officers, and his palace officials. The king of Babylon took

him prisoner in the eighth year of his reign.

Capture of Jerusalem

13 He carried off all the treasures of the house of the LORD, and the treasures of the king's house; he cut in pieces all the vessels of gold in the temple of the LORD, which King Solomon of Israel had made, all this as the LORD had foretold. 14 He carried away all Jerusalem, all the officials, all the warriors, ten thousand captives, all the artisans and the smiths; no one remained, except the poorest people of the land. 15 He carried away Je·hoi'-a·chin to Babylon; the king's mother, the king's wives, his officials, and the elite of the land, he took into captivity from Jerusalem to Babylon. 16 The king of Babylon brought captive to Babylon all the men of valor, seven thousand, the artisans and the smiths, one thousand, all of them strong and fit for war. 17 The king of Babylon made Mat·ta·ni'ah, Je·hoi'a·chin's uncle, king in his place, and changed his name to Zed·e·ki'ah.

Zedekiah Reigns over Judah
(2 Chr 36.11–14; Jer 52.1–3a)

18 Zed·e·ki'ah was twenty-one years old when he began to reign; he reigned eleven years in Jerusalem. His mother's name was Ha·mu'tal daughter of Jer·e·mi'ah of Lib'nah. 19 He did what was evil in the sight of the LORD, just as Je·hoi'a·kim had done. 20 Indeed, Jerusalem and Judah so angered the LORD that he expelled them from his presence.

The Fall and Captivity of Judah
(2 Chr 36.15–21; Jer 52.3b–30)

25 Zed·e·ki'ah rebelled against the king of Babylon. 1 And in the ninth year of his reign, in the tenth month, on the tenth day of the month, King Ne·bu·chad·nez'zar of Babylon came with all his army against Jerusalem, and laid siege to it; they built siegeworks against it all around. 2 So the city was besieged until the eleventh year of King Zed·e·ki'ah. 3 On the ninth day of the fourth month the famine became so severe in the city that there was no food for the people of the land. 4 Then a breach was made in the city wall;[m] the king with all the soldiers fled[n] by night by the way of the gate between the two walls, by the king's garden, though the Chal·de'ans

were all around the city. They went in the direction of the Ar'a·bah. 5 But the army of the Chal·de'ans pursued the king, and overtook him in the plains of Jericho; all his army was scattered, deserting him. 6 Then they captured the king and brought him up to the king of Babylon at Rib'lah, who passed sentence on him. 7 They slaughtered the sons of Zed·e·ki'ah before his eyes, then put out the eyes of Zed·e·ki'ah; they bound him in fetters and took him to Babylon.

8 In the fifth month, on the seventh day of the month—which was the nineteenth year of King Ne·bu·chad·nez'zar, king of Babylon—Ne·bu·za·rad'an, the captain of the bodyguard, a servant of the king of Babylon, came to Jerusalem. 9 He burned the house of the LORD, the king's house, and all the houses of Jerusalem; every great house he burned down. 10 All the army of the Chal·de'ans who were with the captain of the guard broke down the walls around Jerusalem. 11 Ne·bu·za·rad'an the captain of the guard carried into exile the rest of the people who were left in the city and the deserters who had defected to the king of Babylon—all the rest of the population. 12 But the captain of the guard left some of the poorest people of the land to be vinedressers and tillers of the soil.

13 The bronze pillars that were in the house of the LORD, as well as the stands and the bronze sea that were in the house of the LORD, the Chal·de'ans broke in pieces, and carried the bronze to Babylon. 14 They took away the pots, the shovels, the snuffers, the dishes for incense, and all the bronze vessels used in the temple service, 15 as well as the firepans and the basins. What was made of gold the captain of the guard took away for the gold, and what was made of silver, for the silver. 16 As for the two pillars, the one sea, and the stands, which Solomon had made for the house of the LORD, the bronze of all these vessels was beyond weighing. 17 The height of the one pillar was eighteen cubits, and on it was a bronze capital; the height of the capital was three cubits; latticework and pomegranates, all of bronze, were on the capital all

---

m Heb lacks *wall*　　n Gk Compare Jer 39.4; 52.7: Heb lacks *the king* and lacks *fled* around. The second pillar had the same, with the latticework.

18 The captain of the guard took the chief priest Se·rāi′ah, the second priest Zeph·a·nī′ah, and the three guardians of the threshold; 19 from the city he took an officer who had been in command of the soldiers, and five men of the king's council who were found in the city; the secretary who was the commander of the army who mustered the people of the land; and sixty men of the people of the land who were found in the city. 20 Ne·bū·za·rad′an the captain of the guard took them, and brought them to the king of Babylon at Rib′lah. 21 The king of Babylon struck them down and put them to death at Rib′lah in the land of Hā′math. So Judah went into exile out of its land.

Gedaliah Made Governor of Judah
(Jer 40.5—41.18)

22 He appointed Ged·a·lī′ah son of A·hī′kam son of Shaā′phan as governor over the people who remained in the land of Judah, whom King Ne·bū·chad·nez′zar of Babylon had left. 23 Now when all the captains of the forces and their men heard that the king of Babylon had appointed Ged·a·lī′ah as governor, they came with their men to Ged·a·lī′ah at Miz′pah, namely, Ish′ma·el son of Neth·a·nī′ah, Jō·hā′nan son of Ka·rē′ah, Se·rāi′ah son of Tan′hu·meth the Ne·toph′a·thīte, and Jā·az·a·nī′ah

son of the Mā′a·ca·thīte. 24 Ged·a·lī′ah swore to them and their men, saying, "Do not be afraid because of the Chal·dē′an officials; live in the land, serve the king of Babylon, and it shall be well with you." 25 But in the seventh month, Ish′ma·el son of Neth·a·nī′ah son of E·lish′a·ma, of the royal family, came with ten men; they struck down Ged·a·lī′ah so that he died, along with the Judeans and Chal·dē′ans who were with him at Miz′pah. 26 Then all the people, high and low[o] and the captains of the forces set out and went to Egypt; for they were afraid of the Chal·dē′ans.

Jehoiachin Released from Prison
(Jer 52.31—34)

27 In the thirty-seventh year of the exile of King Je·hoi′a·chin of Judah, in the twelfth month, on the twenty-seventh day of the month, King E′vil-me·rō′dach of Babylon, in the year that he began to reign, released King Je·hoi′a·chin of Judah from prison; 28 he spoke kindly to him, and gave him a seat above the other seats of the kings who were with him in Babylon. 29 So Je·hoi′a·chin put aside his prison clothes. Every day of his life he dined regularly in the king's presence. 30 For his allowance, a regular allowance was given him by the king, a portion every day, as long as he lived.

o Or *young and old*

1 CHRONICLES

From Adam to Abraham
(Gen 5.1—32; 10.1—32; 11.10—26; Lk 3.34—38)

1 Adam, Seth, Ē′nosh; 2 Kē′nan, Ma·hal′a·lel, Jar′ed; 3 Ē′noch, Me·thū′se·lah, Lā′mech; 4 Noah, Shem, Ham, and Jā′pheth.

5 The descendants of Jā′pheth: Gō′mer, Mā′gog, Mā′daī, Jā′van, Tū′bal, Mē′shech, and Tī′ras. 6 The descendants of Gō′mer: Ash′ke·naz, Dī′-

phath,[a] and Tō·gar′mah. 7 The descendants of Jā′van: E·li′shah, Tar′shish, Kit′tim, and Rod′a·nim.[b]

8 The descendants of Ham: Cush, Egypt, Put, and Cā′naan. 9 The descendants of Cush: Sē′ba, Hav′i·lah, Sab′ta, Rā′a·ma, and Sab′te·ca. The descendants of Rā′a·mah: Shē′ba and Dē′dan. 10 Cush became the father of

a Gen 10.3 *Ripath;* See Gk Vg　b Gen 10.4 *Dodanim;* See Syr Vg

Nim'rod; he was the first to be a mighty one on the earth.

11 Egypt became the father of Lū'-dim, An'a·mim, Le·hā'bim, Naph'-tū·him, [12] Path·rū'sim, Cas·lū'him, and Caph'to·rim, from whom the Phi·lis'-tines come.[c]

13 Cā'naan became the father of Sī'don his firstborn, and Heth, [14] and the Jeb'ū·sītes, the Am'o·rītes, the Gir'ga·shītes, [15] the Hī'vītes, the Ar'-kītes, the Sī'nītes, [16] the Ar'vad·ītes, the Zem'a·rītes, and the Hā'math·ītes.

17 The descendants of Shem: Ē'lam, As'shur, Ar·pach'shad, Lud, Ar'am, Uz, Hul, Gē'ther, and Mē'-shech.[d] [18] Ar·pach'shad became the father of She'lah; and She'lah became the father of Ē'ber. [19] To Ē'ber were born two sons: the name of the one was Pē'leg (for in his days the earth was divided), and the name of his brother Jok'tan. [20] Jok'tan became the father of Al·mō'dad, She'leph, Hā·zar·mā'veth, Je'rah, [21] Ha·dor'am, Ū'zal, Dik'lah, [22] Ē'bal, A·bim'a·el, She'ba, [23] Ō'phir, Hav'i·lah, and Jō'-bab; all these were the descendants of Jok'tan.

24 Shem, Ar·pach'shad, She'lah; [25] Ē'ber, Pē'leg, Re'ū; [26] Se'rug, Nā'hor, Te'rah; [27] Abram, that is, Abraham.

From Abraham to Jacob
(Gen 25.1–4, 12–16; 36.1–30)

28 The sons of Abraham: Isaac and Ish'ma·el. [29] These are their genealogies: the firstborn of Ish'ma·el, Ne·bā'-i·oth; and Ke'dar, Ad'bē·el, Mib'sam, [30] Mish'ma, Dū'mah, Mas'sa, Hā'dad, Te'ma, [31] Je'tur, Nā'phish, and Ked'e·mah. These are the sons of Ish'ma·el. [32] The sons of Ke·tū'rah, Abraham's concubine: she bore Zim'ran, Jok'-shan, Me'dan, Mid'i·an, Ish'bak, and Shū'ah. The sons of Jok'shan: She'ba and De'dan. [33] The sons of Mid'i·an: E'phah, E'pher, Hā'noch, A·bī'da, and El·dā'ah. All these were the descendants of Ke·tū'rah.

34 Abraham became the father of Isaac. The sons of Isaac: Esau and Israel. [35] The sons of Esau: E·lī'phaz, Reū'el, Je'ush, Ja'lam, and Kō'rah. [36] The sons of E·lī'phaz: Te'man, Ō'mar, Ze'phī, Gā'tam, Ke'naz, Tim'-na, and Am'a·lek. [37] The sons of Reū'-el: Nā'hath, Ze'rah, Sham'mah, and Miz'zah.

38 The sons of Se'ir: Lō'tan, Shō'-bal, Zib'ē·on, An'ah, Dī'shon, Ē'zer, and Dī'shan. [39] The sons of Lō'tan:

Hō'rī and Hō'mam; and Lō'tan's sister was Tim'na. [40] The sons of Shō'bal: Al'i·an, Man'a·hath, Ē'bal, She'phī, and Ō'nam. The sons of Zib'ē·on: Ā'i·ah and An'ah. [41] The sons of An'ah: Dī'shon. The sons of Dī'shon: Ham'-ran, Esh'ban, Ith'ran, and Chē'ran. [42] The sons of Ē'zer: Bil'han, Zā'a·van, and Ja'a·kan.[e] The sons of Dī'shan:[f] Uz and Ar'an.

43 These are the kings who reigned in the land of Ē'dom before any king reigned over the Israelites: Bē'la son of Bē'or, whose city was called Din'-ha·bah. [44] When Bē'la died, Jō'bab son of Ze'rah of Boz'rah succeeded him. [45] When Jō'bab died, Hū'sham of the land of the Te'man·ītes succeeded him. [46] When Hū'sham died, Hā'dad son of Bē'dad, who defeated Mid'i·an in the country of Mō'ab, succeeded him; and the name of his city was A'vith. [47] When Hā'dad died, Sam'lah of Mas·rē'kah succeeded him. [48] When Sam'lah died, Shā'ūl[g] of Re·hō'both on the Euphrates succeeded him. [49] When Shā'ūl[g] died, Bā'al·hā'nan son of Ach'bor succeeded him. [50] When Bā'al·hā'nan died, Hā'dad succeeded him; the name of his city was Pā'ī, and his wife's name Me·het'-a·bel daughter of Ma'tred, daughter of Me·za·hab'. [51] And Hā'dad died.

The clans[h] of Ē'dom were: clans[h] Tim'na, Al'i·ah,[i] Je'theth, [52] Ō·hol-i·bā'mah, Ē'lah, Pī'non, [53] Ke'naz, Te'man, Mib'zar, [54] Mag'di·el, and I'ram; these are the clans[h] of Ē'dom.

The Sons of Israel and the Descendants of Judah
(Gen 29.31—30.24; 35.16–18; 46.8–25; Ruth 4.18–22; Mt 1.2–6; Lk 33.1–33)

2 These are the sons of Israel: Reuben, Sim'ē·on, Levi, Judah, Is'-sa·char, Zeb'ū·lun, [2] Dan, Joseph, Benjamin, Naph'ta·lī, Gad, and Ash'er. [3] The sons of Judah: Er, Ō'nan, and She'lah; these three the Cā'naan·īte woman Bath-shū'a bore to him. Now Er, Judah's firstborn, was wicked in the sight of the LORD, and he put him to death. [4] His daughter-in-law Tā'mar

---

[c] Heb *Casluhim, from which the Philistines come, Caphtorim*; See Am 9.7, Jer 47.4   [d] *Mash* in Gen 10.23   [e] Or *and Akan*; See Gen 36.27   [f] See 1.38: Heb *Dishon*   [g] Or *Saul*   [h] Or *chiefs*   [i] Or *Alvah*; See Gen 36.40

also bore him Per'ez and Ze'rah. Judah had five sons in all.

5 The sons of Per'ez: Hez'ron and Ha'mul. [6] The sons of Ze'rah: Zim'ri, E'than, He'man, Cal'col, and Dar'a,[j] five in all. [7] The sons of Car'mi: A'char, the troubler of Israel, who transgressed in the matter of the devoted thing; [8] and E'than's son was Az-a-ri'ah.

9 The sons of Hez'ron, who were born to him: Je-rah'me-el, Ram, and Che-lu'bai. [10] Ram became the father of Am-min'a-dab, and Am-min'a-dab became the father of Nah'shon, prince of the sons of Judah. [11] Nah'shon became the father of Sal'ma, Sal'ma of Bo'az, [12] Bo'az of O'bed, O'bed of Jesse. [13] Jesse became the father of E-li'ab his firstborn, A-bin'a-dab the second, Shim'e-a the third, [14] Ne-than'el the fourth, Rad'dai the fifth, [15] O'zem the sixth, David the seventh; [16] and their sisters were Ze-ru'i-ah and Ab'i-gail. The sons of Ze-ru'i-ah: A-bi'shai, Jo'ab, and As'a-hel, three. [17] Ab'i-gail bore A-ma'sa, and the father of A-ma'sa was Je'ther the Ish'ma-el-ite.

18 Caleb son of Hez'ron had children by his wife A-zu'bah, and by Jer'i-oth; these were her sons: Je'sher, Sho'bab, and Ar'don. [19] When A-zu'bah died, Caleb married Eph'rath, who bore him Hur. [20] Hur became the father of U'ri, and U'ri became the father of Bez'a-lel.

21 Afterward Hez'ron went in to the daughter of Ma'chir father of Gil'e-ad, whom he married when he was sixty years old; and she bore him Se'gub; [22] and Se'gub became the father of Ja'ir, who had twenty-three towns in the land of Gil'e-ad. [23] But Ge'shur and Ar'am took from them Hav'voth-ja'ir, Ke'nath and its villages, sixty towns. All these were descendants of Ma'chir, father of Gil'e-ad. [24] After the death of Hez'ron, in Ca'leb-eph'ra-thah, A-bi'jah wife of Hez'ron bore him Ash'hur, father of Te-ko'a.

25 The sons of Je-rah'me-el, the firstborn of Hez'ron: Ram his firstborn, Bu'nah, O'ren, O'zem, and A-hi'jah. [26] Je-rah'me-el also had another wife, whose name was At'a-rah; she was the mother of O'nam. [27] The sons of Ram, the firstborn of Je-rah'me-el: Ma'az, Ja'min, and E'ker. [28] The sons of O'nam: Sham'mai and Ja'da. The sons of Sham'mai: Na'dab and A-bi'shur. [29] The name of A-bi'shur's wife

was Ab-i-ha'il, and she bore him Ah'ban and Mo'lid. [30] The sons of Na'dab: Se'led and Ap'pa-im; and Se'led died childless. [31] The son[k] of Ap'pa-im: Ish'i. The son[k] of Ish'i: She'shan. The son[k] of She'shan: Ah'lai. [32] The sons of Ja'da, Sham'mai's brother: Je'ther and Jonathan; and Je'ther died childless. [33] The sons of Jonathan: Pe'leth and Za'za. These were the descendants of Je-rah'me-el. [34] Now She'shan had no sons, only daughters; but She'shan had an Egyptian slave, whose name was Jar'ha. [35] So She'shan gave his daughter in marriage to his slave Jar'ha; and she bore him At'tai. [36] At'tai became the father of Nathan, and Nathan of Za'bad. [37] Za'bad became the father of Eph'lal, and Eph'lal of O'bed. [38] O'bed became the father of Je'hu, and Je'hu of Az-a-ri'ah. [39] Az-a-ri'ah became the father of He'lez, and He'lez of El-e-a'sah. [40] El-e-a'sah became the father of Sis'mai, and Sis'mai of Shal'lum. [41] Shal'lum became the father of Jek-a-mi'ah, and Jek-a-mi'ah of E-lish'a-ma.

42 The sons of Caleb brother of Je-rah'me-el: Me'sha[l] his firstborn, who was father of Ziph. The sons of Ma-re'shah father of He'bron. [43] The sons of He'bron: Ko'rah, Tap'pu-ah, Re'kem, and She'ma. [44] She'ma became father of Ra'ham, father of Jor'ke-am; and Re'kem became the father of Sham'mai. [45] The son of Sham'mai: Ma'on; and Ma'on was the father of Beth-zur. [46] E'phah also, Caleb's concubine, bore Har'an, Mo'za, and Ga'zez; and Har'an became the father of Ga'zez. [47] The sons of Jah'dai: Re'gem, Jo'tham, Ge'shan, Pe'let, E'phah, and Sha'aph. [48] Ma'a-cah, Caleb's concubine, bore She'ber and Tir'ha-nah. [49] She also bore Sha'aph father of Mad-man'nah, She'va father of Mach-be'nah and father of Gib'e-a; and the daughter of Caleb was Ach'sah. [50] These were the descendants of Caleb.

The sons[m] of Hur the firstborn of Eph'ra-thah: Sho'bal father of Kir'i-ath-je'a-rim, [51] Sal'ma father of Bethlehem, and Har'eph father of Beth-ga'der. [52] Sho'bal father of Kir'i-ath-je'a-rim had other sons: Ha-ro'eh, half of the Me-nu'hoth.

---

[j] Or *Darda*; Compare Syr Tg some Gk Mss; See 1 Kings 4.31 [k] Heb *sons*
[l] Gk reads *Mareshah* [m] Gk Vg: Heb *son*

⁵³And the families of Kir'i·ath-jē'a·rim: the Ith'rītes, the Pū'thītes, the Shū'ma·thītes, and the Mish'ra·ītes; from these came the Zō'ra·thītes and the Esh'ta·o·lītes. ⁵⁴The sons of Sal'ma: Bethlehem, the Ne·toph'-a·thītes, At'roth-beth-jō'ab, and half of the Man·a·hā'thītes, the Zō'rītes. ⁵⁵The families also of the scribes that lived at Jā'bez: the Tī'ra·thītes, the Shim'ē·a·thītes, and the Sū'ca·thītes. These are the Ken'ītes who came from Ham'math, father of the house of Rē'-chab.

Descendants of David and Solomon
(Mt 1.6–12)

3 These are the sons of David who were born to him in Hē'bron: the firstborn Am'non, by A·hin'o·am the Jez'rē·el·īte; the second Daniel, by Ab'i·gāil the Car'mel·īte; ²the third Ab'sa·lom, son of Mā'a·cah, daughter of King Tal'mai of Gē'shur; the fourth Ad·o·nī'jah, son of Hag'gith; ³the fifth Sheph·a·tī'ah, by A·bī'tal; the sixth Ith're·am, by his wife Eg'lah; ⁴six were born to him in Hē'bron, where he reigned for seven years and six months. And he reigned thirty-three years in Jerusalem. ⁵These were born to him in Jerusalem: Shim'ē·a, Shō'bab, Nathan, and Solomon, four by Bath-shū'a, daughter of Am'mi·el; ⁶then Ib'har, E·lish'a·ma, E·liph'-e·let, ⁷Nō'gah, Nē'pheg, Ja·phī'a, ⁸E·lish'a·ma, E·lī'a·da, and E·liph'-e·let, nine. ⁹All these were David's sons, besides the sons of the concubines; and Tā'mar was their sister.

10 The descendants of Solomon: Rē·ho·bō'am, A·bī'jah his son, Asa his son, Je·hosh'a·phat his son, ¹¹Jō'ram his son, A·ha·zī'ah his son, Jō'ash his son, ¹²Am·a·zī'ah his son, Az·a·rī'ah his son, Jō'tham his son, ¹³Ā'haz his son, Hez·e·kī'ah his son, Ma·nas'seh his son, ¹⁴Ā'mon his son, Jō·sī'ah his son. ¹⁵The sons of Jō·sī'ah: Jō·hā'nan the firstborn, the second Je·hoi'a·kim, the third Zed·e·kī'ah, the fourth Shal'-lum. ¹⁶The descendants of Je·hoi'-a·kim: Jec·o·nī'ah his son, Zed·e·kī'ah his son; ¹⁷and the sons of Jec·o·nī'ah, the captive: She·al'ti·el his son, ¹⁸Mal·chī'ram, Pe·dāi'ah, Shen·az'-zar, Jek·a·mī'ah, Hosh'a·ma, and Ned·a·bī'ah; ¹⁹The sons of Pe·dāi'ah: Ze·rub'ba·bel and Shim'ē·ī; and the sons of Ze·rub'ba·bel: Me·shul'lam and Han·a·nī'ah, and She·lō'mith was their sister; ²⁰and Ha·shū'bah, O'hel,

Ber·e·chī'ah, Has·a·dī'ah, and Jū'-shab-hē'sed, five. ²¹The sons of Han·a·nī'ah: Pel·a·tī'ah and Je·shā'-i·ah, his sonⁿ Reph·āi'ah, his sonⁿ Ar'nan, his sonⁿ Ō·ba·dī'ah, his sonⁿ Shec·a·nī'ah. ²²The sonᵒ of Shec·a·nī'ah: She·māi'ah. And the sons of She·māi'ah: Hat'tush, I'gal, Ba·rī'ah, Nē·a·rī'ah, and Shā'phat, six. ²³The sons of Nē·a·rī'ah: El·i·ō·ē'naī, Hiz·kī'ah, and Az·rī'kam, three. ²⁴The sons of El·i·ō·ē'naī: Hod·a·vī'ah, E·lī'-a·shib, Pe·lāi'ah, Ak'kub, Jō·hā'nan, De·laī'ah, and A·nā'nī, seven.

Descendants of Judah

4 The sons of Judah: Per'ez, Hez'-ron, Car'mī, Hur, and Shō'bal. ²Rē·āi'ah son of Shō'bal became the father of Jā'hath, and Jā'hath became the father of A·hū'māi and Lā'had. These were the families of the Zō'-ra·thītes. ³These were the sonsᵖ of E'tam: Jez'rē·el, Ish'ma, and Id'bash; and the name of their sister was Haz·ze·lel·pō'nī, ⁴and Pe·nū'el was the father of Gē'dor, and E'zer the father of Hū'shah. These were the sons of Hur, the firstborn of Eph'ra·thah, the father of Bethlehem. ⁵Ash'hur father of Te·kō'a had two wives, Hē'lah and Nā'a·rah; ⁶Nā'a·rah bore him A·huz'-zam, Hē'pher, Tē'me·nī, and Hā·a-hash'ta·rī.�q These were the sons of Nā'a·rah. ⁷The sons of Hē'lah: Zē'-reth, Iz'har,ʳ and Eth'nan. ⁸Koz became the father of Ā'nub, Zō·bē'bah, and the families of A·har'hel son of Har'um. ⁹Jā'bez was honored more than his brothers; and his mother named him Jā'bez, saying, "Because I bore him in pain." ¹⁰Jā'bez called on the God of Israel, saying, "Oh that you would bless me and enlarge my border, and that your hand might be with me, and that you would keep me from hurt and harm!" And God granted what he asked. ¹¹Chē'lub the brother of Shū'hah became the father of Mē'-hir, who was the father of Esh'ton. ¹²Esh'ton became the father of Beth-rā'pha, Pa·sē'ah, and Te·hin'nah the father of Ir-nā'hash. These are the men of Rē'cah. ¹³The sons of Kē'naz: Oth'-ni·el and Se·rāi'ah; and the sons of Oth'ni·el: Hā'thath and Me·ō'no·thaī.ˢ

ⁿGk Compare Syr Vg: Heb *sons of*
ᵒHeb *sons*   ᵖGk Compare Vg: Heb *the father*   qOr *Ahashtari*   ʳAnother reading is *Zohar*   ˢGk Vg: Heb lacks *and Meonothai*

14 Me·ō'no·thaī became the father of Oph'rah; and Se·rāi'ah became the father of Jō'ab father of Ge·har'a·shim, *t* so-called because they were artisans. 15 The sons of Caleb son of Je·phūn'neh: I'rū, E'lah, and Nā'am; and the son *u* of E'lah: Ke'naz. 16 The sons of Je·hal'le·lel: Ziph, Zī'phah, Tir'i·a, and As'a·rel. 17 The sons of Ez'rah: Je'ther, Me'red, E'pher, and Jā'lon. These are the sons of Bith'i·ah, daughter of Pharaoh, whom Me'red married; *v* and she conceived and bore *w* Miriam, Sham'maī, and Ish'bah father of Esh·te·mō'a. 18 And his Judean wife bore Je'red father of Ge'dor, He'ber father of Sō'cō, and Je·kū'thi·el father of Za·nō'ah. 19 The sons of the wife of Hō·dī'ah, the sister of Nā'ham, were the fathers of Ke·ī'lah the Gar'mīte and Esh·te·mō'a the Mā'a·ca·thīte. 20 The sons of Shī'mon: Am'non, Rin'nah, Ben·hā'nan, and Ti'lon. The sons of Ish'ī: Zō'heth and Ben-zō'heth. 21 The sons of She'lah son of Judah: Er father of Le'cah, Lā'a·dah father of Ma·re'shah, and the families of the guild of linen workers at Beth-ash·be'a; 22 and Jō'kim, and the men of Cō·ze'ba, and Jō'ash, and Sar'aph, who married into Mō'ab but returned to Le'hem *x* (now the records *y* are ancient). 23 These were the potters and inhabitants of Ne·tā'im and Ge·de'rah; they lived there with the king in his service.

Descendants of Simeon
(Gen 46.10)

24 The sons of Sim'e·on: Nem'ū·el, Jā'min, Jā'rib, Ze'rah, Shā'ūl; *z* 25 Shal'lum was his son, Mib'sam his son, Mish'ma his son. 26 The sons of Mish'ma: Ham'mū·el his son, Zac'cur his son, Shim'e·ī his son. 27 Shim'e·ī had sixteen sons and six daughters; but his brothers did not have many children, nor did all their family multiply like the Judeans. 28 They lived in Be'er-she'ba, Mō'la·dah, Hā'zar-shū'al, 29 Bil'hah, E'zem, Tō'lad, 30 Be·thū'el, Hor'mah, Zik'lag, 31 Beth-mar'ca·both, Hā'zar-sū'sim, Beth-bi'rī, and Shā·a·rā'im. These were their towns until David became king. 32 And their villages were E'tam, Ā'in, Rim'mon, Tō'chen, and Ā'shan, five towns, 33 along with all their villages that were around these towns as far as Bā'al. These were their settlements. And they kept a genealogical record.

34 Me·shō'bab, Jam'lech, Jō'shah

son of Am·a·zī'ah, 35 Jō'el, Je'hū son of Josh·i·bī'ah son of Se·rāi'ah son of As'i·el, 36 El·i·ō·ē'naī, Jā·a·kō'bah, Jesh·ō·hāi'ah, A·sāi'ah, Ad'i·el, Je·sim'i·el, Be·nā'i·ah, 37 Zī'za son of Shī'phī son of Al'lon son of Je·daī'ah son of Shim'rī son of She·māi'ah— 38 these mentioned by name were leaders in their families, and their clans increased greatly. 39 They journeyed to the entrance of Ge'dor, to the east side of the valley, to seek pasture for their flocks, 40 where they found rich, good pasture, and the land was very broad, quiet, and peaceful; for the former inhabitants there belonged to Ham. 41 These, registered by name, came in the days of King Hez·e·kī'ah of Judah, and attacked their tents and the Me·ū'nim who were found there, and exterminated them to this day, and settled in their place, because there was pasture there for their flocks. 42 And some of them, five hundred men of the Sim'e·on·ītes, went to Mount Se'ir, having as their leaders Pel·a·tī'ah, Ne·a·rī'ah, Reph·āi'ah, and Uz'zi·el, sons of Ish'ī; 43 they destroyed the remnant of the A·mal'e·kītes that had escaped, and they have lived there to this day.

Descendants of Reuben
(Gen 46.8–9)

5 The sons of Reuben the firstborn of Israel. (He was the firstborn, but because he defiled his father's bed his birthright was given to the sons of Joseph son of Israel, so that he is not enrolled in the genealogy according to the birthright; 2 though Judah became prominent among his brothers and a ruler came from him, yet the birthright belonged to Joseph.) 3 The sons of Reuben, the firstborn of Israel: Hā'noch, Pal'lū, Hez'ron, and Car'mī. 4 The sons of Jō'el: She·māi'ah his son, Gog his son, Shim'e·ī his son, 5 Mī'cah his son, Rē·āi'ah his son, Bā'al his son, 6 Be·er'ah his son, whom King Til'gath-pil·ne'ser of Assyria carried away into exile; he was a chieftain of the Reū'ben·ītes. 7 And his kindred by their families, when the genealogy of their generations was reckoned: the chief, Je·ī'el, and Zech·a·rī'ah, 8 and

---

t That is *Valley of artisans*   *u* Heb *sons*
v The clause: *These are ... married* is
transposed from verse 18   *w* Heb lacks
and bore   *x* Vg Compare Gk: Heb *and
Jashubi-lahem*   *y* Or *matters*
z Or *Saul*

Bē'la son of Ā'zaz, son of Shē'ma, son of Jō'el, who lived in A·rō'er, as far as Nē'bo and Ba'al-mē'on. 9 He also lived to the east as far as the beginning of the desert this side of the Euphrates, because their cattle had multiplied in the land of Gil'e·ad. 10 And in the days of Saul they made war on the Hag'-rītes, who fell by their hand; and they lived in their tents throughout all the region east of Gil'e·ad.

Descendants of Gad

11 The sons of Gad lived beside them in the land of Bā'shan as far as Sal'e·cah: 12 Jō'el the chief, Shā'pham the second, Jā'naī, and Shā'phat in Bā'shan. 13 And their kindred according to their clans: Michael, Me·shul'-lam, Shē'ba, Jō'raī, Jā'can, Zī'a, and Ē'ber, seven. 14 These were the sons of Ab·i·hā'il son of Hū'rī, son of Ja·rō'ah, son of Gil'e·ad, son of Michael, son of Je·shish'aī, son of Jah'dō, son of Buz; 15 Ā'hī son of Ab'di·el, son of Gū'nī, was chief in their clan; 16 and they lived in Gil'e·ad, in Bā'shan and in its towns, and in all the pasture lands of Sharon to their limits. 17 All of these were enrolled by genealogies in the days of King Jō'tham of Judah, and in the days of King Jer·o·bō'am of Israel.

18 The Reū'ben·ītes, the Gad'ītes, and the half-tribe of Ma·nas'seh had valiant warriors, who carried shield and sword, and drew the bow, expert in war, forty-four thousand seven hundred sixty, ready for service. 19 They made war on the Hag'rītes, Jē'tur, Nā'-phish, and Nō'dab; 20 and when they received help against them, the Hag'-rītes and all who were with them were given into their hands, for they cried to God in the battle, and he granted their entreaty because they trusted in him. 21 They captured their livestock: fifty thousand of their camels, two hundred fifty thousand sheep, two thousand donkeys, and one hundred thousand captives. 22 Many fell slain, because the war was of God. And they lived in their territory until the exile.

The Half-Tribe of Manasseh

23 The members of the half-tribe of Ma·nas'seh lived in the land; they were very numerous from Bā'shan to Ba'al-her'mon, Sē'nir, and Mount Hermon. 24 These were the heads of their clans: Ē'pher,a Ish'ī, E·lī'el, Az'ri·el, Jer·e·mī'ah, Hod·a·vī'ah, and Jah'-di·el, mighty warriors, famous men,

heads of their clans. 25 But they transgressed against the God of their ancestors, and prostituted themselves to the gods of the peoples of the land, whom God had destroyed before them. 26 So the God of Israel stirred up the spirit of King Pūl of Assyria, the spirit of King Til'gath-pil·nē'ser of Assyria, and he carried them away, namely, the Reū'-ben·ītes, the Gad'ītes, and the half-tribe of Ma·nas'seh, and brought them to Hā'lah, Hā'bor, Hār'a, and the river Gō'zan, to this day.

Descendants of Levi
(Gen 46.11)

6b The sons of Levi: Ger'shom,c Kō'-hath, and Me·rar'ī. 2 The sons of Kō'hath: Am'ram, Iz'har, Hē'bron, and Uz'zi·el. 3 The children of Am'-ram: Aaron, Moses, and Miriam. The sons of Aaron: Nā'dab, A·bī'hū, El·ē·a'zar, and Ith'a·mar. 4 El·ē·a'zar became the father of Phin'e·has, Phin'-e·has of Ab·i·shū'a, 5 Ab·i·shū'a of Buk'kī, Buk'kī of Uz'zī, 6 Uz'zī of Zer·a·hī'ah, Zer·a·hī'ah of Me·rā'i·oth, 7 Me·rā'i·oth of Am·a·rī'ah, Am·a·rī'ah of A·hī'tub, 8 A·hī'tub of Zā'dok, Zā'-dok of A·him'a·az, 9 A·him'a·az of Az·a·rī'ah, Az·a·rī'ah of Jō·hā'nan, 10 and Jō·hā'nan of Az·a·rī'ah (it was he who served as priest in the house that Solomon built in Jerusalem). 11 Az·a·rī'ah became the father of Am·a·rī'ah, Am·a·rī'ah of A·hī'tub, 12 A·hī'tub of Zā'dok, Zā'dok of Shal'-lum, 13 Shal'lum of Hil·kī'ah, Hil·kī'ah of Az·a·rī'ah, 14 Az·a·rī'ah of Se·rāi'-ah, Se·rāi'ah of Je·hoz'a·dak; 15 and Je·hoz'a·dak went into exile when the LORD sent Judah and Jerusalem into exile by the hand of Ne·bū-chad·nez'zar.

16d The sons of Levi: Ger'shom, Kō'-hath, and Me·rar'ī. 17 These are the names of the sons of Ger'shom: Lib'nī and Shim'ē·i. 18 The sons of Kō'hath: Am'ram, Iz'har, Hē'bron, and Uz'zi·el. 19 The sons of Me·rar'ī: Mah'lī and Mū'shī. These are the clans of the Lē'-vites according to their ancestry. 20 Of Ger'shom: Lib'nī his son, Jā'hath his son, Zim'mah his son, 21 Jō'ah his son, Id'dō his son, Zē'rah his son, Jē·ath'-e·raī his son. 22 The sons of Kō'hath: Am·min'a·dab his son, Kō'rah his son, As'sir his son, 23 El·kā'nah his son,

aGk Vg: Heb and Epher   bCh 5.27 in Heb   cHeb Gershon, variant of Gershom; See 6.16   dCh 6.1 in Heb

E·bī′a·saph his son, As′sir his son, [24]Tā′hath his son, Ū·rī′el his son, Uz·zī′ah his son, and Shā′ul his son. [25]The sons of El·kā′nah: A·mā′sai and A·hī′moth, [26]El·kā′nah his son, Zō′phai his son, Nā′hath his son, [27]E·lī′ab his son, Je·rō′ham his son, El·kā′nah his son. [28]The sons of Samuel: Jō′el [e] his firstborn, the second A·bī′jah.[f] [29]The sons of Me·rar′ī: Mah′lī, Lib′nī his son, Shim′e·ī his son, Uz′zah his son, [30]Shim′e·a his son, Hag·gī′ah his son, and A·sāi′ah his son.

Musicians Appointed by David

31 These are the men whom David put in charge of the service of song in the house of the LORD, after the ark came to rest there. [32]They ministered with song before the tabernacle of the tent of meeting, until Solomon had built the house of the LORD in Jerusalem; and they performed their service in due order. [33]These are the men who served; and their sons were: Of the Kō′hath·ites: Hē′man, the singer, son of Jō′el, son of Samuel, [34]son of El·kā′nah, son of Je·rō′ham, son of E·lī′el, son of Tō′ah, [35]son of Zuph, son of El·kā′nah, son of Mā′hath, son of A·mā′sai, [36]son of El·kā′nah, son of Jō′el, son of Az·a·rī′ah, son of Zeph·a·nī′ah, [37]son of Tā′hath, son of As′sir, son of E·bī′a·saph, son of Kō′rah, [38]son of Iz′har, son of Kō′hath, son of Levi, son of Israel; [39]and his brother A′saph, who stood on his right, namely, A′saph son of Ber·e·chī′ah, son of Shim′e·a, [40]son of Michael, son of Bā·a·sē′i·ah, son of Mal·chī′jah, [41]son of Eth′nī, son of Zē′rah, son of A·dāi′ah, [42]son of Ē′than, son of Zim′mah, son of Shim′e·ī, [43]son of Ja′hath, son of Ger′shom, son of Levi. [44]On the left were their kindred the sons of Me·rar′ī: Ē′than son of Kish′ī, son of Ab′dī, son of Mal′luch, [45]son of Hash·a·bī′ah, son of Am·a·zī′ah, son of Hil·kī′ah, [46]son of Am′zī, son of Bā′nī, son of Shē′mer, [47]son of Mah′lī, son of Mū′shī, son of Me·rar′ī, son of Levi; [48]and their kindred the Lē′vītes were appointed for all the service of the tabernacle of the house of God.

49 But Aaron and his sons made offerings on the altar of burnt offering and on the altar of incense, doing all the work of the most holy place, to make atonement for Israel, according to all that Moses the servant of God had commanded. [50]These are the sons of Aaron: El·ē·ā′zar his son, Phin′e·has his son, Ab·i·shū′a his son, [51]Buk′kī his son, Uz′zī his son, Zer·a·hī′ah his son, [52]Me·rā′i·oth his son, Am·a·rī′ah his son, A·hī′tub his son, [53]Zā′dok his son, A·him′a·az his son.

Settlements of the Levites
(Josh 21.1–42)

54 These are their dwelling places according to their settlements within their borders: to the sons of Aaron of the families of Kō′hath·ites—for the lot fell to them first— [55]to them they gave Hē′bron in the land of Judah and its surrounding pasture lands, [56]but the fields of the city and its villages they gave to Caleb son of Je·phūn′neh. [57]To the sons of Aaron they gave the cities of refuge: Hē′bron, Lib′nah with its pasture lands, Jat′tir, Esh·te·mō′a with its pasture lands, [58]Hī′len [g] with its pasture lands, Dē′bir with its pasture lands, [59]A′shan with its pasture lands, and Beth-shē′mesh with its pasture lands. [60]From the tribe of Benjamin, Gē′ba with its pasture lands, Al′e·meth with its pasture lands, and An′a·thoth with its pasture lands. All their towns throughout their families were thirteen.

61 To the rest of the Kō′hath·ites were given by lot out of the family of the tribe, out of the half-tribe, the half of Ma·nas′seh, ten towns. [62]To the Ger′shom·ites according to their families were allotted thirteen towns out of the tribes of Is′sa·char, Ash′er, Naph′ta·lī, and Ma·nas′seh in Bā′shan. [63]To the Me·rar′ītes according to their families were allotted twelve towns out of the tribes of Reuben, Gad, and Zeb′u·lun. [64]So the people of Israel gave the Lē′vītes the towns with their pasture lands. [65]They also gave them by lot out of the tribes of Judah, Sim′e·on, and Benjamin these towns that are mentioned by name.

66 And some of the families of the sons of Kō′hath had towns of their territory out of the tribe of Ē′phra·im. [67]They were given the cities of refuge: Shē′chem with its pasture lands in the hill country of Ē′phra·im, Gē′zer with its pasture lands, [68]Jok′mē·am with its pasture lands, Beth-hō′ron with its

<hr>

[e] Gk Syr Compare verse 33 and 1 Sam 8.2: Heb lacks *Joel*   [f] Heb reads *Vashni, and Abijah* for *the second Abijah,* taking *the second* as a proper name   [g] Other readings *Hilez, Holon*; See Josh 21.15

pasture lands, ⁶⁹Aī'ja·lon with its pasture lands, Gath-rim'mon with its pasture lands; ⁷⁰and out of the half-tribe of Ma·nas'seh, A'ner with its pasture lands, and Bil'ē·am with its pasture lands, for the rest of the families of the Kō'hath·ītes.

71 To the Ger'shom·ites: out of the half-tribe of Ma·nas'seh: Gō'lan in Bā'shan with its pasture lands and Ash'ta·roth with its pasture lands; ⁷²and out of the tribe of Is'sa·char: Kē'desh with its pasture lands, Dab'e·rath ʰ with its pasture lands, ⁷³Rā'moth with its pasture lands, and A'nem with its pasture lands; ⁷⁴out of the tribe of Ash'er: Mā'shal with its pasture lands, Ab'don with its pasture lands, ⁷⁵Hū'kok with its pasture lands, and Rē'hob with its pasture lands; ⁷⁶and out of the tribe of Naph'ta·lī: Kē'desh in Galilee with its pasture lands, Ham'mon with its pasture lands, and Kir·i·a·thā'im with its pasture lands. ⁷⁷To the rest of the Me·rar'-ītes out of the tribe of Zeb'ū·lun: Rim'-mo·nō with its pasture lands, Tā'bor with its pasture lands; ⁷⁸and across the Jordan from Jericho, on the east side of the Jordan, out of the tribe of Reuben: Bē'zer in the steppe with its pasture lands, Jah'zah with its pasture lands, ⁷⁹Ked'e·moth with its pasture lands, and Meph'a·ath with its pasture lands; ⁸⁰and out of the tribe of Gad: Rā'moth in Gil'e·ad with its pasture lands, Mā·ha·nā'im with its pasture lands, and ⁸¹Hesh'bon with its pasture lands, and Jā'zer with its pasture lands.

Descendants of Issachar
(Gen 46.13)

7 The sons ⁱ of Is'sa·char: Tō'la, Pū'ah, Jash'ub, and Shim'ron, four. ²The sons of Tō'la: Uz'zī, Reph·āi'ah, Jē'ri·el, Jah'mai, Ib'sam, and She·mū'el, heads of their ancestral houses, namely of Tō'la, mighty warriors of their generations, their number in the days of David being twenty-two thousand six hundred. ³The son ʲ of Uz'zī: Iz·ra·hī'ah. And the sons of Iz·ra·hī'ah: Michael, Ō·ba·dī'ah, Jō'el, and Is·shī'ah, five, all of them chiefs; ⁴and along with them, by their generations, according to their ancestral houses, were units of the fighting force, thirty-six thousand, for they had many wives and sons. ⁵Their kindred belonging to all the families of Is'sa·char were in all

eighty-seven thousand mighty warriors, enrolled by genealogy.

Descendants of Benjamin
(Gen 46.21)

6 The sons of Benjamin: Bē'la, Bē'cher, and Je·dī'a·el, three. ⁷The sons of Bē'la: Ez'bon, Uz'zī, Uz'zi·el, Jer'i·moth, and I'rī, five, heads of ancestral houses, mighty warriors; and their enrollment by genealogies was twenty-two thousand thirty-four. ⁸The sons of Bē'cher: Ze·mī'rah, Jō'ash, El·i·ē'zer, El·i·ō·ē'naī, Om'rī, Jer'e·moth, A·bī'jah, An'a·thoth, and Al'e·meth. All these were the sons of Bē'cher; ⁹and their enrollment by genealogies, according to their generations, as heads of their ancestral houses, mighty warriors, was twenty thousand two hundred. ¹⁰The sons of Je·dī'a·el: Bil'han. And the sons of Bil'han: Jē'ush, Benjamin, E'hud, Che·nā'a·nah, Zē'than, Tar'shish, and A·hish'a·har. ¹¹All these were the sons of Je·dī'a·el according to the heads of their ancestral houses, mighty warriors, seventeen thousand two hundred, ready for service in war. ¹²And Shup'pim and Hup'pim were the sons of Ir, Hū'shim the son ʲ of A'her.

Descendants of Naphtali
(Gen 46.24)

13 The descendants of Naph'ta·lī: Jah'zi·el, Gū'nī, Jē'zer, and Shal'lum, the descendants of Bil'hah.

Descendants of Manasseh

14 The sons of Ma·nas'seh: As'ri·el, whom his Ar·a·mē'an concubine bore; she bore Mā'chir the father of Gil'e·ad. ¹⁵And Mā'chir took a wife for Hup'pim and for Shup'pim. The name of his sister was Mā'a·cah. And the name of the second was Ze·loph'e·had; and Ze·loph'e·had had daughters. ¹⁶Mā'a·cah the wife of Mā'chir bore a son, and she named him Pē'resh; the name of his brother was Shē'resh; and his sons were Ū'lam and Rē'kem. ¹⁷The son ʲ of Ū'lam: Bē'dan. These were the sons of Gil'e·ad son of Mā'chir, son of Ma·nas'seh. ¹⁸And his sister Ham·mō'le·cheth bore Ish'hod, A·bi·ē'zer, and Mah'lah. ¹⁹The sons of She·mī'da were A·hī'an, Shē'chem, Lik'hī, and A·nī'am.

ʰOr *Dobrath*   ⁱSyr Compare Vg: Heb *And to the sons*   ʲHeb *sons*

Descendants of Ephraim

20 The sons of É'phra·im: Shū·thē'-lah, and Bē'red his son, Tā'hath his son, El·ē·a'dah his son, Tā'hath his son, 21 Zā'bad his son, Shū·thē'lah his son, and É'zer and É'lē·ad. Now the people of Gath, who were born in the land, killed them, because they came down to raid their cattle. 22 And their father É'phra·im mourned many days, and his brothers came to comfort him. 23 É'phra·im *k* went in to his wife, and she conceived and bore a son; and he named him Bē·rī'ah, because disaster*l* had befallen his house. 24 His daughter was Shē'e·rah, who built both Lower and Upper Beth-hō'ron, and Uz'zen-shē'e·rah. 25 Rē'phah was his son, Rē'sheph his son, Tē'lah his son, Tā'han his son, 26 Lā'dan his son, Am·mī'hud his son, E·lish'a·ma his son, 27 Nun *m* his son, Joshua his son. 28 Their possessions and settlements were Beth'el and its towns, and eastward Nā'a·ran, and westward Gē'zer and its towns, Shē'chem and its towns, as far as Åy'yah and its towns; 29 also along the borders of the Ma·nas'sītes, Beth-shē'an and its towns, Tā'a·nach and its towns, Me·gid'dō and its towns, Dor and its towns. In these lived the sons of Joseph son of Israel.

Descendants of Asher
(Gen 46.17)

30 The sons of Ash'er: Im'nah, Ish'-vah, Ish'vī, Bē·rī'ah, and their sister Sē'rah. 31 The sons of Bē·rī'ah: Hē'ber and Mal'chi·el, who was the father of Bir'zā·ith. 32 Hē'ber became the father of Japh'let, Shō'mer, Hō'tham, and their sister Shū'a. 33 The sons of Japh'let: Pā'sach, Bim'hal, and Ash'vath. These are the sons of Japh'let. 34 The sons of Shē'mer: Ā'hī, Rōh'gah, Hub'-bah, and Ar'am. 35 The sons of Hē'-lem *n* his brother: Zō'phah, Im'na, Shē'lesh, and Ā'mal. 36 The sons of Zō'phah: Sū'ah, Har'ne·pher, Shū'-al, Bē'rī, Im'rah, 37 Bē'zer, Hod, Sham'ma, Shil'shah, Ith'ran, and Be·ē'ra. 38 The sons of Jē'ther: Je·phūn'neh, Pis'pa, and Ar'a. 39 The sons of Ul'la: Ā'rah, Han'ni·el, and Rī·zī'a. 40 All of these were men of Ash'er, heads of ancestral houses, select mighty warriors, chief of the princes. Their number enrolled by genealogies, for service in war, was twenty-six thousand men.

Descendants of Benjamin
(Gen 46.21)

8 Benjamin became the father of Bē'la his firstborn, Ash'bel the second, A'har·ah the third, 2 Nō'hah the fourth, and Rā'pha the fifth. 3 And Bē'la had sons: Ad'dar, Gē'ra, A·bī'hud,*o* 4 Ab·i·shū'a, Nā'a·man, A·hō'ah, 5 Gē'ra, She·phū'phan, and Hū'ram. 6 These are the sons of É'hud (they were heads of ancestral houses of the inhabitants of Gē'ba, and they were carried into exile to Man'a·hath): 7 Nā'a·man,*p* A·hī'jah, and Gē'ra, that is, Heg'lam,*q* who became the father of Uz'za and A·hī'hud. 8 And Shā·ha·rā'im had sons in the country of Mō'ab after he had sent away his wives Hū'shim and Bā'a·ra. 9 He had sons by his wife Hō'desh: Jō'bab, Zib'i·a, Mē'sha, Mal'cam, 10 Jē'uz, Sa·chī'a, and Mir'mah. These were his sons, heads of ancestral houses. 11 He also had sons by Hū'shim: A·bī'tub and El·pā'al. 12 The sons of El·pā'al: É'ber, Mī'sham, and Shē'med, who built Ō'nō and Lod with its towns, 13 and Bē·rī'ah and Shē'ma (they were heads of ancestral houses of the inhabitants of Ai'ja·lon, who put to flight the inhabitants of Gath); 14 and A·hī'ō, Shā'shak, and Jer'e·moth. 15 Zeb·a·dī'ah, Ar'ad, É'der, 16 Michael, Ish'pah, and Jō'ha were sons of Bē·rī'ah. 17 Zeb·a·dī'ah, Me·shul'lam, Hiz'kī, Hē'ber, 18 Ish'me·raī, Iz·lī'ah, and Jō'bab were the sons of El·pā'al. 19 Jā'kim, Zich'rī, Zab'dī, 20 E·li·ē'naī, Zil'le·thaī, E·lī'el, 21 A·dāi'ah, Be·rā'-i·ah, and Shim'rath were the sons of Shim'ē·ī. 22 Ish'pan, É'ber, E·lī'el, 23 Ab'don, Zich'rī, Hā'nan, 24 Han·a·nī'ah, É'lam, An·tho·thī'jah, 25 Iph·dē'i·ah, and Pe·nū'el were the sons of Shā'shak. 26 Sham'she·raī, Shē·ha·rī'ah, Ath·a·lī'ah, 27 Jā·ar·e·shī'ah, E·lī'jah, and Zich'rī were the sons of Je·rō'ham. 28 These were the heads of ancestral houses, according to their generations, chiefs. These lived in Jerusalem.

29 Je·ī'el*r* the father of Gib'ē·on lived in Gib'ē·on, and the name of his wife was Mā'a·cah. 30 His firstborn

---

k Heb He *l* Heb beraah *m* Here spelled *Non*; see Ex 33.11 *n* Or *Hotham*; see 7.32 *o* Or *father of Ehud*; see 8.6 *p* Heb *and Naaman* *q* Or *he carried them into exile* *r* Compare 9.35: Heb lacks *Jeiel* son: Ab'don, then Zur, Kish, Ba'al,ˢ Na'dab, 31Ge'dor, A·hi'o, Ze'cher, 32and Mik'loth, who became the father of Shim'e·ah. Now these also lived opposite their kindred in Jerusalem, with their kindred. 33Ner became the father of Kish, Kish of Saul,ᵗ Saulᵗ of Jonathan, Mal·chi·shu'a, A·bin'a·dab, and Esh-ba'al; 34and the son of Jonathan was Mer'ib-ba'al; and Mer'ib-ba'al became the father of Mi'cah. 35The sons of Mi'cah: Pi'thon, Me'lech, Ta·re'a, and A'haz. 36A'haz became the father of Je·ho'ad·dah; and Je·ho'ad·dah became the father of Al'e·meth, and Az'ma·veth, and Zim'ri; Zim'ri became the father of Mo'za. 37Mo'za became the father of Bin'e·a; Ra'phah was his son, El·e·a'sah his son, A'zel his son. 38A'zel had six sons, and these are their names: Az·ri'kam, Bo'che·ru, Ish'ma·el, She·a·ri'ah, O·ba·di'ah, and Ha'nan; all these were the sons of A'zel. 39The sons of his brother E'shek: U'lam his firstborn, Je'ush the second, and E·liph'e·let the third. 40The sons of U'lam were mighty warriors, archers, having many children and grandchildren, one hundred fifty. All these were Ben'ja·min·ites.

9 So all Israel was enrolled by genealogies; and these are written in the Book of the Kings of Israel. And Judah was taken into exile in Babylon because of their unfaithfulness. 2Now the first to live again in their possessions in their towns were Israelites, priests, Le'vites, and temple servants.

Inhabitants of Jerusalem after the Exile

3 And some of the people of Judah, Benjamin, E'phra·im, and Ma·nas'seh lived in Jerusalem: 4U'thai son of Am·mi'hud, son of Om'ri, son of Im'ri, son of Ba'ni, from the sons of Per'ez son of Judah. 5And of the Shi'lo·nites: A·sai'ah the firstborn, and his sons. 6Of the sons of Ze'rah: Je·u'el and their kin, six hundred ninety. 7Of the Ben'ja·min·ites: Sal'lu son of Me·shul'lam, son of Hod·a·vi'ah, son of Has·se·nu'ah, 8Ib·ne'i·ah son of Je·ro'ham, E'lah son of Uz'zi, son of Mich'ri, and Me·shul'lam son of Sheph·a·ti'ah, son of Reu'el, son of Ib·ni'jah; 9and their kindred according to their generations, nine hundred fifty-six. All these were heads of families according to their ancestral houses.

Priestly Families

10 Of the priests: Je·dai'ah, Je·hoi'a·rib, Ja'chin, 11and Az·a·ri'ah son of Hil·ki'ah, son of Me·shul'lam, son of Za'dok, son of Me·ra'i·oth, son of A·hi'tub, the chief officer of the house of God; 12and A·dai'ah son of Je·ro'ham, son of Pash'hur, son of Mal·chi'jah, and Ma'a·sai son of Ad'i·el, son of Jah'ze·rah, son of Me·shul'lam, son of Me·shil'le·mith, son of Im'mer; 13besides their kindred, heads of their ancestral houses, one thousand seven hundred sixty, qualified for the work of the service of the house of God.

Levitical Families

14 Of the Le'vites: She·mai'ah son of Has'shub, son of Az·ri'kam, son of Hash·a·bi'ah, of the sons of Me·rar'i; 15and Bak·bak'kar, He'resh, Ga'lal, and Mat·ta·ni'ah son of Mi'ca, son of Zich'ri, son of A'saph; 16and O·ba·di'ah son of She·mai'ah, son of Ga'lal, son of Je·du'thun, and Ber·e·chi'ah son of Asa, son of El·ka'nah, who lived in the villages of the Ne·toph'a·thites.

17 The gatekeepers were: Shal'lum, Ak'kub, Tal'mon, A·hi'man; and their kindred Shal'lum was the chief, 18stationed previously in the king's gate on the east side. These were the gatekeepers of the camp of the Le'vites. 19Shal'lum son of Ko're, son of E·bi'a·saph, son of Ko'rah, and his kindred of his ancestral house, the Ko'ra·hites, were in charge of the work of the service, guardians of the thresholds of the tent, as their ancestors had been in charge of the camp of the LORD, guardians of the entrance. 20And Phin'e·has son of El·e·a'zar was chief over them in former times; the LORD was with him. 21Zech·a·ri'ah son of Me·shel·e·mi'ah was gatekeeper at the entrance of the tent of meeting. 22All these, who were chosen as gatekeepers at the thresholds, were two hundred twelve. They were enrolled by genealogies in their villages. David and the seer Samuel established them in their office of trust. 23So they and their descendants were in charge of the gates of the house of the LORD, that is, the house of the tent, as guards. 24The gatekeepers were on the four sides, east, west, north, and south; 25and their kindred

who were in their villages were obliged to come in every seven days, in turn, to be with them; ²⁶for the four chief gatekeepers, who were Lē′vītes, were in charge of the chambers and the treasures of the house of God. ²⁷And they would spend the night near the house of God; for on them lay the duty of watching, and they had charge of opening it every morning.

28 Some of them had charge of the utensils of service, for they were required to count them when they were brought in and taken out. ²⁹Others of them were appointed over the furniture, and over all the holy utensils, also over the choice flour, the wine, the oil, the incense, and the spices. ³⁰Others, of the sons of the priests, prepared the mixing of the spices, ³¹and Mat·ti·thī′ah, one of the Lē′vītes, the firstborn of Shal′lum the Kō′ra·hīte, was in charge of making the flat cakes. ³²Also some of their kindred of the Kō′hath·ites had charge of the rows of bread, to prepare them for each sabbath.

33 Now these are the singers, the heads of ancestral houses of the Lē′vītes, living in the chambers of the temple free from other service, for they were on duty day and night. ³⁴These were heads of ancestral houses of the Lē′vītes, according to their generations; these leaders lived in Jerusalem.

The Family of King Saul

35 In Gib′ē·on lived the father of Gib′ē·on, Je·ī′el, and the name of his wife was Mā′a·cah. ³⁶His firstborn son was Ab′don, then Zur, Kish, Bā′-al, Ner, Nā′dab, ³⁷Gē′dor, A·hī′ō, Zech·a·rī′ah, and Mik′loth; ³⁸and Mik′loth became the father of Shim′-ē·am; and these also lived opposite their kindred in Jerusalem, with their kindred. ³⁹Ner became the father of Kish, Kish of Saul, Saul of Jonathan, Mal·chī·shū′a, A·bin′a·dab, and Esh-bā′al; ⁴⁰and the son of Jonathan was Mer′ib-bā′al; and Mer′ib-bā′al became the father of Mī′cah. ⁴¹The sons of Mī′cah: Pī′thon, Me′lech, Tah′rē·a, and Ā′haz;ᵘ ⁴²and Ā′haz became the father of Jar′ah, and Jar′ah of Al′-e·meth, Az′ma·veth, and Zim′rī; and Zim′rī became the father of Mō′za. ⁴³Mō′za became the father of Bin′ē·a; and Reph·ai′ah was his son, El·e·ā′sah his son, Ā′zel his son. ⁴⁴Ā′zel had six sons, and these are their names: Az·rī′-

kam, Bō′che·rū, Ish′ma·el, Shē·a·rī′ah, Ō·ba·dī′ah, and Hā′nan; these were the sons of Ā′zel.

Death of Saul and His Sons
(1 Sam 31.1–13)

10 Now the Phi·lis′tines fought against Israel; and the men of Israel fled before the Phi·lis′tines, and fell slain on Mount Gil·bō′a. ²The Phi·lis′tines overtook Saul and his sons; and the Phi·lis′tines killed Jonathan and A·bin′a·dab and Mal-chī·shū′a, sons of Saul. ³The battle pressed hard on Saul; and the archers found him, and he was wounded by the archers. ⁴Then Saul said to his armor-bearer, "Draw your sword, and thrust me through with it, so that these uncircumcised may not come and make sport of me." But his armor-bearer was unwilling, for he was terrified. So Saul took his own sword and fell on it. ⁵When his armor-bearer saw that Saul was dead, he also fell on his sword and died. ⁶Thus Saul died; he and his three sons and all his house died together. ⁷When all the men of Israel who were in the valley saw that the armyᵛ had fled and that Saul and his sons were dead, they abandoned their towns and fled; and the Phi·lis′-tines came and occupied them.

8 The next day when the Phi·lis′-tines came to strip the dead, they found Saul and his sons fallen on Mount Gil·bō′a. ⁹They stripped him and took his head and his armor, and sent messengers throughout the land of the Phi·lis′tines to carry the good news to their idols and to the people. ¹⁰They put his armor in the temple of their gods, and fastened his head in the temple of Dā′gon. ¹¹But when all Jā′-besh-gil′ē·ad heard everything that the Phi·lis′tines had done to Saul, ¹²all the valiant warriors got up and took away the body of Saul and the bodies of his sons, and brought them to Jā′-besh. Then they buried their bones under the oak in Jā′besh, and fasted seven days.

13 So Saul died for his unfaithfulness; he was unfaithful to the LORD in that he did not keep the command of the LORD; moreover, he had consulted a medium, seeking guidance, ¹⁴and did not seek guidance from the LORD. Therefore the LORDʷ put him to death

ᵘCompare 8.35: Heb lacks and Ahaz
ᵛHeb they　ʷHeb he

and turned the kingdom over to David son of Jesse.

David Anointed King of All Israel
(2 Sam 5.1–3)

11 Then all Israel gathered together to David at Hē′bron and said, "See, we are your bone and flesh. ²For some time now, even while Saul was king, it was you who commanded the army of Israel. The LORD your God said to you: It is you who shall be shepherd of my people Israel, you who shall be ruler over my people Israel." ³So all the elders of Israel came to the king at Hē′bron, and David made a covenant with them at Hē′bron before the LORD. And they anointed David king over Israel, according to the word of the LORD by Samuel.

Jerusalem Captured
(2 Sam 5.6–10)

4 David and all Israel marched to Jerusalem, that is Jē′bus, where the Jeb′ū·sītes were, the inhabitants of the land. ⁵The inhabitants of Jē′bus said to David, "You will not come in here." Nevertheless David took the stronghold of Zion, now the city of David. ⁶David had said, "Whoever attacks the Jeb′ū·sītes first shall be chief and commander." And Jō′ab son of Ze·rū′i·ah went up first, so he became chief. ⁷David resided in the stronghold; therefore it was called the city of David. ⁸He built the city all around, from the Mil′lō in complete circuit; and Jō′ab repaired the rest of the city. ⁹And David became greater and greater, for the LORD of hosts was with him.

David's Mighty Men and Their Exploits
(2 Sam 23.8–39)

10 Now these are the chiefs of David's warriors, who gave him strong support in his kingdom, together with all Israel, to make him king, according to the word of the LORD concerning Israel. ¹¹This is an account of David's mighty warriors: Ja·shō′bē·am, son of Hach′mo·nī,ˣ was chief of the Three;ʸ he wielded his spear against three hundred whom he killed at one time.

12 And next to him among the three warriors was El·e·ā′zar son of Dō′dō, the A·hō′hīte. ¹³He was with David at Pas-dam′mim when the Phi·lis′tines were gathered there for battle. There was a plot of ground full of barley. Now the people had fled from the Phi·lis′tines, ¹⁴but he and David took

their stand in the middle of the plot, defended it, and killed the Phi·lis′-tines; and the LORD saved them by a great victory.

15 Three of the thirty chiefs went down to the rock to David at the cave of A·dul′lam, while the army of Phi·lis′tines was encamped in the valley of Reph′a·im. ¹⁶David was then in the stronghold; and the garrison of the Phi·lis′tines was then at Bethlehem. ¹⁷David said longingly, "O that someone would give me water to drink from the well of Bethlehem that is by the gate!" ¹⁸Then the Three broke through the camp of the Phi·lis′tines, and drew water from the well of Bethlehem that was by the gate, and they brought it to David. But David would not drink of it; he poured it out to the LORD, ¹⁹and said, "My God forbid that I should do this. Can I drink the blood of these men? For at the risk of their lives they brought it." Therefore he would not drink it. The three warriors did these things.

20 Now A·bi′shai,ᶻ the brother of Jō′ab, was chief of the Thirty.ᵃ With his spear he fought against three hundred and killed them, and won a name beside the Three: ²¹He was the most renownedᵇ of the Thirty,ᵃ and became their commander; but he did not attain to the Three.

22 Be·nā′i·ah son of Je·hoi′a·da was a valiant manᶜ of Kab′zē·el, a doer of great deeds; he struck down two sons ofᵈ Ar′i·el of Mō′ab. He also went down and killed a lion in a pit on a day when snow had fallen. ²³And he killed an Egyptian, a man of great stature, five cubits tall. The Egyptian had in his hand a spear like a weaver's beam; but Be·nā′i·ah went against him with a staff, snatched the spear out of the Egyptian's hand, and killed him with his own spear. ²⁴Such were the things Be·nā′i·ah son of Je·hoi′a·da did, and he won a name beside the three warriors. ²⁵He was renowned among the Thirty, but he did not attain to the Three. And David put him in charge of his bodyguard.

ˣOr *a Hachmonite* ʸCompare 2 Sam 23.8: Heb *Thirty* or *captains* ᶻGk Vg Tg Compare 2 Sam 23.18: Heb *Abshai* ᵃSyr: Heb *Three* ᵇCompare 2 Sam 23.19: Heb *more renowned among the two* ᶜSyr: Heb *the son of a valiant man* ᵈSee 2 Sam 23.20: Heb lacks *sons of*

26 The warriors of the armies were As'a·hel brother of Jō'ab, El·hā'nan son of Dō'dō of Bethlehem, 27 Sham'-moth of Har'od, e Hē'lez the Pel'o·nīte, 28 Ira son of Ik'kesh of Te·kō'a, Ā·bi·ē'zer of An'a·thoth, 29 Sib'be·caī the Hū'sha·thīte, I'lai the A·hō'hīte, 30 Mā'ha·raī of Ne·toph'ah, Hē'led son of Bā'a·nah of Ne·toph'ah, 31 Ith'aī son of Rī'baī of Gib'ē·ah of the Ben'-ja·min·ites, Be·nā'i·ah of Pir'a·thon, 32 Hū'raī of the wadis of Gā'ash, A·bī'-el the Ar'ba·thīte, 33 Az'ma·veth of Ba·hā'rum, Ē·lī'ah·ba of Shā·al'-bon, 34 Hā'shem f the Gī'zo·nīte, Jona-than son of Shā'gee the Har'a·rīte, 35 A·hī'am son of Sā'char the Har'-a·rīte, E·lī'phal son of Ur, 36 Hē'pher the Me·chē'ra·thīte, A·hī'jah the Pel'-o·nīte, 37 Hez'rō of Car'mel, Nā'a·raī son of Ez'baī, 38 Jō'el the brother of Nathan, Mib'har son of Hag'rī, 39 Zē'-lek the Am'mon·īte, Nā'ha·raī of Be·er'oth, the armor-bearer of Jō'ab son of Ze·rū'i·ah, 40 Ira the Ith'rīte, Gā'-reb the Ith'rīte, 41 Ū·rī'ah the Hit'tīte, Zā'bad son of Ah'laī, 42 Ad'i·na son of Shī'za the Reū'ben·īte, a leader of the Reū'ben·ītes, and thirty with him, 43 Hā'nan son of Mā'a·cah, and Josh'-a·phat the Mith'nīte, 44 Uz·zī'a the Ash'te·ra·thīte, Sha'ma and Je·ī'el sons of Hō'tham the A·rō'er·īte, 45 Je·dī'a·el son of Shim'rī, and his brother Jō'ha the Tī'zīte, 46 E·lī'el the Mā'ha·vīte, and Jer'i·baī and Josh-a·vī'ah sons of El'nā·am, and Ith'-mah the Mō'ab·īte, 47 E·lī'el, and Ō'bed, and Jā·a·sī'el the Me·zō'ba·īte.

David's Followers in the Wilderness
(1 Sam 22.1–2)

12 The following are those who came to David at Zik'lag, while he could not move about freely be-cause of Saul son of Kish; they were among the mighty warriors who helped him in war. 2 They were arch-ers, and could shoot arrows and sling stones with either the right hand or the left; they were Ben'ja·min·ites, Saul's kindred. 3 The chief was Ā·hī·ē'zer, then Jō'ash, both sons of She·mā'ah of Gib'ē·ah; also Jē'zi·el and Pē'let sons of Az'ma·veth; Ber'a·cah, Jē'hū of An'a·thoth, 4 Ish·mā'i·ah of Gib'ē·on, a warrior among the Thirty and a leader over the Thirty; Jer·e·mī'ah, g Ja·hā'-zi·el, Jō·hā'nan, Joz'a·bad of Ge·dē'-rah, 5 E·lū'zaī, h Jer'i·moth, Be·a·lī'-ah, Shem·a·rī'ah, Sheph·a·tī'ah the Ha·rū'phīte; 6 El·kā'nah, Is·shī'ah,

Az'a·rel, Jō·ē'zer, and Ja·shō'bē·am, the Kō'ra·hītes; 7 and Jō·ē'lah and Zeb·a·dī'ah, sons of Je·rō'ham of Gē'-dor.

8 From the Gad'ītes there went over to David at the stronghold in the wil-derness mighty and experienced war-riors, expert with shield and spear, whose faces were like the faces of lions, and who were swift as ga-zelles on the mountains: 9 Ē'zer the chief, Ō·ba·dī'ah second, E·lī'ab third, 10 Mish·man'nah fourth, Jer·e·mī'ah fifth, 11 At'taī sixth, E·lī'el seventh, 12 Jō·hā'nan eighth, El·zā'bad ninth, 13 Jer·e·mī'ah tenth, Mach'ban·naī eleventh. 14 These Gad'ītes were offi-cers of the army, the least equal to a hundred and the greatest to a thou-sand. 15 These are the men who crossed the Jordan in the first month, when it was overflowing all its banks, and put to flight all those in the valleys, to the east and to the west.

16 Some Ben'ja·min·ites and Jū'-dah·ites came to the stronghold to Da-vid. 17 David went out to meet them and said to them, "If you have come to me in friendship, to help me, then my heart will be knit to you; but if you have come to betray me to my adver-saries, though my hands have done no wrong, then may the God of our ances-tors see and give judgment." 18 Then the spirit came upon A·mā'saī, chief of the Thirty, and he said,

"We are yours, O David;
    and with you, O son of Jesse!
Peace, peace to you,
    and peace to the one who
        helps you!
For your God is the one who
    helps you."

Then David received them, and made them officers of his troops.

19 Some of the Ma·nas'sītes de-serted to David when he came with the Phi·lis'tines for the battle against Saul (Yet he did not help them, for the rul-ers of the Phi·lis'tines took counsel and sent him away, saying, "He will desert to his master Saul at the cost of our heads.") 20 As he went to Zik'lag, these Ma·nas'sītes deserted to him: Ad'nah, Joz'a·bad, Je·dī'a·el, Michael

Joz'a·bad, E·lī'hū, and Zil'le·thaī, chiefs of the thousands in Ma·nas'seh. [21] They helped David against the band of raiders,[i] for they were all warriors and commanders in the army. [22] Indeed from day to day people kept coming to David to help him, until there was a great army, like an army of God.

David's Army at Hebron

[23] These are the numbers of the divisions of the armed troops who came to David in He'bron to turn the kingdom of Saul over to him, according to the word of the LORD. [24] The people of Judah bearing shield and spear numbered six thousand eight hundred armed troops. [25] Of the Sim'e·on·ites, mighty warriors, seven thousand one hundred. [26] Of the Le'vites four thousand six hundred. [27] Je·hoi'a·da, leader of the house of Aaron, and with him three thousand seven hundred. [28] Za'dok, a young warrior, and twenty-two commanders from his own ancestral house. [29] Of the Ben'ja·min·ites, the kindred of Saul, three thousand, of whom the majority had continued to keep their allegiance to the house of Saul. [30] Of the E'phra·im·ites, twenty thousand eight hundred, mighty warriors, notables in their ancestral houses. [31] Of the half-tribe of Ma·nas'seh, eighteen thousand, who were expressly named to come and make David king. [32] Of Is'sa·char, those who had understanding of the times, to know what Israel ought to do, two hundred chiefs, and all their kindred under their command. [33] Of Zeb'u·lun, fifty thousand seasoned troops, equipped for battle with all the weapons of war, to help David[j] with singleness of purpose. [34] Of Naph'ta·lī, a thousand commanders, with whom there were thirty-seven thousand armed with shield and spear. [35] Of the Dan'ites, twenty-eight thousand six hundred equipped for battle. [36] Of Ash'er, forty thousand seasoned troops ready for battle. [37] Of the Reū'ben·ites and Gad'ites and the half-tribe of Ma·nas'seh from beyond the Jordan, one hundred twenty thousand armed with all the weapons of war.

[38] All these, warriors arrayed in battle order, came to He'bron with full intent to make David king over all Israel; likewise all the rest of Israel were of a single mind to make David king. [39] They were there with David for three days, eating and drinking, for their kindred had provided for them. [40] And also their neighbors, from as far away as Is'sa·char and Zeb'u·lun and Naph'ta·lī, came bringing food on donkeys, camels, mules, and oxen—abundant provisions of meal, cakes of figs, clusters of raisins, wine, oil, oxen, and sheep, for there was joy in Israel.

The Ark Brought from Kiriath-jearim
(2 Sam 6.1–11)

13 David consulted with the commanders of the thousands and of the hundreds, with every leader. [2] David said to the whole assembly of Israel, "If it seems good to you, and if it is the will of the LORD our God, let us send abroad to our kindred who remain in all the land of Israel, including the priests and Le'vites in the cities that have pasture lands, that they may come together to us. [3] Then let us bring again the ark of our God to us; for we did not turn to it in the days of Saul." [4] The whole assembly agreed to do so, for the thing pleased all the people.

[5] So David assembled all Israel from the Shī'hor of Egypt to Le'bo-ha'math, to bring the ark of God from Kir'i·ath-je'a·rim. [6] And David and all Israel went up to Ba'a·lah, that is, to Kir'i·ath-je'a·rim, which belongs to Judah, to bring up from there the ark of God, the LORD, who is enthroned on the cherubim, which is called by his[k] name. [7] They carried the ark of God on a new cart, from the house of A·bin'a·dab, and Uz'zah and A·hī'o[l] were driving the cart. [8] David and all Israel were dancing before God with all their might, with song and lyres and harps and tambourines and cymbals and trumpets.

[9] When they came to the threshing floor of Chī'don, Uz'zah put out his hand to hold the ark, for the oxen shook it. [10] The anger of the LORD was kindled against Uz'zah; he struck him down because he put out his hand to the ark; and he died there before God. [11] David was angry because the LORD had burst out against Uz'zah; so that place is called Per'ez-uz'zah[m] to this day. [12] David was afraid of God that day; he said, "How can I bring the ark of God into my care?" [13] So David did not take the ark into his care into the

---

[i] Or as officers of his troops   [j] Gk: Heb lacks David   [k] Heb lacks his   [l] Or and his brother   [m] That is Bursting Out Against Uzzah

city of David; he took it instead to the house of O'bed-e'dom the Git'tīte. [14] The ark of God remained with the household of O'bed-e'dom in his house three months, and the LORD blessed the household of O'bed-e'dom and all that he had.

David Established at Jerusalem
(2 Sam 5.11–16)

14 King Hiram of Tȳre sent messengers to David, along with cedar logs, and masons and carpenters to build a house for him. [2] David then perceived that the LORD had established him as king over Israel, and that his kingdom was highly exalted for the sake of his people Israel.

3 David took more wives in Jerusalem, and David became the father of more sons and daughters. [4] These are the names of the children whom he had in Jerusalem: Sham'mū·a, Shō'bab, and Nathan; Solomon, [5] Ib'har, E·lish'ū·a, and El'pe·let; [6] Nō'gah, Nē'pheg, and Ja·phī'a; [7] E·lish'a·ma, Bē·e·lī'a·da, and E·liph'e·let.

Defeat of the Philistines
(2 Sam 5.17–25)

8 When the Phi·lis'tines heard that David had been anointed king over all Israel, all the Phi·lis'tines went up in search of David; and David heard of it and went out against them. [9] Now the Phi·lis'tines had come and made a raid in the valley of Reph'a·im. [10] David inquired of God, "Shall I go up against the Phi·lis'tines? Will you give them into my hand?" The LORD said to him, "Go up, and I will give them into your hand." [11] So he went up to Bā'al-pe·rā'zim, and David defeated them there. David said, "God has burst out[n] against my enemies by my hand, like a bursting flood." Therefore that place is called Bā'al-pe·rā'zim. [o] [12] They abandoned their gods there, and at David's command they were burned.

13 Once again the Phi·lis'tines made a raid in the valley. [14] When David again inquired of God, God said to him, "You shall not go up after them; go around and come on them opposite the balsam trees. [15] When you hear the sound of marching in the tops of the balsam trees, then go out to battle; for God has gone out before you to strike down the army of the Phi·lis'tines." [16] David did as God had commanded him, and they struck down the Phi·lis'tine army from Gib'e·on to Gē'zer.

[17] The fame of David went out into all lands, and the LORD brought the fear of him on all nations.

The Ark Brought to Jerusalem
(2 Sam 6.12–16)

15 David[p] built houses for himself in the city of David, and he prepared a place for the ark of God and pitched a tent for it. [2] Then David commanded that no one but the Lē'vītes were to carry the ark of God, for the LORD had chosen them to carry the ark of the LORD and to minister to him forever. [3] David assembled all Israel in Jerusalem to bring up the ark of the LORD to its place, which he had prepared for it. [4] Then David gathered together the descendants of Aaron and the Lē'vītes: [5] of the sons of Kō'hath, U·rī'el the chief, with one hundred twenty of his kindred; [6] of the sons of Me·rar'ī, A·sāi'ah the chief, with two hundred twenty of his kindred; [7] of the sons of Ger'shom, Jō'el the chief, with one hundred thirty of his kindred; [8] of the sons of E·li·zā'phan, She·māi'ah the chief, with two hundred of his kindred; [9] of the sons of Hē'bron, E·lī'el the chief, with eighty of his kindred; [10] of the sons of Uz'zi·el, Am·min'a·dab the chief, with one hundred twelve of his kindred.

11 David summoned the priests Zā'dok and A·bī'a·thar, and the Lē'vītes U·rī'el, A·sāi'ah, Jō'el, She·māi'ah, E·lī'el, and Am·min'a·dab. [12] He said to them, "You are the heads of families of the Lē'vītes; sanctify yourselves, you and your kindred, so that you may bring up the ark of the LORD, the God of Israel, to the place that I have prepared for it. [13] Because you did not carry it the first time,[q] the LORD our God burst out against us, because we did not give it proper care." [14] So the priests and the Lē'vītes sanctified themselves to bring up the ark of the LORD, the God of Israel. [15] And the Lē'vītes carried the ark of God on their shoulders with the poles, as Moses had commanded according to the word of the LORD.

16 David also commanded the chiefs of the Lē'vītes to appoint their kindred as the singers to play on musical instruments, on harps and lyres and cymbals, to raise loud sounds of

[n] Heb paraz   [o] That is Lord of Bursting Out   [p] Heb He   [q] Meaning of Heb uncertain

joy. ¹⁷So the Lē′vītes appointed Hē′-man son of Jō′el; and of his kindred Ā′saph son of Ber·e·chī′ah; and of the sons of Me·rar′ī, their kindred, Ē′than son of Kū·shā′i·ah; ¹⁸and with them their kindred of the second order, Zech·a·rī′ah, Ja·ā′zi·el, She·mir′-a·moth, Je·hī′el, Un′nī, E·lī′ab, Be·nā′i·ah, Mā·a·sēi′ah, Mat·ti·thī′ah, E·liph′e·le·hū, and Mik·nē′i·ah, and the gatekeepers Ō′bed-ē′dom and Je·ī′el. ¹⁹The singers Hē′man, Ā′saph, and Ē′than were to sound bronze cymbals; ²⁰Zech·a·rī′ah, Ā′zi·el, She·mir′a·moth, Je·hī′el, Un′nī, E·lī′ab, Mā·a·sēi′ah, and Be·nā′i·ah were to play harps according to Al′a·moth; ²¹but Mat·ti·thī′ah, E·liph′e·le·hū, Mik·nē′i·ah, Ō′bed-ē′dom, Je·ī′el, and Az·a·zī′ah were to lead with lyres according to the Shem′i·nith. ²²Chen·a·nī′ah, leader of the Lē′vītes in music, was to direct the music, for he understood it. ²³Ber·e·chī′ah and El·kā′nah were to be gatekeepers for the ark. ²⁴Sheb·a·nī′ah, Josh′a·phat, Ne·than′el, A·mā′saī, Zech·a·rī′ah, Be·nā′i·ah, and El·ī·ē′zer, the priests, were to blow the trumpets before the ark of God. Ō′bed-ē′dom and Je·hī′ah also were to be gatekeepers for the ark.

25 So David and the elders of Israel, and the commanders of the thousands, went to bring up the ark of the covenant of the LORD from the house of Ō′bed-ē′dom with rejoicing. ²⁶And because God helped the Lē′vītes who were carrying the ark of the covenant of the LORD, they sacrificed seven bulls and seven rams. ²⁷David was clothed with a robe of fine linen, as also were all the Lē′vītes who were carrying the ark, and the singers, and Chen·a·nī′ah the leader of the music of the singers; and David wore a linen ephod. ²⁸So all Israel brought up the ark of the covenant of the LORD with shouting, to the sound of the horn, trumpets, and cymbals, and made loud music on harps and lyres.

29 As the ark of the covenant of the LORD came to the city of David, Mī′chal daughter of Saul looked out of the window, and saw King David leaping and dancing; and she despised him in her heart.

The Ark Placed in the Tent
(2 Sam 6.17–19)

16 They brought in the ark of God, and set it inside the tent that David had pitched for it; and they offered burnt offerings and offerings of well-being before God. ²When David had finished offering the burnt offerings and the offerings of well-being, he blessed the people in the name of the LORD; ³and he distributed to every person in Israel—man and woman alike—to each a loaf of bread, a portion of meat,ʳ and a cake of raisins.

4 He appointed certain of the Lē′-vītes as ministers before the ark of the LORD, to invoke, to thank, and to praise the LORD, the God of Israel. ⁵Ā′saph was the chief, and second to him Zech·a·rī′ah, Je·ī′el, She·mir′-a·moth, Je·hī′el, Mat·ti·thī′ah, E·lī′ab, Be·nā′i·ah, Ō′bed-ē′dom, and Je·ī′el, with harps and lyres; Ā′saph was to sound the cymbals, ⁶and the priests Be·nā′i·ah and Ja·hā′zi·el were to blow trumpets regularly, before the ark of the covenant of God.

David's Psalm of Thanksgiving
(Ps 96.1–13; 105.1–15; 106.1, 47–48)

7 Then on that day David first appointed the singing of praises to the LORD by Ā′saph and his kindred.

8 O give thanks to the LORD, call
      on his name,
    make known his deeds among
      the peoples.
9 Sing to him, sing praises to him,
    tell of all his wonderful works.
10 Glory in his holy name;
    let the hearts of those who
      seek the LORD rejoice.
11 Seek the LORD and his strength,
    seek his presence continually.
12 Remember the wonderful works
      he has done,
    his miracles, and the
      judgments he uttered,
13 O offspring of his servant
      Israel,ˢ
    children of Jacob, his chosen
      ones.

14 He is the LORD our God;
    his judgments are in all the
      earth.
15 Remember his covenant forever,
    the word that he commanded,
      for a thousand generations,
16 the covenant that he made with
      Abraham,

ʳCompare Gk Syr Vg: Meaning of Heb uncertain   ˢAnother reading is *Abraham* (compare Ps 105.6) his sworn promise to Isaac,

17 which he confirmed to Jacob as
a statute,
to Israel as an everlasting
covenant,

18 saying, "To you I will give the
land of Ca'naan
as your portion for an
inheritance."

19 When they were few in number,
of little account, and strangers
in the land,[t]

20 wandering from nation to nation,
from one kingdom to another
people,

21 he allowed no one to oppress
them;
he rebuked kings on their
account,

22 saying, "Do not touch my
anointed ones;
do my prophets no harm."

23 Sing to the LORD, all the earth.
Tell of his salvation from day
to day.

24 Declare his glory among the
nations,
his marvelous works among
all the peoples.

25 For great is the LORD, and
greatly to be praised;
he is to be revered above all
gods.

26 For all the gods of the peoples
are idols,
but the LORD made the
heavens.

27 Honor and majesty are before
him;
strength and joy are in his
place.

28 Ascribe to the LORD, O families
of the peoples,
ascribe to the LORD glory and
strength.

29 Ascribe to the LORD the glory
due his name;
bring an offering, and come
before him.
Worship the LORD in holy
splendor;

30 tremble before him, all the
earth.
The world is firmly
established; it shall never
be moved.

31 Let the heavens be glad, and let
the earth rejoice,
and let them say among the

nations, "The LORD is
king!"

32 Let the sea roar, and all that fills
it;
let the field exult, and
everything in it.

33 Then shall the trees of the forest
sing for joy
before the LORD, for he comes
to judge the earth.

34 O give thanks to the LORD, for
he is good;
for his steadfast love endures
forever.

35 Say also:
"Save us, O God of our
salvation,
and gather and rescue us from
among the nations,
that we may give thanks to your
holy name,
and glory in your praise.

36 Blessed be the LORD, the God of
Israel,
from everlasting to
everlasting."

Then all the people said "Amen!" and
praised the LORD.

Regular Worship Maintained

37 David left A'saph and his kinsfolk there before the ark of the covenant of the LORD to minister regularly
before the ark as each day required,
38 and also O'bed-e'dom and his[u]
sixty-eight kinsfolk; while O'bed-
e'dom son of Je·du'thun and Hō'-
sah were to be gatekeepers. 39 And
he left the priest Za'dok and his kindred the priests before the tabernacle
of the LORD in the high place that was
at Gib'e·on, 40 to offer burnt offerings
to the LORD on the altar of burnt offering regularly, morning and evening,
according to all that is written in the
law of the LORD that he commanded
Israel. 41 With them were He'man and
Je·du'thun, and the rest of those chosen and expressly named to render
thanks to the LORD, for his steadfast
love endures forever. 42 He'man and
Je·du'thun had with them trumpets
and cymbals for the music, and instruments for sacred song. The sons of
Je·du'thun were appointed to the gate.

43 Then all the people departed to
their homes, and David went home to
bless his household.

[t] Heb *in it*   [u] Gk Syr Vg: Heb *their*

God's Covenant with David
(2 Sam 7.1–17)

17 Now when David settled in his house, David said to the prophet Nathan, "I am living in a house of cedar, but the ark of the covenant of the LORD is under a tent." 2 Nathan said to David, "Do all that you have in mind, for God is with you."

3 But that same night the word of the LORD came to Nathan, saying: 4 Go and tell my servant David: Thus says the LORD: You shall not build me a house to live in. 5 For I have not lived in a house since the day I brought out Israel to this very day, but I have lived in a tent and a tabernacle.ᵛ 6 Wherever I have moved about among all Israel, did I ever speak a word with any of the judges of Israel, whom I commanded to shepherd my people, saying, Why have you not built me a house of cedar? 7 Now therefore thus you shall say to my servant David: Thus says the LORD of hosts: I took you from the pasture, from following the sheep, to be ruler over my people Israel; 8 and I have been with you wherever you went, and have cut off all your enemies before you; and I will make for you a name, like the name of the great ones of the earth. 9 I will appoint a place for my people Israel, and will plant them, so that they may live in their own place, and be disturbed no more; and evildoers shall wear them down no more, as they did formerly, 10 from the time that I appointed judges over my people Israel; and I will subdue all your enemies.

Moreover I declare to you that the LORD will build you a house. 11 When your days are fulfilled to go to be with your ancestors, I will raise up your offspring after you, one of your own sons, and I will establish his kingdom. 12 He shall build a house for me, and I will establish his throne forever. 13 I will be a father to him, and he shall be a son to me. I will not take my steadfast love from him, as I took it from him who was before you, 14 but I will confirm him in my house and in my kingdom forever, and his throne shall be established forever. 15 In accordance with all these words and all this vision, Nathan spoke to David.

David's Prayer
(2 Sam 7.18–29)

16 Then King David went in and sat before the LORD, and said, "Who am I, O LORD God, and what is my house, that you have brought me thus far? 17 And even this was a small thing in your sight, O God; you have also spoken of your servant's house for a great while to come. You regard me as someone of high rank,ʷ O LORD God! 18 And what more can David say to you for honoring your servant? You know your servant. 19 For your servant's sake, O LORD, and according to your own heart, you have done all these great deeds, making known all these great things. 20 There is no one like you, O LORD, and there is no God besides you, according to all that we have heard with our ears. 21 Who is like your people Israel, one nation on the earth whom God went to redeem to be his people, making for yourself a name for great and terrible things, in driving out nations before your people whom you redeemed from Egypt? 22 And you made your people Israel to be your people forever; and you, O LORD, became their God.

23 "And now, O LORD, as for the word that you have spoken concerning your servant and concerning his house, let it be established forever, and do as you have promised. 24 Thus your name will be established and magnified forever in the saying, 'The LORD of hosts, the God of Israel, is Israel's God'; and the house of your servant David will be established in your presence. 25 For you, my God, have revealed to your servant that you will build a house for him; therefore your servant has found it possible to pray before you. 26 And now, O LORD, you are God, and you have promised this good thing to your servant; 27 therefore may it please you to bless the house of your servant, that it may continue forever before you. For you, O LORD, have blessed and are blessedˣ forever."

David's Kingdom Established and Extended
(2 Sam 8.1–14)

18 Some time afterward, David attacked the Phi·lis'tines and subdued them; he took Gath and its villages from the Phi·lis'tines.

ᵛ Gk 2 Sam 7.6: Heb *but I have been from tent to tent and from tabernacle* ʷ Meaning of Heb uncertain ˣ Or *and it is blessed*

2 He defeated Mō′ab, and the Mō′-ab·ites became subject to David and brought tribute.

3 David also struck down King Had·a·dē′zer of Zō′bah, toward Hā′-math,ʸ as he went to set up a monument at the river Euphrates. ⁴David took from him one thousand chariots, seven thousand cavalry, and twenty thousand foot soldiers. David hamstrung all the chariot horses, but left one hundred of them. ⁵When the Ar·a·mē′ans of Damascus came to help King Had·a·dē′zer of Zō′bah, David killed twenty-two thousand Ar·a·mē′ans. ⁶Then David put garrisonsᶻ in Ar′am of Damascus; and the Ar·a·mē′ans became subject to David, and brought tribute. The LORD gave victory to David wherever he went. ⁷David took the gold shields that were carried by the servants of Had·a·dē′zer, and brought them to Jerusalem. ⁸From Tib′hath and from Cūn, cities of Had·a·dē′zer, David took a vast quantity of bronze; with it Solomon made the bronze sea and the pillars and the vessels of bronze.

9 When King Tō′ū of Hā′math heard that David had defeated the whole army of King Had·a·dē′zer of Zō′bah, ¹⁰he sent his son Ha·dor′am to King David, to greet him and to congratulate him, because he had fought against Had·a·dē′zer and defeated him. Now Had·a·dē′zer had often been at war with Tō′ū. He sent all sorts of articles of gold, of silver, and of bronze; ¹¹these also King David dedicated to the LORD, together with the silver and gold that he had carried off from all the nations, from E′dom, Mō′ab, the Am′mon·ites, the Phi·lis′-tines, and Am′a·lek.

12 A·bi′shai son of Ze·rū′i·ah killed eighteen thousand E′dom·ites in the Valley of Salt. ¹³He put garrisons in E′dom; and all the E′dom·ites became subject to David. And the LORD gave victory to David wherever he went.

David's Administration
(2 Sam 8.15–18)

14 So David reigned over all Israel; and he administered justice and equity to all his people. ¹⁵Jō′ab son of Ze·rū′-i·ah was over the army; Je·hosh′a·phat son of A·hī′lud was recorder; ¹⁶Zā′dok son of A·hī′tub and A·him′e·lech son of A·bī′a·thar were priests; Shav′sha was secretary; ¹⁷Be·nā′i·ah son of Je·hoi′a·da was over the Cher′e·thītes

and the Pel′eth·ites; and David's sons were the chief officials in the service of the king.

Defeat of the Ammonites
and Arameans
(2 Sam 10.1–19)

19 Some time afterward, King Nā′hash of the Am′mon·ites died, and his son succeeded him. ²David said, "I will deal loyally with Hā′-nun son of Nā′hash, for his father dealt loyally with me." So David sent messengers to console him concerning his father. When David's servants came to Hā′nun in the land of the Am′mon·ites, to console him, ³the officials of the Am′mon·ites said to Hā′nun, "Do you think, because David has sent consolers to you, that he is honoring your father? Have not his servants come to you to search and to overthrow and to spy out the land?" ⁴So Hā′nun seized David's servants, shaved them, cut off their garments in the middle at their hips, and sent them away; ⁵and they departed. When David was told about the men, he sent messengers to them, for they felt greatly humiliated. The king said, "Remain at Jericho until your beards have grown, and then return."

6 When the Am′mon·ites saw that they had made themselves odious to David, Hā′nun and the Am′mon·ites sent a thousand talents of silver to hire chariots and cavalry from Mes·o·po·tā′mi·a, from Ar′am-mā′-a·cah and from Zō′bah. ⁷They hired thirty-two thousand chariots and the king of Mā′a·cah with his army, who came and camped before Med′e·ba. And the Am′mon·ites were mustered from their cities and came to battle. ⁸When David heard of it, he sent Jō′ab and all the army of the warriors. ⁹The Am′mon·ites came out and drew up in battle array at the entrance of the city, and the kings who had come were by themselves in the open country.

10 When Jō′ab saw that the line of battle was set against him both in front and in the rear, he chose some of the picked men of Israel and arrayed them against the Ar·a·mē′ans; ¹¹the rest of his troops he put in the charge of his brother A·bi′shai, and they were arrayed against the Am′mon·ites. ¹²He

---

ʸMeaning of Heb uncertain   ᶻGk Vg 2 Sam 8.6 Compare Syr: Heb lacks *garrisons* said, "If the Ar·a·mēʹans are too strong for me, then you shall help me; but if the Amʹmon·ītes are too strong for you, then I will help you. ¹³Be strong, and let us be courageous for our people and for the cities of our God; and may the LORD do what seems good to him." ¹⁴So Jōʹab and the troops who were with him advanced toward the Ar·a·mēʹans for battle; and they fled before him. ¹⁵When the Amʹmon·ītes saw that the Ar·a·mēʹans fled, they likewise fled before A·biʹshaī, Jōʹab's brother, and entered the city. Then Jōʹab came to Jerusalem.

16 But when the Ar·a·mēʹans saw that they had been defeated by Israel, they sent messengers and brought out the Ar·a·mēʹans who were beyond the Euphrates, with Shōʹphach the commander of the army of Had·a·dēʹzer at their head. ¹⁷When David was informed, he gathered all Israel together, crossed the Jordan, came to them, and drew up his forces against them. When David set the battle in array against the Ar·a·mēʹans, they fought with him. ¹⁸The Ar·a·mēʹans fled before Israel; and David killed seven thousand Ar·a·mēʹan charioteers and forty thousand foot soldiers, and also killed Shōʹphach the commander of their army. ¹⁹When the servants of Had·a·dēʹzer saw that they had been defeated by Israel, they made peace with David, and became subject to him. So the Ar·a·mēʹans were not willing to help the Amʹmon·ītes any more.

Siege and Capture of Rabbah
(2 Sam 11.1; 12.26–31)

20 In the spring of the year, the time when kings go out to battle, Jōʹab led out the army, ravaged the country of the Amʹmon·ītes, and came and besieged Rabʹbah. But David remained at Jerusalem. Jōʹab attacked Rabʹbah, and overthrew it. ²David took the crown of Milʹcom*a* from his head; he found that it weighed a talent of gold, and in it was a precious stone; and it was placed on David's head. He also brought out the booty of the city, a very great amount. ³He brought out the people who were in it, and set them to work*b* with saws and iron picks and axes.*c* Thus David did to all the cities of the Amʹmon·ītes. Then David and all the people returned to Jerusalem.

Exploits against the Philistines
(2 Sam 21.15–22)

4 After this, war broke out with the Phi·lisʹtines at Gēʹzer; then Sibʹbe·caī the Hūʹsha·thīte killed Sipʹpaī, who was one of the descendants of the giants; and the Phi·lisʹtines were subdued. ⁵Again there was war with the Phi·lisʹtines; and El·hāʹnan son of Jāʹir killed Lahʹmī the brother of Goliath the Gitʹtīte, the shaft of whose spear was like a weaver's beam. ⁶Again there was war at Gath, where there was a man of great size, who had six fingers on each hand, and six toes on each foot, twenty-four in number; he also was descended from the giants. ⁷When he taunted Israel, Jonathan son of Shimʹē·a, David's brother, killed him. ⁸These were descended from the giants in Gath; they fell by the hand of David and his servants.

The Census and Plague
(2 Sam 24.1–17)

21 Satan stood up against Israel, and incited David to count the people of Israel. ²So David said to Jōʹab and the commanders of the army, "Go, number Israel, from Bēʹer·shēʹba to Dan, and bring me a report, so that I may know their number." ³But Jōʹab said, "May the LORD increase the number of his people a hundredfold! Are they not, my lord the king, all of them my lord's servants? Why then should my lord require this? Why should he bring guilt on Israel?" ⁴But the king's word prevailed against Jōʹab. So Jōʹab departed and went throughout all Israel, and came back to Jerusalem. ⁵Jōʹab gave the total count of the people to David. In all Israel there were one million one hundred thousand men who drew the sword, and in Judah four hundred seventy thousand who drew the sword. ⁶But he did not include Levi and Benjamin in the numbering, for the king's command was abhorrent to Jōʹab.

7 But God was displeased with this thing, and he struck Israel. ⁸David said to God, "I have sinned greatly in that I have done this thing. But now, I pray you, take away the guilt of your servant; for I have done very foolishly." ⁹The LORD spoke to Gad, David's seer,

---

*a*Gk Vg See 1 Kings 11.5, 33: MT *of their king*   *b*Compare 2 Sam 12.31: Heb *and he sawed*   *c*Compare 2 Sam 12.31: Heb *saws* saying, [10]"Go and say to David, 'Thus says the LORD: Three things I offer you; choose one of them, so that I may do it to you.' " [11]So Gad came to David and said to him, "Thus says the LORD, 'Take your choice; [12]either three years of famine; or three months of devastation by your foes, while the sword of your enemies overtakes you; or three days of the sword of the LORD, pestilence on the land, and the angel of the LORD destroying throughout all the territory of Israel.' Now decide what answer I shall return to the one who sent me." [13]Then David said to Gad, "I am in great distress; let me fall into the hand of the LORD, for his mercy is very great; but let me not fall into human hands."

[14] So the LORD sent a pestilence on Israel; and seventy thousand persons fell in Israel. [15]And God sent an angel to Jerusalem to destroy it; but when he was about to destroy it, the LORD took note and relented concerning the calamity; he said to the destroying angel, "Enough! Stay your hand." The angel of the LORD was then standing by the threshing floor of Or'nan the Jeb'-ū·site. [16]David looked up and saw the angel of the LORD standing between earth and heaven, and in his hand a drawn sword stretched out over Jerusalem. Then David and the elders, clothed in sackcloth, fell on their faces. [17]And David said to God, "Was it not I who gave the command to count the people? It is I who have sinned and done very wickedly. But these sheep, what have they done? Let your hand, I pray, O LORD my God, be against me and against my father's house; but do not let your people be plagued!"

David's Altar and Sacrifice
(2 Sam 24.18–25)

[18] Then the angel of the LORD commanded Gad to tell David that he should go up and erect an altar to the LORD on the threshing floor of Or'nan the Jeb'ū·site. [19]So David went up following Gad's instructions, which he had spoken in the name of the LORD. [20]Or'nan turned and saw the angel; and while his four sons who were with him hid themselves, Or'nan continued to thresh wheat. [21]As David came to Or'nan, Or'nan looked and saw David; he went out from the threshing floor, and did obeisance to David with his face to the ground. [22]David said to Or'-nan, "Give me the site of the threshing floor that I may build on it an altar to the LORD—give it to me at its full price—so that the plague may be averted from the people." [23]Then Or'-nan said to David, "Take it; and let my lord the king do what seems good to him; see, I present the oxen for burnt offerings, and the threshing sledges for the wood, and the wheat for a grain offering. I give it all." [24]But King David said to Or'nan, "No; I will buy them for the full price. I will not take for the LORD what is yours, nor offer burnt offerings that cost me nothing." [25]So David paid Or'nan six hundred shekels of gold by weight for the site. [26]David built there an altar to the LORD and presented burnt offerings and offerings of well-being. He called upon the LORD, and he answered him with fire from heaven on the altar of burnt offering. [27]Then the LORD commanded the angel, and he put his sword back into its sheath.

The Place Chosen for the Temple

[28] At that time, when David saw that the LORD had answered him at the threshing floor of Or'nan the Jeb'-ū·site, he made his sacrifices there. [29]For the tabernacle of the LORD, which Moses had made in the wilderness, and the altar of burnt offering were at that time in the high place at Gib'ē·on; [30]but David could not go before it to inquire of God, for he was afraid of the sword of the angel of the LORD. **22** [1]Then David said, "Here shall be the house of the LORD God and here the altar of burnt offering for Israel."

David Prepares to Build the Temple

[2] David gave orders to gather together the aliens who were residing in the land of Israel, and he set stonecutters to prepare dressed stones for building the house of God. [3]David also provided great stores of iron for nails for the doors of the gates and for clamps, as well as bronze in quantities beyond weighing, [4]and cedar logs without number—for the Sī·dō'ni·ans and Ty'ri·ans brought great quantities of cedar to David. [5]For David said, "My son Solomon is young and inexperienced, and the house that is to be built for the LORD must be exceedingly magnificent, famous and glorified throughout all lands; I will therefore make preparation for it." So David

provided materials in great quantity before his death.

David's Charge to Solomon and the Leaders

6 Then he called for his son Solomon and charged him to build a house for the LORD, the God of Israel. [7] David said to Solomon, "My son, I had planned to build a house to the name of the LORD my God. [8] But the word of the LORD came to me, saying, 'You have shed much blood and have waged great wars; you shall not build a house to my name, because you have shed so much blood in my sight on the earth. [9] See, a son shall be born to you; he shall be a man of peace. I will give him peace from all his enemies on every side; for his name shall be Solomon,[d] and I will give peace[e] and quiet to Israel in his days. [10] He shall build a house for my name. He shall be a son to me, and I will be a father to him, and I will establish his royal throne in Israel forever.' [11] Now, my son, the LORD be with you, so that you may succeed in building the house of the LORD your God, as he has spoken concerning you. [12] Only, may the LORD grant you discretion and understanding, so that when he gives you charge over Israel you may keep the law of the LORD your God. [13] Then you will prosper if you are careful to observe the statutes and the ordinances that the LORD commanded Moses for Israel. Be strong and of good courage. Do not be afraid or dismayed. [14] With great pains I have provided for the house of the LORD one hundred thousand talents of gold, one million talents of silver, and bronze and iron beyond weighing, for there is so much of it; timber and stone too I have provided. To these you must add more. [15] You have an abundance of workers: stonecutters, masons, carpenters, and all kinds of artisans without number, skilled in working [16] gold, silver, bronze, and iron. Now begin the work, and the LORD be with you."

17 David also commanded all the leaders of Israel to help his son Solomon, saying, [18] "Is not the LORD your God with you? Has he not given you peace on every side? For he has delivered the inhabitants of the land into my hand; and the land is subdued before the LORD and his people. [19] Now set your mind and heart to seek the LORD your God. Go and build the sanctuary of the LORD God so that the ark of the covenant of the LORD and the holy vessels of God may be brought into a house built for the name of the LORD."

Families of the Levites and Their Functions

23 When David was old and full of days, he made his son Solomon king over Israel.

2 David assembled all the leaders of Israel and the priests and the Lĕ′vites. [3] The Lĕ′vites, thirty years old and upward, were counted, and the total was thirty-eight thousand. [4] "Twenty-four thousand of these," David said, "shall have charge of the work in the house of the LORD, six thousand shall be officers and judges, [5] four thousand gatekeepers, and four thousand shall offer praises to the LORD with the instruments that I have made for praise." [6] And David organized them in divisions corresponding to the sons of Levi: Ger′shon,[f] Kō′hath, and Merar′ī.

7 The sons of Ger′shon[g] were Lā′dan and Shim′ĕ·ī. [8] The sons of Lā′dan: Je·hī′el the chief, Zē′tham, and Jō′el, three. [9] The sons of Shim′ĕ·ī: She·lō′moth, Hā′zi·el, and Har′an, three. These were the heads of families of Lā′dan. [10] And the sons of Shim′ĕ·ī: Jā′hath, Zī′na, Jĕ′ush, and Bĕ·rī′ah. These four were the sons of Shim′ĕ·ī. [11] Jā′hath was the chief, and Zī′zah the second; but Jĕ′ush and Bĕ·rī′ah did not have many sons, so they were enrolled as a single family.

12 The sons of Kō′hath: Am′ram, Iz′har, Hĕ′bron, and Uz′zi·el, four. [13] The sons of Am′ram: Aaron and Moses. Aaron was set apart to consecrate the most holy things, so that he and his sons forever should make offerings before the LORD, and minister to him and pronounce blessings in his name forever; [14] but as for Moses the man of God, his sons were to be reckoned among the tribe of Levi. [15] The sons of Moses: Ger′shom and El·i·ē′zer. [16] The sons of Ger′shom: She·bū′el the chief. [17] The sons of El·i·ē′zer: Rē·ha·bī′ah the chief; El·i·ē′zer had no other sons, but the sons of Rē·ha·bī′ah were very numerous. [18] The sons of Iz′har: She·lō′mith the chief. [19] The sons of

---

d Heb Shelomoh e Heb shalom
f Or Gershom; See 1 Chr 6.1, note, and 23.15 g Vg Compare Gk Syr: Heb to the Gershonite

Hē'bron: Je·rī'ah the chief, Am·a·rī'ah the second, Ja·hā'zi·el the third, and Jek·a·mē'am the fourth. [20] The sons of Uz'zi·el: Mī'cah the chief and Is·shī'ah the second.

21 The sons of Me·rar'ī: Mah'lī and Mū'shī. The sons of Mah'lī: El·ē·ā'zar and Kish. [22] El·ē·ā'zar died having no sons, but only daughters; their kindred, the sons of Kish, married them. [23] The sons of Mū'shī: Mah'lī, Ē'der, and Jer'e·moth, three.

24 These were the sons of Levi by their ancestral houses, the heads of families as they were enrolled according to the number of the names of the individuals from twenty years old and upward who were to do the work for the service of the house of the LORD. [25] For David said, "The LORD, the God of Israel, has given rest to his people; and he resides in Jerusalem forever. [26] And so the Lē'vītes no longer need to carry the tabernacle or any of the things for its service"— [27] for according to the last words of David these were the number of the Lē'vītes from twenty years old and upward— [28] "but their duty shall be to assist the descendants of Aaron for the service of the house of the LORD, having the care of the courts and the chambers, the cleansing of all that is holy, and any work for the service of the house of God; [29] to assist also with the rows of bread, the choice flour for the grain offering, the wafers of unleavened bread, the baked offering, the offering mixed with oil, and all measures of quantity or size. [30] And they shall stand every morning, thanking and praising the LORD, and likewise at evening, [31] and whenever burnt offerings are offered to the LORD on sabbaths, new moons, and appointed festivals, according to the number required of them, regularly before the LORD. [32] Thus they shall keep charge of the tent of meeting and the sanctuary, and shall attend the descendants of Aaron, their kindred, for the service of the house of the LORD."

Divisions of the Priests

24 The divisions of the descendants of Aaron were these. The sons of Aaron: Nā'dab, A·bī'hū, El·ē·ā'zar, and Ith'a·mar. [2] But Nā'dab and A·bī'hū died before their father, and had no sons; so El·ē·ā'zar and Ith'a·mar became the priests. [3] Along with Zā'dok of the sons of El·ē·ā'zar, and

A·him'e·lech of the sons of Ith'a·mar, David organized them according to the appointed duties in their service. [4] Since more chief men were found among the sons of El·ē·ā'zar than among the sons of Ith'a·mar, they organized them under sixteen heads of ancestral houses of the sons of El·ē·ā'zar, and eight of the sons of Ith'a·mar. [5] They organized them by lot, all alike, for there were officers of the sanctuary and officers of God among both the sons of El·ē·ā'zar and the sons of Ith'a·mar. [6] The scribe She·māi'ah son of Ne·than'el, a Lē'vīte, recorded them in the presence of the king, and the officers, and Zā'dok the priest, and A·him'e·lech son of A·bī'a·thar, and the heads of ancestral houses of the priests and of the Lē'vītes; one ancestral house being chosen for El·ē·ā'zar and one chosen for Ith'a·mar.

7 The first lot fell to Je·hoi'a·rib, the second to Je·daī'ah, [8] the third to Hā'rim, the fourth to Se·ō'rim, [9] the fifth to Mal·chī'jah, the sixth to Mij'a·min, [10] the seventh to Hak'koz, the eighth to A·bī'jah, [11] the ninth to Jesh'ū·a, the tenth to Shec·a·nī'ah, [12] the eleventh to E·lī'a·shib, the twelfth to Jā'kim, [13] the thirteenth to Hup'pah, the fourteenth to Je·sheb'e·ab, [14] the fifteenth to Bil'gah, the sixteenth to Im'mer, [15] the seventeenth to Hē'zir, the eighteenth to Hap'piz·zez, [16] the nineteenth to Peth·a·hī'ah, the twentieth to Je·hez'kel, [17] the twenty-first to Jā'chin, the twenty-second to Gā'mūl, [18] the twenty-third to De·laī'ah, the twenty-fourth to Mā·a·zī'ah. [19] These had as their appointed duty in their service to enter the house of the LORD according to the procedure established for them by their ancestor Aaron, as the LORD God of Israel had commanded him.

Other Levites

20 And of the rest of the sons of Levi: of the sons of Am'ram, Shū'ba·el; of the sons of Shū'ba·el, Jeh·dē'i·ah. [21] Of Rē·ha·bī'ah: of the sons of Rē·ha·bī'ah, Is·shī'ah the chief. [22] Of the Iz'har·ītes, She·lō'moth; of the sons of She·lō'moth, Jā'hath. [23] The sons of Hē'bron:[h] Je·rī'ah the chief,[i] Am·a·rī'ah the second, Ja·hā'zi·el the third, Jek·a·mē'am the fourth. [24] The sons of Uz'zi·el, Mī'cah; of the sons of Mī'cah, Shā'mir. [25] The brother of

---

[h] See 23.19: Heb lacks *Hebron*   [i] See 23.19: Heb lacks *the chief*

Mī'cah, Is·shī'ah; of the sons of Is·shī'ah, Zech·a·rī'ah. 26 The sons of Me·rar'ī: Mah'lī and Mū'shī. The sons of Jā·a·zī'ah: Bē'no.[j] 27 The sons of Me·rar'ī: of Jā·a·zī'ah, Bē'no,[j] Shō'-ham, Zac'cur, and Ib'rī. 28 Of Mah'lī: El·e·ā'zar, who had no sons. 29 Of Kish, the sons of Kish: Je·rah'mē·el. 30 The sons of Mū'shī: Mah'lī, Ē'der, and Jer'i·moth. These were the sons of the Lē'-vites according to their ancestral houses. 31 These also cast lots corresponding to their kindred, the descendants of Aaron, in the presence of King David, Zā'dok, A·him'e·lech, and the heads of ancestral houses of the priests and of the Lē'vites, the chief as well as the youngest brother.

The Temple Musicians

25 David and the officers of the army also set apart for the service the sons of Ā'saph, and of Hē'-man, and of Je·dū'thun, who should prophesy with lyres, harps, and cymbals. The list of those who did the work and of their duties was: 2 Of the sons of Ā'saph: Zac'cur, Joseph, Neth·a·nī'ah, and As·a·rē'lah, sons of Ā'saph, under the direction of Ā'saph, who prophesied under the direction of the king. 3 Of Je·dū'thun, the sons of Je·dū'-thun: Ged·a·lī'ah, Zē'rī, Je·shā'i·ah, Shim'e·ī,[k] Hash·a·bī'ah, and Mat-ti·thī'ah, six, under the direction of their father Je·dū'thun, who prophesied with the lyre in thanksgiving and praise to the LORD. 4 Of Hē'man, the sons of Hē'man: Buk·kī'ah, Mat·ta·nī'ah, Uz'zi·el, She·bū'el, and Jer'i·moth, Han·a·nī'ah, Ha·nā'nī, E·lī'a·thah, Gid·dal'tī, and Rō·mam'-ti·ē'zer, Josh·be·kash'ah, Mal·lō'thī, Hō'thir, Ma·hā'zi·oth. 5 All these were the sons of Hē'man the king's seer, according to the promise of God to exalt him; for God had given Hē'man fourteen sons and three daughters. 6 They were all under the direction of their father for the music in the house of the LORD with cymbals, harps, and lyres for the service of the house of God. Ā'saph, Je·dū'thun, and Hē'man were under the order of the king. 7 They and their kindred, who were trained in singing to the LORD, all of whom were skillful, numbered two hundred eighty-eight. 8 And they cast lots for their duties, small and great, teacher and pupil alike.

9 The first lot fell for Ā'saph to Joseph; the second to Ged·a·lī'ah, to him

and his brothers and his sons, twelve; 10 the third to Zac'cur, his sons and his brothers, twelve; 11 the fourth to Iz'-rī, his sons and his brothers, twelve; 12 the fifth to Neth·a·nī'ah, his sons and his brothers, twelve; 13 the sixth to Buk·kī'ah, his sons and his brothers, twelve; 14 the seventh to Jes·a·rē'lah,[l] his sons and his brothers, twelve; 15 the eighth to Je·shā'i·ah, his sons and his brothers, twelve; 16 the ninth to Mat·ta·nī'ah, his sons and his brothers, twelve; 17 the tenth to Shim'e·ī, his sons and his brothers, twelve; 18 the eleventh to Az'a·rel, his sons and his brothers, twelve; 19 the twelfth to Hash·a·bī'ah, his sons and his brothers, twelve; 20 to the thirteenth, Shū'-ba·el, his sons and his brothers, twelve; 21 to the fourteenth, Mat-ti·thī'ah, his sons and his brothers, twelve; 22 to the fifteenth, to Jer'-e·moth, his sons and his brothers, twelve; 23 to the sixteenth, to Han·a·nī'ah, his sons and his brothers, twelve; 24 to the seventeenth, to Josh·be·kash'ah, his sons and his brothers, twelve; 25 to the eighteenth, to Ha·nā'nī, his sons and his brothers, twelve; 26 to the nineteenth, to Mal·lō'thī, his sons and his brothers, twelve; 27 to the twentieth, to E·lī'-a·thah, his sons and his brothers, twelve; 28 to the twenty-first, to Hō'-thir, his sons and his brothers, twelve; 29 to the twenty-second, to Gid·dal'tī, his sons and his brothers, twelve; 30 to the twenty-third, to Ma·hā'zi·oth, his sons and his brothers, twelve; 31 to the twenty-fourth, to Rō·mam'ti·ē'zer, his sons and his brothers, twelve.

The Gatekeepers

26 As for the divisions of the gatekeepers: of the Kō'ra·hites, Me·shel·e·mī'ah son of Kō're, of the sons of Ā'saph. 2 Me·shel·e·mī'ah had sons: Zech·a·rī'ah the firstborn, Je·dī'-a·el the second, Zeb·a·dī'ah the third, Jath'ni·el the fourth, 3 Ē'lam the fifth, Jē·hō·hā'nan the sixth, El·i·e·hō·ē'naī the seventh. 4 Ō'bed-ē'dom had sons: She·māi'ah the firstborn, Je·hō'za·bad the second, Jō'ah the third, Sā'char the fourth, Ne·than'el the fifth, 5 Am'mi·el the sixth, Is'sa·char the seventh, Pe·ul'le·thaī the eighth; for God blessed him. 6 Also to his son

---

[j] Or his son: Meaning of Heb uncertain
[k] One Ms: Gk: MT lacks Shimei
[l] Or Asarelah; see 25.2

She·mǎi'ah sons were born who exercised authority in their ancestral houses, for they were men of great ability. [7] The sons of She·mǎi'ah: Oth'nī, Reph'a·el, Ō'bed, and El·zā'bad, whose brothers were able men, E·lī'hū and Sem·a·chī'ah. [8] All these, sons of Ō'bed-ē'dom with their sons and brothers, were able men qualified for the service; sixty-two of Ō'bed-ē'dom. [9] Me·shel·e·mī'ah had sons and brothers, able men, eighteen. [10] Hō'sah, of the sons of Me·rar'ī, had sons: Shim'rī the chief (for though he was not the firstborn, his father made him chief), [11] Hil·kī'ah the second, Teb·a·lī'ah the third, Zech·a·rī'ah the fourth: all the sons and brothers of Hō'sah totaled thirteen.

[12] These divisions of the gatekeepers, corresponding to their leaders, had duties, just as their kindred did, ministering in the house of the LORD; [13] and they cast lots by ancestral houses, small and great alike, for their gates. [14] The lot for the east fell to Shel·e·mī'ah. They cast lots also for his son Zech·a·rī'ah, a prudent counselor, and his lot came out for the north [15] Ō'bed-ē'dom's came out for the south, and to his sons was allotted the storehouse. [16] For Shup'pim and Hō'sah it came out for the west, at the gate of Shal'le·cheth on the ascending road. Guard corresponded to guard. [17] On the east there were six Lē'vītes each day, [m] on the north four each day, on the south four each day, as well as two and two at the storehouse; [18] and for the colonnade[n] on the west there were four at the road and two at the colonnade. [n] [19] These were the divisions of the gatekeepers among the Kō'ra·hītes and the sons of Me·rar'ī.

The Treasurers, Officers, and Judges

[20] And of the Lē'vītes, A·hī'jah had charge of the treasuries of the house of God and the treasuries of the dedicated gifts. [21] The sons of Lā'dan, the sons of the Ger'shon·ītes belonging to Lā'dan, the heads of families belonging to Lā'dan the Ger'shon·īte: Je·hī'e·lī. [o] [22] The sons of Je·hī'e·lī, Zē'tham and his brother Jō'el, were in charge of the treasuries of the house of the LORD. [23] Of the Am'ram·ītes, the Iz'har·ītes, the Hē'bron·ītes, and the Uz'zi·el·ītes: [24] She·bū'el son of Ger'shom, son of Moses, was chief officer in charge of the treasuries. [25] His brothers: from

El·i·ē'zer were his son Rē·ha·bī'ah, his son Je·shā'i·ah, his son Jō'ram, his son Zich'rī, and his son She·lō'moth. [26] This She·lō'moth and his brothers were in charge of all the treasuries of the dedicated gifts that King David, and the heads of families, and the officers of the thousands and the hundreds, and the commanders of the army, had dedicated. [27] From booty won in battles they dedicated gifts for the maintenance of the house of the LORD. [28] Also all that Samuel the seer, and Saul son of Kish, and Abner son of Ner, and Jō'ab son of Ze·rū'i·ah had dedicated—all dedicated gifts were in the care of She·lō'moth[p] and his brothers.

[29] Of the Iz'har·ītes, Chen·a·nī'ah and his sons were appointed to outside duties for Israel, as officers and judges. [30] Of the Hē'bron·ītes, Hash·a·bī'ah and his brothers, one thousand seven hundred men of ability, had the oversight of Israel west of the Jordan for all the work of the LORD and for the service of the king. [31] Of the Hē'bron·ītes, Je·rī'jah was chief of the Hē'bron·ītes. (In the fortieth year of David's reign search was made, of whatever genealogy or family, and men of great ability among them were found at Jā'zer in Gil'e·ad.) [32] King David appointed him and his brothers, two thousand seven hundred men of ability, heads of families, to have the oversight of the Reū'ben·ītes, the Gad'ītes, and the half-tribe of the Ma·nas'sītes for everything pertaining to God and for the affairs of the king.

The Military Divisions

27 This is the list of the people of Israel, the heads of families, the commanders of the thousands and the hundreds, and their officers who served the king in all matters concerning the divisions that came and went, month after month throughout the year, each division numbering twenty-four thousand: [2] Ja·shō'be·am son of Zab'di·el was in charge of the first division in the first month; in his division were twenty-four thousand. [3] He was a descendant of Per'ez, and was chief of all

---

[m] Gk: Heb lacks *each day*
[n] Heb *parbar*: meaning uncertain
[o] The Hebrew text of verse 21 is confused [p] Gk Compare 26.28: Heb *Shelomith*

the commanders of the army for the first month. [4] Dō′dai the A·hō′hīte was in charge of the division of the second month; Mik′loth was the chief officer of his division. In his division were twenty-four thousand. [5] The third commander, for the third month, was Be·nā′i·ah son of the priest Je·hoi′a·da, as chief; in his division were twenty-four thousand. [6] This is the Be·nā′i·ah who was a mighty man of the Thirty and in command of the Thirty; his son Am·miz′a·bad was in charge of his division. [q] [7] As′a·hel brother of Jō′ab was fourth, for the fourth month, and his son Zeb·a·dī′ah after him; in his division were twenty-four thousand. [8] The fifth commander, for the fifth month, was Sham′huth, the Iz′ra·hīte; in his division were twenty-four thousand. [9] Sixth, for the sixth month, was Ira son of Ik′kesh the Te·kō′īte; in his division were twenty-four thousand. [10] Seventh, for the seventh month, was Hē′lez the Pel′o·nīte, of the E′phra·im·ites; in his division were twenty-four thousand. [11] Eighth, for the eighth month, was Sib′be·caī the Hū′sha·thīte, of the Zē′ra·hītes; in his division were twenty-four thousand. [12] Ninth, for the ninth month, was A·bi·e′zer of An′a·thoth, a Ben′ja·min·īte; in his division were twenty-four thousand. [13] Tenth, for the tenth month, was Mā′ha·raī of Ne·toph′ah, of the Zē′ra·hītes; in his division were twenty-four thousand. [14] Eleventh, for the eleventh month, was Be·nā′i·ah of Pir′a·thon, of the E′phra·im·ites; in his division were twenty-four thousand. [15] Twelfth, for the twelfth month, was Hel′daī the Ne·toph′a·thīte, of Oth′ni·el; in his division were twenty-four thousand.

Leaders of Tribes

16 Over the tribes of Israel, for the Reū′ben·ites, El·i·e′zer son of Zich′rī was chief officer; for the Sim′e·on·ites, Sheph·a·tī′ah son of Mā′a·cah; [17] for Levi, Hash·a·bī′ah son of Ke·mū′el; for Aaron, Zā′dok; [18] for Judah, E·lī′hū, one of David's brothers; for Is′sa·char, Om′rī son of Michael; [19] for Zeb′u·lun, Ish·mā′i·ah son of Ō·ba·dī′ah; for Naph′ta·lī, Jer′i·moth son of Az′ri·el; [20] for the E′phra·im·ites, Hō·shē′a son of Az·a·zī′ah; for the half-tribe of Ma·nas′seh, Jō′el son of Pe·dai′ah; [21] for the half-tribe of Ma·nas′seh in Gil′e·ad, Id′dō son of Zech·a·rī′ah; for Benjamin, Jā·a·sī′el son of Abner;

[22] for Dan, Az′a·rel son of Je·rō′ham. These were the leaders of the tribes of Israel. [23] David did not count those below twenty years of age, for the LORD had promised to make Israel as numerous as the stars of heaven. [24] Jō′ab son of Ze·rū′i·ah began to count them, but did not finish; yet wrath came upon Israel for this, and the number was not entered into the account of the Annals of King David.

Other Civic Officials

25 Over the king's treasuries was Az′ma·veth son of Ad′i·el. Over the treasuries in the country, in the cities, in the villages and in the towers, was Jonathan son of Uz·zī′ah. [26] Over those who did the work of the field, tilling the soil, was Ez′rī son of Chē′lub. [27] Over the vineyards was Shim′e·ī the Rā′ma·thīte. Over the produce of the vineyards for the wine cellars was Zab′dī the Shiph′mīte. [28] Over the olive and sycamore trees in the She·phē′lah was Bā′al-hā′nan the Ge·dē′rīte. Over the stores of oil was Jō′ash. [29] Over the herds that pastured in Sharon was Shit′raī the Shār′on·īte. Over the herds in the valleys was Shā′phat son of Ad′lā·ī. [30] Over the camels was Ō′bil the Ish′ma·el·īte. Over the donkeys was Jeh·dē′i·ah the Me·ron′o·thīte. Over the flocks was Jā′ziz the Hag′rīte. [31] All these were stewards of King David's property.

32 Jonathan, David's uncle, was a counselor, being a man of understanding and a scribe; Je·hi′el son of Hach′mo·nī attended the king's sons. [33] A·hith′o·phel was the king's counselor, and Hū′shaī the Ar′chīte was the king's friend. [34] After A·hith′o·phel came Je·hoi′a·da son of Be·nā′i·ah, and A·bi′a·thar. Jō′ab was commander of the king's army.

Solomon Instructed to Build the Temple

28 David assembled at Jerusalem all the officials of Israel, the officials of the tribes, the officers of the divisions that served the king, the commanders of the thousands, the commanders of the hundreds, the stewards of all the property and cattle of the king and his sons, together with the palace officials, the mighty warriors, and all the warriors. [2] Then King

q Gk Vg: Heb Ammizabad was his division

David rose to his feet and said: "Hear me, my brothers and my people. I had planned to build a house of rest for the ark of the covenant of the LORD, for the footstool of our God; and I made preparations for building. ³But God said to me, 'You shall not build a house for my name, for you are a warrior and have shed blood.' ⁴Yet the LORD God of Israel chose me from all my ancestral house to be king over Israel forever; for he chose Judah as leader, and in the house of Judah my father's house, and among my father's sons he took delight in making me king over all Israel. ⁵And of all my sons, for the LORD has given me many, he has chosen my son Solomon to sit upon the throne of the kingdom of the LORD over Israel. ⁶He said to me, 'It is your son Solomon who shall build my house and my courts, for I have chosen him to be a son to me, and I will be a father to him. ⁷I will establish his kingdom forever if he continues resolute in keeping my commandments and my ordinances, as he is today.' ⁸Now therefore in the sight of all Israel, the assembly of the LORD, and in the hearing of our God, observe and search out all the commandments of the LORD your God; that you may possess this good land, and leave it for an inheritance to your children after you forever.

9 "And you, my son Solomon, know the God of your father, and serve him with single mind and willing heart; for the LORD searches every mind, and understands every plan and thought. If you seek him, he will be found by you; but if you forsake him, he will abandon you forever. ¹⁰Take heed now, for the LORD has chosen you to build a house as the sanctuary; be strong, and act."

11 Then David gave his son Solomon the plan of the vestibule of the temple, and of its houses, its treasuries, its upper rooms, and its inner chambers, and of the room for the mercy seat;ʳ ¹²and the plan of all that he had in mind: for the courts of the house of the LORD, all the surrounding chambers, the treasuries of the house of God, and the treasuries for dedicated gifts; ¹³for the divisions of the priests and of the Lĕ'vites, and all the work of the service in the house of the LORD; for all the vessels for the service in the house of the LORD, ¹⁴the weight of gold for all golden vessels for each service, the weight of silver vessels for each service, ¹⁵the weight of the golden lampstands and their lamps, the weight of gold for each lampstand and its lamps, the weight of silver for a lampstand and its lamps, according to the use of each in the service, ¹⁶the weight of gold for each table for the rows of bread, the silver for the silver tables, ¹⁷and pure gold for the forks, the basins, and the cups; for the golden bowls and the weight of each; for the silver bowls and the weight of each; ¹⁸for the altar of incense made of refined gold, and its weight; also his plan for the golden chariot of the cherubim that spread their wings and covered the ark of the covenant of the LORD.

19 "All this, in writing at the LORD's direction, he made clear to me—the plan of all the works."

20 David said further to his son Solomon, "Be strong and of good courage, and act. Do not be afraid or dismayed; for the LORD God, my God, is with you. He will not fail you or forsake you, until all the work for the service of the house of the LORD is finished. ²¹Here are the divisions of the priests and the Lĕ'vites for all the service of the house of God; and with you in all the work will be every volunteer who has skill for any kind of service; also the officers and all the people will be wholly at your command."

Offerings for Building the Temple

29 King David said to the whole assembly, "My son Solomon, whom alone God has chosen, is young and inexperienced, and the work is great; for the templeˢ will not be for mortals but for the LORD God. ²So I have provided for the house of my God, so far as I was able, the gold for the things of gold, the silver for the things of silver, and the bronze for the things of bronze, the iron for the things of iron, and wood for the things of wood, besides great quantities of onyx and stones for setting, antimony, colored stones, all sorts of precious stones, and marble in abundance. ³Moreover, in addition to all that I have provided for the holy house, I have a treasure of my own of gold and silver, and because of my devotion to the house of my God I give it to the house of my God: ⁴three thousand talents of gold, of the gold of Ō'phir, and seven thousand talents of refined silver, for overlaying the walls of the

ʳOr *the cover*   ˢHeb *fortress*

house, [5] and for all the work to be done by artisans, gold for the things of gold and silver for the things of silver. Who then will offer willingly, consecrating themselves today to the LORD?"

[6] Then the leaders of ancestral houses made their freewill offerings, as did also the leaders of the tribes, the commanders of the thousands and of the hundreds, and the officers over the king's work. [7] They gave for the service of the house of God five thousand talents and ten thousand darics of gold, ten thousand talents of silver, eighteen thousand talents of bronze, and one hundred thousand talents of iron. [8] Whoever had precious stones gave them to the treasury of the house of the LORD, into the care of Je·hī'el the Ger'shon·ite. [9] Then the people rejoiced because these had given willingly, for with single mind they had offered freely to the LORD; King David also rejoiced greatly.

David's Praise to God

[10] Then David blessed the LORD in the presence of all the assembly; David said: "Blessed are you, O LORD, the God of our ancestor Israel, forever and ever. [11] Yours, O LORD, are the greatness, the power, the glory, the victory, and the majesty; for all that is in the heavens and on the earth is yours; yours is the kingdom, O LORD, and you are exalted as head above all. [12] Riches and honor come from you, and you rule over all. In your hand are power and might; and it is in your hand to make great and to give strength to all. [13] And now, our God, we give thanks to you and praise your glorious name.

[14] "But who am I, and what is my people, that we should be able to make this freewill offering? For all things come from you, and of your own have we given you. [15] For we are aliens and transients before you, as were all our ancestors; our days on the earth are like a shadow, and there is no hope. [16] O LORD our God, all this abundance that we have provided for building you a house for your holy name comes from your hand and is all your own. [17] I know, my God, that you search the heart, and take pleasure in uprightness; in the uprightness of my heart I have freely offered all these things, and now I have seen your people, who are present here, offering freely and joyously to you. [18] O LORD, the God of Abraham, Isaac, and Israel, our ancestors, keep forever such purposes and thoughts in the hearts of your people, and direct their hearts toward you. [19] Grant to my son Solomon that with single mind he may keep your commandments, your decrees, and your statutes, performing all of them, and that he may build the temple[t] for which I have made provision."

[20] Then David said to the whole assembly, "Bless the LORD your God." And all the assembly blessed the LORD, the God of their ancestors, and bowed their heads and prostrated themselves before the LORD and the king. [21] On the next day they offered sacrifices and burnt offerings to the LORD, a thousand bulls, a thousand rams, and a thousand lambs, with their libations, and sacrifices in abundance for all Israel; [22] and they ate and drank before the LORD on that day with great joy.

Solomon Anointed King
(1 Kings 1.38–40; 2.12)

They made David's son Solomon king a second time; they anointed him as the LORD's prince, and Za'dok as priest. [23] Then Solomon sat on the throne of the LORD, succeeding his father David as king; he prospered, and all Israel obeyed him. [24] All the leaders and the mighty warriors, and also all the sons of King David, pledged their allegiance to King Solomon. [25] The LORD highly exalted Solomon in the sight of all Israel, and bestowed upon him such royal majesty as had not been on any king before him in Israel.

Summary of David's Reign

[26] Thus David son of Jesse reigned over all Israel. [27] The period that he reigned over Israel was forty years; he reigned seven years in He'bron, and thirty-three years in Jerusalem. [28] He died in a good old age, full of days, riches, and honor; and his son Solomon succeeded him. [29] Now the acts of King David, from first to last, are written in the records of the seer Samuel, and in the records of the prophet Nathan, and in the records of the seer Gad, [30] with accounts of all his rule and his might and of the events that befell him and Israel and all the kingdoms of the earth.

_t_ Heb _fortress_

1
C
H
R
O
N
I
C
L
E
S

2 CHRONICLES

Solomon Requests Wisdom
(1 Kings 3.1–15)

1 Solomon son of David established himself in his kingdom; the LORD his God was with him and made him exceedingly great.

2 Solomon summoned all Israel, the commanders of the thousands and of the hundreds, the judges, and all the leaders of all Israel, the heads of families. ³Then Solomon, and the whole assembly with him, went to the high place that was at Gib′e·on; for God's tent of meeting, which Moses the servant of the LORD had made in the wilderness, was there. ⁴(But David had brought the ark of God up from Kir′i·ath-je′a·rim to the place that David had prepared for it; for he had pitched a tent for it in Jerusalem.) ⁵Moreover the bronze altar that Bez′a·lel son of U′rī, son of Hur, had made, was there in front of the tabernacle of the LORD. And Solomon and the assembly inquired at it. ⁶Solomon went up there to the bronze altar before the LORD, which was at the tent of meeting, and offered a thousand burnt offerings on it.

7 That night God appeared to Solomon, and said to him, "Ask what I should give you." ⁸Solomon said to God, "You have shown great and steadfast love to my father David, and have made me succeed him as king. ⁹O LORD God, let your promise to my father David now be fulfilled, for you have made me king over a people as numerous as the dust of the earth. ¹⁰Give me now wisdom and knowledge to go out and come in before this people, for who can rule this great people of yours?" ¹¹God answered Solomon, "Because this was in your heart, and you have not asked for possessions, wealth, honor, or the life of those who hate you, and have not even asked for long life, but have asked for wisdom and knowledge for yourself that you may rule my people over whom I have made you king, ¹²wisdom and knowledge are granted to you. I will also give you riches, possessions, and honor, such as none of the kings had who were before you, and none after you shall have the like." ¹³So Solomon came from*a* the high place at Gib′e·on, from the tent of meeting, to Jerusalem. And he reigned over Israel.

Solomon's Military and Commercial Activity
(1 Kings 10.26–29; 2 Chr 9.25–28)

14 Solomon gathered together chariots and horses; he had fourteen hundred chariots and twelve thousand horses, which he stationed in the chariot cities and with the king in Jerusalem. ¹⁵The king made silver and gold as common in Jerusalem as stone, and he made cedar as plentiful as the sycamore of the She·phe′lah. ¹⁶Solomon's horses were imported from Egypt and Ku′e; the king's traders received them from Ku′e at the prevailing price. ¹⁷They imported from Egypt, and then exported, a chariot for six hundred shekels of silver, and a horse for one hundred fifty; so through them these were exported to all the kings of the Hit′tites and the kings of Ar′am.

Preparations for Building the Temple

2 *b*Solomon decided to build a temple for the name of the LORD, and a royal palace for himself. ²*c*Solomon conscripted seventy thousand laborers and eighty thousand stonecutters in the hill country, with three thousand six hundred to oversee them.

Alliance with Huram of Tyre
(1 Kings 5.1–18)

3 Solomon sent word to King Hu′ram of Tyre: "Once you dealt with my

---

*a*Gk Vg: Heb *to*   *b*Ch 1.18 in Heb
*c*Ch 2.1 in Heb

father David and sent him cedar to build himself a house to live in. 4 I am now about to build a house for the name of the LORD my God and dedicate it to him for offering fragrant incense before him, and for the regular offering of the rows of bread, and for burnt offerings morning and evening, on the sabbaths and the new moons and the appointed festivals of the LORD our God, as ordained forever for Israel. 5 The house that I am about to build will be great, for our God is greater than other gods. 6 But who is able to build him a house, since heaven, even highest heaven, cannot contain him? Who am I to build a house for him, except as a place to make offerings before him? 7 So now send me an artisan skilled to work in gold, silver, bronze, and iron, and in purple, crimson, and blue fabrics, trained also in engraving, to join the skilled workers who are with me in Judah and Jerusalem, whom my father David provided. 8 Send me also cedar, cypress, and algum timber from Lebanon, for I know that your servants are skilled in cutting Lebanon timber. My servants will work with your servants 9 to prepare timber for me in abundance, for the house I am about to build will be great and wonderful. 10 I will provide for your servants, those who cut the timber, twenty thousand cors of crushed wheat, twenty thousand cors of barley, twenty thousand baths d of wine, and twenty thousand baths of oil."

11 Then King Hū'ram of Tyre answered in a letter that he sent to Solomon, "Because the LORD loves his people he has made you king over them." 12 Hū'ram also said, "Blessed be the LORD God of Israel, who made heaven and earth, who has given King David a wise son, endowed with discretion and understanding, who will build a temple for the LORD, and a royal palace for himself. 13 "I have dispatched Hū'ram-ā'bī, a skilled artisan, endowed with understanding, 14 the son of one of the Dan'ite women, his father a Ty'ri·an. He is trained to work in gold, silver, bronze, iron, stone, and wood, and in purple, blue, and crimson fabrics and fine linen, and to do all sorts of engraving and execute any design that may be assigned him, with your artisans, the artisans of my lord, your father David. 15 Now, as for the wheat, barley, oil, and wine, of which my lord has

spoken, let him send them to his servants. 16 We will cut whatever timber you need from Lebanon, and bring it to you as rafts by sea to Jop'pa; you will take it up to Jerusalem."

17 Then Solomon took a census of all the aliens who were residing in the land of Israel, after the census that his father David had taken; and there were found to be one hundred fifty-three thousand six hundred. 18 Seventy thousand of them he assigned as laborers, eighty thousand as stonecutters in the hill country, and three thousand six hundred as overseers to make the people work.

Solomon Builds the Temple
(1 Kings 6.1–22)

3 Solomon began to build the house of the LORD in Jerusalem on Mount Mō·rī'ah, where the LORD had appeared to his father David, at the place that David had designated, on the threshing floor of Or'nan the Jeb'-ū·site. 2 He began to build on the second day of the second month of the fourth year of his reign. 3 These are Solomon's measurements e for building the house of God: the length, in cubits of the old standard, was sixty cubits, and the width twenty cubits. 4 The vestibule in front of the nave of the house was twenty cubits long, across the width of the house; f and its height was one hundred twenty cubits. He overlaid it on the inside with pure gold. 5 The nave he lined with cypress, covered it with fine gold, and made palms and chains on it. 6 He adorned the house with settings of precious stones. The gold was gold from Par·vā'im. 7 So he lined the house with gold—its beams, its thresholds, its walls, and its doors; and he carved cherubim on the walls.

8 He made the most holy place; its length, corresponding to the width of the house, was twenty cubits, and its width was twenty cubits; he overlaid it with six hundred talents of fine gold. 9 The weight of the nails was fifty shekels of gold. He overlaid the upper chambers with gold.

10 In the most holy place he made two carved cherubim and overlaid g

---

d A Hebrew measure of volume
e Syr: Heb foundations   f Compare 1 Kings 6.3: Meaning of Heb uncertain
g Heb *they overlaid*

them with gold. 11 The wings of the cherubim together extended twenty cubits: one wing of the one, five cubits long, touched the wall of the house, and its other wing, five cubits long, touched the wing of the other cherub; 12 and of this cherub, one wing, five cubits long, touched the wall of the house, and the other wing, also five cubits long, was joined to the wing of the first cherub. 13 The wings of these cherubim extended twenty cubits; the cherubim *h* stood on their feet, facing the nave. 14 And Solomon *i* made the curtain of blue and purple and crimson fabrics and fine linen, and worked cherubim into it.

15 In front of the house he made two pillars thirty-five cubits high, with a capital of five cubits on the top of each. 16 He made encircling *j* chains and put them on the tops of the pillars; and he made one hundred pomegranates, and put them on the chains. 17 He set up the pillars in front of the temple, one on the right, the other on the left; the one on the right he called Ja′chin, and the one on the left, Bo′az.

Furnishings of the Temple
(1 Kings 6.23–38; 7.13–51)

4 He made an altar of bronze, twenty cubits long, twenty cubits wide, and ten cubits high. 2 Then he made the molten sea; it was round, ten cubits from rim to rim, and five cubits high. A line of thirty cubits would encircle it completely. 3 Under it were panels all around, each of ten cubits, surrounding the sea; there were two rows of panels, cast when it was cast. 4 It stood on twelve oxen, three facing north, three facing west, three facing south, and three facing east; the sea was set on them. The hindquarters of each were toward the inside. 5 Its thickness was a handbreadth; its rim was made like the rim of a cup, like the flower of a lily; it held three thousand baths. *k* 6 He also made ten basins in which to wash, and set five on the right side, and five on the left. In these they were to rinse what was used for the burnt offering. The sea was for the priests to wash in.

7 He made ten golden lampstands as prescribed, and set them in the temple, five on the south side and five on the north. 8 He also made ten tables and placed them in the temple, five on the right side and five on the left. And

he made one hundred basins of gold. 9 He made the court of the priests, and the great court, and doors for the court; he overlaid their doors with bronze. 10 He set the sea at the southeast corner of the house.

11 And Hū′ram made the pots, the shovels, and the basins. Thus Hū′ram finished the work that he did for King Solomon on the house of God: 12 the two pillars, the bowls, and the two capitals on the top of the pillars; and the two latticeworks to cover the two bowls of the capitals that were on the top of the pillars; 13 the four hundred pomegranates for the two latticeworks, two rows of pomegranates for each latticework, to cover the two bowls of the capitals that were on the pillars. 14 He made the stands, the basins on the stands, 15 the one sea, and the twelve oxen underneath it. 16 The pots, the shovels, the forks, and all the equipment for these Hū′ram-ā′bī made of burnished bronze for King Solomon for the house of the LORD. 17 In the plain of the Jordan the king cast them, in the clay ground between Suc′coth and Zer′e·dah. 18 Solomon made all these things in great quantities, so that the weight of the bronze was not determined.

19 So Solomon made all the things that were in the house of God: the golden altar, the tables for the bread of the Presence, 20 the lampstands and their lamps of pure gold to burn before the inner sanctuary, as prescribed; 21 the flowers, the lamps, and the tongs, of purest gold; 22 the snuffers, basins, ladles, and firepans, of pure gold. As for the entrance to the temple: the inner doors to the most holy place and the doors of the nave of the temple were of gold.

5 Thus all the work that Solomon did for the house of the LORD was finished. Solomon brought in the things that his father David had dedicated, and stored the silver, the gold, and all the vessels in the treasuries of the house of God.

The Ark Brought into the Temple
(1 Kings 8.1–11)

2 Then Solomon assembled the el-

h Heb *they* *i* Heb *he* *j* Cn: Heb *in the inner sanctuary* *k* A Hebrew measure of volume ders of Israel and all the heads of the tribes, the leaders of the ancestral houses of the people of Israel, in Jerusalem, to bring up the ark of the covenant of the LORD out of the city of David, which is Zion. ³ And all the Israelites assembled before the king at the festival that is in the seventh month. ⁴ And all the elders of Israel came, and the Lē'vītes carried the ark. ⁵ So they brought up the ark, the tent of meeting, and all the holy vessels that were in the tent; the priests and the Lē'vītes brought them up. ⁶ King Solomon and all the congregation of Israel, who had assembled before him, were before the ark, sacrificing so many sheep and oxen that they could not be numbered or counted. ⁷ Then the priests brought the ark of the covenant of the LORD to its place, in the inner sanctuary of the house, in the most holy place, underneath the wings of the cherubim. ⁸ For the cherubim spread out their wings over the place of the ark, so that the cherubim made a covering above the ark and its poles. ⁹ The poles were so long that the ends of the poles were seen from the holy place in front of the inner sanctuary; but they could not be seen from outside; they are there to this day. ¹⁰ There was nothing in the ark except the two tablets that Moses put there at Hō'reb, where the LORD made a covenant*l* with the people of Israel after they came out of Egypt.

11 Now when the priests came out of the holy place (for all the priests who were present had sanctified themselves, without regard to their divisions, ¹² and all the levitical singers, Ā'saph, Hē'man, and Je·dū'thun, their sons and kindred, arrayed in fine linen, with cymbals, harps, and lyres, stood east of the altar with one hundred twenty priests who were trumpeters). ¹³ It was the duty of the trumpeters and singers to make themselves heard in unison in praise and thanksgiving to the LORD, and when the song was raised, with trumpets and cymbals and other musical instruments, in praise to the LORD,

"For he is good,
   for his steadfast love endures forever,"

the house, the house of the LORD, was filled with a cloud, ¹⁴ so that the priests could not stand to minister because of the cloud; for the glory of the LORD filled the house of God.

Dedication of the Temple
(1 Kings 8.12–21)

6 Then Solomon said, "The LORD has said that he would reside in thick darkness. ² I have built you an exalted house, a place for you to reside in forever."

3 Then the king turned around and blessed all the assembly of Israel, while all the assembly of Israel stood. ⁴ And he said, "Blessed be the LORD, the God of Israel, who with his hand has fulfilled what he promised with his mouth to my father David, saying, ⁵ 'Since the day that I brought my people out of the land of Egypt, I have not chosen a city from any of the tribes of Israel in which to build a house, so that my name might be there, and I chose no one as ruler over my people Israel; ⁶ but I have chosen Jerusalem in order that my name may be there, and I have chosen David to be over my people Israel.' ⁷ My father David had it in mind to build a house for the name of the LORD, the God of Israel. ⁸ But the LORD said to my father David, 'You did well to consider building a house for my name; ⁹ nevertheless you shall not build the house, but your son who shall be born to you shall build the house for my name.' ¹⁰ Now the LORD has fulfilled his promise that he made; for I have succeeded my father David, and sit on the throne of Israel, as the LORD promised, and have built the house for the name of the LORD, the God of Israel. ¹¹ There I have set the ark, in which is the covenant of the LORD that he made with the people of Israel."

Solomon's Prayer of Dedication
(1 Kings 8.22–53)

12 Then Solomon*m* stood before the altar of the LORD in the presence of the whole assembly of Israel, and spread out his hands. ¹³ Solomon had made a bronze platform five cubits long, five cubits wide, and three cubits high, and had set it in the court; and he stood on it. Then he knelt on his knees in the presence of the whole assembly of Israel, and spread out his hands toward heaven. ¹⁴ He said, "O LORD, God of Israel, there is no God like you, in heaven or on earth, keeping covenant in steadfast love with your servants who walk before you with all their heart— ¹⁵ you who have kept for your

l Heb lacks *a covenant*   *m* Heb *he*

servant, my father David, what you promised to him. Indeed, you promised with your mouth and this day have fulfilled with your hand. 16 Therefore, O LORD, God of Israel, keep for your servant, my father David, that which you promised him, saying, 'There shall never fail you a successor before me to sit on the throne of Israel, if only your children keep to their way, to walk in my law as you have walked before me.' 17 Therefore, O LORD, God of Israel, let your word be confirmed, which you promised to your servant David.

18 "But will God indeed reside with mortals on earth? Even heaven and the highest heaven cannot contain you, how much less this house that I have built! 19 Regard your servant's prayer and his plea, O LORD my God, heeding the cry and the prayer that your servant prays to you. 20 May your eyes be open day and night toward this house, the place where you promised to set your name, and may you heed the prayer that your servant prays toward this place. 21 And hear the plea of your servant and of your people Israel, when they pray toward this place; may you hear from heaven your dwelling place; hear and forgive.

22 "If someone sins against another and is required to take an oath and comes and swears before your altar in this house, 23 may you hear from heaven, and act, and judge your servants, repaying the guilty by bringing their conduct on their own head, and vindicating those who are in the right by rewarding them in accordance with their righteousness.

24 "When your people Israel, having sinned against you, are defeated before an enemy but turn again to you, confess your name, pray and plead with you in this house, 25 may you hear from heaven, and forgive the sin of your people Israel, and bring them again to the land that you gave to them and to their ancestors.

26 "When heaven is shut up and there is no rain because they have sinned against you, and then they pray toward this place, confess your name, and turn from their sin, because you punish them, 27 may you hear in heaven, forgive the sin of your servants, your people Israel, when you teach them the good way in which they should walk; and send down rain upon

your land, which you have given to your people as an inheritance.

28 "If there is famine in the land, if there is plague, blight, mildew, locust, or caterpillar; if their enemies besiege them in any of the settlements of the lands; whatever suffering, whatever sickness there is; 29 whatever prayer, whatever plea from any individual or from all your people Israel, all knowing their own suffering and their own sorrows so that they stretch out their hands toward this house; 30 may you hear from heaven, your dwelling place, forgive, and render to all whose heart you know, according to all their ways, for only you know the human heart. 31 Thus may they fear you and walk in your ways all the days that they live in the land that you gave to our ancestors.

32 "Likewise when foreigners, who are not of your people Israel, come from a distant land because of your great name, and your mighty hand, and your outstretched arm, when they come and pray toward this house, 33 may you hear from heaven your dwelling place, and do whatever the foreigners ask of you, in order that all the peoples of the earth may know your name and fear you, as do your people Israel, and that they may know that your name has been invoked on this house that I have built.

34 "If your people go out to battle against their enemies, by whatever way you shall send them, and they pray to you toward this city that you have chosen and the house that I have built for your name, 35 then hear from heaven their prayer and their plea, and maintain their cause.

36 "If they sin against you—for there is no one who does not sin—and you are angry with them and give them to an enemy, so that they are carried away captive to a land far or near; 37 then if they come to their senses in the land to which they have been taken captive, and repent, and plead with you in the land of their captivity, saying, 'We have sinned, and have done wrong; we have acted wickedly'; 38 if they repent with all their heart and soul in the land of their captivity, to which they were taken captive, and pray toward their land, which you gave to their ancestors, the city that you have chosen, and the house that I have built for your name, 39 then hear from heaven your dwelling place their

prayer and their pleas, maintain their cause and forgive your people who have sinned against you. 40 Now, O my God, let your eyes be open and your ears attentive to prayer from this place.

41 "Now rise up, O LORD God, and
     go to your resting place,
   you and the ark of your might.
Let your priests, O LORD God, be
     clothed with salvation,
and let your faithful rejoice in
     your goodness.
42 O LORD God, do not reject your
     anointed one.
Remember your steadfast love
     for your servant David."

Solomon Dedicates the Temple
(1 Kings 8.62–66)

7 When Solomon had ended his prayer, fire came down from heaven and consumed the burnt offering and the sacrifices; and the glory of the LORD filled the temple. 2 The priests could not enter the house of the LORD, because the glory of the LORD filled the LORD's house. 3 When all the people of Israel saw the fire come down and the glory of the LORD on the temple, they bowed down on the pavement with their faces to the ground, and worshiped and gave thanks to the LORD, saying,

"For he is good,
     for his steadfast love endures
     forever."

4 Then the king and all the people offered sacrifice before the LORD. 5 King Solomon offered as a sacrifice twenty-two thousand oxen and one hundred twenty thousand sheep. So the king and all the people dedicated the house of God. 6 The priests stood at their posts; the Lē'vītes also, with the instruments for music to the LORD that King David had made for giving thanks to the LORD—for his steadfast love endures forever—whenever David offered praises by their ministry. Opposite them the priests sounded trumpets; and all Israel stood.

7 Solomon consecrated the middle of the court that was in front of the house of the LORD; for there he offered the burnt offerings and the fat of the offerings of well-being because the bronze altar Solomon had made could not hold the burnt offering and the grain offering and the fat parts.

8 At that time Solomon held the festival for seven days, and all Israel with him, a very great congregation, from Lē'bō-ha'math to the Wadi of Egypt. 9 On the eighth day they held a solemn assembly; for they had observed the dedication of the altar seven days and the festival seven days. 10 On the twenty-third day of the seventh month he sent the people away to their homes, joyful and in good spirits because of the goodness that the LORD had shown to David and to Solomon and to his people Israel.

11 Thus Solomon finished the house of the LORD and the king's house; all that Solomon had planned to do in the house of the LORD and in his own house he successfully accomplished.

God's Second Appearance to Solomon
(1 Kings 9.1–9)

12 Then the LORD appeared to Solomon in the night and said to him: "I have heard your prayer, and have chosen this place for myself as a house of sacrifice. 13 When I shut up the heavens so that there is no rain, or command the locust to devour the land, or send pestilence among my people, 14 if my people who are called by my name humble themselves, pray, seek my face, and turn from their wicked ways, then I will hear from heaven, and will forgive their sin and heal their land. 15 Now my eyes will be open and my ears attentive to the prayer that is made in this place. 16 For now I have chosen and consecrated this house so that my name may be there forever; my eyes and my heart will be there for all time. 17 As for you, if you walk before me, as your father David walked, doing according to all that I have commanded you and keeping my statutes and my ordinances, 18 then I will establish your royal throne, as I made covenant with your father David saying, 'You shall never lack a successor to rule over Israel.'

19 "But if you[n] turn aside and forsake my statutes and my commandments that I have set before you, and go and serve other gods and worship them, 20 then I will pluck you[o] up from the land that I have given you;[o] and this house, which I have consecrated for my name, I will cast out of my sight, and will make it a proverb and a byword among all peoples. 21 And re-

---

n The word *you* in this verse is plural
o Heb *them*

2
C
H
R
O
N
I
C
L
E
S

garding this house, now exalted, everyone passing by will be astonished, and say, 'Why has the LORD done such a thing to this land and to this house?' [22] Then they will say, 'Because they abandoned the LORD the God of their ancestors who brought them out of the land of Egypt, and they adopted other gods, and worshiped them and served them; therefore he has brought all this calamity upon them.' "

Various Activities of Solomon
(1 Kings 9.10–28)

8 At the end of twenty years, during which Solomon had built the house of the LORD and his own house, [2] Solomon rebuilt the cities that Hū'ram had given to him, and settled the people of Israel in them.

[3] Solomon went to Hă'math-zō'bah, and captured it. [4] He built Tad'mor in the wilderness and all the storage towns that he built in Hā'math. [5] He also built Upper Beth-hō'ron and Lower Beth-hō'ron, fortified cities, with walls, gates, and bars, [6] and Bā'a·lath, as well as all Solomon's storage towns, and all the towns for his chariots, the towns for his cavalry, and whatever Solomon desired to build, in Jerusalem, in Lebanon, and in all the land of his dominion. [7] All the people who were left of the Hit'tītes, the Am'o·rītes, the Per'iz·zītes, the Hī'vītes, and the Jeb'ū·sītes, who were not of Israel, [8] from their descendants who were still left in the land, whom the people of Israel had not destroyed—these Solomon conscripted for forced labor, as is still the case today. [9] But of the people of Israel Solomon made no slaves for his work; they were soldiers, and his officers, the commanders of his chariotry and cavalry. [10] These were the chief officers of King Solomon, two hundred fifty of them, who exercised authority over the people.

[11] Solomon brought Pharaoh's daughter from the city of David to the house that he had built for her, for he said, "My wife shall not live in the house of King David of Israel, for the places to which the ark of the LORD has come are holy."

[12] Then Solomon offered up burnt offerings to the LORD on the altar of the LORD that he had built in front of the vestibule, [13] as the duty of each day required, offering according to the commandment of Moses for the sabbaths, the new moons, and the three annual festivals—the festival of unleavened bread, the festival of weeks, and the festival of booths. [14] According to the ordinance of his father David, he appointed the divisions of the priests for their service, and the Lē'vītes for their offices of praise and ministry alongside the priests as the duty of each day required, and the gatekeepers in their divisions for the several gates; for so David the man of God had commanded. [15] They did not turn away from what the king had commanded the priests and Lē'vītes regarding anything at all, or regarding the treasuries.

16 Thus all the work of Solomon was accomplished from[p] the day the foundation of the house of the LORD was laid until the house of the LORD was finished completely.

17 Then Solomon went to Ē'zion-gē'ber and Ē'loth on the shore of the sea, in the land of Ē'dom. [18] Hū'ram sent him, in the care of his servants, ships and servants familiar with the sea. They went to Ō'phir, together with the servants of Solomon, and imported from there four hundred fifty talents of gold and brought it to King Solomon.

Visit of the Queen of Sheba
(1 Kings 10.1–13)

9 When the queen of Shē'ba heard of the fame of Solomon, she came to Jerusalem to test him with hard questions, having a very great retinue and camels bearing spices and very much gold and precious stones. When she came to Solomon, she discussed with him all that was on her mind. [2] Solomon answered all her questions; there was nothing hidden from Solomon that he could not explain to her. [3] When the queen of Shē'ba had observed the wisdom of Solomon, the house that he had built, [4] the food of his table, the seating of his officials, and the attendance of his servants, and their clothing, his valets, and their clothing; and his burnt offerings[q] that he offered at the house of the LORD, there was no more spirit left in her.

5 So she said to the king, "The report was true that I heard in my own land of your accomplishments and of your wisdom, [6] but I did not believe the[r] reports until I came and my own

p Gk Syr Vg: Heb *to*   *q* Gk Syr Vg 1 Kings 10.5: Heb *ascent*   *r* Heb *their* eyes saw it. Not even half of the greatness of your wisdom had been told to me; you far surpass the report that I had heard. [7] Happy are your people! Happy are these your servants, who continually attend you and hear your wisdom! [8] Blessed be the LORD your God, who has delighted in you and set you on his throne as king for the LORD your God. Because your God loved Israel and would establish them forever, he has made you king over them, that you may execute justice and righteousness." [9] Then she gave the king one hundred twenty talents of gold, a very great quantity of spices, and precious stones: there were no spices such as those that the queen of Shē'ba gave to King Solomon.

10 Moreover the servants of Hū'ram and the servants of Solomon who brought gold from Ō'phir brought algum wood and precious stones. [11] From the algum wood, the king made steps[s] for the house of the LORD and for the king's house, lyres also and harps for the singers; there never was seen the like of them before in the land of Judah.

12 Meanwhile King Solomon granted the queen of Shē'ba every desire that she expressed, well beyond what she had brought to the king. Then she returned to her own land, with her servants.

Solomon's Great Wealth
(1 Kings 10.14–29; 2 Chr 1.14–17)

13 The weight of gold that came to Solomon in one year was six hundred sixty-six talents of gold, [14] besides that which the traders and merchants brought; and all the kings of Arabia and the governors of the land brought gold and silver to Solomon. [15] King Solomon made two hundred large shields of beaten gold; six hundred shekels of beaten gold went into each large shield. [16] He made three hundred shields of beaten gold; three hundred shekels of gold went into each shield; and the king put them in the House of the Forest of Lebanon. [17] The king also made a great ivory throne, and overlaid it with pure gold. [18] The throne had six steps and a footstool of gold, which were attached to the throne, and on each side of the seat were arm rests and two lions standing beside the arm rests, [19] while twelve lions were standing, one on each end of a step on the six steps. The like of it was never made in

any kingdom. [20] All King Solomon's drinking vessels were of gold, and all the vessels of the House of the Forest of Lebanon were of pure gold; silver was not considered as anything in the days of Solomon. [21] For the king's ships went to Tar'shish with the servants of Hū'ram; once every three years the ships of Tar'shish used to come bringing gold, silver, ivory, apes, and peacocks.[t]

22 Thus King Solomon excelled all the kings of the earth in riches and in wisdom. [23] All the kings of the earth sought the presence of Solomon to hear his wisdom, which God had put into his mind. [24] Every one of them brought a present, objects of silver and gold, garments, weaponry, spices, horses, and mules, so much year by year. [25] Solomon had four thousand stalls for horses and chariots, and twelve thousand horses, which he stationed in the chariot cities and with the king in Jerusalem. [26] He ruled over all the kings from the Euphrates to the land of the Phi·lis'tines, and to the border of Egypt. [27] The king made silver as common in Jerusalem as stone, and cedar as plentiful as the sycamore of the She·phē'lah. [28] Horses were imported for Solomon from Egypt and from all lands.

Death of Solomon
(1 Kings 11.41–43)

29 Now the rest of the acts of Solomon, from first to last, are they not written in the history of the prophet Nathan, and in the prophecy of A·hī'jah the Shī'lo·nīte, and in the visions of the seer Id'dō concerning Jer·o·bō'am son of Ne'bat? [30] Solomon reigned in Jerusalem over all Israel forty years. [31] Solomon slept with his ancestors and was buried in the city of his father David; and his son Rē·ho·bō'am succeeded him.

The Revolt against Rehoboam
(1 Kings 12.1–19)

10 Rē·ho·bō'am went to Shē'chem, for all Israel had come to Shē'chem to make him king. [2] When Jer·o·bō'am son of Ne'bat heard of it (for he was in Egypt, where he had fled from King Solomon), then Jer·o·bō'am returned from Egypt. [3] They sent and called him; and Jer·o·bō'am and all Is-

[s] Gk Vg: Meaning of Heb uncertain
[t] Or baboons

rael came and said to Rē·ho·bō'am, ⁴"Your father made our yoke heavy. Now therefore lighten the hard service of your father and his heavy yoke that he placed on us, and we will serve you." ⁵He said to them, "Come to me again in three days." So the people went away.

6 Then King Rē·ho·bō'am took counsel with the older men who had attended his father Solomon while he was still alive, saying, "How do you advise me to answer this people?" ⁷They answered him, "If you will be kind to this people and please them, and speak good words to them, then they will be your servants forever." ⁸But he rejected the advice that the older men gave him, and consulted the young men who had grown up with him and now attended him. ⁹He said to them, "What do you advise that we answer this people who have said to me, 'Lighten the yoke that your father put on us'?" ¹⁰The young men who had grown up with him said to him, "Thus should you speak to the people who said to you, 'Your father made our yoke heavy, but you must lighten it for us'; tell them, 'My little finger is thicker than my father's loins. ¹¹Now, whereas my father laid on you a heavy yoke, I will add to your yoke. My father disciplined you with whips, but I will discipline you with scorpions.' "

12 So Jer·o·bō'am and all the people came to Rē·ho·bō'am the third day, as the king had said, "Come to me again the third day." ¹³The king answered them harshly. King Rē·ho·bō'am rejected the advice of the older men; ¹⁴he spoke to them in accordance with the advice of the young men, "My father made your yoke heavy, but I will add to it; my father disciplined you with whips, but I will discipline you with scorpions." ¹⁵So the king did not listen to the people, because it was a turn of affairs brought about by God so that the LORD might fulfill his word, which he had spoken by A·hī'jah the Shī'lo·nīte to Jer·o·bō'am son of Ne'bat.

16 When all Israel saw that the king would not listen to them, the people answered the king,

"What share do we have in
    David?
We have no inheritance in the
    son of Jesse.
Each of you to your tents,
    O Israel!

Look now to your own house,
    O David."

So all Israel departed to their tents. ¹⁷But Rē·ho·bō'am reigned over the people of Israel who were living in the cities of Judah. ¹⁸When King Rē·ho·bō'am sent Ha·dor'am, who was taskmaster over the forced labor, the people of Israel stoned him to death. King Rē·ho·bō'am hurriedly mounted his chariot to flee to Jerusalem. ¹⁹So Israel has been in rebellion against the house of David to this day.

Judah and Benjamin Fortified
(1 Kings 12.20–24)

11 When Rē·ho·bō'am came to Jerusalem, he assembled one hundred eighty thousand chosen troops of the house of Judah and Benjamin to fight against Israel, to restore the kingdom to Rē·ho·bō'am. ²But the word of the LORD came to She·māi'ah the man of God: ³Say to King Rē·ho·bō'am of Judah, son of Solomon, and to all Israel in Judah and Benjamin, ⁴"Thus says the LORD: You shall not go up or fight against your kindred. Let everyone return home, for this thing is from me." So they heeded the word of the LORD and turned back from the expedition against Jer·o·bō'am.

5 Rē·ho·bō'am resided in Jerusalem, and he built cities for defense in Judah. ⁶He built up Bethlehem, Ē'tam, Te·kō'a, ⁷Beth-zur, Sō'cō, A·dul'lam, ⁸Gath, Ma·rē'shah, Ziph, ⁹Ad·o·rā'im, Lā'chish, A·zē'kah, ¹⁰Zō'rah, Ai'ja·lon, and Hē'bron, fortified cities that are in Judah and in Benjamin. ¹¹He made the fortresses strong, and put commanders in them, and stores of food, oil, and wine. ¹²He also put large shields and spears in all the cities, and made them very strong. So he held Judah and Benjamin.

Priests and Levites Support Rehoboam
(1 Kings 14.21–24)

13 The priests and the Lē'vītes who were in all Israel presented themselves to him from all their territories. ¹⁴The Lē'vītes had left their common lands and their holdings and had come to Judah and Jerusalem, because Jer·o·bō'am and his sons had prevented them from serving as priests of the LORD, ¹⁵and had appointed his own priests for the high places, and for the goat-demons, and for the calves that he had made. ¹⁶Those who had set

their hearts to seek the LORD God of Israel came after them from all the tribes of Israel to Jerusalem to sacrifice to the LORD, the God of their ancestors. [17] They strengthened the kingdom of Judah, and for three years they made Rē·ho·bō′am son of Solomon secure, for they walked for three years in the way of David and Solomon.

Rehoboam's Marriages

18 Rē·ho·bō′am took as his wife Mā′ha·lath daughter of Jer′i·moth son of David, and of Ab·i·hā′il daughter of E·lī′ab son of Jesse. [19] She bore him sons: Jē′ush, Shem·a·rī′ah, and Zā′-ham. [20] After her he took Mā′a·cah daughter of Ab′sa·lom, who bore him A·bī′jah, At′tai, Zī′za, and She·lō′-mith. [21] Rē·ho·bō′am loved Mā′a·cah daughter of Ab′sa·lom more than all his other wives and concubines (he took eighteen wives and sixty concubines, and became the father of twenty-eight sons and sixty daughters). [22] Rē·ho·bō′am appointed A·bī′-jah son of Mā′a·cah as chief prince among his brothers, for he intended to make him king. [23] He dealt wisely, and distributed some of his sons through all the districts of Judah and Benjamin, in all the fortified cities; he gave them abundant provisions, and found many wives for them.

Egypt Attacks Judah
(1 Kings 14.25–28)

12 When the rule of Rē·ho·bō′am was established and he grew strong, he abandoned the law of the LORD, he and all Israel with him. [2] In the fifth year of King Rē·ho·bō′am, because they had been unfaithful to the LORD, King Shī′shak of Egypt came up against Jerusalem [3] with twelve hundred chariots and sixty thousand cavalry. A countless army came with him from Egypt—Libyans, Suk′ki·im, and Ethiopians. [u] [4] He took the fortified cities of Judah and came as far as Jerusalem. [5] Then the prophet She·māi′ah came to Rē·ho·bō′am and to the officers of Judah, who had gathered at Jerusalem because of Shī′shak, and said to them, "Thus says the LORD: You abandoned me, so I have abandoned you to the hand of Shī′shak." [6] Then the officers of Israel and the king humbled themselves and said, "The LORD is in the right." [7] When the LORD saw that they humbled themselves, the word of the LORD came to She·māi′ah, saying:

"They have humbled themselves; I will not destroy them, but I will grant them some deliverance, and my wrath shall not be poured out on Jerusalem by the hand of Shī′shak. [8] Nevertheless they shall be his servants, so that they may know the difference between serving me and serving the kingdoms of other lands."

9 So King Shī′shak of Egypt came up against Jerusalem; he took away the treasures of the house of the LORD and the treasures of the king's house; he took everything. He also took away the shields of gold that Solomon had made; [10] but King Rē·ho·bō′am made in place of them shields of bronze, and committed them to the hands of the officers of the guard, who kept the door of the king's house. [11] Whenever the king went into the house of the LORD, the guard would come along bearing them, and would then bring them back to the guardroom. [12] Because he humbled himself the wrath of the LORD turned from him, so as not to destroy them completely; moreover, conditions were good in Judah.

Death of Rehoboam
(1 Kings 14.21–22, 29–31)

13 So King Rē·ho·bō′am established himself in Jerusalem and reigned. Rē·ho·bō′am was forty-one years old when he began to reign; he reigned seventeen years in Jerusalem, the city that the LORD had chosen out of all the tribes of Israel to put his name there. His mother's name was Nā′a·mah the Am′mon·īte. [14] He did evil, for he did not set his heart to seek the LORD.

15 Now the acts of Rē·ho·bō′am, from first to last, are they not written in the records of the prophet She·māi′ah and of the seer Id′dō, recorded by genealogy? There were continual wars between Rē·ho·bō′am and Jer·o·bō′am. [16] Rē·ho·bō′am slept with his ancestors and was buried in the city of David; and his son A·bī′jah succeeded him.

Abijah Reigns over Judah
(1 Kings 15.1–8)

13 In the eighteenth year of King Jer·o·bō′am, A·bī′jah began to reign over Judah. [2] He reigned for three years in Jerusalem. His mother's

u Or Nubians; Heb Cushites

name was Mī·cāi′ah daughter of Ū·rī′el of Gib′e·ah.

Now there was war between A·bī′jah and Jer·o·bō′am. [3] A·bī′jah engaged in battle, having an army of valiant warriors, four hundred thousand picked men; and Jer·o·bō′am drew up his line of battle against him with eight hundred thousand picked mighty warriors. [4] Then A·bī′jah stood on the slope of Mount Zem·a·rā′im that is in the hill country of E′phra·im, and said, "Listen to me, Jer·o·bō′am and all Israel! [5] Do you not know that the LORD God of Israel gave the kingship over Israel forever to David and his sons by a covenant of salt? [6] Yet Jer·o·bō′am son of Ne′bat, a servant of Solomon son of David, rose up and rebelled against his lord; [7] and certain worthless scoundrels gathered around him and defied Rē·ho·bō′am son of Solomon, when Rē·ho·bō′am was young and irresolute and could not withstand them.

[8] "And now you think that you can withstand the kingdom of the LORD in the hand of the sons of David, because you are a great multitude and have with you the golden calves that Jer·o·bō′am made as gods for you. [9] Have you not driven out the priests of the LORD, the descendants of Aaron, and the Lē′vites, and made priests for yourselves like the peoples of other lands? Whoever comes to be consecrated with a young bull or seven rams becomes a priest of what are no gods. [10] But as for us, the LORD is our God, and we have not abandoned him. We have priests ministering to the LORD who are descendants of Aaron, and Lē′vites for their service. [11] They offer to the LORD every morning and every evening burnt offerings and fragrant incense, set out the rows of bread on the table of pure gold, and care for the golden lampstand so that its lamps may burn every evening; for we keep the charge of the LORD our God, but you have abandoned him. [12] See, God is with us at our head, and his priests have their battle trumpets to sound the call to battle against you. O Israelites, do not fight against the LORD, the God of your ancestors; for you cannot succeed."

[13] Jer·o·bō′am had sent an ambush around to come on them from behind; thus his troops[v] were in front of Judah, and the ambush was behind them. [14] When Judah turned, the battle was in front of them and behind them. They cried out to the LORD, and the priests blew the trumpets. [15] Then the people of Judah raised the battle shout. And when the people of Judah shouted, God defeated Jer·o·bō′am and all Israel before A·bī′jah and Judah. [16] The Israelites fled before Judah, and God gave them into their hands. [17] A·bī′jah and his army defeated them with great slaughter; five hundred thousand picked men of Israel fell slain. [18] Thus the Israelites were subdued at that time, and the people of Judah prevailed, because they relied on the LORD, the God of their ancestors. [19] A·bī′jah pursued Jer·o·bō′am, and took cities from him: Beth′el with its villages and Je·shā′nah with its villages and E′phron[w] with its villages. [20] Jer·o·bō′am did not recover his power in the days of A·bī′jah; the LORD struck him down, and he died. [21] But A·bī′jah grew strong. He took fourteen wives, and became the father of twenty-two sons and sixteen daughters. [22] The rest of the acts of A·bī′jah, his behavior and his deeds, are written in the story of the prophet Id′dō.

Asa Reigns
(1 Kings 15.9–15)

14 [x] So A·bī′jah slept with his ancestors, and they buried him in the city of David. His son Asa succeeded him. In his days the land had rest for ten years. [2] [y] Asa did what was good and right in the sight of the LORD his God. [3] He took away the foreign altars and the high places, broke down the pillars, hewed down the sacred poles,[z] [4] and commanded Judah to seek the LORD, the God of their ancestors, and to keep the law and the commandment. [5] He also removed from all the cities of Judah the high places and the incense altars. And the kingdom had rest under him. [6] He built fortified cities in Judah while the land had rest. He had no war in those years, for the LORD gave him peace. [7] He said to Judah, "Let us build these cities, and surround them with walls and towers, gates and bars; the land is still ours because we have sought the LORD our God; we have sought him, and he has given us peace on every side." So they built and prospered. [8] Asa had an army

v Heb *they*   w Another reading is *Ephrain*   x Ch 13.23 in Heb   y Ch 14.1 in Heb   z Heb *Asherim* of three hundred thousand from Judah, armed with large shields and spears, and two hundred eighty thousand troops from Benjamin who carried shields and drew bows; all these were mighty warriors.

Ethiopian Invasion Repulsed

9 Zē'rah the Ethiopian[a] came out against them with an army of a million men and three hundred chariots, and came as far as Ma·rē'shah. [10]Asa went out to meet him, and they drew up their lines of battle in the valley of Zeph'a·thah at Ma·rē'shah. [11]Asa cried to the LORD his God, "O LORD, there is no difference for you between helping the mighty and the weak. Help us, O LORD our God, for we rely on you, and in your name we have come against this multitude. O LORD, you are our God; let no mortal prevail against you." [12]So the LORD defeated the Ethiopians[b] before Asa and before Judah, and the Ethiopians[b] fled. [13]Asa and the army with him pursued them as far as Gē'rar, and the Ethiopians[b] fell until no one remained alive; for they were broken before the LORD and his army. The people of Judah[c] carried away a great quantity of booty. [14]They defeated all the cities around Gē'rar, for the fear of the LORD was on them. They plundered all the cities; for there was much plunder in them. [15]They also attacked the tents of those who had livestock,[d] and carried away sheep and goats in abundance, and camels. Then they returned to Jerusalem.

15 The spirit of God came upon Az·a·rī'ah son of Ō'ded. [2]He went out to meet Asa and said to him, "Hear me, Asa, and all Judah and Benjamin: The LORD is with you, while you are with him. If you seek him, he will be found by you, but if you abandon him, he will abandon you. [3]For a long time Israel was without the true God, and without a teaching priest, and without law; [4]but when in their distress they turned to the LORD, the God of Israel, and sought him, he was found by them. [5]In those times it was not safe for anyone to go or come, for great disturbances afflicted all the inhabitants of the lands. [6]They were broken in pieces, nation against nation and city against city, for God troubled them with every sort of distress. [7]But you, take courage! Do not let your hands be weak, for your work shall be rewarded."

8 When Asa heard these words, the prophecy of Az·a·rī'ah son of Ō'ded,[e] he took courage, and put away the abominable idols from all the land of Judah and Benjamin and from the towns that he had taken in the hill country of Ē'phra·im. He repaired the altar of the LORD that was in front of the vestibule of the house of the LORD.[f] [9]He gathered all Judah and Benjamin, and those from Ē'phra·im, Ma·nas'seh, and Sim'ē·on who were residing as aliens with them, for great numbers had deserted to him from Israel when they saw that the LORD his God was with him. [10]They were gathered at Jerusalem in the third month of the fifteenth year of the reign of Asa. [11]They sacrificed to the LORD on that day, from the booty that they had brought, seven hundred oxen and seven thousand sheep. [12]They entered into a covenant to seek the LORD, the God of their ancestors, with all their heart and with all their soul. [13]Whoever would not seek the LORD, the God of Israel, should be put to death, whether young or old, man or woman. [14]They took an oath to the LORD with a loud voice, and with shouting, and with trumpets, and with horns. [15]All Judah rejoiced over the oath; for they had sworn with all their heart, and had sought him with their whole desire, and he was found by them, and the LORD gave them rest all around.

16 King Asa even removed his mother Mā'a·cah from being queen mother because she had made an abominable image for A·shē'rah. Asa cut down her image, crushed it, and burned it at the Wadi Kid'ron. [17]But the high places were not taken out of Israel. Nevertheless the heart of Asa was true all his days. [18]He brought into the house of God the votive gifts of his father and his own votive gifts—silver, gold, and utensils. [19]And there was no more war until the thirty-fifth year of the reign of Asa.

Alliance with Aram Condemned
(1 Kings 15.16–22)

16 In the thirty-sixth year of the reign of Asa, King Bā'a·sha of Israel went up against Judah, and built

[a] Or Nubian; Heb Cushite
[b] Or Nubians; Heb Cushites　　[c] Heb They
[d] Meaning of Heb uncertain　　[e] Compare Syr Vg: Heb the prophecy, the prophet Obed　　[f] Heb the vestibule of the LORD

Ra′mah, to prevent anyone from going out or coming into the territory of^g King Asa of Judah. 2 Then Asa took silver and gold from the treasures of the house of the LORD and the king's house, and sent them to King Ben-ha′-dad of Ar′am, who resided in Damascus, saying, 3 "Let there be an alliance between me and you, like that between my father and your father; I am sending to you silver and gold; go, break your alliance with King Ba′a·sha of Israel, so that he may withdraw from me." 4 Ben-ha′dad listened to King Asa, and sent the commanders of his armies against the cities of Israel. They conquered I′jon, Dan, A′bel-ma′im, and all the store-cities of Naph′ta·li. 5 When Ba′a·sha heard of it, he stopped building Ra′mah, and let his work cease. 6 Then King Asa brought all Judah, and they carried away the stones of Ra′mah and its timber, with which Ba′a·sha had been building, and with them he built up Ge′ba and Miz′-pah.

7 At that time the seer Ha·na′ni came to King Asa of Judah, and said to him, "Because you relied on the king of Ar′am, and did not rely on the LORD your God, the army of the king of Ar′am has escaped you. 8 Were not the Ethiopians^h and the Libyans a huge army with exceedingly many chariots and cavalry? Yet because you relied on the LORD, he gave them into your hand. 9 For the eyes of the LORD range throughout the entire earth, to strengthen those whose heart is true to him. You have done foolishly in this; for from now on you will have wars." 10 Then Asa was angry with the seer, and put him in the stocks, in prison, for he was in a rage with him because of this. And Asa inflicted cruelties on some of the people at the same time.

Asa's Disease and Death
(1 Kings 15.23–24)

11 The acts of Asa, from first to last, are written in the Book of the Kings of Judah and Israel. 12 In the thirty-ninth year of his reign Asa was diseased in his feet, and his disease became severe; yet even in his disease he did not seek the LORD, but sought help from physicians. 13 Then Asa slept with his ancestors, dying in the forty-first year of his reign. 14 They buried him in the tomb that he had hewn out for himself in the city of David. They laid him on a bier that had been filled with various kinds of spices prepared by the perfumer's art; and they made a very great fire in his honor.

Jehoshaphat's Reign

17 His son Je·hosh′a·phat succeeded him, and strengthened himself against Israel. 2 He placed forces in all the fortified cities of Judah, and set garrisons in the land of Judah, and in the cities of E′phra·im that his father Asa had taken. 3 The LORD was with Je·hosh′a·phat, because he walked in the earlier ways of his father;^{i} he did not seek the Ba′als, 4 but sought the God of his father and walked in his commandments, and not according to the ways of Israel. 5 Therefore the LORD established the kingdom in his hand. All Judah brought tribute to Je·hosh′a·phat, and he had great riches and honor. 6 His heart was courageous in the ways of the LORD; and furthermore he removed the high places and the sacred poles^j from Judah.

7 In the third year of his reign he sent his officials, Ben-ha′il, O·ba·di′ah, Zech·a·ri′ah, Ne·than′el, and Mi·cai′ah, to teach in the cities of Judah. 8 With them were the Le′vites, She·mai′ah, Neth·a·ni′ah, Zeb·a·di′-ah, As′a·hel, She·mir′a·moth, Je·hon′-a·than, Ad·o·ni′jah, To·bi′jah, and Tob-ad·o·ni′jah; and with these Le′-vites, the priests E·lish′a·ma and Je·ho′ram. 9 They taught in Judah, having the book of the law of the LORD with them; they went around through all the cities of Judah and taught among the people.

10 The fear of the LORD fell on all the kingdoms of the lands around Judah, and they did not make war against Je·hosh′a·phat. 11 Some of the Phi·lis′tines brought Je·hosh′a·phat presents, and silver for tribute; and the Arabs also brought him seven thousand seven hundred rams and seven thousand seven hundred male goats. 12 Je·hosh′a·phat grew steadily greater. He built fortresses and storage cities in Judah. 13 He carried out great works in the cities of Judah. He had soldiers, mighty warriors, in Jerusalem. 14 This was the muster of them by ancestral houses: Of Judah, the

---

^{g} Heb lacks *the territory of*
^{h} Or *Nubians;* Heb *Cushites* ^{i} Another reading is *his father David*
^{j} Heb *Asherim*

commanders of the thousands: Ad′nah the commander, with three hundred thousand mighty warriors, 15 and next to him Je·hō·hā′nan the commander, with two hundred eighty thousand, 16 and next to him Am·a·si′ah son of Zich′rī, a volunteer for the service of the LORD, with two hundred thousand mighty warriors. 17 Of Benjamin: E·lī′·a·da, a mighty warrior, with two hundred thousand armed with bow and shield, 18 and next to him Je·hō′za·bad with one hundred eighty thousand armed for war. 19 These were in the service of the king, besides those whom the king had placed in the fortified cities throughout all Judah.

Micaiah Predicts Failure
(1 Kings 22.1–28)

18 Now Je·hosh′a·phat had great riches and honor; and he made a marriage alliance with A′hab. 2 After some years he went down to A′hab in Sa·mār′i·a. A′hab slaughtered an abundance of sheep and oxen for him and for the people who were with him, and induced him to go up against Rā′moth-gil′ē·ad. 3 King A′hab of Israel said to King Je·hosh′a·phat of Judah, "Will you go with me to Rā′moth-gil′ē·ad?" He answered him, "I am with you, my people are your people. We will be with you in the war."

4 But Je·hosh′a·phat also said to the king of Israel, "Inquire first for the word of the LORD." 5 Then the king of Israel gathered the prophets together, four hundred of them, and said to them, "Shall we go to battle against Rā′moth-gil′ē·ad, or shall I refrain?" They said, "Go up; for God will give it into the hand of the king." 6 But Je·hosh′a·phat said, "Is there no other prophet of the LORD here of whom we may inquire?" 7 The king of Israel said to Je·hosh′a·phat, "There is still one other by whom we may inquire of the LORD, Mī·cāi′ah son of Im′lah; but I hate him, for he never prophesies anything favorable about me, but only disaster." Je·hosh′a·phat said, "Let the king not say such a thing." 8 Then the king of Israel summoned an officer and said, "Bring quickly Mī·cāi′ah son of Im′lah." 9 Now the king of Israel and King Je·hosh′a·phat of Judah were sitting on their thrones, arrayed in their robes; and they were sitting at the threshing floor at the entrance of the gate of Sa·mār′i·a; and all the prophets were prophesying before them.

10 Zed·e·kī′ah son of Che·nā′a·nah made for himself horns of iron, and he said, "Thus says the LORD: With these you shall gore the Ar·a·mē′ans until they are destroyed." 11 All the prophets were prophesying the same and saying, "Go up to Rā′moth-gil′ē·ad and triumph; the LORD will give it into the hand of the king."

12 The messenger who had gone to summon Mī·cāi′ah said to him, "Look, the words of the prophets with one accord are favorable to the king; let your word be like the word of one of them, and speak favorably." 13 But Mī·cāi′ah said, "As the LORD lives, whatever my God says, that I will speak."

14 When he had come to the king, the king said to him, "Mī·cāi′ah, shall we go to Rā′moth-gil′ē·ad to battle, or shall I refrain?" He answered, "Go up and triumph; they will be given into your hand." 15 But the king said to him, "How many times must I make you swear to tell me nothing but the truth in the name of the LORD?" 16 Then Mī·cāi′ah[k] said, "I saw all Israel scattered on the mountains, like sheep without a shepherd; and the LORD said, 'These have no master; let each one go home in peace.' " 17 The king of Israel said to Je·hosh′a·phat, "Did I not tell you that he would not prophesy anything favorable about me, but only disaster?"

18 Then Mī·cāi′ah[k] said, "Therefore hear the word of the LORD: I saw the LORD sitting on his throne, with all the host of heaven standing to the right and to the left of him. 19 And the LORD said, 'Who will entice King A′hab of Israel, so that he may go up and fall at Rā′moth-gil′ē·ad?' Then one said one thing, and another said another, 20 until a spirit came forward and stood before the LORD, saying, 'I will entice him.' The LORD asked him, 'How?' 21 He replied, 'I will go out and be a lying spirit in the mouth of all his prophets.' Then the LORD[k] said, 'You are to entice him, and you shall succeed; go out and do it.' 22 So you see, the LORD has put a lying spirit in the mouth of these your prophets; the LORD has decreed disaster for you."

23 Then Zed·e·kī′ah son of Che·nā′a·nah came up to Mī·cāi′ah, slapped him on the cheek, and said, "Which way did the spirit of the LORD pass from me to speak to you?" 24 Mī·cāi′ah

k Heb he

replied, "You will find out on that day when you go in to hide in an inner chamber." 25 The king of Israel then ordered, "Take Mī·cāi'ah, and return him to Ā'mon the governor of the city and to Jō'ash the king's son; 26 and say, 'Thus says the king: Put this fellow in prison, and feed him on reduced rations of bread and water until I return in peace.' " 27 Mī·cāi'ah said, "If you return in peace, the LORD has not spoken by me." And he said, "Hear, you peoples, all of you!"

Defeat and Death of Ahab
(1 Kings 22.29–40)

28 So the king of Israel and King Je·hosh'a·phat of Judah went up to Rā'moth-gil'e·ad. 29 The king of Israel said to Je·hosh'a·phat, "I will disguise myself and go into battle, but you wear your robes." So the king of Israel disguised himself, and they went into battle. 30 Now the king of Ar'am had commanded the captains of his chariots, "Fight with no one small or great, but only with the king of Israel." 31 When the captains of the chariots saw Je·hosh'a·phat, they said, "It is the king of Israel." So they turned to fight against him; and Je·hosh'a·phat cried out, and the LORD helped him. God drew them away from him, 32 for when the captains of the chariots saw that it was not the king of Israel, they turned back from pursuing him. 33 But a certain man drew his bow and unknowingly struck the king of Israel between the scale armor and the breastplate; so he said to the driver of his chariot, "Turn around, and carry me out of the battle, for I am wounded." 34 The battle grew hot that day, and the king of Israel propped himself up in his chariot facing the Ar·a·mē'ans until evening; then at sunset he died.

19 King Je·hosh'a·phat of Judah returned in safety to his house in Jerusalem. 2 Jē'hū son of Ha·nā'nī the seer went out to meet him and said to King Je·hosh'a·phat, "Should you help the wicked and love those who hate the LORD? Because of this, wrath has gone out against you from the LORD. 3 Nevertheless, some good is found in you, for you destroyed the sacred poles*l* out of the land, and have set your heart to seek God."

The Reforms of Jehoshaphat

4 Je·hosh'a·phat resided at Jerusalem; then he went out again among the people, from Bē'er-shē'ba to the hill country of Ē'phra·im, and brought them back to the LORD, the God of their ancestors. 5 He appointed judges in the land in all the fortified cities of Judah, city by city, 6 and said to the judges, "Consider what you are doing, for you judge not on behalf of human beings but on the LORD's behalf; he is with you in giving judgment. 7 Now, let the fear of the LORD be upon you; take care what you do, for there is no perversion of justice with the LORD our God, or partiality, or taking of bribes."

8 Moreover in Jerusalem Je·hosh'a·phat appointed certain Lē'vītes and priests and heads of families of Israel, to give judgment for the LORD and to decide disputed cases. They had their seat at Jerusalem. 9 He charged them: "This is how you shall act: in the fear of the LORD, in faithfulness, and with your whole heart; 10 whenever a case comes to you from your kindred who live in their cities, concerning bloodshed, law or commandment, statutes or ordinances, then you shall instruct them, so that they may not incur guilt before the LORD and wrath may not come on you and your kindred. Do so, and you will not incur guilt. 11 See, Am·a·rī'ah the chief priest is over you in all matters of the LORD; and Zeb·a·dī'ah son of Ish'ma·el, the governor of the house of Judah, in all the king's matters; and the Lē'vītes will serve you as officers. Deal courageously, and may the LORD be with the good!"

Invasion from the East

20 After this the Mō'ab·ītes and Am'mon·ītes, and with them some of the Me·ū'nītes,*m* came against Je·hosh'a·phat for battle. 2 Messengers*n* came and told Je·hosh'a·phat, "A great multitude is coming against you from Ē'dom,*o* from beyond the sea; already they are at Haz'a·zon-tā'mar" (that is, En-ge'di). 3 Je·hosh'a·phat was afraid; he set himself to seek the LORD, and proclaimed a fast throughout all Judah. 4 Judah assembled to seek help from the LORD; from all the towns of Judah they came to seek the LORD.

l Heb *Asheroth*   *m* Compare 26.7: Heb *Ammonites*   *n* Heb *They*   *o* One Ms: MT *Aram*

Jehoshaphat's Prayer and Victory

5 Je·hosh'a·phat stood in the assembly of Judah and Jerusalem, in the house of the LORD, before the new court, 6 and said, "O LORD, God of our ancestors, are you not God in heaven? Do you not rule over all the kingdoms of the nations? In your hand are power and might, so that no one is able to withstand you. 7 Did you not, O our God, drive out the inhabitants of this land before your people Israel, and give it forever to the descendants of your friend Abraham? 8 They have lived in it, and in it have built you a sanctuary for your name, saying, 9 'If disaster comes upon us, the sword, judgment,ᵖ or pestilence, or famine, we will stand before this house, and before you, for your name is in this house, and cry to you in our distress, and you will hear and save.' 10 See now, the people of Am'mon, Mō'ab, and Mount Sē'ir, whom you would not let Israel invade when they came from the land of Egypt, and whom they avoided and did not destroy— 11 they reward us by coming to drive us out of your possession that you have given us to inherit. 12 O our God, will you not execute judgment upon them? For we are powerless against this great multitude that is coming against us. We do not know what to do, but our eyes are on you."

13 Meanwhile all Judah stood before the LORD, with their little ones, their wives, and their children. 14 Then the spirit of the LORD came upon Ja·ha'zi·el son of Zech·a·rī'ah, son of Be·nā'i·ah, son of Je·ī'el, son of Mat·ta·nī'ah, a Lē'vīte of the sons of Ā'saph, in the middle of the assembly. 15 He said, "Listen, all Judah and inhabitants of Jerusalem, and King Je·hosh'a·phat: Thus says the LORD to you: 'Do not fear or be dismayed at this great multitude; for the battle is not yours but God's. 16 Tomorrow go down against them; they will come up by the ascent of Ziz; you will find them at the end of the valley, before the wilderness of Je·rū'el. 17 This battle is not for you to fight; take your position, stand still, and see the victory of the LORD on your behalf, O Judah and Jerusalem.' Do not fear or be dismayed; tomorrow go out against them, and the LORD will be with you."

18 Then Je·hosh'a·phat bowed down with his face to the ground, and all Judah and the inhabitants of Jerusalem fell down before the LORD, worshiping the LORD. 19 And the Lē'vītes, of the Kō'hath·ītes and the Kō'ra·hītes, stood up to praise the LORD, the God of Israel, with a very loud voice.

20 They rose early in the morning and went out into the wilderness of Te·kō'a; and as they went out, Je·hosh'a·phat stood and said, "Listen to me, O Judah and inhabitants of Jerusalem! Believe in the LORD your God and you will be established; believe his prophets." 21 When he had taken counsel with the people, he appointed those who were to sing to the LORD and praise him in holy splendor, as they went before the army, saying,

> "Give thanks to the LORD,
>   for his steadfast love endures
>   forever."

22 As they began to sing and praise, the LORD set an ambush against the Am'mon·ītes, Mō'ab, and Mount Sē'ir, who had come against Judah, so that they were routed. 23 For the Am'mon·ītes and Mō'ab attacked the inhabitants of Mount Sē'ir, destroying them utterly; and when they had made an end of the inhabitants of Sē'ir, they all helped to destroy one another.

24 When Judah came to the watchtower of the wilderness, they looked toward the multitude; they were corpses lying on the ground; no one had escaped. 25 When Je·hosh'a·phat and his people came to take the booty from them, they found livestock�q in great numbers, goods, clothing, and precious things, which they took for themselves until they could carry no more. They spent three days taking the booty, because of its abundance. 26 On the fourth day they assembled in the Valley of Ber'a·cah, for there they blessed the LORD; therefore that place has been called the Valley of Ber'a·cahʳ to this day. 27 Then all the people of Judah and Jerusalem, with Je·hosh'a·phat at their head, returned to Jerusalem with joy, for the LORD had enabled them to rejoice over their enemies. 28 They came to Jerusalem, with harps and lyres and trumpets, to the house of the LORD. 29 The fear of God came on all the kingdoms of the countries when they heard that the LORD had fought against the enemies of Israel. 30 And the realm of Je·hosh'-

---

ᵖ Or *the sword of judgment*   �q Gk: Heb *among them*   ʳ That is *Blessing* a·phat was quiet, for his God gave him rest all around.

The End of Jehoshaphat's Reign
(1 Kings 22.41–50)

31 So Je·hosh′a·phat reigned over Judah. He was thirty-five years old when he began to reign; he reigned twenty-five years in Jerusalem. His mother's name was A·zu′bah daughter of Shil′hi. [32]He walked in the way of his father Asa and did not turn aside from it, doing what was right in the sight of the LORD. [33]Yet the high places were not removed; the people had not yet set their hearts upon the God of their ancestors.

34 Now the rest of the acts of Je·hosh′a·phat, from first to last, are written in the Annals of Je′hu son of Ha·na′ni, which are recorded in the Book of the Kings of Israel.

35 After this King Je·hosh′a·phat of Judah joined with King A·ha·zi′ah of Israel, who did wickedly. [36]He joined him in building ships to go to Tar′shish; they built the ships in E′zi-on-ge′ber. [37]Then El·i·e′zer son of Do·dav′a·hu of Ma·re′shah prophesied against Je·hosh′a·phat, saying, "Because you have joined with A·ha·zi′ah, the LORD will destroy what you have made." And the ships were wrecked and were not able to go to Tar′shish.

Jehoram's Reign
(1 Kings 22.50; 2 Kings 8.16–19)

21 Je·hosh′a·phat slept with his ancestors and was buried with his ancestors in the city of David; his son Je·ho′ram succeeded him. [2]He had brothers, the sons of Je·hosh′a·phat: Az·a·ri′ah, A·zi′el, Zech·a·ri′ah, Az·a·ri′ah, Michael, and Sheph-a·ti′ah; all these were the sons of King Je·hosh′a·phat of Judah.[s] [3]Their father gave them many gifts, of silver, gold, and valuable possessions, together with fortified cities in Judah; but he gave the kingdom to Je·ho′ram, because he was the firstborn. [4]When Je·ho′ram had ascended the throne of his father and was established, he put all his brothers to the sword, and also some of the officials of Israel. [5]Je·ho′ram was thirty-two years old when he began to reign; he reigned eight years in Jerusalem. [6]He walked in the way of the kings of Israel, as the house of A′hab had done; for the daughter of A′hab was his wife. He did what was evil in the sight of the LORD. [7]Yet the

LORD would not destroy the house of David because of the covenant that he had made with David, and since he had promised to give a lamp to him and to his descendants forever.

Revolt of Edom
(2 Kings 8.20–22)

8 In his days E′dom revolted against the rule of Judah and set up a king of their own. [9]Then Je·ho′ram crossed over with his commanders and all his chariots. He set out by night and attacked the E′dom·ites, who had surrounded him and his chariot commanders. [10]So E′dom has been in revolt against the rule of Judah to this day. At that time Lib′nah also revolted against his rule, because he had forsaken the LORD, the God of his ancestors.

Elijah's Letter

11 Moreover he made high places in the hill country of Judah, and led the inhabitants of Jerusalem into unfaithfulness, and made Judah go astray. [12]A letter came to him from the prophet E·li′jah, saying: "Thus says the LORD, the God of your father David: Because you have not walked in the ways of your father Je·hosh′a·phat or in the ways of King Asa of Judah, [13]but have walked in the way of the kings of Israel, and have led Judah and the inhabitants of Jerusalem into unfaithfulness, as the house of A′hab led Israel into unfaithfulness, and because you also have killed your brothers, members of your father's house, who were better than yourself, [14]see, the LORD will bring a great plague on your people, your children, your wives, and all your possessions, [15]and you yourself will have a severe sickness with a disease of your bowels, until your bowels come out, day after day, because of the disease."

16 The LORD aroused against Je·ho′ram the anger of the Phi·lis′tines and of the Arabs who are near the Ethiopians.[t] [17]They came up against Judah, invaded it, and carried away all the possessions they found that belonged to the king's house, along with his sons and his wives, so that no son was left to him except Je·ho′a·haz, his youngest son.

s Gk Syr: Heb Israel   t Or Nubians; Heb Cushites

Disease and Death of Jehoram
(2 Kings 8.23–24)

18 After all this the LORD struck him in his bowels with an incurable disease. 19 In course of time, at the end of two years, his bowels came out because of the disease, and he died in great agony. His people made no fire in his honor, like the fires made for his ancestors. 20 He was thirty-two years old when he began to reign; he reigned eight years in Jerusalem. He departed with no one's regret. They buried him in the city of David, but not in the tombs of the kings.

Ahaziah's Reign
(2 Kings 8.25–29; 9.14–16, 27–29)

22 The inhabitants of Jerusalem made his youngest son A·ha·zī'ah king as his successor; for the troops who came with the Arabs to the camp had killed all the older sons. So A·ha·zī'ah son of Je·hō'ram reigned as king of Judah. 2 A·ha·zī'ah was forty-two years old when he began to reign; he reigned one year in Jerusalem. His mother's name was Ath·a·lī'ah, a granddaughter of Om'rī. 3 He also walked in the ways of the house of A'hab, for his mother was his counselor in doing wickedly. 4 He did what was evil in the sight of the LORD, as the house of A'hab had done; for after the death of his father they were his counselors, to his ruin. 5 He even followed their advice, and went with Je·hō'ram son of King A'hab of Israel to make war against King Haz'a·el of Ar'am at Rā'moth-gil'e·ad. The Ar·a·mē'ans wounded Jō'ram, 6 and he returned to be healed in Jez'rē·el of the wounds that he had received at Rā'mah, when he fought King Haz'a·el of Ar'am. And A·ha·zī'ah son of King Je·hō'ram of Judah went down to see Jō'ram son of A'hab in Jez'rē·el, because he was sick.

7 But it was ordained by God that the downfall of A·ha·zī'ah should come about through his going to visit Jō'ram. For when he came there he went out with Je·hō'ram to meet Jē'hū son of Nim'shī, whom the LORD had anointed to destroy the house of A'hab. 8 When Jē'hū was executing judgment on the house of A'hab, he met the officials of Judah and the sons of A·ha·zī'ah's brothers, who attended A·ha·zī'ah, and he killed them. 9 He searched for A·ha·zī'ah, who was cap-

tured while hiding in Sa·mār'i·a and was brought to Jē'hū, and put to death. They buried him, for they said, "He is the grandson of Je·hosh'a·phat, who sought the LORD with all his heart." And the house of A·ha·zī'ah had no one able to rule the kingdom.

Athaliah Seizes the Throne
(2 Kings 11.1–8)

10 Now when Ath·a·lī'ah, A·ha·zī'ah's mother, saw that her son was dead, she set about to destroy all the royal family of the house of Judah. 11 But Jē·hō·shab'e·ath, the king's daughter, took Jō'ash son of A·ha·zī'ah, and stole him away from among the king's children who were about to be killed; she put him and his nurse in a bedroom. Thus Jē·hō·shab'e·ath, daughter of King Je·hō'ram and wife of the priest Je·hoi'a·da—because she was a sister of A·ha·zī'ah—hid him from Ath·a·lī'ah, so that she did not kill him; 12 he remained with them six years, hidden in the house of God, while Ath·a·lī'ah reigned over the land.

23 But in the seventh year Je·hoi'-a·da took courage, and entered into a compact with the commanders of the hundreds, Az·a·rī'ah son of Je·rō'ham, Ish'ma·el son of Je·hō·hā'nan, Az·a·rī'ah son of O'bed, Mā·a·sēi'ah son of A·dāi'ah, and El·i·shā'phat son of Zich'rī. 2 They went around through Judah and gathered the Lē'vītes from all the towns of Judah, and the heads of families of Israel, and they came to Jerusalem. 3 Then the whole assembly made a covenant with the king in the house of God. Je·hoi'a·da[u] said to them, "Here is the king's son! Let him reign, as the LORD promised concerning the sons of David. 4 This is what you are to do: one third of you, priests and Lē'vītes, who come on duty on the sabbath, shall be gatekeepers, 5 one third shall be at the king's house, and one third at the Gate of the Foundation; and all the people shall be in the courts of the house of the LORD. 6 Do not let anyone enter the house of the LORD except the priests and ministering Lē'vītes; they may enter, for they are holy, but all the other[v] people shall observe the instructions of the LORD. 7 The Lē'vītes shall surround the king, each with his weapons in his hand; and whoever enters the

u Heb *He*   *v* Heb lacks *other*

house shall be killed. Stay with the king in his comings and goings."

Joash Crowned King
(2 Kings 11.9–12)

8 The Lē′vites and all Judah did according to all that the priest Je·hoi′a·da commanded; each brought his men, who were to come on duty on the sabbath, with those who were to go off duty on the sabbath; for the priest Je·hoi′a·da did not dismiss the divisions. 9 The priest Je·hoi′a·da delivered to the captains the spears and the large and small shields that had been King David's, which were in the house of God; 10 and he set all the people as a guard for the king, everyone with weapon in hand, from the south side of the house to the north side of the house, around the altar and the house. 11 Then he brought out the king's son, put the crown on him, and gave him the covenant;ʷ they proclaimed him king, and Je·hoi′a·da and his sons anointed him; and they shouted, "Long live the king!"

Athaliah Murdered
(2 Kings 11.13–20)

12 When Ath·a·lī′ah heard the noise of the people running and praising the king, she went into the house of the LORD to the people; 13 and when she looked, there was the king standing by his pillar at the entrance, and the captains and the trumpeters beside the king, and all the people of the land rejoicing and blowing trumpets, and the singers with their musical instruments leading in the celebration. Ath·a·lī′ah tore her clothes, and cried, "Treason! Treason!" 14 Then the priest Je·hoi′a·da brought out the captains who were set over the army, saying to them, "Bring her out between the ranks; anyone who follows her is to be put to the sword." For the priest said, "Do not put her to death in the house of the LORD." 15 So they laid hands on her; she went into the entrance of the Horse Gate of the king's house, and there they put her to death.

16 Je·hoi′a·da made a covenant between himself and all the people and the king that they should be the LORD's people. 17 Then all the people went to the house of Bā′al, and tore it down; his altars and his images they broke in pieces, and they killed Mat′tan, the priest of Bā′al, in front of the altars. 18 Je·hoi′a·da assigned the care of the

house of the LORD to the levitical priests whom David had organized to be in charge of the house of the LORD, to offer burnt offerings to the LORD, as it is written in the law of Moses, with rejoicing and with singing, according to the order of David. 19 He stationed the gatekeepers at the gates of the house of the LORD so that no one should enter who was in any way unclean. 20 And he took the captains, the nobles, the governors of the people, and all the people of the land, and they brought the king down from the house of the LORD, marching through the upper gate to the king's house. They set the king on the royal throne. 21 So all the people of the land rejoiced, and the city was quiet after Ath·a·lī′ah had been killed with the sword.

Joash Repairs the Temple
(2 Kings 11.21—12.16)

24 Jō′ash was seven years old when he began to reign; he reigned forty years in Jerusalem; his mother's name was Zib′i·ah of Bē′er·shē′ba. 2 Jō′ash did what was right in the sight of the LORD all the days of the priest Je·hoi′a·da. 3 Je·hoi′a·da got two wives for him, and he became the father of sons and daughters.

4 Some time afterward Jō′ash decided to restore the house of the LORD. 5 He assembled the priests and the Lē′vites and said to them, "Go out to the cities of Judah and gather money from all Israel to repair the house of your God, year by year; and see that you act quickly." But the Lē′vites did not act quickly. 6 So the king summoned Je·hoi′a·da the chief, and said to him, "Why have you not required the Lē′vites to bring in from Judah and Jerusalem the tax levied by Moses, the servant of the LORD, onˣ the congregation of Israel for the tent of the covenant?"ʷ 7 For the children of Ath·a·lī′ah, that wicked woman, had broken into the house of God, and had even used all the dedicated things of the house of the LORD for the Bā′als.

8 So the king gave command, and they made a chest, and set it outside the gate of the house of the LORD. 9 A proclamation was made throughout Judah and Jerusalem to bring in for the LORD the tax that Moses the servant of God laid on Israel in the wilder-

ʷ Or *treaty*, or *testimony*; Heb *eduth*
ˣ Compare Vg: Heb *and*

ness. 10 All the leaders and all the people rejoiced and brought their tax and dropped it into the chest until it was full. 11 Whenever the chest was brought to the king's officers by the Le'vites, when they saw that there was a large amount of money in it, the king's secretary and the officer of the chief priest would come and empty the chest and take it and return it to its place. So they did day after day, and collected money in abundance. 12 The king and Je·hoi'a·da gave it to those who had charge of the work of the house of the LORD, and they hired masons and carpenters to restore the house of the LORD, and also workers in iron and bronze to repair the house of the LORD. 13 So those who were engaged in the work labored, and the repairing went forward at their hands, and they restored the house of God to its proper condition and strengthened it. 14 When they had finished, they brought the rest of the money to the king and Je·hoi'a·da, and with it were made utensils for the house of the LORD, utensils for the service and for the burnt offerings, and ladles, and vessels of gold and silver. They offered burnt offerings in the house of the LORD regularly all the days of Je·hoi'-a·da.

Apostasy of Joash

15 But Je·hoi'a·da grew old and full of days, and died; he was one hundred thirty years old at his death. 16 And they buried him in the city of David among the kings, because he had done good in Israel, and for God and his house.

17 Now after the death of Je·hoi'-a·da the officials of Judah came and did obeisance to the king; then the king listened to them. 18 They abandoned the house of the LORD, the God of their ancestors, and served the sacred poles[y] and the idols. And wrath came upon Judah and Jerusalem for this guilt of theirs. 19 Yet he sent prophets among them to bring them back to the LORD; they testified against them, but they would not listen.

20 Then the spirit of God took possession of[z] Zech·a·ri'ah son of the priest Je·hoi'a·da; he stood above the people and said to them, "Thus says God: Why do you transgress the commandments of the LORD, so that you cannot prosper? Because you have forsaken the LORD, he has also forsaken

you." 21 But they conspired against him, and by command of the king they stoned him to death in the court of the house of the LORD. 22 King Jo'ash did not remember the kindness that Je·hoi'a·da, Zech·a·ri'ah's father, had shown him, but killed his son. As he was dying, he said, "May the LORD see and avenge!"

Death of Joash
(2 Kings 12.19–21)

23 At the end of the year the army of Ar'am came up against Jo'ash. They came to Judah and Jerusalem, and destroyed all the officials of the people from among them, and sent all the booty they took to the king of Damascus. 24 Although the army of Ar'am had come with few men, the LORD delivered into their hand a very great army, because they had abandoned the LORD, the God of their ancestors. Thus they executed judgment on Jo'-ash.

25 When they had withdrawn, leaving him severely wounded, his servants conspired against him because of the blood of the son[a] of the priest Je·hoi'a·da, and they killed him on his bed. So he died; and they buried him in the city of David, but they did not bury him in the tombs of the kings. 26 Those who conspired against him were Za'-bad son of Shim'e·ath the Am'mon·ite, and Je·ho'za·bad son of Shim'rith the Mo'ab·ite. 27 Accounts of his sons, and of the many oracles against him, and of the rebuilding[b] of the house of God are written in the Commentary on the Book of the Kings. And his son Am·a·zi'ah succeeded him.

Reign of Amaziah
(2 Kings 14.1–6)

25 Am·a·zi'ah was twenty-five years old when he began to reign, and he reigned twenty-nine years in Jerusalem. His mother's name was Je·ho·ad'dan of Jerusalem. 2 He did what was right in the sight of the LORD, yet not with a true heart. 3 As soon as the royal power was firmly in his hand he killed his servants who had murdered his father the king. 4 But he did not put their children to death, according to what is written in the law, in the book of Moses, where the LORD

y Heb *Asherim*   z Heb *clothed itself with*

a Gk Vg: Heb *sons*   b Heb *founding*

commanded, "The parents shall not be put to death for the children, or the children be put to death for the parents; but all shall be put to death for their own sins."

Slaughter of the Edomites
(2 Kings 14.7)

5 Am·a·zī'ah assembled the people of Judah, and set them by ancestral houses under commanders of the thousands and of the hundreds for all Judah and Benjamin. He mustered those twenty years old and upward, and found that they were three hundred thousand picked troops fit for war, able to handle spear and shield. ⁶He also hired one hundred thousand mighty warriors from Israel for one hundred talents of silver. ⁷But a man of God came to him and said, "O king, do not let the army of Israel go with you, for the LORD is not with Israel—all these Ē'phra·im·ites. ⁸Rather, go by yourself and act; be strong in battle, or God will fling you down before the enemy; for God has power to help or to overthrow." ⁹Am·a·zī'ah said to the man of God, "But what shall we do about the hundred talents that I have given to the army of Israel?" The man of God answered, "The LORD is able to give you much more than this." ¹⁰Then Am·a·zī'ah discharged the army that had come to him from Ē'phra·im, letting them go home again. But they became very angry with Judah, and returned home in fierce anger.

11 Am·a·zī'ah took courage, and led out his people; he went to the Valley of Salt, and struck down ten thousand men of Sē'ir. ¹²The people of Judah captured another ten thousand alive, took them to the top of Sē'la, and threw them down from the top of Sē'la, so that all of them were dashed to pieces. ¹³But the men of the army whom Am·a·zī'ah sent back, not letting them go with him to battle, fell on the cities of Judah from Sa·mār'i·a to Beth-hō'ron; they killed three thousand people in them, and took much booty.

14 Now after Am·a·zī'ah came from the slaughter of the Ē'dom·ites, he brought the gods of the people of Sē'ir, set them up as his gods, and worshiped them, making offerings to them. ¹⁵The LORD was angry with Am·a·zī'ah and sent to him a prophet, who said to him, "Why have you resorted to a people's gods who could not deliver their own

people from your hand?" ¹⁶But as he was speaking the king^c said to him, "Have we made you a royal counselor? Stop! Why should you be put to death?" So the prophet stopped, but said, "I know that God has determined to destroy you, because you have done this and have not listened to my advice."

Israel Defeats Judah
(2 Kings 14.8–14)

17 Then King Am·a·zī'ah of Judah took counsel and sent to King Jō'ash son of Je·hō'a·haz son of Jē'hū of Israel, saying, "Come, let us look one another in the face." ¹⁸King Jō'ash of Israel sent word to King Am·a·zī'ah of Judah, "A thornbush on Lebanon sent to a cedar on Lebanon, saying, 'Give your daughter to my son for a wife'; but a wild animal of Lebanon passed by and trampled down the thornbush. ¹⁹You say, 'See, I have defeated Ē'dom,' and your heart has lifted you up in boastfulness. Now stay at home; why should you provoke trouble so that you fall, you and Judah with you?"

20 But Am·a·zī'ah would not listen—it was God's doing, in order to hand them over, because they had sought the gods of Ē'dom. ²¹So King Jō'ash of Israel went up; he and King Am·a·zī'ah of Judah faced one another in battle at Beth-shē'mesh, which belongs to Judah. ²²Judah was defeated by Israel; everyone fled home. ²³King Jō'ash of Israel captured King Am·a·zī'ah of Judah, son of Jō'ash, son of A·ha·zī'ah, at Beth-shē'mesh; he brought him to Jerusalem, and broke down the wall of Jerusalem from the Ē'phra·im Gate to the Corner Gate, a distance of four hundred cubits. ²⁴He seized all the gold and silver, and all the vessels that were found in the house of God, and Ō'bed-ē'dom with them; he seized also the treasuries of the king's house, also hostages; then he returned to Sa·mār'i·a.

Death of Amaziah
(2 Kings 14.17–20)

25 King Am·a·zī'ah son of Jō'ash of Judah, lived fifteen years after the death of King Jō'ash son of Je·hō'-a·haz of Israel. ²⁶Now the rest of the deeds of Am·a·zī'ah, from first to last, are they not written in the Book of the Kings of Judah and Israel? ²⁷From the

^c Heb *he*

time that Am·a·zī'ah turned away from the LORD they made a conspiracy against him in Jerusalem, and he fled to Lā'chish. But they sent after him to Lā'chish, and killed him there. 28 They brought him back on horses; he was buried with his ancestors in the city of David.

Reign of Uzziah
(2 Kings 14.21–22; 15.1–3)

26 Then all the people of Judah took Uz·zī'ah, who was sixteen years old, and made him king to succeed his father Am·a·zī'ah. 2 He rebuilt Ē'loth and restored it to Judah, after the king slept with his ancestors. 3 Uz·zī'ah was sixteen years old when he began to reign, and he reigned fifty-two years in Jerusalem. His mother's name was Jec·o·lī'ah of Jerusalem. 4 He did what was right in the sight of the LORD, just as his father Am·a·zī'ah had done. 5 He set himself to seek God in the days of Zech·a·rī'ah, who instructed him in the fear of God; and as long as he sought the LORD, God made him prosper.

6 He went out and made war against the Phi·lis'tines, and broke down the wall of Gath and the wall of Jab'neh and the wall of Ash'dod; he built cities in the territory of Ash'dod and elsewhere among the Phi·lis'tines. 7 God helped him against the Phi·lis'-tines, against the Arabs who lived in Gur-bā'al, and against the Me·ū'nītes. 8 The Am'mon·ītes paid tribute to Uz·zī'ah, and his fame spread even to the border of Egypt, for he became very strong. 9 Moreover Uz·zī'ah built towers in Jerusalem at the Corner Gate, at the Valley Gate, and at the Angle, and fortified them. 10 He built towers in the wilderness and hewed out many cisterns, for he had large herds, both in the She·phē'lah and in the plain, and he had farmers and vinedressers in the hills and in the fertile lands, for he loved the soil. 11 Moreover Uz·zī'ah had an army of soldiers, fit for war, in divisions according to the numbers in the muster made by the secretary Je·ī'el and the officer Mā·a·sēi'ah, under the direction of Han·a·nī'ah, one of the king's commanders. 12 The whole number of the heads of ancestral houses of mighty warriors was two thousand six hundred. 13 Under their command was an army of three hundred seven thousand

five hundred, who could make war with mighty power, to help the king against the enemy. 14 Uz·zī'ah provided for all the army the shields, spears, helmets, coats of mail, bows, and stones for slinging. 15 In Jerusalem he set up machines, invented by skilled workers, on the towers and the corners for shooting arrows and large stones. And his fame spread far, for he was marvelously helped until he became strong.

Pride and Apostasy
(2 Kings 15.4–7)

16 But when he had become strong he grew proud, to his destruction. For he was false to the LORD his God, and entered the temple of the LORD to make offering on the altar of incense. 17 But the priest Az·a·rī'ah went in after him, with eighty priests of the LORD who were men of valor; 18 they withstood King Uz·zī'ah, and said to him, "It is not for you, Uz·zī'ah, to make offering to the LORD, but for the priests the descendants of Aaron, who are consecrated to make offering. Go out of the sanctuary; for you have done wrong, and it will bring you no honor from the LORD God." 19 Then Uz·zī'ah was angry. Now he had a censer in his hand to make offering, and when he became angry with the priests a leprous [d] disease broke out on his forehead, in the presence of the priests in the house of the LORD, by the altar of incense. 20 When the chief priest Az·a·rī'ah, and all the priests, looked at him, he was leprous [d] in his forehead. They hurried him out, and he himself hurried to get out, because the LORD had struck him. 21 King Uz·zī'ah was leprous [d] to the day of his death, and being leprous [d] lived in a separate house, for he was excluded from the house of the LORD. His son Jō'tham was in charge of the palace of the king, governing the people of the land.

22 Now the rest of the acts of Uz·zī'ah, from first to last, the prophet Ī·sāi'ah son of Ā'moz wrote. 23 Uz·zī'ah slept with his ancestors; they buried him near his ancestors in the burial field that belonged to the kings, for they said, "He is leprous." [d] His son Jō'tham succeeded him.

[d] A term for several skin diseases; precise meaning uncertain

2 CHRONICLES

Reign of Jotham
(2 Kings 15.32–38)

27 Jō'tham was twenty-five years old when he began to reign; he reigned sixteen years in Jerusalem. His mother's name was Je·rū'shah daughter of Zā'dok. 2 He did what was right in the sight of the LORD just as his father Uz·zī'ah had done—only he did not invade the temple of the LORD. But the people still followed corrupt practices. 3 He built the upper gate of the house of the LORD, and did extensive building on the wall of Ō'phel. 4 Moreover he built cities in the hill country of Judah, and forts and towers on the wooded hills. 5 He fought with the king of the Am'mon·ītes and prevailed against them. The Am'mon·ītes gave him that year one hundred talents of silver, ten thousand cors of wheat and ten thousand of barley. The Am'mon·ītes paid him the same amount in the second and the third years. 6 So Jō'-tham became strong because he ordered his ways before the LORD his God. 7 Now the rest of the acts of Jō'-tham, and all his wars and his ways, are written in the Book of the Kings of Israel and Judah. 8 He was twenty-five years old when he began to reign; he reigned sixteen years in Jerusalem. 9 Jō'tham slept with his ancestors, and they buried him in the city of David; and his son Ā'haz succeeded him.

Reign of Ahaz
(2 Kings 16.1–4)

28 Ā'haz was twenty years old when he began to reign; he reigned sixteen years in Jerusalem. He did not do what was right in the sight of the LORD, as his ancestor David had done, 2 but he walked in the ways of the kings of Israel. He even made cast images for the Bā'als; 3 and he made offerings in the valley of the son of Hin'-nom, and made his sons pass through fire, according to the abominable practices of the nations whom the LORD drove out before the people of Israel. 4 He sacrificed and made offerings on the high places, on the hills, and under every green tree.

Aram and Israel Defeat Judah
(2 Kings 16.5–6; Isa 7.1)

5 Therefore the LORD his God gave him into the hand of the king of Ar'am, who defeated him and took captive a great number of his people and brought them to Damascus. He was also given into the hand of the king of Israel, who defeated him with great slaughter. 6 Pē'kah son of Rem·a·lī'ah killed one hundred twenty thousand in Judah in one day, all of them valiant warriors, because they had abandoned the LORD, the God of their ancestors. 7 And Zich'rī, a mighty warrior of E'phra·im, killed the king's son Mā·a·sēi'ah, Az·rī'kam the commander of the palace, and El·kā'nah the next in authority to the king.

Intervention of Oded

8 The people of Israel took captive two hundred thousand of their kin, women, sons, and daughters; they also took much booty from them and brought the booty to Sa·mār'i·a. 9 But a prophet of the LORD was there, whose name was Ō'ded; he went out to meet the army that came to Sa·mār'i·a, and said to them, "Because the LORD, the God of your ancestors, was angry with Judah, he gave them into your hand, but you have killed them in a rage that has reached up to heaven. 10 Now you intend to subjugate the people of Judah and Jerusalem, male and female, as your slaves. But what have you except sins against the LORD your God? 11 Now hear me, and send back the captives whom you have taken from your kindred, for the fierce wrath of the LORD is upon you." 12 Moreover, certain chiefs of the E'phra·im-ītes, Az·a·rī'ah son of Jō·hā'nan, Ber·e·chī'ah son of Me·shil'le·moth, Jē·hiz·kī'ah son of Shal'lum, and A·mā'sa son of Had'laī, stood up against those who were coming from the war, 13 and said to them, "You shall not bring the captives in here, for you propose to bring on us guilt against the LORD in addition to our present sins and guilt. For our guilt is already great, and there is fierce wrath against Israel." 14 So the warriors left the captives and the booty before the officials and all the assembly. 15 Then those who were mentioned by name got up and took the captives, and with the booty they clothed all that were naked among them; they clothed them, gave them sandals, provided them with food and drink, and anointed them; and carrying all the feeble among them on donkeys, they brought them to their kindred at Jericho, the city of palm trees. Then they returned to Sa·mār'i·a.

Assyria Refuses to Help Judah
(2 Kings 16.7–9)

16 At that time King Āʹhaz sent to the king[e] of Assyria for help. 17 For the Eʹdom·ites had again invaded and defeated Judah, and carried away captives. 18 And the Phi·lisʹtines had made raids on the cities in the She·pheʹlah and the Negʹeb of Judah, and had taken Beth-sheʹmesh, Aiʹja·lon, Ge·deʹroth, Sōʹcō with its villages, Timʹnah with its villages, and Gimʹzō with its villages; and they settled there. 19 For the Lᴏʀᴅ brought Judah low because of King Āʹhaz of Israel, for he had behaved without restraint in Judah and had been faithless to the Lᴏʀᴅ. 20 So King Tilʹgath-pil·neʹser of Assyria came against him, and oppressed him instead of strengthening him. 21 For Āʹhaz plundered the house of the Lᴏʀᴅ and the houses of the king and of the officials, and gave tribute to the king of Assyria; but it did not help him.

Apostasy and Death of Ahaz
(2 Kings 16.12–20)

22 In the time of his distress he became yet more faithless to the Lᴏʀᴅ—this same King Āʹhaz. 23 For he sacrificed to the gods of Damascus, which had defeated him, and said, "Because the gods of the kings of Arʹam helped them, I will sacrifice to them so that they may help me." But they were the ruin of him, and of all Israel. 24 Āʹhaz gathered together the utensils of the house of God, and cut in pieces the utensils of the house of God. He shut up the doors of the house of the Lᴏʀᴅ and made himself altars in every corner of Jerusalem. 25 In every city of Judah he made high places to make offerings to other gods, provoking to anger the Lᴏʀᴅ, the God of his ancestors. 26 Now the rest of his acts and all his ways, from first to last, are written in the Book of the Kings of Judah and Israel. 27 Āʹhaz slept with his ancestors, and they buried him in the city, in Jerusalem; but they did not bring him into the tombs of the kings of Israel. His son Hez·e·kiʹah succeeded him.

Reign of Hezekiah
(2 Kings 18.1–3)

29 Hez·e·kiʹah began to reign when he was twenty-five years old; he reigned twenty-nine years in Jerusalem. His mother's name was A·biʹjah daughter of Zech·a·riʹah. 2 He did what was right in the sight of the Lᴏʀᴅ, just as his ancestor David had done.

The Temple Cleansed

3 In the first year of his reign, in the first month, he opened the doors of the house of the Lᴏʀᴅ and repaired them. 4 He brought in the priests and the Leʹvites and assembled them in the square on the east. 5 He said to them, "Listen to me, Leʹvites! Sanctify yourselves, and sanctify the house of the Lᴏʀᴅ, the God of your ancestors, and carry out the filth from the holy place. 6 For our ancestors have been unfaithful and have done what was evil in the sight of the Lᴏʀᴅ our God; they have forsaken him, and have turned away their faces from the dwelling of the Lᴏʀᴅ, and turned their backs. 7 They also shut the doors of the vestibule and put out the lamps, and have not offered incense or made burnt offerings in the holy place to the God of Israel. 8 Therefore the wrath of the Lᴏʀᴅ came upon Judah and Jerusalem, and he has made them an object of horror, of astonishment, and of hissing, as you see with your own eyes. 9 Our fathers have fallen by the sword and our sons and our daughters and our wives are in captivity for this. 10 Now it is in my heart to make a covenant with the Lᴏʀᴅ, the God of Israel, so that his fierce anger may turn away from us. 11 My sons, do not now be negligent, for the Lᴏʀᴅ has chosen you to stand in his presence to minister to him, and to be his ministers and make offerings to him."

12 Then the Leʹvites arose, Māʹhath son of A·maʹsai, and Jōʹel son of Az·a·riʹah, of the sons of the Kōʹhath·ites; and of the sons of Me·rarʹi, Kish son of Abʹdi, and Az·a·riʹah son of Je·halʹle·lel; and of the Gerʹshon·ites, Jōʹah son of Zimʹmah, and Eden son of Jōʹah; 13 and of the sons of E·li·zaʹphan, Shimʹri and Je·uʹel; and of the sons of Āʹsaph, Zech·a·riʹah and Mat·ta·niʹah; 14 and of the sons of Hēʹman, Je·huʹel and Shimʹe·i; and of the sons of Je·duʹthun, She·maiʹah and Uzʹzi·el. 15 They gathered their brothers, sanctified themselves, and went in as the king had commanded, by the words of the Lᴏʀᴅ, to cleanse the

e Gk Syr Vg Compare 2 Kings 16.7: Heb *kings*

house of the LORD. 16 The priests went into the inner part of the house of the LORD to cleanse it, and they brought out all the unclean things that they found in the temple of the LORD into the court of the house of the LORD; and the Lē'vītes took them and carried them out to the Wadi Kid'ron. 17 They began to sanctify on the first day of the first month, and on the eighth day of the month they came to the vestibule of the LORD; then for eight days they sanctified the house of the LORD, and on the sixteenth day of the first month they finished. 18 Then they went inside to King Hez·e·kī'ah and said, "We have cleansed all the house of the LORD, the altar of burnt offering and all its utensils, and the table for the rows of bread and all its utensils. 19 All the utensils that King A'haz repudiated during his reign when he was faithless, we have made ready and sanctified; see, they are in front of the altar of the LORD."

Temple Worship Restored

20 Then King Hez·e·kī'ah rose early, assembled the officials of the city, and went up to the house of the LORD. 21 They brought seven bulls, seven rams, seven lambs, and seven male goats for a sin offering for the kingdom and for the sanctuary and for Judah. He commanded the priests the descendants of Aaron to offer them on the altar of the LORD. 22 So they slaughtered the bulls, and the priests received the blood and dashed it against the altar; they slaughtered the rams and their blood was dashed against the altar; they also slaughtered the lambs and their blood was dashed against the altar. 23 Then the male goats for the sin offering were brought to the king and the assembly; they laid their hands on them, 24 and the priests slaughtered them and made a sin offering with their blood at the altar, to make atonement for all Israel. For the king commanded that the burnt offering and the sin offering should be made for all Israel.
25 He stationed the Lē'vītes in the house of the LORD with cymbals, harps, and lyres, according to the commandment of David and of Gad the king's seer and of the prophet Nathan, for the commandment was from the LORD through his prophets. 26 The Lē'vītes stood with the instruments of David, and the priests with the trumpets.

27 Then Hez·e·kī'ah commanded that the burnt offering be offered on the altar. When the burnt offering began, the song to the LORD began also, and the trumpets, accompanied by the instruments of King David of Israel. 28 The whole assembly worshiped, the singers sang, and the trumpeters sounded; all this continued until the burnt offering was finished. 29 When the offering was finished, the king and all who were present with him bowed down and worshiped. 30 King Hez·e·kī'ah and the officials commanded the Lē'vītes to sing praises to the LORD with the words of David and of the seer A'saph. They sang praises with gladness, and they bowed down and worshiped.

31 Then Hez·e·kī'ah said, "You have now consecrated yourselves to the LORD; come near, bring sacrifices and thank offerings to the house of the LORD." The assembly brought sacrifices and thank offerings; and all who were of a willing heart brought burnt offerings. 32 The number of the burnt offerings that the assembly brought was seventy bulls, one hundred rams, and two hundred lambs; all these were for a burnt offering to the LORD. 33 The consecrated offerings were six hundred bulls and three thousand sheep. 34 But the priests were too few and could not skin all the burnt offerings, so, until other priests had sanctified themselves, their kindred, the Lē'vītes, helped them until the work was finished—for the Lē'vītes were more conscientious *f* than the priests in sanctifying themselves. 35 Besides the great number of burnt offerings there was the fat of the offerings of well-being, and there were the drink offerings for the burnt offerings. Thus the service of the house of the LORD was restored. 36 And Hez·e·kī'ah and all the people rejoiced because of what God had done for the people; for the thing had come about suddenly.

The Great Passover

30 Hez·e·kī'ah sent word to all Israel and Judah, and wrote letters also to Ē'phra·im and Ma·nas'seh, that they should come to the house of the LORD at Jerusalem, to keep the passover to the LORD the God of Israel. 2 For the king and his officials and all the assembly in Jerusalem had taken

f Heb *upright in heart*

counsel to keep the passover in the second month ³(for they could not keep it at its proper time because the priests had not sanctified themselves in sufficient number, nor had the people assembled in Jerusalem). ⁴The plan seemed right to the king and all the assembly. ⁵So they decreed to make a proclamation throughout all Israel, from Bē′er-shē′ba to Dan, that the people should come and keep the passover to the LORD the God of Israel, at Jerusalem; for they had not kept it in great numbers as prescribed. ⁶So couriers went throughout all Israel and Judah with letters from the king and his officials, as the king had commanded, saying, "O people of Israel, return to the LORD, the God of Abraham, Isaac, and Israel, so that he may turn again to the remnant of you who have escaped from the hand of the kings of Assyria. ⁷Do not be like your ancestors and your kindred, who were faithless to the LORD God of their ancestors, so that he made them a desolation, as you see. ⁸Do not now be stiff-necked as your ancestors were, but yield yourselves to the LORD and come to his sanctuary, which he has sanctified forever, and serve the LORD your God, so that his fierce anger may turn away from you. ⁹For as you return to the LORD, your kindred and your children will find compassion with their captors, and return to this land. For the LORD your God is gracious and merciful, and will not turn away his face from you, if you return to him."

10 So the couriers went from city to city through the country of E′phra·im and Ma·nas′seh, and as far as Zeb′-ū·lun; but they laughed them to scorn, and mocked them. ¹¹Only a few from Ash′er, Ma·nas′seh, and Zeb′ū·lun humbled themselves and came to Jerusalem. ¹²The hand of God was also on Judah to give them one heart to do what the king and the officials commanded by the word of the LORD.

13 Many people came together in Jerusalem to keep the festival of unleavened bread in the second month, a very large assembly. ¹⁴They set to work and removed the altars that were in Jerusalem, and all the altars for offering incense they took away and threw into the Wadi Kid′ron. ¹⁵They slaughtered the passover lamb on the fourteenth day of the second month. The priests and the Lē′vītes were ashamed, and they sanctified them-

selves and brought burnt offerings into the house of the LORD. ¹⁶They took their accustomed posts according to the law of Moses the man of God; the priests dashed the blood that they received ᵍ from the hands of the Lē′-vītes. ¹⁷For there were many in the assembly who had not sanctified themselves; therefore the Lē′vītes had to slaughter the passover lamb for everyone who was not clean, to make it holy to the LORD. ¹⁸For a multitude of the people, many of them from E′phra·im, Ma·nas′seh, Is′sa·char, and Zeb′ū·lun, had not cleansed themselves, yet they ate the passover otherwise than as prescribed. But Hez·e·kī′ah prayed for them, saying, "The good LORD pardon all ¹⁹who set their hearts to seek God, the LORD the God of their ancestors, even though not in accordance with the sanctuary's rules of cleanness." ²⁰The LORD heard Hez·e·kī′ah, and healed the people. ²¹The people of Israel who were present at Jerusalem kept the festival of unleavened bread seven days with great gladness; and the Lē′vītes and the priests praised the LORD day by day, accompanied by loud instruments for the LORD. ²²Hez·e·kī′ah spoke encouragingly to all the Lē′vītes who showed good skill in the service of the LORD. So the people ate the food of the festival for seven days, sacrificing offerings of well-being and giving thanks to the LORD the God of their ancestors.

23 Then the whole assembly agreed together to keep the festival for another seven days; so they kept it for another seven days with gladness. ²⁴For King Hez·e·kī′ah of Judah gave the assembly a thousand bulls and seven thousand sheep for offerings, and the officials gave the assembly a thousand bulls and ten thousand sheep. The priests sanctified themselves in great numbers. ²⁵The whole assembly of Judah, the priests and the Lē′vītes, and the whole assembly that came out of Israel, and the resident aliens who came out of the land of Israel, and the resident aliens who lived in Judah, rejoiced. ²⁶There was great joy in Jerusalem, for since the time of Solomon son of King David of Israel there had been nothing like this in Jerusalem. ²⁷Then the priests and the Lē′vītes stood up and blessed the people, and their voice was heard; their

ᵍ Heb lacks *that they received*

prayer came to his holy dwelling in heaven.

Pagan Shrines Destroyed
(2 Kings 18.4)

31 Now when all this was finished, all Israel who were present went out to the cities of Judah and broke down the pillars, hewed down the sacred poles, *h* and pulled down the high places and the altars throughout all Judah and Benjamin, and in E'phra·im and Ma·nas'seh, until they had destroyed them all. Then all the people of Israel returned to their cities, all to their individual properties.

2 Hez·e·ki'ah appointed the divisions of the priests and of the Le'vites, division by division, everyone according to his service, the priests and the Le'vites, for burnt offerings and offerings of well-being, to minister in the gates of the camp of the LORD and to give thanks and praise. 3 The contribution of the king from his own possessions was for the burnt offerings: the burnt offerings of morning and evening, and the burnt offerings for the sabbaths, the new moons, and the appointed festivals, as it is written in the law of the LORD. 4 He commanded the people who lived in Jerusalem to give the portion due to the priests and the Le'vites, so that they might devote themselves to the law of the LORD. 5 As soon as the word spread, the people of Israel gave in abundance the first fruits of grain, wine, oil, honey, and of all the produce of the field; and they brought in abundantly the tithe of everything. 6 The people of Israel and Judah who lived in the cities of Judah also brought in the tithe of cattle and sheep, and the tithe of the dedicated things that had been consecrated to the LORD their God, and laid them in heaps. 7 In the third month they began to pile up the heaps, and finished them in the seventh month. 8 When Hez·e·ki'ah and the officials came and saw the heaps, they blessed the LORD and his people Israel. 9 Hez·e·ki'ah questioned the priests and the Le'vites about the heaps. 10 The chief priest Az·a·ri'ah, who was of the house of Za'dok, answered him, "Since they began to bring the contributions into the house of the LORD, we have had enough to eat and have plenty to spare; for the LORD has blessed his people, so that we have this great supply left over."

Reorganization of Priests and Levites

11 Then Hez·e·ki'ah commanded them to prepare store-chambers in the house of the LORD; and they prepared them. 12 Faithfully they brought in the contributions, the tithes and the dedicated things. The chief officer in charge of them was Con·a·ni'ah the Le'vite, with his brother Shim'e·i as second; 13 while Je·hi'el, Az·a·zi'ah, Na'hath, As'a·hel, Jer'i·moth, Joz'a·bad, E·li'el, Is·ma·chi'ah, Ma'hath, and Be·na'i·ah were overseers assisting Con·a·ni'ah and his brother Shim'e·i, by the appointment of King Hez·e·ki'ah and of Az·a·ri'ah the chief officer of the house of God. 14 Ko're son of Im'nah the Le'vite, keeper of the east gate, was in charge of the freewill offerings to God, to apportion the contribution reserved for the LORD and the most holy offerings. 15 Eden, Mi·ni'a·min, Jesh'u·a, She·mai'ah, Am·a·ri'ah, and Shec·a·ni'ah were faithfully assisting him in the cities of the priests, to distribute the portions to their kindred, old and young alike, by divisions, 16 except those enrolled by genealogy, males from three years old and upwards, all who entered the house of the LORD as the duty of each day required, for their service according to their offices, by their divisions. 17 The enrollment of the priests was according to their ancestral houses; that of the Le'vites from twenty years old and upwards was according to their offices, by their divisions. 18 The priests were enrolled with all their little children, their wives, their sons, and their daughters, the whole multitude; for they were faithful in keeping themselves holy. 19 And for the descendants of Aaron, the priests, who were in the fields of common land belonging to their towns, town by town, the people designated by name were to distribute portions to every male among the priests and to everyone among the Le'vites who was enrolled.

20 Hez·e·ki'ah did this throughout all Judah; he did what was good and right and faithful before the LORD his God. 21 And every work that he undertook in the service of the house of God, and in accordance with the law and the commandments, to seek his God, he did with all his heart; and he prospered.

h Heb *Asherim*

Sennacherib's Invasion
(2 Kings 18.13—19.34; Isa 36.2–22)

32 After these things and these acts of faithfulness, King Sen·nach'e·rib of Assyria came and invaded Judah and encamped against the fortified cities, thinking to win them for himself. [2] When Hez·e·kī'ah saw that Sen·nach'e·rib had come and intended to fight against Jerusalem, [3] he planned with his officers and his warriors to stop the flow of the springs that were outside the city; and they helped him. [4] A great many people were gathered, and they stopped all the springs and the wadi that flowed through the land, saying, "Why should the Assyrian kings come and find water in abundance?" [5] Hez·e·kī'ah[i] set to work resolutely and built up the entire wall that was broken down, and raised towers on it,[j] and outside it he built another wall; he also strengthened the Mil'lō in the city of David, and made weapons and shields in abundance. [6] He appointed combat commanders over the people, and gathered them together to him in the square at the gate of the city and spoke encouragingly to them, saying, [7] "Be strong and of good courage. Do not be afraid or dismayed before the king of Assyria and all the horde that is with him; for there is one greater with us than with him. [8] With him is an arm of flesh; but with us is the LORD our God, to help us and to fight our battles." The people were encouraged by the words of King Hez·e·kī'ah of Judah.

[9] After this, while King Sen·nach'-e·rib of Assyria was at Lā'chish with all his forces, he sent his servants to Jerusalem to King Hez·e·kī'ah of Judah and to all the people of Judah that were in Jerusalem, saying, [10] "Thus says King Sen·nach'e·rib of Assyria: On what are you relying, that you undergo the siege of Jerusalem? [11] Is not Hez·e·kī'ah misleading you, handing you over to die by famine and by thirst, when he tells you, 'The LORD our God will save us from the hand of the king of Assyria'? [12] Was it not this same Hez·e·kī'ah who took away his high places and his altars and commanded Judah and Jerusalem, saying, 'Before one altar you shall worship, and upon it you shall make your offerings'? [13] Do you not know what I and my ancestors have done to all the peoples of other lands? Were the gods of the nations of those lands at all able to save their lands out of my hand? [14] Who among all the gods of those nations that my ancestors utterly destroyed was able to save his people from my hand, that your God should be able to save you from my hand? [15] Now therefore do not let Hez·e·kī'ah deceive you or mislead you in this fashion, and do not believe him, for no god of any nation or kingdom has been able to save his people from my hand or from the hand of my ancestors. How much less will your God save you out of my hand!"

[16] His servants said still more against the Lord GOD and against his servant Hez·e·kī'ah. [17] He also wrote letters to throw contempt on the LORD the God of Israel and to speak against him, saying, "Just as the gods of the nations in other lands did not rescue their people from my hands, so the God of Hez·e·kī'ah will not rescue his people from my hand." [18] They shouted it with a loud voice in the language of Judah to the people of Jerusalem who were on the wall, to frighten and terrify them, in order that they might take the city. [19] They spoke of the God of Jerusalem as if he were like the gods of the peoples of the earth, which are the work of human hands.

Sennacherib's Defeat and Death
(2 Kings 19.35–37)

[20] Then King Hez·e·kī'ah and the prophet I·sāi'ah son of Ā'moz prayed because of this and cried to heaven. [21] And the LORD sent an angel who cut off all the mighty warriors and commanders and officers in the camp of the king of Assyria. So he returned in disgrace to his own land. When he came into the house of his god, some of his own sons struck him down there with the sword. [22] So the LORD saved Hez·e·kī'ah and the inhabitants of Jerusalem from the hand of King Sen·nach'e·rib of Assyria and from the hand of all his enemies; he gave them rest[k] on every side. [23] Many brought gifts to the LORD in Jerusalem and precious things to King Hez·e·kī'ah of Judah, so that he was exalted in the sight of all nations from that time onward.

Hezekiah's Sickness
(2 Kings 20.1–11; Isa 38.1–8)

[24] In those days Hez·e·kī'ah be-

---

[i] Heb *He* [j] Vg: Heb *and raised on the towers* [k] Gk Vg: Heb *guided them*

came sick and was at the point of death. He prayed to the LORD, and he answered him and gave him a sign. [25] But Hez·e·kī′ah did not respond according to the benefit done to him, for his heart was proud. Therefore wrath came upon him and upon Judah and Jerusalem. [26] Then Hez·e·kī′ah humbled himself for the pride of his heart, both he and the inhabitants of Jerusalem, so that the wrath of the LORD did not come upon them in the days of Hez·e·kī′ah.

Hezekiah's Prosperity and Achievements
(2 Kings 20.12–21; Isa 39.1–8)

[27] Hez·e·kī′ah had very great riches and honor; and he made for himself treasuries for silver, for gold, for precious stones, for spices, for shields, and for all kinds of costly objects; [28] storehouses also for the yield of grain, wine, and oil; and stalls for all kinds of cattle, and sheepfolds.[l] [29] He likewise provided cities for himself, and flocks and herds in abundance; for God had given him very great possessions. [30] This same Hez·e·kī′ah closed the upper outlet of the waters of Gī′hon and directed them down to the west side of the city of David. Hez·e·kī′ah prospered in all his works. [31] So also in the matter of the envoys of the officials of Babylon, who had been sent to him to inquire about the sign that had been done in the land, God left him to himself, in order to test him and to know all that was in his heart.

[32] Now the rest of the acts of Hez·e·kī′ah, and his good deeds, are written in the vision of the prophet I·sāi′ah son of Ā′moz in the Book of the Kings of Judah and Israel. [33] Hez·e·kī′ah slept with his ancestors, and they buried him on the ascent to the tombs of the descendants of David; and all Judah and the inhabitants of Jerusalem did him honor at his death. His son Ma·nas′seh succeeded him.

Reign of Manasseh
(2 Kings 21.1–9)

33 Ma·nas′seh was twelve years old when he began to reign; he reigned fifty-five years in Jerusalem. [2] He did what was evil in the sight of the LORD, according to the abominable practices of the nations whom the LORD drove out before the people of Israel. [3] For he rebuilt the high places that his father Hez·e·kī′ah had pulled

down, and erected altars to the Bā′als, made sacred poles,[m] worshiped all the host of heaven, and served them. [4] He built altars in the house of the LORD, of which the LORD had said, "In Jerusalem shall my name be forever." [5] He built altars for all the host of heaven in the two courts of the house of the LORD. [6] He made his son pass through fire in the valley of the son of Hin′nom, practiced soothsaying and augury and sorcery, and dealt with mediums and with wizards. He did much evil in the sight of the LORD, provoking him to anger. [7] The carved image of the idol that he had made he set in the house of God, of which God said to David and to his son Solomon, "In this house, and in Jerusalem, which I have chosen out of all the tribes of Israel, I will put my name forever; [8] I will never again remove the feet of Israel from the land that I appointed for your ancestors, if only they will be careful to do all that I have commanded them, all the law, the statutes, and the ordinances given through Moses." [9] Ma·nas′seh misled Judah and the inhabitants of Jerusalem, so that they did more evil than the nations whom the LORD had destroyed before the people of Israel.

Manasseh Restored after Repentance

[10] The LORD spoke to Ma·nas′seh and to his people, but they gave no heed. [11] Therefore the LORD brought against them the commanders of the army of the king of Assyria, who took Ma·nas′seh captive in manacles, bound him with fetters, and brought him to Babylon. [12] While he was in distress he entreated the favor of the LORD his God and humbled himself greatly before the God of his ancestors. [13] He prayed to him, and God received his entreaty, heard his plea, and restored him again to Jerusalem and to his kingdom. Then Ma·nas′seh knew that the LORD indeed was God.

[14] Afterward he built an outer wall for the city of David west of Gī′hon, in the valley, reaching the entrance at the Fish Gate; he carried it around Ō′phel, and raised it to a very great height. He also put commanders of the army in all the fortified cities in Judah. [15] He took away the foreign gods and the idol from the house of the LORD, and all the altars that he had built on the moun-

[l] Gk Vg: Heb *flocks for folds*
[m] Heb *Asheroth*

tain of the house of the LORD and in Jerusalem, and he threw them out of the city. [16]He also restored the altar of the LORD and offered on it sacrifices of well-being and of thanksgiving; and he commanded Judah to serve the LORD the God of Israel. [17]The people, however, still sacrificed at the high places, but only to the LORD their God.

Death of Manasseh
(2 Kings 21.17–18)

18 Now the rest of the acts of Ma·nas′seh, his prayer to his God, and the words of the seers who spoke to him in the name of the LORD God of Israel, these are in the Annals of the Kings of Israel. [19]His prayer, and how God received his entreaty, all his sin and his faithlessness, the sites on which he built high places and set up the sacred poles[n] and the images, before he humbled himself, these are written in the records of the seers.[o] [20]So Ma·nas′seh slept with his ancestors, and they buried him in his house. His son Ā′mon succeeded him.

Amon's Reign and Death
(2 Kings 21.19–26)

21 Ā′mon was twenty-two years old when he began to reign; he reigned two years in Jerusalem. [22]He did what was evil in the sight of the LORD, as his father Ma·nas′seh had done. Ā′mon sacrificed to all the images that his father Ma·nas′seh had made, and served them. [23]He did not humble himself before the LORD, as his father Ma·nas′seh had humbled himself, but this Ā′mon incurred more and more guilt. [24]His servants conspired against him and killed him in his house. [25]But the people of the land killed all those who had conspired against King Ā′mon; and the people of the land made his son Jō·sī′ah king to succeed him.

Reign of Josiah
(2 Kings 22.1–2)

34 Jō·sī′ah was eight years old when he began to reign; he reigned thirty-one years in Jerusalem. [2]He did what was right in the sight of the LORD, and walked in the ways of his ancestor David; he did not turn aside to the right or to the left. [3]For in the eighth year of his reign, while he was still a boy, he began to seek the God of his ancestor David, and in the twelfth year he began to purge Judah and Jerusalem of the high places, the sacred poles,[n] and the carved and the cast images. [4]In his presence they pulled down the altars of the Ba′als; he demolished the incense altars that stood above them. He broke down the sacred poles[n] and the carved and the cast images; he made dust of them and scattered it over the graves of those who had sacrificed to them. [5]He also burned the bones of the priests on their altars, and purged Judah and Jerusalem. [6]In the towns of Ma·nas′seh, Ē′phra·im, and Sim′ē·on, and as far as Naph′ta·lī, in their ruins[p] all around, [7]he broke down the altars, beat the sacred poles[n] and the images into powder, and demolished all the incense altars throughout all the land of Israel. Then he returned to Jerusalem.

Discovery of the Book of the Law
(2 Kings 22.3–20)

8 In the eighteenth year of his reign, when he had purged the land and the house, he sent Shā′phan son of Az·a·lī′ah, Mā·a·sēi′ah the governor of the city, and Jō′ah son of Jō′a·haz, the recorder, to repair the house of the LORD his God. [9]They came to the high priest Hil·kī′ah and delivered the money that had been brought into the house of God, which the Lē′vītes, the keepers of the threshold, had collected from Ma·nas′seh and Ē′phra·im and from all the remnant of Israel and from all Judah and Benjamin and from the inhabitants of Jerusalem. [10]They delivered it to the workers who had the oversight of the house of the LORD, and the workers who were working in the house of the LORD gave it for repairing and restoring the house. [11]They gave it to the carpenters and the builders to buy quarried stone, and timber for binders, and beams for the buildings that the kings of Judah had let go to ruin. [12]The people did the work faithfully. Over them were appointed the Lē′vītes Jā′hath and Ō·ba·dī′ah, of the sons of Me·rar′ī, along with Zech·a·rī′ah and Me·shul′lam, of the sons of the Kō′hath·ītes, to have oversight. Other Lē′vītes, all skillful with instruments of music, [13]were over the burden bearers and directed all who did work in every kind of service; and some of the Lē′vītes were scribes, and officials, and gatekeepers.

14 While they were bringing out the

---

[n] Heb *Asherim*   [o] One Ms Gk: MT *of Hozai*   [p] Meaning of Heb uncertain

money that had been brought into the house of the LORD, the priest Hil·ki'ah found the book of the law of the LORD given through Moses. 15 Hil·ki'ah said to the secretary Sha'phan, "I have found the book of the law in the house of the LORD"; and Hil·ki'ah gave the book to Sha'phan. 16 Sha'phan brought the book to the king, and further reported to the king, "All that was committed to your servants they are doing. 17 They have emptied out the money that was found in the house of the LORD and have delivered it into the hand of the overseers and the workers." 18 The secretary Sha'phan informed the king, "The priest Hil·ki'ah has given me a book." Sha'phan then read it aloud to the king.

19 When the king heard the words of the law he tore his clothes. 20 Then the king commanded Hil·ki'ah, A·hi'-kam son of Sha'phan, Ab'don son of Mi'cah, the secretary Sha'phan, and the king's servant A·sai'ah: 21 "Go, inquire of the LORD for me and for those who are left in Israel and in Judah, concerning the words of the book that has been found; for the wrath of the LORD that is poured out on us is great, because our ancestors did not keep the word of the LORD, to act in accordance with all that is written in this book."

The Prophet Huldah Consulted

22 So Hil·ki'ah and those whom the king had sent went to the prophet Hul'-dah, the wife of Shal'lum son of Tok'-hath son of Has'rah, keeper of the wardrobe (who lived in Jerusalem in the Second Quarter) and spoke to her to that effect. 23 She declared to them, "Thus says the LORD, the God of Israel: Tell the man who sent you to me, 24 Thus says the LORD: I will indeed bring disaster upon this place and upon its inhabitants, all the curses that are written in the book that was read before the king of Judah. 25 Because they have forsaken me and have made offerings to other gods, so that they have provoked me to anger with all the works of their hands, my wrath will be poured out on this place and will not be quenched. 26 But as to the king of Judah, who sent you to inquire of the LORD, thus shall you say to him: Thus says the LORD, the God of Israel: Regarding the words that you have heard, 27 because your heart was penitent and you humbled yourself before God when you heard his words against this place and its inhabitants, and you have humbled yourself before me, and have torn your clothes and wept before me, I also have heard you, says the LORD. 28 I will gather you to your ancestors and you shall be gathered to your grave in peace; your eyes shall not see all the disaster that I will bring on this place and its inhabitants." They took the message back to the king.

The Covenant Renewed
(2 Kings 23.1–20)

29 Then the king sent word and gathered together all the elders of Judah and Jerusalem. 30 The king went up to the house of the LORD, with all the people of Judah, the inhabitants of Jerusalem, the priests and the Le'vites, all the people both great and small; he read in their hearing all the words of the book of the covenant that had been found in the house of the LORD. 31 The king stood in his place and made a covenant before the LORD, to follow the LORD, keeping his commandments, his decrees, and his statutes, with all his heart and all his soul, to perform the words of the covenant that were written in this book. 32 Then he made all who were present in Jerusalem and in Benjamin pledge themselves to it. And the inhabitants of Jerusalem acted according to the covenant of God, the God of their ancestors. 33 Jo·si'ah took away all the abominations from all the territory that belonged to the people of Israel, and made all who were in Israel worship the LORD their God. All his days they did not turn away from following the LORD the God of their ancestors.

Celebration of the Passover
(2 Kings 23.21–23)

35 Jo·si'ah kept a passover to the LORD in Jerusalem; they slaughtered the passover lamb on the fourteenth day of the first month. 2 He appointed the priests to their offices and encouraged them in the service of the house of the LORD. 3 He said to the Le'vites who taught all Israel and who were holy to the LORD, "Put the holy ark in the house that Solomon son of David, king of Israel, built; you need no longer carry it on your shoulders. Now serve the LORD your God and his people Israel. 4 Make preparations by your ancestral houses by your divisions, following the written directions of King David of Israel and the written directions of his son Solomon. [5] Take position in the holy place according to the groupings of the ancestral houses of your kindred the people, and let there be Lē′vītes for each division of an ancestral house. [q] [6] Slaughter the passover lamb, sanctify yourselves, and on behalf of your kindred make preparations, acting according to the word of the LORD by Moses."

7 Then Jō·sī′ah contributed to the people, as passover offerings for all that were present, lambs and kids from the flock to the number of thirty thousand, and three thousand bulls; these were from the king's possessions. [8] His officials contributed willingly to the people, to the priests, and to the Lē′-vītes. Hil·kī′ah, Zech·a·rī′ah, and Je·hī′el, the chief officers of the house of God, gave to the priests for the passover offerings two thousand six hundred lambs and kids and three hundred bulls. [9] Con·a·nī′ah also, and his brothers She·māi′ah and Ne·than′el, and Hash·a·bī′ah and Je·ī′el and Joz′-a·bad, the chiefs of the Lē′vītes, gave to the Lē′vītes for the passover offerings five thousand lambs and kids and five hundred bulls.

10 When the service had been prepared for, the priests stood in their place, and the Lē′vītes in their divisions according to the king's command. [11] They slaughtered the passover lamb, and the priests dashed the blood that they received[r] from them, while the Lē′vītes did the skinning. [12] They set aside the burnt offerings so that they might distribute them according to the groupings of the ancestral houses of the people, to offer to the LORD, as it is written in the book of Moses. And they did the same with the bulls. [13] They roasted the passover lamb with fire according to the ordinance; and they boiled the holy offerings in pots, in caldrons, and in pans, and carried them quickly to all the people. [14] Afterward they made preparations for themselves and for the priests, because the priests the descendants of Aaron were occupied in offering the burnt offerings and the fat parts until night; so the Lē′vītes made preparations for themselves and for the priests, the descendants of Aaron. [15] The singers, the descendants of Ā′saph, were in their place according to the command of David, and Ā′saph, and Hē′man, and the king's seer Je·dū′thun. The gatekeepers were at each gate; they did not need to interrupt their service, for their kindred the Lē′vītes made preparations for them.

16 So all the service of the LORD was prepared that day, to keep the passover and to offer burnt offerings on the altar of the LORD, according to the command of King Jō·sī′ah. [17] The people of Israel who were present kept the passover at that time, and the festival of unleavened bread seven days. [18] No passover like it had been kept in Israel since the days of the prophet Samuel; none of the kings of Israel had kept such a passover as was kept by Jō·sī′ah, by the priests and the Lē′-vītes, by all Judah and Israel who were present, and by the inhabitants of Jerusalem. [19] In the eighteenth year of the reign of Jō·sī′ah this passover was kept.

Defeat by Pharaoh Neco and Death of Josiah
(2 Kings 23.28–30)

20 After all this, when Jō·sī′ah had set the temple in order, King Nē′cō of Egypt went up to fight at Car′chem·ish on the Euphrates, and Jō·sī′ah went out against him. [21] But Nē′cō[s] sent envoys to him, saying, "What have I to do with you, king of Judah? I am not coming against you today, but against the house with which I am at war; and God has commanded me to hurry. Cease opposing God, who is with me, so that he will not destroy you." [22] But Jō·sī′ah would not turn away from him, but disguised himself in order to fight with him. He did not listen to the words of Nē′cō from the mouth of God, but joined battle in the plain of Me·gid′dō. [23] The archers shot King Jō·sī′ah; and the king said to his servants, "Take me away, for I am badly wounded." [24] So his servants took him out of the chariot and carried him in his second chariot[t] and brought him to Jerusalem. There he died, and was buried in the tombs of his ancestors. All Judah and Jerusalem mourned for Jō·sī′ah. [25] Jer·e·mī′ah also uttered a lament for Jō·sī′ah; and all the singing men and singing women have spoken of Jō·sī′ah in their laments to this day. They made these a custom in Israel; they are recorded in the Laments. [26] Now the rest of the acts of Jō·sī′ah

[q] Meaning of Heb uncertain
[r] Heb lacks *that they received*   [s] Heb *he*
[t] Or *the chariot of his deputy*

2 CHRONICLES

and his faithful deeds in accordance with what is written in the law of the LORD, 27 and his acts, first and last, are written in the Book of the Kings of Israel and Judah.

Reign of Jehoahaz
(2 Kings 23.31–33)

36 The people of the land took Je·hō′a·haz son of Jō·sī′ah and made him king to succeed his father in Jerusalem. 2 Je·hō′a·haz was twenty-three years old when he began to reign; he reigned three months in Jerusalem. 3 Then the king of Egypt deposed him in Jerusalem and laid on the land a tribute of one hundred talents of silver and one talent of gold. 4 The king of Egypt made his brother E·lī′a·kim king over Judah and Jerusalem, and changed his name to Je·hoi′a·kim; but Nē′cō took his brother Je·hō′a·haz and carried him to Egypt.

Reign and Captivity of Jehoiakim
(2 Kings 23.34—24.7)

5 Je·hoi′a·kim was twenty-five years old when he began to reign; he reigned eleven years in Jerusalem. He did what was evil in the sight of the LORD his God. 6 Against him King Ne·bū·chad·nez′zar of Babylon came up, and bound him with fetters to take him to Babylon. 7 Ne·bū·chad·nez′zar also carried some of the vessels of the house of the LORD to Babylon and put them in his palace in Babylon. 8 Now the rest of the acts of Je·hoi′a·kim, and the abominations that he did, and what was found against him, are written in the Book of the Kings of Israel and Judah; and his son Je·hoi′a·chin succeeded him.

Reign and Captivity of Jehoiachin
(2 Kings 24.8–17)

9 Je·hoi′a·chin was eight years old when he began to reign; he reigned three months and ten days in Jerusalem. He did what was evil in the sight of the LORD. 10 In the spring of the year King Ne·bū·chad·nez′zar sent and brought him to Babylon, along with the precious vessels of the house of the LORD, and made his brother Zed·e·kī′ah king over Judah and Jerusalem.

Reign of Zedekiah
(2 Kings 24.18–20; Jer 52.1–3a)

11 Zed·e·kī′ah was twenty-one years old when he began to reign; he

reigned eleven years in Jerusalem. 12 He did what was evil in the sight of the LORD his God. He did not humble himself before the prophet Jer·e·mī′ah who spoke from the mouth of the LORD. 13 He also rebelled against King Ne·bū·chad·nez′zar, who had made him swear by God; he stiffened his neck and hardened his heart against turning to the LORD, the God of Israel. 14 All the leading priests and the people also were exceedingly unfaithful, following all the abominations of the nations; and they polluted the house of the LORD that he had consecrated in Jerusalem.

The Fall of Jerusalem
(2 Kings 25.1–21; Jer 52.3b–30)

15 The LORD, the God of their ancestors, sent persistently to them by his messengers, because he had compassion on his people and on his dwelling place; 16 but they kept mocking the messengers of God, despising his words, and scoffing at his prophets, until the wrath of the LORD against his people became so great that there was no remedy.

17 Therefore he brought up against them the king of the Chal·dē′ans, who killed their youths with the sword in the house of their sanctuary, and had no compassion on young man or young woman, the aged or the feeble; he gave them all into his hand. 18 All the vessels of the house of God, large and small, and the treasures of the house of the LORD, and the treasures of the king and of his officials, all these he brought to Babylon. 19 They burned the house of God, broke down the wall of Jerusalem, burned all its palaces with fire, and destroyed all its precious vessels. 20 He took into exile in Babylon those who had escaped from the sword, and they became servants to him and to his sons until the establishment of the kingdom of Persia, 21 to fulfill the word of the LORD by the mouth of Jer·e·mī′ah, until the land had made up for its sabbaths. All the days that it lay desolate it kept sabbath, to fulfill seventy years.

Cyrus Proclaims Liberty for the Exiles
(Ezra 1.1–4)

22 In the first year of King Cyrus of Persia, in fulfillment of the word of the LORD spoken by Jer·e·mī′ah, the LORD stirred up the spirit of King Cyrus of

Persia so that he sent a herald throughout all his kingdom and also declared in a written edict: 23 "Thus says King Cyrus of Persia: The LORD, the God of heaven, has given me all the kingdoms of the earth, and he has charged me to build him a house at Jerusalem, which is in Judah. Whoever is among you of all his people, may the LORD his God be with him! Let him go up."

EZRA

End of the Babylonian Captivity
(2 Chr 36.22–23)

1 In the first year of King Cyrus of Persia, in order that the word of the LORD by the mouth of Jer·e·mī'ah might be accomplished, the LORD stirred up the spirit of King Cyrus of Persia so that he sent a herald throughout all his kingdom, and also in a written edict declared:

2 "Thus says King Cyrus of Persia: The LORD, the God of heaven, has given me all the kingdoms of the earth, and he has charged me to build him a house at Jerusalem in Judah. 3 Any of those among you who are of his people—may their God be with them!—are now permitted to go up to Jerusalem in Judah, and rebuild the house of the LORD, the God of Israel—he is the God who is in Jerusalem; 4 and let all survivors, in whatever place they reside, be assisted by the people of their place with silver and gold, with goods and with animals, besides freewill offerings for the house of God in Jerusalem."

5 The heads of the families of Judah and Benjamin, and the priests and the Lē'vītes—everyone whose spirit God had stirred—got ready to go up and rebuild the house of the LORD in Jerusalem. 6 All their neighbors aided them with silver vessels, with gold, with goods, with animals, and with valuable gifts, besides all that was freely offered. 7 King Cyrus himself brought out the vessels of the house of the LORD that Ne·bū·chad·nez'zar had carried away from Jerusalem and placed in the house of his gods. 8 King Cyrus of Persia had them released into the charge of Mith're·dath the treasurer, who counted them out to Shesh·baz'-zar the prince of Judah. 9 And this was the inventory: gold basins, thirty; silver basins, one thousand; knives,a twenty-nine; 10 gold bowls, thirty; other silver bowls, four hundred ten; other vessels, one thousand; 11 the total of the gold and silver vessels was five thousand four hundred. All these Shesh·baz'zar brought up, when the exiles were brought up from Babylonia to Jerusalem.

List of the Returned Exiles
(Neh 7.6–73)

2 Now these were the people of the province who came from those captive exiles whom King Ne·bū·chad·nez'zar of Babylon had carried captive to Babylonia; they returned to Jerusalem and Judah, all to their own towns. 2 They came with Ze·rub'ba·bel, Jesh'ū·a, Nē·he·mī'ah, Se·rāi'ah, Rē·el·āi'ah, Mor'de·caī, Bil'-shan, Mis'par, Big'vaī, Rē'hum, and Bā'a·nah.

The number of the Israelite people: 3 the descendants of Pā'rosh, two thousand one hundred seventy-two. 4 Of Sheph·a·tī'ah, three hundred seventy-two. 5 Of Ā'rah, seven hundred seventy-five. 6 Of Pā'hath-mō'ab, namely the descendants of Jesh'ū·a and Jō'ab, two thousand eight hundred twelve. 7 Of Ē'lam, one thousand two hundred fifty-four. 8 Of Zat'tū, nine hundred forty-five. 9 Of Zac'caī, seven hundred sixty. 10 Of Bā'nī, six hundred forty-two. 11 Of Bē'baī, six hundred twenty-three. 12 Of Az'gad, one thousand two hundred twenty-two. 13 Of Ad·o·nī'kam, six hundred sixty-six. 14 Of Big'vaī, two thousand fifty-six. 15 Of Ā'din, four hundred

a Vg: Meaning of Heb uncertain

422

fifty-four. [16] Of Ā'ter, namely of Hez·e·kī'ah, ninety-eight. [17] Of Bē'zaī, three hundred twenty-three. [18] Of Jō'-rah, one hundred twelve. [19] Of Hā'-shum, two hundred twenty-three. [20] Of Gib'bar, ninety-five. [21] Of Bethlehem, one hundred twenty-three. [22] The people of Ne·toph'ah, fifty-six. [23] Of An'-a·thoth, one hundred twenty-eight. [24] The descendants of Az'ma·veth, forty-two. [25] Of Kir·i·ath·ar'im, Chē·phī'rah, and Be·er'oth, seven hundred forty-three. [26] Of Rā'mah and Gē'ba, six hundred twenty-one. [27] The people of Mich'mas, one hundred twenty-two. [28] Of Beth'el and Aī, two hundred twenty-three. [29] The descendants of Nē'bō, fifty-two. [30] Of Mag'bish, one hundred fifty-six. [31] Of the other Ē'lam, one thousand two hundred fifty-four. [32] Of Hā'rim, three hundred twenty. [33] Of Lod, Hā'did, and Ō'nō, seven hundred twenty-five. [34] Of Jericho, three hundred forty-five. [35] Of Se·nā'ah, three thousand six hundred thirty.

36 The priests: the descendants of Je·daī'ah, of the house of Jesh'ū·a, nine hundred seventy-three. [37] Of Im'-mer, one thousand fifty-two. [38] Of Pash'hur, one thousand two hundred forty-seven. [39] Of Hā'rim, one thousand seventeen.

40 The Lē'vītes: the descendants of Jesh'ū·a and Kad'mi·el, of the descendants of Hod·a·vī'ah, seventy-four. [41] The singers: the descendants of Ā'saph, one hundred twenty-eight. [42] The descendants of the gatekeepers: of Shal'lum, of Ā'ter, of Tal'mon, of Ak'kub, of Ha·tī'ta, and of Shō'baī, in all one hundred thirty-nine.

43 The temple servants: the descendants of Zī'ha, Ha·sū'pha, Tab·bā'oth, [44] Kē'ros, Sī'a·ha, Pā'don, [45] Le·bā'-nah, Hag'a·bah, Ak'kub, [46] Hā'gab, Sham'laī, Hā'nan, [47] Gid'del, Gā'har, Rē·āi'ah, [48] Rē'zin, Ne·kō'da, Gaz'-zam, [49] Uz'za, Pa·sē'ah, Bē'saī, [50] As'-nah, Me·ū'nim, Ne·phī'sim, [51] Bak'-buk, Ha·kū'pha, Har'hur, [52] Baz'luth, Me·hī'da, Har'sha, [53] Bar'kos, Sis'e·ra, Tē'mah, [54] Ne·zī'ah, and Ha·tī'pha.

55 The descendants of Solomon's servants: Sō'taī, Has·sō'phe·reth, Pe·rū'da, [56] Jā'a·lah, Dar'kon, Gid'del, [57] Sheph·a·tī'ah, Hat'til, Pō'che·reth-haz·ze·bā'im, and Ā'mī.

58 All the temple servants and the descendants of Solomon's servants were three hundred ninety-two.

59 The following were those who came up from Tel-mē'lah, Tel-har'sha, Chē'rub, Ad'dan, and Im'mer, though they could not prove their families or their descent, whether they belonged to Israel: [60] the descendants of De·laī'ah, Tō·bī'ah, and Ne·kō'da, six hundred fifty-two. [61] Also, of the descendants of the priests: the descendants of Ha·baī'ah, Hak'koz, and Bar·zil'laī (who had married one of the daughters of Bar·zil'laī the Gil'-e·ad·īte, and was called by their name). [62] These looked for their entries in the genealogical records, but they were not found there, and so they were excluded from the priesthood as unclean; [63] the governor told them that they were not to partake of the most holy food, until there should be a priest to consult Ū'rim and Thum'mim.

64 The whole assembly together was forty-two thousand three hundred sixty, [65] besides their male and female servants, of whom there were seven thousand three hundred thirty-seven; and they had two hundred male and female singers. [66] They had seven hundred thirty-six horses, two hundred forty-five mules, [67] four hundred thirty-five camels, and six thousand seven hundred twenty donkeys.

68 As soon as they came to the house of the LORD in Jerusalem, some of the heads of families made freewill offerings for the house of God, to erect it on its site. [69] According to their resources they gave to the building fund sixty-one thousand darics of gold, five thousand minas of silver, and one hundred priestly robes.

70 The priests, the Lē'vītes, and some of the people lived in Jerusalem and its vicinity;[b] and the singers, the gatekeepers, and the temple servants lived in their towns, and all Israel in their towns.

Worship Restored at Jerusalem

3 When the seventh month came, and the Israelites were in the towns, the people gathered together in Jerusalem. [2] Then Jesh'ū·a son of Jō'-za·dak, with his fellow priests, and Ze·rub'ba·bel son of She·al'ti·el with his kin set out to build the altar of the God of Israel, to offer burnt offerings on it, as prescribed in the law of Moses the man of God. [3] They set up the altar on its foundation, because they were in

b 1 Esdras 5.46: Heb lacks *lived in Jerusalem and its vicinity* dread of the neighboring peoples, and they offered burnt offerings upon it to the LORD, morning and evening. 4 And they kept the festival of booths,[c] as prescribed, and offered the daily burnt offerings by number according to the ordinance, as required for each day, 5 and after that the regular burnt offerings, the offerings at the new moon and at all the sacred festivals of the LORD, and the offerings of everyone who made a freewill offering to the LORD. 6 From the first day of the seventh month they began to offer burnt offerings to the LORD. But the foundation of the temple of the LORD was not yet laid. 7 So they gave money to the masons and the carpenters, and food, drink, and oil to the Si·do'ni·ans and the Ty'ri·ans to bring cedar trees from Lebanon to the sea, to Jop'pa, according to the grant that they had from King Cyrus of Persia.

Foundation Laid for the Temple

8 In the second year after their arrival at the house of God at Jerusalem, in the second month, Ze·rub'ba·bel son of She·al'ti·el and Jesh'u·a son of Jo'za·dak made a beginning, together with the rest of their people, the priests and the Le'vites and all who had come to Jerusalem from the captivity. They appointed the Le'vites, from twenty years old and upward, to have the oversight of the work on the house of the LORD. 9 And Jesh'u·a with his sons and his kin, and Kad'mi·el and his sons, Bin'nu·i and Hod·a·vi'ah[d] along with the sons of Hen'a·dad, the Le'vites, their sons and kin, together took charge of the workers in the house of God.

10 When the builders laid the foundation of the temple of the LORD, the priests in their vestments were stationed to praise the LORD with trumpets, and the Le'vites, the sons of A'saph, with cymbals, according to the directions of King David of Israel; 11 and they sang responsively, praising and giving thanks to the LORD,

"For he is good,
   for his steadfast love endures
         forever toward Israel."
And all the people responded with a great shout when they praised the LORD, because the foundation of the house of the LORD was laid. 12 But many of the priests and Le'vites and heads of families, old people, who had seen the first house on its foundations,

wept with a loud voice when they saw this house, though many shouted aloud for joy, 13 so that the people could not distinguish the sound of the joyful shout from the sound of the people's weeping, for the people shouted so loudly that the sound was heard far away.

Resistance to Rebuilding the Temple

4 When the adversaries of Judah and Benjamin heard that the returned exiles were building a temple to the LORD, the God of Israel, 2 they approached Ze·rub'ba·bel and the heads of families and said to them, "Let us build with you, for we worship your God as you do, and we have been sacrificing to him ever since the days of King E'sar-had'don of Assyria who brought us here." 3 But Ze·rub'ba·bel, Jesh'u·a, and the rest of the heads of families in Israel said to them, "You shall have no part with us in building a house to our God; but we alone will build to the LORD, the God of Israel, as King Cyrus of Persia has commanded us."

4 Then the people of the land discouraged the people of Judah, and made them afraid to build, 5 and they bribed officials to frustrate their plan throughout the reign of King Cyrus of Persia and until the reign of King Da·ri'us of Persia.

Rebuilding of Jerusalem Opposed

6 In the reign of A·has·u·e'rus, in his accession year, they wrote an accusation against the inhabitants of Judah and Jerusalem.

7 And in the days of Ar·ta·xerx'es, Bish'lam and Mith're·dath and Ta'be·el and the rest of their associates wrote to King Ar·ta·xerx'es of Persia; the letter was written in Ar·a·ma'ic and translated.[e] 8 Re'hum the royal deputy and Shim'shai the scribe wrote a letter against Jerusalem to King Ar·ta·xerx'es as follows 9 (then Re'hum the royal deputy, Shim'shai the scribe, and the rest of their associates, the judges, the envoys, the officials, the Persians, the people of E'rech, the

---

[c] Or tabernacles; Heb succoth
[d] Compare 2.40; Neh 7.43; 1 Esdras 5.58: Heb sons of Judah   [e] Heb adds in Aramaic, indicating that 4.8-6.18 is in Aramaic. Another interpretation is The letter was written in the Aramaic script and set forth in the Aramaic language

Babylonians, the people of Su'sa, that is, the E'lam·ites, [10] and the rest of the nations whom the great and noble Os·nap'par deported and settled in the cities of Sa·măr'i·a and in the rest of the province Beyond the River wrote— and now [11] this is a copy of the letter that they sent):

"To King Ar·ta·xerx'ēs: Your servants, the people of the province Beyond the River, send greeting. And now [12] may it be known to the king that the Jews who came up from you to us have gone to Jerusalem. They are rebuilding that rebellious and wicked city; they are finishing the walls and repairing the foundations. [13] Now may it be known to the king that, if this city is rebuilt and the walls finished, they will not pay tribute, custom, or toll, and the royal revenue will be reduced. [14] Now because we share the salt of the palace and it is not fitting for us to witness the king's dishonor, therefore we send and inform the king, [15] so that a search may be made in the annals of your ancestors. You will discover in the annals that this is a rebellious city, hurtful to kings and provinces, and that sedition was stirred up in it from long ago. On that account this city was laid waste. [16] We make known to the king that, if this city is rebuilt and its walls finished, you will then have no possession in the province Beyond the River."

17 The king sent an answer: "To Rē'hum the royal deputy and Shim'-shai the scribe and the rest of their associates who live in Sa·măr'i·a and in the rest of the province Beyond the River, greeting. And now [18] the letter that you sent to us has been read in translation before me. [19] So I made a decree, and someone searched and discovered that this city has risen against kings from long ago, and that rebellion and sedition have been made in it. [20] Jerusalem has had mighty kings who ruled over the whole province Beyond the River, to whom tribute, custom, and toll were paid. [21] Therefore issue an order that these people be made to cease, and that this city not be rebuilt, until I make a decree. [22] Moreover, take care not to be slack in this matter; why should damage grow to the hurt of the king?"

23 Then when the copy of King Ar·ta·xerx'ēs' letter was read before Rē'hum and the scribe Shim'shai and their associates, they hurried to the Jews in Jerusalem and by force and power made them cease. [24] At that time the work on the house of God in Jerusalem stopped and was discontinued until the second year of the reign of King Da·rī'us of Persia.

Restoration of the Temple Resumed
(Hag 1.1; Zech 1.1)

5 Now the prophets, Hag'gai[f] and Zech·a·rī'ah son of Id'do, prophesied to the Jews who were in Judah and Jerusalem, in the name of the God of Israel who was over them. [2] Then Ze·rub'ba·bel son of She·al'ti·el and Jesh'ū·a son of Jŏ'za·dak set out to rebuild the house of God in Jerusalem; and with them were the prophets of God, helping them.

3 At the same time Tat'te·nai the governor of the province Beyond the River and Shē'thar-boz'e·nai and their associates came to them and spoke to them thus, "Who gave you a decree to build this house and to finish this structure?" [4] They[g] also asked them this, "What are the names of the men who are building this building?" [5] But the eye of their God was upon the elders of the Jews, and they did not stop them until a report reached Da·rī'us and then answer was returned by letter in reply to it.

6 The copy of the letter that Tat'-te·nai the governor of the province Beyond the River and Shē'thar-boz'e·nai and his associates the envoys who were in the province Beyond the River sent to King Da·rī'us; [7] they sent him a report, in which was written as follows: "To Da·rī'us the king, all peace! [8] May it be known to the king that we went to the province of Judah, to the house of the great God. It is being built of hewn stone, and timber is laid in the walls; this work is being done diligently and prospers in their hands. [9] Then we spoke to those elders and asked them, 'Who gave you a decree to build this house and to finish this structure?' [10] We also asked them their names, for your information, so that we might write down the names of the men at their head. [11] This was their reply to us: 'We are the servants of the God of heaven and earth, and we are rebuilding the house that was built many years ago, which a great king of Israel built and finished. [12] But because

---

[f] Aram adds *the prophet*   [g] Gk Syr:
Aram *We*

our ancestors had angered the God of heaven, he gave them into the hand of King Ne·bu·chad·nez'zar of Babylon, the Chal·de'an, who destroyed this house and carried away the people to Babylonia. 13 However, King Cyrus of Babylon, in the first year of his reign, made a decree that this house of God should be rebuilt. 14 Moreover, the gold and silver vessels of the house of God, which Ne·bu·chad·nez'zar had taken out of the temple in Jerusalem and had brought into the temple of Babylon, these King Cyrus took out of the temple of Babylon, and they were delivered to a man named Shesh·baz'zar, whom he had made governor. 15 He said to him, "Take these vessels; go and put them in the temple in Jerusalem, and let the house of God be rebuilt on its site." 16 Then this Shesh·baz'zar came and laid the foundations of the house of God in Jerusalem; and from that time until now it has been under construction, and it is not yet finished.' 17 And now, if it seems good to the king, have a search made in the royal archives there in Babylon, to see whether a decree was issued by King Cyrus for the rebuilding of this house of God in Jerusalem. Let the king send us his pleasure in this matter."

The Decree of Darius

6 Then King Da·ri'us made a decree, and they searched the archives where the documents were stored in Babylon. 2 But it was in Ec·bat'a·na, the capital in the province of Med'i·a, that a scroll was found on which this was written: "A record. 3 In the first year of his reign, King Cyrus issued a decree: Concerning the house of God at Jerusalem, let the house be rebuilt, the place where sacrifices are offered and burnt offerings are brought; h its height shall be sixty cubits and its width sixty cubits, 4 with three courses of hewn stones and one course of timber; let the cost be paid from the royal treasury. 5 Moreover, let the gold and silver vessels of the house of God, which Ne·bu·chad·nez'zar took out of the temple in Jerusalem and brought to Babylon, be restored and brought back to the temple in Jerusalem, each to its place; you shall put them in the house of God."

6 "Now you, Tat'te·nai, governor of the province Beyond the River, She'-thar-boz'e·nai, and you, their associates, the envoys in the province Be-

yond the River, keep away; 7 let the work on this house of God alone; let the governor of the Jews and the elders of the Jews rebuild this house of God on its site. 8 Moreover I make a decree regarding what you shall do for these elders of the Jews for the rebuilding of this house of God: the cost is to be paid to these people, in full and without delay, from the royal revenue, the tribute of the province Beyond the River. 9 Whatever is needed—young bulls, rams, or sheep for burnt offerings to the God of heaven, wheat, salt, wine, or oil, as the priests in Jerusalem require—let that be given to them day by day without fail, 10 so that they may offer pleasing sacrifices to the God of heaven, and pray for the life of the king and his children. 11 Furthermore I decree that if anyone alters this edict, a beam shall be pulled out of the house of the perpetrator, who then shall be impaled on it. The house shall be made a dunghill. 12 May the God who has established his name there overthrow any king or people that shall put forth a hand to alter this, or to destroy this house of God in Jerusalem. I, Da·ri'us, make a decree; let it be done with all diligence."

Completion and Dedication of the Temple

13 Then, according to the word sent by King Da·ri'us, Tat'te·nai, the governor of the province Beyond the River, She'thar-boz'e·nai, and their associates did with all diligence what King Da·ri'us had ordered. 14 So the elders of the Jews built and prospered, through the prophesying of the prophet Hag'gai and Zech·a·ri'ah son of Id'do. They finished their building by command of the God of Israel and by decree of Cyrus, Da·ri'us, and King Ar·ta·xerx'es of Persia; 15 and this house was finished on the third day of the month of A'dar, in the sixth year of the reign of King Da·ri'us.

16 The people of Israel, the priests and the Le'vites, and the rest of the returned exiles, celebrated the dedication of this house of God with joy. 17 They offered at the dedication of this house of God one hundred bulls, two hundred rams, four hundred lambs, and as a sin offering for all Israel, twelve male goats, according to the number of the tribes of Israel. 18 Then

h Meaning of Aram uncertain

EZRA

they set the priests in their divisions and the Lē′vītes in their courses for the service of God at Jerusalem, as it is written in the book of Moses.

The Passover Celebrated
(Cp Deut 16.1–8)

19 On the fourteenth day of the first month the returned exiles kept the passover. 20 For both the priests and the Lē′vītes had purified themselves; all of them were clean. So they killed the passover lamb for all the returned exiles, for their fellow priests, and for themselves. 21 It was eaten by the people of Israel who had returned from exile, and also by all who had joined them and separated themselves from the pollutions of the nations of the land to worship the LORD, the God of Israel. 22 With joy they celebrated the festival of unleavened bread seven days; for the LORD had made them joyful, and had turned the heart of the king of Assyria to them, so that he aided them in the work on the house of God, the God of Israel.

The Coming and Work of Ezra

7 After this, in the reign of King Ar·ta·xerx′ēs of Persia, Ezra son of Se·rāi′ah, son of Az·a·rī′ah, son of Hil·kī′ah, 2 son of Shal′lum, son of Zā′dok, son of A·hī′tub, 3 son of Am·a·rī′ah, son of Az·a·rī′ah, son of Me·rā′i·oth, 4 son of Zer·a·hī′ah, son of Uz′zī, son of Buk′kī, 5 son of Ab·i·shū′a, son of Phin′e·has, son of El·ē·ā′zar, son of the chief priest Aaron— 6 this Ezra went up from Babylonia. He was a scribe skilled in the law of Moses that the LORD the God of Israel had given; and the king granted him all that he asked, for the hand of the LORD his God was upon him.

7 Some of the people of Israel, and some of the priests and Lē′vītes, the singers and gatekeepers, and the temple servants also went up to Jerusalem, in the seventh year of King Ar·ta·xerx′ēs. 8 They came to Jerusalem in the fifth month, which was in the seventh year of the king. 9 On the first day of the first month the journey up from Babylon was begun, and on the first day of the fifth month he came to Jerusalem, for the gracious hand of his God was upon him. 10 For Ezra had set his heart to study the law of the LORD, and to do it, and to teach the statutes and ordinances in Israel.

The Letter of Artaxerxes to Ezra

11 This is a copy of the letter that King Ar·ta·xerx′ēs gave to the priest Ezra, the scribe, a scholar of the text of the commandments of the LORD and his statutes for Israel: 12 "Ar·ta·xerx′ēs, king of kings, to the priest Ezra, the scribe of the law of the God of heaven: Peace.[i] And now 13 I decree that any of the people of Israel or their priests or Lē′vītes in my kingdom who freely offers to go to Jerusalem may go with you. 14 For you are sent by the king and his seven counselors to make inquiries about Judah and Jerusalem according to the law of your God, which is in your hand, 15 and also to convey the silver and gold that the king and his counselors have freely offered to the God of Israel, whose dwelling is in Jerusalem, 16 with all the silver and gold that you shall find in the whole province of Babylonia, and with the freewill offerings of the people and the priests, given willingly for the house of their God in Jerusalem. 17 With this money, then, you shall with all diligence buy bulls, rams, and lambs, and their grain offerings and their drink offerings, and you shall offer them on the altar of the house of your God in Jerusalem. 18 Whatever seems good to you and your colleagues to do with the rest of the silver and gold, you may do, according to the will of your God. 19 The vessels that have been given you for the service of the house of your God, you shall deliver before the God of Jerusalem. 20 And whatever else is required for the house of your God, which you are responsible for providing, you may provide out of the king's treasury.

21 "I, King Ar·ta·xerx′ēs, decree to all the treasurers in the province Beyond the River: Whatever the priest Ezra, the scribe of the law of the God of heaven, requires of you, let it be done with all diligence, 22 up to one hundred talents of silver, one hundred cors of wheat, one hundred baths[j] of wine, one hundred baths[j] of oil, and unlimited salt. 23 Whatever is commanded by the God of heaven, let it be done with zeal for the house of the God of heaven, or wrath will come upon the realm of the king and his heirs. 24 We also notify you that it shall not be law-

iSyr Vg 1 Esdras 8.9: Aram *Perfect*   jA Heb measure of volume ful to impose tribute, custom, or toll on any of the priests, the Lē'vītes, the singers, the doorkeepers, the temple servants, or other servants of this house of God.

25 "And you, Ezra, according to the God-given wisdom you possess, appoint magistrates and judges who may judge all the people in the province Beyond the River who know the laws of your God; and you shall teach those who do not know them. 26 All who will not obey the law of your God and the law of the king, let judgment be strictly executed on them, whether for death or for banishment or for confiscation of their goods or for imprisonment."

27 Blessed be the LORD, the God of our ancestors, who put such a thing as this into the heart of the king to glorify the house of the LORD in Jerusalem, 28 and who extended to me steadfast love before the king and his counselors, and before all the king's mighty officers. I took courage, for the hand of the LORD my God was upon me, and I gathered leaders from Israel to go up with me.

Heads of Families Who Returned with Ezra

8 These are their family heads, and this is the genealogy of those who went up with me from Babylonia, in the reign of King Ar·ta·xerx'ēs: 2 Of the descendants of Phin'e·has, Ger'shom. Of Ith'a·mar, Daniel. Of David, Hat'tush, 3 of the descendants of Shec·a·nī'ah. Of Pā'rosh, Zech·a·rī'ah, with whom were registered one hundred fifty males. 4 Of the descendants of Pā'hath-mō'ab, El·i·ē·hō·ē'nai son of Zer·a·hī'ah, and with him two hundred males. 5 Of the descendants of Zat'tū,k Shec·a·nī'ah son of Ja·hā'-zi·el, and with him three hundred males. 6 Of the descendants of Ā'din, Ē'bed son of Jonathan, and with him fifty males. 7 Of the descendants of Ē'lam, Je·shā'i·ah son of Ath·a·lī'ah, and with him seventy males. 8 Of the descendants of Sheph·a·tī'ah, Zeb·a·dī'ah son of Michael, and with him eighty males. 9 Of the descendants of Jō'ab, Ō·ba·dī'ah son of Je·hī'el, and with him two hundred eighteen males. 10 Of the descendants of Bā'nī,l She·lō'mith son of Jos·i·phī'ah, and with him one hundred sixty males. 11 Of the descendants of Bē'bai, Zech·a·rī'ah son of Bē'bai, and with him twenty-eight males. 12 Of the de-

scendants of Az'gad, Jō·hā'nan son of Hak'ka·tan, and with him one hundred ten males. 13 Of the descendants of Ad·o·nī'kam, those who came later, their names being E·liph'e·let, Je·ū'el, and She·māi'ah, and with them sixty males. 14 Of the descendants of Big'vai, Ū'thai and Zac'cur, and with them seventy males.

Servants for the Temple

15 I gathered them by the river that runs to A·hā'va, and there we camped three days. As I reviewed the people and the priests, I found there none of the descendants of Levi. 16 Then I sent for El·i·ē'zer, Ar'i·el, She·māi'ah, El·nā'than, Ja'rib, El·nā'than, Nathan, Zech·a·rī'ah, and Me·shul'lam, who were leaders, and for Joi'a·rib and El·nā'than, who were wise, 17 and sent them to Id'dō, the leader at the place called Cas·i·phī'a, telling them what to say to Id'dō and his colleagues the temple servants at Cas·i·phī'a, namely, to send us ministers for the house of our God. 18 Since the gracious hand of our God was upon us, they brought us a man of discretion, of the descendants of Mah'lī son of Levi son of Israel, namely Sher·e·bī'ah, with his sons and kin, eighteen; 19 also Hash·a·bī'ah and with him Je·shā'i·ah of the descendants of Me·rar'ī, with his kin and their sons, twenty; 20 besides two hundred twenty of the temple servants, whom David and his officials had set apart to attend the Lē'vītes. These were all mentioned by name.

Fasting and Prayer for Protection

21 Then I proclaimed a fast there, at the river A·hā'va, that we might deny ourselvesm before our God, to seek from him a safe journey for ourselves, our children, and all our possessions. 22 For I was ashamed to ask the king for a band of soldiers and cavalry to protect us against the enemy on our way, since we had told the king that the hand of our God is gracious to all who seek him, but his power and his wrath are against all who forsake him. 23 So we fasted and petitioned our God for this, and he listened to our entreaty.

---

k Gk 1 Esdras 8.32: Heb lacks of Zattu
l Gk 1 Esdras 8.36: Heb lacks Bani
m Or might fast

E
Z
R
A

Gifts for the Temple

24 Then I set apart twelve of the leading priests: Sher·e·bi′ah, Hash·a·bi′ah, and ten of their kin with them. 25 And I weighed out to them the silver and the gold and the vessels, the offering for the house of our God that the king, his counselors, his lords, and all Israel there present had offered; 26 I weighed out into their hand six hundred fifty talents of silver, and one hundred silver vessels worth . . . talents, n and one hundred talents of gold, 27 twenty gold bowls worth a thousand darics, and two vessels of fine polished bronze as precious as gold. 28 And I said to them, "You are holy to the LORD, and the vessels are holy; and the silver and the gold are a freewill offering to the LORD, the God of your ancestors. 29 Guard them and keep them until you weigh them before the chief priests and the Le′vites and the heads of families in Israel at Jerusalem, within the chambers of the house of the LORD." 30 So the priests and the Le′vites took over the silver, the gold, and the vessels as they were weighed out, to bring them to Jerusalem, to the house of our God.

The Return to Jerusalem

31 Then we left the river A·ha′va on the twelfth day of the first month, to go to Jerusalem; the hand of our God was upon us, and he delivered us from the hand of the enemy and from ambushes along the way. 32 We came to Jerusalem and remained there three days. 33 On the fourth day, within the house of our God, the silver, the gold, and the vessels were weighed into the hands of the priest Mer′e·moth son of U·ri′ah, and with him was El·e·a′zar son of Phin′e·has, and with them were the Le′vites, Joz′a·bad son of Jesh′u·a and No·a·di′ah son of Bin′nu·i. 34 The total was counted and weighed, and the weight of everything was recorded.

35 At that time those who had come from captivity, the returned exiles, offered burnt offerings to the God of Israel, twelve bulls for all Israel, ninety-six rams, seventy-seven lambs, and as a sin offering twelve male goats; all this was a burnt offering to the LORD. 36 They also delivered the king's commissions to the king's satraps and to the governors of the province Beyond the River; and they supported the people and the house of God.

Denunciation of Mixed Marriages

9 After these things had been done, the officials approached me and said, "The people of Israel, the priests, and the Le′vites have not separated themselves from the peoples of the lands with their abominations, from the Ca′naan·ites, the Hit′tites, the Per′iz·zites, the Jeb′u·sites, the Am′mon·ites, the Mo′ab·ites, the Egyptians, and the Am′o·rites. 2 For they have taken some of their daughters as wives for themselves and for their sons. Thus the holy seed has mixed itself with the peoples of the lands, and in this faithlessness the officials and leaders have led the way." 3 When I heard this, I tore my garment and my mantle, and pulled hair from my head and beard, and sat appalled. 4 Then all who trembled at the words of the God of Israel, because of the faithlessness of the returned exiles, gathered around me while I sat appalled until the evening sacrifice.

Ezra's Prayer

5 At the evening sacrifice I got up from my fasting, with my garments and my mantle torn, and fell on my knees, spread out my hands to the LORD my God, 6 and said,
"O my God, I am too ashamed and embarrassed to lift my face to you, my God, for our iniquities have risen higher than our heads, and our guilt has mounted up to the heavens. 7 From the days of our ancestors to this day we have been deep in guilt, and for our iniquities we, our kings, and our priests have been handed over to the kings of the lands, to the sword, to captivity, to plundering, and to utter shame, as is now the case. 8 But now for a brief moment favor has been shown by the LORD our God, who has left us a remnant, and given us a stake in his holy place, in order that he o may brighten our eyes and grant us a little sustenance in our slavery. 9 For we are slaves; yet our God has not forsaken us in our slavery, but has extended to us his steadfast love before the kings of Persia, to give us new life to set up the house of our God, to repair its ruins, and to give us a wall in Judea and Jerusalem.
10 "And now, our God, what shall

n The number of talents is lacking
o Heb our God

we say after this? For we have forsaken your commandments, [11] which you commanded by your servants the prophets, saying, 'The land that you are entering to possess is a land unclean with the pollutions of the peoples of the lands, with their abominations. They have filled it from end to end with their uncleanness. [12] Therefore do not give your daughters to their sons, neither take their daughters for your sons, and never seek their peace or prosperity, so that you may be strong and eat the good of the land and leave it for an inheritance to your children forever.' [13] After all that has come upon us for our evil deeds and for our great guilt, seeing that you, our God, have punished us less than our iniquities deserved and have given us such a remnant as this, [14] shall we break your commandments again and intermarry with the peoples who practice these abominations? Would you not be angry with us until you destroy us without remnant or survivor? [15] O LORD, God of Israel, you are just, but we have escaped as a remnant, as is now the case. Here we are before you in our guilt, though no one can face you because of this."

The People's Response

10 While Ezra prayed and made confession, weeping and throwing himself down before the house of God, a very great assembly of men, women, and children gathered to him out of Israel; the people also wept bitterly. [2] Shec·a·nī'ah son of Je·hī'el, of the descendants of Ē'lam, addressed Ezra, saying, "We have broken faith with our God and have married foreign women from the peoples of the land, but even now there is hope for Israel in spite of this. [3] So now let us make a covenant with our God to send away all these wives and their children, according to the counsel of my lord and of those who tremble at the commandment of our God; and let it be done according to the law. [4] Take action, for it is your duty, and we are with you; be strong, and do it." [5] Then Ezra stood up and made the leading priests, the Lē'vītes, and all Israel swear that they would do as had been said. So they swore.

Foreign Wives and Their Children Rejected

6 Then Ezra withdrew from before the house of God, and went to the chamber of Jě·hō·hā'nan son of E·lī'-a·shib, where he spent the night. [p] He did not eat bread or drink water, for he was mourning over the faithlessness of the exiles. [7] They made a proclamation throughout Judah and Jerusalem to all the returned exiles that they should assemble at Jerusalem, [8] and that if any did not come within three days, by order of the officials and the elders all their property should be forfeited, and they themselves banned from the congregation of the exiles.

9 Then all the people of Judah and Benjamin assembled at Jerusalem within the three days; it was the ninth month, on the twentieth day of the month. All the people sat in the open square before the house of God, trembling because of this matter and because of the heavy rain. [10] Then Ezra the priest stood up and said to them, "You have trespassed and married foreign women, and so increased the guilt of Israel. [11] Now make confession to the LORD the God of your ancestors, and do his will; separate yourselves from the peoples of the land and from the foreign wives." [12] Then all the assembly answered with a loud voice, "It is so; we must do as you have said. [13] But the people are many, and it is a time of heavy rain; we cannot stand in the open. Nor is this a task for one day or for two, for many of us have transgressed in this matter. [14] Let our officials represent the whole assembly, and let all in our towns who have taken foreign wives come at appointed times, and with them the elders and judges of every town, until the fierce wrath of our God on this account is averted from us." [15] Only Jonathan son of As'a·hel and Jah·zēi'ah son of Tik'-vah opposed this, and Me·shul'lam and Shab'be·thaī the Lē'vītes supported them.

16 Then the returned exiles did so. Ezra the priest selected men, [q] heads of families, according to their families, each of them designated by name. On the first day of the tenth month they sat down to examine the matter. [17] By the first day of the first month they had come to the end of all the men who had married foreign women.

18 There were found of the descen-

---

[p] 1 Esdras 9.2: Heb *where he went*
[q] 1 Esdras 9.16: Syr: Heb *And there were selected Ezra,*

dants of the priests who had married foreign women, of the descendants of Jesh′u·a son of Jŏ′za·dak and his brothers: Mă·a·sēi′ah, El·i·ē′zer, Jă′-rib, and Ged·a·lī′ah. [19]They pledged themselves to send away their wives, and their guilt offering was a ram of the flock for their guilt. [20]Of the descendants of Im′mer: Ha·nă′nī and Zeb·a·dī′ah. [21]Of the descendants of Hā′rim: Mă·a·sēi′ah, E·lī′jah, She·māi′ah, Je·hī′el, and Uz·zī′ah. [22]Of the descendants of Pash′hur: El·i·ō·ē′naī, Mă·a·sēi′ah, Ish′ma·el, Ne·than′el, Joz′a·bad, and El·ă′sah.

23 Of the Lē′vītes: Joz′a·bad, Shim′ē·ī, Ke·lāi′ah (that is, Ke·lī′ta), Peth·a·hī′ah, Judah, and El·i·ē′zer. [24]Of the singers: E·lī′a·shib. Of the gatekeepers: Shal′lum, Tē′lem, and Ū′rī.

25 And of Israel: of the descendants of Pā′rosh: Ra·mī′ah, Iz·zī′-ah, Mal·chī′jah, Mij′a·min, El·ē·ā′zar, Hash·a·bī′ah,[r] and Be·nā′i·ah. [26]Of the descendants of Ē′lam: Mat-ta·nī′ah, Zech·a·rī′ah, Je·hī′el, Ab′dī, Jer′e·moth, and E·lī′jah. [27]Of the descendants of Zat′tū: El·i·ō·ē′naī, E·lī′a·shib, Mat·ta·nī′ah, Jer′e·moth, Ză′bad, and A·zī′za. [28]Of the descendants of Bē′baī: Jē·hō·hā′nan, Han-a·nī′ah, Zab′baī, and Ath′laī. [29]Of the descendants of Bā′nī: Me·shul′lam,

Mal′luch, A·dāi′ah, Jash′ub, Shē′al, and Jer′e·moth. [30]Of the descendants of Pā′hath-mō′ab: Ad′na, Chē′lal, Be·nā′i·ah, Mă·a·sēi′ah, Mat·ta·nī′ah, Bez′a·lel, Bin′nū·ī, and Ma·nas′seh. [31]Of the descendants of Hā′rim: El·i·ē′zer, Is·shī′jah, Mal·chī′jah, She·māi′ah, Shim′ē·on, [32]Benjamin, Mal′luch, and Shem·a·rī′ah. [33]Of the descendants of Hā′shum: Mat·tē′naī, Mat·tat′tah, Ză′bad, E·liph′e·let, Jer′-e·maī, Ma·nas′seh, and Shim′ē·ī. [34]Of the descendants of Bā′nī: Mă·a·dā′ī, Am′ram, Ū′el, [35]Be·nā′i·ah, Bē·dēi′ah, Chel′ū·hī, [36]Va·nī′ah, Mer′e·moth, E·lī′a·shib, [37]Mat·ta·nī′ah, Mat·tē′naī, and Jă·a′sū. [38]Of the descendants of Bin′nū·ī:[s] Shim′ē·ī, [39]Shel·e·mī′ah, Nathan, A·dāi′ah, [40]Mach·nad′e·baī, Shā′shaī, Shā′raī, [41]Az′a·rel, Shel-e·mī′ah, Shem·a·rī′ah, [42]Shal′lum, Am·a·rī′ah, and Joseph. [43]Of the descendants of Nē′bō: Je·ī′el, Mat·ti·thī′-ah, Ză′bad, Ze·bī′na, Jad′daī, Jō′el, and Be·nā′i·ah. [44]All these had married foreign women, and they sent them away with their children.[t]

---

[r] 1 Esdras 9.26 Gk: Heb *Malchijah*
[s] Gk: Heb *Bani, Binnui*   [t] 1 Esdras 9.36; Meaning of Heb uncertain

NEHEMIAH

Nehemiah Prays for His People

1 The words of Nē·he·mī′ah son of Hac·a·lī′ah. In the month of Chis′-lev, in the twentieth year, while I was in Su′sa the capital, [2]one of my broth-ers, Ha·nā′nī, came with certain men from Judah; and I asked them about the Jews that survived, those who had escaped the captivity, and about Jeru-salem. [3]They replied, "The survivors there in the province who escaped cap-tivity are in great trouble and shame; the wall of Jerusalem is broken down, and its gates have been destroyed by fire."

4 When I heard these words I sat down and wept, and mourned for days, fasting and praying before the God of heaven. [5]I said, "O LORD God of heaven, the great and awesome God who keeps covenant and steadfast love with those who love him and keep his commandments; [6]let your ear be attentive and your eyes open to hear the prayer of your servant that I now pray before you day and night for your servants, the people of Israel, confess-ing the sins of the people of Israel, which we have sinned against you. Both I and my family have sinned. [7]We

have offended you deeply, failing to keep the commandments, the statutes, and the ordinances that you commanded your servant Moses. [8] Remember the word that you commanded your servant Moses, 'If you are unfaithful, I will scatter you among the peoples; [9] but if you return to me and keep my commandments and do them, though your outcasts are under the farthest skies, I will gather them from there and bring them to the place at which I have chosen to establish my name.' [10] They are your servants and your people, whom you redeemed by your great power and your strong hand. [11] O Lord, let your ear be attentive to the prayer of your servant, and to the prayer of your servants who delight in revering your name. Give success to your servant today, and grant him mercy in the sight of this man!"

At the time, I was cupbearer to the king.

Nehemiah Sent to Judah

2 In the month of Nī′san, in the twentieth year of King Ar·ta·xerx′es, when wine was served him, I carried the wine and gave it to the king. Now, I had never been sad in his presence before. [2] So the king said to me, "Why is your face sad, since you are not sick? This can only be sadness of the heart." Then I was very much afraid. [3] I said to the king, "May the king live forever! Why should my face not be sad, when the city, the place of my ancestors' graves, lies waste, and its gates have been destroyed by fire?" [4] Then the king said to me, "What do you request?" So I prayed to the God of heaven. [5] Then I said to the king, "If it pleases the king, and if your servant has found favor with you, I ask that you send me to Judah, to the city of my ancestors' graves, so that I may rebuild it." [6] The king said to me (the queen also was sitting beside him), "How long will you be gone, and when will you return?" So it pleased the king to send me, and I set him a date. [7] Then I said to the king, "If it pleases the king, let letters be given me to the governors of the province Beyond the River, that they may grant me passage until I arrive in Judah; [8] and a letter to Ā′saph, the keeper of the king's forest, directing him to give me timber to make beams for the gates of the temple fortress, and for the wall of the city, and for the house that I shall occupy." And

the king granted me what I asked, for the gracious hand of my God was upon me.

[9] Then I came to the governors of the province Beyond the River, and gave them the king's letters. Now the king had sent officers of the army and cavalry with me. [10] When San·bal′lat the Hor′o·nīte and Tō·bī′ah the Am′mon·ite official heard this, it displeased them greatly that someone had come to seek the welfare of the people of Israel.

Nehemiah's Inspection of the Walls

[11] So I came to Jerusalem and was there for three days. [12] Then I got up during the night, I and a few men with me; I told no one what my God had put into my heart to do for Jerusalem. The only animal I took was the animal I rode. [13] I went out by night by the Valley Gate past the Dragon's Spring and to the Dung Gate, and I inspected the walls of Jerusalem that had been broken down and its gates that had been destroyed by fire. [14] Then I went on to the Fountain Gate and to the King's Pool; but there was no place for the animal I was riding to continue. [15] So I went up by way of the valley by night and inspected the wall. Then I turned back and entered by the Valley Gate, and so returned. [16] The officials did not know where I had gone or what I was doing; I had not yet told the Jews, the priests, the nobles, the officials, and the rest that were to do the work.

Decision to Restore the Walls

[17] Then I said to them, "You see the trouble we are in, how Jerusalem lies in ruins with its gates burned. Come, let us rebuild the wall of Jerusalem, so that we may no longer suffer disgrace." [18] I told them that the hand of my God had been gracious upon me, and also the words that the king had spoken to me. Then they said, "Let us start building!" So they committed themselves to the common good. [19] But when San·bal′lat the Hor′o·nīte and Tō·bī′ah the Am′mon·ite official, and Gē′shem the Arab heard of it, they mocked and ridiculed us, saying, "What is this that you are doing? Are you rebelling against the king?" [20] Then I replied to them, "The God of heaven is the one who will give us success, and we his servants are going to start building; but you have no share

or claim or historic right in Jerusa-lem."

Organization of the Work

3 Then the high priest E·li'a·shib set to work with his fellow priests and rebuilt the Sheep Gate. They consecrated it and set up its doors; they consecrated it as far as the Tower of the Hundred and as far as the Tower of Ha·nan'el. [2] And the men of Jericho built next to him. And next to them[a] Zac'cur son of Im'ri built.

[3] The sons of Has·se·na'ah built the Fish Gate; they laid its beams and set up its doors, its bolts, and its bars. [4] Next to them Mer'e·moth son of U·ri'ah son of Hak'koz made repairs. Next to them Me·shul'lam son of Ber·e·chi'ah son of Me·shez'a·bel made repairs. Next to them Za'dok son of Ba'a·na made repairs. [5] Next to them the Te·ko'ites made repairs; but their nobles would not put their shoulders to the work of their Lord.[b]

[6] Joi'a·da son of Pa·se'ah and Me·shul'lam son of Bes·o·dei'ah repaired the Old Gate; they laid its beams and set up its doors, its bolts, and its bars. [7] Next to them repairs were made by Me·la·ti'ah the Gib'e·on·ite and Ja'don the Me·ron'o·thite—the men of Gib'e·on and of Miz'pah—who were under the jurisdiction of[c] the governor of the province Beyond the River. [8] Next to them Uz'zi·el son of Har·hai'ah, one of the goldsmiths, made repairs. Next to him Han·a·ni'ah, one of the perfumers, made repairs; and they restored Jerusalem as far as the Broad Wall. [9] Next to them Reph·ai'ah son of Hur, ruler of half the district of[d] Jerusalem, made repairs. [10] Next to them Je·dai'ah son of Har·u'maph made repairs opposite his house; and next to him Hat'tush son of Hash·ab·nei'ah made repairs. [11] Mal·chi'jah son of Ha'rim and Has'shub son of Pa'hath-mo'ab repaired another section and the Tower of the Ovens. [12] Next to him Shal'lum son of Hal·lo'hesh, ruler of half the district of[d] Jerusalem, made repairs, he and his daughters.

[13] Ha'nun and the inhabitants of Za·no'ah repaired the Valley Gate; they rebuilt it and set up its doors, its bolts, and its bars, and repaired a thousand cubits of the wall, as far as the Dung Gate.

[14] Mal·chi'jah son of Re'chab, ruler of the district of[e] Beth-hac·che'rem, repaired the Dung Gate; he rebuilt it and set up its doors, its bolts, and its bars.

[15] And Shal'lum son of Col-ho'zeh, ruler of the district of[e] Miz'pah, repaired the Fountain Gate; he rebuilt it and covered it and set up its doors, its bolts, and its bars; and he built the wall of the Pool of She'lah of the king's garden, as far as the stairs that go down from the City of David. [16] After him Ne·he·mi'ah son of Az'buk, ruler of half the district of[d] Beth-zur, repaired from a point opposite the graves of David, as far as the artificial pool and the house of the warriors. [17] After him the Le'vites made repairs: Re'hum son of Ba'ni; next to him Hash·a·bi'ah, ruler of half the district of[d] Ke·i'lah, made repairs for his district. [18] After him their kin made repairs: Bin'nu·i,[f] son of Hen'a·dad, ruler of half the district of[d] Ke·i'lah; [19] next to him E'zer son of Jesh'u·a, ruler[g] of Miz'pah, repaired another section opposite the ascent to the armory at the Angle. [20] After him Bar'uch son of Zab'bai repaired another section from the Angle to the door of the house of the high priest E·li'a·shib. [21] After him Mer'e·moth son of U·ri'ah son of Hak'koz repaired another section from the door of the house of E·li'a·shib to the end of the house of E·li'a·shib. [22] After him the priests, the men of the surrounding area, made repairs. [23] After them Benjamin and Has'shub made repairs opposite their house. After them Az·a·ri'ah son of Ma·a·sei'ah son of An·a·ni'ah made repairs beside his own house. [24] After him Bin'nu·i son of Hen'a·dad repaired another section, from the house of Az·a·ri'ah to the Angle and to the corner. [25] Pa'lal son of U'zai repaired opposite the Angle and the tower projecting from the upper house of the king at the court of the guard. After him Pe·dai'ah son of Pa'rosh [26] and the temple servants living[h] on O'phel made repairs up to a point opposite the Water Gate on the east and the projecting tower. [27] After him the Te·ko'ites repaired another section opposite the great projecting tower as far as the wall of O'phel.

---

[a] Heb *him*   [b] Or *lords*   [c] Meaning of Heb uncertain   [d] Or *supervisor of half the portion assigned to*   [e] Or *supervisor of the portion assigned to*   [f] Gk Syr Compare verse 24, 10.9: Heb *Bavvai*   [g] Or *supervisor*   [h] Cn: Heb *were living*

28 Above the Horse Gate the priests made repairs, each one opposite his own house. 29 After them Zā'dok son of Im'mer made repairs opposite his own house. After him She·māi'ah son of Shec·a·nī'ah, the keeper of the East Gate, made repairs. 30 After him Han·a·nī'ah son of Shel·e·mī'ah and Hā'nun sixth son of Zā'laph repaired another section. After him Me·shul'-lam son of Ber·e·chī'ah made repairs opposite his living quarters. 31 After him Mal·chī'jah, one of the gold-smiths, made repairs as far as the house of the temple servants and of the merchants, opposite the Muster Gate, *i* and to the upper room of the corner. 32 And between the upper room of the corner and the Sheep Gate the goldsmiths and the merchants made repairs.

Hostile Plots Thwarted

4 *j* Now when San·bal'lat heard that we were building the wall, he was angry and greatly enraged, and he mocked the Jews. 2 He said in the presence of his associates and of the army of Sa·mār'i·a, "What are these feeble Jews doing? Will they restore things? Will they sacrifice? Will they finish it in a day? Will they revive the stones out of the heaps of rubbish—and burned ones at that?" 3 Tō·bī'ah the Am'mon·ite was beside him, and he said, "That stone wall they are building—any fox going up on it would break it down!" 4 Hear, O our God, for we are despised; turn their taunt back on their own heads, and give them over as plunder in a land of captivity. 5 Do not cover their guilt, and do not let their sin be blotted out from your sight; for they have hurled insults in the face of the builders.

6 So we rebuilt the wall, and all the wall was joined together to half its height; for the people had a mind to work.

7 *k* But when San·bal'lat and Tō·bī'ah and the Arabs and the Am'-mon·ites and the Ash'dod·ites heard that the repairing of the walls of Jeru-salem was going forward and the gaps were beginning to be closed, they were very angry, 8 and all plotted together to come and fight against Jerusalem and to cause confusion in it. 9 So we prayed to our God, and set a guard as a protec-tion against them day and night.

10 But Judah said, "The strength of the burden bearers is failing, and there is too much rubbish so that we are un-able to work on the wall." 11 And our enemies said, "They will not know or see anything before we come upon them and kill them and stop the work." 12 When the Jews who lived near them came, they said to us ten times, "From all the places where they live *l* they will come up against us." *m* 13 So in the lowest parts of the space behind the wall, in open places, I stationed the people according to their families, *n* with their swords, their spears, and their bows. 14 After I looked these things over, I stood up and said to the nobles and the officials and the rest of the people, "Do not be afraid of them. Remember the LORD, who is great and awesome, and fight for your kin, your sons, your daughters, your wives, and your homes."

15 When our enemies heard that their plot was known to us, and that God had frustrated it, we all returned to the wall, each to his work. 16 From that day on, half of my servants worked on construction, and half held the spears, shields, bows, and body-armor; and the leaders posted them-selves behind the whole house of Ju-dah, 17 who were building the wall. The burden bearers carried their loads in such a way that each labored on the work with one hand and with the other held a weapon. 18 And each of the builders had his sword strapped at his side while he built. The man who sounded the trumpet was beside me. 19 And I said to the nobles, the officials, and the rest of the people, "The work is great and widely spread out, and we are separated far from one another on the wall. 20 Rally to us wherever you hear the sound of the trumpet. Our God will fight for us."

21 So we labored at the work, and half of them held the spears from break of dawn until the stars came out. 22 I also said to the people at that time, "Let every man and his servant pass the night inside Jerusalem, so that they may be a guard for us by night and may labor by day." 23 So neither I nor my brothers nor my servants nor the men of the guard who followed me

i Or *Hammiphkad Gate*   *j* Ch 3.33 in Heb   *k* Ch 4.1 in Heb   *l* Cn: Heb *you return*   *m* Compare Gk Syr: Meaning of Heb uncertain   *n* Meaning of Heb uncertain

NEHEMIAH

ever took off our clothes; each kept his weapon in his right hand.[o]

Nehemiah Deals with Oppression

5 Now there was a great outcry of the people and of their wives against their Jewish kin. [2] For there were those who said, "With our sons and our daughters, we are many; we must get grain, so that we may eat and stay alive." [3] There were also those who said, "We are having to pledge our fields, our vineyards, and our houses in order to get grain during the famine." [4] And there were those who said, "We are having to borrow money on our fields and vineyards to pay the king's tax. [5] Now our flesh is the same as that of our kindred; our children are the same as their children; and yet we are forcing our sons and daughters to be slaves, and some of our daughters have been ravished; we are powerless, and our fields and vineyards now belong to others."

[6] I was very angry when I heard their outcry and these complaints. [7] After thinking it over, I brought charges against the nobles and the officials; I said to them, "You are all taking interest from your own people." And I called a great assembly to deal with them, [8] and said to them, "As far as we were able, we have bought back our Jewish kindred who had been sold to other nations; but now you are selling your own kin, who must then be bought back by us!" They were silent, and could not find a word to say. [9] So I said, "The thing that you are doing is not good. Should you not walk in the fear of our God, to prevent the taunts of the nations our enemies? [10] Moreover I and my brothers and my servants are lending them money and grain. Let us stop this taking of interest. [11] Restore to them, this very day, their fields, their vineyards, their olive orchards, and their houses, and the interest on money, grain, wine, and oil that you have been exacting from them." [12] Then they said, "We will restore everything and demand nothing more from them. We will do as you say." And I called the priests, and made them take an oath to do as they had promised. [13] I also shook out the fold of my garment and said, "So may God shake out everyone from house and from property who does not perform this promise. Thus may they be shaken out and emptied." And all the

assembly said, "Amen," and praised the Lord. And the people did as they had promised.

The Generosity of Nehemiah

[14] Moreover from the time that I was appointed to be their governor in the land of Judah, from the twentieth year to the thirty-second year of King Ar·ta·xerx′es, twelve years, neither I nor my brothers ate the food allowance of the governor. [15] The former governors who were before me laid heavy burdens on the people, and took food and wine from them, besides forty shekels of silver. Even their servants lorded it over the people. But I did not do so, because of the fear of God. [16] Indeed, I devoted myself to the work on this wall, and acquired no land; and all my servants were gathered there for the work. [17] Moreover there were at my table one hundred fifty people, Jews and officials, besides those who came to us from the nations around us. [18] Now that which was prepared for one day was one ox and six choice sheep; also fowls were prepared for me, and every ten days skins of wine in abundance; yet with all this I did not demand the food allowance of the governor, because of the heavy burden of labor on the people. [19] Remember for my good, O my God, all that I have done for this people.

Intrigues of Enemies Foiled

6 Now when it was reported to San·bal′lat and Tō·bī′ah and to Gē′shem the Arab and to the rest of our enemies that I had built the wall and that there was no gap left in it (though up to that time I had not set up the doors in the gates), [2] San·bal′lat and Gē′shem sent to me, saying, "Come and let us meet together in one of the villages in the plain of Ō′nō." But they intended to do me harm. [3] So I sent messengers to them, saying, "I am doing a great work and I cannot come down. Why should the work stop while I leave it to come down to you?" [4] They sent to me four times in this way, and I answered them in the same manner. [5] In the same way San·bal′lat for the fifth time sent his servant to me with an open letter in his hand. [6] In it was written, "It is reported among the nations—and Gē′shem[p] also says it—

---

[o] Cn: Heb *each his weapon the water*
[p] Heb *Gashmu*

that you and the Jews intend to rebel; that is why you are building the wall; and according to this report you wish to become their king. ⁷You have also set up prophets to proclaim in Jerusalem concerning you, 'There is a king in Judah!' And now it will be reported to the king according to these words. So come, therefore, and let us confer together." ⁸Then I sent to him, saying, "No such things as you say have been done; you are inventing them out of your own mind" ⁹—for they all wanted to frighten us, thinking, "Their hands will drop from the work, and it will not be done." But now, O God, strengthen my hands.

10 One day when I went into the house of She·mā̄i'ah son of De·lāi'ah son of Me·het'a·bel, who was confined to his house, he said, "Let us meet together in the house of God, within the temple, and let us close the doors of the temple, for they are coming to kill you; indeed, tonight they are coming to kill you." ¹¹But I said, "Should a man like me run away? Would a man like me go into the temple to save his life? I will not go in!" ¹²Then I perceived and saw that God had not sent him at all, but he had pronounced the prophecy against me because Tō·bī'ah and San·bal'lat had hired him. ¹³He was hired for this purpose, to intimidate me and make me sin by acting in this way, and so they could give me a bad name, in order to taunt me. ¹⁴Remember Tō·bī'ah and San·bal'lat, O my God, according to these things that they did, and also the prophetess Nō·a·dī'ah and the rest of the prophets who wanted to make me afraid.

The Wall Completed

15 So the wall was finished on the twenty-fifth day of the month Ē'lul, in fifty-two days. ¹⁶And when all our enemies heard of it, all the nations around us were afraid q and fell greatly in their own esteem; for they perceived that this work had been accomplished with the help of our God. ¹⁷Moreover in those days the nobles of Judah sent many letters to Tō·bī'ah, and Tō·bī'-ah's letters came to them. ¹⁸For many in Judah were bound by oath to him, because he was the son-in-law of Shec·a·nī'ah son of Ā'rah: and his son Jē·hō·hā'nan had married the daughter of Me·shul'lam son of Ber·e·chī'ah. ¹⁹Also they spoke of his good deeds in my presence, and reported my words

to him. And Tō·bī'ah sent letters to intimidate me.

7 Now when the wall had been built and I had set up the doors, and the gatekeepers, the singers, and the Lē'-vites had been appointed, ²I gave my brother Ha·nā'nī charge over Jerusalem, along with Han·a·nī'ah the commander of the citadel—for he was a faithful man and feared God more than many. ³And I said to them, "The gates of Jerusalem are not to be opened until the sun is hot; while the gatekeepers r are still standing guard, let them shut and bar the doors. Appoint guards from among the inhabitants of Jerusalem, some at their watch posts, and others before their own houses." ⁴The city was wide and large, but the people within it were few and no houses had been built.

Lists of the Returned Exiles
(Ezra 2.1–70)

5 Then my God put it into my mind to assemble the nobles and the officials and the people to be enrolled by genealogy. And I found the book of the genealogy of those who were the first to come back, and I found the following written in it:

6 These are the people of the province who came up out of the captivity of those exiles whom King Ne·bū·chad·nez'zar had carried into exile; they returned to Jerusalem and Judah, each to his town. ⁷They came with Ze·rub'ba·bel, Jesh'ū·a, Nē·he·mī'ah, Az·a·rī'ah, Rā·a·mī'ah, Nā·ham'a·nī, Mor'de·caī, Bil'-shan, Mis'pe·reth, Big'vaī, Nē'hum, Bā'a·nah.

The number of the Israelite people: ⁸the descendants of Pā'rosh, two thousand one hundred seventy-two. ⁹Of Sheph·a·tī'ah, three hundred seventy-two. ¹⁰Of Ā'rah, six hundred fifty-two. ¹¹Of Pā'hath-mō'ab, namely the descendants of Jesh'ū·a and Jō'ab, two thousand eight hundred eighteen. ¹²Of Ē'lam, one thousand two hundred fifty-four. ¹³Of Zat'tū, eight hundred forty-five. ¹⁴Of Zac'caī, seven hundred sixty. ¹⁵Of Bin'nū·ī, six hundred forty-eight. ¹⁶Of Bē'baī, six hundred twenty-eight. ¹⁷Of Az'gad, two thousand three hundred twenty-two. ¹⁸Of Ad·o·nī'-kam, six hundred sixty-seven. ¹⁹Of Big'vaī, two thousand sixty-seven.

q Another reading is *saw*   r Heb *while they*

20 Of Ă′din, six hundred fifty-five. 21 Of Ă′ter, namely of Hez·e·kī′ah, ninety-eight. 22 Of Hă′shum, three hundred twenty-eight. 23 Of Bē′zaī, three hundred twenty-four. 24 Of Hă′riph, one hundred twelve. 25 Of Gib′ē·on, ninety-five. 26 The people of Bethlehem and Ne·toph′ah, one hundred eighty-eight. 27 Of An′a·thoth, one hundred twenty-eight. 28 Of Beth-az′ma·veth, forty-two. 29 Of Kir′i·ath-jē′a·rim, Chē·phī′rah, and Be·er′oth, seven hundred forty-three. 30 Of Ră′mah and Gē′ba, six hundred twenty-one. 31 Of Mich′mas, one hundred twenty-two. 32 Of Beth′el and Aī, one hundred twenty-three. 33 Of the other Nē′bō, fifty-two. 34 The descendants of the other Ē′lam, one thousand two hundred fifty-four. 35 Of Hă′rim, three hundred twenty. 36 Of Jericho, three hundred forty-five. 37 Of Lod, Hă′did, and Ō′nō, seven hundred twenty-one. 38 Of Se·nă′ah, three thousand nine hundred thirty.

39 The priests: the descendants of Je·daī′ah, namely the house of Jesh′ū·a, nine hundred seventy-three. 40 Of Im′mer, one thousand fifty-two. 41 Of Pash′hur, one thousand two hundred forty-seven. 42 Of Hă′rim, one thousand seventeen.

43 The Lē′vītes: the descendants of Jesh′ū·a, namely of Kad′mi·el of the descendants of Hō′de·vah, seventy-four. 44 The singers: the descendants of Ă′saph, one hundred forty-eight. 45 The gatekeepers: the descendants of Shal′lum, of Ă′ter, of Tal′mon, of Ak′kub, of Ha·tī′ta, of Shō′baī, one hundred thirty-eight.

46 The temple servants: the descendants of Zī′ha, of Ha·sū′pha, of Tab·bă′oth, 47 of Kē′ros, of Sī′a, of Pă′don, 48 of Le·bă′na, of Hag′a·ba, of Shal′maī, 49 of Hă′nan, of Gid′del, of Gă′har, 50 of Rē·āi′ah, of Rē′zin, of Ne·kō′da, 51 of Gaz′zam, of Uz′za, of Pa·sē′ah, 52 of Bē′saī, of Me·ū′nim, of Ne·phūsh′e·sim, 53 of Bak′buk, of Ha·kū′pha, of Har′hur, 54 of Baz′lith, of Me·hī′da, of Har′sha, 55 of Bar′kos, of Sis′e·ra, of Tē′mah, 56 of Ne·zī′ah, of Ha·tī′pha.

57 The descendants of Solomon's servants: of Sō′taī, of Sō′phe·reth, of Pe·rī′da, 58 of Jă′a·la, of Dar′kon, of Gid′del, 59 of Sheph·a·tī′ah, of Hat′til, of Pō′che·reth-haz·ze·bă′im, of Ă′mon.

60 All the temple servants and the descendants of Solomon's servants were three hundred ninety-two.

61 The following were those who came up from Tel-mē′lah, Tel-har′sha, Chē′rub, Ad′don, and Im′mer, but the could not prove their ancestral house or their descent, whether they be longed to Israel: 62 the descendants o De·laī′ah, of Tō·bī′ah, of Ne·kō′da, si× hundred forty-two. 63 Also, of th priests: the descendants of Hō·baī′ah of Hak′koz, of Bar·zil′laī (who ha married one of the daughters o Bar·zil′laī the Gil′e·ad·īte and wa called by their name). 64 These sough their registration among those en rolled in the genealogies, but it was no found there, so they were exclude from the priesthood as unclean; 65 th governor told them that they were no to partake of the most holy food, unti a priest with Ū′rim and Thum′min should come.

66 The whole assembly togethe was forty-two thousand three hundre sixty, 67 besides their male and femal slaves, of whom there were seve× thousand three hundred thirty-seven and they had two hundred forty-fiv singers, male and female. 68 They ha seven hundred thirty-six horses, tw× hundred forty-five mules, *s* 69 four hun dred thirty-five camels, and six thou sand seven hundred twenty donkeys

70 Now some of the heads of ances tral houses contributed to the work The governor gave to the treasury on thousand darics of gold, fifty basins and five hundred thirty priestly robes 71 And some of the heads of ancestra houses gave into the building fun twenty thousand darics of gold an two thousand two hundred minas o silver. 72 And what the rest of the peo ple gave was twenty thousand daric of gold, two thousand minas of silver and sixty-seven priestly robes.

73 So the priests, the Lē′vītes, th gatekeepers, the singers, some of th people, the temple servants, and all Is rael settled in their towns.

Ezra Summons the People to Obey the Law

When the seventh month came—th people of Israel being settled in thei towns— 1 all the people gathere together into the square before th Water Gate. They told the scribe Ezr to bring the book of the law of Moses which the LORD had given to Israel

---

s Ezra 2.66 and the margins of some Hebrew Mss: MT lacks *They had . . . forty-five mules*

² Accordingly, the priest Ezra brought the law before the assembly, both men and women and all who could hear with understanding. This was on the first day of the seventh month. ³ He read from it facing the square before the Water Gate from early morning until midday, in the presence of the men and the women and those who could understand; and the ears of all the people were attentive to the book of the law. ⁴ The scribe Ezra stood on a wooden platform that had been made for the purpose; and beside him stood Mat·ti·thī'ah, Shē'ma, A·naī'ah, U·rī'ah, Hil·kī'ah, and Mā·a·sēi'ah on his right hand; and Pe·dāi'ah, Mish'-a·el, Mal·chī'jah, Hā'shum, Hash-bad'da·nah, Zech·a·rī'ah, and Me-shul'lam on his left hand. ⁵ And Ezra opened the book in the sight of all the people, for he was standing above all the people; and when he opened it, all the people stood up. ⁶ Then Ezra blessed the LORD, the great God, and all the people answered, "Amen, Amen," lifting up their hands. Then they bowed their heads and worshiped the LORD with their faces to the ground. ⁷ Also Jesh'ū·a, Bā'nī, Sher·e·bī'ah, Jā'min, Ak'kub, Shab'-be·thaī, Hō·dī'ah, Mā·a·sēi'ah, Ke-lī'ta, Az·a·rī'ah, Joz'a·bad, Hā'nan, Pe·lāi'ah, the Lē'vītes,ᵗ helped the people to understand the law, while the people remained in their places. ⁸ So they read from the book, from the law of God, with interpretation. They gave the sense, so that the people understood the reading.

9 And Nē·he·mī'ah, who was the governor, and Ezra the priest and scribe, and the Lē'vītes who taught the people said to all the people. "This day is holy to the LORD your God; do not mourn or weep." For all the people wept when they heard the words of the law. ¹⁰ Then he said to them, "Go your way, eat the fat and drink sweet wine and send portions of them to those for whom nothing is prepared, for this day is holy to our LORD; and do not be grieved, for the joy of the LORD is your strength." ¹¹ So the Lē'vītes stilled all the people, saying, "Be quiet, for this day is holy; do not be grieved." ¹² And all the people went their way to eat and drink and to send portions and to make great rejoicing, because they had understood the words that were declared to them.

The Festival of Booths Celebrated
(Cp Lev 23.33–43)

13 On the second day the heads of ancestral houses of all the people, with the priests and the Lē'vītes, came together to the scribe Ezra in order to study the words of the law. ¹⁴ And they found it written in the law, which the LORD had commanded by Moses, that the people of Israel should live in boothsᵘ during the festival of the seventh month, ¹⁵ and that they should publish and proclaim in all their towns and in Jerusalem as follows, "Go out to the hills and bring branches of olive, wild olive, myrtle, palm, and other leafy trees to make booths,ᵘ as it is written." ¹⁶ So the people went out and brought them, and made boothsᵘ for themselves, each on the roofs of their houses, and in their courts and in the courts of the house of God, and in the square at the Water Gate and in the square at the Gate of E'phra·im. ¹⁷ And all the assembly of those who had returned from the captivity made boothsᵘ and lived in them; for from the days of Jesh'ū·a son of Nun to that day the people of Israel had not done so. And there was very great rejoicing. ¹⁸ And day by day, from the first day to the last day, he read from the book of the law of God. They kept the festival seven days; and on the eighth day there was a solemn assembly, according to the ordinance.

National Confession

9 Now on the twenty-fourth day of this month the people of Israel were assembled with fasting and in sackcloth, and with earth on their heads.ᵛ ² Then those of Israelite descent separated themselves from all foreigners, and stood and confessed their sins and the iniquities of their ancestors. ³ They stood up in their place and read from the book of the law of the LORD their God for a fourth part of the day, and for another fourth they made confession and worshiped LORD their God. ⁴ Then Jesh'ū·a, Bā'-nī, Kad'mi·el, Sheb·a·nī'ah, Bun'nī, Sher·e·bī'ah, Bā'nī, and Che·nā'nī stood on the stairs of the Lē'vītes and cried out with a loud voice to the

---

ᵗ 1 Esdras 9.48 Vg: Heb *and the Levites*
ᵘ Or *tabernacles;* Heb *succoth*
ᵛ Heb *on them*

LORD their God. 5 Then the Lē'vītes, Jesh'ū·a, Kad'mi·el, Bā'nī, Hash·ab·nei'ah, Sher·e·bī'ah, Hō·dī'ah, Sheb·a·nī'ah, and Peth·a·hī'ah, said, "Stand up and bless the LORD your God from everlasting to everlasting. Blessed be your glorious name, which is exalted above all blessing and praise."

6 And Ezra said:ʷ "You are the LORD, you alone; you have made heaven, the heaven of heavens, with all their host, the earth and all that is on it, the seas and all that is in them. To all of them you give life, and the host of heaven worships you. 7 You are the LORD, the God who chose Abram and brought him out of Ur of the Chal·dē'-ans and gave him the name Abraham; 8 and you found his heart faithful before you, and made with him a covenant to give to his descendants the land of the Cā'naan·īte, the Hit'tīte, the Am'o·rīte, the Per'iz·zīte, the Jeb'-ū·sīte, and the Gir'ga·shīte; and you have fulfilled your promise, for you are righteous.

9 "And you saw the distress of our ancestors in Egypt and heard their cry at the Red Sea.ˣ 10 You performed signs and wonders against Pharaoh and all his servants and all the people of his land, for you knew that they acted insolently against our ancestors. You made a name for yourself, which remains to this day. 11 And you divided the sea before them, so that they passed through the sea on dry land, but you threw their pursuers into the depths, like a stone into mighty waters. 12 Moreover, you led them by day with a pillar of cloud, and by night with a pillar of fire, to give them light on the way in which they should go. 13 You came down also upon Mount Sinai, and spoke with them from heaven, and gave them right ordinances and true laws, good statutes and commandments, 14 and you made known your holy sabbath to them and gave them commandments and statutes and a law through your servant Moses. 15 For their hunger you gave them bread from heaven, and for their thirst you brought water for them out of the rock, and you told them to go in to possess the land that you swore to give them.

16 "But they and our ancestors acted presumptuously and stiffened their necks and did not obey your commandments; 17 they refused to obey, and were not mindful of the wonders that you performed among them; but they stiffened their necks and determined to return to their slavery in Egypt. But you are a God ready to forgive, gracious and merciful, slow to anger and abounding in steadfast love, and you did not forsake them. 18 Even when they had cast an image of a calf for themselves and said, 'This is your God who brought you up out of Egypt,' and had committed great blasphemies, 19 you in your great mercies did not forsake them in the wilderness; the pillar of cloud that led them in the way did not leave them by day, nor the pillar of fire by night that gave them light on the way by which they should go. 20 You gave your good spirit to instruct them, and did not withhold your manna from their mouths, and gave them water for their thirst. 21 Forty years you sustained them in the wilderness so that they lacked nothing; their clothes did not wear out and their feet did not swell. 22 And you gave them kingdoms and peoples, and allotted to them every corner,ʸ so they took possession of the land of King Sī'hon of Hesh'bon and the land of King Og of Bā'shan. 23 You multiplied their descendants like the stars of heaven, and brought them into the land that you had told their ancestors to enter and possess. 24 So the descendants went in and possessed the land, and you subdued before them the inhabitants of the land, the Cā'naan·ītes, and gave them into their hands, with their kings and the peoples of the land, to do with them as they pleased. 25 And they captured fortress cities and a rich land, and took possession of houses filled with all sorts of goods, hewn cisterns, vineyards, olive orchards, and fruit trees in abundance; so they ate, and were filled and became fat, and delighted themselves in your great goodness.

26 "Nevertheless they were disobedient and rebelled against you and cast your law behind their backs and killed your prophets, who had warned them in order to turn them back to you, and they committed great blasphemies. 27 Therefore you gave them into the hands of their enemies, who made them suffer. Then in the time of their suffering they cried out to you and you heard them from heaven, and accord-

ʷGk: Heb lacks *And Ezra said*
ˣOr *Sea of Reeds*   ʸMeaning of Heb uncertain

ing to your great mercies you gave them saviors who saved them from the hands of their enemies. 28 But after they had rest, they again did evil before you, and you abandoned them to the hands of their enemies, so that they had dominion over them; yet when they turned and cried to you, you heard from heaven, and many times you rescued them according to your mercies. 29 And you warned them in order to turn them back to your law. Yet they acted presumptuously and did not obey your commandments, but sinned against your ordinances, by the observance of which a person shall live. They turned a stubborn shoulder and stiffened their neck and would not obey. 30 Many years you were patient with them, and warned them by your spirit through your prophets; yet they would not listen. Therefore you handed them over to the peoples of the lands. 31 Nevertheless, in your great mercies you did not make an end of them or forsake them, for you are a gracious and merciful God.

32 "Now therefore, our God—the great and mighty and awesome God, keeping covenant and steadfast love— do not treat lightly all the hardship that has come upon us, upon our kings, our officials, our priests, our prophets, our ancestors, and all your people, since the time of the kings of Assyria until today. 33 You have been just in all that has come upon us, for you have dealt faithfully and we have acted wickedly; 34 our kings, our officials, our priests, and our ancestors have not kept your law or heeded the commandments and the warnings that you gave them. 35 Even in their own kingdom, and in the great goodness you bestowed on them, and in the large and rich land that you set before them, they did not serve you and did not turn from their wicked works. 36 Here we are, slaves to this day—slaves in the land that you gave to our ancestors to enjoy its fruit and its good gifts. 37 Its rich yield goes to the kings whom you have set over us because of our sins; they have power also over our bodies and over our livestock at their pleasure, and we are in great distress."

Those Who Signed the Covenant

38 z Because of all this we make a firm agreement in writing, and on that sealed document are inscribed the names of our officials, our Lĕ′vītes, and our priests.

10 a Upon the sealed document are the names of Nē·he·mī′ah the governor, son of Hac·a·lī′ah, and Zed·e·kī′ah; 2 Se·rāi′ah, Az·a·rī′ah, Jer·e·mī′ah, 3 Pash′hur, Am·a·rī′ah, Mal·chī′jah, 4 Hat′tush, Sheb·a·nī′ah, Mal′luch, 5 Hā′rim, Mer′e·moth, Ō·ba·dī′ah, 6 Daniel, Gin′ne·thon, Bar′uch, 7 Me·shul′lam, A·bī′jah, Mij′a·min, 8 Mā·a·zī′ah, Bil′gaī, She·māi′ah; these are the priests. 9 And the Lĕ′vītes: Jesh′ū·a son of Az·a·nī′ah, Bin′nū·ī of the sons of Hen′a·dad, Kad′mi·el; 10 and their associates, Sheb·a·nī′ah, Hō·dī′ah, Ke·lī′ta, Pe·lāi′ah, Hā′nan, 11 Mī′ca, Rĕ′hob, Hash·a·bī′ah, 12 Zac′cur, Sher·e·bī′ah, Sheb·a·nī′ah, 13 Hō·dī′ah, Bā′nī, Be·nī′nū. 14 The leaders of the people: Pā′rosh, Pā′hath-mō′ab, Ē′lam, Zat′tū, Bā′nī, 15 Bun′nī, Az′gad, Bē′baī, 16 Ad·o·nī′·jah, Big′vaī, Ā′din, 17 Ā′ter, Hez·e·kī′ah, Az′zur, 18 Hō·dī′ah, Hā′shum, Bē′zaī, 19 Hā′riph, An′a·thoth, Nĕ′baī, 20 Mag′pi·ash, Me·shul′lam, Hĕ′zir, 21 Me·shez′a·bel, Zā′dok, Jad′·dū·a, 22 Pel·a·tī′ah, Hā′nan, A·naī′ah, 23 Hō·shē′a, Han·a·nī′ah, Has′shub, 24 Hal·lō′hesh, Pil′ha, Shō′bek, 25 Rĕ′hum, Ha·shab′nah, Mā·a·sēi′ah, 26 A·hī′ah, Hā′nan, Ā′nan, 27 Mal′luch, Hā′rim, and Bā′a·nah.

Summary of the Covenant

28 The rest of the people, the priests, the Lĕ′vītes, the gatekeepers, the singers, the temple servants, and all who have separated themselves from the peoples of the lands to adhere to the law of God, their wives, their sons, their daughters, all who have knowledge and understanding, 29 join with their kin, their nobles, and enter into a curse and an oath to walk in God's law, which was given by Moses the servant of God, and to observe and do all the commandments of the LORD our Lord and his ordinances and his statutes. 30 We will not give our daughters to the peoples of the land or take their daughters for our sons; 31 and if the peoples of the land bring in merchandise or any grain on the sabbath day to sell, we will not buy it from them on the sabbath or on a holy day; and we will forego the crops of the seventh year and the exaction of every debt.

z Ch 10.1 in Heb   a Ch 10.2 in Heb

32 We also lay on ourselves the obligation to charge ourselves yearly one-third of a shekel for the service of the house of our God: 33 for the rows of bread, the regular grain offering, the regular burnt offering, the sabbaths, the new moons, the appointed festivals, the sacred donations, and the sin offerings to make atonement for Israel, and for all the work of the house of our God. 34 We have also cast lots among the priests, the Leʹvites, and the people, for the wood offering, to bring it into the house of our God, by ancestral houses, at appointed times, year by year, to burn on the altar of the LORD our God, as it is written in the law. 35 We obligate ourselves to bring the first fruits of our soil and the first fruits of all fruit of every tree, year by year, to the house of the LORD; 36 also to bring to the house of our God, to the priests who minister in the house of our God, the firstborn of our sons and of our livestock, as it is written in the law, and the firstlings of our herds and of our flocks; 37 and to bring the first of our dough, and our contributions, the fruit of every tree, the wine and the oil, to the priests, to the chambers of the house of our God; and to bring to the Leʹvites the tithes from our soil, for it is the Leʹvites who collect the tithes in all our rural towns. 38 And the priest, the descendant of Aaron, shall be with the Leʹvites when the Leʹvites receive the tithes; and the Leʹvites shall bring up a tithe of the tithes to the house of our God, to the chambers of the storehouse. 39 For the people of Israel and the sons of Levi shall bring the contribution of grain, wine, and oil to the storerooms where the vessels of the sanctuary are, and where the priests that minister, and the gatekeepers and the singers are. We will not neglect the house of our God.

Population of the City Increased

11 Now the leaders of the people lived in Jerusalem; and the rest of the people cast lots to bring one out of ten to live in the holy city Jerusalem, while nine-tenths remained in the other towns. 2 And the people blessed all those who willingly offered to live in Jerusalem.

3 These are the leaders of the province who lived in Jerusalem; but in the towns of Judah all lived on their property in their towns: Israel, the priests, the Leʹvites, the temple servants, and the descendants of Solomon's servants. 4 And in Jerusalem lived some of the Juʹdah-ites and of the Benʹja-min-ites. Of the Juʹdah-ites: A-thaiʹah son of Uz-ziʹah son of Zech-a-riʹah son of Am-a-riʹah son of Sheph-a-tiʹah son of Ma-halʹa-lel, of the descendants of Perʹez; 5 and Ma-a-seiʹah son of Barʹuch son of Col-hoʹzeh son of Ha-zaiʹah son of A-daiʹah son of Joiʹa-rib son of Zech-a-riʹah son of the Shiʹlo-nite. 6 All the descendants of Perʹez who lived in Jerusalem were four hundred sixty-eight valiant warriors.

7 And these are the Benʹja-min-ites: Salʹlu son of Me-shulʹlam son of Joʹed son of Pe-daiʹah son of Koʹlaiʹah son of Ma-a-seiʹah son of Ithʹi-el son of Je-shaʹi-ah. 8 And his brothers[b] Gab-baʹi, Salʹlai: nine hundred twenty-eight. 9 Joʹel son of Zichʹri was their overseer; and Judah son of Has-se-nuʹah was second in charge of the city.

10 Of the priests: Je-daiʹah son of Joiʹa-rib, Jaʹchin, 11 Se-raiʹah son of Hil-kiʹah son of Me-shulʹlam son of Zaʹdok son of Me-raʹi-oth son of A-hiʹtub, officer of the house of God, 12 and their associates who did the work of the house, eight hundred twenty-two; and A-daiʹah son of Je-roʹham son of Pel-a-liʹah son of Amʹzi son of Zech-a-riʹah son of Pashʹhur son of Mal-chiʹjah, 13 and his associates, heads of ancestral houses, two hundred forty-two; and A-mashʹsai son of Azʹa-rel son of Ahʹzai son of Me-shilʹle-moth son of Imʹmer, 14 and their associates, valiant warriors, one hundred twenty-eight; their overseer was Zabʹdi-el son of Hag-ge-doʹlim.

15 And of the Leʹvites: She-maiʹah son of Hasʹshub son of Az-riʹkam son of Hash-a-biʹah son of Bunʹni; 16 and Shabʹbe-thai and Jozʹa-bad, of the leaders of the Leʹvites, who were over the outside work of the house of God; 17 and Mat-ta-niʹah son of Miʹca son of Zabʹdi son of Aʹsaph, who was the leader to begin the thanksgiving in prayer, and Bak-bu-kiʹah, the second among his associates; and Abʹda son of Shamʹmu-a son of Gaʹlal son of Je-duʹthun. 18 All the Leʹvites in the holy city were two hundred eighty-four.

19 The gatekeepers, Akʹkub, Talʹmon and their associates, who kept

b Gk Mss: Heb And after him

watch at the gates, were one hundred seventy-two. 20 And the rest of Israel, and of the priests and the Lĕ′vītes, were in all the towns of Judah, all of them in their inheritance. 21 But the temple servants lived on O′phel; and Zī′ha and Gish′pa were over the temple servants.

22 The overseer of the Lĕ′vītes in Jerusalem was Uz′zī son of Ba′nī son of Hash·a·bī′ah son of Mat·ta·nī′ah son of Mī′ca, of the descendants of Ā′saph, the singers, in charge of the work of the house of God. 23 For there was a command from the king concerning them, and a settled provision for the singers, as was required every day. 24 And Peth·a·hī′ah son of Me·shez′a·bel, of the descendants of Zĕ′rah son of Judah, was at the king's hand in all matters concerning the people.

Villages outside Jerusalem

25 And as for the villages, with their fields, some of the people of Judah lived in Kir′i·ath-ar′ba and its villages, and in Dī′bon and its villages, and in Je·kab′zĕ·el and its villages, 26 and in Jesh′u·a and in Mō′la·dah and Bethpel′et, 27 in Hā′zar-shū′al, in Bĕ′er-shĕ′ba and its villages, 28 in Zik′lag, in Mĕ·cō′nah and its villages, 29 in En-rim′mon, in Zō′rah, in Jar′muth, 30 Za·nō′ah, A·dul′lam, and their villages, La′chish and its fields, and A·zĕ′kah and its villages. So they camped from Bĕ′er-shĕ′ba to the valley of Hin′nom. 31 The people of Benjamin also lived from Gĕ′ba onward, at Mich′mash, Āi′ja, Beth′el and its villages, 32 An′a·thoth, Nob, An·a·nī′ah, 33 Hā′zor, Rā′mah, Git′ta·im, 34 Hā′did, Ze·bō′im, Ne·bal′lat, 35 Lod, and O′nō, the valley of artisans. 36 And certain divisions of the Lĕ′vītes in Judah were joined to Benjamin.

A List of Priests and Levites
(Cp Ezra 2.36–40)

12 These are the priests and the Lĕ′vītes who came up with Ze·rub′ba·bel son of She·al′ti·el, and Jesh′u·a: Se·rāi′ah, Jer·e·mī′ah, Ezra, 2 Am·a·rī′ah, Mal′luch, Hat′tush, 3 Shec·a·nī′ah, Rē′hum, Mer′e·moth, 4 Id′dō, Gin′ne·thoi, A·bī′jah, 5 Mij′a·min, Mā·a·dī′ah, Bil′gah, 6 She·māi′ah, Joi′a·rib, Je·dāi′ah, 7 Sal′lū, Ā′mok, Hil·kī′ah, Je·dāi′ah. These

were the leaders of the priests and of their associates in the days of Jesh′ū·a.

8 And the Lĕ′vītes: Jesh′ū·a, Bin-nū·ī, Kad′mi·el, Sher·e·bī′ah, Judah, and Mat·ta·nī′ah, who with his associates was in charge of the songs of thanksgiving. 9 And Bak·bū·kī′ah and Un′nō their associates stood opposite them in the service. 10 Jesh′ū·a was the father of Joi′a·kim, Joi′a·kim the father of E·lī′a·shib, E·lī′a·shib the father of Joi′a·da, 11 Joi′a·da the father of Jonathan, and Jonathan the father of Jad′dū·a.

12 In the days of Joi′a·kim the priests, heads of ancestral houses, were: of Se·rāi′ah, Me·rāi′ah; of Jer·e·mī′ah, Han·a·nī′ah; 13 of Ezra, Me·shul′lam; of Am·a·rī′ah, Jē·hō·hā′nan; 14 of Mal′lu·chī, Jonathan; of Sheb·a·nī′ah, Joseph; 15 of Hā′rim, Ad′na; of Me·rā′i·oth, Hel′kaī; 16 of Id′dō, Zech·a·rī′ah; of Gin′ne·thon, Me·shul′lam; 17 of A·bī′jah, Zich′rī; of Mi·nī′a·min, of Mō·a·dī′ah, Pil′taī; 18 of Bil′gah, Sham′mū·a; of She·māi′ah, Je·hon′a·than; 19 of Joi′a·rib, Mat-tē′naī; of Je·dāi′ah, Uz′zī; 20 of Sal′laī, Kal′laī; of Ā′mok, Ē′ber; 21 of Hil·kī′ah, Hash·a·bī′ah; of Je·dāi′ah, Ne·than′el.

22 As for the Lĕ′vītes, in the days of E·lī′a·shib, Joi′a·da, Jō·hā′nan, and Jad′dū·a, there were recorded the heads of ancestral houses; also the priests until the reign of Da·rī′us the Persian. 23 The Lĕ′vītes, heads of ancestral houses, were recorded in the Book of the Annals until the days of Jō·hā′nan son of E·lī′a·shib. 24 And the leaders of the Lĕ′vītes: Hash·a·bī′ah, Sher·e·bī′ah, and Jesh′ū·a son of Kad′mi·el, with their associates over against them, to praise and to give thanks, according to the commandment of David the man of God, section opposite to section. 25 Mat·ta·nī′ah, Bak·bū·kī′ah, O·ba·dī′ah, Me·shul′lam, Tal′mon, and Ak′kub were gatekeepers standing guard at the storehouses of the gates. 26 These were in the days of Joi′a·kim son of Jesh′ū·a son of Jō′za·dak, and in the days of the governor Nĕ·he·mī′ah and of the priest Ezra, the scribe.

Dedication of the City Wall

27 Now at the dedication of the wall of Jerusalem they sought out the Lĕ′vītes in all their places, to bring them to Jerusalem to celebrate the dedication with rejoicing, with thanksgivings

and with singing, with cymbals, harps, and lyres. 28 The companies of the singers gathered together from the circuit around Jerusalem and from the villages of the Ne·toph′a·thites; 29 also from Beth-gil′gal and from the region of Ge′ba and Az′ma·veth; for the singers had built for themselves villages around Jerusalem. 30 And the priests and the Le′vites purified themselves; and they purified the people and the gates and the wall.

31 Then I brought the leaders of Judah up onto the wall, and appointed two great companies that gave thanks and went in procession. One went to the right on the wall to the Dung Gate; 32 and after them went Hŏ·shaī′ah and half the officials of Judah, 33 and Az·a·rī′ah, Ezra, Me·shul′lam, 34 Judah, Benjamin, She·māi′ah, and Jer·e·mī′ah, 35 and some of the young priests with trumpets: Zech·a·rī′ah son of Jonathan son of She·māi′ah son of Mat·ta·nī′ah son of Mī·cāi′ah son of Zac′cur son of Ā′saph; 36 and his kindred, She·māi′ah, Az′a·rel, Mil′a·lai, Gil′a·lai, Mā′ai, Ne·than′el, Judah, and Ha·nā′nī, with the musical instruments of David the man of God; and the scribe Ezra went in front of them. 37 At the Fountain Gate, in front of them, they went straight up by the stairs of the city of David, at the ascent of the wall, above the house of David, to the Water Gate on the east.

38 The other company of those who gave thanks went to the left,[c] and I followed them with half of the people on the wall, above the Tower of the Ovens, to the Broad Wall, 39 and above the Gate of Ē′phra·im, and by the Old Gate, and by the Fish Gate and the Tower of Ha·nan′el and the Tower of the Hundred, to the Sheep Gate; and they came to a halt at the Gate of the Guard. 40 So both companies of those who gave thanks stood in the house of God, and I and half of the officials with me; 41 and the priests E·lī′a·kim, Mā·a·sēi′ah, Mi·nī′a·min, Mī·cāi′ah, El·i·o·ē′nai, Zech·a·rī′ah, and Han·a·nī′ah, with trumpets; 42 and Mā·a·sēi′ah, She·māi′ah, El·e·ā′zar, Uz′zī, Jē·hō·hā′nan, Mal·chī′jah, Ē′lam, and Ē′zer. And the singers sang with Jez·ra·hī′ah as their leader. 43 They offered great sacrifices that day and rejoiced, for God had made them rejoice with great joy; the women and children also rejoiced. The joy of Jerusalem was heard far away.

Temple Responsibilities

44 On that day men were appointed over the chambers for the stores, the contributions, the first fruits, and the tithes, to gather into them the portions required by the law for the priests and for the Le′vites from the fields belonging to the towns; for Judah rejoiced over the priests and the Le′vites who ministered. 45 They performed the service of their God and the service of purification, as did the singers and the gatekeepers, according to the command of David and his son Solomon. 46 For in the days of David and Ā′saph long ago there was a leader of the singers, and there were songs of praise and thanksgiving to God. 47 In the days of Ze·rub′ba·bel and in the days of Nē·he·mī′ah all Israel gave the daily portions for the singers and the gatekeepers. They set apart that which was for the Le′vites; and the Le′vites set apart that which was for the descendants of Aaron.

Foreigners Separated from Israel
(Num 22.1—24.25)

13 On that day they read from the book of Moses in the hearing of the people; and in it was found written that no Am′mon·ite or Mō′ab·ite should ever enter the assembly of God, 2 because they did not meet the Israelites with bread and water, but hired Bā′laam against them to curse them— yet our God turned the curse into a blessing. 3 When the people heard the law, they separated from Israel all those of foreign descent.

The Reforms of Nehemiah

4 Now before this, the priest E·lī′a·shib, who was appointed over the chambers of the house of our God, and who was related to Tō·bī′ah, 5 prepared for Tō·bī′ah a large room where they had previously put the grain offering, the frankincense, the vessels, and the tithes of grain, wine, and oil, which were given by commandment to the Le′vites, singers, and gatekeepers, and the contributions for the priests. 6 While this was taking place I was not in Jerusalem, for in the thirty-second year of King Ar·ta·xerx′ēs of Babylon I went to the king. After some time I asked leave of the king 7 and returned to Jerusalem. I then discovered the

[c]Cn: Heb opposite

wrong that E·lī′a·shib had done on behalf of Tō·bī′ah, preparing a room for him in the courts of the house of God. ⁸ And I was very angry, and I threw all the household furniture of Tō·bī′ah out of the room. ⁹ Then I gave orders and they cleansed the chambers, and I brought back the vessels of the house of God, with the grain offering and the frankincense.

10 I also found out that the portions of the Lē′vītes had not been given to them; so that the Lē′vītes and the singers, who had conducted the service, had gone back to their fields. ¹¹ So I remonstrated with the officials and said, "Why is the house of God forsaken?" And I gathered them together and set them in their stations. ¹² Then all Judah brought the tithe of the grain, wine, and oil into the storehouses. ¹³ And I appointed as treasurers over the storehouses the priest Shele·mī′ah, the scribe Zā′dok, and Pedāi′ah of the Lē′vītes, and as their assistant Hā′nan son of Zac′cur son of Mat·ta·nī′ah, for they were considered faithful; and their duty was to distribute to their associates. ¹⁴ Remember me, O my God, concerning this, and do not wipe out my good deeds that I have done for the house of my God and for his service.

Sabbath Reforms Begun

15 In those days I saw in Judah people treading wine presses on the sabbath, and bringing in heaps of grain and loading them on donkeys; and also wine, grapes, figs, and all kinds of burdens, which they brought into Jerusalem on the sabbath day; and I warned them at that time against selling food. ¹⁶ Tȳ′ri·ans also, who lived in the city, brought in fish and all kinds of merchandise and sold them on the sabbath to the people of Judah, and in Jerusalem. ¹⁷ Then I remonstrated with the nobles of Judah and said to them, "What is this evil thing that you are doing, profaning the sabbath day? ¹⁸ Did not your ancestors act in this way, and did not our God bring all this disaster on us and on this city? Yet you bring more wrath on Israel by profaning the sabbath."

19 When it began to be dark at the gates of Jerusalem before the sabbath, I commanded that the doors should be shut and gave orders that they should not be opened until after the sabbath.

And I set some of my servants over the gates, to prevent any burden from being brought in on the sabbath day. ²⁰ Then the merchants and sellers of all kinds of merchandise spent the night outside Jerusalem once or twice. ²¹ But I warned them and said to them, "Why do you spend the night in front of the wall? If you do so again, I will lay hands on you." From that time on they did not come on the sabbath. ²² And I commanded the Lē′vītes that they should purify themselves and come and guard the gates, to keep the sabbath day holy. Remember this also in my favor, O my God, and spare me according to the greatness of your steadfast love.

Mixed Marriages Condemned
(Cp Ezra 9.1–4)

23 In those days also I saw Jews who had married women of Ash′dod, Am′mon, and Mō′ab; ²⁴ and half of their children spoke the language of Ash′dod, and they could not speak the language of Judah, but spoke the language of various peoples. ²⁵ And I contended with them and cursed them and beat some of them and pulled out their hair; and I made them take an oath in the name of God, saying, "You shall not give your daughters to their sons, or take their daughters for your sons or for yourselves. ²⁶ Did not King Solomon of Israel sin on account of such women? Among the many nations there was no king like him, and he was beloved by his God, and God made him king over all Israel; nevertheless, foreign women made even him to sin. ²⁷ Shall we then listen to you and do all this great evil and act treacherously against our God by marrying foreign women?"

28 And one of the sons of Je·hoi′a·da, son of the high priest E·lī′a·shib, was the son-in-law of San·bal′lat the Hor′o·nīte; I chased him away from me. ²⁹ Remember them, O my God, because they have defiled the priesthood, the covenant of the priests and the Lē′vītes.

30 Thus I cleansed them from everything foreign, and I established the duties of the priests and Lē′vītes, each in his work; ³¹ and I provided for the wood offering, at appointed times, and for the first fruits. Remember me, O my God, for good.

TOBIT

1 This book tells the story of Tō′bit son of Tō′bi·el son of Ha·nan′i·el son of A·dū′el son of Gab′a·el son of Raph′a·el[a] of the descendants of As′-i·el, of the tribe of Naph′ta·lī, 2 who in the days of King Shal·man·ē′ser[b] of the Assyrians was taken into captivity from This′bē, which is to the south of Kē′desh Naph′ta·lī in Upper Galilee, above Ash′er toward the west, and north of Phō′gor.

Tobit's Youth and Virtuous Life
(Cp Deut 12.11–14; 16.16; 1 Kings 12.28–29)

3 I, Tō′bit, walked in the ways of truth and righteousness all the days of my life. I performed many acts of charity for my kindred and my people who had gone with me in exile to Nin′e·veh in the land of the Assyrians. 4 When I was in my own country, in the land of Israel, while I was still a young man, the whole tribe of my ancestor Naph′-ta·lī deserted the house of David and Jerusalem. This city had been chosen from among all the tribes of Israel, where all the tribes of Israel should offer sacrifice and where the temple, the dwelling of God, had been conse-crated and established for all genera-tions forever.

5 All my kindred and our ancestral house of Naph′ta·lī sacrificed to the calf[c] that King Jer·o·bō′am of Israel had erected in Dan and on all the mountains of Galilee. 6 But I alone went often to Jerusalem for the festi-vals, as it is prescribed for all Israel by an everlasting decree. I would hurry off to Jerusalem with the first fruits of the crops and the firstlings of the flock, the tithes of the cattle, and the first shearings of the sheep. 7 I would give these to the priests, the sons of Aaron, at the altar; likewise the tenth of the grain, wine, olive oil, pomegranates, figs, and the rest of the fruits to the sons of Levi who ministered at Jerusa-lem. Also for six years I would save up a second tenth in money and go and distribute it in Jerusalem. 8 A third tenth[d] I would give to the orphans and widows and to the converts who had attached themselves to Israel. I would bring it and give it to them in the third year, and we would eat it according to the ordinance decreed concerning it in the law of Moses and according to the instructions of Deb′or·ah, the mother of my father Tō′bi·el,[e] for my father had died and left me an orphan. 9 When I became a man I married a woman,[f] a member of our own family, and by her I became the father of a son whom I named Tō·bī′as.

Taken Captive to Nineveh

10 After I was carried away captive to Assyria and came as a captive to Nin′e·veh, everyone of my kindred and my people ate the food of the Gen-tiles, 11 but I kept myself from eating the food of the Gentiles. 12 Because I was mindful of God with all my heart, 13 the Most High gave me favor and good standing with Shal·man·ē′ser,[b] and I used to buy everything he needed. 14 Until his death I used to go into Mēd′i·a, and buy for him there. While in the country of Mēd′i·a I left bags of silver worth ten talents in trust with Gabael, the brother of Gā′brī. 15 But when Shal·man·ē′ser[b] died, and his son Sen·nach′e·rib reigned in his place, the highways into Mēd′i·a be-came unsafe and I could no longer go there.

Courage in Burying the Dead
(Cp Num 19.11–13)

16 In the days of Shal·man·ē′ser[b] I performed many acts of charity to my

---

[a] Other ancient authorities lack *son of Raphael son of Raguel*
[b] Gk *Enemessaros*   [c] Other ancient authorities read *heifer*   [d] A third tenth added from other ancient authorities
[e] Lat: Gk *Hananiel*   [f] Other ancient authorities add *Anna*

kindred, those of my tribe. [17] I would give my food to the hungry and my clothing to the naked; and if I saw the dead body of any of my people thrown out behind the wall of Nin'e·veh, I would bury it. [18] I also buried any whom King Sen·nach'e·rib put to death when he came fleeing from Judea in those days of judgment that the king of heaven executed upon him because of his blasphemies. For in his anger he put to death many Israelites; but I would secretly remove the bodies and bury them. So when Sen·nach'e·rib looked for them he could not find them. [19] Then one of the Ninevites went and informed the king about me, that I was burying them; so I hid myself. But when I realized that the king knew about me and that I was being searched for to be put to death, I was afraid and ran away. [20] Then all my property was confiscated; nothing was left to me that was not taken into the royal treasury except my wife Anna and my son Tō·bī'as.

[21] But not forty[g] days passed before two of Sen·nach'e·rib's[h] sons killed him, and they fled to the mountains of Ar'a·rat, and his son Ē'sar-had'don[i] reigned after him. He appointed A·hī'kar, the son of my brother Han'a·el[j] over all the accounts of his kingdom, and he had authority over the entire administration. [22] A·hī'kar interceded for me, and I returned to Nin'e·veh. Now A·hī'kar was chief cupbearer, keeper of the signet, and in charge of administrations of the accounts under King Sen·nach'e·rib of Assyria; so Ē'sar-had'don[i] reappointed him. He was my nephew and so a close relative.

2 Then during the reign of Ē'sar-had'don[i] I returned home, and my wife Anna and my son Tō·bī'as were restored to me. At our festival of Pentecost, which is the sacred festival of weeks, a good dinner was prepared for me and I reclined to eat. [2] When the table was set for me and an abundance of food placed before me, I said to my son Tō·bī'as, "Go, my child, and bring whatever poor person you may find of our people among the exiles in Nin'e·veh, who is wholeheartedly mindful of God,[k] and he shall eat together with me. I will wait for you, until you come back." [3] So Tō·bī'as went to look for some poor person of our people. When he had returned he said, "Father!" And I replied, "Here I am, my child." Then he went on to say, "Look, father, one of

our own people has been murdered and thrown into the market place, and now he lies there strangled." [4] Then I sprang up, left the dinner before even tasting it, and removed the body[l] from the square[m] and laid it[l] in one of the rooms until sunset when I might bury it.[l] [5] When I returned, I washed myself and ate my food in sorrow. [6] Then I remembered the prophecy of Ā'mos, how he said against Beth'el,[n]

"Your festivals shall be turned
    into mourning,
and all your songs into
    lamentation."

And I wept.

Tobit Becomes Blind

7 When the sun had set, I went and dug a grave and buried him. [8] And my neighbors laughed and said, "Is he still not afraid? He has already been hunted down to be put to death for doing this, and he ran away; yet here he is again burying the dead!" [9] That same night I washed myself and went into my courtyard and slept by the wall of the courtyard; and my face was uncovered because of the heat. [10] I did not know that there were sparrows on the wall; their fresh droppings fell into my eyes and produced white films. I went to physicians to be healed, but the more they treated me with ointments the more my vision was obscured by the white films, until I became completely blind. For four years I remained unable to see. All my kindred were sorry for me, and A·hī'kar took care of me for two years before he went to El·y·mā'is.

Tobit's Wife Earns Their Livelihood

11 At that time, also, my wife Anna earned money at women's work. [12] She used to send what she made to the owners and they would pay wages to her. One day, the seventh of Dys'trus, when she cut off a piece she had woven and sent it to the owners, they paid her full wages and also gave her a young goat for a meal. [13] When she returned to me, the goat began to bleat. So I

---

[g] Other ancient authorities read either *forty-five* or *fifty*   [h] Gk *his*
[i] Gk *Sacherdonos*   [j] Other authorities read *Hananael*   [k] Lat: Gk *wholeheartedly mindful*   [l] Gk *him*
[m] Other ancient authorities lack *from the square*   [n] Other ancient authorities read *against Bethlehem*

**T
O
B
I
T**

called her and said, "Where did you get this goat? It is surely not stolen, is it? Return it to the owners; for we have no right to eat anything stolen." [14] But she said to me, "It was given to me as a gift in addition to my wages." But I did not believe her, and told her to return it to the owners. I became flushed with anger against her over this. Then she replied to me, "Where are your acts of charity? Where are your righteous deeds? These things are known about you!"[o]

Tobit's Prayer

3 Then with much grief and anguish of heart I wept, and with groaning began to pray:
2 "You are righteous, O Lord,
     and all your deeds are just;
  all your ways are mercy and
     truth;
  you judge the world.[p]
3 And now, O Lord, remember me
     and look favorably upon me.
  Do not punish me for my sins
     and for my unwitting offenses
     and those that my ancestors
        committed before you.
  They sinned against you,
4   and disobeyed your
        commandments.
  So you gave us over to plunder,
     exile, and death,
     to become the talk, the
        byword, and an object of
        reproach
     among all the nations among
        whom you have dispersed
        us.
5 And now your many judgments
     are true
  in exacting penalty from me
     for my sins.
  For we have not kept your
     commandments
  and have not walked in
     accordance with truth
     before you.
6 So now deal with me as you
     will;
  command my spirit to be
     taken from me,
  so that I may be released from
     the face of the earth and
     become dust.
  For it is better for me to die than
     to live,
  because I have had to listen to
     undeserved insults,
  and great is the sorrow within
     me.

Command, O Lord, that I be
     released from this distress;
  release me to go to the eternal
     home,
  and do not, O Lord, turn your
     face away from me.
  For it is better for me to die
     than to see so much distress in
        my life
  and to listen to insults."

Sarah Falsely Accused

7 On the same day, at Ec·bat'a·na in Mēd'i·a, it also happened that Sarah, the daughter of Rag'ū·el, was reproached by one of her father's maids. [8] For she had been married to seven husbands, and the wicked demon As-mō·dē'us had killed each of them before they had been with her as is customary for wives. So the maid said to her, "You are the one who kills[q] your husbands! See, you have already been married to seven husbands and have not borne the name of[r] a single one of them. [9] Why do you beat us? Because your husbands are dead? Go with them! May we never see a son or daughter of yours!"

Sarah's Prayer for Death

10 On that day she was grieved in spirit and wept. When she had gone up to her father's upper room, she intended to hang herself. But she thought it over and said, "Never shall they reproach my father, saying to him, 'You had only one beloved daughter but she hanged herself because of her distress.' And I shall bring my father in his old age down in sorrow to Hades. It is better for me not to hang myself, but to pray the Lord that I may die and not listen to these reproaches anymore." [11] At that same time, with hands outstretched toward the window, she prayed and said,
  "Blessed are you, merciful God!
  Blessed is your name forever;
     let all your works praise you
        forever.
12 And now, Lord,[s] I turn my face
     to you,
  and raise my eyes toward you.

[o] Or to you; Gk with you   [p] Other ancient authorities read you render true and righteous judgment forever
[q] Other ancient authorities read strangles
[r] Other ancient authorities read have had no benefit from   [s] Other ancient authorities lack Lord

13 Command that I be released
    from the earth
  and not listen to such
    reproaches any more.
14 You know, O Master, that I am
    innocent
  of any defilement with a man,
15 and that I have not disgraced my
    name
  or the name of my father in
    the land of my exile.
I am my father's only child;
  he has no other child to be his
    heir;
and he has no close relative or
    other kindred
  for whom I should keep myself
    as wife.
Already seven husbands of mine
    have died.
Why should I still live?
But if it is not pleasing to you,
  O Lord, to take my life,
hear me in my disgrace."

An Answer to Prayer
(Num 36.6–9)

16 At that very moment, the prayers of both of them were heard in the glorious presence of God. 17 So Raph′a·el was sent to heal both of them: Tō′bit, by removing the white films from his eyes, so that he might see God's light with his eyes; and Sarah, daughter of Rag′ū·el, by giving her in marriage to Tō·bī′as son of Tō′bit, and by setting her free from the wicked demon As-mō·dē′us. For Tō·bī′as was entitled to have her before all others who had desired to marry her. At the same time that Tō′bit returned from the courtyard into his house, Sarah daughter of Rag′ū·el came down from her upper room.

Tobit Gives Instructions to His Son
(Deut 15.7–8; Mt 6.2–4)

4 That same day Tō′bit remembered the money that he had left in trust with Gab′a·el at Rā′gēs in Mēd′i·a, 2 and he said to himself, "Now I have asked for death. Why do I not call my son Tō·bī′as and explain to him about the money before I die?" 3 Then he called his son Tō·bī′as, and when he came to him he said, "My son, when I die,[t] give me a proper burial. Honor your mother and do not abandon her all the days of her life. Do whatever pleases her, and do not grieve her in anything. 4 Remember her, my son, because she faced many dangers for you while you were in her womb. And when she dies, bury her beside me in the same grave.

5 "Revere the Lord all your days, my son, and refuse to sin or to transgress his commandments. Live uprightly all the days of your life, and do not walk in the ways of wrongdoing; 6 for those who act in accordance with truth will prosper in all their activities. To all those who practice righteousness[u] 7 give alms from your possessions, and do not let your eye begrudge the gift when you make it. Do not turn your face away from anyone who is poor, and the face of God will not be turned away from you. 8 If you have many possessions, make your gift from them in proportion; if few, do not be afraid to give according to the little you have. 9 So you will be laying up a good treasure for yourself against the day of necessity. 10 For almsgiving delivers from death and keeps you from going into the Darkness. 11 Indeed, almsgiving, for all who practice it, is an excellent offering in the presence of the Most High.

12 "Beware, my son, of every kind of fornication. First of all, marry a woman from among the descendants of your ancestors; do not marry a foreign woman, who is not of your father's tribe; for we are the descendants of the prophets. Remember, my son, that Noah, Abraham, Isaac, and Jacob, our ancestors of old, all took wives from among their kindred. They were blessed in their children, and their posterity will inherit the land. 13 So now, my son, love your kindred, and in your heart do not disdain your kindred, the sons and daughters of your people, by refusing to take a wife for yourself from among them. For in pride there is ruin and great confusion. And in idleness there is loss and dire poverty, because idleness is the mother of famine.

14 "Do not keep over until the next day the wages of those who work for you, but pay them at once. If you serve God you will receive payment. "Watch yourself, my son, in everything you do, and discipline yourself in all your con-

t Lat   u The text of codex Sinaiticus goes directly from verse 6 to verse 19, reading *To those who practice righteousness* 19 *the Lord will give good counsel.* In order to fill the lacuna verses 7 to 18 are derived from other ancient authorities duct. 15 And what you hate, do not do to anyone. Do not drink wine to excess or let drunkenness go with you on your way. 16 Give some of your food to the hungry, and some of your clothing to the naked. Give all your surplus as alms, and do not let your eye begrudge your giving of alms. 17 Place your bread on the grave of the righteous, but give none to sinners. 18 Seek advice from every wise person and do not despise any useful counsel. 19 At all times bless the Lord God, and ask him that your ways may be made straight and that all your paths and plans may prosper. For none of the nations has understanding, but the Lord himself will give them good counsel; but if he chooses otherwise, he casts down to deepest Hades. So now, my child, remember these commandments, and do not let them be erased from your heart.

Money Left in Trust with Gabael

20 "And now, my son, let me explain to you that I left ten talents of silver in trust with Gab'a·el son of Gā'bri·as, at Rā'gēs in Mēd'i·a. 21 Do not be afraid, my son, because we have become poor. You have great wealth if you fear God and flee from every sin and do what is good in the sight of the Lord your God."

The Angel Raphael
(Heb 13.2)

5 Then Tō·bī'as answered his father Tō'bit, "I will do everything that you have commanded me, father; 2 but how can I obtain the money[v] from him, since he does not know me and I do not know him? What evidence[w] am I to give him so that he will recognize and trust me, and give me the money? Also, I do not know the roads to Mēd'i·a, or how to get there." 3 Then Tō'bit answered his son Tō·bī'as, "He gave me his bond and I gave him my bond. I[x] divided his in two; we each took one part, and I put one with the money. And now twenty years have passed since I left this money in trust. So now, my son, find yourself a trustworthy man to go with you, and we will pay him wages until you return. But get back the money from Gab'-a·el."[y]

4 So Tō·bī'as went out to look for a man to go with him to Mēd'i·a, someone who was acquainted with the way. He went out and found the angel Raph'a·el standing in front of him; but he did not perceive that he was an angel of God. 5 Tō·bī'as[z] said to him, "Where do you come from, young man?" "From your kindred, the Israelites," he replied, "and I have come here to work." Then Tō·bī'as[a] said to him, "Do you know the way to go to Mēd'i·a?" 6 "Yes," he replied, "I have been there many times; I am acquainted with it and know all the roads. I have often traveled to Mēd'i·a, and would stay with our kinsman Gab'a·el who lives in Rā'gēs of Mēd'i·a. It is a journey of two days from Ec·bat'a·na to Rā'gēs; for it lies in a mountainous area, while Ec·bat'a·na is in the middle of the plain." 7 Then Tō·bī'as said to him, "Wait for me, young man, until I go in and tell my father; for I do need you to travel with me, and I will pay you your wages." 8 He replied, "All right, I will wait; but do not take too long."

9 So Tō·bī'as[a] went in to tell his father Tō'bit and said to him, "I have just found a man who is one of our own Israelite kindred!" He replied, "Call the man in, my son, so that I may learn about his family and to what tribe he belongs, and whether he is trustworthy enough to go with you."

10 Then Tō·bī'as went out and called him, and said, "Young man, my father is calling for you." So he went in to him, and Tō'bit greeted him first. He replied, "Joyous greetings to you!" But Tō'bit retorted, "What joy is left for me any more? I am a man without eyesight; I cannot see the light of heaven, but I lie in darkness like the dead who no longer see the light. Although still alive, I am among the dead. I hear people but I cannot see them." But the young man[a] said, "Take courage; the time is near for God to heal you; take courage." Then Tō'bit said to him, "My son Tō·bī'as wishes to go to Mēd'i·a. Can you accompany him and guide him? I will pay your wages, brother." He answered, "I can go with him and I know all the roads, for I have often gone to Mēd'i·a and have crossed all its plains, and I am familiar with its mountains and all of its roads."

11 Then Tō'bit[a] said to him, "Brother, of what family are you and from what tribe? Tell me, brother." 12 He replied, "Why do you need to

---

[v] Gk it   [w] Gk sign   [x] Other authorities read He   [y] Gk from him   [z] Gk He   [a] Gk he

know my tribe?" But Tō'bit[b] said, "I want to be sure, brother, whose son you are and what your name is." [13] He replied, "I am Az·a·rī'ah, the son of the great Han·a·nī'ah, one of your relatives." [14] Then Tō'bit said to him, "Welcome! God save you, brother. Do not feel bitter toward me, brother, because I wanted to be sure about your ancestry. It turns out that you are a kinsman, and of good and noble lineage. For I knew Han·a·nī'ah and Nathan,[c] the two sons of Shem·e·lī'ah,[d] and they used to go with me to Jerusalem and worshiped with me there, and were not led astray. Your kindred are good people; you come of good stock. Hearty welcome!"

15 Then he added, "I will pay you a drachma a day as wages, as well as expenses for yourself and my son. So go with my son, [16] and[e] I will add something to your wages." Raph'a·el[f] answered, "I will go with him; so do not fear. We shall leave in good health and return to you in good health, because the way is safe." [17] So Tō'bit[b] said to him, "Blessings be upon you, brother."

Then he called his son and said to him, "Son, prepare supplies for the journey and set out with your brother. May God in heaven bring you safely there and return you in good health to me; and may his angel, my son, accompany you both for your safety."

Before he went out to start his journey, he kissed his father and mother. Tō'bit then said to him, "Have a safe journey."

18 But his mother[g] began to weep, and said to Tō'bit, "Why is it that you have sent my child away? Is he not the staff of our hand as he goes in and out before us? [19] Do not heap money upon money, but let it be a ransom for our child. [20] For the life that is given to us by the Lord is enough for us." [21] Tō'bit[f] said to her, "Do not worry; our child will leave in good health and return to us in good health. Your eyes will see him on the day when he returns to you in good health. Say no more! Do not fear for them, my sister. [22] For a good angel will accompany him; his journey will be successful, and he will come back in good health."

6

[1] So she stopped weeping.

Journey to Rages

The young man went out and the angel went with him; [2] and the dog came out with him and went along with them. So they both journeyed along, and when the first night overtook them they camped by the Tigris river. [3] Then the young man went down to wash his feet in the Tigris river. Suddenly a large fish leaped up from the water and tried to swallow the young man's foot, and he cried out. [4] But the angel said to the young man, "Catch hold of the fish and hang on to it!" So the young man grasped the fish and drew it up on the land. [5] Then the angel said to him, "Cut open the fish and take out its gall, heart, and liver. Keep them with you, but throw away the intestines. For its gall, heart, and liver are useful as medicine." [6] So after cutting open the fish the young man gathered together the gall, heart, and liver; then he roasted and ate some of the fish, and kept some to be salted.

The two continued on their way together until they were near Mēd'i·a.[h] [7] Then the young man questioned the angel and said to him, "Brother Az·a·rī'ah, what medicinal value is there in the fish's heart and liver, and in the gall?" [8] He replied, "As for the fish's heart and liver, you must burn them to make a smoke in the presence of a man or woman afflicted by a demon or evil spirit, and every affliction will flee away and never remain with that person any longer. [9] And as for the gall, anoint a person's eyes where white films have appeared on them; blow upon them, upon the white films, and the eyes[i] will be healed."

Raphael's Instructions
(Num 36.6–9)

10 When he entered Mēd'i·a and already was approaching Ec·bat'a·na,[j] [11] Raph'a·el said to the young man, "Brother Tō·bī'as." "Here I am," he answered. Then Raph'a·el[b] said to him, "We must stay this night in the home of

---

[b]Gk he   [c]Other ancient authorities read *Jathan* or *Nathamiah*   [d]Other ancient authorities read *Shemaiah*   [e]Other ancient authorities add *when you return safely*   [f]Gk *He*   [g]Other ancient authorities add *Anna*   [h]Other ancient authorities read *Ecbatana*   [i]Gk *they*   [j]Other ancient authorities read *Rages*

Rag'ū·el. He is your relative, and he has a daughter named Sarah. [12] He has no male heir and no daughter except Sarah only, and you, as next of kin to her, have before all other men a hereditary claim on her. Also it is right for you to inherit her father's possessions. Moreover, the girl is sensible, brave, and very beautiful, and her father is a good man." [13] He continued, "You have every right to take her in marriage. So listen to me, brother; tonight I will speak to her father about the girl, so that we may take her to be your bride. When we return from Rā'gēs we will celebrate her marriage. For I know that Rag'ū·el can by no means keep her from you or promise her to another man without incurring the penalty of death according to the decree of the book of Moses. Indeed he knows that you, rather than any other man, are entitled to marry his daughter. So now listen to me, brother, and tonight we shall speak concerning the girl and arrange her engagement to you. And when we return from Rā'gēs we will take her and bring her back with us to your house."

14 Then Tō·bī'as said in answer to Raph'a·el, "Brother Az·a·rī'ah, I have heard that she already has been married to seven husbands and that they died in the bridal chamber. On the night when they went in to her, they would die. I have heard people saying that it was a demon that killed them. [15] It does not harm her, but it kills anyone who desires to approach her. So now, since I am the only son my father has, I am afraid that I may die and bring my father's and mother's life down to their grave, grieving for me — and they have no other son to bury them."

16 But Raph'a·el[k] said to him, "Do you not remember your father's orders when he commanded you to take a wife from your father's house? Now listen to me, brother, and say no more about this demon. Take her. I know that this very night she will be given to you in marriage. [17] When you enter the bridal chamber, take some of the fish's liver and heart, and put them on the embers of the incense. An odor will be given off; [18] the demon will smell it and flee, and will never be seen near her any more. Now when you are about to go to bed with her, both of you must first stand up and pray, imploring the Lord of heaven that mercy and safety

may be granted to you. Do not be afraid, for she was set apart for you before the world was made. You will save her, and she will go with you. I presume that you will have children by her, and they will be as brothers to you. Now say no more!" When Tō·bī'as heard the words of Raph'a·el and learned that she was his kinswoman,[l] related through his father's lineage, he loved her very much, and his heart was drawn to her.

Arrival at Home of Raguel

7 Now when they[m] entered Ec·bat'-a·na, Tō·bī'as[k] said to him, "Brother Az·a·rī'ah, take me straight to our brother Rag'ū·el." So he took him to Raguel's house, where they found him sitting beside the courtyard door. They greeted him first, and he replied, "Joyous greetings, brothers; welcome and good health!" Then he brought them into his house. [2] He said to his wife Edna, "How much the young man resembles my kinsman Tō'bit!" [3] Then Edna questioned them, saying, "Where are you from, brothers?" They answered, "We belong to the descendants of Naph'ta·lī who are exiles in Nin'e·veh." [4] She said to them, "Do you know our kinsman Tō'-bit?" And they replied, "Yes, we know him." Then she asked them, "Is he[n] in good health?" [5] They replied, "He is alive and in good health." And Tō·bī'as added, "He is my father!" [6] At that Rag'ū·el jumped up and kissed him and wept. [7] He also spoke to him as follows, "Blessings on you, my child, son of a good and noble father!"[o] "O most miserable of calamities that such an upright and beneficent man has become blind!" He then embraced his kinsman Tō·bī'as and wept. [8] His wife Edna also wept for him, and their daughter Sarah likewise wept. [9] Then Rag'ū·el[k] slaughtered a ram from the flock and received them very warmly.

Marriage of Tobias and Sarah

When they had bathed and washed themselves and had reclined to dine, Tō·bī'as said to Raph'a·el, "Brother

[k] Gk *he*　[l] Gk *sister*　[m] Other ancient authorities read *he*　[n] Other ancient authorities add *alive and*　[o] Other ancient authorities add *When he heard that Tobit had lost his sight, he was stricken with grief and wept. Then he said,*

Az·a·rī'ah, ask Rag'ū·el to give me my kinswoman[p] Sarah." [10]But Rag'ū·el overheard it and said to the lad, "Eat and drink, and be merry tonight. For no one except you, brother, has the right to marry my daughter Sarah. Likewise I am not at liberty to give her to any other man than yourself, because you are my nearest relative. But let me explain to you the true situation more fully, my child. [11]I have given her to seven men of our kinsmen, and all died on the night when they went in to her. But now, my child, eat and drink, and the Lord will act on behalf of you both." But Tō·bī'as said, "I will neither eat nor drink anything until you settle the things that pertain to me." So Rag'ū·el said, "I will do so. She is given to you in accordance with the decree in the book of Moses, and it has been decreed from heaven that she be given to you. Take your kinswoman;[p] from now on you are her brother and she is your sister. She is given to you from today and forever. May the Lord of heaven, my child, guide and prosper you both this night and grant you mercy and peace." [12]Then Rag'ū·el summoned his daughter Sarah. When she came to him he took her by the hand and gave her to Tō·bī'as,[q] saying, "Take her to be your wife in accordance with the law and decree written in the book of Moses. Take her and bring her safely to your father. And may the God of heaven prosper your journey with his peace." [13]Then he called her mother and told her to bring writing material; and he wrote out a copy of a marriage contract, to the effect that he gave her to him as wife according to the decree of the law of Moses. [14]Then they began to eat and drink.

[15] Rag'ū·el called his wife Edna and said to her, "Sister, get the other room ready, and take her there." [16]So she went and made the bed in the room as he had told her, and brought Sarah[r] there. She wept for her daughter.[r] Then, wiping away the tears,[s] she said to her, "Take courage, my daughter; the Lord of heaven grant you joy[t] in place of your sorrow. Take courage, my daughter." Then she went out.

Tobias Routs the Demon
(Cp Mt 12.43–45)

8 When they had finished eating and drinking they wanted to re-tire; so they took the young man and brought him into the bedroom. [2]Then Tō·bī'as remembered the words of Raph'a·el, and he took the fish's liver and heart out of the bag where he had them and put them on the embers of the incense. [3]The odor of the fish so repelled the demon that he fled to the remotest parts[u] of Egypt. But Raph'a·el followed him, and at once bound him there hand and foot.

4 When the parents[v] had gone out and shut the door of the room, Tō·bī'as got out of bed and said to Sarah,[r] "Sister, get up, and let us pray and implore our Lord that he grant us mercy and safety." [5]So she got up, and they began to pray and implore that they might be kept safe. Tō·bī'as[w] began by saying,

"Blessed are you, O God of our
    ancestors,
  and blessed is your name in all
    generations forever.
Let the heavens and the whole
    creation bless you forever.
6 You made Adam, and for him
    you made his wife Eve
  as a helper and support.
From the two of them
    the human race has sprung.
You said, 'It is not good that the
    man should be alone;
  let us make a helper for him
    like himself.'
7 I now am taking this kinswoman
    of mine,
  not because of lust,
  but with sincerity.
Grant that she and I may find
    mercy
  and that we may grow old
    together."

[8]And they both said, "Amen, Amen." [9]Then they went to sleep for the night.

But Rag'ū·el arose and called his servants to him, and they went and dug a grave, [10]for he said, "It is possible that he will die and we will become an object of ridicule and derision." [11]When they had finished digging the grave, Rag'ū·el went into his house and called his wife, [12]saying, "Send one of the maids and have her go in to see if he is alive. But if he is dead, let us bury him without anyone knowing it." [13]So they

---

[p]Gk *sister* [q]Gk *him* [r]Gk *her*
[s]Other ancient authorities read *the tears of her daughter* [t]Other ancient authorities read *favor* [u]Or *fled through the air to the parts* [v]Gk *they*
[w]Gk *He*

sent the maid, lit a lamp, and opened the door; and she went in and found them sound asleep together. 14 Then the maid came out and informed them that he was alive and that nothing was wrong. 15 So they blessed the God of heaven, and Rag′u·el[x] said,

"Blessed are you, O God, with
　　every pure blessing;
let all your chosen ones bless
　　you.[y]
Let them bless you forever.
16　Blessed are you because you
　　have made me glad.
It has not turned out as I
　　expected,
but you have dealt with us
　　according to your great
　　mercy.
17　Blessed are you because you had
　　compassion
　　on two only children.
Be merciful to them, O Master,
　　and keep them safe;
bring their lives to fulfillment
　　in happiness and mercy."

18 Then he ordered his servants to fill in the grave before daybreak.

Wedding Feast

19　After this he asked his wife to bake many loaves of bread; and he went out to the herd and brought two steers and four rams and ordered them to be slaughtered. So they began to make preparations. 20 Then he called for Tō·bī′as and swore on oath to him in these words:[z] "You shall not leave here for fourteen days, but shall stay here eating and drinking with me; and you shall cheer up my daughter, who has been depressed. 21 Take at once half of what I own and return in safety to your father; the other half will be yours when my wife and I die. Take courage, my child. I am your father and Edna is your mother, and we belong to you as well as to your wife[a] now and forever. Take courage, my child."

The Money Recovered

9　Then Tō·bī′as called Raph′a·el and said to him, 2 "Brother Az·a·rī′ah, take four servants and two camels with you and travel to Rā′gēs. Go to the home of Gab′a·el, give him the bond, get the money, and then bring him with you to the wedding celebration. 4 For you know that my father must be counting the days, and if I delay even one day I will upset him very

much. 3 You are witness to the oath Rag′u·el has sworn, and I cannot violate his oath."[b] 5 So Raph′a·el with the four servants and two camels went to Rā′gēs in Mēd′i·a and stayed with Gab′a·el. Raph′a·el[c] gave him the bond and informed him that Tobit's son Tō·bī′as had married and was inviting him to the wedding celebration. So Gab′a·el[d] got up and counted out to him the money bags, with their seals intact; then they loaded them on the camels.[e] 6 In the morning they both got up early and went to the wedding celebration. When they came into Raguel's house they found Tō·bī′as reclining at table. He sprang up and greeted Gab′a·el,[f] who wept and blessed him with the words, "Good and noble son of a father good and noble, upright and generous! May the Lord grant the blessing of heaven to you and your wife, and to your wife's father and mother. Blessed be God, for I see in Tō·bī′as the very image of my cousin Tō′bit."

Anxiety of the Parents

10　Now, day by day, Tō′bit kept counting how many days Tō·bī′as[d] would need for going and for returning. And when the days had passed and his son did not appear, 2 he said, "Is it possible that he has been detained? Or that Gab′a·el has died, and there is no one to give him the money?" 3 And he began to worry. 4 His wife Anna said, "My child has perished and is no longer among the living." And she began to weep and mourn for her son, saying, 5 "Woe to me, my child, the light of my eyes, that I let you make the journey." 6 But Tō′bit kept saying to her, "Be quiet and stop worrying, my dear;[a] he is all right. Probably something unexpected has happened there. The man who went with him is trustworthy and is one of our own kin. Do not grieve for him, my dear;[a] he will soon be here." 7 She answered him, "Be quiet yourself! Stop trying to deceive me! My child has perished." She would rush out every day

---

[x] Gk *they*　　[y] Other ancient authorities lack this line　　[z] Other ancient authorities read *Tobias and said to him*　　[a] Gk *sister*　　[b] In other ancient authorities verse 3 precedes verse 4　　[c] Gk *He*　　[d] Gk *he*　　[e] Other ancient authorities lack *on the camels*　　[f] Gk *him*

and watch the road her son had taken, and would heed no one.[g] When the sun had set she would go in and mourn and weep all night long, getting no sleep at all.

Tobias and Sarah Start for Home

Now when the fourteen days of the wedding celebration had ended that Rag′ū·el had sworn to observe for his daughter, Tō·bī′as came to him and said, "Send me back, for I know that my father and mother do not believe that they will see me again. So I beg of you, father, to let me go so that I may return to my own father. I have already explained to you how I left him." [8] But Rag′ū·el said to Tō·bī′as, "Stay, my child, stay with me; I will send messengers to your father Tō′bit and they will inform him about you." [9] But he said, "No! I beg you to send me back to my father." [10] So Rag′ū·el promptly gave Tō·bī′as his wife Sarah, as well as half of all his property: male and female slaves, oxen and sheep, donkeys and camels, clothing, money, and household goods. [11] Then he saw them safely off; he embraced Tō·bī′as[h] and said, "Farewell, my child; have a safe journey. The Lord of heaven prosper you and your wife Sarah, and may I see children of yours before I die." [12] Then he kissed his daughter Sarah and said to her, "My daughter, honor your father-in-law and your mother-in-law,[i] since from now on they are as much your parents as those who gave you birth. Go in peace, daughter, and may I hear a good report about you as long as I live." Then he bade them farewell and let them go. Then Edna said to Tō·bī′as, "My child and dear brother, the Lord of heaven bring you back safely, and may I live long enough to see children of you and of my daughter Sarah before I die. In the sight of the Lord I entrust my daughter to you; do nothing to grieve her all the days of your life. Go in peace, my child. From now on I am your mother and Sarah is your beloved wife.[j] May we all prosper together all the days of our lives." Then she kissed them both and saw them safely off. [13] Tō·bī′as parted from Rag′ū·el with happiness and joy, praising the Lord of heaven and earth, King over all, because he had made his journey a success. Finally, he blessed Rag′ū·el and his wife Edna, and said, "I have been commanded by the Lord to honor you all the days of my life."[k]

Homeward Journey

11 When they came near to Ka-ser′in, which is opposite Nin′e-veh, Raph′a·el said, [2] "You are aware of how we left your father. [3] Let us run ahead of your wife and prepare the house while they are still on the way." [4] As they went on together Raph′a·el[l] said to him, "Have the gall ready." And the dog[m] went along behind them.

[5] Meanwhile Anna sat looking intently down the road by which her son would come. [6] When she caught sight of him coming, she said to his father, "Look, your son is coming, and the man who went with him!"

Tobit's Sight Restored
(Cp Acts 9.18)

[7] Raph′a·el said to Tō·bī′as, before he had approached his father, "I know that his eyes will be opened. [8] Smear the gall of the fish on his eyes; the medicine will make the white films shrink and peel off from his eyes, and your father will regain his sight and see the light."

[9] Then Anna ran up to her son and threw her arms around him, saying, "Now that I have seen you, my child, I am ready to die." And she wept. [10] Then Tō′bit got up and came stumbling out through the courtyard door. Tō·bī′as went up to him, [11] with the gall of the fish in his hand, and holding him firmly, he blew into his eyes, saying, "Take courage, father." With this he applied the medicine on his eyes, [12] and it made them smart.[k] [13] Next, with both his hands he peeled off the white films from the corners of his eyes. Then Tō′bit[l] saw his son and[n] threw his arms around him, [14] and he wept and said to him, "I see you, my son, the light of my eyes!" Then he said,

> "Blessed be God,
>   and blessed be his great name,
>   and blessed be all his holy
>   angels.
> May his holy name be blessed[o]

[g] Other ancient authorities read *and she would eat nothing*   [h] Gk *him*   [i] Other ancient authorities lack parts of *Then . . . mother-in-law*   [j] Gk *sister*   [k] Lat: Meaning of Gk uncertain   [l] Gk *he*   [m] Codex Sinaiticus reads *And the Lord*   [n] Other ancient authorities lack *saw his son and*   [o] Codex Sinaiticus reads *May his great name be upon us and blessed be all the angels*

throughout all the ages.

15 Though he afflicted me,
he has had mercy upon me.[p]
Now I see my son Tō·bī′as!"

So Tō′bit went in rejoicing and praising God at the top of his voice. Tō·bī′as reported to his father that his journey had been successful, that he had brought the money, that he had married Rag′ūel's daughter Sarah, and that she was, indeed, on her way there, very near to the gate of Nin′e·veh.

16 Then Tō′bit, rejoicing and praising God, went out to meet his daughter-in-law at the gate of Nin′e·veh. When the people of Nin′e·veh saw him coming, walking along in full vigor and with no one leading him, they were amazed. 17 Before them all, Tō′bit acknowledged that God had been merciful to him and had restored his sight. When Tō′bit met Sarah the wife of his son Tō·bī′as, he blessed her saying, "Come in, my daughter, and welcome. Blessed be your God who has brought you to us, my daughter. Blessed be your father and your mother, blessed be my son Tō·bī′as, and blessed be you, my daughter. Come in now to your home, and welcome, with blessing and joy. Come in, my daughter." So on that day there was rejoicing among all the Jews who were in Nin′e·veh. 18 A·hī′kar and his nephew Nā′dab were also present to share Tō′bit's joy. With merriment they celebrated Tō·bī′as's wedding feast for seven days, and many gifts were given to him.[q]

Raphael's Wages

12 When the wedding celebration was ended, Tō′bit called his son Tō·bī′as and said to him, "My child, see to paying the wages of the man who went with you, and give him a bonus as well." 2 He replied, "Father, how much shall I pay him? It would do no harm to give him half of the possessions brought back with me. 3 For he has led me back to you safely, he cured my wife, he brought the money back with me, and he healed you. How much extra shall I give him as a bonus?" 4 Tō′bit said, "He deserves, my child, to receive half of all that he brought back." 5 So Tō·bī′as[r] called him and said, "Take for your wages half of all that you brought back, and farewell."

Raphael's Exhortation
(Sir 29.8–13; Mt 6.1–18)

6 Then Raph′a·el[r] called the two of them privately and said to them, "Bless God and acknowledge him in the presence of all the living for the good things he has done for you. Bless and sing praise to his name. With fitting honor declare to all people the deeds[s] of God. Do not be slow to acknowledge him. 7 It is good to conceal the secret of a king, but to acknowledge and reveal the works of God, and with fitting honor to acknowledge him. Do good and evil will not overtake you. 8 Prayer with fasting[t] is good, but better than both is almsgiving with righteousness. A little with righteousness is better than wealth with wrongdoing.[u] It is better to give alms than to lay up gold. 9 For almsgiving saves from death and purges away every sin. Those who give alms will enjoy a full life, 10 but those who commit sin and do wrong are their own worst enemies.

Raphael Discloses His Identity

11 "I will now declare the whole truth to you and will conceal nothing from you. Already I have declared it to you when I said, 'It is good to conceal the secret of a king, but to reveal with due honor the works of God.' 12 So now when you and Sarah prayed, it was I who brought and read[v] the record of your prayer before the glory of the Lord, and likewise whenever you would bury the dead. 13 And that time when you did not hesitate to get up and leave your dinner to go and bury the dead, 14 I was sent to you to test you. And at the same time God sent me to heal you and Sarah your daughter-in-law. 15 I am Raph′a·el, one of the seven angels who stand ready and enter before the glory of the Lord."

16 The two of them were shaken; they fell face down, for they were afraid. 17 But he said to them, "Do not be afraid; peace be with you. Bless God forevermore. 18 As for me, when I was with you, I was not acting on my own will, but by the will of God. Bless him each and every day; sing his praises. 19 Although you were watching me, I

[p] Lat: Gk lacks this line [q] Other ancient authorities lack parts of this sentence [r] Gk *he* [s] Gk *words*; other ancient authorities read *words of the deeds* [t] Codex Sinaiticus *with sincerity* [u] Lat [v] Lat: Gk lacks *and read*

really did not eat or drink anything — but what you saw was a vision. [20]So now get up from the ground,[w] and acknowledge God. See, I am ascending to him who sent me. Write down all these things that have happened to you." And he ascended. [21]Then they stood up, and could see him no more. [22]They kept blessing God and singing his praises, and they acknowledged God for these marvelous deeds of his, when an angel of God had appeared to them.

Tobit's Thanksgiving to God
(Rev 21.9 – 22.5)

13 Then Tō′bit[x] said:
"Blessed be God who lives forever,
    because his kingdom[y] lasts throughout all ages.
[2] For he afflicts, and he shows mercy;
    he leads down to Hades in the lowest regions of the earth,
    and he brings up from the great abyss,[z]
    and there is nothing that can escape his hand.
[3] Acknowledge him before the nations, O children of Israel;
    for he has scattered you among them.
[4] He has shown you his greatness even there.
Exalt him in the presence of every living being,
    because he is our Lord and he is our God;
    he is our Father and he is God forever.
[5] He will afflict[a] you for your iniquities,
    but he will again show mercy on all of you.
He will gather you from all the nations
    among whom you have been scattered.
[6] If you turn to him with all your heart and with all your soul,
    to do what is true before him,
then he will turn to you
    and will no longer hide his face from you.
So now see what he has done for you;
    acknowledge him at the top of your voice.

Bless the Lord of righteousness,
    and exalt the King of the ages.[b]
In the land of my exile I acknowledge him,
    and show his power and majesty to a nation of sinners:
'Turn back, you sinners, and do what is right before him;
    perhaps he may look with favor upon you and show you mercy.'
[7] As for me, I exalt my God,
    and my soul rejoices in the King of heaven.
[8] Let all people speak of his majesty,
    and acknowledge him in Jerusalem.
[9] O Jerusalem, the holy city,
    he afflicted[c] you for the deeds of your hands,[d]
    but will again have mercy on the children of the righteous.
[10] Acknowledge the Lord, for he is good,[e]
    and bless the King of the ages,
    so that his tent[f] may be rebuilt in you in joy.
May he cheer all those within you who are captives,
    and love all those within you who are distressed,
    to all generations forever.
[11] A bright light will shine to all the ends of the earth;
    many nations will come to you from far away,
the inhabitants of the remotest parts of the earth to your holy name,
    bearing gifts in their hands for the King of heaven.
Generation after generation will give joyful praise in you,
    the name of the chosen city will endure forever.

---

[w] Other ancient authorities read *now bless the Lord on earth*   [x] Gk *he*
[y] Other ancient authorities read *forever, and his kingdom*   [z] Gk *from destruction*
[a] Other ancient authorities read *He afflicted*   [b] The lacuna in codex Sinaiticus, verses 6b to 10a, is filled in from other ancient authorities   [c] Other ancient authorities read *will afflict*
[d] Other ancient authorities read *your children*   [e] Other ancient authorities read *Lord worthily*   [f] Or *tabernacle*

T
O
B
I
T

12 Cursed are all who speak a
  harsh word against you;
cursed are all who conquer
  you
and pull down your walls,
all who overthrow your towers
  and set your homes on fire.
But blessed forever will be all
  who revere you.[g]

13 Go, then, and rejoice over the
  children of the righteous,
for they will be gathered
  together
and will praise the Lord of the
  ages.

14 Happy are those who love you,
  and happy are those who
  rejoice in your prosperity.
Happy also are all people who
  grieve with you
because of your afflictions;
for they will rejoice with you
  and witness all your glory
  forever.

15 My soul blesses[h] the Lord, the
  great King!

16 For Jerusalem will be built[i] as
  his house for all ages.
How happy I will be if a
  remnant of my descendants
  should survive
to see your glory and
  acknowledge the King of
  heaven.
The gates of Jerusalem will be
  built with sapphire and
  emerald,
and all your walls with
  precious stones.
The towers of Jerusalem will be
  built with gold,
and their battlements with
  pure gold.
The streets of Jerusalem will be
  paved
with ruby and with stones of
  Ō'phir.

17 The gates of Jerusalem will sing
  hymns of joy,
and all her houses will cry,
  'Hallelujah!
Blessed be the God of Israel!'
and the blessed will bless the
  holy name forever and
  ever."

Tobit's Final Counsel
(Nah 1.2 – 3.19; Zech 8.20–23)

14 So ended Tō'bit's words of
  praise.
2 Tō'bit[j] died in peace when he
was one hundred twelve years old, and

was buried with great honor in Nin'e-
veh. He was sixty-two[k] years old
when he lost his eyesight, and after
regaining it he lived in prosperity, giving alms and continually blessing God
and acknowledging God's majesty.
3 When he was about to die, he
called his son Tō·bī'as and the seven
sons of Tō·bī'as[l] and gave this command: "My son, take your children
4 and hurry off to Mēd'i·a, for I believe
the word of God that Nā'hum spoke
about Nin'e·veh, that all these things
will take place and overtake Assyria
and Nin'e·veh. Indeed, everything that
was spoken by the prophets of Israel,
whom God sent, will occur. None of all
their words will fail, but all will come
true at their appointed times. So it will
be safer in Mēd'i·a than in Assyria and
Babylon. For I know and believe that
whatever God has said will be fulfilled
and will come true; not a single word
of the prophecies will fail. All of our
kindred, inhabitants of the land of Israel, will be scattered and taken as
captives from the good land; and the
whole land of Israel will be desolate,
even Sa·mār'i·a and Jerusalem will be
desolate. And the temple of God in it
will be burned to the ground, and it
will be desolate for a while.[m]
5 "But God will again have mercy
on them, and God will bring them back
into the land of Israel; and they will
rebuild the temple of God, but not like
the first one until the period when the
times of fulfillment shall come. After
this they all will return from their exile
and will rebuild Jerusalem in splendor; and in it the temple of God will be
rebuilt, just as the prophets of Israel
have said concerning it. 6 Then the nations in the whole world will all be converted and worship God in truth. They
will all abandon their idols, which deceitfully have led them into their error;
7 and in righteousness they will praise
the eternal God. All the Israelites who
are saved in those days and are truly
mindful of God will be gathered together; they will go to Jerusalem and
live in safety forever in the land of

---

[g] Other ancient authorities read *who
build you up*   [h] Or *O my soul, bless*
[i] Other ancient authorities add *for a city*
[j] Gk *He*   [k] Other ancient authorities
read *fifty-eight*   [l] Lat: Gk lacks *and the
seven sons of Tobias*   [m] Lat: Other
ancient authorities read *of God will be in
distress and will be burned for a while*

Abraham, and it will be given over to them. Those who sincerely love God will rejoice, but those who commit sin and injustice will vanish from all the earth. 8,9 So now, my children, I command you, serve God faithfully and do what is pleasing in his sight. Your children are also to be commanded to do what is right and to give alms, and to be mindful of God and to bless his name at all times with sincerity and with all their strength. So now, my son, leave Nin'e·veh; do not remain here. 10 On whatever day you bury your mother beside me, do not stay overnight within the confines of the city. For I see that there is much wickedness within it, and that much deceit is practiced within it, while the people are without shame. See, my son, what Nā'-dab did to A·hī'kar who had reared him. Was he not, while still alive, brought down into the earth? For God repaid him to his face for this shameful treatment. A·hī'kar came out into the light, but Nā'dab went into the eternal darkness, because he tried to kill A·hī'-kar. Because he gave alms, A·hī'kar[n] escaped the fatal trap that Nā'dab had set for him, but Nā'dab fell into it himself, and was destroyed. 11 So now, my children, see what almsgiving accomplishes, and what injustice does—it brings death! But now my breath fails me."

Death of Tobit and Anna

Then they laid him on his bed, and he died; and he received an honorable funeral. 12 When Tō·bī'as's mother died, he buried her beside his father. Then he and his wife and children[o] returned to Mēd'i·a and settled in Ec·bat'a·na with Rag'ū·el his father-in-law. 13 He treated his parents-in-law[p] with great respect in their old age, and buried them in Ec·bat'a·na of Mēd'i·a. He inherited both the property of Rag'ū·el and that of his father Tō'bit. 14 He died highly respected at the age of one hundred seventeen[q] years. 15 Before he died he heard[r] of the destruction of Nin'e·veh, and he saw its prisoners being led into Mēd'i·a, those whom King Cȳ·ax'a·rēs[s] of Mēd'i·a had taken captive. Tō·bī'as[t] praised God for all he had done to the people of Nin'e·veh and Assyria; before he died he rejoiced over Nin'e·veh, and he blessed the Lord God forever and ever. Amen.[u]

[n] Gk he; other ancient authorities read Manasses　[o] Codex Sinaiticus lacks and children　[p] Gk them　[q] Other authorities read other numbers　[r] Codex Sinaiticus reads saw and heard　[s] Cn: Codex Sinaiticus Ahikar; other ancient authorities read Nebuchadnezzar and Ahasuerus　[t] Gk He　[u] Other ancient authorities lack Amen

JUDITH

Arphaxad Fortifies Ecbatana
(Cp Ezra 6.2)

1 It was the twelfth year of the reign of Ne·bū·chad·nez'zar, who ruled over the Assyrians in the great city of Nin'e·veh. In those days Ar·phā'xad ruled over the Mēdes in Ec·bat'a·na. 2 He built walls around Ec·bat'a·na with hewn stones three cubits thick and six cubits long; he made the walls seventy cubits high and fifty cubits wide. 3 At its gates he raised towers one hundred cubits high and sixty cubits wide at the foundations. 4 He made its gates seventy cubits high and forty cubits wide to allow his armies to march out in force and his infantry to form their ranks. 5 Then King Ne·bū·chad·nez'zar made war against King Ar·phā'xad in the great plain that is on the borders of Rā'gau. 6 There rallied to him all the people of the hill country and all those who lived along the Euphrates, the Tigris, and the Hȳ·das'-pēs, and, on the plain, Ar'i·och, king of the El·y·mē'ans. Thus, many nations joined the forces of the Chal·dē'ans.[a]

[a] Syr: Gk Cheleoudites

J
U
D
I
T
H

Nebuchadnezzar Issues Ultimatum

7 Then Ne·bu·chad·nez'zar, king of the Assyrians, sent messengers to all who lived in Persia and to all who lived in the west, those who lived in Ci·li'ci·a and Damascus, Lebanon and An·ti·leb'a·non, and all who lived along the seacoast, 8 and those among the nations of Car'mel and Gil'e·ad, and Upper Galilee and the great plain of Es·dra·ē'lon, 9 and all who were in Samaria and its towns, and beyond the Jordan as far as Jerusalem and Beth'a·ny and Chel'ous and Kā'desh and the river of Egypt, and Tah'pan·hēs and Rā·am'sēs and the whole land of Gō'shen, 10 even beyond Tā'nis and Memphis, and all who lived in Egypt as far as the borders of Ethiopia. 11 But all who lived in the whole region disregarded the summons of Ne·bu·chad·nez'zar, king of the Assyrians, and refused to join him in the war; for they were not afraid of him, but regarded him as only one man.*b* So they sent back his messengers empty-handed and in disgrace.

12 Then Ne·bu·chad·nez'zar became very angry with this whole region, and swore by his throne and kingdom that he would take revenge on the whole territory of Ci·li'ci·a and Damascus and Syria, that he would kill with his sword also all the inhabitants of the land of Mō'ab, and the people of Am'mon, and all Judea, and every one in Egypt, as far as the coasts of the two seas.

Arphaxad Is Defeated

13 In the seventeenth year he led his forces against King Ar·phā'xad and defeated him in battle, overthrowing the whole army of Ar·phā'xad and all his cavalry and all his chariots. 14 Thus he took possession of his towns and came to Ec·bat'a·na, captured its towers, plundered its markets, and turned its glory into disgrace. 15 He captured Ar·phā'xad in the mountains of Rā'gau and struck him down with his spears, thus destroying him once and for all. 16 Then he returned to Nin'e·veh, he and all his combined forces, a vast body of troops; and there he and his forces rested and feasted for one hundred twenty days.

The Expedition against the West

2 In the eighteenth year, on the twenty-second day of the first month, there was talk in the palace of Ne·bu·chad·nez'zar, king of the Assyrians, about carrying out his revenge on the whole region, just as he had said. 2 He summoned all his ministers and all his nobles and set before them his secret plan and recounted fully, with his own lips, all the wickedness of the region.*c* 3 They decided that every one who had not obeyed his command should be destroyed.

4 When he had completed his plan, Ne·bu·chad·nez'zar, king of the Assyrians, called Hol·o·fer'nēs, the chief general of his army, second only to himself, and said to him, 5 "Thus says the Great King, the lord of the whole earth: Leave my presence and take with you men confident in their strength, one hundred twenty thousand foot soldiers and twelve thousand cavalry. 6 March out against all the land to the west, because they disobeyed my orders. 7 Tell them to prepare earth and water, for I am coming against them in my anger, and will cover the whole face of the earth with the feet of my troops, to whom I will hand them over to be plundered. 8 Their wounded shall fill their ravines and gullies, and the swelling river shall be filled with their dead. 9 I will lead them away captive to the ends of the whole earth. 10 You shall go and seize all their territory for me in advance. They must yield themselves to you, and you shall hold them for me until the day of their punishment. 11 But to those who resist show no mercy, but hand them over to slaughter and plunder throughout your whole region. 12 For as I live, and by the power of my kingdom, what I have spoken I will accomplish by my own hand. 13 And you—take care not to transgress any of your lord's commands, but carry them out exactly as I have ordered you; do it without delay."

Campaign of Holofernes

14 So Hol·o·fer'nēs left the presence of his lord, and summoned all the commanders, generals, and officers of the Assyrian army. 15 He mustered the picked troops by divisions as his lord had ordered him to do, one hundred

---

b Or *a man*   *c* Meaning of Gk uncertain

wenty thousand of them, together with twelve thousand archers on horseback, [16] and he organized them as a great army is marshaled for a campaign. [17] He took along a vast number of camels and donkeys and mules for transport, and innumerable sheep and oxen and goats for food; [18] also ample rations for everyone, and a huge amount of gold and silver from the royal palace.

19 Then he set out with his whole army, to go ahead of King Ne·bū·chad·nez′zar and to cover the whole face of the earth to the west with their chariots and cavalry and picked foot soldiers. [20] Along with them went a mixed crowd like a swarm of locusts, like the dust[d] of the earth — a multitude that could not be counted.

21 They marched for three days from Nin′e·veh to the plain of Bec′ti·leth, and camped opposite Bec′ti·leth near the mountain that is to the north of Upper Ci·li′ci·a. [22] From there Hol·o·fer′nēs[e] took his whole army, the infantry, cavalry, and chariots, and went up into the hill country. [23] He ravaged Put and Lud, and plundered all the Ras′si·sītes and the Ish′ma·el·ītes on the border of the desert, south of the country of the Chel′le·ans. [24] Then he followed[f] the Euphrates and passed through Mes·o·po·tā′mi·a and destroyed all the fortified towns along the brook Ab′ron, as far as the sea. [25] He also seized the territory of Ci·li′ci·a, and killed everyone who resisted him. Then he came to the southern borders of Jā′pheth, facing Arabia. [26] He surrounded all the Mid′i·an·ītes, and burned their tents and plundered their sheepfolds. [27] Then he went down into the plain of Damascus during the wheat harvest, and burned all their fields and destroyed their flocks and herds and sacked their towns and ravaged their lands and put all their young men to the sword.

28 So fear and dread of him fell upon all the people who lived along the seacoast, at Sī′don and Tyre, and those who lived in Sur and Ō·cī′na and all who lived in Jam′ni·a. Those who lived in A·zō′tus and As′ca·lon feared him greatly.

Entreaties for Peace
(Cp Dan 3.1–7)

3 They therefore sent messengers to him to sue for peace in these words: [2] "We, the servants of Ne·bū-chad·nez′zar, the Great King, lie prostrate before you. Do with us whatever you will. [3] See, our buildings and all our land and all our wheat fields and our flocks and herds and all our encampments[g] lie before you; do with them as you please. [4] Our towns and their inhabitants are also your slaves; come and deal with them as you see fit."

5 The men came to Hol·o·fer′nēs and told him all this. [6] Then he went down to the seacoast with his army and stationed garrisons in the fortified towns and took picked men from them as auxiliaries. [7] These people and all in the countryside welcomed him with garlands and dances and tambourines. [8] Yet he demolished all their shrines[h] and cut down their sacred groves; for he had been commissioned to destroy all the gods of the land, so that all nations should worship Ne·bū·chad·nez′-zar alone, and that all their dialects and tribes should call upon him as a god.

9 Then he came toward Es·dra·ē′-lon, near Dō′than, facing the great ridge of Judea; [10] he camped between Gē′ba and Scyth·op′o·lis, and remained for a whole month in order to collect all the supplies for his army.

Judea on the Alert

4 When the Israelites living in Judea heard of everything that Hol·o·fer′nēs, the general of Ne·bū·chad·nez′zar, the king of the Assyrians, had done to the nations, and how he had plundered and destroyed all their temples, [2] they were therefore greatly terrified at his approach; they were alarmed both for Jerusalem and for the temple of the Lord their God. [3] For they had only recently returned from exile, and all the people of Judea had just now gathered together, and the sacred vessels and the altar and the temple had been consecrated after their profanation. [4] So they sent word to every district of Sa·mār′i·a, and to Kō′na, Beth·hō′ron, Bel′māin, and Jericho, and to Chō′ba and Aē·sor′a, and the valley of Salem. [5] They immediately seized all the high hilltops and fortified the villages on them and stored up food in preparation for war — since

---

[d] Gk sand　[e] Gk he　[f] Or crossed
[g] Gk all the sheepfolds of our tents
[h] Syr: Gk borders

their fields had recently been harvested.

6 The high priest, Jō'a·kim, who was in Jerusalem at the time, wrote to the people of Beth·ū'li·a and Bet·o·mes·thā'im, which faces Es·dra·ē'lon opposite the plain near Dō'than, 7 ordering them to seize the mountain passes, since by them Judea could be invaded; and it would be easy to stop any who tried to enter, for the approach was narrow, wide enough for only two at a time to pass.

Prayer and Penance

8 So the Israelites did as they had been ordered by the high priest Jō'a·kim and the senate of the whole people of Israel, in session at Jerusalem. 9 And every man of Israel cried out to God with great fervor, and they humbled themselves with much fasting. 10 They and their wives and their children and their cattle and every resident alien and hired laborer and purchased slave—they all put sackcloth around their waists. 11 And all the Israelite men, women, and children living at Jerusalem prostrated themselves before the temple and put ashes on their heads and spread out their sackcloth before the Lord. 12 They even draped the altar with sackcloth and cried out in unison, praying fervently to the God of Israel not to allow their infants to be carried off and their wives to be taken as booty, and the towns they had inherited to be destroyed, and the sanctuary to be profaned and desecrated to the malicious joy of the Gentiles.

13 The Lord heard their prayers and had regard for their distress; for the people fasted many days throughout Judea and in Jerusalem before the sanctuary of the Lord Almighty. 14 The high priest Jō'a·kim and all the priests who stood before the Lord and ministered to the Lord, with sackcloth around their loins, offered the daily burnt offerings, the votive offerings, and freewill offerings of the people. 15 With ashes on their turbans, they cried out to the Lord with all their might to look with favor on the whole house of Israel.

Council against the Israelites

5 It was reported to Hol·o·fer'nēs, the general of the Assyrian army, that the people of Israel had prepared for war and had closed the mountain passes and fortified all the high hill-tops and set up barricades in the plains. 2 In great anger he called together all the princes of Mō'ab and the commanders of Am'mon and all the governors of the coastland, 3 and said to them, "Tell me, you Cā'naan·ites what people is this that lives in the hill country? What towns do they inhabit? How large is their army, and in what does their power and strength consist? Who rules over them as king and leads their army? 4 And why have they alone, of all who live in the west, refused to come out and meet me?"

Achior's Report
(Gen 11.27−12.5; Ex 7.1−12.46; 14.21−22)

5 Then Ā'chi·or, the leader of all the Am'mon·ites, said to him, "May my lord please listen to a report from the mouth of your servant, and I will tell you the truth about this people that lives in the mountain district near you. No falsehood shall come from your servant's mouth. 6 These people are descended from the Chal·dē'ans. 7 At one time they lived in Mes·o·po·tā'mi·a because they did not wish to follow the gods of their ancestors who were in Chal·dē'a. 8 Since they had abandoned the ways of their ancestors, and worshiped the God of heaven, the God they had come to know, their ancestors[i] drove them out from the presence of their gods. So they fled to Mes·o·po·tā'mi·a, and lived there for a long time. 9 Then their God commanded them to leave the place where they were living and go to the land of Cā'naan. There they settled, and grew very prosperous in gold and silver and very much livestock. 10 When a famine spread over the land of Cā'naan they went down to Egypt and lived there as long as they had food. There they became so great a multitude that their race could not be counted. 11 So the king of Egypt became hostile to them; he exploited them and forced them to make bricks. 12 They cried out to their God, and he afflicted the whole land of Egypt with incurable plagues. So the Egyptians drove them out of their sight. 13 Then God dried up the Red Sea before them, 14 and he led them by the way of Sinai and Kā'desh-bar'nē·a. They drove out all the people of the desert, 15 and took up residence in the land of the Am'o·rītes, and by their might destroyed all the inhabitants of

i Gk they

Hesh'bon; and crossing over the Jordan they took possession of all the hill country. [16] They drove out before them the Cā'naan·ites, the Per'iz·zites, the Jeb'u·sites, the Shē'chem·ites, and all the Ger'ge·sites, and lived there a long time.

[17] "As long as they did not sin against their God they prospered, for the God who hates iniquity is with them. [18] But when they departed from the way he had prescribed for them, they were utterly defeated in many battles and were led away captive to a foreign land. The temple of their God was razed to the ground, and their towns were occupied by their enemies. [19] But now they have returned to their God, and have come back from the places where they were scattered, and have occupied Jerusalem, where their sanctuary is, and have settled in the hill country, because it was uninhabited.

[20] "So now, my master and lord, if there is any oversight in this people and they sin against their God and we find out their offense, then we can go up and defeat them. [21] But if they are not a guilty nation, then let my lord pass them by; for their Lord and God will defend them, and we shall become the laughingstock of the whole world."

[22] When Ā'chi·or had finished saying these things, all the people standing around the tent began to complain; Hol·o·fer'nēs' officers and all the inhabitants of the seacoast and Mō'ab insisted that he should be cut to pieces. [23] They said, "We are not afraid of the Israelites; they are a people with no strength or power for making war. [24] Therefore let us go ahead, Lord Hol·o·fer'nēs, and your vast army will swallow them up."

Achior Handed over to the Israelites

6 When the disturbance made by the people outside the council had died down, Hol·o·fer'nēs, the commander of the Assyrian army, said to Ā'chi·or[j] in the presence of all the foreign contingents:

[2] "Who are you, Ā'chi·or and you mercenaries of E'phra·im, to prophesy among us as you have done today and tell us not to make war against the people of Israel because their God will defend them? What god is there except Ne·bū·chad·nez'zar? He will send his forces and destroy them from the face of the earth. Their God will not save

them; [3] we the king's[k] servants will destroy them as one man. They cannot resist the might of our cavalry. [4] We will overwhelm them;[l] their mountains will be drunk with their blood, and their fields will be full of their dead. Not even their footprints will survive our attack; they will utterly perish. So says King Ne·bū·chad·nez'zar, lord of the whole earth. For he has spoken; none of his words shall be in vain.

[5] "As for you, Ā'chi·or, you Am'mon·ite mercenary, you have said these words in a moment of perversity; you shall not see my face again from this day until I take revenge on this race that came out of Egypt. [6] Then at my return the sword of my army and the spear[m] of my servants shall pierce your sides, and you shall fall among their wounded. [7] Now my slaves are going to take you back into the hill country and put you in one of the towns beside the passes. [8] You will not die until you perish along with them. [9] If you really hope in your heart that they will not be taken, then do not look downcast! I have spoken, and none of my words shall fail to come true."

[10] Then Hol·o·fer'nēs ordered his slaves, who waited on him in his tent, to seize Ā'chi·or and take him away to Beth·ū'li·a and hand him over to the Israelites. [11] So the slaves took him and led him out of the camp into the plain, and from the plain they went up into the hill country and came to the springs below Beth·ū'li·a. [12] When the men of the town saw them,[n] they seized their weapons and ran out of the town to the top of the hill, and all the slingers kept them from coming up by throwing stones at them. [13] So having taken shelter below the hill, they bound Ā'chi·or and left him lying at the foot of the hill, and returned to their master.

[14] Then the Israelites came down from their town and found him; they untied him and brought him into Beth·ū'li·a and placed him before the magistrates of their town, [15] who in those days were Uz·zī'ah son of Mī'cah, of the tribe of Sim'ē·on, and Chab'ris son of Gō'thon'i·el, and Char'mis son of

---

[j] Other ancient authorities add *and to all the Moabites*   [k] Gk *his*   [l] Other ancient authorities add *with it*   [m] Lat Syr: Gk *people*   [n] Other ancient authorities add *on the top of the hill*

Mel′chi·el. [16] They called together all the elders of the town, and all their young men and women ran to the assembly. They set Ā′chi·or in the midst of all their people, and Uz·zī′ah questioned him about what had happened. [17] He answered and told them what had taken place at the council of Hol·o·fer′nēs, and all that he had said in the presence of the Assyrian leaders, and all that Hol·o·fer′nēs had boasted he would do against the house of Israel. [18] Then the people fell down and worshiped God, and cried out:

[19] "O Lord God of heaven, see their arrogance, and have pity on our people in their humiliation, and look kindly today on the faces of those who are consecrated to you."

[20] Then they reassured Ā′chi·or, and praised him highly. [21] Uz·zī′ah took him from the assembly to his own house and gave a banquet for the elders; and all that night they called on the God of Israel for help.

The Campaign against Bethulia

7 The next day Hol·o·fer′nēs ordered his whole army, and all the allies who had joined him, to break camp and move against Beth·ū′li·a, and to seize the passes up into the hill country and make war on the Israelites. [2] So all their warriors marched off that day; their fighting forces numbered one hundred seventy thousand infantry and twelve thousand cavalry, not counting the baggage and the foot soldiers handling it, a very great multitude. [3] They encamped in the valley near Beth·ū′li·a, beside the spring, and they spread out in breadth over Dō′than as far as Bal·bā′im and in length from Beth·ū′li·a to Cȳ′a·mon, which faces Es·dra·e′lon. [4] When the Israelites saw their vast numbers, they were greatly terrified and said to one another, "They will now strip clean the whole land; neither the high mountains nor the valleys nor the hills will bear their weight." [5] Yet they all seized their weapons, and when they had kindled fires on their towers, they remained on guard all that night.

[6] On the second day Hol·o·fer′nēs led out all his cavalry in full view of the Israelites in Beth·ū′li·a. [7] He reconnoitered the approaches to their town, and visited the springs that supplied their water; he seized them and set guards of soldiers over them, and then returned to his army.

[8] Then all the chieftains of the Ē′dom·ites and all the leaders of the Mō′ab·ites and the commanders of the coastland came to him and said, [9] "Listen to what we have to say, my lord, and your army will suffer no losses. [10] This people, the Israelites, do not rely on their spears but on the height of the mountains where they live, for it is not easy to reach the tops of their mountains. [11] Therefore, my lord, do not fight against them in regular formation, and not a man of your army will fall. [12] Remain in your camp, and keep all the men in your forces with you; let your servants take possession of the spring of water that flows from the foot of the mountain, [13] for this is where all the people of Beth·ū′li·a get their water. So thirst will destroy them, and they will surrender their town. Meanwhile, we and our people will go up to the tops of the nearby mountains and camp there to keep watch to see that no one gets out of the town. [14] They and their wives and children will waste away with famine, and before the sword reaches them they will be strewn about in the streets where they live. [15] Thus you will pay them back with evil, because they rebelled and did not receive you peaceably."

[16] These words pleased Hol·o·fer′nēs and all his attendants, and he gave orders to do as they had said. [17] So the army of the Am′mon·ites moved forward, together with five thousand Assyrians, and they encamped in the valley and seized the water supply and the springs of the Israelites. [18] And the Ē′dom·ites and Am′mon·ites went up and encamped in the hill country opposite Dō′than; and they sent some of their men toward the south and the east, toward Eg′re·beh, which is near Chū′sī beside the Wadi Moch′mur. The rest of the Assyrian army encamped in the plain, and covered the whole face of the land. Their tents and supply trains spread out in great number, and they formed a vast multitude.

The Distress of the Israelites

[19] The Israelites then cried out to the Lord their God, for their courage failed, because all their enemies had surrounded them, and there was no way of escape from them. [20] The whole Assyrian army, their infantry,

chariots, and cavalry, surrounded them for thirty-four days, until all the water containers of every inhabitant of Beth·u'li·a were empty; 21 their cisterns were going dry, and on no day did they have enough water to drink, for their drinking water was rationed. 22 Their children were listless, and the women and young men fainted from thirst and were collapsing in the streets of the town and in the gateways; they no longer had any strength.

23 Then all the people, the young men, the women, and the children, gathered around Uz·zī'ah and the rulers of the town and cried out with a loud voice, and said before all the elders, 24 "Let God judge between you and us! You have done us a great injury in not making peace with the Assyrians. 25 For now we have no one to help us; God has sold us into their hands, to be strewn before them in thirst and exhaustion. 26 Now summon them and surrender the whole town as booty to the army of Hol·o·fer'nēs and to all his forces. 27 For it would be better for us to be captured by them.º We shall indeed become slaves, but our lives will be spared, and we shall not witness our little ones dying before our eyes, and our wives and children drawing their last breath. 28 We call to witness against you heaven and earth and our God, the Lord of our ancestors, who punishes us for our sins and the sins of our ancestors; do today the things that we have described!"

29 Then great and general lamentation arose throughout the assembly, and they cried out to the Lord God with a loud voice. 30 But Uz·zī'ah said to them, "Courage, my brothers and sisters!ᴾ Let us hold out for five days more; by that time the Lord our God will turn his mercy to us again, for he will not forsake us utterly. 31 But if these days pass by, and no help comes for us, I will do as you say."

32 Then he dismissed the people to their various posts, and they went up on the walls and towers of their town. The women and children he sent home. In the town they were in great misery.

The Character of Judith

8 Now in those days Judith heard about these things: she was the daughter of Me·rar'ī son of Ox son of Joseph son of Ō'zi·el son of El·kī'ah son of An·a·nī'as son of Gideon of

Raph'a·in son of A·hī'tub son of E·lī'jah son of Hil·kī'ah son of E·lī'ab son of Na·than'a·el son of Sa·lā'mi·el son of Sar·a·sad'aī son of Israel. 2 Her husband Ma·nas'seh, who belonged to her tribe and family, had died during the barley harvest. 3 For as he stood overseeing those who were binding sheaves in the field, he was overcome by the burning heat, and took to his bed and died in his town Beth·u'li·a. So they buried him with his ancestors in the field between Dō'than and Bal'a-mon. 4 Judith remained as a widow for three years and four months 5 at home where she set up a tent for herself on the roof of her house. She put sackcloth around her waist and dressed in widow's clothing. 6 She fasted all the days of her widowhood, except the day before the sabbath and the sabbath itself, the day before the new moon and the day of the new moon, and the festivals and days of rejoicing of the house of Israel. 7 She was beautiful in appearance, and was very lovely to behold. Her husband Ma·nas'seh had left her gold and silver, men and women slaves, livestock, and fields; and she maintained this estate. 8 No one spoke ill of her, for she feared God with great devotion.

Judith and the Elders
(Gen 22.1–18; 29.1 – 31.55; Deut 6.16; Rom 11.33–34)

9 When Judith heard the harsh words spoken by the people against the ruler, because they were faint for lack of water, and when she heard all that Uz·zī'ah said to them, and how he promised them under oath to surrender the town to the Assyrians after five days, 10 she sent her maid, who was in charge of all she possessed, to summon Uz·zī'ah and�q Chab'ris and Char'mis, the elders of her town. 11 They came to her, and she said to them,

"Listen to me, rulers of the people of Beth·u'li·a! What you have said to the people today is not right; you have even sworn and pronounced this oath between God and you, promising to surrender the town to our enemies unless the Lord turns and helps us within so many days. 12 Who are you to put

---

º Other ancient authorities add *than to die of thirst* ᴾ Gk *Courage, brothers*
q Other ancient authorities lack *Uzziah and* (see verses 28 and 35)

God to the test today, and to set yourselves up in the place of[r] God in human affairs? [13] You are putting the Lord Almighty to the test, but you will never learn anything! [14] You cannot plumb the depths of the human heart or understand the workings of the human mind; how do you expect to search out God, who made all these things, and find out his mind or comprehend his thought? No, my brothers, do not anger the Lord our God. [15] For if he does not choose to help us within these five days, he has power to protect us within any time he pleases, or even to destroy us in the presence of our enemies. [16] Do not try to bind the purposes of the Lord our God; for God is not like a human being, to be threatened, or like a mere mortal, to be won over by pleading. [17] Therefore, while we wait for his deliverance, let us call upon him to help us, and he will hear our voice, if it pleases him.

18 "For never in our generation, nor in these present days, has there been any tribe or family or people or town of ours that worships gods made with hands, as was done in days gone by. [19] That was why our ancestors were handed over to the sword and to pillage, and so they suffered a great catastrophe before our enemies. [20] But we know no other god but him, and so we hope that he will not disdain us or any of our nation. [21] For if we are captured, all Judea will be captured and our sanctuary will be plundered; and he will make us pay for its desecration with our blood. [22] The slaughter of our kindred and the captivity of the land and the desolation of our inheritance —all this he will bring on our heads among the Gentiles, wherever we serve as slaves; and we shall be an offense and a disgrace in the eyes of those who acquire us. [23] For our slavery will not bring us into favor, but the Lord our God will turn it to dishonor.

24 "Therefore, my brothers, let us set an example for our kindred, for their lives depend upon us, and the sanctuary—both the temple and the altar—rests upon us. [25] In spite of everything let us give thanks to the Lord our God, who is putting us to the test as he did our ancestors. [26] Remember what he did with Abraham, and how he tested Isaac, and what happened to Jacob in Syrian Mes·o·po·tā′mi·a, while he was tending the sheep of Lā′ban, his mother's brother. [27] For

he has not tried us with fire, as he did them, to search their hearts, nor has he taken vengeance on us; but the Lord scourges those who are close to him in order to admonish them."

28 Then Uz·zī′ah said to her, "All that you have said was spoken out of a true heart, and there is no one who can deny your words. [29] Today is not the first time your wisdom has been shown, but from the beginning of your life all the people have recognized your understanding, for your heart's disposition is right. [30] But the people were so thirsty that they compelled us to do for them what we have promised, and made us take an oath that we cannot break. [31] Now since you are a God-fearing woman, pray for us, so that the Lord may send us rain to fill our cisterns. Then we will no longer feel faint from thirst."

32 Then Judith said to them, "Listen to me. I am about to do something that will go down through all generations of our descendants. [33] Stand at the town gate tonight so that I may go out with my maid; and within the days after which you have promised to surrender the town to our enemies, the Lord will deliver Israel by my hand. [34] Only, do not try to find out what I am doing; for I will not tell you until I have finished what I am about to do."

35 Uz·zī′ah and the rulers said to her, "Go in peace, and may the Lord God go before you, to take vengeance on our enemies." [36] So they returned from the tent and went to their posts.

The Prayer of Judith
(Gen 34.1–31)

9 Then Judith prostrated herself, put ashes on her head, and uncovered the sackcloth she was wearing. At the very time when the evening incense was being offered in the house of God in Jerusalem, Judith cried out to the Lord with a loud voice, and said,

2 "O Lord God of my ancestor Sim′-ē·on, to whom you gave a sword to take revenge on those strangers who had torn off a virgin's clothing[s] to defile her, and exposed her thighs to put her to shame, and polluted her womb to disgrace her; for you said, 'It shall not be done'—yet they did it. [3] So you gave up their rulers to be killed, and their bed, which was ashamed of the deceit they had practiced, was stained

[r] Or above   [s] Cn: Gk loosed her womb

with blood, and you struck down slaves along with princes, and princes on their thrones. ⁴You gave up their wives for booty and their daughters to captivity, and all their booty to be divided among your beloved children who burned with zeal for you and abhorred the pollution of their blood and called on you for help — O God, my God, hear me also — a widow.

5 "For you have done these things and those that went before and those that followed. You have designed the things that are now, and those that are to come. What you had in mind has happened; ⁶the things you decided on presented themselves and said, 'Here we are!' For all your ways are prepared in advance, and your judgment is with foreknowledge.

7 "Here now are the Assyrians, a greatly increased force, priding themselves in their horses and riders, boasting in the strength of their foot soldiers, and trusting in shield and spear, in bow and sling. They do not know that you are the Lord who crushes wars; the Lord is your name. ⁸Break their strength by your might, and bring down their power in your anger; for they intend to defile your sanctuary, and to pollute the tabernacle where your glorious name resides, and to break off the horns*t* of your altar with the sword. ⁹Look at their pride, and send your wrath upon their heads. Give to me, a widow, the strong hand to do what I plan. ¹⁰By the deceit of my lips strike down the slave with the prince and the prince with his servant; crush their arrogance by the hand of a woman.

11 "For your strength does not depend on numbers, nor your might on the powerful. But you are the God of the lowly, helper of the oppressed, upholder of the weak, protector of the forsaken, savior of those without hope. ¹²Please, please, God of my father, God of the heritage of Israel, Lord of heaven and earth, Creator of the waters, King of all your creation, hear my prayer! ¹³Make my deceitful words bring wound and bruise on those who have planned cruel things against your covenant, and against your sacred house, and against Mount Zion, and against the house your children possess. ¹⁴Let your whole nation and every tribe know and understand that you are God, the God of all power and might, and that there is no other who protects the people of Israel but you alone!"

Judith Prepares to Go to Holofernes

10 When Judith*u* had stopped crying out to the God of Israel, and had ended all these words, ²she rose from where she lay prostrate. She called her maid and went down into the house where she lived on sabbaths and on her festal days. ³She removed the sackcloth she had been wearing, took off her widow's garments, bathed her body with water, and anointed herself with precious ointment. She combed her hair, put on a tiara, and dressed herself in the festive attire that she used to wear while her husband Ma·nas′seh was living. ⁴She put sandals on her feet, and put on her anklets, bracelets, rings, earrings, and all her other jewelry. Thus she made herself very beautiful, to entice the eyes of all the men who might see her. ⁵She gave her maid a skin of wine and a flask of oil, and filled a bag with roasted grain, dried fig cakes, and fine bread;*v* then she wrapped up all her dishes and gave them to her to carry.

6 Then they went out to the town gate of Beth·u′li·a and found Uz·zi′ah standing there with the elders of the town, Chab′ris and Char′mis. ⁷When they saw her transformed in appearance and dressed differently, they were very greatly astounded at her beauty and said to her, ⁸"May the God of our ancestors grant you favor and fulfill your plans, so that the people of Israel may glory and Jerusalem may be exalted." She bowed down to God.

9 Then she said to them, "Order the gate of the town to be opened for me so that I may go out and accomplish the things you have just said to me." So they ordered the young men to open the gate for her, as she requested. ¹⁰When they had done this, Judith went out, accompanied by her maid. The men of the town watched her until she had gone down the mountain and passed through the valley, where they lost sight of her.

Judith Is Captured

11 As the women*w* were going straight on through the valley, an Assyrian patrol met her ¹²and took her

t Syr: Gk *horn*   *u* Gk *she*   *v* Other ancient authorities add *and cheese*   *w* Gk *they* into custody. They asked her, "To what people do you belong, and where are you coming from, and where are you going?" She replied, "I am a daughter of the Hebrews, but I am fleeing from them, for they are about to be handed over to you to be devoured. ¹³ I am on my way to see Hol·o·fer′nēs the commander of your army, to give him a true report; I will show him a way by which he can go and capture all the hill country without losing one of his men, captured or slain."

14 When the men heard her words, and observed her face — she was in their eyes marvelously beautiful — they said to her, ¹⁵ "You have saved your life by hurrying down to see our lord. Go at once to his tent; some of us will escort you and hand you over to him. ¹⁶ When you stand before him, have no fear in your heart, but tell him what you have just said, and he will treat you well."

17 They chose from their number a hundred men to accompany her and her maid, and they brought them to the tent of Hol·o·fer′nēs. ¹⁸ There was great excitement in the whole camp, for her arrival was reported from tent to tent. They came and gathered around her as she stood outside the tent of Hol·o·fer′nēs, waiting until they told him about her. ¹⁹ They marveled at her beauty and admired the Israelites, judging them by her. They said to one another, "Who can despise these people, who have women like this among them? It is not wise to leave one of their men alive, for if we let them go they will be able to beguile the whole world!"

Judith Is Brought before Holofernes

20 Then the guards of Hol·o·fer′nēs and all his servants came out and led her into the tent. ²¹ Hol·o·fer′nēs was resting on his bed under a canopy that was woven with purple and gold, emeralds and other precious stones. ²² When they told him of her, he came to the front of the tent, with silver lamps carried before him. ²³ When Judith came into the presence of Hol·o·fer′nēsˣ and his servants, they all marveled at the beauty of her face. She prostrated herself and did obeisance to him, but his slaves raised her up.

11 Then Hol·o·fer′nēs said to her, "Take courage, woman, and do not be afraid in your heart, for I have never hurt anyone who chose to serve Ne·bū·chad·nez′zar, king of all the earth. ² Even now, if your people who live in the hill country had not slighted me, I would never have lifted my spear against them. They have brought this on themselves. ³ But now tell me why you have fled from them and have come over to us. In any event, you have come to safety. Take courage! You will live tonight and ever after. ⁴ No one will hurt you. Rather, all will treat you well, as they do the servants of my lord King Ne·bū·chad·nez′zar."

Judith Explains Her Presence

5 Judith answered him, "Accept the words of your slave, and let your servant speak in your presence. I will say nothing false to my lord this night. ⁶ If you follow out the words of your servant, God will accomplish something through you, and my lord will not fail to achieve his purposes. ⁷ By the life of Ne·bū·chad·nez′zar, king of the whole earth, and by the power of him who has sent you to direct every living being! Not only do human beings serve him because of you, but also the animals of the field and the cattle and the birds of the air will live, because of your power, under Ne·bū·chad·nez′zar and all his house. ⁸ For we have heard of your wisdom and skill, and it is reported throughout the whole world that you alone are the best in the whole kingdom, the most informed and the most astounding in military strategy.

9 "Now as for Ā′chi·or′s speech in your council, we have heard his words, for the people of Beth·ū′li·a spared him and he told them all he had said to you. ¹⁰ Therefore, lord and master, do not disregard what he said, but keep it in your mind, for it is true. Indeed our nation cannot be punished, nor can the sword prevail against them, unless they sin against their God.

11 "But now, in order that my lord may not be defeated and his purpose frustrated, death will fall upon them, for a sin has overtaken them by which they are about to provoke their God to anger when they do what is wrong. ¹² Since their food supply is exhausted and their water has almost given out, they have planned to kill their livestock and have determined to use all that God by his laws has forbidden them to eat. ¹³ They have decided to

ˣ Gk *him*

consume the first fruits of the grain and the tithes of the wine and oil, which they had consecrated and set aside for the priests who minister in the presence of our God in Jerusalem — things it is not lawful for any of the people even to touch with their hands. [14] Since even the people in Jerusalem have been doing this, they have sent messengers there in order to bring back permission from the council of the elders. [15] When the response reaches them and they act upon it, on that very day they will be handed over to you to be destroyed.

16 "So when I, your slave, learned all this, I fled from them. God has sent me to accomplish with you things that will astonish the whole world wherever people shall hear about them. [17] Your servant is indeed God-fearing and serves the God of heaven night and day. So, my lord, I will remain with you; but every night your servant will go out into the valley and pray to God. He will tell me when they have committed their sins. [18] Then I will come and tell you, so that you may go out with your whole army, and not one of them will be able to withstand you. [19] Then I will lead you through Judea, until you come to Jerusalem; there I will set your throne.[y] You will drive them like sheep that have no shepherd, and no dog will so much as growl at you. For this was told me to give me foreknowledge; it was announced to me, and I was sent to tell you."

20 Her words pleased Hol·o·fer'nēs and all his servants. They marveled at her wisdom and said, [21] "No other woman from one end of the earth to the other looks so beautiful or speaks so wisely!" [22] Then Hol·o·fer'nēs said to her, "God has done well to send you ahead of the people, to strengthen our hands and bring destruction on those who have despised my lord. [23] You are not only beautiful in appearance, but wise in speech. If you do as you have said, your God shall be my God, and you shall live in the palace of King Ne·bū·chad·nez'zar and be renowned throughout the whole world."

Judith as a Guest of Holofernes
(Cp Dan 1.3–8)

12 Then he commanded them to bring her in where his silver dinnerware was kept, and ordered them to set a table for her with some of his own delicacies, and with some of his own wine to drink. [2] But Judith said, "I cannot partake of them, or it will be an offense; but I will have enough with the things I brought with me." [3] Hol·o·fer'nēs said to her, "If your supply runs out, where can we get you more of the same? For none of your people are here with us." [4] Judith replied, "As surely as you live, my lord, your servant will not use up the supplies I have with me before the Lord carries out by my hand what he has determined."

5 Then the servants of Hol·o·fer'nēs brought her into the tent, and she slept until midnight. Toward the morning watch she got up [6] and sent this message to Hol·o·fer'nēs: "Let my lord now give orders to allow your servant to go out and pray." [7] So Hol·o·fer'nēs commanded his guards not to hinder her. She remained in the camp three days. She went out each night to the valley of Beth·ū'li·a, and bathed at the spring in the camp.[z] [8] After bathing, she prayed the Lord God of Israel to direct her way for the triumph of his[a] people. [9] Then she returned purified and stayed in the tent until she ate her food toward evening.

Judith Attends Holofernes' Banquet

10 On the fourth day Hol·o·fer'nēs held a banquet for his personal attendants only, and did not invite any of his officers. [11] He said to Ba·gō'as, the eunuch who had charge of his personal affairs, "Go and persuade the Hebrew woman who is in your care to join us and to eat and drink with us. [12] For it would be a disgrace if we let such a woman go without having intercourse with her. If we do not seduce her, she will laugh at us."

13 So Ba·gō'as left the presence of Hol·o·fer'nēs, and approached her and said, "Let this pretty girl not hesitate to come to my lord to be honored in his presence, and to enjoy drinking wine with us, and to become today like one of the Assyrian women who serve in the palace of Ne·bū·chad·nez'zar." [14] Judith replied, "Who am I to refuse my lord? Whatever pleases him I will do at once, and it will be a joy to me until the day of my death." [15] So she proceeded to dress herself in all her woman's finery. Her maid went ahead

[y] Or *chariot*   [z] Other ancient authorities lack *in the camp*   [a] Other ancient authorities read *her*

and spread for her on the ground before Hol·o·fer′nēs the lambskins she had received from Ba·gō′as for her daily use in reclining.

16 Then Judith came in and lay down. Hol·o·fer′nēs′ heart was ravished with her and his passion was aroused, for he had been waiting for an opportunity to seduce her from the day he first saw her. 17 So Hol·o·fer′nēs said to her, "Have a drink and be merry with us!" 18 Judith said, "I will gladly drink, my lord, because today is the greatest day in my whole life." 19 Then she took what her maid had prepared and ate and drank before him. 20 Hol·o·fer′nēs was greatly pleased with her, and drank a great quantity of wine, much more than he had ever drunk in any one day since he was born.

Judith Beheads Holofernes

13 When evening came, his slaves quickly withdrew. Ba·gō′as closed the tent from outside and shut out the attendants from his master's presence. They went to bed, for they all were weary because the banquet had lasted so long. 2 But Judith was left alone in the tent, with Hol·o·fer′nēs stretched out on his bed, for he was dead drunk.

3 Now Judith had told her maid to stand outside the bedchamber and to wait for her to come out, as she did on the other days; for she said she would be going out for her prayers. She had said the same thing to Ba·gō′as. 4 So everyone went out, and no one, either small or great, was left in the bedchamber. Then Judith, standing beside his bed, said in her heart, "O Lord God of all might, look in this hour on the work of my hands for the exaltation of Jerusalem. 5 Now indeed is the time to help your heritage and to carry out my design to destroy the enemies who have risen up against us."

6 She went up to the bedpost near Hol·o·fer′nēs′ head, and took down his sword that hung there. 7 She came close to his bed, took hold of the hair of his head, and said, "Give me strength today, O Lord God of Israel!" 8 Then she struck his neck twice with all her might, and cut off his head. 9 Next she rolled his body off the bed and pulled down the canopy from the posts. Soon afterward she went out and gave Hol·o·fer′nēs′ head to her maid, 10 who placed it in her food bag.

Judith Returns to Bethulia

Then the two of them went out together, as they were accustomed to do for prayer. They passed through the camp, circled around the valley, and went up the mountain to Beth·u′li·a, and came to its gates. 11 From a distance Judith called out to the sentries at the gates, "Open, open the gate! God, our God, is with us, still showing his power in Israel and his strength against our enemies, as he has done today!"

12 When the people of her town heard her voice, they hurried down to the town gate and summoned the elders of the town. 13 They all ran together, both small and great, for it seemed unbelievable that she had returned. They opened the gate and welcomed them. Then they lit a fire to give light, and gathered around them. 14 Then she said to them with a loud voice, "Praise God, O praise him! Praise God, who has not withdrawn his mercy from the house of Israel, but has destroyed our enemies by my hand this very night!"

15 Then she pulled the head out of the bag and showed it to them, and said, "See here, the head of Hol·o·fer′nēs, the commander of the Assyrian army, and here is the canopy beneath which he lay in his drunken stupor. The Lord has struck him down by the hand of a woman. 16 As the Lord lives, who has protected me in the way I went, I swear that it was my face that seduced him to his destruction, and that he committed no sin with me, to defile and shame me."

17 All the people were greatly astonished. They bowed down and worshiped God, and said with one accord, "Blessed are you our God, who have this day humiliated the enemies of your people."

18 Then Uz·zī′ah said to her, "O daughter, you are blessed by the Most High God above all other women on earth; and blessed be the Lord God, who created the heavens and the earth, who has guided you to cut off the head of the leader of our enemies. 19 Your praise[b] will never depart from the hearts of those who remember the power of God. 20 May God grant this to be a perpetual honor to you, and may he reward you with blessings, because

b Other ancient authorities read hope

you risked your own life when our nation was brought low, and you averted our ruin, walking in the straight path before our God." And all the people said, "Amen. Amen."

Judith's Counsel

14 Then Judith said to them, "Listen to me, my friends. Take this head and hang it upon the parapet of your wall. [2] As soon as day breaks and the sun rises on the earth, each of you take up your weapons, and let every able-bodied man go out of the town; set a captain over them, as if you were going down to the plain against the Assyrian outpost; only do not go down. [3] Then they will seize their arms and go into the camp and rouse the officers of the Assyrian army. They will rush into the tent of Hol·o·fer′nēs and will not find him. Then panic will come over them, and they will flee before you. [4] Then you and all who live within the borders of Israel will pursue them and cut them down in their tracks. [5] But before you do all this, bring Ā′chi·or the Am′mon·īte to me so that he may see and recognize the man who despised the house of Israel and sent him to us as if to his death."

[6] So they summoned Ā′chi·or from the house of Uz·zī′ah. When he came and saw the head of Hol·o·fer′nēs in the hand of one of the men in the assembly of the people, he fell down on his face in a faint. [7] When they raised him up he threw himself at Judith's feet, and did obeisance to her, and said, "Blessed are you in every tent of Judah! In every nation those who hear your name will be alarmed. [8] Now tell me what you have done during these days."

So Judith told him in the presence of the people all that she had done, from the day she left until the moment she began speaking to them. [9] When she had finished, the people raised a great shout and made a joyful noise in their town. [10] When Ā′chi·or saw all that the God of Israel had done, he believed firmly in God. So he was circumcised, and joined the house of Israel, remaining so to this day.

Holofernes' Death Is Discovered

[11] As soon as it was dawn they hung the head of Hol·o·fer′nēs on the wall. Then they all took their weapons, and they went out in companies to the mountain passes. [12] When the Assyr-ians saw them they sent word to their commanders, who then went to the generals and the captains and to all their other officers. [13] They came to Hol·o·fer′nēs' tent and said to the steward in charge of all his personal affairs, "Wake up our lord, for the slaves have been so bold as to come down against us to give battle, to their utter destruction."

[14] So Ba·gō′as went in and knocked at the entry of the tent, for he supposed that he was sleeping with Judith. [15] But when no one answered, he opened it and went into the bedchamber and found him sprawled on the floor dead, with his head missing. [16] He cried out with a loud voice and wept and groaned and shouted, and tore his clothes. [17] Then he went to the tent where Judith had stayed, and when he did not find her, he rushed out to the people and shouted, [18] "The slaves have tricked us! One Hebrew woman has brought disgrace on the house of King Ne·bū·chad·nez′zar. Look, Hol·o·fer′nēs is lying on the ground, and his head is missing!"

[19] When the leaders of the Assyrian army heard this, they tore their tunics and were greatly dismayed, and their loud cries and shouts rose up throughout the camp.

The Assyrians Flee in Panic

15 When the men in the tents heard it, they were amazed at what had happened. [2] Overcome with fear and trembling, they did not wait for one another, but with one impulse all rushed out and fled by every path across the plain and through the hill country. [3] Those who had camped in the hills around Beth·ū′li·a also took to flight. Then the Israelites, everyone that was a soldier, rushed out upon them. [4] Uz·zī′ah sent men to Bet·o·mas·thā′im[c] and Chō′ba and Kō′la, and to all the frontiers of Israel, to tell what had taken place and to urge all to rush out upon the enemy to destroy them. [5] When the Israelites heard it, with one accord they fell upon the enemy,[d] and cut them down as far as Chō′ba. Those in Jerusalem and all the hill country also came, for they were told what had happened in the camp of the enemy. The men in Gil′e·ad and in Galilee outflanked them with great

[c] Other ancient authorities add *and Bebai*　　[d] Gk *them*

slaughter, even beyond Damascus and its borders. 6 The rest of the people of Beth·ū′li·a fell upon the Assyrian camp and plundered it, acquiring great riches. 7 And the Israelites, when they returned from the slaughter, took possession of what remained. Even the villages and towns in the hill country and in the plain got a great amount of booty, since there was a vast quantity of it.

The Israelites Celebrate Their Victory
(Cp 1 Sam 18.6)

8 Then the high priest Jō′a·kim and the elders of the Israelites who lived in Jerusalem came to witness the good things that the Lord had done for Israel, and to see Judith and to wish her well. 9 When they met her, they all blessed her with one accord and said to her, "You are the glory of Jerusalem, you are the great boast of Israel, you are the great pride of our nation! 10 You have done all this with your own hand; you have done great good to Israel, and God is well pleased with it. May the Almighty Lord bless you forever!" And all the people said, "Amen."

11 All the people plundered the camp for thirty days. They gave Judith the tent of Hol·o·fer′nēs and all his silver dinnerware, his beds, his bowls, and all his furniture. She took them and loaded her mules and hitched up her carts and piled the things on them.

12 All the women of Israel gathered to see her, and blessed her, and some of them performed a dance in her honor. She took ivy-wreathed wands in her hands and distributed them to the women who were with her; 13 and she and those who were with her crowned themselves with olive wreaths. She went before all the people in the dance, leading all the women, while all the men of Israel followed, bearing their arms and wearing garlands and singing hymns.

Judith Offers Her Hymn of Praise
(Cp Ex 15.20–21; Judg 5.1–31; Tob 13.1–17)

14 Judith began this thanksgiving before all Israel, and all the people loudly sang this song of praise.

16 1 And Judith said,
Begin a song to my God with tambourines,
sing to my Lord with cymbals.
Raise to him a new psalm;e
exalt him, and call upon his name.

2 For the Lord is a God who crushes wars;
he sets up his camp among his people;
he delivered me from the hands of my pursuers.
3 The Assyrian came down from the mountains of the north;
he came with myriads of his warriors;
their numbers blocked up the wadis,
and their cavalry covered the hills.
4 He boasted that he would burn up my territory,
and kill my young men with the sword,
and dash my infants to the ground,
and seize my children as booty,
and take my virgins as spoil.
5 But the Lord Almighty has foiled them
by the hand of a woman.f
6 For their mighty one did not fall by the hands of the young men,
nor did the sons of the Titans strike him down,
nor did tall giants set upon him;
but Judith daughter of Me·rar′ī
with the beauty of her countenance undid him.
7 For she put away her widow's clothing
to exalt the oppressed in Israel.
She anointed her face with perfume;
8 she fastened her hair with a tiara
and put on a linen gown to beguile him.
9 Her sandal ravished his eyes,
her beauty captivated his mind,
and the sword severed his neck!
10 The Persians trembled at her boldness,
the Mēdes were daunted at her daring.

e Other ancient authorities read *a psalm and praise* f Other ancient authorities add *he has confounded them*

11 Then my oppressed people
    shouted;
  my weak people cried out,[g]
    and the enemy[h] trembled;
  they lifted up their voices, and
    the enemy[h] were turned
    back.
12 Sons of slave-girls pierced them
    through
  and wounded them like the
    children of fugitives;
  they perished before the army
    of my Lord.

13 I will sing to my God a new
    song:
  O Lord, you are great and
    glorious,
  wonderful in strength,
    invincible.
14 Let all your creatures serve you,
    for you spoke, and they were
    made.
  You sent forth your spirit,[i] and
    it formed them;[j]
  there is none that can resist
    your voice.
15 For the mountains shall be
    shaken to their foundations
    with the waters;
  before your glance the rocks
    shall melt like wax.
  But to those who fear you
    you show mercy.
16 For every sacrifice as a fragrant
    offering is a small thing,
  and the fat of all whole burnt
    offerings to you is a very
    little thing;
  but whoever fears the Lord is
    great forever.

17 Woe to the nations that rise up
    against my people!
  The Lord Almighty will take
    vengeance on them in the
    day of judgment;

he will send fire and worms into
    their flesh;
  they shall weep in pain
    forever.

18 When they arrived at Jerusalem,
they worshiped God. As soon as the
people were purified, they offered
their burnt offerings, their freewill
offerings, and their gifts. 19 Judith also
dedicated to God all the possessions of
Hol·o·fer′nēs, which the people had
given her; and the canopy that she had
taken for herself from his bedchamber
she gave as a votive offering. 20 For
three months the people continued
feasting in Jerusalem before the sanctuary, and Judith remained with them.

The Renown and Death of Judith

21 After this they all returned home
to their own inheritances. Judith went
to Beth·ū′li·a, and remained on her estate. For the rest of her life she was
honored throughout the whole country. 22 Many desired to marry her, but
she gave herself to no man all the days
of her life after her husband Ma·nas′-
seh died and was gathered to his people. 23 She became more and more famous, and grew old in her husband's
house, reaching the age of one hundred five. She set her maid free. She
died in Beth·ū′li·a, and they buried her
in the cave of her husband Ma·nas′seh;
24 and the house of Israel mourned her
for seven days. Before she died she distributed her property to all those who
were next of kin to her husband Ma-
nas′seh, and to her own nearest kindred. 25 No one ever again spread terror among the Israelites during the
lifetime of Judith, or for a long time
after her death.

[g] Other ancient authorities read *feared*
[h] Gk *they*   [i] Or *breath*   [j] Other ancient
authorities read *they were created*

ESTHER

NOTE. The deuterocanonical portions of the Book of Esther are translated from the Greek version (Septuagint) and comprise one hundred and seven additional verses that have been inserted at the appropriate places in the translation of the Hebrew form of the book. The disordered chapter numbers come from the displacement of the additions to the end of the Hebrew form of the Book of Esther by St. Jerome in his Latin Vulgate translation and from the subsequent division of the Bible into chapters by Stephen Langton, who numbered the additions consecutively as though they formed a direct continuation of the Hebrew text. The deuterocanonical portions are given in the order found in the Greek text so that they may be read in their proper context, but the chapter and verse numbers conform to those of the King James or Authorized Version. Proper names are given according to their Hebrew rather than their Greek form; for example, Ahasuerus and Mordecai instead of Artaxerxes and Mardocheus. The additions, conveniently indicated by the letters A—F, are located as follows: A, before 1.1; B, after 3.13; C and D, after 4.17; E, after 8.12; F, after 10.3.

ADDITION A

Mordecai's Dream

11 ^a ² In the second year of the reign of A·has·u·e'rus the Great, on the first day of Ni'san, Mor'de·cai son of Ja'ir son of Shim'e·i^b son of Kish, of the tribe of Benjamin, had a dream. ³ He was a Jew living in the city of Su'sa, a great man, serving in the court of the king. ⁴ He was one of the captives whom King Ne·bu·chad·nez'zar of Babylon had brought from Jerusalem with King Jec·o·ni'ah of Judah. And this was his dream: ⁵ Noises^c and confusion, thunders and earthquake, tumult on the earth! ⁶ Then two great dragons came forward, both ready to fight, and they roared terribly. ⁷ At their roaring every nation prepared for war, to fight against the righteous nation. ⁸ It was a day of darkness and gloom, of tribulation and distress, affliction and great tumult on the earth! ⁹ And the whole righteous nation was troubled; they feared the evils that threatened them,^d and were ready to perish. ¹⁰ Then they cried out to God; and at their outcry, as though from a tiny spring, there came a great river, with abundant water; ¹¹ light came, and the sun rose, and the lowly were exalted and devoured those held in honor.

¹² Mor'de·cai saw in this dream what God had determined to do, and after he awoke he had it on his mind, seeking all day to understand it in every detail.

A Plot against the King

12 Now Mor'de·cai took his rest in the courtyard with Big'than and Te'resh, the two eunuchs of the king who kept watch in the courtyard. ² He overheard their conversation and inquired into their purposes, and learned that they were preparing to lay hands on King A·has·u·e'rus; and he informed the king concerning them. ³ Then the king examined the two eunuchs, and after they had confessed it, they were led away to execution. ⁴ The king made a permanent record of these things, and Mor'de·cai wrote an account of them. ⁵ And the king ordered Mor'de·cai to serve in the court, and rewarded him for these things. ⁶ But Ha'man son of Ham·me·da'tha the Ag'ag·ite, who was in great honor with the king, determined to injure

^a Chapters 11.2—12.6 correspond to chapter A 1-17 in some translations.
^b Gk *Semeios*   ^c Or *Voices*   ^d Gk *their own evils*

Mor'de·caī and his people because of the two eunuchs of the king.

END OF ADDITION A

King Ahasuerus Deposes Queen Vashti

1 This happened in the days of A·has·ū·ē'rus, the same A·has·ū·ē'rus who ruled over one hundred twenty-seven provinces from India to Ethiopia.[e] 2 In those days when King A·has·ū·ē'rus sat on his royal throne in the citadel of Su'sa, 3 in the third year of his reign, he gave a banquet for all his officials and ministers. The army of Persia and Mēd'i·a and the nobles and governors of the provinces were present, 4 while he displayed the great wealth of his kingdom and the splendor and pomp of his majesty for many days, one hundred eighty days in all.

5 When these days were completed, the king gave for all the people present in the citadel of Su'sa, both great and small, a banquet lasting for seven days, in the court of the garden of the king's palace. 6 There were white cotton curtains and blue hangings tied with cords of fine linen and purple to silver rings[f] and marble pillars. There were couches of gold and silver on a mosaic pavement of porphyry, marble, mother-of-pearl, and colored stones. 7 Drinks were served in golden goblets, goblets of different kinds, and the royal wine was lavished according to the bounty of the king. 8 Drinking was by flagons, without restraint; for the king had given orders to all the officials of his palace to do as each one desired. 9 Furthermore, Queen Vash'tī gave a banquet for the women in the palace of King A·has·ū·ē'rus.

10 On the seventh day, when the king was merry with wine, he commanded Me·hū'man, Biz'tha, Har·bō'na, Big'tha and A·bag'tha, Zē'thar and Car'kas, the seven eunuchs who attended him, 11 to bring Queen Vash'tī before the king, wearing the royal crown, in order to show the peoples and the officials her beauty; for she was fair to behold. 12 But Queen Vash'tī refused to come at the king's command conveyed by the eunuchs. At this the king was enraged, and his anger burned within him.

13 Then the king consulted the sages who knew the laws[g] (for this was the king's procedure toward all

who were versed in law and custom, 14 and those next to him were Car·shē'na, Shē'thar, Ad·mā'tha, Tar'·shish, Mē'rēs, Mar·sē'na, and Mē·mū'·can, the seven officials of Persia and Mēd'i·a, who had access to the king, and sat first in the kingdom): 15 "According to the law, what is to be done to Queen Vash'tī because she has not performed the command of King A·has·ū·ē'rus conveyed by the eunuchs?" 16 Then Mē·mū'can said in the presence of the king and the officials, "Not only has Queen Vash'tī done wrong to the king, but also to all the officials and all the peoples who are in all the provinces of King A·has·ū·ē'·rus. 17 For this deed of the queen will be made known to all women, causing them to look with contempt on their husbands, since they will say, 'King A·has·ū·ē'rus commanded Queen Vash'tī to be brought before him, and she did not come.' 18 This very day the noble ladies of Persia and Mēd'i·a who have heard of the queen's behavior will rebel against[h] the king's officials, and there will be no end of contempt and wrath! 19 If it pleases the king, let a royal order go out from him, and let it be written among the laws of the Persians and the Mēdes so that it may not be altered, that Vash'tī is never again to come before King A·has·ū·ē'rus; and let the king give her royal position to another who is better than she. 20 So when the decree made by the king is proclaimed throughout all his kingdom, vast as it is, all women will give honor to their husbands, high and low alike."

21 This advice pleased the king and the officials, and the king did as Mē·mū'can proposed; 22 he sent letters to all the royal provinces, to every province in its own script and to every people in its own language, declaring that every man should be master in his own house.[i]

Esther Becomes Queen

2 After these things, when the anger of King A·has·ū·ē'rus had abated, he remembered Vash'tī and what she had done and what had been decreed against her. 2 Then the king's servants who attended him said, "Let beautiful

---

[e] Or *Nubia*; Heb *Cush*   [f] Or *rods*
[g] Cn: Heb *times*   [h] Cn: Heb *will tell*
[i] Heb adds *and speak according to the language of his people*

young virgins be sought out for the king. ³And let the king appoint commissioners in all the provinces of his kingdom to gather all the beautiful young virgins to the harem in the citadel of Su'sa under custody of Heg'aī, the king's eunuch, who is in charge of the women; let their cosmetic treatments be given them. ⁴And let the girl who pleases the king be queen instead of Vash'tī." This pleased the king, and he did so.

5 Now there was a Jew in the citadel of Su'sa whose name was Mor'de·caī son of Jā'ir son of Shim'e·ī son of Kish, a Ben'ja·min·īte. ⁶Kishʲ had been carried away from Jerusalem among the captives carried away with King Jec·o·nī'ah of Judah, whom King Ne·bū·chad·nez'zar of Babylon had carried away. ⁷Mor'de·caīᵏ had brought up Ha·das'sah, that is Esther, his cousin, for she had neither father nor mother; the girl was fair and beautiful, and when her father and her mother died, Mor'de·caī adopted her as his own daughter. ⁸So when the king's order and his edict were proclaimed, and when many young women were gathered in the citadel of Su'sa in custody of Heg'aī, Esther also was taken into the king's palace and put in custody of Heg'aī, who had charge of the women. ⁹The girl pleased him and won his favor, and he quickly provided her with her cosmetic treatments and her portion of food, and with seven chosen maids from the king's palace, and advanced her and her maids to the best place in the harem. ¹⁰Esther did not reveal her people or kindred, for Mor'de·caī had charged her not to tell. ¹¹Every day Mor'de·caī would walk around in front of the court of the harem, to learn how Esther was and how she fared.

12 The turn came for each girl to go in to King A·has·ū·ē'rus, after being twelve months under the regulations for the women, since this was the regular period of their cosmetic treatment, six months with oil of myrrh and six months with perfumes and cosmetics for women. ¹³When the girl went in to the king she was given whatever she asked for to take with her from the harem to the king's palace. ¹⁴In the evening she went in; then in the morning she came back to the second harem in custody of Sha·ash'gaz, the king's eunuch, who was in charge of the concubines; she did not go in to the king

again, unless the king delighted in her and she was summoned by name.

15 When the turn came for Esther daughter of Ab·i·hā'il the uncle of Mor'de·caī, who had adopted her as his own daughter, to go in to the king, she asked for nothing except what Heg'aī the king's eunuch, who had charge of the women, advised. Now Esther was admired by all who saw her. ¹⁶When Esther was taken to King A·has·ū·ē'rus in his royal palace in the tenth month, which is the month of Tē'beth, in the seventh year of his reign, ¹⁷the king loved Esther more than all the other women; of all the virgins she won his favor and devotion, so that he set the royal crown on her head and made her queen instead of Vash'tī. ¹⁸Then the king gave a great banquet to all his officials and ministers — "Esther's banquet." He also granted a holidayˡ to the provinces, and gave gifts with royal liberality.

Mordecai Discovers a Plot

19 When the virgins were being gathered together,ᵐ Mor'de·caī was sitting at the king's gate. ²⁰Now Esther had not revealed her kindred or her people, as Mor'de·caī had charged her; for Esther obeyed Mor'de·caī just as when she was brought up by him. ²¹In those days, while Mor'de·caī was sitting at the king's gate, Big'than and Tē'resh, two of the king's eunuchs, who guarded the threshold, became angry and conspired to assassinateⁿ King A·has·ū·ē'rus. ²²But the matter came to the knowledge of Mor'de·caī, and he told it to Queen Esther, and Esther told the king in the name of Mor'de·caī. ²³When the affair was investigated and found to be so, both the men were hanged on the gallows. It was recorded in the book of the annals in the presence of the king.

Haman Undertakes to Destroy the Jews

3 After these things King A·has·ū·ē'rus promoted Hā'man son of Ham·me·dā'tha the Ag'ag·īte, and advanced him and set his seat above all the officials who were with him. ²And all the king's servants who were at the king's gate bowed down and did

---

ʲHeb a Benjamite ⁶who   ᵏHeb He
ˡOr an amnesty   ᵐHeb adds a second time   ⁿHeb to lay hands on

beisance to Hā′man; for the king had o commanded concerning him. But Mor′de·caī did not bow down or do beisance. ³ Then the king's servants who were at the king's gate said to Mor′de·caī, "Why do you disobey the king's command?" ⁴ When they spoke o him day after day and he would not listen to them, they told Hā′man, in order to see whether Mor′de·caī's words would avail; for he had told them that he was a Jew. ⁵ When Hā′man saw that Mor′de·caī did not bow down or do obeisance to him, Hā′man was infuriated. ⁶ But he thought it beneath him to lay hands on Mor′de·caī alone. So, having been told who Mor′de·caī's people were, Hā′man plotted to destroy all the Jews, the people of Mor′de·caī, throughout the whole kingdom of A·has·ū·ē′rus.

7 In the first month, which is the month of Nī′san, in the twelfth year of King A·has·ū·ē′rus, they cast Pūr — which means "the lot" — before Hā′man for the day and for the month, and he lot fell on the thirteenth day ° of the twelfth month, which is the month of Ā′dar. ⁸ Then Hā′man said to King A·has·ū·ē′rus, "There is a certain people scattered and separated among the peoples in all the provinces of your kingdom; their laws are different from those of every other people, and they do not keep the king's laws, so that it s not appropriate for the king to tolerate them. ⁹ If it pleases the king, let a decree be issued for their destruction, and I will pay ten thousand talents of silver into the hands of those who have charge of the king's business, so that they may put it into the king's treasuries." ¹⁰ So the king took his signet ring from his hand and gave it to Hā′man son of Ham·me·dā′tha the Ag′ag·ite, the enemy of the Jews. ¹¹ The king said to Hā′man, "The money is given to you, and the people as well, to do with them as it seems good to you."

12 Then the king's secretaries were summoned on the thirteenth day of the first month, and an edict, according to all that Hā′man commanded, was written to the king's satraps and to the governors over all the provinces and to the officials of all the peoples, to every province in its own script and every people in its own language; it was written in the name of King A·has·ū·ē′rus and sealed with the king's ring. ¹³ Letters were sent by couriers to all the king's provinces, giving orders to de-stroy, to kill, and to annihilate all Jews, young and old, women and children, in one day, the thirteenth day of the twelfth month, which is the month of Ā′dar, and to plunder their goods.

Addition B

The King's Letter

13 ᵖ This is a copy of the letter: "The Great King, A·has·ū·ē′rus, writes the following to the governors of the hundred twenty-seven provinces from India to Ethiopia and to the officials under them:

2 "Having become ruler of many nations and master of the whole world (not elated with presumption of authority but always acting reasonably and with kindness), I have determined to settle the lives of my subjects in lasting tranquility and, in order to make my kingdom peaceable and open to travel throughout all its extent, to restore the peace desired by all people.

3 "When I asked my counselors how this might be accomplished, Hā′man — who excels among us in sound judgment, and is distinguished for his unchanging goodwill and steadfast fidelity, and has attained the second place in the kingdom — ⁴ pointed out to us that among all the nations in the world there is scattered a certain hostile people, who have laws contrary to those of every nation and continually disregard the ordinances of kings, so that the unifying of the kingdom that we honorably intend cannot be brought about. ⁵ We understand that this people, and it alone, stands constantly in opposition to every nation, perversely following a strange manner of life and laws, and is ill-disposed to our government, doing all the harm they can so that our kingdom may not attain stability.

6 "Therefore we have decreed that those indicated to you in the letters written by Hā′man, who is in charge of affairs and is our second father, shall all — wives and children included — be utterly destroyed by the swords of their enemies, without pity or restraint, on the fourteenth day of the twelfth month, Ā′dar, of this present year, ⁷ so that those who have long

---

° Cn Compare Gk and verse 13 below: Heb *the twelfth month* ᵖ Chapter 13.1-7 corresponds to chapter B 1-7 in some translations.

been hostile and remain so may in a single day go down in violence to Hades, and leave our government completely secure and untroubled hereafter."

3 14 A copy of the document was to be issued as a decree in every province by proclamation, calling on all the peoples to be ready for that day. 15 The couriers went quickly by order of the king, and the decree was issued in the citadel of Su'sa. The king and Hā'man sat down to drink; but the city of Su'sa was thrown into confusion.

Esther Agrees to Help the Jews

4 When Mor'de·caī learned all that had been done, Mor'de·caī tore his clothes and put on sackcloth and ashes, and went through the city, wailing with a loud and bitter cry; 2 he went up to the entrance of the king's gate, for no one might enter the king's gate clothed with sackcloth. 3 In every province, wherever the king's command and his decree came, there was great mourning among the Jews, with fasting and weeping and lamenting, and most of them lay in sackcloth and ashes.

4 When Esther's maids and her eunuchs came and told her, the queen was deeply distressed; she sent garments to clothe Mor'de·caī, so that he might take off his sackcloth; but he would not accept them. 5 Then Esther called for Hā'thach, one of the king's eunuchs, who had been appointed to attend her, and ordered him to go to Mor'de·caī to learn what was happening and why. 6 Hā'thach went out to Mor'de·caī in the open square of the city in front of the king's gate, 7 and Mor'de·caī told him all that had happened to him, and the exact sum of money that Hā'man had promised to pay into the king's treasuries for the destruction of the Jews. 8 Mor'de·caī also gave him a copy of the written decree issued in Su'sa for their destruction, that he might show it to Esther, explain it to her, and charge her to go to the king to make supplication to him and entreat him for her people. 9 Hā'thach went and told Esther what Mor'de·caī had said. 10 Then Esther spoke to Hā'thach and gave him a message for Mor'de·caī, saying, 11 "All

the king's servants and the people o the king's provinces know that if any man or woman goes to the king inside the inner court without being called there is but one law — all alike are to be put to death. Only if the king holds ou the golden scepter to someone, may that person live. I myself have not been called to come in to the king for thirty days." 12 When they told Mor'de·ca what Esther had said, 13 Mor'de·ca told them to reply to Esther, "Do no think that in the king's palace you wil escape any more than all the othe Jews. 14 For if you keep silence at such a time as this, relief and deliverance will rise for the Jews from anothe quarter, but you and your father's fam ily will perish. Who knows? Perhap you have come to royal dignity for jus such a time as this." 15 Then Esther sai in reply to Mor'de·caī, 16 "Go, gathe all the Jews to be found in Su'sa, and hold a fast on my behalf, and neithe eat nor drink for three days, night o day. I and my maids will also fast a you do. After that I will go to the king though it is against the law; and if perish, I perish." 17 Mor'de·caī the went away and did everything as Es ther had ordered him.

Mordecai's Prayer

13 8q Then Mor'de·caīr prayed t the Lord, calling to remem brance all the works of the Lord.

9 He said, "O Lord, Lord, you rul as King over all things, for the uni verse is in your power and there is n one who can oppose you when it i your will to save Israel, 10 for you hav made heaven and earth and ever wonderful thing under heaven. 11 Yo are Lord of all, and there is no one wh can resist you, the Lord. 12 You knov all things; you know, O Lord, that i was not in insolence or pride or for an love of glory that I did this, and refuse to bow down to this proud Hā'man 13 for I would have been willing to kis the soles of his feet to save Israel! 14 Bu I did this so that I might not set huma glory above the glory of God, and I wil not bow down to anyone but you, wh are my Lord; and I will not do thes

q Chapters 13.8 — 15.16 correspond to chapters C 1-30 and D 1-16 in some translations.   r Gk he hings in pride. [15] And now, O Lord God and King, God of Abraham, spare your people; for the eyes of our foes are upon us[s] to annihilate us, and they desire to destroy the inheritance that has been yours from the beginning. [16] Do not neglect your portion, which you redeemed for yourself out of the land of Egypt. [17] Hear my prayer, and have mercy upon your inheritance; turn our mourning into feasting that we may live and sing praise to your name, O Lord; do not destroy the lips[t] of those who praise you."

18 And all Israel cried out mightily, for their death was before their eyes.

Esther's Prayer

14 Then Queen Esther, seized with deadly anxiety, fled to the Lord. [2] She took off her splendid apparel and put on the garments of distress and mourning, and instead of costly perfumes she covered her head with ashes and dung, and she utterly humbled her body; every part that she loved to adorn she covered with her tangled hair. [3] She prayed to the Lord God of Israel, and said: "O my Lord, you only are our king; help me, who am alone and have no helper but you, [4] for my danger is in my hand. [5] Ever since I was born I have heard in the tribe of my family that you, O Lord, took Israel out of all the nations, and our ancestors from among all their forebears, for an everlasting inheritance, and that you did for them all that you promised. [6] And now we have sinned before you, and you have handed us over to our enemies [7] because we glorified their gods. You are righteous, O Lord! [8] And now they are not satisfied that we are in bitter slavery, but they have covenanted with their idols [9] to abolish what your mouth has ordained, and to destroy your inheritance, to stop the mouths of those who praise you and to quench your altar and the glory of your house, [10] to open the mouths of the nations for the praise of vain idols, and to magnify forever a mortal king.

11 "O Lord, do not surrender your scepter to what has no being; and do not let them laugh at our downfall; but turn their plan against them, and make an example of him who began this against us. [12] Remember, O Lord; make yourself known in this time of our affliction, and give me courage, O King of the gods and Master of all

dominion! [13] Put eloquent speech in my mouth before the lion, and turn his heart to hate the man who is fighting against us, so that there may be an end of him and those who agree with him. [14] But save us by your hand, and help me, who am alone and have no helper but you, O Lord. [15] You have knowledge of all things, and you know that I hate the splendor of the wicked and abhor the bed of the uncircumcised and of any alien. [16] You know my necessity — that I abhor the sign of my proud position, which is upon my head on days when I appear in public. I abhor it like a filthy rag, and I do not wear it on the days when I am at leisure. [17] And your servant has not eaten at Hā′man's table, and I have not honored the king's feast or drunk the wine of libations. [18] Your servant has had no joy since the day that I was brought here until now, except in you, O Lord God of Abraham. [19] O God, whose might is over all, hear the voice of the despairing, and save us from the hands of evildoers. And save me from my fear!"

END OF ADDITION C

ADDITION D

Esther Is Received by the King
(Esth 5.1–2)

15 On the third day, when she ended her prayer, she took off the garments in which she had worshiped, and arrayed herself in splendid attire. [2] Then, majestically adorned, after invoking the aid of the all-seeing God and Savior, she took two maids with her; [3] on one she leaned gently for support, [4] while the other followed, carrying her train. [5] She was radiant with perfect beauty, and she looked happy, as if beloved, but her heart was frozen with fear. [6] When she had gone through all the doors, she stood before the king. He was seated on his royal throne, clothed in the full array of his majesty, all covered with gold and precious stones. He was most terrifying.

7 Lifting his face, flushed with splendor, he looked at her in fierce anger. The queen faltered, and turned pale and faint, and collapsed on the head of the maid who went in front of her. [8] Then God changed the spirit of

---

[s] Gk *for they are eying us*   [t] Gk *mouth*

the king to gentleness, and in alarm he sprang from his throne and took her in his arms until she came to herself. He comforted her with soothing words, and said to her, 9 "What is it, Esther? I am your husband.ᵘ Take courage; 10 You shall not die, for our law applies only to our subjects.ᵛ Come near."

11 Then he raised the golden scepter and touched her neck with it; 12 he embraced her, and said, "Speak to me." 13 She said to him, "I saw you, my lord, like an angel of God, and my heart was shaken with fear at your glory. 14 For you are wonderful, my lord, and your countenance is full of grace." 15 And while she was speaking, she fainted and fell. 16 Then the king was agitated, and all his servants tried to comfort her.

END OF ADDITION D

Esther's Banquet

5 ʷ³ The king said to her, "What is it, Queen Esther? What is your request? It shall be given you, even to the half of my kingdom." 4 Then Esther said, "If it pleases the king, let the king and Hā′man come today to a banquet that I have prepared for the king." 5 Then the king said, "Bring Hā′man quickly, so that we may do as Esther desires." So the king and Hā′man came to the banquet that Esther had prepared. 6 While they were drinking wine, the king said to Esther, "What is your petition? It shall be granted you. And what is your request? Even to the half of my kingdom, it shall be fulfilled." 7 Then Esther said, "This is my petition and request: 8 If I have won the king's favor, and if it pleases the king to grant my petition and fulfill my request, let the king and Hā′man come tomorrow to the banquet that I will prepare for them, and then I will do as the king has said."

Haman Plans to Have Mordecai Hanged

9 Hā′man went out that day happy and in good spirits. But when Hā′man saw Mor′de·caī in the king's gate, and observed that he neither rose nor trembled before him, he was infuriated with Mor′de·caī; 10 nevertheless Hā′man restrained himself and went home. Then he sent and called for his friends and his wife Zē′resh, 11 and

Hā′man recounted to them the splendor of his riches, the number of his sons, all the promotions with which the king had honored him, and how he had advanced him above the officials and the ministers of the king. 12 Hā′man added, "Even Queen Esther let no one but myself come with the king to the banquet that she prepared. Tomorrow also I am invited by her, together with the king. 13 Yet all this does me no good so long as I see the Jew Mor′de·caī sitting at the king's gate.' 14 Then his wife Zē′resh and all his friends said to him, "Let a gallows fifty cubits high be made, and in the morning tell the king to have Mor′de·caī hanged on it; then go with the king to the banquet in good spirits." This advice pleased Hā′man, and he had the gallows made.

The King Honors Mordecai

6 On that night the king could not sleep, and he gave orders to bring the book of records, the annals, and they were read to the king. 2 It was found written how Mor′de·caī had told about Big·thā′na and Tē′resh, two of the king's eunuchs, who guarded the threshold, and who had conspired to assassinateˣ King A·has·ū·ē′rus 3 Then the king said, "What honor or distinction has been bestowed on Mor′de·caī for this?" The king's servants who attended him said, "Nothing has been done for him." 4 The king said, "Who is in the court?" Now Hā′man had just entered the outer court of the king's palace to speak to the king about having Mor′de·caī hanged on the gallows that he had prepared for him. 5 So the king's servants told him, "Hā′man is there, standing in the court." The king said, "Let him come in." 6 So Hā′man came in, and the king said to him, "What shall be done for the man whom the king wishes to honor?" Hā′man said to himself "Whom would the king wish to honor more than me?" 7 So Hā′man said to the king, "For the man whom the king wishes to honor, 8 let royal robes be brought, which the king has worn, and a horse that the king has ridden, with a royal crown on its head. 9 Let the robes and the horse be handed over to

ᵘGk brother   ᵛMeaning of Gk uncertain   ʷIn Greek, Chapter D replaces verses 1 and 2 in Hebrew. ˣHeb to lay hands on one of the king's most noble officials; let him^y robe the man whom the king wishes to honor, and let him^y conduct the man on horseback through the open square of the city, proclaiming before him: 'Thus shall it be done for the man whom the king wishes to honor.'" ¹⁰Then the king said to Hā'-man, "Quickly, take the robes and the horse, as you have said, and do so to the Jew Mor'de·caī who sits at the king's gate. Leave out nothing that you have mentioned." ¹¹So Hā'man took the robes and the horse and robed Mor'de·caī and led him riding through the open square of the city, proclaiming, "Thus shall it be done for the man whom the king wishes to honor."

12 Then Mor'de·caī returned to the king's gate, but Hā'man hurried to his house, mourning and with his head covered. ¹³When Hā'man told his wife Zē'resh and all his friends everything that had happened to him, his advisers and his wife Zē'resh said to him, "If Mor'de·caī, before whom your downfall has begun, is of the Jewish people, you will not prevail against him, but will surely fall before him."

Haman's Downfall and Mordecai's Advancement

14 While they were still talking with him, the king's eunuchs arrived and hurried Hā'man off to the banquet **7** that Esther had prepared. ¹So the king and Hā'man went in to feast with Queen Esther. ²On the second day, as they were drinking wine, the king again said to Esther, "What is your petition, Queen Esther? It shall be granted you. And what is your request? Even to the half of my kingdom, it shall be fulfilled." ³Then Queen Esther answered, "If I have won your favor, O king, and if it pleases the king, let my life be given me—that is my petition—and the lives of my people—that is my request. ⁴For we have been sold, I and my people, to be destroyed, to be killed, and to be annihilated. If we had been sold merely as slaves, men and women, I would have held my peace; but no enemy can compensate for this damage to the king."^z ⁵Then King A·has·ū·ē'rus said to Queen Esther, "Who is he, and where is he, who has presumed to do this?" ⁶Esther said, "A foe and enemy, this wicked Hā'-man!" Then Hā'man was terrified before the king and the queen. ⁷The king rose from the feast in wrath and went into the palace garden, but Hā'man stayed to beg his life from Queen Esther, for he saw that the king had determined to destroy him. ⁸When the king returned from the palace garden to the banquet hall, Hā'man had thrown himself on the couch where Esther was reclining; and the king said, "Will he even assault the queen in my presence, in my own house?" As the words left the mouth of the king, they covered Hā'man's face. ⁹Then Harbō'na, one of the eunuchs in attendance on the king, said, "Look, the very gallows that Hā'man has prepared for Mor'de·caī, whose word saved the king, stands at Hā'man's house, fifty cubits high." And the king said, "Hang him on that." ¹⁰So they hanged Hā'man on the gallows that he had prepared for Mor'de·caī. Then the **8** anger of the king abated. ¹On that day King A·has·ū·ē'rus gave to Queen Esther the house of Hā'man, the enemy of the Jews; and Mor'de·caī came before the king, for Esther had told what he was to her. ²Then the king took off his signet ring, which he had taken from Hā'man, and gave it to Mor'de·caī. So Esther set Mor'de·caī over the house of Hā'man.

Esther Saves the Jews

3 Then Esther spoke again to the king; she fell at his feet, weeping and pleading with him to avert the evil design of Hā'man the Ag'ag·īte and the plot that he had devised against the Jews. ⁴The king held out the golden scepter to Esther, ⁵and Esther rose and stood before the king. She said, "If it pleases the king, and if I have won his favor, and if the thing seems right before the king, and I have his approval, let an order be written to revoke the letters devised by Hā'man son of Hamme·dā'tha the Ag'ag·īte, which he wrote giving orders to destroy the Jews who are in all the provinces of the king. ⁶For how can I bear to see the calamity that is coming on my people? Or how can I bear to see the destruction of my kindred?" ⁷Then King A·has·ū·ē'rus said to Queen Esther and to the Jew Mor'de·caī, "See, I have given Esther the house of Hā'man, and they have hanged him on the gallows, because he plotted to lay hands on the

^yHeb *them*   ^zMeaning of Heb uncertain

Jews. [8] You may write as you please with regard to the Jews, in the name of the king, and seal it with the king's ring; for an edict written in the name of the king and sealed with the king's ring cannot be revoked."

[9] The king's secretaries were summoned at that time, in the third month, which is the month of Sī'van, on the twenty-third day; and an edict was written, according to all that Mor'-de-caī commanded, to the Jews and to the satraps and the governors and the officials of the provinces from India to Ethiopia,[a] one hundred twenty-seven provinces, to every province in its own script and to every people in its own language, and also to the Jews in their script and their language. [10] He wrote letters in the name of King A·has·ū·ē'rus, sealed them with the king's ring, and sent them by mounted couriers riding on fast steeds bred from the royal herd.[b] [11] By these letters the king allowed the Jews who were in every city to assemble and defend their lives, to destroy, to kill, and to annihilate any armed force of any people or province that might attack them, with their children and women, and to plunder their goods [12] on a single day throughout all the provinces of King A·has·ū·ē'rus, on the thirteenth day of the twelfth month, which is the month of Ā'dar.

ADDITION E

The Decree of Ahasuerus

16[c] The following is a copy of this letter:
"The Great King, A·has·ū·ē'rus, to the governors of the provinces from India to Ethiopia, one hundred twenty-seven provinces, and to those who are loyal to our government, greetings.

[2] "Many people, the more they are honored with the most generous kindness of their benefactors, the more proud do they become, [3] and not only seek to injure our subjects, but in their inability to stand prosperity, they even undertake to scheme against their own benefactors. [4] They not only take away thankfulness from others, but, carried away by the boasts of those who know nothing of goodness, they even assume that they will escape the evil-hating justice of God, who always sees everything. [5] And often many of those who are set in places of authority have been made in part responsible for the shedding of innocent blood, and have been involved in irremediable calamities, by the persuasion of friends who have been entrusted with the administration of public affairs, [6] when these persons by the false trickery of their evil natures beguile the sincere good will of their sovereigns.

[7] "What has been wickedly accomplished through the pestilent behavior of those who exercise authority unworthily can be seen, not so much from the more ancient records that we hand on, as from investigation of matters close at hand.[d] [8] In the future we will take care to render our kingdom quiet and peaceable for all, [9] by changing our methods and always judging what comes before our eyes with more equitable consideration. [10] For Hā'man son of Ham·me·dā'tha, a Mac·e·dō'ni·an (really an alien to the Persian blood, and quite devoid of our kindliness), having become our guest, [11] enjoyed so fully the goodwill that we have for every nation that he was called our father and was continually bowed down to by all as the person second to the royal throne. [12] But, unable to restrain his arrogance, he undertook to deprive us of our kingdom and our life,[e] [13] and with intricate craft and deceit asked for the destruction of Mor'de·caī, our savior and perpetual benefactor, and of Esther, the blameless partner of our kingdom, together with their whole nation. [14] He thought that by these methods he would catch us undefended and would transfer the kingdom of the Persians to the Mac·e·dō'ni·ans.

[15] "But we find that the Jews, who were consigned to annihilation by this thrice-accursed man, are not evildoers, but are governed by most righteous laws [16] and are children of the living God, most high, most mighty, who has directed the kingdom both for us and for our ancestors in the most excellent order.

[17] "You will therefore do well not to put in execution the letters sent by Hā'man son of Ham·me·dā'tha, [18] since he the one who did these things, has been hanged at the gate of Su'sa with all his

---

[a] Or *Nubia*; Heb *Cush*   [b] Meaning of Heb uncertain   [c] Chapter 16.1-24 corresponds to chapter E 1-24 in some translations.   [d] Gk *matters beside (your) feet*   [e] Gk *our spirit*   [f] Gk *greatest*

household—for God, who rules over all things, has speedily inflicted on him the punishment that he deserved.

19 "Therefore post a copy of this letter publicly in every place, and permit the Jews to live under their own laws. ²⁰ And give them reinforcements, so that on the thirteenth day of the twelfth month, Ā′dar, on that very day, they may defend themselves against those who attack them at the time of oppression. ²¹ For God, who rules over all things, has made this day to be a joy for his chosen people instead of a day of destruction for them.

22 "Therefore you shall observe this with all good cheer as a notable day among your commemorative festivals, ²³ so that both now and hereafter it may represent deliverance for you[g] and the loyal Persians, but that it may be a reminder of destruction for those who plot against us.

24 "Every city and country, without exception, that does not act accordingly shall be destroyed in wrath with spear and fire. It shall be made not only impassable for human beings, but also most hateful to wild animals and birds for all time."

END OF ADDITION E

8 ¹³ A copy of the writ was to be issued as a decree in every province and published to all peoples, and the Jews were to be ready on that day to take revenge on their enemies. ¹⁴ So the couriers, mounted on their swift royal steeds, hurried out, urged by the king's command. The decree was issued in the citadel of Su′sa.

15 Then Mor′de·caī went out from the presence of the king, wearing royal robes of blue and white, with a great golden crown and a mantle of fine linen and purple, while the city of Su′sa shouted and rejoiced. ¹⁶ For the Jews there was light and gladness, joy and honor. ¹⁷ In every province and in every city, wherever the king's command and his edict came, there was gladness and joy among the Jews, a festival and a holiday. Furthermore, many of the peoples of the country professed to be Jews, because the fear of the Jews had fallen upon them.

Destruction of the Enemies of the Jews
(Cp. 1 Macc 7.49)

9 Now in the twelfth month, which is the month of Ā′dar, on the thirteenth day, when the king's command and edict were about to be executed, on the very day when the enemies of the Jews hoped to gain power over them, but which had been changed to a day when the Jews would gain power over their foes, ² the Jews gathered in their cities throughout all the provinces of King A·has·ū·e′rus to lay hands on those who had sought their ruin; and no one could withstand them, because the fear of them had fallen upon all peoples. ³ All the officials of the provinces, the satraps and the governors, and the royal officials were supporting the Jews, because the fear of Mor′de·caī had fallen upon them. ⁴ For Mor′de·caī was powerful in the king's house, and his fame spread throughout all the provinces as the man Mor′de·caī grew more and more powerful. ⁵ So the Jews struck down all their enemies with the sword, slaughtering, and destroying them, and did as they pleased to those who hated them. ⁶ In the citadel of Su′sa the Jews killed and destroyed five hundred people. ⁷ They killed Par·shan·dā′tha, Dal′phon, As·pā′tha, ⁸ Pō·rā′tha, A·dā′li·a, Ar·i·dā′tha, ⁹ Par·mash′ta, Ar′i·saī, Ar′i·daī, Vaī·zā′tha, ¹⁰ the ten sons of Hā′man son of Ham·me·dā′tha, the enemy of the Jews; but they did not touch the plunder.

11 That very day the number of those killed in the citadel of Su′sa was reported to the king. ¹² The king said to Queen Esther, "In the citadel of Su′sa the Jews have killed five hundred people and also the ten sons of Hā′man. What have they done in the rest of the king's provinces? Now what is your petition? It shall be granted you. And what further is your request? It shall be fulfilled." ¹³ Esther said, "If it pleases the king, let the Jews who are in Su′sa be allowed tomorrow also to do according to this day's edict, and let the ten sons of Hā′man be hanged on the gallows." ¹⁴ So the king commanded this to be done; a decree was issued in Su′sa, and the ten sons of Hā′man were hanged. ¹⁵ The Jews who were in Su′sa gathered also on the fourteenth day of the month of Ā′dar

[g] Other ancient authorities read *for us*

and they killed three hundred persons in Su′sa; but they did not touch the plunder.

16 Now the other Jews who were in the king's provinces also gathered to defend their lives, and gained relief from their enemies, and killed seventy-five thousand of those who hated them; but they laid no hands on the plunder. 17 This was on the thirteenth day of the month of Ā′dar, and on the fourteenth day they rested and made that a day of feasting and gladness.

The Feast of Purim Inaugurated
(Esth 3.7)

18 But the Jews who were in Su′sa gathered on the thirteenth day and on the fourteenth, and rested on the fifteenth day, making that a day of feasting and gladness. 19 Therefore the Jews of the villages, who live in the open towns, hold the fourteenth day of the month of Ā′dar as a day for gladness and feasting, a holiday on which they send gifts of food to one another.

20 Mor′de·cai recorded these things, and sent letters to all the Jews who were in all the provinces of King A·has·u·ē′rus, both near and far, 21 enjoining them that they should keep the fourteenth day of the month Ā′dar and also the fifteenth day of the same month, year by year, 22 as the days on which the Jews gained relief from their enemies, and as the month that had been turned for them from sorrow into gladness and from mourning into a holiday; that they should make them days of feasting and gladness, days for sending gifts of food to one another and presents to the poor. 23 So the Jews adopted as a custom what they had begun to do, as Mor′de·cai had written to them.

24 Hā′man son of Ham·me·dā′tha the Ag′ag·ite, the enemy of all the Jews, had plotted against the Jews to destroy them, and had cast Pūr—that is "the lot"—to crush and destroy them; 25 but when Esther came before the king, he gave orders in writing that the wicked plot that he had devised against the Jews should come upon his own head, and that he and his sons should be hanged on the gallows. 26 Therefore these days are called Pūr′im, from the word Pūr. Thus because of all that was written in this letter, and of what they had faced in this matter, and of what had happened

to them, 27 the Jews established and accepted as a custom for themselves and their descendants and all who joined them, that without fail they would continue to observe these two days every year, as it was written and at the time appointed. 28 These days should be remembered and kept throughout every generation, in every family, province, and city; and these days of Pūr′im should never fall into disuse among the Jews, nor should the commemoration of these days cease among their descendants.

29 Queen Esther daughter of Ab·i·hā′il, along with the Jew Mor′de·cai, gave full written authority, confirming this second letter about Pūr′im. 30 Letters were sent wishing peace and security to all the Jews, to the one hundred twenty-seven provinces of the kingdom of A·has·u·ē′rus, 31 and giving orders that these days of Pūr′im should be observed at their appointed seasons, as the Jew Mor′de·cai and Queen Esther enjoined on the Jews, just as they had laid down for themselves and for their descendants regulations concerning their fasts and their lamentations. 32 The command of Queen Esther fixed these practices of Pūr′im, and it was recorded in writing.

10 King A·has·u·ē′rus laid tribute on the land and on the islands of the sea. 2 All the acts of his power and might, and the full account of the high honor of Mor′de·cai, to which the king advanced him, are they not written in the annals of the kings of Mēd′i·a and Persia? 3 For Mor′de·cai the Jew was next in rank to King A·has·u·ē′rus, and he was powerful among the Jews and popular with his many kindred, for he sought the good of his people and interceded for the welfare of all his descendants.

ADDITION F

Mordecai's Dream Fulfilled

4ʰ And Mor′de·cai said, "These things have come from God; 5 for I remember the dream that I had concerning these matters, and none of them has failed to be fulfilled. 6 There was the little spring that became a river, and there was light and sun and abundant water—the river is Esther, whom

h Chapter 10.4-13 and 11.1 correspond to chapter F 1-11 in some translations.

the king married and made queen. [7] The two dragons are Hā'man and myself. [8] The nations are those that gathered to destroy the name of the Jews. [9] And my nation, this is Israel, who cried out to God and were saved. The Lord has saved his people; the Lord has rescued us from all these evils; God has done great signs and wonders, wonders that have never happened among the nations. [10] For this purpose he made two lots, one for the people of God and one for all the nations, [11] and these two lots came to the hour and moment and day of decision before God and among all the nations. [12] And God remembered his people and vindicated his inheritance. [13] So they will observe these days in the month of Ā'dar, on the fourteenth and fifteenth[i] of that month, with an assembly and joy and gladness before God, from generation to generation forever among his people Israel."

Postscript

11 [1] In the fourth year of the reign of Ptol'e·my and Cleopatra, Dō·sith'e·us, who said that he was a priest and a Lē'vīte,[j] and his son Ptol'e·my brought to Egypt[k] the preceding Letter about Pūr'im, which they said was authentic and had been translated by Lȳ·sim'a·chus son of Ptol'e·my, one of the residents of Jerusalem.

END OF ADDITION F

[i] Other ancient authorities lack *and fifteenth*   [j] Or *priest, and Levitas*   [k] Cn: Gk *brought in*

1 MACCABEES

Alexander the Great

1 After Alexander son of Philip, the Mac·e·dō'ni·an, who came from the land of Kit'tim, had defeated[a] King Da·rī'us of the Persians and the Mēdes, he succeeded him as king. (He had previously become king of Greece.) [2] He fought many battles, conquered strongholds, and put to death the kings of the earth. [3] He advanced to the ends of the earth, and plundered many nations. When the earth became quiet before him, he was exalted, and his heart was lifted up. [4] He gathered a very strong army and ruled over countries, nations, and princes, and they became tributary to him.

[5] After this he fell sick and perceived that he was dying. [6] So he summoned his most honored officers, who had been brought up with him from youth, and divided his kingdom among them while he was still alive. [7] And after Alexander had reigned twelve years, he died.

[8] Then his officers began to rule, each in his own place. [9] They all put on crowns after his death, and so did their descendants after them for many years; and they caused many evils on the earth.

Antiochus Epiphanes and Renegade Jews
(2 Macc 4.7–17)

[10] From them came forth a sinful root, An·tī'o·chus E·piph'a·nēs, son of King An·tī'o·chus; he had been a hostage in Rome. He began to reign in the one hundred thirty-seventh year of the kingdom of the Greeks.[b]

[11] In those days certain renegades came out from Israel and misled many, saying, "Let us go and make a covenant with the Gentiles around us, for since we separated from them many disasters have come upon us." [12] This proposal pleased them, [13] and some of the people eagerly went to the king, who authorized them to observe the ordinances of the Gentiles. [14] So they

[a] Gk adds *and he defeated*   [b] 175 B.C.

built a gymnasium in Jerusalem, according to Gentile custom, [15] and removed the marks of circumcision, and abandoned the holy covenant. They joined with the Gentiles and sold themselves to do evil.

Antiochus in Egypt
(2 Macc 5.1, 11–26)

[16] When An·ti′o·chus saw that his kingdom was established, he determined to become king of the land of Egypt, in order that he might reign over both kingdoms. [17] So he invaded Egypt with a strong force, with chariots and elephants and cavalry and with a large fleet. [18] He engaged King Ptol′e·my of Egypt in battle, and Ptol′e·my turned and fled before him, and many were wounded and fell. [19] They captured the fortified cities in the land of Egypt, and he plundered the land of Egypt.

Persecution of the Jews

[20] After subduing Egypt, An·ti′o·chus returned in the one hundred forty-third year.[c] He went up against Israel and came to Jerusalem with a strong force. [21] He arrogantly entered the sanctuary and took the golden altar, the lampstand for the light, and all its utensils. [22] He took also the table for the bread of the Presence, the cups for drink offerings, the bowls, the golden censers, the curtain, the crowns, and the gold decoration on the front of the temple; he stripped it all off. [23] He took the silver and the gold, and the costly vessels; he took also the hidden treasures that he found. [24] Taking them all, he went into his own land.

He shed much blood,
  and spoke with great
    arrogance.
[25] Israel mourned deeply in every
    community,
[26]   rulers and elders groaned,
  young women and young men
    became faint,
  the beauty of the women
    faded.
[27] Every bridegroom took up the
    lament;
  she who sat in the bridal
    chamber was mourning.
[28] Even the land trembled for its
    inhabitants,
  and all the house of Jacob was
    clothed with shame.

The Occupation of Jerusalem

[29] Two years later the king sent to the cities of Judah a chief collector of tribute, and he came to Jerusalem with a large force. [30] Deceitfully he spoke peaceable words to them, and they believed him; but he suddenly fell upon the city, dealt it a severe blow, and destroyed many people of Israel. [31] He plundered the city, burned it with fire, and tore down its houses and its surrounding walls. [32] They took captive the women and children, and seized the livestock. [33] Then they fortified the city of David with a great strong wall and strong towers, and it became their citadel. [34] They stationed there a sinful people, men who were renegades. These strengthened their position; [35] they stored up arms and food, and collecting the spoils of Jerusalem they stored them there, and became a great menace,

[36]   for the citadel[d] became an
      ambush against the
      sanctuary,
    an evil adversary of Israel at
      all times.
[37] On every side of the sanctuary
      they shed innocent blood;
    they even defiled the
      sanctuary.
[38] Because of them the residents of
      Jerusalem fled;
    she became a dwelling of
      strangers;
  she became strange to her
      offspring,
    and her children forsook her.
[39] Her sanctuary became desolate
      like a desert;
    her feasts were turned into
      mourning,
  her sabbaths into a reproach,
    her honor into contempt.
[40] Her dishonor now grew as great
      as her glory;
    her exaltation was turned into
      mourning.

Installation of Gentile Cults
(Cp 2 Macc 6.1–17; Mt 24.15; Mk 13.14)

[41] Then the king wrote to his whole kingdom that all should be one people, [42] and that all should give up their particular customs. [43] All the Gentiles accepted the command of the king. Many even from Israel gladly adopted his religion; they sacrificed to idols and

c 169 B.C.   d Gk *it*

profaned the sabbath. 44 And the king sent letters by messengers to Jerusalem and the towns of Judah; he directed them to follow customs strange to the land, 45 to forbid burnt offerings and sacrifices and drink offerings in the sanctuary, to profane sabbaths and festivals, 46 to defile the sanctuary and the priests, 47 to build altars and sacred precincts and shrines for idols, to sacrifice swine and other unclean animals, 48 and to leave their sons uncircumcised. They were to make themselves abominable by everything unclean and profane, 49 so that they would forget the law and change all the ordinances. 50 He added,e "And whoever does not obey the command of the king shall die."

51 In such words he wrote to his whole kingdom. He appointed inspectors over all the people and commanded the towns of Judah to offer sacrifice, town by town. 52 Many of the people, everyone who forsook the law, joined them, and they did evil in the land; 53 they drove Israel into hiding in every place of refuge they had.

54 Now on the fifteenth day of Chis'lev, in the one hundred forty-fifth year,f they erected a desolating sacrilege on the altar of burnt offering. They also built altars in the surrounding towns of Judah, 55 and offered incense at the doors of the houses and in the streets. 56 The books of the law that they found they tore to pieces and burned with fire. 57 Anyone found possessing the book of the covenant, or anyone who adhered to the law, was condemned to death by decree of the king. 58 They kept using violence against Israel, against those who were found month after month in the towns. 59 On the twenty-fifth day of the month they offered sacrifice on the altar that was on top of the altar of burnt offering. 60 According to the decree, they put to death the women who had their children circumcised, 61 and their families and those who circumcised them; and they hung the infants from their mothers' necks.

62 But many in Israel stood firm and were resolved in their hearts not to eat unclean food. 63 They chose to die rather than to be defiled by food or to profane the holy covenant; and they did die. 64 Very great wrath came upon Israel.

Mattathias and His Sons

2 In those days Mat·ta·thī'as son of John son of Sim'ē·on, a priest of the family of Jō'a·rib, moved from Jerusalem and settled in Mō'dēin. 2 He had five sons, John surnamed Gad'dī, 3 Simon called Thas'sī, 4 Judas called Mac·ca·bē'us, 5 El·ē·ā'zar called Av'aran, and Jonathan called Ap'phus. 6 He saw the blasphemies being committed in Judah and Jerusalem, 7 and said,
"Alas! Why was I born to see this,
    the ruin of my people, the ruin of the holy city,
and to live there when it was given over to the enemy,
    the sanctuary given over to aliens?
8 Her temple has become like a person without honor;g
9   her glorious vessels have been carried into exile.
Her infants have been killed in her streets,
    her youths by the sword of the foe.
10 What nation has not inherited her palacesh
    and has not seized her spoils?
11 All her adornment has been taken away;
    no longer free, she has become a slave.
12 And see, our holy place, our beauty,
    and our glory have been laid waste;
    the Gentiles have profaned them.
13 Why should we live any longer?"

14 Then Mat·ta·thī'as and his sons tore their clothes, put on sackcloth, and mourned greatly.

Pagan Worship Refused

15 The king's officers who were enforcing the apostasy came to the town of Mō'dēin to make them offer sacrifice. 16 Many from Israel came to them; and Mat·ta·thī'as and his sons were assembled. 17 Then the king's officers spoke to Mat·ta·thī'as as follows: "You are a leader, honored and great in this town, and supported by sons and brothers. 18 Now be the first to come and do what the king commands, as all

e Gk lacks *He added*   f 167 B.C.
g Meaning of Gk uncertain   h Other ancient authorities read *has not had a part in her kingdom*

the Gentiles and the people of Judah and those that are left in Jerusalem have done. Then you and your sons will be numbered among the Friends of the king, and you and your sons will be honored with silver and gold and many gifts."

19 But Mat·ta·thī′as answered and said in a loud voice: "Even if all the nations that live under the rule of the king obey him, and have chosen to obey his commandments, everyone of them abandoning the religion of their ancestors, 20 I and my sons and my brothers will continue to live by the covenant of our ancestors. 21 Far be it from us to desert the law and the ordinances. 22 We will not obey the king's words by turning aside from our religion to the right hand or to the left."

23 When he had finished speaking these words, a Jew came forward in the sight of all to offer sacrifice on the altar in Mō′dēin, according to the king's command. 24 When Mat·ta·thī′as saw it, he burned with zeal and his heart was stirred. He gave vent to righteous anger; he ran and killed him on the altar. 25 At the same time he killed the king's officer who was forcing them to sacrifice, and he tore down the altar. 26 Thus he burned with zeal for the law, just as Phin′e·has did against Zim′ri son of Sa′lū.

27 Then Mat·ta·thī′as cried out in the town with a loud voice, saying: "Let every one who is zealous for the law and supports the covenant come out with me!" 28 Then he and his sons fled to the hills and left all that they had in the town.

29 At that time many who were seeking righteousness and justice went down to the wilderness to live there, 30 they, their sons, their wives, and their livestock, because troubles pressed heavily upon them. 31 And it was reported to the king's officers, and to the troops in Jerusalem the city of David, that those who had rejected the king's command had gone down to the hiding places in the wilderness. 32 Many pursued them, and overtook them; they encamped opposite them and prepared for battle against them on the sabbath day. 33 They said to them, "Enough of this! Come out and do what the king commands, and you will live." 34 But they said, "We will not come out, nor will we do what the king commands and so profane the sabbath day." 35 Then the enemy[i] quickly at-

tacked them. 36 But they did not answer them or hurl a stone at them or block up their hiding places, 37 for they said, "Let us all die in our innocence; heaven and earth testify for us that you are killing us unjustly." 38 So they attacked them on the sabbath, and they died, with their wives and children and livestock, to the number of a thousand persons.

39 When Mat·ta·thī′as and his friends learned of it, they mourned for them deeply. 40 And all said to their neighbors: "If we all do as our kindred have done and refuse to fight with the Gentiles for our lives and for our ordinances, they will quickly destroy us from the earth." 41 So they made this decision that day: "Let us fight against anyone who comes to attack us on the sabbath day; let us not all die as our kindred died in their hiding places."

Counter-Attack

42 Then there united with them a company of Has·i·dē′ans, mighty warriors of Israel, all who offered themselves willingly for the law. 43 And all who became fugitives to escape their troubles joined them and reinforced them. 44 They organized an army, and struck down sinners in their anger and renegades in their wrath; the survivors fled to the Gentiles for safety. 45 And Mat·ta·thī′as and his friends went around and tore down the altars; 46 they forcibly circumcised all the uncircumcised boys that they found within the borders of Israel. 47 They hunted down the arrogant, and the work prospered in their hands. 48 They rescued the law out of the hands of the Gentiles and kings, and they never let the sinner gain the upper hand.

The Last Words of Mattathias
(Gen 22.1–18; 39.1–45.28; Num 13.1–14.10; Josh 1.1–9)

49 Now the days drew near for Mat·ta·thī′as to die, and he said to his sons: "Arrogance and scorn have now become strong; it is a time of ruin and furious anger. 50 Now, my children, show zeal for the law, and give your lives for the covenant of our ancestors.

51 "Remember the deeds of the ancestors, which they did in their generations; and you will receive great honor and an everlasting name. 52 Was not Abraham found faithful when tested,

iGk *they*

and it was reckoned to him as righteousness? [53] Joseph in the time of his distress kept the commandment, and became lord of Egypt. [54] Phin'e·has our ancestor, because he was deeply zealous, received the covenant of everlasting priesthood. [55] Joshua, because he fulfilled the command, became a judge in Israel. [56] Caleb, because he testified in the assembly, received an inheritance in the land. [57] David, because he was merciful, inherited the throne of the kingdom forever. [58] E·li'jah, because of great zeal for the law, was taken up into heaven. [59] Han·a·ni'ah, Az·a·ri'ah, and Mish'a·el believed and were saved from the flame. [60] Daniel, because of his innocence, was delivered from the mouth of the lions.

[61] "And so observe, from generation to generation, that none of those who put their trust in him will lack strength. [62] Do not fear the words of sinners, for their splendor will turn into dung and worms. [63] Today they will be exalted, but tomorrow they will not be found, because they will have returned to the dust, and their plans will have perished. [64] My children, be courageous and grow strong in the law, for by it you will gain honor.

[65] "Here is your brother Sim'e·on who, I know, is wise in counsel; always listen to him; he shall be your father. [66] Judas Mac·ca·be'us has been a mighty warrior from his youth; he shall command the army for you and fight the battle against the peoples.[j] [67] You shall rally around you all who observe the law, and avenge the wrong done to your people. [68] Pay back the Gentiles in full, and obey the commands of the law."

[69] Then he blessed them, and was gathered to his ancestors. [70] He died in the one hundred forty-sixth year[k] and was buried in the tomb of his ancestors at Mō'dein. And all Israel mourned for him with great lamentation.

The Early Victories of Judas
(2 Macc 8.1–7)

3 Then his son Judas, who was called Mac·ca·be'us, took command in his place. [2] All his brothers and all who had joined his father helped him; they gladly fought for Israel.

[3] He extended the glory of his
  people.
Like a giant he put on his
  breastplate;

he bound on his armor of war
  and waged battles,
protecting the camp by his
  sword.
[4] He was like a lion in his deeds,
  like a lion's cub roaring for
  prey.
[5] He searched out and pursued
  those who broke the law;
he burned those who troubled
  his people.
[6] Lawbreakers shrank back for
  fear of him;
all the evildoers were
  confounded;
and deliverance prospered by
  his hand.
[7] He embittered many kings,
  but he made Jacob glad by his
  deeds,
and his memory is blessed
  forever.
[8] He went through the cities of
  Judah;
he destroyed the ungodly out
  of the land;[l]
thus he turned away wrath
  from Israel.
[9] He was renowned to the ends of
  the earth;
he gathered in those who were
  perishing.

[10] Ap·ol·lō'ni·us now gathered together Gentiles and a large force from Samaria to fight against Israel. [11] When Judas learned of it, he went out to meet him, and he defeated and killed him. Many were wounded and fell, and the rest fled. [12] Then they seized their spoils; and Judas took the sword of Ap·ol·lō'ni·us, and used it in battle the rest of his life.

[13] When Sēr'on, the commander of the Syrian army, heard that Judas had gathered a large company, including a body of faithful soldiers who stayed with him and went out to battle, [14] he said, "I will make a name for myself and win honor in the kingdom. I will make war on Judas and his companions, who scorn the king's command." [15] Once again a strong army of godless men went up with him to help him, to take vengeance on the Israelites.

[16] When he approached the ascent of Beth-hō'ron, Judas went out to meet him with a small company. [17] But when they saw the army coming to meet them, they said to Judas, "How can we, few as we are, fight against so great

[j] Or *of the people*   [k] 166 B.C.   [l] Gk *it*

and so strong a multitude? And we are faint, for we have eaten nothing today." [18]Judas replied, "It is easy for many to be hemmed in by few, for in the sight of Heaven there is no difference between saving by many or by few. [19]It is not on the size of the army that victory in battle depends, but strength comes from Heaven. [20]They come against us in great insolence and lawlessness to destroy us and our wives and our children, and to despoil us; [21]but we fight for our lives and our laws. [22]He himself will crush them before us; as for you, do not be afraid of them."

[23]When he finished speaking, he rushed suddenly against Ser′on and his army, and they were crushed before him. [24]They pursued them[m] down the descent of Beth-hō′ron to the plain; eight hundred of them fell, and the rest fled into the land of the Phi·lis′tines. [25]Then Judas and his brothers began to be feared, and terror fell on the Gentiles all around them. [26]His fame reached the king, and the Gentiles talked of the battles of Judas.

The Policy of Antiochus

[27]When King An·tī′o·chus heard these reports, he was greatly angered; and he sent and gathered all the forces of his kingdom, a very strong army. [28]He opened his coffers and gave a year's pay to his forces, and ordered them to be ready for any need. [29]Then he saw that the money in the treasury was exhausted, and that the revenues from the country were small because of the dissension and disaster that he had caused in the land by abolishing the laws that had existed from the earliest days. [30]He feared that he might not have such funds as he had before for his expenses and for the gifts that he used to give more lavishly than preceding kings. [31]He was greatly perplexed in mind; then he determined to go to Persia and collect the revenues from those regions and raise a large fund. [32]He left Lys′i·as, a distinguished man of royal lineage, in charge of the king's affairs from the river Euphrates to the borders of Egypt. [33]Lys′i·as was also to take care of his son An·tī′o·chus until he returned. [34]And he turned over to Lys′i·as[n] half of his forces and the elephants, and gave him orders about all that he wanted done. As for the residents of Judea and Jeru-

salem, [35]Lys′i·as was to send a force against them to wipe out and destroy the strength of Israel and the remnant of Jerusalem; he was to banish the memory of them from the place, [36]settle aliens in all their territory, and distribute their land by lot. [37]Then the king took the remaining half of his forces and left An′ti·och his capital in the one hundred and forty-seventh year.[o] He crossed the Euphrates river and went through the upper provinces.

Preparations for Battle
(2 Macc 8.8–20)

[38]Lys′i·as chose Ptol′e·my son of Dor·ym′e·nēs, and Nī·cā′nor and Gor′-gi·as, able men among the Friends of the king, [39]and sent with them forty thousand infantry and seven thousand cavalry to go into the land of Judah and destroy it, as the king had commanded. [40]So they set out with their entire force, and when they arrived they encamped near Em·mā′us in the plain. [41]When the traders of the region heard what was said to them, they took silver and gold in immense amounts, and fetters,[p] and went to the camp to get the Israelites for slaves. And forces from Syria and the land of the Phi·lis′-tines joined with them.

[42]Now Judas and his brothers saw that misfortunes had increased and that the forces were encamped in their territory. They also learned what the king had commanded to do to the people to cause their final destruction. [43]But they said to one another, "Let us restore the ruins of our people, and fight for our people and the sanctuary." [44]So the congregation assembled to be ready for battle, and to pray and ask for mercy and compassion.

[45]　Jerusalem was uninhabited like
　　　a wilderness;
　　not one of her children went in
　　　or out.
　The sanctuary was trampled
　　　down,
　　and aliens held the citadel;
　　it was a lodging place for the
　　　Gentiles.
　Joy was taken from Jacob;
　　the flute and the harp ceased
　　　to play.

[46]　Then they gathered together and went to Miz′pah, opposite Jerusalem,

[m]Other ancient authorities read *him*
[n]Gk *him*　[o]165 B.C.　[p]Syr: Gk Mss,
Vg *slaves*

because Israel formerly had a place of prayer in Miz′pah. ⁴⁷They fasted that day, put on sackcloth and sprinkled ashes on their heads, and tore their clothes. ⁴⁸And they opened the book of the law to inquire into those matters about which the Gentiles consulted the likenesses of their gods. ⁴⁹They also brought the vestments of the priesthood and the first fruits and the tithes, and they stirred up the nazirites*q* who had completed their days; ⁵⁰and they cried aloud to Heaven, saying,

"What shall we do with these?
　　Where shall we take them?
⁵¹ Your sanctuary is trampled
　　down and profaned,
　　and your priests mourn in
　　humiliation.
⁵² Here the Gentiles are assembled
　　against us to destroy us;
　　you know what they plot
　　against us.
⁵³ How will we be able to
　　withstand them,
　　if you do not help us?"

54 Then they sounded the trumpets and gave a loud shout. ⁵⁵After this Judas appointed leaders of the people, in charge of thousands and hundreds and fifties and tens. ⁵⁶Those who were building houses, or were about to be married, or were planting a vineyard, or were fainthearted, he told to go home again, according to the law. ⁵⁷Then the army marched out and encamped to the south of Em·mā′us.

58 And Judas said, "Arm yourselves and be courageous. Be ready early in the morning to fight with these Gentiles who have assembled against us to destroy us and our sanctuary. ⁵⁹It is better for us to die in battle than to see the misfortunes of our nation and of the sanctuary. ⁶⁰But as his will in heaven may be, so shall he do."

The Battle at Emmaus
(2 Macc 8.21–29, 34–36)

4 Now Gor′gi·as took five thousand infantry and one thousand picked cavalry, and this division moved out by night ²to fall upon the camp of the Jews and attack them suddenly. Men from the citadel were his guides. ³But Judas heard of it, and he and his warriors moved out to attack the king's force in Em·mā′us ⁴while the division was still absent from the camp. ⁵When Gor′gi·as entered the camp of Judas by night, he found no one there, so he looked for them in the hills, because he said, "These men are running away from us."

6 At daybreak Judas appeared in the plain with three thousand men, but they did not have armor and swords such as they desired. ⁷And they saw the camp of the Gentiles, strong and fortified, with cavalry all around it; and these men were trained in war. ⁸But Judas said to those who were with him, "Do not fear their numbers or be afraid when they charge. ⁹Remember how our ancestors were saved at the Red Sea, when Pharaoh with his forces pursued them. ¹⁰And now, let us cry to Heaven, to see whether he will favor us and remember his covenant with our ancestors and crush this army before us today. ¹¹Then all the Gentiles will know that there is one who redeems and saves Israel."

12 When the foreigners looked up and saw them coming against them, ¹³they went out from their camp to battle. Then the men with Judas blew their trumpets ¹⁴and engaged in battle. The Gentiles were crushed, and fled into the plain, ¹⁵and all those in the rear fell by the sword. They pursued them to Ga·zā′ra, and to the plains of Id·u·mē′a, and to A·zō′tus and Jam′ni·a; and three thousand of them fell. ¹⁶Then Judas and his force turned back from pursuing them, ¹⁷and he said to the people, "Do not be greedy for plunder, for there is a battle before us; ¹⁸Gor′gi·as and his force are near us in the hills. But stand now against our enemies and fight them, and afterward seize the plunder boldly."

19 Just as Judas was finishing this speech, a detachment appeared, coming out of the hills. ²⁰They saw that their army*r* had been put to flight, and that the Jews*r* were burning the camp, for the smoke that was seen showed what had happened. ²¹When they perceived this, they were greatly frightened, and when they also saw the army of Judas drawn up in the plain for battle, ²²they all fled into the land of the Phi·lis′tines. ²³Then Judas returned to plunder the camp, and they seized a great amount of gold and silver, and cloth dyed blue and sea purple, and great riches. ²⁴On their return they sang hymns and praises to Heaven—"For he is good, for his

―――――
q That is *those separated* or *those consecrated*　*r* Gk *they*

mercy endures forever." 25 Thus Israel had a great deliverance that day.

First Campaign of Lysias
(2 Macc 11.1–12)

26 Those of the foreigners who escaped went and reported to Lys'i·as all that had happened. 27 When he heard it, he was perplexed and discouraged, for things had not happened to Israel as he had intended, nor had they turned out as the king had ordered. 28 But the next year he mustered sixty thousand picked infantry and five thousand cavalry to subdue them. 29 They came into Id·u·mē'a and encamped at Beth-zur, and Judas met them with ten thousand men.

30 When he saw that their army was strong, he prayed, saying, "Blessed are you, O Savior of Israel, who crushed the attack of the mighty warrior by the hand of your servant David, and gave the camp of the Philis'tines into the hands of Jonathan son of Saul, and of the man who carried his armor. 31 Hem in this army by the hand of your people Israel, and let them be ashamed of their troops and their cavalry. 32 Fill them with cowardice; melt the boldness of their strength; let them tremble in their destruction. 33 Strike them down with the sword of those who love you, and let all who know your name praise you with hymns."

34 Then both sides attacked, and there fell of the army of Lys'i·as five thousand men; they fell in action.s 35 When Lys'i·as saw the rout of his troops and observed the boldness that inspired those of Judas, and how ready they were either to live or to die nobly, he withdrew to An'ti·och and enlisted mercenaries in order to invade Judea again with an even larger army.

Cleansing and Dedication of
the Temple
(2 Macc 10.1–9)

36 Then Judas and his brothers said, "See, our enemies are crushed; let us go up to cleanse the sanctuary and dedicate it." 37 So all the army assembled and went up to Mount Zion. 38 There they saw the sanctuary desolate, the altar profaned, and the gates burned. In the courts they saw bushes sprung up as in a thicket, or as on one of the mountains. They saw also the chambers of the priests in ruins. 39 Then they tore their clothes and

mourned with great lamentation; they sprinkled themselves with ashes 40 and fell face down on the ground. And when the signal was given with the trumpets, they cried out to Heaven. 41 Then Judas detailed men to fight against those in the citadel until he had cleansed the sanctuary. 42 He chose blameless priests devoted to the law, 43 and they cleansed the sanctuary and removed the defiled stones to an unclean place. 44 They deliberated what to do about the altar of burnt offering, which had been profaned. 45 And they thought it best to tear it down, so that it would not be a lasting shame to them that the Gentiles had defiled it. So they tore down the altar, 46 and stored the stones in a convenient place on the temple hill until a prophet should come to tell what to do with them. 47 Then they took unhewn t stones, as the law directs, and built a new altar like the former one. 48 They also rebuilt the sanctuary and the interior of the temple, and consecrated the courts. 49 They made new holy vessels, and brought the lampstand, the altar of incense, and the table into the temple. 50 Then they offered incense on the altar and lit the lamps on the lampstand, and these gave light in the temple. 51 They placed the bread on the table and hung up the curtains. Thus they finished all the work they had undertaken.

52 Early in the morning on the twenty-fifth day of the ninth month, which is the month of Chis'lev, in the one hundred forty-eighth year,u 53 they rose and offered sacrifice, as the law directs, on the new altar of burnt offering that they had built. 54 At the very season and on the very day that the Gentiles had profaned it, it was dedicated with songs and harps and lutes and cymbals. 55 All the people fell on their faces and worshiped and blessed Heaven, who had prospered them. 56 So they celebrated the dedication of the altar for eight days, and joyfully offered burnt offerings; they offered a sacrifice of well-being and a thanksgiving offering. 57 They decorated the front of the temple with golden crowns and small shields; they restored the gates and the chambers for the priests, and fitted them with doors. 58 There was very great joy

s Or and some fell on the opposite side
t Gk whole   u 164 B.C.

mong the people, and the disgrace
rought by the Gentiles was removed.
59 Then Judas and his brothers and
ll the assembly of Israel determined
1at every year at that season the days
f dedication of the altar should be ob-
erved with joy and gladness for eight
ays, beginning with the twenty-fifth
ay of the month of Chis'lev.
60 At that time they fortified Mount
ion with high walls and strong tow-
rs all around, to keep the Gentiles
om coming and trampling them
own as they had done before. 61 Ju-
as[v] stationed a garrison there to
uard it; he also fortified Beth-zur to
uard it, so that the people might have
stronghold that faced Id·ū·mē'a.

Wars with Neighboring Peoples
(2 Macc 10.14–33)

5 When the Gentiles all around
heard that the altar had been re-
uilt and the sanctuary dedicated as it
as before, they became very angry,
and they determined to destroy the
escendants of Jacob who lived
mong them. So they began to kill and
estroy among the people. 3 But Judas
iade war on the descendants of Esau
1 Id·ū·mē'a, at Ak·ra·bat'te·nē, be-
ause they kept lying in wait for Israel.
Ie dealt them a heavy blow and hum-
led them and despoiled them. 4 He
lso remembered the wickedness of
ie sons of Baē'an, who were a trap
nd a snare to the people and am-
ushed them on the highways. 5 They
/ere shut up by him in their[w] towers;
nd he encamped against them, vowed
heir complete destruction, and
urned with fire their towers and all
ho were in them. 6 Then he crossed
ver to attack the Am'mon·ites, where
e found a strong band and many peo-
le, with Timothy as their leader. 7 He
ngaged in many battles with them,
nd they were crushed before him; he
truck them down. 8 He also took Jā'-
er and its villages; then he returned to
udea.

Liberation of Galilean Jews
(2 Macc 12.10–25)

9 Now the Gentiles in Gil'e·ad gath-
red together against the Israelites
/ho lived in their territory, and
lanned to destroy them. But they fled
o the stronghold of Dath'e·ma, 10 and
ent to Judas and his brothers a letter
hat said, "The Gentiles around us
ave gathered together to destroy us.

11 They are preparing to come and capture the stronghold to which we have
fled, and Timothy is leading their
forces. 12 Now then, come and rescue
us from their hands, for many of us
have fallen, 13 and all our kindred who
were in the land of Tob have been
killed; the enemy[x] have captured their
wives and children and goods, and
have destroyed about a thousand persons there."
14 While the letter was still being
read, other messengers, with their garments torn, came from Galilee and
made a similar report; 15 they said that
the people of Ptol·e·mā'is and Tȳre
and Sī'don, and all Galilee of the Gentiles,[y] had gathered together against
them "to annihilate us." 16 When Judas
and the people heard these messages,
a great assembly was called to determine what they should do for their kindred who were in distress and were
being attacked by enemies.[z] 17 Then
Judas said to his brother Simon,
"Choose your men and go and rescue
your kindred in Galilee; Jonathan my
brother and I will go to Gil'e·ad." 18 But
he left Joseph, son of Zech·a·rī'ah, and
Az·a·rī'ah, a leader of the people, with
the rest of the forces, in Judea to guard
it; 19 and he gave them this command,
"Take charge of this people, but do not
engage in battle with the Gentiles until
we return." 20 Then three thousand
men were assigned to Simon to go to
Galilee, and eight thousand to Judas
for Gil'e·ad.
21 So Simon went to Galilee and
fought many battles against the Gentiles, and the Gentiles were crushed
before him. 22 He pursued them to the
gate of Ptol·e·mā'is; as many as three
thousand of the Gentiles fell, and he
despoiled them. 23 Then he took the
Jews[a] of Galilee and Ar·bat'ta, with
their wives and children, and all they
possessed, and led them to Judea with
great rejoicing.

Judas and Jonathan in Gilead

24 Judas Mac·ca·bē'us and his
brother Jonathan crossed the Jordan
and made three days' journey into the
wilderness. 25 They encountered the
Na·ba·tē'ans, who met them peaceably
and told them all that had happened to
their kindred in Gil'e·ad: 26 "Many of
them have been shut up in Boz'rah and

---

[v] Gk He   [w] Gk her   [x] Gk they
[y] Gk aliens   [z] Gk them   [a] Gk those

Bō′sor, in Al′e·ma and Chas′phō, Mā′ked and Car′na·im"—all these towns were strong and large— 27"and some have been shut up in the other towns of Gil′e·ad; the enemy[b] are getting ready to attack the strongholds tomorrow and capture and destroy all these people in a single day."

28 Then Judas and his army quickly turned back by the wilderness road to Boz′rah; and he took the town, and killed every male by the edge of the sword; then he seized all its spoils and burned it with fire. 29 He left the place at night, and they went all the way to the stronghold of Dath′e·ma.[c] 30 At dawn they looked out and saw a large company, which could not be counted, carrying ladders and engines of war to capture the stronghold, and attacking the Jews within.[d] 31 So Judas saw that the battle had begun and that the cry of the town went up to Heaven, with trumpets and loud shouts, 32 and he said to the men of his forces, "Fight today for your kindred!" 33 Then he came up behind them in three companies, who sounded their trumpets and cried aloud in prayer. 34 And when the army of Timothy realized that it was Mac·ca·bē′us, they fled before him, and he dealt them a heavy blow. As many as eight thousand of them fell that day.

35 Next he turned aside to Mā′a-pha,[e] and fought against it and took it; and he killed every male in it, plundered it, and burned it with fire. 36 From there he marched on and took Chas′phō, Mā′ked, and Bō′sor, and the other towns of Gil′e·ad.

37 After these things Timothy gathered another army and encamped opposite Rā′phon, on the other side of the stream. 38 Judas sent men to spy out the camp, and they reported to him, "All the Gentiles around us have gathered to him; it is a very large force. 39 They also have hired A′rabs to help them, and they are encamped across the stream, ready to come and fight against you." And Judas went to meet them.

40 Now as Judas and his army drew near to the stream of water, Timothy said to the officers of his forces, "If he crosses over to us first, we will not be able to resist him, for he will surely defeat us. 41 But if he shows fear and camps on the other side of the river, we will cross over to him and defeat him." 42 When Judas approached the stream

of water, he stationed the officers[f] of the army at the stream and gave them this command, "Permit no one to encamp, but make them all enter the battle." 43 Then he crossed over against them first, and the whole army followed him. All the Gentiles were defeated before him, and they threw away their arms and fled into the sacred precincts at Car′na·im. 44 But he took the town and burned the sacred precincts with fire, together with all who were in them. Thus Car′na·im was conquered; they could stand before Judas no longer.

The Return to Jerusalem
(2 Macc 12.26–31)

45 Then Judas gathered together all the Israelites in Gil′e·ad, the small and the great, with their wives and children and goods, a very large company, to go to the land of Judah. 46 So they came to Ē′phron. This was a large and very strong town on the road, and they could not go around it to the right or to the left; they had to go through it. 47 But the people of the town shut them out and blocked up the gates with stones. 48 Judas sent them this friendly message, "Let us pass through your land to get to our land. No one will do you harm; we will simply pass by on foot." But they refused to open to him. 49 Then Judas ordered proclamation to be made to the army that all should encamp where they were. 50 So the men of the forces encamped, and he fought against the town all that day and all the night, and the town was delivered into his hands. 51 He destroyed every male by the edge of the sword, and razed and plundered the town. Then he passed through the town over the bodies of the dead.

52 Then they crossed the Jordan into the large plain before Beth-shan. 53 Judas kept rallying the laggards and encouraging the people all the way until he came to the land of Judah. 54 So they went up to Mount Zion with joy and gladness, and offered burnt offerings, because they had returned in safety; not one of them had fallen.

[b] Gk they [c] Gk lacks of Dathema. See verse 9 [d] Gk and they were attacking them [e] Other ancient authorities read Alema [f] Or scribes

Joseph and Azariah Defeated

55 Now while Judas and Jonathan were in Gil'e·ad and their brother Simon was in Galilee before Ptol·e·ma'is, 56 Joseph son of Zech·a·ri'ah, and Az·a·ri'ah, the commanders of the forces, heard of their brave deeds and of the heroic war they had fought. 57 So they said, "Let us also make a name for ourselves; let us go and make war on the Gentiles around us." 58 So they issued orders to the men of the forces that were with them and marched against Jam'ni·a. 59 Gor'gi·as and his men came out of the town to meet them in battle. 60 Then Joseph and Az·a·ri'ah were routed, and were pursued to the borders of Judea; as many as two thousand of the people of Israel fell that day. 61 Thus the people suffered a great rout because, thinking to do a brave deed, they did not listen to Judas and his brothers. 62 But they did not belong to the family of those men through whom deliverance was given to Israel. 63 The man Judas and his brothers were greatly honored in all Israel and among all the Gentiles, wherever their name was heard. 64 People gathered to them and praised them.

Success at Hebron and Philistia

65 Then Judas and his brothers went out and fought the descendants of Esau in the land to the south. He struck Hē'bron and its villages and tore down its strongholds and burned its towers on all sides. 66 Then he marched off to go into the land of the Phi·lis'tines, and passed through Mar'i·sa.[h] 67 On that day some priests, who wished to do a brave deed, fell in battle, for they went out to battle unwisely. 68 But Judas turned aside to A·zō'tus in the land of the Phi·lis'tines; he tore down their altars, and the carved images of their gods he burned with fire; he plundered the towns and returned to the land of Judah.

The Last Days of Antiochus Epiphanes
(2 Macc 1.11–17; 9.1–29; 10.9–13)

6 King An·tī'o·chus was going through the upper provinces when he heard that El·y·mā'is in Persia was a city famed for its wealth in silver and gold. 2 Its temple was very rich, containing golden shields, breastplates, and weapons left there by Alexander son of Philip, the Mac·e·dō'ni·an king who first reigned over the Greeks. 3 So

he came and tried to take the city and plunder it, but he could not because his plan had become known to the citizens 4 and they withstood him in battle. So he fled and in great disappointment left there to return to Babylon.

5 Then someone came to him in Persia and reported that the armies that had gone into the land of Judah had been routed, 6 that Lys'i·as had gone first with a strong force, but had turned and fled before the Jews;[i] that the Jews[j] had grown strong from the arms, supplies, and abundant spoils that they had taken from the armies they had cut down; 7 that they had torn down the abomination that he had erected on the altar in Jerusalem; and that they had surrounded the sanctuary with high walls as before, and also Beth-zur, his town.

8 When the king heard this news, he was astounded and badly shaken. He took to his bed and became sick from disappointment, because things had not turned out for him as he had planned. 9 He lay there for many days, because deep disappointment continually gripped him, and he realized that he was dying. 10 So he called all his Friends and said to them, "Sleep has departed from my eyes and I am downhearted with worry. 11 I said to myself, 'To what distress I have come! And into what a great flood I now am plunged! For I was kind and beloved in my power.' 12 But now I remember the wrong I did in Jerusalem. I seized all its vessels of silver and gold, and I sent to destroy the inhabitants of Judah without good reason. 13 I know that it is because of this that these misfortunes have come upon me; here I am, perishing of bitter disappointment in a strange land."

14 Then he called for Philip, one of his Friends, and made him ruler over all his kingdom. 15 He gave him the crown and his robe and the signet, so that he might guide his son An·tī'o·chus and bring him up to be king. 16 Thus King An·tī'o·chus died there in the one hundred forty-ninth year.[k] 17 When Lys'i·as learned that the king was dead, he set up An·tī'o·chus the king's[g] son to reign. Lys'i·as[l] had brought him up from boyhood; he named him Eū'pa·tor.

g Gk his   h Other ancient authorities read Samaria   i Gk them   j Gk they   k 163 B.C.   l Gk He

Renewed Attacks from Syria
(2 Macc 11.22–26; 13.1–26)

18 Meanwhile the garrison in the citadel kept hemming Israel in around the sanctuary. They were trying in every way to harm them and strengthen the Gentiles. [19] Judas therefore resolved to destroy them, and assembled all the people to besiege them. [20] They gathered together and besieged the citadel[m] in the one hundred fiftieth year;[n] and he built siege towers and other engines of war. [21] But some of the garrison escaped from the siege and some of the ungodly Israelites joined them. [22] They went to the king and said, "How long will you fail to do justice and to avenge our kindred? [23] We were happy to serve your father, to live by what he said, and to follow his commands. [24] For this reason the sons of our people besieged the citadel[o] and became hostile to us; moreover, they have put to death as many of us as they have caught, and they have seized our inheritances. [25] It is not against us alone that they have stretched out their hands; they have also attacked all the lands on their borders. [26] And see, today they have encamped against the citadel in Jerusalem to take it; they have fortified both the sanctuary and Beth-zur; [27] unless you quickly prevent them, they will do still greater things, and you will not be able to stop them."

28 The king was enraged when he heard this. He assembled all his Friends, the commanders of his forces and those in authority.[p] [29] Mercenary forces also came to him from other kingdoms and from islands of the seas. [30] The number of his forces was one hundred thousand foot soldiers, twenty thousand horsemen, and thirty-two elephants accustomed to war. [31] They came through Id·u·mē′a and encamped against Beth-zur, and for many days they fought and built engines of war; but the Jews[q] sallied out and burned these with fire, and fought courageously.

The Battle at Beth-zechariah

32 Then Judas marched away from the citadel and encamped at Beth-zech·a·rī′ah, opposite the camp of the king. [33] Early in the morning the king set out and took his army by a forced march along the road to Beth-zech·a·rī′ah, and his troops made ready for battle and sounded their trumpets. [34] They offered the elephants the juice of grapes and mulberries, to arouse them for battle. [35] They distributed the animals among the phalanxes; with each elephant they stationed a thousand men armed with coats of mail and with brass helmets on their heads, and five hundred picked horsemen were assigned to each beast. [36] These took their position beforehand wherever the animal was; wherever it went they went with it, and they never left it. [37] On the elephants[r] were wooden towers, strong and covered; they were fastened on each animal by special harness, and on each were four armed men who fought from there, and also its Indian driver. [38] The rest of the cavalry were stationed on either side, on the two flanks of the army, to harass the enemy while being themselves protected by the phalanxes. [39] When the sun shone on the shields of gold and brass, the hills were ablaze with them and gleamed like flaming torches.

40 Now a part of the king's army was spread out on the high hills, and some troops were on the plain, and they advanced steadily and in good order. [41] All who heard the noise made by their multitude, by the marching of the multitude and the clanking of their arms, trembled, for the army was very large and strong. [42] But Judas and his army advanced to the battle, and six hundred of the king's army fell. [43] Now El·ē·ā′zar, called Av′a·ran, saw that one of the animals was equipped with royal armor. It was taller than all the others, and he supposed that the king was on it. [44] So he gave his life to save his people and to win for himself an everlasting name. [45] He courageously ran into the midst of the phalanx to reach it; he killed men right and left, and they parted before him on both sides. [46] He got under the elephant, stabbed it from beneath, and killed it; but it fell to the ground upon him and he died. [47] When the Jews[q] saw the royal might and the fierce attack of the forces, they turned away in flight.

m Gk *it*　*n* 162 B.C.　*o* Meaning of Gk uncertain　*p* Gk *those over the reins*　*q* Gk *they*　*r* Gk *them*　*s* Cn: Some authorities read *thirty*; others *thirty-two*

The Siege of the Temple

48 The soldiers of the king's army went up to Jerusalem against them, and the king encamped in Judea and at Mount Zion. 49 He made peace with the people of Beth-zur, and they evacuated the town because they had no provisions there to withstand a siege, since it was a sabbatical year for the land. 50 So the king took Beth-zur and stationed a guard there to hold it. 51 Then he encamped before the sanctuary for many days. He set up siege towers, engines of war to throw fire and stones, machines to shoot arrows, and catapults. 52 The Jews[t] also made engines of war to match theirs, and fought for many days. 53 But they had no food in storage,[u] because it was the seventh year; those who had found safety in Judea from the Gentiles had consumed the last of the stores. 54 Only a few men were left in the sanctuary; the rest scattered to their own homes, for the famine proved too much for them.

Syria Offers Terms

55 Then Lys'i·as heard that Philip, whom King An·ti'o·chus while still living had appointed to bring up his son An·ti'o·chus to be king, 56 had returned from Persia and Mēd'i·a with the forces that had gone with the king, and that he was trying to seize control of the government. 57 So he quickly gave orders to withdraw, and said to the king, to the commanders of the forces, and to the troops, men, "Daily we grow weaker, our food supply is scant, the place against which we are fighting is strong, and the affairs of the kingdom press urgently on us. 58 Now then let us come to terms with these people, and make peace with them and with all their nation. 59 Let us agree to let them live by their laws as they did before; for it was on account of their laws that we abolished that they became angry and did all these things."

60 The speech pleased the king and the commanders, and he sent to the Jews[v] an offer of peace, and they accepted it. 61 So the king and the commanders gave them their oath. On these conditions the Jews[t] evacuated the stronghold. 62 But when the king entered Mount Zion and saw what a strong fortress the place was, he broke the oath he had sworn and gave orders to tear down the wall all around.

63 Then he set off in haste and returned to An'ti·och. He found Philip in control of the city, but he fought against him, and took the city by force.

Expedition of Bacchides and Alcimus
(2 Macc 14.1–14)

7 In the one hundred fifty-first year[w] De·mē'tri·us son of Se·leū'cus set out from Rome, sailed with a few men to a town by the sea, and there began to reign. 2 As he was entering the royal palace of his ancestors, the army seized An·ti'o·chus and Lys'i·as to bring them to him. 3 But when this act became known to him, he said, "Do not let me see their faces!" 4 So the army killed them, and De·mē'tri·us took his seat on the throne of his kingdom.

5 Then there came to him all the renegade and godless men of Israel; they were led by Al'ci·mus, who wanted to be high priest. 6 They brought to the king this accusation against the people: "Judas and his brothers have destroyed all your Friends, and have driven us out of our land. 7 Now then send a man whom you trust; let him go and see all the ruin that Judas[x] has brought on us and on the land of the king, and let him punish them and all who help them."

8 So the king chose Bac'chi·dēs, one of the king's Friends, governor of the province Beyond the River; he was a great man in the kingdom and was faithful to the king. 9 He sent him, and with him he sent the ungodly Al'ci·mus, whom he made high priest; and he commanded him to take vengeance on the Israelites. 10 So they marched away and came with a large force into the land of Judah; and he sent messengers to Judas and his brothers with peaceable but treacherous words. 11 But they paid no attention to their words, for they saw that they had come with a large force.

12 Then a group of scribes appeared in a body before Al'ci·mus and Bac'chi·dēs to ask for just terms. 13 The Has·i·dē'ans were first among the Israelites to seek peace from them, 14 for they said, "A priest of the line of Aaron has come with the army, and he will not harm us." 15 Al'ci·mus[y] spoke peaceable words to them and swore

---

t Gk they   u Other ancient authorities read *in the sanctuary*   v Gk *them*
w 161 B.C.   x Gk *he*   y Gk *He*

this oath to them, "We will not seek to injure you or your Friends." [16] So they trusted him; but he seized sixty of them and killed them in one day, in accordance with the word that was written,

[17] "The flesh of your faithful ones
     and their blood
   they poured out all around
        Jerusalem,
   and there was no one to bury
        them."

[18] Then the fear and dread of them fell on all the people, for they said, "There is no truth or justice in them, for they have violated the agreement and the oath that they swore."

[19] Then Bac'chi·des withdrew from Jerusalem and encamped in Beth-zā'-ith. And he sent and seized many of the men who had deserted to him,[z] and some of the people, and killed them and threw them into a great pit. [20] He placed Al'ci·mus in charge of the country and left with him a force to help him; then Bac'chi·des went back to the king.

[21] Al'ci·mus struggled to maintain his high priesthood, [22] and all who were troubling their people joined him. They gained control of the land of Judah and did great damage in Israel. [23] And Judas saw all the wrongs that Al'ci·mus and those with him had done among the Israelites; it was more than the Gentiles had done. [24] So Judas[a] went out into all the surrounding parts of Judea, taking vengeance on those who had deserted and preventing those in the city[b] from going out into the country. [25] When Al'ci·mus saw that Judas and those with him had grown strong, and realized that he could not withstand them, he returned to the king and brought malicious charges against them.

Nicanor in Judea
(2 Macc 14.15 – 15.19)

[26] Then the king sent Nī·cā'nor, one of his honored princes, who hated and detested Israel, and he commanded him to destroy the people. [27] So Nī·cā'nor came to Jerusalem with a large force, and treacherously sent to Judas and his brothers this peaceable message, [28] "Let there be no fighting between you and me; I shall come with a few men to see you face to face in peace."

[29] So he came to Judas, and they greeted one another peaceably; but the enemy were preparing to kidnap Judas. [30] It became known to Judas that Nī·cā'nor[a] had come to him with treacherous intent, and he was afraid of him and would not meet him again. [31] When Nī·cā'nor learned that his plan had been disclosed, he went out to meet Judas in battle near Caph'ar-sala·ma. [32] About five hundred of the army of Nī·cā'nor fell, and the rest fled into the city of David.

Nicanor Threatens the Temple

[33] After these events Nī·cā'nor went up to Mount Zion. Some of the priests from the sanctuary and some of the elders of the people came out to greet him peaceably and to show him the burnt offering that was being offered for the king. [34] But he mocked them and derided them and defiled them and spoke arrogantly, [35] and in anger he swore this oath, "Unless Judas and his army are delivered into my hands this time, then if I return safely I will burn up this house." And he went out in great anger. [36] At this the priests went in and stood before the altar and the temple; they wept and said,

[37] "You chose this house to be
     called by your name,
   and to be for your people a
     house of prayer and
     supplication.

[38] Take vengeance on this man and
     on his army,
   and let them fall by the sword;
   remember their blasphemies,
   and let them live no longer."

The Death of Nicanor
(2 Macc 15.20–37)

[39] Now Nī·cā'nor went out from Jerusalem and encamped in Beth-hō'ron, and the Syrian army joined him. [40] Judas encamped in Ad'a·sa with three thousand men. Then Judas prayed and said, [41] "When the messengers from the king spoke blasphemy, your angel went out and struck down one hundred eighty-five thousand of the Assyrians.[d] [42] So also crush this army before us today; let the rest learn that Nī·cā'nor[a] has spoken wickedly against the sanctuary, and judge him according to this wickedness."

[43] So the armies met in battle on the thirteenth day of the month of Ā'dar,

---

[z] Or *many of his men who had deserted*
[a] Gk *he*   [b] Gk *and they were prevented*
[c] Gk *they*   [d] Gk *of them*

The army of Nī·cā′nor was crushed, and he himself was the first to fall in the battle. ⁴⁴When his army saw that Nī·cā′nor had fallen, they threw down their arms and fled. ⁴⁵The Jews*e* pursued them a day's journey, from Ad′a·sa as far as Ga·zā′ra, and as they followed they kept sounding the battle call on the trumpets. ⁴⁶People came out of all the surrounding villages of Judea, and they outflanked the enemy*f* and drove them back to their pursuers,*g* so that they all fell by the sword; not even one of them was left. ⁴⁷Then the Jews*e* seized the spoils and the plunder; they cut off Nī·cā′nor's head and the right hand that he had so arrogantly stretched out, and brought them and displayed them just outside Jerusalem. ⁴⁸The people rejoiced greatly and celebrated that day as a day of great gladness. ⁴⁹They decreed that this day should be celebrated each year on the thirteenth day of Ā′dar. ⁵⁰So the land of Judah had rest for a few days.

A Eulogy of the Romans

8 Now Judas heard of the fame of the Romans, that they were very strong and were well-disposed toward all who made an alliance with them, that they pledged friendship to those who came to them, ²and that they were very strong. He had been told of their wars and of the brave deeds that they were doing among the Gauls, how they had defeated them and forced them to pay tribute, ³and what they had done in the land of Spain to get control of the silver and gold mines there, ⁴and how they had gained control of the whole region by their planning and patience, even though the place was far distant from them. They also subdued the kings who came against them from the ends of the earth, until they crushed them and inflicted great disaster on them; the rest paid them tribute every year. ⁵They had crushed in battle and conquered Philip, and King Per′sē·us of the Mac·e·dō′ni·ans,*h* and the others who rose up against them. ⁶They also had defeated An·tī′o·chus the Great, king of Asia, who went to fight against them with one hundred twenty elephants and with cavalry and chariots and a very large army. He was crushed by them; ⁷they took him alive and decreed that he and those who would reign after him should pay a heavy tribute and give hostages and surrender some of their best provinces, ⁸the countries of India, Mēd′i·a, and Lyd′i·a. These they took from him and gave to King Eū′me·nēs. ⁹The Greeks planned to come and destroy them, ¹⁰but this became known to them, and they sent a general against the Greeks*f* and attacked them. Many of them were wounded and fell, and the Romans*e* took captive their wives and children; they plundered them, conquered the land, tore down their strongholds, and enslaved them to this day. ¹¹The remaining kingdoms and islands, as many as ever opposed them, they destroyed and enslaved; ¹²but with their friends and those who rely on them they have kept friendship. They have subdued kings far and near, and as many as have heard of their fame have feared them. ¹³Those whom they wish to help and to make kings, they make kings, and those whom they wish to depose; and they have been greatly exalted. ¹⁴Yet for all this not one of them has put on a crown or worn purple as a mark of pride, ¹⁵but they have built for themselves a senate chamber, and every day three hundred twenty senators constantly deliberate concerning the people, to govern them well. ¹⁶They trust one man each year to rule over them and to control all their land; they all heed the one man, and there is no envy or jealousy among them.

An Alliance with Rome

17 So Judas chose Eū·pol′e·mus son of John son of Ac′cos, and Jason son of El·ē·ā′zar, and sent them to Rome to establish friendship and alliance, ¹⁸and to free themselves from the yoke; for they saw that the kingdom of the Greeks was enslaving Israel completely. ¹⁹They went to Rome, a very long journey; and they entered the senate chamber and spoke as follows: ²⁰"Judas, who is also called Mac·ca·bē′us, and his brothers and the people of the Jews have sent us to you to establish alliance and peace with you, so that we may be enrolled as your allies and friends." ²¹The proposal pleased them, ²²and this is a copy of the letter that they wrote in reply, on bronze tablets, and sent to Jerusalem to remain with them there as a memorial of peace and alliance:

e Gk *they*   *f* Gk *them*   *g* Gk *these*   *h* Or *Kittim*

23 "May all go well with the Romans and with the nation of the Jews at sea and on land forever, and may sword and enemy be far from them. 24 If war comes first to Rome or to any of their allies in all their dominion, 25 the nation of the Jews shall act as their allies wholeheartedly, as the occasion may indicate to them. 26 To the enemy that makes war they shall not give or supply grain, arms, money, or ships, just as Rome has decided; and they shall keep their obligations without receiving any return. 27 In the same way, if war comes first to the nation of the Jews, the Romans shall willingly act as their allies, as the occasion may indicate to them. 28 And to their enemies there shall not be given grain, arms, money, or ships, just as Rome has decided; and they shall keep these obligations and do so without deceit. 29 Thus on these terms the Romans make a treaty with the Jewish people. 30 If after these terms are in effect both parties shall determine to add or delete anything, they shall do so at their discretion, and any addition or deletion that they may make shall be valid.

31 "Concerning the wrongs that King De·mē′tri·us is doing to them, we have written to him as follows, 'Why have you made your yoke heavy on our friends and allies the Jews? 32 If now they appeal again for help against you, we will defend their rights and fight you on sea and on land.' "

Bacchides Returns to Judea

9 When De·mē′tri·us heard that Ni·cā′nor and his army had fallen in battle, he sent Bac′chi·dēs and Al′cimus into the land of Judah a second time, and with them the right wing of the army. 2 They went by the road that leads to Gil′gal and encamped against Mes′a·loth in Ar·bē′la, and they took it and killed many people. 3 In the first month of the one hundred fifty-second year[i] they encamped against Jerusalem; 4 then they marched off and went to Be·rē′a with twenty thousand foot soldiers and two thousand cavalry.

5 Now Judas was encamped in El′a·sa, and with him were three thousand picked men. 6 When they saw the huge number of the enemy forces, they were greatly frightened, and many slipped away from the camp, until no more than eight hundred of them were left.

7 When Judas saw that his army had slipped away and the battle was imminent, he was crushed in spirit, for he had no time to assemble them. 8 He became faint, but he said to those who were left, "Let us get up and go against our enemies. We may have the strength to fight them." 9 But they tried to dissuade him, saying, "We do not have the strength. Let us rather save our own lives now, and let us come back with our kindred and fight them; we are too few." 10 But Judas said, "Far be it from us to do such a thing as to flee from them. If our time has come, let us die bravely for our kindred, and leave no cause to question our honor.

The Last Battle of Judas

11 Then the army of Bac′chi·dēs marched out from the camp and took its stand for the encounter. The cavalry was divided into two companies and the slingers and the archers went ahead of the army, as did all the chief warriors. 12 Bac′chi·dēs was on the right wing. Flanked by the two companies, the phalanx advanced to the sound of the trumpets; and the men with Judas also blew their trumpets. 13 The earth was shaken by the noise of the armies, and the battle raged from morning until evening.

14 Judas saw that Bac′chi·dēs and the strength of his army were on the right; then all the stouthearted men went with him, 15 and they crushed the right wing, and he pursued them as far as Mount A·zō′tus. 16 When those on the left wing saw that the right wing was crushed, they turned and followed close behind Judas and his men. 17 The battle became desperate, and many on both sides were wounded and fell. 18 Judas also fell, and the rest fled.

19 Then Jonathan and Simon took their brother Judas and buried him in the tomb of their ancestors at Mō′dēin, 20 and wept for him. All Israel made great lamentation for him; they mourned many days and said,

21 "How is the mighty fallen,
    the savior of Israel!"

22 Now the rest of the acts of Judas, and his wars and the brave deeds that he did, and his greatness, have not been recorded, but they were very many.

i 160 B.C.   j Gk the army

Jonathan Succeeds Judas

23 After the death of Judas, the renegades emerged in all parts of Israel; all the wrongdoers reappeared. 24 In those days a very great famine occurred, and the country went over to their side. 25 Bac′chi·dēs chose the godless and put them in charge of the country. 26 They made inquiry and searched for the friends of Judas, and brought them to Bac′chi·dēs, who took vengeance on them and made sport of them. 27 So there was great distress in Israel, such as had not been since the time that prophets ceased to appear among them.

28 Then all the friends of Judas assembled and said to Jonathan, 29 "Since the death of your brother Judas there has been no one like him to go against our enemies and Bac′chi·dēs, and to deal with those of our nation who hate us. 30 Now therefore we have chosen you today to take his place as our ruler and leader, to fight our battle." 31 So Jonathan accepted the leadership at that time in place of his brother Judas.

The Campaigns of Jonathan

32 When Bac′chi·dēs learned of this, he tried to kill him. 33 But Jonathan and his brother Simon and all who were with him heard of it, and they fled into the wilderness of Te·kō′a and camped by the water of the pool of As′phar. 34 Bac′chi·dēs found this out on the sabbath day, and he with all his army crossed the Jordan.

35 So Jonathan*k* sent his brother as leader of the multitude and begged the Na·ba·tē′ans, who were his friends, for permission to store with them the great amount of baggage that they had. 36 But the family of Jam′brī from Med′e·ba came out and seized John and all that he had, and left with it.

37 After these things it was reported to Jonathan and his brother Simon, "The family of Jam′brī are celebrating a great wedding, and are conducting the bride, a daughter of one of the great nobles of Cā′naan, from Nad′a·bath with a large escort." 38 Remembering how their brother John had been killed, they went up and hid under cover of the mountain. 39 They looked out and saw a tumultuous procession with a great amount of baggage; and the bridegroom came out with his friends and his brothers to

meet them with tambourines and musicians and many weapons. 40 Then they rushed on them from the ambush and began killing them. Many were wounded and fell, and the rest fled to the mountain; and the Jews*l* took all their goods. 41 So the wedding was turned into mourning and the voice of their musicians into a funeral dirge. 42 After they had fully avenged the blood of their brother, they returned to the marshes of the Jordan.

43 When Bac′chi·dēs heard of this, he came with a large force on the sabbath day to the banks of the Jordan. 44 And Jonathan said to those with him, "Let us get up now and fight for our lives, for today things are not as they were before. 45 For look! the battle is in front of us and behind us; the water of the Jordan is on this side and on that, with marsh and thicket; there is no place to turn. 46 Cry out now to Heaven that you may be delivered from the hands of our enemies." 47 So the battle began, and Jonathan stretched out his hand to strike Bac′-chi·dēs, but he eluded him and went to the rear. 48 Then Jonathan and the men with him leaped into the Jordan and swam across to the other side, and the enemy*l* did not cross the Jordan to attack them. 49 And about one thousand of Bac′chi·dēs' men fell that day.

Bacchides Builds Fortifications

50 Then Bac′chi·dēs*k* returned to Jerusalem and built strong cities in Judea: the fortress in Jericho, and Emmā′us, and Beth-hō′ron, and Beth′el, and Tim′nath, and*m* Phar′a·thon, and Tē′phon, with high walls and gates and bars. 51 And he placed garrisons in them to harass Israel. 52 He also fortified the town of Beth-zur, and Ga-zā′ra, and the citadel, and in them he put troops and stores of food. 53 And he took the sons of the leading men of the land as hostages and put them under guard in the citadel at Jerusalem.

54 In the one hundred and fifty-third year,*n* in the second month, Al′-ci·mus gave orders to tear down the wall of the inner court of the sanctuary. He tore down the work of the prophets! 55 But he only began to tear it down, for at that time Al′ci·mus was stricken and his work was hindered; his mouth was stopped and he was

k Gk *he*   *l* Gk *they*   *m* Some authorities omit *and*   *n* 159 B.C.

paralyzed, so that he could no longer say a word or give commands concerning his house. [56] And Al'ci·mus died at that time in great agony. [57] When Bac'chi·dēs saw that Al'cimus was dead, he returned to the king, and the land of Judah had rest for two years.

The End of the War

[58] Then all the lawless plotted and said, "See! Jonathan and his men are living in quiet and confidence. So now let us bring Bac'chi·dēs back, and he will capture them all in one night." [59] And they went and consulted with him. [60] He started to come with a large force, and secretly sent letters to all his allies in Judea, telling them to seize Jonathan and his men; but they were unable to do it, because their plan became known. [61] And Jonathan's men[o] seized about fifty of the men of the country who were leaders in this treachery, and killed them.

[62] Then Jonathan with his men, and Simon, withdrew to Beth·bā'sī in the wilderness; he rebuilt the parts of it that had been demolished, and they fortified it. [63] When Bac'chi·dēs learned of this, he assembled all his forces, and sent orders to the men of Judea. [64] Then he came and encamped against Beth·bā'sī; he fought against it for many days and made machines of war.

[65] But Jonathan left his brother Simon in the town, while he went out into the country; and he went with only a few men. [66] He struck down Od-o·mē'ra and his kindred and the people of Phas'i·ron in their tents. [67] Then he[p] began to attack and went into battle with his forces; and Simon and his men sallied out from the town and set fire to the machines of war. [68] They fought with Bac'chi·dēs, and he was crushed by them. They pressed him very hard, for his plan and his expedition had been in vain. [69] So he was very angry at the renegades who had counseled him to come into the country, and he killed many of them. Then he decided to go back to his own land.

[70] When Jonathan learned of this, he sent ambassadors to him to make peace with him and obtain release of the captives. [71] He agreed, and did as he said; and he swore to Jonathan[q] that he would not try to harm him as long as he lived. [72] He restored to him the captives whom he had taken previ-

ously from the land of Judah; then he turned and went back to his own land, and did not come again into their territory. [73] Thus the sword ceased from Israel. Jonathan settled in Mich'mash and began to judge the people; and he destroyed the godless out of Israel.

Revolt of Alexander Epiphanes

10 In the one hundred sixtieth year[r] Alexander E·piph'a·nēs, son of An·tī'o·chus, landed and occupied Ptol·e·mā'is. They welcomed him, and there he began to reign. [2] When King De·mē'tri·us heard of it, he assembled a very large army and marched out to meet him in battle. [3] De·mē'tri·us sent Jonathan a letter in peaceable words to honor him; [4] for he said to himself, "Let us act first to make peace with him[s] before he makes peace with Alexander against us, [5] for he will remember all the wrongs that we did to him and to his brothers and his nation." [6] So De·mē'tri·us[t] gave him authority to recruit troops, to equip them with arms, and to become his ally; and he commanded that the hostages in the citadel should be released to him.

[7] Then Jonathan came to Jerusalem and read the letter in the hearing of all the people and of those in the citadel. [8] They were greatly alarmed when they heard that the king had given him authority to recruit troops. [9] But those in the citadel released the hostages to Jonathan, and he returned them to their parents.

[10] And Jonathan took up residence in Jerusalem and began to rebuild and restore the city. [11] He directed those who were doing the work to build the walls and encircle Mount Zion with squared stones, for better fortification; and they did so. [12] Then the foreigners who were in the strongholds that Bac'chi·dēs had built fled; [13] all of them left their places and went back to their own lands. [14] Only in Beth-zur did some remain who had forsaken the law and the commandments, for it served as a place of refuge.

[15] Now King Alexander heard of all the promises that De·mē'tri·us had sent to Jonathan, and he heard of the battles that Jonathan[t] and his

[o] Gk they   [p] Other ancient authorities read they   [q] Gk him   [r] 152 B.C.
[s] Gk them   [t] Gk he

brothers had fought, of the brave deeds that they had done, and of the troubles that they had endured. ¹⁶ So he said, "Shall we find another such man? Come now, we will make him our friend and ally." ¹⁷ And he wrote a letter and sent it to him, in the following words:

Jonathan Becomes High Priest

18 "King Alexander to his brother Jonathan, greetings. ¹⁹ We have heard about you, that you are a mighty warrior and worthy to be our friend. ²⁰ And so we have appointed you today to be the high priest of your nation; you are to be called the king's Friend and you are to take our side and keep friendship with us." He also sent him a purple robe and a golden crown.

21 So Jonathan put on the sacred vestments in the seventh month of the one hundred sixtieth year,ᵘ at the festival of booths,ᵛ and he recruited troops and equipped them with arms in abundance. ²² When De·mē′tri·us heard of these things he was distressed and said, ²³ "What is this that we have done? Alexander has gotten ahead of us in forming a friendship with the Jews to strengthen himself. ²⁴ I also will write them words of encouragement and promise them honor and gifts, so that I may have their help." ²⁵ So he sent a message to them in the following words:

A Letter from Demetrius to Jonathan

"King De·mē′tri·us to the nation of the Jews, greetings. ²⁶ Since you have kept your agreement with us and have continued your friendship with us, and have not sided with our enemies, we have heard of it and rejoiced. ²⁷ Now continue still to keep faith with us, and we will repay you with good for what you do for us. ²⁸ We will grant you many immunities and give you gifts.

29 "I now free you and exempt all the Jews from payment of tribute and salt tax and crown levies, ³⁰ and instead of collecting the third of the grain and the half of the fruit of the trees that I should receive, I release them from this day and henceforth. I will not collect them from the land of Judah or from the three districts added to it from Sa·mār′i·a and Galilee, from this day and for all time. ³¹ Jerusalem and its environs, its tithes and its revenues, shall be holy and free from tax. ³² I release also my control of the citadel in Jerusalem and give it to the high priest, so that he may station in it men of his own choice to guard it. ³³ And everyone of the Jews taken as a captive from the land of Judah into any part of my kingdom, I set free without payment; and let all officials cancel also the taxes on their livestock.

34 "All the festivals and sabbaths and new moons and appointed days, and the three days before a festival and the three after a festival — let them all be days of immunity and release for all the Jews who are in my kingdom. ³⁵ No one shall have authority to exact anything from them or annoy any of them about any matter.

36 "Let Jews be enrolled in the king's forces to the number of thirty thousand men, and let the maintenance be given them that is due to all the forces of the king. ³⁷ Let some of them be stationed in the great strongholds of the king, and let some of them be put in positions of trust in the kingdom. Let their officers and leaders be of their own number, and let them live by their own laws, just as the king has commanded in the land of Judah.

38 "As for the three districts that have been added to Judea from the country of Sa·mār′i·a, let them be annexed to Judea so that they may be considered to be under one ruler and obey no other authority than the high priest. ³⁹ Ptol·e·mā′is and the land adjoining it I have given as a gift to the sanctuary in Jerusalem, to meet the necessary expenses of the sanctuary. ⁴⁰ I also grant fifteen thousand shekels of silver yearly out of the king's revenues from appropriate places. ⁴¹ And all the additional funds that the government officials have not paid as they did in the first years,ʷ they shall give from now on for the service of the temple.ˣ ⁴² Moreover, the five thousand shekels of silver that my officialsʸ have received every year from the income of the services of the temple, this too is canceled, because it belongs to the priests who minister there. ⁴³ And all who take refuge at the temple in Jerusalem, or in any of its precincts, because they owe money to the king or are in debt, let them be released and receive back all their property in my kingdom.

44 "Let the cost of rebuilding and

ᵘ 152 B.C.   ᵛ Or *tabernacles*
ʷ Meaning of Gk uncertain   ˣ Gk *house*
ʸ Gk *they*

restoring the structures of the sanctuary be paid from the revenues of the king. ⁴⁵ And let the cost of rebuilding the walls of Jerusalem and fortifying it all around, and the cost of rebuilding the walls in Judea, also be paid from the revenues of the king."

Death of Demetrius

46 When Jonathan and the people heard these words, they did not believe or accept them, because they remembered the great wrongs that De·mē'- tri·us*z* had done in Israel and how much he had oppressed them. ⁴⁷ They favored Alexander, because he had been the first to speak peaceable words to them, and they remained his allies all his days. 48 Now King Alexander assembled large forces and encamped opposite De·mē'tri·us. ⁴⁹ The two kings met in battle, and the army of De·mē'tri·us fled, and Alexander*a* pursued him and defeated them. ⁵⁰ He pressed the battle strongly until the sun set, and on that day De·mē'tri·us fell.

Treaty of Ptolemy and Alexander

51 Then Alexander sent ambassadors to Ptol'e·my king of Egypt with the following message: ⁵² "Since I have returned to my kingdom and have taken my seat on the throne of my ancestors, and established my rule — for I crushed De·mē'tri·us and gained control of our country; ⁵³ I met him in battle, and he and his army were crushed by us, and we have taken our seat on the throne of his kingdom — ⁵⁴ now therefore let us establish friendship with one another; give me now your daughter as my wife, and I will become your son-in-law, and will make gifts to you and to her in keeping with your position."

55 Ptol'e·my the king replied and said, "Happy was the day on which you returned to the land of your ancestors and took your seat on the throne of their kingdom. ⁵⁶ And now I will do for you as you wrote, but meet me at Ptol·e·mā'is, so that we may see one another, and I will become your father-in-law, as you have said."

57 So Ptol'e·my set out from Egypt, he and his daughter Cleopatra, and came to Ptol·e·mā'is in the one hundred sixty-second year.*b* ⁵⁸ King Alexander met him, and Ptol'e·my*z* gave him his daughter Cleopatra in marriage, and celebrated her wedding at Ptol·e·mā'is with great pomp, as kings do.

59 Then King Alexander wrote to Jonathan to come and meet him. ⁶⁰ So he went with pomp to Ptol·e·mā'is and met the two kings; he gave them and their Friends silver and gold and many gifts, and found favor with them. ⁶¹ A group of malcontents from Israel, renegades, gathered together against him to accuse him; but the king paid no attention to them. ⁶² The king gave orders to take off Jonathan's garments and to clothe him in purple, and they did so. ⁶³ The king also seated him at his side; and he said to his officers, "Go out with him into the middle of the city and proclaim that no one is to bring charges against him about any matter, and let no one annoy him for any reason." ⁶⁴ When his accusers saw the honor that was paid him, in accord with the proclamation, and saw him clothed in purple, they all fled. ⁶⁵ Thus the king honored him and enrolled him among his chief*c* Friends, and made him general and governor of the province. ⁶⁶ And Jonathan returned to Jerusalem in peace and gladness.

Apollonius Is Defeated by Jonathan

67 In the one hundred sixty-fifth year*d* De·mē'tri·us son of De·mē'tri·us came from Crete to the land of his ancestors. ⁶⁸ When King Alexander heard of it, he was greatly distressed and returned to An'ti·och. ⁶⁹ And De·mē'tri·us appointed Ap·ol·lō'ni·us the governor of Coē·le·syr'i·a, and he assembled a large force and encamped against Jam'ni·a. Then he sent the following message to the high priest Jonathan:

70 "You are the only one to rise up against us, and I have fallen into ridicule and disgrace because of you. Why do you assume authority against us in the hill country? ⁷¹ If you now have confidence in your forces, come down to the plain to meet us, and let us match strength with each other there, for I have with me the power of the cities. ⁷² Ask and learn who I am and who the others are that are helping us. People will tell you that you cannot stand before us, for your ancestors were twice put to flight in their own land. ⁷³ And now you will not be able to withstand

---

z Gk *he*   *a* Other ancient authorities read *Alexander fled, and Demetrius*   *b* 150 B.C.   *c* Gk *first*   *d* 147 B.C.

my cavalry and such an army in the plain, where there is no stone or pebble, or place to flee."

74 When Jonathan heard the words of Ap·ol·lō'ni·us, his spirit was aroused. He chose ten thousand men and set out from Jerusalem, and his brother Simon met him to help him. 75 He encamped before Jop'pa, but the people of the city closed its gates, for Ap·ol·lō'ni·us had a garrison in Jop'pa. 76 So they fought against it, and the people of the city became afraid and opened the gates, and Jonathan gained possession of Jop'pa.

77 When Ap·ol·lō'ni·us heard of it, he mustered three thousand cavalry and a large army, and went to A·zō'tus as though he were going farther. At the same time he advanced into the plain, for he had a large troop of cavalry and put confidence in it. 78 Jonathan[e] pursued him to A·zō'tus, and the armies engaged in battle. 79 Now Ap·ol·lō'ni·us had secretly left a thousand cavalry behind them. 80 Jonathan learned that there was an ambush behind him, for they surrounded his army and shot arrows at his men from early morning until late afternoon. 81 But his men stood fast, as Jonathan had commanded, and the enemy's[f] horses grew tired.

82 Then Simon brought forward his force and engaged the phalanx in battle (for the cavalry was exhausted); they were overwhelmed by him and fled, 83 and the cavalry was dispersed in the plain. They fled to A·zō'tus and entered Beth-dā'gon, the temple of their idol, for safety. 84 But Jonathan burned A·zō'tus and the surrounding towns and plundered them; and the temple of Dā'gon, and those who had taken refuge in it, he burned with fire. 85 The number of those who fell by the sword, with those burned alive, came to eight thousand.

86 Then Jonathan left there and encamped against As'ka·lon, and the people of the city came out to meet him with great pomp.

87 He and those with him then returned to Jerusalem with a large amount of booty. 88 When King Alexander heard of these things, he honored Jonathan still more; 89 and he sent to him a golden buckle, such as it is the custom to give to the King's Kinsmen. He also gave him Ek'ron and all its environs as his possession.

Ptolemy Invades Syria

11 Then the king of Egypt gathered great forces, like the sand by the seashore, and many ships; and he tried to get possession of Alexander's kingdom by trickery and add it to his own kingdom. 2 He set out for Syria with peaceable words, and the people of the towns opened their gates to him and went to meet him, for King Alexander had commanded them to meet him, since he was Alexander's[g] father-in-law. 3 But when Ptol'e·my entered the towns he stationed forces as a garrison in each town.

4 When he[h] approached A·zō'tus, they showed him the burnt-out temple of Dā'gon, and A·zō'tus and its suburbs destroyed, and the corpses lying about, and the charred bodies of those whom Jonathan[e] had burned in the war, for they had piled them in heaps along his route. 5 They also told the king what Jonathan had done, to throw blame on him; but the king kept silent. 6 Jonathan met the king at Jop'pa with pomp, and they greeted one another and spent the night there. 7 And Jonathan went with the king as far as the river called E·leū'ther·us; then he returned to Jerusalem.

8 So King Ptol'e·my gained control of the coastal cities as far as Se·leū'ci·a by the sea, and he kept devising wicked designs against Alexander. 9 He sent envoys to King De·mē'tri·us, saying, "Come, let us make a covenant with each other, and I will give you in marriage my daughter who was Alexander's wife, and you shall reign over your father's kingdom. 10 I now regret that I gave him my daughter, for he has tried to kill me." 11 He threw blame on Alexander[i] because he coveted his kingdom. 12 So he took his daughter away from him and gave her to De·mē'tri·us. He was estranged from Alexander, and their enmity became manifest.

13 Then Ptol'e·my entered An'ti·och and put on the crown of Asia. Thus he put two crowns on his head, the crown of Egypt and that of Asia. 14 Now King Alexander was in Ci·li'ci·a at that time, because the people of that region were in revolt. 15 When Alexander heard of it, he came against him in battle. Ptol'e·my marched out

[e] Gk *he*   [f] Gk *their*   [g] Gk *his*   [h] Other ancient authorities read *they*   [i] Gk *him*

and met him with a strong force, and put him to flight. ¹⁶ So Alexander fled into Arabia to find protection there, and King Ptol′e·my was triumphant. ¹⁷ Zab′di·el the A′rab cut off the head of Alexander and sent it to Ptol′e·my. ¹⁸ But King Ptol′e·my died three days later, and his troops in the strongholds were killed by the inhabitants of the strongholds. ¹⁹ So De·mē′tri·us became king in the one hundred sixty-seventh year.ʲ

Jonathan's Diplomacy

20 In those days Jonathan assembled the Judeans to attack the citadel in Jerusalem, and he built many engines of war to use against it. ²¹ But certain renegades who hated their nation went to the king and reported to him that Jonathan was besieging the citadel. ²² When he heard this he was angry, and as soon as he heard it he set out and came to Ptol·e·mā′is; and he wrote Jonathan not to continue the siege, but to meet him for a conference at Ptol·e·mā′is as quickly as possible. 23 When Jonathan heard this, he gave orders to continue the siege. He chose some of the elders of Israel and some of the priests, and put himself in danger, ²⁴ for he went to the king at Ptol·e·mā′is, taking silver and gold and clothing and numerous other gifts. And he won his favor. ²⁵ Although certain renegades of his nation kept making complaints against him, ²⁶ the king treated him as his predecessors had treated him; he exalted him in the presence of all his Friends. ²⁷ He confirmed him in the high priesthood and in as many other honors as he had formerly had, and caused him to be reckoned among his chiefᵏ Friends. ²⁸ Then Jonathan asked the king to free Judea and the three districts of Sa·mār′i·aˡ from tribute, and promised him three hundred talents. ²⁹ The king consented, and wrote a letter to Jonathan about all these things; its contents were as follows:

30 "King De·mē′tri·us to his brother Jonathan and to the nation of the Jews, greetings. ³¹ This copy of the letter that we wrote concerning you to our kinsman Las′the·nēs we have written to you also, so that you may know what it says. ³² 'King De·mē′tri·us to his father Las′the·nēs, greetings. ³³ We have determined to do good to the nation of the Jews, who are our friends and fulfill their obligations to us, because of

the goodwill they show toward us. ³⁴ We have confirmed as their possession both the territory of Judea and the three districts of A·phāir′e·ma and Lyd′da and Rath′a·min; the latter, with all the region bordering them, were added to Judea from Samaria. To all those who offer sacrifice in Jerusalem we have granted release fromᵐ the royal taxes that the king formerly received from them each year, from the crops of the land and the fruit of the trees. ³⁵ And the other payments henceforth due to us of the tithes, and the taxes due to us, and the salt pits and the crown taxes due to us — from all these we shall grant them release. ³⁶ And not one of these grants shall be canceled from this time on forever. ³⁷ Now therefore take care to make a copy of this, and let it be given to Jonathan and put up in a conspicuous place on the holy mountain.' "

The Intrigue of Trypho

38 When King De·mē′tri·us saw that the land was quiet before him and that there was no opposition to him, he dismissed all his troops, all of them to their own homes, except the foreign troops that he had recruited from the islands of the nations. So all the troops who had served under his predecessors hated him. ³⁹ A certain Trȳ′phō had formerly been one of Alexander's supporters; he saw that all the troops were grumbling against De·mē′tri·us. So he went to I·mal′kū·ē the Arab, who was bringing up An·tī′o·chus, the young son of Alexander, ⁴⁰ and insistently urged him to hand An·tī′o·chusⁿ over to him, to become king in place of his father. He also reported to I·mal′kū·ē ⁿ what De·mē′tri·us had done and told of the hatred that the troops of De·mē′tri·usº had for him; and he stayed there many days.

41 Now Jonathan sent to King De·mē′tri·us the request that he remove the troops of the citadel from Jerusalem, and the troops in the strongholds; for they kept fighting against Israel. ⁴² And De·mē′tri·us sent this message back to Jonathan: "Not only will I do these things for you and your nation, but I will confer great honor on you

---

ʲ 145 B.C.   ᵏ Gk first   ˡ Cn: Gk the three districts and Samaria
ᵐ Or Samaria, for all those who offer sacrifice in Jerusalem, in place of
ⁿ Gk him   º Gk his troops

and your nation, if I find an opportunity. ⁴³ Now then you will do well to send me men who will help me, for all my troops have revolted." ⁴⁴ So Jonathan sent three thousand stalwart men to him at An'ti·och, and when they came to the king, the king rejoiced at their arrival.

45 Then the people of the city assembled within the city, to the number of a hundred and twenty thousand, and they wanted to kill the king. ⁴⁶ But the king fled into the palace. Then the people of the city seized the main streets of the city and began to fight. ⁴⁷ So the king called the Jews to his aid, and they all rallied around him and then spread out through the city; and they killed on that day about one hundred thousand. ⁴⁸ They set fire to the city and seized a large amount of spoil on that day, and saved the king. ⁴⁹ When the people of the city saw that the Jews had gained control of the city as they pleased, their courage failed and they cried out to the king with this entreaty: ⁵⁰ "Grant us peace, and make the Jews stop fighting against us and our city." ⁵¹ And they threw down their arms and made peace. So the Jews gained glory in the sight of the king and of all the people in his kingdom, and they returned to Jerusalem with a large amount of spoil.

52 So King De·mē'tri·us sat on the throne of his kingdom, and the land was quiet before him. ⁵³ But he broke his word about all that he had promised; he became estranged from Jonathan and did not repay the favors that Jonathan ᵖ had done him, but treated him very harshly.

Trypho Seizes Power

54 After this Trȳ'phō returned, and with him the young boy An·tī'o·chus who began to reign and put on the crown. ⁵⁵ All the troops that De·mē'-tri·us had discharged gathered around him; they fought against De·mē'-tri·us, �q and he fled and was routed. ⁵⁶ Trȳ'phō captured the elephants ʳ and gained control of An'ti·och. ⁵⁷ Then the young An·tī'o·chus wrote to Jonathan, saying, "I confirm you in the high priesthood and set you over the four districts and make you one of the king's Friends." ⁵⁸ He also sent him gold plate and a table service, and granted him the right to drink from gold cups and dress in purple and wear a gold buckle. ⁵⁹ He appointed Jona-

than's ˢ brother Simon governor from the Ladder of Tȳre to the borders of Egypt.

Campaigns of Jonathan and Simon

60 Then Jonathan set out and traveled beyond the river and among the towns, and all the army of Syria gathered to him as allies. When he came to As'ka·lon, the people of the city met him and paid him honor. ⁶¹ From there he went to Gā'za, but the people of Gā'za shut him out. So he besieged it and burned its suburbs with fire and plundered them. ⁶² Then the people of Gā'za pleaded with Jonathan, and he made peace with them, and took the sons of their rulers as hostages and sent them to Jerusalem. And he passed through the country as far as Damascus.

63 Then Jonathan heard that the officers of De·mē'tri·us had come to Kā'-desh in Galilee with a large army, intending to remove him from office. ⁶⁴ He went to meet them, but left his brother Simon in the country. ⁶⁵ Simon encamped before Beth-zur and fought against it for many days and hemmed it in. ⁶⁶ Then they asked him to grant them terms of peace, and he did so. He removed them from there, took possession of the town, and set a garrison over it.

67 Jonathan and his army encamped by the waters of Gen·nes'a·ret. Early in the morning they marched to the plain of Hā'zor, ⁶⁸ and there in the plain the army of the foreigners met him; they had set an ambush against him in the mountains, but they themselves met him face to face. ⁶⁹ Then the men in ambush emerged from their places and joined battle. ⁷⁰ All the men with Jonathan fled; not one of them was left except Mat·ta·thī'as son of Ab'sa·lom and Judas son of Chal'phī, commanders of the forces of the army. ⁷¹ Jonathan tore his clothes, put dust on his head, and prayed. ⁷² Then he turned back to the battle against the enemy ᵗ and routed them, and they fled. ⁷³ When his men who were fleeing saw this, they returned to him and joined him in the pursuit as far as Kā'desh, to their camp, and there they encamped. ⁷⁴ As many as three thousand of the foreign-

ᵖ Gk he   �q Gk him   ʳ Gk animals
ˢ Gk his   ᵗ Gk them

ers fell that day. And Jonathan returned to Jerusalem.

Alliances with Rome and Sparta

12 Now when Jonathan saw that the time was favorable for him, he chose men and sent them to Rome to confirm and renew the friendship with them. ² He also sent letters to the same effect to the Spartans and to other places. ³ So they went to Rome and entered the senate chamber and said, "The high priest Jonathan and the Jewish nation have sent us to renew the former friendship and alliance with them." ⁴ And the Romans[v] gave them letters to the people in every place, asking them to provide for the envoys[v] safe conduct to the land of Judah.

5 This is a copy of the letter that Jonathan wrote to the Spartans: ⁶ "The high priest Jonathan, the senate of the nation, the priests, and the rest of the Jewish people to their brothers the Spartans, greetings. ⁷ Already in time past a letter was sent to the high priest Ō·nī′as from Ar′i·us,[w] who was king among you, stating that you are our brothers, as the appended copy shows. ⁸ Ō·nī′as welcomed the envoy with honor, and received the letter, which contained a clear declaration of alliance and friendship. ⁹ Therefore, though we have no need of these things, since we have as encouragement the holy books that are in our hands, ¹⁰ we have undertaken to send to renew our family ties and friendship with you, so that we may not become estranged from you, for considerable time has passed since you sent your letter to us. ¹¹ We therefore remember you constantly on every occasion, both at our festivals and on other appropriate days, at the sacrifices that we offer and in our prayers, as it is right and proper to remember brothers. ¹² And we rejoice in your glory. ¹³ But as for ourselves, many trials and many wars have encircled us; the kings around us have waged war against us. ¹⁴ We were unwilling to annoy you and our other allies and friends with these wars, ¹⁵ for we have the help that comes from Heaven for our aid, and so we were delivered from our enemies, and our enemies were humbled. ¹⁶ We therefore have chosen Nū·mē′ni·us son of An·tī′o·chus and An·tip′a·ter son of Jason, and have sent them to Rome to renew our former friendship and alli-

ance with them. ¹⁷ We have commanded them to go also to you and greet you and deliver to you this letter from us concerning the renewal of our family ties. ¹⁸ And now please send us a reply to this."

19 This is a copy of the letter that they sent to Ō·nī′as: ²⁰ "King Ar′i·us of the Spartans, to the high priest Ō·nī′as, greetings. ²¹ It has been found in writing concerning the Spartans and the Jews that they are brothers and are of the family of Abraham. ²² And now that we have learned this, please write us concerning your welfare; ²³ we on our part write to you that your livestock and your property belong to us, and ours belong to you. We therefore command that our envoys[u] report to you accordingly."

Further Campaigns of Jonathan and Simon

24 Now Jonathan heard that the commanders of De·mē′tri·us had returned, with a larger force than before, to wage war against him. ²⁵ So he marched away from Jerusalem and met them in the region of Hā′math, for he gave them no opportunity to invade his own country. ²⁶ He sent spies to their camp, and they returned and reported to him that the enemy[u] were being drawn up in formation to attack the Jews[v] by night. ²⁷ So when the sun had set, Jonathan commanded his troops to be alert and to keep their arms at hand so as to be ready all night for battle, and he stationed outposts around the camp. ²⁸ When the enemy heard that Jonathan and his troops were prepared for battle, they were afraid and were terrified at heart; so they kindled fires in their camp and withdrew.[x] ²⁹ But Jonathan and his troops did not know it until morning, for they saw the fires burning. ³⁰ Then Jonathan pursued them, but he did not overtake them, for they had crossed the E·leū′ther·us river. ³¹ So Jonathan turned aside against the A′rabs who are called Zab·a·dē′ans, and he crushed them and plundered them. ³² Then he broke camp and went to Damascus, and marched through all that region.

33 Simon also went out and marched through the country as far as

---

[u] Gk *they*   [v] Gk *them*   [w] Vg Compare verse 20: Gk *Darius*   [x] Other ancient authorities omit *and withdrew*

As'ka·lon and the neighboring strongholds. He turned aside to Jop'pa and took it by surprise, 34 for he had heard that they were ready to hand over the stronghold to those whom De·mē'-ri·us had sent. And he stationed a garrison there to guard it.

35 When Jonathan returned he convened the elders of the people and planned with them to build strongholds in Judea, 36 to build the walls of Jerusalem still higher, and to erect a high barrier between the citadel and the city to separate it from the city, in order to isolate it so that its garrison[y] could neither buy nor sell. 37 So they gathered together to rebuild the city; part of the wall on the valley to the east had fallen, and he repaired the section called Cha·phen'a·tha. 38 Simon also built Ad'i·da in the She·phē'lah; he fortified it and installed gates with bolts.

Trypho Captures Jonathan

39 Then Trȳ'phō attempted to become king in Asia and put on the crown, and to raise his hand against King An·tī'o·chus. 40 He feared that Jonathan might not permit him to do so, but might make war on him, so he kept seeking to seize and kill him, and he marched out and came to Beth-shan. 41 Jonathan went out to meet him with forty thousand picked warriors, and he came to Beth-shan. 42 When Trȳ'phō saw that he had come with a large army, he was afraid to raise his hand against him. 43 So he received him with honor and commended him to all his Friends, and he gave him gifts and commanded his Friends and his troops to obey him as they would himself. 44 Then he said to Jonathan, "Why have you put all these people to so much trouble when we are not at war? 45 Dismiss them now to their homes and choose for yourself a few men to stay with you, and come with me to Ptol·e·mā'is. I will hand it over to you as well as the other strongholds and the remaining troops and all the officials, and will turn around and go home. For that is why I am here."

46 Jonathan[z] trusted him and did as he said; he sent away the troops, and they returned to the land of Judah. 47 He kept with himself three thousand men, two thousand of whom he left in Galilee, while one thousand accompanied him. 48 But when Jonathan entered Ptol·e·mā'is, the people of Ptol·e-mā'is closed the gates and seized him, and they killed with the sword all who had entered with him.

49 Then Trȳ'phō sent troops and cavalry into Galilee and the Great Plain to destroy all Jonathan's soldiers. 50 But they realized that Jonathan had been seized and had perished along with his men, and they encouraged one another and kept marching in close formation, ready for battle. 51 When their pursuers saw that they would fight for their lives, they turned back. 52 So they all reached the land of Judah safely, and they mourned for Jonathan and his companions and were in great fear; and all Israel mourned deeply. 53 All the nations around them tried to destroy them, for they said, "They have no leader or helper. Now therefore let us make war on them and blot out the memory of them from humankind."

Simon Takes Command

13 Simon heard that Trȳ'phō had assembled a large army to invade the land of Judah and destroy it, 2 and he saw that the people were trembling with fear. So he went up to Jerusalem, and gathering the people together 3 he encouraged them, saying to them, "You yourselves know what great things my brothers and I and the house of my father have done for the laws and the sanctuary; you know also the wars and the difficulties that my brothers and I have seen. 4 By reason of this all my brothers have perished for the sake of Israel, and I alone am left. 5 And now, far be it from me to spare my life in any time of distress, for I am not better than my brothers. 6 But I will avenge my nation and the sanctuary and your wives and children, for all the nations have gathered together out of hatred to destroy us."

7 The spirit of the people was rekindled when they heard these words, 8 and they answered in a loud voice, "You are our leader in place of Judas and your brother Jonathan. 9 Fight our battles, and all that you say to us we will do." 10 So he assembled all the warriors and hurried to complete the walls of Jerusalem, and he fortified it on every side. 11 He sent Jonathan son of Ab'sa·lom to Jop'pa, and with him a considerable army; he drove out its occupants and remained there.

y Gk *they*   z Gk *he*

Deceit and Treachery of Trypho

12 Then Trȳ′phō left Ptol·e·mā′is with a large army to invade the land of Judah, and Jonathan was with him under guard. 13 Simon encamped in Ad′i·da, facing the plain. 14 Trȳ′phō learned that Simon had risen up in place of his brother Jonathan, and that he was about to join battle with him, so he sent envoys to him and said, 15 "It is for the money that your brother Jonathan owed the royal treasury, in connection with the offices he held, that we are detaining him. 16 Send now one hundred talents of silver and two of his sons as hostages, so that when released he will not revolt against us, and we will release him."

17 Simon knew that they were speaking deceitfully to him, but he sent to get the money and the sons, so that he would not arouse great hostility among the people, who might say, 18 "It was because Simonª did not send him the money and the sons, that Jonathanᵇ perished." 19 So he sent the sons and the hundred talents, but Trȳ′phōᵇ broke his word and did not release Jonathan.

20 After this Trȳ′phō came to invade the country and destroy it, and he circled around by the way to A·dor′a. But Simon and his army kept marching along opposite him to every place he went. 21 Now the men in the citadel kept sending envoys to Trȳ′phō urging him to come to them by way of the wilderness and to send them food. 22 So Trȳ′phō got all his cavalry ready to go, but that night a very heavy snow fell, and he did not go because of the snow. He marched off and went into the land of Gil′e·ad. 23 When he approached Bas′ka·ma, he killed Jonathan, and he was buried there. 24 Then Trȳ′phō turned and went back to his own land.

Jonathan's Tomb

25 Simon sent and took the bones of his brother Jonathan, and buried him in Mō′dēin, the city of his ancestors. 26 All Israel bewailed him with great lamentation, and mourned for him many days. 27 And Simon built a monument over the tomb of his father and his brothers; he made it high so that it might be seen, with polished stone at the front and back. 28 He also erected seven pyramids, opposite one another, for his father and mother and four

brothers. 29 For the pyramidsᶜ he devised an elaborate setting, erecting about them great columns, and on the columns he put suits of armor for a permanent memorial, and beside the suits of armor he carved ships, so that they could be seen by all who sail the sea. 30 This is the tomb that he built in Mō′dēin; it remains to this day.

Judea Gains Independence

31 Trȳ′phō dealt treacherously with the young King An·ti′o·chus; he killed him 32 and became king in his place, putting on the crown of Asia and he brought great calamity on the land. 33 But Simon built up the strongholds of Judea and walled them all around, with high towers and great walls and gates and bolts, and he stored food in the strongholds. 34 Simon also chose emissaries and sent them to King De·mē′tri·us with a request to grant relief to the country, for all that Trȳ′phō did was to plunder. 35 King De·mē′tri·us sent him a favorable reply to this request, and wrote him a letter as follows, 36 "King Demē′tri·us to Simon, the high priest and friend of kings, and to the elders and nation of the Jews, greetings. 37 We have received the gold crown and the palm branch that youᵈ sent, and we are ready to make a general peace with you and to write to our officials to grant you release from tribute. 38 All the grants that we have made to you remain valid, and let the strongholds that you have built be your possession. 39 We pardon any errors and offenses committed to this day, and cancel the crown tax that you owe; and whatever other tax has been collected in Jerusalem shall be collected no longer. 40 And if any of you are qualified to be enrolled in our bodyguard,ᵉ let them be enrolled, and let there be peace between us."

41 In the one hundred seventieth yearᶠ the yoke of the Gentiles was removed from Israel, 42 and the people began to write in their documents and contracts, "In the first year of Simon the great high priest and commander and leader of the Jews."

ª Gk I   ᵇ Gk he   ᶜ Gk For these
ᵈ The word you in verses 37-40 is plural
ᵉ Or court   ᶠ 142 B.C.

The Capture of Gazara by Simon

43 In those days Simon[g] encamped against Ga·zā′ra[h] and surrounded it with troops. He made a siege engine, brought it up to the city, and battered and captured one tower. 44 The men in the siege engine leaped out into the city, and a great tumult arose in the city. 45 The men in the city, with their wives and children, went up on the wall with their clothes torn, and they cried out with a loud voice, asking Simon to make peace with them; 46 they said, "Do not treat us according to our wicked acts but according to your mercy." 47 So Simon reached an agreement with them and stopped fighting against them. But he expelled them from the city and cleansed the houses in which the idols were located, and then entered it with hymns and praise. 48 He removed all uncleanness from it, and settled in it those who observed the law. He also strengthened its fortifications and built in it a house for himself.

Simon Regains the Citadel at Jerusalem

49 Those who were in the citadel at Jerusalem were prevented from going in and out to buy and sell in the country. So they were very hungry, and many of them perished from famine. 50 Then they cried to Simon to make peace with them, and he did so. But he expelled them from there and cleansed the citadel from its pollutions. 51 On the twenty-third day of the second month, in the one hundred seventy-first year,[i] the Jews[j] entered it with praise and palm branches, and with harps and cymbals and stringed instruments, and with hymns and songs, because a great enemy had been crushed and removed from Israel. 52 Simon[k] decreed that every year they should celebrate this day with rejoicing. He strengthened the fortifications of the temple hill alongside the citadel, and he and his men lived there. 53 Simon saw that his son John had reached manhood, and so he made him commander of all the forces; and he lived at Ga·zā′ra.

Capture of Demetrius

14 In the one hundred seventy-second year[l] King De·mē′-tri·us assembled his forces and marched into Mēd′i·a to obtain help, so that he could make war against Trȳ′phō. 2 When King Ar′sa·cēs of Persia and Mēd′i·a heard that De·mē′-tri·us had invaded his territory, he sent one of his generals to take him alive. 3 The general[k] went and defeated the army of De·mē′tri·us, and seized him and took him to Ar′sa·cēs, who put him under guard.

Eulogy of Simon

4 The land[m] had rest all the days
    of Simon.
  He sought the good of his
    nation;
  his rule was pleasing to them,
    as was the honor shown him,
    all his days.
5 To crown all his honors he took
    Jop′pa for a harbor,
  and opened a way to the isles
    of the sea.
6 He extended the borders of his
    nation,
  and gained full control of the
    country.
7 He gathered a host of captives;
  he ruled over Ga·zā′ra and
    Beth-zur and the citadel,
  and he removed its uncleanness
    from it;
  and there was none to oppose
    him.
8 They tilled their land in peace;
  the ground gave its increase,
  and the trees of the plains
    their fruit.
9 Old men sat in the streets;
  they all talked together of
    good things,
  and the youths put on splendid
    military attire.
10 He supplied the towns with food,
  and furnished them with the
    means of defense,
  until his renown spread to the
    ends of the earth.
11 He established peace in the land,
  and Israel rejoiced with great
    joy.
12 All the people sat under their
    own vines and fig trees,
  and there was none to make
    them afraid.
13 No one was left in the land to
    fight them,
  and the kings were crushed in
    those days.

g Gk he   h Cn: Gk Gaza   i 141 B.C.
j Gk they   k Gk He   l 140 B.C.
m Other ancient authorities add of Judah

14 He gave help to all the humble
   among his people;
  he sought out the law,
   and did away with all the
      renegades and outlaws.
15 He made the sanctuary glorious,
   and added to the vessels of the
      sanctuary.

Diplomacy with Rome and Sparta

16 It was heard in Rome, and as far
away as Sparta, that Jonathan had
died, and they were deeply grieved.
17 When they heard that his brother Simon had become high priest in his
stead, and that he was ruling over the
country and the towns in it, 18 they
wrote to him on bronze tablets to renew with him the friendship and alliance that they had established with his
brothers Judas and Jonathan. 19 And
these were read before the assembly in
Jerusalem.

20 This is a copy of the letter that
the Spartans sent:
"The rulers and the city of the Spartans to the high priest Simon and to the
elders and the priests and the rest of
the Jewish people, our brothers, greetings. 21 The envoys who were sent to
our people have told us about your
glory and honor, and we rejoiced at
their coming. 22 We have recorded
what they said in our public decrees,
as follows, 'Nū·mē′ni·us son of An·tī′-
o·chus and An·tip′a·ter son of Jason,
envoys of the Jews, have come to us to
renew their friendship with us. 23 It has
pleased our people to receive these
men with honor and to put a copy of
their words in the public archives, so
that the people of the Spartans may
have a record of them. And they have
sent a copy of this to the high priest
Simon.' "
24 After this Simon sent Nū·mē′-
ni·us to Rome with a large gold shield
weighing one thousand minas, to confirm the alliance with the Romans.[n]

Official Honors for Simon

25 When the people heard these
things they said, "How shall we thank
Simon and his sons? 26 For he and his
brothers and the house of his father
have stood firm; they have fought and
repulsed Israel's enemies and established its freedom." 27 So they made a
record on bronze tablets and put it on
pillars on Mount Zion.
This is a copy of what they wrote:
"On the eighteenth day of Ē′lul, in the

one hundred seventy-second year,[o]
which is the third year of the great
high priest Simon, 28 in A·sar′a·mel,[p]
in the great assembly of the priests and
the people and the rulers of the nation
and the elders of the country, the following was proclaimed to us:
29 "Since wars often occurred in
the country, Simon son of Mat·ta-
thī′as, a priest of the sons[q] of Jō′a·rib,
and his brothers, exposed themselves
to danger and resisted the enemies of
their nation, in order that their sanctuary and the law might be preserved;
and they brought great glory to their
nation. 30 Jonathan rallied the[r] nation,
became their high priest, and was
gathered to his people. 31 When their
enemies decided to invade their country and lay hands on their sanctuary,
32 then Simon rose up and fought for
his nation. He spent great sums of his
own money; he armed the soldiers of
his nation and paid them wages. 33 He
fortified the towns of Judea, and Beth-
zur on the borders of Judea, where formerly the arms of the enemy had been
stored, and he placed there a garrison
of Jews. 34 He also fortified Jop′pa,
which is by the sea, and Ga·zā′ra,
which is on the borders of A·zō′tus,
where the enemy formerly lived. He
settled Jews there, and provided in
those towns[n] whatever was necessary
for their restoration.
35 "The people saw Simon's faithfulness[s] and the glory that he had resolved to win for his nation, and they
made him their leader and high priest,
because he had done all these things
and because of the justice and loyalty
that he had maintained toward his nation. He sought in every way to exalt
his people. 36 In his days things prospered in his hands, so that the Gentiles
were put out of the[r] country, as were
also those in the city of David in Jerusalem, who had built themselves a citadel from which they used to sally
forth and defile the environs of the
sanctuary, doing great damage to its
purity. 37 He settled Jews in it and fortified it for the safety of the country and
of the city, and built the walls of Jerusalem higher.

[n] Gk *them*   [o] 140 B.C.   [p] This word
resembles the Hebrew words for *the
court of the people of God* or *the prince
of the people of God*   [q] Meaning of Gk
uncertain   [r] Gk *their*   [s] Other ancient
authorities read *conduct*

38 "In view of these things King De·mē′tri·us confirmed him in the high priesthood, 39 made him one of his Friends, and paid him high honors. 40 For he had heard that the Jews were addressed by the Romans as friends and allies and brothers, and that the Romans[t] had received the envoys of Simon with honor.

41 "The Jews and their priests have resolved that Simon should be their leader and high priest forever, until a trustworthy prophet should arise, 42 and that he should be governor over them and that he should take charge of the sanctuary and appoint officials over its tasks and over the country and the weapons and the strongholds, and that he should take charge of the sanctuary, 43 and that he should be obeyed by all, and that all contracts in the country should be written in his name, and that he should be clothed in purple and wear gold.

44 "None of the people or priests shall be permitted to nullify any of these decisions or to oppose what he says, or to convene an assembly in the country without his permission, or to be clothed in purple or put on a gold buckle. 45 Whoever acts contrary to these decisions or rejects any of them shall be liable to punishment."

46 All the people agreed to grant Simon the right to act in accordance with these decisions. 47 So Simon accepted and agreed to be high priest, to be commander and ethnarch of the Jews and priests, and to be protector of them all.[u] 48 And they gave orders to inscribe this decree on bronze tablets, to put them up in a conspicuous place in the precincts of the sanctuary, 49 and to deposit copies of them in the treasury, so that Simon and his sons might have them.

Letter of Antiochus VII

15 An·tī′o·chus, son of King De·mē′tri·us, sent a letter from the islands of the sea to Simon, the priest and ethnarch of the Jews, and to all the nation; 2 its contents were as follows: "King An·tī′o·chus to Simon the high priest and ethnarch and to the nation of the Jews, greetings. 3 Whereas certain scoundrels have gained control of the kingdom of our ancestors, and I intend to lay claim to the kingdom so that I may restore it as it formerly was, and have recruited a host of mercenary troops and have equipped war-

ships, 4 and intend to make a landing in the country so that I may proceed against those who have destroyed our country and those who have devastated many cities in my kingdom, 5 now therefore I confirm to you all the tax remissions that the kings before me have granted you, and a release from all the other payments from which they have released you. 6 I permit you to mint your own coinage as money for your country, 7 and I grant freedom to Jerusalem and the sanctuary. All the weapons that you have prepared and the strongholds that you have built and now hold shall remain yours. 8 Every debt you owe to the royal treasury and any such future debts shall be canceled for you from henceforth and for all time. 9 When we gain control of our kingdom, we will bestow great honor on you and your nation and the temple, so that your glory will become manifest in all the earth."

10 In the one hundred seventy-fourth year[v] An·tī′o·chus set out and invaded the land of his ancestors. All the troops rallied to him, so that there were only a few with Trȳ′phō. 11 An·tī′o·chus pursued him, and Trȳ′phō[w] came in his flight to Dor, which is by the sea; 12 for he knew that troubles had converged on him, and his troops had deserted him. 13 So An·tī′o·chus encamped against Dor, and with him were one hundred twenty thousand warriors and eight thousand cavalry. 14 He surrounded the town, and the ships joined battle from the sea; he pressed the town hard from land and sea, and permitted no one to leave or enter it.

Rome Supports the Jews

15 Then Nū·mē′ni·us and his companions arrived from Rome, with letters to the kings and countries, in which the following was written: 16 "Lucius, consul of the Romans, to King Ptol′e·my, greetings. 17 The envoys of the Jews have come to us as our friends and allies to renew our ancient friendship and alliance. They had been sent by the high priest Simon and by the Jewish people 18 and have brought a gold shield weighing one thousand minas. 19 We therefore have decided to write to the kings and coun-

---

t Gk they   u Or to preside over them all
v 138 B.C.   w Gk he

tries that they should not seek their harm or make war against them and their cities and their country, or make alliance with those who war against them. 20 And it has seemed good to us to accept the shield from them. 21 Therefore if any scoundrels have fled to you from their country, hand them over to the high priest Simon, so that he may punish them according to their law."

22 The consul[x] wrote the same thing to King De·mē'tri·us and to At'-ta·lus and Ar·i·a·rā'thēs and Ar'sa·cēs, 23 and to all the countries, and to Samp'sa·mēs,[y] and to the Spartans, and to Dē'los, and to Myn'dos, and to Si'cy·on, and to Cār'i·a, and to Sā'mos, and to Pam·phyl'i·a, and to Ly'ci·a, and to Hal·i·car·nas'sus, and to Rhōdes, and to Pha·sē'lis, and to Cōs, and to Sī'de, and to Ar'a·dus and Gor-tȳ'na and Cnī'dus and Cyprus and Cȳ-rē'nē. 24 They also sent a copy of these things to the high priest Simon.

Antiochus VII Threatens Simon

25 King An·tī'o·chus besieged Dor for the second time, continually throwing his forces against it and making engines of war; and he shut Trȳ'phō up and kept him from going out or in. 26 And Simon sent to An·tī'o·chus[z] two thousand picked troops, to fight for him, and silver and gold and a large amount of military equipment. 27 But he refused to receive them, and broke all the agreements he formerly had made with Simon, and became estranged from him. 28 He sent to him Ath·e·nō'bi·us, one of his Friends, to confer with him, saying, "You hold control of Jop'pa and Ga·zā'ra and the citadel in Jerusalem; they are cities of my kingdom. 29 You have devastated their territory, you have done great damage in the land, and you have taken possession of many places in my kingdom. 30 Now then, hand over the cities that you have seized and the tribute money of the places that you have conquered outside the borders of Judea; 31 or else pay me five hundred talents of silver for the destruction that you have caused and five hundred talents more for the tribute money of the cities. Otherwise we will come and make war on you."

32 So Ath·e·nō'bi·us, the king's Friend, came to Jerusalem, and when he saw the splendor of Simon, and the sideboard with its gold and silver plate, and his great magnificence, he was amazed. When he reported to him the king's message, 33 Simon said to him in reply: "We have neither taken foreign land nor seized foreign property, but only the inheritance of our ancestors, which at one time had been unjustly taken by our enemies. 34 Now that we have the opportunity, we are firmly holding the inheritance of our ancestors. 35 As for Jop'pa and Ga·zā'ra, which you demand, they were causing great damage among the people and to our land; for them we will give you one hundred talents."

Ath·e·nō'bi·us[x] did not answer him a word, 36 but returned in wrath to the king and reported to him these words, and also the splendor of Simon and all that he had seen. And the king was very angry.

Victory over Cendebeus

37 Meanwhile Trȳ'phō embarked on a ship and escaped to Or·thō'si·a. 38 Then the king made Cen·de·bē'us commander-in-chief of the coastal country, and gave him troops of infantry and cavalry. 39 He commanded him to encamp against Judea, to build up Kēd'ron and fortify its gates, and to make war on the people; but the king pursued Trȳ'phō. 40 So Cen·de·bē'us came to Jam'ni·a and began to provoke the people and invade Judea and take the people captive and kill them. 41 He built up Kēd'ron and stationed horsemen and troops there, so that they might go out and make raids along the highways of Judea, as the king had ordered him.

16 John went up from Ga·zā'ra and reported to his father Simon what Cen·de·bē'us had done. 2 And Simon called in his two eldest sons Judas and John, and said to them: "My brothers and I and my father's house have fought the wars of Israel from our youth until this day, and things have prospered in our hands so that we have delivered Israel many times. 3 But now I have grown old, and you by Heaven's[a] mercy are mature in years. Take my place and my brother's, and go out and fight for our nation, and may the help that comes from Heaven be with you."

4 So John[b] chose out of the country

x Gk He   y The name is uncertain
z Gk him   a Gk his   b Other ancient
authorities read he

twenty thousand warriors and cavalry, and they marched against Cen-de-bē'us and camped for the night in Mō'dēin. [5]Early in the morning they started out and marched into the plain, where a large force of infantry and cavalry was coming to meet them; and a stream lay between them. [6]Then he and his army lined up against them. He saw that the soldiers were afraid to cross the stream, so he crossed over first; and when his troops saw him, they crossed over after him. [7]Then he divided the army and placed the cavalry in the center of the infantry, for the cavalry of the enemy were very numerous. [8]They sounded the trumpets, and Cen-de-bē'us and his army were put to flight; many of them fell wounded and the rest fled into the stronghold. [9]At that time Judas the brother of John was wounded, but John pursued them until Cen-de-bē'us[c] reached Kēd'ron, which he had built. [10]They also fled into the towers that were in the fields of A-zō'tus, and John[c] burned it with fire, and about two thousand of them fell. He then returned to Judea safely.

Murder of Simon and His Sons

[11] Now Ptol'e-my son of A-bū'bus had been appointed governor over the plain of Jericho; he had a large store of silver and gold, [12]for he was son-in-law of the high priest. [13]His heart was lifted up; he determined to get control of the country, and made treacherous plans against Simon and his sons, to do away with them. [14]Now Simon was visiting the towns of the country and attending to their needs, and he went down to Jericho with his sons Mat-ta-thī'as and Judas, in the one hundred seventy-seventh year,[d] in the eleventh month, which is the month of She-bat'. [15]The son of A-bū'bus received them treacherously in the little stronghold called Dok, which he had built; he gave them a great banquet, and hid men there. [16]When Simon and his sons were drunk, Ptol'e-my and his men rose up, took their weapons, rushed in against Simon in the banquet hall and killed him and his two sons, as well as some of his servants. [17]So he committed an act of great treachery and returned evil for good.

John Succeeds Simon

[18] Then Ptol'e-my wrote a report about these things and sent it to the king, asking him to send troops to aid him and to turn over to him the towns and the country. [19]He sent other troops to Ga-zā'ra to do away with John; he sent letters to the captains asking them to come to him so that he might give them silver and gold and gifts; [20]and he sent other troops to take possession of Jerusalem and the temple hill. [21]But someone ran ahead and reported to John at Ga-zā'ra that his father and brothers had perished, and that "he has sent men to kill you also." [22]When he heard this, he was greatly shocked; he seized the men who came to destroy him and killed them, for he had found out that they were seeking to destroy him.

[23] The rest of the acts of John and his wars and the brave deeds that he did, and the building of the walls that he completed, and his achievements, [24]are written in the annals of his high priesthood, from the time that he became high priest after his father.

[c]Gk *he*   [d]134 B.C.

2 MACCABEES

A Letter to the Jews in Egypt

1 The Jews in Jerusalem and those in the land of Judea,
To their Jewish kindred in Egypt,
Greetings and true peace.

[2] May God do good to you, and may he remember his covenant with Abraham and Isaac and Jacob, his faithful servants. [3]May he give you all a heart to worship him and to do his will with

a strong heart and a willing spirit. [4]May he open your heart to his law and his commandments, and may he bring peace. [5]May he hear your prayers and be reconciled to you, and may he not forsake you in time of evil. [6]We are now praying for you here.

[7]In the reign of De·mē′tri·us, in the one hundred sixty-ninth year,[a] we Jews wrote to you, in the critical distress that came upon us in those years after Jason and his company revolted from the holy land and the kingdom [8]and burned the gate and shed innocent blood. We prayed to the Lord and were heard, and we offered sacrifice and grain offering, and we lit the lamps and set out the loaves. [9]And now see that you keep the festival of booths in the month of Chis′lev, in the one hundred eighty-eighth year.[b]

A Letter to Aristobulus
(Cp 1 Macc 6.1–4)

[10]The people of Jerusalem and of Judea and the senate and Judas,

To Ar·is·tob′u·lus, who is of the family of the anointed priests, teacher of King Ptol′e·my, and to the Jews in Egypt,

Greetings and good health.

[11]Having been saved by God out of grave dangers we thank him greatly for taking our side against the king,[c] [12]for he drove out those who fought against the holy city. [13]When the leader reached Persia with a force that seemed irresistible, they were cut to pieces in the temple of Na·nē′a by a deception employed by the priests of the goddess[d] Na·nē′a. [14]On the pretext of intending to marry her, An·tī′o·chus came to the place together with his Friends, to secure most of its treasures as a dowry. [15]When the priests of the temple of Na·nē′a had set out the treasures and An·tī′o·chus had come with a few men inside the wall of the sacred precinct, they closed the temple as soon as he entered it. [16]Opening a secret door in the ceiling, they threw stones and struck down the leader and his men; they dismembered them and cut off their heads and threw them to the people outside. [17]Blessed in every way be our God, who has brought judgment on those who have behaved impiously.

Fire Consumes Nehemiah's Sacrifice

[18]Since on the twenty-fifth day of Chis′lev we shall celebrate the purification of the temple, we thought it necessary to notify you, in order that you also may celebrate the festival of booths and the festival of the fire given when Nē·he·mī′ah, who built the temple and the altar, offered sacrifices.

[19]For when our ancestors were being led captive to Persia, the pious priests of that time took some of the fire of the altar and secretly hid it in the hollow of a dry cistern, where they took such precautions that the place was unknown to anyone. [20]But after many years had passed, when it pleased God, Nē·he·mī′ah, having been commissioned by the king of Persia, sent the descendants of the priests who had hidden the fire to get it. And when they reported to us that they had not found fire but only a thick liquid he ordered them to dip it out and bring it. [21]When the materials for the sacrifices were presented, Nē·he·mī′ah ordered the priests to sprinkle the liquid on the wood and on the things laid upon it. [22]When this had been done and some time had passed, and when the sun, which had been clouded over shone out, a great fire blazed up, so that all marveled. [23]And while the sacrifice was being consumed, the priests offered prayer—the priests and everyone. Jonathan led, and the rest responded, as did Nē·he·mī′ah. [24]The prayer was to this effect:

"O Lord, Lord God, Creator of all things, you are awe-inspiring and strong and just and merciful, you alone are king and are kind, [25]you alone are bountiful, you alone are just and almighty and eternal. You rescue Israel from every evil; you chose the ancestors and consecrated them. [26]Accept this sacrifice on behalf of all your people Israel and preserve your portion and make it holy. [27]Gather together our scattered people, set free those who are slaves among the Gentiles, look on those who are rejected and despised, and let the Gentiles know that you are our God. [28]Punish those who oppress and are insolent with pride. [29]Plant your people in your holy place, as Moses promised."

---

a 143 B.C.　　*b* 124 B.C.　　*c* Cn: Gk *as those who array themselves against a king*　　*d* Gk lacks *the goddess*

30 Then the priests sang the hymns. [31] After the materials of the sacrifice had been consumed, Nē·he·mī'ah ordered that the liquid that was left should be poured on large stones. [32] When this was done, a flame blazed up; but when the light from the altar shone back, it went out. [33] When this matter became known, and it was reported to the king of the Persians that, in the place where the exiled priests had hidden the fire, the liquid had appeared with which Nē·he·mī'ah and his associates had burned the materials of the sacrifice, [34] the king investigated the matter, and enclosed the place and made it sacred. [35] And with those persons whom the king favored he exchanged many excellent gifts. [36] Nē·he·mī'ah and his associates called this "nephthar," which means purification, but by most people it is called naphtha.[e]

Jeremiah Hides the Tent, Ark, and Altar

2 One finds in the records that the prophet Jer·e·mī'ah ordered those who were being deported to take some of the fire, as has been mentioned, [2] and that the prophet, after giving them the law, instructed those who were being deported not to forget the commandments of the Lord, or to be led astray in their thoughts on seeing the gold and silver statues and their adornment. [3] And with other similar words he exhorted them that the law should not depart from their hearts.

4 It was also in the same document that the prophet, having received an oracle, ordered that the tent and the ark should follow with him, and that he went out to the mountain where Moses had gone up and had seen the inheritance of God. [5] Jer·e·mī'ah came and found a cave-dwelling, and he brought there the tent and the ark and the altar of incense; then he sealed up the entrance. [6] Some of those who followed him came up intending to mark the way, but could not find it. [7] When Jer·e·mī'ah learned of it, he rebuked them and declared: "The place shall remain unknown until God gathers his people together again and shows his mercy. [8] Then the Lord will disclose these things, and the glory of the Lord and the cloud will appear, as they were shown in the case of Moses, and as Solomon asked that the place should be specially consecrated."

9 It was also made clear that being possessed of wisdom Solomon[f] offered sacrifice for the dedication and completion of the temple. [10] Just as Moses prayed to the Lord, and fire came down from heaven and consumed the sacrifices, so also Solomon prayed, and the fire came down and consumed the whole burnt offerings. [11] And Moses said, "They were consumed because the sin offering had not been eaten." [12] Likewise Solomon also kept the eight days.

13 The same things are reported in the records and in the memoirs of Nē·he·mī'ah, and also that he founded a library and collected the books about the kings and prophets, and the writings of David, and letters of kings about votive offerings. [14] In the same way Judas also collected all the books that had been lost on account of the war that had come upon us, and they are in our possession. [15] So if you have need of them, send people to get them for you.

16 Since, therefore, we are about to celebrate the purification, we write to you. Will you therefore please keep the days? [17] It is God who has saved all his people, and has returned the inheritance to all, and the kingship and the priesthood and the consecration, [18] as he promised through the law. We have hope in God that he will soon have mercy on us and will gather us from everywhere under heaven into his holy place, for he has rescued us from great evils and has purified the place.

The Compiler's Preface

19 The story of Judas Mac·ca·bē'us and his brothers, and the purification of the great temple, and the dedication of the altar, [20] and further the wars against An·tī'o·chus E·piph'a·nēs and his son Eū'pa·tor, [21] and the appearances that came from heaven to those who fought bravely for Jū'da·ism, so that though few in number they seized the whole land and pursued the barbarian hordes, [22] and regained possession of the temple famous throughout the world, and liberated the city, and re-established the laws that were about to be abolished, while the Lord with great kindness became gracious to them — [23] all this, which has been set forth by Jason of Cȳ·rē'nē in five

[e] Gk nephthai   [f] Gk he

volumes, we shall attempt to condense into a single book. [24] For considering the flood of statistics involved and the difficulty there is for those who wish to enter upon the narratives of history because of the mass of material, [25] we have aimed to please those who wish to read, to make it easy for those who are inclined to memorize, and to profit all readers. [26] For us who have undertaken the toil of abbreviating, it is no light matter but calls for sweat and loss of sleep, [27] just as it is not easy for one who prepares a banquet and seeks the benefit of others. Nevertheless, to secure the gratitude of many we will gladly endure the uncomfortable toil, [28] leaving the responsibility for exact details to the compiler, while devoting our effort to arriving at the outlines of the condensation. [29] For as the master builder of a new house must be concerned with the whole construction, while the one who undertakes its painting and decoration has to consider only what is suitable for its adornment, such in my judgment is the case with us. [30] It is the duty of the original historian to occupy the ground, to discuss matters from every side, and to take trouble with details, [31] but the one who recasts the narrative should be allowed to strive for brevity of expression and to forego exhaustive treatment. [32] At this point therefore let us begin our narrative, without adding any more to what has already been said; for it would be foolish to lengthen the preface while cutting short the history itself.

Arrival of Heliodorus in Jerusalem

3 While the holy city was inhabited in unbroken peace and the laws were strictly observed because of the piety of the high priest Ō·nī'as and his hatred of wickedness, [2] it came about that the kings themselves honored the place and glorified the temple with the finest presents, [3] even to the extent that King Se·leū'cus of Asia defrayed from his own revenues all the expenses connected with the service of the sacrifices.

[4] But a man named Simon, of the tribe of Benjamin, who had been made captain of the temple, had a disagreement with the high priest about the administration of the city market. [5] Since he could not prevail over Ō·nī'as, he went to Ap·ol·lō'ni·us of Tar'sus,[g]

who at that time was governor of Coē·le·syr'i·a and Phoe·ni'ci·a, [6] and reported to him that the treasury in Jerusalem was full of untold sums of money, so that the amount of the funds could not be reckoned, and that they did not belong to the account of the sacrifices, but that it was possible for them to fall under the control of the king. [7] When Ap·ol·lō'ni·us met the king, he told him of the money about which he had been informed. The king[h] chose Hē·li·o·dor'us, who was in charge of his affairs, and sent him with commands to effect the removal of the reported wealth. [8] Hē·li·o·dor'us at once set out on his journey, ostensibly to make a tour of inspection of the cities of Coē·le·syr'i·a and Phoe·ni'ci·a, but in fact to carry out the king's purpose.

[9] When he had arrived at Jerusalem and had been kindly welcomed by the high priest of[i] the city, he told about the disclosure that had been made and stated why he had come, and he inquired whether this really was the situation. [10] The high priest explained that there were some deposits belonging to widows and orphans, [11] and also some money of Hyr·cā'nus son of Tō·bī'as, a man of very prominent position, and that it totaled in all four hundred talents of silver and two hundred of gold. To such an extent the impious Simon had misrepresented the facts. [12] And he said that it was utterly impossible that wrong should be done to those people who had trusted in the holiness of the place and in the sanctity and inviolability of the temple that is honored throughout the whole world.

Heliodorus Plans to Rob the Temple

[13] But Hē·li·o·dor'us, because of the orders he had from the king, said that this money must in any case be confiscated for the king's treasury. [14] So he set a day and went in to direct the inspection of these funds.

There was no little distress throughout the whole city. [15] The priests prostrated themselves before the altar in their priestly vestments and called toward heaven upon him who had given the law about deposits, that he should keep them safe for those who had

g Gk Apollonius son of Tharseas
h Gk He i Other ancient authorities read and

deposited them. 16 To see the appearance of the high priest was to be wounded at heart, for his face and the change in his color disclosed the anguish of his soul. 17 For terror and bodily trembling had come over the man, which plainly showed to those who looked at him the pain lodged in his heart. 18 People also hurried out of their houses in crowds to make a general supplication because the holy place was about to be brought into dishonor. 19 Women, girded with sackcloth under their breasts, thronged the streets. Some of the young women who were kept indoors ran together to the gates, and some to the walls, while others peered out of the windows. 20 And holding up their hands to heaven, they all made supplication. 21 There was something pitiable in the prostration of the whole populace and the anxiety of the high priest in his great anguish.

The Lord Protects His Temple

22 While they were calling upon the Almighty Lord that he would keep what had been entrusted safe and secure for those who had entrusted it, 23 He·li·o·dor′us went on with what had been decided. 24 But when he arrived at the treasury with his bodyguard, then and there the Sovereign of spirits and of all authority caused so great a manifestation that all who had been so bold as to accompany him were astounded by the power of God, and became faint with terror. 25 For there appeared to them a magnificently caparisoned horse, with a rider of frightening mien; it rushed furiously at He·li·o·dor′us and struck at him with its front hoofs. Its rider was seen to have armor and weapons of gold. 26 Two young men also appeared to him, remarkably strong, gloriously beautiful and splendidly dressed, who stood on either side of him and flogged him continuously, inflicting many blows on him. 27 When he suddenly fell to the ground and deep darkness came over him, his men took him up, put him on a stretcher, 28 and carried him away — this man who had just entered the aforesaid treasury with a great retinue and all his bodyguard but was now unable to help himself. They recognized clearly the sovereign power of God.

Onias Prays for Heliodorus

29 While he lay prostrate, speechless because of the divine intervention and deprived of any hope of recovery, 30 they praised the Lord who had acted marvelously for his own place. And the temple, which a little while before was full of fear and disturbance, was filled with joy and gladness, now that the Almighty Lord had appeared.

31 Some of He·li·o·dor′us's friends quickly begged Ō·nī′as to call upon the Most High to grant life to one who was lying quite at his last breath. 32 So the high priest, fearing that the king might get the notion that some foul play had been perpetrated by the Jews with regard to He·li·o·dor′us, offered sacrifice for the man's recovery. 33 While the high priest was making an atonement, the same young men appeared again to He·li·o·dor′us dressed in the same clothing, and they stood and said, "Be very grateful to the high priest Ō·nī′as, since for his sake the Lord has granted you your life. 34 And see that you, who have been flogged by heaven, report to all people the majestic power of God." Having said this they vanished.

The Conversion of Heliodorus

35 Then He·li·o·dor′us offered sacrifice to the Lord and made very great vows to the Savior of his life, and having bidden Ō·nī′as farewell, he marched off with his forces to the king. 36 He bore testimony to all concerning the deeds of the supreme God, which he had seen with his own eyes. 37 When the king asked He·li·o·dor′us what sort of person would be suitable to send on another mission to Jerusalem, he replied, 38 "If you have any enemy or plotter against your government, send him there, for you will get him back thoroughly flogged, if he survives at all; for there is certainly some power of God about the place. 39 For he who has his dwelling in heaven watches over that place himself and brings it aid, and he strikes and destroys those who come to do it injury." 40 This was the outcome of the episode of He·li·o·dor′us and the protection of the treasury.

Simon Accuses Onias

4 The previously mentioned Simon, who had informed about the money against[l] his own country, slandered Ō·nī'as, saying that it was he who had incited Hē·li·o·dor'us and had been the real cause of the misfortune. [2] He dared to designate as a plotter against the government the man who was the benefactor of the city, the protector of his compatriots, and a zealot for the laws. [3] When his hatred progressed to such a degree that even murders were committed by one of Simon's approved agents, [4] Ō·nī'as recognized that the rivalry was serious and that Ap·ol·lō'ni·us son of Me·nes'-thē·us,[k] and governor of Coē·le·syr'i·a and Phoe·ni'ci·a, was intensifying the malice of Simon. [5] So he appealed to the king, not accusing his compatriots but having in view the welfare, both public and private, of all the people. [6] For he saw that without the king's attention public affairs could not again reach a peaceful settlement, and that Simon would not stop his folly.

Jason's Reforms
(Cp 1 Macc 1.10–19)

7 When Se·leū'cus died and An·tī'-o·chus, who was called E·piph'a·nēs, succeeded to the kingdom, Jason the brother of Ō·nī'as obtained the high priesthood by corruption, [8] promising the king at an interview[l] three hundred sixty talents of silver, and from another source of revenue eighty talents. [9] In addition to this he promised to pay one hundred fifty more if permission were given to establish by his authority a gymnasium and a body of youth for it, and to enroll the people of Jerusalem as citizens of An'ti·och. [10] When the king assented and Jason[m] came to office, he at once shifted his compatriots over to the Greek way of life.

11 He set aside the existing royal concessions to the Jews, secured through John the father of Eū·pol'e-mus, who went on the mission to establish friendship and alliance with the Romans; and he destroyed the lawful ways of living and introduced new customs contrary to the law. [12] He took delight in establishing a gymnasium right under the citadel, and he induced the noblest of the young men to wear the Greek hat. [13] There was such an extreme of Hellenization and increase in the adoption of foreign ways because of the surpassing wickedness of Jason, who was ungodly and no true[n] high priest, [14] that the priests were no longer intent upon their service at the altar. Despising the sanctuary and neglecting the sacrifices, they hurried to take part in the unlawful proceedings in the wrestling arena after the signal for the discus-throwing, [15] disdaining the honors prized by their ancestors and putting the highest value upon Greek forms of prestige. [16] For this reason heavy disaster overtook them, and those whose ways of living they admired and wished to imitate completely became their enemies and punished them. [17] It is no light thing to show irreverence to the divine laws — a fact that later events will make clear.

Jason Introduces Greek Customs

18 When the quadrennial games were being held at Tȳre and the king was present, [19] the vile Jason sent envoys, chosen as being An·ti·och'i·an citizens from Jerusalem, to carry three hundred silver drachmas for the sacrifice to Hercules. Those who carried the money, however, thought best not to use it for sacrifice, because that was inappropriate, but to expend it for another purpose. [20] So this money was intended by the sender for the sacrifice to Hercules, but by the decision of its carriers it was applied to the construction of triremes.

21 When Ap·ol·lō'ni·us son of Me-nes'thē·us was sent to Egypt for the coronation[o] of Phil·o·mē'tor as king, An·tī'o·chus learned that Phil·o·mē'-tor[m] had become hostile to his government, and he took measures for his own security. Therefore upon arriving at Jop'pa he proceeded to Jerusalem. [22] He was welcomed magnificently by Jason and the city, and ushered in with a blaze of torches and with shouts. Then he marched his army into Phoe-ni'ci·a.

Menelaus Becomes High Priest

23 After a period of three years Jason sent Men·e·lā'us, the brother of the previously mentioned Simon, to carry the money to the king and to complete the records of essential business. [24] But

he, when presented to the king, extolled him with an air of authority, and secured the high priesthood for himself, outbidding Jason by three hundred talents of silver. ²⁵ After receiving the king's orders he returned, possessing no qualification for the high priesthood, but having the hot temper of a cruel tyrant and the rage of a savage wild beast. ²⁶ So Jason, who after supplanting his own brother was supplanted by another man, was driven as a fugitive into the land of Am'mon. ²⁷ Although Men·e·lā'us continued to hold the office, he did not pay regularly any of the money promised to the king. ²⁸ When Sos'tra·tus the captain of the citadel kept requesting payment—for the collection of the revenue was his responsibility—the two of them were summoned by the king on account of this issue. ²⁹ Men·e·lā'us left his own brother Ly̆·sim'a·chus as deputy in the high priesthood, while Sos'-tra·tus left Crā'tēs, the commander of the Cyp'ri·an troops.

The Murder of Onias

30 While such was the state of affairs, it happened that the people of Tar'sus and of Mal'lus revolted because their cities had been given as a present to An·tī'o·chis, the king's concubine. ³¹ So the king went hurriedly to settle the trouble, leaving An·dron'i·cus, a man of high rank, to act as his deputy. ³² But Men·e·lā'us, thinking he had obtained a suitable opportunity, stole some of the gold vessels of the temple and gave them to An·dron'i·cus; other vessels, as it happened, he had sold to Tȳre and the neighboring cities. ³³ When Ō·nī'as became fully aware of these acts, he publicly exposed them, having first withdrawn to a place of sanctuary at Daphne near An'ti·och. ³⁴ Therefore Men·e·lā'us, taking An·dron'i·cus aside, urged him to kill Ō·nī'as. An·dron'i·cusᵖ came to Ō·nī'as, and resorting to treachery, offered him sworn pledges and gave him his right hand; he persuaded him, though still suspicious, to come out from the place of sanctuary; then, with no regard for justice, he immediately put him out of the way.

Andronicus Is Punished

35 For this reason not only Jews, but many also of other nations, were grieved and displeased at the unjust murder of the man. ³⁶ When the king returned from the region of Ci·li'ci·a, the Jews in the city�q appealed to him with regard to the unreasonable murder of Ō·nī'as, and the Greeks shared their hatred of the crime. ³⁷ Therefore An·tī'o·chus was grieved at heart and filled with pity, and wept because of the moderation and good conduct of the deceased. ³⁸ Inflamed with anger, he immediately stripped off his clothes, from An·dron'i·cus, tore off his purple robe, and led him around the whole city to that very place where he had committed the outrage against Ō·nī'as, and there he dispatched the bloodthirsty fellow. The Lord thus repaid him with the punishment he deserved.

Unpopularity of Lysimachus and Menelaus

39 When many acts of sacrilege had been committed in the city by Ly̆·sim'-a·chus with the connivance of Men·e·lā'us, and when report of them had spread abroad, the populace gathered against Ly̆·sim'a·chus, because many of the gold vessels had already been stolen. ⁴⁰ Since the crowds were becoming aroused and filled with anger, Ly̆·sim'a·chus armed about three thousand men and launched an unjust attack, under the leadership of a certain Au·rā'nus, a man advanced in years and no less advanced in folly. ⁴¹ But when the Jewsʳ became aware that Ly̆·sim'a·chus was attacking them, some picked up stones, some blocks of wood, and others took handfuls of the ashes that were lying around, and threw them in wild confusion at Ly̆·sim'a·chus and his men. ⁴² As a result, they wounded many of them, and killed some, and put all the rest to flight; the temple robber himself they killed close by the treasury.

43 Charges were brought against Men·e·lā'us about this incident. ⁴⁴ When the king came to Tȳre, three men sent by the senate presented the case before him. ⁴⁵ But Men·e·lā'us, already as good as beaten, promised a substantial bribe to Ptol'e·my son of Dor·ym'e·nēs to win over the king. ⁴⁶ Therefore Ptol'e·my, taking the king aside into a colonnade as if for refreshment, induced the king to change his mind. ⁴⁷ Men·e·lā'us, the cause of all the trouble, he acquitted of the charges against him, while he sentenced to

ᵖ Gk *He*   q Or *in each city*   ʳ Gk *they*

death those unfortunate men, who would have been freed uncondemned if they had pleaded even before Scyth′i·ans. 48 And so those who had spoken for the city and the villages[s] and the holy vessels quickly suffered the unjust penalty. 49 Therefore even the Tў′ri·ans, showing their hatred of the crime, provided magnificently for their funeral. 50 But Men·e·lā′us, because of the greed of those in power, remained in office, growing in wickedness, having become the chief plotter against his compatriots.

Jason Tries to Regain Control

5 About this time An·tī′o·chus made his second invasion of Egypt. 2 And it happened that, for almost forty days, there appeared over all the city golden-clad cavalry charging through the air, in companies fully armed with lances and drawn swords — 3 troops of cavalry drawn up, attacks and counterattacks made on this side and on that, brandishing of shields, massing of spears, hurling of missiles, the flash of golden trappings, and armor of all kinds. 4 Therefore everyone prayed that the apparition might prove to have been a good omen.

5 When a false rumor arose that An·tī′o·chus was dead, Jason took no fewer than a thousand men and suddenly made an assault on the city. When the troops on the wall had been forced back and at last the city was being taken, Men·e·lā′us took refuge in the citadel. 6 But Jason kept relentlessly slaughtering his compatriots, not realizing that success at the cost of one's kindred is the greatest misfortune, but imagining that he was setting up trophies of victory over enemies and not over compatriots. 7 He did not, however, gain control of the government; in the end he got only disgrace from his conspiracy, and fled again into the country of the Am′mon·ites. 8 Finally he met a miserable end. Accused[t] before Ar′e·tas the ruler of the A′rabs, fleeing from city to city, pursued by everyone, hated as a rebel against the laws, and abhorred as the executioner of his country and his compatriots, he was cast ashore in Egypt. 9 There he who had driven many from their own country into exile died in exile, having embarked to go to the Lac·e·dae·mō′ni·ans in hope of finding protection because of their kinship. 10 He who had cast out many to lie unburied had no one to mourn for him; he had no funeral of any sort and no place in the tomb of his ancestors.

11 When news of what had happened reached the king, he took it to mean that Judea was in revolt. So, raging inwardly, he left Egypt and took the city by storm. 12 He commanded his soldiers to cut down relentlessly everyone they met and to kill those who went into their houses. 13 Then there was massacre of young and old, destruction of boys, women, and children, and slaughter of young girls and infants. 14 Within the total of three days eighty thousand were destroyed, forty thousand in hand-to-hand fighting, and as many were sold into slavery as were killed.

Pillage of the Temple
(1 Macc 1.20–40)

15 Not content with this, An·tī′o·chus[u] dared to enter the most holy temple in all the world, guided by Men·e·lā′us, who had become a traitor both to the laws and to his country. 16 He took the holy vessels with his polluted hands, and swept away with profane hands the votive offerings that other kings had made to enhance the glory and honor of the place. 17 An·tī′o·chus was elated in spirit, and did not perceive that the Lord was angered for a little while because of the sins of those who lived in the city, and that this was the reason he was disregarding the holy place. 18 But if it had not happened that they were involved in many sins, this man would have been flogged and turned back from his rash act as soon as he came forward, just as Hē·li·o·dor′us had been, whom King Se·leu′cus sent to inspect the treasury. 19 But the Lord did not choose the nation for the sake of the holy place, but the place for the sake of the nation. 20 Therefore the place itself shared in the misfortunes that befell the nation and afterward participated in its benefits; and what was forsaken in the wrath of the Almighty was restored again in all its glory when the great Lord became reconciled.

21 So An·tī′o·chus carried off eighteen hundred talents from the temple, and hurried away to An′ti·och, thinking in his arrogance that he could sail

---

[s] Other ancient authorities read *the people*   [t] Cn: Gk *Imprisoned*   [u] Gk *he*

on the land and walk on the sea, because his mind was elated. [22] He left governors to oppress the people: at Jerusalem, Philip, by birth a Phryg'i·an and in character more barbarous than the man who appointed him; [23] and at Ger'i·zim, An·dron'i·cus; and besides these Men·e·lā'us, who lorded it over his compatriots worse than the others did. In his malice toward the Jewish citizens,[v] [24] An·ti'o·chus[w] sent Ap·ol·lō'ni·us, the captain of the My'si·ans, with an army of twenty-two thousand, and commanded him to kill all the grown men and to sell the women and boys as slaves. [25] When this man arrived in Jerusalem, he pretended to be peaceably disposed and waited until the holy sabbath day; then, finding the Jews not at work, he ordered his troops to parade under arms. [26] He put to the sword all those who came out to see them, then rushed into the city with his armed warriors and killed great numbers of people.

27 But Judas Mac·ca·bē'us, with about nine others, got away to the wilderness, and kept himself and his companions alive in the mountains as wild animals do; they continued to live on what grew wild, so that they might not share in the defilement.

The Suppression of Judaism
(1 Macc 1.41–64)

6 Not long after this, the king sent an Athenian[x] senator[y] to compel the Jews to forsake the laws of their ancestors and no longer to live by the laws of God; [2] also to pollute the temple in Jerusalem and to call it the temple of Olympian Zeūs, and to call the one in Ger'i·zim the temple of Zeūs-the-Friend-of-Strangers, as did the people who lived in that place.

3 Harsh and utterly grievous was the onslaught of evil. [4] For the temple was filled with debauchery and reveling by the Gentiles, who dallied with prostitutes and had intercourse with women within the sacred precincts, and besides brought in things for sacrifice that were unfit. [5] The altar was covered with abominable offerings that were forbidden by the laws. [6] People could neither keep the sabbath, nor observe the festivals of their ancestors, nor so much as confess themselves to be Jews.

7 On the monthly celebration of the king's birthday, the Jews[z] were taken, under bitter constraint, to partake of the sacrifices; and when a festival of Dī·o·nȳ'sus was celebrated, they were compelled to wear wreathes of ivy and to walk in the procession in honor of Dī·o·nȳ'sus. [8] At the suggestion of the people of Ptol·e·mā'is[a] a decree was issued to the neighboring Greek cities that they should adopt the same policy toward the Jews and make them partake of the sacrifices, [9] and should kill those who did not choose to change over to Greek customs. One could see, therefore, the misery that had come upon them. [10] For example, two women were brought in for having circumcised their children. They publicly paraded them around the city, with their babies hanging at their breasts, and then hurled them down headlong from the wall. [11] Others who had assembled in the caves nearby, in order to observe the seventh day secretly, were betrayed to Philip and were all burned together, because their piety kept them from defending themselves, in view of their regard for that most holy day.

Providential Significance of the Persecution

12 Now I urge those who read this book not to be depressed by such calamities, but to recognize that these punishments were designed not to destroy but to discipline our people. [13] In fact, it is a sign of great kindness not to let the impious alone for long, but to punish them immediately. [14] For in the case of the other nations the Lord waits patiently to punish them until they have reached the full measure of their sins; but he does not deal in this way with us, [15] in order that he may not take vengeance on us afterward when our sins have reached their height. [16] Therefore he never withdraws his mercy from us. Although he disciplines us with calamities, he does not forsake his own people. [17] Let what we have said serve as a reminder; we must go on briefly with the story.

[v] Or *worse than the others did in his malice toward the Jewish citizens*　[w] Gk *he*　[x] Other ancient authorities read *Antiochian*　[y] Or *Geron an Athenian*　[z] Gk *they*　[a] Cn: Gk *suggestion of the Ptolemies (or of Ptolemy)*

2 MACCABEES

The Martyrdom of Eleazar
(Lev 11.7–8; 4 Macc 5–7)

18 El·e·ā′zar, one of the scribes in high position, a man now advanced in age and of noble presence, was being forced to open his mouth to eat swine's flesh. 19 But he, welcoming death with honor rather than life with pollution, went up to the rack of his own accord, spitting out the flesh, 20 as all ought to go who have the courage to refuse things that it is not right to taste, even for the natural love of life.

21 Those who were in charge of that unlawful sacrifice took the man aside because of their long acquaintance with him, and privately urged him to bring meat of his own providing, proper for him to use, and to pretend that he was eating the flesh of the sacrificial meal that had been commanded by the king, 22 so that by doing this he might be saved from death, and be treated kindly on account of his old friendship with them. 23 But making a high resolve, worthy of his years and the dignity of his old age and the gray hairs that he had reached with distinction and his excellent life even from childhood, and moreover according to the holy God-given law, he declared himself quickly, telling them to send him to Hades.

24 "Such pretense is not worthy of our time of life," he said, "for many of the young might suppose that El·e·ā′zar in his ninetieth year had gone over to an alien religion, 25 and through my pretense, for the sake of living a brief moment longer, they would be led astray because of me, while I defile and disgrace my old age. 26 Even if for the present I would avoid the punishment of mortals, yet whether I live or die I shall not escape the hands of the Almighty. 27 Therefore, by bravely giving up my life now, I will show myself worthy of my old age 28 and leave to the young a noble example of how to die a good death willingly and nobly for the revered and holy laws."

When he had said this, he went[b] at once to the rack. 29 Those who a little before had acted toward him with goodwill now changed to ill will, because the words he had uttered were in their opinion sheer madness.[c] 30 When he was about to die under the blows, he groaned aloud and said: "It is clear to the Lord in his holy knowledge that, though I might have been saved from death, I am enduring terrible sufferings in my body under this beating, but in my soul I am glad to suffer these things because I fear him."

31 So in this way he died, leaving in his death an example of nobility and a memorial of courage, not only to the young but to the great body of his nation.

The Martyrdom of Seven Brothers
(4 Macc 8–18)

7 It happened also that seven brothers and their mother were arrested and were being compelled by the king, under torture with whips and thongs, to partake of unlawful swine's flesh. 2 One of them, acting as their spokesman, said, "What do you intend to ask and learn from us? For we are ready to die rather than transgress the laws of our ancestors."

3 The king fell into a rage, and gave orders to have pans and caldrons heated. 4 These were heated immediately, and he commanded that the tongue of their spokesman be cut out and that they scalp him and cut off his hands and feet, while the rest of the brothers and the mother looked on. 5 When he was utterly helpless, the king[d] ordered them to take him to the fire, still breathing, and to fry him in a pan. The smoke from the pan spread widely, but the brothers[e] and their mother encouraged one another to die nobly, saying, 6 "The Lord God is watching over us and in truth has compassion on us, as Moses declared in his song that bore witness against the people to their faces, when he said, 'And he will have compassion on his servants.'"[f]

7 After the first brother had died in this way, they brought forward the second for their sport. They tore off the skin of his head with the hair, and asked him, "Will you eat rather than have your body punished limb by limb?" 8 He replied in the language of his ancestors and said to them, "No." Therefore he in turn underwent tortures as the first brother had done. 9 And when he was at his last breath, he said, "You accursed wretch, you dismiss us from this present life, but the King of the universe will raise us

---

[b] Other ancient authorities read *was dragged*   [c] Meaning of Gk uncertain   [d] Gk *he*   [e] Gk *they*   [f] Gk *slaves*

up to an everlasting renewal of life, because we have died for his laws."

10 After him, the third was the victim of their sport. When it was demanded, he quickly put out his tongue and courageously stretched forth his hands, 11 and said nobly, "I got these from Heaven, and because of his laws I disdain them, and from him I hope to get them back again." 12 As a result the king himself and those with him were astonished at the young man's spirit, for he regarded his sufferings as nothing.

13 After he too had died, they maltreated and tortured the fourth in the same way. 14 When he was near death, he said, "One cannot but choose to die at the hands of mortals and to cherish the hope God gives of being raised again by him. But for you there will be no resurrection to life!"

15 Next they brought forward the fifth and maltreated him. 16 But he looked at the king,g and said, "Because you have authority among mortals, though you also are mortal, you do what you please. But do not think that God has forsaken our people. 17 Keep on, and see how his mighty power will torture you and your descendants!"

18 After him they brought forward the sixth. And when he was about to die, he said, "Do not deceive yourself in vain. For we are suffering these things on our own account, because of our sins against our own God. Thereforeh astounding things have happened. 19 But do not think that you will go unpunished for having tried to fight against God!"

20 The mother was especially admirable and worthy of honorable memory. Although she saw her seven sons perish within a single day, she bore it with good courage because of her hope in the Lord. 21 She encouraged each of them in the language of their ancestors. Filled with a noble spirit, she reinforced her woman's reasoning with a man's courage, and said to them, 22 "I do not know how you came into being in my womb. It was not I who gave you life and breath, nor I who set in order the elements within each of you. 23 Therefore the Creator of the world, who shaped the beginning of humankind and devised the origin of all things, will in his mercy give life and breath back to you again, since you now forget yourselves for the sake of his laws."

24 Antiochus felt that he was being treated with contempt, and he was suspicious of her reproachful tone. The youngest brother being still alive, Antiochusi not only appealed to him in words, but promised with oaths that he would make him rich and enviable if he would turn from the ways of his ancestors, and that he would take him for his Friend and entrust him with public affairs. 25 Since the young man would not listen to him at all, the king called the mother to him and urged her to advise the youth to save himself. 26 After much urging on his part, she undertook to persuade her son. 27 But, leaning close to him, she spoke in their native language as follows, deriding the cruel tyrant: "My son, have pity on me. I carried you nine months in my womb, and nursed you for three years, and have reared you and brought you up to this point in your life, and have taken care of you.j 28 I beg you, my child, to look at the heaven and the earth and see everything that is in them, and recognize that God did not make them out of things that existed.k And in the same way the human race came into being. 29 Do not fear this butcher, but prove worthy of your brothers. Accept death, so that in God's mercy I may get you back again along with your brothers."

30 While she was still speaking, the young man said, "What are youl waiting for? I will not obey the king's command, but I obey the command of the law that was given to our ancestors through Moses. 31 But you,m who have contrived all sorts of evil against the Hebrews, will certainly not escape the hands of God. 32 For we are suffering because of our own sins. 33 And if our living Lord is angry for a little while, to rebuke and discipline us, he will again be reconciled with his own servants.n 34 But you, unholy wretch, you most defiled of all mortals, do not be elated in vain and puffed up by uncertain hopes, when you raise your hand against the children of heaven. 35 You

gGk at him   hLat: Other ancient authorities lack Therefore   iGk he   jOr have borne the burden of your education   kOr God made them out of things that did not exist   lThe Gk here for you is plural   mThe Gk here for you is singular   nGk slaves have not yet escaped the judgment of the almighty, all-seeing God. 36 For our brothers after enduring a brief suffering have drunk[o] of ever-flowing life, under God's covenant; but you, by the judgment of God, will receive just punishment for your arrogance. 37 I, like my brothers, give up body and life for the laws of our ancestors, appealing to God to show mercy soon to our nation and by trials and plagues to make you confess that he alone is God, 38 and through me and my brothers to bring to an end the wrath of the Almighty that has justly fallen on our whole nation."

39 The king fell into a rage, and handled him worse than the others, being exasperated at his scorn. 40 So he died in his integrity, putting his whole trust in the Lord.

41 Last of all, the mother died, after her sons.

42 Let this be enough, then, about the eating of sacrifices and the extreme tortures.

The Revolt of Judas Maccabeus
(1 Macc 3.1–26)

8 Meanwhile Judas, who was also called Mac·ca·bē'us, and his companions secretly entered the villages and summoned their kindred and enlisted those who had continued in the Jewish faith, and so they gathered about six thousand. 2 They implored the Lord to look upon the people who were oppressed by all; and to have pity on the temple that had been profaned by the godless; 3 to have mercy on the city that was being destroyed and about to be leveled to the ground; to hearken to the blood that cried out to him; 4 to remember also the lawless destruction of the innocent babies and the blasphemies committed against his name; and to show his hatred of evil.

5 As soon as Mac·ca·bē'us got his army organized, the Gentiles could not withstand him, for the wrath of the Lord had turned to mercy. 6 Coming without warning, he would set fire to towns and villages. He captured strategic positions and put to flight not a few of the enemy. 7 He found the nights most advantageous for such attacks. And talk of his valor spread everywhere.

8 When Philip saw that the man was gaining ground little by little, and that he was pushing ahead with more

frequent successes, he wrote to Ptol'e·my, the governor of Coë·le·syr'i·a and Phoe·ni'ci·a, to come to the aid of the king's government. 9 Then Ptol'e·my[p] promptly appointed Ni·cā'nor son of Pa·trō'clus, one of the king's chief[q] Friends, and sent him, in command of no fewer than twenty thousand Gentiles of all nations, to wipe out the whole race of Judea. He associated with him Gor'gi·as, a general and a man of experience in military service. 10 Ni·cā'nor determined to make up for the king the tribute due to the Romans, two thousand talents, by selling the captured Jews into slavery. 11 So he immediately sent to the towns on the seacoast, inviting them to buy Jewish slaves and promising to hand over ninety slaves for a talent, not expecting the judgment from the Almighty that was about to overtake him.

Preparation for Battle
(1 Macc 3.38–53)

12 Word came to Judas concerning Ni·cā'nor's invasion; and when he told his companions of the arrival of the army, 13 those who were cowardly and distrustful of God's justice ran off and got away. 14 Others sold all their remaining property, and at the same time implored the Lord to rescue those who had been sold by the ungodly Ni·cā'nor before he ever met them, 15 if not for their own sake, then for the sake of the covenants made with their ancestors, and because he had called them by his holy and glorious name. 16 But Mac·ca·bē'us gathered his forces together, to the number six thousand, and exhorted them not to be frightened by the enemy and not to fear the great multitude of Gentiles who were wickedly coming against them, but to fight nobly, 17 keeping before their eyes the lawless outrage that the Gentiles[r] had committed against the holy place, and the torture of the derided city, and besides, the overthrow of their ancestral way of life. 18 "For they trust to arms and acts of daring," he said, "but we trust in the Almighty God, who is able with a single nod to strike down those who are coming against us, and even, if necessary, the whole world."

19 Moreover, he told them of the

o Cn: Gk fallen   p Gk he   q Gk one of the first   r Gk they occasions when help came to their ancestors; how, in the time of Sen·nach'e-rib, when one hundred eighty-five thousand perished, [20] and the time of the battle against the Galatians that took place in Babylonia, when eight thousand Jews[s] fought along with four thousand Mac·e·dō'ni·ans; yet when the Mac·e·dō'ni·ans were hard pressed, the eight thousand, by the help that came to them from heaven, destroyed one hundred twenty thousand Galatians[t] and took a great amount of booty.

Judas Defeats Nicanor
(1 Macc 3.54 – 4.25)

21 With these words he filled them with courage and made them ready to die for their laws and their country; then he divided his army into four parts. [22] He appointed his brothers also, Simon and Joseph and Jonathan, each to command a division, putting fifteen hundred men under each. [23] Besides, he appointed El·ē·ā'zar to read aloud[u] from the holy book, and gave the watchword, "The help of God"; then, leading the first division himself, he joined battle with Nī·cā'nor.

24 With the Almighty as their ally, they killed more than nine thousand of the enemy, and wounded and disabled most of Nī·cā'nor's army, and forced them all to flee. [25] They captured the money of those who had come to buy them as slaves. After pursuing them for some distance, they were obliged to return because the hour was late. [26] It was the day before the sabbath, and for that reason they did not continue their pursuit. [27] When they had collected the arms of the enemy and stripped them of their spoils, they kept the sabbath, giving great praise and thanks to the Lord, who had preserved them for that day and allotted it to them as the beginning of mercy. [28] After the sabbath they gave some of the spoils to those who had been tortured and to the widows and orphans, and distributed the rest among themselves and their children. [29] When they had done this, they made common supplication and implored the merciful Lord to be wholly reconciled with his servants.[v]

Judas Defeats Timothy and Bacchides

30 In encounters with the forces of Timothy and Bac'chi·dēs they killed more than twenty thousand of them

and got possession of some exceedingly high strongholds, and they divided a very large amount of plunder, giving to those who had been tortured and to the orphans and widows, and also to the aged, shares equal to their own. [31] They collected the arms of the enemy,[w] and carefully stored all of them in strategic places; the rest of the spoils they carried to Jerusalem. [32] They killed the commander of Timothy's forces, a most wicked man, and one who had greatly troubled the Jews. [33] While they were celebrating the victory in the city of their ancestors, they burned those who had set fire to the sacred gates, Cal·lis'the·nēs and some others, who had fled into one little house; so these received the proper reward for their impiety.[x]

34 The thrice-accursed Nī·cā'nor, who had brought the thousand merchants to buy the Jews, [35] having been humbled with the help of the Lord by opponents whom he regarded as of the least account, took off his splendid uniform and made his way alone like a runaway slave across the country until he reached An'ti·och, having succeeded chiefly in the destruction of his own army! [36] So he who had undertaken to secure tribute for the Romans by the capture of the people of Jerusalem proclaimed that the Jews had a Defender, and that therefore the Jews were invulnerable, because they followed the laws ordained by him.

The Last Campaign of Antiochus Epiphanes
(1 Macc 6.1–7; 2 Macc 1.11–17)

9 About that time, as it happened, An·tī'o·chus had retreated in disorder from the region of Persia. [2] He had entered the city called Per·sep'o-lis and attempted to rob the temples and control the city. Therefore the people rushed to the rescue with arms, and An·tī'o·chus and his army were defeated,[y] with the result that An·tī'o-chus was put to flight by the inhabitants and beat a shameful retreat. [3] While he was in Ec·bat'a·na, news came to him of what had happened to Nī·cā'nor and the forces of Timothy. [4] Transported with rage, he conceived the idea of turning upon the Jews the

s Gk lacks Jews   t Gk lacks Galatians
u Meaning of Gk uncertain   v Gk slaves
w Gk their arms   x Meaning of Gk
uncertain   y Gk they were defeated

injury done by those who had put him to flight; so he ordered his charioteer to drive without stopping until he completed the journey. But the judgment of heaven rode with him! For in his arrogance he said, "When I get there I will make Jerusalem a cemetery of Jews."

5 But the all-seeing Lord, the God of Israel, struck him with an incurable and invisible blow. As soon as he stopped speaking he was seized with a pain in his bowels, for which there was no relief, and with sharp internal tortures — 6 and that very justly, for he had tortured the bowels of others with many and strange inflictions. 7 Yet he did not in any way stop his insolence, but was even more filled with arrogance, breathing fire in his rage against the Jews, and giving orders to drive even faster. And so it came about that he fell out of his chariot as it was rushing along, and the fall was so hard as to torture every limb of his body. 8 Thus he who only a little while before had thought in his superhuman arrogance that he could command the waves of the sea, and had imagined that he could weigh the high mountains in a balance, was brought down to earth and carried in a litter, making the power of God manifest to all. 9 And so the ungodly man's body swarmed with worms, and while he was still living in anguish and pain, his flesh rotted away, and because of the stench the whole army felt revulsion at his decay. 10 Because of his intolerable stench no one was able to carry the man who a little while before had thought that he could touch the stars of heaven. 11 Then it was that, broken in spirit, he began to lose much of his arrogance and to come to his senses under the scourge of God, for he was tortured with pain every moment. 12 And when he could not endure his own stench, he uttered these words, "It is right to be subject to God; mortals should not think that they are equal to God."z

Antiochus Makes a Promise to God
(1 Macc 6.8–17)

13 Then the abominable fellow made a vow to the Lord, who would no longer have mercy on him, stating 14 that the holy city, which he was hurrying to level to the ground and to make a cemetery, he was now declaring to be free; 15 and the Jews, whom he had not considered worth burying but had planned to throw out with their children for the wild animals and for the birds to eat, he would make, all of them, equal to citizens of Athens 16 and the holy sanctuary, which he had formerly plundered, he would adorn with the finest offerings; and all the holy vessels he would give back many times over; and the expenses incurred for the sacrifices he would provide from his own revenues; 17 and in addition to all this he also would become a Jew and would visit every inhabited place to proclaim the power of God. 18 But when his sufferings did not in any way abate, for the judgment of God had justly come upon him, he gave up all hope for himself and wrote to the Jews the following letter, in the form of a supplication. This was its content:

Antiochus's Letter and Death

19 "To his worthy Jewish citizens An·ti′o·chus their king and general sends hearty greetings and good wishes for their health and prosperity. 20 If you and your children are well and your affairs are as you wish, I am glad. As my hope is in heaven, 21 I remember with affection your esteem and good will. On my way back from the region of Persia I suffered an annoying illness, and I have deemed it necessary to take thought for the general security of all. 22 I do not despair of my condition, for I have good hope of recovering from my illness, 23 but I observed that my father, on the occasions when he made expeditions into the upper country, appointed his successor, 24 so that, if anything unexpected happened or any unwelcome news came, the people throughout the realm would not be troubled, for they would know to whom the government was left. 25 Moreover, I understand how the princes along the borders and the neighbors of my kingdom keep watching for opportunities and waiting to see what will happen. So I have appointed my son An·ti′o·chus to be king, whom I have often entrusted and commended to most of you when I hurried off to the upper provinces; and I have written to him what is written here. 26 I therefore urge and beg you to remember the public and private services rendered to you and to maintain

z Or *not think thoughts proper only to God*

your present goodwill, each of you, toward me and my son. ²⁷For I am sure that he will follow my policy and will treat you with moderation and kindness."

28 So the murderer and blasphemer, having endured the more intense suffering, such as he had inflicted on others, came to the end of his life by a most pitiable fate, among the mountains in a strange land. ²⁹And Philip, one of his courtiers, took his body home; then, fearing the son of An·tī'o·chus, he withdrew to Ptol'e·my Phil·o·mē'tor in Egypt.

Purification of the Temple
(1 Macc 4.36–61)

10 Now Mac·ca·bē'us and his followers, the Lord leading them on, recovered the temple and the city; ²they tore down the altars that had been built in the public square by the foreigners, and also destroyed the sacred precincts. ³They purified the sanctuary, and made another altar of sacrifice; then, striking fire out of flint, they offered sacrifices, after a lapse of two years, and they offered incense and lighted lamps and set out the bread of the Presence. ⁴When they had done this, they fell prostrate and implored the Lord that they might never again fall into such misfortunes, but that, if they should ever sin, they might be disciplined by him with forbearance and not be handed over to blasphemous and barbarous nations. ⁵It happened that on the same day on which the sanctuary had been profaned by the foreigners, the purification of the sanctuary took place, that is, on the twenty-fifth day of the same month, which is Chis'lev. ⁶They celebrated it for eight days with rejoicing, in the manner of the festival of booths, remembering how not long before, during the festival of booths, they had been wandering in the mountains and caves like wild animals. ⁷Therefore, carrying ivy-wreathed wands and beautiful branches and also fronds of palm, they offered hymns of thanksgiving to him who had given success to the purifying of his own holy place. ⁸They decreed by public edict, ratified by vote, that the whole nation of the Jews should observe these days every year.

9 Such then was the end of An·tī'o·chus, who was called E·piph'a·nēs.

Accession of Antiochus Eupator
(1 Macc 6.17)

10 Now we will tell what took place under An·tī'o·chus Eū'pa·tor, who was the son of that ungodly man, and will give a brief summary of the principal calamities of the wars. ¹¹This man, when he succeeded to the kingdom, appointed one Lys'i·as to have charge of the government and to be chief governor of Coē·le·syr'i·a and Phoe·ni'ci·a. ¹²Ptol'e·my, who was called Mā'-cron, took the lead in showing justice to the Jews because of the wrong that had been done to them, and attempted to maintain peaceful relations with them. ¹³As a result he was accused before Eū'pa·tor by the king's Friends. He heard himself called a traitor at every turn, because he had abandoned Cyprus, which Phil·o·mē'tor had entrusted to him, and had gone over to An·tī'o·chus E·piph'a·nēs. Unable to command the respect due his office,ᵃ he took poison and ended his life.

Campaign in Idumea
(1 Macc 5.1–8)

14 When Gor'gi·as became governor of the region, he maintained a force of mercenaries, and at every turn kept attacking the Jews. ¹⁵Besides this, the Id·ū·mē'ans, who had control of important strongholds, were harassing the Jews; they received those who were banished from Jerusalem, and endeavored to keep up the war. ¹⁶But Mac·ca·bē'us and his forces, after making solemn supplication and imploring God to fight on their side, rushed to the strongholds of the Id·ū·mē'ans. ¹⁷Attacking them vigorously, they gained possession of the places, and beat off all who fought upon the wall, and slaughtered those whom they encountered, killing no fewer than twenty thousand.

18 When at least nine thousand took refuge in two very strong towers well equipped to withstand a siege, ¹⁹Mac·ca·bē'us left Simon and Joseph, and also Zac·chaē'us and his troops, a force sufficient to besiege them; and he himself set off for places where he was more urgently needed. ²⁰But those with Simon, who were money-hungry, were bribed by some of those who were in the towers, and on receiving seventy thousand drachmas let some

ᵃCn: Meaning of Gk uncertain

of them slip away. [21] When word of what had happened came to Mac·ca·bē'us, he gathered the leaders of the people, and accused these men of having sold their kindred for money by setting their enemies free to fight against them. [22] Then he killed these men who had turned traitor, and immediately captured the two towers. [23] Having success at arms in everything he undertook, he destroyed more than twenty thousand in the two strongholds.

Judas Defeats Timothy

24 Now Timothy, who had been defeated by the Jews before, gathered a tremendous force of mercenaries and collected the cavalry from Asia in no small number. He came on, intending to take Judea by storm. [25] As he drew near, Mac·ca·bē'us and his men sprinkled dust on their heads and girded their loins with sackcloth, in supplication to God. [26] Falling upon the steps before the altar, they implored him to be gracious to them and to be an enemy to their enemies and an adversary to their adversaries, as the law declares. [27] And rising from their prayer they took up their arms and advanced a considerable distance from the city; and when they came near the enemy they halted. [28] Just as dawn was breaking, the two armies joined battle, the one having as pledge of success and victory not only their valor but also their reliance on the Lord, while the other made rage their leader in the fight.

29 When the battle became fierce, there appeared to the enemy from heaven five resplendent men on horses with golden bridles, and they were leading the Jews. [30] Two of them took Mac·ca·bē'us between them, and shielding him with their own armor and weapons, they kept him from being wounded. They showered arrows and thunderbolts on the enemy, so that, confused and blinded, they were thrown into disorder and cut to pieces. [31] Twenty thousand five hundred were slaughtered, besides six hundred cavalry.

32 Timothy himself fled to a stronghold called Ga·zā'ra, especially well garrisoned, where Chaēr'e·as was commander. [33] Then Mac·ca·bē'us and his men were glad, and they besieged the fort for four days. [34] The men within, relying on the strength of the

place, kept blaspheming terribly and uttering wicked words. [35] But at dawn of the fifth day, twenty young men in the army of Mac·ca·bē'us, fired with anger because of the blasphemies, bravely stormed the wall and with savage fury cut down everyone they met. [36] Others who came up in the same way wheeled around against the defenders and set fire to the towers; they kindled fires and burned the blasphemers alive. Others broke open the gates and let in the rest of the force, and they occupied the city. [37] They killed Timothy, who was hiding in a cistern, and his brother Chaēr'e·as, and Ap·ol·loph'a·nēs. [38] When they had accomplished these things, with hymns and thanksgivings they blessed the Lord who shows great kindness to Israel and gives them the victory.

Lysias Besieges Beth-zur
(1 Macc 4.26–35)

11 Very soon after this, Lys'i·as the king's guardian and kinsman, who was in charge of the government, being vexed at what had happened, [2] gathered about eighty thousand infantry and all his cavalry and came against the Jews. He intended to make the city a home for Greeks, [3] and to levy tribute on the temple as he did on the sacred places of the other nations, and to put up the high priesthood for sale every year. [4] He took no account whatever of the power of God, but was elated with his ten thousands of infantry, and his thousands of cavalry, and his eighty elephants. [5] Invading Judea, he approached Beth-zur, which was a fortified place about five stadia[b] from Jerusalem, and pressed it hard.

6 When Mac·ca·bē'us and his men got word that Lys'i·as[c] was besieging the strongholds, they and all the people, with lamentations and tears, prayed the Lord to send a good angel to save Israel. [7] Mac·ca·bē'us himself was the first to take up arms, and he urged the others to risk their lives with him to aid their kindred. Then they eagerly rushed off together. [8] And there, while they were still near Jerusalem, a horseman appeared at their head, clothed in white and brandishing weapons of gold. [9] And together they all praised the merciful God, and were strengthened in heart, ready to assail

[b] Meaning of Gk uncertain   [c] Gk he

not only humans but the wildest animals or walls of iron. ¹⁰They advanced in battle order, having their heavenly ally, for the Lord had mercy on them. ¹¹They hurled themselves like lions against the enemy, and laid low eleven thousand of them and sixteen hundred cavalry, and forced all the rest to flee. ¹²Most of them got away stripped and wounded, and Lys′i·as himself escaped by disgraceful flight.

Lysias Makes Peace with the Jews
(1 Macc 6.55–63)

13 As he was not without intelligence, he pondered over the defeat that had befallen him, and realized that the Hebrews were invincible because the mighty God fought on their side. So he sent to them ¹⁴and persuaded them to settle everything on just terms, promising that he would persuade the king, constraining him to be their friend.ᵈ ¹⁵Mac·ca·bē′us, having regard for the common good, agreed to all that Lys′i·as urged. For the king granted every request in behalf of the Jews which Mac·ca·bē′us delivered to Lys′i·as in writing.

16 The letter written to the Jews by Lys′i·as was to this effect:

"Lys′i·as to the people of the Jews, greetings. ¹⁷John and Ab′sa·lom, who were sent by you, have delivered your signed communication and have asked about the matters indicated in it. ¹⁸I have informed the king of everything that needed to be brought before him, and he has agreed to what was possible. ¹⁹If you will maintain your goodwill toward the government, I will endeavor in the future to help promote your welfare. ²⁰And concerning such matters and their details, I have ordered these men and my representatives to confer with you. ²¹Farewell. The one hundred forty-eighth year,ᵉ Di·os·co·rin′thi·us twenty-fourth."

22 The king's letter ran thus:

"King An·ti′o·chus to his brother Lys′i·as, greetings. ²³Now that our father has gone on to the gods, we desire that the subjects of the kingdom be undisturbed in caring for their own affairs. ²⁴We have heard that the Jews do not consent to our father's change to Greek customs, but prefer their own way of living and ask that their own customs be allowed them. ²⁵Accordingly, since we choose that this nation also should be free from disturbance, our decision is that their temple be restored to them and that they shall live according to the customs of their ancestors. ²⁶You will do well, therefore, to send word to them and give them pledges of friendship, so that they may know our policy and be of good cheer and go on happily in the conduct of their own affairs."

27 To the nation the king's letter was as follows:

"King An·ti′o·chus to the senate of the Jews and to the other Jews, greetings. ²⁸If you are well, it is as we desire. We also are in good health. ²⁹Men·e·lā′us has informed us that you wish to return home and look after your own affairs. ³⁰Therefore those who go home by the thirtieth of Xan′thi·cus will have our pledge of friendship and full permission ³¹for the Jews to enjoy their own food and laws, just as formerly, and none of them shall be molested in any way for what may have been done in ignorance. ³²And I have also sent Men·e·lā′us to encourage you. ³³Farewell. The one hundred forty-eighth year,ᵉ Xan′thi·cus fifteenth."

34 The Romans also sent them a letter, which read thus:

"Quin′tus Mem′mi·us and Titus Mā′ni·us, envoys of the Romans, to the people of the Jews, greetings. ³⁵With regard to what Lys′i·as the kinsman of the king has granted you, we also give consent. ³⁶But as to the matters that he decided are to be referred to the king, as soon as you have considered them, send some one promptly so that we may make proposals appropriate for you. For we are on our way to An′ti·och. ³⁷Therefore make haste and send messengers so that we may have your judgment. ³⁸Farewell. The one hundred forty-eighth year,ᵉ Xan′thi·cus fifteenth."

Incidents at Joppa and Jamnia

12 When this agreement had been reached, Lys′i·as returned to the king, and the Jews went about their farming.

2 But some of the governors in various places, Timothy and Ap·ol·lō′ni·us son of Gen·naē′us, as well as Hī·e·ron′y·mus and Dem′o·phon, and in addition to these Nī·cā′nor the governor of Cyprus, would not let them live quietly and in peace. ³And the people of

ᵈMeaning of Gk uncertain   ᵉ164 B.C.

Jop'pa did so ungodly a deed as this: they invited the Jews who lived among them to embark, with their wives and children, on boats that they had provided, as though there were no ill will to the Jews;[f] 4 and this was done by public vote of the city. When they accepted, because they wished to live peaceably and suspected nothing, the people of Jop'pa[g] took them out to sea and drowned them, at least two hundred. 5 When Judas heard of the cruelty visited on his compatriots, he gave orders to his men 6 and, calling upon God, the righteous judge, attacked the murderers of his kindred. He set fire to the harbor by night, burned the boats, and massacred those who had taken refuge there. 7 Then, because the city's gates were closed, he withdrew, intending to come again and root out the whole community of Jop'pa. 8 But learning that the people in Jam'ni·a meant in the same way to wipe out the Jews who were living among them, 9 he attacked the Jam'nites by night and set fire to the harbor and the fleet, so that the glow of the light was seen in Jerusalem, thirty miles[h] distant.

The Campaign in Gilead
(1 Macc 5.9–36)

10 When they had gone more than a mile[i] from there, on their march against Timothy, at least five thousand A'rabs with five hundred cavalry attacked them. 11 After a hard fight, Judas and his companions, with God's help, were victorious. The defeated nomads begged Judas to grant them pledges of friendship, promising to give him livestock and to help his people[j] in all other ways. 12 Judas, realizing that they might indeed be useful in many ways, agreed to make peace with them; and after receiving his pledges they went back to their tents.

13 He also attacked a certain town that was strongly fortified with earthworks[k] and walls, and inhabited by all sorts of Gentiles. Its name was Cas'pin. 14 Those who were within, relying on the strength of the walls and on their supply of provisions, behaved most insolently toward Judas and his men, railing at them and even blaspheming and saying unholy things. 15 But Judas and his men, calling against the great Sovereign of the world, who without battering-rams or engines of war overthrew Jericho in the days of Joshua, rushed furiously upon the walls. 16 They took the town by the will of God, and slaughtered untold numbers, so that the adjoining lake, a quarter of a mile[l] wide, appeared to be running over with blood.

Judas Defeats Timothy's Army
(1 Macc 5.37–44)

17 When they had gone ninety-five miles[m] from there, they came to Chār'ax, to the Jews who are called Toū·bi·ā'nī. 18 They did not find Timothy in that region, for he had by then left there without accomplishing anything, though in one place he had left a very strong garrison. 19 Dō·sith'e·us and Sō·sip'a·ter, who were captains under Mac·ca·bē'us, marched out and destroyed those whom Timothy had left in the stronghold, more than ten thousand men. 20 But Mac·ca·bē'us arranged his army in divisions, set men in command of the divisions, and hurried after Timothy, who had with him one hundred twenty thousand infantry and two thousand five hundred cavalry. 21 When Timothy learned of the approach of Judas, he sent off the women and the children and also the baggage to a place called Car'na·im, for that place was hard to besiege and difficult of access because of the narrowness of all the approaches. 22 But when Judas's first division appeared, terror and fear came over the enemy at the manifestation to them of him who sees all things. In their flight they rushed headlong in every direction, so that often they were injured by their own men and pierced by the points of their own swords. 23 Judas pressed the pursuit with the utmost vigor, putting the sinners to the sword, and destroyed as many as thirty thousand.

24 Timothy himself fell into the hands of Dō·sith'e·us and Sō·sip'a·ter and their men. With great guile he begged them to let him go in safety, because he held the parents of most of them, and the brothers of some, to whom no consideration would be shown. 25 And when with many words he had confirmed his solemn promise to restore them unharmed, they let him go, for the sake of saving their kindred.

[f] Gk to them [g] Gk they [h] Gk two hundred forty stadia [i] Gk nine stadia [j] Gk them [k] Meaning of Gk uncertain [l] Gk two stadia [m] Gk seven hundred fifty stadia

Judas Wins Other Victories
(1 Macc 5.45–54)

26 Then Judas[n] marched against Car'na·im and the temple of A·tar'ga·tis, and slaughtered twenty-five thousand people. 27 After the rout and destruction of these, he marched also against Ē'phron, a fortified town where Lys'i·as lived with multitudes of people of all nationalities.[o] Stalwart young men took their stand before the walls and made a vigorous defense; and great stores of war engines and missiles were there. 28 But the Jews[p] called upon the Sovereign who with power shatters the might of his enemies, and they got the town into their hands, and killed as many as twenty-five thousand of those who were in it.

29 Setting out from there, they hastened to Scyth·op'o·lis, which is seventy-five miles[q] from Jerusalem. 30 But when the Jews who lived there bore witness to the goodwill that the people of Scyth·op'o·lis had shown them and their kind treatment of them in times of misfortune, 31 they thanked them and exhorted them to be well disposed to their race in the future also. Then they went up to Jerusalem, as the festival of weeks was close at hand.

Judas Defeats Gorgias

32 After the festival called Pentecost, they hurried against Gor'gi·as, the governor of Id·ū·mē'a, 33 who came out with three thousand infantry and four hundred cavalry. 34 When they joined battle, it happened that a few of the Jews fell. 35 But a certain Dō·sith'e·us, one of Ba·cē'nor's men, who was on horseback and was a strong man, caught hold of Gor'gi·as, and grasping his cloak was dragging him off by main strength, wishing to take the accursed man alive, when one of the Thrā'ci·an cavalry bore down on him and cut off his arm; so Gor'gi·as escaped and reached Mar'i·sa. 36 As Es'dris and his men had been fighting for a long time and were weary, Judas called upon the Lord to show himself their ally and leader in the battle. 37 In the language of their ancestors he raised the battle cry, with hymns; then he charged against Gor'gi·as's troops when they were not expecting it, and put them to flight.

Prayers for Those Killed in Battle

38 Then Judas assembled his army and went to the city of A·dul'lam. As the seventh day was coming on, they purified themselves according to the custom, and kept the sabbath there. 39 On the next day, as had now become necessary, Judas and his men went to take up the bodies of the fallen and to bring them back to lie with their kindred in the sepulchres of their ancestors. 40 Then under the tunic of each one of the dead they found sacred tokens of the idols of Jam'ni·a, which the law forbids the Jews to wear. And it became clear to all that this was the reason these men had fallen. 41 So they all blessed the ways of the Lord, the righteous judge, who reveals the things that are hidden; 42 and they turned to supplication, praying that the sin that had been committed might be wholly blotted out. The noble Judas exhorted the people to keep themselves free from sin, for they had seen with their own eyes what had happened as the result of the sin of those who had fallen. 43 He also took up a collection, man by man, to the amount of two thousand drachmas of silver, and sent it to Jerusalem to provide for a sin offering. In doing this he acted very well and honorably, taking account of the resurrection. 44 For if he were not expecting that those who had fallen would rise again, it would have been superfluous and foolish to pray for the dead. 45 But if he was looking to the splendid reward that is laid up for those who fall asleep in godliness, it was a holy and pious thought. Therefore he made atonement for the dead, so that they might be delivered from their sin.

Menelaus Is Put to Death

13 In the one hundred forty-ninth year[r] word came to Judas and his men that An·tī'o·chus Eū'pa·tor was coming with a great army against Judea, 2 and with him Lys'i·as, his guardian, who had charge of the government. Each of them had a Greek force of one hundred ten thousand infantry, five thousand three hundred cavalry, twenty-two elephants, and

[n] Gk he　[o] Meaning of Gk uncertain
[p] Gk they　[q] Gk six hundred stadia
[r] 163 B.C.

three hundred chariots armed with scythes. 3 Men·e·lā'us also joined them and with utter hypocrisy urged An·tī'o·chus on, not for the sake of his country's welfare, but because he thought that he would be established in office. 4 But the King of kings aroused the anger of An·tī'o·chus against the scoundrel; and when Lys'i·as informed him that this man was to blame for all the trouble, he ordered them to take him to Be·roē'a and to put him to death by the method that is customary in that place. 5 For there is a tower there, fifty cubits high, full of ashes, and it has a rim running around it that on all sides inclines precipitously into the ashes. 6 There they all push to destruction anyone guilty of sacrilege or notorious for other crimes. 7 By such a fate it came about that Men·e·lā'us the lawbreaker died, without even burial in the earth. 8 And this was eminently just; because he had committed many sins against the altar whose fire and ashes were holy, he met his death in ashes.

A Battle Near the City of Modein
(1 Macc 6.43–46)

9 The king with barbarous arrogance was coming to show the Jews things far worse than those that had been done[s] in his father's time. 10 But when Judas heard of this, he ordered the people to call upon the Lord day and night, now if ever to help those who were on the point of being deprived of the law and their country and the holy temple, 11 and not to let the people who had just begun to revive fall into the hands of the blasphemous Gentiles. 12 When they had all joined in the same petition and had implored the merciful Lord with weeping and fasting and lying prostrate for three days without ceasing, Judas exhorted them and ordered them to stand ready.

13 After consulting privately with the elders, he determined to march out and decide the matter by the help of God before the king's army could enter Judea and get possession of the city. 14 So, committing the decision to the Creator of the world and exhorting his troops to fight bravely to the death for the laws, temple, city, country, and commonwealth, he pitched his camp near Mō'dein. 15 He gave his troops the watchword, "God's victory," and with a picked force of the bravest young men, he attacked the king's pavilion at night and killed as many as two thousand men in the camp. He stabbed[t] the leading elephant and its rider. 16 In the end they filled the camp with terror and confusion and withdrew in triumph. 17 This happened, just as day was dawning, because the Lord's help protected him.

Antiochus Makes a Treaty with the Jews
(1 Macc 6.48–63)

18 The king, having had a taste of the daring of the Jews, tried strategy in attacking their positions. 19 He advanced against Beth-zur, a strong fortress of the Jews, was turned back, attacked again,[u] and was defeated. 20 Judas sent in to the garrison whatever was necessary. 21 But Rhod'o·cus, a man from the ranks of the Jews, gave secret information to the enemy; he was sought for, caught, and put in prison. 22 The king negotiated a second time with the people in Beth-zur, gave pledges, received theirs, withdrew, attacked Judas and his men, was defeated; 23 he got word that Philip, who had been left in charge of the government, had revolted in An'ti·och; he was dismayed, called in the Jews yielded and swore to observe all their rights, settled with them and offered sacrifice, honored the sanctuary and showed generosity to the holy place 24 He received Mac·ca·bē'us, left Heg e·mō'ni·dēs as governor from Ptol·e mā'is to Gē'rar, 25 and went to Ptol·e mā'is. The people of Ptol·e·mā'is were indignant over the treaty; in fact they were so angry that they wanted to annul its terms.[t] 26 Lys'i·as took the public platform, made the best possible defense, convinced them, appeased them, gained their goodwill, and se out for An'ti·och. This is how th king's attack and withdrawal turne out.

Alcimus Speaks against Judas
(1 Macc 7.1–25)

14 Three years later, word came t Judas and his men that De·mē tri·us son of Se·leū'cus had sailed int the harbor of Trip'o·lis with a stron army and a fleet, 2 and had take

---

[s] Or the worst of the things that had been done   [t] Meaning of Gk uncertain   [u] Or faltered

possession of the country, having made away with An·tī'o·chus and his guardian Lys'i·as.

3 Now a certain Al'ci·mus, who had formerly been high priest but had willfully defiled himself in the times of separation,[v] realized that there was no way for him to be safe or to have access again to the holy altar, 4 and went to King De·mē'tri·us in about the one hundred fifty-first year,[w] presenting to him a crown of gold and a palm, and besides these some of the customary olive branches from the temple. During that day he kept quiet. 5 But he found an opportunity that furthered his mad purpose when he was invited by De·mē'tri·us to a meeting of the council and was asked about the attitude and intentions of the Jews. He answered:

6 "Those of the Jews who are called Has·i·dē'ans, whose leader is Judas Mac·ca·bē'us, are keeping up war and stirring up sedition, and will not let the kingdom attain tranquility. 7 Therefore I have laid aside my ancestral glory—I mean the high priesthood—and have now come here, 8 first because I am genuinely concerned for the interests of the king, and second because I have regard also for my compatriots. For through the folly of those whom I have mentioned our whole nation is now in no small misfortune. 9 Since you are acquainted, O king, with the details of this matter, may it please you to take thought for our country and our hard-pressed nation with the gracious kindness that you show to all. 10 For as long as Judas lives, it is impossible for the government to find peace." 11 When he had said this, the rest of the king's Friends,[x] who were hostile to Judas, quickly inflamed De·mē'tri·us still more. 12 He immediately chose Nī·cā'nor, who had been in command of the elephants, appointed him governor of Judea, and sent him off 13 with orders to kill Judas and scatter his troops, and to install Al'ci·mus as high priest of the great[y] temple. 14 And the Gentiles throughout Judea, who had fled before[z] Judas, flocked to join Nī·cā'nor, thinking that the misfortunes and calamities of the Jews would mean prosperity for themselves.

Nicanor Makes Friends with Judas
(1 Macc 7.26–28)

15 When the Jews[a] heard of Nicanor's coming and the gathering of the

Gentiles, they sprinkled dust on their heads and prayed to him who established his own people forever and always upholds his own heritage by manifesting himself. 16 At the command of the leader, they[b] set out from there immediately and engaged them in battle at a village called Des'sau.[z] 17 Simon, the brother of Judas, had encountered Nī·cā'nor, but had been temporarily[c] checked because of the sudden consternation created by the enemy.

18 Nevertheless Nī·cā'nor, hearing of the valor of Judas and his troops and their courage in battle for their country, shrank from deciding the issue by bloodshed. 19 Therefore he sent Pos·i·dō'ni·us, Thē·od'o·tus, and Mat·ta·thī'as to give and receive pledges of friendship. 20 When the terms had been fully considered, and the leader had informed the people, and it had appeared that they were of one mind, they agreed to the covenant. 21 The leaders[d] set a day on which to meet by themselves. A chariot came forward from each army; seats of honor were set in place; 22 Judas posted armed men in readiness at key places to prevent sudden treachery on the part of the enemy; so they duly held the consultation.

23 Nī·cā'nor stayed on in Jerusalem and did nothing out of the way, but dismissed the flocks of people that had gathered. 24 And he kept Judas always in his presence; he was warmly attached to the man. 25 He urged him to marry and have children; so Judas[b] married, settled down, and shared the common life.

Nicanor Turns against Judas
(1 Macc 7.29–30)

26 But when Al'ci·mus noticed their goodwill for one another, he took the covenant that had been made and went to De·mē'tri·us. He told him that Nī·cā'nor was disloyal to the government, since he had appointed that conspirator against the kingdom, Judas, to be his successor. 27 The king became excited and, provoked by the false accusations of that depraved man, wrote

[v] Other ancient authorities read *of mixing*   [w] 161 B.C.   [x] Gk *of the Friends*   [y] Gk *greatest*   [z] Meaning of Gk uncertain   [a] Gk *they*   [b] Gk *he*   [c] Other ancient authorities read *slowly*   [d] Gk *They*

to Nĭ·cā′nor, stating that he was displeased with the covenant and commanding him to send Mac·ca·bē′us to An′ti·och as a prisoner without delay.

28 When this message came to Nĭ·cā′nor, he was troubled and grieved that he had to annul their agreement when the man had done no wrong. 29Since it was not possible to oppose the king, he watched for an opportunity to accomplish this by a stratagem. 30But Mac·ca·bē′us, noticing that Nĭ·cā′nor was more austere in his dealings with him and was meeting him more rudely than had been his custom, concluded that this austerity did not spring from the best motives. So he gathered not a few of his men, and went into hiding from Nĭ·cā′nor. 31When the latter became aware that he had been cleverly outwitted by the man, he went to the greate and holy temple while the priests were offering the customary sacrifices, and commanded them to hand the man over. 32When they declared on oath that they did not know where the man was whom he wanted, 33he stretched out his right hand toward the sanctuary, and swore this oath: "If you do not hand Judas over to me as a prisoner, I will level this shrine of God to the ground and tear down the altar, and build here a splendid temple to Dī·o·ny′sus."

34 Having said this, he went away. Then the priests stretched out their hands toward heaven and called upon the constant Defender of our nation, in these words: 35"O Lord of all, though you have need of nothing, you were pleased that there should be a temple for your habitation among us; 36so now, O holy One, Lord of all holiness, keep undefiled forever this house that has been so recently purified."

Razis Dies for His Country

37 A certain Rā′zis, one of the elders of Jerusalem, was denounced to Nĭ·cā′nor as a man who loved his compatriots and was very well thought of and for his goodwill was called father of the Jews. 38In former times, when there was no mingling with the Gentiles, he had been accused of Jū′da·ism, and he had most zealously risked body and life for Jū′da·ism. 39Nĭ·cā′nor, wishing to exhibit the enmity that he had for the Jews, sent more than five hundred soldiers to arrest him; 40for he thought that by arrestingf

him he would do them an injury. 41When the troops were about to capture the tower and were forcing the door of the courtyard, they ordered that fire be brought and the door burned. Being surrounded, Rā′zis fell upon his own sword, 42preferring to die nobly rather than to fall into the hands of sinners and suffer outrage unworthy of his noble birth. 43But in the heat of the struggle he did not hit exactly, and the crowd was now rushing in through the doors. He courageously ran up on the wall, and bravely threw himself down into the crowd. 44But as they quickly drew back, a space opened and he fell in the middle of the empty space. 45Still alive and aflame with anger, he rose, and though his blood gushed forth and his wounds were severe he ran through the crowd; and standing upon a steep rock, 46with his blood now completely drained from him, he tore out his entrails, took them in both hands and hurled them at the crowd, calling upon the Lord of life and spirit to give them back to him again. This was the manner of his death.

Nicanor's Arrogance

15 When Nĭ·cā′nor heard that Judas and his troops were in the region of Samaria, he made plans to attack them with complete safety on the day of rest. 2When the Jews who were compelled to follow him said, "Do not destroy so savagely and barbarously, but show respect for the day that he who sees all things has honored and hallowed above other days, 3the thrice-accursed wretch asked if there were a sovereign in heaven who had commanded the keeping of the sabbath day. 4When they declared, "It is the living Lord himself, the Sovereign in heaven, who ordered us to observe the seventh day," 5he replied, "But I am a sovereign also, on earth and I command you to take up arms and finish the king's business." Nevertheless, he did not succeed in carrying out his abominable design.

Judas Prepares the Jews for Battle

6 This Nĭ·cā′nor in his utter boastfulness and arrogance had determined to erect a public monument of victory over Judas and his forces. 7But

e Gk greatest   f Meaning of Gk uncertain   g Gk he

Mac·ca·bē′us did not cease to trust with all confidence that he would get help from the Lord. [8] He exhorted his troops not to fear the attack of the Gentiles, but to keep in mind the former times when help had come to them from heaven, and so to look for the victory that the Almighty would give them. [9] Encouraging them from the law and the prophets, and reminding them also of the struggles they had won, he made them the more eager. [10] When he had aroused their courage, he issued his orders, at the same time pointing out the perfidy of the Gentiles and their violation of oaths. [11] He armed each of them not so much with confidence in shields and spears as with the inspiration of brave words, and he cheered them all by relating a dream, a sort of vision,[h] which was worthy of belief. [12] What he saw was this: Ō·nī′as, who had been high priest, a noble and good man, of modest bearing and gentle manner, one who spoke fittingly and had been trained from childhood in all that belongs to excellence, was praying with outstretched hands for the whole body of the Jews. [13] Then in the same fashion another appeared, distinguished by his gray hair and dignity, and of marvelous majesty and authority. [14] And Ō·nī′as spoke, saying, "This is a man who loves the family of Israel and prays much for the people and the holy city — Jer·e·mī′ah, the prophet of God." [15] Jer·e·mī′ah stretched out his right hand and gave to Judas a golden sword, and as he gave it he addressed him thus: [16] "Take this holy sword, a gift from God, with which you will strike down your adversaries."

[17] Encouraged by the words of Judas, so noble and so effective in arousing valor and awaking courage in the souls of the young, they determined not to carry on a campaign[i] but to attack bravely, and to decide the matter by fighting hand to hand with all courage, because the city and the sanctuary and the temple were in danger. [18] Their concern for wives and children, and also for brothers and sisters[j] and relatives, lay upon them less heavily; their greatest and first fear was for the consecrated sanctuary. [19] And those who had to remain in the city were in no little distress, being anxious over the encounter in the open country.

The Defeat and Death of Nicanor
(1 Macc 7.39–50)

[20] When all were now looking forward to the coming issue, and the enemy was already close at hand with their army drawn up for battle, the elephants[k] strategically stationed and the cavalry deployed on the flanks, [21] Mac·ca·bē′us, observing the masses that were in front of him and the varied supply of arms and the savagery of the elephants, stretched out his hands toward heaven and called upon the Lord who works wonders; for he knew that it is not by arms, but as the Lord[l] decides, that he gains the victory for those who deserve it. [22] He called upon him in these words: "O Lord, you sent your angel in the time of King Hez·e·kī′ah of Judea, and he killed fully one hundred eighty-five thousand in the camp of Sen·nach′e·rib. [23] So now, O Sovereign of the heavens, send a good angel to spread terror and trembling before us. [24] By the might of your arm may these blasphemers who come against your holy people be struck down." With these words he ended his prayer.

[25] Nī·cā′nor and his troops advanced with trumpets and battle songs, [26] but Judas and his troops met the enemy in battle with invocations to God and prayers. [27] So, fighting with their hands and praying to God in their hearts, they laid low at least thirty-five thousand, and were greatly gladdened by God's manifestation.

[28] When the action was over and they were returning with joy, they recognized Nī·cā′nor, lying dead, in full armor. [29] Then there was shouting and tumult, and they blessed the Sovereign Lord in the language of their ancestors. [30] Then the man who was ever in body and soul the defender of his people, the man who maintained his youthful goodwill toward his compatriots, ordered them to cut off Nī·cā′nor's head and arm and carry them to Jerusalem. [31] When he arrived there and had called his compatriots together and stationed the priests before the altar, he sent for those who were in the citadel. [32] He showed them the vile Nī·cā′nor's head and that profane man's arm, which had been boastfully

[h] Meaning of Gk uncertain   [i] Or *to remain in camp*   [j] Gk *for brothers*
[k] Gk *animals*   [l] Gk *he*

2 MACCABEES

stretched out against the holy house of the Almighty. [33] He cut out the tongue of the ungodly Ni·cā'nor and said that he would feed it piecemeal to the birds and would hang up these rewards of his folly opposite the sanctuary. [34] And they all, looking to heaven, blessed the Lord who had manifested himself, saying, "Blessed is he who has kept his own place undefiled!" [35] Judas*m* hung Ni·cā'nor's head from the citadel, a clear and conspicuous sign to everyone of the help of the Lord. [36] And they all decreed by public vote never to let this day go unobserved, but to celebrate the thirteenth day of the twelfth month—which is called Ā'dar in the Ar·a·mā'ic language—the day before Mordecai's day.

[37] This, then, is how matters turned out with Ni·cā'nor, and from that time the city has been in the possession of the Hebrews. So I will here end my story.

The Compiler's Epilogue

[38] If it is well told and to the point, that is what I myself desired; if it is poorly done and mediocre, that was the best I could do. [39] For just as it is harmful to drink wine alone, or, again, to drink water alone, while wine mixed with water is sweet and delicious and enhances one's enjoyment, so also the style of the story delights the ears of those who read the work. And here will be the end.

m Gk *He*

Wisdom and Poetry

The books of poetry include the Psalms and Song of Solomon. The wisdom books are Job, Proverbs, Ecclesiastes, the Wisdom of Solomon, and Sirach (Ecclesiasticus). This does not mean all poetry in the Bible is found in Psalms and Song of Solomon, nor that all wisdom is found in only five books. Poetry abounds in the Torah and the Prophets. Much of the wisdom literature is written in poetic form. On the other hand, wisdom is also found throughout the Bible.

The Psalms were the hymn book and prayer book of the second temple, and continue to be used in the same way by the Jewish community today. Traditionally, the Psalms were ascribed to David, but a reading of the subheads shows there are several collections of Psalms, including many by David, but also collections credited to the sons of Korah, to Asaph, to Solomon, even to Moses. There are also many kinds of Psalms, just as there are many types of hymns in a modern hymnal. There are songs of praise and thanksgiving, songs of ascent which were sung going up to the temple, royal psalms, prayers, laments, and so on. The Psalms are one of the favorite books for Christians and many of the biblical passages that are most meaningful come from the Psalms.

Song of Solomon is a collection of love poems, which are beautiful expressions of human love at its best. They remind us that God is present in all of life.

Wisdom literature takes several different forms. Sometimes it is short sayings on how to cope with life. The theme is usually how virtue can triumph over wrong. Sometimes wisdom takes the form of riddles. Or wisdom can be reflections on the meaning of life or on the life of faith (what we might call philosophy).

The heart of wisdom literature is a theology of creation and life. God has made the world and everything in it. We can learn something about God and life by observing nature. Because God is in all of life, we are called to live joyfully as well as responsibly. A great deal of wisdom literature deals with how to live the good life, that is, the life God approves.

Job begins with the undeserved suffering of the patriarch Job and reflects on the meaning of suffering and God's relationship to one who suffers unjustly. Job suffers most because he refuses to deny his own integrity or the integrity of God.

Proverbs is a collection of sayings about how to live the good life. It also contains the great passage on the personification of wisdom as God's handmaid, delighting in the works of creation (8.22-31 and ch. 9).

Ecclesiastes reads almost like a diary of a spiritual journey. The author deals with ultimate questions of life and death, while talking about the routines of daily life. He reflects on what his life has meant from youth to old age, and how God has played a part in that life.

The Wisdom of Solomon teaches that the wicked may seem to prosper, but they face a future judgment. The righteous live forever. The book uses wisdom to help Jews face persecution and resist the temptations of a pagan culture.

Sirach (Ecclesiasticus) was written about 180 B.C. in Jerusalem. It is a book about ethics in public and private life. The true measure of character is in virtue rather than money. It relates wisdom to the Torah and to worship.

JOB

Job and His Family

1 There was once a man in the land of Uz whose name was Job. That man was blameless and upright, one who feared God and turned away from evil. [2] There were born to him seven sons and three daughters. [3] He had seven thousand sheep, three thousand camels, five hundred yoke of oxen, five hundred donkeys, and very many servants; so that this man was the greatest of all the people of the east. [4] His sons used to go and hold feasts in one another's houses in turn; and they would send and invite their three sisters to eat and drink with them. [5] And when the feast days had run their course, Job would send and sanctify them, and he would rise early in the morning and offer burnt offerings according to the number of them all; for Job said, "It may be that my children have sinned, and cursed God in their hearts." This is what Job always did.

Attack on Job's Character

6 One day the heavenly beings[a] came to present themselves before the LORD, and Satan[b] also came among them. [7] The LORD said to Satan,[b] "Where have you come from?" Satan[b] answered the LORD, "From going to and fro on the earth, and from walking up and down on it." [8] The LORD said to Satan,[b] "Have you considered my servant Job? There is no one like him on the earth, a blameless and upright man who fears God and turns away from evil." [9] Then Satan[b] answered the LORD, "Does Job fear God for nothing? [10] Have you not put a fence around him and his house and all that he has, on every side? You have blessed the work of his hands, and his possessions have increased in the land. [11] But stretch out your hand now, and touch all that he has, and he will curse you to your face." [12] The LORD said to Satan,[b] "Very well, all that he has is in your power; only do not stretch out your hand against him!" So Satan[b] went out from the presence of the LORD.

Job Loses Property and Children

13 One day when his sons and daughters were eating and drinking wine in the eldest brother's house, [14] a messenger came to Job and said, "The oxen were plowing and the donkeys were feeding beside them, [15] and the Sa·bē'ans fell on them and carried them off, and killed the servants with the edge of the sword; I alone have escaped to tell you." [16] While he was still speaking, another came and said, "The fire of God fell from heaven and burned up the sheep and the servants, and consumed them; I alone have escaped to tell you." [17] While he was still speaking, another came and said, "The Chal·dē'ans formed three columns, made a raid on the camels and carried them off, and killed the servants with the edge of the sword; I alone have escaped to tell you." [18] While he was still speaking, another came and said, "Your sons and daughters were eating and drinking wine in their eldest brother's house, [19] and suddenly a great wind came across the desert, struck the four corners of the house, and it fell on the young people, and they are dead; I alone have escaped to tell you."

20 Then Job arose, tore his robe, shaved his head, and fell on the ground and worshiped. [21] He said, "Naked I came from my mother's womb, and naked shall I return there; the LORD gave, and the LORD has taken away; blessed be the name of the LORD."

22 In all this Job did not sin or charge God with wrongdoing.

---

a Heb *sons of God*   *b* Or *the Accuser;* Heb *ha-satan*

Attack on Job's Health

2 One day the heavenly beings[c] came to present themselves before the LORD, and Satan[d] also came among them to present himself before the LORD. [2]The LORD said to Satan,[d] "Where have you come from?" Satan[e] answered the LORD, "From going to and fro on the earth, and from walking up and down on it." [3]The LORD said to Satan,[d] "Have you considered my servant Job? There is no one like him on the earth, a blameless and upright man who fears God and turns away from evil. He still persists in his integrity, although you incited me against him, to destroy him for no reason." [4]Then Satan[d] answered the LORD, "Skin for skin! All that people have they will give to save their lives.[f] [5]But stretch out your hand now and touch his bone and his flesh, and he will curse you to your face." [6]The LORD said to Satan,[d] "Very well, he is in your power; only spare his life."

7 So Satan[d] went out from the presence of the LORD, and inflicted loathsome sores on Job from the sole of his foot to the crown of his head. [8]Job[g] took a potsherd with which to scrape himself, and sat among the ashes.

9 Then his wife said to him, "Do you still persist in your integrity? Curse[h] God, and die." [10]But he said to her, "You speak as any foolish woman would speak. Shall we receive the good at the hand of God, and not receive the bad?" In all this Job did not sin with his lips.

Job's Three Friends

11 Now when Job's three friends heard of all these troubles that had come upon him, each of them set out from his home—E·li′phaz the Tē′-man·īte, Bil′dad the Shū′hīte, and Zō′-phar the Nā′a·ma·thīte. They met together to go and console and comfort him. [12]When they saw him from a distance, they did not recognize him, and they raised their voices and wept aloud; they tore their robes and threw dust in the air upon their heads. [13]They sat with him on the ground seven days and seven nights, and no one spoke a word to him, for they saw that his suffering was very great.

Job Curses the Day He Was Born

3 After this Job opened his mouth and cursed the day of his birth. [2]Job said:
3 "Let the day perish in which I
    was born,
  and the night that said,
  'A man-child is conceived.'
4 Let that day be darkness!
  May God above not seek it,
  or light shine on it.
5 Let gloom and deep darkness
    claim it.
  Let clouds settle upon it;
  let the blackness of the day
    terrify it.
6 That night—let thick darkness
    seize it!
  let it not rejoice among the
    days of the year;
  let it not come into the number
    of the months.
7 Yes, let that night be barren;
  let no joyful cry be heard[i] in
    it.
8 Let those curse it who curse the
    Sea,[j]
  those who are skilled to rouse
    up Le·vī′a·than.
9 Let the stars of its dawn be
    dark;
  let it hope for light, but have
    none;
  may it not see the eyelids of
    the morning—
10 because it did not shut the doors
    of my mother's womb,
  and hide trouble from my
    eyes.

11 "Why did I not die at birth,
  come forth from the womb
    and expire?
12 Why were there knees to receive
    me,
  or breasts for me to suck?
13 Now I would be lying down and
    quiet;
  I would be asleep; then I
    would be at rest
14 with kings and counselors of the
    earth
  who rebuild ruins for
    themselves,
15 or with princes who have gold,

c Heb *sons of God*   d Or *the Accuser;*
Heb *ha-satan*   e Or *The Accuser;* Heb
ha-satan   f Or *All that the man has he
will give for his life*   g Heb *He*
h Heb *Bless*   i Heb *come*   j Cn: Heb *day*

who fill their houses with
silver.

16 Or why was I not buried like a
stillborn child,
like an infant that never sees
the light?

17 There the wicked cease from
troubling,
and there the weary are at
rest.

18 There the prisoners are at ease
together;
they do not hear the voice of
the taskmaster.

19 The small and the great are
there,
and the slaves are free from
their masters.

20 "Why is light given to one in
misery,
and life to the bitter in soul,

21 who long for death, but it does
not come,
and dig for it more than for
hidden treasures;

22 who rejoice exceedingly,
and are glad when they find
the grave?

23 Why is light given to one who
cannot see the way,
whom God has fenced in?

24 For my sighing comes like*k* my
bread,
and my groanings are poured
out like water.

25 Truly the thing that I fear comes
upon me,
and what I dread befalls me.

26 I am not at ease, nor am I quiet;
I have no rest; but trouble
comes."

Eliphaz Speaks: Job Has Sinned

4 Then E·li′phaz the Tē′man·ite answered:

2 "If one ventures a word with
you, will you be offended?
But who can keep from
speaking?

3 See, you have instructed many;
you have strengthened the
weak hands.

4 Your words have supported
those who were stumbling,
and you have made firm the
feeble knees.

5 But now it has come to you, and
you are impatient;
it touches you, and you are
dismayed.

6 Is not your fear of God your
confidence,
and the integrity of your ways
your hope?

7 "Think now, who that was
innocent ever perished?
Or where were the upright cut
off?

8 As I have seen, those who plow
iniquity
and sow trouble reap the
same.

9 By the breath of God they
perish,
and by the blast of his anger
they are consumed.

10 The roar of the lion, the voice of
the fierce lion,
and the teeth of the young
lions are broken.

11 The strong lion perishes for lack
of prey,
and the whelps of the lioness
are scattered.

12 "Now a word came stealing to
me,
my ear received the whisper of
it.

13 Amid thoughts from visions of
the night,
when deep sleep falls on
mortals,

14 dread came upon me, and
trembling,
which made all my bones
shake.

15 A spirit glided past my face;
the hair of my flesh bristled.

16 It stood still,
but I could not discern its
appearance.
A form was before my eyes;
there was silence, then I heard
a voice:

17 'Can mortals be righteous
before*l* God?
Can human beings be pure
before*l* their Maker?

18 Even in his servants he puts no
trust,
and his angels he charges with
error;

19 how much more those who live
in houses of clay,
whose foundation is in the
dust,
who are crushed like a moth.

k Heb *before*   *l* Or *more than*

20 Between morning and evening
they are destroyed;
they perish forever without
any regarding it.

21 Their tent-cord is plucked up
within them,
and they die devoid of
wisdom.'

Job Is Corrected by God

5 "Call now; is there anyone who
will answer you?
To which of the holy ones will
you turn?

2 Surely vexation kills the fool,
and jealousy slays the simple.

3 I have seen fools taking root,
but suddenly I cursed their
dwelling.

4 Their children are far from
safety,
they are crushed in the gate,
and there is no one to deliver
them.

5 The hungry eat their harvest,
and they take it even out of
the thorns;*m*
and the thirsty*n* pant after
their wealth.

6 For misery does not come from
the earth,
nor does trouble sprout from
the ground;

7 but human beings are born to
trouble
just as sparks*o* fly upward.

8 "As for me, I would seek God,
and to God I would commit
my cause.

9 He does great things and
unsearchable,
marvelous things without
number.

10 He gives rain on the earth
and sends waters on the fields;

11 he sets on high those who are
lowly,
and those who mourn are
lifted to safety.

12 He frustrates the devices of the
crafty,
so that their hands achieve no
success.

13 He takes the wise in their own
craftiness;
and the schemes of the wily
are brought to a quick end.

14 They meet with darkness in the
daytime,
and grope at noonday as in
the night.

15 But he saves the needy from the
sword of their mouth,
from the hand of the mighty.

16 So the poor have hope,
and injustice shuts its mouth.

17 "How happy is the one whom
God reproves;
therefore do not despise the
discipline of the
Almighty.*p*

18 For he wounds, but he binds up;
he strikes, but his hands heal.

19 He will deliver you from six
troubles;
in seven no harm shall touch
you.

20 In famine he will redeem you
from death,
and in war from the power of
the sword.

21 You shall be hidden from the
scourge of the tongue,
and shall not fear destruction
when it comes.

22 At destruction and famine you
shall laugh,
and shall not fear the wild
animals of the earth.

23 For you shall be in league with
the stones of the field,
and the wild animals shall be
at peace with you.

24 You shall know that your tent is
safe,
you shall inspect your fold and
miss nothing.

25 You shall know that your
descendants will be many,
and your offspring like the
grass of the earth.

26 You shall come to your grave in
ripe old age,
as a shock of grain comes up
to the threshing floor in its
season.

27 See, we have searched this out;
it is true.
Hear, and know it for
yourself."

Job Replies: My Complaint Is Just

6 Then Job answered:
2 "O that my vexation were
weighed,

---

m Meaning of Heb uncertain   *n* Aquila
Symmachus Syr Vg: Heb *snare*
o Or *birds*; Heb *sons of Resheph*
p Traditional rendering of Heb *Shaddai*

and all my calamity laid in the
balances!

3 For then it would be heavier
than the sand of the sea;
therefore my words have been
rash.

4 For the arrows of the Almighty[q]
are in me;
my spirit drinks their poison;
the terrors of God are arrayed
against me.

5 Does the wild ass bray over its
grass,
or the ox low over its fodder?

6 Can that which is tasteless be
eaten without salt,
or is there any flavor in the
juice of mallows?[r]

7 My appetite refuses to touch
them;
they are like food that is
loathsome to me.[r]

8 "O that I might have my request,
and that God would grant my
desire;

9 that it would please God to
crush me,
that he would let loose his
hand and cut me off!

10 This would be my consolation;
I would even exult[r] in
unrelenting pain;
for I have not denied the
words of the Holy One.

11 What is my strength, that I
should wait?
And what is my end, that I
should be patient?

12 Is my strength the strength of
stones,
or is my flesh bronze?

13 In truth I have no help in me,
and any resource is driven
from me.

14 "Those who withhold[s] kindness
from a friend
forsake the fear of the
Almighty.[q]

15 My companions are treacherous
like a torrent-bed,
like freshets that pass away,

16 that run dark with ice,
turbid with melting snow.

17 In time of heat they disappear;
when it is hot, they vanish
from their place.

18 The caravans turn aside from
their course;
they go up into the waste, and
perish.

19 The caravans of Tē′ma look,
the travelers of Shē′ba hope.

20 They are disappointed because
they were confident;
they come there and are
confounded.

21 Such you have now become to
me;[t]
you see my calamity, and are
afraid.

22 Have I said, 'Make me a gift'?
Or, 'From your wealth offer a
bribe for me'?

23 Or, 'Save me from an opponent's
hand'?
Or, 'Ransom me from the hand
of oppressors'?

24 "Teach me, and I will be silent;
make me understand how I
have gone wrong.

25 How forceful are honest words!
But your reproof, what does it
reprove?

26 Do you think that you can
reprove words,
as if the speech of the
desperate were wind?

27 You would even cast lots over
the orphan,
and bargain over your friend.

28 "But now, be pleased to look at
me;
for I will not lie to your face.

29 Turn, I pray, let no wrong be
done.
Turn now, my vindication is at
stake.

30 Is there any wrong on my
tongue?
Cannot my taste discern
calamity?

Job: My Suffering Is without End

7 "Do not human beings have a
hard service on earth,
and are not their days like the
days of a laborer?

2 Like a slave who longs for the
shadow,
and like laborers who look for
their wages,

3 so I am allotted months of
emptiness,

[q]Traditional rendering of Heb *Shaddai*
[r]Meaning of Heb uncertain　[s]Syr Vg
Compare Tg: Meaning of Heb uncertain
[t]Cn Compare Gk Syr: Meaning of Heb
uncertain

and nights of misery are apportioned to me.
4 When I lie down I say, 'When shall I rise?'
But the night is long,
and I am full of tossing until dawn.
5 My flesh is clothed with worms and dirt;
my skin hardens, then breaks out again.
6 My days are swifter than a weaver's shuttle,
and come to their end without hope.*u*
7 "Remember that my life is a breath;
my eye will never again see good.
8 The eye that beholds me will see me no more;
while your eyes are upon me, I shall be gone.
9 As the cloud fades and vanishes, so those who go down to Shĕ′ōl do not come up;
10 they return no more to their houses,
nor do their places know them any more.
11 "Therefore I will not restrain my mouth;
I will speak in the anguish of my spirit;
I will complain in the bitterness of my soul.
12 Am I the Sea, or the Dragon, that you set a guard over me?
13 When I say, 'My bed will comfort me,
my couch will ease my complaint,'
14 then you scare me with dreams and terrify me with visions,
15 so that I would choose strangling
and death rather than this body.
16 I loathe my life; I would not live forever.
Let me alone, for my days are a breath.
17 What are human beings, that you make so much of them,
that you set your mind on them,
18 visit them every morning, test them every moment?

19 Will you not look away from me for a while,
let me alone until I swallow my spittle?
20 If I sin, what do I do to you, you watcher of humanity?
Why have you made me your target?
Why have I become a burden to you?
21 Why do you not pardon my transgression
and take away my iniquity?
For now I shall lie in the earth;
you will seek me, but I shall not be."

Bildad Speaks: Job Should Repent

8 Then Bil′dad the Shū′hīte answered:
2 "How long will you say these things,
and the words of your mouth be a great wind?
3 Does God pervert justice?
Or does the Almighty*v* pervert the right?
4 If your children sinned against him,
he delivered them into the power of their transgression.
5 If you will seek God
and make supplication to the Almighty,*v*
6 if you are pure and upright, surely then he will rouse himself for you
and restore to you your rightful place.
7 Though your beginning was small,
your latter days will be very great.

8 "For inquire now of bygone generations,
and consider what their ancestors have found;
9 for we are but of yesterday, and we know nothing,
for our days on earth are but a shadow.
10 Will they not teach you and tell you
and utter words out of their understanding?

u Or as the thread runs out
v Traditional rendering of Heb Shaddai

11 "Can papyrus grow where there
    is no marsh?
    Can reeds flourish where there
    is no water?
12 While yet in flower and not cut
    down,
    they wither before any other
    plant.
13 Such are the paths of all who
    forget God;
    the hope of the godless shall
    perish.
14 Their confidence is gossamer,
    a spider's house their trust.
15 If one leans against its house, it
    will not stand;
    if one lays hold of it, it will not
    endure.
16 The wicked thrivew before the
    sun,
    and their shoots spread over
    the garden.
17 Their roots twine around the
    stoneheap;
    they live among the rocks.x
18 If they are destroyed from their
    place,
    then it will deny them, saying,
    'I have never seen you.'
19 See, these are their happy
    ways,y
    and out of the earth still others
    will spring.

20 "See, God will not reject a
    blameless person,
    nor take the hand of evildoers.
21 He will yet fill your mouth with
    laughter,
    and your lips with shouts of
    joy.
22 Those who hate you will be
    clothed with shame,
    and the tent of the wicked will
    be no more."

Job Replies: There Is No Mediator

9 Then Job answered:
2 "Indeed I know that this is
    so;
    but how can a mortal be just
    before God?
3 If one wished to contend with
    him,
    one could not answer him
    once in a thousand.
4 He is wise in heart, and mighty
    in strength
    —who has resisted him, and
    succeeded?—

5 he who removes mountains, and
    they do not know it,
    when he overturns them in his
    anger;
6 who shakes the earth out of its
    place,
    and its pillars tremble;
7 who commands the sun, and it
    does not rise;
    who seals up the stars;
8 who alone stretched out the
    heavens
    and trampled the waves of the
    Sea;z
9 who made the Bear and Ō·rī'on,
    the Plēi'a·dēs and the
    chambers of the south;
10 who does great things beyond
    understanding,
    and marvelous things without
    number.
11 Look, he passes by me, and I do
    not see him;
    he moves on, but I do not
    perceive him.
12 He snatches away; who can stop
    him?
    Who will say to him, 'What
    are you doing?'

13 "God will not turn back his
    anger;
    the helpers of Rā'hab bowed
    beneath him.
14 How then can I answer him,
    choosing my words with him?
15 Though I am innocent, I cannot
    answer him;
    I must appeal for mercy to my
    accuser.a
16 If I summoned him and he
    answered me,
    I do not believe that he would
    listen to my voice.
17 For he crushes me with a
    tempest,
    and multiplies my wounds
    without cause;
18 he will not let me get my breath,
    but fills me with bitterness.
19 If it is a contest of strength, he is
    the strong one!
    If it is a matter of justice, who
    can summon him?b
20 Though I am innocent, my own
    mouth would condemn me;

wHeb He thrives   xGk Vg: Meaning of
Heb uncertain   yMeaning of Heb
uncertain   zOr trampled the back of
the sea dragon   aOr for my right
bCompare Gk: Heb me

though I am blameless, he
would prove me perverse.
21 I am blameless; I do not know
myself;
I loathe my life.
22 It is all one; therefore I say,
he destroys both the blameless
and the wicked.
23 When disaster brings sudden
death,
he mocks at the calamity[c] of
the innocent.
24 The earth is given into the hand
of the wicked;
he covers the eyes of its
judges —
if it is not he, who then is it?

25 "My days are swifter than a
runner;
they flee away, they see no
good.
26 They go by like skiffs of reed,
like an eagle swooping on the
prey.
27 If I say, 'I will forget my
complaint;
I will put off my sad
countenance and be of
good cheer,'
28 I become afraid of all my
suffering,
for I know you will not hold
me innocent.
29 I shall be condemned;
why then do I labor in vain?
30 If I wash myself with soap
and cleanse my hands with
lye,
31 yet you will plunge me into filth,
and my own clothes will abhor
me.
32 For he is not a mortal, as I am,
that I might answer him,
that we should come to trial
together.
33 There is no umpire[d] between us,
who might lay his hand on us
both.
34 If he would take his rod away
from me,
and not let dread of him
terrify me,
35 then I would speak without fear
of him,
for I know I am not what I am
thought to be.[e]

Job: I Loathe My Life

10 "I loathe my life;
I will give free utterance to
my complaint;
I will speak in the bitterness of
my soul.
2 I will say to God, Do not
condemn me;
let me know why you contend
against me.
3 Does it seem good to you to
oppress,
to despise the work of your
hands
and favor the schemes of the
wicked?
4 Do you have eyes of flesh?
Do you see as humans see?
5 Are your days like the days of
mortals,
or your years like human
years,
6 that you seek out my iniquity
and search for my sin,
7 although you know that I am not
guilty,
and there is no one to deliver
out of your hand?
8 Your hands fashioned and made
me;
and now you turn and destroy
me.[f]
9 Remember that you fashioned
me like clay;
and will you turn me to dust
again?
10 Did you not pour me out like
milk
and curdle me like cheese?
11 You clothed me with skin and
flesh,
and knit me together with
bones and sinews.
12 You have granted me life and
steadfast love,
and your care has preserved
my spirit.
13 Yet these things you hid in your
heart;
I know that this was your
purpose.
14 If I sin, you watch me,
and do not acquit me of my
iniquity.
15 If I am wicked, woe to me!

[c]Meaning of Heb uncertain　　[d]Another
reading is *Would that there were an
umpire*　　[e]Cn: Heb *for I am not so in
myself*　　[f]Cn Compare Gk Syr: Heb
*made me together all around, and you
destroy me*

JOB

If I am righteous, I cannot lift
    up my head,
for I am filled with disgrace
    and look upon my affliction.

16 Bold as a lion you hunt me;
    you repeat your exploits
        against me.

17 You renew your witnesses
        against me,
    and increase your vexation
        toward me;
    you bring fresh troops against
        me.[g]

18 "Why did you bring me forth
        from the womb?
    Would that I had died before
        any eye had seen me,

19 and were as though I had not
        been,
    carried from the womb to the
        grave.

20 Are not the days of my life
        few?[h]
    Let me alone, that I may find a
        little comfort[i]

21 before I go, never to return,
    to the land of gloom and deep
        darkness,

22 the land of gloom[j] and chaos,
    where light is like darkness."

Zophar Speaks: Job's Guilt Deserves Punishment

11 Then Zō′phar the Nā′a·ma-
thīte answered:

2 "Should a multitude of words go
        unanswered,
    and should one full of talk be
        vindicated?

3 Should your babble put others to
        silence,
    and when you mock, shall no
        one shame you?

4 For you say, 'My conduct[k] is
        pure,
    and I am clean in God's[l]
        sight.'

5 But oh, that God would speak,
    and open his lips to you,

6 and that he would tell you the
        secrets of wisdom!
    For wisdom is many-sided.[m]
    Know then that God exacts of
        you less than your guilt
        deserves.

7 "Can you find out the deep
        things of God?
    Can you find out the limit of
        the Almighty?[n]

8 It is higher than heaven[o]—what
        can you do?
    Deeper than Shē′ōl—what can
        you know?

9 Its measure is longer than the
        earth,
    and broader than the sea.

10 If he passes through, and
        imprisons,
    and assembles for judgment,
        who can hinder him?

11 For he knows those who are
        worthless;
    when he sees iniquity, will he
        not consider it?

12 But a stupid person will get
        understanding,
    when a wild ass is born
        human.[m]

13 "If you direct your heart rightly,
    you will stretch out your
        hands toward him.

14 If iniquity is in your hand, put it
        far away,
    and do not let wickedness
        reside in your tents.

15 Surely then you will lift up your
        face without blemish;
    you will be secure, and will
        not fear.

16 You will forget your misery;
    you will remember it as waters
        that have passed away.

17 And your life will be brighter
        than the noonday;
    its darkness will be like the
        morning.

18 And you will have confidence,
        because there is hope;
    you will be protected[p] and
        take your rest in safety.

19 You will lie down, and no one
        will make you afraid;
    many will entreat your favor.

20 But the eyes of the wicked will
        fail;
    all way of escape will be lost
        to them,
    and their hope is to breathe
        their last."

g Cn Compare Gk: Heb *toward me;
changes and a troop are with me*
h Cn Compare Gk Syr: Heb *Are not my
days few? Let him cease!*   i Heb *that I
may brighten up a little*   j Heb *gloom
as darkness, deep darkness*   k Gk: Heb
teaching   l Heb *your*   m Meaning of
Heb uncertain   n Traditional rendering
of Heb *Shaddai*   o Heb *The heights of
heaven*   p Or *you will look around*

Job Replies: I Am a Laughingstock

12

2 "No doubt you are the people,
and wisdom will die with you.
3 But I have understanding as well as you;
I am not inferior to you.
Who does not know such things as these?
4 I am a laughingstock to my friends;
I, who called upon God and he answered me,
a just and blameless man, I am a laughingstock.
5 Those at ease have contempt for misfortune,[q]
but it is ready for those whose feet are unstable.
6 The tents of robbers are at peace,
and those who provoke God are secure,
who bring their god in their hands.[r]
7 "But ask the animals, and they will teach you;
the birds of the air, and they will tell you;
8 ask the plants of the earth,[s] and they will teach you;
and the fish of the sea will declare to you.
9 Who among all these does not know
that the hand of the LORD has done this?
10 In his hand is the life of every living thing
and the breath of every human being.
11 Does not the ear test words
as the palate tastes food?
12 Is wisdom with the aged,
and understanding in length of days?
13 With God[t] are wisdom and strength;
he has counsel and understanding.
14 If he tears down, no one can rebuild;
if he shuts someone in, no one can open up.
15 If he withholds the waters, they dry up;
if he sends them out, they overwhelm the land.

16 With him are strength and wisdom;
the deceived and the deceiver are his.
17 He leads counselors away stripped,
and makes fools of judges.
18 He looses the sash of kings,
and binds a waistcloth on their loins.
19 He leads priests away stripped,
and overthrows the mighty.
20 He deprives of speech those who are trusted,
and takes away the discernment of the elders.
21 He pours contempt on princes,
and looses the belt of the strong.
22 He uncovers the deeps out of darkness,
and brings deep darkness to light.
23 He makes nations great, then destroys them;
he enlarges nations, then leads them away.
24 He strips understanding from the leaders[u] of the earth,
and makes them wander in a pathless waste.
25 They grope in the dark without light;
he makes them stagger like a drunkard.

13

"Look, my eye has seen all this,
my ear has heard and understood it.
2 What you know, I also know;
I am not inferior to you.
3 But I would speak to the Almighty,[v]
and I desire to argue my case with God.
4 As for you, you whitewash with lies;
all of you are worthless physicians.
5 If you would only keep silent,
that would be your wisdom!
6 Hear now my reasoning,
and listen to the pleadings of my lips.

[q]Meaning of Heb uncertain   [r]Or *whom God brought forth by his hand*; Meaning of Heb uncertain   [s]Or *speak to the earth*   [t]Heb *him*   [u]Heb adds *of the people*   [v]Traditional rendering of Heb *Shaddai*

7 Will you speak falsely for God,
    and speak deceitfully for him?
8 Will you show partiality toward
    him,
    will you plead the case for
        God?
9 Will it be well with you when he
    searches you out?
    Or can you deceive him, as
        one person deceives
        another?
10 He will surely rebuke you
    if in secret you show partiality.
11 Will not his majesty terrify you,
    and the dread of him fall upon
        you?
12 Your maxims are proverbs of
        ashes,
    your defenses are defenses of
        clay.

13 "Let me have silence, and I will
        speak,
    and let come on me what may.
14 I will take my flesh in my teeth,
    and put my life in my hand.ʷ
15 See, he will kill me; I have no
        hope;ˣ
    but I will defend my ways to
        his face.
16 This will be my salvation,
    that the godless shall not come
        before him.
17 Listen carefully to my words,
    and let my declaration be in
        your ears.
18 I have indeed prepared my case;
    I know that I shall be
        vindicated.
19 Who is there that will contend
        with me?
    For then I would be silent and
        die.

Job's Despondent Prayer

20 Only grant two things to me,
    then I will not hide myself
        from your face:
21 withdraw your hand far from
        me,
    and do not let dread of you
        terrify me.
22 Then call, and I will answer;
    or let me speak, and you reply
        to me.
23 How many are my iniquities and
        my sins?
    Make me know my
        transgression and my sin.
24 Why do you hide your face,
    and count me as your enemy?

25 Will you frighten a windblown
        leaf
    and pursue dry chaff?
26 For you write bitter things
        against me,
    and make me reapʸ the
        iniquities of my youth.
27 You put my feet in the stocks,
    and watch all my paths;
    you set a bound to the soles of
        my feet.
28 One wastes away like a rotten
        thing,
    like a garment that is
        moth-eaten.

14 "A mortal, born of woman,
    few of days and full of
        trouble,
2   comes up like a flower and
        withers,
    flees like a shadow and does
        not last.
3 Do you fix your eyes on such a
        one?
    Do you bring me into
        judgment with you?
4 Who can bring a clean thing out
        of an unclean?
    No one can.
5 Since their days are determined,
    and the number of their
        months is known to you,
    and you have appointed the
        bounds that they cannot
        pass,
6 look away from them, and
        desist,ᶻ
    that they may enjoy, like
        laborers, their days.

7 "For there is hope for a tree,
    if it is cut down, that it will
        sprout again,
    and that its shoots will not
        cease.
8 Though its root grows old in the
        earth,
    and its stump dies in the
        ground,
9 yet at the scent of water it will
        bud
    and put forth branches like a
        young plant.
10 But mortals die, and are laid
        low;

ʷGk: Heb *Why should I take . . . in my
hand?*   ˣOr *Though he kill me, yet I
will trust in him*   ʸHeb *inherit*
ᶻCn: Heb *that they may desist*

humans expire, and where are
they?

11 As waters fail from a lake,
and a river wastes away and
dries up,

12 so mortals lie down and do not
rise again;
until the heavens are no more,
they will not awake
or be roused out of their sleep.

13 Oh that you would hide me in
Shē'ōl,
that you would conceal me
until your wrath is past,
that you would appoint me a
set time, and remember
me!

14 If mortals die, will they live
again?
All the days of my service I
would wait
until my release should come.

15 You would call, and I would
answer you;
you would long for the work
of your hands.

16 For then you would not*a*
number my steps,
you would not keep watch
over my sin;

17 my transgression would be
sealed up in a bag,
and you would cover over my
iniquity.

18 "But the mountain falls and
crumbles away,
and the rock is removed from
its place;

19 the waters wear away the
stones;
the torrents wash away the
soil of the earth;
so you destroy the hope of
mortals.

20 You prevail forever against
them, and they pass away;
you change their countenance,
and send them away.

21 Their children come to honor,
and they do not know it;
they are brought low, and it
goes unnoticed.

22 They feel only the pain of their
own bodies,
and mourn only for
themselves."

*Eliphaz Speaks: Job
Undermines Religion*

15 Then E·lī'phaz the Tē'man·ite
answered:

2 "Should the wise answer with
windy knowledge,
and fill themselves with the
east wind?

3 Should they argue in
unprofitable talk,
or in words with which they
can do no good?

4 But you are doing away with the
fear of God,
and hindering meditation
before God.

5 For your iniquity teaches your
mouth,
and you choose the tongue of
the crafty.

6 Your own mouth condemns you,
and not I;
your own lips testify against
you.

7 "Are you the firstborn of the
human race?
Were you brought forth before
the hills?

8 Have you listened in the council
of God?
And do you limit wisdom to
yourself?

9 What do you know that we do
not know?
What do you understand that
is not clear to us?

10 The gray-haired and the aged
are on our side,
those older than your father.

11 Are the consolations of God too
small for you,
or the word that deals gently
with you?

12 Why does your heart carry you
away,
and why do your eyes flash,*b*

13 so that you turn your spirit
against God,
and let such words go out of
your mouth?

14 What are mortals, that they can
be clean?
Or those born of woman, that
they can be righteous?

15 God puts no trust even in his
holy ones,

---

*a*Syr: Heb lacks *not*   *b*Meaning of Heb
uncertain

and the heavens are not clean
in his sight;
16 how much less one who is
abominable and corrupt,
one who drinks iniquity like
water!

17 "I will show you; listen to me;
what I have seen I will
declare—
18 what sages have told,
and their ancestors have not
hidden,
19 to whom alone the land was
given,
and no stranger passed among
them.
20 The wicked writhe in pain all
their days,
through all the years that are
laid up for the ruthless.
21 Terrifying sounds are in their
ears;
in prosperity the destroyer will
come upon them.
22 They despair of returning from
darkness,
and they are destined for the
sword.
23 They wander abroad for bread,
saying, 'Where is it?'
They know that a day of
darkness is ready at hand;
24 distress and anguish terrify
them;
they prevail against them, like
a king prepared for battle.
25 Because they stretched out their
hands against God,
and bid defiance to the
Almighty,c
26 running stubbornly against him
with a thick-bossed shield;
27 because they have covered their
faces with their fat,
and gathered fat upon their
loins,
28 they will live in desolate cities,
in houses that no one should
inhabit,
houses destined to become
heaps of ruins;
29 they will not be rich, and their
wealth will not endure,
nor will they strike root in the
earth;d
30 they will not escape from
darkness;
the flame will dry up their
shoots,
and their blossome will be
swept awayf by the wind.

31 Let them not trust in emptiness,
deceiving themselves;
for emptiness will be their
recompense.
32 It will be paid in full before their
time,
and their branch will not be
green.
33 They will shake off their unripe
grape, like the vine,
and cast off their blossoms,
like the olive tree.
34 For the company of the godless
is barren,
and fire consumes the tents of
bribery.
35 They conceive mischief and
bring forth evil
and their heart prepares
deceit."

Job Reaffirms His Innocence

16

Then Job answered:
2 "I have heard many such
things;
miserable comforters are you
all.
3 Have windy words no limit?
Or what provokes you that
you keep on talking?
4 I also could talk as you do,
if you were in my place;
I could join words together
against you,
and shake my head at you.
5 I could encourage you with my
mouth,
and the solace of my lips
would assuage your pain.

6 "If I speak, my pain is not
assuaged,
and if I forbear, how much of
it leaves me?
7 Surely now God has worn me
out;
he hasg made desolate all my
company.
8 And he hasg shriveled me up,
which is a witness against me;
my leanness has risen up against
me,
and it testifies to my face.
9 He has torn me in his wrath, and
hated me;
he has gnashed his teeth at
me;

---

c Traditional rendering of Heb *Shaddai*
d Vg: Meaning of Heb uncertain
e Gk: Heb *mouth*   f Cn: Heb *will depart*
g Heb *you have*

my adversary sharpens his
  eyes against me.
10 They have gaped at me with
    their mouths;
  they have struck me insolently
    on the cheek;
  they mass themselves together
    against me.
11 God gives me up to the ungodly,
  and casts me into the hands of
    the wicked.
12 I was at ease, and he broke me
    in two;
  he seized me by the neck and
    dashed me to pieces;
he set me up as his target;
13   his archers surround me.
He slashes open my kidneys,
  and shows no mercy;
  he pours out my gall on the
    ground.
14 He bursts upon me again and
    again;
  he rushes at me like a warrior.
15 I have sewed sackcloth upon my
    skin,
  and have laid my strength in
    the dust.
16 My face is red with weeping,
  and deep darkness is on my
    eyelids,
17 though there is no violence in
    my hands,
  and my prayer is pure.

18 "O earth, do not cover my blood;
  let my outcry find no resting
    place.
19 Even now, in fact, my witness is
    in heaven,
  and he that vouches for me is
    on high.
20 My friends scorn me;
  my eye pours out tears to God,
21 that he would maintain the right
    of a mortal with God,
  as[h] one does for a neighbor.
22 For when a few years have
    come,
  I shall go the way from which
    I shall not return.

Job Prays for Relief

17 My spirit is broken, my days
    are extinct,
  the grave is ready for me.
2 Surely there are mockers around
    me,
  and my eye dwells on their
    provocation.

3 "Lay down a pledge for me with
    yourself;
  who is there that will give
    surety for me?
4 Since you have closed their
    minds to understanding,
  therefore you will not let them
    triumph.
5 Those who denounce friends for
    reward—
  the eyes of their children will
    fail.

6 "He has made me a byword of
    the peoples,
  and I am one before whom
    people spit.
7 My eye has grown dim from
    grief,
  and all my members are like a
    shadow.
8 The upright are appalled at this,
  and the innocent stir
    themselves up against the
    godless.
9 Yet the righteous hold to their
    way,
  and they that have clean
    hands grow stronger and
    stronger.
10 But you, come back now, all of
    you,
  and I shall not find a sensible
    person among you.
11 My days are past, my plans are
    broken off,
  the desires of my heart.
12 They make night into day;
  'The light,' they say, 'is near to
    the darkness.'[i]
13 If I look for She´ol as my house,
  if I spread my couch in
    darkness,
14 if I say to the Pit, 'You are my
    father,'
  and to the worm, 'My mother,'
    or 'My sister,'
15 where then is my hope?
  Who will see my hope?
16 Will it go down to the bars of
    She´ol?
  Shall we descend together into
    the dust?"

[h]Syr Vg Tg: Heb *and*   [i]Meaning of
Heb uncertain

*Bildad Speaks: God Punishes
the Wicked*

18 Then Bil'dad the Shū'hīte answered:

2 "How long will you hunt for
    words?
  Consider, and then we shall
    speak.

3 Why are we counted as cattle?
  Why are we stupid in your
    sight?

4 You who tear yourself in your
    anger—
  shall the earth be forsaken
    because of you,
  or the rock be removed out of
    its place?

5 "Surely the light of the wicked is
    put out,
  and the flame of their fire does
    not shine.

6 The light is dark in their tent,
  and the lamp above them is
    put out.

7 Their strong steps are shortened,
  and their own schemes throw
    them down.

8 For they are thrust into a net by
    their own feet,
  and they walk into a pitfall.

9 A trap seizes them by the heel;
  a snare lays hold of them.

10 A rope is hid for them in the
    ground,
  a trap for them in the path.

11 Terrors frighten them on every
    side,
  and chase them at their heels.

12 Their strength is consumed by
    hunger,*j*
  and calamity is ready for their
    stumbling.

13 By disease their skin is
    consumed,*k*
  the firstborn of Death
    consumes their limbs.

14 They are torn from the tent in
    which trusted,
  and are brought to the king of
    terrors.

15 In their tents nothing remains;
  sulfur is scattered upon their
    habitations.

16 Their roots dry up beneath,
  and their branches wither
    above.

17 Their memory perishes from the
    earth,
  and they have no name in the
    street.

18 They are thrust from light into
    darkness,
  and driven out of the world.

19 They have no offspring or
    descendant among their
    people,
  and no survivor where they
    used to live.

20 They of the west are appalled at
    their fate,
  and horror seizes those of the
    east.

21 Surely such are the dwellings of
    the ungodly,
  such is the place of those who
    do not know God."

*Job Replies: I Know That My
Redeemer Lives*

19 Then Job answered:

2 "How long will you
    torment me,
  and break me in pieces with
    words?

3 These ten times you have cast
    reproach upon me;
  are you not ashamed to wrong
    me?

4 And even if it is true that I have
    erred,
  my error remains with me.

5 If indeed you magnify yourselves
    against me,
  and make my humiliation an
    argument against me,

6 know then that God has put me
    in the wrong,
  and closed his net around me.

7 Even when I cry out, 'Violence!'
    I am not answered;
  I call aloud, but there is no
    justice.

8 He has walled up my way so
    that I cannot pass,
  and he has set darkness upon
    my paths.

9 He has stripped my glory from
    me,
  and taken the crown from my
    head.

10 He breaks me down on every
    side, and I am gone,
  he has uprooted my hope like
    a tree.

11 He has kindled his wrath against
    me,

j Or *Disaster is hungry for them*
k Cn: Heb *It consumes the limbs of his
skin*

and counts me as his
    adversary.
12 His troops come on together;
    they have thrown up
      siegeworks[l] against me,
    and encamp around my tent.

13 "He has put my family far from
    me,
    and my acquaintances are
      wholly estranged from me.
14 My relatives and my close
    friends have failed me;
15   the guests in my house have
    forgotten me;
my serving girls count me as a
    stranger;
    I have become an alien in their
      eyes.
16 I call to my servant, but he gives
    me no answer;
    I must myself plead with him.
17 My breath is repulsive to my
    wife;
    I am loathsome to my own
      family.
18 Even young children despise me;
    when I rise, they talk against
      me.
19 All my intimate friends abhor
    me,
    and those whom I loved have
      turned against me.
20 My bones cling to my skin and
    to my flesh,
    and I have escaped by the skin
      of my teeth.
21 Have pity on me, have pity on
    me, O you my friends,
    for the hand of God has
      touched me!
22 Why do you, like God, pursue
    me,
    never satisfied with my flesh?

23 "O that my words were written
    down!
    O that they were inscribed in a
      book!
24 O that with an iron pen and with
    lead
    they were engraved on a rock
      forever!
25 For I know that my Redeemer[m]
    lives,
    and that at the last he[n] will
      stand upon the earth;[o]
26 and after my skin has been thus
    destroyed,
    then in[p] my flesh I shall see
      God,[q]
27 whom I shall see on my side,[r]

and my eyes shall behold, and
    not another.
    My heart faints within me!
28 If you say, 'How we will
    persecute him!'
    and, 'The root of the matter is
      found in him';
29 be afraid of the sword,
    for wrath brings the
      punishment of the sword,
    so that you may know there is
      a judgment."

*Zophar Speaks: Wickedness Receives
Just Retribution*

20 Then Zō′phar the Nā′a·ma-
    thīte answered:
2 "Pay attention! My thoughts urge
    me to answer,
    because of the agitation within
      me.
3 I hear censure that insults me,
    and a spirit beyond my
      understanding answers me.
4 Do you not know this from of
    old,
    ever since mortals were placed
      on earth,
5 that the exulting of the wicked is
    short,
    and the joy of the godless is
      but for a moment?
6 Even though they mount up high
    as the heavens,
    and their head reaches to the
      clouds,
7 they will perish forever like their
    own dung;
    those who have seen them will
      say, 'Where are they?'
8 They will fly away like a dream,
    and not be found;
    they will be chased away like
      a vision of the night.
9 The eye that saw them will see
    them no more,
    nor will their place behold
      them any longer.
10 Their children will seek the
    favor of the poor,
    and their hands will give back
      their wealth.
11 Their bodies, once full of youth,
    will lie down in the dust with
      them.

J
O
B

---

*l*Cn: Heb *their way*   *m*Or *Vindicator*
*n*Or *that he the Last*   *o*Heb *dust*
*p*Or *without*   *q*Meaning of Heb of this
verse uncertain   *r*Or *for myself*

12 "Though wickedness is sweet in
their mouth,
though they hide it under their
tongues,
13 though they are loath to let it go,
and hold it in their mouths,
14 yet their food is turned in their
stomachs;
it is the venom of asps within
them.
15 They swallow down riches and
vomit them up again;
God casts them out of their
bellies.
16 They will suck the poison of
asps;
the tongue of a viper will kill
them.
17 They will not look on the rivers,
the streams flowing with
honey and curds.
18 They will give back the fruit of
their toil,
and will not swallow it down;
from the profit of their trading
they will get no enjoyment.
19 For they have crushed and
abandoned the poor,
they have seized a house that
they did not build.

20 "They knew no quiet in their
bellies;
in their greed they let nothing
escape.
21 There was nothing left after they
had eaten;
therefore their prosperity will
not endure.
22 In full sufficiency they will be in
distress;
all the force of misery will
come upon them.
23 To fill their belly to the full
God*s* will send his fierce
anger into them,
and rain it upon them as their
food.*t*
24 They will flee from an iron
weapon;
a bronze arrow will strike
them through.
25 It is drawn forth and comes out
of their body,
and the glittering point comes
out of their gall;
terrors come upon them.
26 Utter darkness is laid up for
their treasures;
a fire fanned by no one will
devour them;

what is left in their tent will be
consumed.
27 The heavens will reveal their
iniquity,
and the earth will rise up
against them.
28 The possessions of their house
will be carried away,
dragged off in the day of
God's*u* wrath.
29 This is the portion of the wicked
from God,
the heritage decreed for them
by God."

Job Replies: The Wicked Often Go Unpunished

21 Then Job answered:
2 "Listen carefully to my
words,
and let this be your
consolation.
3 Bear with me, and I will speak;
then after I have spoken, mock
on.
4 As for me, is my complaint
addressed to mortals?
Why should I not be
impatient?
5 Look at me, and be appalled,
and lay your hand upon your
mouth.
6 When I think of it I am
dismayed,
and shuddering seizes my
flesh.
7 Why do the wicked live on,
reach old age, and grow
mighty in power?
8 Their children are established in
their presence,
and their offspring before their
eyes.
9 Their houses are safe from fear,
and no rod of God is upon
them.
10 Their bull breeds without fail;
their cow calves and never
miscarries.
11 They send out their little ones
like a flock,
and their children dance
around.
12 They sing to the tambourine and
the lyre,
and rejoice to the sound of the
pipe.

s Heb *he*   *t* Cn: Meaning of Heb
uncertain   *u* Heb *his*

13 They spend their days in
prosperity,
and in peace they go down to
Shē′ōl.
14 They say to God, 'Leave us
alone!
We do not desire to know your
ways.
15 What is the Almighty,[v] that we
should serve him?
And what profit do we get if
we pray to him?'
16 Is not their prosperity indeed
their own achievement?[w]
The plans of the wicked are
repugnant to me.

17 "How often is the lamp of the
wicked put out?
How often does calamity come
upon them?
How often does God[x]
distribute pains in his
anger?
18 How often are they like straw
before the wind,
and like chaff that the storm
carries away?
19 You say, 'God stores up their
iniquity for their children.'
Let it be paid back to them, so
that they may know it.
20 Let their own eyes see their
destruction,
and let them drink of the
wrath of the Almighty.[v]
21 For what do they care for their
household after them,
when the number of their
months is cut off?
22 Will any teach God knowledge,
seeing that he judges those
that are on high?
23 One dies in full prosperity,
being wholly at ease and
secure,
24 his loins full of milk
and the marrow of his bones
moist.
25 Another dies in bitterness of
soul,
never having tasted of good.
26 They lie down alike in the dust,
and the worms cover them.

27 "Oh, I know your thoughts,
and your schemes to wrong
me.
28 For you say, 'Where is the house
of the prince?
Where is the tent in which the
wicked lived?'

29 Have you not asked those who
travel the roads,
and do you not accept their
testimony,
30 that the wicked are spared in the
day of calamity,
and are rescued in the day of
wrath?
31 Who declares their way to their
face,
and who repays them for what
they have done?
32 When they are carried to the
grave,
a watch is kept over their
tomb.
33 The clods of the valley are sweet
to them;
everyone will follow after,
and those who went before are
innumerable.
34 How then will you comfort me
with empty nothings?
There is nothing left of your
answers but falsehood."

*Eliphaz Speaks: Job's
Wickedness Is Great*

22 Then E·lī′phaz the Tē′man·īte
answered:
2 "Can a mortal be of use to God?
Can even the wisest be of
service to him?
3 Is it any pleasure to the
Almighty[v] if you are
righteous,
or is it gain to him if you
make your ways
blameless?
4 Is it for your piety that he
reproves you,
and enters into judgment with
you?
5 Is not your wickedness great?
There is no end to your
iniquities.
6 For you have exacted pledges
from your family for no
reason,
and stripped the naked of their
clothing.
7 You have given no water to the
weary to drink,
and you have withheld bread
from the hungry.
8 The powerful possess the land,
and the favored live in it.

[v] Traditional rendering of Heb *Shaddai*
[w] Heb *in their hand*   [x] Heb *he*

9 You have sent widows away
    empty-handed,
  and the arms of the orphans
    you have crushed.ʸ
10 Therefore snares are around
    you,
  and sudden terror overwhelms
    you,
11 or darkness so that you cannot
    see;
  a flood of water covers you.
12 "Is not God high in the heavens?
  See the highest stars, how
    lofty they are!
13 Therefore you say, 'What does
    God know?
  Can he judge through the deep
    darkness?
14 Thick clouds enwrap him, so
    that he does not see,
  and he walks on the dome of
    heaven.'
15 Will you keep to the old way
    that the wicked have trod?
16 They were snatched away before
    their time;
  their foundation was washed
    away by a flood.
17 They said to God, 'Leave us
    alone,'
  and 'What can the Almightyᶻ
    do to us?'ᵃ
18 Yet he filled their houses with
    good things—
  but the plans of the wicked are
    repugnant to me.
19 The righteous see it and are
    glad;
  the innocent laugh them to
    scorn,
20 saying, 'Surely our adversaries
    are cut off,
  and what they left, the fire has
    consumed.'

21 "Agree with God,ᵇ and be at
    peace;
  in this way good will come to
    you.
22 Receive instruction from his
    mouth,
  and lay up his words in your
    heart.
23 If you return to the Almighty,ᶻ
    you will be restored,
  if you remove unrighteousness
    from your tents,
24 if you treat gold like dust,
  and gold of Oʹphir like the
    stones of the torrent-bed,

25 and if the Almightyᶻ is your
    gold
  and your precious silver,
26 then you will delight yourself in
    the Almighty,ᶻ
  and lift up your face to God.
27 You will pray to him, and he
    will hear you,
  and you will pay your vows.
28 You will decide on a matter, and
    it will be established for
    you,
  and light will shine on your
    ways.
29 When others are humiliated, you
    say it is pride;
  for he saves the humble.
30 He will deliver even those who
    are guilty;
  they will escape because of the
    cleanness of your hands."ᶜ

Job Replies: My Complaint Is Bitter

23 Then Job answered:
  2 "Today also my complaint
    is bitter;ᵈ
  hisᵉ hand is heavy despite my
    groaning.
3 Oh, that I knew where I might
    find him,
  that I might come even to his
    dwelling!
4 I would lay my case before him,
  and fill my mouth with
    arguments.
5 I would learn what he would
    answer me,
  and understand what he would
    say to me.
6 Would he contend with me in
    the greatness of his power?
  No; but he would give heed to
    me.
7 There an upright person could
    reason with him,
  and I should be acquitted
    forever by my judge.

8 "If I go forward, he is not there;
  or backward, I cannot perceive
    him;
9 on the left he hides, and I cannot
    behold him;
  I turnᶠ to the right, but I
    cannot see him.

ʸ Gk Syr Tg Vg: Heb *were crushed*
ᶻ Traditional rendering of Heb *Shaddai*
ᵃ Gk Syr: Heb *them*   ᵇ Heb *him*
ᶜ Meaning of Heb uncertain   ᵈ Syr Vg
Tg: Heb *rebellious*   ᵉ Gk Syr: Heb *my*
ᶠ Syr Vg: Heb *he turns*

10 But he knows the way that I
     take;
  when he has tested me, I shall
     come out like gold.
11 My foot has held fast to his
     steps;
  I have kept his way and have
     not turned aside.
12 I have not departed from the
     commandment of his lips;
  I have treasured ing my
     bosom the words of his
     mouth.
13 But he stands alone and who
     can dissuade him?
  What he desires, that he does.
14 For he will complete what he
     appoints for me;
  and many such things are in
     his mind.
15 Therefore I am terrified at his
     presence;
  when I consider, I am in dread
     of him.
16 God has made my heart faint;
  the Almightyh has terrified
     me;
17 If only I could vanish in
     darkness,
  and thick darkness would
     cover my face!i

*Job Complains of Violence
on the Earth*

24 "Why are times not kept by
     the Almighty,h
and why do those who know
     him never see his days?
2 The wickedj remove landmarks;
  they seize flocks and pasture
     them.
3 They drive away the donkey of
     the orphan;
  they take the widow's ox for a
     pledge.
4 They thrust the needy off the
     road;
  the poor of the earth all hide
     themselves.
5 Like wild asses in the desert
     they go out to their toil,
scavenging in the wasteland
     food for their young.
6 They reap in a field not their
     own
  and they glean in the vineyard
     of the wicked.
7 They lie all night naked, without
     clothing,
  and have no covering in the
     cold.

8 They are wet with the rain of the
     mountains,
  and cling to the rock for want
     of shelter.

9 "There are those who snatch the
     orphan child from the
     breast,
  and take as a pledge the infant
     of the poor.
10 They go about naked, without
     clothing;
  though hungry, they carry the
     sheaves;
11 between their terracesk they
     press out oil;
  they tread the wine presses,
     but suffer thirst.
12 From the city the dying groan,
  and the throat of the wounded
     cries for help;
  yet God pays no attention to
     their prayer.

13 "There are those who rebel
     against the light,
  who are not acquainted with
     its ways,
  and do not stay in its paths.
14 The murderer rises at dusk
     to kill the poor and needy,
  and in the night is like a thief.
15 The eye of the adulterer also
     waits for the twilight,
  saying, 'No eye will see me';
  and he disguises his face.
16 In the dark they dig through
     houses;
  by day they shut themselves
     up;
  they do not know the light.
17 For deep darkness is morning to
     all of them;
  for they are friends with the
     terrors of deep darkness.

18 "Swift are they on the face of
     the waters;
  their portion in the land is
     cursed;
  no treader turns toward their
     vineyards.
19 Drought and heat snatch away
     the snow waters;

g Gk Vg: Heb *from*   h Traditional
rendering of Heb *Shaddai*   i Or *But I
am not destroyed by the darkness; he
has concealed the thick darkness from
me*   j Gk: Heb *they*   k Meaning of Heb
uncertain

so does Shē′ol those who have sinned.

20 The womb forgets them;
the worm finds them sweet;
they are no longer remembered;
so wickedness is broken like a tree.

21 "They harm*l* the childless woman,
and do no good to the widow.

22 Yet God*m* prolongs the life of the mighty by his power;
they rise up when they despair of life.

23 He gives them security, and they are supported;
his eyes are upon their ways.

24 They are exalted a little while, and then are gone;
they wither and fade like the mallow;*n*
they are cut off like the heads of grain.

25 If it is not so, who will prove me a liar,
and show that there is nothing in what I say?"

Bildad Speaks: How Can a Mortal Be Righteous Before God?

25 Then Bil′dad the Shū′hīte answered:

2 "Dominion and fear are with God;*o*
he makes peace in his high heaven.

3 Is there any number to his armies?
Upon whom does his light not arise?

4 How then can a mortal be righteous before God?
How can one born of woman be pure?

5 If even the moon is not bright and the stars are not pure in his sight,

6 how much less a mortal, who is a maggot,
and a human being, who is a worm!"

Job Replies: God's Majesty Is Unsearchable

26 Then Job answered:
2 "How you have helped one who has no power!
How you have assisted the arm that has no strength!

3 How you have counseled one who has no wisdom,
and given much good advice!

4 With whose help have you uttered words,
and whose spirit has come forth from you?

5 The shades below tremble, the waters and their inhabitants.

6 Shē′ol is naked before God, and A·bad′don has no covering.

7 He stretches out Zā′phon*p* over the void,
and hangs the earth upon nothing.

8 He binds up the waters in his thick clouds,
and the cloud is not torn open by them.

9 He covers the face of the full moon,
and spreads over it his cloud.

10 He has described a circle on the face of the waters,
at the boundary between light and darkness.

11 The pillars of heaven tremble, and are astounded at his rebuke.

12 By his power he stilled the Sea; by his understanding he struck down Rā′hab.

13 By his wind the heavens were made fair;
his hand pierced the fleeing serpent.

14 These are indeed but the outskirts of his ways;
and how small a whisper do we hear of him!
But the thunder of his power who can understand?"

Job Maintains His Integrity

27 Job again took up his discourse and said:
2 "As God lives, who has taken away my right,
and the Almighty,*q* who has made my soul bitter,

3 as long as my breath is in me and the spirit of God is in my nostrils,

4 my lips will not speak falsehood,

l Gk Tg: Heb *feed on* or *associate with*
m Heb *he*   *n* Gk: Heb *like all others*
o Heb *him*   *p* Or *the North*
q Traditional rendering of Heb *Shaddai*

and my tongue will not utter
deceit.
5 Far be it from me to say that you
are right;
until I die I will not put away
my integrity from me.
6 I hold fast my righteousness, and
will not let it go;
my heart does not reproach
me for any of my days.

7 "May my enemy be like the
wicked,
and may my opponent be like
the unrighteous.
8 For what is the hope of the
godless when God cuts
them off,
when God takes away their
lives?
9 Will God hear their cry
when trouble comes upon
them?
10 Will they take delight in the
Almighty?[r]
Will they call upon God at all
times?
11 I will teach you concerning the
hand of God;
that which is with the
Almighty[r] I will not
conceal.
12 All of you have seen it
yourselves;
why then have you become
altogether vain?

13 This is the portion of the wicked
with God,
and the heritage that
oppressors receive from
the Almighty:[r]
14 If their children are multiplied, it
is for the sword;
and their offspring have not
enough to eat.
15 Those who survive them the
pestilence buries,
and their widows make no
lamentation.
16 Though they heap up silver like
dust,
and pile up clothing like
clay—
17 they may pile it up, but the just
will wear it,
and the innocent will divide
the silver.
18 They build their houses like
nests,
like booths made by sentinels
of the vineyard.

19 They go to bed with wealth, but
will do so no more;
they open their eyes, and it is
gone.
20 Terrors overtake them like a
flood;
in the night a whirlwind
carries them off.
21 The east wind lifts them up and
they are gone;
it sweeps them out of their
place.
22 It[s] hurls at them without pity;
they flee from its[t] power in
headlong flight.
23 It[s] claps its[t] hands at them,
and hisses at them from its[t]
place.

Interlude: Where Wisdom Is Found

28 "Surely there is a mine for
silver,
and a place for gold to be
refined.
2 Iron is taken out of the earth,
and copper is smelted from
ore.
3 Miners put[u] an end to darkness,
and search out to the farthest
bound
the ore in gloom and deep
darkness.
4 They open shafts in a valley
away from human
habitation;
they are forgotten by travelers,
they sway suspended, remote
from people.
5 As for the earth, out of it comes
bread;
but underneath it is turned up
as by fire.
6 Its stones are the place of
sapphires,[v]
and its dust contains gold.

7 "That path no bird of prey
knows,
and the falcon's eye has not
seen it.
8 The proud wild animals have not
trodden it;
the lion has not passed over it.

9 "They put their hand to the flinty
rock,

[r]Traditional rendering of Heb *Shaddai*
[s]Or *He* (that is God)   [t]Or *his*
[u]Heb *He puts*   [v]Or *lapis lazuli*

and overturn mountains by the roots.

10 They cut out channels in the rocks,
and their eyes see every precious thing.

11 The sources of the rivers they probe;*w*
hidden things they bring to light.

12 "But where shall wisdom be found?
And where is the place of understanding?

13 Mortals do not know the way to it,*x*
and it is not found in the land of the living.

14 The deep says, 'It is not in me,'
and the sea says, 'It is not with me.'

15 It cannot be gotten for gold,
and silver cannot be weighed out as its price.

16 It cannot be valued in the gold of Ō'phir,
in precious onyx or sapphire.*y*

17 Gold and glass cannot equal it,
nor can it be exchanged for jewels of fine gold.

18 No mention shall be made of coral or of crystal;
the price of wisdom is above pearls.

19 The chrysolite of Ethiopia*z*
cannot compare with it,
nor can it be valued in pure gold.

20 "Where then does wisdom come from?
And where is the place of understanding?

21 It is hidden from the eyes of all living,
and concealed from the birds of the air.

22 A·bad'don and Death say,
'We have heard a rumor of it with our ears.'

23 "God understands the way to it,
and he knows its place.

24 For he looks to the ends of the earth,
and sees everything under the heavens.

25 When he gave to the wind its weight,
and apportioned out the waters by measure;

26 when he made a decree for the rain,
and a way for the thunderbolt;

27 then he saw it and declared it;
he established it, and searched it out.

28 And he said to humankind,
'Truly, the fear of the Lord, that is wisdom;
and to depart from evil is understanding.' "

Job Finishes His Defense

29 Job again took up his discourse and said:

2 "Oh, that I were as in the months of old,
as in the days when God watched over me;

3 when his lamp shone over my head,
and by his light I walked through darkness;

4 when I was in my prime,
when the friendship of God was upon my tent;

5 when the Almighty*a* was still with me,
when my children were around me;

6 when my steps were washed with milk,
and the rock poured out for me streams of oil!

7 When I went out to the gate of the city,
when I took my seat in the square,

8 the young men saw me and withdrew,
and the aged rose up and stood;

9 the nobles refrained from talking,
and laid their hands on their mouths;

10 the voices of princes were hushed,
and their tongues stuck to the roof of their mouths.

11 When the ear heard, it commended me,
and when the eye saw, it approved;

12 because I delivered the poor who cried,

w Gk Vg: Heb *bind*   *x* Gk: Heb *its price*
y Or *lapis lazuli*   *z* Or *Nubia*; Heb *Cush*
a Traditional rendering of Heb *Shaddai*

and the orphan who had no helper.

13 The blessing of the wretched came upon me,
and I caused the widow's heart to sing for joy.

14 I put on righteousness, and it clothed me;
my justice was like a robe and a turban.

15 I was eyes to the blind,
and feet to the lame.

16 I was a father to the needy,
and I championed the cause of the stranger.

17 I broke the fangs of the unrighteous,
and made them drop their prey from their teeth.

18 Then I thought, 'I shall die in my nest,
and I shall multiply my days like the phoenix;[b]

19 my roots spread out to the waters,
with the dew all night on my branches;

20 my glory was fresh with me,
and my bow ever new in my hand.'

21 "They listened to me, and waited,
and kept silence for my counsel.

22 After I spoke they did not speak again,
and my word dropped upon them like dew.[c]

23 They waited for me as for the rain;
they opened their mouths as for the spring rain.

24 I smiled on them when they had no confidence;
and the light of my countenance they did not extinguish.[d]

25 I chose their way, and sat as chief,
and I lived like a king among his troops,
like one who comforts mourners.

30

"But now they make sport of me,
those who are younger than I,
whose fathers I would have disdained
to set with the dogs of my flock.

2 What could I gain from the strength of their hands?
All their vigor is gone.

3 Through want and hard hunger they gnaw the dry and desolate ground,

4 they pick mallow and the leaves of bushes,
and to warm themselves the roots of broom.

5 They are driven out from society;
people shout after them as after a thief.

6 In the gullies of wadis they must live,
in holes in the ground, and in the rocks.

7 Among the bushes they bray;
under the nettles they huddle together.

8 A senseless, disreputable brood,
they have been whipped out of the land.

9 "And now they mock me in song;
I am a byword to them.

10 They abhor me, they keep aloof from me;
they do not hesitate to spit at the sight of me.

11 Because God has loosed my bowstring and humbled me,
they have cast off restraint in my presence.

12 On my right hand the rabble rise up;
they send me sprawling,
and build roads for my ruin.

13 They break up my path,
they promote my calamity;
no one restrains[e] them.

14 As through a wide breach they come;
amid the crash they roll on.

15 Terrors are turned upon me;
my honor is pursued as by the wind,
and my prosperity has passed away like a cloud.

16 "And now my soul is poured out within me;
days of affliction have taken hold of me.

17 The night racks my bones,

---

[b] Or like sand   [c] Heb lacks like dew
[d] Meaning of Heb uncertain   [e] Cn: Heb helps

and the pain that gnaws me
    takes no rest.
18 With violence he seizes my
    garment;[f]
  he grasps me by[g] the collar of
    my tunic.
19 He has cast me into the mire,
    and I have become like dust
    and ashes.
20 I cry to you and you do not
    answer me;
  I stand, and you merely look
    at me.
21 You have turned cruel to me;
    with the might of your hand
    you persecute me.
22 You lift me up on the wind, you
    make me ride on it,
    and you toss me about in the
    roar of the storm.
23 I know that you will bring me to
    death,
    and to the house appointed for
    all living.

24 "Surely one does not turn
    against the needy,[h]
  when in disaster they cry for
    help.[i]
25 Did I not weep for those whose
    day was hard?
  Was not my soul grieved for
    the poor?
26 But when I looked for good, evil
    came;
    and when I waited for light,
    darkness came.
27 My inward parts are in turmoil,
    and are never still;
    days of affliction come to meet
    me.
28 I go about in sunless gloom;
    I stand up in the assembly and
    cry for help.
29 I am a brother of jackals,
    and a companion of ostriches.
30 My skin turns black and falls
    from me,
    and my bones burn with heat.
31 My lyre is turned to mourning,
    and my pipe to the voice of
    those who weep.

31 "I have made a covenant with
    my eyes;
    how then could I look upon a
    virgin?
2 What would be my portion from
    God above,
    and my heritage from the
    Almighty[j] on high?

3 Does not calamity befall the
    unrighteous,
    and disaster the workers of
    iniquity?
4 Does he not see my ways,
    and number all my steps?

5 "If I have walked with falsehood,
    and my foot has hurried to
    deceit—
6 let me be weighed in a just
    balance,
    and let God know my
    integrity!—
7 if my step has turned aside from
    the way,
    and my heart has followed my
    eyes,
    and if any spot has clung to
    my hands;
8 then let me sow, and another
    eat;
    and let what grows for me be
    rooted out.

9 "If my heart has been enticed by
    a woman,
    and I have lain in wait at my
    neighbor's door;
10 then let my wife grind for
    another,
    and let other men kneel over
    her.
11 For that would be a heinous
    crime;
    that would be a criminal
    offense;
12 for that would be a fire
    consuming down to
    A·bad'don,
    and it would burn to the root
    all my harvest.

13 "If I have rejected the cause of
    my male or female slaves,
    when they brought a
    complaint against me;
14 what then shall I do when God
    rises up?
    When he makes inquiry, what
    shall I answer him?
15 Did not he who made me in the
    womb make them?
    And did not one fashion us in
    the womb?

[f]Gk: Heb my garment is disfigured
[g]Heb like   [h]Heb ruin   [i]Cn: Meaning
of Heb uncertain   [j]Traditional
rendering of Heb Shaddai

16 "If I have withheld anything that
      the poor desired,
   or have caused the eyes of the
      widow to fail,
17 or have eaten my morsel alone,
      and the orphan has not eaten
      from it—
18 for from my youth I reared the
      orphan[k] like a father,
   and from my mother's womb I
      guided the widow[l]—
19 if I have seen anyone perish for
      lack of clothing,
   or a poor person without
      covering,
20 whose loins have not blessed
      me,
   and who was not warmed with
      the fleece of my sheep;
21 if I have raised my hand against
      the orphan,
   because I saw I had supporters
      at the gate;
22 then let my shoulder blade fall
      from my shoulder,
   and let my arm be broken
      from its socket.
23 For I was in terror of calamity
      from God,
   and I could not have faced his
      majesty.

24 "If I have made gold my trust,
   or called fine gold my
      confidence;
25 if I have rejoiced because my
      wealth was great,
   or because my hand had
      gotten much;
26 if I have looked at the sun[m]
      when it shone,
   or the moon moving in
      splendor,
27 and my heart has been secretly
      enticed,
   and my mouth has kissed my
      hand;
28 this also would be an iniquity to
      be punished by the judges,
   for I should have been false to
      God above.

29 "If I have rejoiced at the ruin of
      those who hated me,
   or exulted when evil overtook
      them—
30 I have not let my mouth sin
   by asking for their lives with a
      curse—
31 if those of my tent ever said,
   'O that we might be sated with
      his flesh!'[n]—

32 the stranger has not lodged in
      the street;
   I have opened my doors to the
      traveler—
33 if I have concealed my
      transgressions as others
      do,[o]
   by hiding my iniquity in my
      bosom,
34 because I stood in great fear of
      the multitude,
   and the contempt of families
      terrified me,
   so that I kept silence, and did
      not go out of doors—
35 Oh, that I had one to hear me!
   (Here is my signature! let the
      Almighty[p] answer me!)
   Oh, that I had the indictment
      written by my adversary!
36 Surely I would carry it on my
      shoulder;
   I would bind it on me like a
      crown;
37 I would give him an account of
      all my steps;
   like a prince I would approach
      him.

38 "If my land has cried out against
      me,
   and its furrows have wept
      together;
39 if I have eaten its yield without
      payment,
   and caused the death of its
      owners;
40 let thorns grow instead of wheat,
   and foul weeds instead of
      barley."

The words of Job are ended.

Elihu Rebukes Job's Friends

32 So these three men ceased to
   answer Job, because he was
righteous in his own eyes. ² Then
E·li′hū son of Bar′a·chel the Būz′īte, of
the family of Ram, became angry. He
was angry at Job because he justified
himself rather than God; ³ he was angry also at Job's three friends because
they had found no answer, though
they had declared Job to be in the
wrong.[q] ⁴ Now E·li′hū had waited to

---

[k] Heb *him*   [l] Heb *her*   [m] Heb *the light*
[n] Meaning of Heb uncertain   [o] Or *as
Adam did*   [p] Traditional rendering of
Heb *Shaddai*   [q] Another ancient
tradition reads *answer, and had put God
in the wrong*

speak to Job, because they were older than he. 5 But when E·li′hū saw that there was no answer in the mouths of these three men, he became angry.

6 E·li′hū son of Bar′a·chel the Būz′īte answered:

"I am young in years,
   and you are aged;
therefore I was timid and afraid
   to declare my opinion to you.
7 I said, 'Let days speak,
   and many years teach
     wisdom.'
8 But truly it is the spirit in a
     mortal,
   the breath of the Almighty,[r]
     that makes for
     understanding.
9 It is not the old[s] that are wise,
   nor the aged that understand
     what is right.
10 Therefore I say, 'Listen to me;
   let me also declare my
     opinion.'

11 "See, I waited for your words,
   I listened for your wise
     sayings,
   while you searched out what
     to say.
12 I gave you my attention,
   but there was in fact no one
     that confuted Job,
   no one among you that
     answered his words.
13 Yet do not say, 'We have found
     wisdom;
   God may vanquish him, not a
     human.'
14 He has not directed his words
     against me,
   and I will not answer him with
     your speeches.

15 "They are dismayed, they
     answer no more;
   they have not a word to say.
16 And am I to wait, because they
     do not speak,
   because they stand there, and
     answer no more?
17 I also will give my answer;
   I also will declare my opinion.
18 For I am full of words;
   the spirit within me constrains
     me.
19 My heart is indeed like wine that
     has no vent;
   like new wineskins, it is ready
     to burst.
20 I must speak, so that I may find
     relief;

I must open my lips and
     answer.
21 I will not show partiality to any
     person
   or use flattery toward anyone.
22 For I do not know how to
     flatter—
   or my Maker would soon put
     an end to me!

Elihu Rebukes Job

33 But now, hear my speech,
   O Job,
   and listen to all my words.
2 See, I open my mouth;
   the tongue in my mouth
     speaks.
3 My words declare the
     uprightness of my heart,
   and what my lips know they
     speak sincerely.
4 The spirit of God has made me,
   and the breath of the
     Almighty[r] gives me life.
5 Answer me, if you can;
   set your words in order before
     me; take your stand.
6 See, before God I am as you are;
   I too was formed from a piece
     of clay.
7 No fear of me need terrify you;
   my pressure will not be heavy
     on you.

8 "Surely, you have spoken in my
     hearing,
   and I have heard the sound of
     your words.
9 You say, 'I am clean, without
     transgression;
   I am pure, and there is no
     iniquity in me.
10 Look, he finds occasions against
     me,
   he counts me as his enemy;
11 he puts my feet in the stocks,
   and watches all my paths.'

12 "But in this you are not right. I
     will answer you:
   God is greater than any
     mortal.
13 Why do you contend against
     him,
   saying, 'He will answer none
     of my[t] words'?
14 For God speaks in one way,

[r] Traditional rendering of Heb *Shaddai*
[s] Gk Syr Vg: Heb *many*   [t] Compare Gk:
Heb *his*

and in two, though people do
not perceive it.

15 In a dream, in a vision of the
night,
when deep sleep falls on
mortals,
while they slumber on their
beds,

16 then he opens their ears,
and terrifies them with
warnings,

17 that he may turn them aside
from their deeds,
and keep them from pride,

18 to spare their souls from the Pit,
their lives from traversing the
River.

19 They are also chastened with
pain upon their beds,
and with continual strife in
their bones,

20 so that their lives loathe bread,
and their appetites dainty
food.

21 Their flesh is so wasted away
that it cannot be seen;
and their bones, once invisible,
now stick out.

22 Their souls draw near the Pit,
and their lives to those who
bring death.

23 Then, if there should be for one
of them an angel,
a mediator, one of a thousand,
one who declares a person
upright,

24 and he is gracious to that
person, and says,
'Deliver him from going down
into the Pit;
I have found a ransom;

25 let his flesh become fresh with
youth;
let him return to the days of
his youthful vigor.'

26 Then he prays to God, and is
accepted by him,
he comes into his presence
with joy,
and God*u* repays him for his
righteousness.

27 That person sings to others
and says,
'I sinned, and perverted what
was right,
and it was not paid back to
me.

28 He has redeemed my soul from
going down to the Pit,
and my life shall see the light.'

29 "God indeed does all these
things,
twice, three times, with
mortals,

30 to bring back their souls from
the Pit,
so that they may see the light
of life.*v*

31 Pay heed, Job, listen to me;
be silent, and I will speak.

32 If you have anything to say,
answer me;
speak, for I desire to justify
you.

33 If not, listen to me;
be silent, and I will teach you
wisdom."

Elihu Proclaims God's Justice

34 Then E·li'hu continued and
said:

2 "Hear my words, you wise men,
and give ear to me, you who
know;

3 for the ear tests words
as the palate tastes food.

4 Let us choose what is right;
let us determine among
ourselves what is good.

5 For Job has said, 'I am innocent,
and God has taken away my
right;

6 in spite of being right I am
counted a liar;
my wound is incurable, though
I am without
transgression.'

7 Who is there like Job,
who drinks up scoffing like
water,

8 who goes in company with
evildoers
and walks with the wicked?

9 For he has said, 'It profits one
nothing
to take delight in God.'

10 "Therefore, hear me, you who
have sense,
far be it from God that he
should do wickedness,
and from the Almighty*w* that
he should do wrong.

11 For according to their deeds he
will repay them,
and according to their ways he
will make it befall them.

*u*Heb *he*   *v*Syr: Heb *to be lighted with
the light of life*   *w*Traditional rendering
of Heb *Shaddai*

**J
O
B**

12 Of a truth, God will not do
    wickedly,
    and the Almighty˟ will not
      pervert justice.
13 Who gave him charge over the
    earth
    and who laid on himʸ the
      whole world?
14 If he should take back his
    spiritᶻ to himself,
    and gather to himself his
      breath,
15 all flesh would perish together,
    and all mortals return to dust.

16 "If you have understanding, hear
    this;
    listen to what I say.
17 Shall one who hates justice
    govern?
    Will you condemn one who is
      righteous and mighty,
18 who says to a king, 'You
    scoundrel!'
    and to princes, 'You wicked
      men!';
19 who shows no partiality to
    nobles,
    nor regards the rich more than
      the poor,
    for they are all the work of his
      hands?
20 In a moment they die;
    at midnight the people are
      shaken and pass away,
    and the mighty are taken
      away by no human hand.

21 "For his eyes are upon the ways
    of mortals,
    and he sees all their steps.
22 There is no gloom or deep
    darkness
    where evildoers may hide
      themselves.
23 For he has not appointed a
    timeᵃ for anyone
    to go before God in judgment.
24 He shatters the mighty without
    investigation,
    and sets others in their place.
25 Thus, knowing their works,
    he overturns them in the night,
      and they are crushed.
26 He strikes them for their
    wickedness
    while others look on,
27 because they turned aside from
    following him,
    and had no regard for any of
      his ways,

28 so that they caused the cry of
    the poor to come to him,
    and he heard the cry of the
      afflicted—
29 When he is quiet, who can
    condemn?
    When he hides his face, who
      can behold him,
    whether it be a nation or an
      individual?—
30 so that the godless should not
    reign,
    or those who ensnare the
      people.

31 "For has anyone said to God,
    'I have endured punishment; I
      will not offend any more;
32 teach me what I do not see;
    if I have done iniquity, I will
      do it no more'?
33 Will he then pay back to suit
    you,
    because you reject it?
    For you must choose, and not I;
    therefore declare what you
      know.ᵇ
34 Those who have sense will say
    to me,
    and the wise who hear me will
      say,
35 'Job speaks without knowledge,
    his words are without insight.'
36 Would that Job were tried to the
    limit,
    because his answers are those
      of the wicked.
37 For he adds rebellion to his sin;
    he claps his hands among us,
    and multiplies his words
      against God."

Elihu Condemns Self-Righteousness

35 E·lī′hū continued and said:
2 "Do you think this to be
    just?
    You say, 'I am in the right
      before God.'
3 If you ask, 'What advantage
    have I?
    How am I better off than if I
      had sinned?'
4 I will answer you
    and your friends with you.
5 Look at the heavens and see;
    observe the clouds, which are
      higher than you.

˟Traditional rendering of Heb *Shaddai*
ʸHeb lacks *on him*   ᶻHeb *his heart his*
spirit   ᵃCn: Heb *yet*   ᵇMeaning of
Heb of verses 29-33 uncertain

6 If you have sinned, what do you
accomplish against him?
And if your transgressions are
multiplied, what do you do
to him?
7 If you are righteous, what do
you give to him;
or what does he receive from
your hand?
8 Your wickedness affects others
like you,
and your righteousness, other
human beings.

9 "Because of the multitude of
oppressions people cry out;
they call for help because of
the arm of the mighty.
10 But no one says, 'Where is God
my Maker,
who gives strength in the
night,
11 who teaches us more than the
animals of the earth,
and makes us wiser than the
birds of the air?'
12 There they cry out, but he does
not answer,
because of the pride of
evildoers.
13 Surely God does not hear an
empty cry,
nor does the Almighty^c regard
it.
14 How much less when you say
that you do not see him,
that the case is before him,
and you are waiting for
him!
15 And now, because his anger
does not punish,
and he does not greatly heed
transgression,^{d}
16 Job opens his mouth in empty
talk,
he multiplies words without
knowledge."

Elihu Exalts God's Goodness

36 E·li′hū continued and said:
2 "Bear with me a little, and
I will show you,
for I have yet something to say
on God's behalf.
3 I will bring my knowledge from
far away,
and ascribe righteousness to
my Maker.
4 For truly my words are not false;
one who is perfect in
knowledge is with you.

5 "Surely God is mighty and does
not despise any;
he is mighty in strength of
understanding.
6 He does not keep the wicked
alive,
but gives the afflicted their
right.
7 He does not withdraw his eyes
from the righteous,
but with kings on the throne
he sets them forever, and they
are exalted.
8 And if they are bound in fetters
and caught in the cords of
affliction,
9 then he declares to them their
work
and their transgressions, that
they are behaving
arrogantly.
10 He opens their ears to
instruction,
and commands that they
return from iniquity.
11 If they listen, and serve him,
they complete their days in
prosperity,
and their years in
pleasantness.
12 But if they do not listen, they
shall perish by the sword,
and die without knowledge.

13 "The godless in heart cherish
anger;
they do not cry for help when
he binds them.
14 They die in their youth,
and their life ends in shame.^{e}
15 He delivers the afflicted by their
affliction,
and opens their ear by
adversity.
16 He also allured you out of
distress
into a broad place where there
was no constraint,
and what was set on your
table was full of fatness.

17 "But you are obsessed with the
case of the wicked;
judgment and justice seize
you.
18 Beware that wrath does not
entice you into scoffing,

^{c} Traditional rendering of Heb *Shaddai*
^{d} Theodotion Symmachus Compare Vg:
Meaning of Heb uncertain ^{e} Heb *ends
among the temple prostitutes*

and do not let the greatness of
the ransom turn you aside.

19 Will your cry avail to keep you
from distress,
or will all the force of your
strength?

20 Do not long for the night,
when peoples are cut off in
their place.

21 Beware! Do not turn to iniquity;
because of that you have been
tried by affliction.

22 See, God is exalted in his power;
who is a teacher like him?

23 Who has prescribed for him his
way,
or who can say, 'You have
done wrong'?

Elihu Proclaims God's Majesty

24 "Remember to extol his work,
of which mortals have sung.

25 All people have looked on it;
everyone watches it from far
away.

26 Surely God is great, and we do
not know him;
the number of his years is
unsearchable.

27 For he draws up the drops of
water;
he distills*f* his mist in rain,

28 which the skies pour down
and drop upon mortals
abundantly.

29 Can anyone understand the
spreading of the clouds,
the thunderings of his
pavilion?

30 See, he scatters his lightning
around him
and covers the roots of the
sea.

31 For by these he governs peoples;
he gives food in abundance.

32 He covers his hands with the
lightning,
and commands it to strike the
mark.

33 Its crashing*g* tells about him;
he is jealous*g* with anger
against iniquity.

37
"At this also my heart
trembles,
and leaps out of its place.

2 Listen, listen to the thunder of
his voice
and the rumbling that comes
from his mouth.

3 Under the whole heaven he lets
it loose,
and his lightning to the
corners of the earth.

4 After it his voice roars;
he thunders with his majestic
voice
and he does not restrain the
lightnings*h* when his voice
is heard.

5 God thunders wondrously with
his voice;
he does great things that we
cannot comprehend.

6 For to the snow he says, 'Fall on
the earth';
and the shower of rain, his
heavy shower of rain,

7 serves as a sign on everyone's
hand,
so that all whom he has made
may know it.*i*

8 Then the animals go into their
lairs
and remain in their dens.

9 From its chamber comes the
whirlwind,
and cold from the scattering
winds.

10 By the breath of God ice is
given,
and the broad waters are
frozen fast.

11 He loads the thick cloud with
moisture;
the clouds scatter his
lightning.

12 They turn round and round by
his guidance,
to accomplish all that he
commands them
on the face of the habitable
world.

13 Whether for correction, or for
his land,
or for love, he causes it to
happen.

14 "Hear this, O Job;
stop and consider the
wondrous works of God.

15 Do you know how God lays his
command upon them,
and causes the lightning of his
cloud to shine?

16 Do you know the balancings of
the clouds,

---

*f*Cn: Heb *they distill*   *g*Meaning of Heb
uncertain   *h*Heb *them*   *i*Meaning of
Heb of verse 7 uncertain

the wondrous works of the one
whose knowledge is
perfect,

17 you whose garments are hot
when the earth is still because
of the south wind?

18 Can you, like him, spread out
the skies,
hard as a molten mirror?

19 Teach us what we shall say to
him;
we cannot draw up our case
because of darkness.

20 Should he be told that I want to
speak?
Did anyone ever wish to be
swallowed up?

21 Now, no one can look on the
light
when it is bright in the skies,
when the wind has passed and
cleared them.

22 Out of the north comes golden
splendor;
around God is awesome
majesty.

23 The Almighty*j* — we cannot find
him;
he is great in power and
justice,
and abundant righteousness he
will not violate.

24 Therefore mortals fear him;
he does not regard any who
are wise in their own
conceit."

The LORD Answers Job
(Cp Gen 1.1–10)

38 Then the LORD answered Job
out of the whirlwind:

2 "Who is this that darkens
counsel by words without
knowledge?

3 Gird up your loins like a man,
I will question you, and you
shall declare to me.

4 "Where were you when I laid the
foundation of the earth?
Tell me, if you have
understanding.

5 Who determined its
measurements — surely you
know!
Or who stretched the line upon
it?

6 On what were its bases sunk,
or who laid its cornerstone

7 when the morning stars sang
together

and all the heavenly beings*k*
shouted for joy?

8 "Or who shut in the sea with
doors
when it burst out from the
womb? —

9 when I made the clouds its
garment,
and thick darkness its
swaddling band,

10 and prescribed bounds for it,
and set bars and doors,

11 and said, 'Thus far shall you
come, and no farther,
and here shall your proud
waves be stopped'?

12 "Have you commanded the
morning since your days
began,
and caused the dawn to know
its place,

13 so that it might take hold of the
skirts of the earth,
and the wicked be shaken out
of it?

14 It is changed like clay under the
seal,
and it is dyed*l* like a garment.

15 Light is withheld from the
wicked,
and their uplifted arm is
broken.

16 "Have you entered into the
springs of the sea,
or walked in the recesses of
the deep?

17 Have the gates of death been
revealed to you,
or have you seen the gates of
deep darkness?

18 Have you comprehended the
expanse of the earth?
Declare, if you know all this.

19 "Where is the way to the
dwelling of light,
and where is the place of
darkness,

20 that you may take it to its
territory
and that you may discern the
paths to its home?

21 Surely you know, for you were
born then,

---

*j*Traditional rendering of Heb *Shaddai*
*k*Heb *sons of God*   *l*Cn: Heb *and they
stand forth*

and the number of your days
is great!

22 "Have you entered the
storehouses of the snow,
or have you seen the
storehouses of the hail,
23 which I have reserved for the
time of trouble,
for the day of battle and war?
24 What is the way to the place
where the light is
distributed,
or where the east wind is
scattered upon the earth?

25 "Who has cut a channel for the
torrents of rain,
and a way for the thunderbolt,
26 to bring rain on a land where no
one lives,
on the desert, which is empty
of human life,
27 to satisfy the waste and desolate
land,
and to make the ground put
forth grass?

28 "Has the rain a father,
or who has begotten the drops
of dew?
29 From whose womb did the ice
come forth,
and who has given birth to the
hoarfrost of heaven?
30 The waters become hard like
stone,
and the face of the deep is
frozen.

31 "Can you bind the chains of the
Plēi′a·dēs,
or loose the cords of Ō·rī′on?
32 Can you lead forth the
Maz′za·roth in their season,
or can you guide the Bear with
its children?
33 Do you know the ordinances of
the heavens?
Can you establish their rule on
the earth?

34 "Can you lift up your voice to
the clouds,
so that a flood of waters may
cover you?
35 Can you send forth lightnings,
so that they may go
and say to you, 'Here we are'?
36 Who has put wisdom in the
inward parts,[m]

or given understanding to the
mind?[m]
37 Who has the wisdom to number
the clouds?
Or who can tilt the waterskins
of the heavens,
38 when the dust runs into a mass
and the clods cling together?

39 "Can you hunt the prey for the
lion,
or satisfy the appetite of the
young lions,
40 when they crouch in their dens,
or lie in wait in their covert?
41 Who provides for the raven its
prey,
when its young ones cry to
God,
and wander about for lack of
food?

39 "Do you know when the
mountain goats give birth?
Do you observe the calving of
the deer?
2 Can you number the months that
they fulfill,
and do you know the time
when they give birth,
3 when they crouch to give birth
to their offspring,
and are delivered of their
young?
4 Their young ones become
strong, they grow up in the
open;
they go forth, and do not
return to them.

5 "Who has let the wild ass go
free?
Who has loosed the bonds of
the swift ass,
6 to which I have given the steppe
for its home,
the salt land for its dwelling
place?
7 It scorns the tumult of the city;
it does not hear the shouts of
the driver.
8 It ranges the mountains as its
pasture,
and it searches after every
green thing.

9 "Is the wild ox willing to serve
you?
Will it spend the night at your
crib?

[m] Meaning of Heb uncertain

10 Can you tie it in the furrow with
     ropes,
        or will it harrow the valleys
        after you?
11 Will you depend on it because
        its strength is great,
        and will you hand over your
        labor to it?
12 Do you have faith in it that it
        will return,
        and bring your grain to your
        threshing floor?[n]

13 "The ostrich's wings flap wildly,
        though its pinions lack
        plumage.[o]
14 For it leaves its eggs to the
        earth,
        and lets them be warmed on
        the ground,
15 forgetting that a foot may crush
        them,
        and that a wild animal may
        trample them.
16 It deals cruelly with its young, as
        if they were not its own;
        though its labor should be in
        vain, yet it has no fear;
17 because God has made it forget
        wisdom,
        and given it no share in
        understanding.
18 When it spreads its plumes
        aloft,[o]
        it laughs at the horse and its
        rider.

19 "Do you give the horse its
        might?
        Do you clothe its neck with
        mane?
20 Do you make it leap like the
        locust?
        Its majestic snorting is terrible.
21 It paws[p] violently, exults
        mightily;
        it goes out to meet the
        weapons.
22 It laughs at fear, and is not
        dismayed;
        it does not turn back from the
        sword.
23 Upon it rattle the quiver,
        the flashing spear, and the
        javelin.
24 With fierceness and rage it
        swallows the ground;
        it cannot stand still at the
        sound of the trumpet.
25 When the trumpet sounds, it
        says 'Aha!'

From a distance it smells the
        battle,
        the thunder of the captains,
        and the shouting.

26 "Is it by your wisdom that the
        hawk soars,
        and spreads its wings toward
        the south?
27 Is it at your command that the
        eagle mounts up
        and makes its nest on high?
28 It lives on the rock and makes
        its home
        in the fastness of the rocky
        crag.
29 From there it spies the prey;
        its eyes see it from far away.
30 Its young ones suck up blood;
        and where the slain are, there
        it is."

40 And the LORD said to Job:
  2   "Shall a faultfinder
        contend with the
        Almighty?[q]
        Anyone who argues with God
        must respond."

Job's Response to God

3 Then Job answered the LORD:
4 "See, I am of small account;
        what shall I answer you?
        I lay my hand on my mouth.
5 I have spoken once, and I will
        not answer;
        twice, but will proceed no
        further."

God's Challenge to Job

6 Then the LORD answered Job out
of the whirlwind:
7 "Gird up your loins like a man;
        I will question you, and you
        declare to me.
8 Will you even put me in the
        wrong?
        Will you condemn me that you
        may be justified?
9 Have you an arm like God,
        and can you thunder with a
        voice like his?

10 "Deck yourself with majesty and
        dignity;

[n] Heb *your grain and your threshing floor*
[o] Meaning of Heb uncertain   [p] Gk Syr
Vg: Heb *they dig*   [q] Traditional
rendering of Heb *Shaddai*

clothe yourself with glory and splendor.

11 Pour out the overflowings of your anger,
and look on all who are proud, and abase them.

12 Look on all who are proud, and bring them low;
tread down the wicked where they stand.

13 Hide them all in the dust together;
bind their faces in the world below.[r]

14 Then I will also acknowledge to you
that your own right hand can give you victory.

15 "Look at Bē′he·moth,
which I made just as I made you;
it eats grass like an ox.

16 Its strength is in its loins,
and its power in the muscles of its belly.

17 It makes its tail stiff like a cedar;
the sinews of its thighs are knit together.

18 Its bones are tubes of bronze,
its limbs like bars of iron.

19 "It is the first of the great acts of God—
only its Maker can approach it with the sword.

20 For the mountains yield food for it
where all the wild animals play.

21 Under the lotus plants it lies,
in the covert of the reeds and in the marsh.

22 The lotus trees cover it for shade;
the willows of the wadi surround it.

23 Even if the river is turbulent, it is not frightened;
it is confident though Jordan rushes against its mouth.

24 Can one take it with hooks[s]
or pierce its nose with a snare?

41 [t] "Can you draw out Le·vī′a·than[u] with a fishhook,
or press down its tongue with a cord?

2 Can you put a rope in its nose,
or pierce its jaw with a hook?

3 Will it make many supplications to you?
Will it speak soft words to you?

4 Will it make a covenant with you
to be taken as your servant forever?

5 Will you play with it as with a bird,
or will you put it on leash for your girls?

6 Will traders bargain over it?
Will they divide it up among the merchants?

7 Can you fill its skin with harpoons,
or its head with fishing spears?

8 Lay hands on it;
think of the battle; you will not do it again!

9[v] Any hope of capturing it[w] will be disappointed;
were not even the gods[x] overwhelmed at the sight of it?

10 No one is so fierce as to dare to stir it up.
Who can stand before it?[y]

11 Who can confront it[y] and be safe?[z]
—under the whole heaven, who?[a]

12 "I will not keep silence concerning its limbs,
or its mighty strength, or its splendid frame.

13 Who can strip off its outer garment?
Who can penetrate its double coat of mail?[b]

14 Who can open the doors of its face?
There is terror all around its teeth.

15 Its back[c] is made of shields in rows,
shut up closely as with a seal.

16 One is so near to another
that no air can come between them.

17 They are joined one to another;

[r] Heb *the hidden place*   [s] Cn: Heb *in his eyes*   [t] Ch 40.25 in Heb   [u] Or *the crocodile*   [v] Ch 41.1 in Heb   [w] Heb *of it*   [x] Cn Compare Symmachus Syr: Heb *one is*   [y] Heb *me*   [z] Gk: Heb *that I shall repay*   [a] Heb *to me*   [b] Gk: Heb *bridle*   [c] Cn Compare Gk Vg: Heb *pride*

they clasp each other and
cannot be separated.
18 Its sneezes flash forth light,
and its eyes are like the
eyelids of the dawn.
19 From its mouth go flaming
torches;
sparks of fire leap out.
20 Out of its nostrils comes smoke,
as from a boiling pot and
burning rushes.
21 Its breath kindles coals,
and a flame comes out of its
mouth.
22 In its neck abides strength,
and terror dances before it.
23 The folds of its flesh cling
together;
it is firmly cast and
immovable.
24 Its heart is as hard as stone,
as hard as the lower millstone.
25 When it raises itself up the gods
are afraid;
at the crashing they are beside
themselves.
26 Though the sword reaches it, it
does not avail,
nor does the spear, the dart, or
the javelin.
27 It counts iron as straw,
and bronze as rotten wood.
28 The arrow cannot make it flee;
slingstones, for it, are turned
to chaff.
29 Clubs are counted as chaff;
it laughs at the rattle of
javelins.
30 Its underparts are like sharp
potsherds;
it spreads itself like a
threshing sledge on the
mire.
31 It makes the deep boil like a pot;
it makes the sea like a pot of
ointment.
32 It leaves a shining wake behind
it;
one would think the deep to be
white-haired.
33 On earth it has no equal,
a creature without fear.
34 It surveys everything that is
lofty;
it is king over all that are
proud.”

Job Is Humbled and Satisfied

42 Then Job answered the LORD:
2 “I know that you can do
all things,

and that no purpose of yours
can be thwarted.
3 ‘Who is this that hides counsel
without knowledge?’
Therefore I have uttered what I
did not understand,
things too wonderful for me,
which I did not know.
4 ‘Hear, and I will speak;
I will question you, and you
declare to me.’
5 I had heard of you by the
hearing of the ear,
but now my eye sees you;
6 therefore I despise myself,
and repent in dust and ashes.”

Job's Friends Are Humiliated

7 After the LORD had spoken these
words to Job, the LORD said to E·li′-
phaz the Te′man·ite: “My wrath is kindled against you and against your two
friends; for you have not spoken of me
what is right, as my servant Job has.
8 Now therefore take seven bulls and
seven rams, and go to my servant Job,
and offer up for yourselves a burnt
offering; and my servant Job shall
pray for you, for I will accept his
prayer not to deal with you according
to your folly; for you have not spoken
of me what is right, as my servant Job
has done.” 9 So E·li′phaz the Te′-
man·ite and Bil′dad the Shu′hite and
Zo′phar the Na′a·ma·thite went and
did what the LORD had told them; and
the LORD accepted Job's prayer.

Job's Fortunes Are Restored Twofold

10 And the LORD restored the fortunes of Job when he had prayed for
his friends; and the LORD gave Job
twice as much as he had before.
11 Then there came to him all his
brothers and sisters and all who had
known him before, and they ate bread
with him in his house; they showed
him sympathy and comforted him for all
the evil that the LORD had brought
upon him; and each of them gave him
a piece of money[d] and a gold ring.
12 The LORD blessed the latter days of
Job more than his beginning; and he
had fourteen thousand sheep, six thousand camels, a thousand yoke of oxen,
and a thousand donkeys. 13 He also
had seven sons and three daughters.
14 He named the first Je·mi′mah, the

---

d Heb a qesitah

second Ke·zī′ah, and the third Ker′en-hap′puch. ¹⁵ In all the land there were no women so beautiful as Job's daughters; and their father gave them an inheritance along with their brothers.

¹⁶ After this Job lived one hundred and forty years, and saw his children, and his children's children, four generations. ¹⁷ And Job died, old and full of days.

THE PSALMS

BOOK I
(Psalms 1–41)

Psalm 1

The Two Ways

1 Happy are those
    who do not follow the advice
        of the wicked,
    or take the path that sinners
        tread,
    or sit in the seat of scoffers;
2 but their delight is in the law of
        the LORD,
    and on his law they meditate
        day and night.
3 They are like trees
    planted by streams of water,
  which yield their fruit in its
        season,
    and their leaves do not wither.
  In all that they do, they prosper.

4 The wicked are not so,
    but are like chaff that the wind
        drives away.
5 Therefore the wicked will not
        stand in the judgment,
    nor sinners in the
        congregation of the
        righteous;
6 for the LORD watches over the
        way of the righteous,
    but the way of the wicked will
        perish.

Psalm 2

God's Promise to His Anointed
(Acts 4.23–31)

1 Why do the nations conspire,
    and the peoples plot in vain?
2 The kings of the earth set
        themselves,
    and the rulers take counsel
        together,
    against the LORD and his
        anointed, saying,
3 "Let us burst their bonds
        asunder,
    and cast their cords from us."

4 He who sits in the heavens
        laughs;
    the LORD has them in derision.
5 Then he will speak to them in
        his wrath,
    and terrify them in his fury,
        saying,
6 "I have set my king on Zion, my
        holy hill."

7 I will tell of the decree of the
        LORD:
    He said to me, "You are my son;
        today I have begotten you.
8 Ask of me, and I will make the
        nations your heritage,
    and the ends of the earth your
        possession.
9 You shall break them with a rod
        of iron,
    and dash them in pieces like a
        potter's vessel."

10 Now therefore, O kings, be wise;
    be warned, O rulers of the
        earth.
11 Serve the LORD with fear,
    with trembling ¹²kiss his feet,ᵃ
    or he will be angry, and you will
        perish in the way;
    for his wrath is quickly
        kindled.

ᵃ Cn: Meaning of Heb of verses 11b and 12a is uncertain

Happy are all who take refuge in him.

Psalm 3

Trust in God under Adversity

A Psalm of David, when he fled from his son Ab'sa·lom.

1 O LORD, how many are my foes!
  Many are rising against me;
2 many are saying to me,
  "There is no help for you[b] in
    God."   *Sē'lah*

3 But you, O LORD, are a shield
    around me,
  my glory, and the one who
    lifts up my head.
4 I cry aloud to the LORD,
  and he answers me from his
    holy hill.   *Sē'lah*

5 I lie down and sleep;
  I wake again, for the LORD
    sustains me.
6 I am not afraid of ten thousands
    of people
  who have set themselves
    against me all around.

7 Rise up, O LORD!
  Deliver me, O my God!
  For you strike all my enemies on
    the cheek;
  you break the teeth of the
    wicked.

8 Deliverance belongs to the
    LORD;
  may your blessing be on your
    people!   *Sē'lah*

Psalm 4

*Confident Plea for Deliverance
from Enemies*

To the leader: with stringed
instruments. A Psalm of David.

1 Answer me when I call, O God
    of my right!
  You gave me room when I was
    in distress.
  Be gracious to me, and hear
    my prayer.

2 How long, you people, shall my
    honor suffer shame?
  How long will you love vain
    words, and seek after lies?
           Sē'lah

3 But know that the LORD has set
    apart the faithful for
    himself;
  the LORD hears when I call to
    him.

4 When you are disturbed,[c] do
    not sin;
  ponder it on your beds, and be
    silent.   *Sē'lah*
5 Offer right sacrifices,
  and put your trust in the
    LORD.

6 There are many who say,
  "O that we might see some
    good!
  Let the light of your face shine
    on us, O LORD!"
7 You have put gladness in my
    heart
  more than when their grain
    and wine abound.

8 I will both lie down and sleep in
    peace;
  for you alone, O LORD, make
    me lie down in safety.

Psalm 5

*Trust in God for Deliverance
from Enemies*

To the leader: for the flutes.
A Psalm of David.

1 Give ear to my words, O LORD;
  give heed to my sighing.
2 Listen to the sound of my cry,
  my King and my God,
  for to you I pray.
3 O LORD, in the morning you
    hear my voice;
  in the morning I plead my case
    to you, and watch.

4 For you are not a God who
    delights in wickedness;
  evil will not sojourn with you.
5 The boastful will not stand
    before your eyes;
  you hate all evildoers.
6 You destroy those who speak
    lies;
  the LORD abhors the
    bloodthirsty and deceitful.

7 But I, through the abundance of
    your steadfast love,
  will enter your house,

b Syr: Heb *him*   c Or *are angry*

I will bow down toward your
holy temple
in awe of you.
8 Lead me, O LORD, in your
righteousness
because of my enemies;
make your way straight before
me.

9 For there is no truth in their
mouths;
their hearts are destruction;
their throats are open graves;
they flatter with their tongues.
10 Make them bear their guilt,
O God;
let them fall by their own
counsels;
because of their many
transgressions cast them
out,
for they have rebelled against
you.

11 But let all who take refuge in
you rejoice;
let them ever sing for joy.
Spread your protection over
them,
so that those who love your
name may exult in you.
12 For you bless the righteous,
O LORD;
you cover them with favor as
with a shield.

Psalm 6

Prayer for Recovery from Grave Illness

To the leader: with stringed
instruments; according to The
Shem′i·nith. A Psalm of David.

1 O LORD, do not rebuke me in
your anger,
or discipline me in your wrath.
2 Be gracious to me, O LORD, for I
am languishing;
O LORD, heal me, for my
bones are shaking with
terror.
3 My soul also is struck with
terror,
while you, O LORD—how
long?

4 Turn, O LORD, save my life;
deliver me for the sake of your
steadfast love.
5 For in death there is no
remembrance of you;

in Shē′ōl who can give you
praise?

6 I am weary with my moaning;
every night I flood my bed
with tears;
I drench my couch with my
weeping.
7 My eyes waste away because of
grief;
they grow weak because of all
my foes.

8 Depart from me, all you workers
of evil,
for the LORD has heard the
sound of my weeping.
9 The LORD has heard my
supplication;
the LORD accepts my prayer.
10 All my enemies shall be
ashamed and struck with
terror;
they shall turn back, and in a
moment be put to shame.

Psalm 7

Plea for Help against Persecutors

A Shig·gāi′on of David, which he sang
to the LORD concerning Cush,
a Ben′ja·min·īte.

1 O LORD my God, in you I take
refuge;
save me from all my pursuers,
and deliver me,
2 or like a lion they will tear me
apart;
they will drag me away, with
no one to rescue.

3 O LORD my God, if I have done
this,
if there is wrong in my hands,
4 if I have repaid my ally with
harm
or plundered my foe without
cause,
5 then let the enemy pursue and
overtake me,
trample my life to the ground,
and lay my soul in the dust.
Sē′lah

6 Rise up, O LORD, in your anger;
lift yourself up against the fury
of my enemies;
awake, O my God;[d] you have
appointed a judgment.

d Or *awake for me*

7 Let the assembly of the peoples
        be gathered around you,
     and over it take your seat[e] on
        high.
8 The LORD judges the peoples;
     judge me, O LORD, according
        to my righteousness
     and according to the integrity
        that is in me.

9 O let the evil of the wicked come
        to an end,
     but establish the righteous,
   you who test the minds and
        hearts,
     O righteous God.
10 God is my shield,
     who saves the upright in heart.
11 God is a righteous judge,
     and a God who has
        indignation every day.

12 If one does not repent, God[f]
        will whet his sword;
     he has bent and strung his
        bow;
13 he has prepared his deadly
        weapons,
     making his arrows fiery shafts.
14 See how they conceive evil,
     and are pregnant with
        mischief,
     and bring forth lies.
15 They make a pit, digging it out,
     and fall into the hole that they
        have made.
16 Their mischief returns upon their
        own heads,
     and on their own heads their
        violence descends.

17 I will give to the LORD the
        thanks due to his
        righteousness,
     and sing praise to the name of
        the LORD, the Most High.

Psalm 8

Divine Majesty and Human Dignity

To the leader: according to The Git'tith.
     A Psalm of David.

1 O LORD, our Sovereign,
     how majestic is your name in
        all the earth!

   You have set your glory above
        the heavens.
2 Out of the mouths of babes
        and infants

   you have founded a bulwark
        because of your foes,
     to silence the enemy and the
        avenger.

3 When I look at your heavens,
        the work of your fingers,
     the moon and the stars that
        you have established;
4 what are human beings that you
        are mindful of them,
     mortals[g] that you care for
        them?

5 Yet you have made them a little
        lower than God,[h]
     and crowned them with glory
        and honor.
6 You have given them dominion
        over the works of your
        hands;
     you have put all things under
        their feet,
7 all sheep and oxen,
     and also the beasts of the field,
8 the birds of the air, and the fish
        of the sea,
     whatever passes along the
        paths of the seas.

9 O LORD, our Sovereign,
     how majestic is your name in
        all the earth!

Psalm 9

God's Power and Justice

To the leader: according to
Muth-lab'ben. A Psalm of David.

1 I will give thanks to the LORD
        with my whole heart;
     I will tell of all your wonderful
        deeds.
2 I will be glad and exult in you;
     I will sing praise to your
        name, O Most High.

3 When my enemies turned back,
     they stumbled and perished
        before you.
4 For you have maintained my just
        cause;
     you have sat on the throne
        giving righteous judgment.

5 You have rebuked the nations,
     you have destroyed the
        wicked;

[e] Cn: Heb *return*   [f] Heb *he*   [g] Heb *ben
adam*, lit. *son of man*   [h] Or *than the
divine beings* or *angels*: Heb *elohim*

P
S
A
L
M
S

you have blotted out their
    name forever and ever.
6 The enemies have vanished in
    everlasting ruins;
  their cities you have rooted
    out;
  the very memory of them has
    perished.

7 But the LORD sits enthroned
    forever,
  he has established his throne
    for judgment.
8 He judges the world with
    righteousness;
  he judges the peoples with
    equity.

9 The LORD is a stronghold for the
    oppressed,
  a stronghold in times of
    trouble.
10 And those who know your name
    put their trust in you,
  for you, O LORD, have not
    forsaken those who seek
    you.

11 Sing praises to the LORD, who
    dwells in Zion.
  Declare his deeds among the
    peoples.
12 For he who avenges blood is
    mindful of them;
  he does not forget the cry of
    the afflicted.

13 Be gracious to me, O LORD.
  See what I suffer from those
    who hate me;
  you are the one who lifts me
    up from the gates of death,
14 so that I may recount all your
    praises,
  and, in the gates of daughter
    Zion,
  rejoice in your deliverance.

15 The nations have sunk in the pit
    that they made;
  in the net that they hid has
    their own foot been caught.
16 The LORD has made himself
    known, he has executed
    judgment;
  the wicked are snared in the
    work of their own hands.
              Hig·gāi'on. Sē'lah

17 The wicked shall depart to
    Shē'ōl,
  all the nations that forget God.

18 For the needy shall not always
    be forgotten,
  nor the hope of the poor
    perish forever.

19 Rise up, O LORD! Do not let
    mortals prevail;
  let the nations be judged
    before you.
20 Put them in fear, O LORD;
  let the nations know that they
    are only human.   *Sē'lah*

Psalm 10

Prayer for Deliverance from Enemies

1 Why, O LORD, do you stand far
    off?
  Why do you hide yourself in
    times of trouble?
2 In arrogance the wicked
    persecute the poor—
  let them be caught in the
    schemes they have devised.

3 For the wicked boast of the
    desires of their heart,
  those greedy for gain curse
    and renounce the LORD.
4 In the pride of their countenance
    the wicked say, "God will
    not seek it out";
  all their thoughts are, "There
    is no God."

5 Their ways prosper at all times;
  your judgments are on high,
    out of their sight;
  as for their foes, they scoff at
    them.
6 They think in their heart, "We
    shall not be moved;
  throughout all generations we
    shall not meet adversity."

7 Their mouths are filled with
    cursing and deceit and
    oppression;
  under their tongues are
    mischief and iniquity.
8 They sit in ambush in the
    villages;
  in hiding places they murder
    the innocent.

  Their eyes stealthily watch for
    the helpless;
9   they lurk in secret like a lion
    in its covert;
  they lurk that they may seize the
    poor;

they seize the poor and drag
them off in their net.
10 They stoop, they crouch,
and the helpless fall by their
might.
11 They think in their heart, "God
has forgotten,
he has hidden his face, he will
never see it."

12 Rise up, O LORD; O God, lift up
your hand;
do not forget the oppressed.
13 Why do the wicked renounce
God,
and say in their hearts, "You
will not call us to account"?

14 But you do see! Indeed you note
trouble and grief,
that you may take it into your
hands;
the helpless commit themselves
to you;
you have been the helper of
the orphan.

15 Break the arm of the wicked and
evildoers;
seek out their wickedness until
you find none.
16 The LORD is king forever and
ever;
the nations shall perish from
his land.

17 O LORD, you will hear the desire
of the meek;
you will strengthen their heart,
you will incline your ear
18 to do justice for the orphan and
the oppressed,
so that those from earth may
strike terror no more.[i]

Psalm 11

Song of Trust in God

To the leader. Of David.

1 In the LORD I take refuge; how
can you say to me,
"Flee like a bird to the
mountains;[j]
2 for look, the wicked bend the
bow,
they have fitted their arrow to
the string,
to shoot in the dark at the
upright in heart.
3 If the foundations are destroyed,

what can the righteous do?"

4 The LORD is in his holy temple;
the LORD's throne is in
heaven.
His eyes behold, his gaze
examines humankind.
5 The LORD tests the righteous
and the wicked,
and his soul hates the lover of
violence.
6 On the wicked he will rain coals
of fire and sulfur;
a scorching wind shall be the
portion of their cup.
7 For the LORD is righteous;
he loves righteous deeds;
the upright shall behold his
face.

Psalm 12

Plea for Help in Evil Times

To the leader: according to The
Shem'i·nith. A Psalm of David.

1 Help, O LORD, for there is no
longer anyone who is
godly;
the faithful have disappeared
from humankind.
2 They utter lies to each other;
with flattering lips and a
double heart they speak.

3 May the LORD cut off all
flattering lips,
the tongue that makes great
boasts,
4 those who say, "With our
tongues we will prevail;
our lips are our own — who is
our master?"

5 "Because the poor are despoiled,
because the needy groan,
I will now rise up," says the
LORD;
"I will place them in the safety
for which they long."
6 The promises of the LORD are
promises that are pure,
silver refined in a furnace on
the ground,
purified seven times.

7 You, O LORD, will protect us;
you will guard us from this
generation forever.

[i]Meaning of Heb uncertain   [j]Gk Syr
Jerome Tg: Heb *flee to your mountain,
O bird*

P
S
A
L
M
S

8 On every side the wicked prowl,
   as vileness is exalted among
   humankind.

Psalm 13

Prayer for Deliverance from Enemies

To the leader. A Psalm of David.

1 How long, O LORD? Will you
   forget me forever?
   How long will you hide your
   face from me?
2 How long must I bear pain[k] in
   my soul,
   and have sorrow in my heart
   all day long?
   How long shall my enemy be
   exalted over me?

3 Consider and answer me,
   O LORD my God!
   Give light to my eyes, or I will
   sleep the sleep of death,
4 and my enemy will say, "I have
   prevailed";
   my foes will rejoice because I
   am shaken.

5 But I trusted in your steadfast
   love;
   my heart shall rejoice in your
   salvation.
6 I will sing to the LORD,
   because he has dealt
   bountifully with me.

Psalm 14

Denunciation of Godlessness
(Ps 53.1–6)

To the leader. Of David.

1 Fools say in their hearts, "There
   is no God."
   They are corrupt, they do
   abominable deeds;
   there is no one who does good.

2 The LORD looks down from
   heaven on humankind
   to see if there are any who are
   wise,
   who seek after God.

3 They have all gone astray, they
   are all alike perverse;
   there is no one who does good,
   no, not one.

4 Have they no knowledge, all the
   evildoers

who eat up my people as they
   eat bread,
   and do not call upon the
   LORD?

5 There they shall be in great
   terror,
   for God is with the company
   of the righteous.
6 You would confound the plans
   of the poor,
   but the LORD is their refuge.

7 O that deliverance for Israel
   would come from Zion!
   When the LORD restores the
   fortunes of his people,
   Jacob will rejoice; Israel will
   be glad.

Psalm 15

Who Shall Abide in God's Sanctuary?

A Psalm of David.

1 O LORD, who may abide in your
   tent?
   Who may dwell on your holy
   hill?

2 Those who walk blamelessly,
   and do what is right,
   and speak the truth from their
   heart;
3 who do not slander with their
   tongue,
   and do no evil to their friends,
   nor take up a reproach against
   their neighbors;
4 in whose eyes the wicked are
   despised,
   but who honor those who fear
   the LORD;
   who stand by their oath even to
   their hurt;
5 who do not lend money at
   interest,
   and do not take a bribe
   against the innocent.

Those who do these things shall
   never be moved.

[k] Syr: Heb *hold counsels*

Psalm 16

Song of Trust and Security in God

A Mik'tam of David.

1 Protect me, O God, for in you I
    take refuge.
2 I say to the LORD, "You are my
    Lord;
    I have no good apart from
        you."[l]

3 As for the holy ones in the land,
        they are the noble,
    in whom is all my delight.

4 Those who choose another god
        multiply their sorrows;[m]
    their drink offerings of blood I
        will not pour out
    or take their names upon my
        lips.

5 The LORD is my chosen portion
        and my cup;
    you hold my lot.
6 The boundary lines have fallen
        for me in pleasant places;
    I have a goodly heritage.

7 I bless the LORD who gives me
        counsel;
    in the night also my heart
        instructs me.
8 I keep the LORD always before
        me;
    because he is at my right
        hand, I shall not be moved.

9 Therefore my heart is glad, and
        my soul rejoices;
    my body also rests secure.
10 For you do not give me up to
        Shē′ōl,
    or let your faithful one see the
        Pit.

11 You show me the path of life.
    In your presence there is
        fullness of joy;
    in your right hand are
        pleasures forevermore.

Psalm 17

*Prayer for Deliverance
from Persecutors*

A Prayer of David.

1 Hear a just cause, O LORD;
        attend to my cry;
    give ear to my prayer from
        lips free of deceit.

2 From you let my vindication
        come;
    let your eyes see the right.

3 If you try my heart, if you visit
        me by night,
    if you test me, you will find no
        wickedness in me;
    my mouth does not transgress.
4 As for what others do, by the
        word of your lips
    I have avoided the ways of the
        violent.
5 My steps have held fast to your
        paths;
    my feet have not slipped.

6 I call upon you, for you will
        answer me, O God;
    incline your ear to me, hear
        my words.
7 Wondrously show your steadfast
        love,
    O savior of those who seek
        refuge
    from their adversaries at your
        right hand.

8 Guard me as the apple of the
        eye;
    hide me in the shadow of your
        wings,
9 from the wicked who despoil me,
    my deadly enemies who
        surround me.
10 They close their hearts to pity;
    with their mouths they speak
        arrogantly.
11 They track me down;[n] now they
        surround me;
    they set their eyes to cast me
        to the ground.
12 They are like a lion eager to
        tear,
    like a young lion lurking in
        ambush.

13 Rise up, O LORD, confront them,
        overthrow them!
    By your sword deliver my life
        from the wicked,
14 from mortals — by your hand,
        O LORD —
    from mortals whose portion in
        life is in this world.
    May their bellies be filled with
        what you have stored up
        for them;

l Jerome Tg: Meaning of Heb uncertain
m Cn: Meaning of Heb uncertain   *n* One
Ms Compare Syr: MT *Our steps*

may their children have more
than enough;
may they leave something over
to their little ones.

15 As for me, I shall behold your
face in righteousness;
when I awake I shall be
satisfied, beholding your
likeness.

Psalm 18

Royal Thanksgiving for Victory
(2 Sam 22.1–51)

To the leader. A Psalm of David the
servant of the LORD, who addressed the
words of this song to the LORD on the
day when the LORD delivered him from
the hand of all his enemies, and from
the hand of Saul. He said:

1 I love you, O LORD, my strength.
2 The LORD is my rock, my
fortress, and my deliverer,
my God, my rock in whom I
take refuge,
my shield, and the horn of my
salvation, my stronghold.
3 I call upon the LORD, who is
worthy to be praised,
so I shall be saved from my
enemies.

4 The cords of death encompassed
me;
the torrents of perdition
assailed me;
5 the cords of She′ōl entangled
me;
the snares of death confronted
me.

6 In my distress I called upon the
LORD;
to my God I cried for help.
From his temple he heard my
voice,
and my cry to him reached his
ears.

7 Then the earth reeled and
rocked;
the foundations also of the
mountains trembled
and quaked, because he was
angry.
8 Smoke went up from his nostrils,
and devouring fire from his
mouth;
glowing coals flamed forth
from him.

9 He bowed the heavens, and
came down;
thick darkness was under his
feet.
10 He rode on a cherub, and flew;
he came swiftly upon the
wings of the wind.
11 He made darkness his covering
around him,
his canopy thick clouds dark
with water.
12 Out of the brightness before him
there broke through his clouds
hailstones and coals of fire.
13 The LORD also thundered in the
heavens,
and the Most High uttered his
voice.º
14 And he sent out his arrows, and
scattered them;
he flashed forth lightnings,
and routed them.
15 Then the channels of the sea
were seen,
and the foundations of the
world were laid bare
at your rebuke, O LORD,
at the blast of the breath of
your nostrils.

16 He reached down from on high,
he took me;
he drew me out of mighty
waters.
17 He delivered me from my strong
enemy,
and from those who hated me;
for they were too mighty for
me.
18 They confronted me in the day
of my calamity;
but the LORD was my support.
19 He brought me out into a broad
place;
he delivered me, because he
delighted in me.

20 The LORD rewarded me
according to my
righteousness;
according to the cleanness of
my hands he recompensed
me.
21 For I have kept the ways of the
LORD,
and have not wickedly
departed from my God.
22 For all his ordinances were
before me,

º Gk See 2 Sam 22.14: Heb adds
hailstones and coals of fire

and his statutes I did not put
away from me.
23 I was blameless before him,
and I kept myself from guilt.
24 Therefore the LORD has
recompensed me according
to my righteousness,
according to the cleanness of
my hands in his sight.

25 With the loyal you show
yourself loyal;
with the blameless you show
yourself blameless;
26 with the pure you show yourself
pure;
and with the crooked you
show yourself perverse.
27 For you deliver a humble people,
but the haughty eyes you
bring down.
28 It is you who light my lamp;
the LORD, my God, lights up
my darkness.
29 By you I can crush a troop,
and by my God I can leap over
a wall.
30 This God—his way is perfect;
the promise of the LORD
proves true;
he is a shield for all who take
refuge in him.

31 For who is God except the
LORD?
And who is a rock besides our
God?—
32 the God who girded me with
strength,
and made my way safe.
33 He made my feet like the feet of
a deer,
and set me secure on the
heights.
34 He trains my hands for war,
so that my arms can bend a
bow of bronze.
35 You have given me the shield of
your salvation,
and your right hand has
supported me;
your help[p] has made me
great.
36 You gave me a wide place for
my steps under me,
and my feet did not slip.
37 I pursued my enemies and
overtook them;
and did not turn back until
they were consumed.
38 I struck them down, so that they
were not able to rise;

they fell under my feet.
39 For you girded me with strength
for the battle;
you made my assailants sink
under me.
40 You made my enemies turn their
backs to me,
and those who hated me I
destroyed.
41 They cried for help, but there
was no one to save them;
they cried to the LORD, but he
did not answer them.
42 I beat them fine, like dust before
the wind;
I cast them out like the mire of
the streets.

43 You delivered me from strife
with the peoples;[q]
you made me head of the
nations;
people whom I had not known
served me.
44 As soon as they heard of me
they obeyed me;
foreigners came cringing to
me.
45 Foreigners lost heart,
and came trembling out of
their strongholds.

46 The LORD lives! Blessed be my
rock,
and exalted be the God of my
salvation,
47 the God who gave me vengeance
and subdued peoples under
me;
48 who delivered me from my
enemies;
indeed, you exalted me above
my adversaries;
you delivered me from the
violent.

49 For this I will extol you, O LORD,
among the nations,
and sing praises to your name.
50 Great triumphs he gives to his
king,
and shows steadfast love to his
anointed,
to David and his descendants
forever.

p Or gentleness   q Gk Tg: Heb people

Psalm 19

God's Glory in Creation and the Law

To the leader. A Psalm of David.

1 The heavens are telling the glory
    of God;
    and the firmament[r] proclaims
        his handiwork.
2 Day to day pours forth speech,
    and night to night declares
        knowledge.
3 There is no speech, nor are there
        words;
    their voice is not heard;
4 yet their voice[s] goes out
        through all the earth,
    and their words to the end of
        the world.

In the heavens[t] he has set a
    tent for the sun,
5 which comes out like a
        bridegroom from his
        wedding canopy,
    and like a strong man runs its
        course with joy.
6 Its rising is from the end of the
        heavens,
    and its circuit to the end of
        them;
    and nothing is hid from its
        heat.

7 The law of the LORD is perfect,
        reviving the soul;
    the decrees of the LORD are sure,
        making wise the simple;
8 the precepts of the LORD are
        right,
        rejoicing the heart;
    the commandment of the LORD
        is clear,
        enlightening the eyes;
9 the fear of the LORD is pure,
        enduring forever;
    the ordinances of the LORD are
        true
        and righteous altogether.
10 More to be desired are they than
        gold,
        even much fine gold;
    sweeter also than honey,
        and drippings of the
        honeycomb.

11 Moreover by them is your
        servant warned;
    in keeping them there is great
        reward.
12 But who can detect their errors?
    Clear me from hidden faults.

13 Keep back your servant also
        from the insolent;[u]
    do not let them have dominion
        over me.
    Then I shall be blameless,
        and innocent of great
        transgression.

14 Let the words of my mouth and
        the meditation of my heart
    be acceptable to you,
        O LORD, my rock and my
        redeemer.

Psalm 20

Prayer for Victory

To the leader. A Psalm of David.

1 The LORD answer you in the day
        of trouble!
    The name of the God of Jacob
        protect you!
2 May he send you help from the
        sanctuary,
    and give you support from
        Zion.
3 May he remember all your
        offerings,
    and regard with favor your
        burnt sacrifices.   *Se'lah*

4 May he grant you your heart's
        desire,
    and fulfill all your plans.
5 May we shout for joy over your
        victory,
    and in the name of our God
        set up our banners.
    May the LORD fulfill all your
        petitions.

6 Now I know that the LORD will
        help his anointed;
    he will answer him from his
        holy heaven
    with mighty victories by his
        right hand.
7 Some take pride in chariots, and
        some in horses,
    but our pride is in the name of
        the LORD our God.
8 They will collapse and fall,
    but we shall rise and stand
        upright.

9 Give victory to the king,
        O LORD;

[r] Or *dome*   [s] Gk Jerome Compare Syr:
Heb *line*   [t] Heb *In them*   [u] Or *from
proud thoughts*

answer us when we call.[v]

Psalm 21

Thanksgiving for Victory

To the leader. A Psalm of David.

1 In your strength the king
        rejoices, O LORD,
    and in your help how greatly
        he exults!
2 You have given him his heart's
        desire,
    and have not withheld the
        request of his lips.   *Sĕ'lah*
3 For you meet him with rich
        blessings;
    you set a crown of fine gold
        on his head.
4 He asked you for life; you gave
        it to him —
    length of days forever and
        ever.
5 His glory is great through your
        help;
    splendor and majesty you
        bestow on him.
6 You bestow on him blessings
        forever;
    you make him glad with the
        joy of your presence.
7 For the king trusts in the LORD,
        and through the steadfast love
        of the Most High he shall
        not be moved.

8 Your hand will find out all your
        enemies;
    your right hand will find out
        those who hate you.
9 You will make them like a fiery
        furnace
    when you appear.
    The LORD will swallow them up
        in his wrath,
    and fire will consume them.
10 You will destroy their offspring
        from the earth,
    and their children from among
        humankind.
11 If they plan evil against you,
    if they devise mischief, they
        will not succeed.
12 For you will put them to flight;
    you will aim at their faces with
        your bows.

13 Be exalted, O LORD, in your
        strength!
    We will sing and praise your
        power.

Psalm 22

*Plea for Deliverance from Suffering
and Hostility*

To the leader: according to The Deer of
the Dawn. A Psalm of David.

1 My God, my God, why have you
        forsaken me?
    Why are you so far from
        helping me, from the words
        of my groaning?
2 O my God, I cry by day, but you
        do not answer;
    and by night, but find no rest.

3 Yet you are holy,
    enthroned on the praises of
        Israel.
4 In you our ancestors trusted;
    they trusted, and you delivered
        them.
5 To you they cried, and were
        saved;
    in you they trusted, and were
        not put to shame.

6 But I am a worm, and not
        human;
    scorned by others, and
        despised by the people.
7 All who see me mock at me;
    they make mouths at me, they
        shake their heads;
8 "Commit your cause to the
        LORD; let him deliver —
    let him rescue the one in
        whom he delights!"

9 Yet it was you who took me
        from the womb;
    you kept me safe on my
        mother's breast.
10 On you I was cast from my
        birth,
    and since my mother bore me
        you have been my God.
11 Do not be far from me,
    for trouble is near
    and there is no one to help.

12 Many bulls encircle me,
    strong bulls of Bā'shan
        surround me;
13 they open wide their mouths at
        me,
    like a ravening and roaring
        lion.

14 I am poured out like water,

v Gk: Heb *give victory, O LORD; let the
King answer us when we call*

P
S
A
L
M
S

and all my bones are out of
        joint;
my heart is like wax;
        it is melted within my breast;
15   my mouth[w] is dried up like a
            potsherd,
        and my tongue sticks to my
            jaws;
        you lay me in the dust of
            death.

16   For dogs are all around me;
        a company of evildoers
            encircles me.
    My hands and feet have
        shriveled;[x]
17   I can count all my bones.
    They stare and gloat over me;
18   they divide my clothes among
        themselves,
        and for my clothing they cast
            lots.

19   But you, O LORD, do not be far
            away!
        O my help, come quickly to
            my aid!
20   Deliver my soul from the sword,
        my life[y] from the power of the
            dog!
21   Save me from the mouth of
            the lion!

    From the horns of the wild oxen
        you have rescued[z] me.
22   I will tell of your name to my
        brothers and sisters;[a]
    in the midst of the
        congregation I will praise
        you:
23   You who fear the LORD, praise
        him!
        All you offspring of Jacob,
            glorify him;
        stand in awe of him, all you
            offspring of Israel!
24   For he did not despise or abhor
        the affliction of the afflicted;
    he did not hide his face from
        me,[b]
        but heard when I[c] cried to
            him.

25   From you comes my praise in
        the great congregation;
        my vows I will pay before
            those who fear him.
26   The poor[d] shall eat and be
        satisfied;
        those who seek him shall
            praise the LORD.
        May your hearts live forever!

27   All the ends of the earth shall
        remember
        and turn to the LORD;
    and all the families of the
        nations
        shall worship before him.[e]
28   For dominion belongs to the
        LORD,
        and he rules over the nations.

29   To him,[f] indeed, shall all who
        sleep in[g] the earth bow
        down;
        before him shall bow all who
            go down to the dust,
        and I shall live for him.[h]
30   Posterity will serve him;
        future generations will be told
            about the Lord,
31   and[i] proclaim his deliverance to
        a people yet unborn,
        saying that he has done it.

Psalm 23

The Divine Shepherd

A Psalm of David.

1   The LORD is my shepherd, I
        shall not want.
2   He makes me lie down in
            green pastures;
    he leads me beside still waters;[j]
3   he restores my soul.[k]
    He leads me in right paths[l]
        for his name's sake.

4   Even though I walk through the
        darkest valley,[m]
        I fear no evil;
    for you are with me;
        your rod and your staff—
            they comfort me.

5   You prepare a table before me
        in the presence of my enemies;
    you anoint my head with oil;
        my cup overflows.

w Cn: Heb *strength*   *x* Meaning of Heb
uncertain   *y* Heb *my only one*
z Heb *answered*   *a* Or *kindred*
b Heb *him*   *c* Heb *he*   *d* Or *afflicted*
e Gk Syr Jerome: Heb *you*   *f* Cn: Heb
They have eaten and   *g* Cn: Heb *all the*
fat ones   *h* Compare Gk Syr Vg: Heb
and he who cannot keep himself alive
i Compare Gk: Heb *it will be told about*
the Lord to the generation, *31they will*
come and   *j* Heb *waters of rest*
k Or *life*   *l* Or *paths of righteousness*
m Or *the valley of the shadow of death*

[5] Surely[n] goodness and mercy[o]
    shall follow me
all the days of my life,
and I shall dwell in the house of
    the LORD
    my whole life long.[p]

Psalm 24

Entrance into the Temple

Of David. A Psalm.

1 The earth is the LORD's and all
    that is in it,
    the world, and those who live
      in it;
2 for he has founded it on the
    seas,
    and established it on the
      rivers.

3 Who shall ascend the hill of the
    LORD?
    And who shall stand in his
      holy place?
4 Those who have clean hands
    and pure hearts,
    who do not lift up their souls
      to what is false,
    and do not swear deceitfully.
5 They will receive blessing from
    the LORD,
    and vindication from the God
      of their salvation.
6 Such is the company of those
    who seek him,
    who seek the face of the God
      of Jacob.[q]   Sĕ'lah

7 Lift up your heads, O gates!
    and be lifted up, O ancient
      doors!
    that the King of glory may
      come in.
8 Who is the King of glory?
    The LORD, strong and mighty,
    the LORD, mighty in battle.
9 Lift up your heads, O gates!
    and be lifted up, O ancient
      doors!
    that the King of glory may
      come in.
10 Who is this King of glory?
    The LORD of hosts,
    he is the King of glory.   Sĕ'lah

Psalm 25

Prayer for Guidance and
for Deliverance

Of David.

1 To you, O LORD, I lift up my
    soul.
2 O my God, in you I trust;
    do not let me be put to shame;
    do not let my enemies exult
      over me.
3 Do not let those who wait for
    you be put to shame;
    let them be ashamed who are
      wantonly treacherous.

4 Make me to know your ways,
    O LORD;
    teach me your paths.
5 Lead me in your truth, and teach
    me,
    for you are the God of my
      salvation;
    for you I wait all day long.

6 Be mindful of your mercy,
    O LORD, and of your
      steadfast love,
    for they have been from of old.
7 Do not remember the sins of my
    youth or my
      transgressions;
    according to your steadfast
      love remember me,
    for your goodness' sake,
      O LORD!

8 Good and upright is the LORD;
    therefore he instructs sinners
      in the way.
9 He leads the humble in what is
    right,
    and teaches the humble his
      way.
10 All the paths of the LORD are
    steadfast love and
      faithfulness,
    for those who keep his
      covenant and his decrees.

11 For your name's sake, O LORD,
    pardon my guilt, for it is great.
12 Who are they that fear the
    LORD?
    He will teach them the way
      that they should choose.

[n]Or Only   [o]Or kindness   [p]Heb for
length of days   [q]Gk Syr: Heb your
face, O Jacob

P
S
A
L
M
S

13 They will abide in prosperity,
  and their children shall
    possess the land.
14 The friendship of the LORD is for
    those who fear him,
  and he makes his covenant
    known to them.
15 My eyes are ever toward the
    LORD,
  for he will pluck my feet out of
    the net.

16 Turn to me and be gracious to
    me,
  for I am lonely and afflicted.
17 Relieve the troubles of my heart,
  and bring me*r* out of my
    distress.
18 Consider my affliction and my
    trouble,
  and forgive all my sins.

19 Consider how many are my foes,
  and with what violent hatred
    they hate me.
20 O guard my life, and deliver me;
  do not let me be put to shame,
  for I take refuge in you.
21 May integrity and uprightness
    preserve me,
  for I wait for you.

22 Redeem Israel, O God,
  out of all its troubles.

Psalm 26

*Plea for Justice and Declaration
of Righteousness*

Of David.

1 Vindicate me, O LORD,
  for I have walked in my
    integrity,
  and I have trusted in the LORD
    without wavering.
2 Prove me, O LORD, and try me;
  test my heart and mind.
3 For your steadfast love is before
    my eyes,
  and I walk in faithfulness to
    you.*s*

4 I do not sit with the worthless,
  nor do I consort with
    hypocrites;
5 I hate the company of evildoers,
  and will not sit with the
    wicked.

6 I wash my hands in innocence,
  and go around your altar,
    O LORD,
7 singing aloud a song of
    thanksgiving,
  and telling all your wondrous
    deeds.

8 O LORD, I love the house in
    which you dwell,
  and the place where your
    glory abides.
9 Do not sweep me away with
    sinners,
  nor my life with the
    bloodthirsty,
10 those in whose hands are evil
    devices,
  and whose right hands are full
    of bribes.

11 But as for me, I walk in my
    integrity;
  redeem me, and be gracious to
    me.
12 My foot stands on level ground;
  in the great congregation I will
    bless the LORD.

Psalm 27

Triumphant Song of Confidence

Of David.

1 The LORD is my light and my
    salvation;
  whom shall I fear?
  The LORD is the stronghold*t* of
    my life;
  of whom shall I be afraid?

2 When evildoers assail me
    to devour my flesh—
  my adversaries and foes—
    they shall stumble and fall.

3 Though an army encamp against
    me,
  my heart shall not fear;
  though war rise up against me,
    yet I will be confident.

4 One thing I asked of the LORD,
    that will I seek after:
  to live in the house of the LORD
    all the days of my life,
  to behold the beauty of the
    LORD,
  and to inquire in his temple.

*rOr The troubles of my heart are
enlarged; bring me   sOr in your
faithfulness   tOr refuge*

5 For he will hide me in his shelter
    in the day of trouble;
  he will conceal me under the
      cover of his tent;
    he will set me high on a rock.

6 Now my head is lifted up
    above my enemies all around
      me,
  and I will offer in his tent
    sacrifices with shouts of joy;
  I will sing and make melody to
      the LORD.

7 Hear, O LORD, when I cry aloud,
    be gracious to me and answer
      me!
8 "Come," my heart says, "seek his
      face!"
    Your face, LORD, do I seek.
9   Do not hide your face from
      me.

  Do not turn your servant away
      in anger,
    you who have been my help.
  Do not cast me off, do not
      forsake me,
    O God of my salvation!
10 If my father and mother forsake
      me,
    the LORD will take me up.

11 Teach me your way, O LORD,
    and lead me on a level path
      because of my enemies.
12 Do not give me up to the will of
      my adversaries,
    for false witnesses have risen
      against me,
    and they are breathing out
      violence.

13 I believe that I shall see the
      goodness of the LORD
    in the land of the living.
14 Wait for the LORD;
    be strong, and let your heart
      take courage;
    wait for the LORD!

Psalm 28

Prayer for Help and Thanksgiving for It

Of David.

1 To you, O LORD, I call;
    my rock, do not refuse to hear
      me,
  for if you are silent to me,
    I shall be like those who go
      down to the Pit.

2 Hear the voice of my
      supplication,
    as I cry to you for help,
  as I lift up my hands
    toward your most holy
      sanctuary.[u]

3 Do not drag me away with the
      wicked,
    with those who are workers of
      evil,
  who speak peace with their
      neighbors,
    while mischief is in their
      hearts.
4 Repay them according to their
      work,
    and according to the evil of
      their deeds;
  repay them according to the
      work of their hands;
    render them their due reward.
5 Because they do not regard the
      works of the LORD,
    or the work of his hands,
  he will break them down and
      build them up no more.

6 Blessed be the LORD,
    for he has heard the sound of
      my pleadings.
7 The LORD is my strength and my
      shield;
    in him my heart trusts;
  so I am helped, and my heart
      exults,
    and with my song I give
      thanks to him.

8 The LORD is the strength of his
      people;
    he is the saving refuge of his
      anointed.
9 O save your people, and bless
      your heritage;
    be their shepherd, and carry
      them forever.

Psalm 29

The Voice of God in a Great Storm

A Psalm of David.

1 Ascribe to the LORD, O heavenly
      beings,[v]
    ascribe to the LORD glory and
      strength.
2 Ascribe to the LORD the glory of
      his name;

u Heb *your innermost sanctuary*
v Heb *sons of gods*

worship the LORD in holy
splendor.

3 The voice of the LORD is over
the waters;
the God of glory thunders,
the LORD, over mighty waters.
4 The voice of the LORD is
powerful;
the voice of the LORD is full of
majesty.

5 The voice of the LORD breaks
the cedars;
the LORD breaks the cedars of
Lebanon.
6 He makes Lebanon skip like a
calf,
and Sir'i·on like a young wild
ox.

7 The voice of the LORD flashes
forth flames of fire.
8 The voice of the LORD shakes
the wilderness;
the LORD shakes the
wilderness of Kā'desh.

9 The voice of the LORD causes
the oaks to whirl,w
and strips the forest bare;
and in his temple all say,
"Glory!"

10 The LORD sits enthroned over
the flood;
the LORD sits enthroned as
king forever.
11 May the LORD give strength to
his people!
May the LORD bless his people
with peace!

Psalm 30

*Thanksgiving for Recovery from
Grave Illness*

A Psalm. A Song at the dedication of
the temple. Of David.

1 I will extol you, O LORD, for you
have drawn me up,
and did not let my foes rejoice
over me.
2 O LORD my God, I cried to you
for help,
and you have healed me.
3 O LORD, you brought up my soul
from Shē'ōl,
restored me to life from among
those gone down to the
Pit.x

4 Sing praises to the LORD, O you
his faithful ones,
and give thanks to his holy
name.
5 For his anger is but for a
moment;
his favor is for a lifetime.
Weeping may linger for the
night,
but joy comes with the
morning.

6 As for me, I said in my
prosperity,
"I shall never be moved."
7 By your favor, O LORD,
you had established me as a
strong mountain;
you hid your face;
I was dismayed.

8 To you, O LORD, I cried,
and to the LORD I made
supplication:
9 "What profit is there in my
death,
if I go down to the Pit?
Will the dust praise you?
Will it tell of your faithfulness?
10 Hear, O LORD, and be gracious
to me!
O LORD, be my helper!"

11 You have turned my mourning
into dancing;
you have taken off my
sackcloth
and clothed me with joy,
12 so that my souly may praise you
and not be silent.
O LORD my God, I will give
thanks to you forever.

Psalm 31

*Prayer and Praise for Deliverance
from Enemies*

To the leader. A Psalm of David.

1 In you, O LORD, I seek refuge;
do not let me ever be put to
shame;
in your righteousness deliver
me.
2 Incline your ear to me;
rescue me speedily.
Be a rock of refuge for me,
a strong fortress to save me.

w Or *causes the deer to calve*   x Or *that
I should not go down to the Pit*
y Heb *that glory*

3 You are indeed my rock and my
      fortress;
    for your name's sake lead me
      and guide me,
4 take me out of the net that is
      hidden for me,
    for you are my refuge.
5 Into your hand I commit my
      spirit;
    you have redeemed me,
      O LORD, faithful God.

6 You hate[z] those who pay regard
      to worthless idols,
    but I trust in the LORD.
7 I will exult and rejoice in your
      steadfast love,
    because you have seen my
      affliction;
    you have taken heed of my
      adversities,
8 and have not delivered me into
      the hand of the enemy;
    you have set my feet in a
      broad place.

9 Be gracious to me, O LORD, for I
      am in distress;
    my eye wastes away from
      grief,
    my soul and body also.
10 For my life is spent with sorrow,
    and my years with sighing;
    my strength fails because of my
      misery,[a]
    and my bones waste away.

11 I am the scorn of all my
      adversaries,
    a horror[b] to my neighbors,
    an object of dread to my
      acquaintances;
    those who see me in the street
      flee from me.
12 I have passed out of mind like
      one who is dead;
    I have become like a broken
      vessel.
13 For I hear the whispering of
      many—
    terror all around!—
    as they scheme together against
      me,
    as they plot to take my life.

14 But I trust in you, O LORD;
    I say, "You are my God."
15 My times are in your hand;
    deliver me from the hand of
      my enemies and
      persecutors.

16 Let your face shine upon your
      servant;
    save me in your steadfast love.
17 Do not let me be put to shame,
      O LORD,
    for I call on you;
    let the wicked be put to shame;
    let them go dumbfounded to
      Shě′ōl.
18 Let the lying lips be stilled
    that speak insolently against
      the righteous
    with pride and contempt.

19 O how abundant is your
      goodness
    that you have laid up for those
      who fear you,
    and accomplished for those who
      take refuge in you,
    in the sight of everyone!
20 In the shelter of your presence
      you hide them
    from human plots;
    you hold them safe under your
      shelter
    from contentious tongues.

21 Blessed be the LORD,
    for he has wondrously shown
      his steadfast love to me
    when I was beset as a city
      under seige.
22 I had said in my alarm,
    "I am driven far[c] from your
      sight."
    But you heard my supplications
    when I cried out to you for
      help.

23 Love the LORD, all you his
      saints.
    The LORD preserves the
      faithful,
    but abundantly repays the one
      who acts haughtily.
24 Be strong, and let your heart
      take courage,
    all you who wait for the LORD.

Psalm 32

The Joy of Forgiveness

Of David. A Mas′kil.

1 Happy are those whose
      transgression is forgiven,
    whose sin is covered.

z One Heb Ms Gk Syr Jerome: MT *I hate*
a Gk Syr: Heb *my iniquity*　b Cn: Heb
exceedingly　c Another reading is *cut
off*

P
S
A
L
M
S

2 Happy are those to whom the
      LORD imputes no iniquity,
   and in whose spirit there is no
      deceit.

3 While I kept silence, my body
      wasted away
   through my groaning all day
      long.
4 For day and night your hand
      was heavy upon me;
   my strength was dried up[d] as
      by the heat of summer.
                              Sē'lah

5 Then I acknowledged my sin to
      you,
   and I did not hide my iniquity;
   I said, "I will confess my
      transgressions to the
      LORD,"
   and you forgave the guilt of
      my sin.   *Sē'lah*

6 Therefore let all who are faithful
      offer prayer to you;
   at a time of distress,[e] the rush
      of mighty waters
   shall not reach them.
7 You are a hiding place for me;
   you preserve me from trouble;
   you surround me with glad
      cries of deliverance. *Sē'lah*

8 I will instruct you and teach you
      the way you should go;
   I will counsel you with my eye
      upon you.
9 Do not be like a horse or a mule,
      without understanding,
   whose temper must be curbed
      with bit and bridle,
   else it will not stay near you.

10 Many are the torments of the
      wicked,
   but steadfast love surrounds
      those who trust in the
      LORD.
11 Be glad in the LORD and rejoice,
      O righteous,
   and shout for joy, all you
      upright in heart.

Psalm 33

The Greatness and Goodness of God

1 Rejoice in the LORD, O you
      righteous.
   Praise befits the upright.
2 Praise the LORD with the lyre;

make melody to him with the
      harp of ten strings.
3 Sing to him a new song;
   play skillfully on the strings,
      with loud shouts.

4 For the word of the LORD is
      upright,
   and all his work is done in
      faithfulness.
5 He loves righteousness and
      justice;
   the earth is full of the
      steadfast love of the LORD.

6 By the word of the LORD the
      heavens were made,
   and all their host by the breath
      of his mouth.
7 He gathered the waters of the
      sea as in a bottle;
   he put the deeps in
      storehouses.

8 Let all the earth fear the LORD;
   let all the inhabitants of the
      world stand in awe of him.
9 For he spoke, and it came to be;
   he commanded, and it stood
      firm.

10 The LORD brings the counsel of
      the nations to nothing;
   he frustrates the plans of the
      peoples.
11 The counsel of the LORD stands
      forever,
   the thoughts of his heart to all
      generations.
12 Happy is the nation whose God
      is the LORD,
   the people whom he has
      chosen as his heritage.

13 The LORD looks down from
      heaven;
   he sees all humankind.
14 From where he sits enthroned he
      watches
   all the inhabitants of the
      earth—
15 he who fashions the hearts of
      them all,
   and observes all their deeds.
16 A king is not saved by his great
      army;
   a warrior is not delivered by
      his great strength.

[d]Meaning of Heb uncertain   [e]Cn: Heb
at a time of finding only

17 The war horse is a vain hope for
       victory,
    and by its great might it
       cannot save.

18 Truly the eye of the LORD is on
       those who fear him,
    on those who hope in his
       steadfast love,
19 to deliver their soul from death,
    and to keep them alive in
       famine.

20 Our soul waits for the LORD;
    he is our help and shield.
21 Our heart is glad in him,
    because we trust in his holy
       name.
22 Let your steadfast love, O LORD,
    be upon us,
    even as we hope in you.

Psalm 34

Praise for Deliverance from Trouble

Of David, when he feigned madness
before A·bim'e·lech, so that he drove
   him out, and he went away.

1 I will bless the LORD at all times;
    his praise shall continually be
       in my mouth.
2 My soul makes its boast in the
       LORD;
    let the humble hear and be
       glad.
3 O magnify the LORD with me,
    and let us exalt his name
       together.

4 I sought the LORD, and he
       answered me,
    and delivered me from all my
       fears.
5 Look to him, and be radiant;
    so your*f* faces shall never be
       ashamed.
6 This poor soul cried, and was
       heard by the LORD,
    and was saved from every
       trouble.
7 The angel of the LORD encamps
       around those who fear him,
    and delivers them.
8 O taste and see that the LORD is
       good;
    happy are those who take
       refuge in him.
9 O fear the LORD, you his holy
       ones,
    for those who fear him have
       no want.

10 The young lions suffer want and
       hunger,
    but those who seek the LORD
       lack no good thing.
11 Come, O children, listen to me;
    I will teach you the fear of the
       LORD.
12 Which of you desires life,
    and covets many days to enjoy
       good?
13 Keep your tongue from evil,
    and your lips from speaking
       deceit.
14 Depart from evil, and do good;
    seek peace, and pursue it.
15 The eyes of the LORD are on the
       righteous,
    and his ears are open to their
       cry.
16 The face of the LORD is against
       evildoers,
    to cut off the remembrance of
       them from the earth.
17 When the righteous cry for help,
       the LORD hears,
    and rescues them from all
       their troubles.
18 The LORD is near to the
       brokenhearted,
    and saves the crushed in spirit.

19 Many are the afflictions of the
       righteous,
    but the LORD rescues them
       from them all.
20 He keeps all their bones;
    not one of them will be
       broken.
21 Evil brings death to the wicked,
    and those who hate the
       righteous will be
       condemned.
22 The LORD redeems the life of his
       servants;
    none of those who take refuge
       in him will be condemned.

Psalm 35

Prayer for Deliverance from Enemies

Of David.

1 Contend, O LORD, with those
       who contend with me;
    fight against those who fight
       against me!
2 Take hold of shield and buckler,
    and rise up to help me!

f Gk Syr Jerome: Heb *their*

3 Draw the spear and javelin
    against my pursuers;
  say to my soul,
  "I am your salvation."

4 Let them be put to shame and
    dishonor
    who seek after my life.
  Let them be turned back and
    confounded
    who devise evil against me.
5 Let them be like chaff before the
    wind,
    with the angel of the LORD
      driving them on.
6 Let their way be dark and
    slippery,
    with the angel of the LORD
      pursuing them.

7 For without cause they hid their
    net[g] for me;
    without cause they dug a pit[h]
      for my life.
8 Let ruin come on them
    unawares.
  And let the net that they hid
    ensnare them;
    let them fall in it—to their
      ruin.

9 Then my soul shall rejoice in the
    LORD,
    exulting in his deliverance.
10 All my bones shall say,
    "O LORD, who is like you?
  You deliver the weak
    from those too strong for
      them,
    the weak and needy from
      those who despoil them."

11 Malicious witnesses rise up;
    they ask me about things I do
      not know.
12 They repay me evil for good;
    my soul is forlorn.
13 But as for me, when they were
    sick,
    I wore sackcloth;
    I afflicted myself with fasting.
  I prayed with head bowed[i] on
    my bosom,
14   as though I grieved for a
      friend or a brother;
  I went about as one who laments
    for a mother,
    bowed down and in mourning.

15 But at my stumbling they
    gathered in glee,

they gathered together against
  me;
ruffians whom I did not know
  tore at me without ceasing;
16 they impiously mocked more
    and more,[j]
    gnashing at me with their
      teeth.

17 How long, O LORD, will you look
    on?
  Rescue me from their ravages,
    my life from the lions!
18 Then I will thank you in the
    great congregation;
  in the mighty throng I will
    praise you.

19 Do not let my treacherous
    enemies rejoice over me,
    or those who hate me without
      cause wink the eye.
20 For they do not speak peace,
    but they conceive deceitful
      words
    against those who are quiet in
      the land.
21 They open wide their mouths
    against me;
    they say, "Aha, Aha,
      our eyes have seen it."

22 You have seen, O LORD; do not
    be silent!
  O Lord, do not be far from me!
23 Wake up! Bestir yourself for my
    defense,
    for my cause, my God and my
      Lord!
24 Vindicate me, O LORD, my God,
    according to your
      righteousness,
    and do not let them rejoice
      over me.
25 Do not let them say to
    themselves,
    "Aha, we have our heart's
      desire."
  Do not let them say, "We have
    swallowed you[k] up."

26 Let all those who rejoice at my
    calamity
    be put to shame and
      confusion;

[g]Heb a pit, their net   [h]The word pit is
transposed from the preceding line
[i]Or My prayer turned back
[j]Cn Compare Gk: Heb like the profanest
of mockers of a cake   [k]Heb him

let those who exalt themselves
    against me
  be clothed with shame and
    dishonor.
27 Let those who desire my
    vindication
  shout for joy and be glad,
  and say evermore,
"Great is the LORD,
  who delights in the welfare of
    his servant."
28 Then my tongue shall tell of
    your righteousness
  and of your praise all day
    long.

Psalm 36

*Human Wickedness and
Divine Goodness*

To the leader. Of David,
  the servant of the LORD.

1 Transgression speaks to the
    wicked
  deep in their hearts;
there is no fear of God
  before their eyes.
2 For they flatter themselves in
    their own eyes
  that their iniquity cannot be
    found out and hated.
3 The words of their mouths are
    mischief and deceit;
  they have ceased to act wisely
    and do good.
4 They plot mischief while on their
    beds;
  they are set on a way that is
    not good;
  they do not reject evil.

5 Your steadfast love, O LORD,
    extends to the heavens,
  your faithfulness to the clouds.
6 Your righteousness is like the
    mighty mountains,
  your judgments are like the
    great deep;
  you save humans and animals
    alike, O LORD.

7 How precious is your steadfast
    love, O God!
  All people may take refuge in
    the shadow of your wings.
8 They feast on the abundance of
    your house,
  and you give them drink from
    the river of your delights.

9 For with you is the fountain of
    life;
  in your light we see light.

10 O continue your steadfast love to
    those who know you,
  and your salvation to the
    upright of heart!
11 Do not let the foot of the
    arrogant tread on me,
  or the hand of the wicked
    drive me away.
12 There the evildoers lie prostrate;
  they are thrust down, unable
    to rise.

Psalm 37

Exhortation to Patience and Trust

Of David.

1 Do not fret because of the
    wicked;
  do not be envious of
    wrongdoers,
2 for they will soon fade like the
    grass,
  and wither like the green herb.

3 Trust in the LORD, and do good;
  so you will live in the land,
    and enjoy security.
4 Take delight in the LORD,
  and he will give you the
    desires of your heart.

5 Commit your way to the LORD;
  trust in him, and he will act.
6 He will make your vindication
    shine like the light,
  and the justice of your cause
    like the noonday.

7 Be still before the LORD, and
    wait patiently for him;
  do not fret over those who
    prosper in their way,
  over those who carry out evil
    devices.

8 Refrain from anger, and forsake
    wrath.
  Do not fret — it leads only to
    evil.
9 For the wicked shall be cut off,
  but those who wait for the
    LORD shall inherit the land.

10 Yet a little while, and the wicked
  will be no more;

P
S
A
L
M
S

though you look diligently for
their place, they will not be
there.
11 But the meek shall inherit the
land,
and delight themselves in
abundant prosperity.

12 The wicked plot against the
righteous,
and gnash their teeth at them;
13 but the LORD laughs at the
wicked,
for he sees that their day is
coming.

14 The wicked draw the sword and
bend their bows
to bring down the poor and
needy,
to kill those who walk
uprightly;
15 their sword shall enter their own
heart,
and their bows shall be
broken.

16 Better is a little that the
righteous person has
than the abundance of many
wicked.
17 For the arms of the wicked shall
be broken,
but the LORD upholds the
righteous.

18 The LORD knows the days of the
blameless,
and their heritage will abide
forever;
19 they are not put to shame in evil
times,
in the days of famine they
have abundance.

20 But the wicked perish,
and the enemies of the LORD
are like the glory of the
pastures;
they vanish—like smoke they
vanish away.

21 The wicked borrow, and do not
pay back,
but the righteous are generous
and keep giving;
22 for those blessed by the LORD
shall inherit the land,
but those cursed by him shall
be cut off.

23 Our steps*l* are made firm by the
LORD,
when he delights in our*m* way;
24 though we stumble,*n* we*o* shall
not fall headlong,
for the LORD holds us*p* by the
hand.

25 I have been young, and now am
old,
yet I have not seen the
righteous forsaken
or their children begging
bread.
26 They are ever giving liberally
and lending,
and their children become a
blessing.

27 Depart from evil, and do good;
so you shall abide forever.
28 For the LORD loves justice;
he will not forsake his faithful
ones.

The righteous shall be kept safe
forever,
but the children of the wicked
shall be cut off.
29 The righteous shall inherit the
land,
and live in it forever.

30 The mouths of the righteous
utter wisdom,
and their tongues speak
justice.
31 The law of their God is in their
hearts;
their steps do not slip.

32 The wicked watch for the
righteous,
and seek to kill them.
33 The LORD will not abandon them
to their power,
or let them be condemned
when they are brought to
trial.

34 Wait for the LORD, and keep to
his way,
and he will exalt you to inherit
the land;
you will look on the
destruction of the wicked.

l Heb *a man's steps*   *m* Heb *his*
n Heb *he stumbles*   *o* Heb *he*
p Heb *him*

35 I have seen the wicked
       oppressing,
    and towering like a cedar of
       Lebanon.*q*
36 Again I*r* passed by, and they
       were no more;
    though I sought them, they
       could not be found.

37 Mark the blameless, and behold
       the upright,
    for there is posterity for the
       peaceable.
38 But transgressors shall be
       altogether destroyed;
    the posterity of the wicked
       shall be cut off.

39 The salvation of the righteous is
       from the LORD;
    he is their refuge in the time of
       trouble.
40 The LORD helps them and
       rescues them;
    he rescues them from the
       wicked, and saves them,
    because they take refuge in
       him.

Psalm 38

A Penitent Sufferer's Plea for Healing

    A Psalm of David, for the
       memorial offering.

1 O LORD, do not rebuke me in
       your anger,
    or discipline me in your wrath.
2 For your arrows have sunk into
       me,
    and your hand has come down
       on me.

3 There is no soundness in my
       flesh
       because of your indignation;
    there is no health in my bones
       because of my sin.
4 For my iniquities have gone over
       my head;
    they weigh like a burden too
       heavy for me.

5 My wounds grow foul and fester
       because of my foolishness;
6 I am utterly bowed down and
       prostrate;
    all day long I go around
       mourning.
7 For my loins are filled with
       burning,

and there is no soundness in
       my flesh.
8 I am utterly spent and crushed;
    I groan because of the tumult
       of my heart.

9 O Lord, all my longing is known
       to you;
    my sighing is not hidden from
       you.
10 My heart throbs, my strength
       fails me;
    as for the light of my eyes—it
       also has gone from me.
11 My friends and companions
       stand aloof from my
       affliction,
    and my neighbors stand far
       off.

12 Those who seek my life lay their
       snares;
    those who seek to hurt me
       speak of ruin,
    and meditate treachery all day
       long.

13 But I am like the deaf, I do not
       hear;
    like the mute, who cannot
       speak.
14 Truly, I am like one who does
       not hear,
    and in whose mouth is no
       retort.

15 But it is for you, O LORD, that I
       wait;
    it is you, O LORD my God,
       who will answer.
16 For I pray, "Only do not let them
       rejoice over me,
    those who boast against me
       when my foot slips."

17 For I am ready to fall,
    and my pain is ever with me.
18 I confess my iniquity;
    I am sorry for my sin.
19 Those who are my foes without
       cause*s* are mighty,
    and many are those who hate
       me wrongfully.
20 Those who render me evil for
       good
    are my adversaries because I
       follow after good.

q Gk: Meaning of Heb uncertain
r Gk Syr Jerome: Heb *he*   *s* Q Ms: MT
my living foes

21 Do not forsake me, O LORD;
O my God, do not be far from
me;
22 make haste to help me,
O Lord, my salvation.

Psalm 39

Prayer for Wisdom and Forgiveness

To the leader: to Je·dú'thun.
A Psalm of David.

1 I said, "I will guard my ways
that I may not sin with my
tongue;
I will keep a muzzle on my
mouth
as long as the wicked are in
my presence."
2 I was silent and still;
I held my peace to no avail;
my distress grew worse,
3 my heart became hot within
me.
While I mused, the fire burned;
then I spoke with my tongue:

4 "LORD, let me know my end,
and what is the measure of my
days;
let me know how fleeting my
life is.
5 You have made my days a few
handbreadths,
and my lifetime is as nothing
in your sight.
Surely everyone stands as a
mere breath.   *Sē'lah*
6 Surely everyone goes about
like a shadow.
Surely for nothing they are in
turmoil;
they heap up, and do not
know who will gather.

7 "And now, O Lord, what do I
wait for?
My hope is in you.
8 Deliver me from all my
transgressions.
Do not make me the scorn of
the fool.
9 I am silent; I do not open my
mouth,
for it is you who have done it.
10 Remove your stroke from me;
I am worn down by the
blows[t] of your hand.

11 "You chastise mortals
in punishment for sin,

consuming like a moth what is
dear to them;
surely everyone is a mere
breath.   *Sē'lah*

12 "Hear my prayer, O LORD,
and give ear to my cry;
do not hold your peace at my
tears.
For I am your passing guest,
an alien, like all my forebears.
13 Turn your gaze away from me,
that I may smile again,
before I depart and am no
more."

Psalm 40

*Thanksgiving for Deliverance and
Prayer for Help*
(Ps 70.1–5)

To the leader. Of David. A Psalm.

1 I waited patiently for the LORD;
he inclined to me and heard
my cry.
2 He drew me up from the
desolate pit,[u]
out of the miry bog,
and set my feet upon a rock,
making my steps secure.
3 He put a new song in my mouth,
a song of praise to our God.
Many will see and fear,
and put their trust in the
LORD.

4 Happy are those who make
the LORD their trust,
who do not turn to the proud,
to those who go astray after
false gods.
5 You have multiplied, O LORD my
God,
your wondrous deeds and your
thoughts toward us;
none can compare with you.
Were I to proclaim and tell of
them,
they would be more than can
be counted.

6 Sacrifice and offering you do not
desire,
but you have given me an
open ear.[v]
Burnt offering and sin offering
you have not required.
7 Then I said, "Here I am;

t Heb *hostility*   *u* Cn: Heb *pit of tumult*
v Heb *ears you have dug for me*

in the scroll of the book it is
written of me.*w*
8 I delight to do your will, O my
God;
    your law is within my heart."

9 I have told the glad news of
deliverance
    in the great congregation;
see, I have not restrained my
lips,
    as you know, O LORD.
10 I have not hidden your saving
help within my heart,
    I have spoken of your
faithfulness and your
salvation;
I have not concealed your
steadfast love and your
faithfulness
    from the great congregation.

11 Do not, O LORD, withhold
your mercy from me;
    let your steadfast love and your
faithfulness
    keep me safe forever.
12 For evils have encompassed me
without number;
    my iniquities have overtaken me,
until I cannot see;
they are more than the hairs of
my head,
    and my heart fails me.

13 Be pleased, O LORD, to deliver
me;
    O LORD, make haste to help
me.
14 Let all those be put to shame
and confusion
    who seek to snatch away my
life;
let those be turned back and
brought to dishonor
    who desire my hurt.
15 Let those be appalled because of
their shame
    who say to me, "Aha, Aha!"

16 But may all who seek you
rejoice and be glad in you;
    may those who love your
salvation
    say continually, "Great is the
LORD!"
17 As for me, I am poor and needy,
but the Lord takes thought for
me.
    You are my help and my
deliverer;
do not delay, O my God.

Psalm 41

*Assurance of God's Help and
a Plea for Healing*

To the leader. A Psalm of David.

1 Happy are those who consider
the poor;*x*
    the LORD delivers them in the
day of trouble.
2 The LORD protects them and
keeps them alive;
    they are called happy in the
land.
You do not give them up to
the will of their enemies.
3 The LORD sustains them on their
sickbed;
    in their illness you heal all
their infirmities.*y*

4 As for me, I said, "O LORD, be
gracious to me;
    heal me, for I have sinned
against you."
5 My enemies wonder in malice
    when I will die, and my name
perish.
6 And when they come to see me,
they utter empty words,
    while their hearts gather
mischief;
    when they go out, they tell it
abroad.
7 All who hate me whisper
together about me;
    they imagine the worst for me.

8 They think that a deadly thing
has fastened on me,
    that I will not rise again from
where I lie.
9 Even my bosom friend in whom
I trusted,
    who ate of my bread, has
lifted the heel against me.
10 But you, O LORD, be gracious to
me,
    and raise me up, that I may
repay them.

11 By this I know that you are
pleased with me;
    because my enemy has not
triumphed over me.
12 But you have upheld me because
of my integrity,
    and set me in your presence
forever.

P
S
A
L
M
S

---

w Meaning of Heb uncertain   *x* Or *weak*
y Heb *you change all his bed*

13 Blessed be the LORD, the God of
Israel,
from everlasting to everlasting.
Amen and Amen.

BOOK II

(Psalms 42–72)

Psalm 42

*Longing for God and His
Help in Distress*

To the leader. A Mas'kil
of the Kō'ra·hītes.

1 As a deer longs for flowing
streams,
so my soul longs for you,
O God.
2 My soul thirsts for God,
for the living God.
When shall I come and behold
the face of God?
3 My tears have been my food
day and night,
while people say to me
continually,
"Where is your God?"

4 These things I remember,
as I pour out my soul:
how I went with the throng,z
and led them in procession to
the house of God,
with glad shouts and songs of
thanksgiving,
a multitude keeping festival.
5 Why are you cast down, O my
soul,
and why are you disquieted
within me?
Hope in God; for I shall again
praise him,
my help 6 and my God.

My soul is cast down within me;
therefore I remember you
from the land of Jordan and of
Hermon,
from Mount Mī'zar.
7 Deep calls to deep
at the thunder of your
cataracts;
all your waves and your billows
have gone over me.
8 By day the LORD commands his
steadfast love,
and at night his song is with
me,
a prayer to the God of my life.

9 I say to God, my rock,

"Why have you forgotten me?
Why must I walk about
mournfully
because the enemy oppresses
me?"
10 As with a deadly wound in my
body,
my adversaries taunt me,
while they say to me continually,
"Where is your God?"

11 Why are you cast down, O my
soul,
and why are you disquieted
within me?
Hope in God; for I shall again
praise him,
my help and my God.

Psalm 43

Prayer to God in Time of Trouble

1 Vindicate me, O God, and defend
my cause
against an ungodly people;
from those who are deceitful and
unjust
deliver me!
2 For you are the God in whom I
take refuge;
why have you cast me off?
Why must I walk about
mournfully
because of the oppression of
the enemy?

3 O send out your light and your
truth;
let them lead me;
let them bring me to your holy
hill
and to your dwelling.
4 Then I will go to the altar of
God,
to God my exceeding joy;
and I will praise you with the
harp,
O God, my God.

5 Why are you cast down, O my
soul,
and why are you disquieted
within me?
Hope in God; for I shall again
praise him,
my help and my God.

z Meaning of Heb uncertain

Psalm 44

National Lament and Prayer for Help

To the leader. Of the Kō′ra·hītes.
A Mas′kil.

1 We have heard with our ears,
    O God,
  our ancestors have told us,
 what deeds you performed in
    their days,
  in the days of old:
2 you with your own hand drove
    out the nations,
  but them you planted;
 you afflicted the peoples,
  but them you set free;
3 for not by their own sword did
    they win the land,
  nor did their own arm give
    them victory;
 but your right hand, and your
    arm,
  and the light of your
    countenance,
  for you delighted in them.

4 You are my King and my God;
  you command*a* victories for
    Jacob.
5 Through you we push down our
    foes;
  through your name we tread
    down our assailants.
6 For not in my bow do I trust,
  nor can my sword save me.
7 But you have saved us from our
    foes,
  and have put to confusion
    those who hate us.
8 In God we have boasted
    continually,
  and we will give thanks to
    your name forever. *Sē′lah*

9 Yet you have rejected us and
    abased us,
  and have not gone out with
    our armies.
10 You made us turn back from the
    foe,
  and our enemies have gotten
    spoil.
11 You have made us like sheep for
    slaughter,
  and have scattered us among
    the nations.
12 You have sold your people for a
    trifle,
  demanding no high price for
    them.

13 You have made us the taunt of
    our neighbors,
  the derision and scorn of those
    around us.
14 You have made us a byword
    among the nations,
  a laughingstock*b* among the
    peoples.
15 All day long my disgrace is
    before me,
  and shame has covered my
    face
16 at the words of the taunters and
    revilers,
  at the sight of the enemy and
    the avenger.

17 All this has come upon us,
  yet we have not forgotten you,
  or been false to your covenant.
18 Our heart has not turned back,
  nor have our steps departed
    from your way,
19 yet you have broken us in the
    haunt of jackals,
  and covered us with deep
    darkness.

20 If we had forgotten the name of
    our God,
  or spread out our hands to a
    strange god,
21 would not God discover this?
  For he knows the secrets of
    the heart.
22 Because of you we are being
    killed all day long,
  and accounted as sheep for the
    slaughter.

23 Rouse yourself! Why do you
    sleep, O Lord?
  Awake, do not cast us off
    forever!
24 Why do you hide your face?
  Why do you forget our
    affliction and oppression?
25 For we sink down to the dust;
  our bodies cling to the ground.
26 Rise up, come to our help.
  Redeem us for the sake of
    your steadfast love.

a Gk Syr: Heb *You are my King, O God;*
command   *b* Heb *a shaking of the head*

Psalm 45

Ode for a Royal Wedding

To the leader: according to Lilies. Of
the Kō'ra·hītes. A Mas'kil, A love song.

1 My heart overflows with a
goodly theme;
 I address my verses to the
king;
 my tongue is like the pen of a
ready scribe.

2 You are the most handsome of
men;
 grace is poured upon your lips;
 therefore God has blessed you
forever.

3 Gird your sword on your thigh,
O mighty one,
 in your glory and majesty.

4 In your majesty ride on
victoriously
 for the cause of truth and to
defend[c] the right;
 let your right hand teach you
dread deeds.

5 Your arrows are sharp
 in the heart of the king's
enemies;
 the peoples fall under you.

6 Your throne, O God,[d] endures
forever and ever.
 Your royal scepter is a scepter
of equity;

7 you love righteousness and
hate wickedness.
 Therefore God, your God, has
anointed you
 with the oil of gladness
beyond your companions;

8 your robes are all fragrant
with myrrh and aloes and
cassia.
 From ivory palaces stringed
instruments make you
glad;

9 daughters of kings are among
your ladies of honor;
 at your right hand stands the
queen in gold of Ō'phir.

10 Hear, O daughter, consider and
incline your ear;
 forget your people and your
father's house,

11 and the king will desire your
beauty.
 Since he is your lord, bow to
him;

12 the people[e] of Tyre will seek
your favor with gifts,
 the richest of the people [13]with
all kinds of wealth.

 The princess is decked in her
chamber with gold-woven
robes;[f]

14 in many-colored robes she is
led to the king;
 behind her the virgins, her
companions, follow.

15 With joy and gladness they are
led along
 as they enter the palace of the
king.

16 In the place of ancestors you,
O king,[g] shall have sons;
 you will make them princes in
all the earth.

17 I will cause your name to be
celebrated in all
generations;
 therefore the peoples will
praise you forever and
ever.

Psalm 46

God's Defense of His City and People

To the leader. Of the Kō'ra·hītes.
According to Al'a·moth. A Song.

1 God is our refuge and strength,
 a very present[h] help in
trouble.

2 Therefore we will not fear,
 though the earth should
change,
 though the mountains shake in
the heart of the sea;

3 though its waters roar and foam,
 though the mountains tremble
with its tumult. *Sē'lah*

4 There is a river whose streams
 make glad the city of God,
 the holy habitation of the Most
High.

5 God is in the midst of the city;[i]
 it shall not be moved;
 God will help it when the
morning dawns.

6 The nations are in an uproar, the
kingdoms totter;

[c] Cn: Heb *and the meekness of*
[d] Or *Your throne is a throne of God, it*
[e] Heb *daughter* [f] Or *people.* [13]All
*glorious is the princess within, gold
embroidery is her clothing* [g] Heb lacks
O king [h] Or *well proved* [i] Heb *of it*

he utters his voice, the earth
  melts.
7 The LORD of hosts is with us;
    the God of Jacob is our
      refuge.*j*   *Sē'lah*

8 Come, behold the works of the
    LORD;
  see what desolations he has
    brought on the earth.
9 He makes wars cease to the end
    of the earth;
  he breaks the bow, and
    shatters the spear;
  he burns the shields with fire.
10 "Be still, and know that I am
    God!
  I am exalted among the
    nations,
  I am exalted in the earth."
11 The LORD of hosts is with us;
    the God of Jacob is our
      refuge.*j*   *Sē'lah*

Psalm 47

God's Rule over the Nations

To the leader. Of the Kō'ra·hītes.
A Psalm.

1 Clap your hands, all you
    peoples;
  shout to God with loud songs
    of joy.
2 For the LORD, the Most High, is
    awesome,
  a great king over all the earth.
3 He subdued peoples under us,
  and nations under our feet.
4 He chose our heritage for us,
  the pride of Jacob whom he
    loves.   *Sē'lah*

5 God has gone up with a shout,
  the LORD with the sound of a
    trumpet.
6 Sing praises to God, sing
    praises;
  sing praises to our King, sing
    praises.
7 For God is the king of all the
    earth;
  sing praises with a psalm.*k*

8 God is king over the nations;
  God sits on his holy throne.
9 The princes of the peoples
    gather
  as the people of the God of
    Abraham.
For the shields of the earth
  belong to God;

he is highly exalted.

Psalm 48

The Glory and Strength of Zion

A Song. A Psalm of the Kō'ra·hītes.

1 Great is the LORD and greatly to
    be praised
  in the city of our God.
His holy mountain, 2 beautiful in
    elevation,
  is the joy of all the earth,
Mount Zion, in the far north,
  the city of the great King.
3 Within its citadels God
  has shown himself a sure
    defense.

4 Then the kings assembled,
  they came on together.
5 As soon as they saw it, they
    were astounded;
  they were in panic, they took
    to flight;
6 trembling took hold of them
    there,
  pains as of a woman in labor,
7 as when an east wind shatters
  the ships of Tar'shish.
8 As we have heard, so have we
    seen
  in the city of the LORD of
    hosts,
in the city of our God,
  which God establishes forever.
                            Sē'lah

9 We ponder your steadfast love,
    O God,
  in the midst of your temple.
10 Your name, O God, like your
    praise,
  reaches to the ends of the
    earth.
Your right hand is filled with
    victory.
11 Let Mount Zion be glad,
let the towns*l* of Judah rejoice
  because of your judgments.

12 Walk about Zion, go all around
    it,
  count its towers,
13 consider well its ramparts;
  go through its citadels,
that you may tell the next
    generation
14   that this is God,

j Or *fortress*   *k* Heb *Maskil*
l Heb *daughters*

our God forever and ever.
He will be our guide forever.

Psalm 49

The Folly of Trust in Riches

To the leader. Of the Kō′ra·hītes.
A Psalm.

1 Hear this, all you peoples;
  give ear, all inhabitants of the
    world,
2 both low and high,
  rich and poor together.
3 My mouth shall speak wisdom;
  the meditation of my heart
    shall be understanding.
4 I will incline my ear to a
    proverb;
  I will solve my riddle to the
    music of the harp.

5 Why should I fear in times of
    trouble,
  when the iniquity of my
    persecutors surrounds me,
6 those who trust in their wealth
  and boast of the abundance of
    their riches?
7 Truly, no ransom avails for one's
    life,*m*
  there is no price one can give
    to God for it.
8 For the ransom of life is costly,
  and can never suffice
9 that one should live on forever
  and never see the grave.*n*

10 When we look at the wise, they
    die;
  fool and dolt perish together
  and leave their wealth to
    others.
11 Their graves*o* are their homes
    forever,
  their dwelling places to all
    generations,
  though they named lands their
    own.
12 Mortals cannot abide in their
    pomp;
  they are like the animals that
    perish.

13 Such is the fate of the foolhardy,
  the end of those*p* who are
    pleased with their lot.
                              Se′lah
14 Like sheep they are appointed
    for Shē′ōl;
  Death shall be their shepherd;

straight to the grave they
    descend,*q*
  and their form shall waste
    away;
  Shē′ōl shall be their home.*r*
15 But God will ransom my soul
    from the power of Shē′ōl,
  for he will receive me.   *Se′lah*

16 Do not be afraid when some
    become rich,
  when the wealth of their
    houses increases.
17 For when they die they will
    carry nothing away;
  their wealth will not go down
    after them.
18 Though in their lifetime they
    count themselves happy
  —for you are praised when
    you do well for yourself—
19 they*s* will go to the company of
    their ancestors,
  who will never again see the
    light.
20 Mortals cannot abide in their
    pomp;
  they are like the animals that
    perish.

Psalm 50

The Acceptable Sacrifice

A Psalm of Ā′saph.

1 The mighty one, God the LORD,
  speaks and summons the earth
  from the rising of the sun to
    its setting.
2 Out of Zion, the perfection of
    beauty,
  God shines forth.

3 Our God comes and does not
    keep silence,
  before him is a devouring fire,
  and a mighty tempest all
    around him.
4 He calls to the heavens above
  and to the earth, that he may
    judge his people:
5 "Gather to me my faithful ones,
  who made a covenant with me
    by sacrifice!"

m Another reading is *no one can ransom
a brother*   *n* Heb *the pit*   *o* Gk Syr
Compare Tg: Heb *their inward* (thought)
p Tg: Heb *after them*   *q* Cn: Heb *the
upright shall have dominion over them
in the morning*   *r* Meaning of Heb
uncertain   *s* Cn: Heb *you*

6 The heavens declare his
    righteousness,
    for God himself is judge.

Sĕ′lah

7 "Hear, O my people, and I will
    speak,
    O Israel, I will testify against
        you.
    I am God, your God.
8 Not for your sacrifices do I
    rebuke you;
    your burnt offerings are
        continually before me.
9 I will not accept a bull from your
    house,
    or goats from your folds.
10 For every wild animal of the
    forest is mine,
    the cattle on a thousand hills.
11 I know all the birds of the air, [t]
    and all that moves in the field
        is mine.

12 "If I were hungry, I would not
    tell you,
    for the world and all that is in
        it is mine.
13 Do I eat the flesh of bulls,
    or drink the blood of goats?
14 Offer to God a sacrifice of
    thanksgiving, [u]
    and pay your vows to the Most
        High.
15 Call on me in the day of trouble;
    I will deliver you, and you
        shall glorify me."

16 But to the wicked God says:
    "What right have you to recite
        my statutes,
    or take my covenant on your
        lips?
17 For you hate discipline,
    and you cast my words behind
        you.
18 You make friends with a thief
    when you see one,
    and you keep company with
        adulterers.

19 "You give your mouth free rein
    for evil,
    and your tongue frames deceit.
20 You sit and speak against your
    kin;
    you slander your own mother's
        child.
21 These things you have done and
    I have been silent;
    you thought that I was one
        just like yourself.

But now I rebuke you, and lay
    the charge before you.

22 "Mark this, then, you who forget
    God,
    or I will tear you apart, and
        there will be no one to
        deliver.
23 Those who bring thanksgiving
    as their sacrifice honor me;
    to those who go the right
        way [v]
    I will show the salvation of
        God."

Psalm 51

Prayer for Cleansing and Pardon

To the leader. A Psalm of David, when
the prophet Nathan came to him, after
he had gone in to Bath·shē′ba.

1 Have mercy on me, O God,
    according to your steadfast
        love;
    according to your abundant
        mercy
    blot out my transgressions.
2 Wash me thoroughly from my
    iniquity,
    and cleanse me from my sin.

3 For I know my transgressions,
    and my sin is ever before me.
4 Against you, you alone, have I
    sinned,
    and done what is evil in your
        sight,
    so that you are justified in your
        sentence
    and blameless when you pass
        judgment.
5 Indeed, I was born guilty,
    a sinner when my mother
        conceived me.

6 You desire truth in the inward
    being; [w]
    therefore teach me wisdom in
        my secret heart.
7 Purge me with hyssop, and I
    shall be clean;
    wash me, and I shall be whiter
        than snow.
8 Let me hear joy and gladness;
    let the bones that you have
        crushed rejoice.
9 Hide your face from my sins,

t Gk Syr Tg: Heb *mountains*   u Or *make
thanksgiving your sacrifice to God*
v Heb *who set a way*   w Meaning of
Heb uncertain

and blot out all my iniquities.

10 Create in me a clean heart,
O God,
and put a new and right[x]
spirit within me.
11 Do not cast me away from your
presence,
and do not take your holy
spirit from me.
12 Restore to me the joy of your
salvation,
and sustain in me a willing[y]
spirit.

13 Then I will teach transgressors
your ways,
and sinners will return to you.
14 Deliver me from bloodshed,
O God,
O God of my salvation,
and my tongue will sing aloud
of your deliverance.

15 O Lord, open my lips,
and my mouth will declare
your praise.
16 For you have no delight in
sacrifice;
if I were to give a burnt
offering, you would not be
pleased.
17 The sacrifice acceptable to God[z]
is a broken spirit;
a broken and contrite heart,
O God, you will not
despise.

18 Do good to Zion in your good
pleasure;
rebuild the walls of Jerusalem,
19 then you will delight in right
sacrifices,
in burnt offerings and whole
burnt offerings;
then bulls will be offered on
your altar.

Psalm 52

Judgment on the Deceitful

To the leader. A Mas′kil of David,
when Dō′eg the E′dom·ite came to Saul
and said to him, "David has come to
the house of A·him′e·lech."

1 Why do you boast, O mighty
one,
of mischief done against the
godly?[a]
All day long [2]you are plotting
destruction.

Your tongue is like a sharp
razor,
you worker of treachery.
3 You love evil more than good,
and lying more than speaking
the truth.   *Se′lah*
4 You love all words that devour,
O deceitful tongue.

5 But God will break you down
forever;
he will snatch and tear you
from your tent;
he will uproot you from the
land of the living.   *Se′lah*
6 The righteous will see, and fear,
and will laugh at the
evildoer,[b] saying,
7 "See the one who would not take
refuge in God,
but trusted in abundant riches,
and sought refuge in wealth!"[c]

8 But I am like a green olive tree
in the house of God.
I trust in the steadfast love of
God
forever and ever.
9 I will thank you forever,
because of what you have
done.
In the presence of the faithful
I will proclaim[d] your name,
for it is good.

Psalm 53

Denunciation of Godlessness
(Ps 14.1–7)

To the leader: according to Mā′ha·lath.
A Mas′kil of David.

1 Fools say in their hearts, "There
is no God."
They are corrupt, they commit
abominable acts;
there is no one who does good.

2 God looks down from heaven on
humankind
to see if there are any who are
wise,
who seek after God.

3 They have all fallen away, they
are all alike perverse;
there is no one who does good,

x Or *steadfast*   y Or *generous*   z Or *My
sacrifice, O God,*   a Cn Compare Syr:
Heb *the kindness of God*   b Heb *him*
c Syr Tg: Heb *in his destruction*
d Cn: Heb *wait for*

no, not one.

4 Have they no knowledge, those
    evildoers,
    who eat up my people as they
      eat bread,
    and do not call upon God?

5 There they shall be in great
      terror,
    in terror such as has not been.
  For God will scatter the bones of
      the ungodly;[e]
    they will be put to shame,[f] for
      God has rejected them.

6 O that deliverance for Israel
      would come from Zion!
  When God restores the
      fortunes of his people,
    Jacob will rejoice; Israel will
      be glad.

Psalm 54

Prayer for Vindication

To the leader: with stringed
instruments. A Mas′kil of David, when
the Ziph′ites went and told Saul,
"David is in hiding among us."

1 Save me, O God, by your name,
    and vindicate me by your
      might.
2 Hear my prayer, O God;
    give ear to the words of my
      mouth.
3 For the insolent have risen
      against me,
    the ruthless seek my life;
    they do not set God before
      them.   Se′lah

4 But surely, God is my helper;
    the Lord is the upholder of[g]
      my life.
5 He will repay my enemies for
      their evil.
    In your faithfulness, put an
      end to them.

6 With a freewill offering I will
      sacrifice to you;
    I will give thanks to your
      name, O LORD, for it is
      good.
7 For he has delivered me from
      every trouble,
    and my eye has looked in
      triumph on my enemies.

Psalm 55

Complaint about a Friend's Treachery

To the leader: with stringed
instruments. A Mas′kil of David.

1 Give ear to my prayer, O God;
    do not hide yourself from my
      supplication.
2 Attend to me, and answer me;
    I am troubled in my complaint.
  I am distraught [3] by the noise of
      the enemy,
    because of the clamor of the
      wicked.
  For they bring[h] trouble upon
      me,
    and in anger they cherish
      enmity against me.

4 My heart is in anguish within
      me,
    the terrors of death have fallen
      upon me.
5 Fear and trembling come upon
      me,
    and horror overwhelms me.
6 And I say, "O that I had wings
      like a dove!
    I would fly away and be at
      rest;
7 truly, I would flee far away;
    I would lodge in the
      wilderness;   Se′lah
8 I would hurry to find a shelter
      for myself
    from the raging wind and
      tempest."

9 Confuse, O Lord, confound their
      speech;
    for I see violence and strife in
      the city.
10 Day and night they go around it
      on its walls,
  and iniquity and trouble are
      within it;
11   ruin is in its midst;
  oppression and fraud
    do not depart from its
      marketplace.

12 It is not enemies who taunt me—
    I could bear that;

e Cn Compare Gk Syr: Heb *him who
encamps against you*   f Gk: Heb *you
will put to shame*   g Gk Syr Jerome:
Heb *is of those who uphold* or *is with
those who uphold*   h Cn Compare Gk:
Heb *they cause to totter*

it is not adversaries who deal
    insolently with me —
    I could hide from them.
13 But it is you, my equal,
    my companion, my familiar
      friend,
14 with whom I kept pleasant
    company;
    we walked in the house of God
      with the throng.
15 Let death come upon them;
    let them go down alive to
      Shē′ōl;
    for evil is in their homes and
      in their hearts.

16 But I call upon God,
    and the LORD will save me.
17 Evening and morning and at
    noon
    I utter my complaint and
      moan,
    and he will hear my voice.
18 He will redeem me unharmed
    from the battle that I wage,
    for many are arrayed against
      me.
19 God, who is enthroned from of
    old,   *Sē′lah*
    will hear, and will humble
      them —
  because they do not change,
    and do not fear God.

20 My companion laid hands on a
    friend
    and violated a covenant with
      me*i*
21 with speech smoother than
    butter,
    but with a heart set on war;
  with words that were softer than
    oil,
    but in fact were drawn swords.

22 Cast your burden*j* on the LORD,
    and he will sustain you;
  he will never permit
    the righteous to be moved.

23 But you, O God, will cast them
    down
    into the lowest pit;
  the bloodthirsty and treacherous
    shall not live out half their
      days.
  But I will trust in you.

Psalm 56

Trust in God under Persecution

To the leader: according to The Dove
on Far-off Terebinths. Of David. A
Mik′tam, when the Phi·lis′tines seized
him in Gath.

1 Be gracious to me, O God, for
    people trample on me;
    all day long foes oppress me;
2 my enemies trample on me all
    day long,
    for many fight against me.
  O Most High, 3when I am afraid,
    I put my trust in you.
4 In God, whose word I praise,
    in God I trust; I am not afraid;
    what can flesh do to me?

5 All day long they seek to injure
    my cause;
    all their thoughts are against
      me for evil.
6 They stir up strife, they lurk,
    they watch my steps.
  As they hoped to have my life,
7   so repay*k* them for their
      crime;
    in wrath cast down the
      peoples, O God!

8 You have kept count of my
    tossings;
    put my tears in your bottle.
    Are they not in your record?
9 Then my enemies will retreat
    in the day when I call.
    This I know, that*l* God is for
      me.
10 In God, whose word I praise,
    in the LORD, whose word I
      praise,
11 in God I trust; I am not afraid.
    What can a mere mortal do to
      me?

12 My vows to you I must perform,
    O God;
    I will render thank offerings to
      you.
13 For you have delivered my soul
    from death,
    and my feet from falling,
  so that I may walk before God
    in the light of life.

*i*Heb lacks *with me*   *j*Or *Cast what he
has given you*   *k*Cn: Heb *rescue*
*l*Or *because*

Psalm 57

*Praise and Assurance
under Persecution*
(Cp Ps 108.1–5)

To the leader: Do Not Destroy. Of
David. A Mik′tam, when he fled from
Saul, in the cave.

1 Be merciful to me, O God, be
        merciful to me,
    for in you my soul takes
        refuge;
  in the shadow of your wings I
        will take refuge,
    until the destroying storms
        pass by.
2 I cry to God Most High,
    to God who fulfills his purpose
        for me.
3 He will send from heaven and
        save me,
    he will put to shame those
        who trample on me. *Sē′lah*
  God will send forth his steadfast
        love and his faithfulness.

4 I lie down among lions
    that greedily devour[m] human
        prey;
  their teeth are spears and
        arrows,
    their tongues sharp swords.

5 Be exalted, O God, above the
        heavens.
    Let your glory be over all the
        earth.

6 They set a net for my steps;
    my soul was bowed down.
  They dug a pit in my path,
    but they have fallen into it
        themselves.   *Sē′lah*
7 My heart is steadfast, O God,
    my heart is steadfast.
  I will sing and make melody.
8   Awake, my soul!
  Awake, O harp and lyre!
    I will awake the dawn.
9 I will give thanks to you,
        O Lord, among the
        peoples;
    I will sing praises to you
        among the nations.
10 For your steadfast love is as
        high as the heavens;
    your faithfulness extends to
        the clouds.

11 Be exalted, O God, above the
        heavens.

Let your glory be over all the
        earth.

Psalm 58

Prayer for Vengeance

To the leader: Do Not Destroy.
Of David. A Mik′tam.

1 Do you indeed decree what is
        right, you gods?[n]
    Do you judge people fairly?
2 No, in your hearts you devise
        wrongs;
    your hands deal out violence
        on earth.

3 The wicked go astray from the
        womb;
    they err from their birth,
        speaking lies.
4 They have venom like the venom
        of a serpent,
    like the deaf adder that stops
        its ear,
5 so that it does not hear the voice
        of charmers
    or of the cunning enchanter.

6 O God, break the teeth in their
        mouths;
    tear out the fangs of the young
        lions, O LORD!
7 Let them vanish like water that
        runs away;
    like grass let them be trodden
        down[o] and wither.
8 Let them be like the snail that
        dissolves into slime;
    like the untimely birth that
        never sees the sun.
9 Sooner than your pots can feel
        the heat of thorns,
    whether green or ablaze, may
        he sweep them away!

10 The righteous will rejoice when
        they see vengeance done;
    they will bathe their feet in the
        blood of the wicked.
11 People will say, "Surely there is
        a reward for the righteous;
    surely there is a God who
        judges on earth."

m Cn: Heb *are aflame for*   *n* Or *mighty
lords*   *o* Cn: Meaning of Heb uncertain

P
S
A
L
M
S

Psalm 59

Prayer for Deliverance from Enemies

To the leader: Do Not Destroy. Of
David. A Mik'tam, when Saul ordered
his house to be watched in order
to kill him.

1 Deliver me from my enemies,
        O my God;
    protect me from those who
        rise up against me.
2 Deliver me from those who work
        evil;
    from the bloodthirsty save me.

3 Even now they lie in wait for my
        life;
    the mighty stir up strife
        against me.
  For no transgression or sin of
        mine, O LORD,
4   for no fault of mine, they run
        and make ready.

  Rouse yourself, come to my help
        and see!
5   You, LORD God of hosts, are
        God of Israel.
  Awake to punish all the nations;
    spare none of those who
        treacherously plot evil.
                        Sē′lah

6 Each evening they come back,
    howling like dogs
  and prowling about the city.
7 There they are, bellowing with
        their mouths,
    with sharp words*p* on their
        lips —
    for "Who," they think,*q* "will
        hear us?"

8 But you laugh at them, O LORD;
    you hold all the nations in
        derision.
9 O my strength, I will watch for
        you;
    for you, O God, are my
        fortress.
10 My God in his steadfast love will
        meet me;
    my God will let me look in
        triumph on my enemies.

11 Do not kill them, or my people
        may forget;
    make them totter by your
        power, and bring them
        down,
    O Lord, our shield.

12 For the sin of their mouths, the
        words of their lips,
    let them be trapped in their
        pride.
  For the cursing and lies that they
        utter,
13   consume them in wrath;
    consume them until they are
        no more.
  Then it will be known to the
        ends of the earth
    that God rules over Jacob.
                        Sē′lah

14 Each evening they come back,
    howling like dogs
  and prowling about the city.
15 They roam about for food,
    and growl if they do not get
        their fill.

16 But I will sing of your might;
    I will sing aloud of your
        steadfast love in the
        morning.
  For you have been a fortress for
        me
    and a refuge in the day of my
        distress.
17 O my strength, I will sing
        praises to you,
    for you, O God, are my
        fortress,
    the God who shows me
        steadfast love.

Psalm 60

*Prayer for National Victory
after Defeat*
(Cp Ps 108.6–13)

To the leader: according to the Lily of
the Covenant. A Mik'tam of David; for
instruction; when he struggled with
Ar′am-nā·ha·rā′im and with
Ar′am-zō′bah, and when Jō′ab on his
return killed twelve thousand
Ē′dom·ites in the Valley of Salt.

1 O God, you have rejected us,
        broken our defenses;
    you have been angry; now
        restore us!
2 You have caused the land to
        quake; you have torn it
        open;
    repair the cracks in it, for it is
        tottering.
3 You have made your people
        suffer hard things;

p Heb *with swords*   *q* Heb lacks *they
think*

you have given us wine to
　　drink that made us reel.

4 You have set up a banner for
　　those who fear you,
　　to rally to it out of bowshot.*r*
　　　　　　　　　Sē′lah
5 Give victory with your right
　　hand, and answer us,*s*
　　so that those whom you love
　　　may be rescued.

6 God has promised in his
　　　sanctuary:*t*
　　"With exultation I will divide
　　　up Shē′chem,
　　and portion out the Vale of
　　　Suc′coth.
7 Gil′e·ad is mine, and Ma·nas′seh
　　　is mine;
　　Ē′phra·im is my helmet;
　　Judah is my scepter.
8 Mō′ab is my washbasin;
　　on Ē′dom I hurl my shoe;
　　over Phi·lis′ti·a I shout in
　　　triumph."

9 Who will bring me to the
　　　fortified city?
　　Who will lead me to Ē′dom?
10 Have you not rejected us,
　　　O God?
　　You do not go out, O God,
　　　with our armies.
11 O grant us help against the foe,
　　for human help is worthless.
12 With God we shall do valiantly;
　　it is he who will tread down
　　　our foes.

Psalm 61

Assurance of God's Protection

To the leader: with stringed
　　instruments. Of David.

1 Hear my cry, O God;
　　listen to my prayer.
2 From the end of the earth I call
　　to you,
　　when my heart is faint.

Lead me to the rock
　　that is higher than I;
3 for you are my refuge,
　　a strong tower against the
　　　enemy.

4 Let me abide in your tent
　　forever,
　　find refuge under the shelter
　　of your wings.　　　*Sē′lah*

5 For you, O God, have heard my
　　　vows;
　　you have given me the
　　　heritage of those who fear
　　　your name.

6 Prolong the life of the king;
　　may his years endure to all
　　　generations!
7 May he be enthroned forever
　　　before God;
　　appoint steadfast love and
　　　faithfulness to watch over
　　　him!

8 So I will always sing praises to
　　　your name,
　　as I pay my vows day after
　　　day.

Psalm 62

Song of Trust in God Alone

To the leader: according to Je·dū′thun.
　　A Psalm of David.

1 For God alone my soul waits in
　　　silence;
　　from him comes my salvation.
2 He alone is my rock and my
　　　salvation,
　　my fortress; I shall never be
　　　shaken.

3 How long will you assail a
　　　person,
　　will you batter your victim, all
　　　of you,
　　as you would a leaning wall, a
　　　tottering fence?
4 Their only plan is to bring down
　　　a person of prominence.
　　They take pleasure in
　　　falsehood;
　　they bless with their mouths,
　　but inwardly they curse. *Sē′lah*

5 For God alone my soul waits in
　　　silence,
　　for my hope is from him.
6 He alone is my rock and my
　　　salvation,
　　my fortress; I shall not be
　　　shaken.
7 On God rests my deliverance
　　　and my honor;
　　my mighty rock, my refuge is
　　　in God.

*r*Gk Syr Jerome: Heb *because of the
truth*　　*s*Another reading is *me*
*t*Or *by his holiness*

8 Trust in him at all times,
   O people;
pour out your heart before
   him;
God is a refuge for us.   *Se'lah*

9 Those of low estate are but a
   breath,
those of high estate are a
   delusion;
in the balances they go up;
   they are together lighter than
   a breath.
10 Put no confidence in extortion,
   and set no vain hopes on
   robbery;
if riches increase, do not set
   your heart on them.

11 Once God has spoken;
   twice have I heard this:
that power belongs to God,
12   and steadfast love belongs to
   you, O Lord.
For you repay to all
   according to their work.

Psalm 63

Comfort and Assurance in
God's Presence

A Psalm of David, when he was in the
Wilderness of Judah.

1 O God, you are my God, I seek
   you,
my soul thirsts for you;
my flesh faints for you,
   as in a dry and weary land
   where there is no water.
2 So I have looked upon you in
   the sanctuary,
beholding your power and
   glory.
3 Because your steadfast love is
   better than life,
my lips will praise you.
4 So I will bless you as long as I
   live;
I will lift up my hands and call
   on your name.

5 My soul is satisfied as with a
   rich feast,[u]
and my mouth praises you
   with joyful lips
6 when I think of you on my bed,
   and meditate on you in the
   watches of the night;
7 for you have been my help,
   and in the shadow of your
   wings I sing for joy.

8 My soul clings to you;
   your right hand upholds me.
9 But those who seek to destroy
   my life
shall go down into the depths
   of the earth;
10 they shall be given over to the
   power of the sword,
they shall be prey for jackals.
11 But the king shall rejoice in God;
   all who swear by him shall
   exult,
for the mouths of liars will be
   stopped.

Psalm 64

Prayer for Protection from Enemies

To the leader. A Psalm of David.

1 Hear my voice, O God, in my
   complaint;
preserve my life from the
   dread enemy.
2 Hide me from the secret plots of
   the wicked,
from the scheming of
   evildoers,
3 who whet their tongues like
   swords,
who aim bitter words like
   arrows,
4 shooting from ambush at the
   blameless;
they shoot suddenly and
   without fear.
5 They hold fast to their evil
   purpose;
they talk of laying snares
   secretly,
thinking, "Who can see us?[v]
6   Who can search out our
   crimes?[w]
We have thought out a
   cunningly conceived plot."
For the human heart and mind
   are deep.

7 But God will shoot his arrow at
   them;
they will be wounded
   suddenly.
8 Because of their tongue he will
   bring them to ruin;[x]
all who see them will shake
   with horror.
9 Then everyone will fear;

[u] Heb *with fat and fatness*   [v] Syr: Heb
them   [w] Cn: Heb *They search out
crimes*   [x] Cn: Heb *They will bring him
to ruin, their tongue being against them*

they will tell what God has
brought about,
and ponder what he has done.

10 Let the righteous rejoice in the
LORD
and take refuge in him.
Let all the upright in heart glory.

Psalm 65

Thanksgiving for Earth's Bounty

To the leader. A Psalm of David.
A Song.

1 Praise is due to you,
O God, in Zion;
and to you shall vows be
performed,
2 O you who answer prayer!
To you all flesh shall come.
3 When deeds of iniquity
overwhelm us,
you forgive our transgressions.
4 Happy are those whom you
choose and bring near
to live in your courts.
We shall be satisfied with the
goodness of your house,
your holy temple.

5 By awesome deeds you answer
us with deliverance,
O God of our salvation;
you are the hope of all the ends
of the earth
and of the farthest seas.
6 By your[y] strength you
established the mountains;
you are girded with might.
7 You silence the roaring of the
seas,
the roaring of their waves,
the tumult of the peoples.
8 Those who live at earth's
farthest bounds are awed
by your signs;
you make the gateways of the
morning and the evening
shout for joy.

9 You visit the earth and water it,
you greatly enrich it;
the river of God is full of water;
you provide the people with
grain,
for so you have prepared it.
10 You water its furrows
abundantly,
settling its ridges,
softening it with showers,
and blessing its growth.

11 You crown the year with your
bounty;
your wagon tracks overflow
with richness.
12 The pastures of the wilderness
overflow,
the hills gird themselves with
joy,
13 the meadows clothe themselves
with flocks,
the valleys deck themselves
with grain,
they shout and sing together
for joy.

Psalm 66

Praise for God's Goodness to Israel

To the leader. A Song. A Psalm.

1 Make a joyful noise to God, all
the earth;
2 sing the glory of his name;
give to him glorious praise.
3 Say to God, "How awesome are
your deeds!
Because of your great power,
your enemies cringe before
you.
4 All the earth worships you;
they sing praises to you,
sing praises to your name."
Se'lah

5 Come and see what God has
done:
he is awesome in his deeds
among mortals.
6 He turned the sea into dry land;
they passed through the river
on foot.
There we rejoiced in him,
7 who rules by his might
forever,
whose eyes keep watch on the
nations —
let the rebellious not exalt
themselves.   *Se'lah*

8 Bless our God, O peoples,
let the sound of his praise be
heard,
9 who has kept us among the
living,
and has not let our feet slip.
10 For you, O God, have tested us;
you have tried us as silver is
tried.
11 You brought us into the net;
you laid burdens on our backs;

[y] Gk Jerome: Heb *his*

PSALMS

12 you let people ride over our
heads;
we went through fire and
through water;
yet you have brought us out to a
spacious place.z

13 I will come into your house with
burnt offerings;
I will pay you my vows,
14 those that my lips uttered
and my mouth promised when
I was in trouble.
15 I will offer to you burnt offerings
of fatlings,
with the smoke of the sacrifice
of rams;
I will make an offering of bulls
and goats.   *Sē'lah*

16 Come and hear, all you who fear
God,
and I will tell what he has
done for me.
17 I cried aloud to him,
and he was extolled with my
tongue.
18 If I had cherished iniquity in my
heart,
the Lord would not have
listened.
19 But truly God has listened;
he has given heed to the
words of my prayer.

20 Blessed be God,
because he has not rejected
my prayer
or removed his steadfast love
from me.

Psalm 67

The Nations Called to Praise God

To the leader: with stringed
instruments. A Psalm. A Song.

1 May God be gracious to us and
bless us
and make his face to shine
upon us,   *Sē'lah*
2 that your way may be known
upon earth,
your saving power among all
nations.
3 Let the peoples praise you,
O God;
let all the peoples praise you.

4 Let the nations be glad and sing
for joy,

for you judge the peoples with
equity
and guide the nations upon
earth.   *Sē'lah*
5 Let the peoples praise you,
O God;
let all the peoples praise you.

6 The earth has yielded its
increase;
God, our God, has blessed us.
7 May God continue to bless us;
let all the ends of the earth
revere him.

Psalm 68

Praise and Thanksgiving

To the leader. Of David. A Psalm.
A Song.

1 Let God rise up, let his enemies
be scattered;
let those who hate him flee
before him.
2 As smoke is driven away, so
drive them away;
as wax melts before the fire,
let the wicked perish before
God.
3 But let the righteous be joyful;
let them exult before God;
let them be jubilant with joy.

4 Sing to God, sing praises to his
name;
lift up a song to him who rides
upon the cloudsa—
his name is the LORD—
be exultant before him.

5 Father of orphans and protector
of widows
is God in his holy habitation.
6 God gives the desolate a home to
live in;
he leads out the prisoners to
prosperity,
but the rebellious live in a
parched land.

7 O God, when you went out
before your people,
when you marched through
the wilderness,   *Sē'lah*
8 the earth quaked, the heavens
poured down rain
at the presence of God, the
God of Sinai,

z Cn Compare Gk Syr Jerome Tg: Heb *to
a saturation*   a Or *cast up a highway
for him who rides through the deserts*

at the presence of God, the
God of Israel.
9 Rain in abundance, O God, you
showered abroad;
you restored your heritage
when it languished;
10 your flock found a dwelling in it;
in your goodness, O God, you
provided for the needy.

11 The Lord gives the command;
great is the company of those[b]
who bore the tidings:
12 "The kings of the armies, they
flee, they flee!"
The women at home divide the
spoil,
13 though they stay among the
sheepfolds—
the wings of a dove covered with
silver,
its pinions with green gold.
14 When the Almighty[c] scattered
kings there,
snow fell on Zal'mon.

15 O mighty mountain, mountain of
Bā'shan;
O many-peaked mountain,
mountain of Bā'shan!
16 Why do you look with envy,
O many-peaked mountain,
at the mount that God desired
for his abode,
where the LORD will reside
forever?

17 With mighty chariotry, twice ten
thousand,
thousands upon thousands,
the Lord came from Sinai into
the holy place.[d]
18 You ascended the high mount,
leading captives in your train
and receiving gifts from
people,
even from those who rebel
against the LORD God's
abiding there.

19 Blessed be the Lord,
who daily bears us up;
God is our salvation.   *Sē'lah*
20 Our God is a God of salvation,
and to GOD, the Lord, belongs
escape from death.

21 But God will shatter the heads of
his enemies,
the hairy crown of those who
walk in their guilty ways.
22 The Lord said,

"I will bring them back from
Bā'shan,
I will bring them back from the
depths of the sea,
23 so that you may bathe[e] your
feet in blood,
so that the tongues of your
dogs may have their share
from the foe."

24 Your solemn processions are
seen,[f] O God,
the processions of my God, my
King, into the sanctuary—
25 the singers in front, the
musicians last,
between them girls playing
tambourines:
26 "Bless God in the great
congregation,
the LORD, O you who are of
Israel's fountain!"
27 There is Benjamin, the least of
them, in the lead,
the princes of Judah in a body,
the princes of Zeb'ū·lun, the
princes of Naph'ta·lī.

28 Summon your might, O God;
show your strength, O God, as
you have done for us
before.
29 Because of your temple at
Jerusalem
kings bear gifts to you.
30 Rebuke the wild animals that
live among the reeds,
the herd of bulls with the
calves of the peoples.
Trample[g] under foot those who
lust after tribute;
scatter the peoples who delight
in war.[h]
31 Let bronze be brought from
Egypt;
let Ethiopia[i] hasten to stretch
out its hands to God.

32 Sing to God, O kingdoms of the
earth;
sing praises to the Lord,   *Sē'lah*
33 O rider in the heavens, the
ancient heavens;

[b]Or *company of the women*
[c]Traditional rendering of Heb *Shaddai*
[d]Cn: Heb *The Lord among them Sinai in
the holy* (place)   [e]Gk Syr Tg: Heb
shatter   [f]Or *have been seen*
[g]Cn: Heb *Trampling*   [h]Meaning of Heb
of verse 30 is uncertain   [i]Or *Nubia*;
Heb *Cush*

listen, he sends out his voice,
   his mighty voice.
34 Ascribe power to God,
   whose majesty is over Israel;
   and whose power is in the
      skies.
35 Awesome is God in his[l]
      sanctuary,
   the God of Israel;
   he gives power and strength to
      his people.

Blessed be God!

Psalm 69

*Prayer for Deliverance
from Persecution*

To the leader: according to Lilies.
Of David.

1 Save me, O God,
   for the waters have come up to
      my neck.
2 I sink in deep mire,
   where there is no foothold;
I have come into deep waters,
   and the flood sweeps over me.
3 I am weary with my crying;
   my throat is parched.
My eyes grow dim
   with waiting for my God.

4 More in number than the hairs
      of my head
   are those who hate me without
      cause;
many are those who would
      destroy me,
   my enemies who accuse me
      falsely.
What I did not steal
   must I now restore?
5 O God, you know my folly;
   the wrongs I have done are
      not hidden from you.

6 Do not let those who hope in
      you be put to shame
      because of me,
   O Lord GOD of hosts;
do not let those who seek you be
      dishonored because of me,
   O God of Israel.
7 It is for your sake that I have
      borne reproach,
   that shame has covered my
      face.
8 I have become a stranger to my
      kindred,
   an alien to my mother's
      children.

9 It is zeal for your house that has
      consumed me;
   the insults of those who insult
      you have fallen on me.
10 When I humbled my soul with
      fasting,[k]
   they insulted me for doing so.
11 When I made sackcloth my
      clothing,
   I became a byword to them.
12 I am the subject of gossip for
      those who sit in the gate,
   and the drunkards make songs
      about me.

13 But as for me, my prayer is to
      you, O LORD.
   At an acceptable time, O God,
   in the abundance of your
      steadfast love, answer me.
With your faithful help [14]rescue
      me
   from sinking in the mire;
let me be delivered from my
      enemies
   and from the deep waters.
15 Do not let the flood sweep over
      me,
   or the deep swallow me up,
   or the Pit close its mouth over
      me.

16 Answer me, O LORD, for your
      steadfast love is good;
   according to your abundant
      mercy, turn to me.
17 Do not hide your face from your
      servant,
   for I am in distress—make
      haste to answer me.
18 Draw near to me, redeem me,
   set me free because of my
      enemies.

19 You know the insults I receive,
   and my shame and dishonor;
   my foes are all known to you.
20 Insults have broken my heart,
   so that I am in despair.
I looked for pity, but there was
      none;
   and for comforters, but I found
      none.
21 They gave me poison for food,
   and for my thirst they gave me
      vinegar to drink.

*l*Gk: Heb *from your*   *k*Gk Syr: Heb *I
wept, with fasting my soul, or I made
my soul mourn with fasting*

22 Let their table be a trap for
      them,
    a snare for their allies.
23 Let their eyes be darkened so
      that they cannot see,
    and make their loins tremble
      continually.
24 Pour out your indignation upon
      them,
    and let your burning anger
      overtake them.
25 May their camp be a desolation;
    let no one live in their tents.
26 For they persecute those whom
      you have struck down,
    and those whom you have
      wounded, they attack still
      more.[l]
27 Add guilt to their guilt;
    may they have no acquittal
      from you.
28 Let them be blotted out of the
      book of the living;
    let them not be enrolled
      among the righteous.
29 But I am lowly and in pain;
    let your salvation, O God,
      protect me.

30 I will praise the name of God
      with a song;
    I will magnify him with
      thanksgiving.
31 This will please the LORD more
      than an ox
    or a bull with horns and hoofs.
32 Let the oppressed see it and be
      glad;
    you who seek God, let your
      hearts revive.
33 For the LORD hears the needy,
    and does not despise his own
      that are in bonds.

34 Let heaven and earth praise him,
    the seas and everything that
      moves in them.
35 For God will save Zion
    and rebuild the cities of Judah;
    and his servants shall live[m]
      there and possess it;
36 the children of his servants
      shall inherit it,
    and those who love his name
      shall live in it.

Psalm 70

Prayer for Deliverance from Enemies
(Ps 40.13–17)

To the leader. Of David,
for the memorial offering.

1 Be pleased, O God, to deliver
      me.
    O LORD, make haste to help
      me!
2 Let those be put to shame and
      confusion
    who seek my life.
  Let those be turned back and
      brought to dishonor
    who desire to hurt me.
3 Let those who say, "Aha, Aha!"
    turn back because of their
      shame.

4 Let all who seek you
    rejoice and be glad in you.
  Let those who love your
      salvation
    say evermore, "God is great!"
5 But I am poor and needy;
    hasten to me, O God!
  You are my help and my
      deliverer;
    O LORD, do not delay!

Psalm 71

Prayer for Lifelong Protection and Help

1 In you, O LORD, I take refuge;
    let me never be put to shame.
2 In your righteousness deliver me
      and rescue me;
    incline your ear to me and
      save me.
3 Be to me a rock of refuge,
    a strong fortress,[n] to save me,
    for you are my rock and my
      fortress.

4 Rescue me, O my God, from the
      hand of the wicked,
    from the grasp of the unjust
      and cruel.
5 For you, O Lord, are my hope,
    my trust, O LORD, from my
      youth.
6 Upon you I have leaned from my
      birth;
    it was you who took me from
      my mother's womb.
  My praise is continually of you.

[l] Gk Syr: Heb *recount the pain of*
[m] Syr: Heb *and they shall live*
[n] Gk Compare 31.3: Heb *to come*
continually you have commanded

7 I have been like a portent to
    many,
    but you are my strong refuge.
8 My mouth is filled with your
    praise,
    and with your glory all day
    long.
9 Do not cast me off in the time of
    old age;
    do not forsake me when my
    strength is spent.
10 For my enemies speak
    concerning me,
    and those who watch for my
    life consult together.
11 They say, "Pursue and seize that
    person
    whom God has forsaken,
    for there is no one to deliver."

12 O God, do not be far from me;
    O my God, make haste to help
    me!
13 Let my accusers be put to shame
    and consumed;
    let those who seek to hurt me
    be covered with scorn and
    disgrace.
14 But I will hope continually,
    and will praise you yet more
    and more.
15 My mouth will tell of your
    righteous acts,
    of your deeds of salvation all
    day long,
    though their number is past
    my knowledge.
16 I will come praising the mighty
    deeds of the Lord GOD,
    I will praise your
    righteousness, yours alone.

17 O God, from my youth you have
    taught me,
    and I still proclaim your
    wondrous deeds.
18 So even to old age and gray
    hairs,
    O God, do not forsake me,
    until I proclaim your might
    to all the generations to
    come.º
    Your power 19 and your
    righteousness, O God,
    reach the high heavens.

    You who have done great things,
    O God, who is like you?
20 You who have made me see
    many troubles and
    calamities
    will revive me again;

from the depths of the earth
    you will bring me up again.
21 You will increase my honor,
    and comfort me once again.

22 I will also praise you with the
    harp
    for your faithfulness, O my
    God;
    I will sing praises to you with
    the lyre,
    O Holy One of Israel.
23 My lips will shout for joy
    when I sing praises to you;
    my soul also, which you have
    rescued.
24 All day long my tongue will talk
    of your righteous help,
for those who tried to do me
    harm
    have been put to shame, and
    disgraced.

Psalm 72

*Prayer for Guidance and Support
for the King*

Of Solomon.

1 Give the king your justice,
    O God,
    and your righteousness to a
    king's son.
2 May he judge your people with
    righteousness,
    and your poor with justice.
3 May the mountains yield
    prosperity for the people,
    and the hills, in righteousness.
4 May he defend the cause of the
    poor of the people,
    give deliverance to the needy,
    and crush the oppressor.

5 May he liveᵖ while the sun
    endures,
    and as long as the moon,
    throughout all generations.
6 May he be like rain that falls on
    the mown grass,
    like showers that water the
    earth.
7 In his days may righteousness
    flourish
    and peace abound, until the
    moon is no more.

ºGk Compare Syr: Heb *to a generation,
to all that come*   ᵖGk: Heb *may they
fear you*

8 May he have dominion from sea
to sea,
and from the River to the ends
of the earth.
9 May his foes[q] bow down before
him,
and his enemies lick the dust.
10 May the kings of Tar'shish and
of the isles
render him tribute,
may the kings of Shē'ba and
Sē'ba
bring gifts.
11 May all kings fall down before
him,
all nations give him service.

12 For he delivers the needy when
they call,
the poor and those who have
no helper.
13 He has pity on the weak and the
needy,
and saves the lives of the
needy.
14 From oppression and violence he
redeems their life;
and precious is their blood in
his sight.

15 Long may he live!
May gold of Shē'ba be given
to him.
May prayer be made for him
continually,
and blessings invoked for him
all day long.
16 May there be abundance of
grain in the land;
may it wave on the tops of the
mountains;
may its fruit be like Lebanon;
and may people blossom in the
cities
like the grass of the field.
17 May his name endure forever,
his fame continue as long as
the sun.
May all nations be blessed in
him;[r]
may they pronounce him
happy.

18 Blessed be the LORD, the God of
Israel,
who alone does wondrous
things.
19 Blessed be his glorious name
forever;
may his glory fill the whole
earth.
Amen and Amen.

20 The prayers of David son of
Jesse are ended.

BOOK III

(Psalms 73–89)

Psalm 73

Plea for Relief from Oppressors

A Psalm of Ā'saph.

1 Truly God is good to the
upright,[s]
to those who are pure in heart.
2 But as for me, my feet had
almost stumbled;
my steps had nearly slipped.
3 For I was envious of the
arrogant;
I saw the prosperity of the
wicked.

4 For they have no pain;
their bodies are sound and
sleek.
5 They are not in trouble as others
are;
they are not plagued like other
people.
6 Therefore pride is their necklace;
violence covers them like a
garment.
7 Their eyes swell out with
fatness;
their hearts overflow with
follies.
8 They scoff and speak with
malice;
loftily they threaten
oppression.
9 They set their mouths against
heaven,
and their tongues range over
the earth.

10 Therefore the people turn and
praise them,[t]
and find no fault in them.[u]
11 And they say, "How can God
know?
Is there knowledge in the Most
High?"
12 Such are the wicked;
always at ease, they increase
in riches.

[q] Cn: Heb *those who live in the
wilderness*   [r] Or *bless themselves by
him*   [s] Or *good to Israel*   [t] Cn: Heb *his
people return here*   [u] Cn: Heb
abundant waters are drained by them

P
S
A
L
M
S

13 All in vain I have kept my heart
      clean
      and washed my hands in
      innocence.
14 For all day long I have been
      plagued,
      and am punished every
      morning.

15 If I had said, "I will talk on in
      this way,"
      I would have been untrue to
      the circle of your children.
16 But when I thought how to
      understand this,
      it seemed to me a wearisome
      task,
17 until I went into the sanctuary of
      God;
      then I perceived their end.
18 Truly you set them in slippery
      places;
      you make them fall to ruin.
19 How they are destroyed in a
      moment,
      swept away utterly by terrors!
20 They are[v] like a dream when
      one awakes;
      on awaking you despise their
      phantoms.

21 When my soul was embittered,
      when I was pricked in heart,
22 I was stupid and ignorant;
      I was like a brute beast toward
      you.
23 Nevertheless I am continually
      with you;
      you hold my right hand.
24 You guide me with your counsel,
      and afterward you will receive
      me with honor.[w]
25 Whom have I in heaven but you?
      And there is nothing on earth
      that I desire other than
      you.
26 My flesh and my heart may fail,
      but God is the strength[x] of my
      heart and my portion
      forever.

27 Indeed, those who are far from
      you will perish;
      you put an end to those who
      are false to you.
28 But for me it is good to be near
      God;
      I have made the Lord GOD my
      refuge,
      to tell of all your works.

Psalm 74

*Plea for Help in Time of
National Humiliation*

A Mas'kil of Ā'saph.

1 O God, why do you cast us off
      forever?
      Why does your anger smoke
      against the sheep of your
      pasture?
2 Remember your congregation,
      which you acquired long
      ago,
      which you redeemed to be the
      tribe of your heritage.
      Remember Mount Zion, where
      you came to dwell.
3 Direct your steps to the
      perpetual ruins;
      the enemy has destroyed
      everything in the
      sanctuary.

4 Your foes have roared within
      your holy place;
      they set up their emblems
      there.
5 At the upper entrance they
      hacked
      the wooden trellis with axes.[y]
6 And then, with hatchets and
      hammers,
      they smashed all its carved
      work.
7 They set your sanctuary on fire;
      they desecrated the dwelling
      place of your name,
      bringing it to the ground.
8 They said to themselves, "We
      will utterly subdue them";
      they burned all the meeting
      places of God in the land.

9 We do not see our emblems;
      there is no longer any prophet,
      and there is no one among us
      who knows how long.
10 How long, O God, is the foe to
      scoff?
      Is the enemy to revile your
      name forever?
11 Why do you hold back your
      hand;
      why do you keep your hand
      in[z] your bosom?

12 Yet God my King is from of old,

vCn: Heb *Lord*   wOr *to glory*
xHeb *rock*   yCn Compare Gk Syr:
Meaning of Heb uncertain   zCn: Heb
do you consume your right hand from

working salvation in the earth.
13 You divided the sea by your
       might;
   you broke the heads of the
       dragons in the waters.
14 You crushed the heads of
       Le·vi′a·than;
   you gave him as food[a] for the
       creatures of the wilderness.
15 You cut openings for springs
       and torrents;
   you dried up ever-flowing
       streams.
16 Yours is the day, yours also the
       night;
   you established the
       luminaries[b] and the sun.
17 You have fixed all the bounds of
       the earth;
   you made summer and winter.

18 Remember this, O LORD, how
       the enemy scoffs,
   and an impious people reviles
       your name.
19 Do not deliver the soul of your
       dove to the wild animals;
   do not forget the life of your
       poor forever.

20 Have regard for your[c] covenant,
   for the dark places of the land
       are full of the haunts of
       violence.
21 Do not let the downtrodden be
       put to shame;
   let the poor and needy praise
       your name.
22 Rise up, O God, plead your
       cause;
   remember how the impious
       scoff at you all day long.
23 Do not forget the clamor of your
       foes,
   the uproar of your adversaries
       that goes up continually.

Psalm 75

Thanksgiving for God's Wondrous Deeds

To the leader: Do Not Destroy. A Psalm
   of A′saph. A Song.

1 We give thanks to you, O God;
   we give thanks; your name is
       near.
   People tell of your wondrous
       deeds.

2 At the set time that I appoint
   I will judge with equity.

3 When the earth totters, with all
       its inhabitants,
   it is I who keep its pillars
       steady.   Se′lah
4 I say to the boastful, "Do not
       boast,"
   and to the wicked, "Do not lift
       up your horn;
5 do not lift up your horn on high,
   or speak with insolent neck."

6 For not from the east or from
       the west
   and not from the wilderness
       comes lifting up;
7 but it is God who executes
       judgment,
   putting down one and lifting
       up another.
8 For in the hand of the LORD
       there is a cup
   with foaming wine, well
       mixed;
   he will pour a draught from it,
   and all the wicked of the earth
       shall drain it down to the
       dregs.
9 But I will rejoice[d] forever;
   I will sing praises to the God
       of Jacob.

10 All the horns of the wicked I will
       cut off,
   but the horns of the righteous
       shall be exalted.

Psalm 76

Israel's God—Judge of All the Earth

To the leader: with stringed
instruments. A Psalm of A′saph.
   A Song.

1 In Judah God is known,
   his name is great in Israel.
2 His abode has been established
       in Salem,
   his dwelling place in Zion.
3 There he broke the flashing
       arrows,
   the shield, the sword, and the
       weapons of war.   Se′lah

4 Glorious are you, more majestic
       than the everlasting
       mountains.[e]
5 The stouthearted were stripped
       of their spoil;

[a] Heb food for the people   [b] Or moon;
Heb light   [c] Gk Syr: Heb the
[d] Gk: Heb declare   [e] Gk: Heb the
mountains of prey

they sank into sleep;
  none of the troops
    was able to lift a hand.
6 At your rebuke, O God of Jacob,
  both rider and horse lay
    stunned.

7 But you indeed are awesome!
  Who can stand before you
  when once your anger is
    roused?
8 From the heavens you uttered
    judgment;
  the earth feared and was still
9 when God rose up to establish
    judgment,
  to save all the oppressed of the
    earth.   *Sĕ'lah*

10 Human wrath serves only to
    praise you,
  when you bind the last bit of
    your[f] wrath around you.
11 Make vows to the LORD your
    God, and perform them;
  let all who are around him
    bring gifts
  to the one who is awesome,
12 who cuts off the spirit of princes,
  who inspires fear in the kings
    of the earth.

Psalm 77

God's Mighty Deeds Recalled

To the leader: according to Je·dū'thun.
Of Ā'saph. A Psalm.

1 I cry aloud to God,
  aloud to God, that he may
    hear me.
2 In the day of my trouble I seek
    the Lord;
  in the night my hand is
    stretched out without
    wearying;
  my soul refuses to be
    comforted.
3 I think of God, and I moan;
  I meditate, and my spirit
    faints.   *Sĕ'lah*

4 You keep my eyelids from
    closing;
  I am so troubled that I cannot
    speak.
5 I consider the days of old,
  and remember the years of
    long ago.
6 I commune[g] with my heart in
    the night;

I meditate and search my
    spirit:[h]
7 "Will the Lord spurn forever,
  and never again be favorable?
8 Has his steadfast love ceased
    forever?
  Are his promises at an end for
    all time?
9 Has God forgotten to be
    gracious?
  Has he in anger shut up his
    compassion?"   *Sĕ'lah*
10 And I say, "It is my grief
  that the right hand of the Most
    High has changed."

11 I will call to mind the deeds of
    the LORD;
  I will remember your wonders
    of old.
12 I will meditate on all your work,
  and muse on your mighty
    deeds.
13 Your way, O God, is holy.
  What god is so great as our
    God?
14 You are the God who works
    wonders;
  you have displayed your might
    among the peoples.
15 With your strong arm you
    redeemed your people,
  the descendants of Jacob and
    Joseph.   *Sĕ'lah*

16 When the waters saw you,
    O God,
  when the waters saw you, they
    were afraid;
  the very deep trembled.
17 The clouds poured out water;
  the skies thundered;
  your arrows flashed on every
    side.
18 The crash of your thunder was
    in the whirlwind;
  your lightnings lit up the
    world;
  the earth trembled and shook.
19 Your way was through the sea,
  your path, through the mighty
    waters;
  yet your footprints were
    unseen.
20 You led your people like a flock
  by the hand of Moses and
    Aaron.

[f] Heb lacks *your*   [g] Gk Syr: Heb *My
music*   [h] Syr Jerome: Heb *my spirit
searches*

Psalm 78

*God's Goodness and
Israel's Ingratitude*

A Mas'kil of Ā'saph.

1 Give ear, O my people, to my
    teaching;
    incline your ears to the words
      of my mouth.
2 I will open my mouth in a
    parable;
    I will utter dark sayings from
      of old,
3 things that we have heard and
    known,
    that our ancestors have told
      us.
4 We will not hide them from their
    children;
    we will tell to the coming
      generation
the glorious deeds of the LORD,
    and his might,
    and the wonders that he has
      done.

5 He established a decree in
    Jacob,
    and appointed a law in Israel,
which he commanded our
    ancestors
    to teach to their children;
6 that the next generation might
    know them,
    the children yet unborn,
and rise up and tell them to their
    children,
7 so that they should set their
    hope in God,
and not forget the works of God,
    but keep his commandments;
8 and that they should not be like
    their ancestors,
    a stubborn and rebellious
      generation,
a generation whose heart was
    not steadfast,
    whose spirit was not faithful to
      God.

9 The Ē'phra·im·ites, armed with[i]
    the bow,
    turned back on the day of
      battle.
10 They did not keep God's
    covenant,
    but refused to walk according
      to his law.
11 They forgot what he had done,
    and the miracles that he had
      shown them.

12 In the sight of their ancestors he
    worked marvels
    in the land of Egypt, in the
      fields of Zō'an.
13 He divided the sea and let them
    pass through it,
    and made the waters stand
      like a heap.
14 In the daytime he led them with
    a cloud,
    and all night long with a fiery
      light.
15 He split rocks open in the
    wilderness,
    and gave them drink
      abundantly as from the
      deep.
16 He made streams come out of
    the rock,
    and caused waters to flow
      down like rivers.

17 Yet they sinned still more
    against him,
    rebelling against the Most
      High in the desert.
18 They tested God in their heart
    by demanding the food they
      craved.
19 They spoke against God, saying,
    "Can God spread a table in the
      wilderness?
20 Even though he struck the rock
    so that water gushed out
    and torrents overflowed,
can he also give bread,
    or provide meat for his
      people?"

21 Therefore, when the LORD
    heard, he was full of rage;
    a fire was kindled against
      Jacob,
    his anger mounted against
      Israel,
22 because they had no faith in
    God,
    and did not trust his saving
      power.
23 Yet he commanded the skies
    above,
    and opened the doors of
      heaven;
24 he rained down on them manna
    to eat,
    and gave them the grain of
      heaven.
25 Mortals ate of the bread of
    angels;

[i]Heb *armed with shooting*

PSALMS

he sent them food in abundance.

26 He caused the east wind to blow
      in the heavens,
   and by his power he led out
      the south wind;

27 he rained flesh upon them like
      dust,
   winged birds like the sand of
      the seas;

28 he let them fall within their
      camp,
   all around their dwellings.

29 And they ate and were well
      filled,
   for he gave them what they
      craved.

30 But before they had satisfied
      their craving,
   while the food was still in their
      mouths,

31 the anger of God rose against
      them
   and he killed the strongest of
      them,
   and laid low the flower of
      Israel.

32 In spite of all this they still
      sinned;
   they did not believe in his
      wonders.

33 So he made their days vanish
      like a breath,
   and their years in terror.

34 When he killed them, they
      sought for him;
   they repented and sought God
      earnestly.

35 They remembered that God was
      their rock,
   the Most High God their
      redeemer.

36 But they flattered him with their
      mouths;
   they lied to him with their
      tongues.

37 Their heart was not steadfast
      toward him;
   they were not true to his
      covenant.

38 Yet he, being compassionate,
      forgave their iniquity,
   and did not destroy them;
   often he restrained his anger,
   and did not stir up all his
      wrath.

39 He remembered that they were
      but flesh,
   a wind that passes and does
      not come again.

40 How often they rebelled against
      him in the wilderness
   and grieved him in the desert!

41 They tested God again and
      again,
   and provoked the Holy One of
      Israel.

42 They did not keep in mind his
      power,
   or the day when he redeemed
      them from the foe;

43 when he displayed his signs in
      Egypt,
   and his miracles in the fields
      of Zō'an.

44 He turned their rivers to blood,
   so that they could not drink of
      their streams.

45 He sent among them swarms of
      flies, which devoured them,
   and frogs, which destroyed
      them.

46 He gave their crops to the
      caterpillar,
   and the fruit of their labor to
      the locust.

47 He destroyed their vines with
      hail,
   and their sycamores with frost.

48 He gave over their cattle to the
      hail,
   and their flocks to
      thunderbolts.

49 He let loose on them his fierce
      anger,
   wrath, indignation, and
      distress,
   a company of destroying
      angels.

50 He made a path for his anger;
   he did not spare them from
      death,
   but gave their lives over to the
      plague.

51 He struck all the firstborn in
      Egypt,
   the first issue of their strength
      in the tents of Ham.

52 Then he led out his people like
      sheep,
   and guided them in the
      wilderness like a flock.

53 He led them in safety, so that
      they were not afraid;
   but the sea overwhelmed their
      enemies.

54 And he brought them to his holy
      hill,
   to the mountain that his right
      hand had won.

55 He drove out nations before
      them;

he apportioned them for a
   possession
   and he settled the tribes of Israel
   in their tents.

56 Yet they tested the Most High
   God,
   and rebelled against him.
   They did not observe his
   decrees,
57 but turned away and were
   faithless like their
   ancestors;
   they twisted like a treacherous
   bow.
58 For they provoked him to anger
   with their high places;
   they moved him to jealousy
   with their idols.
59 When God heard, he was full of
   wrath,
   and he utterly rejected Israel.
60 He abandoned his dwelling at
   Shī′lōh,
   the tent where he dwelt among
   mortals,
61 and delivered his power to
   captivity,
   his glory to the hand of the
   foe.
62 He gave his people to the sword,
   and vented his wrath on his
   heritage.
63 Fire devoured their young men,
   and their girls had no
   marriage song.
64 Their priests fell by the sword,
   and their widows made no
   lamentation.
65 Then the Lord awoke as from
   sleep,
   like a warrior shouting
   because of wine.
66 He put his adversaries to rout;
   he put them to everlasting
   disgrace.

67 He rejected the tent of Joseph,
   he did not choose the tribe of
   Ē′phra·im;
68 but he chose the tribe of Judah,
   Mount Zion, which he loves.
69 He built his sanctuary like the
   high heavens,
   like the earth, which he has
   founded forever.
70 He chose his servant David,
   and took him from the
   sheepfolds;
71 from tending the nursing ewes
   he brought him

to be the shepherd of his
   people Jacob,
   of Israel, his inheritance.
72 With upright heart he tended
   them,
   and guided them with skillful
   hand.

Psalm 79

Plea for Mercy for Jerusalem

A Psalm of Ā′saph.

1 O God, the nations have come
   into your inheritance;
   they have defiled your holy
   temple;
   they have laid Jerusalem in
   ruins.
2 They have given the bodies of
   your servants
   to the birds of the air for food,
   the flesh of your faithful to the
   wild animals of the earth.
3 They have poured out their
   blood like water
   all around Jerusalem,
   and there was no one to bury
   them.
4 We have become a taunt to our
   neighbors,
   mocked and derided by those
   around us.

5 How long, O LORD? Will you be
   angry forever?
   Will your jealous wrath burn
   like fire?
6 Pour out your anger on the
   nations
   that do not know you,
   and on the kingdoms
   that do not call on your name.
7 For they have devoured Jacob
   and laid waste his habitation.

8 Do not remember against us the
   iniquities of our ancestors;
   let your compassion come
   speedily to meet us,
   for we are brought very low.
9 Help us, O God of our salvation,
   for the glory of your name;
   deliver us, and forgive our sins,
   for your name's sake.
10 Why should the nations say,
   "Where is their God?"
   Let the avenging of the
   outpoured blood of your
   servants
   be known among the nations
   before our eyes.

PSALMS

11 Let the groans of the prisoners
     come before you;
   according to your great power
     preserve those doomed to
     die.
12 Return sevenfold into the bosom
     of our neighbors
   the taunts with which they
     taunted you, O Lord!
13 Then we your people, the flock
     of your pasture,
   will give thanks to you
     forever;
   from generation to generation
     we will recount your
     praise.

Psalm 80

Prayer for Israel's Restoration

To the leader: on Lilies, a Covenant.
Of Ā′saph. A Psalm.

1 Give ear, O Shepherd of Israel,
     you who lead Joseph like a
     flock!
   You who are enthroned upon the
     cherubim, shine forth
2   before Ē′phra·im and
     Benjamin and Ma·nas′seh.
   Stir up your might,
     and come to save us!

3 Restore us, O God;
     let your face shine, that we
     may be saved.

4 O LORD God of hosts,
     how long will you be angry
     with your people's prayers?
5 You have fed them with the
     bread of tears,
   and given them tears to drink
     in full measure.
6 You make us the scorn[j] of our
     neighbors;
   our enemies laugh among
     themselves.

7 Restore us, O God of hosts;
     let your face shine, that we
     may be saved.

8 You brought a vine out of Egypt;
     you drove out the nations and
     planted it.
9 You cleared the ground for it;
     it took deep root and filled the
     land.
10 The mountains were covered
     with its shade,

the mighty cedars with its
     branches;
11 it sent out its branches to the
     sea,
   and its shoots to the River.
12 Why then have you broken
     down its walls,
   so that all who pass along the
     way pluck its fruit?
13 The boar from the forest ravages
     it,
   and all that move in the field
     feed on it.

14 Turn again, O God of hosts;
     look down from heaven, and
     see;
   have regard for this vine,
15   the stock that your right hand
     planted.[k]
16 They have burned it with fire,
     they have cut it down;[l]
   may they perish at the rebuke
     of your countenance.
17 But let your hand be upon the
     one at your right hand,
   the one whom you made
     strong for yourself.
18 Then we will never turn back
     from you;
   give us life, and we will call on
     your name.

19 Restore us, O LORD God of
     hosts;
   let your face shine, that we
     may be saved.

Psalm 81

God's Appeal to Stubborn Israel

To the leader: according to The Git′tith.
Of Ā′saph.

1 Sing aloud to God our strength;
     shout for joy to the God of
     Jacob.
2 Raise a song, sound the
     tambourine,
   the sweet lyre with the harp.
3 Blow the trumpet at the new
     moon,
   at the full moon, on our festal
     day.
4 For it is a statute for Israel,
     an ordinance of the God of
     Jacob.
5 He made it a decree in Joseph,

j Syr: Heb *strife*   *k* Heb adds *from verse
17 and upon the one whom you made
strong for yourself*   *l* Cn: Heb *it is cut
down*

when he went out over^m the
land of Egypt.

I hear a voice I had not known:
6 "I relieved your^n shoulder of the
    burden;
    your^n hands were freed from
        the basket.
7 In distress you called, and I
        rescued you;
    I answered you in the secret
        place of thunder;
    I tested you at the waters of
        Mer'i·bah.   Se'lah
8 Hear, O my people, while I
        admonish you;
    O Israel, if you would but
        listen to me!
9 There shall be no strange god
        among you;
    you shall not bow down to a
        foreign god.
10 I am the LORD your God,
    who brought you up out of the
        land of Egypt.
    Open your mouth wide and I
        will fill it.

11 "But my people did not listen to
        my voice;
    Israel would not submit to me.
12 So I gave them over to their
        stubborn hearts,
    to follow their own counsels.
13 O that my people would listen to
        me,
    that Israel would walk in my
        ways!
14 Then I would quickly subdue
        their enemies,
    and turn my hand against
        their foes.
15 Those who hate the LORD would
        cringe before him,
    and their doom would last
        forever.
16 I would feed you^o with the
        finest of the wheat,
    and with honey from the rock
        I would satisfy you."

Psalm 82

A Plea for Justice

A Psalm of Ā'saph.

1 God has taken his place in the
        divine council;
    in the midst of the gods he
        holds judgment:
2 "How long will you judge
        unjustly

and show partiality to the
    wicked?   Se'lah
3 Give justice to the weak and the
        orphan;
    maintain the right of the lowly
        and the destitute.
4 Rescue the weak and the needy;
    deliver them from the hand of
        the wicked."

5 They have neither knowledge
        nor understanding,
    they walk around in darkness;
    all the foundations of the earth
        are shaken.

6 I say, "You are gods,
    children of the Most High, all
        of you;
7 nevertheless, you shall die like
        mortals,
    and fall like any prince."^{p}

8 Rise up, O God, judge the earth;
    for all the nations belong to
        you!

Psalm 83

Prayer for Judgment on Israel's Foes

A Song. A Psalm of Ā'saph.

1 O God, do not keep silence;
    do not hold your peace or be
        still, O God!
2 Even now your enemies are in
        tumult;
    those who hate you have
        raised their heads.
3 They lay crafty plans against
        your people;
    they consult together against
        those you protect.
4 They say, "Come, let us wipe
        them out as a nation;
    let the name of Israel be
        remembered no more."
5 They conspire with one accord;
    against you they make a
        covenant—
6 the tents of Ē'dom and the
        Ish'ma·el·ites,
    Mō'ab and the Hag'rites,
7 Gē'bal and Am'mon and
        Am'a·lek,
    Phi·lis'ti·a with the inhabitants
        of Tȳre;
8 Assyria also has joined them;

^{m} Or *against* ^{n} Heb *his* ^{o} Cn Compare
verse 16b: Heb *he would feed him*
^{p} Or *fall as one man, O princes*

they are the strong arm of the
children of Lot.   *Sē'lah*

9 Do to them as you did to Mid'-
    i·an,
    as to Sis'e·ra and Jā'bin at the
        Wadi Kī'shon,
10 who were destroyed at En-dor,
    who became dung for the
        ground.
11 Make their nobles like Or'eb and
        Zē'eb,
    all their princes like Zē'bah
        and Zal·mun'na,
12 who said, "Let us take the
        pastures of God
    for our own possession."

13 O my God, make them like
        whirling dust,*q*
    like chaff before the wind.
14 As fire consumes the forest,
    as the flame sets the
        mountains ablaze,
15 so pursue them with your
        tempest
    and terrify them with your
        hurricane.
16 Fill their faces with shame,
    so that they may seek your
        name, O LORD.
17 Let them be put to shame and
        dismayed forever;
    let them perish in disgrace.
18 Let them know that you alone,
    whose name is the LORD,
    are the Most High over all the
        earth.

Psalm 84

The Joy of Worship in the Temple

To the leader: according to The Git'tith.
Of the Kō'ra·hītes. A Psalm.

1 How lovely is your dwelling
        place,
    O LORD of hosts!
2 My soul longs, indeed it faints
    for the courts of the LORD;
    my heart and my flesh sing for
        joy
    to the living God.

3 Even the sparrow finds a home,
    and the swallow a nest for
        herself,
    where she may lay her young,
    at your altars, O LORD of hosts,
    my King and my God.
4 Happy are those who live in
        your house,

ever singing your praise.
                        Sē'lah

5 Happy are those whose strength
        is in you,
    in whose heart are the
        highways to Zion.*r*
6 As they go through the valley of
        Bā'ca
    they make it a place of
        springs;
    the early rain also covers it
        with pools.
7 They go from strength to
        strength;
    the God of gods will be seen in
        Zion.

8 O LORD God of hosts, hear my
        prayer;
    give ear, O God of Jacob!
                        Sē'lah
9 Behold our shield, O God;
    look on the face of your
        anointed.

10 For a day in your courts is better
        than a thousand elsewhere.
    I would rather be a doorkeeper
        in the house of my God
    than live in the tents of
        wickedness.
11 For the LORD God is a sun and
        shield;
    he bestows favor and honor.
    No good thing does the LORD
        withhold
    from those who walk
        uprightly.
12 O LORD of hosts,
    happy is everyone who trusts
        in you.

Psalm 85

*Prayer for the Restoration
of God's Favor*

To the leader. Of the Kō'ra·hītes.
A Psalm.

1 LORD, you were favorable to
        your land;
    you restored the fortunes of
        Jacob.
2 You forgave the iniquity of your
        people;
    you pardoned all their sin.
                        Sē'lah
3 You withdrew all your wrath;

*q*Or *a tumbleweed*   *r*Heb lacks *to Zion*

you turned from your hot
anger.

4 Restore us again, O God of our
salvation,
and put away your indignation
toward us.
5 Will you be angry with us
forever?
Will you prolong your anger to
all generations?
6 Will you not revive us again,
so that your people may
rejoice in you?
7 Show us your steadfast love,
O LORD,
and grant us your salvation.

8 Let me hear what God the LORD
will speak,
for he will speak peace to his
people,
to his faithful, to those who
turn to him in their
hearts.[s]
9 Surely his salvation is at hand
for those who fear him,
that his glory may dwell in our
land.

10 Steadfast love and faithfulness
will meet;
righteousness and peace will
kiss each other.
11 Faithfulness will spring up from
the ground,
and righteousness will look
down from the sky.
12 The LORD will give what is good,
and our land will yield its
increase.
13 Righteousness will go before
him,
and will make a path for his
steps.

Psalm 86

Supplication for Help against Enemies

A Prayer of David.

1 Incline your ear, O LORD, and
answer me,
for I am poor and needy.
2 Preserve my life, for I am
devoted to you;
save your servant who trusts
in you.
You are my God; 3 be gracious to
me, O Lord,
for to you do I cry all day
long.

4 Gladden the soul of your
servant,
for to you, O Lord, I lift up my
soul.
5 For you, O Lord, are good and
forgiving,
abounding in steadfast love to
all who call on you.
6 Give ear, O LORD, to my prayer;
listen to my cry of
supplication.
7 In the day of my trouble I call
on you,
for you will answer me.

8 There is none like you among
the gods, O Lord,
nor are there any works like
yours.
9 All the nations you have made
shall come
and bow down before you,
O Lord,
and shall glorify your name.
10 For you are great and do
wondrous things;
you alone are God.
11 Teach me your way, O LORD,
that I may walk in your truth;
give me an undivided heart to
revere your name.
12 I give thanks to you, O Lord my
God, with my whole heart,
and I will glorify your name
forever.
13 For great is your steadfast love
toward me;
you have delivered my soul
from the depths of Shē′ōl.

14 O God, the insolent rise up
against me;
a band of ruffians seeks my
life,
and they do not set you before
them.
15 But you, O Lord, are a God
merciful and gracious,
slow to anger and abounding
in steadfast love and
faithfulness.
16 Turn to me and be gracious to
me;
give your strength to your
servant;
save the child of your serving
girl.
17 Show me a sign of your favor,

[s] Gk: Heb *but let them not turn back to
folly*

so that those who hate me
    may see it and be put to
    shame,
because you, LORD, have
    helped me and comforted
    me.

Psalm 87

The Joy of Living in Zion

Of the Kō'ra·hītes. A Psalm. A Song.

1 On the holy mount stands the
    city he founded;
2   the LORD loves the gates of
    Zion
    more than all the dwellings of
    Jacob.
3 Glorious things are spoken of
    you,
    O city of God.   *Sĕ'lah*

4 Among those who know me I
    mention Rā'hab and
    Babylon;
    Phi·lis'ti·a too, and Tȳre, with
    Ethiopia[t] —
    "This one was born there,"
    they say.

5 And of Zion it shall be said,
    "This one and that one were
    born in it";
    for the Most High himself will
    establish it.
6 The LORD records, as he
    registers the peoples,
    "This one was born there."
         Sĕ'lah

7 Singers and dancers alike say,
    "All my springs are in you."

Psalm 88

Prayer for Help in Despondency

A Song. A Psalm of the Kō'ra·hītes. To
the leader: according to Mā'ha·lath
Le·an'noth. A Mas'kil of Hē'man
    the Ez'ra·hīte.

1 O LORD, God of my salvation,
    when, at night, I cry out in
    your presence,
2 let my prayer come before you;
    incline your ear to my cry.

3 For my soul is full of troubles,
    and my life draws near to
    Shē'ōl.
4 I am counted among those who
    go down to the Pit;

I am like those who have no
    help,
5 like those forsaken among the
    dead,
    like the slain that lie in the
    grave,
    like those whom you remember
    no more,
    for they are cut off from your
    hand.
6 You have put me in the depths
    of the Pit,
    in the regions dark and deep.
7 Your wrath lies heavy upon me,
    and you overwhelm me with
    all your waves.   *Sĕ'lah*

8 You have caused my
    companions to shun me;
    you have made me a thing of
    horror to them.
I am shut in so that I cannot
    escape;
9   my eye grows dim through
    sorrow.
Every day I call on you, O LORD;
    I spread out my hands to you.
10 Do you work wonders for the
    dead?
    Do the shades rise up to praise
    you?   *Sĕ'lah*
11 Is your steadfast love declared in
    the grave,
    or your faithfulness in
    A·bad'don?
12 Are your wonders known in the
    darkness,
    or your saving help in the land
    of forgetfulness?

13 But I, O LORD, cry out to you;
    in the morning my prayer
    comes before you.
14 O LORD, why do you cast me
    off?
    Why do you hide your face
    from me?
15 Wretched and close to death
    from my youth up,
    I suffer your terrors; I am
    desperate.[u]
16 Your wrath has swept over me;
    your dread assaults destroy
    me.
17 They surround me like a flood
    all day long;
    from all sides they close in on
    me.

[t] Or *Nubia*; Heb *Cush*   [u] Meaning of
Heb uncertain

18 You have caused friend and
    neighbor to shun me;
  my companions are in
    darkness.

Psalm 89

God's Covenant with David

A Mas'kil of Ē'than the Ez'ra·hīte.

1 I will sing of your steadfast love,
    O LORD,ᵛ forever;
  with my mouth I will proclaim
    your faithfulness to all
    generations.

2 I declare that your steadfast love
    is established forever;
  your faithfulness is as firm as
    the heavens.

3 You said, "I have made a
    covenant with my chosen
    one,
  I have sworn to my servant
    David:

4 'I will establish your descendants
    forever,
  and build your throne for all
    generations.' "   Sē'lah

5 Let the heavens praise your
    wonders, O LORD,
  your faithfulness in the
    assembly of the holy ones.

6 For who in the skies can be
    compared to the LORD?
  Who among the heavenly
    beings is like the LORD,

7 a God feared in the council of
    the holy ones,
  great and awesomeʷ above all
    that are around him?

8 O LORD God of hosts,
    who is as mighty as you,
    O LORD?
  Your faithfulness surrounds
    you.

9 You rule the raging of the sea;
  when its waves rise, you still
    them.

10 You crushed Rā'hab like a
    carcass;
  you scattered your enemies
    with your mighty arm.

11 The heavens are yours, the earth
    also is yours;
  the world and all that is in it —
    you have founded them.

12 The north and the southˣ — you
    created them;
  Tā'bor and Hermon joyously
    praise your name.

13 You have a mighty arm;
  strong is your hand, high your
    right hand.

14 Righteousness and justice are
    the foundation of your
    throne;
  steadfast love and faithfulness
    go before you.

15 Happy are the people who know
    the festal shout,
  who walk, O LORD, in the light
    of your countenance;

16 they exult in your name all day
    long,
  and extolʸ your righteousness.

17 For you are the glory of their
    strength;
  by your favor our horn is
    exalted.

18 For our shield belongs to the
    LORD,
  our king to the Holy One of
    Israel.

19 Then you spoke in a vision to
    your faithful one, and said:
  "I have set the crownᶻ on one
    who is mighty,
  I have exalted one chosen
    from the people.

20 I have found my servant David;
  with my holy oil I have
    anointed him;

21 my hand shall always remain
    with him;
  my arm also shall strengthen
    him.

22 The enemy shall not outwit him,
  the wicked shall not humble
    him.

23 I will crush his foes before him
  and strike down those who
    hate him.

24 My faithfulness and steadfast
    love shall be with him;
  and in my name his horn shall
    be exalted.

25 I will set his hand on the sea
  and his right hand on the
    rivers.

26 He shall cry to me, 'You are my
    Father,
  my God, and the Rock of my
    salvation!'

27 I will make him the firstborn,
  the highest of the kings of the
    earth.

ᵛ Gk: Heb *the steadfast love of the* LORD
ʷ Gk Syr: Heb *greatly awesome*
ˣ Or *Zaphon and Yamin*   ʸ Cn: Heb *are
exalted in*   ᶻ Cn: Heb *help*

28 Forever I will keep my steadfast
      love for him,
   and my covenant with him will
      stand firm.
29 I will establish his line forever,
   and his throne as long as the
      heavens endure.
30 If his children forsake my law
   and do not walk according to
      my ordinances,
31 if they violate my statutes
   and do not keep my
      commandments,
32 then I will punish their
      transgression with the rod
   and their iniquity with
      scourges;
33 but I will not remove from him
      my steadfast love,
   or be false to my faithfulness.
34 I will not violate my covenant,
   or alter the word that went
      forth from my lips.
35 Once and for all I have sworn by
      my holiness;
   I will not lie to David.
36 His line shall continue forever,
   and his throne endure before
      me like the sun.
37 It shall be established forever
      like the moon,
   an enduring witness in the
      skies."   *Sē'lah*

38 But now you have spurned and
      rejected him;
   you are full of wrath against
      your anointed.
39 You have renounced the
      covenant with your
      servant;
   you have defiled his crown in
      the dust.
40 You have broken through all his
      walls;
   you have laid his strongholds
      in ruins.
41 All who pass by plunder him;
   he has become the scorn of his
      neighbors.
42 You have exalted the right hand
      of his foes;
   you have made all his enemies
      rejoice.
43 Moreover, you have turned back
      the edge of his sword,
   and you have not supported
      him in battle.
44 You have removed the scepter
      from his hand,[a]
   and hurled his throne to the
      ground.

45 You have cut short the days of
      his youth;
   you have covered him with
      shame.   *Sē'lah*

46 How long, O LORD? Will you
      hide yourself forever?
   How long will your wrath burn
      like fire?
47 Remember how short my time
      is — [b]
   for what vanity you have
      created all mortals!
48 Who can live and never see
      death?
   Who can escape the power of
      Shē'ōl?   *Sē'lah*

49 Lord, where is your steadfast
      love of old,
   which by your faithfulness you
      swore to David?
50 Remember, O Lord, how your
      servant is taunted;
   how I bear in my bosom the
      insults of the peoples,[c]
51 with which your enemies taunt,
      O LORD,
   with which they taunted the
      footsteps of your anointed.

52 Blessed be the LORD forever.
   Amen and Amen.

BOOK IV

(Psalms 90–106)

Psalm 90

God's Eternity and Human Frailty

A Prayer of Moses, the man of God.

1 Lord, you have been our
      dwelling place[d]
   in all generations.
2 Before the mountains were
      brought forth,
   or ever you had formed the
      earth and the world,
   from everlasting to everlasting
      you are God.

3 You turn us[e] back to dust,
   and say, "Turn back, you
      mortals."
4 For a thousand years in your
      sight

[a] Cn: Heb *removed his cleanness*
[b] Meaning of Heb uncertain   [c] Cn: Heb
bosom all of many peoples   [d] Another
reading is *our refuge*   [e] Heb *humankind*

are like yesterday when it is
past,
or like a watch in the night.

5 You sweep them away; they are
like a dream,
like grass that is renewed in
the morning;
6 in the morning it flourishes and
is renewed;
in the evening it fades and
withers.

7 For we are consumed by your
anger;
by your wrath we are
overwhelmed.
8 You have set our iniquities
before you,
our secret sins in the light of
your countenance.

9 For all our days pass away
under your wrath;
our years come to an end[f]
like a sigh.
10 The days of our life are seventy
years,
or perhaps eighty, if we are
strong;
even then their span[g] is only
toil and trouble;
they are soon gone, and we fly
away.

11 Who considers the power of
your anger?
Your wrath is as great as the
fear that is due you.
12 So teach us to count our days
that we may gain a wise heart.

13 Turn, O LORD! How long?
Have compassion on your
servants!
14 Satisfy us in the morning with
your steadfast love,
so that we may rejoice and be
glad all our days.
15 Make us glad as many days as
you have afflicted us,
and as many years as we have
seen evil.
16 Let your work be manifest to
your servants,
and your glorious power to
their children.
17 Let the favor of the Lord our
God be upon us,
and prosper for us the work of
our hands—

O prosper the work of our
hands!

Psalm 91

Assurance of God's Protection

1 You who live in the shelter of
the Most High,
who abide in the shadow of
the Almighty,[h]
2 will say to the LORD, "My refuge
and my fortress;
my God, in whom I trust."

3 For he will deliver you from the
snare of the fowler
and from the deadly
pestilence;
4 he will cover you with his
pinions,
and under his wings you will
find refuge;
his faithfulness is a shield and
buckler.
5 You will not fear the terror of
the night,
or the arrow that flies by day,
6 or the pestilence that stalks in
darkness,
or the destruction that wastes
at noonday.

7 A thousand may fall at your
side,
ten thousand at your right
hand,
but it will not come near you.
8 You will only look with your
eyes
and see the punishment of the
wicked.

9 Because you have made the
LORD your refuge,[i]
the Most High your dwelling
place,
10 no evil shall befall you,
no scourge come near your
tent.

11 For he will command his angels
concerning you
to guard you in all your ways.
12 On their hands they will bear
you up,
so that you will not dash your
foot against a stone.

f Syr: Heb *we bring our years to an end*
g Cn Compare Gk Syr Jerome Tg: Heb
pride   h Traditional rendering of Heb
Shaddai   i Cn: Heb *Because you, LORD,
are my refuge; you have made*

13 You will tread on the lion and
    the adder,
  the young lion and the serpent
    you will trample under
    foot.

14 Those who love me, I will
    deliver;
  I will protect those who know
    my name.
15 When they call to me, I will
    answer them;
  I will be with them in trouble,
  I will rescue them and honor
    them.
16 With long life I will satisfy them,
  and show them my salvation.

Psalm 92

Thanksgiving for Vindication

A Psalm. A Song for the Sabbath Day.

1 It is good to give thanks to the
    LORD,
  to sing praises to your name,
    O Most High;
2 to declare your steadfast love in
    the morning,
  and your faithfulness by night,
3 to the music of the lute and the
    harp,
  to the melody of the lyre.
4 For you, O LORD, have made me
    glad by your work;
  at the works of your hands I
    sing for joy.

5 How great are your works,
    O LORD!
  Your thoughts are very deep!
6 The dullard cannot know,
  the stupid cannot understand
    this:
7 though the wicked sprout like
    grass
  and all evildoers flourish,
  they are doomed to destruction
    forever,
8 but you, O LORD, are on high
    forever.
9 For your enemies, O LORD,
  for your enemies shall perish;
  all evildoers shall be scattered.

10 But you have exalted my horn
    like that of the wild ox;
  you have poured over me[j]
    fresh oil.
11 My eyes have seen the downfall
    of my enemies;

my ears have heard the doom
    of my evil assailants.

12 The righteous flourish like the
    palm tree,
  and grow like a cedar in
    Lebanon.
13 They are planted in the house of
    the LORD;
  they flourish in the courts of
    our God.
14 In old age they still produce
    fruit;
  they are always green and full
    of sap,
15 showing that the LORD is
    upright;
  he is my rock, and there is no
    unrighteousness in him.

Psalm 93

The Majesty of God's Rule

1 The LORD is king, he is robed in
    majesty;
  the LORD is robed, he is girded
    with strength.
  He has established the world; it
    shall never be moved;
2   your throne is established
    from of old;
  you are from everlasting.

3 The floods have lifted up,
    O LORD,
  the floods have lifted up their
    voice;
  the floods lift up their roaring.
4 More majestic than the thunders
    of mighty waters,
  more majestic than the
    waves[k] of the sea,
  majestic on high is the LORD!

5 Your decrees are very sure;
  holiness befits your house,
  O LORD, forevermore.

Psalm 94

God the Avenger of the Righteous

1 O LORD, you God of vengeance,
  you God of vengeance, shine
    forth!
2 Rise up, O judge of the earth;
  give to the proud what they
    deserve!
3 O LORD, how long shall the
    wicked,

---

j Syr: Meaning of Heb uncertain
k Cn: Heb *majestic are the waves*

how long shall the wicked
exult?

4 They pour out their arrogant
words;
all the evildoers boast.
5 They crush your people,
O LORD,
and afflict your heritage.
6 They kill the widow and the
stranger,
they murder the orphan,
7 and they say, "The LORD does
not see;
the God of Jacob does not
perceive."

8 Understand, O dullest of the
people;
fools, when will you be wise?
9 He who planted the ear, does he
not hear?
He who formed the eye, does he
not see?
10 He who disciplines the nations,
he who teaches knowledge to
humankind,
does he not chastise?
11 The LORD knows our thoughts,[l]
that they are but an empty
breath.

12 Happy are those whom you
discipline, O LORD,
and whom you teach out of
your law,
13 giving them respite from days of
trouble,
until a pit is dug for the
wicked.
14 For the LORD will not forsake
his people;
he will not abandon his
heritage;
15 for justice will return to the
righteous,
and all the upright in heart
will follow it.

16 Who rises up for me against the
wicked?
Who stands up for me against
evildoers?
17 If the LORD had not been my
help,
my soul would soon have lived
in the land of silence.
18 When I thought, "My foot is
slipping,"
your steadfast love, O LORD,
held me up.

19 When the cares of my heart are
many,
your consolations cheer my
soul.
20 Can wicked rulers be allied with
you,
those who contrive mischief by
statute?
21 They band together against the
life of the righteous,
and condemn the innocent to
death.
22 But the LORD has become my
stronghold,
and my God the rock of my
refuge.
23 He will repay them for their
iniquity
and wipe them out for their
wickedness;
the LORD our God will wipe
them out.

Psalm 95

A Call to Worship and Obedience

1 O come, let us sing to the LORD;
let us make a joyful noise to
the rock of our salvation!
2 Let us come into his presence
with thanksgiving;
let us make a joyful noise to
him with songs of praise!
3 For the LORD is a great God,
and a great King above all
gods.
4 In his hand are the depths of the
earth;
the heights of the mountains
are his also.
5 The sea is his, for he made it,
and the dry land, which his
hands have formed.

6 O come, let us worship and bow
down,
let us kneel before the LORD,
our Maker!
7 For he is our God,
and we are the people of his
pasture,
and the sheep of his hand.

O that today you would listen to
his voice!
8 Do not harden your hearts, as
at Mer'i·bah,
as on the day at Mas'sah in
the wilderness,
9 when your ancestors tested me,

[l]Heb *the thoughts of humankind*

and put me to the proof,
  though they had seen my
  work.

10 For forty years I loathed that
  generation
  and said, "They are a people
  whose hearts go astray,
  and they do not regard my
  ways."

11 Therefore in my anger I swore,
  "They shall not enter my rest."

Psalm 96

Praise to God Who Comes in Judgment
  (1 Chr 16.23–33)

1 O sing to the LORD a new song;
  sing to the LORD, all the earth.
2 Sing to the LORD, bless his
  name;
  tell of his salvation from day
  to day.
3 Declare his glory among the
  nations,
  his marvelous works among
  all the peoples.
4 For great is the LORD, and
  greatly to be praised;
  he is to be revered above all
  gods.
5 For all the gods of the peoples
  are idols,
  but the LORD made the
  heavens.
6 Honor and majesty are before
  him;
  strength and beauty are in his
  sanctuary.

7 Ascribe to the LORD, O families
  of the peoples,
  ascribe to the LORD glory and
  strength.
8 Ascribe to the LORD the glory
  due his name;
  bring an offering, and come
  into his courts.
9 Worship the LORD in holy
  splendor;
  tremble before him, all the
  earth.

10 Say among the nations, "The
  LORD is king!
  The world is firmly
  established; it shall never
  be moved.
  He will judge the peoples with
  equity."
11 Let the heavens be glad, and let
  the earth rejoice;

let the sea roar, and all that
  fills it;
12 let the field exult, and
  everything in it.
Then shall all the trees of the
  forest sing for joy
13 before the LORD; for he is
  coming,
  for he is coming to judge the
  earth.
He will judge the world with
  righteousness,
  and the peoples with his truth.

Psalm 97

The Glory of God's Reign

1 The LORD is king! Let the earth
  rejoice;
  let the many coastlands be
  glad!
2 Clouds and thick darkness are
  all around him;
  righteousness and justice are
  the foundation of his
  throne.
3 Fire goes before him,
  and consumes his adversaries
  on every side.
4 His lightnings light up the world;
  the earth sees and trembles.
5 The mountains melt like wax
  before the LORD,
  before the Lord of all the
  earth.

6 The heavens proclaim his
  righteousness;
  and all the peoples behold his
  glory.
7 All worshipers of images are put
  to shame,
  those who make their boast in
  worthless idols;
  all gods bow down before him.
8 Zion hears and is glad,
  and the towns[m] of Judah
  rejoice,
  because of your judgments,
  O God.
9 For you, O LORD, are most high
  over all the earth;
  you are exalted far above all
  gods.

10 The LORD loves those who hate[n]
  evil;
  he guards the lives of his
  faithful;

[m] Heb *daughters*   [n] Cn: Heb *You who*
love the LORD hate

he rescues them from the hand
    of the wicked.
11 Light dawns° for the righteous,
    and joy for the upright in
      heart.
12 Rejoice in the LORD, O you
    righteous,
    and give thanks to his holy
      name!

Psalm 98

Praise the Judge of the World

A Psalm.

1 O sing to the LORD a new song,
    for he has done marvelous
      things.
   His right hand and his holy arm
    have gotten him victory.
2 The LORD has made known his
    victory;
    he has revealed his vindication
      in the sight of the nations.
3 He has remembered his steadfast
    love and faithfulness
   to the house of Israel.
   All the ends of the earth have
    seen
      the victory of our God.

4 Make a joyful noise to the LORD,
    all the earth;
    break forth into joyous song
      and sing praises.
5 Sing praises to the LORD with
    the lyre,
    with the lyre and the sound of
      melody.
6 With trumpets and the sound of
    the horn
    make a joyful noise before the
      King, the LORD.

7 Let the sea roar, and all that fills
    it;
    the world and those who live
      in it.
8 Let the floods clap their hands;
    let the hills sing together for
      joy
9 at the presence of the LORD, for
    he is coming
   to judge the earth.
   He will judge the world with
    righteousness,
    and the peoples with equity.

Psalm 99

Praise to God for His Holiness

1 The LORD is king; let the peoples
    tremble!
   He sits enthroned upon the
    cherubim; let the earth
      quake!
2 The LORD is great in Zion;
    he is exalted over all the
      peoples.
3 Let them praise your great and
    awesome name.
   Holy is he!
4 Mighty King,ᴾ lover of justice,
    you have established equity;
   you have executed justice
    and righteousness in Jacob.
5 Extol the LORD our God;
    worship at his footstool.
   Holy is he!

6 Moses and Aaron were among
    his priests,
    Samuel also was among those
      who called on his name.
   They cried to the LORD, and
    he answered them.
7 He spoke to them in the pillar of
    cloud;
    they kept his decrees,
    and the statutes that he gave
      them.

8 O LORD our God, you answered
    them;
    you were a forgiving God to
      them,
    but an avenger of their
      wrongdoings.
9 Extol the LORD our God,
    and worship at his holy
      mountain;
    for the LORD our God is holy.

Psalm 100

All Lands Summoned to Praise God

A Psalm of thanksgiving.

1 Make a joyful noise to the LORD,
    all the earth.
2   Worship the LORD with
    gladness;
    come into his presence with
      singing.

3 Know that the LORD is God.

° Gk Syr Jerome: Heb *is sown*
ᴾ Cn: Heb *And a king's strength*

PSALMS

It is he that made us, and we
are his;[q]
we are his people, and the
sheep of his pasture.

4 Enter his gates with
thanksgiving,
and his courts with praise.
Give thanks to him, bless his
name.

5 For the LORD is good;
his steadfast love endures
forever,
and his faithfulness to all
generations.

Psalm 101

*A Sovereign's Pledge of Integrity
and Justice*

Of David. A Psalm.

1 I will sing of loyalty and of
justice;
to you, O LORD, I will sing.
2 I will study the way that is
blameless.
When shall I attain it?

I will walk with integrity of
heart
within my house;
3 I will not set before my eyes
anything that is base.

I hate the work of those who fall
away;
it shall not cling to me.
4 Perverseness of heart shall be
far from me;
I will know nothing of evil.

5 One who secretly slanders a
neighbor
I will destroy.
A haughty look and an arrogant
heart
I will not tolerate.

6 I will look with favor on the
faithful in the land,
so that they may live with me;
whoever walks in the way that is
blameless
shall minister to me.

7 No one who practices deceit
shall remain in my house;
no one who utters lies
shall continue in my presence.

8 Morning by morning I will
destroy
all the wicked in the land,
cutting off all evildoers
from the city of the LORD.

Psalm 102

Prayer to the Eternal King for Help

A prayer of one afflicted, when faint
and pleading before the LORD.

1 Hear my prayer, O LORD;
let my cry come to you.
2 Do not hide your face from me
in the day of my distress.
Incline your ear to me;
answer me speedily in the day
when I call.

3 For my days pass away like
smoke,
and my bones burn like a
furnace.
4 My heart is stricken and
withered like grass;
I am too wasted to eat my
bread.
5 Because of my loud groaning
my bones cling to my skin.
6 I am like an owl of the
wilderness,
like a little owl of the waste
places.
7 I lie awake;
I am like a lonely bird on the
housetop.
8 All day long my enemies taunt
me;
those who deride me use my
name for a curse.
9 For I eat ashes like bread,
and mingle tears with my
drink,
10 because of your indignation and
anger;
for you have lifted me up and
thrown me aside.
11 My days are like an evening
shadow;
I wither away like grass.

12 But you, O LORD, are enthroned
forever;
your name endures to all
generations.
13 You will rise up and have
compassion on Zion,
for it is time to favor it;
the appointed time has come.

[q] Another reading is *and not we
ourselves*

14 For your servants hold its stones
      dear,
     and have pity on its dust.
15 The nations will fear the name
      of the LORD,
     and all the kings of the earth
      your glory.
16 For the LORD will build up Zion;
     he will appear in his glory.
17 He will regard the prayer of the
      destitute,
     and will not despise their
      prayer.

18 Let this be recorded for a
      generation to come,
     so that a people yet unborn
      may praise the LORD:
19 that he looked down from his
      holy height,
     from heaven the LORD looked
      at the earth,
20 to hear the groans of the
      prisoners,
     to set free those who were
      doomed to die;
21 so that the name of the LORD
      may be declared in Zion,
     and his praise in Jerusalem,
22 when peoples gather together,
     and kingdoms, to worship the
      LORD.

23 He has broken my strength in
      midcourse;
     he has shortened my days.
24 "O my God," I say, "do not take
      me away
     at the mid-point of my life,
you whose years endure
     throughout all generations."

25 Long ago you laid the
      foundation of the earth,
     and the heavens are the work
      of your hands.
26 They will perish, but you
      endure;
     they will all wear out like a
      garment.
You change them like clothing,
     and they pass away;
27 but you are the same, and
     your years have no end.
28 The children of your servants
      shall live secure;
     their offspring shall be
      established in your
      presence.

Psalm 103

Thanksgiving for God's Goodness

Of David.

1 Bless the LORD, O my soul,
     and all that is within me,
     bless his holy name.
2 Bless the LORD, O my soul,
     and do not forget all his
      benefits—
3 who forgives all your iniquity,
     who heals all your diseases,
4 who redeems your life from the
      Pit,
     who crowns you with steadfast
      love and mercy,
5 who satisfies you with good as
     long as you live[r]
     so that your youth is renewed
      like the eagle's.

6 The LORD works vindication
     and justice for all who are
      oppressed.
7 He made known his ways to
      Moses,
     his acts to the people of Israel.
8 The LORD is merciful and
      gracious,
     slow to anger and abounding
      in steadfast love.
9 He will not always accuse,
     nor will he keep his anger
      forever.
10 He does not deal with us
      according to our sins,
     nor repay us according to our
      iniquities.
11 For as the heavens are high
      above the earth,
     so great is his steadfast love
      toward those who fear him;
12 as far as the east is from the
      west,
     so far he removes our
      transgressions from us.
13 As a father has compassion for
      his children,
     so the LORD has compassion
      for those who fear him.
14 For he knows how we were
      made;
     he remembers that we are
      dust.

15 As for mortals, their days are
      like grass;
     they flourish like a flower of
      the field;

[r] Meaning of Heb uncertain

PSALMS

16 for the wind passes over it, and
      it is gone,
   and its place knows it no
      more.
17 But the steadfast love of the
      LORD is from everlasting to
      everlasting
   on those who fear him,
   and his righteousness to
      children's children,
18 to those who keep his covenant
   and remember to do his
      commandments.

19 The LORD has established his
      throne in the heavens,
   and his kingdom rules over all.
20 Bless the LORD, O you his
      angels,
   you mighty ones who do his
      bidding,
   obedient to his spoken word.
21 Bless the LORD, all his hosts,
   his ministers that do his will.
22 Bless the LORD, all his works,
   in all places of his dominion.
   Bless the LORD, O my soul.

Psalm 104

God the Creator and Provider
(Cp Gen 1.1–31)

1 Bless the LORD, O my soul.
   O LORD my God, you are very
      great.
   You are clothed with honor and
      majesty,
2   wrapped in light as with a
      garment.
   You stretch out the heavens like
      a tent,
3   you set the beams of your[s]
      chambers on the waters,
   you make the clouds your[s]
      chariot,
   you ride on the wings of the
      wind,
4 you make the winds your[s]
      messengers,
   fire and flame your[s]
      ministers.

5 You set the earth on its
      foundations,
   so that it shall never be
      shaken.
6 You cover it with the deep as
      with a garment;
   the waters stood above the
      mountains.
7 At your rebuke they flee;

   at the sound of your thunder
      they take to flight.
8 They rose up to the mountains,
      ran down to the valleys
   to the place that you appointed
      for them.
9 You set a boundary that they
      may not pass,
   so that they might not again
      cover the earth.

10 You make springs gush forth in
      the valleys;
   they flow between the hills,
11 giving drink to every wild
      animal;
   the wild asses quench their
      thirst.
12 By the streams[t] the birds of the
      air have their habitation;
   they sing among the branches.
13 From your lofty abode you water
      the mountains;
   the earth is satisfied with the
      fruit of your work.

14 You cause the grass to grow for
      the cattle,
   and plants for people to use,[u]
   to bring forth food from the
      earth,
15   and wine to gladden the
      human heart,
   oil to make the face shine,
   and bread to strengthen the
      human heart.
16 The trees of the LORD are
      watered abundantly,
   the cedars of Lebanon that he
      planted.
17 In them the birds build their
      nests;
   the stork has its home in the
      fir trees.
18 The high mountains are for the
      wild goats;
   the rocks are a refuge for the
      coneys.
19 You have made the moon to
      mark the seasons;
   the sun knows its time for
      setting.
20 You make darkness, and it is
      night,
   when all the animals of the
      forest come creeping out.
21 The young lions roar for their
      prey,
   seeking their food from God.

[s] Heb *his*   [t] Heb *By them*   [u] Or *to*
cultivate

22 When the sun rises, they
withdraw
and lie down in their dens.
23 People go out to their work
and to their labor until the
evening.

24 O LORD, how manifold are your
works!
In wisdom you have made
them all;
the earth is full of your
creatures.
25 Yonder is the sea, great and
wide,
creeping things innumerable
are there,
living things both small and
great.
26 There go the ships,
and Le·vī′a·than that you
formed to sport in it.

27 These all look to you
to give them their food in due
season;
28 when you give to them, they
gather it up;
when you open your hand,
they are filled with good
things.
29 When you hide your face, they
are dismayed;
when you take away their
breath, they die
and return to their dust.
30 When you send forth your
spirit,ᵛ they are created;
and you renew the face of the
ground.

31 May the glory of the LORD
endure forever;
may the LORD rejoice in his
works—
32 who looks on the earth and it
trembles,
who touches the mountains
and they smoke.
33 I will sing to the LORD as long
as I live;
I will sing praise to my God
while I have being.
34 May my meditation be pleasing
to him,
for I rejoice in the LORD.
35 Let sinners be consumed from
the earth,
and let the wicked be no more.
Bless the LORD, O my soul.
Praise the LORD!

Psalm 105

God's Faithfulness to Israel
(Ex 7.8 – 11.10; 1 Chr 16.8–22)

1 O give thanks to the LORD, call
on his name,
make known his deeds among
the peoples.
2 Sing to him, sing praises to him;
tell of all his wonderful works.
3 Glory in his holy name;
let the hearts of those who
seek the LORD rejoice.
4 Seek the LORD and his strength;
seek his presence continually.
5 Remember the wonderful works
he has done,
his miracles, and the
judgments he uttered,
6 O offspring of his servant
Abraham,ʷ
children of Jacob, his chosen
ones.

7 He is the LORD our God;
his judgments are in all the
earth.
8 He is mindful of his covenant
forever,
of the word that he
commanded, for a
thousand generations,
9 the covenant that he made with
Abraham,
his sworn promise to Isaac,
10 which he confirmed to Jacob as
a statute,
to Israel as an everlasting
covenant,
11 saying, "To you I will give the
land of Cā′naan
as your portion for an
inheritance."

12 When they were few in number,
of little account, and strangers
in it,
13 wandering from nation to nation,
from one kingdom to another
people,
14 he allowed no one to oppress
them;
he rebuked kings on their
account,
15 saying, "Do not touch my
anointed ones;
do my prophets no harm."

ᵛ Or *your breath*   ʷ Another reading is
Israel (compare 1 Chr 16.13)

16 When he summoned famine
   against the land,
   and broke every staff of bread,
17 he had sent a man ahead of
   them,
   Joseph, who was sold as a
   slave.
18 His feet were hurt with fetters,
   his neck was put in a collar of
   iron;
19 until what he had said came to
   pass,
   the word of the LORD kept
   testing him.
20 The king sent and released him;
   the ruler of the peoples set
   him free.
21 He made him lord of his house,
   and ruler of all his
   possessions,
22 to instruct[x] his officials at his
   pleasure,
   and to teach his elders
   wisdom.

23 Then Israel came to Egypt;
   Jacob lived as an alien in the
   land of Ham.
24 And the LORD made his people
   very fruitful,
   and made them stronger than
   their foes,
25 whose hearts he then turned to
   hate his people,
   to deal craftily with his
   servants.

26 He sent his servant Moses,
   and Aaron whom he had
   chosen.
27 They performed his signs among
   them,
   and miracles in the land of
   Ham.
28 He sent darkness, and made the
   land dark;
   they rebelled[y] against his
   words.
29 He turned their waters into
   blood,
   and caused their fish to die.
30 Their land swarmed with frogs,
   even in the chambers of their
   kings.
31 He spoke, and there came
   swarms of flies,
   and gnats throughout their
   country.
32 He gave them hail for rain,
   and lightning that flashed
   through their land.

33 He struck their vines and fig
   trees,
   and shattered the trees of their
   country.
34 He spoke, and the locusts came,
   and young locusts without
   number;
35 they devoured all the vegetation
   in their land,
   and ate up the fruit of their
   ground.
36 He struck down all the firstborn
   in their land,
   the first issue of all their
   strength.

37 Then he brought Israel[z] out
   with silver and gold,
   and there was no one among
   their tribes who stumbled.
38 Egypt was glad when they
   departed,
   for dread of them had fallen
   upon it.
39 He spread a cloud for a
   covering,
   and fire to give light by night.
40 They asked, and he brought
   quails,
   and gave them food from
   heaven in abundance.
41 He opened the rock, and water
   gushed out;
   it flowed through the desert
   like a river.
42 For he remembered his holy
   promise,
   and Abraham, his servant.

43 So he brought his people out
   with joy,
   his chosen ones with singing.
44 He gave them the lands of the
   nations,
   and they took possession of
   the wealth of the peoples,
45 that they might keep his statutes
   and observe his laws.
   Praise the LORD!

Psalm 106

A Confession of Israel's Sins

1 Praise the LORD!
   O give thanks to the LORD, for
   he is good;
   for his steadfast love endures
   forever.

x Gk Syr Jerome: Heb *to bind*
y Cn Compare Gk Syr: Heb *they did not
rebel*   z Heb *them*

2 Who can utter the mighty doings
of the LORD,
or declare all his praise?
3 Happy are those who observe
justice,
who do righteousness at all
times.

4 Remember me, O LORD, when
you show favor to your
people;
help me when you deliver
them;
5 that I may see the prosperity of
your chosen ones,
that I may rejoice in the
gladness of your nation,
that I may glory in your
heritage.

6 Both we and our ancestors have
sinned;
we have committed iniquity,
have done wickedly.
7 Our ancestors, when they were
in Egypt,
did not consider your
wonderful works;
they did not remember the
abundance of your
steadfast love,
but rebelled against the Most
High[a] at the Red Sea.[b]
8 Yet he saved them for his
name's sake,
so that he might make known
his mighty power.
9 He rebuked the Red Sea,[b] and it
became dry;
he led them through the deep
as through a desert.
10 So he saved them from the hand
of the foe,
and delivered them from the
hand of the enemy.
11 The waters covered their
adversaries;
not one of them was left.
12 Then they believed his words;
they sang his praise.

13 But they soon forgot his works;
they did not wait for his
counsel.
14 But they had a wanton craving
in the wilderness,
and put God to the test in the
desert;
15 he gave them what they asked,
but sent a wasting disease
among them.

16 They were jealous of Moses in
the camp,
and of Aaron, the holy one of
the LORD.
17 The earth opened and swallowed
up Dā'than,
and covered the faction of
A·bī'ram.
18 Fire also broke out in their
company;
the flame burned up the
wicked.

19 They made a calf at Hō'reb
and worshiped a cast image.
20 They exchanged the glory of
God[c]
for the image of an ox that
eats grass.
21 They forgot God, their Savior,
who had done great things in
Egypt,
22 wondrous works in the land of
Ham,
and awesome deeds by the
Red Sea.[b]
23 Therefore he said he would
destroy them—
had not Moses, his chosen one,
stood in the breach before him,
to turn away his wrath from
destroying them.

24 Then they despised the pleasant
land,
having no faith in his promise.
25 They grumbled in their tents,
and did not obey the voice of
the LORD.
26 Therefore he raised his hand
and swore to them
that he would make them fall
in the wilderness,
27 and would disperse[d] their
descendants among the
nations,
scattering them over the lands.

28 Then they attached themselves
to the Bā'al of Pē'or,
and ate sacrifices offered to
the dead;
29 they provoked the LORD to
anger with their deeds,
and a plague broke out among
them.

P
S
A
L
M
S

a Cn Compare 78.17, 56: Heb *rebelled at
the sea*   b Or *Sea of Reeds*   c Compare
Gk Mss: Heb *exchanged their glory*
d Syr Compare Ezek 20.23: Heb *cause to
fall*

30 Then Phin'e·has stood up and
   interceded,
   and the plague was stopped.
31 And that has been reckoned to
   him as righteousness
   from generation to generation
   forever.
32 They angered the LORD*e* at the
   waters of Mer'i·bah,
   and it went ill with Moses on
   their account;
33 for they made his spirit bitter,
   and he spoke words that were
   rash.

34 They did not destroy the
   peoples,
   as the LORD commanded them,
35 but they mingled with the
   nations
   and learned to do as they did.
36 They served their idols,
   which became a snare to them.
37 They sacrificed their sons
   and their daughters to the
   demons;
38 they poured out innocent blood,
   the blood of their sons and
   daughters,
   whom they sacrificed to the idols
   of Ca'naan;
   and the land was polluted with
   blood.
39 Thus they became unclean by
   their acts,
   and prostituted themselves in
   their doings.

40 Then the anger of the LORD was
   kindled against his people,
   and he abhorred his heritage;
41 he gave them into the hand of
   the nations,
   so that those who hated them
   ruled over them.
42 Their enemies oppressed them,
   and they were brought into
   subjection under their
   power.
43 Many times he delivered them,
   but they were rebellious in
   their purposes,
   and were brought low through
   their iniquity.
44 Nevertheless he regarded their
   distress
   when he heard their cry.
45 For their sake he remembered
   his covenant,

   and showed compassion
   according to the abundance
   of his steadfast love.
46 He caused them to be pitied
   by all who held them captive.

47 Save us, O LORD our God,
   and gather us from among the
   nations,
   that we may give thanks to your
   holy name
   and glory in your praise.

48 Blessed be the LORD, the God of
   Israel,
   from everlasting to everlasting.
   And let all the people say,
   "Amen."
   Praise the LORD!

BOOK V

(Psalms 107–150)

Psalm 107

*Thanksgiving for Deliverance from
Many Troubles*

1 O give thanks to the LORD, for
   he is good;
   for his steadfast love endures
   forever.
2 Let the redeemed of the LORD
   say so,
   those he redeemed from
   trouble
3 and gathered in from the lands,
   from the east and from the
   west,
   from the north and from the
   south.*f*

4 Some wandered in desert
   wastes,
   finding no way to an inhabited
   town;
5 hungry and thirsty,
   their soul fainted within them.
6 Then they cried to the LORD in
   their trouble,
   and he delivered them from
   their distress;
7 he led them by a straight way,
   until they reached an
   inhabited town.
8 Let them thank the LORD for his
   steadfast love,
   for his wonderful works to
   humankind.
9 For he satisfies the thirsty,

e Heb *him*   *f* Cn: Heb *sea*

and the hungry he fills with
good things.

10 Some sat in darkness and in
gloom,
prisoners in misery and in
irons,
11 for they had rebelled against the
words of God,
and spurned the counsel of the
Most High.
12 Their hearts were bowed down
with hard labor;
they fell down, with no one to
help.
13 Then they cried to the LORD in
their trouble,
and he saved them from their
distress;
14 he brought them out of darkness
and gloom,
and broke their bonds
asunder.
15 Let them thank the LORD for his
steadfast love,
for his wonderful works to
humankind.
16 For he shatters the doors of
bronze,
and cuts in two the bars of
iron.

17 Some were sick[g] through their
sinful ways,
and because of their iniquities
endured affliction;
18 they loathed any kind of food,
and they drew near to the
gates of death.
19 Then they cried to the LORD in
their trouble,
and he saved them from their
distress;
20 he sent out his word and healed
them,
and delivered them from
destruction.
21 Let them thank the LORD for his
steadfast love,
for his wonderful works to
humankind.
22 And let them offer thanksgiving
sacrifices,
and tell of his deeds with
songs of joy.

23 Some went down to the sea in
ships,
doing business on the mighty
waters;
24 they saw the deeds of the LORD,

his wondrous works in the
deep.
25 For he commanded and raised
the stormy wind,
which lifted up the waves of
the sea.
26 They mounted up to heaven,
they went down to the
depths;
their courage melted away in
their calamity;
27 they reeled and staggered like
drunkards,
and were at their wits' end.
28 Then they cried to the LORD in
their trouble,
and he brought them out from
their distress;
29 he made the storm be still,
and the waves of the sea were
hushed.
30 Then they were glad because
they had quiet,
and he brought them to their
desired haven.
31 Let them thank the LORD for his
steadfast love,
for his wonderful works to
humankind.
32 Let them extol him in the
congregation of the people,
and praise him in the
assembly of the elders.

33 He turns rivers into a desert,
springs of water into thirsty
ground,
34 a fruitful land into a salty waste,
because of the wickedness of
its inhabitants.
35 He turns a desert into pools of
water,
a parched land into springs of
water.
36 And there he lets the hungry
live,
and they establish a town to
live in;
37 they sow fields, and plant
vineyards,
and get a fruitful yield.
38 By his blessing they multiply
greatly,
and he does not let their cattle
decrease.

39 When they are diminished and
brought low
through oppression, trouble,
and sorrow,

g Cn: Heb *fools*

40 he pours contempt on princes
    and makes them wander in
        trackless wastes;
41 but he raises up the needy out of
        distress,
    and makes their families like
        flocks.
42 The upright see it and are glad;
    and all wickedness stops its
        mouth.
43 Let those who are wise give
        heed to these things,
    and consider the steadfast love
        of the LORD.

Psalm 108

Praise and Prayer for Victory
(Ps 57.7–11; 60.5–12)

A Song. A Psalm of David.

1 My heart is steadfast, O God, my
        heart is steadfast;[h]
    I will sing and make melody.
    Awake, my soul![i]
2 Awake, O harp and lyre!
    I will awake the dawn.
3 I will give thanks to you,
        O LORD, among the
        peoples,
    and I will sing praises to you
        among the nations.
4 For your steadfast love is higher
        than the heavens,
    and your faithfulness reaches
        to the clouds.

5 Be exalted, O God, above the
        heavens,
    and let your glory be over all
        the earth.
6 Give victory with your right
        hand, and answer me,
    so that those whom you love
        may be rescued.

7 God has promised in his
        sanctuary:[j]
    "With exultation I will divide
        up Shē'chem,
    and portion out the Vale of
        Suc'coth.
8 Gil'e·ad is mine; Ma·nas'seh is
        mine;
    Ē'phra·im is my helmet;
    Judah is my scepter.
9 Mō'ab is my washbasin;
    on Ē'dom I hurl my shoe;
    over Phi·lis'ti·a I shout in
        triumph."

10 Who will bring me to the
        fortified city?
    Who will lead me to Ē'dom?
11 Have you not rejected us,
        O God?
    You do not go out, O God,
        with our armies.
12 O grant us help against the foe,
    for human help is worthless.
13 With God we shall do valiantly;
    it is he who will tread down
        our foes.

Psalm 109

Prayer for Vindication and Vengeance

To the leader. Of David. A Psalm.

1 Do not be silent, O God of my
        praise.
2 For wicked and deceitful mouths
        are opened against me,
    speaking against me with lying
        tongues.
3 They beset me with words of
        hate,
    and attack me without cause.
4 In return for my love they
        accuse me,
    even while I make prayer for
        them.[k]
5 So they reward me evil for good,
    and hatred for my love.

6 They say,[l] "Appoint a wicked
        man against him;
    let an accuser stand on his
        right.
7 When he is tried, let him be
        found guilty;
    let his prayer be counted as
        sin.
8 May his days be few;
    may another seize his position.
9 May his children be orphans,
    and his wife a widow.
10 May his children wander about
        and beg;
    may they be driven out of[m]
        the ruins they inhabit.
11 May the creditor seize all that he
        has;
    may strangers plunder the
        fruits of his toil.
12 May there be no one to do him a
        kindness,

h Heb Mss Gk Syr: MT lacks *my heart is
steadfast*   i Compare 57.8: Heb *also my
soul*   j Or *by his holiness*   k Syr: Heb *I
prayer*   l Heb lacks *They say*
m Gk: Heb *and seek*

nor anyone to pity his
orphaned children.

13 May his posterity be cut off;
may his name be blotted out in
the second generation.

14 May the iniquity of his father[n]
be remembered before the
LORD,
and do not let the sin of his
mother be blotted out.

15 Let them be before the LORD
continually,
and may his[o] memory be cut
off from the earth.

16 For he did not remember to
show kindness,
but pursued the poor and
needy
and the brokenhearted to their
death.

17 He loved to curse; let curses
come on him.
He did not like blessing; may
it be far from him.

18 He clothed himself with cursing
as his coat,
may it soak into his body like
water,
like oil into his bones.

19 May it be like a garment that he
wraps around himself,
like a belt that he wears every
day."

20 May that be the reward of my
accusers from the LORD,
of those who speak evil
against my life.

21 But you, O LORD my Lord,
act on my behalf for your
name's sake;
because your steadfast love is
good, deliver me.

22 For I am poor and needy,
and my heart is pierced within
me.

23 I am gone like a shadow at
evening;
I am shaken off like a locust.

24 My knees are weak through
fasting;
my body has become gaunt.

25 I am an object of scorn to my
accusers;
when they see me, they shake
their heads.

26 Help me, O LORD my God!
Save me according to your
steadfast love.

27 Let them know that this is your
hand;

you, O LORD, have done it.

28 Let them curse, but you will
bless.
Let my assailants be put to
shame;[p] may your servant
be glad.

29 May my accusers be clothed
with dishonor;
may they be wrapped in their
own shame as in a mantle.

30 With my mouth I will give great
thanks to the LORD;
I will praise him in the midst
of the throng.

31 For he stands at the right hand
of the needy,
to save them from those who
would condemn them to
death.

Psalm 110

*Assurance of Victory for God's
Priest-King*
(Mt 22.44; Acts 2.34–35)

Of David. A Psalm.

1 The LORD says to my lord,
"Sit at my right hand
until I make your enemies your
footstool."

2 The LORD sends out from Zion
your mighty scepter.
Rule in the midst of your foes.

3 Your people will offer
themselves willingly
on the day you lead your
forces
on the holy mountains.[q]
From the womb of the morning,
like dew, your youth[r] will
come to you.

4 The LORD has sworn and will
not change his mind,
"You are a priest forever
according to the order of
Mel·chiz′e·dek."[s]

5 The Lord is at your right hand;
he will shatter kings on the
day of his wrath.

6 He will execute judgment among
the nations,
filling them with corpses;
he will shatter heads

n Cn: Heb *fathers*   *o* Gk: Heb *their*
p Gk: Heb *They have risen up and have
been put to shame*   *q* Another reading
is *in holy splendor*   *r* Cn: Heb *the dew
of your youth*   *s* Or *forever, a rightful
king by my edict*

over the wide earth.
7 He will drink from the stream by
the path;
therefore he will lift up his
head.

Psalm 111

Praise for God's Wonderful Works

1 Praise the LORD!
I will give thanks to the LORD
with my whole heart,
in the company of the upright,
in the congregation.
2 Great are the works of the LORD,
studied by all who delight in
them.
3 Full of honor and majesty is his
work,
and his righteousness endures
forever.
4 He has gained renown by his
wonderful deeds;
the LORD is gracious and
merciful.
5 He provides food for those who
fear him;
he is ever mindful of his
covenant.
6 He has shown his people the
power of his works,
in giving them the heritage of
the nations.
7 The works of his hands are
faithful and just;
all his precepts are
trustworthy.
8 They are established forever and
ever,
to be performed with
faithfulness and
uprightness.
9 He sent redemption to his
people;
he has commanded his
covenant forever.
Holy and awesome is his
name.
10 The fear of the LORD is the
beginning of wisdom;
all those who practice it*t* have
a good understanding.
His praise endures forever.

Psalm 112

Blessings of the Righteous

1 Praise the LORD!
Happy are those who fear the
LORD,
who greatly delight in his
commandments.

2 Their descendants will be mighty
in the land;
the generation of the upright
will be blessed.
3 Wealth and riches are in their
houses,
and their righteousness
endures forever.
4 They rise in the darkness as a
light for the upright;
they are gracious, merciful,
and righteous.
5 It is well with those who deal
generously and lend,
who conduct their affairs with
justice.
6 For the righteous will never be
moved;
they will be remembered
forever.
7 They are not afraid of evil
tidings;
their hearts are firm, secure in
the LORD.
8 Their hearts are steady, they will
not be afraid;
in the end they will look in
triumph on their foes.
9 They have distributed freely,
they have given to the
poor;
their righteousness endures
forever;
their horn is exalted in honor.
10 The wicked see it and are angry;
they gnash their teeth and
melt away;
the desire of the wicked comes
to nothing.

Psalm 113

God the Helper of the Needy

1 Praise the LORD!
Praise, O servants of the LORD;
praise the name of the LORD.

2 Blessed be the name of the LORD
from this time on and
forevermore.
3 From the rising of the sun to its
setting
the name of the LORD is to be
praised.
4 The LORD is high above all
nations,
and his glory above the
heavens.

5 Who is like the LORD our God,

t Gk Syr: Heb *them*

who is seated on high,

6 who looks far down
on the heavens and the earth?

7 He raises the poor from the dust,
and lifts the needy from the
ash heap,

8 to make them sit with princes,
with the princes of his people.

9 He gives the barren woman a
home,
making her the joyous mother
of children.
Praise the LORD!

Psalm 114

*God's Wonders at the Exodus
(Cp Ex 14.1–31)*

1 When Israel went out from
Egypt,
the house of Jacob from a
people of strange language,

2 Judah became God's[u] sanctuary,
Israel his dominion.

3 The sea looked and fled;
Jordan turned back.

4 The mountains skipped like
rams,
the hills like lambs.

5 Why is it, O sea, that you flee?
O Jordan, that you turn back?

6 O mountains, that you skip like
rams?
O hills, like lambs?

7 Tremble, O earth, at the
presence of the LORD,
at the presence of the God of
Jacob,

8 who turns the rock into a pool of
water,
the flint into a spring of water.

Psalm 115

*The Impotence of Idols and the
Greatness of God*

1 Not to us, O LORD, not to us, but
to your name give glory,
for the sake of your steadfast
love and your faithfulness.

2 Why should the nations say,
"Where is their God?"

3 Our God is in the heavens;
he does whatever he pleases.

4 Their idols are silver and gold,
the work of human hands.

5 They have mouths, but do not
speak;

eyes, but do not see.

6 They have ears, but do not hear;
noses, but do not smell.

7 They have hands, but do not
feel;
feet, but do not walk;
they make no sound in their
throats.

8 Those who make them are like
them;
so are all who trust in them.

9 O Israel, trust in the LORD!
He is their help and their
shield.

10 O house of Aaron, trust in the
LORD!
He is their help and their
shield.

11 You who fear the LORD, trust in
the LORD!
He is their help and their
shield.

12 The LORD has been mindful of
us; he will bless us;
he will bless the house of
Israel;
he will bless the house of
Aaron;

13 he will bless those who fear the
LORD,
both small and great.

14 May the LORD give you increase,
both you and your children.

15 May you be blessed by the
LORD,
who made heaven and earth.

16 The heavens are the LORD's
heavens,
but the earth he has given to
human beings.

17 The dead do not praise the
LORD,
nor do any that go down into
silence.

18 But we will bless the LORD
from this time on and
forevermore.
Praise the LORD!

Psalm 116

Thanksgiving for Recovery from Illness

1 I love the LORD, because he has
heard
my voice and my
supplications.

u Heb *his*

P
S
A
L
M
S

2 Because he inclined his ear to
    me,
    therefore I will call on him as
      long as I live.
3 The snares of death
      encompassed me;
    the pangs of Shē′ōl laid hold
      on me;
    I suffered distress and
      anguish.
4 Then I called on the name of the
    LORD:
    "O LORD, I pray, save my life!"

5 Gracious is the LORD, and
      righteous;
    our God is merciful.
6 The LORD protects the simple;
    when I was brought low, he
      saved me.
7 Return, O my soul, to your rest,
    for the LORD has dealt
      bountifully with you.

8 For you have delivered my soul
      from death,
    my eyes from tears,
    my feet from stumbling.
9 I walk before the LORD
    in the land of the living.
10 I kept my faith, even when I
      said,
    "I am greatly afflicted";
11 I said in my consternation,
    "Everyone is a liar."

12 What shall I return to the LORD
    for all his bounty to me?
13 I will lift up the cup of salvation
    and call on the name of the
      LORD,
14 I will pay my vows to the LORD
    in the presence of all his
      people.
15 Precious in the sight of the LORD
    is the death of his faithful
      ones.
16 O LORD, I am your servant;
    I am your servant, the child of
      your serving girl.
    You have loosed my bonds.
17 I will offer to you a thanksgiving
      sacrifice
    and call on the name of the
      LORD.
18 I will pay my vows to the LORD
    in the presence of all his
      people,
19 in the courts of the house of the
      LORD,
    in your midst, O Jerusalem.
    Praise the LORD!

Psalm 117

Universal Call to Worship

1 Praise the LORD, all you nations!
    Extol him, all you peoples!
2 For great is his steadfast love
      toward us,
    and the faithfulness of the
      LORD endures forever.
Praise the LORD!

Psalm 118

A Song of Victory

1 O give thanks to the LORD, for
      he is good;
    his steadfast love endures
      forever!

2 Let Israel say,
    "His steadfast love endures
      forever."
3 Let the house of Aaron say,
    "His steadfast love endures
      forever."
4 Let those who fear the LORD
      say,
    "His steadfast love endures
      forever."

5 Out of my distress I called on
      the LORD;
    the LORD answered me and set
      me in a broad place.
6 With the LORD on my side I do
      not fear.
    What can mortals do to me?
7 The LORD is on my side to help
      me;
    I shall look in triumph on
      those who hate me.
8 It is better to take refuge in the
      LORD
    than to put confidence in
      mortals.
9 It is better to take refuge in the
      LORD
    than to put confidence in
      princes.

10 All nations surrounded me;
    in the name of the LORD I cut
      them off!
11 They surrounded me,
      surrounded me on every
      side;
    in the name of the LORD I cut
      them off!
12 They surrounded me like bees;

they blazed[v] like a fire of
thorns;
in the name of the LORD I cut
them off!

13 I was pushed hard,[w] so that I
was falling,
but the LORD helped me.

14 The LORD is my strength and my
might;
he has become my salvation.

15 There are glad songs of victory
in the tents of the
righteous:
"The right hand of the LORD
does valiantly;

16 the right hand of the LORD is
exalted;
the right hand of the LORD
does valiantly."

17 I shall not die, but I shall live,
and recount the deeds of the
LORD.

18 The LORD has punished me
severely,
but he did not give me over to
death.

19 Open to me the gates of
righteousness,
that I may enter through them
and give thanks to the LORD.

20 This is the gate of the LORD;
the righteous shall enter
through it.

21 I thank you that you have
answered me
and have become my
salvation.

22 The stone that the builders
rejected
has become the chief
cornerstone.

23 This is the LORD's doing;
it is marvelous in our eyes.

24 This is the day that the LORD
has made;
let us rejoice and be glad in
it.[x]

25 Save us, we beseech you,
O LORD!
O LORD, we beseech you, give
us success!

26 Blessed is the one who comes in
the name of the LORD.[y]
We bless you from the house
of the LORD.

27 The LORD is God,
and he has given us light.

Bind the festal procession with
branches,
up to the horns of the altar.[z]

28 You are my God, and I will give
thanks to you;
you are my God, I will extol
you.

29 O give thanks to the LORD, for
he is good,
for his steadfast love endures
forever.

Psalm 119

The Glories of God's Law

1 Happy are those whose way is
blameless,
who walk in the law of the
LORD.

2 Happy are those who keep his
decrees,
who seek him with their whole
heart,

3 who also do no wrong,
but walk in his ways.

4 You have commanded your
precepts
to be kept diligently.

5 O that my ways may be
steadfast
in keeping your statutes!

6 Then I shall not be put to shame,
having my eyes fixed on all
your commandments.

7 I will praise you with an upright
heart,
when I learn your righteous
ordinances.

8 I will observe your statutes;
do not utterly forsake me.

9 How can young people keep
their way pure?
By guarding it according to
your word.

10 With my whole heart I seek you;
do not let me stray from your
commandments.

11 I treasure your word in my
heart,
so that I may not sin against
you.

12 Blessed are you, O LORD;
teach me your statutes.

v Gk: Heb *were extinguished*　w Gk Syr
Jerome: Heb *You pushed me hard*
x Or *in him*　y Or *Blessed in the name of
the LORD is the one who comes*
z Meaning of Heb uncertain

13 With my lips I declare
all the ordinances of your
mouth.
14 I delight in the way of your
decrees
as much as in all riches.
15 I will meditate on your precepts,
and fix my eyes on your ways.
16 I will delight in your statutes;
I will not forget your word.

17 Deal bountifully with your
servant,
so that I may live and observe
your word.
18 Open my eyes, so that I may
behold
wondrous things out of your
law.
19 I live as an alien in the land;
do not hide your
commandments from me.
20 My soul is consumed with
longing
for your ordinances at all
times.
21 You rebuke the insolent,
accursed ones,
who wander from your
commandments;
22 take away from me their scorn
and contempt,
for I have kept your decrees.
23 Even though princes sit plotting
against me,
your servant will meditate on
your statutes.
24 Your decrees are my delight,
they are my counselors.

25 My soul clings to the dust;
revive me according to your
word.
26 When I told of my ways, you
answered me;
teach me your statutes.
27 Make me understand the way of
your precepts,
and I will meditate on your
wondrous works.
28 My soul melts away for sorrow;
strengthen me according to
your word.
29 Put false ways far from me;
and graciously teach me your
law.
30 I have chosen the way of
faithfulness;
I set your ordinances before
me.
31 I cling to your decrees, O LORD;
let me not be put to shame.

32 I run the way of your
commandments,
for you enlarge my
understanding.

33 Teach me, O LORD, the way of
your statutes,
and I will observe it to the
end.
34 Give me understanding, that I
may keep your law
and observe it with my whole
heart.
35 Lead me in the path of your
commandments,
for I delight in it.
36 Turn my heart to your decrees,
and not to selfish gain.
37 Turn my eyes from looking at
vanities;
give me life in your ways.
38 Confirm to your servant your
promise,
which is for those who fear
you.
39 Turn away the disgrace that I
dread,
for your ordinances are good.
40 See, I have longed for your
precepts;
in your righteousness give me
life.

41 Let your steadfast love come to
me, O LORD,
your salvation according to
your promise.
42 Then I shall have an answer for
those who taunt me,
for I trust in your word.
43 Do not take the word of truth
utterly out of my mouth,
for my hope is in your
ordinances.
44 I will keep your law continually,
forever and ever.
45 I shall walk at liberty,
for I have sought your
precepts.
46 I will also speak of your decrees
before kings,
and shall not be put to shame;
47 I find my delight in your
commandments,
because I love them.
48 I revere your commandments,
which I love,
and I will meditate on your
statutes.

49 Remember your word to your
servant,

in which you have made me
hope.

50 This is my comfort in my
distress,
that your promise gives me
life.

51 The arrogant utterly deride me,
but I do not turn away from
your law.

52 When I think of your ordinances
from of old,
I take comfort, O LORD.

53 Hot indignation seizes me
because of the wicked,
those who forsake your law.

54 Your statutes have been my
songs
wherever I make my home.

55 I remember your name in the
night, O LORD,
and keep your law.

56 This blessing has fallen to me,
for I have kept your precepts.

57 The LORD is my portion;
I promise to keep your words.

58 I implore your favor with all my
heart;
be gracious to me according to
your promise.

59 When I think of your ways,
I turn my feet to your decrees;

60 I hurry and do not delay
to keep your commandments.

61 Though the cords of the wicked
ensnare me,
I do not forget your law.

62 At midnight I rise to praise you,
because of your righteous
ordinances.

63 I am a companion of all who
fear you,
of those who keep your
precepts.

64 The earth, O LORD, is full of
your steadfast love;
teach me your statutes.

65 You have dealt well with your
servant,
O LORD, according to your
word.

66 Teach me good judgment and
knowledge,
for I believe in your
commandments.

67 Before I was humbled I went
astray,
but now I keep your word.

68 You are good and do good;
teach me your statutes.

69 The arrogant smear me with lies,

but with my whole heart I
keep your precepts.

70 Their hearts are fat and gross,
but I delight in your law.

71 It is good for me that I was
humbled,
so that I might learn your
statutes.

72 The law of your mouth is better
to me
than thousands of gold and
silver pieces.

73 Your hands have made and
fashioned me;
give me understanding that I
may learn your
commandments.

74 Those who fear you shall see me
and rejoice,
because I have hoped in your
word.

75 I know, O LORD, that your
judgments are right,
and that in faithfulness you
have humbled me.

76 Let your steadfast love become
my comfort
according to your promise to
your servant.

77 Let your mercy come to me, that
I may live;
for your law is my delight.

78 Let the arrogant be put to
shame,
because they have subverted
me with guile;
as for me, I will meditate on
your precepts.

79 Let those who fear you turn to
me,
so that they may know your
decrees.

80 May my heart be blameless in
your statutes,
so that I may not be put to
shame.

81 My soul languishes for your
salvation;
I hope in your word.

82 My eyes fail with watching for
your promise;
I ask, "When will you comfort
me?"

83 For I have become like a
wineskin in the smoke,
yet I have not forgotten your
statutes.

84 How long must your servant
endure?

When will you judge those
   who persecute me?
85 The arrogant have dug pitfalls
   for me;
   they flout your law.
86 All your commandments are
   enduring;
   I am persecuted without cause;
   help me!
87 They have almost made an end
   of me on earth;
   but I have not forsaken your
   precepts.
88 In your steadfast love spare my
   life,
   so that I may keep the decrees
   of your mouth.

89 The LORD exists forever;
   your word is firmly fixed in
   heaven.
90 Your faithfulness endures to all
   generations;
   you have established the earth,
   and it stands fast.
91 By your appointment they stand
   today,
   for all things are your
   servants.
92 If your law had not been my
   delight,
   I would have perished in my
   misery.
93 I will never forget your precepts,
   for by them you have given
   me life.
94 I am yours; save me,
   for I have sought your
   precepts.
95 The wicked lie in wait to destroy
   me,
   but I consider your decrees.
96 I have seen a limit to all
   perfection,
   but your commandment is
   exceedingly broad.

97 Oh, how I love your law!
   It is my meditation all day long.
98 Your commandment makes me
   wiser than my enemies,
   for it is always with me.
99 I have more understanding than
   all my teachers,
   for your decrees are my
   meditation.
100 I understand more than the
   aged,
   for I keep your precepts.
101 I hold back my feet from every
   evil way,
   in order to keep your word.

102 I do not turn away from your
   ordinances,
   for you have taught me.
103 How sweet are your words to
   my taste,
   sweeter than honey to my
   mouth!
104 Through your precepts I get
   understanding;
   therefore I hate every false way.

105 Your word is a lamp to my feet
   and a light to my path.
106 I have sworn an oath and
   confirmed it,
   to observe your righteous
   ordinances.
107 I am severely afflicted;
   give me life, O LORD, according
   to your word.
108 Accept my offerings of praise,
   O LORD,
   and teach me your ordinances.
109 I hold my life in my hand
   continually,
   but I do not forget your law.
110 The wicked have laid a snare
   for me,
   but I do not stray from your
   precepts.
111 Your decrees are my heritage
   forever;
   they are the joy of my heart.
112 I incline my heart to perform
   your statutes
   forever, to the end.

113 I hate the double-minded,
   but I love your law.
114 You are my hiding place and
   my shield;
   I hope in your word.
115 Go away from me, you
   evildoers,
   that I may keep the
   commandments of my God.
116 Uphold me according to your
   promise, that I may live,
   and let me not be put to shame
   in my hope.
117 Hold me up, that I may be safe
   and have regard for your
   statutes continually.
118 You spurn all who go astray
   from your statutes;
   for their cunning is in vain.
119 All the wicked of the earth you
   count as dross;
   therefore I love your decrees.
120 My flesh trembles for fear of
   you,

and I am afraid of your
    judgments.

121 I have done what is just and
    right;
    do not leave me to my
      oppressors.
122 Guarantee your servant's
    well-being;
    do not let the godless oppress
      me.
123 My eyes fail from watching for
    your salvation,
    and for the fulfillment of your
      righteous promise.
124 Deal with your servant
    according to your steadfast
      love,
    and teach me your statutes.
125 I am your servant; give me
    understanding,
    so that I may know your
      decrees.
126 It is time for the LORD to act,
    for your law has been broken.
127 Truly I love your
    commandments
    more than gold, more than fine
      gold.
128 Truly I direct my steps by all
    your precepts;[a]
    I hate every false way.

129 Your decrees are wonderful;
    therefore my soul keeps them.
130 The unfolding of your words
    gives light;
    it imparts understanding to the
      simple.
131 With open mouth I pant,
    because I long for your
      commandments.
132 Turn to me and be gracious to
    me,
    as is your custom toward those
      who love your name.
133 Keep my steps steady according
    to your promise,
    and never let iniquity have
      dominion over me.
134 Redeem me from human
    oppression,
    that I may keep your precepts.
135 Make your face shine upon
    your servant,
    and teach me your statutes.
136 My eyes shed streams of tears
    because your law is not kept.

137 You are righteous, O LORD,
    and your judgments are right.

138 You have appointed your
    decrees in righteousness
    and in all faithfulness.
139 My zeal consumes me
    because my foes forget your
      words.
140 Your promise is well tried,
    and your servant loves it.
141 I am small and despised,
    yet I do not forget your
      precepts.
142 Your righteousness is an
    everlasting righteousness,
    and your law is the truth.
143 Trouble and anguish have come
    upon me,
    but your commandments are my
      delight.
144 Your decrees are righteous
    forever;
    give me understanding that I
      may live.

145 With my whole heart I cry;
    answer me, O LORD.
    I will keep your statutes.
146 I cry to you; save me,
    that I may observe your decrees.
147 I rise before dawn and cry for
    help;
    I put my hope in your words.
148 My eyes are awake before each
    watch of the night,
    that I may meditate on your
      promise.
149 In your steadfast love hear my
    voice;
    O LORD, in your justice preserve
      my life.
150 Those who persecute me with
    evil purpose draw near;
    they are far from your law.
151 Yet you are near, O LORD,
    and all your commandments are
      true.
152 Long ago I learned from your
    decrees
    that you have established them
      forever.

153 Look on my misery and rescue
    me,
    for I do not forget your law.
154 Plead my cause and redeem me;
    give me life according to your
      promise.
155 Salvation is far from the
    wicked,
    for they do not seek your
      statutes.

PSALMS

a Gk Jerome: Meaning of Heb uncertain

156 Great is your mercy, O LORD;
   give me life according to your
      justice.
157 Many are my persecutors and
      my adversaries,
   yet I do not swerve from your
      decrees.
158 I look at the faithless with
      disgust,
   because they do not keep your
      commands.
159 Consider how I love your
      precepts;
   preserve my life according to
      your steadfast love.
160 The sum of your word is truth;
   and every one of your righteous
      ordinances endures
         forever.

161 Princes persecute me without
      cause,
   but my heart stands in awe of
      your words.
162 I rejoice at your word
   like one who finds great spoil.
163 I hate and abhor falsehood,
   but I love your law.
164 Seven times a day I praise you
   for your righteous ordinances.
165 Great peace have those who
      love your law;
   nothing can make them stumble.
166 I hope for your salvation,
      O LORD,
   and I fulfill your
      commandments.
167 My soul keeps your decrees;
   I love them exceedingly.
168 I keep your precepts and
      decrees,
   for all my ways are before you.

169 Let my cry come before you,
      O LORD;
   give me understanding
      according to your word.
170 Let my supplication come
      before you;
   deliver me according to your
      promise.
171 My lips will pour forth praise,
   because you teach me your
      statutes.
172 My tongue will sing of your
      promise,
   for all your commandments are
      right.
173 Let your hand be ready to help
      me,
   for I have chosen your precepts.

174 I long for your salvation,
      O LORD,
   and your law is my delight.
175 Let me live that I may praise
      you,
   and let your ordinances help
      me.
176 I have gone astray like a lost
      sheep; seek out your
         servant,
   for I do not forget your
      commandments.

Psalm 120

Prayer for Deliverance from Slanderers

A Song of Ascents.

1 In my distress I cry to the LORD,
   that he may answer me:
2 "Deliver me, O LORD,
   from lying lips,
   from a deceitful tongue."

3 What shall be given to you?
   And what more shall be done
      to you,
   you deceitful tongue?
4 A warrior's sharp arrows,
   with glowing coals of the
      broom tree!

5 Woe is me, that I am an alien in
      Mē′shech,
   that I must live among the
      tents of Kē′dar.
6 Too long have I had my dwelling
   among those who hate peace.
7 I am for peace;
   but when I speak,
   they are for war.

Psalm 121

Assurance of God's Protection

A Song of Ascents.

1 I lift up my eyes to the hills —
   from where will my help
      come?
2 My help comes from the LORD,
   who made heaven and earth.

3 He will not let your foot be
      moved;
   he who keeps you will not
      slumber.
4 He who keeps Israel
   will neither slumber nor sleep.

5 The LORD is your keeper;
   the LORD is your shade at your
      right hand.

6 The sun shall not strike you by
    day,
  nor the moon by night.

7 The LORD will keep you from all
    evil;
  he will keep your life.
8 The LORD will keep
  your going out and your
    coming in
  from this time on and
    forevermore.

Psalm 122

*Song of Praise and Prayer
for Jerusalem*

A Song of Ascents. Of David.

1 I was glad when they said to me,
  "Let us go to the house of the
    LORD!"
2 Our feet are standing
  within your gates,
    O Jerusalem.

3 Jerusalem—built as a city
  that is bound firmly together.
4 To it the tribes go up,
  the tribes of the LORD,
  as was decreed for Israel,
    to give thanks to the name of
    the LORD.
5 For there the thrones for
    judgment were set up,
  the thrones of the house of
    David.

6 Pray for the peace of Jerusalem:
  "May they prosper who love
    you.
7 Peace be within your walls,
  and security within your
    towers."
8 For the sake of my relatives and
    friends
  I will say, "Peace be within
    you."
9 For the sake of the house of the
    LORD our God,
  I will seek your good.

Psalm 123

Supplication for Mercy

A Song of Ascents.

1 To you I lift up my eyes,
  O you who are enthroned in
    the heavens!
2 As the eyes of servants
  look to the hand of their
    master,

as the eyes of a maid
  to the hand of her mistress,
so our eyes look to the LORD our
    God,
  until he has mercy upon us.

3 Have mercy upon us, O LORD,
  have mercy upon us,
  for we have had more than
    enough of contempt.
4 Our soul has had more than its
    fill
  of the scorn of those who are
    at ease,
  of the contempt of the proud.

Psalm 124

Thanksgiving for Israel's Deliverance

A Song of Ascents. Of David.

1 If it had not been the LORD who
    was on our side
  —let Israel now say—
2 if it had not been the LORD who
    was on our side,
  when our enemies attacked us,
3 then they would have swallowed
    us up alive,
  when their anger was kindled
    against us;
4 then the flood would have swept
    us away,
  the torrent would have gone
    over us;
5 then over us would have gone
  the raging waters.

6 Blessed be the LORD,
  who has not given us
  as prey to their teeth.
7 We have escaped like a bird
  from the snare of the fowlers;
  the snare is broken,
  and we have escaped.

8 Our help is in the name of the
    LORD,
  who made heaven and earth.

Psalm 125

The Security of God's People

A Song of Ascents.

1 Those who trust in the LORD are
    like Mount Zion,
  which cannot be moved, but
    abides forever.
2 As the mountains surround
    Jerusalem,
  so the LORD surrounds his
    people,

from this time on and
forevermore.
3 For the scepter of wickedness
shall not rest
on the land allotted to the
righteous,
so that the righteous might not
stretch out
their hands to do wrong.
4 Do good, O LORD, to those who
are good,
and to those who are upright
in their hearts.
5 But those who turn aside to their
own crooked ways
the LORD will lead away with
evildoers.
Peace be upon Israel!

Psalm 126

A Harvest of Joy

A Song of Ascents.

1 When the LORD restored the
fortunes of Zion,[b]
we were like those who dream.
2 Then our mouth was filled with
laughter,
and our tongue with shouts of
joy;
then it was said among the
nations,
"The LORD has done great
things for them."
3 The LORD has done great things
for us,
and we rejoiced.

4 Restore our fortunes, O LORD,
like the watercourses in the
Neg'eb.
5 May those who sow in tears
reap with shouts of joy.
6 Those who go out weeping,
bearing the seed for sowing,
shall come home with shouts of
joy,
carrying their sheaves.

Psalm 127

God's Blessings in the Home

A Song of Ascents. Of Solomon.

1 Unless the LORD builds the
house,
those who build it labor in
vain.
Unless the LORD guards the city,
the guard keeps watch in vain.
2 It is in vain that you rise up
early

and go late to rest,
eating the bread of anxious toil;
for he gives sleep to his
beloved.[c]

3 Sons are indeed a heritage from
the LORD,
the fruit of the womb a
reward.
4 Like arrows in the hand of a
warrior
are the sons of one's youth.
5 Happy is the man who has
his quiver full of them.
He shall not be put to shame
when he speaks with his
enemies in the gate.

Psalm 128

The Happy Home of the Faithful

A Song of Ascents.

1 Happy is everyone who fears the
LORD,
who walks in his ways.
2 You shall eat the fruit of the
labor of your hands;
you shall be happy, and it
shall go well with you.

3 Your wife will be like a fruitful
vine
within your house;
your children will be like olive
shoots
around your table.
4 Thus shall the man be blessed
who fears the LORD.

5 The LORD bless you from Zion.
May you see the prosperity of
Jerusalem
all the days of your life.
6 May you see your children's
children.
Peace be upon Israel!

Psalm 129

Prayer for the Downfall of
Israel's Enemies

A Song of Ascents.

1 "Often have they attacked me
from my youth"
—let Israel now say—
2 "often have they attacked me
from my youth,

[b] *Or brought back those who returned to
Zion*   [c] *Or for he provides for his
beloved during sleep*

yet they have not prevailed
     against me.
3 The plowers plowed on my back;
     they made their furrows long."
4 The LORD is righteous;
     he has cut the cords of the
         wicked.
5 May all who hate Zion
     be put to shame and turned
         backward.
6 Let them be like the grass on the
         housetops
     that withers before it grows
         up,
7 with which reapers do not fill
         their hands
     or binders of sheaves their
         arms,
8 while those who pass by do not
         say,
     "The blessing of the LORD be
         upon you!
     We bless you in the name of
         the LORD!"

Psalm 130

Waiting for Divine Redemption

A Song of Ascents.

1 Out of the depths I cry to you,
     O LORD.
2   Lord, hear my voice!
Let your ears be attentive
     to the voice of my
         supplications!

3 If you, O LORD, should mark
         iniquities,
     Lord, who could stand?
4 But there is forgiveness with
         you,
     so that you may be revered.

5 I wait for the LORD, my soul
         waits,
     and in his word I hope;
6 my soul waits for the Lord
     more than those who watch
         for the morning,
     more than those who watch
         for the morning.

7 O Israel, hope in the LORD!
     For with the LORD there is
         steadfast love,
     and with him is great power to
         redeem.
8 It is he who will redeem Israel
     from all its iniquities.

Psalm 131

Song of Quiet Trust

A Song of Ascents. Of David.

1 O LORD, my heart is not lifted
         up,
     my eyes are not raised too
         high;
I do not occupy myself with
         things
     too great and too marvelous
         for me.
2 But I have calmed and quieted
         my soul,
     like a weaned child with its
         mother;
     my soul is like the weaned
         child that is with me.*d*

3 O Israel, hope in the LORD
     from this time on and
         forevermore.

Psalm 132

The Eternal Dwelling of God in Zion

A Song of Ascents.

1 O LORD, remember in David's
         favor
     all the hardships he endured;
2 how he swore to the LORD
     and vowed to the Mighty One
         of Jacob,
3 "I will not enter my house
     or get into my bed;
4 I will not give sleep to my eyes
     or slumber to my eyelids,
5 until I find a place for the LORD,
     a dwelling place for the
         Mighty One of Jacob."

6 We heard of it in Eph·ra·thah;
     we found it in the fields of
         Jā'ar.
7 "Let us go to his dwelling place;
     let us worship at his footstool."

8 Rise up, O LORD, and go to your
         resting place,
     you and the ark of your might.
9 Let your priests be clothed with
         righteousness,
     and let your faithful shout for
         joy.
10 For your servant David's sake
     do not turn away the face of
         your anointed one.

d Or *my soul within me is like a weaned child*

11 The LORD swore to David a sure
oath
from which he will not turn
back:
"One of the sons of your body
I will set on your throne.
12 If your sons keep my covenant
and my decrees that I shall
teach them,
their sons also, forevermore,
shall sit on your throne."

13 For the LORD has chosen Zion;
he has desired it for his
habitation:
14 "This is my resting place
forever;
here I will reside, for I have
desired it.
15 I will abundantly bless its
provisions;
I will satisfy its poor with
bread.
16 Its priests I will clothe with
salvation,
and its faithful will shout for
joy.
17 There I will cause a horn to
sprout up for David;
I have prepared a lamp for my
anointed one.
18 His enemies I will clothe with
disgrace,
but on him, his crown will
gleam."

Psalm 133

The Blessedness of Unity

A Song of Ascents.

1 How very good and pleasant it is
when kindred live together in
unity!
2 It is like the precious oil on the
head,
running down upon the beard,
on the beard of Aaron,
running down over the collar
of his robes.
3 It is like the dew of Hermon,
which falls on the mountains
of Zion.
For there the LORD ordained his
blessing,
life forevermore.

Psalm 134

Praise in the Night

A Song of Ascents.

1 Come, bless the LORD, all you
servants of the LORD,
who stand by night in the
house of the LORD!
2 Lift up your hands to the holy
place,
and bless the LORD.

3 May the LORD, maker of heaven
and earth,
bless you from Zion.

Psalm 135

Praise for God's Goodness and Might

1 Praise the LORD!
Praise the name of the LORD;
give praise, O servants of the
LORD,
2 you that stand in the house of
the LORD,
in the courts of the house of
our God.
3 Praise the LORD, for the LORD is
good;
sing to his name, for he is
gracious.
4 For the LORD has chosen Jacob
for himself,
Israel as his own possession.

5 For I know that the LORD is
great;
our Lord is above all gods.
6 Whatever the LORD pleases he
does,
in heaven and on earth,
in the seas and all deeps.
7 He it is who makes the clouds
rise at the end of the earth;
he makes lightnings for the
rain
and brings out the wind from
his storehouses.

8 He it was who struck down the
firstborn of Egypt,
both human beings and
animals;
9 he sent signs and wonders
into your midst, O Egypt,
against Pharaoh and all his
servants.
10 He struck down many nations
and killed mighty kings—
11 Si'hon, king of the Am'o·rites,
and Og, king of Bā'shan,

and all the kingdoms of
Cā'naan—
12 and gave their land as a
heritage,
a heritage to his people Israel.

13 Your name, O LORD, endures
forever,
your renown, O LORD,
throughout all ages.
14 For the LORD will vindicate his
people,
and have compassion on his
servants.

15 The idols of the nations are
silver and gold,
the work of human hands.
16 They have mouths, but they do
not speak;
they have eyes, but they do
not see;
17 they have ears, but they do not
hear,
and there is no breath in their
mouths.
18 Those who make them
and all who trust them
shall become like them.

19 O house of Israel, bless the
LORD!
O house of Aaron, bless the
LORD!
20 O house of Levi, bless the LORD!
You that fear the LORD, bless
the LORD!
21 Blessed be the LORD from Zion,
he who resides in Jerusalem.
Praise the LORD!

Psalm 136

God's Work in Creation and in History

1 O give thanks to the LORD, for
he is good,
for his steadfast love endures
forever.
2 O give thanks to the God of
gods,
for his steadfast love endures
forever.
3 O give thanks to the Lord of
lords,
for his steadfast love endures
forever;

4 who alone does great wonders,
for his steadfast love endures
forever;
5 who by understanding made the
heavens,

for his steadfast love endures
forever;
6 who spread out the earth on the
waters,
for his steadfast love endures
forever;
7 who made the great lights,
for his steadfast love endures
forever;
8 the sun to rule over the day,
for his steadfast love endures
forever;
9 the moon and stars to rule over
the night,
for his steadfast love endures
forever;

10 who struck Egypt through their
firstborn,
for his steadfast love endures
forever;
11 and brought Israel out from
among them,
for his steadfast love endures
forever;
12 with a strong hand and an
outstretched arm,
for his steadfast love endures
forever;
13 who divided the Red Sea*e* in
two,
for his steadfast love endures
forever;
14 and made Israel pass through
the midst of it,
for his steadfast love endures
forever;
15 but overthrew Pharaoh and his
army in the Red Sea,*e*
for his steadfast love endures
forever;
16 who led his people through the
wilderness,
for his steadfast love endures
forever;
17 who struck down great kings,
for his steadfast love endures
forever;
18 and killed famous kings,
for his steadfast love endures
forever;
19 Sī'hon, king of the Am'o·rītes,
for his steadfast love endures
forever;
20 and Og, king of Bā'shan,
for his steadfast love endures
forever;
21 and gave their land as a
heritage,

e Or *Sea of Reeds*

for his steadfast love endures
forever;
22 a heritage to his servant Israel,
for his steadfast love endures
forever.

23 It is he who remembered us in
our low estate,
for his steadfast love endures
forever;
24 and rescued us from our foes,
for his steadfast love endures
forever;
25 who gives food to all flesh,
for his steadfast love endures
forever.

26 O give thanks to the God of
heaven,
for his steadfast love endures
forever.

Psalm 137

*Lament over the Destruction
of Jerusalem*

1 By the rivers of Babylon —
there we sat down and there
we wept
when we remembered Zion.
2 On the willows*f* there
we hung up our harps.
3 For there our captors
asked us for songs,
and our tormentors asked for
mirth, saying,
"Sing us one of the songs of
Zion!"

4 How could we sing the LORD's
song
in a foreign land?
5 If I forget you, O Jerusalem,
let my right hand wither!
6 Let my tongue cling to the roof
of my mouth,
if I do not remember you,
if I do not set Jerusalem
above my highest joy.

7 Remember, O LORD, against the
E'dom·ites
the day of Jerusalem's fall,
how they said, "Tear it down!
Tear it down!
Down to its foundations!"
8 O daughter Babylon, you
devastator!*g*
Happy shall they be who pay
you back
what you have done to us!

9 Happy shall they be who take
your little ones
and dash them against the
rock!

Psalm 138

Thanksgiving and Praise
Of David.

1 I give you thanks, O LORD, with
my whole heart;
before the gods I sing your
praise;
2 I bow down toward your holy
temple
and give thanks to your name
for your steadfast love and
your faithfulness;
for you have exalted your
name and your word
above everything.*h*
3 On the day I called, you
answered me,
you increased my strength of
soul.*i*

4 All the kings of the earth shall
praise you, O LORD,
for they have heard the words
of your mouth.
5 They shall sing of the ways of
the LORD,
for great is the glory of the
LORD.
6 For though the LORD is high, he
regards the lowly;
but the haughty he perceives
from far away.

7 Though I walk in the midst of
trouble,
you preserve me against the
wrath of my enemies;
you stretch out your hand,
and your right hand delivers
me.
8 The LORD will fulfill his purpose
for me;
your steadfast love, O LORD,
endures forever.
Do not forsake the work of
your hands.

f Or *poplars*   *g* Or *you who are*
devastated   *h* Cn: Heb *you have*
exalted your word above all your name
i Syr Compare Gk Tg: Heb *you made me*
arrogant in my soul with strength

Psalm 139

The Inescapable God

To the leader. Of David. A Psalm.

1 O LORD, you have searched me
     and known me.
2 You know when I sit down and
     when I rise up;
   you discern my thoughts from
     far away.
3 You search out my path and my
     lying down,
   and are acquainted with all my
     ways.
4 Even before a word is on my
     tongue,
   O LORD, you know it
     completely.
5 You hem me in, behind and
     before,
   and lay your hand upon me.
6 Such knowledge is too
     wonderful for me;
   it is so high that I cannot
     attain it.

7 Where can I go from your spirit?
   Or where can I flee from your
     presence?
8 If I ascend to heaven, you are
     there;
   if I make my bed in Shē′ōl,
     you are there.
9 If I take the wings of the
     morning
   and settle at the farthest limits
     of the sea,
10 even there your hand shall lead
     me,
   and your right hand shall hold
     me fast.
11 If I say, "Surely the darkness
     shall cover me,
   and the light around me
     become night,"
12 even the darkness is not dark to
     you;
   the night is as bright as the
     day,
   for darkness is as light to you.

13 For it was you who formed my
     inward parts;
   you knit me together in my
     mother's womb.
14 I praise you, for I am fearfully
     and wonderfully made.
   Wonderful are your works;
   that I know very well.
15 My frame was not hidden from
     you,

   when I was being made in
     secret,
   intricately woven in the depths
     of the earth.
16 Your eyes beheld my unformed
     substance.
   In your book were written
     all the days that were formed
       for me,
   when none of them as yet
     existed.
17 How weighty to me are your
     thoughts, O God!
   How vast is the sum of them!
18 I try to count them—they are
     more than the sand;
   I come to the end[j] —I am still
     with you.

19 O that you would kill the
     wicked, O God,
   and that the bloodthirsty
     would depart from me—
20 those who speak of you
     maliciously,
   and lift themselves up against
     you for evil![k]
21 Do I not hate those who hate
     you, O LORD?
   And do I not loathe those who
     rise up against you?
22 I hate them with perfect hatred;
   I count them my enemies.
23 Search me, O God, and know
     my heart;
   test me and know my
     thoughts.
24 See if there is any wicked[l] way
     in me,
   and lead me in the way
     everlasting.[m]

Psalm 140

Prayer for Deliverance from Enemies

To the leader. A Psalm of David.

1 Deliver me, O LORD, from
     evildoers;
   protect me from those who are
     violent,
2 who plan evil things in their
     minds
   and stir up wars continually.
3 They make their tongue sharp as
     a snake's,
   and under their lips is the
     venom of vipers.   *Sē′lah*

j Or *I awake*   *k* Cn: Meaning of Heb
uncertain   *l* Heb *hurtful*   *m* Or *the
ancient way.* Compare Jer 6.16

4 Guard me, O LORD, from the
     hands of the wicked;
  protect me from the violent
     who have planned my
     downfall.
5 The arrogant have hidden a trap
     for me,
  and with cords they have
     spread a net,[n]
  along the road they have set
     snares for me.   *Sē'lah*

6 I say to the LORD, "You are my
     God;
  give ear, O LORD, to the voice
     of my supplications."
7 O LORD, my Lord, my strong
     deliverer,
  you have covered my head in
     the day of battle.
8 Do not grant, O LORD, the
     desires of the wicked;
  do not further their evil plot.[o]
                              Sē'lah

9 Those who surround me lift up
     their heads;[p]
  let the mischief of their lips
     overwhelm them!
10 Let burning coals fall on them!
   Let them be flung into pits, no
     more to rise!
11 Do not let the slanderer be
     established in the land;
   let evil speedily hunt down the
     violent!

12 I know that the LORD maintains
     the cause of the needy,
   and executes justice for the
     poor.
13 Surely the righteous shall give
     thanks to your name;
   the upright shall live in your
     presence.

Psalm 141

Prayer for Preservation from Evil

A Psalm of David.

1 I call upon you, O LORD; come
     quickly to me;
  give ear to my voice when I
     call to you.
2 Let my prayer be counted as
     incense before you,
  and the lifting up of my hands
     as an evening sacrifice.

3 Set a guard over my mouth,
     O LORD;

keep watch over the door of
     my lips.
4 Do not turn my heart to any evil,
     to busy myself with wicked
     deeds
  in company with those who
     work iniquity;
  do not let me eat of their
     delicacies.

5 Let the righteous strike me;
   let the faithful correct me.
  Never let the oil of the wicked
     anoint my head,[q]
  for my prayer is continually[r]
     against their wicked deeds.
6 When they are given over to
     those who shall condemn
     them,
  then they shall learn that my
     words were pleasant.
7 Like a rock that one breaks
     apart and shatters on the
     land,
  so shall their bones be strewn
     at the mouth of Shē'ōl.[s]

8 But my eyes are turned toward
     you, O GOD, my Lord;
  in you I seek refuge; do not
     leave me defenseless.
9 Keep me from the trap that they
     have laid for me,
  and from the snares of
     evildoers.
10 Let the wicked fall into their
     own nets,
   while I alone escape.

Psalm 142

*Prayer for Deliverance
from Persecutors*

A Mas'kil of David. When he was in
     the cave. A Prayer.

1 With my voice I cry to the LORD;
   with my voice I make
     supplication to the LORD.
2 I pour out my complaint before
     him;
   I tell my trouble before him.
3 When my spirit is faint,

n Or *they have spread cords as a net*
o Heb adds *they are exalted*
p Cn Compare Gk: Heb *those who
surround me are uplifted in head*; Heb
divides verses 8 and 9 differently
q Gk: Meaning of Heb uncertain
r Cn: Heb *for continually and my prayer*
s Meaning of Heb of verses 5-7 is
uncertain

you know my way.

In the path where I walk
  they have hidden a trap for
    me.
4 Look on my right hand and
    see—
  there is no one who takes
    notice of me;
no refuge remains to me;
  no one cares for me.

5 I cry to you, O LORD;
  I say, "You are my refuge,
    my portion in the land of the
      living."
6 Give heed to my cry,
  for I am brought very low.

Save me from my persecutors,
  for they are too strong for me.
7 Bring me out of prison,
  so that I may give thanks to
    your name.
The righteous will surround me,
  for you will deal bountifully
    with me.

Psalm 143

Prayer for Deliverance from Enemies

A Psalm of David.

1 Hear my prayer, O LORD;
  give ear to my supplications in
    your faithfulness;
  answer me in your
    righteousness.
2 Do not enter into judgment with
    your servant,
  for no one living is righteous
    before you.

3 For the enemy has pursued me,
  crushing my life to the ground,
  making me sit in darkness like
    those long dead.
4 Therefore my spirit faints within
    me;
  my heart within me is
    appalled.

5 I remember the days of old,
  I think about all your deeds,
  I meditate on the works of
    your hands.
6 I stretch out my hands to you;
  my soul thirsts for you like a
    parched land.   *Sĕ'lah*

7 Answer me quickly, O LORD;
  my spirit fails.

Do not hide your face from me,
  or I shall be like those who go
    down to the Pit.
8 Let me hear of your steadfast
    love in the morning,
  for in you I put my trust.
Teach me the way I should go,
  for to you I lift up my soul.

9 Save me, O LORD, from my
    enemies;
  I have fled to you for refuge.[t]
10 Teach me to do your will,
  for you are my God.
Let your good spirit lead me
  on a level path.

11 For your name's sake, O LORD,
    preserve my life.
  In your righteousness bring
    me out of trouble.
12 In your steadfast love cut off my
    enemies,
  and destroy all my
    adversaries,
  for I am your servant.

Psalm 144

*Prayer for National Deliverance
and Security*

Of David.

1 Blessed be the LORD, my rock,
  who trains my hands for war,
    and my fingers for battle;
2 my rock[u] and my fortress,
  my stronghold and my
    deliverer,
my shield, in whom I take
    refuge,
  who subdues the peoples[v]
    under me.

3 O LORD, what are human beings
    that you regard them,
  or mortals that you think of
    them?
4 They are like a breath;
  their days are like a passing
    shadow.

5 Bow your heavens, O LORD, and
    come down;
  touch the mountains so that
    they smoke.
6 Make the lightning flash and
    scatter them;

t One Heb Ms Gk: MT *to you I have
hidden*   *u* With 18.2 and 2 Sam 22.2:
Heb *my steadfast love*   *v* Heb Mss Syr
Aquila Jerome: MT *my people*

send out your arrows and rout
  them.
7 Stretch out your hand from on
    high;
  set me free and rescue me
    from the mighty waters,
    from the hand of aliens,
8 whose mouths speak lies,
  and whose right hands are
    false.

9 I will sing a new song to you,
    O God;
  upon a ten-stringed harp I will
    play to you,
10 the one who gives victory to
    kings,
  who rescues his servant David.
11 Rescue me from the cruel sword,
  and deliver me from the hand
    of aliens,
  whose mouths speak lies,
    and whose right hands are
    false.

12 May our sons in their youth
    be like plants full grown,
  our daughters like corner pillars,
    cut for the building of a
    palace.
13 May our barns be filled,
    with produce of every kind;
  may our sheep increase by
    thousands,
    by tens of thousands in our
    fields,
14 and may our cattle be heavy
    with young.
  May there be no breach in the
    walls,^{w} no exile,
  and no cry of distress in our
    streets.

15 Happy are the people to whom
    such blessings fall;
  happy are the people whose
    God is the LORD.

Psalm 145

*The Greatness and the Goodness
of God*

Praise. Of David.

1 I will extol you, my God and
    King,
  and bless your name forever
    and ever.
2 Every day I will bless you,
  and praise your name forever
    and ever.

3 Great is the LORD, and greatly to
    be praised;
  his greatness is unsearchable.

4 One generation shall laud your
    works to another,
  and shall declare your mighty
    acts.
5 On the glorious splendor of your
    majesty,
  and on your wondrous works,
    I will meditate.
6 The might of your awesome
    deeds shall be proclaimed,
  and I will declare your
    greatness.
7 They shall celebrate the fame of
    your abundant goodness,
  and shall sing aloud of your
    righteousness.

8 The LORD is gracious and
    merciful,
  slow to anger and abounding
    in steadfast love.
9 The LORD is good to all,
  and his compassion is over all
    that he has made.

10 All your works shall give thanks
    to you, O LORD,
  and all your faithful shall bless
    you.
11 They shall speak of the glory of
    your kingdom,
  and tell of your power,
12 to make known to all people
    your^x mighty deeds,
  and the glorious splendor of
    your^y kingdom.
13 Your kingdom is an everlasting
    kingdom,
  and your dominion endures
    throughout all generations.

The LORD is faithful in all his
    words,
  and gracious in all his deeds.^{z}
14 The LORD upholds all who are
    falling,
  and raises up all who are
    bowed down.
15 The eyes of all look to you,
  and you give them their food
    in due season.
16 You open your hand,
  satisfying the desire of every
    living thing.

^{w} Heb lacks *in the walls* ^{x} Gk Jerome
Syr: Heb *his* ^{y} Heb *his* ^{z} These two
lines supplied by Q Ms Gk Syr

17 The LORD is just in all his ways,
   and kind in all his doings.
18 The LORD is near to all who call
   on him,
   to all who call on him in truth.
19 He fulfills the desire of all who
   fear him;
   he also hears their cry, and
   saves them.
20 The LORD watches over all who
   love him,
   but all the wicked he will
   destroy.

21 My mouth will speak the praise
   of the LORD,
   and all flesh will bless his holy
   name forever and ever.

Psalm 146

Praise for God's Help

1 Praise the LORD!
   Praise the LORD, O my soul!
2 I will praise the LORD as long as
   I live;
   I will sing praises to my God
   all my life long.

3 Do not put your trust in princes,
   in mortals, in whom there is
   no help.
4 When their breath departs, they
   return to the earth;
   on that very day their plans
   perish.

5 Happy are those whose help is
   the God of Jacob,
   whose hope is in the LORD
   their God,
6 who made heaven and earth,
   the sea, and all that is in them;
who keeps faith forever;
7 who executes justice for the
   oppressed;
   who gives food to the hungry.

The LORD sets the prisoners
   free;
8 the LORD opens the eyes of the
   blind.
The LORD lifts up those who are
   bowed down;
   the LORD loves the righteous.
9 The LORD watches over the
   strangers;
   he upholds the orphan and the
   widow,
   but the way of the wicked he
   brings to ruin.

10 The LORD will reign forever,
   your God, O Zion, for all
   generations.
   Praise the LORD!

Psalm 147

Praise for God's Care for Jerusalem

1 Praise the LORD!
   How good it is to sing praises to
   our God;
   for he is gracious, and a song
   of praise is fitting.
2 The LORD builds up Jerusalem;
   he gathers the outcasts of
   Israel.
3 He heals the brokenhearted,
   and binds up their wounds.
4 He determines the number of the
   stars;
   he gives to all of them their
   names.
5 Great is our Lord, and abundant
   in power;
   his understanding is beyond
   measure.
6 The LORD lifts up the
   downtrodden;
   he casts the wicked to the
   ground.

7 Sing to the LORD with
   thanksgiving;
   make melody to our God on
   the lyre.
8 He covers the heavens with
   clouds,
   prepares rain for the earth,
   makes grass grow on the hills.
9 He gives to the animals their
   food,
   and to the young ravens when
   they cry.
10 His delight is not in the strength
   of the horse,
   nor his pleasure in the speed
   of a runner;[a]
11 but the LORD takes pleasure in
   those who fear him,
   in those who hope in his
   steadfast love.

12 Praise the LORD, O Jerusalem!
   Praise your God, O Zion!
13 For he strengthens the bars of
   your gates;
   he blesses your children within
   you.
14 He grants peace[b] within your
   borders;

[a] Heb *legs of a person*   [b] Or *prosperity*

P
S
A
L
M
S

he fills you with the finest of
wheat.

15 He sends out his command to
the earth;
his word runs swiftly.

16 He gives snow like wool;
he scatters frost like ashes.

17 He hurls down hail like
crumbs —
who can stand before his cold?

18 He sends out his word, and
melts them;
he makes his wind blow, and
the waters flow.

19 He declares his word to Jacob,
his statutes and ordinances to
Israel.

20 He has not dealt thus with any
other nation;
they do not know his
ordinances.
Praise the LORD!

Psalm 148

Praise for God's Universal Glory

1 Praise the LORD!
Praise the LORD from the
heavens;
praise him in the heights!

2 Praise him, all his angels;
praise him, all his host!

3 Praise him, sun and moon;
praise him, all you shining
stars!

4 Praise him, you highest heavens,
and you waters above the
heavens!

5 Let them praise the name of the
LORD,
for he commanded and they
were created.

6 He established them forever and
ever;
he fixed their bounds, which
cannot be passed.c

7 Praise the LORD from the earth,
you sea monsters and all
deeps,

8 fire and hail, snow and frost,
stormy wind fulfilling his
command!

9 Mountains and all hills,
fruit trees and all cedars!

10 Wild animals and all cattle,
creeping things and flying
birds!

11 Kings of the earth and all
peoples,
princes and all rulers of the
earth!

12 Young men and women alike,
old and young together!

13 Let them praise the name of the
LORD,
for his name alone is exalted;
his glory is above earth and
heaven.

14 He has raised up a horn for his
people,
praise for all his faithful,
for the people of Israel who
are close to him.
Praise the LORD!

Psalm 149

Praise for God's Goodness to Israel

1 Praise the LORD!
Sing to the LORD a new song,
his praise in the assembly of
the faithful.

2 Let Israel be glad in its Maker;
let the children of Zion rejoice
in their King.

3 Let them praise his name with
dancing,
making melody to him with
tambourine and lyre.

4 For the LORD takes pleasure in
his people;
he adorns the humble with
victory.

5 Let the faithful exult in glory;
let them sing for joy on their
couches.

6 Let the high praises of God be in
their throats
and two-edged swords in their
hands,

7 to execute vengeance on the
nations
and punishment on the
peoples,

8 to bind their kings with fetters
and their nobles with chains of
iron,

9 to execute on them the judgment
decreed.
This is glory for all his faithful
ones.
Praise the LORD!

cOr *he set a law that cannot pass away*

Psalm 150

Praise for God's Surpassing Greatness

1 Praise the LORD!
  Praise God in his sanctuary;
    praise him in his mighty
      firmament![d]
2 Praise him for his mighty deeds;
    praise him according to his
      surpassing greatness!

3 Praise him with trumpet sound;
    praise him with lute and harp!

4 Praise him with tambourine and
      dance;
    praise him with strings and
      pipe!
5 Praise him with clanging
      cymbals;
    praise him with loud clashing
      cymbals!
6 Let everything that breathes
      praise the LORD!
  Praise the LORD!

[d] Or *dome*

PROVERBS

1 The proverbs of Solomon son of
  David, king of Israel:

Prologue

2 For learning about wisdom and
    instruction,
    for understanding words of
      insight,
3 for gaining instruction in wise
    dealing,
    righteousness, justice, and
      equity;
4 to teach shrewdness to the
    simple,
    knowledge and prudence to
      the young —
5 Let the wise also hear and gain
    in learning,
    and the discerning acquire
      skill,
6 to understand a proverb and a
    figure,
    the words of the wise and
      their riddles.

7 The fear of the LORD is the
    beginning of knowledge;
    fools despise wisdom and
      instruction.

Warnings against Evil Companions

8 Hear, my child, your father's
    instruction,
    and do not reject your
      mother's teaching;
9 for they are a fair garland for
      your head,
    and pendants for your neck.
10 My child, if sinners entice you,
    do not consent.
11 If they say, "Come with us, let us
      lie in wait for blood;
    let us wantonly ambush the
      innocent;
12 like Shē′ōl let us swallow them
      alive
    and whole, like those who go
      down to the Pit.
13 We shall find all kinds of costly
      things;
    we shall fill our houses with
      booty.
14 Throw in your lot among us;
    we will all have one purse" —
15 my child, do not walk in their
      way,
    keep your foot from their
      paths;
16 for their feet run to evil,
    and they hurry to shed blood.
17 For in vain is the net baited
    while the bird is looking on;
18 yet they lie in wait — to kill
      themselves!
    and set an ambush — for their
      own lives!
19 Such is the end[a] of all who are
      greedy for gain;
    it takes away the life of its
      possessors.

[a] Gk: Heb *ways*

The Call of Wisdom

20 Wisdom cries out in the street;
   in the squares she raises her
   voice.
21 At the busiest corner she cries
   out;
   at the entrance of the city
   gates she speaks:
22 "How long, O simple ones, will
   you love being simple?
   How long will scoffers delight in
   their scoffing
   and fools hate knowledge?
23 Give heed to my reproof;
   I will pour out my thoughts to
   you;
   I will make my words known
   to you.
24 Because I have called and you
   refused,
   have stretched out my hand
   and no one heeded,
25 and because you have ignored
   all my counsel
   and would have none of my
   reproof,
26 I also will laugh at your
   calamity;
   I will mock when panic strikes
   you,
27 when panic strikes you like a
   storm,
   and your calamity comes like
   a whirlwind,
   when distress and anguish
   come upon you.
28 Then they will call upon me, but
   I will not answer;
   they will seek me diligently,
   but will not find me.
29 Because they hated knowledge
   and did not choose the fear of
   the LORD,
30 would have none of my counsel,
   and despised all my reproof,
31 therefore they shall eat the fruit
   of their way
   and be sated with their own
   devices.
32 For waywardness kills the
   simple,
   and the complacency of fools
   destroys them;
33 but those who listen to me will
   be secure
   and will live at ease, without
   dread of disaster."

The Value of Wisdom

2 My child, if you accept my
   words
   and treasure up my
   commandments within you,
2 making your ear attentive to
   wisdom
   and inclining your heart to
   understanding;
3 if you indeed cry out for insight,
   and raise your voice for
   understanding;
4 if you seek it like silver,
   and search for it as for hidden
   treasures—
5 then you will understand the
   fear of the LORD
   and find the knowledge of
   God.
6 For the LORD gives wisdom;
   from his mouth come
   knowledge and
   understanding;
7 he stores up sound wisdom for
   the upright;
   he is a shield to those who
   walk blamelessly,
8 guarding the paths of justice
   and preserving the way of his
   faithful ones.
9 Then you will understand
   righteousness and justice
   and equity, every good path;
10 for wisdom will come into your
   heart,
   and knowledge will be
   pleasant to your soul;
11 prudence will watch over you;
   and understanding will guard
   you.
12 It will save you from the way of
   evil,
   from those who speak
   perversely,
13 who forsake the paths of
   uprightness
   to walk in the ways of
   darkness,
14 who rejoice in doing evil
   and delight in the perverseness
   of evil;
15 those whose paths are crooked,
   and who are devious in their
   ways.

16 You will be saved from the
   loose[b] woman,
   from the adulteress with her
   smooth words,

[b] Heb *strange*

17 who forsakes the partner of her
youth
and forgets her sacred
covenant;

18 for her way[c] leads down to
death,
and her paths to the shades;

19 those who go to her never come
back,
nor do they regain the paths of
life.

20 Therefore walk in the way of the
good,
and keep to the paths of the
just.

21 For the upright will abide in the
land,
and the innocent will remain
in it;

22 but the wicked will be cut off
from the land,
and the treacherous will be
rooted out of it.

Admonition to Trust and Honor God

3 My child, do not forget my
teaching,
but let your heart keep my
commandments;

2 for length of days and years of
life
and abundant welfare they will
give you.

3 Do not let loyalty and
faithfulness forsake you;
bind them around your neck,
write them on the tablet of
your heart.

4 So you will find favor and good
repute
in the sight of God and of
people.

5 Trust in the LORD with all your
heart,
and do not rely on your own
insight.

6 In all your ways acknowledge
him,
and he will make straight your
paths.

7 Do not be wise in your own
eyes;
fear the LORD, and turn away
from evil.

8 It will be a healing for your flesh
and a refreshment for your
body.

9 Honor the LORD with your
substance
and with the first fruits of all
your produce;

10 then your barns will be filled
with plenty,
and your vats will be bursting
with wine.

11 My child, do not despise the
LORD's discipline
or be weary of his reproof,

12 for the LORD reproves the one
he loves,
as a father the son in whom he
delights.

The True Wealth

13 Happy are those who find
wisdom,
and those who get
understanding,

14 for her income is better than
silver,
and her revenue better than
gold.

15 She is more precious than
jewels,
and nothing you desire can
compare with her.

16 Long life is in her right hand;
in her left hand are riches and
honor.

17 Her ways are ways of
pleasantness,
and all her paths are peace.

18 She is a tree of life to those who
lay hold of her;
those who hold her fast are
called happy.

God's Wisdom in Creation

19 The LORD by wisdom founded
the earth;
by understanding he
established the heavens;

20 by his knowledge the deeps
broke open,
and the clouds drop down the
dew.

The True Security

21 My child, do not let these escape
from your sight:
keep sound wisdom and
prudence,

22 and they will be life for your
soul
and adornment for your neck.

c Cn: Heb *house*

23 Then you will walk on your way
    securely
    and your foot will not stumble.
24 If you sit down,*d* you will not be
    afraid;
    when you lie down, your sleep
    will be sweet.
25 Do not be afraid of sudden
    panic,
    or of the storm that strikes the
    wicked;
26 for the LORD will be your
    confidence
    and will keep your foot from
    being caught.

27 Do not withhold good from
    those to whom it is due,*e*
    when it is in your power to do
    it.
28 Do not say to your neighbor,
    "Go, and come again,
    tomorrow I will give it"—when
    you have it with you.
29 Do not plan harm against your
    neighbor
    who lives trustingly beside
    you.
30 Do not quarrel with anyone
    without cause,
    when no harm has been done
    to you.
31 Do not envy the violent
    and do not choose any of their
    ways;
32 for the perverse are an
    abomination to the LORD,
    but the upright are in his
    confidence.
33 The LORD's curse is on the
    house of the wicked,
    but he blesses the abode of the
    righteous.
34 Toward the scorners he is
    scornful,
    but to the humble he shows
    favor.
35 The wise will inherit honor,
    but stubborn fools, disgrace.

Parental Advice

4 Listen, children, to a father's
    instruction,
    and be attentive, that you may
    gain*f* insight;
2 for I give you good precepts:
    do not forsake my teaching.
3 When I was a son with my
    father,
    tender, and my mother's
    favorite,

4 he taught me, and said to me,
    "Let your heart hold fast my
    words;
    keep my commandments, and
    live.
5 Get wisdom; get insight: do not
    forget, nor turn away
    from the words of my mouth.
6 Do not forsake her, and she will
    keep you;
    love her, and she will guard
    you.
7 The beginning of wisdom is this:
    Get wisdom,
    and whatever else you get, get
    insight.
8 Prize her highly, and she will
    exalt you;
    she will honor you if you
    embrace her.
9 She will place on your head a
    fair garland;
    she will bestow on you a
    beautiful crown."

Admonition to Keep to the Right Path

10 Hear, my child, and accept my
    words,
    that the years of your life may
    be many.
11 I have taught you the way of
    wisdom;
    I have led you in the paths of
    uprightness.
12 When you walk, your step will
    not be hampered;
    and if you run, you will not
    stumble.
13 Keep hold of instruction; do not
    let go;
    guard her, for she is your life.
14 Do not enter the path of the
    wicked,
    and do not walk in the way of
    evildoers.
15 Avoid it; do not go on it;
    turn away from it and pass on.
16 For they cannot sleep unless
    they have done wrong;
    they are robbed of sleep unless
    they have made someone
    stumble.
17 For they eat the bread of
    wickedness
    and drink the wine of violence.
18 But the path of the righteous is
    like the light of dawn,

*d*Gk: Heb *lie down*   *e*Heb *from its
owners*   *f*Heb *know*

which shines brighter and
brighter until full day.
19 The way of the wicked is like
deep darkness;
they do not know what they
stumble over.
20 My child, be attentive to my
words;
incline your ear to my sayings.
21 Do not let them escape from
your sight;
keep them within your heart.
22 For they are life to those who
find them,
and healing to all their flesh.
23 Keep your heart with all
vigilance,
for from it flow the springs of
life.
24 Put away from you crooked
speech,
and put devious talk far from
you.
25 Let your eyes look directly
forward,
and your gaze be straight
before you.
26 Keep straight the path of your
feet,
and all your ways will be sure.
27 Do not swerve to the right or to
the left;
turn your foot away from evil.

Warning against Impurity and Infidelity

5 My child, be attentive to my
wisdom;
incline your ear to my
understanding,
2 so that you may hold on to
prudence,
and your lips may guard
knowledge.
3 For the lips of a loose*g* woman
drip honey,
and her speech is smoother
than oil;
4 but in the end she is bitter as
wormwood,
sharp as a two-edged sword.
5 Her feet go down to death;
her steps follow the path to
She′ōl.
6 She does not keep straight to the
path of life;
her ways wander, and she
does not know it.
7 And now, my child,*h* listen to
me,

and do not depart from the
words of my mouth.
8 Keep your way far from her,
and do not go near the door of
her house;
9 or you will give your honor to
others,
and your years to the
merciless,
10 and strangers will take their fill
of your wealth,
and your labors will go to the
house of an alien;
11 and at the end of your life you
will groan,
when your flesh and body are
consumed,
12 and you say, "Oh, how I hated
discipline,
and my heart despised
reproof!
13 I did not listen to the voice of
my teachers
or incline my ear to my
instructors.
14 Now I am at the point of utter
ruin
in the public assembly."

15 Drink water from your own
cistern,
flowing water from your own
well.
16 Should your springs be scattered
abroad,
streams of water in the
streets?
17 Let them be for yourself alone,
and not for sharing with
strangers.
18 Let your fountain be blessed,
and rejoice in the wife of your
youth,
19 a lovely deer, a graceful doe.
May her breasts satisfy you at
all times;
may you be intoxicated always
by her love.
20 Why should you be intoxicated,
my son, by another woman
and embrace the bosom of an
adulteress?
21 For human ways are under the
eyes of the LORD,
and he examines all their
paths.
22 The iniquities of the wicked
ensnare them,
and they are caught in the
toils of their sin.

g Heb *strange*   *h* Gk Vg: Heb *children*

P
R
O
V
E
R
B
S

23 They die for lack of discipline,
and because of their great
folly they are lost.

Practical Admonitions

6 My child, if you have given your
pledge to your neighbor,
if you have bound yourself to
another,[i]
2 you are snared by the utterance
of your lips,[j]
caught by the words of your
mouth.
3 So do this, my child, and save
yourself,
for you have come into your
neighbor's power:
go, hurry,[k] and plead with
your neighbor.
4 Give your eyes no sleep
and your eyelids no slumber;
5 save yourself like a gazelle from
the hunter,[l]
like a bird from the hand of
the fowler.

6 Go to the ant, you lazybones;
consider its ways, and be wise.
7 Without having any chief
or officer or ruler,
8 it prepares its food in summer,
and gathers its sustenance in
harvest.
9 How long will you lie there,
O lazybones?
When will you rise from your
sleep?
10 A little sleep, a little slumber,
a little folding of the hands to
rest,
11 and poverty will come upon you
like a robber,
and want, like an armed
warrior.

12 A scoundrel and a villain
goes around with crooked
speech,
13 winking the eyes, shuffling the
feet,
pointing the fingers,
14 with perverted mind devising
evil,
continually sowing discord;
15 on such a one calamity will
descend suddenly;
in a moment, damage beyond
repair.

16 There are six things that the
LORD hates,
seven that are an abomination
to him:
17 haughty eyes, a lying tongue,
and hands that shed innocent
blood,
18 a heart that devises wicked
plans,
feet that hurry to run to evil,
19 a lying witness who testifies
falsely,
and one who sows discord in a
family.

20 My child, keep your father's
commandment,
and do not forsake your
mother's teaching.
21 Bind them upon your heart
always;
tie them around your neck.
22 When you walk, they[m] will lead
you;
when you lie down, they[m] will
watch over you;
and when you awake, they[m]
will talk with you.
23 For the commandment is a lamp
and the teaching a light,
and the reproofs of discipline
are the way of life,
24 to preserve you from the wife of
another,[n]
from the smooth tongue of the
adulteress.
25 Do not desire her beauty in your
heart,
and do not let her capture you
with her eyelashes;
26 for a prostitute's fee is only a
loaf of bread,[o]
but the wife of another stalks
a man's very life.
27 Can fire be carried in the bosom
without burning one's clothes?
28 Or can one walk on hot coals
without scorching the feet?
29 So is he who sleeps with his
neighbor's wife;
no one who touches her will
go unpunished.
30 Thieves are not despised who
steal only
to satisfy their appetite when
they are hungry.

[i]Or a stranger   [j]Cn Compare Gk Syr:
Heb the words of your mouth
[k]Or humble yourself   [l]Cn: Heb from
the hand   [m]Heb it   [n]Gk: MT the evil
woman   [o]Cn Compare Gk Syr Vg Tg:
Heb for because of a harlot to a piece of
bread

31 Yet if they are caught, they will
       pay sevenfold;
     they will forfeit all the goods
       of their house.
32 But he who commits adultery
     has no sense;
   he who does it destroys
     himself.
33 He will get wounds and
     dishonor,
   and his disgrace will not be
     wiped away.
34 For jealousy arouses a husband's
     fury,
   and he shows no restraint
     when he takes revenge.
35 He will accept no compensation,
   and refuses a bribe no matter
     how great.

The False Attractions of Adultery

7 My child, keep my words
     and store up my
       commandments with you;
2 keep my commandments and
     live,
   keep my teachings as the
     apple of your eye;
3 bind them on your fingers,
   write them on the tablet of
     your heart.
4 Say to wisdom, "You are my
     sister,"
   and call insight your intimate
     friend,
5 that they may keep you from the
     loose^p woman,
   from the adulteress with her
     smooth words.

6 For at the window of my house
     I looked out through my
       lattice,
7 and I saw among the simple
     ones,
   I observed among the youths,
   a young man without sense,
8 passing along the street near her
     corner,
   taking the road to her house
9 in the twilight, in the evening,
   at the time of night and
     darkness.

10 Then a woman comes toward
     him,
   decked out like a prostitute,
     wily of heart.^{q}
11 She is loud and wayward;
   her feet do not stay at home;

12 now in the street, now in the
     squares,
   and at every corner she lies in
     wait.
13 She seizes him and kisses him,
   and with impudent face she
     says to him:
14 "I had to offer sacrifices,
   and today I have paid my
     vows;
15 so now I have come out to meet
     you,
   to seek you eagerly, and I
     have found you!
16 I have decked my couch with
     coverings,
   colored spreads of Egyptian
     linen;
17 I have perfumed my bed with
     myrrh,
   aloes, and cinnamon.
18 Come, let us take our fill of love
     until morning;
   let us delight ourselves with
     love.
19 For my husband is not at home;
   he has gone on a long journey.
20 He took a bag of money with
     him;
   he will not come home until
     full moon."

21 With much seductive speech she
     persuades him;
   with her smooth talk she
     compels him.
22 Right away he follows her,
   and goes like an ox to the
     slaughter,
   or bounds like a stag toward the
     trap^r
23   until an arrow pierces its
        entrails.
   He is like a bird rushing into a
     snare,
   not knowing that it will cost
     him his life.

24 And now, my children, listen to
     me,
   and be attentive to the words
     of my mouth.
25 Do not let your hearts turn aside
     to her ways;
   do not stray into her paths.
26 for many are those she has laid
     low,
   and numerous are her victims.

^{p} Heb strange ^{q} Meaning of Heb
uncertain ^{r} Cn Compare Gk: Meaning
of Heb uncertain

27 Her house is the way to Shē′ōl,
    going down to the chambers of
    death.

The Gifts of Wisdom

8 Does not wisdom call,
    and does not understanding
    raise her voice?
2 On the heights, beside the way,
    at the crossroads she takes her
    stand;
3 beside the gates in front of the
    town,
    at the entrance of the portals
    she cries out:
4 "To you, O people, I call,
    and my cry is to all that live.
5 O simple ones, learn prudence;
    acquire intelligence, you who
    lack it.
6 Hear, for I will speak noble
    things,
    and from my lips will come
    what is right;
7 for my mouth will utter truth;
    wickedness is an abomination
    to my lips.
8 All the words of my mouth are
    righteous;
    there is nothing twisted or
    crooked in them.
9 They are all straight to one who
    understands
    and right to those who find
    knowledge.
10 Take my instruction instead of
    silver,
    and knowledge rather than
    choice gold;
11 for wisdom is better than jewels,
    and all that you may desire
    cannot compare with her.
12 I, wisdom, live with prudence,*s*
    and I attain knowledge and
    discretion.
13 The fear of the LORD is hatred of
    evil.
    Pride and arrogance and the
    way of evil
    and perverted speech I hate.
14 I have good advice and sound
    wisdom;
    I have insight, I have strength.
15 By me kings reign,
    and rulers decree what is just;
16 by me rulers rule,
    and nobles, all who govern
    rightly.
17 I love those who love me,
    and those who seek me
    diligently find me.

18 Riches and honor are with me,
    enduring wealth and
    prosperity.
19 My fruit is better than gold, even
    fine gold,
    and my yield than choice
    silver.
20 I walk in the way of
    righteousness,
    along the paths of justice,
21 endowing with wealth those who
    love me,
    and filling their treasuries.

Wisdom's Part in Creation
(Cp Jn 1.1–3)

22 The LORD created me at the
    beginning*t* of his work,*u*
    the first of his acts of long
    ago.
23 Ages ago I was set up,
    at the first, before the
    beginning of the earth.
24 When there were no depths I
    was brought forth,
    when there were no springs
    abounding with water.
25 Before the mountains had been
    shaped,
    before the hills, I was brought
    forth—
26 when he had not yet made earth
    and fields,*s*
    or the world's first bits of soil.
27 When he established the
    heavens, I was there,
    when he drew a circle on the
    face of the deep,
28 when he made firm the skies
    above,
    when he established the
    fountains of the deep,
29 when he assigned to the sea its
    limit,
    so that the waters might not
    transgress his command,
    when he marked out the
    foundations of the earth,
30 then I was beside him, like a
    master worker;*v*
    and I was daily his*w* delight,
    rejoicing before him always,
31 rejoicing in his inhabited world
    and delighting in the human
    race.

*s*Meaning of Heb uncertain   *t*Or *me as
the beginning*   *u*Heb *way*   *v*Another
reading is *little child*   *w*Gk: Heb lacks
his

32 And now, my children, listen to
me:
 happy are those who keep my
 ways.
33 Hear instruction and be wise,
 and do not neglect it.
34 Happy is the one who listens to
me,
 watching daily at my gates,
 waiting beside my doors.
35 For whoever finds me finds life
 and obtains favor from the
 LORD;
36 but those who miss me injure
 themselves;
 all who hate me love death."

Wisdom's Feast

9 Wisdom has built her house,
 she has hewn her seven
 pillars.
2 She has slaughtered her animals,
 she has mixed her wine,
 she has also set her table.
3 She has sent out her
 servant-girls, she calls
 from the highest places in the
 town,
4 "You that are simple, turn in
here!"
 To those without sense she
 says,
5 "Come, eat of my bread
 and drink of the wine I have
 mixed.
6 Lay aside immaturity,x and live,
 and walk in the way of
 insight."

General Maxims

7 Whoever corrects a scoffer wins
 abuse;
 whoever rebukes the wicked
 gets hurt.
8 A scoffer who is rebuked will
 only hate you;
 the wise, when rebuked, will
 love you.
9 Give instructiony to the wise,
 and they will become wiser
 still;
 teach the righteous and they
 will gain in learning.
10 The fear of the LORD is the
 beginning of wisdom,
 and the knowledge of the Holy
 One is insight.
11 For by me your days will be
 multiplied,
 and years will be added to
 your life.

12 If you are wise, you are wise for
 yourself;
 if you scoff, you alone will
 bear it.

Folly's Invitation and Promise

13 The foolish woman is loud;
 she is ignorant and knows
 nothing.
14 She sits at the door of her house,
 on a seat at the high places of
 the town,
15 calling to those who pass by,
 who are going straight on their
 way,
16 "You who are simple, turn in
here!"
 And to those without sense
 she says,
17 "Stolen water is sweet,
 and bread eaten in secret is
 pleasant."
18 But they do not know that the
 deadz are there,
 that her guests are in the
 depths of Shēʹōl.

Wise Sayings of Solomon

10 The proverbs of Solomon.

 A wise child makes a glad
 father,
 but a foolish child is a
 mother's grief.
2 Treasures gained by wickedness
 do not profit,
 but righteousness delivers
 from death.
3 The LORD does not let the
 righteous go hungry,
 but he thwarts the craving of
 the wicked.
4 A slack hand causes poverty,
 but the hand of the diligent
 makes rich.
5 A child who gathers in summer
 is prudent,
 but a child who sleeps in
 harvest brings shame.
6 Blessings are on the head of the
 righteous,
 but the mouth of the wicked
 conceals violence.
7 The memory of the righteous is
 a blessing,
 but the name of the wicked
 will rot.

x Or simpleness y Heb lacks instruction
z Heb shades

8 The wise of heart will heed
commandments,
but a babbling fool will come
to ruin.
9 Whoever walks in integrity
walks securely,
but whoever follows perverse
ways will be found out.
10 Whoever winks the eye causes
trouble,
but the one who rebukes
boldly makes peace.[a]
11 The mouth of the righteous is a
fountain of life,
but the mouth of the wicked
conceals violence.
12 Hatred stirs up strife,
but love covers all offenses.
13 On the lips of one who has
understanding wisdom is
found,
but a rod is for the back of
one who lacks sense.
14 The wise lay up knowledge,
but the babbling of a fool
brings ruin near.
15 The wealth of the rich is their
fortress;
the poverty of the poor is their
ruin.
16 The wage of the righteous leads
to life,
the gain of the wicked to sin.
17 Whoever heeds instruction is on
the path to life,
but one who rejects a rebuke
goes astray.
18 Lying lips conceal hatred,
and whoever utters slander is
a fool.
19 When words are many,
transgression is not
lacking,
but the prudent are restrained
in speech.
20 The tongue of the righteous is
choice silver;
the mind of the wicked is of
little worth.
21 The lips of the righteous feed
many,
but fools die for lack of sense.
22 The blessing of the LORD makes
rich,
and he adds no sorrow with
it.[b]
23 Doing wrong is like sport to a
fool,
but wise conduct is pleasure to
a person of understanding.
24 What the wicked dread will
come upon them,

but the desire of the righteous
will be granted.
25 When the tempest passes, the
wicked are no more,
but the righteous are
established forever.
26 Like vinegar to the teeth, and
smoke to the eyes,
so are the lazy to their
employers.
27 The fear of the LORD prolongs
life,
but the years of the wicked
will be short.
28 The hope of the righteous ends
in gladness,
but the expectation of the
wicked comes to nothing.
29 The way of the LORD is a
stronghold for the upright,
but destruction for evildoers.
30 The righteous will never be
removed,
but the wicked will not remain
in the land.
31 The mouth of the righteous
brings forth wisdom,
but the perverse tongue will be
cut off.
32 The lips of the righteous know
what is acceptable,
but the mouth of the wicked
what is perverse.

11 A false balance is an
abomination to the LORD,
but an accurate weight is his
delight.
2 When pride comes, then comes
disgrace;
but wisdom is with the
humble.
3 The integrity of the upright
guides them,
but the crookedness of the
treacherous destroys them.
4 Riches do not profit in the day
of wrath,
but righteousness delivers
from death.
5 The righteousness of the
blameless keeps their ways
straight,
but the wicked fall by their
own wickedness.
6 The righteousness of the upright
saves them,
but the treacherous are taken
captive by their schemes.

[a] Gk: Heb *but a babbling fool will come
to ruin*   [b] Or *and toil adds nothing to it*

7 When the wicked die, their hope
        perishes,
    and the expectation of the
        godless comes to nothing.
8 The righteous are delivered from
        trouble,
    and the wicked get into it
        instead.
9 With their mouths the godless
        would destroy their
        neighbors,
    but by knowledge the
        righteous are delivered.
10 When it goes well with the
        righteous, the city rejoices;
    and when the wicked perish,
        there is jubilation.
11 By the blessing of the upright a
        city is exalted,
    but it is overthrown by the
        mouth of the wicked.
12 Whoever belittles another lacks
        sense,
    but an intelligent person
        remains silent.
13 A gossip goes about telling
        secrets,
    but one who is trustworthy in
        spirit keeps a confidence.
14 Where there is no guidance, a
        nation*c* falls,
    but in an abundance of
        counselors there is safety.
15 To guarantee loans for a
        stranger brings trouble,
    but there is safety in refusing
        to do so.
16 A gracious woman gets honor,
    but she who hates virtue is
        covered with shame.*d*
    The timid become destitute,*e*
    but the aggressive gain riches.
17 Those who are kind reward
        themselves,
    but the cruel do themselves
        harm.
18 The wicked earn no real gain,
    but those who sow
        righteousness get a true
        reward.
19 Whoever is steadfast in
        righteousness will live,
    but whoever pursues evil will
        die.
20 Crooked minds are an
        abomination to the LORD,
    but those of blameless ways
        are his delight.
21 Be assured, the wicked will not
        go unpunished,
    but those who are righteous
        will escape.

22 Like a gold ring in a pig's snout
    is a beautiful woman without
        good sense.
23 The desire of the righteous ends
        only in good;
    the expectation of the wicked
        in wrath.
24 Some give freely, yet grow all
        the richer;
    others withhold what is due,
        and only suffer want.
25 A generous person will be
        enriched,
    and one who gives water will
        get water.
26 The people curse those who hold
        back grain,
    but a blessing is on the head
        of those who sell it.
27 Whoever diligently seeks good
        seeks favor,
    but evil comes to the one who
        searches for it.
28 Those who trust in their riches
        will wither,*f*
    but the righteous will flourish
        like green leaves.
29 Those who trouble their
        households will inherit
        wind,
    and the fool will be servant to
        the wise.
30 The fruit of the righteous is a
        tree of life,
    but violence*g* takes lives
        away.
31 If the righteous are repaid on
        earth,
    how much more the wicked
        and the sinner!

12 Whoever loves discipline
        loves knowledge,
    but those who hate to be
        rebuked are stupid.
2 The good obtain favor from the
        LORD,
    but those who devise evil he
        condemns.
3 No one finds security by
        wickedness,
    but the root of the righteous
        will never be moved.
4 A good wife is the crown of her
        husband,

---

c Or *an army*   *d* Compare Gk Syr: Heb
lacks *but she . . . shame*   *e* Gk: Heb
lacks *The timid . . . destitute*   *f* Cn: Heb
fall   *g* Cn Compare Gk Syr: Heb *a wise
man*

but she who brings shame is
like rottenness in his
bones.

5 The thoughts of the righteous
are just;
the advice of the wicked is
treacherous.

6 The words of the wicked are a
deadly ambush,
but the speech of the upright
delivers them.

7 The wicked are overthrown and
are no more,
but the house of the righteous
will stand.

8 One is commended for good
sense,
but a perverse mind is
despised.

9 Better to be despised and have a
servant,
than to be self-important and
lack food.

10 The righteous know the needs of
their animals,
but the mercy of the wicked is
cruel.

11 Those who till their land will
have plenty of food,
but those who follow
worthless pursuits have no
sense.

12 The wicked covet the proceeds
of wickedness,*h*
but the root of the righteous
bears fruit.

13 The evil are ensnared by the
transgression of their lips,
but the righteous escape from
trouble.

14 From the fruit of the mouth one
is filled with good things,
and manual labor has its
reward.

15 Fools think their own way is
right,
but the wise listen to advice.

16 Fools show their anger at once,
but the prudent ignore an
insult.

17 Whoever speaks the truth gives
honest evidence,
but a false witness speaks
deceitfully.

18 Rash words are like sword
thrusts,
but the tongue of the wise
brings healing.

19 Truthful lips endure forever,
but a lying tongue lasts only a
moment.

20 Deceit is in the mind of those
who plan evil,
but those who counsel peace
have joy.

21 No harm happens to the
righteous,
but the wicked are filled with
trouble.

22 Lying lips are an abomination to
the LORD,
but those who act faithfully
are his delight.

23 One who is clever conceals
knowledge,
but the mind of a fool*i*
broadcasts folly.

24 The hand of the diligent will
rule,
while the lazy will be put to
forced labor.

25 Anxiety weighs down the human
heart,
but a good word cheers it up.

26 The righteous gives good advice
to friends,*j*
but the way of the wicked
leads astray.

27 The lazy do not roast*k* their
game,
but the diligent obtain precious
wealth.*k*

28 In the path of righteousness
there is life,
in walking its path there is no
death.

13 A wise child loves
discipline,*l*
but a scoffer does not listen to
rebuke.

2 From the fruit of their words
good persons eat good
things,
but the desire of the
treacherous is for
wrongdoing.

3 Those who guard their mouths
preserve their lives;
those who open wide their lips
come to ruin.

4 The appetite of the lazy craves,
and gets nothing,
while the appetite of the
diligent is richly supplied.

5 The righteous hate falsehood,
but the wicked act shamefully
and disgracefully.

h Or *covet the catch of the wicked*
i Heb *the heart of fools*   *j* Syr: Meaning
of Heb uncertain   *k* Meaning of Heb
uncertain   *l* Cn: Heb *A wise child the
discipline of his father*

6 Righteousness guards one whose
way is upright,
but sin overthrows the wicked.
7 Some pretend to be rich, yet
have nothing;
others pretend to be poor, yet
have great wealth.
8 Wealth is a ransom for a
person's life,
but the poor get no threats.
9 The light of the righteous
rejoices,
but the lamp of the wicked
goes out.
10 By insolence the heedless make
strife,
but wisdom is with those who
take advice.
11 Wealth hastily gotten[m] will
dwindle,
but those who gather little by
little will increase it.
12 Hope deferred makes the heart
sick,
but a desire fulfilled is a tree
of life.
13 Those who despise the word
bring destruction on
themselves,
but those who respect the
commandment will be
rewarded.
14 The teaching of the wise is a
fountain of life,
so that one may avoid the
snares of death.
15 Good sense wins favor,
but the way of the faithless is
their ruin.[n]
16 The clever do all things
intelligently,
but the fool displays folly.
17 A bad messenger brings trouble,
but a faithful envoy, healing.
18 Poverty and disgrace are for the
one who ignores
instruction,
but one who heeds reproof is
honored.
19 A desire realized is sweet to the
soul,
but to turn away from evil is
an abomination to fools.
20 Whoever walks with the wise
becomes wise,
but the companion of fools
suffers harm.
21 Misfortune pursues sinners,
but prosperity rewards the
righteous.
22 The good leave an inheritance to
their children's children,

but the sinner's wealth is laid
up for the righteous.
23 The field of the poor may yield
much food,
but it is swept away through
injustice.
24 Those who spare the rod hate
their children,
but those who love them are
diligent to discipline them.
25 The righteous have enough to
satisfy their appetite,
but the belly of the wicked is
empty.

14 The wise woman[o] builds her
house,
but the foolish tears it down
with her own hands.
2 Those who walk uprightly fear
the LORD,
but one who is devious in
conduct despises him.
3 The talk of fools is a rod for
their backs,[p]
but the lips of the wise
preserve them.
4 Where there are no oxen, there
is no grain;
abundant crops come by the
strength of the ox.
5 A faithful witness does not lie,
but a false witness breathes
out lies.
6 A scoffer seeks wisdom in vain,
but knowledge is easy for one
who understands.
7 Leave the presence of a fool,
for there you do not find
words of knowledge.
8 It is the wisdom of the clever to
understand where they go,
but the folly of fools misleads.
9 Fools mock at the guilt
offering,[q]
but the upright enjoy God's
favor.
10 The heart knows its own
bitterness,
and no stranger shares its joy.
11 The house of the wicked is
destroyed,
but the tent of the upright
flourishes.
12 There is a way that seems right
to a person,

---

[m] Gk Vg: Heb *from vanity*
[n] Cn Compare Gk Syr Vg Tg: Heb *is
enduring* [o] Heb *Wisdom of women*
[p] Cn: Heb *a rod of pride* [q] Meaning of
Heb uncertain

but its end is the way to
    death.[r]

13 Even in laughter the heart is
      sad,
    and the end of joy is grief.

14 The perverse get what their
      ways deserve,
    and the good, what their deeds
      deserve.[s]

15 The simple believe everything,
    but the clever consider their
      steps.

16 The wise are cautious and turn
      away from evil,
    but the fool throws off
      restraint and is careless.

17 One who is quick-tempered acts
      foolishly,
    and the schemer is hated.

18 The simple are adorned with[t]
      folly,
    but the clever are crowned
      with knowledge.

19 The evil bow down before the
      good,
    the wicked at the gates of the
      righteous.

20 The poor are disliked even by
      their neighbors,
    but the rich have many
      friends.

21 Those who despise their
      neighbors are sinners,
    but happy are those who are
      kind to the poor.

22 Do they not err that plan evil?
    Those who plan good find
      loyalty and faithfulness.

23 In all toil there is profit,
    but mere talk leads only to
      poverty.

24 The crown of the wise is their
      wisdom,[u]
    but folly is the garland[v] of
      fools.

25 A truthful witness saves lives,
    but one who utters lies is a
      betrayer.

26 In the fear of the LORD one has
      strong confidence,
    and one's children will have a
      refuge.

27 The fear of the LORD is a
      fountain of life,
    so that one may avoid the
      snares of death.

28 The glory of a king is a
      multitude of people;
    without people a prince is
      ruined.

29 Whoever is slow to anger has
      great understanding,

but one who has a hasty
    temper exalts folly.

30 A tranquil mind gives life to the
      flesh,
    but passion makes the bones
      rot.

31 Those who oppress the poor
      insult their Maker,
    but those who are kind to the
      needy honor him.

32 The wicked are overthrown by
      their evildoing,
    but the righteous find a refuge
      in their integrity.[w]

33 Wisdom is at home in the mind
      of one who has
      understanding,
    but it is not[x] known in the
      heart of fools.

34 Righteousness exalts a nation,
    but sin is a reproach to any
      people.

35 A servant who deals wisely has
      the king's favor,
    but his wrath falls on one who
      acts shamefully.

15 A soft answer turns away
      wrath,
    but a harsh word stirs up
      anger.

2 The tongue of the wise dispenses
      knowledge,[y]
    but the mouths of fools pour
      out folly.

3 The eyes of the LORD are in
      every place,
    keeping watch on the evil and
      the good.

4 A gentle tongue is a tree of life,
    but perverseness in it breaks
      the spirit.

5 A fool despises a parent's
      instruction,
    but the one who heeds
      admonition is prudent.

6 In the house of the righteous
      there is much treasure,
    but trouble befalls the income
      of the wicked.

7 The lips of the wise spread
      knowledge;
    not so the minds of fools.

8 The sacrifice of the wicked is an
      abomination to the LORD,

---

[r]Heb ways of death   [s]Cn: Heb from
upon him   [t]Or inherit   [u]Cn Compare
Gk: Heb riches   [v]Cn: Heb is the folly
[w]Gk Syr: Heb in their death   [x]Gk Syr:
Heb lacks not   [y]Cn: Heb makes
knowledge good

but the prayer of the upright is
his delight.

9 The way of the wicked is an
abomination to the LORD,
but he loves the one who
pursues righteousness.

10 There is severe discipline for one
who forsakes the way,
but one who hates a rebuke
will die.

11 Shē′ōl and A·bad′don lie open
before the LORD,
how much more human
hearts!

12 Scoffers do not like to be
rebuked;
they will not go to the wise.

13 A glad heart makes a cheerful
countenance,
but by sorrow of heart the
spirit is broken.

14 The mind of one who has
understanding seeks
knowledge,
but the mouths of fools feed
on folly.

15 All the days of the poor are
hard,
but a cheerful heart has a
continual feast.

16 Better is a little with the fear of
the LORD
than great treasure and trouble
with it.

17 Better is a dinner of vegetables
where love is
than a fatted ox and hatred
with it.

18 Those who are hot-tempered stir
up strife,
but those who are slow to
anger calm contention.

19 The way of the lazy is
overgrown with thorns,
but the path of the upright is a
level highway.

20 A wise child makes a glad
father,
but the foolish despise their
mothers.

21 Folly is a joy to one who has no
sense,
but a person of understanding
walks straight ahead.

22 Without counsel, plans go
wrong,
but with many advisers they
succeed.

23 To make an apt answer is a joy
to anyone,
and a word in season, how
good it is!

24 For the wise the path of life
leads upward,
in order to avoid Shē′ōl below.

25 The LORD tears down the house
of the proud,
but maintains the widow's
boundaries.

26 Evil plans are an abomination to
the LORD,
but gracious words are pure.

27 Those who are greedy for unjust
gain make trouble for their
households,
but those who hate bribes will
live.

28 The mind of the righteous
ponders how to answer,
but the mouth of the wicked
pours out evil.

29 The LORD is far from the
wicked,
but he hears the prayer of the
righteous.

30 The light of the eyes rejoices the
heart,
and good news refreshes the
body.

31 The ear that heeds wholesome
admonition
will lodge among the wise.

32 Those who ignore instruction
despise themselves,
but those who heed
admonition gain
understanding.

33 The fear of the LORD is
instruction in wisdom,
and humility goes before
honor.

16 The plans of the mind belong
to mortals,
but the answer of the tongue is
from the LORD.

2 All one's ways may be pure in
one's own eyes,
but the LORD weighs the spirit.

3 Commit your work to the LORD,
and your plans will be
established.

4 The LORD has made everything
for its purpose,
even the wicked for the day of
trouble.

5 All those who are arrogant are
an abomination to the
LORD;
be assured, they will not go
unpunished.

6 By loyalty and faithfulness
iniquity is atoned for,

and by the fear of the LORD
one avoids evil.

7 When the ways of people please
the LORD,
he causes even their enemies
to be at peace with them.

8 Better is a little with
righteousness
than large income with
injustice.

9 The human mind plans the way,
but the LORD directs the steps.

10 Inspired decisions are on the lips
of a king;
his mouth does not sin in
judgment.

11 Honest balances and scales are
the LORD's;
all the weights in the bag are
his work.

12 It is an abomination to kings to
do evil,
for the throne is established by
righteousness.

13 Righteous lips are the delight of
a king,
and he loves those who speak
what is right.

14 A king's wrath is a messenger of
death,
and whoever is wise will
appease it.

15 In the light of a king's face there
is life,
and his favor is like the clouds
that bring the spring rain.

16 How much better to get wisdom
than gold!
To get understanding is to be
chosen rather than silver.

17 The highway of the upright
avoids evil;
those who guard their way
preserve their lives.

18 Pride goes before destruction,
and a haughty spirit before a
fall.

19 It is better to be of a lowly spirit
among the poor
than to divide the spoil with
the proud.

20 Those who are attentive to a
matter will prosper,
and happy are those who trust
in the LORD.

21 The wise of heart is called
perceptive,
and pleasant speech increases
persuasiveness.

22 Wisdom is a fountain of life to
one who has it,

but folly is the punishment of
fools.

23 The mind of the wise makes
their speech judicious,
and adds persuasiveness to
their lips.

24 Pleasant words are like a
honeycomb,
sweetness to the soul and
health to the body.

25 Sometimes there is a way that
seems to be right,
but in the end it is the way to
death.

26 The appetite of workers works
for them;
their hunger urges them on.

27 Scoundrels concoct evil,
and their speech is like a
scorching fire.

28 A perverse person spreads strife,
and a whisperer separates
close friends.

29 The violent entice their
neighbors,
and lead them in a way that is
not good.

30 One who winks the eyes plans z
perverse things;
one who compresses the lips
brings evil to pass.

31 Gray hair is a crown of glory;
it is gained in a righteous life.

32 One who is slow to anger is
better than the mighty,
and one whose temper is
controlled than one who
captures a city.

33 The lot is cast into the lap,
but the decision is the LORD's
alone.

17 Better is a dry morsel with
quiet
than a house full of feasting
with strife.

2 A slave who deals wisely will
rule over a child who acts
shamefully,
and will share the inheritance
as one of the family.

3 The crucible is for silver, and the
furnace is for gold,
but the LORD tests the heart.

4 An evildoer listens to wicked
lips;
and a liar gives heed to a
mischievous tongue.

5 Those who mock the poor insult
their Maker;

z Gk Syr Vg Tg: Heb *to plan*

those who are glad at calamity
  will not go unpunished.

6 Grandchildren are the crown of
    the aged,
  and the glory of children is
    their parents.

7 Fine speech is not becoming to a
    fool;
  still less is false speech to a
    ruler.^a

8 A bribe is like a magic stone in
    the eyes of those who give
    it;
  wherever they turn they
    prosper.

9 One who forgives an affront
    fosters friendship,
  but one who dwells on
    disputes will alienate a
    friend.

10 A rebuke strikes deeper into a
    discerning person
  than a hundred blows into a
    fool.

11 Evil people seek only rebellion,
  but a cruel messenger will be
    sent against them.

12 Better to meet a she-bear robbed
    of its cubs
  than to confront a fool
    immersed in folly.

13 Evil will not depart from the
    house
  of one who returns evil for
    good.

14 The beginning of strife is like
    letting out water;
  so stop before the quarrel
    breaks out.

15 One who justifies the wicked
    and one who condemns the
    righteous
  are both alike an abomination
    to the LORD.

16 Why should fools have a price in
    hand
  to buy wisdom, when they
    have no mind to learn?

17 A friend loves at all times,
  and kinsfolk are born to share
    adversity.

18 It is senseless to give a pledge,
  to become surety for a
    neighbor.

19 One who loves transgression
    loves strife;
  one who builds a high
    threshold invites broken
    bones.

20 The crooked of mind do not
    prosper,

and the perverse of tongue fall
  into calamity.

21 The one who begets a fool gets
    trouble;
  the parent of a fool has no joy.

22 A cheerful heart is a good
    medicine,
  but a downcast spirit dries up
    the bones.

23 The wicked accept a concealed
    bribe
  to pervert the ways of justice.

24 The discerning person looks to
    wisdom,
  but the eyes of a fool to the
    ends of the earth.

25 Foolish children are a grief to
    their father
  and bitterness to her who bore
    them.

26 To impose a fine on the innocent
    is not right,
  or to flog the noble for their
    integrity.

27 One who spares words is
    knowledgeable;
  one who is cool in spirit has
    understanding.

28 Even fools who keep silent are
    considered wise;
  when they close their lips, they
    are deemed intelligent.

18

The one who lives alone is
  self-indulgent,
  showing contempt for all who
    have sound judgment.^b

2 A fool takes no pleasure in
    understanding,
  but only in expressing
    personal opinion.

3 When wickedness comes,
    contempt comes also;
  and with dishonor comes
    disgrace.

4 The words of the mouth are
    deep waters;
  the fountain of wisdom is a
    gushing stream.

5 It is not right to be partial to the
    guilty,
  or to subvert the innocent in
    judgment.

6 A fool's lips bring strife,
  and a fool's mouth invites a
    flogging.

7 The mouths of fools are their
    ruin,
  and their lips a snare to
    themselves.

^aOr *a noble person*   ^bMeaning of Heb
uncertain

8 The words of a whisperer are
    like delicious morsels;
  they go down into the inner
    parts of the body.
9 One who is slack in work
  is close kin to a vandal.
10 The name of the LORD is a
    strong tower;
  the righteous run into it and
    are safe.
11 The wealth of the rich is their
    strong city;
  in their imagination it is like a
    high wall.
12 Before destruction one's heart is
    haughty,
  but humility goes before
    honor.
13 If one gives answer before
    hearing,
  it is folly and shame.
14 The human spirit will endure
    sickness;
  but a broken spirit—who can
    bear?
15 An intelligent mind acquires
    knowledge,
  and the ear of the wise seeks
    knowledge.
16 A gift opens doors;
  it gives access to the great.
17 The one who first states a case
    seems right,
  until the other comes and
    cross-examines.
18 Casting the lot puts an end to
    disputes
  and decides between powerful
    contenders.
19 An ally offended is stronger than
    a city;c
  such quarreling is like the bars
    of a castle.
20 From the fruit of the mouth
    one's stomach is satisfied;
  the yield of the lips brings
    satisfaction.
21 Death and life are in the power
    of the tongue,
  and those who love it will eat
    its fruits.
22 He who finds a wife finds a good
    thing,
  and obtains favor from the
    LORD.
23 The poor use entreaties,
  but the rich answer roughly.
24 Somed friends play at
    friendshipe
  but a true friend sticks closer
    than one's nearest kin.

19 Better the poor walking in
    integrity
  than one perverse of speech
    who is a fool.
2 Desire without knowledge is not
    good,
  and one who moves too
    hurriedly misses the way.
3 One's own folly leads to ruin,
  yet the heart rages against the
    LORD.
4 Wealth brings many friends,
  but the poor are left friendless.
5 A false witness will not go
    unpunished,
  and a liar will not escape.
6 Many seek the favor of the
    generous,
  and everyone is a friend to a
    giver of gifts.
7 If the poor are hated even by
    their kin,
  how much more are they
    shunned by their friends!
  When they call after them, they
    are not there.f
8 To get wisdom is to love oneself;
  to keep understanding is to
    prosper.
9 A false witness will not go
    unpunished,
  and the liar will perish.
10 It is not fitting for a fool to live
    in luxury,
  much less for a slave to rule
    over princes.
11 Those with good sense are slow
    to anger,
  and it is their glory to
    overlook an offense.
12 A king's anger is like the
    growling of a lion,
  but his favor is like dew on the
    grass.
13 A stupid child is ruin to a father,
  and a wife's quarreling is a
    continual dripping of rain.
14 House and wealth are inherited
    from parents,
  but a prudent wife is from the
    LORD.
15 Laziness brings on deep sleep;
  an idle person will suffer
    hunger.
16 Those who keep the
    commandment will live;

cGk Syr Vg Tg: Meaning of Heb
uncertain   dSyr Tg: Heb A man of
eCn Compare Syr Vg Tg: Meaning of
Heb uncertain   fMeaning of Heb
uncertain

those who are heedless of their
ways will die.

17 Whoever is kind to the poor
    lends to the LORD,
  and will be repaid in full.

18 Discipline your children while
    there is hope;
  do not set your heart on their
    destruction.

19 A violent tempered person will
    pay the penalty;
  if you effect a rescue, you will
    only have to do it again.*g*

20 Listen to advice and accept
    instruction,
  that you may gain wisdom for
    the future.

21 The human mind may devise
    many plans,
  but it is the purpose of the
    LORD that will be
    established.

22 What is desirable in a person is
    loyalty,
  and it is better to be poor than
    a liar.

23 The fear of the LORD is life
    indeed;
  filled with it one rests secure
    and suffers no harm.

24 The lazy person buries a hand in
    the dish,
  and will not even bring it back
    to the mouth.

25 Strike a scoffer, and the simple
    will learn prudence;
  reprove the intelligent, and
    they will gain knowledge.

26 Those who do violence to their
    father and chase away
    their mother
  are children who cause shame
    and bring reproach.

27 Cease straying, my child, from
    the words of knowledge,
  in order that you may hear
    instruction.

28 A worthless witness mocks at
    justice,
  and the mouth of the wicked
    devours iniquity.

29 Condemnation is ready for
    scoffers,
  and flogging for the backs of
    fools.

20 Wine is a mocker, strong
    drink a brawler,
  and whoever is led astray by it
    is not wise.

2 The dread anger of a king is like
    the growling of a lion;

anyone who provokes him to
    anger forfeits life itself.

3 It is honorable to refrain from
    strife,
  but every fool is quick to
    quarrel.

4 The lazy person does not plow
    in season;
  harvest comes, and there is
    nothing to be found.

5 The purposes in the human mind
    are like deep water,
  but the intelligent will draw
    them out.

6 Many proclaim themselves loyal,
  but who can find one worthy
    of trust?

7 The righteous walk in
    integrity—
  happy are the children who
    follow them!

8 A king who sits on the throne of
    judgment
  winnows all evil with his eyes.

9 Who can say, "I have made my
    heart clean;
  I am pure from my sin"?

10 Diverse weights and diverse
    measures
  are both alike an abomination
    to the LORD.

11 Even children make themselves
    known by their acts,
  by whether what they do is
    pure and right.

12 The hearing ear and the seeing
    eye—
  the LORD has made them both.

13 Do not love sleep, or else you
    will come to poverty;
  open your eyes, and you will
    have plenty of bread.

14 "Bad, bad," says the buyer,
  then goes away and boasts.

15 There is gold, and abundance of
    costly stones;
  but the lips informed by
    knowledge are a precious
    jewel.

16 Take the garment of one who
    has given surety for a
    stranger;
  seize the pledge given as
    surety for foreigners.

17 Bread gained by deceit is sweet,
  but afterward the mouth will
    be full of gravel.

18 Plans are established by taking
    advice;

g Meaning of Heb uncertain

wage war by following wise
guidance.

19 A gossip reveals secrets;
therefore do not associate with
a babbler.

20 If you curse father or mother,
your lamp will go out in utter
darkness.

21 An estate quickly acquired in the
beginning
will not be blessed in the end.

22 Do not say, "I will repay evil";
wait for the LORD, and he will
help you.

23 Differing weights are an
abomination to the LORD,
and false scales are not good.

24 All our steps are ordered by the
LORD;
how then can we understand
our own ways?

25 It is a snare for one to say
rashly, "It is holy,"
and begin to reflect only after
making a vow.

26 A wise king winnows the
wicked,
and drives the wheel over
them.

27 The human spirit is the lamp of
the LORD,
searching every inmost part.

28 Loyalty and faithfulness
preserve the king,
and his throne is upheld by
righteousness.*h*

29 The glory of youths is their
strength,
but the beauty of the aged is
their gray hair.

30 Blows that wound cleanse away
evil;
beatings make clean the
innermost parts.

21 The king's heart is a stream
of water in the hand of the
LORD;
he turns it wherever he will.

2 All deeds are right in the sight
of the doer,
but the LORD weighs the heart.

3 To do righteousness and justice
is more acceptable to the LORD
than sacrifice.

4 Haughty eyes and a proud
heart—
the lamp of the wicked—are
sin.

5 The plans of the diligent lead
surely to abundance,
but everyone who is hasty
comes only to want.

6 The getting of treasures by a
lying tongue
is a fleeting vapor and a
snare*i* of death.

7 The violence of the wicked will
sweep them away,
because they refuse to do what
is just.

8 The way of the guilty is crooked,
but the conduct of the pure is
right.

9 It is better to live in a corner of
the housetop
than in a house shared with a
contentious wife.

10 The souls of the wicked desire
evil;
their neighbors find no mercy
in their eyes.

11 When a scoffer is punished, the
simple become wiser;
when the wise are instructed,
they increase in
knowledge.

12 The Righteous One observes the
house of the wicked;
he casts the wicked down to
ruin.

13 If you close your ear to the cry
of the poor,
you will cry out and not be
heard.

14 A gift in secret averts anger;
and a concealed bribe in the
bosom, strong wrath.

15 When justice is done, it is a joy
to the righteous,
but dismay to evildoers.

16 Whoever wanders from the way
of understanding
will rest in the assembly of the
dead.

17 Whoever loves pleasure will
suffer want;
whoever loves wine and oil
will not be rich.

18 The wicked is a ransom for the
righteous,
and the faithless for the
upright.

19 It is better to live in a desert
land
than with a contentious and
fretful wife.

20 Precious treasure remains*j* in
the house of the wise,
but the fool devours it.

21 Whoever pursues righteousness
and kindness

h Gk: Heb *loyalty*   *i* Gk: Heb *seekers*
j Gk: Heb *and oil*

will find life[k] and honor.

2 One wise person went up against
 a city of warriors
 and brought down the
 stronghold in which they
 trusted.

3 To watch over mouth and
 tongue
 is to keep out of trouble.

4 The proud, haughty person,
 named "Scoffer,"
 acts with arrogant pride.

5 The craving of the lazy person is
 fatal,
 for lazy hands refuse to labor.

6 All day long the wicked covet,[l]
 but the righteous give and do
 not hold back.

7 The sacrifice of the wicked is an
 abomination;
 how much more when brought
 with evil intent.

8 A false witness will perish,
 but a good listener will testify
 successfully.

9 The wicked put on a bold face,
 but the upright give thought
 to[m] their ways.

10 No wisdom, no understanding,
 no counsel,
 can avail against the LORD.

11 The horse is made ready for the
 day of battle,
 but the victory belongs to the
 LORD.

22 A good name is to be chosen
 rather than great riches,
 and favor is better than silver
 or gold.

2 The rich and the poor have this
 in common:
 the LORD is the maker of them
 all.

3 The clever see danger and hide;
 but the simple go on, and
 suffer for it.

4 The reward for humility and fear
 of the LORD
 is riches and honor and life.

5 Thorns and snares are in the
 way of the perverse;
 the cautious will keep far from
 them.

6 Train children in the right way,
 and when old, they will not
 stray.

7 The rich rules over the poor,
 and the borrower is the slave
 of the lender.

8 Whoever sows injustice will reap
 calamity,
 and the rod of anger will fail.

9 Those who are generous are
 blessed,
 for they share their bread with
 the poor.

10 Drive out a scoffer, and strife
 goes out;
 quarreling and abuse will
 cease.

11 Those who love a pure heart and
 are gracious in speech
 will have the king as a friend.

12 The eyes of the LORD keep
 watch over knowledge,
 but he overthrows the words
 of the faithless.

13 The lazy person says, "There is a
 lion outside!
 I shall be killed in the streets!"

14 The mouth of a loose[n] woman is
 a deep pit;
 he with whom the LORD is
 angry falls into it.

15 Folly is bound up in the heart of
 a boy,
 but the rod of discipline drives
 it far away.

16 Oppressing the poor in order to
 enrich oneself,
 and giving to the rich, will
 lead only to loss.

Sayings of the Wise

17   The words of the wise:

Incline your ear and hear my
 words,[o]
 and apply your mind to my
 teaching;

18 for it will be pleasant if you
 keep them within you,
 if all of them are ready on
 your lips.

19 So that your trust may be in the
 LORD,
 I have made them known to
 you today—yes, to you.

20 Have I not written for you thirty
 sayings
 of admonition and knowledge,

21 to show you what is right and
 true,
 so that you may give a true
 answer to those who sent
 you?

k Gk: Heb *life and righteousness*
l Gk: Heb *all day long one covets
covetously*   m Another reading is
establish   n Heb *strange*
o Cn Compare Gk: Heb *Incline your ear,
and hear the words of the wise*

P
R
O
V
E
R
B
S

22 Do not rob the poor because
       they are poor,
    or crush the afflicted at the
       gate;
23 for the LORD pleads their cause
    and despoils of life those who
       despoil them.
24 Make no friends with those
       given to anger,
    and do not associate with
       hotheads,
25 or you may learn their ways
    and entangle yourself in a
       snare.
26 Do not be one of those who give
       pledges,
    who become surety for debts.
27 If you have nothing with which
       to pay,
    why should your bed be taken
       from under you?
28 Do not remove the ancient
       landmark
    that your ancestors set up.
29 Do you see those who are
       skillful in their work?
    they will serve kings;
    they will not serve common
       people.

23 When you sit down to eat
    with a ruler,
    observe carefully what*p* is
       before you,
2 and put a knife to your throat
    if you have a big appetite.
3 Do not desire the ruler's*q*
       delicacies,
    for they are deceptive food.
4 Do not wear yourself out to get
       rich;
    be wise enough to desist.
5 When your eyes light upon it, it
       is gone;
    for suddenly it takes wings to
       itself,
    flying like an eagle toward
       heaven.
6 Do not eat the bread of the
       stingy;
    do not desire their delicacies;
7 for like a hair in the throat, so
    are they.*r*
    "Eat and drink!" they say to
       you;
    but they do not mean it.
8 You will vomit up the little you
       have eaten,
    and you will waste your
       pleasant words.
9 Do not speak in the hearing of a
       fool,

who will only despise the
       wisdom of your words.
10 Do not remove an ancient
       landmark
    or encroach on the fields of
       orphans;
11 for their redeemer is strong;
    he will plead their cause
       against you.
12 Apply your mind to instruction
    and your ear to words of
       knowledge.
13 Do not withhold discipline from
       your children;
    if you beat them with a rod,
       they will not die.
14 If you beat them with the rod,
    you will save their lives from
       Shē'ōl.
15 My child, if your heart is wise,
    my heart too will be glad.
16 My soul will rejoice
    when your lips speak what is
       right.
17 Do not let your heart envy
       sinners,
    but always continue in the fear
       of the LORD.
18 Surely there is a future,
    and your hope will not be cut
       off.

19 Hear, my child, and be wise,
    and direct your mind in the
       way.
20 Do not be among winebibbers,
    or among gluttonous eaters of
       meat;
21 for the drunkard and the glutton
    will come to poverty,
    and drowsiness will clothe
       them with rags.

22 Listen to your father who begot
       you,
    and do not despise your
       mother when she is old.
23 Buy truth, and do not sell it;
    buy wisdom, instruction, and
       understanding.
24 The father of the righteous will
       greatly rejoice;
    he who begets a wise son will
       be glad in him.
25 Let your father and mother be
       glad;
    let her who bore you rejoice.

26 My child, give me your heart,

p Or *who*   *q* Heb *his*   *r* Meaning of Heb
uncertain

and let your eyes observe[s] my
    ways.
7 For a prostitute is a deep pit;
    an adulteress[t] is a narrow
      well.
8 She lies in wait like a robber
    and increases the number of
      the faithless.

9 Who has woe? Who has sorrow?
    Who has strife? Who has
      complaining?
    Who has wounds without cause?
    Who has redness of eyes?
10 Those who linger late over wine,
    those who keep trying mixed
      wines.
11 Do not look at wine when it is
    red,
    when it sparkles in the cup
    and goes down smoothly.
12 At the last it bites like a serpent,
    and stings like an adder.
13 Your eyes will see strange
    things,
    and your mind utter perverse
      things.
14 You will be like one who lies
    down in the midst of the
      sea,
    like one who lies on the top of
      a mast.[u]
15 "They struck me," you will say,[v]
    "but I was not hurt;
    they beat me, but I did not feel
      it.
    When shall I awake?
    I will seek another drink."

24 Do not envy the wicked,
    nor desire to be with them;
2 for their minds devise violence,
    and their lips talk of mischief.

3 By wisdom a house is built,
    and by understanding it is
      established;
4 by knowledge the rooms are
    filled
    with all precious and pleasant
      riches.
5 Wise warriors are mightier than
    strong ones,[w]
    and those who have
      knowledge than those who
      have strength;
6 for by wise guidance you can
    wage your war,
    and in abundance of
      counselors there is victory.
7 Wisdom is too high for fools;
    in the gate they do not open
      their mouths.

8 Whoever plans to do evil
    will be called a
      mischief-maker.
9 The devising of folly is sin,
    and the scoffer is an
      abomination to all.

10 If you faint in the day of
    adversity,
    your strength being small;
11 if you hold back from rescuing
    those taken away to death,
    those who go staggering to the
      slaughter;
12 if you say, "Look, we did not
    know this" —
    does not he who weighs the
      heart perceive it?
    Does not he who keeps watch
      over your soul know it?
    And will he not repay all
      according to their deeds?

13 My child, eat honey, for it is
    good,
    and the drippings of the
      honeycomb are sweet to
      your taste.
14 Know that wisdom is such to
    your soul;
    if you find it, you will find a
      future,
    and your hope will not be cut
      off.

15 Do not lie in wait like an outlaw
    against the home of the
      righteous;
    do no violence to the place
      where the righteous live;
16 for though they fall seven times,
    they will rise again;
    but the wicked are overthrown
      by calamity.

17 Do not rejoice when your
    enemies fall,
    and do not let your heart be
      glad when they stumble,
18 or else the LORD will see it and
    be displeased,
    and turn away his anger from
      them.

19 Do not fret because of evildoers.
    Do not envy the wicked;

[s] Another reading is *delight in*
[t] Heb *an alien woman*   [u] Meaning of
Heb uncertain   [v] Gk Syr Vg Tg: Heb
lacks *you will say*   [w] Gk Compare Syr
Tg: Heb *A wise man is strength*

20 for the evil have no future;
   the lamp of the wicked will go
      out.

21 My child, fear the LORD and the
      king,
   and do not disobey either of
      them;[x]
22 for disaster comes from them
      suddenly,
   and who knows the ruin that
      both can bring?

Further Sayings of the Wise

23 These also are sayings of the
      wise:

Partiality in judging is not good.
24 Whoever says to the wicked,
   "You are innocent,"
   will be cursed by peoples,
   abhorred by nations;
25 but those who rebuke the
      wicked will have delight,
   and a good blessing will come
      upon them.
26 One who gives an honest answer
   gives a kiss on the lips.

27 Prepare your work outside,
   get everything ready for you in
      the field;
   and after that build your
      house.

28 Do not be a witness against your
      neighbor without cause,
   and do not deceive with your
      lips.
29 Do not say, "I will do to others
      as they have done to me;
   I will pay them back for what
      they have done."

30 I passed by the field of one who
      was lazy,
   by the vineyard of a stupid
      person;
31 and see, it was all overgrown
      with thorns;
   the ground was covered with
      nettles,
   and its stone wall was broken
      down.
32 Then I saw and considered it;
   I looked and received
      instruction.
33 A little sleep, a little slumber,
   a little folding of the hands to
      rest,

34 and poverty will come upon you
      like a robber,
   and want, like an armed
      warrior.

Further Wise Sayings of Solomon

25 These are other proverbs o
   Solomon that the officials o
King Hez·e·ki′ah of Judah copied.

2 It is the glory of God to conceal
      things,
   but the glory of kings is to
      search things out.
3 Like the heavens for height, like
      the earth for depth,
   so the mind of kings is
      unsearchable.
4 Take away the dross from the
      silver,
   and the smith has material for
      a vessel;
5 take away the wicked from the
      presence of the king,
   and his throne will be
      established in
      righteousness.
6 Do not put yourself forward in
      the king's presence
   or stand in the place of the
      great;
7 for it is better to be told, "Come
      up here,"
   than to be put lower in the
      presence of a noble.

What your eyes have seen
8   do not hastily bring into court;
   for[y] what will you do in the
      end,
   when your neighbor puts you
      to shame?
9 Argue your case with your
      neighbor directly,
   and do not disclose another's
      secret;
10 or else someone who hears you
      will bring shame upon you,
   and your ill repute will have
      no end.

11 A word fitly spoken
   is like apples of gold in a
      setting of silver.
12 Like a gold ring or an ornament
      of gold
   is a wise rebuke to a listening
      ear.

x Gk: Heb *do not associate with those
who change*   y Cn: Heb *or else*

13 Like the cold of snow in the time
    of harvest
    are faithful messengers to
        those who send them;
    they refresh the spirit of their
        masters.
14 Like clouds and wind without
    rain
    is one who boasts of a gift
        never given.
15 With patience a ruler may be
        persuaded,
    and a soft tongue can break
        bones.
16 If you have found honey, eat
        only enough for you,
    or else, having too much, you
        will vomit it.
17 Let your foot be seldom in your
        neighbor's house,
    otherwise the neighbor will
        become weary of you and
        hate you.
18 Like a war club, a sword, or a
        sharp arrow
    is one who bears false witness
        against a neighbor.
19 Like a bad tooth or a lame foot
    is trust in a faithless person in
        time of trouble.
20 Like vinegar on a wound[z]
    is one who sings songs to a
        heavy heart.
    Like a moth in clothing or a
        worm in wood,
    sorrow gnaws at the human
        heart.[a]
21 If your enemies are hungry, give
        them bread to eat;
    and if they are thirsty, give
        them water to drink;
22 for you will heap coals of fire on
        their heads,
    and the LORD will reward you.
23 The north wind produces rain,
    and a backbiting tongue,
        angry looks.
24 It is better to live in a corner of
        the housetop
    than in a house shared with a
        contentious wife.
25 Like cold water to a thirsty soul,
    so is good news from a far
        country.
26 Like a muddied spring or a
        polluted fountain
    are the righteous who give
        way before the wicked.
27 It is not good to eat much honey,
    or to seek honor on top of
        honor.

28 Like a city breached, without
        walls,
    is one who lacks self-control.

26 Like snow in summer or rain
    in harvest,
    so honor is not fitting for a
        fool.
2 Like a sparrow in its flitting, like
        a swallow in its flying,
    an undeserved curse goes
        nowhere.
3 A whip for the horse, a bridle
        for the donkey,
    and a rod for the back of fools.
4 Do not answer fools according
        to their folly,
    or you will be a fool yourself.
5 Answer fools according to their
        folly,
    or they will be wise in their
        own eyes.
6 It is like cutting off one's foot
        and drinking down
        violence,
    to send a message by a fool.
7 The legs of a disabled person
        hang limp;
    so does a proverb in the
        mouth of a fool.
8 It is like binding a stone in a
        sling
    to give honor to a fool.
9 Like a thornbush brandished by
        the hand of a drunkard
    is a proverb in the mouth of a
        fool.
10 Like an archer who wounds
        everybody
    is one who hires a passing fool
        or drunkard.[b]
11 Like a dog that returns to its
        vomit
    is a fool who reverts to his
        folly.
12 Do you see persons wise in their
        own eyes?
    There is more hope for fools
        than for them.
13 The lazy person says, "There is a
        lion in the road!
    There is a lion in the streets!"
14 As a door turns on its hinges,
    so does a lazy person in bed.
15 The lazy person buries a hand in
        the dish,

z Gk: Heb *Like one who takes off a
garment on a cold day, like vinegar on
lye*   a Gk Syr Tg: Heb lacks *Like a
moth... human heart*   b Meaning of
Heb uncertain

and is too tired to bring it
    back to the mouth.
16 The lazy person is wiser in
    self-esteem
    than seven who can answer
    discreetly.
17 Like somebody who takes a
    passing dog by the ears
    is one who meddles in the
    quarrel of another.
18 Like a maniac who shoots
    deadly firebrands and
    arrows,
19 so is one who deceives a
    neighbor
    and says, "I am only joking!"
20 For lack of wood the fire goes
    out,
    and where there is no
    whisperer, quarreling
    ceases.
21 As charcoal is to hot embers and
    wood to fire,
    so is a quarrelsome person for
    kindling strife.
22 The words of a whisperer are
    like delicious morsels;
    they go down into the inner
    parts of the body.
23 Like the glaze[c] covering an
    earthen vessel
    are smooth[d] lips with an evil
    heart.
24 An enemy dissembles in
    speaking
    while harboring deceit within;
25 when an enemy speaks
    graciously, do not believe
    it,
    for there are seven
    abominations concealed
    within;
26 though hatred is covered with
    guile,
    the enemy's wickedness will
    be exposed in the
    assembly.
27 Whoever digs a pit will fall into
    it,
    and a stone will come back on
    the one who starts it
    rolling.
28 A lying tongue hates its victims,
    and a flattering mouth works
    ruin.

27 Do not boast about tomorrow,
    for you do not know what a
    day may bring.
2 Let another praise you, and not
    your own mouth—
    a stranger, and not your own
    lips.

3 A stone is heavy, and sand is
    weighty,
    but a fool's provocation is
    heavier than both.
4 Wrath is cruel, anger is
    overwhelming,
    but who is able to stand before
    jealousy?
5 Better is open rebuke
    than hidden love.
6 Well meant are the wounds a
    friend inflicts,
    but profuse are the kisses of
    an enemy.
7 The sated appetite spurns honey,
    but to a ravenous appetite
    even the bitter is sweet.
8 Like a bird that strays from its
    nest
    is one who strays from home.
9 Perfume and incense make the
    heart glad,
    but the soul is torn by
    trouble.[e]
10 Do not forsake your friend or
    the friend of your parent;
    do not go to the house of your
    kindred in the day of your
    calamity.
    Better is a neighbor who is
    nearby
    than kindred who are far
    away.
11 Be wise, my child, and make my
    heart glad,
    so that I may answer whoever
    reproaches me.
12 The clever see danger and hide;
    but the simple go on, and
    suffer for it.
13 Take the garment of one who
    has given surety for a
    stranger;
    seize the pledge given as
    surety for foreigners.[f]
14 Whoever blesses a neighbor with
    a loud voice,
    rising early in the morning,
    will be counted as cursing.
15 A continual dripping on a rainy
    day
    and a contentious wife are
    alike;
16 to restrain her is to restrain the
    wind

*c*Cn: Heb *silver of dross*   *d*Gk: Heb
burning   *e*Gk: Heb *the sweetness of a*
friend is better than one's own counsel
*f*Vg and 20.16: Heb *for a foreign woman*

or to grasp oil in the right
    hand.[g]

7 Iron sharpens iron,
    and one person sharpens the
      wits[h] of another.

8 Anyone who tends a fig tree will
    eat its fruit,
    and anyone who takes care of
      a master will be honored.

9 Just as water reflects the face,
    so one human heart reflects
      another.

10 Shē′ōl and A·bad′don are never
    satisfied,
    and human eyes are never
      satisfied.

11 The crucible is for silver, and the
    furnace is for gold,
    so a person is tested[i] by
      being praised.

12 Crush a fool in a mortar with a
    pestle
    along with crushed grain,
    but the folly will not be driven
      out.

13 Know well the condition of your
    flocks,
    and give attention to your
      herds;

14 for riches do not last forever,
    nor a crown for all
      generations.

15 When the grass is gone, and
    new growth appears,
    and the herbage of the
      mountains is gathered,

16 the lambs will provide your
    clothing,
    and the goats the price of a
      field;

17 there will be enough goats' milk
    for your food,
    for the food of your household
    and nourishment for your
      servant-girls.

28 The wicked flee when no one
    pursues,
    but the righteous are as bold
      as a lion.

2 When a land rebels
    it has many rulers;
    but with an intelligent ruler
      there is lasting order.[g]

3 A ruler[j] who oppresses the poor
    is a beating rain that leaves no
      food.

4 Those who forsake the law
    praise the wicked,
    but those who keep the law
      struggle against them.

5 The evil do not understand
    justice,
    but those who seek the LORD
      understand it completely.

6 Better to be poor and walk in
    integrity
    than to be crooked in one's
      ways even though rich.

7 Those who keep the law are
    wise children,
    but companions of gluttons
      shame their parents.

8 One who augments wealth by
    exorbitant interest
    gathers it for another who is
      kind to the poor.

9 When one will not listen to the
    law,
    even one's prayers are an
      abomination.

10 Those who mislead the upright
    into evil ways
    will fall into pits of their own
      making,
    but the blameless will have a
      goodly inheritance.

11 The rich is wise in self-esteem,
    but an intelligent poor person
      sees through the pose.

12 When the righteous triumph,
    there is great glory,
    but when the wicked prevail,
      people go into hiding.

13 No one who conceals
    transgressions will prosper,
    but one who confesses and
      forsakes them will obtain
      mercy.

14 Happy is the one who is never
    without fear,
    but one who is hard-hearted
      will fall into calamity.

15 Like a roaring lion or a charging
    bear
    is a wicked ruler over a poor
      people.

16 A ruler who lacks understanding
    is a cruel oppressor;
    but one who hates unjust gain
      will enjoy a long life.

17 If someone is burdened with the
    blood of another,
    let that killer be a fugitive
      until death;
    let no one offer assistance.

18 One who walks in integrity will
    be safe,

[g] Meaning of Heb uncertain   [h] Heb *face*
[i] Heb lacks *is tested*   [j] Cn: Heb *A poor
person*

P
R
O
V
E
R
B
S

but whoever follows crooked
ways will fall into the Pit.*k*

19 Anyone who tills the land will
have plenty of bread,
but one who follows worthless
pursuits will have plenty of
poverty.

20 The faithful will abound with
blessings,
but one who is in a hurry to be
rich will not go
unpunished.

21 To show partiality is not good—
yet for a piece of bread a
person may do wrong.

22 The miser is in a hurry to get
rich
and does not know that loss is
sure to come.

23 Whoever rebukes a person will
afterward find more favor
than one who flatters with the
tongue.

24 Anyone who robs father or
mother
and says, "That is no crime,"
is partner to a thug.

25 The greedy person stirs up strife,
but whoever trusts in the LORD
will be enriched.

26 Those who trust in their own
wits are fools;
but those who walk in wisdom
come through safely.

27 Whoever gives to the poor will
lack nothing,
but one who turns a blind eye
will get many a curse.

28 When the wicked prevail, people
go into hiding;
but when they perish, the
righteous increase.

29 One who is often reproved,
yet remains stubborn,
will suddenly be broken
beyond healing.

2 When the righteous are in
authority, the people
rejoice;
but when the wicked rule, the
people groan.

3 A child who loves wisdom
makes a parent glad,
but to keep company with
prostitutes is to squander
one's substance.

4 By justice a king gives stability
to the land,
but one who makes heavy
exactions ruins it.

5 Whoever flatters a neighbor
is spreading a net for the
neighbor's feet.

6 In the transgression of the evil
there is a snare,
but the righteous sing and
rejoice.

7 The righteous know the rights of
the poor;
the wicked have no such
understanding.

8 Scoffers set a city aflame,
but the wise turn away wrath.

9 If the wise go to law with fools,
there is ranting and ridicule
without relief.

10 The bloodthirsty hate the
blameless,
and they seek the life of the
upright.

11 A fool gives full vent to anger,
but the wise quietly holds it
back.

12 If a ruler listens to falsehood,
all his officials will be wicked.

13 The poor and the oppressor have
this in common:
the LORD gives light to the
eyes of both.

14 If a king judges the poor with
equity,
his throne will be established
forever.

15 The rod and reproof give
wisdom,
but a mother is disgraced by a
neglected child.

16 When the wicked are in
authority, transgression
increases,
but the righteous will look
upon their downfall.

17 Discipline your children, and
they will give you rest;
they will give delight to your
heart.

18 Where there is no prophecy, the
people cast off restraint,
but happy are those who keep
the law.

19 By mere words servants are not
disciplined,
for though they understand,
they will not give heed.

20 Do you see someone who is
hasty in speech?
There is more hope for a fool
than for anyone like that.

21 A slave pampered from
childhood

k Syr: Heb *fall all at once*

will come to a bad end.[l]

2 One given to anger stirs up
    strife,
    and the hothead causes much
        transgression.

3 A person's pride will bring
    humiliation,
    but one who is lowly in spirit
        will obtain honor.

4 To be a partner of a thief is to
    hate one's own life;
    one hears the victim's curse,
    but discloses nothing.[m]

5 The fear of others[n] lays a snare,
    but one who trusts in the
        LORD is secure.

6 Many seek the favor of a ruler,
    but it is from the LORD that
        one gets justice.

7 The unjust are an abomination
    to the righteous,
    but the upright are an
        abomination to the wicked.

Sayings of Agur

30 The words of Ā'gur son of Jā'-
    keh. An oracle.

Thus says the man: I am weary,
    O God,
    I am weary, O God. How can I
        prevail?[o]

2 Surely I am too stupid to be
    human;
    I do not have human
        understanding.

3 I have not learned wisdom,
    nor have I knowledge of the
        holy ones.[p]

4 Who has ascended to heaven
    and come down?
    Who has gathered the wind in
        the hollow of the hand?
    Who has wrapped up the waters
        in a garment?
    Who has established all the
        ends of the earth?
    What is the person's name?
    And what is the name of the
        person's child?
    Surely you know!

5 Every word of God proves true;
    he is a shield to those who
        take refuge in him.

6 Do not add to his words,
    or else he will rebuke you, and
        you will be found a liar.

7 Two things I ask of you;

do not deny them to me before
    I die:

8 Remove far from me falsehood
    and lying;
    give me neither poverty nor
        riches;
    feed me with the food that I
        need,

9 or I shall be full, and deny you,
    and say, "Who is the LORD?"
    or I shall be poor, and steal,
    and profane the name of my
        God.

10 Do not slander a servant to a
    master,
    or the servant will curse you,
    and you will be held guilty.

11 There are those who curse their
    fathers
    and do not bless their mothers.

12 There are those who are pure in
    their own eyes
    yet are not cleansed of their
        filthiness.

13 There are those—how lofty are
    their eyes,
    how high their eyelids lift!

14 There are those whose teeth are
    swords,
    whose teeth are knives,
    to devour the poor from off the
        earth,
    the needy from among
        mortals.

15 The leech[m] has two daughters;
    "Give, give," they cry.
    Three things are never satisfied;
    four never say, "Enough":

16 Shē'ōl, the barren womb,
    the earth ever thirsty for
        water,
    and the fire that never says,
        "Enough."[m]

17 The eye that mocks a father
    and scorns to obey a mother
    will be pecked out by the ravens
        of the valley
    and eaten by the vultures.

18 Three things are too wonderful
    for me;
    four I do not understand:

[l]Vg: Meaning of Heb uncertain
[m]Meaning of Heb uncertain
[n]Or *human fear*   [o]Or *I am spent.*
Meaning of Heb uncertain   [p]Or *Holy One*

19 the way of an eagle in the sky,
    the way of a snake on a rock,
the way of a ship on the high
    seas,
    and the way of a man with a
    girl.

20 This is the way of an adulteress:
    she eats, and wipes her mouth,
    and says, "I have done no
    wrong."

21 Under three things the earth
    trembles;
    under four it cannot bear up:
22 a slave when he becomes king,
    and a fool when glutted with
    food;
23 an unloved woman when she
    gets a husband,
    and a maid when she succeeds
    her mistress.

24 Four things on earth are small,
    yet they are exceedingly wise:
25 the ants are a people without
    strength,
    yet they provide their food in
    the summer;
26 the badgers are a people without
    power,
    yet they make their homes in
    the rocks;
27 the locusts have no king,
    yet all of them march in rank;
28 the lizard*q* can be grasped in
    the hand,
    yet it is found in kings'
    palaces.

29 Three things are stately in their
    stride;
    four are stately in their gait:
30 the lion, which is mightiest
    among wild animals
    and does not turn back before
    any;
31 the strutting rooster,*r* the
    he-goat,
    and a king striding before*s* his
    people.

32 If you have been foolish,
    exalting yourself,
    or if you have been devising
    evil,
    put your hand on your mouth.
33 For as pressing milk produces
    curds,
    and pressing the nose
    produces blood,

    so pressing anger produces
    strife.

The Teaching of King Lemuel's Mother

31 The words of King Lem′u·el.
    An oracle that his mother
taught him:

2 No, my son! No, son of my
    womb!
    No, son of my vows!
3 Do not give your strength to
    women,
    your ways to those who
    destroy kings.
4 It is not for kings, O Lem′u·el,
    it is not for kings to drink
    wine,
    or for rulers to desire*t* strong
    drink;
5 or else they will drink and forget
    what has been decreed,
    and will pervert the rights of
    all the afflicted.
6 Give strong drink to one who is
    perishing,
    and wine to those in bitter
    distress;
7 let them drink and forget their
    poverty,
    and remember their misery no
    more.
8 Speak out for those who cannot
    speak,
    for the rights of all the
    destitute.*u*
9 Speak out, judge righteously,
    defend the rights of the poor
    and needy.

Ode to a Capable Wife

10 A capable wife who can find?
    She is far more precious than
    jewels.
11 The heart of her husband trusts
    in her,
    and he will have no lack of
    gain.
12 She does him good, and not
    harm,
    all the days of her life.
13 She seeks wool and flax,
    and works with willing hands.
14 She is like the ships of the
    merchant,

q Or *spider*   *r* Gk Syr Tg Compare Vg:
Meaning of Heb uncertain   *s* Meaning
of Heb uncertain   *t* Cn: Heb *where*
u Heb *all children of passing away*

she brings her food from far
   away.
15 She rises while it is still night
   and provides food for her
      household
   and tasks for her servant-girls.
16 She considers a field and buys
    it;
   with the fruit of her hands she
      plants a vineyard.
17 She girds herself with strength,
   and makes her arms strong.
18 She perceives that her
      merchandise is profitable.
   Her lamp does not go out at
      night.
19 She puts her hands to the
      distaff,
   and her hands hold the
      spindle.
20 She opens her hand to the poor,
   and reaches out her hands to
      the needy.
21 She is not afraid for her
      household when it snows,
   for all her household are
      clothed in crimson.
22 She makes herself coverings;
   her clothing is fine linen and
      purple.
23 Her husband is known in the
      city gates,

taking his seat among the
      elders of the land.
24 She makes linen garments and
      sells them;
   she supplies the merchant with
      sashes.
25 Strength and dignity are her
      clothing,
   and she laughs at the time to
      come.
26 She opens her mouth with
      wisdom,
   and the teaching of kindness is
      on her tongue.
27 She looks well to the ways of
      her household,
   and does not eat the bread of
      idleness.
28 Her children rise up and call her
      happy;
   her husband too, and he
      praises her:
29 "Many women have done
      excellently,
   but you surpass them all."
30 Charm is deceitful, and beauty is
      vain,
   but a woman who fears the
      LORD is to be praised.
31 Give her a share in the fruit of
      her hands,
   and let her works praise her in
      the city gates.

ECCLESIASTES

Reflections of a Royal Philosopher

1 The words of the Teacher,[a] the
son of David, king in Jerusalem.
2 Vanity of vanities, says the
      Teacher,[a]
   vanity of vanities! All is
      vanity.
3 What do people gain from all the
      toil
   at which they toil under the
      sun?
4 A generation goes, and a
      generation comes,
   but the earth remains forever.
5 The sun rises and the sun goes
      down,

and hurries to the place where
      it rises.
6 The wind blows to the south,
   and goes around to the north;
   round and round goes the wind,
   and on its circuits the wind
      returns.
7 All streams run to the sea,
   but the sea is not full;
   to the place where the streams
      flow,
   there they continue to flow.
8 All things[b] are wearisome;

---

aHeb *Qoheleth*, traditionally rendered
Preacher   bOr *words*

more than one can express;
the eye is not satisfied with
        seeing,
    or the ear filled with hearing.
9 What has been is what will be,
    and what has been done is
        what will be done;
    there is nothing new under the
        sun.
10 Is there a thing of which it is
        said,
    "See, this is new"?
    It has already been,
        in the ages before us.
11 The people of long ago are not
        remembered,
    nor will there be any
        remembrance
of people yet to come
    by those who come after them.

The Futility of Seeking Wisdom

12 I, the Teacher,[c] when king over
Israel in Jerusalem, 13 applied my mind
to seek and to search out by wisdom all
that is done under heaven; it is an unhappy business that God has given to
human beings to be busy with. 14 I saw
all the deeds that are done under the
sun; and see, all is vanity and a chasing
after wind.[d]
15 What is crooked cannot be made
        straight,
    and what is lacking cannot be
        counted.
16 I said to myself, "I have acquired
great wisdom, surpassing all who were
over Jerusalem before me; and my
mind has had great experience of wisdom and knowledge." 17 And I applied
my mind to know wisdom and to know
madness and folly. I perceived that
this also is but a chasing after wind.[d]
18 For in much wisdom is much
        vexation,
    and those who increase
        knowledge increase
        sorrow.

The Futility of Self-Indulgence
(Cp 1 Kings 4.20–28)

2 I said to myself, "Come now, I will
    make a test of pleasure; enjoy
yourself." But again, this also was vanity. 2 I said of laughter, "It is mad," and
of pleasure, "What use is it?" 3 I
searched with my mind how to cheer
my body with wine—my mind still
guiding me with wisdom—and how to
lay hold on folly, until I might see what
was good for mortals to do under
heaven during the few days of their

life. 4 I made great works; I built
houses and planted vineyards for myself; 5 I made myself gardens and
parks, and planted in them all kinds of
fruit trees. 6 I made myself pools from
which to water the forest of growing
trees. 7 I bought male and female
slaves, and had slaves who were born
in my house; I also had great possessions of herds and flocks, more than
any who had been before me in Jerusalem. 8 I also gathered for myself silver
and gold and the treasure of kings and
of the provinces; I got singers, both
men and women, and delights of the
flesh, and many concubines.[e]
9 So I became great and surpassed
all who were before me in Jerusalem;
also my wisdom remained with me.
10 Whatever my eyes desired I did not
keep from them; I kept my heart from
no pleasure, for my heart found pleasure in all my toil, and this was my
reward for all my toil. 11 Then I considered all that my hands had done and
the toil I had spent in doing it, and
again, all was vanity and a chasing after wind,[d] and there was nothing to be
gained under the sun.

Wisdom and Joy Given to One
Who Pleases God

12 So I turned to consider wisdom
and madness and folly; for what can
the one who comes after the king do?
Only what has already been done.
13 Then I saw that wisdom excels folly
as light excels darkness.
14 The wise have eyes in their
        head,
    but fools walk in darkness.
Yet I perceived that the same fate
befalls all of them. 15 Then I said to myself, "What happens to the fool will
happen to me also; why then have I
been so very wise?" And I said to myself that this also is vanity. 16 For there
is no enduring remembrance of the
wise or of fools, seeing that in the days
to come all will have been long forgotten. How can the wise die just like
fools? 17 So I hated life, because what is
done under the sun was grievous to
me; for all is vanity and a chasing after
wind.[d]
18 I hated all my toil in which I had
toiled under the sun, seeing that I must
leave it to those who come after me

c Heb *Qoheleth*, traditionally rendered
Preacher   d Or *a feeding on wind.* See
Hos 12.1   e Meaning of Heb uncertain

19 — and who knows whether they will be wise or foolish? Yet they will be master of all for which I toiled and used my wisdom under the sun. This also is vanity. 20 So I turned and gave my heart up to despair concerning all the toil of my labors under the sun, 21 because sometimes one who has toiled with wisdom and knowledge and skill must leave all to be enjoyed by another who did not toil for it. This also is vanity and a great evil. 22 What do mortals get from all the toil and strain with which they toil under the sun? 23 For all their days are full of pain, and their work is a vexation; even at night their minds do not rest. This also is vanity.

24 There is nothing better for mortals than to eat and drink, and find enjoyment in their toil. This also, I saw, is from the hand of God; 25 for apart from him*f* who can eat or who can have enjoyment? 26 For to the one who pleases him God gives wisdom and knowledge and joy; but to the sinner he gives the work of gathering and heaping, only to give to one who pleases God. This also is vanity and a chasing after wind.*g*

Everything Has Its Time

3 For everything there is a season, and a time for every matter under heaven:

2 a time to be born, and a time to die;
a time to plant, and a time to pluck up what is planted;

3 a time to kill, and a time to heal;
a time to break down, and a time to build up;

4 a time to weep, and a time to laugh;
a time to mourn, and a time to dance;

5 a time to throw away stones, and a time to gather stones together;
a time to embrace, and a time to refrain from embracing;

6 a time to seek, and a time to lose;
a time to keep, and a time to throw away;

7 a time to tear, and a time to sew;
a time to keep silence, and a time to speak;

8 a time to love, and a time to hate;

a time for war, and a time for peace.

The God-Given Task

9 What gain have the workers from their toil? 10 I have seen the business that God has given to everyone to be busy with. 11 He has made everything suitable for its time; moreover he has put a sense of past and future into their minds, yet they cannot find out what God has done from the beginning to the end. 12 I know that there is nothing better for them than to be happy and enjoy themselves as long as they live; 13 moreover, it is God's gift that all should eat and drink and take pleasure in all their toil. 14 I know that whatever God does endures forever; nothing can be added to it, nor anything taken from it; God has done this, so that all should stand in awe before him. 15 That which is, already has been; that which is to be, already is; and God seeks out what has gone by.*h*

Judgment and the Future Belong to God

16 Moreover I saw under the sun that in the place of justice, wickedness was there, and in the place of righteousness, wickedness was there as well. 17 I said in my heart, God will judge the righteous and the wicked, for he has appointed a time for every matter, and for every work. 18 I said in my heart with regard to human beings that God is testing them to show that they are but animals. 19 For the fate of humans and the fate of animals is the same; as one dies, so dies the other. They all have the same breath, and humans have no advantage over the animals; for all is vanity. 20 All go to one place; all are from the dust, and all turn to dust again. 21 Who knows whether the human spirit goes upward and the spirit of animals goes downward to the earth? 22 So I saw that there is nothing better than that all should enjoy their work, for that is their lot; who can bring them to see what will be after them?

4 Again I saw all the oppressions that are practiced under the sun. Look, the tears of the oppressed — with no one to comfort them! On the side of their oppressors there was power —

f Gk Syr: Heb *apart from me* *g* Or *a feeding on wind.* See Hos 12.1
h Heb *what is pursued*

with no one to comfort them. 2 And I thought the dead, who have already died, more fortunate than the living, who are still alive; 3 but better than both is the one who has not yet been, and has not seen the evil deeds that are done under the sun.

4 Then I saw that all toil and all skill in work come from one person's envy of another. This also is vanity and a chasing after wind.[i]

5 Fools fold their hands
and consume their own flesh.
6 Better is a handful with quiet
than two handfuls with toil,
and a chasing after wind.[i]

7 Again, I saw vanity under the sun: 8 the case of solitary individuals, without sons or brothers; yet there is no end to all their toil, and their eyes are never satisfied with riches. "For whom am I toiling," they ask, "and depriving myself of pleasure?" This also is vanity and an unhappy business.

The Value of a Friend

9 Two are better than one, because they have a good reward for their toil. 10 For if they fall, one will lift up the other; but woe to one who is alone and falls and does not have another to help. 11 Again, if two lie together, they keep warm; but how can one keep warm alone? 12 And though one might prevail against another, two will withstand one. A threefold cord is not quickly broken.

13 Better is a poor but wise youth than an old but foolish king, who will no longer take advice. 14 One can indeed come out of prison to reign, even though born poor in the kingdom. 15 I saw all the living who, moving about under the sun, follow that[j] youth who replaced the king;[k] 16 there was no end to all those people whom he led. Yet those who come later will not rejoice in him. Surely this also is vanity and a chasing after wind.[i]

Reverence, Humility, and Contentment

5 [l] Guard your steps when you go to the house of God; to draw near to listen is better than the sacrifice offered by fools; for they do not know how to keep from doing evil.[m] 2 n Never be rash with your mouth, nor let your heart be quick to utter a word before God, for God is in heaven, and you upon earth; therefore let your words be few.

3 For dreams come with many cares, and a fool's voice with many words.

4 When you make a vow to God, do not delay fulfilling it; for he has no pleasure in fools. Fulfill what you vow. 5 It is better that you should not vow than that you should vow and not fulfill it. 6 Do not let your mouth lead you into sin, and do not say before the messenger that it was a mistake; why should God be angry at your words, and destroy the work of your hands?

7 With many dreams come vanities and a multitude of words;[o] but fear God.

8 If you see in a province the oppression of the poor and the violation of justice and right, do not be amazed at the matter; for the high official is watched by a higher, and there are yet higher ones over them. 9 But all things considered, this is an advantage for a land: a king for a plowed field.[o]

10 The lover of money will not be satisfied with money; nor the lover of wealth, with gain. This also is vanity.

11 When goods increase, those who eat them increase; and what gain has their owner but to see them with his eyes?

12 Sweet is the sleep of laborers, whether they eat little or much; but the surfeit of the rich will not let them sleep.

13 There is a grievous ill that I have seen under the sun: riches were kept by their owners to their hurt, 14 and those riches were lost in a bad venture; though they are parents of children, they have nothing in their hands. 15 As they came from their mother's womb, so they shall go again, naked as they came; they shall take nothing for their toil, which they may carry away with their hands. 16 This also is a grievous ill: just as they came, so shall they go; and what gain do they have from toiling for the wind? 17 Besides, all their days they eat in darkness, in much vexation and sickness and resentment.

18 This is what I have seen to be good: it is fitting to eat and drink and find enjoyment in all the toil with which one toils under the sun the few days of the life God gives us; for this is our lot. 19 Likewise all to whom God

i Or a feeding on wind. See Hos 12.1
j Heb the second   k Heb him   l Ch 4.17
in Heb   m Cn: Heb they do not know
how to do evil   n Ch 5.1 in Heb
o Meaning of Heb uncertain

gives wealth and possessions and whom he enables to enjoy them, and to accept their lot and find enjoyment in their toil — this is the gift of God. 20 For they will scarcely brood over the days of their lives, because God keeps them occupied with the joy of their hearts.

The Frustration of Desires

6 There is an evil that I have seen under the sun, and it lies heavy upon humankind: 2 those to whom God gives wealth, possessions, and honor, so that they lack nothing of all that they desire, yet God does not enable them to enjoy these things, but a stranger enjoys them. This is vanity; it is a grievous ill. 3 A man may beget a hundred children, and live many years; but however many are the days of his years, if he does not enjoy life's good things, or has no burial, I say that a stillborn child is better off than he. 4 For it comes into vanity and goes into darkness, and in darkness its name is covered; 5 moreover it has not seen the sun or known anything; yet it finds rest rather than he. 6 Even though he should live a thousand years twice over, yet enjoy no good — do not all go to one place?

7 All human toil is for the mouth, yet the appetite is not satisfied. 8 For what advantage have the wise over fools? And what do the poor have who know how to conduct themselves before the living? 9 Better is the sight of the eyes than the wandering of desire; this also is vanity and a chasing after wind. *p*

10 Whatever has come to be has already been named, and it is known what human beings are, and that they are not able to dispute with those who are stronger. 11 The more words, the more vanity, so how is one the better? 12 For who knows what is good for mortals while they live the few days of their vain life, which they pass like a shadow? For who can tell them what will be after them under the sun?

A Disillusioned View of Life

7 A good name is better than precious ointment,
    and the day of death, than the day of birth.
2 It is better to go to the house of mourning
    than to go to the house of feasting;
for this is the end of everyone,

    and the living will lay it to heart.
3 Sorrow is better than laughter,
    for by sadness of countenance the heart is made glad.
4 The heart of the wise is in the house of mourning;
    but the heart of fools is in the house of mirth.
5 It is better to hear the rebuke of the wise
    than to hear the song of fools.
6 For like the crackling of thorns under a pot,
    so is the laughter of fools;
    this also is vanity.
7 Surely oppression makes the wise foolish,
    and a bribe corrupts the heart.
8 Better is the end of a thing than its beginning;
    the patient in spirit are better than the proud in spirit.
9 Do not be quick to anger,
    for anger lodges in the bosom of fools.
10 Do not say, "Why were the former days better than these?"
    For it is not from wisdom that you ask this.
11 Wisdom is as good as an inheritance,
    an advantage to those who see the sun.
12 For the protection of wisdom is like the protection of money,
    and the advantage of knowledge is that wisdom gives life to the one who possesses it.
13 Consider the work of God;
    who can make straight what he has made crooked?

14 In the day of prosperity be joyful, and in the day of adversity consider; God has made the one as well as the other, so that mortals may not find out anything that will come after them.

The Riddles of Life

15 In my vain life I have seen everything; there are righteous people who perish in their righteousness, and there are wicked people who prolong their life in their evildoing. 16 Do not be too righteous, and do not act too wise; why should you destroy yourself? 17 Do not be too wicked, and do not be

p Or *a feeding on wind.* See Hos 12.1

a fool; why should you die before your time? [18] It is good that you should take hold of the one, without letting go of the other; for the one who fears God shall succeed with both.

19 Wisdom gives strength to the wise more than ten rulers that are in a city.

20 Surely there is no one on earth so righteous as to do good without ever sinning.

21 Do not give heed to everything that people say, or you may hear your servant cursing you; [22] your heart knows that many times you have yourself cursed others.

23 All this I have tested by wisdom; I said, "I will be wise," but it was far from me. [24] That which is, is far off, and deep, very deep; who can find it out? [25] I turned my mind to know and to search out and to seek wisdom and the sum of things, and to know that wickedness is folly and that foolishness is madness. [26] I found more bitter than death the woman who is a trap, whose heart is snares and nets, whose hands are fetters; one who pleases God escapes her, but the sinner is taken by her. [27] See, this is what I found, says the Teacher,[q] adding one thing to another to find the sum, [28] which my mind has sought repeatedly, but I have not found. One man among a thousand I found, but a woman among all these I have not found. [29] See, this alone I found, that God made human beings straightforward, but they have devised many schemes.

Obey the King and Enjoy Yourself

8 Who is like the wise man?
  And who knows the
      interpretation of a thing?
Wisdom makes one's face shine,
  and the hardness of one's
      countenance is changed.

2 Keep[r] the king's command because of your sacred oath. [3] Do not be terrified; go from his presence, do not delay when the matter is unpleasant, for he does whatever he pleases. [4] For the word of the king is powerful, and who can say to him, "What are you doing?" [5] Whoever obeys a command will meet no harm, and the wise mind will know the time and way. [6] For every matter has its time and way, although the troubles of mortals lie heavy upon them. [7] Indeed, they do not know what is to be, for who can tell

them how it will be? [8] No one has power over the wind[s] to restrain the wind,[s] or power over the day of death; there is no discharge from the battle, nor does wickedness deliver those who practice it. [9] All this I observed, applying my mind to all that is done under the sun, while one person exercises authority over another to the other's hurt.

God's Ways Are Inscrutable

10 Then I saw the wicked buried; they used to go in and out of the holy place, and were praised in the city where they had done such things.[t] This also is vanity. [11] Because sentence against an evil deed is not executed speedily, the human heart is fully set to do evil. [12] Though sinners do evil a hundred times and prolong their lives, yet I know that it will be well with those who fear God, because they stand in fear before him, [13] but it will not be well with the wicked, neither will they prolong their days like a shadow, because they do not stand in fear before God.

14 There is a vanity that takes place on earth, that there are righteous people who are treated according to the conduct of the wicked, and there are wicked people who are treated according to the conduct of the righteous. I said that this also is vanity. [15] So I commend enjoyment, for there is nothing better for people under the sun than to eat, and drink, and enjoy themselves, for this will go with them in their toil through the days of life that God gives them under the sun.

16 When I applied my mind to know wisdom, and to see the business that is done on earth, how one's eyes see sleep neither day nor night, [17] then I saw all the work of God, that no one can find out what is happening under the sun. However much they may toil in seeking, they will not find it out; even though those who are wise claim to know, they cannot find it out.

Take Life as It Comes

9 All this I laid to heart, examining it all, how the righteous and the wise and their deeds are in the hand of God; whether it is love or hate one

[q] Qoheleth, traditionally rendered *Preacher*   [r] Heb I keep   [s] Or breath
[t] Meaning of Heb uncertain

does not know. Everything that confronts them [2]is vanity,[u] since the same fate comes to all, to the righteous and the wicked, to the good and the evil,[v] to the clean and the unclean, to those who sacrifice and those who do not sacrifice. As are the good, so are the sinners; those who swear are like those who shun an oath. [3]This is an evil in all that happens under the sun, that the same fate comes to everyone. Moreover, the hearts of all are full of evil; madness is in their hearts while they live, and after that they go to the dead. [4]But whoever is joined with all the living has hope, for a living dog is better than a dead lion. [5]The living know that they will die, but the dead know nothing; they have no more reward, and even the memory of them is lost. [6]Their love and their hate and their envy have already perished; never again will they have any share in all that happens under the sun.

7 Go, eat your bread with enjoyment, and drink your wine with a merry heart; for God has long ago approved what you do. [8]Let your garments always be white; do not let oil be lacking on your head. [9]Enjoy life with the wife whom you love, all the days of your vain life that are given you under the sun, because that is your portion in life and in your toil at which you toil under the sun. [10]Whatever your hand finds to do, do with your might; for there is no work or thought or knowledge or wisdom in Shĕʹōl, to which you are going.

11 Again I saw that under the sun the race is not to the swift, nor the battle to the strong, nor bread to the wise, nor riches to the intelligent, nor favor to the skillful; but time and chance happen to them all. [12]For no one can anticipate the time of disaster. Like fish taken in a cruel net, and like birds caught in a snare, so mortals are snared at a time of calamity, when it suddenly falls upon them.

Wisdom Superior to Folly

13 I have also seen this example of wisdom under the sun, and it seemed great to me. [14]There was a little city with few people in it. A great king came against it and besieged it, building great siegeworks against it. [15]Now there was found in it a poor wise man, and he by his wisdom delivered the city. Yet no one remembered that poor man. [16]So I said, "Wisdom is better than might; yet the poor man's wisdom is despised, and his words are not heeded."

17 The quiet words of the wise are
    more to be heeded
  than the shouting of a ruler
    among fools.
18 Wisdom is better than weapons
    of war,
  but one bungler destroys much
    good.

Miscellaneous Observations

10 Dead flies make the
    perfumer's ointment give
    off a foul odor;
  so a little folly outweighs
    wisdom and honor.
2 The heart of the wise inclines to
    the right,
  but the heart of a fool to the
    left.
3 Even when fools walk on the
    road, they lack sense,
  and show to everyone that
    they are fools.
4 If the anger of the ruler rises
    against you, do not leave
    your post,
  for calmness will undo great
    offenses.

5 There is an evil that I have seen under the sun, as great an error as if it proceeded from the ruler: [6]folly is set in many high places, and the rich sit in a low place. [7]I have seen slaves on horseback, and princes walking on foot like slaves.

8 Whoever digs a pit will fall into it;
  and whoever breaks through a
    wall will be bitten by a
    snake.
9 Whoever quarries stones will be
    hurt by them;
  and whoever splits logs will be
    endangered by them.
10 If the iron is blunt, and one does
    not whet the edge,
  then more strength must be
    exerted;
  but wisdom helps one to
    succeed.
11 If the snake bites before it is
    charmed,
  there is no advantage in a
    charmer.

[u]Syr Compare Gk: Heb *Everything that confronts them* [2]*is everything*   [v]Gk Syr Vg: Heb lacks *and the evil*

ECCLESIASTES

12 Words spoken by the wise bring
        them favor,
    but the lips of fools consume
        them.
13 The words of their mouths begin
        in foolishness,
    and their talk ends in wicked
        madness;
14 yet fools talk on and on.
    No one knows what is to
        happen,
    and who can tell anyone what
        the future holds?
15 The toil of fools wears them out,
    for they do not even know the
        way to town.

16 Alas for you, O land, when your
        king is a servant,[w]
    and your princes feast in the
        morning!
17 Happy are you, O land, when
        your king is a nobleman,
    and your princes feast at the
        proper time—
    for strength, and not for
        drunkenness!
18 Through sloth the roof sinks in,
    and through indolence the
        house leaks.
19 Feasts are made for laughter;
    wine gladdens life,
    and money meets every need.
20 Do not curse the king, even in
        your thoughts,
    or curse the rich, even in your
        bedroom;
    for a bird of the air may carry
        your voice,
    or some winged creature tell
        the matter.

The Value of Diligence

11 Send out your bread upon
        the waters,
    for after many days you will
        get it back.
2 Divide your means seven ways,
        or even eight,
    for you do not know what
        disaster may happen on
        earth.
3 When clouds are full,
    they empty rain on the earth;
    whether a tree falls to the south
        or to the north,
    in the place where the tree
        falls, there it will lie.
4 Whoever observes the wind will
        not sow;
    and whoever regards the
        clouds will not reap.

5 Just as you do not know how the
breath comes to the bones in the
mother's womb, so you do not know
the work of God, who makes everything.
6 In the morning sow your seed,
and at evening do not let your hands be
idle; for you do not know which will
prosper, this or that, or whether both
alike will be good.

Youth and Old Age

7 Light is sweet, and it is pleasant
for the eyes to see the sun.
8 Even those who live many years
should rejoice in them all; yet let them
remember that the days of darkness
will be many. All that comes is vanity.
9 Rejoice, young man, while you
are young, and let your heart cheer
you in the days of your youth. Follow
the inclination of your heart and the
desire of your eyes, but know that for
all these things God will bring you into
judgment.
10 Banish anxiety from your mind,
and put away pain from your body; for
youth and the dawn of life are vanity.

12 Remember your creator in the
        days of your youth, before the
days of trouble come, and the years
draw near when you will say, "I have
no pleasure in them"; 2before the sun
and the light and the moon and the
stars are darkened and the clouds return with[x] the rain; 3in the day when
the guards of the house tremble, and
the strong men are bent, and the
women who grind cease working because they are few, and those who look
through the windows see dimly;
4when the doors on the street are shut,
and the sound of the grinding is low,
and one rises up at the sound of a bird,
and all the daughters of song are
brought low; 5when one is afraid of
heights, and terrors are in the road; the
almond tree blossoms, the grasshopper drags itself along[y] and desire
fails; because all must go to their eternal home, and the mourners will go
about the streets; 6before the silver
cord is snapped,[z] and the golden bowl
is broken, and the pitcher is broken at
the fountain, and the wheel broken at
the cistern, 7and the dust returns to the
earth as it was, and the breath[a] returns to God who gave it. 8Vanity of

[w] Or *a child*   [x] Or *after*; Heb '*ahar*
[y] Or *is a burden*   [z] Syr Vg Compare Gk:
Heb *is removed*   [a] Or *the spirit*

vanities, says the Teacher;[b] all is van-
ty.

Epilogue

9 Besides being wise, the Teacher[b]
also taught the people knowledge,
weighing and studying and arrang-
ng many proverbs. [10] The Teacher[b]
sought to find pleasing words, and he
wrote words of truth plainly.

11 The sayings of the wise are like
goads, and like nails firmly fixed are
the collected sayings that are given by
one shepherd.[c] [12] Of anything beyond

these, my child, beware. Of making
many books there is no end, and much
study is a weariness of the flesh.
13 The end of the matter; all has
been heard. Fear God, and keep his
commandments; for that is the whole
duty of everyone. [14] For God will bring
every deed into judgment, including[d]
every secret thing, whether good or
evil.

[b] Qoheleth, traditionally rendered
Preacher   [c] Meaning of Heb uncertain
[d] Or into the judgment on

The

SONG OF SOLOMON

1 The Song of Songs, which is Solomon's.

Colloquy of Bride and Friends

2 Let him kiss me with the kisses
     of his mouth!
   For your love is better than
     wine,
3   your anointing oils are
          fragrant,
   your name is perfume poured
     out;
       therefore the maidens love
          you.
4 Draw me after you, let us make
     haste.
   The king has brought me into
     his chambers.
   We will exult and rejoice in you;
     we will extol your love more
       than wine;
     rightly do they love you.

5 I am black and beautiful,
     O daughters of Jerusalem,
   like the tents of Kē′dar,
     like the curtains of Solomon.
6 Do not gaze at me because I am
     dark,
       because the sun has gazed on
          me.
   My mother's sons were angry
     with me;
       they made me keeper of the
          vineyards,

   but my own vineyard I have
     not kept!
7 Tell me, you whom my soul
     loves,
     where you pasture your flock,
     where you make it lie down at
       noon;
   for why should I be like one who
       is veiled
     beside the flocks of your
       companions?

8 If you do not know,
     O fairest among women,
   follow the tracks of the flock,
     and pasture your kids
     beside the shepherds' tents.

Colloquy of Bridegroom, Friends, and Bride

9 I compare you, my love,
     to a mare among Pharaoh's
       chariots.
10 Your cheeks are comely with
       ornaments,
     your neck with strings of
       jewels.
11 We will make you ornaments of
       gold,
     studded with silver.

12 While the king was on his
       couch,
     my nard gave forth its
       fragrance.

13 My beloved is to me a bag of
    myrrh
      that lies between my breasts.
14 My beloved is to me a cluster of
    henna blossoms
      in the vineyards of En-gedi.

15 Ah, you are beautiful, my love;
    ah, you are beautiful;
      your eyes are doves.
16 Ah, you are beautiful, my
    beloved,
      truly lovely.
    Our couch is green;
17   the beams of our house are
      cedar,
        our rafters*a* are pine.

2 I am a rose*b* of Sharon,
    a lily of the valleys.

2 As a lily among brambles,
    so is my love among maidens.

3 As an apple tree among the trees
    of the wood,
      so is my beloved among young
      men.
    With great delight I sat in his
      shadow,
        and his fruit was sweet to my
        taste.
4 He brought me to the banqueting
    house,
      and his intention toward me
      was love.
5 Sustain me with raisins,
    refresh me with apples;
      for I am faint with love.
6 O that his left hand were under
    my head,
      and that his right hand
      embraced me!
7 I adjure you, O daughters of
    Jerusalem,
      by the gazelles or the wild
      does:
    do not stir up or awaken love
      until it is ready!

Springtime Rhapsody

8 The voice of my beloved!
    Look, he comes,
  leaping upon the mountains,
    bounding over the hills.
9 My beloved is like a gazelle
    or a young stag.
  Look, there he stands
    behind our wall,
  gazing in at the windows,
    looking through the lattice.

10 My beloved speaks and says to
    me:
  "Arise, my love, my fair one,
    and come away;
11 for now the winter is past,
    the rain is over and gone.
12 The flowers appear on the earth;
    the time of singing has come,
  and the voice of the turtledove
    is heard in our land.
13 The fig tree puts forth its figs,
    and the vines are in blossom;
      they give forth fragrance.
  Arise, my love, my fair one,
    and come away.
14 O my dove, in the clefts of the
    rock,
      in the covert of the cliff,
  let me see your face,
    let me hear your voice;
  for your voice is sweet,
    and your face is lovely.
15 Catch us the foxes,
    the little foxes,
  that ruin the vineyards—
    for our vineyards are in
    blossom."

16 My beloved is mine and I am
    his;
      he pastures his flock among
      the lilies.
17 Until the day breathes
    and the shadows flee,
  turn, my beloved, be like a
    gazelle
      or a young stag on the cleft
      mountains.*c*

Love's Dream

3 Upon my bed at night
    I sought him whom my soul
    loves;
  I sought him, but found him not;
    I called him, but he gave no
    answer.*d*
2 "I will rise now and go about the
    city,
      in the streets and in the
      squares;
  I will seek him whom my soul
    loves."
  I sought him, but found him
    not.
3 The sentinels found me,
    as they went about in the city.

*a*Meaning of Heb uncertain
*b*Heb *crocus*   *c*Or *on the mountains of
Bether*: meaning of Heb uncertain
*d*Gk: Heb lacks this line

"Have you seen him whom my
soul loves?"
4 Scarcely had I passed them,
when I found him whom my
soul loves.
I held him, and would not let
him go
until I brought him into my
mother's house,
and into the chamber of her
that conceived me.
5 I adjure you, O daughters of
Jerusalem,
by the gazelles or the wild
does:
do not stir up or awaken love
until it is ready!

The Groom and His Party Approach

6 What is that coming up from the
wilderness,
like a column of smoke,
perfumed with myrrh and
frankincense,
with all the fragrant powders
of the merchant?
7 Look, it is the litter of Solomon!
Around it are sixty mighty men
of the mighty men of Israel,
8 all equipped with swords
and expert in war,
each with his sword at his thigh
because of alarms by night.
9 King Solomon made himself a
palanquin
from the wood of Lebanon.
10 He made its posts of silver,
its back of gold, its seat of
purple;
its interior was inlaid with
love.*e*
11 Daughters of Jerusalem,
come out.
Look, O daughters of Zion,
at King Solomon,
at the crown with which his
mother crowned him
on the day of his wedding,
on the day of the gladness of
his heart.

The Bride's Beauty Extolled

4 How beautiful you are, my love,
how very beautiful!
Your eyes are doves
behind your veil.
Your hair is like a flock of goats,
moving down the slopes of
Gil'e·ad.
2 Your teeth are like a flock of
shorn ewes

that have come up from the
washing,
all of which bear twins,
and not one among them is
bereaved.
3 Your lips are like a crimson
thread,
and your mouth is lovely.
Your cheeks are like halves of a
pomegranate
behind your veil.
4 Your neck is like the tower of
David,
built in courses;
on it hang a thousand bucklers,
all of them shields of warriors.
5 Your two breasts are like two
fawns,
twins of a gazelle,
that feed among the lilies.
6 Until the day breathes
and the shadows flee,
I will hasten to the mountain of
myrrh
and the hill of frankincense.
7 You are altogether beautiful, my
love;
there is no flaw in you.
8 Come with me from Lebanon,
my bride;
come with me from Lebanon.
Depart*f* from the peak of
A·ma'na,
from the peak of Sē'nir and
Hermon,
from the dens of lions,
from the mountains of
leopards.

9 You have ravished my heart, my
sister, my bride,
you have ravished my heart
with a glance of your eyes,
with one jewel of your
necklace.
10 How sweet is your love, my
sister, my bride!
how much better is your love
than wine,
and the fragrance of your oils
than any spice!
11 Your lips distill nectar, my bride;
honey and milk are under
your tongue;
the scent of your garments is
like the scent of Lebanon.
12 A garden locked is my sister, my
bride,
a garden locked, a fountain
sealed.

*e*Meaning of Heb uncertain　　*f*Or *Look*

13 Your channel[g] is an orchard of
     pomegranates
   with all choicest fruits,
   henna with nard,
14 nard and saffron, calamus and
     cinnamon,
   with all trees of frankincense,
   myrrh and aloes,
   with all chief spices —
15 a garden fountain, a well of
     living water,
   and flowing streams from
     Lebanon.

16 Awake, O north wind,
   and come, O south wind!
   Blow upon my garden
     that its fragrance may be
       wafted abroad.
   Let my beloved come to his
     garden,
     and eat its choicest fruits.

5 I come to my garden, my sister,
     my bride;
   I gather my myrrh with my
     spice,
   I eat my honeycomb with my
     honey,
   I drink my wine with my milk.

Eat, friends, drink,
   and be drunk with love.

Another Dream

2 I slept, but my heart was awake.
   Listen! my beloved is knocking.
   "Open to me, my sister, my love,
     my dove, my perfect one;
   for my head is wet with dew,
     my locks with the drops of the
       night."
3 I had put off my garment;
     how could I put it on again?
   I had bathed my feet;
     how could I soil them?
4 My beloved thrust his hand into
     the opening,
     and my inmost being yearned
       for him.
5 I arose to open to my beloved,
     and my hands dripped with
       myrrh,
   my fingers with liquid myrrh,
     upon the handles of the bolt.
6 I opened to my beloved,
     but my beloved had turned
       and was gone.
   My soul failed me when he
     spoke.

I sought him, but did not find
     him;
   I called him, but he gave no
     answer.
7 Making their rounds in the city
     the sentinels found me;
   they beat me, they wounded me,
     they took away my mantle,
     those sentinels of the walls.
8 I adjure you, O daughters of
     Jerusalem,
   if you find my beloved,
     tell him this:
   I am faint with love.

Colloquy of Friends and Bride

9 What is your beloved more than
     another beloved,
   O fairest among women?
   What is your beloved more than
     another beloved,
     that you thus adjure us?

10 My beloved is all radiant and
     ruddy,
     distinguished among ten
       thousand.
11 His head is the finest gold;
     his locks are wavy,
     black as a raven.
12 His eyes are like doves
     beside springs of water,
   bathed in milk,
     fitly set.[g]
13 His cheeks are like beds of
     spices,
     yielding fragrance.
   His lips are lilies,
     distilling liquid myrrh.
14 His arms are rounded gold,
     set with jewels.
   His body is ivory work,[g]
     encrusted with sapphires.[h]
15 His legs are alabaster columns,
     set upon bases of gold.
   His appearance is like Lebanon,
     choice as the cedars.
16 His speech is most sweet,
     and he is altogether desirable.
   This is my beloved and this is
     my friend,
     O daughters of Jerusalem.

6 Where has your beloved gone,
     O fairest among women?
   Which way has your beloved
     turned,

[g] Meaning of Heb uncertain   [h] Heb lapis
lazuli

that we may seek him with
you?

2 My beloved has gone down to
his garden,
to the beds of spices,
to pasture his flock in the
gardens,
and to gather lilies.

3 I am my beloved's and my
beloved is mine;
he pastures his flock among
the lilies.

The Bride's Matchless Beauty

4 You are beautiful as Tir'zah, my
love,
comely as Jerusalem,
terrible as an army with
banners.

5 Turn away your eyes from me,
for they overwhelm me!
Your hair is like a flock of goats,
moving down the slopes of
Gil'e·ad.

6 Your teeth are like a flock of
ewes,
that have come up from the
washing;
all of them bear twins,
and not one among them is
bereaved.

7 Your cheeks are like halves of a
pomegranate
behind your veil.

8 There are sixty queens and
eighty concubines,
and maidens without number.

9 My dove, my perfect one, is the
only one,
the darling of her mother,
flawless to her that bore her.
The maidens saw her and called
her happy;
the queens and concubines
also, and they praised her.

10 "Who is this that looks forth like
the dawn,
fair as the moon, bright as the
sun,
terrible as an army with
banners?"

11 I went down to the nut orchard,
to look at the blossoms of the
valley,
to see whether the vines had
budded,
whether the pomegranates
were in bloom.

12 Before I was aware, my fancy
set me
in a chariot beside my
prince.[i]

13[j] Return, return, O Shū'lam·mīte!
Return, return, that we may
look upon you.

Why should you look upon the
Shū'lam·mīte,
as upon a dance before two
armies?[k]

Expressions of Praise

7 How graceful are your feet in
sandals,
O queenly maiden!
Your rounded thighs are like
jewels,
the work of a master hand.

2 Your navel is a rounded bowl
that never lacks mixed wine.
Your belly is a heap of wheat,
encircled with lilies.

3 Your two breasts are like two
fawns,
twins of a gazelle.

4 Your neck is like an ivory tower.
Your eyes are pools in
Hesh'bon,
by the gate of Bath-rab'bim.
Your nose is like a tower of
Lebanon,
overlooking Damascus.

5 Your head crowns you like
Car'mel,
and your flowing locks are
like purple;
a king is held captive in the
tresses.[l]

6 How fair and pleasant you are,
O loved one, delectable
maiden![m]

7 You are stately[n] as a palm tree,
and your breasts are like its
clusters.

8 I say I will climb the palm tree
and lay hold of its branches.
Oh, may your breasts be like
clusters of the vine,
and the scent of your breath
like apples,

9 and your kisses[o] like the best
wine

---

[i] Cn: Meaning of Heb uncertain   [j] Ch
7.1 in Heb   [k] Or *dance of Mahanaim*
[l] Meaning of Heb uncertain   [m] Syr: Heb
in delights   [n] Heb *This your stature is*
[o] Heb *palate*

that goes down[p] smoothly,
    gliding over lips and teeth.[q]

10 I am my beloved's,
    and his desire is for me.
11 Come, my beloved,
    let us go forth into the fields,
    and lodge in the villages;
12 let us go out early to the
        vineyards,
    and see whether the vines
        have budded,
    whether the grape blossoms
        have opened
    and the pomegranates are in
        bloom.
    There I will give you my love.
13 The mandrakes give forth
        fragrance,
    and over our doors are all
        choice fruits,
    new as well as old,
        which I have laid up for you,
        O my beloved.

8 O that you were like a brother to
        me,
    who nursed at my mother's
        breast!
    If I met you outside, I would kiss
        you,
    and no one would despise me.
2 I would lead you and bring you
        into the house of my mother,
    and into the chamber of the
        one who bore me.[r]
    I would give you spiced wine to
        drink,
    the juice of my pomegranates.
3 O that his left hand were under
        my head,
    and that his right hand
        embraced me!
4 I adjure you, O daughters of
        Jerusalem,
    do not stir up or awaken love
    until it is ready!

Homecoming

5 Who is that coming up from the
        wilderness,
    leaning upon her beloved?

Under the apple tree I awakened
        you.
There your mother was in labor
        with you;
    there she who bore you was in
        labor.

6 Set me as a seal upon your
        heart,
    as a seal upon your arm;
    for love is strong as death,
        passion fierce as the grave.
    Its flashes are flashes of fire,
        a raging flame.
7 Many waters cannot quench
        love,
    neither can floods drown it.
    If one offered for love
        all the wealth of his house,
    it would be utterly scorned.

8 We have a little sister,
    and she has no breasts.
    What shall we do for our sister,
        on the day when she is spoken
        for?
9 If she is a wall,
    we will build upon her a
        battlement of silver;
    but if she is a door,
        we will enclose her with
        boards of cedar.
10 I was a wall,
    and my breasts were like
        towers;
    then I was in his eyes
        as one who brings[s] peace.
11 Solomon had a vineyard at
        Bā′al-hā′mon;
    he entrusted the vineyard to
        keepers;
    each one was to bring for its
        fruit a thousand pieces of
        silver.
12 My vineyard, my very own, is
        for myself;
    you, O Solomon, may have the
        thousand,
    and the keepers of the fruit
        two hundred!

13 O you who dwell in the gardens,
    my companions are listening
        for your voice;
    let me hear it.

14 Make haste, my beloved,
    and be like a gazelle
    or a young stag
        upon the mountains of spices!

[p] Heb *down for my lover*   [q] Gk Syr Vg:
Heb *lips of sleepers*   [r] Gk Syr: Heb *my
mother; she* (or *you*) *will teach me*
[s] Or *finds*

THE WISDOM OF SOLOMON

Exhortation to Uprightness
(Wis 6.1–11)

1 Love righteousness, you rulers
  of the earth,
think of the Lord in goodness
and seek him with sincerity of
  heart;

2 because he is found by those
  who do not put him to the
  test,
and manifests himself to those
  who do not distrust him.

3 For perverse thoughts separate
  people from God,
and when his power is tested, it
  exposes the foolish;

4 because wisdom will not enter a
  deceitful soul,
or dwell in a body enslaved to
  sin.

5 For a holy and disciplined spirit
  will flee from deceit,
and will leave foolish thoughts
  behind,
and will be ashamed at the
  approach of
  unrighteousness.

6 For wisdom is a kindly spirit,
but will not free blasphemers
  from the guilt of their
  words;
because God is witness of their
  inmost feelings,
and a true observer of their
  hearts, and a hearer of
  their tongues.

7 Because the spirit of the Lord
  has filled the world,
and that which holds all things
  together knows what is
  said,

8 therefore those who utter
  unrighteous things will not
  escape notice,
and justice, when it punishes,
  will not pass them by.

9 For inquiry will be made into the
  counsels of the ungodly,
and a report of their words will
  come to the Lord,
to convict them of their lawless
  deeds;

10 because a jealous ear hears all
  things,
and the sound of grumbling does
  not go unheard.

11 Beware then of useless
  grumbling,
and keep your tongue from
  slander;
because no secret word is
  without result,[a]
and a lying mouth destroys the
  soul.

12 Do not invite death by the error
  of your life,
or bring on destruction by the
  works of your hands;

13 because God did not make
  death,
and he does not delight in the
  death of the living.

14 For he created all things so that
  they might exist;
the generative forces[b] of the
  world are wholesome,
and there is no destructive
  poison in them,
and the dominion[c] of Hades is
  not on earth.

15 For righteousness is immortal.

Life as the Ungodly See It

16 But the ungodly by their words
  and deeds summoned
  death;[d]
considering him a friend, they
  pined away
and made a covenant with him,
because they are fit to belong to
  his company.

2 For they reasoned unsoundly,
  saying to themselves,

---

a Or *will go unpunished*   b Or *the
creatures*   c Or *palace*   d Gk *him*

W
I
S
D
O
M

"Short and sorrowful is our life,
  and there is no remedy when a
    life comes to its end,
  and no one has been known to
    return from Hades.
2 For we were born by mere
    chance,
  and hereafter we shall be as
    though we had never been,
  for the breath in our nostrils is
    smoke,
  and reason is a spark kindled by
    the beating of our hearts;
3 when it is extinguished, the body
    will turn to ashes,
  and the spirit will dissolve like
    empty air.
4 Our name will be forgotten in
    time,
  and no one will remember our
    works;
  our life will pass away like the
    traces of a cloud,
  and be scattered like mist
  that is chased by the rays of the
    sun
  and overcome by its heat.
5 For our allotted time is the
    passing of a shadow,
  and there is no return from our
    death,
  because it is sealed up and no
    one turns back.

6 "Come, therefore, let us enjoy
    the good things that exist,
  and make use of the creation to
    the full as in youth.
7 Let us take our fill of costly wine
    and perfumes,
  and let no flower of spring pass
    us by.
8 Let us crown ourselves with
    rosebuds before they
    wither.
9 Let none of us fail to share in
    our revelry;
  everywhere let us leave signs of
    enjoyment,
  because this is our portion, and
    this our lot.
10 Let us oppress the righteous
    poor man;
  let us not spare the widow
  or regard the gray hairs of the
    aged.
11 But let our might be our law of
    right,
  for what is weak proves itself to
    be useless.

12 "Let us lie in wait for the
    righteous man,
  because he is inconvenient to us
    and opposes our actions;
  he reproaches us for sins against
    the law,
  and accuses us of sins against
    our training.
13 He professes to have knowledge
    of God,
  and calls himself a child*e* of the
    Lord.
14 He became to us a reproof of
    our thoughts;
15 the very sight of him is a burden
    to us,
  because his manner of life is
    unlike that of others,
  and his ways are strange.
16 We are considered by him as
    something base,
  and he avoids our ways as
    unclean;
  he calls the last end of the
    righteous happy,
  and boasts that God is his father.
17 Let us see if his words are true,
  and let us test what will happen
    at the end of his life;
18 for if the righteous man is God's
    child, he will help him,
  and will deliver him from the
    hand of his adversaries.
19 Let us test him with insult and
    torture,
  so that we may find out how
    gentle he is,
  and make trial of his
    forbearance.
20 Let us condemn him to a
    shameful death,
  for, according to what he says,
    he will be protected."

Error of the Wicked
(Cp Gen 1.26–27)

21 Thus they reasoned, but they
    were led astray,
  for their wickedness blinded
    them,
22 and they did not know the secret
    purposes of God,
  nor hoped for the wages of
    holiness,
  nor discerned the prize for
    blameless souls;
23 for God created us for
    incorruption,

e Or *servant*

and made us in the image of his
own eternity,[f]

24 but through the devil's envy
death entered the world,
and those who belong to his
company experience it.

The Destiny of the Righteous
(Wis 4.17)

3 But the souls of the righteous
are in the hand of God,
and no torment will ever touch
them.

2 In the eyes of the foolish they
seemed to have died,
and their departure was thought
to be a disaster,

3 and their going from us to be
their destruction;
but they are at peace.

4 For though in the sight of others
they were punished,
their hope is full of immortality.

5 Having been disciplined a little,
they will receive great
good,
because God tested them and
found them worthy of
himself;

6 like gold in the furnace he tried
them,
and like a sacrificial burnt
offering he accepted them.

7 In the time of their visitation
they will shine forth,
and will run like sparks through
the stubble.

8 They will govern nations and
rule over peoples,
and the Lord will reign over
them forever.

9 Those who trust in him will
understand truth,
and the faithful will abide with
him in love,
because grace and mercy are
upon his holy ones,
and he watches over his elect.[g]

The Destiny of the Ungodly

10 But the ungodly will be punished
as their reasoning
deserves,
those who disregarded the
righteous[h]
and rebelled against the Lord;

11 for those who despise wisdom
and instruction are
miserable.
Their hope is vain, their labors
are unprofitable,

and their works are useless.

12 Their wives are foolish, and
their children evil;

13 their offspring are accursed.

On Childlessness
(Sir 16.3)

For blessed is the barren woman
who is undefiled,
who has not entered into a sinful
union;
she will have fruit when God
examines souls.

14 Blessed also is the eunuch
whose hands have done no
lawless deed,
and who has not devised wicked
things against the Lord;
for special favor will be shown
him for his faithfulness,
and a place of great delight in
the temple of the Lord.

15 For the fruit of good labors is
renowned,
and the root of understanding
does not fail.

16 But children of adulterers will
not come to maturity,
and the offspring of an unlawful
union will perish.

17 Even if they live long they will
be held of no account,
and finally their old age will be
without honor.

18 If they die young, they will have
no hope
and no consolation on the day of
judgment.

19 For the end of an unrighteous
generation is grievous.

4 Better than this is childlessness
with virtue,
for in the memory of virtue[i] is
immortality,
because it is known both by God
and by mortals.

2 When it is present, people
imitate[j] it,
and they long for it when it has
gone;
throughout all time it marches,
crowned in triumph,
victor in the contest for prizes
that are undefiled.

---

[f] Other ancient authorities read *nature*
[g] Text of this line uncertain; omitted by
some ancient authorities. Compare 4.15
[h] Or *what is right*   [i] Gk it   [j] Other
ancient authorities read *honor*

3 But the prolific brood of the
  ungodly will be of no use,
and none of their illegitimate
  seedlings will strike a deep
  root
or take a firm hold.
4 For even if they put forth boughs
  for a while,
standing insecurely they will be
  shaken by the wind,
and by the violence of the winds
  they will be uprooted.
5 The branches will be broken off
  before they come to
  maturity,
and their fruit will be useless,
not ripe enough to eat, and good
  for nothing.
6 For children born of unlawful
  unions
are witnesses of evil against
  their parents when God
  examines them.^{k}
7 But the righteous, though they
  die early, will be at rest.
8 For old age is not honored for
  length of time,
or measured by number of
  years;
9 but understanding is gray hair
  for anyone,
and a blameless life is ripe old
  age.
10 There were some who pleased
  God and were loved by
  him,
and while living among sinners
  were taken up.
11 They were caught up so that evil
  might not change their
  understanding
or guile deceive their souls.
12 For the fascination of
  wickedness obscures what
  is good,
and roving desire perverts the
  innocent mind.
13 Being perfected in a short time,
  they fulfilled long years;
14 for their souls were pleasing to
  the Lord,
therefore he took them quickly
  from the midst of
  wickedness.
15 Yet the peoples saw and did not
  understand,
or take such a thing to heart,
that God's grace and mercy are
  with his elect,
and that he watches over his
  holy ones.

The Triumph of the Righteous

16 The righteous who have died
  will condemn the ungodly
  who are living,
and youth that is quickly
  perfected^l will condemn
  the prolonged old age of
  the unrighteous.
17 For they will see the end of the
  wise,
and will not understand what the
  Lord purposed for them,
and for what he kept them safe.
18 The unrighteous^m will see, and
  will have contempt for them,
but the Lord will laugh them to
  scorn.
After this they will become
  dishonored corpses,
and an outrage among the dead
  forever;
19 because he will dash them
  speechless to the ground,
and shake them from the
  foundations;
they will be left utterly dry and
  barren,
and they will suffer anguish,
and the memory of them will
  perish.

The Final Judgment

20 They will come with dread when
  their sins are reckoned up,
and their lawless deeds will
  convict them to their face.
5 Then the righteous will stand
  with great confidence
in the presence of those who
  have oppressed them
and those who make light of
  their labors.
2 When the unrighteous^n see
  them, they will be shaken
  with dreadful fear,
and they will be amazed at the
  unexpected salvation of the
  righteous.
3 They will speak to one another
  in repentance,
and in anguish of spirit they will
  groan, and say,
4 "These are persons whom we
  once held in derision
and made a byword of
  reproach—fools that we
  were!

We thought that their lives were
madness
and that their end was without
honor.
5 Why have they been numbered
among the children of
God?
And why is their lot among the
saints?
6 So it was we who strayed from
the way of truth,
and the light of righteousness
did not shine on us,
and the sun did not rise upon us.
7 We took our fill of the paths of
lawlessness and
destruction,
and we journeyed through
trackless deserts,
but the way of the Lord we have
not known.
8 What has our arrogance profited
us?
And what good has our boasted
wealth brought us?

9 "All those things have vanished
like a shadow,
and like a rumor that passes by;
10 like a ship that sails through the
billowy water,
and when it has passed no trace
can be found,
no track of its keel in the waves;
11 or as, when a bird flies through
the air,
no evidence of its passage is
found;
the light air, lashed by the beat
of its pinions
and pierced by the force of its
rushing flight,
is traversed by the movement of
its wings,
and afterward no sign of its
coming is found there;
12 or as, when an arrow is shot at a
target,
the air, thus divided, comes
together at once,
so that no one knows its
pathway.
13 So we also, as soon as we were
born, ceased to be,
and we had no sign of virtue to
show,
but were consumed in our
wickedness."
14 Because the hope of the ungodly
is like thistledown[o] carried
by the wind,

and like a light frost[p] driven
away by a storm;
it is dispersed like smoke before
the wind,
and it passes like the
remembrance of a guest
who stays but a day.

The Reward of the Righteous
(Eph 6.10–20)

15 But the righteous live forever,
and their reward is with the
Lord;
the Most High takes care of
them.
16 Therefore they will receive a
glorious crown
and a beautiful diadem from the
hand of the Lord,
because with his right hand he
will cover them,
and with his arm he will shield
them.
17 The Lord[q] will take his zeal as
his whole armor,
and will arm all creation to
repel[r] his enemies;
18 he will put on righteousness as a
breastplate,
and wear impartial justice as a
helmet;
19 he will take holiness as an
invincible shield,
20 and sharpen stern wrath for a
sword,
and creation will join with him
to fight against his frenzied
foes.
21 Shafts of lightning will fly with
true aim,
and will leap from the clouds to
the target, as from a
well-drawn bow,
22 and hailstones full of wrath will
be hurled as from a
catapult;
the water of the sea will rage
against them,
and rivers will relentlessly
overwhelm them;
23 a mighty wind will rise against
them,
and like a tempest it will
winnow them away.
Lawlessness will lay waste the
whole earth,

o Other ancient authorities read *dust*
p Other ancient authorities read *spider's*
web   q Gk *He*   r Or *punish*

and evildoing will overturn the
thrones of rulers.

Kings Should Seek Wisdom
(Rom 13.1)

6 Listen therefore, O kings, and
understand;
learn, O judges of the ends of
the earth.
2 Give ear, you that rule over
multitudes,
and boast of many nations.
3 For your dominion was given
you from the Lord,
and your sovereignty from the
Most High;
he will search out your works
and inquire into your
plans.
4 Because as servants of his
kingdom you did not rule
rightly,
or keep the law,
or walk according to the purpose
of God,
5 he will come upon you terribly
and swiftly,
because severe judgment falls on
those in high places.
6 For the lowliest may be
pardoned in mercy,
but the mighty will be mightily
tested.
7 For the Lord of all will not stand
in awe of anyone,
or show deference to greatness;
because he himself made both
small and great,
and he takes thought for all
alike.
8 But a strict inquiry is in store for
the mighty.
9 To you then, O monarchs, my
words are directed,
so that you may learn wisdom
and not transgress.
10 For they will be made holy who
observe holy things in
holiness,
and those who have been taught
them will find a defense.
11 Therefore set your desire on my
words;
long for them, and you will be
instructed.

Description of Wisdom
(Cp Prov 8.1–36)

12 Wisdom is radiant and unfading,
and she is easily discerned by
those who love her,

and is found by those who seek
her.
13 She hastens to make herself
known to those who desire
her.
14 One who rises early to seek her
will have no difficulty,
for she will be found sitting at
the gate.
15 To fix one's thought on her is
perfect understanding,
and one who is vigilant on her
account will soon be free
from care,
16 because she goes about seeking
those worthy of her,
and she graciously appears to
them in their paths,
and meets them in every
thought.

17 The beginning of wisdom[s] is the
most sincere desire for
instruction,
and concern for instruction is
love of her,
18 and love of her is the keeping of
her laws,
and giving heed to her laws is
assurance of immortality,
19 and immortality brings one near
to God;
20 so the desire for wisdom leads to
a kingdom.

21 Therefore if you delight in
thrones and scepters,
O monarchs over the
peoples,
honor wisdom, so that you may
reign forever.
22 I will tell you what wisdom is
and how she came to be,
and I will hide no secrets from
you,
but I will trace her course from
the beginning of creation,
and make knowledge of her
clear,
and I will not pass by the truth;
23 nor will I travel in the company
of sickly envy,
for envy[t] does not associate
with wisdom.
24 The multitude of the wise is the
salvation of the world,
and a sensible king is the
stability of any people.
25 Therefore be instructed by my
words, and you will profit.

[s] Gk *Her beginning*   [t] Gk *this*

Solomon Like Other Mortals

7 I also am mortal, like everyone
     else,
a descendant of the first-formed
     child of earth;
and in the womb of a mother I
     was molded into flesh,
2 within the period of ten months,
     compacted with blood,
from the seed of a man and the
     pleasure of marriage.
3 And when I was born, I began to
     breathe the common air,
and fell upon the kindred earth;
my first sound was a cry, as is
     true of all.
4 I was nursed with care in
     swaddling cloths.
5 For no king has had a different
     beginning of existence;
6 there is for all one entrance into
     life, and one way out.

Solomon's Respect for Wisdom
(1 Kings 3.3–9; Wis 9.1–18)

7 Therefore I prayed, and
     understanding was given
     me;
I called on God, and the spirit of
     wisdom came to me.
8 I preferred her to scepters and
     thrones,
and I accounted wealth as
     nothing in comparison with
     her.
9 Neither did I liken to her any
     priceless gem,
because all gold is but a little
     sand in her sight,
and silver will be accounted as
     clay before her.
10 I loved her more than health and
     beauty,
and I chose to have her rather
     than light,
because her radiance never
     ceases.
11 All good things came to me
     along with her,
and in her hands uncounted
     wealth.
12 I rejoiced in them all, because
     wisdom leads them;
but I did not know that she was
     their mother.
13 I learned without guile and I
     impart without grudging;
I do not hide her wealth,
14 for it is an unfailing treasure for
     mortals;

those who get it obtain
     friendship with God,
commended for the gifts that
     come from instruction.

Solomon Prays for Wisdom

15 May God grant me to speak with
     judgment,
and to have thoughts worthy of
     what I have received;
for he is the guide even of
     wisdom
and the corrector of the wise.
16 For both we and our words are
     in his hand,
as are all understanding and
     skill in crafts.
17 For it is he who gave me
     unerring knowledge of
     what exists,
to know the structure of the
     world and the activity of
     the elements;
18 the beginning and end and
     middle of times,
the alternations of the solstices
     and the changes of the
     seasons,
19 the cycles of the year and the
     constellations of the stars,
20 the natures of animals and the
     tempers of wild animals,
the powers of spirits[u] and the
     thoughts of human beings,
the varieties of plants and the
     virtues of roots;
21 I learned both what is secret and
     what is manifest,
22 for wisdom, the fashioner of all
     things, taught me.

The Nature of Wisdom
(Jn 1.1–14; Heb 1.1–4)

There is in her a spirit that is
     intelligent, holy,
unique, manifold, subtle,
mobile, clear, unpolluted,
distinct, invulnerable, loving the
     good, keen,
irresistible, 23 beneficent,
     humane,
steadfast, sure, free from
     anxiety,
all-powerful, overseeing all,
and penetrating through all
     spirits
that are intelligent, pure, and
     altogether subtle.

[u] Or *winds*

WISDOM

24 For wisdom is more mobile than
any motion;
because of her pureness she
pervades and penetrates all
things.
25 For she is a breath of the power
of God,
and a pure emanation of the
glory of the Almighty;
therefore nothing defiled gains
entrance into her.
26 For she is a reflection of eternal
light,
a spotless mirror of the working
of God,
and an image of his goodness.
27 Although she is but one, she can
do all things,
and while remaining in herself,
she renews all things;
in every generation she passes
into holy souls
and makes them friends of God,
and prophets;
28 for God loves nothing so much
as the person who lives
with wisdom.
29 She is more beautiful than the
sun,
and excels every constellation of
the stars.
Compared with the light she is
found to be superior,
30 for it is succeeded by the night,
but against wisdom evil does not
prevail.

8 She reaches mightily from one
end of the earth to the
other,
and she orders all things well.

Solomon's Love for Wisdom
(Cp Prov 8.22–31)

2 I loved her and sought her from
my youth;
I desired to take her for my
bride,
and became enamored of her
beauty.
3 She glorifies her noble birth by
living with God,
and the Lord of all loves her.
4 For she is an initiate in the
knowledge of God,
and an associate in his works.
5 If riches are a desirable
possession in life,
what is richer than wisdom, the
active cause of all things?
6 And if understanding is effective,
who more than she is fashioner
of what exists?

7 And if anyone loves
righteousness,
her labors are virtues;
for she teaches self-control and
prudence,
justice and courage;
nothing in life is more profitable
for mortals than these.
8 And if anyone longs for wide
experience,
she knows the things of old, and
infers the things to come;
she understands turns of speech
and the solutions of
riddles;
she has foreknowledge of signs
and wonders
and of the outcome of seasons
and times.

Wisdom Indispensible to Rulers

9 Therefore I determined to take
her to live with me,
knowing that she would give me
good counsel
and encouragement in cares and
grief.
10 Because of her I shall have glory
among the multitudes
and honor in the presence of the
elders, though I am young.
11 I shall be found keen in
judgment,
and in the sight of rulers I shall
be admired.
12 When I am silent they will wait
for me,
and when I speak they will give
heed;
if I speak at greater length,
they will put their hands on their
mouths.
13 Because of her I shall have
immortality,
and leave an everlasting
remembrance to those who
come after me.
14 I shall govern peoples,
and nations will be subject to
me;
15 dread monarchs will be afraid of
me when they hear of me;
among the people I shall show
myself capable, and
courageous in war.
16 When I enter my house, I shall
find rest with her;
for companionship with her has
no bitterness,
and life with her has no pain,
but gladness and joy.

17 When I considered these things
   inwardly,
   and pondered in my heart
that in kinship with wisdom
   there is immortality,
18 and in friendship with her, pure
   delight,
and in the labors of her hands,
   unfailing wealth,
and in the experience of her
   company, understanding,
and renown in sharing her
   words,
I went about seeking how to get
   her for myself.
19 As a child I was naturally gifted,
and a good soul fell to my lot;
20 or rather, being good, I entered
   an undefiled body.
21 But I perceived that I would not
   possess wisdom unless God
   gave her to me—
and it was a mark of insight to
   know whose gift she was—
so I appealed to the Lord and
   implored him,
and with my whole heart I said:

Solomon's Prayer for Wisdom
(1 Kings 3.3–9; Wis 7.7–22a)

9 "O God of my ancestors and
   Lord of mercy,
who have made all things by
   your word,
2 and by your wisdom have
   formed humankind
to have dominion over the
   creatures you have made,
3 and rule the world in holiness
   and righteousness,
and pronounce judgment in
   uprightness of soul,
4 give me the wisdom that sits by
   your throne,
and do not reject me from
   among your servants.
5 For I am your servant[v] the son
   of your serving girl,
a man who is weak and
   short-lived,
with little understanding of
   judgment and laws;
6 for even one who is perfect
   among human beings
will be regarded as nothing
   without the wisdom that
   comes from you.
7 You have chosen me to be king
   of your people
and to be judge over your sons
   and daughters.

8 You have given command to
   build a temple on your
   holy mountain,
and an altar in the city of your
   habitation,
a copy of the holy tent that you
   prepared from the
   beginning.
9 With you is wisdom, she who
   knows your works
and was present when you made
   the world;
she understands what is pleasing
   in your sight
and what is right according to
   your commandments.
10 Send her forth from the holy
   heavens,
and from the throne of your
   glory send her,
that she may labor at my side,
and that I may learn what is
   pleasing to you.
11 For she knows and understands
   all things,
and she will guide me wisely in
   my actions
and guard me with her glory.
12 Then my works will be
   acceptable,
and I shall judge your people
   justly,
and shall be worthy of the
   throne[w] of my father.
13 For who can learn the counsel of
   God?
Or who can discern what the
   Lord wills?
14 For the reasoning of mortals is
   worthless,
and our designs are likely to fail;
15 for a perishable body weighs
   down the soul,
and this earthy tent burdens the
   thoughtful[x] mind.
16 We can hardly guess at what is
   on earth,
and what is at hand we find with
   labor;
but who has traced out what is
   in the heavens?
17 Who has learned your counsel,
   unless you have given wisdom
and sent your holy spirit from
   on high?
18 And thus the paths of those on
   earth were set right,
and people were taught what
   pleases you,
and were saved by wisdom."

v Gk *slave*   *w* Gk *thrones*   *x* Or *anxious*

W
I
S
D
O
M

*The Work of Wisdom
from Adam to Moses*

10 Wisdom[y] protected the first-formed father of the world, when he alone had been created;
she delivered him from his transgression,

2 and gave him strength to rule all things.

3 But when an unrighteous man departed from her in his anger,
he perished because in rage he killed his brother.

4 When the earth was flooded because of him, wisdom again saved it,
steering the righteous man by a paltry piece of wood.

5 Wisdom[y] also, when the nations in wicked agreement had been put to confusion,
recognized the righteous man and preserved him blameless before God,
and kept him strong in the face of his compassion for his child.

6 Wisdom[y] rescued a righteous man when the ungodly were perishing;
he escaped the fire that descended on the Five Cities.[z]

7 Evidence of their wickedness still remains:
a continually smoking wasteland,
plants bearing fruit that does not ripen,
and a pillar of salt standing as a monument to an unbelieving soul.

8 For because they passed wisdom by,
they not only were hindered from recognizing the good,
but also left for humankind a reminder of their folly,
so that their failures could never go unnoticed.

9 Wisdom rescued from troubles those who served her.

10 When a righteous man fled from his brother's wrath,
she guided him on straight paths;

she showed him the kingdom of God,
and gave him knowledge of holy things;
she prospered him in his labors,
and increased the fruit of his toil.

11 When his oppressors were covetous,
she stood by him and made him rich.

12 She protected him from his enemies,
and kept him safe from those who lay in wait for him;
in his arduous contest she gave him the victory,
so that he might learn that godliness is more powerful than anything else.

13 When a righteous man was sold, wisdom[a] did not desert him,
but delivered him from sin.
She descended with him into the dungeon,

14 and when he was in prison she did not leave him,
until she brought him the scepter of a kingdom
and authority over his masters.
Those who accused him she showed to be false,
and she gave him everlasting honor.

Wisdom Led the Israelites out of Egypt
(Ex 13 – 15)

15 A holy people and blameless race
wisdom delivered from a nation of oppressors.

16 She entered the soul of a servant of the Lord,
and withstood dread kings with wonders and signs.

17 She gave to holy people the reward of their labors;
she guided them along a marvelous way,
and became a shelter to them by day,
and a starry flame through the night.

18 She brought them over the Red Sea,
and led them through deep waters;

[y] Gk *She*   [z] Or *on Pentapolis*   [a] Gk *she*

19 but she drowned their enemies,
and cast them up from the depth
of the sea.
20 Therefore the righteous
plundered the ungodly;
they sang hymns, O Lord, to
your holy name,
and praised with one accord
your defending hand;
21 for wisdom opened the mouths
of those who were mute,
and made the tongues of infants
speak clearly.

Wisdom Led the Israelites through the Desert
(Ex 15 – 17)

11 Wisdom[b] prospered their
works by the hand of a
holy prophet.
2 They journeyed through an
uninhabited wilderness,
and pitched their tents in
untrodden places.
3 They withstood their enemies
and fought off their foes.
4 When they were thirsty, they
called upon you,
and water was given them out of
flinty rock,
and from hard stone a remedy
for their thirst.
5 For through the very things by
which their enemies were
punished,
they themselves received benefit
in their need.
6 Instead of the fountain of an
ever-flowing river,
stirred up and defiled with blood
7 in rebuke for the decree to kill
the infants,
you gave them abundant water
unexpectedly,
8 showing by their thirst at that
time
how you punished their enemies.
9 For when they were tried,
though they were being
disciplined in mercy,
they learned how the ungodly
were tormented when
judged in wrath.
10 For you tested them as a
parent[c] does in warning,
but you examined the ungodly[d]
as a stern king does in
condemnation.
11 Whether absent or present, they
were equally distressed,

12 for a twofold grief possessed
them,
and a groaning at the memory of
what had occurred.
13 For when they heard that
through their own
punishments
the righteous[e] had received
benefit, they perceived it
was the Lord's doing.
14 For though they had mockingly
rejected him who long
before had been cast out
and exposed,
at the end of the events they
marveled at him,
when they felt thirst in a
different way from the
righteous.

Punishment of the Wicked
(Ex 7 – 11)

15 In return for their foolish and
wicked thoughts,
which led them astray to
worship irrational serpents
and worthless animals,
you sent upon them a multitude
of irrational creatures to
punish them,
16 so that they might learn that one
is punished by the very
things by which one sins.
17 For your all-powerful hand,
which created the world out of
formless matter,
did not lack the means to send
upon them a multitude of
bears, or bold lions,
18 or newly-created unknown
beasts full of rage,
or such as breathe out fiery
breath,
or belch forth a thick pall of
smoke,
or flash terrible sparks from
their eyes;
19 not only could the harm they did
destroy people,[f]
but the mere sight of them could
kill by fright.
20 Even apart from these, people[e]
could fall at a single breath
when pursued by justice
and scattered by the breath of
your power.

b Gk *She*   *c* Gk *a father*   *d* Gk *those*
e Gk *they*   *f* Gk *them*

But you have arranged all things
   by measure and number
   and weight.

God Is Powerful and Merciful

21 For it is always in your power to
      show great strength,
   and who can withstand the
      might of your arm?

22 Because the whole world before
      you is like a speck that tips
      the scales,
   and like a drop of morning dew
      that falls on the ground.

23 But you are merciful to all, for
      you can do all things,
   and you overlook people's sins,
      so that they may repent.

24 For you love all things that exist,
   and detest none of the things
      that you have made,
   for you would not have made
      anything if you had hated
      it.

25 How would anything have
      endured if you had not
      willed it?
   Or how would anything not
      called forth by you have
      been preserved?

26 You spare all things, for they are
      yours, O Lord, you who
      love the living.

12 For your immortal spirit is in
         all things.
2 Therefore you correct little by
      little those who trespass,
   and you remind and warn them
      of the things through
      which they sin,
   so that they may be freed from
      wickedness and put their
      trust in you, O Lord.

The Sins of the Canaanites
(Ex 23.20–33; Deut 18.9–14)

3 Those who lived long ago in
      your holy land

4 you hated for their detestable
      practices,
   their works of sorcery and
      unholy rites,

5 their merciless slaughter^g of
      children,
   and their sacrificial feasting on
      human flesh and blood.
   These initiates from the midst of
      a heathen cult,^{h}

6 these parents who murder
      helpless lives,

you willed to destroy by the
   hands of our ancestors,

7 so that the land most precious of
      all to you
   might receive a worthy colony of
      the servants^i of God.

8 But even these you spared, since
      they were but mortals,
   and sent wasps^j as forerunners
      of your army
   to destroy them little by little,

9 though you were not unable to
      give the ungodly into the
      hands of the righteous in
      battle,
   or to destroy them at one blow
      by dread wild animals or
      your stern word.

10 But judging them little by little
      you gave them an
      opportunity to repent,
   though you were not unaware
      that their origin^k was evil
   and their wickedness inborn,
   and that their way of thinking
      would never change.

11 For they were an accursed race
      from the beginning,
   and it was not through fear of
      anyone that you left them
      unpunished for their sins.

God Is Sovereign

12 For who will say, "What have
      you done?"
   Or will resist your judgment?
   Who will accuse you for the
      destruction of nations that
      you made?
   Or who will come before you to
      plead as an advocate for
      the unrighteous?

13 For neither is there any god
      besides you, whose care is
      for all people,^{l}
   to whom you should prove that
      you have not judged
      unjustly;

14 nor can any king or monarch
      confront you about those
      whom you have punished.

15 You are righteous and you rule
      all things righteously,
   deeming it alien to your power
   to condemn anyone who does
      not deserve to be punished.

^{g} Gk *slaughterers* ^{h} Meaning of Gk
uncertain ^{i} Or *children* ^{j} Or *hornets*
^{k} Or *nature* ^{l} Or *all things*

16 For your strength is the source
of righteousness,
and your sovereignty over all
causes you to spare all.
17 For you show your strength
when people doubt the
completeness of your
power,
and you rebuke any insolence
among those who know
it.*m*
18 Although you are sovereign in
strength, you judge with
mildness,
and with great forbearance you
govern us;
for you have power to act
whenever you choose.

God's Lessons for Israel

19 Through such works you have
taught your people
that the righteous must be kind,
and you have filled your
children with good hope,
because you give repentance for
sins.
20 For if you punished with such
great care and indulgence*n*
the enemies of your servants*o*
and those deserving of
death,
granting them time and
opportunity to give up their
wickedness,
21 with what strictness you have
judged your children,
to whose ancestors you gave
oaths and covenants full of
good promises!
22 So while chastening us you
scourge our enemies ten
thousand times more,
so that, when we judge, we may
meditate upon your
goodness,
and when we are judged, we
may expect mercy.

The Punishment of the Egyptians

23 Therefore those who lived
unrighteously, in a life of
folly,
you tormented through their
own abominations.
24 For they went far astray on the
paths of error,
accepting as gods those animals
that even their enemies*p*
despised;

they were deceived like foolish
infants.
25 Therefore, as though to children
who cannot reason,
you sent your judgment to mock
them.
26 But those who have not heeded
the warning of mild
rebukes
will experience the deserved
judgment of God.
27 For when in their suffering they
became incensed
at those creatures that they had
thought to be gods, being
punished by means of
them,
they saw and recognized as the
true God the one whom
they had before refused to
know.
Therefore the utmost
condemnation came upon
them.

The Foolishness of Nature Worship

13 For all people who were
ignorant of God were
foolish by nature;
and they were unable from the
good things that are seen
to know the one who
exists,
nor did they recognize the
artisan while paying heed
to his works;
2 but they supposed that either
fire or wind or swift air,
or the circle of the stars, or
turbulent water,
or the luminaries of heaven were
the gods that rule the
world.
3 If through delight in the beauty
of these things people
assumed them to be gods,
let them know how much better
than these is their Lord,
for the author of beauty created
them.
4 And if people*p* were amazed at
their power and working,
let them perceive from them
how much more powerful is the
one who formed them.
5 For from the greatness and
beauty of created things

m Meaning of Gk uncertain   *n* Other
ancient authorities lack *and indulgence*;
others read *and entreaty*   *o* Or *children*
p Gk *they*

comes a corresponding
perception of their Creator.
6 Yet these people are little to be
blamed,
for perhaps they go astray
while seeking God and desiring
to find him.
7 For while they live among his
works, they keep
searching,
and they trust in what they see,
because the things that are
seen are beautiful.
8 Yet again, not even they are to
be excused;
9 for if they had the power to
know so much
that they could investigate the
world,
how did they fail to find sooner
the Lord of these things?

The Foolishness of Idolatry
(Isa 44.9–20; Jer 10.1–16; Let Jer 8–73)

10 But miserable, with their hopes
set on dead things, are
those
who give the name "gods" to the
works of human hands,
gold and silver fashioned with
skill,
and likenesses of animals,
or a useless stone, the work of
an ancient hand.
11 A skilled woodcutter may saw
down a tree easy to handle
and skillfully strip off all its
bark,
and then with pleasing
workmanship
make a useful vessel that serves
life's needs,
12 and burn the cast-off pieces of
his work
to prepare his food, and eat his
fill.
13 But a cast-off piece from among
them, useful for nothing,
a stick crooked and full of knots,
he takes and carves with care in
his leisure,
and shapes it with skill gained in
idleness;[q]
he forms it in the likeness of a
human being,
14 or makes it like some worthless
animal,
giving it a coat of red paint and
coloring its surface red
and covering every blemish in it
with paint;

15 then he makes a suitable niche
for it,
and sets it in the wall, and
fastens it there with iron.
16 He takes thought for it, so that it
may not fall,
because he knows that it cannot
help itself,
for it is only an image and has
need of help.
17 When he prays about
possessions and his
marriage and children,
he is not ashamed to address a
lifeless thing.
18 For health he appeals to a thing
that is weak;
for life he prays to a thing that
is dead;
for aid he entreats a thing that is
utterly inexperienced;
for a prosperous journey, a thing
that cannot take a step;
19 for money-making and work and
success with his hands
he asks strength of a thing
whose hands have no
strength.

Folly of a Navigator Praying to an Idol

14 Again, one preparing to sail
and about to voyage over
raging waves
calls upon a piece of wood more
fragile than the ship that
carries him.
2 For it was desire for gain that
planned that vessel,
and wisdom was the artisan who
built it;
3 but it is your providence,
O Father, that steers its
course,
because you have given it a path
in the sea,
and a safe way through the
waves,
4 showing that you can save from
every danger,
so that even a person who lacks
skill may put to sea.
5 It is your will that works of your
wisdom should not be
without effect;
therefore people trust their lives
even to the smallest piece
of wood,

[q] Other ancient authorities read *with intelligent skill*

and passing through the billows
on a raft they come safely
to land.
6 For even in the beginning, when
arrogant giants were
perishing,
the hope of the world took
refuge on a raft,
and guided by your hand left to
the world the seed of a
new generation.
7 For blessed is the wood by
which righteousness
comes.

8 But the idol made with hands is
accursed, and so is the one
who made it—
he for having made it, and the
perishable thing because it
was named a god.
9 For equally hateful to God are
the ungodly and their
ungodliness;
10 for what was done will be
punished together with the
one who did it.
11 Therefore there will be a
visitation also upon the
heathen idols,
because, though part of what
God created, they became
an abomination,
snares for human souls
and a trap for the feet of the
foolish.

The Origin and Evils of Idolatry

12 For the idea of making idols was
the beginning of
fornication,
and the invention of them was
the corruption of life;
13 for they did not exist from the
beginning,
nor will they last forever.
14 For through human vanity they
entered the world,
and therefore their speedy end
has been planned.

15 For a father, consumed with
grief at an untimely
bereavement,
made an image of his child, who
had been suddenly taken
from him;
he now honored as a god what
was once a dead human
being,

and handed on to his dependents
secret rites and initiations.
16 Then the ungodly custom, grown
strong with time, was kept
as a law,
and at the command of
monarchs carved images
were worshiped.
17 When people could not honor
monarchs[r] in their
presence, since they lived
at a distance,
they imagined their appearance
far away,
and made a visible image of the
king whom they honored,
so that by their zeal they might
flatter the absent one as
though present.
18 Then the ambition of the artisan
impelled
even those who did not know
the king to intensify their
worship.
19 For he, perhaps wishing to
please his ruler,
skillfully forced the likeness to
take more beautiful form,
20 and the multitude, attracted by
the charm of his work,
now regarded as an object of
worship the one whom
shortly before they had
honored as a human being.
21 And this became a hidden trap
for humankind,
because people, in bondage to
misfortune or to royal
authority,
bestowed on objects of stone or
wood the name that ought
not to be shared.

22 Then it was not enough for them
to err about the knowledge
of God,
but though living in great strife
due to ignorance,
they call such great evils peace.
23 For whether they kill children in
their initiations, or
celebrate secret mysteries,
or hold frenzied revels with
strange customs,
24 they no longer keep either their
lives or their marriages
pure,

[r] Gk *them*

but they either treacherously kill
one another, or grieve one
another by adultery,
25 and all is a raging riot of blood
and murder, theft and
deceit, corruption,
faithlessness, tumult,
perjury,
26 confusion over what is good,
forgetfulness of favors,
defiling of souls, sexual
perversion,
disorder in marriages, adultery,
and debauchery.
27 For the worship of idols not to
be named
is the beginning and cause and
end of every evil.
28 For their worshipers[s] either
rave in exultation,
or prophesy lies, or live
unrighteously, or readily
commit perjury;
29 for because they trust in lifeless
idols
they swear wicked oaths and
expect to suffer no harm.
30 But just penalties will overtake
them on two counts:
because they thought wrongly
about God in devoting
themselves to idols,
and because in deceit they swore
unrighteously through
contempt for holiness.
31 For it is not the power of the
things by which people
swear,[t]
but the just penalty for those
who sin,
that always pursues the
transgression of the
unrighteous.

Benefits of Worshiping the True God

15 But you, our God, are kind
and true,
patient, and ruling all things[u] in
mercy.
2 For even if we sin we are yours,
knowing your power;
but we will not sin, because we
know that you
acknowledge us as yours.
3 For to know you is complete
righteousness,
and to know your power is the
root of immortality.
4 For neither has the evil intent of
human art misled us,
nor the fruitless toil of painters,

a figure stained with varied
colors,
5 whose appearance arouses
yearning in fools,
so that they desire[v] the lifeless
form of a dead image.
6 Lovers of evil things and fit for
such objects of hope[w]
are those who either make or
desire or worship them.

The Foolishness of Worshiping Clay Idols

7 A potter kneads the soft earth
and laboriously molds each
vessel for our service,
fashioning out of the same clay
both the vessels that serve clean
uses
and those for contrary uses,
making all alike;
but which shall be the use of
each of them
the worker in clay decides.
8 With misspent toil, these
workers form a futile god
from the same clay—
these mortals who were made of
earth a short time before
and after a little while go to the
earth from which all
mortals are taken,
when the time comes to return
the souls that were
borrowed.
9 But the workers are not
concerned that mortals are
destined to die
or that their life is brief,
but they compete with workers
in gold and silver,
and imitate workers in copper;
and they count it a glorious
thing to mold counterfeit
gods.
10 Their heart is ashes, their hope
is cheaper than dirt,
and their lives are of less worth
than clay,
11 because they failed to know the
one who formed them
and inspired them with active
souls
and breathed a living spirit into
them.
12 But they considered our
existence an idle game,

s Gk *they*   *t* Or *of the oaths people
swear*   *u* Or *ruling the universe*
v Gk *and he desires*   *w* Gk *such hopes*

and life a festival held for profit,
for they say one must get money
     however one can, even by
     base means.

13 For these persons, more than all
          others, know that they sin
when they make from earthy
     matter fragile vessels and
     carved images.

14 But most foolish, and more
          miserable than an infant,
are all the enemies who
     oppressed your people.

15 For they thought that all their
          heathen idols were gods,
though these have neither the
     use of their eyes to see
     with,
nor nostrils with which to draw
     breath,
nor ears with which to hear,
nor fingers to feel with,
and their feet are of no use for
     walking.

16 For a human being made them,
and one whose spirit is
          borrowed formed them;
for none can form gods that are
     like themselves.

17 People are mortal, and what
          they make with lawless
          hands is dead;
for they are better than the
     objects they worship,
since*x* they have life, but the
     idols*y* never had.

Serpents in the Desert
(Num 11.31–35; 21.6–9)

18 Moreover, they worship even the
          most hateful animals,
which are worse than all others
          when judged by their lack
          of intelligence;

19 and even as animals they are not
          so beautiful in appearance
          that one would desire
          them,
but they have escaped both the
     praise of God and his
     blessing.

16 Therefore those people*z* were
          deservedly punished
          through such creatures,
and were tormented by a
     multitude of animals.

2 Instead of this punishment you
          showed kindness to your
          people,
and you prepared quails to eat,

a delicacy to satisfy the desire of
     appetite;

3 in order that those people, when
          they desired food,
might lose the least remnant of
     appetite*a*
because of the odious creatures
     sent to them,
while your people,*z* after
     suffering want a short
     time,
might partake of delicacies.

4 For it was necessary that upon
          those oppressors
          inescapable want should
          come,
while to these others it was
     merely shown how their
     enemies were being
     tormented.

5 For when the terrible rage of
          wild animals came upon
          your people*b*
and they were being destroyed
     by the bites of writhing
     serpents,
your wrath did not continue to
     the end;

6 they were troubled for a little
          while as a warning,
and received a symbol of
     deliverance to remind them
     of your law's command.

7 For the one who turned toward
          it was saved, not by the
          thing that was beheld,
but by you, the Savior of all.

8 And by this also you convinced
          our enemies
that it is you who deliver from
     every evil.

9 For they were killed by the bites
          of locusts and flies,
and no healing was found for
     them,
because they deserved to be
     punished by such things.

10 But your children were not
          conquered even by the
          fangs of venomous
          serpents,
for your mercy came to their
     help and healed them.

11 To remind them of your oracles
          they were bitten,
and then were quickly delivered,

---

x Other ancient authorities read *of which*
y Gk *but they*   *z* Gk *they*   *a* Gk *loathed*
the necessary appetite   *b* Gk *them*

W
I
S
D
O
M

so that they would not fall into
deep forgetfulness
and become unresponsive[c] to
your kindness.
12 For neither herb nor poultice
cured them,
but it was your word, O Lord,
that heals all people.
13 For you have power over life
and death;
you lead mortals down to the
gates of Hades and back
again.
14 A person in wickedness kills
another,
but cannot bring back the
departed spirit,
or set free the imprisoned soul.

Disastrous Storms Strike Egypt

15 To escape from your hand is
impossible;
16 for the ungodly, refusing to
know you,
were flogged by the strength of
your arm,
pursued by unusual rains and
hail and relentless storms,
and utterly consumed by fire.
17 For — most incredible of all — in
water, which quenches all
things,
the fire had still greater effect,
for the universe defends the
righteous.
18 At one time the flame was
restrained,
so that it might not consume the
creatures sent against the
ungodly,
but that seeing this they might
know
that they were being pursued by
the judgment of God;
19 and at another time even in the
midst of water it burned
more intensely than fire,
to destroy the crops of the
unrighteous land.

The Israelites Receive Manna
(Ex 16.1–21)

20 Instead of these things you gave
your people food of angels,
and without their toil you
supplied them from heaven
with bread ready to eat,
providing every pleasure and
suited to every taste.

21 For your sustenance manifested
your sweetness toward
your children;
and the bread, ministering[d] to
the desire of the one who
took it,
was changed to suit everyone's
liking.
22 Snow and ice withstood fire
without melting,
so that they might know that the
crops of their enemies
were being destroyed by the fire
that blazed in the hail
and flashed in the showers of
rain;
23 whereas the fire,[e] in order that
the righteous might be fed,
even forgot its native power.

24 For creation, serving you who
made it,
exerts itself to punish the
unrighteous,
and in kindness relaxes on
behalf of those who trust in
you.
25 Therefore at that time also,
changed into all forms,
it served your all-nourishing
bounty,
according to the desire of those
who had need,[f]
26 so that your children, whom you
loved, O Lord, might learn
that it is not the production of
crops that feeds
humankind
but that your word sustains
those who trust in you.
27 For what was not destroyed by
fire
was melted when simply
warmed by a fleeting ray
of the sun,
28 to make it known that one must
rise before the sun to give
you thanks,
and must pray to you at the
dawning of the light;
29 for the hope of an ungrateful
person will melt like wintry
frost,
and flow away like waste water.

[c] Meaning of Gk uncertain   [d] Gk and it,
ministering   [e] Gk this   [f] Or who made
supplication

Terror Strikes the Egyptians at Night
(Ex 10.21–23)

17 Great are your judgments and
hard to describe;
therefore uninstructed souls
have gone astray.
2 For when lawless people
supposed that they held the
holy nation in their power,
they themselves lay as captives
of darkness and prisoners
of long night,
shut in under their roofs, exiles
from eternal providence,
3 For thinking that in their secret
sins they were unobserved
behind a dark curtain of
forgetfulness,
they were scattered, terribly[g]
alarmed,
and appalled by specters.
4 For not even the inner chamber
that held them protected
them from fear,
but terrifying sounds rang out
around them,
and dismal phantoms with
gloomy faces appeared.
5 And no power of fire was able to
give light,
nor did the brilliant flames of
the stars
avail to illumine that hateful
night.
6 Nothing was shining through to
them
except a dreadful, self-kindled
fire,
and in terror they deemed the
things that they saw
to be worse than that unseen
appearance.
7 The delusions of their magic art
lay humbled,
and their boasted wisdom was
scornfully rebuked.
8 For those who promised to drive
off the fears and disorders
of a sick soul
were sick themselves with
ridiculous fear.
9 For even if nothing disturbing
frightened them,
yet, scared by the passing of
wild animals and the
hissing of snakes
10 they perished in trembling fear,
refusing to look even at the air,
though it nowhere could be
avoided.

11 For wickedness is a cowardly
thing, condemned by its
own testimony;[h]
distressed by conscience, it has
always exaggerated[i] the
difficulties.
12 For fear is nothing but a giving
up of the helps that come
from reason;
13 and hope, defeated by this
inward weakness,
prefers ignorance of what causes
the torment.
14 But throughout the night, which
was really powerless
and which came upon them from
the recesses of powerless
Hades,
they all slept the same sleep,
15 and now were driven by
monstrous specters,
and now were paralyzed by their
souls' surrender;
for sudden and unexpected fear
overwhelmed them.
16 And whoever was there fell
down,
and thus was kept shut up in a
prison not made of iron;
17 for whether they were farmers
or shepherds
or workers who toiled in the
wilderness,
they were seized, and endured
the inescapable fate;
for with one chain of darkness
they all were bound.
18 Whether there came a whistling
wind,
or a melodious sound of birds in
wide-spreading branches,
or the rhythm of violently
rushing water,
19 or the harsh crash of rocks
hurled down,
or the unseen running of leaping
animals,
or the sound of the most savage
roaring beasts,
or an echo thrown back from a
hollow of the mountains,
it paralyzed them with terror.
20 For the whole world was
illumined with brilliant
light,

g Other ancient authorities read
unobserved, they were darkened behind
a dark curtain of forgetfulness, terribly
h Meaning of Gk uncertain   i Other
ancient authorities read anticipated

and went about its work
    unhindered,
21 while over those people alone
    heavy night was spread,
an image of the darkness that
    was destined to receive
    them;
but still heavier than darkness
    were they to themselves.

Light Shines on the Israelites
(Ex 13.17–22)

18 But for your holy ones there
    was very great light.
Their enemies[j] heard their
    voices but did not see their
    forms,
and counted them happy for not
    having suffered,
2 and were thankful that your holy
    ones,[k] though previously
    wronged, were doing them
    no injury;
and they begged their pardon for
    having been at variance
    with them.[k]
3 Therefore you provided a
    flaming pillar of fire
as a guide for your people's[l]
    unknown journey,
and a harmless sun for their
    glorious wandering.
4 For their enemies[m] deserved to
    be deprived of light and
    imprisoned in darkness,
those who had kept your
    children imprisoned,
through whom the imperishable
    light of the law was to be
    given to the world.

The Death of the Egyptian Firstborn
(Ex 12.29–30; 14.26–31)

5 When they had resolved to kill
    the infants of your holy
    ones,
and one child had been
    abandoned and rescued,
you in punishment took away a
    multitude of their children;
and you destroyed them all
    together by a mighty flood.
6 That night was made known
    beforehand to our
    ancestors,
so that they might rejoice in sure
    knowledge of the oaths in
    which they trusted.
7 The deliverance of the righteous
    and the destruction of their
    enemies

were expected by your people.
8 For by the same means by which
    you punished our enemies
you called us to yourself and
    glorified us.
9 For in secret the holy children of
    good people offered
    sacrifices,
and with one accord agreed to
    the divine law,
so that the saints would share
    alike the same things,
both blessings and dangers;
and already they were singing
    the praises of the
    ancestors.[n]
10 But the discordant cry of their
    enemies echoed back,
and their piteous lament for
    their children was spread
    abroad.
11 The slave was punished with the
    same penalty as the
    master,
and the commoner suffered the
    same loss as the king;
12 and they all together, by the one
    form[o] of death,
had corpses too many to count.
For the living were not sufficient
    even to bury them,
since in one instant their most
    valued children had been
    destroyed.
13 For though they had disbelieved
    everything because of their
    magic arts,
yet, when their firstborn were
    destroyed, they
    acknowledged your people
    to be God's child.
14 For while gentle silence
    enveloped all things,
and night in its swift course was
    now half gone,
15 your all-powerful word leaped
    from heaven, from the
    royal throne,
into the midst of the land that
    was doomed,
a stern warrior
16 carrying the sharp sword of your
    authentic command,
and stood and filled all things
    with death,

j Gk *They*   *k* Meaning of Gk uncertain
l Gk *their*   *m* Gk *those persons*
n Other ancient authorities read *dangers,
the ancestors already leading the songs
of praise*   *o* Gk *name*

and touched heaven while
   standing on the earth.
17 Then at once apparitions in
      dreadful dreams greatly
      troubled them,
   and unexpected fears assailed
      them;
18 and one here and another there,
      hurled down half dead,
   made known why they were
      dying;
19 for the dreams that disturbed
      them forewarned them of
      this,
   so that they might not perish
      without knowing why they
      suffered.

Threat of Annihilation in the Desert
(Num 16.41–50)

20 The experience of death touched
      also the righteous,
   and a plague came upon the
      multitude in the desert,
   but the wrath did not long
      continue.
21 For a blameless man was quick
      to act as their champion;
   he brought forward the shield of
      his ministry,
   prayer and propitiation by
      incense;
   he withstood the anger and put
      an end to the disaster,
   showing that he was your
      servant.
22 He conquered the wrath[p] not by
      strength of body,
   not by force of arms,
   but by his word he subdued the
      avenger,
   appealing to the oaths and
      covenants given to our
      ancestors.
23 For when the dead had already
      fallen on one another in
      heaps,
   he intervened and held back the
      wrath,
   and cut off its way to the living.
24 For on his long robe the whole
      world was depicted,
   and the glories of the ancestors
      were engraved on the four
      rows of stones,
   and your majesty was on the
      diadem upon his head.
25 To these the destroyer yielded,
      these he[q] feared;
   for merely to test the wrath was
      enough.

The Red Sea

19 But the ungodly were assailed
      to the end by pitiless
      anger,
   for God[r] knew in advance even
      their future actions:
2 how, though they themselves
      had permitted[s] your
      people to depart
   and hastily sent them out,
   they would change their minds
      and pursue them.
3 For while they were still
      engaged in mourning,
   and were lamenting at the
      graves of their dead,
   they reached another foolish
      decision,
   and pursued as fugitives those
      whom they had begged and
      compelled to leave.
4 For the fate they deserved drew
      them on to this end,
   and made them forget what had
      happened,
   in order that they might fill up
      the punishment that their
      torments still lacked,
5 and that your people might
      experience[t] an incredible
      journey,
   but they themselves might meet
      a strange death.

God Guides and Protects His People
(Num 11.1–35)

6 For the whole creation in its
      nature was fashioned
      anew,
   complying with your commands,
   so that your children[u] might be
      kept unharmed.
7 The cloud was seen
      overshadowing the camp,
   and dry land emerging where
      water had stood before,
   an unhindered way out of the
      Red Sea,
   and a grassy plain out of the
      raging waves,
8 where those protected by your
      hand passed through as
      one nation,

---

p Cn: Gk *multitude*   q Other ancient
authorities read *they*   r Gk *he*   s Other
ancient authorities read *had changed
their minds to permit*   t Other ancient
authorities read *accomplish*
u Or *servants*

**W
I
S
D
O
M**

after gazing on marvelous
    wonders.

9 For they ranged like horses,
    and leaped like lambs,
praising you, O Lord, who
    delivered them.

10 For they still recalled the events
    of their sojourn,
how instead of producing
    animals the earth brought
    forth gnats,
and instead of fish the river
    spewed out vast numbers
    of frogs.

11 Afterward they saw also a new
    kind^v of birds,
when desire led them to ask for
    luxurious food;

12 for, to give them relief, quails
    came up from the sea.

The Punishment of the Egyptians

13 The punishments did not come
    upon the sinners
without prior signs in the
    violence of thunder,
for they justly suffered because
    of their wicked acts;
for they practiced a more bitter
    hatred of strangers.

14 Others had refused to receive
    strangers when they came
    to them,
but these made slaves of guests
    who were their
    benefactors.

15 And not only so—but, while
    punishment of some sort
    will come upon the former
for having received strangers
    with hostility,

16 the latter, having first received
    them with festal
    celebrations,
afterward afflicted with terrible
    sufferings
those who had already shared
    the same rights.

17 They were stricken also with
    loss of sight—
just as were those at the door of
    the righteous man—
when, surrounded by yawning
    darkness,
all of them tried to find the way
    through their own doors.

A New Harmony in Nature

18 For the elements changed^w
    places with one another,
as on a harp the notes vary the
    nature of the rhythm,
while each note remains the
    same.^{x}
This may be clearly inferred
    from the sight of what took
    place.

19 For land animals were
    transformed into water
    creatures,
and creatures that swim moved
    over to the land.

20 Fire even in water retained its
    normal power,
and water forgot its
    fire-quenching nature.

21 Flames, on the contrary, failed to
    consume
the flesh of perishable creatures
    that walked among them,
nor did they melt^y the
    crystalline, quick-melting
    kind of heavenly food.

Conclusion

22 For in everything, O Lord, you
    have exalted and glorified
    your people,
and you have not neglected to
    help them at all times and
    in all places.

^{v} Or production ^{w} Gk changing
^{x} Meaning of Gk uncertain ^{y} Cn: Gk
nor could be melted

Ecclesiasticus, or The Wisdom of Jesus Son of

SIRACH

THE PROLOGUE

Many great teachings have been given to us through the Law and the Prophets and the others[a] that followed them, and for these we should praise Israel for instruction and wisdom. Now, those who read the scriptures must not only themselves understand them, but must also as lovers of learning be able through the spoken and written word to help the outsiders. So my grandfather Jesus, who had devoted himself especially to the reading of the Law and the Prophets and the other books of our ancestors, and had acquired considerable proficiency in them, was himself also led to write something pertaining to instruction and wisdom, so that by becoming familiar also with his book[b] those who love learning might make even greater progress in living according to the law.

You are invited therefore to read it with goodwill and attention, and to be indulgent in cases where, despite our diligent labor in translating, we may seem to have rendered some phrases imperfectly. For what was originally expressed in Hebrew does not have exactly the same sense when translated into another language. Not only this book, but even the Law itself, the Prophecies, and the rest of the books differ not a little when read in the original.

When I came to Egypt in the thirty-eighth year of the reign of Eū·er'ge·tēs and stayed for some time, I found opportunity for no little instruction.[c] It seemed highly necessary that I should myself devote some diligence and labor to the translation of this book. During that time I have applied my skill day and night to complete and publish the book for those living abroad who wished to gain learning and are disposed to live according to the law.

In Praise of Wisdom
(Cp Prov 3.13–20; 8.22–31; Rom 11.33)

1 All wisdom is from the Lord,
  and with him it remains
    forever.
2 The sand of the sea, the drops of
    rain,
  and the days of eternity — who
    can count them?
3 The height of heaven, the
    breadth of the earth,
  the abyss, and wisdom[d]
    — who can search them
    out?
4 Wisdom was created before all
    other things,
  and prudent understanding
    from eternity.[e]
6 The root of wisdom — to whom
    has it been revealed?
  Her subtleties — who knows
    them?[f]
8 There is but one who is wise,
    greatly to be feared,
  seated upon his throne — the
    Lord.
9 It is he who created her;
  he saw her and took her
    measure;
  he poured her out upon all his
    works,
10 upon all the living according to
    his gift;

a Or *other books*   b Gk *with these things*   c Other ancient authorities read *I found a copy affording no little instruction*   d Other ancient authorities read *the depth of the abyss*   e Other ancient authorities add as verse 5, *The source of wisdom is God's word in the highest heaven, and her ways are the eternal commandments.*   f Other ancient authorities add as verse 7, *The knowledge of wisdom — to whom was it manifested? And her abundant experience — who has understood it?*

SIRACH

he lavished her upon those
who love him.^g

Fear of the Lord Is True Wisdom
(Job 28.28; Prov 1.7)

11 The fear of the Lord is glory and
exultation,
and gladness and a crown of
rejoicing.
12 The fear of the Lord delights the
heart,
and gives gladness and joy
and long life.^h
13 Those who fear the Lord will
have a happy end;
on the day of their death they
will be blessed.

14 To fear the Lord is the beginning
of wisdom;
she is created with the faithful
in the womb.
15 She madeⁱ among human
beings an eternal
foundation,
and among their descendants
she will abide faithfully.
16 To fear the Lord is fullness of
wisdom;
she inebriates mortals with her
fruits;
17 she fills their^j whole house with
desirable goods,
and their^j storehouses with
her produce.
18 The fear of the Lord is the
crown of wisdom,
making peace and perfect
health to flourish.^k
19 She rained down knowledge and
discerning comprehension,
and she heightened the glory
of those who held her fast.
20 To fear the Lord is the root of
wisdom,
and her branches are long
life.^l

22 Unjust anger cannot be justified,
for anger tips the scale to
one's ruin.
23 Those who are patient stay calm
until the right moment,
and then cheerfulness comes
back to them.
24 They hold back their words until
the right moment;
then the lips of many tell of
their good sense.

25 In the treasuries of wisdom are
wise sayings,
but godliness is an
abomination to a sinner.
26 If you desire wisdom, keep the
commandments,
and the Lord will lavish her
upon you.
27 For the fear of the Lord is
wisdom and discipline,
fidelity and humility are his
delight.

28 Do not disobey the fear of the
Lord;
do not approach him with a
divided mind.
29 Do not be a hypocrite before
others,
and keep watch over your lips.
30 Do not exalt yourself, or you
may fall
and bring dishonor upon
yourself.
The Lord will reveal your secrets
and overthrow you before the
whole congregation,
because you did not come in the
fear of the Lord,
and your heart was full of
deceit.

Duties toward God
(Jas 1.2–4, 12–16; Wis 3.1–9)

2 My child, when you come to
serve the Lord,
prepare yourself for testing.^m
2 Set your heart right and be
steadfast,
and do not be impetuous in
time of calamity.
3 Cling to him and do not depart,
so that your last days may be
prosperous.
4 Accept whatever befalls you,

^gOther ancient authorities add *Love of
the Lord is glorious wisdom; to those to
whom he appears he apportions her,
that they may see him.*   ^hOther
ancient authorities add *The fear of the
Lord is a gift from the Lord; also for
love he makes firm paths.*   ⁱGk *made
as a nest*   ^jOther ancient authorities
read *her*   ^kOther ancient authorities
add *Both are gifts of God for peace;
glory opens out for those who love him.
He saw her and took her measure.*
^lOther ancient authorities add as verse
21, *The fear of the Lord drives away
sins; and where it abides, it will turn
away all anger.*   ^mOr *trials*

and in times of humiliation be
  patient.
5 For gold is tested in the fire,
  and those found acceptable, in
    the furnace of
    humiliation.[n]
6 Trust in him, and he will help
    you;
  make your ways straight, and
    hope in him.

7 You who fear the Lord, wait for
    his mercy;
  do not stray, or else you may
    fall.
8 You who fear the Lord, trust in
    him,
  and your reward will not be
    lost.
9 You who fear the Lord, hope for
    good things,
  for lasting joy and mercy.[o]
10 Consider the generations of old
    and see:
  has anyone trusted in the Lord
    and been disappointed?
  Or has anyone persevered in the
    fear of the Lord[p] and been
    forsaken?
  Or has anyone called upon
    him and been neglected?
11 For the Lord is compassionate
    and merciful;
  he forgives sins and saves in
    time of distress.

12 Woe to timid hearts and to slack
    hands,
  and to the sinner who walks a
    double path!
13 Woe to the fainthearted who
    have no trust!
  Therefore they will have no
    shelter.
14 Woe to you who have lost your
    nerve!
  What will you do when the
    Lord's reckoning comes?

15 Those who fear the Lord do not
    disobey his words,
  and those who love him keep
    his ways.
16 Those who fear the Lord seek to
    please him,
  and those who love him are
    filled with his law.
17 Those who fear the Lord prepare
    their hearts,
  and humble themselves before
    him.

18 Let us fall into the hands of the
    Lord,
  but not into the hands of
    mortals;
  for equal to his majesty is his
    mercy,
  and equal to his name are his
    works.[q]

Duties toward Parents
(Ex 20.12; Deut 5.16; Eph 6.1–3)

3 Listen to me your father,
    O children;
  act accordingly, that you may
    be kept in safety.
2 For the Lord honors a father
    above his children,
  and he confirms a mother's
    right over her children.
3 Those who honor their father
    atone for sins,
4   and those who respect their
    mother are like those who
    lay up treasure.
5 Those who honor their father
    will have joy in their own
    children,
  and when they pray they will
    be heard.
6 Those who respect their father
    will have long life,
  and those who honor[r] their
    mother obey the Lord;
7   they will serve their parents as
    their masters.[s]
8 Honor your father by word and
    deed,
  that his blessing may come
    upon you.
9 For a father's blessing
    strengthens the houses of
    the children,
  but a mother's curse uproots
    their foundations.
10 Do not glorify yourself by
    dishonoring your father,
  for your father's dishonor is
    no glory to you.
11 The glory of one's father is one's
    own glory,

n Other ancient authorities add *in
sickness and poverty put your trust in
him* o Other ancient authorities add
*For his reward is an everlasting gift with
joy.* p Gk *of him* q Syr: Gk lacks this
line r Heb: Other ancient authorities
read *comfort* s In other ancient
authorities this line is preceded by
*Those who fear the Lord honor their
father,*

and it is a disgrace for
children not to respect
their mother.

12 My child, help your father in his
old age,
and do not grieve him as long
as he lives;
13 even if his mind fails, be patient
with him;
because you have all your
faculties do not despise
him.
14 For kindness to a father will not
be forgotten,
and will be credited to you
against your sins;
15 in the day of your distress it will
be remembered in your
favor;
like frost in fair weather, your
sins will melt away.
16 Whoever forsakes a father is
like a blasphemer,
and whoever angers a mother
is cursed by the Lord.

Humility
(Mt 20.26–28; Phil 2.3–8)

17 My child, perform your tasks
with humility;[t]
then you will be loved by
those whom God accepts.
18 The greater you are, the more
you must humble yourself;
so you will find favor in the
sight of the Lord.[u]
20 For great is the might of the
Lord;
but by the humble he is
glorified.
21 Neither seek what is too difficult
for you,
nor investigate what is beyond
your power.
22 Reflect upon what you have
been commanded,
for what is hidden is not your
concern.
23 Do not meddle in matters that
are beyond you,
for more than you can
understand has been
shown you.
24 For their conceit has led many
astray,
and wrong opinion has
impaired their judgment.

25 Without eyes there is no light;

without knowledge there is no
wisdom.[v]
26 A stubborn mind will fare badly
at the end,
and whoever loves danger will
perish in it.
27 A stubborn mind will be
burdened by troubles,
and the sinner adds sin to sins.
28 When calamity befalls the proud,
there is no healing,
for an evil plant has taken root
in him.
29 The mind of the intelligent
appreciates proverbs,
and an attentive ear is the
desire of the wise.

Alms for the Poor
(Tob 4.7–11)

30 As water extinguishes a blazing
fire,
so almsgiving atones for sin.
31 Those who repay favors give
thought to the future;
when they fall they will find
support.

*Duties toward the Poor and the
Oppressed*
(Deut 15.7–11)

4 My child, do not cheat the poor
of their living,
and do not keep needy eyes
waiting.
2 Do not grieve the hungry,
or anger one in need.
3 Do not add to the troubles of the
desperate,
or delay giving to the needy.
4 Do not reject a suppliant in
distress,
or turn your face away from
the poor.
5 Do not avert your eye from the
needy,
and give no one reason to
curse you;
6 for if in bitterness of soul some
should curse you,
their Creator will hear their
prayer.

7 Endear yourself to the
congregation;

---

[t]Heb: Gk *meekness*   [u]Other ancient
authorities add as verse 19, *Many are
lofty and renowned, but to the humble
he reveals his secrets.*   [v]Heb: Other
ancient authorities lack verse 25

bow your head low to the great.

8 Give a hearing to the poor, and return their greeting politely.

9 Rescue the oppressed from the oppressor; and do not be hesitant in giving a verdict.

10 Be a father to orphans, and be like a husband to their mother; you will then be like a son of the Most High, and he will love you more than does your mother.

The Rewards of Wisdom
(Prov 3.13–18; Wis 8.17–18)

11 Wisdom teaches[w] her children and gives help to those who seek her.

12 Whoever loves her loves life, and those who seek her from early morning are filled with joy.

13 Whoever holds her fast inherits glory, and the Lord blesses the place she[x] enters.

14 Those who serve her minister to the Holy One; the Lord loves those who love her.

15 Those who obey her will judge the nations, and all who listen to her will live secure.

16 If they remain faithful, they will inherit her; their descendants will also obtain her.

17 For at first she will walk with them on tortuous paths; she will bring fear and dread upon them, and will torment them by her discipline until she trusts them,[y] and she will test them with her ordinances.

18 Then she will come straight back to them again and gladden them, and will reveal her secrets to them.

19 If they go astray she will forsake them, and hand them over to their ruin.

20 Watch for the opportune time, and beware of evil, and do not be ashamed to be yourself.

21 For there is a shame that leads to sin, and there is a shame that is glory and favor.

22 Do not show partiality, to your own harm, or deference, to your downfall.

23 Do not refrain from speaking at the proper moment,[z] and do not hide your wisdom.[a]

24 For wisdom becomes known through speech, and education through the words of the tongue.

25 Never speak against the truth, but be ashamed of your ignorance.

26 Do not be ashamed to confess your sins, and do not try to stop the current of a river.

27 Do not subject yourself to a fool, or show partiality to a ruler.

28 Fight to the death for truth, and the Lord God will fight for you.

29 Do not be reckless in your speech, or sluggish and remiss in your deeds.

30 Do not be like a lion in your home, or suspicious of your servants.

31 Do not let your hand be stretched out to receive and closed when it is time to give.

Precepts for Everyday Living

5 Do not rely on your wealth, or say, "I have enough."

2 Do not follow your inclination and strength in pursuing the desires of your heart.

3 Do not say, "Who can have power over me?" for the Lord will surely punish you.

---

w Heb Syr: Gk *exalts*   x Or *he*
y Or *until they remain faithful in their heart*   z Heb: Gk *at a time of salvation*
a So some Gk Mss and Heb Syr Lat: Other Gk Mss lack *and do not hide your wisdom*

S
I
R
A
C
H

4 Do not say, "I sinned, yet what
     has happened to me?"
   for the Lord is slow to anger.
5 Do not be so confident of
     forgiveness[b]
   that you add sin to sin.
6 Do not say, "His mercy is great,
     he will forgive[c] the multitude
     of my sins,"
   for both mercy and wrath are
     with him,
   and his anger will rest on
     sinners.
7 Do not delay to turn back to the
     Lord,
   and do not postpone it from
     day to day;
   for suddenly the wrath of the
     Lord will come upon you,
   and at the time of punishment
     you will perish.
8 Do not depend on dishonest
     wealth,
   for it will not benefit you on
     the day of calamity.

9 Do not winnow in every wind,
     or follow every path.[d]
10 Stand firm for what you know,
     and let your speech be
     consistent.
11 Be quick to hear,
     but deliberate in answering.
12 If you know what to say, answer
     your neighbor;
   but if not, put your hand over
     your mouth.

13 Honor and dishonor come from
     speaking,
   and the tongue of mortals may
     be their downfall.
14 Do not be called
     double-tongued[e]
   and do not lay traps with your
     tongue;
   for shame comes to the thief,
   and severe condemnation to
     the double-tongued.
15 In great and small matters cause
     no harm,[f]

6 1 and do not become an enemy
       instead of a friend;
   for a bad name incurs shame
     and reproach;
   so it is with the
     double-tongued sinner.

2 Do not fall into the grip of
     passion,[g]
   or you may be torn apart as
     by a bull.[h]

3 Your leaves will be devoured
     and your fruit destroyed,
   and you will be left like a
     withered tree.
4 Evil passion destroys those who
     have it,
   and makes them the
     laughingstock of their
     enemies.

Friendship, False and True

5 Pleasant speech multiplies
     friends,
   and a gracious tongue
     multiplies courtesies.
6 Let those who are friendly with
     you be many,
   but let your advisers be one in
     a thousand.
7 When you gain friends, gain
     them through testing,
   and do not trust them hastily.
8 For there are friends who are
     such when it suits them,
   but they will not stand by you
     in time of trouble.
9 And there are friends who
     change into enemies,
   and tell of the quarrel to your
     disgrace.
10 And there are friends who sit at
     your table,
   but they will not stand by you
     in time of trouble.
11 When you are prosperous, they
     become your second self,
   and lord it over your servants;
12 but if you are brought low, they
     turn against you,
   and hide themselves from you.
13 Keep away from your enemies,
   and be on guard with your
     friends.

14 Faithful friends are a sturdy
     shelter:
   whoever finds one has found a
     treasure.
15 Faithful friends are beyond
     price;
   no amount can balance their
     worth.
16 Faithful friends are life-saving
     medicine;

b Heb: Gk *atonement*   c Heb: Gk *he* (or
it) *will atone for*   d Gk adds *so it is
with the double-tongued sinner* (see 6.1)
e Heb: Gk *a slanderer*   f Heb Syr: Gk *be
ignorant*   g Heb: Meaning of Gk
uncertain   h Meaning of Gk uncertain

and those who fear the Lord
will find them.
17 Those who fear the Lord direct
their friendship aright,
for as they are, so are their
neighbors also.

Blessings of Wisdom

18 My child, from your youth
choose discipline,
and when you have gray hair
you will still find wisdom.
19 Come to her like one who plows
and sows,
and wait for her good harvest.
For when you cultivate her you
will toil but little,
and soon you will eat of her
produce.
20 She seems very harsh to the
undisciplined;
fools cannot remain with her.
21 She will be like a heavy stone to
test them,
and they will not delay in
casting her aside.
22 For wisdom is like her name;
she is not readily perceived by
many.

23 Listen, my child, and accept my
judgment;
do not reject my counsel.
24 Put your feet into her fetters,
and your neck into her collar.
25 Bend your shoulders and carry
her,
and do not fret under her
bonds.
26 Come to her with all your soul,
and keep her ways with all
your might.
27 Search out and seek, and she
will become known to you;
and when you get hold of her,
do not let her go.
28 For at last you will find the rest
she gives,
and she will be changed into
joy for you.
29 Then her fetters will become for
you a strong defense,
and her collar a glorious robe.
30 Her yoke[i] is a golden ornament,
and her bonds a purple cord.
31 You will wear her like a glorious
robe,
and put her on like a splendid
crown.[j]

32 If you are willing, my child, you
can be disciplined,
and if you apply yourself you
will become clever.
33 If you love to listen you will gain
knowledge,
and if you pay attention you
will become wise.
34 Stand in the company of the
elders.
Who is wise? Attach yourself
to such a one.
35 Be ready to listen to every godly
discourse,
and let no wise proverbs
escape you.
36 If you see an intelligent person,
rise early to visit him;
let your foot wear out his
doorstep.
37 Reflect on the statutes of the
Lord,
and meditate at all times on
his commandments.
It is he who will give insight to[k]
your mind,
and your desire for wisdom
will be granted.

Miscellaneous Advice

7 Do no evil, and evil will never
overtake you.
2 Stay away from wrong, and it
will turn away from you.
3 Do[l] not sow in the furrows of
injustice,
and you will not reap a
sevenfold crop.

4 Do not seek from the Lord high
office,
or the seat of honor from the
king.
5 Do not assert your righteousness
before the Lord,
or display your wisdom before
the king.
6 Do not seek to become a judge,
or you may be unable to root
out injustice;
you may be partial to the
powerful,
and so mar your integrity.
7 Commit no offense against the
public,
and do not disgrace yourself
among the people.

i Heb: Gk *Upon her*   j Heb: Gk *crown of
gladness*   k Heb: Gk *will confirm*
l Gk *My child, do*

S
I
R
A
C
H

8 Do not commit a sin twice;
  not even for one will you go
    unpunished.
9 Do not say, "He will consider the
    great number of my gifts,
  and when I make an offering
    to the Most High God, he
      will accept it."
10 Do not grow weary when you
    pray;
  do not neglect to give alms.
11 Do not ridicule a person who is
    embittered in spirit,
  for there is One who humbles
    and exalts.
12 Do not devise*m* a lie against
    your brother,
  or do the same to a friend.
13 Refuse to utter any lie,
  for it is a habit that results in
    no good.
14 Do not babble in the assembly of
    the elders,
  and do not repeat yourself
    when you pray.

15 Do not hate hard labor
  or farm work, which was
    created by the Most High.
16 Do not enroll in the ranks of
    sinners;
  remember that retribution does
    not delay.
17 Humble yourself to the utmost,
  for the punishment of the
    ungodly is fire and
      worms.*n*

Relations with Others

18 Do not exchange a friend for
    money,
  or a real brother for the gold
    of Ō'phir.
19 Do not dismiss*o* a wise and
    good wife,
  for her charm is worth more
    than gold.
20 Do not abuse slaves who work
    faithfully,
  or hired laborers who devote
    themselves to their task.
21 Let your soul love intelligent
    slaves;*p*
  do not withhold from them
    their freedom.

22 Do you have cattle? Look after
    them;
  if they are profitable to you,
    keep them.

23 Do you have children? Discipline
    them,
  and make them obedient*q*
    from their youth.
24 Do you have daughters? Be
    concerned for their
      chastity,*r*
  and do not show yourself too
    indulgent with them.
25 Give a daughter in marriage,
    and you complete a great
      task;
  but give her to a sensible man.
26 Do you have a wife who pleases
    you?*s* Do not divorce her;
  but do not trust yourself to one
    whom you detest.

27 With all your heart honor your
    father,
  and do not forget the birth
    pangs of your mother.
28 Remember that it was of your
    parents*t* you were born;
  how can you repay what they
    have given to you?

29 With all your soul fear the Lord,
    and revere his priests.
30 With all your might love your
    Maker,
  and do not neglect his
    ministers.
31 Fear the Lord and honor the
    priest,
  and give him his portion, as
    you have been
      commanded:
  the first fruits, the guilt offering,
    the gift of the shoulders,
  the sacrifice of sanctification,
    and the first fruits of the
      holy things.

32 Stretch out your hand to the
    poor,
  so that your blessing may be
    complete.
33 Give graciously to all the living;
  do not withhold kindness even
    from the dead.
34 Do not avoid those who weep,
  but mourn with those who
    mourn.

m Heb: Gk *plow*   *n* Heb *for the*
expectation of mortals is worms
o Heb: Gk *deprive yourself of*
p Heb *Love a wise slave as yourself*
q Gk *bend their necks*   *r* Gk *body*
s Heb Syr *lack who pleases you*
t Gk *them*

35 Do not hesitate to visit the sick,
    because for such deeds you
        will be loved.
36 In all you do, remember the end
    of your life,
    and then you will never sin.

Prudence and Common Sense

8 Do not contend with the
    powerful,
    or you may fall into their
        hands.
2 Do not quarrel with the rich,
    in case their resources
        outweigh yours;
    for gold has ruined many,
        and has perverted the minds of
            kings.
3 Do not argue with the loud of
        mouth,
    and do not heap wood on their
        fire.

4 Do not make fun of one who is
        ill-bred,
    or your ancestors may be
        insulted.
5 Do not reproach one who is
        turning away from sin;
    remember that we all deserve
        punishment.
6 Do not disdain one who is old,
    for some of us are also
        growing old.
7 Do not rejoice over any one's
        death;
    remember that we must all die.

8 Do not slight the discourse of
        the sages,
    but busy yourself with their
        maxims;
    because from them you will
        learn discipline
    and how to serve princes.
9 Do not ignore the discourse of
        the aged,
    for they themselves learned
        from their parents;[u]
    from them you learn how to
        understand
    and to give an answer when
        the need arises.

10 Do not kindle the coals of
        sinners,
    or you may be burned in their
        flaming fire.
11 Do not let the insolent bring you
    to your feet,

or they may lie in ambush
    against your words.
12 Do not lend to one who is
        stronger than you;
    but if you do lend anything,
        count it as a loss.
13 Do not give surety beyond your
        means;
    but if you give surety, be
        prepared to pay.

14 Do not go to law against a
        judge,
    for the decision will favor him
        because of his standing.
15 Do not go traveling with the
        reckless,
    or they will be burdensome to
        you;
    for they will act as they please,
        and through their folly you
            will perish with them.
16 Do not pick a fight with the
        quick-tempered,
    and do not journey with them
        through lonely country,
    because bloodshed means
        nothing to them,
    and where no help is at hand,
        they will strike you down.
17 Do not consult with fools,
    for they cannot keep a secret.
18 In the presence of strangers do
        nothing that is to be kept
            secret,
    for you do not know what they
        will divulge.[v]
19 Do not reveal your thoughts to
        anyone,
    or you may drive away your
        happiness.[w]

Advice Concerning Women
(Cp Num 5.11–15)

9 Do not be jealous of the wife of
    your bosom,
    or you will teach her an evil
        lesson to your own hurt.
2 Do not give yourself to a woman
    and let her trample down your
        strength.
3 Do not go near a loose woman,
    or you will fall into her snares.
4 Do not dally with a singing girl,
    or you will be caught by her
        tricks.
5 Do not look intently at a virgin,

u Or *ancestors* v Or *it will bring forth*
w Heb: Gk *and let him not return a favor
to you*

or you may stumble and incur
   penalties for her.
6 Do not give yourself to
      prostitutes,
   or you may lose your
      inheritance.
7 Do not look around in the streets
      of a city,
   or wander about in its
      deserted sections.
8 Turn away your eyes from a
      shapely woman,
   and do not gaze at beauty
      belonging to another;
many have been seduced by a
      woman's beauty,
   and by it passion is kindled
      like a fire.
9 Never dine with another man's
      wife,
   or revel with her at wine;
or your heart may turn aside to
      her,
   and in blood*x* you may be
      plunged into destruction.

Choice of Friends

10 Do not abandon old friends,
   for new ones cannot equal
      them.
A new friend is like new wine;
   when it has aged, you can
      drink it with pleasure.

11 Do not envy the success of
      sinners,
   for you do not know what
      their end will be like.
12 Do not delight in what pleases
      the ungodly;
   remember that they will not be
      held guiltless all their lives.

13 Keep far from those who have
      power to kill,
   and you will not be haunted
      by the fear of death.
But if you approach them, make
      no misstep,
   or they may rob you of your
      life.
Know that you are stepping
      among snares,
   and that you are walking on
      the city battlements.

14 As much as you can, aim to
      know your neighbors,
   and consult with the wise.
15 Let your conversation be with
      intelligent people,

and let all your discussion be
   about the law of the Most
      High.
16 Let the righteous be your dinner
      companions,
   and let your glory be in the
      fear of the Lord.

Concerning Rulers
(Prov 8.15–16; Wis 6.1–11)

17 A work is praised for the skill of
      the artisan;
   so a people's leader is proved
      wise by his words.
18 The loud of mouth are feared in
      their city,
   and the one who is reckless in
      speech is hated.

10 A wise magistrate educates
      his people,
   and the rule of an intelligent
      person is well ordered.
2 As the people's judge is, so are
      his officials;
   as the ruler of the city is, so
      are all its inhabitants.
3 An undisciplined king ruins his
      people,
   but a city becomes fit to live in
      through the understanding
      of its rulers.
4 The government of the earth is
      in the hand of the Lord,
   and over it he will raise up the
      right leader for the time.
5 Human success is in the hand of
      the Lord,
   and it is he who confers honor
      upon the lawgiver.*y*

The Sin of Pride

6 Do not get angry with your
      neighbor for every injury,
   and do not resort to acts of
      insolence.
7 Arrogance is hateful to the Lord
      and to mortals,
   and injustice is outrageous to
      both.
8 Sovereignty passes from nation
      to nation
   on account of injustice and
      insolence and wealth.*z*

x Heb: Gk *by your spirit*   *y* Heb: Gk
scribe   *z* Other ancient authorities add
here or after verse 9a, *Nothing is more
wicked than one who loves money, for
such a person puts his own soul up for
sale.*

9 How can dust and ashes be
proud?
Even in life the human body
decays.*a*
10 A long illness baffles the
physician;*b*
the king of today will die
tomorrow.
11 For when one is dead
he inherits maggots and
vermin*c* and worms.
12 The beginning of human pride is
to forsake the Lord;
the heart has withdrawn from
its Maker.
13 For the beginning of pride is sin,
and the one who clings to it
pours out abominations.
Therefore the Lord brings upon
them unheard-of
calamities,
and destroys them completely.
14 The Lord overthrows the thrones
of rulers,
and enthrones the lowly in
their place.
15 The Lord plucks up the roots of
the nations,*d*
and plants the humble in their
place.
16 The Lord lays waste the lands of
the nations,
and destroys them to the
foundations of the earth.
17 He removes some of them and
destroys them,
and erases the memory of
them from the earth.
18 Pride was not created for human
beings,
or violent anger for those born
of women.

Persons Deserving Honor
(Cp Jer 9.23–24; 1 Cor 1.26–31)

19 Whose offspring are worthy of
honor?
Human offspring.
Whose offspring are worthy of
honor?
Those who fear the Lord.
Whose offspring are unworthy
of honor?
Human offspring.
Whose offspring are unworthy
of honor?
Those who break the
commandments.
20 Among family members their
leader is worthy of honor,

but those who fear the Lord
are worthy of honor in his
eyes.*e*
22 The rich, and the eminent, and
the poor —
their glory is the fear of the
Lord.
23 It is not right to despise one who
is intelligent but poor,
and it is not proper to honor
one who is sinful.
24 The prince and the judge and
the ruler are honored,
but none of them is greater
than the one who fears the
Lord.
25 Free citizens will serve a wise
servant,
and an intelligent person will
not complain.

Concerning Humility

26 Do not make a display of your
wisdom when you do your
work,
and do not boast when you are
in need.
27 Better is the worker who has
goods in plenty
than the boaster who lacks
bread.

28 My child, honor yourself with
humility,
and give yourself the esteem
you deserve.
29 Who will acquit those who
condemn*f* themselves?
And who will honor those who
dishonor themselves?*g*
30 The poor are honored for their
knowledge,
while the rich are honored for
their wealth.
31 One who is honored in poverty,
how much more in wealth!
And one dishonored in wealth,
how much more in
poverty!

a Heb: Meaning of Gk uncertain
b Heb Lat: Meaning of Gk uncertain
c Heb: Gk *wild animals*   *d* Other ancient
authorities read *proud nations*   *e* Other
ancient authorities add as verse 21, *The
fear of the Lord is the beginning of
acceptance; obduracy and pride are the
beginning of rejection.*   *f* Heb: Gk *sin
against*   *g* Heb Lat: Gk *their own life*

S
I
R
A
C
H

The Deceptiveness of Appearances

11 The wisdom of the humble
lifts their heads high,
and seats them among the
great.

2 Do not praise individuals for
their good looks,
or loathe anyone because of
appearance alone.

3 The bee is small among flying
creatures,
but what it produces is the
best of sweet things.

4 Do not boast about wearing fine
clothes,
and do not exalt yourself when
you are honored;
for the works of the Lord are
wonderful,
and his works are concealed
from humankind.

5 Many kings have had to sit on
the ground,
but one who was never
thought of has worn a
crown.

6 Many rulers have been utterly
disgraced,
and the honored have been
handed over to others.

Deliberation and Caution
(Prov 18.13)

7 Do not find fault before you
investigate;
examine first, and then
criticize.

8 Do not answer before you listen,
and do not interrupt when
another is speaking.

9 Do not argue about a matter that
does not concern you,
and do not sit with sinners
when they judge a case.

10 My child, do not busy yourself
with many matters;
if you multiply activities, you
will not be held blameless.
If you pursue, you will not
overtake,
and by fleeing you will not
escape.

11 There are those who work and
struggle and hurry,
but are so much the more in
want.

12 There are others who are slow
and need help,
who lack strength and abound
in poverty;

but the eyes of the Lord look
kindly upon them;
he lifts them out of their lowly
condition

13 and raises up their heads
to the amazement of the many.

14 Good things and bad, life and
death,
poverty and wealth, come
from the Lord.^{h}

17 The Lord's gift remains with the
devout,
and his favor brings lasting
success.

18 One becomes rich through
diligence and self-denial,
and the reward allotted to him
is this:

19 when he says, "I have found
rest,
and now I shall feast on my
goods!"
he does not know how long it
will be
until he leaves them to others
and dies.

20 Stand by your agreement and
attend to it,
and grow old in your work.

21 Do not wonder at the works of a
sinner,
but trust in the Lord and keep
at your job;
for it is easy in the sight of the
Lord
to make the poor rich
suddenly, in an instant.

22 The blessing of the Lord is^i the
reward of the pious,
and quickly God causes his
blessing to flourish.

23 Do not say, "What do I need,
and what further benefit can
be mine?"

24 Do not say, "I have enough,
and what harm can come to
me now?"

25 In the day of prosperity,
adversity is forgotten,

^{h}Other ancient authorities add as verses
15 and 16, *15Wisdom, understanding,
and knowledge of the law come from
the Lord; affection and the ways of good
works come from him. 16Error and
darkness were created with sinners; evil
grows old with those who take pride in
malice.* ^{i}Heb: Gk *is in*

and in the day of adversity,
  prosperity is not
  remembered.
26 For it is easy for the Lord on the
  day of death
  to reward individuals
  according to their conduct.
27 An hour's misery makes one
  forget past delights,
  and at the close of one's life
  one's deeds are revealed.
28 Call no one happy before his
  death;
  by how he ends, a person
  becomes known.[j]

Care in Choosing Friends
(Prov 19.4, 6)

29 Do not invite everyone into your
  home,
  for many are the tricks of the
  crafty.
30 Like a decoy partridge in a cage,
  so is the mind of the proud,
  and like spies they observe
  your weakness;[k]
31 for they lie in wait, turning good
  into evil,
  and to worthy actions they
  attach blame.
32 From a spark many coals are
  kindled,
  and a sinner lies in wait to
  shed blood.
33 Beware of scoundrels, for they
  devise evil,
  and they may ruin your
  reputation forever.
34 Receive strangers into your
  home and they will stir up
  trouble for you,
  and will make you a stranger
  to your own family.

12 If you do good, know to
  whom you do it,
  and you will be thanked for
  your good deeds.
2 Do good to the devout, and you
  will be repaid —
  if not by them, certainly by the
  Most High.
3 No good comes to one who
  persists in evil
  or to one who does not give
  alms.
4 Give to the devout, but do not
  help the sinner.
5 Do good to the humble, but do
  not give to the ungodly;

hold back their bread, and do
  not give it to them,
  for by means of it they might
  subdue you;
  then you will receive twice as
  much evil
  for all the good you have done
  to them.
6 For the Most High also hates
  sinners
  and will inflict punishment on
  the ungodly.[l]
7 Give to the one who is good, but
  do not help the sinner.
8 A friend is not known[m] in
  prosperity,
  nor is an enemy hidden in
  adversity.
9 One's enemies are friendly[n]
  when one prospers,
  but in adversity even one's
  friend disappears.
10 Never trust your enemy,
  for like corrosion in copper, so
  is his wickedness.
11 Even if he humbles himself and
  walks bowed down,
  take care to be on your guard
  against him.
  Be to him like one who polishes
  a mirror,
  to be sure it does not become
  completely tarnished.
12 Do not put him next to you,
  or he may overthrow you and
  take your place.
  Do not let him sit at your right
  hand,
  or else he may try to take your
  own seat,
  and at last you will realize the
  truth of my words,
  and be stung by what I have
  said.
13 Who pities a snake charmer
  when he is bitten,
  or all those who go near wild
  animals?
14 So no one pities a person who
  associates with a sinner
  and becomes involved in the
  other's sins.
15 He stands by you for a while,

[j]Heb: Gk and through his children a
person becomes known   [k]Heb: Gk
downfall   [l]Other ancient authorities
add and he is keeping them for the day
of their punishment   [m]Other ancient
authorities read punished   [n]Heb: Gk
grieved

but if you falter, he will not be there."

16 An enemy speaks sweetly with his lips,
   but in his heart he plans to throw you into a pit;
an enemy may have tears in his eyes,
   but if he finds an opportunity he will never have enough of your blood.
17 If evil comes upon you, you will find him there ahead of you;
   pretending to help, he will trip you up.
18 Then he will shake his head, and clap his hands,
   and whisper much, and show his true face.

Caution Regarding Associates

13 Whoever touches pitch gets dirty,
   and whoever associates with a proud person becomes like him.
2 Do not lift a weight too heavy for you,
   or associate with one mightier and richer than you.
How can the clay pot associate with the iron kettle?
   The pot will strike against it and be smashed.
3 A rich person does wrong, and even adds insults;
   a poor person suffers wrong, and must add apologies.
4 A rich person[o] will exploit you if you can be of use to him,
   but if you are in need he will abandon you.
5 If you own something, he will live with you;
   he will drain your resources without a qualm.
6 When he needs you he will deceive you,
   and will smile at you and encourage you;
   he will speak to you kindly and say, "What do you need?"
7 He will embarrass you with his delicacies,
   until he has drained you two or three times,
   and finally he will laugh at you.

Should he see you afterwards, he will pass you by
   and shake his head at you.

8 Take care not to be led astray and humiliated when you are enjoying yourself.[p]
9 When an influential person invites you, be reserved,
   and he will invite you more insistently.
10 Do not be forward, or you may be rebuffed;
   do not stand aloof, or you will be forgotten.
11 Do not try to treat him as an equal,
   or trust his lengthy conversations;
for he will test you by prolonged talk,
   and while he smiles he will be examining you.
12 Cruel are those who do not keep your secrets;
   they will not spare you harm or imprisonment.
13 Be on your guard and very careful,
   for you are walking about with your own downfall.[q]

15 Every creature loves its like,
   and every person the neighbor.
16 All living beings associate with their own kind,
   and people stick close to those like themselves.
17 What does a wolf have in common with a lamb?
   No more has a sinner with the devout.
18 What peace is there between a hyena and a dog?
   And what peace between the rich and the poor?
19 Wild asses in the wilderness are the prey of lions;
   likewise the poor are feeding grounds for the rich.
20 Humility is an abomination to the proud;
   likewise the poor are an abomination to the rich.

[o] Gk *He*   [p] Other ancient authorities read *in your folly*   [q] Other ancient authorities add as verse 14, *When you hear these things in your sleep, wake up! During all your life love the Lord, and call on him for your salvation.*

21 When the rich person totters, he
     is supported by friends,
   but when the humble[r] falls,
     he is pushed away even by
     friends.
22 If the rich person slips, many
     come to the rescue;
   he speaks unseemly words, but
     they justify him.
   If the humble person slips, they
     even criticize him;
   he talks sense, but is not given
     a hearing.
23 The rich person speaks and all
     are silent;
   they extol to the clouds what
     he says.
   The poor person speaks and
     they say, "Who is this
     fellow?"
   And should he stumble, they
     even push him down.
24 Riches are good if they are free
     from sin;
   poverty is evil only in the
     opinion of the ungodly.

25 The heart changes the
     countenance,
   either for good or for evil.[s]
26 The sign of a happy heart is a
     cheerful face,
   but to devise proverbs requires
     painful thinking.

14 Happy are those who do not
     blunder with their lips,
   and need not suffer remorse
     for sin.
2 Happy are those whose hearts
     do not condemn them,
   and who have not given up
     their hope.

Responsible Use of Wealth

3 Riches are inappropriate for a
     small-minded person;
   and of what use is wealth to a
     miser?
4 What he denies himself he
     collects for others;
   and others will live in luxury
     on his goods.
5 If one is mean to himself, to
     whom will he be generous?
   He will not enjoy his own
     riches.
6 No one is worse than one who is
     grudging to himself;
   this is the punishment for his
     meanness.

7 If ever he does good, it is by
     mistake;
   and in the end he reveals his
     meanness.
8 The miser is an evil person;
   he turns away and disregards
     people.
9 The eye of the greedy person is
     not satisfied with his share;
   greedy injustice withers the
     soul.
10 A miser begrudges bread,
   and it is lacking at his table.

11 My child, treat yourself well,
     according to your means,
   and present worthy offerings
     to the Lord.
12 Remember that death does not
     tarry,
   and the decree[t] of Hades has
     not been shown to you.
13 Do good to friends before you
     die,
   and reach out and give to
     them as much as you can.
14 Do not deprive yourself of a
     day's enjoyment;
   do not let your share of
     desired good pass by you.
15 Will you not leave the fruit of
     your labors to another,
   and what you acquired by toil
     to be divided by lot?
16 Give, and take, and indulge
     yourself,
   because in Hades one cannot
     look for luxury.
17 All living beings become old like
     a garment,
   for the decree[u] from of old is,
     "You must die!"
18 Like abundant leaves on a
     spreading tree
   that sheds some and puts forth
     others,
   so are the generations of flesh
     and blood:
   one dies and another is born.
19 Every work decays and ceases to
     exist,
   and the one who made it will
     pass away with it.

[r] Other ancient authorities read poor
[s] Other ancient authorities add and a
glad heart makes a cheerful
countenance   [t] Heb Syr: Gk covenant
[u] Heb: Gk covenant

The Happiness of Seeking Wisdom
(Prov 8.32–36)

20 Happy is the person who
meditates on[v] wisdom
and reasons intelligently,
21 who[w] reflects in his heart on her
ways
and ponders her secrets,
22 pursuing her like a hunter,
and lying in wait on her paths;
23 who peers through her windows
and listens at her doors;
24 who camps near her house
and fastens his tent peg to her
walls;
25 who pitches his tent near her,
and so occupies an excellent
lodging place;
26 who places his children under
her shelter,
and lodges under her boughs;
27 who is sheltered by her from the
heat,
and dwells in the midst of her
glory.

15 Whoever fears the Lord will
do this,
and whoever holds to the law
will obtain wisdom.[x]
2 She will come to meet him like a
mother,
and like a young bride she will
welcome him.
3 She will feed him with the bread
of learning,
and give him the water of
wisdom to drink.
4 He will lean on her and not fall,
and he will rely on her and not
be put to shame.
5 She will exalt him above his
neighbors,
and will open his mouth in the
midst of the assembly.
6 He will find gladness and a
crown of rejoicing,
and will inherit an everlasting
name.
7 The foolish will not obtain her,
and sinners will not see her.
8 She is far from arrogance,
and liars will never think of
her.
9 Praise is unseemly on the lips of
a sinner,
for it has not been sent from
the Lord.
10 For in wisdom must praise be
uttered,

and the Lord will make it
prosper.

Freedom of Choice
(Cp Sir 17.1–12)

11 Do not say, "It was the Lord's
doing that I fell away";
for he does not do[y] what he
hates.
12 Do not say, "It was he who led
me astray";
for he has no need of the
sinful.
13 The Lord hates all abominations;
such things are not loved by
those who fear him.
14 It was he who created
humankind in the
beginning,
and he left them in the power
of their own free choice.
15 If you choose, you can keep the
commandments,
and to act faithfully is a matter
of your own choice.
16 He has placed before you fire
and water;
stretch out your hand for
whichever you choose.
17 Before each person are life and
death,
and whichever one chooses
will be given.
18 For great is the wisdom of the
Lord;
he is mighty in power and sees
everything;
19 his eyes are on those who fear
him,
and he knows every human
action.
20 He has not commanded anyone
to be wicked,
and he has not given anyone
permission to sin.

God's Punishment of Sinners

16 Do not desire a multitude of
worthless[z] children,
and do not rejoice in ungodly
offspring.
2 If they multiply, do not rejoice in
them,
unless the fear of the Lord is
in them.

---

v Other ancient authorities read *dies in*
w The structure adopted in verses 21-27
follows the Heb   x Gk *her*   y Heb: Gk
you ought not do   z Heb: Gk
unprofitable

3 Do not trust in their survival,
   or rely on their numbers;[a]
for one can be better than a
      thousand,
   and to die childless better than
      to have ungodly children.
4 For through one intelligent
      person a city can be filled
      with people,
   but through a clan of outlaws
      it becomes desolate.

5 Many such things my eye has
      seen,
   and my ear has heard things
      more striking than these.
6 In an assembly of sinners a fire
      is kindled,
   and in a disobedient nation
      wrath blazes up.
7 He did not forgive the ancient
      giants
   who revolted in their might.
8 He did not spare the neighbors
      of Lot,
   whom he loathed on account
      of their arrogance.
9 He showed no pity on the
      doomed nation,
   on those dispossessed because
      of their sins;[b]
10 or on the six hundred thousand
      foot soldiers
   who assembled in their
      stubbornness.[c]
11 Even if there were only one
      stiff-necked person,
   it would be a wonder if he
      remained unpunished.
For mercy and wrath are with
      the Lord;[d]
   he is mighty to forgive—but
      he also pours out wrath.
12 Great as his mercy, so also is his
      chastisement;
   he judges a person according
      to one's deeds.
13 The sinner will not escape with
      plunder,
   and the patience of the godly
      will not be frustrated.
14 He makes room for every act of
      mercy;
   everyone receives in
      accordance with one's
      deeds.[e]

17 Do not say, "I am hidden from
      the Lord,
   and who from on high has me
      in mind?

Among so many people I am
      unknown,
   for what am I in a boundless
      creation?
18 Lo, heaven and the highest
      heaven,
   the abyss and the earth,
      tremble at his visitation![f]
19 The very mountains and the
      foundations of the earth
   quiver and quake when he
      looks upon them.
20 But no human mind can grasp
      this,
   and who can comprehend his
      ways?
21 Like a tempest that no one can
      see,
   so most of his works are
      concealed.[g]
22 Who is to announce his acts of
      justice?
   Or who can await them? For
      his decree[h] is far off."[i]
23 Such are the thoughts of one
      devoid of understanding;
   a senseless and misguided
      person thinks foolishly.

God's Wisdom Seen in Creation
         (Gen 1.1 – 2.4a)

24 Listen to me, my child, and
      acquire knowledge,
   and pay close attention to my
      words.

[a] Other ancient authorities add *For you
will groan in untimely mourning, and
will know of their sudden end.*   [b] Other
ancient authorities add *All these things
he did to the hard-hearted nations, and
by the multitude of his holy ones he was
not appeased.*   [c] Other ancient
authorities add *Chastising, showing
mercy, striking, healing, the Lord
persisted in mercy and discipline.*
[d] Gk *him*   [e] Other ancient authorities
add [15] *The Lord hardened Pharaoh so
that he did not recognize him, in order
that his works might be known under
heaven.* [16] *His mercy is manifest to the
whole of creation, and he divided his
light and darkness with a plumb line.*
[f] Other ancient authorities add *The
whole world past and present is in his
will.*   [g] Meaning of Gk uncertain: Heb
Syr *If I sin, no eye can see me, and if I
am disloyal all in secret, who is to
know?*   [h] Heb *the decree:* Gk *the
covenant*   [i] Other ancient authorities
add *and a scrutiny for all comes at the
end*

25 I will impart discipline
   precisely[j]
   and declare knowledge
   accurately.

26 When the Lord created[k] his
   works from the beginning,
   and, in making them,
   determined their
   boundaries,
27 he arranged his works in an
   eternal order,
   and their dominion[l] for all
   generations.
   They neither hunger nor grow
   weary,
   and they do not abandon their
   tasks.
28 They do not crowd one another,
   and they never disobey his
   word.
29 Then the Lord looked upon the
   earth,
   and filled it with his good
   things.
30 With all kinds of living beings
   he covered its surface,
   and into it they must return.

17 The Lord created human
   beings out of earth,
   and makes them return to it
   again.
2 He gave them a fixed number of
   days,
   but granted them authority
   over everything on the
   earth.[m]
3 He endowed them with strength
   like his own,[n]
   and made them in his own
   image.
4 He put the fear of them[o] in all
   living beings,
   and gave them dominion over
   beasts and birds.[p]
6 Discretion and tongue and eyes,
   ears and a mind for thinking
   he gave them.
7 He filled them with knowledge
   and understanding,
   and showed them good and
   evil.
8 He put the fear of him into[q]
   their hearts
   to show them the majesty of
   his works.[r]
10 And they will praise his holy
   name,
9 to proclaim the grandeur of his
   works.

11 He bestowed knowledge upon
   them,
   and allotted to them the law of
   life.[s]
12 He established with them an
   eternal covenant,
   and revealed to them his
   decrees.
13 Their eyes saw his glorious
   majesty,
   and their ears heard the glory
   of his voice.
14 He said to them, "Beware of all
   evil."
   And he gave commandment to
   each of them concerning
   the neighbor.
15 Their ways are always known to
   him;
   they will not be hid from his
   eyes.[t]
17 He appointed a ruler for every
   nation,
   but Israel is the Lord's own
   portion.[u]
19 All their works are as clear as
   the sun before him,
   and his eyes are ever upon
   their ways.
20 Their iniquities are not hidden
   from him,
   and all their sins are before
   the Lord.[v]

[j] Gk by weight   [k] Heb: Gk judged
[l] Or elements   [m] Lat: Gk it   [n] Lat: Gk
proper to them   [o] Syr: Gk him
[p] Other ancient authorities add as verse
5, They obtained the use of the five
faculties of the Lord; as sixth he
distributed to them the gift of mind, and
as seventh, reason, the interpreter of
one's faculties.   [q] Other ancient
authorities read He set his eye upon
[r] Other ancient authorities add and he
gave them to boast of his marvels
forever   [s] Other ancient authorities add
so that they may know that they who
are alive now are mortal   [t] Other
ancient authorities add 16Their ways
from youth tend toward evil, and they
are unable to make for themselves
hearts of flesh in place of their stony
hearts. 17For in the division of the
nations of the whole earth, he appointed
[u] Other ancient authorities add as verse
18, whom, being his firstborn, he brings
up with discipline, and allotting to him
the light of his love, he does not neglect
him.   [v] Other ancient authorities add as
verse 21, But the Lord, who is gracious
and knows how they are formed, has
neither left them nor abandoned them,
but has spared them.

22 One's almsgiving is like a signet
ring with the Lord,[w]
and he will keep a person's
kindness like the apple of
his eye.[x]
23 Afterward he will rise up and
repay them,
and he will bring their
recompense on their heads.
24 Yet to those who repent he
grants a return,
and he encourages those who
are losing hope.

A Call to Repentance

25 Turn back to the Lord and
forsake your sins;
pray in his presence and
lessen your offense.
26 Return to the Most High and
turn away from iniquity,[y]
and hate intensely what he
abhors.
27 Who will sing praises to the
Most High in Hades
in place of the living who give
thanks?
28 From the dead, as from one who
does not exist,
thanksgiving has ceased;
those who are alive and well
sing the Lord's praises.
29 How great is the mercy of the
Lord,
and his forgiveness for those
who return to him!
30 For not everything is within
human capability,
since human beings are not
immortal.
31 What is brighter than the sun?
Yet it can be eclipsed.
So flesh and blood devise evil.
32 He marshals the host of the
height of heaven;
but all human beings are dust
and ashes.

The Majesty of God

18 He who lives forever created
the whole universe;
2 the Lord alone is just.[z]
4 To none has he given power to
proclaim his works;
and who can search out his
mighty deeds?
5 Who can measure his majestic
power?
And who can fully recount his
mercies?

6 It is not possible to diminish or
increase them,
nor is it possible to fathom the
wonders of the Lord.
7 When human beings have
finished, they are just
beginning,
and when they stop, they are
still perplexed.
8 What are human beings, and of
what use are they?
What is good in them, and
what is evil?
9 The number of days in their life
is great if they reach one
hundred years.[a]
10 Like a drop of water from the
sea and a grain of sand,
so are a few years among the
days of eternity.
11 That is why the Lord is patient
with them
and pours out his mercy upon
them.
12 He sees and recognizes that
their end is miserable;
therefore he grants them
forgiveness all the more.
13 The compassion of human
beings is for their
neighbors,
but the compassion of the
Lord is for every living
thing.
He rebukes and trains and
teaches them,
and turns them back, as a
shepherd his flock.
14 He has compassion on those
who accept his discipline
and who are eager for his
precepts.

---

[w] Gk *him*   [x] Other ancient authorities
add *apportioning repentance to his sons
and daughters*   [y] Other ancient
authorities add *for he will lead you out
of darkness to the light of health.*
[z] Other ancient authorities add *and there
is no other beside him; 3he steers the
world with the span of his hand, and all
things obey his will; for he is king of all
things by his power, separating among
them the holy things from the profane.*
[a] Other ancient authorities add *but the
death of each one is beyond the
calculation of all*

S
I
R
A
C
H

The Right Spirit in Giving Alms

15 My child, do not mix reproach
    with your good deeds,
    or spoil your gift by harsh
    words.
16 Does not the dew give relief
    from the scorching heat?
    So a word is better than a gift.
17 Indeed, does not a word surpass
    a good gift?
    Both are to be found in a
    gracious person.
18 A fool is ungracious and
    abusive,
    and the gift of a grudging
    giver makes the eyes dim.

*The Need of Reflection and
    Self-control*

19 Before you speak, learn;
    and before you fall ill, take
    care of your health.
20 Before judgment comes, examine
    yourself;
    and at the time of scrutiny you
    will find forgiveness.
21 Before falling ill, humble
    yourself;
    and when you have sinned,
    repent.
22 Let nothing hinder you from
    paying a vow promptly,
    and do not wait until death to
    be released from it.
23 Before making a vow, prepare
    yourself;
    do not be like one who puts
    the Lord to the test.
24 Think of his wrath on the day of
    death,
    and of the moment of
    vengeance when he turns
    away his face.
25 In the time of plenty think of the
    time of hunger;
    in days of wealth think of
    poverty and need.
26 From morning to evening
    conditions change;
    all things move swiftly before
    the Lord.

27 One who is wise is cautious in
    everything;
    when sin is all around, one
    guards against
    wrongdoing.
28 Every intelligent person knows
    wisdom,
    and praises the one who finds
    her.

29 Those who are skilled in words
    become wise themselves,
    and pour forth apt proverbs.*b*

SELF-CONTROL*c*

30 Do not follow your base desires,
    but restrain your appetites.
31 If you allow your soul to take
    pleasure in base desire,
    it will make you the
    laughingstock of your
    enemies.
32 Do not revel in great luxury,
    or you may become
    impoverished by its
    expense.
33 Do not become a beggar by
    feasting with borrowed
    money,
    when you have nothing in
    your purse.*d*

19 The one who does this*e* will
    not become rich;
    one who despises small things
    will fail little by little.
2 Wine and women lead intelligent
    men astray,
    and the man who consorts
    with prostitutes is reckless.
3 Decay and worms will take
    possession of him,
    and the reckless person will be
    snatched away.

Against Loose Talk

4 One who trusts others too
    quickly has a shallow
    mind,
    and one who sins does wrong
    to oneself.
5 One who rejoices in
    wickedness*f* will be
    condemned,*g*
6 but one who hates gossip has
    less evil.
7 Never repeat a conversation,
    and you will lose nothing at
    all.

b Other ancient authorities add *Better is
confidence in the one Lord than clinging
with a dead heart to a dead one.*
c This heading is included in the Gk text.
d Other ancient authorities add *for you
will be plotting against your own life*
e Heb: Gk *A worker who is a drunkard*
f Other ancient authorities read *heart*
g Other ancient authorities add *but one
who withstands pleasures crowns his
life. 6One who controls the tongue will
live without strife,*

8 With friend or foe do not report
     it,
   and unless it would be a sin
     for you, do not reveal it;
9 for someone may have heard
     you and watched you,
   and in time will hate you.
10 Have you heard something? Let
     it die with you.
   Be brave, it will not make you
     burst!
11 Having heard something, the
     fool suffers birth pangs
   like a woman in labor with a
     child.
12 Like an arrow stuck in a
     person's thigh,
   so is gossip inside a fool.

13 Question a friend; perhaps he
     did not do it;
   or if he did, so that he may not
     do it again.
14 Question a neighbor; perhaps he
     did not say it;
   or if he said it, so that he may
     not repeat it.
15 Question a friend, for often it is
     slander;
   so do not believe everything
     you hear.
16 A person may make a slip
     without intending it.
   Who has not sinned with his
     tongue?
17 Question your neighbor before
     you threaten him;
   and let the law of the Most
     High take its course.^h

True and False Wisdom

20 The whole of wisdom is fear of
     the Lord,
   and in all wisdom there is the
     fulfillment of the law.^i
22 The knowledge of wickedness is
     not wisdom,
   nor is there prudence in the
     counsel of sinners.
23 There is a cleverness that is
     detestable,
   and there is a fool who merely
     lacks wisdom.
24 Better are the God-fearing who
     lack understanding
   than the highly intelligent who
     transgress the law.
25 There is a cleverness that is
     exact but unjust,

and there are people who
     abuse favors to gain a
     verdict.
26 There is the villain bowed down
     in mourning,
   but inwardly he is full of deceit.
27 He hides his face and pretends
     not to hear,
   but when no one notices, he
     will take advantage of you.
28 Even if lack of strength keeps
     him from sinning,
   he will nevertheless do evil
     when he finds the
     opportunity.
29 A person is known by his
     appearance,
   and a sensible person is
     known when first met, face
     to face.
30 A person's attire and hearty
     laughter,
   and the way he walks, show
     what he is.

Silence and Speech

20 There is a rebuke that is
     untimely,
   and there is the person who is
     wise enough to keep silent.
2 How much better it is to rebuke
     than to fume!
3 And the one who admits his
     fault will be kept from
     failure.
4 Like a eunuch lusting to violate
     a girl
   is the person who does right
     under compulsion.
5 Some people keep silent and are
     thought to be wise,
   while others are detested for
     being talkative.
6 Some people keep silent because
     they have nothing to say,
   while others keep silent
     because they know when
     to speak.

^h Other ancient authorities add *and do
not be angry.* 18*The fear of the Lord is
the beginning of acceptance, and
wisdom obtains his love.* 19*The
knowledge of the Lord's commandments
is life-giving discipline; and those who
do what is pleasing to him enjoy the
fruit of the tree of immortality.* ^i Other
ancient authorities add *and the
knowledge of his omnipotence.* 21*When
a slave says to his master, "I will not
act as you wish," even if later he does it,
he angers the one who supports him.*

S
I
R
A
C
H

7 The wise remain silent until the
right moment,
but a boasting fool misses the
right moment.
8 Whoever talks too much is
detested,
and whoever pretends to
authority is hated.[j]

Paradoxes

9 There may be good fortune for a
person in adversity,
and a windfall may result in a
loss.
10 There is the gift that profits you
nothing,
and the gift to be paid back
double.
11 There are losses for the sake of
glory,
and there are some who have
raised their heads from
humble circumstances.
12 Some buy much for little,
but pay for it seven times over.
13 The wise make themselves
beloved by only few
words,[k]
but the courtesies of fools are
wasted.
14 A fool's gift will profit you
nothing,[l]
for he looks for recompense
sevenfold.[m]
15 He gives little and upbraids
much;
he opens his mouth like a
town crier.
Today he lends and tomorrow he
asks it back;
such a one is hateful to God
and humans.[n]
16 The fool says, "I have no friends,
and I get no thanks for my
good deeds.
Those who eat my bread are
evil-tongued."
17 How many will ridicule him, and
how often![o]

Inappropriate Speech

18 A slip on the pavement is better
than a slip of the tongue;
the downfall of the wicked will
occur just as speedily.
19 A coarse person is like an
inappropriate story,
continually on the lips of the
ignorant.
20 A proverb from a fool's lips will
be rejected,

for he does not tell it at the
proper time.
21 One may be prevented from
sinning by poverty;
so when he rests he feels no
remorse.
22 One may lose his life through
shame,
or lose it because of human
respect.[p]
23 Another out of shame makes
promises to a friend,
and so makes an enemy for
nothing.

Lying

24 A lie is an ugly blot on a person;
it is continually on the lips of
the ignorant.
25 A thief is preferable to a
habitual liar,
but the lot of both is ruin.
26 A liar's way leads to disgrace,
and his shame is ever with
him.

PROVERBIAL SAYINGS[q]

27 The wise person advances
himself by his words,
and one who is sensible
pleases the great.
28 Those who cultivate the soil
heap up their harvest,
and those who please the great
atone for injustice.
29 Favors and gifts blind the eyes
of the wise;
like a muzzle on the mouth
they stop reproofs.
30 Hidden wisdom and unseen
treasure,
of what value is either?
31 Better are those who hide their
folly

[j]Other ancient authorities add *How good
it is to show repentance when you are
reproved, for so you will escape
deliberate sin!*   [k]Heb: Gk *by words*
[l]Other ancient authorities add *so it is
with the envious who give under
compulsion*   [m]Syr: Gk *he has many
eyes instead of one*   [n]Other ancient
authorities lack *to God and humans*
[o]Other ancient authorities add *for he
has not honestly received what he has,
and what he does not have is
unimportant to him*   [p]Other ancient
authorities read *his foolish look*   [q]This
heading is included in the Gk text.

than those who hide their
wisdom.*r*

Various Sins

21 Have you sinned, my child?
Do so no more,
but ask forgiveness for your
past sins.
2 Flee from sin as from a snake;
for if you approach sin, it will
bite you.
Its teeth are lion's teeth,
and can destroy human lives.
3 All lawlessness is like a
two-edged sword;
there is no healing for the
wound it inflicts.

4 Panic and insolence will waste
away riches;
thus the house of the proud
will be laid waste.*s*
5 The prayer of the poor goes
from their lips to the ears
of God,*t*
and his judgment comes
speedily.
6 Those who hate reproof walk in
the sinner's steps,
but those who fear the Lord
repent in their heart.
7 The mighty in speech are widely
known;
when they slip, the sensible
person knows it.

8 Whoever builds his house with
other people's money
is like one who gathers stones
for his burial mound.*u*
9 An assembly of the wicked is
like a bundle of tow,
and their end is a blazing fire.
10 The way of sinners is paved with
smooth stones,
but at its end is the pit of
Hades.

Wisdom and Foolishness

11 Whoever keeps the law controls
his thoughts,
and the fulfillment of the fear
of the Lord is wisdom.
12 The one who is not clever
cannot be taught,
but there is a cleverness that
increases bitterness.
13 The knowledge of the wise will
increase like a flood,
and their counsel like a
life-giving spring.

14 The mind*v* of a fool is like a
broken jar;
it can hold no knowledge.

15 When an intelligent person
hears a wise saying,
he praises it and adds to it;
when a fool*w* hears it, he laughs
at*x* it
and throws it behind his back.
16 A fool's chatter is like a burden
on a journey,
but delight is found in the
speech of the intelligent.
17 The utterance of a sensible
person is sought in the
assembly,
and they ponder his words in
their minds.

18 Like a house in ruins is wisdom
to a fool,
and to the ignorant,
knowledge is talk that has
no meaning.
19 To a senseless person education
is fetters on his feet,
and like manacles on his right
hand.
20 A fool raises his voice when he
laughs,
but the wise*y* smile quietly.
21 To the sensible person education
is like a golden ornament,
and like a bracelet on the right
arm.

22 The foot of a fool rushes into a
house,
but an experienced person
waits respectfully outside.
23 A boor peers into the house
from the door,
but a cultivated person
remains outside.
24 It is ill-mannered for a person to
listen at a door;
the discreet would be grieved
by the disgrace.

---

r Other ancient authorities add
*32Unwearied endurance in seeking the
Lord is better than a masterless
charioteer of one's own life.*   *s* Other
ancient authorities read *uprooted*
t Gk *his ears*   *u* Other ancient
authorities read *for the winter*   *v* Syr
Lat: Gk *entrails*   *w* Syr: Gk *reveler*
x Syr: Gk *dislikes*   *y* Syr Lat: Gk *clever*

25 The lips of babblers speak of
    what is not their concern,[z]
  but the words of the prudent
    are weighed in the balance.
26 The mind of fools is in their
    mouth,
  but the mouth of the wise is
    in[a] their mind.
27 When an ungodly person curses
    an adversary,[b]
  he curses himself.
28 A whisperer degrades himself
    and is hated in his
    neighborhood.

The Idler

22 The idler is like a filthy stone,
    and every one hisses at his
    disgrace.
2 The idler is like the filth of
    dunghills;
  anyone that picks it up will
    shake it off his hand.

Degenerate Children

3 It is a disgrace to be the father
    of an undisciplined son,
  and the birth of a daughter is
    a loss.
4 A sensible daughter obtains a
    husband of her own,
  but one who acts shamefully is
    a grief to her father.
5 An impudent daughter disgraces
    father and husband,
  and is despised by both.
6 Like music in time of mourning
    is ill-timed conversation,
  but a thrashing and discipline
    are at all times wisdom.[c]

Wisdom and Folly

9 Whoever teaches a fool is like
    one who glues potsherds
    together,
  or who rouses a sleeper from
    deep slumber.
10 Whoever tells a story to a fool
    tells it to a drowsy man;
  and at the end he will say,
    "What is it?"
11 Weep for the dead, for he has
    left the light behind;
  and weep for the fool, for he
    has left intelligence behind.
  Weep less bitterly for the dead,
    for he is at rest;
  but the life of the fool is worse
    than death.

12 Mourning for the dead lasts
    seven days,
  but for the foolish or the
    ungodly it lasts all the days
    of their lives.

13 Do not talk much with a
    senseless person
  or visit an unintelligent
    person.[d]
  Stay clear of him, or you may
    have trouble,
  and be spattered when he
    shakes himself off.
  Avoid him and you will find rest,
    and you will never be wearied
    by his lack of sense.
14 What is heavier than lead?
    And what is its name except
    "Fool"?
15 Sand, salt, and a piece of iron
    are easier to bear than a
    stupid person.

16 A wooden beam firmly bonded
    into a building
  is not loosened by an
    earthquake;
  so the mind firmly resolved after
    due reflection
  will not be afraid in a crisis.
17 A mind settled on an intelligent
    thought
  is like stucco decoration that
    makes a wall smooth.
18 Fences[e] set on a high place
    will not stand firm against the
    wind;
  so a timid mind with a fool's
    resolve
  will not stand firm against any
    fear.

The Preservation of Friendship

19 One who pricks the eye brings
    tears,
  and one who pricks the heart
    makes clear its feelings.

[z] Other ancient authorities read *of
strangers speak of these things*
[a] Other ancient authorities omit *in*
[b] Or *curses Satan*   [c] Other ancient
authorities add *7Children who are
brought up in a good life, conceal the
lowly birth of their parents. 8Children
who are disdainfully and boorishly
haughty stain the nobility of their
kindred.*   [d] Other ancient authorities
add *For being without sense he will
despise everything about you*   [e] Other
ancient authorities read *Pebbles*

20 One who throws a stone at birds
    scares them away,
  and one who reviles a friend
    destroys a friendship.
21 Even if you draw your sword
    against a friend,
  do not despair, for there is a
    way back.
22 If you open your mouth against
    your friend,
  do not worry, for
    reconciliation is possible.
But as for reviling, arrogance,
    disclosure of secrets, or a
    treacherous blow —
in these cases any friend will
    take to flight.

23 Gain the trust of your neighbor
    in his poverty,
  so that you may rejoice with
    him in his prosperity.
Stand by him in time of distress,
  so that you may share with
    him in his inheritance.f
24 The vapor and smoke of the
    furnace precede the fire;
  so insults precede bloodshed.
25 I am not ashamed to shelter a
    friend,
  and I will not hide from him.
26 But if harm should come to me
    because of him,
  whoever hears of it will
    beware of him.

A Prayer for Help against Sinning

27 Who will set a guard over my
    mouth,
  and an effective seal upon my
    lips,
so that I may not fall because of
    them,
  and my tongue may not
    destroy me?

23 O Lord, Father and Master of
    my life,
  do not abandon me to their
    designs,
  and do not let me fall because
    of them!
2 Who will set whips over my
    thoughts,
  and the discipline of wisdom
    over my mind,
so as not to spare me in my
    errors,
  and not overlook myg sins?
3 Otherwise my mistakes may be
    multiplied,
  and my sins may abound,

and I may fall before my
    adversaries,
  and my enemy may rejoice
    over me.h
4 O Lord, Father and God of my
    life,
  do not give me haughty eyes,
5 and remove evil desire from
    me.
6 Let neither gluttony nor lust
    overcome me,
  and do not give me over to
    shameless passion.

DISCIPLINE OF THE TONGUEi

7 Listen, my children, to
    instruction concerning the
    mouth;
  the one who observes it will
    never be caught.
8 Sinners are overtaken through
    their lips;
  by them the reviler and the
    arrogant are tripped up.
9 Do not accustom your mouth to
    oaths,
  nor habitually utter the name
    of the Holy One;
10 for as a servant who is
    constantly under scrutiny
    will not lack bruises,
so also the person who always
    swears and utters the
    Name
will never be cleansedj from
    sin.
11 The one who swears many oaths
    is full of iniquity,
  and the scourge will not leave
    his house.
If he swears in error, his sin
    remains on him,
  and if he disregards it, he sins
    doubly;
if he swears a false oath, he will
    not be justified,
  for his house will be filled with
    calamities.

fOther ancient authorities add *For one
should not always despise restricted
circumstances, or admire a rich person
who is stupid.*   gGk *their*   hOther
ancient authorities add *From them the
hope of your mercy is remote*   iThis
heading is included in the Gk text.
jSyr *be free*

Foul Language

12 There is a manner of speaking
　　comparable to death;[k]
　　may it never be found in the
　　　inheritance of Jacob!
　Such conduct will be far from
　　the godly,
　　and they will not wallow in
　　　sins.
13 Do not accustom your mouth to
　　coarse, foul language,
　for it involves sinful speech.
14 Remember your father and
　　mother
　　when you sit among the great,
　or you may forget yourself in
　　their presence,
　　and behave like a fool through
　　　bad habit;
　then you will wish that you had
　　never been born,
　　and you will curse the day of
　　　your birth.
15 Those who are accustomed to
　　using abusive language
　will never become disciplined
　　as long as they live.

Concerning Sexual Sins

16 Two kinds of individuals
　　multiply sins,
　　and a third incurs wrath.
　Hot passion that blazes like a
　　fire
　　will not be quenched until it
　　　burns itself out;
　one who commits fornication
　　with his near of kin
　　will never cease until the fire
　　　burns him up.
17 To a fornicator all bread is
　　sweet;
　　he will never weary until he
　　　dies.
18 The one who sins against his
　　marriage bed
　　says to himself, "Who can see
　　　me?
　Darkness surrounds me, the
　　walls hide me,
　　and no one sees me. Why
　　　should I worry?
　The Most High will not
　　remember sins."
19 His fear is confined to human
　　eyes
　　and he does not realize that
　　　the eyes of the Lord
　are ten thousand times
　　brighter than the sun;

they look upon every aspect of
　　human behavior
　and see into hidden corners.
20 Before the universe was created,
　　it was known to him,
　　and so it is since its
　　　completion.
21 This man will be punished in the
　　streets of the city,
　　and where he least suspects it,
　　　he will be seized.

22 So it is with a woman who
　　leaves her husband
　　and presents him with an heir
　　　by another man.
23 For first of all, she has
　　disobeyed the law of the
　　　Most High;
　second, she has committed an
　　offense against her
　　　husband;
　and third, through her
　　fornication she has
　　　committed adultery
　　and brought forth children by
　　　another man.
24 She herself will be brought
　　before the assembly,
　　and her punishment will
　　　extend to her children.
25 Her children will not take root,
　　and her branches will not bear
　　　fruit.
26 She will leave behind an
　　accursed memory
　　and her disgrace will never be
　　　blotted out.
27 Those who survive her will
　　recognize
　　that nothing is better than the
　　　fear of the Lord,
　and nothing sweeter than to
　　heed the commandments of
　　　the Lord.[l]

THE PRAISE OF WISDOM[m]

24 Wisdom praises herself,
　　and tells of her glory in the
　　　midst of her people.
2 In the assembly of the Most
　　High she opens her mouth,
　　and in the presence of his
　　　hosts she tells of her glory:

k Other ancient authorities read *clothed
about with death*　l Other ancient
authorities add as verse 28, *It is a great
honor to follow God, and to be received
by him is long life.*　m This heading is
included in the Gk text.

3 "I came forth from the mouth of
the Most High,
and covered the earth like a
mist.
4 I dwelt in the highest heavens,
and my throne was in a pillar
of cloud.
5 Alone I compassed the vault of
heaven
and traversed the depths of the
abyss.
6 Over waves of the sea, over all
the earth,
and over every people and
nation I have held sway.[n]
7 Among all these I sought a
resting place;
in whose territory should I
abide?

8 "Then the Creator of all things
gave me a command,
and my Creator chose the
place for my tent.
He said, 'Make your dwelling in
Jacob,
and in Israel receive your
inheritance.'
9 Before the ages, in the
beginning, he created me,
and for all the ages I shall not
cease to be.
10 In the holy tent I ministered
before him,
and so I was established in
Zion.
11 Thus in the beloved city he gave
me a resting place,
and in Jerusalem was my
domain.
12 I took root in an honored people,
in the portion of the Lord, his
heritage.

13 "I grew tall like a cedar in
Lebanon,
and like a cypress on the
heights of Hermon.
14 I grew tall like a palm tree in
En-ge'di,[o]
and like rosebushes in Jericho;
like a fair olive tree in the field,
and like a plane tree beside
water[p] I grew tall.
15 Like cassia and camel's thorn I
gave forth perfume,
and like choice myrrh I spread
my fragrance,
like galbanum, onycha, and
stacte,
and like the odor of incense in
the tent.

16 Like a terebinth I spread out my
branches,
and my branches are glorious
and graceful.
17 Like the vine I bud forth
delights,
and my blossoms become
glorious and abundant
fruit.[q]

19 "Come to me, you who desire
me,
and eat your fill of my fruits.
20 For the memory of me is sweeter
than honey,
and the possession of me
sweeter than the
honeycomb.
21 Those who eat of me will hunger
for more,
and those who drink of me
will thirst for more.
22 Whoever obeys me will not be
put to shame,
and those who work with me
will not sin."

Wisdom and the Law

23 All this is the book of the
covenant of the Most High
God,
the law that Moses
commanded us
as an inheritance for the
congregations of Jacob.[r]
25 It overflows, like the Pi'shon,
with wisdom,
and like the Tigris at the time
of the first fruits.
26 It runs over, like the Euphrates,
with understanding,
and like the Jordan at harvest
time.
27 It pours forth instruction like the
Nile,[s]

[n] Other ancient authorities read *I have
acquired a possession* [o] Other ancient
authorities read *on the beaches*
[p] Other ancient authorities omit *beside
water* [q] Other ancient authorities add
as verse 18, *I am the mother of beautiful
love, of fear, of knowledge, and of holy
hope; being eternal, I am given to all my
children, to those who are named by
him.* [r] Other ancient authorities add as
verse 24, "Do not cease to be strong in
the Lord, cling to him so that he may
strengthen you; the Lord Almighty alone
is God, and besides him there is no
savior." [s] Syr: Gk It makes instruction
shine forth like light

like the Gĭ'hon at the time of
vintage.

28 The first man did not know
wisdom[t] fully,
nor will the last one fathom
her.

29 For her thoughts are more
abundant than the sea,
and her counsel deeper than
the great abyss.

30 As for me, I was like a canal
from a river,
like a water channel into a
garden.

31 I said, "I will water my garden
and drench my flower-beds."
And lo, my canal became a river,
and my river a sea.

32 I will again make instruction
shine forth like the dawn,
and I will make it clear from
far away.

33 I will again pour out teaching
like prophecy,
and leave it to all future
generations.

34 Observe that I have not labored
for myself alone,
but for all who seek wisdom.[t]

Those Who Are Worthy of Praise

25 I take pleasure in three
things,
and they are beautiful in the
sight of God and of
mortals:[u]
agreement among brothers and
sisters, friendship among
neighbors,
and a wife and a husband who
live in harmony.

2 I hate three kinds of people,
and I loathe their manner of
life:
a pauper who boasts, a rich
person who lies,
and an old fool who commits
adultery.

3 If you gathered nothing in your
youth,
how can you find anything in
your old age?

4 How attractive is sound
judgment in the
gray-haired,
and for the aged to possess
good counsel!

5 How attractive is wisdom in the
aged,

and understanding and
counsel in the venerable!

6 Rich experience is the crown of
the aged,
and their boast is the fear of
the Lord.

7 I can think of nine whom I
would call blessed,
and a tenth my tongue
proclaims:
a man who can rejoice in his
children;
a man who lives to see the
downfall of his foes.

8 Happy the man who lives with a
sensible wife,
and the one who does not
plow with ox and ass
together.[v]
Happy is the one who does not
sin with the tongue,
and the one who has not
served an inferior.

9 Happy is the one who finds a
friend,[w]
and the one who speaks to
attentive listeners.

10 How great is the one who finds
wisdom!
But none is superior to the one
who fears the Lord.

11 Fear of the Lord surpasses
everything;
to whom can we compare the
one who has it?[x]

Some Extreme Forms of Evil

13 Any wound, but not a wound of
the heart!
Any wickedness, but not the
wickedness of a woman!

14 Any suffering, but not suffering
from those who hate!
And any vengeance, but not
the vengeance of enemies!

15 There is no venom[y] worse than
a snake's venom,[y]

[t] Gk *her*   [u] Syr Lat: Gk *In three things I
was beautiful and I stood in beauty
before the Lord and mortals.*
[v] Heb Syr: Gk lacks *and the one who
does not plow with ox and ass together*
[w] Lat Syr: Gk *good sense*   [x] Other
ancient authorities add as verse 12, *The
fear of the Lord is the beginning of love
for him, and faith is the beginning of
clinging to him.*   [y] Syr: Gk *head*

and no anger worse than a
  woman's[z] wrath.

The Evil of a Wicked Woman

16 I would rather live with a lion
      and a dragon
    than live with an evil woman.
17 A woman's wickedness changes
      her appearance,
    and darkens her face like that
      of a bear.
18 Her husband sits[a] among the
      neighbors,
    and he cannot help sighing[b]
      bitterly.
19 Any iniquity is small compared
      to a woman's iniquity;
    may a sinner's lot befall her!
20 A sandy ascent for the feet of
      the aged—
    such is a garrulous wife to a
      quiet husband.
21 Do not be ensnared by a
      woman's beauty,
    and do not desire a woman for
      her possessions.[c]
22 There is wrath and impudence
      and great disgrace
    when a wife supports her
      husband.
23 Dejected mind, gloomy face,
      and wounded heart come from
      an evil wife.
    Drooping hands and weak knees
      come from the wife who does
      not make her husband
      happy.
24 From a woman sin had its
      beginning,
    and because of her we all die.
25 Allow no outlet to water,
    and no boldness of speech to
      an evil wife.
26 If she does not go as you direct,
    separate her from yourself.

The Joy of a Good Wife

26 Happy is the husband of a
      good wife;
    the number of his days will be
      doubled.
2 A loyal wife brings joy to her
      husband,
    and he will complete his years
      in peace.
3 A good wife is a great blessing;
    she will be granted among the
      blessings of the man who
      fears the Lord.
4 Whether rich or poor, his heart
    is content,

and at all times his face is
  cheerful.

The Worst of Evils: A Wicked Wife

5 Of three things my heart is
      frightened,
    and of a fourth I am in great
      fear:[d]
    Slander in the city, the gathering
      of a mob,
    and false accusation—all these
      are worse than death.
6 But it is heartache and sorrow
      when a wife is jealous of a
      rival,
    and a tongue-lashing makes it
      known to all.
7 A bad wife is a chafing yoke;
    taking hold of her is like
      grasping a scorpion.
8 A drunken wife arouses great
      anger;
    she cannot hide her shame.
9 The haughty stare betrays an
      unchaste wife;
    her eyelids give her away.
10 Keep strict watch over a
      headstrong daughter,
    or else, when she finds liberty,
      she will make use of it.
11 Be on guard against her
      impudent eye,
    and do not be surprised if she
      sins against you.
12 As a thirsty traveler opens his
      mouth
    and drinks from any water
      near him,
    so she will sit in front of every
      tent peg
    and open her quiver to the
      arrow.

The Blessing of a Good Wife

13 A wife's charm delights her
      husband,
    and her skill puts flesh on his
      bones.
14 A silent wife is a gift from the
      Lord,
    and nothing is so precious as
      her self-discipline.
15 A modest wife adds charm to
      charm,

z Other ancient authorities read *an
enemy's*   a Heb Syr: Gk *loses heart*
b Other ancient authorities read *and
listening he sighs*   c Heb Syr: Other Gk
authorities read *for her beauty*
d Syr: Meaning of Gk uncertain

and no scales can weigh the
value of her chastity.

16 Like the sun rising in the heights
of the Lord,
so is the beauty of a good wife
in her well-ordered home.

17 Like the shining lamp on the
holy lampstand,
so is a beautiful face on a
stately figure.

18 Like golden pillars on silver
bases,
so are shapely legs and
steadfast feet.

Other ancient authorities add verses
19–27:

19 *My child, keep sound the bloom
of your youth,
and do not give your strength
to strangers.*

20 *Seek a fertile field within the
whole plain,
and sow it with your own
seed, trusting in your fine
stock.*

21 *So your offspring will prosper,
and, having confidence in their
good descent, will grow
great.*

22 *A prostitute is regarded as
spittle,
and a married woman as a
tower of death to her
lovers.*

23 *A godless wife is given as a
portion to a lawless man,
but a pious wife is given to the
man who fears the Lord.*

24 *A shameless woman constantly
acts disgracefully,
but a modest daughter will
even be embarrassed
before her husband.*

25 *A headstrong wife is regarded as
a dog,
but one who has a sense of
shame will fear the Lord.*

26 *A wife honoring her husband
will seem wise to all,
but if she dishonors him in her
pride she will be known to
all as ungodly.
Happy is the husband of a
good wife;
for the number of his years
will be doubled.*

27 *A loud-voiced and garrulous
wife is like a trumpet
sounding the charge,*

*and every person like this lives
in the anarchy of war.*

Three Depressing Things

28 At two things my heart is
grieved,
and because of a third anger
comes over me:
a warrior in want through
poverty,
intelligent men who are
treated contemptuously,
and a man who turns back from
righteousness to sin—
the Lord will prepare him for
the sword!

The Temptations of Commerce

29 A merchant can hardly keep
from wrongdoing,
nor is a tradesman innocent of
sin.

27 Many have committed sin for
gain,[e]
and those who seek to get rich
will avert their eyes.

2 As a stake is driven firmly into a
fissure between stones,
so sin is wedged in between
selling and buying.

3 If a person is not steadfast in the
fear of the Lord,
his house will be quickly
overthrown.

Tests in Life

4 When a sieve is shaken, the
refuse appears;
so do a person's faults when
he speaks.

5 The kiln tests the potter's
vessels;
so the test of a person is in his
conversation.

6 Its fruit discloses the cultivation
of a tree;
so a person's speech discloses
the cultivation of his mind.

7 Do not praise anyone before he
speaks,
for this is the way people are
tested.

[e] Other ancient authorities read *a trifle*

Reward and Retribution

8 If you pursue justice, you will
attain it
and wear it like a glorious
robe.
9 Birds roost with their own kind,
so honesty comes home to
those who practice it.
10 A lion lies in wait for prey;
so does sin for evildoers.

Varieties of Speech

11 The conversation of the godly is
always wise,
but the fool changes like the
moon.
12 Among stupid people limit your
time,
but among thoughtful people
linger on.
13 The talk of fools is offensive,
and their laughter is wantonly
sinful.
14 Their cursing and swearing
make one's hair stand on
end,
and their quarrels make others
stop their ears.
15 The strife of the proud leads to
bloodshed,
and their abuse is grievous to
hear.

Betraying Secrets
(Prov 20.19; 25.9)

16 Whoever betrays secrets
destroys confidence,
and will never find a congenial
friend.
17 Love your friend and keep faith
with him;
but if you betray his secrets,
do not follow after him.
18 For as a person destroys his
enemy,
so you have destroyed the
friendship of your
neighbor.
19 And as you allow a bird to
escape from your hand,
so you have let your neighbor
go, and will not catch him
again.
20 Do not go after him, for he is too
far off,
and has escaped like a gazelle
from a snare.
21 For a wound may be bandaged,
and there is reconciliation
after abuse,

but whoever has betrayed
secrets is without hope.

Hypocrisy and Retribution

22 Whoever winks the eye plots
mischief,
and those who know him will
keep their distance.
23 In your presence his mouth is all
sweetness,
and he admires your words;
but later he will twist his speech
and with your own words he
will trip you up.
24 I have hated many things, but
him above all;
even the Lord hates him.
25 Whoever throws a stone straight
up throws it on his own
head,
and a treacherous blow opens
up many wounds.
26 Whoever digs a pit will fall into
it,
and whoever sets a snare will
be caught in it.
27 If a person does evil, it will roll
back upon him,
and he will not know where it
came from.
28 Mockery and abuse issue from
the proud,
but vengeance lies in wait for
them like a lion.
29 Those who rejoice in the fall of
the godly will be caught in
a snare,
and pain will consume them
before their death.

Anger and Vengeance

30 Anger and wrath, these also are
abominations,
yet a sinner holds on to them.

28 The vengeful will face the
Lord's vengeance,
for he keeps a strict account
of[f] their sins.
2 Forgive your neighbor the wrong
he has done,
and then your sins will be
pardoned when you pray.
3 Does anyone harbor anger
against another,
and expect healing from the
Lord?
4 If one has no mercy toward
another like himself,

---

[f] Other ancient authorities read *for he
firmly establishes*

can he then seek pardon for
his own sins?

5 If a mere mortal harbors wrath,
who will make an atoning
sacrifice for his sins?

6 Remember the end of your life,
and set enmity aside;
remember corruption and
death, and be true to the
commandments.

7 Remember the commandments,
and do not be angry with
your neighbor;
remember the covenant of the
Most High, and overlook
faults.

8 Refrain from strife, and your
sins will be fewer;
for the hot-tempered kindle
strife,

9 and the sinner disrupts
friendships
and sows discord among those
who are at peace.

10 In proportion to the fuel, so will
the fire burn,
and in proportion to the
obstinacy, so will strife
increase;[g]
in proportion to a person's
strength will be his anger,
and in proportion to his wealth
he will increase his wrath.

11 A hasty quarrel kindles a fire,
and a hasty dispute sheds
blood.

The Evil Tongue
(Jas 3.1–12)

12 If you blow on a spark, it will
glow;
if you spit on it, it will be put
out;
yet both come out of your
mouth.

13 Curse the gossips and the
double-tongued,
for they destroy the peace of
many.

14 Slander[h] has shaken many,
and scattered them from
nation to nation;
it has destroyed strong cities,
and overturned the houses of
the great.

15 Slander[i] has driven virtuous
women from their homes,
and deprived them of the fruit
of their toil.

16 Those who pay heed to slander[j]
will not find rest,
nor will they settle down in
peace.

17 The blow of a whip raises a
welt,
but a blow of the tongue
crushes the bones.

18 Many have fallen by the edge of
the sword,
but not as many as have fallen
because of the tongue.

19 Happy is the one who is
protected from it,
who has not been exposed to
its anger,
who has not borne its yoke,
and has not been bound with
its fetters.

20 For its yoke is a yoke of iron,
and its fetters are fetters of
bronze;

21 its death is an evil death,
and Hades is preferable to it.

22 It has no power over the godly;
they will not be burned in its
flame.

23 Those who forsake the Lord will
fall into its power;
it will burn among them and
will not be put out.
It will be sent out against them
like a lion;
like a leopard it will mangle
them.

24a As you fence in your property
with thorns,

25b so make a door and a bolt for
your mouth.

24b As you lock up your silver and
gold,

25a so make balances and scales
for your words.

26 Take care not to err with your
tongue,[k]
and fall victim to one lying in
wait.

On Lending and Borrowing
(Cp Ex 22.25; Lev 25.35–38)

29 The merciful lend to their
neighbors;
by holding out a helping hand
they keep the
commandments.

2 Lend to your neighbor in his
time of need;

g Other ancient authorities read *burn*
h Gk *A third tongue* i Gk *a third
tongue* j Gk *it* k Gk *with it*

repay your neighbor when a loan falls due.

3 Keep your promise and be honest with him,
    and on every occasion you will find what you need.

4 Many regard a loan as a windfall,
    and cause trouble to those who help them.

5 One kisses another's hands until he gets a loan,
    and is deferential in speaking of his neighbor's money;
but at the time for repayment he delays,
    and pays back with empty promises,
    and finds fault with the time.

6 If he can pay, his creditor[l] will hardly get back half,
    and will regard that as a windfall.
If he cannot pay, the borrower[l] has robbed the other of his money,
    and he has needlessly made him an enemy;
he will repay him with curses and reproaches,
    and instead of glory will repay him with dishonor.

7 Many refuse to lend, not because of meanness,
    but from fear[m] of being defrauded needlessly.

8 Nevertheless, be patient with someone in humble circumstances,
    and do not keep him waiting for your alms.

9 Help the poor for the commandment's sake,
    and in their need do not send them away empty-handed.

10 Lose your silver for the sake of a brother or a friend,
    and do not let it rust under a stone and be lost.

11 Lay up your treasure according to the commandments of the Most High,
    and it will profit you more than gold.

12 Store up almsgiving in your treasury,
    and it will rescue you from every disaster;

13 better than a stout shield and a sturdy spear,

it will fight for you against the enemy.

On Guaranteeing Debts

14 A good person will be surety for his neighbor,
    but the one who has lost all sense of shame will fail him.

15 Do not forget the kindness of your guarantor,
    for he has given his life for you.

16 A sinner wastes the property of his guarantor,

17 and the ungrateful person abandons his rescuer.

18 Being surety has ruined many who were prosperous,
    and has tossed them about like waves of the sea;
it has driven the influential into exile,
    and they have wandered among foreign nations.

19 The sinner comes to grief through surety;
    his pursuit of gain involves him in lawsuits.

20 Assist your neighbor to the best of your ability,
    but be careful not to fall yourself.

Home and Hospitality

21 The necessities of life are water, bread, and clothing,
    and also a house to assure privacy.

22 Better is the life of the poor under their own crude roof
    than sumptuous food in the house of others.

23 Be content with little or much,
    and you will hear no reproach for being a guest.[n]

24 It is a miserable life to go from house to house;
    as a guest you should not open your mouth;

25 you will play the host and provide drink without being thanked,

[l]Gk he   [m]Other ancient authorities read *many refuse to lend, therefore, because of such meanness; they are afraid*   [n]Lat: Gk *reproach from your family;* other ancient authorities lack this line

and besides this you will hear
rude words like these:

26 "Come here, stranger, prepare
the table;
let me eat what you have
there."

27 "Be off, stranger, for an honored
guest is here;
my brother has come for a
visit, and I need the
guest-room."

28 It is hard for a sensible person
to bear
scolding about lodging[o] and
the insults of the
moneylender.

CONCERNING CHILDREN[p]

30 He who loves his son will
whip him often,
so that he may rejoice at the
way he turns out.

2 He who disciplines his son will
profit by him,
and will boast of him among
acquaintances.

3 He who teaches his son will
make his enemies envious,
and will glory in him among
his friends.

4 When the father dies he will not
seem to be dead,
for he has left behind him one
like himself,

5 whom in his life he looked upon
with joy
and at death, without grief.

6 He has left behind him an
avenger against his
enemies,
and one to repay the kindness
of his friends.

7 Whoever spoils his son will bind
up his wounds,
and will suffer heartache at
every cry.

8 An unbroken horse turns out
stubborn,
and an unchecked son turns
out headstrong.

9 Pamper a child, and he will
terrorize you;
play with him, and he will
grieve you.

10 Do not laugh with him, or you
will have sorrow with him,
and in the end you will gnash
your teeth.

11 Give him no freedom in his
youth,

and do not ignore his errors.

12 Bow down his neck in his
youth,[q]
and beat his sides while he is
young,
or else he will become stubborn
and disobey you,
and you will have sorrow of
soul from him.[r]

13 Discipline your son and make
his yoke heavy,[s]
so that you may not be
offended by his
shamelessness.

14 Better off poor, healthy, and fit
than rich and afflicted in body.

15 Health and fitness are better
than any gold,
and a robust body than
countless riches.

16 There is no wealth better than
health of body,
and no gladness above joy of
heart.

17 Death is better than a life of
misery,
and eternal sleep[t] than
chronic sickness.

CONCERNING FOODS[u]

18 Good things poured out upon a
mouth that is closed
are like offerings of food
placed upon a grave.

19 Of what use to an idol is a
sacrifice?
For it can neither eat nor
smell.
So is the one punished by the
Lord;

20 he sees with his eyes and groans
as a eunuch groans when
embracing a girl.[v]

21 Do not give yourself over to
sorrow,
and do not distress yourself
deliberately.

[o] Or scolding from the household
[p] This heading is included in the Gk text.
[q] Other ancient authorities lack this line
and the preceding line   [r] Other ancient
authorities lack this line   [s] Heb: Gk
take pains with him   [t] Other ancient
authorities lack eternal sleep   [u] This
heading is included in the Gk text; other
ancient authorities place the heading
before verse 16   [v] Other ancient
authorities add So is the person who
does right under compulsion

22 A joyful heart is life itself,
   and rejoicing lengthens one's
      life span.
23 Indulge yourself[w] and take
      comfort,
   and remove sorrow far from
      you,
   for sorrow has destroyed many,
   and no advantage ever comes
      from it.
24 Jealousy and anger shorten life,
   and anxiety brings on
      premature old age.
25 Those who are cheerful and
      merry at table
   will benefit from their food.

Right Attitude toward Riches

31 Wakefulness over wealth
         wastes away one's flesh,
   and anxiety about it drives
      away sleep.
2 Wakeful anxiety prevents
      slumber,
   and a severe illness carries off
      sleep.[x]
3 The rich person toils to amass a
      fortune,
   and when he rests he fills
      himself with his dainties.
4 The poor person toils to make a
      meager living,
   and if ever he rests he
      becomes needy.

5 One who loves gold will not be
      justified;
   one who pursues money will
      be led astray[y] by it.
6 Many have come to ruin because
      of gold,
   and their destruction has met
      them face to face.
7 It is a stumbling block to those
      who are avid for it,
   and every fool will be taken
      captive by it.
8 Blessed is the rich person who is
      found blameless,
   and who does not go after
      gold.
9 Who is he, that we may praise
      him?
   For he has done wonders
      among his people.
10 Who has been tested by it and
      been found perfect?
   Let it be for him a ground for
      boasting.

Who has had the power to
   transgress and did not
      transgress,
and to do evil and did not do
   it?
11 His prosperity will be
      established,[z]
   and the assembly will proclaim
      his acts of charity.

Table Etiquette

12 Are you seated at the table of
      the great?[a]
   Do not be greedy at it,
   and do not say, "How much
      food there is here!"
13 Remember that a greedy eye is a
      bad thing.
   What has been created more
      greedy than the eye?
   Therefore it sheds tears for
      any reason.
14 Do not reach out your hand for
      everything you see,
   and do not crowd your
      neighbor[b] at the dish.
15 Judge your neighbor's feelings
      by your own,
   and in every matter be
      thoughtful.
16 Eat what is set before you like a
      well brought-up person,[c]
   and do not chew greedily, or
      you will give offense.
17 Be the first to stop, as befits
      good manners,
   and do not be insatiable, or
      you will give offense.
18 If you are seated among many
      persons,
   do not help yourself[d] before
      they do.

19 How ample a little is for a
      well-disciplined person!
   He does not breathe heavily
      when in bed.
20 Healthy sleep depends on
      moderate eating;
   he rises early, and feels fit.
   The distress of sleeplessness and
      of nausea

---

[w] Other ancient authorities read *Beguile
yourself*   [x] Other ancient authorities
read *sleep carries off a severe illness*
[y] Heb Syr: Gk *pursues destruction will
be filled*   [z] Other ancient authorities
add *because of this*   [a] Heb Syr: Gk *at a
great table*   [b] Gk *him*   [c] Heb: Gk *like
a human being*   [d] Gk *reach out your
hand*

and colic are with the glutton.

21 If you are overstuffed with food,
     get up to vomit, and you will
     have relief.

22 Listen to me, my child, and do
     not disregard me,
   and in the end you will
     appreciate my words.
   In everything you do be
     moderate,*e*
   and no sickness will overtake
     you.

23 People bless the one who is
     liberal with food,
   and their testimony to his
     generosity is trustworthy.

24 The city complains of the one
     who is stingy with food,
   and their testimony to his
     stinginess is accurate.

Temperance in Drinking Wine

25 Do not try to prove your
     strength by wine-drinking,
   for wine has destroyed many.

26 As the furnace tests the work of
     the smith,*f*
   so wine tests hearts when the
     insolent quarrel.

27 Wine is very life to human
     beings
   if taken in moderation.
   What is life to one who is
     without wine?
   It has been created to make
     people happy.

28 Wine drunk at the proper time
     and in moderation
   is rejoicing of heart and
     gladness of soul.

29 Wine drunk to excess leads to
     bitterness of spirit,
   to quarrels and stumbling.

30 Drunkenness increases the anger
     of a fool to his own hurt,
   reducing his strength and
     adding wounds.

31 Do not reprove your neighbor at
     a banquet of wine,
   and do not despise him in his
     merrymaking;
   speak no word of reproach to
     him,
   and do not distress him by
     making demands of him.

Etiquette at a Banquet

32 If they make you master of
       the feast, do not exalt
       yourself;

be among them as one of their
     number.
   Take care of them first and then
     sit down;

2 when you have fulfilled all
     your duties, take your
     place,
   so that you may be merry along
     with them
   and receive a wreath for your
     excellent leadership.

3 Speak, you who are older, for it
     is your right,
   but with accurate knowledge,
     and do not interrupt the
     music.

4 Where there is entertainment, do
     not pour out talk;
   do not display your cleverness
     at the wrong time.

5 A ruby seal in a setting of gold
   is a concert of music at a
     banquet of wine.

6 A seal of emerald in a rich
     setting of gold
   is the melody of music with
     good wine.

7 Speak, you who are young, if
     you are obliged to,
   but no more than twice, and
     only if asked.

8 Be brief; say much in few words;
   be as one who knows and can
     still hold his tongue.

9 Among the great do not act as
     their equal;
   and when another is speaking,
     do not babble.

10 Lightning travels ahead of the
     thunder,
   and approval goes before one
     who is modest.

11 Leave in good time and do not
     be the last;
   go home quickly and do not
     linger.

12 Amuse yourself there to your
     heart's content,
   but do not sin through proud
     speech.

13 But above all bless your Maker,
   who fills you with his good
     gifts.

e Heb Syr: Gk *industrious*   *f* Heb: Gk
tests the hardening of steel by dipping

The Providence of God

14 The one who seeks God[g] will
  accept his discipline,
  and those who rise early to
  seek him[h] will find favor.
15 The one who seeks the law will
  be filled with it,
  but the hypocrite will stumble
  at it.
16 Those who fear the Lord will
  form true judgments,
  and they will kindle righteous
  deeds like a light.
17 The sinner will shun reproof,
  and will find a decision
  according to his liking.

18 A sensible person will not
  overlook a thoughtful
  suggestion;
  an insolent[i] and proud person
  will not be deterred by
  fear.[j]
19 Do nothing without deliberation,
  but when you have acted, do
  not regret it.
20 Do not go on a path full of
  hazards,
  and do not stumble at an
  obstacle twice.[k]
21 Do not be overconfident on a
  smooth[l] road,
22 and give good heed to your
  paths.[m]
23 Guard[n] yourself in every act,
  for this is the keeping of the
  commandments.

24 The one who keeps the law
  preserves himself,[o]
  and the one who trusts the
  Lord will not suffer loss.

33 No evil will befall the one
  who fears the Lord,
  but in trials such a one will be
  rescued again and again.
2 The wise will not hate the law,
  but the one who is hypocritical
  about it is like a boat in a
  storm.
3 The sensible person will trust in
  the law;
  for such a one the law is as
  dependable as a divine
  oracle.

4 Prepare what to say, and then
  you will be listened to;
  draw upon your training, and
  give your answer.

5 The heart of a fool is like a cart
  wheel,
  and his thoughts like a turning
  axle.
6 A mocking friend is like a
  stallion
  that neighs no matter who the
  rider is.

Differences in Nature and in Humankind

7 Why is one day more important
  than another,
  when all the daylight in the
  year is from the sun?
8 By the Lord's wisdom they were
  distinguished,
  and he appointed the different
  seasons and festivals.
9 Some days he exalted and
  hallowed,
  and some he made ordinary
  days.
10 All human beings come from the
  ground,
  and humankind[p] was created
  out of the dust.
11 In the fullness of his knowledge
  the Lord distinguished
  them
  and appointed their different
  ways.
12 Some he blessed and exalted,
  and some he made holy and
  brought near to himself;
  but some he cursed and brought
  low,
  and turned them out of their
  place.
13 Like clay in the hand of the
  potter,
  to be molded as he pleases,
  so all are in the hand of their
  Maker,
  to be given whatever he
  decides.

14 Good is the opposite of evil,
  and life the opposite of death;

[g] Heb: Gk *who fears the Lord*   [h] Other
ancient authorities lack *to seek him*
[i] Heb: Gk *alien*   [j] Meaning of Gk
uncertain. Other ancient authorities add
*and after acting, with him, without
deliberation*   [k] Heb: Gk *stumble on
stony ground*   [l] Or *an unexplored*
[m] Heb Syr: Gk *and beware of your
children*   [n] Heb Syr: Gk *Trust*   [o] Heb:
Gk *who believes the law heeds the
commandments*   [p] Heb: Gk *Adam*

so the sinner is the opposite of
the godly.

15 Look at all the works of the
Most High;
they come in pairs, one the
opposite of the other.

16 Now I was the last to keep vigil;
I was like a gleaner following
the grape-pickers;
17 by the blessing of the Lord I
arrived first,
and like a grape-picker I filled
my wine press.
18 Consider that I have not labored
for myself alone,
but for all who seek
instruction.
19 Hear me, you who are great
among the people,
and you leaders of the
congregation, pay heed!

The Advantage of Independence

20 To son or wife, to brother or
friend,
do not give power over
yourself, as long as you
live;
and do not give your property to
another,
in case you change your mind
and must ask for it.
21 While you are still alive and
have breath in you,
do not let anyone take your
place.
22 For it is better that your children
should ask from you
than that you should look to
the hand of your children.
23 Excel in all that you do;
bring no stain upon your
honor.
24 At the time when you end the
days of your life,
in the hour of death, distribute
your inheritance.

The Treatment of Slaves

25 Fodder and a stick and burdens
for a donkey;
bread and discipline and work
for a slave.
26 Set your slave to work, and you
will find rest;
leave his hands idle, and he
will seek liberty.
27 Yoke and thong will bow the
neck,

and for a wicked slave there
are racks and tortures.
28 Put him to work, in order that
he may not be idle,
29 for idleness teaches much evil.
30 Set him to work, as is fitting for
him,
and if he does not obey, make
his fetters heavy.
Do not be overbearing toward
anyone,
and do nothing unjust.

31 If you have but one slave, treat
him like yourself,
because you have bought him
with blood.
If you have but one slave, treat
him like a brother,
for you will need him as you
need your life.
32 If you ill-treat him, and he
leaves you and runs away,
33 which way will you go to seek
him?

Dreams Mean Nothing
(Deut 13.1–5; 18.9–14)

34 The senseless have vain and
false hopes,
and dreams give wings to
fools.
2 As one who catches at a shadow
and pursues the wind,
so is anyone who believes in*q*
dreams.
3 What is seen in dreams is but a
reflection,
the likeness of a face looking
at itself.
4 From an unclean thing what can
be clean?
And from something false
what can be true?
5 Divinations and omens and
dreams are unreal,
and like a woman in labor, the
mind has fantasies.
6 Unless they are sent by
intervention from the Most
High,
pay no attention to them.
7 For dreams have deceived many,
and those who put their hope
in them have perished.
8 Without such deceptions the law
will be fulfilled,
and wisdom is complete in the
mouth of the faithful.

q Syr: Gk *pays heed to*

Experience as a Teacher

9 An educated[r] person knows
  many things,
  and one with much experience
  knows what he is talking
  about.
10 An inexperienced person knows
  few things,
11 but he that has traveled
  acquires much cleverness.
12 I have seen many things in my
  travels,
  and I understand more than I
  can express.
13 I have often been in danger of
  death,
  but have escaped because of
  these experiences.

Fear the Lord

14 The spirit of those who fear the
  Lord will live,
15 for their hope is in him who
  saves them.
16 Those who fear the Lord will not
  be timid,
  or play the coward, for he is
  their hope.
17 Happy is the soul that fears the
  Lord!
18 To whom does he look? And
  who is his support?
19 The eyes of the Lord are on
  those who love him,
  a mighty shield and strong
  support,
  a shelter from scorching wind
  and a shade from noonday
  sun,
  a guard against stumbling and
  a help against falling.
20 He lifts up the soul and makes
  the eyes sparkle;
  he gives health and life and
  blessing.

Offering Sacrifices

21 If one sacrifices ill-gotten goods,
  the offering is blemished;[s]
22 the gifts[t] of the lawless are
  not acceptable.
23 The Most High is not pleased
  with the offerings of the
  ungodly,
  nor for a multitude of
  sacrifices does he forgive
  sins.
24 Like one who kills a son before
  his father's eyes

is the person who offers a
  sacrifice from the property
  of the poor.
25 The bread of the needy is the life
  of the poor;
  whoever deprives them of it is
  a murderer.
26 To take away a neighbor's living
  is to commit murder;
27 to deprive an employee of
  wages is to shed blood.
28 When one builds and another
  tears down,
  what do they gain but hard
  work?
29 When one prays and another
  curses,
  to whose voice will the Lord
  listen?
30 If one washes after touching a
  corpse, and touches it
  again,
  what has been gained by
  washing?
31 So if one fasts for his sins,
  and goes again and does the
  same things,
  who will listen to his prayer?
  And what has he gained by
  humbling himself?

The Law and Sacrifices
(Cp 2 Cor 9.7)

35 The one who keeps the law
  makes many offerings;
2 one who heeds the
  commandments makes an
  offering of well-being.
3 The one who returns a kindness
  offers choice flour,
4 and one who gives alms
  sacrifices a thank offering.
5 To keep from wickedness is
  pleasing to the Lord,
  and to forsake
  unrighteousness is an
  atonement.
6 Do not appear before the Lord
  empty-handed,
7 for all that you offer is in
  fulfillment of the
  commandment.
8 The offering of the righteous
  enriches the altar,
  and its pleasing odor rises
  before the Most High.

r Other ancient authorities read *A
traveled*　s Other ancient authorities
read *is made in mockery*　t Other
ancient authorities read *mockeries*

S
I
R
A
C
H

9 The sacrifice of the righteous is
acceptable,
and it will never be forgotten.
10 Be generous when you worship
the Lord,
and do not stint the first fruits
of your hands.
11 With every gift show a cheerful
face,
and dedicate your tithe with
gladness.
12 Give to the Most High as he has
given to you,
and as generously as you can
afford.
13 For the Lord is the one who
repays,
and he will repay you
sevenfold.

Divine Justice

14 Do not offer him a bribe, for he
will not accept it;
15 and do not rely on a dishonest
sacrifice;
for the Lord is the judge,
and with him there is no
partiality.
16 He will not show partiality to the
poor;
but he will listen to the prayer
of one who is wronged.
17 He will not ignore the
supplication of the orphan,
or the widow when she pours
out her complaint.
18 Do not the tears of the widow
run down her cheek
19 as she cries out against the
one who causes them to
fall?
20 The one whose service is
pleasing to the Lord will be
accepted,
and his prayer will reach to
the clouds.
21 The prayer of the humble
pierces the clouds,
and it will not rest until it
reaches its goal;
it will not desist until the Most
High responds
22 and does justice for the
righteous, and executes
judgment.
Indeed, the Lord will not delay,
and like a warrior[u] will not be
patient
until he crushes the loins of the
unmerciful
23 and repays vengeance on the
nations;

until he destroys the multitude of
the insolent,
and breaks the scepters of the
unrighteous;
24 until he repays mortals
according to their deeds,
and the works of all according
to their thoughts;
25 until he judges the case of his
people
and makes them rejoice in his
mercy.
26 His mercy is as welcome in time
of distress
as clouds of rain in time of
drought.

A Prayer for God's People

36 Have mercy upon us, O God[v]
of all,
2 and put all the nations in fear
of you.
3 Lift up your hand against
foreign nations
and let them see your might.
4 As you have used us to show
your holiness to them,
so use them to show your
glory to us.
5 Then they will know,[w] as we
have known
that there is no God but you,
O Lord.
6 Give new signs, and work other
wonders;
7 make your hand and right arm
glorious.
8 Rouse your anger and pour out
your wrath;
9 destroy the adversary and
wipe out the enemy.
10 Hasten the day, and remember
the appointed time,[x]
and let people recount your
mighty deeds.
11 Let survivors be consumed in
the fiery wrath,
and may those who harm your
people meet destruction.
12 Crush the heads of hostile rulers
who say, "There is no one but
ourselves."
13 Gather all the tribes of Jacob,[y]

[u]Heb: Gk *and with them*   [v]Heb: Gk
O Master, the God   [w]Heb: Gk *And let
them know you*   [x]Other ancient
authorities read *remember your oath*
[y]Owing to a dislocation in the Greek
Mss of Sirach, the verse numbers 14 and
15 are not used in chapter 36, though no
text is missing.

16 and give them their
   inheritance, as at the
   beginning.
17 Have mercy, O Lord, on the
   people called by your
   name,
      on Israel, whom you have
      named^z your firstborn,
18 Have pity on the city of your
   sanctuary,^{a}
      Jerusalem, the place of your
      dwelling.^{b}
19 Fill Zion with your majesty,^{c}
      and your temple^d with your
      glory.
20 Bear witness to those whom you
   created in the beginning,
      and fulfill the prophecies
      spoken in your name.
21 Reward those who wait for you
      and let your prophets be found
      trustworthy.
22 Hear, O Lord, the prayer of your
   servants, according to your
   goodwill toward^e your
   people,
   and all who are on the earth will
   know
      that you are the Lord, the God
      of the ages.

Concerning Discrimination

23 The stomach will take any food,
      yet one food is better than
      another.
24 As the palate tastes the kinds of
   game,
      so an intelligent mind detects
      false words.
25 A perverse mind will cause grief,
      but a person with experience
      will pay him back.
26 A woman will accept any man
   as a husband,
      but one girl is preferable to
      another.
27 A woman's beauty lights up a
   man's face,
      and there is nothing he desires
      more.
28 If kindness and humility mark
   her speech,
      her husband is more fortunate
      than other men.
29 He who acquires a wife gets his
   best possession,^{f}
      a helper fit for him and a
      pillar of support.^{g}
30 Where there is no fence, the
   property will be plundered;

and where there is no wife, a
man will become a fugitive
and a wanderer.^{h}
31 For who will trust a nimble
   robber
      that skips from city to city?
   So who will trust a man that has
   no nest,
      but lodges wherever night
      overtakes him?

False Friends

37 Every friend says, "I too am a
      friend";
      but some friends are friends
      only in name.
2 Is it not a sorrow like that for
   death itself
      when a dear friend turns into
      an enemy?
3 O inclination to evil, why were
   you formed
      to cover the land with deceit?
4 Some companions rejoice in the
   happiness of a friend,
      but in time of trouble they are
      against him.
5 Some companions help a friend
   for their stomachs' sake,
      yet in battle they will carry his
      shield.
6 Do not forget a friend during the
   battle,^{i}
      and do not be unmindful of
      him when you distribute
      your spoils.^{j}

Caution in Taking Advice

7 All counselors praise the counsel
   they give,
      but some give counsel in their
      own interest.
8 Be wary of a counselor,
      and learn first what is his
      interest,
      for he will take thought for
      himself.
   He may cast the lot against you

^{z} Other ancient authorities read *you have
likely to* ^{a} Or *on your holy city*
^{b} Heb: Gk *your rest* ^{c} Heb Syr: Gk *the
celebration of your wondrous deeds*
^{d} Heb Syr: Gk Lat *people* ^{e} Heb and
two Gk witnesses: Lat and most Gk
witnesses read *according to the blessing
of Aaron for* ^{f} Heb: Gk *enters upon a
possession* ^{g} Heb: Gk *rest* ^{h} Heb: Gk
wander about and sigh ^{i} Heb: Gk *in
your heart* ^{j} Heb: Gk *him in your
wealth*

9 and tell you, "Your way is
good,"
and then stand aside to see
what happens to you.
10 Do not consult the one who
regards you with suspicion;
hide your intentions from
those who are jealous of
you.
11 Do not consult with a woman
about her rival
or with a coward about war,
with a merchant about business
or with a buyer about selling,
with a miser about generosity[k]
or with the merciless about
kindness,
with an idler about any work
or with a seasonal laborer
about completing his work,
with a lazy servant about a big
task—
pay no attention to any advice
they give.
12 But associate with a godly
person
whom you know to be a
keeper of the
commandments,
who is like-minded with
yourself,
and who will grieve with you
if you fail.
13 And heed[l] the counsel of your
own heart,
for no one is more faithful to
you than it is.
14 For our own mind sometimes
keeps us better informed
than seven sentinels sitting
high on a watchtower.
15 But above all pray to the Most
High
that he may direct your way in
truth.

True and False Wisdom

16 Discussion is the beginning of
every work,
and counsel precedes every
undertaking.
17 The mind is the root of all
conduct;
18 it sprouts four branches,[m]
good and evil, life and death;
and it is the tongue that
continually rules them.
19 Some people may be clever
enough to teach many,
and yet be useless to
themselves.

20 A skillful speaker may be hated;
he will be destitute of all food,
21 for the Lord has withheld the
gift of charm,
since he is lacking in all
wisdom.
22 If a person is wise to his own
advantage,
the fruits of his good sense
will be praiseworthy.[n]
23 A wise person instructs his own
people,
and the fruits of his good
sense will endure.
24 A wise person will have praise
heaped upon him,
and all who see him will call
him happy.
25 The days of a person's life are
numbered,
but the days of Israel are
without number.
26 One who is wise among his
people will inherit honor,[o]
and his name will live forever.

Concerning Moderation

27 My child, test yourself while you
live;
see what is bad for you and do
not give in to it.
28 For not everything is good for
everyone,
and no one enjoys everything.
29 Do not be greedy for every
delicacy,
and do not eat without
restraint;
30 for overeating brings sickness,
and gluttony leads to nausea.
31 Many have died of gluttony,
but the one who guards
against it prolongs his life.

Concerning Physicians and Health

38 Honor physicians for their
services,
for the Lord created them;
2 for their gift of healing comes
from the Most High,
and they are rewarded by the
king.
3 The skill of physicians makes
them distinguished,

---

k Heb: Gk *gratitude*   l Heb: Gk
establish   m Heb: Gk *As a clue to
changes of heart four kinds of destiny
appear*   n Other ancient witnesses read
trustworthy   o Other ancient
authorities read *confidence*

and in the presence of the
great they are admired.

4 The Lord created medicines out
of the earth,
and the sensible will not
despise them.

5 Was not water made sweet with
a tree
in order that its^p power might
be known?

6 And he gave skill to human
beings
that he^q might be glorified in
his marvelous works.

7 By them the physician^r heals
and takes away pain;

8 the pharmacist makes a
mixture from them.
God's^s works will never be
finished;
and from him health^t spreads
over all the earth.

9 My child, when you are ill, do
not delay,
but pray to the Lord, and he
will heal you.

10 Give up your faults and direct
your hands rightly,
and cleanse your heart from
all sin.

11 Offer a sweet-smelling sacrifice,
and a memorial portion of
choice flour,
and pour oil on your offering,
as much as you can
afford.^{u}

12 Then give the physician his
place, for the Lord created
him;
do not let him leave you, for
you need him.

13 There may come a time when
recovery lies in the hands
of physicians,^{v}

14 for they too pray to the Lord
that he grant them success in
diagnosis^w
and in healing, for the sake of
preserving life.

15 He who sins against his Maker,
will be defiant toward the
physician.^{x}

On Mourning for the Dead
(Cp Sir 22.11–12)

16 My child, let your tears fall for
the dead,
and as one in great pain begin
the lament.

Lay out the body with due
ceremony,
and do not neglect the burial.

17 Let your weeping be bitter and
your wailing fervent;
make your mourning worthy
of the departed,
for one day, or two, to avoid
criticism;
then be comforted for your
grief.

18 For grief may result in death,
and a sorrowful heart saps
one's strength.

19 When a person is taken away,
sorrow is over;
but the life of the poor weighs
down the heart.

20 Do not give your heart to grief;
drive it away, and remember
your own end.

21 Do not forget, there is no
coming back;
you do the dead^y no good,
and you injure yourself.

22 Remember his^z fate, for yours is
like it;
yesterday it was his,^{a} and
today it is yours.

23 When the dead is at rest, let his
remembrance rest too,
and be comforted for him
when his spirit has
departed.

Trades and Crafts

24 The wisdom of the scribe
depends on the opportunity
of leisure;
only the one who has little
business can become wise.

25 How can one become wise who
handles the plow,
and who glories in the shaft of
a goad,
who drives oxen and is occupied
with their work,
and whose talk is about bulls?

26 He sets his heart on plowing
furrows,
and he is careful about fodder
for the heifers.

^{p} Or *his* ^{q} Or *they* ^{r} Heb: Gk *he*
^{s} Gk *His* ^{t} Or *peace* ^{u} Heb: Lat lacks
as much as you can afford; Meaning of
Gk uncertain ^{v} Gk *in their hands*
^{w} Heb: Gk *rest* ^{x} Heb: Gk *may he fall
into the hands of the physician*
^{y} Gk *him* ^{z} Heb: Gk *my* ^{a} Heb: Gk
mine

27 So too is every artisan and
    master artisan
    who labors by night as well as
        by day;
    those who cut the signets of
        seals,
        each is diligent in making a
            great variety;
    they set their heart on painting a
        lifelike image,
        and they are careful to finish
            their work.
28 So too is the smith, sitting by the
        anvil,
    intent on his iron-work;
    the breath of the fire melts his
        flesh,
        and he struggles with the heat
            of the furnace;
    the sound of the hammer
        deafens his ears,[b]
        and his eyes are on the pattern
            of the object.
    He sets his heart on finishing his
        handiwork,
        and he is careful to complete
            its decoration.
29 So too is the potter sitting at his
        work
    and turning the wheel with his
        feet;
    he is always deeply concerned
        over his products,
        and he produces them in
            quantity.
30 He molds the clay with his arm
    and makes it pliable with his
        feet;
    he sets his heart to finish the
        glazing,
        and he takes care in firing[c]
            the kiln.

31 All these rely on their hands,
    and all are skillful in their own
        work.
32 Without them no city can be
        inhabited,
    and wherever they live, they
        will not go hungry.[d]
    Yet they are not sought out for
        the council of the people,[e]
33   nor do they attain eminence in
            the public assembly.
    They do not sit in the judge's
        seat,
        nor do they understand the
            decisions of the courts;
    they cannot expound discipline
        or judgment,
        and they are not found among
            the rulers.[f]

34 But they maintain the fabric of
        the world,
    and their concern is for[g] the
        exercise of their trade.

The Activity of the Scribe

How different the one who
        devotes himself
    to the study of the law of the
        Most High!

39 He seeks out the wisdom of
    all the ancients,
    and is concerned with
        prophecies;
2 he preserves the sayings of the
        famous
    and penetrates the subtleties of
        parables;
3 he seeks out the hidden
        meanings of proverbs
    and is at home with the
        obscurities of parables.
4 He serves among the great
    and appears before rulers;
    he travels in foreign lands
    and learns what is good and
        evil in the human lot.
5 He sets his heart to rise early
    to seek the Lord who made
        him,
    and to petition the Most High;
    he opens his mouth in prayer
    and asks pardon for his sins.

6 If the great Lord is willing,
    he will be filled with the spirit
        of understanding;
    he will pour forth words of
        wisdom of his own
    and give thanks to the Lord in
        prayer.
7 The Lord[h] will direct his
        counsel and knowledge,
    as he meditates on his
        mysteries.
8 He will show the wisdom of
        what he has learned,
    and will glory in the law of the
        Lord's covenant.
9 Many will praise his
        understanding;
    it will never be blotted out.
    His memory will not disappear,
    and his name will live through
        all generations.

---

[b] Cn: Gk *renews his ear*   [c] Cn: Gk
cleaning   [d] Syr: Gk *and people can
neither live nor walk there*   [e] Most
ancient authorities lack this line
[f] Cn: Gk *among parables*   [g] Syr: Gk
prayer is in   [h] Gk *He himself*

10 Nations will speak of his
    wisdom,
    and the congregation will
      proclaim his praise.
11 If he lives long, he will leave a
    name greater than a
    thousand,
    and if he goes to rest, it is
      enough[i] for him.

A Hymn of Praise to God

12 I have more on my mind to
    express;
    I am full like the full moon.
13 Listen to me, my faithful
    children, and blossom
    like a rose growing by a
      stream of water.
14 Send out fragrance like incense,
    and put forth blossoms like a
      lily.
    Scatter the fragrance, and sing a
      hymn of praise;
    bless the Lord for all his
      works.
15 Ascribe majesty to his name
    and give thanks to him with
      praise,
    with songs on your lips, and
      with harps;
    this is what you shall say in
      thanksgiving:

16 "All the works of the Lord are
    very good,
    and whatever he commands
      will be done at the
      appointed time.
17 No one can say, 'What is this?'
    or 'Why is that?' —
    for at the appointed time all
      such questions will be
      answered.
    At his word the waters stood in
      a heap,
    and the reservoirs of water at
      the word of his mouth.
18 When he commands, his every
    purpose is fulfilled,
    and none can limit his saving
      power.
19 The works of all are before him,
    and nothing can be hidden
      from his eyes.
20 From the beginning to the end of
    time he can see everything,
    and nothing is too marvelous
      for him.
21 No one can say, 'What is this?'
    or 'Why is that?' —

    for everything has been
      created for its own
      purpose.
22 "His blessing covers the dry land
    like a river,
    and drenches it like a flood.
23 But his wrath drives out the
    nations,
    as when he turned a watered
      land into salt.
24 To the faithful his ways are
    straight,
    but full of pitfalls for the
      wicked.
25 From the beginning good things
    were created for the good,
    but for sinners good things
      and bad.[j]
26 The basic necessities of human
    life
    are water and fire and iron
      and salt
    and wheat flour and milk and
      honey,
    the blood of the grape and oil
      and clothing.
27 All these are good for the godly,
    but for sinners they turn into
      evils.

28 "There are winds created for
    vengeance,
    and in their anger they can
      dislodge mountains;[k]
    on the day of reckoning they
      will pour out their strength
      and calm the anger of their
      Maker.
29 Fire and hail and famine and
    pestilence,
    all these have been created for
      vengeance;
30 the fangs of wild animals and
    scorpions and vipers,
    and the sword that punishes
      the ungodly with
      destruction.
31 They take delight in doing his
    bidding,
    always ready for his service
      on earth;
    and when their time comes
      they never disobey his
      command."

32 So from the beginning I have
    been convinced of all this

i Cn: Meaning of Gk uncertain
j Heb Lat: Gk *sinners bad things*
k Heb Syr: Gk *can scourge mightily*

and have thought it out and
left it in writing:
33 All the works of the Lord are
good,
and he will supply every need
in its time.
34 No one can say, "This is not as
good as that,"
for everything proves good in
its appointed time.
35 So now sing praise with all your
heart and voice,
and bless the name of the
Lord.

Human Wretchedness

40 Hard work was created for
everyone,
and a heavy yoke is laid on
the children of Adam,
from the day they come forth
from their mother's womb
until the day they return to[l]
the mother of all the
living.[m]
2 Perplexities and fear of heart are
theirs,
and anxious thought of the
day of their death.
3 From the one who sits on a
splendid throne
to the one who grovels in dust
and ashes,
4 from the one who wears purple
and a crown
to the one who is clothed in
burlap,
5 there is anger and envy and
trouble and unrest,
and fear of death, and fury
and strife.
And when one rests upon his
bed,
his sleep at night confuses his
mind.
6 He gets little or no rest;
he struggles in his sleep as he
did by day.[n]
He is troubled by the visions of
his mind
like one who has escaped from
the battlefield.
7 At the moment he reaches safety
he wakes up,
astonished that his fears were
groundless.
8 To all creatures, human and
animal,
but to sinners seven times
more,
9 come death and bloodshed and
strife and sword,
calamities and famine and ruin
and plague.
10 All these were created for the
wicked,
and on their account the flood
came.
11 All that is of earth returns to
earth,
and what is from above
returns above.[o]

Injustice Will Not Prosper

12 All bribery and injustice will be
blotted out,
but good faith will last forever.
13 The wealth of the unjust will dry
up like a river,
and crash like a loud clap of
thunder in a storm.
14 As a generous person has cause
to rejoice,
so lawbreakers will utterly fail.
15 The children of the ungodly put
out few branches;
they are unhealthy roots on
sheer rock.
16 The reeds by any water or river
bank
are plucked up before any
grass;
17 but kindness is like a garden of
blessings,
and almsgiving endures
forever.

The Joys of Life

18 Wealth and wages make life
sweet,[p]
but better than either is
finding a treasure.
19 Children and the building of a
city establish one's name,
but better than either is the
one who finds wisdom.
Cattle and orchards make one
prosperous;[q]
but a blameless wife is
accounted better than
either.
20 Wine and music gladden the
heart,

[l]Other Gk and Lat authorities read *are
buried in*   [m]Heb: Gk *of all*   [n]Arm:
Meaning of Gk uncertain   [o]Heb Syr:
Gk Lat *from the waters returns to the
sea*   [p]Heb: Gk *Life is sweet for the
self-reliant worker*   [q]Heb Syr: Gk lacks
but better . . . prosperous

but the love of friends[r] is
     better than either.
21 The flute and the harp make
     sweet melody,
     but a pleasant voice is better
        than either.
22 The eye desires grace and
     beauty,
     but the green shoots of grain
        more than either.
23 A friend or companion is always
     welcome,
     but a sensible wife[s] is better
        than either.
24 Kindred and helpers are for a
     time of trouble,
     but almsgiving rescues better
        than either.
25 Gold and silver make one stand
     firm,
     but good counsel is esteemed
        more than either.
26 Riches and strength build up
     confidence,
     but the fear of the Lord is
        better than either.
There is no want in the fear of
     the Lord,
     and with it there is no need to
        seek for help.
27 The fear of the Lord is like a
     garden of blessing,
     and covers a person better
        than any glory.

The Disgrace of Begging

28 My child, do not lead the life of
     a beggar;
     it is better to die than to beg.
29 When one looks to the table of
     another,
     one's way of life cannot be
        considered a life.
One loses self-respect with
     another person's food,
     but one who is intelligent and
        well instructed guards
        against that.
30 In the mouth of the shameless
     begging is sweet,
     but it kindles a fire inside him.

Concerning Death

41 O death, how bitter is the
     thought of you
to the one at peace among
     possessions,
who has nothing to worry about
     and is prosperous in
     everything,

and still is vigorous enough to
     enjoy food!
2 O death, how welcome is your
     sentence
     to one who is needy and
        failing in strength,
worn down by age and anxious
     about everything;
     to one who is contrary, and
        has lost all patience!
3 Do not fear death's decree for
     you;
     remember those who went
        before you and those who
        will come after.
4 This is the Lord's decree for all
     flesh;
     why then should you reject the
        will of the Most High?
Whether life lasts for ten years
     or a hundred or a
     thousand,
     there are no questions asked
        in Hades.

The Fate of the Wicked

5 The children of sinners are
     abominable children,
     and they frequent the haunts
        of the ungodly.
6 The inheritance of the children
     of sinners will perish,
     and on their offspring will be a
        perpetual disgrace.
7 Children will blame an ungodly
     father,
     for they suffer disgrace
        because of him.
8 Woe to you, the ungodly,
     who have forsaken the law of
        the Most High God!
9 If you have children, calamity
     will be theirs;
     you will beget them only for
        groaning.
When you stumble, there is
     lasting joy;[t]
     and when you die, a curse is
        your lot.
10 Whatever comes from earth
     returns to earth;
     so the ungodly go from curse
        to destruction.
11 The human body is a fleeting
     thing,

[r] Heb: Gk *wisdom*   [s] Heb Compare Syr:
Gk *wife with her husband*   [t] Heb:
Meaning of Gk uncertain

but a virtuous name will never
be blotted out.[u]

12 Have regard for your name,
since it will outlive you
longer than a thousand hoards
of gold.
13 The days of a good life are
numbered,
but a good name lasts forever.

14 My children, be true to your
training and be at peace;
hidden wisdom and unseen
treasure —
of what value is either?

A Series of Contrasts

15 Better are those who hide their
folly
than those who hide their
wisdom.
16 Therefore show respect for my
words;
for it is not good to feel shame
in every circumstance,
nor is every kind of
abashment to be
approved.[v]

17 Be ashamed of sexual
immorality, before your
father or mother;
and of a lie, before a prince or
a ruler;
18 of a crime, before a judge or
magistrate;
and of a breach of the law,
before the congregation
and the people;
of unjust dealing, before your
partner or your friend;
19 and of theft, in the place
where you live.
Be ashamed of breaking an oath
or agreement,[w]
and of leaning on your elbow
at meals;
of surliness in receiving or
giving,
20 and of silence, before those
who greet you;
of looking at a prostitute,
21 and of rejecting the appeal of
a relative;
of taking away someone's
portion or gift,
and of gazing at another man's
wife;
22 of meddling with his
servant-girl —
and do not approach her bed;

of abusive words, before
friends —
and do not be insulting after
making a gift.

42 Be ashamed of repeating what
you hear,
and of betraying secrets.
Then you will show proper
shame,
and will find favor with
everyone.

Of the following things do not be
ashamed,
and do not sin to save face:
2 Do not be ashamed of the law of
the Most High and his
covenant,
and of rendering judgment to
acquit the ungodly;
3 of keeping accounts with a
partner or with traveling
companions,
and of dividing the inheritance
of friends;
4 of accuracy with scales and
weights,
and of acquiring much or
little;
5 of profit from dealing with
merchants,
and of frequent disciplining of
children,
and of drawing blood from the
back of a wicked slave.
6 Where there is an untrustworthy
wife, a seal is a good thing;
and where there are many
hands, lock things up.
7 When you make a deposit, be
sure it is counted and
weighed,
and when you give or receive,
put it all in writing.
8 Do not be ashamed to correct
the stupid or foolish
or the aged who are guilty of
sexual immorality.
Then you will show your sound
training,
and will be approved by all.

[u] Heb: Gk *People grieve over the death
of the body, but the bad name of sinners
will be blotted out*   [v] Heb: Gk *and not
everything is confidently esteemed by
everyone*   [w] Heb: Gk *before the truth
of God and the covenant*

Daughters and Fathers
(Sir 7.24–25; 26.10–12)

9 A daughter is a secret anxiety to
her father,
   and worry over her robs him
of sleep;
when she is young, for fear she
may not marry,
   or if married, for fear she may
be disliked;
10 while a virgin, for fear she may
be seduced
   and become pregnant in her
father's house;
or having a husband, for fear
she may go astray,
   or, though married, for fear
she may be barren.
11 Keep strict watch over a
headstrong daughter,
   or she may make you a
laughingstock to your
enemies,
a byword in the city and the
assembly of[x] the people,
   and put you to shame in public
gatherings.[y]
See that there is no lattice in her
room,
   no spot that overlooks the
approaches to the house.[z]
12 Do not let her parade her beauty
before any man,
   or spend her time among
married women;[x]
13 for from garments comes the
moth,
   and from a woman comes
woman's wickedness.
14 Better is the wickedness of a
man than a woman who
does good;
   it is woman who brings shame
and disgrace.

The Works of God in Nature

15 I will now call to mind the
works of the Lord,
   and will declare what I have
seen.
By the word of the Lord his
works are made;
   and all his creatures do his
will.[a]
16 The sun looks down on
everything with its light,
   and the work of the Lord is
full of his glory.
17 The Lord has not empowered
even his holy ones

to recount all his marvelous
works,
which the Lord the Almighty has
established
   so that the universe may stand
firm in his glory.
18 He searches out the abyss and
the human heart;
   he understands their
innermost secrets.
For the Most High knows all that
may be known;
   he sees from of old the things
that are to come.[b]
19 He discloses what has been and
what is to be,
   and he reveals the traces of
hidden things.
20 No thought escapes him,
   and nothing is hidden from
him.
21 He has set in order the splendors
of his wisdom;
   he is from all eternity one and
the same.
Nothing can be added or taken
away,
   and he needs no one to be his
counselor.
22 How desirable are all his works,
   and how sparkling they are to
see![c]
23 All these things live and remain
forever;
   each creature is preserved to
meet a particular need.[d]
24 All things come in pairs, one
opposite the other,
   and he has made nothing
incomplete.
25 Each supplements the virtues of
the other.
   Who could ever tire of seeing
his glory?

The Splendor of the Sun

43 The pride of the higher
realms is the clear vault of
the sky,
   as glorious to behold as the
sight of the heavens.
2 The sun, when it appears,
proclaims as it rises

---

[x] Heb: Meaning of Gk uncertain   [y] Heb:
Gk *to shame before the great multitude*
[z] Heb: Gk lacks *See . . . house*   [a] Syr
Compare Heb: most Gk witnesses lack
and all . . . will   [b] Heb: Gk *he sees the
sign(s) of the age*   [c] Meaning of Gk
uncertain   [d] Heb: Gk *forever for every
need, and all are obedient*

what a marvelous instrument
    it is, the work of the Most
    High.
3 At noon it parches the land,
    and who can withstand its
    burning heat?
4 A man tending*e* a furnace
    works in burning heat,
  but three times as hot is the
    sun scorching the
    mountains;
it breathes out fiery vapors,
  and its bright rays blind the
    eyes.
5 Great is the Lord who made it;
  at his orders it hurries on its
    course.

The Splendor of the Moon

6 It is the moon that marks the
    changing seasons,*f*
  governing the times, their
    everlasting sign.
7 From the moon comes the sign
    for festal days,
  a light that wanes when it
    completes its course.
8 The new moon, as its name
    suggests, renews itself;*g*
how marvelous it is in this
    change,
a beacon to the hosts on high,
  shining in the vault of the
    heavens!

*The Glory of the Stars and the
Rainbow*

9 The glory of the stars is the
    beauty of heaven,
  a glittering array in the
    heights of the Lord.
10 On the orders of the Holy One
    they stand in their
    appointed places;
  they never relax in their
    watches.
11 Look at the rainbow, and praise
    him who made it;
  it is exceedingly beautiful in
    its brightness.
12 It encircles the sky with its
    glorious arc;
  the hands of the Most High
    have stretched it out.

The Marvels of Nature

13 By his command he sends the
    driving snow
  and speeds the lightnings of
    his judgment.

14 Therefore the storehouses are
    opened,
  and the clouds fly out like
    birds.
15 In his majesty he gives the
    clouds their strength,
  and the hailstones are broken
    in pieces.
17a The voice of his thunder
    rebukes the earth;
16 when he appears, the
    mountains shake.
At his will the south wind blows;
17b   so do the storm from the
    north and the whirlwind.
He scatters the snow like birds
    flying down,
  and its descent is like locusts
    alighting.
18 The eye is dazzled by the beauty
    of its whiteness,
  and the mind is amazed as it
    falls.
19 He pours frost over the earth
    like salt,
  and icicles form like pointed
    thorns.
20 The cold north wind blows,
  and ice freezes on the water;
it settles on every pool of water,
  and the water puts it on like a
    breastplate.
21 He consumes the mountains and
    burns up the wilderness,
  and withers the tender grass
    like fire.
22 A mist quickly heals all things;
  the falling dew gives
    refreshment from the heat.

23 By his plan he stilled the deep
  and planted islands in it.
24 Those who sail the sea tell of its
    dangers,
  and we marvel at what we
    hear.
25 In it are strange and marvelous
    creatures,
  all kinds of living things, and
    huge sea-monsters.
26 Because of him each of his
    messengers succeeds,
  and by his word all things
    hold together.

27 We could say more but could
    never say enough;

e Other ancient authorities read *blowing
upon*   *f* Heb: Meaning of Gk uncertain
g Heb: Gk *The month is named after the
moon*

let the final word be: "He is the all."

28 Where can we find the strength to praise him?
For he is greater than all his works.
29 Awesome is the Lord and very great,
and marvelous is his power.
30 Glorify the Lord and exalt him as much as you can,
for he surpasses even that.
When you exalt him, summon all your strength,
and do not grow weary, for you cannot praise him enough.
31 Who has seen him and can describe him?
Or who can extol him as he is?
32 Many things greater than these lie hidden,
for I[h] have seen but few of his works.
33 For the Lord has made all things,
and to the godly he has given wisdom.

HYMN IN HONOR OF OUR ANCESTORS[i]

44 Let us now sing the praises of famous men,
our ancestors in their generations.
2 The Lord apportioned to them[j] great glory,
his majesty from the beginning.
3 There were those who ruled in their kingdoms,
and made a name for themselves by their valor;
those who gave counsel because they were intelligent;
those who spoke in prophetic oracles;
4 those who led the people by their counsels
and by their knowledge of the people's lore;
they were wise in their words of instruction;
5 those who composed musical tunes,
or put verses in writing;
6 rich men endowed with resources,
living peacefully in their homes —

7 all these were honored in their generations,
and were the pride of their times.
8 Some of them have left behind a name,
so that others declare their praise.
9 But of others there is no memory;
they have perished as though they had never existed;
they have become as though they had never been born,
they and their children after them.
10 But these also were godly men, whose righteous deeds have not been forgotten;
11 their wealth will remain with their descendants,
and their inheritance with their children's children.[k]
12 Their descendants stand by the covenants;
their children also, for their sake.
13 Their offspring will continue forever,
and their glory will never be blotted out.
14 Their bodies are buried in peace, but their name lives on generation after generation.
15 The assembly declares[l] their wisdom,
and the congregation proclaims their praise.

Enoch
(Gen 5.24; Heb 11.5)

16 E'noch pleased the Lord and was taken up,
an example of repentance to all generations.

Noah
(Gen 6.9 – 9.17)

17 Noah was found perfect and righteous;
in the time of wrath he kept the race alive;[m]
therefore a remnant was left on the earth

h Heb: Gk *we*   i This title is included in the Gk text.   j Heb: Gk *created*
k Heb Compare Lat Syr: Meaning of Gk uncertain   l Heb: Gk *Peoples declare*
m Heb: Gk *was taken in exchange*

when the flood came.

18 Everlasting covenants were
made with him
that all flesh should never
again be blotted out by a
flood.

Abraham
(Gen 15.1–17.27; 22.1–18)

19 Abraham was the great father of
a multitude of nations,
and no one has been found
like him in glory.

20 He kept the law of the Most
High,
and entered into a covenant
with him;
he certified the covenant in his
flesh,
and when he was tested he
proved faithful.

21 Therefore the Lord[n] assured
him with an oath
that the nations would be
blessed through his
offspring;
that he would make him as
numerous as the dust of
the earth,
and exalt his offspring like the
stars,
and give them an inheritance
from sea to sea
and from the Euphrates[o] to
the ends of the earth.

Isaac and Jacob
(Gen 26.1–5; 27.1–29)

22 To Isaac also he gave the same
assurance
for the sake of his father
Abraham.
The blessing of all people and
the covenant

23 he made to rest on the head of
Jacob;
he acknowledged him with his
blessings,
and gave him his inheritance;
he divided his portions,
and distributed them among
twelve tribes.

Moses
(Ex 6.28–11.10; 20.1–21)

From his descendants the Lord[n]
brought forth a godly man,
who found favor in the sight of
all

45 1 and was beloved by God
and people,

Moses, whose memory is
blessed.

2 He made him equal in glory to
the holy ones,
and made him great, to the
terror of his enemies.

3 By his words he performed swift
miracles;[p]
the Lord[n] glorified him in the
presence of kings.
He gave him commandments for
his people,
and revealed to him his glory.

4 For his faithfulness and
meekness he consecrated
him,
choosing him out of all
humankind.

5 He allowed him to hear his
voice,
and led him into the dark
cloud,
and gave him the
commandments face to
face,
the law of life and knowledge,
so that he might teach Jacob the
covenant,
and Israel his decrees.

Aaron
(Ex 28.1–43; Lev 8.1–36; Num 16.1–35)

6 He exalted Aaron, a holy man
like Moses[q]
who was his brother, of the
tribe of Levi.

7 He made an everlasting
covenant with him,
and gave him the priesthood
of the people.
He blessed him with stateliness,
and put a glorious robe on
him.

8 He clothed him in perfect
splendor,
and strengthened him with the
symbols of authority,
the linen undergarments, the
long robe, and the ephod.

9 And he encircled him with
pomegranates,
with many golden bells all
around,
to send forth a sound as he
walked,
to make their ringing heard in
the temple
as a reminder to his people;

[n] Gk *he*   [o] Syr: Heb Gk *River*   [p] Heb:
Gk *caused signs to cease*   [q] Gk *him*

10 with the sacred vestment, of gold
and violet
and purple, the work of an
embroiderer;
with the oracle of judgment,
U'rim and Thum'mim;
11 with twisted crimson, the work
of an artisan;
with precious stones engraved
like seals,
in a setting of gold, the work
of a jeweler,
to commemorate in engraved
letters
each of the tribes of Israel;
12 with a gold crown upon his
turban,
inscribed like a seal with
"Holiness,"
a distinction to be prized, the
work of an expert,
a delight to the eyes, richly
adorned.
13 Before him such beautiful things
did not exist.
No outsider ever put them on,
but only his sons
and his descendants in
perpetuity.
14 His sacrifices shall be wholly
burned
twice every day continually.
15 Moses ordained him,
and anointed him with holy
oil;
it was an everlasting covenant
for him
and for his descendants as
long as the heavens
endure,
to minister to the Lord[r] and
serve as priest
and bless his people in his
name.
16 He chose him out of all the
living
to offer sacrifice to the Lord,
incense and a pleasing odor as a
memorial portion,
to make atonement for the[s]
people.
17 In his commandments he gave
him
authority and statutes and[t]
judgments,
to teach Jacob the testimonies,
and to enlighten Israel with his
law.
18 Outsiders conspired against him,
and envied him in the
wilderness,
Dā'than and A·bī'ram and their
followers
and the company of Kō'rah, in
wrath and anger.
19 The Lord saw it and was not
pleased,
and in the heat of his anger
they were destroyed;
he performed wonders against
them
to consume them in flaming
fire.
20 He added glory to Aaron
and gave him a heritage;
he allotted to him the best of the
first fruits,
and prepared bread of first
fruits in abundance;
21 for they eat the sacrifices of the
Lord,
which he gave to him and his
descendants.
22 But in the land of the people he
has no inheritance,
and he has no portion among
the people;
for the Lord[u] himself is his[v]
portion and inheritance.

Phinehas
(Num 25.7–13)

23 Phin'e·has son of El·ē·ā'zar
ranks third in glory
for being zealous in the fear of
the Lord,
and standing firm, when the
people turned away,
in the noble courage of his
soul;
and he made atonement for
Israel.
24 Therefore a covenant of
friendship was established
with him,
that he should be leader of the
sanctuary and of his
people,
that he and his descendants
should have
the dignity of the priesthood
forever.
25 Just as a covenant was
established with David
son of Jesse of the tribe of
Judah,
that the king's heritage passes
only from son to son,

[r] Gk him   [s] Other ancient authorities
read *his* or *your*   [t] Heb: Gk *authority in
covenants of*   [u] Gk *he*   [v] Other ancient
authorities read *your*

so the heritage of Aaron is for
his descendants alone.

26 And now bless the Lord
who has crowned you with
glory.*w*
May the Lord*x* grant you
wisdom of mind
to judge his people with
justice,
so that their prosperity may not
vanish,
and that their glory may
endure through all their
generations.

Joshua and Caleb
(Josh 6 — 11)

46 Joshua son of Nun was
mighty in war,
and was the successor of
Moses in the prophetic
office.
He became, as his name implies,
a great savior of God's*y* elect,
to take vengeance on the
enemies that rose against
them,
so that he might give Israel its
inheritance.
2 How glorious he was when he
lifted his hands
and brandished his sword
against the cities!
3 Who before him ever stood so
firm?
For he waged the wars of the
Lord.
4 Was it not through him that the
sun stood still
and one day become as long
as two?
5 He called upon the Most High,
the Mighty One,
when enemies pressed him on
every side,
and the great Lord answered
him
with hailstones of mighty
power.
6 He overwhelmed that nation in
battle,
and on the slope he destroyed
his opponents,
so that the nations might know
his armament,
that he was fighting in the
sight of the Lord;
for he was a devoted follower
of the Mighty One.

7 And in the days of Moses he
proved his loyalty,
he and Caleb son of
Je·phŭn'neh:
they opposed the congregation,*z*
restrained the people from sin,
and stilled their wicked
grumbling.
8 And these two alone were
spared
out of six hundred thousand
infantry,
to lead the people*a* into their
inheritance,
the land flowing with milk and
honey.
9 The Lord gave Caleb strength,
which remained with him in
his old age,
so that he went up to the hill
country,
and his children obtained it for
an inheritance,
10 so that all the Israelites might
see
how good it is to follow the
Lord.

The Judges
(Judg 1 — 16; 1 Sam 3.19—20)

11 The judges also, with their
respective names,
whose hearts did not fall into
idolatry
and who did not turn away from
the Lord —
may their memory be blessed!
12 May their bones send forth new
life from where they lie,
and may the names of those
who have been honored
live again in their children!

13 Samuel was beloved by his
Lord;
a prophet of the Lord, he
established the kingdom
and anointed rulers over his
people.
14 By the law of the Lord he judged
the congregation,
and the Lord watched over
Jacob.
15 By his faithfulness he was
proved to be a prophet,

*w*Heb: Gk lacks *who ... glory*   *x*Gk *he*
*y*Gk *his*   *z*Other ancient authorities
read *the enemy*   *a*Gk *them*

and by his words he became
known as a trustworthy
seer.

16 He called upon the Lord, the
Mighty One,
when his enemies pressed him
on every side,
and he offered in sacrifice a
suckling lamb.

17 Then the Lord thundered from
heaven,
and made his voice heard with
a mighty sound;

18 he subdued the leaders of the
enemy[b]
and all the rulers of the
Phi·lis′tines.

19 Before the time of his eternal
sleep,
Samuel[c] bore witness before
the Lord and his anointed:
"No property, not so much as a
pair of shoes,
have I taken from anyone!"
And no one accused him.

20 Even after he had fallen asleep,
he prophesied
and made known to the king
his death,
and lifted up his voice from the
ground
in prophecy, to blot out the
wickedness of the people.

Nathan
(2 Sam 7.1–3; 12.1–14)

47 After him Nathan rose up
to prophesy in the days of
David.

David
(1 Sam 17.12 – 18.7)

2 As the fat is set apart from the
offering of well-being,
so David was set apart from
the Israelites.

3 He played with lions as though
they were young goats,
and with bears as though they
were lambs of the flock.

4 In his youth did he not kill a
giant,
and take away the people's
disgrace,
when he whirled the stone in the
sling
and struck down the boasting
Goliath?

5 For he called on the Lord, the
Most High,

and he gave strength to his
right arm
to strike down a mighty warrior,
and to exalt the power[d] of his
people.

6 So they glorified him for the
tens of thousands he
conquered,
and praised him for the
blessings bestowed by the
Lord,
when the glorious diadem was
given to him.

7 For he wiped out his enemies on
every side,
and annihilated his adversaries
the Phi·lis′tines;
he crushed their power[d] to
our own day.

8 In all that he did he gave thanks
to the Holy One, the Most
High, proclaiming his
glory;
he sang praise with all his heart,
and he loved his Maker.

9 He placed singers before the
altar,
to make sweet melody with
their voices.[e]

10 He gave beauty to the festivals,
and arranged their times
throughout the year,[f]
while they praised God's[g] holy
name,
and the sanctuary resounded
from early morning.

11 The Lord took away his sins,
and exalted his power[d]
forever;
he gave him a covenant of
kingship
and a glorious throne in Israel.

Solomon
(1 Kings 4.20–34)

12 After him a wise son rose up
who because of him lived in
security:[h]

13 Solomon reigned in an age of
peace,
because God made all his
borders tranquil,
so that he might build a house in
his name
and provide a sanctuary to
stand forever.

[b]Heb: Gk *leaders of the people of Tyre*
[c]Gk *he*   [d]Gk *horn*   [e]Other ancient
authorities add *and daily they sing his
praises*   [f]Gk *to completion*   [g]Gk *his*
[h]Heb: Gk *in a broad place*

14 How wise you were when you
    were young!
    You overflowed like the Nile[i]
      with understanding.
15 Your influence spread
    throughout the earth,
  and you filled it with proverbs
    having deep meaning.
16 Your fame reached to far-off
    islands,
  and you were loved for your
    peaceful reign.
17 Your songs, proverbs, and
    parables,
  and the answers you gave
    astounded the nations.
18 In the name of the Lord God,
  who is called the God of Israel,
  you gathered gold like tin
  and amassed silver like lead.
19 But you brought in women to lie
    at your side,
  and through your body you
    were brought into
    subjection.
20 You stained your honor,
  and defiled your family line,
  so that you brought wrath upon
    your children,
  and they were grieved[j] at
    your folly.
21 because the sovereignty was
    divided
  and a rebel kingdom arose out
    of E'phra·im.
22 But the Lord will never give up
    his mercy,
  or cause any of his works to
    perish;
  he will never blot out the
    descendants of his chosen
    one,
  or destroy the family line of
    him who loved him.
  So he gave a remnant to Jacob,
  and to David a root from his
    own family.

Rehoboam and Jeroboam
(1 Kings 12.6–33)

23 Solomon rested with his
    ancestors,
  and left behind him one of his
    sons,
  broad in[k] folly and lacking in
    sense,
  Rē·ho·bō'am, whose policy
    drove the people to revolt.
  Then Jer·o·bō'am son of Nē'bat
    led Israel into sin

and started E'phra·im on its
    sinful ways.
24 Their sins increased more and
    more,
  until they were exiled from
    their land.
25 For they sought out every kind
    of wickedness,
  until vengeance came upon
    them.

Elijah
(1 Kings 17.1 – 19.18)

48 Then E·lī'jah arose, a prophet
    like fire,
  and his word burned like a
    torch.
2 He brought a famine upon them,
  and by his zeal he made them
    few in number.
3 By the word of the Lord he shut
    up the heavens,
  and also three times brought
    down fire.
4 How glorious you were, E·lī'jah,
    in your wondrous deeds!
  Whose glory is equal to yours?
5 You raised a corpse from death
  and from Hades, by the word
    of the Most High.
6 You sent kings down to
    destruction,
  and famous men, from their
    sickbeds.
7 You heard rebuke at Sinai
  and judgments of vengeance at
    Hō'reb.
8 You anointed kings to inflict
    retribution,
  and prophets to succeed you.[l]
9 You were taken up by a
    whirlwind of fire,
  in a chariot with horses of fire.
10 At the appointed time, it is
    written, you are destined[m]
  to calm the wrath of God
    before it breaks out in fury,
  to turn the hearts of parents to
    their children,
  and to restore the tribes of
    Jacob.
11 Happy are those who saw you
  and were adorned[n] with your
    love!

[i]Heb: Gk *a river* [j]Other ancient
authorities read *I was grieved*
[k]Heb (with a play on the name
Rehoboam) Syr: Gk *the people's*
[l]Heb: Gk *him* [m]Heb: Gk *are for
reproofs* [n]Other ancient authorities
read *and have died*

For we also shall surely live.[o]

Elisha
(2 Kings 2.9–13)

12 When E·lī′jah was enveloped in
   the whirlwind,
   E·lī′sha was filled with his
   spirit.
He performed twice as many
   signs,
   and marvels with every
   utterance of his mouth.[p]
Never in his lifetime did he
   tremble before any ruler,
   nor could anyone intimidate
   him at all.
13 Nothing was too hard for him,
   and when he was dead, his
   body prophesied.
14 In his life he did wonders,
   and in death his deeds were
   marvelous.

15 Despite all this the people did
   not repent,
   nor did they forsake their sins,
until they were carried off as
   plunder from their land,
   and were scattered over all the
   earth.
The people were left very few in
   number,
   but with a ruler from the
   house of David.
16 Some of them did what was
   right,
   but others sinned more and
   more.

Hezekiah
(2 Kings 18.1 – 20.21)

17 Hez·e·kī′ah fortified his city,
   and brought water into its
   midst;
he tunneled the rock with iron
   tools,
   and built cisterns for the
   water.
18 In his days Sen·nach′e·rib
   invaded the country;
he sent his commander[q] and
   departed;
he shook his fist against Zion,
   and made great boasts in his
   arrogance.
19 Then their hearts were shaken
   and their hands trembled,
   and they were in anguish, like
   women in labor.
20 But they called upon the Lord
   who is merciful,

spreading out their hands
   toward him.
The Holy One quickly heard
   them from heaven,
   and delivered them through
   Ī·sāi′ah.
21 The Lord[r] struck down the
   camp of the Assyrians,
   and his angel wiped them out.
22 For Hez·e·kī′ah did what was
   pleasing to the Lord,
   and he kept firmly to the ways
   of his ancestor David,
as he was commanded by the
   prophet Ī·sāi′ah,
   who was great and
   trustworthy in his visions.

Isaiah
(2 Kings 20.10–11)

23 In Isaiah's[s] days the sun went
   backward,
   and he prolonged the life of
   the king.
24 By his dauntless spirit he saw
   the future,
   and comforted the mourners in
   Zion.
25 He revealed what was to occur
   to the end of time,
   and the hidden things before
   they happened.

Josiah and Other Worthies

49 The name[t] of Jō·sī′ah is like
   blended incense
prepared by the skill of the
   perfumer;
his memory[u] is as sweet as
   honey to every mouth,
   and like music at a banquet of
   wine.
2 He did what was right by
   reforming the people,
   and removing the wicked
   abominations.
3 He kept his heart fixed on the
   Lord;
   in lawless times he made
   godliness prevail.

4 Except for David and
   Hez·e·kī′ah and Jō·sī′ah,
all of them were great sinners,
   for they abandoned the law of
   the Most High;

o Text and meaning of Gk uncertain
p Heb: Gk lacks *He performed . . . mouth*
q Other ancient authorities add *from
Lachish*   r Gk *He*   s Gk *his*   t Heb:
Gk *memory*   u Heb: Gk *it*

the kings of Judah came to an
end.

5 They[v] gave their power to
others,
and their glory to a foreign
nation,

6 who set fire to the chosen city of
the sanctuary,
and made its streets desolate,
as Jer·e·mī'ah had foretold.[w]

7 For they had mistreated him,
who even in the womb had
been consecrated a
prophet,
to pluck up and ruin and
destroy,
and likewise to build and to
plant.

8 It was E·zēk'i·el who saw the
vision of glory,
which God[x] showed him
above the chariot of the
cherubim.

9 For God[y] also mentioned Job
who held fast to all the ways
of justice.[z]

10 May the bones of the Twelve
Prophets
send forth new life from where
they lie,
for they comforted the people of
Jacob
and delivered them with
confident hope.

11 How shall we magnify
Ze·rub'ba·bel?
He was like a signet ring on
the right hand,

12 and so was Jesh'ū·a son of
Jō'za·dak;
in their days they built the house
and raised a temple[a] holy to
the Lord,
destined for everlasting glory.

13 The memory of Nē·he·mī'ah also
is lasting;
he raised our fallen walls,
and set up gates and bars,
and rebuilt our ruined houses.

Retrospect

14 Few have[b] ever been created on
earth like E'noch,
for he was taken up from the
earth.

15 Nor was anyone ever born like
Joseph;[c]
even his bones were cared for.

16 Shem and Seth and E'nosh were
honored,[d]
but above every other created
living being was Adam.

Simon Son of Onias

50 The leader of his brothers and
the pride of his people[e]
was the high priest, Simon son
of Ō·nī'as,
who in his life repaired the
house,
and in his time fortified the
temple.

2 He laid the foundations for the
high double walls,
the high retaining walls for the
temple enclosure.

3 In his days a water cistern was
dug,[f]
a reservoir like the sea in
circumference.

4 He considered how to save his
people from ruin,
and fortified the city against
siege.

5 How glorious he was,
surrounded by the people,
as he came out of the house of
the curtain.

6 Like the morning star among the
clouds,
like the full moon at the festal
season;[f]

7 like the sun shining on the
temple of the Most High,
like the rainbow gleaming in
splendid clouds;

8 like roses in the days of first
fruits,
like lilies by a spring of water,
like a green shoot on Lebanon
on a summer day;

9 like fire and incense in the
censer,
like a vessel of hammered gold
studded with all kinds of
precious stones;

10 like an olive tree laden with
fruit,

v Heb He   w Gk by the hand of Jeremiah
x Gk He   y Gk he   z Heb Compare Syr:
Meaning of Gk uncertain   a Other
ancient authorities read people
b Heb Syr: Gk No one has   c Heb Syr:
Gk adds the leader of his brothers, the
support of the people   d Heb: Gk Shem
and Seth were honored by people
e Heb Syr: Gk lacks this line. Compare
49.15   f Heb: Meaning of Gk uncertain

and like a cypress towering in
the clouds.
11 When he put on his glorious
robe
and clothed himself in perfect
splendor,
when he went up to the holy
altar,
he made the court of the
sanctuary glorious.

12 When he received the portions
from the hands of the
priests,
as he stood by the hearth of
the altar
with a garland of brothers
around him,
he was like a young cedar on
Lebanon
surrounded by the trunks of
palm trees.
13 All the sons of Aaron in their
splendor
held the Lord's offering in
their hands
before the whole congregation
of Israel.
14 Finishing the service at the
altars,g
and arranging the offering to
the Most High, the
Almighty,
15 he held out his hand for the cup
and poured a drink offering of
the blood of the grape;
he poured it out at the foot of
the altar,
a pleasing odor to the Most
High, the king of all.
16 Then the sons of Aaron shouted;
they blew their trumpets of
hammered metal;
they sounded a mighty fanfare
as a reminder before the Most
High.
17 Then all the people together
quickly
fell to the ground on their
faces
to worship their Lord,
the Almighty, God Most High.

18 Then the singers praised him
with their voices
in sweet and full-toned
melody.h
19 And the people of the Lord Most
High offered
their prayers before the
Merciful One,

until the order of worship of the
Lord was ended,
and they completed his ritual.
20 Then Simon$i$ came down and
raised his hands
over the whole congregation of
Israelites,
to pronounce the blessing of the
Lord with his lips,
and to glory in his name;
21 and they bowed down in
worship a second time,
to receive the blessing from
the Most High.

A Benediction

22 And now bless the God of all,
who everywhere works great
wonders,
who fosters our growth from
birth,
and deals with us according to
his mercy.
23 May he give us$j$ gladness of
heart,
and may there be peace in
our$k$ days
in Israel, as in the days of old.
24 May he entrust to us his mercy,
and may he deliver us in our$l$
days!

Epilogue

25 Two nations my soul detests,
and the third is not even a
people:
26 Those who live in Sē'ir,m and
the Phi·lis'tines,
and the foolish people that live
in Shē'chem.

27 Instruction in understanding and
knowledge
I have written in this book,
Jesus son of El·ē·ā'zar son of
Sī'rach$n$ of Jerusalem,
whose mind poured forth
wisdom.
28 Happy are those who concern
themselves with these
things,

g Other ancient authorities read *altar*
h Other ancient authorities read *in sweet
melody throughout the house* i Gk *he*
j Other ancient authorities read *you*
k Other ancient authorities read *your*
l Other ancient authorities read *his*
m Heb Compare Lat: Gk *on the mountain
of Samaria* n Heb: Meaning of Gk
uncertain

and those who lay them to
    heart will become wise.
29 For if they put them into
        practice, they will be equal
        to anything,
    for the fear⁰ of the Lord is
        their path.

PRAYER OF JESUS SON OF SIRACHᴾ

51 I give you thanks, O Lord and
            King,
    and praise you, O God my
        Savior.
    I give thanks to your name,
2   for you have been my
            protector and helper
    and have delivered me from
            destruction
        and from the trap laid by a
            slanderous tongue,
    from lips that fabricate lies.
    In the face of my adversaries
        you have been my helper ³and
            delivered me,
        in the greatness of your mercy
            and of your name,
    from grinding teeth about to
        devour me,
        from the hand of those seeking
            my life,
        from the many troubles I
            endured,
4   from choking fire on every side,
        and from the midst of fire that
            I had not kindled,
5   from the deep belly of Hades,
        from an unclean tongue and
            lying words —
6   the slander of an unrighteous
            tongue to the king.
    My soul drew near to death,
        and my life was on the brink
            of Hades below.
7   They surrounded me on every
            side,
        and there was no one to help
            me;
    I looked for human assistance,
        and there was none.
8   Then I remembered your mercy,
            O Lord,
        and your kindness�q from of
            old,
    for you rescue those who wait
        for you
    and save them from the hand
        of their enemies.
9   And I sent up my prayer from
            the earth,
        and begged for rescue from
            death.

10   I cried out, "Lord, you are my
            Father;ʳ
        do not forsake me in the days
            of trouble,
        when there is no help against
            the proud.
11   I will praise your name
            continually,
        and will sing hymns of
            thanksgiving."
    My prayer was heard,
12   for you saved me from
            destruction
        and rescued me in time of
            trouble.
    For this reason I thank you and
        praise you,
        and I bless the name of the
            Lord.

Heb adds:

*Give thanks to the LORD, for he
    is good,
    for his mercy endures forever;*

*Give thanks to the God of
        praises,
    for his mercy endures forever;*

*Give thanks to the guardian of
        Israel,
    for his mercy endures forever;*

*Give thanks to him who formed
        all things,
    for his mercy endures forever;*

*Give thanks to the redeemer of
        Israel,
    for his mercy endures forever;*

*Give thanks to him who gathers
        the dispersed of Israel,
    for his mercy endures forever;*

*Give thanks to him who rebuilt
        his city and his sanctuary,
    for his mercy endures forever;*

*Give thanks to him who makes a
        horn to sprout for the
        house of David,
    for his mercy endures forever;*

o Heb: Other ancient authorities read
light   p This title is included in the Gk
text.   q Other ancient authorities read
work   r Heb: Gk the Father of my lord

Give thanks to him who has
    chosen the sons of Zā'dok
    to be priests,
for his mercy endures forever;

Give thanks to the shield of
    Abraham,
for his mercy endures forever;

Give thanks to the rock of Isaac,
    for his mercy endures forever;

Give thanks to the mighty one
    of Jacob,
for his mercy endures forever;

Give thanks to him who has
    chosen Zion,
for his mercy endures forever;

Give thanks to the King of the
    kings of kings,
for his mercy endures forever;

He has raised up a horn for his
    people,
praise for all his loyal ones.

For the children of Israel, the
    people close to him.
Praise the LORD!

Autobiographical Poem on Wisdom

13 While I was still young, before I
    went on my travels,
    I sought wisdom openly in my
    prayer.
14 Before the temple I asked for
    her,
    and I will search for her until
    the end.

15 From the first blossom to the
    ripening grape
    my heart delighted in her;
my foot walked on the straight
    path;
    from my youth I followed her
    steps.

16 I inclined my ear a little and
    received her,
    and I found for myself much
    instruction.
17 I made progress in her;
    to him who gives wisdom I
    will give glory.

18 For I resolved to live according
    to wisdom,[s]

and I was zealous for the
    good,
and I shall never be
    disappointed.
19 My soul grappled with wisdom,[s]
    and in my conduct I was
    strict;[t]

I spread out my hands to the
    heavens,
    and lamented my ignorance of
    her.
20 I directed my soul to her,
    and in purity I found her.

With her I gained understanding
    from the first;
    therefore I will never be
    forsaken.
21 My heart was stirred to seek
    her;
    therefore I have gained a prize
    possession.
22 The Lord gave me my tongue as
    a reward,
    and I will praise him with it.

23 Draw near to me, you who are
    uneducated,
    and lodge in the house of
    instruction.
24 Why do you say you are lacking
    in these things,[u]
    and why do you endure such
    great thirst?
25 I opened my mouth and said,
    Acquire wisdom[v] for
    yourselves without money.

26 Put your neck under her[w] yoke,
    and let your souls receive
    instruction;
    it is to be found close by.

27 See with your own eyes that I
    have labored but little
    and found for myself much
    serenity.
28 Hear but a little of my
    instruction,
    and through me you will
    acquire silver and gold.[x]

---

[s] Gk *her*   [t] Meaning of Gk uncertain
[u] Cn Compare Heb Syr: Meaning of Gk
uncertain   [v] Heb: Gk lacks *wisdom*
[w] Heb: other ancient authorities read *the*
[x] Syr Compare Heb: Gk *Get instruction
with a large sum of silver, and you will
gain by it much gold.*

29 May your soul rejoice in God's[y]
   mercy,
   and may you never be
   ashamed to praise him.
30 Do your work in good time,

and in his own time God[z] will
give you your reward.

[y] Gk *his*   [z] Gk *he*

Prophecy

Prophets in Israel were persons who interpreted the actions of God in the events of history. They tried to keep alive the memory of the Exodus and re-interpret the meaning of the ancient faith for new times, to proclaim God's will (based on the Sinai covenant) in national crises. After the national disasters of the fall of Israel (722) and Judah (598–586) they began to speak words of hope and comfort.

The writings are called the major and minor prophets. The terms 'major' and 'minor' have to do with the size of the books, and not the importance of the message. In the Hebrew canon, the prophets are Isaiah, Jeremiah, Ezekiel, and the Book of the Twelve. Daniel is included among the writings in the Jewish Scripture, but we list that book with the prophets.

In roughly chronological order, the prophets are:

Amos preached in the northern kingdom of Israel around 750 B.C. His message included an emphasis on social justice as an expression of the covenant, the idea of the coming Day of the Lord, and the hope of a remnant. He emphasized that the covenant with God carried obligations as well as promises.

Hosea was active from about 745 to perhaps 722 B.C. He described the relationship between God and Israel as a marriage. His social themes were the danger of injustice at home and reliance on military alliances abroad. He talked about the compassion of God, and of God's tender longing for God's people.

Isaiah of Jerusalem was a counselor to kings from 740–701 B.C. During this time there were two major crises—the war with Syria in 734 and the Assyrian threats from 734–701. Isaiah saw those events as expressions of God's rule over the nations. The cause of the wars, he said, is social injustice. God is working out punishment for his people in the international arena. Some of the best-known passages in this book are those dealing with the longing for a Messiah and Isaiah's description of his own call.

The latter part of the book of Isaiah is a collection of great hymns and poems about the hope of restoration at the end of the Exile. Included in the hymns are four about the Servant of God, who suffers for the sake of Israel.

Micah preached in Jerusalem somewhere between 725–705 B.C. He cried out against the injustice practiced in both Samaria and Jerusalem but also lifted the vision of a great day of peace and salvation, with Jerusalem as the center of God's Kingdom. Micah 6.8 is a good summary of the teachings of the prophets of the eighth century.

Zephaniah For sixty years after Micah the kings of Judah practiced idolatry and oppression. Zephaniah's preaching began the great reform that culminated in the finding of Deuteronomy and national covenant-renewal. His message was one of condemnation of idolatry and injustice.

Jeremiah preached from 627–586, the longest career of any of the prophets. Over so long a career, his message changed as world events changed and called forth new understandings of the work of God. It was a time of trouble for Judah and Jerusalem, ending with the destruction of the city and the temple. Jeremiah continued the great themes of the earlier prophets, calling for true piety, social justice, and loyalty to God rather than military alliances. His teaching deepened the idea of repentance, and he introduced the vision of a new covenant written on the heart. After 598, he began to preach of hope and new beginnings following a time of punishment.

Lamentations is a collection of poems of deep bitterness and grief over the destruction of Jerusalem and the temple by the Babylonians in 586 B.C. It is traditionally attributed to Jeremiah and is printed immediately after his book in most Bibles.

Baruch contains four major sections. One has reflections on repentance after the fall of Jerusalem. Another is a poem on wisdom, and the third offers words of hope in a time of despair and persecution. The fourth is the Letter of Jeremiah, which was written in Jeremiah's name in the 4th century B.C. The theme is that idols are not real.

Joel lived in a time of a great locust plague, which he saw as the beginning of the judgment of God. His message is primarily a call to national repentance.

Habakkuk preached between 625–600, a time when the Babylonians were on the march and overrunning all the little kingdoms of the Middle East. He questioned the justice of God in allowing the Babylonians to triumph, and finally received the answer that "the righteous live by their faith."

Nahum was written at the time of the fall of Nineveh in 612. His work includes a hymn about a God who is slow to anger but who will punish those who defy him.

Ezekiel was a priest taken to Babylon in 598. Before 586, he preached a message of judgment and doom. After 586 he focused on hope and salvation. The source of his hope is not in any of the political powers of his day, but in God's own nature and purpose. The temple is destroyed, but God is not bound by a temple and has moved into exile with his people. The sins of the past will not keep the present generation from choosing life and salvation. The book ends with a great vision of the future restoration of the people and the temple.

Haggai and **Zechariah** preached in Jerusalem around 520 B.C., in the reign of Darius of Persia. Their message was that the temple was to be rebuilt and the people were to come together into a purified and faithful community. The source of hope was that God does keep his promises. When work on the temple is begun, then God will raise up the glory of the house of David in Zerubbabel, the last known prince of David's line.

Malachi told of the coming day of the Lord, and accused the people and priests of indifference, doubt, and immorality.

Opinion is divided as to the chronological places of the following prophets:

Obadiah is the shortest book in the Old Testament. It is a song of anger toward the Edomites for their part in the destruction of Jerusalem.

Jonah is the story of a prophet driven by God to proclaim salvation and mercy even to Israel's enemies.

Daniel was written to offer hope and consolation to Jews who were suffering persecution. The accounts of Daniel and his friends in the first half of the book show how loyalty to God brings victory over one's persecutors. The second part of the book (chs. 7–12) says, in a series of visions, that the fate of the righteous is in the hands of God and that God can be trusted to keep the future safe for his people. Susanna is an addition to Daniel. It tells of Daniel's rescue of Susanna, a beautiful young woman who has been falsely accused of adultery, and is a victim of blackmail. The message is how God defends the righteous who call on him. Bel and the Dragon is the last of the additions to Daniel. It is a series of satires and humorous stories directed against idolatry. The point is that only God is God.

ISAIAH

1 The vision of Ī·sāi′ah son of
Ā′moz, which he saw concerning
Judah and Jerusalem in the days of
Uz·zi′ah, Jō′tham, Ā′haz, and
Hez·e·kī′ah, kings of Judah.

The Wickedness of Judah

2 Hear, O heavens, and listen,
  O earth;
  for the LORD has spoken:
I reared children and brought
    them up,
  but they have rebelled against
    me.
3 The ox knows its owner,
  and the donkey its master's
    crib;
but Israel does not know,
  my people do not understand.

4 Ah, sinful nation,
  people laden with iniquity,
offspring who do evil,
  children who deal corruptly,
who have forsaken the LORD,
  who have despised the Holy
    One of Israel,
who are utterly estranged!

5 Why do you seek further
    beatings?
  Why do you continue to rebel?
The whole head is sick,
  and the whole heart faint.
6 From the sole of the foot even to
    the head,
  there is no soundness in it,
but bruises and sores
  and bleeding wounds;
they have not been drained, or
    bound up,
  or softened with oil.

7 Your country lies desolate,
  your cities are burned with
    fire;
in your very presence
  aliens devour your land;
  it is desolate, as overthrown
    by foreigners.

8 And daughter Zion is left
  like a booth in a vineyard,
like a shelter in a cucumber
    field,
  like a besieged city.
9 If the LORD of hosts
  had not left us a few survivors,
we would have been like
    Sod′om,
  and become like Go·mor′rah.

10 Hear the word of the LORD,
  you rulers of Sod′om!
Listen to the teaching of our
    God,
  you people of Go·mor′rah!
11 What to me is the multitude of
    your sacrifices?
  says the LORD;
I have had enough of burnt
    offerings of rams
  and the fat of fed beasts;
I do not delight in the blood of
    bulls,
  or of lambs, or of goats.

12 When you come to appear
    before me,*a*
  who asked this from your
    hand?
  Trample my courts no more;
13 bringing offerings is futile;
  incense is an abomination to
    me.
New moon and sabbath and
    calling of convocation —
  I cannot endure solemn
    assemblies with iniquity.
14 Your new moons and your
    appointed festivals
  my soul hates;
they have become a burden to
    me,
  I am weary of bearing them.
15 When you stretch out your
    hands,
  I will hide my eyes from you;

a Or see my face

even though you make many
  prayers,
    I will not listen;
  your hands are full of blood.
16 Wash yourselves; make
    yourselves clean;
  remove the evil of your doings
    from before my eyes;
cease to do evil,
17   learn to do good;
seek justice,
  rescue the oppressed,
defend the orphan,
  plead for the widow.

18 Come now, let us argue it out,
    says the LORD:
  though your sins are like scarlet,
    they shall be like snow;
  though they are red like
    crimson,
    they shall become like wool.
19 If you are willing and obedient,
    you shall eat the good of the
      land;
20 but if you refuse and rebel,
    you shall be devoured by the
      sword;
  for the mouth of the LORD has
    spoken.

The Degenerate City

21 How the faithful city
    has become a whore!
  She that was full of justice,
righteousness lodged in her—
  but now murderers!
22 Your silver has become dross,
    your wine is mixed with water.
23 Your princes are rebels
    and companions of thieves.
  Everyone loves a bribe
    and runs after gifts.
  They do not defend the orphan,
    and the widow's cause does
      not come before them.

24 Therefore says the Sovereign,
    the LORD of hosts, the
    Mighty One of Israel:
  Ah, I will pour out my wrath on
    my enemies,
    and avenge myself on my foes!
25 I will turn my hand against you;
  I will smelt away your dross
    as with lye
  and remove all your alloy.
26 And I will restore your judges as
    at the first,
    and your counselors as at the
      beginning.

Afterward you shall be called
    the city of righteousness,
    the faithful city.

27 Zion shall be redeemed by
    justice,
  and those in her who repent,
    by righteousness.
28 But rebels and sinners shall be
    destroyed together,
  and those who forsake the
    LORD shall be consumed.
29 For you shall be ashamed of the
    oaks
    in which you delighted;
  and you shall blush for the
    gardens
    that you have chosen.
30 For you shall be like an oak
    whose leaf withers,
  and like a garden without
    water.
31 The strong shall become like
    tinder,
  and their work[b] like a spark;
  they and their work shall burn
    together,
  with no one to quench them.

The Future House of God
(Mic 4.1–5)

2 The word that Ī·sāi′ah son of
  Ā′moz saw concerning Judah and
Jerusalem.

2 In days to come
    the mountain of the LORD's
      house
  shall be established as the
    highest of the mountains,
    and shall be raised above the
      hills;
  all the nations shall stream to it.
3   Many peoples shall come and
      say,
  "Come, let us go up to the
    mountain of the LORD,
    to the house of the God of
      Jacob;
  that he may teach us his ways
    and that we may walk in his
      paths."
  For out of Zion shall go forth
    instruction,
    and the word of the LORD
      from Jerusalem.
4 He shall judge between the
    nations,

b Or its makers

and shall arbitrate for many
  peoples;
they shall beat their swords into
  plowshares,
and their spears into pruning
  hooks;
nation shall not lift up sword
  against nation,
neither shall they learn war
  any more.

Judgment Pronounced on Arrogance

5 O house of Jacob,
  come, let us walk
  in the light of the LORD!
6 For you have forsaken the ways
    ofc your people,
  O house of Jacob.
  Indeed they are full of divinersd
    from the east
  and of soothsayers like the
    Phi·lis'tines,
  and they clasp hands with
    foreigners.
7 Their land is filled with silver
    and gold,
  and there is no end to their
    treasures;
  their land is filled with horses,
  and there is no end to their
    chariots.
8 Their land is filled with idols;
    they bow down to the work of
    their hands,
  to what their own fingers have
    made.
9 And so people are humbled,
  and everyone is brought low—
  do not forgive them!
10 Enter into the rock,
  and hide in the dust
  from the terror of the LORD,
  and from the glory of his
    majesty.
11 The haughty eyes of people shall
    be brought low,
  and the pride of everyone shall
    be humbled;
  and the LORD alone will be
    exalted
  in that day.
12 For the LORD of hosts has a day
  against all that is proud and
    lofty,
  against all that is lifted up and
    high;e
13 against all the cedars of
    Lebanon,
  lofty and lifted up;
  and against all the oaks of
    Bā'shan;

14 against all the high mountains,
  and against all the lofty hills;
15 against every high tower,
  and against every fortified
    wall;
16 against all the ships of Tar'shish,
  and against all the beautiful
    craft.f
17 The haughtiness of people shall
    be humbled,
  and the pride of everyone shall
    be brought low;
  and the LORD alone will be
    exalted on that day.
18 The idols shall utterly pass
    away.
19 Enter the caves of the rocks
  and the holes of the ground,
  from the terror of the LORD,
  and from the glory of his
    majesty,
  when he rises to terrify the
    earth.
20 On that day people will throw
    away
  to the moles and to the bats
  their idols of silver and their
    idols of gold,
  which they made for
    themselves to worship,
21 to enter the caverns of the rocks
  and the clefts in the crags,
  from the terror of the LORD,
  and from the glory of his
    majesty,
  when he rises to terrify the
    earth.
22 Turn away from mortals,
  who have only breath in their
    nostrils,
  for of what account are they?

3 For now the Sovereign, the
    LORD of hosts,
  is taking away from Jerusalem
    and from Judah
  support and staff—
    all support of bread,
    and all support of water—
2 warrior and soldier,
    judge and prophet,
    diviner and elder,
3 captain of fifty
    and dignitary,
  counselor and skillful magician
    and expert enchanter.
4 And I will make boys their
    princes,

cHeb lacks the ways of   dCn: Heb
lacks of diviners   eCn Compare Gk:
Heb low   fCompare Gk: Meaning of
Heb uncertain

and babes shall rule over
them.

5 The people will be oppressed,
everyone by another
and everyone by a neighbor;
the youth will be insolent to the
elder,
and the base to the honorable.

6 Someone will even seize a
relative,
a member of the clan, saying,
"You have a cloak;
you shall be our leader,
and this heap of ruins
shall be under your rule."
7 But the other will cry out on that
day, saying,
"I will not be a healer;
in my house there is neither
bread nor cloak;
you shall not make me
leader of the people."
8 For Jerusalem has stumbled
and Judah has fallen,
because their speech and their
deeds are against the
LORD,
defying his glorious presence.

9 The look on their faces bears
witness against them;
they proclaim their sin like
Sod'om,
they do not hide it.
Woe to them!
For they have brought evil on
themselves.
10 Tell the innocent how fortunate
they are,
for they shall eat the fruit of
their labors.
11 Woe to the guilty! How
unfortunate they are,
for what their hands have
done shall be done to them.
12 My people—children are their
oppressors,
and women rule over them.
O my people, your leaders
mislead you,
and confuse the course of your
paths.

13 The LORD rises to argue his
case;
he stands to judge the peoples.
14 The LORD enters into judgment
with the elders and princes of
his people:
It is you who have devoured the
vineyard;
the spoil of the poor is in your
houses.
15 What do you mean by crushing
my people,
by grinding the face of the
poor? says the Lord GOD of
hosts.

16 The LORD said:
Because the daughters of Zion
are haughty
and walk with outstretched
necks,
glancing wantonly with their
eyes,
mincing along as they go,
tinkling with their feet;
17 the Lord will afflict with scabs
the heads of the daughters of
Zion,
and the LORD will lay bare
their secret parts.

18 In that day the Lord will take
away the finery of the anklets, the
headbands, and the crescents; 19 the
pendants, the bracelets, and the scarfs;
20 the headdresses, the armlets, the
sashes, the perfume boxes, and the
amulets; 21 the signet rings and nose
rings; 22 the festal robes, the mantles,
the cloaks, and the handbags; 23 the
garments of gauze, the linen garments,
the turbans, and the veils.
24 Instead of perfume there will be
a stench;
and instead of a sash, a rope;
and instead of well-set hair,
baldness;
and instead of a rich robe, a
binding of sackcloth;
instead of beauty, shame.^{g}
25 Your men shall fall by the sword
and your warriors in battle.
26 And her gates shall lament and
mourn;
ravaged, she shall sit upon the
ground.

4 Seven women shall take hold of
one man in that day, saying,
"We will eat our own bread and
wear our own clothes;
just let us be called by your
name;
take away our disgrace."

^{g}Q Ms: MT lacks *shame*

The Future Glory of the Survivors in Zion

2 On that day the branch of the LORD shall be beautiful and glorious, and the fruit of the land shall be the pride and glory of the survivors of Israel. ³Whoever is left in Zion and remains in Jerusalem will be called holy, everyone who has been recorded for life in Jerusalem, ⁴once the Lord has washed away the filth of the daughters of Zion and cleansed the bloodstains of Jerusalem from its midst by a spirit of judgment and by a spirit of burning. ⁵Then the LORD will create over the whole site of Mount Zion and over its places of assembly a cloud by day and smoke and the shining of a flaming fire by night. Indeed over all the glory there will be a canopy. ⁶It will serve as a pavilion, a shade by day from the heat, and a refuge and a shelter from the storm and rain.

The Song of the Unfruitful Vineyard

5 Let me sing for my beloved
   my love-song concerning his
      vineyard:
   My beloved had a vineyard
      on a very fertile hill.
2 He dug it and cleared it of
      stones,
   and planted it with choice
      vines;
   he built a watchtower in the
      midst of it,
   and hewed out a wine vat in it;
   he expected it to yield grapes,
      but it yielded wild grapes.

3 And now, inhabitants of
      Jerusalem
   and people of Judah,
   judge between me
      and my vineyard.
4 What more was there to do for
      my vineyard
   that I have not done in it?
   When I expected it to yield
      grapes,
   why did it yield wild grapes?

5 And now I will tell you
   what I will do to my vineyard.
   I will remove its hedge,
      and it shall be devoured;
   I will break down its wall,
      and it shall be trampled down.
6 I will make it a waste;
   it shall not be pruned or hoed,

and it shall be overgrown with
      briers and thorns;
   I will also command the clouds
      that they rain no rain upon it.

7 For the vineyard of the LORD of
      hosts
   is the house of Israel,
   and the people of Judah
      are his pleasant planting;
   he expected justice,
      but saw bloodshed;
   righteousness,
      but heard a cry!

Social Injustice Denounced

8 Ah, you who join house to
      house,
   who add field to field,
   until there is room for no one
      but you,
   and you are left to live alone
      in the midst of the land!
9 The LORD of hosts has sworn in
      my hearing:
   Surely many houses shall be
      desolate,
   large and beautiful houses,
      without inhabitant.
10 For ten acres of vineyard shall
      yield but one bath,
   and a homer of seed shall
      yield a mere ephah.ʰ

11 Ah, you who rise early in the
      morning
   in pursuit of strong drink,
   who linger in the evening
      to be inflamed by wine,
12 whose feasts consist of lyre and
      harp,
   tambourine and flute and
      wine,
   but who do not regard the deeds
      of the LORD,
   or see the work of his hands!
13 Therefore my people go into
      exile without knowledge;
   their nobles are dying of hunger,
   and their multitude is parched
      with thirst.

14 Therefore She'ōl has enlarged its
      appetite
   and opened its mouth beyond
      measure;
   the nobility of Jerusalemⁱ and
      her multitude go down,

ʰThe Heb *bath, homer,* and *ephah* are measures of quantity   ⁱHeb *her nobility*

her throng and all who exult
in her.

15 People are bowed down,
everyone is brought low,
and the eyes of the haughty
are humbled.

16 But the LORD of hosts is exalted
by justice,
and the Holy God shows
himself holy by
righteousness.

17 Then the lambs shall graze as in
their pasture,
fatlings and kids*j* shall feed
among the ruins.

18 Ah, you who drag iniquity along
with cords of falsehood,
who drag sin along as with
cart ropes,

19 who say, "Let him make haste,
let him speed his work
that we may see it;
let the plan of the Holy One of
Israel hasten to fulfillment,
that we may know it!"

20 Ah, you who call evil good
and good evil,
who put darkness for light
and light for darkness,
who put bitter for sweet
and sweet for bitter!

21 Ah, you who are wise in your
own eyes,
and shrewd in your own sight!

22 Ah, you who are heroes in
drinking wine
and valiant at mixing drink,

23 who acquit the guilty for a bribe,
and deprive the innocent of
their rights!

Foreign Invasion Predicted

24 Therefore, as the tongue of fire
devours the stubble,
and as dry grass sinks down
in the flame,
so their root will become rotten,
and their blossom go up like
dust;
for they have rejected the
instruction of the LORD of
hosts,
and have despised the word of
the Holy One of Israel.

25 Therefore the anger of the LORD
was kindled against his
people,
and he stretched out his hand
against them and struck
them;

the mountains quaked,
and their corpses were like
refuse
in the streets.
For all this his anger has not
turned away,
and his hand is stretched out
still.

26 He will raise a signal for a
nation far away,
and whistle for a people at the
ends of the earth;
Here they come, swiftly,
speedily!

27 None of them is weary, none
stumbles,
none slumbers or sleeps,
not a loincloth is loose,
not a sandal-thong broken;

28 their arrows are sharp,
all their bows bent,
their horses' hoofs seem like
flint,
and their wheels like the
whirlwind.

29 Their roaring is like a lion,
like young lions they roar;
they growl and seize their prey,
they carry it off, and no one
can rescue.

30 They will roar over it on that
day,
like the roaring of the sea.
And if one look to the land —
only darkness and distress;
and the light grows dark with
clouds.

A Vision of God in the Temple
(Cp Ezek 1.4–28)

6 In the year that King Uz·zi′ah
died, I saw the Lord sitting on a
throne, high and lofty; and the hem of
his robe filled the temple. 2 Seraphs
were in attendance above him; each
had six wings: with two they covered
their faces, and with two they covered
their feet, and with two they flew.
3 And one called to another and said:

"Holy, holy, holy is the LORD of
hosts;
the whole earth is full of his
glory."

4 The pivots*k* on the thresholds shook
at the voices of those who called, and
the house filled with smoke. 5 And I
said: "Woe is me! I am lost, for I am a

j Cn Compare Gk: Heb *aliens*
k Meaning of Heb uncertain

man of unclean lips, and I live among a people of unclean lips; yet my eyes have seen the King, the LORD of hosts!"

6 Then one of the seraphs flew to me, holding a live coal that had been taken from the altar with a pair of tongs. 7 The seraph[l] touched my mouth with it and said: "Now that this has touched your lips, your guilt has departed and your sin is blotted out." 8 Then I heard the voice of the Lord saying, "Whom shall I send, and who will go for us?" And I said, "Here am I; send me!" 9 And he said, "Go and say to this people:

'Keep listening, but do not
        comprehend;
keep looking, but do not
        understand.'
10 Make the mind of this people
        dull,
    and stop their ears,
    and shut their eyes,
so that they may not look with
        their eyes,
    and listen with their ears,
and comprehend with their
        minds,
    and turn and be healed."
11 Then I said, "How long,
        O Lord?" And he said:
"Until cities lie waste
    without inhabitant,
and houses without people,
    and the land is utterly
        desolate;
12 until the LORD sends everyone
        far away,
    and vast is the emptiness in
        the midst of the land.
13 Even if a tenth part remain in it,
    it will be burned again,
like a terebinth or an oak
    whose stump remains standing
        when it is felled."[m]
The holy seed is its stump.

Isaiah Reassures King Ahaz
(2 Kings 16.5; 2 Chr 28.5–15)

7 In the days of Ā′haz son of Jō′-tham son of Uz·zī′ah, king of Judah, King Rē′zin of Ar′am and King Pē′kah son of Rem·a·lī′ah of Israel went up to attack Jerusalem, but could not mount an attack against it. 2 When the house of David heard that Ar′am had allied itself with Ē′phra·im, the heart of Ā′haz[n] and the heart of his people shook as the trees of the forest shake before the wind.

3 Then the LORD said to Ī·sāi′ah, Go out to meet Ā′haz, you and your son Shē′ar-jash′ub,[o] at the end of the conduit of the upper pool on the highway to the Fuller's Field, 4 and say to him, Take heed, be quiet, do not fear, and do not let your heart be faint because of these two smoldering stumps of firebrands, because of the fierce anger of Rē′zin and Ar′am and the son of Rem·a·lī′ah. 5 Because Ar′am—with Ē′phra·im and the son of Rem·a·lī′ah—has plotted evil against you, saying, 6 Let us go up against Judah and cut off Jerusalem[p] and conquer it for ourselves and make the son of Tā′-bē·el king in it; 7 therefore thus says the Lord GOD:

It shall not stand,
    and it shall not come to pass.
8   For the head of Ar′am is
        Damascus,
    and the head of Damascus is
        Rē′zin.
(Within sixty-five years Ē′phra·im will be shattered, no longer a people.)
9   The head of Ē′phra·im is
        Samaria,
    and the head of Samaria is the
        son of Rem·a·lī′ah.
If you do not stand firm in faith,
    you shall not stand at all.

Isaiah Gives Ahaz the Sign
of Immanuel

10 Again the LORD spoke to Ā′haz, saying, 11 Ask a sign of the LORD your God; let it be deep as Shē′ōl or high as heaven. 12 But Ā′haz said, I will not ask, and I will not put the LORD to the test. 13 Then Ī·sāi′ah[q] said: "Hear then, O house of David! Is it too little for you to weary mortals, that you weary my God also? 14 Therefore the Lord himself will give you a sign. Look, the young woman[r] is with child and shall bear a son, and shall name him Im·man′ū·el.[s] 15 He shall eat curds and honey by the time he knows how to refuse the evil and choose the good. 16 For before the child knows how to refuse the evil and choose the good, the land before whose two kings you are in dread will be deserted. 17 The LORD will bring on you and on your people and on your ancestral house such days as have not come since the

[l] Heb He   [m] Meaning of Heb uncertain
[n] Heb his heart   [o] That is A remnant
shall return   [p] Heb cut it off   [q] Heb he
[r] Gk the virgin   [s] That is God is with us

I
S
A
I
A
H

day that Ē′phra·im departed from Judah — the king of Assyria."

18 On that day the LORD will whistle for the fly that is at the sources of the streams of Egypt, and for the bee that is in the land of Assyria. 19 And they will all come and settle in the steep ravines, and in the clefts of the rocks, and on all the thornbushes, and on all the pastures.

20 On that day the Lord will shave with a razor hired beyond the River — with the king of Assyria — the head and the hair of the feet, and it will take off the beard as well.

21 On that day one will keep alive a young cow and two sheep, 22 and will eat curds because of the abundance of milk that they give; for everyone that is left in the land shall eat curds and honey.

23 On that day every place where there used to be a thousand vines, worth a thousand shekels of silver, will become briers and thorns. 24 With bow and arrows one will go there, for all the land will be briers and thorns; 25 and as for all the hills that used to be hoed with a hoe, you will not go there for fear of briers and thorns; but they will become a place where cattle are let loose and where sheep tread.

Isaiah's Son a Sign of the Assyrian Invasion

8 Then the LORD said to me, Take a large tablet and write on it in common characters, "Belonging to Mā′her-shal′al-hash-baz,"[t] 2 and have it attested[u] for me by reliable witnesses, the priest Ū·rī′ah and Zech·a·rī′ah son of Je·ber·e·chī′ah. 3 And I went to the prophetess, and she conceived and bore a son. Then the LORD said to me, Name him Mā′her-shal′al-hash-baz; 4 for before the child knows how to call "My father" or "My mother," the wealth of Damascus and the spoil of Samaria will be carried away by the king of Assyria.

5 The LORD spoke to me again: 6 Because this people has refused the waters of Shī·lō′ah that flow gently, and melt in fear before[v] Rē′zin and the son of Rem·a·lī′ah; 7 therefore, the Lord is bringing up against it the mighty flood waters of the River, the king of Assyria and all his glory; it will rise above all its channels and overflow all its banks; 8 it will sweep on into Judah as a flood, and, pouring over, it will reach up to

the neck; and its outspread wings will fill the breadth of your land, O Im·man′ū·el.

9 Band together, you peoples, and be dismayed;
  listen, all you far countries;
gird yourselves and be dismayed;
  gird yourselves and be dismayed!
10 Take counsel together, but it shall be brought to naught;
  speak a word, but it will not stand,
  for God is with us.[w]

11 For the LORD spoke thus to me while his hand was strong upon me, and warned me not to walk in the way of this people, saying: 12 Do not call conspiracy all that this people calls conspiracy, and do not fear what it fears, or be in dread. 13 But the LORD of hosts, him you shall regard as holy; let him be your fear, and let him be your dread. 14 He will become a sanctuary, a stone one strikes against; for both houses of Israel he will become a rock one stumbles over — a trap and a snare for the inhabitants of Jerusalem. 15 And many among them shall stumble; they shall fall and be broken; they shall be snared and taken.

Disciples of Isaiah

16 Bind up the testimony, seal the teaching among my disciples. 17 I will wait for the LORD, who is hiding his face from the house of Jacob, and I will hope in him. 18 See, I and the children whom the LORD has given me are signs and portents in Israel from the LORD of hosts, who dwells on Mount Zion. 19 Now if people say to you, "Consult the ghosts and the familiar spirits that chirp and mutter; should not a people consult their gods, the dead on behalf of the living, 20 for teaching and for instruction?" Surely, those who speak like this will have no dawn! 21 They will pass through the land,[x] greatly distressed and hungry; when they are hungry, they will be enraged and will curse[y] their king and their gods. They will turn their faces upward, 22 or they will look to the earth, but will see only

t That is *The spoil speeds, the prey hastens*   u Q Ms Gk Syr: MT *and I caused to be attested*   v Cn: Meaning of Heb uncertain   w Heb *immanu el*   x Heb *it*   y Or *curse by* distress and darkness, the gloom of anguish; and they will be thrust into thick darkness.[z]

The Righteous Reign
of the Coming King
(Isa 11.1–9)

9 [a] But there will be no gloom for those who were in anguish. In the former time he brought into contempt the land of Zeb′u·lun and the land of Naph′ta·li, but in the latter time he will make glorious the way of the sea, the land beyond the Jordan, Galilee of the nations.

2 [b] The people who walked in darkness
      have seen a great light;
those who lived in a land of
      deep darkness—
on them light has shined.
3 You have multiplied the nation,
      you have increased its joy;
they rejoice before you
      as with joy at the harvest,
      as people exult when dividing
      plunder.
4 For the yoke of their burden,
      and the bar across their
      shoulders,
      the rod of their oppressor,
      you have broken as on the day
      of Mid′i·an.
5 For all the boots of the tramping
      warriors
      and all the garments rolled in
      blood
shall be burned as fuel for the
      fire.
6 For a child has been born for us,
      a son given to us;
authority rests upon his
      shoulders;
and he is named
Wonderful Counselor, Mighty
      God,
      Everlasting Father, Prince of
      Peace.
7 His authority shall grow
      continually,
      and there shall be endless
      peace
for the throne of David and his
      kingdom.
He will establish and uphold it
with justice and with
      righteousness
from this time onward and
      forevermore.
The zeal of the LORD of hosts
      will do this.

Judgment on Arrogance
and Oppression

8 The Lord sent a word against
      Jacob,
      and it fell on Israel;
9 and all the people knew it—
      E′phra·im and the inhabitants
      of Samaria—
but in pride and arrogance of
      heart they said:
10 "The bricks have fallen,
      but we will build with dressed
      stones;
the sycamores have been cut
      down,
      but we will put cedars in their
      place."
11 So the LORD raised adversaries[c]
      against them,
      and stirred up their enemies,
12 the Ar·a·me′ans on the east and
      the Phi·lis′tines on the
      west,
      and they devoured Israel with
      open mouth.
For all this his anger has not
      turned away;
      his hand is stretched out still.

13 The people did not turn to him
      who struck them,
      or seek the LORD of hosts.
14 So the LORD cut off from Israel
      head and tail,
      palm branch and reed in one
      day—
15 elders and dignitaries are the
      head,
      and prophets who teach lies
      are the tail;
16 for those who led this people led
      them astray,
      and those who were led by
      them were left in
      confusion.
17 That is why the Lord did not
      have pity on[d] their young
      people,
      or compassion on their
      orphans and widows;
for everyone was godless and an
      evildoer,
      and every mouth spoke folly.
For all this his anger has not
      turned away,
      his hand is stretched out still.

I
S
A
I
A
H

---

[z] Meaning of Heb uncertain   [a] Ch 8.23 in Heb   [b] Ch 9.1 in Heb   [c] Cn: Heb *the adversaries of Rezin*   [d] Q Ms: MT *rejoice over*

18 For wickedness burned like a
    fire,
      consuming briers and thorns;
  it kindled the thickets of the
    forest,
  and they swirled upward in a
    column of smoke.
19 Through the wrath of the LORD
    of hosts
  the land was burned,
  and the people became like fuel
    for the fire;
  no one spared another.
20 They gorged on the right, but
    still were hungry,
  and they devoured on the left,
    but were not satisfied;
  they devoured the flesh of their
    own kindred;*e*
21 Ma·nas′seh devoured E′phra·im,
    and E′phra·im Ma·nas′seh,
  and together they were against
    Judah.
For all this his anger has not
    turned away;
  his hand is stretched out still.

10   Ah, you who make iniquitous
    decrees,
  who write oppressive statutes,
2 to turn aside the needy from
    justice
  and to rob the poor of my
    people of their right,
  that widows may be your spoil,
  and that you may make the
    orphans your prey!
3 What will you do on the day of
    punishment,
  in the calamity that will come
    from far away?
To whom will you flee for help,
  and where will you leave your
    wealth,
4 so as not to crouch among the
    prisoners
  or fall among the slain?
For all this his anger has not
    turned away;
  his hand is stretched out still.

Arrogant Assyria Also Judged

5 Ah, Assyria, the rod of my
    anger—
  the club in their hands is my
    fury!
6 Against a godless nation I send
    him,
  and against the people of my
    wrath I command him,
to take spoil and seize plunder,

  and to tread them down like
    the mire of the streets.
7 But this is not what he intends,
  nor does he have this in mind;
but it is in his heart to destroy,
  and to cut off nations not a
    few.
8 For he says:
"Are not my commanders all
    kings?
9 Is not Cal′nō like Car′chem·ish?
  Is not Hā′math like Ar′pad?
  Is not Samaria like Damascus?
10 As my hand has reached to the
    kingdoms of the idols
  whose images were greater
    than those of Jerusalem
    and Samaria,
11 shall I not do to Jerusalem and
    her idols
  what I have done to Sa·mār′i·a
    and her images?"

12 When the Lord has finished all
his work on Mount Zion and on Jerusalem, he*f* will punish the arrogant
boasting of the king of Assyria and his
haughty pride. 13 For he says:
"By the strength of my hand I
    have done it,
  and by my wisdom, for I have
    understanding;
I have removed the boundaries
    of peoples,
  and have plundered their
    treasures;
  like a bull I have brought
    down those who sat on
    thrones.
14 My hand has found, like a nest,
  the wealth of the peoples;
and as one gathers eggs that
    have been forsaken,
  so I have gathered all the
    earth;
and there was none that moved
    a wing,
  or opened its mouth, or
    chirped."

15 Shall the ax vaunt itself over the
    one who wields it,
  or the saw magnify itself
    against the one who
    handles it?
As if a rod should raise the one
    who lifts it up,
  or as if a staff should lift the
    one who is not wood!

e Or *arm*   *f* Heb *I*

¹⁶ Therefore the Sovereign, the
   LORD of hosts,
   will send wasting sickness
      among his stout warriors,
   and under his glory a burning
      will be kindled,
      like the burning of fire.
¹⁷ The light of Israel will become a
      fire,
   and his Holy One a flame;
   and it will burn and devour
      his thorns and briers in one
      day.
¹⁸ The glory of his forest and his
      fruitful land
   the LORD will destroy, both
      soul and body,
   and it will be as when an
      invalid wastes away.
¹⁹ The remnant of the trees of his
      forest will be so few
   that a child can write them
      down.

The Repentant Remnant of Israel

²⁰ On that day the remnant of Israel
and the survivors of the house of Jacob
will no more lean on the one who
struck them, but will lean on the LORD,
the Holy One of Israel, in truth. ²¹ A
remnant will return, the remnant of Jacob, to the mighty God. ²² For though
your people Israel were like the sand
of the sea, only a remnant of them will
return. Destruction is decreed, overflowing with righteousness. ²³ For the
Lord GOD of hosts will make a full end,
as decreed, in all the earth.^g

²⁴ Therefore thus says the Lord
GOD of hosts: O my people, who live in
Zion, do not be afraid of the Assyrians
when they beat you with a rod and lift
up their staff against you as the Egyp-
tians did. ²⁵ For in a very little while my
indignation will come to an end, and
my anger will be directed to their destruction. ²⁶ The LORD of hosts will
wield a whip against them, as when he
struck Mid'i·an at the rock of Or'eb;
his staff will be over the sea, and he
will lift it as he did in Egypt. ²⁷ On that
day his burden will be removed from
your shoulder, and his yoke will be destroyed from your neck.

   He has gone up from Rim'mon,^h
²⁸   he has come to Ai'ath;
   he has passed through Mig'ron,
      at Mich'mash he stores his
      baggage;
²⁹ they have crossed over the pass,

   at Ge'ba they lodge for the
      night;
   Ra'mah trembles,
   Gib'e·ah of Saul has fled.
³⁰ Cry aloud, O daughter Gal'lim!
   Listen, O La'i·shah!
   Answer her, O An'a·thoth!
³¹ Mad·me'nah is in flight,
   the inhabitants of Ge'bim flee
      for safety.
³² This very day he will halt at
      Nob,
   he will shake his fist
   at the mount of daughter Zion,
   the hill of Jerusalem.

³³ Look, the Sovereign, the LORD
      of hosts,
   will lop the boughs with
      terrifying power;
   the tallest trees will be cut down,
   and the lofty will be brought
      low.
³⁴ He will hack down the thickets
      of the forest with an ax,
   and Lebanon with its majestic
      treesⁱ will fall.

The Peaceful Kingdom
(Isa 9.1–7)

11 A shoot shall come out from
      the stump of Jesse,
   and a branch shall grow out of
      his roots.
² The spirit of the LORD shall rest
      on him,
   the spirit of wisdom and
      understanding,
   the spirit of counsel and might,
   the spirit of knowledge and
      the fear of the LORD.
³ His delight shall be in the fear of
      the LORD.

   He shall not judge by what his
      eyes see,
   or decide by what his ears
      hear;
⁴ but with righteousness he shall
      judge the poor,
   and decide with equity for the
      meek of the earth;
   he shall strike the earth with the
      rod of his mouth,
   and with the breath of his lips
      he shall kill the wicked.

^gOr land ^hCn: Heb and his yoke from
your neck, and a yoke will be destroyed
because of fatness ⁱCn Compare Gk
Vg: Heb with a majestic one

5 Righteousness shall be the belt
       around his waist,
   and faithfulness the belt
       around his loins.

6 The wolf shall live with the
       lamb,
   the leopard shall lie down with
       the kid,
   the calf and the lion and the
       fatling together,
   and a little child shall lead
       them.
7 The cow and the bear shall
       graze,
   their young shall lie down
       together;
   and the lion shall eat straw
       like the ox.
8 The nursing child shall play over
       the hole of the asp,
   and the weaned child shall put
       its hand on the adder's
       den.
9 They will not hurt or destroy
   on all my holy mountain;
   for the earth will be full of the
       knowledge of the LORD
   as the waters cover the sea.

Return of the Remnant of
Israel and Judah

10 On that day the root of Jesse
shall stand as a signal to the peoples;
the nations shall inquire of him, and
his dwelling shall be glorious.
11 On that day the Lord will extend
his hand yet a second time to recover
the remnant that is left of his people,
from Assyria, from Egypt, from Path'-
ros, from Ethiopia,ⁱ from Ē'lam, from
Shī'nar, from Hā'math, and from the
coastlands of the sea.
12 He will raise a signal for the
       nations,
   and will assemble the outcasts
       of Israel,
   and gather the dispersed of
       Judah
   from the four corners of the
       earth.
13 The jealousy of Ē'phra·im shall
       depart,
   the hostility of Judah shall be
       cut off;
   Ē'phra·im shall not be jealous of
       Judah,
   and Judah shall not be hostile
       towards Ē'phra·im.

14 But they shall swoop down on
       the backs of the
       Phi·lis'tines in the west,
   together they shall plunder the
       people of the east.
   They shall put forth their hand
       against Ē'dom and Mō'ab,
   and the Am'mon·ites shall
       obey them.
15 And the LORD will utterly
       destroy
   the tongue of the sea of Egypt;
   and will wave his hand over the
       River
   with his scorching wind;
   and will split it into seven
       channels,
   and make a way to cross on
       foot;
16 so there shall be a highway from
       Assyria
   for the remnant that is left of
       his people,
   as there was for Israel
   when they came up from the
       land of Egypt.

Thanksgiving and Praise

12 You will say in that day:
   I will give thanks to you,
       O LORD,
   for though you were angry
       with me,
   your anger turned away,
   and you comforted me.

2 Surely God is my salvation;
   I will trust, and will not be
       afraid,
   for the LORD GODᵏ is my
       strength and my might;
   he has become my salvation.

3 With joy you will draw water
from the wells of salvation. 4 And you
will say in that day:
   Give thanks to the LORD,
       call on his name;
   make known his deeds among
       the nations;
   proclaim that his name is
       exalted.

5 Sing praises to the LORD, for he
       has done gloriously;
   let this be knownⁱ in all the
       earth.

ⁱOr Nubia; Heb Cush   ᵏHeb for Yah,
the LORD   ⁱOr this is made known

6 Shout aloud and sing for joy,
    O royal[m] Zion,
  for great in your midst is the
    Holy One of Israel.

Proclamation against Babylon

13 The oracle concerning Babylon
    that Ī·sāi′ah son of Ā′moz saw.

2 On a bare hill raise a signal,
    cry aloud to them;
  wave the hand for them to enter
    the gates of the nobles.
3 I myself have commanded my
    consecrated ones,
  have summoned my warriors,
    my proudly exulting ones,
    to execute my anger.

4 Listen, a tumult on the
    mountains
    as of a great multitude!
  Listen, an uproar of kingdoms,
    of nations gathering together!
  The LORD of hosts is mustering
    an army for battle.
5 They come from a distant land,
    from the end of the heavens,
  the LORD and the weapons of his
    indignation,
    to destroy the whole earth.

6 Wail, for the day of the LORD is
    near;
    it will come like destruction
    from the Almighty![n]
7 Therefore all hands will be
    feeble,
    and every human heart will
    melt,
8   and they will be dismayed.
  Pangs and agony will seize
    them;
    they will be in anguish like a
    woman in labor.
  They will look aghast at one
    another;
    their faces will be aflame.
9 See, the day of the LORD comes,
    cruel, with wrath and fierce
    anger,
  to make the earth a desolation,
    and to destroy its sinners from
    it.
10 For the stars of the heavens and
    their constellations
    will not give their light;
  the sun will be dark at its rising,
    and the moon will not shed its
    light.

11 I will punish the world for its
    evil,
    and the wicked for their
    iniquity;
  I will put an end to the pride of
    the arrogant,
    and lay low the insolence of
    tyrants.
12 I will make mortals more rare
    than fine gold,
    and humans than the gold of
    Ō′phir.
13 Therefore I will make the
    heavens tremble,
    and the earth will be shaken
    out of its place,
  at the wrath of the LORD of
    hosts
    in the day of his fierce anger.
14 Like a hunted gazelle,
    or like sheep with no one to
    gather them,
  all will turn to their own people,
    and all will flee to their own
    lands.
15 Whoever is found will be thrust
    through,
    and whoever is caught will fall
    by the sword.
16 Their infants will be dashed to
    pieces
    before their eyes;
  their houses will be plundered,
    and their wives ravished.
17 See, I am stirring up the Mēdes
    against them,
    who have no regard for silver
    and do not delight in gold.
18 Their bows will slaughter the
    young men;
    they will have no mercy on the
    fruit of the womb;
    their eyes will not pity
    children.
19 And Babylon, the glory of
    kingdoms,
    the splendor and pride of the
    Chal·dē′ans,
  will be like Sod′om and
    Go·mor′rah
    when God overthrew them.
20 It will never be inhabited
    or lived in for all generations;
  Arabs will not pitch their tents
    there,
    shepherds will not make their
    flocks lie down there.
21 But wild animals will lie down
    there,

m Or O inhabitant of   *n Traditional
rendering of Heb Shaddai*

and its houses will be full of
   howling creatures;
there ostriches will live,
   and there goat-demons will
      dance.
22 Hyenas will cry in its towers,
   and jackals in the pleasant
      palaces;
its time is close at hand,
   and its days will not be
      prolonged.

Restoration of Judah

14 But the LORD will have compassion on Jacob and will again
choose Israel, and will set them in their
own land; and aliens will join them
and attach themselves to the house of
Jacob. 2 And the nations will take them
and bring them to their place, and the
house of Israel will possess the nations*o* as male and female slaves in the
LORD's land; they will take captive
those who were their captors, and rule
over those who oppressed them.

Downfall of the King of Babylon

3 When the LORD has given you rest
from your pain and turmoil and the
hard service with which you were
made to serve, 4 you will take up this
taunt against the king of Babylon:
How the oppressor has ceased!
   How his insolence*p* has
      ceased!
5 The LORD has broken the staff
      of the wicked,
   the scepter of rulers,
6 that struck down the peoples in
      wrath
   with unceasing blows,
that ruled the nations in anger
   with unrelenting persecution.
7 The whole earth is at rest and
      quiet;
   they break forth into singing.
8 The cypresses exult over you,
   the cedars of Lebanon, saying,
"Since you were laid low,
   no one comes to cut us down."
9 Shē'ōl beneath is stirred up
   to meet you when you come;
it rouses the shades to greet you,
   all who were leaders of the
      earth;
it raises from their thrones
   all who were kings of the
      nations.
10 All of them will speak
   and say to you:
"You too have become as weak
   as we!

You have become like us!"
11 Your pomp is brought down to
      Shē'ōl,
   and the sound of your harps;
maggots are the bed beneath
      you,
   and worms are your covering.
12 How you are fallen from heaven,
   O Day Star, son of Dawn!
How you are cut down to the
      ground,
   you who laid the nations low!
13 You said in your heart,
   "I will ascend to heaven;
I will raise my throne
   above the stars of God;
I will sit on the mount of
      assembly
   on the heights of Zā'phon;*q*
14 I will ascend to the tops of the
      clouds,
   I will make myself like the
      Most High."
15 But you are brought down to
      Shē'ōl,
   to the depths of the Pit.
16 Those who see you will stare at
      you,
   and ponder over you:
"Is this the man who made the
      earth tremble,
   who shook kingdoms,
17 who made the world like a
      desert
   and overthrew its cities,
   who would not let his
      prisoners go home?"
18 All the kings of the nations lie in
      glory,
   each in his own tomb;
19 but you are cast out, away from
      your grave,
   like loathsome carrion,*r*
clothed with the dead, those
      pierced by the sword,
   who go down to the stones of
      the Pit,
   like a corpse trampled
      underfoot.
20 You will not be joined with them
      in burial,
   because you have destroyed
      your land,
   you have killed your people.

o Heb *them*   *p* Q Ms Compare Gk Syr
Vg: Meaning of MT uncertain
q Or *assembly in the far north*
r Cn Compare Gk: Heb *like a loathed
branch*

May the descendants of
    evildoers
    nevermore be named!
21 Prepare slaughter for his sons
    because of the guilt of their
        father.*s*
Let them never rise to possess
    the earth
    or cover the face of the world
        with cities.

22 I will rise up against them, says
the LORD of hosts, and will cut off from
Babylon name and remnant, offspring
and posterity, says the LORD. 23 And I
will make it a possession of the hedge-
hog, and pools of water, and I will
sweep it with the broom of destruction,
says the LORD of hosts.

An Oracle concerning Assyria

24 The LORD of hosts has sworn:
As I have designed,
    so shall it be;
and as I have planned,
    so shall it come to pass:
25 I will break the Assyrian in my
    land,
and on my mountains trample
    him under foot;
his yoke shall be removed from
    them,
and his burden from their
        shoulders.
26 This is the plan that is planned
    concerning the whole earth;
and this is the hand that is
        stretched out
    over all the nations.
27 For the LORD of hosts has
        planned,
and who will annul it?
His hand is stretched out,
    and who will turn it back?

An Oracle concerning Philistia

28 In the year that King Ā'haz died this
oracle came:

29 Do not rejoice, all you
        Phi·lis'tines,
that the rod that struck you is
        broken,
for from the root of the snake
        will come forth an adder,
and its fruit will be a flying
        fiery serpent.
30 The firstborn of the poor will
        graze,
and the needy lie down in
        safety;

but I will make your root die of
        famine,
and your remnant I*t* will kill.
31 Wail, O gate; cry, O city;
    melt in fear, O Phi·lis'ti·a, all
        of you!
For smoke comes out of the
        north,
and there is no straggler in its
        ranks.

32 What will one answer the
        messengers of the nation?
"The LORD has founded Zion,
    and the needy among his
        people
will find refuge in her."

An Oracle concerning Moab

15 An oracle concerning Mō'ab.

Because Ar is laid waste in a
        night,
    Mō'ab is undone;
because Kir is laid waste in a
        night,
    Mō'ab is undone.
2 Dī'bon*u* has gone up to the
        temple,
    to the high places to weep;
over Nē'bō and over Med'e·ba
    Mō'ab wails.
On every head is baldness,
    every beard is shorn;
3 in the streets they bind on
        sackcloth;
on the housetops and in the
        squares
everyone wails and melts in
        tears.
4 Hesh'bon and Ē·le·ā'leh cry out,
    their voices are heard as far as
        Jā'haz;
therefore the loins of Mō'ab
        quiver;*v*
his soul trembles.
5 My heart cries out for Mō'ab;
    his fugitives flee to Zō'ar,
    to Eg'lath-she·lish'i·yah.
For at the ascent of Lū'hith
    they go up weeping;
on the road to Hor·ō·nā'im
    they raise a cry of destruction;
6 the waters of Nim'rim
    are a desolation;
the grass is withered, the new
        growth fails,

s Syr Compare Gk: Heb *fathers*   *t* Q Ms
Vg: MT *he*   *u* Cn: Heb *the house and
Dibon*   *v* Cn Compare Gk Syr: Heb *the
armed men of Moab cry aloud*

the verdure is no more.

7 Therefore the abundance they
        have gained
    and what they have laid up
they carry away
    over the Wadi of the Willows.

8 For a cry has gone
        around the land of Mō'ab;
the wailing reaches to Eg·lā'im,
    the wailing reaches to
        Bē'er-ē'lim.

9 For the waters of Dī'bon[w] are
        full of blood;
    yet I will bring upon Dī'bon[w]
        even more—
a lion for those of Mō'ab who
        escape,
    for the remnant of the land.

16 Send lambs
        to the ruler of the land,
from Sē'la, by way of the desert,
    to the mount of daughter Zion.

2 Like fluttering birds,
    like scattered nestlings,
so are the daughters of Mō'ab
    at the fords of the Ar'non.

3 "Give counsel,
        grant justice;
make your shade like night
    at the height of noon;
hide the outcasts,
    do not betray the fugitive;

4 let the outcasts of Mō'ab
        settle among you;
be a refuge to them
    from the destroyer."

When the oppressor is no more,
    and destruction has ceased,
and marauders have vanished
        from the land,

5 then a throne shall be
        established in steadfast
        love
    in the tent of David,
    and on it shall sit in
        faithfulness
a ruler who seeks justice
    and is swift to do what is
        right.

6 We have heard of the pride of
        Mō'ab
    —how proud he is!—
of his arrogance, his pride, and
        his insolence;
    his boasts are false.

7 Therefore let Mō'ab wail,
    let everyone wail for Mō'ab.
Mourn, utterly stricken,
    for the raisin cakes of
        Kir-har'e·seth.

8 For the fields of Hesh'bon
        languish,
    and the vines of Sib'mah,
whose clusters once made drunk
    the lords of the nations,
reached to Jā'zer
    and strayed to the desert;
their shoots once spread abroad
    and crossed over the sea.

9 Therefore I weep with the
        weeping of Jā'zer
    for the vines of Sib'mah;
I drench you with my tears,
    O Hesh'bon and Ē·le·ā'leh;
for the shout over your fruit
        harvest
    and your grain harvest has
        ceased.

10 Joy and gladness are taken
        away
    from the fruitful field;
and in the vineyards no songs
        are sung,
    no shouts are raised;
no treader treads out wine in the
        presses;
    the vintage-shout is hushed.[x]

11 Therefore my heart throbs like a
        harp for Mō'ab,
    and my very soul for
        Kir-hē'res.

12 When Mō'ab presents himself,
when he wearies himself upon the
high place, when he comes to his sanctuary to pray, he will not prevail.

13 This was the word that the LORD
spoke concerning Mō'ab in the past.
14 But now the LORD says, In three
years, like the years of a hired worker,
the glory of Mō'ab will be brought into
contempt, in spite of all its great multitude; and those who survive will be
very few and feeble.

An Oracle concerning Damascus

17 An oracle concerning Damascus.

See, Damascus will cease to be a
        city,
    and will become a heap of
        ruins.

2 Her towns will be deserted
        forever;[y]
    they will be places for flocks,
    which will lie down, and no
        one will make them afraid.

[w] Q Ms Vg Compare Syr: MT *Dimon*
[x] Gk: Heb *I have hushed*   [y] Cn Compare
Gk: Heb *the cities of Aroer are deserted*

3 The fortress will disappear from
        Ē'phra·im,
    and the kingdom from
        Damascus;
    and the remnant of Ar'am will
        be
    like the glory of the children
        of Israel,
            says the LORD of hosts.

4 On that day
        the glory of Jacob will be
            brought low,
        and the fat of his flesh will
            grow lean.
5 And it shall be as when reapers
            gather standing grain
        and their arms harvest the
            ears,
    and as when one gleans the ears
        of grain
    in the Valley of Reph'a·im.
6 Gleanings will be left in it,
        as when an olive tree is
            beaten—
    two or three berries
        in the top of the highest
            bough,
    four or five
        on the branches of a fruit tree,
            says the LORD God of Israel.

7 On that day people will regard
their Maker, and their eyes will look to
the Holy One of Israel; 8 they will not
have regard for the altars, the work of
their hands, and they will not look to
what their own fingers have made, either the sacred poles[z] or the altars of
incense.
9 On that day their strong cities will
be like the deserted places of the
Hi'vites and the Am'o·rites,[a] which
they deserted because of the children
of Israel, and there will be desolation.

10 For you have forgotten the God
        of your salvation,
    and have not remembered the
        Rock of your refuge;
    therefore, though you plant
        pleasant plants
    and set out slips of an alien
        god,
11 though you make them grow on
        the day that you plant
        them,
    and make them blossom in the
        morning that you sow;
    yet the harvest will flee away
        in a day of grief and incurable
            pain.

12 Ah, the thunder of many
        peoples,
    they thunder like the
        thundering of the sea!
    Ah, the roar of nations,
        they roar like the roaring of
            mighty waters!
13 The nations roar like the roaring
        of many waters,
    but he will rebuke them, and
        they will flee far away,
    chased like chaff on the
        mountains before the wind
    and whirling dust before the
        storm.
14 At evening time, lo, terror!
    Before morning, they are no
        more.
    This is the fate of those who
        despoil us,
    and the lot of those who
        plunder us.

An Oracle concerning Ethiopia

18 Ah, land of whirring wings
        beyond the rivers of
            Ethiopia,[b]
2 sending ambassadors by the Nile
        in vessels of papyrus on the
            waters!
    Go, you swift messengers,
        to a nation tall and smooth,
    to a people feared near and far,
    a nation mighty and
        conquering,
    whose land the rivers divide.

3 All you inhabitants of the world,
        you who live on the earth,
    when a signal is raised on the
        mountains, look!
    When a trumpet is blown,
        listen!
4 For thus the LORD said to me:
    I will quietly look from my
        dwelling
        like clear heat in sunshine,
        like a cloud of dew in the heat
            of harvest.
5 For before the harvest, when the
        blossom is over
    and the flower becomes a
        ripening grape,
    he will cut off the shoots with
        pruning hooks,
    and the spreading branches he
        will hew away.

z Heb *Asherim*   a Cn Compare Gk: Heb
*places of the wood and the highest
bough*   b Or *Nubia*; Heb *Cush*

6 They shall all be left
   to the birds of prey of the
      mountains
   and to the animals of the
      earth.
And the birds of prey will
      summer on them,
   and all the animals of the
      earth will winter on them.

7 At that time gifts will be brought to the LORD of hosts from[c] a people tall and smooth, from a people feared near and far, a nation mighty and conquering, whose land the rivers divide, to Mount Zion, the place of the name of the LORD of hosts.

An Oracle concerning Egypt

19 An oracle concerning Egypt.

See, the LORD is riding on a
      swift cloud
   and comes to Egypt;
the idols of Egypt will tremble at
      his presence,
   and the heart of the Egyptians
      will melt within them.
2 I will stir up Egyptians against
      Egyptians,
   and they will fight, one against
      the other,
   neighbor against neighbor,
   city against city, kingdom
      against kingdom;
3 the spirit of the Egyptians within
      them will be emptied out,
   and I will confound their
      plans;
they will consult the idols and
      the spirits of the dead
   and the ghosts and the
      familiar spirits;
4 I will deliver the Egyptians
      into the hand of a hard
      master;
a fierce king will rule over them,
   says the Sovereign, the LORD
      of hosts.

5 The waters of the Nile will be
      dried up,
   and the river will be parched
      and dry;
6 its canals will become foul,
   and the branches of Egypt's
      Nile will diminish and dry
      up,
reeds and rushes will rot
      away.

7 There will be bare places by the
      Nile,
   on the brink of the Nile;
and all that is sown by the Nile
      will dry up,
   be driven away, and be no
      more.
8 Those who fish will mourn;
   all who cast hooks in the Nile
      will lament,
   and those who spread nets on
      the water will languish.
9 The workers in flax will be in
      despair,
   and the carders and those at
      the loom will grow pale.
10 Its weavers will be dismayed,
   and all who work for wages
      will be grieved.

11 The princes of Zō'an are utterly
      foolish;
   the wise counselors of
      Pharaoh give stupid
      counsel.
How can you say to Pharaoh,
   "I am one of the sages,
   a descendant of ancient
      kings"?
12 Where now are your sages?
   Let them tell you and make
      known
   what the LORD of hosts has
      planned against Egypt.
13 The princes of Zō'an have
      become fools,
   and the princes of Memphis
      are deluded;
those who are the cornerstones
      of its tribes
   have led Egypt astray.
14 The LORD has poured into
      them[d]
   a spirit of confusion;
and they have made Egypt
      stagger in all its doings
   as a drunkard staggers around
      in vomit.
15 Neither head nor tail, palm
      branch or reed,
   will be able to do anything for
      Egypt.

16 On that day the Egyptians will be like women, and tremble with fear before the hand that the LORD of hosts raises against them. 17And the land of Judah will become a terror to the Egyptians; everyone to whom it is

[c]Q Ms Gk Vg: MT *of*   [d]Gk Compare Tg: Heb *it*

mentioned will fear because of the plan that the LORD of hosts is planning against them.

Egypt, Assyria, and Israel Blessed

18 On that day there will be five cities in the land of Egypt that speak the language of Cā′naan and swear allegiance to the LORD of hosts. One of these will be called the City of the Sun.

19 On that day there will be an altar to the LORD in the center of the land of Egypt, and a pillar to the LORD at its border. 20 It will be a sign and a witness to the LORD of hosts in the land of Egypt; when they cry to the LORD because of oppressors, he will send them a savior, and will defend and deliver them. 21 The LORD will make himself known to the Egyptians; and the Egyptians will know the LORD on that day, and will worship with sacrifice and burnt offering, and they will make vows to the LORD and perform them. 22 The LORD will strike Egypt, striking and healing; they will return to the LORD, and he will listen to their supplications and heal them.

23 On that day there will be a highway from Egypt to Assyria, and the Assyrian will come into Egypt, and the Egyptian into Assyria, and the Egyptians will worship with the Assyrians.

24 On that day Israel will be the third with Egypt and Assyria, a blessing in the midst of the earth, 25 whom the LORD of hosts has blessed, saying, "Blessed be Egypt my people, and Assyria the work of my hands, and Israel my heritage."

Isaiah Dramatizes the Conquest of Egypt and Ethiopia

20 In the year that the commander-in-chief, who was sent by King Sar′gon of Assyria, came to Ash′dod and fought against it and took it — 2 at that time the LORD had spoken to Ī·sāi′ah son of Ā′moz, saying, "Go, and loose the sackcloth from your loins and take your sandals off your feet," and he had done so, walking naked and barefoot. 3 Then the LORD said, "Just as my servant Ī·sāi′ah has walked naked and barefoot for three years as a sign and a portent against Egypt and Ethiopia,e 4 so shall the king of Assyria lead away the Egyptians as captives and the Ethiopiansf as exiles, both the young and the old, naked and barefoot, with buttocks

uncovered, to the shame of Egypt. 5 And they shall be dismayed and confounded because of Ethiopiae their hope and of Egypt their boast. 6 In that day the inhabitants of this coastland will say, 'See, this is what has happened to those in whom we hoped and to whom we fled for help and deliverance from the king of Assyria! And we, how shall we escape?' "

Oracles concerning Babylon, Edom, and Arabia

21 The oracle concerning the wilderness of the sea.

As whirlwinds in the Neg′eb
　　sweep on,
　　it comes from the desert,
　　from a terrible land.
2 A stern vision is told to me;
　　the betrayer betrays,
　　and the destroyer destroys.
Go up, O Ē′lam,
　　lay siege, O Mēd′i·a;
all the sighing she has caused
　　I bring to an end.
3 Therefore my loins are filled
　　with anguish;
　　pangs have seized me,
　　like the pangs of a woman in
　　　labor;
I am bowed down so that I
　　cannot hear,
　　I am dismayed so that I cannot
　　see.
4 My mind reels, horror has
　　appalled me;
　　the twilight I longed for
　　has been turned for me into
　　　trembling.
5 They prepare the table,
　　they spread the rugs,
　　they eat, they drink.
Rise up, commanders,
　　oil the shield!
6 For thus the Lord said to me:
"Go, post a lookout,
　　let him announce what he
　　sees.
7 When he sees riders, horsemen
　　in pairs,
　　riders on donkeys, riders on
　　camels,
let him listen diligently,
　　very diligently."
8 Then the watcherg called out:

e Or Nubia; Heb Cush　f Or Nubians; Heb Cushites　g Q Ms: MT a lion

"Upon a watchtower I stand,
   O Lord,
   continually by day,
and at my post I am stationed
   throughout the night.
9 Look, there they come, riders,
   horsemen in pairs!"
Then he responded,
   "Fallen, fallen is Babylon;
and all the images of her gods
   lie shattered on the ground."
10 O my threshed and winnowed
   one,
   what I have heard from the
   LORD of hosts,
the God of Israel, I announce
   to you.

11 The oracle concerning Dū'mah.

One is calling to me from Se'ir,
   "Sentinel, what of the night?
Sentinel, what of the night?"
12 The sentinel says:
"Morning comes, and also the
   night.
If you will inquire, inquire;
   come back again."

13 The oracle concerning the desert
   plain.

In the scrub of the desert plain
   you will lodge,
   O caravans of Ded'an·ites.
14 Bring water to the thirsty,
   meet the fugitive with bread,
O inhabitants of the land of
   Te'ma.
15 For they have fled from the
   swords,
   from the drawn sword,
from the bent bow,
   and from the stress of battle.

16 For thus the Lord said to me:
Within a year, according to the years
of a hired worker, all the glory of Ke'-
dar will come to an end; 17 and the remaining bows of Ke'dar's warriors
will be few; for the LORD, the God of
Israel, has spoken.

A Warning of Destruction of Jerusalem

22 The oracle concerning the val-
      ley of vision.

What do you mean that you
   have gone up,
   all of you, to the housetops,
2 you that are full of shoutings,
tumultuous city, exultant
   town?
Your slain are not slain by the
   sword,
   nor are they dead in battle.
3 Your rulers have all fled
   together;
   they were captured without
   the use of a bow.ʰ
All of you who were found were
   captured,
   though they had fled far
   away.ⁱ
4 Therefore I said:
Look away from me,
   let me weep bitter tears;
do not try to comfort me
   for the destruction of my
   beloved people.

5 For the Lord GOD of hosts has a
   day
   of tumult and trampling and
   confusion
in the valley of vision,
   a battering down of walls
   and a cry for help to the
   mountains.
6 E'lam bore the quiver
   with chariots and cavalry,ʲ
   and Kir uncovered the shield.
7 Your choicest valleys were full
   of chariots,
   and the cavalry took their
   stand at the gates.
8 He has taken away the covering
   of Judah.

On that day you looked to the weapons of the House of the Forest, 9 and
you saw that there were many
breaches in the city of David, and you
collected the waters of the lower pool.
10 You counted the houses of Jerusalem, and you broke down the houses to
fortify the wall. 11 You made a reservoir between the two walls for the water of the old pool. But you did not look
to him who did it, or have regard for
him who planned it long ago.

12 In that day the Lord GOD of
   hosts
   called to weeping and
   mourning,
to baldness and putting on
   sackcloth;

ʰ Or *without their bows*   ⁱ Gk Syr Vg:
Heb *fled from far away*   ʲ Meaning of
Heb uncertain

◀13 but instead there was joy and
festivity,
 killing oxen and slaughtering
  sheep,
 eating meat and drinking
  wine.
"Let us eat and drink,
 for tomorrow we die."
14 The LORD of hosts has revealed
  himself in my ears:
Surely this iniquity will not be
  forgiven you until you die,
 says the Lord GOD of hosts.

Denunciation of Self-Seeking Officials

15 Thus says the Lord GOD of hosts:
Come, go to this steward, to Sheb'na,
who is master of the household, and
say to him: 16 What right do you have
here? Who are your relatives here, that
you have cut out a tomb here for yourself, cutting a tomb on the height, and
carving a habitation for yourself in the
rock? 17 The LORD is about to hurl you
away violently, my fellow. He will
seize firm hold on you, 18 whirl you
round and round, and throw you like a
ball into a wide land; there you shall
die, and there your splendid chariots
shall lie, O you disgrace to your master's house! 19 I will thrust you from
your office, and you will be pulled
down from your post.

20 On that day I will call my servant
E·li'a·kim son of Hil·ki'ah, 21 and will
clothe him with your robe and bind
your sash on him. I will commit your
authority to his hand, and he shall be
a father to the inhabitants of Jerusalem and to the house of Judah. 22 I will
place on his shoulder the key of the
house of David; he shall open, and no
one shall shut; he shall shut, and no
one shall open. 23 I will fasten him like
a peg in a secure place, and he will
become a throne of honor to his ancestral house. 24 And they will hang on
him the whole weight of his ancestral
house, the offspring and issue, every
small vessel, from the cups to all the
flagons. 25 On that day, says the LORD
of hosts, the peg that was fastened in a
secure place will give way; it will be
cut down and fall, and the load that
was on it will perish, for the LORD has
spoken.

An Oracle concerning Tyre

23 The oracle concerning Tyre.

Wail, O ships of Tar'shish,
 for your fortress is
  destroyed.[k]
When they came in from Cyprus
 they learned of it.
2 Be still, O inhabitants of the
  coast,
 O merchants of Si'don,
your messengers crossed over
 the sea[l]
3 and were on the mighty
  waters;
your revenue was the grain of
 Shi'hor,
 the harvest of the Nile;
 you were the merchant of the
  nations.
4 Be ashamed, O Si'don, for the
  sea has spoken,
 the fortress of the sea, saying:
"I have neither labored nor given
  birth,
 I have neither reared young
  men
 nor brought up young
  women."
5 When the report comes to Egypt,
 they will be in anguish over
  the report about Tyre.
6 Cross over to Tar'shish—
 wail, O inhabitants of the
  coast!
7 Is this your exultant city
 whose origin is from days of
  old,
whose feet carried her
 to settle far away?
8 Who has planned this
 against Tyre, the bestower of
  crowns,
whose merchants were princes,
 whose traders were the
  honored of the earth?
9 The LORD of hosts has planned
  it—
 to defile the pride of all glory,
 to shame all the honored of
  the earth.
10 Cross over to your own land,
 O ships of[m] Tar'shish;
 this is a harbor[n] no more.
11 He has stretched out his hand
  over the sea,

[k] Cn Compare verse 14: Heb *for it is
destroyed, without houses*   [l] Q Ms: MT
*crossing over the sea, they replenished
you*   [m] Cn Compare Gk: Heb *like the
Nile, daughter*   [n] Cn: Heb *restraint*

he has shaken the kingdoms;
the LORD has given command
    concerning Cā′naan
to destroy its fortresses.
12 He said:
You will exult no longer,
    O oppressed virgin daughter
        Si′don;
rise, cross over to Cyprus—
    even there you will have no
        rest.

13 Look at the land of the Chal·dē′-
ans! This is the people; it was not Assyria. They destined Tyre for wild animals. They erected their siege towers,
they tore down her palaces, they made
her a ruin.[o]
14 Wail, O ships of Tar′shish,
    for your fortress is destroyed.
15 From that day Tyre will be forgotten
for seventy years, the lifetime of one
king. At the end of seventy years, it
will happen to Tyre as in the song
about the prostitute:
16 Take a harp,
    go about the city,
    you forgotten prostitute!
Make sweet melody,
    sing many songs,
    that you may be remembered.
17 At the end of seventy years, the
LORD will visit Tyre, and she will return to her trade, and will prostitute
herself with all the kingdoms of the
world on the face of the earth. 18 Her
merchandise and her wages will be
dedicated to the LORD; her profits[p]
will not be stored or hoarded, but her
merchandise will supply abundant
food and fine clothing for those who
live in the presence of the LORD.

Impending Judgment on the Earth

24 Now the LORD is about to
    lay waste the earth and
    make it desolate,
and he will twist its surface
    and scatter its inhabitants.
2 And it shall be, as with the
        people, so with the priest;
    as with the slave, so with his
        master;
    as with the maid, so with her
        mistress;
    as with the buyer, so with the
        seller;
    as with the lender, so with the
        borrower;
    as with the creditor, so with
        the debtor.

3 The earth shall be utterly laid
        waste and utterly
        despoiled;
    for the LORD has spoken this
        word.

4 The earth dries up and withers,
    the world languishes and
        withers;
    the heavens languish together
        with the earth.
5 The earth lies polluted
    under its inhabitants;
    for they have transgressed laws,
        violated the statutes,
        broken the everlasting
            covenant.
6 Therefore a curse devours the
        earth,
    and its inhabitants suffer for
        their guilt;
    therefore the inhabitants of the
        earth dwindled,
    and few people are left.
7 The wine dries up,
    the vine languishes,
    all the merry-hearted sigh.
8 The mirth of the timbrels is
        stilled,
    the noise of the jubilant has
        ceased,
    the mirth of the lyre is stilled.
9 No longer do they drink wine
        with singing;
    strong drink is bitter to those
        who drink it.
10 The city of chaos is broken
        down,
    every house is shut up so that
        no one can enter.
11 There is an outcry in the streets
        for lack of wine;
    all joy has reached its
        eventide;
    the gladness of the earth is
        banished.
12 Desolation is left in the city,
    the gates are battered into
        ruins.
13 For thus it shall be on the earth
        and among the nations,
    as when an olive tree is beaten,
    as at the gleaning when the
        grape harvest is ended.

14 They lift up their voices, they
        sing for joy;
    they shout from the west over
        the majesty of the LORD.

[o] Meaning of Heb uncertain   [p] Heb it

and no one is born to inhabit
the world.
19 Your dead shall live, their
corpses[s] shall rise.
O dwellers in the dust, awake
and sing for joy!
For your dew is a radiant dew,
and the earth will give birth to
those long dead.[t]

20 Come, my people, enter your
chambers,
and shut your doors behind
you;
hide yourselves for a little while
until the wrath is past.
21 For the LORD comes out from his
place
to punish the inhabitants of
the earth for their iniquity;
the earth will disclose the blood
shed on it,
and will no longer cover its
slain.

Israel's Redemption

27 On that day the LORD with his
cruel and great and strong
sword will punish Le·vi′a·than the
fleeing serpent, Le·vi′a·than the twisting serpent, and he will kill the dragon
that is in the sea.

2 On that day:
A pleasant vineyard, sing about
it!
3 I, the LORD, am its keeper;
every moment I water it.
I guard it night and day
so that no one can harm it;
4 I have no wrath.
If it gives me thorns and briers,
I will march to battle against
it.
I will burn it up.
5 Or else let it cling to me for
protection,
let it make peace with me,
let it make peace with me.

6 In days to come[u] Jacob shall
take root,
Israel shall blossom and put
forth shoots,
and fill the whole world with
fruit.

7 Has he struck them down as he
struck down those who
struck them?

Or have they been killed as
their killers were killed?
8 By expulsion,[v] by exile you
struggled against them;
with his fierce blast he
removed them in the day of
the east wind.
9 Therefore by this the guilt of
Jacob will be expiated,
and this will be the full fruit of
the removal of his sin:
when he makes all the stones of
the altars
like chalkstones crushed to
pieces,
no sacred poles[w] or incense
altars will remain standing.
10 For the fortified city is solitary,
a habitation deserted and
forsaken, like the
wilderness;
the calves graze there,
there they lie down, and strip
its branches.
11 When its boughs are dry, they
are broken;
women come and make a fire
of them.
For this is a people without
understanding;
therefore he that made them
will not have compassion
on them,
he that formed them will show
them no favor.

12 On that day the LORD will thresh
from the channel of the Euphrates to
the Wadi of Egypt, and you will be
gathered one by one, O people of Israel. 13 And on that day a great trumpet
will be blown, and those who were lost
in the land of Assyria and those who
were driven out to the land of Egypt
will come and worship the LORD on the
holy mountain at Jerusalem.

Judgment on Corrupt Rulers, Priests, and Prophets

28 Ah, the proud garland of the
drunkards of E′phra·im,
and the fading flower of its
glorious beauty,
which is on the head of those
bloated with rich food, of
those overcome with wine!

s Cn Compare Syr Tg: Heb *my corpse*
t Heb *to the shades*   u Heb *Those to
come*   v Meaning of Heb uncertain
w Heb *Asherim*

2 See, the Lord has one who is
  mighty and strong;
  like a storm of hail, a
    destroying tempest,
  like a storm of mighty,
    overflowing waters;
  with his hand he will hurl
    them down to the earth.
3 Trampled under foot will be
    the proud garland of the
    drunkards of Ē'phra·im.
4 And the fading flower of its
    glorious beauty,
  which is on the head of those
    bloated with rich food,
  will be like a first-ripe fig before
    the summer;
  whoever sees it, eats it up
    as soon as it comes to hand.

5 In that day the LORD of hosts
    will be a garland of glory,
  and a diadem of beauty, to the
    remnant of his people;
6 and a spirit of justice to the one
    who sits in judgment,
  and strength to those who turn
    back the battle at the gate.

7 These also reel with wine
    and stagger with strong drink;
  the priest and the prophet reel
    with strong drink,
  they are confused with wine,
    they stagger with strong drink;
  they err in vision,
    they stumble in giving
    judgment.
8 All tables are covered with filthy
    vomit;
  no place is clean.

9 "Whom will he teach knowledge,
    and to whom will he explain
    the message?
  Those who are weaned from
    milk,
  those taken from the breast?
10 For it is precept upon precept,
    precept upon precept,
  line upon line, line upon line,
  here a little, there a little."ˣ

11 Truly, with stammering lip
    and with alien tongue
  he will speak to this people,
12   to whom he has said,
  "This is rest;
    give rest to the weary;
  and this is repose";
    yet they would not hear.

13 Therefore the word of the LORD
    will be to them,
  "Precept upon precept, precept
    upon precept,
  line upon line, line upon line,
  here a little, there a little;"ˣ
  in order that they may go, and
    fall backward,
  and be broken, and snared,
    and taken.

14 Therefore hear the word of the
    LORD, you scoffers
  who rule this people in
    Jerusalem.
15 Because you have said, "We
    have made a covenant with
    death,
  and with Shē'ōl we have an
    agreement;
  when the overwhelming scourge
    passes through
  it will not come to us;
  for we have made lies our
    refuge,
  and in falsehood we have
    taken shelter";
16 therefore thus says the Lord
    GOD,
  See, I am laying in Zion a
    foundation stone,
  a tested stone,
  a precious cornerstone, a sure
    foundation:
  "One who trusts will not
    panic."
17 And I will make justice the line,
    and righteousness the
    plummet;
  hail will sweep away the refuge
    of lies,
  and waters will overwhelm the
    shelter.
18 Then your covenant with death
    will be annulled,
  and your agreement with
    Shē'ōl will not stand;
  when the overwhelming scourge
    passes through
  you will be beaten down by it.
19 As often as it passes through, it
    will take you;
  for morning by morning it will
    pass through,
  by day and by night;
  and it will be sheer terror to
    understand the message.
20 For the bed is too short to
    stretch oneself on it,

ˣMeaning of Heb of this verse uncertain

and the covering too narrow to
wrap oneself in it.

21 For the LORD will rise up as on
Mount Pe·rā′zim,
he will rage as in the valley of
Gib′e·on;
to do his deed — strange is his
deed!
and to work his work — alien is
his work!

22 Now therefore do not scoff,
or your bonds will be made
stronger;
for I have heard a decree of
destruction
from the Lord GOD of hosts
upon the whole land.

23 Listen, and hear my voice;
Pay attention, and hear my
speech.

24 Do those who plow for sowing
plow continually?
Do they continually open and
harrow their ground?

25 When they have leveled its
surface,
do they not scatter dill, sow
cummin,
and plant wheat in rows
and barley in its proper place,
and spelt as the border?

26 For they are well instructed;
their God teaches them.

27 Dill is not threshed with a
threshing sledge,
nor is a cart wheel rolled over
cummin;
but dill is beaten out with a
stick,
and cummin with a rod.

28 Grain is crushed for bread,
but one does not thresh it
forever;
one drives the cart wheel and
horses over it,
but does not pulverize it.

29 This also comes from the LORD
of hosts;
he is wonderful in counsel,
and excellent in wisdom.

The Siege of Jerusalem

29 Ah, Ar′i·el, Ar′i·el,
the city where David
encamped!
Add year to year;
let the festivals run their
round.

2 Yet I will distress Ar′i·el,

and there shall be moaning
and lamentation,
and Jerusalem[y] shall be to me
like an Ar′i·el.[z]

3 And like David[a] I will encamp
against you;
I will besiege you with towers
and raise siegeworks against
you.

4 Then deep from the earth you
shall speak,
from low in the dust your
words shall come;
your voice shall come from the
ground like the voice of a
ghost,
and your speech shall whisper
out of the dust.

5 But the multitude of your foes[b]
shall be like small dust,
and the multitude of tyrants
like flying chaff.
And in an instant, suddenly,
6   you will be visited by the
LORD of hosts
with thunder and earthquake
and great noise,
with whirlwind and tempest,
and the flame of a
devouring fire.

7 And the multitude of all the
nations that fight against
Ar′i·el,
all that fight against her and
her stronghold, and who
distress her,
shall be like a dream, a vision
of the night.

8 Just as when a hungry person
dreams of eating
and wakes up still hungry,
or a thirsty person dreams of
drinking
and wakes up faint, still
thirsty,
so shall the multitude of all the
nations
that fight against Mount Zion.

9 Stupefy yourselves and be in a
stupor,
blind yourselves and be blind!
Be drunk, but not from wine;
stagger, but not from strong
drink!

y Heb *she*   z Probable meaning, *altar
hearth*; compare Ezek 43.15
a Gk: Meaning of Heb uncertain
b Cn: Heb *strangers*

10 For the LORD has poured out
        upon you
    a spirit of deep sleep;
    he has closed your eyes, you
        prophets,
        and covered your heads, you
        seers.

11 The vision of all this has become
for you like the words of a sealed document. If it is given to those who can
read, with the command, "Read this,"
they say, "We cannot, for it is sealed."
12 And if it is given to those who cannot
read, saying, "Read this," they say,
"We cannot read."

13 The Lord said:
    Because these people draw near
        with their mouths
        and honor me with their lips,
        while their hearts are far from
        me,
    and their worship of me is a
        human commandment
        learned by rote;
14 so I will again do
        amazing things with this
        people,
        shocking and amazing.
    The wisdom of their wise shall
        perish,
        and the discernment of the
        discerning shall be hidden.

15 Ha! You who hide a plan too
        deep for the LORD,
    whose deeds are in the dark,
    and who say, "Who sees us?
        Who knows us?"
16 You turn things upside down!
    Shall the potter be regarded as
        the clay?
    Shall the thing made say of its
        maker,
        "He did not make me";
    or the thing formed say of the
        one who formed it,
        "He has no understanding"?

Hope for the Future

17 Shall not Lebanon in a very little
        while
    become a fruitful field,
    and the fruitful field be
        regarded as a forest?
18 On that day the deaf shall hear
        the words of a scroll,
    and out of their gloom and
        darkness
    the eyes of the blind shall see.

19 The meek shall obtain fresh joy
        in the LORD,
    and the neediest people shall
        exult in the Holy One of
        Israel.
20 For the tyrant shall be no more,
        and the scoffer shall cease to
        be;
    all those alert to do evil shall
        be cut off—
21 those who cause a person to lose
        a lawsuit,
    who set a trap for the arbiter
        in the gate,
    and without grounds deny
        justice to the one in the
        right.

22 Therefore thus says the LORD,
who redeemed Abraham, concerning
the house of Jacob:
    No longer shall Jacob be
        ashamed,
    no longer shall his face grow
        pale.
23 For when he sees his children,
        the work of my hands, in his
        midst,
    they will sanctify my name;
    they will sanctify the Holy One
        of Jacob,
    and will stand in awe of the
        God of Israel.
24 And those who err in spirit will
        come to understanding,
    and those who grumble will
        accept instruction.

The Futility of Reliance on Egypt

30 Oh, rebellious children, says
    the LORD,
    who carry out a plan, but not
        mine;
    who make an alliance, but
        against my will,
        adding to sin;
2 who set out to go down to Egypt
        without asking for my counsel,
    to take refuge in the protection
        of Pharaoh,
    and to seek shelter in the
        shadow of Egypt;
3 Therefore the protection of
        Pharaoh shall become your
        shame,
    and the shelter in the shadow
        of Egypt your humiliation.
4 For though his officials are at
        Zō'an
    and his envoys reach Hā'nēs,
5 everyone comes to shame

through a people that cannot
profit them,
that brings neither help nor
profit,
but shame and disgrace.

6 An oracle concerning the animals
of the Neg'eb.
Through a land of trouble and
distress,
of lioness and roaring[c] lion,
of viper and flying serpent,
they carry their riches on the
backs of donkeys,
and their treasures on the
humps of camels,
to a people that cannot profit
them.
7 For Egypt's help is worthless
and empty,
therefore I have called her,
"Rā'hab who sits still."[d]

A Rebellious People

8 Go now, write it before them on
a tablet,
and inscribe it in a book,
so that it may be for the time to
come
as a witness forever.
9 For they are a rebellious people,
faithless children,
children who will not hear
the instruction of the LORD;
10 who say to the seers, "Do not
see";
and to the prophets, "Do not
prophesy to us what is
right;
speak to us smooth things,
prophesy illusions,
11 leave the way, turn aside from
the path,
let us hear no more about the
Holy One of Israel."
12 Therefore thus says the Holy
One of Israel:
Because you reject this word,
and put your trust in
oppression and deceit,
and rely on them;
13 therefore this iniquity shall
become for you
like a break in a high wall,
bulging out, and about to
collapse,
whose crash comes suddenly,
in an instant;
14 its breaking is like that of a
potter's vessel
that is smashed so ruthlessly

that among its fragments not a
sherd is found
for taking fire from the hearth,
or dipping water out of the
cistern.

15 For thus said the Lord GOD, the
Holy One of Israel:
In returning and rest you shall
be saved;
in quietness and in trust shall
be your strength.
But you refused 16 and said,
"No! We will flee upon horses"—
therefore you shall flee!
and, "We will ride upon swift
steeds"—
therefore your pursuers shall
be swift!
17 A thousand shall flee at the
threat of one,
at the threat of five you shall
flee,
until you are left
like a flagstaff on the top of a
mountain,
like a signal on a hill.

God's Promise to Zion

18 Therefore the LORD waits to be
gracious to you;
therefore he will rise up to
show mercy to you.
For the LORD is a God of justice;
blessed are all those who wait
for him.
19 Truly, O people in Zion, inhabitants of Jerusalem, you shall weep no
more. He will surely be gracious to you
at the sound of your cry; when he
hears it, he will answer you. 20 Though
the Lord may give you the bread of
adversity and the water of affliction,
yet your Teacher will not hide himself
any more, but your eyes shall see your
Teacher. 21 And when you turn to the
right or when you turn to the left, your
ears shall hear a word behind you, saying, "This is the way; walk in it."
22 Then you will defile your silver-covered idols and your gold-plated images. You will scatter them like filthy
rags; you will say to them, "Away with
you!"
23 He will give rain for the seed
with which you sow the ground, and
grain, the produce of the ground,
which will be rich and plenteous. On

c Cn: Heb *from them*   *d* Meaning of Heb
uncertain

that day your cattle will graze in broad pastures; 24 and the oxen and donkeys that till the ground will eat silage, which has been winnowed with shovel and fork. 25 On every lofty mountain and every high hill there will be brooks running with water—on a day of the great slaughter, when the towers fall. 26 Moreover the light of the moon will be like the light of the sun, and the light of the sun will be sevenfold, like the light of seven days, on the day when the LORD binds up the injuries of his people, and heals the wounds inflicted by his blow.

Judgment on Assyria

27 See, the name of the LORD
     comes from far away,
     burning with his anger, and in
       thick rising smoke;e
his lips are full of indignation,
     and his tongue is like a
       devouring fire;
28 his breath is like an overflowing
     stream
     that reaches up to the neck—
to sift the nations with the sieve
     of destruction,
     and to place on the jaws of the
       peoples a bridle that leads
       them astray.

29 You shall have a song as in the night when a holy festival is kept; and gladness of heart, as when one sets out to the sound of the flute to go to the mountain of the LORD, to the Rock of Israel. 30 And the LORD will cause his majestic voice to be heard and the descending blow of his arm to be seen, in furious anger and a flame of devouring fire, with a cloudburst and tempest and hailstones. 31 The Assyrian will be terror-stricken at the voice of the LORD, when he strikes with his rod. 32 And every stroke of the staff of punishment that the LORD lays upon him will be to the sound of timbrels and lyres; battling with brandished arm he will fight with him. 33 For his burning placef has long been prepared; truly it is made ready for the king,g its pyre made deep and wide, with fire and wood in abundance; the breath of the LORD, like a stream of sulfur, kindles it.

Alliance with Egypt Is Futile

31 Alas for those who go down
     to Egypt for help
and who rely on horses,
who trust in chariots because
     they are many
     and in horsemen because they
       are very strong,
but do not look to the Holy One
     of Israel
or consult the LORD!
2 Yet he too is wise and brings
     disaster;
     he does not call back his
       words,
but will rise against the house of
     the evildoers,
     and against the helpers of
       those who work iniquity.
3 The Egyptians are human, and
     not God;
     their horses are flesh, and not
       spirit.
When the LORD stretches out his
     hand,
     the helper will stumble, and
       the one helped will fall,
     and they will all perish
       together.

4 For thus the LORD said to me,
As a lion or a young lion growls
       over its prey,
     and—when a band of
       shepherds is called out
       against it—
is not terrified by their shouting
     or daunted at their noise,
so the LORD of hosts will come
     down
     to fight upon Mount Zion and
       upon its hill.
5 Like birds hovering overhead, so
     the LORD of hosts
will protect Jerusalem;
he will protect and deliver it,
     he will spare and rescue it.

6 Turn back to him whom youh have deeply betrayed, O people of Israel. 7 For on that day all of you shall throw away your idols of silver and idols of gold, which your hands have sinfully made for you.
8 "Then the Assyrian shall fall by
       a sword, not of mortals;
     and a sword, not of humans,
       shall devour him;

e Meaning of Heb uncertain
f Or Topheth   g Or Molech   h Heb they

he shall flee from the sword,
and his young men shall be
put to forced labor.
9 His rock shall pass away in
terror,
and his officers desert the
standard in panic,"
says the LORD, whose fire is in
Zion,
and whose furnace is in
Jerusalem.

Government with Justice Predicted

32 See, a king will reign in
righteousness,
and princes will rule with
justice.
2 Each will be like a hiding place
from the wind,
a covert from the tempest,
like streams of water in a dry
place,
like the shade of a great rock
in a weary land.
3 Then the eyes of those who have
sight will not be closed,
and the ears of those who
have hearing will listen.
4 The minds of the rash will have
good judgment,
and the tongues of stammerers
will speak readily and
distinctly.
5 A fool will no longer be called
noble,
nor a villain said to be
honorable.
6 For fools speak folly,
and their minds plot iniquity:
to practice ungodliness,
to utter error concerning the
LORD,
to leave the craving of the
hungry unsatisfied,
and to deprive the thirsty of
drink.
7 The villainies of villains are evil;
they devise wicked devices
to ruin the poor with lying
words,
even when the plea of the
needy is right.
8 But those who are noble plan
noble things,
and by noble things they
stand.

Complacent Women Warned of Disaster

9 Rise up, you women who are at
ease, hear my voice;
you complacent daughters,
listen to my speech.
10 In little more than a year
you will shudder, you
complacent ones;
for the vintage will fail,
the fruit harvest will not come.
11 Tremble, you women who are at
ease,
shudder, you complacent ones;
strip, and make yourselves bare,
and put sackcloth on your
loins.
12 Beat your breasts for the
pleasant fields,
for the fruitful vine,
13 for the soil of my people
growing up in thorns and
briers;
yes, for all the joyous houses
in the jubilant city.
14 For the palace will be forsaken,
the populous city deserted;
the hill and the watchtower
will become dens forever,
the joy of wild asses,
a pasture for flocks;
15 until a spirit from on high is
poured out on us,
and the wilderness becomes a
fruitful field,
and the fruitful field is deemed
a forest.

The Peace of God's Reign

16 Then justice will dwell in the
wilderness,
and righteousness abide in the
fruitful field.
17 The effect of righteousness will
be peace,
and the result of
righteousness, quietness
and trust forever.
18 My people will abide in a
peaceful habitation,
in secure dwellings, and in
quiet resting places.
19 The forest will disappear
completely,[i]
and the city will be utterly laid
low.
20 Happy will you be who sow
beside every stream,

iCn: Heb And it will hail when the forest
comes down

who let the ox and the donkey
range freely.

A Prophecy of Deliverance from Foes

33 Ah, you destroyer,
who yourself have not been
destroyed;
you treacherous one,
with whom no one has dealt
treacherously!
When you have ceased to
destroy,
you will be destroyed;
and when you have stopped
dealing treacherously,
you will be dealt with
treacherously.

2 O LORD, be gracious to us; we
wait for you.
Be our arm every morning,
our salvation in the time of
trouble.
3 At the sound of tumult, peoples
fled;
before your majesty, nations
scattered.
4 Spoil was gathered as the
caterpillar gathers;
as locusts leap, they leaped*j*
upon it.
5 The LORD is exalted, he dwells
on high;
he filled Zion with justice and
righteousness;
6 he will be the stability of your
times,
abundance of salvation,
wisdom, and knowledge;
the fear of the LORD is Zion's
treasure.*k*

7 Listen! the valiant*j* cry in the
streets;
the envoys of peace weep
bitterly.
8 The highways are deserted,
travelers have quit the road.
The treaty is broken,
its oaths*l* are despised,
its obligation*m* is disregarded.
9 The land mourns and
languishes;
Lebanon is confounded and
withers away;
Sharon is like a desert;
and Bā'shan and Car'mel
shake off their leaves.

10 "Now I will arise," says the
LORD,

"now I will lift myself up;
now I will be exalted.
11 You conceive chaff, you bring
forth stubble;
your breath is a fire that will
consume you.
12 And the peoples will be as if
burned to lime,
like thorns cut down, that are
burned in the fire."

13 Hear, you who are far away,
what I have done;
and you who are near,
acknowledge my might.
14 The sinners in Zion are afraid;
trembling has seized the
godless:
"Who among us can live with
the devouring fire?
Who among us can live with
everlasting flames?"
15 Those who walk righteously and
speak uprightly,
who despise the gain of
oppression,
who wave away a bribe instead
of accepting it,
who stop their ears from
hearing of bloodshed
and shut their eyes from
looking on evil,
16 they will live on the heights;
their refuge will be the
fortresses of rocks;
their food will be supplied,
their water assured.

The Land of the Majestic King

17 Your eyes will see the king in
his beauty;
they will behold a land that
stretches far away.
18 Your mind will muse on the
terror:
"Where is the one who
counted?
Where is the one who weighed
the tribute?
Where is the one who counted
the towers?"
19 No longer will you see the
insolent people,
the people of an obscure
speech that you cannot
comprehend,

j Meaning of Heb uncertain　　*k* Heb *his*
treasure; meaning of Heb uncertain
l Q Ms: MT *cities*　　*m* Or *everyone*

stammering in a language that
    you cannot understand.
20 Look on Zion, the city of our
    appointed festivals!
    Your eyes will see Jerusalem,
    a quiet habitation, an
        immovable tent,
    whose stakes will never be
        pulled up,
    and none of whose ropes will
        be broken.
21 But there the LORD in majesty
        will be for us
    a place of broad rivers and
        streams,
    where no galley with oars can
        go,
    nor stately ship can pass.
22 For the LORD is our judge, the
        LORD is our ruler,
    the LORD is our king; he will
        save us.

23 Your rigging hangs loose;
    it cannot hold the mast firm in
        its place,
    or keep the sail spread out.

    Then prey and spoil in
        abundance will be divided;
    even the lame will fall to
        plundering.
24 And no inhabitant will say, "I
        am sick";
    the people who live there will
        be forgiven their iniquity.

Judgment on the Nations

34 Draw near, O nations, to
        hear;
    O peoples, give heed!
    Let the earth hear, and all that
        fills it;
    the world, and all that comes
        from it.
2 For the LORD is enraged against
        all the nations,
    and furious against all their
        hoards;
    he has doomed them, has
        given them over for
        slaughter.
3 Their slain shall be cast out,
    and the stench of their corpses
        shall rise;
    the mountains shall flow with
        their blood.
4 All the host of heaven shall rot
        away,
    and the skies roll up like a
        scroll.
    All their host shall wither

like a leaf withering on a vine,
    or fruit withering on a fig tree.

5 When my sword has drunk its
        fill in the heavens,
    lo, it will descend upon Ē′dom,
    upon the people I have
        doomed to judgment.
6 The LORD has a sword; it is
        sated with blood,
    it is gorged with fat,
    with the blood of lambs and
        goats,
    with the fat of the kidneys of
        rams.
    For the LORD has a sacrifice in
        Boz′rah,
    a great slaughter in the land of
        Ē′dom.
7 Wild oxen shall fall with them,
    and young steers with the
        mighty bulls.
    Their land shall be soaked with
        blood,
    and their soil made rich with
        fat.

8 For the LORD has a day of
        vengeance,
    a year of vindication by Zion's
        cause.[n]
9 And the streams of Ē′dom[o] shall
        be turned into pitch,
    and her soil into sulfur;
    her land shall become burning
        pitch.
10 Night and day it shall not be
        quenched;
    its smoke shall go up forever.
    From generation to generation it
        shall lie waste;
    no one shall pass through it
        forever and ever.
11 But the hawk[p] and the
        hedgehog[p] shall possess it;
    the owl[p] and the raven shall
        live in it.
    He shall stretch the line of
        confusion over it,
    and the plummet of chaos
        over[q] its nobles.
12 They shall name it No Kingdom
        There,
    and all its princes shall be
        nothing.
13 Thorns shall grow over its
        strongholds,

---

n Or of recompense by Zion's defender
o Heb her streams   p Identification
uncertain   q Heb lacks over

nettles and thistles in its
fortresses.
It shall be the haunt of jackals,
an abode for ostriches.
14 Wildcats shall meet with hyenas,
goat-demons shall call to each
other;
there too Lil'ith shall repose,
and find a place to rest.
15 There shall the owl nest
and lay and hatch and brood
in its shadow;
there too the buzzards shall
gather,
each one with its mate.
16 Seek and read from the book of
the LORD:
Not one of these shall be
missing;
none shall be without its mate.
For the mouth of the LORD has
commanded,
and his spirit has gathered
them.
17 He has cast the lot for them,
his hand has portioned it out
to them with the line;
they shall possess it forever,
from generation to generation
they shall live in it.

The Return of the Redeemed to Zion

35 The wilderness and the dry
land shall be glad,
the desert shall rejoice and
blossom;
like the crocus [2] it shall blossom
abundantly,
and rejoice with joy and
singing.
The glory of Lebanon shall be
given to it,
the majesty of Car'mel and
Sharon.
They shall see the glory of the
LORD,
the majesty of our God.

3 Strengthen the weak hands,
and make firm the feeble
knees.
4 Say to those who are of a fearful
heart,
"Be strong, do not fear!
Here is your God.
He will come with vengeance,
with terrible recompense.
He will come and save you."

5 Then the eyes of the blind shall
be opened,

and the ears of the deaf
unstopped;
6 then the lame shall leap like a
deer,
and the tongue of the
speechless sing for joy.
For waters shall break forth in
the wilderness,
and streams in the desert;
7 the burning sand shall become a
pool,
and the thirsty ground springs
of water;
the haunt of jackals shall
become a swamp,[r]
the grass shall become reeds
and rushes.

8 A highway shall be there,
and it shall be called the Holy
Way;
the unclean shall not travel on
it,[s]
but it shall be for God's
people;[t]
no traveler, not even fools,
shall go astray.
9 No lion shall be there,
nor shall any ravenous beast
come up on it;
they shall not be found there,
but the redeemed shall walk
there.
10 And the ransomed of the LORD
shall return,
and come to Zion with
singing;
everlasting joy shall be upon
their heads;
they shall obtain joy and
gladness,
and sorrow and sighing shall
flee away.

Sennacherib Threatens Jerusalem
(2 Kings 18.13–37; 2 Chr 32.1–19)

36 In the fourteenth year of King
Hez·e·kī'ah, King Sen·nach'-
e·rib of Assyria came up against all the
fortified cities of Judah and captured
them. [2] The king of Assyria sent the
Rab'sha·keh from Lā'chish to King
Hez·e·kī'ah at Jerusalem, with a great
army. He stood by the conduit of the
upper pool on the highway to the Fuller's Field. [3] And there came out to him
E·lī'a·kim son of Hil·kī'ah, who was in

r Cn: Heb *in the haunt of jackals is her
resting place*   s Or *pass it by*
t Cn: Heb *for them*

charge of the palace, and Sheb'na the secretary, and Jō'ah son of Ā'saph, the recorder.

4 The Rab'sha·keh said to them, "Say to Hez·e·kī'ah: Thus says the great king, the king of Assyria: On what do you base this confidence of yours? 5 Do you think that mere words are strategy and power for war? On whom do you now rely, that you have rebelled against me? 6 See, you are relying on Egypt, that broken reed of a staff, which will pierce the hand of anyone who leans on it. Such is Pharaoh king of Egypt to all who rely on him. 7 But if you say to me, 'We rely on the LORD our God,' is it not he whose high places and altars Hez·e·kī'ah has removed, saying to Judah and to Jerusalem, 'You shall worship before this altar'? 8 Come now, make a wager with my master the king of Assyria: I will give you two thousand horses, if you are able on your part to set riders on them. 9 How then can you repulse a single captain among the least of my master's servants, when you rely on Egypt for chariots and for horsemen? 10 Moreover, is it without the LORD that I have come up against this land to destroy it? The LORD said to me, Go up against this land, and destroy it."

11 Then E·lī'a·kim, Sheb'na, and Jō'ah said to the Rab'sha·keh, "Please speak to your servants in Ar·a·mā'ic, for we understand it; do not speak to us in the language of Judah within the hearing of the people who are on the wall." 12 But the Rab'sha·keh said, "Has my master sent me to speak these words to your master and to you, and not to the people sitting on the wall, who are doomed with you to eat their own dung and drink their own urine?"

13 Then the Rab'sha·keh stood and called out in a loud voice in the language of Judah, "Hear the words of the great king, the king of Assyria! 14 Thus says the king: 'Do not let Hez·e·kī'ah deceive you, for he will not be able to deliver you. 15 Do not let Hez·e·kī'ah make you rely on the LORD by saying, The LORD will surely deliver us; this city will not be given into the hand of the king of Assyria.' 16 Do not listen to Hez·e·kī'ah; for thus says the king of Assyria: 'Make your peace with me and come out to me; then everyone of you will eat from your own vine and your own fig tree and drink water from your own cistern, 17 until I come and take you away to a land like your own

land, a land of grain and wine, a land of bread and vineyards. 18 Do not let Hez·e·kī'ah mislead you by saying, The LORD will save us. Has any of the gods of the nations saved their land out of the hand of the king of Assyria? 19 Where are the gods of Hā'math and Ar'pad? Where are the gods of Seph·ar·vā'im? Have they delivered Samaria out of my hand? 20 Who among all the gods of these countries have saved their countries out of my hand, that the LORD should save Jerusalem out of my hand?' "

21 But they were silent and answered him not a word, for the king's command was, "Do not answer him." 22 Then E·lī'a·kim son of Hil·kī'ah, who was in charge of the palace, and Sheb'na the secretary, and Jō'ah son of Ā'saph, the recorder, came to Hez·e·kī'ah with their clothes torn, and told him the words of the Rab'-sha·keh.

Hezekiah Consults Isaiah
(2 Kings 19.1–13)

37 When King Hez·e·kī'ah heard it, he tore his clothes, covered himself with sackcloth, and went into the house of the LORD. 2 And he sent E·lī'a·kim, who was in charge of the palace, and Sheb'na the secretary, and the senior priests, covered with sackcloth, to the prophet Ī·sāi'ah son of Ā'moz. 3 They said to him, "Thus says Hez·e·kī'ah, This day is a day of distress, of rebuke, and of disgrace; children have come to the birth, and there is no strength to bring them forth. 4 It may be that the LORD your God heard the words of the Rab'sha·keh, whom his master the king of Assyria has sent to mock the living God, and will rebuke the words that the LORD your God has heard; therefore lift up your prayer for the remnant that is left."

5 When the servants of King Hez·e·kī'ah came to Ī·sāi'ah, 6 Ī·sāi'ah said to them, "Say to your master, 'Thus says the LORD: Do not be afraid because of the words that you have heard, with which the servants of the king of Assyria have reviled me. 7 I myself will put a spirit in him, so that he shall hear a rumor, and return to his own land; I will cause him to fall by the sword in his own land.' "

8 The Rab'sha·keh returned, and found the king of Assyria fighting against Lib'nah; for he had heard that the king had left Lā'chish. 9 Now the

king[u] heard concerning King Tir·hā'-kah of Ethiopia,[v] "He has set out to fight against you." When he heard it, he sent messengers to Hez·e·kī'ah, saying, 10 "Thus shall you speak to King Hez·e·kī'ah of Judah: Do not let your God on whom you rely deceive you by promising that Jerusalem will not be given into the hand of the king of Assyria. 11 See, you have heard what the kings of Assyria have done to all lands, destroying them utterly. Shall you be delivered? 12 Have the gods of the nations delivered them, the nations that my predecessors destroyed, Gō'-zan, Har'an, Rē'zeph, and the people of Eden who were in Te·las'sar? 13 Where is the king of Hā'math, the king of Ar'pad, the king of the city of Seph·ar·vā'im, the king of Hē'na, or the king of Iv'vah?"

Hezekiah's Prayer
(2 Kings 19.14–34)

14 Hez·e·kī'ah received the letter from the hand of the messengers and read it; then Hez·e·kī'ah went up to the house of the LORD and spread it before the LORD. 15 And Hez·e·kī'ah prayed to the LORD, saying: 16 "O LORD of hosts, God of Israel, who are enthroned above the cherubim, you are God, you alone, of all the kingdoms of the earth; you have made heaven and earth. 17 Incline your ear, O LORD, and hear; open your eyes, O LORD, and see; hear all the words of Sen·nach'e·rib, which he has sent to mock the living God. 18 Truly, O LORD, the kings of Assyria have laid waste all the nations and their lands, 19 and have hurled their gods into the fire, though they were no gods, but the work of human hands — wood and stone — and so they were destroyed. 20 So now, O LORD our God, save us from his hand, so that all the kingdoms of the earth may know that you alone are the LORD."

21 Then Ī·sāi'ah son of Ā'moz sent to Hez·e·kī'ah, saying: "Thus says the LORD, the God of Israel: Because you have prayed to me concerning King Sen·nach'e·rib of Assyria, 22 this is the word that the LORD has spoken concerning him:

She despises you, she scorns you —
  virgin daughter Zion;
she tosses her head — behind your back,
  daughter Jerusalem.

23 Whom have you mocked and reviled?
  Against whom have you raised your voice
and haughtily lifted your eyes?
  Against the Holy One of Israel!
24 By your servants you have mocked the Lord,
  and you have said, 'With my many chariots
I have gone up the heights of the mountains,
  to the far recesses of Lebanon;
I felled its tallest cedars,
  its choicest cypresses;
I came to its remotest height,
  its densest forest.
25 I dug wells
  and drank waters,
I dried up with the sole of my foot
  all the streams of Egypt.'
26 Have you not heard
  that I determined it long ago?
I planned from days of old
  what now I bring to pass,
that you should make fortified cities
  crash into heaps of ruins,
27 while their inhabitants, shorn of strength,
  are dismayed and confounded;
they have become like plants of the field
  and like tender grass,
like grass on the housetops,
  blighted[w] before it is grown.

28 I know your rising up[x] and your sitting down,
  your going out and coming in,
  and your raging against me.
29 Because you have raged against me
  and your arrogance has come to my ears,
I will put my hook in your nose
  and my bit in your mouth;
I will turn you back on the way
  by which you came.

30 "And this shall be the sign for you: This year eat what grows of itself, and in the second year what springs from that; then in the third year sow, reap, plant vineyards, and eat their

---

u Heb *he*   v Or Nubia; Heb *Cush*
w With 2 Kings 19.26: Heb *field*   x Q Ms
Gk: MT lacks *your rising up*

fruit. [31]The surviving remnant of the house of Judah shall again take root downward, and bear fruit upward; [32]for from Jerusalem a remnant shall go out, and from Mount Zion a band of survivors. The zeal of the LORD of hosts will do this.

33 "Therefore thus says the LORD concerning the king of Assyria: He shall not come into this city, shoot an arrow there, come before it with a shield, or cast up a siege ramp against it. [34]By the way that he came, by the same he shall return; he shall not come into this city, says the LORD. [35]For I will defend this city to save it, for my own sake and for the sake of my servant David."

Sennacherib's Defeat and Death
(2 Kings 19.35–37)

36 Then the angel of the LORD set out and struck down one hundred eighty-five thousand in the camp of the Assyrians; when morning dawned, they were all dead bodies. [37]Then King Sen·nach′e·rib of Assyria left, went home, and lived at Nin′e·veh. [38]As he was worshiping in the house of his god Nis′roch, his sons A·dram′me·lech and Sha·rē′zer killed him with the sword, and they escaped into the land of Ar′a·rat. His son Ē′sar-had′don succeeded him.

Hezekiah's Illness
(2 Kings 20.1–11; 2 Chr 32.24–26)

38 In those days Hez·e·kī′ah became sick and was at the point of death. The prophet Ī·sāi′ah son of Ā′moz came to him, and said to him, "Thus says the LORD: Set your house in order, for you shall die; you shall not recover." [2]Then Hez·e·kī′ah turned his face to the wall, and prayed to the LORD: [3]"Remember now, O LORD, I implore you, how I have walked before you in faithfulness with a whole heart, and have done what is good in your sight." And Hez·e·kī′ah wept bitterly.

4 Then the word of the LORD came to Ī·sāi′ah: [5]"Go and say to Hez·e·kī′ah, Thus says the LORD, the God of your ancestor David: I have heard your prayer, I have seen your tears; I will add fifteen years to your life. [6]I will deliver you and this city out of the hand of the king of Assyria, and defend this city.

7 "This is the sign to you from the LORD, that the LORD will do this thing that he has promised: [8]See, I will make the shadow cast by the declining sun on the dial of Ā′haz turn back ten steps." So the sun turned back on the dial the ten steps by which it had declined.[y]

9 A writing of King Hez·e·kī′ah of Judah, after he had been sick and had recovered from his sickness:

[10] I said: In the noontide of my
           days
        I must depart;
     I am consigned to the gates of
           Shē′ōl
        for the rest of my years.
[11] I said, I shall not see the LORD
        in the land of the living;
     I shall look upon mortals no
           more
        among the inhabitants of the
           world.
[12] My dwelling is plucked up and
           removed from me
        like a shepherd's tent;
     like a weaver I have rolled up
           my life;
     he cuts me off from the loom;
     from day to night you bring me
           to an end;[y]
[13]   I cry for help[z] until morning;
     like a lion he breaks all my
           bones;
        from day to night you bring
           me to an end.[y]

[14] Like a swallow or a crane[y] I
           clamor,
        I moan like a dove.
     My eyes are weary with looking
           upward.
        O Lord, I am oppressed; be my
           security!
[15] But what can I say? For he has
           spoken to me,
        and he himself has done it.
     All my sleep has fled[a]
        because of the bitterness of my
           soul.

[16] O Lord, by these things people
           live,
        and in all these is the life of
           my spirit.[y]
        Oh, restore me to health and
           make me live!
[17] Surely it was for my welfare

[y]Meaning of Heb uncertain
[z]Cn: Meaning of Heb uncertain
[a]Cn Compare Syr: Heb *I will walk
slowly all my years*

that I had great bitterness;
but you have held back[b] my life
  from the pit of destruction,
for you have cast all my sins
  behind your back.
18 For She'ol cannot thank you,
    death cannot praise you;
  those who go down to the Pit
    cannot hope
    for your faithfulness.
19 The living, the living, they thank
    you,
    as I do this day;
  fathers make known to children
    your faithfulness.

20 The LORD will save me,
    and we will sing to stringed
      instruments[c]
  all the days of our lives,
    at the house of the LORD.

21 Now Ī·sāi'ah had said, "Let them take a lump of figs, and apply it to the boil, so that he may recover." 22 Hez·e·kī'ah also had said, "What is the sign that I shall go up to the house of the LORD?"

Envoys from Babylon Welcomed
(2 Kings 20.12–19)

39 At that time King Mer'o·dach-bal'a·dan son of Bal'a·dan of Babylon sent envoys with letters and a present to Hez·e·kī'ah, for he heard that he had been sick and had recovered. 2 Hez·e·kī'ah welcomed them; he showed them his treasure house, the silver, the gold, the spices, the precious oil, his whole armory, all that was found in his storehouses. There was nothing in his house or in all his realm that Hez·e·kī'ah did not show them. 3 Then the prophet Ī·sāi'ah came to King Hez·e·kī'ah and said to him, "What did these men say? From where did they come to you?" Hez·e·kī'ah answered, "They have come to me from a far country, from Babylon." 4 He said, "What have they seen in your house?" Hez·e·kī'ah answered, "They have seen all that is in my house; there is nothing in my storehouses that I did not show them."

5 Then Ī·sāi'ah said to Hez·e·kī'ah, "Hear the word of the LORD of hosts: 6 Days are coming when all that is in your house, and that which your ancestors have stored up until this day, shall be carried to Babylon; nothing shall be left, says the LORD. 7 Some of your own sons who are born to you

shall be taken away; they shall be eunuchs in the palace of the king of Babylon." 8 Then Hez·e·kī'ah said to Ī·sāi'ah, "The word of the LORD that you have spoken is good." For he thought, "There will be peace and security in my days."

God's People Are Comforted
(Cp Lk 3.4–6)

40 Comfort, O comfort my
      people,
    says your God.
2 Speak tenderly to Jerusalem,
    and cry to her
  that she has served her term,
    that her penalty is paid,
  that she has received from the
    LORD's hand
    double for all her sins.

3 A voice cries out:
  "In the wilderness prepare the
      way of the LORD,
    make straight in the desert a
      highway for our God.
4 Every valley shall be lifted up,
    and every mountain and hill
      be made low;
  the uneven ground shall become
      level,
    and the rough places a plain.
5 Then the glory of the LORD shall
      be revealed,
    and all people shall see it
      together,
  for the mouth of the LORD has
      spoken."

6 A voice says, "Cry out!"
    And I said, "What shall I cry?"
  All people are grass,
    their constancy is like the
      flower of the field.
7 The grass withers, the flower
      fades,
    when the breath of the LORD
      blows upon it;
  surely the people are grass.
8 The grass withers, the flower
      fades;
    but the word of our God will
      stand forever.
9 Get you up to a high mountain,
    O Zion, herald of good
      tidings;[d]
  lift up your voice with strength,

b Cn Compare Gk Vg: Heb *loved*
c Heb *my stringed instruments*
d Or *O herald of good tidings to Zion*

O Jerusalem, herald of good
     tidings,*e*
lift it up, do not fear;
say to the cities of Judah,
     "Here is your God!"
10 See, the Lord GOD comes with
     might,
     and his arm rules for him;
his reward is with him,
     and his recompense before
     him.
11 He will feed his flock like a
     shepherd;
he will gather the lambs in his
     arms,
and carry them in his bosom,
     and gently lead the mother
     sheep.

12 Who has measured the waters in
     the hollow of his hand
     and marked off the heavens
     with a span,
enclosed the dust of the earth in
     a measure,
     and weighed the mountains in
     scales
     and the hills in a balance?
13 Who has directed the spirit of
     the LORD,
     or as his counselor has
     instructed him?
14 Whom did he consult for his
     enlightenment,
     and who taught him the path
     of justice?
Who taught him knowledge,
     and showed him the way of
     understanding?
15 Even the nations are like a drop
     from a bucket,
     and are accounted as dust on
     the scales;
     see, he takes up the isles like
     fine dust.
16 Lebanon would not provide fuel
     enough,
     nor are its animals enough for
     a burnt offering.
17 All the nations are as nothing
     before him;
     they are accounted by him as
     less than nothing and
     emptiness.

18 To whom then will you liken
     God,
     or what likeness compare with
     him?
19 An idol? —A workman casts it,
     and a goldsmith overlays it
     with gold,

and casts for it silver chains.
20 As a gift one chooses mulberry
     wood*f*
     —wood that will not rot—
then seeks out a skilled artisan
     to set up an image that will
     not topple.

21 Have you not known? Have you
     not heard?
     Has it not been told you from
     the beginning?
     Have you not understood from
     the foundations of the
     earth?
22 It is he who sits above the circle
     of the earth,
     and its inhabitants are like
     grasshoppers;
who stretches out the heavens
     like a curtain,
     and spreads them like a tent to
     live in;
23 who brings princes to naught,
     and makes the rulers of the
     earth as nothing.

24 Scarcely are they planted,
     scarcely sown,
     scarcely has their stem taken
     root in the earth,
when he blows upon them, and
     they wither,
     and the tempest carries them
     off like stubble.

25 To whom then will you compare
     me,
     or who is my equal? says the
     Holy One.
26 Lift up your eyes on high and
     see:
     Who created these?
He who brings out their host and
     numbers them,
     calling them all by name;
because he is great in strength,
     mighty in power,
     not one is missing.

27 Why do you say, O Jacob,
     and speak, O Israel,
"My way is hidden from the
     LORD,
     and my right is disregarded by
     my God"?
28 Have you not known? Have you
     not heard?
The LORD is the everlasting God,

I
S
A
I
A
H

e Or *O herald of good tidings to
Jerusalem*   *f* Meaning of Heb uncertain

the Creator of the ends of the
earth.
He does not faint or grow weary;
his understanding is
unsearchable.
29 He gives power to the faint,
and strengthens the powerless.
30 Even youths will faint and be
weary,
and the young will fall
exhausted;
31 but those who wait for the LORD
shall renew their strength,
they shall mount up with
wings like eagles,
they shall run and not be weary,
they shall walk and not faint.

Israel Assured of God's Help

41 Listen to me in silence,
O coastlands;
let the peoples renew their
strength;
let them approach, then let them
speak;
let us together draw near for
judgment.

2 Who has roused a victor from
the east,
summoned him to his service?
He delivers up nations to him,
and tramples kings under foot;
he makes them like dust with his
sword,
like driven stubble with his
bow.
3 He pursues them and passes on
safely,
scarcely touching the path
with his feet.
4 Who has performed and done
this,
calling the generations from
the beginning?
I, the LORD, am first,
and will be with the last.
5 The coastlands have seen and
are afraid,
the ends of the earth tremble;
they have drawn near and
come.
6 Each one helps the other,
saying to one another, "Take
courage!"
7 The artisan encourages the
goldsmith,
and the one who smooths with
the hammer encourages
the one who strikes the
anvil,

saying of the soldering, "It is
good";
and they fasten it with nails so
that it cannot be moved.
8 But you, Israel, my servant,
Jacob, whom I have chosen,
the offspring of Abraham, my
friend;
9 you whom I took from the ends
of the earth,
and called from its farthest
corners,
saying to you, "You are my
servant,
I have chosen you and not cast
you off";
10 do not fear, for I am with you,
do not be afraid, for I am your
God;
I will strengthen you, I will help
you,
I will uphold you with my
victorious right hand.

11 Yes, all who are incensed
against you
shall be ashamed and
disgraced;
those who strive against you
shall be as nothing and shall
perish.
12 You shall seek those who
contend with you,
but you shall not find them;
those who war against you
shall be as nothing at all.
13 For I, the LORD your God,
hold your right hand;
it is I who say to you, "Do not
fear,
I will help you."

14 Do not fear, you worm Jacob,
you insect[g] Israel!
I will help you, says the LORD;
your Redeemer is the Holy
One of Israel.
15 Now, I will make of you a
threshing sledge,
sharp, new, and having teeth;
you shall thresh the mountains
and crush them,
and you shall make the hills
like chaff.
16 You shall winnow them and the
wind shall carry them
away,
and the tempest shall scatter
them.

g Syr: Heb *men of*

Then you shall rejoice in the
  LORD;
   in the Holy One of Israel you
     shall glory.

17 When the poor and needy seek
     water,
   and there is none,
   and their tongue is parched
     with thirst,
 I the LORD will answer them,
   I the God of Israel will not
     forsake them.
18 I will open rivers on the bare
     heights,[h]
   and fountains in the midst of
     the valleys;
 I will make the wilderness a pool
     of water,
   and the dry land springs of
     water.
19 I will put in the wilderness the
     cedar,
   the acacia, the myrtle, and the
     olive;
 I will set in the desert the
     cypress,
   the plane and the pine
     together,
20 so that all may see and know,
   all may consider and
     understand,
 that the hand of the LORD has
     done this,
   the Holy One of Israel has
     created it.

The Futility of Idols

21 Set forth your case, says the
     LORD;
   bring your proofs, says the
     King of Jacob.
22 Let them bring them, and tell us
     what is to happen.
 Tell us the former things, what
     they are,
   so that we may consider them,
 and that we may know their
     outcome;
   or declare to us the things to
     come.
23 Tell us what is to come
     hereafter,
   that we may know that you
     are gods;
 do good, or do harm,
   that we may be afraid and
     terrified.
24 You, indeed, are nothing
   and your work is nothing at
     all;

whoever chooses you is an
  abomination.

25 I stirred up one from the north,
     and he has come,
   from the rising of the sun he
     was summoned by name.[i]
 He shall trample[j] on rulers as
     on mortar,
   as the potter treads clay.
26 Who declared it from the
     beginning, so that we
     might know,
   and beforehand, so that we
     might say, "He is right"?
 There was no one who declared
     it, none who proclaimed,
   none who heard your words.
27 I first have declared it to Zion,[k]
   and I give to Jerusalem a
     herald of good tidings.
28 But when I look there is no one;
   among these there is no
     counselor
 who, when I ask, gives an
     answer.
29 No, they are all a delusion;
   their works are nothing;
   their images are empty wind.

The Servant, a Light to the Nations

42 Here is my servant, whom I
     uphold,
   my chosen, in whom my soul
     delights;
 I have put my spirit upon him;
   he will bring forth justice to
     the nations.
2 He will not cry or lift up his
     voice,
   or make it heard in the street;
3 a bruised reed he will not break,
   and a dimly burning wick he
     will not quench;
   he will faithfully bring forth
     justice.
4 He will not grow faint or be
     crushed
   until he has established justice
     in the earth;
   and the coastlands wait for his
     teaching.

5 Thus says God, the LORD,
   who created the heavens and
     stretched them out,

I
S
A
I
A
H

h Or *trails*   i Cn Compare Q Ms Gk: MT
and he shall call on my name
j Cn: Heb *come*   k Cn: Heb *First to
Zion—Behold, behold them*

who spread out the earth and
what comes from it,
who gives breath to the people
upon it
and spirit to those who walk
in it:

6 I am the LORD, I have called you
in righteousness,
I have taken you by the hand
and kept you;
I have given you as a covenant
to the people,^{l}
a light to the nations,

7 to open the eyes that are blind,
to bring out the prisoners from
the dungeon,
from the prison those who sit
in darkness.

8 I am the LORD, that is my name;
my glory I give to no other,
nor my praise to idols.

9 See, the former things have
come to pass,
and new things I now declare;
before they spring forth,
I tell you of them.

A Hymn of Praise

10 Sing to the LORD a new song,
his praise from the end of the
earth!
Let the sea roar^m and all that
fills it,
the coastlands and their
inhabitants.

11 Let the desert and its towns lift
up their voice,
the villages that Kē′dar
inhabits;
let the inhabitants of Sē′la sing
for joy,
let them shout from the tops of
the mountains.

12 Let them give glory to the LORD,
and declare his praise in the
coastlands.

13 The LORD goes forth like a
soldier,
like a warrior he stirs up his
fury;
he cries out, he shouts aloud,
he shows himself mighty
against his foes.

14 For a long time I have held my
peace,
I have kept still and restrained
myself;
now I will cry out like a woman
in labor,
I will gasp and pant.

15 I will lay waste mountains and
hills,
and dry up all their herbage;
I will turn the rivers into islands,
and dry up the pools.

16 I will lead the blind
by a road they do not know,
by paths they have not known
I will guide them.
I will turn the darkness before
them into light,
the rough places into level
ground.
These are the things I will do,
and I will not forsake them.

17 They shall be turned back and
utterly put to shame—
those who trust in carved
images,
who say to cast images,
"You are our gods."

18 Listen, you that are deaf;
and you that are blind, look up
and see!

19 Who is blind but my servant,
or deaf like my messenger
whom I send?
Who is blind like my dedicated
one,
or blind like the servant of the
LORD?

20 He sees many things, but does^n
not observe them;
his ears are open, but he does
not hear.

Israel's Disobedience

21 The LORD was pleased, for the
sake of his righteousness,
to magnify his teaching and
make it glorious.

22 But this is a people robbed and
plundered,
all of them are trapped in
holes
and hidden in prisons;
they have become a prey with
no one to rescue,
a spoil with no one to say,
"Restore!"

23 Who among you will give heed
to this,
who will attend and listen for
the time to come?

24 Who gave up Jacob to the
spoiler,

^{l}Meaning of Heb uncertain
^{m}Cn Compare Ps 96.11; 98.7: Heb *Those
who go down to the sea* ^{n}Heb *You
see many things but do*

and Israel to the robbers?
Was it not the LORD, against
    whom we have sinned,
    in whose ways they would not
        walk,
    and whose law they would not
        obey?
25 So he poured upon him the heat
        of his anger
    and the fury of war;
    it set him on fire all around, but
        he did not understand;
    it burned him, but he did not
        take it to heart.

Restoration and Protection Promised

43 But now thus says the LORD,
        he who created you,
            O Jacob,
        he who formed you, O Israel:
Do not fear, for I have redeemed
        you;
    I have called you by name,
        you are mine.
2 When you pass through the
            waters, I will be with you;
    and through the rivers, they
            shall not overwhelm you;
    when you walk through fire you
            shall not be burned,
    and the flame shall not
            consume you.
3 For I am the LORD your God,
        the Holy One of Israel, your
            Savior.
    I give Egypt as your ransom,
    Ethiopia° and Se′ba in
            exchange for you.
4 Because you are precious in my
            sight,
    and honored, and I love you,
    I give people in return for you,
        nations in exchange for your
            life.
5 Do not fear, for I am with you;
    I will bring your offspring
            from the east,
    and from the west I will gather
        you;
6 I will say to the north, "Give
            them up,"
    and to the south, "Do not
            withhold;
    bring my sons from far away
    and my daughters from the
            end of the earth—
7 everyone who is called by my
            name,
        whom I created for my glory,
        whom I formed and made."

8 Bring forth the people who are
            blind, yet have eyes,
        who are deaf, yet have ears!
9 Let all the nations gather
            together,
        and let the peoples assemble.
    Who among them declared this,
        and foretold to us the former
            things?
    Let them bring their witnesses to
            justify them,
        and let them hear and say, "It
            is true."
10 You are my witnesses, says the
            LORD,
        and my servant whom I have
            chosen,
    so that you may know and
            believe me
    and understand that I am he.
    Before me no god was formed,
        nor shall there be any after
            me.
11 I, I am the LORD,
        and besides me there is no
            savior.
12 I declared and saved and
            proclaimed,
        when there was no strange
            god among you;
        and you are my witnesses,
            says the LORD.
13 I am God, and also henceforth I
            am He;
        there is no one who can
            deliver from my hand;
        I work and who can hinder it?

14 Thus says the LORD,
        your Redeemer, the Holy One
            of Israel:
    For your sake I will send to
            Babylon
        and break down all the bars,
        and the shouting of the
            Chal·de′ans will be turned
                to lamentation.ᴾ
15 I am the LORD, your Holy One,
        the Creator of Israel, your
            King.
16 Thus says the LORD,
        who makes a way in the sea,
        a path in the mighty waters,
17 who brings out chariot and
            horse,
        army and warrior;
    they lie down, they cannot rise,
        they are extinguished,
            quenched like a wick:

°Or Nubia; Heb Cush   ᴾMeaning of
Heb uncertain

I
S
A
I
A
H

18 Do not remember the former
      things,
    or consider the things of old.
19 I am about to do a new thing;
      now it springs forth, do you
         not perceive it?
    I will make a way in the
      wilderness
    and rivers in the desert.
20 The wild animals will honor me,
      the jackals and the ostriches;
    for I give water in the
      wilderness,
      rivers in the desert,
    to give drink to my chosen
      people,
21   the people whom I formed for
         myself
    so that they might declare my
         praise.

22 Yet you did not call upon me,
      O Jacob;
    but you have been weary of
      me, O Israel!
23 You have not brought me your
      sheep for burnt offerings,
    or honored me with your
         sacrifices.
    I have not burdened you with
         offerings,
      or wearied you with
         frankincense.
24 You have not bought me sweet
      cane with money,
    or satisfied me with the fat of
      your sacrifices.
    But you have burdened me with
      your sins;
      you have wearied me with
         your iniquities.

25 I, I am He
    who blots out your
      transgressions for my own
         sake,
    and I will not remember your
         sins.
26 Accuse me, let us go to trial;
    set forth your case, so that you
      may be proved right.
27 Your first ancestor sinned,
    and your interpreters
      transgressed against me.
28 Therefore I profaned the princes
      of the sanctuary,
    I delivered Jacob to utter
         destruction,
    and Israel to reviling.

God's Blessing on Israel

44 But now hear, O Jacob my
      servant,
    Israel whom I have chosen!
2 Thus says the LORD who made
      you,
    who formed you in the womb
      and will help you:
    Do not fear, O Jacob my servant,
    Jesh′ū·run whom I have
      chosen.
3 For I will pour water on the
      thirsty land,
    and streams on the dry
      ground;
    I will pour my spirit upon your
      descendants,
    and my blessing on your
      offspring.
4 They shall spring up like a green
      tamarisk,
    like willows by flowing
      streams.
5 This one will say, "I am the
      LORD's,"
    another will be called by the
      name of Jacob,
    yet another will write on the
      hand, "The LORD's,"
    and adopt the name of Israel.

6 Thus says the LORD, the King of
      Israel,
    and his Redeemer, the LORD of
      hosts:
    I am the first and I am the last;
    besides me there is no god.
7 Who is like me? Let them
      proclaim it,
    let them declare and set it
      forth before me.
    Who has announced from of old
      the things to come?q
    Let them tell usr what is yet
      to be.
8 Do not fear, or be afraid;
    have I not told you from of old
      and declared it?
    You are my witnesses!
    Is there any god besides me?
    There is no other rock; I know
      not one.

The Absurdity of Idol Worship

9 All who make idols are nothing,
and the things they delight in do not
profit; their witnesses neither see nor

q Cn: Heb *from my placing an eternal
people and things to come*   r Tg: Heb
them

know. And so they will be put to shame. ¹⁰Who would fashion a god or cast an image that can do no good? ¹¹Look, all its devotees shall be put to shame; the artisans too are merely human. Let them all assemble, let them stand up; they shall be terrified, they shall all be put to shame.

12 The ironsmith fashions it[s] and works it over the coals, shaping it with hammers, and forging it with his strong arm; he becomes hungry and his strength fails, he drinks no water and is faint. ¹³The carpenter stretches a line, marks it out with a stylus, fashions it with planes, and marks it with a compass; he makes it in human form, with human beauty, to be set up in a shrine. ¹⁴He cuts down cedars or chooses a holm tree or an oak and lets it grow strong among the trees of the forest. He plants a cedar and the rain nourishes it. ¹⁵Then it can be used as fuel. Part of it he takes and warms himself; he kindles a fire and bakes bread. Then he makes a god and worships it, makes it a carved image and bows down before it. ¹⁶Half of it he burns in the fire; over this half he roasts meat, eats it and is satisfied. He also warms himself and says, "Ah, I am warm, I can feel the fire!" ¹⁷The rest of it he makes into a god, his idol, bows down to it and worships it; he prays to it and says, "Save me, for you are my god!"

18 They do not know, nor do they comprehend; for their eyes are shut, so that they cannot see, and their minds as well, so that they cannot understand. ¹⁹No one considers, nor is there knowledge or discernment to say, "Half of it I burned in the fire; I also baked bread on its coals, I roasted meat and have eaten. Now shall I make the rest of it an abomination? Shall I fall down before a block of wood?" ²⁰He feeds on ashes; a deluded mind has led him astray, and he cannot save himself or say, "Is not this thing in my right hand a fraud?"

Israel Is Not Forgotten

21 Remember these things,
    O Jacob,
and Israel, for you are my
    servant;
I formed you, you are my
    servant;
O Israel, you will not be
    forgotten by me.

22 I have swept away your
    transgressions like a cloud,
    and your sins like mist;
return to me, for I have
    redeemed you.

23 Sing, O heavens, for the LORD
    has done it;
    shout, O depths of the earth;
break forth into singing,
    O mountains,
    O forest, and every tree in it!
For the LORD has redeemed
    Jacob,
    and will be glorified in Israel.

24 Thus says the LORD, your
    Redeemer,
    who formed you in the womb:
I am the LORD, who made all
    things,
    who alone stretched out the
    heavens,
    who by myself spread out the
    earth;
25 who frustrates the omens of
    liars,
    and makes fools of diviners;
who turns back the wise,
    and makes their knowledge
    foolish;
26 who confirms the word of his
    servant,
    and fulfills the prediction of
    his messengers;
who says of Jerusalem, "It shall
    be inhabited,"
    and of the cities of Judah,
    "They shall be rebuilt,
    and I will raise up their ruins";
27 who says to the deep, "Be dry—
    I will dry up your rivers";
28 who says of Cyrus, "He is my
    shepherd,
    and he shall carry out all my
    purpose";
and who says of Jerusalem, "It
    shall be rebuilt,"
    and of the temple, "Your
    foundation shall be laid."

Cyrus, God's Instrument

45 Thus says the LORD to his anointed, to Cyrus,
whose right hand I have
    grasped
to subdue nations before him
    and strip kings of their robes,
to open doors before him—

[s] Cn: Heb an ax

and the gates shall not be
closed:
2 I will go before you
and level the mountains,[t]
I will break in pieces the doors
of bronze
and cut through the bars of
iron,
3 I will give you the treasures of
darkness
and riches hidden in secret
places,
so that you may know that it is
I, the LORD,
the God of Israel, who call you
by your name.
4 For the sake of my servant
Jacob,
and Israel my chosen,
I call you by your name,
I surname you, though you do
not know me.
5 I am the LORD, and there is no
other;
besides me there is no god.
I arm you, though you do not
know me,
6 so that they may know, from the
rising of the sun
and from the west, that there
is no one besides me;
I am the LORD, and there is no
other.
7 I form light and create darkness,
I make weal and create woe;
I the LORD do all these things.

8 Shower, O heavens, from above,
and let the skies rain down
righteousness;
let the earth open, that salvation
may spring up,[u]
and let it cause righteousness
to sprout up also;
I the LORD have created it.

9 Woe to you who strive with your
Maker,
earthen vessels with the
potter![v]
Does the clay say to the one
who fashions it, "What are
you making"?
or "Your work has no
handles"?
10 Woe to anyone who says to a
father, "What are you
begetting?"
or to a woman, "With what are
you in labor?"
11 Thus says the LORD,

the Holy One of Israel, and its
Maker:
Will you question me[w] about my
children,
or command me concerning
the work of my hands?
12 I made the earth,
and created humankind upon
it;
it was my hands that stretched
out the heavens,
and I commanded all their
host.
13 I have aroused Cyrus[x] in
righteousness,
and I will make all his paths
straight;
he shall build my city
and set my exiles free,
not for price or reward,
says the LORD of hosts.
14 Thus says the LORD:
The wealth of Egypt and the
merchandise of Ethiopia,[y]
and the Sa·bē′ans, tall of
stature,
shall come over to you and be
yours,
they shall follow you;
they shall come over in chains
and bow down to you.
They will make supplication to
you, saying,
"God is with you alone, and
there is no other;
there is no god besides him."
15 Truly, you are a God who hides
himself,
O God of Israel, the Savior.
16 All of them are put to shame
and confounded,
the makers of idols go in
confusion together.
17 But Israel is saved by the LORD
with everlasting salvation;
you shall not be put to shame or
confounded
to all eternity.

18 For thus says the LORD,
who created the heavens
(he is God!),
who formed the earth and
made it
(he established it;

[t] Q Ms Gk: MT the swellings   [u] Q Ms:
MT that they may bring forth salvation
[v] Cn: Heb with the potsherds, or with
the potters   [w] Cn: Heb Ask me of
things to come   [x] Heb him
[y] Or Nubia; Heb Cush

he did not create it a chaos,
    he formed it to be inhabited!):
I am the LORD, and there is no
    other.
19 I did not speak in secret,
    in a land of darkness;
I did not say to the offspring of
    Jacob,
    "Seek me in chaos."
I the LORD speak the truth,
    I declare what is right.

Idols Cannot Save Babylon

20 Assemble yourselves and come
    together,
    draw near, you survivors of
      the nations!
They have no knowledge—
    those who carry about their
      wooden idols,
and keep on praying to a god
    that cannot save.
21 Declare and present your case;
    let them take counsel together!
Who told this long ago?
    Who declared it of old?
Was it not I, the LORD?
    There is no other god besides
      me,
a righteous God and a Savior;
    there is no one besides me.

22 Turn to me and be saved,
    all the ends of the earth!
For I am God, and there is no
    other.
23 By myself I have sworn,
    from my mouth has gone forth
      in righteousness
a word that shall not return:
"To me every knee shall bow,
    every tongue shall swear."

24 Only in the LORD, it shall be
    said of me,
    are righteousness and
      strength;
all who were incensed against
    him
    shall come to him and be
      ashamed.
25 In the LORD all the offspring of
    Israel
    shall triumph and glory.

46 Bel bows down, Nē′bō stoops,
    their idols are on beasts and
      cattle;
these things you carry are
    loaded
    as burdens on weary animals.

2 They stoop, they bow down
    together;
    they cannot save the burden,
    but themselves go into
      captivity.

3 Listen to me, O house of Jacob,
    all the remnant of the house of
      Israel,
who have been borne by me
    from your birth,
    carried from the womb;
4 even to your old age I am he,
    even when you turn gray I will
      carry you.
I have made, and I will bear;
    I will carry and will save.

5 To whom will you liken me and
    make me equal,
    and compare me, as though
      we were alike?
6 Those who lavish gold from the
    purse,
    and weigh out silver in the
      scales—
they hire a goldsmith, who
    makes it into a god;
    then they fall down and
      worship!
7 They lift it to their shoulders,
    they carry it,
    they set it in its place, and it
      stands there;
    it cannot move from its place.
If one cries out to it, it does not
    answer
    or save anyone from trouble.

8 Remember this and consider,[z]
    recall it to mind, you
      transgressors,
9   remember the former things of
      old;
for I am God, and there is no
    other;
    I am God, and there is no one
      like me,
10 declaring the end from the
    beginning
    and from ancient times things
      not yet done,
saying, "My purpose shall stand,
    and I will fulfill my intention,"
11 calling a bird of prey from the
    east,
    the man for my purpose from
      a far country.
I have spoken, and I will bring it
    to pass;

z Meaning of Heb uncertain

I
S
A
I
A
H

I have planned, and I will do
it.
12 Listen to me, you stubborn of
heart,
you who are far from
deliverance:
13 I bring near my deliverance, it is
not far off,
and my salvation will not
tarry;
I will put salvation in Zion,
for Israel my glory.

The Humiliation of Babylon

47 Come down and sit in the
dust,
virgin daughter Babylon!
Sit on the ground without a
throne,
daughter Chal·dē′a!
For you shall no more be called
tender and delicate.
2 Take the millstones and grind
meal,
remove your veil,
strip off your robe, uncover your
legs,
pass through the rivers.
3 Your nakedness shall be
uncovered,
and your shame shall be seen.
I will take vengeance,
and I will spare no one.
4 Our Redeemer—the LORD of
hosts is his name—
is the Holy One of Israel.

5 Sit in silence, and go into
darkness,
daughter Chal·dē′a!
For you shall no more be called
the mistress of kingdoms.
6 I was angry with my people,
I profaned my heritage;
I gave them into your hand,
you showed them no mercy;
on the aged you made your yoke
exceedingly heavy.
7 You said, "I shall be mistress
forever,"
so that you did not lay these
things to heart
or remember their end.

8 Now therefore hear this, you
lover of pleasures,
who sit securely,
who say in your heart,
"I am, and there is no one
besides me;

I shall not sit as a widow
or know the loss of
children"—
9 both these things shall come
upon you
in a moment, in one day:
the loss of children and
widowhood
shall come upon you in full
measure,
in spite of your many sorceries
and the great power of your
enchantments.

10 You felt secure in your
wickedness;
you said, "No one sees me."
Your wisdom and your
knowledge
led you astray,
and you said in your heart,
"I am, and there is no one
besides me."
11 But evil shall come upon you,
which you cannot charm
away;
disaster shall fall upon you,
which you will not be able to
ward off;
and ruin shall come on you
suddenly,
of which you know nothing.

12 Stand fast in your enchantments
and your many sorceries,
with which you have labored
from your youth;
perhaps you may be able to
succeed,
perhaps you may inspire
terror.
13 You are wearied with your many
consultations;
let those who study[a] the
heavens
stand up and save you,
those who gaze at the stars,
and at each new moon predict
what[b] shall befall you.

14 See, they are like stubble,
the fire consumes them;
they cannot deliver themselves
from the power of the flame.
No coal for warming oneself is
this,
no fire to sit before!
15 Such to you are those with
whom you have labored,

---

[a] Meaning of Heb uncertain   [b] Gk Syr
Compare Vg: Heb *from what*

who have trafficked with you
　　from your youth;
they all wander about in their
　　own paths;
　　there is no one to save you.

God the Creator and Redeemer

48 Hear this, O house of Jacob,
　　who are called by the name
　　　of Israel,
　　and who came forth from the
　　　loins*c* of Judah;
who swear by the name of the
　　LORD,
　　and invoke the God of Israel,
　　but not in truth or right.

2 For they call themselves after
　　　the holy city,
　　and lean on the God of Israel;
　　the LORD of hosts is his name.

3 The former things I declared
　　　long ago,
　　they went out from my mouth
　　　and I made them known;
　　then suddenly I did them and
　　　they came to pass.
4 Because I know that you are
　　　obstinate,
　　and your neck is an iron sinew
　　and your forehead brass,
5 I declared them to you from long
　　　ago,
　　before they came to pass I
　　　announced them to you,
so that you would not say, "My
　　　idol did them,
　　my carved image and my cast
　　　image commanded them."

6 You have heard; now see all
　　　this;
　　and will you not declare it?
From this time forward I make
　　　you hear new things,
　　hidden things that you have
　　　not known.
7 They are created now, not long
　　　ago;
　　before today you have never
　　　heard of them,
　　so that you could not say, "I
　　　already knew them."
8 You have never heard, you have
　　　never known,
　　from of old your ear has not
　　　been opened.
For I knew that you would deal
　　　very treacherously,
　　and that from birth you were
　　　called a rebel.

9 For my name's sake I defer my
　　　anger,
　　for the sake of my praise I
　　　restrain it for you,
　　so that I may not cut you off.
10 See, I have refined you, but not
　　　like*d* silver;
　　I have tested you in the
　　　furnace of adversity.
11 For my own sake, for my own
　　　sake, I do it,
　　for why should my name*e* be
　　　profaned?
　　My glory I will not give to
　　　another.

12 Listen to me, O Jacob,
　　and Israel, whom I called:
I am He; I am the first,
　　and I am the last.
13 My hand laid the foundation of
　　　the earth,
　　and my right hand spread out
　　　the heavens;
when I summon them,
　　they stand at attention.

14 Assemble, all of you, and hear!
　　Who among them has declared
　　　these things?
The LORD loves him;
　　he shall perform his purpose
　　　on Babylon,
　　and his arm shall be against
　　　the Chal·dē'ans.
15 I, even I, have spoken and called
　　　him,
　　I have brought him, and he
　　　will prosper in his way.
16 Draw near to me, hear this!
　　From the beginning I have not
　　　spoken in secret,
　　from the time it came to be I
　　　have been there.
And now the Lord GOD has sent
　　　me and his spirit.

17 Thus says the LORD,
　　your Redeemer, the Holy One
　　　of Israel:
I am the LORD your God,
　　who teaches you for your own
　　　good,
　　who leads you in the way you
　　　should go.
18 O that you had paid attention to
　　　my commandments!
　　Then your prosperity would
　　　have been like a river,

---

*c*Cn: Heb *waters*　*d*Cn: Heb *with*
*e*Gk Old Latin: Heb *for why should it*

and your success like the
waves of the sea;
19 your offspring would have been
like the sand,
and your descendants like its
grains;
their name would never be cut
off
or destroyed from before me.

20 Go out from Babylon, flee from
Chal·dē′a,
declare this with a shout of
joy, proclaim it,
send it forth to the end of the
earth;
say, "The LORD has redeemed
his servant Jacob!"
21 They did not thirst when he led
them through the deserts;
he made water flow for them
from the rock;
he split open the rock and the
water gushed out.

22 "There is no peace," says the
LORD, "for the wicked."

The Servant's Mission

49 Listen to me, O coastlands,
pay attention, you peoples
from far away!
The LORD called me before I was
born,
while I was in my mother's
womb he named me.
2 He made my mouth like a sharp
sword,
in the shadow of his hand he
hid me;
he made me a polished arrow,
in his quiver he hid me away.
3 And he said to me, "You are my
servant,
Israel, in whom I will be
glorified."
4 But I said, "I have labored in
vain,
I have spent my strength for
nothing and vanity;
yet surely my cause is with the
LORD,
and my reward with my God."

5 And now the LORD says,
who formed me in the womb
to be his servant,
to bring Jacob back to him,
and that Israel might be
gathered to him,

for I am honored in the sight of
the LORD,
and my God has become my
strength—
6 he says,
"It is too light a thing that you
should be my servant
to raise up the tribes of Jacob
and to restore the survivors of
Israel;
I will give you as a light to the
nations,
that my salvation may reach to
the end of the earth."

7 Thus says the LORD,
the Redeemer of Israel and his
Holy One,
to one deeply despised, abhorred
by the nations,
the slave of rulers,
"Kings shall see and stand up,
princes, and they shall
prostrate themselves,
because of the LORD, who is
faithful,
the Holy One of Israel, who
has chosen you."

Zion's Children to Be Brought Home

8 Thus says the LORD:
In a time of favor I have
answered you,
on a day of salvation I have
helped you;
I have kept you and given you
as a covenant to the people,[f]
to establish the land,
to apportion the desolate
heritages;
9 saying to the prisoners, "Come
out,"
to those who are in darkness,
"Show yourselves."
They shall feed along the ways,
on all the bare heights[g] shall
be their pasture;
10 they shall not hunger or thirst,
neither scorching wind nor
sun shall strike them down,
for he who has pity on them will
lead them,
and by springs of water will
guide them.
11 And I will turn all my mountains
into a road,
and my highways shall be
raised up.

[f]Meaning of Heb uncertain   [g]Or the
trails

12 Lo, these shall come from far
        away,
    and lo, these from the north
            and from the west,
    and these from the land of
            Sў·ē′nē.ʰ

13 Sing for joy, O heavens, and
            exult, O earth;
    break forth, O mountains, into
            singing!
    For the LORD has comforted his
            people,
        and will have compassion on
            his suffering ones.

14 But Zion said, "The LORD has
            forsaken me,
        my Lord has forgotten me."
15 Can a woman forget her nursing
            child,
        or show no compassion for the
            child of her womb?
    Even these may forget,
        yet I will not forget you.
16 See, I have inscribed you on the
            palms of my hands;
        your walls are continually
            before me.
17 Your builders outdo your
            destroyers,ⁱ
        and those who laid you waste
            go away from you.
18 Lift up your eyes all around and
            see;
        they all gather, they come to
            you.
    As I live, says the LORD,
        you shall put all of them on
            like an ornament,
        and like a bride you shall bind
            them on.

19 Surely your waste and your
            desolate places
        and your devastated land—
    surely now you will be too
            crowded for your
            inhabitants,
        and those who swallowed you
            up will be far away.
20 The children born in the time of
            your bereavement
        will yet say in your hearing:
    "The place is too crowded for
            me;
        make room for me to settle."
21 Then you will say in your heart,
    "Who has borne me these?
    I was bereaved and barren,
            exiled and put away—
        so who has reared these?

I was left all alone—
        where then have these come
            from?"

22 Thus says the Lord GOD:
    I will soon lift up my hand to the
            nations,
        and raise my signal to the
            peoples;
    and they shall bring your sons in
            their bosom,
        and your daughters shall be
            carried on their shoulders.
23 Kings shall be your foster
            fathers,
        and their queens your nursing
            mothers.
    With their faces to the ground
            they shall bow down to
            you,
        and lick the dust of your feet.
    Then you will know that I am
            the LORD;
        those who wait for me shall
            not be put to shame.

24 Can the prey be taken from the
            mighty,
        or the captives of a tyrantʲ be
            rescued?
25 But thus says the LORD:
    Even the captives of the mighty
            shall be taken,
        and the prey of the tyrant be
            rescued;
    for I will contend with those
            who contend with you,
        and I will save your children.
26 I will make your oppressors eat
            their own flesh,
        and they shall be drunk with
            their own blood as with
            wine.
    Then all flesh shall know
        that I am the LORD your
            Savior,
        and your Redeemer, the
            Mighty One of Jacob.

50 Thus says the LORD:
    Where is your mother's bill
            of divorce
    with which I put her away?
    Or which of my creditors is it
        to whom I have sold you?
    No, because of your sins you
            were sold,

ʰ Q Ms: MT *Sinim*   ⁱ Or *Your children
come swiftly; your destroyers*   ʲ Q Ms
Syr Vg: MT *of a righteous person*

and for your transgressions
　　your mother was put away.
2 Why was no one there when I
　　came?
　　Why did no one answer when
　　　I called?
　Is my hand shortened, that it
　　cannot redeem?
　　Or have I no power to deliver?
　By my rebuke I dry up the sea,
　　I make the rivers a desert;
　their fish stink for lack of water,
　　and die of thirst.*k*
3 I clothe the heavens with
　　blackness,
　　and make sackcloth their
　　　covering.

The Servant's Humiliation and Vindication

4 The Lord GOD has given me
　　the tongue of a teacher,*l*
　that I may know how to sustain
　　the weary with a word.
　Morning by morning he
　　wakens—
　　wakens my ear
　to listen as those who are
　　taught.
5 The Lord GOD has opened my
　　ear,
　　and I was not rebellious,
　　I did not turn backward.
6 I gave my back to those who
　　struck me,
　　and my cheeks to those who
　　　pulled out the beard;
　I did not hide my face
　　from insult and spitting.

7 The Lord GOD helps me;
　　therefore I have not been
　　　disgraced;
　therefore I have set my face like
　　flint,
　　and I know that I shall not be
　　　put to shame;
8 he who vindicates me is near.
　Who will contend with me?
　　Let us stand up together.
　Who are my adversaries?
　　Let them confront me.
9 It is the Lord GOD who helps
　　me;
　　who will declare me guilty?
　All of them will wear out like a
　　garment;
　　the moth will eat them up.

10 Who among you fears the LORD

and obeys the voice of his
　　servant,
　who walks in darkness
　　and has no light,
　yet trusts in the name of the
　　LORD
　　and relies upon his God?
11 But all of you are kindlers of
　　fire,
　　lighters of firebrands.*m*
　Walk in the flame of your fire,
　　and among the brands that
　　　you have kindled!
　This is what you shall have from
　　my hand:
　　you shall lie down in torment.

Blessings in Store for God's People
(Cp Gen 12.1–3)

51 Listen to me, you that pursue
　　righteousness,
　　you that seek the LORD.
　Look to the rock from which you
　　were hewn,
　　and to the quarry from which
　　　you were dug.
2 Look to Abraham your father
　　and to Sarah who bore you;
　for he was but one when I called
　　him,
　　but I blessed him and made
　　　him many.
3 For the LORD will comfort Zion;
　　he will comfort all her waste
　　　places,
　and will make her wilderness
　　like Eden,
　　her desert like the garden of
　　　the LORD;
　joy and gladness will be found in
　　her,
　　thanksgiving and the voice of
　　　song.

4 Listen to me, my people,
　　and give heed to me, my
　　　nation;
　for a teaching will go out from
　　me,
　　and my justice for a light to
　　　the peoples.
5 I will bring near my deliverance
　　swiftly,
　　my salvation has gone out
　　and my arms will rule the
　　　peoples;
　　the coastlands wait for me,

---

k Or *die on the thirsty ground*
l Cn: Heb *of those who are taught*
m Syr: Heb *you gird yourselves with firebrands*

and for my arm they hope.
6 Lift up your eyes to the heavens,
   and look at the earth beneath;
for the heavens will vanish like
      smoke,
   the earth will wear out like a
      garment,
   and those who live on it will
      die like gnats;[n]
but my salvation will be forever,
   and my deliverance will never
      be ended.

7 Listen to me, you who know
      righteousness,
   you people who have my
      teaching in your hearts;
do not fear the reproach of
      others,
   and do not be dismayed when
      they revile you.
8 For the moth will eat them up
      like a garment,
   and the worm will eat them
      like wool;
but my deliverance will be
      forever,
   and my salvation to all
      generations.

9 Awake, awake, put on strength,
      O arm of the LORD!
Awake, as in days of old,
   the generations of long ago!
Was it not you who cut Rā′hab
      in pieces,
   who pierced the dragon?
10 Was it not you who dried up the
      sea,
   the waters of the great deep;
who made the depths of the sea
      a way
   for the redeemed to cross
      over?
11 So the ransomed of the LORD
      shall return,
   and come to Zion with
      singing;
everlasting joy shall be upon
      their heads;
   they shall obtain joy and
      gladness,
   and sorrow and sighing shall
      flee away.

12 I, I am he who comforts you;
   why then are you afraid of a
      mere mortal who must die,
   a human being who fades like
      grass?
13 You have forgotten the LORD,
      your Maker,

who stretched out the heavens
   and laid the foundations of the
      earth.
You fear continually all day long
   because of the fury of the
      oppressor,
who is bent on destruction.
   But where is the fury of the
      oppressor?
14 The oppressed shall speedily be
      released;
   they shall not die and go down
      to the Pit,
   nor shall they lack bread.
15 For I am the LORD your God,
   who stirs up the sea so that its
      waves roar—
   the LORD of hosts is his name.
16 I have put my words in your
      mouth,
   and hidden you in the shadow
      of my hand,
stretching out[o] the heavens
   and laying the foundations of
      the earth,
   and saying to Zion, "You are
      my people."

17 Rouse yourself, rouse yourself!
      Stand up, O Jerusalem,
you who have drunk at the hand
      of the LORD
   the cup of his wrath,
who have drunk to the dregs
   the bowl of staggering.
18 There is no one to guide her
   among all the children she has
      borne;
there is no one to take her by
      the hand
   among all the children she has
      brought up.
19 These two things have befallen
      you
   —who will grieve with you?—
devastation and destruction,
      famine and sword—
   who will comfort you?[p]
20 Your children have fainted,
   they lie at the head of every
      street
   like an antelope in a net;
they are full of the wrath of the
      LORD,
   the rebuke of your God.

21 Therefore hear this, you who are
      wounded,[q]

n Or in like manner   o Syr: Heb planting
p Q Ms Gk Syr Vg: MT how may I
comfort you?   q Or humbled

who are drunk, but not with
wine:

22 Thus says your Sovereign, the
LORD,
your God who pleads the
cause of his people:
See, I have taken from your
hand the cup of staggering;
you shall drink no more
from the bowl of my wrath.

23 And I will put it into the hand of
your tormentors,
who have said to you,
"Bow down, that we may walk
on you";
and you have made your back
like the ground
and like the street for them to
walk on.

Let Zion Rejoice

52 Awake, awake,
put on your strength, O Zion!
Put on your beautiful garments,
O Jerusalem, the holy city;
for the uncircumcised and the
unclean
shall enter you no more.

2 Shake yourself from the dust,
rise up,
O captive[r] Jerusalem;
loose the bonds from your neck,
O captive daughter Zion!

3 For thus says the LORD: You were
sold for nothing, and you shall be redeemed without money. [4] For thus says
the Lord GOD: Long ago, my people
went down into Egypt to reside there
as aliens; the Assyrian, too, has oppressed them without cause. [5] Now
therefore what am I doing here, says
the LORD, seeing that my people are
taken away without cause? Their rulers howl, says the LORD, and continually, all day long, my name is despised.
[6] Therefore my people shall know my
name; therefore in that day they shall
know that it is I who speak; here am I.

7 How beautiful upon the
mountains
are the feet of the messenger
who announces peace,
who brings good news,
who announces salvation,
who says to Zion, "Your God
reigns."

8 Listen! Your sentinels lift up
their voices,
together they sing for joy;

for in plain sight they see
the return of the LORD to Zion.

9 Break forth together into
singing,
you ruins of Jerusalem;
for the LORD has comforted his
people,
he has redeemed Jerusalem.

10 The LORD has bared his holy
arm
before the eyes of all the
nations;
and all the ends of the earth
shall see
the salvation of our God.

11 Depart, depart, go out from
there!
Touch no unclean thing;
go out from the midst of it,
purify yourselves,
you who carry the vessels of
the LORD.

12 For you shall not go out in haste,
and you shall not go in flight;
for the LORD will go before you,
and the God of Israel will be
your rear guard.

The Suffering Servant

13 See, my servant shall prosper;
he shall be exalted and lifted
up,
and shall be very high.

14 Just as there were many who
were astonished at him[s]
—so marred was his
appearance, beyond human
semblance,
and his form beyond that of
mortals—

15 so he shall startle[t] many
nations;
kings shall shut their mouths
because of him;
for that which had not been told
them they shall see,
and that which they had not
heard they shall
contemplate.

53 Who has believed what we
have heard?
And to whom has the arm of
the LORD been revealed?

2 For he grew up before him like a
young plant,
and like a root out of dry
ground;

r Cn: Heb *rise up, sit*   s Syr Tg: Heb *you*
t Meaning of Heb uncertain

he had no form or majesty that
  we should look at him,
  nothing in his appearance that
  we should desire him.
3 He was despised and rejected by
    others;
  a man of suffering[u] and
    acquainted with infirmity;
and as one from whom others
    hide their faces[v]
  he was despised, and we held
    him of no account.

4 Surely he has borne our
    infirmities
  and carried our diseases;
yet we accounted him stricken,
  struck down by God, and
    afflicted.
5 But he was wounded for our
    transgressions,
  crushed for our iniquities;
upon him was the punishment
    that made us whole,
  and by his bruises we are
    healed.
6 All we like sheep have gone
    astray;
  we have all turned to our own
    way,
and the LORD has laid on him
  the iniquity of us all.

7 He was oppressed, and he was
    afflicted,
  yet he did not open his mouth;
like a lamb that is led to the
    slaughter,
  and like a sheep that before its
    shearers is silent,
  so he did not open his mouth.
8 By a perversion of justice he was
    taken away.
  Who could have imagined his
    future?
For he was cut off from the land
    of the living,
  stricken for the transgression
    of my people.
9 They made his grave with the
    wicked
  and his tomb[w] with the rich,[x]
although he had done no
    violence,
  and there was no deceit in his
    mouth.

10 Yet it was the will of the LORD
    to crush him with pain.[y]
When you make his life an
  offering for sin,[z]

he shall see his offspring, and
  shall prolong his days;
through him the will of the LORD
  shall prosper.
11 Out of his anguish he shall see
    light;[a]
he shall find satisfaction through
  his knowledge.
  The righteous one,[b] my
    servant, shall make many
    righteous,
  and he shall bear their
    iniquities.
12 Therefore I will allot him a
    portion with the great,
  and he shall divide the spoil
    with the strong;
because he poured out himself to
    death,
  and was numbered with the
    transgressors;
yet he bore the sin of many,
  and made intercession for the
    transgressors.

The Eternal Covenant of Peace

54 Sing, O barren one who did
    not bear;
  burst into song and shout,
  you who have not been in
    labor!
For the children of the desolate
    woman will be more
  than the children of her that is
    married, says the LORD.
2 Enlarge the site of your tent,
  and let the curtains of your
    habitations be stretched
    out;
do not hold back; lengthen your
    cords
  and strengthen your stakes.
3 For you will spread out to the
    right and to the left,
  and your descendants will
    possess the nations
  and will settle the desolate
    towns.

4 Do not fear, for you will not be
    ashamed;

[u]Or *a man of sorrows*   [v]Or *as one who
hides his face from us*   [w]Q Ms: MT *and
in his death*   [x]Cn: Heb *with a rich
person*   [y]Or *by disease*; meaning of
Heb uncertain   [z]Meaning of Heb
uncertain   [a]Q Mss: MT lacks *light*
[b]Or *and he shall find satisfaction.
Through his knowledge, the righteous
one*

do not be discouraged, for you
will not suffer disgrace;
for you will forget the shame of
your youth,
and the disgrace of your
widowhood you will
remember no more.
5 For your Maker is your husband,
the LORD of hosts is his name;
the Holy One of Israel is your
Redeemer,
the God of the whole earth he
is called.
6 For the LORD has called you
like a wife forsaken and
grieved in spirit,
like the wife of a man's youth
when she is cast off,
says your God.
7 For a brief moment I abandoned
you,
but with great compassion I
will gather you.
8 In overflowing wrath for a
moment
I hid my face from you,
but with everlasting love I will
have compassion on you,
says the LORD, your
Redeemer.

9 This is like the days of Noah to
me:
Just as I swore that the waters
of Noah
would never again go over the
earth,
so I have sworn that I will not
be angry with you
and will not rebuke you.
10 For the mountains may depart
and the hills be removed,
but my steadfast love shall not
depart from you,
and my covenant of peace
shall not be removed,
says the LORD, who has
compassion on you.

11 O afflicted one, storm-tossed,
and not comforted,
I am about to set your stones
in antimony,
and lay your foundations with
sapphires.c
12 I will make your pinnacles of
rubies,
your gates of jewels,
and all your wall of precious
stones.
13 All your children shall be taught
by the LORD,
and great shall be the
prosperity of your children.
14 In righteousness you shall be
established;
you shall be far from
oppression, for you shall
not fear;
and from terror, for it shall not
come near you.
15 If anyone stirs up strife,
it is not from me;
whoever stirs up strife with you
shall fall because of you.
16 See it is I who have created the
smith
who blows the fire of coals,
and produces a weapon fit for
its purpose;
I have also created the ravager
to destroy.
17 No weapon that is fashioned
against you shall prosper,
and you shall confute every
tongue that rises against
you in judgment.
This is the heritage of the
servants of the LORD
and their vindication from me,
says the LORD.

An Invitation to Abundant Life

55 Ho, everyone who thirsts,
come to the waters;
and you that have no money,
come, buy and eat!
Come, buy wine and milk
without money and without
price.
2 Why do you spend your money
for that which is not bread,
and your labor for that which
does not satisfy?
Listen carefully to me, and eat
what is good,
and delight yourselves in rich
food.
3 Incline your ear, and come to
me;
listen, so that you may live.
I will make with you an
everlasting covenant,
my steadfast, sure love for
David.
4 See, I made him a witness to the
peoples,
a leader and commander for
the peoples.
5 See, you shall call nations that
you do not know,

c Or *lapis lazuli*

and nations that do not know
    you shall run to you,
because of the LORD your God,
    the Holy One of Israel,
    for he has glorified you.

6 Seek the LORD while he may be
        found,
    call upon him while he is near;
7 let the wicked forsake their way,
    and the unrighteous their
        thoughts;
let them return to the LORD, that
        he may have mercy on
        them,
    and to our God, for he will
        abundantly pardon.
8 For my thoughts are not your
        thoughts,
    nor are your ways my ways,
        says the LORD.
9 For as the heavens are higher
        than the earth,
    so are my ways higher than
        your ways
    and my thoughts than your
        thoughts.

10 For as the rain and the snow
        come down from heaven,
    and do not return there until
        they have watered the
        earth,
making it bring forth and sprout,
    giving seed to the sower and
        bread to the eater,
11 so shall my word be that goes
        out from my mouth;
    it shall not return to me
        empty,
but it shall accomplish that
        which I purpose,
    and succeed in the thing for
        which I sent it.

12 For you shall go out in joy,
    and be led back in peace;
the mountains and the hills
        before you
    shall burst into song,
    and all the trees of the field
        shall clap their hands.
13 Instead of the thorn shall come
        up the cypress;
    instead of the brier shall come
        up the myrtle;
and it shall be to the LORD for a
        memorial,
    for an everlasting sign that
        shall not be cut off.

The Covenant Extended
to All Who Obey

56 Thus says the LORD:
    Maintain justice, and do
        what is right,
for soon my salvation will come,
    and my deliverance be
        revealed.

2 Happy is the mortal who does
        this,
    the one who holds it fast,
who keeps the sabbath, not
        profaning it,
    and refrains from doing any
        evil.

3 Do not let the foreigner joined to
        the LORD say,
    "The LORD will surely separate
        me from his people";
and do not let the eunuch say,
    "I am just a dry tree."
4 For thus says the LORD:
To the eunuchs who keep my
        sabbaths,
    who choose the things that
        please me
    and hold fast my covenant,
5 I will give, in my house and
        within my walls,
    a monument and a name
    better than sons and
        daughters;
I will give them an everlasting
        name
    that shall not be cut off.

6 And the foreigners who join
        themselves to the LORD,
    to minister to him, to love the
        name of the LORD,
    and to be his servants,
all who keep the sabbath, and do
        not profane it,
    and hold fast my covenant—
7 these I will bring to my holy
        mountain,
    and make them joyful in my
        house of prayer;
their burnt offerings and their
        sacrifices
    will be accepted on my altar;
for my house shall be called a
        house of prayer
    for all peoples.
8 Thus says the Lord GOD,
    who gathers the outcasts of
        Israel,
I will gather others to them

besides those already
gathered.[d]

The Corruption of Israel's Rulers

9 All you wild animals,
    all you wild animals in the
        forest, come to devour!
10 Israel's[e] sentinels are blind,
    they are all without
        knowledge;
they are all silent dogs
    that cannot bark;
dreaming, lying down,
    loving to slumber.
11 The dogs have a mighty
        appetite;
    they never have enough.
The shepherds also have no
        understanding;
    they have all turned to their
        own way,
    to their own gain, one and all.
12 "Come," they say, "let us[f] get
        wine;
    let us fill ourselves with strong
        drink.
And tomorrow will be like today,
    great beyond measure."

Israel's Futile Idolatry

57 The righteous perish,
    and no one takes it to heart;
the devout are taken away,
    while no one understands.
For the righteous are taken away
        from calamity,
2   and they enter into peace;
those who walk uprightly
    will rest on their couches.
3 But as for you, come here,
    you children of a sorceress,
    you offspring of an adulterer
        and a whore.[g]
4 Whom are you mocking?
    Against whom do you open
        your mouth wide
    and stick out your tongue?
Are you not children of
        transgression,
    the offspring of deceit —
5 you that burn with lust among
        the oaks,
    under every green tree;
you that slaughter your children
        in the valleys,
    under the clefts of the rocks?
6 Among the smooth stones of the
        valley is your portion;
    they, they, are your lot;
to them you have poured out a
        drink offering,

you have brought a grain
    offering.
Shall I be appeased for these
    things?
7 Upon a high and lofty mountain
    you have set your bed,
    and there you went up to offer
        sacrifice.
8 Behind the door and the
        doorpost
    you have set up your symbol;
for, in deserting me,[h] you have
        uncovered your bed,
    you have gone up to it,
    you have made it wide;
and you have made a bargain
        for yourself with them,
    you have loved their bed,
    you have gazed on their
        nakedness.[i]
9 You journeyed to Mō'lech[j] with
        oil,
    and multiplied your perfumes;
you sent your envoys far away,
    and sent down even to Shē'ōl.
10 You grew weary from your
        many wanderings,
    but you did not say, "It is
        useless."
You found your desire rekindled,
    and so you did not weaken.

11 Whom did you dread and fear
        so that you lied,
and did not remember me
    or give me a thought?
Have I not kept silent and closed
        my eyes,[k]
    and so you do not fear me?
12 I will concede your
        righteousness and your
        works,
    but they will not help you.
13 When you cry out, let your
        collection of idols deliver
        you!
The wind will carry them off,
    a breath will take them away.
But whoever takes refuge in me
        shall possess the land
    and inherit my holy mountain.

---

[d] Heb besides his gathered ones
[e] Heb His   [f] Q Ms Syr Vg Tg: MT me
[g] Heb an adulterer and she plays the
whore   [h] Meaning of Heb uncertain
[i] Or their phallus; Heb the hand
[j] Or the king   [k] Gk Vg: Heb silent even
for a long time

A Promise of Help and Healing

14 It shall be said,
"Build up, build up, prepare the
way,
remove every obstruction from
my people's way."
15 For thus says the high and lofty
one
who inhabits eternity, whose
name is Holy:
I dwell in the high and holy
place,
and also with those who are
contrite and humble in
spirit,
to revive the spirit of the
humble,
and to revive the heart of the
contrite.
16 For I will not continually accuse,
nor will I always be angry;
for then the spirits would grow
faint before me,
even the souls that I have
made.
17 Because of their wicked
covetousness I was angry;
I struck them, I hid and was
angry;
but they kept turning back to
their own ways.
18 I have seen their ways, but I will
heal them;
I will lead them and repay
them with comfort,
creating for their mourners the
fruit of the lips.*l*
19 Peace, peace, to the far and the
near, says the LORD;
and I will heal them.
20 But the wicked are like the
tossing sea
that cannot keep still;
its waters toss up mire and
mud.
21 There is no peace, says my God,
for the wicked.

False and True Worship

58 Shout out, do not hold back!
Lift up your voice like a
trumpet!
Announce to my people their
rebellion,
to the house of Jacob their
sins.
2 Yet day after day they seek me
and delight to know my ways,
as if they were a nation that
practiced righteousness

and did not forsake the
ordinance of their God;
they ask of me righteous
judgments,
they delight to draw near to
God.
3 "Why do we fast, but you do not
see?
Why humble ourselves, but
you do not notice?"
Look, you serve your own
interest on your fast day,
and oppress all your workers.
4 Look, you fast only to quarrel
and to fight
and to strike with a wicked
fist.
Such fasting as you do today
will not make your voice
heard on high.
5 Is such the fast that I choose,
a day to humble oneself?
Is it to bow down the head like a
bulrush,
and to lie in sackcloth and
ashes?
Will you call this a fast,
a day acceptable to the LORD?

6 Is not this the fast that I choose:
to loose the bonds of injustice,
to undo the thongs of the
yoke,
to let the oppressed go free,
and to break every yoke?
7 Is it not to share your bread with
the hungry,
and bring the homeless poor
into your house;
when you see the naked, to
cover them,
and not to hide yourself from
your own kin?
8 Then your light shall break forth
like the dawn,
and your healing shall spring
up quickly;
your vindicator*m* shall go before
you,
the glory of the LORD shall be
your rear guard.
9 Then you shall call, and the
LORD will answer;
you shall cry for help, and he
will say, Here I am.

If you remove the yoke from
among you,

*l*Meaning of Heb uncertain
*m*Or *vindication*

I
S
A
I
A
H

the pointing of the finger, the
speaking of evil,
10 if you offer your food to the
hungry
and satisfy the needs of the
afflicted,
then your light shall rise in the
darkness
and your gloom be like the
noonday.
11 The LORD will guide you
continually,
and satisfy your needs in
parched places,
and make your bones strong;
and you shall be like a watered
garden,
like a spring of water,
whose waters never fail.
12 Your ancient ruins shall be
rebuilt;
you shall raise up the
foundations of many
generations;
you shall be called the repairer
of the breach,
the restorer of streets to live
in.
13 If you refrain from trampling the
sabbath,
from pursuing your own
interests on my holy day;
if you call the sabbath a delight
and the holy day of the LORD
honorable;
if you honor it, not going your
own ways,
serving your own interests, or
pursuing your own
affairs;[n]
14 then you shall take delight in the
LORD,
and I will make you ride upon
the heights of the earth;
I will feed you with the heritage
of your ancestor Jacob,
for the mouth of the LORD has
spoken.

Injustice and Oppression to Be Punished

59 See, the LORD's hand is not
too short to save,
nor his ear too dull to hear.
2 Rather, your iniquities have been
barriers
between you and your God,
and your sins have hidden his
face from you
so that he does not hear.

3 For your hands are defiled with
blood,
and your fingers with iniquity;
your lips have spoken lies,
your tongue mutters
wickedness.
4 No one brings suit justly,
no one goes to law honestly;
they rely on empty pleas, they
speak lies,
conceiving mischief and
begetting iniquity.
5 They hatch adders' eggs,
and weave the spider's web;
whoever eats their eggs dies,
and the crushed egg hatches
out a viper.
6 Their webs cannot serve as
clothing;
they cannot cover themselves
with what they make.
Their works are works of
iniquity,
and deeds of violence are in
their hands.
7 Their feet run to evil,
and they rush to shed innocent
blood;
their thoughts are thoughts of
iniquity,
desolation and destruction are
in their highways.
8 The way of peace they do not
know,
and there is no justice in their
paths.
Their roads they have made
crooked;
no one who walks in them
knows peace.
9 Therefore justice is far from us,
and righteousness does not
reach us;
we wait for light, and lo! there is
darkness;
and for brightness, but we
walk in gloom.
10 We grope like the blind along a
wall,
groping like those who have
no eyes;
we stumble at noon as in the
twilight,
among the vigorous[o] as
though we were dead.
11 We all growl like bears;
like doves we moan
mournfully.

[n] Heb or speaking words　　　[o] Meaning of Heb uncertain

We wait for justice, but there is
none;
for salvation, but it is far from
us.
12 For our transgressions before
you are many,
and our sins testify against us.
Our transgressions indeed are
with us,
and we know our iniquities:
13 transgressing, and denying the
LORD,
and turning away from
following our God,
talking oppression and revolt,
conceiving lying words and
uttering them from the
heart.
14 Justice is turned back,
and righteousness stands at a
distance;
for truth stumbles in the public
square,
and uprightness cannot enter.
15 Truth is lacking,
and whoever turns from evil is
despoiled.

The LORD saw it, and it
displeased him
that there was no justice.
16 He saw that there was no one,
and was appalled that there
was no one to intervene;
so his own arm brought him
victory,
and his righteousness upheld
him.
17 He put on righteousness like a
breastplate,
and a helmet of salvation on
his head;
he put on garments of vengeance
for clothing,
and wrapped himself in fury
as in a mantle.
18 According to their deeds, so will
he repay;
wrath to his adversaries,
requital to his enemies;
to the coastlands he will
render requital.
19 So those in the west shall fear
the name of the LORD,
and those in the east, his
glory;
for he will come like a pent-up
stream
that the wind of the LORD
drives on.

20 And he will come to Zion as
Redeemer,
to those in Jacob who turn
from transgression, says
the LORD.
21 And as for me, this is my covenant
with them, says the LORD: my spirit
that is upon you, and my words that I
have put in your mouth, shall not depart out of your mouth, or out of the
mouths of your children, or out of the
mouths of your children's children,
says the LORD, from now on and forever.

The Ingathering of the Dispersed

60 Arise, shine; for your light
has come,
and the glory of the LORD has
risen upon you.
2 For darkness shall cover the
earth,
and thick darkness the
peoples;
but the LORD will arise upon
you,
and his glory will appear over
you.
3 Nations shall come to your light,
and kings to the brightness of
your dawn.

4 Lift up your eyes and look
around;
they all gather together, they
come to you;
your sons shall come from far
away,
and your daughters shall be
carried on their nurses'
arms.
5 Then you shall see and be
radiant;
your heart shall thrill and
rejoice,*p*
because the abundance of the
sea shall be brought to
you,
the wealth of the nations shall
come to you.
6 A multitude of camels shall
cover you,
the young camels of Mid'i·an
and E'phah;
all those from She'ba shall
come.
They shall bring gold and
frankincense,

ISAIAH

p Heb *be enlarged*

and shall proclaim the praise
    of the LORD.

7 All the flocks of Kē′dar shall be
    gathered to you,
    the rams of Ne·bā′i·oth shall
      minister to you;
  they shall be acceptable on my
      altar,
    and I will glorify my glorious
      house.

8 Who are these that fly like a
    cloud,
    and like doves to their
      windows?

9 For the coastlands shall wait for
    me,
    the ships of Tar′shish first,
  to bring your children from far
      away,
    their silver and gold with
      them,
  for the name of the LORD your
      God,
    and for the Holy One of Israel,
      because he has glorified you.

10 Foreigners shall build up your
      walls,
    and their kings shall minister
      to you;
  for in my wrath I struck you
      down,
    but in my favor I have had
      mercy on you.

11 Your gates shall always be open;
    day and night they shall not
      be shut,
  so that nations shall bring you
      their wealth,
    with their kings led in
      procession.

12 For the nation and kingdom
    that will not serve you shall
      perish;
    those nations shall be utterly
      laid waste.

13 The glory of Lebanon shall come
    to you,
    the cypress, the plane, and the
      pine,
  to beautify the place of my
      sanctuary;
    and I will glorify where my
      feet rest.

14 The descendants of those who
      oppressed you
    shall come bending low to you,
  and all who despised you
    shall bow down at your feet;
  they shall call you the City of
    the LORD,

the Zion of the Holy One of
  Israel.

15 Whereas you have been
    forsaken and hated,
    with no one passing through,
  I will make you majestic forever,
    a joy from age to age.

16 You shall suck the milk of
      nations,
    you shall suck the breasts of
      kings;
  and you shall know that I, the
      LORD, am your Savior
    and your Redeemer, the
      Mighty One of Jacob.

17 Instead of bronze I will bring
      gold,
    instead of iron I will bring
      silver;
  instead of wood, bronze,
    instead of stones, iron.
  I will appoint Peace as your
      overseer
    and Righteousness as your
      taskmaster.

18 Violence shall no more be heard
    in your land,
    devastation or destruction
      within your borders;
  you shall call your walls
      Salvation,
    and your gates Praise.

God the Glory of Zion

19 The sun shall no longer be
    your light by day,
  nor for brightness shall the
      moon
    give light to you by night;*q*
  but the LORD will be your
      everlasting light,
    and your God will be your
      glory.

20 Your sun shall no more go
      down,
    or your moon withdraw itself;
  for the LORD will be your
      everlasting light,
    and your days of mourning
      shall be ended.

21 Your people shall all be
      righteous;
    they shall possess the land
      forever.
  They are the shoot that I
    planted, the work of my
      hands,
    so that I might be glorified.

q Q Ms Gk Old Latin Tg: MT lacks *by
night*

22 The least of them shall become a
     clan,
    and the smallest one a mighty
     nation;
  I am the LORD;
    in its time I will accomplish it
     quickly.

The Good News of Deliverance

61 The spirit of the Lord GOD is
   upon me,
    because the LORD has
     anointed me;
  he has sent me to bring good
     news to the oppressed,
  to bind up the brokenhearted,
  to proclaim liberty to the
     captives,
    and release to the prisoners;
2 to proclaim the year of the
     LORD's favor,
    and the day of vengeance of
     our God;
    to comfort all who mourn;
3 to provide for those who mourn
     in Zion—
    to give them a garland instead
     of ashes,
  the oil of gladness instead of
     mourning,
    the mantle of praise instead of
     a faint spirit.
  They will be called oaks of
     righteousness,
    the planting of the LORD, to
     display his glory.
4 They shall build up the ancient
     ruins,
    they shall raise up the former
     devastations;
  they shall repair the ruined
     cities,
    the devastations of many
     generations.

5 Strangers shall stand and feed
     your flocks,
    foreigners shall till your land
     and dress your vines;
6 but you shall be called priests of
     the LORD,
    you shall be named ministers
     of our God;
  you shall enjoy the wealth of the
     nations,
    and in their riches you shall
     glory.
7 Because their[r] shame was
     double,
    and dishonor was proclaimed
     as their lot,

therefore they shall possess a
     double portion;
  everlasting joy shall be theirs.

8 For I the LORD love justice,
    I hate robbery and
     wrongdoing;[s]
  I will faithfully give them their
     recompense,
    and I will make an everlasting
     covenant with them.
9 Their descendants shall be
     known among the nations,
    and their offspring among the
     peoples;
  all who see them shall
     acknowledge
    that they are a people whom
     the LORD has blessed.
10 I will greatly rejoice in the
     LORD,
    my whole being shall exult in
     my God;
  for he has clothed me with the
     garments of salvation,
    he has covered me with the
     robe of righteousness,
  as a bridegroom decks himself
     with a garland,
    and as a bride adorns herself
     with her jewels.
11 For as the earth brings forth its
     shoots,
    and as a garden causes what is
     sown in it to spring up,
  so the Lord GOD will cause
     righteousness and praise
    to spring up before all the
     nations.

The Vindication and Salvation of Zion

62 For Zion's sake I will not
   keep silent,
    and for Jerusalem's sake I will
     not rest,
  until her vindication shines out
     like the dawn,
    and her salvation like a
     burning torch.
2 The nations shall see your
     vindication,
    and all the kings your glory;
  and you shall be called by a new
     name
    that the mouth of the LORD
     will give.
3 You shall be a crown of beauty
     in the hand of the LORD,

___
r Heb your   s Or robbery with a burnt
offering

and a royal diadem in the
hand of your God.
4 You shall no more be termed
Forsaken,[t]
and your land shall no more
be termed Desolate;[u]
but you shall be called My
Delight Is in Her,[v]
and your land Married;[w]
for the LORD delights in you,
and your land shall be
married.
5 For as a young man marries a
young woman,
so shall your builder[x] marry
you,
and as the bridegroom rejoices
over the bride,
so shall your God rejoice over
you.
6 Upon your walls, O Jerusalem,
I have posted sentinels;
all day and all night
they shall never be silent.
You who remind the LORD,
take no rest,
7 and give him no rest
until he establishes Jerusalem
and makes it renowned
throughout the earth.
8 The LORD has sworn by his right
hand
and by his mighty arm:
I will not again give your grain
to be food for your enemies,
and foreigners shall not drink
the wine
for which you have labored;
9 but those who garner it shall
eat it
and praise the LORD,
and those who gather it shall
drink it
in my holy courts.

10 Go through, go through the
gates,
prepare the way for the
people;
build up, build up the highway,
clear it of stones,
lift up an ensign over the
peoples.
11 The LORD has proclaimed
to the end of the earth:
Say to daughter Zion,
"See, your salvation comes;
his reward is with him,
and his recompense before
him."
12 They shall be called, "The Holy
People,

The Redeemed of the LORD";
and you shall be called, "Sought
Out,
A City Not Forsaken."

Vengeance on Edom

63 "Who is this that comes from
Ē'dom,
from Boz'rah in garments
stained crimson?
Who is this so splendidly robed,
marching in his great might?"

"It is I, announcing vindication,
mighty to save."

2 "Why are your robes red,
and your garments like theirs
who tread the wine press?"

3 "I have trodden the wine press
alone,
and from the peoples no one
was with me;
I trod them in my anger
and trampled them in my
wrath;
their juice spattered on my
garments,
and stained all my robes.
4 For the day of vengeance was in
my heart,
and the year for my redeeming
work had come.
5 I looked, but there was no
helper;
I stared, but there was no one
to sustain me;
so my own arm brought me
victory,
and my wrath sustained me.
6 I trampled down peoples in my
anger,
I crushed them in my wrath,
and I poured out their
lifeblood on the earth."

God's Mercy Remembered

7 I will recount the gracious deeds
of the LORD,
the praiseworthy acts of the
LORD,
because of all that the LORD has
done for us,
and the great favor to the
house of Israel

---

[t] Heb *Azubah*   [u] Heb *Shemamah*
[v] Heb *Hephzibah*   [w] Heb *Beulah*
[x] Cn: Heb *your sons*

that he has shown them
    according to his mercy,
    according to the abundance of
    his steadfast love.
8 For he said, "Surely they are my
    people,
    children who will not deal
    falsely";
and he became their savior
9   in all their distress.
It was no messenger[y] or angel
    but his presence that saved
    them;[z]
in his love and in his pity he
    redeemed them;
    he lifted them up and carried
    them all the days of old.

10 But they rebelled
    and grieved his holy spirit;
therefore he became their
    enemy;
    he himself fought against
    them.
11 Then they[a] remembered the
    days of old,
    of Moses his servant.[b]
Where is the one who brought
    them up out of the sea
    with the shepherds of his
    flock?
Where is the one who put within
    them
    his holy spirit,
12 who caused his glorious arm
    to march at the right hand of
    Moses,
who divided the waters before
    them
    to make for himself an
    everlasting name,
13 who led them through the
    depths?
Like a horse in the desert,
    they did not stumble.
14 Like cattle that go down into the
    valley,
    the spirit of the LORD gave
    them rest.
Thus you led your people,
    to make for yourself a glorious
    name.

A Prayer of Penitence

15 Look down from heaven and
    see,
    from your holy and glorious
    habitation.
Where are your zeal and your
    might?
The yearning of your heart
    and your compassion?

They are withheld from me.
16 For you are our father,
    though Abraham does not
    know us
    and Israel does not
    acknowledge us;
you, O LORD, are our father;
    our Redeemer from of old is
    your name.
17 Why, O LORD, do you make us
    stray from your ways
    and harden our heart, so that
    we do not fear you?
Turn back for the sake of your
    servants,
    for the sake of the tribes that
    are your heritage.
18 Your holy people took
    possession for a little
    while;
    but now our adversaries have
    trampled down your
    sanctuary.
19 We have long been like those
    whom you do not rule,
    like those not called by your
    name.

64 O that you would tear open
    the heavens and come
    down,
    so that the mountains would
    quake at your presence —
2[c] as when fire kindles brushwood
    and the fire causes water to
    boil —
to make your name known to
    your adversaries,
    so that the nations might
    tremble at your presence!
3 When you did awesome deeds
    that we did not expect,
    you came down, the mountains
    quaked at your presence.
4 From ages past no one has
    heard,
    no ear has perceived,
no eye has seen any God besides
    you,
    who works for those who wait
    for him.
5 You meet those who gladly do
    right,
    those who remember you in
    your ways.

y Gk: Heb *anguish*   z Or *savior.* 9*In all
their distress he was distressed; the
angel of his presence saved them;*
a Heb *he*   b Cn: Heb *his people*   c Ch
64.1 in Heb

I
S
A
I
A
H

But you were angry, and we
    sinned;
    because you hid yourself we
      transgressed.*d*

6 We have all become like one
    who is unclean,
    and all our righteous deeds are
      like a filthy cloth.
We all fade like a leaf,
    and our iniquities, like the
      wind, take us away.

7 There is no one who calls on
    your name,
    or attempts to take hold of
      you;
for you have hidden your face
    from us,
    and have delivered*e* us into
      the hand of our iniquity.

8 Yet, O LORD, you are our Father;
    we are the clay, and you are
      our potter;
    we are all the work of your
      hand.

9 Do not be exceedingly angry,
    O LORD,
    and do not remember iniquity
      forever.
    Now consider, we are all your
      people.

10 Your holy cities have become a
    wilderness,
    Zion has become a wilderness,
    Jerusalem a desolation.

11 Our holy and beautiful house,
    where our ancestors praised
      you,
has been burned by fire,
    and all our pleasant places
      have become ruins.

12 After all this, will you restrain
    yourself, O LORD?
Will you keep silent, and
    punish us so severely?

The Righteousness of God's Judgment

65 I was ready to be sought out
    by those who did not ask,
to be found by those who did
    not seek me.
I said, "Here I am, here I am,"
    to a nation that did not call on
    my name.

2 I held out my hands all day long
    to a rebellious people,
who walk in a way that is not
    good,
    following their own devices;

3 a people who provoke me
    to my face continually,
sacrificing in gardens

and offering incense on bricks;
4 who sit inside tombs,
    and spend the night in secret
      places;
who eat swine's flesh,
    with broth of abominable
      things in their vessels;

5 who say, "Keep to yourself,
    do not come near me, for I am
      too holy for you."
These are a smoke in my
    nostrils,
    a fire that burns all day long.

6 See, it is written before me:
    I will not keep silent, but I will
      repay;
I will indeed repay into their
    laps
7   their*f* iniquities and their*f*
      ancestors' iniquities
      together,
                 says the LORD;
because they offered incense on
    the mountains
    and reviled me on the hills,
I will measure into their laps
    full payment for their actions.

8 Thus says the LORD:
As the wine is found in the
    cluster,
    and they say, "Do not destroy
      it,
    for there is a blessing in it,"
so I will do for my servants'
    sake,
    and not destroy them all.

9 I will bring forth descendants*g*
    from Jacob,
    and from Judah inheritors*h* of
      my mountains;
my chosen shall inherit it,
    and my servants shall settle
      there.

10 Sharon shall become a pasture
    for flocks,
    and the Valley of A'chor a
      place for herds to lie down,
    for my people who have
      sought me.

11 But you who forsake the LORD,
    who forget my holy mountain,
who set a table for Fortune
    and fill cups of mixed wine for
      Destiny;

12 I will destine you to the sword,
    and all of you shall bow down
      to the slaughter;

d Meaning of Heb uncertain   *e* Gk Syr
Old Latin Tg: Heb *melted*   *f* Gk Syr:
Heb *your*   *g* Or *a descendant*   *h* Or *an
inheritor*

because, when I called, you did
  not answer,
    when I spoke, you did not
      listen,
but you did what was evil in my
  sight,
    and chose what I did not
      delight in.

13 Therefore thus says the Lord
    GOD:
My servants shall eat,
  but you shall be hungry;
my servants shall drink,
  but you shall be thirsty;
my servants shall rejoice,
  but you shall be put to shame;
14 my servants shall sing for
    gladness of heart,
  but you shall cry out for pain
    of heart,
  and shall wail for anguish of
    spirit.
15 You shall leave your name to my
    chosen to use as a curse,
  and the Lord GOD will put you
    to death;
  but to his servants he will give
    a different name.
16 Then whoever invokes a
    blessing in the land
  shall bless by the God of
    faithfulness,
  and whoever takes an oath in
    the land
  shall swear by the God of
    faithfulness;
because the former troubles are
    forgotten
  and are hidden from my sight.

The Glorious New Creation

17 For I am about to create new
    heavens
  and a new earth;
the former things shall not be
    remembered
  or come to mind.
18 But be glad and rejoice forever
    in what I am creating;
for I am about to create
    Jerusalem as a joy,
  and its people as a delight.
19 I will rejoice in Jerusalem,
  and delight in my people;
no more shall the sound of
    weeping be heard in it,
  or the cry of distress.
20 No more shall there be in it
    an infant that lives but a few
      days,

or an old person who does not
    live out a lifetime;
for one who dies at a hundred
    years will be considered a
      youth,
  and one who falls short of a
    hundred will be considered
      accursed.
21 They shall build houses and
    inhabit them;
  they shall plant vineyards and
    eat their fruit.
22 They shall not build and another
    inhabit;
  they shall not plant and
    another eat;
for like the days of a tree shall
    the days of my people be,
  and my chosen shall long
    enjoy the work of their
      hands.
23 They shall not labor in vain,
  or bear children for calamity;[i]
for they shall be offspring
    blessed by the LORD—
  and their descendants as well.
24 Before they call I will answer,
  while they are yet speaking I
    will hear.
25 The wolf and the lamb shall feed
    together,
  the lion shall eat straw like the
    ox;
  but the serpent—its food shall
    be dust!
They shall not hurt or destroy
  on all my holy mountain,
                    says the LORD.

The Worship God Demands

66 Thus says the LORD:
    Heaven is my throne
  and the earth is my footstool;
what is the house that you
    would build for me,
  and what is my resting place?
2 All these things my hand has
    made,
  and so all these things are
    mine,[j]
                    says the LORD.
But this is the one to whom I
    will look,
  to the humble and contrite in
    spirit,
  who trembles at my word.

---

*i*Or *sudden terror*   *j*Gk Syr: Heb *these
things came to be*

3 Whoever slaughters an ox is like
    one who kills a human
    being;
  whoever sacrifices a lamb, like
    one who breaks a dog's
    neck;
  whoever presents a grain
    offering, like one who
    offers swine's blood;*k*
  whoever makes a memorial
    offering of frankincense,
    like one who blesses an
    idol.
  These have chosen their own
    ways,
    and in their abominations they
      take delight;
4 I also will choose to mock*l*
    them,
    and bring upon them what
      they fear;
  because, when I called, no one
    answered,
    when I spoke, they did not
      listen;
  but they did what was evil in my
    sight,
    and chose what did not please
      me.

The LORD Vindicates Zion

5 Hear the word of the LORD,
    you who tremble at his word:
  Your own people who hate you
    and reject you for my name's
      sake
  have said, "Let the LORD be
    glorified,
    so that we may see your joy";
    but it is they who shall be put
      to shame.

6 Listen, an uproar from the city!
    A voice from the temple!
  The voice of the LORD,
    dealing retribution to his
      enemies!

7 Before she was in labor
    she gave birth;
  before her pain came upon her
    she delivered a son.
8 Who has heard of such a thing?
    Who has seen such things?
  Shall a land be born in one day?
    Shall a nation be delivered in
      one moment?
  Yet as soon as Zion was in labor
    she delivered her children.
9 Shall I open the womb and not
    deliver?
    says the LORD;

shall I, the one who delivers,
    shut the womb?
    says your God.

10 Rejoice with Jerusalem, and be
    glad for her,
    all you who love her;
  rejoice with her in joy,
    all you who mourn over her—
11 that you may nurse and be
    satisfied
    from her consoling breast;
  that you may drink deeply with
    delight
    from her glorious bosom.

12 For thus says the LORD:
  I will extend prosperity to her
    like a river,
    and the wealth of the nations
      like an overflowing stream;
  and you shall nurse and be
    carried on her arm,
    and dandled on her knees.
13 As a mother comforts her child,
    so I will comfort you;
    you shall be comforted in
      Jerusalem.

The Reign and Indignation of God

14 You shall see, and your heart
    shall rejoice;
    your bodies*m* shall flourish
      like the grass;
  and it shall be known that the
    hand of the LORD is with
      his servants,
    and his indignation is against
      his enemies.
15 For the LORD will come in fire,
    and his chariots like the
      whirlwind,
  to pay back his anger in fury,
    and his rebuke in flames of
      fire.
16 For by fire will the LORD execute
    judgment,
    and by his sword, on all flesh;
    and those slain by the LORD
      shall be many.

17 Those who sanctify and purify
themselves to go into the gardens, following the one in the center, eating the
flesh of pigs, vermin, and rodents,
shall come to an end together, says the
LORD.

k Meaning of Heb uncertain   *l* Or *to
punish*   *m* Heb *bones*

18 For I know[n] their works and their thoughts, and I am[o] coming to gather all nations and tongues; and they shall come and shall see my glory, [19] and I will set a sign among them. From them I will send survivors to the nations, to Tar'shish, Put,[p] and Lud—which draw the bow—to Tū'bal and Jā'van, to the coastlands far away that have not heard of my fame or seen my glory; and they shall declare my glory among the nations. [20] They shall bring all your kindred from all the nations as an offering to the LORD, on horses, and in chariots, in litters, and on mules, and on dromedaries, to my holy mountain Jerusalem, says the LORD, just as the Israelites bring a grain offering in a clean vessel to the house of the LORD. [21] And I will also take some of them as priests and as Lē'-vītes, says the LORD.

22 For as the new heavens and the
　　new earth,
　　which I will make,
　shall remain before me, says the
　　LORD;
　　so shall your descendants and
　　　your name remain.
23 From new moon to new moon,
　　and from sabbath to sabbath,
　all flesh shall come to worship
　　before me,
　says the LORD.

24 And they shall go out and look at the dead bodies of the people who have rebelled against me; for their worm shall not die, their fire shall not be quenched, and they shall be an abhorrence to all flesh.

[n] Gk Syr: Heb lacks *know*　　[o] Gk Syr Vg Tg: Heb *it is*　　[p] Gk: Heb *Pul*

JEREMIAH

1 The words of Jer·e·mī'ah son of Hil·kī'ah, of the priests who were in An'a·thoth in the land of Benjamin, [2] to whom the word of the LORD came in the days of King Jō·sī'ah son of Ā'mon of Judah, in the thirteenth year of his reign. [3] It came also in the days of King Je·hoi'a·kim son of Jō·sī'ah of Judah, and until the end of the eleventh year of King Zed·e·kī'ah son of Jō·sī'ah of Judah, until the captivity of Jerusalem in the fifth month.

Jeremiah's Call and Commission

4 Now the word of the LORD came to me saying,
5 　"Before I formed you in the
　　womb I knew you,
　and before you were born I
　　consecrated you;
　I appointed you a prophet to the
　　nations."
6 Then I said, "Ah, Lord GOD! Truly I do not know how to speak, for I am only a boy." [7] But the LORD said to me,
　"Do not say, 'I am only a boy';
　for you shall go to all to whom I
　　send you,
and you shall speak whatever I
　　command you,
8 　Do not be afraid of them,
　for I am with you to deliver you,
　　says the LORD."
[9] Then the LORD put out his hand and touched my mouth; and the LORD said to me,
　"Now I have put my words in
　　your mouth.
10 　See, today I appoint you over
　　nations and over
　　　kingdoms,
　to pluck up and to pull down,
　to destroy and to overthrow,
　to build and to plant."
11 The word of the LORD came to me, saying, "Jer·e·mī'ah, what do you see?" And I said, "I see a branch of an almond tree."[a] [12] Then the LORD said to me, "You have seen well, for I am watching[b] over my word to perform it." [13] The word of the LORD came to me a second time, saying, "What do you see?" And I said, "I see a boiling pot, tilted away from the north."

[a] Heb *shaqed*　　[b] Heb *shoqed*

14 Then the LORD said to me: Out of the north disaster shall break out on all the inhabitants of the land. 15 For now I am calling all the tribes of the kingdoms of the north, says the LORD; and they shall come and all of them shall set their thrones at the entrance of the gates of Jerusalem, against all its surrounding walls and against all the cities of Judah. 16 And I will utter my judgments against them, for all their wickedness in forsaking me; they have made offerings to other gods, and worshiped the works of their own hands. 17 But you, gird up your loins; stand up and tell them everything that I command you. Do not break down before them, or I will break you before them. 18 And I for my part have made you today a fortified city, an iron pillar, and a bronze wall, against the whole land — against the kings of Judah, its princes, its priests, and the people of the land. 19 They will fight against you; but they shall not prevail against you, for I am with you, says the LORD, to deliver you.

God Pleads with Israel to Repent

2 The word of the LORD came to me, saying: 2 Go and proclaim in the hearing of Jerusalem, Thus says the LORD:

I remember the devotion of your youth,
  your love as a bride,
how you followed me in the wilderness,
  in a land not sown.
3 Israel was holy to the LORD,
  the first fruits of his harvest.
All who ate of it were held guilty;
  disaster came upon them,
        says the LORD.

4 Hear the word of the LORD, O house of Jacob, and all the families of the house of Israel. 5 Thus says the LORD:

What wrong did your ancestors find in me
  that they went far from me,
and went after worthless things,
  and became worthless themselves?
6 They did not say, "Where is the LORD
  who brought us up from the land of Egypt,
who led us in the wilderness,
  in a land of deserts and pits,

in a land of drought and deep darkness,
  in a land that no one passes through,
  where no one lives?"
7 I brought you into a plentiful land
  to eat its fruits and its good things.
But when you entered you defiled my land,
  and made my heritage an abomination.
8 The priests did not say, "Where is the LORD?"
  Those who handle the law did not know me;
the rulers[c] transgressed against me;
  the prophets prophesied by Bā'al,
  and went after things that do not profit.

9 Therefore once more I accuse you,
        says the LORD,
  and I accuse your children's children.
10 Cross to the coasts of Cyprus and look,
  send to Kē'dar and examine with care;
  see if there has ever been such a thing.
11 Has a nation changed its gods,
  even though they are no gods?
But my people have changed their glory
  for something that does not profit.
12 Be appalled, O heavens, at this,
  be shocked, be utterly desolate,
        says the LORD,
13 for my people have committed two evils:
  they have forsaken me,
the fountain of living water,
  and dug out cisterns for themselves,
cracked cisterns
  that can hold no water.

14 Is Israel a slave? Is he a homeborn servant?
  Why then has he become plunder?
15 The lions have roared against him,

---

c Heb shepherds

they have roared loudly.
They have made his land a
   waste;
   his cities are in ruins, without
     inhabitant.
16 Moreover, the people of
     Memphis and Tah′pan·hēs
   have broken the crown of your
     head.
17 Have you not brought this upon
     yourself
   by forsaking the LORD your
     God,
   while he led you in the way?
18 What then do you gain by going
     to Egypt,
   to drink the waters of the
     Nile?
Or what do you gain by going to
     Assyria,
   to drink the waters of the
     Euphrates?
19 Your wickedness will punish
     you,
   and your apostasies will
     convict you.
Know and see that it is evil and
     bitter
   for you to forsake the LORD
     your God;
   the fear of me is not in you,
     says the Lord GOD of hosts.

20 For long ago you broke your
     yoke
   and burst your bonds,
   and you said, "I will not
     serve!"
On every high hill
   and under every green tree
   you sprawled and played the
     whore.
21 Yet I planted you as a choice
     vine,
   from the purest stock.
How then did you turn
     degenerate
   and become a wild vine?
22 Though you wash yourself with
     lye
   and use much soap,
   the stain of your guilt is still
     before me,
        says the Lord GOD.
23 How can you say, "I am not
     defiled,
   I have not gone after the
     Bā′als"?
Look at your way in the valley;
   know what you have done —
   a restive young camel interlacing
     her tracks,

24   a wild ass at home in the
     wilderness,
   in her heat sniffing the wind!
   Who can restrain her lust?
None who seek her need weary
     themselves;
   in her month they will find
     her.
25 Keep your feet from going
     unshod
   and your throat from thirst.
But you said, "It is hopeless,
   for I have loved strangers,
   and after them I will go."

26 As a thief is shamed when
     caught,
   so the house of Israel shall be
     shamed —
they, their kings, their officials,
   their priests, and their
     prophets,
27 who say to a tree, "You are my
     father,"
   and to a stone, "You gave me
     birth."
For they have turned their backs
     to me,
   and not their faces.
But in the time of their trouble
     they say,
   "Come and save us!"
28 But where are your gods
   that you made for yourself?
Let them come, if they can save
     you,
   in your time of trouble;
for you have as many gods
   as you have towns, O Judah.

29 Why do you complain against
     me?
   You have all rebelled against
     me,
        says the LORD.
30 In vain I have struck down your
     children;
   they accepted no correction.
Your own sword devoured your
     prophets
   like a ravening lion.
31 And you, O generation, behold
     the word of the LORD![d]
Have I been a wilderness to
     Israel,
   or a land of thick darkness?
Why then do my people say,
   "We are free,
   we will come to you no more"?
32 Can a girl forget her ornaments,

[d]Meaning of Heb uncertain

or a bride her attire?
Yet my people have forgotten
me,
days without number.

33 How well you direct your course
to seek lovers!
So that even to wicked women
you have taught your ways.
34 Also on your skirts is found
the lifeblood of the innocent
poor,
though you did not catch them
breaking in.
Yet in spite of all these
things[e]
35 you say, "I am innocent;
surely his anger has turned
from me."
Now I am bringing you to
judgment
for saying, "I have not sinned."
36 How lightly you gad about,
changing your ways!
You shall be put to shame by
Egypt
as you were put to shame by
Assyria.
37 From there also you will come
away
with your hands on your head;
for the LORD has rejected those
in whom you trust,
and you will not prosper
through them.

Unfaithful Israel

3 If[f] a man divorces his wife
and she goes from him
and becomes another man's
wife,
will he return to her?
Would not such a land be
greatly polluted?
You have played the whore with
many lovers;
and would you return to me?
says the LORD.
2 Look up to the bare heights,[g]
and see!
Where have you not been lain
with?
By the waysides you have sat
waiting for lovers,
like a nomad in the
wilderness.
You have polluted the land
with your whoring and
wickedness.
3 Therefore the showers have been
withheld,

and the spring rain has not
come;
yet you have the forehead of a
whore,
you refuse to be ashamed.
4 Have you not just now called to
me,
"My Father, you are the friend
of my youth —
5 will he be angry forever,
will he be indignant to the
end?"
This is how you have spoken,
but you have done all the evil
that you could.

A Call to Repentance

6 The LORD said to me in the days of
King Jō·sī'ah: Have you seen what she
did, that faithless one, Israel, how she
went up on every high hill and under
every green tree, and played the whore
there? 7 And I thought, "After she has
done all this she will return to me"; but
she did not return, and her false sister
Judah saw it. 8 She[h] saw that for all the
adulteries of that faithless one, Israel,
I had sent her away with a decree of
divorce; yet her false sister Judah did
not fear, but she too went and played
the whore. 9 Because she took her
whoredom so lightly, she polluted the
land, committing adultery with stone
and tree. 10 Yet for all this her false sister Judah did not return to me with her
whole heart, but only in pretense, says
the LORD.

11 Then the LORD said to me: Faithless Israel has shown herself less
guilty than false Judah. 12 Go, and proclaim these words toward the north,
and say:

Return, faithless Israel,
says the LORD.
I will not look on you in anger,
for I am merciful,
says the LORD;
I will not be angry forever.
13 Only acknowledge your guilt,
that you have rebelled against
the LORD your God,
and scattered your favors among
strangers under every
green tree,
and have not obeyed my voice,
says the LORD.
14 Return, O faithless children,

[e] Meaning of Heb uncertain   [f] Q Ms Gk
Syr: MT Saying, If   [g] Or the trails
[h] Q Ms Gk Mss Syr: MT I

says the LORD,
for I am your master;
I will take you, one from a city
and two from a family,
and I will bring you to Zion.

15 I will give you shepherds after
my own heart, who will feed you with
knowledge and understanding. 16 And
when you have multiplied and increased in the land, in those days, says
the LORD, they shall no longer say,
"The ark of the covenant of the LORD."
It shall not come to mind, or be remembered, or missed; nor shall another one
be made. 17 At that time Jerusalem
shall be called the throne of the LORD,
and all nations shall gather to it, to the
presence of the LORD in Jerusalem,
and they shall no longer stubbornly
follow their own evil will. 18 In those
days the house of Judah shall join the
house of Israel, and together they shall
come from the land of the north to the
land that I gave your ancestors for a
heritage.

19 I thought
how I would set you among
my children,
and give you a pleasant land,
the most beautiful heritage of
all the nations.
And I thought you would call
me, My Father,
and would not turn from
following me.
20 Instead, as a faithless wife
leaves her husband,
so you have been faithless to
me, O house of Israel,
says the LORD.

21 A voice on the bare heights[i] is
heard,
the plaintive weeping of
Israel's children,
because they have perverted
their way,
they have forgotten the LORD
their God:
22 Return, O faithless children,
I will heal your faithlessness.

"Here we come to you;
for you are the LORD our God.
23 Truly the hills are[j] a delusion,
the orgies on the mountains.
Truly in the LORD our God
is the salvation of Israel.
24 "But from our youth the shameful thing has devoured all for which

our ancestors had labored, their flocks
and their herds, their sons and their
daughters. 25 Let us lie down in our
shame, and let our dishonor cover us;
for we have sinned against the LORD
our God, we and our ancestors, from
our youth even to this day; and we
have not obeyed the voice of the LORD
our God."

4 If you return, O Israel,
says the LORD,
if you return to me,
if you remove your abominations
from my presence,
and do not waver,
2 and if you swear, "As the LORD
lives!"
in truth, in justice, and in
uprightness,
then nations shall be blessed[k]
by him,
and by him they shall boast.

3 For thus says the LORD to the people of Judah and to the inhabitants of
Jerusalem:
Break up your fallow ground,
and do not sow among thorns.
4 Circumcise yourselves to the
LORD,
remove the foreskin of your
hearts,
O people of Judah and
inhabitants of Jerusalem,
or else my wrath will go forth
like fire,
and burn with no one to
quench it,
because of the evil of your
doings.

*Invasion and Desolation of
Judah Threatened*

5 Declare in Judah, and proclaim in
Jerusalem, and say:
Blow the trumpet through the
land;
shout aloud[l] and say,
"Gather together, and let us go
into the fortified cities!"
6 Raise a standard toward Zion,
flee for safety, do not delay,
for I am bringing evil from the
north,
and a great destruction.
7 A lion has gone up from its
thicket,

---

[i]Or *the trails*   [j]Gk Syr Vg: Heb *Truly
from the hills is*   [k]Or *shall bless
themselves*   [l]Or *shout, take your
weapons*: Heb *shout, fill* (your hand)

a destroyer of nations has set
out;
he has gone out from his place
to make your land a waste;
your cities will be ruins
without inhabitant.
8 Because of this put on sackcloth,
lament and wail:
"The fierce anger of the LORD
has not turned away from us."

9 On that day, says the LORD, courage shall fail the king and the officials; the priests shall be appalled and the prophets astounded. 10 Then I said, "Ah, Lord GOD, how utterly you have deceived this people and Jerusalem, saying, 'It shall be well with you,' even while the sword is at the throat!"

11 At that time it will be said to this people and to Jerusalem: A hot wind comes from me out of the bare heights^m in the desert toward my poor people, not to winnow or cleanse — 12 a wind too strong for that. Now it is I who speak in judgment against them.
13 Look! He comes up like clouds,
his chariots like the whirlwind;
his horses are swifter than
eagles —
woe to us, for we are ruined!
14 O Jerusalem, wash your heart
clean of wickedness
so that you may be saved.
How long shall your evil
schemes
lodge within you?
15 For a voice declares from Dan
and proclaims disaster from
Mount E'phra-im.
16 Tell the nations, "Here they are!"
Proclaim against Jerusalem,
"Besiegers come from a distant
land;
they shout against the cities of
Judah.
17 They have closed in around her
like watchers of a field,
because she has rebelled
against me,
says the LORD.
18 Your ways and your doings
have brought this upon you.
This is your doom; how bitter it
is!
It has reached your very
heart."

Sorrow for a Doomed Nation

19 My anguish, my anguish! I
writhe in pain!
Oh, the walls of my heart!
My heart is beating wildly;
I cannot keep silent;
for I^n hear the sound of the
trumpet,
the alarm of war.
20 Disaster overtakes disaster,
the whole land is laid waste.
Suddenly my tents are
destroyed,
my curtains in a moment.
21 How long must I see the
standard,
and hear the sound of the
trumpet?
22 "For my people are foolish,
they do not know me;
they are stupid children,
they have no understanding.
They are skilled in doing evil,
but do not know how to do
good."

23 I looked on the earth, and lo, it
was waste and void;
and to the heavens, and they
had no light.
24 I looked on the mountains, and
lo, they were quaking,
and all the hills moved to and
fro.
25 I looked, and lo, there was no
one at all,
and all the birds of the air had
fled.
26 I looked, and lo, the fruitful land
was a desert,
and all its cities were laid in
ruins
before the LORD, before his
fierce anger.
27 For thus says the LORD: The whole land shall be a desolation; yet I will not make a full end.
28 Because of this the earth shall
mourn,
and the heavens above grow
black;
for I have spoken, I have
purposed;
I have not relented nor will I
turn back.

29 At the noise of horseman and
archer

^m Or *the trails*   ^n Another reading is *for you, O my soul,*

every town takes to flight;
they enter thickets; they climb
    among rocks;
    all the towns are forsaken,
    and no one lives in them.
30 And you, O desolate one,
    what do you mean that you
        dress in crimson,
        that you deck yourself with
            ornaments of gold,
        that you enlarge your eyes
            with paint?
In vain you beautify yourself.
    Your lovers despise you;
    they seek your life.
31 For I heard a cry as of a woman
    in labor,
    anguish as of one bringing
        forth her first child,
the cry of daughter Zion gasping
    for breath,
    stretching out her hands,
    "Woe is me! I am fainting before
        killers!"

The Utter Corruption of God's People

5 Run to and fro through the
    streets of Jerusalem,
    look around and take note!
Search its squares and see
    if you can find one person
who acts justly
    and seeks truth —
so that I may pardon
    Jerusalem.*o*
2 Although they say, "As the LORD
    lives,"
    yet they swear falsely.
3 O LORD, do your eyes not look
    for truth?
You have struck them,
    but they felt no anguish;
you have consumed them,
    but they refused to take
        correction.
They have made their faces
    harder than rock;
    they have refused to turn
        back.

4 Then I said, "These are only the
    poor,
    they have no sense;
for they do not know the way of
    the LORD,
    the law of their God.
5 Let me go to the rich*p*
    and speak to them;
    surely they know the way of the
        LORD,
    the law of their God."

But they all alike had broken the
    yoke,
    they had burst the bonds.

6 Therefore a lion from the forest
    shall kill them,
    a wolf from the desert shall
        destroy them.
A leopard is watching against
    their cities;
    everyone who goes out of
        them shall be torn in
        pieces —
because their transgressions are
    many,
    their apostasies are great.

7 How can I pardon you?
    Your children have forsaken
        me,
    and have sworn by those who
        are no gods.
When I fed them to the full,
    they committed adultery
    and trooped to the houses of
        prostitutes.
8 They were well-fed lusty
    stallions,
    each neighing for his
        neighbor's wife.
9 Shall I not punish them for these
    things?
                        says the LORD;
    and shall I not bring
        retribution
    on a nation such as this?

10 Go up through her vine-rows
        and destroy,
    but do not make a full end;
strip away her branches,
    for they are not the LORD's.
11 For the house of Israel and the
        house of Judah
    have been utterly faithless to
        me,
                        says the LORD.
12 They have spoken falsely of the
        LORD,
    and have said, "He will do
        nothing.
No evil will come upon us,
    and we shall not see sword or
        famine."
13 The prophets are nothing but
        wind,
    for the word is not in them.
Thus shall it be done to them!

o Heb *it*   p Or *the great*

14 Therefore thus says the LORD,
　　　the God of hosts:
Because they*q* have spoken this
　　　word,
I am now making my words in
　　　your mouth a fire,
　　and this people wood, and the
　　　fire shall devour them.
15 I am going to bring upon you
　　　a nation from far away,
　　　　O house of Israel,
　　　　　　　　says the LORD.
It is an enduring nation,
　　it is an ancient nation,
a nation whose language you do
　　　not know,
　　nor can you understand what
　　　they say.
16 Their quiver is like an open
　　　tomb;
　　all of them are mighty
　　　warriors.
17 They shall eat up your harvest
　　　and your food;
　　they shall eat up your sons
　　　and your daughters;
they shall eat up your flocks and
　　　your herds;
　　they shall eat up your vines
　　　and your fig trees;
they shall destroy with the
　　　sword
　　your fortified cities in which
　　　you trust.

18　But even in those days, says the
LORD, I will not make a full end of you.
19 And when your people say, "Why
has the LORD our God done all these
things to us?" you shall say to them,
"As you have forsaken me and served
foreign gods in your land, so you shall
serve strangers in a land that is not
yours."

20 Declare this in the house of
　　　Jacob,
　　proclaim it in Judah:
21 Hear this, O foolish and
　　　senseless people,
　　who have eyes, but do not see,
　　who have ears, but do not
　　　hear.
22 Do you not fear me? says the
　　　LORD;
　　Do you not tremble before me?
I placed the sand as a boundary
　　　for the sea,
　　a perpetual barrier that it
　　　cannot pass;
though the waves toss, they
　　　cannot prevail,

　　though they roar, they cannot
　　　pass over it.
23 But this people has a stubborn
　　　and rebellious heart;
　　they have turned aside and
　　　gone away.
24 They do not say in their hearts,
　　　"Let us fear the LORD our God,
who gives the rain in its season,
　　the autumn rain and the spring
　　　rain,
and keeps for us
　　the weeks appointed for the
　　　harvest."
25 Your iniquities have turned
　　　these away,
　　and your sins have deprived
　　　you of good.
26 For scoundrels are found among
　　　my people;
　　they take over the goods of
　　　others.
Like fowlers they set a trap;*r*
　　they catch human beings.
27 Like a cage full of birds,
　　their houses are full of
　　　treachery;
therefore they have become
　　　great and rich,
28　they have grown fat and sleek.
They know no limits in deeds of
　　　wickedness;
　　they do not judge with justice
the cause of the orphan, to make
　　　it prosper,
　　and they do not defend the
　　　rights of the needy.
29 Shall I not punish them for these
　　　things?
　　　　　　　　says the LORD,
　　and shall I not bring
　　　retribution
　　on a nation such as this?

30 An appalling and horrible thing
　　　has happened in the land:
31 the prophets prophesy falsely,
　　and the priests rule as the
　　　prophets direct;*s*
my people love to have it so,
　　but what will you do when the
　　　end comes?

*The Imminence and Horror
of the Invasion*

6 Flee for safety, O children of
　　　Benjamin,
　　from the midst of Jerusalem!

q Heb *you*　　*r* Meaning of Heb uncertain
s Or *rule by their own authority*

Blow the trumpet in Te·kō′a,
  and raise a signal on
    Beth-hac·chē′rem;
for evil looms out of the north,
  and great destruction.
2 I have likened daughter Zion
    to the loveliest pasture.[t]
3 Shepherds with their flocks shall
    come against her.
  They shall pitch their tents
    around her;
    they shall pasture, all in their
      places.
4 "Prepare war against her;
    up, and let us attack at noon!"
  "Woe to us, for the day declines,
    the shadows of evening
      lengthen!"
5 "Up, and let us attack by night,
    and destroy her palaces!"
6 For thus says the LORD of hosts:
  Cut down her trees;
    cast up a siege ramp against
      Jerusalem.
  This is the city that must be
    punished;[u]
    there is nothing but oppression
      within her.
7 As a well keeps its water fresh,
    so she keeps fresh her
      wickedness;
  violence and destruction are
    heard within her;
    sickness and wounds are ever
      before me.
8 Take warning, O Jerusalem,
    or I shall turn from you in
      disgust,
  and make you a desolation,
    an uninhabited land.

9 Thus says the LORD of hosts:
  Glean[v] thoroughly as a vine
    the remnant of Israel;
  like a grape-gatherer, pass your
    hand again
    over its branches.

10 To whom shall I speak and give
      warning,
    that they may hear?
  See, their ears are closed,[w]
    they cannot listen.
  The word of the LORD is to them
    an object of scorn;
    they take no pleasure in it.
11 But I am full of the wrath of the
      LORD;
    I am weary of holding it in.

  Pour it out on the children in the
    street,

and on the gatherings of
  young men as well;
both husband and wife shall be
  taken,
  the old folk and the very aged.
12 Their houses shall be turned
    over to others,
  their fields and wives together;
for I will stretch out my hand
  against the inhabitants of the
    land,
                          says the LORD.

13 For from the least to the greatest
      of them,
    everyone is greedy for unjust
      gain;
  and from prophet to priest,
    everyone deals falsely.
14 They have treated the wound of
    my people carelessly,
    saying, "Peace, peace,"
    when there is no peace.
15 They acted shamefully, they
      committed abomination;
    yet they were not ashamed,
    they did not know how to
      blush.
  Therefore they shall fall among
    those who fall;
    at the time that I punish them,
    they shall be overthrown,
                          says the LORD.
16 Thus says the LORD:
  Stand at the crossroads, and
    look,
    and ask for the ancient paths,
  where the good way lies; and
    walk in it,
    and find rest for your souls.
  But they said, "We will not walk
    in it."
17 Also I raised up sentinels for
      you:
    "Give heed to the sound of the
      trumpet!"
  But they said, "We will not give
    heed."
18 Therefore hear, O nations,
    and know, O congregation,
      what will happen to them.
19 Hear, O earth; I am going to
    bring disaster on this
      people,
    the fruit of their schemes,
  because they have not given
    heed to my words;

t Or I will destroy daughter Zion, the
loveliest pasture   u Or the city of
license   v Cn: Heb They shall glean
w Heb are uncircumcised

and as for my teaching, they
have rejected it.

20 Of what use to me is
frankincense that comes
from Shē′ba,
or sweet cane from a distant
land?
Your burnt offerings are not
acceptable,
nor are your sacrifices
pleasing to me.

21 Therefore thus says the LORD:
See, I am laying before this
people
stumbling blocks against
which they shall stumble;
parents and children together,
neighbor and friend shall
perish.

22 Thus says the LORD:
See, a people is coming from the
land of the north,
a great nation is stirring from
the farthest parts of the
earth.

23 They grasp the bow and the
javelin,
they are cruel and have no
mercy,
their sound is like the roaring
sea;
they ride on horses,
equipped like a warrior for
battle,
against you, O daughter Zion!

24 "We have heard news of them,
our hands fall helpless;
anguish has taken hold of us,
pain as of a woman in labor.

25 Do not go out into the field,
or walk on the road;
for the enemy has a sword,
terror is on every side."

26 O my poor people, put on
sackcloth,
and roll in ashes;
make mourning as for an only
child,
most bitter lamentation:
for suddenly the destroyer
will come upon us.

27 I have made you a tester and a
refiner[x] among my people
so that you may know and test
their ways.

28 They are all stubbornly
rebellious,
going about with slanders;

they are bronze and iron,
all of them act corruptly.

29 The bellows blow fiercely,
the lead is consumed by the
fire;
in vain the refining goes on,
for the wicked are not
removed.

30 They are called "rejected silver,"
for the LORD has rejected
them.

Jeremiah Proclaims God's Judgment
on the Nation
(Cp Jer 26.4–6)

7 The word that came to Jer·e·mī′ah
from the LORD: 2 Stand in the gate
of the LORD's house, and proclaim
there this word, and say, Hear the
word of the LORD, all you people of
Judah, you that enter these gates to
worship the LORD. 3 Thus says the
LORD of hosts, the God of Israel:
Amend your ways and your doings,
and let me dwell with you[y] in this
place. 4 Do not trust in these deceptive
words: "This is[z] the temple of the
LORD, the temple of the LORD, the temple of the LORD."

5 For if you truly amend your ways
and your doings, if you truly act justly
one with another, 6 if you do not oppress the alien, the orphan, and the
widow, or shed innocent blood in this
place, and if you do not go after other
gods to your own hurt, 7 then I will
dwell with you in this place, in the land
that I gave of old to your ancestors forever and ever.

8 Here you are, trusting in deceptive words to no avail. 9 Will you steal,
murder, commit adultery, swear
falsely, make offerings to Bā′al, and go
after other gods that you have not
known, 10 and then come and stand before me in this house, which is called
by my name, and say, "We are safe!" —
only to go on doing all these abominations? 11 Has this house, which is called
by my name, become a den of robbers
in your sight? You know, I too am
watching, says the LORD. 12 Go now to
my place that was in Shī′lōh, where I
made my name dwell at first, and see
what I did to it for the wickedness of
my people Israel. 13 And now, because
you have done all these things, says
the LORD, and when I spoke to you

x Or *a fortress*   y Or *and I will let you*
dwell   z Heb *They are*

persistently, you did not listen, and when I called you, you did not answer, [14]therefore I will do to the house that is called by my name, in which you trust, and to the place that I gave to you and to your ancestors, just what I did to Shi′lōh. [15]And I will cast you out of my sight, just as I cast out all your kinsfolk, all the offspring of E′phra·im.

The People's Disobedience

16 As for you, do not pray for this people, do not raise a cry or prayer on their behalf, and do not intercede with me, for I will not hear you. [17]Do you not see what they are doing in the towns of Judah and in the streets of Jerusalem? [18]The children gather wood, the fathers kindle fire, and the women knead dough, to make cakes for the queen of heaven; and they pour out drink offerings to other gods, to provoke me to anger. [19]Is it I whom they provoke? says the LORD. Is it not themselves, to their own hurt? [20]Therefore thus says the Lord GOD: My anger and my wrath shall be poured out on this place, on human beings and animals, on the trees of the field and the fruit of the ground; it will burn and not be quenched.

21 Thus says the LORD of hosts, the God of Israel: Add your burnt offerings to your sacrifices, and eat the flesh. [22]For in the day that I brought your ancestors out of the land of Egypt, I did not speak to them or command them concerning burnt offerings and sacrifices. [23]But this command I gave them, "Obey my voice, and I will be your God, and you shall be my people; and walk only in the way that I command you, so that it may be well with you." [24]Yet they did not obey or incline their ear, but, in the stubbornness of their evil will, they walked in their own counsels, and looked backward rather than forward. [25]From the day that your ancestors came out of the land of Egypt until this day, I have persistently sent all my servants the prophets to them, day after day; [26]yet they did not listen to me, or pay attention, but they stiffened their necks. They did worse than their ancestors did.

27 So you shall speak all these words to them, but they will not listen to you. You shall call to them, but they will not answer you. [28]You shall say to them: This is the nation that did not obey the voice of the LORD their God, and did not accept discipline; truth has perished; it is cut off from their lips.
[29] Cut off your hair and throw it away;
raise a lamentation on the bare heights,[a]
for the LORD has rejected and forsaken
the generation that provoked his wrath.

30 For the people of Judah have done evil in my sight, says the LORD; they have set their abominations in the house that is called by my name, defiling it. [31]And they go on building the high place[b] of Tō′pheth, which is in the valley of the son of Hin′nom, to burn their sons and their daughters in the fire—which I did not command, nor did it come into my mind. [32]Therefore, the days are surely coming, says the LORD, when it will no more be called Tō′pheth, or the valley of the son of Hin′nom, but the valley of Slaughter: for they will bury in Tō′pheth until there is no more room. [33]The corpses of this people will be food for the birds of the air, and for the animals of the earth; and no one will frighten them away. [34]And I will bring to an end the sound of mirth and gladness, the voice of the bride and bridegroom in the cities of Judah and in the streets of Jerusalem; for the land shall become a waste.

8 At that time, says the LORD, the bones of the kings of Judah, the bones of its officials, the bones of the priests, the bones of the prophets, and the bones of the inhabitants of Jerusalem shall be brought out of their tombs; [2]and they shall be spread before the sun and the moon and all the host of heaven, which they have loved and served, which they have followed, and which they have inquired of and worshiped; and they shall not be gathered or buried; they shall be like dung on the surface of the ground. [3]Death shall be preferred to life by all the remnant that remains of this evil family in all the places where I have driven them, says the LORD of hosts.

aOr the trails   bGk Tg: Heb high places

*The Blind Perversity of the
Whole Nation*

4 You shall say to them, Thus says
   the LORD:
When people fall, do they not
   get up again?
   If they go astray, do they not
   turn back?
5 Why then has this people[c]
   turned away
in perpetual backsliding?
They have held fast to deceit,
   they have refused to return.
6 I have given heed and listened,
   but they do not speak
   honestly;
no one repents of wickedness,
   saying, "What have I done!"
All of them turn to their own
   course,
   like a horse plunging headlong
   into battle.
7 Even the stork in the heavens
   knows its times;
and the turtledove, swallow, and
   crane[d]
   observe the time of their
   coming;
but my people do not know
   the ordinance of the LORD.

8 How can you say, "We are wise,
   and the law of the LORD is
   with us,"
when, in fact, the false pen of
   the scribes
   has made it into a lie?
9 The wise shall be put to shame,
   they shall be dismayed and
   taken;
since they have rejected the
   word of the LORD,
   what wisdom is in them?
10 Therefore I will give their wives
   to others
and their fields to conquerors,
because from the least to the
   greatest
   everyone is greedy for unjust
   gain;
from prophet to priest
   everyone deals falsely.
11 They have treated the wound of
   my people carelessly,
   saying, "Peace, peace,"
   when there is no peace.
12 They acted shamefully, they
   committed abomination;
yet they were not at all
   ashamed,

they did not know how to
   blush.
Therefore they shall fall among
   those who fall;
   at the time when I punish
   them, they shall be
   overthrown,
                    says the LORD.
13 When I wanted to gather them,
   says the LORD,
   there are[e] no grapes on the
   vine,
   nor figs on the fig tree;
even the leaves are withered,
   and what I gave them has
   passed away from them.[d]

14 Why do we sit still?
Gather together, let us go into
   the fortified cities
   and perish there;
for the LORD our God has
   doomed us to perish,
   and has given us poisoned
   water to drink,
   because we have sinned
   against the LORD.
15 We look for peace, but find no
   good,
   for a time of healing, but there
   is terror instead.

16 The snorting of their horses is
   heard from Dan;
   at the sound of the neighing of
   their stallions
   the whole land quakes.
They come and devour the land
   and all that fills it,
   the city and those who live in
   it.
17 See, I am letting snakes loose
   among you,
   adders that cannot be
   charmed,
   and they shall bite you,
                    says the LORD.

The Prophet Mourns for the People

18 My joy is gone, grief is upon me,
   my heart is sick.
19 Hark, the cry of my poor people
   from far and wide in the land:
"Is the LORD not in Zion?
   Is her King not in her?"
("Why have they provoked me to
   anger with their images,

[c] One Ms Gk: MT *this people, Jerusalem,*
[d] Meaning of Heb uncertain   [e] Or *I will
make an end of them, says the LORD.
There are*

20 "The harvest is past, the summer
   is ended,
   and we are not saved."
21 For the hurt of my poor people I
   am hurt,
   I mourn, and dismay has taken
   hold of me.

22 Is there no balm in Gil·e·ad?
   Is there no physician there?
   Why then has the health of my
   poor people
   not been restored?

9 [f] O that my head were a spring
   of water,
   and my eyes a fountain of
   tears,
   so that I might weep day and
   night
   for the slain of my poor
   people!
2 [g] O that I had in the desert
   a traveler's lodging place,
   that I might leave my people
   and go away from them!
   For they are all adulterers,
   a band of traitors.
3 They bend their tongues like
   bows;
   they have grown strong in the
   land for falsehood, and not
   for truth;
   for they proceed from evil to
   evil,
   and they do not know me,
   says the LORD.

4 Beware of your neighbors,
   and put no trust in any of your
   kin;[h]
   for all your kin[i] are
   supplanters,
   and every neighbor goes
   around like a slanderer.
5 They all deceive their neighbors,
   and no one speaks the truth;
   they have taught their tongues to
   speak lies;
   they commit iniquity and are
   too weary to repent.[j]
6 Oppression upon oppression,
   deceit[k] upon deceit!
   They refuse to know me, says
   the LORD.

7 Therefore thus says the LORD of
   hosts:
   I will now refine and test them,
   for what else can I do with my
   sinful people?[l]
8 Their tongue is a deadly arrow;
   it speaks deceit through the
   mouth.
   They all speak friendly words to
   their neighbors,
   but inwardly are planning to
   lay an ambush.
9 Shall I not punish them for these
   things? says the LORD;
   and shall I not bring
   retribution
   on a nation such as this?

10 Take up[m] weeping and wailing
   for the mountains,
   and a lamentation for the
   pastures of the wilderness,
   because they are laid waste so
   that no one passes through,
   and the lowing of cattle is not
   heard;
   both the birds of the air and the
   animals
   have fled and are gone.
11 I will make Jerusalem a heap of
   ruins,
   a lair of jackals;
   and I will make the towns of
   Judah a desolation,
   without inhabitant.

12 Who is wise enough to understand this? To whom has the mouth of
the LORD spoken, so that they may declare it? Why is the land ruined and
laid waste like a wilderness, so that no
one passes through? 13 And the LORD
says: Because they have forsaken my
law that I set before them, and have
not obeyed my voice, or walked in accordance with it, 14 but have stubbornly followed their own hearts and
have gone after the Bā'als, as their ancestors taught them. 15 Therefore thus
says the LORD of hosts, the God of Israel: I am feeding this people with
wormwood, and giving them poisonous water to drink. 16 I will scatter
them among nations that neither they
nor their ancestors have known; and I
will send the sword after them, until I
have consumed them.

f Ch 8.23 in Heb   g Ch 9.1 in Heb
h Heb in a brother   i Heb for every
brother   j Cn Compare Gk: Heb they
weary themselves with iniquity. 6 Your
dwelling   k Cn: Heb Your dwelling in
the midst of deceit   l Or my poor
people   m Gk Syr: Heb I will take up

J
E
R
E
M
I
A
H

The People Mourn in Judgment

17 Thus says the LORD of hosts:
Consider, and call for the
      mourning women to come;
   send for the skilled women to
      come;
18 let them quickly raise a dirge
      over us,
   so that our eyes may run down
      with tears,
   and our eyelids flow with
      water.
19 For a sound of wailing is heard
      from Zion:
   "How we are ruined!
   We are utterly shamed,
   because we have left the land,
   because they have cast down
      our dwellings."

20 Hear, O women, the word of the
      LORD,
   and let your ears receive the
      word of his mouth;
   teach to your daughters a dirge,
   and each to her neighbor a
      lament.
21 "Death has come up into our
      windows,
   it has entered our palaces,
   to cut off the children from the
      streets
   and the young men from the
      squares."
22 Speak! Thus says the LORD:
   "Human corpses shall fall
   like dung upon the open field,
   like sheaves behind the reaper,
   and no one shall gather them."

23 Thus says the LORD: Do not let
the wise boast in their wisdom, do not
let the mighty boast in their might, do
not let the wealthy boast in their
wealth; 24 but let those who boast boast
in this, that they understand and know
me, that I am the LORD; I act with
steadfast love, justice, and righteousness in the earth, for in these things I
delight, says the LORD.
25 The days are surely coming, says
the LORD, when I will attend to all
those who are circumcised only in the
foreskin: 26 Egypt, Judah, Ē'dom, the
Am'mon·ites, Mō'ab, and all those
with shaven temples who live in the
desert. For all these nations are uncircumcised, and all the house of Israel is
uncircumcised in heart.

Idolatry Has Brought Ruin on Israel

10 Hear the word that the LORD
speaks to you, O house of Israel. 2 Thus says the LORD:
   Do not learn the way of the
      nations,
   or be dismayed at the signs of
      the heavens;
   for the nations are dismayed
      at them.
3 For the customs of the peoples
      are false:
   a tree from the forest is cut
      down,
   and worked with an ax by the
      hands of an artisan;
4 people deck it with silver and
      gold;
   they fasten it with hammer
      and nails
   so that it cannot move.
5 Their idols[n] are like scarecrows
      in a cucumber field,
   and they cannot speak;
   they have to be carried,
   for they cannot walk.
   Do not be afraid of them,
   for they cannot do evil,
   nor is it in them to do good.

6 There is none like you, O LORD;
   you are great, and your name
      is great in might.
7 Who would not fear you, O King
      of the nations?
   For that is your due;
   among all the wise ones of the
      nations
   and in all their kingdoms
   there is no one like you.
8 They are both stupid and foolish;
   the instruction given by idols
   is no better than wood![o]
9 Beaten silver is brought from
      Tar'shish,
   and gold from Ū'phaz.
   They are the work of the artisan
   and of the hands of the
      goldsmith;
   their clothing is blue and
      purple;
   they are all the product of
      skilled workers.
10 But the LORD is the true God;
   he is the living God and the
      everlasting King.
   At his wrath the earth quakes,

n Heb They   o Meaning of Heb
uncertain

and the nations cannot endure
his indignation.

11 Thus shall you say to them: The
gods who did not make the heavens
and the earth shall perish from the
earth and from under the heavens.p

12 It is he who made the earth by
his power,
who established the world by
his wisdom,
and by his understanding
stretched out the heavens.
13 When he utters his voice, there
is a tumult of waters in the
heavens,
and he makes the mist rise
from the ends of the earth.
He makes lightnings for the rain,
and he brings out the wind
from his storehouses.
14 Everyone is stupid and without
knowledge;
goldsmiths are all put to
shame by their idols;
for their images are false,
and there is no breath in them.
15 They are worthless, a work of
delusion;
at the time of their punishment
they shall perish.
16 Not like these is the LORD,q the
portion of Jacob,
for he is the one who formed
all things,
and Israel is the tribe of his
inheritance;
the LORD of hosts is his name.

The Coming Exile

17 Gather up your bundle from the
ground,
O you who live under siege!
18 For thus says the LORD:
I am going to sling out the
inhabitants of the land
at this time,
and I will bring distress on them,
so that they shall feel it.

19 Woe is me because of my hurt!
My wound is severe.
But I said, "Truly this is my
punishment,
and I must bear it."

20 My tent is destroyed,
and all my cords are broken;
my children have gone from me,
and they are no more;

there is no one to spread my tent
again,
and to set up my curtains.
21 For the shepherds are stupid,
and do not inquire of the
LORD;
therefore they have not
prospered,
and all their flock is scattered.

22 Hear, a noise! Listen, it is
coming—
a great commotion from the
land of the north
to make the cities of Judah a
desolation,
a lair of jackals.

23 I know, O LORD, that the way of
human beings is not in
their control,
that mortals as they walk
cannot direct their steps.
24 Correct me, O LORD, but in just
measure;
not in your anger, or you will
bring me to nothing.

25 Pour out your wrath on the
nations that do not know
you,
and on the peoples that do not
call on your name;
for they have devoured Jacob;
they have devoured him and
consumed him,
and have laid waste his
habitation.

Israel and Judah Have Broken
the Covenant

11 The word that came to
Jer·e·mi'ah from the LORD:
2 Hear the words of this covenant, and
speak to the people of Judah and the
inhabitants of Jerusalem. 3 You shall
say to them, Thus says the LORD, the
God of Israel: Cursed be anyone who
does not heed the words of this covenant, 4 which I commanded your ancestors when I brought them out of the
land of Egypt, from the iron-smelter,
saying, Listen to my voice, and do all
that I command you. So shall you be
my people, and I will be your God,
5 that I may perform the oath that I
swore to your ancestors, to give them
a land flowing with milk and honey, as

p This verse is in Aramaic   q Heb lacks
the LORD

at this day. Then I answered, "So be it, LORD."

6 And the LORD said to me: Proclaim all these words in the cities of Judah, and in the streets of Jerusalem: Hear the words of this covenant and do them. ⁷For I solemnly warned your ancestors when I brought them up out of the land of Egypt, warning them persistently, even to this day, saying, Obey my voice. ⁸Yet they did not obey or incline their ear, but everyone walked in the stubbornness of an evil will. So I brought upon them all the words of this covenant, which I commanded them to do, but they did not.

9 And the LORD said to me: Conspiracy exists among the people of Judah and the inhabitants of Jerusalem. ¹⁰They have turned back to the iniquities of their ancestors of old, who refused to heed my words; they have gone after other gods to serve them; the house of Israel and the house of Judah have broken the covenant that I made with their ancestors. ¹¹Therefore, thus says the LORD, assuredly I am going to bring disaster upon them that they cannot escape; though they cry out to me, I will not listen to them. ¹²Then the cities of Judah and the inhabitants of Jerusalem will go and cry out to the gods to whom they make offerings, but they will never save them in the time of their trouble. ¹³For your gods have become as many as your towns, O Judah; and as many as the streets of Jerusalem are the altars you have set up to shame, altars to make offerings to Bā′al.

14 As for you, do not pray for this people, or lift up a cry or prayer on their behalf, for I will not listen when they call to me in the time of their trouble. ¹⁵What right has my beloved in my house, when she has done vile deeds? Can vowsʳ and sacrificial flesh avert your doom? Can you then exult? ¹⁶The LORD once called you, "A green olive tree, fair with goodly fruit"; but with the roar of a great tempest he will set fire to it, and its branches will be consumed. ¹⁷The LORD of hosts, who planted you, has pronounced evil against you, because of the evil that the house of Israel and the house of Judah have done, provoking me to anger by making offerings to Bā′al.

Jeremiah's Life Threatened

18 It was the LORD who made it
    known to me, and I knew;
  then you showed me their evil
    deeds.
19 But I was like a gentle lamb
    led to the slaughter.
  And I did not know it was
    against me
  that they devised schemes,
    saying,
  "Let us destroy the tree with its
    fruit,
  let us cut him off from the
    land of the living,
  so that his name will no longer
    be remembered!"
20 But you, O LORD of hosts, who
    judge righteously,
  who try the heart and the
    mind,
  let me see your retribution upon
    them,
  for to you I have committed
    my cause.

21 Therefore thus says the LORD concerning the people of An′a·thoth, who seek your life, and say, "You shall not prophesy in the name of the LORD, or you will die by our hand" — ²²therefore thus says the LORD of hosts: I am going to punish them; the young men shall die by the sword; their sons and their daughters shall die by famine; ²³and not even a remnant shall be left of them. For I will bring disaster upon the people of An′a·thoth, the year of their punishment.

Jeremiah Complains to God

12 You will be in the right,
    O LORD,
  when I lay charges against
    you;
  but let me put my case to you.
  Why does the way of the guilty
    prosper?
  Why do all who are
    treacherous thrive?
2 You plant them, and they take
    root;
  they grow and bring forth
    fruit;
  you are near in their mouths
    yet far from their hearts.
3 But you, O LORD, know me;
  You see me and test me — my
    heart is with you.

ʳGk: Heb *Can many*

Pull them out like sheep for the
　　slaughter,
　　and set them apart for the day
　　　of slaughter.
4 How long will the land mourn,
　　and the grass of every field
　　　wither?
For the wickedness of those who
　　live in it
　　the animals and the birds are
　　　swept away,
　　and because people said, "He
　　　is blind to our ways."[s]

God Replies to Jeremiah

5 If you have raced with
　　　foot-runners and they have
　　　wearied you,
　　how will you compete with
　　　horses?
And if in a safe land you fall
　　down,
　　how will you fare in the
　　　thickets of the Jordan?
6 For even your kinsfolk and your
　　　own family,
　　even they have dealt
　　　treacherously with you;
　　they are in full cry after you;
do not believe them,
　　though they speak friendly
　　　words to you.

7 I have forsaken my house,
　　I have abandoned my heritage;
I have given the beloved of my
　　heart
　　into the hands of her enemies.
8 My heritage has become to me
　　like a lion in the forest;
she has lifted up her voice
　　against me —
　　therefore I hate her.
9 Is the hyena greedy[t] for my
　　　heritage at my command?
　　Are the birds of prey all
　　　around her?
Go, assemble all the wild
　　animals;
　　bring them to devour her.
10 Many shepherds have destroyed
　　my vineyard,
　　they have trampled down my
　　　portion,
they have made my pleasant
　　portion
　　a desolate wilderness.
11 They have made it a desolation;
　　desolate, it mourns to me.
The whole land is made
　　desolate,

but no one lays it to heart.
12 Upon all the bare heights[u] in
　　　the desert
　　spoilers have come;
for the sword of the LORD
　　devours
　　from one end of the land to
　　　the other;
　　no one shall be safe.
13 They have sown wheat and have
　　reaped thorns,
　　they have tired themselves out
　　　but profit nothing.
They shall be ashamed of their[v]
　　harvests
　　because of the fierce anger of
　　　the LORD.

14 Thus says the LORD concerning
all my evil neighbors who touch the
heritage that I have given my people
Israel to inherit: I am about to pluck
them up from their land, and I will
pluck up the house of Judah from
among them. 15 And after I have
plucked them up, I will again have
compassion on them, and I will bring
them again to their heritage and to
their land, everyone of them. 16 And
then, if they will diligently learn the
ways of my people, to swear by my
name, "As the LORD lives," as they
taught my people to swear by Bā′al,
then they shall be built up in the midst
of my people. 17 But if any nation will
not listen, then I will completely uproot it and destroy it, says the LORD.

The Linen Loincloth

13 Thus said the LORD to me, "Go
and buy yourself a linen loincloth, and put it on your loins, but do
not dip it in water." 2 So I bought a loincloth according to the word of the
LORD, and put it on my loins. 3 And the
word of the LORD came to me a second
time, saying, 4 "Take the loincloth that
you bought and are wearing, and go
now to the Euphrates,[w] and hide it
there in a cleft of the rock." 5 So I went,
and hid it by the Euphrates,[x] as the
LORD commanded me. 6 And after
many days the LORD said to me, "Go
now to the Euphrates,[w] and take from
there the loincloth that I commanded
you to hide there." 7 Then I went to the
Euphrates,[w] and dug, and I took the

[s] Gk: Heb *to our future*　[t] Cn: Heb *Is
the hyena, the bird of prey*　[u] Or *the
trails*　[v] Heb *your*　[w] Or *to Parah*; Heb
perath　[x] Or *by Parah*; Heb *perath*

loincloth from the place where I had hidden it. But now the loincloth was ruined; it was good for nothing.

8 Then the word of the LORD came to me: [9]Thus says the LORD: Just so I will ruin the pride of Judah and the great pride of Jerusalem. [10]This evil people, who refuse to hear my words, who stubbornly follow their own will and have gone after other gods to serve them and worship them, shall be like this loincloth, which is good for nothing. [11]For as the loincloth clings to one's loins, so I made the whole house of Israel and the whole house of Judah cling to me, says the LORD, in order that they might be for me a people, a name, a praise, and a glory. But they would not listen.

Symbol of the Wine-Jars

12 You shall speak to them this word: Thus says the LORD, the God of Israel: Every wine-jar should be filled with wine. And they will say to you, "Do you think we do not know that every wine-jar should be filled with wine?" [13]Then you shall say to them: Thus says the LORD: I am about to fill all the inhabitants of this land — the kings who sit on David's throne, the priests, the prophets, and all the inhabitants of Jerusalem — with drunkenness. [14]And I will dash them one against another, parents and children together, says the LORD. I will not pity or spare or have compassion when I destroy them.

Exile Threatened

15 Hear and give ear; do not be haughty,
for the LORD has spoken.
16 Give glory to the LORD your God
before he brings darkness,
and before your feet stumble
on the mountains at twilight;
while you look for light,
he turns it into gloom
and makes it deep darkness.
17 But if you will not listen,
my soul will weep in secret for
your pride;
my eyes will weep bitterly and
run down with tears,
because the LORD's flock has
been taken captive.

18 Say to the king and the queen
mother;
"Take a lowly seat,

for your beautiful crown
has come down from your
head."[y]
19 The towns of the Neg'eb are
shut up
with no one to open them;
all Judah is taken into exile,
wholly taken into exile.

20 Lift up your eyes and see
those who come from the
north.
Where is the flock that was
given you,
your beautiful flock?
21 What will you say when they set
as head over you
those whom you have trained
to be your allies?
Will not pangs take hold of you,
like those of a woman in
labor?
22 And if you say in your heart,
"Why have these things come
upon me?"
it is for the greatness of your
iniquity
that your skirts are lifted up,
and you are violated.
23 Can Ethiopians[z] change their
skin
or leopards their spots?
Then also you can do good
who are accustomed to do evil.
24 I will scatter you[a] like chaff
driven by the wind from the
desert.
25 This is your lot,
the portion I have measured
out to you, says the LORD,
because you have forgotten me
and trusted in lies.
26 I myself will lift up your skirts
over your face,
and your shame will be seen.
27 I have seen your abominations,
your adulteries and neighings,
your shameless
prostitutions
on the hills of the countryside.
Woe to you, O Jerusalem!
How long will it be
before you are made clean?

[y] Gk Syr Vg: Meaning of Heb uncertain
[z] Or *Nubians*; Heb *Cushites*
[a] Heb *them*

The Great Drought

14 The word of the LORD that came to Jer·e·mi'ah concerning the drought:

2 Judah mourns
   and her gates languish;
   they lie in gloom on the ground,
      and the cry of Jerusalem goes
         up.
3 Her nobles send their servants
      for water;
   they come to the cisterns,
   they find no water,
      they return with their vessels
         empty.
They are ashamed and dismayed
      and cover their heads,
4 because the ground is cracked.
   Because there has been no
      rain on the land
   the farmers are dismayed;
      they cover their heads.
5 Even the doe in the field
      forsakes her newborn fawn
   because there is no grass.
6 The wild asses stand on the bare
      heights,[b]
   they pant for air like jackals;
   their eyes fail
      because there is no herbage.

7 Although our iniquities testify
      against us,
   act, O LORD, for your name's
         sake;
   our apostasies indeed are many,
      and we have sinned against
         you.
8 O hope of Israel,
   its savior in time of trouble,
   why should you be like a
      stranger in the land,
   like a traveler turning aside
      for the night?
9 Why should you be like someone
      confused,
   like a mighty warrior who
      cannot give help?
Yet you, O LORD, are in the
      midst of us,
   and we are called by your
      name;
   do not forsake us!

10 Thus says the LORD concerning
      this people:
Truly they have loved to wander,
   they have not restrained their
      feet;
therefore the LORD does not
   accept them,

now he will remember their
   iniquity
and punish their sins.

11 The LORD said to me: Do not pray for the welfare of this people. 12 Although they fast, I do not hear their cry, and although they offer burnt offering and grain offering, I do not accept them; but by the sword, by famine, and by pestilence I consume them.

Denunciation of Lying Prophets

13 Then I said: "Ah, Lord GOD! Here are the prophets saying to them, 'You shall not see the sword, nor shall you have famine, but I will give you true peace in this place.'" 14 And the LORD said to me: The prophets are prophesying lies in my name; I did not send them, nor did I command them or speak to them. They are prophesying to you a lying vision, worthless divination, and the deceit of their own minds. 15 Therefore thus says the LORD concerning the prophets who prophesy in my name though I did not send them, and who say, "Sword and famine shall not come on this land": By sword and famine those prophets shall be consumed. 16 And the people to whom they prophesy shall be thrown out into the streets of Jerusalem, victims of famine and sword. There shall be no one to bury them—themselves, their wives, their sons, and their daughters. For I will pour out their wickedness upon them.

17 You shall say to them this word:
   Let my eyes run down with tears
      night and day,
   and let them not cease,
   for the virgin daughter—my
      people—is struck down
      with a crushing blow,
   with a very grievous wound.
18 If I go out into the field,
   look—those killed by the
      sword!
And if I enter the city,
   look—those sick with[c]
      famine!
For both prophet and priest ply
      their trade throughout the
         land,
   and have no knowledge.

---

[b] Or *the trails*　　[c] Heb *look—the sicknesses of*

The People Plead for Mercy

19 Have you completely rejected
    Judah?
    Does your heart loathe Zion?
    Why have you struck us down
        so that there is no healing for
        us?
    We look for peace, but find no
        good;
        for a time of healing, but there
        is terror instead.
20 We acknowledge our
        wickedness, O LORD,
    the iniquity of our ancestors,
    for we have sinned against
        you.
21 Do not spurn us, for your name's
        sake;
    do not dishonor your glorious
        throne;
    remember and do not break
        your covenant with us.
22 Can any idols of the nations
        bring rain?
    Or can the heavens give
        showers?
    Is it not you, O LORD our God?
    We set our hope on you,
    for it is you who do all this.

Punishment Is Inevitable

15 Then the LORD said to me:
    Though Moses and Samuel
stood before me, yet my heart would
not turn toward this people. Send them
out of my sight, and let them go! 2 And
when they say to you, "Where shall we
go?" you shall say to them: Thus says
the LORD:
    Those destined for pestilence, to
        pestilence,
    and those destined for the
        sword, to the sword;
    those destined for famine, to
        famine,
    and those destined for
        captivity, to captivity.
3 And I will appoint over them four
kinds of destroyers, says the LORD: the
sword to kill, the dogs to drag away,
and the birds of the air and the wild
animals of the earth to devour and destroy. 4 I will make them a horror to all
the kingdoms of the earth because of
what King Ma·nas′seh son of
Hez·e·ki′ah of Judah did in Jerusalem.

5 Who will have pity on you,
        O Jerusalem,
    or who will bemoan you?
    Who will turn aside

    to ask about your welfare?
6 You have rejected me, says the
        LORD,
    you are going backward;
    so I have stretched out my hand
        against you and destroyed
        you—
    I am weary of relenting.
7 I have winnowed them with a
        winnowing fork
    in the gates of the land;
    I have bereaved them, I have
        destroyed my people;
    they did not turn from their
        ways.
8 Their widows became more
        numerous
    than the sand of the seas;
    I have brought against the
        mothers of youths
    a destroyer at noonday;
    I have made anguish and terror
    fall upon her suddenly.
9 She who bore seven has
        languished;
    she has swooned away;
    her sun went down while it was
        yet day;
    she has been shamed and
        disgraced.
    And the rest of them I will give
        to the sword
    before their enemies,
                    says the LORD.

*Jeremiah Complains Again
and Is Reassured*

10 Woe is me, my mother, that you
ever bore me, a man of strife and contention to the whole land! I have not
lent, nor have I borrowed, yet all of
them curse me. 11 The LORD said:
Surely I have intervened in your life[d]
for good, surely I have imposed enemies on you in a time of trouble and in
a time of distress.[e] 12 Can iron and
bronze break iron from the north?
13 Your wealth and your treasures
I will give as plunder, without price,
for all your sins, throughout all your
territory. 14 I will make you serve your
enemies in a land that you do not
know, for in my anger a fire is kindled
that shall burn forever.
15 O LORD, you know;
    remember me and visit me,
    and bring down retribution for
        me on my persecutors.

dHeb *intervened with you*   eMeaning
of Heb uncertain

In your forbearance do not take
    me away;
    know that on your account I
        suffer insult.
16 Your words were found, and I
    ate them,
    and your words became to me
        a joy
    and the delight of my heart;
for I am called by your name,
    O LORD, God of hosts.
17 I did not sit in the company of
    merrymakers,
    nor did I rejoice;
under the weight of your hand I
    sat alone,
    for you had filled me with
        indignation.
18 Why is my pain unceasing,
    my wound incurable,
    refusing to be healed?
Truly, you are to me like a
    deceitful brook,
    like waters that fail.

19 Therefore thus says the LORD:
If you turn back, I will take you
    back,
    and you shall stand before me.
If you utter what is precious, and
    not what is worthless,
    you shall serve as my mouth.
It is they who will turn to you,
    not you who will turn to them.
20 And I will make you to this
    people
    a fortified wall of bronze;
they will fight against you,
    but they shall not prevail over
        you,
for I am with you
    to save you and deliver you,
            says the LORD.
21 I will deliver you out of the hand
    of the wicked,
    and redeem you from the
        grasp of the ruthless.

Jeremiah's Celibacy and Message

16 The word of the LORD came to
me: 2 You shall not take a wife,
nor shall you have sons or daughters
in this place. 3 For thus says the LORD
concerning the sons and daughters
who are born in this place, and concerning the mothers who bear them
and the fathers who beget them in this
land: 4 They shall die of deadly diseases. They shall not be lamented, nor
shall they be buried; they shall become
like dung on the surface of the ground.
They shall perish by the sword and by

famine, and their dead bodies shall become food for the birds of the air and
for the wild animals of the earth.
   5 For thus says the LORD: Do not
enter the house of mourning, or go to
lament, or bemoan them; for I have
taken away my peace from this people,
says the LORD, my steadfast love and
mercy. 6 Both great and small shall die
in this land; they shall not be buried,
and no one shall lament for them;
there shall be no gashing, no shaving
of the head for them. 7 No one shall
break bread*f* for the mourner, to offer
comfort for the dead; nor shall anyone
give them the cup of consolation to
drink for their fathers or their mothers. 8 You shall not go into the house of
feasting to sit with them, to eat and
drink. 9 For thus says the LORD of
hosts, the God of Israel: I am going
to banish from this place, in your
days and before your eyes, the voice
of mirth and the voice of gladness, the
voice of the bridegroom and the voice
of the bride.
   10 And when you tell this people all
these words, and they say to you,
"Why has the LORD pronounced all
this great evil against us? What is our
iniquity? What is the sin that we have
committed against the LORD our God?"
11 then you shall say to them: It is because your ancestors have forsaken
me, says the LORD, and have gone after other gods and have served and
worshiped them, and have forsaken
me and have not kept my law; 12 and
because you have behaved worse than
your ancestors, for here you are, every
one of you, following your stubborn
evil will, refusing to listen to me.
13 Therefore I will hurl you out of this
land into a land that neither you nor
your ancestors have known, and there
you shall serve other gods day and
night, for I will show you no favor.

God Will Restore Israel
(Cp Jer 23.7–8)

14 Therefore, the days are surely
coming, says the LORD, when it shall
no longer be said, "As the LORD lives
who brought the people of Israel up
out of the land of Egypt," 15 but "As the
LORD lives who brought the people of
Israel up out of the land of the north
and out of all the lands where he had
driven them." For I will bring them

f Two Mss Gk: MT *break for them*

back to their own land that I gave to their ancestors.

16 I am now sending for many fishermen, says the LORD, and they shall catch them; and afterward I will send for many hunters, and they shall hunt them from every mountain and every hill, and out of the clefts of the rocks. 17For my eyes are on all their ways; they are not hidden from my presence, nor is their iniquity concealed from my sight. 18Andg I will doubly repay their iniquity and their sin, because they have polluted my land with the carcasses of their detestable idols, and have filled my inheritance with their abominations.

19 O LORD, my strength and my
        stronghold,
    my refuge in the day of
        trouble,
  to you shall the nations come
    from the ends of the earth and
        say:
  Our ancestors have inherited
        nothing but lies,
    worthless things in which
        there is no profit.
20 Can mortals make for
        themselves gods?
    Such are no gods!

21 "Therefore I am surely going to teach them, this time I am going to teach them my power and my might, and they shall know that my name is the LORD."

Judah's Sin and Punishment

17 The sin of Judah is written with an iron pen; with a diamond point it is engraved on the tablet of their hearts, and on the horns of their altars, 2while their children remember their altars and their sacred poles,h beside every green tree, and on the high hills, 3on the mountains in the open country. Your wealth and all your treasures I will give for spoil as the price of your sini throughout all your territory. 4By your own act you shall lose the heritage that I gave you, and I will make you serve your enemies in a land that you do not know, for in my anger a fire is kindledj that shall burn forever.

5 Thus says the LORD:
  Cursed are those who trust in
        mere mortals

  and make mere flesh their
        strength,
  whose hearts turn away from
        the LORD.
6 They shall be like a shrub in the
        desert,
    and shall not see when relief
        comes.
  They shall live in the parched
        places of the wilderness,
    in an uninhabited salt land.

7 Blessed are those who trust in
        the LORD,
    whose trust is the LORD.
8 They shall be like a tree planted
        by water,
    sending out its roots by the
        stream.
  It shall not fear when heat
        comes,
    and its leaves shall stay green;
  in the year of drought it is not
        anxious,
    and it does not cease to bear
        fruit.

9 The heart is devious above all
        else;
    it is perverse—
  who can understand it?
10 I the LORD test the mind
        and search the heart,
  to give to all according to their
        ways,
    according to the fruit of their
        doings.

11 Like the partridge hatching what
        it did not lay,
    so are all who amass wealth
        unjustly;
  in mid-life it will leave them,
    and at their end they will
        prove to be fools.

12 O glorious throne, exalted from
        the beginning,
    shrine of our sanctuary!
13 O hope of Israel! O LORD!
  All who forsake you shall be
        put to shame;
    those who turn away from youk
        shall be recorded in the
        underworld,l

g Gk: Heb *And first*   h Heb *Asherim*
i Cn: Heb *spoil your high places for sin*
j Two Mss Theodotion: *you kindled*
k Heb *me*   l Or *in the earth*

for they have forsaken the
  fountain of living water,
  the LORD.

Jeremiah Prays for Vindication

4 Heal me, O LORD, and I shall be
    healed;
  save me, and I shall be saved;
    for you are my praise.
5 See how they say to me,
    "Where is the word of the
    LORD?
    Let it come!"
6 But I have not run away from
    being a shepherd[m] in your
    service,
  nor have I desired the fatal
    day.
  You know what came from my
    lips;
  it was before your face.
7 Do not become a terror to me;
    you are my refuge in the day
    of disaster;
8 Let my persecutors be shamed,
    but do not let me be shamed;
  let them be dismayed,
    but do not let me be dismayed;
  bring on them the day of
    disaster;
  destroy them with double
    destruction!

Hallow the Sabbath Day

19 Thus said the LORD to me: Go
and stand in the People's Gate, by
which the kings of Judah enter and by
which they go out, and in all the gates
of Jerusalem, 20 and say to them: Hear
the word of the LORD, you kings of
Judah, and all Judah, and all the inhabitants of Jerusalem, who enter by
these gates. 21 Thus says the LORD: For
the sake of your lives, take care that
you do not bear a burden on the sabbath day or bring it in by the gates of
Jerusalem. 22 And do not carry a burden out of your houses on the sabbath
or do any work, but keep the sabbath
day holy, as I commanded your ancestors. 23 Yet they did not listen or incline
their ear; they stiffened their necks
and would not hear or receive instruction.
24 But if you listen to me, says the
LORD, and bring in no burden by the
gates of this city on the sabbath day,
but keep the sabbath day holy and do
no work on it, 25 then there shall enter
by the gates of this city kings[n] who sit
on the throne of David, riding in chari-

ots and on horses, they and their officials, the people of Judah and the inhabitants of Jerusalem; and this city
shall be inhabited forever. 26 And people shall come from the towns of Judah
and the places around Jerusalem, from
the land of Benjamin, from the
She·phē'lah, from the hill country, and
from the Neg'eb, bringing burnt offerings and sacrifices, grain offerings and
frankincense, and bringing thank
offerings to the house of the LORD.
27 But if you do not listen to me, to keep
the sabbath day holy, and to carry in
no burden through the gates of Jerusalem on the sabbath day, then I will kindle a fire in its gates; it shall devour the
palaces of Jerusalem and shall not be
quenched.

The Potter and the Clay

18 The word that came to
    Jer·e·mī'ah from the LORD:
2 "Come, go down to the potter's house,
and there I will let you hear my
words." 3 So I went down to the potter's
house, and there he was working at his
wheel. 4 The vessel he was making of
clay was spoiled in the potter's hand,
and he reworked it into another vessel,
as seemed good to him.
5 Then the word of the LORD came
to me: 6 Can I not do with you, O house
of Israel, just as this potter has done?
says the LORD. Just like the clay in the
potter's hand, so are you in my hand,
O house of Israel. 7 At one moment I
may declare concerning a nation or a
kingdom, that I will pluck up and
break down and destroy it, 8 but if that
nation, concerning which I have spoken, turns from its evil, I will change
my mind about the disaster that I intended to bring on it. 9 And at another
moment I may declare concerning a
nation or a kingdom that I will build
and plant it, 10 but if it does evil in my
sight, not listening to my voice, then I
will change my mind about the good
that I had intended to do to it. 11 Now,
therefore, say to the people of Judah
and the inhabitants of Jerusalem: Thus
says the LORD: Look, I am a potter
shaping evil against you and devising
a plan against you. Turn now, all of
you from your evil way, and amend
your ways and your doings.

J
E
R
E
M
I
A
H

---

m Meaning of Heb uncertain   n Cn: Heb
kings and officials

Israel's Stubborn Idolatry

12 But they say, "It is no use! We will follow our own plans, and each of us will act according to the stubbornness of our evil will."

13 Therefore thus says the LORD:
Ask among the nations:
Who has heard the like of
this?
The virgin Israel has done
a most horrible thing.
14 Does the snow of Lebanon leave
the crags of Sir'i·on?*o*
Do the mountain*p* waters run
dry,*q*
the cold flowing streams?
15 But my people have forgotten
me,
they burn offerings to a
delusion;
they have stumbled*r* in their
ways,
in the ancient roads,
and have gone into bypaths,
not the highway,
16 making their land a horror,
a thing to be hissed at forever.
All who pass by it are horrified
and shake their heads.
17 Like the wind from the east,
I will scatter them before the
enemy.
I will show them my back, not
my face,
in the day of their calamity.

A Plot against Jeremiah

18 Then they said, "Come, let us make plots against Jer·e·mī'ah — for instruction shall not perish from the priest, nor counsel from the wise, nor the word from the prophet. Come, let us bring charges against him,*s* and let us not heed any of his words."

19 Give heed to me, O LORD,
and listen to what my
adversaries say!
20 Is evil a recompense for good?
Yet they have dug a pit for my
life.
Remember how I stood before
you
to speak good for them,
to turn away your wrath from
them.
21 Therefore give their children
over to famine;
hurl them out to the power of
the sword,

let their wives become childless
and widowed.
May their men meet death by
pestilence,
their youths be slain by the
sword in battle.
22 May a cry be heard from their
houses,
when you bring the marauder
suddenly upon them!
For they have dug a pit to catch
me,
and laid snares for my feet.
23 Yet you, O LORD, know
all their plotting to kill me.
Do not forgive their iniquity,
do not blot out their sin from
your sight.
Let them be tripped up before
you;
deal with them while you are
angry.

The Broken Earthenware Jug

19 Thus said the LORD: Go an buy a potter's earthenware jug Take with you*t* some of the elders o the people and some of the senio priests, 2 and go out to the valley of th son of Hin'nom at the entry of the Pot sherd Gate, and proclaim there th words that I tell you. 3 You shall say Hear the word of the LORD, O kings o Judah and inhabitants of Jerusalem Thus says the LORD of hosts, the Go of Israel: I am going to bring such di saster upon this place that the ears c everyone who hears of it will tingle 4 Because the people have forsake me, and have profaned this place b making offerings in it to other god whom neither they nor their ancestor nor the kings of Judah have known and because they have filled this plac with the blood of the innocent, 5 an gone on building the high places o Bā'al to burn their children in the fir as burnt offerings to Bā'al, which I di not command or decree, nor did it en ter my mind. 6 Therefore the days ar surely coming, says the LORD, whe this place shall no more be called Tō pheth, or the valley of the son of Hin nom, but the valley of Slaughter. 7 An in this place I will make void the plan

*o*Cn: Heb *of the field*   *p*Cn: Heb *foreign*
*q*Cn: Heb *Are . . . plucked up?*   *r*Gk Syr
Vg: Heb *they made them stumble*
*s*Heb *strike him with the tongue*   *t*Syr
Tg Compare Gk: Heb lacks *take with*
you

of Judah and Jerusalem, and will make them fall by the sword before their enemies, and by the hand of those who seek their life. I will give their dead bodies for food to the birds of the air and to the wild animals of the earth. 8 And I will make this city a horror, a thing to be hissed at; everyone who passes by it will be horrified and will hiss because of all its disasters. 9 And I will make them eat the flesh of their sons and the flesh of their daughters, and all shall eat the flesh of their neighbors in the siege, and in the distress with which their enemies and those who seek their life afflict them.

10 Then you shall break the jug in the sight of those who go with you, 11 and shall say to them: Thus says the LORD of hosts: So will I break this people and this city, as one breaks a potter's vessel, so that it can never be mended. In Tō'pheth they shall bury until there is no more room to bury. 12 Thus will I do to this place, says the LORD, and to its inhabitants, making this city like Tō'pheth. 13 And the houses of Jerusalem and the houses of the kings of Judah shall be defiled like the place of Tō'pheth — all the houses upon whose roofs offerings have been made to the whole host of heaven, and libations have been poured out to other gods.

14 When Jer·e·mī'ah came from Tō'pheth, where the LORD had sent him to prophesy, he stood in the court of the LORD's house and said to all the people: 15 Thus says the LORD of hosts, the God of Israel: I am now bringing upon this city and upon all its towns all the disaster that I have pronounced against it, because they have stiffened their necks, refusing to hear my words.

Jeremiah Persecuted by Pashhur

20 Now the priest Pash'hur son of Im'mer, who was chief officer in the house of the LORD, heard Jer·e·mī'ah prophesying these things. 2 Then Pash'hur struck the prophet Jer·e·mī'ah, and put him in the stocks that were in the upper Benjamin Gate of the house of the LORD. 3 The next morning when Pash'hur released Jer·e·mī'ah from the stocks, Jer·e·mī'ah said to him, The LORD has named you not Pash'hur but "Terror-all-around." 4 For thus says the LORD: I am making you a terror to yourself and to all your friends; and they shall fall by the sword of their enemies

while you look on. And I will give all Judah into the hand of the king of Babylon; he shall carry them captive to Babylon, and shall kill them with the sword. 5 I will give all the wealth of this city, all its gains, all its prized belongings, and all the treasures of the kings of Judah into the hand of their enemies, who shall plunder them, and seize them, and carry them to Babylon. 6 And you, Pash'hur, and all who live in your house, shall go into captivity, and to Babylon you shall go; there you shall die, and there you shall be buried, you and all your friends, to whom you have prophesied falsely.

Jeremiah Denounces His Persecutors

7 O LORD, you have enticed me,
   and I was enticed;
you have overpowered me,
   and you have prevailed.
I have become a laughingstock
   all day long;
   everyone mocks me.
8 For whenever I speak, I must cry out,
   I must shout, "Violence and destruction!"
For the word of the LORD has become for me
   a reproach and derision all day long.
9 If I say, "I will not mention him, or speak any more in his name,"
then within me there is something like a burning fire
   shut up in my bones;
I am weary with holding it in,
   and I cannot.
10 For I hear many whispering:
   "Terror is all around!
Denounce him! Let us denounce him!"
   All my close friends
   are watching for me to stumble.
"Perhaps he can be enticed,
   and we can prevail against him,
   and take our revenge on him."
11 But the LORD is with me like a dread warrior;
   therefore my persecutors will stumble,
   and they will not prevail.
They will be greatly shamed,
   for they will not succeed.
Their eternal dishonor

will never be forgotten.

12 O LORD of hosts, you test the
righteous,
you see the heart and the
mind;
let me see your retribution upon
them,
for to you I have committed
my cause.

13 Sing to the LORD;
praise the LORD!
For he has delivered the life of
the needy
from the hands of evildoers.

14 Cursed be the day
on which I was born!
The day when my mother bore
me,
let it not be blessed!
15 Cursed be the man
who brought the news to my
father, saying,
"A child is born to you, a son,"
making him very glad.
16 Let that man be like the cities
that the LORD overthrew
without pity;
let him hear a cry in the
morning
and an alarm at noon,
17 because he did not kill me in the
womb;
so my mother would have
been my grave,
and her womb forever great.
18 Why did I come forth from the
womb
to see toil and sorrow,
and spend my days in shame?

Jerusalem Will Fall to Nebuchadrezzar

21 This is the word that came to
Jer·e·mī′ah from the LORD,
when King Zed·e·kī′ah sent to him
Pash′hur son of Mal·chī′ah and the
priest Zeph·a·nī′ah son of Mā·a·sēi′
ah, saying, 2 "Please inquire of the
LORD on our behalf, for King Ne-
bū·chad·rez′zar of Babylon is making
war against us; perhaps the LORD will
perform a wonderful deed for us, as he
has often done, and will make him
withdraw from us."

3 Then Jer·e·mī′ah said to them:
4 Thus you shall say to Zed·e·kī′ah:
Thus says the LORD, the God of Israel:
I am going to turn back the weapons of
war that are in your hands and with
which you are fighting against the
king of Babylon and against the
Chal·dē′ans who are besieging you
outside the walls; and I will bring them
together into the center of this city. 5 I
myself will fight against you with outstretched hand and mighty arm, in anger, in fury, and in great wrath. 6 And
I will strike down the inhabitants of
this city, both human beings and animals; they shall die of a great pestilence. 7 Afterward, says the LORD, I
will give King Zed·e·kī′ah of Judah,
and his servants, and the people in this
city—those who survive the pestilence, sword, and famine—into the
hands of King Ne·bū·chad·rez′zar of
Babylon, into the hands of their enemies, into the hands of those who seek
their lives. He shall strike them down
with the edge of the sword; he shall not
pity them, or spare them, or have compassion.

8 And to this people you shall say:
Thus says the LORD: See, I am setting
before you the way of life and the way
of death. 9 Those who stay in this city
shall die by the sword, by famine, and
by pestilence; but those who go out
and surrender to the Chal·dē′ans who
are besieging you shall live and shall
have their lives as a prize of war. 10 For
I have set my face against this city for
evil and not for good, says the LORD: it
shall be given into the hands of the
king of Babylon, and he shall burn it
with fire.

Message to the House of David

11 To the house of the king of Judah
say: Hear the word of the LORD,
12 O house of David! Thus says the
LORD:
Execute justice in the morning,
and deliver from the hand of
the oppressor
anyone who has been robbed,
or else my wrath will go forth
like fire,
and burn, with no one to
quench it,
because of your evil doings.

13 See, I am against you,
O inhabitant of the valley,
O rock of the plain,
says the LORD;
you who say, "Who can come
down against us,
or who can enter our places of
refuge?"

¹⁴ I will punish you according to
   the fruit of your doings,
                    says the LORD;
   I will kindle a fire in its forest,
   and it shall devour all that is
      around it.

Exhortation to Repent

22 Thus says the LORD: Go down
   to the house of the king of Judah, and speak there this word, ² and
say: Hear the word of the LORD,
O King of Judah sitting on the throne
of David — you, and your servants, and
your people who enter these gates.
³ Thus says the LORD: Act with justice
and righteousness, and deliver from
the hand of the oppressor anyone who
has been robbed. And do no wrong or
violence to the alien, the orphan, and
the widow, or shed innocent blood in
this place. ⁴ For if you will indeed obey
this word, then through the gates of
this house shall enter kings who sit on
the throne of David, riding in chariots
and on horses, they, and their servants, and their people. ⁵ But if you will
not heed these words, I swear by myself, says the LORD, that this house
shall become a desolation. ⁶ For thus
says the LORD concerning the house of
the king of Judah:
   You are like Gil′e·ad to me,
      like the summit of Lebanon;
   but I swear that I will make you
      a desert,
      an uninhabited city.^u
⁷ I will prepare destroyers against
      you,
      all with their weapons;
   they shall cut down your
      choicest cedars
      and cast them into the fire.

⁸ And many nations will pass by
this city, and all of them will say one to
another, "Why has the LORD dealt in
this way with that great city?" ⁹ And
they will answer, "Because they abandoned the covenant of the LORD their
God, and worshiped other gods and
served them."

¹⁰ Do not weep for him who is dead,
      nor bemoan him;
   weep rather for him who goes
      away,
   for he shall return no more
      to see his native land.

Message to the Sons of Josiah

¹¹ For thus says the LORD concerning Shal′lum son of King Jō·sī′ah of
Judah, who succeeded his father
Jō·sī′ah, and who went away from this
place: He shall return here no more,
¹² but in the place where they have carried him captive he shall die, and he
shall never see this land again.

¹³ Woe to him who builds his
      house by unrighteousness,
   and his upper rooms by
      injustice;
   who makes his neighbors work
      for nothing,
   and does not give them their
      wages;
¹⁴ who says, "I will build myself a
      spacious house
   with large upper rooms,"
   and who cuts out windows for it,
      paneling it with cedar,
   and painting it with vermilion.
¹⁵ Are you a king
   because you compete in cedar?
Did not your father eat and
      drink
   and do justice and
      righteousness?
   Then it was well with him.
¹⁶ He judged the cause of the poor
      and needy;
   then it was well.
Is not this to know me?
   says the LORD.
¹⁷ But your eyes and heart
   are only on your dishonest
      gain,
   for shedding innocent blood,
   and for practicing oppression
      and violence.
¹⁸ Therefore thus says the LORD
concerning King Je·hoi′a·kim son of
Jō·sī′ah of Judah:
   They shall not lament for him,
      saying,
   "Alas, my brother!" or "Alas,
      sister!"
   They shall not lament for him,
      saying,
   "Alas, lord!" or "Alas, his
      majesty!"
¹⁹ With the burial of a donkey he
      shall be buried —
   dragged off and thrown out
      beyond the gates of
      Jerusalem.

^u Cn: Heb *uninhabited cities*

20 Go up to Lebanon, and cry out,
   and lift up your voice in
   Bā'shan;
   cry out from Ab'a·rim,
   for all your lovers are crushed.
21 I spoke to you in your
   prosperity,
   but you said, "I will not listen."
   This has been your way from
   your youth,
   for you have not obeyed my
   voice.
22 The wind shall shepherd all your
   shepherds,
   and your lovers shall go into
   captivity;
   then you will be ashamed and
   dismayed
   because of all your
   wickedness.
23 O inhabitant of Lebanon,
   nested among the cedars,
   how you will groan[v] when
   pangs come upon you,
   pain as of a woman in labor!

Judgment on Coniah (Jehoiachin)

24 As I live, says the LORD, even if King Cō·nī'ah son of Je·hoi'a·kim of Judah were the signet ring on my right hand, even from there I would tear you off 25 and give you into the hands of those who seek your life, into the hands of those of whom you are afraid, even into the hands of King Ne·bū-chad·rez'zar of Babylon and into the hands of the Chal·dē'ans. 26 I will hurl you and the mother who bore you into another country, where you were not born, and there you shall die. 27 But they shall not return to the land to which they long to return.
28 Is this man Cō·nī'ah a despised
   broken pot,
   a vessel no one wants?
   Why are he and his offspring
   hurled out
   and cast away in a land that
   they do not know?
29 O land, land, land,
   hear the word of the LORD!
30 Thus says the LORD:
   Record this man as childless,
   a man who shall not succeed
   in his days;
   for none of his offspring shall
   succeed
   in sitting on the throne of
   David,
   and ruling again in Judah.

Restoration after Exile

23 Woe to the shepherds who destroy and scatter the sheep of my pasture! says the LORD. 2 Therefore thus says the LORD, the God of Israel, concerning the shepherds who shepherd my people: It is you who have scattered my flock, and have driven them away, and you have not attended to them. So I will attend to you for your evil doings, says the LORD. 3 Then I myself will gather the remnant of my flock out of all the lands where I have driven them, and I will bring them back to their fold, and they shall be fruitful and multiply. 4 I will raise up shepherds over them who will shepherd them, and they shall not fear any longer, or be dismayed, nor shall any be missing, says the LORD.

The Righteous Branch of David
(Cp Jer 16.14–15)

5 The days are surely coming, says the LORD, when I will raise up for David a righteous Branch, and he shall reign as king and deal wisely, and shall execute justice and righteousness in the land. 6 In his days Judah will be saved and Israel will live in safety. And this is the name by which he will be called: "The LORD is our righteousness."

7 Therefore, the days are surely coming, says the LORD, when it shall no longer be said, "As the LORD lives who brought the people of Israel up out of the land of Egypt," 8 but "As the LORD lives who brought out and led the offspring of the house of Israel out of the land of the north and out of all the lands where he[w] had driven them." Then they shall live in their own land.

False Prophets of Hope Denounced

9 Concerning the prophets:
   My heart is crushed within me,
   all my bones shake;
   I have become like a drunkard,
   like one overcome by wine,
   because of the LORD
   and because of his holy words.
10 For the land is full of adulterers;
   because of the curse the land
   mourns,
   and the pastures of the
   wilderness are dried up.
   Their course has been evil,

v Gk Vg Syr: Heb *will be pitied*
w Gk: Heb *I*

and their might is not right.

11 Both prophet and priest are
ungodly;
even in my house I have found
their wickedness,
says the LORD.
12 Therefore their way shall be to
them
like slippery paths in the
darkness,
into which they shall be driven
and fall;
for I will bring disaster upon
them
in the year of their
punishment,
says the LORD.
13 In the prophets of Sa·mār′i·a
I saw a disgusting thing:
they prophesied by Bā′al
and led my people Israel
astray.
14 But in the prophets of Jerusalem
I have seen a more shocking
thing:
they commit adultery and walk
in lies;
they strengthen the hands of
evildoers,
so that no one turns from
wickedness;
all of them have become like
Sod′om to me,
and its inhabitants like
Go·mor′rah.
15 Therefore thus says the LORD of
hosts concerning the
prophets:
"I am going to make them eat
wormwood,
and give them poisoned water
to drink;
for from the prophets of
Jerusalem
ungodliness has spread
throughout the land."

16 Thus says the LORD of hosts: Do not listen to the words of the prophets who prophesy to you; they are deluding you. They speak visions of their own minds, not from the mouth of the LORD. 17 They keep saying to those who despise the word of the LORD, "It shall be well with you"; and to all who stubbornly follow their own stubborn hearts, they say, "No calamity shall come upon you."

18 For who has stood in the council of the LORD

so as to see and to hear his
word?
Who has given heed to his
word so as to proclaim it?
19 Look, the storm of the LORD!
Wrath has gone forth,
a whirling tempest;
it will burst upon the head of
the wicked.
20 The anger of the LORD will not
turn back
until he has executed and
accomplished
the intents of his mind.
In the latter days you will
understand it clearly.

21 I did not send the prophets,
yet they ran;
I did not speak to them,
yet they prophesied.
22 But if they had stood in my
council,
then they would have
proclaimed my words to
my people,
and they would have turned
them from their evil way,
and from the evil of their
doings.

23 Am I a God near by, says the LORD, and not a God far off? 24 Who can hide in secret places so that I cannot see them? says the LORD. Do I not fill heaven and earth? says the LORD. 25 I have heard what the prophets have said who prophesy lies in my name, saying, "I have dreamed, I have dreamed!" 26 How long? Will the hearts of the prophets ever turn back—those who prophesy lies, and who prophesy the deceit of their own heart? 27 They plan to make my people forget my name by their dreams that they tell one another, just as their ancestors forgot my name for Bā′al. 28 Let the prophet who has a dream tell the dream, but let the one who has my word speak my word faithfully. What has straw in common with wheat? says the LORD. 29 Is not my word like fire, says the LORD, and like a hammer that breaks a rock in pieces? 30 See, therefore, I am against the prophets, says the LORD, who steal my words from one another. 31 See, I am against the prophets, says the LORD, who use their own tongues and say, "Says the LORD." 32 See, I am against those who prophesy lying dreams, says the LORD, and who tell them, and who lead my people astray

by their lies and their recklessness, when I did not send them or appoint them; so they do not profit this people at all, says the LORD.

33 When this people, or a prophet, or a priest asks you, "What is the burden of the LORD?" you shall say to them, "You are the burden,[x] and I will cast you off, says the LORD." 34 And as for the prophet, priest, or the people who say, "The burden of the LORD," I will punish them and their households. 35 Thus shall you say to one another, among yourselves, "What has the LORD answered?" or "What has the LORD spoken?" 36 But "the burden of the LORD" you shall mention no more, for the burden is everyone's own word, and so you pervert the words of the living God, the LORD of hosts, our God. 37 Thus you shall ask the prophet, "What has the LORD answered you?" or "What has the LORD spoken?" 38 But if you say, "the burden of the LORD," thus says the LORD: Because you have said these words, "the burden of the LORD," when I sent to you, saying, You shall not say, "the burden of the LORD," 39 therefore, I will surely lift you up[y] and cast you away from my presence, you and the city that I gave to you and your ancestors. 40 And I will bring upon you everlasting disgrace and perpetual shame, which shall not be forgotten.

The Good and the Bad Figs

24 The LORD showed me two baskets of figs placed before the temple of the LORD. This was after King Ne·bu·chad·rez'zar of Babylon had taken into exile from Jerusalem King Jec·o·ni'ah son of Je·hoi'a·kim of Judah, together with the officials of Judah, the artisans, and the smiths, and had brought them to Babylon. 2 One basket had very good figs, like first-ripe figs, but the other basket had very bad figs, so bad that they could not be eaten. 3 And the LORD said to me, "What do you see, Jer·e·mi'ah?" I said, "Figs, the good figs very good, and the bad figs very bad, so bad that they cannot be eaten."

4 Then the word of the LORD came to me: 5 Thus says the LORD, the God of Israel: Like these good figs, so I will regard as good the exiles from Judah, whom I have sent away from this place to the land of the Chal·de'ans. 6 I will set my eyes upon them for good, and I

will bring them back to this land. I will build them up, and not tear them down; I will plant them, and not pluck them up. 7 I will give them a heart to know that I am the LORD; and they shall be my people and I will be their God, for they shall return to me with their whole heart.

8 But thus says the LORD: Like the bad figs that are so bad they cannot be eaten, so will I treat King Zed·e·ki'ah of Judah, his officials, the remnant of Jerusalem who remain in this land, and those who live in the land of Egypt. 9 I will make them a horror, an evil thing, to all the kingdoms of the earth—a disgrace, a byword, a taunt, and a curse in all the places where I shall drive them. 10 And I will send sword, famine, and pestilence upon them, until they are utterly destroyed from the land that I gave to them and their ancestors.

The Babylonian Captivity Foretold

25 The word that came to Jer·e·mi'ah concerning all the people of Judah, in the fourth year of King Je·hoi'a·kim son of Jo·si'ah of Judah (that was the first year of King Ne·bu·chad·rez'zar of Babylon), 2 which the prophet Jer·e·mi'ah spoke to all the people of Judah and all the inhabitants of Jerusalem: 3 For twenty-three years, from the thirteenth year of King Jo·si'ah son of A'mon of Judah, to this day, the word of the LORD has come to me, and I have spoken persistently to you, but you have not listened. 4 And though the LORD persistently sent you all his servants the prophets, you have neither listened nor inclined your ears to hear 5 when they said, "Turn now, everyone of you, from your evil way and wicked doings, and you will remain upon the land that the LORD has given to you and your ancestors from of old and forever; 6 do not go after other gods to serve and worship them, and do not provoke me to anger with the work of your hands. Then I will do you no harm." 7 Yet you did not listen to me, says the LORD, and so you have provoked me to anger with the work of your hands to your own harm.

8 Therefore thus says the LORD of hosts: Because you have not obeyed my words, 9 I am going to send for all

---

[x] Gk Vg: Heb *What burden*   [y] Heb Mss Gk Vg: MT *forget you*

the tribes of the north, says the LORD, even for King Ne·bu·chad·rez'zar of Babylon, my servant, and I will bring them against this land and its inhabitants, and against all these nations around; I will utterly destroy them, and make them an object of horror and of hissing, and an everlasting disgrace.[z] 10 And I will banish from them the sound of mirth and the sound of gladness, the voice of the bridegroom and the voice of the bride, the sound of the millstones and the light of the lamp. 11 This whole land shall become a ruin and a waste, and these nations shall serve the king of Babylon seventy years. 12 Then after seventy years are completed, I will punish the king of Babylon and that nation, the land of the Chal·de'ans, for their iniquity, says the LORD, making the land an everlasting waste. 13 I will bring upon that land all the words that I have uttered against it, everything written in this book, which Jer·e·mi'ah prophesied against all the nations. 14 For many nations and great kings shall make slaves of them also; and I will repay them according to their deeds and the work of their hands.

The Cup of God's Wrath

15 For thus the LORD, the God of Israel, said to me: Take from my hand this cup of the wine of wrath, and make all the nations to whom I send you drink it. 16 They shall drink and stagger and go out of their minds because of the sword that I am sending among them.

17 So I took the cup from the LORD's hand, and made all the nations to whom the LORD sent me drink it: 18 Jerusalem and the towns of Judah, its kings and officials, to make them a desolation and a waste, an object of hissing and of cursing, as they are today; 19 Pharaoh king of Egypt, his servants, his officials, and all his people; 20 all the mixed people;[a] all the kings of the land of Uz; all the kings of the land of the Phi·lis'tines — Ash'ke·lon, Ga'za, Ek'ron, and the remnant of Ash'dod; 21 E'dom, Mo'ab, and the Am'mon·ites; 22 all the kings of Tyre, all the kings of Si'don, and the kings of the coastland across the sea; 23 De'dan, Te'ma, Buz, and all who have shaven temples; 24 all the kings of Arabia and all the kings of the mixed peoples[a] that live in the desert; 25 all the kings of Zim'ri, all the kings of E'lam, and all

the kings of Med'i·a; 26 all the kings of the north, far and near, one after another, and all the kingdoms of the world that are on the face of the earth. And after them the king of She'shach[b] shall drink.

27 Then you shall say to them, Thus says the LORD of hosts, the God of Israel: Drink, get drunk and vomit, fall and rise no more, because of the sword that I am sending among you.

28 And if they refuse to accept the cup from your hand to drink, then you shall say to them: Thus says the LORD of hosts: You must drink! 29 See, I am beginning to bring disaster on the city that is called by my name, and how can you possibly avoid punishment? You shall not go unpunished, for I am summoning a sword against all the inhabitants of the earth, says the LORD of hosts.

30 You, therefore, shall prophesy against them all these words, and say to them:

The LORD will roar from on
    high,
  and from his holy habitation
    utter his voice;
he will roar mightily against his
    fold,
  and shout, like those who
    tread grapes,
  against all the inhabitants of
    the earth.
31 The clamor will resound to the
    ends of the earth,
  for the LORD has an
    indictment against the
    nations;
he is entering into judgment
    with all flesh,
  and the guilty he will put to
    the sword,
        says the LORD.

32 Thus says the LORD of hosts:
See, disaster is spreading
  from nation to nation,
and a great tempest is stirring
  from the farthest parts of the
    earth!
33 Those slain by the LORD on that day shall extend from one end of the earth to the other. They shall not be lamented, or gathered, or buried; they

[z] Gk Compare Syr: Heb and everlasting desolations   [a] Meaning of Heb uncertain   [b] Sheshach is a cryptogram for Babel, Babylon

shall become dung on the surface of the ground.

34 Wail, you shepherds, and cry
    out;
    roll in ashes, you lords of the
      flock,
for the days of your slaughter
    have come — and your
    dispersions,c
and you shall fall like a choice
    vessel.
35 Flight shall fail the shepherds,
    and there shall be no escape
      for the lords of the flock.
36 Hark! the cry of the shepherds,
    and the wail of the lords of the
      flock!
For the LORD is despoiling their
    pasture,
37 and the peaceful folds are
    devastated,
    because of the fierce anger of
      the LORD.
38 Like a lion he has left his covert;
    for their land has become a
      waste
because of the cruel sword,
    and because of his fierce
      anger.

Jeremiah's Prophecies in the Temple
(Cp Jer 7.1–15)

26 At the beginning of the reign of King Je·hoi′a·kim son of Jō·sī′ah of Judah, this word came from the LORD: 2 Thus says the LORD: Stand in the court of the LORD's house, and speak to all the cities of Judah that come to worship in the house of the LORD; speak to them all the words that I command you; do not hold back a word. 3 It may be that they will listen, all of them, and will turn from their evil way, that I may change my mind about the disaster that I intend to bring on them because of their evil doings. 4 You shall say to them: Thus says the LORD: If you will not listen to me, to walk in my law that I have set before you, 5 and to heed the words of my servants the prophets whom I send to you urgently — though you have not heeded — 6 then I will make this house like Shī′lōh, and I will make this city a curse for all the nations of the earth.

7 The priests and the prophets and all the people heard Jer·e·mī′ah speaking these words in the house of the LORD. 8 And when Jer·e·mī′ah had finished speaking all that the LORD had commanded him to speak to all the people, then the priests and the prophets and all the people laid hold of him, saying, "You shall die! 9 Why have you prophesied in the name of the LORD, saying, 'This house shall be like Shī′lōh, and this city shall be desolate, without inhabitant'?" And all the people gathered around Jer·e·mī′ah in the house of the LORD.

10 When the officials of Judah heard these things, they came up from the king's house to the house of the LORD and took their seat in the entry of the New Gate of the house of the LORD. 11 Then the priests and the prophets said to the officials and to all the people, "This man deserves the sentence of death because he has prophesied against this city, as you have heard with your own ears."

12 Then Jer·e·mī′ah spoke to all the officials and all the people, saying, "It is the LORD who sent me to prophesy against this house and this city all the words you have heard. 13 Now therefore amend your ways and your doings, and obey the voice of the LORD your God, and the LORD will change his mind about the disaster that he has pronounced against you. 14 But as for me, here I am in your hands. Do with me as seems good and right to you. 15 Only know for certain that if you put me to death, you will be bringing innocent blood upon yourselves and upon this city and its inhabitants, for in truth the LORD sent me to you to speak all these words in your ears."

16 Then the officials and all the people said to the priests and the prophets, "This man does not deserve the sentence of death, for he has spoken to us in the name of the LORD our God." 17 And some of the elders of the land arose and said to all the assembled people, 18 "Mī′cah of Mō′re·sheth, who prophesied during the days of King Hez·e·kī′ah of Judah, said to all the people of Judah: 'Thus says the LORD of hosts,

Zion shall be plowed as a field;
    Jerusalem shall become a heap
      of ruins,
    and the mountain of the house
      a wooded height.'

19 Did King Hez·e·kī′ah of Judah and all Judah actually put him to death? Did he not fear the LORD and entreat the favor of the LORD, and did not the LORD change his mind about the

cMeaning of Heb uncertain

disaster that he had pronounced against them? But we are about to bring great disaster on ourselves!"

20 There was another man prophesying in the name of the LORD, Ū·rī'ah son of She·māi'ah from Kir'-i·ath-jē'a·rim. He prophesied against this city and against this land in words exactly like those of Jer·e·mī'ah. 21 And when King Je·hoi'a·kim, with all his warriors and all the officials, heard his words, the king sought to put him to death; but when Ū·rī'ah heard of it, he was afraid and fled and escaped to Egypt. 22 Then King Je·hoi'-a·kim sent*d* El·nā'than son of Ach'bor and men with him to Egypt, 23 and they took Ū·rī'ah from Egypt and brought him to King Je·hoi'a·kim, who struck him down with the sword and threw his dead body into the burial place of the common people.

24 But the hand of A·hī'kam son of Shā'phan was with Jer·e·mī'ah so that he was not given over into the hands of the people to be put to death.

The Sign of the Yoke

27 In the beginning of the reign of King Zed·e·kī'ah*e* son of Jō·sī'ah of Judah, this word came to Jer·e·mī'ah from the LORD. 2 Thus the LORD said to me: Make yourself a yoke of straps and bars, and put them on your neck. 3 Send word*f* to the king of Ē'dom, the king of Mō'ab, the king of the Am'mon·ites, the king of Tȳre, and the king of Sī'don by the hand of the envoys who have come to Jerusalem to King Zed·e·kī'ah of Judah. 4 Give them this charge for their masters: Thus says the LORD of hosts, the God of Israel: This is what you shall say to your masters: 5 It is I who by my great power and my outstretched arm have made the earth, with the people and animals that are on the earth, and I give it to whomever I please. 6 Now I have given all these lands into the hand of King Ne·bū·chad·nez'zar of Babylon, my servant, and I have given him even the wild animals of the field to serve him. 7 All the nations shall serve him and his son and his grandson, until the time of his own land comes; then many nations and great kings shall make him their slave.

8 But if any nation or kingdom will not serve this king, Ne·bū·chad·nez'-zar of Babylon, and put its neck under the yoke of the king of Babylon, then

I will punish that nation with the sword, with famine, and with pestilence, says the LORD, until I have completed its*g* destruction by his hand. 9 You, therefore, must not listen to your prophets, your diviners, your dreamers,*h* your soothsayers, or your sorcerers, who are saying to you, 'You shall not serve the king of Babylon.' 10 For they are prophesying a lie to you, with the result that you will be removed far from your land; I will drive you out, and you will perish. 11 But any nation that will bring its neck under the yoke of the king of Babylon and serve him, I will leave on its own land, says the LORD, to till it and live there.

12 I spoke to King Zed·e·kī'ah of Judah in the same way: Bring your necks under the yoke of the king of Babylon, and serve him and his people, and live. 13 Why should you and your people die by the sword, by famine, and by pestilence, as the LORD has spoken concerning any nation that will not serve the king of Babylon? 14 Do not listen to the words of the prophets who are telling you not to serve the king of Babylon, for they are prophesying a lie to you. 15 I have not sent them, says the LORD, but they are prophesying falsely in my name, with the result that I will drive you out and you will perish, you and the prophets who are prophesying to you.

16 Then I spoke to the priests and to all this people, saying, Thus says the LORD: Do not listen to the words of your prophets who are prophesying to you, saying, "The vessels of the LORD's house will soon be brought back from Babylon," for they are prophesying a lie to you. 17 Do not listen to them; serve the king of Babylon and live. Why should this city become a desolation? 18 If indeed they are prophets, and if the word of the LORD is with them, then let them intercede with the LORD of hosts, that the vessels left in the house of the LORD, in the house of the king of Judah, and in Jerusalem may not go to Babylon. 19 For thus says the LORD of hosts concerning the pillars, the sea, the stands, and the rest of the vessels that are left in this city, 20 which King Ne·bū·chad·nez'zar of Babylon did not take away when he

---

d Heb adds *men to Egypt*   *e* Another reading is *Jehoiakim*   *f* Cn: Heb *send them*   *g* Heb *their*   *h* Gk Syr Vg: Heb *dreams* took into exile from Jerusalem to Babylon King Jec·o·nī′ah son of Je·hoi′-a·kim of Judah, and all the nobles of Judah and Jerusalem— 21thus says the LORD of hosts, the God of Israel, concerning the vessels left in the house of the LORD, in the house of the king of Judah, and in Jerusalem: 22They shall be carried to Babylon, and there they shall stay, until the day when I give attention to them, says the LORD. Then I will bring them up and restore them to this place.

Hananiah Opposes Jeremiah and Dies

28 In that same year, at the beginning of the reign of King Zed·e·kī′ah of Judah, in the fifth month of the fourth year, the prophet Han·a·nī′ah son of Az′zur, from Gib′-ē·on, spoke to me in the house of the LORD, in the presence of the priests and all the people, saying, 2 "Thus says the LORD of hosts, the God of Israel: I have broken the yoke of the king of Babylon. 3 Within two years I will bring back to this place all the vessels of the LORD's house, which King Ne·bu·chad·nez′zar of Babylon took away from this place and carried to Babylon. 4I will also bring back to this place King Jec·o·nī′ah son of Je·hoi′-a·kim of Judah, and all the exiles from Judah who went to Babylon, says the LORD, for I will break the yoke of the king of Babylon."

5 Then the prophet Jer·e·mī′ah spoke to the prophet Han·a·nī′ah in the presence of the priests and all the people who were standing in the house of the LORD; 6and the prophet Jer·e·mī′ah said, "Amen! May the LORD do so; may the LORD fulfill the words that you have prophesied, and bring back to this place from Babylon the vessels of the house of the LORD, and all the exiles. 7But listen now to this word that I speak in your hearing and in the hearing of all the people. 8The prophets who preceded you and me from ancient times prophesied war, famine, and pestilence against many countries and great kingdoms. 9As for the prophet who prophesies peace, when the word of that prophet comes true, then it will be known that the LORD has truly sent the prophet."

10 Then the prophet Han·a·nī′ah took the yoke from the neck of the prophet Jer·e·mī′ah, and broke it. 11And Han·a·nī′ah spoke in the presence of all the people, saying, "Thus says the LORD: This is how I will break the yoke of King Ne·bu·chad·nez′zar of Babylon from the neck of all the nations within two years." At this, the prophet Jer·e·mī′ah went his way.

12 Sometime after the prophet Han·a·nī′ah had broken the yoke from the neck of the prophet Jer·e·mī′ah, the word of the LORD came to Jer·e·mī′ah: 13Go, tell Han·a·nī′ah, Thus says the LORD: You have broken wooden bars only to forge iron bars in place of them! 14For thus says the LORD of hosts, the God of Israel: I have put an iron yoke on the neck of all these nations so that they may serve King Ne·bu·chad·nez′zar of Babylon, and they shall indeed serve him; I have even given him the wild animals. 15And the prophet Jer·e·mī′ah said to the prophet Han·a·nī′ah, "Listen, Han·a·nī′ah, the LORD has not sent you, and you made this people trust in a lie. 16Therefore thus says the LORD: I am going to send you off the face of the earth. Within this year you will be dead, because you have spoken rebellion against the LORD."

17 In that same year, in the seventh month, the prophet Han·a·nī′ah died.

Jeremiah's Letter to the Exiles in Babylon

29 These are the words of the letter that the prophet Jer·e·mī′ah sent from Jerusalem to the remaining elders among the exiles, and to the priests, the prophets, and all the people, whom Ne·bu·chad·nez′zar had taken into exile from Jerusalem to Babylon. 2This was after King Jec·o·nī′ah, and the queen mother, the court officials, the leaders of Judah and Jerusalem, the artisans, and the smiths had departed from Jerusalem. 3The letter was sent by the hand of El·ā′sah son of Shā′phan and Gem·a·rī′ah son of Hil·kī′ah, whom King Zed·e·kī′ah of Judah sent to Babylon to King Ne·bu·chad·nez′zar of Babylon. It said: 4Thus says the LORD of hosts, the God of Israel, to all the exiles whom I have sent into exile from Jerusalem to Babylon: 5Build houses and live in them; plant gardens and eat what they produce. 6Take wives and have sons and daughters; take wives for your sons, and give your daughters in marriage, that they may bear sons and daughters; multiply there, and do not decrease. 7But seek the welfare of the city where I have sent you into exile, and pray to the LORD on its behalf, for in its welfare you will find your welfare. [8] For thus says the LORD of hosts, the God of Israel: Do not let the prophets and the diviners who are among you deceive you, and do not listen to the dreams that they dream,[i] [9] for it is a lie that they are prophesying to you in my name; I did not send them, says the LORD.

10 For thus says the LORD: Only when Babylon's seventy years are completed will I visit you, and I will fulfill to you my promise and bring you back to this place. [11] For surely I know the plans I have for you, says the LORD, plans for your welfare and not for harm, to give you a future with hope. [12] Then when you call upon me and come and pray to me, I will hear you. [13] When you search for me, you will find me; if you seek me with all your heart, [14] I will let you find me, says the LORD, and I will restore your fortunes and gather you from all the nations and all the places where I have driven you, says the LORD, and I will bring you back to the place from which I sent you into exile.

15 Because you have said, "The LORD has raised up prophets for us in Babylon," — [16] Thus says the LORD concerning the king who sits on the throne of David, and concerning all the people who live in this city, your kinsfolk who did not go out with you into exile: [17] Thus says the LORD of hosts, I am going to let loose on them sword, famine, and pestilence, and I will make them like rotten figs that are so bad they cannot be eaten. [18] I will pursue them with the sword, with famine, and with pestilence, and will make them a horror to all the kingdoms of the earth, to be an object of cursing, and horror, and hissing, and a derision among all the nations where I have driven them, [19] because they did not heed my words, says the LORD, when I persistently sent to you my servants the prophets, but they[j] would not listen, says the LORD. [20] But now, all you exiles whom I sent away from Jerusalem to Babylon, hear the word of the LORD: [21] Thus says the LORD of hosts, the God of Israel, concerning Ā'hab son of Kō·laī'ah and Zed·e·kī'ah son of Mā·a·sēi'ah, who are prophesying a lie to you in my name: I am going to deliver them into the hand of King Ne·bū·chad·rez'zar of Babylon, and he shall kill them before your eyes. [22] And on account of them this curse shall be used by all the exiles from Judah in Babylon: "The LORD make you like Zed·e·kī'ah and Ā'hab, whom the king of Babylon roasted in the fire," [23] because they have perpetrated outrage in Israel and have committed adultery with their neighbors' wives, and have spoken in my name lying words that I did not command them; I am the one who knows and bears witness, says the LORD.

The Letter of Shemaiah

24 To She·māi'ah of Ne·hel'am you shall say: [25] Thus says the LORD of hosts, the God of Israel: In your own name you sent a letter to all the people who are in Jerusalem, and to the priest Zeph·a·nī'ah son of Mā·a·sēi'ah, and to all the priests, saying, [26] The LORD himself has made you priest instead of the priest Je·hoi'a·da, so that there may be officers in the house of the LORD to control any madman who plays the prophet, to put him in the stocks and the collar. [27] So now why have you not rebuked Jer·e·mī'ah of An'a·thoth who plays the prophet for you? [28] For he has actually sent to us in Babylon, saying, "It will be a long time; build houses and live in them, and plant gardens and eat what they produce."

29 The priest Zeph·a·nī'ah read this letter in the hearing of the prophet Jer·e·mī'ah. [30] Then the word of the LORD came to Jer·e·mī'ah: [31] Send to all the exiles, saying, Thus says the LORD concerning She·māi'ah of Ne·hel'am: Because She·māi'ah has prophesied to you, though I did not send him, and has led you to trust in a lie, [32] therefore thus says the LORD: I am going to punish She·māi'ah of Ne·hel'am and his descendants; he shall not have anyone living among this people to see[k] the good that I am going to do to my people, says the LORD, for he has spoken rebellion against the LORD.

Restoration Promised for Israel and Judah

30 The word that came to Jer·e·mī'ah from the LORD: [2] Thus says the LORD, the God of Israel:

---

[i] Cn: Heb *your dreams that you cause to dream*   [j] Syr: Heb *you*   [k] Gk: Heb *and he shall not see*

Write in a book all the words that I have spoken to you. ³For the days are surely coming, says the LORD, when I will restore the fortunes of my people, Israel and Judah, says the LORD, and I will bring them back to the land that I gave to their ancestors and they shall take possession of it.

4 These are the words that the LORD spoke concerning Israel and Judah:
5 Thus says the LORD:
We have heard a cry of panic,
    of terror, and no peace.
6 Ask now, and see,
    can a man bear a child?
Why then do I see every man
    with his hands on his loins
        like a woman in labor?
Why has every face turned
    pale?
7 Alas! that day is so great
    there is none like it;
it is a time of distress for Jacob;
    yet he shall be rescued from it.

8 On that day, says the LORD of hosts, I will break the yoke from off his[l] neck, and I will burst his[l] bonds, and strangers shall no more make a servant of him. ⁹But they shall serve the LORD their God and David their king, whom I will raise up for them.

10 But as for you, have no fear, my
        servant Jacob, says the
        LORD,
    and do not be dismayed,
        O Israel;
for I am going to save you from
        far away,
    and your offspring from the
        land of their captivity.
Jacob shall return and have
        quiet and ease,
    and no one shall make him
        afraid.
11 For I am with you, says the
        LORD, to save you;
I will make an end of all the
        nations
    among which I scattered you,
    but of you I will not make an
        end.
I will chastise you in just
        measure,
    and I will by no means leave
        you unpunished.

12 For thus says the LORD:
Your hurt is incurable,
    your wound is grievous.
13 There is no one to uphold your
        cause,

    no medicine for your wound,
        no healing for you.
14 All your lovers have forgotten
        you;
    they care nothing for you;
for I have dealt you the blow of
        an enemy,
    the punishment of a merciless
        foe,
because your guilt is great,
    because your sins are so
        numerous.
15 Why do you cry out over your
        hurt?
    Your pain is incurable.
Because your guilt is great,
    because your sins are so
        numerous,
    I have done these things to
        you.
16 Therefore all who devour you
        shall be devoured,
    and all your foes, everyone of
        them, shall go into
        captivity;
those who plunder you shall be
        plundered,
    and all who prey on you I will
        make a prey.
17 For I will restore health to you,
    and your wounds I will heal,
                    says the LORD,
because they have called you an
        outcast:
    "It is Zion; no one cares for
        her!"

18 Thus says the LORD:
I am going to restore the
        fortunes of the tents of
        Jacob,
    and have compassion on his
        dwellings;
the city shall be rebuilt upon its
        mound,
    and the citadel set on its
        rightful site.
19 Out of them shall come
        thanksgiving,
    and the sound of
        merrymakers.
I will make them many, and they
        shall not be few;
    I will make them honored, and
        they shall not be disdained.
20 Their children shall be as of old,
    their congregation shall be
        established before me;
    and I will punish all who
        oppress them.

_l_Cn: Heb _your_

21 Their prince shall be one of their
   own,
      their ruler shall come from
      their midst;
   I will bring him near, and he
      shall approach me,
      for who would otherwise dare
      to approach me?
                    says the LORD.
22 And you shall be my people,
   and I will be your God.

23 Look, the storm of the LORD!
   Wrath has gone forth,
   a whirling*m* tempest;
      it will burst upon the head of
      the wicked.
24 The fierce anger of the LORD
   will not turn back
   until he has executed and
   accomplished
      the intents of his mind.
   In the latter days you will
      understand this.

The Joyful Return of the Exiles

31 At that time, says the LORD, I
   will be the God of all the families of Israel, and they shall be my people.
2 Thus says the LORD:
   The people who survived the
      sword
         found grace in the wilderness;
   when Israel sought for rest,
3   the LORD appeared to him*n*
         from far away.*o*
   I have loved you with an
      everlasting love;
      therefore I have continued my
      faithfulness to you.
4 Again I will build you, and you
      shall be built,
      O virgin Israel!
   Again you shall take*p* your
      tambourines,
      and go forth in the dance of
      the merrymakers.
5 Again you shall plant vineyards
      on the mountains of Sa·mār′i·a;
   the planters shall plant,
      and shall enjoy the fruit.
6 For there shall be a day when
      sentinels will call
   in the hill country of
      E′phra·im:
   "Come, let us go up to Zion,
      to the LORD our God."

7 For thus says the LORD:
   Sing aloud with gladness for
      Jacob,

   and raise shouts for the chief
      of the nations;
   proclaim, give praise, and say,
      "Save, O LORD, your people,
      the remnant of Israel."
8 See, I am going to bring them
      from the land of the north,
   and gather them from the
      farthest parts of the earth,
   among them the blind and the
      lame,
      those with child and those in
      labor, together;
      a great company, they shall
      return here.
9 With weeping they shall come,
      and with consolations*q* I will
      lead them back,
   I will let them walk by brooks of
      water,
      in a straight path in which
      they shall not stumble;
   for I have become a father to
      Israel,
      and E′phra·im is my firstborn.

10 Hear the word of the LORD,
      O nations,
      and declare it in the
      coastlands far away;
   say, "He who scattered Israel
      will gather him,
      and will keep him as a
      shepherd a flock."
11 For the LORD has ransomed
      Jacob,
      and has redeemed him from
      hands too strong for him.
12 They shall come and sing aloud
      on the height of Zion,
      and they shall be radiant over
      the goodness of the LORD,
   over the grain, the wine, and the
      oil,
      and over the young of the
      flock and the herd;
   their life shall become like a
      watered garden,
      and they shall never languish
      again.
13 Then shall the young women
      rejoice in the dance,
      and the young men and the
      old shall be merry.
   I will turn their mourning into
      joy,

*m*One Ms: Meaning of MT uncertain
*n*Gk: Heb *me*   *o*Or *to him long ago*
*p*Or *adorn yourself with*   *q*Gk Compare
Vg Tg: Heb *supplications*

I will comfort them, and give
them gladness for sorrow.
14 I will give the priests their fill of
fatness,
and my people shall be
satisfied with my bounty,
says the LORD.

15 Thus says the LORD:
A voice is heard in Rā'mah,
lamentation and bitter
weeping.
Rachel is weeping for her
children;
she refuses to be comforted for
her children,
because they are no more.
16 Thus says the LORD:
Keep your voice from weeping,
and your eyes from tears;
for there is a reward for your
work,
says the LORD:
they shall come back from the
land of the enemy;
17 there is hope for your future,
says the LORD:
your children shall come back
to their own country.

18 Indeed I heard Ē'phra·im
pleading:
"You disciplined me, and I took
the discipline;
I was like a calf untrained.
Bring me back, let me come
back,
for you are the LORD my God.
19 For after I had turned away I
repented;
and after I was discovered, I
struck my thigh;
I was ashamed, and I was
dismayed
because I bore the disgrace of
my youth."
20 Is Ē'phra·im my dear son?
Is he the child I delight in?
As often as I speak against him,
I still remember him.
Therefore I am deeply moved for
him;
I will surely have mercy on
him,
says the LORD.

21 Set up road markers for
yourself,
make yourself guideposts;
consider well the highway,
the road by which you went.
Return, O virgin Israel,

return to these your cities.
22 How long will you waver,
O faithless daughter?
For the LORD has created a new
thing on the earth:
a woman encompasses[r] a
man.

23 Thus says the LORD of hosts, the
God of Israel: Once more they shall
use these words in the land of Judah
and in its towns when I restore their
fortunes:
"The LORD bless you, O abode of
righteousness,
O holy hill!"
24 And Judah and all its towns shall live
there together, and the farmers and
those who wander[s] with their flocks.
25 I will satisfy the weary,
and all who are faint I will
replenish.
26 Thereupon I awoke and looked,
and my sleep was pleasant to me.

Individual Retribution

27 The days are surely coming, says
the LORD, when I will sow the house of
Israel and the house of Judah with the
seed of humans and the seed of animals. 28 And just as I have watched
over them to pluck up and break down,
to overthrow, destroy, and bring evil,
so I will watch over them to build and
to plant, says the LORD. 29 In those days
they shall no longer say:
"The parents have eaten sour
grapes,
and the children's teeth are set
on edge."
30 But all shall die for their own sins;
the teeth of everyone who eats sour
grapes shall be set on edge.

A New Covenant

31 The days are surely coming, says
the LORD, when I will make a new covenant with the house of Israel and the
house of Judah. 32 It will not be like the
covenant that I made with their ancestors when I took them by the hand to
bring them out of the land of Egypt — a
covenant that they broke, though I was
their husband,[t] says the LORD. 33 But
this is the covenant that I will make
with the house of Israel after those
days, says the LORD: I will put my law
within them, and I will write it on their

r Meaning of Heb uncertain
s Cn Compare Syr Vg Tg: Heb and they
shall wander   t Or master

hearts; and I will be their God, and they shall be my people. ³⁴No longer shall they teach one another, or say to each other, "Know the LORD," for they shall all know me, from the least of them to the greatest, says the LORD; for I will forgive their iniquity, and remember their sin no more.

³⁵ Thus says the LORD,
  who gives the sun for light by
    day
    and the fixed order of the
      moon and the stars for
      light by night,
  who stirs up the sea so that its
    waves roar—
    the LORD of hosts is his name:
³⁶ If this fixed order were ever to
    cease
  from my presence, says the
    LORD,
  then also the offspring of Israel
    would cease
    to be a nation before me
      forever.

³⁷ Thus says the LORD:
  If the heavens above can be
    measured,
    and the foundations of the
      earth below can be
      explored,
  then I will reject all the offspring
    of Israel
  because of all they have done,
          says the LORD.

Jerusalem to Be Enlarged

38 The days are surely coming, says the LORD, when the city shall be rebuilt for the LORD from the tower of Ha·nan′el to the Corner Gate. ³⁹And the measuring line shall go out farther, straight to the hill Gā′reb, and shall then turn to Gō′ah. ⁴⁰The whole valley of the dead bodies and the ashes, and all the fields as far as the Wadi Kid′-ron, to the corner of the Horse Gate toward the east, shall be sacred to the LORD. It shall never again be uprooted or overthrown.

Jeremiah Buys a Field During the Siege

32 The word that came to Jer·e·mī′ah from the LORD in the tenth year of King Zed·e·kī′ah of Judah, which was the eighteenth year of Ne·bū·chad·rez′zar. ²At that time the army of the king of Babylon was besieging Jerusalem, and the prophet Jer·e·mī′ah was confined in the court of the guard that was in the palace of the king of Judah, ³where King Zed·e·kī′ah of Judah had confined him. Zed·e·kī′ah had said, "Why do you prophesy and say: Thus says the LORD: I am going to give this city into the hand of the king of Babylon, and he shall take it; ⁴King Zed·e·kī′ah of Judah shall not escape out of the hands of the Chal·dē′ans, but shall surely be given into the hands of the king of Babylon, and shall speak with him face to face and see him eye to eye; ⁵and he shall take Zed·e·kī′ah to Babylon, and there he shall remain until I attend to him, says the LORD; though you fight against the Chal·dē′ans, you shall not succeed?"

6 Jer·e·mī′ah said, The word of the LORD came to me: ⁷Han′a·mel son of your uncle Shal′lum is going to come to you and say, "Buy my field that is at An′a·thoth, for the right of redemption by purchase is yours." ⁸Then my cousin Han′a·mel came to me in the court of the guard, in accordance with the word of the LORD, and said to me, "Buy my field that is at An′a·thoth in the land of Benjamin, for the right of possession and redemption is yours; buy it for yourself." Then I knew that this was the word of the LORD.

9 And I bought the field at An′-a·thoth from my cousin Han′a·mel, and weighed out the money to him, seventeen shekels of silver. ¹⁰I signed the deed, sealed it, got witnesses, and weighed the money on scales. ¹¹Then I took the sealed deed of purchase, containing the terms and conditions, and the open copy; ¹²and I gave the deed of purchase to Bar′uch son of Ne·rī′ah son of Mah′sēi·ah, in the presence of my cousin Han′a·mel, in the presence of the witnesses who signed the deed of purchase, and in the presence of all the Judeans who were sitting in the court of the guard. ¹³In their presence I charged Bar′uch, saying, ¹⁴Thus says the LORD of hosts, the God of Israel: Take these deeds, both this sealed deed of purchase and this open deed, and put them in an earthenware jar, in order that they may last for a long time. ¹⁵For thus says the LORD of hosts, the God of Israel: Houses and fields and vineyards shall again be bought in this land.

Jeremiah Prays for Understanding

16 After I had given the deed of purchase to Bar'uch son of Ne·rī'ah, I prayed to the LORD, saying: [17] Ah Lord GOD! It is you who made the heavens and the earth by your great power and by your outstretched arm! Nothing is too hard for you. [18] You show steadfast love to the thousandth generation,[u] but repay the guilt of parents into the laps of their children after them, O great and mighty God whose name is the LORD of hosts, [19] great in counsel and mighty in deed; whose eyes are open to all the ways of mortals, rewarding all according to their ways and according to the fruit of their doings. [20] You showed signs and wonders in the land of Egypt, and to this day in Israel and among all humankind, and have made yourself a name that continues to this very day. [21] You brought your people Israel out of the land of Egypt with signs and wonders, with a strong hand and outstretched arm, and with great terror; [22] and you gave them this land, which you swore to their ancestors to give them, a land flowing with milk and honey; [23] and they entered and took possession of it. But they did not obey your voice or follow your law; of all you commanded them to do, they did nothing. Therefore you have made all these disasters come upon them. [24] See, the siege ramps have been cast up against the city to take it, and the city, faced with sword, famine, and pestilence, has been given into the hands of the Chal·dē'ans who are fighting against it. What you spoke has happened, as you yourself can see. [25] Yet you, O Lord GOD, have said to me, "Buy the field for money and get witnesses"—though the city has been given into the hands of the Chal·dē'ans.

God's Assurance of the People's Return

26 The word of the LORD came to Jer·e·mī'ah: [27] See, I am the LORD, the God of all flesh; is anything too hard for me? [28] Therefore, thus says the LORD: I am going to give this city into the hands of the Chal·dē'ans and into the hand of King Ne·bū·chad·rez'zar of Babylon, and he shall take it. [29] The Chal·dē'ans who are fighting against this city shall come, set it on fire, and burn it, with the houses on whose roofs offerings have been made to Bā'al and libations have been poured out to other gods, to provoke me to anger. [30] For the people of Israel and the people of Judah have done nothing but evil in my sight from their youth; the people of Israel have done nothing but provoke me to anger by the work of their hands, says the LORD. [31] This city has aroused my anger and wrath, from the day it was built until this day, so that I will remove it from my sight [32] because of all the evil of the people of Israel and the people of Judah that they did to provoke me to anger—they, their kings and their officials, their priests and their prophets, the citizens of Judah and the inhabitants of Jerusalem. [33] They have turned their backs to me, not their faces; though I have taught them persistently, they would not listen and accept correction. [34] They set up their abominations in the house that bears my name, and defiled it. [35] They built the high places of Bā'al in the valley of the son of Hin'nom, to offer up their sons and daughters to Mō'lech, though I did not command them, nor did it enter my mind that they should do this abomination, causing Judah to sin.

36 Now therefore thus says the LORD, the God of Israel, concerning this city of which you say, "It is being given into the hand of the king of Babylon by the sword, by famine, and by pestilence": [37] See, I am going to gather them from all the lands to which I drove them in my anger and my wrath and in great indignation; I will bring them back to this place, and I will settle them in safety. [38] They shall be my people, and I will be their God. [39] I will give them one heart and one way, that they may fear me for all time, for their own good and the good of their children after them. [40] I will make an everlasting covenant with them, never to draw back from doing good to them; and I will put the fear of me in their hearts, so that they may not turn from me. [41] I will rejoice in doing good to them, and I will plant them in this land in faithfulness, with all my heart and all my soul.

42 For thus says the LORD: Just as I have brought all this great disaster upon this people, so I will bring upon them all the good fortune that I now promise them. [43] Fields shall be bought in this land of which you are saying, It is a desolation, without human beings

[u] Or *to thousands*

or animals; it has been given into the hands of the Chal·dē'ans. [44] Fields shall be bought for money, and deeds shall be signed and sealed and witnessed, in the land of Benjamin, in the places around Jerusalem, and in the cities of Judah, of the hill country, of the She·phē'lah, and of the Neg'eb; for I will restore their fortunes, says the LORD.

Healing after Punishment

33 The word of the LORD came to Jer·e·mī'ah a second time, while he was still confined in the court of the guard: [2] Thus says the LORD who made the earth,[v] the LORD who formed it to establish it—the LORD is his name: [3] Call to me and I will answer you, and will tell you great and hidden things that you have not known. [4] For thus says the LORD, the God of Israel, concerning the houses of this city and the houses of the kings of Judah that were torn down to make a defense against the siege ramps and before the sword:[w] [5] The Chal·dē'ans are coming in to fight[x] and to fill them with the dead bodies of those whom I shall strike down in my anger and my wrath, for I have hidden my face from this city because of all their wickedness. [6] I am going to bring it recovery and healing; I will heal them and reveal to them abundance[w] of prosperity and security. [7] I will restore the fortunes of Judah and the fortunes of Israel, and rebuild them as they were at first. [8] I will cleanse them from all the guilt of their sin against me, and I will forgive all the guilt of their sin and rebellion against me. [9] And this city[y] shall be to me a name of joy, a praise and a glory before all the nations of the earth who shall hear of all the good that I do for them; they shall fear and tremble because of all the good and all the prosperity I provide for it. [10] Thus says the LORD: In this place of which you say, "It is a waste without human beings or animals," in the towns of Judah and the streets of Jerusalem that are desolate, without inhabitants, human or animal, there shall once more be heard [11] the voice of mirth and the voice of gladness, the voice of the bridegroom and the voice of the bride, the voices of those who sing, as they bring thank offerings to the house of the LORD:

"Give thanks to the LORD of hosts,

for the LORD is good,
　for his steadfast love endures forever!"

For I will restore the fortunes of the land as at first, says the LORD. [12] Thus says the LORD of hosts: In this place that is waste, without human beings or animals, and in all its towns there shall again be pasture for shepherds resting their flocks. [13] In the towns of the hill country, of the She·phē'lah, and of the Neg'eb, in the land of Benjamin, the places around Jerusalem, and in the towns of Judah, flocks shall again pass under the hands of the one who counts them, says the LORD.

The Righteous Branch and the Covenant with David

[14] The days are surely coming, says the LORD, when I will fulfill the promise I made to the house of Israel and the house of Judah. [15] In those days and at that time I will cause a righteous Branch to spring up for David; and he shall execute justice and righteousness in the land. [16] In those days Judah will be saved and Jerusalem will live in safety. And this is the name by which it will be called: "The LORD is our righteousness."

[17] For thus says the LORD: David shall never lack a man to sit on the throne of the house of Israel, [18] and the levitical priests shall never lack a man in my presence to offer burnt offerings, to make grain offerings, and to make sacrifices for all time.

[19] The word of the LORD came to Jer·e·mī'ah: [20] Thus says the LORD: If any of you could break my covenant with the day and my covenant with the night, so that day and night would not come at their appointed time, [21] only then could my covenant with my servant David be broken, so that he would not have a son to reign on his throne, and my covenant with my ministers the Lē'vites. [22] Just as the host of heaven cannot be numbered and the sands of the sea cannot be measured, so I will increase the offspring of my servant David, and the Lē'vites who minister to me.

[23] The word of the LORD came to Jer·e·mī'ah: [24] Have you not observed

---

[v] Gk: Heb *it*　　[w] Meaning of Heb uncertain　　[x] Cn: Heb *They are coming in to fight against the Chaldeans*　　[y] Heb *And it*

how these people say, "The two families that the LORD chose have been rejected by him," and how they hold my people in such contempt that they no longer regard them as a nation? 25 Thus says the LORD: Only if I had not established my covenant with day and night and the ordinances of heaven and earth, 26 would I reject the offspring of Jacob and of my servant David and not choose any of his descendants as rulers over the offspring of Abraham, Isaac, and Jacob. For I will restore their fortunes, and will have mercy upon them.

Death in Captivity Predicted for Zedekiah

34 The word that came to Jer·e·mī'ah from the LORD, when King Ne·bū·chad·rez'zar of Babylon and all his army and all the kingdoms of the earth and all the peoples under his dominion were fighting against Jerusalem and all its cities: 2 "Thus says the LORD, the God of Israel: Go and speak to King Zed·e·kī'ah of Judah and say to him: Thus says the LORD: I am going to give this city into the hand of the king of Babylon, and he shall burn it with fire. 3 And you yourself shall not escape from his hand, but shall surely be captured and handed over to him; you shall see the king of Babylon eye to eye and speak with him face to face; and you shall go to Babylon. 4 Yet hear the word of the LORD, O King Zed·e·kī'ah of Judah! Thus says the LORD concerning you: You shall not die by the sword; 5 you shall die in peace. And as spices were burnedᶻ for your ancestors, the earlier kings who preceded you, so they shall burn spicesᵃ for you and lament for you, saying, "Alas, lord!" For I have spoken the word, says the LORD.

6 Then the prophet Jer·e·mī'ah spoke all these words to Zed·e·kī'ah king of Judah, in Jerusalem, 7 when the army of the king of Babylon was fighting against Jerusalem and against all the cities of Judah that were left, Lā'chish and A·zē'kah; for these were the only fortified cities of Judah that remained.

Treacherous Treatment of Slaves

8 The word that came to Jer·e·mī'ah from the LORD, after King Zed·e·kī'ah had made a covenant with all the people in Jerusalem to make a proclamation of liberty to them, 9 that all should set free their Hebrew slaves, male and female, so that no one should hold another Judean in slavery. 10 And they obeyed, all the officials and all the people who had entered into the covenant that all would set free their slaves, male or female, so that they would not be enslaved again; they obeyed and set them free. 11 But afterward they turned around and took back the male and female slaves they had set free, and brought them again into subjection as slaves. 12 The word of the LORD came to Jer·e·mī'ah from the LORD: 13 Thus says the LORD, the God of Israel: I myself made a covenant with your ancestors when I brought them out of the land of Egypt, out of the house of slavery, saying, 14 "Every seventh year each of you must set free any Hebrews who have been sold to you and have served you six years; you must set them free from your service." But your ancestors did not listen to me or incline their ears to me. 15 You yourselves recently repented and did what was right in my sight by proclaiming liberty to one another, and you made a covenant before me in the house that is called by my name; 16 but then you turned around and profaned my name when each of you took back your male and female slaves, whom you had set free according to their desire, and you brought them again into subjection to be your slaves. 17 Therefore, thus says the LORD: You have not obeyed me by granting a release to your neighbors and friends; I am going to grant a release to you, says the LORD — a release to the sword, to pestilence, and to famine. I will make you a horror to all the kingdoms of the earth. 18 And those who transgressed my covenant and did not keep the terms of the covenant that they made before me, I will make likeᵇ the calf when they cut it in two and passed between its parts: 19 the officials of Judah, the officials of Jerusalem, the eunuchs, the priests, and all the people of the land who passed between the parts of the calf 20 shall be handed over to their enemies and to those who seek their lives. Their corpses shall become food for the birds of the air and the wild animals of the earth. 21 And as for King Zed·e·kī'ah of Judah and his officials,

ᶻ Heb *as there was burning*   ᵃ Heb *shall burn*   ᵇ Cn: Heb lacks *like*

I will hand them over to their enemies and to those who seek their lives, to the army of the king of Babylon, which has withdrawn from you. ²² I am going to command, says the LORD, and will bring them back to this city; and they will fight against it, and take it, and burn it with fire. The towns of Judah I will make a desolation without inhabitant.

The Rechabites Commended

35 The word that came to Jer·e·mī'ah from the LORD in the days of King Je·hoi'a·kim son of Jō·sī'ah of Judah: ² Go to the house of the Rē'chab·ītes, and speak with them, and bring them to the house of the LORD, into one of the chambers; then offer them wine to drink. ³ So I took Jā·az·a·nī'ah son of Jer·e·mī'ah son of Ha·baz·zi·nī'ah, and his brothers, and all his sons, and the whole house of the Rē'chab·ītes. ⁴ I brought them to the house of the LORD into the chamber of the sons of Hā'nan son of Ig·da·lī'ah, the man of God, which was near the chamber of the officials, above the chamber of Mā·a·sēi'ah son of Shal'lum, keeper of the threshold. ⁵ Then I set before the Rē'chab·ītes pitchers full of wine, and cups; and I said to them, "Have some wine." ⁶ But they answered, "We will drink no wine, for our ancestor Jon'a·dab son of Rē'chab commanded us, 'You shall never drink wine, neither you nor your children; ⁷ nor shall you ever build a house, or sow seed; nor shall you plant a vineyard, or even own one; but you shall live in tents all your days, that you may live many days in the land where you reside.' ⁸ We have obeyed the charge of our ancestor Jon'a·dab son of Rē'chab in all that he commanded us, to drink no wine all our days, ourselves, our wives, our sons, or our daughters, ⁹ and not to build houses to live in. We have no vineyard or field or seed; ¹⁰ but we have lived in tents, and have obeyed and done all that our ancestor Jon'a·dab commanded us. ¹¹ But when King Ne·bū·chad·rez'zar of Babylon came up against the land, we said, 'Come, and let us go to Jerusalem for fear of the army of the Chal·dē'ans and the army of the Ar·a·mē'ans.' That is why we are living in Jerusalem."

¹² Then the word of the LORD came to Jer·e·mī'ah: ¹³ Thus says the LORD of hosts, the God of Israel: Go and say to the people of Judah and the inhabitants of Jerusalem, Can you not learn a lesson and obey my words? says the LORD. ¹⁴ The command has been carried out that Jon'a·dab son of Rē'chab gave to his descendants to drink no wine; and they drink none to this day, for they have obeyed their ancestor's command. But I myself have spoken to you persistently, and you have not obeyed me. ¹⁵ I have sent to you all my servants the prophets, sending them persistently, saying, 'Turn now everyone of you from your evil way, and amend your doings, and do not go after other gods to serve them, and then you shall live in the land that I gave to you and your ancestors.' But you did not incline your ear or obey me. ¹⁶ The descendants of Jon'a·dab son of Rē'chab have carried out the command that their ancestor gave them, but this people has not obeyed me. ¹⁷ Therefore, thus says the LORD, the God of hosts, the God of Israel: I am going to bring on Judah and on all the inhabitants of Jerusalem every disaster that I have pronounced against them; because I have spoken to them and they have not listened, I have called to them and they have not answered.

¹⁸ But to the house of the Rē'chab·ītes Jer·e·mī'ah said: Thus says the LORD of hosts, the God of Israel: Because you have obeyed the command of your ancestor Jon'a·dab, and kept all his precepts, and done all that he commanded you, ¹⁹ therefore thus says the LORD of hosts, the God of Israel: Jon'a·dab son of Rē'chab shall not lack a descendant to stand before me for all time.

The Scroll Read in the Temple

36 In the fourth year of King Je·hoi'a·kim son of Jō·sī'ah of Judah, this word came to Jer·e·mī'ah from the LORD: ² Take a scroll and write on it all the words that I have spoken to you against Israel and Judah and all the nations, from the day I spoke to you, from the days of Jō·sī'ah until today. ³ It may be that when the house of Judah hears of all the disasters that I intend to do to them, all of them may turn from their evil ways, so that I may forgive their iniquity and their sin.

⁴ Then Jer·e·mī'ah called Bar'uch son of Ne·rī'ah, and Bar'uch wrote on a scroll at Jer·e·mī'ah's dictation all

J
E
R
E
M
I
A
H

the words of the LORD that he had spoken to him. ⁵ And Jer·e·mi′ah ordered Bar′uch, saying, "I am prevented from entering the house of the LORD; ⁶ so you go yourself, and on a fast day in the hearing of the people in the LORD's house you shall read the words of the LORD from the scroll that you have written at my dictation. You shall read them also in the hearing of all the people of Judah who come up from their towns. ⁷ It may be that their plea will come before the LORD, and that all of them will turn from their evil ways, for great is the anger and wrath that the LORD has pronounced against this people." ⁸ And Bar′uch son of Ne·ri′ah did all that the prophet Jer·e·mi′ah ordered him about reading from the scroll the words of the LORD in the LORD's house.

9 In the fifth year of King Je·hoi′a·kim son of Jo·si′ah of Judah, in the ninth month, all the people in Jerusalem and all the people who came from the towns of Judah to Jerusalem proclaimed a fast before the LORD. ¹⁰ Then, in the hearing of all the people, Bar′uch read the words of Jer·e·mi′ah from the scroll, in the house of the LORD, in the chamber of Gem·a·ri′ah son of Sha′phan the secretary, which was in the upper court, at the entry of the New Gate of the LORD's house.

The Scroll Read in the Palace

11 When Mi·cai′ah son of Gem·a·ri′ah son of Sha′phan heard all the words of the LORD from the scroll, ¹² he went down to the king's house, into the secretary's chamber; and all the officials were sitting there: E·lish′a·ma the secretary, De·lai′ah son of She·mai′ah, El·na′than son of Ach′bor, Gem·a·ri′ah son of Sha′phan, Zed·e·ki′ah son of Han·a·ni′ah, and all the officials. ¹³ And Mi·cai′ah told them all the words that he had heard, when Bar′uch read the scroll in the hearing of the people. ¹⁴ Then all the officials sent Je·hu′di son of Neth·a·ni′ah son of Shel·e·mi′ah son of Cu′shi to say to Bar′uch, "Bring the scroll that you read in the hearing of the people, and come." So Bar′uch son of Ne·ri′ah took the scroll in his hand and came to them. ¹⁵ And they said to him, "Sit down and read it to us." So Bar′uch read it to them. ¹⁶ When they heard all the words, they turned to one another in alarm, and said to Bar′uch, "We certainly must report all these

words to the king." ¹⁷ Then they questioned Bar′uch, "Tell us now, how did you write all these words? Was it at his dictation?" ¹⁸ Bar′uch answered them, "He dictated all these words to me, and I wrote them with ink on the scroll." ¹⁹ Then the officials said to Bar′uch, "Go and hide, you and Jer·e·mi′ah, and let no one know where you are."

Jehoiakim Burns the Scroll

20 Leaving the scroll in the chamber of E·lish′a·ma the secretary, they went to the court of the king; and they reported all the words to the king. ²¹ Then the king sent Je·hu′di to get the scroll, and he took it from the chamber of E·lish′a·ma the secretary; and Je·hu′di read it to the king and all the officials who stood beside the king. ²² Now the king was sitting in his winter apartment (it was the ninth month), and there was a fire burning in the brazier before him. ²³ As Je·hu′di read three or four columns, the king^c would cut them off with a penknife and throw them into the fire in the brazier, until the entire scroll was consumed in the fire that was in the brazier. ²⁴ Yet neither the king, nor any of his servants who heard all these words, was alarmed, nor did they tear their garments. ²⁵ Even when El·na′than and De·lai′ah and Gem·a·ri′ah urged the king not to burn the scroll, he would not listen to them. ²⁶ And the king commanded Je·rah′me·el the king's son and Se·rai′ah son of Az′ri·el and Shel·e·mi′ah son of Ab·de′el to arrest the secretary Bar′uch and the prophet Jer·e·mi′ah. But the LORD hid them.

Jeremiah Dictates Another

27 Now, after the king had burned the scroll with the words that Bar′uch wrote at Jer·e·mi′ah's dictation, the word of the LORD came to Jer·e·mi′ah: ²⁸ Take another scroll and write on it all the former words that were in the first scroll, which King Je·hoi′a·kim of Judah has burned. ²⁹ And concerning King Je·hoi′a·kim of Judah you shall say: Thus says the LORD, You have dared to burn this scroll, saying, Why have you written in it that the king of Babylon will certainly come and destroy this land, and will cut off from it human beings and animals? ³⁰ Therefore thus says the LORD concerning King Je·hoi′a·kim of Judah: He shall

---

^c Heb *he*

have no one to sit upon the throne of David, and his dead body shall be cast out to the heat by day and the frost by night. ³¹ And I will punish him and his offspring and his servants for their iniquity; I will bring on them, and on the inhabitants of Jerusalem, and on the people of Judah, all the disasters with which I have threatened them — but they would not listen.

32 Then Jer·e·mī′ah took another scroll and gave it to the secretary Bar′uch son of Ne·rī′ah, who wrote on it at Jer·e·mī′ah's dictation all the words of the scroll that King Je·hoi′a·kim of Judah had burned in the fire; and many similar words were added to them.

Zedekiah's Vain Hope
(2 Kings 24.17; 2 Chr 36.10)

37 Zed·e·kī′ah son of Jō·sī′ah, whom King Ne·bū·chad·rez′zar of Babylon made king in the land of Judah, succeeded Cō·nī′ah son of Je·hoi′a·kim. ² But neither he nor his servants nor the people of the land listened to the words of the LORD that he spoke through the prophet Jer·e·mī′ah.

3 King Zed·e·kī′ah sent Je·hū′cal son of Shel·e·mī′ah and the priest Zeph·a·nī′ah son of Mā·a·sēi′ah to the prophet Jer·e·mī′ah saying, "Please pray for us to the LORD our God." ⁴ Now Jer·e·mī′ah was still going in and out among the people, for he had not yet been put in prison. ⁵ Meanwhile, the army of Pharaoh had come out of Egypt; and when the Chal·dē′ans who were besieging Jerusalem heard news of them, they withdrew from Jerusalem.

6 Then the word of the LORD came to the prophet Jer·e·mī′ah: ⁷ Thus says the LORD, God of Israel: This is what the two of you shall say to the king of Judah, who sent you to me to inquire of me, Pharaoh's army, which set out to help you, is going to return to its own land, to Egypt. ⁸ And the Chal·dē′ans shall return and fight against this city; they shall take it and burn it with fire. ⁹ Thus says the LORD: Do not deceive yourselves, saying, "The Chal·dē′ans will surely go away from us," for they will not go away. ¹⁰ Even if you defeated the whole army of Chal·dē′ans who are fighting against you, and there remained of them only wounded men in their tents, they

would rise up and burn this city with fire.

Jeremiah Is Imprisoned

11 Now when the Chal·dē′an army had withdrawn from Jerusalem at the approach of Pharaoh's army, ¹² Jer·e·mī′ah set out from Jerusalem to go to the land of Benjamin to receive his share of property*d* among the people there. ¹³ When he reached the Benjamin Gate, a sentinel there named I·rī′jah son of Shel·e·mī′ah son of Han·a·nī′ah arrested the prophet Jer·e·mī′ah saying, "You are deserting to the Chal·dē′ans." ¹⁴ And Jer·e·mī′ah said, "That is a lie; I am not deserting to the Chal·dē′ans." But I·rī′jah would not listen to him, and arrested Jer·e·mī′ah and brought him to the officials. ¹⁵ The officials were enraged at Jer·e·mī′ah, and they beat him and imprisoned him in the house of the secretary Jonathan, for it had been made a prison. ¹⁶ Thus Jer·e·mī′ah was put in the cistern house, in the cells, and remained there many days.

17 Then King Zed·e·kī′ah sent for him, and received him. The king questioned him secretly in his house, and said, "Is there any word from the LORD?" Jer·e·mī′ah said, "There is!" Then he said, "You shall be handed over to the king of Babylon." ¹⁸ Jer·e·mī′ah also said to King Zed·e·kī′ah, "What wrong have I done to you or your servants or this people, that you have put me in prison? ¹⁹ Where are your prophets who prophesied to you, saying, 'The king of Babylon will not come against you and against this land'? ²⁰ Now please hear me, my lord king: be good enough to listen to my plea, and do not send me back to the house of the secretary Jonathan to die there." ²¹ So King Zed·e·kī′ah gave orders, and they committed Jer·e·mī′ah to the court of the guard; and a loaf of bread was given him daily from the bakers' street, until all the bread of the city was gone. So Jer·e·mī′ah remained in the court of the guard.

Jeremiah in the Cistern

38 Now Sheph·a·tī′ah son of Mat′tan, Ged·a·lī′ah son of Pash′hur, Jū′cal son of Shel·e·mī′ah, and Pash′hur son of Mal·chī′ah heard the words that Jer·e·mī′ah was saying to

d Meaning of Heb uncertain

all the people, 2 Thus says the LORD, Those who stay in this city shall die by the sword, by famine, and by pestilence; but those who go out to the Chal·dē′ans shall live; they shall have their lives as a prize of war, and live. 3 Thus says the LORD, This city shall surely be handed over to the army of the king of Babylon and be taken. 4 Then the officials said to the king, "This man ought to be put to death, because he is discouraging the soldiers who are left in this city, and all the people, by speaking such words to them. For this man is not seeking the welfare of this people, but their harm." 5 King Zed·e·kī′ah said, "Here he is; he is in your hands; for the king is powerless against you." 6 So they took Jer·e·mī′ah and threw him into the cistern of Mal·chī′ah, the king's son, which was in the court of the guard, letting Jer·e·mī′ah down by ropes. Now there was no water in the cistern, but only mud, and Jer·e·mī′ah sank in the mud.

Jeremiah Is Rescued by Ebed-melech

7 Ē′bed-mē′lech the Ethiopian,[e] a eunuch in the king's house, heard that they had put Jer·e·mī′ah into the cistern. The king happened to be sitting at the Benjamin Gate, 8 So Ē′bed-mē′lech left the king's house and spoke to the king, 9 "My lord king, these men have acted wickedly in all they did to the prophet Jer·e·mī′ah by throwing him into the cistern to die there of hunger, for there is no bread left in the city." 10 Then the king commanded Ē′bed-mē′lech the Ethiopian,[e] "Take three men with you from here, and pull the prophet Jer·e·mī′ah up from the cistern before he dies." 11 So Ē′bed-mē′lech took the men with him and went to the house of the king, to a wardrobe of[f] the storehouse, and took from there old rags and worn-out clothes, which he let down to Jer·e·mī′ah in the cistern by ropes. 12 Then Ē′bed-mē′lech the Ethiopian[e] said to Jer·e·mī′ah, "Just put the rags and clothes between your armpits and the ropes." Jer·e·mī′ah did so. 13 Then they drew Jer·e·mī′ah up by the ropes and pulled him out of the cistern. And Jer·e·mī′ah remained in the court of the guard.

Zedekiah Consults Jeremiah Again

14 King Zed·e·kī′ah sent for the prophet Jer·e·mī′ah and received him at the third entrance of the temple of the LORD. The king said to Jer·e·mī′ah, "I have something to ask you; do not hide anything from me." 15 Jer·e·mī′ah said to Zed·e·kī′ah, "If I tell you, you will put me to death, will you not? And if I give you advice, you will not listen to me." 16 So King Zed·e·kī′ah swore an oath in secret to Jer·e·mī′ah, "As the LORD lives, who gave us our lives, I will not put you to death or hand you over to these men who seek your life."

17 Then Jer·e·mī′ah said to Zed·e·kī′ah, "Thus says the LORD, the God of hosts, the God of Israel, If you will only surrender to the officials of the king of Babylon, then your life shall be spared, and this city shall not be burned with fire, and you and your house shall live. 18 But if you do not surrender to the officials of the king of Babylon, then this city shall be handed over to the Chal·dē′ans, and they shall burn it with fire, and you yourself shall not escape from their hand." 19 King Zed·e·kī′ah said to Jer·e·mī′ah, "I am afraid of the Judeans who have deserted to the Chal·dē′ans, for I might be handed over to them and they would abuse me." 20 Jer·e·mī′ah said, "That will not happen. Just obey the voice of the LORD in what I say to you, and it shall go well with you, and your life shall be spared. 21 But if you are determined not to surrender, this is what the LORD has shown me — 22 a vision of all the women remaining in the house of the king of Judah being led out to the officials of the king of Babylon and saying,

'Your trusted friends have
　　seduced you
　　and have overcome you;
Now that your feet are stuck in
　　the mud,
　　they desert you.'

23 All your wives and your children shall be led out to the Chal·dē′ans, and you yourself shall not escape from their hand, but shall be seized by the king of Babylon; and this city shall be burned with fire."

24 Then Zed·e·kī′ah said to Jer·e·mī′ah, "Do not let anyone else know of this conversation, or you will

e Or *Nubian*; Heb *Cushite*　　*f* Cn: Heb *to under*

die. 25 If the officials should hear that I have spoken with you, and they should come and say to you, 'Just tell us what you said to the king; do not conceal it from us, or we will put you to death. What did the king say to you?' 26 then you shall say to them, 'I was presenting my plea to the king not to send me back to the house of Jonathan to die there.' " 27 All the officials did come to Jer·e·mī′ah and questioned him; and he answered them in the very words the king had commanded. So they stopped questioning him, for the conversation had not been overheard. 28 And Jer·e·mī′ah remained in the court of the guard until the day that Jerusalem was taken.

The Fall of Jerusalem
(2 Kings 25.1–12; Jer 52.4–16)

39 In the ninth year of King Zed·e·kī′ah of Judah, in the tenth month, King Ne·bū·chad·rez′zar of Babylon and all his army came against Jerusalem and besieged it; 2 in the eleventh year of Zed·e·kī′ah, in the fourth month, on the ninth day of the month, a breach was made in the city. 3 When Jerusalem was taken,g all the officials of the king of Babylon came and sat in the middle gate: Ner′gal-sha·rē′zer, Sam′gar-nē′bō, Sar′se-chim the Rab·sar′is, Ner′gal-sha-rē′zer the Rab′mag, with all the rest of the officials of the king of Babylon. 4 When King Zed·e·kī′ah of Judah and all the soldiers saw them, they fled, going out of the city at night by way of the king's garden through the gate between the two walls; and they went toward the Ar′a·bah. 5 But the army of the Chal·dē′ans pursued them, and overtook Zed·e·kī′ah in the plains of Jericho; and when they had taken him, they brought him up to King Ne·bū·chad·rez′zar of Babylon, at Rib′lah, in the land of Hā′math; and he passed sentence on him. 6 The king of Babylon slaughtered the sons of Zed·e·kī′ah at Rib′lah before his eyes; also the king of Babylon slaughtered all the nobles of Judah. 7 He put out the eyes of Zed·e·kī′ah, and bound him in fetters to take him to Babylon. 8 The Chal·dē′ans burned the king's house and the houses of the people, and broke down the walls of Jerusalem. 9 Then Ne·bū·za·rad′an the captain of the guard exiled to Babylon the rest of the people who were left in the city, those who had deserted to him, and the people who remained. 10 Ne·bū·za·rad′an the captain of the guard left in the land of Judah some of the poor people who owned nothing, and gave them vineyards and fields at the same time.

Jeremiah, Set Free, Remembers Ebed-melech

11 King Ne·bū·chad·rez′zar of Babylon gave command concerning Jer·e·mī′ah through Ne·bū·za·rad′an, the captain of the guard, saying, 12 "Take him, look after him well and do him no harm, but deal with him as he may ask you." 13 So Ne·bū·za·rad′an the captain of the guard, Ne·bū·shaz′ban the Rab·sar′is, Ner′gal-sha·rē′zer the Rab·mag, and all the chief officers of the king of Babylon sent 14 and took Jer·e·mī′ah from the court of the guard. They entrusted him to Ged·a·lī′ah son of A·hī′kam son of Shā′phan to be brought home. So he stayed with his own people.

15 The word of the LORD came to Jer·e·mī′ah while he was confined in the court of the guard: 16 Go and say to Ē′bed-mē′lech the Ethiopian:h Thus says the LORD of hosts, the God of Israel: I am going to fulfill my words against this city for evil and not for good, and they shall be accomplished in your presence on that day. 17 But I will save you on that day, says the LORD, and you shall not be handed over to those whom you dread. 18 For I will surely save you, and you shall not fall by the sword; but you shall have your life as a prize of war, because you have trusted in me, says the LORD.

Jeremiah with Gedaliah the Governor
(2 Kings 25.22–26)

40 The word that came to Jer·e·mī′ah from the LORD after Ne·bū·za·rad′an the captain of the guard had let him go from Rā′mah, when he took him bound in fetters along with all the captives of Jerusalem and Judah who were being exiled to Babylon. 2 The captain of the guard took Jer·e·mī′ah and said to him, "The LORD your God threatened this place with this disaster; 3 and now the LORD has brought it about, and has done as he said, because all of you sinned against the LORD and did not obey his

g This clause has been transposed from 38.28   h Or Nubian; Heb Cushite voice. Therefore this thing has come upon you. 4 Now look, I have just released you today from the fetters on your hands. If you wish to come with me to Babylon, come, and I will take good care of you; but if you do not wish to come with me to Babylon, you need not come. See, the whole land is before you; go wherever you think it good and right to go. 5 If you remain,[i] then return to Ged·a·lī'ah son of A·hī'kam son of Shā'phan, whom the king of Babylon appointed governor of the towns of Judah, and stay with him among the people; or go wherever you think it right to go." So the captain of the guard gave him an allowance of food and a present, and let him go. 6 Then Jer·e·mī'ah went to Ged·a·lī'ah son of A·hī'kam at Miz'pah, and stayed with him among the people who were left in the land.

7 When all the leaders of the forces in the open country and their troops heard that the king of Babylon had appointed Ged·a·lī'ah son of A·hī'kam governor in the land, and had committed to him men, women, and children, those of the poorest of the land who had not been taken into exile to Babylon, 8 they went to Ged·a·lī'ah at Miz'pah—Ish'ma·el son of Neth·a·nī'ah, Jō·hā'nan son of Ka·rē'ah, Se·rāi'ah son of Tan'hu·meth, the sons of Ē'phai the Ne·toph'a·thīte, Jez·a·nī'ah son of the Mā'a·ca·thīte, they and their troops. 9 Ged·a·lī'ah son of A·hī'kam son of Shā'phan swore to them and their troops, saying, "Do not be afraid to serve the Chal·dē'ans. Stay in the land and serve the king of Babylon, and it shall go well with you. 10 As for me, I am staying at Miz'pah to represent you before the Chal·dē'ans who come to us; but as for you, gather wine and summer fruits and oil, and store them in your vessels, and live in the towns that you have taken over." 11 Likewise, when all the Judeans who were in Mō'ab and among the Am'mon·ites and in Ē'dom and in other lands heard that the king of Babylon had left a remnant in Judah and had appointed Ged·a·lī'ah son of A·hī'kam son of Shā'phan as governor over them, 12 then all the Judeans returned from all the places to which they had been scattered and came to the land of Judah, to Ged·a·lī'ah at Miz'pah; and they gathered wine and summer fruits in great abundance.

13 Now Jō·hā'nan son of Ka·rē'ah and all the leaders of the forces in the open country came to Ged·a·lī'ah at Miz'pah 14 and said to him, "Are you at all aware that Bā'a·lis king of the Am'mon·ites has sent Ish'ma·el son of Neth·a·nī'ah to take your life?" But Ged·a·lī'ah son of A·hī'kam would not believe them. 15 Then Jō·hā'nan son of Ka·rē'ah spoke secretly to Ged·a·lī'ah at Miz'pah, "Please let me go and kill Ish'ma·el son of Neth·a·nī'ah, and no one else will know. Why should he take your life, so that all the Judeans who are gathered around you would be scattered, and the remnant of Judah would perish?" 16 But Ged·a·lī'ah son of A·hī'kam said to Jō·hā'nan son of Ka·rē'ah, "Do not do such a thing, for you are telling a lie about Ish'ma·el."

Insurrection against Gedaliah

41 In the seventh month, Ish'ma·el son of Neth·a·nī'ah son of E·lish'a·ma, of the royal family, one of the chief officers of the king, came with ten men to Ged·a·lī'ah son of A·hī'kam, at Miz'pah. As they ate bread together there at Miz'pah, 2 Ish'ma·el son of Neth·a·nī'ah and the ten men with him got up and struck down Ged·a·lī'ah son of A·hī'kam son of Shā'phan with the sword and killed him, because the king of Babylon had appointed him governor in the land. 3 Ish'ma·el also killed all the Judeans who were with Ged·a·lī'ah at Miz'pah, and the Chal·dē'an soldiers who happened to be there.

4 On the day after the murder of Ged·a·lī'ah, before anyone knew of it, 5 eighty men arrived from Shē'chem and Shī'lōh and Samaria, with their beards shaved and their clothes torn, and their bodies gashed, bringing grain offerings and incense to present at the temple of the LORD. 6 And Ish'ma·el son of Neth·a·nī'ah came out from Miz'pah to meet them, weeping as he came. As he met them, he said to them, "Come to Ged·a·lī'ah son of A·hī'kam." 7 When they reached the middle of the city, Ish'ma·el son of Neth·a·nī'ah and the men with him slaughtered them, and threw them[j] into a cistern. 8 But there were ten men among them who said to Ish'ma·el, "Do not kill us, for we have stores of wheat, barley, oil, and honey hidden in

---

i Syr: Meaning of Heb uncertain
j Syr: Heb lacks *and threw them*; compare verse 9

the fields." So he refrained, and did not kill them along with their companions.

9 Now the cistern into which Ish'-ma·el had thrown all the bodies of the men whom he had struck down was the large cistern[k] that King Asa had made for defense against King Bā'-a·sha of Israel; Ish'ma·el son of Neth·a·nī'ah filled that cistern with those whom he had killed. 10 Then Ish'-ma·el took captive all the rest of the people who were in Miz'pah, the king's daughters and all the people who were left at Miz'pah, whom Ne·bū·za·rad'an, the captain of the guard, had committed to Ged·a·lī'ah son of A·hī'kam. Ish'ma·el son of Neth·a·nī'ah took them captive and set out to cross over to the Am'mon·ītes.

11 But when Jō·hā'nan son of Ka·rē'ah and all the leaders of the forces with him heard of all the crimes that Ish'ma·el son of Neth·a·nī'ah had done, 12 they took all their men and went to fight against Ish'ma·el son of Neth·a·nī'ah. They came upon him at the great pool that is in Gib'ē·on. 13 And when all the people who were with Ish'ma·el saw Jō·hā'nan son of Ka·rē'ah and all the leaders of the forces with him, they were glad. 14 So all the people whom Ish'ma·el had carried away captive from Miz'pah turned around and came back, and went to Jō·hā'nan son of Ka·rē'ah. 15 But Ish'ma·el son of Neth·a·nī'ah escaped from Jō·hā'nan with eight men, and went to the Am'mon·ītes. 16 Then Jō·hā'nan son of Ka·rē'ah and all the leaders of the forces with him took all the rest of the people whom Ish'ma·el son of Neth·a·nī'ah had carried away captive[l] from Miz'pah after he had slain Ged·a·lī'ah son of A·hī'kam—soldiers, women, children, and eunuchs, whom Jō·hā'nan brought back from Gib'ē·on.[m] 17 And they set out, and stopped at Gē'rūth Chim'ham near Bethlehem, intending to go to Egypt 18 because of the Chal·dē'ans; for they were afraid of them, because Ish'ma·el son of Neth·a·nī'ah had killed Ged·a·lī'ah son of A·hī'kam, whom the king of Babylon had made governor over the land.

Jeremiah Advises Survivors Not to Migrate

42 Then all the commanders of the forces, and Jō·hā'nan son of Ka·rē'ah and Az·a·rī'ah[n] son of Hō·shaī'ah, and all the people from the least to the greatest, approached 2 the prophet Jer·e·mī'ah and said, "Be good enough to listen to our plea, and pray to the LORD your God for us—for all this remnant. For there are only a few of us left out of many, as your eyes can see. 3 Let the LORD your God show us where we should go and what we should do." 4 The prophet Jer·e·mī'ah said to them, "Very well: I am going to pray to the LORD your God as you request, and whatever the LORD answers you I will tell you; I will keep nothing back from you." 5 They in their turn said to Jer·e·mī'ah, "May the LORD be a true and faithful witness against us if we do not act according to everything that the LORD your God sends us through you. 6 Whether it is good or bad, we will obey the voice of the LORD our God to whom we are sending you, in order that it may go well with us when we obey the voice of the LORD our God."

7 At the end of ten days the word of the LORD came to Jer·e·mī'ah. 8 Then he summoned Jō·hā'nan son of Ka·rē'ah and all the commanders of the forces who were with him, and all the people from the least to the greatest, 9 and said to them, "Thus says the LORD, the God of Israel, to whom you sent me to present your plea before him: 10 If you will only remain in this land, then I will build you up and not pull you down; I will plant you, and not pluck you up; for I am sorry for the disaster that I have brought upon you. 11 Do not be afraid of the king of Babylon, as you have been; do not be afraid of him, says the LORD, for I am with you, to save you and to rescue you from his hand. 12 I will grant you mercy, and he will have mercy on you and restore you to your native soil. 13 But if you continue to say, 'We will not stay in this land,' thus disobeying the voice of the LORD your God 14 and saying, 'No, we will go to the land of Egypt, where we shall not see war, or hear the sound of the trumpet, or be hungry for bread, and there we will stay,' 15 then hear the word of the LORD, O remnant of Judah. Thus says the LORD of hosts, the God of Israel: If you are determined to enter Egypt and

---

[k] Gk: Heb whom he had killed by the hand of Gedaliah   [l] Cn: Heb whom he recovered from Ishmael son of Nethaniah   [m] Meaning of Heb uncertain   [n] Gk: Heb Jezaniah

go to settle there, [16] then the sword that you fear shall overtake you there, in the land of Egypt; and the famine that you dread shall follow close after you into Egypt; and there you shall die. [17] All the people who have determined to go to Egypt to settle there shall die by the sword, by famine, and by pestilence; they shall have no remnant or survivor from the disaster that I am bringing upon them.

[18] "For thus says the LORD of hosts, the God of Israel: Just as my anger and my wrath were poured out on the inhabitants of Jerusalem, so my wrath will be poured out on you when you go to Egypt. You shall become an object of execration and horror, of cursing and ridicule. You shall see this place no more. [19] The LORD has said to you, O remnant of Judah, Do not go to Egypt. Be well aware that I have warned you today [20] that you have made a fatal mistake. For you yourselves sent me to the LORD your God, saying, 'Pray for us to the LORD our God, and whatever the LORD our God says, tell us and we will do it.' [21] So I have told you today, but you have not obeyed the voice of the LORD your God in anything that he sent me to tell you. [22] Be well aware, then, that you shall die by the sword, by famine, and by pestilence in the place where you desire to go and settle."

Taken to Egypt, Jeremiah Warns of Judgment

43 When Jer·e·mī′ah finished speaking to all the people all these words of the LORD their God, with which the LORD their God had sent him to them, [2] Az·a·rī′ah son of Hō·shaī′ah and Jō·hā′nan son of Ka·rē′ah and all the other insolent men said to Jer·e·mī′ah, "You are telling a lie. The LORD our God did not send you to say, 'Do not go to Egypt to settle there'; [3] but Bar′uch son of Ne·rī′ah is inciting you against us, to hand us over to the Chal·dē′ans, in order that they may kill us or take us into exile in Babylon." [4] So Jō·hā′nan son of Ka·rē′ah and all the commanders of the forces and all the people did not obey the voice of the LORD, to stay in the land of Judah. [5] But Jō·hā′nan son of Ka·rē′ah and all the commanders of the forces took all the remnant of Judah who had returned to settle in the land of Judah from all the nations to which they had been driven— [6] the men, the women,

the children, the princesses, and everyone whom Ne·bū·za·rad′an the captain of the guard had left with Ged·a·lī′ah son of A·hī′kam son of Shā′phan; also the prophet Jer·e·mī′ah and Bar′uch son of Ne·rī′ah. [7] And they came into the land of Egypt, for they did not obey the voice of the LORD. And they arrived at Tah′-pan·hēs.

[8] Then the word of the LORD came to Jer·e·mī′ah in Tah′pan·hēs: [9] Take some large stones in your hands, and bury them in the clay pavement[o] that is at the entrance to Pharaoh's palace in Tah′pan·hēs. Let the Judeans see you do it, [10] and say to them, Thus says the LORD of hosts, the God of Israel: I am going to send and take my servant King Ne·bū·chad·rez′zar of Babylon, and he[p] will set his throne above these stones that I have buried, and he will spread his royal canopy over them. [11] He shall come and ravage the land of Egypt, giving

those who are destined for
  pestilence, to pestilence,
and those who are destined for
  captivity, to captivity,
and those who are destined for
  the sword, to the sword.

[12] He[q] shall kindle a fire in the temples of the gods of Egypt; and he shall burn them and carry them away captive; and he shall pick clean the land of Egypt, as a shepherd picks his cloak clean of vermin; and he shall depart from there safely. [13] He shall break the obelisks of Hē·li·op′o·lis, which is in the land of Egypt; and the temples of the gods of Egypt he shall burn with fire.

Denunciation of Persistent Idolatry

44 The word that came to Jer·e·mī′ah for all the Judeans living in the land of Egypt, at Mig′dōl, at Tah′pan·hēs, at Memphis, and in the land of Path′ros, [2] Thus says the LORD of hosts, the God of Israel: You yourselves have seen all the disaster that I have brought on Jerusalem and on all the towns of Judah. Look at them; today they are a desolation, without an inhabitant in them, [3] because of the wickedness that they committed, provoking me to anger, in that they went to make offerings and serve other gods

o Meaning of Heb uncertain   p Gk Syr: Heb I   q Gk Syr Vg: Heb I that they had not known, neither they, nor you, nor your ancestors. 4 Yet I persistently sent to you all my servants the prophets, saying, "I beg you not to do this abominable thing that I hate!" 5 But they did not listen or incline their ear, to turn from their wickedness and make no offerings to other gods. 6 So my wrath and my anger were poured out and kindled in the towns of Judah and in the streets of Jerusalem; and they became a waste and a desolation, as they still are today. 7 And now thus says the LORD God of hosts, the God of Israel: Why are you doing such great harm to yourselves, to cut off man and woman, child and infant, from the midst of Judah, leaving yourselves without a remnant? 8 Why do you provoke me to anger with the works of your hands, making offerings to other gods in the land of Egypt where you have come to settle? Will you be cut off and become an object of cursing and ridicule among all the nations of the earth? 9 Have you forgotten the crimes of your ancestors, of the kings of Judah, of their[r] wives, your own crimes and those of your wives, which they committed in the land of Judah and in the streets of Jerusalem? 10 They have shown no contrition or fear to this day, nor have they walked in my law and my statutes that I set before you and before your ancestors.

11　Therefore thus says the LORD of hosts, the God of Israel: I am determined to bring disaster on you, to bring all Judah to an end. 12 I will take the remnant of Judah who are determined to come to the land of Egypt to settle, and they shall perish, everyone; in the land of Egypt they shall fall; by the sword and by famine they shall perish; from the least to the greatest, they shall die by the sword and by famine; and they shall become an object of execration and horror, of cursing and ridicule. 13 I will punish those who live in the land of Egypt, as I have punished Jerusalem, with the sword, with famine, and with pestilence, 14 so that none of the remnant of Judah who have come to settle in the land of Egypt shall escape or survive or return to the land of Judah. Although they long to go back to live there, they shall not go back, except some fugitives.

15　Then all the men who were aware that their wives had been making offerings to other gods, and all the women who stood by, a great assembly, all the people who lived in Path'ros in the land of Egypt, answered Jer·e·mi'ah: 16 "As for the word that you have spoken to us in the name of the LORD, we are not going to listen to you. 17 Instead, we will do everything that we have vowed, make offerings to the queen of heaven and pour out libations to her, just as we and our ancestors, our kings and our officials, used to do in the towns of Judah and in the streets of Jerusalem. We used to have plenty of food, and prospered, and saw no misfortune. 18 But from the time we stopped making offerings to the queen of heaven and pouring out libations to her, we have lacked everything and have perished by the sword and by famine." 19 And the women said,[s] "Indeed we will go on making offerings to the queen of heaven and pouring out libations to her; do you think that we made cakes for her, marked with her image, and poured out libations to her without our husbands' being involved?"

20　Then Jer·e·mi'ah said to all the people, men and women, all the people who were giving him this answer: 21 "As for the offerings that you made in the towns of Judah and in the streets of Jerusalem, you and your ancestors, your kings and your officials, and the people of the land, did not the LORD remember them? Did it not come into his mind? 22 The LORD could no longer bear the sight of your evil doings, the abominations that you committed; therefore your land became a desolation and a waste and a curse, without inhabitant, as it is to this day. 23 It is because you burned offerings, and because you sinned against the LORD and did not obey the voice of the LORD or walk in his law and in his statutes and in his decrees, that this disaster has befallen you, as is still evident today."

24　Jer·e·mi'ah said to all the people and all the women, "Hear the word of the LORD, all you Judeans who are in the land of Egypt, 25 Thus says the LORD of hosts, the God of Israel: You and your wives have accomplished in deeds what you declared in words, saying, 'We are determined to perform the vows that we have made, to make offerings to the queen of heaven and to pour out libations to her.' By all means, keep your vows and make your liba-

---

[r] Heb *his*　　[s] Compare Syr: Heb lacks *And the women said*

tions! 26 Therefore hear the word of the LORD, all you Judeans who live in the land of Egypt: Lo, I swear by my great name, says the LORD, that my name shall no longer be pronounced on the lips of any of the people of Judah in all the land of Egypt, saying, 'As the Lord GOD lives.' 27 I am going to watch over them for harm and not for good; all the people of Judah who are in the land of Egypt shall perish by the sword and by famine, until not one is left. 28 And those who escape the sword shall return from the land of Egypt to the land of Judah, few in number; and all the remnant of Judah, who have come to the land of Egypt to settle, shall know whose words will stand, mine or theirs! 29 This shall be the sign to you, says the LORD, that I am going to punish you in this place, in order that you may know that my words against you will surely be carried out: 30 Thus says the LORD, I am going to give Pharaoh Hoph'ra, king of Egypt, into the hands of his enemies, those who seek his life, just as I gave King Zed·e·kī'ah of Judah into the hand of King Ne·bū·chad·rez'zar of Babylon, his enemy who sought his life."

A Word of Comfort to Baruch

45 The word that the prophet Jer·e·mī'ah spoke to Bar'uch son of Ne·rī'ah, when he wrote these words in a scroll at the dictation of Jer·e·mī'ah, in the fourth year of King Je·hoi'a·kim son of Jō·sī'ah of Judah: 2 Thus says the LORD, the God of Israel, to you, O Bar'uch: 3 You said, "Woe is me! The LORD has added sorrow to my pain; I am weary with my groaning, and I find no rest." 4 Thus you shall say to him, "Thus says the LORD: I am going to break down what I have built, and pluck up what I have planted — that is, the whole land. 5 And you, do you seek great things for yourself? Do not seek them; for I am going to bring disaster upon all flesh, says the LORD; but I will give you your life as a prize of war in every place to which you may go."

Judgment on Egypt

46 The word of the LORD that came to the prophet Jer·e·mī'ah concerning the nations.

2 Concerning Egypt, about the army of Pharaoh Nē'cō, king of Egypt, which was by the river Euphrates at Car'chem·ish and which King Ne·bū·chad·rez'zar of Babylon defeated in the fourth year of King Je·hoi'a·kim son of Jō·sī'ah of Judah:

3 Prepare buckler and shield,
    and advance for battle!
4 Harness the horses;
    mount the steeds!
Take your stations with your
    helmets,
    whet your lances,
    put on your coats of mail!
5 Why do I see them terrified?
    They have fallen back;
their warriors are beaten down,
    and have fled in haste.
They do not look back —
    terror is all around!
              says the LORD.
6 The swift cannot flee away,
    nor can the warrior escape;
in the north by the river
    Euphrates
    they have stumbled and fallen.

7 Who is this, rising like the Nile,
    like rivers whose waters
        surge?
8 Egypt rises like the Nile,
    like rivers whose waters surge.
It said, Let me rise, let me cover
    the earth,
    let me destroy cities and their
        inhabitants.
9 Advance, O horses,
    and dash madly, O chariots!
Let the warriors go forth:
    Ethiopia[t] and Put who carry
        the shield,
    the Lū'dim, who draw[u] the
        bow.
10 That day is the day of the Lord
    GOD of hosts,
    a day of retribution,
    to gain vindication from his
        foes.
The sword shall devour and be
    sated,
    and drink its fill of their blood.
For the Lord GOD of hosts holds
    a sacrifice
    in the land of the north by the
        river Euphrates.
11 Go up to Gil'e·ad, and take
    balm,
    O virgin daughter Egypt!
In vain you have used many
    medicines;
    there is no healing for you.

t Or Nubia; Heb Cush   u Cn: Heb who grasp, who draw

12 The nations have heard of your
    shame,
    and the earth is full of your
        cry;
    for warrior has stumbled against
        warrior;
    both have fallen together.

Babylonia Will Strike Egypt

13 The word that the LORD spoke to
the prophet Jer·e·mī′ah about the coming of King Ne·bū·chad·rez′zar of Babylon to attack the land of Egypt:
14 Declare in Egypt, and proclaim
        in Mig′dōl;
    proclaim in Memphis and
        Tah′pan·hēs;
    Say, "Take your stations and be
        ready,
    for the sword shall devour
        those around you."
15 Why has Ā′pis fled?ᵛ
    Why did your bull not stand?
    —because the LORD thrust him
        down.
16 Your multitude stumbledʷ and
        fell,
    and one said to another,ˣ
    "Come, let us go back to our
        own people
    and to the land of our birth,
    because of the destroying
        sword."
17 Give Pharaoh, king of Egypt, the
        name
    "Braggart who missed his
        chance."

18 As I live, says the King,
    whose name is the LORD of
        hosts,
    one is coming
    like Tā′bor among the
        mountains,
    and like Car′mel by the sea.
19 Pack your bags for exile,
    sheltered daughter Egypt!
    For Memphis shall become a
        waste,
    a ruin, without inhabitant.

20 A beautiful heifer is Egypt—
    a gadfly from the north lights
        upon her.
21 Even her mercenaries in her
        midst
    are like fatted calves;
    they too have turned and fled
        together,
    they did not stand;

for the day of their calamity has
    come upon them,
the time of their punishment.

22 She makes a sound like a snake
        gliding away;
    for her enemies march in
        force,
    and come against her with axes,
    like those who fell trees.
23 They shall cut down her forest,
                says the LORD,
    though it is impenetrable,
    because they are more numerous
        than locusts;
    they are without number.
24 Daughter Egypt shall be put to
        shame;
    she shall be handed over to a
        people from the north.

25 The LORD of hosts, the God of
Israel, said: See, I am bringing punishment upon Ā′mon of Thēbes, and
Pharaoh, and Egypt and her gods and
her kings, upon Pharaoh and those
who trust in him. 26 I will hand them
over to those who seek their life, to
King Ne·bū·chad·rez′zar of Babylon
and his officers. Afterward Egypt shall
be inhabited as in the days of old, says
the LORD.

God Will Save Israel
(Cp Jer 30.10–11)

27 But as for you, have no fear, my
        servant Jacob,
    and do not be dismayed,
        O Israel;
    for I am going to save you from
        far away,
    and your offspring from the
        land of their captivity.
    Jacob shall return and have
        quiet and ease,
    and no one shall make him
        afraid.
28 As for you, have no fear, my
        servant Jacob,
                says the LORD,
    for I am with you.
    I will make an end of all the
        nations
    among which I have banished
        you,
    but I will not make an end of
        you!

ᵛ Gk: Heb *Why was it swept away*
ʷ Gk: Heb *Meaning of Heb uncertain*
ˣ Gk: Heb *and fell one to another and*
    they said

I will chastise you in just
        measure,
    and I will by no means leave
        you unpunished.

Judgment on the Philistines

47 The word of the LORD that came
to the prophet Jer·e·mī′ah concerning the Phi·lis′tines, before Pharaoh attacked Gā′za:

2 Thus says the LORD:
    See, waters are rising out of the
        north
    and shall become an
        overflowing torrent;
    they shall overflow the land and
        all that fills it,
    the city and those who live in
        it.
    People shall cry out,
    and all the inhabitants of the
        land shall wail.

3 At the noise of the stamping of
        the hoofs of his stallions,
    at the clatter of his chariots, at
        the rumbling of their
        wheels,
    parents do not turn back for
        children,
    so feeble are their hands,

4 because of the day that is
        coming
    to destroy all the Phi·lis′tines,
    to cut off from Tȳre and Sī′don
        every helper that remains.
    For the LORD is destroying the
        Phi·lis′tines,
    the remnant of the coastland
        of Caph′tor.

5 Baldness has come upon Gā′za,
    Ash′ke·lon is silenced.
    O remnant of their power![y]
    How long will you gash
        yourselves?

6 Ah, sword of the LORD!
    How long until you are quiet?
    Put yourself into your scabbard,
        rest and be still!

7 How can it[z] be quiet,
    when the LORD has given it an
        order?
    Against Ash′ke·lon and against
        the seashore —
    there he has appointed it.

Judgment on Moab

48 Concerning Mō′ab.
Thus says the LORD of hosts, the God
of Israel:
    Alas for Nē′bo, it is laid waste!

Kir·i·a·thā′im is put to shame,
        it is taken;
    the fortress is put to shame and
        broken down;
2   the renown of Mō′ab is no
        more.
    In Hesh′bon they planned evil
        against her:
    "Come, let us cut her off from
        being a nation!"
    You also, O Mad′men, shall be
        brought to silence;[a]
    the sword shall pursue you.

3 Hark! a cry from Hor·ō·nā′im,
    "Desolation and great
        destruction!"
4 "Mō′ab is destroyed!"
    her little ones cry out.
5 For at the ascent of Lū′hith
    they go[b] up weeping bitterly;
    for at the descent of Hor·ō·nā′im
    they have heard the
        distressing cry of anguish.
6 Flee! Save yourselves!
    Be like a wild ass[c] in the
        desert!

7 Surely, because you trusted in
        your strongholds[d] and
        your treasures,
    you also shall be taken;
    Chē′mosh shall go out into exile,
    with his priests and his
        attendants.
8 The destroyer shall come upon
        every town,
    and no town shall escape;
    the valley shall perish,
    and the plain shall be
        destroyed,
    as the LORD has spoken.

9 Set aside salt for Mō′ab,
    for she will surely fall;
    her towns shall become a
        desolation,
    with no inhabitant in them.

10 Accursed is the one who is slack
in doing the work of the LORD; and
accursed is the one who keeps back
the sword from bloodshed.

11 Mō′ab has been at ease from his
        youth,

[y] Gk: Heb *their valley*   [z] Gk Vg: Heb
you   [a] The place-name *Madmen* sounds
like the Hebrew verb *to be silent*
[b] Cn: Heb *he goes*   [c] Gk Aquila: Heb
like Aroer   [d] Gk: Heb *works*

settled like wine[e] on its dregs;
he has not been emptied from
vessel to vessel,
nor has he gone into exile;
therefore his flavor has
remained
and his aroma is unspoiled.

12 Therefore, the time is surely
coming, says the LORD, when I shall
send to him decanters to decant him,
and empty his vessels, and break his[f]
jars in pieces. 13 Then Mō'ab shall be
ashamed of Chē'mosh, as the house of
Israel was ashamed of Beth'el, their
confidence.

14 How can you say, "We are
heroes
and mighty warriors"?
15 The destroyer of Mō'ab and his
towns has come up,
and the choicest of his young
men have gone down to
slaughter,
says the King, whose name is
the LORD of hosts.
16 The calamity of Mō'ab is near at
hand
and his doom approaches
swiftly.
17 Mourn over him, all you his
neighbors,
and all who know his name;
say, "How the mighty scepter is
broken,
the glorious staff!"

18 Come down from glory,
and sit on the parched ground,
enthroned daughter Dī'bon!
For the destroyer of Mō'ab has
come up against you;
he has destroyed your
strongholds.
19 Stand by the road and watch,
you inhabitant of A·rō'er!
Ask the man fleeing and the
woman escaping;
say, "What has happened?"
20 Mō'ab is put to shame, for it is
broken down;
wail and cry!
Tell it by the Ar'non,
that Mō'ab is laid waste.

21 Judgment has come upon the tableland, upon Hō'lon, and Jah'zah,
and Meph'a·ath, 22 and Dī'bon, and
Nē'bō, and Beth-dib·la·thā'im, 23 and
Kir·i·a·thā'im, and Beth-gā'mul, and
Beth-mē'on, 24 and Ker'i·oth, and Boz'-
rah, and all the towns of the land of
Mō'ab, far and near. 25 The horn of
Mō'ab is cut off, and his arm is broken,
says the LORD.
26 Make him drunk, because he
magnified himself against the LORD;
let Mō'ab wallow in his vomit; he too
shall become a laughingstock. 27 Israel
was a laughingstock for you, though
he was not caught among thieves; but
whenever you spoke of him you shook
your head!

28 Leave the towns, and live on the
rock,
O inhabitants of Mō'ab!
Be like the dove that nests
on the sides of the mouth of a
gorge.
29 We have heard of the pride of
Mō'ab—
he is very proud—
of his loftiness, his pride, and his
arrogance,
and the haughtiness of his
heart.
30 I myself know his insolence,
says the LORD;
his boasts are false,
his deeds are false.
31 Therefore I wail for Mō'ab;
I cry out for all Mō'ab;
for the people of Kir-hē'res I
mourn.
32 More than for Jā'zer I weep for
you,
O vine of Sib'mah!
Your branches crossed over the
sea,
reached as far as Jā'zer;[g]
upon your summer fruits and
your vintage
the destroyer has fallen.
33 Gladness and joy have been
taken away
from the fruitful land of
Mō'ab;
I have stopped the wine from the
wine presses;
no one treads them with
shouts of joy;
the shouting is not the shout of
joy.

34 Hesh'bon and Ē·le·ā'leh cry
out;[h] as far as Jā'haz they utter their
voice, from Zō'ar to Hor·ō·nā'im and
Eg'lath-she·lish'i·yah. For even the

_e_ Heb lacks _like wine_　　_f_ Gk Aquila: Heb
their　　_g_ Two Mss and Isa 16.8: MT _the
sea of Jazer_　　_h_ Cn: Heb _From the cry of
Heshbon to Elealeh_

waters of Nim'rim have become desolate. ³⁵ And I will bring to an end in Mō'ab, says the LORD, those who offer sacrifice at a high place and make offerings to their gods. ³⁶ Therefore my heart moans for Mō'ab like a flute, and my heart moans like a flute for the people of Kir-hē'res; for the riches they gained have perished.

37　For every head is shaved and every beard cut off; on all the hands there are gashes, and on the loins sackcloth. ³⁸ On all the housetops of Mō'ab and in the squares there is nothing but lamentation; for I have broken Mō'ab like a vessel that no one wants, says the LORD. ³⁹ How it is broken! How they wail! How Mō'ab has turned his back in shame! So Mō'ab has become a derision and a horror to all his neighbors.

40　For thus says the LORD:
　　Look, he shall swoop down like
　　　　an eagle,
　　　and spread his wings against
　　　　Mō'ab;
41　the towns*ⁱ* shall be taken
　　　and the strongholds seized.
　　The hearts of the warriors of
　　　　Mō'ab, on that day,
　　　shall be like the heart of a
　　　　woman in labor.
42　Mō'ab shall be destroyed as a
　　　　people,
　　　because he magnified himself
　　　　against the LORD.
43　Terror, pit, and trap
　　　are before you, O inhabitants
　　　　of Mō'ab!
　　　　　　　says the LORD.
44　Everyone who flees from the
　　　　terror
　　　shall fall into the pit,
　　and everyone who climbs out of
　　　　the pit
　　　shall be caught in the trap.
　　For I will bring these things*ⁱ*
　　　　upon Mō'ab
　　　in the year of their
　　　　punishment,
　　　　　　　says the LORD.

45　In the shadow of Hesh'bon
　　　fugitives stop exhausted;
　　for a fire has gone out from
　　　　Hesh'bon,
　　　a flame from the house of
　　　　Sī'hon;
　　it has destroyed the forehead of
　　　　Mō'ab,
　　　the scalp of the people of
　　　　tumult.*ᵏ*
46　Woe to you, O Mō'ab!

　　The people of Chē'mosh have
　　　　perished,
　　for your sons have been taken
　　　　captive,
　　　and your daughters into
　　　　captivity.
47　Yet I will restore the fortunes of
　　　　Mō'ab
　　　in the latter days, says the
　　　　LORD.
　　Thus far is the judgment on
　　　　Mō'ab.

Judgment on the Ammonites

49　Concerning the Am'mon·ites.
Thus says the LORD:
　　Has Israel no sons?
　　　Has he no heir?
　　Why then has Mil'com
　　　　dispossessed Gad,
　　　and his people settled in its
　　　　towns?
2　Therefore, the time is surely
　　　　coming,
　　　says the LORD,
　　when I will sound the battle
　　　　alarm
　　　against Rab'bah of the
　　　　Am'mon·ites;
　　it shall become a desolate
　　　　mound,
　　　and its villages shall be burned
　　　　with fire;
　　then Israel shall dispossess those
　　　　who dispossessed him,
　　　says the LORD.

3　Wail, O Hesh'bon, for Aī is laid
　　　　waste!
　　　Cry out, O daughters*ⁱ* of
　　　　Rab'bah!
　　Put on sackcloth,
　　　lament, and slash yourselves
　　　　with whips!*ᵐ*
　　For Mil'com shall go into exile,
　　　with his priests and his
　　　　attendants.
4　Why do you boast in your
　　　　strength?
　　　Your strength is ebbing,
　　O faithless daughter.
　　　You trusted in your treasures,
　　　　saying,
　　　"Who will attack me?"
5　I am going to bring terror upon
　　　　you,

ⁱ Or *Kerioth*　*ʲ* Gk Syr: Heb *bring upon it*　*ᵏ* Or *of Shaon*　*ˡ* Or *villages*
ᵐ Cn: Meaning of Heb uncertain

says the Lord GOD of hosts,
from all your neighbors,
and you will be scattered, each
    headlong,
with no one to gather the
    fugitives.
6 But afterward I will restore the
fortunes of the Am'mon·ites, says the
LORD.

Judgment on Edom

7 Concerning Ē'dom.

Thus says the LORD of hosts:
Is there no longer wisdom in
    Tē'man?
    Has counsel perished from the
        prudent?
    Has their wisdom vanished?
8 Flee, turn back, get down low,
    inhabitants of Dē'dan!
For I will bring the calamity of
    Esau upon him,
    the time when I punish him.
9 If grape-gatherers came to you,
    would they not leave
        gleanings?
If thieves came by night,
    even they would pillage only
        what they wanted.
10 But as for me, I have stripped
    Esau bare,
    I have uncovered his hiding
        places,
and he is not able to conceal
    himself.
His offspring are destroyed, his
    kinsfolk
and his neighbors; and he is
    no more.
11 Leave your orphans, I will keep
    them alive;
    and let your widows trust in
        me.
12 For thus says the LORD: If those
who do not deserve to drink the cup
still have to drink it, shall you be the
one to go unpunished? You shall not
go unpunished; you must drink it.
13 For by myself I have sworn, says the
LORD, that Boz'rah shall become an
object of horror and ridicule, a waste,
and an object of cursing; and all her
towns shall be perpetual wastes.
14 I have heard tidings from the
    LORD,
    and a messenger has been sent
        among the nations:
"Gather yourselves together and
    come against her,
and rise up for battle!"

15 For I will make you least among
    the nations,
    despised by humankind.
16 The terror you inspire
    and the pride of your heart
        have deceived you,
you who live in the clefts of the
    rock,[n]
    who hold the height of the hill.
Although you make your nest as
    high as the eagle's,
    from there I will bring you
        down,
                        says the LORD.
17 Ē'dom shall become an object of
horror; everyone who passes by it will
be horrified and will hiss because of all
its disasters. 18 As when Sod'om and
Go·mor'rah and their neighbors were
overthrown, says the LORD, no one
shall live there, nor shall anyone settle
in it. 19 Like a lion coming up from the
thickets of the Jordan against a peren-
nial pasture, I will suddenly chase
Ē'dom[o] away from it; and I will appoint over it whomever I choose.[p] For
who is like me? Who can summon me?
Who is the shepherd who can stand
before me? 20 Therefore hear the plan
that the LORD has made against Ē'dom
and the purposes that he has formed
against the inhabitants of Tē'man:
Surely the little ones of the flock shall
be dragged away; surely their fold
shall be appalled at their fate. 21 At the
sound of their fall the earth shall tremble; the sound of their cry shall be
heard at the Red Sea.[q] 22 Look, he
shall mount up and swoop down like
an eagle, and spread his wings against
Boz'rah, and the heart of the warriors
of Ē'dom in that day shall be like the
heart of a woman in labor.

Judgment on Damascus

23 Concerning Damascus.

Hā'math and Ar'pad are
    confounded,
    for they have heard bad news;
they melt in fear, they are
    troubled like the sea[r]
    that cannot be quiet.
24 Damascus has become feeble,
    she turned to flee,
    and panic seized her;

n Or of Sela   o Heb him   p Or and I will
single out the choicest of his rams:
Meaning of Heb uncertain   q Or Sea of
Reeds   r Cn: Heb there is trouble in the
sea

anguish and sorrows have taken
hold of her,
as of a woman in labor.
25 How the famous city is
forsaken,[s]
the joyful town![t]
26 Therefore her young men shall
fall in her squares,
and all her soldiers shall be
destroyed in that day,
says the LORD of hosts.
27 And I will kindle a fire at the
wall of Damascus,
and it shall devour the
strongholds of Ben-hā′dad.

Judgment on Kedar and Hazor

28 Concerning Kē′dar and the kingdoms of Hā′zor that King Ne·bu-
chad·rez′zar of Babylon defeated.

Thus says the LORD:
Rise up, advance against Kē′dar!
Destroy the people of the east!
29 Take their tents and their flocks,
their curtains and all their
goods;
carry off their camels for
yourselves,
and a cry shall go up: "Terror
is all around!"
30 Flee, wander far away, hide in
deep places,
O inhabitants of Hā′zor!
says the LORD.
For King Ne·bu·chad·rez′zar of
Babylon
has made a plan against you
and formed a purpose against
you.
31 Rise up, advance against a
nation at ease,
that lives secure,
says the LORD,
that has no gates or bars,
that lives alone.
32 Their camels shall become
booty,
their herds of cattle a spoil.
I will scatter to every wind
those who have shaven
temples,
and I will bring calamity
against them from every side,
says the LORD.
33 Hā′zor shall become a lair of
jackals,
an everlasting waste;
no one shall live there,
nor shall anyone settle in it.

Judgment on Elam

34 The word of the LORD that came
to the prophet Jer·e·mī′ah concerning
Ē′lam, at the beginning of the reign of
King Zed·e·kī′ah of Judah.

35 Thus says the LORD of hosts: I
am going to break the bow of Ē′lam,
the mainstay of their might; 36 and I
will bring upon Ē′lam the four winds
from the four quarters of heaven; and
I will scatter them to all these winds,
and there shall be no nation to which
the exiles from Ē′lam shall not come.
37 I will terrify Ē′lam before their enemies, and before those who seek their
life; I will bring disaster upon them,
my fierce anger, says the LORD. I will
send the sword after them, until I have
consumed them; 38 and I will set my
throne in Ē′lam, and destroy their king
and officials, says the LORD.
39 But in the latter days I will restore the fortunes of Ē′lam, says the
LORD.

Judgment on Babylon

50 The word that the LORD spoke
concerning Babylon, concern-
ing the land of the Chal·dē′ans, by the
prophet Jer·e·mī′ah:
2 Declare among the nations and
proclaim,
set up a banner and proclaim,
do not conceal it, say:
Babylon is taken,
Bel is put to shame,
Mer′o·dach is dismayed.
Her images are put to shame,
her idols are dismayed.
3 For out of the north a nation has
come up against her; it shall make her
land a desolation, and no one shall live
in it; both human beings and animals
shall flee away.

4 In those days and in that time,
says the LORD, the people of Israel
shall come, they and the people of Judah together; they shall come weeping
as they seek the LORD their God.
5 They shall ask the way to Zion, with
faces turned toward it, and they shall
come and join[u] themselves to the
LORD by an everlasting covenant that
will never be forgotten.

_s_ Vg: Heb _is not forsaken_   _t_ Syr Vg Tg:
Heb _the town of my joy_   _u_ Gk: Heb
toward it. Come! They shall join

6 My people have been lost sheep;
their shepherds have led them astray,
turning them away on the mountains;
from mountain to hill they have gone,
they have forgotten their fold. ⁷ All
who found them have devoured them,
and their enemies have said, "We are
not guilty, because they have sinned
against the LORD, the true pasture, the
LORD, the hope of their ancestors."

8 Flee from Babylon, and go out of
the land of the Chal·dē'ans, and be like
male goats leading the flock. ⁹ For I am
going to stir up and bring against Babylon a company of great nations from
the land of the north; and they shall
array themselves against her; from
there she shall be taken. Their arrows
are like the arrows of a skilled warrior
who does not return empty-handed.
¹⁰ Chal·dē'a shall be plundered; all
who plunder her shall be sated, says
the LORD.

11 Though you rejoice, though you
        exult,
    O plunderers of my heritage,
  though you frisk about like a
        heifer on the grass,
    and neigh like stallions,
12 your mother shall be utterly
        shamed,
    and she who bore you shall be
        disgraced.
  Lo, she shall be the last of the
        nations,
    a wilderness, dry land, and a
        desert.
13 Because of the wrath of the
        LORD she shall not be
        inhabited,
    but shall be an utter
        desolation;
  everyone who passes by Babylon
        shall be appalled
    and hiss because of all her
        wounds.
14 Take up your positions around
        Babylon,
    all you that bend the bow;
  shoot at her, spare no arrows,
    for she has sinned against the
        LORD.
15 Raise a shout against her from
        all sides,
    "She has surrendered;
  her bulwarks have fallen,
    her walls are thrown down."
  For this is the vengeance of the
        LORD:
    take vengeance on her,

  do to her as she has done.
16 Cut off from Babylon the sower,
    and the wielder of the sickle in
        time of harvest;
  because of the destroying sword
    all of them shall return to their
        own people,
    and all of them shall flee to
        their own land.

17 Israel is a hunted sheep driven
away by lions. First the king of Assyria
devoured it, and now at the end King
Ne·bu·chad·rez'zar of Babylon has
gnawed its bones. ¹⁸ Therefore, thus
says the LORD of hosts, the God of Israel: I am going to punish the king of
Babylon and his land, as I punished the
king of Assyria. ¹⁹ I will restore Israel
to its pasture, and it shall feed on Car'-
mel and in Bā'shan, and on the hills of
Ē'phra·im and in Gil'e·ad its hunger
shall be satisfied. ²⁰ In those days and
at that time, says the LORD, the iniquity of Israel shall be sought, and there
shall be none; and the sins of Judah,
and none shall be found; for I will pardon the remnant that I have spared.

21 Go up to the land of
        Mer·a·thā'im;ᵛ
    go up against her,
  and attack the inhabitants of
        Pē'kodʷ
    and utterly destroy the last of
        them,ˣ
                    says the LORD;
    do all that I have commanded
        you.
22 The noise of battle is in the land,
    and great destruction!
23 How the hammer of the whole
        earth
    is cut down and broken!
  How Babylon has become
    a horror among the nations!
24 You set a snare for yourself and
        you were caught,
        O Babylon,
    but you did not know it;
  you were discovered and seized,
    because you challenged the
        LORD.
25 The LORD has opened his
        armory,
    and brought out the weapons
        of his wrath,

ᵛ Or of Double Rebellion   ʷ Or of
Punishment   ˣ Tg: Heb destroy after
them

for the Lord GOD of hosts has a
task to do
in the land of the Chal·dē′ans.
26 Come against her from every
quarter;
open her granaries;
pile her up like heaps of grain,
and destroy her utterly;
let nothing be left of her.
27 Kill all her bulls,
let them go down to the
slaughter.
Alas for them, their day has
come,
the time of their punishment!

28 Listen! Fugitives and refugees
from the land of Babylon are coming to
declare in Zion the vengeance of the
LORD our God, vengeance for his temple.

29 Summon archers against Babylon, all who bend the bow. Encamp
all around her; let no one escape. Repay her according to her deeds; just as
she has done, do to her—for she has
arrogantly defied the LORD, the Holy
One of Israel. 30Therefore her young
men shall fall in her squares, and all
her soldiers shall be destroyed on that
day, says the LORD.

31 I am against you, O arrogant
one,
says the Lord GOD of hosts;
for your day has come,
the time when I will punish
you.
32 The arrogant one shall stumble
and fall,
with no one to raise him up,
and I will kindle a fire in his
cities,
and it will devour everything
around him.

33 Thus says the LORD of hosts: The
people of Israel are oppressed, and so
too are the people of Judah; all their
captors have held them fast and refuse
to let them go. 34Their Redeemer is
strong; the LORD of hosts is his name.
He will surely plead their cause, that
he may give rest to the earth, but unrest to the inhabitants of Babylon.

35 A sword against the Chal·dē′ans,
says the LORD,
and against the inhabitants of
Babylon,

and against her officials and
her sages!
36 A sword against the diviners,
so that they may become fools!
A sword against her warriors,
so that they may be destroyed!
37 A sword against her[y] horses
and against her[y] chariots,
and against all the foreign
troops in her midst,
so that they may become
women!
A sword against all her
treasures,
that they may be plundered!
38 A drought[z] against her waters,
that they may be dried up!
For it is a land of images,
and they go mad over idols.

39 Therefore wild animals shall live
with hyenas in Babylon,[a] and ostriches shall inhabit her; she shall
never again be peopled, or inhabited
for all generations. 40As when God
overthrew Sod′om and Go·mor′rah
and their neighbors, says the LORD, so
no one shall live there, nor shall anyone settle in her.

41 Look, a people is coming from
the north;
a mighty nation and many
kings
are stirring from the farthest
parts of the earth.
42 They wield bow and spear,
they are cruel and have no
mercy.
The sound of them is like the
roaring sea;
they ride upon horses,
set in array as a warrior for
battle,
against you, O daughter
Babylon!

43 The king of Babylon heard news
of them,
and his hands fell helpless;
anguish seized him,
pain like that of a woman in
labor.

44 Like a lion coming up from the
thickets of the Jordan against a peren-
nial pasture, I will suddenly chase
them away from her; and I will appoint

[y] Cn: Heb *his*   [z] Another reading is *A
sword*   [a] Heb lacks *in Babylon*

over her whomever I choose.[b] For
who is like me? Who can summon me?
Who is the shepherd who can stand
before me? [45] Therefore hear the plan
that the LORD has made against Babylon, and the purposes that he has
formed against the land of the
Chal·dē′ans: Surely the little ones of
the flock shall be dragged away;
surely their[c] fold shall be appalled at
their fate. [46] At the sound of the capture
of Babylon the earth shall tremble, and
her cry shall be heard among the nations.

51 Thus says the LORD:
I am going to stir up a
destructive wind[d]
against Babylon
and against the inhabitants of
Leb-qā′maī;[e]
[2] and I will send winnowers to
Babylon,
and they shall winnow her.
They shall empty her land
when they come against her
from every side
on the day of trouble.
[3] Let not the archer bend his bow,
and let him not array himself
in his coat of mail.
Do not spare her young men;
utterly destroy her entire
army.
[4] They shall fall down slain in the
land of the Chal·dē′ans,
and wounded in her streets.
[5] Israel and Judah have not been
forsaken
by their God, the LORD of
hosts,
though their land is full of guilt
before the Holy One of Israel.

[6] Flee from the midst of Babylon,
save your lives, each of you!
Do not perish because of her
guilt,
for this is the time of the
LORD's vengeance;
he is repaying her what is due.
[7] Babylon was a golden cup in the
LORD's hand,
making all the earth drunken;
the nations drank of her wine,
and so the nations went mad.
[8] Suddenly Babylon has fallen and
is shattered;
wail for her!
Bring balm for her wound;
perhaps she may be healed.
[9] We tried to heal Babylon,

but she could not be healed.
Forsake her, and let each of us
go
to our own country;
for her judgment has reached up
to heaven
and has been lifted up even to
the skies.
[10] The LORD has brought forth our
vindication;
come, let us declare in Zion
the work of the LORD our God.

[11] Sharpen the arrows!
Fill the quivers!
The LORD has stirred up the spirit of
the kings of the Mēdes, because his
purpose concerning Babylon is to destroy it, for that is the vengeance of the
LORD, vengeance for his temple.
[12] Raise a standard against the
walls of Babylon;
make the watch strong;
post sentinels;
prepare the ambushes;
for the LORD has both planned
and done
what he spoke concerning the
inhabitants of Babylon.
[13] You who live by mighty waters,
rich in treasures,
your end has come,
the thread of your life is cut.
[14] The LORD of hosts has sworn by
himself:
Surely I will fill you with troops
like a swarm of locusts,
and they shall raise a shout of
victory over you.

[15] It is he who made the earth by
his power,
who established the world by
his wisdom,
and by his understanding
stretched out the heavens.
[16] When he utters his voice there is
a tumult of waters in the
heavens,
and he makes the mist rise
from the ends of the earth.
He makes lightnings for the rain,
and he brings out the wind
from his storehouses.

[b] Or and I will single out the choicest of
her rams: Meaning of Heb uncertain
[c] Syr Gk Tg Compare 49.20: Heb lacks
their   [d] Or stir up the spirit of a
destroyer   [e] Leb-qamai is a cryptogram
for Kasdim, Chaldea

17 Everyone is stupid and without
knowledge;
goldsmiths are all put to
shame by their idols;
for their images are false,
and there is no breath in them.
18 They are worthless, a work of
delusion;
at the time of their punishment
they shall perish.
19 Not like these is the LORD,*f* the
portion of Jacob,
for he is the one who formed
all things,
and Israel is the tribe of his
inheritance;
the LORD of hosts is his name.

Israel the Creator's Instrument

20 You are my war club, my
weapon of battle:
with you I smash nations;
with you I destroy kingdoms;
21 with you I smash the horse and
its rider;
with you I smash the chariot
and the charioteer;
22 with you I smash man and
woman;
with you I smash the old man
and the boy;
with you I smash the young man
and the girl;
23 with you I smash shepherds
and their flocks;
with you I smash farmers and
their teams;
with you I smash governors
and deputies.

The Doom of Babylon

24 I will repay Babylon and all the
inhabitants of Chal·dē′a before your
very eyes for all the wrong that they
have done in Zion, says the LORD.

25 I am against you, O destroying
mountain,
says the LORD,
that destroys the whole earth;
I will stretch out my hand
against you,
and roll you down from the
crags,
and make you a burned-out
mountain.
26 No stone shall be taken from
you for a corner
and no stone for a foundation,
but you shall be a perpetual
waste,

says the LORD.

27 Raise a standard in the land,
blow the trumpet among the
nations;
prepare the nations for war
against her,
summon against her the
kingdoms,
Ar′a·rat, Min′nī, and
Ash′ke·naz;
appoint a marshal against her,
bring up horses like bristling
locusts.
28 Prepare the nations for war
against her,
the kings of the Mēdes, with
their governors and
deputies,
and every land under their
dominion.
29 The land trembles and writhes,
for the LORD's purposes
against Babylon stand,
to make the land of Babylon a
desolation,
without inhabitant.
30 The warriors of Babylon have
given up fighting,
they remain in their
strongholds;
their strength has failed,
they have become women;
her buildings are set on fire,
her bars are broken.
31 One runner runs to meet
another,
and one messenger to meet
another,
to tell the king of Babylon
that his city is taken from end
to end:
32 the fords have been seized,
the marshes have been burned
with fire,
and the soldiers are in panic.
33 For thus says the LORD of hosts,
the God of Israel:
Daughter Babylon is like a
threshing floor
at the time when it is trodden;
yet a little while
and the time of her harvest
will come.

34 "King Ne·bū·chad·rez′zar of
Babylon has devoured me,
he has crushed me;
he has made me an empty
vessel,

f Heb lacks *the* LORD

he has swallowed me like a
monster;
he has filled his belly with my
delicacies,
he has spewed me out.
35 May my torn flesh be avenged
on Babylon,"
the inhabitants of Zion shall
say.
"May my blood be avenged on
the inhabitants of
Chal·dē′a,"
Jerusalem shall say.
36 Therefore thus says the LORD:
I am going to defend your cause
and take vengeance for you.
I will dry up her sea
and make her fountain dry;
37 and Babylon shall become a
heap of ruins,
a den of jackals,
an object of horror and of
hissing,
without inhabitant.

38 Like lions they shall roar
together;
they shall growl like lions'
whelps.
39 When they are inflamed, I will
set out their drink
and make them drunk, until
they become merry
and then sleep a perpetual sleep
and never wake, says the
LORD.
40 I will bring them down like
lambs to the slaughter,
like rams and goats.

41 How Shē′shach g is taken,
the pride of the whole earth
seized!
How Babylon has become
an object of horror among the
nations!
42 The sea has risen over Babylon;
she has been covered by its
tumultuous waves.
43 Her cities have become an object
of horror,
a land of drought and a desert,
a land in which no one lives,
and through which no mortal
passes.
44 I will punish Bel in Babylon,
and make him disgorge what
he has swallowed.
The nations shall no longer
stream to him;
the wall of Babylon has fallen.

45 Come out of her, my people!
Save your lives, each of you,
from the fierce anger of the
LORD!
46 Do not be fainthearted or fearful
at the rumors heard in the
land—
one year one rumor comes,
the next year another,
rumors of violence in the land
and of ruler against ruler.

47 Assuredly, the days are coming
when I will punish the images
of Babylon;
her whole land shall be put to
shame,
and all her slain shall fall in
her midst.
48 Then the heavens and the earth,
and all that is in them,
shall shout for joy over Babylon;
for the destroyers shall come
against them out of the
north,
says the LORD.
49 Babylon must fall for the slain of
Israel,
as the slain of all the earth
have fallen because of
Babylon.

50 You survivors of the sword,
go, do not linger!
Remember the LORD in a distant
land,
and let Jerusalem come into
your mind:
51 We are put to shame, for we
have heard insults;
dishonor has covered our face,
for aliens have come
into the holy places of the
LORD's house.

52 Therefore the time is surely
coming, says the LORD,
when I will punish her idols,
and through all her land
the wounded shall groan.
53 Though Babylon should mount
up to heaven,
and though she should fortify
her strong height,
from me destroyers would come
upon her,
says the LORD.

54 Listen!—a cry from Babylon!

g *Sheshach* is a cryptogram for *Babel,*
Babylon

A great crashing from the land
    of the Chal·dē′ans!
55 For the LORD is laying Babylon
    waste,
    and stilling her loud clamor.
Their waves roar like mighty
    waters,
    the sound of their clamor
    resounds;
56 for a destroyer has come against
    her,
    against Babylon;
her warriors are taken,
    their bows are broken;
for the LORD is a God of
    recompense,
he will repay in full.
57 I will make her officials and her
    sages drunk,
    also her governors, her
    deputies, and her warriors;
they shall sleep a perpetual sleep
    and never wake,
    says the King, whose name is
    the LORD of hosts.

58 Thus says the LORD of hosts:
The broad wall of Babylon
    shall be leveled to the ground,
and her high gates
    shall be burned with fire.
The peoples exhaust themselves
    for nothing,
and the nations weary
    themselves only for fire.[h]

Jeremiah's Command to Seraiah

59 The word that the prophet
Jer·e·mī′ah commanded Se·rāi′ah son
of Ne·rī′ah son of Mah′sēi·ah, when he
went with King Zed·e·kī′ah of Judah to
Babylon, in the fourth year of his
reign. Se·rāi′ah was the quartermas-
ter. 60 Jer·e·mī′ah wrote in a[i] scroll all
the disasters that would come on
Babylon, all these words that are
written concerning Babylon. 61 And
Jer·e·mī′ah said to Se·rāi′ah: "When
you come to Babylon, see that you read
all these words, 62 and say, 'O LORD,
you yourself threatened to destroy this
place so that neither human beings nor
animals shall live in it, and it shall be
desolate forever.' 63 When you finish
reading this scroll, tie a stone to it, and
throw it into the middle of the Euphrates, 64 and say, 'Thus shall Babylon
sink, to rise no more, because of the
disasters that I am bringing on her.'"[j]
    Thus far are the words of Jer-
e·mī′ah.

The Destruction of Jerusalem Reviewed
(2 Kings 24.18–25.26; 2 Chr 36.11–20; Jer 39.1–10)

52 Zed·e·kī′ah was twenty-one
years old when he began to
reign; he reigned eleven years in Jerusalem. His mother's name was
Ha·mū′tal daughter of Jer·e·mī′ah of
Lib′nah. 2 He did what was evil in the
sight of the LORD, just as Je·hoi′a·kim
had done. 3 Indeed, Jerusalem and Judah so angered the LORD that he expelled them from his presence.
    Zed·e·kī′ah rebelled against the king
of Babylon. 4 And in the ninth year of
his reign, in the tenth month, on the
tenth day of the month, King
Ne·bū·chad·rez′zar of Babylon came
with all his army against Jerusalem,
and they laid siege to it; they built
siegeworks against it all around. 5 So
the city was besieged until the eleventh year of King Zed·e·kī′ah. 6 On the
ninth day of the fourth month the famine became so severe in the city that
there was no food for the people of the
land. 7 Then a breach was made in the
city wall;[k] and all the soldiers fled and
went out from the city by night by the
way of the gate between the two walls,
by the king's garden, though the
Chal·dē′ans were all around the city.
They went in the direction of the Ar′-
a·bah. 8 But the army of the Chal·dē′-
ans pursued the king, and overtook
Zed·e·kī′ah in the plains of Jericho;
and all his army was scattered, deserting him. 9 Then they captured the king,
and brought him up to the king of Babylon at Rib′lah in the land of Hā′math,
and he passed sentence on him. 10 The
king of Babylon killed the sons of
Zed·e·kī′ah before his eyes, and also
killed all the officers of Judah at
Rib′lah. 11 He put out the eyes of
Zed·e·kī′ah, and bound him in fetters,
and the king of Babylon took him to
Babylon, and put him in prison until
the day of his death.
    12 In the fifth month, on the tenth
day of the month—which was the
nineteenth year of King Ne·bū-
chad·rez′zar, king of Babylon—
Ne·bū·za·rad′an the captain of the
bodyguard who served the king of
Babylon, entered Jerusalem. 13 He

---

[h] Gk Syr Compare Hab 2.13: Heb and
the nations for fire, and they are weary
[i] Or one [j] Gk: Heb on her. And they
shall weary themselves [k] Heb lacks
wall

burned the house of the LORD, the king's house, and all the houses of Jerusalem; every great house he burned down. [14] All the army of the Chal·dē'ans, who were with the captain of the guard, broke down all the walls around Jerusalem. [15] Ne·bū·za·rad'an the captain of the guard carried into exile some of the poorest of the people and the rest of the people who were left in the city and the deserters who had defected to the king of Babylon, together with the rest of the artisans. [16] But Ne·bū·za·rad'an the captain of the guard left some of the poorest people of the land to be vinedressers and tillers of the soil.

17 The pillars of bronze that were in the house of the LORD, and the stands and the bronze sea that were in the house of the LORD, the Chal·dē'ans broke in pieces, and carried all the bronze to Babylon. [18] They took away the pots, the shovels, the snuffers, the basins, the ladles, and all the vessels of bronze used in the temple service. [19] The captain of the guard took away the small bowls also, the firepans, the basins, the pots, the lampstands, the ladles, and the bowls for libation, both those of gold and those of silver. [20] As for the two pillars, the one sea, the twelve bronze bulls that were under the sea, and the stands,[l] which King Solomon had made for the house of the LORD, the bronze of all these vessels was beyond weighing. [21] As for the pillars, the height of the one pillar was eighteen cubits, its circumference was twelve cubits; it was hollow and its thickness was four fingers. [22] Upon it was a capital of bronze; the height of the one capital was five cubits; latticework and pomegranates, all of bronze, encircled the top of the capital. And the second pillar had the same, with pomegranates. [23] There were ninety-six pomegranates on the sides; all the pomegranates encircling the latticework numbered one hundred.

24 The captain of the guard took the chief priest Se·rāi'ah, the second priest

Zeph·a·nī'ah, and the three guardians of the threshold; [25] and from the city he took an officer who had been in command of the soldiers, and seven men of the king's council who were found in the city; the secretary of the commander of the army who mustered the people of the land; and sixty men of the people of the land who were found inside the city. [26] Then Ne·bū·za·rad'an the captain of the guard took them, and brought them to the king of Babylon at Rib'lah. [27] And the king of Babylon struck them down, and put them to death at Rib'lah in the land of Hā'math. So Judah went into exile out of its land.

28 This is the number of the people whom Ne·bū·chad·rez'zar took into exile: in the seventh year, three thousand twenty-three Judeans; [29] in the eighteenth year of Ne·bū·chad·rez'zar he took into exile from Jerusalem eight hundred thirty-two persons; [30] in the twenty-third year of Ne·bū·chad·rez'zar, Ne·bū·za·rad'an the captain of the guard took into exile of the Judeans seven hundred forty-five persons; all the persons were four thousand six hundred.

Jehoiachin Favored in Captivity
(2 Kings 25.27–30)

31 In the thirty-seventh year of the exile of King Je·hoi'a·chin of Judah, in the twelfth month, on the twenty-fifth day of the month, King Ē'vil-me-rō'dach of Babylon, in the year he began to reign, showed favor to King Je·hoi'a·chin of Judah and brought him out of prison; [32] he spoke kindly to him, and gave him a seat above the seats of the other kings who were with him in Babylon. [33] So Je·hoi'a·chin put aside his prison clothes, and every day of his life he dined regularly at the king's table. [34] For his allowance, a regular daily allowance was given him by the king of Babylon, as long as he lived, up to the day of his death.

l Cn: Heb *that were under the stands*

LAMENTATIONS

The Deserted City

1 How lonely sits the city
　　that once was full of people!
How like a widow she has
　　become,
　　she that was great among the
　　　　nations!
She that was a princess among
　　　　the provinces
　　has become a vassal.

2 She weeps bitterly in the night,
　　with tears on her cheeks;
among all her lovers
　　she has no one to comfort her;
all her friends have dealt
　　treacherously with her,
　　they have become her
　　　　enemies.

3 Judah has gone into exile with
　　　　suffering
　　and hard servitude;
she lives now among the
　　　　nations,
　　and finds no resting place;
her pursuers have all overtaken
　　her
　　in the midst of her distress.

4 The roads to Zion mourn,
　　for no one comes to the
　　　　festivals;
all her gates are desolate,
　　her priests groan;
her young girls grieve,[a]
　　and her lot is bitter.

5 Her foes have become the
　　　　masters,
　　her enemies prosper,
because the LORD has made her
　　　　suffer
　　for the multitude of her
　　　　transgressions;
her children have gone away,
　　captives before the foe.

6 From daughter Zion has
　　　　departed
　　all her majesty.
Her princes have become like
　　　　stags
　　that find no pasture;
they fled without strength
　　before the pursuer.

7 Jerusalem remembers,
　　in the days of her affliction
　　　　and wandering,
all the precious things
　　that were hers in days of old.
When her people fell into the
　　　　hand of the foe,
　　and there was no one to help
　　　　her,
the foe looked on mocking
　　over her downfall.

8 Jerusalem sinned grievously,
　　so she has become a mockery;
all who honored her despise her,
　　for they have seen her
　　　　nakedness;
she herself groans,
　　and turns her face away.

9 Her uncleanness was in her
　　　　skirts;
　　she took no thought of her
　　　　future;
her downfall was appalling,
　　with none to comfort her.
"O LORD, look at my affliction,
　　for the enemy has triumphed!"

10 Enemies have stretched out their
　　　　hands
　　over all her precious things;
she has even seen the nations
　　invade her sanctuary,
those whom you forbade
　　to enter your congregation.

11 All her people groan
　　as they search for bread;

[a] Meaning of Heb uncertain

they trade their treasures for
    food
      to revive their strength.
Look, O LORD, and see
    how worthless I have become.

12 Is it nothing to you,*b* all you
    who pass by?
    Look and see
if there is any sorrow like my
    sorrow,
    which was brought upon me,
which the LORD inflicted
    on the day of his fierce anger.

13 From on high he sent fire;
    it went deep into my bones;
he spread a net for my feet;
    he turned me back;
he has left me stunned,
    faint all day long.

14 My transgressions were bound*b*
    into a yoke;
    by his hand they were
      fastened together;
they weigh on my neck,
    sapping my strength;
the Lord handed me over
    to those whom I cannot
      withstand.

15 The LORD has rejected
    all my warriors in the midst of
      me;
he proclaimed a time against me
    to crush my young men;
the Lord has trodden as in a
    wine press
    the virgin daughter Judah.

16 For these things I weep;
    my eyes flow with tears;
for a comforter is far from me,
    one to revive my courage;
my children are desolate,
    for the enemy has prevailed.

17 Zion stretches out her hands,
    but there is no one to comfort
      her;
the LORD has commanded
    against Jacob
    that his neighbors should
      become his foes;
Jerusalem has become
    a filthy thing among them.

18 The LORD is in the right,
    for I have rebelled against his
      word;
but hear, all you peoples,

and behold my suffering;
my young women and young
    men
    have gone into captivity.

19 I called to my lovers
    but they deceived me;
my priests and elders
    perished in the city
while seeking food
    to revive their strength.

20 See, O LORD, how distressed I
    am;
    my stomach churns,
my heart is wrung within me,
    because I have been very
      rebellious.
In the street the sword bereaves;
    in the house it is like death.

21 They heard how I was groaning,
    with no one to comfort me.
All my enemies heard of my
    trouble;
    they are glad that you have
      done it.
Bring on the day you have
    announced,
    and let them be as I am.

22 Let all their evil doing come
    before you;
    and deal with them
as you have dealt with me
    because of all my
      transgressions;
for my groans are many
    and my heart is faint.

God's Warnings Fulfilled

2 How the Lord in his anger
    has humiliated*b* daughter
    Zion!
He has thrown down from
    heaven to earth
    the splendor of Israel;
he has not remembered his
    footstool
    in the day of his anger.

2 The Lord has destroyed without
    mercy
    all the dwellings of Jacob;
in his wrath he has broken down
    the strongholds of daughter
      Judah;
he has brought down to the
    ground in dishonor

b Meaning of Heb uncertain

LAMENTATIONS

the kingdom and its rulers.

3 He has cut down in fierce anger
    all the might of Israel;
  he has withdrawn his right hand
    from them
    in the face of the enemy;
  he has burned like a flaming fire
    in Jacob,
    consuming all around.

4 He has bent his bow like an
    enemy,
    with his right hand set like a
    foe;
  he has killed all in whom we
    took pride
    in the tent of daughter Zion;
  he has poured out his fury like
    fire.

5 The Lord has become like an
    enemy;
    he has destroyed Israel;
  He has destroyed all its palaces,
    laid in ruins its strongholds,
  and multiplied in daughter
    Judah
    mourning and lamentation.

6 He has broken down his booth
    like a garden,
  he has destroyed his
    tabernacle;
  the LORD has abolished in Zion
    festival and sabbath,
  and in his fierce indignation has
    spurned
    king and priest.

7 The Lord has scorned his altar,
    disowned his sanctuary;
  he has delivered into the hand of
    the enemy
    the walls of her palaces;
  a clamor was raised in the house
    of the LORD
    as on a day of festival.

8 The LORD determined to lay in
    ruins
    the wall of daughter Zion;
  he stretched the line;
  he did not withhold his hand
    from destroying;
  he caused rampart and wall to
    lament;
    they languish together.

9 Her gates have sunk into the
    ground;

he has ruined and broken her
    bars;
  her king and princes are among
    the nations;
  guidance is no more,
  and her prophets obtain
    no vision from the LORD.

10 The elders of daughter Zion
    sit on the ground in silence;
  they have thrown dust on their
    heads
    and put on sackcloth;
  the young girls of Jerusalem
    have bowed their heads to the
    ground.

11 My eyes are spent with weeping;
    my stomach churns;
  my bile is poured out on the
    ground
    because of the destruction of
    my people,
  because infants and babes faint
    in the streets of the city.

12 They cry to their mothers,
    "Where is bread and wine?"
  as they faint like the wounded
    in the streets of the city,
  as their life is poured out
    on their mothers' bosom.

13 What can I say for you, to what
    compare you,
    O daughter Jerusalem?
  To what can I liken you, that I
    may comfort you,
    O virgin daughter Zion?
  For vast as the sea is your ruin;
    who can heal you?

14 Your prophets have seen for you
    false and deceptive visions;
  they have not exposed your
    iniquity
    to restore your fortunes,
  but have seen oracles for you
    that are false and misleading.

15 All who pass along the way
    clap their hands at you;
  they hiss and wag their heads
    at daughter Jerusalem;
  "Is this the city that was called
    the perfection of beauty,
    the joy of all the earth?"

16 All your enemies
    open their mouths against you;
  they hiss, they gnash their teeth,

they cry: "We have devoured
  her!
Ah, this is the day we longed
  for;
  at last we have seen it!"

17 The LORD has done what he
    purposed,
  he has carried out his threat;
as he ordained long ago,
  he has demolished without
    pity;
he has made the enemy rejoice
    over you,
  and exalted the might of your
    foes.

18 Cry aloud[c] to the Lord!
  O wall of daughter Zion!
Let tears stream down like a
    torrent
  day and night!
Give yourself no rest,
  your eyes no respite!

19 Arise, cry out in the night,
  at the beginning of the
    watches!
Pour out your heart like water
  before the presence of the
    Lord!
Lift your hands to him
  for the lives of your children,
who faint for hunger
  at the head of every street.

20 Look, O LORD, and consider!
  To whom have you done this?
Should women eat their
    offspring,
  the children they have borne?
Should priest and prophet be
    killed
  in the sanctuary of the Lord?

21 The young and the old are lying
  on the ground in the streets;
my young women and my young
    men
  have fallen by the sword;
in the day of your anger you
    have killed them,
  slaughtering without mercy.

22 You invited my enemies from all
    around
  as if for a day of festival;
and on the day of the anger of
    the LORD
  no one escaped or survived;
those whom I bore and reared
  my enemy has destroyed.

God's Steadfast Love Endures

3 I am one who has seen affliction
  under the rod of God's[d]
    wrath;
2 he has driven and brought me
  into darkness without any
    light;
3 against me alone he turns his
    hand,
  again and again, all day long.

4 He has made my flesh and my
    skin waste away,
  and broken my bones;
5 he has besieged and enveloped
    me
  with bitterness and tribulation;
6 he has made me sit in darkness
  like the dead of long ago.

7 He has walled me about so that I
    cannot escape;
  he has put heavy chains on
    me;
8 though I call and cry for help,
  he shuts out my prayer;
9 he has blocked my ways with
    hewn stones,
  he has made my paths
    crooked.

10 He is a bear lying in wait for
    me,
  a lion in hiding;
11 he led me off my way and tore
    me to pieces;
  he has made me desolate;
12 he bent his bow and set me
  as a mark for his arrow.

13 He shot into my vitals
  the arrows of his quiver;
14 I have become the laughingstock
    of all my people,
  the object of their taunt-songs
    all day long.
15 He has filled me with bitterness,
  he has sated me with
    wormwood.

16 He has made my teeth grind on
    gravel,
  and made me cower in ashes;
17 my soul is bereft of peace;
  I have forgotten what
    happiness is;
18 so I say, "Gone is my glory,
  and all that I had hoped for
    from the LORD."

c Cn: Heb *Their heart cried*   d Heb *his*

19 The thought of my affliction and
    my homelessness
    is wormwood and gall!
20 My soul continually thinks of it
    and is bowed down within me.
21 But this I call to mind,
    and therefore I have hope:

22 The steadfast love of the LORD
    never ceases,*e*
    his mercies never come to an
    end;
23 they are new every morning;
    great is your faithfulness.
24 "The LORD is my portion," says
    my soul,
    "therefore I will hope in him."

25 The LORD is good to those who
    wait for him,
    to the soul that seeks him.
26 It is good that one should wait
    quietly
    for the salvation of the LORD.
27 It is good for one to bear
    the yoke in youth,
28 to sit alone in silence
    when the Lord has imposed it,
29 to put one's mouth to the dust
    (there may yet be hope),
30 to give one's cheek to the smiter,
    and be filled with insults.

31 For the Lord will not
    reject forever.
32 Although he causes grief, he will
    have compassion
    according to the abundance of
    his steadfast love;
33 for he does not willingly afflict
    or grieve anyone.

34 When all the prisoners of the
    land
    are crushed under foot,
35 when human rights are
    perverted
    in the presence of the Most
    High,
36 when one's case is subverted
    —does the Lord not see it?

37 Who can command and have it
    done,
    if the Lord has not ordained
    it?
38 Is it not from the mouth of the
    Most High
    that good and bad come?
39 Why should any who draw
    breath complain

about the punishment of their
    sins?

40 Let us test and examine our
    ways,
    and return to the LORD.
41 Let us lift up our hearts as well
    as our hands
    to God in heaven.
42 We have transgressed and
    rebelled,
    and you have not forgiven.

43 You have wrapped yourself with
    anger and pursued us,
    killing without pity;
44 you have wrapped yourself with
    a cloud
    so that no prayer can pass
    through.
45 You have made us filth and
    rubbish
    among the peoples.

46 All our enemies
    have opened their mouths
    against us;
47 panic and pitfall have come
    upon us,
    devastation and destruction.
48 My eyes flow with rivers of tears
    because of the destruction of
    my people.

49 My eyes will flow without
    ceasing,
    without respite,
50 until the LORD from heaven
    looks down and sees.
51 My eyes cause me grief
    at the fate of all the young
    women in my city.

52 Those who were my enemies
    without cause
    have hunted me like a bird;
53 they flung me alive into a pit
    and hurled stones on me;
54 water closed over my head;
    I said, "I am lost."

55 I called on your name, O LORD,
    from the depths of the pit;
56 you heard my plea, "Do not
    close your ear
    to my cry for help, but give me
    relief!"
57 You came near when I called on
    you;
    you said, "Do not fear!"

e Syr Tg: Heb LORD, *we are not cut off*

58 You have taken up my cause,
O Lord,
  you have redeemed my life.
59 You have seen the wrong done
to me, O LORD;
  judge my cause.
60 You have seen all their malice,
  all their plots against me.

61 You have heard their taunts,
O LORD,
  all their plots against me.
62 The whispers and murmurs of
my assailants
  are against me all day long.
63 Whether they sit or rise—see,
  I am the object of their
taunt-songs.

64 Pay them back for their deeds,
O LORD,
  according to the work of their
hands!
65 Give them anguish of heart;
  your curse be on them!
66 Pursue them in anger and
destroy them
  from under the LORD's
heavens.

The Punishment of Zion

4 How the gold has grown dim,
  how the pure gold is changed!
The sacred stones lie scattered
  at the head of every street.

2 The precious children of Zion,
  worth their weight in fine
gold—
how they are reckoned as
earthen pots,
  the work of a potter's hands!

3 Even the jackals offer the breast
  and nurse their young,
but my people has become cruel,
  like the ostriches in the
wilderness.

4 The tongue of the infant sticks
  to the roof of its mouth for
thirst;
the children beg for food,
  but no one gives them
anything.

5 Those who feasted on delicacies
  perish in the streets;
those who were brought up in
purple
  cling to ash heaps.

6 For the chastisement[f] of my
people has been greater
  than the punishment[g] of
Sod'om,
which was overthrown in a
moment,
  though no hand was laid on
it.[h]

7 Her princes were purer than
snow,
  whiter than milk;
their bodies were more ruddy
than coral,
  their hair[h] like sapphire.[i]

8 Now their visage is blacker than
soot;
  they are not recognized in the
streets.
Their skin has shriveled on their
bones;
  it has become as dry as wood.

9 Happier were those pierced by
the sword
  than those pierced by hunger,
whose life drains away, deprived
  of the produce of the field.

10 The hands of compassionate
women
  have boiled their own
children;
they became their food
  in the destruction of my
people.

11 The LORD gave full vent to his
wrath;
  he poured out his hot anger,
and kindled a fire in Zion
  that consumed its foundations.

12 The kings of the earth did not
believe,
  nor did any of the inhabitants
of the world,
that foe or enemy could enter
  the gates of Jerusalem.

13 It was for the sins of her
prophets
  and the iniquities of her
priests,
who shed the blood of the
righteous
  in the midst of her.

f Or *iniquity*   g Or *sin*   h Meaning of
Heb uncertain   i Or *lapis lazuli*

14 Blindly they wandered through
the streets,
so defiled with blood
that no one was able
to touch their garments.

15 "Away! Unclean!" people
shouted at them;
"Away! Away! Do not touch!"
So they became fugitives and
wanderers;
it was said among the nations,
"They shall stay here no
longer."

16 The LORD himself has scattered
them,
he will regard them no more;
no honor was shown to the
priests,
no favor to the elders.

17 Our eyes failed, ever watching
vainly for help;
we were watching eagerly
for a nation that could not
save.

18 They dogged our steps
so that we could not walk in
our streets;
our end drew near; our days
were numbered;
for our end had come.

19 Our pursuers were swifter
than the eagles in the heavens;
they chased us on the
mountains,
they lay in wait for us in the
wilderness.

20 The LORD's anointed, the breath
of our life,
was taken in their pits —
the one of whom we said,
"Under his shadow
we shall live among the
nations."

21 Rejoice and be glad, O daughter
Ē′dom,
you that live in the land of Uz;
but to you also the cup shall
pass;
you shall become drunk and
strip yourself bare.

22 The punishment of your iniquity,
O daughter Zion, is
accomplished,

he will keep you in exile no
longer;
but your iniquity, O daughter
Ē′dom, he will punish,
he will uncover your sins.

A Plea for Mercy

5 Remember, O LORD, what has
befallen us;
look, and see our disgrace!
2 Our inheritance has been turned
over to strangers,
our homes to aliens.
3 We have become orphans,
fatherless;
our mothers are like widows.
4 We must pay for the water we
drink;
the wood we get must be
bought.
5 With a yoke[j] on our necks we
are hard driven;
we are weary, we are given no
rest.
6 We have made a pact with[k]
Egypt and Assyria,
to get enough bread.
7 Our ancestors sinned; they are
no more,
and we bear their iniquities.
8 Slaves rule over us;
there is no one to deliver us
from their hand.
9 We get our bread at the peril of
our lives,
because of the sword in the
wilderness.
10 Our skin is black as an oven
from the scorching heat of
famine.
11 Women are raped in Zion,
virgins in the towns of Judah.
12 Princes are hung up by their
hands;
no respect is shown to the
elders.
13 Young men are compelled to
grind,
and boys stagger under loads
of wood.
14 The old men have left the city
gate,
the young men their music.
15 The joy of our hearts has
ceased;
our dancing has been turned
to mourning.

_____
j Symmachus: Heb lacks *With a yoke*
k Heb *have given the hand to*

16 The crown has fallen from our
    head;
    woe to us, for we have sinned!
17 Because of this our hearts are
    sick,
    because of these things our
    eyes have grown dim:
18 because of Mount Zion, which
    lies desolate;
    jackals prowl over it.

19 But you, O LORD, reign forever;

your throne endures to all
    generations.
20 Why have you forgotten us
    completely?
    Why have you forsaken us
    these many days?
21 Restore us to yourself, O LORD,
    that we may be restored;
    renew our days as of old—
22 unless you have utterly rejected
    us,
    and are angry with us beyond
    measure.

BARUCH

Baruch and the Jews in Babylon
(Cp 2 Kings 24.8–17; Ezra 1.7–11; Jer 36.4)

1 These are the words of the book
that Bar'uch son of Ne·rī'ah son of
Mah·sēi·ah son of Zed·e·kī'ah son of
Has·a·dī'ah son of Hil·kī'ah wrote in
Babylon, 2 in the fifth year, on the seventh day of the month, at the time when
the Chal·dē'ans took Jerusalem and
burned it with fire.
3 Bar'uch read the words of this
book to Jec·o·nī'ah son of Je·hoi'a·kim,
king of Judah, and to all the people
who came to hear the book, 4 and to the
nobles and the princes, and to the elders, and to all the people, small and
great, all who lived in Babylon by the
river Sud.
5 Then they wept, and fasted, and
prayed before the Lord; 6 they collected
as much money as each could give,
7 and sent it to Jerusalem to the high
priest[a] Je·hoi'a·kim son of Hil·kī'ah
son of Shal'lum, and to the priests, and
to all the people who were present with
him in Jerusalem. 8 At the same time,
on the tenth day of Sī'van, Bar'uch[b]
took the vessels of the house of the
Lord, which had been carried away
from the temple, to return them to the
land of Judah—the silver vessels that
Zed·e·kī'ah son of Jō·sī'ah, king of Judah, had made, 9 after King Ne·bū-
chad·nez'zar of Babylon had carried
away from Jerusalem Jec·o·nī'ah and
the princes and the prisoners and the

nobles and the people of the land, and
brought them to Babylon.

A Letter to Jerusalem

10 They said: Here we send you
money; so buy with the money burnt
offerings and sin offerings and incense, and prepare a grain offering,
and offer them on the altar of the Lord
our God; 11 and pray for the life of King
Ne·bū·chad·nez'zar of Babylon, and
for the life of his son Bel·shaz'zar, so
that their days on earth may be like the
days of heaven. 12 The Lord will give us
strength, and light to our eyes; we shall
live under the protection[c] of King Ne-
bū·chad·nez'zar of Babylon, and under
the protection of his son Bel·shaz'zar,
and we shall serve them many days
and find favor in their sight. 13 Pray
also for us to the Lord our God, for we
have sinned against the Lord our God,
and to this day the anger of the Lord
and his wrath have not turned away
from us. 14 And you shall read aloud
this scroll that we are sending you, to
make your confession in the house of
the Lord on the days of the festivals
and at appointed seasons.

Confession of Sins
(Cp Deut 28.15–68; Jer 11.3–5)

15 And you shall say: The Lord our
God is in the right, but there is open
shame on us today, on the people of

a Gk *the priest*   b Gk *he*   c Gk *in the
shadow*

Judah, on the inhabitants of Jerusalem, 16 and on our kings, our rulers, our priests, our prophets, and our ancestors, 17 because we have sinned before the Lord. 18 We have disobeyed him, and have not heeded the voice of the Lord our God, to walk in the statutes of the Lord that he set before us. 19 From the time when the Lord brought our ancestors out of the land of Egypt until today, we have been disobedient to the Lord our God, and we have been negligent, in not heeding his voice. 20 So to this day there have clung to us the calamities and the curse that the Lord declared through his servant Moses at the time when he brought our ancestors out of the land of Egypt to give to us a land flowing with milk and honey. 21 We did not listen to the voice of the Lord our God in all the words of the prophets whom he sent to us, 22 but all of us followed the intent of our own wicked hearts by serving other gods and doing what is evil in the sight of the Lord our God.

2 So the Lord carried out the threat he spoke against us: against our judges who ruled Israel, and against our kings and our rulers and the people of Israel and Judah. 2 Under the whole heaven there has not been done the like of what he has done in Jerusalem, in accordance with the threats that were[d] written in the law of Moses. 3 Some of us ate the flesh of their sons and others the flesh of their daughters. 4 He made them subject to all the kingdoms around us, to be an object of scorn and a desolation among all the surrounding peoples, where the Lord has scattered them. 5 They were brought down and not raised up, because our nation[e] sinned against the Lord our God, in not heeding his voice.

6 The Lord our God is in the right, but there is open shame on us and our ancestors this very day. 7 All those calamities with which the Lord threatened us have come upon us. 8 Yet we have not entreated the favor of the Lord by turning away, each of us, from the thoughts of our wicked hearts. 9 And the Lord has kept the calamities ready, and the Lord has brought them upon us, for the Lord is just in all the works that he has commanded us to do. 10 Yet we have not obeyed his voice, to walk in the statutes of the Lord that he set before us.

Prayer for Deliverance
(Cp Dan 9.15–17)

11 And now, O Lord God of Israel, who brought your people out of the land of Egypt with a mighty hand and with signs and wonders and with great power and outstretched arm, and made yourself a name that continues to this day, 12 we have sinned, we have been ungodly, we have done wrong, O Lord our God, against all your ordinances. 13 Let your anger turn away from us, for we are left, few in number, among the nations where you have scattered us. 14 Hear, O Lord, our prayer and our supplication, and for your own sake deliver us, and grant us favor in the sight of those who have carried us into exile; 15 so that all the earth may know that you are the Lord our God, for Israel and his descendants are called by your name.

16 O Lord, look down from your holy dwelling, and consider us. Incline your ear, O Lord, and hear; 17 open your eyes, O Lord, and see, for the dead who are in Hades, whose spirit has been taken from their bodies, will not ascribe glory or justice to the Lord; 18 but the person who is deeply grieved, who walks bowed and feeble, with failing eyes and famished soul, will declare your glory and righteousness, O Lord.

19 For it is not because of any righteous deeds of our ancestors or our kings that we bring before you our prayer for mercy, O Lord our God. 20 For you have sent your anger and your wrath upon us, as you declared by your servants the prophets, saying: 21 Thus says the Lord: Bend your shoulders and serve the king of Babylon, and you will remain in the land that I gave to your ancestors. 22 But if you will not obey the voice of the Lord and will not serve the king of Babylon, 23 I will make to cease from the towns of Judah and from the region around Jerusalem the voice of mirth and the voice of gladness, the voice of the bridegroom and the voice of the bride, and the whole land will be a desolation without inhabitants.

24 But we did not obey your voice, to serve the king of Babylon; and you have carried out your threats, which you spoke by your servants the prophets, that the bones of our kings and the

---

[d] Gk *in accordance with what is*
[e] Gk *because we*

bones of our ancestors would be brought out of their resting place; 25 and indeed they have been thrown out to the heat of day and the frost of night. They perished in great misery, by famine and sword and pestilence. 26 And the house that is called by your name you have made as it is today, because of the wickedness of the house of Israel and the house of Judah.

God's Promise Recalled
(Deut 28.58–62; Cp Jer 32.38–40)

27 Yet you have dealt with us, O Lord our God, in all your kindness and in all your great compassion, 28 as you spoke by your servant Moses on the day when you commanded him to write your law in the presence of the people of Israel, saying, 29 "If you will not obey my voice, this very great multitude will surely turn into a small number among the nations, where I will scatter them. 30 For I know that they will not obey me, for they are a stiff-necked people. But in the land of their exile they will come to themselves 31 and know that I am the Lord their God. I will give them a heart that obeys and ears that hear; 32 they will praise me in the land of their exile, and will remember my name 33 and turn from their stubbornness and their wicked deeds; for they will remember the ways of their ancestors, who sinned before the Lord. 34 I will bring them again into the land that I swore to give to their ancestors, to Abraham, Isaac, and Jacob, and they will rule over it; and I will increase them, and they will not be diminished. 35 I will make an everlasting covenant with them to be their God and they shall be my people; and I will never again remove my people Israel from the land that I have given them."

3 O Lord Almighty, God of Israel, the soul in anguish and the wearied spirit cry out to you. 2 Hear, O Lord, and have mercy, for we have sinned before you. 3 For you are enthroned forever, and we are perishing forever. 4 O Lord Almighty, God of Israel, hear now the prayer of the people[f] of Israel, the children of those who sinned before you, who did not heed the voice of the Lord their God, so that calamities have clung to us. 5 Do not remember the iniquities of our ancestors, but in this crisis remember your power and your name. 6 For you are the Lord our God, and it is you, O Lord, whom we will praise. 7 For you

have put the fear of you in our hearts so that we would call upon your name; and we will praise you in our exile, for we have put away from our hearts all the iniquity of our ancestors who sinned against you. 8 See, we are today in our exile where you have scattered us, to be reproached and cursed and punished for all the iniquities of our ancestors, who forsook the Lord our God.

In Praise of Wisdom
(Cp Job 28.23–28; Prov 8.22–31; Sir 24.1–22)

9 Hear the commandments of life, O Israel;
give ear, and learn wisdom!

10 Why is it, O Israel, why is it that you are in the land of your enemies,
that you are growing old in a foreign country,
that you are defiled with the dead,

11 that you are counted among those in Hades?

12 You have forsaken the fountain of wisdom.

13 If you had walked in the way of God,
you would be living in peace forever.

14 Learn where there is wisdom,
where there is strength,
where there is understanding,
so that you may at the same time discern
where there is length of days, and life,
where there is light for the eyes, and peace.

15 Who has found her place?
And who has entered her storehouses?

16 Where are the rulers of the nations,
and those who lorded it over the animals on earth;

17 those who made sport of the birds of the air,
and who hoarded up silver and gold
in which people trust,
and there is no end to their getting;

18 those who schemed to get silver, and were anxious,
but there is no trace of their works?

---

[f] Gk *dead*

19 They have vanished and gone
down to Hades,
    and others have arisen in their
place.
20 Later generations have seen the
light of day,
    and have lived upon the earth;
but they have not learned the way
to knowledge,
    nor understood her paths,
    nor laid hold of her.
21 Their descendants have strayed
far from her^g way.
22 She has not been heard of in
Cā′naan,
    or seen in Tē′man;
23 the descendants of Hā′gar, who
seek for understanding on
the earth,
    the merchants of Mer′ran and
Tē′man,
    the story-tellers and the seekers
for understanding,
have not learned the way to
wisdom,
    or given thought to her paths.
24 O Israel, how great is the house
of God,
    how vast the territory that he
possesses!
25 It is great and has no bounds;
    it is high and immeasurable.
26 The giants were born there, who
were famous of old,
    great in stature, expert in war.
27 God did not choose them,
    or give them the way to
knowledge;
28 so they perished because they
had no wisdom,
    they perished through their
folly.
29 Who has gone up into heaven,
and taken her,
    and brought her down from the
clouds?
30 Who has gone over the sea, and
found her,
    and will buy her for pure gold?
31 No one knows the way to her,
    or is concerned about the path
to her.
32 But the one who knows all things
knows her,
    he found her by his
understanding.
The one who prepared the earth
for all time
    filled it with four-footed
creatures;

33 the one who sends forth the light,
and it goes;
    he called it, and it obeyed him,
trembling;
34 the stars shone in their watches,
and were glad;
    he called them, and they said,
"Here we are!"
    They shone with gladness for
him who made them.
35 This is our God;
    no other can be compared to
him.
36 He found the whole way to
knowledge,
    and gave her to his servant
Jacob
    and to Israel, whom he loved.
37 Afterward she appeared on earth
and lived with humankind.

4 She is the book of the
    commandments of God,
    the law that endures forever.
All who hold her fast will live,
    and those who forsake her will
die.
2 Turn, O Jacob, and take her;
    walk toward the shining of her
light.
3 Do not give your glory to another,
    or your advantages to an alien
people.
4 Happy are we, O Israel,
    for we know what is pleasing to
God.

Encouragement for Israel

5 Take courage, my people,
    who perpetuate Israel's name!
6 It was not for destruction
    that you were sold to the
nations,
but you were handed over to your
enemies
    because you angered God.
7 For you provoked the one who
made you
    by sacrificing to demons and
not to God.
8 You forgot the everlasting God,
    who brought you up,
    and you grieved Jerusalem,
who reared you.
9 For she saw the wrath that came
upon you from God,
    and she said:
Listen, you neighbors of Zion,
    God has brought great sorrow
upon me;

^g Other ancient authorities read *their*

10 for I have seen the exile of my
   sons and daughters,
   which the Everlasting brought
   upon them.
11 With joy I nurtured them,
   but I sent them away with
   weeping and sorrow.
12 Let no one rejoice over me, a
   widow
   and bereaved of many;
   I was left desolate because of the
   sins of my children,
   because they turned away from
   the law of God.
13 They had no regard for his
   statutes;
   they did not walk in the ways
   of God's commandments,
   or tread the paths his
   righteousness showed them.
14 Let the neighbors of Zion come;
   remember the capture of my
   sons and daughters,
   which the Everlasting brought
   upon them.
15 For he brought a distant nation
   against them,
   a nation ruthless and of a
   strange language,
   which had no respect for the aged
   and no pity for a child.
16 They led away the widow's
   beloved sons,
   and bereaved the lonely woman
   of her daughters.
17 But I, how can I help you?
18 For he who brought these
   calamities upon you
   will deliver you from the hand
   of your enemies.
19 Go, my children, go;
   for I have been left desolate.
20 I have taken off the robe of peace
   and put on sackcloth for my
   supplication;
   I will cry to the Everlasting all
   my days.
21 Take courage, my children, cry to
   God,
   and he will deliver you from the
   power and hand of the
   enemy.
22 For I have put my hope in the
   Everlasting to save you,
   and joy has come to me from
   the Holy One,
   because of the mercy that will
   soon come to you
   from your everlasting savior.[h]
23 For I sent you out with sorrow
   and weeping,

but God will give you back to
   me with joy and gladness
   forever.
24 For as the neighbors of Zion have
   now seen your capture,
   so they soon will see your
   salvation by God,
   which will come to you with great
   glory
   and with the splendor of the
   Everlasting.
25 My children, endure with patience
   the wrath that has come
   upon you from God.
   Your enemy has overtaken you,
   but you will soon see their
   destruction
   and will tread upon their necks.
26 My pampered children have
   traveled rough roads;
   they were taken away like a
   flock carried off by the
   enemy.
27 Take courage, my children, and
   cry to God,
   for you will be remembered by
   the one who brought this
   upon you.
28 For just as you were disposed to
   go astray from God,
   return with tenfold zeal to seek
   him.
29 For the one who brought these
   calamities upon you
   will bring you everlasting joy
   with your salvation.

Jerusalem Is Assured of Help
(Cp Isa 52.1–10)

30 Take courage, O Jerusalem,
   for the one who named you will
   comfort you.
31 Wretched will be those who
   mistreated you
   and who rejoiced at your fall.
32 Wretched will be the cities that
   your children served as
   slaves;
   wretched will be the city that
   received your offspring.
33 For just as she rejoiced at your
   fall
   and was glad for your ruin,
   so she will be grieved at her
   own desolation.
34 I will take away her pride in her
   great population,
   and her insolence will be turned
   to grief.

h Or from the Everlasting, your savior

35 For fire will come upon her from
the Everlasting for many
days,
and for a long time she will be
inhabited by demons.
36 Look toward the east,
O Jerusalem,
and see the joy that is coming
to you from God.
37 Look, your children are coming,
whom you sent away;
they are coming, gathered from
east and west,
at the word of the Holy One,
rejoicing in the glory of God.

5 Take off the garment of your
sorrow and affliction,
O Jerusalem,
and put on forever the beauty
of the glory from God.
2 Put on the robe of the
righteousness that comes
from God;
put on your head the diadem of
the glory of the Everlasting;
3 for God will show your splendor
everywhere under heaven.
4 For God will give you evermore
the name,
"Righteous Peace, Godly Glory."

5 Arise, O Jerusalem, stand upon
the height;
look toward the east,
and see your children gathered
from west and east
at the word of the Holy One,
rejoicing that God has
remembered them.
6 For they went out from you on
foot,
led away by their enemies;
but God will bring them back to
you,
carried in glory, as on a royal
throne.
7 For God has ordered that every
high mountain and the
everlasting hills be made
low
and the valleys filled up, to
make level ground,
so that Israel may walk safely
in the glory of God.
8 The woods and every fragrant
tree
have shaded Israel at God's
command.
9 For God will lead Israel with joy,
in the light of his glory,

with the mercy and
righteousness that come
from him.

The Letter of Jeremiah

6 [i] A copy of a letter that Jer·e·mī'ah
sent to those who were to be taken
to Babylon as exiles by the king of the
Babylonians, to give them the message
that God had commanded him.

The People Face a Long Captivity
(Cp Jer 29.1–23)

2 Because of the sins that you have
committed before God, you will be
taken to Babylon as exiles by Ne·bū-
chad·nez'zar, king of the Babylonians.
3 Therefore when you have come to
Babylon you will remain there for
many years, for a long time, up to seven
generations; after that I will bring you
away from there in peace. 4 Now in
Babylon you will see gods made of silver and gold and wood, which people
carry on their shoulders, and which
cause the heathen to fear. 5 So beware
of becoming at all like the foreigners or
of letting fear for these gods[j] possess
you 6 when you see the multitude before and behind them worshiping
them. But say in your heart, "It is you,
O Lord, whom we must worship." 7 For
my angel is with you, and he is watching over your lives.

The Helplessness of Idols

8 Their tongues are smoothed by the
carpenter, and they themselves are
overlaid with gold and silver; but they
are false and cannot speak. 9 People[k]
take gold and make crowns for the
heads of their gods, as they might for a
girl who loves ornaments. 10 Sometimes the priests secretly take gold and
silver from their gods and spend it on
themselves, 11 or even give some of it to
the prostitutes on the terrace. They
deck their gods[l] out with garments
like human beings—these gods of silver and gold and wood 12 that cannot
save themselves from rust and corrosion. When they have been dressed in
purple robes, 13 their faces are wiped
because of the dust from the temple,

[i] The King James Version (like the Latin
Vulgate) prints The Letter of Jeremiah as
Chapter 6 of the Book of Baruch, and the
chapter and verse numbers are here
retained. In the Greek Septuagint, the Letter
is separated from Baruch by the Book of
Lamentations. [j] Gk for them [k] Gk They
[l] Gk them

which is thick upon them. [14]One of them holds a scepter, like a district judge, but is unable to destroy anyone who offends it. [15]Another has a dagger in its right hand, and an ax, but cannot defend itself from war and robbers. [16]From this it is evident that they are not gods; so do not fear them.

[17] For just as someone's dish is useless when it is broken, [18]so are their gods when they have been set up in the temples. Their eyes are full of the dust raised by the feet of those who enter. And just as the gates are shut on every side against anyone who has offended a king, as though under sentence of death, so the priests make their temples secure with doors and locks and bars, in order that they may not be plundered by robbers. [19]They light more lamps for them than they light for themselves, though their gods[m] can see none of them. [20]They are[n] just like a beam of the temple, but their hearts, it is said, are eaten away when crawling creatures from the earth devour them and their robes. They do not notice [21]when their faces have been blackened by the smoke of the temple. [22]Bats, swallows, and birds alight on their bodies and heads; and so do cats. [23]From this you will know that they are not gods; so do not fear them.

[24] As for the gold that they wear for beauty — it[o] will not shine unless someone wipes off the tarnish; for even when they were being cast, they did not feel it. [25]They are bought without regard to cost, but there is no breath in them. [26]Having no feet, they are carried on the shoulders of others, revealing to humankind their worthlessness. And those who serve them are put to shame [27]because, if any of these gods falls[p] to the ground, they themselves must pick it up. If anyone sets it upright, it cannot move itself; and if it is tipped over, it cannot straighten itself. Gifts are placed before them just as before the dead. [28]The priests sell the sacrifices that are offered to these gods[q] and use the money themselves. Likewise their wives preserve some of the meat[r] with salt, but give none to the poor or helpless. [29]Sacrifices to them may even be touched by women in their periods or at childbirth. Since you know by these things that they are not gods, do not fear them.

[30] For how can they be called gods? Women serve meals for gods of silver and gold and wood; [31]and in their tem-

ples the priests sit with their clothes torn, their heads and beards shaved, and their heads uncovered. [32]They howl and shout before their gods as some do at a funeral banquet. [33]The priests take some of the clothing of their gods[s] to clothe their wives and children. [34]Whether one does evil to them or good, they will not be able to repay it. They cannot set up a king or depose one. [35]Likewise they are not able to give either wealth or money; if one makes a vow to them and does not keep it, they will not require it. [36]They cannot save anyone from death or rescue the weak from the strong. [37]They cannot restore sight to the blind; they cannot rescue one who is in distress. [38]They cannot take pity on a widow or do good to an orphan. [39]These things that are made of wood and overlaid with gold and silver are like stones from the mountain, and those who serve them will be put to shame. [40]Why then must anyone think that they are gods, or call them gods?

The Foolishness of Worshiping Idols
(Cp Isa 46.1–13)

Besides, even the Chal·dē'ans themselves dishonor them; for when they see someone who cannot speak, they bring Bel and pray that the mute may speak, as though Bel[t] were able to understand! [41]Yet they themselves cannot perceive this and abandon them, for they have no sense. [42]And the women, with cords around them, sit along the passageways, burning bran for incense. [43]When one of them is led off by one of the passers-by and is taken to bed by him, she derides the woman next to her, because she was not as attractive as herself and her cord was not broken. [44]Whatever is done for these idols[u] is false. Why then must anyone think that they are gods, or call them gods?

[45] They are made by carpenters and goldsmiths; they can be nothing but what the artisans wish them to be. [46]Those who make them will certainly not live very long themselves; [47]how then can the things that are made by them be gods? They have left only lies and reproach for those who come after. [48]For when war or calamity comes

---

[m]Gk *they*   [n]Gk *It is*   [o]Lat Syr: Gk *they*
[p]Gk *if they fall*   [q]Gk *to them*   [r]Gk *of them*   [s]Gk *some of their clothing*
[t]Gk *he*   [u]Gk *them*

upon them, the priests consult together as to where they can hide themselves and their gods.ᵛ ⁴⁹How then can one fail to see that these are not gods, for they cannot save themselves from war or calamity? ⁵⁰Since they are made of wood and overlaid with gold and silver, it will afterward be known that they are false. ⁵¹It will be manifest to all the nations and kings that they are not gods but the work of human hands, and that there is no work of God in them. ⁵²Who then can fail to know that they are not gods?ʷ

53 For they cannot set up a king over a country or give rain to people. ⁵⁴They cannot judge their own cause or deliver one who is wronged, for they have no power; ⁵⁵they are like crows between heaven and earth. When fire breaks out in a temple of wooden gods overlaid with gold or silver, their priests will flee and escape, but the godsˣ will be burned up like timbers. ⁵⁶Besides, they can offer no resistance to king or enemy. Why then must anyone admit or think that they are gods?

57 Gods made of wood and overlaid with silver and gold are unable to save themselves from thieves or robbers. ⁵⁸Anyone who can will strip them of their gold and silver and of the robes they wear, and go off with this booty, and they will not be able to help themselves. ⁵⁹So it is better to be a king who shows his courage, or a household utensil that serves its owner's need, than to be these false gods; better even the door of a house that protects its contents, than these false gods; better also a wooden pillar in a palace, than these false gods.

60 For sun and moon and stars are bright, and when sent to do a service,

they are obedient. ⁶¹So also the lightning, when it flashes, is widely seen; and the wind likewise blows in every land. ⁶²When God commands the clouds to go over the whole world, they carry out his command. ⁶³And the fire sent from above to consume mountains and woods does what it is ordered. But these idolsʸ are not to be compared with them in appearance or power. ⁶⁴Therefore one must not think that they are gods, nor call them gods, for they are not able either to decide a case or to do good to anyone. ⁶⁵Since you know then that they are not gods, do not fear them.

66 They can neither curse nor bless kings; ⁶⁷they cannot show signs in the heavens for the nations, or shine like the sun or give light like the moon. ⁶⁸The wild animals are better than they are, for they can flee to shelter and help themselves. ⁶⁹So we have no evidence whatever that they are gods; therefore do not fear them.

70 Like a scarecrow in a cucumber bed, which guards nothing, so are their gods of wood, overlaid with gold and silver. ⁷¹In the same way, their gods of wood, overlaid with gold and silver, are like a thornbush in a garden on which every bird perches; or like a corpse thrown out in the darkness. ⁷²From the purple and linenᶻ that rot upon them you will know that they are not gods; and they will finally be consumed themselves, and be a reproach in the land. ⁷³Better, therefore, is someone upright who has no idols; such a person will be far above reproach.

ᵛGk them ʷMeaning of Gk uncertain ˣGk they ʸGk these things ᶻCn: Gk marble, Syr silk

EZEKIEL

The Vision of the Chariot

1 In the thirtieth year, in the fourth month, on the fifth day of the month, as I was among the exiles by the river Chē'bar, the heavens were opened, and I saw visions of God. ²On the fifth day of the month (it was the

fifth year of the exile of King Je·hoi'-a·chin), ³the word of the LORD came to the priest E·zēk'i·el son of Bū'zī, in the land of the Chal·dē'ans by the river Chē'bar; and the hand of the LORD was on him there.

4 As I looked, a stormy wind came out of the north: a great cloud with

brightness around it and fire flashing forth continually, and in the middle of the fire, something like gleaming amber. 5 In the middle of it was something like four living creatures. This was their appearance: they were of human form. 6 Each had four faces, and each of them had four wings. 7 Their legs were straight, and the soles of their feet were like the sole of a calf's foot; and they sparkled like burnished bronze. 8 Under their wings on their four sides they had human hands. And the four had their faces and their wings thus: 9 their wings touched one another; each of them moved straight ahead, without turning as they moved. 10 As for the appearance of their faces: the four had the face of a human being, the face of a lion on the right side, the face of an ox on the left side, and the face of an eagle; 11 such were their faces. Their wings were spread out above; each creature had two wings, each of which touched the wing of another, while two covered their bodies. 12 Each moved straight ahead; wherever the spirit would go, they went, without turning as they went. 13 In the middle of*a* the living creatures there was something that looked like burning coals of fire, like torches moving to and fro among the living creatures; the fire was bright, and lightning issued from the fire. 14 The living creatures darted to and fro, like a flash of lightning.

15 As I looked at the living creatures, I saw a wheel on the earth beside the living creatures, one for each of the four of them.*b* 16 As for the appearance of the wheels and their construction: their appearance was like the gleaming of beryl; and the four had the same form, their construction being something like a wheel within a wheel. 17 When they moved, they moved in any of the four directions without veering as they moved. 18 Their rims were tall and awesome, for the rims of all four were full of eyes all around. 19 When the living creatures moved, the wheels moved beside them; and when the living creatures rose from the earth, the wheels rose. 20 Wherever the spirit would go, they went, and the wheels rose along with them; for the spirit of the living creatures was in the wheels. 21 When they moved, the others moved; when they stopped, the others stopped; and when they rose from the earth, the wheels rose along

with them; for the spirit of the living creatures was in the wheels.

22 Over the heads of the living creatures there was something like a dome, shining like crystal,*c* spread out above their heads. 23 Under the dome their wings were stretched out straight, one toward another; and each of the creatures had two wings covering its body. 24 When they moved, I heard the sound of their wings like the sound of mighty waters, like the thunder of the Almighty,*d* a sound of tumult like the sound of an army; when they stopped, they let down their wings. 25 And there came a voice from above the dome over their heads; when they stopped, they let down their wings.

26 And above the dome over their heads there was something like a throne, in appearance like sapphire;*e* and seated above the likeness of a throne was something that seemed like a human form. 27 Upward from what appeared like the loins I saw something like gleaming amber, something that looked like fire enclosed all around; and downward from what looked like the loins I saw something that looked like fire, and there was a splendor all around. 28 Like the bow in a cloud on a rainy day, such was the appearance of the splendor all around. This was the appearance of the likeness of the glory of the LORD.

When I saw it, I fell on my face, and I heard the voice of someone speaking.

The Vision of the Scroll

2 He said to me: O mortal,*f* stand up on your feet, and I will speak with you. 2 And when he spoke to me, a spirit entered into me and set me on my feet; and I heard him speaking to me. 3 He said to me, Mortal, I am sending you to the people of Israel, to a nation*g* of rebels who have rebelled against me; they and their ancestors have transgressed against me to this very day. 4 The descendants are impudent and stubborn I am sending you to them, and you shall say to them, "Thus says the Lord GOD." 5 Whether they

a Gk OL: Heb *And the appearance of*
b Heb *of their faces*   *c* Gk: Heb *like the awesome crystal*   *d* Traditional rendering of Heb *Shaddai*   *e* Or *lapis lazuli*   *f* Or *son of man*; Heb *ben adam* (and so throughout the book when Ezekiel is addressed)   *g* Syr: Heb *to nations*

hear or refuse to hear (for they are a rebellious house), they shall know that there has been a prophet among them. [6]And you, O mortal, do not be afraid of them, and do not be afraid of their words, though briers and thorns surround you and you live among scorpions; do not be afraid of their words, and do not be dismayed at their looks, for they are a rebellious house. [7]You shall speak my words to them, whether they hear or refuse to hear; for they are a rebellious house.

8 But you, mortal, hear what I say to you; do not be rebellious like that rebellious house; open your mouth and eat what I give you. [9]I looked, and a hand was stretched out to me, and a written scroll was in it. [10]He spread it before me; it had writing on the front and on the back, and written on it were words of lamentation and mourning and woe.

3 He said to me, O mortal, eat what is offered to you; eat this scroll, and go, speak to the house of Israel. [2]So I opened my mouth, and he gave me the scroll to eat. [3]He said to me, Mortal, eat this scroll that I give you and fill your stomach with it. Then I ate it; and in my mouth it was as sweet as honey.

4 He said to me: Mortal, go to the house of Israel and speak my very words to them. [5]For you are not sent to a people of obscure speech and difficult language, but to the house of Israel— [6]not to many peoples of obscure speech and difficult language, whose words you cannot understand. Surely, if I sent you to them, they would listen to you. [7]But the house of Israel will not listen to you, for they are not willing to listen to me; because all the house of Israel have a hard forehead and a stubborn heart. [8]See, I have made your face hard against their faces, and your forehead hard against their foreheads. [9]Like the hardest stone, harder than flint, I have made your forehead; do not fear them or be dismayed at their looks, for they are a rebellious house. [10]He said to me: Mortal, all my words that I shall speak to you receive in your heart and hear with your ears; [11]then go to the exiles, to your people, and speak to them. Say to them, "Thus says the Lord GOD"; whether they hear or refuse to hear.

Ezekiel at the River Chebar

12 Then the spirit lifted me up, and as the glory of the LORD rose[h] from its place, I heard behind me the sound of loud rumbling; [13]it was the sound of the wings of the living creatures brushing against one another, and the sound of the wheels beside them, that sounded like a loud rumbling. [14]The spirit lifted me up and bore me away; I went in bitterness in the heat of my spirit, the hand of the LORD being strong upon me. [15]I came to the exiles at Tel-a·bib', who lived by the river Chē'bar.[i] And I sat there among them, stunned, for seven days.

16 At the end of seven days, the word of the LORD came to me: [17]Mortal, I have made you a sentinel for the house of Israel; whenever you hear a word from my mouth, you shall give them warning from me. [18]If I say to the wicked, "You shall surely die," and you give them no warning, or speak to warn the wicked from their wicked way, in order to save their life, those wicked persons shall die for their iniquity; but their blood I will require at your hand. [19]But if you warn the wicked, and they do not turn from their wickedness, or from their wicked way, they shall die for their iniquity, but you will have saved your life. [20]Again, if the righteous turn from their righteousness and commit iniquity, and I lay a stumbling block before them, they shall die; because you have not warned them, they shall die for their sin, and their righteous deeds that they have done shall not be remembered; but their blood I will require at your hand. [21]If, however, you warn the righteous not to sin, and they do not sin, they shall surely live, because they took warning; and you will have saved your life.

Ezekiel Isolated and Silenced

22 Then the hand of the LORD was upon me there; and he said to me, Rise up, go out into the valley, and there I will speak with you. [23]So I rose up and went out into the valley; and the glory of the LORD stood there, like the glory that I had seen by the river Chē'bar; and I fell on my face. [24]The spirit entered into me, and set me on my feet;

[h]Cn: Heb *and blessed be the glory of the* LORD   [i]Two Mss Syr: Heb *Chebar, and to where they lived. Another reading is Chebar, and I sat where they sat*

and he spoke with me and said to me: Go, shut yourself inside your house. 25 As for you, mortal, cords shall be placed on you, and you shall be bound with them, so that you cannot go out among the people; 26 and I will make your tongue cling to the roof of your mouth, so that you shall be speechless and unable to reprove them; for they are a rebellious house. 27 But when I speak with you, I will open your mouth, and you shall say to them, "Thus says the Lord GOD"; let those who will hear, hear; and let those who refuse to hear, refuse; for they are a rebellious house.

The Siege of Jerusalem Portrayed

4 And you, O mortal, take a brick and set it before you. On it portray a city, Jerusalem; 2 and put siegeworks against it, and build a siege wall against it, and cast up a ramp against it; set camps also against it, and plant battering rams against it all around. 3 Then take an iron plate and place it as an iron wall between you and the city; set your face toward it, and let it be in a state of siege, and press the siege against it. This is a sign for the house of Israel.

4 Then lie on your left side, and place the punishment of the house of Israel upon it; you shall bear their punishment for the number of the days that you lie there. 5 For I assign to you a number of days, three hundred ninety days, equal to the number of the years of their punishment; and so you shall bear the punishment of the house of Israel. 6 When you have completed these, you shall lie down a second time, but on your right side, and bear the punishment of the house of Judah; forty days I assign you, one day for each year. 7 You shall set your face toward the siege of Jerusalem, and with your arm bared you shall prophesy against it. 8 See, I am putting cords on you so that you cannot turn from one side to the other until you have completed the days of your siege.

9 And you, take wheat and barley, beans and lentils, millet and spelt; put them into one vessel, and make bread for yourself. During the number of days that you lie on your side, three hundred ninety days, you shall eat it. 10 The food that you eat shall be twenty shekels a day by weight; at fixed times you shall eat it. 11 And you shall drink water by measure, one-sixth of a hin;

at fixed times you shall drink. 12 You shall eat it as a barley-cake, baking it in their sight on human dung. 13 The LORD said, "Thus shall the people of Israel eat their bread, unclean, among the nations to which I will drive them." 14 Then I said, "Ah Lord GOD! I have never defiled myself; from my youth up until now I have never eaten what died of itself or was torn by animals, nor has carrion flesh come into my mouth." 15 Then he said to me, "See, I will let you have cow's dung instead of human dung, on which you may prepare your bread."

16 Then he said to me, Mortal, I am going to break the staff of bread in Jerusalem; they shall eat bread by weight and with fearfulness; and they shall drink water by measure and in dismay. 17 Lacking bread and water, they will look at one another in dismay, and waste away under their punishment.

A Sword against Jerusalem

5 And you, O mortal, take a sharp sword; use it as a barber's razor and run it over your head and your beard; then take balances for weighing, and divide the hair. 2 One third of the hair you shall burn in the fire inside the city, when the days of the siege are completed; one third you shall take and strike with the sword all around the city;_j_ and one third you shall scatter to the wind, and I will unsheathe the sword after them. 3 Then you shall take from these a small number, and bind them in the skirts of your robe. 4 From these, again, you shall take some, throw them into the fire and burn them up; from there a fire will come out against all the house of Israel.

5 Thus says the Lord GOD: This is Jerusalem; I have set her in the center of the nations, with countries all around her. 6 But she has rebelled against my ordinances and my statutes, becoming more wicked than the nations and the countries all around her, rejecting my ordinances and not following my statutes. 7 Therefore thus says the Lord GOD: Because you are more turbulent than the nations that are all around you, and have not followed my statutes or kept my ordinances, but have acted according to the ordinances of the nations that are

_j_ Heb _it_

all around you; [8]therefore thus says the Lord GOD: I, I myself, am coming against you; I will execute judgments among you in the sight of the nations. [9]And because of all your abominations, I will do to you what I have never yet done, and the like of which I will never do again. [10]Surely, parents shall eat their children in your midst, and children shall eat their parents; I will execute judgments on you, and any of you who survive I will scatter to every wind. [11]Therefore, as I live, says the Lord GOD, surely, because you have defiled my sanctuary with all your detestable things and with all your abominations—therefore I will cut you down;[k] my eye will not spare, and I will have no pity. [12]One third of you shall die of pestilence or be consumed by famine among you; one third shall fall by the sword around you; and one third I will scatter to every wind and will unsheathe the sword after them.

13 My anger shall spend itself, and I will vent my fury on them and satisfy myself; and they shall know that I, the LORD, have spoken in my jealousy, when I spend my fury on them. [14]Moreover I will make you a desolation and an object of mocking among the nations around you, in the sight of all that pass by. [15]You shall be[l] a mockery and a taunt, a warning and a horror, to the nations around you, when I execute judgments on you in anger and fury, and with furious punishments—I, the LORD, have spoken— [16]when I loose against you[m] my deadly arrows of famine, arrows for destruction, which I will let loose to destroy you, and when I bring more and more famine upon you, and break your staff of bread. [17]I will send famine and wild animals against you, and they will rob you of your children; pestilence and bloodshed shall pass through you; and I will bring the sword upon you. I, the LORD, have spoken.

Judgment on Idolatrous Israel

6 The word of the LORD came to me: [2]O mortal, set your face toward the mountains of Israel, and prophesy against them, [3]and say, You mountains of Israel, hear the word of the Lord GOD! Thus says the Lord GOD to the mountains and the hills, to the ravines and the valleys: I, I myself will bring a sword upon you, and I will destroy your high places. [4]Your altars shall become desolate, and your in-

cense stands shall be broken; and I will throw down your slain in front of your idols. [5]I will lay the corpses of the people of Israel in front of their idols; and I will scatter your bones around your altars. [6]Wherever you live, your towns shall be waste and your high places ruined, so that your altars will be waste and ruined,[n] your idols broken and destroyed, your incense stands cut down, and your works wiped out. [7]The slain shall fall in your midst; then you shall know that I am the LORD.

8 But I will spare some. Some of you shall escape the sword among the nations and be scattered through the countries. [9]Those of you who escape shall remember me among the nations where they are carried captive, how I was crushed by their wanton heart that turned away from me, and their wanton eyes that turned after their idols. Then they will be loathsome in their own sight for the evils that they have committed, for all their abominations. [10]And they shall know that I am the LORD; I did not threaten in vain to bring this disaster upon them.

11 Thus says the Lord GOD: Clap your hands and stamp your foot, and say, Alas for all the vile abominations of the house of Israel! For they shall fall by the sword, by famine, and by pestilence. [12]Those far off shall die of pestilence; those nearby shall fall by the sword; and any who are left and are spared shall die of famine. Thus I will spend my fury upon them. [13]And you shall know that I am the LORD, when their slain lie among their idols around their altars, on every high hill, on all the mountain tops, under every green tree, and under every leafy oak, wherever they offered pleasing odor to all their idols. [14]I will stretch out my hand against them, and make the land desolate and waste, throughout all their settlements, from the wilderness to Rib′lah.[o] Then they shall know that I am the LORD.

Impending Disaster

7 The word of the LORD came to me: [2]You, O mortal, thus says the Lord GOD to the land of Israel:
An end! The end has come

---

[k] Another reading is *I will withdraw*
[l] Gk Syr Vg Tg: Heb *It shall be*
[m] Heb *them*   [n] Syr Vg Tg: Heb *and be made guilty*   [o] Another reading is *Diblah*

upon the four corners of the
　　land.

3　Now the end is upon you,
　　I will let loose my anger upon
　　　　you;
　I will judge you according to
　　　　your ways,
　　I will punish you for all your
　　　　abominations.
4　My eye will not spare you, I will
　　　　have no pity.
　I will punish you for your
　　　　ways,
　　while your abominations are
　　　　among you.
Then you shall know that I am the
LORD.
5　Thus says the Lord GOD:
　Disaster after disaster! See, it
　　　　comes.
6　　An end has come, the end has
　　　　come.
　It has awakened against you;
　　　　see, it comes!
7　Your doom[p] has come to you,
　　　　O inhabitant of the land.
　The time has come, the day is
　　　　near—
　　of tumult, not of reveling on
　　　　the mountains.
8　Soon now I will pour out my
　　　　wrath upon you;
　　I will spend my anger against
　　　　you.
　I will judge you according to
　　　　your ways,
　　and punish you for all your
　　　　abominations.
9　My eye will not spare; I will
　　　　have no pity.
　I will punish you according to
　　　　your ways,
　　while your abominations are
　　　　among you.
Then you shall know that it is I the
LORD who strike.
10　See, the day! See, it comes!
　　　　Your doom[p] has gone out.
　The rod has blossomed, pride
　　　　has budded.
11　　Violence has grown into a rod
　　　　of wickedness.
　None of them shall remain,
　　　not their abundance, not their
　　　　wealth;
　　no pre-eminence among
　　　　them.[p]
12　The time has come, the day
　　　　draws near;
　　let not the buyer rejoice, nor
　　　　the seller mourn,

for wrath is upon all their
　　multitude.

13 For the sellers shall not return to
what has been sold as long as they remain alive. For the vision concerns all
their multitude; it shall not be revoked.
Because of their iniquity, they cannot
maintain their lives.[p]
14　They have blown the horn and
　　　　made everything ready;
　　but no one goes to battle,
　　for my wrath is upon all their
　　　　multitude.
15　The sword is outside, pestilence
　　　　and famine are inside;
　　those in the field die by the
　　　　sword;
　　those in the city—famine and
　　　　pestilence devour them.
16　If any survivors escape,
　　　they shall be found on the
　　　　mountains
　　like doves of the valleys,
　　all of them moaning over their
　　　　iniquity.
17　All hands shall grow feeble,
　　　　all knees turn to water.
18　They shall put on sackcloth,
　　　　horror shall cover them.
　Shame shall be on all faces,
　　　　baldness on all their heads.
19　They shall fling their silver into
　　　　the streets,
　　their gold shall be treated as
　　　　unclean.
Their silver and gold cannot save them
on the day of the wrath of the LORD.
They shall not satisfy their hunger or
fill their stomachs with it. For it was
the stumbling block of their iniquity.
20 From their[q] beautiful ornament, in
which they took pride, they made their
abominable images, their detestable
things; therefore I will make of it an
unclean thing to them.
21　I will hand it over to strangers
　　　　as booty,
　　to the wicked of the earth as
　　　　plunder;
　　they shall profane it.
22　I will avert my face from them,
　　　so that they may profane my
　　　　treasured[r] place;
　　the violent shall enter it,
　　　　they shall profane it.
23　Make a chain![p]
　For the land is full of bloody
　　　　crimes;
　　the city is full of violence.

E
Z
E
K
I
E
L

24 I will bring the worst of the
        nations
    to take possession of their
        houses.
    I will put an end to the
        arrogance of the strong,
    and their holy places shall be
        profaned.
25 When anguish comes, they will
        seek peace,
    but there shall be none.
26 Disaster comes upon disaster,
        rumor follows rumor;
    they shall keep seeking a vision
        from the prophet;
    instruction shall perish from
        the priest,
    and counsel from the elders.
27 The king shall mourn,
        the prince shall be wrapped in
            despair,
    and the hands of the people of
        the land shall tremble.
    According to their way I will
        deal with them;
    according to their own
        judgments I will judge
            them.
And they shall know that I am the
LORD.

Abominations in the Temple

8 In the sixth year, in the sixth
    month, on the fifth day of the
month, as I sat in my house, with the
elders of Judah sitting before me,
the hand of the Lord GOD fell upon me
there. 2 I looked, and there was a figure
that looked like a human being;[s] below what appeared to be its loins it was
fire, and above the loins it was like the
appearance of brightness, like gleaming amber. 3 It stretched out the form of
a hand, and took me by a lock of my
head; and the spirit lifted me up between earth and heaven, and brought
me in visions of God to Jerusalem, to
the entrance of the gateway of the inner court that faces north, to the seat of
the image of jealousy, which provokes
to jealousy. 4 And the glory of the God
of Israel was there, like the vision that
I had seen in the valley.

5 Then God[t] said to me, "O mortal,
lift up your eyes now in the direction of
the north." So I lifted up my eyes toward the north, and there, north of the
altar gate, in the entrance, was this image of jealousy. 6 He said to me, "Mortal, do you see what they are doing, the
great abominations that the house of
Israel are committing here, to drive me

far from my sanctuary? Yet you will
see still greater abominations."
7 And he brought me to the entrance of the court; I looked, and there
was a hole in the wall. 8 Then he said to
me, "Mortal, dig through the wall"; and
when I dug through the wall, there was
an entrance. 9 He said to me, "Go in
and see the vile abominations that they
are committing here." 10 So I went in
and looked; there, portrayed on the
wall all around, were all kinds of
creeping things, and loathsome animals, and all the idols of the house of
Israel. 11 Before them stood seventy of
the elders of the house of Israel, with
Jā·az·a·nī'ah son of Shā'phan standing among them. Each had his censer
in his hand, and the fragrant cloud of
incense was ascending. 12 Then he said
to me, "Mortal, have you seen what the
elders of the house of Israel are doing
in the dark, each in his room of images? For they say, 'The LORD does not
see us, the LORD has forsaken the
land.' " 13 He said also to me, "You will
see still greater abominations that they
are committing."
14 Then he brought me to the entrance of the north gate of the house of
the LORD; women were sitting there
weeping for Tam'mūz. 15 Then he said
to me, "Have you seen this, O mortal?
You will see still greater abominations
than these."
16 And he brought me into the inner
court of the house of the LORD; there
at the entrance of the temple of the
LORD, between the porch and the altar
were about twenty-five men, with their
backs to the temple of the LORD, and
their faces toward the east, prostrating
themselves to the sun toward the east.
17 Then he said to me, "Have you seen
this, O mortal? Is it not bad enough
that the house of Judah commits the
abominations done here? Must they
fill the land with violence, and provoke
my anger still further? See, they are
putting the branch to their nose!
18 Therefore I will act in wrath; my eye
will not spare, nor will I have pity; and
though they cry in my hearing with a
loud voice, I will not listen to them."

The Slaughter of the Idolaters

9 Then he cried in my hearing with
    a loud voice, saying, "Draw near,
you executioners of the city, each with
his destroying weapon in his hand."

s Gk: Heb *like fire*   t Heb *he*

² And six men came from the direction of the upper gate, which faces north, each with his weapon for slaughter in his hand; among them was a man clothed in linen, with a writing case at his side. They went in and stood beside the bronze altar.

3 Now the glory of the God of Israel had gone up from the cherub on which it rested to the threshold of the house. The LORD called to the man clothed in linen, who had the writing case at his side; ⁴ and said to him, "Go through the city, through Jerusalem, and put a mark on the foreheads of those who sigh and groan over all the abominations that are committed in it." ⁵ To the others he said in my hearing, "Pass through the city after him, and kill; your eye shall not spare, and you shall show no pity. ⁶ Cut down old men, young men and young women, little children and women, but touch no one who has the mark. And begin at my sanctuary." So they began with the elders who were in front of the house. ⁷ Then he said to them, "Defile the house, and fill the courts with the slain. Go!" So they went out and killed in the city. ⁸ While they were killing, and I was left alone, I fell prostrate on my face and cried out, "Ah Lord GOD! will you destroy all who remain of Israel as you pour out your wrath upon Jerusalem?" ⁹ He said to me, "The guilt of the house of Israel and Judah is exceedingly great; the land is full of bloodshed and the city full of perversity; for they say, 'The LORD has forsaken the land, and the LORD does not see.' ¹⁰ As for me, my eye will not spare, nor will I have pity, but I will bring down their deeds upon their heads."

11 Then the man clothed in linen, with the writing case at his side, brought back word, saying, "I have done as you commanded me."

God's Glory Leaves Jerusalem

10 Then I looked, and above the dome that was over the heads of the cherubim there appeared above them something like a sapphire,ᵘ in form resembling a throne. ² He said to the man clothed in linen, "Go within the wheelwork underneath the cherubim; fill your hands with burning coals from among the cherubim, and scatter them over the city." He went in as I looked on. ³ Now the cherubim were standing on the south side of the house when the man went in; and a cloud filled the inner court. ⁴ Then the glory of the LORD rose up from the cherub to the threshold of the house; the house was filled with the cloud, and the court was full of the brightness of the glory of the LORD. ⁵ The sound of the wings of the cherubim was heard as far as the outer court, like the voice of God Almightyᵛ when he speaks.

6 When he commanded the man clothed in linen, "Take fire from within the wheelwork, from among the cherubim," he went in and stood beside a wheel. ⁷ And a cherub stretched out his hand from among the cherubim to the fire that was among the cherubim, took some of it and put it into the hands of the man clothed in linen, who took it and went out. ⁸ The cherubim appeared to have the form of a human hand under their wings.

9 I looked, and there were four wheels beside the cherubim, one beside each cherub; and the appearance of the wheels was like gleaming beryl. ¹⁰ And as for their appearance, the four looked alike, something like a wheel within a wheel. ¹¹ When they moved, they moved in any of the four directions without veering as they moved; but in whatever direction the front wheel faced, the others followed without veering as they moved. ¹² Their entire body, their rims, their spokes, their wings, and the wheels — the wheels of the four of them — were full of eyes all around. ¹³ As for the wheels, they were called in my hearing "the wheelwork." ¹⁴ Each one had four faces: the first face was that of the cherub, the second face was that of a human being, the third that of a lion, and the fourth that of an eagle.

15 The cherubim rose up. These were the living creatures that I saw by the river Chē'bar. ¹⁶ When the cherubim moved, the wheels moved beside them; and when the cherubim lifted up their wings to rise up from the earth, the wheels at their side did not veer. ¹⁷ When they stopped, the others stopped, and when they rose up, the others rose up with them; for the spirit of the living creatures was in them.

18 Then the glory of the LORD went out from the threshold of the house and stopped above the cherubim. ¹⁹ The cherubim lifted up their wings and rose up from the earth in my sight

E
Z
E
K
I
E
L

ᵘ Or *lapis lazuli*   ᵛ Traditional rendering of Heb *El Shaddai* as they went out with the wheels beside them. They stopped at the entrance of the east gate of the house of the LORD; and the glory of the God of Israel was above them.

20 These were the living creatures that I saw underneath the God of Israel by the river Chē'bar; and I knew that they were cherubim. 21 Each had four faces, each four wings, and underneath their wings something like human hands. 22 As for what their faces were like, they were the same faces whose appearance I had seen by the river Chē'bar. Each one moved straight ahead.

Judgment on Wicked Counselors

11 The spirit lifted me up and brought me to the east gate of the house of the LORD, which faces east. There, at the entrance of the gateway, were twenty-five men; among them I saw Jā·az·a·nī'ah son of Az'zur, and Pel·a·tī'ah son of Be·nā'i·ah, officials of the people. 2 He said to me, "Mortal, these are the men who devise iniquity and who give wicked counsel in this city; 3 they say, 'The time is not near to build houses; this city is the pot, and we are the meat.' 4 Therefore prophesy against them; prophesy, O mortal."

5 Then the spirit of the LORD fell upon me, and he said to me, "Say, Thus says the LORD: This is what you think, O house of Israel; I know the things that come into your mind. 6 You have killed many in this city, and have filled its streets with the slain. 7 Therefore thus says the Lord GOD: The slain whom you have placed within it are the meat, and this city is the pot; but you shall be taken out of it. 8 You have feared the sword; and I will bring the sword upon you, says the Lord GOD. 9 I will take you out of it and give you over to the hands of foreigners, and execute judgments upon you. 10 You shall fall by the sword; I will judge you at the border of Israel. And you shall know that I am the LORD. 11 This city shall not be your pot, and you shall not be the meat inside it; I will judge you at the border of Israel. 12 Then you shall know that I am the LORD, whose statutes you have not followed, and whose ordinances you have not kept, but you have acted according to the ordinances of the nations that are around you."

13 Now, while I was prophesying, Pel·a·tī'ah son of Be·nā'i·ah died. Then I fell down on my face, cried with a loud voice, and said, "Ah Lord GOD! will you make a full end of the remnant of Israel?"

God Will Restore Israel

14 Then the word of the LORD came to me: 15 Mortal, your kinsfolk, your own kin, your fellow exiles, *w* the whole house of Israel, all of them, are those of whom the inhabitants of Jerusalem have said, "They have gone far from the LORD; to us this land is given for a possession." 16 Therefore say: Thus says the Lord GOD: Though I removed them far away among the nations, and though I scattered them among the countries, yet I have been a sanctuary to them for a little while *x* in the countries where they have gone. 17 Therefore say: Thus says the Lord GOD: I will gather you from the peoples, and assemble you out of the countries where you have been scattered, and I will give you the land of Israel. 18 When they come there, they will remove from it all its detestable things and all its abominations. 19 I will give them one *y* heart, and put a new spirit within them; I will remove the heart of stone from their flesh and give them a heart of flesh, 20 so that they may follow my statutes and keep my ordinances and obey them. Then they shall be my people, and I will be their God. 21 But as for those whose heart goes after their detestable things and their abominations, *z* I will bring their deeds upon their own heads, says the Lord GOD.

22 Then the cherubim lifted up their wings, with the wheels beside them; and the glory of the God of Israel was above them. 23 And the glory of the LORD ascended from the middle of the city, and stopped on the mountain east of the city. 24 The spirit lifted me up and brought me in a vision by the spirit of God into Chal·dē'a, to the exiles. Then the vision that I had seen left me. 25 And I told the exiles all the things that the LORD had shown me.

---

w Gk Syr: Heb *people of your kindred*
x Or *to some extent*   *y* Another reading is *a new*   *z* Cn: Heb *And to the heart of their detestable things and their abominations their heart goes*

Judah's Captivity Portrayed

12 The word of the LORD came to me: [2] Mortal, you are living in the midst of a rebellious house, who have eyes to see but do not see, who have ears to hear but do not hear; [3] for they are a rebellious house. Therefore, mortal, prepare for yourself an exile's baggage, and go into exile by day in their sight; you shall go like an exile from your place to another place in their sight. Perhaps they will understand, though they are a rebellious house. [4] You shall bring out your baggage by day in their sight, as baggage for exile; and you shall go out yourself at evening in their sight, as those do who go into exile. [5] Dig through the wall in their sight, and carry the baggage through it. [6] In their sight you shall lift the baggage on your shoulder, and carry it out in the dark; you shall cover your face, so that you may not see the land; for I have made you a sign for the house of Israel.

[7] I did just as I was commanded. I brought out my baggage by day, as baggage for exile, and in the evening I dug through the wall with my own hands; I brought it out in the dark, carrying it on my shoulder in their sight.

[8] In the morning the word of the LORD came to me: [9] Mortal, has not the house of Israel, the rebellious house, said to you, "What are you doing?" [10] Say to them, "Thus says the Lord GOD: This oracle concerns the prince in Jerusalem and all the house of Israel in it." [11] Say, "I am a sign for you: as I have done, so shall it be done to them; they shall go into exile, into captivity." [12] And the prince who is among them shall lift his baggage on his shoulder in the dark, and shall go out; hea shall dig through the wall and carry it through; he shall cover his face, so that he may not see the land with his eyes. [13] I will spread my net over him, and he shall be caught in my snare; and I will bring him to Babylon, the land of the Chal·dē'ans, yet he shall not see it; and he shall die there. [14] I will scatter to every wind all who are around him, his helpers and all his troops; and I will unsheathe the sword behind them. [15] And they shall know that I am the LORD, when I disperse them among the nations and scatter them through the countries. [16] But I will let a few of them escape from the sword, from famine and pestilence, so that they may tell of all their abominations among the nations where they go; then they shall know that I am the LORD.

Judgment Not Postponed

[17] The word of the LORD came to me: [18] Mortal, eat your bread with quaking, and drink your water with trembling and with fearfulness; [19] and say to the people of the land, Thus says the Lord GOD concerning the inhabitants of Jerusalem in the land of Israel: They shall eat their bread with fearfulness, and drink their water in dismay, because their land shall be stripped of all it contains, on account of the violence of all those who live in it. [20] The inhabited cities shall be laid waste, and the land shall become a desolation; and you shall know that I am the LORD.

[21] The word of the LORD came to me: [22] Mortal, what is this proverb of yours about the land of Israel, which says, "The days are prolonged, and every vision comes to nothing"? [23] Tell them therefore, "Thus says the Lord GOD: I will put an end to this proverb, and they shall use it no more as a proverb in Israel." But say to them, The days are near, and the fulfillment of every vision. [24] For there shall no longer be any false vision or flattering divination within the house of Israel. [25] But I the LORD will speak the word that I speak, and it will be fulfilled. It will no longer be delayed; but in your days, O rebellious house, I will speak the word and fulfill it, says the Lord GOD.

[26] The word of the LORD came to me: [27] Mortal, the house of Israel is saying, "The vision that he sees is for many years ahead; he prophesies for distant times." [28] Therefore say to them, Thus says the Lord GOD: None of my words will be delayed any longer, but the word that I speak will be fulfilled, says the Lord GOD.

False Prophets Condemned

13 The word of the LORD came to me: [2] Mortal, prophesy against the prophets of Israel who are prophesying; say to those who prophesy out of their own imagination: "Hear the word of the LORD!" [3] Thus says the Lord GOD, Alas for the senseless prophets who follow their own spirit, and have seen nothing! [4] Your proph-

aGk Syr: Heb *they*

ets have been like jackals among ruins, O Israel. 5 You have not gone up into the breaches, or repaired a wall for the house of Israel, so that it might stand in battle on the day of the LORD. 6 They have envisioned falsehood and lying divination; they say, "Says the LORD," when the LORD has not sent them, and yet they wait for the fulfillment of their word! 7 Have you not seen a false vision or uttered a lying divination, when you have said, "Says the LORD," even though I did not speak?

8 Therefore thus says the Lord GOD: Because you have uttered falsehood and envisioned lies, I am against you, says the Lord GOD. 9 My hand will be against the prophets who see false visions and utter lying divinations; they shall not be in the council of my people, nor be enrolled in the register of the house of Israel, nor shall they enter the land of Israel; and you shall know that I am the Lord GOD. 10 Because, in truth, because they have misled my people, saying, "Peace," when there is no peace; and because, when the people build a wall, these prophets*b* smear whitewash on it. 11 Say to those who smear whitewash on it that it shall fall. There will be a deluge of rain,*c* great hailstones will fall, and a stormy wind will break out. 12 When the wall falls, will it not be said to you, "Where is the whitewash you smeared on it?" 13 Therefore thus says the Lord GOD: In my wrath I will make a stormy wind break out, and in my anger there shall be a deluge of rain, and hailstones in wrath to destroy it. 14 I will break down the wall that you have smeared with whitewash, and bring it to the ground, so that its foundation will be laid bare; when it falls, you shall perish within it; and you shall know that I am the LORD. 15 Thus I will spend my wrath upon the wall, and upon those who have smeared it with whitewash; and I will say to you, The wall is no more, nor those who smeared it— 16 the prophets of Israel who prophesied concerning Jerusalem and saw visions of peace for it, when there was no peace, says the Lord GOD.

17 As for you, mortal, set your face against the daughters of your people, who prophesy out of their own imagination; prophesy against them 18 and say, Thus says the Lord GOD: Woe to the women who sew bands on all wrists, and make veils for the heads of persons of every height, in the hunt for human lives! Will you hunt down lives among my people, and maintain your own lives? 19 You have profaned me among my people for handfuls of barley and for pieces of bread, putting to death persons who should not die and keeping alive persons who should not live, by your lies to my people, who listen to lies.

20 Therefore thus says the Lord GOD: I am against your bands with which you hunt lives;*d* I will tear them from your arms, and let the lives go free, the lives that you hunt down like birds. 21 I will tear off your veils, and save my people from your hands; they shall no longer be prey in your hands; and you shall know that I am the LORD. 22 Because you have disheartened the righteous falsely, although I have not disheartened them, and you have encouraged the wicked not to turn from their wicked way and save their lives; 23 therefore you shall no longer see false visions or practice divination; I will save my people from your hand. Then you will know that I am the LORD.

God's Judgments Justified

14 Certain elders of Israel came to me and sat down before me. 2 And the word of the LORD came to me: 3 Mortal, these men have taken their idols into their hearts, and placed their iniquity as a stumbling block before them; shall I let myself be consulted by them? 4 Therefore speak to them, and say to them, Thus says the Lord GOD: Any of those of the house of Israel who take their idols into their hearts and place their iniquity as a stumbling block before them, and yet come to the prophet—I the LORD will answer those who come with the multitude of their idols, 5 in order that I may take hold of the hearts of the house of Israel, all of whom are estranged from me through their idols.

6 Therefore say to the house of Israel, Thus says the Lord GOD: Repent and turn away from your idols; and turn away your faces from all your abominations. 7 For any of those of the house of Israel, or of the aliens who reside in Israel, who separate themselves from me, taking their idols into

b Heb *they*   *c* Heb *rain and you*
d Gk Syr: Heb *lives for birds*

their hearts and placing their iniquity as a stumbling block before them, and yet come to a prophet to inquire of me by him, I the LORD will answer them myself. [8] I will set my face against them; I will make them a sign and a byword and cut them off from the midst of my people; and you shall know that I am the LORD.

9 If a prophet is deceived and speaks a word, I, the LORD, have deceived that prophet, and I will stretch out my hand against him, and will destroy him from the midst of my people Israel. [10] And they shall bear their punishment—the punishment of the inquirer and the punishment of the prophet shall be the same— [11] so that the house of Israel may no longer go astray from me, nor defile themselves any more with all their transgressions. Then they shall be my people, and I will be their God, says the Lord GOD.

12 The word of the LORD came to me: [13] Mortal, when a land sins against me by acting faithlessly, and I stretch out my hand against it, and break its staff of bread and send famine upon it, and cut off from it human beings and animals, [14] even if Noah, Daniel,[e] and Job, these three, were in it, they would save only their own lives by their righteousness, says the Lord GOD. [15] If I send wild animals through the land to ravage it, so that it is made desolate, and no one may pass through because of the animals; [16] even if these three men were in it, as I live, says the Lord GOD, they would save neither sons nor daughters; they alone would be saved, but the land would be desolate. [17] Or if I bring a sword upon that land and say, 'Let a sword pass through the land,' and I cut off human beings and animals from it; [18] though these three men were in it, as I live, says the Lord GOD, they would save neither sons nor daughters, but they alone would be saved. [19] Or if I send a pestilence into that land, and pour out my wrath upon it with blood, to cut off humans and animals from it; [20] even if Noah, Daniel,[e] and Job were in it, as I live, says the Lord GOD, they would save neither son nor daughter; they would save only their own lives by their righteousness.

21 For thus says the Lord GOD: How much more when I send upon Jerusalem my four deadly acts of judgment, sword, famine, wild animals, and pestilence, to cut off humans and animals

from it! [22] Yet, survivors shall be left in it, sons and daughters who will be brought out; they will come out to you. When you see their ways and their deeds, you will be consoled for the evil that I have brought upon Jerusalem, for all that I have brought upon it. [23] They shall console you, when you see their ways and their deeds; and you shall know that it was not without cause that I did all that I have done in it, says the Lord GOD.

The Useless Vine

15 The word of the LORD came to me:
2 O mortal, how does the wood of
    the vine surpass all other
    wood—
the vine branch that is among
    the trees of the forest?
3 Is wood taken from it to make
    anything?
Does one take a peg from it on
    which to hang any object?
4 It is put in the fire for fuel;
when the fire has consumed
    both ends of it
and the middle of it is charred,
    is it useful for anything?
5 When it was whole it was used
    for nothing;
how much less—when the fire
    has consumed it,
and it is charred—
can it ever be used for
    anything!

6 Therefore thus says the Lord GOD: Like the wood of the vine among the trees of the forest, which I have given to the fire for fuel, so I will give up the inhabitants of Jerusalem. [7] I will set my face against them; although they escape from the fire, the fire shall still consume them; and you shall know that I am the LORD, when I set my face against them. [8] And I will make the land desolate, because they have acted faithlessly, says the Lord GOD.

God's Faithless Bride

16 The word of the LORD came to me: [2] Mortal, make known to Jerusalem her abominations, [3] and say, Thus says the Lord GOD to Jerusalem: Your origin and your birth were in the land of the Cā'naan·ites; your father was an Am'o·rīte, and your mother a Hit'tīte. [4] As for your birth, on

e Or, as otherwise read, *Danel*

the day you were born your navel cord was not cut, nor were you washed with water to cleanse you, nor rubbed with salt, nor wrapped in cloths. [5]No eye pitied you, to do any of these things for you out of compassion for you; but you were thrown out in the open field, for you were abhorred on the day you were born.

6 I passed by you, and saw you flailing about in your blood. As you lay in your blood, I said to you, "Live! [7]and grow up[f] like a plant of the field." You grew up and became tall and arrived at full womanhood;[g] your breasts were formed, and your hair had grown; yet you were naked and bare.

8 I passed by you again and looked on you; you were at the age for love. I spread the edge of my cloak over you, and covered your nakedness: I pledged myself to you and entered into a covenant with you, says the Lord GOD, and you became mine. [9]Then I bathed you with water and washed off the blood from you, and anointed you with oil. [10]I clothed you with embroidered cloth and with sandals of fine leather; I bound you in fine linen and covered you with rich fabric.[h] [11]I adorned you with ornaments: I put bracelets on your arms, a chain on your neck, [12]a ring on your nose, earrings in your ears, and a beautiful crown upon your head. [13]You were adorned with gold and silver, while your clothing was of fine linen, rich fabric,[h] and embroidered cloth. You had choice flour and honey and oil for food. You grew exceedingly beautiful, fit to be a queen. [14]Your fame spread among the nations on account of your beauty, for it was perfect because of my splendor that I had bestowed on you, says the Lord GOD.

15 But you trusted in your beauty, and played the whore because of your fame, and lavished your whorings on any passer-by.[i] [16]You took some of your garments, and made for yourself colorful shrines, and on them played the whore; nothing like this has ever been or ever shall be.[h] [17]You also took your beautiful jewels of my gold and my silver that I had given you, and made for yourself male images, and with them played the whore; [18]and you took your embroidered garments to cover them, and set my oil and my incense before them. [19]Also my bread that I gave you—I fed you with choice flour and oil and honey—you set it be-

fore them as a pleasing odor; and so it was, says the Lord GOD. [20]You took your sons and your daughters, whom you had borne to me, and these you sacrificed to them to be devoured. As if your whorings were not enough! [21]You slaughtered my children and delivered them up as an offering to them. [22]And in all your abominations and your whorings you did not remember the days of your youth, when you were naked and bare, flailing about in your blood.

23 After all your wickedness (woe, woe to you! says the Lord GOD), [24]you built yourself a platform and made yourself a lofty place in every square; [25]at the head of every street you built your lofty place and prostituted your beauty, offering yourself to every passer-by, and multiplying your whoring. [26]You played the whore with the Egyptians, your lustful neighbors, multiplying your whoring, to provoke me to anger. [27]Therefore I stretched out my hand against you, reduced your rations, and gave you up to the will of your enemies, the daughters of the Phi·lis′tines, who were ashamed of your lewd behavior. [28]You played the whore with the Assyrians, because you were insatiable; you played the whore with them, and still you were not satisfied. [29]You multiplied your whoring with Chal·dē′a, the land of merchants; and even with this you were not satisfied.

30 How sick is your heart, says the Lord GOD, that you did all these things, the deeds of a brazen whore; [31]building your platform at the head of every street, and making your lofty place in every square! Yet you were not like a whore, because you scorned payment. [32]Adulterous wife, who receives strangers instead of her husband! [33]Gifts are given to all whores; but you gave your gifts to all your lovers, bribing them to come to you from all around for your whorings. [34]So you were different from other women in your whorings: no one solicited you to play the whore; and you gave payment, while no payment was given to you; you were different.

35 Therefore, O whore, hear the word of the LORD: [36]Thus says the

f Gk Syr: Heb *Live! I made you a myriad*
g Cn: Heb *ornament of ornaments*
h Meaning of Heb uncertain   i Heb adds *let it be his*

Lord GOD, Because your lust was poured out and your nakedness uncovered in your whoring with your lovers, and because of all your abominable idols, and because of the blood of your children that you gave to them, 37therefore, I will gather all your lovers, with whom you took pleasure, all those you loved and all those you hated; I will gather them against you from all around, and will uncover your nakedness to them, so that they may see all your nakedness. 38 I will judge you as women who commit adultery and shed blood are judged, and bring blood upon you in wrath and jealousy. 39 I will deliver you into their hands, and they shall throw down your platform and break down your lofty places; they shall strip you of your clothes and take your beautiful objects and leave you naked and bare. 40 They shall bring up a mob against you, and they shall stone you and cut you to pieces with their swords. 41 They shall burn your houses and execute judgments on you in the sight of many women; I will stop you from playing the whore, and you shall also make no more payments. 42 So I will satisfy my fury on you, and my jealousy shall turn away from you; I will be calm, and will be angry no longer. 43 Because you have not remembered the days of your youth, but have enraged me with all these things; therefore, I have returned your deeds upon your head, says the Lord GOD.

Have you not committed lewdness beyond all your abominations? 44 See, everyone who uses proverbs will use this proverb about you, "Like mother, like daughter." 45 You are the daughter of your mother, who loathed her husband and her children; and you are the sister of your sisters, who loathed their husbands and their children. Your mother was a Hit'tite and your father an Am'o·rite. 46 Your elder sister is Samaria, who lived with her daughters to the north of you; and your younger sister, who lived to the south of you, is Sod'om with her daughters. 47 You not only followed their ways, and acted according to their abominations; within a very little time you were more corrupt than they in all your ways. 48 As I live, says the Lord GOD, your sister Sod'om and her daughters have not done as you and your daughters have done. 49 This was the guilt of your sister Sod'om: she and her daughters had

pride, excess of food, and prosperous ease, but did not aid the poor and needy. 50 They were haughty, and did abominable things before me; therefore I removed them when I saw it. 51 Samaria has not committed half your sins; you have committed more abominations than they, and have made your sisters appear righteous by all the abominations that you have committed. 52 Bear your disgrace, you also, for you have brought about for your sisters a more favorable judgment; because of your sins in which you acted more abominably than they, they are more in the right than you. So be ashamed, you also, and bear your disgrace, for you have made your sisters appear righteous.

53 I will restore their fortunes, the fortunes of Sod'om and her daughters and the fortunes of Samaria and her daughters, and I will restore your own fortunes along with theirs, 54 in order that you may bear your disgrace and be ashamed of all that you have done, becoming a consolation to them. 55 As for your sisters, Sod'om and her daughters shall return to their former state, Samaria and her daughters shall return to their former state, and you and your daughters shall return to your former state. 56 Was not your sister Sod'om a byword in your mouth in the day of your pride, 57 before your wickedness was uncovered? Now you are a mockery to the daughters of Ar'am[j] and all her neighbors, and to the daughters of the Phi·lis'tines, those all around who despise you. 58 You must bear the penalty of your lewdness and your abominations, says the LORD.

An Everlasting Covenant

59 Yes, thus says the Lord GOD: I will deal with you as you have done, you who have despised the oath, breaking the covenant; 60 yet I will remember my covenant with you in the days of your youth, and I will establish with you an everlasting covenant. 61 Then you will remember your ways, and be ashamed when I[k] take your sisters, both your elder and your younger, and give them to you as daughters, but not on account of my[l] covenant with you. 62 I will establish my covenant with you, and you shall know that

j Another reading is Edom   k Syr: Heb you   l Heb lacks my

I am the LORD, 63 in order that you may remember and be confounded, and never open your mouth again because of your shame, when I forgive you all that you have done, says the Lord GOD.

The Two Eagles and the Vine

17 The word of the LORD came to me: 2 O mortal, propound a riddle, and speak an allegory to the house of Israel. 3 Say: Thus says the Lord GOD:

A great eagle, with great wings
    and long pinions,
rich in plumage of many
    colors,
came to the Lebanon.
He took the top of the cedar,
4   broke off its topmost shoot;
He carried it to a land of trade,
    set it in a city of merchants.
5 Then he took a seed from the
    land,
    placed it in fertile soil;
A plant^m by abundant waters,
    he set it like a willow twig.
6 It sprouted and became a vine
    spreading out, but low;
Its branches turned toward him,
    its roots remained where it
    stood.
So it became a vine;
    it brought forth branches,
    put forth foliage.

7 There was another great eagle,
    with great wings and much
    plumage.
And see! This vine stretched out
    its roots toward him;
It shot out its branches toward
    him,
    so that he might water it.
From the bed where it was
    planted
8   it was transplanted
to good soil by abundant waters,
    so that it might produce
    branches
    and bear fruit
    and become a noble vine.
9 Say: Thus says the Lord GOD:
    Will it prosper?
Will he not pull up its roots,
    cause its fruit to rot^m and
    wither,
    its fresh sprouting leaves to
    fade?
No strong arm or mighty army
    will be needed
    to pull it from its roots.

10 When it is transplanted, will it
    thrive?
When the east wind strikes it,
    will it not utterly wither,
    wither on the bed where it
    grew?

11 Then the word of the LORD came to me: 12 Say now to the rebellious house: Do you not know what these things mean? Tell them: The king of Babylon came to Jerusalem, took its king and its officials, and brought them back with him to Babylon. 13 He took one of the royal offspring and made a covenant with him, putting him under oath (he had taken away the chief men of the land), 14 so that the kingdom might be humble and not lift itself up, and that by keeping his covenant it might stand. 15 But he rebelled against him by sending ambassadors to Egypt, in order that they might give him horses and a large army. Will he succeed? Can one escape who does such things? Can he break the covenant and yet escape? 16 As I live, says the Lord GOD, surely in the place where the king resides who made him king, whose oath he despised, and whose covenant with him he broke—in Babylon he shall die. 17 Pharaoh with his mighty army and great company will not help him in war, when ramps are cast up and siege walls built to cut off many lives. 18 Because he despised the oath and broke the covenant, because he gave his hand and yet did all these things, he shall not escape. 19 Therefore thus says the Lord GOD: As I live, I will surely return upon his head my oath that he despised, and my covenant that he broke. 20 I will spread my net over him, and he shall be caught in my snare; I will bring him to Babylon and enter into judgment with him there for the treason he has committed against me. 21 All the pick^n of his troops shall fall by the sword, and the survivors shall be scattered to every wind; and you shall know that I, the LORD, have spoken.

Israel Exalted at Last
(Cp Ezek 31.1–9)

22 Thus says the Lord GOD:
I myself will take a sprig
    from the lofty top of a cedar;
    I will set it out.
I will break off a tender one

---

^{m} Meaning of Heb uncertain ^{n} Another reading is *fugitives*

from the topmost of its young
    twigs;
I myself will plant it
    on a high and lofty mountain.
23 On the mountain height of Israel
    I will plant it,
in order that it may produce
    boughs and bear fruit,
    and become a noble cedar.
Under it every kind of bird will
    live;
    in the shade of its branches
    will nest
winged creatures of every
    kind.
24 All the trees of the field shall
    know
    that I am the LORD.
I bring low the high tree,
    I make high the low tree;
I dry up the green tree
    and make the dry tree flourish.
I the LORD have spoken;
    I will accomplish it.

Individual Retribution

18 The word of the LORD came to
me: 2 What do you mean by repeating this proverb concerning the
land of Israel, "The parents have eaten
sour grapes, and the children's teeth
are set on edge"? 3 As I live, says the
Lord GOD, this proverb shall no more
be used by you in Israel. 4 Know that all
lives are mine; the life of the parent as
well as the life of the child is mine: it is
only the person who sins that shall die.

5 If a man is righteous and does
what is lawful and right— 6 if he does
not eat upon the mountains or lift up
his eyes to the idols of the house of
Israel, does not defile his neighbor's
wife or approach a woman during her
menstrual period, 7 does not oppress
anyone, but restores to the debtor his
pledge, commits no robbery, gives his
bread to the hungry and covers the naked with a garment, 8 does not take advance or accrued interest, withholds
his hand from iniquity, executes true
justice between contending parties,
9 follows my statutes, and is careful to
observe my ordinances, acting
faithfully—such a one is righteous; he
shall surely live, says the Lord GOD.

10 If he has a son who is violent, a
shedder of blood, 11 who does any of
these things (though his father° does
none of them), who eats upon the
mountains, defiles his neighbor's wife,
12 oppresses the poor and needy, commits robbery, does not restore the

pledge, lifts up his eyes to the idols,
commits abomination, 13 takes advance or accrued interest; shall he
then live? He shall not. He has done all
these abominable things; he shall
surely die; his blood shall be upon himself.

14 But if this man has a son who
sees all the sins that his father has
done, considers, and does not do likewise, 15 who does not eat upon the
mountains or lift up his eyes to the
idols of the house of Israel, does not
defile his neighbor's wife, 16 does not
wrong anyone, exacts no pledge, commits no robbery, but gives his bread to
the hungry and covers the naked with
a garment, 17 withholds his hand from
iniquity,ᵖ takes no advance or accrued interest, observes my ordinances, and follows my statutes; he
shall not die for his father's iniquity;
he shall surely live. 18 As for his father,
because he practiced extortion,
robbed his brother, and did what is not
good among his people, he dies for his
iniquity.

19 Yet you say, "Why should not
the son suffer for the iniquity of the
father?" When the son has done what
is lawful and right, and has been careful to observe all my statutes, he shall
surely live. 20 The person who sins
shall die. A child shall not suffer for
the iniquity of a parent, nor a parent
suffer for the iniquity of a child; the
righteousness of the righteous shall be
his own, and the wickedness of the
wicked shall be his own.

21 But if the wicked turn away from
all their sins that they have committed
and keep all my statutes and do what
is lawful and right, they shall surely
live; they shall not die. 22 None of the
transgressions that they have committed shall be remembered against them;
for the righteousness that they have
done they shall live. 23 Have I any pleasure in the death of the wicked, says
the Lord GOD, and not rather that they
should turn from their ways and live?
24 But when the righteous turn away
from their righteousness and commit
iniquity and do the same abominable
things that the wicked do, shall they
live? None of the righteous deeds that
they have done shall be remembered;
for the treachery of which they are
guilty and the sin they have committed, they shall die.

o Heb *he*   p Gk: Heb *the poor*

25 Yet you say, "The way of the Lord is unfair." Hear now, O house of Israel: Is my way unfair? Is it not your ways that are unfair? 26 When the righteous turn away from their righteousness and commit iniquity, they shall die for it; for the iniquity that they have committed they shall die. 27 Again, when the wicked turn away from the wickedness they have committed and do what is lawful and right, they shall save their life. 28 Because they considered and turned away from all the transgressions that they had committed, they shall surely live; they shall not die. 29 Yet the house of Israel says, "The way of the Lord is unfair." O house of Israel, are my ways unfair? Is it not your ways that are unfair?

30 Therefore I will judge you, O house of Israel, all of you according to your ways, says the Lord GOD. Repent and turn from all your transgressions; otherwise iniquity will be your ruin.*q* 31 Cast away from you all the transgressions that you have committed against me, and get yourselves a new heart and a new spirit! Why will you die, O house of Israel? 32 For I have no pleasure in the death of anyone, says the Lord GOD. Turn, then, and live.

Israel Degraded

19 As for you, raise up a lamentation for the princes of Israel, 2 and say:
What a lioness was your mother among lions!
She lay down among young lions,
rearing her cubs.
3 She raised up one of her cubs;
he became a young lion,
and he learned to catch prey;
he devoured humans.
4 The nations sounded an alarm against him;
he was caught in their pit;
and they brought him with hooks
to the land of Egypt.
5 When she saw that she was thwarted,
that her hope was lost,
she took another of her cubs
and made him a young lion.
6 He prowled among the lions;
he became a young lion,
and he learned to catch prey;
he devoured people.

7 And he ravaged their strongholds,*r*
and laid waste their towns;
the land was appalled, and all in it,
at the sound of his roaring.
8 The nations set upon him
from the provinces all around;
they spread their net over him;
he was caught in their pit.
9 With hooks they put him in a cage,
and brought him to the king of Babylon;
they brought him into custody,
so that his voice should be heard no more
on the mountains of Israel.
10 Your mother was like a vine in a vineyard*s*
transplanted by the water,
fruitful and full of branches
from abundant water.
11 Its strongest stem became
a ruler's scepter;*t*
it towered aloft
among the thick boughs;
it stood out in its height
with its mass of branches.
12 But it was plucked up in fury,
cast down to the ground;
the east wind dried it up;
its fruit was stripped off,
its strong stem was withered;
the fire consumed it.
13 Now it is transplanted into the wilderness,
into a dry and thirsty land.
14 And fire has gone out from its stem,
has consumed its branches and fruit,
so that there remains in it no strong stem,
no scepter for ruling.

This is a lamentation, and it is used as a lamentation.

Israel's Continuing Rebellion

20 In the seventh year, in the fifth month, on the tenth day of the month, certain elders of Israel came to consult the LORD, and sat down before me. 2 And the word of the LORD came to me: 3 Mortal, speak to the elders of

q Or *so that they shall not be a stumbling block of iniquity to you* *r* Heb *his widows* *s* Cn: Heb *in your blood* *t* Heb *Its strongest stems became rulers' scepters*

Israel, and say to them: Thus says the Lord GOD: Why are you coming? To consult me? As I live, says the Lord GOD, I will not be consulted by you. [4] Will you judge them, mortal, will you judge them? Then let them know the abominations of their ancestors, [5] and say to them: Thus says the Lord GOD: On the day when I chose Israel, I swore to the offspring of the house of Jacob — making myself known to them in the land of Egypt — I swore to them, saying, I am the LORD your God. [6] On that day I swore to them that I would bring them out of the land of Egypt into a land that I had searched out for them, a land flowing with milk and honey, the most glorious of all lands. [7] And I said to them, Cast away the detestable things your eyes feast on, every one of you, and do not defile yourselves with the idols of Egypt; I am the LORD your God. [8] But they rebelled against me and would not listen to me; not one of them cast away the detestable things their eyes feasted on, nor did they forsake the idols of Egypt.

Then I thought I would pour out my wrath upon them and spend my anger against them in the midst of the land of Egypt. [9] But I acted for the sake of my name, that it should not be profaned in the sight of the nations among whom they lived, in whose sight I made myself known to them in bringing them out of the land of Egypt. [10] So I led them out of the land of Egypt and brought them into the wilderness. [11] I gave them my statutes and showed them my ordinances, by whose observance everyone shall live. [12] Moreover I gave them my sabbaths, as a sign between me and them, so that they might know that I the LORD sanctify them. [13] But the house of Israel rebelled against me in the wilderness; they did not observe my statutes but rejected my ordinances, by whose observance everyone shall live; and my sabbaths they greatly profaned.

Then I thought I would pour out my wrath upon them in the wilderness, to make an end of them. [14] But I acted for the sake of my name, so that it should not be profaned in the sight of the nations, in whose sight I had brought them out. [15] Moreover I swore to them in the wilderness that I would not bring them into the land that I had given them, a land flowing with milk and honey, the most glorious of all lands, [16] because they rejected my ordinances and did not observe my statutes, and profaned my sabbaths; for their heart went after their idols. [17] Nevertheless my eye spared them, and I did not destroy them or make an end of them in the wilderness.

[18] I said to their children in the wilderness, Do not follow the statutes of your parents, nor observe their ordinances, nor defile yourselves with their idols. [19] I the LORD am your God; follow my statutes, and be careful to observe my ordinances, [20] and hallow my sabbaths that they may be a sign between me and you, so that you may know that I the LORD am your God. [21] But the children rebelled against me; they did not follow my statutes, and were not careful to observe my ordinances, by whose observance everyone shall live; they profaned my sabbaths.

Then I thought I would pour out my wrath upon them and spend my anger against them in the wilderness. [22] But I withheld my hand, and acted for the sake of my name, so that it should not be profaned in the sight of the nations, in whose sight I had brought them out. [23] Moreover I swore to them in the wilderness that I would scatter them among the nations and disperse them through the countries, [24] because they had not executed my ordinances, but had rejected my statutes and profaned my sabbaths, and their eyes were set on their ancestors' idols. [25] Moreover I gave them statutes that were not good and ordinances by which they could not live. [26] I defiled them through their very gifts, in their offering up all their firstborn, in order that I might horrify them, so that they might know that I am the LORD.

[27] Therefore, mortal, speak to the house of Israel and say to them, Thus says the Lord GOD: In this again your ancestors blasphemed me, by dealing treacherously with me. [28] For when I had brought them into the land that I swore to give them, then wherever they saw any high hill or any leafy tree, there they offered their sacrifices and presented the provocation of their offering; there they sent up their pleasing odors, and there they poured out their drink offerings. [29] (I said to them, What is the high place to which you go? So it is called Bā′mah[u] to this day.) [30] Therefore say to the house of

[u] That is High Place

Israel, Thus says the Lord GOD: Will you defile yourselves after the manner of your ancestors and go astray after their detestable things? 31 When you offer your gifts and make your children pass through the fire, you defile yourselves with all your idols to this day. And shall I be consulted by you, O house of Israel? As I live, says the Lord GOD, I will not be consulted by you.

32 What is in your mind shall never happen—the thought, "Let us be like the nations, like the tribes of the countries, and worship wood and stone."

God Will Restore Israel

33 As I live, says the Lord GOD, surely with a mighty hand and an outstretched arm, and with wrath poured out, I will be king over you. 34 I will bring you out from the peoples and gather you out of the countries where you are scattered, with a mighty hand and an outstretched arm, and with wrath poured out; 35 and I will bring you into the wilderness of the peoples, and there I will enter into judgment with you face to face. 36 As I entered into judgment with your ancestors in the wilderness of the land of Egypt, so I will enter into judgment with you, says the Lord GOD. 37 I will make you pass under the staff, and will bring you within the bond of the covenant. 38 I will purge out the rebels among you, and those who transgress against me; I will bring them out of the land where they reside as aliens, but they shall not enter the land of Israel. Then you shall know that I am the LORD.

39 As for you, O house of Israel, thus says the Lord GOD: Go serve your idols, everyone of you now and hereafter, if you will not listen to me; but my holy name you shall no more profane with your gifts and your idols.

40 For on my holy mountain, the mountain height of Israel, says the Lord GOD, there all the house of Israel, all of them, shall serve me in the land; there I will accept them, and there I will require your contributions and the choicest of your gifts, with all your sacred things. 41 As a pleasing odor I will accept you, when I bring you out from the peoples, and gather you out of the countries where you have been scattered; and I will manifest my holiness among you in the sight of the nations. 42 You shall know that I am the LORD, when I bring you into the land of Is-

rael, the country that I swore to give to your ancestors. 43 There you shall remember your ways and all the deeds by which you have polluted yourselves; and you shall loathe yourselves for all the evils that you have committed. 44 And you shall know that I am the LORD, when I deal with you for my name's sake, not according to your evil ways, or corrupt deeds, O house of Israel, says the Lord GOD.

A Prophecy against the Negeb

45[v] The word of the LORD came to me: 46 Mortal, set your face toward the south, preach against the south, and prophesy against the forest land in the Neg'eb; 47 say to the forest of the Neg'eb, Hear the word of the LORD: Thus says the Lord GOD, I will kindle a fire in you, and it shall devour every green tree in you and every dry tree; the blazing flame shall not be quenched, and all faces from south to north shall be scorched by it. 48 All flesh shall see that I the LORD have kindled it; it shall not be quenched. 49 Then I said, "Ah Lord GOD! they are saying of me, 'Is he not a maker of allegories?' "

The Drawn Sword of God

21 [w] The word of the LORD came to me: 2 Mortal, set your face toward Jerusalem and preach against the sanctuaries; prophesy against the land of Israel 3 and say to the land of Israel, Thus says the LORD: I am coming against you, and will draw my sword out of its sheath, and will cut off from you both righteous and wicked. 4 Because I will cut off from you both righteous and wicked, therefore my sword shall go out of its sheath against all flesh from south to north; 5 and all flesh shall know that I the LORD have drawn my sword out of its sheath; it shall not be sheathed again. 6 Moan therefore, mortal; moan with breaking heart and bitter grief before their eyes. 7 And when they say to you, "Why do you moan?" you shall say, "Because of the news that has come. Every heart will melt and all hands will be feeble, every spirit will faint and all knees will turn to water. See, it comes and it will be fulfilled," says the Lord GOD.

8 And the word of the LORD came to me: 9 Mortal, prophesy and say: Thus says the Lord; Say:

[v] Ch 21.1 in Heb   [w] Ch 21.6 in Heb

A sword, a sword is sharpened,
   it is also polished;
10 It is sharpened for slaughter,
   honed to flash like lightning!
How can we make merry?
   You have despised the rod,
   and all discipline.[x]
11 The sword[y] is given to be
     polished,
   to be grasped in the hand;
It is sharpened, the sword is
     polished,
   to be placed in the slayer's
     hand.
12 Cry and wail, O mortal,
   for it is against my people;
it is against all Israel's princes;
   they are thrown to the sword,
   together with my people.
   Ah! Strike the thigh!
13 For consider: What! If you despise
the rod, will it not happen?[x] says the
Lord GOD.
14 And you, mortal, prophesy;
   Strike hand to hand.
Let the sword fall twice, thrice;
   it is a sword for killing.
A sword for great slaughter—
   it surrounds them;
15 therefore hearts melt
   and many stumble.
At all their gates I have set
   the point[x] of the sword.
Ah! It is made for flashing,
   it is polished[z] for slaughter.
16 Attack to the right!
   Engage to the left!
Wherever your edge is
     directed.
17 I too will strike hand to hand,
   I will satisfy my fury;
   I the LORD have spoken.

18 The word of the LORD came to
me: 19 Mortal, mark out two roads for
the sword of the king of Babylon to
come; both of them shall issue from
the same land. And make a signpost,
make it for a fork in the road leading
to a city; 20 mark out the road for the
sword to come to Rab'bah of the Am'-
mon·ites or to Judah and to[a] Jerusalem the fortified. 21 For the king of Babylon stands at the parting of the way,
at the fork in the two roads, to use divination; he shakes the arrows, he consults the teraphim,[b] he inspects the
liver. 22 Into his right hand comes the
lot for Jerusalem, to set battering
rams, to call out for slaughter, for raising the battle cry, to set battering rams
against the gates, to cast up ramps, to
build siege towers. 23 But to them it will

seem like a false divination; they have
sworn solemn oaths; but he brings
their guilt to remembrance, bringing
about their capture.
24 Therefore thus says the Lord
GOD: Because you have brought your
guilt to remembrance, in that your
transgressions are uncovered, so that
in all your deeds your sins appear—
because you have come to remembrance, you shall be taken in hand.[c]
25 As for you, vile, wicked prince
     of Israel,
   you whose day has come,
   the time of final punishment,
26 thus says the Lord GOD:
Remove the turban, take off the
     crown;
   things shall not remain as they
     are.
Exalt that which is low,
   abase that which is high.
27 A ruin, a ruin, a ruin—
   I will make it!
(Such has never occurred.)
Until he comes whose right it is;
   to him I will give it.
28 As for you, mortal, prophesy,
and say, Thus says the Lord GOD concerning the Am'mon·ites, and concerning their reproach; say:
A sword, a sword! Drawn for
     slaughter
   Polished to consume,[d] to flash
     like lightning.
29 Offering false visions for you,
   divining lies for you,
they place you over the necks
   of the vile, wicked ones—
those whose day has come,
   the time of final punishment.
30 Return it to its sheath!
In the place where you were
     created,
   in the land of your origin,
   I will judge you.
31 I will pour out my indignation
     upon you,
   with the fire of my wrath
   I will blow upon you.
I will deliver you into brutish
     hands,
   those skillful to destroy.
32 You shall be fuel for the fire,
   your blood shall enter the
     earth;

x Meaning of Heb uncertain   y Heb It
z Tg: Heb wrapped up   a Gk Syr: Heb
Judah in   b Or the household gods
c Or be taken captive   d Cn: Heb to
contain

You shall be remembered no
more,
for I the LORD have spoken.

The Bloody City

22 The word of the LORD came to me: [2] You, mortal, will you judge, will you judge the bloody city? Then declare to it all its abominable deeds. [3] You shall say, Thus says the Lord GOD: A city! Shedding blood within itself; its time has come; making its idols, defiling itself. [4] You have become guilty by the blood that you have shed, and defiled by the idols that you have made; you have brought your day near, the appointed time of your years has come. Therefore I have made you a disgrace before the nations, and a mockery to all the countries. [5] Those who are near and those who are far from you will mock you, you infamous one, full of tumult.

[6] The princes of Israel in you, everyone according to his power, have been bent on shedding blood. [7] Father and mother are treated with contempt in you; the alien residing within you suffers extortion; the orphan and the widow are wronged in you. [8] You have despised my holy things, and profaned my sabbaths. [9] In you are those who slander to shed blood, those in you who eat upon the mountains, who commit lewdness in your midst. [10] In you they uncover their fathers' nakedness; in you they violate women in their menstrual periods. [11] One commits abomination with his neighbor's wife; another lewdly defiles his daughter-in-law; another in you defiles his sister, his father's daughter. [12] In you, they take bribes to shed blood; you take both advance interest and accrued interest, and make gain of your neighbors by extortion; and you have forgotten me, says the Lord GOD.

[13] See, I strike my hands together at the dishonest gain you have made, and at the blood that has been shed within you. [14] Can your courage endure, or can your hands remain strong in the days when I shall deal with you? I the LORD have spoken, and I will do it. [15] I will scatter you among the nations and disperse you through the countries, and I will purge your filthiness out of you. [16] And I[e] shall be profaned through you in the sight of the nations; and you shall know that I am the LORD.

[17] The word of the LORD came to me: [18] Mortal, the house of Israel has become dross to me; all of them, silver,[f] bronze, tin, iron, and lead. In the smelter they have become dross. [19] Therefore thus says the Lord GOD: Because you have all become dross, I will gather you into the midst of Jerusalem. [20] As one gathers silver, bronze, iron, lead, and tin into a smelter, to blow the fire upon them in order to melt them; so I will gather you in my anger and in my wrath, and I will put you in and melt you. [21] I will gather you and blow upon you with the fire of my wrath, and you shall be melted within it. [22] As silver is melted in a smelter, so you shall be melted in it; and you shall know that I the LORD have poured out my wrath upon you.

[23] The word of the LORD came to me: [24] Mortal, say to it: You are a land that is not cleansed, not rained upon in the day of indignation. [25] Its princes[g] within it are like a roaring lion tearing the prey; they have devoured human lives; they have taken treasure and precious things; they have made many widows within it. [26] Its priests have done violence to my teaching and have profaned my holy things; they have made no distinction between the holy and the common, neither have they taught the difference between the unclean and the clean, and they have disregarded my sabbaths, so that I am profaned among them. [27] Its officials within it are like wolves tearing the prey, shedding blood, destroying lives to get dishonest gain. [28] Its prophets have smeared whitewash on their behalf, seeing false visions and divining lies for them, saying, "Thus says the Lord GOD," when the LORD has not spoken. [29] The people of the land have practiced extortion and committed robbery; they have oppressed the poor and needy, and have extorted from the alien without redress. [30] And I sought for anyone among them who would repair the wall and stand in the breach before me on behalf of the land, so that I would not destroy it; but I found no one. [31] Therefore I have poured out my indignation upon them; I have consumed them with the fire of my wrath; I have returned their conduct upon their heads, says the Lord GOD.

e Gk Syr Vg: Heb you   f Transposed from the end of the verse; compare verse 20   g Gk: Heb indignation. 25 A conspiracy of its prophets

Oholah and Oholibah

23 The word of the LORD came to me: [2] Mortal, there were two women, the daughters of one mother; [3] they played the whore in Egypt; they played the whore in their youth; their breasts were caressed there, and their virgin bosoms were fondled. [4] Ō·hō′lah was the name of the elder and Ō·hol′i·bah the name of her sister. They became mine, and they bore sons and daughters. As for their names, Ō·hō′lah is Samaria, and Ō·hol′i·bah is Jerusalem.

[5] Ō·hō′lah played the whore while she was mine; she lusted after her lovers the Assyrians, warriors[h] [6] clothed in blue, governors and commanders, all of them handsome young men, mounted horsemen. [7] She bestowed her favors upon them, the choicest men of Assyria all of them; and she defiled herself with all the idols of everyone for whom she lusted. [8] She did not give up her whorings that she had practiced since Egypt; for in her youth men had lain with her and fondled her virgin bosom and poured out their lust upon her. [9] Therefore I delivered her into the hands of her lovers, into the hands of the Assyrians, for whom she lusted. [10] These uncovered her nakedness; they seized her sons and her daughters; and they killed her with the sword. Judgment was executed upon her, and she became a byword among women.

[11] Her sister Ō·hol′i·bah saw this, yet she was more corrupt than she in her lusting and in her whorings, which were worse than those of her sister. [12] She lusted after the Assyrians, governors and commanders, warriors[h] clothed in full armor, mounted horsemen, all of them handsome young men. [13] And I saw that she was defiled; they both took the same way. [14] But she carried her whorings further; she saw male figures carved on the wall, images of the Chal·dē′ans portrayed in vermilion, [15] with belts around their waists, with flowing turbans on their heads, all of them looking like officers —a picture of Babylonians whose native land was Chal·dē′a. [16] When she saw them she lusted after them, and sent messengers to them in Chal·dē′a. [17] And the Babylonians came to her into the bed of love, and they defiled her with their lust; and after she defiled herself with them, she turned from them in disgust. [18] When she carried on her whorings so openly and flaunted her nakedness, I turned in disgust from her, as I had turned from her sister. [19] Yet she increased her whorings, remembering the days of her youth, when she played the whore in the land of Egypt [20] and lusted after her paramours there, whose members were like those of donkeys, and whose emission was like that of stallions. [21] Thus you longed for the lewdness of your youth, when the Egyptians[i] fondled your bosom and caressed[j] your young breasts.

[22] Therefore, O Ō·hol′i·bah, thus says the Lord GOD: I will rouse against you your lovers from whom you turned in disgust, and I will bring them against you from every side: [23] the Babylonians and all the Chal·dē′ans, Pē′kod and Shō′a and Kō′a, and all the Assyrians with them, handsome young men, governors and commanders all of them, officers and warriors,[k] all of them riding on horses. [24] They shall come against you from the north[l] with chariots and wagons and a host of peoples; they shall set themselves against you on every side with buckler, shield, and helmet, and I will commit the judgment to them, and they shall judge you according to their ordinances. [25] I will direct my indignation against you, in order that they may deal with you in fury. They shall cut off your nose and your ears, and your survivors shall fall by the sword. They shall seize your sons and your daughters, and your survivors shall be devoured by fire. [26] They shall also strip you of your clothes and take away your fine jewels. [27] So I will put an end to your lewdness and your whoring brought from the land of Egypt; you shall not long for them, or remember Egypt any more. [28] For thus says the Lord GOD: I will deliver you into the hands of those whom you hate, into the hands of those from whom you turned in disgust; [29] and they shall deal with you in hatred, and take away all the fruit of your labor, and leave you naked and bare, and the nakedness of your whorings shall be exposed. Your lewdness and your whorings [30] have

[h] Meaning of Heb uncertain   [i] Two Mss: MT *from Egypt*   [j] Cn: Heb *for the sake of*   [k] Compare verses 6 and 12: Heb *officers and called ones*   [l] Gk: Meaning of Heb uncertain

brought this upon you, because you played the whore with the nations, and polluted yourself with their idols. ³¹You have gone the way of your sister; therefore I will give her cup into your hand. ³²Thus says the Lord GOD:

You shall drink your sister's cup,
   deep and wide;
you shall be scorned and
      derided,
   it holds so much.
³³ You shall be filled with
      drunkenness and sorrow.
   A cup of horror and desolation
      is the cup of your sister
      Samaria;
³⁴ you shall drink it and drain it
      out,
      and gnaw its sherds;
   and tear out your breasts;

for I have spoken, says the Lord GOD. ³⁵Therefore thus says the Lord GOD: Because you have forgotten me and cast me behind your back, therefore bear the consequences of your lewdness and whorings.

36 The LORD said to me: Mortal, will you judge Ō·hō′lah and Ō·hol′-i·bah? Then declare to them their abominable deeds. ³⁷For they have committed adultery, and blood is on their hands; with their idols they have committed adultery; and they have even offered up to them for food the children whom they had borne to me. ³⁸Moreover this they have done to me: they have defiled my sanctuary on the same day and profaned my sabbaths. ³⁹For when they had slaughtered their children for their idols, on the same day they came into my sanctuary to profane it. This is what they did in my house.

40 They even sent for men to come from far away, to whom a messenger was sent, and they came. For them you bathed yourself, painted your eyes, and decked yourself with ornaments; ⁴¹you sat on a stately couch, with a table spread before it on which you had placed my incense and my oil. ⁴²The sound of a raucous multitude was around her, with many of the rabble brought in drunken from the wilderness; and they put bracelets on the arms[m] of the women, and beautiful crowns upon their heads. 43 Then I said, Ah, she is worn out with adulteries, but they carry on their sexual acts with her. ⁴⁴For they have gone in to her, as one goes in to a whore. Thus they went in to Ō·hō′lah and to Ō·hol′i·bah, wanton women. ⁴⁵But righteous judges shall declare them guilty of adultery and of bloodshed; because they are adulteresses and blood is on their hands.

46 For thus says the Lord GOD: Bring up an assembly against them, and make them an object of terror and of plunder. ⁴⁷The assembly shall stone them and with their swords they shall cut them down; they shall kill their sons and their daughters, and burn up their houses. ⁴⁸Thus will I put an end to lewdness in the land, so that all women may take warning and not commit lewdness as you have done. ⁴⁹They shall repay you for your lewdness, and you shall bear the penalty for your sinful idolatry; and you shall know that I am the Lord GOD.

The Boiling Pot
(Cp Jer 1.13–19)

24 In the ninth year, in the tenth month, on the tenth day of the month, the word of the LORD came to me: ²Mortal, write down the name of this day, this very day. The king of Babylon has laid siege to Jerusalem this very day. ³And utter an allegory to the rebellious house and say to them, Thus says the Lord GOD:

Set on the pot, set it on,
   pour in water also;
4 put in it the pieces,
      all the good pieces, the thigh
         and the shoulder;
   fill it with choice bones.
5 Take the choicest one of the
      flock,
      pile the logs[n] under it;
   boil its pieces,[o]
      seethe[p] also its bones in it.

6 Therefore thus says the Lord GOD:

Woe to the bloody city,
   the pot whose rust is in it,
      whose rust has not gone out of
         it!
Empty it piece by piece,
   making no choice at all.[q]
7 For the blood she shed is inside
      it;
   she placed it on a bare rock;
she did not pour it out on the
      ground,

m Heb hands   n Compare verse 10: Heb the bones   o Two Mss: Heb its boilings   p Cn: Heb its bones seethe   q Heb piece, no lot has fallen on it to cover it with earth.

8 To rouse my wrath, to take
    vengeance,
  I have placed the blood she
    shed
    on a bare rock,
  so that it may not be covered.

9 Therefore thus says the Lord GOD:
  Woe to the bloody city!
  I will even make the pile great.

10 Heap up the logs, kindle the fire;
  boil the meat well, mix in the
    spices,
  let the bones be burned.

11 Stand it empty upon the coals,
  so that it may become hot, its
    copper glow,
  its filth melt in it, its rust be
    consumed.

12 In vain I have wearied myself;[r]
  its thick rust does not depart.
  To the fire with its rust![s]

13 Yet, when I cleansed you in your
    filthy lewdness,
  you did not become clean from
    your filth;
  you shall not again be cleansed
    until I have satisfied my fury
    upon you.

14 I the LORD have spoken; the time is coming, I will act. I will not refrain, I will not spare, I will not relent. According to your ways and your doings I will judge you, says the Lord GOD.

Ezekiel's Bereavement

15 The word of the LORD came to me: 16 Mortal, with one blow I am about to take from you the delight of your eyes; yet you shall not mourn or weep, nor shall your tears run down. 17 Sigh, but not aloud; make no mourning for the dead. Bind on your turban, and put your sandals on your feet; do not cover your upper lip or eat the bread of mourners.[t] 18 So I spoke to the people in the morning, and at evening my wife died. And on the next morning I did as I was commanded.

19 Then the people said to me, "Will you not tell us what these things mean for us, that you are acting this way?" 20 Then I said to them: The word of the LORD came to me: 21 Say to the house of Israel, Thus says the Lord GOD: I will profane my sanctuary, the pride of your power, the delight of your eyes, and your heart's desire; and your sons and your daughters whom you left behind shall fall by the sword. 22 And you shall do as I have done; you shall not

cover your upper lip or eat the bread of mourners.[t] 23 Your turbans shall be on your heads and your sandals on your feet; you shall not mourn or weep, but you shall pine away in your iniquities and groan to one another. 24 Thus E·zēk'i·el shall be a sign to you; you shall do just as he has done. When this comes, then you shall know that I am the Lord GOD.

25 And you, mortal, on the day when I take from them their stronghold, their joy and glory, the delight of their eyes and their heart's affection, and also[u] their sons and their daughters, 26 on that day, one who has escaped will come to you to report to you the news. 27 On that day your mouth shall be opened to the one who has escaped, and you shall speak and no longer be silent. So you shall be a sign to them; and they shall know that I am the LORD.

Proclamation against Ammon

25 The word of the LORD came to me: 2 Mortal, set your face toward the Am'mon·ites and prophesy against them. 3 Say to the Am'mon·ites, Hear the word of the Lord GOD: Thus says the Lord GOD, Because you said, "Aha!" over my sanctuary when it was profaned, and over the land of Israel when it was made desolate, and over the house of Judah when it went into exile; 4 therefore I am handing you over to the people of the east for a possession. They shall set their encampments among you and pitch their tents in your midst; they shall eat your fruit, and they shall drink your milk. 5 I will make Rab'bah a pasture for camels and Am'mon a fold for flocks. Then you shall know that I am the LORD. 6 For thus says the Lord GOD: Because you have clapped your hands and stamped your feet and rejoiced with all the malice within you against the land of Israel, 7 therefore I have stretched out my hand against you, and will hand you over as plunder to the nations. I will cut you off from the peoples and will make you perish out of the countries; I will destroy you. Then you shall know that I am the LORD.

r Cn: Meaning of Heb uncertain
s Meaning of Heb uncertain   t Vg Tg:
Heb *of men*   u Heb lacks *and also*

Proclamation against Moab

8 Thus says the Lord GOD: Because Mō'ab[v] said, The house of Judah is like all the other nations, [9]therefore I will lay open the flank of Mō'ab from the towns[w] on its frontier, the glory of the country, Beth-jesh'i·moth, Bā'al-mē'on, and Kir·i·a·thā'im. [10]I will give it along with Am'mon to the people of the east as a possession. Thus Am'mon shall be remembered no more among the nations, [11]and I will execute judgments upon Mō'ab. Then they shall know that I am the LORD.

Proclamation against Edom

12 Thus says the Lord GOD: Because Ē'dom acted revengefully against the house of Judah and has grievously offended in taking vengeance upon them, [13]therefore thus says the Lord GOD, I will stretch out my hand against Ē'dom, and cut off from it humans and animals, and I will make it desolate; from Tē'man even to Dē'dan they shall fall by the sword. [14]I will lay my vengeance upon Ē'dom by the hand of my people Israel; and they shall act in Ē'dom according to my anger and according to my wrath; and they shall know my vengeance, says the Lord GOD.

Proclamation against Philistia

15 Thus says the Lord GOD: Because with unending hostilities the Phi·lis'tines acted in vengeance, and with malice of heart took revenge in destruction; [16]therefore thus says the Lord GOD, I will stretch out my hand against the Phi·lis'tines, cut off the Cher'e·thītes, and destroy the rest of the seacoast. [17]I will execute great vengeance on them with wrathful punishments. Then they shall know that I am the LORD, when I lay my vengeance on them.

Proclamation against Tyre

26 In the eleventh year, on the first day of the month, the word of the LORD came to me: [2]Mortal, because Tyre said concerning Jerusalem, "Aha, broken is the gateway of the peoples;
it has swung open to me;
I shall be replenished,
now that it is wasted."
[3]Therefore, thus says the Lord GOD: See, I am against you, O Tyre!

I will hurl many nations
against you,
as the sea hurls its waves.
4 They shall destroy the walls of Tyre
and break down its towers.
I will scrape its soil from it
and make it a bare rock.
5 It shall become, in the midst of the sea,
a place for spreading nets.
I have spoken, says the Lord GOD.
It shall become plunder for the nations,
6 and its daughter-towns in the country
shall be killed by the sword.
Then they shall know that I am the LORD.
7 For thus says the Lord GOD: I will bring against Tyre from the north King Ne·bū·chad·rez'zar of Babylon, king of kings, together with horses, chariots, cavalry, and a great and powerful army.
8 Your daughter-towns in the country
he shall put to the sword.
He shall set up a siege wall against you,
cast up a ramp against you,
and raise a roof of shields against you.
9 He shall direct the shock of his battering rams against your walls
and break down your towers with his axes.
10 His horses shall be so many
that their dust shall cover you.
At the noise of cavalry, wheels, and chariots
your very walls shall shake,
when he enters your gates
like those entering a breached city.
11 With the hoofs of his horses
he shall trample all your streets.
He shall put your people to the sword,
and your strong pillars shall fall to the ground.
12 They will plunder your riches
and loot your merchandise;
they shall break down your walls
and destroy your fine houses.
Your stones and timber and soil

[v]Gk Old Latin: Heb *Moab and Seir*
[w]Heb *towns from its towns*

they shall cast into the water.
13 I will silence the music of your
   songs;
   the sound of your lyres shall
      be heard no more.
14 I will make you a bare rock;
   you shall be a place for
      spreading nets.
   You shall never again be rebuilt,
      for I the LORD have spoken,
   says the Lord GOD.

15 Thus says the Lord GOD to Tȳre:
Shall not the coastlands shake at the
sound of your fall, when the wounded
groan, when slaughter goes on within
you? 16 Then all the princes of the sea
shall step down from their thrones;
they shall remove their robes and strip
off their embroidered garments. They
shall clothe themselves with trembling, and shall sit on the ground; they
shall tremble every moment, and be
appalled at you. 17 And they shall raise
a lamentation over you, and say to
you:

How you have vanishedˣ from
   the seas,
O city renowned,
once mighty on the sea,
   you and your inhabitants,ʸ
who imposed yourᶻ terror
   on all the mainland!ᵃ
18 Now the coastlands tremble
   on the day of your fall;
   the coastlands by the sea
      are dismayed at your passing.

19 For thus says the Lord GOD:
When I make you a city laid waste, like
cities that are not inhabited, when I
bring up the deep over you, and the
great waters cover you, 20 then I will
thrust you down with those who descend into the Pit, to the people of long
ago, and I will make you live in the
world below, among primeval ruins,
with those who go down to the Pit, so
that you will not be inhabited or have
a placeᵇ in the land of the living. 21 I
will bring you to a dreadful end, and
you shall be no more; though sought
for, you will never be found again, says
the Lord GOD.

Lamentation over Tyre

27 The word of the LORD came to
   me: 2 Now you, mortal, raise a
lamentation over Tȳre, 3 and say to
Tȳre, which sits at the entrance to the
sea, merchant of the peoples on many
coastlands, Thus says the Lord GOD:
O Tȳre, you have said,
   "I am perfect in beauty."

4 Your borders are in the heart of
   the seas;
   your builders made perfect
      your beauty.
5 They made all your planks
   of fir trees from Sē′nir;
   they took a cedar from Lebanon
      to make a mast for you.
6 From oaks of Bā′shan
   they made your oars;
   they made your deck of pinesᶜ
      from the coasts of Cyprus,
      inlaid with ivory.
7 Of fine embroidered linen from
   Egypt
      was your sail,
      serving as your ensign;
   blue and purple from the coasts
      of E·li′shah
      was your awning.
8 The inhabitants of Sī′don and
   Ar′vad
      were your rowers;
   skilled men of Zē′merᵈ were
      within you,
      they were your pilots.
9 The elders of Gē′bal and its
      artisans were within you,
      caulking your seams;
   all the ships of the sea with their
      mariners were within you,
      to barter for your wares.
10 Par′aseᵉ and Lud and Put
      were in your army,
      your mighty warriors;
   they hung shield and helmet in
      you;
      they gave you splendor.
11 Men of Ar′vad and Hē′lechᶠ
      were on your walls all around;
   men of Gā′mad were at your
      towers.
   They hung their quivers all
      around your walls;
      they made perfect your beauty.

12 Tar′shish did business with you
out of the abundance of your great
wealth; silver, iron, tin, and lead they
exchanged for your wares. 13 Jā′van,
Tū′bal, and Mē′shech traded with you;
they exchanged human beings and
vessels of bronze for your merchandise. 14 Beth-tō·gar′mah exchanged for
your wares horses, war horses, and

ˣ Gk OL Aquila: Heb *have vanished,
O inhabited one,*   ʸ Heb *it and its
inhabitants*   ᶻ Heb *their*   ᵃ Cn: Heb *its
inhabitants*   ᵇ Gk: Heb *I will give
beauty*   ᶜ Or *boxwood*   ᵈ Cn Compare
Gen 10.18: Heb *your skilled men, O Tyre*
ᵉ Or *Persia*   ᶠ Or *and your army*

mules. 15 The Rhō′di·ans[g] traded with you; many coastlands were your own special markets; they brought you in payment ivory tusks and ebony. 16 E′dom[h] did business with you because of your abundant goods; they exchanged for your wares turquoise, purple, embroidered work, fine linen, coral, and rubies. 17 Judah and the land of Israel traded with you; they exchanged for your merchandise wheat from Min′nith, millet,[i] honey, oil, and balm. 18 Damascus traded with you for your abundant goods—because of your great wealth of every kind—wine of Hel′bon, and white wool. 19 Vē′dan and Jā′van from Ū′zal[i] entered into trade for your wares; wrought iron, cassia, and sweet cane were bartered for your merchandise. 20 Dē′dan traded with you in saddlecloths for riding. 21 Arabia and all the princes of Kē′dar were your favored dealers in lambs, rams, and goats; in these they did business with you. 22 The merchants of Shē′ba and Rā′a·mah traded with you; they exchanged for your wares the best of all kinds of spices, and all precious stones, and gold. 23 Har′an, Can′neh, Eden, the merchants of Shē′ba, As′shur, and Chil′mad traded with you. 24 These traded with you in choice garments, in clothes of blue and embroidered work, and in carpets of colored material, bound with cords and made secure; in these they traded with you.[j] 25 The ships of Tar′shish traveled for you in your trade.

So you were filled and heavily laden
　　in the heart of the seas.
26 Your rowers have brought you
　　into the high seas.
The east wind has wrecked you
　　in the heart of the seas.
27 Your riches, your wares, your
　　merchandise,
　　your mariners and your pilots,
your caulkers, your dealers in
　　merchandise,
　　and all your warriors within
　　　you,
with all the company
　　that is with you,
sink into the heart of the seas
　　on the day of your ruin.
28 At the sound of the cry of your
　　pilots
　　the countryside shakes,
29 and down from their ships
　　come all that handle the oar.

The mariners and all the pilots
　　of the sea
　　stand on the shore
30 and wail aloud over you,
　　and cry bitterly.
They throw dust on their heads
　　and wallow in ashes;
31 they make themselves bald for
　　you,
　　and put on sackcloth,
and they weep over you in
　　bitterness of soul,
　　with bitter mourning.
32 In their wailing they raise a
　　lamentation for you,
　　and lament over you:
"Who was ever destroyed[k] like
　　Tyre
　　in the midst of the sea?
33 When your wares came from the
　　seas,
　　you satisfied many peoples;
with your abundant wealth and
　　merchandise
　　you enriched the kings of the
　　　earth.
34 Now you are wrecked by the
　　seas,
　　in the depths of the waters;
your merchandise and all your
　　crew
　　have sunk with you.
35 All the inhabitants of the
　　coastlands
　　are appalled at you;
and their kings are horribly
　　afraid,
　　their faces are convulsed.
36 The merchants among the
　　peoples hiss at you;
you have come to a dreadful
　　end
　　and shall be no more forever."

Proclamation against the King of Tyre

28 The word of the LORD came to me: 2 Mortal, say to the prince of Tyre, Thus says the Lord GOD:
Because your heart is proud
　　and you have said, "I am a
　　　god;
I sit in the seat of the gods,
　　in the heart of the seas,"
yet you are but a mortal, and no
　　god,
　　though you compare your
　　　mind

[g] Gk: Heb *The Dedanites*　[h] Another reading is *Aram*　[i] Meaning of Heb uncertain　[j] Cn: Heb *in your market*　[k] Tg Vg: Heb *like silence*

with the mind of a god.
3 You are indeed wiser than
Daniel;[l]
no secret is hidden from you;
4 by your wisdom and your
understanding
you have amassed wealth for
yourself,
and have gathered gold and
silver
into your treasuries.
5 By your great wisdom in trade
you have increased your
wealth,
and your heart has become
proud in your wealth.
6 Therefore thus says the Lord
GOD:
Because you compare your mind
with the mind of a god,
7 therefore, I will bring strangers
against you,
the most terrible of the
nations;
they shall draw their swords
against the beauty of your
wisdom
and defile your splendor.
8 They shall thrust you down to
the Pit,
and you shall die a violent
death
in the heart of the seas.
9 Will you still say, "I am a god,"
in the presence of those who
kill you,
though you are but a mortal, and
no god,
in the hands of those who
wound you?
10 You shall die the death of the
uncircumcised
by the hand of foreigners;
for I have spoken, says the
Lord GOD.

Lamentation over the King of Tyre

11 Moreover the word of the LORD
came to me: 12 Mortal, raise a lamentation over the king of Tyre, and say to
him, Thus says the Lord GOD:
You were the signet of
perfection,[m]
full of wisdom and perfect in
beauty.
13 You were in Eden, the garden of
God;
every precious stone was your
covering,
carnelian, chrysolite, and
moonstone,
beryl, onyx, and jasper,

sapphire,[n] turquoise, and
emerald;
and worked in gold were your
settings
and your engravings.[m]
On the day that you were
created
they were prepared.
14 With an anointed cherub as
guardian I placed you;[m]
you were on the holy
mountain of God;
you walked among the stones
of fire.
15 You were blameless in your
ways
from the day that you were
created,
until iniquity was found in
you.
16 In the abundance of your trade
you were filled with violence,
and you sinned;
so I cast you as a profane thing
from the mountain of God,
and the guardian cherub drove
you out
from among the stones of fire.
17 Your heart was proud because
of your beauty;
you corrupted your wisdom for
the sake of your splendor.
I cast you to the ground;
I exposed you before kings,
to feast their eyes on you.
18 By the multitude of your
iniquities,
in the unrighteousness of your
trade,
you profaned your sanctuaries.
So I brought out fire from within
you;
it consumed you,
and I turned you to ashes on the
earth
in the sight of all who saw
you.
19 All who know you among the
peoples
are appalled at you;
you have come to a dreadful end
and shall be no more forever.

Proclamation against Sidon

20 The word of the LORD came to
me: 21 Mortal, set your face toward
Si'don, and prophesy against it, 22 and
say, Thus says the Lord GOD:

[l] Or, as otherwise read, *Danel*
[m] Meaning of Heb uncertain   [n] Or *lapis lazuli*

I am against you, O Sī′don,
and I will gain glory in your
midst.
They shall know that I am the
LORD
when I execute judgments in
it,
and manifest my holiness in it;
23 for I will send pestilence into it,
and bloodshed into its streets;
and the dead shall fall in its
midst,
by the sword that is against it
on every side.
And they shall know that I am
the LORD.

24 The house of Israel shall no longer find a pricking brier or a piercing
thorn among all their neighbors who
have treated them with contempt. And
they shall know that I am the Lord
GOD.

Future Blessing for Israel

25 Thus says the Lord GOD: When I
gather the house of Israel from the
peoples among whom they are scattered, and manifest my holiness in
them in the sight of the nations, then
they shall settle on their own soil that
I gave to my servant Jacob. 26 They
shall live in safety in it, and shall build
houses and plant vineyards. They shall
live in safety, when I execute judgments upon all their neighbors who
have treated them with contempt. And
they shall know that I am the LORD
their God.

Proclamation against Egypt

29 In the tenth year, in the tenth
month, on the twelfth day of the
month, the word of the LORD came to
me: 2 Mortal, set your face against
Pharaoh king of Egypt, and prophesy
against him and against all Egypt;
3 speak, and say, Thus says the Lord
GOD:
I am against you,
Pharaoh king of Egypt,
the great dragon sprawling
in the midst of its channels,
saying, "My Nile is my own;
I made it for myself."
4 I will put hooks in your jaws,
and make the fish of your
channels stick to your
scales.
I will draw you up from your
channels,
with all the fish of your
channels

sticking to your scales.
5 I will fling you into the
wilderness,
you and all the fish of your
channels;
you shall fall in the open field,
and not be gathered and
buried.
To the animals of the earth and
to the birds of the air
I have given you as food.
6 Then all the inhabitants of Egypt
shall know
that I am the LORD
because you⁰ were a staff of
reed
to the house of Israel;
7 when they grasped you with the
hand, you broke,
and tore all their shoulders;
and when they leaned on you,
you broke,
and made all their legs
unsteady.ᵖ
8 Therefore, thus says the Lord
GOD: I will bring a sword upon you,
and will cut off from you human being
and animal; 9 and the land of Egypt
shall be a desolation and a waste. Then
they shall know that I am the LORD.
Because you�q said, "The Nile is
mine, and I made it," 10 therefore, I am
against you, and against your channels, and I will make the land of Egypt
an utter waste and desolation, from
Mig′dōl to Sȳ·ē′nē, as far as the border
of Ethiopia.ʳ 11 No human foot shall
pass through it, and no animal foot
shall pass through it; it shall be uninhabited forty years. 12 I will make the
land of Egypt a desolation among desolated countries; and her cities shall be
a desolation forty years among cities
that are laid waste. I will scatter the
Egyptians among the nations, and disperse them among the countries.
13 Further, thus says the Lord GOD:
At the end of forty years I will gather
the Egyptians from the peoples among
whom they were scattered; 14 and I will
restore the fortunes of Egypt, and
bring them back to the land of Path′-
ros, the land of their origin; and there
they shall be a lowly kingdom. 15 It
shall be the most lowly of the kingdoms, and never again exalt itself
above the nations; and I will make
them so small that they will never

⁰Gk Syr Vg: Heb they   ᵖSyr: Heb
stand   qGk Syr Vg: Heb he
ʳOr Nubia; Heb Cush

again rule over the nations. 16 The Egyptians[s] shall never again be the reliance of the house of Israel; they will recall their iniquity, when they turned to them for aid. Then they shall know that I am the Lord GOD.

Babylonia Will Plunder Egypt

17 In the twenty-seventh year, in the first month, on the first day of the month, the word of the LORD came to me: 18 Mortal, King Ne·bū·chad·rez'-zar of Babylon made his army labor hard against Tȳre; every head was made bald and every shoulder was rubbed bare; yet neither he nor his army got anything from Tȳre to pay for the labor that he had expended against it. 19 Therefore thus says the Lord GOD: I will give the land of Egypt to King Ne·bū·chad·rez'zar of Babylon; and he shall carry off its wealth and despoil it and plunder it; and it shall be the wages for his army. 20 I have given him the land of Egypt as his payment for which he labored, because they worked for me, says the Lord GOD.

21 On that day I will cause a horn to sprout up for the house of Israel, and I will open your lips among them. Then they shall know that I am the LORD.

Lamentation for Egypt

30 The word of the LORD came to me: 2 Mortal, prophesy, and say, Thus says the Lord GOD:
Wail, "Alas for the day!"
3 For a day is near,
  the day of the LORD is near;
it will be a day of clouds,
  a time of doom[t] for the
    nations.
4 A sword shall come upon Egypt,
  and anguish shall be in
    Ethiopia,[u]
when the slain fall in Egypt,
  and its wealth is carried away,
  and its foundations are torn
    down.
5 Ethiopia,[u] and Put, and Lud, and all Arabia, and Lib'ya,[v] and the people of the allied land[w] shall fall with them by the sword.

6 Thus says the LORD:
Those who support Egypt shall
    fall,
  and its proud might shall come
    down;
from Mig'dōl to Sȳ·ē'nē

they shall fall within it by the
    sword,
says the Lord GOD.
7 They shall be desolated among
    other desolated countries,
  and their cities shall lie among
    cities laid waste.
8 Then they shall know that I am
    the LORD,
  when I have set fire to Egypt,
  and all who help it are broken.
9 On that day, messengers shall go out from me in ships to terrify the unsuspecting Ethiopians;[x] and anguish shall come upon them on the day of Egypt's doom;[y] for it is coming!

10 Thus says the Lord GOD:
I will put an end to the hordes of
    Egypt,
  by the hand of King
    Ne·bū·chad·rez'zar of
    Babylon.
11 He and his people with him, the
    most terrible of the
    nations,
  shall be brought in to destroy
    the land;
and they shall draw their swords
    against Egypt,
  and fill the land with the slain.
12 I will dry up the channels,
  and will sell the land into the
    hand of evildoers;
I will bring desolation upon the
    land and everything in it
  by the hand of foreigners;
I the LORD have spoken.

13 Thus says the Lord GOD:
I will destroy the idols
  and put an end to the images
    in Memphis;
there shall no longer be a prince
    in the land of Egypt;
  so I will put fear in the land of
    Egypt.
14 I will make Path'ros a
    desolation,
  and will set fire to Zō'an,
  and will execute acts of
    judgment on Thēbes.
15 I will pour my wrath upon
    Pe·lū'si·um,
  the stronghold of Egypt,

s Heb It   t Heb lacks of doom
u Or Nubia; Heb Cush   v Compare Gk
Syr Vg: Heb Cub   w Meaning of Heb
uncertain   x Or Nubians; Heb Cush
y Heb the day of Egypt

and cut off the hordes of
    Thēbes.
16 I will set fire to Egypt;
    Pe·lū′si·um shall be in great
        agony;
    Thēbes shall be breached,
        and Memphis face adversaries
            by day.
17 The young men of On and of
        Pī-bē′seth shall fall by the
            sword;
    and the cities themselves[z]
        shall go into captivity.
18 At Te·haph′ne·hēs the day shall
        be dark,
    when I break there the
        dominion of Egypt,
    and its proud might shall come
        to an end;
    the city[a] shall be covered by a
        cloud,
    and its daughter-towns shall
        go into captivity.
19 Thus I will execute acts of
        judgment on Egypt.
    Then they shall know that I
        am the LORD.

Proclamation against Pharaoh

20 In the eleventh year, in the first
month, on the seventh day of the
month, the word of the LORD came to
me: [21] Mortal, I have broken the arm of
Pharaoh king of Egypt; it has not been
bound up for healing or wrapped with
a bandage, so that it may become
strong to wield the sword. [22] Therefore
thus says the Lord GOD: I am against
Pharaoh king of Egypt, and will break
his arms, both the strong arm and the
one that was broken; and I will make
the sword fall from his hand. [23] I will
scatter the Egyptians among the nations, and disperse them throughout
the lands. [24] I will strengthen the arms
of the king of Babylon, and put my
sword in his hand; but I will break the
arms of Pharaoh, and he will groan
before him with the groans of one mortally wounded. [25] I will strengthen the
arms of the king of Babylon, but the
arms of Pharaoh shall fall. And they
shall know that I am the LORD, when
I put my sword into the hand of the
king of Babylon. He shall stretch it out
against the land of Egypt, [26] and I will
scatter the Egyptians among the nations and disperse them throughout
the countries. Then they shall know
that I am the LORD.

The Lofty Cedar
(Cp Ezek 17.22–24)

31 In the eleventh year, in the
third month, on the first day of
the month, the word of the LORD came
to me: [2] Mortal, say to Pharaoh king of
Egypt and to his hordes:
    Whom are you like in your
        greatness?
3 Consider Assyria, a cedar of
        Lebanon,
    with fair branches and forest
        shade,
    and of great height,
        its top among the clouds.[b]
4 The waters nourished it,
        the deep made it grow tall,
    making its rivers flow[c]
        around the place it was
            planted,
    sending forth its streams
        to all the trees of the field.
5 So it towered high
        above all the trees of the field;
    its boughs grew large
        and its branches long,
    from abundant water in its
        shoots.
6 All the birds of the air
        made their nests in its boughs;
    under its branches all the
        animals of the field
    gave birth to their young;
    and in its shade
        all great nations lived.
7 It was beautiful in its greatness,
        in the length of its branches;
    for its roots went down
        to abundant water.
8 The cedars in the garden of God
        could not rival it,
    nor the fir trees equal its
        boughs;
    the plane trees were as nothing
        compared with its branches;
    no tree in the garden of God
        was like it in beauty.
9 I made it beautiful
        with its mass of branches,
    the envy of all the trees of Eden
        that were in the garden of
            God.
10 Therefore thus says the Lord
GOD: Because it[d] towered high and set
its top among the clouds,[b] and its
heart was proud of its height, [11] I gave
it into the hand of the prince of the

---

[z] Heb and they   [a] Heb she   [b] Gk: Heb
thick boughs   [c] Gk: Heb rivers going
[d] Syr Vg: Heb you

nations; he has dealt with it as its wickedness deserves. I have cast it out. [12]Foreigners from the most terrible of the nations have cut it down and left it. On the mountains and in all the valleys its branches have fallen, and its boughs lie broken in all the watercourses of the land; and all the peoples of the earth went away from its shade and left it.

[13] On its fallen trunk settle
    all the birds of the air,
    and among its boughs lodge
    all the wild animals.

[14]All this is in order that no trees by the waters may grow to lofty height or set their tops among the clouds,[e] and that no trees that drink water may reach up to them in height.

    For all of them are handed over
      to death,
    to the world below;
    along with all mortals,
      with those who go down to the
      Pit.

[15] Thus says the Lord GOD: On the day it went down to Shĕ′ōl I closed the deep over it and covered it; I restrained its rivers, and its mighty waters were checked. I clothed Lebanon in gloom for it, and all the trees of the field fainted because of it. [16]I made the nations quake at the sound of its fall, when I cast it down to Shĕ′ōl with those who go down to the Pit; and all the trees of Eden, the choice and best of Lebanon, all that were well watered, were consoled in the world below. [17]They also went down to Shĕ′ōl with it, to those killed by the sword, along with its allies,[f] those who lived in its shade among the nations.

[18] Which among the trees of Eden was like you in glory and in greatness? Now you shall be brought down with the trees of Eden to the world below; you shall lie among the uncircumcised, with those who are killed by the sword. This is Pharaoh and all his horde, says the Lord GOD.

Lamentation over Pharaoh and Egypt

32 In the twelfth year, in the twelfth month, on the first day of the month, the word of the LORD came to me: [2]Mortal, raise a lamentation over Pharaoh king of Egypt, and say to him:

    You consider yourself a lion
      among the nations,
    but you are like a dragon in
      the seas;

    you thrash about in your
      streams,
    trouble the water with your
      feet,
    and foul your[g] streams.

[3] Thus says the Lord GOD:
    In an assembly of many
      peoples
    I will throw my net over you;
    and I[h] will haul you up in my
      dragnet.

[4] I will throw you on the ground,
    on the open field I will fling
      you,
    and will cause all the birds of
      the air to settle on you,
      and I will let the wild animals
      of the whole earth gorge
      themselves with you.

[5] I will strew your flesh on the
      mountains,
    and fill the valleys with your
      carcass.[i]

[6] I will drench the land with your
      flowing blood
    up to the mountains,
    and the watercourses will be
      filled with you.

[7] When I blot you out, I will cover
      the heavens,
    and make their stars dark;
    I will cover the sun with a cloud,
      and the moon shall not give its
      light.

[8] All the shining lights of the
      heavens
    I will darken above you,
    and put darkness on your
      land,
          says the Lord GOD.

[9] I will trouble the hearts of many
      peoples,
    as I carry you captive[j] among
      the nations,
    into countries you have not
      known.

[10] I will make many peoples
      appalled at you;
    their kings shall shudder
      because of you.
    When I brandish my sword
      before them,
    they shall tremble every
      moment
    for their lives, each one of them,
      on the day of your downfall.

[11] For thus says the Lord GOD:

[e]Gk: Heb *thick boughs*   [f]Heb *its arms*
[g]Heb *their*   [h]Gk Vg: Heb *they*
[i]Symmachus Syr Vg: Heb *your height*
[j]Gk: Heb *bring your destruction*

The sword of the king of
Babylon shall come against
you.
12 I will cause your hordes to fall
by the swords of mighty ones,
all of them most terrible
among the nations.
They shall bring to ruin the
pride of Egypt,
and all its hordes shall perish.
13 I will destroy all its livestock
from beside abundant waters;
and no human foot shall trouble
them any more,
nor shall the hoofs of cattle
trouble them.
14 Then I will make their waters
clear,
and cause their streams to run
like oil, says the Lord GOD.
15 When I make the land of Egypt
desolate
and when the land is stripped
of all that fills it,
when I strike down all who live
in it,
then they shall know that I am
the LORD.
16 This is a lamentation; it shall be
chanted.
The women of the nations
shall chant it.
Over Egypt and all its hordes
they shall chant it,
says the Lord GOD.

Dirge over Egypt

17 In the twelfth year, in the first
month,[k] on the fifteenth day of the
month, the word of the LORD came to
me:
18 Mortal, wail over the hordes of
Egypt,
and send them down,
with Egypt[l] and the daughters
of majestic nations,
to the world below,
with those who go down to the
Pit.
19 "Whom do you surpass in
beauty?
Go down! Be laid to rest with
the uncircumcised!"
20 They shall fall among those who are
killed by the sword. Egypt[m] has been
handed over to the sword; carry away
both it and its hordes. 21 The mighty
chiefs shall speak of them, with their
helpers, out of the midst of Shē'ōl:
"They have come down, they lie still,
the uncircumcised, killed by the
sword."

22 Assyria is there, and all its company, their graves all around it, all of
them killed, fallen by the sword.
23 Their graves are set in the uttermost
parts of the Pit. Its company is all
around its grave, all of them killed,
fallen by the sword, who spread terror
in the land of the living.
24 Ē'lam is there, and all its hordes
around its grave; all of them killed,
fallen by the sword, who went down
uncircumcised into the world below,
who spread terror in the land of the
living. They bear their shame with
those who go down to the Pit. 25 They
have made Ē'lam[l] a bed among the
slain with all its hordes, their graves
all around it, all of them uncircumcised, killed by the sword; for terror of
them was spread in the land of the living, and they bear their shame with
those who go down to the Pit; they are
placed among the slain.
26 Mē'shech and Tū'bal are there,
and all their multitude, their graves all
around them, all of them uncircumcised, killed by the sword; for they
spread terror in the land of the living.
27 And they do not lie with the fallen
warriors of long ago[n] who went down
to Shē'ōl with their weapons of war,
whose swords were laid under their
heads, and whose shields[o] are upon
their bones; for the terror of the warriors was in the land of the living. 28 So
you shall be broken and lie among the
uncircumcised, with those who are
killed by the sword.
29 Ē'dom is there, its kings and all
its princes, who for all their might are
laid with those who are killed by the
sword; they lie with the uncircumcised, with those who go down to the
Pit.
30 The princes of the north are
there, all of them, and all the Sī·dō'-
ni·ans, who have gone down in shame
with the slain, for all the terror that
they caused by their might; they lie uncircumcised with those who are killed
by the sword, and bear their shame
with those who go down to the Pit.
31 When Pharaoh sees them, he
will be consoled for all his hordes—
Pharaoh and all his army, killed by the
sword, says the Lord GOD. 32 For he[p]
spread terror in the land of the living;

k Gk: Heb lacks *in the first month*
l Heb *it*   m Heb *It*   n Gk Old Latin: Heb
of the uncircumcised   o Cn: Heb
iniquities   p Cn: Heb *I*

therefore he shall be laid to rest among the uncircumcised, with those who are slain by the sword—Pharaoh and all his multitude, says the Lord GOD.

Ezekiel Israel's Sentry

33 The word of the LORD came to me: [2] O Mortal, speak to your people and say to them, If I bring the sword upon a land, and the people of the land take one of their number as their sentinel; [3] and if the sentinel sees the sword coming upon the land and blows the trumpet and warns the people; [4] then if any who hear the sound of the trumpet do not take warning, and the sword comes and takes them away, their blood shall be upon their own heads. [5] They heard the sound of the trumpet and did not take warning; their blood shall be upon themselves. But if they had taken warning, they would have saved their lives. [6] But if the sentinel sees the sword coming and does not blow the trumpet, so that the people are not warned, and the sword comes and takes any of them, they are taken away in their iniquity, but their blood I will require at the sentinel's hand.

[7] So you, mortal, I have made a sentinel for the house of Israel; whenever you hear a word from my mouth, you shall give them warning from me. [8] If I say to the wicked, "O wicked ones, you shall surely die," and you do not speak to warn the wicked to turn from their ways, the wicked shall die in their iniquity, but their blood I will require at your hand. [9] But if you warn the wicked to turn from their ways, and they do not turn from their ways, the wicked shall die in their iniquity, but you will have saved your life.

God's Justice and Mercy

[10] Now you, mortal, say to the house of Israel, Thus you have said: "Our transgressions and our sins weigh upon us, and we waste away because of them; how then can we live?" [11] Say to them, As I live, says the Lord GOD, I have no pleasure in the death of the wicked, but that the wicked turn from their ways and live; turn back, turn back from your evil ways; for why will you die, O house of Israel? [12] And you, mortal, say to your people, The righteousness of the righteous shall not save them when they transgress; and as for the wickedness of the wicked, it shall not make them stumble when they turn from their wickedness; and the righteous shall not be able to live by their righteousness[q] when they sin. [13] Though I say to the righteous that they shall surely live, yet if they trust in their righteousness and commit iniquity, none of their righteous deeds shall be remembered; but in the iniquity that they have committed they shall die. [14] Again, though I say to the wicked, "You shall surely die," yet if they turn from their sin and do what is lawful and right— [15] if the wicked restore the pledge, give back what they have taken by robbery, and walk in the statutes of life, committing no iniquity—they shall surely live, they shall not die. [16] None of the sins that they have committed shall be remembered against them; they have done what is lawful and right, they shall surely live.

[17] Yet your people say, "The way of the Lord is not just," when it is their own way that is not just. [18] When the righteous turn from their righteousness, and commit iniquity, they shall die for it.[r] [19] And when the wicked turn from their wickedness, and do what is lawful and right, they shall live by it.[r] [20] Yet you say, "The way of the Lord is not just." O house of Israel, I will judge all of you according to your ways!

The Fall of Jerusalem

[21] In the twelfth year of our exile, in the tenth month, on the fifth day of the month, someone who had escaped from Jerusalem came to me and said, "The city has fallen." [22] Now the hand of the LORD had been upon me the evening before the fugitive came; but he had opened my mouth by the time the fugitive came to me in the morning; so my mouth was opened, and I was no longer unable to speak.

The Survivors in Judah

[23] The word of the LORD came to me: [24] Mortal, the inhabitants of these waste places in the land of Israel keep saying, "Abraham was only one man, yet he got possession of the land; but we are many; the land is surely given us to possess." [25] Therefore say to them, Thus says the Lord GOD: You eat flesh with the blood, and lift up your eyes to your idols, and shed blood; shall you then possess the land?

[q]Heb *by it*   [r]Heb *them*

26 You depend on your swords, you commit abominations, and each of you defiles his neighbor's wife; shall you then possess the land? 27 Say this to them, Thus says the Lord GOD: As I live, surely those who are in the waste places shall fall by the sword; and those who are in the open field I will give to the wild animals to be devoured; and those who are in strongholds and in caves shall die by pestilence. 28 I will make the land a desolation and a waste, and its proud might shall come to an end; and the mountains of Israel shall be so desolate that no one will pass through. 29 Then they shall know that I am the LORD, when I have made the land a desolation and a waste because of all their abominations that they have committed.

30 As for you, mortal, your people who talk together about you by the walls, and at the doors of the houses, say to one another, each to a neighbor, "Come and hear what the word is that comes from the LORD." 31 They come to you as people come, and they sit before you as my people, and they hear your words, but they will not obey them. For flattery is on their lips, but their heart is set on their gain. 32 To them you are like a singer of love songs,s one who has a beautiful voice and plays well on an instrument; they hear what you say, but they will not do it. 33 When this comes — and come it will! — then they shall know that a prophet has been among them.

Israel's False Shepherds

34 The word of the LORD came to me: 2 Mortal, prophesy against the shepherds of Israel: prophesy, and say to them — to the shepherds: Thus says the Lord GOD: Ah, you shepherds of Israel who have been feeding yourselves! Should not shepherds feed the sheep? 3 You eat the fat, you clothe yourselves with the wool, you slaughter the fatlings; but you do not feed the sheep. 4 You have not strengthened the weak, you have not healed the sick, you have not bound up the injured, you have not brought back the strayed, you have not sought the lost, but with force and harshness you have ruled them. 5 So they were scattered, because there was no shepherd; and scattered, they became food for all the wild animals. 6 My sheep were scattered, they wandered over all the mountains and on every high hill; my sheep were scattered over all the face of the earth, with no one to search or seek for them.

7 Therefore, you shepherds, hear the word of the LORD: 8 As I live, says the Lord GOD, because my sheep have become a prey, and my sheep have become food for all the wild animals, since there was no shepherd; and because my shepherds have not searched for my sheep, but the shepherds have fed themselves, and have not fed my sheep; 9 therefore, you shepherds, hear the word of the LORD: 10 Thus says the Lord GOD, I am against the shepherds; and I will demand my sheep at their hand, and put a stop to their feeding the sheep; no longer shall the shepherds feed themselves. I will rescue my sheep from their mouths, so that they may not be food for them.

God, the True Shepherd

11 For thus says the Lord GOD: I myself will search for my sheep, and will seek them out. 12 As shepherds seek out their flocks when they are among their scattered sheep, so I will seek out my sheep. I will rescue them from all the places to which they have been scattered on a day of clouds and thick darkness. 13 I will bring them out from the peoples and gather them from the countries, and will bring them into their own land; and I will feed them on the mountains of Israel, by the watercourses, and in all the inhabited parts of the land. 14 I will feed them with good pasture, and the mountain heights of Israel shall be their pasture; there they shall lie down in good grazing land, and they shall feed on rich pasture on the mountains of Israel. 15 I myself will be the shepherd of my sheep, and I will make them lie down, says the Lord GOD. 16 I will seek the lost, and I will bring back the strayed, and I will bind up the injured, and I will strengthen the weak, but the fat and the strong I will destroy. I will feed them with justice.

17 As for you, my flock, thus says the Lord GOD: I shall judge between sheep and sheep, between rams and goats: 18 Is it not enough for you to feed on the good pasture, but you must tread down with your feet the rest of your pasture? When you drink of clear water, must you foul the rest with your feet? 19 And must my sheep eat what

s Cn: Heb *like a love song*

you have trodden with your feet, and drink what you have fouled with your feet?

20 Therefore, thus says the Lord GOD to them: I myself will judge between the fat sheep and the lean sheep. 21 Because you pushed with flank and shoulder, and butted at all the weak animals with your horns until you scattered them far and wide, 22 I will save my flock, and they shall no longer be ravaged; and I will judge between sheep and sheep.

23 I will set up over them one shepherd, my servant David, and he shall feed them: he shall feed them and be their shepherd. 24 And I, the LORD, will be their God, and my servant David shall be prince among them; I, the LORD, have spoken.

25 I will make with them a covenant of peace and banish wild animals from the land, so that they may live in the wild and sleep in the woods securely. 26 I will make them and the region around my hill a blessing; and I will send down the showers in their season; they shall be showers of blessing. 27 The trees of the field shall yield their fruit, and the earth shall yield its increase. They shall be secure on their soil; and they shall know that I am the LORD, when I break the bars of their yoke, and save them from the hands of those who enslaved them. 28 They shall no more be plunder for the nations, nor shall the animals of the land devour them; they shall live in safety, and no one shall make them afraid. 29 I will provide for them a splendid vegetation so that they shall no more be consumed with hunger in the land, and no longer suffer the insults of the nations. 30 They shall know that I, the LORD their God, am with them, and that they, the house of Israel, are my people, says the Lord GOD. 31 You are my sheep, the sheep of my pasture[t] and I am your God, says the Lord GOD.

Judgment on Mount Seir

35 The word of the LORD came to me: 2 Mortal, set your face against Mount Sē'ir, and prophesy against it, 3 and say to it, Thus says the Lord GOD:

I am against you, Mount Sē'ir;
    I stretch out my hand against
        you
    to make you a desolation and
        a waste.
4 I lay your towns in ruins;

you shall become a desolation,
    and you shall know that I am
        the LORD.

5 Because you cherished an ancient enmity, and gave over the people of Israel to the power of the sword at the time of their calamity, at the time of their final punishment; 6 therefore, as I live, says the Lord GOD, I will prepare you for blood, and blood shall pursue you; since you did not hate bloodshed, bloodshed shall pursue you. 7 I will make Mount Sē'ir a waste and a desolation; and I will cut off from it all who come and go. 8 I will fill its mountains with the slain; on your hills and in your valleys and in all your watercourses those killed with the sword shall fall. 9 I will make you a perpetual desolation, and your cities shall never be inhabited. Then you shall know that I am the LORD.

10 Because you said, "These two nations and these two countries shall be mine, and we will take possession of them,"—although the LORD was there— 11 therefore, as I live, says the Lord GOD, I will deal with you according to the anger and envy that you showed because of your hatred against them; and I will make myself known among you,[u] when I judge you. 12 You shall know that I, the LORD, have heard all the abusive speech that you uttered against the mountains of Israel, saying, "They are laid desolate, they are given us to devour." 13 And you magnified yourselves against me with your mouth, and multiplied your words against me; I heard it. 14 Thus says the Lord GOD: As the whole earth rejoices, I will make you desolate. 15 As you rejoiced over the inheritance of the house of Israel, because it was desolate, so I will deal with you; you shall be desolate, Mount Sē'ir, and all Ē'dom, all of it. Then they shall know that I am the LORD.

Blessing on Israel

36 And you, mortal, prophesy to the mountains of Israel, and say: O mountains of Israel, hear the word of the LORD. 2 Thus says the Lord GOD: Because the enemy said of you, "Aha!" and, "The ancient heights have become our possession," 3 therefore prophesy, and say: Thus says the Lord GOD: Because they made you desolate

---

[t] Gk OL: Heb *pasture, you are people*
[u] Gk: Heb *them*

indeed, and crushed you from all sides, so that you became the possession of the rest of the nations, and you became an object of gossip and slander among the people; 4therefore, O mountains of Israel, hear the word of the Lord GOD: Thus says the Lord GOD to the mountains and the hills, the watercourses and the valleys, the desolate wastes and the deserted towns, which have become a source of plunder and an object of derision to the rest of the nations all around; 5therefore thus says the Lord GOD: I am speaking in my hot jealousy against the rest of the nations, and against all É'dom, who, with wholehearted joy and utter contempt, took my land as their possession, because of its pasture, to plunder it. 6Therefore prophesy concerning the land of Israel, and say to the mountains and hills, to the watercourses and valleys, Thus says the Lord GOD: I am speaking in my jealous wrath, because you have suffered the insults of the nations; 7therefore thus says the Lord GOD: I swear that the nations that are all around you shall themselves suffer insults.

8 But you, O mountains of Israel, shall shoot out your branches, and yield your fruit to my people Israel; for they shall soon come home. 9See now, I am for you; I will turn to you, and you shall be tilled and sown; 10and I will multiply your population, the whole house of Israel, all of it; the towns shall be inhabited and the waste places rebuilt; 11and I will multiply human beings and animals upon you. They shall increase and be fruitful; and I will cause you to be inhabited as in your former times, and will do more good to you than ever before. Then you shall know that I am the LORD. 12I will lead people upon you—my people Israel—and they shall possess you, and you shall be their inheritance. No longer shall you bereave them of children.

13 Thus says the Lord GOD: Because they say to you, "You devour people, and you bereave your nation of children," 14therefore you shall no longer devour people and no longer bereave your nation of children, says the Lord GOD; 15and no longer will I let you hear the insults of the nations, no longer shall you bear the disgrace of the peoples; and no longer shall you cause your nation to stumble, says the Lord GOD.

The Renewal of Israel

16 The word of the LORD came to me: 17Mortal, when the house of Israel lived on their own soil, they defiled it with their ways and their deeds; their conduct in my sight was like the uncleanness of a woman in her menstrual period. 18So I poured out my wrath upon them for the blood that they had shed upon the land, and for the idols with which they had defiled it. 19I scattered them among the nations, and they were dispersed through the countries; in accordance with their conduct and their deeds I judged them. 20But when they came to the nations, wherever they came, they profaned my holy name, in that it was said of them, "These are the people of the LORD, and yet they had to go out of his land." 21But I had concern for my holy name, which the house of Israel had profaned among the nations to which they came.

22 Therefore say to the house of Israel, Thus says the Lord GOD: It is not for your sake, O house of Israel, that I am about to act, but for the sake of my holy name, which you have profaned among the nations to which you came. 23I will sanctify my great name, which has been profaned among the nations, and which you have profaned among them; and the nations shall know that I am the LORD, says the Lord GOD, when through you I display my holiness before their eyes. 24I will take you from the nations, and gather you from all the countries, and bring you into your own land. 25I will sprinkle clean water upon you, and you shall be clean from all your uncleannesses, and from all your idols I will cleanse you. 26A new heart I will give you, and a new spirit I will put within you; and I will remove from your body the heart of stone and give you a heart of flesh. 27I will put my spirit within you, and make you follow my statutes and be careful to observe my ordinances. 28Then you shall live in the land that I gave to your ancestors; and you shall be my people, and I will be your God. 29I will save you from all your uncleannesses, and I will summon the grain and make it abundant and lay no famine upon you. 30I will make the fruit of the tree and the produce of the field abundant, so that you may never again suffer the disgrace of famine among the nations. 31Then you shall remember your evil ways, and your dealings that were not

good; and you shall loathe yourselves for your iniquities and your abominable deeds. ³²It is not for your sake that I will act, says the Lord GOD; let that be known to you. Be ashamed and dismayed for your ways, O house of Israel.

33 Thus says the Lord GOD: On the day that I cleanse you from all your iniquities, I will cause the towns to be inhabited, and the waste places shall be rebuilt. ³⁴The land that was desolate shall be tilled, instead of being the desolation that it was in the sight of all who passed by. ³⁵And they will say, "This land that was desolate has become like the garden of Eden; and the waste and desolate and ruined towns are now inhabited and fortified." ³⁶Then the nations that are left all around you shall know that I, the LORD, have rebuilt the ruined places, and replanted that which was desolate; I, the LORD, have spoken, and I will do it.

37 Thus says the Lord GOD: I will also let the house of Israel ask me to do this for them: to increase their population like a flock. ³⁸Like the flock for sacrifices,ᵛ like the flock at Jerusalem during her appointed festivals, so shall the ruined towns be filled with flocks of people. Then they shall know that I am the LORD.

The Valley of Dry Bones

37 The hand of the LORD came upon me, and he brought me out by the spirit of the LORD and set me down in the middle of a valley; it was full of bones. ²He led me all around them; there were very many lying in the valley, and they were very dry. ³He said to me, "Mortal, can these bones live?" I answered, "O Lord GOD, you know." ⁴Then he said to me, "Prophesy to these bones, and say to them: O dry bones, hear the word of the LORD. ⁵Thus says the Lord GOD to these bones: I will cause breathʷ to enter you, and you shall live. ⁶I will lay sinews on you, and will cause flesh to come upon you, and cover you with skin, and put breathʷ in you, and you shall live; and you shall know that I am the LORD."

7 So I prophesied as I had been commanded; and as I prophesied, suddenly there was a noise, a rattling, and the bones came together, bone to its bone. ⁸I looked, and there were sinews on them, and flesh had come upon

them, and skin had covered them; but there was no breath in them. ⁹Then he said to me, "Prophesy to the breath, prophesy, mortal, and say to the breath:ˣ Thus says the Lord GOD: Come from the four winds, O breath,ˣ and breathe upon these slain, that they may live." ¹⁰I prophesied as he commanded me, and the breath came into them, and they lived, and stood on their feet, a vast multitude.

11 Then he said to me, "Mortal, these bones are the whole house of Israel. They say, 'Our bones are dried up, and our hope is lost; we are cut off completely.' ¹²Therefore prophesy, and say to them, Thus says the Lord GOD: I am going to open your graves, and bring you up from your graves, O my people; and I will bring you back to the land of Israel. ¹³And you shall know that I am the LORD, when I open your graves, and bring you up from your graves, O my people. ¹⁴I will put my spirit within you, and you shall live, and I will place you on your own soil; then you shall know that I, the LORD, have spoken and will act," says the LORD.

The Two Sticks

15 The word of the LORD came to me: ¹⁶Mortal, take a stick and write on it, "For Judah, and the Israelites associated with it"; then take another stick and write on it, "For Joseph (the stick of Éʹphra·im) and all the house of Israel associated with it"; ¹⁷and join them together into one stick, so that they may become one in your hand. ¹⁸And when your people say to you, "Will you not show us what you mean by these?" ¹⁹say to them, Thus says the Lord GOD: I am about to take the stick of Joseph (which is in the hand of Éʹphra·im) and the tribes of Israel associated with it; and I will put the stick of Judah upon it,ʸ and make them one stick, in order that they may be one in my hand. ²⁰When the sticks on which you write are in your hand before their eyes, ²¹then say to them, Thus says the Lord GOD: I will take the people of Israel from the nations among which they have gone, and will gather them from every quarter, and bring them to their own land. ²²I will make them one

---

ᵛHeb *flock of holy things*   ʷOr *spirit*
ˣOr *wind* or *spirit*   ʸHeb *I will put them upon it*

nation in the land, on the mountains of Israel; and one king shall be king over them all. Never again shall they be two nations, and never again shall they be divided into two kingdoms. 23 They shall never again defile themselves with their idols and their detestable things, or with any of their transgressions. I will save them from all the apostasies into which they have fallen,z and will cleanse them. Then they shall be my people, and I will be their GOD.

24 My servant David shall be king over them; and they shall all have one shepherd. They shall follow my ordinances and be careful to observe my statutes. 25 They shall live in the land that I gave to my servant Jacob, in which your ancestors lived; they and their children and their children's children shall live there forever; and my servant David shall be their prince forever. 26 I will make a covenant of peace with them; it shall be an everlasting covenant with them; and I will blessa them and multiply them, and will set my sanctuary among them forevermore. 27 My dwelling place shall be with them; and I will be their God, and they shall be my people. 28 Then the nations shall know that I the LORD sanctify Israel, when my sanctuary is among them forevermore.

Invasion by Gog

38 The word of the LORD came to me: 2 Mortal, set your face toward Gog, of the land of Mā'gog, the chief prince of Mē'shech and Tū'bal. Prophesy against him 3 and say: Thus says the Lord GOD: I am against you, O Gog, chief prince of Mē'shech and Tū'bal; 4 I will turn you around and put hooks into your jaws, and I will lead you out with all your army, horses and horsemen, all of them clothed in full armor, a great company, all of them with shield and buckler, wielding swords. 5 Persia, Ethiopia,b and Put are with them, all of them with buckler and helmet; 6 Gō'mer and all its troops; Beth-tō·gar'mah from the remotest parts of the north with all its troops — many peoples are with you.

7 Be ready and keep ready, you and all the companies that are assembled around you, and hold yourselves in reserve for them. 8 After many days you shall be mustered; in the latter years you shall go against a land restored from war, a land where people were gathered from many nations on the mountains of Israel, which had long lain waste; its people were brought out from the nations and now are living in safety, all of them. 9 You shall advance, coming on like a storm; you shall be like a cloud covering the land, you and all your troops, and many peoples with you.

10 Thus says the Lord GOD: On that day thoughts will come into your mind, and you will devise an evil scheme. 11 You will say, "I will go up against the land of unwalled villages; I will fall upon the quiet people who live in safety, all of them living without walls, and having no bars or gates"; 12 to seize spoil and carry off plunder; to assail the waste places that are now inhabited, and the people who were gathered from the nations, who are acquiring cattle and goods, who live at the centerc of the earth. 13 Shē'ba and Dē'dan and the merchants of Tar'shish and all its young warriorsd will say to you, "Have you come to seize spoil? Have you assembled your horde to carry off plunder, to carry away silver and gold, to take away cattle and goods, to seize a great amount of booty?"

14 Therefore, mortal, prophesy, and say to Gog: Thus says the Lord GOD: On that day when my people Israel are living securely, you will rouse yourselfe 15 and come from your place out of the remotest parts of the north, you and many peoples with you, all of them riding on horses, a great horde, a mighty army; 16 you will come up against my people Israel, like a cloud covering the earth. In the latter days I will bring you against my land, so that the nations may know me, when through you, O Gog, I display my holiness before their eyes.

Judgment on Gog

17 Thus says the Lord GOD: Are you he of whom I spoke in former days by my servants the prophets of Israel, who in those days prophesied for years that I would bring you against them? 18 On that day, when Gog comes against the land of Israel, says the Lord GOD, my wrath shall be aroused.

z Another reading is from all the settlements in which they have sinned
a Tg: Heb give   b Or Nubia; Heb Cush
c Heb navel   d Heb young lions
e Gk: Heb will you not know?

19 For in my jealousy and in my blazing wrath I declare: On that day there shall be a great shaking in the land of Israel; 20 the fish of the sea, and the birds of the air, and the animals of the field, and all creeping things that creep on the ground, and all human beings that are on the face of the earth, shall quake at my presence, and the mountains shall be thrown down, and the cliffs shall fall, and every wall shall tumble to the ground. 21 I will summon the sword against Gog*f* in*g* all my mountains, says the Lord GOD; the swords of all will be against their comrades. 22 With pestilence and bloodshed I will enter into judgment with him; and I will pour down torrential rains and hailstones, fire and sulfur, upon him and his troops and the many peoples that are with him. 23 So I will display my greatness and my holiness and make myself known in the eyes of many nations. Then they shall know that I am the LORD.

Gog's Armies Destroyed

39 And you, mortal, prophesy against Gog, and say: Thus says the Lord GOD: I am against you, O Gog, chief prince of Mē'shech and Tū'bal! 2 I will turn you around and drive you forward, and bring you up from the remotest parts of the north, and lead you against the mountains of Israel. 3 I will strike your bow from your left hand, and will make your arrows drop out of your right hand. 4 You shall fall upon the mountains of Israel, you and all your troops and the peoples that are with you; I will give you to birds of prey of every kind and to the wild animals to be devoured. 5 You shall fall in the open field; for I have spoken, says the Lord GOD. 6 I will send fire on Mā'gog and on those who live securely in the coastlands; and they shall know that I am the LORD.

7 My holy name I will make known among my people Israel; and I will not let my holy name be profaned any more; and the nations shall know that I am the LORD, the Holy One in Israel. 8 It has come! It has happened, says the Lord GOD. This is the day of which I have spoken.

9 Then those who live in the towns of Israel will go out and make fires of the weapons and burn them — bucklers and shields, bows and arrows, handpikes and spears — and they will make fires of them for seven years. 10 They will not need to take wood out of the field or cut down any trees in the forests, for they will make their fires of the weapons; they will despoil those who despoiled them, and plunder those who plundered them, says the Lord GOD.

The Burial of Gog

11 On that day I will give to Gog a place for burial in Israel, the Valley of the Travelers*h* east of the sea; it shall block the path of the travelers, for there Gog and all his horde will be buried; it shall be called the Valley of Hā'-mon-gog.*i* 12 Seven months the house of Israel shall spend burying them, in order to cleanse the land. 13 All the people of the land shall bury them; and it will bring them honor on the day that I show my glory, says the Lord GOD. 14 They will set apart men to pass through the land regularly and bury any invaders*j* who remain on the face of the land, so as to cleanse it; for seven months they shall make their search. 15 As the searchers*j* pass through the land, anyone who sees a human bone shall set up a sign by it, until the buriers have buried it in the Valley of Hā'mon-gog.*i* 16 (A city Ha·mō'nah*k* is there also.) Thus they shall cleanse the land.

17 As for you, mortal, thus says the Lord GOD: Speak to the birds of every kind and to all the wild animals: Assemble and come, gather from all around to the sacrificial feast that I am preparing for you, a great sacrificial feast on the mountains of Israel, and you shall eat flesh and drink blood. 18 You shall eat the flesh of the mighty, and drink the blood of the princes of the earth — of rams, of lambs, and of goats, of bulls, all of them fatlings of Bā'shan. 19 You shall eat fat until you are filled, and drink blood until you are drunk, at the sacrificial feast that I am preparing for you. 20 And you shall be filled at my table with horses and charioteers,*l* with warriors and all kinds of soldiers, says the Lord GOD.

Israel Restored to the Land

21 I will display my glory among the nations; and all the nations shall see my judgment that I have executed,

---

f Heb *him*   *g* Heb *to* or *for*   *h* Or *of the Abarim*   *i* That is, *the Horde of Gog*
j Heb *travelers*   *k* That is *The Horde*
l Heb *chariots*

and my hand that I have laid on them. [22] The house of Israel shall know that I am the LORD their God, from that day forward. [23] And the nations shall know that the house of Israel went into captivity for their iniquity, because they dealt treacherously with me. So I hid my face from them and gave them into the hand of their adversaries, and they all fell by the sword. [24] I dealt with them according to their uncleanness and their transgressions, and hid my face from them.

25 Therefore thus says the Lord GOD: Now I will restore the fortunes of Jacob, and have mercy on the whole house of Israel; and I will be jealous for my holy name. [26] They shall forget[m] their shame, and all the treachery they have practiced against me, when they live securely in their land with no one to make them afraid, [27] when I have brought them back from the peoples and gathered them from their enemies' lands, and through them have displayed my holiness in the sight of many nations. [28] Then they shall know that I am the LORD their God because I sent them into exile among the nations, and then gathered them into their own land. I will leave none of them behind; [29] and I will never again hide my face from them, when I pour out my spirit upon the house of Israel, says the Lord GOD.

The Vision of the New Temple

40 In the twenty-fifth year of our exile, at the beginning of the year, on the tenth day of the month, in the fourteenth year after the city was struck down, on that very day, the hand of the LORD was upon me, and he brought me there. [2] He brought me, in visions of God, to the land of Israel, and set me down upon a very high mountain, on which was a structure like a city to the south. [3] When he brought me there, a man was there, whose appearance shone like bronze, with a linen cord and a measuring reed in his hand; and he was standing in the gateway. [4] The man said to me, "Mortal, look closely and listen attentively, and set your mind upon all that I shall show you, for you were brought here in order that I might show it to you; declare all that you see to the house of Israel."

5 Now there was a wall all around the outside of the temple area. The length of the measuring reed in the man's hand was six long cubits, each being a cubit and a handbreadth in length; so he measured the thickness of the wall, one reed; and the height, one reed. [6] Then he went into the gateway facing east, going up its steps, and measured the threshold of the gate, one reed deep.[n] There were [7] recesses, and each recess was one reed wide and one reed deep; and the space between the recesses, five cubits; and the threshold of the gate by the vestibule of the gate at the inner end was one reed deep. [8] Then he measured the inner vestibule of the gateway, one cubit. [9] Then he measured the vestibule of the gateway, eight cubits; and its pilasters, two cubits; and the vestibule of the gate was at the inner end. [10] There were three recesses on either side of the east gate; the three were of the same size; and the pilasters on either side were of the same size. [11] Then he measured the width of the opening of the gateway, ten cubits; and the width of the gateway, thirteen cubits. [12] There was a barrier before the recesses, one cubit on either side; and the recesses were six cubits on either side. [13] Then he measured the gate from the back[o] of the one recess to the back[o] of the other, a width of twenty-five cubits, from wall to wall.[p] [14] He measured[q] also the vestibule, twenty cubits; and the gate next to the pilaster on every side of the court.[r] [15] From the front of the gate at the entrance to the end of the inner vestibule of the gate was fifty cubits. [16] The recesses and their pilasters had windows, with shutters[r] on the inside of the gateway all around, and the vestibules also had windows on the inside all around; and on the pilasters were palm trees.

17 Then he brought me into the outer court; there were chambers there, and a pavement, all around the court; thirty chambers fronted on the pavement. [18] The pavement ran along the side of the gates, corresponding to the length of the gates; this was the lower pavement. [19] Then he measured the distance from the inner front of[s]

[m] Another reading is *They shall bear*
[n] Heb *deep, and one threshold, one reed deep*   [o] Gk: Heb *roof*   [p] Heb *opening facing opening*   [q] Heb *made*
[r] Meaning of Heb uncertain   [s] Compare Gk: Heb *from before*

the lower gate to the outer front of the inner court, one hundred cubits.[t]

20 Then he measured the gate of the outer court that faced north — its depth and width. [21]Its recesses, three on either side, and its pilasters and its vestibule were of the same size as those of the first gate; its depth was fifty cubits, and its width twenty-five cubits. [22]Its windows, its vestibule, and its palm trees were of the same size as those of the gate that faced toward the east. Seven steps led up to it; and its vestibule was on the inside.[u] [23]Opposite the gate on the north, as on the east, was a gate to the inner court; he measured from gate to gate, one hundred cubits.

24 Then he led me toward the south, and there was a gate on the south; and he measured its pilasters and its vestibule; they had the same dimensions as the others. [25]There were windows all around in it and in its vestibule, like the windows of the others; its depth was fifty cubits, and its width twenty-five cubits. [26]There were seven steps leading up to it; its vestibule was on the inside.[u] It had palm trees on its pilasters, one on either side. [27]There was a gate on the south of the inner court; and he measured from gate to gate toward the south, one hundred cubits.

28 Then he brought me to the inner court by the south gate, and he measured the south gate; it was of the same dimensions as the others. [29]Its recesses, its pilasters, and its vestibule were of the same size as the others; and there were windows all around in it and in its vestibule; its depth was fifty cubits, and its width twenty-five cubits. [30]There were vestibules all around, twenty-five cubits deep and five cubits wide. [31]Its vestibule faced the outer court, and palm trees were on its pilasters, and its stairway had eight steps.

32 Then he brought me to the inner court on the east side, and he measured the gate; it was of the same size as the others. [33]Its recesses, its pilasters, and its vestibule were of the same dimensions as the others; and there were windows all around in it and in its vestibule; its depth was fifty cubits, and its width twenty-five cubits. [34]Its vestibule faced the outer court, and it had palm trees on its pilasters, on either side; and its stairway had eight steps.

35 Then he brought me to the north gate, and he measured it; it had the same dimensions as the others. [36]Its recesses, its pilasters, and its vestibule were of the same size as the others;[v] and it had windows all around. Its depth was fifty cubits, and its width twenty-five cubits. [37]Its vestibule[w] faced the outer court, and it had palm trees on its pilasters, on either side; and its stairway had eight steps.

38 There was a chamber with its door in the vestibule of the gate,[x] where the burnt offering was to be washed. [39]And in the vestibule of the gate were two tables on either side, on which the burnt offering and the sin offering and the guilt offering were to be slaughtered. [40]On the outside of the vestibule[y] at the entrance of the north gate were two tables; and on the other side of the vestibule of the gate were two tables. [41]Four tables were on the inside, and four tables on the outside of the side of the gate, eight tables, on which the sacrifices were to be slaughtered. [42]There were also four tables of hewn stone for the burnt offering, a cubit and a half long, and one cubit and a half wide, and one cubit high, on which the instruments were to be laid with which the burnt offerings and the sacrifices were slaughtered. [43]There were pegs, one handbreadth long, fastened all around the inside. And on the tables the flesh of the offering was to be laid.

44 On the outside of the inner gateway there were chambers for the singers in the inner court, one[z] at the side of the north gate facing south, the other at the side of the east gate facing north. [45]He said to me, "This chamber that faces south is for the priests who have charge of the temple, [46]and the chamber that faces north is for the priests who have charge of the altar; these are the descendants of Zā′dok, who alone among the descendants of Levi may come near to the LORD to minister to him." [47]He measured the court, one hundred cubits deep, and one hundred cubits wide, a square; and the altar was in front of the temple.

---

[t] Heb adds *the east and the north*
[u] Gk: Heb *before them*   [v] One Ms: Compare verses 29 and 33: MT lacks *were of the same size as the others*
[w] Gk Vg Compare verses 26, 31, 34: Heb *pilasters*   [x] Cn: Heb *at the pilasters of the gates*   [y] Cn: Heb *to him who goes up*   [z] Heb lacks *one*

The Temple
(Cp 1 Kings 7.14–22)

48 Then he brought me to the vestibule of the temple and measured the pilasters of the vestibule, five cubits on either side; and the width of the gate was fourteen cubits; and the sidewalls of the gate were three cubits*a* on either side. 49 The depth of the vestibule was twenty cubits, and the width twelve*b* cubits; ten steps led up*c* to it; and there were pillars beside the pilasters on either side.

41 Then he brought me to the nave, and measured the pilasters; on each side six cubits was the width of the pilasters.*d* 2 The width of the entrance was ten cubits; and the sidewalls of the entrance were five cubits on either side. He measured the length of the nave, forty cubits, and its width, twenty cubits. 3 Then he went into the inner room and measured the pilasters of the entrance, two cubits; and the width of the entrance, six cubits; and the sidewalls*e* of the entrance, seven cubits. 4 He measured the depth of the room, twenty cubits, and its width, twenty cubits, beyond the nave. And he said to me, This is the most holy place.

5 Then he measured the wall of the temple, six cubits thick; and the width of the side chambers, four cubits, all around the temple. 6 The side chambers were in three stories, one over another, thirty in each story. There were offsets*f* all around the wall of the temple to serve as supports for the side chambers, so that they should not be supported by the wall of the temple. 7 The passageway*g* of the side chambers widened from story to story; for the structure was supplied with a stairway all around the temple. For this reason the structure became wider from story to story. One ascended from the bottom story to the uppermost story by way of the middle one. 8 I saw also that the temple had a raised platform all around; the foundations of the side chambers measured a full reed of six long cubits. 9 The thickness of the outer wall of the side chambers was five cubits; and the free space between the side chambers of the temple 10 and the chambers of the court was a width of twenty cubits all around the temple on every side. 11 The side chambers opened onto the area left free, one door toward the north, and another door toward the south; and the width of the part that was left free was five cubits all around.

12 The building that was facing the temple yard on the west side was seventy cubits wide; and the wall of the building was five cubits thick all around, and its depth ninety cubits.

13 Then he measured the temple, one hundred cubits deep; and the yard and the building with its walls, one hundred cubits deep; 14 also the width of the east front of the temple and the yard, one hundred cubits.

15 Then he measured the depth of the building facing the yard at the west, together with its galleries*h* on either side, one hundred cubits.

The nave of the temple and the inner room and the outer*i* vestibule 16 were paneled,*j* and, all around, all three had windows with recessed*k* frames. Facing the threshold the temple was paneled with wood all around, from the floor up to the windows (now the windows were covered), 17 to the space above the door, even to the inner room, and on the outside. And on all the walls all around in the inner room and the nave there was a pattern.*l* 18 It was formed of cherubim and palm trees, a palm tree between cherub and cherub. Each cherub had two faces: 19 a human face turned toward the palm tree on the one side, and the face of a young lion turned toward the palm tree on the other side. They were carved on the whole temple all around; 20 from the floor to the area above the door, cherubim and palm trees were carved on the wall.*m*

21 The doorposts of the nave were square. In front of the holy place was something resembling 22 an altar of wood, three cubits high, two cubits long, and two cubits wide;*n* its corners, its base,*o* and its walls were of wood. He said to me, "This is the table

a Gk: Heb *and the width of the gate was three cubits*   *b* Gk: Heb *eleven*
c Gk: Heb *and by steps that went up*
d Compare Gk: Heb *tent*   *e* Gk: Heb *width*   *f* Gk Compare 1 Kings 6.6: Heb *they entered*   *g* Cn: Heb *it was surrounded*   *h* Cn: Meaning of Heb uncertain   *i* Gk: Heb *of the court*
j Gk: Heb *the thresholds*   *k* Cn Compare Gk 1 Kings 6.4: Meaning of Heb uncertain   *l* Heb *measures*
m Cn Compare verse 25: Heb *and the wall*   *n* Gk: Heb lacks *two cubits wide*   *o* Gk: Heb *length*

that stands before the LORD." ²³The nave and the holy place had each a double door. ²⁴The doors had two leaves apiece, two swinging leaves for each door. ²⁵On the doors of the nave were carved cherubim and palm trees, such as were carved on the walls; and there was a canopy of wood in front of the vestibule outside. ²⁶And there were recessed windows and palm trees on either side, on the sidewalls of the vestibule.ᵖ

The Holy Chambers and the Outer Wall

42 Then he led me out into the outer court, toward the north, and he brought me to the chambers that were opposite the temple yard and opposite the building on the north. ²The length of the building that was on the north side�q wasʳ one hundred cubits, and the width fifty cubits. ³Across the twenty cubits that belonged to the inner court, and facing the pavement that belonged to the outer court, the chambers roseˢ galleryᵗ by galleryᵗ in three stories. ⁴In front of the chambers was a passage on the inner side, ten cubits wide and one hundred cubits deep,ᵘ and itsᵛ entrances were on the north. ⁵Now the upper chambers were narrower, for the galleriesᵗ took more away from them than from the lower and middle chambers in the building. ⁶For they were in three stories, and they had no pillars like the pillars of the outerʷ court; for this reason the upper chambers were set back from the ground more than the lower and the middle ones. ⁷There was a wall outside parallel to the chambers, toward the outer court, opposite the chambers, fifty cubits long. ⁸For the chambers on the outer court were fifty cubits long, while those opposite the temple were one hundred cubits long. ⁹At the foot of these chambers ran a passage that one entered from the east in order to enter them from the outer court. ¹⁰The width of the passageˣ is fixed by the wall of the court.

On the southʸ also, opposite the vacant area and opposite the building, there were chambers ¹¹with a passage in front of them; they were similar to the chambers on the north, of the same length and width, with the same exitsᶻ and arrangements and doors. ¹²So the entrances of the chambers to the south were entered through the entrance at the head of the corresponding pas-

sage, from the east, along the matching wall.ᵗ
¹³Then he said to me, "The north chambers and the south chambers opposite the vacant area are the holy chambers, where the priests who approach the LORD shall eat the most holy offerings; there they shall deposit the most holy offerings—the grain offering, the sin offering, and the guilt offering, for the place is holy. ¹⁴When the priests enter the holy place, they shall not go out of it into the outer court without laying there the vestments in which they minister, for these are holy; they shall put on other garments before they go near to the area open to the people."
¹⁵When he had finished measuring the interior of the temple area, he led me out by the gate that faces east, and measured the temple area all around. ¹⁶He measured the east side with the measuring reed, five hundred cubits by the measuring reed. ¹⁷Then he turned and measuredᵃ the north side, five hundred cubits by the measuring reed. ¹⁸Then he turned and measuredᵃ the south side, five hundred cubits by the measuring reed. ¹⁹Then he turned to the west side and measured, five hundred cubits by the measuring reed. ²⁰He measured it on the four sides. It had a wall around it, five hundred cubits long and five hundred cubits wide, to make a separation between the holy and the common.

The Divine Glory Returns to the Temple

43 Then he brought me to the gate, the gate facing east. ²And there, the glory of the God of Israel was coming from the east; the sound was like the sound of mighty waters; and the earth shone with his glory. ³Theᵇ vision I saw was like the vision that I had seen when he came to destroy the city, andᶜ like the vision that I had seen by the river Chē'bar; and I

p Cn: Heb *vestibule. And the side chambers of the temple and the canopies*   q Gk: Heb *door*   r Gk: Heb *before the length*   s Heb lacks *the chambers rose*   t Meaning of Heb uncertain   u Gk Syr: Heb *a way of one cubit*   v Heb *their*   w Gk: Heb lacks *outer*   x Heb lacks *of the passage*   y Gk: Heb *east*   z Heb *and all their exits*   a Gk: Heb *measuring reed all around. He measured*   b Gk: Heb *Like the vision*   c Syr: Heb *and the visions* fell upon my face. [4] As the glory of the LORD entered the temple by the gate facing east, [5] the spirit lifted me up, and brought me into the inner court; and the glory of the LORD filled the temple.

6 While the man was standing beside me, I heard someone speaking to me out of the temple. [7] He said to me: Mortal, this is the place of my throne and the place for the soles of my feet, where I will reside among the people of Israel forever. The house of Israel shall no more defile my holy name, neither they nor their kings, by their whoring, and by the corpses of their kings at their death.[d] [8] When they placed their threshold by my threshold and their doorposts beside my doorposts, with only a wall between me and them, they were defiling my holy name by their abominations that they committed; therefore I have consumed them in my anger. [9] Now let them put away their idolatry and the corpses of their kings far from me, and I will reside among them forever.

10 As for you, mortal, describe the temple to the house of Israel, and let them measure the pattern; and let them be ashamed of their iniquities. [11] When they are ashamed of all that they have done, make known to them the plan of the temple, its arrangement, its exits and its entrances, and its whole form — all its ordinances and its entire plan and all its laws; and write it down in their sight, so that they may observe and follow the entire plan and all its ordinances. [12] This is the law of the temple: the whole territory on the top of the mountain all around shall be most holy. This is the law of the temple.

The Altar

13 These are the dimensions of the altar by cubits (the cubit being one cubit and a handbreadth): its base shall be one cubit high,[e] and one cubit wide, with a rim of one span around its edge. This shall be the height of the altar: [14] From the base on the ground to the lower ledge, two cubits, with a width of one cubit; and from the smaller ledge to the larger ledge, four cubits, with a width of one cubit; [15] and the altar hearth, four cubits; and from the altar hearth projecting upward, four horns. [16] The altar hearth shall be square, twelve cubits long by twelve wide. [17] The ledge also shall be square, fourteen cubits long by fourteen wide,

with a rim around it half a cubit wide, and its surrounding base, one cubit. Its steps shall face east.

18 Then he said to me: Mortal, thus says the Lord GOD: These are the ordinances for the altar: On the day when it is erected for offering burnt offerings upon it and for dashing blood against it, [19] you shall give to the levitical priests of the family of Zā'dok, who draw near to me to minister to me, says the Lord GOD, a bull for a sin offering. [20] And you shall take some of its blood, and put it on the four horns of the altar, and on the four corners of the ledge, and upon the rim all around; thus shall purify it and make atonement for it. [21] You shall also take the bull of the sin offering, and it shall be burnt in the appointed place belonging to the temple, outside the sacred area.

22 On the second day you shall offer a male goat without blemish for a sin offering; and the altar shall be purified, as it was purified with the bull. [23] When you have finished purifying it, you shall offer a bull without blemish and a ram from the flock without blemish. [24] You shall present them before the LORD, and the priests shall throw salt on them and offer them up as a burnt offering to the LORD. [25] For seven days you shall provide daily a goat for a sin offering; also a bull and a ram from the flock, without blemish, shall be provided. [26] Seven days shall they make atonement for the altar and cleanse it, and so consecrate it. [27] When these days are over, then from the eighth day onward the priests shall offer upon the altar your burnt offerings and your offerings of well-being; and I will accept you, says the Lord GOD.

The Closed Gate

44 Then he brought me back to the outer gate of the sanctuary, which faces east; and it was shut. [2] The LORD said to me: This gate shall remain shut; it shall not be opened, and no one shall enter by it; for the LORD, the God of Israel, has entered by it; therefore it shall remain shut. [3] Only the prince, because he is a prince, may sit in it to eat food before the LORD; he shall enter by way of the vestibule of the gate, and shall go out by the same way.

[d] Or *on their high places*   [e] Gk: Heb lacks *high*

Admission to the Temple

4 Then he brought me by way of the north gate to the front of the temple; and I looked, and lo! the glory of the LORD filled the temple of the LORD; and I fell upon my face. 5 The LORD said to me: Mortal, mark well, look closely, and listen attentively to all that I shall tell you concerning all the ordinances of the temple of the LORD and all its laws; and mark well those who may be admitted to*f* the temple and all those who are to be excluded from the sanctuary. 6 Say to the rebellious house,*g* to the house of Israel, Thus says the Lord GOD: O house of Israel, let there be an end to all your abominations 7 in admitting foreigners, uncircumcised in heart and flesh, to be in my sanctuary, profaning my temple when you offer to me my food, the fat and the blood. You*h* have broken my covenant with all your abominations. 8 And you have not kept charge of my sacred offerings; but you have appointed foreigners*i* to act for you in keeping my charge in my sanctuary.

9 Thus says the Lord GOD: No foreigner, uncircumcised in heart and flesh, of all the foreigners who are among the people of Israel, shall enter my sanctuary. 10 But the Lē'vītes who went far from me, going astray from me after their idols when Israel went astray, shall bear their punishment. 11 They shall be ministers in my sanctuary, having oversight at the gates of the temple, and serving in the temple; they shall slaughter the burnt offering and the sacrifice for the people, and they shall attend on them and serve them. 12 Because they ministered to them before their idols and made the house of Israel stumble into iniquity, therefore I have sworn concerning them, says the Lord GOD, that they shall bear their punishment. 13 They shall not come near to me, to serve me as priest, nor come near any of my sacred offerings, the things that are most sacred; but they shall bear their shame, and the consequences of the abominations that they have committed. 14 Yet I will appoint them to keep charge of the temple, to do all its chores, all that is to be done in it.

The Levitical Priests

15 But the levitical priests, the descendants of Zā'dok, who kept the charge of my sanctuary when the people of Israel went astray from me, shall come near to me to minister to me; and they shall attend me to offer me the fat and the blood, says the Lord GOD. 16 It is they who shall enter my sanctuary, it is they who shall approach my table, to minister to me, and they shall keep my charge. 17 When they enter the gates of the inner court, they shall wear linen vestments; they shall have nothing of wool on them, while they minister at the gates of the inner court, and within. 18 They shall have linen turbans on their heads, and linen undergarments on their loins; they shall not bind themselves with anything that causes sweat. 19 When they go out into the outer court to the people, they shall remove the vestments in which they have been ministering, and lay them in the holy chambers; and they shall put on other garments, so that they may not communicate holiness to the people with their vestments. 20 They shall not shave their heads or let their locks grow long; they shall only trim the hair of their heads. 21 No priest shall drink wine when he enters the inner court. 22 They shall not marry a widow, or a divorced woman, but only a virgin of the stock of the house of Israel, or a widow who is the widow of a priest. 23 They shall teach my people the difference between the holy and the common, and show them how to distinguish between the unclean and the clean. 24 In a controversy they shall act as judges, and they shall decide it according to my judgments. They shall keep my laws and my statutes regarding all my appointed festivals, and they shall keep my sabbaths holy. 25 They shall not defile themselves by going near to a dead person; for father or mother, however, and for son or daughter, and for brother or unmarried sister they may defile themselves. 26 After he has become clean, they shall count seven days for him. 27 On the day that he goes into the holy place, into the inner court, to minister in the holy place, he shall offer his sin offering, says the Lord GOD.

f Cn: Heb *the entrance of*   *g* Gk: Heb lacks *house*   *h* Gk Syr Vg: Heb *They* *i* Heb lacks *foreigners*

28 This shall be their inheritance: I am their inheritance; and you shall give them no holding in Israel; I am their holding. 29 They shall eat the grain offering, the sin offering, and the guilt offering; and every devoted thing in Israel shall be theirs. 30 The first of all the first fruits of all kinds, and every offering of all kinds from all your offerings, shall belong to the priests; you shall also give to the priests the first of your dough, in order that a blessing may rest on your house. 31 The priests shall not eat of anything, whether bird or animal, that died of itself or was torn by animals.

The Holy District

45 When you allot the land as an inheritance, you shall set aside for the LORD a portion of the land as a holy district, twenty-five thousand cubits long and twenty*j* thousand cubits wide; it shall be holy throughout its entire extent. 2 Of this, a square plot of five hundred by five hundred cubits shall be for the sanctuary, with fifty cubits for an open space around it. 3 In the holy district you shall measure off a section twenty-five thousand cubits long and ten thousand wide, in which shall be the sanctuary, the most holy place. 4 It shall be a holy portion of the land; it shall be for the priests, who minister in the sanctuary and approach the LORD to minister to him; and it shall be both a place for their houses and a holy place for the sanctuary. 5 Another section, twenty-five thousand cubits long and ten thousand cubits wide, shall be for the Lē'vītes who minister at the temple, as their holding for cities to live in.*k*

6 Alongside the portion set apart as the holy district you shall assign as a holding for the city an area five thousand cubits wide, and twenty-five thousand cubits long; it shall belong to the whole house of Israel.

7 And to the prince shall belong the land on both sides of the holy district and the holding of the city, alongside the holy district and the holding of the city, on the west and on the east, corresponding in length to one of the tribal portions, and extending from the western to the eastern boundary 8 of the land. It is to be his property in Israel. And my princes shall no longer oppress my people; but they shall let the house of Israel have the land according to their tribes.

9 Thus says the Lord GOD: Enough, O princes of Israel! Put away violence and oppression, and do what is just and right. Cease your evictions of my people, says the Lord GOD.

Weights and Measures

10 You shall have honest balances, an honest ephah, and an honest bath.*l* 11 The ephah and the bath shall be of the same measure, the bath containing one-tenth of a homer, and the ephah one-tenth of a homer; the homer shall be the standard measure. 12 The shekel shall be twenty gerahs. Twenty shekels, twenty-five shekels, and fifteen shekels shall make a mina for you.

Offerings

13 This is the offering that you shall make: one-sixth of an ephah from each homer of wheat, and one-sixth of an ephah from each homer of barley, 14 and as the fixed portion of oil,*m* one-tenth of a bath from each cor (the cor,*n* like the homer, contains ten baths); 15 and one sheep from every flock of two hundred, from the pastures of Israel. This is the offering for grain offerings, burnt offerings, and offerings of well-being, to make atonement for them, says the Lord GOD. 16 All the people of the land shall join with the prince in Israel in making this offering. 17 But this shall be the obligation of the prince regarding the burnt offerings, grain offerings, and drink offerings, at the festivals, the new moons, and the sabbaths, all the appointed festivals of the house of Israel: he shall provide the sin offerings, grain offerings, the burnt offerings, and the offerings of well-being, to make atonement for the house of Israel.

Festivals
(Ex 12.1–20; Lev 23.33–43)

18 Thus says the Lord GOD: In the first month, on the first day of the month, you shall take a young bull without blemish, and purify the sanctuary. 19 The priest shall take some of the blood of the sin offering and put it on the doorposts of the temple, the four corners of the ledge of the altar, and the posts of the gate of the inner court. 20 You shall do the same on the

j Gk: Heb *ten* *k* Gk: Heb *as their holding, twenty chambers* *l* A Heb measure of volume *m* Cn: Heb *oil, the bath the oil* *n* Vg: Heb *homer* seventh day of the month for anyone who has sinned through error or ignorance; so you shall make atonement for the temple.

21 In the first month, on the fourteenth day of the month, you shall celebrate the festival of the passover, and for seven days unleavened bread shall be eaten. 22 On that day the prince shall provide for himself and all the people of the land a young bull for a sin offering. 23 And during the seven days of the festival he shall provide as a burnt offering to the LORD seven young bulls and seven rams without blemish, on each of the seven days; and a male goat daily for a sin offering. 24 He shall provide as a grain offering an ephah for each bull, an ephah for each ram, and a hin of oil to each ephah. 25 In the seventh month, on the fifteenth day of the month and for the seven days of the festival, he shall make the same provision for sin offerings, burnt offerings, and grain offerings, and for the oil.

Miscellaneous Regulations

46 Thus says the Lord GOD: The gate of the inner court that faces east shall remain closed on the six working days; but on the sabbath day it shall be opened and on the day of the new moon it shall be opened. 2 The prince shall enter by the vestibule of the gate from outside, and shall take his stand by the post of the gate. The priests shall offer his burnt offering and his offerings of well-being, and he shall bow down at the threshold of the gate. Then he shall go out, but the gate shall not be closed until evening. 3 The people of the land shall bow down at the entrance of that gate before the LORD on the sabbaths and on the new moons. 4 The burnt offering that the prince offers to the LORD on the sabbath day shall be six lambs without blemish and a ram without blemish; 5 and the grain offering with the ram shall be an ephah, and the grain offering with the lambs shall be as much as he wishes to give, together with a hin of oil to each ephah. 6 On the day of the new moon he shall offer a young bull without blemish, and six lambs and a ram, which shall be without blemish; 7 as a grain offering he shall provide an ephah with the bull and an ephah with the ram, and with the lambs as much as he wishes, together with a hin of oil to each ephah.

8 When the prince enters, he shall come in by the vestibule of the gate, and he shall go out by the same way.

9 When the people of the land come before the LORD at the appointed festivals, whoever enters by the north gate to worship shall go out by the south gate; and whoever enters by the south gate shall go out by the north gate: they shall not return by way of the gate by which they entered, but shall go out straight ahead. 10 When they come in, the prince shall come in with them; and when they go out, he shall go out.

11 At the festivals and the appointed seasons the grain offering with a young bull shall be an ephah, and with a ram an ephah, and with the lambs as much as one wishes to give, together with a hin of oil to an ephah. 12 When the prince provides a freewill offering, either a burnt offering or offerings of well-being as a freewill offering to the LORD, the gate facing east shall be opened for him; and he shall offer his burnt offering or his offerings of well-being as he does on the sabbath day. Then he shall go out, and after he has gone out the gate shall be closed.

13 He shall provide a lamb, a yearling, without blemish, for a burnt offering to the LORD daily; morning by morning he shall provide it. 14 And he shall provide a grain offering with it morning by morning regularly, one-sixth of an ephah, and one-third of a hin of oil to moisten the choice flour, as a grain offering to the LORD; this is the ordinance for all time. 15 Thus the lamb and the grain offering and the oil shall be provided, morning by morning, as a regular burnt offering.

16 Thus says the Lord GOD: If the prince makes a gift to any of his sons out of his inheritance,ᵒ it shall belong to his sons, it is their holding by inheritance. 17 But if he makes a gift out of his inheritance to one of his servants, it shall be his to the year of liberty; then it shall revert to the prince; only his sons may keep a gift from his inheritance. 18 The prince shall not take any of the inheritance of the people, thrusting them out of their holding; he shall give his sons their inheritance out of his own holding, so that none of my people shall be dispossessed of their holding.

19 Then he brought me through the

ᵒGk: Heb *it is his inheritance*

entrance, which was at the side of the gate, to the north row of the holy chambers for the priests; and there I saw a place at the extreme western end of them. 20 He said to me, "This is the place where the priests shall boil the guilt offering and the sin offering, and where they shall bake the grain offering, in order not to bring them out into the outer court and so communicate holiness to the people."

21 Then he brought me out to the outer court, and led me past the four corners of the court; and in each corner of the court there was a court— 22 in the four corners of the court were small[p] courts, forty cubits long and thirty wide; the four were of the same size. 23 On the inside, around each of the four courts[q] was a row of masonry, with hearths made at the bottom of the rows all around. 24 Then he said to me, "These are the kitchens where those who serve at the temple shall boil the sacrifices of the people."

Water Flowing from the Temple

47 Then he brought me back to the entrance of the temple; there, water was flowing from below the threshold of the temple toward the east (for the temple faced east); and the water was flowing down from below the south end of the threshold of the temple, south of the altar. 2 Then he brought me out by way of the north gate, and led me around on the outside to the outer gate that faces toward the east;[r] and the water was coming out on the south side.

3 Going on eastward with a cord in his hand, the man measured one thousand cubits, and then led me through the water; and it was ankle-deep. 4 Again he measured one thousand, and led me through the water; and it was knee-deep. Again he measured one thousand, and led me through the water; and it was up to the waist. 5 Again he measured one thousand, and it was a river that I could not cross, for the water had risen; it was deep enough to swim in, a river that could not be crossed. 6 He said to me, "Mortal, have you seen this?"

Then he led me back along the bank of the river. 7 As I came back, I saw on the bank of the river a great many trees on the one side and on the other. 8 He said to me, "This water flows toward the eastern region and goes down into the Ar'a·bah; and when it enters the sea, the sea of stagnant waters, the water will become fresh. 9 Wherever the river goes,[s] every living creature that swarms will live, and there will be very many fish, once these waters reach there. It will become fresh; and everything will live where the river goes. 10 People will stand fishing beside the sea[t] from En·ge'di to En-eg'la·im; it will be a place for the spreading of nets; its fish will be of a great many kinds, like the fish of the Great Sea. 11 But its swamps and marshes will not become fresh; they are to be left for salt. 12 On the banks, on both sides of the river, there will grow all kinds of trees for food. Their leaves will not wither nor their fruit fail, but they will bear fresh fruit every month, because the water for them flows from the sanctuary. Their fruit will be for food, and their leaves for healing."

The New Boundaries of the Land
(Cp Num 34.1–12)

13 Thus says the Lord GOD: These are the boundaries by which you shall divide the land for inheritance among the twelve tribes of Israel. Joseph shall have two portions. 14 You shall divide it equally; I swore to give it to your ancestors, and this land shall fall to you as your inheritance.

15 This shall be the boundary of the land: On the north side, from the Great Sea by way of Heth'lon to Le'bo-ha'math, and on to Ze'dad,[u] 16 Be·ro'thah, Sib'ra·im (which lies between the border of Damascus and the border of Ha'math), as far as Ha'zer-hat'-ti·con, which is on the border of Hau'ran. 17 So the boundary shall run from the sea to Ha'zar-e'non, which is north of the border of Damascus, with the border of Ha'math to the north.[r] This shall be the north side.

18 On the east side, between Hau'ran and Damascus; along the Jordan between Gil'e·ad and the land of Israel; to the eastern sea and as far as Ta'mar.[v] This shall be the east side.

19 On the south side, it shall run from Ta'mar as far as the waters of Mer'i·bath-ka'desh, from there along

---

[p] Gk Syr Vg: Meaning of Heb uncertain
[q] Heb *the four of them*   [r] Meaning of Heb uncertain   [s] Gk Syr Vg Tg: Heb *the two rivers go*   [t] Heb *it*   [u] Gk: Heb *Lebo-zedad,* [16] *Hamath*   [v] Compare Syr: Heb *you shall measure*

the Wadi of Egypt[w] to the Great Sea. This shall be the south side.

20 On the west side, the Great Sea shall be the boundary to a point opposite Lē'bō-hā'math. This shall be the west side.

21 So you shall divide this land among you according to the tribes of Israel. [22] You shall allot it as an inheritance for yourselves and for the aliens who reside among you and have begotten children among you. They shall be to you as citizens of Israel; with you they shall be allotted an inheritance among the tribes of Israel. [23] In whatever tribe aliens reside, there you shall assign them their inheritance, says the Lord GOD.

The Tribal Portions

48 These are the names of the tribes: Beginning at the northern border, on the Heth'lon road,[x] from Lē'bō-hā'math, as far as Hā'zar-ē'non (which is on the border of Damascus, with Hā'math to the north), and[y] extending from the east side to the west,[z] Dan, one portion. [2] Adjoining the territory of Dan, from the east side to the west, Ash'er, one portion. [3] Adjoining the territory of Ash'er, from the east side to the west, Naph'-ta·lī, one portion. [4] Adjoining the territory of Naph'ta·lī, from the east side to the west, Ma·nas'seh, one portion. [5] Adjoining the territory of Ma·nas'-seh, from the east side to the west, Ē'phra·im, one portion. [6] Adjoining the territory of Ē'phra·im, from the east side to the west, Reuben, one portion. [7] Adjoining the territory of Reuben, from the east side to the west, Judah, one portion.

8 Adjoining the territory of Judah, from the east side to the west, shall be the portion that you shall set apart, twenty-five thousand cubits in width, and in length equal to one of the tribal portions, from the east side to the west, with the sanctuary in the middle of it. [9] The portion that you shall set apart for the LORD shall be twenty-five thousand cubits in length, and twenty[a] thousand in width. [10] These shall be the allotments of the holy portion: the priests shall have an allotment measuring twenty-five thousand cubits on the northern side, ten thousand cubits in width on the western side, ten thousand in width on the eastern side, and twenty-five thousand in length on the southern side, with the sanctuary of

the LORD in the middle of it. [11] This shall be for the consecrated priests, the descendants[b] of Zā'dok, who kept my charge, who did not go astray when the people of Israel went astray, as the Lē'vītes did. [12] It shall belong to them as a special portion from the holy portion of the land, a most holy place, adjoining the territory of the Lē'vītes. [13] Alongside the territory of the priests, the Lē'vītes shall have an allotment twenty-five thousand cubits in length and ten thousand in width. The whole length shall be twenty-five thousand cubits and the width twenty[c] thousand. [14] They shall not sell or exchange any of it; they shall not transfer this choice portion of the land, for it is holy to the LORD.

15 The remainder, five thousand cubits in width and twenty-five thousand in length, shall be for ordinary use for the city, for dwellings and for open country. In the middle of it shall be the city; [16] and these shall be its dimensions: the north side four thousand five hundred cubits, the south side four thousand five hundred, the east side four thousand five hundred, and the west side four thousand and five hundred. [17] The city shall have open land: on the north two hundred fifty cubits, on the south two hundred fifty, on the east two hundred fifty, on the west two hundred fifty. [18] The remainder of the length alongside the holy portion shall be ten thousand cubits to the east, and ten thousand to the west, and it shall be alongside the holy portion. Its produce shall be food for the workers of the city. [19] The workers of the city, from all the tribes of Israel, shall cultivate it. [20] The whole portion that you shall set apart shall be twenty-five thousand cubits square, that is, the holy portion together with the property of the city.

21 What remains on both sides of the holy portion and of the property of the city shall belong to the prince. Extending from the twenty-five thousand cubits of the holy portion to the east border, and westward from the twenty-five thousand cubits to the west border, parallel to the tribal por-

---

[w] Heb lacks *of Egypt*   [x] Compare 47.15: Heb *by the side of the way*   [y] Cn: Heb *and they shall be his*   [z] Gk Compare verses 2-8: Heb *the east side the west*   [a] Compare 45.1: Heb *ten*   [b] One Ms Gk: Heb *of the descendants*   [c] Gk: Heb *ten*

tions, it shall belong to the prince. The holy portion with the sanctuary of the temple in the middle of it, 22 and the property of the Lē'vītes and of the city, shall be in the middle of that which belongs to the prince. The portion of the prince shall lie between the territory of Judah and the territory of Benjamin.

23 As for the rest of the tribes: from the east side to the west, Benjamin, one portion. 24 Adjoining the territory of Benjamin, from the east side to the west, Sim'ē·on, one portion. 25 Adjoining the territory of Sim'ē·on, from the east side to the west, Is'sa·char, one portion. 26 Adjoining the territory of Is'sa·char, from the east side to the west, Zeb'ū·lun, one portion. 27 Adjoining the territory of Zeb'ū·lun, from the east side to the west, Gad, one portion. 28 And adjoining the territory of Gad to the south, the boundary shall run from Tā'mar to the waters of Mer'i·bath-kā'desh, from there along the Wadi of Egypt[d] to the Great Sea. 29 This is the land that you shall allot as an inheritance among the tribes of Israel, and these are their portions, says the Lord God.

30 These shall be the exits of the city: On the north side, which is to be four thousand five hundred cubits by measure, 31 three gates, the gate of Reuben, the gate of Judah, and the gate of Levi, the gates of the city being named after the tribes of Israel. 32 On the east side, which is to be four thousand five hundred cubits, three gates, the gate of Joseph, the gate of Benjamin, and the gate of Dan. 33 On the south side, which is to be four thousand five hundred cubits by measure, three gates, the gate of Sim'ē·on, the gate of Is'sa·char, and the gate of Zeb'-ū·lun. 34 On the west side, which is to be four thousand five hundred cubits, three gates,[e] the gate of Gad, the gate of Ash'er, and the gate of Naph'ta·lī. 35 The circumference of the city shall be eighteen thousand cubits. And the name of the city from that time on shall be, The Lord is There.

[d] Heb lacks *of Egypt*   [e] One Ms Gk Syr: MT *their gates three*

DANIEL

Four Young Israelites at the Babylonian Court
(Cp. 2 Kings 24.10–17)

1 In the third year of the reign of King Je·hoi'a·kim of Judah, King Ne·bū·chad·nez'zar of Babylon came to Jerusalem and besieged it. 2 The Lord let King Je·hoi'a·kim of Judah fall into his power, as well as some of the vessels of the house of God. These he brought to the land of Shī'nar,[a] and placed the vessels in the treasury of his gods.

3 Then the king commanded his palace master Ash'pe·naz to bring some of the Israelites of the royal family and of the nobility, 4 young men without physical defect and handsome, versed in every branch of wisdom, endowed with knowledge and insight, and competent to serve in the king's palace; they were to be taught the literature and language of the Chal·dē'ans. 5 The king assigned them a daily portion of the royal rations of food and wine. They were to be educated for three years, so that at the end of that time they could be stationed in the king's court. 6 Among them were Daniel, Han·a·nī'ah, Mish'a·el, and Az·a·rī'ah, from the tribe of Judah. 7 The palace master gave them other names: Daniel he called Bel·te·shaz'-zar, Han·a·nī'ah he called Shad'rach, Mish'a·el he called Mē'shach, and Az·a·rī'ah he called A·bed'ne·gō.

8 But Daniel resolved that he would not defile himself with the royal rations of food and wine; so he asked the

[a] Gk Theodotion: Heb adds *to the house of his own gods*

palace master to allow him not to defile himself. [9] Now God allowed Daniel to receive favor and compassion from the palace master. [10] The palace master said to Daniel, "I am afraid of my lord the king; he has appointed your food and your drink. If he should see you in poorer condition than the other young men of your own age, you would endanger my head with the king." [11] Then Daniel asked the guard whom the palace master had appointed over Daniel, Han·a·nī′ah, Mish′a·el, and Az·a·rī′ah: [12] "Please test your servants for ten days. Let us be given vegetables to eat and water to drink. [13] You can then compare our appearance with the appearance of the young men who eat the royal rations, and deal with your servants according to what you observe." [14] So he agreed to this proposal and tested them for ten days. [15] At the end of ten days it was observed that they appeared better and fatter than all the young men who had been eating the royal rations. [16] So the guard continued to withdraw their royal rations and the wine they were to drink, and gave them vegetables. [17] To these four young men God gave knowledge and skill in every aspect of literature and wisdom; Daniel also had insight into all visions and dreams.

[18] At the end of the time that the king had set for them to be brought in, the palace master brought them into the presence of Ne·bū·chad·nez′zar, [19] and the king spoke with them. And among them all, no one was found to compare with Daniel, Han·a·nī′ah, Mish′a·el, and Az·a·rī′ah; therefore they were stationed in the king's court. [20] In every matter of wisdom and understanding concerning which the king inquired of them, he found them ten times better than all the magicians and enchanters in his whole kingdom. [21] And Daniel continued there until the first year of King Cyrus.

Nebuchadnezzar's Dream

2 In the second year of Ne·bū·chad·nez′zar's reign, Ne·bū·chad·nez′zar dreamed such dreams that his spirit was troubled and his sleep left him. [2] So the king commanded that the magicians, the enchanters, the sorcerers, and the Chal·dē′ans be summoned to tell the king his dreams. When they came in and stood before the king, [3] he said to them, "I have had such a dream that my spirit is troubled by the desire to understand it." [4] The Chal·dē′ans said to the king (in Ar·a·mā′ic),[b] "O king, live forever! Tell your servants the dream, and we will reveal the interpretation." [5] The king answered the Chal·dē′ans, "This is a public decree: if you do not tell me both the dream and its interpretation, you shall be torn limb from limb, and your houses shall be laid in ruins. [6] But if you do tell me the dream and its interpretation, you shall receive from me gifts and rewards and great honor. Therefore tell me the dream and its interpretation." [7] They answered a second time, "Let the king first tell his servants the dream, then we can give its interpretation." [8] The king answered, "I know with certainty that you are trying to gain time, because you see I have firmly decreed: [9] if you do not tell me the dream, there is but one verdict for you. You have agreed to speak lying and misleading words to me until things take a turn. Therefore, tell me the dream, and I shall know that you can give me its interpretation." [10] The Chal·dē′ans answered the king, "There is no one on earth who can reveal what the king demands! In fact no king, however great and powerful, has ever asked such a thing of any magician or enchanter or Chal·dē′an. [11] The thing that the king is asking is too difficult, and no one can reveal it to the king except the gods, whose dwelling is not with mortals."

[12] Because of this the king flew into a violent rage and commanded that all the wise men of Babylon be destroyed. [13] The decree was issued, and the wise men were about to be executed; and they looked for Daniel and his companions, to execute them. [14] Then Daniel responded with prudence and discretion to Ar′i·och, the king's chief executioner, who had gone out to execute the wise men of Babylon; [15] he asked Ar′i·och, the royal official, "Why is the decree of the king so urgent?" Ar′i·och then explained the matter to Daniel. [16] So Daniel went in and requested that the king give him time and he would tell the king the interpretation.

[b] The text from this point to the end of chapter 7 is in Aramaic, except for 3.24-91a, the text of which is in Greek

God Reveals Nebuchadnezzar's Dream

17 Then Daniel went to his home and informed his companions, Han·a·ni′ah, Mish′a·el, and Az·a·ri′ah, 18 and told them to seek mercy from the God of heaven concerning this mystery, so that Daniel and his companions with the rest of the wise men of Babylon might not perish. 19 Then the mystery was revealed to Daniel in a vision of the night, and Daniel blessed the God of heaven.

20 Daniel said:
"Blessed be the name of God
      from age to age,
   for wisdom and power are his.
21 He changes times and seasons,
   deposes kings and sets up
      kings;
   he gives wisdom to the wise
      and knowledge to those who
         have understanding.
22 He reveals deep and hidden
      things;
   he knows what is in the
      darkness,
   and light dwells with him.
23 To you, O God of my ancestors,
   I give thanks and praise,
   for you have given me wisdom
      and power,
   and have now revealed to me
      what we asked of you,
   for you have revealed to us
      what the king ordered."

Daniel Interprets the Dream

24 Therefore Daniel went to Ar′-i·och, whom the king had appointed to destroy the wise men of Babylon, and said to him, "Do not destroy the wise men of Babylon; bring me in before the king, and I will give the king the interpretation." 25 Then Ar′i·och quickly brought Daniel before the king and said to him: "I have found among the exiles from Judah a man who can tell the king the interpretation." 26 The king said to Daniel, whose name was Bel·te·shaz′-zar, "Are you able to tell me the dream that I have seen and its interpretation?" 27 Daniel answered the king, "No wise men, enchanters, magicians, or diviners can show to the king the mystery that the king is asking, 28 but there is a God in heaven who reveals mysteries, and he has disclosed to King Ne·bu·chad·nez′zar what will happen at the end of days. Your dream and the visions of your head as you lay in bed

were these: 29 To you, O king, as you lay in bed, came thoughts of what would be hereafter, and the revealer of mysteries disclosed to you what is to be. 30 But as for me, this mystery has not been revealed to me because of any wisdom that I have more than any other living being, but in order that the interpretation may be known to the king and that you may understand the thoughts of your mind.

31 "You were looking, O king, and lo! there was a great statue. This statue was huge, its brilliance extraordinary; it was standing before you, and its appearance was frightening. 32 The head of that statue was of fine gold, its chest and arms of silver, its middle and thighs of bronze, 33 its legs of iron, its feet partly of iron and partly of clay. 34 As you looked on, a stone was cut out, not by human hands, and it struck the statue on its feet of iron and clay and broke them in pieces. 35 Then the iron, the clay, the bronze, the silver, and the gold, were all broken in pieces and became like the chaff of the summer threshing floors; and the wind carried them away, so that not a trace of them could be found. But the stone that struck the statue became a great mountain and filled the whole earth.

36 "This was the dream; now we will tell the king its interpretation. 37 You, O king, the king of kings—to whom the God of heaven has given the kingdom, the power, the might, and the glory, 38 into whose hand he has given human beings, wherever they live, the wild animals of the field, and the birds of the air, and whom he has established as ruler over them all—you are the head of gold. 39 After you shall arise another kingdom inferior to yours, and yet a third kingdom of bronze, which shall rule over the whole earth. 40 And there shall be a fourth kingdom, strong as iron; just as iron crushes and smashes everything,ᶜ it shall crush and shatter all these. 41 As you saw the feet and toes partly of potter's clay and partly of iron, it shall be a divided kingdom; but some of the strength of iron shall be in it, as you saw the iron mixed with the clay. 42 As the toes of the feet were part iron and part clay, so the kingdom shall be partly strong and partly brittle. 43 As you saw the iron mixed with

ᶜ Gk Theodotion Syr Vg: Aram adds *and like iron that crushes* clay, so will they mix with one another in marriage,[d] but they will not hold together, just as iron does not mix with clay. 44 And in the days of those kings the God of heaven will set up a kingdom that shall never be destroyed, nor shall this kingdom be left to another people. It shall crush all these kingdoms and bring them to an end, and it shall stand forever; 45 just as you saw that a stone was cut from the mountain not by hands, and that it crushed the iron, the bronze, the clay, the silver, and the gold. The great God has informed the king what shall be hereafter. The dream is certain, and its interpretation trustworthy."

Daniel and His Friends Promoted

46 Then King Ne·bu·chad·nez'zar fell on his face, worshiped Daniel, and commanded that a grain offering and incense be offered to him. 47 The king said to Daniel, "Truly, your God is God of gods and Lord of kings and a revealer of mysteries, for you have been able to reveal this mystery!" 48 Then the king promoted Daniel, gave him many great gifts, and made him ruler over the whole province of Babylon and chief prefect over all the wise men of Babylon. 49 Daniel made a request of the king, and he appointed Shad'rach, Me'shach, and A·bed'ne·go over the affairs of the province of Babylon. But Daniel remained at the king's court.

The Golden Image

3 King Ne·bu·chad·nez'zar made a golden statue whose height was sixty cubits and whose width was six cubits; he set it up on the plain of Du'ra in the province of Babylon. 2 Then King Ne·bu·chad·nez'zar sent for the satraps, the prefects, and the governors, the counselors, the treasurers, the justices, the magistrates, and all the officials of the provinces to assemble and come to the dedication of the statue that King Ne·bu·chad·nez'zar had set up. 3 So the satraps, the prefects, and the governors, the counselors, the treasurers, the justices, the magistrates, and all the officials of the provinces, assembled for the dedication of the statue that King Ne·bu·chad·nez'zar had set up. When they were standing before the statue that Ne·bu·chad·nez'zar had set up, 4 the herald proclaimed aloud, "You are commanded, O peoples, nations, and languages, 5 that when you hear

the sound of the horn, pipe, lyre, trigon, harp, drum, and entire musical ensemble, you are to fall down and worship the golden statue that King Ne·bu·chad·nez'zar has set up. 6 Whoever does not fall down and worship shall immediately be thrown into a furnace of blazing fire." 7 Therefore, as soon as all the peoples heard the sound of the horn, pipe, lyre, trigon, harp, drum, and entire musical ensemble, all the peoples, nations, and languages fell down and worshiped the golden statue that King Ne·bu·chad·nez'zar had set up.

8 Accordingly, at this time certain Chal·de'ans came forward and denounced the Jews. 9 They said to King Ne·bu·chad·nez'zar, "O king, live forever! 10 You, O king, have made a decree, that everyone who hears the sound of the horn, pipe, lyre, trigon, harp, drum, and entire musical ensemble, shall fall down and worship the golden statue, 11 and whoever does not fall down and worship shall be thrown into a furnace of blazing fire. 12 There are certain Jews whom you have appointed over the affairs of the province of Babylon: Shad'rach, Me'shach, and A·bed'ne·go. These pay no heed to you, O King. They do not serve your gods and they do not worship the golden statue that you have set up."

13 Then Ne·bu·chad·nez'zar in furious rage commanded that Shad'rach, Me'shach, and A·bed'ne·go be brought in; so they brought those men before the king. 14 Ne·bu·chad·nez'zar said to them, "Is it true, O Shad'rach, Me'shach, and A·bed'ne·go, that you do not serve my gods and you do not worship the golden statue that I have set up? 15 Now if you are ready when you hear the sound of the horn, pipe, lyre, trigon, harp, drum, and entire musical ensemble to fall down and worship the statue that I have made, well and good.[e] But if you do not worship, you shall immediately be thrown into a furnace of blazing fire, and who is the god that will deliver you out of my hands?"

16 Shad'rach, Me'shach, and A·bed'ne·go answered the king, "O Ne·bu·chad·nez'zar, we have no need to present a defense to you in this matter. 17 If our God whom we serve is able to deliver us from the furnace of

D A N I E L

d Aram by human seed   e Aram lacks well and good

blazing fire and out of your hand, O king, let him deliver us./ ¹⁸ But if not, be it known to you, O king, that we will not serve your gods and we will not worship the golden statue that you have set up."

The Fiery Furnace

19 Then Ne·bū·chad·nez′zar was so filled with rage against Shad′rach, Mē′shach, and A·bed′ne·gō that his face was distorted. He ordered the furnace heated up seven times more than was customary, ²⁰ and ordered some of the strongest guards in his army to bind Shad′rach, Mē′shach, and A·bed′ne·gō and to throw them into the furnace of blazing fire. ²¹ So the men were bound, still wearing their tunics,ᵍ their trousers,ᵍ their hats, and their other garments, and they were thrown into the furnace of blazing fire. ²² Because the king's command was urgent and the furnace was so overheated, the raging flames killed the men who lifted Shad′rach, Mē′shach, and A·bed′ne·gō. ²³ But the three men, Shad′rach, Mē′shach, and A·bed′ne·gō, fell down, bound, into the furnace of blazing fire.

The Prayer of Azariah in the Furnace

24 They walked around in the midst of the flames, singing hymns to God and blessing the Lord. ²⁵ Then Az·a·rī′ah stood still in the fire and prayed aloud:
²⁶ "Blessed are you, O Lord, God of our ancestors, and worthy of praise;
and glorious is your name forever!
²⁷ For you are just in all you have done;
all your works are true and your ways right,
and all your judgments are true.
²⁸ You have executed true judgments in all you have brought upon us
and upon Jerusalem, the holy city of our ancestors;
by a true judgment you have brought all this upon us because of our sins.
²⁹ For we have sinned and broken your law in turning away from you;
in all matters we have sinned grievously.

³⁰ We have not obeyed your commandments,
we have not kept them or done what you have commanded us for our own good.
³¹ So all that you have brought upon us,
and all that you have done to us,
you have done by a true judgment.
³² You have handed us over to our enemies, lawless and hateful rebels,
and to an unjust king, the most wicked in all the world.
³³ And now we cannot open our mouths;
we, your servants who worship you, have become a shame and a reproach.
³⁴ For your name's sake do not give us up forever,
and do not annul your covenant.
³⁵ Do not withdraw your mercy from us,
for the sake of Abraham your beloved
and for the sake of your servant Isaac
and Israel your holy one,
³⁶ to whom you promised
to multiply their descendants like the stars of heaven
and like the sand on the shore of the sea.
³⁷ For we, O Lord, have become fewer than any other nation,
and are brought low this day in all the world because of our sins.
³⁸ In our day we have no ruler, or prophet, or leader,
no burnt offering, or sacrifice, or oblation, or incense,
no place to make an offering before you and to find mercy.
³⁹ Yet with a contrite heart and a humble spirit may we be accepted,

f Or *If our God whom we serve is able to deliver us, he will deliver us from the furnace of blazing fire and out of your hand, O king.*   *ᵍ* Meaning of Aram word uncertain

40 as though it were with burnt
        offerings of rams and bulls,
    or with tens of thousands of
        fat lambs;
    such may our sacrifice be in
        your sight today,
    and may we unreservedly
        follow you,[h]
    for no shame will come to
        those who trust in you.
41 And now with all our heart we
        follow you;
    we fear you and seek your
        presence.
42 Do not put us to shame,
    but deal with us in your
        patience
    and in your abundant mercy.
43 Deliver us in accordance with
        your marvelous works,
    and bring glory to your name,
        O Lord.
44 Let all who do harm to your
        servants be put to shame;
    let them be disgraced and
        deprived of all power,
    and let their strength be
        broken.
45 Let them know that you alone
        are the Lord God,
    glorious over the whole
        world."

The Song of the Three Jews

46 Now the king's servants who
threw them in kept stoking the furnace
with naphtha, pitch, tow, and brushwood. 47 And the flames poured out
above the furnace forty-nine cubits,
48 and spread out and burned those
Chal·dē′ans who were caught near the
furnace. 49 But the angel of the Lord
came down into the furnace to be with
Az·a·ri′ah and his companions, and
drove the fiery flame out of the furnace, 50 and made the inside of the furnace as though a moist wind were
whistling through it. The fire did not
touch them at all and caused them no
pain or distress.
51 Then the three with one voice
praised and glorified and blessed God
in the furnace:
52 "Blessed are you, O Lord, God of
        our ancestors,
    and to be praised and highly
        exalted forever;
    And blessed is your glorious,
        holy name,
    and to be highly praised and
        highly exalted forever.

53 Blessed are you in the temple of
        your holy glory,
    and to be extolled and highly
        glorified forever.
54 Blessed are you who look into
        the depths from your
        throne on the cherubim,
    and to be praised and highly
        exalted forever.
55 Blessed are you on the throne of
        your kingdom,
    and to be extolled and highly
        exalted forever.
56 Blessed are you in the firmament
        of heaven,
    and to be sung and glorified
        forever.

57 "Bless the Lord, all you works of
        the Lord;
    sing praise to him and highly
        exalt him forever.
58 Bless the Lord, you heavens;
    sing praise to him and highly
        exalt him forever.
59 Bless the Lord, you angels of the
        Lord;
    sing praise to him and highly
        exalt him forever.
60 Bless the Lord, all you waters
        above the heavens;
    sing praise to him and highly
        exalt him forever.
61 Bless the Lord, all you powers of
        the Lord;
    sing praise to him and highly
        exalt him forever.
62 Bless the Lord, sun and moon;
    sing praise to him and highly
        exalt him forever.
63 Bless the Lord, stars of heaven;
    sing praise to him and highly
        exalt him forever.

64 "Bless the Lord, all rain and
        dew;
    sing praise to him and highly
        exalt him forever.
65 Bless the Lord, all you winds;
    sing praise to him and highly
        exalt him forever.
66 Bless the Lord, fire and heat;
    sing praise to him and highly
        exalt him forever.
67 Bless the Lord, winter cold and
        summer heat;
    sing praise to him and highly
        exalt him forever.
68 Bless the Lord, dews and falling
        snow;

[h] Meaning of Gk uncertain

D
A
N
I
E
L

sing praise to him and highly
exalt him forever.
69 Bless the Lord, ice and cold;
sing praise to him and highly
exalt him forever.
70 Bless the Lord, frosts and snows;
sing praise to him and highly
exalt him forever.
71 Bless the Lord, nights and days;
sing praise to him and highly
exalt him forever.
72 Bless the Lord, light and
darkness;
sing praise to him and highly
exalt him forever.
73 Bless the Lord, lightnings and
clouds;
sing praise to him and highly
exalt him forever.

74 "Let the earth bless the Lord;
let it sing praise to him and
highly exalt him forever.
75 Bless the Lord, mountains and
hills;
sing praise to him and highly
exalt him forever.
76 Bless the Lord, all that grows in
the ground;
sing praise to him and highly
exalt him forever.
77 Bless the Lord, you springs;
sing praise to him and highly
exalt him forever.
78 Bless the Lord, seas and rivers;
sing praise to him and highly
exalt him forever.
79 Bless the Lord, you whales and
all that swim in the waters;
sing praise to him and highly
exalt him forever.
80 Bless the Lord, all birds of the
air;
sing praise to him and highly
exalt him forever.
81 Bless the Lord, all wild animals
and cattle;
sing praise to him and highly
exalt him forever.

82 "Bless the Lord, all people on
earth;
sing praise to him and highly
exalt him forever.
83 Bless the Lord, O Israel;
sing praise to him and highly
exalt him forever.
84 Bless the Lord, you priests of the
Lord;
sing praise to him and highly
exalt him forever.

85 Bless the Lord, you servants of
the Lord;
sing praise to him and highly
exalt him forever.
86 Bless the Lord, spirits and souls
of the righteous;
sing praise to him and highly
exalt him forever.
87 Bless the Lord, you who are holy
and humble in heart;
sing praise to him and highly
exalt him forever.

88 "Bless the Lord, Han·a·nī′ah,
Az·a·rī′ah, and Mish′a·el;
sing praise to him and highly
exalt him forever.
For he has rescued us from
Hades and saved us from
the power[i] of death,
and delivered us from the
midst of the burning fiery
furnace;
from the midst of the fire he
has delivered us.
89 Give thanks to the Lord, for he
is good,
for his mercy endures forever.
90 All who worship the Lord, bless
the God of gods,
sing praise to him and give
thanks to him,
for his mercy endures forever."

91 Hearing them sing, and amazed
at seeing them alive, King Ne·
bū·chad·nez′zar rose up quickly. He
said to his counselors, "Was it not
three men that we threw bound into
the fire?" They answered the king,
"True, O king." 92 He replied, "But I see
four men unbound, walking in the
middle of the fire, and they are not
hurt; and the fourth has the appearance of a god."[j] 93 Ne·bū·chad·nez′zar
then approached the door of the furnace of blazing fire and said, "Shad′-
rach, Mē′shach, and A·bed′ne·gō, servants of the Most High God, come out!
Come here!" So Shad′rach, Mē′shach,
and A·bed′ne·gō came out from the
fire. 94 And the satraps, the prefects,
the governors, and the king's counselors gathered together and saw that the
fire had not had any power over the
bodies of those men; the hair of their
heads was not singed, their tunics[k]
were not harmed, and not even the
smell of fire came from them.
95 Ne·bū·chad·nez′zar said, "Blessed

----

[i]Gk *hand* [j]Aram *a son of the gods*
[k]Meaning of Aram word uncertain

be the God of Shad′rach, Mē′shach, and A·bed′ne·gō, who has sent his angel and delivered his servants who trusted in him. They disobeyed the king's command and yielded up their bodies rather than serve and worship any god except their own God. [96]Therefore I make a decree: Any people, nation, or language that utters blasphemy against the God of Shad′rach, Mē′shach, and A·bed′ne·gō shall be torn limb from limb, and their houses laid in ruins; for there is no other god who is able to deliver in this way." [97]Then the king promoted Shad′rach, Mē′shach, and A·bed′ne·gō in the province of Babylon.

Nebuchadnezzar's Second Dream

4 [l] King Ne·bū·chad·nez′zar to all peoples, nations, and languages that live throughout the earth: May you have abundant prosperity! [2]The signs and wonders that the Most High God has worked for me I am pleased to recount.

[3] How great are his signs,
    how mighty his wonders!
His kingdom is an everlasting
    kingdom,
  and his sovereignty is from
      generation to generation.

[4m] I, Ne·bū·chad·nez′zar, was living at ease in my home and prospering in my palace. [5]I saw a dream that frightened me; my fantasies in bed and the visions of my head terrified me. [6]So I made a decree that all the wise men of Babylon should be brought before me, in order that they might tell me the interpretation of the dream. [7]Then the magicians, the enchanters, the Chal·dē′ans, and the diviners came in, and I told them the dream, but they could not tell me its interpretation. [8]At last Daniel came in before me—he who was named Bel·te·shaz′zar after the name of my god, and who is endowed with a spirit of the holy gods[n]—and I told him the dream: [9]"O Bel·te·shaz′zar, chief of the magicians, I know that you are endowed with a spirit of the holy gods[n] and that no mystery is too difficult for you. Hear[o] the dream that I saw; tell me its interpretation.

[10p] Upon my bed this is what I saw;
    there was a tree at the center
      of the earth,
    and its height was great.
[11] The tree grew great and strong,
    its top reached to heaven,

    and it was visible to the ends
      of the whole earth.
[12] Its foliage was beautiful,
    its fruit abundant,
    and it provided food for all.
The animals of the field found
      shade under it,
    the birds of the air nested in
      its branches,
  and from it all living beings
      were fed.

[13]I continued looking, in the visions of my head as I lay in bed, and there was a holy watcher, coming down from heaven. [14]He cried aloud and said:
'Cut down the tree and chop off
    its branches,
  strip off its foliage and scatter
    its fruit.
Let the animals flee from
      beneath it
  and the birds from its
      branches.
[15] But leave its stump and roots in
      the ground,
  with a band of iron and
      bronze,
  in the tender grass of the field.
Let him be bathed with the dew
      of heaven.
  and let his lot be with the
      animals of the field
  in the grass of the earth.
[16] Let his mind be changed from
      that of a human,
  and let the mind of an animal
      be given to him.
  And let seven times pass
      over him.
[17] The sentence is rendered by
      decree of the watchers,
  the decision is given by order
      of the holy ones,
in order that all who live
      may know
  that the Most High is
      sovereign over the
      kingdom of mortals;
he gives it to whom he will
    and sets over it the lowliest of
      human beings.'

[18]This is the dream that I, King Ne·bū·chad·nez′zar, saw. Now you,

[l]Ch 3.31 in Aram   [m]Ch 4.1 in Aram
[n]Or *a holy, divine spirit*   [o]Theodotion: Aram *The visions of*   [p]Theodotion Syr Compare Gk: Aram adds *The visions of my head*

Bel·te·shaz'zar, declare the interpretation, since all the wise men of my kingdom are unable to tell me the interpretation. You are able, however, for you are endowed with a spirit of the holy gods."q

Daniel Interprets the Second Dream

19 Then Daniel, who was called Bel·te·shaz'zar, was severely distressed for a while. His thoughts terrified him. The king said, "Bel·te·shaz'zar, do not let the dream or the interpretation terrify you." Bel·te·shaz'zar answered, "My lord, may the dream be for those who hate you, and its interpretation for your enemies! 20 The tree that you saw, which grew great and strong, so that its top reached to heaven and was visible to the end of the whole earth, 21 whose foliage was beautiful and its fruit abundant, and which provided food for all, under which animals of the field lived, and in whose branches the birds of the air had nests — 22 it is you, O king! You have grown great and strong. Your greatness has increased and reaches to heaven, and your sovereignty to the ends of the earth. 23 And whereas the king saw a holy watcher coming down from heaven and saying, 'Cut down the tree and destroy it, but leave its stump and roots in the ground, with a band of iron and bronze, in the grass of the field; and let him be bathed with the dew of heaven, and let his lot be with the animals of the field, until seven times pass over him' — 24 this is the interpretation, O king, and it is a decree of the Most High that has come upon my lord the king: 25 You shall be driven away from human society, and your dwelling shall be with the wild animals. You shall be made to eat grass like oxen, you shall be bathed with the dew of heaven, and seven times shall pass over you, until you have learned that the Most High has sovereignty over the kingdom of mortals, and gives it to whom he will. 26 As it was commanded to leave the stump and roots of the tree, your kingdom shall be reestablished for you from the time that you learn that Heaven is sovereign. 27 Therefore, O king, may my counsel be acceptable to you: atone forr your sins with righteousness, and your iniquities with mercy to the oppressed, so that your prosperity may be prolonged."

Nebuchadnezzar's Humiliation

28 All this came upon King Ne·bu·chad·nez'zar. 29 At the end of twelve months he was walking on the roof of the royal palace of Babylon, 30 and the king said, "Is this not magnificent Babylon, which I have built as a royal capital by my mighty power and for my glorious majesty?" 31 While the words were still in the king's mouth, a voice came from heaven: "O King Ne·bu·chad·nez'zar, to you it is declared: The kingdom has departed from you! 32 You shall be driven away from human society, and your dwelling shall be with the animals of the field. You shall be made to eat grass like oxen, and seven times shall pass over you, until you have learned that the Most High has sovereignty over the kingdom of mortals and gives it to whom he will." 33 Immediately the sentence was fulfilled against Ne·bu·chad·nez'zar. He was driven away from human society, ate grass like oxen, and his body was bathed with the dew of heaven, until his hair grew as long as eagles' feathers and his nails became like birds' claws.

Nebuchadnezzar Praises God

34 When that period was over, I, Ne·bu·chad·nez'zar, lifted my eyes to heaven, and my reason returned to me.
I blessed the Most High,
    and praised and honored the
        one who lives forever.
For his sovereignty is an
        everlasting sovereignty,
    and his kingdom endures from
        generation to generation.
35 All the inhabitants of the earth
        are accounted as nothing,
    and he does what he wills with
        the host of heaven
    and the inhabitants of the
        earth.
There is no one who can stay
        his hand
    or say to him, "What are you
        doing?"
36 At that time my reason returned to me; and my majesty and splendor were restored to me for the glory of my kingdom. My counselors and my lords sought me out, I was re-established over my kingdom, and still more greatness was added to me. 37 Now I,

q Or a holy, divine spirit   r Aram break off

Ne·bu·chad·nez'zar, praise and extol
and honor the King of heaven,
     for all his works are truth,
          and his ways are justice;
     and he is able to bring low
          those who walk in pride.

Belshazzar's Feast

5 King Bel·shaz'zar made a great
festival for a thousand of his lords,
and he was drinking wine in the presence of the thousand.
2 Under the influence of the wine,
Bel·shaz'zar commanded that they
bring in the vessels of gold and silver
that his father Ne·bu·chad·nez'zar had
taken out of the temple in Jerusalem,
so that the king and his lords, his
wives, and his concubines might drink
from them. 3 So they brought in the
vessels of gold and silver[s] that had
been taken out of the temple, the house
of God in Jerusalem, and the king and
his lords, his wives, and his concubines drank from them. 4 They drank
the wine and praised the gods of gold
and silver, bronze, iron, wood, and
stone.

The Writing on the Wall

5 Immediately the fingers of a human hand appeared and began writing
on the plaster of the wall of the royal
palace, next to the lampstand. The
king was watching the hand as it
wrote. 6 Then the king's face turned
pale, and his thoughts terrified him.
His limbs gave way, and his knees
knocked together. 7 The king cried
aloud to bring in the enchanters, the
Chal·de'ans, and the diviners; and the
king said to the wise men of Babylon,
"Whoever can read this writing and
tell me its interpretation shall be
clothed in purple, have a chain of gold
around his neck, and rank third in the
kingdom." 8 Then all the king's wise
men came in, but they could not read
the writing or tell the king the interpretation. 9 Then King Bel·shaz'zar became greatly terrified and his face
turned pale, and his lords were perplexed.
10 The queen, when she heard the
discussion of the king and his lords,
came into the banqueting hall. The
queen said, "O king, live forever! Do
not let your thoughts terrify you or
your face grow pale. 11 There is a man
in your kingdom who is endowed with
a spirit of the holy gods.[t] In the days

of your father he was found to have
enlightenment, understanding, and
wisdom like the wisdom of the gods.
Your father, King Ne·bu·chad·nez'zar,
made him chief of the magicians, enchanters, Chal·de'ans, and diviners,[u]
12 because an excellent spirit, knowledge, and understanding to interpret
dreams, explain riddles, and solve
problems were found in this Daniel,
whom the king named Bel·te·shaz'zar.
Now let Daniel be called, and he will
give the interpretation."

The Writing on the Wall Interpreted

13 Then Daniel was brought in before the king. The king said to Daniel,
"So you are Daniel, one of the exiles of
Judah, whom my father the king
brought from Judah? 14 I have heard of
you that a spirit of the gods[v] is in you,
and that enlightenment, understanding, and excellent wisdom are found in
you. 15 Now the wise men, the enchanters, have been brought in before me to
read this writing and tell me its interpretation, but they were not able to
give the interpretation of the matter.
16 But I have heard that you can give
interpretations and solve problems.
Now if you are able to read the writing
and tell me its interpretation, you shall
be clothed in purple, have a chain of
gold around your neck, and rank third
in the kingdom."
17 Then Daniel answered in the
presence of the king, "Let your gifts be
for yourself, or give your rewards to
someone else! Nevertheless I will read
the writing to the king and let him
know the interpretation. 18 O king, the
Most High God gave your father
Ne·bu·chad·nez'zar kingship, greatness, glory, and majesty. 19 And because of the greatness that he gave
him, all peoples, nations, and languages trembled and feared before
him. He killed those he wanted to kill,
kept alive those he wanted to keep
alive, honored those he wanted to
honor, and degraded those he wanted
to degrade. 20 But when his heart was
lifted up and his spirit was hardened so
that he acted proudly, he was deposed
from his kingly throne, and his glory
was stripped from him. 21 He was
driven from human society, and his

---

[s] Theodotion Vg: Aram lacks *and silver*
[t] Or *a holy, divine spirit*   [u] Aram adds
the king your father   [v] Or *a divine
spirit*

mind was made like that of an animal. His dwelling was with the wild asses, he was fed grass like oxen, and his body was bathed with the dew of heaven, until he learned that the Most High God has sovereignty over the kingdom of mortals, and sets over it whomever he will. 22 And you, Bel·shaz'zar his son, have not humbled your heart, even though you knew all this! 23 You have exalted yourself against the Lord of heaven! The vessels of his temple have been brought in before you, and you and your lords, your wives and your concubines have been drinking wine from them. You have praised the gods of silver and gold, of bronze, iron, wood, and stone, which do not see or hear or know; but the God in whose power is your very breath, and to whom belong all your ways, you have not honored.

24 "So from his presence the hand was sent and this writing was inscribed. 25 And this is the writing that was inscribed: MENE, MENE, TEKEL, and PARSIN. 26 This is the interpretation of the matter: MENE, God has numbered the days of[w] your kingdom and brought it to an end; 27 TEKEL, you have been weighed on the scales and found wanting; 28 PERES,[x] your kingdom is divided and given to the Medes and Persians."

29 Then Bel·shaz'zar gave the command, and Daniel was clothed in purple, a chain of gold was put around his neck, and a proclamation was made concerning him that he should rank third in the kingdom.

30 That very night Bel·shaz'zar, the Chal·de'an king, was killed. 31[y] And Da·ri'us the Mede received the kingdom, being about sixty-two years old.

The Plot against Daniel

6 It pleased Da·ri'us to set over the kingdom one hundred twenty satraps, stationed throughout the whole kingdom, 2 and over them three presidents, including Daniel; to these the satraps gave account, so that the king might suffer no loss. 3 Soon Daniel distinguished himself above all the other presidents and satraps because an excellent spirit was in him, and the king planned to appoint him over the whole kingdom. 4 So the presidents and the satraps tried to find grounds for complaint against Daniel in connection with the kingdom. But they could find no grounds for complaint or any corruption, because he was faithful, and no negligence or corruption could be found in him. 5 The men said, "We shall not find any ground for complaint against this Daniel unless we find it in connection with the law of his God."

6 So the presidents and satraps conspired and came to the king and said to him, "O King Da·ri'us, live forever! 7 All the presidents of the kingdom, the prefects and the satraps, the counselors and the governors are agreed that the king should establish an ordinance and enforce an interdict, that whoever prays to anyone, divine or human, for thirty days, except to you, O king, shall be thrown into a den of lions. 8 Now, O king, establish the interdict and sign the document, so that it cannot be changed, according to the law of the Medes and the Persians, which cannot be revoked." 9 Therefore King Da·ri'us signed the document and interdict.

Daniel in the Lions' Den

10 Although Daniel knew that the document had been signed, he continued to go to his house, which had windows in its upper room open toward Jerusalem, and to get down on his knees three times a day to pray to his God and praise him, just as he had done previously. 11 The conspirators came and found Daniel praying and seeking mercy before his God. 12 Then they approached the king and said concerning the interdict, "O king! Did you not sign an interdict, that anyone who prays to anyone, divine or human, within thirty days except to you, O king, shall be thrown into a den of lions?" The king answered, "The thing stands fast, according to the law of the Medes and Persians, which cannot be revoked." 13 Then they responded to the king, "Daniel, one of the exiles from Judah, pays no attention to you, O king, or to the interdict you have signed, but he is saying his prayers three times a day."

14 When the king heard the charge, he was very much distressed. He was determined to save Daniel, and until the sun went down he made every effort to rescue him. 15 Then the conspirators came to the king and said to him, "Know, O king, that it is a law of the

---

w Aram lacks *the days of*
x The singular of *Parsin*   y Ch 6.1 in Aram

Mēdes and Persians that no interdict or ordinance that the king establishes can be changed."

16 Then the king gave the command, and Daniel was brought and thrown into the den of lions. The king said to Daniel, "May your God, whom you faithfully serve, deliver you!" 17 A stone was brought and laid on the mouth of the den, and the king sealed it with his own signet and with the signet of his lords, so that nothing might be changed concerning Daniel. 18 Then the king went to his palace and spent the night fasting; no food was brought to him, and sleep fled from him.

Daniel Saved from the Lions

19 Then, at break of day, the king got up and hurried to the den of lions. 20 When he came near the den where Daniel was, he cried out anxiously to Daniel, "O Daniel, servant of the living God, has your God whom you faithfully serve been able to deliver you from the lions?" 21 Daniel then said to the king, "O king, live forever! 22 My God sent his angel and shut the lions' mouths so that they would not hurt me, because I was found blameless before him; and also before you, O king, I have done no wrong." 23 Then the king was exceedingly glad and commanded that Daniel be taken up out of the den. So Daniel was taken up out of the den, and no kind of harm was found on him, because he had trusted in his God. 24 The king gave a command, and those who had accused Daniel were brought and thrown into the den of lions — they, their children, and their wives. Before they reached the bottom of the den the lions overpowered them and broke all their bones in pieces.

25 Then King Da·rī′us wrote to all peoples and nations of every language throughout the whole world: "May you have abundant prosperity! 26 I make a decree, that in all my royal dominion people should tremble and fear before the God of Daniel:

> For he is the living God,
>   enduring forever.
> His kingdom shall never be
>   destroyed,
> and his dominion has no end.

27 He delivers and rescues,
>   he works signs and wonders in
>   heaven and on earth;
> for he has saved Daniel
>   from the power of the lions."

28 So this Daniel prospered during the reign of Da·rī′us and the reign of Cyrus the Persian.

Visions of the Four Beasts

7 In the first year of King Bel·shaz′-zar of Babylon, Daniel had a dream and visions of his head as he lay in bed. Then he wrote down the dream:[z] 2 I,[a] Daniel, saw in my vision by night the four winds of heaven stirring up the great sea, 3 and four great beasts came up out of the sea, different from one another. 4 The first was like a lion and had eagles' wings. Then, as I watched, its wings were plucked off, and it was lifted up from the ground and made to stand on two feet like a human being; and a human mind was given to it. 5 Another beast appeared, a second one, that looked like a bear. It was raised up on one side, had three tusks[b] in its mouth among its teeth and was told, "Arise, devour many bodies!" 6 After this, as I watched, another appeared, like a leopard. The beast had four wings of a bird on its back and four heads; and dominion was given to it. 7 After this I saw in the visions by night a fourth beast, terrifying and dreadful and exceedingly strong. It had great iron teeth and was devouring, breaking in pieces, and stamping what was left with its feet. It was different from all the beasts that preceded it, and it had ten horns. 8 I was considering the horns, when another horn appeared, a little one coming up among them; to make room for it, three of the earlier horns were plucked up by the roots. There were eyes like human eyes in this horn, and a mouth speaking arrogantly.

Judgment before the Ancient One

9   As I watched,
> thrones were set in place,
>   and an Ancient One[c] took
>   his throne,
> his clothing was white as snow,
>   and the hair of his head like
>   pure wool;
> his throne was fiery flames,
>   and its wheels were burning
>   fire.

10   A stream of fire issued

---

[z] Q Ms Theodotion: MT adds *the beginning of the words; he said*
[a] Theodotion: Aram *Daniel answered and said,* "I   [b] Or *ribs*   [c] Aram *an Ancient of Days*

D
A
N
I
E
L

and flowed out from his
    presence.
A thousand thousands served
    him,
and ten thousand times ten
    thousand stood
    attending him.
The court sat in judgment,
    and the books were opened.
[11] I watched then because of the noise
of the arrogant words that the horn
was speaking. And as I watched, the
beast was put to death, and its body
destroyed and given over to be burned
with fire. [12] As for the rest of the beasts,
their dominion was taken away, but
their lives were prolonged for a season
and a time. [13] As I watched in the night
visions,
I saw one like a human being[d]
    coming with the clouds
    of heaven.
And he came to the Ancient
    One[e]
    and was presented before him.
[14] To him was given dominion
    and glory and kingship,
    that all peoples, nations, and
        languages
    should serve him.
His dominion is an everlasting
    dominion
    that shall not pass away,
and his kingship is one
    that shall never be destroyed.

Daniel's Visions Interpreted

15 As for me, Daniel, my spirit was
troubled within me,[f] and the visions
of my head terrified me. [16] I approached one of the attendants to ask
him the truth concerning all this. So he
said that he would disclose to me the
interpretation of the matter: [17] "As for
these four great beasts, four kings
shall arise out of the earth. [18] But the
holy ones of the Most High shall receive the kingdom and possess the
kingdom forever—forever and ever."
19 Then I desired to know the truth
concerning the fourth beast, which
was different from all the rest, exceedingly terrifying, with its teeth of iron
and claws of bronze, and which devoured and broke in pieces, and
stamped what was left with its feet;
[20] and concerning the ten horns that
were on its head, and concerning the
other horn, which came up and to
make room for which three of them fell
out—the horn that had eyes and a
mouth that spoke arrogantly, and that

seemed greater than the others. [21] As I
looked, this horn made war with the
holy ones and was prevailing over
them, [22] until the Ancient One[e] came;
then judgment was given for the holy
ones of the Most High, and the time
arrived when the holy ones gained
possession of the kingdom.
23 This is what he said: "As for the
fourth beast,
there shall be a fourth kingdom
    on earth
    that shall be different from all
        the other kingdoms;
it shall devour the whole earth,
    and trample it down, and
        break it to pieces.
24 As for the ten horns,
out of this kingdom ten kings
        shall arise,
    and another shall arise after
        them.
This one shall be different from
        the former ones,
    and shall put down three
        kings.
25 He shall speak words against the
        Most High,
    shall wear out the holy ones of
        the Most High,
    and shall attempt to change
        the sacred seasons and the
        law;
and they shall be given into
        his power
    for a time, two times,[g] and
        half a time.
26 Then the court shall sit in
        judgment,
    and his dominion shall be
        taken away,
    to be consumed and totally
        destroyed.
27 The kingship and dominion
    and the greatness of the
        kingdoms under the
        whole heaven
    shall be given to the people of
        the holy ones of the
        Most High;
their kingdom shall be an
        everlasting kingdom,
    and all dominions shall serve
        and obey them."
28 Here the account ends. As for
me, Daniel, my thoughts greatly terrified me, and my face turned pale; but
I kept the matter in my mind.

[d] Aram *one like a son of man* [e] Aram
the Ancient of Days [f] Aram *troubled
in its sheath* [g] Aram *a time, times*

Vision of a Ram and a Goat

8 In the third year of the reign of King Bel·shaz'zar a vision appeared to me, Daniel, after the one that had appeared to me at first. ²In the vision I was looking and saw myself in Su'sa the capital, in the province of E'lam,[h] and I was by the river U'lai.[i] ³I looked up and saw a ram standing beside the river.[j] It had two horns. Both horns were long, but one was longer than the other, and the longer one came up second. ⁴I saw the ram charging westward and northward and southward. All beasts were powerless to withstand it, and no one could rescue from its power; it did as it pleased and became strong.

5 As I was watching, a male goat appeared from the west, coming across the face of the whole earth without touching the ground. The goat had a horn[k] between its eyes. ⁶It came toward the ram with the two horns that I had seen standing beside the river,[j] and it ran at it with savage force. ⁷I saw it approaching the ram. It was enraged against it and struck the ram, breaking its two horns. The ram did not have power to withstand it; it threw the ram down to the ground and trampled upon it, and there was no one who could rescue the ram from its power. ⁸Then the male goat grew exceedingly great; but at the height of its power, the great horn was broken, and in its place there came up four prominent horns toward the four winds of heaven.

9 Out of one of them came another[l] horn, a little one, which grew exceedingly great toward the south, toward the east, and toward the beautiful land. ¹⁰It grew as high as the host of heaven. It threw down to the earth some of the host and some of the stars, and trampled on them. ¹¹Even against the prince of the host it acted arrogantly; it took the regular burnt offering away from him and overthrew the place of his sanctuary. ¹²Because of wickedness, the host was given over to it together with the regular burnt offering;[m] it cast truth to the ground, and kept prospering in what it did. ¹³Then I heard a holy one speaking, and another holy one said to the one that spoke, "For how long is this vision concerning the regular burnt offering, the transgression that makes desolate, and the giving over of the sanctuary

and host to be trampled?"[m] ¹⁴And he answered him,[n] "For two thousand three hundred evenings and mornings; then the sanctuary shall be restored to its rightful state."

Gabriel Interprets the Vision

15 When I, Daniel, had seen the vision, I tried to understand it. Then someone appeared standing before me, having the appearance of a man, ¹⁶and I heard a human voice by the U'lai, calling, "Gabriel, help this man understand the vision." ¹⁷So he came near where I stood; and when he came, I became frightened and fell prostrate. But he said to me, "Understand, O mortal,[o] that the vision is for the time of the end."

18 As he was speaking to me, I fell into a trance, face to the ground; then he touched me and set me on my feet. ¹⁹He said, "Listen, and I will tell you what will take place later in the period of wrath; for it refers to the appointed time of the end. ²⁰As for the ram that you saw with the two horns, these are the kings of Med'i·a and Persia. ²¹The male goat[p] is the king of Greece, and the great horn between its eyes is the first king. ²²As for the horn that was broken, in place of which four others arose, four kingdoms shall arise from his[q] nation, but not with his power.
23   At the end of their rule,
       when the transgressions have
          reached their full measure,
     a king of bold countenance
          shall arise,
       skilled in intrigue.
24   He shall grow strong in power,[r]
       shall cause fearful destruction,
       and shall succeed in what
          he does.
     He shall destroy the powerful
       and the people of the holy
          ones.
25   By his cunning
       he shall make deceit prosper
          under his hand,

---

[h] Gk Theodotion: MT Q Ms repeat *in the vision I was looking*   [i] Or *the Ulai Gate*   [j] Or *gate*   [k] Theodotion: Gk *one horn*; Heb *a horn of vision*   [l] Cn Compare 7.8: Heb *one*   [m] Meaning of Heb uncertain   [n] Gk Theodotion Syr Vg: Heb *me*   [o] Heb *son of man*   [p] Or *shaggy male goat*   [q] Gk Theodotion Vg: Heb *the*   [r] Theodotion and one Gk Ms: Heb repeats (from 8.22) *but not with his power*

and in his own mind he shall
    be great.
Without warning he shall
    destroy many
and shall even rise up against
    the Prince of princes.
But he shall be broken, and not
    by human hands.

26 The vision of the evenings and the mornings that has been told is true. As for you, seal up the vision, for it refers to many days from now."

27 So I, Daniel, was overcome and lay sick for some days; then I arose and went about the king's business. But I was dismayed by the vision and did not understand it.

Daniel's Prayer for the People

9 In the first year of Da·rī′us son of A·has·ū·ē′rus, by birth a Mēde, who became king over the realm of the Chal·dē′ans — 2 in the first year of his reign, I, Daniel, perceived in the books the number of years that, according to the word of the LORD to the prophet Jer·e·mī′ah, must be fulfilled for the devastation of Jerusalem, namely, seventy years. 3 Then I turned to the Lord God, to seek an answer by prayer and supplication with fasting and sackcloth and ashes. 4 I prayed to the LORD my God and made confession, saying,

"Ah, Lord, great and awesome God, keeping covenant and steadfast love with those who love you and keep your commandments, 5 we have sinned and done wrong, acted wickedly and rebelled, turning aside from your commandments and ordinances. 6 We have not listened to your servants the prophets, who spoke in your name to our kings, our princes, and our ancestors, and to all the people of the land. 7 "Righteousness is on your side, O Lord, but open shame, as at this day, falls on us, the people of Judah, the inhabitants of Jerusalem, and all Israel, those who are near and those who are far away, in all the lands to which you have driven them, because of the treachery that they have committed against you. 8 Open shame, O LORD, falls on us, our kings, our officials, and our ancestors, because we have sinned against you. 9 To the Lord our God belong mercy and forgiveness, for we have rebelled against him, 10 and have not obeyed the voice of the LORD our God by following his laws, which he set before us by his servants the prophets.

11 "All Israel has transgressed your law and turned aside, refusing to obey your voice. So the curse and the oath written in the law of Moses, the servant of God, have been poured out upon us, because we have sinned against you. 12 He has confirmed his words, which he spoke against us and against our rulers, by bringing upon us a calamity so great that what has been done against Jerusalem has never before been done under the whole heaven. 13 Just as it is written in the law of Moses, all this calamity has come upon us. We did not entreat the favor of the LORD our God, turning from our iniquities and reflecting on his[s] fidelity. 14 So the LORD kept watch over this calamity until he brought it upon us. Indeed, the LORD our God is right in all that he has done; for we have disobeyed his voice.

15 "And now, O Lord our God, who brought your people out of the land of Egypt with a mighty hand and made your name renowned even to this day — we have sinned, we have done wickedly. 16 O Lord, in view of all your righteous acts, let your anger and wrath, we pray, turn away from your city Jerusalem, your holy mountain; because of our sins and the iniquities of our ancestors, Jerusalem and your people have become a disgrace among all our neighbors. 17 Now therefore, O our God, listen to the prayer of your servant and to his supplication, and for your own sake, Lord,[t] let your face shine upon your desolated sanctuary. 18 Incline your ear, O my God, and hear. Open your eyes and look at our desolation and the city that bears your name. We do not present our supplication before you on the ground of our righteousness, but on the ground of your great mercies. 19 O Lord, hear; O Lord, forgive; O Lord, listen and act and do not delay! For your own sake, O my God, because your city and your people bear your name!"

The Seventy Weeks

20 While I was speaking, and was praying and confessing my sin and the sin of my people Israel, and presenting my supplication before the LORD my God on behalf of the holy mountain of

---

s Heb your   t Theodotion Vg Compare
Syr: Heb for the Lord's sake

my God— ²¹while I was speaking in prayer, the man Gabriel, whom I had seen before in a vision, came to me in swift flight at the time of the evening sacrifice. ²²He came ͧ and said to me, "Daniel, I have now come out to give you wisdom and understanding. ²³At the beginning of your supplications a word went out, and I have come to declare it, for you are greatly beloved. So consider the word and understand the vision:

24 "Seventy weeks are decreed for your people and your holy city: to finish the transgression, to put an end to sin, and to atone for iniquity, to bring in everlasting righteousness, to seal both vision and prophet, and to anoint a most holy place.ᵛ ²⁵Know therefore and understand: from the time that the word went out to restore and rebuild Jerusalem until the time of an anointed prince, there shall be seven weeks; and for sixty-two weeks it shall be built again with streets and moat, but in a troubled time. ²⁶After the sixty-two weeks, an anointed one shall be cut off and shall have nothing, and the troops of the prince who is to come shall destroy the city and the sanctuary. Itsʷ end shall come with a flood, and to the end there shall be war. Desolations are decreed. ²⁷He shall make a strong covenant with many for one week, and for half of the week he shall make sacrifice and offering cease; and in their placeˣ shall be an abomination that desolates, until the decreed end is poured out upon the desolator."

Conflict of Nations and Heavenly Powers

10 In the third year of King Cyrus of Persia a word was revealed to Daniel, who was named Bel·te-shaz'zar. The word was true, and it concerned a great conflict. He understood the word, having received understanding in the vision.

2 At that time I, Daniel, had been mourning for three weeks. ³I had eaten no rich food, no meat or wine had entered my mouth, and I had not anointed myself at all, for the full three weeks. ⁴On the twenty-fourth day of the first month, as I was standing on the bank of the great river (that is, the Tigris), ⁵I looked up and saw a man clothed in linen, with a belt of gold from U'phaz around his waist. ⁶His body was like beryl, his face like lightning, his eyes like flaming torches, his arms and legs like the gleam of burnished bronze, and the sound of his words like the roar of a multitude. ⁷I, Daniel, alone saw the vision; the people who were with me did not see the vision, though a great trembling fell upon them, and they fled and hid themselves. ⁸So I was left alone to see this great vision. My strength left me, and my complexion grew deathly pale, and I retained no strength. ⁹Then I heard the sound of his words; and when I heard the sound of his words, I fell into a trance, face to the ground.

10 But then a hand touched me and roused me to my hands and knees. ¹¹He said to me, "Daniel, greatly beloved, pay attention to the words that I am going to speak to you. Stand on your feet, for I have now been sent to you." So while he was speaking this word to me, I stood up trembling. ¹²He said to me, "Do not fear, Daniel, for from the first day that you set your mind to gain understanding and to humble yourself before your God, your words have been heard, and I have come because of your words. ¹³But the prince of the kingdom of Persia opposed me twenty-one days. So Michael, one of the chief princes, came to help me, and I left him there with the prince of the kingdom of Persia,ʸ ¹⁴and have come to help you understand what is to happen to your people at the end of days. For there is a further vision for those days."

15 While he was speaking these words to me, I turned my face toward the ground and was speechless. ¹⁶Then one in human form touched my lips, and I opened my mouth to speak, and said to the one who stood before me, "My lord, because of the vision such pains have come upon me that I retain no strength. ¹⁷How can my lord's servant talk with my lord? For I am shaking,ᶻ no strength remains in me, and no breath is left in me."

18 Again one in human form touched me and strengthened me. ¹⁹He said, "Do not fear, greatly beloved, you are safe. Be strong and courageous!" When he spoke to me, I was strengthened and said, "Let my lord

ͧGk Syr: Heb *He made to understand*
ᵛOr *thing* or *one*   ʷOr *His*
ˣCn: Meaning of Heb uncertain
ʸGk Theodotion: Heb *I was left there with the kings of Persia*   ᶻGk: Heb *from now*

speak, for you have strengthened me."
20 Then he said, "Do you know why I have come to you? Now I must return to fight against the prince of Persia, and when I am through with him, the prince of Greece will come. 21 But I am to tell you what is inscribed in the book of truth. There is no one with me who contends against these princes except Michael, your prince. 11 1 As for me, in the first year of Da·rī′us the Mēde, I stood up to support and strengthen him.

2 "Now I will announce the truth to you. Three more kings shall arise in Persia. The fourth shall be far richer than all of them, and when he has become strong through his riches, he shall stir up all against the kingdom of Greece. 3 Then a warrior king shall arise, who shall rule with great dominion and take action as he pleases. 4 And while still rising in power, his kingdom shall be broken and divided toward the four winds of heaven, but not to his posterity, nor according to the dominion with which he ruled; for his kingdom shall be uprooted and go to others besides these.

5 "Then the king of the south shall grow strong, but one of his officers shall grow stronger than he and shall rule a realm greater than his own realm. 6 After some years they shall make an alliance, and the daughter of the king of the south shall come to the king of the north to ratify the agreement. But she shall not retain her power, and his offspring shall not endure. She shall be given up, she and her attendants and her child and the one who supported her.

"In those times 7 a branch from her roots shall rise up in his place. He shall come against the army and enter the fortress of the king of the north, and he shall take action against them and prevail. 8 Even their gods, with their idols and with their precious vessels of silver and gold, he shall carry off to Egypt as spoils of war. For some years he shall refrain from attacking the king of the north; 9 then the latter shall invade the realm of the king of the south, but will return to his own land.

10 "His sons shall wage war and assemble a multitude of great forces, which shall advance like a flood and pass through, and again shall carry the war as far as his fortress. 11 Moved with rage, the king of the south shall go out and do battle against the king of the north, who shall muster a great multitude, which shall, however, be defeated by his enemy. 12 When the multitude has been carried off, his heart shall be exalted, and he shall overthrow tens of thousands, but he shall not prevail. 13 For the king of the north shall again raise a multitude, larger than the former, and after some years[a] he shall advance with a great army and abundant supplies.

14 "In those times many shall rise against the king of the south. The lawless among your own people shall lift themselves up in order to fulfill the vision, but they shall fail. 15 Then the king of the north shall come and throw up siegeworks, and take a well-fortified city. And the forces of the south shall not stand, not even his picked troops, for there shall be no strength to resist. 16 But he who comes against him shall take the actions he pleases, and no one shall withstand him. He shall take a position in the beautiful land, and all of it shall be in his power. 17 He shall set his mind to come with the strength of his whole kingdom, and he shall bring terms of peace[b] and perform them. In order to destroy the kingdom,[c] he shall give him a woman in marriage; but it shall not succeed or be to his advantage. 18 Afterward he shall turn to the coastlands, and shall capture many. But a commander shall put an end to his insolence; indeed,[d] he shall turn his insolence back upon him. 19 Then he shall turn back toward the fortresses of his own land, but he shall stumble and fall, and shall not be found.

20 "Then shall arise in his place one who shall send an official for the glory of the kingdom; but within a few days he shall be broken, though not in anger or in battle. 21 In his place shall arise a contemptible person on whom royal majesty had not been conferred; he shall come in without warning and obtain the kingdom through intrigue. 22 Armies shall be utterly swept away and broken before him, and the prince of the covenant as well. 23 And after an alliance is made with him, he shall act deceitfully and become strong with a small party. 24 Without warning he shall come into the richest parts[e] of

a Heb and at the end of the times years b Gk: Heb kingdom, and upright ones with him   c Heb it   d Meaning of Heb uncertain   e Or among the richest men the province and do what none of his predecessors had ever done, lavishing plunder, spoil, and wealth on them. He shall devise plans against strongholds, but only for a time. [25] He shall stir up his power and determination against the king of the south with a great army, and the king of the south shall wage war with a much greater and stronger army. But he shall not succeed, for plots shall be devised against him [26] by those who eat of the royal rations. They shall break him, his army shall be swept away, and many shall fall slain. [27] The two kings, their minds bent on evil, shall sit at one table and exchange lies. But it shall not succeed, for there remains an end at the time appointed. [28] He shall return to his land with great wealth, but his heart shall be set against the holy covenant. He shall work his will, and return to his own land.

29 "At the time appointed he shall return and come into the south, but this time it shall not be as it was before. [30] For ships of Kit′tim shall come against him, and he shall lose heart and withdraw. He shall be enraged and take action against the holy covenant. He shall turn back and pay heed to those who forsake the holy covenant. [31] Forces sent by him shall occupy and profane the temple and fortress. They shall abolish the regular burnt offering and set up the abomination that makes desolate. [32] He shall seduce with intrigue those who violate the covenant; but the people who are loyal to their God shall stand firm and take action. [33] The wise among the people shall give understanding to many; for some days, however, they shall fall by sword and flame, and suffer captivity and plunder. [34] When they fall victim, they shall receive a little help, and many shall join them insincerely. [35] Some of the wise shall fall, so that they may be refined, purified, and cleansed,[f] until the time of the end, for there is still an interval until the time appointed.

36 "The king shall act as he pleases. He shall exalt himself and consider himself greater than any god, and shall speak horrendous things against the God of gods. He shall prosper until the period of wrath is completed, for what is determined shall be done. [37] He shall pay no respect to the gods of his ancestors, or to the one beloved by women; he shall pay no respect to any other

god, for he shall consider himself greater than all. [38] He shall honor the god of fortresses instead of these; a god whom his ancestors did not know he shall honor with gold and silver, with precious stones and costly gifts. [39] He shall deal with the strongest fortresses by the help of a foreign god. Those who acknowledge him he shall make more wealthy, and shall appoint them as rulers over many, and shall distribute the land for a price.

The Time of the End

40 "At the time of the end the king of the south shall attack him. But the king of the north shall rush upon him like a whirlwind, with chariots and horsemen, and with many ships. He shall advance against countries and pass through like a flood. [41] He shall come into the beautiful land, and tens of thousands shall fall victim, but E′dom and Mō′ab and the main part of the Am′mon·ites shall escape from his power. [42] He shall stretch out his hand against the countries, and the land of Egypt shall not escape. [43] He shall become ruler of the treasures of gold and of silver, and all the riches of Egypt; and the Libyans and the Ethiopians[g] shall follow in his train. [44] But reports from the east and the north shall alarm him, and he shall go out with great fury to bring ruin and complete destruction to many. [45] He shall pitch his palatial tents between the sea and the beautiful holy mountain. Yet he shall come to his end, with no one to help him.

The Resurrection of the Dead

12 "At that time Michael, the great prince, the protector of your people, shall arise. There shall be a time of anguish, such as has never occurred since nations first came into existence. But at that time your people shall be delivered, everyone who is found written in the book. [2] Many of those who sleep in the dust of the earth[h] shall awake, some to everlasting life, and some to shame and everlasting contempt. [3] Those who are wise shall shine like the brightness of the sky,[i] and those who lead many to righteousness, like the stars forever and ever. [4] But you, Daniel, keep the words secret and the book sealed until

D
A
N
I
E
L

---

[f] Heb *made them white*   [g] Or *Nubians;*
Heb *Cushites*   [h] Or *the land of dust*
[i] Or *dome*

the time of the end. Many shall be running back and forth, and evil[j] shall increase."

5 Then I, Daniel, looked, and two others appeared, one standing on this bank of the stream and one on the other. 6 One of them said to the man clothed in linen, who was upstream, "How long shall it be until the end of these wonders?" 7 The man clothed in linen, who was upstream, raised his right hand and his left hand toward heaven. And I heard him swear by the one who lives forever that it would be for a time, two times, and half a time,[k] and that when the shattering of the power of the holy people comes to an end, all these things would be accomplished. 8 I heard but could not understand; so I said, "My lord, what shall be the outcome of these things?" 9 He said, "Go your way, Daniel, for the words are to remain secret and sealed until the time of the end. 10 Many shall be purified, cleansed, and refined, but the wicked shall continue to act wickedly. None of the wicked shall understand, but those who are wise shall understand. 11 From the time that the regular burnt offering is taken away and the abomination that desolates is set up, there shall be one thousand two hundred ninety days. 12 Happy are those who persevere and attain the thousand three hundred thirty-five days. 13 But you, go your way,[l] and rest; you shall rise for your reward at the end of the days."

Susanna's Beauty Attracts Two Elders

13 There was a man living in Babylon whose name was Jō'-a·kim. 2 He married the daughter of Hil·ki'ah, named Susanna, a very beautiful woman and one who feared the Lord. 3 Her parents were righteous, and had trained their daughter according to the law of Moses. 4 Jō'a·kim was very rich, and had a fine garden adjoining his house; the Jews used to come to him because he was the most honored of them all.

5 That year two elders from the people were appointed as judges. Concerning them the Lord had said: "Wickedness came forth from Babylon, from elders who were judges, who were supposed to govern the people." 6 These men were frequently at Jō'a·kim's house, and all who had a case to be tried came to them there.

7 When the people left at noon, Susanna would go into her husband's garden to walk. 8 Every day the two elders used to see her, going in and walking about, and they began to lust for her. 9 They suppressed their consciences and turned away their eyes from looking to Heaven or remembering their duty to administer justice. 10 Both were overwhelmed with passion for her, but they did not tell each other of their distress, 11 for they were ashamed to disclose their lustful desire to seduce her. 12 Day after day they watched eagerly to see her.

13 One day they said to each other, "Let us go home, for it is time for lunch." So they both left and parted from each other. 14 But turning back, they met again; and when each pressed the other for the reason, they confessed their lust. Then together they arranged for a time when they could find her alone.

The Elders Attempt to Seduce Susanna

15 Once, while they were watching for an opportune day, she went in as before with only two maids, and wished to bathe in the garden, for it was a hot day. 16 No one was there except the two elders, who had hidden themselves and were watching her. 17 She said to her maids, "Bring me olive oil and ointments, and shut the garden doors so that I can bathe." 18 They did as she told them: they shut the doors of the garden and went out by the side doors to bring what they had been commanded; they did not see the elders, because they were hiding.

19 When the maids had gone out, the two elders got up and ran to her. 20 They said, "Look, the garden doors are shut, and no one can see us. We are burning with desire for you; so give your consent, and lie with us. 21 If you refuse, we will testify against you that a young man was with you, and this was why you sent your maids away."

22 Susanna groaned and said, "I am completely trapped. For if I do this, it will mean death for me; if I do not, I cannot escape your hands. 23 I choose not to do it; I will fall into your hands, rather than sin in the sight of the Lord."

24 Then Susanna cried out with a

---

[j] Cn Compare Gk: Heb *knowledge*
[k] Heb *a time, times, and a half*
[l] Gk Theodotion: Heb adds *to the end*

loud voice, and the two elders shouted against her. 25 And one of them ran and opened the garden doors. 26 When the people in the house heard the shouting in the garden, they rushed in at the side door to see what had happened to her. 27 And when the elders told their story, the servants felt very much ashamed, for nothing like this had ever been said about Susanna.

The Elders Testify against Susanna

28 The next day, when the people gathered at the house of her husband Jō'a·kim, the two elders came, full of their wicked plot to have Susanna put to death. In the presence of the people they said, 29 "Send for Susanna daughter of Hil·kī'ah, the wife of Jō'a·kim." So they sent for her. 30 And she came with her parents, her children, and all her relatives.

31 Now Susanna was a woman of great refinement and beautiful in appearance. 32 As she was veiled, the scoundrels ordered her to be unveiled, so that they might feast their eyes on her beauty. 33 Those who were with her and all who saw her were weeping.

34 Then the two elders stood up before the people and laid their hands on her head. 35 Through her tears she looked up toward Heaven, for her heart trusted in the Lord. 36 The elders said, "While we were walking in the garden alone, this woman came in with two maids, shut the garden doors, and dismissed the maids. 37 Then a young man, who was hiding there, came to her and lay with her. 38 We were in a corner of the garden, and when we saw this wickedness we ran to them. 39 Although we saw them embracing, we could not hold the man, because he was stronger than we, and he opened the doors and got away. 40 We did, however, seize this woman and asked who the young man was, 41 but she would not tell us. These things we testify."

Because they were elders of the people and judges, the assembly believed them and condemned her to death.

42 Then Susanna cried out with a loud voice, and said, "O eternal God, you know what is secret and are aware of all things before they come to be; 43 you know that these men have given false evidence against me. And now I am to die, though I have done none of the wicked things that they have charged against me!"

44 The Lord heard her cry. 45 Just as she was being led off to execution, God stirred up the holy spirit of a young lad named Daniel, 46 and he shouted with a loud voice, "I want no part in shedding this woman's blood!"

Daniel Rescues Susanna

47 All the people turned to him and asked, "What is this you are saying?" 48 Taking his stand among them he said, "Are you such fools, O Israelites, as to condemn a daughter of Israel without examination and without learning the facts? 49 Return to court, for these men have given false evidence against her."

50 So all the people hurried back. And the rest of them[m] elders said to him, "Come, sit among us and inform us, for God has given you the standing of an elder." 51 Daniel said to them, "Separate them far from each other, and I will examine them."

52 When they were separated from each other, he summoned one of them and said to him, "You old relic of wicked days, your sins have now come home, which you have committed in the past, 53 pronouncing unjust judgments, condemning the innocent and acquitting the guilty, though the Lord said, 'You shall not put an innocent and righteous person to death.' 54 Now then, if you really saw this woman, tell me this: Under what tree did you see them being intimate with each other?" He answered, "Under a mastic tree."[n] 55 And Daniel said, "Very well! This lie has cost you your head, for the angel of God has received the sentence from God and will immediately cut[n] you in two."

56 Then, putting him to one side, he ordered them to bring the other. And he said to him, "You offspring of Cā'-naan and not of Judah, beauty has beguiled you and lust has perverted your heart. 57 This is how you have been treating the daughters of Israel, and they were intimate with you through fear; but a daughter of Judah would not tolerate your wickedness. 58 Now then, tell me: Under what tree did you catch them being intimate with each other?" He answered, "Under an ever-

---

m Gk lacks rest of the   n The Greek words for mastic tree and cut are similar, thus forming an ironic wordplay green oak."o 59 Daniel said to him, "Very well! This lie has cost you also your head, for the angel of God is waiting with his sword to splito you in two, so as to destroy you both."

60 Then the whole assembly raised a great shout and blessed God, who saves those who hope in him. 61 And they took action against the two elders, because out of their own mouths Daniel had convicted them of bearing false witness; they did to them as they had wickedly planned to do to their neighbor. 62 Acting in accordance with the law of Moses, they put them to death. Thus innocent blood was spared that day.

63 Hil·kī′ah and his wife praised God for their daughter Susanna, and so did her husband Jō′a·kim and all her relatives, because she was found innocent of a shameful deed. 64 And from that day onward Daniel had a great reputation among the people.

Daniel and the Priests of Bel

14 When King As·tȳ′a·ges was laid to rest with his ancestors, Cyrus the Persian succeeded to his kingdom. 2 Daniel was a companion of the king, and was the most honored of all his friends.

3 Now the Babylonians had an idol called Bel, and every day they provided for it twelve bushels of choice flour and forty sheep and six measuresp of wine. 4 The king revered it and went every day to worship it. But Daniel worshiped his own God.

So the king said to him, "Why do you not worship Bel?" 5 He answered, "Because I do not revere idols made with hands, but the living God, who created heaven and earth and has dominion over all living creatures."

6 The king said to him, "Do you not think that Bel is a living god? Do you not see how much he eats and drinks every day?" 7 And Daniel laughed, and said, "Do not be deceived, O king, for this thing is only clay inside and bronze outside, and it never ate or drank anything."

8 Then the king was angry and called the priests of Belq and said to them, "If you do not tell me who is eating these provisions, you shall die. 9 But if you prove that Bel is eating them, Daniel shall die, because he has spoken blasphemy against Bel." Daniel said to the king, "Let it be done as you have said."

10 Now there were seventy priests of Bel, besides their wives and children. So the king went with Daniel into the temple of Bel. 11 The priests of Bel said, "See, we are now going outside; you yourself, O king, set out the food and prepare the wine, and shut the door and seal it with your signet. 12 When you return in the morning, if you do not find that Bel has eaten it all, we will die; otherwise Daniel will, who is telling lies about us." 13 They were unconcerned, for beneath the table they had made a hidden entrance, through which they used to go in regularly and consume the provisions. 14 After they had gone out, the king set out the food for Bel. Then Daniel ordered his servants to bring ashes, and they scattered them throughout the whole temple in the presence of the king alone. Then they went out, shut the door and sealed it with the king's signet, and departed. 15 During the night the priests came as usual, with their wives and children, and they ate and drank everything.

16 Early in the morning the king rose and came, and Daniel with him. 17 The king said, "Are the seals unbroken, Daniel?" He answered, "They are unbroken, O king." 18 As soon as the doors were opened, the king looked at the table, and shouted in a loud voice, "You are great, O Bel, and in you there is no deceit at all!"

19 But Daniel laughed and restrained the king from going in. "Look at the floor," he said, "and notice whose footprints these are." 20 The king said, "I see the footprints of men and women and children."

21 Then the king was enraged, and he arrested the priests and their wives and children. They showed him the secret doors through which they used to enter to consume what was on the table. 22 Therefore the king put them to death, and gave Bel over to Daniel, who destroyed it and its temple.

Daniel Kills the Dragon

23 Now in that placer there was a great dragon, which the Babylonians revered. 24 The king said to Daniel, "You cannot deny that this is a living

---

o The Greek words for *evergreen oak* and *split* are similar, thus forming an ironic wordplay   p A little more than fifty gallons   q Gk *his priests*   r Other ancient authorities lack *in that place* god; so worship him." ²⁵ Daniel said, "I worship the Lord my God, for he is the living God. ²⁶ But give me permission, O king, and I will kill the dragon without sword or club." The king said, "I give you permission."

27 Then Daniel took pitch, fat, and hair, and boiled them together and made cakes, which he fed to the dragon. The dragon ate them, and burst open. Then Daniel said, "See what you have been worshiping!"

28 When the Babylonians heard about it, they were very indignant and conspired against the king, saying, "The king has become a Jew; he has destroyed Bel, and killed the dragon, and slaughtered the priests." ²⁹ Going to the king, they said, "Hand Daniel over to us, or else we will kill you and your household." ³⁰ The king saw that they were pressing him hard, and under compulsion he handed Daniel over to them.

Daniel in the Lions' Den

31 They threw Daniel into the lions' den, and he was there for six days. ³² There were seven lions in the den, and every day they had been given two human bodies and two sheep; but now they were given nothing, so that they would devour Daniel.

33 Now the prophet Ha·bak'kuk was in Judea; he had made a stew and had broken bread into a bowl, and was going into the field to take it to the reapers. ³⁴ But the angel of the Lord said to Ha·bak'kuk, "Take the food that you have to Babylon, to Daniel, in the lions' den." ³⁵ Ha·bak'kuk said, "Sir, I have never seen Babylon, and I know nothing about the den." ³⁶ Then the angel of the Lord took him by the crown of his head and carried him by his hair; with the speed of the wind[s] he set him down in Babylon, right over the den.

37 Then Ha·bak'kuk shouted, "Daniel, Daniel! Take the food that God has sent you." ³⁸ Daniel said, "You have remembered me, O God, and have not forsaken those who love you." ³⁹ So Daniel got up and ate. And the angel of God immediately returned Ha·bak'kuk to his own place.

40 On the seventh day the king came to mourn for Daniel. When he came to the den he looked in, and there sat Daniel! ⁴¹ The king shouted with a loud voice, "You are great, O Lord, the God of Daniel, and there is no other besides you!" ⁴² Then he pulled Daniel[t] out, and threw into the den those who had attempted his destruction, and they were instantly eaten before his eyes.

[s] Or *by the power of his spirit* [t] Gk *him*

HOSEA

1 The word of the LORD that came to Hō·sē'a son of Be·ē'rī, in the days of Kings Uz·zī'ah, Jō'tham, Ā'haz, and Hez·e·kī'ah of Judah, and in the days of King Jer·o·bō'am son of Jō'ash of Israel.

The Family of Hosea
(Cp 2 Kings 24.10–17)

2 When the LORD first spoke through Hō·sē'a, the LORD said to Hō·sē'a, "Go, take for yourself a wife of whoredom and have children of whoredom, for the land commits great whoredom by forsaking the LORD." ³ So he went and took Gō'mer daughter of Dib·lā'im, and she conceived and bore him a son.

4 And the LORD said to him, "Name him Jez'rē·el;[a] for in a little while I will punish the house of Jē'hū for the blood of Jez'rē·el, and I will put an end to the kingdom of the house of Israel. ⁵ On that day I will break the bow of Israel in the valley of Jez'rē·el."

6 She conceived again and bore a

[a] That is *God sows*

daughter. Then the LORD said to him, "Name her Lō-rū·ha′mah,[b] for I will no longer have pity on the house of Israel or forgive them. [7] But I will have pity on the house of Judah, and I will save them by the LORD their God; I will not save them by bow, or by sword, or by war, or by horses, or by horsemen."

8 When she had weaned Lō-rū·ha′-mah, she conceived and bore a son. [9] Then the LORD said, "Name him Lō-am′mī,[c] for you are not my people and I am not your God."[d]

The Restoration of Israel

10[e] Yet the number of the people of Israel shall be like the sand of the sea, which can be neither measured nor numbered; and in the place where it was said to them, "You are not my people," it shall be said to them, "Children of the living God." [11] The people of Judah and the people of Israel shall be gathered together, and they shall appoint for themselves one head; and they shall take possession of[f] the land, for great shall be the day of Jez′re·el.

2 [g] Say to your brother,[h] Am′mī,[i] and to your sister,[j] Rū·ha′mah.[k]

Israel's Infidelity, Punishment, and Redemption

2 Plead with your mother, plead —
  for she is not my wife,
  and I am not her husband —
that she put away her whoring
    from her face,
  and her adultery from between
    her breasts,
3 or I will strip her naked
  and expose her as in the day
    she was born,
and make her like a wilderness,
  and turn her into a parched
    land,
  and kill her with thirst.
4 Upon her children also I will
    have no pity,
  because they are children of
    whoredom.
5 For their mother has played the
    whore;
  she who conceived them has
    acted shamefully.
For she said, "I will go after my
    lovers;
  they give me my bread and my
    water,
my wool and my flax, my oil
    and my drink."

6 Therefore I will hedge up her[l]
    way with thorns;
  and I will build a wall against
    her,
  so that she cannot find her
    paths.
7 She shall pursue her lovers,
  but not overtake them;
and she shall seek them,
  but shall not find them.
Then she shall say, "I will go
  and return to my first
    husband,
  for it was better with me then
    than now."
8 She did not know
  that it was I who gave her
  the grain, the wine, and the
    oil,
and who lavished upon her
    silver
  and gold that they used for
    Bā′al.
9 Therefore I will take back
  my grain in its time,
  and my wine in its season;
and I will take away my wool
    and my flax,
  which were to cover her
    nakedness.
10 Now I will uncover her shame
  in the sight of her lovers,
  and no one shall rescue her
    out of my hand.
11 I will put an end to all her mirth,
  her festivals, her new moons,
    her sabbaths,
  and all her appointed festivals.
12 I will lay waste her vines and
    her fig trees,
  of which she said,
"These are my pay,
  which my lovers have given
    me."
I will make them a forest,
  and the wild animals shall
    devour them.
13 I will punish her for the festival
    days of the Bā′als,
  when she offered incense to
    them
and decked herself with her ring
    and jewelry,
  and went after her lovers,
  and forgot me, says the LORD.

[b] That is *Not pitied* [c] That is *Not my people* [d] Heb *I am not yours* [e] Ch 2.1 in Heb [f] Heb *rise up from* [g] Ch 2.3 in Heb [h] Gk: Heb *brothers* [i] That is *My People* [j] Gk Vg: Heb *sisters* [k] That is *Pitied* [l] Gk Syr: Heb *your*

H
O
S
E
A

14 Therefore, I will now allure her,
    and bring her into the
    wilderness,
    and speak tenderly to her.
15 From there I will give her her
    vineyards,
    and make the Valley of Ā'chor
    a door of hope.
    There she shall respond as in the
    days of her youth,
    as at the time when she came
    out of the land of Egypt.
16 On that day, says the LORD, you will call me, "My husband," and no longer will you call me, "My Bā'al."[m] 17 For I will remove the names of the Bā'als from her mouth, and they shall be mentioned by name no more. 18 I will make for you[n] a covenant on that day with the wild animals, the birds of the air, and the creeping things of the ground; and I will abolish[o] the bow, the sword, and war from the land; and I will make you lie down in safety. 19 And I will take you for my wife forever; I will take you for my wife in righteousness and in justice, in steadfast love, and in mercy. 20 I will take you for my wife in faithfulness; and you shall know the LORD.
21 On that day I will answer, says
        the LORD,
    I will answer the heavens
    and they shall answer the
        earth;
22 and the earth shall answer the
        grain, the wine, and the oil,
    and they shall answer
        Jez'rē·el;[p]
23 and I will sow him[q] for myself
    in the land.
    And I will have pity on
        Lō·rū·ha'mah,[r]
    and I will say to Lō-am'mī,[s]
        "You are my people";
    and he shall say, "You are my
        God."

Further Assurances of God's Redeeming Love

3 The LORD said to me again, "Go, love a woman who has a lover and is an adulteress, just as the LORD loves the people of Israel, though they turn to other gods and love raisin cakes." 2 So I bought her for fifteen shekels of silver and a homer of barley and a measure of wine.[t] 3 And I said to her, "You must remain as mine for many days; you shall not play the whore, nor shall you have intercourse with a man, nor I with you." 4 For the Israelites shall remain many days without king or prince, without sacrifice or pillar, without ephod or teraphim. 5 Afterward the Israelites shall return and seek the LORD their God, and David their king; they shall come in awe to the LORD and to his goodness in the latter days.

God Accuses Israel

4 Hear the word of the LORD,
        O people of Israel;
    for the LORD has an
        indictment against the
        inhabitants of the land.
    There is no faithfulness or
        loyalty,
    and no knowledge of God in
        the land.
2 Swearing, lying, and murder,
    and stealing and adultery
        break out;
    bloodshed follows bloodshed.
3 Therefore the land mourns,
    and all who live in it languish;
    together with the wild animals
        and the birds of the air,
    even the fish of the sea are
        perishing.

4 Yet let no one contend,
    and let none accuse,
    for with you is my contention,
        O priest.[u]
5 You shall stumble by day;
    the prophet also shall stumble
        with you by night,
    and I will destroy your mother.
6 My people are destroyed for lack
        of knowledge;
    because you have rejected
        knowledge,
    I reject you from being a priest
        to me.
    And since you have forgotten
        the law of your God,
    I also will forget your children.

7 The more they increased,
    the more they sinned against
        me;
    they changed[v] their glory into
        shame.

[m] That is, "My master" [n] Heb them
[o] Heb break [p] That is God sows
[q] Cn: Heb her [r] That is Not pitied
[s] That is Not my people [t] Gk: Heb a homer of barley and a lethech of barley
[u] Cn: Meaning of Heb uncertain
[v] Ancient Heb tradition: MT I will change

H
O
S
E
A

8 They feed on the sin of my
    people;
    they are greedy for their
      iniquity.
9 And it shall be like people, like
    priest;
    I will punish them for their
      ways,
    and repay them for their
      deeds.
10 They shall eat, but not be
    satisfied;
    they shall play the whore, but
      not multiply;
because they have forsaken the
    LORD
    to devote themselves to
    11 whoredom.

The Idolatry of Israel

Wine and new wine
    take away the understanding.
12 My people consult a piece of
    wood,
    and their divining rod gives
      them oracles.
For a spirit of whoredom has led
    them astray,
    and they have played the
      whore, forsaking their God.
13 They sacrifice on the tops of the
    mountains,
    and make offerings upon the
      hills,
under oak, poplar, and terebinth,
    because their shade is good.

Therefore your daughters play
    the whore,
    and your daughters-in-law
      commit adultery.
14 I will not punish your daughters
    when they play the whore,
    nor your daughters-in-law
      when they commit
      adultery;
for the men themselves go aside
    with whores,
    and sacrifice with temple
      prostitutes;
thus a people without
    understanding comes to
    ruin.

15 Though you play the whore,
    O Israel,
    do not let Judah become
      guilty.
Do not enter into Gil'gal,
    or go up to Beth-a'ven,

and do not swear, "As the
    LORD lives."
16 Like a stubborn heifer,
    Israel is stubborn;
can the LORD now feed them
    like a lamb in a broad pasture?

17 E'phra·im is joined to idols—
    let him alone.
18 When their drinking is ended,
    they indulge in sexual
      orgies;
    they love lewdness more than
      their glory.w
19 A wind has wrapped themx in
    its wings,
    and they shall be ashamed
      because of their altars.y

Impending Judgment on Israel and Judah

5 Hear this, O priests!
    Give heed, O house of Israel!
Listen, O house of the king!
    For the judgment pertains to
      you;
for you have been a snare at
    Miz'pah,
    and a net spread upon Tā'bor,
2 and a pit dug deep in Shit'tim;z
    but I will punish all of them.

3 I know E'phra·im,
    and Israel is not hidden from
      me;
for now, O E'phra·im, you have
    played the whore;
    Israel is defiled.
4 Their deeds do not permit them
    to return to their God.
For the spirit of whoredom is
    within them,
    and they do not know the
      LORD.

5 Israel's pride testifies against
    him;
    E'phra·ima stumbles in his
      guilt;
    Judah also stumbles with
      them.
6 With their flocks and herds they
    shall go
    to seek the LORD,
but they will not find him;
    he has withdrawn from them.

w Cn Compare Gk: Meaning of Heb
uncertain   x Heb her   y Gk Syr: Heb
sacrifices   z Cn: Meaning of Heb
uncertain   a Heb Israel and Ephraim

7 They have dealt faithlessly with
  the LORD;
    for they have borne
      illegitimate children.
  Now the new moon shall
    devour them along with
      their fields.

8 Blow the horn in Gib'e·ah,
    the trumpet in Rā'mah.
  Sound the alarm at Beth-ā'ven;
    look behind you, Benjamin!
9 Ē'phra·im shall become a
    desolation
  in the day of punishment;
    among the tribes of Israel
      I declare what is sure.
10 The princes of Judah have
      become
    like those who remove the
      landmark;
  on them I will pour out
    my wrath like water.
11 Ē'phra·im is oppressed, crushed
      in judgment,
    because he was determined to
      go after vanity.b
12 Therefore I am like maggots to
      Ē'phra·im,
    and like rottenness to the
      house of Judah.
13 When Ē'phra·im saw his
      sickness,
    and Judah his wound,
  then Ē'phra·im went to Assyria,
    and sent to the great king.c
  But he is not able to cure you
    or heal your wound.
14 For I will be like a lion to
      Ē'phra·im,
    and like a young lion to the
      house of Judah.
  I myself will tear and go away;
    I will carry off, and no one
      shall rescue.
15 I will return again to my place
    until they acknowledge their
      guilt and seek my face.
  In their distress they will beg
    my favor:

A Call to Repentance

6 "Come, let us return to the
    LORD;
  for it is he who has torn, and
    he will heal us;
  he has struck down, and he
    will bind us up.
2 After two days he will revive us;
    on the third day he will raise
      us up,
  that we may live before him.

3 Let us know, let us press on to
    know the LORD;
  his appearing is as sure as the
    dawn;
  he will come to us like the
    showers,
    like the spring rains that water
      the earth."

Impenitence of Israel and Judah

4 What shall I do with you,
    O Ē'phra·im?
  What shall I do with you,
    O Judah?
  Your love is like a morning
    cloud,
    like the dew that goes away
      early.
5 Therefore I have hewn them by
    the prophets,
  I have killed them by the
    words of my mouth,
  and myd judgment goes forth
    as the light.
6 For I desire steadfast love and
    not sacrifice,
  the knowledge of God rather
    than burnt offerings.

7 But ate Adam they transgressed
    the covenant;
  there they dealt faithlessly
    with me.
8 Gil'e·ad is a city of evildoers,
    tracked with blood.
9 As robbers lie in waitf for
    someone,
  so the priests are banded
    together;g
  they murder on the road to
    Shē'chem,
  they commit a monstrous
    crime.
10 In the house of Israel I have
    seen a horrible thing;
  Ē'phra·im's whoredom is
    there, Israel is defiled.

11 For you also, O Judah, a harvest
    is appointed.

  When I would restore the
    fortunes of my people,
7 1when I would heal Israel,
    the corruption of Ē'phra·im is
      revealed,

bGk: Meaning of Heb uncertain
cCn: Heb to a king who will contend
dGk Syr: Heb your   eCn: Heb like
fCn: Meaning of Heb uncertain
gSyr: Heb are a company

and the wicked deeds of
Samaria;
for they deal falsely,
the thief breaks in,
and the bandits raid outside.
2 But they do not consider
that I remember all their
wickedness.
Now their deeds surround them,
they are before my face.
3 By their wickedness they make
the king glad,
and the officials by their
treachery.
4 They are all adulterers;
they are like a heated oven,
whose baker does not need to
stir the fire,
from the kneading of the
dough until it is leavened.
5 On the day of our king the
officials
became sick with the heat of
wine;
he stretched out his hand with
mockers.
6 For they are kindled[h] like an
oven, their heart burns
within them;
all night their anger smolders;
in the morning it blazes like a
flaming fire.
7 All of them are hot as an oven,
and they devour their rulers.
All their kings have fallen;
none of them calls upon me.

8 Ē'phra·im mixes himself with
the peoples;
Ē'phra·im is a cake not turned.
9 Foreigners devour his strength,
but he does not know it;
gray hairs are sprinkled upon
him,
but he does not know it.
10 Israel's pride testifies against[i]
him;
yet they do not return to the
LORD their God,
or seek him, for all this.

Futile Reliance on the Nations

11 Ē'phra·im has become like a
dove,
silly and without sense;
they call upon Egypt, they go
to Assyria.
12 As they go, I will cast my net
over them;
I will bring them down like
birds of the air;

I will discipline them
according to the report
made to their assembly.[j]
13 Woe to them, for they have
strayed from me!
Destruction to them, for they
have rebelled against me!
I would redeem them,
but they speak lies against me.
14 They do not cry to me from the
heart,
but they wail upon their beds;
they gash themselves for grain
and wine;
they rebel against me.
15 It was I who trained and
strengthened their arms,
yet they plot evil against me.
16 They turn to that which does not
profit;[k]
they have become like a
defective bow;
their officials shall fall by the
sword
because of the rage of their
tongue.
So much for their babbling in
the land of Egypt.

Israel's Apostasy

8 Set the trumpet to your lips!
One like a vulture[j] is over the
house of the LORD,
because they have broken my
covenant,
and transgressed my law.
2 Israel cries to me,
"My God, we—Israel—know
you!"
3 Israel has spurned the good;
the enemy shall pursue him.

4 They made kings, but not
through me;
they set up princes, but
without my knowledge.
With their silver and gold they
made idols
for their own destruction.
5 Your calf is rejected, O Samaria.
My anger burns against them.
How long will they be incapable
of innocence?
6 For it is from Israel,
an artisan made it;
it is not God.

h Gk Syr: Heb *brought near*
i Or *humbles* j Meaning of Heb
uncertain   k Cn: Meaning of Heb
uncertain

The calf of Samaria
　　shall be broken to pieces.[l]

7　For they sow the wind,
　　　and they shall reap the
　　　　whirlwind.
　The standing grain has no
　　　heads,
　　　it shall yield no meal;
　if it were to yield,
　　　foreigners would devour it.
8　Israel is swallowed up;
　　　now they are among the
　　　　nations
　　　as a useless vessel.
9　For they have gone up to
　　　Assyria,
　　　a wild ass wandering alone;
　　Eʹphra·im has bargained for
　　　　lovers.
10　Though they bargain with the
　　　nations,
　　　I will now gather them up.
　They shall soon writhe
　　　under the burden of kings and
　　　　princes.

11　When Eʹphra·im multiplied
　　　altars to expiate sin,
　　　they became to him altars for
　　　　sinning.
12　Though I write for him the
　　　multitude of my
　　　　instructions,
　　　they are regarded as a strange
　　　　thing.
13　Though they offer choice
　　　sacrifices,[m]
　　　though they eat flesh,
　　　the LORD does not accept
　　　　them.
　Now he will remember their
　　　iniquity,
　　　and punish their sins;
　　　they shall return to Egypt.
14　Israel has forgotten his Maker,
　　　and built palaces;
　and Judah has multiplied
　　　fortified cities;
　　　but I will send a fire upon his
　　　　cities,
　　　and it shall devour his
　　　　strongholds.

Punishment for Israel's Sin

9　Do not rejoice, O Israel!
　　Do not exult[n] as other nations
　　　do;
　for you have played the whore,
　　　departing from your God.
　You have loved a prostitute's
　　　pay
　　on all threshing floors.
2　Threshing floor and wine vat
　　　shall not feed them,
　　　and the new wine shall fail
　　　　them.
3　They shall not remain in the
　　　land of the LORD;
　　　but Eʹphra·im shall return to
　　　　Egypt,
　　　and in Assyria they shall eat
　　　　unclean food.

4　They shall not pour drink
　　　offerings of wine to the
　　　　LORD,
　　　and their sacrifices shall not
　　　　please him.
　Such sacrifices shall be like
　　　mourners' bread;
　　　all who eat of it shall be
　　　　defiled;
　for their bread shall be for their
　　　hunger only;
　　　it shall not come to the house
　　　　of the LORD.

5　What will you do on the day of
　　　appointed festival,
　　　and on the day of the festival
　　　　of the LORD?
6　For even if they escape
　　　destruction,
　　　Egypt shall gather them,
　　　Memphis shall bury them.
　Nettles shall possess their
　　　precious things of silver;[o]
　　　thorns shall be in their tents.

7　The days of punishment have
　　　come,
　　　the days of recompense have
　　　　come;
　　　Israel cries,[p]
　"The prophet is a fool,
　　　the man of the spirit is mad!"
　Because of your great iniquity,
　　　your hostility is great.
8　The prophet is a sentinel for my
　　　God over Eʹphra·im,
　　　yet a fowler's snare is on all his
　　　　ways,
　　　and hostility in the house of
　　　　his God.

[l] Or *shall go up in flames*
[m] Cn: Meaning of Heb uncertain
[n] Gk: Heb *To exultation*　[o] Meaning of
Heb uncertain　[p] Cn Compare Gk: Heb
shall know

9 They have deeply corrupted
     themselves
     as in the days of Gib′e·ah;
he will remember their iniquity,
     he will punish their sins.

10 Like grapes in the wilderness,
     I found Israel.
Like the first fruit on the fig
     tree,
     in its first season,
     I saw your ancestors.
But they came to Ba′al-pe′or,
     and consecrated themselves to
     a thing of shame,
     and became detestable like the
     thing they loved.
11 E′phra·im's glory shall fly away
     like a bird—
     no birth, no pregnancy, no
     conception!
12 Even if they bring up children,
     I will bereave them until no
     one is left.
Woe to them indeed
     when I depart from them!
13 Once I saw E′phra·im as a
     young palm planted in a
     lovely meadow,q
     but now E′phra·im must lead
     out his children for
     slaughter.
14 Give them, O LORD—
     what will you give?
Give them a miscarrying womb
     and dry breasts.

15 Every evil of theirs began at
     Gil′gal;
     there I came to hate them.
Because of the wickedness of
     their deeds
     I will drive them out of my
     house.
I will love them no more;
     all their officials are rebels.

16 E′phra·im is stricken,
     their root is dried up,
     they shall bear no fruit.
Even though they give birth,
     I will kill the cherished
     offspring of their womb.
17 Because they have not listened
     to him,
     my God will reject them;
they shall become wanderers
     among the nations.

Israel's Sin and Captivity

10 Israel is a luxuriant vine
     that yields its fruit.
The more his fruit increased
     the more altars he built;
as his country improved,
     he improved his pillars.
2 Their heart is false;
     now they must bear their guilt.
The LORDr will break down
     their altars,
     and destroy their pillars.

3 For now they will say:
     "We have no king,
for we do not fear the LORD,
     and a king—what could he do
     for us?"
4 They utter mere words;
     with empty oaths they make
     covenants;
so litigation springs up like
     poisonous weeds
     in the furrows of the field.
5 The inhabitants of Samaria
     tremble
     for the calfs of Beth-a′ven.
Its people shall mourn for it,
     and its idolatrous priests shall
     wailt over it,
     over its glory that has
     departed from it.
6 The thing itself shall be carried
     to Assyria
     as tribute to the great king.u
E′phra·im shall be put to shame,
     and Israel shall be ashamed of
     his idol.v

7 Samaria's king shall perish
     like a chip on the face of the
     waters.
8 The high places of A′ven, the sin
     of Israel,
     shall be destroyed.
Thorn and thistle shall grow up
     on their altars.
They shall say to the mountains,
     Cover us,
     and to the hills, Fall on us.

9 Since the days of Gib′e·ah you
     have sinned, O Israel;
     there they have continued.
     Shall not war overtake them in
     Gib′e·ah?

q Meaning of Heb uncertain   r Heb *he*
s Gk Syr: Heb *calves*   t Cn: Heb *exult*
u Cn: Heb *to a king who will contend*
v Cn: Heb *counsel*

10 I will come[w] against the
         wayward people to punish
         them;
     and nations shall be gathered
         against them
     when they are punished[x] for
         their double iniquity.
11 Ē′phra·im was a trained heifer
         that loved to thresh,
     and I spared her fair neck;
     but I will make Ē′phra·im break
         the ground;
         Judah must plow;
         Jacob must harrow for himself.
12 Sow for yourselves
         righteousness;
     reap steadfast love;
     break up your fallow ground;
     for it is time to seek the LORD,
         that he may come and rain
         righteousness upon you.

13 You have plowed wickedness,
         you have reaped injustice,
         you have eaten the fruit of lies.
     Because you have trusted in
         your power
     and in the multitude of your
         warriors,
14 therefore the tumult of war shall
         rise against your people,
     and all your fortresses shall be
         destroyed,
     as Shal′man destroyed
         Beth-ar′bel on the day of
         battle
     when mothers were dashed in
         pieces with their children.
15 Thus it shall be done to you,
         O Beth′el,
     because of your great
         wickedness.
     At dawn the king of Israel
         shall be utterly cut off.

*God's Compassion Despite
Israel's Ingratitude*

11 When Israel was a child, I
         loved him,
     and out of Egypt I called my
         son.
2 The more I[y] called them,
         the more they went from me;[z]
     they kept sacrificing to the
         Bā′als,
     and offering incense to idols.

3 Yet it was I who taught
         Ē′phra·im to walk,
     I took them up in my[a] arms;

     but they did not know that I
         healed them.
4 I led them with cords of human
         kindness,
     with bands of love.
     I was to them like those
         who lift infants to their
         cheeks.[b]
     I bent down to them and fed
         them.

5 They shall return to the land of
         Egypt,
     and Assyria shall be their
         king,
     because they have refused to
         return to me.
6 The sword rages in their cities,
     it consumes their
         oracle-priests,
     and devours because of their
         schemes.
7 My people are bent on turning
         away from me.
     To the Most High they call,
     but he does not raise them up
         at all.[c]

8 How can I give you up,
         Ē′phra·im?
     How can I hand you over,
         O Israel?
     How can I make you like
         Ad′mah?
     How can I treat you like
         Ze·bo′im?
     My heart recoils within me;
         my compassion grows warm
         and tender.
9 I will not execute my fierce
         anger;
     I will not again destroy
         Ē′phra·im;
     for I am God and no mortal,
         the Holy One in your midst,
     and I will not come in wrath.[c]

10 They shall go after the LORD,
         who roars like a lion;
     when he roars,
         his children shall come
         trembling from the west.
11 They shall come trembling like
         birds from Egypt,
     and like doves from the land
         of Assyria;

H
O
S
E
A

---

w Cn Compare Gk: Heb *In my desire*
x Gk: Heb *bound*   y Gk: Heb *they*
z Gk: Heb *them*   a Gk Syr Vg: Heb *his*
b Or *who ease the yoke on their jaws*
c Meaning of Heb uncertain

and I will return them to their homes, says the LORD.

12d E′phra·im has surrounded me with lies,
and the house of Israel with deceit;
but Judah still walks*e* with God,
and is faithful to the Holy One.

12 E′phra·im herds the wind,
and pursues the east wind all day long;
they multiply falsehood and violence;
they make a treaty with Assyria,
and oil is carried to Egypt.

The Long History of Rebellion
(Cp Gen 25 − 32)

2 The LORD has an indictment against Judah,
and will punish Jacob according to his ways,
and repay him according to his deeds.

3 In the womb he tried to supplant his brother,
and in his manhood he strove with God.

4 He strove with the angel and prevailed,
he wept and sought his favor;
he met him at Beth′el,
and there he spoke with him.*f*

5 The LORD the God of hosts,
the LORD is his name!

6 But as for you, return to your God,
hold fast to love and justice,
and wait continually for your God.

7 A trader, in whose hands are false balances,
he loves to oppress.

8 E′phra·im has said, "Ah, I am rich,
I have gained wealth for myself;
in all of my gain
no offense has been found in me
that would be sin."*g*

9 I am the LORD your God
from the land of Egypt;
I will make you live in tents again,
as in the days of the appointed festival.

10 I spoke to the prophets;
it was I who multiplied visions,
and through the prophets I will bring destruction.

11 In Gil′e·ad*h* there is iniquity,
they shall surely come to nothing.
In Gil′gal they sacrifice bulls,
so their altars shall be like stone heaps
on the furrows of the field.

12 Jacob fled to the land of Ar′am,
there Israel served for a wife,
and for a wife he guarded sheep.*i*

13 By a prophet the LORD brought Israel up from Egypt,
and by a prophet he was guarded.

14 E′phra·im has given bitter offense,
so his Lord will bring his crimes down on him
and pay him back for his insults.

Relentless Judgment on Israel

13 When E′phra·im spoke, there was trembling;
he was exalted in Israel;
but he incurred guilt through Ba′al and died.

2 And now they keep on sinning
and make a cast image for themselves,
idols of silver made according to their understanding,
all of them the work of artisans.
"Sacrifice to these," they say.*j*
People are kissing calves!

3 Therefore they shall be like the morning mist
or like the dew that goes away early,
like chaff that swirls from the threshing floor
or like smoke from a window.

4 Yet I have been the LORD your God
ever since the land of Egypt;
you know no God but me,
and besides me there is no savior.

---

d Ch 12.1 in Heb   *e* Heb *roams* or *rules*
f Gk Syr: Heb *us*   *g* Meaning of Heb uncertain   *h* Compare Syr: Heb *Gilead*
i Heb lacks *sheep*   *j* Cn Compare Gk: Heb *To these they say sacrifices of people*

5 It was I who fed[k] you in the
      wilderness,
   in the land of drought.
6 When I fed[l] them, they were
      satisfied;
   they were satisfied, and their
      heart was proud;
   therefore they forgot me.
7 So I will become like a lion to
      them,
   like a leopard I will lurk
      beside the way.
8 I will fall upon them like a bear
      robbed of her cubs,
   and will tear open the
      covering of their heart;
   there I will devour them like a
      lion,
   as a wild animal would
      mangle them.

9 I will destroy you, O Israel;
   who can help you?[m]
10 Where now is[n] your king, that
      he may save you?
   Where in all your cities are
      your rulers,
   of whom you said,
      "Give me a king and rulers"?
11 I gave you a king in my anger,
   and I took him away in my
      wrath.

12 Ē'phra·im's iniquity is bound up;
   his sin is kept in store.
13 The pangs of childbirth come for
      him,
   but he is an unwise son;
   for at the proper time he does
      not present himself
   at the mouth of the womb.

14 Shall I ransom them from the
      power of Shē'ōl?
   Shall I redeem them from
      Death?
   O Death, where are[o] your
      plagues?
   O Shē'ōl, where is[o] your
      destruction?
   Compassion is hidden from my
      eyes.

15 Although he may flourish among
      rushes,[p]
   the east wind shall come, a
      blast from the LORD,
   rising from the wilderness;
   and his fountain shall dry up,
   his spring shall be parched.
   It shall strip his treasury
   of every precious thing.

16[q] Samaria shall bear her guilt,
   because she has rebelled
      against her God;
   they shall fall by the sword,
   their little ones shall be
      dashed in pieces,
   and their pregnant women
      ripped open.

A Plea for Repentance

14 Return, O Israel, to the LORD
      your God,
   for you have stumbled because
      of your iniquity.
2 Take words with you
   and return to the LORD;
   say to him,
      "Take away all guilt;
   accept that which is good,
   and we will offer
      the fruit[r] of our lips.
3 Assyria shall not save us;
   we will not ride upon horses;
   we will say no more, 'Our God,'
   to the work of our hands.
   In you the orphan finds mercy."

Assurance of Forgiveness

4 I will heal their disloyalty;
   I will love them freely,
   for my anger has turned from
      them.
5 I will be like the dew to Israel;
   he shall blossom like the lily,
   he shall strike root like the
      forests of Lebanon.[s]
6 His shoots shall spread out;
   his beauty shall be like the
      olive tree,
   and his fragrance like that of
      Lebanon.
7 They shall again live beneath
      my[t] shadow,
   they shall flourish as a
      garden;[u]
   they shall blossom like the vine,
   their fragrance shall be like
      the wine of Lebanon.

8 O Ē'phra·im, what have I[v] to do
      with idols?

k Gk Syr: Heb knew   l Cn: Heb
according to their pasture   m Gk Syr:
Heb for in me is your help   n Gk Syr
Vg: Heb I will be   o Gk Syr: Heb I will
be   p Or among brothers   q Ch 14.1 in
Heb   r Gk Syr: Heb bulls   s Cn: Heb
like Lebanon   t Heb his   u Cn: Heb
they shall grow grain   v Or What more
has Ephraim

H
O
S
E
A

It is I who answer and look
after you.*w*
I am like an evergreen cypress;
your faithfulness*x* comes from
me.
9 Those who are wise understand
these things;
those who are discerning
know them.

For the ways of the LORD are
right,
and the upright walk in them,
but transgressors stumble in
them.

w Heb *him*   *x* Heb *your fruit*

JOEL

1 The word of the LORD that came to
Jō′el son of Pe·thū′el:

Lament over the Ruin of the Country
(Ex 10.1–20)

2 Hear this, O elders,
give ear, all inhabitants of the
land!
Has such a thing happened in
your days,
or in the days of your
ancestors?
3 Tell your children of it,
and let your children tell their
children,
and their children another
generation.

4 What the cutting locust left,
the swarming locust has eaten.
What the swarming locust left,
the hopping locust has eaten,
and what the hopping locust left,
the destroying locust has
eaten.

5 Wake up, you drunkards, and
weep;
and wail, all you
wine-drinkers,
over the sweet wine,
for it is cut off from your
mouth.
6 For a nation has invaded my
land,
powerful and innumerable;
its teeth are lions' teeth,
and it has the fangs of a
lioness.
7 It has laid waste my vines,

and splintered my fig trees;
it has stripped off their bark and
thrown it down;
their branches have turned
white.

8 Lament like a virgin dressed in
sackcloth
for the husband of her youth.
9 The grain offering and the drink
offering are cut off
from the house of the LORD.
The priests mourn,
the ministers of the LORD.
10 The fields are devastated,
the ground mourns;
for the grain is destroyed,
the wine dries up,
the oil fails.

11 Be dismayed, you farmers,
wail, you vinedressers,
over the wheat and the barley;
for the crops of the field are
ruined.
12 The vine withers,
the fig tree droops.
Pomegranate, palm, and apple —
all the trees of the field are
dried up;
surely, joy withers away
among the people.

A Call to Repentance and Prayer

13 Put on sackcloth and lament,
you priests;
wail, you ministers of the
altar.
Come, pass the night in
sackcloth,

you ministers of my God!
Grain offering and drink offering
  are withheld from the house of
    your God.

14 Sanctify a fast,
  call a solemn assembly.
Gather the elders
  and all the inhabitants of the
    land
to the house of the LORD your
    God,
  and cry out to the LORD.

15 Alas for the day!
For the day of the LORD is near,
  and as destruction from the
    Almighty*a* it comes.
16 Is not the food cut off
  before our eyes,
joy and gladness
  from the house of our God?

17 The seed shrivels under the
    clods,*b*
  the storehouses are desolate;
the granaries are ruined
  because the grain has failed.
18 How the animals groan!
  The herds of cattle wander
    about
because there is no pasture for
    them;
  even the flocks of sheep are
    dazed.*c*

19 To you, O LORD, I cry.
For fire has devoured
  the pastures of the wilderness,
and flames have burned
  all the trees of the field.
20 Even the wild animals cry to you
  because the watercourses are
    dried up,
and fire has devoured
  the pastures of the wilderness.

2 Blow the trumpet in Zion;
  sound the alarm on my holy
    mountain!
Let all the inhabitants of the
    land tremble,
  for the day of the LORD is
    coming, it is near—
2 a day of darkness and gloom,
  a day of clouds and thick
    darkness!
Like blackness spread upon the
    mountains
  a great and powerful army
    comes;

their like has never been from of
    old,
  nor will be again after them
  in ages to come.

3 Fire devours in front of them,
  and behind them a flame
    burns.
Before them the land is like the
    garden of Eden,
  but after them a desolate
    wilderness,
  and nothing escapes them.

4 They have the appearance of
    horses,
  and like war-horses they
    charge.
5 As with the rumbling of chariots,
  they leap on the tops of the
    mountains,
like the crackling of a flame of
    fire
  devouring the stubble,
like a powerful army
  drawn up for battle.

6 Before them peoples are in
    anguish,
  all faces grow pale.*b*
7 Like warriors they charge,
  like soldiers they scale the
    wall.
Each keeps to its own course,
  they do not swerve from*d*
    their paths.
8 They do not jostle one another,
  each keeps to its own track;
they burst through the weapons
  and are not halted.
9 They leap upon the city,
  they run upon the walls;
they climb up into the houses,
  they enter through the
    windows like a thief.

10 The earth quakes before them,
  the heavens tremble.
The sun and the moon are
    darkened,
  and the stars withdraw their
    shining.
11 The LORD utters his voice
  at the head of his army;
how vast is his host!

*a*Traditional rendering of Heb *Shaddai*
*b*Meaning of Heb uncertain   *c*Compare
Gk Syr Vg: Meaning of Heb uncertain
*d*Gk Syr Vg: Heb *they do not take a
pledge along*

J
O
E
L

Numberless are those who
  obey his command.
Truly the day of the LORD is
  great;
  terrible indeed—who can
  endure it?

12 Yet even now, says the LORD,
  return to me with all your
  heart,
with fasting, with weeping, and
  with mourning;
13 rend your hearts and not your
  clothing.
Return to the LORD, your God,
  for he is gracious and
  merciful,
slow to anger, and abounding in
  steadfast love,
  and relents from punishing.
14 Who knows whether he will not
  turn and relent,
  and leave a blessing behind
  him,
a grain offering and a drink
  offering
  for the LORD, your God?

15 Blow the trumpet in Zion;
  sanctify a fast;
call a solemn assembly;
16 gather the people.
Sanctify the congregation;
  assemble the aged;
gather the children,
  even infants at the breast.
Let the bridegroom leave his
  room,
  and the bride her canopy.

17 Between the vestibule and the
  altar
  let the priests, the ministers of
  the LORD, weep.
Let them say, "Spare your
  people, O LORD,
and do not make your heritage
  a mockery,
  a byword among the nations.
Why should it be said among the
  peoples,
  'Where is their God?' "

God's Response and Promise
(Acts 2.17)

18 Then the LORD became jealous
  for his land,
  and had pity on his people.
19 In response to his people the
  LORD said:
I am sending you

grain, wine, and oil,
  and you will be satisfied;
and I will no more make you
  a mockery among the nations.

20 I will remove the northern army
  far from you,
  and drive it into a parched and
  desolate land,
its front into the eastern sea,
  and its rear into the western
  sea;
its stench and foul smell will rise
  up.
  Surely he has done great
  things!

21 Do not fear, O soil;
  be glad and rejoice,
  for the LORD has done great
  things!
22 Do not fear, you animals of the
  field,
  for the pastures of the
  wilderness are green;
the tree bears its fruit,
  the fig tree and vine give their
  full yield.

23 O children of Zion, be glad
  and rejoice in the LORD your
  God;
for he has given the early rain*e*
  for your vindication,
he has poured down for you
  abundant rain,
  the early and the later rain, as
  before.
24 The threshing floors shall be full
  of grain,
  the vats shall overflow with
  wine and oil.

25 I will repay you for the years
  that the swarming locust has
  eaten,
the hopper, the destroyer, and
  the cutter,
  my great army, which I sent
  against you.

26 You shall eat in plenty and be
  satisfied,
  and praise the name of the
  LORD your God,
who has dealt wondrously
  with you.
And my people shall never again
  be put to shame.

e Meaning of Heb uncertain

27 You shall know that I am in the
    midst of Israel,
  and that I, the LORD, am your
    God and there is no other.
And my people shall never again
  be put to shame.

God's Spirit Poured Out

28f Then afterward
  I will pour out my spirit on all
    flesh;
  your sons and your daughters
    shall prophesy,
  your old men shall dream
    dreams,
  and your young men shall see
    visions.
29 Even on the male and female
    slaves,
  in those days, I will pour out
    my spirit.

30 I will show portents in the heavens and on the earth, blood and fire and columns of smoke. 31 The sun shall be turned to darkness, and the moon to blood, before the great and terrible day of the LORD comes. 32 Then everyone who calls on the name of the LORD shall be saved; for in Mount Zion and in Jerusalem there shall be those who escape, as the LORD has said, and among the survivors shall be those whom the LORD calls.

3 g For then, in those days and at that time, when I restore the fortunes of Judah and Jerusalem, 2 I will gather all the nations and bring them down to the valley of Je·hosh′a·phat, and I will enter into judgment with them there, on account of my people and my heritage Israel, because they have scattered them among the nations. They have divided my land, 3 and cast lots for my people, and traded boys for prostitutes, and sold girls for wine, and drunk it down.

4 What are you to me, O Tȳre and Sī′don, and all the regions of Phi·lis′-ti·a? Are you paying me back for something? If you are paying me back, I will turn your deeds back upon your own heads swiftly and speedily. 5 For you have taken my silver and my gold, and have carried my rich treasures into your temples.h 6 You have sold the people of Judah and Jerusalem to the Greeks, removing them far from their own border. 7 But now I will rouse them to leave the places to which you have sold them, and I will turn your

deeds back upon your own heads. 8 I will sell your sons and your daughters into the hand of the people of Judah, and they will sell them to the Sa·bē′-ans, to a nation far away; for the LORD has spoken.

Judgment in the Valley of Jehoshaphat
(Cp Isa 2.4; Mic 4.3)

9 Proclaim this among the nations:
  Prepare war,i
    stir up the warriors.
  Let all the soldiers draw near,
    let them come up.
10 Beat your plowshares into
    swords,
    and your pruning hooks into
      spears;
  let the weakling say, "I am a
    warrior."

11 Come quickly,j
  all you nations all around,
  gather yourselves there.
Bring down your warriors,
  O LORD.
12 Let the nations rouse
    themselves,
  and come up to the valley of
    Je·hosh′a·phat;
for there I will sit to judge
  all the neighboring nations.
13 Put in the sickle,
  for the harvest is ripe.
Go in, tread,
  for the wine press is full.
The vats overflow,
  for their wickedness is great.

14 Multitudes, multitudes,
  in the valley of decision!
For the day of the LORD is near
  in the valley of decision.
15 The sun and the moon are
    darkened,
  and the stars withdraw their
    shining.

16 The LORD roars from Zion,
  and utters his voice from
    Jerusalem,
  and the heavens and the earth
    shake.
But the LORD is a refuge for his
  people,

f Ch 3.1 in Heb   g Ch 4.1 in Heb
h Or palaces   i Heb sanctify war
j Meaning of Heb uncertain

J
O
E
L

a stronghold for the people of
Israel.

The Glorious Future of Judah

17 So you shall know that I, the
LORD your God,
dwell in Zion, my holy
mountain.
And Jerusalem shall be holy,
and strangers shall never
again pass through it.

18 In that day
the mountains shall drip sweet
wine,
the hills shall flow with milk,
and all the stream beds of Judah
shall flow with water;
a fountain shall come forth from
the house of the LORD

and water the Wadi Shit′tim.

19 Egypt shall become a desolation
and E′dom a desolate
wilderness,
because of the violence done to
the people of Judah,
in whose land they have shed
innocent blood.

20 But Judah shall be inhabited
forever,
and Jerusalem to all
generations.

21 I will avenge their blood, and I
will not clear the guilty,[k]
for the LORD dwells in Zion.

[k] Gk Syr: Heb *I will hold innocent their
blood that I have not held innocent*

AMOS

1 The words of Ā′mos, who was
among the shepherds of Te·kō′a,
which he saw concerning Israel in the
days of King Uz·zī′ah of Judah and in
the days of King Jer·o·bō′am son of
Jō′ash of Israel, two years[a] before the
earthquake.

Judgment on Israel's Neighbors

2 And he said:
The LORD roars from Zion,
and utters his voice from
Jerusalem;
the pastures of the shepherds
wither,
and the top of Car′mel dries
up.

3 Thus says the LORD:
For three transgressions of
Damascus,
and for four, I will not revoke
the punishment;[b]
because they have threshed
Gil′e·ad
with threshing sledges of iron.

4 So I will send a fire on the house
of Haz′a·el,

and it shall devour the
strongholds of Ben-hā′dad.

5 I will break the gate bars of
Damascus,
and cut off the inhabitants
from the Valley of Ā′ven,
and the one who holds the
scepter from Beth-ē′den;
and the people of Ar′am shall
go into exile to Kir,
says the LORD.

6 Thus says the LORD:
For three transgressions of
Gā′za,
and for four, I will not revoke
the punishment;[b]
because they carried into exile
entire communities,
to hand them over to E′dom.

7 So I will send a fire on the wall
of Gā′za,
fire that shall devour its
strongholds.

8 I will cut off the inhabitants
from Ash′dod,

[a] Or *during two years* [b] Heb *cause it to
return*

and the one who holds the
    scepter from Ash'ke·lon;
I will turn my hand against
    Ek'ron,
    and the remnant of the
        Phi·lis'tines shall perish,
            says the Lord GOD.

9 Thus says the LORD:
For three transgressions of Tȳre,
    and for four, I will not revoke
        the punishment;[c]
because they delivered entire
    communities over to
    Ē'dom,
    and did not remember the
        covenant of kinship.
10 So I will send a fire on the wall
    of Tȳre,
    fire that shall devour its
        strongholds.

11 Thus says the LORD:
For three transgressions of
    Ē'dom,
    and for four, I will not revoke
        the punishment;[c]
because he pursued his brother
    with the sword
    and cast off all pity;
he maintained his anger
    perpetually,[d]
    and kept his wrath[e] forever.
12 So I will send a fire on Tē'man,
    and it shall devour the
        strongholds of Boz'rah.

13 Thus says the LORD:
For three transgressions of the
    Am'mon·ites,
    and for four, I will not revoke
        the punishment;[c]
because they have ripped open
    pregnant women in
    Gil'e·ad
    in order to enlarge their
        territory.
14 So I will kindle a fire against the
    wall of Rab'bah,
    fire that shall devour its
        strongholds,
with shouting on the day of
    battle,
    with a storm on the day of the
        whirlwind;
15 then their king shall go into
    exile,
    he and his officials together,
            says the LORD.

2 Thus says the LORD:
For three transgressions of
    Mō'ab,
    and for four, I will not revoke
        the punishment;[c]
because he burned to lime
    the bones of the king of
    Ē'dom.
2 So I will send a fire on Mō'ab,
    and it shall devour the
        strongholds of Ker'i·oth,
and Mō'ab shall die amid
    uproar,
    amid shouting and the sound
        of the trumpet;
3 I will cut off the ruler from its
    midst,
    and will kill all its officials
    with him,
            says the LORD.

Judgment on Judah

4 Thus says the LORD:
For three transgressions of
    Judah,
    and for four, I will not revoke
        the punishment;[c]
because they have rejected the
    law of the LORD,
    and have not kept his statutes,
but they have been led astray by
    the same lies
    after which their ancestors
        walked.
5 So I will send a fire on Judah,
    and it shall devour the
        strongholds of Jerusalem.

Judgment on Israel

6 Thus says the LORD:
For three transgressions of
    Israel,
    and for four, I will not revoke
        the punishment;[c]
because they sell the righteous
    for silver,
    and the needy for a pair of
        sandals—
7 they who trample the head of
    the poor into the dust of
    the earth,
    and push the afflicted out of
    the way;
father and son go in to the same
    girl,
    so that my holy name is
    profaned;

A
M
O
S

[c] Heb *cause it to return*   [d] Syr Vg: Heb
and his anger tore perpetually
[e] Gk Syr Vg: Heb *and his wrath kept*

8   they lay themselves down beside
        every altar
    on garments taken in pledge;
    and in the house of their God
        they drink
        wine bought with fines they
            imposed.

9   Yet I destroyed the Am'o·rīte
        before them,
        whose height was like the
            height of cedars,
        and who was as strong as
            oaks;
    I destroyed his fruit above,
        and his roots beneath.
10 Also I brought you up out of the
        land of Egypt,
        and led you forty years in the
            wilderness,
        to possess the land of the
            Am'o·rīte.
11 And I raised up some of your
        children to be prophets
        and some of your youths to be
            nazirites.*f*
        Is it not indeed so, O people of
            Israel?
                            says the LORD.

12 But you made the nazirites*f*
        drink wine,
        and commanded the prophets,
            saying, "You shall not
            prophesy."

13 So, I will press you down in
        your place,
        just as a cart presses down
        when it is full of sheaves.*g*
14 Flight shall perish from the
        swift,
        and the strong shall not retain
            their strength,
        nor shall the mighty save their
            lives;
15 those who handle the bow shall
        not stand,
        and those who are swift of
            foot shall not save
            themselves,
        nor shall those who ride
            horses save their lives;
16 and those who are stout of heart
        among the mighty
        shall flee away naked in that
            day,
                            says the LORD.

Israel's Guilt and Punishment

3   Hear this word that the LORD has
    spoken against you, O people of
    Israel, against the whole family that I
    brought up out of the land of Egypt:
2   You only have I known
        of all the families of the earth;
    therefore I will punish you
        for all your iniquities.

3   Do two walk together
        unless they have made an
            appointment?
4   Does a lion roar in the forest,
        when it has no prey?
    Does a young lion cry out from
        its den,
        if it has caught nothing?
5   Does a bird fall into a snare on
        the earth,
        when there is no trap for it?
    Does a snare spring up from the
        ground,
        when it has taken nothing?
6   Is a trumpet blown in a city,
        and the people are not afraid?
    Does disaster befall a city,
        unless the LORD has done it?
7   Surely the Lord GOD does
        nothing,
        without revealing his secret
        to his servants the prophets.
8   The lion has roared;
        who will not fear?
    The Lord GOD has spoken;
        who can but prophesy?

9   Proclaim to the strongholds in
        Ash'dod,
        and to the strongholds in the
            land of Egypt,
    and say, "Assemble yourselves
        on Mount*h* Samaria,
        and see what great tumults are
            within it,
        and what oppressions are in
            its midst."
10 They do not know how to do
        right, says the LORD,
        those who store up violence
        and robbery in their
            strongholds.
11 Therefore thus says the Lord
        GOD:
    An adversary shall surround the
        land,
        and strip you of your defense;

*f*That is, *those separated* or *those
consecrated*   *g*Meaning of Heb
uncertain   *h*Gk Syr: Heb *the
mountains of*

and your strongholds shall be
plundered.

12 Thus says the LORD: As the shepherd rescues from the mouth of the lion two legs, or a piece of an ear, so shall the people of Israel who live in Samaria be rescued, with the corner of a couch and part*i* of a bed.

13 Hear, and testify against the
house of Jacob,
says the Lord GOD, the God of
hosts:
14 On the day I punish Israel for its
transgressions,
I will punish the altars of
Beth′el,
and the horns of the altar shall
be cut off
and fall to the ground.
15 I will tear down the winter
house as well as the
summer house;
and the houses of ivory shall
perish,
and the great houses*j* shall
come to an end,
says the LORD.

4 Hear this word, you cows of
Bā′shan
who are on Mount Samaria,
who oppress the poor, who
crush the needy,
who say to their husbands,
"Bring something to drink!"
2 The Lord GOD has sworn by his
holiness:
The time is surely coming
upon you,
when they shall take you away
with hooks,
even the last of you with
fishhooks.
3 Through breaches in the wall
you shall leave,
each one straight ahead;
and you shall be flung out into
Har′mon,*i*
says the LORD.
4 Come to Beth′el—and
transgress;
to Gil′gal—and multiply
transgression;
bring your sacrifices every
morning,
your tithes every three days;
5 bring a thank offering of
leavened bread,
and proclaim freewill
offerings, publish them;

for so you love to do, O people
of Israel!
says the Lord GOD.

Israel Rejects Correction

6 I gave you cleanness of teeth in
all your cities,
and lack of bread in all your
places,
yet you did not return to me,
says the LORD.

7 And I also withheld the rain
from you
when there were still three
months to the harvest;
I would send rain on one city,
and send no rain on another
city;
one field would be rained upon,
and the field on which it did
not rain withered;
8 so two or three towns wandered
to one town
to drink water, and were not
satisfied;
yet you did not return to me,
says the LORD.

9 I struck you with blight and
mildew;
I laid waste*k* your gardens
and your vineyards;
the locust devoured your fig
trees and your olive trees;
yet you did not return to me,
says the LORD.

10 I sent among you a pestilence
after the manner of Egypt;
I killed your young men with
the sword;
I carried away your horses;*l*
and I made the stench of your
camp go up into your
nostrils;
yet you did not return to me,
says the LORD.

11 I overthrew some of you,
as when God overthrew
Sod′om and Go·mor′rah,
and you were like a brand
snatched from the fire;
yet you did not return to me,
says the LORD.

A
M
O
S

*i*Meaning of Heb uncertain   *j*Or *many houses*   *k*Cn: Heb *the multitude of*   *l*Heb *with the captivity of your horses*

12 Therefore thus I will do to you,
       O Israel;
   because I will do this to you,
       prepare to meet your God,
           O Israel!

13 For lo, the one who forms the
       mountains, creates the
       wind,
   reveals his thoughts to
       mortals,
   makes the morning darkness,
       and treads on the heights of
       the earth —
       the LORD, the God of hosts, is
       his name!

A Lament for Israel's Sin

5 Hear this word that I take up over
   you in lamentation, O house of Israel:
2 Fallen, no more to rise,
       is maiden Israel;
   forsaken on her land,
       with no one to raise her up.

3 For thus says the Lord GOD:
   The city that marched out a
       thousand
       shall have a hundred left,
   and that which marched out a
       hundred
       shall have ten left.*m*

4 For thus says the LORD to the
       house of Israel:
   Seek me and live;
5   but do not seek Beth'el,
   and do not enter into Gil'gal
       or cross over to Bē'er-shē'ba;
   for Gil'gal shall surely go into
       exile,
   and Beth'el shall come to
       nothing.

6 Seek the LORD and live,
       or he will break out against
           the house of Joseph like
           fire,
   and it will devour Beth'el, with
       no one to quench it.
7 Ah, you that turn justice to
       wormwood,
   and bring righteousness to the
       ground!

8 The one who made the Plēi'a·dēs
       and Ō·rī'on,
   and turns deep darkness into
       the morning,

and darkens the day into
       night,
   who calls for the waters of the
       sea,
       and pours them out on the
           surface of the earth,
   the LORD is his name,
9 who makes destruction flash out
       against the strong,
       so that destruction comes upon
           the fortress.

10 They hate the one who reproves
       in the gate,
   and they abhor the one who
       speaks the truth.
11 Therefore because you trample
       on the poor
   and take from them levies of
       grain,
   you have built houses of hewn
       stone,
       but you shall not live in them;
   you have planted pleasant
       vineyards,
       but you shall not drink their
           wine.
12 For I know how many are your
       transgressions,
   and how great are your sins —
   you who afflict the righteous,
       who take a bribe,
       and push aside the needy in
           the gate.
13 Therefore the prudent will keep
       silent in such a time;
   for it is an evil time.

14 Seek good and not evil,
       that you may live;
   and so the LORD, the God of
       hosts, will be with you,
       just as you have said.
15 Hate evil and love good,
       and establish justice in the
           gate;
   it may be that the LORD, the God
       of hosts,
   will be gracious to the
       remnant of Joseph.

16 Therefore thus says the LORD,
       the God of hosts, the Lord:
   In all the squares there shall be
       wailing;
   and in all the streets they shall
       say, "Alas! alas!"
   They shall call the farmers to
       mourning,

m Heb adds *to the house of Israel*

and those skilled in
lamentation, to wailing;
17 in all the vineyards there shall
be wailing,
for I will pass through the
midst of you,
says the LORD.

The Day of the LORD a Dark Day

18 Alas for you who desire the day
of the LORD!
Why do you want the day of
the LORD?
It is darkness, not light;
19 as if someone fled from a lion,
and was met by a bear;
or went into the house and
rested a hand against the
wall,
and was bitten by a snake.
20 Is not the day of the LORD
darkness, not light,
and gloom with no brightness
in it?

21 I hate, I despise your festivals,
and I take no delight in your
solemn assemblies.
22 Even though you offer me your
burnt offerings and grain
offerings,
I will not accept them;
and the offerings of well-being
of your fatted animals
I will not look upon.
23 Take away from me the noise of
your songs;
I will not listen to the melody
of your harps.
24 But let justice roll down like
waters,
and righteousness like an
ever-flowing stream.

25 Did you bring to me sacrifices
and offerings the forty years in the wilderness, O house of Israel? 26 You shall
take up Sak′kuth your king, and Kaī′-
wan your star-god, your images,[n]
which you made for yourselves;
27 therefore I will take you into exile
beyond Damascus, says the LORD,
whose name is the God of hosts.

Complacent Self-Indulgence Will Be Punished

6 Alas for those who are at ease
in Zion,
and for those who feel secure
on Mount Samaria,

the notables of the first of the
nations,
to whom the house of Israel
resorts!
2 Cross over to Cal′neh, and see;
from there go to Hā′math the
great;
then go down to Gath of the
Phi·lis′tines.
Are you better[o] than these
kingdoms?
Or is your[p] territory greater
than their[q] territory,
3 O you that put far away the evil
day,
and bring near a reign of
violence?

4 Alas for those who lie on beds of
ivory,
and lounge on their couches,
and eat lambs from the flock,
and calves from the stall;
5 who sing idle songs to the sound
of the harp,
and like David improvise on
instruments of music;
6 who drink wine from bowls,
and anoint themselves with the
finest oils,
but are not grieved over the
ruin of Joseph!
7 Therefore they shall now be the
first to go into exile,
and the revelry of the loungers
shall pass away.

8 The Lord GOD has sworn by
himself
(says the LORD, the God of
hosts):
I abhor the pride of Jacob
and hate his strongholds;
and I will deliver up the city
and all that is in it.

9 If ten people remain in one house,
they shall die. 10 And if a relative, one
who burns the dead,[r] shall take up the
body to bring it out of the house, and
shall say to someone in the innermost
parts of the house, "Is anyone else with
you?" the answer will come, "No."
Then the relative[s] shall say, "Hush!
We must not mention the name of the
LORD."

n Heb your images, your star-god
o Or Are they better   p Heb their
q Heb your   r Or who makes a burning
for him   s Heb he

A
M
O
S

11 See, the LORD commands,
   and the great house shall be
     shattered to bits,
   and the little house to pieces.
12 Do horses run on rocks?
   Does one plow the sea with
     oxen?[t]
But you have turned justice into
   poison
and the fruit of righteousness
   into wormwood—
13 you who rejoice in Lō-dē'bar,[u]
   who say, "Have we not by our
     own strength
   taken Kar·nā'im[v] for
     ourselves?"
14 Indeed, I am raising up against
     you a nation,
   O house of Israel, says the
     LORD, the God of hosts,
and they shall oppress you from
   Lē'bō-hā'math
to the Wadi Ar'a·bah.

Locusts, Fire, and a Plumb Line

7 This is what the Lord GOD showed me: he was forming locusts at the time the latter growth began to sprout (it was the latter growth after the king's mowings). 2 When they had finished eating the grass of the land, I said,
  "O Lord GOD, forgive, I beg you!
   How can Jacob stand?
   He is so small!"
3 The LORD relented concerning
   this;
   "It shall not be," said the
    LORD.

4 This is what the Lord GOD showed me: the Lord GOD was calling for a shower of fire,[w] and it devoured the great deep and was eating up the land. 5 Then I said,
  "O Lord GOD, cease, I beg you!
   How can Jacob stand?
   He is so small!"
6 The LORD relented concerning
   this;
   "This also shall not be," said
    the Lord GOD.

7 This is what he showed me: the Lord was standing beside a wall built with a plumb line, with a plumb line in his hand. 8 And the LORD said to me, "Ā'mos, what do you see?" And I said, "A plumb line." Then the Lord said, "See, I am setting a plumb line

   in the midst of my people
    Israel;
   I will never again pass them
    by;
9 the high places of Isaac shall be
    made desolate,
   and the sanctuaries of Israel
    shall be laid waste,
   and I will rise against the
    house of Jer·o·bō'am with
    the sword."

Amaziah Complains to the King

10 Then Am·a·zī'ah, the priest of Beth'el, sent to King Jer·o·bō'am of Israel, saying, "Ā'mos has conspired against you in the very center of the house of Israel; the land is not able to bear all his words. 11 For thus Ā'mos has said,
  'Jer·o·bō'am shall die by the
    sword,
   and Israel must go into exile
    away from his land.' "
12 And Am·a·zī'ah said to Ā'mos, "O seer, go, flee away to the land of Judah, earn your bread there, and prophesy there; 13 but never again prophesy at Beth'el, for it is the king's sanctuary, and it is a temple of the kingdom."
14 Then Ā'mos answered Am·a·zī'ah, "I am[x] no prophet, nor a prophet's son; but I am[x] a herdsman, and a dresser of sycamore trees, 15 and the LORD took me from following the flock, and the LORD said to me, 'Go, prophesy to my people Israel.'
16 "Now therefore hear the word of
    the LORD.
  You say, 'Do not prophesy
    against Israel,
   and do not preach against the
    house of Isaac.'
17 Therefore thus says the LORD:
  'Your wife shall become a
    prostitute in the city,
   and your sons and your
    daughters shall fall by the
    sword,
   and your land shall be
    parceled out by line;
  you yourself shall die in an
    unclean land,
   and Israel shall surely go into
    exile away from its land.' "

t Or *Does one plow them with oxen*
u Or *in a thing of nothingness*
v Or *horns*   w Or *for a judgment by fire*
x Or *was*

The Basket of Fruit

8 This is what the Lord GOD showed me—a basket of summer fruit.*y* [2] He said, "Ā′mos, what do you see?" And I said, "A basket of summer fruit."*y* Then the LORD said to me,

"The end*z* has come upon my
  people Israel;
I will never again pass them
  by.

3 The songs of the temple*a* shall
    become wailings in that
    day,"

          says the Lord GOD;
"the dead bodies shall be many,
  cast out in every place. Be
  silent!"

4 Hear this, you that trample on
    the needy,
  and bring to ruin the poor of
    the land,
5 saying, "When will the new
    moon be over
  so that we may sell grain;
and the sabbath,
  so that we may offer wheat for
    sale?
We will make the ephah small
    and the shekel great,
  and practice deceit with false
    balances,
6 buying the poor for silver
  and the needy for a pair of
    sandals,
  and selling the sweepings of
    the wheat."

7 The LORD has sworn by the
    pride of Jacob:
Surely I will never forget any of
  their deeds.

8 Shall not the land tremble on
    this account,
  and everyone mourn who lives
    in it,
and all of it rise like the Nile,
  and be tossed about and sink
    again, like the Nile of
    Egypt?

9 On that day, says the Lord GOD,
  I will make the sun go down at
    noon,
  and darken the earth in broad
    daylight.
10 I will turn your feasts into
     mourning,
  and all your songs into
    lamentation;

I will bring sackcloth on all
    loins,
  and baldness on every head;
I will make it like the mourning
    for an only son,
  and the end of it like a bitter
    day.

11 The time is surely coming, says
     the Lord GOD,
  when I will send a famine on
    the land;
not a famine of bread, or a thirst
    for water,
  but of hearing the words of the
    LORD.
12 They shall wander from sea to
     sea,
  and from north to east;
they shall run to and fro,
    seeking the word of the
    LORD,
  but they shall not find it.

13 In that day the beautiful young
     women and the young men
     shall faint for thirst.
14 Those who swear by Ash′i·mah
     of Samaria,
  and say, "As your god lives,
    O Dan,"
and, "As the way of Bē′er-shē′ba
    lives"—
  they shall fall, and never rise
    again.

The Destruction of Israel

9 I saw the LORD standing beside*b* the altar, and he said:
Strike the capitals until the
    thresholds shake,
  and shatter them on the heads
    of all the people;*c*
and those who are left I will kill
    with the sword;
  not one of them shall flee
    away,
  not one of them shall escape.

2 Though they dig into Shē′ōl,
    from there shall my hand take
    them;
though they climb up to heaven,
  from there I will bring them
    down.
3 Though they hide themselves on
    the top of Car′mel,

---

y Heb *qayits*   *z* Heb *qets*   *a* Or *palace*
b Or *on*   *c* Heb *all of them*

A
M
O
S

from there I will search out
and take them;
and though they hide from my
sight at the bottom of the
sea,
there I will command the
sea-serpent, and it shall
bite them.
4 And though they go into
captivity in front of their
enemies,
there I will command the
sword, and it shall kill
them;
and I will fix my eyes on them
for harm and not for good.

5 The Lord, GOD of hosts,
he who touches the earth and it
melts,
and all who live in it mourn,
and all of it rises like the Nile,
and sinks again, like the Nile
of Egypt;
6 who builds his upper chambers
in the heavens,
and founds his vault upon the
earth;
who calls for the waters of the
sea,
and pours them out upon the
surface of the earth —
the LORD is his name.

7 Are you not like the Ethiopians[d]
to me,
O people of Israel? says the
LORD.
Did I not bring Israel up from
the land of Egypt,
and the Phi·lis'tines from
Caph'tor and the
Ar·a·mē'ans from Kir?
8 The eyes of the Lord GOD are
upon the sinful kingdom,
and I will destroy it from the
face of the earth
— except that I will not utterly
destroy the house of Jacob,
says the LORD.

9 For lo, I will command,
and shake the house of Israel
among all the nations

as one shakes with a sieve,
but no pebble shall fall to the
ground.
10 All the sinners of my people
shall die by the sword,
who say, "Evil shall not
overtake or meet us."

The Restoration of
David's Kingdom
(Cp Acts 15.16–17)

11 On that day I will raise up
the booth of David that is
fallen,
and repair its[e] breaches,
and raise up its[f] ruins,
and rebuild it as in the days of
old;
12 in order that they may possess
the remnant of E'dom
and all the nations who are
called by my name,
says the LORD who does this.

13 The time is surely coming, says
the LORD,
when the one who plows shall
overtake the one who
reaps,
and the treader of grapes the
one who sows the seed;
the mountains shall drip sweet
wine,
and all the hills shall flow with
it.
14 I will restore the fortunes of my
people Israel,
and they shall rebuild the
ruined cities and inhabit
them;
they shall plant vineyards and
drink their wine,
and they shall make gardens
and eat their fruit.
15 I will plant them upon their land,
and they shall never again be
plucked up
out of the land that I have
given them,
says the LORD your God.

d Or Nubians; Heb Cushites　　e Gk: Heb
their　　f Gk: Heb his

A
M
O
S

OBADIAH

Proud Edom Will Be Brought Low

1 The vision of Ō·ba·dī′ah.

Thus says the Lord GOD
    concerning Ē′dom:
We have heard a report from the
    LORD,
    and a messenger has been sent
        among the nations:
"Rise up! Let us rise against it
    for battle!"
2 I will surely make you least
    among the nations;
    you shall be utterly despised.
3 Your proud heart has deceived
    you,
    you that live in the clefts of
        the rock,*a*
    whose dwelling is in the
        heights.
You say in your heart,
    "Who will bring me down to
        the ground?"
4 Though you soar aloft like the
    eagle,
    though your nest is set among
        the stars,
    from there I will bring you
        down,
                says the LORD.

*Pillage and Slaughter Will Repay
Edom's Cruelty*

5 If thieves came to you,
    if plunderers by night
    —how you have been
        destroyed!—
    would they not steal only what
        they wanted?
If grape-gatherers came to you,
    would they not leave
        gleanings?
6 How Esau has been pillaged,
    his treasures searched out!
7 All your allies have deceived
    you,
    they have driven you to the
        border;

your confederates have prevailed
    against you;
    those who ate*b* your bread
        have set a trap for you—
    there is no understanding of it.
8 On that day, says the LORD,
    I will destroy the wise out of
        Ē′dom,
    and understanding out of
        Mount Esau.
9 Your warriors shall be shattered,
    O Tē′man,
    so that everyone from Mount
        Esau will be cut off.

Edom Mistreated His Brother

10 For the slaughter and violence
    done to your brother
        Jacob,
    shame shall cover you,
    and you shall be cut off
        forever.
11 On the day that you stood aside,
    on the day that strangers
        carried off his wealth,
    and foreigners entered his gates
    and cast lots for Jerusalem,
    you too were like one of them.
12 But you should not have
    gloated*c* over*d* your
        brother
    on the day of his misfortune;
    you should not have rejoiced
        over the people of Judah
    on the day of their ruin;
    you should not have boasted
    on the day of distress.
13 You should not have entered the
    gate of my people
    on the day of their calamity;
    you should not have joined in
        the gloating over Judah's*e*
        disaster
    on the day of his calamity;

a Or *clefts of Sela*   *b* Cn: Heb lacks
those who ate   *c* Heb *But do not gloat*
(and similarly through verse 14)
d Heb *on the day of*   *e* Heb *his*

you should not have looted his
goods
on the day of his calamity.
14 You should not have stood at the
crossings
to cut off his fugitives;
you should not have handed
over his survivors
on the day of distress.

15 For the day of the LORD is near
against all the nations.
As you have done, it shall be
done to you;
your deeds shall return on
your own head.
16 For as you have drunk on my
holy mountain,
all the nations around you
shall drink;
they shall drink and gulp
down,*f*
and shall be as though they
had never been.

Israel's Final Triumph

17 But on Mount Zion there shall
be those that escape,
and it shall be holy;
and the house of Jacob shall
take possession of those
who dispossessed them.
18 The house of Jacob shall be a
fire,

the house of Joseph a flame,
and the house of Esau stubble;
they shall burn them and
consume them,
and there shall be no survivor
of the house of Esau;
for the LORD has spoken.
19 Those of the Neg'eb shall
possess Mount Esau,
and those of the She·phē'lah
the land of the Phi·lis'tines;
they shall possess the land of
E'phra·im and the land of
Samaria,
and Benjamin shall possess
Gil'e·ad.
20 The exiles of the Israelites who
are in Hā'lah*g*
shall possess*h* Phoe·ni'ci·a as
far as Zar'e·phath;
and the exiles of Jerusalem who
are in Se·phar'ad
shall possess the towns of the
Neg'eb.
21 Those who have been saved*i*
shall go up to Mount Zion
to rule Mount Esau;
and the kingdom shall be the
LORD's.

f Meaning of Heb uncertain   *g* Cn: Heb
in this army   *h* Cn: Meaning of Heb
uncertain   *i* Or *Saviors*

JONAH

Jonah Tries to Run Away from God

1 Now the word of the LORD came to Jonah son of A·mit'tai, saying, 2 "Go at once to Nin'e·veh, that great city, and cry out against it; for their wickedness has come up before me." 3 But Jonah set out to flee to Tar'shish from the presence of the LORD. He went down to Jop'pa and found a ship going to Tar'shish; so he paid his fare and went on board, to go with them to Tar'shish, away from the presence of the LORD.

4 But the LORD hurled a great wind

upon the sea, and such a mighty storm came upon the sea that the ship threatened to break up. 5 Then the mariners were afraid, and each cried to his god. They threw the cargo that was in the ship into the sea, to lighten it for them. Jonah, meanwhile, had gone down into the hold of the ship and had lain down, and was fast asleep. 6 The captain came and said to him, "What are you doing sound asleep? Get up, call on your god! Perhaps the god will spare us a thought so that we do not perish."

7 The sailors[a] said to one another, "Come, let us cast lots, so that we may know on whose account this calamity has come upon us." So they cast lots, and the lot fell on Jonah. 8 Then they said to him, "Tell us why this calamity has come upon us. What is your occupation? Where do you come from? What is your country? And of what people are you?" 9 "I am a Hebrew," he replied. "I worship the LORD, the God of heaven, who made the sea and the dry land." 10 Then the men were even more afraid, and said to him, "What is this that you have done!" For the men knew that he was fleeing from the presence of the LORD, because he had told them so.

11 Then they said to him, "What shall we do to you, that the sea may quiet down for us?" For the sea was growing more and more tempestuous. 12 He said to them, "Pick me up and throw me into the sea; then the sea will quiet down for you; for I know it is because of me that this great storm has come upon you." 13 Nevertheless the men rowed hard to bring the ship back to land, but they could not, for the sea grew more and more stormy against them. 14 Then they cried out to the LORD, "Please, O LORD, we pray, do not let us perish on account of this man's life. Do not make us guilty of innocent blood; for you, O LORD, have done as it pleased you." 15 So they picked Jonah up and threw him into the sea; and the sea ceased from its raging. 16 Then the men feared the LORD even more, and they offered a sacrifice to the LORD and made vows.

17[b] But the LORD provided a large fish to swallow up Jonah; and Jonah was in the belly of the fish three days and three nights.

A Psalm of Thanksgiving

2 Then Jonah prayed to the LORD his God from the belly of the fish, 2 saying,

"I called to the LORD out of my
   distress,
  and he answered me;
out of the belly of Sheʹol I cried,
  and you heard my voice.
3 You cast me into the deep,
  into the heart of the seas,
  and the flood surrounded me;
all your waves and your billows
  passed over me.
4 Then I said, 'I am driven away
  from your sight;

how[c] shall I look again
  upon your holy temple?'
5 The waters closed in over me;
  the deep surrounded me;
weeds were wrapped around my
  head
6   at the roots of the mountains.
I went down to the land
  whose bars closed upon me
   forever;
yet you brought up my life from
  the Pit,
  O LORD my God.
7 As my life was ebbing away,
  I remembered the LORD;
and my prayer came to you,
  into your holy temple.
8 Those who worship vain idols
  forsake their true loyalty.
9 But I with the voice of
   thanksgiving
  will sacrifice to you;
what I have vowed I will pay.
  Deliverance belongs to the
   LORD!"

10 Then the LORD spoke to the fish, and it spewed Jonah out upon the dry land.

Conversion of Nineveh

3 The word of the LORD came to Jonah a second time, saying, 2 "Get up, go to Ninʹeveh, that great city, and proclaim to it the message that I tell you." 3 So Jonah set out and went to Ninʹeveh, according to the word of the LORD. Now Ninʹeveh was an exceedingly large city, a three days' walk across. 4 Jonah began to go into the city, going a day's walk. And he cried out, "Forty days more, and Ninʹeveh shall be overthrown!" 5 And the people of Ninʹeveh believed God; they proclaimed a fast, and everyone, great and small, put on sackcloth.

6 When the news reached the king of Ninʹeveh, he rose from his throne, removed his robe, covered himself with sackcloth, and sat in ashes. 7 Then he had a proclamation made in Ninʹeveh: "By the decree of the king and his nobles: No human being or animal, no herd or flock, shall taste anything. They shall not feed, nor shall they drink water. 8 Human beings and animals shall be covered with sackcloth, and they shall cry mightily to God. All shall turn from their evil ways and from the violence that is in their hands.

---

a Heb *They*   b Ch 2.1 in Heb
c Theodotion: Heb *surely*

**J
O
N
A
H**

9 Who knows? God may relent and change his mind; he may turn from his fierce anger, so that we do not perish."

10 When God saw what they did, how they turned from their evil ways, God changed his mind about the calamity that he had said he would bring upon them; and he did not do it.

Jonah's Anger

4 But this was very displeasing to Jonah, and he became angry. ²He prayed to the LORD and said, "O LORD! Is not this what I said while I was still in my own country? That is why I fled to Tar′shish at the beginning; for I knew that you are a gracious God and merciful, slow to anger, and abounding in steadfast love, and ready to relent from punishing. ³And now, O LORD, please take my life from me, for it is better for me to die than to live." ⁴And the LORD said, "Is it right for you to be angry?" ⁵Then Jonah went out of the city and sat down east of the city, and made a booth for himself there. He sat under it in the shade, waiting to see what would become of the city.

6 The LORD God appointed a bush,^{d} and made it come up over Jonah, to give shade over his head, to save him from his discomfort; so Jonah was very happy about the bush. ⁷But when dawn came up the next day, God appointed a worm that attacked the bush, so that it withered. ⁸When the sun rose, God prepared a sultry east wind, and the sun beat down on the head of Jonah so that he was faint and asked that he might die. He said, "It is better for me to die than to live."

Jonah Is Reproved

9 But God said to Jonah, "Is it right for you to be angry about the bush?" And he said, "Yes, angry enough to die." ¹⁰Then the LORD said, "You are concerned about the bush, for which you did not labor and which you did not grow; it came into being in a night and perished in a night. ¹¹And should I not be concerned about Nin′e·veh, that great city, in which there are more than a hundred and twenty thousand persons who do not know their right hand from their left, and also many animals?"

^{d}Heb *qiqayon,* possibly *the castor bean plant*

MICAH

1 The word of the LORD that came to Mī′cah of Mō′re·sheth in the days of Kings Jō′tham, Ā′haz, and Hez·e·kī′ah of Judah, which he saw concerning Samaria and Jerusalem.

Judgment Pronounced against Samaria

2 Hear, you peoples, all of you;
   listen, O earth, and all that is in it;
and let the Lord GOD be a
   witness against you,
   the Lord from his holy temple.
3 For lo, the LORD is coming out of his place,
   and will come down and tread upon the high places of the earth.

4 Then the mountains will melt under him
   and the valleys will burst open,
like wax near the fire,
   like waters poured down a steep place.
5 All this is for the transgression of Jacob
   and for the sins of the house of Israel.
What is the transgression of Jacob?
   Is it not Samaria?
And what is the high place^a of Judah?
   Is it not Jerusalem?

^{a}Heb *what are the high places*

6 Therefore I will make Samaria a
    heap in the open country,
    a place for planting vineyards.
I will pour down her stones into
    the valley,
    and uncover her foundations.
7 All her images shall be beaten to
    pieces,
    all her wages shall be burned
      with fire,
    and all her idols I will lay
      waste;
for as the wages of a prostitute
    she gathered them,
    and as the wages of a
      prostitute they shall again
      be used.

The Doom of the Cities of Judah

8 For this I will lament and wail;
    I will go barefoot and naked;
I will make lamentation like the
    jackals,
    and mourning like the
      ostriches.
9 For her wound[b] is incurable.
    It has come to Judah.
it has reached to the gate of my
      people,
    to Jerusalem.

10 Tell it not in Gath,
    weep not at all;
in Beth-le·aph′rah
    roll yourselves in the dust.
11 Pass on your way,
    inhabitants of Shā′phir,
    in nakedness and shame;
the inhabitants of Zā′a·nan
    do not come forth;
Beth-ē′zel is wailing
    and shall remove its support
      from you.
12 For the inhabitants of Mā′roth
    wait anxiously for good,
yet disaster has come down from
    the LORD
    to the gate of Jerusalem.
13 Harness the steeds to the
    chariots,
    inhabitants of Lā′chish;
it was the beginning of sin
    to daughter Zion,
for in you were found
    the transgressions of Israel.
14 Therefore you shall give parting
    gifts
    to Mō′re·sheth-gath;
the houses of Ach′zib shall be a
    deception
    to the kings of Israel.

15 I will again bring a conqueror
    upon you,
    inhabitants of Ma·rē′shah;
the glory of Israel
    shall come to A·dul′lam.
16 Make yourselves bald and cut
    off your hair
    for your pampered children;
make yourselves as bald as the
    eagle,
    for they have gone from you
      into exile.

Social Evils Denounced

2 Alas for those who devise
    wickedness
    and evil deeds[c] on their beds!
When the morning dawns, they
    perform it,
    because it is in their power.
2 They covet fields, and seize
    them;
    houses, and take them away;
they oppress householder and
    house,
    people and their inheritance.
3 Therefore thus says the LORD:
Now, I am devising against this
    family an evil
    from which you cannot
      remove your necks;
and you shall not walk
    haughtily,
    for it will be an evil time.
4 On that day they shall take up a
    taunt song against you,
    and wail with bitter
      lamentation,
and say, "We are utterly ruined;
    the LORD[d] alters the
      inheritance of my people;
how he removes it from me!
    Among our captors[e] he
      parcels out our fields."
5 Therefore you will have no one
    to cast the line by lot
    in the assembly of the LORD.

6 "Do not preach"—thus they
    preach—
    "one should not preach of such
      things;
    disgrace will not overtake us."
7 Should this be said, O house of
    Jacob?
    Is the LORD's patience
      exhausted?

---

[b] Gk Syr Vg: Heb *wounds*   [c] Cn: Heb
work evil   [d] Heb *he*   [e] Cn: Heb *the
rebellious*

Are these his doings?
Do not my words do good
to one who walks uprightly?

8 But you rise up against my
people[f] as an enemy;
you strip the robe from the
peaceful,[g]
from those who pass by
trustingly
with no thought of war.

9 The women of my people you
drive out
from their pleasant houses;
from their young children you
take away
my glory forever.

10 Arise and go;
for this is no place to rest,
because of uncleanness that
destroys
with a grievous destruction.[h]

11 If someone were to go about
uttering empty falsehoods,
saying, "I will preach to you of
wine and strong drink,"
such a one would be the
preacher for this people!

A Promise for the Remnant of Israel

12 I will surely gather all of you,
O Jacob,
I will gather the survivors of
Israel;
I will set them together
like sheep in a fold,
like a flock in its pasture;
it will resound with people.

13 The one who breaks out will go
up before them;
they will break through and
pass the gate,
going out by it.
Their king will pass on before
them,
the LORD at their head.

Wicked Rulers and Prophets

3 And I said:
Listen, you heads of Jacob
and rulers of the house of
Israel!
Should you not know justice? —

2 you who hate the good and
love the evil,
who tear the skin off my
people,[i]
and the flesh off their bones;

3 who eat the flesh of my people,
flay their skin off them,
break their bones in pieces,

and chop them up like meat[j]
in a kettle,
like flesh in a caldron.

4 Then they will cry to the LORD,
but he will not answer them;
he will hide his face from them
at that time,
because they have acted
wickedly.

5 Thus says the LORD concerning
the prophets
who lead my people astray,
who cry "Peace"
when they have something to
eat,
but declare war against those
who put nothing into their
mouths.

6 Therefore it shall be night to
you, without vision,
and darkness to you, without
revelation.
The sun shall go down upon the
prophets,
and the day shall be black
over them;

7 the seers shall be disgraced,
and the diviners put to shame;
they shall all cover their lips,
for there is no answer from
God.

8 But as for me, I am filled with
power,
with the spirit of the LORD,
and with justice and might,
to declare to Jacob his
transgression
and to Israel his sin.

9 Hear this, you rulers of the
house of Jacob
and chiefs of the house of
Israel,
who abhor justice
and pervert all equity,

10 who build Zion with blood
and Jerusalem with wrong!

11 Its rulers give judgment for a
bribe,
its priests teach for a price,
its prophets give oracles for
money;
yet they lean upon the LORD and
say,
"Surely the LORD is with us!

f Cn: Heb *But yesterday my people rose*
g Cn: Heb *from before a garment*
h Meaning of Heb uncertain   i Heb *from them*   j Gk: Heb *as*

No harm shall come upon us."
12 Therefore because of you
    Zion shall be plowed as a
        field;
    Jerusalem shall become a heap
        of ruins,
        and the mountain of the house
        a wooded height.

Peace and Security through Obedience
(Cp Isa 2.2–4)

4 In days to come
    the mountain of the LORD's
      house
    shall be established as the
      highest of the mountains,
      and shall be raised up above
      the hills.
    Peoples shall stream to it,
2   and many nations shall come
      and say:
    "Come, let us go up to the
      mountain of the LORD,
    to the house of the God of
      Jacob;
    that he may teach us his ways
      and that we may walk in his
      paths."
    For out of Zion shall go forth
      instruction,
      and the word of the LORD
      from Jerusalem.
3 He shall judge between many
      peoples,
      and shall arbitrate between
      strong nations far away;
    they shall beat their swords into
      plowshares,
      and their spears into pruning
      hooks;
    nation shall not lift up sword
      against nation,
      neither shall they learn war
      any more;
4 but they shall all sit under their
      own vines and under their
      own fig trees,
      and no one shall make them
      afraid;
    for the mouth of the LORD of
      hosts has spoken.

5 For all the peoples walk,
    each in the name of its god,
    but we will walk in the name of
      the LORD our God
      forever and ever.

Restoration Promised after Exile

6 In that day, says the LORD,
    I will assemble the lame
    and gather those who have been
      driven away,
      and those whom I have
      afflicted.
7 The lame I will make the
      remnant,
      and those who were cast off, a
      strong nation;
    and the LORD will reign over
      them in Mount Zion
      now and forevermore.

8 And you, O tower of the flock,
    hill of daughter Zion,
    to you it shall come,
      the former dominion shall
      come,
      the sovereignty of daughter
      Jerusalem.

9 Now why do you cry aloud?
    Is there no king in you?
    Has your counselor perished,
      that pangs have seized you
      like a woman in labor?
10 Writhe and groan,*k* O daughter
      Zion,
      like a woman in labor;
    for now you shall go forth from
      the city
      and camp in the open country;
    you shall go to Babylon.
    There you shall be rescued,
      there the LORD will redeem
      you
      from the hands of your
      enemies.

11 Now many nations
    are assembled against you,
    saying, "Let her be profaned,
      and let our eyes gaze upon
      Zion."
12 But they do not know
      the thoughts of the LORD;
    they do not understand his plan,
      that he has gathered them as
      sheaves to the threshing
      floor.
13 Arise and thresh,
    O daughter Zion,
    for I will make your horn iron
    and your hoofs bronze;
    you shall beat in pieces many
      peoples,

k Meaning of Heb uncertain

M
I
C
A
H

and shall[l] devote their gain to
the LORD,
their wealth to the Lord of the
whole earth.

5 [m]Now you are walled around with
a wall;[n]
siege is laid against us;
with a rod they strike the ruler
of Israel
upon the cheek.

The Ruler from Bethlehem

2 [o] But you, O Bethlehem of
Eph´ra·thah,
who are one of the little clans
of Judah,
from you shall come forth for
me
one who is to rule in Israel,
whose origin is from of old,
from ancient days.
3 Therefore he shall give them up
until the time
when she who is in labor has
brought forth;
then the rest of his kindred shall
return
to the people of Israel.
4 And he shall stand and feed his
flock in the strength of the
LORD,
in the majesty of the name of
the LORD his God.
And they shall live secure, for
now he shall be great
to the ends of the earth;
5 and he shall be the one of peace.

If the Assyrians come into our
land
and tread upon our soil,[p]
we will raise against them seven
shepherds
and eight installed as rulers.
6 They shall rule the land of
Assyria with the sword,
and the land of Nim´rod with
the drawn sword;[q]
they[r] shall rescue us from the
Assyrians
if they come into our land
or tread within our border.

The Future Role of the Remnant

7 Then the remnant of Jacob,
surrounded by many peoples,
shall be like dew from the LORD,
like showers on the grass,
which do not depend upon
people

or wait for any mortal.
8 And among the nations the
remnant of Jacob,
surrounded by many peoples,
shall be like a lion among the
animals of the forest,
like a young lion among the
flocks of sheep,
which, when it goes through,
treads down
and tears in pieces, with no
one to deliver.
9 Your hand shall be lifted up over
your adversaries,
and all your enemies shall be
cut off.

10 In that day, says the LORD,
I will cut off your horses from
among you
and will destroy your chariots;
11 and I will cut off the cities of
your land
and throw down all your
strongholds;
12 and I will cut off sorceries from
your hand,
and you shall have no more
soothsayers;
13 and I will cut off your images
and your pillars from among
you,
and you shall bow down no
more
to the work of your hands;
14 and I will uproot your sacred
poles[s] from among you
and destroy your towns.
15 And in anger and wrath I will
execute vengeance
on the nations that did not
obey.

God Challenges Israel

6 Hear what the LORD says:
Rise, plead your case before
the mountains,
and let the hills hear your
voice.
2 Hear, you mountains, the
controversy of the LORD,
and you enduring foundations
of the earth;
for the LORD has a controversy
with his people,

[l]Gk Syr Tg: Heb *and I will*   [m]Ch 4.14
in Heb   [n]Cn Compare Gk: Meaning of
Heb uncertain   [o]Ch 5.1 in Heb
[p]Gk: Heb *in our palaces*   [q]Cn: Heb *in
its entrances*   [r]Heb *he*
[s]Heb *Asherim*

and he will contend with Israel.

3 "O my people, what have I done to you?
    In what have I wearied you?
    Answer me!
4 For I brought you up from the land of Egypt,
    and redeemed you from the house of slavery;
    and I sent before you Moses, Aaron, and Miriam.
5 O my people, remember now what King Bā′lak of Mō′ab devised,
    what Bā′laam son of Bē′or answered him,
    and what happened from Shit′tim to Gil′gal,
    that you may know the saving acts of the LORD."

What God Requires
(Cp Am 5.24)

6 "With what shall I come before the LORD,
    and bow myself before God on high?
    Shall I come before him with burnt offerings,
    with calves a year old?
7 Will the LORD be pleased with thousands of rams,
    with ten thousands of rivers of oil?
    Shall I give my firstborn for my transgression,
    the fruit of my body for the sin of my soul?"
8 He has told you, O mortal, what is good;
    and what does the LORD require of you
    but to do justice, and to love kindness,
    and to walk humbly with your God?

Cheating and Violence to Be Punished

9 The voice of the LORD cries to the city
    (it is sound wisdom to fear your name):
    Hear, O tribe and assembly of the city![t]
10 Can I forget[u] the treasures of wickedness in the house of the wicked,
    and the scant measure that is accursed?

11 Can I tolerate wicked scales and a bag of dishonest weights?
12 Your[v] wealthy are full of violence;
    your[w] inhabitants speak lies, with tongues of deceit in their mouths.
13 Therefore I have begun[x] to strike you down,
    making you desolate because of your sins.
14 You shall eat, but not be satisfied,
    and there shall be a gnawing hunger within you;
    you shall put away, but not save,
    and what you save, I will hand over to the sword.
15 You shall sow, but not reap;
    you shall tread olives, but not anoint yourselves with oil;
    you shall tread grapes, but not drink wine.
16 For you have kept the statutes of Om′ri[y]
    and all the works of the house of Ā′hab,
    and you have followed their counsels.
    Therefore I will make you a desolation, and your[z] inhabitants an object of hissing;
    so you shall bear the scorn of my people.

The Total Corruption of the People

7 Woe is me! For I have become like one who,
    after the summer fruit has been gathered,
    after the vintage has been gleaned,
    finds no cluster to eat;
    there is no first-ripe fig for which I hunger.
2 The faithful have disappeared from the land,
    and there is no one left who is upright;
    they all lie in wait for blood,
    and they hunt each other with nets.

[t] Cn Compare Gk: Heb *tribe, and who has appointed it yet?* [u] Cn: Meaning of Heb uncertain [v] Heb *Whose* [w] Heb *whose* [x] Gk Syr Vg: Heb *have made sick* [y] Gk Syr Vg Tg: Heb *the statutes of Omri are kept* [z] Heb *its*

3 Their hands are skilled to do
      evil;
   the official and the judge ask
      for a bribe,
and the powerful dictate what
      they desire;
   thus they pervert justice.[a]
4 The best of them is like a brier,
   the most upright of them a
      thorn hedge.
The day of their[b] sentinels, of
      their[b] punishment, has
      come;
   now their confusion is at hand.
5 Put no trust in a friend,
   have no confidence in a loved
      one;
guard the doors of your mouth
   from her who lies in your
      embrace;
6 for the son treats the father with
      contempt,
   the daughter rises up against
      her mother,
the daughter-in-law against her
      mother-in-law;
   your enemies are members of
      your own household.
7 But as for me, I will look to the
      LORD,
   I will wait for the God of my
      salvation;
   my God will hear me.

Penitence and Trust in God

8 Do not rejoice over me, O my
      enemy;
   when I fall, I shall rise;
when I sit in darkness,
   the LORD will be a light to me.
9 I must bear the indignation of
      the LORD,
   because I have sinned against
      him,
until he takes my side
   and executes judgment for me.
He will bring me out to the light;
   I shall see his vindication.
10 Then my enemy will see,
   and shame will cover her who
      said to me,
   "Where is the LORD your
      God?"
My eyes will see her downfall;[c]
   now she will be trodden down
   like the mire of the streets.

A Prophecy of Restoration

11 A day for the building of your
      walls!
   In that day the boundary shall
      be far extended.
12 In that day they will come to
      you
   from Assyria to[d] Egypt,
and from Egypt to the River,
   from sea to sea and from
      mountain to mountain.
13 But the earth will be desolate
   because of its inhabitants,
   for the fruit of their doings.

14 Shepherd your people with your
      staff,
   the flock that belongs to you,
which lives alone in a forest
   in the midst of a garden land;
let them feed in Bā'shan and
      Gil'e·ad
   as in the days of old.
15 As in the days when you came
      out of the land of Egypt,
   show us[e] marvelous things.
16 The nations shall see and be
      ashamed
   of all their might;
they shall lay their hands on
      their mouths;
   their ears shall be deaf;
17 they shall lick dust like a snake,
   like the crawling things of the
      earth;
they shall come trembling out of
      their fortresses;
   they shall turn in dread to the
      LORD our God,
   and they shall stand in fear of
      you.

God's Compassion and Steadfast Love

18 Who is a God like you,
      pardoning iniquity
   and passing over the
      transgression
   of the remnant of your[f]
      possession?
He does not retain his anger
      forever,
   because he delights in showing
      clemency.
19 He will again have compassion
      upon us;

---

[a]Cn: Heb *they weave it*   [b]Heb *your*
[c]Heb lacks *downfall*   [d]One Ms: MT
Assyria and cities of   [e]Cn: Heb *I will*
show him   [f]Heb *his*

he will tread our iniquities
under foot.
You will cast all our^g sins
into the depths of the sea.
20 You will show faithfulness to
Jacob

and unswerving loyalty to
Abraham,
as you have sworn to our
ancestors
from the days of old.

^gGk Syr Vg Tg: Heb *their*

NAHUM

1 An oracle concerning Nin′e·veh.
The book of the vision of Nā′hum
of El′kosh.

The Consuming Wrath of God

2 A jealous and avenging God is
the LORD,
the LORD is avenging and
wrathful;
the LORD takes vengeance on his
adversaries
and rages against his enemies.
3 The LORD is slow to anger but
great in power,
and the LORD will by no
means clear the guilty.

His way is in whirlwind and
storm,
and the clouds are the dust of
his feet.
4 He rebukes the sea and makes it
dry,
and he dries up all the rivers;
Bā′shan and Car′mel wither,
and the bloom of Lebanon
fades.
5 The mountains quake before
him,
and the hills melt;
the earth heaves before him,
the world and all who live in
it.
6 Who can stand before his
indignation?
Who can endure the heat of
his anger?
His wrath is poured out like fire,
and by him the rocks are
broken in pieces.
7 The LORD is good,

a stronghold in a day of
trouble;
he protects those who take
refuge in him,
8 even in a rushing flood.
He will make a full end of his
adversaries,^a
and will pursue his enemies
into darkness.
9 Why do you plot against the
LORD?
He will make an end;
no adversary will rise up
twice.
10 Like thorns they are entangled,
like drunkards they are drunk;
they are consumed like dry
straw.
11 From you one has gone out
who plots evil against the
LORD,
who counsels wickedness.

Good News for Judah

12 Thus says the LORD,
"Though they are at full strength
and many,^b
they will be cut off and pass
away.
Though I have afflicted you,
I will afflict you no more.
13 And now I will break off his
yoke from you
and snap the bonds that bind
you."

14 The LORD has commanded
concerning you:

^aGk: Heb *of her place*   ^bMeaning of
Heb uncertain

"Your name shall be
　perpetuated no longer;
from the house of your gods I
　will cut off
　the carved image and the cast
　image.
I will make your grave, for you
　are worthless."

[15c] Look! On the mountains the feet
　of one
　who brings good tidings,
　who proclaims peace!
Celebrate your festivals,
　O Judah,
　fulfill your vows,
for never again shall the wicked
　invade you;
　they are utterly cut off.

The Destruction of the Wicked City

2 A shatterer[d] has come up
　against you.
　Guard the ramparts;
　watch the road;
gird your loins;
　collect all your strength.

2 (For the LORD is restoring the
　majesty of Jacob,
　as well as the majesty of
　Israel,
though ravagers have ravaged
　them
　and ruined their branches.)

3 The shields of his warriors are
　red;
　his soldiers are clothed in
　crimson.
The metal on the chariots flashes
　on the day when he musters
　them;
　the chargers[e] prance.
4 The chariots race madly through
　the streets,
　they rush to and fro through
　the squares;
their appearance is like torches,
　they dart like lightning.
5 He calls his officers;
　they stumble as they come
　forward;
they hasten to the wall,
　and the mantelet[f] is set up.
6 The river gates are opened,
　the palace trembles.
7 It is decreed[f] that the city[g] be
　exiled,
　its slave women led away,
moaning like doves
　and beating their breasts.

8 Nin'e·veh is like a pool
　whose waters[h] run away.
　"Halt! Halt!" —
　but no one turns back.
9 "Plunder the silver,
　plunder the gold!
There is no end of treasure!
　An abundance of every
　precious thing!"

10 Devastation, desolation, and
　destruction!
　Hearts faint and knees
　tremble,
all loins quake,
　all faces grow pale!
11 What became of the lions' den,
　the cave[i] of the young lions,
where the lion goes,
　and the lion's cubs, with no
　one to disturb them?
12 The lion has torn enough for his
　whelps
　and strangled prey for his
　lionesses;
he has filled his caves with prey
　and his dens with torn flesh.

13 See, I am against you, says the
LORD of hosts, and I will burn your[j]
chariots in smoke, and the sword shall
devour your young lions; I will cut off
your prey from the earth, and the voice
of your messengers shall be heard no
more.

Ruin Imminent and Inevitable

3 Ah! City of bloodshed,
　utterly deceitful, full of
　booty —
　no end to the plunder!
2 The crack of whip and rumble of
　wheel,
　galloping horse and bounding
　chariot!
3 Horsemen charging,
　flashing sword and glittering
　spear,
piles of dead,
　heaps of corpses,
dead bodies without end —
　they stumble over the bodies!
4 Because of the countless
　debaucheries of the
　prostitute,

[c] Ch 2.1 in Heb　　[d] Cn: Heb *scatterer*
[e] Cn Compare Gk Syr: Heb *cypresses*
[f] Meaning of Heb uncertain　　[g] Heb *it*
[h] Cn Compare Gk: Heb *a pool, from the*
days that she has become, and they
[i] Cn: Heb *pasture*　　[j] Heb *her*

gracefully alluring, mistress of
    sorcery,
who enslaves[k] nations through
    her debaucheries,
    and peoples through her
      sorcery,
5 I am against you,
    says the LORD of hosts,
    and will lift up your skirts
      over your face;
    and I will let nations look on
      your nakedness
    and kingdoms on your shame.
6 I will throw filth at you
    and treat you with contempt,
    and make you a spectacle.
7 Then all who see you will shrink
    from you and say,
"Nin'e·veh is devastated; who
    will bemoan her?"
    Where shall I seek comforters
      for you?

8 Are you better than Thēbes[l]
    that sat by the Nile,
with water around her,
    her rampart a sea,
    water her wall?
9 Ethiopia[m] was her strength,
    Egypt too, and that without
      limit;
    Put and the Libyans were
      her[n] helpers.

10 Yet she became an exile,
    she went into captivity;
even her infants were dashed in
    pieces
    at the head of every street;
lots were cast for her nobles,
    all her dignitaries were bound
      in fetters.
11 You also will be drunken,
    you will go into hiding;[o]
you will seek
    a refuge from the enemy.
12 All your fortresses are like fig
    trees
    with first-ripe figs —
if shaken they fall
    into the mouth of the eater.
13 Look at your troops:

they are women in your midst.
The gates of your land
    are wide open to your foes;
    fire has devoured the bars of
      your gates.

14 Draw water for the siege,
    strengthen your forts;
trample the clay,
    tread the mortar,
    take hold of the brick mold!
15 There the fire will devour you,
    the sword will cut you off.
    It will devour you like the
      locust.

Multiply yourselves like the
    locust,
    multiply like the grasshopper!
16 You increased your merchants
    more than the stars of the
      heavens.
    The locust sheds its skin and
      flies away.
17 Your guards are like
    grasshoppers,
    your scribes like swarms[o] of
      locusts
settling on the fences
    on a cold day —
when the sun rises, they fly
    away;
    no one knows where they have
      gone.

18 Your shepherds are asleep,
    O king of Assyria;
    your nobles slumber.
Your people are scattered on the
    mountains
    with no one to gather them.
19 There is no assuaging your hurt,
    your wound is mortal.
All who hear the news about
    you
    clap their hands over you.
For who has ever escaped
    your endless cruelty?

k Heb *sells*   l Heb *No-amon*
m Or *Nubia*; Heb *Cush*   n Gk: Heb *your*
o Meaning of Heb uncertain

N
A
H
U
M

HABAKKUK

1

The oracle that the prophet Ha·bak'kuk saw.

The Prophet's Complaint

2 O LORD, how long shall I cry for
    help,
  and you will not listen?
  Or cry to you "Violence!"
  and you will not save?
3 Why do you make me see
    wrongdoing
  and look at trouble?
  Destruction and violence are
    before me;
  strife and contention arise.
4 So the law becomes slack
  and justice never prevails.
  The wicked surround the
    righteous—
  therefore judgment comes
    forth perverted.

5 Look at the nations, and see!
  Be astonished! Be astounded!
  For a work is being done in your
    days
  that you would not believe if
    you were told.
6 For I am rousing the
    Chal·dē'ans,
  that fierce and impetuous
    nation,
  who march through the breadth
    of the earth
  to seize dwellings not their
    own.
7 Dread and fearsome are they;
  their justice and dignity
  proceed from themselves.
8 Their horses are swifter than
    leopards,
  more menacing than wolves at
    dusk;
  their horses charge.
  Their horsemen come from far
    away;
  they fly like an eagle swift to
    devour.
9 They all come for violence,
  with faces pressing[a] forward;
  they gather captives like sand.
10 At kings they scoff,
  and of rulers they make sport.
  They laugh at every fortress,
  and heap up earth to take it.
11 Then they sweep by like the
    wind;
  they transgress and become
    guilty;
  their own might is their god!

12 Are you not from of old,
  O LORD my God, my Holy
    One?
  You[b] shall not die.
  O LORD, you have marked them
    for judgment;
  and you, O Rock, have
    established them for
    punishment.
13 Your eyes are too pure to behold
    evil,
  and you cannot look on
    wrongdoing;
  why do you look on the
    treacherous,
  and are silent when the
    wicked swallow
  those more righteous than
    they?
14 You have made people like the
    fish of the sea,
  like crawling things that have
    no ruler.

15 The enemy[c] brings all of them
    up with a hook;
  he drags them out with his net,
  he gathers them in his seine;
  so he rejoices and exults.
16 Therefore he sacrifices to his net
  and makes offerings to his
    seine;
  for by them his portion is lavish,
  and his food is rich.

a Meaning of Heb uncertain   b Ancient
Heb tradition: MT *We*   c Heb *He*

17 Is he then to keep on emptying
    his net,
    and destroying nations without
      mercy?

God's Reply to the Prophet's Complaint

2 I will stand at my watchpost,
  and station myself on the
    rampart;
I will keep watch to see what he
    will say to me,
    and what he[d] will answer
      concerning my complaint.
2 Then the LORD answered me
    and said:
Write the vision;
    make it plain on tablets,
    so that a runner may read it.
3 For there is still a vision for the
    appointed time;
    it speaks of the end, and does
      not lie.
If it seems to tarry, wait for it;
    it will surely come, it will not
      delay.
4 Look at the proud!
    Their spirit is not right in
      them,
    but the righteous live by their
      faith.[e]
5 Moreover, wealth[f] is
    treacherous;
    the arrogant do not endure.
They open their throats wide as
    Shē′ōl;
    like Death they never have
      enough.
They gather all nations for
    themselves,
    and collect all peoples as their
      own.

The Woes of the Wicked

6 Shall not everyone taunt such
people and, with mocking riddles, say
about them,
    "Alas for you who heap up what
      is not your own!"
    How long will you load
      yourselves with goods
      taken in pledge?
7 Will not your own creditors
    suddenly rise,
    and those who make you
      tremble wake up?
    Then you will be booty for
      them.
8 Because you have plundered
    many nations,

all that survive of the peoples
    shall plunder you—
because of human bloodshed,
    and violence to the earth,
to cities and all who live in
    them.

9 "Alas for you who get evil gain
    for your houses,
    setting your nest on high
    to be safe from the reach of
      harm!"
10 You have devised shame for
    your house
    by cutting off many peoples;
    you have forfeited your life.
11 The very stones will cry out
    from the wall,
    and the plaster[g] will respond
      from the woodwork.

12 "Alas for you who build a town
    by bloodshed,
    and found a city on iniquity!"
13 Is it not from the LORD of hosts
    that peoples labor only to feed
      the flames,
    and nations weary themselves
      for nothing?
14 But the earth will be filled
    with the knowledge of the
      glory of the LORD,
    as the waters cover the sea.

15 "Alas for you who make your
    neighbors drink,
    pouring out your wrath[h] until
      they are drunk,
    in order to gaze on their
      nakedness!"
16 You will be sated with contempt
    instead of glory.
    Drink, you yourself, and
      stagger![i]
The cup in the LORD's right
    hand
    will come around to you,
    and shame will come upon
      your glory!
17 For the violence done to
    Lebanon will overwhelm
      you;
    the destruction of the animals
      will terrify you—[j]
because of human bloodshed
    and violence to the earth,

---

[d] Syr: Heb I   [e] Or *faithfulness*   [f] Other
Heb Mss read *wine*   [g] Or *beam*
[h] Or *poison*   [i] Q Ms Gk: MT *be
uncircumcised*   [j] Gk Syr: Meaning of
Heb uncertain

H
A
B
A
K
K
U
K

to cities and all who live in
them.

18 What use is an idol
once its maker has shaped it —
a cast image, a teacher of lies?
For its maker trusts in what has
been made,
though the product is only an
idol that cannot speak!
19 Alas for you who say to the
wood, "Wake up!"
to silent stone, "Rouse
yourself!"
Can it teach?
See, it is gold and silver plated,
and there is no breath in it at
all.
20 But the LORD is in his holy
temple;
let all the earth keep silence
before him!

3 A prayer of the prophet Ha·bak´-
kuk according to Shig·i·ōn´oth.

The Prophet's Prayer

2 O LORD, I have heard of your
renown,
and I stand in awe, O LORD, of
your work.
In our own time revive it;
in our own time make it
known;
in wrath may you remember
mercy.
3 God came from Tē´man,
the Holy One from Mount
Par´an.   *Sē´lah*
His glory covered the heavens,
and the earth was full of his
praise.
4 The brightness was like the sun;
rays came forth from his hand,
where his power lay hidden.
5 Before him went pestilence,
and plague followed close
behind.
6 He stopped and shook the earth;
he looked and made the
nations tremble.
The eternal mountains were
shattered;
along his ancient pathways
the everlasting hills sank low.
7 I saw the tents of Cūsh´an under
affliction;
the tent-curtains of the land of
Mid´i·an trembled.

8 Was your wrath against the
rivers,*k* O LORD?
Or your anger against the
rivers,*k*
or your rage against the sea,*l*
when you drove your horses,
your chariots to victory?
9 You brandished your naked
bow,
sated*m* were the arrows at
your command.*n*   *Sē´lah*
You split the earth with rivers.
10 The mountains saw you, and
writhed;
a torrent of water swept by;
the deep gave forth its voice.
The sun*o* raised high its
hands;
11 the moon*p* stood still in its
exalted place,
at the light of your arrows
speeding by,
at the gleam of your flashing
spear.
12 In fury you trod the earth,
in anger you trampled nations.
13 You came forth to save your
people,
to save your anointed.
You crushed the head of the
wicked house,
laying it bare from foundation
to roof.*n*   *Sē´lah*
14 You pierced with his own
arrows the head*q* of his
warriors,*r*
who came like a whirlwind to
scatter us,*s*
gloating as if ready to devour
the poor who were in
hiding.
15 You trampled the sea with your
horses,
churning the mighty waters.

16 I hear, and I tremble within;
my lips quiver at the sound.
Rottenness enters into my bones,
and my steps tremble*t*
beneath me.
I wait quietly for the day of
calamity
to come upon the people who
attack us.

---

k Or *against River*   *l* Or *against Sea*
m Cn: Heb *oaths*   *n* Meaning of Heb
uncertain   *o* Heb *It*   *p* Heb *sun, moon*
q Or *leader*   *r* Vg Compare Gk Syr:
Meaning of Heb uncertain   *s* Heb *me*
t Cn Compare Gk: Meaning of Heb
uncertain

Trust and Joy in the Midst of Trouble

17 Though the fig tree does not
         blossom,
      and no fruit is on the vines;
   though the produce of the olive
         fails
      and the fields yield no food;
   though the flock is cut off from
         the fold
      and there is no herd in the
         stalls,
18 yet I will rejoice in the LORD;

I will exult in the God of my
      salvation.
19 GOD, the Lord, is my strength;
      he makes my feet like the feet
         of a deer,
      and makes me tread upon the
         heights.ᵘ

To the leader: with stringedᵛ
      instruments.

ᵘHeb *my heights*   ᵛHeb *my stringed*

ZEPHANIAH

1 The word of the LORD that came to
   Zeph·a·ni′ah son of Cū′shī son of
Ged·a·lī′ah son of Am·a·rī′ah son of
Hez·e·kī′ah, in the days of King
Jō·sī′ah son of Ā′mon of Judah.

The Coming Judgment on Judah

2 I will utterly sweep away
      everything
      from the face of the earth,
         says the LORD.
3 I will sweep away humans and
         animals;
      I will sweep away the birds of
         the air
      and the fish of the sea.
   I will make the wicked
         stumble.ᵃ
      I will cut off humanity
      from the face of the earth,
         says the LORD.
4 I will stretch out my hand
         against Judah,
      and against all the inhabitants
         of Jerusalem;
   and I will cut off from this place
      every remnant of Bā′al
      and the name of the idolatrous
         priests;ᵇ
5 those who bow down on the
         roofs
      to the host of the heavens;
   those who bow down and swear
      to the LORD,
      but also swear by Mil′com;ᶜ

6 those who have turned back
         from following the LORD,
      who have not sought the LORD
         or inquired of him.

7 Be silent before the Lord GOD!
      For the day of the LORD is at
         hand;
   the LORD has prepared a
         sacrifice,
      he has consecrated his guests.
8 And on the day of the LORD's
         sacrifice
   I will punish the officials and the
         king's sons
      and all who dress themselves
         in foreign attire.
9 On that day I will punish
      all who leap over the
         threshold,
   who fill their master's house
      with violence and fraud.

10 On that day, says the LORD,
      a cry will be heard from the
         Fish Gate,
   a wail from the Second Quarter,
      a loud crash from the hills.
11 The inhabitants of the Mortar
         wail,

ᵃCn: Heb *sea, and those who cause the
wicked to stumble*   ᵇCompare Gk: Heb
the idolatrous priests with the priests
ᶜGk Mss Syr Vg: Heb *Malcam* (or, *their
king*)

Z
E
P
H
A
N
I
A
H

for all the traders have
  perished;
all who weigh out silver are
  cut off.

12 At that time I will search
  Jerusalem with lamps,
and I will punish the people
who rest complacently[d] on their
  dregs,
  those who say in their hearts,
"The LORD will not do good,
  nor will he do harm."

13 Their wealth shall be plundered,
  and their houses laid waste.
Though they build houses,
  they shall not inhabit them;
though they plant vineyards,
  they shall not drink wine from
    them.

The Great Day of the LORD
(Cp Am 5.18–20)

14 The great day of the LORD is
    near,
  near and hastening fast;
the sound of the day of the LORD
    is bitter,
  the warrior cries aloud there.

15 That day will be a day of wrath,
  a day of distress and anguish,
a day of ruin and devastation,
  a day of darkness and gloom,
a day of clouds and thick
    darkness,

16   a day of trumpet blast and
    battle cry
against the fortified cities
  and against the lofty
    battlements.

17 I will bring such distress upon
    people
  that they shall walk like the
    blind;
  because they have sinned
    against the LORD,
their blood shall be poured out
    like dust,
  and their flesh like dung.

18 Neither their silver nor their
    gold
  will be able to save them
  on the day of the LORD's
    wrath;
in the fire of his passion
  the whole earth shall be
    consumed;
for a full, a terrible end
  he will make of all the
    inhabitants of the earth.

Judgment on Israel's Enemies

2 Gather together, gather,
  O shameless nation,
2 before you are driven away
    like the drifting chaff,[e]
before there comes upon you
    the fierce anger of the LORD,
before there comes upon you
    the day of the LORD's wrath.

3 Seek the LORD, all you humble
    of the land,
  who do his commands;
seek righteousness, seek
    humility;
  perhaps you may be hidden
  on the day of the LORD's
    wrath.

4 For Gā′za shall be deserted,
    and Ash′ke·lon shall become a
    desolation;
  Ash′dod's people shall be driven
    out at noon,
    and Ek′ron shall be uprooted.

5 Ah, inhabitants of the seacoast,
    you nation of the Cher′e·thītes!
  The word of the LORD is against
    you,
    O Cā′naan, land of the
      Phi·lis′tines;
    and I will destroy you until no
      inhabitant is left.

6 And you, O seacoast, shall be
    pastures,
  meadows for shepherds
    and folds for flocks.

7 The seacoast shall become the
    possession
  of the remnant of the house of
    Judah,
  on which they shall pasture,
  and in the houses of Ash′ke·lon
    they shall lie down at evening.
  For the LORD their God will be
    mindful of them
    and restore their fortunes.

8 I have heard the taunts of Mō′ab
    and the revilings of the
      Am′mon·ites,
  how they have taunted my
    people
    and made boasts against their
      territory.

9 Therefore, as I live, says the
    LORD of hosts,
    the God of Israel,

d Heb who thicken   e Cn Compare Gk
Syr: Heb before a decree is born; like
chaff a day has passed away

Mō'ab shall become like Sod'om
and the Am'mon·ites like
Go·mor'rah,
a land possessed by nettles and
salt pits,
and a waste forever.
The remnant of my people shall
plunder them,
and the survivors of my nation
shall possess them.

10 This shall be their lot in return
for their pride,
because they scoffed and
boasted
against the people of the LORD
of hosts.

11 The LORD will be terrible against
them;
he will shrivel all the gods of
the earth,
and to him shall bow down,
each in its place,
all the coasts and islands of
the nations.

12 You also, O Ethiopians,*f*
shall be killed by my sword.

13 And he will stretch out his hand
against the north,
and destroy Assyria;
and he will make Nin'e·veh a
desolation,
a dry waste like the desert.

14 Herds shall lie down in it,
every wild animal;*g*
the desert owl*h* and the screech
owl*h*
shall lodge on its capitals;
the owl*i* shall hoot at the
window,
the raven*j* croak on the
threshold;
for its cedar work will be laid
bare.

15 Is this the exultant city
that lived secure,
that said to itself,
"I am, and there is no one
else"?
What a desolation it has become,
a lair for wild animals!
Everyone who passes by it
hisses and shakes the fist.

The Wickedness of Jerusalem

3 Ah, soiled, defiled,
oppressing city!

2 It has listened to no voice;
it has accepted no correction.
It has not trusted in the LORD;

it has not drawn near to its
God.

3 The officials within it
are roaring lions;
its judges are evening wolves
that leave nothing until the
morning.

4 Its prophets are reckless,
faithless persons;
its priests have profaned what is
sacred,
they have done violence to the
law.

5 The LORD within it is righteous;
he does no wrong.
Every morning he renders his
judgment,
each dawn without fail;
but the unjust knows no
shame.

6 I have cut off nations;
their battlements are in ruins;
I have laid waste their streets
so that no one walks in them;
their cities have been made
desolate,
without people, without
inhabitants.

7 I said, "Surely the city*k* will fear
me,
it will accept correction;
it will not lose sight*l*
of all that I have brought upon
it."
But they were the more eager
to make all their deeds
corrupt.

*Punishment and Conversion
of the Nations*
(Cp Gen 11.1–9; Acts 2.1–11)

8 Therefore wait for me, says the
LORD,
for the day when I arise as a
witness.
For my decision is to gather
nations,
to assemble kingdoms,
to pour out upon them my
indignation,
all the heat of my anger;
for in the fire of my passion

---

f Or *Nubians*; Heb *Cushites*
g Tg Compare Gk: Heb *nation*
h Meaning of Heb uncertain   *i* Cn: Heb
a voice   *j* Gk Vg: Heb *desolation*
k Heb *it*   *l* Gk Syr: Heb *its dwelling will
not be cut off*

all the earth shall be
consumed.

9 At that time I will change the
speech of the peoples
to a pure speech,
that all of them may call on the
name of the LORD
and serve him with one
accord.
10 From beyond the rivers of
Ethiopia*m*
my suppliants, my scattered
ones,
shall bring my offering.

11 On that day you shall not be put
to shame
because of all the deeds by
which you have rebelled
against me;
for then I will remove from your
midst
your proudly exultant ones,
and you shall no longer be
haughty
in my holy mountain.
12 For I will leave in the midst of
you
a people humble and lowly.
They shall seek refuge in the
name of the LORD —
13 the remnant of Israel;
they shall do no wrong
and utter no lies,
nor shall a deceitful tongue
be found in their mouths.
Then they will pasture and lie
down,
and no one shall make them
afraid.

A Song of Joy

14 Sing aloud, O daughter Zion;
shout, O Israel!
Rejoice and exult with all your
heart,
O daughter Jerusalem!

15 The LORD has taken away the
judgments against you,
he has turned away your
enemies.
The king of Israel, the LORD, is
in your midst;
you shall fear disaster no
more.
16 On that day it shall be said to
Jerusalem:
Do not fear, O Zion;
do not let your hands grow
weak.
17 The LORD, your God, is in your
midst,
a warrior who gives victory;
he will rejoice over you with
gladness,
he will renew you*n* in his love;
he will exult over you with loud
singing
18 as on a day of festival.*o*
I will remove disaster from
you,*p*
so that you will not bear
reproach for it.
19 I will deal with all your
oppressors
at that time.
And I will save the lame
and gather the outcast,
and I will change their shame
into praise
and renown in all the earth.
20 At that time I will bring you
home,
at the time when I gather you;
for I will make you renowned
and praised
among all the peoples of the
earth,
when I restore your fortunes
before your eyes, says the
LORD.

*m Or Nubia; Heb Cush   n Gk Syr: Heb
he will be silent   o Gk Syr: Meaning of
Heb uncertain   p Cn: Heb I will remove
from you; they were*

HAGGAI

The Command to Rebuild the Temple
(Ezra 5.1)

1 In the second year of King Da·ri'us, in the sixth month, on the first day of the month, the word of the LORD came by the prophet Hag'gai to Ze·rub'ba·bel son of She·al'ti·el, governor of Judah, and to Joshua son of Je·hoz'a·dak, the high priest: ²Thus says the LORD of hosts: These people say the time has not yet come to rebuild the LORD's house. ³Then the word of the LORD came by the prophet Hag'gai, saying: ⁴Is it a time for you yourselves to live in your paneled houses, while this house lies in ruins? ⁵Now therefore thus says the LORD of hosts: Consider how you have fared. ⁶You have sown much, and harvested little; you eat, but you never have enough; you drink, but you never have your fill; you clothe yourselves, but no one is warm; and you that earn wages earn wages to put them into a bag with holes.

7 Thus says the LORD of hosts: Consider how you have fared. ⁸Go up to the hills and bring wood and build the house, so that I may take pleasure in it and be honored, says the LORD. ⁹You have looked for much, and, lo, it came to little; and when you brought it home, I blew it away. Why? says the LORD of hosts. Because my house lies in ruins, while all of you hurry off to your own houses. ¹⁰Therefore the heavens above you have withheld the dew, and the earth has withheld its produce. ¹¹And I have called for a drought on the land and the hills, on the grain, the new wine, the oil, on what the soil produces, on human beings and animals, and on all their labors.

12 Then Ze·rub'ba·bel son of She·al'ti·el, and Joshua son of Je·hoz'a·dak, the high priest, with all the remnant of the people, obeyed the voice of the LORD their God, and the words of the prophet Hag'gai, as the LORD their God had sent him; and the people feared the LORD. ¹³Then Hag'gai, the messenger of the LORD, spoke to the people with the LORD's message, saying, I am with you, says the LORD. ¹⁴And the LORD stirred up the spirit of Ze·rub'ba·bel son of She·al'ti·el, governor of Judah, and the spirit of Joshua son of Je·hoz'a·dak, the high priest, and the spirit of all the remnant of the people; and they came and worked on the house of the LORD of hosts, their God, ¹⁵on the twenty-fourth day of the month, in the sixth month.

The Future Glory of the Temple

2 In the second year of King Da·ri'us, ¹in the seventh month, on the twenty-first day of the month, the word of the LORD came by the prophet Hag'gai, saying: ²Speak now to Ze·rub'ba·bel son of She·al'ti·el, governor of Judah, and to Joshua son of Je·hoz'a·dak, the high priest, and to the remnant of the people, and say, ³Who is left among you that saw this house in its former glory? How does it look to you now? Is it not in your sight as nothing? ⁴Yet now take courage, O Ze·rub'ba·bel, says the LORD; take courage, O Joshua, son of Je·hoz'-a·dak, the high priest; take courage, all you people of the land, says the LORD; work, for I am with you, says the LORD of hosts, ⁵according to the promise that I made you when you came out of Egypt. My spirit abides among you; do not fear. ⁶For thus says the LORD of hosts: Once again, in a little while, I will shake the heavens and the earth and the sea and the dry land; ⁷and I will shake all the nations, so that the treasure of all nations shall come, and I will fill this house with splendor, says the LORD of hosts. ⁸The silver is mine, and the gold is mine, says the LORD of hosts. ⁹The latter splendor of this house shall be greater than the former, says the LORD of hosts; and in this place I will give prosperity, says the LORD of hosts.

A Rebuke and a Promise

10 On the twenty-fourth day of the ninth month, in the second year of Da·rī′us, the word of the LORD came by the prophet Hag′gaī, saying: 11 Thus says the LORD of hosts: Ask the priests for a ruling: 12 If one carries conse-crated meat in the fold of one's gar-ment, and with the fold touches bread, or stew, or wine, or oil, or any kind of food, does it become holy? The priests answered, "No." 13 Then Hag′gaī said, "If one who is unclean by contact with a dead body touches any of these, does it become unclean?" The priests an-swered, "Yes, it becomes unclean." 14 Hag′gaī then said, So is it with this people, and with this nation before me, says the LORD; and so with every work of their hands; and what they offer there is unclean. 15 But now, consider what will come to pass from this day on. Before a stone was placed upon a stone in the LORD's temple, 16 how did you fare?*a* When one came to a heap of twenty measures, there were but ten; when one came to the winevat to draw fifty measures, there were but twenty. 17 I struck you and all the prod-

ucts of your toil with blight and mil-dew and hail; yet you did not return to me, says the LORD. 18 Consider from this day on, from the twenty-fourth day of the ninth month. Since the day that the foundation of the LORD's tem-ple was laid, consider: 19 Is there any seed left in the barn? Do the vine, the fig tree, the pomegranate, and the ol-ive tree still yield nothing? From this day on I will bless you.

God's Promise to Zerubbabel

20 The word of the LORD came a second time to Hag′gaī on the twenty-fourth day of the month: 21 Speak to Ze·rub′ba·bel, governor of Judah, say-ing, I am about to shake the heavens and the earth, 22 and to overthrow the throne of kingdoms; I am about to de-stroy the strength of the kingdoms of the nations, and overthrow the chari-ots and their riders; and the horses and their riders shall fall, every one by the sword of a comrade. 23 On that day, says the LORD of hosts, I will take you, O Ze·rub′ba·bel my servant, son of She·al′ti·el, says the LORD, and make you like a signet ring; for I have chosen you, says the LORD of hosts.

a Gk: Heb *since they were*

ZECHARIAH

Israel Urged to Repent

1 In the eighth month, in the second year of Da·rī′us, the word of the LORD came to the prophet Zech·a·rī′ah son of Ber·e·chī′ah son of Id′dō, say-ing: 2 The LORD was very angry with your ancestors. 3 Therefore say to them, Thus says the LORD of hosts: Re-turn to me, says the LORD of hosts, and I will return to you, says the LORD of hosts. 4 Do not be like your ancestors, to whom the former prophets pro-claimed, "Thus says the LORD of hosts, Return from your evil ways and from your evil deeds." But they did not hear or heed me, says the LORD. 5 Your an-cestors, where are they? And the

prophets, do they live forever? 6 But my words and my statutes, which I commanded my servants the prophets, did they not overtake your ancestors? So they repented and said, "The LORD of hosts has dealt with us according to our ways and deeds, just as he planned to do."

First Vision: The Horsemen

7 On the twenty-fourth day of the eleventh month, the month of She·bat′, in the second year of Da·rī′us, the word of the LORD came to the prophet Zech·a·rī′ah son of Ber·e·chī′ah son of Id′dō; and Zech·a·rī′ah*a* said, 8 In the

a Heb *and he*

night I saw a man riding on a red horse! He was standing among the myrtle trees in the glen; and behind him were red, sorrel, and white horses. [9] Then I said, "What are these, my lord?" The angel who talked with me said to me, "I will show you what they are." [10] So the man who was standing among the myrtle trees answered, "They are those whom the LORD has sent to patrol the earth." [11] Then they spoke to the angel of the LORD who was standing among the myrtle trees, "We have patrolled the earth, and lo, the whole earth remains at peace." [12] Then the angel of the LORD said, "O LORD of hosts, how long will you withhold mercy from Jerusalem and the cities of Judah, with which you have been angry these seventy years?" [13] Then the LORD replied with gracious and comforting words to the angel who talked with me. [14] So the angel who talked with me said to me, Proclaim this message: Thus says the LORD of hosts; I am very jealous for Jerusalem and for Zion. [15] And I am extremely angry with the nations that are at ease; for while I was only a little angry, they made the disaster worse. [16] Therefore, thus says the LORD, I have returned to Jerusalem with compassion; my house shall be built in it, says the LORD of hosts, and the measuring line shall be stretched out over Jerusalem. [17] Proclaim further: Thus says the LORD of hosts: My cities shall again overflow with prosperity; the LORD will again comfort Zion and again choose Jerusalem.

Second Vision: The Horns and the Smiths

[18b] And I looked up and saw four horns. [19] I asked the angel who talked with me, "What are these?" And he answered me, "These are the horns that have scattered Judah, Israel, and Jerusalem." [20] Then the LORD showed me four blacksmiths. [21] And I asked, "What are they coming to do?" He answered, "These are the horns that scattered Judah, so that no head could be raised; but these have come to terrify them, to strike down the horns of the nations that lifted up their horns against the land of Judah to scatter its people."[c]

Third Vision: The Man with a Measuring Line

2 [d] I looked up and saw a man with a measuring line in his hand. [2] Then I asked, "Where are you going?" He answered me, "To measure Jerusalem, to see what is its width and what is its length." [3] Then the angel who talked with me came forward, and another angel came forward to meet him, [4] and said to him, "Run, say to that young man: Jerusalem shall be inhabited like villages without walls, because of the multitude of people and animals in it. [5] For I will be a wall of fire all around it, says the LORD, and I will be the glory within it."

Interlude: An Appeal to the Exiles

[6] Up, up! Flee from the land of the north, says the LORD; for I have spread you abroad like the four winds of heaven, says the LORD. [7] Up! Escape to Zion, you that live with daughter Babylon. [8] For thus said the LORD of hosts (after his glory[e] sent me) regarding the nations that plundered you: Truly, one who touches you touches the apple of my eye.[f] [9] See now, I am going to raise[g] my hand against them, and they shall become plunder for their own slaves. Then you will know that the LORD of hosts has sent me. [10] Sing and rejoice, O daughter Zion! For lo, I will come and dwell in your midst, says the LORD. [11] Many nations shall join themselves to the LORD on that day, and shall be my people; and I will dwell in your midst. And you shall know that the LORD of hosts has sent me to you. [12] The LORD will inherit Judah as his portion in the holy land, and will again choose Jerusalem.

[13] Be silent, all people, before the LORD; for he has roused himself from his holy dwelling.

Fourth Vision: Joshua and Satan

3 Then he showed me the high priest Joshua standing before the angel of the LORD, and Satan[h] standing at his right hand to accuse him. [2] And the LORD said to Satan,[h] "The LORD rebuke you, O Satan![h] The LORD who has chosen Jerusalem rebuke you! Is not this man a brand plucked from the fire?" [3] Now Joshua

b Ch 2.1 in Heb   c Heb it   d Ch 2.5 in Heb   e Cn: Heb after glory he   f Heb his eye   g Or wave   h Or the Accuser; Heb the Adversary was dressed with filthy clothes as he stood before the angel. 4 The angel said to those who were standing before him, "Take off his filthy clothes." And to him he said, "See, I have taken your guilt away from you, and I will clothe you with festal apparel." 5 And I said, "Let them put a clean turban on his head." So they put a clean turban on his head and clothed him with the apparel; and the angel of the LORD was standing by.

6 Then the angel of the LORD assured Joshua, saying 7 "Thus says the LORD of hosts: If you will walk in my ways and keep my requirements, then you shall rule my house and have charge of my courts, and I will give you the right of access among those who are standing here. 8 Now listen, Joshua, high priest, you and your colleagues who sit before you! For they are an omen of things to come: I am going to bring my servant the Branch. 9 For on the stone that I have set before Joshua, on a single stone with seven facets, I will engrave its inscription, says the LORD of hosts, and I will remove the guilt of this land in a single day. 10 On that day, says the LORD of hosts, you shall invite each other to come under your vine and fig tree."

Fifth Vision: The Lampstand and Olive Trees

4 The angel who talked with me came again, and wakened me, as one is wakened from sleep. 2 He said to me, "What do you see?" And I said, "I see a lampstand all of gold, with a bowl on the top of it; there are seven lamps on it, with seven lips on each of the lamps that are on the top of it. 3 And by it there are two olive trees, one on the right of the bowl and the other on its left." 4 I said to the angel who talked with me, "What are these, my lord?" 5 Then the angel who talked with me answered me, "Do you not know what these are?" I said, "No, my lord." 6 He said to me, "This is the word of the LORD to Ze·rub′ba·bel: Not by might, nor by power, but by my spirit, says the LORD of hosts. 7 What are you, O great mountain? Before Ze·rub′ba·bel you shall become a plain; and he shall bring out the top stone amid shouts of 'Grace, grace to it!' "

8 Moreover the word of the LORD came to me, saying, 9 "The hands of Ze·rub′ba·bel have laid the foundation of this house; his hands shall also com-

plete it. Then you will know that the LORD of hosts has sent me to you. 10 For whoever has despised the day of small things shall rejoice, and shall see the plummet in the hand of Ze·rub′ba·bel.

"These seven are the eyes of the LORD, which range through the whole earth." 11 Then I said to him, "What are these two olive trees on the right and the left of the lampstand?" 12 And a second time I said to him, "What are these two branches of the olive trees, which pour out the oil[i] through the two golden pipes?" 13 He said to me, "Do you not know what these are?" I said, "No, my lord." 14 Then he said, "These are the two anointed ones who stand by the Lord of the whole earth."

Sixth Vision: The Flying Scroll

5 Again I looked up and saw a flying scroll. 2 And he said to me, "What do you see?" I answered, "I see a flying scroll; its length is twenty cubits, and its width ten cubits." 3 Then he said to me, "This is the curse that goes out over the face of the whole land; for everyone who steals shall be cut off according to the writing on one side, and everyone who swears falsely[j] shall be cut off according to the writing on the other side. 4 I have sent it out, says the LORD of hosts, and it shall enter the house of the thief, and the house of anyone who swears falsely by my name; and it shall abide in that house and consume it, both timber and stones."

Seventh Vision: The Woman in a Basket

5 Then the angel who talked with me came forward and said to me, "Look up and see what this is that is coming out." 6 I said, "What is it?" He said, "This is a basket[k] coming out." And he said, "This is their iniquity[l] in all the land." 7 Then a leaden cover was lifted, and there was a woman sitting in the basket![k] 8 And he said, "This is Wickedness." So he thrust her back into the basket,[k] and pressed the leaden weight down on its mouth. 9 Then I looked up and saw two women coming forward. The wind was in their wings; they had wings like the wings of a stork, and they lifted up the

<hr>

i Cn: Heb gold   j The word falsely added from verse 4   k Heb ephah
l Gk Compare Syr: Heb their eye

basket[m] between earth and sky. [10]Then I said to the angel who talked with me, "Where are they taking the basket?"[m] [11]He said to me, "To the land of Shī'nar, to build a house for it; and when this is prepared, they will set the basket[m] down there on its base."

Eighth Vision: Four Chariots

6 And again I looked up and saw four chariots coming out from between two mountains—mountains of bronze. [2]The first chariot had red horses, the second chariot black horses, [3]the third chariot white horses, and the fourth chariot dappled gray[n] horses. [4]Then I said to the angel who talked with me, "What are these, my lord?" [5]The angel answered me, "These are the four winds[o] of heaven going out, after presenting themselves before the LORD of all the earth. [6]The chariot with the black horses goes toward the north country, the white ones go toward the west country,[p] and the dappled ones go toward the south country." [7]When the steeds came out, they were impatient to get off and patrol the earth. And he said, "Go, patrol the earth." So they patrolled the earth. [8]Then he cried out to me, "Lo, those who go toward the north country have set my spirit at rest in the north country."

The Coronation of the Branch

[9] The word of the LORD came to me: [10]Collect silver and gold[q] from the exiles—from Hel'daī, Tō-bī'jah, and Je·daī'ah—who have arrived from Babylon; and go the same day to the house of Jō·sī'ah son of Zeph·a·nī'ah. [11]Take the silver and gold and make a crown,[r] and set it on the head of the high priest Joshua son of Je·hoz'-a·dak; [12]say to him: Thus says the LORD of hosts: Here is a man whose name is Branch: for he shall branch out in his place, and he shall build the temple of the LORD. [13]It is he that shall build the temple of the LORD; he shall bear royal honor, and shall sit and rule on his throne. There shall be a priest by his throne, with peaceful understanding between the two of them. [14]And the crown[s] shall be in the care of Hel'daī,[t] Tō-bī'jah, Je·daī'ah, and Jō·sī'ah[u] son of Zeph·a·nī'ah, as a memorial in the temple of the LORD. [15] Those who are far off shall come and help to build the temple of the LORD; and you shall know that the

LORD of hosts has sent me to you. This will happen if you diligently obey the voice of the LORD your God.

Hypocritical Fasting Condemned

7 In the fourth year of King Da·rī'us, the word of the LORD came to Zech·a·rī'ah on the fourth day of the ninth month, which is Chis'lev. [2]Now the people of Beth'el had sent Sha·rē'-zer and Reg'em-mel'ech and their men, to entreat the favor of the LORD, [3]and to ask the priests of the house of the LORD of hosts and the prophets, "Should I mourn and practice abstinence in the fifth month, as I have done for so many years?" [4]Then the word of the LORD of hosts came to me: [5]Say to all the people of the land and the priests: When you fasted and lamented in the fifth month and in the seventh, for these seventy years, was it for me that you fasted? [6]And when you eat and when you drink, do you not eat and drink only for yourselves? [7]Were not these the words that the LORD proclaimed by the former prophets, when Jerusalem was inhabited and in prosperity, along with the towns around it, and when the Neg'eb and the She·phē'lah were inhabited?

Punishment for Rejecting God's Demands

[8] The word of the LORD came to Zech·a·rī'ah, saying: [9]Thus says the LORD of hosts: Render true judgments, show kindness and mercy to one another; [10]do not oppress the widow, the orphan, the alien, or the poor; and do not devise evil in your hearts against one another. [11]But they refused to listen, and turned a stubborn shoulder, and stopped their ears in order not to hear. [12]They made their hearts adamant in order not to hear the law and the words that the LORD of hosts had sent by his spirit through the former prophets. Therefore great wrath came from the LORD of hosts. [13]Just as, when I[v] called, they would not hear, so, when they called, I would not hear, says the LORD of hosts, [14]and I scat-

[m]Heb *ephah*   [n]Compare Gk: Meaning of Heb uncertain   [o]Or *spirits* [p]Cn: Heb *go after them*   [q]Cn Compare verse 11: Heb lacks *silver and gold* [r]Gk Mss Syr Tg: Heb *crowns*   [s]Gk Syr: Heb *crowns*   [t]Syr Compare verse 10: Heb *Helem*   [u]Syr Compare verse 10: Heb *Hen*   [v]Heb *he*

tered them with a whirlwind among all the nations that they had not known. Thus the land they left was desolate, so that no one went to and fro, and a pleasant land was made desolate.

God's Promises to Zion

8 The word of the LORD of hosts came to me, saying: ²Thus says the LORD of hosts: I am jealous for Zion with great jealousy, and I am jealous for her with great wrath. ³Thus says the LORD: I will return to Zion, and will dwell in the midst of Jerusalem; Jerusalem shall be called the faithful city, and the mountain of the LORD of hosts shall be called the holy mountain. ⁴Thus says the LORD of hosts: Old men and old women shall again sit in the streets of Jerusalem, each with staff in hand because of their great age. ⁵And the streets of the city shall be full of boys and girls playing in its streets. ⁶Thus says the LORD of hosts: Even though it seems impossible to the remnant of this people in these days, should it also seem impossible to me, says the LORD of hosts? ⁷Thus says the LORD of hosts: I will save my people from the east country and from the west country; ⁸and I will bring them to live in Jerusalem. They shall be my people and I will be their God, in faithfulness and in righteousness.

9 Thus says the LORD of hosts: Let your hands be strong—you that have recently been hearing these words from the mouths of the prophets who were present when the foundation was laid for the rebuilding of the temple, the house of the LORD of hosts. ¹⁰For before those days there were no wages for people or for animals, nor was there any safety from the foe for those who went out or came in, and I set them all against one other. ¹¹But now I will not deal with the remnant of this people as in the former days, says the LORD of hosts. ¹²For there shall be a sowing of peace; the vine shall yield its fruit, the ground shall give its produce, and the skies shall give their dew; and I will cause the remnant of this people to possess all these things. ¹³Just as you have been a cursing among the nations, O house of Judah and house of Israel, so I will save you and you shall be a blessing. Do not be afraid, but let your hands be strong.

14 For thus says the LORD of hosts: Just as I purposed to bring disaster upon you, when your ancestors provoked me to wrath, and I did not relent, says the LORD of hosts, ¹⁵so again I have purposed in these days to do good to Jerusalem and to the house of Judah; do not be afraid. ¹⁶These are the things that you shall do: Speak the truth to one another, render in your gates judgments that are true and make for peace, ¹⁷do not devise evil in your hearts against one another, and love no false oath; for all these are things that I hate, says the LORD.

Joyful Fasting

18 The word of the LORD of hosts came to me, saying: ¹⁹Thus says the LORD of hosts: The fast of the fourth month, and the fast of the fifth, and the fast of the seventh, and the fast of the tenth, shall be seasons of joy and gladness, and cheerful festivals for the house of Judah: therefore love truth and peace.

Many Peoples Drawn to Jerusalem

20 Thus says the LORD of hosts: Peoples shall yet come, the inhabitants of many cities; ²¹the inhabitants of one city shall go to another, saying, "Come, let us go to entreat the favor of the LORD, and to seek the LORD of hosts; I myself am going." ²²Many peoples and strong nations shall come to seek the LORD of hosts in Jerusalem, and to entreat the favor of the LORD. ²³Thus says the LORD of hosts: In those days ten men from nations of every language shall take hold of a Jew, grasping his garment and saying, "Let us go with you, for we have heard that God is with you."

Judgment on Israel's Enemies

9 An Oracle.

The word of the LORD is against
    the land of Had′rach
and will rest upon Damascus.
For to the LORD belongs the
    capitalʷ of Ar′am,ˣ
    as do all the tribes of Israel;
² Hā′math also, which borders on
    it,
    Tyre and Si′don, though they
    are very wise.
³ Tyre has built itself a rampart,
    and heaped up silver like dust,

ʷHeb *eye* ˣCn: Heb *of Adam* (or *of humankind*)

and gold like the dirt of the
streets.
4 But now, the Lord will strip it of
its possessions
and hurl its wealth into the
sea,
and it shall be devoured by
fire.

5 Ash′ke·lon shall see it and be
afraid;
Gä′za too, and shall writhe in
anguish;
Ek′ron also, because its hopes
are withered.
The king shall perish from
Gä′za;
Ash′ke·lon shall be
uninhabited;
6 a mongrel people shall settle in
Ash′dod,
and I will make an end of the
pride of Phi·lis′ti·a.
7 I will take away its blood from
its mouth,
and its abominations from
between its teeth;
it too shall be a remnant for our
God;
it shall be like a clan in Judah,
and Ek′ron shall be like the
Jeb′u·sites.
8 Then I will encamp at my house
as a guard,
so that no one shall march to
and fro;
no oppressor shall again overrun
them,
for now I have seen with my
own eyes.

The Coming Ruler of God's People
(Mt 21.5; Jn 12.14–15)

9 Rejoice greatly, O daughter
Zion!
Shout aloud, O daughter
Jerusalem!
Lo, your king comes to you;
triumphant and victorious is
he,
humble and riding on a donkey,
on a colt, the foal of a donkey.
10 He^y will cut off the chariot from
E′phra·im
and the war horse from
Jerusalem;
and the battle bow shall be cut
off,
and he shall command peace
to the nations;

his dominion shall be from sea
to sea,
and from the River to the ends
of the earth.

11 As for you also, because of the
blood of my covenant with
you,
I will set your prisoners free
from the waterless pit.
12 Return to your stronghold,
O prisoners of hope;
today I declare that I will
restore to you double.
13 For I have bent Judah as my
bow;
I have made E′phra·im its
arrow.
I will arouse your sons, O Zion,
against your sons, O Greece,
and wield you like a warrior's
sword.

14 Then the LORD will appear over
them,
and his arrow go forth like
lightning;
the Lord GOD will sound the
trumpet
and march forth in the
whirlwinds of the south.
15 The LORD of hosts will protect
them,
and they shall devour and
tread down the slingers;^z
they shall drink their blood^a
like wine,
and be full like a bowl,
drenched like the corners of
the altar.
16 On that day the LORD their God
will save them
for they are the flock of his
people;
for like the jewels of a crown
they shall shine on his land.
17 For what goodness and beauty
are his!
Grain shall make the young
men flourish,
and new wine the young
women.

Restoration of Judah and Israel

10 Ask rain from the LORD
in the season of the spring
rain,

y Gk: Heb I　　z Cn: Heb *the slingstones*
a Gk: Heb *shall drink*

from the LORD who makes the
storm clouds,
who gives showers of rain to
you,*b*
the vegetation in the field to
everyone.

2 For the teraphim*c* utter
nonsense,
and the diviners see lies;
the dreamers tell false dreams,
and give empty consolation.
Therefore the people wander like
sheep;
they suffer for lack of a
shepherd.

3 My anger is hot against the
shepherds,
and I will punish the leaders;*d*
for the LORD of hosts cares for
his flock, the house of
Judah,
and will make them like his
proud war horse.

4 Out of them shall come the
cornerstone,
out of them the tent peg,
out of them the battle bow,
out of them every commander.

5 Together they shall be like
warriors in battle,
trampling the foe in the mud
of the streets;
they shall fight, for the LORD is
with them,
and they shall put to shame
the riders on horses.

6 I will strengthen the house of
Judah,
and I will save the house of
Joseph.
I will bring them back because I
have compassion on them,
and they shall be as though I
had not rejected them;
for I am the LORD their God
and I will answer them.

7 Then the people of Ē′phra·im
shall become like warriors,
and their hearts shall be glad
as with wine.
Their children shall see it and
rejoice,
their hearts shall exult in the
LORD.

8 I will signal for them and gather
them in,
for I have redeemed them,
and they shall be as numerous
as they were before.

9 Though I scattered them among
the nations,
yet in far countries they shall
remember me,
and they shall rear their
children and return.

10 I will bring them home from the
land of Egypt,
and gather them from Assyria;
I will bring them to the land of
Gil′e·ad and to Lebanon,
until there is no room for
them.

11 They*e* shall pass through the
sea of distress,
and the waves of the sea shall
be struck down,
and all the depths of the Nile
dried up.
The pride of Assyria shall be
laid low,
and the scepter of Egypt shall
depart.

12 I will make them strong in the
LORD,
and they shall walk in his
name,
says the LORD.

11 Open your doors, O Lebanon,
so that fire may devour your
cedars!

2 Wail, O cypress, for the cedar
has fallen,
for the glorious trees are
ruined!
Wail, oaks of Bā′shan,
for the thick forest has been
felled!

3 Listen, the wail of the shepherds,
for their glory is despoiled!
Listen, the roar of the lions,
for the thickets of the Jordan
are destroyed!

Two Kinds of Shepherds

4 Thus said the LORD my God: Be a
shepherd of the flock doomed to
slaughter. 5 Those who buy them kill
them and go unpunished; and those
who sell them say, "Blessed be the
LORD, for I have become rich"; and
their own shepherds have no pity on
them. 6 For I will no longer have pity on
the inhabitants of the earth, says the
LORD. I will cause them, every one, to
fall each into the hand of a neighbor,
and each into the hand of the king; and

b Heb *them*   *c* Or *household gods*
d Or *male goats*   *e* Gk: Heb *He*

they shall devastate the earth, and I will deliver no one from their hand.

7 So, on behalf of the sheep merchants, I became the shepherd of the flock doomed to slaughter. I took two staffs; one I named Favor, the other I named Unity, and I tended the sheep. 8 In one month I disposed of the three shepherds, for I had become impatient with them, and they also detested me. 9 So I said, "I will not be your shepherd. What is to die, let it die; what is to be destroyed, let it be destroyed; and let those that are left devour the flesh of one another!" 10 I took my staff Favor and broke it, annulling the covenant that I had made with all the peoples. 11 So it was annulled on that day, and the sheep merchants, who were watching me, knew that it was the word of the LORD. 12 I then said to them, "If it seems right to you, give me my wages; but if not, keep them." So they weighed out as my wages thirty shekels of silver. 13 Then the LORD said to me, "Throw it into the treasury" *f* —this lordly price at which I was valued by them. So I took the thirty shekels of silver and threw them into the treasury *f* in the house of the LORD. 14 Then I broke my second staff Unity, annulling the family ties between Judah and Israel.

15 Then the LORD said to me: Take once more the implements of a worthless shepherd. 16 For I am now raising up in the land a shepherd who does not care for the perishing, or seek the wandering,*g* or heal the maimed, or nourish the healthy,*h* but devours the flesh of the fat ones, tearing off even their hoofs.

17 Oh, my worthless shepherd,
 who deserts the flock!
May the sword strike his arm
 and his right eye!
Let his arm be completely
 withered,
 his right eye utterly blinded!

Jerusalem's Victory

12

An Oracle.

The word of the LORD concerning Israel: Thus says the LORD, who stretched out the heavens and founded the earth and formed the human spirit within: 2 See, I am about to make Jerusalem a cup of reeling for all the surrounding peoples; it will be against Judah also in the siege against Jerusalem. 3 On that day I will make Jerusalem a heavy stone for all the peoples; all who lift it shall grievously hurt themselves. And all the nations of the earth shall come together against it. 4 On that day, says the LORD, I will strike every horse with panic, and its rider with madness. But on the house of Judah I will keep a watchful eye, when I strike every horse of the peoples with blindness. 5 Then the clans of Judah shall say to themselves, "The inhabitants of Jerusalem have strength through the LORD of hosts, their God."

6 On that day I will make the clans of Judah like a blazing pot on a pile of wood, like a flaming torch among sheaves; and they shall devour to the right and to the left all the surrounding peoples, while Jerusalem shall again be inhabited in its place, in Jerusalem.

7 And the LORD will give victory to the tents of Judah first, that the glory of the house of David and the glory of the inhabitants of Jerusalem may not be exalted over that of Judah. 8 On that day the LORD will shield the inhabitants of Jerusalem so that the feeblest among them on that day shall be like David, and the house of David shall be like God, like the angel of the LORD, at their head. 9 And on that day I will seek to destroy all the nations that come against Jerusalem.

Mourning for the Pierced One

10 And I will pour out a spirit of compassion and supplication on the house of David and the inhabitants of Jerusalem, so that, when they look on the one*i* whom they have pierced, they shall mourn for him, as one mourns for an only child, and weep bitterly over him, as one weeps over a firstborn. 11 On that day the mourning in Jerusalem will be as great as the mourning for Hā′dad-rim′mon in the plain of Me·gid′dō. 12 The land shall mourn, each family by itself; the family of the house of David by itself, and their wives by themselves; the family of the house of Nathan by itself, and their wives by themselves; 13 the family of the house of Levi by itself, and their wives by themselves; the family of the Shim′e-ītes by itself, and their

f Syr: Heb *it to the potter* *g* Syr Compare Gk Vg: Heb *the youth* *h* Meaning of Heb uncertain *i* Heb *on me* wives by themselves; [14] and all the families that are left, each by itself, and their wives by themselves.

13 On that day a fountain shall be opened for the house of David and the inhabitants of Jerusalem, to cleanse them from sin and impurity.

Idolatry Cut Off

2 On that day, says the LORD of hosts, I will cut off the names of the idols from the land, so that they shall be remembered no more; and also I will remove from the land the prophets and the unclean spirit. [3] And if any prophets appear again, their fathers and mothers who bore them will say to them, "You shall not live, for you speak lies in the name of the LORD"; and their fathers and their mothers who bore them shall pierce them through when they prophesy. [4] On that day the prophets will be ashamed, every one, of their visions when they prophesy; they will not put on a hairy mantle in order to deceive, [5] but each of them will say, "I am no prophet, I am a tiller of the soil; for the land has been my possession[j] since my youth." [6] And if anyone asks them, "What are these wounds on your chest?"[k] the answer will be "The wounds I received in the house of my friends."

The Shepherd Struck,
the Flock Scattered

7 "Awake, O sword, against my shepherd,
   against the man who is my associate,"
       says the LORD of hosts.
Strike the shepherd, that the sheep may be scattered;
   I will turn my hand against the little ones.
8 In the whole land, says the LORD,
   two-thirds shall be cut off and perish,
   and one-third shall be left alive.
9 And I will put this third into the fire,
   refine them as one refines silver,
   and test them as gold is tested.
They will call on my name,
   and I will answer them.
I will say, "They are my people";
   and they will say, "The LORD is our God."

Future Warfare and Final Victory
(Cp Ezek 38 – 39; Mk 13; Rev 20 – 22)

14 See, a day is coming for the LORD, when the plunder taken from you will be divided in your midst. [2] For I will gather all the nations against Jerusalem to battle, and the city shall be taken and the houses looted and the women raped; half the city shall go into exile, but the rest of the people shall not be cut off from the city. [3] Then the LORD will go forth and fight against those nations as when he fights on a day of battle. [4] On that day his feet shall stand on the Mount of Olives, which lies before Jerusalem on the east; and the Mount of Olives shall be split in two from east to west by a very wide valley; so that one half of the Mount shall withdraw northward, and the other half southward. [5] And you shall flee by the valley of the LORD's mountain,[l] for the valley between the mountains shall reach to Ā'zal;[m] and you shall flee as you fled from the earthquake in the days of King Uz·zī'ah of Judah. Then the LORD my God will come, and all the holy ones with him.

6 On that day there shall not be[n] either cold or frost.[o] [7] And there shall be continuous day (it is known to the LORD), not day and not night, for at evening time there shall be light.

8 On that day living waters shall flow out from Jerusalem, half of them to the eastern sea and half of them to the western sea; it shall continue in summer as in winter.

9 And the LORD will become king over all the earth; on that day the LORD will be one and his name one.

10 The whole land shall be turned into a plain from Gē'ba to Rim'mon south of Jerusalem. But Jerusalem shall remain aloft on its site from the Gate of Benjamin to the place of the former gate, to the Corner Gate, and from the Tower of Ha·nan'el to the king's wine presses. [11] And it shall be inhabited, for never again shall it be doomed to destruction; Jerusalem shall abide in security.

12 This shall be the plague with which the LORD will strike all the

[j] Cn: Heb *for humankind has caused me to possess*   [k] Heb *wounds between your hands*   [l] Heb *my mountains*   [m] Meaning of Heb uncertain   [n] Cn: Heb *there shall not be light*   [o] Compare Gk Syr Vg Tg: Meaning of Heb uncertain

peoples that wage war against Jerusalem: their flesh shall rot while they are still on their feet; their eyes shall rot in their sockets, and their tongues shall rot in their mouths. [13] On that day a great panic from the LORD shall fall on them, so that each will seize the hand of a neighbor, and the hand of the one will be raised against the hand of the other; [14] even Judah will fight at Jerusalem. And the wealth of all the surrounding nations shall be collected — gold, silver, and garments in great abundance. [15] And a plague like this plague shall fall on the horses, the mules, the camels, the donkeys, and whatever animals may be in those camps.

16 Then all who survive of the nations that have come against Jerusalem shall go up year after year to worship the King, the LORD of hosts, and to keep the festival of booths.[p] [17] If any of the families of the earth do not go up to Jerusalem to worship the King, the LORD of hosts, there will be no rain upon them. [18] And if the family of Egypt do not go up and present themselves, then on them shall[q] come the plague that the LORD inflicts on the nations that do not go up to keep the festival of booths.[p] [19] Such shall be the punishment of Egypt and the punishment of all the nations that do not go up to keep the festival of booths.[p]

20 On that day there shall be inscribed on the bells of the horses, "Holy to the LORD." And the cooking pots in the house of the LORD shall be as holy as[r] the bowls in front of the altar; [21] and every cooking pot in Jerusalem and Judah shall be sacred to the LORD of hosts, so that all who sacrifice may come and use them to boil the flesh of the sacrifice. And there shall no longer be traders[s] in the house of the LORD of hosts on that day.

[p] Or *tabernacles*; Heb *succoth*
[q] Gk Syr: Heb *shall not*   [r] Heb *shall be like*   [s] Or *Canaanites*

MALACHI

M A L A C H I

1 An oracle. The word of the LORD to Israel by Mal'a·chī.[a]

Israel Preferred to Edom

2 I have loved you, says the LORD. But you say, "How have you loved us?" Is not Esau Jacob's brother? says the LORD. Yet I have loved Jacob [3] but I have hated Esau; I have made his hill country a desolation and his heritage a desert for jackals. [4] If Ē'dom says, "We are shattered but we will rebuild the ruins," the LORD of hosts says: They may build, but I will tear down, until they are called the wicked country, the people with whom the LORD is angry forever. [5] Your own eyes shall see this, and you shall say, "Great is the LORD beyond the borders of Israel!"

Corruption of the Priesthood

6 A son honors his father, and servants their master. If then I am a father, where is the honor due me? And if I am a master, where is the respect due me? says the LORD of hosts to you, O priests, who despise my name. You say, "How have we despised your name?" [7] By offering polluted food on my altar. And you say, "How have we polluted it?"[b] By thinking that the LORD's table may be despised. [8] When you offer blind animals in sacrifice, is that not wrong? And when you offer those that are lame or sick, is that not wrong? Try presenting that to your governor; will he be pleased with you or show you favor? says the LORD of hosts. [9] And now implore the favor of God, that he may be gracious to us. The fault is yours. Will he show favor

[a] Or *by my messenger*   [b] Gk: Heb *you*

to any of you? says the LORD of hosts. [10] Oh, that someone among you would shut the temple[c] doors, so that you would not kindle fire on my altar in vain! I have no pleasure in you, says the LORD of hosts, and I will not accept an offering from your hands. [11] For from the rising of the sun to its setting my name is great among the nations, and in every place incense is offered to my name, and a pure offering; for my name is great among the nations, says the LORD of hosts. [12] But you profane it when you say that the Lord's table is polluted, and the food for it[d] may be despised. [13] "What a weariness this is," you say, and you sniff at me,[e] says the LORD of hosts. You bring what has been taken by violence or is lame or sick, and this you bring as your offering! Shall I accept that from your hand? says the LORD. [14] Cursed be the cheat who has a male in the flock and vows to give it, and yet sacrifices to the Lord what is blemished; for I am a great King, says the LORD of hosts, and my name is reverenced among the nations.

2 And now, O priests, this command is for you. [2] If you will not listen, if you will not lay it to heart to give glory to my name, says the LORD of hosts, then I will send the curse on you and I will curse your blessings; indeed I have already cursed them,[f] because you do not lay it to heart. [3] I will rebuke your offspring, and spread dung on your faces, the dung of your offerings, and I will put you out of my presence.[g]

[4] Know, then, that I have sent this command to you, that my covenant with Levi may hold, says the LORD of hosts. [5] My covenant with him was a covenant of life and well-being, which I gave him; this called for reverence, and he revered me and stood in awe of my name. [6] True instruction was in his mouth, and no wrong was found on his lips. He walked with me in integrity and uprightness, and he turned many from iniquity. [7] For the lips of a priest should guard knowledge, and people should seek instruction from his mouth, for he is the messenger of the LORD of hosts. [8] But you have turned aside from the way; you have caused many to stumble by your instruction; you have corrupted the covenant of Levi, says the LORD of hosts, [9] and so I make you despised and abased before all the people, inasmuch as you have

not kept my ways but have shown partiality in your instruction.

The Covenant Profaned by Judah

10 Have we not all one father? Has not one God created us? Why then are we faithless to one another, profaning the covenant of our ancestors? [11] Judah has been faithless, and abomination has been committed in Israel and in Jerusalem; for Judah has profaned the sanctuary of the LORD, which he loves, and has married the daughter of a foreign god. [12] May the LORD cut off from the tents of Jacob anyone who does this—any to witness[h] or answer, or to bring an offering to the LORD of hosts.

13 And this you do as well: You cover the LORD's altar with tears, with weeping and groaning because he no longer regards the offering or accepts it with favor at your hand. [14] You ask, "Why does he not?" Because the LORD was a witness between you and the wife of your youth, to whom you have been faithless, though she is your companion and your wife by covenant. [15] Did not one God make her?[i] Both flesh and spirit are his.[j] And what does the one God[k] desire? Godly offspring. So look to yourselves, and do not let anyone be faithless to the wife of his youth. [16] For I hate[l] divorce, says the LORD, the God of Israel, and covering one's garment with violence, says the LORD of hosts. So take heed to yourselves and do not be faithless.

17 You have wearied the LORD with your words. Yet you say, "How have we wearied him?" By saying, "All who do evil are good in the sight of the LORD, and he delights in them." Or by asking, "Where is the God of justice?"

The Coming Messenger

3 See, I am sending my messenger to prepare the way before me, and the Lord whom you seek will suddenly come to his temple. The messenger of the covenant in whom you delight—indeed, he is coming, says the LORD of hosts. [2] But who can endure the day of

[c] Heb lacks *temple* [d] Compare Syr Tg: Heb *its fruit, its food* [e] Another reading is *at it* [f] Heb *it* [g] Cn Compare Gk Syr: Heb *and he shall bear you to it* [h] Cn Compare Gk: Heb *arouse* [i] Or *Has he not made one?* [j] Cn: Heb *and a remnant of spirit was his* [k] Heb *he* [l] Cn: Heb *he hates*

his coming, and who can stand when he appears? For he is like a refiner's fire and like fullers' soap; [3] he will sit as a refiner and purifier of silver, and he will purify the descendants of Levi and refine them like gold and silver, until they present offerings to the LORD in righteousness.[m] [4] Then the offering of Judah and Jerusalem will be pleasing to the LORD as in the days of old and as in former years.

5 Then I will draw near to you for judgment; I will be swift to bear witness against the sorcerers, against the adulterers, against those who swear falsely, against those who oppress the hired workers in their wages, the widow and the orphan, against those who thrust aside the alien, and do not fear me, says the LORD of hosts.

6 For I the LORD do not change; therefore you, O children of Jacob, have not perished. [7] Ever since the days of your ancestors you have turned aside from my statutes and have not kept them. Return to me, and I will return to you, says the LORD of hosts. But you say, "How shall we return?"

Do Not Rob God

8 Will anyone rob God? Yet you are robbing me! But you say, "How are we robbing you?" In your tithes and offerings! [9] You are cursed with a curse, for you are robbing me—the whole nation of you! [10] Bring the full tithe into the storehouse, so that there may be food in my house, and thus put me to the test, says the LORD of hosts; see if I will not open the windows of heaven for you and pour down for you an overflowing blessing. [11] I will rebuke the locust[n] for you, so that it will not destroy the produce of your soil; and your vine in the field shall not be barren, says the LORD of hosts. [12] Then all nations will count you happy, for you will be a land of delight, says the LORD of hosts.

13 You have spoken harsh words against me, says the LORD. Yet you say, "How have we spoken against you?" [14] You have said, "It is vain to serve God. What do we profit by keeping his command or by going about as mourners before the LORD of hosts? [15] Now we count the arrogant happy; evildoers not only prosper, but when they put God to the test they escape."

The Reward of the Faithful

16 Then those who revered the LORD spoke with one another. The LORD took note and listened, and a book of remembrance was written before him of those who revered the LORD and thought on his name. [17] They shall be mine, says the LORD of hosts, my special possession on the day when I act, and I will spare them as parents spare their children who serve them. [18] Then once more you shall see the difference between the righteous and the wicked, between one who serves God and one who does not serve him.

The Great Day of the LORD

4[o] See, the day is coming, burning like an oven, when all the arrogant and all evildoers will be stubble; the day that comes shall burn them up, says the LORD of hosts, so that it will leave them neither root nor branch. [2] But for you who revere my name the sun of righteousness shall rise, with healing in its wings. You shall go out leaping like calves from the stall. [3] And you shall tread down the wicked, for they will be ashes under the soles of your feet, on the day when I act, says the LORD of hosts.

4 Remember the teaching of my servant Moses, the statutes and ordinances that I commanded him at Hō'reb for all Israel.

5 Lo, I will send you the prophet E·lī'jah before the great and terrible day of the LORD comes. [6] He will turn the hearts of parents to their children and the hearts of children to their parents, so that I will not come and strike the land with a curse.[p]

M
A
L
A
C
H
I

[m] Or *right offerings to the* LORD
[n] Heb *devourer* [o] Ch 4.1-6 are Ch 3.19-24 in Heb [p] Or *a ban of utter destruction*

THE NEW COVENANT
commonly called

THE NEW TESTAMENT

of
OUR LORD AND SAVIOR
JESUS CHRIST

New Revised Standard Version

Gospels

The word Gospel is from the Anglo-Saxon "godspell", meaning good news. Ultimately the word comes from the Greek **euangelion**, also meaning good news. Gospel can mean the good news preached by Jesus, or the good news preached about Jesus. These two meanings are the ones found in the Bible. Gospel can also mean the books that contain the memories of Jesus, the gospels we find in our New Testaments.

Gospels are not biographies. They are accounts of the life and teaching of Jesus, but they are also reflections on who Jesus is and what he means for the world. Each of the gospel writers wanted to say something specific about the meaning of Jesus and carefully selected materials and arranged them to carry his own particular emphasis. The gospels contain a great deal of historical information, but that information is always interpreted by the writers to show Jesus as Son of God and Savior of the world.

There are four gospels. Matthew, Mark, and Luke are called **Synoptic** gospels, because they follow a common synopsis, or outline. These three gospels can be studied in parallel because they follow the same basic outline, use many of the same words and the same order. Much of modern biblical study is based on the assumption that Matthew and Luke used Mark as a basic source and outline. The Gospel of John is entirely different from the other three. It does not follow the same outline, has a three-year ministry for Jesus instead of one year, and contains long reflections about the meaning of Jesus instead of short sayings and parables.

Mark is probably the oldest of the gospels. Tradition says it was written in Rome by John Mark and contains the memories of Peter. The crucifixion and resurrection are the key to understanding who Jesus is — nearly one-half of the gospel deals with these events. Mark does not have any birth narratives, but begins with the preaching of John the Baptist.

Matthew begins by placing Jesus within the whole story of salvation. Jesus is son of Abraham and son of David, the fulfillment of all the promises to God's people. The teaching material in Matthew is organized into five great sections, the best-known of which is the Sermon on the Mount. Many have said Matthew saw Jesus as a second Moses, giving a new Torah to God's people.

Luke's special interest is in the oppressed and outcasts of society, especially women and the poor. His gospel begins with the births of John the Baptist and of Jesus. It has the only story of Jesus between his birth and ministry, the episode in the temple at the age of twelve. Some of the best-loved parables — the good Samaritan, the prodigal son, the rich man and Lazarus — are found only in Luke's gospel.

John has less narrative and no parables, but a series of long reflections on Jesus as divine Son of God. The gospel begins with a great hymn on the "Word" who was always God and became flesh for the salvation of the world. That word is Jesus. John also contains a series of miracles as signs pointing to Jesus, and the "I AM" sayings, which express what Jesus means in a series of striking metaphors.

PALESTINE IN THE TIME OF JESUS

The Gospel According to
MATTHEW

The Genealogy of Jesus the Messiah
(Ruth 4.18–22; 1 Chr 2.1–15; Lk 3.23–38)

1 An account of the genealogy*a* of Jesus the Messiah,*b* the son of David, the son of Abraham.

2 Abraham was the father of Isaac, and Isaac the father of Jacob, and Jacob the father of Judah and his brothers, 3 and Judah the father of Per′ez and Ze′rah by Ta′mar, and Per′ez the father of Hez′ron, and Hez′ron the father of Ar′am, 4 and Ar′am the father of A·min′a·dab, and A·min′a·dab the father of Nah′shon, and Nah′shon the father of Sal′mon, 5 and Sal′mon the father of Bo′az by Ra′hab, and Bo′az the father of O′bed by Ruth, and O′bed the father of Jesse, 6 and Jesse the father of King David.

And David was the father of Solomon by the wife of U·ri′ah, 7 and Solomon the father of Re·ho·bo′am, and Re·ho·bo′am the father of A·bi′jah, and A·bi′jah the father of A′saph,*c* 8 and A′saph*c* the father of Je·hosh′a·phat, and Je·hosh′a·phat the father of Jo′ram, and Jo′ram the father of Uz·zi′ah, 9 and Uz·zi′ah the father of Jo′tham, and Jo′tham the father of A′haz, and A′haz the father of Hez·e·ki′ah, 10 and Hez·e·ki′ah the father of Ma·nas′seh, and Ma·nas′seh the father of A′mos,*d* and A′mos*d* the father of Jo·si′ah, 11 and Jo·si′ah the father of Jech·o·ni′ah and his brothers, at the time of the deportation to Babylon.

12 And after the deportation to Babylon: Jech·o·ni′ah was the father of Sa·la′thi·el, and Sa·la′thi·el the father of Ze·rub′ba·bel, 13 and Ze·rub′ba·bel the father of A·bi′ud, and A·bi′ud the father of E·li′a·kim, and E·li′a·kim the father of A′zor, 14 and A′zor the father of Za′dok, and Za′dok the father of A′chim, and A′chim the father of E·li′ud, 15 and E·li′ud the father of El·e·a′zar, and El·e·a′zar the father of Mat′than, and Mat′than the father of Jacob, 16 and Jacob the father of Joseph the husband of Mary, of whom Jesus was born, who is called the Messiah.*e*

17 So all the generations from Abraham to David are fourteen generations; and from David to the deportation to Babylon, fourteen generations; and from the deportation to Babylon to the Messiah,*e* fourteen generations.

The Birth of Jesus the Messiah
(Lk 2.1–7)

18 Now the birth of Jesus the Messiah*b* took place in this way. When his mother Mary had been engaged to Joseph, but before they lived together, she was found to be with child from the Holy Spirit. 19 Her husband Joseph, being a righteous man and unwilling to expose her to public disgrace, planned to dismiss her quietly. 20 But just when he had resolved to do this, an angel of the Lord appeared to him in a dream and said, "Joseph, son of David, do not be afraid to take Mary as your wife, for the child conceived in her is from the Holy Spirit. 21 She will bear a son, and you are to name him Jesus, for he will save his people from their sins." 22 All this took place to fulfill what had been spoken by the Lord through the prophet:

23 "Look, the virgin shall conceive
   and bear a son,
 and they shall name him
     Em·man′u·el,"

which means, "God is with us." 24 When Joseph awoke from sleep, he did as the angel of the Lord commanded him; he took her as his wife, 25 but had no marital relations with her until she had borne a son;*f* and he named him Jesus.

---

a Or *birth*   *b* Or *Jesus Christ*   *c* Other ancient authorities read *Asa*   *d* Other ancient authorities read *Amon*   *e* Or *the Christ*   *f* Other ancient authorities read *her firstborn son*

MATTHEW

The Visit of the Wise Men

2 In the time of King Her′od, after Jesus was born in Bethlehem of Judea, wise men[g] from the East came to Jerusalem, [2]asking, "Where is the child who has been born king of the Jews? For we observed his star at its rising,[h] and have come to pay him homage." [3]When King Her′od heard this, he was frightened, and all Jerusalem with him; [4]and calling together all the chief priests and scribes of the people, he inquired of them where the Messiah[i] was to be born. [5]They told him, "In Bethlehem of Judea; for so it has been written by the prophet:
[6] 'And you, Bethlehem, in the land
     of Judah,
   are by no means least among
     the rulers of Judah;
   for from you shall come a ruler
     who is to shepherd[j] my
      people Israel.' "
[7] Then Her′od secretly called for the wise men[g] and learned from them the exact time when the star had appeared. [8]Then he sent them to Bethlehem, saying, "Go and search diligently for the child; and when you have found him, bring me word so that I may also go and pay him homage." [9]When they had heard the king, they set out; and there, ahead of them, went the star that they had seen at its rising,[h] until it stopped over the place where the child was. [10]When they saw that the star had stopped,[k] they were overwhelmed with joy. [11]On entering the house, they saw the child with Mary his mother; and they knelt down and paid him homage. Then, opening their treasure chests, they offered him gifts of gold, frankincense, and myrrh. [12]And having been warned in a dream not to return to Her′od, they left for their own country by another road.

The Escape to Egypt

[13] Now after they had left, an angel of the Lord appeared to Joseph in a dream and said, "Get up, take the child and his mother, and flee to Egypt, and remain there until I tell you; for Her′od is about to search for the child, to destroy him." [14]Then Joseph[l] got up, took the child and his mother by night, and went to Egypt, [15]and remained there until the death of Her′od. This was to fulfill what had been spoken by the Lord through the prophet, "Out of Egypt I have called my son."

The Massacre of the Infants

[16] When Her′od saw that he had been tricked by the wise men,[g] he was infuriated, and he sent and killed all the children in and around Bethlehem who were two years old or under, according to the time that he had learned from the wise men.[g] [17]Then was fulfilled what had been spoken through the prophet Jer·e·mi′ah:
[18] "A voice was heard in Ra′mah,
   wailing and loud lamentation,
   Rachel weeping for her children;
   she refused to be consoled,
     because they are no more."

The Return from Egypt
(Lk 2.39)

[19] When Her′od died, an angel of the Lord suddenly appeared in a dream to Joseph in Egypt and said, [20]"Get up, take the child and his mother, and go to the land of Israel, for those who were seeking the child's life are dead." [21]Then Joseph[l] got up, took the child and his mother, and went to the land of Israel. [22]But when he heard that Ar·che·la′us was ruling over Judea in place of his father Her′od, he was afraid to go there. And after being warned in a dream, he went away to the district of Galilee. [23]There he made his home in a town called Nazareth, so that what had been spoken through the prophets might be fulfilled, "He will be called a Naz·o·re′an."

The Proclamation of John the Baptist
(Mk 1.2–8; Lk 3.1–20)

3 In those days John the Baptist appeared in the wilderness of Judea, proclaiming, [2]"Repent, for the kingdom of heaven has come near."[m] [3]This is the one of whom the prophet I·sai′ah spoke when he said,
   "The voice of one crying out in
     the wilderness:
   'Prepare the way of the Lord,
     make his paths straight.' "
[4]Now John wore clothing of camel's hair with a leather belt around his waist, and his food was locusts and wild honey. [5]Then the people of Jerusalem and all Judea were going out to him, and all the region along the Jor-

[g]Or astrologers; Gk magi   [h]Or in the East   [i]Or the Christ   [j]Or rule   [k]Gk saw the star   [l]Gk he   [m]Or is at hand

dan, [6] and they were baptized by him in the river Jordan, confessing their sins.

7 But when he saw many Phar'i·sees and Sad'du·cees coming for baptism, he said to them, "You brood of vipers! Who warned you to flee from the wrath to come? [8] Bear fruit worthy of repentance. [9] Do not presume to say to yourselves, 'We have Abraham as our ancestor'; for I tell you, God is able from these stones to raise up children to Abraham. [10] Even now the ax is lying at the root of the trees; every tree therefore that does not bear good fruit is cut down and thrown into the fire.

11 "I baptize you with[n] water for repentance, but one who is more powerful than I is coming after me; I am not worthy to carry his sandals. He will baptize you with[n] the Holy Spirit and fire. [12] His winnowing fork is in his hand, and he will clear his threshing floor and will gather his wheat into the granary; but the chaff he will burn with unquenchable fire."

The Baptism of Jesus
(Mk 1.9–11; Lk 3.21–22; Jn 1.29–34)

13 Then Jesus came from Galilee to John at the Jordan, to be baptized by him. [14] John would have prevented him, saying, "I need to be baptized by you, and do you come to me?" [15] But Jesus answered him, "Let it be so now; for it is proper for us in this way to fulfill all righteousness." Then he consented. [16] And when Jesus had been baptized, just as he came up from the water, suddenly the heavens were opened to him and he saw the Spirit of God descending like a dove and alighting on him. [17] And a voice from heaven said, "This is my Son, the Beloved,[o] with whom I am well pleased."

The Temptation of Jesus
(Mk 1.12–13; Lk 4.1–13)

4 Then Jesus was led up by the Spirit into the wilderness to be tempted by the devil. [2] He fasted forty days and forty nights, and afterwards he was famished. [3] The tempter came and said to him, "If you are the Son of God, command these stones to become loaves of bread." [4] But he answered, "It is written,

'One does not live by bread alone,
    but by every word that comes from the mouth of God.' "

5 Then the devil took him to the holy city and placed him on the pinnacle of the temple, [6] saying to him, "If you are the Son of God, throw yourself down; for it is written,

'He will command his angels concerning you,'
and 'On their hands they will bear you up,
so that you will not dash your foot against a stone.' "

7 Jesus said to him, "Again it is written, 'Do not put the Lord your God to the test.' "

8 Again, the devil took him to a very high mountain and showed him all the kingdoms of the world and their splendor; [9] and he said to him, "All these I will give you, if you will fall down and worship me." [10] Jesus said to him, "Away with you, Satan! for it is written,

'Worship the Lord your God, and serve only him.' "

11 Then the devil left him, and suddenly angels came and waited on him.

Jesus Begins His Ministry in Galilee
(Mk 1.14–15; Lk 4.14–15)

12 Now when Jesus[p] heard that John had been arrested, he withdrew to Galilee. [13] He left Nazareth and made his home in Ca·per'na·um by the sea, in the territory of Zeb'u·lun and Naph'ta·li, [14] so that what had been spoken through the prophet I·sai'ah might be fulfilled:
15 "Land of Zeb'u·lun, land of Naph'ta·li,
    on the road by the sea, across the Jordan, Galilee of the Gentiles—
16 the people who sat in darkness have seen a great light,
    and for those who sat in the region and shadow of death
light has dawned."
17 From that time Jesus began to proclaim, "Repent, for the kingdom of heaven has come near."[q]

Jesus Calls the First Disciples
(Mk 1.16–20; Lk 5.1–11)

18 As he walked by the Sea of Galilee, he saw two brothers, Simon, who is called Peter, and Andrew his brother, casting a net into the sea—for they were fishermen. [19] And he said to

---

[n] Or *in*   [o] Or *my beloved Son*   [p] Gk *he*
[q] Or *is at hand*

them, "Follow me, and I will make you fish for people." [20]Immediately they left their nets and followed him. [21]As he went from there, he saw two other brothers, James son of Zeb'e·dee and his brother John, in the boat with their father Zeb'e·dee, mending their nets, and he called them. [22]Immediately they left the boat and their father, and followed him.

Jesus Ministers to Crowds of People
(Mk 1.35–39; Lk 4.44; 6.17–19)

23 Jesus[r] went throughout Galilee, teaching in their synagogues and proclaiming the good news[s] of the kingdom and curing every disease and every sickness among the people. [24]So his fame spread throughout all Syria, and they brought to him all the sick, those who were afflicted with various diseases and pains, demoniacs, epileptics, and paralytics, and he cured them. [25]And great crowds followed him from Galilee, the De·cap'o·lis, Jerusalem, Judea, and from beyond the Jordan.

The Beatitudes
(Lk 6.20–26)

5 When Jesus[t] saw the crowds, he went up the mountain; and after he sat down, his disciples came to him. [2]Then he began to speak, and taught them, saying:

3 "Blessed are the poor in spirit, for theirs is the kingdom of heaven.

4 "Blessed are those who mourn, for they will be comforted.

5 "Blessed are the meek, for they will inherit the earth.

6 "Blessed are those who hunger and thirst for righteousness, for they will be filled.

7 "Blessed are the merciful, for they will receive mercy.

8 "Blessed are the pure in heart, for they will see God.

9 "Blessed are the peacemakers, for they will be called children of God.

10 "Blessed are those who are persecuted for righteousness' sake, for theirs is the kingdom of heaven.

11 "Blessed are you when people revile you and persecute you and utter all kinds of evil against you falsely[u] on my account. [12]Rejoice and be glad, for your reward is great in heaven, for in the same way they persecuted the prophets who were before you.

Salt and Light
(Mk 9.50; Lk 14.34–35)

13 "You are the salt of the earth; but if salt has lost its taste, how can its saltiness be restored? It is no longer good for anything, but is thrown out and trampled under foot.

14 "You are the light of the world. A city built on a hill cannot be hid. [15]No one after lighting a lamp puts it under the bushel basket, but on the lampstand, and it gives light to all in the house. [16]In the same way, let your light shine before others, so that they may see your good works and give glory to your Father in heaven.

The Law and the Prophets

17 "Do not think that I have come to abolish the law or the prophets; I have come not to abolish but to fulfill. [18]For truly I tell you, until heaven and earth pass away, not one letter,[v] not one stroke of a letter, will pass from the law until all is accomplished. [19]Therefore, whoever breaks[w] one of the least of these commandments, and teaches others to do the same, will be called least in the kingdom of heaven; but whoever does them and teaches them will be called great in the kingdom of heaven. [20]For I tell you, unless your righteousness exceeds that of the scribes and Phar'i·sees, you will never enter the kingdom of heaven.

Concerning Anger
(Lk 12.57–59)

21 "You have heard that it was said to those of ancient times, 'You shall not murder'; and 'whoever murders shall be liable to judgment.' [22]But I say to you that if you are angry with a brother or sister,[x] you will be liable to judgment; and if you insult[y] a brother or sister,[z] you will be liable to the council; and if you say, 'You fool,' you will be liable to the hell[a] of fire. [23]So when you are offering your gift at the altar, if you remember that your brother or sister[b] has something against you, [24]leave your gift there before the altar and go; first be reconciled to your brother or sister,[b] and

[r]Gk He　　[s]Gk gospel　　[t]Gk he
[u]Other ancient authorities lack *falsely*
[v]Gk *one iota*　　[w]Or *annuls*　　[x]Gk *a brother*; other ancient authorities add *without cause*　　[y]Gk *say Raca to* (an obscure term of abuse)　　[z]Gk *a brother*
[a]Gk *Gehenna*　　[b]Gk *your brother*

then come and offer your gift. 25 Come to terms quickly with your accuser while you are on the way to court[c] with him, or your accuser may hand you over to the judge, and the judge to the guard, and you will be thrown into prison. 26 Truly I tell you, you will never get out until you have paid the last penny.

Concerning Adultery

27 "You have heard that it was said, 'You shall not commit adultery.' 28 But I say to you that everyone who looks at a woman with lust has already committed adultery with her in his heart. 29 If your right eye causes you to sin, tear it out and throw it away; it is better for you to lose one of your members than for your whole body to be thrown into hell.[d] 30 And if your right hand causes you to sin, cut it off and throw it away; it is better for you to lose one of your members than for your whole body to go into hell.[d]

Concerning Divorce
(Mt 19.9; Mk 10.11–12; Lk 16.18)

31 "It was also said, 'Whoever divorces his wife, let him give her a certificate of divorce.' 32 But I say to you that anyone who divorces his wife, except on the ground of unchastity, causes her to commit adultery; and whoever marries a divorced woman commits adultery.

Concerning Oaths

33 "Again, you have heard that it was said to those of ancient times, 'You shall not swear falsely, but carry out the vows you have made to the Lord.' 34 But I say to you, Do not swear at all, either by heaven, for it is the throne of God, 35 or by the earth, for it is his footstool, or by Jerusalem, for it is the city of the great King. 36 And do not swear by your head, for you cannot make one hair white or black. 37 Let your word be 'Yes, Yes' or 'No, No'; anything more than this comes from the evil one.[e]

Concerning Retaliation
(Lk 6.29–31)

38 "You have heard that it was said, 'An eye for an eye and a tooth for a tooth.' 39 But I say to you, Do not resist an evildoer. But if anyone strikes you on the right cheek, turn the other also; 40 and if anyone wants to sue you and take your coat, give your cloak as well;

41 and if anyone forces you to go one mile, go also the second mile. 42 Give to everyone who begs from you, and do not refuse anyone who wants to borrow from you.

Love for Enemies
(Lk 6.27–28, 32–36)

43 "You have heard that it was said, 'You shall love your neighbor and hate your enemy.' 44 But I say to you, Love your enemies and pray for those who persecute you, 45 so that you may be children of your Father in heaven; for he makes his sun rise on the evil and on the good, and sends rain on the righteous and on the unrighteous. 46 For if you love those who love you, what reward do you have? Do not even the tax collectors do the same? 47 And if you greet only your brothers and sisters,[f] what more are you doing than others? Do not even the Gentiles do the same? 48 Be perfect, therefore, as your heavenly Father is perfect.

Concerning Almsgiving

6 "Beware of practicing your piety before others in order to be seen by them; for then you have no reward from your Father in heaven.

2 "So whenever you give alms, do not sound a trumpet before you, as the hypocrites do in the synagogues and in the streets, so that they may be praised by others. Truly I tell you, they have received their reward. 3 But when you give alms, do not let your left hand know what your right hand is doing, 4 so that your alms may be done in secret; and your Father who sees in secret will reward you.[g]

Concerning Prayer
(Lk 11.2–4)

5 "And whenever you pray, do not be like the hypocrites; for they love to stand and pray in the synagogues and at the street corners, so that they may be seen by others. Truly I tell you, they have received their reward. 6 But whenever you pray, go into your room and shut the door and pray to your Father who is in secret; and your Father who sees in secret will reward you.[g]

7 "When you are praying, do not heap up empty phrases as the Gentiles

---

[c] Gk lacks *to court*   [d] Gk *Gehenna*
[e] Or *evil*   [f] Gk *your brothers*   [g] Other ancient authorities add *openly*

do; for they think that they will be heard because of their many words. [8]Do not be like them, for your Father knows what you need before you ask him.

9 "Pray then in this way:

Our Father in heaven,
   hallowed be your name.
10   Your kingdom come.
   Your will be done,
     on earth as it is in heaven.
11   Give us this day our daily
     bread.[h]
12   And forgive us our debts,
     as we also have forgiven our
     debtors.
13   And do not bring us to the
     time of trial,[i]
     but rescue us from the evil
     one.[j]

[14]For if you forgive others their trespasses, your heavenly Father will also forgive you; [15]but if you do not forgive others, neither will your Father forgive your trespasses.

Concerning Fasting

16 "And whenever you fast, do not look dismal, like the hypocrites, for they disfigure their faces so as to show others that they are fasting. Truly I tell you, they have received their reward. [17]But when you fast, put oil on your head and wash your face, [18]so that your fasting may be seen not by others but by your Father who is in secret; and your Father who sees in secret will reward you.[k]

Concerning Treasures
(Lk 12.33–34)

19 "Do not store up for yourselves treasures on earth, where moth and rust[l] consume and where thieves break in and steal; [20]but store up for yourselves treasures in heaven, where neither moth nor rust[l] consumes and where thieves do not break in and steal. [21]For where your treasure is, there your heart will be also.

The Sound Eye
(Lk 11.34–36)

22 "The eye is the lamp of the body. So, if your eye is healthy, your whole body will be full of light; [23]but if your eye is unhealthy, your whole body will be full of darkness. If then the light in you is darkness, how great is the darkness!

Serving Two Masters

24 "No one can serve two masters; for a slave will either hate the one and love the other, or be devoted to the one and despise the other. You cannot serve God and wealth.[m]

Do Not Worry
(Lk 12.22–31)

25 "Therefore I tell you, do not worry about your life, what you will eat or what you will drink,[n] or about your body, what you will wear. Is not life more than food, and the body more than clothing? [26]Look at the birds of the air; they neither sow nor reap nor gather into barns, and yet your heavenly Father feeds them. Are you not of more value than they? [27]And can any of you by worrying add a single hour to your span of life?[o] [28]And why do you worry about clothing? Consider the lilies of the field, how they grow; they neither toil nor spin, [29]yet I tell you, even Solomon in all his glory was not clothed like one of these. [30]But if God so clothes the grass of the field, which is alive today and tomorrow is thrown into the oven, will he not much more clothe you—you of little faith? [31]Therefore do not worry, saying, 'What will we eat?' or 'What will we drink?' or 'What will we wear?' [32]For it is the Gentiles who strive for all these things; and indeed your heavenly Father knows that you need all these things. [33]But strive first for the kingdom of God[p] and his[q] righteousness, and all these things will be given to you as well.

34 "So do not worry about tomorrow, for tomorrow will bring worries of its own. Today's trouble is enough for today.

Judging Others
(Lk 6.37–42)

7 "Do not judge, so that you may not be judged. [2]For with the judgment you make you will be judged, and the

[h]Or *our bread for tomorrow*   [i]Or *us into temptation*   [j]Or *from evil.* Other ancient authorities add, in some form, *For the kingdom and the power and the glory are yours forever. Amen.*   [k]Other ancient authorities add *openly*   [l]Gk *eating*   [m]Gk *mammon*   [n]Other ancient authorities lack *or what you will drink*   [o]Or *add one cubit to your height*   [p]Other ancient authorities lack *of God*   [q]Or *its*

measure you give will be the measure you get. ³Why do you see the speck in your neighbor's^r eye, but do not notice the log in your own eye? ⁴Or how can you say to your neighbor,^s 'Let me take the speck out of your eye,' while the log is in your own eye? ⁵You hypocrite, first take the log out of your own eye, and then you will see clearly to take the speck out of your neighbor's^r eye.

Profaning the Holy

6 "Do not give what is holy to dogs; and do not throw your pearls before swine, or they will trample them under foot and turn and maul you.

Ask, Search, Knock
(Lk 11.9–13)

7 "Ask, and it will be given you; search, and you will find; knock, and the door will be opened for you. ⁸For everyone who asks receives, and everyone who searches finds, and for everyone who knocks, the door will be opened. ⁹Is there anyone among you who, if your child asks for bread, will give a stone? ¹⁰Or if the child asks for a fish, will give a snake? ¹¹If you then, who are evil, know how to give good gifts to your children, how much more will your Father in heaven give good things to those who ask him!

The Golden Rule
(Lk 6.31)

12 "In everything do to others as you would have them do to you; for this is the law and the prophets.

The Narrow Gate
(Lk 13.24)

13 "Enter through the narrow gate; for the gate is wide and the road is easy^t that leads to destruction, and there are many who take it. ¹⁴For the gate is narrow and the road is hard that leads to life, and there are few who find it.

A Tree and Its Fruit
(Mt 12.33; Lk 6.43–45)

15 "Beware of false prophets, who come to you in sheep's clothing but inwardly are ravenous wolves. ¹⁶You will know them by their fruits. Are grapes gathered from thorns, or figs from thistles? ¹⁷In the same way, every good tree bears good fruit, but the bad tree bears bad fruit. ¹⁸A good tree cannot bear bad fruit, nor can a bad tree

bear good fruit. ¹⁹Every tree that does not bear good fruit is cut down and thrown into the fire. ²⁰Thus you will know them by their fruits.

Concerning Self-Deception
(Lk 6.46; 13.26–27)

21 "Not everyone who says to me, 'Lord, Lord,' will enter the kingdom of heaven, but only the one who does the will of my Father in heaven. ²²On that day many will say to me, 'Lord, Lord, did we not prophesy in your name, and cast out demons in your name, and do many deeds of power in your name?' ²³Then I will declare to them, 'I never knew you; go away from me, you evildoers.'

Hearers and Doers
(Lk 6.47–49)

24 "Everyone then who hears these words of mine and acts on them will be like a wise man who built his house on rock. ²⁵The rain fell, the floods came, and the winds blew and beat on that house, but it did not fall, because it had been founded on rock. ²⁶And everyone who hears these words of mine and does not act on them will be like a foolish man who built his house on sand. ²⁷The rain fell, and the floods came, and the winds blew and beat against that house, and it fell—and great was its fall!"

28 Now when Jesus had finished saying these things, the crowds were astounded at his teaching, ²⁹for he taught them as one having authority, and not as their scribes.

Jesus Cleanses a Leper
(Mk 1.40–45; Lk 5.12–16)

8 When Jesus^u had come down from the mountain, great crowds followed him; ²and there was a leper^v who came to him and knelt before him, saying, "Lord, if you choose, you can make me clean." ³He stretched out his hand and touched him, saying, "I do choose. Be made clean!" Immediately his leprosy^v was cleansed. ⁴Then Jesus said to him, "See that you say nothing to anyone; but go, show yourself to the priest, and offer the gift that

^rGk brother's   ^sGk brother   ^tOther ancient authorities read *for the road is wide and easy*   ^uGk he   ^vThe terms *leper* and *leprosy* can refer to several diseases

Moses commanded, as a testimony to them."

Jesus Heals a Centurion's Servant
(Lk 7.1–10)

5 When he entered Ca·per'na·um, a centurion came to him, appealing to him 6 and saying, "Lord, my servant is lying at home paralyzed, in terrible distress." 7 And he said to him, "I will come and cure him." 8 The centurion answered, "Lord, I am not worthy to have you come under my roof; but only speak the word, and my servant will be healed. 9 For I also am a man under authority, with soldiers under me; and I say to one, 'Go,' and he goes, and to another, 'Come,' and he comes, and to my slave, 'Do this,' and the slave does it." 10 When Jesus heard him, he was amazed and said to those who followed him, "Truly I tell you, in no one w in Israel have I found such faith. 11 I tell you, many will come from east and west and will eat with Abraham and Isaac and Jacob in the kingdom of heaven, 12 while the heirs of the kingdom will be thrown into the outer darkness, where there will be weeping and gnashing of teeth." 13 And to the centurion Jesus said, "Go; let it be done for you according to your faith." And the servant was healed in that hour.

Jesus Heals Many at Peter's House
(Mk 1.29–34; Lk 4.38–41)

14 When Jesus entered Peter's house, he saw his mother-in-law lying in bed with a fever; 15 he touched her hand, and the fever left her, and she got up and began to serve him. 16 That evening they brought to him many who were possessed with demons; and he cast out the spirits with a word, and cured all who were sick. 17 This was to fulfill what had been spoken through the prophet I·sai'ah, "He took our infirmities and bore our diseases."

Would-Be Followers of Jesus
(Lk 9.57–62)

18 Now when Jesus saw great crowds around him, he gave orders to go over to the other side. 19 A scribe then approached and said, "Teacher, I will follow you wherever you go." 20 And Jesus said to him, "Foxes have holes, and birds of the air have nests; but the Son of Man has nowhere to lay his head." 21 Another of his disciples said to him, "Lord, first let me go and bury my father." 22 But Jesus said to him, "Follow me, and let the dead bury their own dead."

Jesus Stills the Storm
(Mk 4.35–41; Lk 8.22–25)

23 And when he got into the boat, his disciples followed him. 24 A windstorm arose on the sea, so great that the boat was being swamped by the waves; but he was asleep. 25 And they went and woke him up, saying, "Lord, save us! We are perishing!" 26 And he said to them, "Why are you afraid, you of little faith?" Then he got up and rebuked the winds and the sea; and there was a dead calm. 27 They were amazed, saying, "What sort of man is this, that even the winds and the sea obey him?"

Jesus Heals the Gadarene Demoniacs
(Mk 5.1–20; Lk 8.26–39)

28 When he came to the other side, to the country of the Gad'a·renes, x two demoniacs coming out of the tombs met him. They were so fierce that no one could pass that way. 29 Suddenly they shouted, "What have you to do with us, Son of God? Have you come here to torment us before the time?" 30 Now a large herd of swine was feeding at some distance from them. 31 The demons begged him, "If you cast us out, send us into the herd of swine." 32 And he said to them, "Go!" So they came out and entered the swine; and suddenly, the whole herd rushed down the steep bank into the sea and perished in the water. 33 The swineherds ran off, and on going into the town, they told the whole story about what had happened to the demoniacs. 34 Then the whole town came out to meet Jesus; and when they saw him, they begged him to leave their neighborhood. 1 And after getting into a boat he crossed the sea and came to his own town.

Jesus Heals a Paralytic
(Mk 2.1–12; Lk 5.17–26)

2 And just then some people were carrying a paralyzed man lying on a bed. When Jesus saw their faith, he said to the paralytic, "Take heart, son; your sins are forgiven." 3 Then some of the scribes said to themselves, "This

w Other ancient authorities read *Truly I tell you, not even* x Other ancient authorities read *Gergesenes*; others, *Gerasenes* man is blaspheming." [4]But Jesus, perceiving their thoughts, said, "Why do you think evil in your hearts? [5]For which is easier, to say, 'Your sins are forgiven,' or to say, 'Stand up and walk'? [6]But so that you may know that the Son of Man has authority on earth to forgive sins"—he then said to the paralytic—"Stand up, take your bed and go to your home." [7]And he stood up and went to his home. [8]When the crowds saw it, they were filled with awe, and they glorified God, who had given such authority to human beings.

The Call of Matthew
(Mk 2.13–17; Lk 5.27–32)

9 As Jesus was walking along, he saw a man called Matthew sitting at the tax booth; and he said to him, "Follow me." And he got up and followed him.

10 And as he sat at dinner[y] in the house, many tax collectors and sinners came and were sitting[z] with him and his disciples. [11]When the Phar′i·sees saw this, they said to his disciples, "Why does your teacher eat with tax collectors and sinners?" [12]But when he heard this, he said, "Those who are well have no need of a physician, but those who are sick. [13]Go and learn what this means, 'I desire mercy, not sacrifice.' For I have come to call not the righteous but sinners."

The Question about Fasting
(Mk 2.18–22; Lk 5.33–39)

14 Then the disciples of John came to him, saying, "Why do we and the Phar′i·sees fast often,[a] but your disciples do not fast?" [15]And Jesus said to them, "The wedding guests cannot mourn as long as the bridegroom is with them, can they? The days will come when the bridegroom is taken away from them, and then they will fast. [16]No one sews a piece of unshrunk cloth on an old cloak, for the patch pulls away from the cloak, and a worse tear is made. [17]Neither is new wine put into old wineskins; otherwise, the skins burst, and the wine is spilled, and the skins are destroyed; but new wine is put into fresh wineskins, and so both are preserved."

A Girl Restored to Life and a Woman Healed
(Mk 5.21–43; Lk 8.40–56)

18 While he was saying these things to them, suddenly a leader of the synagogue[b] came in and knelt before him, saying, "My daughter has just died; but come and lay your hand on her, and she will live." [19]And Jesus got up and followed him, with his disciples. [20]Then suddenly a woman who had been suffering from hemorrhages for twelve years came up behind him and touched the fringe of his cloak, [21]for she said to herself, "If I only touch his cloak, I will be made well." [22]Jesus turned, and seeing her he said, "Take heart, daughter; your faith has made you well." And instantly the woman was made well. [23]When Jesus came to the leader's house and saw the flute players and the crowd making a commotion, [24]he said, "Go away; for the girl is not dead but sleeping." And they laughed at him. [25]But when the crowd had been put outside, he went in and took her by the hand, and the girl got up. [26]And the report of this spread throughout that district.

Jesus Heals Two Blind Men

27 As Jesus went on from there, two blind men followed him, crying loudly, "Have mercy on us, Son of David!" [28]When he entered the house, the blind men came to him; and Jesus said to them, "Do you believe that I am able to do this?" They said to him, "Yes, Lord." [29]Then he touched their eyes and said, "According to your faith let it be done to you." [30]And their eyes were opened. Then Jesus sternly ordered them, "See that no one knows of this." [31]But they went away and spread the news about him throughout that district.

Jesus Heals One Who Was Mute

32 After they had gone away, a demoniac who was mute was brought to him. [33]And when the demon had been cast out, the one who had been mute spoke; and the crowds were amazed and said, "Never has anything like this been seen in Israel." [34]But the Phar′i·sees said, "By the ruler of the demons he casts out the demons."[c]

The Harvest Is Great, the Laborers Few
(Lk 10.2–3)

35 Then Jesus went about all the cit-

---

[y]Gk *reclined*   [z]Gk *were reclining*
[a]Other ancient authorities lack *often*
[b]Gk lacks *of the synagogue*   [c]Other ancient authorities lack this verse

MATTHEW

ies and villages, teaching in their synagogues, and proclaiming the good news of the kingdom, and curing every disease and every sickness. 36When he saw the crowds, he had compassion for them, because they were harassed and helpless, like sheep without a shepherd. 37Then he said to his disciples, "The harvest is plentiful, but the laborers are few; 38therefore ask the Lord of the harvest to send out laborers into his harvest."

The Twelve Apostles
(Mk 3.13–19a; Lk 6.12–16)

10 Then Jesus[d] summoned his twelve disciples and gave them authority over unclean spirits, to cast them out, and to cure every disease and every sickness. 2These are the names of the twelve apostles: first, Simon, also known as Peter, and his brother Andrew; James son of Zeb'-e·dee, and his brother John; 3Philip and Bartholomew; Thomas and Matthew the tax collector; James son of Al·phae'us, and Thad·dae'us;[e] 4Simon the Ca·na·nae'an, and Judas Is·car'i·ot, the one who betrayed him.

The Mission of the Twelve
(Mk 6.6b–13; Lk 9.1–6)

5 These twelve Jesus sent out with the following instructions: "Go nowhere among the Gentiles, and enter no town of the Sa·mar'i·tans, 6but go rather to the lost sheep of the house of Israel. 7As you go, proclaim the good news, 'The kingdom of heaven has come near.'[f] 8Cure the sick, raise the dead, cleanse the lepers,[g] cast out demons. You received without payment; give without payment. 9Take no gold, or silver, or copper in your belts, 10no bag for your journey, or two tunics, or sandals, or a staff; for laborers deserve their food. 11Whatever town or village you enter, find out who in it is worthy, and stay there until you leave. 12As you enter the house, greet it. 13If the house is worthy, let your peace come upon it; but if it is not worthy, let your peace return to you. 14If anyone will not welcome you or listen to your words, shake off the dust from your feet as you leave that house or town. 15Truly I tell you, it will be more tolerable for the land of Sod'om and Go·mor'rah on the day of judgment than for that town.

Coming Persecutions
(Mk 13.9–13; Lk 21.12–17)

16 "See, I am sending you out like sheep into the midst of wolves; so be wise as serpents and innocent as doves. 17Beware of them, for they will hand you over to councils and flog you in their synagogues; 18and you will be dragged before governors and kings because of me, as a testimony to them and the Gentiles. 19When they hand you over, do not worry about how you are to speak or what you are to say; for what you are to say will be given to you at that time; 20for it is not you who speak, but the Spirit of your Father speaking through you. 21Brother will betray brother to death, and a father his child, and children will rise against parents and have them put to death; 22and you will be hated by all because of my name. But the one who endures to the end will be saved. 23When they persecute you in one town, flee to the next; for truly I tell you, you will not have gone through all the towns of Israel before the Son of Man comes.

24 "A disciple is not above the teacher, nor a slave above the master; 25it is enough for the disciple to be like the teacher, and the slave like the master. If they have called the master of the house Be·el'ze·bul, how much more will they malign those of his household!

Whom to Fear
(Lk 12.2–7)

26 "So have no fear of them; for nothing is covered up that will not be uncovered, and nothing secret that will not become known. 27What I say to you in the dark, tell in the light; and what you hear whispered, proclaim from the housetops. 28Do not fear those who kill the body but cannot kill the soul; rather fear him who can destroy both soul and body in hell.[h] 29Are not two sparrows sold for a penny? Yet not one of them will fall to the ground apart from your Father. 30And even the hairs of your head are all counted. 31So do not be afraid; you are of more value than many sparrows.

32 "Everyone therefore who ac-

---

[d] Gk he   [e] Other ancient authorities read Lebbaeus, or Lebbaeus called Thaddaeus   [f] Or is at hand   [g] The terms leper and leprosy can refer to several diseases   [h] Gk Gehenna

**M
A
T
T
H
E
W**

knowledges me before others, I also will acknowledge before my Father in heaven; 33 but whoever denies me before others, I also will deny before my Father in heaven.

Not Peace, but a Sword
(Lk 12.51–53; 14.26–27)

34 "Do not think that I have come to bring peace to the earth; I have not come to bring peace, but a sword. 35 For I have come to set a man
against his father,
and a daughter against her
mother,
and a daughter-in-law against
her mother-in-law;
36 and one's foes will be members
of one's own household.
37 Whoever loves father or mother more than me is not worthy of me; and whoever loves son or daughter more than me is not worthy of me; 38 and whoever does not take up the cross and follow me is not worthy of me. 39 Those who find their life will lose it, and those who lose their life for my sake will find it.

Rewards
(Mk 9.41)

40 "Whoever welcomes you welcomes me, and whoever welcomes me welcomes the one who sent me. 41 Whoever welcomes a prophet in the name of a prophet will receive a prophet's reward; and whoever welcomes a righteous person in the name of a righteous person will receive the reward of the righteous; 42 and whoever gives even a cup of cold water to one of these little ones in the name of a disciple—truly I tell you, none of these will lose their reward."

11 Now when Jesus had finished instructing his twelve disciples, he went on from there to teach and proclaim his message in their cities.

Messengers from John the Baptist
(Lk 7.18–23)

2 When John heard in prison what the Messiah[i] was doing, he sent word by his[j] disciples 3 and said to him, "Are you the one who is to come, or are we to wait for another?" 4 Jesus answered them, "Go and tell John what you hear and see: 5 the blind receive their sight, the lame walk, the lepers[k] are cleansed, the deaf hear, the dead are raised, and the poor have good

news brought to them. 6 And blessed is anyone who takes no offense at me."

Jesus Praises John the Baptist
(Lk 7.24–35)

7 As they went away, Jesus began to speak to the crowds about John: "What did you go out into the wilderness to look at? A reed shaken by the wind? 8 What then did you go out to see? Someone[l] dressed in soft robes? Look, those who wear soft robes are in royal palaces. 9 What then did you go out to see? A prophet?[m] Yes, I tell you, and more than a prophet. 10 This is the one about whom it is written,
'See, I am sending my
messenger ahead of you,
who will prepare your way
before you.'
11 Truly I tell you, among those born of women no one has arisen greater than John the Baptist; yet the least in the kingdom of heaven is greater than he. 12 From the days of John the Baptist until now the kingdom of heaven has suffered violence,[n] and the violent take it by force. 13 For all the prophets and the law prophesied until John came; 14 and if you are willing to accept it, he is E·li'jah who is to come. 15 Let anyone with ears[o] listen!

16 "But to what will I compare this generation? It is like children sitting in the marketplaces and calling to one another,
17 'We played the flute for you, and
you did not dance;
we wailed, and you did not
mourn.'
18 For John came neither eating nor drinking, and they say, 'He has a demon'; 19 the Son of Man came eating and drinking, and they say, 'Look, a glutton and a drunkard, a friend of tax collectors and sinners!' Yet wisdom is vindicated by her deeds."[p]

Woes to Unrepentant Cities
(Gen 19.12–14; Lk 10.13–15)

20 Then he began to reproach the

i Or *the Christ*   j Other ancient authorities read *two of his*   k The terms *leper* and *leprosy* can refer to several diseases   l Or *Why then did you go out? To see someone*   m Other ancient authorities read *Why then did you go out? To see a prophet?*   n Or *has been coming violently*   o Other ancient authorities add *to hear*   p Other ancient authorities read *children* cities in which most of his deeds of power had been done, because they did not repent. 21 "Woe to you, Chō·rā'-zin! Woe to you, Beth·sā'i·da! For if the deeds of power done in you had been done in Tyre and Si'don, they would have repented long ago in sackcloth and ashes. 22 But I tell you, on the day of judgment it will be more tolerable for Tyre and Si'don than for you. 23 And you, Ca·per'na·um,

will you be exalted to heaven?
No, you will be brought down
to Hades.

For if the deeds of power done in you had been done in Sod'om, it would have remained until this day. 24 But I tell you that on the day of judgment it will be more tolerable for the land of Sod'om than for you."

Jesus Thanks His Father
(Lk 10.21–22)

25 At that time Jesus said, "I thank q you, Father, Lord of heaven and earth, because you have hidden these things from the wise and the intelligent and have revealed them to infants; 26 yes, Father, for such was your gracious will. r 27 All things have been handed over to me by my Father; and no one knows the Son except the Father, and no one knows the Father except the Son and anyone to whom the Son chooses to reveal him.

28 "Come to me, all you that are weary and are carrying heavy burdens, and I will give you rest. 29 Take my yoke upon you, and learn from me; for I am gentle and humble in heart, and you will find rest for your souls. 30 For my yoke is easy, and my burden is light."

Plucking Grain on the Sabbath
(Mk 2.23–28; Lk 6.1–5)

12 At that time Jesus went through the grainfields on the sabbath; his disciples were hungry, and they began to pluck heads of grain and to eat. 2 When the Phar'i·sees saw it, they said to him, "Look, your disciples are doing what is not lawful to do on the sabbath." 3 He said to them, "Have you not read what David did when he and his companions were hungry? 4 He entered the house of God and ate the bread of the Presence, which it was not lawful for him or his companions to eat, but only for the priests. 5 Or have you not read in the law that on the sabbath the priests in

the temple break the sabbath and yet are guiltless? 6 I tell you, something greater than the temple is here. 7 But if you had known what this means, 'I desire mercy and not sacrifice,' you would not have condemned the guiltless. 8 For the Son of Man is lord of the sabbath."

The Man with a Withered Hand
(Mk 3.1–6; Lk 6.6–11)

9 He left that place and entered their synagogue; 10 a man was there with a withered hand, and they asked him, "Is it lawful to cure on the sabbath?" so that they might accuse him. 11 He said to them, "Suppose one of you has only one sheep and it falls into a pit on the sabbath; will you not lay hold of it and lift it out? 12 How much more valuable is a human being than a sheep! So it is lawful to do good on the sabbath." 13 Then he said to the man, "Stretch out your hand." He stretched it out, and it was restored, as sound as the other. 14 But the Phar'i·sees went out and conspired against him, how to destroy him.

God's Chosen Servant

15 When Jesus became aware of this, he departed. Many crowds s followed him, and he cured all of them, 16 and he ordered them not to make him known. 17 This was to fulfill what had been spoken through the prophet I·sāi'ah:

18 "Here is my servant, whom I
have chosen,
my beloved, with whom my
soul is well pleased.
I will put my Spirit upon him,
and he will proclaim justice to
the Gentiles.
19 He will not wrangle or cry
aloud,
nor will anyone hear his voice
in the streets.
20 He will not break a bruised reed
or quench a smoldering wick
until he brings justice to victory.
21 And in his name the Gentiles
will hope."

Jesus and Beelzebul
(Mk 3.19b–30; Lk 11.14–23)

22 Then they brought to him a demoniac who was blind and mute; and

q Or *praise* 　 r Or *for so it was well-pleasing in your sight* 　 s Other ancient authorities lack *crowds* he cured him, so that the one who had been mute could speak and see. 23 All the crowds were amazed and said, "Can this be the Son of David?" 24 But when the Phar'i·sees heard it, they said, "It is only by Be·el'ze·bul, the ruler of the demons, that this fellow casts out the demons." 25 He knew what they were thinking and said to them, "Every kingdom divided against itself is laid waste, and no city or house divided against itself will stand. 26 If Satan casts out Satan, he is divided against himself; how then will his kingdom stand? 27 If I cast out demons by Be·el'ze·bul, by whom do your own exorcists *t* cast them out? Therefore they will be your judges. 28 But if it is by the Spirit of God that I cast out demons, then the kingdom of God has come to you. 29 Or how can one enter a strong man's house and plunder his property, without first tying up the strong man? Then indeed the house can be plundered. 30 Whoever is not with me is against me, and whoever does not gather with me scatters. 31 Therefore I tell you, people will be forgiven for every sin and blasphemy, but blasphemy against the Spirit will not be forgiven. 32 Whoever speaks a word against the Son of Man will be forgiven, but whoever speaks against the Holy Spirit will not be forgiven, either in this age or in the age to come.

A Tree and Its Fruit
(Mt 7.15–20)

33 "Either make the tree good, and its fruit good; or make the tree bad, and its fruit bad; for the tree is known by its fruit. 34 You brood of vipers! How can you speak good things, when you are evil? For out of the abundance of the heart the mouth speaks. 35 The good person brings good things out of a good treasure, and the evil person brings evil things out of an evil treasure. 36 I tell you, on the day of judgment you will have to give an account for every careless word you utter; 37 for by your words you will be justified, and by your words you will be condemned."

The Sign of Jonah
(Lk 11.29–32)

38 Then some of the scribes and Phar'i·sees said to him, "Teacher, we wish to see a sign from you." 39 But he answered them, "An evil and adulterous generation asks for a sign, but no sign will be given to it except the sign of the prophet Jonah. 40 For just as Jonah was three days and three nights in the belly of the sea monster, so for three days and three nights the Son of Man will be in the heart of the earth. 41 The people of Nin'e·veh will rise up at the judgment with this generation and condemn it, because they repented at the proclamation of Jonah, and see, something greater than Jonah is here! 42 The queen of the South will rise up at the judgment with this generation and condemn it, because she came from the ends of the earth to listen to the wisdom of Solomon, and see, something greater than Solomon is here!

The Return of the Unclean Spirit
(Lk 11.24–26)

43 "When the unclean spirit has gone out of a person, it wanders through waterless regions looking for a resting place, but it finds none. 44 Then it says, 'I will return to my house from which I came.' When it comes, it finds it empty, swept, and put in order. 45 Then it goes and brings along seven other spirits more evil than itself, and they enter and live there; and the last state of that person is worse than the first. So will it be also with this evil generation."

The True Kindred of Jesus
(Mk 3.31–35; Lk 8.19–21)

46 While he was still speaking to the crowds, his mother and his brothers were standing outside, wanting to speak to him. 47 Someone told him, "Look, your mother and your brothers are standing outside, wanting to speak to you." *u* 48 But to the one who had told him this, Jesus *v* replied, "Who is my mother, and who are my brothers?" 49 And pointing to his disciples, he said, "Here are my mother and my brothers! 50 For whoever does the will of my Father in heaven is my brother and sister and mother."

The Parable of the Sower
(Mk 4.1–9, 13–20; Lk 8.4–8, 11–15)

13 That same day Jesus went out of the house and sat beside the sea. 2 Such great crowds gathered around him that he got into a boat and

---

t Gk *sons*   *u* Other ancient authorities lack verse 47   *v* Gk *he* sat there, while the whole crowd stood on the beach. ³And he told them many things in parables, saying: "Listen! A sower went out to sow. ⁴And as he sowed, some seeds fell on the path, and the birds came and ate them up. ⁵Other seeds fell on rocky ground, where they did not have much soil, and they sprang up quickly, since they had no depth of soil. ⁶But when the sun rose, they were scorched; and since they had no root, they withered away. ⁷Other seeds fell among thorns, and the thorns grew up and choked them. ⁸Other seeds fell on good soil and brought forth grain, some a hundredfold, some sixty, some thirty. ⁹Let anyone with ears *w* listen!"

The Purpose of the Parables
(Mk 4.10–12; Lk 8.9–10)

10 Then the disciples came and asked him, "Why do you speak to them in parables?" ¹¹He answered, "To you it has been given to know the secrets *x* of the kingdom of heaven, but to them it has not been given. ¹²For to those who have, more will be given, and they will have an abundance; but from those who have nothing, even what they have will be taken away. ¹³The reason I speak to them in parables is that 'seeing they do not perceive, and hearing they do not listen, nor do they understand.' ¹⁴With them indeed is fulfilled the prophecy of I·sāi'ah that says:

'You will indeed listen, but never understand,
and you will indeed look, but never perceive.
¹⁵ For this people's heart has grown dull,
and their ears are hard of hearing,
and they have shut their eyes;
so that they might not look with their eyes,
and listen with their ears,
and understand with their heart and turn—
and I would heal them.'

¹⁶But blessed are your eyes, for they see, and your ears, for they hear. ¹⁷Truly I tell you, many prophets and righteous people longed to see what you see, but did not see it, and to hear what you hear, but did not hear it.

The Parable of the Sower Explained

18 "Hear then the parable of the sower. ¹⁹When anyone hears the word of the kingdom and does not understand it, the evil one comes and snatches away what is sown in the heart; this is what was sown on the path. ²⁰As for what was sown on rocky ground, this is the one who hears the word and immediately receives it with joy; ²¹yet such a person has no root, but endures only for a while, and when trouble or persecution arises on account of the word, that person immediately falls away. *y* ²²As for what was sown among thorns, this is the one who hears the word, but the cares of the world and the lure of wealth choke the word, and it yields nothing. ²³But as for what was sown on good soil, this is the one who hears the word and understands it, who indeed bears fruit and yields, in one case a hundredfold, in another sixty, and in another thirty."

The Parable of Weeds among the Wheat

24 He put before them another parable: "The kingdom of heaven may be compared to someone who sowed good seed in his field; ²⁵but while everybody was asleep, an enemy came and sowed weeds among the wheat, and then went away. ²⁶So when the plants came up and bore grain, then the weeds appeared as well. ²⁷And the slaves of the householder came and said to him, 'Master, did you not sow good seed in your field? Where, then, did these weeds come from?' ²⁸He answered, 'An enemy has done this.' The slaves said to him, 'Then do you want us to go and gather them?' ²⁹But he replied, 'No; for in gathering the weeds you would uproot the wheat along with them. ³⁰Let both of them grow together until the harvest; and at harvest time I will tell the reapers, Collect the weeds first and bind them in bundles to be burned, but gather the wheat into my barn.'"

The Parable of the Mustard Seed
(Mk 4.30–32; Lk 13.18–19)

31 He put before them another parable: "The kingdom of heaven is like a mustard seed that someone took and sowed in his field; ³²it is the smallest of all the seeds, but when it has grown it is the greatest of shrubs and becomes

---

w Other ancient authorities add *to hear*
x Or *mysteries*   *y* Gk *stumbles*

a tree, so that the birds of the air come and make nests in its branches."

The Parable of the Yeast
(Lk 13.20–21)

33 He told them another parable: "The kingdom of heaven is like yeast that a woman took and mixed in with z three measures of flour until all of it was leavened."

The Use of Parables

34 Jesus told the crowds all these things in parables; without a parable he told them nothing. 35 This was to fulfill what had been spoken through the prophet: a

"I will open my mouth to speak
    in parables;
I will proclaim what has been
    hidden from the foundation
    of the world." b

Jesus Explains the Parable
of the Weeds

36 Then he left the crowds and went into the house. And his disciples approached him, saying, "Explain to us the parable of the weeds of the field." 37 He answered, "The one who sows the good seed is the Son of Man; 38 the field is the world, and the good seed are the children of the kingdom; the weeds are the children of the evil one, 39 and the enemy who sowed them is the devil; the harvest is the end of the age, and the reapers are angels. 40 Just as the weeds are collected and burned up with fire, so will it be at the end of the age. 41 The Son of Man will send his angels, and they will collect out of his kingdom all causes of sin and all evildoers, 42 and they will throw them into the furnace of fire, where there will be weeping and gnashing of teeth. 43 Then the righteous will shine like the sun in the kingdom of their Father. Let anyone with ears c listen!

Three Parables

44 "The kingdom of heaven is like treasure hidden in a field, which someone found and hid; then in his joy he goes and sells all that he has and buys that field.
45 "Again, the kingdom of heaven is like a merchant in search of fine pearls; 46 on finding one pearl of great value, he went and sold all that he had and bought it.
47 "Again, the kingdom of heaven is like a net that was thrown into the sea and caught fish of every kind; 48 when it was full, they drew it ashore, sat down, and put the good into baskets but threw out the bad. 49 So it will be at the end of the age. The angels will come out and separate the evil from the righteous 50 and throw them into the furnace of fire, where there will be weeping and gnashing of teeth.

Treasures New and Old

51 "Have you understood all this?" They answered, "Yes." 52 And he said to them, "Therefore every scribe who has been trained for the kingdom of heaven is like the master of a household who brings out of his treasure what is new and what is old." 53 When Jesus had finished these parables, he left that place.

The Rejection of Jesus at Nazareth
(Mk 6.1–6; Lk 4.16–30)

54 He came to his hometown and began to teach the people d in their synagogue, so that they were astounded and said, "Where did this man get this wisdom and these deeds of power? 55 Is not this the carpenter's son? Is not his mother called Mary? And are not his brothers James and Joseph and Simon and Judas? 56 And are not all his sisters with us? Where then did this man get all this?" 57 And they took offense at him. But Jesus said to them, "Prophets are not without honor except in their own country and in their own house." 58 And he did not do many deeds of power there, because of their unbelief.

The Death of John the Baptist
(Lk 9.7–9; Mk 6.14–29)

14 At that time Her'od the ruler e heard reports about Jesus; 2 and he said to his servants, "This is John the Baptist; he has been raised from the dead, and for this reason these powers are at work in him." 3 For Her'od had arrested John, bound him, and put him in prison on account of He·rō'di·as, his brother Philip's wife, f 4 because John had been telling him, "It is not lawful for you to have her."

z Gk hid in   a Other ancient authorities read the prophet Isaiah   b Other ancient authorities lack of the world   c Other ancient authorities add to hear   d Gk them   e Gk tetrarch   f Other ancient authorities read his brother's wife

M
A
T
T
H
E
W

5 Though Her′od g wanted to put him to death, he feared the crowd, because they regarded him as a prophet. 6 But when Her′od's birthday came, the daughter of He·rō′di·as danced before the company, and she pleased Her′od 7 so much that he promised on oath to grant her whatever she might ask. 8 Prompted by her mother, she said, "Give me the head of John the Baptist here on a platter." 9 The king was grieved, yet out of regard for his oaths and for the guests, he commanded it to be given; 10 he sent and had John beheaded in the prison. 11 The head was brought on a platter and given to the girl, who brought it to her mother. 12 His disciples came and took the body and buried it; then they went and told Jesus.

Feeding the Five Thousand
(Mk 6.30–44; Lk 9.10–17; Jn 6.1–14)

13 Now when Jesus heard this, he withdrew from there in a boat to a deserted place by himself. But when the crowds heard it, they followed him on foot from the towns. 14 When he went ashore, he saw a great crowd; and he had compassion for them and cured their sick. 15 When it was evening, the disciples came to him and said, "This is a deserted place, and the hour is now late; send the crowds away so that they may go into the villages and buy food for themselves." 16 Jesus said to them, "They need not go away; you give them something to eat." 17 They replied, "We have nothing here but five loaves and two fish." 18 And he said, "Bring them here to me." 19 Then he ordered the crowds to sit down on the grass. Taking the five loaves and the two fish, he looked up to heaven, and blessed and broke the loaves, and gave them to the disciples, and the disciples gave them to the crowds. 20 And all ate and were filled; and they took up what was left over of the broken pieces, twelve baskets full. 21 And those who ate were about five thousand men, besides women and children.

Jesus Walks on the Water
(Mk 6.45–52; Jn 6.15–21)

22 Immediately he made the disciples get into the boat and go on ahead to the other side, while he dismissed the crowds. 23 And after he had dismissed the crowds, he went up the mountain by himself to pray. When evening came, he was there alone,

24 but by this time the boat, battered by the waves, was far from the land, h for the wind was against them. 25 And early in the morning he came walking toward them on the sea. 26 But when the disciples saw him walking on the sea, they were terrified, saying, "It is a ghost!" And they cried out in fear. 27 But immediately Jesus spoke to them and said, "Take heart, it is I; do not be afraid."

28 Peter answered him, "Lord, if it is you, command me to come to you on the water." 29 He said, "Come." So Peter got out of the boat, started walking on the water, and came toward Jesus. 30 But when he noticed the strong wind, i he became frightened, and beginning to sink, he cried out, "Lord, save me!" 31 Jesus immediately reached out his hand and caught him, saying to him, "You of little faith, why did you doubt?" 32 When they got into the boat, the wind ceased. 33 And those in the boat worshiped him, saying, "Truly you are the Son of God."

Jesus Heals the Sick in Gennesaret
(Mk 6.53–56)

34 When they had crossed over, they came to land at Gen·nes′a·ret. 35 After the people of that place recognized him, they sent word throughout the region and brought all who were sick to him, 36 and begged him that they might touch even the fringe of his cloak; and all who touched it were healed.

The Tradition of the Elders
(Mk 7.1–13)

15 Then Phar′i·sees and scribes came to Jesus from Jerusalem and said, 2 "Why do your disciples break the tradition of the elders? For they do not wash their hands before they eat." 3 He answered them, "And why do you break the commandment of God for the sake of your tradition? 4 For God said, j 'Honor your father and your mother,' and, 'Whoever speaks evil of father or mother must surely die.' 5 But you say that whoever tells father or mother, 'Whatever support you might have had from me is given to God,' k then that person need

g Gk *he*   h Other ancient authorities read *was out on the sea*   i Other ancient authorities read *the wind*   j Other ancient authorities read *commanded, saying*   k Or *is an offering* not honor the father.[l] [6]So, for the sake of your tradition, you make void the word[m] of God. [7]You hypocrites! I·sai'ah prophesied rightly about you when he said:

[8] 'This people honors me with their lips,
　　but their hearts are far from me;
[9] in vain do they worship me,
　　teaching human precepts as doctrines.' "

Things That Defile
(Mk 7.14–23)

[10] Then he called the crowd to him and said to them, "Listen and understand: [11]it is not what goes into the mouth that defiles a person, but it is what comes out of the mouth that defiles." [12]Then the disciples approached and said to him, "Do you know that the Phar'i·sees took offense when they heard what you said?" [13]He answered, "Every plant that my heavenly Father has not planted will be uprooted. [14]Let them alone; they are blind guides of the blind.[n] And if one blind person guides another, both will fall into a pit." [15]But Peter said to him, "Explain this parable to us." [16]Then he said, "Are you also still without understanding? [17]Do you not see that whatever goes into the mouth enters the stomach, and goes out into the sewer? [18]But what comes out of the mouth proceeds from the heart, and this is what defiles. [19]For out of the heart come evil intentions, murder, adultery, fornication, theft, false witness, slander. [20]These are what defile a person, but to eat with unwashed hands does not defile."

The Canaanite Woman's Faith
(Mk 7.24–30)

[21] Jesus left that place and went away to the district of Tyre and Si'don. [22]Just then a Ca'naan·ite woman from that region came out and started shouting, "Have mercy on me, Lord, Son of David; my daughter is tormented by a demon." [23]But he did not answer her at all. And his disciples came and urged him, saying, "Send her away, for she keeps shouting after us." [24]He answered, "I was sent only to the lost sheep of the house of Israel." [25]But she came and knelt before him, saying, "Lord, help me." [26]He answered, "It is not fair to take the children's food and throw it to the dogs." [27]She said, "Yes, Lord, yet even the dogs eat the crumbs that fall from their masters' table." [28]Then Jesus answered her, "Woman, great is your faith! Let it be done for you as you wish." And her daughter was healed instantly.

Jesus Cures Many People
(Mk 7.31–37)

[29] After Jesus had left that place, he passed along the Sea of Galilee, and he went up the mountain, where he sat down. [30]Great crowds came to him, bringing with them the lame, the maimed, the blind, the mute, and many others. They put them at his feet, and he cured them, [31]so that the crowd was amazed when they saw the mute speaking, the maimed whole, the lame walking, and the blind seeing. And they praised the God of Israel.

Feeding the Four Thousand
(Mk 8.1–10)

[32] Then Jesus called his disciples to him and said, "I have compassion for the crowd, because they have been with me now for three days and have nothing to eat; and I do not want to send them away hungry, for they might faint on the way." [33]The disciples said to him, "Where are we to get enough bread in the desert to feed so great a crowd?" [34]Jesus asked them, "How many loaves have you?" They said, "Seven, and a few small fish." [35]Then ordering the crowd to sit down on the ground, [36]he took the seven loaves and the fish; and after giving thanks he broke them and gave them to the disciples, and the disciples gave them to the crowds. [37]And all of them ate and were filled; and they took up the broken pieces left over, seven baskets full. [38]Those who had eaten were four thousand men, besides women and children. [39]After sending away the crowds, he got into the boat and went to the region of Mag'a·dan.[o]

The Demand for a Sign
(Mk 8.11–13; Lk 12.54–56)

16 The Phar'i·sees and Sad'du·cees came, and to test Jesus[p] they asked him to show them a

[l]Other ancient authorities add *or the mother*　[m]Other ancient authorities read *law*; others, *commandment*
[n]Other ancient authorities lack *of the blind*　[o]Other ancient authorities read *Magdala* or *Magdalan*　[p]Gk *him*

M
A
T
T
H
E
W

sign from heaven. [2] He answered them, "When it is evening, you say, 'It will be fair weather, for the sky is red.' [3] And in the morning, 'It will be stormy today, for the sky is red and threatening.' You know how to interpret the appearance of the sky, but you cannot interpret the signs of the times.[q] [4] An evil and adulterous generation asks for a sign, but no sign will be given to it except the sign of Jonah." Then he left them and went away.

The Yeast of the Pharisees and Sadducees
(Mk 8.14–21)

5 When the disciples reached the other side, they had forgotten to bring any bread. [6] Jesus said to them, "Watch out, and beware of the yeast of the Phar′i·sees and Sad′du·cees." [7] They said to one another, "It is because we have brought no bread." [8] And becoming aware of it, Jesus said, "You of little faith, why are you talking about having no bread? [9] Do you still not perceive? Do you not remember the five loaves for the five thousand, and how many baskets you gathered? [10] Or the seven loaves for the four thousand, and how many baskets you gathered? [11] How could you fail to perceive that I was not speaking about bread? Beware of the yeast of the Phar′i·sees and Sad′du·cees!" [12] Then they understood that he had not told them to beware of the yeast of bread, but of the teaching of the Phar′i·sees and Sad′du·cees.

Peter's Declaration about Jesus
(Mk 8.27–30; Lk 9.18–20)

13 Now when Jesus came into the district of Caes·a·re′a Phi·lip′pi, he asked his disciples, "Who do people say that the Son of Man is?" [14] And they said, "Some say John the Baptist, but others E·li′jah, and still others Jer·e·mi′ah or one of the prophets." [15] He said to them, "But who do you say that I am?" [16] Simon Peter answered, "You are the Messiah,[r] the Son of the living God." [17] And Jesus answered him, "Blessed are you, Simon son of Jonah! For flesh and blood has not revealed this to you, but my Father in heaven. [18] And I tell you, you are Peter,[s] and on this rock[t] I will build my church, and the gates of Hades will not prevail against it. [19] I will give you the keys of the kingdom of heaven, and whatever you bind on earth will be bound in heaven, and whatever you loose on earth will be loosed in heaven." [20] Then he sternly ordered the disciples not to tell anyone that he was[u] the Messiah.[r]

Jesus Foretells His Death and Resurrection
(Mk 8.31–33; Lk 9.21–22)

21 From that time on, Jesus began to show his disciples that he must go to Jerusalem and undergo great suffering at the hands of the elders and chief priests and scribes, and be killed, and on the third day be raised. [22] And Peter took him aside and began to rebuke him, saying, "God forbid it, Lord! This must never happen to you." [23] But he turned and said to Peter, "Get behind me, Satan! You are a stumbling block to me; for you are setting your mind not on divine things but on human things."

The Cross and Self-Denial
(Mk 8.34—9.1; Lk 9.23–27)

24 Then Jesus told his disciples, "If any want to become my followers, let them deny themselves and take up their cross and follow me. [25] For those who want to save their life will lose it, and those who lose their life for my sake will find it. [26] For what will it profit them if they gain the whole world but forfeit their life? Or what will they give in return for their life? 27 "For the Son of Man is to come with his angels in the glory of his Father, and then he will repay everyone for what has been done. [28] Truly I tell you, there are some standing here who will not taste death before they see the Son of Man coming in his kingdom."

The Transfiguration
(Mk 9.2–13; Lk 9.28–36; 2 Pet 1.16–18)

17 Six days later, Jesus took with him Peter and James and his brother John and led them up a high mountain, by themselves. [2] And he was transfigured before them, and his face shone like the sun, and his clothes became dazzling white. [3] Suddenly there appeared to them Moses and E·li′jah, talking with him. [4] Then Peter said to Jesus, "Lord, it is good for us to be

[q] Other ancient authorities lack *2When it is . . . of the times*   [r] Or *the Christ*   [s] Gk *Petros*   [t] Gk *petra*   [u] Other ancient authorities add *Jesus*

here; if you wish, I[v] will make three dwellings[w] here, one for you, one for Moses, and one for E·li′jah." [5]While he was still speaking, suddenly a bright cloud overshadowed them, and from the cloud a voice said, "This is my Son, the Beloved;[x] with him I am well pleased; listen to him!" [6]When the disciples heard this, they fell to the ground and were overcome by fear. [7]But Jesus came and touched them, saying, "Get up and do not be afraid." [8]And when they looked up, they saw no one except Jesus himself alone.

[9] As they were coming down the mountain, Jesus ordered them, "Tell no one about the vision until after the Son of Man has been raised from the dead." [10]And the disciples asked him, "Why, then, do the scribes say that E·li′jah must come first?" [11]He replied, "E·li′jah is indeed coming and will restore all things; [12]but I tell you that E·li′jah has already come, and they did not recognize him, but they did to him whatever they pleased. So also the Son of Man is about to suffer at their hands." [13]Then the disciples understood that he was speaking to them about John the Baptist.

Jesus Cures a Boy with a Demon
(Mk 9.14–29; Lk 9.37–43a)

[14] When they came to the crowd, a man came to him, knelt before him, [15]and said, "Lord, have mercy on my son, for he is an epileptic and he suffers terribly; he often falls into the fire and often into the water. [16]And I brought him to your disciples, but they could not cure him." [17]Jesus answered, "You faithless and perverse generation, how much longer must I be with you? How much longer must I put up with you? Bring him here to me." [18]And Jesus rebuked the demon,[y] and it[z] came out of him, and the boy was cured instantly. [19]Then the disciples came to Jesus privately and said, "Why could we not cast it out?" [20]He said to them, "Because of your little faith. For truly I tell you, if you have faith the size of a[a] mustard seed, you will say to this mountain, 'Move from here to there,' and it will move; and nothing will be impossible for you."[b]

Jesus Again Foretells His Death and Resurrection
(Mk 9.30–32; Lk 9.43b–45)

[22] As they were gathering[c] in Galilee, Jesus said to them, "The Son of Man is going to be betrayed into human hands, [23]and they will kill him, and on the third day he will be raised." And they were greatly distressed.

Jesus and the Temple Tax

[24] When they reached Ca·per′na·um, the collectors of the temple tax[d] came to Peter and said, "Does your teacher not pay the temple tax?"[d] [25]He said, "Yes, he does." And when he came home, Jesus spoke of it first, asking, "What do you think, Simon? From whom do kings of the earth take toll or tribute? From their children or from others?" [26]When Peter[e] said, "From others," Jesus said to him, "Then the children are free. [27]However, so that we do not give offense to them, go to the sea and cast a hook; take the first fish that comes up; and when you open its mouth, you will find a coin;[f] take that and give it to them for you and me."

True Greatness
(Mk 9.33–37; Lk 9.46–48)

18 At that time the disciples came to Jesus and asked, "Who is the greatest in the kingdom of heaven?" [2]He called a child, whom he put among them, [3]and said, "Truly I tell you, unless you change and become like children, you will never enter the kingdom of heaven. [4]Whoever becomes humble like this child is the greatest in the kingdom of heaven. [5]Whoever welcomes one such child in my name welcomes me.

Temptations to Sin
(Mk 9.42–48; Lk 17.1–2)

[6] "If any of you put a stumbling block before one of these little ones who believe in me, it would be better for you if a great millstone were fastened around your neck and you were drowned in the depth of the sea. [7]Woe to the world because of stumbling blocks! Occasions for stumbling are

[v]Other ancient authorities read *we*
[w]Or *tents*   [x]Or *my beloved Son*
[y]Gk *it* or *him*   [z]Gk *the demon*
[a]Gk *faith as a grain of*   [b]Other ancient authorities add verse 21, *But this kind does not come out except by prayer and fasting*   [c]Other ancient authorities read *living*   [d]Gk *didrachma*   [e]Gk *he* [f]Gk *stater*; the stater was worth two didrachmas

M
A
T
T
H
E
W

bound to come, but woe to the one by whom the stumbling block comes!

8 "If your hand or your foot causes you to stumble, cut it off and throw it away; it is better for you to enter life maimed or lame than to have two hands or two feet and to be thrown into the eternal fire. 9 And if your eye causes you to stumble, tear it out and throw it away; it is better for you to enter life with one eye than to have two eyes and to be thrown into the hell g of fire.

The Parable of the Lost Sheep
(Lk 15.1–7)

10 "Take care that you do not despise one of these little ones; for, I tell you, in heaven their angels continually see the face of my Father in heaven. h 12 What do you think? If a shepherd has a hundred sheep, and one of them has gone astray, does he not leave the ninety-nine on the mountains and go in search of the one that went astray? 13 And if he finds it, truly I tell you, he rejoices over it more than over the ninety-nine that never went astray. 14 So it is not the will of your i Father in heaven that one of these little ones should be lost.

Reproving Another Who Sins

15 "If another member of the church j sins against you, k go and point out the fault when the two of you are alone. If the member listens to you, you have regained that one. l 16 But if you are not listened to, take one or two others along with you, so that every word may be confirmed by the evidence of two or three witnesses. 17 If the member refuses to listen to them, tell it to the church; and if the offender refuses to listen even to the church, let such a one be to you as a Gentile and a tax collector. 18 Truly I tell you, whatever you bind on earth will be bound in heaven, and whatever you loose on earth will be loosed in heaven. 19 Again, truly I tell you, if two of you agree on earth about anything you ask, it will be done for you by my Father in heaven. 20 For where two or three are gathered in my name, I am there among them."

Forgiveness

21 Then Peter came and said to him, "Lord, if another member of the church m sins against me, how often should I forgive? As many as seven times?" 22 Jesus said to him, "Not seven times, but, I tell you, seventy-seven n times.

The Parable of the Unforgiving Servant

23 "For this reason the kingdom of heaven may be compared to a king who wished to settle accounts with his slaves. 24 When he began the reckoning, one who owed him ten thousand talents o was brought to him; 25 and, as he could not pay, his lord ordered him to be sold, together with his wife and children and all his possessions, and payment to be made. 26 So the slave fell on his knees before him, saying, 'Have patience with me, and I will pay you everything.' 27 And out of pity for him, the lord of that slave released him and forgave him the debt. 28 But that same slave, as he went out, came upon one of his fellow slaves who owed him a hundred denarii; p and seizing him by the throat, he said, 'Pay what you owe.' 29 Then his fellow slave fell down and pleaded with him, 'Have patience with me, and I will pay you.' 30 But he refused; then he went and threw him into prison until he would pay the debt. 31 When his fellow slaves saw what had happened, they were greatly distressed, and they went and reported to their lord all that had taken place. 32 Then his lord summoned him and said to him, 'You wicked slave! I forgave you all that debt because you pleaded with me. 33 Should you not have had mercy on your fellow slave, as I had mercy on you?' 34 And in anger his lord handed him over to be tortured until he would pay his entire debt. 35 So my heavenly Father will also do to every one of you, if you do not forgive your brother or sister q from your heart."

g Gk Gehenna   h Other ancient authorities add verse 11, *For the Son of Man came to save the lost*   i Other ancient authorities read *my*   j Gk *If your brother*   k Other ancient authorities lack *against you*   l Gk *the brother*   m Gk *if my brother*   n Or *seventy times seven*   o A talent was worth more than fifteen years' wages of a laborer   p The denarius was the usual day's wage for a laborer   q Gk *brother*

Teaching about Divorce
(Mk 10.1–12)

19 When Jesus had finished saying these things, he left Galilee and went to the region of Judea beyond the Jordan. 2 Large crowds followed him, and he cured them there. 3 Some Phar′i·sees came to him, and to test him they asked, "Is it lawful for a man to divorce his wife for any cause?" 4 He answered, "Have you not read that the one who made them at the beginning 'made them male and female,' 5 and said, 'For this reason a man shall leave his father and mother and be joined to his wife, and the two shall become one flesh'? 6 So they are no longer two, but one flesh. Therefore what God has joined together, let no one separate." 7 They said to him, "Why then did Moses command us to give a certificate of dismissal and to divorce her?" 8 He said to them, "It was because you were so hard-hearted that Moses allowed you to divorce your wives, but from the beginning it was not so. 9 And I say to you, whoever divorces his wife, except for unchastity, and marries another commits adultery."*r*

10 His disciples said to him, "If such is the case of a man with his wife, it is better not to marry." 11 But he said to them, "Not everyone can accept this teaching, but only those to whom it is given. 12 For there are eunuchs who have been so from birth, and there are eunuchs who have been made eunuchs by others, and there are eunuchs who have made themselves eunuchs for the sake of the kingdom of heaven. Let anyone accept this who can."

Jesus Blesses Little Children
(Mk 10.13–16; Lk 18.15–17)

13 Then little children were being brought to him in order that he might lay his hands on them and pray. The disciples spoke sternly to those who brought them; 14 but Jesus said, "Let the little children come to me, and do not stop them; for it is to such as these that the kingdom of heaven belongs." 15 And he laid his hands on them and went on his way.

The Rich Young Man
(Mk 10.17–31; Lk 18.18–30)

16 Then someone came to him and said, "Teacher, what good deed must I do to have eternal life?" 17 And he said to him, "Why do you ask me about what is good? There is only one who is good. If you wish to enter into life, keep the commandments." 18 He said to him, "Which ones?" And Jesus said, "You shall not murder; You shall not commit adultery; You shall not steal; You shall not bear false witness; 19 Honor your father and mother; also, You shall love your neighbor as yourself." 20 The young man said to him, "I have kept all these;*s* what do I still lack?" 21 Jesus said to him, "If you wish to be perfect, go, sell your possessions, and give the money*t* to the poor, and you will have treasure in heaven; then come, follow me." 22 When the young man heard this word, he went away grieving, for he had many possessions.

23 Then Jesus said to his disciples, "Truly I tell you, it will be hard for a rich person to enter the kingdom of heaven. 24 Again I tell you, it is easier for a camel to go through the eye of a needle than for someone who is rich to enter the kingdom of God." 25 When the disciples heard this, they were greatly astounded and said, "Then who can be saved?" 26 But Jesus looked at them and said, "For mortals it is impossible, but for God all things are possible."

27 Then Peter said in reply, "Look, we have left everything and followed you. What then will we have?" 28 Jesus said to them, "Truly I tell you, at the renewal of all things, when the Son of Man is seated on the throne of his glory, you who have followed me will also sit on twelve thrones, judging the twelve tribes of Israel. 29 And everyone who has left houses or brothers or sisters or father or mother or children or fields, for my name's sake, will receive a hundredfold,*u* and will inherit eternal life. 30 But many who are first will be last, and the last will be first.

The Laborers in the Vineyard

20 "For the kingdom of heaven is like a landowner who went out early in the morning to hire laborers

---

r Other ancient authorities read *except on the ground of unchastity, causes her to commit adultery*; others add at the end of the verse *and he who marries a divorced woman commits adultery*　*s* Other ancient authorities add *from my youth*　*t* Gk lacks *the money*　*u* Other ancient authorities read *manifold* for his vineyard. ²After agreeing with the laborers for the usual daily wage,ᵛ he sent them into his vineyard. ³When he went out about nine o'clock, he saw others standing idle in the marketplace; ⁴and he said to them, 'You also go into the vineyard, and I will pay you whatever is right.' So they went. ⁵When he went out again about noon and about three o'clock, he did the same. ⁶And about five o'clock he went out and found others standing around; and he said to them, 'Why are you standing here idle all day?' ⁷They said to him, 'Because no one has hired us.' He said to them, 'You also go into the vineyard.' ⁸When evening came, the owner of the vineyard said to his manager, 'Call the laborers and give them their pay, beginning with the last and then going to the first.' ⁹When those hired about five o'clock came, each of them received the usual daily wage.ᵛ ¹⁰Now when the first came, they thought they would receive more; but each of them also received the usual daily wage.ᵛ ¹¹And when they received it, they grumbled against the landowner, ¹²saying, 'These last worked only one hour, and you have made them equal to us who have borne the burden of the day and the scorching heat.' ¹³But he replied to one of them, 'Friend, I am doing you no wrong; did you not agree with me for the usual daily wage?ᵛ ¹⁴Take what belongs to you and go; I choose to give to this last the same as I give to you. ¹⁵Am I not allowed to do what I choose with what belongs to me? Or are you envious because I am generous?'ʷ ¹⁶So the last will be first, and the first will be last."ˣ

A Third Time Jesus Foretells His Death and Resurrection
(Mk 10.32–34; Lk 18.31–34)

17 While Jesus was going up to Jerusalem, he took the twelve disciples aside by themselves, and said to them on the way, ¹⁸"See, we are going up to Jerusalem, and the Son of Man will be handed over to the chief priests and scribes, and they will condemn him to death; ¹⁹then they will hand him over to the Gentiles to be mocked and flogged and crucified; and on the third day he will be raised."

The Request of the Mother of James and John
(Mk 10.35–45)

20 Then the mother of the sons of Zeb'e·dee came to him with her sons, and kneeling before him, she asked a favor of him. ²¹And he said to her, "What do you want?" She said to him, "Declare that these two sons of mine will sit, one at your right hand and one at your left, in your kingdom." ²²But Jesus answered, "You do not know what you are asking. Are you able to drink the cup that I am about to drink?"ʸ They said to him, "We are able." ²³He said to them, "You will indeed drink my cup, but to sit at my right hand and at my left, this is not mine to grant, but it is for those for whom it has been prepared by my Father."

24 When the ten heard it, they were angry with the two brothers. ²⁵But Jesus called them to him and said, "You know that the rulers of the Gentiles lord it over them, and their great ones are tyrants over them. ²⁶It will not be so among you; but whoever wishes to be great among you must be your servant, ²⁷and whoever wishes to be first among you must be your slave; ²⁸just as the Son of Man came not to be served but to serve, and to give his life a ransom for many."

Jesus Heals Two Blind Men
(Mk 10.46–52; Lk 18.35–43)

29 As they were leaving Jericho, a large crowd followed him. ³⁰There were two blind men sitting by the roadside. When they heard that Jesus was passing by, they shouted, "Lord,ᶻ have mercy on us, Son of David!" ³¹The crowd sternly ordered them to be quiet; but they shouted even more loudly, "Have mercy on us, Lord, Son of David!" ³²Jesus stood still and called them, saying, "What do you want me to do for you?" ³³They said to him, "Lord, let our eyes be opened." ³⁴Moved with compassion, Jesus touched their eyes. Immediately they regained their sight and followed him.

ᵛGk *a denarius*   ʷGk *is your eye evil because I am good?*   ˣOther ancient authorities add *for many are called but few are chosen*   ʸOther ancient authorities add *or to be baptized with the baptism that I am baptized with?*   ᶻOther ancient authorities lack *Lord*

Jesus' Triumphal Entry into Jerusalem
(Mk 11.1–10; Lk 19.28–40; Jn 12.12–19)

21 When they had come near Jerusalem and had reached Beth'pha·ge, at the Mount of Olives, Jesus sent two disciples, ²saying to them, "Go into the village ahead of you, and immediately you will find a donkey tied, and a colt with her; untie them and bring them to me. ³If anyone says anything to you, just say this, 'The Lord needs them.' And he will send them immediately. *ᵃ* ⁴This took place to fulfill what had been spoken through the prophet, saying,

⁵ "Tell the daughter of Zion,
    Look, your king is coming to
        you,
      humble, and mounted on a
        donkey,
          and on a colt, the foal of a
            donkey."

⁶The disciples went and did as Jesus had directed them; ⁷they brought the donkey and the colt, and put their cloaks on them, and he sat on them. ⁸A very large crowd *ᵇ* spread their cloaks on the road, and others cut branches from the trees and spread them on the road. ⁹The crowds that went ahead of him and that followed were shouting,

  "Hosanna to the Son of David!
    Blessed is the one who comes
      in the name of the Lord!
    Hosanna in the highest heaven!"

¹⁰When he entered Jerusalem, the whole city was in turmoil, asking, "Who is this?" ¹¹The crowds were saying, "This is the prophet Jesus from Nazareth in Galilee."

Jesus Cleanses the Temple
(Mk 11.15–19; Lk 19.45–48; Jn 2.13–25)

12 Then Jesus entered the temple *ᶜ* and drove out all who were selling and buying in the temple, and he overturned the tables of the money changers and the seats of those who sold doves. ¹³He said to them, "It is written,

  'My house shall be called a
    house of prayer';
  but you are making it a den of
    robbers."

14 The blind and the lame came to him in the temple, and he cured them. ¹⁵But when the chief priests and the scribes saw the amazing things that he did, and heard *ᵈ* the children crying out in the temple, "Hosanna to the Son of David," they became angry ¹⁶and said to him, "Do you hear what these

are saying?" Jesus said to them, "Yes; have you never read,

  'Out of the mouths of infants
      and nursing babies
    you have prepared praise for
        yourself'?"

¹⁷He left them, went out of the city to Beth'a·ny, and spent the night there.

Jesus Curses the Fig Tree
(Mk 11.12–14, 20–25)

18 In the morning, when he returned to the city, he was hungry. ¹⁹And seeing a fig tree by the side of the road, he went to it and found nothing at all on it but leaves. Then he said to it, "May no fruit ever come from you again!" And the fig tree withered at once. ²⁰When the disciples saw it, they were amazed, saying, "How did the fig tree wither at once?" ²¹Jesus answered them, "Truly I tell you, if you have faith and do not doubt, not only will you do what has been done to the fig tree, but even if you say to this mountain, 'Be lifted up and thrown into the sea,' it will be done. ²²Whatever you ask for in prayer with faith, you will receive."

The Authority of Jesus Questioned
(Mk 11.27–33; Lk 20.1–8)

23 When he entered the temple, the chief priests and the elders of the people came to him as he was teaching, and said, "By what authority are you doing these things, and who gave you this authority?" ²⁴Jesus said to them, "I will also ask you one question; if you tell me the answer, then I will also tell you by what authority I do these things. ²⁵Did the baptism of John come from heaven, or was it of human origin?" And they argued with one another, "If we say, 'From heaven,' he will say to us, 'Why then did you not believe him?' ²⁶But if we say, 'Of human origin,' we are afraid of the crowd; for all regard John as a prophet." ²⁷So they answered Jesus, "We do not know." And he said to them, "Neither will I tell you by what authority I am doing these things.

The Parable of the Two Sons

28 "What do you think? A man had two sons; he went to the first and said, 'Son, go and work in the vineyard to-

---

*ᵃ*Or *'The Lord needs them and will send them back immediately.'*   *ᵇ*Or *Most of the crowd*   *ᶜ*Other ancient authorities add *of God*   *ᵈ*Gk lacks *heard* day.' 29 He answered, 'I will not'; but later he changed his mind and went. 30 The father*e* went to the second and said the same; and he answered, 'I go, sir'; but he did not go. 31 Which of the two did the will of his father?" They said, "The first." Jesus said to them, "Truly I tell you, the tax collectors and the prostitutes are going into the kingdom of God ahead of you. 32 For John came to you in the way of righteousness and you did not believe him, but the tax collectors and the prostitutes believed him; and even after you saw it, you did not change your minds and believe him.

The Parable of the Wicked Tenants
(Mk 12.1–12; Lk 20.9–19)

33 "Listen to another parable. There was a landowner who planted a vineyard, put a fence around it, dug a wine press in it, and built a watchtower. Then he leased it to tenants and went to another country. 34 When the harvest time had come, he sent his slaves to the tenants to collect his produce. 35 But the tenants seized his slaves and beat one, killed another, and stoned another. 36 Again he sent other slaves, more than the first; and they treated them in the same way. 37 Finally he sent his son to them, saying, 'They will respect my son.' 38 But when the tenants saw the son, they said to themselves, 'This is the heir; come, let us kill him and get his inheritance.' 39 So they seized him, threw him out of the vineyard, and killed him. 40 Now when the owner of the vineyard comes, what will he do to those tenants?" 41 They said to him, "He will put those wretches to a miserable death, and lease the vineyard to other tenants who will give him the produce at the harvest time."

42 Jesus said to them, "Have you never read in the scriptures:

'The stone that the builders rejected
has become the cornerstone;*f*
this was the Lord's doing,
and it is amazing in our eyes'?

43 Therefore I tell you, the kingdom of God will be taken away from you and given to a people that produces the fruits of the kingdom.*g* 44 The one who falls on this stone will be broken to pieces; and it will crush anyone on whom it falls."*h*

45 When the chief priests and the Phar'i·sees heard his parables, they realized that he was speaking about them. 46 They wanted to arrest him, but they feared the crowds, because they regarded him as a prophet.

The Parable of the Wedding Banquet
(Lk 14.15–24)

22 Once more Jesus spoke to them in parables, saying: 2 "The kingdom of heaven may be compared to a king who gave a wedding banquet for his son. 3 He sent his slaves to call those who had been invited to the wedding banquet, but they would not come. 4 Again he sent other slaves, saying, 'Tell those who have been invited: Look, I have prepared my dinner, my oxen and my fat calves have been slaughtered, and everything is ready; come to the wedding banquet.' 5 But they made light of it and went away, one to his farm, another to his business, 6 while the rest seized his slaves, mistreated them, and killed them. 7 The king was enraged. He sent his troops, destroyed those murderers, and burned their city. 8 Then he said to his slaves, 'The wedding is ready, but those invited were not worthy. 9 Go therefore into the main streets, and invite everyone you find to the wedding banquet.' 10 Those slaves went out into the streets and gathered all whom they found, both good and bad; so the wedding hall was filled with guests.

11 "But when the king came in to see the guests, he noticed a man there who was not wearing a wedding robe, 12 and he said to him, 'Friend, how did you get in here without a wedding robe?' And he was speechless. 13 Then the king said to the attendants, 'Bind him hand and foot, and throw him into the outer darkness, where there will be weeping and gnashing of teeth.' 14 For many are called, but few are chosen."

The Question about Paying Taxes
(Mk 12.13–17; Lk 20.20–26)

15 Then the Phar'i·sees went and plotted to entrap him in what he said. 16 So they sent their disciples to him, along with the He·ro'di·ans, saying, "Teacher, we know that you are sincere, and teach the way of God in accordance with truth, and show deference to no one; for you do not regard people with partiality. 17 Tell us, then,

e Gk He *f* Or *keystone* *g* Gk *the fruits of it* *h* Other ancient authorities lack verse 44 what you think. Is it lawful to pay taxes to the emperor, or not?" [18] But Jesus, aware of their malice, said, "Why are you putting me to the test, you hypocrites? [19] Show me the coin used for the tax." And they brought him a denarius. [20] Then he said to them, "Whose head is this, and whose title?" [21] They answered, "The emperor's." Then he said to them, "Give therefore to the emperor the things that are the emperor's, and to God the things that are God's." [22] When they heard this, they were amazed; and they left him and went away.

The Question about the Resurrection
(Mk 12.18–27; Lk 20.27–40)

23 The same day some Sad'du·cees came to him, saying there is no resurrection; [i] and they asked him a question, saying, [24] "Teacher, Moses said, 'If a man dies childless, his brother shall marry the widow, and raise up children for his brother.' [25] Now there were seven brothers among us; the first married, and died childless, leaving the widow to his brother. [26] The second did the same, so also the third, down to the seventh. [27] Last of all, the woman herself died. [28] In the resurrection, then, whose wife of the seven will she be? For all of them had married her."

29 Jesus answered them, "You are wrong, because you know neither the scriptures nor the power of God. [30] For in the resurrection they neither marry nor are given in marriage, but are like angels [j] in heaven. [31] And as for the resurrection of the dead, have you not read what was said to you by God, [32] 'I am the God of Abraham, the God of Isaac, and the God of Jacob'? He is God not of the dead, but of the living." [33] And when the crowd heard it, they were astounded at his teaching.

The Greatest Commandment
(Mk 12.28–34; Lk 10.25–28)

34 When the Phar'i·sees heard that he had silenced the Sad'du·cees, they gathered together, [35] and one of them, a lawyer, asked him a question to test him. [36] "Teacher, which commandment in the law is the greatest?" [37] He said to him, " 'You shall love the Lord your God with all your heart, and with all your soul, and with all your mind.' [38] This is the greatest and first commandment. [39] And a second is like it: 'You shall love your neighbor as your-

self.' [40] On these two commandments hang all the law and the prophets."

The Question about David's Son
(Mk 12.35–37; Lk 20.41–44)

41 Now while the Phar'i·sees were gathered together, Jesus asked them this question: [42] "What do you think of the Messiah? [k] Whose son is he?" They said to him, "The son of David." [43] He said to them, "How is it then that David by the Spirit [l] calls him Lord, saying,
[44] 'The Lord said to my Lord,
"Sit at my right hand,
    until I put your enemies under
        your feet" '?
[45] If David thus calls him Lord, how can he be his son?" [46] No one was able to give him an answer, nor from that day did anyone dare to ask him any more questions.

Jesus Denounces Scribes and Pharisees
(Mk 12.38–40; Lk 20.45–47)

23 Then Jesus said to the crowds and to his disciples, [2] "The scribes and the Phar'i·sees sit on Moses' seat; [3] therefore, do whatever they teach you and follow it; but do not do as they do, for they do not practice what they teach. [4] They tie up heavy burdens, hard to bear, [m] and lay them on the shoulders of others; but they themselves are unwilling to lift a finger to move them. [5] They do all their deeds to be seen by others; for they make their phylacteries broad and their fringes long. [6] They love to have the place of honor at banquets and the best seats in the synagogues, [7] and to be greeted with respect in the marketplaces, and to have people call them rabbi. [8] But you are not to be called rabbi, for you have one teacher, and you are all students. [n] [9] And call no one your father on earth, for you have one Father—the one in heaven. [10] Nor are you to be called instructors, for you have one instructor, the Messiah. [o] [11] The greatest among you will be your servant. [12] All who exalt themselves will be humbled, and all who humble themselves will be exalted.

13 "But woe to you, scribes and Phar'i·sees, hypocrites! For you lock

[i] Other ancient authorities read *who say that there is no resurrection*   [j] Other ancient authorities add *of God*   [k] Or *Christ*   [l] Gk *in spirit*   [m] Other ancient authorities lack *hard to bear*   [n] Gk *brothers*   [o] Or *the Christ*

people out of the kingdom of heaven. For you do not go in yourselves, and when others are going in, you stop them. *p* 15 Woe to you, scribes and Phar'i·sees, hypocrites! For you cross sea and land to make a single convert, and you make the new convert twice as much a child of hell *q* as yourselves.

16 "Woe to you, blind guides, who say, 'Whoever swears by the sanctuary is bound by nothing, but whoever swears by the gold of the sanctuary is bound by the oath.' 17 You blind fools! For which is greater, the gold or the sanctuary that has made the gold sacred? 18 And you say, 'Whoever swears by the altar is bound by nothing, but whoever swears by the gift that is on the altar is bound by the oath.' 19 How blind you are! For which is greater, the gift or the altar that makes the gift sacred? 20 So whoever swears by the altar, swears by it and by everything on it; 21 and whoever swears by the sanctuary, swears by it and by the one who dwells in it; 22 and whoever swears by heaven, swears by the throne of God and by the one who is seated upon it.

23 "Woe to you, scribes and Phar'-i·sees, hypocrites! For you tithe mint, dill, and cummin, and have neglected the weightier matters of the law: justice and mercy and faith. It is these you ought to have practiced without neglecting the others. 24 You blind guides! You strain out a gnat but swallow a camel!

25 "Woe to you, scribes and Phar'-i·sees, hypocrites! For you clean the outside of the cup and of the plate, but inside they are full of greed and self-indulgence. 26 You blind Phar'i·see! First clean the inside of the cup, *r* so that the outside also may become clean.

27 "Woe to you, scribes and Phar'-i·sees, hypocrites! For you are like whitewashed tombs, which on the outside look beautiful, but inside they are full of the bones of the dead and of all kinds of filth. 28 So you also on the outside look righteous to others, but inside you are full of hypocrisy and lawlessness.

29 "Woe to you, scribes and Phar'-i·sees, hypocrites! For you build the tombs of the prophets and decorate the graves of the righteous, 30 and you say, 'If we had lived in the days of our ancestors, we would not have taken part with them in shedding the blood of the prophets.' 31 Thus you testify against

yourselves that you are descendants of those who murdered the prophets. 32 Fill up, then, the measure of your ancestors. 33 You snakes, you brood of vipers! How can you escape being sentenced to hell? *q* 34 Therefore I send you prophets, sages, and scribes, some of whom you will kill and crucify, and some you will flog in your synagogues and pursue from town to town, 35 so that upon you may come all the righteous blood shed on earth, from the blood of righteous Abel to the blood of Zech·a·ri'ah son of Bar·a·chi'ah, whom you murdered between the sanctuary and the altar. 36 Truly I tell you, all this will come upon this generation.

The Lament over Jerusalem
(Lk 13.34–35)

37 "Jerusalem, Jerusalem, the city that kills the prophets and stones those who are sent to it! How often have I desired to gather your children together as a hen gathers her brood under her wings, and you were not willing! 38 See, your house is left to you, desolate. *s* 39 For I tell you, you will not see me again until you say, 'Blessed is the one who comes in the name of the Lord.' "

The Destruction of the
Temple Foretold
(Mk 13.1–2; Lk 21.5–6)

24 As Jesus came out of the temple and was going away, his disciples came to point out to him the buildings of the temple. 2 Then he asked them, "You see all these, do you not? Truly I tell you, not one stone will be left here upon another; all will be thrown down."

Signs of the End of the Age
(Mk 13.3–8; Lk 21.7–11)

3 When he was sitting on the Mount of Olives, the disciples came to him privately, saying, "Tell us, when will this be, and what will be the sign of your coming and of the end of the

p Other authorities add here (or after verse 12) verse 14, *Woe to you, scribes and Pharisees, hypocrites! For you devour widows' houses and for the sake of appearance you make long prayers; therefore you will receive the greater condemnation*   *q* Gk *Gehenna*   *r* Other ancient authorities add *and of the plate*   *s* Other ancient authorities lack *desolate* age?" [4] Jesus answered them, "Beware that no one leads you astray. [5] For many will come in my name, saying, 'I am the Messiah!'[t] and they will lead many astray. [6] And you will hear of wars and rumors of wars; see that you are not alarmed; for this must take place, but the end is not yet. [7] For nation will rise against nation, and kingdom against kingdom, and there will be famines[u] and earthquakes in various places: [8] all this is but the beginning of the birth pangs.

Persecutions Foretold
(Mk 13.9–13; Lk 21.12–19)

9 "Then they will hand you over to be tortured and will put you to death, and you will be hated by all nations because of my name. [10] Then many will fall away,[v] and they will betray one another and hate one another. [11] And many false prophets will arise and lead many astray. [12] And because of the increase of lawlessness, the love of many will grow cold. [13] But the one who endures to the end will be saved. [14] And this good news[w] of the kingdom will be proclaimed throughout the world, as a testimony to all the nations; and then the end will come.

The Desolating Sacrilege
(Mk 13.14–23; Lk 17.23–24, 37; 21.20–24)

15 "So when you see the desolating sacrilege standing in the holy place, as was spoken of by the prophet Daniel (let the reader understand), [16] then those in Judea must flee to the mountains; [17] the one on the housetop must not go down to take what is in the house; [18] the one in the field must not turn back to get a coat. [19] Woe to those who are pregnant and to those who are nursing infants in those days! [20] Pray that your flight may not be in winter or on a sabbath. [21] For at that time there will be great suffering, such as has not been from the beginning of the world until now, no, and never will be. [22] And if those days had not been cut short, no one would be saved; but for the sake of the elect those days will be cut short. [23] Then if anyone says to you, 'Look! Here is the Messiah!'[t] or 'There he is!'—do not believe it. [24] For false messiahs[x] and false prophets will appear and produce great signs and omens, to lead astray, if possible, even the elect. [25] Take note, I have told you beforehand. [26] So, if they say to you, 'Look! He is in the wilderness,' do not go out.

If they say, 'Look! He is in the inner rooms,' do not believe it. [27] For as the lightning comes from the east and flashes as far as the west, so will be the coming of the Son of Man. [28] Wherever the corpse is, there the vultures will gather.

The Coming of the Son of Man
(Mk 13.24–27; Lk 21.25–28)

29 "Immediately after the suffering of those days
> the sun will be darkened,
>   and the moon will not give its light;
> the stars will fall from heaven,
>   and the powers of heaven will be shaken.

[30] Then the sign of the Son of Man will appear in heaven, and then all the tribes of the earth will mourn, and they will see 'the Son of Man coming on the clouds of heaven' with power and great glory. [31] And he will send out his angels with a loud trumpet call, and they will gather his elect from the four winds, from one end of heaven to the other.

The Lesson of the Fig Tree
(Mk 13.28–31; Lk 21.29–33)

32 "From the fig tree learn its lesson: as soon as its branch becomes tender and puts forth its leaves, you know that summer is near. [33] So also, when you see all these things, you know that he[y] is near, at the very gates. [34] Truly I tell you, this generation will not pass away until all these things have taken place. [35] Heaven and earth will pass away, but my words will not pass away.

The Necessity for Watchfulness
(Mk 13.32–37; Lk 17.26–27, 34–35; 21.34–36)

36 "But about that day and hour no one knows, neither the angels of heaven, nor the Son,[z] but only the Father. [37] For as the days of Noah were, so will be the coming of the Son of Man. [38] For as in those days before the flood they were eating and drinking, marrying and giving in marriage, until the day Noah entered the ark, [39] and they knew nothing until the flood came and swept them all away, so too

---

[t] Or the Christ   [u] Other ancient authorities add and pestilences
[v] Or stumble   [w] Or gospel   [x] Or christs
[y] Or it   [z] Other ancient authorities lack nor the Son

will be the coming of the Son of Man. 40 Then two will be in the field; one will be taken and one will be left. 41 Two women will be grinding meal together; one will be taken and one will be left. 42 Keep awake therefore, for you do not know on what day[a] your Lord is coming. 43 But understand this: if the owner of the house had known in what part of the night the thief was coming, he would have stayed awake and would not have let his house be broken into. 44 Therefore you also must be ready, for the Son of Man is coming at an unexpected hour.

The Faithful or the Unfaithful Slave
(Lk 12.41–48)

45 "Who then is the faithful and wise slave, whom his master has put in charge of his household, to give the other slaves[b] their allowance of food at the proper time? 46 Blessed is that slave whom his master will find at work when he arrives. 47 Truly I tell you, he will put that one in charge of all his possessions. 48 But if that wicked slave says to himself, 'My master is delayed,' 49 and he begins to beat his fellow slaves, and eats and drinks with drunkards, 50 the master of that slave will come on a day when he does not expect him and at an hour that he does not know. 51 He will cut him in pieces[c] and put him with the hypocrites, where there will be weeping and gnashing of teeth.

The Parable of the Ten Bridesmaids

25 "Then the kingdom of heaven will be like this. Ten bridesmaids[d] took their lamps and went to meet the bridegroom.[e] 2 Five of them were foolish, and five were wise. 3 When the foolish took their lamps, they took no oil with them; 4 but the wise took flasks of oil with their lamps. 5 As the bridegroom was delayed, all of them became drowsy and slept. 6 But at midnight there was a shout, 'Look! Here is the bridegroom! Come out to meet him.' 7 Then all those bridesmaids[d] got up and trimmed their lamps. 8 The foolish said to the wise, 'Give us some of your oil, for our lamps are going out.' 9 But the wise replied, 'No! there will not be enough for you and for us; you had better go to the dealers and buy some for yourselves.' 10 And while they went to buy it, the bridegroom came, and those who were ready went with him into the wedding banquet; and the door was shut. 11 Later the other bridesmaids[d] came also, saying, 'Lord, lord, open to us.' 12 But he replied, 'Truly I tell you, I do not know you.' 13 Keep awake therefore, for you know neither the day nor the hour.[f]

The Parable of the Talents
(Lk 19.11–27)

14 "For it is as if a man, going on a journey, summoned his slaves and entrusted his property to them; 15 to one he gave five talents,[g] to another two, to another one, to each according to his ability. Then he went away. 16 The one who had received the five talents went off at once and traded with them, and made five more talents. 17 In the same way, the one who had the two talents made two more talents. 18 But the one who had received the one talent went off and dug a hole in the ground and hid his master's money. 19 After a long time the master of those slaves came and settled accounts with them. 20 Then the one who had received the five talents came forward, bringing five more talents, saying, 'Master, you handed over to me five talents; see, I have made five more talents.' 21 His master said to him, 'Well done, good and trustworthy slave; you have been trustworthy in a few things, I will put you in charge of many things; enter into the joy of your master.' 22 And the one with the two talents also came forward, saying, 'Master, you handed over to me two talents; see, I have made two more talents.' 23 His master said to him, 'Well done, good and trustworthy slave; you have been trustworthy in a few things, I will put you in charge of many things; enter into the joy of your master.' 24 Then the one who had received the one talent also came forward, saying, 'Master, I knew that you were a harsh man, reaping where you did not sow, and gathering where you did not scatter seed; 25 so I was afraid, and I went and hid your talent in the ground. Here you have what is yours.' 26 But his master

---

[a] Other ancient authorities read *at what hour*   [b] Gk *to give them*   [c] Or *cut him off*   [d] Gk *virgins*   [e] Other ancient authorities add *and the bride*   [f] Other ancient authorities add *in which the Son of Man is coming*   [g] A talent was worth more than fifteen years' wages of a laborer

replied, 'You wicked and lazy slave! You knew, did you, that I reap where I did not sow, and gather where I did not scatter? ²⁷Then you ought to have invested my money with the bankers, and on my return I would have received what was my own with interest. ²⁸So take the talent from him, and give it to the one with the ten talents. ²⁹For to all those who have, more will be given, and they will have an abundance; but from those who have nothing, even what they have will be taken away. ³⁰As for this worthless slave, throw him into the outer darkness, where there will be weeping and gnashing of teeth.'

The Judgment of the Nations

31 "When the Son of Man comes in his glory, and all the angels with him, then he will sit on the throne of his glory. ³²All the nations will be gathered before him, and he will separate people one from another as a shepherd separates the sheep from the goats, ³³and he will put the sheep at his right hand and the goats at the left. ³⁴Then the king will say to those at his right hand, 'Come, you that are blessed by my Father, inherit the kingdom prepared for you from the foundation of the world; ³⁵for I was hungry and you gave me food, I was thirsty and you gave me something to drink, I was a stranger and you welcomed me, ³⁶I was naked and you gave me clothing, I was sick and you took care of me, I was in prison and you visited me.' ³⁷Then the righteous will answer him, 'Lord, when was it that we saw you hungry and gave you food, or thirsty and gave you something to drink? ³⁸And when was it that we saw you a stranger and welcomed you, or naked and gave you clothing? ³⁹And when was it that we saw you sick or in prison and visited you?' ⁴⁰And the king will answer them, 'Truly I tell you, just as you did it to one of the least of these who are members of my family,ʰ you did it to me.' ⁴¹Then he will say to those at his left hand, 'You that are accursed, depart from me into the eternal fire prepared for the devil and his angels; ⁴²for I was hungry and you gave me no food, I was thirsty and you gave me nothing to drink, ⁴³I was a stranger and you did not welcome me, naked and you did not give me clothing, sick and in prison and you did not visit me.' ⁴⁴Then they also will answer, 'Lord, when was it that we saw you hungry or thirsty or a stranger or naked or sick or in prison, and did not take care of you?' ⁴⁵Then he will answer them, 'Truly I tell you, just as you did not do it to one of the least of these, you did not do it to me.' ⁴⁶And these will go away into eternal punishment, but the righteous into eternal life."

The Plot to Kill Jesus
(Mk 14.1–2; Lk 22.1–2; Jn 11.45–53)

26 When Jesus had finished saying all these things, he said to his disciples, ²"You know that after two days the Passover is coming, and the Son of Man will be handed over to be crucified."

3 Then the chief priests and the elders of the people gathered in the palace of the high priest, who was called Ca'i·a·phas, ⁴and they conspired to arrest Jesus by stealth and kill him. ⁵But they said, "Not during the festival, or there may be a riot among the people."

The Anointing at Bethany
(Mk 14.3–9; Jn 12.1–8)

6 Now while Jesus was at Beth'a·ny in the house of Simon the leper,ⁱ ⁷a woman came to him with an alabaster jar of very costly ointment, and she poured it on his head as he sat at the table. ⁸But when the disciples saw it, they were angry and said, "Why this waste? ⁹For this ointment could have been sold for a large sum, and the money given to the poor." ¹⁰But Jesus, aware of this, said to them, "Why do you trouble the woman? She has performed a good service for me. ¹¹For you always have the poor with you, but you will not always have me. ¹²By pouring this ointment on my body she has prepared me for burial. ¹³Truly I tell you, wherever this good newsʲ is proclaimed in the whole world, what she has done will be told in remembrance of her."

Judas Agrees to Betray Jesus
(Mk 14.10–11; Lk 22.3–6)

14 Then one of the twelve, who was called Judas Is·car'i·ot, went to the chief priests ¹⁵and said, "What will you give me if I betray him to you?" They paid him thirty pieces of silver.

ʰGk *these my brothers*   ⁱThe terms *leper* and *leprosy* can refer to several diseases   ʲOr *gospel*

M
A
T
T
H
E
W

16 And from that moment he began to look for an opportunity to betray him.

The Passover with the Disciples
(Mk 14.12–21; Lk 22.7–13)

17 On the first day of Unleavened Bread the disciples came to Jesus, saying, "Where do you want us to make the preparations for you to eat the Passover?" 18 He said, "Go into the city to a certain man, and say to him, 'The Teacher says, My time is near; I will keep the Passover at your house with my disciples.' " 19 So the disciples did as Jesus had directed them, and they prepared the Passover meal.

20 When it was evening, he took his place with the twelve;*k* 21 and while they were eating, he said, "Truly I tell you, one of you will betray me." 22 And they became greatly distressed and began to say to him one after another, "Surely not I, Lord?" 23 He answered, "The one who has dipped his hand into the bowl with me will betray me. 24 The Son of Man goes as it is written of him, but woe to that one by whom the Son of Man is betrayed! It would have been better for that one not to have been born." 25 Judas, who betrayed him, said, "Surely not I, Rabbi?" He replied, "You have said so."

The Institution of the Lord's Supper
(Mk 14.22–26; Lk 22.14–23; 1 Cor 11.23–26)

26 While they were eating, Jesus took a loaf of bread, and after blessing it he broke it, gave it to the disciples, and said, "Take, eat; this is my body." 27 Then he took a cup, and after giving thanks he gave it to them, saying, "Drink from it, all of you; 28 for this is my blood of the*l* covenant, which is poured out for many for the forgiveness of sins. 29 I tell you, I will never again drink of this fruit of the vine until that day when I drink it new with you in my Father's kingdom."

30 When they had sung the hymn, they went out to the Mount of Olives.

Peter's Denial Foretold
(Mk 14.27–31; Lk 22.31–34; Jn 13.36–38)

31 Then Jesus said to them, "You will all become deserters because of me this night; for it is written,

'I will strike the shepherd,
    and the sheep of the flock will
        be scattered.'

32 But after I am raised up, I will go ahead of you to Galilee." 33 Peter said to him, "Though all become deserters because of you, I will never desert you." 34 Jesus said to him, "Truly I tell you, this very night, before the cock crows, you will deny me three times." 35 Peter said to him, "Even though I must die with you, I will not deny you." And so said all the disciples.

Jesus Prays in Gethsemane
(Mk 14.32–42; Lk 22.39–46)

36 Then Jesus went with them to a place called Geth·sem'a·nē; and he said to his disciples, "Sit here while I go over there and pray." 37 He took with him Peter and the two sons of Zeb'e·dee, and began to be grieved and agitated. 38 Then he said to them, "I am deeply grieved, even to death; remain here, and stay awake with me." 39 And going a little farther, he threw himself on the ground and prayed, "My Father, if it is possible, let this cup pass from me; yet not what I want but what you want." 40 Then he came to the disciples and found them sleeping; and he said to Peter, "So, could you not stay awake with me one hour? 41 Stay awake and pray that you may not come into the time of trial;*m* the spirit indeed is willing, but the flesh is weak." 42 Again he went away for the second time and prayed, "My Father, if this cannot pass unless I drink it, your will be done." 43 Again he came and found them sleeping, for their eyes were heavy. 44 So leaving them again, he went away and prayed for the third time, saying the same words. 45 Then he came to the disciples and said to them, "Are you still sleeping and taking your rest? See, the hour is at hand, and the Son of Man is betrayed into the hands of sinners. 46 Get up, let us be going. See, my betrayer is at hand."

The Betrayal and Arrest of Jesus
(Mk 14.43–52; Lk 22.47–53; Jn 18.1–11)

47 While he was still speaking, Judas, one of the twelve, arrived; with him was a large crowd with swords and clubs, from the chief priests and the elders of the people. 48 Now the betrayer had given them a sign, saying, "The one I will kiss is the man; arrest him." 49 At once he came up to Jesus and said, "Greetings, Rabbi!" and kissed him. 50 Jesus said to him, "Friend, do what you are here to do."

k Other ancient authorities add *disciples*
l Other ancient authorities add *new*
m Or *into temptation*

Then they came and laid hands on Jesus and arrested him. 51 Suddenly, one of those with Jesus put his hand on his sword, drew it, and struck the slave of the high priest, cutting off his ear. 52 Then Jesus said to him, "Put your sword back into its place; for all who take the sword will perish by the sword. 53 Do you think that I cannot appeal to my Father, and he will at once send me more than twelve legions of angels? 54 But how then would the scriptures be fulfilled, which say it must happen in this way?" 55 At that hour Jesus said to the crowds, "Have you come out with swords and clubs to arrest me as though I were a bandit? Day after day I sat in the temple teaching, and you did not arrest me. 56 But all this has taken place, so that the scriptures of the prophets may be fulfilled." Then all the disciples deserted him and fled.

Jesus before the High Priest
(Mk 14.53–65; Lk 22.66–71;
Jn 18.12–14, 19–24)

57 Those who had arrested Jesus took him to Ca'i·a·phas the high priest, in whose house the scribes and the elders had gathered. 58 But Peter was following him at a distance, as far as the courtyard of the high priest; and going inside, he sat with the guards in order to see how this would end. 59 Now the chief priests and the whole council were looking for false testimony against Jesus so that they might put him to death, 60 but they found none, though many false witnesses came forward. At last two came forward 61 and said, "This fellow said, 'I am able to destroy the temple of God and to build it in three days.'" 62 The high priest stood up and said, "Have you no answer? What is it that they testify against you?" 63 But Jesus was silent. Then the high priest said to him, "I put you under oath before the living God, tell us if you are the Messiah, n the Son of God." 64 Jesus said to him, "You have said so. But I tell you,

From now on you will see the
Son of Man
seated at the right hand of
Power
and coming on the clouds of
heaven."

65 Then the high priest tore his clothes and said, "He has blasphemed! Why do we still need witnesses? You have now heard his blasphemy. 66 What is

your verdict?" They answered, "He deserves death." 67 Then they spat in his face and struck him; and some slapped him, 68 saying, "Prophesy to us, you Messiah! n Who is it that struck you?"

Peter's Denial of Jesus
(Mk 14.66–72; Lk 22.54–62;
Jn 18.15–18, 25–27)

69 Now Peter was sitting outside in the courtyard. A servant-girl came to him and said, "You also were with Jesus the Galilean." 70 But he denied it before all of them, saying, "I do not know what you are talking about." 71 When he went out to the porch, another servant-girl saw him, and she said to the bystanders, "This man was with Jesus of Nazareth." o 72 Again he denied it with an oath, "I do not know the man." 73 After a little while the bystanders came up and said to Peter, "Certainly you are also one of them, for your accent betrays you." 74 Then he began to curse, and he swore an oath, "I do not know the man!" At that moment the cock crowed. 75 Then Peter remembered what Jesus had said: "Before the cock crows, you will deny me three times." And he went out and wept bitterly.

Jesus Brought before Pilate
(Mk 15.1; Lk 23.1; Jn 18.28)

27 When morning came, all the chief priests and the elders of the people conferred together against Jesus in order to bring about his death. 2 They bound him, led him away, and handed him over to Pilate the governor.

The Suicide of Judas
(Acts 1.18–19)

3 When Judas, his betrayer, saw that Jesus p was condemned, he repented and brought back the thirty pieces of silver to the chief priests and the elders. 4 He said, "I have sinned by betraying innocent q blood." But they said, "What is that to us? See to it yourself." 5 Throwing down the pieces of silver in the temple, he departed; and he went and hanged himself. 6 But the chief priests, taking the pieces of silver, said, "It is not lawful to put them into the treasury, since they are blood money." 7 After conferring together,

n Or Christ   o Gk the Nazorean
p Gk he   q Other ancient authorities
read *righteous*

they used them to buy the potter's field as a place to bury foreigners. [8] For this reason that field has been called the Field of Blood to this day. [9] Then was fulfilled what had been spoken through the prophet Jer·e·mi'ah,[r] "And they took[s] the thirty pieces of silver, the price of the one on whom a price had been set,[t] on whom some of the people of Israel had set a price, [10] and they gave[u] them for the potter's field, as the Lord commanded me."

Pilate Questions Jesus
(Mk 15.2–5; Lk 23.2–5; Jn 18.29–38a)

11 Now Jesus stood before the governor; and the governor asked him, "Are you the King of the Jews?" Jesus said, "You say so." [12] But when he was accused by the chief priests and elders, he did not answer. [13] Then Pilate said to him, "Do you not hear how many accusations they make against you?" [14] But he gave him no answer, not even to a single charge, so that the governor was greatly amazed.

Barabbas or Jesus?
(Mk 15.6–14; Lk 23.13–24; Jn 18.39–40)

15 Now at the festival the governor was accustomed to release a prisoner for the crowd, anyone whom they wanted. [16] At that time they had a notorious prisoner, called Jesus[v] Ba·rab'bas. [17] So after they had gathered, Pilate said to them, "Whom do you want me to release for you, Jesus[v] Ba·rab'bas or Jesus who is called the Messiah?"[w] [18] For he realized that it was out of jealousy that they had handed him over. [19] While he was sitting on the judgment seat, his wife sent word to him, "Have nothing to do with that innocent man, for today I have suffered a great deal because of a dream about him." [20] Now the chief priests and the elders persuaded the crowds to ask for Ba·rab'bas and to have Jesus killed. [21] The governor again said to them, "Which of the two do you want me to release for you?" And they said, "Ba·rab'bas." [22] Pilate said to them, "Then what should I do with Jesus who is called the Messiah?"[w] All of them said, "Let him be crucified!" [23] Then he asked, "Why, what evil has he done?" But they shouted all the more, "Let him be crucified!"

Pilate Hands Jesus over to Be Crucified
(Mk 15.15; Lk 23.25; Jn 19.16)

24 So when Pilate saw that he could do nothing, but rather that a riot was beginning, he took some water and washed his hands before the crowd, saying, "I am innocent of this man's blood;[x] see to it yourselves." [25] Then the people as a whole answered, "His blood be on us and on our children!" [26] So he released Ba·rab'bas for them; and after flogging Jesus, he handed him over to be crucified.

The Soldiers Mock Jesus
(Mk 15.16–20)

27 Then the soldiers of the governor took Jesus into the governor's headquarters,[y] and they gathered the whole cohort around him. [28] They stripped him and put a scarlet robe on him, [29] and after twisting some thorns into a crown, they put it on his head. They put a reed in his right hand and knelt before him and mocked him, saying, "Hail, King of the Jews!" [30] They spat on him, and took the reed and struck him on the head. [31] After mocking him, they stripped him of the robe and put his own clothes on him. Then they led him away to crucify him.

The Crucifixion of Jesus
(Mk 15.21–32; Lk 23.26–43; Jn 19.16b–27)

32 As they went out, they came upon a man from Cy·re'ne named Simon; they compelled this man to carry his cross. [33] And when they came to a place called Gol'go·tha (which means Place of a Skull), [34] they offered him wine to drink, mixed with gall; but when he tasted it, he would not drink it. [35] And when they had crucified him, they divided his clothes among themselves by casting lots;[z] [36] then they sat down there and kept watch over him. [37] Over his head they put the charge against him, which read, "This is Jesus, the King of the Jews."

38 Then two bandits were crucified with him, one on his right and one on

r Other ancient authorities read *Zechariah* or *Isaiah*   s Or *I took*   t Or *the price of the precious One*   u Other ancient authorities read *I gave*   v Other ancient authorities lack *Jesus*   w Or *the Christ*   x Other ancient authorities read *this righteous blood*, or *this righteous man's blood*   y Gk *the praetorium*   z Other ancient authorities add *in order that what had been spoken through the prophet might be fulfilled*, "They divided my clothes among themselves, and for my clothing they cast lots."

his left. ³⁹Those who passed by derided[a] him, shaking their heads ⁴⁰and saying, "You who would destroy the temple and build it in three days, save yourself! If you are the Son of God, come down from the cross." ⁴¹In the same way the chief priests also, along with the scribes and elders, were mocking him, saying, ⁴²"He saved others; he cannot save himself.[b] He is the King of Israel; let him come down from the cross now, and we will believe in him. ⁴³He trusts in God; let God deliver him now, if he wants to; for he said, 'I am God's Son.'" ⁴⁴The bandits who were crucified with him also taunted him in the same way.

The Death of Jesus
(Mk 15.33–41; Lk 23.44–49; Jn 19.28–30)

45 From noon on, darkness came over the whole land[c] until three in the afternoon. ⁴⁶And about three o'clock Jesus cried with a loud voice, "Ē′li, Ē′li, le·ma′ sa·bach′tha·ni?" that is, "My God, my God, why have you forsaken me?" ⁴⁷When some of the bystanders heard it, they said, "This man is calling for E·li′jah." ⁴⁸At once one of them ran and got a sponge, filled it with sour wine, put it on a stick, and gave it to him to drink. ⁴⁹But the others said, "Wait, let us see whether E·li′jah will come to save him."[d] ⁵⁰Then Jesus cried again with a loud voice, and breathed his last.[e] ⁵¹At that moment the curtain of the temple was torn in two, from top to bottom. The earth shook, and the rocks were split. ⁵²The tombs also were opened, and many bodies of the saints who had fallen asleep were raised. ⁵³After his resurrection they came out of the tombs and entered the holy city and appeared to many. ⁵⁴Now when the centurion and those with him, who were keeping watch over Jesus, saw the earthquake and what took place, they were terrified and said, "Truly this man was God's Son!"[f]

55 Many women were also there, looking on from a distance; they had followed Jesus from Galilee and had provided for him. ⁵⁶Among them were Mary Mag′da·lēne, and Mary the mother of James and Joseph, and the mother of the sons of Zeb′e·dee.

The Burial of Jesus
(Mk 15.42–47; Lk 23.50–56; Jn 19.38–42)

57 When it was evening, there came a rich man from Ar·i·ma·thē′a, named Joseph, who was also a disciple of Jesus. ⁵⁸He went to Pilate and asked for the body of Jesus; then Pilate ordered it to be given to him. ⁵⁹So Joseph took the body and wrapped it in a clean linen cloth ⁶⁰and laid it in his own new tomb, which he had hewn in the rock. He then rolled a great stone to the door of the tomb and went away. ⁶¹Mary Mag′da·lēne and the other Mary were there, sitting opposite the tomb.

The Guard at the Tomb

62 The next day, that is, after the day of Preparation, the chief priests and the Phar′i·sees gathered before Pilate ⁶³and said, "Sir, we remember what that impostor said while he was still alive, 'After three days I will rise again.' ⁶⁴Therefore command the tomb to be made secure until the third day; otherwise his disciples may go and steal him away, and tell the people, 'He has been raised from the dead,' and the last deception would be worse than the first." ⁶⁵Pilate said to them, "You have a guard[g] of soldiers; go, make it as secure as you can."[h] ⁶⁶So they went with the guard and made the tomb secure by sealing the stone.

The Resurrection of Jesus
(Mk 16.1–8; Lk 24.1–12; Jn 20.1–10)

28 After the sabbath, as the first day of the week was dawning, Mary Mag′da·lēne and the other Mary went to see the tomb. ²And suddenly there was a great earthquake; for an angel of the Lord, descending from heaven, came and rolled back the stone and sat on it. ³His appearance was like lightning, and his clothing white as snow. ⁴For fear of him the guards shook and became like dead men. ⁵But the angel said to the women, "Do not be afraid; I know that you are looking for Jesus who was crucified. ⁶He is not here; for he has been raised, as he said. Come, see the place where he[i] lay. ⁷Then go quickly and tell his disciples, 'He has been raised from the

---

[a] Or *blasphemed*   [b] Or *is he unable to save himself?*   [c] Or *earth*   [d] Other ancient authorities add *And another took a spear and pierced his side, and out came water and blood*   [e] Or *gave up his spirit*   [f] Or *a son of God*   [g] Or *Take a guard*   [h] Gk *you know how*   [i] Other ancient authorities read *the Lord*

dead,[j] and indeed he is going ahead of you to Galilee; there you will see him.' This is my message for you." [8] So they left the tomb quickly with fear and great joy, and ran to tell his disciples. [9] Suddenly Jesus met them and said, "Greetings!" And they came to him, took hold of his feet, and worshiped him. [10] Then Jesus said to them, "Do not be afraid; go and tell my brothers to go to Galilee; there they will see me."

The Report of the Guard

11 While they were going, some of the guard went into the city and told the chief priests everything that had happened. [12] After the priests[k] had assembled with the elders, they devised a plan to give a large sum of money to the soldiers, [13] telling them, "You must say, 'His disciples came by night and stole him away while we were asleep.' [14] If this comes to the governor's ears, we will satisfy him and keep you out of trouble." [15] So they took the money and did as they were directed. And this story is still told among the Jews to this day.

The Commissioning of the Disciples
(Mk 16.14–18; Lk 24.36–49; Jn 20.19–23; Acts 1.6–8)

16 Now the eleven disciples went to Galilee, to the mountain to which Jesus had directed them. [17] When they saw him, they worshiped him; but some doubted. [18] And Jesus came and said to them, "All authority in heaven and on earth has been given to me. [19] Go therefore and make disciples of all nations, baptizing them in the name of the Father and of the Son and of the Holy Spirit, [20] and teaching them to obey everything that I have commanded you. And remember, I am with you always, to the end of the age."[l]

[j] Other ancient authorities lack *from the dead* [k] Gk *they* [l] Other ancient authorities add *Amen*

The Gospel According to

MARK

The Proclamation of John the Baptist
(Mt 3.1–12; Lk 3.1–20; Jn 1.19–28)

1 The beginning of the good news[a] of Jesus Christ, the Son of God.[b]
2 As it is written in the prophet I·sai'ah,[c]

"See, I am sending my
    messenger ahead of you,[d]
who will prepare your way;
3 the voice of one crying out in the wilderness:
'Prepare the way of the Lord,
    make his paths straight,' "

[4] John the baptizer appeared[e] in the wilderness, proclaiming a baptism of repentance for the forgiveness of sins. [5] And people from the whole Judean countryside and all the people of Jerusalem were going out to him, and were baptized by him in the river Jordan, confessing their sins. [6] Now John was clothed with camel's hair, with a leather belt around his waist, and he ate locusts and wild honey. [7] He proclaimed, "The one who is more powerful than I is coming after me; I am not worthy to stoop down and untie the thong of his sandals. [8] I have baptized you with[f] water; but he will baptize you with[f] the Holy Spirit."

The Baptism of Jesus
(Mt 3.13–17; Lk 3.21–22; Jn 1.29–34)

9 In those days Jesus came from Nazareth of Galilee and was baptized by John in the Jordan. [10] And just as he was coming up out of the water, he saw the heavens torn apart and the Spirit

[a] Or *gospel* [b] Other ancient authorities lack *the Son of God* [c] Other ancient authorities read *in the prophets* [d] Gk *before your face* [e] Other ancient authorities read *John was baptizing* [f] Or *in*

descending like a dove on him. ¹¹And a voice came from heaven, "You are my Son, the Beloved;*g* with you I am well pleased."

The Temptation of Jesus
(Mt 4.1–11; Lk 4.1–13)

12 And the Spirit immediately drove him out into the wilderness. ¹³He was in the wilderness forty days, tempted by Satan; and he was with the wild beasts; and the angels waited on him.

The Beginning of the Galilean Ministry
(Mt 4.12–17; Lk 4.14–15)

14 Now after John was arrested, Jesus came to Galilee, proclaiming the good news*h* of God,*i* ¹⁵and saying, "The time is fulfilled, and the kingdom of God has come near;*j* repent, and believe in the good news."*h*

Jesus Calls the First Disciples
(Mt 4.18–22; Lk 5.1–11)

16 As Jesus passed along the Sea of Galilee, he saw Simon and his brother Andrew casting a net into the sea—for they were fishermen. ¹⁷And Jesus said to them, "Follow me and I will make you fish for people." ¹⁸And immediately they left their nets and followed him. ¹⁹As he went a little farther, he saw James son of Zeb′e·dee and his brother John, who were in their boat mending the nets. ²⁰Immediately he called them; and they left their father Zeb′e·dee in the boat with the hired men, and followed him.

The Man with an Unclean Spirit
(Lk 4.31–37)

21 They went to Ca·per′na·um; and when the sabbath came, he entered the synagogue and taught. ²²They were astounded at his teaching, for he taught them as one having authority, and not as the scribes. ²³Just then there was in their synagogue a man with an unclean spirit, ²⁴and he cried out, "What have you to do with us, Jesus of Nazareth? Have you come to destroy us? I know who you are, the Holy One of God." ²⁵But Jesus rebuked him, saying, "Be silent, and come out of him!" ²⁶And the unclean spirit, convulsing him and crying with a loud voice, came out of him. ²⁷They were all amazed, and they kept on asking one another, "What is this? A new teaching—with authority! He*k* com-

mands even the unclean spirits, and they obey him." ²⁸At once his fame began to spread throughout the surrounding region of Galilee.

Jesus Heals Many at Simon's House
(Mt. 8.14–17; Lk 4.38–41)

29 As soon as they*l* left the synagogue, they entered the house of Simon and Andrew, with James and John. ³⁰Now Simon's mother-in-law was in bed with a fever, and they told him about her at once. ³¹He came and took her by the hand and lifted her up. Then the fever left her, and she began to serve them.

32 That evening, at sundown, they brought to him all who were sick or possessed with demons. ³³And the whole city was gathered around the door. ³⁴And he cured many who were sick with various diseases, and cast out many demons; and he would not permit the demons to speak, because they knew him.

A Preaching Tour in Galilee
(Mt 4.23–25; Lk 4.42–44)

35 In the morning, while it was still very dark, he got up and went out to a deserted place, and there he prayed. ³⁶And Simon and his companions hunted for him. ³⁷When they found him, they said to him, "Everyone is searching for you." ³⁸He answered, "Let us go on to the neighboring towns, so that I may proclaim the message there also; for that is what I came out to do." ³⁹And he went throughout Galilee, proclaiming the message in their synagogues and casting out demons.

Jesus Cleanses a Leper
(Mt 8.1–4; Lk 5.12–16)

40 A leper*m* came to him begging him, and kneeling*n* he said to him, "If you choose, you can make me clean." ⁴¹Moved with pity,*o* Jesus*p* stretched out his hand and touched him, and said to him, "I do choose. Be made clean!" ⁴²Immediately the leprosy*m* left him, and he was made clean. ⁴³After sternly

*g*Or *my beloved Son*   *h*Or *gospel*
*i*Other ancient authorities read *of the kingdom*   *j*Or *is at hand*   *k*Or *A new teaching! With authority he*   *l*Other ancient authorities read *he*
*m*The terms *leper* and *leprosy* can refer to several diseases   *n*Other ancient authorities lack *kneeling*   *o*Other ancient authorities read *anger*   *p*Gk *he*

warning him he sent him away at once, [44] saying to him, "See that you say nothing to anyone; but go, show yourself to the priest, and offer for your cleansing what Moses commanded, as a testimony to them." [45] But he went out and began to proclaim it freely, and to spread the word, so that Jesus[q] could no longer go into a town openly, but stayed out in the country; and people came to him from every quarter.

Jesus Heals a Paralytic
(Mt 9.2–8; Lk 5.17–26)

2 When he returned to Ca·per'-na·um after some days, it was reported that he was at home. [2] So many gathered around that there was no longer room for them, not even in front of the door; and he was speaking the word to them. [3] Then some people[r] came, bringing to him a paralyzed man, carried by four of them. [4] And when they could not bring him to Jesus because of the crowd, they removed the roof above him; and after having dug through it, they let down the mat on which the paralytic lay. [5] When Jesus saw their faith, he said to the paralytic, "Son, your sins are forgiven." [6] Now some of the scribes were sitting there, questioning in their hearts, [7] "Why does this fellow speak in this way? It is blasphemy! Who can forgive sins but God alone?" [8] At once Jesus perceived in his spirit that they were discussing these questions among themselves; and he said to them, "Why do you raise such questions in your hearts? [9] Which is easier, to say to the paralytic, 'Your sins are forgiven,' or to say, 'Stand up and take your mat and walk'? [10] But so that you may know that the Son of Man has authority on earth to forgive sins"—he said to the paralytic— [11] "I say to you, stand up, take your mat and go to your home." [12] And he stood up, and immediately took the mat and went out before all of them; so that they were all amazed and glorified God, saying, "We have never seen anything like this!"

Jesus Calls Levi
(Mt 9.9–13; Lk 5.27–32)

[13] Jesus[s] went out again beside the sea; the whole crowd gathered around him, and he taught them. [14] As he was walking along, he saw Levi son of Al·phae'us sitting at the tax booth, and he said to him, "Follow me." And he got up and followed him.

[15] And as he sat at dinner[t] in Levi's[u] house, many tax collectors and sinners were also sitting[v] with Jesus and his disciples—for there were many who followed him. [16] When the scribes of[w] the Phar'i·sees saw that he was eating with sinners and tax collectors, they said to his disciples, "Why does he eat[x] with tax collectors and sinners?" [17] When Jesus heard this, he said to them, "Those who are well have no need of a physician, but those who are sick; I have come to call not the righteous but sinners."

The Question about Fasting
(Mt 9.14–17; Lk 5.33–39)

[18] Now John's disciples and the Phar'i·sees were fasting; and people came and said to him, "Why do John's disciples and the disciples of the Phar'-i·sees fast, but your disciples do not fast?" [19] Jesus said to them, "The wedding guests cannot fast while the bridegroom is with them, can they? As long as they have the bridegroom with them, they cannot fast. [20] The days will come when the bridegroom is taken away from them, and then they will fast on that day.

[21] "No one sews a piece of unshrunk cloth on an old cloak; otherwise, the patch pulls away from it, the new from the old, and a worse tear is made. [22] And no one puts new wine into old wineskins; otherwise, the wine will burst the skins, and the wine is lost, and so are the skins; but one puts new wine into fresh wineskins."[y]

Pronouncement about the Sabbath
(Mt 12.1–8; Lk 6.1–5)

[23] One sabbath he was going through the grainfields; and as they made their way his disciples began to pluck heads of grain. [24] The Phar'i·sees said to him, "Look, why are they doing what is not lawful on the sabbath?" [25] And he said to them, "Have you never read what David did when he and his companions were hungry and in need of food? [26] He entered the house of God, when A·bi'a·thar was

[q] Gk he [r] Gk they [s] Gk He
[t] Gk reclined [u] Gk his [v] Gk reclining
[w] Other ancient authorities read *and*
[x] Other ancient authorities add *and drink*
[y] Other ancient authorities lack *but one puts new wine into fresh wineskins*

high priest, and ate the bread of the Presence, which it is not lawful for any but the priests to eat, and he gave some to his companions." 27 Then he said to them, "The sabbath was made for humankind, and not humankind for the sabbath; 28 so the Son of Man is lord even of the sabbath."

The Man with a Withered Hand
(Mt 12.9–14; Lk 6.6–11)

3 Again he entered the synagogue, and a man was there who had a withered hand. 2 They watched him to see whether he would cure him on the sabbath, so that they might accuse him. 3 And he said to the man who had the withered hand, "Come forward." 4 Then he said to them, "Is it lawful to do good or to do harm on the sabbath, to save life or to kill?" But they were silent. 5 He looked around at them with anger; he was grieved at their hardness of heart and said to the man, "Stretch out your hand." He stretched it out, and his hand was restored. 6 The Phar'i·sees went out and immediately conspired with the He·rō'di·ans against him, how to destroy him.

A Multitude at the Seaside
(Mt 12.15–21)

7 Jesus departed with his disciples to the sea, and a great multitude from Galilee followed him; 8 hearing all that he was doing, they came to him in great numbers from Judea, Jerusalem, Id·u·mē'a, beyond the Jordan, and the region around Tȳre and Sī'don. 9 He told his disciples to have a boat ready for him because of the crowd, so that they would not crush him; 10 for he had cured many, so that all who had diseases pressed upon him to touch him. 11 Whenever the unclean spirits saw him, they fell down before him and shouted, "You are the Son of God!" 12 But he sternly ordered them not to make him known.

Jesus Appoints the Twelve
(Mt 10.1–4; Lk 6.12–16)

13 He went up the mountain and called to him those whom he wanted, and they came to him. 14 And he appointed twelve, whom he also named apostles, z to be with him, and to be sent out to proclaim the message, 15 and to have authority to cast out demons. 16 So he appointed the twelve: a Simon (to whom he gave the name Pe-

ter); 17 James son of Zeb'e·dee and John the brother of James (to whom he gave the name Bō·a·ner'gēs, that is, Sons of Thunder); 18 and Andrew, and Philip, and Bartholomew, and Matthew, and Thomas, and James son of Al·phae'us, and Thad·dae'us, and Simon the Cā·na·nae'an, 19 and Judas Is·car'i·ot, who betrayed him.

Jesus and Beelzebul
(Mt 12.22–32; Lk 11.14–23)

Then he went home; 20 and the crowd came together again, so that they could not even eat. 21 When his family heard it, they went out to restrain him, for people were saying, "He has gone out of his mind." 22 And the scribes who came down from Jerusalem said, "He has Bē·el'ze·bul, and by the ruler of the demons he casts out demons." 23 And he called them to him, and spoke to them in parables, "How can Satan cast out Satan? 24 If a kingdom is divided against itself, that kingdom cannot stand. 25 And if a house is divided against itself, that house will not be able to stand. 26 And if Satan has risen up against himself and is divided, he cannot stand, but his end has come. 27 But no one can enter a strong man's house and plunder his property without first tying up the strong man; then indeed the house can be plundered. 28 "Truly I tell you, people will be forgiven for their sins and whatever blasphemies they utter; 29 but whoever blasphemes against the Holy Spirit can never have forgiveness, but is guilty of an eternal sin"— 30 for they had said, "He has an unclean spirit."

The True Kindred of Jesus
(Mt 12.46–50; Lk 8.19–21)

31 Then his mother and his brothers came; and standing outside, they sent to him and called him. 32 A crowd was sitting around him; and they said to him, "Your mother and your brothers and sisters b are outside, asking for you." 33 And he replied, "Who are my mother and my brothers?" 34 And looking at those who sat around him, he said, "Here are my mother and my brothers! 35 Whoever does the will of

---

z Other ancient authorities lack *whom he also named apostles*   a Other ancient authorities lack *So he appointed the twelve*   b Other ancient authorities lack *and sisters*

God is my brother and sister and mother."

The Parable of the Sower
(Mt 13.1–23; Lk 8.4–15)

**M
A
R
K**

4 Again he began to teach beside the sea. Such a very large crowd gathered around him that he got into a boat on the sea and sat there, while the whole crowd was beside the sea on the land. 2He began to teach them many things in parables, and in his teaching he said to them: 3"Listen! A sower went out to sow. 4And as he sowed, some seed fell on the path, and the birds came and ate it up. 5Other seed fell on rocky ground, where it did not have much soil, and it sprang up quickly, since it had no depth of soil. 6And when the sun rose, it was scorched; and since it had no root, it withered away. 7Other seed fell among thorns, and the thorns grew up and choked it, and it yielded no grain. 8Other seed fell into good soil and brought forth grain, growing up and increasing and yielding thirty and sixty and a hundredfold." 9And he said, "Let anyone with ears to hear listen!"

The Purpose of the Parables
(Mt 13.10–17; Lk 8.9–10)

10 When he was alone, those who were around him along with the twelve asked him about the parables. 11And he said to them, "To you has been given the secret c of the kingdom of God, but for those outside, everything comes in parables; 12in order that

'they may indeed look, but not perceive,
and may indeed listen, but not understand;
so that they may not turn again and be forgiven.' "

13 And he said to them, "Do you not understand this parable? Then how will you understand all the parables? 14The sower sows the word. 15These are the ones on the path where the word is sown: when they hear, Satan immediately comes and takes away the word that is sown in them. 16And these are the ones sown on rocky ground: when they hear the word, they immediately receive it with joy. 17But they have no root, and endure only for a while; then, when trouble or persecution arises on account of the word, immediately they fall away. d 18And oth-

ers are those sown among the thorns: these are the ones who hear the word, 19but the cares of the world, and the lure of wealth, and the desire for other things come in and choke the word, and it yields nothing. 20And these are the ones sown on the good soil: they hear the word and accept it and bear fruit, thirty and sixty and a hundredfold."

A Lamp under a Bushel Basket
(Lk 8.16–18)

21 He said to them, "Is a lamp brought in to be put under the bushel basket, or under the bed, and not on the lampstand? 22For there is nothing hidden, except to be disclosed; nor is anything secret, except to come to light. 23Let anyone with ears to hear listen!" 24And he said to them, "Pay attention to what you hear; the measure you give will be the measure you get, and still more will be given you. 25For to those who have, more will be given; and from those who have nothing, even what they have will be taken away."

The Parable of the Growing Seed

26 He also said, "The kingdom of God is as if someone would scatter seed on the ground, 27and would sleep and rise night and day, and the seed would sprout and grow, he does not know how. 28The earth produces of itself, first the stalk, then the head, then the full grain in the head. 29But when the grain is ripe, at once he goes in with his sickle, because the harvest has come."

The Parable of the Mustard Seed
(Mt 13.31–32; Lk 13.18–19)

30 He also said, "With what can we compare the kingdom of God, or what parable will we use for it? 31It is like a mustard seed, which, when sown upon the ground, is the smallest of all the seeds on earth; 32yet when it is sown it grows up and becomes the greatest of all shrubs, and puts forth large branches, so that the birds of the air can make nests in its shade."

The Use of Parables

33 With many such parables he spoke the word to them, as they were able to hear it; 34he did not speak to them except in parables, but he ex-

c Or *mystery* d Or *stumble*

plained everything in private to his disciples.

Jesus Stills a Storm
(Mt 8.23–27; Lk 8.22–25)

35 On that day, when evening had come, he said to them, "Let us go across to the other side." 36 And leaving the crowd behind, they took him with them in the boat, just as he was. Other boats were with him. 37 A great windstorm arose, and the waves beat into the boat, so that the boat was already being swamped. 38 But he was in the stern, asleep on the cushion; and they woke him up and said to him, "Teacher, do you not care that we are perishing?" 39 He woke up and rebuked the wind, and said to the sea, "Peace! Be still!" Then the wind ceased, and there was a dead calm. 40 He said to them, "Why are you afraid? Have you still no faith?" 41 And they were filled with great awe and said to one another, "Who then is this, that even the wind and the sea obey him?"

Jesus Heals the Gerasene Demoniac
(Mt 8.28—9.1; Lk 8.26–39)

5 They came to the other side of the sea, to the country of the Ger'-a·senes.e 2 And when he had stepped out of the boat, immediately a man out of the tombs with an unclean spirit met him. 3 He lived among the tombs; and no one could restrain him any more, even with a chain; 4 for he had often been restrained with shackles and chains, but the chains he wrenched apart, and the shackles he broke in pieces; and no one had the strength to subdue him. 5 Night and day among the tombs and on the mountains he was always howling and bruising himself with stones. 6 When he saw Jesus from a distance, he ran and bowed down before him; 7 and he shouted at the top of his voice, "What have you to do with me, Jesus, Son of the Most High God? I adjure you by God, do not torment me." 8 For he had said to him, "Come out of the man, you unclean spirit!" 9 Then Jesusf asked him, "What is your name?" He replied, "My name is Legion; for we are many." 10 He begged him earnestly not to send them out of the country. 11 Now there on the hillside a great herd of swine was feeding; 12 and the unclean spirits g begged him, "Send us into the swine; let us enter them." 13 So he gave

them permission. And the unclean spirits came out and entered the swine; and the herd, numbering about two thousand, rushed down the steep bank into the sea, and were drowned in the sea.

14 The swineherds ran off and told it in the city and in the country. Then people came to see what it was that had happened. 15 They came to Jesus and saw the demoniac sitting there, clothed and in his right mind, the very man who had had the legion; and they were afraid. 16 Those who had seen what had happened to the demoniac and to the swine reported it. 17 Then they began to beg Jesus h to leave their neighborhood. 18 As he was getting into the boat, the man who had been possessed by demons begged him that he might be with him. 19 But Jesusf refused, and said to him, "Go home to your friends, and tell them how much the Lord has done for you, and what mercy he has shown you." 20 And he went away and began to proclaim in the De·cap'o·lis how much Jesus had done for him; and everyone was amazed.

A Girl Restored to Life and a Woman Healed
(Mt 9.18–26; Lk 8.40–56)

21 When Jesus had crossed again in the boat i to the other side, a great crowd gathered around him; and he was by the sea. 22 Then one of the leaders of the synagogue named Ja·i'rus came and, when he saw him, fell at his feet 23 and begged him repeatedly, "My little daughter is at the point of death. Come and lay your hands on her, so that she may be made well, and live." 24 So he went with him.

And a large crowd followed him and pressed in on him. 25 Now there was a woman who had been suffering from hemorrhages for twelve years. 26 She had endured much under many physicians, and had spent all that she had; and she was no better, but rather grew worse. 27 She had heard about Jesus, and came up behind him in the crowd and touched his cloak, 28 for she said, "If I but touch his clothes, I will be made well." 29 Immediately her hemorrhage stopped; and she felt in her body

eOther ancient authorities read Gergesenes; others, Gadarenes   fGk he gGk they   hGk him   iOther ancient authorities lack in the boat that she was healed of her disease. [30]Immediately aware that power had gone forth from him, Jesus turned about in the crowd and said, "Who touched my clothes?" [31]And his disciples said to him, "You see the crowd pressing in on you; how can you say, 'Who touched me?'" [32]He looked all around to see who had done it. [33]But the woman, knowing what had happened to her, came in fear and trembling, fell down before him, and told him the whole truth. [34]He said to her, "Daughter, your faith has made you well; go in peace, and be healed of your disease."

[35] While he was still speaking, some people came from the leader's house to say, "Your daughter is dead. Why trouble the teacher any further?" [36]But overhearing[j] what they said, Jesus said to the leader of the synagogue, "Do not fear, only believe." [37]He allowed no one to follow him except Peter, James, and John, the brother of James. [38]When they came to the house of the leader of the synagogue, he saw a commotion, people weeping and wailing loudly. [39]When he had entered, he said to them, "Why do you make a commotion and weep? The child is not dead but sleeping." [40]And they laughed at him. Then he put them all outside, and took the child's father and mother and those who were with him, and went in where the child was. [41]He took her by the hand and said to her, "Tal'i·tha cūm," which means, "Little girl, get up!" [42]And immediately the girl got up and began to walk about (she was twelve years of age). At this they were overcome with amazement. [43]He strictly ordered them that no one should know this, and told them to give her something to eat.

The Rejection of Jesus at Nazareth
(Mt 13.54–58; Lk 4.16–30)

6 He left that place and came to his hometown, and his disciples followed him. [2]On the sabbath he began to teach in the synagogue, and many who heard him were astounded. They said, "Where did this man get all this? What is this wisdom that has been given to him? What deeds of power are being done by his hands! [3]Is not this the carpenter, the son of Mary[k] and brother of James and Jō'sēs and Judas and Simon, and are not his sisters here with us?" And they took offense[l] at

him. [4]Then Jesus said to them, "Prophets are not without honor, except in their hometown, and among their own kin, and in their own house." [5]And he could do no deed of power there, except that he laid his hands on a few sick people and cured them. [6]And he was amazed at their unbelief.

The Mission of the Twelve
(Mt 10.5–15; Lk 9.1–6)

Then he went about among the villages teaching. [7]He called the twelve and began to send them out two by two, and gave them authority over the unclean spirits. [8]He ordered them to take nothing for their journey except a staff; no bread, no bag, no money in their belts; [9]but to wear sandals and not to put on two tunics. [10]He said to them, "Wherever you enter a house, stay there until you leave the place. [11]If any place will not welcome you and they refuse to hear you, as you leave, shake off the dust that is on your feet as a testimony against them." [12]So they went out and proclaimed that all should repent. [13]They cast out many demons, and anointed with oil many who were sick and cured them.

The Death of John the Baptist
(Mt 14.1–12; Lk 9.7–9)

[14] King Her'od heard of it, for Jesus'[m] name had become known. Some were[n] saying, "John the baptizer has been raised from the dead; and for this reason these powers are at work in him." [15]But others said, "It is E·lī'jah." And others said, "It is a prophet, like one of the prophets of old." [16]But when Her'od heard of it, he said, "John, whom I beheaded, has been raised."

[17] For Her'od himself had sent men who arrested John, bound him, and put him in prison on account of He·rō'di·as, his brother Philip's wife, because Her'od[o] had married her. [18]For John had been telling Her'od, "It is not lawful for you to have your brother's wife." [19]And He·rō'di·as had a grudge against him, and wanted to kill him. But she could not, [20]for Her'od feared John, knowing that he was a righteous

[j]Or *ignoring*; other ancient authorities read *hearing*   [k]Other ancient authorities read *son of the carpenter and of Mary*   [l]Or *stumbled*   [m]Gk *his*   [n]Other ancient authorities read *He was*   [o]Gk *he*

and holy man, and he protected him. When he heard him, he was greatly perplexed;*p* and yet he liked to listen to him. ²¹But an opportunity came when Her′od on his birthday gave a banquet for his courtiers and officers and for the leaders of Galilee. ²²When his daughter He·rō′di·as*q* came in and danced, she pleased Her′od and his guests; and the king said to the girl, "Ask me for whatever you wish, and I will give it." ²³And he solemnly swore to her, "Whatever you ask me, I will give you, even half of my kingdom." ²⁴She went out and said to her mother, "What should I ask for?" She replied, "The head of John the baptizer." ²⁵Immediately she rushed back to the king and requested, "I want you to give me at once the head of John the Baptist on a platter." ²⁶The king was deeply grieved; yet out of regard for his oaths and for the guests, he did not want to refuse her. ²⁷Immediately the king sent a soldier of the guard with orders to bring John′s*r* head. He went and beheaded him in the prison, ²⁸brought his head on a platter, and gave it to the girl. Then the girl gave it to her mother. ²⁹When his disciples heard about it, they came and took his body, and laid it in a tomb.

Feeding the Five Thousand
(Mt 14.13–21; Lk 9.10–17; Jn 6.1–14)

30 The apostles gathered around Jesus, and told him all that they had done and taught. ³¹He said to them, "Come away to a deserted place all by yourselves and rest a while." For many were coming and going, and they had no leisure even to eat. ³²And they went away in the boat to a deserted place by themselves. ³³Now many saw them going and recognized them, and they hurried there on foot from all the towns and arrived ahead of them. ³⁴As he went ashore, he saw a great crowd; and he had compassion for them, because they were like sheep without a shepherd; and he began to teach them many things. ³⁵When it grew late, his disciples came to him and said, "This is a deserted place, and the hour is now very late; ³⁶send them away so that they may go into the surrounding country and villages and buy something for themselves to eat." ³⁷But he answered them, "You give them something to eat." They said to him, "Are we to go and buy two hundred denarii*s*

worth of bread, and give it to them to eat?" ³⁸And he said to them, "How many loaves have you? Go and see." When they had found out, they said, "Five, and two fish." ³⁹Then he ordered them to get all the people to sit down in groups on the green grass. ⁴⁰So they sat down in groups of hundreds and of fifties. ⁴¹Taking the five loaves and the two fish, he looked up to heaven, and blessed and broke the loaves, and gave them to his disciples to set before the people; and he divided the two fish among them all. ⁴²And all ate and were filled; ⁴³and they took up twelve baskets full of broken pieces and of the fish. ⁴⁴Those who had eaten the loaves numbered five thousand men.

Jesus Walks on the Water
(Mt 14.22–33; Jn 6.15–21)

45 Immediately he made his disciples get into the boat and go on ahead to the other side, to Beth·sa′i·da, while he dismissed the crowd. ⁴⁶After saying farewell to them, he went up on the mountain to pray.

47 When evening came, the boat was out on the sea, and he was alone on the land. ⁴⁸When he saw that they were straining at the oars against an adverse wind, he came towards them early in the morning, walking on the sea. He intended to pass them by. ⁴⁹But when they saw him walking on the sea, they thought it was a ghost and cried out; ⁵⁰for they all saw him and were terrified. But immediately he spoke to them and said, "Take heart, it is I; do not be afraid." ⁵¹Then he got into the boat with them and the wind ceased. And they were utterly astounded, ⁵²for they did not understand about the loaves, but their hearts were hardened.

Healing the Sick in Gennesaret
(Mt 14.34–36)

53 When they had crossed over, they came to land at Gen·nes′a·ret and moored the boat. ⁵⁴When they got out of the boat, people at once recognized him, ⁵⁵and rushed about that whole region and began to bring the sick on mats to wherever they heard he was.

---

*p*Other ancient authorities read *he did many things* *q*Other ancient authorities read *the daughter of Herodias herself* *r*Gk *his* *s*The denarius was the usual day's wage for a laborer

56 And wherever he went, into villages or cities or farms, they laid the sick in the marketplaces, and begged him that they might touch even the fringe of his cloak; and all who touched it were healed.

The Tradition of the Elders
(Mt 15.1–20)

7 Now when the Phar′i·sees and some of the scribes who had come from Jerusalem gathered around him, 2 they noticed that some of his disciples were eating with defiled hands, that is, without washing them. 3 (For the Phar′i·sees, and all the Jews, do not eat unless they thoroughly wash their hands,[t] thus observing the tradition of the elders; 4 and they do not eat anything from the market unless they wash it;[u] and there are also many other traditions that they observe, the washing of cups, pots, and bronze kettles.[v]) 5 So the Phar′i·sees and the scribes asked him, "Why do your disciples not live[w] according to the tradition of the elders, but eat with defiled hands?" 6 He said to them, "I·sai′ah prophesied rightly about you hypocrites, as it is written,

'This people honors me with
     their lips,
but their hearts are far from
     me;
7 in vain do they worship me,
     teaching human precepts as
          doctrines.'

8 You abandon the commandment of God and hold to human tradition."

9 Then he said to them, "You have a fine way of rejecting the commandment of God in order to keep your tradition! 10 For Moses said, 'Honor your father and your mother'; and, 'Whoever speaks evil of father or mother must surely die.' 11 But you say that if anyone tells father or mother, 'Whatever support you might have had from me is Cor′ban' (that is, an offering to God[x])— 12 then you no longer permit doing anything for a father or mother, 13 thus making void the word of God through your tradition that you have handed on. And you do many things like this."

14 Then he called the crowd again and said to them, "Listen to me, all of you, and understand: 15 there is nothing outside a person that by going in can defile, but the things that come out are what defile."[y]
17 When he had left the crowd and entered the house, his disciples asked him about the parable. 18 He said to them, "Then do you also fail to understand? Do you not see that whatever goes into a person from outside cannot defile, 19 since it enters, not the heart but the stomach, and goes out into the sewer?" (Thus he declared all foods clean.) 20 And he said, "It is what comes out of a person that defiles. 21 For it is from within, from the human heart, that evil intentions come: fornication, theft, murder, 22 adultery, avarice, wickedness, deceit, licentiousness, envy, slander, pride, folly. 23 All these evil things come from within, and they defile a person."

The Syrophoenician Woman's Faith
(Mt 15.21–28)

24 From there he set out and went away to the region of Tyre.[z] He entered a house and did not want anyone to know he was there. Yet he could not escape notice, 25 but a woman whose little daughter had an unclean spirit immediately heard about him, and she came and bowed down at his feet. 26 Now the woman was a Gentile, of Sy·ro·phoe·ni′ci·an origin. She begged him to cast the demon out of her daughter. 27 He said to her, "Let the children be fed first, for it is not fair to take the children's food and throw it to the dogs." 28 But she answered him, "Sir,[a] even the dogs under the table eat the children's crumbs." 29 Then he said to her, "For saying that, you may go—the demon has left your daughter." 30 So she went home, found the child lying on the bed, and the demon gone.

Jesus Cures a Deaf Man
(Mt 15.29–31)

31 Then he returned from the region of Tyre, and went by way of Si′don towards the Sea of Galilee, in the region of the De·cap′o·lis. 32 They brought to him a deaf man who had an

---

[t] Meaning of Gk uncertain   [u] Other ancient authorities read *and when they come from the marketplace, they do not eat unless they purify themselves*
[v] Other ancient authorities add *and beds*
[w] Gk *walk*   [x] Gk lacks *to God*   [y] Other ancient authorities add verse 16, *"Let anyone with ears to hear listen"*
[z] Other ancient authorities add *and Sidon*   [a] Or *Lord*; other ancient authorities prefix *Yes*

impediment in his speech; and they begged him to lay his hand on him. 33 He took him aside in private, away from the crowd, and put his fingers into his ears, and he spat and touched his tongue. 34 Then looking up to heaven, he sighed and said to him, "Eph'pha·tha," that is, "Be opened." 35 And immediately his ears were opened, his tongue was released, and he spoke plainly. 36 Then Jesus *b* ordered them to tell no one; but the more he ordered them, the more zealously they proclaimed it. 37 They were astounded beyond measure, saying, "He has done everything well; he even makes the deaf to hear and the mute to speak."

Feeding the Four Thousand
(Mt 15.32–39)

8 In those days when there was again a great crowd without anything to eat, he called his disciples and said to them, 2 "I have compassion for the crowd, because they have been with me now for three days and have nothing to eat. 3 If I send them away hungry to their homes, they will faint on the way—and some of them have come from a great distance." 4 His disciples replied, "How can one feed these people with bread here in the desert?" 5 He asked them, "How many loaves do you have?" They said, "Seven." 6 Then he ordered the crowd to sit down on the ground; and he took the seven loaves, and after giving thanks he broke them and gave them to his disciples to distribute; and they distributed them to the crowd. 7 They had also a few small fish; and after blessing them, he ordered that these too should be distributed. 8 They ate and were filled; and they took up the broken pieces left over, seven baskets full. 9 Now there were about four thousand people. And he sent them away. 10 And immediately he got into the boat with his disciples and went to the district of Dal·ma·nu'tha. *c*

The Demand for a Sign
(Mt 16.1–4)

11 The Phar'i·sees came and began to argue with him, asking him for a sign from heaven, to test him. 12 And he sighed deeply in his spirit and said, "Why does this generation ask for a sign? Truly I tell you, no sign will be given to this generation." 13 And he left

them, and getting into the boat again, he went across to the other side.

The Yeast of the Pharisees and of Herod
(Mt 16.5–12)

14 Now the disciples *d* had forgotten to bring any bread; and they had only one loaf with them in the boat. 15 And he cautioned them, saying, "Watch out—beware of the yeast of the Phar'i·sees and the yeast of Her'od." *e* 16 They said to one another, "It is because we have no bread." 17 And becoming aware of it, Jesus said to them, "Why are you talking about having no bread? Do you still not perceive or understand? Are your hearts hardened? 18 Do you have eyes, and fail to see? Do you have ears, and fail to hear? And do you not remember? 19 When I broke the five loaves for the five thousand, how many baskets full of broken pieces did you collect?" They said to him, "Twelve." 20 "And the seven for the four thousand, how many baskets full of broken pieces did you collect?" And they said to him, "Seven." 21 Then he said to them, "Do you not yet understand?"

Jesus Cures a Blind Man at Bethsaida

22 They came to Beth·sa'i·da. Some people *f* brought a blind man to him and begged him to touch him. 23 He took the blind man by the hand and led him out of the village; and when he had put saliva on his eyes and laid his hands on him, he asked him, "Can you see anything?" 24 And the man *b* looked up and said, "I can see people, but they look like trees, walking." 25 Then Jesus *b* laid his hands on his eyes again; and he looked intently and his sight was restored, and he saw everything clearly. 26 Then he sent him away to his home, saying, "Do not even go into the village." *g*

Peter's Declaration about Jesus
(Mt 16.13–20; Lk 9.18–20)

27 Jesus went on with his disciples to the villages of Caes·a·re'a Phi·lip'pi; and on the way he asked his disciples,

b Gk *he*   *c* Other ancient authorities read *Mageda* or *Magdala*   *d* Gk *they*   *e* Other ancient authorities read *the Herodians*   *f* Gk *They*   *g* Other ancient authorities add *or tell anyone in the village*

"Who do people say that I am?" [28] And they answered him, "John the Baptist; and others, E·li'jah; and still others, one of the prophets." [29] He asked them, "But who do you say that I am?" Peter answered him, "You are the Messiah." [h] [30] And he sternly ordered them not to tell anyone about him.

Jesus Foretells His Death and Resurrection
(Mt 16.21–28; Lk 9.21–27)

[31] Then he began to teach them that the Son of Man must undergo great suffering, and be rejected by the elders, the chief priests, and the scribes, and be killed, and after three days rise again. [32] He said all this quite openly. And Peter took him aside and began to rebuke him. [33] But turning and looking at his disciples, he rebuked Peter and said, "Get behind me, Satan! For you are setting your mind not on divine things but on human things."

[34] He called the crowd with his disciples, and said to them, "If any want to become my followers, let them deny themselves and take up their cross and follow me. [35] For those who want to save their life will lose it, and those who lose their life for my sake, and for the sake of the gospel, [i] will save it. [36] For what will it profit them to gain the whole world and forfeit their life? [37] Indeed, what can they give in return for their life? [38] Those who are ashamed of me and of my words [j] in this adulterous and sinful generation, of them the Son of Man will also be ashamed when he comes in the glory of his Father with the holy angels."

9 [1] And he said to them, "Truly I tell you, there are some standing here who will not taste death until they see that the kingdom of God has come with [k] power."

The Transfiguration
(Mt 17.1–8; Lk 9.28–36; 2 Pet 1.16–18)

[2] Six days later, Jesus took with him Peter and James and John, and led them up a high mountain apart, by themselves. And he was transfigured before them, [3] and his clothes became dazzling white, such as no one [l] on earth could bleach them. [4] And there appeared to them E·li'jah with Moses, who were talking with Jesus. [5] Then Peter said to Jesus, "Rabbi, it is good for us to be here; let us make three dwellings, [m] one for you, one for Mo-

ses, and one for E·li'jah." [6] He did not know what to say, for they were terrified. [7] Then a cloud overshadowed them, and from the cloud there came a voice, "This is my Son, the Beloved; [n] listen to him!" [8] Suddenly when they looked around, they saw no one with them any more, but only Jesus.

The Coming of Elijah
(Mt 17.9–13)

[9] As they were coming down the mountain, he ordered them to tell no one about what they had seen, until after the Son of Man had risen from the dead. [10] So they kept the matter to themselves, questioning what this rising from the dead could mean. [11] Then they asked him, "Why do the scribes say that E·li'jah must come first?" [12] He said to them, "E·li'jah is indeed coming first to restore all things. How then is it written about the Son of Man, that he is to go through many sufferings and be treated with contempt? [13] But I tell you that E·li'jah has come, and they did to him whatever they pleased, as it is written about him."

The Healing of a Boy with a Spirit
(Mt 17.14–21; Lk 9.37–43a)

[14] When they came to the disciples, they saw a great crowd around them, and some scribes arguing with them. [15] When the whole crowd saw him, they were immediately overcome with awe, and they ran forward to greet him. [16] He asked them, "What are you arguing about with them?" [17] Someone from the crowd answered him, "Teacher, I brought you my son; he has a spirit that makes him unable to speak; [18] and whenever it seizes him, it dashes him down; and he foams and grinds his teeth and becomes rigid; and I asked your disciples to cast it out, but they could not do so." [19] He answered them, "You faithless generation, how much longer must I be among you? How much longer must I put up with you? Bring him to me." [20] And they brought the boy [o] to him. When the spirit saw him, immediately it convulsed the boy, [o] and he fell on the ground and rolled about, foaming

---

[h] Or the Christ [i] Other ancient authorities read lose their life for the sake of the gospel [j] Other ancient authorities read and of mine [k] Or in [l] Gk no fuller [m] Or tents [n] Or my beloved Son [o] Gk him

at the mouth. 21 Jesus[p] asked the father, "How long has this been happening to him?" And he said, "From childhood. 22 It has often cast him into the fire and into the water, to destroy him; but if you are able to do anything, have pity on us and help us." 23 Jesus said to him, "If you are able!—All things can be done for the one who believes." 24 Immediately the father of the child cried out,[q] "I believe; help my unbelief!" 25 When Jesus saw that a crowd came running together, he rebuked the unclean spirit, saying to it, "You spirit that keeps this boy from speaking and hearing, I command you, come out of him, and never enter him again!" 26 After crying out and convulsing him terribly, it came out, and the boy was like a corpse, so that most of them said, "He is dead." 27 But Jesus took him by the hand and lifted him up, and he was able to stand. 28 When he had entered the house, his disciples asked him privately, "Why could we not cast it out?" 29 He said to them, "This kind can come out only through prayer."[r]

Jesus Again Foretells His Death and Resurrection
(Mt 17.22–23; Lk 9.43b–45)

30 They went on from there and passed through Galilee. He did not want anyone to know it; 31 for he was teaching his disciples, saying to them, "The Son of Man is to be betrayed into human hands, and they will kill him, and three days after being killed, he will rise again." 32 But they did not understand what he was saying and were afraid to ask him.

Who Is the Greatest?
(Mt 18.1–5; Lk 9.46–48)

33 Then they came to Ca·per'-na·um; and when he was in the house he asked them, "What were you arguing about on the way?" 34 But they were silent, for on the way they had argued with one another who was the greatest. 35 He sat down, called the twelve, and said to them, "Whoever wants to be first must be last of all and servant of all." 36 Then he took a little child and put it among them; and taking it in his arms, he said to them, 37 "Whoever welcomes one such child in my name welcomes me, and whoever welcomes me welcomes not me but the one who sent me."

Another Exorcist
(Mt 10.40–42; Lk 9.49–50)

38 John said to him, "Teacher, we saw someone[s] casting out demons in your name, and we tried to stop him, because he was not following us." 39 But Jesus said, "Do not stop him; for no one who does a deed of power in my name will be able soon afterward to speak evil of me. 40 Whoever is not against us is for us. 41 For truly I tell you, whoever gives you a cup of water to drink because you bear the name of Christ will by no means lose the reward.

Temptations to Sin
(Mt 18.6–9; Lk 17.1–2)

42 "If any of you put a stumbling block before one of these little ones who believe in me,[t] it would be better for you if a great millstone were hung around your neck and you were thrown into the sea. 43 If your hand causes you to stumble, cut it off; it is better for you to enter life maimed than to have two hands and to go to hell,[u] to the unquenchable fire.[v] 45 And if your foot causes you to stumble, cut it off; it is better for you to enter life lame than to have two feet and to be thrown into hell.[u,v] 47 And if your eye causes you to stumble, tear it out; it is better for you to enter the kingdom of God with one eye than to have two eyes and to be thrown into hell,[u] 48 where their worm never dies, and the fire is never quenched.

49 "For everyone will be salted with fire.[w] 50 Salt is good; but if salt has lost its saltiness, how can you season it?[x] Have salt in yourselves, and be at peace with one another."

Teaching about Divorce
(Mt 19.1–9)

10 He left that place and went to the region of Judea and[y] be-

[p] Gk *He* [q] Other ancient authorities add *with tears* [r] Other ancient authorities add *and fasting* [s] Other ancient authorities add *who does not follow us* [t] Other ancient authorities lack *in me* [u] Gk *Gehenna* [v] Verses 44 and 46 (which are identical with verse 48) are lacking in the best ancient authorities [w] Other ancient authorities either add or substitute *and every sacrifice will be salted with salt* [x] Or *how can you restore its saltiness?* [y] Other ancient authorities lack *and*

yond the Jordan. And crowds again gathered around him; and, as was his custom, he again taught them.

2 Some Phar'i·sees came, and to test him they asked, "Is it lawful for a man to divorce his wife?" 3 He answered them, "What did Moses command you?" 4 They said, "Moses allowed a man to write a certificate of dismissal and to divorce her." 5 But Jesus said to them, "Because of your hardness of heart he wrote this commandment for you. 6 But from the beginning of creation, 'God made them male and female.' 7 'For this reason a man shall leave his father and mother and be joined to his wife,^{z} 8 and the two shall become one flesh.' So they are no longer two, but one flesh. 9 Therefore what God has joined together, let no one separate."

10 Then in the house the disciples asked him again about this matter. 11 He said to them, "Whoever divorces his wife and marries another commits adultery against her; 12 and if she divorces her husband and marries another, she commits adultery."

Jesus Blesses Little Children
(Mt 19.13–15; Lk 18.15–17)

13 People were bringing little children to him in order that he might touch them; and the disciples spoke sternly to them. 14 But when Jesus saw this, he was indignant and said to them, "Let the little children come to me; do not stop them; for it is to such as these that the kingdom of God belongs. 15 Truly I tell you, whoever does not receive the kingdom of God as a little child will never enter it." 16 And he took them up in his arms, laid his hands on them, and blessed them.

The Rich Man
(Mt 19.16–30; Lk 18.18–30)

17 As he was setting out on a journey, a man ran up and knelt before him, and asked him, "Good Teacher, what must I do to inherit eternal life?" 18 Jesus said to him, "Why do you call me good? No one is good but God alone. 19 You know the commandments: 'You shall not murder; You shall not commit adultery; You shall not steal; You shall not bear false witness; You shall not defraud; Honor your father and mother.' " 20 He said to him, "Teacher, I have kept all these since my youth." 21 Jesus, looking at him, loved him and said, "You lack one thing; go, sell what you own, and give the money^a to the poor, and you will have treasure in heaven; then come, follow me." 22 When he heard this, he was shocked and went away grieving, for he had many possessions.

23 Then Jesus looked around and said to his disciples, "How hard it will be for those who have wealth to enter the kingdom of God!" 24 And the disciples were perplexed at these words. But Jesus said to them again, "Children, how hard it is^b to enter the kingdom of God! 25 It is easier for a camel to go through the eye of a needle than for someone who is rich to enter the kingdom of God." 26 They were greatly astounded and said to one another,^{c} "Then who can be saved?" 27 Jesus looked at them and said, "For mortals it is impossible, but not for God; for God all things are possible."

28 Peter began to say to him, "Look, we have left everything and followed you." 29 Jesus said, "Truly I tell you, there is no one who has left house or brothers or sisters or mother or father or children or fields, for my sake and for the sake of the good news,^{d} 30 who will not receive a hundredfold now in this age—houses, brothers and sisters, mothers and children, and fields with persecutions—and in the age to come eternal life. 31 But many who are first will be last, and the last will be first."

A Third Time Jesus Foretells His Death and Resurrection
(Mt 20.17–19; Lk 18.31–34)

32 They were on the road, going up to Jerusalem, and Jesus was walking ahead of them; they were amazed, and those who followed were afraid. He took the twelve aside again and began to tell them what was to happen to him, 33 saying, "See, we are going up to Jerusalem, and the Son of Man will be handed over to the chief priests and the scribes, and they will condemn him to death; then they will hand him over to the Gentiles; 34 they will mock him, and spit upon him, and flog him, and kill him; and after three days he will rise again."

^{z} Other ancient authorities lack *and be joined to his wife* ^{a} Gk lacks *the money* ^{b} Other ancient authorities add *for those who trust in riches* ^{c} Other ancient authorities read *to him* ^{d} Or *gospel*

The Request of James and John
(Mt 20.20–28)

35 James and John, the sons of Zeb'e·dee, came forward to him and said to him, "Teacher, we want you to do for us whatever we ask of you." 36 And he said to them, "What is it you want me to do for you?" 37 And they said to him, "Grant us to sit, one at your right hand and one at your left, in your glory." 38 But Jesus said to them, "You do not know what you are asking. Are you able to drink the cup that I drink, or be baptized with the baptism that I am baptized with?" 39 They replied, "We are able." Then Jesus said to them, "The cup that I drink you will drink; and with the baptism with which I am baptized, you will be baptized; 40 but to sit at my right hand or at my left is not mine to grant, but it is for those for whom it has been prepared."

41 When the ten heard this, they began to be angry with James and John. 42 So Jesus called them and said to them, "You know that among the Gentiles those whom they recognize as their rulers lord it over them, and their great ones are tyrants over them. 43 But it is not so among you; but whoever wishes to become great among you must be your servant, 44 and whoever wishes to be first among you must be slave of all. 45 For the Son of Man came not to be served but to serve, and to give his life a ransom for many."

The Healing of Blind Bartimaeus
(Mt 20.29–34; Lk 18.35–43)

46 They came to Jericho. As he and his disciples and a large crowd were leaving Jericho, Bar·ti·mae'us son of Ti·mae'us, a blind beggar, was sitting by the roadside. 47 When he heard that it was Jesus of Nazareth, he began to shout out and say, "Jesus, Son of David, have mercy on me!" 48 Many sternly ordered him to be quiet, but he cried out even more loudly, "Son of David, have mercy on me!" 49 Jesus stood still and said, "Call him here." And they called the blind man, saying to him, "Take heart; get up, he is calling you." 50 So throwing off his cloak, he sprang up and came to Jesus. 51 Then Jesus said to him, "What do you want me to do for you?" The blind man said to him, "My teacher,[e] let me see again." 52 Jesus said to him, "Go; your faith has made you well." Imme-diately he regained his sight and followed him on the way.

Jesus' Triumphal Entry into Jerusalem
(Mt 21.1–11; Lk 19.28–40; Jn 12.12–19)

11 When they were approaching Jerusalem, at Beth'pha·gē and Beth'a·ny, near the Mount of Olives, he sent two of his disciples 2 and said to them, "Go into the village ahead of you, and immediately as you enter it, you will find there a colt that has never been ridden; untie it and bring it. 3 If anyone says to you, 'Why are you doing this?' just say this, 'The Lord needs it and will send it back here immediately.'" 4 They went away and found a colt tied near a door, outside in the street. As they were untying it, 5 some of the bystanders said to them, "What are you doing, untying the colt?" 6 They told them what Jesus had said; and they allowed them to take it. 7 Then they brought the colt to Jesus and threw their cloaks on it; and he sat on it. 8 Many people spread their cloaks on the road, and others spread leafy branches that they had cut in the fields. 9 Then those who went ahead and those who followed were shouting,

"Hosanna!
　Blessed is the one who comes
　　in the name of the Lord!
10　Blessed is the coming kingdom
　　of our ancestor David!
Hosanna in the highest heaven!"

11 Then he entered Jerusalem and went into the temple; and when he had looked around at everything, as it was already late, he went out to Beth'a·ny with the twelve.

Jesus Curses the Fig Tree
(Mt 21.18–19)

12 On the following day, when they came from Beth'a·ny, he was hungry. 13 Seeing in the distance a fig tree in leaf, he went to see whether perhaps he would find anything on it. When he came to it, he found nothing but leaves, for it was not the season for figs. 14 He said to it, "May no one ever eat fruit from you again." And his disciples heard it.

Jesus Cleanses the Temple
(Mt 21.12–17; Lk 19.45–48; Jn 2.13–22)

15 Then they came to Jerusalem.

[e] Aramaic *Rabbouni*

And he entered the temple and began to drive out those who were selling and those who were buying in the temple, and he overturned the tables of the money changers and the seats of those who sold doves; [16]and he would not allow anyone to carry anything through the temple. [17]He was teaching and saying, "Is it not written,

'My house shall be called a
house of prayer for all the
nations'?
But you have made it a den of
robbers."

[18]And when the chief priests and the scribes heard it, they kept looking for a way to kill him; for they were afraid of him, because the whole crowd was spellbound by his teaching. [19]And when evening came, Jesus and his disciples[f] went out of the city.

The Lesson from the Withered Fig Tree
(Mt 21.20–22)

[20] In the morning as they passed by, they saw the fig tree withered away to its roots. [21]Then Peter remembered and said to him, "Rabbi, look! The fig tree that you cursed has withered." [22]Jesus answered them, "Have[g] faith in God. [23]Truly I tell you, if you say to this mountain, 'Be taken up and thrown into the sea,' and if you do not doubt in your heart, but believe that what you say will come to pass, it will be done for you. [24]So I tell you, whatever you ask for in prayer, believe that you have received[h] it, and it will be yours. [25] "Whenever you stand praying, forgive, if you have anything against anyone; so that your Father in heaven may also forgive you your trespasses."[i]

Jesus' Authority Is Questioned
(Mt 21.23–27; Lk 20.1–8)

[27] Again they came to Jerusalem. As he was walking in the temple, the chief priests, the scribes, and the elders came to him [28]and said, "By what authority are you doing these things? Who gave you this authority to do them?" [29]Jesus said to them, "I will ask you one question; answer me, and I will tell you by what authority I do these things. [30]Did the baptism of John come from heaven, or was it of human origin? Answer me." [31]They argued with one another, "If we say, 'From heaven,' he will say, 'Why then did you not believe him?' [32]But shall we say, 'Of human origin'?"—they were afraid of the crowd, for all regarded John as truly a prophet. [33]So they answered Jesus, "We do not know." And Jesus said to them, "Neither will I tell you by what authority I am doing these things."

The Parable of the Wicked Tenants
(Mt 21.33–46; Lk 20.9–19)

12 Then he began to speak to them in parables. "A man planted a vineyard, put a fence around it, dug a pit for the wine press, and built a watchtower; then he leased it to tenants and went to another country. [2]When the season came, he sent a slave to the tenants to collect from them his share of the produce of the vineyard. [3]But they seized him, and beat him, and sent him away empty-handed. [4]And again he sent another slave to them; this one they beat over the head and insulted. [5]Then he sent another, and that one they killed. And so it was with many others; some they beat, and others they killed. [6]He had still one other, a beloved son. Finally he sent him to them, saying, 'They will respect my son.' [7]But those tenants said to one another, 'This is the heir; come, let us kill him, and the inheritance will be ours.' [8]So they seized him, killed him, and threw him out of the vineyard. [9]What then will the owner of the vineyard do? He will come and destroy the tenants and give the vineyard to others. [10]Have you not read this scripture:

'The stone that the builders
rejected
has become the cornerstone;[j]
[11] this was the Lord's doing,
and it is amazing in our
eyes'?"

[12] When they realized that he had told this parable against them, they wanted to arrest him, but they feared the crowd. So they left him and went away.

---

[f]Gk they: other ancient authorities read he [g]Other ancient authorities read "If you have [h]Other ancient authorities read are receiving [i]Other ancient authorities add verse 26, "But if you do not forgive, neither will your Father in heaven forgive your trespasses." [j]Or keystone

The Question about Paying Taxes
(Mt 22.15–22; Lk 20.20–26)

13 Then they sent to him some Phar′i·sees and some He·rō′di·ans to trap him in what he said. 14 And they came and said to him, "Teacher, we know that you are sincere, and show deference to no one; for you do not regard people with partiality, but teach the way of God in accordance with truth. Is it lawful to pay taxes to the emperor, or not? 15 Should we pay them, or should we not?" But knowing their hypocrisy, he said to them, "Why are you putting me to the test? Bring me a denarius and let me see it." 16 And they brought one. Then he said to them, "Whose head is this, and whose title?" They answered, "The emperor's." 17 Jesus said to them, "Give to the emperor the things that are the emperor's, and to God the things that are God's." And they were utterly amazed at him.

The Question about the Resurrection
(Mt 22.23–33; Lk 20.27–40)

18 Some Sad′du·cees, who say there is no resurrection, came to him and asked him a question, saying, 19 "Teacher, Moses wrote for us that 'if a man's brother dies, leaving a wife but no child, the man*k* shall marry the widow and raise up children for his brother.' 20 There were seven brothers; the first married and, when he died, left no children; 21 and the second married her and died, leaving no children; and the third likewise; 22 none of the seven left children. Last of all the woman herself died. 23 In the resurrection*l* whose wife will she be? For the seven had married her."

24 Jesus said to them, "Is not this the reason you are wrong, that you know neither the scriptures nor the power of God? 25 For when they rise from the dead, they neither marry nor are given in marriage, but are like angels in heaven. 26 And as for the dead being raised, have you not read in the book of Moses, in the story about the bush, how God said to him, 'I am the God of Abraham, the God of Isaac, and the God of Jacob'? 27 He is God not of the dead, but of the living; you are quite wrong."

The First Commandment
(Mt 22.34–40; Lk 10.25–28)

28 One of the scribes came near and heard them disputing with one another, and seeing that he answered them well, he asked him, "Which commandment is the first of all?" 29 Jesus answered, "The first is, 'Hear, O Israel: the Lord our God, the Lord is one; 30 you shall love the Lord your God with all your heart, and with all your soul, and with all your mind, and with all your strength.' 31 The second is this, 'You shall love your neighbor as yourself.' There is no other commandment greater than these." 32 Then the scribe said to him, "You are right, Teacher; you have truly said that 'he is one, and besides him there is no other'; 33 and 'to love him with all the heart, and with all the understanding, and with all the strength,' and 'to love one's neighbor as oneself,'—this is much more important than all whole burnt offerings and sacrifices." 34 When Jesus saw that he answered wisely, he said to him, "You are not far from the kingdom of God." After that no one dared to ask him any question.

The Question about David's Son
(Mt 22.41–46; Lk 20.41–44)

35 While Jesus was teaching in the temple, he said, "How can the scribes say that the Messiah*m* is the son of David? 36 David himself, by the Holy Spirit, declared,

'The Lord said to my Lord,
"Sit at my right hand,
    until I put your enemies under
        your feet." '

37 David himself calls him Lord; so how can he be his son?" And the large crowd was listening to him with delight.

Jesus Denounces the Scribes
(Mt 23.1–7; Lk 20.45–47)

38 As he taught, he said, "Beware of the scribes, who like to walk around in long robes, and to be greeted with respect in the marketplaces, 39 and to have the best seats in the synagogues and places of honor at banquets! 40 They devour widows' houses and for the sake of appearance say long prayers. They will receive the greater condemnation."

k Gk *his brother*   *l* Other ancient authorities add *when they rise*   *m* Or *the Christ*

MARK

The Widow's Offering
(Lk 21.1–4)

41 He sat down opposite the treasury, and watched the crowd putting money into the treasury. Many rich people put in large sums. 42 A poor widow came and put in two small copper coins, which are worth a penny. 43 Then he called his disciples and said to them, "Truly I tell you, this poor widow has put in more than all those who are contributing to the treasury. 44 For all of them have contributed out of their abundance; but she out of her poverty has put in everything she had, all she had to live on."

The Destruction of the Temple Foretold
(Mt 24.1–8; Lk 21.5–11)

13 As he came out of the temple, one of his disciples said to him, "Look, Teacher, what large stones and what large buildings!" 2 Then Jesus asked him, "Do you see these great buildings? Not one stone will be left here upon another; all will be thrown down."

3 When he was sitting on the Mount of Olives opposite the temple, Peter, James, John, and Andrew asked him privately, 4 "Tell us, when will this be, and what will be the sign that all these things are about to be accomplished?" 5 Then Jesus began to say to them, "Beware that no one leads you astray. 6 Many will come in my name and say, 'I am he!'[n] and they will lead many astray. 7 When you hear of wars and rumors of wars, do not be alarmed; this must take place, but the end is still to come. 8 For nation will rise against nation, and kingdom against kingdom; there will be earthquakes in various places; there will be famines. This is but the beginning of the birth pangs.

Persecution Foretold
(Mt 24.9–14; Lk 21.12–19)

9 "As for yourselves, beware; for they will hand you over to councils; and you will be beaten in synagogues; and you will stand before governors and kings because of me, as a testimony to them. 10 And the good news[o] must first be proclaimed to all nations. 11 When they bring you to trial and hand you over, do not worry beforehand about what you are to say; but say whatever is given you at that time, for it is not you who speak, but the Holy Spirit. 12 Brother will betray brother to death, and a father his child, and children will rise against parents and have them put to death; 13 and you will be hated by all because of my name. But the one who endures to the end will be saved.

The Desolating Sacrilege
(Mt 24.15–28; Lk 21.20–24)

14 "But when you see the desolating sacrilege set up where it ought not to be (let the reader understand), then those in Judea must flee to the mountains; 15 the one on the housetop must not go down or enter the house to take anything away; 16 the one in the field must not turn back to get a coat. 17 Woe to those who are pregnant and to those who are nursing infants in those days! 18 Pray that it may not be in winter. 19 For in those days there will be suffering, such as has not been from the beginning of the creation that God created until now, no, and never will be. 20 And if the Lord had not cut short those days, no one would be saved; but for the sake of the elect, whom he chose, he has cut short those days. 21 And if anyone says to you at that time, 'Look! Here is the Messiah!'[p] or 'Look! There he is!'—do not believe it. 22 False messiahs[q] and false prophets will appear and produce signs and omens, to lead astray, if possible, the elect. 23 But be alert; I have already told you everything.

The Coming of the Son of Man
(Mt 24.29–31; Lk 21.25–28)

24 "But in those days, after that suffering,
the sun will be darkened,
    and the moon will not give its
    light,
25 and the stars will be falling from
heaven,
    and the powers in the heavens
    will be shaken.

26 Then they will see 'the Son of Man coming in clouds' with great power and glory. 27 Then he will send out the angels, and gather his elect from the four winds, from the ends of the earth to the ends of heaven.

The Lesson of the Fig Tree
(Mt 24.32–35; Lk 21.29–33)

28 "From the fig tree learn its les-

[n] Gk *I am*   [o] Gk *gospel*   [p] Or *the Christ*   [q] Or *christs*

son: as soon as its branch becomes tender and puts forth its leaves, you know that summer is near. 29 So also, when you see these things taking place, you know that he[r] is near, at the very gates. 30 Truly I tell you, this generation will not pass away until all these things have taken place. 31 Heaven and earth will pass away, but my words will not pass away.

The Necessity for Watchfulness
(Mt 24.36–44; Lk 21.34–36)

32 "But about that day or hour no one knows, neither the angels in heaven, nor the Son, but only the Father. 33 Beware, keep alert;[s] for you do not know when the time will come. 34 It is like a man going on a journey, when he leaves home and puts his slaves in charge, each with his work, and commands the doorkeeper to be on the watch. 35 Therefore, keep awake—for you do not know when the master of the house will come, in the evening, or at midnight, or at cockcrow, or at dawn, 36 or else he may find you asleep when he comes suddenly. 37 And what I say to you I say to all: Keep awake."

The Plot to Kill Jesus
(Mt 26.1–5; Lk 22.1–2; Jn 11.45–53)

14 It was two days before the Passover and the festival of Unleavened Bread. The chief priests and the scribes were looking for a way to arrest Jesus[t] by stealth and kill him; 2 for they said, "Not during the festival, or there may be a riot among the people."

The Anointing at Bethany
(Mt 26.6–13; Jn 12.1–8)

3 While he was at Beth'a·ny in the house of Simon the leper,[u] as he sat at the table, a woman came with an alabaster jar of very costly ointment of nard, and she broke open the jar and poured the ointment on his head. 4 But some were there who said to one another in anger, "Why was the ointment wasted in this way? 5 For this ointment could have been sold for more than three hundred denarii,[v] and the money given to the poor." And they scolded her. 6 But Jesus said, "Let her alone; why do you trouble her? She has performed a good service for me. 7 For you always have the poor with you, and you can show kindness to them whenever you wish; but you will

not always have me. 8 She has done what she could; she has anointed my body beforehand for its burial. 9 Truly I tell you, wherever the good news[w] is proclaimed in the whole world, what she has done will be told in remembrance of her."

Judas Agrees to Betray Jesus
(Mt 26.14–16; Lk 22.3–6)

10 Then Judas Is·car'i·ot, who was one of the twelve, went to the chief priests in order to betray him to them. 11 When they heard it, they were greatly pleased, and promised to give him money. So he began to look for an opportunity to betray him.

The Passover with the Disciples
(Mt 26.17–25; Lk 22.7–13; Jn 13.21–30)

12 On the first day of Unleavened Bread, when the Passover lamb is sacrificed, his disciples said to him, "Where do you want us to go and make the preparations for you to eat the Passover?" 13 So he sent two of his disciples, saying to them, "Go into the city, and a man carrying a jar of water will meet you; follow him, 14 and wherever he enters, say to the owner of the house, 'The Teacher asks, Where is my guest room where I may eat the Passover with my disciples?' 15 He will show you a large room upstairs, furnished and ready. Make preparations for us there." 16 So the disciples set out and went to the city, and found everything as he had told them; and they prepared the Passover meal.

17 When it was evening, he came with the twelve. 18 And when they had taken their places and were eating, Jesus said, "Truly I tell you, one of you will betray me, one who is eating with me." 19 They began to be distressed and to say to him one after another, "Surely, not I?" 20 He said to them, "It is one of the twelve, one who is dipping bread[x] into the bowl[y] with me. 21 For the Son of Man goes as it is written of him, but woe to that one by whom the Son of Man is betrayed! It would have been better for that one not to have been born."

---

[r] Or *it*   [s] Other ancient authorities add *and pray*   [t] Gk *him*   [u] The terms *leper* and *leprosy* can refer to several diseases   [v] The denarius was the usual day's wage for a laborer   [w] Or *gospel*   [x] Gk lacks *bread*   [y] Other ancient authorities read *same bowl*

The Institution of the Lord's Supper
(Mt 26.26–29; Lk 22.14–23; 1 Cor 11.23–26)

22 While they were eating, he took a loaf of bread, and after blessing it he broke it, gave it to them, and said, "Take; this is my body." ²³Then he took a cup, and after giving thanks he gave it to them, and all of them drank from it. ²⁴He said to them, "This is my blood of the ᶻ covenant, which is poured out for many. ²⁵Truly I tell you, I will never again drink of the fruit of the vine until that day when I drink it new in the kingdom of God."

Peter's Denial Foretold
(Mt 26.30–35; Lk 22.31–34; Jn 13.36–38)

26 When they had sung the hymn, they went out to the Mount of Olives. ²⁷And Jesus said to them, "You will all become deserters; for it is written,

'I will strike the shepherd,
    and the sheep will be
        scattered.'

²⁸But after I am raised up, I will go before you to Galilee." ²⁹Peter said to him, "Even though all become deserters, I will not." ³⁰Jesus said to him, "Truly I tell you, this day, this very night, before the cock crows twice, you will deny me three times." ³¹But he said vehemently, "Even though I must die with you, I will not deny you." And all of them said the same.

Jesus Prays in Gethsemane
(Mt 26.36–46; Lk 22.39–46)

32 They went to a place called Geth·sem´a·ne; and he said to his disciples, "Sit here while I pray." ³³He took with him Peter and James and John, and began to be distressed and agitated. ³⁴And he said to them, "I am deeply grieved, even to death; remain here, and keep awake." ³⁵And going a little farther, he threw himself on the ground and prayed that, if it were possible, the hour might pass from him. ³⁶He said, "Abba,ᵃ Father, for you all things are possible; remove this cup from me; yet, not what I want, but what you want." ³⁷He came and found them sleeping; and he said to Peter, "Simon, are you asleep? Could you not keep awake one hour? ³⁸Keep awake and pray that you may not come into the time of trial;ᵇ the spirit indeed is willing, but the flesh is weak." ³⁹And again he went away and prayed, saying the same words. ⁴⁰And once more he came and found them sleeping, for their eyes were very heavy; and they did not know what to say to him. ⁴¹He came a third time and said to them, "Are you still sleeping and taking your rest? Enough! The hour has come; the Son of Man is betrayed into the hands of sinners. ⁴²Get up, let us be going. See, my betrayer is at hand."

The Betrayal and Arrest of Jesus
(Mt 26.47–56; Lk 22.47–53; Jn 18.1–11)

43 Immediately, while he was still speaking, Judas, one of the twelve, arrived; and with him there was a crowd with swords and clubs, from the chief priests, the scribes, and the elders. ⁴⁴Now the betrayer had given them a sign, saying, "The one I will kiss is the man; arrest him and lead him away under guard." ⁴⁵So when he came, he went up to him at once and said, "Rabbi!" and kissed him. ⁴⁶Then they laid hands on him and arrested him. ⁴⁷But one of those who stood near drew his sword and struck the slave of the high priest, cutting off his ear. ⁴⁸Then Jesus said to them, "Have you come out with swords and clubs to arrest me as though I were a bandit? ⁴⁹Day after day I was with you in the temple teaching, and you did not arrest me. But let the scriptures be fulfilled." ⁵⁰All of them deserted him and fled.

51 A certain young man was following him, wearing nothing but a linen cloth. They caught hold of him, ⁵²but he left the linen cloth and ran off naked.

Jesus before the Council
*(Mt 26.57–68; Lk 22.66–71;
Jn 18.12–14, 19–24)*

53 They took Jesus to the high priest; and all the chief priests, the elders, and the scribes were assembled. ⁵⁴Peter had followed him at a distance, right into the courtyard of the high priest; and he was sitting with the guards, warming himself at the fire. ⁵⁵Now the chief priests and the whole council were looking for testimony against Jesus to put him to death; but they found none. ⁵⁶For many gave false testimony against him, and their testimony did not agree. ⁵⁷Some stood up and gave false testimony against him, saying, ⁵⁸"We heard him say, 'I

ᶻ Other ancient authorities add *new*
ᵃ Aramaic for *Father*   ᵇ Or *into temptation*

will destroy this temple that is made with hands, and in three days I will build another, not made with hands.' " ⁵⁹But even on this point their testimony did not agree. ⁶⁰Then the high priest stood up before them and asked Jesus, "Have you no answer? What is it that they testify against you?" ⁶¹But he was silent and did not answer. Again the high priest asked him, "Are you the Messiah,ᶜ the Son of the Blessed One?" ⁶²Jesus said, "I am; and

> 'you will see the Son of Man
>   seated at the right hand of the
>   Power,'
> and 'coming with the clouds of
>   heaven.' "

⁶³Then the high priest tore his clothes and said, "Why do we still need witnesses? ⁶⁴You have heard his blasphemy! What is your decision?" All of them condemned him as deserving death. ⁶⁵Some began to spit on him, to blindfold him, and to strike him, saying to him, "Prophesy!" The guards also took him over and beat him.

Peter Denies Jesus
(Mt 26.69–75; Lk 22.54–62;
Jn 18.15–18, 25–27)

66 While Peter was below in the courtyard, one of the servant-girls of the high priest came by. ⁶⁷When she saw Peter warming himself, she stared at him and said, "You also were with Jesus, the man from Nazareth." ⁶⁸But he denied it, saying, "I do not know or understand what you are talking about." And he went out into the forecourt.ᵈ Then the cock crowed.ᵉ ⁶⁹And the servant-girl, on seeing him, began again to say to the bystanders, "This man is one of them." ⁷⁰But again he denied it. Then after a little while the bystanders again said to Peter, "Certainly you are one of them; for you are a Galilean." ⁷¹But he began to curse, and he swore an oath, "I do not know this man you are talking about." ⁷²At that moment the cock crowed for the second time. Then Peter remembered that Jesus had said to him, "Before the cock crows twice, you will deny me three times." And he broke down and wept.

Jesus before Pilate
(Mt 27.1–2, 11–14; Lk 23.1–5, 13–16;
Jn 18.28–38a)

15 As soon as it was morning, the chief priests held a consultation with the elders and scribes and the whole council. They bound Jesus, led him away, and handed him over to Pilate. ²Pilate asked him, "Are you the King of the Jews?" He answered him, "You say so." ³Then the chief priests accused him of many things. ⁴Pilate asked him again, "Have you no answer? See how many charges they bring against you." ⁵But Jesus made no further reply, so that Pilate was amazed.

Pilate Hands Jesus over to Be Crucified
(Mt 27.15–26; Lk 23.18–25; Jn 18.38b—19.16)

6 Now at the festival he used to release a prisoner for them, anyone for whom they asked. ⁷Now a man called Ba·rab′bas was in prison with the rebels who had committed murder during the insurrection. ⁸So the crowd came and began to ask Pilate to do for them according to his custom. ⁹Then he answered them, "Do you want me to release for you the King of the Jews?" ¹⁰For he realized that it was out of jealousy that the chief priests had handed him over. ¹¹But the chief priests stirred up the crowd to have him release Ba·rab′bas for them instead. ¹²Pilate spoke to them again, "Then what do you wish me to doᶠ with the man you callᵍ the King of the Jews?" ¹³They shouted back, "Crucify him!" ¹⁴Pilate asked them, "Why, what evil has he done?" But they shouted all the more, "Crucify him!" ¹⁵So Pilate, wishing to satisfy the crowd, released Ba·rab′bas for them; and after flogging Jesus, he handed him over to be crucified.

The Soldiers Mock Jesus
(Mt 27.27–31)

16 Then the soldiers led him into the courtyard of the palace (that is, the governor's headquartersʰ); and they called together the whole cohort. ¹⁷And they clothed him in a purple cloak; and after twisting some thorns into a crown, they put it on him. ¹⁸And they began saluting him, "Hail, King of the Jews!" ¹⁹They struck his head with a reed, spat upon him, and knelt down in homage to him. ²⁰After mocking him, they stripped him of the purple cloak and put his own clothes on him.

ᶜOr *the Christ*　ᵈOr *gateway*　ᵉOther ancient authorities lack *Then the cock crowed*　ᶠOther ancient authorities read *what should I do*　ᵍOther ancient authorities lack *the man you call*　ʰGk *the praetorium*

Then they led him out to crucify him.

The Crucifixion of Jesus
(Mt 27.32–44; Lk 23.26–43; Jn 19.16b–27)

21 They compelled a passer-by, who was coming in from the country, to carry his cross; it was Simon of Cy·rē′ne, the father of Alexander and Rufus. 22 Then they brought Jesus[i] to the place called Gol′go·tha (which means the place of a skull). 23 And they offered him wine mixed with myrrh; but he did not take it. 24 And they crucified him, and divided his clothes among them, casting lots to decide what each should take.

25 It was nine o'clock in the morning when they crucified him. 26 The inscription of the charge against him read, "The King of the Jews." 27 And with him they crucified two bandits, one on his right and one on his left.[j] 29 Those who passed by derided[k] him, shaking their heads and saying, "Aha! You who would destroy the temple and build it in three days, 30 save yourself, and come down from the cross!" 31 In the same way the chief priests, along with the scribes, were also mocking him among themselves and saying, "He saved others; he cannot save himself. 32 Let the Messiah,[l] the King of Israel, come down from the cross now, so that we may see and believe." Those who were crucified with him also taunted him.

The Death of Jesus
(Mt 27.45–56; Lk 23.44–49; Jn 19.28–30)

33 When it was noon, darkness came over the whole land[m] until three in the afternoon. 34 At three o'clock Jesus cried out with a loud voice, "E′lo·i, E′lo·i, le·ma′ sa·bach′tha·ni?" which means, "My God, my God, why have you forsaken me?"[n] 35 When some of the bystanders heard it, they said, "Listen, he is calling for E·li′jah." 36 And someone ran, filled a sponge with sour wine, put it on a stick, and gave it to him to drink, saying, "Wait, let us see whether E·li′jah will come to take him down." 37 Then Jesus gave a loud cry and breathed his last. 38 And the curtain of the temple was torn in two, from top to bottom. 39 Now when the centurion, who stood facing him, saw that in this way he[o] breathed his last, he said, "Truly this man was God's Son!"[p]

40 There were also women looking on from a distance; among them were Mary Mag′da·lēne, and Mary the mother of James the younger and of Jō′ses, and Sa·lō′me. 41 These used to follow him and provided for him when he was in Galilee; and there were many other women who had come up with him to Jerusalem.

The Burial of Jesus
(Mt 27.57–61; Lk 23.50–56; Jn 19.38–42)

42 When evening had come, and since it was the day of Preparation, that is, the day before the sabbath, 43 Joseph of Ar·i·ma·thē′a, a respected member of the council, who was also himself waiting expectantly for the kingdom of God, went boldly to Pilate and asked for the body of Jesus. 44 Then Pilate wondered if he were already dead; and summoning the centurion, he asked him whether he had been dead for some time. 45 When he learned from the centurion that he was dead, he granted the body to Joseph. 46 Then Joseph[q] bought a linen cloth, and taking down the body,[r] wrapped it in the linen cloth, and laid it in a tomb that had been hewn out of the rock. He then rolled a stone against the door of the tomb. 47 Mary Mag′da·lēne and Mary the mother of Jō′ses saw where the body[r] was laid.

The Resurrection of Jesus
(Mt 28.1–10; Lk 24.1–12; Jn 20.1–10)

16 When the sabbath was over, Mary Mag′da·lēne, and Mary the mother of James, and Sa·lō′me bought spices, so that they might go and anoint him. 2 And very early on the first day of the week, when the sun had risen, they went to the tomb. 3 They had been saying to one another, "Who will roll away the stone for us from the entrance to the tomb?" 4 When they looked up, they saw that the stone, which was very large, had already been rolled back. 5 As they entered the tomb, they saw a young man, dressed in a white robe, sitting on the right side; and they were alarmed. 6 But he said to them, "Do not be alarmed; you

---

[i] Gk him   [j] Other ancient authorities add verse 28, *And the scripture was fulfilled that says, "And he was counted among the lawless."*   [k] Or blasphemed   [l] Or *the Christ*   [m] Or *earth*   [n] Other ancient authorities read *made me a reproach*   [o] Other ancient authorities add *cried out and*   [p] Or *a son of God*   [q] Gk *he*   [r] Gk *it*

are looking for Jesus of Nazareth, who was crucified. He has been raised; he is not here. Look, there is the place they laid him. 7 But go, tell his disciples and Peter that he is going ahead of you to Galilee; there you will see him, just as he told you." 8 So they went out and fled from the tomb, for terror and amazement had seized them; and they said nothing to anyone, for they were afraid. *s*

THE SHORTER ENDING OF MARK

〚And all that had been commanded them they told briefly to those around Peter. And afterward Jesus himself sent out through them, from east to west, the sacred and imperishable proclamation of eternal salvation. *t* 〛

THE LONGER ENDING OF MARK

Jesus Appears to Mary Magdalene
(Jn 20.11–18)

9 〚Now after he rose early on the first day of the week, he appeared first to Mary Mag'da·lēne, from whom he had cast out seven demons. 10 She went out and told those who had been with him, while they were mourning and weeping. 11 But when they heard that he was alive and had been seen by her, they would not believe it.

Jesus Appears to Two Disciples
(Lk 24.13–43; Jn 20.19–23)

12 After this he appeared in another form to two of them, as they were walking into the country. 13 And they went back and told the rest, but they did not believe them.

Jesus Commissions the Disciples
(Mt 28.16–20; Lk 24.44–49; Jn 20.19–23; Acts 1.6–8)

14 Later he appeared to the eleven themselves as they were sitting at the table; and he upbraided them for their lack of faith and stubbornness, because they had not believed those who saw him after he had risen. *u* 15 And he said to them, "Go into all the world and proclaim the good news *v* to the whole creation. 16 The one who believes and is baptized will be saved; but the one who does not believe will be condemned. 17 And these signs will accompany those who believe: by using my name they will cast out demons; they will speak in new tongues; 18 they will pick up snakes in their hands, *w* and if they drink any deadly thing, it will not hurt them; they will lay their hands on the sick, and they will recover."

The Ascension of Jesus
(Lk 24.50–53)

19 So then the Lord Jesus, after he had spoken to them, was taken up into heaven and sat down at the right hand of God. 20 And they went out and proclaimed the good news everywhere, while the Lord worked with them and confirmed the message by the signs that accompanied it. *t* 〛

s Some of the most ancient authorities bring the book to a close at the end of verse 8. One authority concludes the book with the shorter ending; others include the shorter ending and then continue with verses 9-20. In most authorities verses 9-20 follow immediately after verse 8, though in some of these authorities the passage is marked as being doubtful.   *t* Other ancient authorities add *Amen*   *u* Other ancient authorities add, in whole or in part, *And they excused themselves, saying, "This age of lawlessness and unbelief is under Satan, who does not allow the truth and power of God to prevail over the unclean things of the spirits. Therefore reveal your righteousness now"—thus they spoke to Christ. And Christ replied to them, "The term of years of Satan's power has been fulfilled, but other terrible things draw near. And for those who have sinned I was handed over to death, that they may return to the truth and sin no more, that they may inherit the spiritual and imperishable glory of righteousness that is in heaven."*   *v* Or *gospel*   *w* Other ancient authorities lack *in their hands*

The Gospel According to

LUKE

Dedication to Theophilus

1 Since many have undertaken to set down an orderly account of the events that have been fulfilled among us, [2] just as they were handed on to us by those who from the beginning were eyewitnesses and servants of the word, [3] I too decided, after investigating everything carefully from the very first, [a] to write an orderly account for you, most excellent Thē·oph'i·lus, [4] so that you may know the truth concerning the things about which you have been instructed.

The Birth of John the Baptist Foretold

5 In the days of King Her'od of Judea, there was a priest named Zech·a·rī'ah, who belonged to the priestly order of A·bī'jah. His wife was a descendant of Aaron, and her name was Elizabeth. [6] Both of them were righteous before God, living blamelessly according to all the commandments and regulations of the Lord. [7] But they had no children, because Elizabeth was barren, and both were getting on in years.

8 Once when he was serving as priest before God and his section was on duty, [9] he was chosen by lot, according to the custom of the priesthood, to enter the sanctuary of the Lord and offer incense. [10] Now at the time of the incense offering, the whole assembly of the people was praying outside. [11] Then there appeared to him an angel of the Lord, standing at the right side of the altar of incense. [12] When Zech·a·rī'ah saw him, he was terrified; and fear overwhelmed him. [13] But the angel said to him, "Do not be afraid, Zech·a·rī'ah, for your prayer has been heard. Your wife Elizabeth will bear you a son, and you will name him John. [14] You will have joy and gladness, and many will rejoice at his birth, [15] for he will be great in the sight of the Lord. He must never drink wine or strong drink; even before his birth he will be filled with the Holy Spirit. [16] He will turn many of the people of Israel to the Lord their God. [17] With the spirit and power of E·lī'jah he will go before him, to turn the hearts of parents to their children, and the disobedient to the wisdom of the righteous, to make ready a people prepared for the Lord." [18] Zech·a·rī'ah said to the angel, "How will I know that this is so? For I am an old man, and my wife is getting on in years." [19] The angel replied, "I am Gabriel. I stand in the presence of God, and I have been sent to speak to you and to bring you this good news. [20] But now, because you did not believe my words, which will be fulfilled in their time, you will become mute, unable to speak, until the day these things occur."

21 Meanwhile the people were waiting for Zech·a·rī'ah, and wondered at his delay in the sanctuary. [22] When he did come out, he could not speak to them, and they realized that he had seen a vision in the sanctuary. He kept motioning to them and remained unable to speak. [23] When his time of service was ended, he went to his home.

24 After those days his wife Elizabeth conceived, and for five months she remained in seclusion. She said, [25] "This is what the Lord has done for me when he looked favorably on me and took away the disgrace I have endured among my people."

The Birth of Jesus Foretold

26 In the sixth month the angel Gabriel was sent by God to a town in Galilee called Nazareth, [27] to a virgin engaged to a man whose name was Joseph, of the house of David. The virgin's name was Mary. [28] And he came to her and said, "Greetings, favored

[a] Or for a long time

one! The Lord is with you."[b] 29 But she was much perplexed by his words and pondered what sort of greeting this might be. 30 The angel said to her, "Do not be afraid, Mary, for you have found favor with God. 31 And now, you will conceive in your womb and bear a son, and you will name him Jesus. 32 He will be great, and will be called the Son of the Most High, and the Lord God will give to him the throne of his ancestor David. 33 He will reign over the house of Jacob forever, and of his kingdom there will be no end." 34 Mary said to the angel, "How can this be, since I am a virgin?"[c] 35 The angel said to her, "The Holy Spirit will come upon you, and the power of the Most High will overshadow you; therefore the child to be born[d] will be holy; he will be called Son of God. 36 And now, your relative Elizabeth in her old age has also conceived a son; and this is the sixth month for her who was said to be barren. 37 For nothing will be impossible with God." 38 Then Mary said, "Here am I, the servant of the Lord; let it be with me according to your word." Then the angel departed from her.

Mary Visits Elizabeth

39 In those days Mary set out and went with haste to a Judean town in the hill country, 40 where she entered the house of Zech·a·ri′ah and greeted Elizabeth. 41 When Elizabeth heard Mary's greeting, the child leaped in her womb. And Elizabeth was filled with the Holy Spirit 42 and exclaimed with a loud cry, "Blessed are you among women, and blessed is the fruit of your womb. 43 And why has this happened to me, that the mother of my Lord comes to me? 44 For as soon as I heard the sound of your greeting, the child in my womb leaped for joy. 45 And blessed is she who believed that there would be[e] a fulfillment of what was spoken to her by the Lord."

Mary's Song of Praise

46 And Mary[f] said,
"My soul magnifies the Lord,
47   and my spirit rejoices in God
        my Savior,
48   for he has looked with favor on
        the lowliness of his
        servant.
      Surely, from now on all
        generations will call me
        blessed;

49   for the Mighty One has done
        great things for me,
      and holy is his name.
50   His mercy is for those who fear
        him
      from generation to generation.
51   He has shown strength with his
        arm;
      he has scattered the proud in
        the thoughts of their
        hearts.
52   He has brought down the
        powerful from their
        thrones,
      and lifted up the lowly;
53   he has filled the hungry with
        good things,
      and sent the rich away empty.
54   He has helped his servant Israel,
      in remembrance of his mercy,
55   according to the promise he
        made to our ancestors,
      to Abraham and to his
        descendants forever."

56 And Mary remained with her about three months and then returned to her home.

The Birth of John the Baptist

57 Now the time came for Elizabeth to give birth, and she bore a son. 58 Her neighbors and relatives heard that the Lord had shown his great mercy to her, and they rejoiced with her. 59 On the eighth day they came to circumcise the child, and they were going to name him Zech·a·ri′ah after his father. 60 But his mother said, "No; he is to be called John." 61 They said to her, "None of your relatives has this name." 62 Then they began motioning to his father to find out what name he wanted to give him. 63 He asked for a writing tablet and wrote, "His name is John." And all of them were amazed. 64 Immediately his mouth was opened and his tongue freed, and he began to speak, praising God. 65 Fear came over all their neighbors, and all these things were talked about throughout the entire hill country of Judea. 66 All who heard them pondered them and said, "What then will this child become?" For, indeed, the hand of the Lord was with him.

b Other ancient authorities add *Blessed are you among women*   c Gk *I do not know a man*   d Other ancient authorities add *of you*   e Or *believed, for there will be*   f Other ancient authorities read *Elizabeth*

Zechariah's Prophecy

67 Then his father Zech·a·rī′ah was filled with the Holy Spirit and spoke this prophecy:

68 "Blessed be the Lord God of
    Israel,
    for he has looked favorably on
      his people and redeemed
      them.
69 He has raised up a mighty
    savior[g] for us
    in the house of his servant
      David,
70 as he spoke through the mouth
    of his holy prophets from
    of old,
71 that we would be saved from
    our enemies and from the
    hand of all who hate us.
72 Thus he has shown the mercy
    promised to our ancestors,
    and has remembered his holy
      covenant,
73 the oath that he swore to our
    ancestor Abraham,
    to grant us 74that we, being
      rescued from the hands of
      our enemies,
    might serve him without fear,
      75in holiness and
      righteousness
    before him all our days.
76 And you, child, will be called the
    prophet of the Most High;
    for you will go before the Lord
      to prepare his ways,
77 to give knowledge of salvation to
    his people
    by the forgiveness of their
      sins.
78 By the tender mercy of our God,
    the dawn from on high will
      break upon[h] us,
79 to give light to those who sit in
    darkness and in the
      shadow of death,
    to guide our feet into the way
      of peace."

80 The child grew and became strong in spirit, and he was in the wilderness until the day he appeared publicly to Israel.

The Birth of Jesus
(Mt 1.18–25)

2 In those days a decree went out from Emperor Augustus that all the world should be registered. 2This was the first registration and was taken while Quī·rin′i·us was governor of Syria. 3All went to their own towns to be registered. 4Joseph also went from the town of Nazareth in Galilee to Judea, to the city of David called Bethlehem, because he was descended from the house and family of David. 5He went to be registered with Mary, to whom he was engaged and who was expecting a child. 6While they were there, the time came for her to deliver her child. 7And she gave birth to her firstborn son and wrapped him in bands of cloth, and laid him in a manger, because there was no place for them in the inn.

The Shepherds and the Angels

8 In that region there were shepherds living in the fields, keeping watch over their flock by night. 9Then an angel of the Lord stood before them, and the glory of the Lord shone around them, and they were terrified. 10But the angel said to them, "Do not be afraid; for see—I am bringing you good news of great joy for all the people: 11to you is born this day in the city of David a Savior, who is the Messiah,[i] the Lord. 12This will be a sign for you: you will find a child wrapped in bands of cloth and lying in a manger." 13And suddenly there was with the angel a multitude of the heavenly host,[j] praising God and saying,

14 "Glory to God in the highest
      heaven,
    and on earth peace among
      those whom he favors!"[k]

15 When the angels had left them and gone into heaven, the shepherds said to one another, "Let us go now to Bethlehem and see this thing that has taken place, which the Lord has made known to us." 16So they went with haste and found Mary and Joseph, and the child lying in the manger. 17When they saw this, they made known what had been told them about this child; 18and all who heard it were amazed at what the shepherds told them. 19But Mary treasured all these words and pondered them in her heart. 20The shepherds returned, glorifying and praising God for all they had heard and seen, as it had been told them.

g Gk *a horn of salvation*   h Other ancient authorities read *has broken upon*   i Or *the Christ*   j Gk *army*   k Other ancient authorities read *peace, goodwill among people*

Jesus Is Named

21 After eight days had passed, it was time to circumcise the child; and he was called Jesus, the name given by the angel before he was conceived in the womb.

Jesus Is Presented in the Temple

22 When the time came for their purification according to the law of Moses, they brought him up to Jerusalem to present him to the Lord 23 (as it is written in the law of the Lord, "Every firstborn male shall be designated as holy to the Lord"), 24 and they offered a sacrifice according to what is stated in the law of the Lord, "a pair of turtledoves or two young pigeons."

25 Now there was a man in Jerusalem whose name was Sim′e·on;[l] this man was righteous and devout, looking forward to the consolation of Israel, and the Holy Spirit rested on him. 26 It had been revealed to him by the Holy Spirit that he would not see death before he had seen the Lord's Messiah.[m] 27 Guided by the Spirit, Sim′e·on[n] came into the temple; and when the parents brought in the child Jesus, to do for him what was customary under the law, 28 Sim′e·on[o] took him in his arms and praised God, saying,
29 "Master, now you are dismissing
        your servant [p] in peace,
        according to your word;
30 for my eyes have seen your
        salvation,
31 which you have prepared in
        the presence of all peoples,
32 a light for revelation to the
        Gentiles
    and for glory to your people
        Israel."

33 And the child's father and mother were amazed at what was being said about him. 34 Then Sim′e·on[l] blessed them and said to his mother Mary, "This child is destined for the falling and the rising of many in Israel, and to be a sign that will be opposed 35 so that the inner thoughts of many will be revealed—and a sword will pierce your own soul too."

36 There was also a prophet, Anna[q] the daughter of Phan′u·el, of the tribe of Ash′er. She was of a great age, having lived with her husband seven years after her marriage, 37 then as a widow to the age of eighty-four. She never left the temple but worshiped there with fasting and prayer night and day. 38 At that moment she came, and began to praise God and to speak about the child[r] to all who were looking for the redemption of Jerusalem.

The Return to Nazareth

39 When they had finished everything required by the law of the Lord, they returned to Galilee, to their own town of Nazareth. 40 The child grew and became strong, filled with wisdom; and the favor of God was upon him.

The Boy Jesus in the Temple

41 Now every year his parents went to Jerusalem for the festival of the Passover. 42 And when he was twelve years old, they went up as usual for the festival. 43 When the festival was ended and they started to return, the boy Jesus stayed behind in Jerusalem, but his parents did not know it. 44 Assuming that he was in the group of travelers, they went a day's journey. Then they started to look for him among their relatives and friends. 45 When they did not find him, they returned to Jerusalem to search for him. 46 After three days they found him in the temple, sitting among the teachers, listening to them and asking them questions. 47 And all who heard him were amazed at his understanding and his answers. 48 When his parents[s] saw him they were astonished; and his mother said to him, "Child, why have you treated us like this? Look, your father and I have been searching for you in great anxiety." 49 He said to them, "Why were you searching for me? Did you not know that I must be in my Father's house?"[t] 50 But they did not understand what he said to them. 51 Then he went down with them and came to Nazareth, and was obedient to them. His mother treasured all these things in her heart.

52 And Jesus increased in wisdom and in years,[u] and in divine and human favor.

---

[l] Gk *Symeon*   [m] Or *the Lord's Christ*
[n] Gk *In the Spirit, he*   [o] Gk *he*
[p] Gk *slave*   [q] Gk *Hanna*   [r] Gk *him*
[s] Gk *they*   [t] Or *be about my Father's
interests?*   [u] Or *in stature*

The Proclamation of John the Baptist
(Mt 3.1–12; Mk 1.1–8; Jn 1.19–28)

3 In the fifteenth year of the reign of Emperor Tī·bē´ri·us, when Pon´·ti·us Pilate was governor of Judea, and Her´od was ruler[v] of Galilee, and his brother Philip ruler[v] of the region of Ī·tu·raē´a and Trach·o·nī´tis, and Ly̆·sā´ni·as ruler[v] of Ab·i·lē´nē, 2 during the high priesthood of An´nas and Cā´i·a·phas, the word of God came to John son of Zech·a·rī´ah in the wilderness. 3 He went into all the region around the Jordan, proclaiming a baptism of repentance for the forgiveness of sins, 4 as it is written in the book of the words of the prophet Ī·sāi´ah,

"The voice of one crying out in
    the wilderness:
'Prepare the way of the Lord,
    make his paths straight.
5 Every valley shall be filled,
    and every mountain and hill
        shall be made low,
and the crooked shall be made
        straight,
    and the rough ways made
        smooth;
6 and all flesh shall see the
        salvation of God.' "

7 John said to the crowds that came out to be baptized by him, "You brood of vipers! Who warned you to flee from the wrath to come? 8 Bear fruits worthy of repentance. Do not begin to say to yourselves, 'We have Abraham as our ancestor'; for I tell you, God is able from these stones to raise up children to Abraham. 9 Even now the ax is lying at the root of the trees; every tree therefore that does not bear good fruit is cut down and thrown into the fire."

10 And the crowds asked him, "What then should we do?" 11 In reply he said to them, "Whoever has two coats must share with anyone who has none; and whoever has food must do likewise." 12 Even tax collectors came to be baptized, and they asked him, "Teacher, what should we do?" 13 He said to them, "Collect no more than the amount prescribed for you." 14 Soldiers also asked him, "And we, what should we do?" He said to them, "Do not extort money from anyone by threats or false accusation, and be satisfied with your wages."

15 As the people were filled with expectation, and all were questioning in their hearts concerning John, whether he might be the Messiah,[w]

16 John answered all of them by saying, "I baptize you with water; but one who is more powerful than I is coming; I am not worthy to untie the thong of his sandals. He will baptize you with[x] the Holy Spirit and fire. 17 His winnowing fork is in his hand, to clear his threshing floor and to gather the wheat into his granary; but the chaff he will burn with unquenchable fire."

18 So, with many other exhortations, he proclaimed the good news to the people. 19 But Her´od the ruler,[v] who had been rebuked by him because of He·rō´di·as, his brother's wife, and because of all the evil things that Her´od had done, 20 added to them all by shutting up John in prison.

The Baptism of Jesus
(Mt 3.13–17; Mk 1.9–11; Jn 1.29–34)

21 Now when all the people were baptized, and when Jesus also had been baptized and was praying, the heaven was opened, 22 and the Holy Spirit descended upon him in bodily form like a dove. And a voice came from heaven, "You are my Son, the Beloved;[y] with you I am well pleased."[z]

The Ancestors of Jesus
(Gen 5.1–32; 11.10–26; Ruth 4.18–22; 1 Chr 1.1–4, 24–27, 34; 2.1–15; Mt 1.2–16)

23 Jesus was about thirty years old when he began his work. He was the son (as was thought) of Joseph son of Hē´lī, 24 son of Mat´that, son of Levi, son of Mel´chī, son of Jan´naī, son of Joseph, 25 son of Mat·ta·thī´as, son of Ā´mos, son of Nā´hum, son of Es´lī, son of Nag´ga·ī, 26 son of Mā´ath, son of Mat·ta·thī´as, son of Sem´ē·in, son of Jō´sech, son of Jō´da, 27 son of Jō·an´an, son of Rhē´sa, son of Ze·rub´ba·bel, son of She·al´ti·el,[a] son of Nē´rī, 28 son of Mel´chī, son of Ad´dī, son of Cō´sam, son of El·mā´dam, son of Er, 29 son of Joshua, son of El·i·e´zer, son of Jō´rim, son of Mat´that, son of Levi, 30 son of Sim´e·on, son of Judah, son of Joseph, son of Jō´nam, son of E·lī´a·kim, 31 son of Mē´le·a, son of Men´na, son of Mat´ta·tha, son of Nathan, son of David, 32 son of Jesse, son of Ō´bed, son of Bō´az, son of Sā´la,[b] son of Nah´shon, 33 son of Am·min´-

---

[v] Gk *tetrarch*   [w] Or *the Christ*   [x] Or *in*
[y] Or *my beloved Son*   [z] Other ancient authorities read *You are my Son, today I have begotten you*   [a] Gk *Salathiel*
[b] Other ancient authorities read *Salmon*

a·dab, son of Ad·min, son of Ar'nī,[c] son of Hez'ron, son of Per'ez, son of Judah, 34 son of Jacob, son of Isaac, son of Abraham, son of Tē'rah, son of Nā'-hor, 35 son of Sē'rug, son of Rē'ū, son of Pē'leg, son of Ē'ber, son of Shē'lah, 36 son of Cā·ī'nan, son of Ar·phả'xad, son of Shem, son of Noah, son of Lā'-mech, 37 son of Me·thū'se·lah, son of Ē'noch, son of Jar'ed, son of Ma·hā'-la·lē·el, son of Cā·ī'nan, 38 son of Ē'nos, son of Seth, son of Adam, son of God.

The Temptation of Jesus
(Mt 4.1–11; Mk 1.12–13)

4 Jesus, full of the Holy Spirit, re-turned from the Jordan and was led by the Spirit in the wilderness, 2 where for forty days he was tempted by the devil. He ate nothing at all dur-ing those days, and when they were over, he was famished. 3 The devil said to him, "If you are the Son of God, com-mand this stone to become a loaf of bread." 4 Jesus answered him, "It is written, 'One does not live by bread alone.' "

5 Then the devil[d] led him up and showed him in an instant all the king-doms of the world. 6 And the devil[d] said to him, "To you I will give their glory and all this authority; for it has been given over to me, and I give it to anyone I please. 7 If you, then, will wor-ship me, it will all be yours." 8 Jesus answered him, "It is written,

'Worship the Lord your God,
    and serve only him.' "

9 Then the devil[d] took him to Jeru-salem, and placed him on the pinnacle of the temple, saying to him, "If you are the Son of God, throw yourself down from here, 10 for it is written,

'He will command his angels
        concerning you,
    to protect you,'

11 and

'On their hands they will bear
        you up,
    so that you will not dash your
        foot against a stone.' "

12 Jesus answered him, "It is said, 'Do not put the Lord your God to the test.' " 13 When the devil had finished every test, he departed from him until an op-portune time.

The Beginning of the Galilean Ministry
(Mt 4.17; Mk 1.14–15)

14 Then Jesus, filled with the power of the Spirit, returned to Galilee, and a report about him spread through all the surrounding country. 15 He began to teach in their synagogues and was praised by everyone.

The Rejection of Jesus at Nazareth
(Mt 13.54–58; Mk 6.1–6)

16 When he came to Nazareth, where he had been brought up, he went to the synagogue on the sabbath day, as was his custom. He stood up to read, 17 and the scroll of the prophet Ī·sai'ah was given to him. He unrolled the scroll and found the place where it was written:

18 "The Spirit of the Lord is upon
        me,
    because he has anointed me
        to bring good news to the
            poor.
He has sent me to proclaim
        release to the captives
    and recovery of sight to the
            blind,
        to let the oppressed go free,
19   to proclaim the year of the
        Lord's favor."

20 And he rolled up the scroll, gave it back to the attendant, and sat down. The eyes of all in the synagogue were fixed on him. 21 Then he began to say to them, "Today this scripture has been fulfilled in your hearing." 22 All spoke well of him and were amazed at the gracious words that came from his mouth. They said, "Is not this Joseph's son?" 23 He said to them, "Doubtless you will quote to me this proverb, 'Doctor, cure yourself!' And you will say, 'Do here also in your hometown the things that we have heard you did at Ca·per'na·um.' " 24 And he said, "Truly I tell you, no prophet is ac-cepted in the prophet's hometown. 25 But the truth is, there were many widows in Israel in the time of E·lī'jah, when the heaven was shut up three years and six months, and there was a severe famine over all the land; 26 yet E·lī'jah was sent to none of them ex-cept to a widow at Zar'e·phath in Si'don. 27 There were also many lep-ers[e] in Israel in the time of the prophet E·lī'sha, and none of them was cleansed except Nā'a·man the Syrian." 28 When they heard this, all in the syna-gogue were filled with rage. 29 They got

---

[c] Other ancient authorities read *Amminadab, son of Aram*; others vary widely   [d] Gk *he*   [e] The terms *leper* and *leprosy* can refer to several diseases

up, drove him out of the town, and led him to the brow of the hill on which their town was built, so that they might hurl him off the cliff. ³⁰But he passed through the midst of them and went on his way.

The Man with an Unclean Spirit
(Mk 1.21–28)

31 He went down to Ca·per′na·um, a city in Galilee, and was teaching them on the sabbath. ³²They were astounded at his teaching, because he spoke with authority. ³³In the synagogue there was a man who had the spirit of an unclean demon, and he cried out with a loud voice, ³⁴"Let us alone! What have you to do with us, Jesus of Nazareth? Have you come to destroy us? I know who you are, the Holy One of God." ³⁵But Jesus rebuked him, saying, "Be silent, and come out of him!" When the demon had thrown him down before them, he came out of him without having done him any harm. ³⁶They were all amazed and kept saying to one another, "What kind of utterance is this? For with authority and power he commands the unclean spirits, and out they come!" ³⁷And a report about him began to reach every place in the region.

Healings at Simon's House
(Mt 8.14–17; Mk 1.29–34)

38 After leaving the synagogue he entered Simon's house. Now Simon's mother-in-law was suffering from a high fever, and they asked him about her. ³⁹Then he stood over her and rebuked the fever, and it left her. Immediately she got up and began to serve them.

40 As the sun was setting, all those who had any who were sick with various kinds of diseases brought them to him; and he laid his hands on each of them and cured them. ⁴¹Demons also came out of many, shouting, "You are the Son of God!" But he rebuked them and would not allow them to speak, because they knew that he was the Messiah.*f*

Jesus Preaches in the Synagogues
(Mt 4.23–25; Mk 1.35–39)

42 At daybreak he departed and went into a deserted place. And the crowds were looking for him; and when they reached him, they wanted to prevent him from leaving them. ⁴³But he said to them, "I must proclaim the good news of the kingdom of God to the other cities also; for I was sent for this purpose." ⁴⁴So he continued proclaiming the message in the synagogues of Judea.*g*

Jesus Calls the First Disciples
(Mt 4.18–22; Mk 1.16–20)

5 Once while Jesus*h* was standing beside the lake of Gen·nes′a·ret, and the crowd was pressing in on him to hear the word of God, ²he saw two boats there at the shore of the lake; the fishermen had gone out of them and were washing their nets. ³He got into one of the boats, the one belonging to Simon, and asked him to put out a little way from the shore. Then he sat down and taught the crowds from the boat. ⁴When he had finished speaking, he said to Simon, "Put out into the deep water and let down your nets for a catch." ⁵Simon answered, "Master, we have worked all night long but have caught nothing. Yet if you say so, I will let down the nets." ⁶When they had done this, they caught so many fish that their nets were beginning to break. ⁷So they signaled their partners in the other boat to come and help them. And they came and filled both boats, so that they began to sink. ⁸But when Simon Peter saw it, he fell down at Jesus' knees, saying, "Go away from me, Lord, for I am a sinful man!" ⁹For he and all who were with him were amazed at the catch of fish that they had taken; ¹⁰and so also were James and John, sons of Zeb′e·dee, who were partners with Simon. Then Jesus said to Simon, "Do not be afraid; from now on you will be catching people." ¹¹When they had brought their boats to shore, they left everything and followed him.

Jesus Cleanses a Leper
(Mt 8.1–4; Mk 1.40–45)

12 Once, when he was in one of the cities, there was a man covered with leprosy.*i* When he saw Jesus, he bowed with his face to the ground and begged him, "Lord, if you choose, you can make me clean." ¹³Then Jesus*h* stretched out his hand, touched him, and said, "I do choose. Be made clean." Immediately the leprosy*i* left him.

---

*f*Or the Christ　　*g*Other ancient authorities read *Galilee*　　*h*Gk *he*
*i*The terms *leper* and *leprosy* can refer to several diseases

¹⁴And he ordered him to tell no one. "Go," he said, "and show yourself to the priest, and, as Moses commanded, make an offering for your cleansing, for a testimony to them." ¹⁵But now more than ever the word about Jesus*j* spread abroad; many crowds would gather to hear him and to be cured of their diseases. ¹⁶But he would withdraw to deserted places and pray.

Jesus Heals a Paralytic
(Mt 9.2–8; Mk 2.1–12)

17 One day, while he was teaching, Phar′i·sees and teachers of the law were sitting near by (they had come from every village of Galilee and Judea and from Jerusalem); and the power of the Lord was with him to heal.*k* ¹⁸Just then some men came, carrying a paralyzed man on a bed. They were trying to bring him in and lay him before Jesus;*j* ¹⁹but finding no way to bring him in because of the crowd, they went up on the roof and let him down with his bed through the tiles into the middle of the crowd*l* in front of Jesus. ²⁰When he saw their faith, he said, "Friend,*m* your sins are forgiven you." ²¹Then the scribes and the Phar′i·sees began to question, "Who is this who is speaking blasphemies? Who can forgive sins but God alone?" ²²When Jesus perceived their questionings, he answered them, "Why do you raise such questions in your hearts? ²³Which is easier, to say, 'Your sins are forgiven you,' or to say, 'Stand up and walk'? ²⁴But so that you may know that the Son of Man has authority on earth to forgive sins"—he said to the one who was paralyzed—"I say to you, stand up and take your bed and go to your home." ²⁵Immediately he stood up before them, took what he had been lying on, and went to his home, glorifying God. ²⁶Amazement seized all of them, and they glorified God and were filled with awe, saying, "We have seen strange things today."

Jesus Calls Levi
(Mt 9.9–13; Mk 2.13–17)

27 After this he went out and saw a tax collector named Levi, sitting at the tax booth; and he said to him, "Follow me." ²⁸And he got up, left everything, and followed him.
²⁹Then Levi gave a great banquet for him in his house; and there was a large crowd of tax collectors and others sitting at the table*n* with them.

³⁰The Phar′i·sees and their scribes were complaining to his disciples, saying, "Why do you eat and drink with tax collectors and sinners?" ³¹Jesus answered, "Those who are well have no need of a physician, but those who are sick; ³²I have come to call not the righteous but sinners to repentance."

The Question about Fasting
(Mt 9.14–17; Mk 2.18–22)

33 Then they said to him, "John's disciples, like the disciples of the Phar′i·sees, frequently fast and pray, but your disciples eat and drink." ³⁴Jesus said to them, "You cannot make wedding guests fast while the bridegroom is with them, can you? ³⁵The days will come when the bridegroom will be taken away from them, and then they will fast in those days." ³⁶He also told them a parable: "No one tears a piece from a new garment and sews it on an old garment; otherwise the new will be torn, and the piece from the new will not match the old. ³⁷And no one puts new wine into old wineskins; otherwise the new wine will burst the skins and will be spilled, and the skins will be destroyed. ³⁸But new wine must be put into fresh wineskins. ³⁹And no one after drinking old wine desires new wine, but says, 'The old is good.' "*o*

The Question about the Sabbath
(Mt 12.1–8; Mk 2.23–28)

6 One sabbath*p* while Jesus*q* was going through the grainfields, his disciples plucked some heads of grain, rubbed them in their hands, and ate them. ²But some of the Phar′i·sees said, "Why are you doing what is not lawful*r* on the sabbath?" ³Jesus answered, "Have you not read what David did when he and his companions were hungry? ⁴He entered the house of God and took and ate the bread of the Presence, which it is not lawful for any but the priests to eat, and gave some to his companions?" ⁵Then he said to them, "The Son of Man is lord of the sabbath."

---

*j*Gk *him*   *k*Other ancient authorities read *was present to heal them*
*l*Gk *into the midst*   *m*Gk *Man*
*n*Gk *reclining*   *o*Other ancient authorities read *better*; others lack verse 39   *p*Other ancient authorities read *On the second first sabbath*   *q*Gk *he*
*r*Other ancient authorities add *to do*

The Man with a Withered Hand
(Mt 12.9–14; Mk 3.1–6)

6 On another sabbath he entered the synagogue and taught, and there was a man there whose right hand was withered. [7] The scribes and the Phar'i·sees watched him to see whether he would cure on the sabbath, so that they might find an accusation against him. [8] Even though he knew what they were thinking, he said to the man who had the withered hand, "Come and stand here." He got up and stood there. [9] Then Jesus said to them, "I ask you, is it lawful to do good or to do harm on the sabbath, to save life or to destroy it?" [10] After looking around at all of them, he said to him, "Stretch out your hand." He did so, and his hand was restored. [11] But they were filled with fury and discussed with one another what they might do to Jesus.

Jesus Chooses the Twelve Apostles
(Mt 10.1–4; Mk 3.13–19a)

12 Now during those days he went out to the mountain to pray; and he spent the night in prayer to God. [13] And when day came, he called his disciples and chose twelve of them, whom he also named apostles: [14] Simon, whom he named Peter, and his brother Andrew, and James, and John, and Philip, and Bartholomew, [15] and Matthew, and Thomas, and James son of Al·phae'us, and Simon, who was called the Zealot, [16] and Judas son of James, and Judas Is·car'i·ot, who became a traitor.

Jesus Teaches and Heals
(Mt 4.23–25; Mk 1.35–39; Lk 4.44)

17 He came down with them and stood on a level place, with a great crowd of his disciples and a great multitude of people from all Judea, Jerusalem, and the coast of Tyre and Si'don. [18] They had come to hear him and to be healed of their diseases; and those who were troubled with unclean spirits were cured. [19] And all in the crowd were trying to touch him, for power came out from him and healed all of them.

Blessings and Woes
(Mt 5.1–12)

20 Then he looked up at his disciples and said:
"Blessed are you who are poor,
for yours is the kingdom of God.
21 "Blessed are you who are hungry now,
for you will be filled.
"Blessed are you who weep now,
for you will laugh.
22 "Blessed are you when people hate you, and when they exclude you, revile you, and defame you[s] on account of the Son of Man. [23] Rejoice in that day and leap for joy, for surely your reward is great in heaven; for that is what their ancestors did to the prophets.
24 "But woe to you who are rich,
for you have received your consolation.
25 "Woe to you who are full now,
for you will be hungry.
"Woe to you who are laughing now,
for you will mourn and weep.
26 "Woe to you when all speak well of you, for that is what their ancestors did to the false prophets.

Love for Enemies
(Mt 5.33–48)

27 "But I say to you that listen, Love your enemies, do good to those who hate you, [28] bless those who curse you, pray for those who abuse you. [29] If anyone strikes you on the cheek, offer the other also; and from anyone who takes away your coat do not withhold even your shirt. [30] Give to everyone who begs from you; and if anyone takes away your goods, do not ask for them again. [31] Do to others as you would have them do to you.
32 "If you love those who love you, what credit is that to you? For even sinners love those who love them. [33] If you do good to those who do good to you, what credit is that to you? For even sinners do the same. [34] If you lend to those from whom you hope to receive, what credit is that to you? Even sinners lend to sinners, to receive as much again. [35] But love your enemies, do good, and lend, expecting nothing in return.[t] Your reward will be great, and you will be children of the Most High; for he is kind to the ungrateful and the wicked. [36] Be merciful, just as your Father is merciful.

---

[s] Gk *cast out your name as evil*   [t] Other ancient authorities read *despairing of no one*

Judging Others
(Mt 7.1–5)

37 "Do not judge, and you will not be judged; do not condemn, and you will not be condemned. Forgive, and you will be forgiven; 38 give, and it will be given to you. A good measure, pressed down, shaken together, running over, will be put into your lap; for the measure you give will be the measure you get back."

39 He also told them a parable: "Can a blind person guide a blind person? Will not both fall into a pit? 40 A disciple is not above the teacher, but everyone who is fully qualified will be like the teacher. 41 Why do you see the speck in your neighbor's *u* eye, but do not notice the log in your own eye? 42 Or how can you say to your neighbor, *v* 'Friend, *v* let me take out the speck in your eye,' when you yourself do not see the log in your own eye? You hypocrite, first take the log out of your own eye, and then you will see clearly to take the speck out of your neighbor's *u* eye.

A Tree and Its Fruit
(Mt 7.15–20)

43 "No good tree bears bad fruit, nor again does a bad tree bear good fruit; 44 for each tree is known by its own fruit. Figs are not gathered from thorns, nor are grapes picked from a bramble bush. 45 The good person out of the good treasure of the heart produces good, and the evil person out of evil treasure produces evil; for it is out of the abundance of the heart that the mouth speaks.

The Two Foundations
(Mt 7.21–27)

46 "Why do you call me 'Lord, Lord,' and do not do what I tell you? 47 I will show you what someone is like who comes to me, hears my words, and acts on them. 48 That one is like a man building a house, who dug deeply and laid the foundation on rock; when a flood arose, the river burst against that house but could not shake it, because it had been well built. *w* 49 But the one who hears and does not act is like a man who built a house on the ground without a foundation. When the river burst against it, immediately it fell, and great was the ruin of that house."

Jesus Heals a Centurion's Servant
(Mt 8.5–13)

7 After Jesus *x* had finished all his sayings in the hearing of the people, he entered Ca·per′na·um. 2 A centurion there had a slave whom he valued highly, and who was ill and close to death. 3 When he heard about Jesus, he sent some Jewish elders to him, asking him to come and heal his slave. 4 When they came to Jesus, they appealed to him earnestly, saying, "He is worthy of having you do this for him, 5 for he loves our people, and it is he who built our synagogue for us." 6 And Jesus went with them, but when he was not far from the house, the centurion sent friends to say to him, "Lord, do not trouble yourself, for I am not worthy to have you come under my roof; 7 therefore I did not presume to come to you. But only speak the word, and let my servant be healed. 8 For I also am a man set under authority, with soldiers under me; and I say to one, 'Go,' and he goes, and to another, 'Come,' and he comes, and to my slave, 'Do this,' and the slave does it." 9 When Jesus heard this he was amazed at him, and turning to the crowd that followed him, he said, "I tell you, not even in Israel have I found such faith." 10 When those who had been sent returned to the house, they found the slave in good health.

Jesus Raises the Widow's Son at Nain

11 Soon afterwards *y* he went to a town called Na′in, and his disciples and a large crowd went with him. 12 As he approached the gate of the town, a man who had died was being carried out. He was his mother's only son, and she was a widow; and with her was a large crowd from the town. 13 When the Lord saw her, he had compassion for her and said to her, "Do not weep." 14 Then he came forward and touched the bier, and the bearers stood still. And he said, "Young man, I say to you, rise!" 15 The dead man sat up and began to speak, and Jesus *x* gave him to his mother. 16 Fear seized all of them; and they glorified God, saying, "A great prophet has risen among us!" and "God has looked favorably on his people!" 17 This word about him spread

---

u Gk *brother's*   *v* Gk *brother*   *w* Other ancient authorities read *founded upon the rock*   *x* Gk *he*   *y* Other ancient authorities read *Next day* throughout Judea and all the surrounding country.

Messengers from John the Baptist
(Mt 11.2–19)

18 The disciples of John reported all these things to him. So John summoned two of his disciples [19] and sent them to the Lord to ask, "Are you the one who is to come, or are we to wait for another?" [20] When the men had come to him, they said, "John the Baptist has sent us to you to ask, 'Are you the one who is to come, or are we to wait for another?' " [21] Jesus[z] had just then cured many people of diseases, plagues, and evil spirits, and had given sight to many who were blind. [22] And he answered them, "Go and tell John what you have seen and heard: the blind receive their sight, the lame walk, the lepers[a] are cleansed, the deaf hear, the dead are raised, the poor have good news brought to them. [23] And blessed is anyone who takes no offense at me."

24 When John's messengers had gone, Jesus[b] began to speak to the crowds about John:[c] "What did you go out into the wilderness to look at? A reed shaken by the wind? [25] What then did you go out to see? Someone[d] dressed in soft robes? Look, those who put on fine clothing and live in luxury are in royal palaces. [26] What then did you go out to see? A prophet? Yes, I tell you, and more than a prophet. [27] This is the one about whom it is written,

'See, I am sending my
     messenger ahead of you,
who will prepare your way
     before you.'

[28] I tell you, among those born of women no one is greater than John; yet the least in the kingdom of God is greater than he." [29] (And all the people who heard this, including the tax collectors, acknowledged the justice of God,[e] because they had been baptized with John's baptism. [30] But by refusing to be baptized by him, the Phar'i·sees and the lawyers rejected God's purpose for themselves.)

31 "To what then will I compare the people of this generation, and what are they like? [32] They are like children sitting in the marketplace and calling to one another,

'We played the flute for you, and
     you did not dance;
we wailed, and you did not
     weep.'

[33] For John the Baptist has come eating no bread and drinking no wine, and you say, 'He has a demon'; [34] the Son of Man has come eating and drinking, and you say, 'Look, a glutton and a drunkard, a friend of tax collectors and sinners!' [35] Nevertheless, wisdom is vindicated by all her children."

A Sinful Woman Forgiven

36 One of the Phar'i·sees asked Jesus[c] to eat with him, and he went into the Phar'i·see's house and took his place at the table. [37] And a woman in the city, who was a sinner, having learned that he was eating in the Phar'i·see's house, brought an alabaster jar of ointment. [38] She stood behind him at his feet, weeping, and began to bathe his feet with her tears and to dry them with her hair. Then she continued kissing his feet and anointing them with the ointment. [39] Now when the Phar'i·see who had invited him saw it, he said to himself, "If this man were a prophet, he would have known who and what kind of woman this is who is touching him—that she is a sinner." [40] Jesus spoke up and said to him, "Simon, I have something to say to you." "Teacher," he replied, "Speak." [41] "A certain creditor had two debtors; one owed five hundred denarii,[f] and the other fifty. [42] When they could not pay, he canceled the debts for both of them. Now which of them will love him more?" [43] Simon answered, "I suppose the one for whom he canceled the greater debt." And Jesus[b] said to him, "You have judged rightly." [44] Then turning toward the woman, he said to Simon, "Do you see this woman? I entered your house; you gave me no water for my feet, but she has bathed my feet with her tears and dried them with her hair. [45] You gave me no kiss, but from the time I came in she has not stopped kissing my feet. [46] You did not anoint my head with oil, but she has anointed my feet with ointment. [47] Therefore, I tell you, her sins, which were many, have been forgiven; hence she has shown great love. But the one to whom little is forgiven, loves little." [48] Then he said to her, "Your sins are

---

[z] Gk He   [a] The terms *leper* and *leprosy* can refer to several diseases   [b] Gk he   [c] Gk him   [d] Or *Why then did you go out? To see someone*   [e] Or *praised God*   [f] The denarius was the usual day's wage for a laborer

forgiven." 49 But those who were at the table with him began to say among themselves, "Who is this who even forgives sins?" 50 And he said to the woman, "Your faith has saved you; go in peace."

Some Women Accompany Jesus

8 Soon afterwards he went on through cities and villages, proclaiming and bringing the good news of the kingdom of God. The twelve were with him, 2 as well as some women who had been cured of evil spirits and infirmities: Mary, called Mag'da·lēne, from whom seven demons had gone out, 3 and Jō·an'na, the wife of Herod's steward Chū'za, and Susanna, and many others, who provided for them g out of their resources.

The Parable of the Sower
(Mt 13.1–9; Mk 4.1–9)

4 When a great crowd gathered and people from town after town came to him, he said in a parable: 5 "A sower went out to sow his seed; and as he sowed, some fell on the path and was trampled on, and the birds of the air ate it up. 6 Some fell on the rock; and as it grew up, it withered for lack of moisture. 7 Some fell among thorns, and the thorns grew with it and choked it. 8 Some fell into good soil, and when it grew, it produced a hundredfold." As he said this, he called out, "Let anyone with ears to hear listen!"

The Purpose of the Parables
(Mt 13.10–17; Mk 4.10–12)

9 Then his disciples asked him what this parable meant. 10 He said, "To you it has been given to know the secrets h of the kingdom of God; but to others I speak i in parables, so that
'looking they may not perceive,
   and listening they may not
      understand.'

The Parable of the Sower Explained
(Mt 13.18–23; Mk 4.13–20)

11 "Now the parable is this: The seed is the word of God. 12 The ones on the path are those who have heard; then the devil comes and takes away the word from their hearts, so that they may not believe and be saved. 13 The ones on the rock are those who, when they hear the word, receive it with joy.

But these have no root; they believe only for a while and in a time of testing fall away. 14 As for what fell among the thorns, these are the ones who hear; but as they go on their way, they are choked by the cares and riches and pleasures of life, and their fruit does not mature. 15 But as for that in the good soil, these are the ones who, when they hear the word, hold it fast in an honest and good heart, and bear fruit with patient endurance.

A Lamp under a Jar
(Mt 4.21–25)

16 "No one after lighting a lamp hides it under a jar, or puts it under a bed, but puts it on a lampstand, so that those who enter may see the light. 17 For nothing is hidden that will not be disclosed, nor is anything secret that will not become known and come to light. 18 Then pay attention to how you listen; for to those who have, more will be given; and from those who do not have, even what they seem to have will be taken away."

The True Kindred of Jesus
(Mt 12.46–50; Mk 3.31–35)

19 Then his mother and his brothers came to him, but they could not reach him because of the crowd. 20 And he was told, "Your mother and your brothers are standing outside, wanting to see you." 21 But he said to them, "My mother and my brothers are those who hear the word of God and do it."

Jesus Calms a Storm
(Mt 8.23–27; Mk 4.35–41)

22 One day he got into a boat with his disciples, and he said to them, "Let us go across to the other side of the lake." So they put out, 23 and while they were sailing he fell asleep. A windstorm swept down on the lake, and the boat was filling with water, and they were in danger. 24 They went to him and woke him up, shouting, "Master, Master, we are perishing!" And he woke up and rebuked the wind and the raging waves; they ceased, and there was a calm. 25 He said to them, "Where is your faith?" They were afraid and amazed, and said to one another,

g Other ancient authorities read him
h Or mysteries   i Gk lacks I speak

"Who then is this, that he commands even the winds and the water, and they obey him?"

Jesus Heals the Gerasene Demoniac
(Mt 8.28—9.1; Mk 5.1–20)

26 Then they arrived at the country of the Ger'a·senes, [j] which is opposite Galilee. 27 As he stepped out on land, a man of the city who had demons met him. For a long time he had worn [k] no clothes, and he did not live in a house but in the tombs. 28 When he saw Jesus, he fell down before him and shouted at the top of his voice, "What have you to do with me, Jesus, Son of the Most High God? I beg you, do not torment me"— 29 for Jesus [l] had commanded the unclean spirit to come out of the man. (For many times it had seized him; he was kept under guard and bound with chains and shackles, but he would break the bonds and be driven by the demon into the wilds.) 30 Jesus then asked him, "What is your name?" He said, "Legion"; for many demons had entered him. 31 They begged him not to order them to go back into the abyss.

32 Now there on the hillside a large herd of swine was feeding; and the demons [m] begged Jesus [n] to let them enter these. So he gave them permission. 33 Then the demons came out of the man and entered the swine, and the herd rushed down the steep bank into the lake and was drowned.

34 When the swineherds saw what had happened, they ran off and told it in the city and in the country. 35 Then people came out to see what had happened, and when they came to Jesus, they found the man from whom the demons had gone sitting at the feet of Jesus, clothed and in his right mind. And they were afraid. 36 Those who had seen it told them how the one who had been possessed by demons had been healed. 37 Then all the people of the surrounding country of the Ger'-a·senes [j] asked Jesus [n] to leave them; for they were seized with great fear. So he got into the boat and returned. 38 The man from whom the demons had gone begged that he might be with him; but Jesus [l] sent him away, saying, 39 "Return to your home, and declare how much God has done for you." So he went away, proclaiming throughout the city how much Jesus had done for him.

A Girl Restored to Life and a Woman Healed
(Mt 9.18–26; Mk 5.21–43)

40 Now when Jesus returned, the crowd welcomed him, for they were all waiting for him. 41 Just then there came a man named Ja·i'rus, a leader of the synagogue. He fell at Jesus' feet and begged him to come to his house, 42 for he had an only daughter, about twelve years old, who was dying.

As he went, the crowds pressed in on him. 43 Now there was a woman who had been suffering from hemorrhages for twelve years; and though she had spent all she had on physicians, [o] no one could cure her. 44 She came up behind him and touched the fringe of his clothes, and immediately her hemorrhage stopped. 45 Then Jesus asked, "Who touched me?" When all denied it, Peter [p] said, "Master, the crowds surround you and press in on you." 46 But Jesus said, "Someone touched me; for I noticed that power had gone out from me." 47 When the woman saw that she could not remain hidden, she came trembling; and falling down before him, she declared in the presence of all the people why she had touched him, and how she had been immediately healed. 48 He said to her, "Daughter, your faith has made you well; go in peace."

49 While he was still speaking, someone came from the leader's house to say, "Your daughter is dead; do not trouble the teacher any longer." 50 When Jesus heard this, he replied, "Do not fear. Only believe, and she will be saved." 51 When he came to the house, he did not allow anyone to enter with him, except Peter, John, and James, and the child's father and mother. 52 They were all weeping and wailing for her; but he said, "Do not weep; for she is not dead but sleeping." 53 And they laughed at him, knowing that she was dead. 54 But he took her by the hand and called out, "Child, get up!" 55 Her spirit returned,

---

[j] Other ancient authorities read *Gadarenes*; others, *Gergesenes*   [k] Other ancient authorities read *a man of the city who had had demons for a long time met him. He wore*   [l] Gk *he*   [m] Gk *they*   [n] Gk *him*   [o] Other ancient authorities lack *and had spent all she had on physicians*   [p] Other ancient authorities add *and those who were with him*

and she got up at once. Then he directed them to give her something to eat. [56]Her parents were astounded; but he ordered them to tell no one what had happened.

The Mission of the Twelve
(Mt 10.5–15)

9 Then Jesus[q] called the twelve together and gave them power and authority over all demons and to cure diseases, [2]and he sent them out to proclaim the kingdom of God and to heal. [3]He said to them, "Take nothing for your journey, no staff, nor bag, nor bread, nor money—not even an extra tunic. [4]Whatever house you enter, stay there, and leave from there. [5]Wherever they do not welcome you, as you are leaving that town shake the dust off your feet as a testimony against them." [6]They departed and went through the villages, bringing the good news and curing diseases everywhere.

Herod's Perplexity
(Mt 14.1–12; Mk 6.14–29)

[7] Now Her'od the ruler[r] heard about all that had taken place, and he was perplexed, because it was said by some that John had been raised from the dead, [8]by some that E·li'jah had appeared, and by others that one of the ancient prophets had arisen. [9]Her'od said, "John I beheaded; but who is this about whom I hear such things?" And he tried to see him.

Feeding the Five Thousand
(Mt 14.13–21; Mk 6.30–44; Jn 6.1–15)

[10] On their return the apostles told Jesus[s] all they had done. He took them with him and withdrew privately to a city called Beth·sa'i·da. [11]When the crowds found out about it, they followed him; and he welcomed them, and spoke to them about the kingdom of God, and healed those who needed to be cured.

[12] The day was drawing to a close, and the twelve came to him and said, "Send the crowd away, so that they may go into the surrounding villages and countryside, to lodge and get provisions; for we are here in a deserted place." [13]But he said to them, "You give them something to eat." They said, "We have no more than five loaves and two fish—unless we are to go and buy food for all these people." [14]For there were about five thousand

men. And he said to his disciples, "Make them sit down in groups of about fifty each." [15]They did so and made them all sit down. [16]And taking the five loaves and the two fish, he looked up to heaven, and blessed and broke them, and gave them to the disciples to set before the crowd. [17]And all ate and were filled. What was left over was gathered up, twelve baskets of broken pieces.

Peter's Declaration about Jesus
(Mt 16.13–20; Mk 8.27–30)

[18] Once when Jesus[q] was praying alone, with only the disciples near him, he asked them, "Who do the crowds say that I am?" [19]They answered, "John the Baptist; but others, E·li'jah; and still others, that one of the ancient prophets has arisen." [20]He said to them, "But who do you say that I am?" Peter answered, "The Messiah[t] of God."

Jesus Foretells His Death and Resurrection
(Mt 16.24–28; Mk 8.31—9.1)

[21] He sternly ordered and commanded them not to tell anyone, [22]saying, "The Son of Man must undergo great suffering, and be rejected by the elders, chief priests, and scribes, and be killed, and on the third day be raised."

[23] Then he said to them all, "If any want to become my followers, let them deny themselves and take up their cross daily and follow me. [24]For those who want to save their life will lose it, and those who lose their life for my sake will save it. [25]What does it profit them if they gain the whole world, but lose or forfeit themselves? [26]Those who are ashamed of me and of my words, of them the Son of Man will be ashamed when he comes in his glory and the glory of the Father and of the holy angels. [27]But truly I tell you, there are some standing here who will not taste death before they see the kingdom of God."

The Transfiguration
(Mt 17.1–8; Mk 9.2–8; 2 Pet 1.16–18)

[28] Now about eight days after these sayings Jesus[q] took with him Peter and John and James, and went up on the mountain to pray. [29]And while he

[q]Gk *he*   [r]Gk *tetrarch*   [s]Gk *him*
[t]Or *The Christ*

was praying, the appearance of his face changed, and his clothes became dazzling white. 30 Suddenly they saw two men, Moses and E·li′jah, talking to him. 31 They appeared in glory and were speaking of his departure, which he was about to accomplish at Jerusalem. 32 Now Peter and his companions were weighed down with sleep; but since they had stayed awake, u they saw his glory and the two men who stood with him. 33 Just as they were leaving him, Peter said to Jesus, "Master, it is good for us to be here; let us make three dwellings, v one for you, one for Moses, and one for E·li′jah"— not knowing what he said. 34 While he was saying this, a cloud came and overshadowed them; and they were terrified as they entered the cloud. 35 Then from the cloud came a voice that said, "This is my Son, my Chosen; w listen to him!" 36 When the voice had spoken, Jesus was found alone. And they kept silent and in those days told no one any of the things they had seen.

Jesus Heals a Boy with a Demon
(Mt 17.14–21; Mk 9.14–29)

37 On the next day, when they had come down from the mountain, a great crowd met him. 38 Just then a man from the crowd shouted, "Teacher, I beg you to look at my son; he is my only child. 39 Suddenly a spirit seizes him, and all at once he x shrieks. It convulses him until he foams at the mouth; it mauls him and will scarcely leave him. 40 I begged your disciples to cast it out, but they could not." 41 Jesus answered, "You faithless and perverse generation, how much longer must I be with you and bear with you? Bring your son here." 42 While he was coming, the demon dashed him to the ground in convulsions. But Jesus rebuked the unclean spirit, healed the boy, and gave him back to his father. 43 And all were astounded at the greatness of God.

Jesus Again Foretells His Death
(Mt 17.22–23; Mk 9.30–32)

While everyone was amazed at all that he was doing, he said to his disciples, 44 "Let these words sink into your ears: The Son of Man is going to be betrayed into human hands." 45 But they did not understand this saying; its meaning was concealed from them, so that they could not perceive it. And

they were afraid to ask him about this saying.

True Greatness
(Mt 18.1–5; Mk 9.33–37)

46 An argument arose among them as to which one of them was the greatest. 47 But Jesus, aware of their inner thoughts, took a little child and put it by his side, 48 and said to them, "Whoever welcomes this child in my name welcomes me, and whoever welcomes me welcomes the one who sent me; for the least among all of you is the greatest."

Another Exorcist
(Mk 9.38–41)

49 John answered, "Master, we saw someone casting out demons in your name, and we tried to stop him, because he does not follow with us." 50 But Jesus said to him, "Do not stop him; for whoever is not against you is for you."

A Samaritan Village Refuses to Receive Jesus

51 When the days drew near for him to be taken up, he set his face to go to Jerusalem. 52 And he sent messengers ahead of him. On their way they entered a village of the Sa·mar′i·tans to make ready for him; 53 but they did not receive him, because his face was set toward Jerusalem. 54 When his disciples James and John saw it, they said, "Lord, do you want us to command fire to come down from heaven and consume them?" y 55 But he turned and rebuked them. 56 Then z they went on to another village.

Would-Be Followers of Jesus
(Mt 8.18–22)

57 As they were going along the road, someone said to him, "I will follow you wherever you go." 58 And Jesus said to him, "Foxes have holes, and birds of the air have nests; but the Son of Man has nowhere to lay his head." 59 To another he said, "Follow

u Or but when they were fully awake
v Or tents   w Other ancient authorities read my Beloved   x Or it   y Other ancient authorities add as Elijah did
z Other ancient authorities read rebuked them, and said, "You do not know what spirit you are of, 56 for the Son of Man has not come to destroy the lives of human beings but to save them." Then

me." But he said, "Lord, first let me go and bury my father." ⁶⁰ But Jesus^a said to him, "Let the dead bury their own dead; but as for you, go and proclaim the kingdom of God." ⁶¹ Another said, "I will follow you, Lord; but let me first say farewell to those at my home." ⁶² Jesus said to him, "No one who puts a hand to the plow and looks back is fit for the kingdom of God."

The Mission of the Seventy

10 After this the Lord appointed seventy^b others and sent them on ahead of him in pairs to every town and place where he himself intended to go. ² He said to them, "The harvest is plentiful, but the laborers are few; therefore ask the Lord of the harvest to send out laborers into his harvest. ³ Go on your way. See, I am sending you out like lambs into the midst of wolves. ⁴ Carry no purse, no bag, no sandals; and greet no one on the road. ⁵ Whatever house you enter, first say, 'Peace to this house!' ⁶ And if anyone is there who shares in peace, your peace will rest on that person; but if not, it will return to you. ⁷ Remain in the same house, eating and drinking whatever they provide, for the laborer deserves to be paid. Do not move about from house to house. ⁸ Whenever you enter a town and its people welcome you, eat what is set before you; ⁹ cure the sick who are there, and say to them, 'The kingdom of God has come near to you.' ^c ¹⁰ But whenever you enter a town and they do not welcome you, go out into its streets and say, ¹¹ 'Even the dust of your town that clings to our feet, we wipe off in protest against you. Yet know this: the kingdom of God has come near.' ^d ¹² I tell you, on that day it will be more tolerable for Sod'om than for that town.

Woes to Unrepentant Cities
(Mt 11.20–24)

13 "Woe to you, Chō·ra'zin! Woe to you, Beth·sa'i·da! For if the deeds of power done in you had been done in Tyre and Sī'don, they would have repented long ago, sitting in sackcloth and ashes. ¹⁴ But at the judgment it will be more tolerable for Tyre and Sī'don than for you. ¹⁵ And you, Ca·per'na·um,

will you be exalted to heaven?
No, you will be brought down
to Hades.

16 "Whoever listens to you listens

to me, and whoever rejects you rejects me, and whoever rejects me rejects the one who sent me."

The Return of the Seventy

17 The seventy^b returned with joy, saying, "Lord, in your name even the demons submit to us!" ¹⁸ He said to them, "I watched Satan fall from heaven like a flash of lightning. ¹⁹ See, I have given you authority to tread on snakes and scorpions, and over all the power of the enemy; and nothing will hurt you. ²⁰ Nevertheless, do not rejoice at this, that the spirits submit to you, but rejoice that your names are written in heaven."

Jesus Rejoices
(Mt 11.25–27)

21 At that same hour Jesus^a rejoiced in the Holy Spirit^e and said, "I thank^f you, Father, Lord of heaven and earth, because you have hidden these things from the wise and the intelligent and have revealed them to infants; yes, Father, for such was your gracious will. ^g ²² All things have been handed over to me by my Father; and no one knows who the Son is except the Father, or who the Father is except the Son and anyone to whom the Son chooses to reveal him."

23 Then turning to the disciples, Jesus^a said to them privately, "Blessed are the eyes that see what you see! ²⁴ For I tell you that many prophets and kings desired to see what you see, but did not see it, and to hear what you hear, but did not hear it."

The Parable of the Good Samaritan
(Mt 22.34–40; Mk 12.28–34)

25 Just then a lawyer stood up to test Jesus.^h "Teacher," he said, "what must I do to inherit eternal life?" ²⁶ He said to him, "What is written in the law? What do you read there?" ²⁷ He answered, "You shall love the Lord your God with all your heart, and with all your soul, and with all your strength, and with all your mind; and your neighbor as yourself." ²⁸ And he said to him, "You have given the right answer; do this, and you will live."

---

^a Gk he   ^b Other ancient authorities read *seventy-two*   ^c Or *is at hand for you*   ^d Or *is at hand*   ^e Other authorities read *in the spirit*   ^f Or *praise*   ^g Or *for so it was well-pleasing in your sight*   ^h Gk *him*

L U K E

29 But wanting to justify himself, he asked Jesus, "And who is my neighbor?" 30 Jesus replied, "A man was going down from Jerusalem to Jericho, and fell into the hands of robbers, who stripped him, beat him, and went away, leaving him half dead. 31 Now by chance a priest was going down that road; and when he saw him, he passed by on the other side. 32 So likewise a Lē'vīte, when he came to the place and saw him, passed by on the other side. 33 But a Sa·mar'i·tan while traveling came near him; and when he saw him, he was moved with pity. 34 He went to him and bandaged his wounds, having poured oil and wine on them. Then he put him on his own animal, brought him to an inn, and took care of him. 35 The next day he took out two denarii,[i] gave them to the innkeeper, and said, 'Take care of him; and when I come back, I will repay you whatever more you spend.' 36 Which of these three, do you think, was a neighbor to the man who fell into the hands of the robbers?" 37 He said, "The one who showed him mercy." Jesus said to him, "Go and do likewise."

Jesus Visits Martha and Mary

38 Now as they went on their way, he entered a certain village, where a woman named Martha welcomed him into her home. 39 She had a sister named Mary, who sat at the Lord's feet and listened to what he was saying. 40 But Martha was distracted by her many tasks; so she came to him and asked, "Lord, do you not care that my sister has left me to do all the work by myself? Tell her then to help me." 41 But the Lord answered her, "Martha, Martha, you are worried and distracted by many things; 42 there is need of only one thing.[j] Mary has chosen the better part, which will not be taken away from her."

The Lord's Prayer
(Mt 6.9–15)

11 He was praying in a certain place, and after he had finished, one of his disciples said to him, "Lord, teach us to pray, as John taught his disciples." 2 He said to them, "When you pray, say:

Father,[k] hallowed be your
     name.
Your kingdom come.[l]
3   Give us each day our daily
     bread.[m]

4   And forgive us our sins,
        for we ourselves forgive
        everyone indebted to us.
     And do not bring us to the
        time of trial."[n]

Perseverance in Prayer
(Mt 7.7–11)

5 And he said to them, "Suppose one of you has a friend, and you go to him at midnight and say to him, 'Friend, lend me three loaves of bread; 6 for a friend of mine has arrived, and I have nothing to set before him.' 7 And he answers from within, 'Do not bother me; the door has already been locked, and my children are with me in bed; I cannot get up and give you anything.' 8 I tell you, even though he will not get up and give him anything because he is his friend, at least because of his persistence he will get up and give him whatever he needs.

9 "So I say to you, Ask, and it will be given you; search, and you will find; knock, and the door will be opened for you. 10 For everyone who asks receives, and everyone who searches finds, and for everyone who knocks, the door will be opened. 11 Is there anyone among you who, if your child asks for[o] a fish, will give a snake instead of a fish? 12 Or if the child asks for an egg, will give a scorpion? 13 If you then, who are evil, know how to give good gifts to your children, how much more will the heavenly Father give the Holy Spirit[p] to those who ask him!"

Jesus and Beelzebul
(Mt 12.22–32; Mk 3.19b–30)

14 Now he was casting out a demon that was mute; when the demon had gone out, the one who had been mute spoke, and the crowds were amazed.

[i] The denarius was the usual day's wage for a laborer   [j] Other ancient authorities read *few things are necessary, or only one*   [k] Other ancient authorities read *Our Father in heaven*   [l] A few ancient authorities read *Your Holy Spirit come upon us and cleanse us.* Other ancient authorities add *Your will be done, on earth as in heaven*   [m] Or *our bread for tomorrow*   [n] Or *us into temptation.* Other ancient authorities add *but rescue us from the evil one* (or *from evil*)   [o] Other ancient authorities add *bread, will give a stone; or if your child asks for*   [p] Other ancient authorities read *the Father give the Holy Spirit from heaven*

15 But some of them said, "He casts out demons by Bē·el′ze·bul, the ruler of the demons." 16 Others, to test him, kept demanding from him a sign from heaven. 17 But he knew what they were thinking and said to them, "Every kingdom divided against itself becomes a desert, and house falls on house. 18 If Satan also is divided against himself, how will his kingdom stand? —for you say that I cast out the demons by Bē·el′ze·bul. 19 Now if I cast out the demons by Bē·el′ze·bul, by whom do your exorcists q cast them out? Therefore they will be your judges. 20 But if it is by the finger of God that I cast out the demons, then the kingdom of God has come to you. 21 When a strong man, fully armed, guards his castle, his property is safe. 22 But when one stronger than he attacks him and overpowers him, he takes away his armor in which he trusted and divides his plunder. 23 Whoever is not with me is against me, and whoever does not gather with me scatters.

The Return of the Unclean Spirit
(Mt 12.43–45)

24 "When the unclean spirit has gone out of a person, it wanders through waterless regions looking for a resting place, but not finding any, it says, 'I will return to my house from which I came.' 25 When it comes, it finds it swept and put in order. 26 Then it goes and brings seven other spirits more evil than itself, and they enter and live there; and the last state of that person is worse than the first."

True Blessedness

27 While he was saying this, a woman in the crowd raised her voice and said to him, "Blessed is the womb that bore you and the breasts that nursed you!" 28 But he said, "Blessed rather are those who hear the word of God and obey it!"

The Sign of Jonah
(Mt 12.38–42)

29 When the crowds were increasing, he began to say, "This generation is an evil generation; it asks for a sign, but no sign will be given to it except the sign of Jonah. 30 For just as Jonah became a sign to the people of Nin′e·veh, so the Son of Man will be to this generation. 31 The queen of the South will rise at the judgment with the people of this generation and condemn them, because she came from the ends of the earth to listen to the wisdom of Solomon, and see, something greater than Solomon is here! 32 The people of Nin′e·veh will rise up at the judgment with this generation and condemn it, because they repented at the proclamation of Jonah, and see, something greater than Jonah is here!

The Light of the Body
(Mt 6.22–23)

33 "No one after lighting a lamp puts it in a cellar, r but on the lampstand so that those who enter may see the light. 34 Your eye is the lamp of your body. If your eye is healthy, your whole body is full of light; but if it is not healthy, your body is full of darkness. 35 Therefore consider whether the light in you is not darkness. 36 If then your whole body is full of light, with no part of it in darkness, it will be as full of light as when a lamp gives you light with its rays."

Jesus Denounces Pharisees
and Lawyers

37 While he was speaking, a Phar′i·see invited him to dine with him; so he went in and took his place at the table. 38 The Phar′i·see was amazed to see that he did not first wash before dinner. 39 Then the Lord said to him, "Now you Phar′i·sees clean the outside of the cup and of the dish, but inside you are full of greed and wickedness. 40 You fools! Did not the one who made the outside make the inside also? 41 So give for alms those things that are within; and see, everything will be clean for you.

42 "But woe to you Phar′i·sees! For you tithe the mint and rue and herbs of all kinds, and neglect justice and the love of God; it is these you ought to have practiced, without neglecting the others. 43 Woe to you Phar′i·sees! For you love to have the seat of honor in the synagogues and to be greeted with respect in the marketplaces. 44 Woe to you! For you are like unmarked graves, and people walk over them without realizing it."

45 One of the lawyers answered him, "Teacher, when you say these things, you insult us too." 46 And he said, "Woe also to you lawyers! For

q Gk sons   r Other ancient authorities add or under the bushel basket you load people with burdens hard to bear, and you yourselves do not lift a finger to ease them. 47 Woe to you! For you build the tombs of the prophets whom your ancestors killed. 48 So you are witnesses and approve of the deeds of your ancestors; for they killed them, and you build their tombs. 49 Therefore also the Wisdom of God said, 'I will send them prophets and apostles, some of whom they will kill and persecute,' 50 so that this generation may be charged with the blood of all the prophets shed since the foundation of the world, 51 from the blood of Abel to the blood of Zech·a·rī'ah, who perished between the altar and the sanctuary. Yes, I tell you, it will be charged against this generation. 52 Woe to you lawyers! For you have taken away the key of knowledge; you did not enter yourselves, and you hindered those who were entering."

53 When he went outside, the scribes and the Phar'i·sees began to be very hostile toward him and to cross-examine him about many things, 54 lying in wait for him, to catch him in something he might say.

A Warning against Hypocrisy

12 Meanwhile, when the crowd gathered by the thousands, so that they trampled on one another, he began to speak first to his disciples, "Beware of the yeast of the Phar'i·sees, that is, their hypocrisy. 2 Nothing is covered up that will not be uncovered, and nothing secret that will not become known. 3 Therefore whatever you have said in the dark will be heard in the light, and what you have whispered behind closed doors will be proclaimed from the housetops.

Exhortation to Fearless Confession
(Mt 10.26–33)

4 "I tell you, my friends, do not fear those who kill the body, and after that can do nothing more. 5 But I will warn you whom to fear: fear him who, after he has killed, has authority[s] to cast into hell.[t] Yes, I tell you, fear him! 6 Are not five sparrows sold for two pennies? Yet not one of them is forgotten in God's sight. 7 But even the hairs of your head are all counted. Do not be afraid; you are of more value than many sparrows.

8 "And I tell you, everyone who acknowledges me before others, the Son of Man also will acknowledge before the angels of God; 9 but whoever denies me before others will be denied before the angels of God. 10 And everyone who speaks a word against the Son of Man will be forgiven; but whoever blasphemes against the Holy Spirit will not be forgiven. 11 When they bring you before the synagogues, the rulers, and the authorities, do not worry about how[u] you are to defend yourselves or what you are to say; 12 for the Holy Spirit will teach you at that very hour what you ought to say."

The Parable of the Rich Fool

13 Someone in the crowd said to him, "Teacher, tell my brother to divide the family inheritance with me." 14 But he said to him, "Friend, who set me to be a judge or arbitrator over you?" 15 And he said to them, "Take care! Be on your guard against all kinds of greed; for one's life does not consist in the abundance of possessions." 16 Then he told them a parable: "The land of a rich man produced abundantly. 17 And he thought to himself, 'What should I do, for I have no place to store my crops?' 18 Then he said, 'I will do this: I will pull down my barns and build larger ones, and there I will store all my grain and my goods. 19 And I will say to my soul, 'Soul, you have ample goods laid up for many years; relax, eat, drink, be merry.' 20 But God said to him, 'You fool! This very night your life is being demanded of you. And the things you have prepared, whose will they be?' 21 So it is with those who store up treasures for themselves but are not rich toward God."

Do Not Worry
(Mt 6.19–21, 25–34)

22 He said to his disciples, "Therefore I tell you, do not worry about your life, what you will eat, or about your body, what you will wear. 23 For life is more than food, and the body more than clothing. 24 Consider the ravens: they neither sow nor reap, they have neither storehouse nor barn, and yet God feeds them. Of how much more value are you than the birds! 25 And can any of you by worrying add a single hour to your span of life?[v] 26 If then you are not able to do so small a thing

---

[s] Or *power*   [t] Gk *Gehenna*   [u] Other ancient authorities add *or what*
[v] Or *add a cubit to your stature*

as that, why do you worry about the rest? 27Consider the lilies, how they grow: they neither toil nor spin;w yet I tell you, even Solomon in all his glory was not clothed like one of these. 28But if God so clothes the grass of the field, which is alive today and tomorrow is thrown into the oven, how much more will he clothe you—you of little faith! 29And do not keep striving for what you are to eat and what you are to drink, and do not keep worrying. 30For it is the nations of the world that strive after all these things, and your Father knows that you need them. 31Instead, strive for hisx kingdom, and these things will be given to you as well.

32 "Do not be afraid, little flock, for it is your Father's good pleasure to give you the kingdom. 33Sell your possessions, and give alms. Make purses for yourselves that do not wear out, an unfailing treasure in heaven, where no thief comes near and no moth destroys. 34For where your treasure is, there your heart will be also.

Watchful Slaves

35 "Be dressed for action and have your lamps lit; 36be like those who are waiting for their master to return from the wedding banquet, so that they may open the door for him as soon as he comes and knocks. 37Blessed are those slaves whom the master finds alert when he comes; truly I tell you, he will fasten his belt and have them sit down to eat, and he will come and serve them. 38If he comes during the middle of the night, or near dawn, and finds them so, blessed are those slaves.

"But know this: if the owner of the house had known at what hour the thief was coming, hey would not have let his house be broken into. 40You also must be ready, for the Son of Man is coming at an unexpected hour."

The Faithful or the Unfaithful Slave
(Mt 24.45–51)

41 Peter said, "Lord, are you telling this parable for us or for everyone?" 42And the Lord said, "Who then is the faithful and prudent manager whom his master will put in charge of his slaves, to give them their allowance of food at the proper time? 43Blessed is that slave whom his master will find at work when he arrives. 44Truly I tell you, he will put that one in charge of all his possessions. 45But if that slave says to himself, 'My master is delayed in coming,' and if he begins to beat the other slaves, men and women, and to eat and drink and get drunk, 46the master of that slave will come on a day when he does not expect him and at an hour that he does not know, and will cut him in pieces,z and put him with the unfaithful. 47That slave who knew what his master wanted, but did not prepare himself or do what was wanted, will receive a severe beating. 48But the one who did not know and did what deserved a beating will receive a light beating. From everyone to whom much has been given, much will be required; and from the one to whom much has been entrusted, even more will be demanded.

Jesus the Cause of Division
(Mt 10.34–39)

49 "I came to bring fire to the earth, and how I wish it were already kindled! 50I have a baptism with which to be baptized, and what stress I am under until it is completed! 51Do you think that I have come to bring peace to the earth? No, I tell you, but rather division! 52From now on five in one household will be divided, three against two and two against three; 53they will be divided:
father against son
and son against father,
mother against daughter
and daughter against mother,
mother-in-law against her
daughter-in-law
and daughter-in-law against
mother-in-law."

Interpreting the Time
(Mt 16.1–4)

54 He also said to the crowds, "When you see a cloud rising in the west, you immediately say, 'It is going to rain'; and so it happens. 55And when you see the south wind blowing, you say, 'There will be scorching heat'; and it happens. 56You hypocrites! You know how to interpret the appearance of earth and sky, but why do you not know how to interpret the present time?

wOther ancient authorities read *Consider the lilies; they neither spin nor weave* xOther ancient authorities read *God's* yOther ancient authorities add *would have watched and* zOr *cut him off*

Settling with Your Opponent

57 "And why do you not judge for yourselves what is right? 58 Thus, when you go with your accuser before a magistrate, on the way make an effort to settle the case,ᵃ or you may be dragged before the judge, and the judge hand you over to the officer, and the officer throw you in prison. 59 I tell you, you will never get out until you have paid the very last penny."

Repent or Perish

13 At that very time there were some present who told him about the Galileans whose blood Pilate had mingled with their sacrifices. 2 He asked them, "Do you think that because these Galileans suffered in this way they were worse sinners than all other Galileans? 3 No, I tell you; but unless you repent, you will all perish as they did. 4 Or those eighteen who were killed when the tower of Si·lo'am fell on them— do you think that they were worse offenders than all the others living in Jerusalem? 5 No, I tell you; but unless you repent, you will all perish just as they did."

The Parable of the Barren Fig Tree

6 Then he told this parable: "A man had a fig tree planted in his vineyard; and he came looking for fruit on it and found none. 7 So he said to the gardener, 'See here! For three years I have come looking for fruit on this fig tree, and still I find none. Cut it down! Why should it be wasting the soil?' 8 He replied, 'Sir, let it alone for one more year, until I dig around it and put manure on it. 9 If it bears fruit next year, well and good; but if not, you can cut it down.' "

Jesus Heals a Crippled Woman

10 Now he was teaching in one of the synagogues on the sabbath. 11 And just then there appeared a woman with a spirit that had crippled her for eighteen years. She was bent over and was quite unable to stand up straight. 12 When Jesus saw her, he called her over and said, "Woman, you are set free from your ailment." 13 When he laid his hands on her, immediately she stood up straight and began praising God. 14 But the leader of the synagogue, indignant because Jesus had cured on the sabbath, kept saying to the crowd, "There are six days on which work ought to be done; come on those days and be cured, and not on the sabbath day." 15 But the Lord answered him and said, "You hypocrites! Does not each of you on the sabbath untie his ox or his donkey from the manger, and lead it away to give it water? 16 And ought not this woman, a daughter of Abraham whom Satan bound for eighteen long years, be set free from this bondage on the sabbath day?" 17 When he said this, all his opponents were put to shame; and the entire crowd was rejoicing at all the wonderful things that he was doing.

The Parable of the Mustard Seed
(Mt 13.31–32; Mk 4.30–32)

18 He said therefore, "What is the kingdom of God like? And to what should I compare it? 19 It is like a mustard seed that someone took and sowed in the garden; it grew and became a tree, and the birds of the air made nests in its branches."

The Parable of the Yeast
(Mt 13.33)

20 And again he said, "To what should I compare the kingdom of God? 21 It is like yeast that a woman took and mixed in with ᵇ three measures of flour until all of it was leavened."

The Narrow Door
(Mt 7.13–14)

22 Jesusᶜ went through one town and village after another, teaching as he made his way to Jerusalem. 23 Someone asked him, "Lord, will only a few be saved?" He said to them, 24 "Strive to enter through the narrow door; for many, I tell you, will try to enter and will not be able. 25 When once the owner of the house has got up and shut the door, and you begin to stand outside and to knock at the door, saying, 'Lord, open to us,' then in reply he will say to you, 'I do not know where you come from.' 26 Then you will begin to say, 'We ate and drank with you, and you taught in our streets.' 27 But he will say, 'I do not know where you come from; go away from me, all you evildoers!' 28 There will be weeping and gnashing of teeth when you see Abraham and Isaac and Jacob and all the prophets in the kingdom of God, and you yourselves thrown out.

ᵃ Gk settle with him   ᵇ Gk hid in
ᶜ Gk He

29 Then people will come from east and west, from north and south, and will eat in the kingdom of God. 30 Indeed, some are last who will be first, and some are first who will be last."

The Lament over Jerusalem
(Mt 23.37–39)

31 At that very hour some Phar'-i·sees came and said to him, "Get away from here, for Her'od wants to kill you." 32 He said to them, "Go and tell that fox for me,d 'Listen, I am casting out demons and performing cures today and tomorrow, and on the third day I finish my work. 33 Yet today, tomorrow, and the next day I must be on my way, because it is impossible for a prophet to be killed outside of Jerusalem.' 34 Jerusalem, Jerusalem, the city that kills the prophets and stones those who are sent to it! How often have I desired to gather your children together as a hen gathers her brood under her wings, and you were not willing! 35 See, your house is left to you. And I tell you, you will not see me until the time comes whene you say, 'Blessed is the one who comes in the name of the Lord.' "

Jesus Heals the Man with Dropsy

14 On one occasion when Jesusf was going to the house of a leader of the Phar'i·sees to eat a meal on the sabbath, they were watching him closely. 2 Just then, in front of him, there was a man who had dropsy. 3 And Jesus asked the lawyers and Phar'i·sees, "Is it lawful to cure people on the sabbath, or not?" 4 But they were silent. So Jesusf took him and healed him, and sent him away. 5 Then he said to them, "If one of you has a childg or an ox that has fallen into a well, will you not immediately pull it out on a sabbath day?" 6 And they could not reply to this.

Humility and Hospitality

7 When he noticed how the guests chose the places of honor, he told them a parable. 8 "When you are invited by someone to a wedding banquet, do not sit down at the place of honor, in case someone more distinguished than you has been invited by your host; 9 and the host who invited both of you may come and say to you, 'Give this person your place,' and then in disgrace you would start to take the lowest place. 10 But when you are invited, go and sit down at the lowest place, so that when your host comes, he may say to you, 'Friend, move up higher'; then you will be honored in the presence of all who sit at the table with you. 11 For all who exalt themselves will be humbled, and those who humble themselves will be exalted."

12 He said also to the one who had invited him, "When you give a luncheon or a dinner, do not invite your friends or your brothers or your relatives or rich neighbors, in case they may invite you in return, and you would be repaid. 13 But when you give a banquet, invite the poor, the crippled, the lame, and the blind. 14 And you will be blessed, because they cannot repay you, for you will be repaid at the resurrection of the righteous."

The Parable of the Great Dinner
(Mt 22.1–14)

15 One of the dinner guests, on hearing this, said to him, "Blessed is anyone who will eat bread in the kingdom of God!" 16 Then Jesusf said to him, "Someone gave a great dinner and invited many. 17 At the time for the dinner he sent his slave to say to those who had been invited, 'Come; for everything is ready now.' 18 But they all alike began to make excuses. The first said to him, 'I have bought a piece of land, and I must go out and see it; please accept my regrets.' 19 Another said, 'I have bought five yoke of oxen, and I am going to try them out; please accept my regrets.' 20 Another said, 'I have just been married, and therefore I cannot come.' 21 So the slave returned and reported this to his master. Then the owner of the house became angry and said to his slave, 'Go out at once into the streets and lanes of the town and bring in the poor, the crippled, the blind, and the lame.' 22 And the slave said, 'Sir, what you ordered has been done, and there is still room.' 23 Then the master said to the slave, 'Go out into the roads and lanes, and compel people to come in, so that my house may be filled. 24 For I tell you,h none of those who were invited will taste my dinner.' "

dGk lacks *for me*   eOther ancient authorities lack *the time comes when*   fGk he   gOther ancient authorities read *a donkey*   hThe Greek word for *you* here is plural

The Cost of Discipleship
(Mt 10.34–39)

25 Now large crowds were traveling with him; and he turned and said to them, 26 "Whoever comes to me and does not hate father and mother, wife and children, brothers and sisters, yes, and even life itself, cannot be my disciple. 27 Whoever does not carry the cross and follow me cannot be my disciple. 28 For which of you, intending to build a tower, does not first sit down and estimate the cost, to see whether he has enough to complete it? 29 Otherwise, when he has laid a foundation and is not able to finish, all who see it will begin to ridicule him, 30 saying, 'This fellow began to build and was not able to finish.' 31 Or what king, going out to wage war against another king, will not sit down first and consider whether he is able with ten thousand to oppose the one who comes against him with twenty thousand? 32 If he cannot, then, while the other is still far away, he sends a delegation and asks for the terms of peace. 33 So therefore, none of you can become my disciple if you do not give up all your possessions.

About Salt
(Mt 5.13; Mk 9.50)

34 "Salt is good; but if salt has lost its taste, how can its saltiness be restored?[i] 35 It is fit neither for the soil nor for the manure pile; they throw it away. Let anyone with ears to hear listen!"

The Parable of the Lost Sheep
(Mt 18.10–14)

15 Now all the tax collectors and sinners were coming near to listen to him. 2 And the Phar'i·sees and the scribes were grumbling and saying, "This fellow welcomes sinners and eats with them."

3 So he told them this parable: 4 "Which one of you, having a hundred sheep and losing one of them, does not leave the ninety-nine in the wilderness and go after the one that is lost until he finds it? 5 When he has found it, he lays it on his shoulders and rejoices. 6 And when he comes home, he calls together his friends and neighbors, saying to them, 'Rejoice with me, for I have found my sheep that was lost.' 7 Just so, I tell you, there will be more joy in heaven over one sinner who repents than over ninety-nine righteous persons who need no repentance.

The Parable of the Lost Coin

8 "Or what woman having ten silver coins,[j] if she loses one of them, does not light a lamp, sweep the house, and search carefully until she finds it? 9 When she has found it, she calls together her friends and neighbors, saying, 'Rejoice with me, for I have found the coin that I had lost.' 10 Just so, I tell you, there is joy in the presence of the angels of God over one sinner who repents."

The Parable of the Prodigal and His Brother

11 Then Jesus[k] said, "There was a man who had two sons. 12 The younger of them said to his father, 'Father, give me the share of the property that will belong to me.' So he divided his property between them. 13 A few days later the younger son gathered all he had and traveled to a distant country, and there he squandered his property in dissolute living. 14 When he had spent everything, a severe famine took place throughout that country, and he began to be in need. 15 So he went and hired himself out to one of the citizens of that country, who sent him to his fields to feed the pigs. 16 He would gladly have filled himself with[l] the pods that the pigs were eating; and no one gave him anything. 17 But when he came to himself he said, 'How many of my father's hired hands have bread enough and to spare, but here I am dying of hunger! 18 I will get up and go to my father, and I will say to him, "Father, I have sinned against heaven and before you; 19 I am no longer worthy to be called your son; treat me like one of your hired hands." ' 20 So he set off and went to his father. But while he was still far off, his father saw him and was filled with compassion; he ran and put his arms around him and kissed him. 21 Then the son said to him, 'Father, I have sinned against heaven and before you; I am no longer worthy to be called your son.'[m] 22 But the father said to his

---

[i] Or how can it be used for seasoning?
[j] Gk drachmas, each worth about a day's wage for a laborer [k] Gk he [l] Other ancient authorities read filled his stomach with [m] Other ancient authorities add treat me as one of your hired servants

slaves, 'Quickly, bring out a robe—the best one—and put it on him; put a ring on his finger and sandals on his feet. 23 And get the fatted calf and kill it, and let us eat and celebrate; 24 for this son of mine was dead and is alive again; he was lost and is found!' And they began to celebrate.

25 "Now his elder son was in the field; and when he came and approached the house, he heard music and dancing. 26 He called one of the slaves and asked what was going on. 27 He replied, 'Your brother has come, and your father has killed the fatted calf, because he has got him back safe and sound.' 28 Then he became angry and refused to go in. His father came out and began to plead with him. 29 But he answered his father, 'Listen! For all these years I have been working like a slave for you, and I have never disobeyed your command; yet you have never given me even a young goat so that I might celebrate with my friends. 30 But when this son of yours came back, who has devoured your property with prostitutes, you killed the fatted calf for him!' 31 Then the father[n] said to him, 'Son, you are always with me, and all that is mine is yours. 32 But we had to celebrate and rejoice, because this brother of yours was dead and has come to life; he was lost and has been found.' "

The Parable of the Dishonest Manager

16 Then Jesus[n] said to the disciples, "There was a rich man who had a manager, and charges were brought to him that this man was squandering his property. 2 So he summoned him and said to him, 'What is this that I hear about you? Give me an accounting of your management, because you cannot be my manager any longer.' 3 Then the manager said to himself, 'What will I do, now that my master is taking the position away from me? I am not strong enough to dig, and I am ashamed to beg. 4 I have decided what to do so that, when I am dismissed as manager, people may welcome me into their homes.' 5 So, summoning his master's debtors one by one, he asked the first, 'How much do you owe my master?' 6 He answered, 'A hundred jugs of olive oil.' He said to him, 'Take your bill, sit down quickly, and make it fifty.' 7 Then he asked another, 'And how much do you owe?' He replied, 'A hun-

dred containers of wheat.' He said to him, 'Take your bill and make it eighty.' 8 And his master commended the dishonest manager because he had acted shrewdly; for the children of this age are more shrewd in dealing with their own generation than are the children of light. 9 And I tell you, make friends for yourselves by means of dishonest wealth[o] so that when it is gone, they may welcome you into the eternal homes.[p]

10 "Whoever is faithful in a very little is faithful also in much; and whoever is dishonest in a very little is dishonest also in much. 11 If then you have not been faithful with the dishonest wealth,[o] who will entrust to you the true riches? 12 And if you have not been faithful with what belongs to another, who will give you what is your own? 13 No slave can serve two masters; for a slave will either hate the one and love the other, or be devoted to the one and despise the other. You cannot serve God and wealth."[o]

The Law and the Kingdom of God

14 The Phar'i·sees, who were lovers of money, heard all this, and they ridiculed him. 15 So he said to them, "You are those who justify yourselves in the sight of others; but God knows your hearts; for what is prized by human beings is an abomination in the sight of God.

16 "The law and the prophets were in effect until John came; since then the good news of the kingdom of God is proclaimed, and everyone tries to enter it by force.[q] 17 But it is easier for heaven and earth to pass away, than for one stroke of a letter in the law to be dropped.

18 "Anyone who divorces his wife and marries another commits adultery, and whoever marries a woman divorced from her husband commits adultery.

The Rich Man and Lazarus

19 "There was a rich man who was dressed in purple and fine linen and who feasted sumptuously every day. 20 And at his gate lay a poor man named Laz'a·rus, covered with sores, 21 who longed to satisfy his hunger with what fell from the rich man's ta-

---

[n] Gk he   [o] Gk mammon   [p] Gk tents
[q] Or everyone is strongly urged to enter it

L
U
K
E

ble; even the dogs would come and lick his sores. 22 The poor man died and was carried away by the angels to be with Abraham.*r* The rich man also died and was buried. 23 In Hades, where he was being tormented, he looked up and saw Abraham far away with Laz'a·rus by his side.*s* 24 He called out, 'Father Abraham, have mercy on me, and send Laz'a·rus to dip the tip of his finger in water and cool my tongue; for I am in agony in these flames.' 25 But Abraham said, 'Child, remember that during your lifetime you received your good things, and Laz'a·rus in like manner evil things; but now he is comforted here, and you are in agony. 26 Besides all this, between you and us a great chasm has been fixed, so that those who might want to pass from here to you cannot do so, and no one can cross from there to us.' 27 He said, 'Then, father, I beg you to send him to my father's house— 28 for I have five brothers—that he may warn them, so that they will not also come into this place of torment.' 29 Abraham replied, 'They have Moses and the prophets; they should listen to them.' 30 He said, 'No, father Abraham; but if someone goes to them from the dead, they will repent.' 31 He said to him, 'If they do not listen to Moses and the prophets, neither will they be convinced even if someone rises from the dead.' "

Some Sayings of Jesus
(Mt 18.6–9; Mk 9.42–48)

17 Jesus*t* said to his disciples, "Occasions for stumbling are bound to come, but woe to anyone by whom they come! 2 It would be better for you if a millstone were hung around your neck and you were thrown into the sea than for you to cause one of these little ones to stumble. 3 Be on your guard! If another disciple*u* sins, you must rebuke the offender, and if there is repentance, you must forgive. 4 And if the same person sins against you seven times a day, and turns back to you seven times and says, 'I repent,' you must forgive."

5 The apostles said to the Lord, "Increase our faith!" 6 The Lord replied, "If you had faith the size of a*v* mustard seed, you could say to this mulberry tree, 'Be uprooted and planted in the sea,' and it would obey you.

7 "Who among you would say to your slave who has just come in from plowing or tending sheep in the field, 'Come here at once and take your place at the table'? 8 Would you not rather say to him, 'Prepare supper for me, put on your apron and serve me while I eat and drink; later you may eat and drink'? 9 Do you thank the slave for doing what was commanded? 10 So you also, when you have done all that you were ordered to do, say, 'We are worthless slaves; we have done only what we ought to have done!' "

Jesus Cleanses Ten Lepers

11 On the way to Jerusalem Jesus*w* was going through the region between Sa·mar'i·a and Galilee. 12 As he entered a village, ten lepers*x* approached him. Keeping their distance, 13 they called out, saying, "Jesus, Master, have mercy on us!" 14 When he saw them, he said to them, "Go and show yourselves to the priests." And as they went, they were made clean. 15 Then one of them, when he saw that he was healed, turned back, praising God with a loud voice. 16 He prostrated himself at Jesus'*y* feet and thanked him. And he was a Sa·mar'i·tan. 17 Then Jesus asked, "Were not ten made clean? But the other nine, where are they? 18 Was none of them found to return and give praise to God except this foreigner?" 19 Then he said to him, "Get up and go on your way; your faith has made you well."

The Coming of the Kingdom
(Gen 6.5—8.22; 19.12–14)

20 Once Jesus*w* was asked by the Phar'i·sees when the kingdom of God was coming, and he answered, "The kingdom of God is not coming with things that can be observed; 21 nor will they say, 'Look, here it is!' or 'There it is!' For, in fact, the kingdom of God is among*z* you."

22 Then he said to the disciples, "The days are coming when you will long to see one of the days of the Son of Man, and you will not see it. 23 They will say to you, 'Look there!' or 'Look here!' Do not go, do not set off in pursuit. 24 For as the lightning flashes and

---

r Gk *to Abraham's bosom*   *s* Gk *in his bosom*   *t* Gk *He*   *u* Gk *your brother*
v Gk *faith as a grain of*   *w* Gk *he*
x The terms *leper* and *leprosy* can refer to several diseases   *y* Gk *his*
z Or *within*

lights up the sky from one side to the other, so will the Son of Man be in his day.[a] 25 But first he must endure much suffering and be rejected by this generation. 26 Just as it was in the days of Noah, so too it will be in the days of the Son of Man. 27 They were eating and drinking, and marrying and being given in marriage, until the day Noah entered the ark, and the flood came and destroyed all of them. 28 Likewise, just as it was in the days of Lot: they were eating and drinking, buying and selling, planting and building, 29 but on the day that Lot left Sod'om, it rained fire and sulfur from heaven and destroyed all of them 30 —it will be like that on the day that the Son of Man is revealed. 31 On that day, anyone on the housetop who has belongings in the house must not come down to take them away; and likewise anyone in the field must not turn back. 32 Remember Lot's wife. 33 Those who try to make their life secure will lose it, but those who lose their life will keep it. 34 I tell you, on that night there will be two in one bed; one will be taken and the other left. 35 There will be two women grinding meal together; one will be taken and the other left."[b] 37 Then they asked him, "Where, Lord?" He said to them, "Where the corpse is, there the vultures will gather."

The Parable of the Widow and the Unjust Judge

18 Then Jesus[c] told them a parable about their need to pray always and not to lose heart. 2 He said, "In a certain city there was a judge who neither feared God nor had respect for people. 3 In that city there was a widow who kept coming to him and saying, 'Grant me justice against my opponent.' 4 For a while he refused; but later he said to himself, 'Though I have no fear of God and no respect for anyone, 5 yet because this widow keeps bothering me, I will grant her justice, so that she may not wear me out by continually coming.' "[d] 6 And the Lord said, "Listen to what the unjust judge says. 7 And will not God grant justice to his chosen ones who cry to him day and night? Will he delay long in helping them? 8 I tell you, he will quickly grant justice to them. And yet, when the Son of Man comes, will he find faith on earth?"

The Parable of the Pharisee and the Tax Collector

9 He also told this parable to some who trusted in themselves that they were righteous and regarded others with contempt: 10 "Two men went up to the temple to pray, one a Phar'i·see and the other a tax collector. 11 The Phar'i·see, standing by himself, was praying thus, 'God, I thank you that I am not like other people: thieves, rogues, adulterers, or even like this tax collector. 12 I fast twice a week; I give a tenth of all my income.' 13 But the tax collector, standing far off, would not even look up to heaven, but was beating his breast and saying, 'God, be merciful to me, a sinner!' 14 I tell you, this man went down to his home justified rather than the other; for all who exalt themselves will be humbled, but all who humble themselves will be exalted."

Jesus Blesses Little Children
(Mt 19.13–15; Mk 10.13–16)

15 People were bringing even infants to him that he might touch them; and when the disciples saw it, they sternly ordered them not to do it. 16 But Jesus called for them and said, "Let the little children come to me, and do not stop them; for it is to such as these that the kingdom of God belongs. 17 Truly I tell you, whoever does not receive the kingdom of God as a little child will never enter it."

The Rich Ruler
(Mt 19.16–30; Mk 10.17–31)

18 A certain ruler asked him, "Good Teacher, what must I do to inherit eternal life?" 19 Jesus said to him, "Why do you call me good? No one is good but God alone. 20 You know the commandments: 'You shall not commit adultery; You shall not murder; You shall not steal; You shall not bear false witness; Honor your father and mother.' " 21 He replied, "I have kept all these since my youth." 22 When Jesus heard this, he said to him, "There is still one thing lacking. Sell all that you own and dis-

---

a Other ancient authorities lack *in his day*   b Other ancient authorities add verse 36, *"Two will be in the field; one will be taken and the other left."*   c Gk *he*   d Or *so that she may not finally come and slap me in the face* tribute the money[e] to the poor, and you will have treasure in heaven; then come, follow me." [23] But when he heard this, he became sad; for he was very rich. [24] Jesus looked at him and said, "How hard it is for those who have wealth to enter the kingdom of God! [25] Indeed, it is easier for a camel to go through the eye of a needle than for someone who is rich to enter the kingdom of God."

[26] Those who heard it said, "Then who can be saved?" [27] He replied, "What is impossible for mortals is possible for God."

[28] Then Peter said, "Look, we have left our homes and followed you." [29] And he said to them, "Truly I tell you, there is no one who has left house or wife or brothers or parents or children, for the sake of the kingdom of God, [30] who will not get back very much more in this age, and in the age to come eternal life."

A Third Time Jesus Foretells His Death and Resurrection
(Mt 20.17–19; Mk 10.32–34)

[31] Then he took the twelve aside and said to them, "See, we are going up to Jerusalem, and everything that is written about the Son of Man by the prophets will be accomplished. [32] For he will be handed over to the Gentiles; and he will be mocked and insulted and spat upon. [33] After they have flogged him, they will kill him, and on the third day he will rise again." [34] But they understood nothing about all these things; in fact, what he said was hidden from them, and they did not grasp what was said.

Jesus Heals a Blind Beggar Near Jericho
(Mt 20.29–34; Mk 10.46–52)

[35] As he approached Jericho, a blind man was sitting by the roadside begging. [36] When he heard a crowd going by, he asked what was happening. [37] They told him, "Jesus of Nazareth[f] is passing by." [38] Then he shouted, "Jesus, Son of David, have mercy on me!" [39] Those who were in front sternly ordered him to be quiet; but he shouted even more loudly, "Son of David, have mercy on me!" [40] Jesus stood still and ordered the man to be brought to him; and when he came near, he asked him, [41] "What do you want me to do for you?" He said, "Lord, let me see again."

[42] Jesus said to him, "Receive your sight; your faith has saved you." [43] Immediately he regained his sight and followed him, glorifying God; and all the people, when they saw it, praised God.

Jesus and Zacchaeus

19 He entered Jericho and was passing through it. [2] A man was there named Zac·chae′us; he was a chief tax collector and was rich. [3] He was trying to see who Jesus was, but on account of the crowd he could not, because he was short in stature. [4] So he ran ahead and climbed a sycamore tree to see him, because he was going to pass that way. [5] When Jesus came to the place, he looked up and said to him, "Zac·chae′us, hurry and come down; for I must stay at your house today." [6] So he hurried down and was happy to welcome him. [7] All who saw it began to grumble and said, "He has gone to be the guest of one who is a sinner." [8] Zac·chae′us stood there and said to the Lord, "Look, half of my possessions, Lord, I will give to the poor; and if I have defrauded anyone of anything, I will pay back four times as much." [9] Then Jesus said to him, "Today salvation has come to this house, because he too is a son of Abraham. [10] For the Son of Man came to seek out and to save the lost."

The Parable of the Ten Pounds
(Mt 25.14–30)

[11] As they were listening to this, he went on to tell a parable, because he was near Jerusalem, and because they supposed that the kingdom of God was to appear immediately. [12] So he said, "A nobleman went to a distant country to get royal power for himself and then return. [13] He summoned ten of his slaves, and gave them ten pounds,[g] and said to them, 'Do business with these until I come back.' [14] But the citizens of his country hated him and sent a delegation after him, saying, 'We do not want this man to rule over us.' [15] When he returned, having received royal power, he ordered these slaves, to whom he had given the money, to be summoned so that he might find out what they had gained by trading.

[e] Gk lacks *the money* [f] Gk *the Nazorean* [g] The mina, rendered here by *pound*, was about three months' wages for a laborer

**L
U
K
E**

[16]The first came forward and said, 'Lord, your pound has made ten more pounds.' [17]He said to him, 'Well done, good slave! Because you have been trustworthy in a very small thing, take charge of ten cities.' [18]Then the second came, saying, 'Lord, your pound has made five pounds.' [19]He said to him, 'And you, rule over five cities.' [20]Then the other came, saying, 'Lord, here is your pound. I wrapped it up in a piece of cloth, [21]for I was afraid of you, because you are a harsh man; you take what you did not deposit, and reap what you did not sow.' [22]He said to him, 'I will judge you by your own words, you wicked slave! You knew, did you, that I was a harsh man, taking what I did not deposit and reaping what I did not sow? [23]Why then did you not put my money into the bank? Then when I returned, I could have collected it with interest.' [24]He said to the bystanders, 'Take the pound from him and give it to the one who has ten pounds.' [25](And they said to him, 'Lord, he has ten pounds!') [26]'I tell you, to all those who have, more will be given; but from those who have nothing, even what they have will be taken away. [27]But as for these enemies of mine who did not want me to be king over them—bring them here and slaughter them in my presence.' "

Jesus' Triumphal Entry into Jerusalem
(Mt 21.1–11; Mk 11.1–11; Jn 12.12–19)

[28]After he had said this, he went on ahead, going up to Jerusalem.

[29]When he had come near Beth'-pha·gē and Beth'a·ny, at the place called the Mount of Olives, he sent two of the disciples, [30]saying, "Go into the village ahead of you, and as you enter it you will find tied there a colt that has never been ridden. Untie it and bring it here. [31]If anyone asks you, 'Why are you untying it?' just say this, 'The Lord needs it.' " [32]So those who were sent departed and found it as he had told them. [33]As they were untying the colt, its owners asked them, "Why are you untying the colt?" [34]They said, "The Lord needs it." [35]Then they brought it to Jesus; and after throwing their cloaks on the colt, they set Jesus on it. [36]As he rode along, people kept spreading their cloaks on the road. [37]As he was now approaching the path down from the Mount of Olives, the whole multitude of the disciples began to praise God joyfully with a loud voice

for all the deeds of power that they had seen, [38]saying,

"Blessed is the king
who comes in the name of the Lord!
Peace in heaven,
and glory in the highest heaven!"

[39]Some of the Phar'i·sees in the crowd said to him, "Teacher, order your disciples to stop." [40]He answered, "I tell you, if these were silent, the stones would shout out."

Jesus Weeps over Jerusalem

[41]As he came near and saw the city, he wept over it, [42]saying, "If you, even you, had only recognized on this day the things that make for peace! But now they are hidden from your eyes. [43]Indeed, the days will come upon you, when your enemies will set up ramparts around you and surround you, and hem you in on every side. [44]They will crush you to the ground, you and your children within you, and they will not leave within you one stone upon another; because you did not recognize the time of your visitation from God."[h]

Jesus Cleanses the Temple
(Mt 21.12–17; Mk 11.15–19; Jn 2.12–25)

[45]Then he entered the temple and began to drive out those who were selling things there; [46]and he said, "It is written,

'My house shall be a house of prayer';
but you have made it a den of robbers."

[47]Every day he was teaching in the temple. The chief priests, the scribes, and the leaders of the people kept looking for a way to kill him; [48]but they did not find anything they could do, for all the people were spellbound by what they heard.

The Authority of Jesus Questioned
(Mt 21.23–27; Mk 11.27–33)

20 One day, as he was teaching the people in the temple and telling the good news, the chief priests and the scribes came with the elders [2]and said to him, "Tell us, by what authority are you doing these things? Who is it who gave you this authority?" [3]He answered them, "I will also ask you a question, and you tell me: [4]Did the

h Gk lacks *from God*

baptism of John come from heaven, or was it of human origin?" ⁵They discussed it with one another, saying, "If we say, 'From heaven,' he will say, 'Why did you not believe him?' ⁶But if we say, 'Of human origin,' all the people will stone us; for they are convinced that John was a prophet." ⁷So they answered that they did not know where it came from. ⁸Then Jesus said to them, "Neither will I tell you by what authority I am doing these things."

The Parable of the Wicked Tenants
(Mt 21.33–46; Mk 12.1–12)

9 He began to tell the people this parable: "A man planted a vineyard, and leased it to tenants, and went to another country for a long time. ¹⁰When the season came, he sent a slave to the tenants in order that they might give him his share of the produce of the vineyard; but the tenants beat him and sent him away empty-handed. ¹¹Next he sent another slave; that one also they beat and insulted and sent away empty-handed. ¹²And he sent still a third; this one also they wounded and threw out. ¹³Then the owner of the vineyard said, 'What shall I do? I will send my beloved son; perhaps they will respect him.' ¹⁴But when the tenants saw him, they discussed it among themselves and said, 'This is the heir; let us kill him so that the inheritance may be ours.' ¹⁵So they threw him out of the vineyard and killed him. What then will the owner of the vineyard do to them? ¹⁶He will come and destroy those tenants and give the vineyard to others." When they heard this, they said, "Heaven forbid!" ¹⁷But he looked at them and said, "What then does this text mean:
'The stone that the builders rejected
has become the cornerstone'?ⁱ
¹⁸Everyone who falls on that stone will be broken to pieces; and it will crush anyone on whom it falls." ¹⁹When the scribes and chief priests realized that he had told this parable against them, they wanted to lay hands on him at that very hour, but they feared the people.

The Question about Paying Taxes
(Mt 22.15–22; Mk 12.13–17)

20 So they watched him and sent spies who pretended to be honest, in order to trap him by what he said, so as to hand him over to the jurisdiction and authority of the governor. ²¹So they asked him, "Teacher, we know that you are right in what you say and teach, and you show deference to no one, but teach the way of God in accordance with truth. ²²Is it lawful for us to pay taxes to the emperor, or not?" ²³But he perceived their craftiness and said to them, ²⁴"Show me a denarius. Whose head and whose title does it bear?" They said, "The emperor's." ²⁵He said to them, "Then give to the emperor the things that are the emperor's, and to God the things that are God's." ²⁶And they were not able in the presence of the people to trap him by what he said; and being amazed by his answer, they became silent.

The Question about the Resurrection
(Mt 22.23–33; Mk 12.18–27)

27 Some Sad′du·cees, those who say there is no resurrection, came to him ²⁸and asked him a question, "Teacher, Moses wrote for us that if a man's brother dies, leaving a wife but no children, the manʲ shall marry the widow and raise up children for his brother. ²⁹Now there were seven brothers; the first married, and died childless; ³⁰then the second ³¹and the third married her, and so in the same way all seven died childless. ³²Finally the woman also died. ³³In the resurrection, therefore, whose wife will the woman be? For the seven had married her."

34 Jesus said to them, "Those who belong to this age marry and are given in marriage; ³⁵but those who are considered worthy of a place in that age and in the resurrection from the dead neither marry nor are given in marriage. ³⁶Indeed they cannot die anymore, because they are like angels and are children of God, being children of the resurrection. ³⁷And the fact that the dead are raised Moses himself showed, in the story about the bush, where he speaks of the Lord as the God of Abraham, the God of Isaac, and the God of Jacob. ³⁸Now he is God not of the dead, but of the living; for to him all of them are alive." ³⁹Then some of the scribes answered, "Teacher, you have spoken well." ⁴⁰For they no longer dared to ask him another question.

ⁱOr *keystone*   ʲGk *his brother*

The Question about David's Son
(Mt 22.41–46; Mk 12.35–37)

41 Then he said to them, "How can they say that the Messiah[k] is David's son? 42 For David himself says in the book of Psalms,

'The Lord said to my Lord,
"Sit at my right hand,
43 until I make your enemies
     your footstool." '

44 David thus calls him Lord; so how can he be his son?"

Jesus Denounces the Scribes
(Mt 23.1–7; Mk 12.38–40)

45 In the hearing of all the people he said to the[l] disciples, 46 "Beware of the scribes, who like to walk around in long robes, and love to be greeted with respect in the marketplaces, and to have the best seats in the synagogues and places of honor at banquets. 47 They devour widows' houses and for the sake of appearance say long prayers. They will receive the greater condemnation."

The Widow's Offering
(Mk 12.41–44)

21 He looked up and saw rich people putting their gifts into the treasury; 2 he also saw a poor widow put in two small copper coins. 3 He said, "Truly I tell you, this poor widow has put in more than all of them; 4 for all of them have contributed out of their abundance, but she out of her poverty has put in all she had to live on."

The Destruction of the Temple Foretold
(Mt 24.1–2; Mk 13.1–2)

5 When some were speaking about the temple, how it was adorned with beautiful stones and gifts dedicated to God, he said, 6 "As for these things that you see, the days will come when not one stone will be left upon another; all will be thrown down."

Signs and Persecutions
(Mt 24.3–14; Mk 13.3–13)

7 They asked him, "Teacher, when will this be, and what will be the sign that this is about to take place?" 8 And he said, "Beware that you are not led astray; for many will come in my name and say, 'I am he!'[m] and, 'The time is near!'[n] Do not go after them. 9 "When you hear of wars and in-

surrections, do not be terrified; for these things must take place first, but the end will not follow immediately." 10 Then he said to them, "Nation will rise against nation, and kingdom against kingdom; 11 there will be great earthquakes, and in various places famines and plagues; and there will be dreadful portents and great signs from heaven.

12 "But before all this occurs, they will arrest you and persecute you; they will hand you over to synagogues and prisons, and you will be brought before kings and governors because of my name. 13 This will give you an opportunity to testify. 14 So make up your minds not to prepare your defense in advance; 15 for I will give you words[o] and a wisdom that none of your opponents will be able to withstand or contradict. 16 You will be betrayed even by parents and brothers, by relatives and friends; and they will put some of you to death. 17 You will be hated by all because of my name. 18 But not a hair of your head will perish. 19 By your endurance you will gain your souls.

The Destruction of Jerusalem Foretold
(Mt 24.15–28; Mk 13.14–23)

20 "When you see Jerusalem surrounded by armies, then know that its desolation has come near.[p] 21 Then those in Judea must flee to the mountains, and those inside the city must leave it, and those out in the country must not enter it; 22 for these are days of vengeance, as a fulfillment of all that is written. 23 Woe to those who are pregnant and to those who are nursing infants in those days! For there will be great distress on the earth and wrath against this people; 24 they will fall by the edge of the sword and be taken away as captives among all nations; and Jerusalem will be trampled on by the Gentiles, until the times of the Gentiles are fulfilled.

The Coming of the Son of Man
(Mt 24.29–31; Mk 13.24–27)

25 "There will be signs in the sun, the moon, and the stars, and on the earth distress among nations confused by the roaring of the sea and the waves. 26 People will faint from fear

[k] Or *the Christ*   [l] Other ancient authorities read *his*   [m] Gk *I am*   [n] Or *at hand*   [o] Gk *a mouth*   [p] Or *is at hand*

and foreboding of what is coming upon the world, for the powers of the heavens will be shaken. 27 Then they will see 'the Son of Man coming in a cloud' with power and great glory. 28 Now when these things begin to take place, stand up and raise your heads, because your redemption is drawing near."

The Lesson of the Fig Tree
(Mt 24.32–35; Mk 13.28–31)

29 Then he told them a parable: "Look at the fig tree and all the trees; 30 as soon as they sprout leaves you can see for yourselves and know that summer is already near. 31 So also, when you see these things taking place, you know that the kingdom of God is near. 32 Truly I tell you, this generation will not pass away until all things have taken place. 33 Heaven and earth will pass away, but my words will not pass away.

Exhortation to Watch
(Mt 24.36–44; Mk 13.32–37)

34 "Be on guard so that your hearts are not weighed down with dissipation and drunkenness and the worries of this life, and that day catch you unexpectedly, 35 like a trap. For it will come upon all who live on the face of the whole earth. 36 Be alert at all times, praying that you may have the strength to escape all these things that will take place, and to stand before the Son of Man."

37 Every day he was teaching in the temple, and at night he would go out and spend the night on the Mount of Olives, as it was called. 38 And all the people would get up early in the morning to listen to him in the temple.

The Plot to Kill Jesus
(Mt 26.1–5, 14–16; Mk 14.1–2, 10–11; Jn 11.45–53)

22 Now the festival of Unleavened Bread, which is called the Passover, was near. 2 The chief priests and the scribes were looking for a way to put Jesus*q* to death, for they were afraid of the people.

3 Then Satan entered into Judas called Is·car'i·ot, who was one of the twelve; 4 he went away and conferred with the chief priests and officers of the temple police about how he might betray him to them. 5 They were greatly pleased and agreed to give him

money. 6 So he consented and began to look for an opportunity to betray him to them when no crowd was present.

The Preparation of the Passover
(Mt 26.17–19; Mk 14.12–16)

7 Then came the day of Unleavened Bread, on which the Passover lamb had to be sacrificed. 8 So Jesus*r* sent Peter and John, saying, "Go and prepare the Passover meal for us that we may eat it." 9 They asked him, "Where do you want us to make preparations for it?" 10 "Listen," he said to them, "when you have entered the city, a man carrying a jar of water will meet you; follow him into the house he enters 11 and say to the owner of the house, 'The teacher asks you, "Where is the guest room, where I may eat the Passover with my disciples?"' 12 He will show you a large room upstairs, already furnished. Make preparations for us there." 13 So they went and found everything as he had told them; and they prepared the Passover meal.

The Institution of the Lord's Supper
(Mt 26.20–30; Mk 14.17–26; Jn 13.21–30)

14 When the hour came, he took his place at the table, and the apostles with him. 15 He said to them, "I have eagerly desired to eat this Passover with you before I suffer; 16 for I tell you, I will not eat it*s* until it is fulfilled in the kingdom of God." 17 Then he took a cup, and after giving thanks he said, "Take this and divide it among yourselves; 18 for I tell you that from now on I will not drink of the fruit of the vine until the kingdom of God comes." 19 Then he took a loaf of bread, and when he had given thanks, he broke it and gave it to them, saying, "This is my body, which is given for you. Do this in remembrance of me." 20 And he did the same with the cup after supper, saying, "This cup that is poured out for you is the new covenant in my blood.*t* 21 But see, the one who betrays me is with me, and his hand is on the table. 22 For the Son of Man is going as it has been determined, but woe to that one by whom he is betrayed!" 23 Then they began to ask one another, which one of them it could be who would do this.

q Gk *him*   *r* Gk *he*   *s* Other ancient authorities read *never eat it again*   *t* Other ancient authorities lack, in whole or in part, verses 19b-20 (*which is given . . . in my blood*)

The Dispute about Greatness

24 A dispute also arose among them as to which one of them was to be regarded as the greatest. 25 But he said to them, "The kings of the Gentiles lord it over them; and those in authority over them are called benefactors. 26 But not so with you; rather the greatest among you must become like the youngest, and the leader like one who serves. 27 For who is greater, the one who is at the table or the one who serves? Is it not the one at the table? But I am among you as one who serves.

28 "You are those who have stood by me in my trials; 29 and I confer on you, just as my Father has conferred on me, a kingdom, 30 so that you may eat and drink at my table in my kingdom, and you will sit on thrones judging the twelve tribes of Israel.

Jesus Predicts Peter's Denial
(Mt 26.31–35; Mk 14.27–31; Jn 13.36–38)

31 "Simon, Simon, listen! Satan has demanded u to sift all of you like wheat, 32 but I have prayed for you that your own faith may not fail; and you, when once you have turned back, strengthen your brothers." 33 And he said to him, "Lord, I am ready to go with you to prison and to death!" 34 Jesus v said, "I tell you, Peter, the cock will not crow this day, until you have denied three times that you know me."

Purse, Bag, and Sword

35 He said to them, "When I sent you out without a purse, bag, or sandals, did you lack anything?" They said, "No, not a thing." 36 He said to them, "But now, the one who has a purse must take it, and likewise a bag. And the one who has no sword must sell his cloak and buy one. 37 For I tell you, this scripture must be fulfilled in me, 'And he was counted among the lawless'; and indeed what is written about me is being fulfilled." 38 They said, "Lord, look, here are two swords." He replied, "It is enough."

Jesus Prays on the Mount of Olives
(Mt 26.36–46; Mk 14.32–42; Jn 18.1)

39 He came out and went, as was his custom, to the Mount of Olives; and the disciples followed him. 40 When he reached the place, he said to them, "Pray that you may not come into the time of trial." w 41 Then he withdrew from them about a stone's throw, knelt down, and prayed, 42 "Father, if you are willing, remove this cup from me; yet, not my will but yours be done." ⟦43 Then an angel from heaven appeared to him and gave him strength. 44 In his anguish he prayed more earnestly, and his sweat became like great drops of blood falling down on the ground.⟧ x 45 When he got up from prayer, he came to the disciples and found them sleeping because of grief, 46 and he said to them, "Why are you sleeping? Get up and pray that you may not come into the time of trial." w

The Betrayal and Arrest of Jesus
(Mt 26.47–56; Mk 14.43–52; Jn 18.1–11)

47 While he was still speaking, suddenly a crowd came, and the one called Judas, one of the twelve, was leading them. He approached Jesus to kiss him; 48 but Jesus said to him, "Judas, is it with a kiss that you are betraying the Son of Man?" 49 When those who were around him saw what was coming, they asked, "Lord, should we strike with the sword?" 50 Then one of them struck the slave of the high priest and cut off his right ear. 51 But Jesus said, "No more of this!" And he touched his ear and healed him. 52 Then Jesus said to the chief priests, the officers of the temple police, and the elders who had come for him, "Have you come out with swords and clubs as if I were a bandit? 53 When I was with you day after day in the temple, you did not lay hands on me. But this is your hour, and the power of darkness!"

Peter Denies Jesus
(Mt 25.69–75; Mk 14.66–72; Jn 18.15–18, 25–27)

54 Then they seized him and led him away, bringing him into the high priest's house. But Peter was following at a distance. 55 When they had kindled a fire in the middle of the courtyard and sat down together, Peter sat among them. 56 Then a servant-girl, seeing him in the firelight, stared at him and said, "This man also was with him." 57 But he denied it, saying, "Woman, I do not know him." 58 A little later someone else, on seeing him,

---

u Or *has obtained permission*   v Gk *He*
w Or *into temptation*   x Other ancient authorities lack verses 43 and 44

said, "You also are one of them." But Peter said, "Man, I am not!" 59 Then about an hour later still another kept insisting, "Surely this man also was with him; for he is a Galilean." 60 But Peter said, "Man, I do not know what you are talking about!" At that moment, while he was still speaking, the cock crowed. 61 The Lord turned and looked at Peter. Then Peter remembered the word of the Lord, how he had said to him, "Before the cock crows today, you will deny me three times." 62 And he went out and wept bitterly.

The Mocking and Beating of Jesus
(Mt 26.67–68; Mk 14.65)

63 Now the men who were holding Jesus began to mock him and beat him; 64 they also blindfolded him and kept asking him, "Prophesy! Who is it that struck you?" 65 They kept heaping many other insults on him.

Jesus before the Council
(Mt 26.57–68; Mk 14.61–64; Jn 18.12–14, 19–24)

66 When day came, the assembly of the elders of the people, both chief priests and scribes, gathered together, and they brought him to their council. 67 They said, "If you are the Messiah,*y* tell us." He replied, "If I tell you, you will not believe; 68 and if I question you, you will not answer. 69 But from now on the Son of Man will be seated at the right hand of the power of God." 70 All of them asked, "Are you, then, the Son of God?" He said to them, "You say that I am." 71 Then they said, "What further testimony do we need? We have heard it ourselves from his own lips!"

Jesus before Pilate
(Mt 27.1–2, 11–14; Mk 15.1–5; Jn 18.28–38)

23 Then the assembly rose as a body and brought Jesus*z* before Pilate. 2 They began to accuse him, saying, "We found this man perverting our nation, forbidding us to pay taxes to the emperor, and saying that he himself is the Messiah, a king."*a* 3 Then Pilate asked him, "Are you the king of the Jews?" He answered, "You say so." 4 Then Pilate said to the chief priests and the crowds, "I find no basis for an accusation against this man." 5 But they were insistent and said, "He stirs up the people by teaching throughout all Judea, from Galilee

where he began even to this place."

Jesus before Herod

6 When Pilate heard this, he asked whether the man was a Galilean. 7 And when he learned that he was under Herod's jurisdiction, he sent him off to Her'od, who was himself in Jerusalem at that time. 8 When Her'od saw Jesus, he was very glad, for he had been wanting to see him for a long time, because he had heard about him and was hoping to see him perform some sign. 9 He questioned him at some length, but Jesus*b* gave him no answer. 10 The chief priests and the scribes stood by, vehemently accusing him. 11 Even Her'od with his soldiers treated him with contempt and mocked him; then he put an elegant robe on him, and sent him back to Pilate. 12 That same day Her'od and Pilate became friends with each other; before this they had been enemies.

Jesus Sentenced to Death
(Mt 27.15–26; Mk 15.6–15; Jn 18.38b—19.16a)

13 Pilate then called together the chief priests, the leaders, and the people, 14 and said to them, "You brought me this man as one who was perverting the people; and here I have examined him in your presence and have not found this man guilty of any of your charges against him. 15 Neither has Her'od, for he sent him back to us. Indeed, he has done nothing to deserve death. 16 I will therefore have him flogged and release him."*c* 18 Then they all shouted out together, "Away with this fellow! Release Ba·rab'bas for us!" 19 (This was a man who had been put in prison for an insurrection that had taken place in the city, and for murder.) 20 Pilate, wanting to release Jesus, addressed them again; 21 but they kept shouting, "Crucify, crucify him!" 22 A third time he said to them, "Why, what evil has he done? I have found in him no ground for the sentence of death; I will therefore have him flogged and then release him." 23 But they kept urgently demanding with loud shouts that he should be crucified; and their voices

y Or *the Christ*　　*z* Gk *him*　　*a* Or *is an anointed king*　　*b* Gk *he*　　*c* Here, or after verse 19, other ancient authorities add verse 17, *Now he was obliged to release someone for them at the festival* prevailed. 24 So Pilate gave his verdict that their demand should be granted. 25 He released the man they asked for, the one who had been put in prison for insurrection and murder, and he handed Jesus over as they wished.

The Crucifixion of Jesus
(Mt 27.32–44; Mk 15.21–32; Jn 19.16b–24)

26 As they led him away, they seized a man, Simon of Cy·rē'nē, who was coming from the country, and they laid the cross on him, and made him carry it behind Jesus. 27 A great number of the people followed him, and among them were women who were beating their breasts and wailing for him. 28 But Jesus turned to them and said, "Daughters of Jerusalem, do not weep for me, but weep for yourselves and for your children. 29 For the days are surely coming when they will say, 'Blessed are the barren, and the wombs that never bore, and the breasts that never nursed.' 30 Then they will begin to say to the mountains, 'Fall on us'; and to the hills, 'Cover us.' 31 For if they do this when the wood is green, what will happen when it is dry?"

32 Two others also, who were criminals, were led away to be put to death with him. 33 When they came to the place that is called The Skull, they crucified Jesus *d* there with the criminals, one on his right and one on his left. [⟦34 Then Jesus said, "Father, forgive them; for they do not know what they are doing."⟧ *e* And they cast lots to divide his clothing. 35 And the people stood by, watching; but the leaders scoffed at him, saying, "He saved others; let him save himself if he is the Messiah *f* of God, his chosen one!" 36 The soldiers also mocked him, coming up and offering him sour wine, 37 and saying, "If you are the King of the Jews, save yourself!" 38 There was also an inscription over him, *g* "This is the King of the Jews."

39 One of the criminals who were hanged there kept deriding *h* him and saying, "Are you not the Messiah? *f* Save yourself and us!" 40 But the other rebuked him, saying, "Do you not fear God, since you are under the same sentence of condemnation? 41 And we indeed have been condemned justly, for we are getting what we deserve for our deeds, but this man has done nothing wrong." 42 Then he said, "Jesus, re-member me when you come into *i* your kingdom." 43 He replied, "Truly I tell you, today you will be with me in Paradise."

The Death of Jesus
(Mt 27.45–56; Mk 15.33–41; Jn 19.25–30)

44 It was now about noon, and darkness came over the whole land *j* until three in the afternoon, 45 while the sun's light failed; *k* and the curtain of the temple was torn in two. 46 Then Jesus, crying with a loud voice, said, "Father, into your hands I commend my spirit." Having said this, he breathed his last. 47 When the centurion saw what had taken place, he praised God and said, "Certainly this man was innocent." *l* 48 And when all the crowds who had gathered there for this spectacle saw what had taken place, they returned home, beating their breasts. 49 But all his acquaintances, including the women who had followed him from Galilee, stood at a distance, watching these things.

The Burial of Jesus
(Mt 27.57–61; Mk 15.42–47; Jn 19.38–42)

50 Now there was a good and righteous man named Joseph, who, though a member of the council, 51 had not agreed to their plan and action. He came from the Jewish town of Ar·i·ma·thē'a, and he was waiting expectantly for the kingdom of God. 52 This man went to Pilate and asked for the body of Jesus. 53 Then he took it down, wrapped it in a linen cloth, and laid it in a rock-hewn tomb where no one had ever been laid. 54 It was the day of Preparation, and the sabbath was beginning. *m* 55 The women who had come with him from Galilee followed, and they saw the tomb and how his body was laid. 56 Then they returned, and prepared spices and ointments.

On the sabbath they rested according to the commandment.

d Gk *him*   *e* Other ancient authorities lack the sentence *Then Jesus . . . what they are doing*   *f* Or *the Christ*   *g* Other ancient authorities add *written in Greek and Latin and Hebrew* (that is, Aramaic)   *h* Or *blaspheming*   *i* Other ancient authorities read *in*   *j* Or *earth*   *k* Or *the sun was eclipsed.* Other ancient authorities read *the sun was darkened*   *l* Or *righteous*   *m* Gk *was dawning*

The Resurrection of Jesus
(Mt 28.1–10; Mk 16.1–8; Jn 20.1–10)

24 But on the first day of the week, at early dawn, they came to the tomb, taking the spices that they had prepared. 2 They found the stone rolled away from the tomb, 3 but when they went in, they did not find the body.[n] 4 While they were perplexed about this, suddenly two men in dazzling clothes stood beside them. 5 The women[o] were terrified and bowed their faces to the ground, but the men[p] said to them, "Why do you look for the living among the dead? He is not here, but has risen.[q] 6 Remember how he told you, while he was still in Galilee, 7 that the Son of Man must be handed over to sinners, and be crucified, and on the third day rise again." 8 Then they remembered his words, 9 and returning from the tomb, they told all this to the eleven and to all the rest. 10 Now it was Mary Mag′da·lēne, Jō·an′na, Mary the mother of James, and the other women with them who told this to the apostles. 11 But these words seemed to them an idle tale, and they did not believe them. 12 But Peter got up and ran to the tomb; stooping and looking in, he saw the linen cloths by themselves; then he went home, amazed at what had happened.[r]

The Walk to Emmaus
(Mt 16.12–13)

13 Now on that same day two of them were going to a village called Em·mā′us, about seven miles[s] from Jerusalem, 14 and talking with each other about all these things that had happened. 15 While they were talking and discussing, Jesus himself came near and went with them, 16 but their eyes were kept from recognizing him. 17 And he said to them, "What are you discussing with each other while you walk along?" They stood still, looking sad.[t] 18 Then one of them, whose name was Clē′o·pas, answered him, "Are you the only stranger in Jerusalem who does not know the things that have taken place there in these days?" 19 He asked them, "What things?" They replied, "The things about Jesus of Nazareth,[u] who was a prophet mighty in deed and word before God and all the people, 20 and how our chief priests and leaders handed him over to be condemned to death and crucified him. 21 But we had hoped that he was

the one to redeem Israel.[v] Yes, and besides all this, it is now the third day since these things took place. 22 Moreover, some women of our group astounded us. They were at the tomb early this morning, 23 and when they did not find his body there, they came back and told us that they had indeed seen a vision of angels who said that he was alive. 24 Some of those who were with us went to the tomb and found it just as the women had said; but they did not see him." 25 Then he said to them, "Oh, how foolish you are, and how slow of heart to believe all that the prophets have declared! 26 Was it not necessary that the Messiah[w] should suffer these things and then enter into his glory?" 27 Then beginning with Moses and all the prophets, he interpreted to them the things about himself in all the scriptures.

28 As they came near the village to which they were going, he walked ahead as if he were going on. 29 But they urged him strongly, saying, "Stay with us, because it is almost evening and the day is now nearly over." So he went in to stay with them. 30 When he was at the table with them, he took bread, blessed and broke it, and gave it to them. 31 Then their eyes were opened, and they recognized him; and he vanished from their sight. 32 They said to each other, "Were not our hearts burning within us[x] while he was talking to us on the road, while he was opening the scriptures to us?" 33 That same hour they got up and returned to Jerusalem; and they found the eleven and their companions gathered together. 34 They were saying, "The Lord has risen indeed, and he has appeared to Simon!" 35 Then they told what had happened on the road, and how he had been made known to them in the breaking of the bread.

---

[n] Other ancient authorities add *of the Lord Jesus*   [o] Gk *They*   [p] Gk *but they*   [q] Other ancient authorities lack *He is not here, but has risen*   [r] Other ancient authorities lack verse 12   [s] Gk *sixty stadia*; other ancient authorities read *a hundred sixty stadia*   [t] Other ancient authorities read *walk along, looking sad?"*   [u] Other ancient authorities read *Jesus the Nazorean*   [v] Or *to set Israel free*   [w] Or *the Christ*   [x] Other ancient authorities lack *within us*

Jesus Appears to His Disciples
(Jn 20.19–23; Acts 1.3–5; 1 Cor 15.5)

36 While they were talking about this, Jesus himself stood among them and said to them, "Peace be with you."*y* 37 They were startled and terrified, and thought that they were seeing a ghost. 38 He said to them, "Why are you frightened, and why do doubts arise in your hearts? 39 Look at my hands and my feet; see that it is I myself. Touch me and see; for a ghost does not have flesh and bones as you see that I have." 40 And when he had said this, he showed them his hands and his feet. *z* 41 While in their joy they were disbelieving and still wondering, he said to them, "Have you anything here to eat?" 42 They gave him a piece of broiled fish, 43 and he took it and ate in their presence.

44 Then he said to them, "These are my words that I spoke to you while I was still with you—that everything written about me in the law of Moses, the prophets, and the psalms must be fulfilled." 45 Then he opened their minds to understand the scriptures, 46 and he said to them, "Thus it is written, that the Messiah *a* is to suffer and to rise from the dead on the third day, 47 and that repentance and forgiveness of sins is to be proclaimed in his name to all nations, *b* beginning from Jerusalem. 48 You are witnesses of these things. 49 And see, I am sending upon you what my Father promised; so stay here in the city until you have been clothed with power from on high."

The Ascension of Jesus
(Mk 16.19–20; Acts 1.9)

50 Then he led them out as far as Beth′a·ny, and, lifting up his hands, he blessed them. 51 While he was blessing them, he withdrew from them and was carried up into heaven. *c* 52 And they worshiped him, and *d* returned to Jerusalem with great joy; 53 and they were continually in the temple blessing God. *e*

---

y Other ancient authorities lack *and said to them, "Peace be with you."*   *z* Other ancient authorities lack verse 40   *a* Or *the Christ*   *b* Or *nations. Beginning from Jerusalem you are witnesses*   *c* Other ancient authorities lack *and was carried up into heaven*   *d* Other ancient authorities lack *worshiped him, and*   *e* Other ancient authorities add *Amen*

The Gospel According to

JOHN

The Word Became Flesh
(Gen 1.1—2.4a)

1 In the beginning was the Word, and the Word was with God, and the Word was God. 2 He was in the beginning with God. 3 All things came into being through him, and without him not one thing came into being. What has come into being 4 in him was life, *a* and the life was the light of all people. 5 The light shines in the darkness, and the darkness did not overcome it.

6 There was a man sent from God, whose name was John. 7 He came as a witness to testify to the light, so that all might believe through him. 8 He himself was not the light, but he came to testify to the light. 9 The true light, which enlightens everyone, was coming into the world. *b*

10 He was in the world, and the world came into being through him; yet the world did not know him. 11 He came to what was his own, *c* and his own people did not accept him. 12 But to all who received him, who believed in his name, he gave power to become children of God, 13 who were born, not

---

a Or *3through him. And without him not one thing came into being that has come into being. 4In him was life*   *b* Or *He was the true light that enlightens everyone coming into the world*   *c* Or *to his own home* of blood or of the will of the flesh or of the will of man, but of God.

14 And the Word became flesh and lived among us, and we have seen his glory, the glory as of a father's only son,[d] full of grace and truth. [15] (John testified to him and cried out, "This was he of whom I said, 'He who comes after me ranks ahead of me because he was before me.' ") [16] From his fullness we have all received, grace upon grace. [17] The law indeed was given through Moses; grace and truth came through Jesus Christ. [18] No one has ever seen God. It is God the only Son,[e] who is close to the Father's heart,[f] who has made him known.

The Testimony of John the Baptist
(Mt 3.1–12; Mk 1.1–8; Lk 3.1–20)

19 This is the testimony given by John when the Jews sent priests and Le′vites from Jerusalem to ask him, "Who are you?" [20] He confessed and did not deny it, but confessed, "I am not the Messiah."[g] [21] And they asked him, "What then? Are you E·li′jah?" He said, "I am not." "Are you the prophet?" He answered, "No." [22] Then they said to him, "Who are you? Let us have an answer for those who sent us. What do you say about yourself?" [23] He said,

"I am the voice of one crying out
     in the wilderness,
'Make straight the way of the
     Lord,' "

as the prophet I·sai′ah said.

24 Now they had been sent from the Phar′i·sees. [25] They asked him, "Why then are you baptizing if you are neither the Messiah,[g] nor E·li′jah, nor the prophet?" [26] John answered them, "I baptize with water. Among you stands one whom you do not know, [27] the one who is coming after me; I am not worthy to untie the thong of his sandal." [28] This took place in Beth′a·ny across the Jordan where John was baptizing.

The Lamb of God
(Mt 3.13–17; Mk 1.9–11; Lk 3.21–22)

29 The next day he saw Jesus coming toward him and declared, "Here is the Lamb of God who takes away the sin of the world! [30] This is he of whom I said, 'After me comes a man who ranks ahead of me because he was before me.' [31] I myself did not know him; but I came baptizing with water for this reason, that he might be revealed to Israel." [32] And John testified, "I saw the Spirit descending from heaven like a dove, and it remained on him. [33] I myself did not know him, but the one who sent me to baptize with water said to me, 'He on whom you see the Spirit descend and remain is the one who baptizes with the Holy Spirit.' [34] And I myself have seen and have testified that this is the Son of God."[h]

The First Disciples of Jesus

35 The next day John again was standing with two of his disciples, [36] and as he watched Jesus walk by, he exclaimed, "Look, here is the Lamb of God!" [37] The two disciples heard him say this, and they followed Jesus. [38] When Jesus turned and saw them following, he said to them, "What are you looking for?" They said to him, "Rabbi" (which translated means Teacher), "where are you staying?" [39] He said to them, "Come and see." They came and saw where he was staying, and they remained with him that day. It was about four o'clock in the afternoon. [40] One of the two who heard John speak and followed him was Andrew, Simon Peter's brother. [41] He first found his brother Simon and said to him, "We have found the Messiah" (which is translated Anointed[i]). [42] He brought Simon[j] to Jesus, who looked at him and said, "You are Simon son of John. You are to be called Ce′phas" (which is translated Peter[k]).

Jesus Calls Philip and Nathanael

43 The next day Jesus decided to go to Galilee. He found Philip and said to him, "Follow me." [44] Now Philip was from Beth·sa′i·da, the city of Andrew and Peter. [45] Philip found Na·than′a·el and said to him, "We have found him about whom Moses in the law and also the prophets wrote, Jesus son of Joseph from Nazareth." [46] Na·than′a·el said to him, "Can anything good come out of Nazareth?" Philip said to him, "Come and see." [47] When Jesus saw Na·than′a·el coming toward him, he said of him, "Here is truly an Israelite

---

[d] Or *the Father's only Son*   [e] Other ancient authorities read *It is an only Son, God,* or *It is the only Son*   [f] Gk *bosom*   [g] Or *the Christ*   [h] Other ancient authorities read *is God's chosen one*   [i] Or *Christ*   [j] Gk *him*   [k] From the word for *rock* in Aramaic (*kepha*) and Greek (*petra*), respectively

in whom there is no deceit!" [48] Na·than'a·el asked him, "Where did you get to know me?" Jesus answered, "I saw you under the fig tree before Philip called you." [49] Na·than'a·el replied, "Rabbi, you are the Son of God! You are the King of Israel!" [50] Jesus answered, "Do you believe because I told you that I saw you under the fig tree? You will see greater things than these." [51] And he said to him, "Very truly, I tell you,[l] you will see heaven opened and the angels of God ascending and descending upon the Son of Man."

The Wedding at Cana

2 On the third day there was a wedding in Ca'na of Galilee, and the mother of Jesus was there. [2] Jesus and his disciples had also been invited to the wedding. [3] When the wine gave out, the mother of Jesus said to him, "They have no wine." [4] And Jesus said to her, "Woman, what concern is that to you and to me? My hour has not yet come." [5] His mother said to the servants, "Do whatever he tells you." [6] Now standing there were six stone water jars for the Jewish rites of purification, each holding twenty or thirty gallons. [7] Jesus said to them, "Fill the jars with water." And they filled them up to the brim. [8] He said to them, "Now draw some out, and take it to the chief steward." So they took it. [9] When the steward tasted the water that had become wine, and did not know where it came from (though the servants who had drawn the water knew), the steward called the bridegroom [10] and said to him, "Everyone serves the good wine first, and then the inferior wine after the guests have become drunk. But you have kept the good wine until now." [11] Jesus did this, the first of his signs, in Ca'na of Galilee, and revealed his glory; and his disciples believed in him.

[12] After this he went down to Ca·per'na·um with his mother, his brothers, and his disciples; and they remained there a few days.

Jesus Cleanses the Temple
(Mt 21.12–17; Mk 11.15–19; Lk 19.45–48)

[13] The Passover of the Jews was near, and Jesus went up to Jerusalem. [14] In the temple he found people selling cattle, sheep, and doves, and the money changers seated at their tables. [15] Making a whip of cords, he drove all of them out of the temple, both the sheep and the cattle. He also poured out the coins of the money changers and overturned their tables. [16] He told those who were selling the doves, "Take these things out of here! Stop making my Father's house a marketplace!" [17] His disciples remembered that it was written, "Zeal for your house will consume me." [18] The Jews then said to him, "What sign can you show us for doing this?" [19] Jesus answered them, "Destroy this temple, and in three days I will raise it up." [20] The Jews then said, "This temple has been under construction for forty-six years, and will you raise it up in three days?" [21] But he was speaking of the temple of his body. [22] After he was raised from the dead, his disciples remembered that he had said this; and they believed the scripture and the word that Jesus had spoken.

[23] When he was in Jerusalem during the Passover festival, many believed in his name because they saw the signs that he was doing. [24] But Jesus on his part would not entrust himself to them, because he knew all people [25] and needed no one to testify about anyone; for he himself knew what was in everyone.

Nicodemus Visits Jesus

3 Now there was a Phar'i·see named Nic·o·de'mus, a leader of the Jews. [2] He came to Jesus[m] by night and said to him, "Rabbi, we know that you are a teacher who has come from God; for no one can do these signs that you do apart from the presence of God." [3] Jesus answered him, "Very truly, I tell you, no one can see the kingdom of God without being born from above."[n] [4] Nic·o·de'mus said to him, "How can anyone be born after having grown old? Can one enter a second time into the mother's womb and be born?" [5] Jesus answered, "Very truly, I tell you, no one can enter the kingdom of God without being born of water and Spirit. [6] What is born of the flesh is flesh, and what is born of the Spirit is spirit.[o] [7] Do not be astonished that I said to you, 'You[p] must be born

---

[l] Both instances of the Greek word for *you* in this verse are plural   [m] Gk *him*   [n] Or *born anew*   [o] The same Greek word means both *wind* and *spirit*   [p] The Greek word for *you* here is plural

from above.'[q] [8]The wind[r] blows where it chooses, and you hear the sound of it, but you do not know where it comes from or where it goes. So it is with everyone who is born of the Spirit." [9]Nic·o·dē'mus said to him, "How can these things be?" [10]Jesus answered him, "Are you a teacher of Israel, and yet you do not understand these things?

[11] "Very truly, I tell you, we speak of what we know and testify to what we have seen; yet you[s] do not receive our testimony. [12]If I have told you about earthly things and you do not believe, how can you believe if I tell you about heavenly things? [13]No one has ascended into heaven except the one who descended from heaven, the Son of Man.[t] [14]And just as Moses lifted up the serpent in the wilderness, so must the Son of Man be lifted up, [15]that whoever believes in him may have eternal life.[u]

[16] "For God so loved the world that he gave his only Son, so that everyone who believes in him may not perish but may have eternal life.

[17] "Indeed, God did not send the Son into the world to condemn the world, but in order that the world might be saved through him. [18]Those who believe in him are not condemned; but those who do not believe are condemned already, because they have not believed in the name of the only Son of God. [19]And this is the judgment, that the light has come into the world, and people loved darkness rather than light because their deeds were evil. [20]For all who do evil hate the light and do not come to the light, so that their deeds may not be exposed. [21]But those who do what is true come to the light, so that it may be clearly seen that their deeds have been done in God."[u]

Jesus and John the Baptist

[22] After this Jesus and his disciples went into the Judean countryside, and he spent some time there with them and baptized. [23]John also was baptizing at Ae'non near Să'lim because water was abundant there; and people kept coming and were being baptized [24]—John, of course, had not yet been thrown into prison.

[25] Now a discussion about purification arose between John's disciples and a Jew.[v] [26]They came to John and

said to him, "Rabbi, the one who was with you across the Jordan, to whom you testified, here he is baptizing, and all are going to him." [27]John answered, "No one can receive anything except what has been given from heaven. [28]You yourselves are my witnesses that I said, 'I am not the Messiah,[w] but I have been sent ahead of him.' [29]He who has the bride is the bridegroom. The friend of the bridegroom, who stands and hears him, rejoices greatly at the bridegroom's voice. For this reason my joy has been fulfilled. [30]He must increase, but I must decrease."[x]

The One Who Comes from Heaven

[31] The one who comes from above is above all; the one who is of the earth belongs to the earth and speaks about earthly things. The one who comes from heaven is above all. [32]He testifies to what he has seen and heard, yet no one accepts his testimony. [33]Whoever has accepted his testimony has certified[y] this, that God is true. [34]He whom God has sent speaks the words of God, for he gives the Spirit without measure. [35]The Father loves the Son and has placed all things in his hands. [36]Whoever believes in the Son has eternal life; whoever disobeys the Son will not see life, but must endure God's wrath.

Jesus and the Woman of Samaria

4 Now when Jesus[z] learned that the Phar'i·sees had heard, "Jesus is making and baptizing more disciples than John" [2]—although it was not Jesus himself but his disciples who baptized— [3]he left Judea and started back to Galilee. [4]But he had to go through Sa·măr'i·a. [5]So he came to a Sa·măr'i·tan city called Sў'char, near the plot of ground that Jacob had given to his son Joseph. [6]Jacob's well was there, and Jesus, tired out by his journey, was sitting by the well. It was about noon.

[q]Or *anew* [r]The same Greek word means both *wind* and *spirit*
[s]The Greek word for *you* here and in verse 12 is plural [t]Other ancient authorities add *who is in heaven*
[u]Some interpreters hold that the quotation concludes with verse 15
[v]Other ancient authorities read *the Jews*
[w]Or *the Christ* [x]Some interpreters hold that the quotation continues through verse 36 [y]Gk *set a seal to*
[z]Other ancient authorities read *the Lord*

7 A Sa·măr′i·tan woman came to draw water, and Jesus said to her, "Give me a drink." 8(His disciples had gone to the city to buy food.) 9The Sa·măr′i·tan woman said to him, "How is it that you, a Jew, ask a drink of me, a woman of Sa·măr′i·a?" (Jews do not share things in common with Sa·măr′-i·tans.)ª 10Jesus answered her, "If you knew the gift of God, and who it is that is saying to you, 'Give me a drink,' you would have asked him, and he would have given you living water." 11The woman said to him, "Sir, you have no bucket, and the well is deep. Where do you get that living water? 12Are you greater than our ancestor Jacob, who gave us the well, and with his sons and his flocks drank from it?" 13Jesus said to her, "Everyone who drinks of this water will be thirsty again, 14but those who drink of the water that I will give them will never be thirsty. The water that I will give will become in them a spring of water gushing up to eternal life." 15The woman said to him, "Sir, give me this water, so that I may never be thirsty or have to keep coming here to draw water."

16 Jesus said to her, "Go, call your husband, and come back." 17The woman answered him, "I have no husband." Jesus said to her, "You are right in saying, 'I have no husband'; 18for you have had five husbands, and the one you have now is not your husband. What you have said is true!" 19The woman said to him, "Sir, I see that you are a prophet. 20Our ancestors worshiped on this mountain, but youᵇ say that the place where people must worship is in Jerusalem." 21Jesus said to her, "Woman, believe me, the hour is coming when you will worship the Father neither on this mountain nor in Jerusalem. 22You worship what you do not know; we worship what we know, for salvation is from the Jews. 23But the hour is coming, and is now here, when the true worshipers will worship the Father in spirit and truth, for the Father seeks such as these to worship him. 24God is spirit, and those who worship him must worship in spirit and truth." 25The woman said to him, "I know that Messiah is coming" (who is called Christ). "When he comes, he will proclaim all things to us." 26Jesus said to her, "I am he,ᶜ the one who is speaking to you."

27 Just then his disciples came. They were astonished that he was speaking with a woman, but no one said, "What do you want?" or, "Why are you speaking with her?" 28Then the woman left her water jar and went back to the city. She said to the people, 29"Come and see a man who told me everything I have ever done! He cannot be the Messiah,ᵈ can he?" 30They left the city and were on their way to him.

31 Meanwhile the disciples were urging him, "Rabbi, eat something." 32But he said to them, "I have food to eat that you do not know about." 33So the disciples said to one another, "Surely no one has brought him something to eat?" 34Jesus said to them, "My food is to do the will of him who sent me and to complete his work. 35Do you not say, 'Four months more, then comes the harvest'? But I tell you, look around you, and see how the fields are ripe for harvesting. 36The reaper is already receivingᵉ wages and is gathering fruit for eternal life, so that sower and reaper may rejoice together. 37For here the saying holds true, 'One sows and another reaps.' 38I sent you to reap that for which you did not labor. Others have labored, and you have entered into their labor."

39 Many Sa·măr′i·tans from that city believed in him because of the woman's testimony, "He told me everything I have ever done." 40So when the Sa·măr′i·tans came to him, they asked him to stay with them; and he stayed there two days. 41And many more believed because of his word. 42They said to the woman, "It is no longer because of what you said that we believe, for we have heard for ourselves, and we know that this is truly the Savior of the world."

Jesus Returns to Galilee

43 When the two days were over, he went from that place to Galilee 44(for Jesus himself had testified that a prophet has no honor in the prophet's own country). 45When he came to Galilee, the Galileans welcomed him, since they had seen all that he had done in Jerusalem at the festival; for they too had gone to the festival.

ªOther ancient authorities lack this sentence   ᵇThe Greek word for you here and in verses 21 and 22 is plural   ᶜGk I am   ᵈOr the Christ   ᵉOr 35. . . the fields are already ripe for harvesting. 36The reaper is receiving

Jesus Heals an Official's Son

46 Then he came again to Cā′na in Galilee where he had changed the water into wine. Now there was a royal official whose son lay ill in Ca·per′na·um. 47 When he heard that Jesus had come from Judea to Galilee, he went and begged him to come down and heal his son, for he was at the point of death. 48 Then Jesus said to him, "Unless youᶠ see signs and wonders you will not believe." 49 The official said to him, "Sir, come down before my little boy dies." 50 Jesus said to him, "Go; your son will live." The man believed the word that Jesus spoke to him and started on his way. 51 As he was going down, his slaves met him and told him that his child was alive. 52 So he asked them the hour when he began to recover, and they said to him, "Yesterday at one in the afternoon the fever left him." 53 The father realized that this was the hour when Jesus had said to him, "Your son will live." So he himself believed, along with his whole household. 54 Now this was the second sign that Jesus did after coming from Judea to Galilee.

Jesus Heals on the Sabbath

5 After this there was a festival of the Jews, and Jesus went up to Jerusalem. 2 Now in Jerusalem by the Sheep Gate there is a pool, called in Hebrewᵍ Beth-zā′tha,ʰ which has five porticoes. 3 In these lay many invalids—blind, lame, and paralyzed.ⁱ 5 One man was there who had been ill for thirty-eight years. 6 When Jesus saw him lying there and knew that he had been there a long time, he said to him, "Do you want to be made well?" 7 The sick man answered him, "Sir, I have no one to put me into the pool when the water is stirred up; and while I am making my way, someone else steps down ahead of me." 8 Jesus said to him, "Stand up, take your mat and walk." 9 At once the man was made well, and he took up his mat and began to walk.
Now that day was a sabbath. 10 So the Jews said to the man who had been cured, "It is the sabbath; it is not lawful for you to carry your mat." 11 But he answered them, "The man who made me well said to me, 'Take up your mat and walk.'" 12 They asked him, "Who is the man who said to you, 'Take it up and walk'?" 13 Now the man who had

been healed did not know who it was, for Jesus had disappeared inʲ the crowd that was there. 14 Later Jesus found him in the temple and said to him, "See, you have been made well! Do not sin any more, so that nothing worse happens to you." 15 The man went away and told the Jews that it was Jesus who had made him well. 16 Therefore the Jews started persecuting Jesus, because he was doing such things on the sabbath. 17 But Jesus answered them, "My Father is still working, and I also am working." 18 For this reason the Jews were seeking all the more to kill him, because he was not only breaking the sabbath, but was also calling God his own Father, thereby making himself equal to God.

The Authority of the Son

19 Jesus said to them, "Very truly, I tell you, the Son can do nothing on his own, but only what he sees the Father doing; for whatever the Fatherᵏ does, the Son does likewise. 20 The Father loves the Son and shows him all that he himself is doing; and he will show him greater works than these, so that you will be astonished. 21 Indeed, just as the Father raises the dead and gives them life, so also the Son gives life to whomever he wishes. 22 The Father judges no one but has given all judgment to the Son, 23 so that all may honor the Son just as they honor the Father. Anyone who does not honor the Son does not honor the Father who sent him. 24 Very truly, I tell you, anyone who hears my word and believes him who sent me has eternal life, and does not come under judgment, but has passed from death to life.
25 "Very truly, I tell you, the hour is coming, and is now here, when the dead will hear the voice of the Son of God, and those who hear will live.

ᶠ Both instances of the Greek word for you in this verse are plural   ᵍ That is, Aramaic   ʰ Other ancient authorities read Bethesda, others Bethsaida
ⁱ Other ancient authorities add, wholly or in part, waiting for the stirring of the water; 4 for an angel of the Lord went down at certain seasons into the pool, and stirred up the water; whoever stepped in first after the stirring of the water was made well from whatever disease that person had.   ʲ Or had left because of   ᵏ Gk that one

26 For just as the Father has life in himself, so he has granted the Son also to have life in himself; 27 and he has given him authority to execute judgment, because he is the Son of Man. 28 Do not be astonished at this; for the hour is coming when all who are in their graves will hear his voice 29 and will come out—those who have done good, to the resurrection of life, and those who have done evil, to the resurrection of condemnation.

Witnesses to Jesus

30 "I can do nothing on my own. As I hear, I judge; and my judgment is just, because I seek to do not my own will but the will of him who sent me. 31 "If I testify about myself, my testimony is not true. 32 There is another who testifies on my behalf, and I know that his testimony is true. 33 You sent messengers to John, and he testified to the truth. 34 Not that I accept such human testimony, but I say these things so that you may be saved. 35 He was a burning and shining lamp, and you were willing to rejoice for a while in his light. 36 But I have a testimony greater than John's. The works that the Father has given me to complete, the very works that I am doing, testify on my behalf that the Father has sent me. 37 And the Father who sent me has himself testified on my behalf. You have never heard his voice or seen his form, 38 and you do not have his word abiding in you, because you do not believe him whom he has sent.

39 "You search the scriptures because you think that in them you have eternal life; and it is they that testify on my behalf. 40 Yet you refuse to come to me to have life. 41 I do not accept glory from human beings. 42 But I know that you do not have the love of God in[l] you. 43 I have come in my Father's name, and you do not accept me; if another comes in his own name, you will accept him. 44 How can you believe when you accept glory from one another and do not seek the glory that comes from the one who alone is God? 45 Do not think that I will accuse you before the Father; your accuser is Moses, on whom you have set your hope. 46 If you believed Moses, you would believe me, for he wrote about me. 47 But if you do not believe what he wrote, how will you believe what I say?"

Feeding the Five Thousand
(Mt 14.13–21; Mk 6.30–44; Lk 9.10–17)

6 After this Jesus went to the other side of the Sea of Galilee, also called the Sea of Tī-bē'ri-as.[m] 2 A large crowd kept following him, because they saw the signs that he was doing for the sick. 3 Jesus went up the mountain and sat down there with his disciples. 4 Now the Passover, the festival of the Jews, was near. 5 When he looked up and saw a large crowd coming toward him, Jesus said to Philip, "Where are we to buy bread for these people to eat?" 6 He said this to test him, for he himself knew what he was going to do. 7 Philip answered him, "Six months' wages[n] would not buy enough bread for each of them to get a little." 8 One of his disciples, Andrew, Simon Peter's brother, said to him, 9 "There is a boy here who has five barley loaves and two fish. But what are they among so many people?" 10 Jesus said, "Make the people sit down." Now there was a great deal of grass in the place; so they[o] sat down, about five thousand in all. 11 Then Jesus took the loaves, and when he had given thanks, he distributed them to those who were seated; so also the fish, as much as they wanted. 12 When they were satisfied, he told his disciples, "Gather up the fragments left over, so that nothing may be lost." 13 So they gathered them up, and from the fragments of the five barley loaves, left by those who had eaten, they filled twelve baskets. 14 When the people saw the sign that he had done, they began to say, "This is indeed the prophet who is to come into the world."

15 When Jesus realized that they were about to come and take him by force to make him king, he withdrew again to the mountain by himself.

Jesus Walks on the Water
(Mt 14.22–33; Mk 6.45–52)

16 When evening came, his disciples went down to the sea, 17 got into a boat, and started across the sea to Ca·per'na·um. It was now dark, and Jesus had not yet come to them. 18 The sea became rough because a strong wind was blowing. 19 When they had

---

[l] Or *among*   [m] Gk *of Galilee of Tiberius*
[n] Gk *Two hundred denarii*; the denarius was the usual day's wage for a laborer
[o] Gk *the men*

rowed about three or four miles,ᵖ they saw Jesus walking on the sea and coming near the boat, and they were terrified. ²⁰ But he said to them, "It is I;�q do not be afraid." ²¹ Then they wanted to take him into the boat, and immediately the boat reached the land toward which they were going.

The Bread from Heaven

22 The next day the crowd that had stayed on the other side of the sea saw that there had been only one boat there. They also saw that Jesus had not got into the boat with his disciples, but that his disciples had gone away alone. ²³ Then some boats from Ti·bē′ri·as came near the place where they had eaten the bread after the Lord had given thanks.ʳ ²⁴ So when the crowd saw that neither Jesus nor his disciples were there, they themselves got into the boats and went to Ca·per′na·um looking for Jesus.

25 When they found him on the other side of the sea, they said to him, "Rabbi, when did you come here?" ²⁶ Jesus answered them, "Very truly, I tell you, you are looking for me, not because you saw signs, but because you ate your fill of the loaves. ²⁷ Do not work for the food that perishes, but for the food that endures for eternal life, which the Son of Man will give you. For it is on him that God the Father has set his seal." ²⁸ Then they said to him, "What must we do to perform the works of God?" ²⁹ Jesus answered them, "This is the work of God, that you believe in him whom he has sent." ³⁰ So they said to him, "What sign are you going to give us then, so that we may see it and believe you? What work are you performing? ³¹ Our ancestors ate the manna in the wilderness; as it is written, 'He gave them bread from heaven to eat.' " ³² Then Jesus said to them, "Very truly, I tell you, it was not Moses who gave you the bread from heaven, but it is my Father who gives you the true bread from heaven. ³³ For the bread of God is that whichˢ comes down from heaven and gives life to the world." ³⁴ They said to him, "Sir, give us this bread always."

35 Jesus said to them, "I am the bread of life. Whoever comes to me will never be hungry, and whoever believes in me will never be thirsty. ³⁶ But I said to you that you have seen me and yet do not believe. ³⁷ Everything that the Father gives me will come to me,

and anyone who comes to me I will never drive away; ³⁸ for I have come down from heaven, not to do my own will, but the will of him who sent me. ³⁹ And this is the will of him who sent me, that I should lose nothing of all that he has given me, but raise it up on the last day. ⁴⁰ This is indeed the will of my Father, that all who see the Son and believe in him may have eternal life; and I will raise them up on the last day."

41 Then the Jews began to complain about him because he said, "I am the bread that came down from heaven." ⁴² They were saying, "Is not this Jesus, the son of Joseph, whose father and mother we know? How can he now say, 'I have come down from heaven'?" ⁴³ Jesus answered them, "Do not complain among yourselves. ⁴⁴ No one can come to me unless drawn by the Father who sent me; and I will raise that person up on the last day. ⁴⁵ It is written in the prophets, 'And they shall all be taught by God.' Everyone who has heard and learned from the Father comes to me. ⁴⁶ Not that anyone has seen the Father except the one who is from God; he has seen the Father. ⁴⁷ Very truly, I tell you, whoever believes has eternal life. ⁴⁸ I am the bread of life. ⁴⁹ Your ancestors ate the manna in the wilderness, and they died. ⁵⁰ This is the bread that comes down from heaven, so that one may eat of it and not die. ⁵¹ I am the living bread that came down from heaven. Whoever eats of this bread will live forever; and the bread that I will give for the life of the world is my flesh."

52 The Jews then disputed among themselves, saying, "How can this man give us his flesh to eat?" ⁵³ So Jesus said to them, "Very truly, I tell you, unless you eat the flesh of the Son of Man and drink his blood, you have no life in you. ⁵⁴ Those who eat my flesh and drink my blood have eternal life, and I will raise them up on the last day; ⁵⁵ for my flesh is true food and my blood is true drink. ⁵⁶ Those who eat my flesh and drink my blood abide in me, and I in them. ⁵⁷ Just as the living Father sent me, and I live because of the Father, so whoever eats me will live because of me. ⁵⁸ This is the bread

ᵖ Gk *about twenty-five or thirty stadia*
q Gk *I am* ʳ Other ancient authorities lack *after the Lord had given thanks*
ˢ Or *he who*

that came down from heaven, not like that which your ancestors ate, and they died. But the one who eats this bread will live forever." [59]He said these things while he was teaching in the synagogue at Ca·per′na·um.

The Words of Eternal Life

[60] When many of his disciples heard it, they said, "This teaching is difficult; who can accept it?" [61]But Jesus, being aware that his disciples were complaining about it, said to them, "Does this offend you? [62]Then what if you were to see the Son of Man ascending to where he was before? [63]It is the spirit that gives life; the flesh is useless. The words that I have spoken to you are spirit and life. [64]But among you there are some who do not believe." For Jesus knew from the first who were the ones that did not believe, and who was the one that would betray him. [65]And he said, "For this reason I have told you that no one can come to me unless it is granted by the Father."

[66] Because of this many of his disciples turned back and no longer went about with him. [67]So Jesus asked the twelve, "Do you also wish to go away?" [68]Simon Peter answered him, "Lord, to whom can we go? You have the words of eternal life. [69]We have come to believe and know that you are the Holy One of God." [t] [70]Jesus answered them, "Did I not choose you, the twelve? Yet one of you is a devil." [71]He was speaking of Judas son of Simon Is·car′i·ot, [u] for he, though one of the twelve, was going to betray him.

The Unbelief of Jesus' Brothers

7 After this Jesus went about in Galilee. He did not wish [v] to go about in Judea because the Jews were looking for an opportunity to kill him. [2]Now the Jewish festival of Booths [w] was near. [3]So his brothers said to him, "Leave here and go to Judea so that your disciples also may see the works you are doing; [4]for no one who wants [x] to be widely known acts in secret. If you do these things, show yourself to the world." [5](For not even his brothers believed in him.) [6]Jesus said to them, "My time has not yet come, but your time is always here. [7]The world cannot hate you, but it hates me because I testify against it that its works are evil. [8]Go to the festival yourselves. I am not [y] going to this festival, for my time has not yet fully come." [9]After saying this, he remained in Galilee.

Jesus at the Festival of Booths

[10] But after his brothers had gone to the festival, then he also went, not publicly but as it were [z] in secret. [11]The Jews were looking for him at the festival and saying, "Where is he?" [12]And there was considerable complaining about him among the crowds. While some were saying, "He is a good man," others were saying, "No, he is deceiving the crowd." [13]Yet no one would speak openly about him for fear of the Jews.

[14] About the middle of the festival Jesus went up into the temple and began to teach. [15]The Jews were astonished at it, saying, "How does this man have such learning, [a] when he has never been taught?" [16]Then Jesus answered them, "My teaching is not mine but his who sent me. [17]Anyone who resolves to do the will of God will know whether the teaching is from God or whether I am speaking on my own. [18]Those who speak on their own seek their own glory; but the one who seeks the glory of him who sent him is true, and there is nothing false in him.

[19] "Did not Moses give you the law? Yet none of you keeps the law. Why are you looking for an opportunity to kill me?" [20]The crowd answered, "You have a demon! Who is trying to kill you?" [21]Jesus answered them, "I performed one work, and all of you are astonished. [22]Moses gave you circumcision (it is, of course, not from Moses, but from the patriarchs), and you circumcise a man on the sabbath. [23]If a man receives circumcision on the sabbath in order that the law of Moses may not be broken, are you angry with me because I healed a man's whole body on the sabbath? [24]Do not judge by appearances, but judge with right judgment."

JOHN (side tab)

---

[t] Other ancient authorities read *the Christ, the Son of the living God*
[u] Other ancient authorities read *Judas Iscariot son of Simon;* others, *Judas son of Simon from Karyot* (Kerioth)
[v] Other ancient authorities read *was not at liberty*   [w] Or *Tabernacles*   [x] Other ancient authorities read *wants it*
[y] Other ancient authorities add *yet*
[z] Other ancient authorities lack *as it were*   [a] Or *this man know his letters*

Is This the Christ?

25 Now some of the people of Jerusalem were saying, "Is not this the man whom they are trying to kill? 26 And here he is, speaking openly, but they say nothing to him! Can it be that the authorities really know that this is the Messiah?[b] 27 Yet we know where this man is from; but when the Messiah[b] comes, no one will know where he is from." 28 Then Jesus cried out as he was teaching in the temple, "You know me, and you know where I am from. I have not come on my own. But the one who sent me is true, and you do not know him. 29 I know him, because I am from him, and he sent me." 30 Then they tried to arrest him, but no one laid hands on him, because his hour had not yet come. 31 Yet many in the crowd believed in him and were saying, "When the Messiah[b] comes, will he do more signs than this man has done?"[c]

Officers Are Sent to Arrest Jesus

32 The Phar'i·sees heard the crowd muttering such things about him, and the chief priests and Phar'i·sees sent temple police to arrest him. 33 Jesus then said, "I will be with you a little while longer, and then I am going to him who sent me. 34 You will search for me, but you will not find me; and where I am, you cannot come." 35 The Jews said to one another, "Where does this man intend to go that we will not find him? Does he intend to go to the Dispersion among the Greeks and teach the Greeks? 36 What does he mean by saying, 'You will search for me and you will not find me' and 'Where I am, you cannot come'?"

Rivers of Living Water

37 On the last day of the festival, the great day, while Jesus was standing there, he cried out, "Let anyone who is thirsty come to me, 38 and let the one who believes in me drink. As[d] the scripture has said, 'Out of the believer's heart[e] shall flow rivers of living water.'" 39 Now he said this about the Spirit, which believers in him were to receive; for as yet there was no Spirit,[f] because Jesus was not yet glorified.

Division among the People

40 When they heard these words, some in the crowd said, "This is really the prophet." 41 Others said, "This is

the Messiah."[b] But some asked, "Surely the Messiah[b] does not come from Galilee, does he? 42 Has not the scripture said that the Messiah[b] is descended from David and comes from Bethlehem, the village where David lived?" 43 So there was a division in the crowd because of him. 44 Some of them wanted to arrest him, but no one laid hands on him.

The Unbelief of Those in Authority

45 Then the temple police went back to the chief priests and Phar'i·sees, who asked them, "Why did you not arrest him?" 46 The police answered, "Never has anyone spoken like this!" 47 Then the Phar'i·sees replied, "Surely you have not been deceived too, have you? 48 Has any one of the authorities or of the Phar'i·sees believed in him? 49 But this crowd, which does not know the law—they are accursed." 50 Nic·o·de'mus, who had gone to Jesus[g] before, and who was one of them, asked, 51 "Our law does not judge people without first giving them a hearing to find out what they are doing, does it?" 52 They replied, "Surely you are not also from Galilee, are you? Search and you will see that no prophet is to arise from Galilee."

The Woman Caught in Adultery

⟦ 53 Then each of them went home, 8 1 while Jesus went to the Mount of Olives. 2 Early in the morning he came again to the temple. All the people came to him and he sat down and began to teach them. 3 The scribes and the Phar'i·sees brought a woman who had been caught in adultery; and making her stand before all of them, 4 they said to him, "Teacher, this woman was caught in the very act of committing adultery. 5 Now in the law Moses commanded us to stone such women. Now what do you say?" 6 They said this to test him, so that they might have some charge to bring against him. Jesus bent down and wrote with his finger on the ground. 7 When they kept on questioning him, he straightened up and said to them, "Let anyone among

b Or the Christ　　c Other ancient authorities read is doing　　d Or come to me and drink.　38 The one who believes in me, as　　e Gk out of his belly　f Other ancient authorities read for as yet the Spirit (others, Holy Spirit) had not been given　g Gk him you who is without sin be the first to throw a stone at her." [8] And once again he bent down and wrote on the ground.[h] [9] When they heard it, they went away, one by one, beginning with the elders; and Jesus was left alone with the woman standing before him. [10] Jesus straightened up and said to her, "Woman, where are they? Has no one condemned you?" [11] She said, "No one, sir."[i] And Jesus said, "Neither do I condemn you. Go your way, and from now on do not sin again."[j]

Jesus the Light of the World

12 Again Jesus spoke to them, saying, "I am the light of the world. Whoever follows me will never walk in darkness but will have the light of life." [13] Then the Phar'i-sees said to him, "You are testifying on your own behalf; your testimony is not valid." [14] Jesus answered, "Even if I testify on my own behalf, my testimony is valid because I know where I have come from and where I am going, but you do not know where I come from or where I am going. [15] You judge by human standards;[k] I judge no one. [16] Yet even if I do judge, my judgment is valid; for it is not I alone who judge, but I and the Father[l] who sent me. [17] In your law it is written that the testimony of two witnesses is valid. [18] I testify on my own behalf, and the Father who sent me testifies on my behalf." [19] Then they said to him, "Where is your Father?" Jesus answered, "You know neither me nor my Father. If you knew me, you would know my Father also." [20] He spoke these words while he was teaching in the treasury of the temple, but no one arrested him, because his hour had not yet come.

Jesus Foretells His Death

21 Again he said to them, "I am going away, and you will search for me, but you will die in your sin. Where I am going, you cannot come." [22] Then the Jews said, "Is he going to kill himself? Is that what he means by saying, 'Where I am going, you cannot come'?" [23] He said to them, "You are from below, I am from above; you are of this world, I am not of this world. [24] I told you that you would die in your sins, for you will die in your sins unless you believe that I am he."[m] [25] They said to him, "Who are you?" Jesus said to them, "Why do I speak to you at all?[n]

[26] I have much to say about you and much to condemn; but the one who sent me is true, and I declare to the world what I have heard from him." [27] They did not understand that he was speaking to them about the Father. [28] So Jesus said, "When you have lifted up the Son of Man, then you will realize that I am he,[m] and that I do nothing on my own, but I speak these things as the Father instructed me. [29] And the one who sent me is with me; he has not left me alone, for I always do what is pleasing to him." [30] As he was saying these things, many believed in him.

True Disciples

31 Then Jesus said to the Jews who had believed in him, "If you continue in my word, you are truly my disciples; [32] and you will know the truth, and the truth will make you free." [33] They answered him, "We are descendants of Abraham and have never been slaves to anyone. What do you mean by saying, 'You will be made free'?" [34] Jesus answered them, "Very truly, I tell you, everyone who commits sin is a slave to sin. [35] The slave does not have a permanent place in the household; the son has a place there forever. [36] So if the Son makes you free, you will be free indeed. [37] I know that you are descendants of Abraham; yet you look for an opportunity to kill me, because there is no place in you for my word. [38] I declare what I have seen in the Father's presence; as for you, you should do what you have heard from the Father."[o]

Jesus and Abraham

39 They answered him, "Abraham is our father." Jesus said to them, "If you were Abraham's children, you would be doing[p] what Abraham did,

---

[h] Other ancient authorities add *the sins of each of them*　[i] Or *Lord*　[j] The most ancient authorities lack 7.53—8.11; other authorities add the passage here or after 7.36 or after 21.25 or after Luke 21.38, with variations of text; some mark the passage as doubtful.　[k] Gk *according to the flesh*　[l] Other ancient authorities read *he*　[m] Gk *I am*　[n] Or *What I have told you from the beginning*　[o] Other ancient authorities read *you do what you have heard from your father*　[p] Other ancient authorities read *If you are Abraham's children, then do*

⁴⁰ but now you are trying to kill me, a man who has told you the truth that I heard from God. This is not what Abraham did. ⁴¹ You are indeed doing what your father does." They said to him, "We are not illegitimate children; we have one father, God himself." ⁴² Jesus said to them, "If God were your Father, you would love me, for I came from God and now I am here. I did not come on my own, but he sent me. ⁴³ Why do you not understand what I say? It is because you cannot accept my word. ⁴⁴ You are from your father the devil, and you choose to do your father's desires. He was a murderer from the beginning and does not stand in the truth, because there is no truth in him. When he lies, he speaks according to his own nature, for he is a liar and the father of lies. ⁴⁵ But because I tell the truth, you do not believe me. ⁴⁶ Which of you convicts me of sin? If I tell the truth, why do you not believe me? ⁴⁷ Whoever is from God hears the words of God. The reason you do not hear them is that you are not from God."

48 The Jews answered him, "Are we not right in saying that you are a Sa·mar′i·tan and have a demon?" ⁴⁹ Jesus answered, "I do not have a demon; but I honor my Father, and you dishonor me. ⁵⁰ Yet I do not seek my own glory; there is one who seeks it and he is the judge. ⁵¹ Very truly, I tell you, whoever keeps my word will never see death." ⁵² The Jews said to him, "Now we know that you have a demon. Abraham died, and so did the prophets; yet you say, 'Whoever keeps my word will never taste death.' ⁵³ Are you greater than our father Abraham, who died? The prophets also died. Who do you claim to be?" ⁵⁴ Jesus answered, "If I glorify myself, my glory is nothing. It is my Father who glorifies me, he of whom you say, 'He is our God,' ⁵⁵ though you do not know him. But I know him; if I would say that I do not know him, I would be a liar like you. But I do know him and I keep his word. ⁵⁶ Your ancestor Abraham rejoiced that he would see my day; he saw it and was glad." ⁵⁷ Then the Jews said to him, "You are not yet fifty years old, and have you seen Abraham?"*q* ⁵⁸ Jesus said to them, "Very truly, I tell you, before Abraham was, I am." ⁵⁹ So they picked up stones to throw at him, but Jesus hid himself and went out of the temple.

A Man Born Blind Receives Sight

9 As he walked along, he saw a man blind from birth. ² His disciples asked him, "Rabbi, who sinned, this man or his parents, that he was born blind?" ³ Jesus answered, "Neither this man nor his parents sinned; he was born blind so that God's works might be revealed in him. ⁴ We*r* must work the works of him who sent me*s* while it is day; night is coming when no one can work. ⁵ As long as I am in the world, I am the light of the world." ⁶ When he had said this, he spat on the ground and made mud with the saliva and spread the mud on the man's eyes, ⁷ saying to him, "Go, wash in the pool of Si·lo′am" (which means Sent). Then he went and washed and came back able to see. ⁸ The neighbors and those who had seen him before as a beggar began to ask, "Is this not the man who used to sit and beg?" ⁹ Some were saying, "It is he." Others were saying, "No, but it is someone like him." He kept saying, "I am the man." ¹⁰ But they kept asking him, "Then how were your eyes opened?" ¹¹ He answered, "The man called Jesus made mud, spread it on my eyes, and said to me, 'Go to Si·lo′am and wash.' Then I went and washed and received my sight." ¹² They said to him, "Where is he?" He said, "I do not know."

The Pharisees Investigate the Healing

13 They brought to the Phar′i·sees the man who had formerly been blind. ¹⁴ Now it was a sabbath day when Jesus made the mud and opened his eyes. ¹⁵ Then the Phar′i·sees also began to ask him how he had received his sight. He said to them, "He put mud on my eyes. Then I washed, and now I see." ¹⁶ Some of the Phar′i·sees said, "This man is not from God, for he does not observe the sabbath." But others said, "How can a man who is a sinner perform such signs?" And they were divided. ¹⁷ So they said again to the blind man, "What do you say about him? It was your eyes he opened." He said, "He is a prophet."

18 The Jews did not believe that he had been blind and had received his sight until they called the parents of the man who had received his sight

q Other ancient authorities read *has Abraham seen you?* *r* Other ancient authorities read *I* *s* Other ancient authorities read *us*

19 and asked them, "Is this your son, who you say was born blind? How then does he now see?" 20 His parents answered, "We know that this is our son, and that he was born blind; 21 but we do not know how it is that now he sees, nor do we know who opened his eyes. Ask him; he is of age. He will speak for himself." 22 His parents said this because they were afraid of the Jews; for the Jews had already agreed that anyone who confessed Jesus*t* to be the Messiah*u* would be put out of the synagogue. 23 Therefore his parents said, "He is of age; ask him."

24 So for the second time they called the man who had been blind, and they said to him, "Give glory to God! We know that this man is a sinner." 25 He answered, "I do not know whether he is a sinner. One thing I do know, that though I was blind, now I see." 26 They said to him, "What did he do to you? How did he open your eyes?" 27 He answered them, "I have told you already, and you would not listen. Why do you want to hear it again? Do you also want to become his disciples?" 28 Then they reviled him, saying, "You are his disciple, but we are disciples of Moses. 29 We know that God has spoken to Moses, but as for this man, we do not know where he comes from." 30 The man answered, "Here is an astonishing thing! You do not know where he comes from, and yet he opened my eyes. 31 We know that God does not listen to sinners, but he does listen to one who worships him and obeys his will. 32 Never since the world began has it been heard that anyone opened the eyes of a person born blind. 33 If this man were not from God, he could do nothing." 34 They answered him, "You were born entirely in sins, and are you trying to teach us?" And they drove him out.

Spiritual Blindness

35 Jesus heard that they had driven him out, and when he found him, he said, "Do you believe in the Son of Man?"*v* 36 He answered, "And who is he, sir?*w* Tell me, so that I may believe in him." 37 Jesus said to him, "You have seen him, and the one speaking with you is he." 38 He said, "Lord,*w* I believe." And he worshiped him. 39 Jesus said, "I came into this world for judgment so that those who do not see may see, and those who do see may become blind." 40 Some of the Phar′i·sees near

him heard this and said to him, "Surely we are not blind, are we?" 41 Jesus said to them, "If you were blind, you would not have sin. But now that you say, 'We see,' your sin remains.

Jesus the Good Shepherd

10 "Very truly, I tell you, anyone who does not enter the sheepfold by the gate but climbs in by another way is a thief and a bandit. 2 The one who enters by the gate is the shepherd of the sheep. 3 The gatekeeper opens the gate for him, and the sheep hear his voice. He calls his own sheep by name and leads them out. 4 When he has brought out all his own, he goes ahead of them, and the sheep follow him because they know his voice. 5 They will not follow a stranger, but they will run from him because they do not know the voice of strangers." 6 Jesus used this figure of speech with them, but they did not understand what he was saying to them.

7 So again Jesus said to them, "Very truly, I tell you, I am the gate for the sheep. 8 All who came before me are thieves and bandits; but the sheep did not listen to them. 9 I am the gate. Whoever enters by me will be saved, and will come in and go out and find pasture. 10 The thief comes only to steal and kill and destroy. I came that they may have life, and have it abundantly.

11 "I am the good shepherd. The good shepherd lays down his life for the sheep. 12 The hired hand, who is not the shepherd and does not own the sheep, sees the wolf coming and leaves the sheep and runs away—and the wolf snatches them and scatters them. 13 The hired hand runs away because a hired hand does not care for the sheep. 14 I am the good shepherd. I know my own and my own know me, 15 just as the Father knows me and I know the Father. And I lay down my life for the sheep. 16 I have other sheep that do not belong to this fold. I must bring them also, and they will listen to my voice. So there will be one flock, one shepherd. 17 For this reason the Father loves me, because I lay down my life in order to take it up again. 18 No one takes*x* it from me, but I lay it down of

t Gk *him*   *u* Or *the Christ*   *v* Other ancient authorities read *the Son of God* *w* Sir and *Lord* translate the same Greek word   *x* Other ancient authorities read *has taken* my own accord. I have power to lay it down, and I have power to take it up again. I have received this command from my Father."

19 Again the Jews were divided because of these words. [20] Many of them were saying, "He has a demon and is out of his mind. Why listen to him?" [21] Others were saying, "These are not the words of one who has a demon. Can a demon open the eyes of the blind?"

Jesus Is Rejected by the Jews

22 At that time the festival of the Dedication took place in Jerusalem. It was winter, [23] and Jesus was walking in the temple, in the portico of Solomon. [24] So the Jews gathered around him and said to him, "How long will you keep us in suspense? If you are the Messiah,[y] tell us plainly." [25] Jesus answered, "I have told you, and you do not believe. The works that I do in my Father's name testify to me; [26] but you do not believe, because you do not belong to my sheep. [27] My sheep hear my voice. I know them, and they follow me. [28] I give them eternal life, and they will never perish. No one will snatch them out of my hand. [29] What my Father has given me is greater than all else, and no one can snatch it out of the Father's hand. [z] [30] The Father and I are one."

31 The Jews took up stones again to stone him. [32] Jesus replied, "I have shown you many good works from the Father. For which of these are you going to stone me?" [33] The Jews answered, "It is not for a good work that we are going to stone you, but for blasphemy, because you, though only a human being, are making yourself God." [34] Jesus answered, "Is it not written in your law,[a] 'I said, you are gods'? [35] If those to whom the word of God came were called 'gods'—and the scripture cannot be annulled— [36] can you say that the one whom the Father has sanctified and sent into the world is blaspheming because I said, 'I am God's Son'? [37] If I am not doing the works of my Father, then do not believe me. [38] But if I do them, even though you do not believe me, believe the works, so that you may know and understand[b] that the Father is in me and I am in the Father." [39] Then they tried to arrest him again, but he escaped from their hands.

40 He went away again across the Jordan to the place where John had been baptizing earlier, and he remained there. [41] Many came to him, and they were saying, "John performed no sign, but everything that John said about this man was true." [42] And many believed in him there.

The Death of Lazarus

11 Now a certain man was ill, Laz'a·rus of Beth'a·ny, the village of Mary and her sister Martha. [2] Mary was the one who anointed the Lord with perfume and wiped his feet with her hair; her brother Laz'a·rus was ill. [3] So the sisters sent a message to Jesus, [c] "Lord, he whom you love is ill." [4] But when Jesus heard it, he said, "This illness does not lead to death; rather it is for God's glory, so that the Son of God may be glorified through it." [5] Accordingly, though Jesus loved Martha and her sister and Laz'a·rus, [6] after having heard that Laz'a·rus[d] was ill, he stayed two days longer in the place where he was.

7 Then after this he said to the disciples, "Let us go to Judea again." [8] The disciples said to him, "Rabbi, the Jews were just now trying to stone you, and are you going there again?" [9] Jesus answered, "Are there not twelve hours of daylight? Those who walk during the day do not stumble, because they see the light of this world. [10] But those who walk at night stumble, because the light is not in them." [11] After saying this, he told them, "Our friend Laz'a·rus has fallen asleep, but I am going there to awaken him." [12] The disciples said to him, "Lord, if he has fallen asleep, he will be all right." [13] Jesus, however, had been speaking about his death, but they thought that he was referring merely to sleep. [14] Then Jesus told them plainly, "Laz'a·rus is dead. [15] For your sake I am glad I was not there, so that you may believe. But let us go to him." [16] Thomas, who was called the Twin,[e] said to his fellow disciples, "Let us also go, that we may die with him."

Jesus the Resurrection and the Life

17 When Jesus arrived, he found that Laz′a·rus[f] had already been in the tomb four days. 18 Now Beth′a·ny was near Jerusalem, some two miles[g] away, 19 and many of the Jews had come to Martha and Mary to console them about their brother. 20 When Martha heard that Jesus was coming, she went and met him, while Mary stayed at home. 21 Martha said to Jesus, "Lord, if you had been here, my brother would not have died. 22 But even now I know that God will give you whatever you ask of him." 23 Jesus said to her, "Your brother will rise again." 24 Martha said to him, "I know that he will rise again in the resurrection on the last day." 25 Jesus said to her, "I am the resurrection and the life.[h] Those who believe in me, even though they die, will live, 26 and everyone who lives and believes in me will never die. Do you believe this?" 27 She said to him, "Yes, Lord, I believe that you are the Messiah,[i] the Son of God, the one coming into the world."

Jesus Weeps

28 When she had said this, she went back and called her sister Mary, and told her privately, "The Teacher is here and is calling for you." 29 And when she heard it, she got up quickly and went to him. 30 Now Jesus had not yet come to the village, but was still at the place where Martha had met him. 31 The Jews who were with her in the house, consoling her, saw Mary get up quickly and go out. They followed her because they thought that she was going to the tomb to weep there. 32 When Mary came where Jesus was and saw him, she knelt at his feet and said to him, "Lord, if you had been here, my brother would not have died." 33 When Jesus saw her weeping, and the Jews who came with her also weeping, he was greatly disturbed in spirit and deeply moved. 34 He said, "Where have you laid him?" They said to him, "Lord, come and see." 35 Jesus began to weep. 36 So the Jews said, "See how he loved him!" 37 But some of them said, "Could not he who opened the eyes of the blind man have kept this man from dying?"

Jesus Raises Lazarus to Life

38 Then Jesus, again greatly disturbed, came to the tomb. It was a cave, and a stone was lying against it. 39 Jesus said, "Take away the stone." Martha, the sister of the dead man, said to him, "Lord, already there is a stench because he has been dead four days." 40 Jesus said to her, "Did I not tell you that if you believed, you would see the glory of God?" 41 So they took away the stone. And Jesus looked upward and said, "Father, I thank you for having heard me. 42 I knew that you always hear me, but I have said this for the sake of the crowd standing here, so that they may believe that you sent me." 43 When he had said this, he cried with a loud voice, "Laz′a·rus, come out!" 44 The dead man came out, his hands and feet bound with strips of cloth, and his face wrapped in a cloth. Jesus said to them, "Unbind him, and let him go."

The Plot to Kill Jesus
(Mt 26.1–5; Mk 14.1–2; Lk 22.1–2)

45 Many of the Jews therefore, who had come with Mary and had seen what Jesus did, believed in him. 46 But some of them went to the Phar′i·sees and told them what he had done. 47 So the chief priests and the Phar′i·sees called a meeting of the council, and said, "What are we to do? This man is performing many signs. 48 If we let him go on like this, everyone will believe in him, and the Romans will come and destroy both our holy place[j] and our nation." 49 But one of them, Ca′-i·a·phas, who was high priest that year, said to them, "You know nothing at all! 50 You do not understand that it is better for you to have one man die for the people than to have the whole nation destroyed." 51 He did not say this on his own, but being high priest that year he prophesied that Jesus was about to die for the nation, 52 and not for the nation only, but to gather into one the dispersed children of God. 53 So from that day on they planned to put him to death.

54 Jesus therefore no longer walked about openly among the Jews, but went from there to a town called E′phra·im in the region near the wilderness; and he remained there with the disciples.

55 Now the Passover of the Jews

---

[f] Gk *he*   [g] Gk *fifteen stadia*   [h] Other ancient authorities lack *and the life*
[i] Or *the Christ*   [j] Or *our temple*; Greek *our place*

was near, and many went up from the country to Jerusalem before the Passover to purify themselves. 56 They were looking for Jesus and were asking one another as they stood in the temple, "What do you think? Surely he will not come to the festival, will he?" 57 Now the chief priests and the Phar'i-sees had given orders that anyone who knew where Jesus*k* was should let them know, so that they might arrest him.

Mary Anoints Jesus
(Mt 26.6–13; Mk 14.3–9)

12 Six days before the Passover Jesus came to Beth'a-ny, the home of Laz'a-rus, whom he had raised from the dead. 2 There they gave a dinner for him. Martha served, and Laz'a-rus was one of those at the table with him. 3 Mary took a pound of costly perfume made of pure nard, anointed Jesus' feet, and wiped them*l* with her hair. The house was filled with the fragrance of the perfume. 4 But Judas Is-car'i-ot, one of his disciples (the one who was about to betray him), said, 5 "Why was this perfume not sold for three hundred denarii*m* and the money given to the poor?" 6 (He said this not because he cared about the poor, but because he was a thief; he kept the common purse and used to steal what was put into it.) 7 Jesus said, "Leave her alone. She bought it*n* so that she might keep it for the day of my burial. 8 You always have the poor with you, but you do not always have me."

The Plot to Kill Lazarus

9 When the great crowd of the Jews learned that he was there, they came not only because of Jesus but also to see Laz'a-rus, whom he had raised from the dead. 10 So the chief priests planned to put Laz'a-rus to death as well, 11 since it was on account of him that many of the Jews were deserting and were believing in Jesus.

Jesus' Triumphal Entry into Jerusalem
(Mt 21.1–11; Mk 11.1–11; Lk 19.28–40)

12 The next day the great crowd that had come to the festival heard that Jesus was coming to Jerusalem. 13 So they took branches of palm trees and went out to meet him, shouting,
"Hosanna!
Blessed is the one who comes in
  the name of the Lord—
  the King of Israel!"

14 Jesus found a young donkey and sat on it; as it is written:
15 "Do not be afraid, daughter of
  Zion.
Look, your king is coming,
  sitting on a donkey's colt!"
16 His disciples did not understand these things at first; but when Jesus was glorified, then they remembered that these things had been written of him and had been done to him. 17 So the crowd that had been with him when he called Laz'a-rus out of the tomb and raised him from the dead continued to testify.*o* 18 It was also because they heard that he had performed this sign that the crowd went to meet him. 19 The Phar'i-sees then said to one another, "You see, you can do nothing. Look, the world has gone after him!"

Some Greeks Wish to See Jesus

20 Now among those who went up to worship at the festival were some Greeks. 21 They came to Philip, who was from Beth-sa'i-da in Galilee, and said to him, "Sir, we wish to see Jesus." 22 Philip went and told Andrew; then Andrew and Philip went and told Jesus. 23 Jesus answered them, "The hour has come for the Son of Man to be glorified. 24 Very truly, I tell you, unless a grain of wheat falls into the earth and dies, it remains just a single grain; but if it dies, it bears much fruit. 25 Those who love their life lose it, and those who hate their life in this world will keep it for eternal life. 26 Whoever serves me must follow me, and where I am, there will my servant be also. Whoever serves me, the Father will honor.

Jesus Speaks about His Death

27 "Now my soul is troubled. And what should I say—'Father, save me from this hour'? No, it is for this reason that I have come to this hour. 28 Father, glorify your name." Then a voice came from heaven, "I have glorified it, and I will glorify it again." 29 The crowd standing there heard it and said that it was thunder. Others said, "An angel

k Gk *he* *l* Gk *his feet* *m* Three hundred denarii would be nearly a year's wages for a laborer *n* Gk lacks *She bought it* *o* Other ancient authorities read *with him began to testify that he had called. . .from the dead* has spoken to him." ³⁰Jesus answered, "This voice has come for your sake, not for mine. ³¹Now is the judgment of this world; now the ruler of this world will be driven out. ³²And I, when I am lifted up from the earth, will draw all people*p* to myself." ³³He said this to indicate the kind of death he was to die. ³⁴The crowd answered him, "We have heard from the law that the Messiah*q* remains forever. How can you say that the Son of Man must be lifted up? Who is this Son of Man?" ³⁵Jesus said to them, "The light is with you for a little longer. Walk while you have the light, so that the darkness may not overtake you. If you walk in the darkness, you do not know where you are going. ³⁶While you have the light, believe in the light, so that you may become children of light."

The Unbelief of the People

After Jesus had said this, he departed and hid from them. ³⁷Although he had performed so many signs in their presence, they did not believe in him. ³⁸This was to fulfill the word spoken by the prophet I·sāi′ah:
"Lord, who has believed our
        message,
    and to whom has the arm of
        the Lord been revealed?"
³⁹And so they could not believe, because I·sāi′ah also said,
⁴⁰   "He has blinded their eyes
        and hardened their heart,
    so that they might not look with
        their eyes,
    and understand with their
        heart and turn—
    and I would heal them."
⁴¹I·sāi′ah said this because*r* he saw his glory and spoke about him. ⁴²Nevertheless many, even of the authorities, believed in him. But because of the Phar′i·sees they did not confess it, for fear that they would be put out of the synagogue; ⁴³for they loved human glory more than the glory that comes from God.

Summary of Jesus' Teaching

44 Then Jesus cried aloud: "Whoever believes in me believes not in me but in him who sent me. ⁴⁵And whoever sees me sees him who sent me. ⁴⁶I have come as light into the world, so that everyone who believes in me should not remain in the darkness. ⁴⁷I do not judge anyone who hears my words and does not keep them, for I

came not to judge the world, but to save the world. ⁴⁸The one who rejects me and does not receive my word has a judge; on the last day the word that I have spoken will serve as judge, ⁴⁹for I have not spoken on my own, but the Father who sent me has himself given me a commandment about what to say and what to speak. ⁵⁰And I know that his commandment is eternal life. What I speak, therefore, I speak just as the Father has told me."

Jesus Washes the Disciples' Feet

13 Now before the festival of the Passover, Jesus knew that his hour had come to depart from this world and go to the Father. Having loved his own who were in the world, he loved them to the end. ²The devil had already put it into the heart of Judas son of Simon Is·car′i·ot to betray him. And during supper ³Jesus, knowing that the Father had given all things into his hands, and that he had come from God and was going to God, ⁴got up from the table,*s* took off his outer robe, and tied a towel around himself. ⁵Then he poured water into a basin and began to wash the disciples' feet and to wipe them with the towel that was tied around him. ⁶He came to Simon Peter, who said to him, "Lord, are you going to wash my feet?" ⁷Jesus answered, "You do not know now what I am doing, but later you will understand." ⁸Peter said to him, "You will never wash my feet." Jesus answered, "Unless I wash you, you have no share with me." ⁹Simon Peter said to him, "Lord, not my feet only but also my hands and my head!" ¹⁰Jesus said to him, "One who has bathed does not need to wash, except for the feet,*t* but is entirely clean. And you*u* are clean, though not all of you." ¹¹For he knew who was to betray him; for this reason he said, "Not all of you are clean."

12 After he had washed their feet, had put on his robe, and had returned to the table, he said to them, "Do you know what I have done to you? ¹³You call me Teacher and Lord—and you are right, for that is what I am. ¹⁴So if I, your Lord and Teacher, have washed

J
O
H
N

your feet, you also ought to wash one another's feet. [15]For I have set you an example, that you also should do as I have done to you. [16]Very truly, I tell you, servants[v] are not greater than their master, nor are messengers greater than the one who sent them. [17]If you know these things, you are blessed if you do them. [18]I am not speaking of all of you; I know whom I have chosen. But it is to fulfill the scripture, 'The one who ate my bread[w] has lifted his heel against me.' [19]I tell you this now, before it occurs, so that when it does occur, you may believe that I am he.[x] [20]Very truly, I tell you, whoever receives one whom I send receives me; and whoever receives me receives him who sent me."

Jesus Foretells His Betrayal
(Mt 26.21–25; Mk 14.18–19; Lk 22.21–23)

21 After saying this Jesus was troubled in spirit, and declared, "Very truly, I tell you, one of you will betray me." [22]The disciples looked at one another, uncertain of whom he was speaking. [23]One of his disciples—the one whom Jesus loved—was reclining next to him; [24]Simon Peter therefore motioned to him to ask Jesus of whom he was speaking. [25]So while reclining next to Jesus, he asked him, "Lord, who is it?" [26]Jesus answered, "It is the one to whom I give this piece of bread when I have dipped it in the dish."[y] So when he had dipped the piece of bread, he gave it to Judas son of Simon Is·car'i·ot.[z] [27]After he received the piece of bread,[a] Satan entered into him. Jesus said to him, "Do quickly what you are going to do." [28]Now no one at the table knew why he said this to him. [29]Some thought that, because Judas had the common purse, Jesus was telling him, "Buy what we need for the festival"; or, that he should give something to the poor. [30]So, after receiving the piece of bread, he immediately went out. And it was night.

The New Commandment

31 When he had gone out, Jesus said, "Now the Son of Man has been glorified, and God has been glorified in him. [32]If God has been glorified in him,[b] God will also glorify him in himself and will glorify him at once. [33]Little children, I am with you only a little longer. You will look for me; and as I said to the Jews so now I say to you, 'Where I am going, you cannot come.'

[34]I give you a new commandment, that you love one another. Just as I have loved you, you also should love one another. [35]By this everyone will know that you are my disciples, if you have love for one another."

Jesus Foretells Peter's Denial

36 Simon Peter said to him, "Lord, where are you going?" Jesus answered, "Where I am going, you cannot follow me now; but you will follow afterward." [37]Peter said to him, "Lord, why can I not follow you now? I will lay down my life for you." [38]Jesus answered, "Will you lay down your life for me? Very truly, I tell you, before the cock crows, you will have denied me three times.

Jesus the Way to the Father

14 "Do not let your hearts be troubled. Believe[c] in God, believe also in me. [2]In my Father's house there are many dwelling places. If it were not so, would I have told you that I go to prepare a place for you?[d] [3]And if I go and prepare a place for you, I will come again and will take you to myself, so that where I am, there you may be also. [4]And you know the way to the place where I am going."[e] [5]Thomas said to him, "Lord, we do not know where you are going. How can we know the way?" [6]Jesus said to him, "I am the way, and the truth, and the life. No one comes to the Father except through me. [7]If you know me, you will know[f] my Father also. From now on you do know him and have seen him."

8 Philip said to him, "Lord, show us the Father, and we will be satisfied." [9]Jesus said to him, "Have I been with you all this time, Philip, and you still do not know me? Whoever has seen me has seen the Father. How can you say, 'Show us the Father'? [10]Do you

---

[v] Gk slaves [w] Other ancient authorities read ate bread with me [x] Gk I am [y] Gk dipped it [z] Other ancient authorities read Judas Iscariot son of Simon; others, Judas son of Simon from Karyot (Kerioth) [a] Gk After the piece of bread [b] Other ancient authorities lack If God has been glorified in him [c] Or You believe [d] Or If it were not so, I would have told you; for I go to prepare a place for you [e] Other ancient authorities read Where I am going you know, and the way you know [f] Other ancient authorities read If you had known me, you would have known

not believe that I am in the Father and the Father is in me? The words that I say to you I do not speak on my own; but the Father who dwells in me does his works. 11 Believe me that I am in the Father and the Father is in me; but if you do not, then believe me because of the works themselves. 12 Very truly, I tell you, the one who believes in me will also do the works that I do and, in fact, will do greater works than these, because I am going to the Father. 13 I will do whatever you ask in my name, so that the Father may be glorified in the Son. 14 If in my name you ask me [g] for anything, I will do it.

The Promise of the Holy Spirit

15 "If you love me, you will keep [h] my commandments. 16 And I will ask the Father, and he will give you another Advocate, [i] to be with you forever. 17 This is the Spirit of truth, whom the world cannot receive, because it neither sees him nor knows him. You know him, because he abides with you, and he will be in [j] you.

18 "I will not leave you orphaned; I am coming to you. 19 In a little while the world will no longer see me, but you will see me; because I live, you also will live. 20 On that day you will know that I am in my Father, and you in me, and I in you. 21 They who have my commandments and keep them are those who love me; and those who love me will be loved by my Father, and I will love them and reveal myself to them." 22 Judas (not Is·car'i·ot) said to him, "Lord, how is it that you will reveal yourself to us, and not to the world?" 23 Jesus answered him, "Those who love me will keep my word, and my Father will love them, and we will come to them and make our home with them. 24 Whoever does not love me does not keep my words; and the word that you hear is not mine, but is from the Father who sent me.

25 "I have said these things to you while I am still with you. 26 But the Advocate, [i] the Holy Spirit, whom the Father will send in my name, will teach you everything, and remind you of all that I have said to you. 27 Peace I leave with you; my peace I give to you. I do not give to you as the world gives. Do not let your hearts be troubled, and do not let them be afraid. 28 You heard me say to you, 'I am going away, and I am coming to you.' If you loved me, you would rejoice that I am going to

the Father, because the Father is greater than I. 29 And now I have told you this before it occurs, so that when it does occur, you may believe. 30 I will no longer talk much with you, for the ruler of this world is coming. He has no power over me; 31 but I do as the Father has commanded me, so that the world may know that I love the Father. Rise, let us be on our way.

Jesus the True Vine

15 "I am the true vine, and my Father is the vinegrower. 2 He removes every branch in me that bears no fruit. Every branch that bears fruit he prunes [k] to make it bear more fruit. 3 You have already been cleansed [k] by the word that I have spoken to you. 4 Abide in me as I abide in you. Just as the branch cannot bear fruit by itself unless it abides in the vine, neither can you unless you abide in me. 5 I am the vine, you are the branches. Those who abide in me and I in them bear much fruit, because apart from me you can do nothing. 6 Whoever does not abide in me is thrown away like a branch and withers; such branches are gathered, thrown into the fire, and burned. 7 If you abide in me, and my words abide in you, ask for whatever you wish, and it will be done for you. 8 My Father is glorified by this, that you bear much fruit and become [l] my disciples. 9 As the Father has loved me, so I have loved you; abide in my love. 10 If you keep my commandments, you will abide in my love, just as I have kept my Father's commandments and abide in his love. 11 I have said these things to you so that my joy may be in you, and that your joy may be complete.

12 "This is my commandment, that you love one another as I have loved you. 13 No one has greater love than this, to lay down one's life for one's friends. 14 You are my friends if you do what I command you. 15 I do not call you servants [m] any longer, because the servant [n] does not know what the master is doing; but I have called you friends, because I have made known to you everything that I have heard from my Father. 16 You did not choose me

[g] Other ancient authorities lack *me*
[h] Other ancient authorities read *me, keep*
[i] Or *Helper*　[j] Or *among*　[k] The same Greek root refers to pruning and cleansing　[l] Or *be*　[m] Gk *slaves*
[n] Gk *slave*

but I chose you. And I appointed you to go and bear fruit, fruit that will last, so that the Father will give you whatever you ask him in my name. [17] I am giving you these commands so that you may love one another.

The World's Hatred

18 "If the world hates you, be aware that it hated me before it hated you. [19] If you belonged to the world,[o] the world would love you as its own. Because you do not belong to the world, but I have chosen you out of the world—therefore the world hates you. [20] Remember the word that I said to you, 'Servants[p] are not greater than their master.' If they persecuted me, they will persecute you; if they kept my word, they will keep yours also. [21] But they will do all these things to you on account of my name, because they do not know him who sent me. [22] If I had not come and spoken to them, they would not have sin; but now they have no excuse for their sin. [23] Whoever hates me hates my Father also. [24] If I had not done among them the works that no one else did, they would not have sin. But now they have seen and hated both me and my Father. [25] It was to fulfill the word that is written in their law, 'They hated me without a cause.'

26 "When the Advocate[q] comes, whom I will send to you from the Father, the Spirit of truth who comes from the Father, he will testify on my behalf. [27] You also are to testify because you have been with me from the beginning.

16 "I have said these things to you to keep you from stumbling. [2] They will put you out of the synagogues. Indeed, an hour is coming when those who kill you will think that by doing so they are offering worship to God. [3] And they will do this because they have not known the Father or me. [4] But I have said these things to you so that when their hour comes you may remember that I told you about them.

The Work of the Spirit

"I did not say these things to you from the beginning, because I was with you. [5] But now I am going to him who sent me; yet none of you asks me, 'Where are you going?' [6] But because I have said these things to you, sorrow has filled your hearts. [7] Nevertheless I tell you the truth: it is to your advantage that I go away, for if I do not go away, the Advocate[q] will not come to you; but if I go, I will send him to you. [8] And when he comes, he will prove the world wrong about[r] sin and righteousness and judgment: [9] about sin, because they do not believe in me; [10] about righteousness, because I am going to the Father and you will see me no longer; [11] about judgment, because the ruler of this world has been condemned.

12 "I still have many things to say to you, but you cannot bear them now. [13] When the Spirit of truth comes, he will guide you into all the truth; for he will not speak on his own, but will speak whatever he hears, and he will declare to you the things that are to come. [14] He will glorify me, because he will take what is mine and declare it to you. [15] All that the Father has is mine. For this reason I said that he will take what is mine and declare it to you.

Sorrow Will Turn into Joy

16 "A little while, and you will no longer see me, and again a little while, and you will see me." [17] Then some of his disciples said to one another, "What does he mean by saying to us, 'A little while, and you will no longer see me, and again a little while, and you will see me'; and 'Because I am going to the Father'?" [18] They said, "What does he mean by this 'a little while'? We do not know what he is talking about." [19] Jesus knew that they wanted to ask him, so he said to them, "Are you discussing among yourselves what I meant when I said, 'A little while, and you will no longer see me, and again a little while, and you will see me'? [20] Very truly, I tell you, you will weep and mourn, but the world will rejoice; you will have pain, but your pain will turn into joy. [21] When a woman is in labor, she has pain, because her hour has come. But when her child is born, she no longer remembers the anguish because of the joy of having brought a human being into the world. [22] So you have pain now; but I will see you again, and your hearts will rejoice, and no one will take your joy from you. [23] On that day you will ask nothing of me.[s] Very truly, I tell you, if you ask anything of the Father in my

---

[o] Gk were of the world   [p] Gk Slaves
[q] Or Helper   [r] Or convict the world of
[s] Or will ask me no question

name, he will give it to you. *t* 24 Until now you have not asked for anything in my name. Ask and you will receive, so that your joy may be complete.

Peace for the Disciples

25 "I have said these things to you in figures of speech. The hour is coming when I will no longer speak to you in figures, but will tell you plainly of the Father. 26 On that day you will ask in my name. I do not say to you that I will ask the Father on your behalf; 27 for the Father himself loves you, because you have loved me and have believed that I came from God. *u* 28 I came from the Father and have come into the world; again, I am leaving the world and am going to the Father."

29 His disciples said, "Yes, now you are speaking plainly, not in any figure of speech! 30 Now we know that you know all things, and do not need to have anyone question you; by this we believe that you came from God." 31 Jesus answered them, "Do you now believe? 32 The hour is coming, indeed it has come, when you will be scattered, each one to his home, and you will leave me alone. Yet I am not alone because the Father is with me. 33 I have said this to you, so that in me you may have peace. In the world you face persecution. But take courage; I have conquered the world!"

Jesus Prays for His Disciples

17 After Jesus had spoken these words, he looked up to heaven and said, "Father, the hour has come; glorify your Son so that the Son may glorify you, 2 since you have given him authority over all people, *v* to give eternal life to all whom you have given him. 3 And this is eternal life, that they may know you, the only true God, and Jesus Christ whom you have sent. 4 I glorified you on earth by finishing the work that you gave me to do. 5 So now, Father, glorify me in your own presence with the glory that I had in your presence before the world existed.

6 "I have made your name known to those whom you gave me from the world. They were yours, and you gave them to me, and they have kept your word. 7 Now they know that everything you have given me is from you; 8 for the words that you gave to me I have given to them, and they have received them and know in truth that I came from you; and they have be-

lieved that you sent me. 9 I am asking on their behalf; I am not asking on behalf of the world, but on behalf of those whom you gave me, because they are yours. 10 All mine are yours, and yours are mine; and I have been glorified in them. 11 And now I am no longer in the world, but they are in the world, and I am coming to you. Holy Father, protect them in your name that *w* you have given me, so that they may be one, as we are one. 12 While I was with them, I protected them in your name that *w* you have given me. I guarded them, and not one of them was lost except the one destined to be lost, *x* so that the scripture might be fulfilled. 13 But now I am coming to you, and I speak these things in the world so that they may have my joy made complete in themselves. *y* 14 I have given them your word, and the world has hated them because they do not belong to the world, just as I do not belong to the world. 15 I am not asking you to take them out of the world, but I ask you to protect them from the evil one. *z* 16 They do not belong to the world, just as I do not belong to the world. 17 Sanctify them in the truth; your word is truth. 18 As you have sent me into the world, so I have sent them into the world. 19 And for their sakes I sanctify myself, so that they also may be sanctified in truth.

20 "I ask not only on behalf of these, but also on behalf of those who will believe in me through their word, 21 that they may all be one. As you, Father, are in me and i am in you, may they also be in us, *a* so that the world may believe that you have sent me. 22 The glory that you have given me I have given them, so that they may be one, as we are one, 23 I in them and you in me, that they may become completely one, so that the world may know that you have sent me and have loved them even as you have loved me. 24 Father, I desire that those also, whom you have given me, may be with me where I am, to see my glory, which

---

t Other ancient authorities read *Father, he will give it to you in my name*
u Other ancient authorities read *the Father* *v* Gk *flesh* *w* Other ancient authorities read *protected in your name those whom* *x* Gk *except the son of destruction* *y* Or *among themselves* *z* Or *from evil* *a* Other ancient authorities read *be one in us*

you have given me because you loved me before the foundation of the world. 25 "Righteous Father, the world does not know you, but I know you; and these know that you have sent me. 26 I made your name known to them, and I will make it known, so that the love with which you have loved me may be in them, and I in them."

The Betrayal and Arrest of Jesus
(Mt 26.47–56; Mk 14.43–52; Lk 22.47–53)

18 After Jesus had spoken these words, he went out with his disciples across the Kid′ron valley to a place where there was a garden, which he and his disciples entered. 2 Now Judas, who betrayed him, also knew the place, because Jesus often met there with his disciples. 3 So Judas brought a detachment of soldiers together with police from the chief priests and the Phar′i·sees, and they came there with lanterns and torches and weapons. 4 Then Jesus, knowing all that was to happen to him, came forward and asked them, "Whom are you looking for?" 5 They answered, "Jesus of Nazareth." *b* Jesus replied, "I am he." *c* Judas, who betrayed him, was standing with them. 6 When Jesus *d* said to them, "I am he," *c* they stepped back and fell to the ground. 7 Again he asked them, "Whom are you looking for?" And they said, "Jesus of Nazareth." *b* 8 Jesus answered, "I told you that I am he. *c* So if you are looking for me, let these men go." 9 This was to fulfill the word that he had spoken, "I did not lose a single one of those whom you gave me." 10 Then Simon Peter, who had a sword, drew it, struck the high priest's slave, and cut off his right ear. The slave's name was Mal′chus. 11 Jesus said to Peter, "Put your sword back into its sheath. Am I not to drink the cup that the Father has given me?"

Jesus before the High Priest

12 So the soldiers, their officer, and the Jewish police arrested Jesus and bound him. 13 First they took him to An′nas, who was the father-in-law of Ca′i·a·phas, the high priest that year. 14 Ca′i·a·phas was the one who had advised the Jews that it was better to have one person die for the people.

Peter Denies Jesus
(Mt 26.69–75; Mk 14.66–72; Lk 22.54–62)

15 Simon Peter and another disciple followed Jesus. Since that disciple was known to the high priest, he went with Jesus into the courtyard of the high priest, 16 but Peter was standing outside at the gate. So the other disciple, who was known to the high priest, went out, spoke to the woman who guarded the gate, and brought Peter in. 17 The woman said to Peter, "You are not also one of this man's disciples, are you?" He said, "I am not." 18 Now the slaves and the police had made a charcoal fire because it was cold, and they were standing around it and warming themselves. Peter also was standing with them and warming himself.

The High Priest Questions Jesus

19 Then the high priest questioned Jesus about his disciples and about his teaching. 20 Jesus answered, "I have spoken openly to the world; I have always taught in synagogues and in the temple, where all the Jews come together. I have said nothing in secret. 21 Why do you ask me? Ask those who heard what I said to them; they know what I said." 22 When he had said this, one of the police standing nearby struck Jesus on the face, saying, "Is that how you answer the high priest?" 23 Jesus answered, "If I have spoken wrongly, testify to the wrong. But if I have spoken rightly, why do you strike me?" 24 Then An′nas sent him bound to Ca′i·a·phas the high priest.

Peter Denies Jesus Again

25 Now Simon Peter was standing and warming himself. They asked him, "You are not also one of his disciples, are you?" He denied it and said, "I am not." 26 One of the slaves of the high priest, a relative of the man whose ear Peter had cut off, asked, "Did I not see you in the garden with him?" 27 Again Peter denied it, and at that moment the cock crowed.

Jesus before Pilate
(Mt 27.1–2, 11–14; Mk 15.1–5; Lk 23.1–5)

28 Then they took Jesus from Ca′i·a·phas to Pilate's headquarters. *e* It was early in the morning. They themselves did not enter the headquarters, *e* so as to avoid ritual defilement and to be able to eat the Passover. 29 So Pilate went out to them and said, "What accusation do you bring against

b Gk *the Nazorean*   *c* Gk *I am*   *d* Gk *he*
e Gk *the praetorium*

this man?" [30] They answered, "If this man were not a criminal, we would not have handed him over to you." [31] Pilate said to them, "Take him yourselves and judge him according to your law." The Jews replied, "We are not permitted to put anyone to death." [32] (This was to fulfill what Jesus had said when he indicated the kind of death he was to die.)

[33] Then Pilate entered the headquarters[f] again, summoned Jesus, and asked him, "Are you the King of the Jews?" [34] Jesus answered, "Do you ask this on your own, or did others tell you about me?" [35] Pilate replied, "I am not a Jew, am I? Your own nation and the chief priests have handed you over to me. What have you done?" [36] Jesus answered, "My kingdom is not from this world. If my kingdom were from this world, my followers would be fighting to keep me from being handed over to the Jews. But as it is, my kingdom is not from here." [37] Pilate asked him, "So you are a king?" Jesus answered, "You say that I am a king. For this I was born, and for this I came into the world, to testify to the truth. Everyone who belongs to the truth listens to my voice." [38] Pilate asked him, "What is truth?"

Jesus Sentenced to Death
(Mt 27.15–31; Mk 15.6–20; Lk 23.13–25)

After he had said this, he went out to the Jews again and told them, "I find no case against him. [39] But you have a custom that I release someone for you at the Passover. Do you want me to release for you the King of the Jews?" [40] They shouted in reply, "Not this man, but Ba·rab′bas!" Now Ba·rab′bas was a bandit.

19 Then Pilate took Jesus and had him flogged. [2] And the soldiers wove a crown of thorns and put it on his head, and they dressed him in a purple robe. [3] They kept coming up to him, saying, "Hail, King of the Jews!" and striking him on the face. [4] Pilate went out again and said to them, "Look, I am bringing him out to you to let you know that I find no case against him." [5] So Jesus came out, wearing the crown of thorns and the purple robe. Pilate said to them, "Here is the man!" [6] When the chief priests and the police saw him, they shouted, "Crucify him! Crucify him!" Pilate said to them, "Take him yourselves and crucify him; I find no case against him." [7] The Jews answered him, "We have a law, and according to that law he ought to die because he has claimed to be the Son of God."

[8] Now when Pilate heard this, he was more afraid than ever. [9] He entered his headquarters[f] again and asked Jesus, "Where are you from?" But Jesus gave him no answer. [10] Pilate therefore said to him, "Do you refuse to speak to me? Do you not know that I have power to release you, and power to crucify you?" [11] Jesus answered him, "You would have no power over me unless it had been given you from above; therefore the one who handed me over to you is guilty of a greater sin." [12] From then on Pilate tried to release him, but the Jews cried out, "If you release this man, you are no friend of the emperor. Everyone who claims to be a king sets himself against the emperor."

[13] When Pilate heard these words, he brought Jesus outside and sat[g] on the judge's bench at a place called The Stone Pavement, or in Hebrew[h] Gab′-ba·tha. [14] Now it was the day of Preparation for the Passover; and it was about noon. He said to the Jews, "Here is your King!" [15] They cried out, "Away with him! Away with him! Crucify him!" Pilate asked them, "Shall I crucify your King?" The chief priests answered, "We have no king but the emperor." [16] Then he handed him over to them to be crucified.

The Crucifixion of Jesus
(Mt 27.32–56; Mk 15.21–41; Lk 23.26–49)

So they took Jesus; [17] and carrying the cross by himself, he went out to what is called The Place of the Skull, which in Hebrew[h] is called Gol′-go·tha. [18] There they crucified him, and with him two others, one on either side, with Jesus between them. [19] Pilate also had an inscription written and put on the cross. It read, "Jesus of Nazareth,[i] the King of the Jews." [20] Many of the Jews read this inscription, because the place where Jesus was crucified was near the city; and it was written in Hebrew,[h] in Latin, and in Greek. [21] Then the chief priests of the Jews said to Pilate, "Do not write, 'The King of the Jews,' but, 'This man said, I am King of the Jews.'" [22] Pilate answered, "What I have written I have

---

[f] Gk *the praetorium*   [g] Or *seated him*
[h] That is, *Aramaic*   [i] Gk *the Nazorean*

written." 23 When the soldiers had crucified Jesus, they took his clothes and divided them into four parts, one for each soldier. They also took his tunic; now the tunic was seamless, woven in one piece from the top. 24 So they said to one another, "Let us not tear it, but cast lots for it to see who will get it." This was to fulfill what the scripture says,

"They divided my clothes among themselves,
and for my clothing they cast lots."

25 And that is what the soldiers did.

Meanwhile, standing near the cross of Jesus were his mother, and his mother's sister, Mary the wife of Cloʹpas, and Mary Magʹda·lēne. 26 When Jesus saw his mother and the disciple whom he loved standing beside her, he said to his mother, "Woman, here is your son." 27 Then he said to the disciple, "Here is your mother." And from that hour the disciple took her into his own home.

28 After this, when Jesus knew that all was now finished, he said (in order to fulfill the scripture), "I am thirsty." 29 A jar full of sour wine was standing there. So they put a sponge full of the wine on a branch of hyssop and held it to his mouth. 30 When Jesus had received the wine, he said, "It is finished." Then he bowed his head and gave up his spirit.

Jesus' Side Is Pierced

31 Since it was the day of Preparation, the Jews did not want the bodies left on the cross during the sabbath, especially because that sabbath was a day of great solemnity. So they asked Pilate to have the legs of the crucified men broken and the bodies removed. 32 Then the soldiers came and broke the legs of the first and of the other who had been crucified with him. 33 But when they came to Jesus and saw that he was already dead, they did not break his legs. 34 Instead, one of the soldiers pierced his side with a spear, and at once blood and water came out. 35 (He who saw this has testified so that you also may believe. His testimony is true, and he knowsʲ that he tells the truth.) 36 These things occurred so that the scripture might be fulfilled, "None of his bones shall be broken." 37 And again another passage of scripture says, "They will look on the one whom they have pierced."

The Burial of Jesus
(Mt 27.57–61; Mk 15.42–47; Lk 23.50–56)

38 After these things, Joseph of Ar·i·ma·theʹa, who was a disciple of Jesus, though a secret one because of his fear of the Jews, asked Pilate to let him take away the body of Jesus. Pilate gave him permission; so he came and removed his body. 39 Nic·o·deʹmus, who had at first come to Jesus by night, also came, bringing a mixture of myrrh and aloes, weighing about a hundred pounds. 40 They took the body of Jesus and wrapped it with the spices in linen cloths, according to the burial custom of the Jews. 41 Now there was a garden in the place where he was crucified, and in the garden there was a new tomb in which no one had ever been laid. 42 And so, because it was the Jewish day of Preparation, and the tomb was nearby, they laid Jesus there.

The Resurrection of Jesus
(Mt 28.1–10; Mk 16.1–8; Lk 24.1–12)

20 Early on the first day of the week, while it was still dark, Mary Magʹda·lēne came to the tomb and saw that the stone had been removed from the tomb. 2 So she ran and went to Simon Peter and the other disciple, the one whom Jesus loved, and said to them, "They have taken the Lord out of the tomb, and we do not know where they have laid him." 3 Then Peter and the other disciple set out and went toward the tomb. 4 The two were running together, but the other disciple outran Peter and reached the tomb first. 5 He bent down to look in and saw the linen wrappings lying there, but he did not go in. 6 Then Simon Peter came, following him, and went into the tomb. He saw the linen wrappings lying there, 7 and the cloth that had been on Jesus' head, not lying with the linen wrappings but rolled up in a place by itself. 8 Then the other disciple, who reached the tomb first, also went in, and he saw and believed; 9 for as yet they did not understand the scripture, that he must rise from the dead. 10 Then the disciples returned to their homes.

Jesus Appears to Mary Magdalene

11 But Mary stood weeping outside the tomb. As she wept, she bent over to

ʲ Or *there is one who knows*

look[k] into the tomb; [12] and she saw two angels in white, sitting where the body of Jesus had been lying, one at the head and the other at the feet. [13] They said to her, "Woman, why are you weeping?" She said to them, "They have taken away my Lord, and I do not know where they have laid him." [14] When she had said this, she turned around and saw Jesus standing there, but she did not know that it was Jesus. [15] Jesus said to her, "Woman, why are you weeping? Whom are you looking for?" Supposing him to be the gardener, she said to him, "Sir, if you have carried him away, tell me where you have laid him, and I will take him away." [16] Jesus said to her, "Mary!" She turned and said to him in Hebrew,[l] "Rab·boū′ni!" (which means Teacher). [17] Jesus said to her, "Do not hold on to me, because I have not yet ascended to the Father. But go to my brothers and say to them, 'I am ascending to my Father and your Father, to my God and your God.'" [18] Mary Mag′da·lēne went and announced to the disciples, "I have seen the Lord"; and she told them that he had said these things to her.

Jesus Appears to the Disciples
(Lk 24.36–43; 1 Cor 15.5)

19 When it was evening on that day, the first day of the week, and the doors of the house where the disciples had met were locked for fear of the Jews, Jesus came and stood among them and said, "Peace be with you." [20] After he said this, he showed them his hands and his side. Then the disciples rejoiced when they saw the Lord. [21] Jesus said to them again, "Peace be with you. As the Father has sent me, so I send you." [22] When he had said this, he breathed on them and said to them, "Receive the Holy Spirit. [23] If you forgive the sins of any, they are forgiven them; if you retain the sins of any, they are retained."

Jesus and Thomas

24 But Thomas (who was called the Twin[m]), one of the twelve, was not with them when Jesus came. [25] So the other disciples told him, "We have seen the Lord." But he said to them, "Unless I see the mark of the nails in his hands, and put my finger in the mark of the nails and my hand in his side, I will not believe."

26 A week later his disciples were again in the house, and Thomas was with them. Although the doors were shut, Jesus came and stood among them and said, "Peace be with you." [27] Then he said to Thomas, "Put your finger here and see my hands. Reach out your hand and put it in my side. Do not doubt but believe." [28] Thomas answered him, "My Lord and my God!" [29] Jesus said to him, "Have you believed because you have seen me? Blessed are those who have not seen and yet have come to believe."

The Purpose of This Book

30 Now Jesus did many other signs in the presence of his disciples, which are not written in this book. [31] But these are written so that you may come to believe[n] that Jesus is the Messiah,[o] the Son of God, and that through believing you may have life in his name.

Jesus Appears to Seven Disciples

21 After these things Jesus showed himself again to the disciples by the Sea of Ti·bē′ri·as; and he showed himself in this way. [2] Gathered there together were Simon Peter, Thomas called the Twin,[m] Na·than′a·el of Ca′na in Galilee, the sons of Zeb′e·dee, and two others of his disciples. [3] Simon Peter said to them, "I am going fishing." They said to him, "We will go with you." They went out and got into the boat, but that night they caught nothing.

4 Just after daybreak, Jesus stood on the beach; but the disciples did not know that it was Jesus. [5] Jesus said to them, "Children, you have no fish, have you?" They answered him, "No." [6] He said to them, "Cast the net to the right side of the boat, and you will find some." So they cast it, and now they were not able to haul it in because there were so many fish. [7] That disciple whom Jesus loved said to Peter, "It is the Lord!" When Simon Peter heard that it was the Lord, he put on some clothes, for he was naked, and jumped into the sea. [8] But the other disciples came in the boat, dragging the net full of fish, for they were not far from the land, only about a hundred yards[p] off.

9 When they had gone ashore, they

---

[k] Gk lacks *to look*   [l] That is, *Aramaic*
[m] Gk *Didymus*   [n] Other ancient authorities read *may continue to believe*
[o] Or *the Christ*   [p] Gk *two hundred cubits*

saw a charcoal fire there, with fish on it, and bread. [10] Jesus said to them, "Bring some of the fish that you have just caught." [11] So Simon Peter went aboard and hauled the net ashore, full of large fish, a hundred fifty-three of them; and though there were so many, the net was not torn. [12] Jesus said to them, "Come and have breakfast." Now none of the disciples dared to ask him, "Who are you?" because they knew it was the Lord. [13] Jesus came and took the bread and gave it to them, and did the same with the fish. [14] This was now the third time that Jesus appeared to the disciples after he was raised from the dead.

Jesus and Peter

15 When they had finished breakfast, Jesus said to Simon Peter, "Simon son of John, do you love me more than these?" He said to him, "Yes, Lord; you know that I love you." Jesus said to him, "Feed my lambs." [16] A second time he said to him, "Simon son of John, do you love me?" He said to him, "Yes, Lord; you know that I love you." Jesus said to him, "Tend my sheep." [17] He said to him the third time, "Simon son of John, do you love me?" Peter felt hurt because he said to him the third time, "Do you love me?" And he said to him, "Lord, you know everything; you know that I love you." Jesus said to him, "Feed my sheep. [18] Very truly, I tell you, when you were younger, you used to fasten your own belt and to go wherever you wished. But when you grow old, you will stretch out your hands, and someone else will fasten a belt around you and take you where you do not wish to go." [19] (He said this to indicate the kind of death by which he would glorify God.) After this he said to him, "Follow me."

Jesus and the Beloved Disciple

20 Peter turned and saw the disciple whom Jesus loved following them; he was the one who had reclined next to Jesus at the supper and had said, "Lord, who is it that is going to betray you?" [21] When Peter saw him, he said to Jesus, "Lord, what about him?" [22] Jesus said to him, "If it is my will that he remain until I come, what is that to you? Follow me!" [23] So the rumor spread in the community*q* that this disciple would not die. Yet Jesus did not say to him that he would not die, but, "If it is my will that he remain until I come, what is that to you?"*r*

24 This is the disciple who is testifying to these things and has written them, and we know that his testimony is true. [25] But there are also many other things that Jesus did; if every one of them were written down, I suppose that the world itself could not contain the books that would be written.

q Gk *among the brothers*   *r* Other ancient authorities lack *what is that to you*

History: The Acts of the Apostles

Acts is a unique book in the Scripture. It is really volume 2 of Luke's work and tells the story of the beginnings of the church. It begins with the ascension of Jesus, has the record of the giving of the Spirit at Pentecost, and the life of the early church. It is not, however, the story of the whole church, or even of all the apostles. It focuses on the beginnings of the church, then on the work of Peter, and finally on the work of Paul. Luke wanted to show how the church spread from Jerusalem all over Palestine and then to the Gentiles.

Luke reports a series of episodes in the life and faith of the early church to show how Christianity rose out of Judaism and has deep roots in the Jewish faith. He shows something of the struggle the disciples felt in moving out in a mission to Gentiles. One of the major themes in the book is the role of the Holy Spirit in guiding and strengthening the church as it spread across the Mediterranean world. Another theme is the message that Christianity is not dangerous to the authority or power of the Roman Empire. More than one-half of Acts is devoted to the ministry of Paul and his travels to preach the good news.

THE JOURNEYS OF PAUL

The

ACTS

of the Apostles

The Promise of the Holy Spirit

1 In the first book, Thē·oph'i·lus, I wrote about all that Jesus did and taught from the beginning 2until the day when he was taken up to heaven, after giving instructions through the Holy Spirit to the apostles whom he had chosen. 3After his suffering he presented himself alive to them by many convincing proofs, appearing to them during forty days and speaking about the kingdom of God. 4While staying*a* with them, he ordered them not to leave Jerusalem, but to wait there for the promise of the Father. "This," he said, "is what you have heard from me; 5for John baptized with water, but you will be baptized with*b* the Holy Spirit not many days from now."

The Ascension of Jesus
(Mk 16.19–20; Lk 24.50–53)

6 So when they had come together, they asked him, "Lord, is this the time when you will restore the kingdom to Israel?" 7He replied, "It is not for you to know the times or periods that the Father has set by his own authority. 8But you will receive power when the Holy Spirit has come upon you; and you will be my witnesses in Jerusalem, in all Judea and Sa·mãr'i·a, and to the ends of the earth." 9When he had said this, as they were watching, he was lifted up, and a cloud took him out of their sight. 10While he was going and they were gazing up toward heaven, suddenly two men in white robes stood by them. 11They said, "Men of Galilee, why do you stand looking up toward heaven? This Jesus, who has been taken up from you into heaven, will come in the same way as you saw him go into heaven."

Matthias Chosen to Replace Judas
(Cp Ps 109.8)

12 Then they returned to Jerusalem from the mount called Ol'i·vet, which is near Jerusalem, a sabbath day's journey away. 13When they had entered the city, they went to the room upstairs where they were staying, Peter, and John, and James, and Andrew, Philip and Thomas, Bartholomew and Matthew, James son of Al·phaē'us, and Simon the Zealot, and Judas son of*c* James. 14All these were constantly devoting themselves to prayer, together with certain women, including Mary the mother of Jesus, as well as his brothers.

15 In those days Peter stood up among the believers*d* (together the crowd numbered about one hundred twenty persons) and said, 16"Friends,*e* the scripture had to be fulfilled, which the Holy Spirit through David foretold concerning Judas, who became a guide for those who arrested Jesus— 17for he was numbered among us and was allotted his share in this ministry." 18(Now this man acquired a field with the reward of his wickedness; and falling headlong,*f* he burst open in the middle and all his bowels gushed out. 19This became known to all the residents of Jerusalem, so that the field was called in their language Ha·kel'-da·ma, that is, Field of Blood.) 20"For it is written in the book of Psalms,

'Let his homestead become
      desolate,
    and let there be no one to live
      in it';

and

'Let another take his position of
      overseer.'

21So one of the men who have accompanied us during all the time that the Lord Jesus went in and out among us, 22beginning from the baptism of John until the day when he was taken up from us—one of these must become a

---

*a*Or *eating*   *b*Or *by*   *c*Or *the brother of*   *d*Gk *brothers*   *e*Gk *Men, brothers*   *f*Or *swelling up* witness with us to his resurrection." [23] So they proposed two, Joseph called Bar·sab′bas, who was also known as Justus, and Mat·thi′as. [24] Then they prayed and said, "Lord, you know everyone's heart. Show us which one of these two you have chosen [25] to take the place [g] in this ministry and apostleship from which Judas turned aside to go to his own place." [26] And they cast lots for them, and the lot fell on Mat·thi′as; and he was added to the eleven apostles.

The Coming of the Holy Spirit

2 When the day of Pentecost had come, they were all together in one place. [2] And suddenly from heaven there came a sound like the rush of a violent wind, and it filled the entire house where they were sitting. [3] Divided tongues, as of fire, appeared among them, and a tongue rested on each of them. [4] All of them were filled with the Holy Spirit and began to speak in other languages, as the Spirit gave them ability.

[5] Now there were devout Jews from every nation under heaven living in Jerusalem. [6] And at this sound the crowd gathered and was bewildered, because each one heard them speaking in the native language of each. [7] Amazed and astonished, they asked, "Are not all these who are speaking Galileans? [8] And how is it that we hear, each of us, in our own native language? [9] Par′thi·ans, Medes, E′lam·ites, and residents of Mes·o·po·ta′mi·a, Judea and Cap·pa·do′ci·a, Pon′tus and Asia, [10] Phryg′i·a and Pam·phyl′i·a, Egypt and the parts of Lib′ya belonging to Cy·re′ne, and visitors from Rome, both Jews and proselytes, [11] Cre′tans and Arabs—in our own languages we hear them speaking about God's deeds of power." [12] All were amazed and perplexed, saying to one another, "What does this mean?" [13] But others sneered and said, "They are filled with new wine."

Peter Addresses the Crowd
(Joel 2.28–32)

[14] But Peter, standing with the eleven, raised his voice and addressed them, "Men of Judea and all who live in Jerusalem, let this be known to you, and listen to what I say. [15] Indeed, these are not drunk, as you suppose, for it is only nine o'clock in the morning. [16] No, this is what was spoken through the prophet Jo′el:

[17]   'In the last days it will be, God
            declares,
        that I will pour out my Spirit
            upon all flesh,
        and your sons and your
            daughters shall prophesy,
        and your young men shall see
            visions,
        and your old men shall dream
            dreams.
[18]   Even upon my slaves, both men
            and women,
        in those days I will pour out
            my Spirit;
        and they shall prophesy.
[19]   And I will show portents in the
            heaven above
        and signs on the earth below,
            blood, and fire, and smoky
            mist.
[20]   The sun shall be turned to
            darkness
        and the moon to blood,
            before the coming of the
            Lord's great and glorious
            day.
[21]   Then everyone who calls on the
            name of the Lord shall be
            saved.'

[22] "You that are Israelites,[h] listen to what I have to say: Jesus of Nazareth,[i] a man attested to you by God with deeds of power, wonders, and signs that God did through him among you, as you yourselves know— [23] this man, handed over to you according to the definite plan and foreknowledge of God, you crucified and killed by the hands of those outside the law. [24] But God raised him up, having freed him from death,[j] because it was impossible for him to be held in its power. [25] For David says concerning him,

        'I saw the Lord always before
            me,
        for he is at my right hand so
            that I will not be shaken;
[26]   therefore my heart was glad,
            and my tongue rejoiced;
        moreover my flesh will live in
            hope.
[27]   For you will not abandon my
            soul to Hades,
        or let your Holy One
            experience corruption.

[g] Other ancient authorities read *the share* [h] Gk *Men, Israelites* [i] Gk *the Nazorean* [j] Gk *the pains of death*

28 You have made known to me the
    ways of life;
    you will make me full of
    gladness with your
    presence.'
29 "Fellow Israelites,*k* I may say to
you confidently of our ancestor David
that he both died and was buried, and
his tomb is with us to this day. 30 Since
he was a prophet, he knew that God
had sworn with an oath to him that he
would put one of his descendants on
his throne. 31 Foreseeing this, David*l*
spoke of the resurrection of the Messiah,*m* saying,

'He was not abandoned to
    Hades,
    nor did his flesh experience
    corruption.'
32 This Jesus God raised up, and of that
all of us are witnesses. 33 Being therefore exalted at*n* the right hand of God,
and having received from the Father
the promise of the Holy Spirit, he has
poured out this that you both see and
hear. 34 For David did not ascend into
the heavens, but he himself says,

'The Lord said to my Lord,
    "Sit at my right hand,
35   until I make your enemies
    your footstool." '
36 Therefore let the entire house of Israel know with certainty that God has
made him both Lord and Messiah,*o*
this Jesus whom you crucified."

The First Converts

37 Now when they heard this, they
were cut to the heart and said to Peter
and to the other apostles, "Brothers,*k*
what should we do?" 38 Peter said to
them, "Repent, and be baptized every
one of you in the name of Jesus Christ
so that your sins may be forgiven; and
you will receive the gift of the Holy
Spirit. 39 For the promise is for you, for
your children, and for all who are far
away, everyone whom the Lord our
God calls to him." 40 And he testified
with many other arguments and exhorted them, saying, "Save yourselves
from this corrupt generation." 41 So
those who welcomed his message
were baptized, and that day about
three thousand persons were added.
42 They devoted themselves to the
apostles' teaching and fellowship, to
the breaking of bread and the prayers.

Life among the Believers

43 Awe came upon everyone, because many wonders and signs were
being done by the apostles. 44 All who
believed were together and had all
things in common; 45 they would sell
their possessions and goods and distribute the proceeds*p* to all, as any had
need. 46 Day by day, as they spent
much time together in the temple, they
broke bread at home*q* and ate their
food with glad and generous*r* hearts,
47 praising God and having the goodwill of all the people. And day by day
the Lord added to their number those
who were being saved.

Peter Heals a Crippled Beggar

3 One day Peter and John were going up to the temple at the hour of
prayer, at three o'clock in the afternoon. 2 And a man lame from birth was
being carried in. People would lay him
daily at the gate of the temple called
the Beautiful Gate so that he could ask
for alms from those entering the temple. 3 When he saw Peter and John
about to go into the temple, he asked
them for alms. 4 Peter looked intently
at him, as did John, and said, "Look at
us." 5 And he fixed his attention on
them, expecting to receive something
from them. 6 But Peter said, "I have no
silver or gold, but what I have I give
you; in the name of Jesus Christ of
Nazareth,*s* stand up and walk." 7 And
he took him by the right hand and
raised him up; and immediately his
feet and ankles were made strong.
8 Jumping up, he stood and began to
walk, and he entered the temple with
them, walking and leaping and praising God. 9 All the people saw him walking and praising God, 10 and they recognized him as the one who used to sit
and ask for alms at the Beautiful Gate
of the temple; and they were filled with
wonder and amazement at what had
happened to him.

Peter Speaks in Solomon's Portico

11 While he clung to Peter and
John, all the people ran together to
them in the portico called Solomon's
Portico, utterly astonished. 12 When
Peter saw it, he addressed the people,
"You Israelites,*t* why do you wonder
at this, or why do you stare at us, as
though by our own power or piety we

k Gk Men, brothers   *l* Gk he   *m* Or the
Christ   *n* Or by   *o* Or Christ
p Gk them   *q* Or from house to house
r Or sincere   *s* Gk the Nazorean
t Gk Men, Israelites

had made him walk? [13] The God of Abraham, the God of Isaac, and the God of Jacob, the God of our ancestors has glorified his servant[u] Jesus, whom you handed over and rejected in the presence of Pilate, though he had decided to release him. [14] But you rejected the Holy and Righteous One and asked to have a murderer given to you, [15] and you killed the Author of life, whom God raised from the dead. To this we are witnesses. [16] And by faith in his name, his name itself has made this man strong, whom you see and know; and the faith that is through Jesus[v] has given him this perfect health in the presence of all of you.

17 "And now, friends,[w] I know that you acted in ignorance, as did also your rulers. [18] In this way God fulfilled what he had foretold through all the prophets, that his Messiah[x] would suffer. [19] Repent therefore, and turn to God so that your sins may be wiped out, [20] so that times of refreshing may come from the presence of the Lord, and that he may send the Messiah[y] appointed for you, that is, Jesus, [21] who must remain in heaven until the time of universal restoration that God announced long ago through his holy prophets. [22] Moses said, 'The Lord your God will raise up for you from your own people[w] a prophet like me. You must listen to whatever he tells you. [23] And it will be that everyone who does not listen to that prophet will be utterly rooted out of the people.' [24] And all the prophets, as many as have spoken, from Samuel and those after him, also predicted these days. [25] You are the descendants of the prophets and of the covenant that God gave to your ancestors, saying to Abraham, 'And in your descendants all the families of the earth shall be blessed.' [26] When God raised up his servant,[u] he sent him first to you, to bless you by turning each of you from your wicked ways."

Peter and John before the Council

4 While Peter and John[z] were speaking to the people, the priests, the captain of the temple, and the Sad′·dū·cees came to them, [2] much annoyed because they were teaching the people and proclaiming that in Jesus there is the resurrection of the dead. [3] So they arrested them and put them in custody until the next day, for it was already evening. [4] But many of those who

heard the word believed; and they numbered about five thousand.

5 The next day their rulers, elders, and scribes assembled in Jerusalem, [6] with An′nas the high priest, Ca′i·a·phas, John,[a] and Alexander, and all who were of the high-priestly family. [7] When they had made the prisoners[b] stand in their midst, they inquired, "By what power or by what name did you do this?" [8] Then Peter, filled with the Holy Spirit, said to them, "Rulers of the people and elders, [9] if we are questioned today because of a good deed done to someone who was sick and are asked how this man has been healed, [10] let it be known to all of you, and to all the people of Israel, that this man is standing before you in good health by the name of Jesus Christ of Nazareth,[c] whom you crucified, whom God raised from the dead. [11] This Jesus[d] is

'the stone that was rejected by
    you, the builders;
it has become the
    cornerstone.'[e]

[12] There is salvation in no one else, for there is no other name under heaven given among mortals by which we must be saved."

13 Now when they saw the boldness of Peter and John and realized that they were uneducated and ordinary men, they were amazed and recognized them as companions of Jesus. [14] When they saw the man who had been cured standing beside them, they had nothing to say in opposition. [15] So they ordered them to leave the council while they discussed the matter with one another. [16] They said, "What will we do with them? For it is obvious to all who live in Jerusalem that a notable sign has been done through them; we cannot deny it. [17] But to keep it from spreading further among the people, let us warn them to speak no more to anyone in this name." [18] So they called them and ordered them not to speak or teach at all in the name of Jesus. [19] But Peter and John answered them, "Whether it is right in God's sight to listen to you rather than to God, you must judge; [20] for we cannot keep from

u Or child v Gk him w Gk brothers
x Or his Christ y Or the Christ
z Gk While they a Other ancient
authorities read Jonathan b Gk them
c Gk the Nazorean d Gk This
e Or keystone

speaking about what we have seen and heard." 21 After threatening them again, they let them go, finding no way to punish them because of the people, for all of them praised God for what had happened. 22 For the man on whom this sign of healing had been performed was more than forty years old.

The Believers Pray for Boldness
(Cp Ps 2.1–2)

23 After they were released, they went to their friends[f] and reported what the chief priests and the elders had said to them. 24 When they heard it, they raised their voices together to God and said, "Sovereign Lord, who made the heaven and the earth, the sea, and everything in them, 25 it is you who said by the Holy Spirit through our ancestor David, your servant:[g]

'Why did the Gentiles rage,
     and the peoples imagine vain
          things?
26 The kings of the earth took their
          stand,
     and the rulers have gathered
          together
          against the Lord and against
          his Messiah.'[h]

27 For in this city, in fact, both Her'od and Pon'ti·us Pilate, with the Gentiles and the peoples of Israel, gathered together against your holy servant[g] Jesus, whom you anointed, 28 to do whatever your hand and your plan had predestined to take place. 29 And now, Lord, look at their threats, and grant to your servants[i] to speak your word with all boldness, 30 while you stretch out your hand to heal, and signs and wonders are performed through the name of your holy servant[g] Jesus." 31 When they had prayed, the place in which they were gathered together was shaken; and they were all filled with the Holy Spirit and spoke the word of God with boldness.

The Believers Share Their Possessions

32 Now the whole group of those who believed were of one heart and soul, and no one claimed private ownership of any possessions, but everything they owned was held in common. 33 With great power the apostles gave their testimony to the resurrection of the Lord Jesus, and great grace was upon them all. 34 There was not a needy person among them, for as many as owned lands or houses sold them and brought the proceeds of what was sold. 35 They laid it at the apostles' feet, and it was distributed to each as any had need. 36 There was a Le'vite, a native of Cyprus, Joseph, to whom the apostles gave the name Bar'na·bas (which means "son of encouragement"). 37 He sold a field that belonged to him, then brought the money, and laid it at the apostles' feet.

Ananias and Sapphira

5 But a man named An·a·ni'as, with the consent of his wife Sap·phi'ra, sold a piece of property; 2 with his wife's knowledge, he kept back some of the proceeds, and brought only a part and laid it at the apostles' feet. 3 "An·a·ni'as," Peter asked, "why has Satan filled your heart to lie to the Holy Spirit and to keep back part of the proceeds of the land? 4 While it remained unsold, did it not remain your own? And after it was sold, were not the proceeds at your disposal? How is it that you have contrived this deed in your heart? You did not lie to us[i] but to God!" 5 Now when An·a·ni'as heard these words, he fell down and died. And great fear seized all who heard of it. 6 The young men came and wrapped up his body,[k] then carried him out and buried him.

7 After an interval of about three hours his wife came in, not knowing what had happened. 8 Peter said to her, "Tell me whether you and your husband sold the land for such and such a price." And she said, "Yes, that was the price." 9 Then Peter said to her, "How is it that you have agreed together to put the Spirit of the Lord to the test? Look, the feet of those who have buried your husband are at the door, and they will carry you out." 10 Immediately she fell down at his feet and died. When the young men came in they found her dead, so they carried her out and buried her beside her husband. 11 And great fear seized the whole church and all who heard of these things.

The Apostles Heal Many

12 Now many signs and wonders were done among the people through the apostles. And they were all together in Solomon's Portico. 13 None of the rest dared to join them, but the peo-

---

[f] Gk *their own*   [g] Or *child*   [h] Or *his Christ*   [i] Gk *slaves*   [j] Gk *to men*
[k] Meaning of Gk uncertain

ple held them in high esteem. [14] Yet more than ever believers were added to the Lord, great numbers of both men and women, [15] so that they even carried out the sick into the streets, and laid them on cots and mats, in order that Peter's shadow might fall on some of them as he came by. [16] A great number of people would also gather from the towns around Jerusalem, bringing the sick and those tormented by unclean spirits, and they were all cured.

The Apostles Are Persecuted

17 Then the high priest took action; he and all who were with him (that is, the sect of the Sad'du·cees), being filled with jealousy, [18] arrested the apostles and put them in the public prison. [19] But during the night an angel of the Lord opened the prison doors, brought them out, and said, [20] "Go, stand in the temple and tell the people the whole message about this life." [21] When they heard this, they entered the temple at daybreak and went on with their teaching.

When the high priest and those with him arrived, they called together the council and the whole body of the elders of Israel, and sent to the prison to have them brought. [22] But when the temple police went there, they did not find them in the prison; so they returned and reported, [23] "We found the prison securely locked and the guards standing at the doors, but when we opened them, we found no one inside." [24] Now when the captain of the temple and the chief priests heard these words, they were perplexed about them, wondering what might be going on. [25] Then someone arrived and announced, "Look, the men whom you put in prison are standing in the temple and teaching the people!" [26] Then the captain went with the temple police and brought them, but without violence, for they were afraid of being stoned by the people.

27 When they had brought them, they had them stand before the council. The high priest questioned them, [28] saying, "We gave you strict orders not to teach in this name,[l] yet here you have filled Jerusalem with your teaching and you are determined to bring this man's blood on us." [29] But Peter and the apostles answered, "We must obey God rather than any human authority.[m] [30] The God of our ancestors raised up Jesus, whom you had killed by hanging him on a tree. [31] God exalted him at his right hand as Leader and Savior that he might give repentance to Israel and forgiveness of sins. [32] And we are witnesses to these things, and so is the Holy Spirit whom God has given to those who obey him."

33 When they heard this, they were enraged and wanted to kill them. [34] But a Phar'i·see in the council named Ga·ma'li·el, a teacher of the law, respected by all the people, stood up and ordered the men to be put outside for a short time. [35] Then he said to them, "Fellow Israelites,[n] consider carefully what you propose to do to these men. [36] For some time ago Theu'das rose up, claiming to be somebody, and a number of men, about four hundred, joined him; but he was killed, and all who followed him were dispersed and disappeared. [37] After him Judas the Galilean rose up at the time of the census and got people to follow him; he also perished, and all who followed him were scattered. [38] So in the present case, I tell you, keep away from these men and let them alone; because if this plan or this undertaking is of human origin, it will fail; [39] but if it is of God, you will not be able to overthrow them—in that case you may even be found fighting against God!"

They were convinced by him, [40] and when they had called in the apostles, they had them flogged. Then they ordered them not to speak in the name of Jesus, and let them go. [41] As they left the council, they rejoiced that they were considered worthy to suffer dishonor for the sake of the name. [42] And every day in the temple and at home[o] they did not cease to teach and proclaim Jesus as the Messiah.[p]

Seven Chosen to Serve

6 Now during those days, when the disciples were increasing in number, the Hellenists complained against the Hebrews because their widows were being neglected in the daily distribution of food. [2] And the twelve called together the whole community of the disciples and said, "It is not right that we should neglect the word of God

---

[l] Other ancient authorities read *Did we not give you strict orders not to teach in this name?*   [m] Gk *than men*
[n] Gk *Men, Israelites*   [o] Or *from house to house*   [p] Or *the Christ*

in order to wait on tables.[q] [3]Therefore, friends,[r] select from among yourselves seven men of good standing, full of the Spirit and of wisdom, whom we may appoint to this task, [4]while we, for our part, will devote ourselves to prayer and to serving the word." [5]What they said pleased the whole community, and they chose Stephen, a man full of faith and the Holy Spirit, together with Philip, Proch'o·rus, Ni·ca'nor, Ti'mon, Par'me·nas, and Nic·o·la'us, a proselyte of An'ti·och. [6]They had these men stand before the apostles, who prayed and laid their hands on them.

7 The word of God continued to spread; the number of the disciples increased greatly in Jerusalem, and a great many of the priests became obedient to the faith.

The Arrest of Stephen

8 Stephen, full of grace and power, did great wonders and signs among the people. [9]Then some of those who belonged to the synagogue of the Freedmen (as it was called), Cy·rē'ni·ans, Alexandrians, and others of those from Ci·li'ci·a and Asia, stood up and argued with Stephen. [10]But they could not withstand the wisdom and the Spirit[s] with which he spoke. [11]Then they secretly instigated some men to say, "We have heard him speak blasphemous words against Moses and God." [12]They stirred up the people as well as the elders and the scribes; then they suddenly confronted him, seized him, and brought him before the council. [13]They set up false witnesses who said, "This man never stops saying things against this holy place and the law; [14]for we have heard him say that this Jesus of Nazareth[t] will destroy this place and will change the customs that Moses handed on to us." [15]And all who sat in the council looked intently at him, and they saw that his face was like the face of an angel.

Stephen's Speech to the Council
(Gen 12.1—50.26)

7 Then the high priest asked him, "Are these things so?" [2]And Stephen replied:

"Brothers[u] and fathers, listen to me. The God of glory appeared to our ancestor Abraham when he was in Mes·o·po·tā'mi·a, before he lived in Har'an, [3]and said to him, 'Leave your country and your relatives and go to the land that I will show you.' [4]Then he left the country of the Chal·dē'ans and settled in Har'an. After his father died, God had him move from there to this country in which you are now living. [5]He did not give him any of it as a heritage, not even a foot's length, but promised to give it to him as his possession and to his descendants after him, even though he had no child. [6]And God spoke in these terms, that his descendants would be resident aliens in a country belonging to others, who would enslave them and mistreat them during four hundred years. [7]'But I will judge the nation that they serve,' said God, 'and after that they shall come out and worship me in this place.' [8]Then he gave him the covenant of circumcision. And so Abraham[v] became the father of Isaac and circumcised him on the eighth day; and Isaac became the father of Jacob, and Jacob of the twelve patriarchs.

9 "The patriarchs, jealous of Joseph, sold him into Egypt; but God was with him, [10]and rescued him from all his afflictions, and enabled him to win favor and to show wisdom when he stood before Pharaoh, king of Egypt, who appointed him ruler over Egypt and over all his household. [11]Now there came a famine throughout Egypt and Ca'naan, and great suffering, and our ancestors could find no food. [12]But when Jacob heard that there was grain in Egypt, he sent our ancestors there on their first visit. [13]On the second visit Joseph made himself known to his brothers, and Joseph's family became known to Pharaoh. [14]Then Joseph sent and invited his father Jacob and all his relatives to come to him, seventy-five in all; [15]so Jacob went down to Egypt. He himself died there as well as our ancestors, [16]and their bodies[w] were brought back to Shē'chem and laid in the tomb that Abraham had bought for a sum of silver from the sons of Hā'mor in Shē'chem.

17 "But as the time drew near for the fulfillment of the promise that God had made to Abraham, our people in Egypt increased and multiplied [18]until another king who had not known Joseph ruled over Egypt. [19]He dealt

---

[q] Or keep accounts   [r] Gk brothers
[s] Or spirit   [t] Gk the Nazorean
[u] Gk Men, brothers   [v] Gk he
[w] Gk they

craftily with our race and forced our ancestors to abandon their infants so that they would die. 20 At this time Moses was born, and he was beautiful before God. For three months he was brought up in his father's house; 21 and when he was abandoned, Pharaoh's daughter adopted him and brought him up as her own son. 22 So Moses was instructed in all the wisdom of the Egyptians and was powerful in his words and deeds.

23 "When he was forty years old, it came into his heart to visit his relatives, the Israelites. *x* 24 When he saw one of them being wronged, he defended the oppressed man and avenged him by striking down the Egyptian. 25 He supposed that his kinsfolk would understand that God through him was rescuing them, but they did not understand. 26 The next day he came to some of them as they were quarreling and tried to reconcile them, saying, 'Men, you are brothers; why do you wrong each other?' 27 But the man who was wronging his neighbor pushed Moses *y* aside, saying, 'Who made you a ruler and a judge over us? 28 Do you want to kill me as you killed the Egyptian yesterday?' 29 When he heard this, Moses fled and became a resident alien in the land of Mid′i·an. There he became the father of two sons.

30 "Now when forty years had passed, an angel appeared to him in the wilderness of Mount Sinai, in the flame of a burning bush. 31 When Moses saw it, he was amazed at the sight; and as he approached to look, there came the voice of the Lord: 32 'I am the God of your ancestors, the God of Abraham, Isaac, and Jacob.' Moses began to tremble and did not dare to look. 33 Then the Lord said to him, 'Take off the sandals from your feet, for the place where you are standing is holy ground. 34 I have surely seen the mistreatment of my people who are in Egypt and have heard their groaning, and I have come down to rescue them. Come now, I will send you to Egypt.'

35 "It was this Moses whom they rejected when they said, 'Who made you a ruler and a judge?' and whom God now sent as both ruler and liberator through the angel who appeared to him in the bush. 36 He led them out, having performed wonders and signs in Egypt, at the Red Sea, and in the wilderness for forty years. 37 This is the Moses who said to the Israelites, 'God will raise up a prophet for you from your own people *z* as he raised me up.' 38 He is the one who was in the congregation in the wilderness with the angel who spoke to him at Mount Sinai, and with our ancestors; and he received living oracles to give to us. 39 Our ancestors were unwilling to obey him; instead, they pushed him aside, and in their hearts they turned back to Egypt, 40 saying to Aaron, 'Make gods for us who will lead the way for us; as for this Moses who led us out from the land of Egypt, we do not know what has happened to him.' 41 At that time they made a calf, offered a sacrifice to the idol, and reveled in the works of their hands. 42 But God turned away from them and handed them over to worship the host of heaven, as it is written in the book of the prophets:

> 'Did you offer to me slain
> > victims and sacrifices
> forty years in the wilderness,
> > O house of Israel?
> 43 No; you took along the tent of
> > Mo′loch,
> > and the star of your god
> > > Re′phan,
> > > the images that you made to
> > > > worship;
> so I will remove you beyond
> > Babylon.'

44 "Our ancestors had the tent of testimony in the wilderness, as God *a* directed when he spoke to Moses, ordering him to make it according to the pattern he had seen. 45 Our ancestors in turn brought it in with Joshua when they dispossessed the nations that God drove out before our ancestors. And it was there until the time of David, 46 who found favor with God and asked that he might find a dwelling place for the house of Jacob. *b* 47 But it was Solomon who built a house for him. 48 Yet the Most High does not dwell in houses made with human hands; *c* as the prophet says,

> 49 'Heaven is my throne,
> > and the earth is my footstool.
> What kind of house will you
> > build for me, says the Lord,
> > or what is the place of my
> > > rest?

x Gk *his brothers, the sons of Israel*
y Gk *him*   *z* Gk *your brothers*   *a* Gk *he*
b Other ancient authorities read *for the God of Jacob*   *c* Gk *with hands*

50 Did not my hand make all these things?'

51 "You stiff-necked people, uncircumcised in heart and ears, you are forever opposing the Holy Spirit, just as your ancestors used to do. 52 Which of the prophets did your ancestors not persecute? They killed those who foretold the coming of the Righteous One, and now you have become his betrayers and murderers. 53 You are the ones that received the law as ordained by angels, and yet you have not kept it."

The Stoning of Stephen

54 When they heard these things, they became enraged and ground their teeth at Stephen.*d* 55 But filled with the Holy Spirit, he gazed into heaven and saw the glory of God and Jesus standing at the right hand of God. 56 "Look," he said, "I see the heavens opened and the Son of Man standing at the right hand of God!" 57 But they covered their ears, and with a loud shout all rushed together against him. 58 Then they dragged him out of the city and began to stone him; and the witnesses laid their coats at the feet of a young man named Saul. 59 While they were stoning Stephen, he prayed, "Lord Jesus, receive my spirit." 60 Then he knelt down and cried out in a loud voice, "Lord, do not hold this sin against them." When he had said this, he died.*e* 8 1 And Saul approved of their killing him.

Saul Persecutes the Church

That day a severe persecution began against the church in Jerusalem, and all except the apostles were scattered throughout the countryside of Judea and Sa·mār'i·a. 2 Devout men buried Stephen and made loud lamentation over him. 3 But Saul was ravaging the church by entering house after house; dragging off both men and women, he committed them to prison.

Philip Preaches in Samaria

4 Now those who were scattered went from place to place, proclaiming the word. 5 Philip went down to the city*f* of Sa·mār'i·a and proclaimed the Messiah*g* to them. 6 The crowds with one accord listened eagerly to what was said by Philip, hearing and seeing the signs that he did, 7 for unclean spirits, crying with loud shrieks, came out of many who were possessed; and many others who were paralyzed or lame were cured. 8 So there was great joy in that city.

9 Now a certain man named Simon had previously practiced magic in the city and amazed the people of Sa·mār'i·a, saying that he was someone great. 10 All of them, from the least to the greatest, listened to him eagerly, saying, "This man is the power of God that is called Great." 11 And they listened eagerly to him because for a long time he had amazed them with his magic. 12 But when they believed Philip, who was proclaiming the good news about the kingdom of God and the name of Jesus Christ, they were baptized, both men and women. 13 Even Simon himself believed. After being baptized, he stayed constantly with Philip and was amazed when he saw the signs and great miracles that took place.

14 Now when the apostles at Jerusalem heard that Sa·mār'i·a had accepted the word of God, they sent Peter and John to them. 15 The two went down and prayed for them that they might receive the Holy Spirit 16 (for as yet the Spirit had not come*h* upon any of them; they had only been baptized in the name of the Lord Jesus). 17 Then Peter and John*i* laid their hands on them, and they received the Holy Spirit. 18 Now when Simon saw that the Spirit was given through the laying on of the apostles' hands, he offered them money, 19 saying, "Give me also this power so that anyone on whom I lay my hands may receive the Holy Spirit." 20 But Peter said to him, "May your silver perish with you, because you thought you could obtain God's gift with money! 21 You have no part or share in this, for your heart is not right before God. 22 Repent therefore of this wickedness of yours, and pray to the Lord that, if possible, the intent of your heart may be forgiven you. 23 For I see that you are in the gall of bitterness and the chains of wickedness." 24 Simon answered, "Pray for me to the Lord, that nothing of what you*j* have said may happen to me."

25 Now after Peter and John*k* had testified and spoken the word of the Lord, they returned to Jerusalem, pro-

d Gk him   *e* Gk fell asleep   *f* Other ancient authorities read *a city*   *g* Or the Christ   *h* Gk fallen   *i* Gk they   *j* The Greek word for *you* and the verb *pray* are plural   *k* Gk after they claiming the good news to many villages of the Sa·măr'i·tans.

Philip and the Ethiopian Eunuch
(Cp Isa 53.7–8)

26 Then an angel of the Lord said to Philip, "Get up and go toward the south[l] to the road that goes down from Jerusalem to Gă'za." (This is a wilderness road.) 27 So he got up and went. Now there was an Ethiopian eunuch, a court official of the Can·dă'cē, queen of the Ethiopians, in charge of her entire treasury. He had come to Jerusalem to worship 28 and was returning home; seated in his chariot, he was reading the prophet I·săi'ah. 29 Then the Spirit said to Philip, "Go over to this chariot and join it." 30 So Philip ran up to it and heard him reading the prophet I·săi'ah. He asked, "Do you understand what you are reading?" 31 He replied, "How can I, unless someone guides me?" And he invited Philip to get in and sit beside him. 32 Now the passage of the scripture that he was reading was this:

"Like a sheep he was led to the
　　slaughter,
and like a lamb silent before
　　its shearer,
so he does not open his
　　mouth.
33 In his humiliation justice was
　　denied him.
Who can describe his
　　generation?
For his life is taken away
　　from the earth."

34 The eunuch asked Philip, "About whom, may I ask you, does the prophet say this, about himself or about someone else?" 35 Then Philip began to speak, and starting with this scripture, he proclaimed to him the good news about Jesus. 36 As they were going along the road, they came to some water; and the eunuch said, "Look, here is water! What is to prevent me from being baptized?"[m] 38 He commanded the chariot to stop, and both of them, Philip and the eunuch, went down into the water, and Philip[n] baptized him. 39 When they came up out of the water, the Spirit of the Lord snatched Philip away; the eunuch saw him no more, and went on his way rejoicing. 40 But Philip found himself at A·zō'tus, and as he was passing through the region, he proclaimed the good news to all the towns until he came to Caes·a·rē'a.

The Conversion of Saul
(Acts 22.6–16; 26.12–18)

9 Meanwhile Saul, still breathing threats and murder against the disciples of the Lord, went to the high priest 2 and asked him for letters to the synagogues at Damascus, so that if he found any who belonged to the Way, men or women, he might bring them bound to Jerusalem. 3 Now as he was going along and approaching Damascus, suddenly a light from heaven flashed around him. 4 He fell to the ground and heard a voice saying to him, "Saul, Saul, why do you persecute me?" 5 He asked, "Who are you, Lord?" The reply came, "I am Jesus, whom you are persecuting. 6 But get up and enter the city, and you will be told what you are to do." 7 The men who were traveling with him stood speechless because they heard the voice but saw no one. 8 Saul got up from the ground, and though his eyes were open, he could see nothing; so they led him by the hand and brought him into Damascus. 9 For three days he was without sight, and neither ate nor drank.

10 Now there was a disciple in Damascus named An·a·nī'as. The Lord said to him in a vision, "An·a·nī'as." He answered, "Here I am, Lord." 11 The Lord said to him, "Get up and go to the street called Straight, and at the house of Judas look for a man of Tar'sus named Saul. At this moment he is praying, 12 and he has seen in a vision[o] a man named An·a·nī'as come in and lay his hands on him so that he might regain his sight." 13 But An·a·nī'as answered, "Lord, I have heard from many about this man, how much evil he has done to your saints in Jerusalem; 14 and here he has authority from the chief priests to bind all who invoke your name." 15 But the Lord said to him, "Go, for he is an instrument whom I have chosen to bring my name before Gentiles and kings and before the people of Israel; 16 I myself will show him how much he must suffer for the sake of my name." 17 So An·a·nī'as went and entered the house. He laid

---

[l] Or *go at noon*　[m] Other ancient authorities add all or most of verse 37, *And Philip said, "If you believe with all your heart, you may." And he replied, "I believe that Jesus Christ is the Son of God."*　[n] Gk *he*　[o] Other ancient authorities lack *in a vision*

his hands on Saul[p] and said, "Brother Saul, the Lord Jesus, who appeared to you on your way here, has sent me so that you may regain your sight and be filled with the Holy Spirit." [18] And immediately something like scales fell from his eyes, and his sight was restored. Then he got up and was baptized, [19] and after taking some food, he regained his strength.

Saul Preaches in Damascus

For several days he was with the disciples in Damascus, [20] and immediately he began to proclaim Jesus in the synagogues, saying, "He is the Son of God." [21] All who heard him were amazed and said, "Is not this the man who made havoc in Jerusalem among those who invoked this name? And has he not come here for the purpose of bringing them bound before the chief priests?" [22] Saul became increasingly more powerful and confounded the Jews who lived in Damascus by proving that Jesus[q] was the Messiah.[r]

Saul Escapes from the Jews

23 After some time had passed, the Jews plotted to kill him, [24] but their plot became known to Saul. They were watching the gates day and night so that they might kill him; [25] but his disciples took him by night and let him down through an opening in the wall,[s] lowering him in a basket.

Saul in Jerusalem

26 When he had come to Jerusalem, he attempted to join the disciples; and they were all afraid of him, for they did not believe that he was a disciple. [27] But Bar'na·bas took him, brought him to the apostles, and described for them how on the road he had seen the Lord, who had spoken to him, and how in Damascus he had spoken boldly in the name of Jesus. [28] So he went in and out among them in Jerusalem, speaking boldly in the name of the Lord. [29] He spoke and argued with the Hellenists; but they were attempting to kill him. [30] When the believers[t] learned of it, they brought him down to Caes·a·re'a and sent him off to Tar'sus.

31 Meanwhile the church throughout Judea, Galilee, and Sa·mar'i·a had peace and was built up. Living in the fear of the Lord and in the comfort of the Holy Spirit, it increased in numbers.

The Healing of Aeneas

32 Now as Peter went here and there among all the believers,[u] he came down also to the saints living in Lyd'da. [33] There he found a man named Ae·ne'as, who had been bedridden for eight years, for he was paralyzed. [34] Peter said to him, "Ae·ne'as, Jesus Christ heals you; get up and make your bed!" And immediately he got up. [35] And all the residents of Lyd'da and Sharon saw him and turned to the Lord.

Peter in Lydda and Joppa

36 Now in Jop'pa there was a disciple whose name was Tab'i·tha, which in Greek is Dor'cas.[v] She was devoted to good works and acts of charity. [37] At that time she became ill and died. When they had washed her, they laid her in a room upstairs. [38] Since Lyd'da was near Jop'pa, the disciples, who heard that Peter was there, sent two men to him with the request, "Please come to us without delay." [39] So Peter got up and went with them; and when he arrived, they took him to the room upstairs. All the widows stood beside him, weeping and showing tunics and other clothing that Dor'cas had made while she was with them. [40] Peter put all of them outside, and then he knelt down and prayed. He turned to the body and said, "Tab'i·tha, get up." Then she opened her eyes, and seeing Peter, she sat up. [41] He gave her his hand and helped her up. Then calling the saints and widows, he showed her to be alive. [42] This became known throughout Jop'pa, and many believed in the Lord. [43] Meanwhile he stayed in Jop'pa for some time with a certain Simon, a tanner.

Peter and Cornelius

10 In Caes·a·re'a there was a man named Cornelius, a centurion of the Italian Cohort, as it was called. [2] He was a devout man who feared God with all his household; he gave alms generously to the people and prayed constantly to God. [3] One afternoon at about three o'clock he had a vision in which he clearly saw an angel of God coming in and saying to him, "Cornel-

[p] Gk him   [q] Gk that this   [r] Or the Christ   [s] Gk through the wall
[t] Gk brothers   [u] Gk all of them
[v] The name Tabitha in Aramaic and the name Dorcas in Greek mean a gazelle

ius." ⁴He stared at him in terror and said, "What is it, Lord?" He answered, "Your prayers and your alms have ascended as a memorial before God. ⁵Now send men to Jop'pa for a certain Simon who is called Peter; ⁶he is lodging with Simon, a tanner, whose house is by the seaside." ⁷When the angel who spoke to him had left, he called two of his slaves and a devout soldier from the ranks of those who served him, ⁸and after telling them everything, he sent them to Jop'pa.

9 About noon the next day, as they were on their journey and approaching the city, Peter went up on the roof to pray. ¹⁰He became hungry and wanted something to eat; and while it was being prepared, he fell into a trance. ¹¹He saw the heaven opened and something like a large sheet coming down, being lowered to the ground by its four corners. ¹²In it were all kinds of four-footed creatures and reptiles and birds of the air. ¹³Then he heard a voice saying, "Get up, Peter; kill and eat." ¹⁴But Peter said, "By no means, Lord; for I have never eaten anything that is profane or unclean." ¹⁵The voice said to him again, a second time, "What God has made clean, you must not call profane." ¹⁶This happened three times, and the thing was suddenly taken up to heaven.

17 Now while Peter was greatly puzzled about what to make of the vision that he had seen, suddenly the men sent by Cornelius appeared. They were asking for Simon's house and were standing by the gate. ¹⁸They called out to ask whether Simon, who was called Peter, was staying there. ¹⁹While Peter was still thinking about the vision, the Spirit said to him, "Look, three *w* men are searching for you. ²⁰Now get up, go down, and go with them without hesitation; for I have sent them." ²¹So Peter went down to the men and said, "I am the one you are looking for; what is the reason for your coming?" ²²They answered, "Cornelius, a centurion, an upright and God-fearing man, who is well spoken of by the whole Jewish nation, was directed by a holy angel to send for you to come to his house and to hear what you have to say." ²³So Peter *x* invited them in and gave them lodging.

The next day he got up and went with them, and some of the believers *y* from Jop'pa accompanied him. ²⁴The following day they came to Caes·a·re'a. Cornelius was expecting them and had called together his relatives and close friends. ²⁵On Peter's arrival Cornelius met him, and, falling at his feet, worshiped him. ²⁶But Peter made him get up, saying, "Stand up; I am only a mortal." ²⁷And as he talked with him, he went in and found that many had assembled; ²⁸and he said to them, "You yourselves know that it is unlawful for a Jew to associate with or to visit a Gentile; but God has shown me that I should not call anyone profane or unclean. ²⁹So when I was sent for, I came without objection. Now may I ask why you sent for me?"

30 Cornelius replied, "Four days ago at this very hour, at three o'clock, I was praying in my house when suddenly a man in dazzling clothes stood before me. ³¹He said, 'Cornelius, your prayer has been heard and your alms have been remembered before God. ³²Send therefore to Jop'pa and ask for Simon, who is called Peter; he is staying in the home of Simon, a tanner, by the sea.' ³³Therefore I sent for you immediately, and you have been kind enough to come. So now all of us are here in the presence of God to listen to all that the Lord has commanded you to say."

Gentiles Hear the Good News

34 Then Peter began to speak to them: "I truly understand that God shows no partiality, ³⁵but in every nation anyone who fears him and does what is right is acceptable to him. ³⁶You know the message he sent to the people of Israel, preaching peace by Jesus Christ—he is Lord of all. ³⁷That message spread throughout Judea, beginning in Galilee after the baptism that John announced: ³⁸how God anointed Jesus of Nazareth with the Holy Spirit and with power; how he went about doing good and healing all who were oppressed by the devil, for God was with him. ³⁹We are witnesses to all that he did both in Judea and in Jerusalem. They put him to death by hanging him on a tree; ⁴⁰but God raised him on the third day and allowed him to appear, ⁴¹not to all the people but to us who were chosen by God as witnesses, and who ate and drank with him after he rose from the

w One ancient authority reads *two*; others lack the word　*x* Gk *he*　*y* Gk *brothers* dead. 42 He commanded us to preach to the people and to testify that he is the one ordained by God as judge of the living and the dead. 43 All the prophets testify about him that everyone who believes in him receives forgiveness of sins through his name."

Gentiles Receive the Holy Spirit

44 While Peter was still speaking, the Holy Spirit fell upon all who heard the word. 45 The circumcised believers who had come with Peter were astounded that the gift of the Holy Spirit had been poured out even on the Gentiles, 46 for they heard them speaking in tongues and extolling God. Then Peter said, 47 "Can anyone withhold the water for baptizing these people who have received the Holy Spirit just as we have?" 48 So he ordered them to be baptized in the name of Jesus Christ. Then they invited him to stay for several days.

Peter's Report to the Church at Jerusalem

11 Now the apostles and the believers z who were in Judea heard that the Gentiles had also accepted the word of God. 2 So when Peter went up to Jerusalem, the circumcised believers a criticized him, 3 saying, "Why did you go to uncircumcised men and eat with them?" 4 Then Peter began to explain it to them, step by step, saying, 5 "I was in the city of Jop'pa praying, and in a trance I saw a vision. There was something like a large sheet coming down from heaven, being lowered by its four corners; and it came close to me. 6 As I looked at it closely I saw four-footed animals, beasts of prey, reptiles, and birds of the air. 7 I also heard a voice saying to me, 'Get up, Peter; kill and eat.' 8 But I replied, 'By no means, Lord; for nothing profane or unclean has ever entered my mouth.' 9 But a second time the voice answered from heaven, 'What God has made clean, you must not call profane.' 10 This happened three times; then everything was pulled up again to heaven. 11 At that very moment three men, sent to me from Caes·a·re'a, arrived at the house where we were. 12 The Spirit told me to go with them and not to make a distinction between them and us. b These six brothers also accompanied me, and we entered the man's house. 13 He told us how he had seen the angel standing

in his house and saying, 'Send to Jop'pa and bring Simon, who is called Peter; 14 he will give you a message by which you and your entire household will be saved.' 15 And as I began to speak, the Holy Spirit fell upon them just as it had upon us at the beginning. 16 And I remembered the word of the Lord, how he had said, 'John baptized with water, but you will be baptized with the Holy Spirit.' 17 If then God gave them the same gift that he gave us when we believed in the Lord Jesus Christ, who was I that I could hinder God?" 18 When they heard this, they were silenced. And they praised God, saying, "Then God has given even to the Gentiles the repentance that leads to life."

The Church in Antioch

19 Now those who were scattered because of the persecution that took place over Stephen traveled as far as Phoe·ni'ci·a, Cyprus, and An'ti·och, and they spoke the word to no one except Jews. 20 But among them were some men of Cyprus and Cy·re'ne who, on coming to An'ti·och, spoke to the Hellenists c also, proclaiming the Lord Jesus. 21 The hand of the Lord was with them, and a great number became believers and turned to the Lord. 22 News of this came to the ears of the church in Jerusalem, and they sent Bar'na·bas to An'ti·och. 23 When he came and saw the grace of God, he rejoiced, and he exhorted them all to remain faithful to the Lord with steadfast devotion; 24 for he was a good man, full of the Holy Spirit and of faith. And a great many people were brought to the Lord. 25 Then Bar'na·bas went to Tar'sus to look for Saul, 26 and when he had found him, he brought him to An'ti·och. So it was that for an entire year they met with d the church and taught a great many people, and it was in An'ti·och that the disciples were first called "Christians."

27 At that time prophets came down from Jerusalem to An'ti·och. 28 One of them named Ag'a·bus stood up and predicted by the Spirit that there would be a severe famine over all the world; and this took place during the reign of Clau'di·us. 29 The disciples

z Gk brothers   a Gk lacks believers
b Or not to hesitate   c Other ancient authorities read Greeks   d Or were guests of

determined that according to their ability, each would send relief to the believers[e] living in Judea; [30]this they did, sending it to the elders by Bar'-na·bas and Saul.

James Killed and Peter Imprisoned

12 About that time King Her'od laid violent hands upon some who belonged to the church. [2]He had James, the brother of John, killed with the sword. [3]After he saw that it pleased the Jews, he proceeded to arrest Peter also. (This was during the festival of Unleavened Bread.) [4]When he had seized him, he put him in prison and handed him over to four squads of soldiers to guard him, intending to bring him out to the people after the Passover. [5]While Peter was kept in prison, the church prayed fervently to God for him.

Peter Delivered from Prison

[6] The very night before Her'od was going to bring him out, Peter, bound with two chains, was sleeping between two soldiers, while guards in front of the door were keeping watch over the prison. [7]Suddenly an angel of the Lord appeared and a light shone in the cell. He tapped Peter on the side and woke him, saying, "Get up quickly." And the chains fell off his wrists. [8]The angel said to him, "Fasten your belt and put on your sandals." He did so. Then he said to him, "Wrap your cloak around you and follow me." [9]Peter[f] went out and followed him; he did not realize that what was happening with the angel's help was real; he thought he was seeing a vision. [10]After they had passed the first and the second guard, they came before the iron gate leading into the city. It opened for them of its own accord, and they went outside and walked along a lane, when suddenly the angel left him. [11]Then Peter came to himself and said, "Now I am sure that the Lord has sent his angel and rescued me from the hands of Her'od and from all that the Jewish people were expecting."

[12] As soon as he realized this, he went to the house of Mary, the mother of John whose other name was Mark, where many had gathered and were praying. [13]When he knocked at the outer gate, a maid named Rhō'da came to answer. [14]On recognizing Peter's voice, she was so overjoyed that, instead of opening the gate, she ran in

and announced that Peter was standing at the gate. [15]They said to her, "You are out of your mind!" But she insisted that it was so. They said, "It is his angel." [16]Meanwhile Peter continued knocking; and when they opened the gate, they saw him and were amazed. [17]He motioned to them with his hand to be silent, and described for them how the Lord had brought him out of the prison. And he added, "Tell this to James and to the believers."[e] Then he left and went to another place.

[18] When morning came, there was no small commotion among the soldiers over what had become of Peter. [19]When Her'od had searched for him and could not find him, he examined the guards and ordered them to be put to death. Then Peter[g] went down from Judea to Caes·a·rē'a and stayed there.

The Death of Herod

[20] Now Her'od was angry with the people of Tyre and Sī'don. So they came to him in a body; and after winning over Blas'tus, the king's chamberlain, they asked for a reconciliation, because their country depended on the king's country for food. [21]On an appointed day Her'od put on his royal robes, took his seat on the platform, and delivered a public address to them. [22]The people kept shouting, "The voice of a god, and not of a mortal!" [23]And immediately, because he had not given the glory to God, an angel of the Lord struck him down, and he was eaten by worms and died.

[24] But the word of God continued to advance and gain adherents. [25]Then after completing their mission Bar'-na·bas and Saul returned to[h] Jerusalem and brought with them John, whose other name was Mark.

Barnabas and Saul Commissioned

13 Now in the church at An'ti·och there were prophets and teachers: Bar'na·bas, Sim'ē·on who was called Nī'ger, Lucius of Cy·rē'nē, Man'a·en a member of the court of Her'od the ruler,[i] and Saul. [2]While they were worshiping the Lord and fasting, the Holy Spirit said, "Set apart for me Bar'na·bas and Saul for the work to which I have called them."

e Gk brothers   *f* Gk He   *g* Gk he
h Other ancient authorities read *from*
i Gk tetrarch

[3] Then after fasting and praying they laid their hands on them and sent them off.

The Apostles Preach in Cyprus

[4] So, being sent out by the Holy Spirit, they went down to Se·leū'ci·a; and from there they sailed to Cyprus. [5] When they arrived at Sal'a·mis, they proclaimed the word of God in the synagogues of the Jews. And they had John also to assist them. [6] When they had gone through the whole island as far as Pā'phos, they met a certain magician, a Jewish false prophet, named Bar-Jesus. [7] He was with the proconsul, Ser'gi·us Paul'us, an intelligent man, who summoned Bar'na·bas and Saul and wanted to hear the word of God. [8] But the magician El'y·mas (for that is the translation of his name) opposed them and tried to turn the proconsul away from the faith. [9] But Saul, also known as Paul, filled with the Holy Spirit, looked intently at him [10] and said, "You son of the devil, you enemy of all righteousness, full of all deceit and villainy, will you not stop making crooked the straight paths of the Lord? [11] And now listen—the hand of the Lord is against you, and you will be blind for a while, unable to see the sun." Immediately mist and darkness came over him, and he went about groping for someone to lead him by the hand. [12] When the proconsul saw what had happened, he believed, for he was astonished at the teaching about the Lord.

Paul and Barnabas in Antioch of Pisidia

[13] Then Paul and his companions set sail from Pā'phos and came to Per'ga in Pam·phyl'i·a. John, however, left them and returned to Jerusalem; [14] but they went on from Per'ga and came to An'ti·och in Pi·sid'i·a. And on the sabbath day they went into the synagogue and sat down. [15] After the reading of the law and the prophets, the officials of the synagogue sent them a message, saying, "Brothers, if you have any word of exhortation for the people, give it." [16] So Paul stood up and with a gesture began to speak:

"You Israelites,[j] and others who fear God, listen. [17] The God of this people Israel chose our ancestors and made the people great during their stay in the land of Egypt, and with uplifted arm he led them out of it. [18] For about forty years he put up with[k] them in the wilderness. [19] After he had destroyed seven nations in the land of Cā'naan, he gave them their land as an inheritance [20] for about four hundred fifty years. After that he gave them judges until the time of the prophet Samuel. [21] Then they asked for a king; and God gave them Saul son of Kish, a man of the tribe of Benjamin, who reigned for forty years. [22] When he had removed him, he made David their king. In his testimony about him he said, 'I have found David, son of Jesse, to be a man after my heart, who will carry out all my wishes.' [23] Of this man's posterity God has brought to Israel a Savior, Jesus, as he promised; [24] before his coming John had already proclaimed a baptism of repentance to all the people of Israel. [25] And as John was finishing his work, he said, 'What do you suppose that I am? I am not he. No, but one is coming after me; I am not worthy to untie the thong of the sandals[l] on his feet.'

[26] "My brothers, you descendants of Abraham's family, and others who fear God, to us[m] the message of this salvation has been sent. [27] Because the residents of Jerusalem and their leaders did not recognize him or understand the words of the prophets that are read every sabbath, they fulfilled those words by condemning him. [28] Even though they found no cause for a sentence of death, they asked Pilate to have him killed. [29] When they had carried out everything that was written about him, they took him down from the tree and laid him in a tomb. [30] But God raised him from the dead; [31] and for many days he appeared to those who came up with him from Galilee to Jerusalem, and they are now his witnesses to the people. [32] And we bring you the good news that what God promised to our ancestors [33] he has fulfilled for us, their children, by raising Jesus; as also it is written in the second psalm,

'You are my Son;
     today I have begotten you.'
[34] As to his raising him from the dead, no more to return to corruption, he has spoken in this way,

---

[j] Gk Men, Israelites   [k] Other ancient authorities read cared for   [l] Gk untie the sandals   [m] Other ancient authorities read you

'I will give you the holy
  promises made to David.'
35 Therefore he has also said in another
psalm,
'You will not let your Holy One
  experience corruption.'
36 For David, after he had served the
purpose of God in his own generation,
died,n was laid beside his ancestors,
and experienced corruption; 37 but he
whom God raised up experienced no
corruption. 38 Let it be known to you
therefore, my brothers, that through
this man forgiveness of sins is proclaimed to you; 39 by this Jesus o everyone who believes is set free from all
those sins p from which you could not
be freed by the law of Moses. 40 Beware, therefore, that what the prophets said does not happen to you:
41 'Look, you scoffers!
  Be amazed and perish,
  for in your days I am doing a
    work,
  a work that you will never
    believe, even if someone
    tells you.' "
42 As Paul and Bar′na·bas q were
going out, the people urged them to
speak about these things again the
next sabbath. 43 When the meeting of
the synagogue broke up, many Jews
and devout converts to Ju′da·ism followed Paul and Bar′na·bas, who spoke
to them and urged them to continue in
the grace of God.
44 The next sabbath almost the
whole city gathered to hear the word
of the Lord.r 45 But when the Jews saw
the crowds, they were filled with jealousy; and blaspheming, they contra-
dicted what was spoken by Paul.
46 Then both Paul and Bar′na·bas
spoke out boldly, saying, "It was necessary that the word of God should be
spoken first to you. Since you reject it
and judge yourselves to be unworthy
of eternal life, we are now turning to
the Gentiles. 47 For so the Lord has
commanded us, saying,
'I have set you to be a light for
  the Gentiles,
so that you may bring
  salvation to the ends of the
    earth.' "
48 When the Gentiles heard this,
they were glad and praised the word of
the Lord; and as many as had been
destined for eternal life became believers. 49 Thus the word of the Lord
spread throughout the region. 50 But
the Jews incited the devout women of

high standing and the leading men of
the city, and stirred up persecution
against Paul and Bar′na·bas, and
drove them out of their region. 51 So
they shook the dust off their feet in
protest against them, and went to
I·cō′ni·um. 52 And the disciples were
filled with joy and with the Holy Spirit.

Paul and Barnabas in Iconium

14 The same thing occurred in
I·cō′ni·um, where Paul and
Bar′na·bas q went into the Jewish synagogue and spoke in such a way that a
great number of both Jews and Greeks
became believers. 2 But the unbelieving Jews stirred up the Gentiles and
poisoned their minds against the
brothers. 3 So they remained for a long
time, speaking boldly for the Lord,
who testified to the word of his grace
by granting signs and wonders to be
done through them. 4 But the residents
of the city were divided; some sided
with the Jews, and some with the apostles. 5 And when an attempt was made
by both Gentiles and Jews, with their
rulers, to mistreat them and to stone
them, 6 the apostles q learned of it and
fled to Lys′tra and Der′bē, cities of
Lyc·a·ō′ni·a, and to the surrounding
country; 7 and there they continued
proclaiming the good news.

Paul and Barnabas in Lystra and Derbe

8 In Lys′tra there was a man sitting
who could not use his feet and had
never walked, for he had been crippled
from birth. 9 He listened to Paul as he
was speaking. And Paul, looking at
him intently and seeing that he had
faith to be healed, 10 said in a loud
voice, "Stand upright on your feet."
And the man s sprang up and began to
walk. 11 When the crowds saw what
Paul had done, they shouted in the
Lyc·a·ō′ni·an language, "The gods
have come down to us in human form!"
12 Bar′na·bas they called Zeūs, and
Paul they called Her′mēs, because he
was the chief speaker. 13 The priest of
Zeūs, whose temple was just outside
the city, t brought oxen and garlands
to the gates; he and the crowds wanted
to offer sacrifice. 14 When the apostles
Bar′na·bas and Paul heard of it, they
tore their clothes and rushed out into

n Gk *fell asleep*   o Gk *this*   p Gk *all*
q Gk *they*   r Other ancient authorities
read *God*   s Gk *he*   t Or *The priest of
Zeus-Outside-the-City*

ACTS

the crowd, shouting, [15] "Friends, *u* why are you doing this? We are mortals just like you, and we bring you good news, that you should turn from these worthless things to the living God, who made the heaven and the earth and the sea and all that is in them. [16] In past generations he allowed all the nations to follow their own ways; [17] yet he has not left himself without a witness in doing good—giving you rains from heaven and fruitful seasons, and filling you with food and your hearts with joy." [18] Even with these words, they scarcely restrained the crowds from offering sacrifice to them.

19 But Jews came there from An′ti·och and I·cō′ni·um and won over the crowds. Then they stoned Paul and dragged him out of the city, supposing that he was dead. [20] But when the disciples surrounded him, he got up and went into the city. The next day he went on with Bar′na·bas to Der′bē.

The Return to Antioch in Syria

21 After they had proclaimed the good news to that city and had made many disciples, they returned to Lys′tra, then on to I·cō′ni·um and An′ti·och. [22] There they strengthened the souls of the disciples and encouraged them to continue in the faith, saying, "It is through many persecutions that we must enter the kingdom of God." [23] And after they had appointed elders for them in each church, with prayer and fasting they entrusted them to the Lord in whom they had come to believe.

24 Then they passed through Pi·sid′i·a and came to Pam·phyl′i·a. [25] When they had spoken the word in Per′ga, they went down to At·ta·li′a. [26] From there they sailed back to An′ti·och, where they had been commended to the grace of God for the work *v* that they had completed. [27] When they arrived, they called the church together and related all that God had done with them, and how he had opened a door of faith for the Gentiles. [28] And they stayed there with the disciples for some time.

The Council at Jerusalem

15 Then certain individuals came down from Judea and were teaching the brothers, "Unless you are circumcised according to the custom of Moses, you cannot be saved." [2] And after Paul and Bar′na·bas had no small

dissension and debate with them, Paul and Bar′na·bas and some of the others were appointed to go up to Jerusalem to discuss this question with the apostles and the elders. [3] So they were sent on their way by the church, and as they passed through both Phoe·ni′ci·a and Sa·mar′i·a, they reported the conversion of the Gentiles, and brought great joy to all the believers. *w* [4] When they came to Jerusalem, they were welcomed by the church and the apostles and the elders, and they reported all that God had done with them. [5] But some believers who belonged to the sect of the Phar′i·sees stood up and said, "It is necessary for them to be circumcised and ordered to keep the law of Moses."

6 The apostles and the elders met together to consider this matter. [7] After there had been much debate, Peter stood up and said to them, "My brothers, *x* you know that in the early days God made a choice among you, that I should be the one through whom the Gentiles would hear the message of the good news and become believers. [8] And God, who knows the human heart, testified to them by giving them the Holy Spirit, just as he did to us; [9] and in cleansing their hearts by faith he has made no distinction between them and us. [10] Now therefore why are you putting God to the test by placing on the neck of the disciples a yoke that neither our ancestors nor we have been able to bear? [11] On the contrary, we believe that we will be saved through the grace of the Lord Jesus, just as they will."

12 The whole assembly kept silence, and listened to Bar′na·bas and Paul as they told of all the signs and wonders that God had done through them among the Gentiles. [13] After they finished speaking, James replied, "My brothers, *x* listen to me. [14] Sim′e·on has related how God first looked favorably on the Gentiles, to take from among them a people for his name. [15] This agrees with the words of the prophets, as it is written,

16 'After this I will return,
    and I will rebuild the dwelling of
         David, which has fallen;
    from its ruins I will rebuild it,
         and I will set it up,

u Gk Men   *v* Or committed in the grace of God to the work   *w* Gk brothers
x Gk Men, brothers

17 so that all other peoples may
        seek the Lord—
    even all the Gentiles over
        whom my name has been
        called.
    Thus says the Lord, who has
        been making these things
        18known from long ago.' y
19Therefore I have reached the decision that we should not trouble those Gentiles who are turning to God, 20but we should write to them to abstain only from things polluted by idols and from fornication and from whatever has been strangled z and from blood. 21For in every city, for generations past, Moses has had those who proclaim him, for he has been read aloud every sabbath in the synagogues."

The Council's Letter to
Gentile Believers

22 Then the apostles and the elders, with the consent of the whole church, decided to choose men from among their members a and to send them to An·ti·och with Paul and Bar′na·bas. They sent Judas called Bar·sab′bas, and Silas, leaders among the brothers, 23with the following letter: "The brothers, both the apostles and the elders, to the believers b of Gentile origin in An′-ti·och and Syria and Ci·li′ci·a, greetings. 24Since we have heard that certain persons who have gone out from us, though with no instructions from us, have said things to disturb you and have unsettled your minds, c 25we have decided unanimously to choose representatives d and send them to you, along with our beloved Bar′-na·bas and Paul, 26who have risked their lives for the sake of our Lord Jesus Christ. 27We have therefore sent Judas and Silas, who themselves will tell you the same things by word of mouth. 28For it has seemed good to the Holy Spirit and to us to impose on you no further burden than these essentials: 29that you abstain from what has been sacrificed to idols and from blood and from what is strangled e and from fornication. If you keep yourselves from these, you will do well. Farewell."

30 So they were sent off and went down to An·ti·och. When they gathered the congregation together, they delivered the letter. 31When its members f read it, they rejoiced at the exhortation. 32Judas and Silas, who were themselves prophets, said much to encourage and strengthen the believ-

ers. b 33After they had been there for some time, they were sent off in peace by the believers b to those who had sent them. g 35But Paul and Bar′na·bas remained in An′ti·och, and there, with many others, they taught and proclaimed the word of the Lord.

Paul and Barnabas Separate

36 After some days Paul said to Bar′na·bas, "Come, let us return and visit the believers b in every city where we proclaimed the word of the Lord and see how they are doing." 37Bar′na·bas wanted to take with them John called Mark. 38But Paul decided not to take with them one who had deserted them in Pam·phyl′i·a and had not accompanied them in the work. 39The disagreement became so sharp that they parted company; Bar′na·bas took Mark with him and sailed away to Cyprus. 40But Paul chose Silas and set out, the believers b commending him to the grace of the Lord. 41He went through Syria and Ci·li′ci·a, strengthening the churches.

Timothy Joins Paul and Silas

16 Paul h went on also to Der′bē and to Lys′tra, where there was a disciple named Timothy, the son of a Jewish woman who was a believer; but his father was a Greek. 2He was well spoken of by the believers b in Lys′tra and I·cō′ni·um. 3Paul wanted Timothy to accompany him; and he took him and had him circumcised because of the Jews who were in those places, for they all knew that his father was a Greek. 4As they went from town to town, they delivered to them for observance the decisions that had been reached by the apostles and elders who were in Jerusalem. 5So the churches were strengthened in the faith and increased in numbers daily.

y Other ancient authorities read *things.* *18Known to God from of old are all his works.'* z Other ancient authorities lack *and from whatever has been* *strangled* a Gk *from among them* b Gk *brothers* c Other ancient authorities add *saying, 'You must be circumcised and keep the law,'* d Gk *men* e Other ancient authorities lack *and from what is strangled* f Gk *When they* g Other ancient authorities add verse 34, *But it seemed good to Silas to remain there* h Gk *He*

A
C
T
S

Paul's Vision of the Man of Macedonia

6 They went through the region of Phryg′i·a and Galatia, having been forbidden by the Holy Spirit to speak the word in Asia. 7 When they had come opposite My′si·a, they attempted to go into Bi·thyn′i·a, but the Spirit of Jesus did not allow them; 8 so, passing by My′si·a, they went down to Tro′as. 9 During the night Paul had a vision: there stood a man of Mac·e·dō′ni·a pleading with him and saying, "Come over to Mac·e·dō′ni·a and help us." 10 When he had seen the vision, we immediately tried to cross over to Mac·e·dō′ni·a, being convinced that God had called us to proclaim the good news to them.

The Conversion of Lydia

11 We set sail from Tro′as and took a straight course to Sam′o·thrāce, the following day to Nē·ap′o·lis, 12 and from there to Phi·lip′pī, which is a leading city of the district *i* of Mac·e·dō′ni·a and a Roman colony. We remained in this city for some days. 13 On the sabbath day we went outside the gate by the river, where we supposed there was a place of prayer; and we sat down and spoke to the women who had gathered there. 14 A certain woman named Lyd′i·a, a worshiper of God, was listening to us; she was from the city of Thȳ·a·tī′ra and a dealer in purple cloth. The Lord opened her heart to listen eagerly to what was said by Paul. 15 When she and her household were baptized, she urged us, saying, "If you have judged me to be faithful to the Lord, come and stay at my home." And she prevailed upon us.

Paul and Silas in Prison

16 One day, as we were going to the place of prayer, we met a slave-girl who had a spirit of divination and brought her owners a great deal of money by fortune-telling. 17 While she followed Paul and us, she would cry out, "These men are slaves of the Most High God, who proclaim to you *j* a way of salvation." 18 She kept doing this for many days. But Paul, very much annoyed, turned and said to the spirit, "I order you in the name of Jesus Christ to come out of her." And it came out that very hour.

19 But when her owners saw that their hope of making money was gone,

they seized Paul and Silas and dragged them into the marketplace before the authorities. 20 When they had brought them before the magistrates, they said, "These men are disturbing our city; they are Jews 21 and are advocating customs that are not lawful for us as Romans to adopt or observe." 22 The crowd joined in attacking them, and the magistrates had them stripped of their clothing and ordered them to be beaten with rods. 23 After they had given them a severe flogging, they threw them into prison and ordered the jailer to keep them securely. 24 Following these instructions, he put them in the innermost cell and fastened their feet in the stocks.

25 About midnight Paul and Silas were praying and singing hymns to God, and the prisoners were listening to them. 26 Suddenly there was an earthquake, so violent that the foundations of the prison were shaken; and immediately all the doors were opened and everyone's chains were unfastened. 27 When the jailer woke up and saw the prison doors wide open, he drew his sword and was about to kill himself, since he supposed that the prisoners had escaped. 28 But Paul shouted in a loud voice, "Do not harm yourself, for we are all here." 29 The jailer *k* called for lights, and rushing in, he fell down trembling before Paul and Silas. 30 Then he brought them outside and said, "Sirs, what must I do to be saved?" 31 They answered, "Believe on the Lord Jesus, and you will be saved, you and your household." 32 They spoke the word of the Lord *l* to him and to all who were in his house. 33 At the same hour of the night he took them and washed their wounds; then he and his entire family were baptized without delay. 34 He brought them up into the house and set food before them; and he and his entire household rejoiced that he had become a believer in God.

35 When morning came, the magistrates sent the police, saying, "Let those men go." 36 And the jailer reported the message to Paul, saying, "The magistrates sent word to let you go; therefore come out now and go in peace." 37 But Paul replied, "They have

i Other authorities read *a city of the first district*   *j* Other ancient authorities read *to us*   *k* Gk *He*   *l* Other ancient authorities read *word of God* beaten us in public, uncondemned, men who are Roman citizens; and have thrown us into prison; and now are they going to discharge us in secret? Certainly not! Let them come and take us out themselves." [38] The police reported these words to the magistrates, and they were afraid when they heard that they were Roman citizens; [39] so they came and apologized to them. And they took them out and asked them to leave the city. [40] After leaving the prison they went to Lydia's home; and when they had seen and encouraged the brothers and sisters[m] there, they departed.

The Uproar in Thessalonica

17 After Paul and Silas[n] had passed through Am·phip′o·lis and Ap·ol·lo′ni·a, they came to Thes·sa·lo·ni′ca, where there was a synagogue of the Jews. [2] And Paul went in, as was his custom, and on three sabbath days argued with them from the scriptures, [3] explaining and proving that it was necessary for the Messiah[o] to suffer and to rise from the dead, and saying, "This is the Messiah,[o] Jesus whom I am proclaiming to you." [4] Some of them were persuaded and joined Paul and Silas, as did a great many of the devout Greeks and not a few of the leading women. [5] But the Jews became jealous, and with the help of some ruffians in the marketplaces they formed a mob and set the city in an uproar. While they were searching for Paul and Silas to bring them out to the assembly, they attacked Jason's house. [6] When they could not find them, they dragged Jason and some believers[m] before the city authorities,[p] shouting, "These people who have been turning the world upside down have come here also, [7] and Jason has entertained them as guests. They are all acting contrary to the decrees of the emperor, saying that there is another king named Jesus." [8] The people and the city officials were disturbed when they heard this, [9] and after they had taken bail from Jason and the others, they let them go.

Paul and Silas in Beroea

[10] That very night the believers[m] sent Paul and Silas off to Be·roe′a; and when they arrived, they went to the Jewish synagogue. [11] These Jews were more receptive than those in Thes·sa·lo·ni′ca, for they welcomed the message very eagerly and examined the scriptures every day to see whether these things were so. [12] Many of them therefore believed, including not a few Greek women and men of high standing. [13] But when the Jews of Thes·sa·lo·ni′ca learned that the word of God had been proclaimed by Paul in Be·roe′a as well, they came there too, to stir up and incite the crowds. [14] Then the believers[m] immediately sent Paul away to the coast, but Silas and Timothy remained behind. [15] Those who conducted Paul brought him as far as Athens; and after receiving instructions to have Silas and Timothy join him as soon as possible, they left him.

Paul in Athens

[16] While Paul was waiting for them in Athens, he was deeply distressed to see that the city was full of idols. [17] So he argued in the synagogue with the Jews and the devout persons, and also in the marketplace[q] every day with those who happened to be there. [18] Also some Ep·i·cu·re′an and Stoic philosophers debated with him. Some said, "What does this babbler want to say?" Others said, "He seems to be a proclaimer of foreign divinities." (This was because he was telling the good news about Jesus and the resurrection.) [19] So they took him and brought him to the Ar·e·op′a·gus and asked him, "May we know what this new teaching is that you are presenting? [20] It sounds rather strange to us, so we would like to know what it means." [21] Now all the Athenians and the foreigners living there would spend their time in nothing but telling or hearing something new.

[22] Then Paul stood in front of the Ar·e·op′a·gus and said, "Athenians, I see how extremely religious you are in every way. [23] For as I went through the city and looked carefully at the objects of your worship, I found among them an altar with the inscription, 'To an unknown god.' What therefore you worship as unknown, this I proclaim to you. [24] The God who made the world and everything in it, he who is Lord of heaven and earth, does not live in shrines made by human hands, [25] nor is he served by human hands, as

A
C
T
S

m Gk brothers   *n* Gk they   *o* Or the Christ   *p* Gk politarchs   *q* Or civic center; Gk agora though he needed anything, since he himself gives to all mortals life and breath and all things. 26 From one ancestor[r] he made all nations to inhabit the whole earth, and he allotted the times of their existence and the boundaries of the places where they would live, 27 so that they would search for God[s] and perhaps grope for him and find him—though indeed he is not far from each one of us. 28 For 'In him we live and move and have our being'; as even some of your own poets have said,

'For we too are his offspring.'

29 Since we are God's offspring, we ought not to think that the deity is like gold, or silver, or stone, an image formed by the art and imagination of mortals. 30 While God has overlooked the times of human ignorance, now he commands all people everywhere to repent, 31 because he has fixed a day on which he will have the world judged in righteousness by a man whom he has appointed, and of this he has given assurance to all by raising him from the dead."

32 When they heard of the resurrection of the dead, some scoffed; but others said, "We will hear you again about this." 33 At that point Paul left them. 34 But some of them joined him and became believers, including Dī·o·nys'i·us the Ar·e·op'a·gīte and a woman named Dam'a·ris, and others with them.

Paul in Corinth

18 After this Paul[t] left Athens and went to Corinth. 2 There he found a Jew named A·qui'la, a native of Pon'tus, who had recently come from Italy with his wife Priscilla, because Clau'di·us had ordered all Jews to leave Rome. Paul[u] went to see them, 3 and, because he was of the same trade, he stayed with them, and they worked together—by trade they were tentmakers. 4 Every sabbath he would argue in the synagogue and would try to convince Jews and Greeks.

5 When Silas and Timothy arrived from Mac·e·dō'ni·a, Paul was occupied with proclaiming the word,[v] testifying to the Jews that the Messiah[w] was Jesus. 6 When they opposed and reviled him, in protest he shook the dust from his clothes[x] and said to them, "Your blood be on your own heads! I am innocent. From now on I will go to the Gentiles." 7 Then he left the synagogue[y] and went to the house of a man named Tit'i·us[z] Justus, a worshiper of God; his house was next door to the synagogue. 8 Cris'pus, the official of the synagogue, became a believer in the Lord, together with all his household; and many of the Corinthians who heard Paul became believers and were baptized. 9 One night the Lord said to Paul in a vision, "Do not be afraid, but speak and do not be silent; 10 for I am with you, and no one will lay a hand on you to harm you, for there are many in this city who are my people." 11 He stayed there a year and six months, teaching the word of God among them.

12 But when Gal'li·ō was proconsul of A·chā'i·a, the Jews made a united attack on Paul and brought him before the tribunal. 13 They said, "This man is persuading people to worship God in ways that are contrary to the law." 14 Just as Paul was about to speak, Gal'li·ō said to the Jews, "If it were a matter of crime or serious villainy, I would be justified in accepting the complaint of you Jews; 15 but since it is a matter of questions about words and names and your own law, see to it yourselves; I do not wish to be a judge of these matters." 16 And he dismissed them from the tribunal. 17 Then all of them[a] seized Sos'the·nēs, the official of the synagogue, and beat him in front of the tribunal. But Gal'li·ō paid no attention to any of these things.

Paul's Return to Antioch

18 After staying there for a considerable time, Paul said farewell to the believers[b] and sailed for Syria, accompanied by Priscilla and A·qui'la. At Cen'chrē·ae he had his hair cut, for he was under a vow. 19 When they reached Eph'e·sus, he left them there, but first he himself went into the synagogue and had a discussion with the Jews. 20 When they asked him to stay longer, he declined; 21 but on taking

r Gk From one; other ancient authorities read From one blood   s Other ancient authorities read the Lord   t Gk he   u Gk He   v Gk with the word   w Or the Christ   x Gk reviled him, he shook out his clothes   y Gk left there   z Other ancient authorities read Titus   a Other ancient authorities read all the Greeks   b Gk brothers leave of them, he said, "I*c* will return to you, if God wills." Then he set sail from Eph'e·sus.

22 When he had landed at Caes·a·re'a, he went up to Jerusalem*d* and greeted the church, and then went down to An'ti·och. 23 After spending some time there he departed and went from place to place through the region of Galatia*e* and Phryg'i·a, strengthening all the disciples.

Ministry of Apollos

24 Now there came to Eph'e·sus a Jew named A·pol'los, a native of Alexandria. He was an eloquent man, well-versed in the scriptures. 25 He had been instructed in the Way of the Lord; and he spoke with burning enthusiasm and taught accurately the things concerning Jesus, though he knew only the baptism of John. 26 He began to speak boldly in the synagogue; but when Priscilla and A·qui'la heard him, they took him aside and explained the Way of God to him more accurately. 27 And when he wished to cross over to A·cha'i·a, the believers*f* encouraged him and wrote to the disciples to welcome him. On his arrival he greatly helped those who through grace had become believers, 28 for he powerfully refuted the Jews in public, showing by the scriptures that the Messiah*g* is Jesus.

Paul in Ephesus

19 While A·pol'los was in Corinth, Paul passed through the interior regions and came to Eph'e·sus, where he found some disciples. 2 He said to them, "Did you receive the Holy Spirit when you became believers?" They replied, "No, we have not even heard that there is a Holy Spirit." 3 Then he said, "Into what then were you baptized?" They answered, "Into John's baptism." 4 Paul said, "John baptized with the baptism of repentance, telling the people to believe in the one who was to come after him, that is, in Jesus." 5 On hearing this, they were baptized in the name of the Lord Jesus. 6 When Paul had laid his hands on them, the Holy Spirit came upon them, and they spoke in tongues and prophesied— 7 altogether there were about twelve of them.

8 He entered the synagogue and for three months spoke out boldly, and argued persuasively about the kingdom of God. 9 When some stubbornly re-fused to believe and spoke evil of the Way before the congregation, he left them, taking the disciples with him, and argued daily in the lecture hall of Ty·ran'nus.*h* 10 This continued for two years, so that all the residents of Asia, both Jews and Greeks, heard the word of the Lord.

The Sons of Sceva

11 God did extraordinary miracles through Paul, 12 so that when the handkerchiefs or aprons that had touched his skin were brought to the sick, their diseases left them, and the evil spirits came out of them. 13 Then some itinerant Jewish exorcists tried to use the name of the Lord Jesus over those who had evil spirits, saying, "I adjure you by the Jesus whom Paul proclaims." 14 Seven sons of a Jewish high priest named Sce'va were doing this. 15 But the evil spirit said to them in reply, "Jesus I know, and Paul I know; but who are you?" 16 Then the man with the evil spirit leaped on them, mastered them all, and so overpowered them that they fled out of the house naked and wounded. 17 When this became known to all residents of Eph'e·sus, both Jews and Greeks, everyone was awestruck; and the name of the Lord Jesus was praised. 18 Also many of those who became believers confessed and disclosed their practices. 19 A number of those who practiced magic collected their books and burned them publicly; when the value of these books*i* was calculated, it was found to come to fifty thousand silver coins. 20 So the word of the Lord grew mightily and prevailed.

The Riot in Ephesus

21 Now after these things had been accomplished, Paul resolved in the Spirit to go through Mac·e·do'ni·a and A·cha'i·a, and then to go on to Jerusalem. He said, "After I have gone there, I must also see Rome." 22 So he sent two of his helpers, Timothy and E·ras'-tus, to Mac·e·do'ni·a, while he himself

c Other ancient authorities read *I must at all costs keep the approaching festival in Jerusalem, but I*   *d* Gk *went up*   *e* Gk *the Galatian region*   *f* Gk *brothers*   *g* Or *the Christ*   *h* Other ancient authorities read *of a certain Tyrannus, from eleven o'clock in the morning to four in the afternoon*   *i* Gk *them*

stayed for some time longer in Asia.
23 About that time no little disturbance broke out concerning the Way. [24] A man named De·mē′tri·us, a silversmith who made silver shrines of Ar′te·mis, brought no little business to the artisans. [25] These he gathered together, with the workers of the same trade, and said, "Men, you know that we get our wealth from this business. [26] You also see and hear that not only in Eph′e·sus but in almost the whole of Asia this Paul has persuaded and drawn away a considerable number of people by saying that gods made with hands are not gods. [27] And there is danger not only that this trade of ours may come into disrepute but also that the temple of the great goddess Ar′te·mis will be scorned, and she will be deprived of her majesty that brought all Asia and the world to worship her."

28 When they heard this, they were enraged and shouted, "Great is Ar′te·mis of the E·phē′si·ans!" [29] The city was filled with the confusion; and people[j] rushed together to the theater, dragging with them Gā′i·us and Ar·is·tar′chus, Mac·e·dō′ni·ans who were Paul's travel companions. [30] Paul wished to go into the crowd, but the disciples would not let him; [31] even some officials of the province of Asia,[k] who were friendly to him, sent him a message urging him not to venture into the theater. [32] Meanwhile, some were shouting one thing, some another; for the assembly was in confusion, and most of them did not know why they had come together. [33] Some of the crowd gave instructions to Alexander, whom the Jews had pushed forward. And Alexander motioned for silence and tried to make a defense before the people. [34] But when they recognized that he was a Jew, for about two hours all of them shouted in unison, "Great is Ar′te·mis of the E·phē′si·ans!" [35] But when the town clerk had quieted the crowd, he said, "Citizens of Eph′e·sus, who is there that does not know that the city of the E·phē′si·ans is the temple keeper of the great Ar′te·mis and of the statue that fell from heaven?[l] [36] Since these things cannot be denied, you ought to be quiet and do nothing rash. [37] You have brought these men here who are neither temple robbers nor blasphemers of our[m] goddess. [38] If therefore De·mē′tri·us and the artisans with him have a complaint against anyone, the courts are open, and there are proconsuls; let them bring charges there against one another. [39] If there is anything further[n] you want to know, it must be settled in the regular assembly. [40] For we are in danger of being charged with rioting today, since there is no cause that we can give to justify this commotion." [41] When he had said this, he dismissed the assembly.

Paul Goes to Macedonia and Greece

20 After the uproar had ceased, Paul sent for the disciples; and after encouraging them and saying farewell, he left for Mac·e·dō′ni·a. [2] When he had gone through those regions and had given the believers[o] much encouragement, he came to Greece, [3] where he stayed for three months. He was about to set sail for Syria when a plot was made against him by the Jews, and so he decided to return through Mac·e·dō′ni·a. [4] He was accompanied by Sop′a·ter son of Pyr′rhus from Be·roē′a, by Ar·is·tar′chus and Se·cun′dus from Thes·sa·lo·nī′ca, by Gā′i·us from Der′bē, and by Timothy, as well as by Tych′i·cus and Troph′i·mus from Asia. [5] They went ahead and were waiting for us in Trō′as; [6] but we sailed from Phi·lip′pī after the days of Unleavened Bread, and in five days we joined them in Trō′as, where we stayed for seven days.

Paul's Farewell Visit to Troas

7 On the first day of the week, when we met to break bread, Paul was holding a discussion with them; since he intended to leave the next day, he continued speaking until midnight. [8] There were many lamps in the room upstairs where we were meeting. [9] A young man named Eū′ty·chus, who was sitting in the window, began to sink off into a deep sleep while Paul talked still longer. Overcome by sleep, he fell to the ground three floors below and was picked up dead. [10] But Paul went down, and bending over him took him in his arms, and said, "Do not be alarmed, for his life is in him." [11] Then Paul went upstairs, and after he had broken bread and eaten, he

[j] Gk they   [k] Gk some of the Asiarchs
[l] Meaning of Gk uncertain   [m] Other ancient authorities read your   [n] Other ancient authorities read about other matters   [o] Gk given them

continued to converse with them until dawn; then he left. [12]Meanwhile they had taken the boy away alive and were not a little comforted.

The Voyage from Troas to Miletus

13 We went ahead to the ship and set sail for As'sos, intending to take Paul on board there; for he had made this arrangement, intending to go by land himself. [14]When he met us in As'sos, we took him on board and went to Mit·y·le'ne. [15]We sailed from there, and on the following day we arrived opposite Chi'os. The next day we touched at Sa'mos, and*p* the day after that we came to Mi·le'tus. [16]For Paul had decided to sail past Eph'e·sus, so that he might not have to spend time in Asia; he was eager to be in Jerusalem, if possible, on the day of Pentecost.

Paul Speaks to the Ephesian Elders

17 From Mi·le'tus he sent a message to Eph'e·sus, asking the elders of the church to meet him. [18]When they came to him, he said to them:
"You yourselves know how I lived among you the entire time from the first day that I set foot in Asia, [19]serving the Lord with all humility and with tears, enduring the trials that came to me through the plots of the Jews. [20]I did not shrink from doing anything helpful, proclaiming the message to you and teaching you publicly and from house to house, [21]as I testified to both Jews and Greeks about repentance toward God and faith toward our Lord Jesus. [22]And now, as a captive to the Spirit,*q* I am on my way to Jerusalem, not knowing what will happen to me there, [23]except that the Holy Spirit testifies to me in every city that imprisonment and persecutions are waiting for me. [24]But I do not count my life of any value to myself, if only I may finish my course and the ministry that I received from the Lord Jesus, to testify to the good news of God's grace.
25 "And now I know that none of you, among whom I have gone about proclaiming the kingdom, will ever see my face again. [26]Therefore I declare to you this day that I am not responsible for the blood of any of you, [27]for I did not shrink from declaring to you the whole purpose of God. [28]Keep watch over yourselves and over all the flock, of which the Holy Spirit has made you overseers, to shepherd the church of God*r* that he obtained with the blood

of his own Son.*s* [29]I know that after I have gone, savage wolves will come in among you, not sparing the flock. [30]Some even from your own group will come distorting the truth in order to entice the disciples to follow them. [31]Therefore be alert, remembering that for three years I did not cease night or day to warn everyone with tears. [32]And now I commend you to God and to the message of his grace, a message that is able to build you up and to give you the inheritance among all who are sanctified. [33]I coveted no one's silver or gold or clothing. [34]You know for yourselves that I worked with my own hands to support myself and my companions. [35]In all this I have given you an example that by such work we must support the weak, remembering the words of the Lord Jesus, for he himself said, 'It is more blessed to give than to receive.' "
36 When he had finished speaking, he knelt down with them all and prayed. [37]There was much weeping among them all; they embraced Paul and kissed him, [38]grieving especially because of what he had said, that they would not see him again. Then they brought him to the ship.

Paul's Journey to Jerusalem

21 When we had parted from them and set sail, we came by a straight course to Cos, and the next day to Rhodes, and from there to Pat'a·ra.*t* [2]When we found a ship bound for Phoe·ni'ci·a, we went on board and set sail. [3]We came in sight of Cyprus; and leaving it on our left, we sailed to Syria and landed at Tyre, because the ship was to unload its cargo there. [4]We looked up the disciples and stayed there for seven days. Through the Spirit they told Paul not to go on to Jerusalem. [5]When our days there were ended, we left and proceeded on our journey; and all of them, with wives and children, escorted us outside the city. There we knelt down on the beach and prayed [6]and said farewell to one another. Then we went on board the ship, and they returned home.

p Other ancient authorities add *after remaining at Trogyllium*   *q* Or *And now, bound in the spirit*   *r* Other ancient authorities read *of the Lord*   *s* Or *with his own blood*; Gk *with the blood of his Own*   *t* Other ancient authorities add *and Myra*

7 When we had finished[u] the voyage from Tyre, we arrived at Ptolemais; and we greeted the believers[v] and stayed with them for one day. [8] The next day we left and came to Caes·a·rē′a; and we went into the house of Philip the evangelist, one of the seven, and stayed with him. [9] He had four unmarried daughters[w] who had the gift of prophecy. [10] While we were staying there for several days, a prophet named Ag′a·bus came down from Judea. [11] He came to us and took Paul's belt, bound his own feet and hands with it, and said, "Thus says the Holy Spirit, 'This is the way the Jews in Jerusalem will bind the man who owns this belt and will hand him over to the Gentiles.' " [12] When we heard this, we and the people there urged him not to go up to Jerusalem. [13] Then Paul answered, "What are you doing, weeping and breaking my heart? For I am ready not only to be bound but even to die in Jerusalem for the name of the Lord Jesus." [14] Since he would not be persuaded, we remained silent except to say, "The Lord's will be done."

15 After these days we got ready and started to go up to Jerusalem. [16] Some of the disciples from Caes·a·rē′a also came along and brought us to the house of Mnā′son of Cyprus, an early disciple, with whom we were to stay.

Paul Visits James at Jerusalem

17 When we arrived in Jerusalem, the brothers welcomed us warmly. [18] The next day Paul went with us to visit James; and all the elders were present. [19] After greeting them, he related one by one the things that God had done among the Gentiles through his ministry. [20] When they heard it, they praised God. Then they said to him, "You see, brother, how many thousands of believers there are among the Jews, and they are all zealous for the law. [21] They have been told about you that you teach all the Jews living among the Gentiles to forsake Moses, and that you tell them not to circumcise their children or observe the customs. [22] What then is to be done? They will certainly hear that you have come. [23] So do what we tell you. We have four men who are under a vow. [24] Join these men, go through the rite of purification with them, and pay for the shaving of their heads.

Thus all will know that there is nothing in what they have been told about you, but that you yourself observe and guard the law. [25] But as for the Gentiles who have become believers, we have sent a letter with our judgment that they should abstain from what has been sacrificed to idols and from blood and from what is strangled[x] and from fornication." [26] Then Paul took the men, and the next day, having purified himself, he entered the temple with them, making public the completion of the days of purification when the sacrifice would be made for each of them.

Paul Arrested in the Temple

27 When the seven days were almost completed, the Jews from Asia, who had seen him in the temple, stirred up the whole crowd. They seized him, [28] shouting, "Fellow Israelites, help! This is the man who is teaching everyone everywhere against our people, our law, and this place; more than that, he has actually brought Greeks into the temple and has defiled this holy place." [29] For they had previously seen Troph′i·mus the E·phē′-si·an with him in the city, and they supposed that Paul had brought him into the temple. [30] Then all the city was aroused, and the people rushed together. They seized Paul and dragged him out of the temple, and immediately the doors were shut. [31] While they were trying to kill him, word came to the tribune of the cohort that all Jerusalem was in an uproar. [32] Immediately he took soldiers and centurions and ran down to them. When they saw the tribune and the soldiers, they stopped beating Paul. [33] Then the tribune came, arrested him, and ordered him to be bound with two chains; he inquired who he was and what he had done. [34] Some in the crowd shouted one thing, some another; and as he could not learn the facts because of the uproar, he ordered him to be brought into the barracks. [35] When Paul[y] came to the steps, the violence of the mob was so great that he had to be carried by the soldiers. [36] The crowd that followed kept shouting, "Away with him!"

---

[u] Or *continued*   [v] Gk *brothers*
[w] Gk *four daughters, virgins,*   [x] Other ancient authorities lack *and from what is strangled*   [y] Gk *he*

Paul Defends Himself

37 Just as Paul was about to be brought into the barracks, he said to the tribune, "May I say something to you?" The tribune[z] replied, "Do you know Greek? 38 Then you are not the Egyptian who recently stirred up a revolt and led the four thousand assassins out into the wilderness?" 39 Paul replied, "I am a Jew, from Tar'sus in Ci·li'ci·a, a citizen of an important city; I beg you, let me speak to the people." 40 When he had given him permission, Paul stood on the steps and motioned to the people for silence; and when there was a great hush, he addressed them in the Hebrew[a] language, saying:

22 "Brothers and fathers, listen to the defense that I now make before you."

2 When they heard him addressing them in Hebrew,[a] they became even more quiet. Then he said:

3 "I am a Jew, born in Tar'sus in Ci·li'ci·a, but brought up in this city at the feet of Ga·ma'li·el, educated strictly according to our ancestral law, being zealous for God, just as all of you are today. 4 I persecuted this Way up to the point of death by binding both men and women and putting them in prison, 5 as the high priest and the whole council of elders can testify about me. From them I also received letters to the brothers in Damascus, and I went there in order to bind those who were there and to bring them back to Jerusalem for punishment.

Paul Tells of His Conversion
(Acts 9.1–19a; 26.12–18)

6 "While I was on my way and approaching Damascus, about noon a great light from heaven suddenly shone about me. 7 I fell to the ground and heard a voice saying to me, 'Saul, Saul, why are you persecuting me?' 8 I answered, 'Who are you, Lord?' Then he said to me, 'I am Jesus of Nazareth[b] whom you are persecuting.' 9 Now those who were with me saw the light but did not hear the voice of the one who was speaking to me. 10 I asked, 'What am I to do, Lord?' The Lord said to me, 'Get up and go to Damascus; there you will be told everything that has been assigned to you to do.' 11 Since I could not see because of the brightness of that light, those who

were with me took my hand and led me to Damascus.

12 "A certain An·a·ni'as, who was a devout man according to the law and well spoken of by all the Jews living there, 13 came to me; and standing beside me, he said, 'Brother Saul, regain your sight!' In that very hour I regained my sight and saw him. 14 Then he said, 'The God of our ancestors has chosen you to know his will, to see the Righteous One and to hear his own voice; 15 for you will be his witness to all the world of what you have seen and heard. 16 And now why do you delay? Get up, be baptized, and have your sins washed away, calling on his name.'

Paul Sent to the Gentiles

17 "After I had returned to Jerusalem and while I was praying in the temple, I fell into a trance 18 and saw Jesus[c] saying to me, 'Hurry and get out of Jerusalem quickly, because they will not accept your testimony about me.' 19 And I said, 'Lord, they themselves know that in every synagogue I imprisoned and beat those who believed in you. 20 And while the blood of your witness Stephen was shed, I myself was standing by, approving and keeping the coats of those who killed him.' 21 Then he said to me, 'Go, for I will send you far away to the Gentiles.'"

Paul and the Roman Tribune

22 Up to this point they listened to him, but then they shouted, "Away with such a fellow from the earth! For he should not be allowed to live." 23 And while they were shouting, throwing off their cloaks, and tossing dust into the air, 24 the tribune directed that he was to be brought into the barracks, and ordered him to be examined by flogging, to find out the reason for this outcry against him. 25 But when they had tied him up with thongs,[d] Paul said to the centurion who was standing by, "Is it legal for you to flog a Roman citizen who is uncondemned?" 26 When the centurion heard that, he went to the tribune and said to him, "What are you about to do? This man is a Roman citizen." 27 The tribune came and asked Paul,[c] "Tell me, are

---

[z] Gk He [a] That is, *Aramaic* [b] Gk *the Nazorean* [c] Gk *him* [d] Or *up for the lashes*

you a Roman citizen?" And he said, "Yes." 28 The tribune answered, "It cost me a large sum of money to get my citizenship." Paul said, "But I was born a citizen." 29 Immediately those who were about to examine him drew back from him; and the tribune also was afraid, for he realized that Paul was a Roman citizen and that he had bound him.

Paul before the Council

30 Since he wanted to find out what Paul*e* was being accused of by the Jews, the next day he released him and ordered the chief priests and the entire council to meet. He brought Paul down and had him stand before them.

23 While Paul was looking intently at the council he said, "Brothers,*f* up to this day I have lived my life with a clear conscience before God." 2 Then the high priest An·a·ni'as ordered those standing near him to strike him on the mouth. 3 At this Paul said to him, "God will strike you, you whitewashed wall! Are you sitting there to judge me according to the law, and yet in violation of the law you order me to be struck?" 4 Those standing nearby said, "Do you dare to insult God's high priest?" 5 And Paul said, "I did not realize, brothers, that he was high priest; for it is written, 'You shall not speak evil of a leader of your people.' "

6 When Paul noticed that some were Sad'du·cees and others were Phar'i·sees, he called out in the council, "Brothers, I am a Phar'i·see, a son of Phar'i·sees. I am on trial concerning the hope of the resurrection*g* of the dead." 7 When he said this, a dissension began between the Phar'i·sees and the Sad'du·cees, and the assembly was divided. 8 (The Sad'du·cees say that there is no resurrection, or angel, or spirit; but the Phar'i·sees acknowledge all three.) 9 Then a great clamor arose, and certain scribes of the Phar'i·sees' group stood up and contended, "We find nothing wrong with this man. What if a spirit or an angel has spoken to him?" 10 When the dissension became violent, the tribune, fearing that they would tear Paul to pieces, ordered the soldiers to go down, take him by force, and bring him into the barracks.

11 That night the Lord stood near him and said, "Keep up your courage! For just as you have testified for me in Jerusalem, so you must bear witness also in Rome."

The Plot to Kill Paul

12 In the morning the Jews joined in a conspiracy and bound themselves by an oath neither to eat nor drink until they had killed Paul. 13 There were more than forty who joined in this conspiracy. 14 They went to the chief priests and elders and said, "We have strictly bound ourselves by an oath to taste no food until we have killed Paul. 15 Now then, you and the council must notify the tribune to bring him down to you, on the pretext that you want to make a more thorough examination of his case. And we are ready to do away with him before he arrives."

16 Now the son of Paul's sister heard about the ambush; so he went and gained entrance to the barracks and told Paul. 17 Paul called one of the centurions and said, "Take this young man to the tribune, for he has something to report to him." 18 So he took him, brought him to the tribune, and said, "The prisoner Paul called me and asked me to bring this young man to you; he has something to tell you." 19 The tribune took him by the hand, drew him aside privately, and asked, "What is it that you have to report to me?" 20 He answered, "The Jews have agreed to ask you to bring Paul down to the council tomorrow, as though they were going to inquire more thoroughly into his case. 21 But do not be persuaded by them, for more than forty of their men are lying in ambush for him. They have bound themselves by an oath neither to eat nor drink until they kill him. They are ready now and are waiting for your consent." 22 So the tribune dismissed the young man, ordering him, "Tell no one that you have informed me of this."

Paul Sent to Felix the Governor

23 Then he summoned two of the centurions and said, "Get ready to leave by nine o'clock tonight for Caes·a·re'a with two hundred soldiers, seventy horsemen, and two hundred spearmen. 24 Also provide mounts for Paul to ride, and take him safely to Felix the governor." 25 He wrote a letter to this effect:

26 "Clau'di·us Lys'i·as to his Excel-

e Gk he   *f* Gk Men, brothers
g Gk concerning hope and resurrection

lency the governor Felix, greetings. [27] This man was seized by the Jews and was about to be killed by them, but when I had learned that he was a Roman citizen, I came with the guard and rescued him. [28] Since I wanted to know the charge for which they accused him, I had him brought to their council. [29] I found that he was accused concerning questions of their law, but was charged with nothing deserving death or imprisonment. [30] When I was informed that there would be a plot against the man, I sent him to you at once, ordering his accusers also to state before you what they have against him. [h]"

31 So the soldiers, according to their instructions, took Paul and brought him during the night to An·tip′a·tris. [32] The next day they let the horsemen go on with him, while they returned to the barracks. [33] When they came to Caes·a·re′a and delivered the letter to the governor, they presented Paul also before him. [34] On reading the letter, he asked what province he belonged to, and when he learned that he was from Ci·li′ci·a, [35] he said, "I will give you a hearing when your accusers arrive." Then he ordered that he be kept under guard in Herod's headquarters. [i]

Paul before Felix at Caesarea

24 Five days later the high priest An·a·ni′as came down with some elders and an attorney, a certain Ter·tul′lus, and they reported their case against Paul to the governor. [2] When Paul[j] had been summoned, Ter·tul′lus began to accuse him, saying:

"Your Excellency,[k] because of you we have long enjoyed peace, and reforms have been made for this people because of your foresight. [3] We welcome this in every way and everywhere with utmost gratitude. [4] But, to detain you no further, I beg you to hear us briefly with your customary graciousness. [5] We have, in fact, found this man a pestilent fellow, an agitator among all the Jews throughout the world, and a ringleader of the sect of the Naz′a·renes.[l] [6] He even tried to profane the temple, and so we seized him.[m] [8] By examining him yourself you will be able to learn from him concerning everything of which we accuse him."

9 The Jews also joined in the charge by asserting that all this was true.

Paul's Defense before Felix

10 When the governor motioned to him to speak, Paul replied:

"I cheerfully make my defense, knowing that for many years you have been a judge over this nation. [11] As you can find out, it is not more than twelve days since I went up to worship in Jerusalem. [12] They did not find me disputing with anyone in the temple or stirring up a crowd either in the synagogues or throughout the city. [13] Neither can they prove to you the charge that they now bring against me. [14] But this I admit to you, that according to the Way, which they call a sect, I worship the God of our ancestors, believing everything laid down according to the law or written in the prophets. [15] I have a hope in God—a hope that they themselves also accept—that there will be a resurrection of both[n] the righteous and the unrighteous. [16] Therefore I do my best always to have a clear conscience toward God and all people. [17] Now after some years I came to bring alms to my nation and to offer sacrifices. [18] While I was doing this, they found me in the temple, completing the rite of purification, without any crowd or disturbance. [19] But there were some Jews from Asia—they ought to be here before you to make an accusation, if they have anything against me. [20] Or let these men here tell what crime they had found when I stood before the council, [21] unless it was this one sentence that I called out while standing before them, 'It is about the resurrection of the dead that I am on trial before you today.' "

22 But Felix, who was rather well informed about the Way, adjourned the hearing with the comment, "When Lys′i·as the tribune comes down, I will decide your case." [23] Then he ordered the centurion to keep him in custody, but to let him have some liberty and

[h] Other ancient authorities add *Farewell*
[i] Gk *praetorium*   [j] Gk *he*   [k] Gk lacks *Your Excellency*   [l] Gk *Nazoreans*
[m] Other ancient authorities add *and we would have judged him according to our law.* [7] *But the chief captain Lysias came and with great violence took him out of our hands,* [8] *commanding his accusers to come before you.*   [n] Other ancient authorities read *of the dead, both of*

not to prevent any of his friends from taking care of his needs.

Paul Held in Custody

24 Some days later when Felix came with his wife Drū·sil'la, who was Jewish, he sent for Paul and heard him speak concerning faith in Christ Jesus. 25 And as he discussed justice, self-control, and the coming judgment, Felix became frightened and said, "Go away for the present; when I have an opportunity, I will send for you." 26 At the same time he hoped that money would be given him by Paul, and for that reason he used to send for him very often and converse with him. 27 After two years had passed, Felix was succeeded by Por'ci·us Fes'tus; and since he wanted to grant the Jews a favor, Felix left Paul in prison.

Paul Appeals to the Emperor

25 Three days after Fes'tus had arrived in the province, he went up from Caes·a·rē'a to Jerusalem 2 where the chief priests and the leaders of the Jews gave him a report against Paul. They appealed to him 3 and requested, as a favor to them against Paul,o to have him transferred to Jerusalem. They were, in fact, planning an ambush to kill him along the way. 4 Fes'tus replied that Paul was being kept at Caes·a·rē'a, and that he himself intended to go there shortly. 5 "So," he said, "let those of you who have the authority come down with me, and if there is anything wrong about the man, let them accuse him."

6 After he had stayed among them not more than eight or ten days, he went down to Caes·a·rē'a; the next day he took his seat on the tribunal and ordered Paul to be brought. 7 When he arrived, the Jews who had gone down from Jerusalem surrounded him, bringing many serious charges against him, which they could not prove. 8 Paul said in his defense, "I have in no way committed an offense against the law of the Jews, or against the temple, or against the emperor." 9 But Fes'tus, wishing to do the Jews a favor, asked Paul, "Do you wish to go up to Jerusalem and be tried there before me on these charges?" 10 Paul said, "I am appealing to the emperor's tribunal; this is where I should be tried. I have done no wrong to the Jews, as you very well know. 11 Now if I am in the wrong and have committed something for which I

deserve to die, I am not trying to escape death; but if there is nothing to their charges against me, no one can turn me over to them. I appeal to the emperor." 12 Then Fes'tus, after he had conferred with his council, replied, "You have appealed to the emperor; to the emperor you will go."

Festus Consults King Agrippa

13 After several days had passed, King A·grip'pa and Ber·nī'cē arrived at Caes·a·rē'a to welcome Fes'tus. 14 Since they were staying there several days, Fes'tus laid Paul's case before the king, saying, "There is a man here who was left in prison by Felix. 15 When I was in Jerusalem, the chief priests and the elders of the Jews informed me about him and asked for a sentence against him. 16 I told them that it was not the custom of the Romans to hand over anyone before the accused had met the accusers face to face and had been given an opportunity to make a defense against the charge. 17 So when they met here, I lost no time, but on the next day took my seat on the tribunal and ordered the man to be brought. 18 When the accusers stood up, they did not charge him with any of the crimesp that I was expecting. 19 Instead they had certain points of disagreement with him about their own religion and about a certain Jesus, who had died, but whom Paul asserted to be alive. 20 Since I was at a loss how to investigate these questions, I asked whether he wished to go to Jerusalem and be tried there on these charges.q 21 But when Paul had appealed to be kept in custody for the decision of his Imperial Majesty, I ordered him to be held until I could send him to the emperor." 22 A·grip'pa said to Fes'tus, "I would like to hear the man myself." "Tomorrow," he said, "you will hear him."

Paul Brought before Agrippa

23 So on the next day A·grip'pa and Ber·nī'cē came with great pomp, and they entered the audience hall with the military tribunes and the prominent men of the city. Then Fes'tus gave the order and Paul was brought in. 24 And Fes'tus said, "King A·grip'pa and all here present with us, you see this man about whom the whole Jewish com-

o Gk him　p Other ancient authorities read with anything　q Gk on them munity petitioned me, both in Jerusalem and here, shouting that he ought not to live any longer. 25 But I found that he had done nothing deserving death; and when he appealed to his Imperial Majesty, I decided to send him. 26 But I have nothing definite to write to our sovereign about him. Therefore I have brought him before all of you, and especially before you, King A·grip′pa, so that, after we have examined him, I may have something to write— 27 for it seems to me unreasonable to send a prisoner without indicating the charges against him."

Paul Defends Himself before Agrippa

26 A·grip′pa said to Paul, "You have permission to speak for yourself." Then Paul stretched out his hand and began to defend himself:

2 "I consider myself fortunate that it is before you, King A·grip′pa, I am to make my defense today against all the accusations of the Jews, 3 because you are especially familiar with all the customs and controversies of the Jews; therefore I beg of you to listen to me patiently.

4 "All the Jews know my way of life from my youth, a life spent from the beginning among my own people and in Jerusalem. 5 They have known for a long time, if they are willing to testify, that I have belonged to the strictest sect of our religion and lived as a Phar′i·see. 6 And now I stand here on trial on account of my hope in the promise made by God to our ancestors, 7 a promise that our twelve tribes hope to attain, as they earnestly worship day and night. It is for this hope, your Excellency,[r] that I am accused by Jews! 8 Why is it thought incredible by any of you that God raises the dead?

9 "Indeed, I myself was convinced that I ought to do many things against the name of Jesus of Nazareth.[s] 10 And that is what I did in Jerusalem; with authority received from the chief priests, I not only locked up many of the saints in prison, but I also cast my vote against them when they were being condemned to death. 11 By punishing them often in all the synagogues I tried to force them to blaspheme; and since I was so furiously enraged at them, I pursued them even to foreign cities.

Paul Tells of His Conversion
(Acts 9.1–19; 22.6–16)

12 "With this in mind, I was traveling to Damascus with the authority and commission of the chief priests, 13 when at midday along the road, your Excellency,[r] I saw a light from heaven, brighter than the sun, shining around me and my companions. 14 When we had all fallen to the ground, I heard a voice saying to me in the Hebrew[t] language, 'Saul, Saul, why are you persecuting me? It hurts you to kick against the goads.' 15 I asked, 'Who are you, Lord?' The Lord answered, 'I am Jesus whom you are persecuting. 16 But get up and stand on your feet; for I have appeared to you for this purpose, to appoint you to serve and testify to the things in which you have seen me[u] and to those in which I will appear to you. 17 I will rescue you from your people and from the Gentiles—to whom I am sending you 18 to open their eyes so that they may turn from darkness to light and from the power of Satan to God, so that they may receive forgiveness of sins and a place among those who are sanctified by faith in me.'

Paul Tells of His Preaching

19 "After that, King A·grip′pa, I was not disobedient to the heavenly vision, 20 but declared first to those in Damascus, then in Jerusalem and throughout the countryside of Judea, and also to the Gentiles, that they should repent and turn to God and do deeds consistent with repentance. 21 For this reason the Jews seized me in the temple and tried to kill me. 22 To this day I have had help from God, and so I stand here, testifying to both small and great, saying nothing but what the prophets and Moses said would take place: 23 that the Messiah[v] must suffer, and that, by being the first to rise from the dead, he would proclaim light both to our people and to the Gentiles."

Paul Appeals to Agrippa to Believe

24 While he was making this defense, Fes′tus exclaimed, "You are out of your mind, Paul! Too much learning is driving you insane!" 25 But Paul said, "I am not out of my mind, most excel-

---

[r]Gk O king   [s]Gk the Nazorean   [t]That is, Aramaic   [u]Other ancient authorities read *the things that you have seen*   [v]Or *the Christ*

lent Fes'tus, but I am speaking the sober truth. [26] Indeed the king knows about these things, and to him I speak freely; for I am certain that none of these things has escaped his notice, for this was not done in a corner. [27] King A·grip'pa, do you believe the prophets? I know that you believe." [28] A·grip'pa said to Paul, "Are you so quickly persuading me to become a Christian?"[w] [29] Paul replied, "Whether quickly or not, I pray to God that not only you but also all who are listening to me today might become such as I am—except for these chains."

30 Then the king got up, and with him the governor and Ber·ni'cē and those who had been seated with them; [31] and as they were leaving, they said to one another, "This man is doing nothing to deserve death or imprisonment." [32] A·grip'pa said to Fes'tus, "This man could have been set free if he had not appealed to the emperor."

Paul Sails for Rome

27 When it was decided that we were to sail for Italy, they transferred Paul and some other prisoners to a centurion of the Augustan Cohort, named Julius. [2] Embarking on a ship of Ad·ra·myt'ti·um that was about to set sail to the ports along the coast of Asia, we put to sea, accompanied by Ar·is·tar'chus, a Mac·e·do'ni·an from Thes·sa·lo·ni'ca. [3] The next day we put in at Si'don; and Julius treated Paul kindly, and allowed him to go to his friends to be cared for. [4] Putting out to sea from there, we sailed under the lee of Cyprus, because the winds were against us. [5] After we had sailed across the sea that is off Ci·li'ci·a and Pam·phyl'i·a, we came to My'ra in Ly'ci·a. [6] There the centurion found an Alexandrian ship bound for Italy and put us on board. [7] We sailed slowly for a number of days and arrived with difficulty off Cni'dus, and as the wind was against us, we sailed under the lee of Crete off Sal·mo'nē. [8] Sailing past it with difficulty, we came to a place called Fair Havens, near the city of La·sē'a.

9 Since much time had been lost and sailing was now dangerous, because even the Fast had already gone by, Paul advised them, [10] saying, "Sirs, I can see that the voyage will be with danger and much heavy loss, not only of the cargo and the ship, but also of our lives." [11] But the centurion paid more attention to the pilot and to the owner of the ship than to what Paul said. [12] Since the harbor was not suitable for spending the winter, the majority was in favor of putting to sea from there, on the chance that somehow they could reach Phoenix, where they could spend the winter. It was a harbor of Crete, facing southwest and northwest.

The Storm at Sea

13 When a moderate south wind began to blow, they thought they could achieve their purpose; so they weighed anchor and began to sail past Crete, close to the shore. [14] But soon a violent wind, called the northeaster, rushed down from Crete.[x] [15] Since the ship was caught and could not be turned head-on into the wind, we gave way to it and were driven. [16] By running under the lee of a small island called Cau'da[y] we were scarcely able to get the ship's boat under control. [17] After hoisting it up they took measures[z] to undergird the ship; then, fearing that they would run on the Syr'tis, they lowered the sea anchor and so were driven. [18] We were being pounded by the storm so violently that on the next day they began to throw the cargo overboard, [19] and on the third day with their own hands they threw the ship's tackle overboard. [20] When neither sun nor stars appeared for many days, and no small tempest raged, all hope of our being saved was at last abandoned.

21 Since they had been without food for a long time, Paul then stood up among them and said, "Men, you should have listened to me and not have set sail from Crete and thereby avoided this damage and loss. [22] I urge you now to keep up your courage, for there will be no loss of life among you, but only of the ship. [23] For last night there stood by me an angel of the God to whom I belong and whom I worship, [24] and he said, 'Do not be afraid, Paul; you must stand before the emperor; and indeed, God has granted safety to all those who are sailing with you.' [25] So keep up your courage, men, for I have faith in God that it will be exactly as I have been told. [26] But we will have to run aground on some island."

w Or *Quickly you will persuade me to play the Christian*   *x* Gk it   *y* Other ancient authorities read *Clauda*   *z* Gk *helps*

27 When the fourteenth night had come, as we were drifting across the sea of Ā′dri·a, about midnight the sailors suspected that they were nearing land. 28 So they took soundings and found twenty fathoms; a little farther on they took soundings again and found fifteen fathoms. 29 Fearing that we might run on the rocks, they let down four anchors from the stern and prayed for day to come. 30 But when the sailors tried to escape from the ship and had lowered the boat into the sea, on the pretext of putting out anchors from the bow, 31 Paul said to the centurion and the soldiers, "Unless these men stay in the ship, you cannot be saved." 32 Then the soldiers cut away the ropes of the boat and set it adrift.

33 Just before daybreak, Paul urged all of them to take some food, saying, "Today is the fourteenth day that you have been in suspense and remaining without food, having eaten nothing. 34 Therefore I urge you to take some food, for it will help you survive; for none of you will lose a hair from your heads." 35 After he had said this, he took bread; and giving thanks to God in the presence of all, he broke it and began to eat. 36 Then all of them were encouraged and took food for themselves. 37 (We were in all two hundred seventy-six [a] persons in the ship.) 38 After they had satisfied their hunger, they lightened the ship by throwing the wheat into the sea.

The Shipwreck

39 In the morning they did not recognize the land, but they noticed a bay with a beach, on which they planned to run the ship ashore, if they could. 40 So they cast off the anchors and left them in the sea. At the same time they loosened the ropes that tied the steering-oars; then hoisting the foresail to the wind, they made for the beach. 41 But striking a reef, [b] they ran the ship aground; the bow stuck and remained immovable, but the stern was being broken up by the force of the waves. 42 The soldiers' plan was to kill the prisoners, so that none might swim away and escape; 43 but the centurion, wishing to save Paul, kept them from carrying out their plan. He ordered those who could swim to jump overboard first and make for the land, 44 and the rest to follow, some on planks and others on pieces of the ship. And so it was that all were brought safely to land.

Paul on the Island of Malta

28 After we had reached safety, we then learned that the island was called Malta. 2 The natives showed us unusual kindness. Since it had begun to rain and was cold, they kindled a fire and welcomed all of us around it. 3 Paul had gathered a bundle of brushwood and was putting it on the fire, when a viper, driven out by the heat, fastened itself on his hand. 4 When the natives saw the creature hanging from his hand, they said to one another, "This man must be a murderer; though he has escaped from the sea, justice has not allowed him to live." 5 He, however, shook off the creature into the fire and suffered no harm. 6 They were expecting him to swell up or drop dead, but after they had waited a long time and saw that nothing unusual had happened to him, they changed their minds and began to say that he was a god.

7 Now in the neighborhood of that place were lands belonging to the leading man of the island, named Pub′li·us, who received us and entertained us hospitably for three days. 8 It so happened that the father of Pub′li·us lay sick in bed with fever and dysentery. Paul visited him and cured him by praying and putting his hands on him. 9 After this happened, the rest of the people on the island who had diseases also came and were cured. 10 They bestowed many honors on us, and when we were about to sail, they put on board all the provisions we needed.

Paul Arrives at Rome

11 Three months later we set sail on a ship that had wintered at the island, an Alexandrian ship with the Twin Brothers as its figurehead. 12 We put in at Syracuse and stayed there for three days; 13 then we weighed anchor and came to Rhe′gi·um. After one day there a south wind sprang up, and on the second day we came to Pu·te′o·li. 14 There we found believers [c] and were invited to stay with them for seven days. And so we came to Rome. 15 The believers [c] from there, when they heard of us, came as far as the Forum

A
C
T
S

---

[a] Other ancient authorities read *seventy-six*; others, *about seventy-six*
[b] Gk *place of two seas*   [c] Gk *brothers*

of Ap'pi·us and Three Taverns to meet us. On seeing them, Paul thanked God and took courage.

16 When we came into Rome, Paul was allowed to live by himself, with the soldier who was guarding him.

Paul and Jewish Leaders in Rome

17 Three days later he called together the local leaders of the Jews. When they had assembled, he said to them, "Brothers, though I had done nothing against our people or the customs of our ancestors, yet I was arrested in Jerusalem and handed over to the Romans. [18] When they had examined me, the Romans[d] wanted to release me, because there was no reason for the death penalty in my case. [19] But when the Jews objected, I was compelled to appeal to the emperor— even though I had no charge to bring against my nation. [20] For this reason therefore I have asked to see you and speak with you,[e] since it is for the sake of the hope of Israel that I am bound with this chain." [21] They replied, "We have received no letters from Judea about you, and none of the brothers coming here has reported or spoken anything evil about you. [22] But we would like to hear from you what you think, for with regard to this sect we know that everywhere it is spoken against."

Paul Preaches in Rome
(Isa 6.9–10)

23 After they had set a day to meet with him, they came to him at his lodgings in great numbers. From morning until evening he explained the matter to them, testifying to the kingdom of God and trying to convince them about Jesus both from the law of Moses and from the prophets. [24] Some were convinced by what he had said, while others refused to believe. [25] So they disagreed with each other; and as they were leaving, Paul made one further statement: "The Holy Spirit was right in saying to your ancestors through the prophet I·sai'ah,

26 'Go to this people and say,
  You will indeed listen, but never understand,
    and you will indeed look, but never perceive.
27 For this people's heart has grown dull,
    and their ears are hard of hearing,
      and they have shut their eyes;
    so that they might not look with their eyes,
  and listen with their ears,
  and understand with their heart and turn—
    and I would heal them.'

[28] Let it be known to you then that this salvation of God has been sent to the Gentiles; they will listen."[f]

30 He lived there two whole years at his own expense[g] and welcomed all who came to him, [31] proclaiming the kingdom of God and teaching about the Lord Jesus Christ with all boldness and without hindrance.

[d] Gk they   [e] Or I have asked you to see me and speak with me   [f] Other ancient authorities add verse 29, And when he had said these words, the Jews departed, arguing vigorously among themselves   [g] Or in his own hired dwelling

Pauline and Other Letters

P aul's letters are the oldest Christian documents we have. The first of them was written within 25 years of Jesus' death, and the last may have been written before any of the gospels. These letters are also the largest collection of writings by any one person in the New Testament. They are in order of length, with the longest letter to a church first, and the letters to individuals last.

We can learn from Paul's letters a great deal about Paul's faith and his understanding of what Jesus Christ means for the life of the ordinary Christian. We can learn some of the problems that churches and persons were facing because of their faith and what Paul said was an answer to the problem. We can learn a lot about Paul as a person and how his faith can help us as persons.

Romans was written to pave the way for Paul's visit to a church he had never seen, but whose help he needed as he began to preach the gospel in the western Mediterranean world. Romans is one of the fullest statements of Paul's faith. He tries to show how Christianity is rooted in Judaism, but is a faith for all of humanity. Romans is a book full of the power and grace of God and has been a source of inspiration and renewal in the church from earliest times to the present.

1 and 2 Corinthians are the most typical of Paul's letters. They were written in response to specific concerns, in this case division in the church and how Christians are called to live a way of life different from pagans. 1 Corinthians has great sections on love in the church (12—14) and the resurrection (15). The accounts of the resurrection and of the Last Supper in 1 Corinthians are the oldest written accounts of those events we have. 2 Corinthians is a combination of harsh differences and rejoicing over reconciliation. Because of the differences in tone, many scholars believe that parts of at least two letters are in our present 2 Corinthians. Chapters 3—5 are a meditation on what it means to be an apostle.

Galatians contains important information about Paul's own life and about the beginnings of the church. It is also a key to understanding Paul's faith in Christ, justification, and the relationship between Judaism and Christianity.

Ephesians is a meditation on the purpose of God in reconciling all things in Christ. The church is a part of the purpose of God, called to bring unity to the world, as Christ brought unity to the church.

Philippians is a warm, personal letter giving thanks for a gift from the church and encouraging the church to be faithful. The hymn quoted in 2:5–11 is a powerful statement about Christ coming into the world for salvation.

Colossians was a church confused by false teaching. Paul wrote to try to straighten out that confusion. He says that Christ is the ruling power in the universe. He also gives guidance for the true spiritual life.

1 and 2 Thessalonians are possibly the earliest writings of the New Testament. Persecution had compelled Paul to leave Thessalonica, and in his letters he tells Christians there how they ought to live, and to await the Lord's return with constant diligence.

1 and 2 Timothy and **Titus** are known as the "Pastoral Epistles", since they are concerned about the care of the church. They reflect the beginnings of organizational life in the church. Paul wants to show how true faith results in a way of life in both the church and the world. There is guidance for the young pastors who are trying to lead the church.

Philemon is the only surviving private letter of Paul. It is a plea for Philemon to forgive the runaway slave Onesimus and receive him back as a brother in Christ.

Hebrews was written to Jewish Christians, saying that Christ is the perfect sacrifice and the true High Priest. Hebrews emphasizes the humanity of Jesus more than any other book in the New Testament, except the gospels. It also emphasizes the role of Jesus as the mediator between God and humanity, the one who brings forgiveness once and for all.

The Letter of Paul to the

ROMANS

Salutation

1 Paul, a servant[a] of Jesus Christ, called to be an apostle, set apart for the gospel of God, 2 which he promised beforehand through his prophets in the holy scriptures, 3 the gospel concerning his Son, who was descended from David according to the flesh 4 and was declared to be Son of God with power according to the spirit[b] of holiness by resurrection from the dead, Jesus Christ our Lord, 5 through whom we have received grace and apostleship to bring about the obedience of faith among all the Gentiles for the sake of his name, 6 including yourselves who are called to belong to Jesus Christ,

7 To all God's beloved in Rome, who are called to be saints:

Grace to you and peace from God our Father and the Lord Jesus Christ.

Prayer of Thanksgiving

8 First, I thank my God through Jesus Christ for all of you, because your faith is proclaimed throughout the world. 9 For God, whom I serve with my spirit by announcing the gospel[c] of his Son, is my witness that without ceasing I remember you always in my prayers, 10 asking that by God's will I may somehow at last succeed in coming to you. 11 For I am longing to see you so that I may share with you some spiritual gift to strengthen you— 12 or rather so that we may be mutually encouraged by each other's faith, both yours and mine. 13 I want you to know, brothers and sisters,[d] that I have often intended to come to you (but thus far have been prevented), in order that I may reap some harvest among you as I have among the rest of the Gentiles. 14 I am a debtor both to Greeks and to barbarians, both to the wise and to the foolish 15— hence my eagerness to proclaim the gospel to you also who are in Rome.

The Power of the Gospel

16 For I am not ashamed of the gospel; it is the power of God for salvation to everyone who has faith, to the Jew first and also to the Greek. 17 For in it the righteousness of God is revealed through faith for faith; as it is written, "The one who is righteous will live by faith."[e]

The Guilt of Humankind

18 For the wrath of God is revealed from heaven against all ungodliness and wickedness of those who by their wickedness suppress the truth. 19 For what can be known about God is plain to them, because God has shown it to them. 20 Ever since the creation of the world his eternal power and divine nature, invisible though they are, have been understood and seen through the things he has made. So they are without excuse; 21 for though they knew God, they did not honor him as God or give thanks to him, but they became futile in their thinking, and their senseless minds were darkened. 22 Claiming to be wise, they became fools; 23 and they exchanged the glory of the immortal God for images resembling a mortal human being or birds or four-footed animals or reptiles.

24 Therefore God gave them up in the lusts of their hearts to impurity, to the degrading of their bodies among themselves, 25 because they exchanged the truth about God for a lie and worshiped and served the creature rather than the Creator, who is blessed forever! Amen.

26 For this reason God gave them up to degrading passions. Their women exchanged natural intercourse for unnatural, 27 and in the same way also the men, giving up natural inter-

---

[a] Gk slave   [b] Or Spirit   [c] Gk my spirit in the gospel   [d] Gk brothers   [e] Or The one who is righteous through faith will live

course with women, were consumed with passion for one another. Men committed shameless acts with men and received in their own persons the due penalty for their error.

28 And since they did not see fit to acknowledge God, God gave them up to a debased mind and to things that should not be done. 29 They were filled with every kind of wickedness, evil, covetousness, malice. Full of envy, murder, strife, deceit, craftiness, they are gossips, 30 slanderers, God-haters,*f* insolent, haughty, boastful, inventors of evil, rebellious toward parents, 31 foolish, faithless, heartless, ruthless. 32 They know God's decree, that those who practice such things deserve to die—yet they not only do them but even applaud others who practice them.

The Righteous Judgment of God

2 Therefore you have no excuse, whoever you are, when you judge others; for in passing judgment on another you condemn yourself, because you, the judge, are doing the very same things. 2 You say,*g* "We know that God's judgment on those who do such things is in accordance with truth." 3 Do you imagine, whoever you are, that when you judge those who do such things and yet do them yourself, you will escape the judgment of God? 4 Or do you despise the riches of his kindness and forbearance and patience? Do you not realize that God's kindness is meant to lead you to repentance? 5 But by your hard and impenitent heart you are storing up wrath for yourself on the day of wrath, when God's righteous judgment will be revealed. 6 For he will repay according to each one's deeds: 7 to those who by patiently doing good seek for glory and honor and immortality, he will give eternal life; 8 while for those who are self-seeking and who obey not the truth but wickedness, there will be wrath and fury. 9 There will be anguish and distress for everyone who does evil, the Jew first and also the Greek, 10 but glory and honor and peace for everyone who does good, the Jew first and also the Greek. 11 For God shows no partiality.

12 All who have sinned apart from the law will also perish apart from the law, and all who have sinned under the law will be judged by the law. 13 For it is not the hearers of the law who are

righteous in God's sight, but the doers of the law who will be justified. 14 When Gentiles, who do not possess the law, do instinctively what the law requires, these, though not having the law, are a law to themselves. 15 They show that what the law requires is written on their hearts, to which their own conscience also bears witness; and their conflicting thoughts will accuse or perhaps excuse them 16 on the day when, according to my gospel, God, through Jesus Christ, will judge the secret thoughts of all.

The Jews and the Law

17 But if you call yourself a Jew and rely on the law and boast of your relation to God 18 and know his will and determine what is best because you are instructed in the law, 19 and if you are sure that you are a guide to the blind, a light to those who are in darkness, 20 a corrector of the foolish, a teacher of children, having in the law the embodiment of knowledge and truth, 21 you, then, that teach others, will you not teach yourself? While you preach against stealing, do you steal? 22 You that forbid adultery, do you commit adultery? You that abhor idols, do you rob temples? 23 You that boast in the law, do you dishonor God by breaking the law? 24 For, as it is written, "The name of God is blasphemed among the Gentiles because of you."

25 Circumcision indeed is of value if you obey the law; but if you break the law, your circumcision has become uncircumcision. 26 So, if those who are uncircumcised keep the requirements of the law, will not their uncircumcision be regarded as circumcision? 27 Then those who are physically uncircumcised but keep the law will condemn you that have the written code and circumcision but break the law. 28 For a person is not a Jew who is one outwardly, nor is true circumcision something external and physical. 29 Rather, a person is a Jew who is one inwardly, and real circumcision is a matter of the heart—it is spiritual and not literal. Such a person receives praise not from others but from God.

3 Then what advantage has the Jew? Or what is the value of circumcision? 2 Much, in every way. For

f Or *God-hated*   *g* Gk lacks *You say*

R O M A N S

in the first place the Jews[h] were entrusted with the oracles of God. [3]What if some were unfaithful? Will their faithlessness nullify the faithfulness of God? [4]By no means! Although everyone is a liar, let God be proved true, as it is written,

"So that you may be justified in
  your words,
  and prevail in your judging."[i]

[5]But if our injustice serves to confirm the justice of God, what should we say? That God is unjust to inflict wrath on us? (I speak in a human way.) [6]By no means! For then how could God judge the world? [7]But if through my falsehood God's truthfulness abounds to his glory, why am I still being condemned as a sinner? [8]And why not say (as some people slander us by saying that we say), "Let us do evil so that good may come"? Their condemnation is deserved!

None Is Righteous
(Ps 14.1–3; 53.1–4)

[9]What then? Are we any better off?[j] No, not at all; for we have already charged that all, both Jews and Greeks, are under the power of sin, [10]as it is written:

"There is no one who is
  righteous, not even one;
[11] there is no one who has
    understanding,
  there is no one who seeks
    God.
[12] All have turned aside, together
    they have become
    worthless;
  there is no one who shows
    kindness,
  there is not even one."
[13] "Their throats are opened
    graves;
  they use their tongues to
    deceive."
  "The venom of vipers is under
    their lips."
[14] "Their mouths are full of
    cursing and bitterness."
[15] "Their feet are swift to shed
    blood;
[16] ruin and misery are in their
    paths,
[17] and the way of peace they have
    not known."
[18] "There is no fear of God
    before their eyes."

[19]Now we know that whatever the law says, it speaks to those who are under the law, so that every mouth may be silenced, and the whole world may be held accountable to God. [20]For "no human being will be justified in his sight" by deeds prescribed by the law, for through the law comes the knowledge of sin.

Righteousness through Faith

[21]But now, apart from law, the righteousness of God has been disclosed, and is attested by the law and the prophets, [22]the righteousness of God through faith in Jesus Christ[k] for all who believe. For there is no distinction, [23]since all have sinned and fall short of the glory of God; [24]they are now justified by his grace as a gift, through the redemption that is in Christ Jesus, [25]whom God put forward as a sacrifice of atonement[l] by his blood, effective through faith. He did this to show his righteousness, because in his divine forbearance he had passed over the sins previously committed; [26]it was to prove at the present time that he himself is righteous and that he justifies the one who has faith in Jesus.[m]

[27]Then what becomes of boasting? It is excluded. By what law? By that of works? No, but by the law of faith. [28]For we hold that a person is justified by faith apart from works prescribed by the law. [29]Or is God the God of Jews only? Is he not the God of Gentiles also? Yes, of Gentiles also, [30]since God is one; and he will justify the circumcised on the ground of faith and the uncircumcised through that same faith. [31]Do we then overthrow the law by this faith? By no means! On the contrary, we uphold the law.

The Example of Abraham
(Gen 17.10)

4 What then are we to say was gained by[n] Abraham, our ancestor according to the flesh? [2]For if Abraham was justified by works, he has something to boast about, but not before God. [3]For what does the scripture say? "Abraham believed God, and it was reckoned to him as righteousness." [4]Now to one who works, wages are not reckoned as a gift but as some-

---

[h]Gk they [i]Gk when you are being judged [j]Or at any disadvantage? [k]Or through the faith of Jesus Christ [l]Or a place of atonement [m]Or who has the faith of Jesus [n]Other ancient authorities read say about

thing due. [5] But to one who without works trusts him who justifies the ungodly, such faith is reckoned as righteousness. [6] So also David speaks of the blessedness of those to whom God reckons righteousness apart from works:

[7] "Blessed are those whose
    iniquities are forgiven,
and whose sins are covered;
[8] blessed is the one against whom
    the Lord will not reckon
    sin."

[9] Is this blessedness, then, pronounced only on the circumcised, or also on the uncircumcised? We say, "Faith was reckoned to Abraham as righteousness." [10] How then was it reckoned to him? Was it before or after he had been circumcised? It was not after, but before he was circumcised. [11] He received the sign of circumcision as a seal of the righteousness that he had by faith while he was still uncircumcised. The purpose was to make him the ancestor of all who believe without being circumcised and who thus have righteousness reckoned to them, [12] and likewise the ancestor of the circumcised who are not only circumcised but who also follow the example of the faith that our ancestor Abraham had before he was circumcised.

God's Promise Realized through Faith

[13] For the promise that he would inherit the world did not come to Abraham or to his descendants through the law but through the righteousness of faith. [14] If it is the adherents of the law who are to be the heirs, faith is null and the promise is void. [15] For the law brings wrath; but where there is no law, neither is there violation.

[16] For this reason it depends on faith, in order that the promise may rest on grace and be guaranteed to all his descendants, not only to the adherents of the law but also to those who share the faith of Abraham (for he is the father of all of us, [17] as it is written, "I have made you the father of many nations")—in the presence of the God in whom he believed, who gives life to the dead and calls into existence the things that do not exist. [18] Hoping against hope, he believed that he would become "the father of many nations," according to what was said, "So numerous shall your descendants be." [19] He did not weaken in faith when he

considered his own body, which was already[o] as good as dead (for he was about a hundred years old), or when he considered the barrenness of Sarah's womb. [20] No distrust made him waver concerning the promise of God, but he grew strong in his faith as he gave glory to God, [21] being fully convinced that God was able to do what he had promised. [22] Therefore his faith[p] "was reckoned to him as righteousness." [23] Now the words, "it was reckoned to him," were written not for his sake alone, [24] but for ours also. It will be reckoned to us who believe in him who raised Jesus our Lord from the dead, [25] who was handed over to death for our trespasses and was raised for our justification.

Results of Justification

5 Therefore, since we are justified by faith, we[q] have peace with God through our Lord Jesus Christ, [2] through whom we have obtained access[r] to this grace in which we stand; and we[s] boast in our hope of sharing the glory of God. [3] And not only that, but we[s] also boast in our sufferings, knowing that suffering produces endurance, [4] and endurance produces character, and character produces hope, [5] and hope does not disappoint us, because God's love has been poured into our hearts through the Holy Spirit that has been given to us.

[6] For while we were still weak, at the right time Christ died for the ungodly. [7] Indeed, rarely will anyone die for a righteous person—though perhaps for a good person someone might actually dare to die. [8] But God proves his love for us in that while we still were sinners Christ died for us. [9] Much more surely then, now that we have been justified by his blood, will we be saved through him from the wrath of God.[t] [10] For if while we were enemies, we were reconciled to God through the death of his Son, much more surely, having been reconciled, will we be saved by his life. [11] But more than that, we even boast in God through our Lord Jesus Christ, through whom we have now received reconciliation.

o Other ancient authorities lack *already*
p Gk *Therefore it* q Other ancient authorities read *let us* r Other ancient authorities add *by faith* s Or *let us*
t Gk *the wrath*

Adam and Christ
(Gen 3.1–19)

12 Therefore, just as sin came into the world through one man, and death came through sin, and so death spread to all because all have sinned— 13 sin was indeed in the world before the law, but sin is not reckoned when there is no law. 14 Yet death exercised dominion from Adam to Moses, even over those whose sins were not like the transgression of Adam, who is a type of the one who was to come.

15 But the free gift is not like the trespass. For if the many died through the one man's trespass, much more surely have the grace of God and the free gift in the grace of the one man, Jesus Christ, abounded for the many. 16 And the free gift is not like the effect of the one man's sin. For the judgment following one trespass brought condemnation, but the free gift following many trespasses brings justification. 17 If, because of the one man's trespass, death exercised dominion through that one, much more surely will those who receive the abundance of grace and the free gift of righteousness exercise dominion in life through the one man, Jesus Christ.

18 Therefore just as one man's trespass led to condemnation for all, so one man's act of righteousness leads to justification and life for all. 19 For just as by the one man's disobedience the many were made sinners, so by the one man's obedience the many will be made righteous. 20 But law came in, with the result that the trespass multiplied; but where sin increased, grace abounded all the more, 21 so that, just as sin exercised dominion in death, so grace might also exercise dominion through justification[u] leading to eternal life through Jesus Christ our Lord.

Dying and Rising with Christ

6 What then are we to say? Should we continue in sin in order that grace may abound? 2 By no means! How can we who died to sin go on living in it? 3 Do you not know that all of us who have been baptized into Christ Jesus were baptized into his death? 4 Therefore we have been buried with him by baptism into death, so that, just as Christ was raised from the dead by the glory of the Father, so we too might walk in newness of life.

5 For if we have been united with him in a death like his, we will certainly be united with him in a resurrection like his. 6 We know that our old self was crucified with him so that the body of sin might be destroyed, and we might no longer be enslaved to sin. 7 For whoever has died is freed from sin. 8 But if we have died with Christ, we believe that we will also live with him. 9 We know that Christ, being raised from the dead, will never die again; death no longer has dominion over him. 10 The death he died, he died to sin, once for all; but the life he lives, he lives to God. 11 So you also must consider yourselves dead to sin and alive to God in Christ Jesus.

12 Therefore, do not let sin exercise dominion in your mortal bodies, to make you obey their passions. 13 No longer present your members to sin as instruments[v] of wickedness, but present yourselves to God as those who have been brought from death to life, and present your members to God as instruments[v] of righteousness. 14 For sin will have no dominion over you, since you are not under law but under grace.

Slaves of Righteousness

15 What then? Should we sin because we are not under law but under grace? By no means! 16 Do you not know that if you present yourselves to anyone as obedient slaves, you are slaves of the one whom you obey, either of sin, which leads to death, or of obedience, which leads to righteousness? 17 But thanks be to God that you, having once been slaves of sin, have become obedient from the heart to the form of teaching to which you were entrusted, 18 and that you, having been set free from sin, have become slaves of righteousness. 19 I am speaking in human terms because of your natural limitations.[w] For just as you once presented your members as slaves to impurity and to greater and greater iniquity, so now present your members as slaves to righteousness for sanctification.

20 When you were slaves of sin, you were free in regard to righteousness. 21 So what advantage did you then get from the things of which you now are ashamed? The end of those things is death. 22 But now that you have been

---

u Or *righteousness*   v Or *weapons*
w Gk *the weakness of your flesh*

freed from sin and enslaved to God, the advantage you get is sanctification. The end is eternal life. [23] For the wages of sin is death, but the free gift of God is eternal life in Christ Jesus our Lord.

An Analogy from Marriage

7 Do you not know, brothers and sisters[x]—for I am speaking to those who know the law—that the law is binding on a person only during that person's lifetime? [2] Thus a married woman is bound by the law to her husband as long as he lives; but if her husband dies, she is discharged from the law concerning the husband. [3] Accordingly, she will be called an adulteress if she lives with another man while her husband is alive. But if her husband dies, she is free from that law, and if she marries another man, she is not an adulteress.

[4] In the same way, my friends,[x] you have died to the law through the body of Christ, so that you may belong to another, to him who has been raised from the dead in order that we may bear fruit for God. [5] While we were living in the flesh, our sinful passions, aroused by the law, were at work in our members to bear fruit for death. [6] But now we are discharged from the law, dead to that which held us captive, so that we are slaves not under the old written code but in the new life of the Spirit.

The Law and Sin

[7] What then should we say? That the law is sin? By no means! Yet, if it had not been for the law, I would not have known sin. I would not have known what it is to covet if the law had not said, "You shall not covet." [8] But sin, seizing an opportunity in the commandment, produced in me all kinds of covetousness. Apart from the law sin lies dead. [9] I was once alive apart from the law, but when the commandment came, sin revived [10] and I died, and the very commandment that promised life proved to be death to me. [11] For sin, seizing an opportunity in the commandment, deceived me and through it killed me. [12] So the law is holy, and the commandment is holy and just and good.

[13] Did what is good, then, bring death to me? By no means! It was sin, working death in me through what is good, in order that sin might be shown to be sin, and through the command-ment might become sinful beyond measure.

The Inner Conflict

[14] For we know that the law is spiri-tual; but I am of the flesh, sold into slavery under sin.[y] [15] I do not under-stand my own actions. For I do not do what I want, but I do the very thing I hate. [16] Now if I do what I do not want, I agree that the law is good. [17] But in fact it is no longer I that do it, but sin that dwells within me. [18] For I know that nothing good dwells within me, that is, in my flesh. I can will what is right, but I cannot do it. [19] For I do not do the good I want, but the evil I do not want is what I do. [20] Now if I do what I do not want, it is no longer I that do it, but sin that dwells within me.

[21] So I find it to be a law that when I want to do what is good, evil lies close at hand. [22] For I delight in the law of God in my inmost self, [23] but I see in my members another law at war with the law of my mind, making me captive to the law of sin that dwells in my mem-bers. [24] Wretched man that I am! Who will rescue me from this body of death? [25] Thanks be to God through Jesus Christ our Lord!

So then, with my mind I am a slave to the law of God, but with my flesh I am a slave to the law of sin.

Life in the Spirit

8 There is therefore now no con-demnation for those who are in Christ Jesus. [2] For the law of the Spirit[z] of life in Christ Jesus has set you[a] free from the law of sin and of death. [3] For God has done what the law, weakened by the flesh, could not do: by sending his own Son in the like-ness of sinful flesh, and to deal with sin,[b] he condemned sin in the flesh, [4] so that the just requirement of the law might be fulfilled in us, who walk not according to the flesh but according to the Spirit.[z] [5] For those who live ac-cording to the flesh set their minds on the things of the flesh, but those who live according to the Spirit[z] set their minds on the things of the Spirit.[z] [6] To set the mind on the flesh is death, but to set the mind on the Spirit[z] is life and

x Gk brothers   y Gk sold under sin
z Or spirit   a Here the Greek word you is singular number; other ancient authorities read me or us   b Or and as a sin offering

peace. [7] For this reason the mind that is set on the flesh is hostile to God; it does not submit to God's law—indeed it cannot, [8] and those who are in the flesh cannot please God.

9 But you are not in the flesh; you are in the Spirit,[c] since the Spirit of God dwells in you. Anyone who does not have the Spirit of Christ does not belong to him. [10] But if Christ is in you, though the body is dead because of sin, the Spirit[c] is life because of righteousness. [11] If the Spirit of him who raised Jesus from the dead dwells in you, he who raised Christ[d] from the dead will give life to your mortal bodies also through[e] his Spirit that dwells in you.

12 So then, brothers and sisters,[f] we are debtors, not to the flesh, to live according to the flesh— [13] for if you live according to the flesh, you will die; but if by the Spirit you put to death the deeds of the body, you will live. [14] For all who are led by the Spirit of God are children of God. [15] For you did not receive a spirit of slavery to fall back into fear, but you have received a spirit of adoption. When we cry, "Abba![g] Father!" [16] it is that very Spirit bearing witness[h] with our spirit that we are children of God, [17] and if children, then heirs, heirs of God and joint heirs with Christ—if, in fact, we suffer with him so that we may also be glorified with him.

Future Glory

18 I consider that the sufferings of this present time are not worth comparing with the glory about to be revealed to us. [19] For the creation waits with eager longing for the revealing of the children of God; [20] for the creation was subjected to futility, not of its own will but by the will of the one who subjected it, in hope [21] that the creation itself will be set free from its bondage to decay and will obtain the freedom of the glory of the children of God. [22] We know that the whole creation has been groaning in labor pains until now; [23] and not only the creation, but we ourselves, who have the first fruits of the Spirit, groan inwardly while we wait for adoption, the redemption of our bodies. [24] For in[i] hope we were saved. Now hope that is seen is not hope. For who hopes[j] for what is seen? [25] But if we hope for what we do not see, we wait for it with patience.

26 Likewise the Spirit helps us in our weakness; for we do not know how to pray as we ought, but that very Spirit intercedes[k] with sighs too deep for words. [27] And God,[l] who searches the heart, knows what is the mind of the Spirit, because the Spirit[m] intercedes for the saints according to the will of God.[n]

28 We know that all things work together for good[o] for those who love God, who are called according to his purpose. [29] For those whom he foreknew he also predestined to be conformed to the image of his Son, in order that he might be the firstborn within a large family.[p] [30] And those whom he predestined he also called; and those whom he called he also justified; and those whom he justified he also glorified.

God's Love in Christ Jesus

31 What then are we to say about these things? If God is for us, who is against us? [32] He who did not withhold his own Son, but gave him up for all of us, will he not with him also give us everything else? [33] Who will bring any charge against God's elect? It is God who justifies. [34] Who is to condemn? It is Christ Jesus, who died, yes, who was raised, who is at the right hand of God, who indeed intercedes for us.[q] [35] Who will separate us from the love of Christ? Will hardship, or distress, or persecution, or famine, or nakedness, or peril, or sword? [36] As it is written,

"For your sake we are being
killed all day long;
we are accounted as sheep to
be slaughtered."

[37] No, in all these things we are more than conquerors through him who loved us. [38] For I am convinced that neither death, nor life, nor angels, nor rulers, nor things present, nor things to come, nor powers, [39] nor height, nor

c Or *spirit*   d Other ancient authorities read *the Christ* or *Christ Jesus* or *Jesus Christ*   e Other ancient authorities read *on account of*   f Gk *brothers*   g Aramaic for *Father*   h Or [15] *a spirit of adoption, by which we cry, "Abba! Father!"* [16] *The Spirit itself bears witness*   i Or *by*   j Other ancient authorities read *awaits*   k Other ancient authorities add *for us*   l Gk *the one*   m Gk *he* or *it*   n Gk *according to God*   o Other ancient authorities read *God makes all things work together for good*, or *in all things God works for good*   p Gk *among many brothers*   q Or *Is it Christ Jesus . . . for us?*

depth, nor anything else in all creation, will be able to separate us from the love of God in Christ Jesus our Lord.

God's Election of Israel
(Gen 25.19–23)

9 I am speaking the truth in Christ— I am not lying; my conscience confirms it by the Holy Spirit— ²I have great sorrow and unceasing anguish in my heart. ³For I could wish that I myself were accursed and cut off from Christ for the sake of my own people,*r* my kindred according to the flesh. ⁴They are Israelites, and to them belong the adoption, the glory, the covenants, the giving of the law, the worship, and the promises; ⁵to them belong the patriarchs, and from them, according to the flesh, comes the Messiah,*s* who is over all, God blessed forever.*t* Amen.

6 It is not as though the word of God had failed. For not all Israelites truly belong to Israel, ⁷and not all of Abraham's children are his true descendants; but "It is through Isaac that descendants shall be named for you." ⁸This means that it is not the children of the flesh who are the children of God, but the children of the promise are counted as descendants. ⁹For this is what the promise said, "About this time I will return and Sarah shall have a son." ¹⁰Nor is that all; something similar happened to Rebecca when she had conceived children by one husband, our ancestor Isaac. ¹¹Even before they had been born or had done anything good or bad (so that God's purpose of election might continue, ¹²not by works but by his call) she was told, "The elder shall serve the younger." ¹³As it is written,

"I have loved Jacob,
but I have hated Esau."

14 What then are we to say? Is there injustice on God's part? By no means! ¹⁵For he says to Moses,

"I will have mercy on whom I
have mercy,
and I will have compassion on
whom I have compassion."

¹⁶So it depends not on human will or exertion, but on God who shows mercy. ¹⁷For the scripture says to Pharaoh, "I have raised you up for the very purpose of showing my power in you, so that my name may be proclaimed in all the earth." ¹⁸So then he has mercy on whomever he chooses, and he hardens the heart of whomever he chooses.

God's Wrath and Mercy

19 You will say to me then, "Why then does he still find fault? For who can resist his will?" ²⁰But who indeed are you, a human being, to argue with God? Will what is molded say to the one who molds it, "Why have you made me like this?" ²¹Has the potter no right over the clay, to make out of the same lump one object for special use and another for ordinary use? ²²What if God, desiring to show his wrath and to make known his power, has endured with much patience the objects of wrath that are made for destruction; ²³and what if he has done so in order to make known the riches of his glory for the objects of mercy, which he has prepared beforehand for glory— ²⁴including us whom he has called, not from the Jews only but also from the Gentiles? ²⁵As indeed he says in Hō·sē'a,

"Those who were not my people
I will call 'my people,'
and her who was not beloved I
will call 'beloved.' "

26 "And in the very place where it
was said to them, 'You are
not my people,'
there they shall be called
children of the living God."

27 And Ī·sāi'ah cries out concerning Israel, "Though the number of the children of Israel were like the sand of the sea, only a remnant of them will be saved; ²⁸for the Lord will execute his sentence on the earth quickly and decisively."*u* ²⁹And as Ī·sāi'ah predicted,

"If the Lord of hosts had not left
survivors*v* to us,
we would have fared like
Sod'om
and been made like
Go·mor'rah."

Israel's Unbelief

30 What then are we to say? Gen-

---

r Gk *my brothers*   *s* Or *the Christ*
t Or *Messiah, who is God over all,*
*blessed forever; or Messiah. May he who
is God over all be blessed forever*
u Other ancient authorities read *for he
will finish his work and cut it short in
righteousness, because the Lord will
make the sentence shortened on the
earth*   *v* Or *descendants; Gk seed*

tiles, who did not strive for righteousness, have attained it, that is, righteousness through faith; 31 but Israel, who did strive for the righteousness that is based on the law, did not succeed in fulfilling that law. 32 Why not? Because they did not strive for it on the basis of faith, but as if it were based on works. They have stumbled over the stumbling stone, 33 as it is written,

"See, I am laying in Zion a stone
     that will make people
     stumble, a rock that will
     make them fall,
and whoever believes in him w
     will not be put to shame."

10 Brothers and sisters, x my heart's desire and prayer to God for them is that they may be saved. 2 I can testify that they have a zeal for God, but it is not enlightened. 3 For, being ignorant of the righteousness that comes from God, and seeking to establish their own, they have not submitted to God's righteousness. 4 For Christ is the end of the law so that there may be righteousness for everyone who believes.

Salvation Is for All

5 Moses writes concerning the righteousness that comes from the law, that "the person who does these things will live by them." 6 But the righteousness that comes from faith says, "Do not say in your heart, 'Who will ascend into heaven?' " (that is, to bring Christ down) 7 "or 'Who will descend into the abyss?' " (that is, to bring Christ up from the dead). 8 But what does it say?

"The word is near you,
     on your lips and in your heart"
(that is, the word of faith that we proclaim); 9 because y if you confess with your lips that Jesus is Lord and believe in your heart that God raised him from the dead, you will be saved. 10 For one believes with the heart and so is justified, and one confesses with the mouth and so is saved. 11 The scripture says, "No one who believes in him will be put to shame." 12 For there is no distinction between Jew and Greek; the same Lord is Lord of all and is generous to all who call on him. 13 For, "Everyone who calls on the name of the Lord shall be saved."

14 But how are they to call on one in whom they have not believed? And how are they to believe in one of whom they have never heard? And how are they to hear without someone to pro-

claim him? 15 And how are they to proclaim him unless they are sent? As it is written, "How beautiful are the feet of those who bring good news!" 16 But not all have obeyed the good news; z for I·sāi′ah says, "Lord, who has believed our message?" 17 So faith comes from what is heard, and what is heard comes through the word of Christ. a

18 But I ask, have they not heard? Indeed they have; for

"Their voice has gone out to all
     the earth,
and their words to the ends of
     the world."

19 Again I ask, did Israel not understand? First Moses says,

"I will make you jealous of those
     who are not a nation;
with a foolish nation I will
     make you angry."

20 Then I·sāi′ah is so bold as to say,

"I have been found by those who
     did not seek me;
I have shown myself to those
     who did not ask for me."

21 But of Israel he says, "All day long I have held out my hands to a disobedient and contrary people."

Israel's Rejection Is Not Final
(Cp Ps 69.22–23; Isa 29.10)

11 I ask, then, has God rejected his people? By no means! I myself am an Israelite, a descendant of Abraham, a member of the tribe of Benjamin. 2 God has not rejected his people whom he foreknew. Do you not know what the scripture says of E·lī′jah, how he pleads with God against Israel? 3 "Lord, they have killed your prophets, they have demolished your altars; I alone am left, and they are seeking my life." 4 But what is the divine reply to him? "I have kept for myself seven thousand who have not bowed the knee to Ba′al." 5 So too at the present time there is a remnant, chosen by grace. 6 But if it is by grace, it is no longer on the basis of works, otherwise grace would no longer be grace. b

7 What then? Israel failed to obtain what it was seeking. The elect ob-

w Or *trusts in it*   x Gk *Brothers*
y Or *namely, that*   z Or *gospel*
a Or *about Christ;* other ancient
authorities read *of God*   b Other
ancient authorities add *But if it is by*
works, it is no longer on the basis of
grace, otherwise work would no longer
be work

tained it, but the rest were hardened, [8] as it is written,

> "God gave them a sluggish spirit,
>   eyes that would not see
>   and ears that would not hear,
>   down to this very day."

[9] And David says,

> "Let their table become a snare
>   and a trap,
>   a stumbling block and a
>   retribution for them;
> [10]   let their eyes be darkened so
>   that they cannot see,
>   and keep their backs forever
>   bent."

The Salvation of the Gentiles

[11] So I ask, have they stumbled so as to fall? By no means! But through their stumbling[c] salvation has come to the Gentiles, so as to make Israel[d] jealous. [12] Now if their stumbling[c] means riches for the world, and if their defeat means riches for Gentiles, how much more will their full inclusion mean!

[13] Now I am speaking to you Gentiles. Inasmuch then as I am an apostle to the Gentiles, I glorify my ministry [14] in order to make my own people[e] jealous, and thus save some of them. [15] For if their rejection is the reconciliation of the world, what will their acceptance be but life from the dead! [16] If the part of the dough offered as first fruits is holy, then the whole batch is holy; and if the root is holy, then the branches also are holy.

[17] But if some of the branches were broken off, and you, a wild olive shoot, were grafted in their place to share the rich root[f] of the olive tree, [18] do not boast over the branches. If you do boast, remember that it is not you that support the root, but the root that supports you. [19] You will say, "Branches were broken off so that I might be grafted in." [20] That is true. They were broken off because of their unbelief, but you stand only through faith. So do not become proud, but stand in awe. [21] For if God did not spare the natural branches, perhaps he will not spare you.[g] [22] Note then the kindness and the severity of God: severity toward those who have fallen, but God's kindness toward you, provided you continue in his kindness; otherwise you also will be cut off. [23] And even those of Israel,[h] if they do not persist in unbelief, will be grafted in, for God has the power to graft them in again. [24] For if

you have been cut from what is by nature a wild olive tree and grafted, contrary to nature, into a cultivated olive tree, how much more will these natural branches be grafted back into their own olive tree.

All Israel Will Be Saved

[25] So that you may not claim to be wiser than you are, brothers and sisters,[i] I want you to understand this mystery: a hardening has come upon part of Israel, until the full number of the Gentiles has come in. [26] And so all Israel will be saved; as it is written,

> "Out of Zion will come the
>   Deliverer;
>   he will banish ungodliness
>   from Jacob."
> [27] "And this is my covenant with
>   them,
>   when I take away their sins."

[28] As regards the gospel they are enemies of God[j] for your sake; but as regards election they are beloved, for the sake of their ancestors; [29] for the gifts and the calling of God are irrevocable. [30] Just as you were once disobedient to God but have now received mercy because of their disobedience, [31] so they have now been disobedient in order that, by the mercy shown to you, they too may now[k] receive mercy. [32] For God has imprisoned all in disobedience so that he may be merciful to all.

[33] O the depth of the riches and wisdom and knowledge of God! How unsearchable are his judgments and how inscrutable his ways!

> [34] "For who has known the mind of
>   the Lord?
>   Or who has been his
>   counselor?"
> [35] "Or who has given a gift to him,
>   to receive a gift in return?"

[36] For from him and through him and to him are all things. To him be the glory forever. Amen.

The New Life in Christ

12 I appeal to you therefore, brothers and sisters,[i] by the mercies of God, to present your bodies as a living sacrifice, holy and acceptable to

---

[c] Gk transgression   [d] Gk them
[e] Gk my flesh   [f] Other ancient authorities read the richness   [g] Other ancient authorities read neither will he spare you   [h] Gk lacks of Israel
[i] Gk brothers   [j] Gk lacks of God
[k] Other ancient authorities lack now

God, which is your spiritual[l] worship. [2]Do not be conformed to this world,[m] but be transformed by the renewing of your minds, so that you may discern what is the will of God—what is good and acceptable and perfect.[n]

3 For by the grace given to me I say to everyone among you not to think of yourself more highly than you ought to think, but to think with sober judgment, each according to the measure of faith that God has assigned. [4]For as in one body we have many members, and not all the members have the same function, [5]so we, who are many, are one body in Christ, and individually we are members one of another. [6]We have gifts that differ according to the grace given to us: prophecy, in proportion to faith; [7]ministry, in ministering; the teacher, in teaching; [8]the exhorter, in exhortation; the giver, in generosity; the leader, in diligence; the compassionate, in cheerfulness.

Marks of the True Christian

9 Let love be genuine; hate what is evil, hold fast to what is good; [10]love one another with mutual affection; outdo one another in showing honor. [11]Do not lag in zeal, be ardent in spirit, serve the Lord.[o] [12]Rejoice in hope, be patient in suffering, persevere in prayer. [13]Contribute to the needs of the saints; extend hospitality to strangers.

14 Bless those who persecute you; bless and do not curse them. [15]Rejoice with those who rejoice, weep with those who weep. [16]Live in harmony with one another; do not be haughty, but associate with the lowly;[p] do not claim to be wiser than you are. [17]Do not repay anyone evil for evil, but take thought for what is noble in the sight of all. [18]If it is possible, so far as it depends on you, live peaceably with all. [19]Beloved, never avenge yourselves, but leave room for the wrath of God;[q] for it is written, "Vengeance is mine, I will repay, says the Lord." [20]No, "if your enemies are hungry, feed them; if they are thirsty, give them something to drink; for by doing this you will heap burning coals on their heads." [21]Do not be overcome by evil, but overcome evil with good.

Being Subject to Authorities

13 Let every person be subject to the governing authorities; for there is no authority except from God,

and those authorities that exist have been instituted by God. [2]Therefore whoever resists authority resists what God has appointed, and those who resist will incur judgment. [3]For rulers are not a terror to good conduct, but to bad. Do you wish to have no fear of the authority? Then do what is good, and you will receive its approval; [4]for it is God's servant for your good. But if you do what is wrong, you should be afraid, for the authority[r] does not bear the sword in vain! It is the servant of God to execute wrath on the wrongdoer. [5]Therefore one must be subject, not only because of wrath but also because of conscience. [6]For the same reason you also pay taxes, for the authorities are God's servants, busy with this very thing. [7]Pay to all what is due them—taxes to whom taxes are due, revenue to whom revenue is due, respect to whom respect is due, honor to whom honor is due.

Love for One Another
(Cp Mk 12.31; Jas 2.8)

8 Owe no one anything, except to love one another; for the one who loves another has fulfilled the law. [9]The commandments, "You shall not commit adultery; You shall not murder; You shall not steal; You shall not covet"; and any other commandment, are summed up in this word, "Love your neighbor as yourself." [10]Love does no wrong to a neighbor; therefore, love is the fulfilling of the law.

An Urgent Appeal

11 Besides this, you know what time it is, how it is now the moment for you to wake from sleep. For salvation is nearer to us now than when we became believers; [12]the night is far gone, the day is near. Let us then lay aside the works of darkness and put on the armor of light; [13]let us live honorably as in the day, not in reveling and drunkenness, not in debauchery and licentiousness, not in quarreling and jealousy. [14]Instead, put on the Lord Jesus Christ, and make no provision for the flesh, to gratify its desires.

[l]Or *reasonable*   [m]Gk *age*   [n]Or *what is the good and acceptable and perfect will of God*   [o]Other ancient authorities read *serve the opportune time*   [p]Or *give yourselves to humble tasks*   [q]Gk *the wrath*   [r]Gk *it*

Do Not Judge Another

14 Welcome those who are weak in faith,[s] but not for the purpose of quarreling over opinions. [2] Some believe in eating anything, while the weak eat only vegetables. [3] Those who eat must not despise those who abstain, and those who abstain must not pass judgment on those who eat; for God has welcomed them. [4] Who are you to pass judgment on servants of another? It is before their own lord that they stand or fall. And they will be upheld, for the Lord[t] is able to make them stand.

5 Some judge one day to be better than another, while others judge all days to be alike. Let all be fully convinced in their own minds. [6] Those who observe the day, observe it in honor of the Lord. Also those who eat, eat in honor of the Lord, since they give thanks to God; while those who abstain, abstain in honor of the Lord and give thanks to God.

7 We do not live to ourselves, and we do not die to ourselves. [8] If we live, we live to the Lord, and if we die, we die to the Lord; so then, whether we live or whether we die, we are the Lord's. [9] For to this end Christ died and lived again, so that he might be Lord of both the dead and the living.

10 Why do you pass judgment on your brother or sister?[u] Or you, why do you despise your brother or sister?[u] For we will all stand before the judgment seat of God.[v] [11] For it is written,

"As I live, says the Lord, every
    knee shall bow to me,
and every tongue shall give
        praise to[w] God."

[12] So then, each of us will be accountable to God.[x]

Do Not Make Another Stumble

13 Let us therefore no longer pass judgment on one another, but resolve instead never to put a stumbling block or hindrance in the way of another.[y] [14] I know and am persuaded in the Lord Jesus that nothing is unclean in itself; but it is unclean for anyone who thinks it unclean. [15] If your brother or sister[u] is being injured by what you eat, you are no longer walking in love. Do not let what you eat cause the ruin of one for whom Christ died. [16] So do not let your good be spoken of as evil. [17] For the kingdom of God is not food

and drink but righteousness and peace and joy in the Holy Spirit. [18] The one who thus serves Christ is acceptable to God and has human approval. [19] Let us then pursue what makes for peace and for mutual upbuilding. [20] Do not, for the sake of food, destroy the work of God. Everything is indeed clean, but it is wrong for you to make others fall by what you eat; [21] it is good not to eat meat or drink wine or do anything that makes your brother or sister[u] stumble.[z] [22] The faith that you have, have as your own conviction before God. Blessed are those who have no reason to condemn themselves because of what they approve. [23] But those who have doubts are condemned if they eat, because they do not act from faith;[s] for whatever does not proceed from faith[s] is sin.[a]

Please Others, Not Yourselves

15 We who are strong ought to put up with the failings of the weak, and not to please ourselves. [2] Each of us must please our neighbor for the good purpose of building up the neighbor. [3] For Christ did not please himself; but, as it is written, "The insults of those who insult you have fallen on me." [4] For whatever was written in former days was written for our instruction, so that by steadfastness and by the encouragement of the scriptures we might have hope. [5] May the God of steadfastness and encouragement grant you to live in harmony with one another, in accordance with Christ Jesus, [6] so that together you may with one voice glorify the God and Father of our Lord Jesus Christ.

The Gospel for Jews and Gentiles Alike

7 Welcome one another, therefore, just as Christ has welcomed you, for the glory of God. [8] For I tell you that Christ has become a servant of the circumcised on behalf of the truth of God in order that he might confirm the promises given to the patriarchs, [9] and

[s] Or *conviction*   [t] Other ancient authorities read *for God*   [u] Gk *brother*
[v] Other ancient authorities read *of Christ*
[w] Or *confess*   [x] Other ancient authorities lack *to God*   [y] Gk *of a brother*   [z] Other ancient authorities add *or be upset or be weakened*
[a] Other authorities, some ancient, add here 16.25-27

in order that the Gentiles might glorify God for his mercy. As it is written,

"Therefore I will confess[b] you
    among the Gentiles,
and sing praises to your
    name";

10 and again he says,

"Rejoice, O Gentiles, with his
    people";

11 and again,

"Praise the Lord, all you
    Gentiles,
and let all the peoples praise
    him";

12 and again I·sāi'ah says,

"The root of Jesse shall come,
    the one who rises to rule the
        Gentiles;
in him the Gentiles shall hope."

13 May the God of hope fill you with all joy and peace in believing, so that you may abound in hope by the power of the Holy Spirit.

Paul's Reason for Writing So Boldly

14 I myself feel confident about you, my brothers and sisters,[c] that you yourselves are full of goodness, filled with all knowledge, and able to instruct one another. 15 Nevertheless on some points I have written to you rather boldly by way of reminder, because of the grace given me by God 16 to be a minister of Christ Jesus to the Gentiles in the priestly service of the gospel of God, so that the offering of the Gentiles may be acceptable, sanctified by the Holy Spirit. 17 In Christ Jesus, then, I have reason to boast of my work for God. 18 For I will not venture to speak of anything except what Christ has accomplished[d] through me to win obedience from the Gentiles, by word and deed, 19 by the power of signs and wonders, by the power of the Spirit of God,[e] so that from Jerusalem and as far around as Il·lyr'i·cum I have fully proclaimed the good news[f] of Christ. 20 Thus I make it my ambition to proclaim the good news,[f] not where Christ has already been named, so that I do not build on someone else's foundation, 21 but as it is written,

"Those who have never been
    told of him shall see,
and those who have never
    heard of him shall
        understand."

Paul's Plan to Visit Rome

22 This is the reason that I have so often been hindered from coming to you. 23 But now, with no further place for me in these regions, I desire, as I have for many years, to come to you 24 when I go to Spain. For I do hope to see you on my journey and to be sent on by you, once I have enjoyed your company for a little while. 25 At present, however, I am going to Jerusalem in a ministry to the saints; 26 for Mac·e·dō'ni·a and A·chā'i·a have been pleased to share their resources with the poor among the saints at Jerusalem. 27 They were pleased to do this, and indeed they owe it to them; for if the Gentiles have come to share in their spiritual blessings, they ought also to be of service to them in material things. 28 So, when I have completed this, and have delivered to them what has been collected,[g] I will set out by way of you to Spain; 29 and I know that when I come to you, I will come in the fullness of the blessing[h] of Christ.

30 I appeal to you, brothers and sisters,[c] by our Lord Jesus Christ and by the love of the Spirit, to join me in earnest prayer to God on my behalf, 31 that I may be rescued from the unbelievers in Judea, and that my ministry[i] to Jerusalem may be acceptable to the saints, 32 so that by God's will I may come to you with joy and be refreshed in your company. 33 The God of peace be with all of you.[j] Amen.

Personal Greetings

16 I commend to you our sister Phoe'be, a deacon[k] of the church at Cen'chre·ae, 2 so that you may welcome her in the Lord as is fitting for the saints, and help her in whatever she may require from you, for she has been a benefactor of many and of myself as well.

3 Greet Pris'ca and A·qui'la, who work with me in Christ Jesus, 4 and who risked their necks for my life, to whom not only I give thanks, but also all the churches of the Gentiles. 5 Greet

---

b Or *thank*   *c* Gk *brothers*   *d* Gk *speak of those things that Christ has not accomplished*   *e* Other ancient authorities read *of the Spirit* or *of the Holy Spirit*   *f* Or *gospel*   *g* Gk *have sealed to them this fruit*   *h* Other ancient authorities add *of the gospel*   *i* Other ancient authorities read *my bringing of a gift*   *j* One ancient authority adds 16.25-27 here   *k* Or *minister* also the church in their house. Greet my beloved E·paē′ne·tus, who was the first convert[l] in Asia for Christ. [6]Greet Mary, who has worked very hard among you. [7]Greet An·dron′i·cus and Jū′ni·a,[m] my relatives[n] who were in prison with me; they are prominent among the apostles, and they were in Christ before I was. [8]Greet Am·pli·ā′tus, my beloved in the Lord. [9]Greet Ur·bā′nus, our co-worker in Christ, and my beloved Stā′chys. [10]Greet A·pel′lēs, who is approved in Christ. Greet those who belong to the family of Ar·is·tob′ū·lus. [11]Greet my relative[o] He·rō′di·on. Greet those in the Lord who belong to the family of Nar·cis′sus. [12]Greet those workers in the Lord, Trȳ·phaē′na and Trȳ·phō′sa. Greet the beloved Per′sis, who has worked hard in the Lord. [13]Greet Rufus, chosen in the Lord; and greet his mother—a mother to me also. [14]Greet A·syn′cri·tus, Phlē′gon, Her′mēs, Pat′ro·bas, Her′mas, and the brothers and sisters[p] who are with them. [15]Greet Phi·lol′o·gus, Julia, Nē′re·us and his sister, and O·lym′pas, and all the saints who are with them. [16]Greet one another with a holy kiss. All the churches of Christ greet you.

Final Instructions

[17] I urge you, brothers and sisters,[p] to keep an eye on those who cause dissensions and offenses, in opposition to the teaching that you have learned; avoid them. [18]For such people do not serve our Lord Christ, but their own appetites,[q] and by smooth talk and flattery they deceive the hearts of the simple-minded. [19]For while your obedience is known to all, so that I rejoice over you, I want you to be wise in what is good and guileless in what is evil.

[20]The God of peace will shortly crush Satan under your feet. The grace of our Lord Jesus Christ be with you.[r]

[21] Timothy, my co-worker, greets you; so do Lucius and Jason and Sō·sip′a·ter, my relatives.[n]

[22] I Ter′ti·us, the writer of this letter, greet you in the Lord.[s]

[23] Gā′i·us, who is host to me and to the whole church, greets you. E·ras′tus, the city treasurer, and our brother Quar′tus, greet you.[t]

Final Doxology

[25] Now to God[u] who is able to strengthen you according to my gospel and the proclamation of Jesus Christ, according to the revelation of the mystery that was kept secret for long ages [26]but is now disclosed, and through the prophetic writings is made known to all the Gentiles, according to the command of the eternal God, to bring about the obedience of faith— [27]to the only wise God, through Jesus Christ, to whom[v] be the glory forever! Amen.[w]

[l]Gk first fruits   [m]Or Junias; other ancient authorities read Julia   [n]Or compatriots   [o]Or compatriot   [p]Gk brothers   [q]Gk their own belly   [r]Other ancient authorities lack this sentence   [s]Or I Tertius, writing this letter in the Lord, greet you   [t]Other ancient authorities add verse 24, The grace of our Lord Jesus Christ be with all of you. Amen.   [u]Gk the one   [v]Other ancient authorities lack to whom. The verse then reads, to the only wise God be the glory through Jesus Christ forever. Amen.   [w]Other ancient authorities lack 16.25-27 or include it after 14.23 or 15.33; others put verse 24 after verse 27

The First Letter of Paul to the

CORINTHIANS

Salutation

1 Paul, called to be an apostle of Christ Jesus by the will of God, and our brother Sos′the·nēs,

[2] To the church of God that is in Corinth, to those who are sanctified in Christ Jesus, called to be saints, together with all those who in every place call on the name of our Lord

Jesus Christ, both their Lord*a* and ours:

3 Grace to you and peace from God our Father and the Lord Jesus Christ.

4 I give thanks to my*b* God always for you because of the grace of God that has been given you in Christ Jesus, [5] for in every way you have been enriched in him, in speech and knowledge of every kind— [6] just as the testimony of*c* Christ has been strengthened among you— [7] so that you are not lacking in any spiritual gift as you wait for the revealing of our Lord Jesus Christ. [8] He will also strengthen you to the end, so that you may be blameless on the day of our Lord Jesus Christ. [9] God is faithful; by him you were called into the fellowship of his Son, Jesus Christ our Lord.

Divisions in the Church

10 Now I appeal to you, brothers and sisters,*d* by the name of our Lord Jesus Christ, that all of you be in agreement and that there be no divisions among you, but that you be united in the same mind and the same purpose. [11] For it has been reported to me by Chlō′ē′s people that there are quarrels amoung you, my brothers and sisters.*e* [12] What I mean is that each of you says, "I belong to Paul," or "I belong to A·pol′los," or "I belong to Cē′-phas," or "I belong to Christ." [13] Has Christ been divided? Was Paul crucified for you? Or were you baptized in the name of Paul? [14] I thank God*f* that I baptized none of you except Cris′pus and Gāi′·us, [15] so that no one can say that you were baptized in my name. [16] (I did baptize also the household of Steph′a·nas; beyond that, I do not know whether I baptized anyone else.) [17] For Christ did not send me to baptize but to proclaim the gospel, and not with eloquent wisdom, so that the cross of Christ might not be emptied of its power.

Christ the Power and Wisdom of God
(Cp Isa 29.14)

18 For the message about the cross is foolishness to those who are perishing, but to us who are being saved it is the power of God. [19] For it is written,
 "I will destroy the wisdom of the wise,
 and the discernment of the discerning I will thwart."
[20] Where is the one who is wise? Where is the scribe? Where is the debater of this age? Has not God made foolish the wisdom of the world? [21] For since, in the wisdom of God, the world did not know God through wisdom, God decided, through the foolishness of our proclamation, to save those who believe. [22] For Jews demand signs and Greeks desire wisdom, [23] but we proclaim Christ crucified, a stumbling block to Jews and foolishness to Gentiles, [24] but to those who are the called, both Jews and Greeks, Christ the power of God and the wisdom of God. [25] For God's foolishness is wiser than human wisdom, and God's weakness is stronger than human strength.

26 Consider your own call, brothers and sisters: *d* not many of you were wise by human standards,*g* not many were powerful, not many were of noble birth. [27] But God chose what is foolish in the world to shame the wise; God chose what is weak in the world to shame the strong; [28] God chose what is low and despised in the world, things that are not, to reduce to nothing things that are, [29] so that no one*h* might boast in the presence of God. [30] He is the source of your life in Christ Jesus, who became for us wisdom from God, and righteousness and sanctification and redemption, [31] in order that, as it is written, "Let the one who boasts, boast in*i* the Lord."

Proclaiming Christ Crucified

2 When I came to you, brothers and sisters, *d* I did not come proclaiming the mystery*j* of God to you in lofty words or wisdom. [2] For I decided to know nothing among you except Jesus Christ, and him crucified. [3] And I came to you in weakness and in fear and in much trembling. [4] My speech and my proclamation were not with plausible

---

a Gk *theirs*   *b* Other ancient authorities lack *my*   *c* Or *to*   *d* Gk *brothers*
e Gk *my brothers*   *f* Other ancient authorities read *I am thankful*
g Gk *according to the flesh*   *h* Gk *no flesh*   *i* Or *of*   *j* Other ancient authorities read *testimony*

words of wisdom,[k] but with a demonstration of the Spirit and of power, [5]so that your faith might rest not on human wisdom but on the power of God.

The True Wisdom of God

6 Yet among the mature we do speak wisdom, though it is not a wisdom of this age or of the rulers of this age, who are doomed to perish. [7]But we speak God's wisdom, secret and hidden, which God decreed before the ages for our glory. [8]None of the rulers of this age understood this; for if they had, they would not have crucified the Lord of glory. [9]But, as it is written,

"What no eye has seen, nor ear heard,
　nor the human heart conceived,
　what God has prepared for those who love him"—

[10]these things God has revealed to us through the Spirit; for the Spirit searches everything, even the depths of God. [11]For what human being knows what is truly human except the human spirit that is within? So also no one comprehends what is truly God's except the Spirit of God. [12]Now we have received not the spirit of the world, but the Spirit that is from God, so that we may understand the gifts bestowed on us by God. [13]And we speak of these things in words not taught by human wisdom but taught by the Spirit, interpreting spiritual things to those who are spiritual.[l]

14 Those who are unspiritual[m] do not receive the gifts of God's Spirit, for they are foolishness to them, and they are unable to understand them because they are spiritually discerned. [15]Those who are spiritual discern all things, and they are themselves subject to no one else's scrutiny.

16 "For who has known the mind of the Lord
　so as to instruct him?"
But we have the mind of Christ.

On Divisions in the Corinthian Church

3 And so, brothers and sisters,[n] I could not speak to you as spiritual people, but rather as people of the flesh, as infants in Christ. [2]I fed you with milk, not solid food, for you were not ready for solid food. Even now you are still not ready, [3]for you are still of the flesh. For as long as there is jealousy and quarreling among you, are you not of the flesh, and behaving according to human inclinations? [4]For when one says, "I belong to Paul," and another, "I belong to A·pol'los," are you not merely human?

5 What then is A·pol'los? What is Paul? Servants through whom you came to believe, as the Lord assigned to each. [6]I planted, A·pol'los watered, but God gave the growth. [7]So neither the one who plants nor the one who waters is anything, but only God who gives the growth. [8]The one who plants and the one who waters have a common purpose, and each will receive wages according to the labor of each. [9]For we are God's servants, working together; you are God's field, God's building.

10 According to the grace of God given to me, like a skilled master builder I laid a foundation, and someone else is building on it. Each builder must choose with care how to build on it. [11]For no one can lay any foundation other than the one that has been laid; that foundation is Jesus Christ. [12]Now if anyone builds on the foundation with gold, silver, precious stones, wood, hay, straw— [13]the work of each builder will become visible, for the Day will disclose it, because it will be revealed with fire, and the fire will test what sort of work each has done. [14]If what has been built on the foundation survives, the builder will receive a reward. [15]If the work is burned up, the builder will suffer loss; the builder will be saved, but only as through fire.

16 Do you not know that you are God's temple and that God's Spirit dwells in you?[o] [17]If anyone destroys God's temple, God will destroy that person. For God's temple is holy, and you are that temple.

18 Do not deceive yourselves. If you think that you are wise in this age, you should become fools so that you may become wise. [19]For the wisdom of this world is foolishness with God. For it is written,

---

[k]Other ancient authorities read *the persuasiveness of wisdom*
[l]Or *interpreting spiritual things in spiritual language,* or *comparing spiritual things with spiritual*
[m]Or *natural*　[n]Gk *brothers*
[o]In verses 16 and 17 the Greek word for *you* is plural

1 CORINTHIANS

"He catches the wise in their
   craftiness,"
20 and again,
"The Lord knows the thoughts of
   the wise,
   that they are futile."
21 So let no one boast about human leaders. For all things are yours, 22 whether Paul or A·pol′los or Ce′phas or the world or life or death or the present or the future—all belong to you, 23 and you belong to Christ, and Christ belongs to God.

The Ministry of the Apostles

4 Think of us in this way, as servants of Christ and stewards of God's mysteries. 2 Moreover, it is required of stewards that they be found trustworthy. 3 But with me it is a very small thing that I should be judged by you or by any human court. I do not even judge myself. 4 I am not aware of anything against myself, but I am not thereby acquitted. It is the Lord who judges me. 5 Therefore do not pronounce judgment before the time, before the Lord comes, who will bring to light the things now hidden in darkness and will disclose the purposes of the heart. Then each one will receive commendation from God.

6 I have applied all this to A·pol′los and myself for your benefit, brothers and sisters, p so that you may learn through us the meaning of the saying, "Nothing beyond what is written," so that none of you will be puffed up in favor of one against another. 7 For who sees anything different in you? q What do you have that you did not receive? And if you received it, why do you boast as if it were not a gift?

8 Already you have all you want! Already you have become rich! Quite apart from us you have become kings! Indeed, I wish that you had become kings, so that we might be kings with you! 9 For I think that God has exhibited us apostles as last of all, as though sentenced to death, because we have become a spectacle to the world, to angels and to mortals. 10 We are fools for the sake of Christ, but you are wise in Christ. We are weak, but you are strong. You are held in honor, but we in disrepute. 11 To the present hour we are hungry and thirsty, and we are poorly clothed and beaten and homeless, 12 and we grow weary from the work of our own hands. When reviled, we bless; when persecuted, we endure;

13 when slandered, we speak kindly. We have become like the rubbish of the world, the dregs of all things, to this very day.

Fatherly Admonition

14 I am not writing this to make you ashamed, but to admonish you as my beloved children. 15 For though you might have ten thousand guardians in Christ, you do not have many fathers. Indeed, in Christ Jesus I became your father through the gospel. 16 I appeal to you, then, be imitators of me. 17 For this reason I sent r you Timothy, who is my beloved and faithful child in the Lord, to remind you of my ways in Christ Jesus, as I teach them everywhere in every church. 18 But some of you, thinking that I am not coming to you, have become arrogant. 19 But I will come to you soon, if the Lord wills, and I will find out not the talk of these arrogant people but their power. 20 For the kingdom of God depends not on talk but on power. 21 What would you prefer? Am I to come to you with a stick, or with love in a spirit of gentleness?

Sexual Immorality Defiles the Church

5 It is actually reported that there is sexual immorality among you, and of a kind that is not found even among pagans; for a man is living with his father's wife. 2 And you are arrogant! Should you not rather have mourned, so that he who has done this would have been removed from among you?

3 For though absent in body, I am present in spirit; and as if present I have already pronounced judgment 4 in the name of the Lord Jesus on the man who has done such a thing. s When you are assembled, and my spirit is present with the power of our Lord Jesus, 5 you are to hand this man over to Satan for the destruction of the flesh, so that his spirit may be saved in the day of the Lord. t

6 Your boasting is not a good thing. Do you not know that a little yeast leavens the whole batch of dough? 7 Clean out the old yeast so that you may be a new batch, as you really are

unleavened. For our paschal lamb, Christ, has been sacrificed. [8] Therefore, let us celebrate the festival, not with the old yeast, the yeast of malice and evil, but with the unleavened bread of sincerity and truth.

Sexual Immorality Must Be Judged

9 I wrote to you in my letter not to associate with sexually immoral persons— [10] not at all meaning the immoral of this world, or the greedy and robbers, or idolaters, since you would then need to go out of the world. [11] But now I am writing to you not to associate with anyone who bears the name of brother or sister[u] who is sexually immoral or greedy, or is an idolater, reviler, drunkard, or robber. Do not even eat with such a one. [12] For what have I to do with judging those outside? Is it not those who are inside that you are to judge? [13] God will judge those outside. "Drive out the wicked person from among you."

Lawsuits among Believers

6 When any of you has a grievance against another, do you dare to take it to court before the unrighteous, instead of taking it before the saints? [2] Do you not know that the saints will judge the world? And if the world is to be judged by you, are you incompetent to try trivial cases? [3] Do you not know that we are to judge angels—to say nothing of ordinary matters? [4] If you have ordinary cases, then, do you appoint as judges those who have no standing in the church? [5] I say this to your shame. Can it be that there is no one among you wise enough to decide between one believer[u] and another, [6] but a believer[u] goes to court against a believer[u] —and before unbelievers at that?

7 In fact, to have lawsuits at all with one another is already a defeat for you. Why not rather be wronged? Why not rather be defrauded? [8] But you yourselves wrong and defraud—and believers[v] at that.

9 Do you not know that wrongdoers will not inherit the kingdom of God? Do not be deceived! Fornicators, idolaters, adulterers, male prostitutes, sodomites, [10] thieves, the greedy, drunkards, revilers, robbers—none of these will inherit the kingdom of God. [11] And this is what some of you used to be. But you were washed, you were sanctified,

you were justified in the name of the Lord Jesus Christ and in the Spirit of our God.

Glorify God in Body and Spirit

12 "All things are lawful for me," but not all things are beneficial. "All things are lawful for me," but I will not be dominated by anything. [13] "Food is meant for the stomach and the stomach for food,"[w] and God will destroy both one and the other. The body is meant not for fornication but for the Lord, and the Lord for the body. [14] And God raised the Lord and will also raise us by his power. [15] Do you not know that your bodies are members of Christ? Should I therefore take the members of Christ and make them members of a prostitute? Never! [16] Do you not know that whoever is united to a prostitute becomes one body with her? For it is said, "The two shall be one flesh." [17] But anyone united to the Lord becomes one spirit with him. [18] Shun fornication! Every sin that a person commits is outside the body; but the fornicator sins against the body itself. [19] Or do you not know that your body is a temple[x] of the Holy Spirit within you, which you have from God, and that you are not your own? [20] For you were bought with a price; therefore glorify God in your body.

Directions concerning Marriage

7 Now concerning the matters about which you wrote: "It is well for a man not to touch a woman." [2] But because of cases of sexual immorality, each man should have his own wife and each woman her own husband. [3] The husband should give to his wife her conjugal rights, and likewise the wife to her husband. [4] For the wife does not have authority over her own body, but the husband does; likewise the husband does not have authority over his own body, but the wife does. [5] Do not deprive one another except perhaps by agreement for a set time, to devote yourselves to prayer, and then come together again, so that Satan may not tempt you because of your lack of self-control. [6] This I say by way of concession, not of command. [7] I

---

[u] Gk brother　　[v] Gk brothers
[w] The quotation may extend to the word other　[x] Or sanctuary

wish that all were as I myself am. But each has a particular gift from God, one having one kind and another a different kind.

8 To the unmarried and the widows I say that it is well for them to remain unmarried as I am. [9] But if they are not practicing self-control, they should marry. For it is better to marry than to be aflame with passion.

10 To the married I give this command—not I but the Lord—that the wife should not separate from her husband [11] (but if she does separate, let her remain unmarried or else be reconciled to her husband), and that the husband should not divorce his wife. 12 To the rest I say—I and not the Lord—that if any believer[y] has a wife who is an unbeliever, and she consents to live with him, he should not divorce her. [13] And if any woman has a husband who is an unbeliever, and he consents to live with her, she should not divorce him. [14] For the unbelieving husband is made holy through his wife, and the unbelieving wife is made holy through her husband. Otherwise, your children would be unclean, but as it is, they are holy. [15] But if the unbelieving partner separates, let it be so; in such a case the brother or sister is not bound. It is to peace that God has called you.[z] [16] Wife, for all you know, you might save your husband. Husband, for all you know, you might save your wife.

The Life That the Lord Has Assigned

17 However that may be, let each of you lead the life that the Lord has assigned, to which God called you. This is my rule in all the churches. [18] Was anyone at the time of his call already circumcised? Let him not seek to remove the marks of circumcision. Was anyone at the time of his call uncircumcised? Let him not seek circumcision. [19] Circumcision is nothing, and uncircumcision is nothing; but obeying the commandments of God is everything. [20] Let each of you remain in the condition in which you were called. 21 Were you a slave when called? Do not be concerned about it. Even if you can gain your freedom, make use of your present condition now more than ever.[a] [22] For whoever was called in the Lord as a slave is a freed person belonging to the Lord, just as whoever was free when called is a slave of Christ. [23] You were bought with a price; do not become slaves of human masters. [24] In whatever condition you were called, brothers and sisters,[b] there remain with God.

The Unmarried and the Widows

25 Now concerning virgins, I have no command of the Lord. I give my opinion as one who by the Lord's mercy is trustworthy. [26] I think that, in view of the impending[c] crisis, it is well for you to remain as you are. 27 Are you bound to a wife? Do not seek to be free. Are you free from a wife? Do not seek a wife. [28] But if you marry, you do not sin, and if a virgin marries, she does not sin. Yet those who marry will experience distress in this life,[d] and I would spare you that. [29] I mean, brothers and sisters,[b] the appointed time has grown short; from now on, let even those who have wives be as though they had none, [30] and those who mourn as though they were not mourning, and those who rejoice as though they were not rejoicing, and those who buy as though they had no possessions, [31] and those who deal with the world as though they had no dealings with it. For the present form of this world is passing away.

32 I want you to be free from anxieties. The unmarried man is anxious about the affairs of the Lord, how to please the Lord; [33] but the married man is anxious about the affairs of the world, how to please his wife, [34] and his interests are divided. And the unmarried woman and the virgin are anxious about the affairs of the Lord, so that they may be holy in body and spirit; but the married woman is anxious about the affairs of the world, how to please her husband. [35] I say this for your own benefit, not to put any restraint upon you, but to promote good order and unhindered devotion to the Lord.

36 If anyone thinks that he is not behaving properly toward his fiancée,[e] if his passions are strong, and so it has to be, let him marry as he wishes; it is no sin. Let them marry. [37] But if someone stands firm in his resolve, being under no necessity but having his

---

[y] Gk *brother*   [z] Other ancient authorities read *us*   [a] Or *avail yourself of the opportunity*   [b] Gk *brothers*   [c] Or *present*   [d] Gk *in the flesh*   [e] Gk *virgin*

own desire under control, and has determined in his own mind to keep her as his fiancée,[f] he will do well. 38 So then, he who marries his fiancée[f] does well; and he who refrains from marriage will do better.

39 A wife is bound as long as her husband lives. But if the husband dies,[g] she is free to marry anyone she wishes, only in the Lord. 40 But in my judgment she is more blessed if she remains as she is. And I think that I too have the Spirit of God.

Food Offered to Idols

8 Now concerning food sacrificed to idols: we know that "all of us possess knowledge." Knowledge puffs up, but love builds up. 2 Anyone who claims to know something does not yet have the necessary knowledge; 3 but anyone who loves God is known by him.

4 Hence, as to the eating of food offered to idols, we know that "no idol in the world really exists," and that "there is no God but one." 5 Indeed, even though there may be so-called gods in heaven or on earth—as in fact there are many gods and many lords— 6 yet for us there is one God, the Father, from whom are all things and for whom we exist, and one Lord, Jesus Christ, through whom are all things and through whom we exist.

7 It is not everyone, however, who has this knowledge. Since some have become so accustomed to idols until now, they still think of the food they eat as food offered to an idol; and their conscience, being weak, is defiled. 8 "Food will not bring us close to God."[h] We are no worse off if we do not eat, and no better off if we do. 9 But take care that this liberty of yours does not somehow become a stumbling block to the weak. 10 For if others see you, who possess knowledge, eating in the temple of an idol, might they not, since their conscience is weak, be encouraged to the point of eating food sacrificed to idols? 11 So by your knowledge those weak believers for whom Christ died are destroyed.[i] 12 But when you thus sin against members of your family,[j] and wound their conscience when it is weak, you sin against Christ. 13 Therefore, if food is a cause of their falling,[k] I will never eat meat, so that I may not cause one of them[l] to fall.

The Rights of an Apostle

9 Am I not free? Am I not an apostle? Have I not seen Jesus our Lord? Are you not my work in the Lord? 2 If I am not an apostle to others, at least I am to you; for you are the seal of my apostleship in the Lord.

3 This is my defense to those who would examine me. 4 Do we not have the right to our food and drink? 5 Do we not have the right to be accompanied by a believing wife,[m] as do the other apostles and the brothers of the Lord and Cē′phas? 6 Or is it only Bar′na·bas and I who have no right to refrain from working for a living? 7 Who at any time pays the expenses for doing military service? Who plants a vineyard and does not eat any of its fruit? Or who tends a flock and does not get any of its milk?

8 Do I say this on human authority? Does not the law also say the same? 9 For it is written in the law of Moses, "You shall not muzzle an ox while it is treading out the grain." Is it for oxen that God is concerned? 10 Or does he not speak entirely for our sake? It was indeed written for our sake, for whoever plows should plow in hope and whoever threshes should thresh in hope of a share in the crop. 11 If we have sown spiritual good among you, is it too much if we reap your material benefits? 12 If others share this rightful claim on you, do not we still more?

Nevertheless, we have not made use of this right, but we endure anything rather than put an obstacle in the way of the gospel of Christ. 13 Do you not know that those who are employed in the temple service get their food from the temple, and those who serve at the altar share in what is sacrificed on the altar? 14 In the same way, the Lord commanded that those who proclaim the gospel should get their living by the gospel.

15 But I have made no use of any of these rights, nor am I writing this so that they may be applied in my case. Indeed, I would rather die than that— no one will deprive me of my ground for boasting! 16 If I proclaim the gospel, this gives me no ground for boasting,

---

[f] Gk virgin   [g] Gk falls asleep
[h] The quotation may extend to the end of the verse   [i] Gk the weak brother . . . is destroyed   [j] Gk against the brothers
[k] Gk my brother's falling   [l] Gk cause my brother   [m] Gk a sister as wife

for an obligation is laid on me, and woe to me if I do not proclaim the gospel! [17]For if I do this of my own will, I have a reward; but if not of my own will, I am entrusted with a commission. [18]What then is my reward? Just this: that in my proclamation I may make the gospel free of charge, so as not to make full use of my rights in the gospel.

19 For though I am free with respect to all, I have made myself a slave to all, so that I might win more of them. [20]To the Jews I became as a Jew, in order to win Jews. To those under the law I became as one under the law (though I myself am not under the law) so that I might win those under the law. [21]To those outside the law I became as one outside the law (though I am not free from God's law but am under Christ's law) so that I might win those outside the law. [22]To the weak I became weak, so that I might win the weak. I have become all things to all people, that I might by all means save some. [23]I do it all for the sake of the gospel, so that I may share in its blessings.

24 Do you not know that in a race the runners all compete, but only one receives the prize? Run in such a way that you may win it. [25]Athletes exercise self-control in all things; they do it to receive a perishable wreath, but we an imperishable one. [26]So I do not run aimlessly, nor do I box as though beating the air; [27]but I punish my body and enslave it, so that after proclaiming to others I myself should not be disqualified.

Warnings from Israel's History

10 I do not want you to be unaware, brothers and sisters,[n] that our ancestors were all under the cloud, and all passed through the sea, [2]and all were baptized into Moses in the cloud and in the sea, [3]and all ate the same spiritual food, [4]and all drank the same spiritual drink. For they drank from the spiritual rock that followed them, and the rock was Christ. [5]Nevertheless, God was not pleased with most of them, and they were struck down in the wilderness.

6 Now these things occurred as examples for us, so that we might not desire evil as they did. [7]Do not become idolaters as some of them did; as it is written, "The people sat down to eat and drink, and they rose up to play."

[8]We must not indulge in sexual immorality as some of them did, and twenty-three thousand fell in a single day. [9]We must not put Christ[o] to the test, as some of them did, and were destroyed by serpents. [10]And do not complain as some of them did, and were destroyed by the destroyer. [11]These things happened to them to serve as an example, and they were written down to instruct us, on whom the ends of the ages have come. [12]So if you think you are standing, watch out that you do not fall. [13]No testing has overtaken you that is not common to everyone. God is faithful, and he will not let you be tested beyond your strength, but with the testing he will also provide the way out so that you may be able to endure it.

14 Therefore, my dear friends,[p] flee from the worship of idols. [15]I speak as to sensible people; judge for yourselves what I say. [16]The cup of blessing that we bless, is it not a sharing in the blood of Christ? The bread that we break, is it not a sharing in the body of Christ? [17]Because there is one bread, we who are many are one body, for we all partake of the one bread. [18]Consider the people of Israel;[q] are not those who eat the sacrifices partners in the altar? [19]What do I imply then? That food sacrificed to idols is anything, or that an idol is anything? [20]No, I imply that what pagans sacrifice, they sacrifice to demons and not to God. I do not want you to be partners with demons. [21]You cannot drink the cup of the Lord and the cup of demons. You cannot partake of the table of the Lord and the table of demons. [22]Or are we provoking the Lord to jealousy? Are we stronger than he?

Do All to the Glory of God
(Cp Ps 24.1)

23 "All things are lawful," but not all things are beneficial. "All things are lawful," but not all things build up. [24]Do not seek your own advantage, but that of the other. [25]Eat whatever is sold in the meat market without raising any question on the ground of conscience, [26]for "the earth and its fullness are the Lord's." [27]If an unbeliever invites you to a meal and you are disposed to go, eat whatever is set before

[n]Gk brothers   [o]Other ancient authorities read the Lord   [p]Gk my beloved   [q]Gk Israel according to the flesh

you without raising any question on the ground of conscience. 28 But if someone says to you, "This has been offered in sacrifice," then do not eat it, out of consideration for the one who informed you, and for the sake of conscience— 29 I mean the other's conscience, not your own. For why should my liberty be subject to the judgment of someone else's conscience? 30 If I partake with thankfulness, why should I be denounced because of that for which I give thanks?

31 So, whether you eat or drink, or whatever you do, do everything for the glory of God. 32 Give no offense to Jews or to Greeks or to the church of God, 33 just as I try to please everyone in everything I do, not seeking my own advantage, but that of many, so that 11 they may be saved. 1 Be imitators of me, as I am of Christ.

Head Coverings

2 I commend you because you remember me in everything and maintain the traditions just as I handed them on to you. 3 But I want you to understand that Christ is the head of every man, and the husband*r* is the head of his wife,*s* and God is the head of Christ. 4 Any man who prays or prophesies with something on his head disgraces his head, 5 but any woman who prays or prophesies with her head unveiled disgraces her head—it is one and the same thing as having her head shaved. 6 For if a woman will not veil herself, then she should cut off her hair; but if it is disgraceful for a woman to have her hair cut off or to be shaved, she should wear a veil. 7 For a man ought not to have his head veiled, since he is the image and reflection*t* of God; but woman is the reflection*t* of man. 8 Indeed, man was not made from woman, but woman from man. 9 Neither was man created for the sake of woman, but woman for the sake of man. 10 For this reason a woman ought to have a symbol of*u* authority on her head,*v* because of the angels. 11 Nevertheless, in the Lord woman is not independent of man or man independent of woman. 12 For just as woman came from man, so man comes through woman; but all things come from God. 13 Judge for yourselves: is it proper for a woman to pray to God with her head unveiled? 14 Does not nature itself teach you that

if a man wears long hair, it is degrading to him, 15 but if a woman has long hair, it is her glory? For her hair is given to her for a covering. 16 But if anyone is disposed to be contentious— we have no such custom, nor do the churches of God.

Abuses at the Lord's Supper

17 Now in the following instructions I do not commend you, because when you come together it is not for the better but for the worse. 18 For, to begin with, when you come together as a church, I hear that there are divisions among you; and to some extent I believe it. 19 Indeed, there have to be factions among you, for only so will it become clear who among you are genuine. 20 When you come together, it is not really to eat the Lord's supper. 21 For when the time comes to eat, each of you goes ahead with your own supper, and one goes hungry and another becomes drunk. 22 What! Do you not have homes to eat and drink in? Or do you show contempt for the church of God and humiliate those who have nothing? What should I say to you? Should I commend you? In this matter I do not commend you!

The Institution of the Lord's Supper
(Mt 26.26–29; Mk 14.22–25; Lk 22.14–23)

23 For I received from the Lord what I also handed on to you, that the Lord Jesus on the night when he was betrayed took a loaf of bread, 24 and when he had given thanks, he broke it and said, "This is my body that is for*w* you. Do this in remembrance of me." 25 In the same way he took the cup also, after supper, saying, "This cup is the new covenant in my blood. Do this, as often as you drink it, in remembrance of me." 26 For as often as you eat this bread and drink the cup, you proclaim the Lord's death until he comes.

Partaking of the Supper Unworthily

27 Whoever, therefore, eats the bread or drinks the cup of the Lord in an unworthy manner will be answerable for the body and blood of the Lord. 28 Examine yourselves, and only

---

r The same Greek word means *man* or *husband*   *s* Or *head of the woman*
t Or *glory*   *u* Gk lacks *a symbol of*
v Or *have freedom of choice regarding her head*   *w* Other ancient authorities read *is broken for*

then eat of the bread and drink of the cup. [29] For all who eat and drink[x] without discerning the body,[y] eat and drink judgment against themselves. [30] For this reason many of you are weak and ill, and some have died.[z] [31] But if we judged ourselves, we would not be judged. [32] But when we are judged by the Lord, we are disciplined[a] so that we may not be condemned along with the world.

[33] So then, my brothers and sisters,[b] when you come together to eat, wait for one another. [34] If you are hungry, eat at home, so that when you come together, it will not be for your condemnation. About the other things I will give instructions when I come.

Spiritual Gifts

12 Now concerning spiritual gifts,[c] brothers and sisters,[b] I do not want you to be uninformed. [2] You know that when you were pagans, you were enticed and led astray to idols that could not speak. [3] Therefore I want you to understand that no one speaking by the Spirit of God ever says "Let Jesus be cursed!" and no one can say "Jesus is Lord" except by the Holy Spirit.

[4] Now there are varieties of gifts, but the same Spirit; [5] and there are varieties of services, but the same Lord; [6] and there are varieties of activities, but it is the same God who activates all of them in everyone. [7] To each is given the manifestation of the Spirit for the common good. [8] To one is given through the Spirit the utterance of wisdom, and to another the utterance of knowledge according to the same Spirit, [9] to another faith by the same Spirit, to another gifts of healing by the one Spirit, [10] to another the working of miracles, to another prophecy, to another the discernment of spirits, to another various kinds of tongues, to another the interpretation of tongues. [11] All these are activated by one and the same Spirit, who allots to each one individually just as the Spirit chooses.

One Body with Many Members
(Cp Eph 4.1–16)

[12] For just as the body is one and has many members, and all the members of the body, though many, are one body, so it is with Christ. [13] For in the one Spirit we were all baptized into one body—Jews or Greeks, slaves or free—and we were all made to drink of one Spirit.

[14] Indeed, the body does not consist of one member but of many. [15] If the foot would say, "Because I am not a hand, I do not belong to the body," that would not make it any less a part of the body. [16] And if the ear would say, "Because I am not an eye, I do not belong to the body," that would not make it any less a part of the body. [17] If the whole body were an eye, where would the hearing be? If the whole body were hearing, where would the sense of smell be? [18] But as it is, God arranged the members in the body, each one of them, as he chose. [19] If all were a single member, where would the body be? [20] As it is, there are many members, yet one body. [21] The eye cannot say to the hand, "I have no need of you," nor again the head to the feet, "I have no need of you." [22] On the contrary, the members of the body that seem to be weaker are indispensable, [23] and those members of the body that we think less honorable we clothe with greater honor, and our less respectable members are treated with greater respect; [24] whereas our more respectable members do not need this. But God has so arranged the body, giving the greater honor to the inferior member, [25] that there may be no dissension within the body, but the members may have the same care for one another. [26] If one member suffers, all suffer together with it; if one member is honored, all rejoice together with it.

[27] Now you are the body of Christ and individually members of it. [28] And God has appointed in the church first apostles, second prophets, third teachers; then deeds of power, then gifts of healing, forms of assistance, forms of leadership, various kinds of tongues. [29] Are all apostles? Are all prophets? Are all teachers? Do all work miracles? [30] Do all possess gifts of healing? Do all speak in tongues? Do all interpret? [31] But strive for the greater gifts. And I will show you a still more excellent way.

---

[x] Other ancient authorities add *in an unworthy manner,*   [y] Other ancient authorities read *the Lord's body*   [z] Gk *fallen asleep*   [a] Or *When we are judged, we are being disciplined by the Lord*   [b] Gk *brothers*   [c] Or *spiritual persons*

The Gift of Love

13 If I speak in the tongues of mortals and of angels, but do not have love, I am a noisy gong or a clanging cymbal. ²And if I have prophetic powers, and understand all mysteries and all knowledge, and if I have all faith, so as to remove mountains, but do not have love, I am nothing. ³If I give away all my possessions, and if I hand over my body so that I may boast,^d but do not have love, I gain nothing.

4 Love is patient; love is kind; love is not envious or boastful or arrogant ⁵or rude. It does not insist on its own way; it is not irritable or resentful; ⁶it does not rejoice in wrongdoing, but rejoices in the truth. ⁷It bears all things, believes all things, hopes all things, endures all things.

8 Love never ends. But as for prophecies, they will come to an end; as for tongues, they will cease; as for knowledge, it will come to an end. ⁹For we know only in part, and we prophesy only in part; ¹⁰but when the complete comes, the partial will come to an end. ¹¹When I was a child, I spoke like a child, I thought like a child, I reasoned like a child; when I became an adult, I put an end to childish ways. ¹²For now we see in a mirror, dimly,^e but then we will see face to face. Now I know only in part; then I will know fully, even as I have been fully known. ¹³And now faith, hope, and love abide, these three; and the greatest of these is love.

Gifts of Prophecy and Tongues

14 Pursue love and strive for the spiritual gifts, and especially that you may prophesy. ²For those who speak in a tongue do not speak to other people but to God; for nobody understands them, since they are speaking mysteries in the Spirit. ³On the other hand, those who prophesy speak to other people for their upbuilding and encouragement and consolation. ⁴Those who speak in a tongue build up themselves, but those who prophesy build up the church. ⁵Now I would like all of you to speak in tongues, but even more to prophesy. One who prophesies is greater than one who speaks in tongues, unless someone interprets, so that the church may be built up.

6 Now, brothers and sisters,^f if I come to you speaking in tongues, how will I benefit you unless I speak to you in some revelation or knowledge or prophecy or teaching? ⁷It is the same way with lifeless instruments that produce sound, such as the flute or the harp. If they do not give distinct notes, how will anyone know what is being played? ⁸And if the bugle gives an indistinct sound, who will get ready for battle? ⁹So with yourselves; if in a tongue you utter speech that is not intelligible, how will anyone know what is being said? For you will be speaking into the air. ¹⁰There are doubtless many different kinds of sounds in the world, and nothing is without sound. ¹¹If then I do not know the meaning of a sound, I will be a foreigner to the speaker and the speaker a foreigner to me. ¹²So with yourselves; since you are eager for spiritual gifts, strive to excel in them for building up the church.

13 Therefore, one who speaks in a tongue should pray for the power to interpret. ¹⁴For if I pray in a tongue, my spirit prays but my mind is unproductive. ¹⁵What should I do then? I will pray with the spirit, but I will pray with the mind also; I will sing praise with the spirit, but I will sing praise with the mind also. ¹⁶Otherwise, if you say a blessing with the spirit, how can anyone in the position of an outsider say the "Amen" to your thanksgiving, since the outsider does not know what you are saying? ¹⁷For you may give thanks well enough, but the other person is not built up. ¹⁸I thank God that I speak in tongues more than all of you; ¹⁹nevertheless, in church I would rather speak five words with my mind, in order to instruct others also, than ten thousand words in a tongue.

20 Brothers and sisters,^f do not be children in your thinking; rather, be infants in evil, but in thinking be adults. ²¹In the law it is written,

"By people of strange tongues
   and by the lips of foreigners
I will speak to this people;
   yet even then they will not
      listen to me,"

says the Lord. ²²Tongues, then, are a sign not for believers but for unbelievers, while prophecy is not for unbelievers but for believers. ²³If, therefore, the whole church comes together and all

---

^d Other ancient authorities read *body to be burned*   ^e Gk *in a riddle*   ^f Gk *brothers* speak in tongues, and outsiders or unbelievers enter, will they not say that you are out of your mind? [24]But if all prophesy, an unbeliever or outsider who enters is reproved by all and called to account by all. [25]After the secrets of the unbeliever's heart are disclosed, that person will bow down before God and worship him, declaring, "God is really among you."

Orderly Worship

26 What should be done then, my friends?[g] When you come together, each one has a hymn, a lesson, a revelation, a tongue, or an interpretation. Let all things be done for building up. [27]If anyone speaks in a tongue, let there be only two or at most three, and each in turn; and let one interpret. [28]But if there is no one to interpret, let them be silent in church and speak to themselves and to God. [29]Let two or three prophets speak, and let the others weigh what is said. [30]If a revelation is made to someone else sitting nearby, let the first person be silent. [31]For you can all prophesy one by one, so that all may learn and all be encouraged. [32]And the spirits of prophets are subject to the prophets, [33]for God is a God not of disorder but of peace.

(As in all the churches of the saints, [34]women should be silent in the churches. For they are not permitted to speak, but should be subordinate, as the law also says. [35]If there is anything they desire to know, let them ask their husbands at home. For it is shameful for a woman to speak in church.[h] [36]Or did the word of God originate with you? Or are you the only ones it has reached?)

37 Anyone who claims to be a prophet, or to have spiritual powers, must acknowledge that what I am writing to you is a command of the Lord. [38]Anyone who does not recognize this is not to be recognized. [39]So, my friends,[i] be eager to prophesy, and do not forbid speaking in tongues; [40]but all things should be done decently and in order.

The Resurrection of Christ
(Cp Mk 16.9–20)

15 Now I would remind you, brothers and sisters,[g] of the good news[j] that I proclaimed to you, which you in turn received, in which also you stand, [2]through which also you are being saved, if you hold firmly to the message that I proclaimed to you—unless you have come to believe in vain.

3 For I handed on to you as of first importance what I in turn had received: that Christ died for our sins in accordance with the scriptures, [4]and that he was buried, and that he was raised on the third day in accordance with the scriptures, [5]and that he appeared to Ce′phas, then to the twelve. [6]Then he appeared to more than five hundred brothers and sisters[g] at one time, most of whom are still alive, though some have died.[k] [7]Then he appeared to James, then to all the apostles. [8]Last of all, as to one untimely born, he appeared also to me. [9]For I am the least of the apostles, unfit to be called an apostle, because I persecuted the church of God. [10]But by the grace of God I am what I am, and his grace toward me has not been in vain. On the contrary, I worked harder than any of them—though it was not I, but the grace of God that is with me. [11]Whether then it was I or they, so we proclaim and so you have come to believe.

The Resurrection of the Dead
(Cp 1 Thess 4.13–18)

12 Now if Christ is proclaimed as raised from the dead, how can some of you say there is no resurrection of the dead? [13]If there is no resurrection of the dead, then Christ has not been raised; [14]and if Christ has not been raised, then our proclamation has been in vain and your faith has been in vain. [15]We are even found to be misrepresenting God, because we testified of God that he raised Christ—whom he did not raise if it is true that the dead are not raised. [16]For if the dead are not raised, then Christ has not been raised. [17]If Christ has not been raised, your faith is futile and you are still in your sins. [18]Then those also who have died[k] in Christ have perished. [19]If for this life only we have hoped in Christ, we are of all people most to be pitied.

20 But in fact Christ has been raised from the dead, the first fruits of those who have died.[k] [21]For since death came through a human being, the res-

[g]Gk brothers   [h]Other ancient authorities put verses 34-35 after verse 40   [i]Gk my brothers   [j]Or gospel   [k]Gk fallen asleep

urrection of the dead has also come through a human being; [22] for as all die in Adam, so all will be made alive in Christ. [23] But each in his own order: Christ the first fruits, then at his coming those who belong to Christ. [24] Then comes the end,[l] when he hands over the kingdom to God the Father, after he has destroyed every ruler and every authority and power. [25] For he must reign until he has put all his enemies under his feet. [26] The last enemy to be destroyed is death. [27] For "God[m] has put all things in subjection under his feet." But when it says, "All things are put in subjection," it is plain that this does not include the one who put all things in subjection under him. [28] When all things are subjected to him, then the Son himself will also be subjected to the one who put all things in subjection under him, so that God may be all in all.

29 Otherwise, what will those people do who receive baptism on behalf of the dead? If the dead are not raised at all, why are people baptized on their behalf?

30 And why are we putting ourselves in danger every hour? [31] I die every day! That is as certain, brothers and sisters,[n] as my boasting of you—a boast that I make in Christ Jesus our Lord. [32] If with merely human hopes I fought with wild animals at Eph'e·sus, what would I have gained by it? If the dead are not raised,

"Let us eat and drink,
    for tomorrow we die."

[33] Do not be deceived:
"Bad company ruins good
    morals."

[34] Come to a sober and right mind, and sin no more; for some people have no knowledge of God. I say this to your shame.

The Resurrection Body

35 But someone will ask, "How are the dead raised? With what kind of body do they come?" [36] Fool! What you sow does not come to life unless it dies. [37] And as for what you sow, you do not sow the body that is to be, but a bare seed, perhaps of wheat or of some other grain. [38] But God gives it a body as he has chosen, and to each kind of seed its own body. [39] Not all flesh is alike, but there is one flesh for human beings, another for animals, another for birds, and another for fish. [40] There are both heavenly bodies and earthly bodies, but the glory of the heavenly is one thing, and that of the earthly is another. [41] There is one glory of the sun, and another glory of the moon, and another glory of the stars; indeed, star differs from star in glory.

42 So it is with the resurrection of the dead. What is sown is perishable, what is raised is imperishable. [43] It is sown in dishonor, it is raised in glory. It is sown in weakness, it is raised in power. [44] It is sown a physical body, it is raised a spiritual body. If there is a physical body, there is also a spiritual body. [45] Thus it is written, "The first man, Adam, became a living being"; the last Adam became a life-giving spirit. [46] But it is not the spiritual that is first, but the physical, and then the spiritual. [47] The first man was from the earth, a man of dust; the second man is[o] from heaven. [48] As was the man of dust, so are those who are of the dust; and as is the man of heaven, so are those who are of heaven. [49] Just as we have borne the image of the man of dust, we will[p] also bear the image of the man of heaven.

50 What I am saying, brothers and sisters,[n] is this: flesh and blood cannot inherit the kingdom of God, nor does the perishable inherit the imperishable. [51] Listen, I will tell you a mystery! We will not all die,[q] but we will all be changed, [52] in a moment, in the twinkling of an eye, at the last trumpet. For the trumpet will sound, and the dead will be raised imperishable, and we will be changed. [53] For this perishable body must put on imperishability, and this mortal body must put on immortality. [54] When this perishable body puts on imperishability, and this mortal body puts on immortality, then the saying that is written will be fulfilled:

"Death has been swallowed up
    in victory."

55 "Where, O death, is your
        victory?
    Where, O death, is your
        sting?"

[56] The sting of death is sin, and the power of sin is the law. [57] But thanks be to God, who gives us the victory through our Lord Jesus Christ.

58 Therefore, my beloved,[r] be

l Or Then come the rest   m Gk he
n Gk brothers   o Other ancient
authorities add the Lord   p Other
ancient authorities read let us   q Gk fall
asleep   r Gk beloved brothers

steadfast, immovable, always excelling in the work of the Lord, because you know that in the Lord your labor is not in vain.

The Collection for the Saints

16 Now concerning the collection for the saints: you should follow the directions I gave to the churches of Galatia. ² On the first day of every week, each of you is to put aside and save whatever extra you earn, so that collections need not be taken when I come. ³ And when I arrive, I will send any whom you approve with letters to take your gift to Jerusalem. ⁴ If it seems advisable that I should go also, they will accompany me.

Plans for Travel
(Cp Acts 19.21)

5 I will visit you after passing through Mac·e·dō′ni·a—for I intend to pass through Mac·e·dō′ni·a— ⁶ and perhaps I will stay with you or even spend the winter, so that you may send me on my way, wherever I go. ⁷ I do not want to see you now just in passing, for I hope to spend some time with you, if the Lord permits. ⁸ But I will stay in Eph′e·sus until Pentecost, ⁹ for a wide door for effective work has opened to me, and there are many adversaries.

10 If Timothy comes, see that he has nothing to fear among you, for he is doing the work of the Lord just as I am; ¹¹ therefore let no one despise him. Send him on his way in peace, so that he may come to me; for I am expecting him with the brothers.

12 Now concerning our brother A·pol′los, I strongly urged him to visit you with the other brothers, but he was not at all willing *s* to come now. He will come when he has the opportunity.

Final Messages and Greetings

13 Keep alert, stand firm in your faith, be courageous, be strong. ¹⁴ Let all that you do be done in love.

15 Now, brothers and sisters, *t* you know that members of the household of Steph′a·nas were the first converts in A·chā′i·a, and they have devoted themselves to the service of the saints; ¹⁶ I urge you to put yourselves at the service of such people, and of everyone who works and toils with them. ¹⁷ I rejoice at the coming of Steph′a·nas and For·tu·nā′tus and A·chā′i·cus, because they have made up for your absence; ¹⁸ for they refreshed my spirit as well as yours. So give recognition to such persons.

19 The churches of Asia send greetings. A·qui′la and Pris′ca, together with the church in their house, greet you warmly in the Lord. ²⁰ All the brothers and sisters *t* send greetings. Greet one another with a holy kiss.

21 I, Paul, write this greeting with my own hand. ²² Let anyone be accursed who has no love for the Lord. Our Lord, come! *u* ²³ The grace of the Lord Jesus be with you. ²⁴ My love be with all of you in Christ Jesus. *v*

s Or *it was not at all God's will for him* *t* Gk *brothers* *u* Gk *Marana tha.* These Aramaic words can also be read *Maran atha,* meaning *Our Lord has come* *v* Other ancient authorities add *Amen*

The Second Letter of Paul to the

CORINTHIANS

Salutation

1 Paul, an apostle of Christ Jesus by the will of God, and Timothy our brother,
To the church of God that is in Corinth, including all the saints throughout A·chā′i·a:

2 Grace to you and peace from God our Father and the Lord Jesus Christ.

Paul's Thanksgiving after Affliction

3 Blessed be the God and Father of our Lord Jesus Christ, the Father of mercies and the God of all consolation, [4] who consoles us in all our affliction, so that we may be able to console those who are in any affliction with the consolation with which we ourselves are consoled by God. [5] For just as the sufferings of Christ are abundant for us, so also our consolation is abundant through Christ. [6] If we are being afflicted, it is for your consolation and salvation; if we are being consoled, it is for your consolation, which you experience when you patiently endure the same sufferings that we are also suffering. [7] Our hope for you is unshaken; for we know that as you share in our sufferings, so also you share in our consolation.

8 We do not want you to be unaware, brothers and sisters,[a] of the affliction we experienced in Asia; for we were so utterly, unbearably crushed that we despaired of life itself. [9] Indeed, we felt that we had received the sentence of death so that we would rely not on ourselves but on God who raises the dead. [10] He who rescued us from so deadly a peril will continue to rescue us; on him we have set our hope that he will rescue us again, [11] as you also join in helping us by your prayers, so that many will give thanks on our[b] behalf for the blessing granted us through the prayers of many.

The Postponement of Paul's Visit

12 Indeed, this is our boast, the testimony of our conscience: we have behaved in the world with frankness[c] and godly sincerity, not by earthly wisdom but by the grace of God—and all the more toward you. [13] For we write you nothing other than what you can read and also understand; I hope you will understand until the end— [14] as you have already understood us in part—that on the day of the Lord Jesus we are your boast even as you are our boast.

15 Since I was sure of this, I wanted to come to you first, so that you might have a double favor;[d] [16] I wanted to visit you on my way to Mac·e·do′ni·a, and to come back to you from Mac·e·do′ni·a and have you send me on to Judea. [17] Was I vacillating when I wanted to do this? Do I make my plans according to ordinary human

standards,[e] ready to say "Yes, yes" and "No, no" at the same time? [18] As surely as God is faithful, our word to you has not been "Yes and No." [19] For the Son of God, Jesus Christ, whom we proclaimed among you, Sil·va′nus and Timothy and I, was not "Yes and No"; but in him it is always "Yes." [20] For in him every one of God's promises is a "Yes." For this reason it is through him that we say the "Amen," to the glory of God. [21] But it is God who establishes us with you in Christ and has anointed us, [22] by putting his seal on us and giving us his Spirit in our hearts as a first installment.

23 But I call on God as witness against me: it was to spare you that I did not come again to Corinth. [24] I do not mean to imply that we lord it over your faith; rather, we are workers with you for your joy, because you stand firm in the faith. [2] [1] So I made up my mind not to make you another painful visit. [2] For if I cause you pain, who is there to make me glad but the one whom I have pained? [3] And I wrote as I did, so that when I came, I might not suffer pain from those who should have made me rejoice; for I am confident about all of you, that my joy would be the joy of all of you. [4] For I wrote you out of much distress and anguish of heart and with many tears, not to cause you pain, but to let you know the abundant love that I have for you.

Forgiveness for the Offender

5 But if anyone has caused pain, he has caused it not to me, but to some extent—not to exaggerate it—to all of you. [6] This punishment by the majority is enough for such a person; [7] so now instead you should forgive and console him, so that he may not be overwhelmed by excessive sorrow. [8] So I urge you to reaffirm your love for him. [9] I wrote for this reason: to test you and to know whether you are obedient in everything. [10] Anyone whom you forgive, I also forgive. What I have forgiven, if I have forgiven anything, has been for your sake in the presence of Christ. [11] And we do this so that we may not be outwitted by Satan; for we are not ignorant of his designs.

---

[a] Gk *brothers*   [b] Other ancient authorities read *your*   [c] Other ancient authorities read *holiness*   [d] Other ancient authorities read *pleasure*   [e] Gk *according to the flesh*

Paul's Anxiety in Troas

12 When I came to Trō'as to proclaim the good news of Christ, a door was opened for me in the Lord; [13]but my mind could not rest because I did not find my brother Titus there. So I said farewell to them and went on to Mac·e·dō'ni·a.

14 But thanks be to God, who in Christ always leads us in triumphal procession, and through us spreads in every place the fragrance that comes from knowing him. [15]For we are the aroma of Christ to God among those who are being saved and among those who are perishing; [16]to the one a fragrance from death to death, to the other a fragrance from life to life. Who is sufficient for these things? [17]For we are not peddlers of God's word like so many;[f] but in Christ we speak as persons of sincerity, as persons sent from God and standing in his presence.

Ministers of the New Covenant
(Cp Jer 31.31–34)

3 Are we beginning to commend ourselves again? Surely we do not need, as some do, letters of recommendation to you or from you, do we? [2]You yourselves are our letter, written on our[g] hearts, to be known and read by all; [3]and you show that you are a letter of Christ, prepared by us, written not with ink but with the Spirit of the living God, not on tablets of stone but on tablets of human hearts.

4 Such is the confidence that we have through Christ toward God. [5]Not that we are competent of ourselves to claim anything as coming from us; our competence is from God, [6]who has made us competent to be ministers of a new covenant, not of letter but of spirit; for the letter kills, but the Spirit gives life.

7 Now if the ministry of death, chiseled in letters on stone tablets,[h] came in glory so that the people of Israel could not gaze at Moses' face because of the glory of his face, a glory now set aside, [8]how much more will the ministry of the Spirit come in glory? [9]For if there was glory in the ministry of condemnation, much more does the ministry of justification abound in glory! [10]Indeed, what once had glory has lost its glory because of the greater glory; [11]for if what was set aside came through glory, much more has the permanent come in glory!

12 Since, then, we have such a hope, we act with great boldness, [13]not like Moses, who put a veil over his face to keep the people of Israel from gazing at the end of the glory that[i] was being set aside. [14]But their minds were hardened. Indeed, to this very day, when they hear the reading of the old covenant, that same veil is still there, since only in Christ is it set aside. [15]Indeed, to this very day whenever Moses is read, a veil lies over their minds; [16]but when one turns to the Lord, the veil is removed. [17]Now the Lord is the Spirit, and where the Spirit of the Lord is, there is freedom. [18]And all of us, with unveiled faces, seeing the glory of the Lord as though reflected in a mirror, are being transformed into the same image from one degree of glory to another; for this comes from the Lord, the Spirit.

Treasure in Clay Jars

4 Therefore, since it is by God's mercy that we are engaged in this ministry, we do not lose heart. [2]We have renounced the shameful things that one hides; we refuse to practice cunning or to falsify God's word; but by the open statement of the truth we commend ourselves to the conscience of everyone in the sight of God. [3]And even if our gospel is veiled, it is veiled to those who are perishing. [4]In their case the god of this world has blinded the minds of the unbelievers, to keep them from seeing the light of the gospel of the glory of Christ, who is the image of God. [5]For we do not proclaim ourselves; we proclaim Jesus Christ as Lord and ourselves as your slaves for Jesus' sake. [6]For it is the God who said, "Let light shine out of darkness," who has shone in our hearts to give the light of the knowledge of the glory of God in the face of Jesus Christ.

7 But we have this treasure in clay jars, so that it may be made clear that this extraordinary power belongs to God and does not come from us. [8]We are afflicted in every way, but not crushed; perplexed, but not driven to despair; [9]persecuted, but not forsaken; struck down, but not destroyed; [10]always carrying in the body the death of Jesus, so that the life of Jesus may also be made visible in our bodies.

---

[f]Other ancient authorities read *like the others*　[g]Other ancient authorities read *your*　[h]Gk *on stones*　[i]Gk *of what*

11 For while we live, we are always being given up to death for Jesus' sake, so that the life of Jesus may be made visible in our mortal flesh. 12 So death is at work in us, but life in you.

13 But just as we have the same spirit of faith that is in accordance with scripture—"I believed, and so I spoke"—we also believe, and so we speak, 14 because we know that the one who raised the Lord Jesus will raise us also with Jesus, and will bring us with you into his presence. 15 Yes, everything is for your sake, so that grace, as it extends to more and more people, may increase thanksgiving, to the glory of God.

Living by Faith

16 So we do not lose heart. Even though our outer nature is wasting away, our inner nature is being renewed day by day. 17 For this slight momentary affliction is preparing us for an eternal weight of glory beyond all measure, 18 because we look not at what can be seen but at what cannot be seen; for what can be seen is temporary, but what cannot be seen is eternal.

5 For we know that if the earthly tent we live in is destroyed, we have a building from God, a house not made with hands, eternal in the heavens. 2 For in this tent we groan, longing to be clothed with our heavenly dwelling— 3 if indeed, when we have taken it off[j] we will not be found naked. 4 For while we are still in this tent, we groan under our burden, because we wish not to be unclothed but to be further clothed, so that what is mortal may be swallowed up by life. 5 He who has prepared us for this very thing is God, who has given us the Spirit as a guarantee.

6 So we are always confident; even though we know that while we are at home in the body we are away from the Lord— 7 for we walk by faith, not by sight. 8 Yes, we do have confidence, and we would rather be away from the body and at home with the Lord. 9 So whether we are at home or away, we make it our aim to please him. 10 For all of us must appear before the judgment seat of Christ, so that each may receive recompense for what has been done in the body, whether good or evil.

The Ministry of Reconciliation

11 Therefore, knowing the fear of the Lord, we try to persuade others; but we ourselves are well known to God, and I hope that we are also well known to your consciences. 12 We are not commending ourselves to you again, but giving you an opportunity to boast about us, so that you may be able to answer those who boast in outward appearance and not in the heart. 13 For if we are beside ourselves, it is for God; if we are in our right mind, it is for you. 14 For the love of Christ urges us on, because we are convinced that one has died for all; therefore all have died. 15 And he died for all, so that those who live might live no longer for themselves, but for him who died and was raised for them.

16 From now on, therefore, we regard no one from a human point of view;[k] even though we once knew Christ from a human point of view,[k] we know him no longer in that way. 17 So if anyone is in Christ, there is a new creation: everything old has passed away; see, everything has become new! 18 All this is from God, who reconciled us to himself through Christ, and has given us the ministry of reconciliation; 19 that is, in Christ God was reconciling the world to himself,[l] not counting their trespasses against them, and entrusting the message of reconciliation to us. 20 So we are ambassadors for Christ, since God is making his appeal through us; we entreat you on behalf of Christ, be reconciled to God. 21 For our sake he made him to be sin who knew no sin, so that in him we might become the righteousness of God.

6 As we work together with him,[m] we urge you also not to accept the grace of God in vain. 2 For he says,

"At an acceptable time I have
    listened to you,
and on a day of salvation I
    have helped you."

See, now is the acceptable time; see, now is the day of salvation! 3 We are putting no obstacle in anyone's way, so that no fault may be found with our ministry, 4 but as servants of God we have commended ourselves in every way: through great endurance, in afflictions, hardships, calamities, 5 beatings, imprisonments, riots, labors,

---

j Other ancient authorities read *put it on*   k Gk *according to the flesh*   l Or *God was in Christ reconciling the world to himself*   m Gk *As we work together* sleepless nights, hunger; 6by purity, knowledge, patience, kindness, holiness of spirit, genuine love, 7truthful speech, and the power of God; with the weapons of righteousness for the right hand and for the left; 8in honor and dishonor, in ill repute and good repute. We are treated as impostors, and yet are true; 9as unknown, and yet are well known; as dying, and see—we are alive; as punished, and yet not killed; 10as sorrowful, yet always rejoicing; as poor, yet making many rich; as having nothing, and yet possessing everything.

11 We have spoken frankly to you Corinthians; our heart is wide open to you. 12There is no restriction in our affections, but only in yours. 13In return—I speak as to children—open wide your hearts also.

The Temple of the Living God

14 Do not be mismatched with unbelievers. For what partnership is there between righteousness and lawlessness? Or what fellowship is there between light and darkness? 15What agreement does Christ have with Bē'-li·ar? Or what does a believer share with an unbeliever? 16What agreement has the temple of God with idols? For we[n] are the temple of the living God; as God said,
"I will live in them and walk
          among them,
      and I will be their God,
      and they shall be my people.
17 Therefore come out from them,
      and be separate from them,
          says the Lord,
      and touch nothing unclean;
      then I will welcome you,
18 and I will be your father,
      and you shall be my sons and
          daughters,
      says the Lord Almighty."

7 Since we have these promises, beloved, let us cleanse ourselves from every defilement of body and of spirit, making holiness perfect in the fear of God.

Paul's Joy at the Church's Repentance

2 Make room in your hearts[o] for us; we have wronged no one, we have corrupted no one, we have taken advantage of no one. 3I do not say this to condemn you, for I said before that you are in our hearts, to die together and to live together. 4I often boast about you; I have great pride in you; I am filled with consolation; I am overjoyed in all our affliction.

5 For even when we came into Mac·e·dō'ni·a, our bodies had no rest, but we were afflicted in every way—disputes without and fears within. 6But God, who consoles the downcast, consoled us by the arrival of Titus, 7and not only by his coming, but also by the consolation with which he was consoled about you, as he told us of your longing, your mourning, your zeal for me, so that I rejoiced still more. 8For even if I made you sorry with my letter, I do not regret it (though I did regret it, for I see that I grieved you with that letter, though only briefly). 9Now I rejoice, not because you were grieved, but because your grief led to repentance; for you felt a godly grief, so that you were not harmed in any way by us. 10For godly grief produces a repentance that leads to salvation and brings no regret, but worldly grief produces death. 11For see what earnestness this godly grief has produced in you, what eagerness to clear yourselves, what indignation, what alarm, what longing, what zeal, what punishment! At every point you have proved yourselves guiltless in the matter. 12So although I wrote to you, it was not on account of the one who did the wrong, nor on account of the one who was wronged, but in order that your zeal for us might be made known to you before God. 13In this we find comfort.

In addition to our own consolation, we rejoiced still more at the joy of Titus, because his mind has been set at rest by all of you. 14For if I have been somewhat boastful about you to him, I was not disgraced; but just as everything we said to you was true, so our boasting to Titus has proved true as well. 15And his heart goes out all the more to you, as he remembers the obedience of all of you, and how you welcomed him with fear and trembling. 16I rejoice, because I have complete confidence in you.

Encouragement to Be Generous

8 We want you to know, brothers and sisters,[p] about the grace of God that has been granted to the

---

[n]Other ancient authorities read *you*
[o]Gk lacks *in your hearts*   [p]Gk *brothers*

churches of Mac·e·dō′ni·a; [2] for during a severe ordeal of affliction, their abundant joy and their extreme poverty have overflowed in a wealth of generosity on their part. [3] For, as I can testify, they voluntarily gave according to their means, and even beyond their means, [4] begging us earnestly for the privilege[q] of sharing in this ministry to the saints— [5] and this, not merely as we expected; they gave themselves first to the Lord and, by the will of God, to us, [6] so that we might urge Titus that, as he had already made a beginning, so he should also complete this generous undertaking[r] among you. [7] Now as you excel in everything—in faith, in speech, in knowledge, in utmost eagerness, and in our love for you[s]—so we want you to excel also in this generous undertaking.[r]

[8] I do not say this as a command, but I am testing the genuineness of your love against the earnestness of others. [9] For you know the generous act[t] of our Lord Jesus Christ, that though he was rich, yet for your sakes he became poor, so that by his poverty you might become rich. [10] And in this matter I am giving my advice: it is appropriate for you who began last year not only to do something but even to desire to do something— [11] now finish doing it, so that your eagerness may be matched by completing it according to your means. [12] For if the eagerness is there, the gift is acceptable according to what one has—not according to what one does not have. [13] I do not mean that there should be relief for others and pressure on you, but it is a question of a fair balance between [14] your present abundance and their need, so that their abundance may be for your need, in order that there may be a fair balance. [15] As it is written,

"The one who had much did not have too much,
and the one who had little did not have too little."

Commendation of Titus

[16] But thanks be to God who put in the heart of Titus the same eagerness for you that I myself have. [17] For he not only accepted our appeal, but since he is more eager than ever, he is going to you of his own accord. [18] With him we are sending the brother who is famous among all the churches for his proclaiming of the good news;[u] [19] and not only that, but he has also been appointed by the churches to travel with us while we are administering this generous undertaking[r] for the glory of the Lord himself[v] and to show our goodwill. [20] We intend that no one should blame us about this generous gift that we are administering, [21] for we intend to do what is right not only in the Lord's sight but also in the sight of others. [22] And with them we are sending our brother whom we have often tested and found eager in many matters, but who is now more eager than ever because of his great confidence in you. [23] As for Titus, he is my partner and co-worker in your service; as for our brothers, they are messengers[w] of the churches, the glory of Christ. [24] Therefore openly before the churches, show them the proof of your love and of our reason for boasting about you.

The Collection for Christians at Jerusalem

9 Now it is not necessary for me to write you about the ministry to the saints, [2] for I know your eagerness, which is the subject of my boasting about you to the people of Mac·e·dō′ni·a, saying that A·chā′i·a has been ready since last year; and your zeal has stirred up most of them. [3] But I am sending the brothers in order that our boasting about you may not prove to have been empty in this case, so that you may be ready, as I said you would be; [4] otherwise, if some Mac·e·dō′ni·ans come with me and find that you are not ready, we would be humiliated—to say nothing of you—in this undertaking.[x] [5] So I thought it necessary to urge the brothers to go on ahead to you, and arrange in advance for this bountiful gift that you have promised, so that it may be ready as a voluntary gift and not as an extortion.

[6] The point is this: the one who sows sparingly will also reap sparingly, and the one who sows bountifully will also reap bountifully. [7] Each of you must give as you have made up your mind, not reluctantly or under

2 CORINTHIANS

compulsion, for God loves a cheerful giver. [8] And God is able to provide you with every blessing in abundance, so that by always having enough of everything, you may share abundantly in every good work. [9] As it is written,

"He scatters abroad, he gives to
      the poor;
   his righteousness[y] endures
      forever."

[10] He who supplies seed to the sower and bread for food will supply and multiply your seed for sowing and increase the harvest of your righteousness.[y] [11] You will be enriched in every way for your great generosity, which will produce thanksgiving to God through us; [12] for the rendering of this ministry not only supplies the needs of the saints but also overflows with many thanksgivings to God. [13] Through the testing of this ministry you glorify God by your obedience to the confession of the gospel of Christ and by the generosity of your sharing with them and with all others, [14] while they long for you and pray for you because of the surpassing grace of God that he has given you. [15] Thanks be to God for his indescribable gift!

Paul Defends His Ministry

10 I myself, Paul, appeal to you by the meekness and gentleness of Christ—I who am humble when face to face with you, but bold toward you when I am away!— [2] I ask that when I am present I need not show boldness by daring to oppose those who think we are acting according to human standards.[z] [3] Indeed, we live as human beings,[a] but we do not wage war according to human standards;[z] [4] for the weapons of our warfare are not merely human,[b] but they have divine power to destroy strongholds. We destroy arguments [5] and every proud obstacle raised up against the knowledge of God, and we take every thought captive to obey Christ. [6] We are ready to punish every disobedience when your obedience is complete.

[7] Look at what is before your eyes. If you are confident that you belong to Christ, remind yourself of this, that just as you belong to Christ, so also do we. [8] Now, even if I boast a little too much of our authority, which the Lord gave for building you up and not for tearing you down, I will not be ashamed of it. [9] I do not want to seem as though I am trying to frighten you with my letters. [10] For they say, "His letters are weighty and strong, but his bodily presence is weak, and his speech contemptible." [11] Let such people understand that what we say by letter when absent, we will also do when present.

[12] We do not dare to classify or compare ourselves with some of those who commend themselves. But when they measure themselves by one another, and compare themselves with one another, they do not show good sense. [13] We, however, will not boast beyond limits, but will keep within the field that God has assigned to us, to reach out even as far as you. [14] For we were not overstepping our limits when we reached you; we were the first to come all the way to you with the good news[c] of Christ. [15] We do not boast beyond limits, that is, in the labors of others; but our hope is that, as your faith increases, our sphere of action among you may be greatly enlarged, [16] so that we may proclaim the good news[c] in lands beyond you, without boasting of work already done in someone else's sphere of action. [17] "Let the one who boasts, boast in the Lord." [18] For it is not those who commend themselves that are approved, but those whom the Lord commends.

Paul and the False Apostles

11 I wish you would bear with me in a little foolishness. Do bear with me! [2] I feel a divine jealousy for you, for I promised you in marriage to one husband, to present you as a chaste virgin to Christ. [3] But I am afraid that as the serpent deceived Eve by its cunning, your thoughts will be led astray from a sincere and pure[d] devotion to Christ. [4] For if someone comes and proclaims another Jesus than the one we proclaimed, or if you receive a different spirit from the one you received, or a different gospel from the one you accepted, you submit to it readily enough. [5] I think that I am not in the least inferior to these superapostles. [6] I may be untrained in speech, but not in knowledge; certainly in every way and in all things we have made this evident to you.

---

[y] Or *benevolence*   [z] Gk *according to the flesh*   [a] Gk *in the flesh*   [b] Gk *fleshly*   [c] Or *the gospel*   [d] Other ancient authorities lack *and pure*

7 Did I commit a sin by humbling myself so that you might be exalted, because I proclaimed God's good news[e] to you free of charge? [8]I robbed other churches by accepting support from them in order to serve you. [9]And when I was with you and was in need, I did not burden anyone, for my needs were supplied by the friends[f] who came from Mac·e·dō'ni·a. So I refrained and will continue to refrain from burdening you in any way. [10]As the truth of Christ is in me, this boast of mine will not be silenced in the regions of A·chā'i·a. [11]And why? Because I do not love you? God knows I do!

12 And what I do I will also continue to do, in order to deny an opportunity to those who want an opportunity to be recognized as our equals in what they boast about. [13]For such boasters are false apostles, deceitful workers, disguising themselves as apostles of Christ. [14]And no wonder! Even Satan disguises himself as an angel of light. [15]So it is not strange if his ministers also disguise themselves as ministers of righteousness. Their end will match their deeds.

Paul's Sufferings as an Apostle

16 I repeat, let no one think that I am a fool; but if you do, then accept me as a fool, so that I too may boast a little. [17]What I am saying in regard to this boastful confidence, I am saying not with the Lord's authority, but as a fool; [18]since many boast according to human standards,[g] I will also boast. [19]For you gladly put up with fools, being wise yourselves! [20]For you put up with it when someone makes slaves of you, or preys upon you, or takes advantage of you, or puts on airs, or gives you a slap in the face. [21]To my shame, I must say, we were too weak for that!

But whatever anyone dares to boast of—I am speaking as a fool—I also dare to boast of that. [22]Are they Hebrews? So am I. Are they Israelites? So am I. Are they descendants of Abraham? So am I. [23]Are they ministers of Christ? I am talking like a madman—I am a better one: with far greater labors, far more imprisonments, with countless floggings, and often near death. [24]Five times I have received from the Jews the forty lashes minus one. [25]Three times I was beaten with rods. Once I received a stoning. Three times I was shipwrecked; for a night and a day I was adrift at sea; [26]on frequent journeys, in danger from rivers, danger from bandits, danger from my own people, danger from Gentiles, danger in the city, danger in the wilderness, danger at sea, danger from false brothers and sisters;[f] [27]in toil and hardship, through many a sleepless night, hungry and thirsty, often without food, cold and naked. [28]And, besides other things, I am under daily pressure because of my anxiety for all the churches. [29]Who is weak, and I am not weak? Who is made to stumble, and I am not indignant?

30 If I must boast, I will boast of the things that show my weakness. [31]The God and Father of the Lord Jesus (blessed be he forever!) knows that I do not lie. [32]In Damascus, the governor[h] under King Ar'e·tas guarded the city of Damascus in order to[i] seize me, [33]but I was let down in a basket through a window in the wall,[j] and escaped from his hands.

Paul's Visions and Revelations

12 It is necessary to boast; nothing is to be gained by it, but I will go on to visions and revelations of the Lord. [2]I know a person in Christ who fourteen years ago was caught up to the third heaven—whether in the body or out of the body I do not know; God knows. [3]And I know that such a person—whether in the body or out of the body I do not know; God knows— [4]was caught up into Paradise and heard things that are not to be told, that no mortal is permitted to repeat. [5]On behalf of such a one I will boast, but on my own behalf I will not boast, except of my weaknesses. [6]But if I wish to boast, I will not be a fool, for I will be speaking the truth. But I refrain from it, so that no one may think better of me than what is seen in me or heard from me, [7]even considering the exceptional character of the revelations. Therefore, to keep[k] me from being too elated, a thorn was given me in the flesh, a messenger of Satan to torment me, to keep me from being too elated.[l]

[e] Gk the gospel of God   [f] Gk brothers
[g] Gk according to the flesh
[h] Gk ethnarch   [i] Other ancient authorities read and wanted to
[j] Gk through the wall   [k] Other ancient authorities read To keep   [l] Other ancient authorities lack to keep me from being too elated

2 CORINTHIANS

8 Three times I appealed to the Lord about this, that it would leave me, 9 but he said to me, "My grace is sufficient for you, for power *m* is made perfect in weakness." So, I will boast all the more gladly of my weaknesses, so that the power of Christ may dwell in me. 10 Therefore I am content with weaknesses, insults, hardships, persecutions, and calamities for the sake of Christ; for whenever I am weak, then I am strong.

Paul's Concern for the Corinthian Church

11 I have been a fool! You forced me to it. Indeed you should have been the ones commending me, for I am not at all inferior to these super-apostles, even though I am nothing. 12 The signs of a true apostle were performed among you with utmost patience, signs and wonders and mighty works. 13 How have you been worse off than the other churches, except that I myself did not burden you? Forgive me this wrong!

14 Here I am, ready to come to you this third time. And I will not be a burden, because I do not want what is yours but you; for children ought not to lay up for their parents, but parents for their children. 15 I will most gladly spend and be spent for you. If I love you more, am I to be loved less? 16 Let it be assumed that I did not burden you. Nevertheless (you say) since I was crafty, I took you in by deceit. 17 Did I take advantage of you through any of those whom I sent to you? 18 I urged Titus to go, and sent the brother with him. Titus did not take advantage of you, did he? Did we not conduct ourselves with the same spirit? Did we not take the same steps?

19 Have you been thinking all along that we have been defending ourselves before you? We are speaking in Christ before God. Everything we do, beloved, is for the sake of building you up. 20 For I fear that when I come, I may find you not as I wish, and that you may find me not as you wish; I fear that there may perhaps be quarreling, jealousy, anger, selfishness, slander, gossip, conceit, and disorder. 21 I fear that when I come again, my God may humble me before you, and that I may have to mourn over many who previously sinned and have not repented of the impurity, sexual immorality, and licentiousness that they have practiced.

Further Warning

13 This is the third time I am coming to you. "Any charge must be sustained by the evidence of two or three witnesses." 2 I warned those who sinned previously and all the others, and I warn them now while absent, as I did when present on my second visit, that if I come again, I will not be lenient— 3 since you desire proof that Christ is speaking in me. He is not weak in dealing with you, but is powerful in you. 4 For he was crucified in weakness, but lives by the power of God. For we are weak in him, *n* but in dealing with you we will live with him by the power of God.

5 Examine yourselves to see whether you are living in the faith. Test yourselves. Do you not realize that Jesus Christ is in you?—unless, indeed, you fail to meet the test! 6 I hope you will find out that we have not failed. 7 But we pray to God that you may not do anything wrong—not that we may appear to have met the test, but that you may do what is right, though we may seem to have failed. 8 For we cannot do anything against the truth, but only for the truth. 9 For we rejoice when we are weak and you are strong. This is what we pray for, that you may become perfect. 10 So I write these things while I am away from you, so that when I come, I may not have to be severe in using the authority that the Lord has given me for building up and not for tearing down.

Final Greetings and Benediction

11 Finally, brothers and sisters, *o* farewell. *p* Put things in order, listen to my appeal, *q* agree with one another, live in peace; and the God of love and peace will be with you. 12 Greet one another with a holy kiss. All the saints greet you.

13 The grace of the Lord Jesus Christ, the love of God, and the communion of *r* the Holy Spirit be with all of you.

---

m Other ancient authorities read *my power*   *n* Other ancient authorities read *with him*   *o* Gk *brothers*   *p* Or *rejoice*   *q* Or *encourage one another*   *r* Or *and the sharing in*

The Letter of Paul to the

GALATIANS

Salutation

1 Paul an apostle—sent neither by human commission nor from human authorities, but through Jesus Christ and God the Father, who raised him from the dead— [2] and all the members of God's family[a] who are with me,

To the churches of Galatia:

3 Grace to you and peace from God our Father and the Lord Jesus Christ, [4] who gave himself for our sins to set us free from the present evil age, according to the will of our God and Father, [5] to whom be the glory forever and ever. Amen.

There Is No Other Gospel

6 I am astonished that you are so quickly deserting the one who called you in the grace of Christ and are turning to a different gospel— [7] not that there is another gospel, but there are some who are confusing you and want to pervert the gospel of Christ. [8] But even if we or an angel[b] from heaven should proclaim to you a gospel contrary to what we proclaimed to you, let that one be accursed! [9] As we have said before, so now I repeat, if anyone proclaims to you a gospel contrary to what you received, let that one be accursed!

10 Am I now seeking human approval, or God's approval? Or am I trying to please people? If I were still pleasing people, I would not be a servant[c] of Christ.

Paul's Vindication of His Apostleship
(Cp Acts 9)

11 For I want you to know, brothers and sisters,[d] that the gospel that was proclaimed by me is not of human origin; [12] for I did not receive it from a human source, nor was I taught it, but I received it through a revelation of Jesus Christ.
13 You have heard, no doubt, of my earlier life in Jū′da·ism. I was violently persecuting the church of God and was trying to destroy it. [14] I advanced in Jū′da·ism beyond many among my people of the same age, for I was far more zealous for the traditions of my ancestors. [15] But when God, who had set me apart before I was born and called me through his grace, was pleased [16] to reveal his Son to me,[e] so that I might proclaim him among the Gentiles, I did not confer with any human being, [17] nor did I go up to Jerusalem to those who were already apostles before me, but I went away at once into Arabia, and afterwards I returned to Damascus.

18 Then after three years I did go up to Jerusalem to visit Cē′phas and stayed with him fifteen days; [19] but I did not see any other apostle except James the Lord's brother. [20] In what I am writing to you, before God, I do not lie! [21] Then I went into the regions of Syria and Ci·li′ci·a, [22] and I was still unknown by sight to the churches of Judea that are in Christ; [23] they only heard it said, "The one who formerly was persecuting us is now proclaiming the faith he once tried to destroy." [24] And they glorified God because of me.

Paul and the Other Apostles
(Cp Acts 15.1–21)

2 Then after fourteen years I went up again to Jerusalem with Bar′na·bas, taking Titus along with me. [2] I went up in response to a revelation. Then I laid before them (though only in a private meeting with the acknowledged leaders) the gospel that I proclaim among the Gentiles, in order to make sure that I was not running, or had not run, in vain. [3] But even Titus, who was with me, was not compelled to be circumcised, though he was a

---

[a] Gk *all the brothers* [b] Or *a messenger*
[c] Gk *slave* [d] Gk *brothers* [e] Gk *in me*

Greek. [4] But because of false believers[f] secretly brought in, who slipped in to spy on the freedom we have in Christ Jesus, so that they might enslave us— [5] we did not submit to them even for a moment, so that the truth of the gospel might always remain with you. [6] And from those who were supposed to be acknowledged leaders (what they actually were makes no difference to me; God shows no partiality)—those leaders contributed nothing to me. [7] On the contrary, when they saw that I had been entrusted with the gospel for the uncircumcised, just as Peter had been entrusted with the gospel for the circumcised [8] (for he who worked through Peter making him an apostle to the circumcised also worked through me in sending me to the Gentiles), [9] and when James and Cĕ'phas and John, who were acknowledged pillars, recognized the grace that had been given to me, they gave to Bar'na·bas and me the right hand of fellowship, agreeing that we should go to the Gentiles and they to the circumcised. [10] They asked only one thing, that we remember the poor, which was actually what I was[g] eager to do.

Paul Rebukes Peter at Antioch

11 But when Cĕ'phas came to An'ti·och, I opposed him to his face, because he stood self-condemned; [12] for until certain people came from James, he used to eat with the Gentiles. But after they came, he drew back and kept himself separate for fear of the circumcision faction. [13] And the other Jews joined him in this hypocrisy, so that even Bar'na·bas was led astray by their hypocrisy. [14] But when I saw that they were not acting consistently with the truth of the gospel, I said to Cĕ'phas before them all, "If you, though a Jew, live like a Gentile and not like a Jew, how can you compel the Gentiles to live like Jews?"[h]

Jews and Gentiles Are Saved by Faith

15 We ourselves are Jews by birth and not Gentile sinners; [16] yet we know that a person is justified[i] not by the works of the law but through faith in Jesus Christ.[j] And we have come to believe in Christ Jesus, so that we might be justified by faith in Christ,[k] and not by doing the works of the law, because no one will be justified by the works of the law. [17] But if, in our effort to be justified in Christ, we ourselves have been found to be sinners, is Christ then a servant of sin? Certainly not! [18] But if I build up again the very things that I once tore down, then I demonstrate that I am a transgressor. [19] For through the law I died to the law, so that I might live to God. I have been crucified with Christ; [20] and it is no longer I who live, but it is Christ who lives in me. And the life I now live in the flesh I live by faith in the Son of God,[l] who loved me and gave himself for me. [21] I do not nullify the grace of God; for if justification[m] comes through the law, then Christ died for nothing.

Law or Faith
(Cp Rom 4.1–25)

3 You foolish Galatians! Who has bewitched you? It was before your eyes that Jesus Christ was publicly exhibited as crucified! [2] The only thing I want to learn from you is this: Did you receive the Spirit by doing the works of the law or by believing what you heard? [3] Are you so foolish? Having started with the Spirit, are you now ending with the flesh? [4] Did you experience so much for nothing?—if it really was for nothing. [5] Well then, does God[n] supply you with the Spirit and work miracles among you by your doing the works of the law, or by your believing what you heard?

6 Just as Abraham "believed God, and it was reckoned to him as righteousness," [7] so, you see, those who believe are the descendants of Abraham. [8] And the scripture, foreseeing that God would justify the Gentiles by faith, declared the gospel beforehand to Abraham, saying, "All the Gentiles shall be blessed in you." [9] For this reason, those who believe are blessed with Abraham who believed.

10 For all who rely on the works of the law are under a curse; for it is written, "Cursed is everyone who does not observe and obey all the things written in the book of the law." [11] Now it is evident that no one is justified before God by the law; for "The one who is

---

[f] Gk *false brothers*   [g] Or *had been*
[h] Some interpreters hold that the quotation extends into the following paragraph   [i] Or *reckoned as righteous; and so elsewhere*   [j] Or *the faith of Jesus Christ*   [k] Or *the faith of Christ*
[l] Or *by the faith of the Son of God*
[m] Or *righteousness*   [n] Gk *he*

righteous will live by faith."ᵒ ¹²But the law does not rest on faith; on the contrary, "Whoever does the works of the lawᵖ will live by them." ¹³Christ redeemed us from the curse of the law by becoming a curse for us—for it is written, "Cursed is everyone who hangs on a tree"— ¹⁴in order that in Christ Jesus the blessing of Abraham might come to the Gentiles, so that we might receive the promise of the Spirit through faith.

The Promise to Abraham
(Cp Gen 12.1–3)

15 Brothers and sisters,�q I give an example from daily life: once a person's willʳ has been ratified, no one adds to it or annuls it. ¹⁶Now the promises were made to Abraham and to his offspring;ˢ it does not say, "And to offsprings,"ᵗ as of many; but it says, "And to your offspring,"ˢ that is, to one person, who is Christ. ¹⁷My point is this: the law, which came four hundred thirty years later, does not annul a covenant previously ratified by God, so as to nullify the promise. ¹⁸For if the inheritance comes from the law, it no longer comes from the promise; but God granted it to Abraham through the promise.

The Purpose of the Law

19 Why then the law? It was added because of transgressions, until the offspringˢ would come to whom the promise had been made; and it was ordained through angels by a mediator. ²⁰Now a mediator involves more than one party; but God is one. 21 Is the law then opposed to the promises of God? Certainly not! For if a law had been given that could make alive, then righteousness would indeed come through the law. ²²But the scripture has imprisoned all things under the power of sin, so that what was promised through faith in Jesus Christᵘ might be given to those who believe. 23 Now before faith came, we were imprisoned and guarded under the law until faith would be revealed. ²⁴Therefore the law was our disciplinarian until Christ came, so that we might be justified by faith. ²⁵But now that faith has come, we are no longer subject to a disciplinarian, ²⁶for in Christ Jesus you are all children of God through faith. ²⁷As many of you as were bap-

tized into Christ have clothed yourselves with Christ. ²⁸There is no longer Jew or Greek, there is no longer slave or free, there is no longer male and female; for all of you are one in Christ Jesus. ²⁹And if you belong to Christ, then you are Abraham's offspring,ˢ heirs according to the promise.

4 My point is this: heirs, as long as they are minors, are no better than slaves, though they are the owners of all the property; ²but they remain under guardians and trustees until the date set by the father. ³So with us; while we were minors, we were enslaved to the elemental spiritsᵛ of the world. ⁴But when the fullness of time had come, God sent his Son, born of a woman, born under the law, ⁵in order to redeem those who were under the law, so that we might receive adoption as children. ⁶And because you are children, God has sent the Spirit of his Son into ourʷ hearts, crying, "Abba!ˣ Father!" ⁷So you are no longer a slave but a child, and if a child then also an heir, through God.ʸ

Paul Reproves the Galatians

8 Formerly, when you did not know God, you were enslaved to beings that by nature are not gods. ⁹Now, however, that you have come to know God, or rather to be known by God, how can you turn back again to the weak and beggarly elemental spirits?ᶻ How can you want to be enslaved to them again? ¹⁰You are observing special days, and months, and seasons, and years. ¹¹I am afraid that my work for you may have been wasted. 12 Friends,q I beg you, become as I am, for I also have become as you are. You have done me no wrong. ¹³You know that it was because of a physical infirmity that I first announced the gospel to you; ¹⁴though my condition put you to the test, you did not scorn or despise me, but welcomed me as an angel of God, as Christ Jesus. ¹⁵What has become of the goodwill you felt?

ᵒOr The one who is righteous through faith will live   ᵖGk does them
qGk Brothers   ʳOr covenant (as in verse 17)   ˢGk seed   ᵗGk seeds
ᵘOr through the faith of Jesus Christ
ᵛOr the rudiments   ʷOther ancient authorities read your   ˣAramaic for Father   ʸOther ancient authorities read an heir of God through Christ
ᶻOr beggarly rudiments

For I testify that, had it been possible, you would have torn out your eyes and given them to me. [16]Have I now become your enemy by telling you the truth? [17]They make much of you, but for no good purpose; they want to exclude you, so that you may make much of them. [18]It is good to be made much of for a good purpose at all times, and not only when I am present with you. [19]My little children, for whom I am again in the pain of childbirth until Christ is formed in you, [20]I wish I were present with you now and could change my tone, for I am perplexed about you.

The Allegory of Hagar and Sarah
(Gen 21.8–21; Isa 54.1)

21 Tell me, you who desire to be subject to the law, will you not listen to the law? [22]For it is written that Abraham had two sons, one by a slave woman and the other by a free woman. [23]One, the child of the slave, was born according to the flesh; the other, the child of the free woman, was born through the promise. [24]Now this is an allegory: these women are two covenants. One woman, in fact, is Hā´gar, from Mount Sinai, bearing children for slavery. [25]Now Hā´gar is Mount Sinai in Arabia[a] and corresponds to the present Jerusalem, for she is in slavery with her children. [26]But the other woman corresponds to the Jerusalem above; she is free, and she is our mother. [27]For it is written,

"Rejoice, you childless one, you
   who bear no children,
burst into song and shout, you
   who endure no birth pangs;
for the children of the desolate
   woman are more numerous
than the children of the one
   who is married."

[28]Now you,[b] my friends,[c] are children of the promise, like Isaac. [29]But just as at that time the child who was born according to the flesh persecuted the child who was born according to the Spirit, so it is now also. [30]But what does the scripture say? "Drive out the slave and her child; for the child of the slave will not share the inheritance with the child of the free woman." [31]So then, friends,[c] we are children, not of the slave but of the free woman.

5 [1]For freedom Christ has set us free. Stand firm, therefore, and do not submit again to a yoke of slavery.

The Nature of Christian Freedom

2 Listen! I, Paul, am telling you that if you let yourselves be circumcised, Christ will be of no benefit to you. [3]Once again I testify to every man who lets himself be circumcised that he is obliged to obey the entire law. [4]You who want to be justified by the law have cut yourselves off from Christ; you have fallen away from grace. [5]For through the Spirit, by faith, we eagerly wait for the hope of righteousness. [6]For in Christ Jesus neither circumcision nor uncircumcision counts for anything; the only thing that counts is faith working[d] through love.

7 You were running well; who prevented you from obeying the truth? [8]Such persuasion does not come from the one who calls you. [9]A little yeast leavens the whole batch of dough. [10]I am confident about you in the Lord that you will not think otherwise. But whoever it is that is confusing you will pay the penalty. [11]But my friends,[c] why am I still being persecuted if I am still preaching circumcision? In that case the offense of the cross has been removed. [12]I wish those who unsettle you would castrate themselves!

13 For you were called to freedom, brothers and sisters;[c] only do not use your freedom as an opportunity for self-indulgence,[e] but through love become slaves to one another. [14]For the whole law is summed up in a single commandment, "You shall love your neighbor as yourself." [15]If, however, you bite and devour one another, take care that you are not consumed by one another.

The Works of the Flesh

16 Live by the Spirit, I say, and do not gratify the desires of the flesh. [17]For what the flesh desires is opposed to the Spirit, and what the Spirit desires is opposed to the flesh; for these are opposed to each other, to prevent you from doing what you want. [18]But if you are led by the Spirit, you are not subject to the law. [19]Now the works of the flesh are obvious: fornication, impurity, licentiousness, [20]idolatry, sorcery, enmities, strife, jealousy, anger, quarrels, dissensions, factions,

---

[a]Other ancient authorities read *For Sinai is a mountain in Arabia*   [b]Other ancient authorities read *we*   [c]Gk *brothers*   [d]Or *made effective*   [e]Gk *the flesh*

21 envy,ᶠ drunkenness, carousing, and things like these. I am warning you, as I warned you before: those who do such things will not inherit the kingdom of God.

The Fruit of the Spirit
(Cp Col 3.12–13)

22　By contrast, the fruit of the Spirit is love, joy, peace, patience, kindness, generosity, faithfulness, 23 gentleness, and self-control. There is no law against such things. 24 And those who belong to Christ Jesus have crucified the flesh with its passions and desires. 25 If we live by the Spirit, let us also be guided by the Spirit. 26 Let us not become conceited, competing against one another, envying one another.

Bear One Another's Burdens

6 My friends,ᵍ if anyone is detected in a transgression, you who have received the Spirit should restore such a one in a spirit of gentleness. Take care that you yourselves are not tempted. 2 Bear one another's burdens, and in this way you will fulfill ʰ the law of Christ. 3 For if those who are nothing think they are something, they deceive themselves. 4 All must test their own work; then that work, rather than their neighbor's work, will become a cause for pride. 5 For all must carry their own loads.

6　Those who are taught the word must share in all good things with their teacher.

7　Do not be deceived; God is not mocked, for you reap whatever you sow. 8 If you sow to your own flesh, you will reap corruption from the flesh; but if you sow to the Spirit, you will reap eternal life from the Spirit. 9 So let us not grow weary in doing what is right, for we will reap at harvest time, if we do not give up. 10 So then, whenever we have an opportunity, let us work for the good of all, and especially for those of the family of faith.

Final Admonitions and Benediction

11　See what large letters I make when I am writing in my own hand! 12 It is those who want to make a good showing in the flesh that try to compel you to be circumcised—only that they may not be persecuted for the cross of Christ. 13 Even the circumcised do not themselves obey the law, but they want you to be circumcised so that they may boast about your flesh. 14 May I never boast of anything except the cross of our Lord Jesus Christ, by whichⁱ the world has been crucified to me, and I to the world. 15 Forʲ neither circumcision nor uncircumcision is anything; but a new creation is everything! 16 As for those who will follow this rule—peace be upon them, and mercy, and upon the Israel of God.

17　From now on, let no one make trouble for me; for I carry the marks of Jesus branded on my body.

18　May the grace of our Lord Jesus Christ be with your spirit, brothers and sisters.ᵏ Amen.

ᶠ Other ancient authorities add *murder*
ᵍ Gk *Brothers*　ʰ Other ancient authorities read *in this way fulfill*
ⁱ Or *through whom*　ʲ Other ancient authorities add *in Christ Jesus*
ᵏ Gk *brothers*

The Letter of Paul to the

EPHESIANS

Salutation

1 Paul, an apostle of Christ Jesus by the will of God,
To the saints who are in Eph'e·sus and are faithfulᵃ in Christ Jesus:
2　Grace to you and peace from God our Father and the Lord Jesus Christ.

ᵃ Other ancient authorities lack *in Ephesus*, reading *saints who are also faithful*

Spiritual Blessings in Christ

3 Blessed be the God and Father of our Lord Jesus Christ, who has blessed us in Christ with every spiritual blessing in the heavenly places, [4]just as he chose us in Christ[b] before the foundation of the world to be holy and blameless before him in love. [5]He destined us for adoption as his children through Jesus Christ, according to the good pleasure of his will, [6]to the praise of his glorious grace that he freely bestowed on us in the Beloved. [7]In him we have redemption through his blood, the forgiveness of our trespasses, according to the riches of his grace [8]that he lavished on us. With all wisdom and insight [9]he has made known to us the mystery of his will, according to his good pleasure that he set forth in Christ, [10]as a plan for the fullness of time, to gather up all things in him, things in heaven and things on earth. [11]In Christ we have also obtained an inheritance,[c] having been destined according to the purpose of him who accomplishes all things according to his counsel and will, [12]so that we, who were the first to set our hope on Christ, might live for the praise of his glory. [13]In him you also, when you had heard the word of truth, the gospel of your salvation, and had believed in him, were marked with the seal of the promised Holy Spirit; [14]this[d] is the pledge of our inheritance toward redemption as God's own people, to the praise of his glory.

Paul's Prayer

15 I have heard of your faith in the Lord Jesus and your love[e] toward all the saints, and for this reason [16]I do not cease to give thanks for you as I remember you in my prayers. [17]I pray that the God of our Lord Jesus Christ, the Father of glory, may give you a spirit of wisdom and revelation as you come to know him, [18]so that, with the eyes of your heart enlightened, you may know what is the hope to which he has called you, what are the riches of his glorious inheritance among the saints, [19]and what is the immeasurable greatness of his power for us who believe, according to the working of his great power. [20]God[f] put this power to work in Christ when he raised him from the dead and seated him at his right hand in the heavenly places, [21]far above all rule and authority and power

and dominion, and above every name that is named, not only in this age but also in the age to come. [22]And he has put all things under his feet and has made him the head over all things for the church, [23]which is his body, the fullness of him who fills all in all.

From Death to Life

2 You were dead through the trespasses and sins [2]in which you once lived, following the course of this world, following the ruler of the power of the air, the spirit that is now at work among those who are disobedient. [3]All of us once lived among them in the passions of our flesh, following the desires of flesh and senses, and we were by nature children of wrath, like everyone else. [4]But God, who is rich in mercy, out of the great love with which he loved us [5]even when we were dead through our trespasses, made us alive together with Christ[g]—by grace you have been saved—[6]and raised us up with him and seated us with him in the heavenly places in Christ Jesus, [7]so that in the ages to come he might show the immeasurable riches of his grace in kindness toward us in Christ Jesus. [8]For by grace you have been saved through faith, and this is not your own doing; it is the gift of God— [9]not the result of works, so that no one may boast. [10]For we are what he has made us, created in Christ Jesus for good works, which God prepared beforehand to be our way of life.

One in Christ

11 So then, remember that at one time you Gentiles by birth,[h] called "the uncircumcision" by those who are called "the circumcision"—a physical circumcision made in the flesh by human hands— [12]remember that you were at that time without Christ, being aliens from the commonwealth of Israel, and strangers to the covenants of promise, having no hope and without God in the world. [13]But now in Christ Jesus you who once were far off have been brought near by the blood of Christ. [14]For he is our peace; in his flesh he has made both groups into one

[b]Gk *in him*   [c]Or *been made a heritage*
[d]Other ancient authorities read *who*
[e]Other ancient authorities lack *and your love*   [f]Gk *He*   [g]Other ancient authorities read *in Christ*   [h]Gk *in the flesh*

and has broken down the dividing wall, that is, the hostility between us. [15]He has abolished the law with its commandments and ordinances, that he might create in himself one new humanity in place of the two, thus making peace, [16]and might reconcile both groups to God in one body[i] through the cross, thus putting to death that hostility through it.[j] [17]So he came and proclaimed peace to you who were far off and peace to those who were near; [18]for through him both of us have access in one Spirit to the Father. [19]So then you are no longer strangers and aliens, but you are citizens with the saints and also members of the household of God, [20]built upon the foundation of the apostles and prophets, with Christ Jesus himself as the cornerstone.[k] [21]In him the whole structure is joined together and grows into a holy temple in the Lord; [22]in whom you also are built together spiritually[l] into a dwelling place for God.

Paul's Ministry to the Gentiles

3 This is the reason that I Paul am a prisoner for[m] Christ Jesus for the sake of you Gentiles— [2]for surely you have already heard of the commission of God's grace that was given me for you, [3]and how the mystery was made known to me by revelation, as I wrote above in a few words, [4]a reading of which will enable you to perceive my understanding of the mystery of Christ. [5]In former generations this mystery[n] was not made known to humankind, as it has now been revealed to his holy apostles and prophets by the Spirit: [6]that is, the Gentiles have become fellow heirs, members of the same body, and sharers in the promise in Christ Jesus through the gospel.

[7] Of this gospel I have become a servant according to the gift of God's grace that was given me by the working of his power. [8]Although I am the very least of all the saints, this grace was given to me to bring to the Gentiles the news of the boundless riches of Christ, [9]and to make everyone see[o] what is the plan of the mystery hidden for ages in[p] God who created all things; [10]so that through the church the wisdom of God in its rich variety might now be made known to the rulers and authorities in the heavenly places. [11]This was in accordance with the eternal purpose that he has carried out in Christ Jesus our Lord, [12]in

whom we have access to God in boldness and confidence through faith in him.[q] [13]I pray therefore that you[r] may not lose heart over my sufferings for you; they are your glory.

Prayer for the Readers

[14] For this reason I bow my knees before the Father,[s] [15]from whom every family[t] in heaven and on earth takes its name. [16]I pray that, according to the riches of his glory, he may grant that you may be strengthened in your inner being with power through his Spirit, [17]and that Christ may dwell in your hearts through faith, as you are being rooted and grounded in love. [18]I pray that you may have the power to comprehend, with all the saints, what is the breadth and length and height and depth, [19]and to know the love of Christ that surpasses knowledge, so that you may be filled with all the fullness of God.

[20] Now to him who by the power at work within us is able to accomplish abundantly far more than all we can ask or imagine, [21]to him be glory in the church and in Christ Jesus to all generations, forever and ever. Amen.

Unity in the Body of Christ

4 I therefore, the prisoner in the Lord, beg you to lead a life worthy of the calling to which you have been called, [2]with all humility and gentleness, with patience, bearing with one another in love, [3]making every effort to maintain the unity of the Spirit in the bond of peace. [4]There is one body and one Spirit, just as you were called to the one hope of your calling, [5]one Lord, one faith, one baptism, [6]one God and Father of all, who is above all and through all and in all.

[7] But each of us was given grace according to the measure of Christ's gift. [8]Therefore it is said,
> "When he ascended on high he
>> made captivity itself a
>> captive;
> he gave gifts to his people."

[9](When it says, "He ascended," what

does it mean but that he had also descended[u] into the lower parts of the earth? [10]He who descended is the same one who ascended far above all the heavens, so that he might fill all things.) [11]The gifts he gave were that some would be apostles, some prophets, some evangelists, some pastors and teachers, [12]to equip the saints for the work of ministry, for building up the body of Christ, [13]until all of us come to the unity of the faith and of the knowledge of the Son of God, to maturity, to the measure of the full stature of Christ. [14]We must no longer be children, tossed to and fro and blown about by every wind of doctrine, by people's trickery, by their craftiness in deceitful scheming. [15]But speaking the truth in love, we must grow up in every way into him who is the head, into Christ, [16]from whom the whole body, joined and knit together by every ligament with which it is equipped, as each part is working properly, promotes the body's growth in building itself up in love.

The Old Life and the New

17 Now this I affirm and insist on in the Lord: you must no longer live as the Gentiles live, in the futility of their minds. [18]They are darkened in their understanding, alienated from the life of God because of their ignorance and hardness of heart. [19]They have lost all sensitivity and have abandoned themselves to licentiousness, greedy to practice every kind of impurity. [20]That is not the way you learned Christ! [21]For surely you have heard about him and were taught in him, as truth is in Jesus. [22]You were taught to put away your former way of life, your old self, corrupt and deluded by its lusts, [23]and to be renewed in the spirit of your minds, [24]and to clothe yourselves with the new self, created according to the likeness of God in true righteousness and holiness.

Rules for the New Life

25 So then, putting away falsehood, let all of us speak the truth to our neighbors, for we are members of one another. [26]Be angry but do not sin; do not let the sun go down on your anger, [27]and do not make room for the devil. [28]Thieves must give up stealing; rather let them labor and work honestly with their own hands, so as to have something to share with the needy. [29]Let no

evil talk come out of your mouths, but only what is useful for building up,[v] as there is need, so that your words may give grace to those who hear. [30]And do not grieve the Holy Spirit of God, with which you were marked with a seal for the day of redemption. [31]Put away from you all bitterness and wrath and anger and wrangling and slander, together with all malice, [32]and be kind to one another, tenderhearted, forgiving one another, as God in Christ has forgiven you.[w] 5 [1]Therefore be imitators of God, as beloved children, [2]and live in love, as Christ loved us[x] and gave himself up for us, a fragrant offering and sacrifice to God.

Renounce Pagan Ways

3 But fornication and impurity of any kind, or greed, must not even be mentioned among you, as is proper among saints. [4]Entirely out of place is obscene, silly, and vulgar talk; but instead, let there be thanksgiving. [5]Be sure of this, that no fornicator or impure person, or one who is greedy (that is, an idolater), has any inheritance in the kingdom of Christ and of God.

6 Let no one deceive you with empty words, for because of these things the wrath of God comes on those who are disobedient. [7]Therefore do not be associated with them. [8]For once you were darkness, but now in the Lord you are light. Live as children of light— [9]for the fruit of the light is found in all that is good and right and true. [10]Try to find out what is pleasing to the Lord. [11]Take no part in the unfruitful works of darkness, but instead expose them. [12]For it is shameful even to mention what such people do secretly; [13]but everything exposed by the light becomes visible, [14]for everything that becomes visible is light. Therefore it says,
"Sleeper, awake!
    Rise from the dead,
    and Christ will shine on you."
15 Be careful then how you live, not as unwise people but as wise, [16]making the most of the time, because the days are evil. [17]So do not be foolish, but understand what the will of the Lord is. [18]Do not get drunk with wine,

u Other ancient authorities add *first*
v Other ancient authorities read *building up faith*   w Other ancient authorities read *us*   x Other ancient authorities read *you*

for that is debauchery; but be filled with the Spirit, [19]as you sing psalms and hymns and spiritual songs among yourselves, singing and making melody to the Lord in your hearts, [20]giving thanks to God the Father at all times and for everything in the name of our Lord Jesus Christ.

The Christian Household
(Cp Col 3.18–19)

21 Be subject to one another out of reverence for Christ.

22 Wives, be subject to your husbands as you are to the Lord. [23]For the husband is the head of the wife just as Christ is the head of the church, the body of which he is the Savior. [24]Just as the church is subject to Christ, so also wives ought to be, in everything, to their husbands.

25 Husbands, love your wives, just as Christ loved the church and gave himself up for her, [26]in order to make her holy by cleansing her with the washing of water by the word, [27]so as to present the church to himself in splendor, without a spot or wrinkle or anything of the kind—yes, so that she may be holy and without blemish. [28]In the same way, husbands should love their wives as they do their own bodies. He who loves his wife loves himself. [29]For no one ever hates his own body, but he nourishes and tenderly cares for it, just as Christ does for the church, [30]because we are members of his body.[y] [31]"For this reason a man will leave his father and mother and be joined to his wife, and the two will become one flesh." [32]This is a great mystery, and I am applying it to Christ and the church. [33]Each of you, however, should love his wife as himself, and a wife should respect her husband.

Children and Parents
(Ex 20.12; Deut 5.16)

6 Children, obey your parents in the Lord,[z] for this is right. [2]"Honor your father and mother"—this is the first commandment with a promise: [3]"so that it may be well with you and you may live long on the earth."

4 And, fathers, do not provoke your children to anger, but bring them up in the discipline and instruction of the Lord.

Slaves and Masters

5 Slaves, obey your earthly masters with fear and trembling, in singleness of heart, as you obey Christ; [6]not only while being watched, and in order to please them, but as slaves of Christ, doing the will of God from the heart. [7]Render service with enthusiasm, as to the Lord and not to men and women, [8]knowing that whatever good we do, we will receive the same again from the Lord, whether we are slaves or free.

9 And, masters, do the same to them. Stop threatening them, for you know that both of you have the same Master in heaven, and with him there is no partiality.

The Whole Armor of God

10 Finally, be strong in the Lord and in the strength of his power. [11]Put on the whole armor of God, so that you may be able to stand against the wiles of the devil. [12]For our[a] struggle is not against enemies of blood and flesh, but against the rulers, against the authorities, against the cosmic powers of this present darkness, against the spiritual forces of evil in the heavenly places. [13]Therefore take up the whole armor of God, so that you may be able to withstand on that evil day, and having done everything, to stand firm. [14]Stand therefore, and fasten the belt of truth around your waist, and put on the breastplate of righteousness. [15]As shoes for your feet put on whatever will make you ready to proclaim the gospel of peace. [16]With all of these,[b] take the shield of faith, with which you will be able to quench all the flaming arrows of the evil one. [17]Take the helmet of salvation, and the sword of the Spirit, which is the word of God.

18 Pray in the Spirit at all times in every prayer and supplication. To that end keep alert and always persevere in supplication for all the saints. [19]Pray also for me, so that when I speak, a message may be given to me to make known with boldness the mystery of the gospel,[c] [20]for which I am an ambassador in chains. Pray that I may declare it boldly, as I must speak.

Personal Matters and Benediction

21 So that you also may know how

yOther ancient authorities add *of his flesh and of his bones*   zOther ancient authorities lack *in the Lord*   aOther ancient authorities read *your*   bOr *In all circumstances*   cOther ancient authorities lack *of the gospel*

I am and what I am doing, Tych′i·cus will tell you everything. He is a dear brother and a faithful minister in the Lord. 22 I am sending him to you for this very purpose, to let you know how we are, and to encourage your hearts.

23 Peace be to the whole commu-

nity, *d* and love with faith, from God the Father and the Lord Jesus Christ. 24 Grace be with all who have an undying love for our Lord Jesus Christ. *e*

d Gk *to the brothers*   *e* Other ancient authorities add *Amen*

The Letter of Paul to the

PHILIPPIANS

Salutation

1 Paul and Timothy, servants*a* of Christ Jesus,

To all the saints in Christ Jesus who are in Phi·lip′pi, with the bishops*b* and deacons: *c*

2 Grace to you and peace from God our Father and the Lord Jesus Christ.

Paul's Prayer for the Philippians

3 I thank my God every time I remember you, 4 constantly praying with joy in every one of my prayers for all of you, 5 because of your sharing in the gospel from the first day until now. 6 I am confident of this, that the one who began a good work among you will bring it to completion by the day of Jesus Christ. 7 It is right for me to think this way about all of you, because you hold me in your heart, *d* for all of you share in God's grace*e* with me, both in my imprisonment and in the defense and confirmation of the gospel. 8 For God is my witness, how I long for all of you with the compassion of Christ Jesus. 9 And this is my prayer, that your love may overflow more and more with knowledge and full insight 10 to help you to determine what is best, so that in the day of Christ you may be pure and blameless, 11 having produced the harvest of righteousness that comes through Jesus Christ for the glory and praise of God.

Paul's Present Circumstances

12 I want you to know, beloved, *f* that what has happened to me has actually helped to spread the gospel, 13 so that it has become known throughout

the whole imperial guard*g* and to everyone else that my imprisonment is for Christ; 14 and most of the brothers and sisters, *f* having been made confident in the Lord by my imprisonment, dare to speak the word*h* with greater boldness and without fear.

15 Some proclaim Christ from envy and rivalry, but others from goodwill. 16 These proclaim Christ out of love, knowing that I have been put here for the defense of the gospel; 17 the others proclaim Christ out of selfish ambition, not sincerely but intending to increase my suffering in my imprisonment. 18 What does it matter? Just this, that Christ is proclaimed in every way, whether out of false motives or true; and in that I rejoice.

Yes, and I will continue to rejoice, 19 for I know that through your prayers and the help of the Spirit of Jesus Christ this will turn out for my deliverance. 20 It is my eager expectation and hope that I will not be put to shame in any way, but that by my speaking with all boldness, Christ will be exalted now as always in my body, whether by life or by death. 21 For to me, living is Christ and dying is gain. 22 If I am to live in the flesh, that means fruitful labor for me; and I do not know which I prefer. 23 I am hard pressed between the two: my desire is to depart and be with Christ, for that is far better; 24 but

a Gk *slaves*   *b* Or *overseers*
c Or *overseers and helpers*
d Or *because I hold you in my heart*
e Gk *in grace*   *f* Gk *brothers*
g Gk *whole praetorium*   *h* Other ancient authorities read *word of God*

to remain in the flesh is more necessary for you. 25 Since I am convinced of this, I know that I will remain and continue with all of you for your progress and joy in faith, 26 so that I may share abundantly in your boasting in Christ Jesus when I come to you again.

27 Only, live your life in a manner worthy of the gospel of Christ, so that, whether I come and see you or am absent and hear about you, I will know that you are standing firm in one spirit, striving side by side with one mind for the faith of the gospel, 28 and are in no way intimidated by your opponents. For them this is evidence of their destruction, but of your salvation. And this is God's doing. 29 For he has graciously granted you the privilege not only of believing in Christ, but of suffering for him as well— 30 since you are having the same struggle that you saw I had and now hear that I still have.

Imitating Christ's Humility

2 If then there is any encouragement in Christ, any consolation from love, any sharing in the Spirit, any compassion and sympathy, 2 make my joy complete: be of the same mind, having the same love, being in full accord and of one mind. 3 Do nothing from selfish ambition or conceit, but in humility regard others as better than yourselves. 4 Let each of you look not to your own interests, but to the interests of others. 5 Let the same mind be in you that was[i] in Christ Jesus,

6 who, though he was in the form
       of God,
   did not regard equality with
       God
   as something to be exploited,
7 but emptied himself,
   taking the form of a slave,
   being born in human likeness.
   And being found in human form,
8 he humbled himself
   and became obedient to the
       point of death—
   even death on a cross.

9 Therefore God also highly
       exalted him
   and gave him the name
   that is above every name,
10 so that at the name of Jesus
   every knee should bend,
   in heaven and on earth and
       under the earth,
11 and every tongue should confess

that Jesus Christ is Lord,
   to the glory of God the Father.

Shining as Lights in the World

12 Therefore, my beloved, just as you have always obeyed me, not only in my presence, but much more now in my absence, work out your own salvation with fear and trembling; 13 for it is God who is at work in you, enabling you both to will and to work for his good pleasure.

14 Do all things without murmuring and arguing, 15 so that you may be blameless and innocent, children of God without blemish in the midst of a crooked and perverse generation, in which you shine like stars in the world. 16 It is by your holding fast to the word of life that I can boast on the day of Christ that I did not run in vain or labor in vain. 17 But even if I am being poured out as a libation over the sacrifice and the offering of your faith, I am glad and rejoice with all of you— 18 and in the same way you also must be glad and rejoice with me.

Timothy and Epaphroditus

19 I hope in the Lord Jesus to send Timothy to you soon, so that I may be cheered by news of you. 20 I have no one like him who will be genuinely concerned for your welfare. 21 All of them are seeking their own interests, not those of Jesus Christ. 22 But Timothy's[j] worth you know, how like a son with a father he has served with me in the work of the gospel. 23 I hope therefore to send him as soon as I see how things go with me; 24 and I trust in the Lord that I will also come soon.

25 Still, I think it necessary to send to you E·paph·ro·di'tus—my brother and co-worker and fellow soldier, your messenger[k] and minister to my need; 26 for he has been longing for[l] all of you, and has been distressed because you heard that he was ill. 27 He was indeed so ill that he nearly died. But God had mercy on him, and not only on him but on me also, so that I would not have one sorrow after another. 28 I am the more eager to send him, therefore, in order that you may rejoice at seeing him again, and that I may be less anxious. 29 Welcome him then in

iOr that you have   jGk his
kGk apostle   lOther ancient authorities
read longing to see

the Lord with all joy, and honor such people, 30 because he came close to death for the work of Christ,*m* risking his life to make up for those services that you could not give me.

3 Finally, my brothers and sisters,*n* rejoice*o* in the Lord.

Breaking with the Past

To write the same things to you is not troublesome to me, and for you it is a safeguard.

2 Beware of the dogs, beware of the evil workers, beware of those who mutilate the flesh!*p* 3 For it is we who are the circumcision, who worship in the Spirit of God*q* and boast in Christ Jesus and have no confidence in the flesh— 4 even though I, too, have reason for confidence in the flesh.

If anyone else has reason to be confident in the flesh, I have more: 5 circumcised on the eighth day, a member of the people of Israel, of the tribe of Benjamin, a Hebrew born of Hebrews; as to the law, a Phar'i·see; 6 as to zeal, a persecutor of the church; as to righteousness under the law, blameless.

7 Yet whatever gains I had, these I have come to regard as loss because of Christ. 8 More than that, I regard everything as loss because of the surpassing value of knowing Christ Jesus my Lord. For his sake I have suffered the loss of all things, and I regard them as rubbish, in order that I may gain Christ 9 and be found in him, not having a righteousness of my own that comes from the law, but one that comes through faith in Christ,*r* the righteousness from God based on faith. 10 I want to know Christ*s* and the power of his resurrection and the sharing of his sufferings by becoming like him in his death, 11 if somehow I may attain the resurrection from the dead.

Pressing toward the Goal

12 Not that I have already obtained this or have already reached the goal;*t* but I press on to make it my own, because Christ Jesus has made me his own. 13 Beloved,*u* I do not consider that I have made it my own;*v* but this one thing I do: forgetting what lies behind and straining forward to what lies ahead, 14 I press on toward the goal for the prize of the heavenly*w* call of God in Christ Jesus. 15 Let those of us then who are mature be of the same mind; and if you think differently

about anything, this too God will reveal to you. 16 Only let us hold fast to what we have attained.

17 Brothers and sisters,*u* join in imitating me, and observe those who live according to the example you have in us. 18 For many live as enemies of the cross of Christ; I have often told you of them, and now I tell you even with tears. 19 Their end is destruction; their god is the belly; and their glory is in their shame; their minds are set on earthly things. 20 But our citizenship*x* is in heaven, and it is from there that we are expecting a Savior, the Lord Jesus Christ. 21 He will transform the body of our humiliation*y* that it may be conformed to the body of his glory,*z* by the power that also enables him to make all things subject to himself.

4 Therefore, my brothers and sisters,*n* whom I love and long for, my joy and crown, stand firm in the Lord in this way, my beloved.

Exhortations

2 I urge Eū·o'di·a and I urge Syn'ty·chē to be of the same mind in the Lord. 3 Yes, and I ask you also, my loyal companion,*a* help these women, for they have struggled beside me in the work of the gospel, together with Clement and the rest of my co-workers, whose names are in the book of life.

4 Rejoice*b* in the Lord always; again I will say, Rejoice.*b* 5 Let your gentleness be known to everyone. The Lord is near. 6 Do not worry about anything, but in everything by prayer and supplication with thanksgiving let your requests be made known to God. 7 And the peace of God, which surpasses all understanding, will guard your hearts and your minds in Christ Jesus.

8 Finally, beloved,*c* whatever is true, whatever is honorable, whatever is just, whatever is pure, whatever is

m Other ancient authorities read *of the Lord*　*n* Gk *my brothers*　*o* Or *farewell*　*p* Gk *the mutilation*　*q* Other ancient authorities read *worship God in spirit*　*r* Or *through the faith of Christ*　*s* Gk *him*　*t* Or *have already been made perfect*　*u* Gk *Brothers*　*v* Other ancient authorities read *my own yet*　*w* Gk *upward*　*x* Or *commonwealth*　*y* Or *our humble bodies*　*z* Or *his glorious body*　*a* Or *loyal Syzygus*　*b* Or *Farewell*　*c* Gk *brothers* pleasing, whatever is commendable, if there is any excellence and if there is anything worthy of praise, think about[d] these things. [9]Keep on doing the things that you have learned and received and heard and seen in me, and the God of peace will be with you.

Acknowledgment of the Philippians' Gift

10 I rejoice[e] in the Lord greatly that now at last you have revived your concern for me; indeed, you were concerned for me, but had no opportunity to show it.[f] [11]Not that I am referring to being in need; for I have learned to be content with whatever I have. [12]I know what it is to have little, and I know what it is to have plenty. In any and all circumstances I have learned the secret of being well-fed and of going hungry, of having plenty and of being in need. [13]I can do all things through him who strengthens me. [14]In any case, it was kind of you to share my distress.

15 You Phi·lip'pi·ans indeed know that in the early days of the gospel, when I left Mac·e·do'ni·a, no church shared with me in the matter of giving

and receiving, except you alone. [16]For even when I was in Thes·sa·lo·ni'ca, you sent me help for my needs more than once. [17]Not that I seek the gift, but I seek the profit that accumulates to your account. [18]I have been paid in full and have more than enough; I am fully satisfied, now that I have received from E·paph·ro·di'tus the gifts you sent, a fragrant offering, a sacrifice acceptable and pleasing to God. [19]And my God will fully satisfy every need of yours according to his riches in glory in Christ Jesus. [20]To our God and Father be glory forever and ever. Amen.

Final Greetings and Benediction

21 Greet every saint in Christ Jesus. The friends[g] who are with me greet you. [22]All the saints greet you, especially those of the emperor's household.

23 The grace of the Lord Jesus Christ be with your spirit.[h]

*d*Gk *take account of*   *e*Gk *I rejoiced*
*f*Gk lacks *to show it*   *g*Gk *brothers*
*h*Other ancient authorities add *Amen*

The Letter of Paul to the

COLOSSIANS

Salutation

1 Paul, an apostle of Christ Jesus by the will of God, and Timothy our brother,

2 To the saints and faithful brothers and sisters[a] in Christ in Co·los'sae:
Grace to you and peace from God our Father.

Paul Thanks God for the Colossians

3 In our prayers for you we always thank God, the Father of our Lord Jesus Christ, [4]for we have heard of your faith in Christ Jesus and of the love that you have for all the saints, [5]because of the hope laid up for you in heaven. You have heard of this hope before in the word of the truth, the gos-

pel [6]that has come to you. Just as it is bearing fruit and growing in the whole world, so it has been bearing fruit among yourselves from the day you heard it and truly comprehended the grace of God. [7]This you learned from Ep'a·phras, our beloved fellow servant.[b] He is a faithful minister of Christ on your[c] behalf, [8]and he has made known to us your love in the Spirit.

9 For this reason, since the day we heard it, we have not ceased praying for you and asking that you may be filled with the knowledge of God's[d] will in all spiritual wisdom and under-

*a*Gk *brothers*   *b*Gk *slave*   *c*Other
ancient authorities read *our*   *d*Gk *his*

standing, [10] so that you may lead lives worthy of the Lord, fully pleasing to him, as you bear fruit in every good work and as you grow in the knowledge of God. [11] May you be made strong with all the strength that comes from his glorious power, and may you be prepared to endure everything with patience, while joyfully [12] giving thanks to the Father, who has enabled[e] you[f] to share in the inheritance of the saints in the light. [13] He has rescued us from the power of darkness and transferred us into the kingdom of his beloved Son, [14] in whom we have redemption, the forgiveness of sins.[g]

The Supremacy of Christ
(Cp Jn 1.1–5)

15 He is the image of the invisible God, the firstborn of all creation; [16] for in[h] him all things in heaven and on earth were created, things visible and invisible, whether thrones or dominions or rulers or powers—all things have been created through him and for him. [17] He himself is before all things, and in[h] him all things hold together. [18] He is the head of the body, the church; he is the beginning, the firstborn from the dead, so that he might come to have first place in everything. [19] For in him all the fullness of God was pleased to dwell, [20] and through him God was pleased to reconcile to himself all things, whether on earth or in heaven, by making peace through the blood of his cross.

21 And you who were once estranged and hostile in mind, doing evil deeds, [22] he has now reconciled[i] in his fleshly body[j] through death, so as to present you holy and blameless and irreproachable before him— [23] provided that you continue securely established and steadfast in the faith, without shifting from the hope promised by the gospel that you heard, which has been proclaimed to every creature under heaven. I, Paul, became a servant of this gospel.

Paul's Interest in the Colossians

24 I am now rejoicing in my sufferings for your sake, and in my flesh I am completing what is lacking in Christ's afflictions for the sake of his body, that is, the church. [25] I became its servant according to God's commission that was given to me for you, to make the word of God fully known, [26] the mystery that has been hidden throughout the ages and generations but has now been revealed to his saints. [27] To them God chose to make known how great among the Gentiles are the riches of the glory of this mystery, which is Christ in you, the hope of glory. [28] It is he whom we proclaim, warning everyone and teaching everyone in all wisdom, so that we may present everyone mature in Christ. [29] For this I toil and struggle with all the energy that he powerfully inspires within me.

2 For I want you to know how much I am struggling for you, and for those in Lā·o·di·cē'a, and for all who have not seen me face to face. [2] I want their hearts to be encouraged and united in love, so that they may have all the riches of assured understanding and have the knowledge of God's mystery, that is, Christ himself,[k] [3] in whom are hidden all the treasures of wisdom and knowledge. [4] I am saying this so that no one may deceive you with plausible arguments. [5] For though I am absent in body, yet I am with you in spirit, and I rejoice to see your morale and the firmness of your faith in Christ.

Fullness of Life in Christ

6 As you therefore have received Christ Jesus the Lord, continue to live your lives[l] in him, [7] rooted and built up in him and established in the faith, just as you were taught, abounding in thanksgiving.

8 See to it that no one takes you captive through philosophy and empty deceit, according to human tradition, according to the elemental spirits of the universe,[m] and not according to Christ. [9] For in him the whole fullness of deity dwells bodily, [10] and you have come to fullness in him, who is the head of every ruler and authority. [11] In him also you were circumcised with a spiritual circumcision,[n] by putting off the body of the flesh in the circumcision of Christ; [12] when you were buried

[e] Other ancient authorities read *called*
[f] Other ancient authorities read *us*
[g] Other ancient authorities add *through his blood* [h] Or *by* [i] Other ancient authorities read *you have now been reconciled* [j] Gk *in the body of his flesh* [k] Other ancient authorities read *of the mystery of God, both of the Father and of Christ* [l] Gk *to walk* [m] Or *the rudiments of the world* [n] Gk *a circumcision made without hands*

with him in baptism, you were also raised with him through faith in the power of God, who raised him from the dead. [13] And when you were dead in trespasses and the uncircumcision of your flesh, God[o] made you[p] alive together with him, when he forgave us all our trespasses, [14] erasing the record that stood against us with its legal demands. He set this aside, nailing it to the cross. [15] He disarmed[q] the rulers and authorities and made a public example of them, triumphing over them in it.

[16] Therefore do not let anyone condemn you in matters of food and drink or of observing festivals, new moons, or sabbaths. [17] These are only a shadow of what is to come, but the substance belongs to Christ. [18] Do not let anyone disqualify you, insisting on self-abasement and worship of angels, dwelling[r] on visions,[s] puffed up without cause by a human way of thinking,[t] [19] and not holding fast to the head, from whom the whole body, nourished and held together by its ligaments and sinews, grows with a growth that is from God.

Warnings against False Teachers

[20] If with Christ you died to the elemental spirits of the universe,[u] why do you live as if you still belonged to the world? Why do you submit to regulations, [21] "Do not handle, Do not taste, Do not touch"? [22] All these regulations refer to things that perish with use; they are simply human commands and teachings. [23] These have indeed an appearance of wisdom in promoting self-imposed piety, humility, and severe treatment of the body, but they are of no value in checking self-indulgence.[v]

The New Life in Christ

3 So if you have been raised with Christ, seek the things that are above, where Christ is, seated at the right hand of God. [2] Set your minds on things that are above, not on things that are on earth, [3] for you have died, and your life is hidden with Christ in God. [4] When Christ who is your[w] life is revealed, then you also will be revealed with him in glory.

[5] Put to death, therefore, whatever in you is earthly: fornication, impurity, passion, evil desire, and greed (which is idolatry). [6] On account of these the wrath of God is coming on those who

are disobedient.[x] [7] These are the ways you also once followed, when you were living that life.[y] [8] But now you must get rid of all such things—anger, wrath, malice, slander, and abusive[z] language from your mouth. [9] Do not lie to one another, seeing that you have stripped off the old self with its practices [10] and have clothed yourselves with the new self, which is being renewed in knowledge according to the image of its creator. [11] In that renewal[a] there is no longer Greek and Jew, circumcised and uncircumcised, barbarian, Scyth'i·an, slave and free; but Christ is all and in all!

[12] As God's chosen ones, holy and beloved, clothe yourselves with compassion, kindness, humility, meekness, and patience. [13] Bear with one another and, if anyone has a complaint against another, forgive each other; just as the Lord[b] has forgiven you, so you also must forgive. [14] Above all, clothe yourselves with love, which binds everything together in perfect harmony. [15] And let the peace of Christ rule in your hearts, to which indeed you were called in the one body. And be thankful. [16] Let the word of Christ[c] dwell in you richly; teach and admonish one another in all wisdom; and with gratitude in your hearts sing psalms, hymns, and spiritual songs to God.[d] [17] And whatever you do, in word or deed, do everything in the name of the Lord Jesus, giving thanks to God the Father through him.

Rules for Christian Households
(Cp Eph 5.21—6.9)

[18] Wives, be subject to your husbands, as is fitting in the Lord. [19] Hus-

[o] Gk *he*　[p] Other ancient authorities read *made us*; others, *made*
[q] Or *divested himself of*　[r] Other ancient authorities read *not dwelling*
[s] Meaning of Gk uncertain　[t] Gk *by the mind of his flesh*　[u] Or *the rudiments of the world*　[v] Or *are of no value, serving only to indulge the flesh*　[w] Other authorities read *our*　[x] Other ancient authorities lack *on those who are disobedient* (Gk *the children of disobedience*)　[y] Or *living among such people*　[z] Or *filthy*　[a] Gk *its creator,* [11] *where*　[b] Other ancient authorities read *just as Christ*　[c] Other ancient authorities read *of God,* or *of the Lord*　[d] Other ancient authorities read *to the Lord*

bands, love your wives and never treat them harshly.

20 Children, obey your parents in everything, for this is your acceptable duty in the Lord. [21] Fathers, do not provoke your children, or they may lose heart. [22] Slaves, obey your earthly masters[e] in everything, not only while being watched and in order to please them, but wholeheartedly, fearing the Lord.[e] [23] Whatever your task, put yourselves into it, as done for the Lord and not for your masters,[f] [24] since you know that from the Lord you will receive the inheritance as your reward; you serve[g] the Lord Christ. [25] For the wrongdoer will be paid back for whatever wrong has been done, and there is no partiality. [1] Masters, treat your 4 slaves justly and fairly, for you know that you also have a Master in heaven.

Further Instructions

2 Devote yourselves to prayer, keeping alert in it with thanksgiving. [3] At the same time pray for us as well that God will open to us a door for the word, that we may declare the mystery of Christ, for which I am in prison, [4] so that I may reveal it clearly, as I should.

5 Conduct yourselves wisely toward outsiders, making the most of the time.[h] [6] Let your speech always be gracious, seasoned with salt, so that you may know how you ought to answer everyone.

Final Greetings and Benediction
(Cp Eph 6.21–22)

7 Tych'i·cus will tell you all the news about me; he is a beloved brother, a faithful minister, and a fellow servant[i] in the Lord. [8] I have sent him to you for this very purpose, so that you may know how we are[j] and

that he may encourage your hearts; [9] he is coming with O·nes'i·mus, the faithful and beloved brother, who is one of you. They will tell you about everything here.

10 Ar·is·tar'chus my fellow prisoner greets you, as does Mark the cousin of Bar'na·bas, concerning whom you have received instructions—if he comes to you, welcome him. [11] And Jesus who is called Justus greets you. These are the only ones of the circumcision among my co-workers for the kingdom of God, and they have been a comfort to me. [12] Ep'a·phras, who is one of you, a servant[i] of Christ Jesus, greets you. He is always wrestling in his prayers on your behalf, so that you may stand mature and fully assured in everything that God wills. [13] For I testify for him that he has worked hard for you and for those in La·o·di·ce'a and in Hi·er·ap'o·lis. [14] Luke, the beloved physician, and De'mas greet you. [15] Give my greetings to the brothers and sisters[k] in La·o·di·ce'a, and to Nym'pha and the church in her house. [16] And when this letter has been read among you, have it read also in the church of the La·o·di·ce'ans; and see that you read also the letter from La·o·di·ce'a. [17] And say to Ar·chip'pus, "See that you complete the task that you have received in the Lord."

18 I, Paul, write this greeting with my own hand. Remember my chains. Grace be with you.[l]

---

[e] In Greek the same word is used for *master* and *Lord*   [f] Gk *not for men*
[g] Or *you are slaves of,* or *be slaves of*
[h] Or *opportunity*   [i] Gk *slave*   [j] Other authorities read *that I may know how you are*   [k] Gk *brothers*   [l] Other ancient authorities add *Amen*

The First Letter of Paul to the

THESSALONIANS

Salutation

1 Paul, Sil·va′nus, and Timothy,
To the church of the Thes-sa·lo′ni·ans in God the Father and the Lord Jesus Christ:
Grace to you and peace.

The Thessalonians' Faith and Example

2 We always give thanks to God for all of you and mention you in our prayers, constantly ³remembering before our God and Father your work of faith and labor of love and steadfast-ness of hope in our Lord Jesus Christ. ⁴For we know, brothers and sisters[a] beloved by God, that he has chosen you, ⁵because our message of the gos-pel came to you not in word only, but also in power and in the Holy Spirit and with full conviction; just as you know what kind of persons we proved to be among you for your sake. ⁶And you became imitators of us and of the Lord, for in spite of persecution you received the word with joy inspired by the Holy Spirit, ⁷so that you became an example to all the believers in Mac·e·do′ni·a and in A·cha′i·a. ⁸For the word of the Lord has sounded forth from you not only in Mac·e·do′ni·a and A·cha′i·a, but in every place your faith in God has become known, so that we have no need to speak about it. ⁹For the people of those regions[b] report about us what kind of welcome we had among you, and how you turned to God from idols, to serve a living and true God, ¹⁰and to wait for his Son from heaven, whom he raised from the dead—Jesus, who rescues us from the wrath that is coming.

Paul's Ministry in Thessalonica
(Cp Acts 17.1–9)

2 You yourselves know, brothers and sisters,[a] that our coming to you was not in vain, ²but though we had already suffered and been shame-fully mistreated at Phi·lip′pi, as you know, we had courage in our God to declare to you the gospel of God in spite of great opposition. ³For our ap-peal does not spring from deceit or im-pure motives or trickery, ⁴but just as we have been approved by God to be entrusted with the message of the gos-pel, even so we speak, not to please mortals, but to please God who tests our hearts. ⁵As you know and as God is our witness, we never came with words of flattery or with a pretext for greed; ⁶nor did we seek praise from mortals, whether from you or from others, ⁷though we might have made demands as apostles of Christ. But we were gentle[c] among you, like a nurse tenderly caring for her own children. ⁸So deeply do we care for you that we are determined to share with you not only the gospel of God but also our own selves, because you have become very dear to us.

9 You remember our labor and toil, brothers and sisters;[a] we worked night and day, so that we might not burden any of you while we pro-claimed to you the gospel of God. ¹⁰You are witnesses, and God also, how pure, upright, and blameless our conduct was toward you believers. ¹¹As you know, we dealt with each one of you like a father with his children, ¹²urging and encouraging you and pleading that you lead a life worthy of God, who calls you into his own king-dom and glory.

13 We also constantly give thanks to God for this, that when you received the word of God that you heard from us, you accepted it not as a human word but as what it really is, God's word, which is also at work in you be-lievers. ¹⁴For you, brothers and sis-ters,[a] became imitators of the churches of God in Christ Jesus that are in Judea, for you suffered the same

---

[a] Gk brothers   [b] Gk For they   [c] Other ancient authorities read infants

things from your own compatriots as they did from the Jews, [15]who killed both the Lord Jesus and the prophets,[d] and drove us out; they displease God and oppose everyone [16]by hindering us from speaking to the Gentiles so that they may be saved. Thus they have constantly been filling up the measure of their sins; but God's wrath has overtaken them at last.[e]

Paul's Desire to Visit the Thessalonians Again

17 As for us, brothers and sisters,[f] when, for a short time, we were made orphans by being separated from you—in person, not in heart—we longed with great eagerness to see you face to face. [18]For we wanted to come to you—certainly I, Paul, wanted to again and again—but Satan blocked our way. [19]For what is our hope or joy or crown of boasting before our Lord Jesus at his coming? Is it not you? [20]Yes, you are our glory and joy!

3 Therefore when we could bear it no longer, we decided to be left alone in Athens; [2]and we sent Timothy, our brother and co-worker for God in proclaiming[g] the gospel of Christ, to strengthen and encourage you for the sake of your faith, [3]so that no one would be shaken by these persecutions. Indeed, you yourselves know that this is what we are destined for. [4]In fact, when we were with you, we told you beforehand that we were to suffer persecution; so it turned out, as you know. [5]For this reason, when I could bear it no longer, I sent to find out about your faith; I was afraid that somehow the tempter had tempted you and that our labor had been in vain.

Timothy's Encouraging Report

6 But Timothy has just now come to us from you, and has brought us the good news of your faith and love. He has told us also that you always remember us kindly and long to see us— just as we long to see you. [7]For this reason, brothers and sisters,[f] during all our distress and persecution we have been encouraged about you through your faith. [8]For we now live, if you continue to stand firm in the Lord. [9]How can we thank God enough for you in return for all the joy that we feel before our God because of you? [10]Night and day we pray most earnestly that we may see you face to face

and restore whatever is lacking in your faith.

11 Now may our God and Father himself and our Lord Jesus direct our way to you. [12]And may the Lord make you increase and abound in love for one another and for all, just as we abound in love for you. [13]And may he so strengthen your hearts in holiness that you may be blameless before our God and Father at the coming of our Lord Jesus with all his saints.

A Life Pleasing to God

4 Finally, brothers and sisters,[f] we ask and urge you in the Lord Jesus that, as you learned from us how you ought to live and to please God (as, in fact, you are doing), you should do so more and more. [2]For you know what instructions we gave you through the Lord Jesus. [3]For this is the will of God, your sanctification: that you abstain from fornication; [4]that each one of you know how to control your own body[h] in holiness and honor, [5]not with lustful passion, like the Gentiles who do not know God; [6]that no one wrong or exploit a brother or sister[i] in this matter, because the Lord is an avenger in all these things, just as we have already told you beforehand and solemnly warned you. [7]For God did not call us to impurity but in holiness. [8]Therefore whoever rejects this rejects not human authority but God, who also gives his Holy Spirit to you.

9 Now concerning love of the brothers and sisters,[f] you do not need to have anyone write to you, for you yourselves have been taught by God to love one another; [10]and indeed you do love all the brothers and sisters[f] throughout Mac·e·dō'ni·a. But we urge you, beloved,[f] to do so more and more, [11]to aspire to live quietly, to mind your own affairs, and to work with your own hands, as we directed you, [12]so that you may behave properly toward outsiders and be dependent on no one.

The Coming of the Lord

13 But we do not want you to be uninformed, brothers and sisters,[f]

[d]Other ancient authorities read *their own prophets*   [e]Or *completely* or *forever*   [f]Gk *brothers*   [g]Gk lacks *proclaiming*   [h]Or *how to take a wife for himself*   [i]Gk *brother*

about those who have died,^{j} so that you may not grieve as others do who have no hope. ^{14}For since we believe that Jesus died and rose again, even so, through Jesus, God will bring with him those who have died.^{j} ^{15}For this we declare to you by the word of the Lord, that we who are alive, who are left until the coming of the Lord, will by no means precede those who have died.^{j} ^{16}For the Lord himself, with a cry of command, with the archangel's call and with the sound of God's trumpet, will descend from heaven, and the dead in Christ will rise first. ^{17}Then we who are alive, who are left, will be caught up in the clouds together with them to meet the Lord in the air; and so we will be with the Lord forever. ^{18}Therefore encourage one another with these words.

5 Now concerning the times and the seasons, brothers and sisters,^{k} you do not need to have anything written to you. ^{2}For you yourselves know very well that the day of the Lord will come like a thief in the night. ^{3}When they say, "There is peace and security," then sudden destruction will come upon them, as labor pains come upon a pregnant woman, and there will be no escape! ^{4}But you, beloved,^{k} are not in darkness, for that day to surprise you like a thief; ^{5}for you are all children of light and children of the day; we are not of the night or of darkness. ^{6}So then let us not fall asleep as others do, but let us keep awake and be sober; ^{7}for those who sleep sleep at night, and those who are drunk get drunk at night. ^{8}But since we belong to the day, let us be sober, and put on the breastplate of faith and love, and for a helmet the hope of salvation. ^{9}For God has destined us not for wrath but for obtaining salvation through our Lord Jesus Christ, ^{10}who died for us, so that whether we are awake or asleep we may live with him. ^{11}Therefore encourage one another and build up each other, as indeed you are doing.

*Final Exhortations, Greetings,
and Benediction*

12 But we appeal to you, brothers and sisters,^{k} to respect those who labor among you, and have charge of you in the Lord and admonish you; ^{13}esteem them very highly in love because of their work. Be at peace among yourselves. ^{14}And we urge you, beloved,^{k} to admonish the idlers, encourage the faint hearted, help the weak, be patient with all of them. ^{15}See that none of you repays evil for evil, but always seek to do good to one another and to all. ^{16}Rejoice always, ^{17}pray without ceasing, ^{18}give thanks in all circumstances; for this is the will of God in Christ Jesus for you. ^{19}Do not quench the Spirit. ^{20}Do not despise the words of prophets,^{l} ^{21}but test everything; hold fast to what is good; ^{22}abstain from every form of evil.

23 May the God of peace himself sanctify you entirely; and may your spirit and soul and body be kept sound^m and blameless at the coming of our Lord Jesus Christ. ^{24}The one who calls you is faithful, and he will do this.

25 Beloved,^{n} pray for us.

26 Greet all the brothers and sisters^k with a holy kiss. ^{27}I solemnly command you by the Lord that this letter be read to all of them.^{o}

28 The grace of our Lord Jesus Christ be with you.^{p}

^{j} Gk *fallen asleep* ^{k} Gk *brothers*
^{l} Gk *despise prophecies* ^{m} Or *complete*
^{n} Gk *Brothers* ^{o} Gk *to all the brothers*
^{p} Other ancient authorities add *Amen*

The Second Letter of Paul to the

THESSALONIANS

Salutation

1 Paul, Sil·va′nus, and Timothy,
To the church of the Thes-sa·lo′ni·ans in God our Father and the Lord Jesus Christ:

2 Grace to you and peace from God our^a Father and the Lord Jesus Christ.

^{a} Other ancient authorities read *the*

2 THESSALONIANS

Thanksgiving

3 We must always give thanks to God for you, brothers and sisters,[b] as is right, because your faith is growing abundantly, and the love of everyone of you for one another is increasing. [4]Therefore we ourselves boast of you among the churches of God for your steadfastness and faith during all your persecutions and the afflictions that you are enduring.

The Judgment at Christ's Coming

5 This is evidence of the righteous judgment of God, and is intended to make you worthy of the kingdom of God, for which you are also suffering. [6]For it is indeed just of God to repay with affliction those who afflict you, [7]and to give relief to the afflicted as well as to us, when the Lord Jesus is revealed from heaven with his mighty angels [8]in flaming fire, inflicting vengeance on those who do not know God and on those who do not obey the gospel of our Lord Jesus. [9]These will suffer the punishment of eternal destruction, separated from the presence of the Lord and from the glory of his might, [10]when he comes to be glorified by his saints and to be marveled at on that day among all who have believed, because our testimony to you was believed. [11]To this end we always pray for you, asking that our God will make you worthy of his call and will fulfill by his power every good resolve and work of faith, [12]so that the name of our Lord Jesus may be glorified in you, and you in him, according to the grace of our God and the Lord Jesus Christ.

The Man of Lawlessness

2 As to the coming of our Lord Jesus Christ and our being gathered together to him, we beg you, brothers and sisters,[b] [2]not to be quickly shaken in mind or alarmed, either by spirit or by word or by letter, as though from us, to the effect that the day of the Lord is already here. [3]Let no one deceive you in any way; for that day will not come unless the rebellion comes first and the lawless one[c] is revealed, the one destined for destruction.[d] [4]He opposes and exalts himself above every so-called god or object of worship, so that he takes his seat in the temple of God, declaring himself to be God. [5]Do you not remember that I told you these things when I was still with you? [6]And you know what is now restraining him, so that he may be revealed when his time comes. [7]For the mystery of lawlessness is already at work, but only until the one who now restrains it is removed. [8]And then the lawless one will be revealed, whom the Lord Jesus[e] will destroy[f] with the breath of his mouth, annihilating him by the manifestation of his coming. [9]The coming of the lawless one is apparent in the working of Satan, who uses all power, signs, lying wonders, [10]and every kind of wicked deception for those who are perishing, because they refused to love the truth and so be saved. [11]For this reason God sends them a powerful delusion, leading them to believe what is false, [12]so that all who have not believed the truth but took pleasure in unrighteousness will be condemned.

Chosen for Salvation

13 But we must always give thanks to God for you, brothers and sisters[b] beloved by the Lord, because God chose you as the first fruits[g] for salvation through sanctification by the Spirit and through belief in the truth. [14]For this purpose he called you through our proclamation of the good news,[h] so that you may obtain the glory of our Lord Jesus Christ. [15]So then, brothers and sisters,[b] stand firm and hold fast to the traditions that you were taught by us, either by word of mouth or by our letter.

16 Now may our Lord Jesus Christ himself and God our Father, who loved us and through grace gave us eternal comfort and good hope, [17]comfort your hearts and strengthen them in every good work and word.

Request for Prayer

3 Finally, brothers and sisters,[b] pray for us, so that the word of the Lord may spread rapidly and be glorified everywhere, just as it is among you, [2]and that we may be rescued from

---

[b]Gk *brothers*   [c]Gk *the man of lawlessness*; other ancient authorities read *the man of sin*   [d]Gk *the son of destruction*   [e]Other ancient authorities lack *Jesus*   [f]Other ancient authorities read *consume*   [g]Other ancient authorities read *from the beginning*   [h]Or *through our gospel*

wicked and evil people; for not all have faith. [3] But the Lord is faithful; he will strengthen you and guard you from the evil one.[i] [4] And we have confidence in the Lord concerning you, that you are doing and will go on doing the things that we command. [5] May the Lord direct your hearts to the love of God and to the steadfastness of Christ.

Warning against Idleness

[6] Now we command you, beloved,[j] in the name of our Lord Jesus Christ, to keep away from believers who are[k] living in idleness and not according to the tradition that they[l] received from us. [7] For you yourselves know how you ought to imitate us; we were not idle when we were with you, [8] and we did not eat anyone's bread without paying for it; but with toil and labor we worked night and day, so that we might not burden any of you. [9] This was not because we do not have that right, but in order to give you an example to imitate. [10] For even when we were with you, we gave you this command: Anyone unwilling to work should not eat. [11] For we hear that some of you are living in idleness, mere busybodies, not doing any work. [12] Now such persons we command and exhort in the Lord Jesus Christ to do their work quietly and to earn their own living. [13] Brothers and sisters,[m] do not be weary in doing what is right.

14 Take note of those who do not obey what we say in this letter; have nothing to do with them, so that they may be ashamed. [15] Do not regard them as enemies, but warn them as believers.[n]

Final Greetings and Benediction

16 Now may the Lord of peace himself give you peace at all times in all ways. The Lord be with all of you.
17 I, Paul, write this greeting with my own hand. This is the mark in every letter of mine; it is the way I write. [18] The grace of our Lord Jesus Christ be with all of you.[o]

[i] Or *from evil* [j] Gk *brothers* [k] Gk *from every brother who is* [l] Other ancient authorities read *you* [m] Gk *Brothers* [n] Gk *a brother* [o] Other ancient authorities add *Amen*

The First Letter of Paul to
TIMOTHY

Salutation

1 Paul, an apostle of Christ Jesus by the command of God our Savior and of Christ Jesus our hope,
2 To Timothy, my loyal child in the faith:
Grace, mercy, and peace from God the Father and Christ Jesus our Lord.

Warning against False Teachers

3 I urge you, as I did when I was on my way to Mac·e·dō′ni·a, to remain in Eph′e·sus so that you may instruct certain people not to teach any different doctrine, [4] and not to occupy themselves with myths and endless genealogies that promote speculations rather than the divine training[a] that is known by faith. [5] But the aim of such instruction is love that comes from a pure heart, a good conscience, and sincere faith. [6] Some people have deviated from these and turned to meaningless talk, [7] desiring to be teachers of the law, without understanding either what they are saying or the things about which they make assertions.

8 Now we know that the law is good, if one uses it legitimately. [9] This means understanding that the law is laid down not for the innocent but for the lawless and disobedient, for the godless and sinful, for the unholy and profane, for those who kill their father or mother, for murderers, [10] fornicators, sodomites, slave traders, liars, perjurers, and whatever else is con-

[a] Or *plan*

trary to the sound teaching [11] that conforms to the glorious gospel of the blessed God, which he entrusted to me.

Gratitude for Mercy
(Cp Acts 8.1–3; 9.1–19)

12 I am grateful to Christ Jesus our Lord, who has strengthened me, because he judged me faithful and appointed me to his service, [13] even though I was formerly a blasphemer, a persecutor, and a man of violence. But I received mercy because I had acted ignorantly in unbelief, [14] and the grace of our Lord overflowed for me with the faith and love that are in Christ Jesus. [15] The saying is sure and worthy of full acceptance, that Christ Jesus came into the world to save sinners—of whom I am the foremost. [16] But for that very reason I received mercy, so that in me, as the foremost, Jesus Christ might display the utmost patience, making me an example to those who would come to believe in him for eternal life. [17] To the King of the ages, immortal, invisible, the only God, be honor and glory forever and ever.[b] Amen.

18 I am giving you these instructions, Timothy, my child, in accordance with the prophecies made earlier about you, so that by following them you may fight the good fight, [19] having faith and a good conscience. By rejecting conscience, certain persons have suffered shipwreck in the faith; [20] among them are Hy·me·naeʹus and Alexander, whom I have turned over to Satan, so that they may learn not to blaspheme.

Instructions concerning Prayer

2 First of all, then, I urge that supplications, prayers, intercessions, and thanksgivings be made for everyone, [2] for kings and all who are in high positions, so that we may lead a quiet and peaceable life in all godliness and dignity. [3] This is right and is acceptable in the sight of God our Savior, [4] who desires everyone to be saved and to come to the knowledge of the truth. [5] For

there is one God;
there is also one mediator
between God and
humankind,
Christ Jesus, himself human,
6 who gave himself a ransom for
all

—this was attested at the right time. [7] For this I was appointed a herald and an apostle (I am telling the truth,[c] I am not lying), a teacher of the Gentiles in faith and truth.

8 I desire, then, that in every place the men should pray, lifting up holy hands without anger or argument; [9] also that the women should dress themselves modestly and decently in suitable clothing, not with their hair braided, or with gold, pearls, or expensive clothes, [10] but with good works, as is proper for women who profess reverence for God. [11] Let a woman[d] learn in silence with full submission. [12] I permit no woman[d] to teach or to have authority over a man;[e] she is to keep silent. [13] For Adam was formed first, then Eve; [14] and Adam was not deceived, but the woman was deceived and became a transgressor. [15] Yet she will be saved through childbearing, provided they continue in faith and love and holiness, with modesty.

Qualifications of Bishops

3 The saying is sure:[f] whoever aspires to the office of bishop[g] desires a noble task. [2] Now a bishop[h] must be above reproach, married only once,[i] temperate, sensible, respectable, hospitable, an apt teacher, [3] not a drunkard, not violent but gentle, not quarrelsome, and not a lover of money. [4] He must manage his own household well, keeping his children submissive and respectful in every way— [5] for if someone does not know how to manage his own household, how can he take care of God's church? [6] He must not be a recent convert, or he may be puffed up with conceit and fall into the condemnation of the devil. [7] Moreover, he must be well thought of by outsiders, so that he may not fall into disgrace and the snare of the devil.

Qualifications of Deacons

8 Deacons likewise must be serious, not double-tongued, not indulging in much wine, not greedy for money;

---

[b] Gk to the ages of the ages   [c] Other ancient authorities add in Christ
[d] Or wife   [e] Or her husband   [f] Some interpreters place these words at the end of the previous paragraph. Other ancient authorities read The saying is commonly accepted   [g] Or overseer   [h] Or an overseer   [i] Gk the husband of one wife

9 they must hold fast to the mystery of the faith with a clear conscience. 10 And let them first be tested; then, if they prove themselves blameless, let them serve as deacons. 11 Women[j] likewise must be serious, not slanderers, but temperate, faithful in all things. 12 Let deacons be married only once,[k] and let them manage their children and their households well; 13 for those who serve well as deacons gain a good standing for themselves and great boldness in the faith that is in Christ Jesus.

The Mystery of Our Religion

14 I hope to come to you soon, but I am writing these instructions to you so that, 15 if I am delayed, you may know how one ought to behave in the household of God, which is the church of the living God, the pillar and bulwark of the truth. 16 Without any doubt, the mystery of our religion is great:

He[l] was revealed in flesh,
vindicated[m] in spirit,[n]
    seen by angels,
proclaimed among Gentiles,
    believed in throughout the
        world,
        taken up in glory.

False Asceticism

4 Now the Spirit expressly says that in later[o] times some will renounce the faith by paying attention to deceitful spirits and teachings of demons, 2 through the hypocrisy of liars whose consciences are seared with a hot iron. 3 They forbid marriage and demand abstinence from foods, which God created to be received with thanksgiving by those who believe and know the truth. 4 For everything created by God is good, and nothing is to be rejected, provided it is received with thanksgiving; 5 for it is sanctified by God's word and by prayer.

A Good Minister of Jesus Christ

6 If you put these instructions before the brothers and sisters,[p] you will be a good servant[q] of Christ Jesus, nourished on the words of the faith and of the sound teaching that you have followed. 7 Have nothing to do with profane myths and old wives' tales. Train yourself in godliness, 8 for, while physical training is of some value, godliness is valuable in every way, holding promise for both the present life and the life to come. 9 The saying is sure and worthy of full acceptance. 10 For to this end we toil and struggle,[r] because we have our hope set on the living God, who is the Savior of all people, especially of those who believe.

11 These are the things you must insist on and teach. 12 Let no one despise your youth, but set the believers an example in speech and conduct, in love, in faith, in purity. 13 Until I arrive, give attention to the public reading of scripture,[s] to exhorting, to teaching. 14 Do not neglect the gift that is in you, which was given to you through prophecy with the laying on of hands by the council of elders.[t] 15 Put these things into practice, devote yourself to them, so that all may see your progress. 16 Pay close attention to yourself and to your teaching; continue in these things, for in doing this you will save both yourself and your hearers.

Duties toward Believers

5 Do not speak harshly to an older man,[u] but speak to him as to a father, to younger men as brothers, 2 to older women as mothers, to younger women as sisters—with absolute purity.

3 Honor widows who are really widows. 4 If a widow has children or grandchildren, they should first learn their religious duty to their own family and make some repayment to their parents; for this is pleasing in God's sight. 5 The real widow, left alone, has set her hope on God and continues in supplications and prayers night and day; 6 but the widow[v] who lives for pleasure is dead even while she lives. 7 Give these commands as well, so that they may be above reproach. 8 And whoever does not provide for relatives, and especially for family members, has denied the faith and is worse than an unbeliever.

9 Let a widow be put on the list if

---

j Or *Their wives*, or *Women deacons*
k Gk *be husbands of one wife*
l Gk *Who*; other ancient authorities read *God*; others, *Which*   m Or *justified*
n Or *by the Spirit*   o Or *the last*
p Gk *brothers*   q Or *deacon*   r Other ancient authorities read *suffer reproach*
s Gk *to the reading*   t Gk *by the presbytery*   u Or *an elder*, or *a presbyter*   v Gk *she*

she is not less than sixty years old and has been married only once;[w] [10]she must be well attested for her good works, as one who has brought up children, shown hospitality, washed the saints' feet, helped the afflicted, and devoted herself to doing good in every way. [11]But refuse to put younger widows on the list; for when their sensual desires alienate them from Christ, they want to marry, [12]and so they incur condemnation for having violated their first pledge. [13]Besides that, they learn to be idle, gadding about from house to house; and they are not merely idle, but also gossips and busybodies, saying what they should not say. [14]So I would have younger widows marry, bear children, and manage their households, so as to give the adversary no occasion to revile us. [15]For some have already turned away to follow Satan. [16]If any believing woman[x] has relatives who are really widows, let her assist them; let the church not be burdened, so that it can assist those who are real widows.

[17] Let the elders who rule well be considered worthy of double honor,[y] especially those who labor in preaching and teaching; [18]for the scripture says, "You shall not muzzle an ox while it is treading out the grain," and, "The laborer deserves to be paid." [19]Never accept any accusation against an elder except on the evidence of two or three witnesses. [20]As for those who persist in sin, rebuke them in the presence of all, so that the rest also may stand in fear. [21]In the presence of God and of Christ Jesus and of the elect angels, I warn you to keep these instructions without prejudice, doing nothing on the basis of partiality. [22]Do not ordain[z] anyone hastily, and do not participate in the sins of others; keep yourself pure.

[23] No longer drink only water, but take a little wine for the sake of your stomach and your frequent ailments.

[24] The sins of some people are conspicuous and precede them to judgment, while the sins of others follow them there. [25]So also good works are conspicuous; and even when they are not, they cannot remain hidden.

6 Let all who are under the yoke of slavery regard their masters as worthy of all honor, so that the name of God and the teaching may not be blasphemed. [2]Those who have believing masters must not be disrespectful to them on the ground that they are members of the church;[a] rather they must serve them all the more, since those who benefit by their service are believers and beloved.[b]

False Teaching and True Riches

Teach and urge these duties. [3]Whoever teaches otherwise and does not agree with the sound words of our Lord Jesus Christ and the teaching that is in accordance with godliness, [4]is conceited, understanding nothing, and has a morbid craving for controversy and for disputes about words. From these come envy, dissension, slander, base suspicions, [5]and wrangling among those who are depraved in mind and bereft of the truth, imagining that godliness is a means of gain.[c] [6]Of course, there is great gain in godliness combined with contentment; [7]for we brought nothing into the world, so that[d] we can take nothing out of it; [8]but if we have food and clothing, we will be content with these. [9]But those who want to be rich fall into temptation and are trapped by many senseless and harmful desires that plunge people into ruin and destruction. [10]For the love of money is a root of all kinds of evil, and in their eagerness to be rich some have wandered away from the faith and pierced themselves with many pains.

The Good Fight of Faith

[11] But as for you, man of God, shun all this; pursue righteousness, godliness, faith, love, endurance, gentleness. [12]Fight the good fight of the faith; take hold of the eternal life, to which you were called and for which you made[e] the good confession in the presence of many witnesses. [13]In the presence of God, who gives life to all things, and of Christ Jesus, who in his testimony before Pon'ti·us Pilate made the good confession, I charge you [14]to

---

[w] Gk *the wife of one husband*   [x] Other ancient authorities read *believing man or woman*; others, *believing man*
[y] Or *compensation*   [z] Gk *Do not lay hands on*   [a] Gk *are brothers*
[b] Or *since they are believers and beloved, who devote themselves to good deeds*
[c] Other ancient authorities add *Withdraw yourself from such people*
[d] Other ancient authorities read *world—it is certain that*
[e] Gk *confessed*

keep the commandment without spot or blame until the manifestation of our Lord Jesus Christ, [15]which he will bring about at the right time—he who is the blessed and only Sovereign, the King of kings and Lord of lords. [16]It is he alone who has immortality and dwells in unapproachable light, whom no one has ever seen or can see; to him be honor and eternal dominion. Amen.

[17] As for those who in the present age are rich, command them not to be haughty, or to set their hopes on the uncertainty of riches, but rather on God who richly provides us with everything for our enjoyment. [18]They are to do good, to be rich in good works, generous, and ready to share, [19]thus storing up for themselves the treasure of a good foundation for the future, so that they may take hold of the life that really is life.

Personal Instructions and Benediction

[20] Timothy, guard what has been entrusted to you. Avoid the profane chatter and contradictions of what is falsely called knowledge; [21]by professing it some have missed the mark as regards the faith.

Grace be with you.[f]

[f]The Greek word for you here is plural; in other ancient authorities it is singular. Other ancient authorities add Amen

The Second Letter of Paul to

TIMOTHY

Salutation

1 Paul, an apostle of Christ Jesus by the will of God, for the sake of the promise of life that is in Christ Jesus, 2 To Timothy, my beloved child:

Grace, mercy, and peace from God the Father and Christ Jesus our Lord.

Thanksgiving and Encouragement

3 I am grateful to God—whom I worship with a clear conscience, as my ancestors did—when I remember you constantly in my prayers night and day. [4]Recalling your tears, I long to see you so that I may be filled with joy. [5]I am reminded of your sincere faith, a faith that lived first in your grandmother Lō'is and your mother Eū'nice and now, I am sure, lives in you. [6]For this reason I remind you to rekindle the gift of God that is within you through the laying on of my hands; [7]for God did not give us a spirit of cowardice, but rather a spirit of power and of love and of self-discipline.

8 Do not be ashamed, then, of the testimony about our Lord or of me his prisoner, but join with me in suffering for the gospel, relying on the power of God, [9]who saved us and called us with a holy calling, not according to our works but according to his own purpose and grace. This grace was given to us in Christ Jesus before the ages began, [10]but it has now been revealed through the appearing of our Savior Christ Jesus, who abolished death and brought life and immortality to light through the gospel. [11]For this gospel I was appointed a herald and an apostle and a teacher,[a] [12]and for this reason I suffer as I do. But I am not ashamed, for I know the one in whom I have put my trust, and I am sure that he is able to guard until that day what I have entrusted to him.[b] [13]Hold to the standard of sound teaching that you have heard from me, in the faith and love that are in Christ Jesus. [14]Guard the good treasure entrusted to you, with the help of the Holy Spirit living in us.

15 You are aware that all who are in Asia have turned away from me, including Phÿ'ge·lus and Her-mog'e·nēs. [16]May the Lord grant mercy to the household of One-e·siph'o·rus, because he often refreshed me and was not ashamed of

[a]Other ancient authorities add of the Gentiles   [b]Or what has been entrusted to me

my chain; [17]when he arrived in Rome, he eagerly[c] searched for me and found me [18]—may the Lord grant that he will find mercy from the Lord on that day! And you know very well how much service he rendered in Eph′-e·sus.

A Good Soldier of Christ Jesus

2 You then, my child, be strong in the grace that is in Christ Jesus; [2]and what you have heard from me through many witnesses entrust to faithful people who will be able to teach others as well. [3]Share in suffering like a good soldier of Christ Jesus. [4]No one serving in the army gets entangled in everyday affairs; the soldier's aim is to please the enlisting officer. [5]And in the case of an athlete, no one is crowned without competing according to the rules. [6]It is the farmer who does the work who ought to have the first share of the crops. [7]Think over what I say, for the Lord will give you understanding in all things.

[8] Remember Jesus Christ, raised from the dead, a descendant of David—that is my gospel, [9]for which I suffer hardship, even to the point of being chained like a criminal. But the word of God is not chained. [10]Therefore I endure everything for the sake of the elect, so that they may also obtain the salvation that is in Christ Jesus, with eternal glory. [11]The saying is sure:

If we have died with him, we
　　will also live with him;
[12] if we endure, we will also reign
　　with him;
if we deny him, he will also deny
　　us;
[13] if we are faithless, he remains
　　faithful—
for he cannot deny himself.

A Worker Approved by God

[14] Remind them of this, and warn them before God[d] that they are to avoid wrangling over words, which does no good but only ruins those who are listening. [15]Do your best to present yourself to God as one approved by him, a worker who has no need to be ashamed, rightly explaining the word of truth. [16]Avoid profane chatter, for it will lead people into more and more impiety, [17]and their talk will spread like gangrene. Among them are Hy̆·me·naē′us and Phi·lē′tus, [18]who have swerved from the truth by claiming that the resurrection has already taken place. They are upsetting the faith of some. [19]But God's firm foundation stands, bearing this inscription: "The Lord knows those who are his," and, "Let everyone who calls on the name of the Lord turn away from wickedness."

[20] In a large house there are utensils not only of gold and silver but also of wood and clay, some for special use, some for ordinary. [21]All who cleanse themselves of the things I have mentioned[e] will become special utensils, dedicated and useful to the owner of the house, ready for every good work. [22]Shun youthful passions and pursue righteousness, faith, love, and peace, along with those who call on the Lord from a pure heart. [23]Have nothing to do with stupid and senseless controversies; you know that they breed quarrels. [24]And the Lord's servant[f] must not be quarrelsome but kindly to everyone, an apt teacher, patient, [25]correcting opponents with gentleness. God may perhaps grant that they will repent and come to know the truth, [26]and that they may escape from the snare of the devil, having been held captive by him to do his will.[g]

Godlessness in the Last Days

3 You must understand this, that in the last days distressing times will come. [2]For people will be lovers of themselves, lovers of money, boasters, arrogant, abusive, disobedient to their parents, ungrateful, unholy, [3]inhuman, implacable, slanderers, profligates, brutes, haters of good, [4]treacherous, reckless, swollen with conceit, lovers of pleasure rather than lovers of God, [5]holding to the outward form of godliness but denying its power. Avoid them! [6]For among them are those who make their way into households and captivate silly women, overwhelmed by their sins and swayed by all kinds of desires, [7]who are always being instructed and can never arrive at a knowledge of the truth. [8]As Jan′nēs and Jam′brēs opposed Moses, so these people, of corrupt mind and counterfeit faith, also oppose the truth. [9]But they will not make much progress, be-

---

[c]Or *promptly*　[d]Other ancient authorities read *the Lord*　[e]Gk *of these things*　[f]Gk *slave*　[g]Or *by him, to do his* (that is, God's) *will*

cause, as in the case of those two men,[h] their folly will become plain to everyone.

Paul's Charge to Timothy

10 Now you have observed my teaching, my conduct, my aim in life, my faith, my patience, my love, my steadfastness, [11] my persecutions and suffering the things that happened to me in An'ti·och, I·cō'ni·um, and Lys'-tra. What persecutions I endured! Yet the Lord rescued me from all of them. [12] Indeed, all who want to live a godly life in Christ Jesus will be persecuted. [13] But wicked people and impostors will go from bad to worse, deceiving others and being deceived. [14] But as for you, continue in what you have learned and firmly believed, knowing from whom you learned it, [15] and how from childhood you have known the sacred writings that are able to instruct you for salvation through faith in Christ Jesus. [16] All scripture is inspired by God and is[i] useful for teaching, for reproof, for correction, and for training in righteousness, [17] so that everyone who belongs to God may be proficient, equipped for every good work.

4 In the presence of God and of Christ Jesus, who is to judge the living and the dead, and in view of his appearing and his kingdom, I solemnly urge you: [2] proclaim the message; be persistent whether the time is favorable or unfavorable; convince, rebuke, and encourage, with the utmost patience in teaching. [3] For the time is coming when people will not put up with sound doctrine, but having itching ears, they will accumulate for themselves teachers to suit their own desires, [4] and will turn away from listening to the truth and wander away to myths. [5] As for you, always be sober, endure suffering, do the work of an evangelist, carry out your ministry fully.

6 As for me, I am already being poured out as a libation, and the time of my departure has come. [7] I have fought the good fight, I have finished the race, I have kept the faith. [8] From

now on there is reserved for me the crown of righteousness, which the Lord, the righteous judge, will give me on that day, and not only to me but also to all who have longed for his appearing.

Personal Instructions

9 Do your best to come to me soon, [10] for Dē'mas, in love with this present world, has deserted me and gone to Thes·sa·lo·ni'ca; Cres'cens has gone to Galatia,[j] Titus to Dal·ma'tia. [11] Only Luke is with me. Get Mark and bring him with you, for he is useful in my ministry. [12] I have sent Tych'i·cus to Eph'e·sus. [13] When you come, bring the cloak that I left with Car'pus at Trō'as, also the books, and above all the parchments. [14] Alexander the coppersmith did me great harm; the Lord will pay him back for his deeds. [15] You also must beware of him, for he strongly opposed our message.

16 At my first defense no one came to my support, but all deserted me. May it not be counted against them! [17] But the Lord stood by me and gave me strength, so that through me the message might be fully proclaimed and all the Gentiles might hear it. So I was rescued from the lion's mouth. [18] The Lord will rescue me from every evil attack and save me for his heavenly kingdom. To him be the glory forever and ever. Amen.

Final Greetings and Benediction

19 Greet Pris'ca and A·qui'la, and the household of On·e·siph'o·rus. [20] E·ras'tus remained in Corinth; Troph'i·mus I left ill in Mī·lē'tus. [21] Do your best to come before winter. Eū·bū'lus sends greetings to you, as do Pū'dens and Lī'nus and Clau'di·a and all the brothers and sisters.[k]

22 The Lord be with your spirit. Grace be with you.[l]

[h] Gk lacks *two men*　[i] Or *Every scripture inspired by God is also*　[j] Other ancient authorities read *Gaul*　[k] Gk *all the brothers*　[l] The Greek word for *you* here is plural. Other ancient authorities add *Amen*

The Letter of Paul to

TITUS

Salutation

1 Paul, a servant*a* of God and an apostle of Jesus Christ, for the sake of the faith of God's elect and the knowledge of the truth that is in accordance with godliness, [2] in the hope of eternal life that God, who never lies, promised before the ages began— [3] in due time he revealed his word through the proclamation with which I have been entrusted by the command of God our Savior,

4 To Titus, my loyal child in the faith we share:

Grace*b* and peace from God the Father and Christ Jesus our Savior.

Titus in Crete

5 I left you behind in Crete for this reason, so that you should put in order what remained to be done, and should appoint elders in every town, as I directed you: [6] someone who is blameless, married only once,*c* whose children are believers, not accused of debauchery and not rebellious. [7] For a bishop,*d* as God's steward, must be blameless; he must not be arrogant or quick-tempered or addicted to wine or violent or greedy for gain; [8] but he must be hospitable, a lover of goodness, prudent, upright, devout, and self-controlled. [9] He must have a firm grasp of the word that is trustworthy in accordance with the teaching, so that he may be able both to preach with sound doctrine and to refute those who contradict it.

10 There are also many rebellious people, idle talkers and deceivers, especially those of the circumcision; [11] they must be silenced, since they are upsetting whole families by teaching for sordid gain what it is not right to teach. [12] It was one of them, their very own prophet, who said,

> "Crē'tans are always liars,
> vicious brutes, lazy
> gluttons."

[13] That testimony is true. For this reason rebuke them sharply, so that they may become sound in the faith, [14] not paying attention to Jewish myths or to commandments of those who reject the truth. [15] To the pure all things are pure, but to the corrupt and unbelieving nothing is pure. Their very minds and consciences are corrupted. [16] They profess to know God, but they deny him by their actions. They are detestable, disobedient, unfit for any good work.

Teach Sound Doctrine

2 But as for you, teach what is consistent with sound doctrine. [2] Tell the older men to be temperate, serious, prudent, and sound in faith, in love, and in endurance.

3 Likewise, tell the older women to be reverent in behavior, not to be slanderers or slaves to drink; they are to teach what is good, [4] so that they may encourage the young women to love their husbands, to love their children, [5] to be self-controlled, chaste, good managers of the household, kind, being submissive to their husbands, so that the word of God may not be discredited.

6 Likewise, urge the younger men to be self-controlled. [7] Show yourself in all respects a model of good works, and in your teaching show integrity, gravity, [8] and sound speech that cannot be censured; then any opponent will be put to shame, having nothing evil to say of us.

9 Tell slaves to be submissive to their masters and to give satisfaction in every respect; they are not to talk back, [10] not to pilfer, but to show complete and perfect fidelity, so that in everything they may be an ornament

---

a Gk *slave*   *b* Other ancient authorities read *Grace, mercy,*   *c* Gk *husband of one wife*   *d* Or *an overseer* to the doctrine of God our Savior.

11 For the grace of God has appeared, bringing salvation to all,[e] [12]training us to renounce impiety and worldly passions, and in the present age to live lives that are self-controlled, upright, and godly, [13]while we wait for the blessed hope and the manifestation of the glory of our great God and Savior,[f] Jesus Christ. [14]He it is who gave himself for us that he might redeem us from all iniquity and purify for himself a people of his own who are zealous for good deeds.

15 Declare these things; exhort and reprove with all authority.[g] Let no one look down on you.

Maintain Good Deeds

3 Remind them to be subject to rulers and authorities, to be obedient, to be ready for every good work, [2]to speak evil of no one, to avoid quarreling, to be gentle, and to show every courtesy to everyone. [3]For we ourselves were once foolish, disobedient, led astray, slaves to various passions and pleasures, passing our days in malice and envy, despicable, hating one another. [4]But when the goodness and loving kindness of God our Savior appeared, [5]he saved us, not because of any works of righteousness that we had done, but according to his mercy, through the water[h] of rebirth and renewal by the Holy Spirit. [6]This Spirit he poured out on us richly through Jesus Christ our Savior, [7]so that, having been justified by his grace, we

might become heirs according to the hope of eternal life. [8]The saying is sure.

I desire that you insist on these things, so that those who have come to believe in God may be careful to devote themselves to good works; these things are excellent and profitable to everyone. [9]But avoid stupid controversies, genealogies, dissensions, and quarrels about the law, for they are unprofitable and worthless. [10]After a first and second admonition, have nothing more to do with anyone who causes divisions, [11]since you know that such a person is perverted and sinful, being self-condemned.

Final Messages and Benediction

12 When I send Ar·te·mas to you, or Tych·i·cus, do your best to come to me at Ni·cop·o·lis, for I have decided to spend the winter there. [13]Make every effort to send Ze·nas the lawyer and A·pol·los on their way, and see that they lack nothing. [14]And let people learn to devote themselves to good works in order to meet urgent needs, so that they may not be unproductive.

15 All who are with me send greetings to you. Greet those who love us in the faith.

Grace be with all of you.[i]

[e]Or *has appeared to all, bringing salvation* [f]Or *of the great God and our Savior* [g]Gk *commandment* [h]Gk *washing* [i]Other ancient authorities add *Amen*

The Letter of Paul to

PHILEMON

Salutation

1 Paul, a prisoner of Christ Jesus, and Timothy our brother,[a]

To Phi·le·mon our dear friend and co-worker, [2]to Ap·phi·a our sister,[b] to Ar·chip·pus our fellow soldier, and to the church in your house:

3 Grace to you and peace from God our Father and the Lord Jesus Christ.

Philemon's Love and Faith

4 When I remember you[c] in my prayers, I always thank my God [5]because I hear of your love for all the saints and your faith toward the Lord

[a]Gk *the brother*   [b]Gk *the sister*
[c]From verse 4 through verse 21, *you* is singular

Jesus. 6 I pray that the sharing of your faith may become effective when you perceive all the good that we d may do for Christ. 7 I have indeed received much joy and encouragement from your love, because the hearts of the saints have been refreshed through you, my brother.

Paul's Plea for Onesimus

8 For this reason, though I am bold enough in Christ to command you to do your duty, 9 yet I would rather appeal to you on the basis of love—and I, Paul, do this as an old man, and now also as a prisoner of Christ Jesus. e 10 I am appealing to you for my child, O·nes′i·mus, whose father I have become during my imprisonment. 11 Formerly he was useless to you, but now he is indeed useful f both to you and to me. 12 I am sending him, that is, my own heart, back to you. 13 I wanted to keep him with me, so that he might be of service to me in your place during my imprisonment for the gospel; 14 but I preferred to do nothing without your consent, in order that your good deed might be voluntary and not something forced. 15 Perhaps this is the reason he was separated from you for a while, so that you might have him back forever, 16 no longer as a slave but more than a slave, a beloved brother—especially to

me but how much more to you, both in the flesh and in the Lord.

17 So if you consider me your partner, welcome him as you would welcome me. 18 If he has wronged you in any way, or owes you anything, charge that to my account. 19 I, Paul, am writing this with my own hand: I will repay it. I say nothing about your owing me even your own self. 20 Yes, brother, let me have this benefit from you in the Lord! Refresh my heart in Christ. 21 Confident of your obedience, I am writing to you, knowing that you will do even more than I say.

22 One thing more—prepare a guest room for me, for I am hoping through your prayers to be restored to you.

Final Greetings and Benediction

23 Ep′a·phras, my fellow prisoner in Christ Jesus, sends greetings to you, g 24 and so do Mark, Ar·is·tar′-chus, De′mas, and Luke, my fellow workers.

25 The grace of the Lord Jesus Christ be with your spirit. h

d Other ancient authorities read you (plural)   e Or as an ambassador of Christ Jesus, and now also his prisoner   f The name Onesimus means useful or (compare verse 20) beneficial   g Here you is singular   h Other ancient authorities add Amen

The Letter to the

HEBREWS

God Has Spoken by His Son
(Cp Jn 1.1–4)

1 Long ago God spoke to our ancestors in many and various ways by the prophets, [2] but in these last days he has spoken to us by a Son,[a] whom he appointed heir of all things, through whom he also created the worlds. [3] He is the reflection of God's glory and the exact imprint of God's very being, and he sustains[b] all things by his powerful word. When he had made purification for sins, he sat down at the right hand of the Majesty on high, [4] having become as much superior to angels as the name he has inherited is more excellent than theirs.

The Son Is Superior to Angels

[5] For to which of the angels did God ever say,
"You are my Son;
today I have begotten you?"
Or again,
"I will be his Father,
and he will be my Son"?
[6] And again, when he brings the firstborn into the world, he says,
"Let all God's angels worship him."
[7] Of the angels he says,
"He makes his angels winds,
and his servants flames of fire."
[8] But of the Son he says,
"Your throne, O God,[c] is forever and ever,
and the righteous scepter is the scepter of your[d] kingdom.
[9] You have loved righteousness and hated wickedness;
therefore God, your God, has anointed you
with the oil of gladness beyond your companions."
[10] And,
"In the beginning, Lord, you founded the earth,
and the heavens are the work of your hands;
[11] they will perish, but you remain;
they will all wear out like clothing;
[12] like a cloak you will roll them up,
and like clothing[e] they will be changed.
But you are the same,
and your years will never end."
[13] But to which of the angels has he ever said,
"Sit at my right hand
until I make your enemies a footstool for your feet"?
[14] Are not all angels[f] spirits in the divine service, sent to serve for the sake of those who are to inherit salvation?

Warning to Pay Attention

2 Therefore we must pay greater attention to what we have heard, so that we do not drift away from it. [2] For if the message declared through angels was valid, and every transgression or disobedience received a just penalty, [3] how can we escape if we neglect so great a salvation? It was declared at first through the Lord, and it was attested to us by those who heard him, [4] while God added his testimony by signs and wonders and various miracles, and by gifts of the Holy Spirit, distributed according to his will.

Exaltation through Abasement
(Cp Ps 8.1–9)

[5] Now God[g] did not subject the

[a] Or *the Son*   [b] Or *bears along*
[c] Or *God is your throne*   [d] Other ancient authorities read *his*   [e] Other ancient authorities lack *like clothing*   [f] Gk *all of them*   [g] Gk *he*

coming world, about which we are speaking, to angels. [6]But someone has testified somewhere,

"What are human beings that
    you are mindful of them,[h]
or mortals, that you care for
    them?[i]
[7] You have made them for a little
    while lower[j] than the
    angels;
you have crowned them with
    glory and honor,[k]
[8]   subjecting all things under
    their feet."

Now in subjecting all things to them, God[l] left nothing outside their control. As it is, we do not yet see everything in subjection to them, [9]but we do see Jesus, who for a little while was made lower[m] than the angels, now crowned with glory and honor because of the suffering of death, so that by the grace of God[n] he might taste death for everyone.

[10] It was fitting that God,[l] for whom and through whom all things exist, in bringing many children to glory, should make the pioneer of their salvation perfect through sufferings. [11]For the one who sanctifies and those who are sanctified all have one Father.[o] For this reason Jesus[l] is not ashamed to call them brothers and sisters,[p] [12]saying,

"I will proclaim your name to
    my brothers and sisters,[p]
in the midst of the
    congregation I will praise
    you."

[13]And again,

"I will put my trust in him."

And again,

"Here am I and the children
    whom God has given me."

[14] Since, therefore, the children share flesh and blood, he himself likewise shared the same things, so that through death he might destroy the one who has the power of death, that is, the devil, [15]and free those who all their lives were held in slavery by the fear of death. [16]For it is clear that he did not come to help angels, but the descendants of Abraham. [17]Therefore he had to become like his brothers and sisters[p] in every respect, so that he might be a merciful and faithful high priest in the service of God, to make a sacrifice of atonement for the sins of the people. [18]Because he himself was tested by what he suffered, he is able to help those who are being tested.

Moses a Servant, Christ a Son

3 Therefore, brothers and sisters,[p] holy partners in a heavenly calling, consider that Jesus, the apostle and high priest of our confession, [2]was faithful to the one who appointed him, just as Moses also "was faithful in all[q] God's[r] house." [3]Yet Jesus[s] is worthy of more glory than Moses, just as the builder of a house has more honor than the house itself. [4](For every house is built by someone, but the builder of all things is God.) [5]Now Moses was faithful in all God's[r] house as a servant, to testify to the things that would be spoken later. [6]Christ, however, was faithful over God's[r] house as a son, and we are his house if we hold firm[t] the confidence and the pride that belong to hope.

Warning against Unbelief
(Ps 95.7b–11)

[7] Therefore, as the Holy Spirit says,
    "Today, if you hear his voice,
[8] do not harden your hearts as in
    the rebellion,
    as on the day of testing in the
    wilderness,
[9] where your ancestors put me to
    the test,
    though they had seen my
    works [10]for forty years.
Therefore I was angry with that
    generation,
and I said, 'They always go
    astray in their hearts,
    and they have not known my
    ways.'
[11] As in my anger I swore,
    'They will not enter my rest.' "

[12]Take care, brothers and sisters,[p] that none of you may have an evil, unbelieving heart that turns away from the living God. [13]But exhort one another every day, as long as it is called

[h]Gk *What is man that you are mindful of him?* [i]Gk *or the son of man that you care for him?* In the Hebrew of Psalm 8.4-6 both *man* and *son of man* refer to all humankind [j]Or *them only a little lower* [k]Other ancient authorities add *and set them over the works of your hands* [l]Gk *he* [m]Or *who was made a little lower* [n]Other ancient authorities read *apart from God* [o]Gk *are all of one* [p]Gk *brothers* [q]Other ancient authorities lack *all* [r]Gk *his* [s]Gk *this one* [t]Other ancient authorities add *to the end*

"today," so that none of you may be hardened by the deceitfulness of sin. [14] For we have become partners of Christ, if only we hold our first confidence firm to the end. [15] As it is said,

"Today, if you hear his voice,
　do not harden your hearts as in
　　the rebellion."

[16] Now who were they who heard and yet were rebellious? Was it not all those who left Egypt under the leadership of Moses? [17] But with whom was he angry forty years? Was it not those who sinned, whose bodies fell in the wilderness? [18] And to whom did he swear that they would not enter his rest, if not to those who were disobedient? [19] So we see that they were unable to enter because of unbelief.

The Rest That God Promised

4 Therefore, while the promise of entering his rest is still open, let us take care that none of you should seem to have failed to reach it. [2] For indeed the good news came to us just as to them; but the message they heard did not benefit them, because they were not united by faith with those who listened. [u] [3] For we who have believed enter that rest, just as God[v] has said,

"As in my anger I swore,
'They shall not enter my rest,' "
though his works were finished at the foundation of the world. [4] For in one place it speaks about the seventh day as follows, "And God rested on the seventh day from all his works." [5] And again in this place it says, "They shall not enter my rest." [6] Since therefore it remains open for some to enter it, and those who formerly received the good news failed to enter because of disobedience, [7] again he sets a certain day—"today"—saying through David much later, in the words already quoted,

"Today, if you hear his voice,
　do not harden your hearts."

[8] For if Joshua had given them rest, God[v] would not speak later about another day. [9] So then, a sabbath rest still remains for the people of God; [10] for those who enter God's rest also cease from their labors as God did from his. [11] Let us therefore make every effort to enter that rest, so that no one may fall through such disobedience as theirs.

[12] Indeed, the word of God is living and active, sharper than any two-edged sword, piercing until it divides soul from spirit, joints from marrow; it is able to judge the thoughts and intentions of the heart. [13] And before him no creature is hidden, but all are naked and laid bare to the eyes of the one to whom we must render an account.

Jesus the Great High Priest

14 Since, then, we have a great high priest who has passed through the heavens, Jesus, the Son of God, let us hold fast to our confession. [15] For we do not have a high priest who is unable to sympathize with our weaknesses, but we have one who in every respect has been tested[w] as we are, yet without sin. [16] Let us therefore approach the throne of grace with boldness, so that we may receive mercy and find grace to help in time of need.

5 Every high priest chosen from among mortals is put in charge of things pertaining to God on their behalf, to offer gifts and sacrifices for sins. [2] He is able to deal gently with the ignorant and wayward, since he himself is subject to weakness; [3] and because of this he must offer sacrifice for his own sins as well as for those of the people. [4] And one does not presume to take this honor, but takes it only when called by God, just as Aaron was.

5 So also Christ did not glorify himself in becoming a high priest, but was appointed by the one who said to him,

"You are my Son,
　today I have begotten you";
[6] as he says also in another place,

"You are a priest forever,
　according to the order of
　　Mel·chiz'e·dek."

7 In the days of his flesh, Jesus[v] offered up prayers and supplications, with loud cries and tears, to the one who was able to save him from death, and he was heard because of his reverent submission. [8] Although he was a Son, he learned obedience through what he suffered; [9] and having been made perfect, he became the source of eternal salvation for all who obey him, [10] having been designated by God a high priest according to the order of Mel·chiz'e·dek.

Warning against Falling Away

11 About this[x] we have much to say that is hard to explain, since you have

---

u Other ancient authorities read *it did not meet with faith in those who listened*　v Gk *he*　w Or *tempted*
x Or *him*

become dull in understanding. ¹²For though by this time you ought to be teachers, you need someone to teach you again the basic elements of the oracles of God. You need milk, not solid food; ¹³for everyone who lives on milk, being still an infant, is unskilled in the word of righteousness. ¹⁴But solid food is for the mature, for those whose faculties have been trained by practice to distinguish good from evil.

The Peril of Falling Away

6 Therefore let us go on toward perfection,ʸ leaving behind the basic teaching about Christ, and not laying again the foundation: repentance from dead works and faith toward God, ²instruction about baptisms, laying on of hands, resurrection of the dead, and eternal judgment. ³And we will doᶻ this, if God permits. ⁴For it is impossible to restore again to repentance those who have once been enlightened, and have tasted the heavenly gift, and have shared in the Holy Spirit, ⁵and have tasted the goodness of the word of God and the powers of the age to come, ⁶and then have fallen away, since on their own they are crucifying again the Son of God and are holding him up to contempt. ⁷Ground that drinks up the rain falling on it repeatedly, and that produces a crop useful to those for whom it is cultivated, receives a blessing from God. ⁸But if it produces thorns and thistles, it is worthless and on the verge of being cursed; its end is to be burned over.

⁹ Even though we speak in this way, beloved, we are confident of better things in your case, things that belong to salvation. ¹⁰For God is not unjust; he will not overlook your work and the love that you showed for his sakeᵃ in serving the saints, as you still do. ¹¹And we want each one of you to show the same diligence so as to realize the full assurance of hope to the very end, ¹²so that you may not become sluggish, but imitators of those who through faith and patience inherit the promises.

The Certainty of God's Promise
(Cp Gen 12.1–3)

13 When God made a promise to Abraham, because he had no one greater by whom to swear, he swore by himself, ¹⁴saying, "I will surely bless you and multiply you." ¹⁵And thus Abraham,ᵇ having patiently endured, obtained the promise. ¹⁶Human beings, of course, swear by someone greater than themselves, and an oath given as confirmation puts an end to all dispute. ¹⁷In the same way, when God desired to show even more clearly to the heirs of the promise the unchangeable character of his purpose, he guaranteed it by an oath, ¹⁸so that through two unchangeable things, in which it is impossible that God would prove false, we who have taken refuge might be strongly encouraged to seize the hope set before us. ¹⁹We have this hope, a sure and steadfast anchor of the soul, a hope that enters the inner shrine behind the curtain, ²⁰where Jesus, a forerunner on our behalf, has entered, having become a high priest forever according to the order of Mel·chiz′e·dek.

The Priestly Order of Melchizedek
(Gen 14.17–20)

7 This "King Mel·chiz′e·dek of Salem, priest of the Most High God, met Abraham as he was returning from defeating the kings and blessed him"; ²and to him Abraham apportioned "one-tenth of everything." His name, in the first place, means "king of righteousness"; next he is also king of Salem, that is, "king of peace." ³Without father, without mother, without genealogy, having neither beginning of days nor end of life, but resembling the Son of God, he remains a priest forever.

4 See how great he is! Evenᶜ Abraham the patriarch gave him a tenth of the spoils. ⁵And those descendants of Levi who receive the priestly office have a commandment in the law to collect tithesᵈ from the people, that is, from their kindred,ᵉ though these also are descended from Abraham. ⁶But this man, who does not belong to their ancestry, collected tithesᵈ from Abraham and blessed him who had received the promises. ⁷It is beyond dispute that the inferior is blessed by the superior. ⁸In the one case, tithes are received by those who are mortal; in the other, by one of whom it is testified that he lives. ⁹One might even say that Levi himself, who receives tithes, paid

ʸOr *toward maturity*   ᶻOther ancient authorities read *let us do*   ᵃGk *for his name*   ᵇGk *he*   ᶜOther ancient authorities lack *Even*   ᵈOr *a tenth*   ᵉGk *brothers* tithes through Abraham, [10] for he was still in the loins of his ancestor when Mel·chiz'e·dek met him.

Another Priest, Like Melchizedek
(Ps 110.4)

11 Now if perfection had been attainable through the levitical priesthood—for the people received the law under this priesthood—what further need would there have been to speak of another priest arising according to the order of Mel·chiz'e·dek, rather than one according to the order of Aaron? [12] For when there is a change in the priesthood, there is necessarily a change in the law as well. [13] Now the one of whom these things are spoken belonged to another tribe, from which no one has ever served at the altar. [14] For it is evident that our Lord was descended from Judah, and in connection with that tribe Moses said nothing about priests.

15 It is even more obvious when another priest arises, resembling Mel·chiz'e·dek, [16] one who has become a priest, not through a legal requirement concerning physical descent, but through the power of an indestructible life. [17] For it is attested of him,
"You are a priest forever,
    according to the order of
        Mel·chiz'e·dek."
[18] There is, on the one hand, the abrogation of an earlier commandment because it was weak and ineffectual [19] (for the law made nothing perfect); there is, on the other hand, the introduction of a better hope, through which we approach God.
20 This was confirmed with an oath; for others who became priests took their office without an oath, [21] but this one became a priest with an oath, because of the one who said to him,
"The Lord has sworn
    and will not change his mind,
'You are a priest forever' "—
[22] accordingly Jesus has also become the guarantee of a better covenant.
23 Furthermore, the former priests were many in number, because they were prevented by death from continuing in office; [24] but he holds his priesthood permanently, because he continues forever. [25] Consequently he is able for all time to save[f] those who approach God through him, since he always lives to make intercession for them.
26 For it was fitting that we should

have such a high priest, holy, blameless, undefiled, separated from sinners, and exalted above the heavens. [27] Unlike the other[g] high priests, he has no need to offer sacrifices day after day, first for his own sins, and then for those of the people; this he did once for all when he offered himself. [28] For the law appoints as high priests those who are subject to weakness, but the word of the oath, which came later than the law, appoints a Son who has been made perfect forever.

Mediator of a Better Covenant
(Jer 31.31–34)

8 Now the main point in what we are saying is this: we have such a high priest, one who is seated at the right hand of the throne of the Majesty in the heavens, [2] a minister in the sanctuary and the true tent[h] that the Lord, and not any mortal, has set up. [3] For every high priest is appointed to offer gifts and sacrifices; hence it is necessary for this priest also to have something to offer. [4] Now if he were on earth, he would not be a priest at all, since there are priests who offer gifts according to the law. [5] They offer worship in a sanctuary that is a sketch and shadow of the heavenly one; for Moses, when he was about to erect the tent,[h] was warned, "See that you make everything according to the pattern that was shown you on the mountain." [6] But Jesus[i] has now obtained a more excellent ministry, and to that degree he is the mediator of a better covenant, which has been enacted through better promises. [7] For if that first covenant had been faultless, there would have been no need to look for a second one.

8 God[j] finds fault with them when he says:
"The days are surely coming,
        says the Lord,
    when I will establish a new
        covenant with the house of
        Israel
    and with the house of Judah;
[9] not like the covenant that I made
        with their ancestors,
    on the day when I took them
        by the hand to lead them
        out of the land of Egypt;

---

[f] Or *able to save completely*   [g] Gk lacks *other*   [h] Or *tabernacle*   [i] Gk *he*
[j] Gk *He*

for they did not continue in my
    covenant,
and so I had no concern for
    them, says the Lord.
10 This is the covenant that I will
    make with the house of
    Israel
after those days, says the
    Lord:
I will put my laws in their
    minds,
and write them on their hearts,
and I will be their God,
and they shall be my people.
11 And they shall not teach one
    another
or say to each other, 'Know
    the Lord,'
for they shall all know me,
from the least of them to the
    greatest.
12 For I will be merciful toward
    their iniquities,
and I will remember their sins
    no more."
13 In speaking of "a new covenant," he
has made the first one obsolete. And
what is obsolete and growing old will
soon disappear.

The Earthly and the Heavenly Sanctuaries
(Cp Ex 25.10–40)

9 Now even the first covenant had
    regulations for worship and an
earthly sanctuary. 2 For a tent k was
constructed, the first one, in which
were the lampstand, the table, and the
bread of the Presence; l this is called
the Holy Place. 3 Behind the second
curtain was a tent k called the Holy of
Holies. 4 In it stood the golden altar of
incense and the ark of the covenant
overlaid on all sides with gold, in
which there were a golden urn holding
the manna, and Aaron's rod that budded, and the tablets of the covenant;
5 above it were the cherubim of glory
overshadowing the mercy seat. m Of
these things we cannot speak now in
detail.

6 Such preparations having been
made, the priests go continually into
the first tent k to carry out their ritual
duties; 7 but only the high priest goes
into the second, and he but once a
year, and not without taking the blood
that he offers for himself and for the
sins committed unintentionally by the
people. 8 By this the Holy Spirit indicates that the way into the sanctuary
has not yet been disclosed as long as

the first tent k is still standing. 9 This is
a symbol n of the present time, during
which gifts and sacrifices are offered
that cannot perfect the conscience of
the worshiper, 10 but deal only with
food and drink and various baptisms,
regulations for the body imposed until
the time comes to set things right.

11 But when Christ came as a high
priest of the good things that have
come, o then through the greater and
perfect p tent k (not made with hands,
that is, not of this creation), 12 he entered once for all into the Holy Place,
not with the blood of goats and calves,
but with his own blood, thus obtaining
eternal redemption. 13 For if the blood
of goats and bulls, with the sprinkling
of the ashes of a heifer, sanctifies those
who have been defiled so that their
flesh is purified, 14 how much more will
the blood of Christ, who through the
eternal Spirit q offered himself without
blemish to God, purify our r conscience from dead works to worship
the living God!

15 For this reason he is the mediator of a new covenant, so that those
who are called may receive the promised eternal inheritance, because a
death has occurred that redeems them
from the transgressions under the first
covenant. s 16 Where a will s is involved, the death of the one who made
it must be established. 17 For a will s
takes effect only at death, since it is not
in force as long as the one who made
it is alive. 18 Hence not even the first
covenant was inaugurated without
blood. 19 For when every commandment had been told to all the people by
Moses in accordance with the law, he
took the blood of calves and goats, t
with water and scarlet wool and hyssop, and sprinkled both the scroll itself
and all the people, 20 saying, "This is
the blood of the covenant that God has
ordained for you." 21 And in the same
way he sprinkled with the blood both
the tent k and all the vessels used in
worship. 22 Indeed, under the law al-

k Or tabernacle   l Gk the presentation
of the loaves   m Or the place of
atonement   n Gk parable   o Other
ancient authorities read good things to
come   p Gk more perfect   q Other
ancient authorities read Holy Spirit
r Other ancient authorities read your
s The Greek word used here means both
covenant and will   t Other ancient
authorities lack and goats

most everything is purified with blood, and without the shedding of blood there is no forgiveness of sins.

Christ's Sacrifice Takes Away Sin

23 Thus it was necessary for the sketches of the heavenly things to be purified with these rites, but the heavenly things themselves need better sacrifices than these. 24 For Christ did not enter a sanctuary made by human hands, a mere copy of the true one, but he entered into heaven itself, now to appear in the presence of God on our behalf. 25 Nor was it to offer himself again and again, as the high priest enters the Holy Place year after year with blood that is not his own; 26 for then he would have had to suffer again and again since the foundation of the world. But as it is, he has appeared once for all at the end of the age to remove sin by the sacrifice of himself. 27 And just as it is appointed for mortals to die once, and after that the judgment, 28 so Christ, having been offered once to bear the sins of many, will appear a second time, not to deal with sin, but to save those who are eagerly waiting for him.

Christ's Sacrifice Once for All
(Cp Ps 40.6–8)

10 Since the law has only a shadow of the good things to come and not the true form of these realities, it *u* can never, by the same sacrifices that are continually offered year after year, make perfect those who approach. 2 Otherwise, would they not have ceased being offered, since the worshipers, cleansed once for all, would no longer have any consciousness of sin? 3 But in these sacrifices there is a reminder of sin year after year. 4 For it is impossible for the blood of bulls and goats to take away sins. 5 Consequently, when Christ *v* came into the world, he said,
"Sacrifices and offerings you
   have not desired,
but a body you have prepared
   for me;
6 in burnt offerings and sin
   offerings
you have taken no pleasure.
7 Then I said, 'See, God, I have
   come to do your will, O
   God'
(in the scroll of the book *w* it is
   written of me)."
8 When he said above, "You have nei-

ther desired nor taken pleasure in sacrifices and offerings and burnt offerings and sin offerings" (these are offered according to the law), 9 then he added, "See, I have come to do your will." He abolishes the first in order to establish the second. 10 And it is by God's will *x* that we have been sanctified through the offering of the body of Jesus Christ once for all.

11 And every priest stands day after day at his service, offering again and again the same sacrifices that can never take away sins. 12 But when Christ *y* had offered for all time a single sacrifice for sins, "he sat down at the right hand of God," 13 and since then has been waiting "until his enemies would be made a footstool for his feet." 14 For by a single offering he has perfected for all time those who are sanctified. 15 And the Holy Spirit also testifies to us, for after saying,
16 "This is the covenant that I will
     make with them
   after those days, says the
     Lord:
I will put my laws in their
     hearts,
and I will write them on their
     minds,"
17 he also adds,
"I will remember *z* their sins and
   their lawless deeds no
     more."
18 Where there is forgiveness of these, there is no longer any offering for sin.

A Call to Persevere

19 Therefore, my friends, *a* since we have confidence to enter the sanctuary by the blood of Jesus, 20 by the new and living way that he opened for us through the curtain (that is, through his flesh), 21 and since we have a great priest over the house of God, 22 let us approach with a true heart in full assurance of faith, with our hearts sprinkled clean from an evil conscience and our bodies washed with pure water. 23 Let us hold fast to the confession of our hope without wavering, for he who has promised is faithful. 24 And let us consider how to provoke one another to love and good deeds, 25 not neglecting to meet together, as is the habit of

u Other ancient authorities read *they*
v Gk *he*   *w* Meaning of Gk uncertain
x Gk *by that will*   *y* Gk *this one*
z Gk *on their minds and I will remember*
a Gk *Therefore, brothers*

some, but encouraging one another, and all the more as you see the Day approaching.

26 For if we willfully persist in sin after having received the knowledge of the truth, there no longer remains a sacrifice for sins, 27 but a fearful prospect of judgment, and a fury of fire that will consume the adversaries. 28 Anyone who has violated the law of Moses dies without mercy "on the testimony of two or three witnesses." 29 How much worse punishment do you think will be deserved by those who have spurned the Son of God, profaned the blood of the covenant by which they were sanctified, and outraged the Spirit of grace? 30 For we know the one who said, "Vengeance is mine, I will repay." And again, "The Lord will judge his people." 31 It is a fearful thing to fall into the hands of the living God.

32 But recall those earlier days when, after you had been enlightened, you endured a hard struggle with sufferings, 33 sometimes being publicly exposed to abuse and persecution, and sometimes being partners with those so treated. 34 For you had compassion for those who were in prison, and you cheerfully accepted the plundering of your possessions, knowing that you yourselves possessed something better and more lasting. 35 Do not, therefore, abandon that confidence of yours; it brings a great reward. 36 For you need endurance, so that when you have done the will of God, you may receive what was promised.

37 For yet "in a very little while,
  the one who is coming will
    come and will not delay;
38 but my righteous one will live by
  faith.
My soul takes no pleasure in
  anyone who shrinks back."
39 But we are not among those who shrink back and so are lost, but among those who have faith and so are saved.

The Meaning of Faith

11 Now faith is the assurance of things hoped for, the conviction of things not seen. 2 Indeed, by faith *b* our ancestors received approval. 3 By faith we understand that the worlds were prepared by the word of God, so that what is seen was made from things that are not visible. *c*

The Examples of Abel, Enoch, and Noah
(Gen 4.1–16; 6.5—8.22)

4 By faith Abel offered to God a more acceptable *d* sacrifice than Cain's. Through this he received approval as righteous, God himself giving approval to his gifts; he died, but through his faith *e* he still speaks. 5 By faith E′noch was taken so that he did not experience death; and "he was not found, because God had taken him." For it was attested before he was taken away that "he had pleased God." 6 And without faith it is impossible to please God, for whoever would approach him must believe that he exists and that he rewards those who seek him. 7 By faith Noah, warned by God about events as yet unseen, respected the warning and built an ark to save his household; by this he condemned the world and became an heir to the righteousness that is in accordance with faith.

The Faith of Abraham
(Gen 15.1–6; 21.1–7; 22.1–14; 48.8–16; 50.22–25)

8 By faith Abraham obeyed when he was called to set out for a place that he was to receive as an inheritance; and he set out, not knowing where he was going. 9 By faith he stayed for a time in the land he had been promised, as in a foreign land, living in tents, as did Isaac and Jacob, who were heirs with him of the same promise. 10 For he looked forward to the city that has foundations, whose architect and builder is God. 11 By faith he received power of procreation, even though he was too old—and Sarah herself was barren—because he considered him faithful who had promised. *f* 12 Therefore from one person, and this one as good as dead, descendants were born, "as many as the stars of heaven and as the innumerable grains of sand by the seashore."

13 All of these died in faith without having received the promises, but from a distance they saw and greeted them. They confessed that they were

b Gk by this   *c* Or was not made out of visible things   *d* Gk greater *e* Gk through it   *f* Other ancient authorities read *By faith Sarah herself, though barren, received power to conceive, even when she was too old, because she considered him faithful who had promised.*

strangers and foreigners on the earth, [14]for people who speak in this way make it clear that they are seeking a homeland. [15]If they had been thinking of the land that they had left behind, they would have had opportunity to return. [16]But as it is, they desire a better country, that is, a heavenly one. Therefore God is not ashamed to be called their God; indeed, he has prepared a city for them.

[17] By faith Abraham, when put to the test, offered up Isaac. He who had received the promises was ready to offer up his only son, [18]of whom he had been told, "It is through Isaac that descendants shall be named for you." [19]He considered the fact that God is able even to raise someone from the dead—and figuratively speaking, he did receive him back. [20]By faith Isaac invoked blessings for the future on Jacob and Esau. [21]By faith Jacob, when dying, blessed each of the sons of Joseph, "bowing in worship over the top of his staff." [22]By faith Joseph, at the end of his life, made mention of the exodus of the Israelites and gave instructions about his burial.[g]

The Faith of Moses
(Ex 2.1–10; 12.31–51)

[23] By faith Moses was hidden by his parents for three months after his birth, because they saw that the child was beautiful; and they were not afraid of the king's edict.[h] [24]By faith Moses, when he was grown up, refused to be called a son of Pharaoh's daughter, [25]choosing rather to share ill-treatment with the people of God than to enjoy the fleeting pleasures of sin. [26]He considered abuse suffered for the Christ[i] to be greater wealth than the treasures of Egypt, for he was looking ahead to the reward. [27]By faith he left Egypt, unafraid of the king's anger; for he persevered as though[j] he saw him who is invisible. [28]By faith he kept the Passover and the sprinkling of blood, so that the destroyer of the firstborn would not touch the firstborn of Israel.[k]

The Faith of Other Israelite Heroes

[29] By faith the people passed through the Red Sea as if it were dry land, but when the Egyptians attempted to do so they were drowned. [30]By faith the walls of Jericho fell after they had been encircled for seven days. [31]By faith Ra′hab the prostitute

did not perish with those who were disobedient,[l] because she had received the spies in peace.

[32] And what more should I say? For time would fail me to tell of Gideon, Bar′ak, Samson, Jeph′thah, of David and Samuel and the prophets— [33]who through faith conquered kingdoms, administered justice, obtained promises, shut the mouths of lions, [34]quenched raging fire, escaped the edge of the sword, won strength out of weakness, became mighty in war, put foreign armies to flight. [35]Women received their dead by resurrection. Others were tortured, refusing to accept release, in order to obtain a better resurrection. [36]Others suffered mocking and flogging, and even chains and imprisonment. [37]They were stoned to death, they were sawn in two,[m] they were killed by the sword; they went about in skins of sheep and goats, destitute, persecuted, tormented— [38]of whom the world was not worthy. They wandered in deserts and mountains, and in caves and holes in the ground.

[39] Yet all these, though they were commended for their faith, did not receive what was promised, [40]since God had provided something better so that they would not, apart from us, be made perfect.

The Example of Jesus
(Prov 3.11–12)

12 Therefore, since we are surrounded by so great a cloud of witnesses, let us also lay aside every weight and the sin that clings so closely,[n] and let us run with perseverance the race that is set before us, [2]looking to Jesus the pioneer and perfecter of our faith, who for the sake of[o] the joy that was set before him endured the cross, disregarding its shame, and has taken his seat at the right hand of the throne of God.

[3] Consider him who endured such hostility against himself from sin-

[g]Gk his bones [h]Other ancient authorities add By faith Moses, when he was grown up, killed the Egyptian, because he observed the humiliation of his people (Gk brothers) [i]Or the Messiah [j]Or because [k]Gk would not touch them [l]Or unbelieving [m]Other ancient authorities add they were tempted [n]Other ancient authorities read sin that easily distracts [o]Or who instead of

ners,[p] so that you may not grow weary or lose heart. [4] In your struggle against sin you have not yet resisted to the point of shedding your blood. [5] And you have forgotten the exhortation that addresses you as children—

"My child, do not regard lightly
the discipline of the Lord,
or lose heart when you are
punished by him;
[6] for the Lord disciplines those
whom he loves,
and chastises every child
whom he accepts."

[7] Endure trials for the sake of discipline. God is treating you as children; for what child is there whom a parent does not discipline? [8] If you do not have that discipline in which all children share, then you are illegitimate and not his children. [9] Moreover, we had human parents to discipline us, and we respected them. Should we not be even more willing to be subject to the Father of spirits and live? [10] For they disciplined us for a short time as seemed best to them, but he disciplines us for our good, in order that we may share his holiness. [11] Now, discipline always seems painful rather than pleasant at the time, but later it yields the peaceful fruit of righteousness to those who have been trained by it.

12 Therefore lift your drooping hands and strengthen your weak knees, [13] and make straight paths for your feet, so that what is lame may not be put out of joint, but rather be healed.

*Warnings against Rejecting
God's Grace
(Gen 25.29–34; 27.30–40)*

14 Pursue peace with everyone, and the holiness without which no one will see the Lord. [15] See to it that no one fails to obtain the grace of God; that no root of bitterness springs up and causes trouble, and through it many become defiled. [16] See to it that no one becomes like Esau, an immoral and godless person, who sold his birthright for a single meal. [17] You know that later, when he wanted to inherit the blessing, he was rejected, for he found no chance to repent,[q] even though he sought the blessing[r] with tears.

18 You have not come to something[s] that can be touched, a blazing fire, and darkness, and gloom, and a tempest, [19] and the sound of a trumpet, and a voice whose words made the

hearers beg that not another word be spoken to them. [20] (For they could not endure the order that was given, "If even an animal touches the mountain, it shall be stoned to death." [21] Indeed, so terrifying was the sight that Moses said, "I tremble with fear.") [22] But you have come to Mount Zion and to the city of the living God, the heavenly Jerusalem, and to innumerable angels in festal gathering, [23] and to the assembly[t] of the firstborn who are enrolled in heaven, and to God the judge of all, and to the spirits of the righteous made perfect, [24] and to Jesus, the mediator of a new covenant, and to the sprinkled blood that speaks a better word than the blood of Abel.

25 See that you do not refuse the one who is speaking; for if they did not escape when they refused the one who warned them on earth, how much less will we escape if we reject the one who warns from heaven? [26] At that time his voice shook the earth; but now he has promised, "Yet once more I will shake not only the earth but also the heaven." [27] This phrase, "Yet once more," indicates the removal of what is shaken—that is, created things—so that what cannot be shaken may remain. [28] Therefore, since we are receiving a kingdom that cannot be shaken, let us give thanks, by which we offer to God an acceptable worship with reverence and awe; [29] for indeed our God is a consuming fire.

Service Well-Pleasing to God

13 Let mutual love continue. [2] Do not neglect to show hospitality to strangers, for by doing that some have entertained angels without knowing it. [3] Remember those who are in prison, as though you were in prison with them; those who are being tortured, as though you yourselves were being tortured.[u] [4] Let marriage be held in honor by all, and let the marriage bed be kept undefiled; for God will judge fornicators and adulterers. [5] Keep your lives free from the love of money, and be content with what you have; for he has said, "I will never

[p] Other ancient authorities read *such
hostility from sinners against themselves*
[q] *or no chance to change his father's
mind*   [r] Gk *it*   [s] Other ancient
authorities read *a mountain*
[t] Or *angels, and to the festal gathering*
23*and assembly*   [u] Gk *were in the body*

leave you or forsake you." ⁶So we can say with confidence,

"The Lord is my helper;
I will not be afraid.
What can anyone do to me?"

7 Remember your leaders, those who spoke the word of God to you; consider the outcome of their way of life, and imitate their faith. ⁸Jesus Christ is the same yesterday and today and forever. ⁹Do not be carried away by all kinds of strange teachings; for it is well for the heart to be strengthened by grace, not by regulations about food,ᵛ which have not benefited those who observe them. ¹⁰We have an altar from which those who officiate in the tentʷ have no right to eat. ¹¹For the bodies of those animals whose blood is brought into the sanctuary by the high priest as a sacrifice for sin are burned outside the camp. ¹²Therefore Jesus also suffered outside the city gate in order to sanctify the people by his own blood. ¹³Let us then go to him outside the camp and bear the abuse he endured. ¹⁴For here we have no lasting city, but we are looking for the city that is to come. ¹⁵Through him, then, let us continually offer a sacrifice of praise to God, that is, the fruit of lips that confess his name. ¹⁶Do not neglect to do good and to share what you have, for such sacrifices are pleasing to God.

17 Obey your leaders and submit to them, for they are keeping watch over your souls and will give an account.

Let them do this with joy and not with sighing—for that would be harmful to you.

18 Pray for us; we are sure that we have a clear conscience, desiring to act honorably in all things. ¹⁹I urge you all the more to do this, so that I may be restored to you very soon.

Benediction

20 Now may the God of peace, who brought back from the dead our Lord Jesus, the great shepherd of the sheep, by the blood of the eternal covenant, ²¹make you complete in everything good so that you may do his will, working among usˣ that which is pleasing in his sight, through Jesus Christ, to whom be the glory forever and ever. Amen.

Final Exhortation and Greetings

22 I appeal to you, brothers and sisters,ʸ bear with my word of exhortation, for I have written to you briefly. ²³I want you to know that our brother Timothy has been set free; and if he comes in time, he will be with me when I see you. ²⁴Greet all your leaders and all the saints. Those from Italy send you greetings. ²⁵Grace be with all of you.ᶻ

ᵛGk not by foods   ʷOr tabernacle
ˣOther ancient authorities read you
ʸGk brothers   ᶻOther ancient
authorities add Amen

Catholic Letters
and Apocalypse

James was written to Jewish Christians to remind them that faith, if it is real faith, leads to faithful living. We are to show our faith in the little acts of daily living. Church tradition says the book was written by James, a relative of Jesus (see Mt. 13:55).

1 Peter was written to encourage the church in Asia Minor in a time of persecution. The key idea of the book is hope in Christ. It is this hope that sees us through tough times. Because we have hope in Christ, we are called to live a life of hope and love in the world.

2 Peter is a reflection of the belief in the early church that Jesus would return at any moment. It calls the church to be faithful and continue to expect Jesus to return.

1, 2, and **3 John** are (1) a sermon, (2) a letter to a church, and (3) a letter to an individual. 1 John urges Christians to return to fundamental loyalties. It stresses that Jesus came in the flesh, probably against heretics who were teaching that Jesus only seemed to be human. The writer says that believers experience eternal life now, that to know God is to obey God's commandments, and that the mark of eternal life is love. 2 John was written to a church to emphasize the commandment of love. 3 John is a letter to a church leader warning against a false teacher.

Jude was written to warn against a doctrine that said God's grace is an excuse for immoral living.

Revelation is a book about the struggle between good and evil and the ultimate triumph of Christ and the church. It was written in a time of persecution, probably around A.D. 95. Writing in code, the author encourages his readers to stand fast in the face of persecution, for only the faithful will share in the final triumph of Christ. Yes, he says, things are bad and they will get worse, but Christ will triumph. Some of the great hymns and prayers of the early church are found in this book.

The Letter of
JAMES

Salutation

1 James, a servant*a* of God and of the Lord Jesus Christ,
To the twelve tribes in the Dispersion:
Greetings.

Faith and Wisdom

2 My brothers and sisters,*b* whenever you face trials of any kind, consider it nothing but joy, 3 because you know that the testing of your faith produces endurance; 4 and let endurance have its full effect, so that you may be mature and complete, lacking in nothing.

5 If any of you is lacking in wisdom, ask God, who gives to all generously and ungrudgingly, and it will be given you. 6 But ask in faith, never doubting, for the one who doubts is like a wave of the sea, driven and tossed by the wind; 7, 8 for the doubter, being

a Gk *slave*   *b* Gk *brothers*

double-minded and unstable in every way, must not expect to receive anything from the Lord.

Poverty and Riches

9 Let the believer[c] who is lowly boast in being raised up, [10] and the rich in being brought low, because the rich will disappear like a flower in the field. [11] For the sun rises with its scorching heat and withers the field; its flower falls, and its beauty perishes. It is the same way with the rich; in the midst of a busy life, they will wither away.

Trial and Temptation

12 Blessed is anyone who endures temptation. Such a one has stood the test and will receive the crown of life that the Lord[d] has promised to those who love him. [13] No one, when tempted, should say, "I am being tempted by God"; for God cannot be tempted by evil and he himself tempts no one. [14] But one is tempted by one's own desire, being lured and enticed by it; [15] then, when that desire has conceived, it gives birth to sin, and that sin, when it is fully grown, gives birth to death. [16] Do not be deceived, my beloved.[e] 17 Every generous act of giving, with every perfect gift, is from above, coming down from the Father of lights, with whom there is no variation or shadow due to change.[f] [18] In fulfillment of his own purpose he gave us birth by the word of truth, so that we would become a kind of first fruits of his creatures.

Hearing and Doing the Word

19 You must understand this, my beloved:[e] let everyone be quick to listen, slow to speak, slow to anger; [20] for your anger does not produce God's righteousness. [21] Therefore rid yourselves of all sordidness and rank growth of wickedness, and welcome with meekness the implanted word that has the power to save your souls. 22 But be doers of the word, and not merely hearers who deceive themselves. [23] For if any are hearers of the word and not doers, they are like those who look at themselves[g] in a mirror; [24] for they look at themselves and, on going away, immediately forget what they were like. [25] But those who look into the perfect law, the law of liberty, and persevere, being not hearers who

forget but doers who act—they will be blessed in their doing.

26 If any think they are religious, and do not bridle their tongues but deceive their hearts, their religion is worthless. [27] Religion that is pure and undefiled before God, the Father, is this: to care for orphans and widows in their distress, and to keep oneself unstained by the world.

Warning against Partiality

2 My brothers and sisters,[h] do you with your acts of favoritism really believe in our glorious Lord Jesus Christ?[i] [2] For if a person with gold rings and in fine clothes comes into your assembly, and if a poor person in dirty clothes also comes in, [3] and if you take notice of the one wearing the fine clothes and say, "Have a seat here, please," while to the one who is poor you say, "Stand there," or, "Sit at my feet,"[j] [4] have you not made distinctions among yourselves, and become judges with evil thoughts? [5] Listen, my beloved brothers and sisters. [k] Has not God chosen the poor in the world to be rich in faith and to be heirs of the kingdom that he has promised to those who love him? [6] But you have dishonored the poor. Is it not the rich who oppress you? Is it not they who drag you into court? [7] Is it not they who blaspheme the excellent name that was invoked over you?

8 You do well if you really fulfill the royal law according to the scripture, "You shall love your neighbor as yourself." [9] But if you show partiality, you commit sin and are convicted by the law as transgressors. [10] For whoever keeps the whole law but fails in one point has become accountable for all of it. [11] For the one who said, "You shall not commit adultery," also said, "You shall not murder." Now if you do not commit adultery but if you murder, you have become a transgressor of the law. [12] So speak and so act as those who are to be judged by the law of liberty. [13] For judgment will be without

[c] Gk brother   [d] Gk he; other ancient authorities read God   [e] Gk my beloved brothers   [f] Other ancient authorities read variation due to a shadow of turning   [g] Gk at the face of his birth   [h] Gk My brothers   [i] Or hold the faith of our glorious Lord Jesus Christ without acts of favoritism   [j] Gk Sit under my footstool   [k] Gk brothers

mercy to anyone who has shown no mercy; mercy triumphs over judgment.

Faith without Works Is Dead
(Cp Gen 22; Josh 2)

14 What good is it, my brothers and sisters,[l] if you say you have faith but do not have works? Can faith save you? 15 If a brother or sister is naked and lacks daily food, 16 and one of you says to them, "Go in peace; keep warm and eat your fill," and yet you do not supply their bodily needs, what is the good of that? 17 So faith by itself, if it has no works, is dead.

18 But someone will say, "You have faith and I have works." Show me your faith apart from your works, and I by my works will show you my faith. 19 You believe that God is one; you do well. Even the demons believe—and shudder. 20 Do you want to be shown, you senseless person, that faith apart from works is barren? 21 Was not our ancestor Abraham justified by works when he offered his son Isaac on the altar? 22 You see that faith was active along with his works, and faith was brought to completion by the works. 23 Thus the scripture was fulfilled that says, "Abraham believed God, and it was reckoned to him as righteousness," and he was called the friend of God. 24 You see that a person is justified by works and not by faith alone. 25 Likewise, was not Rā′hab the prostitute also justified by works when she welcomed the messengers and sent them out by another road? 26 For just as the body without the spirit is dead, so faith without works is also dead.

Taming the Tongue

3 Not many of you should become teachers, my brothers and sisters,[l] for you know that we who teach will be judged with greater strictness. 2 For all of us make many mistakes. Anyone who makes no mistakes in speaking is perfect, able to keep the whole body in check with a bridle. 3 If we put bits into the mouths of horses to make them obey us, we guide their whole bodies. 4 Or look at ships: though they are so large that it takes strong winds to drive them, yet they are guided by a very small rudder wherever the will of the pilot directs. 5 So also the tongue is a small member, yet it boasts of great exploits.

How great a forest is set ablaze by a small fire! 6 And the tongue is a fire. The tongue is placed among our members as a world of iniquity; it stains the whole body, sets on fire the cycle of nature,[m] and is itself set on fire by hell.[n] 7 For every species of beast and bird, of reptile and sea creature, can be tamed and has been tamed by the human species, 8 but no one can tame the tongue—a restless evil, full of deadly poison. 9 With it we bless the Lord and Father, and with it we curse those who are made in the likeness of God. 10 From the same mouth come blessing and cursing. My brothers and sisters,[o] this ought not to be so. 11 Does a spring pour forth from the same opening both fresh and brackish water? 12 Can a fig tree, my brothers and sisters,[p] yield olives, or a grapevine figs? No more can salt water yield fresh.

Two Kinds of Wisdom

13 Who is wise and understanding among you? Show by your good life that your works are done with gentleness born of wisdom. 14 But if you have bitter envy and selfish ambition in your hearts, do not be boastful and false to the truth. 15 Such wisdom does not come down from above, but is earthly, unspiritual, devilish. 16 For where there is envy and selfish ambition, there will also be disorder and wickedness of every kind. 17 But the wisdom from above is first pure, then peaceable, gentle, willing to yield, full of mercy and good fruits, without a trace of partiality or hypocrisy. 18 And a harvest of righteousness is sown in peace for[q] those who make peace.

Friendship with the World

4 Those conflicts and disputes among you, where do they come from? Do they not come from your cravings that are at war within you? 2 You want something and do not have it; so you commit murder. And you covet[r] something and cannot obtain it; so you engage in disputes and conflicts. You do not have, because you do not ask. 3 You ask and do not receive, because you ask wrongly, in order to spend what you get on your pleasures. 4 Adulterers! Do you not know that

---

l Gk *brothers*　　*m* Or *wheel of birth*
n Gk *Gehenna*　　*o* Gk *My brothers*
p Gk *my brothers*　　*q* Or *by*　　*r* Or *you murder and you covet*

friendship with the world is enmity with God? Therefore whoever wishes to be a friend of the world becomes an enemy of God. [5] Or do you suppose that it is for nothing that the scripture says, "God[s] yearns jealously for the spirit that he has made to dwell in us"? [6] But he gives all the more grace; therefore it says,

"God opposes the proud,
    but gives grace to the humble."

[7] Submit yourselves therefore to God. Resist the devil, and he will flee from you. [8] Draw near to God, and he will draw near to you. Cleanse your hands, you sinners, and purify your hearts, you double-minded. [9] Lament and mourn and weep. Let your laughter be turned into mourning and your joy into dejection. [10] Humble yourselves before the Lord, and he will exalt you.

Warning against Judging Another

11 Do not speak evil against one another, brothers and sisters.[t] Whoever speaks evil against another or judges another, speaks evil against the law and judges the law; but if you judge the law, you are not a doer of the law but a judge. [12] There is one lawgiver and judge who is able to save and to destroy. So who, then, are you to judge your neighbor?

Boasting about Tomorrow

13 Come now, you who say, "Today or tomorrow we will go to such and such a town and spend a year there, doing business and making money." [14] Yet you do not even know what tomorrow will bring. What is your life? For you are a mist that appears for a little while and then vanishes. [15] Instead you ought to say, "If the Lord wishes, we will live and do this or that." [16] As it is, you boast in your arrogance; all such boasting is evil. [17] Anyone, then, who knows the right thing to do and fails to do it, commits sin.

Warning to Rich Oppressors

5 Come now, you rich people, weep and wail for the miseries that are coming to you. [2] Your riches have rotted, and your clothes are moth-eaten. [3] Your gold and silver have rusted, and their rust will be evidence against you, and it will eat your flesh like fire. You have laid up treasure[u] for the last days. [4] Listen! The wages of the laborers who mowed your fields, which you

kept back by fraud, cry out, and the cries of the harvesters have reached the ears of the Lord of hosts. [5] You have lived on the earth in luxury and in pleasure; you have fattened your hearts in a day of slaughter. [6] You have condemned and murdered the righteous one, who does not resist you.

Patience in Suffering

7 Be patient, therefore, beloved,[t] until the coming of the Lord. The farmer waits for the precious crop from the earth, being patient with it until it receives the early and the late rains. [8] You also must be patient. Strengthen your hearts, for the coming of the Lord is near.[v] [9] Beloved,[w] do not grumble against one another, so that you may not be judged. See, the Judge is standing at the doors! [10] As an example of suffering and patience, beloved,[t] take the prophets who spoke in the name of the Lord. [11] Indeed we call blessed those who showed endurance. You have heard of the endurance of Jōb, and you have seen the purpose of the Lord, how the Lord is compassionate and merciful.

12 Above all, my beloved,[t] do not swear, either by heaven or by earth or by any other oath, but let your "Yes" be yes and your "No" be no, so that you may not fall under condemnation.

The Prayer of Faith
(Cp 1 Kings 18.41–46)

13 Are any among you suffering? They should pray. Are any cheerful? They should sing songs of praise. [14] Are any among you sick? They should call for the elders of the church and have them pray over them, anointing them with oil in the name of the Lord. [15] The prayer of faith will save the sick, and the Lord will raise them up; and anyone who has committed sins will be forgiven. [16] Therefore confess your sins to one another, and pray for one another, so that you may be healed. The prayer of the righteous is powerful and effective. [17] E·li'jah was a human being like us, and he prayed fervently that it might not rain, and for three years and six months it did not rain on the earth. [18] Then he prayed again, and the heaven gave rain and the earth yielded its harvest.

[s] Gk He   [t] Gk brothers   [u] Or will eat your flesh, since you have stored up fire   [v] Or is at hand   [w] Gk Brothers

J
A
M
E
S

19 My brothers and sisters,[x] if anyone among you wanders from the truth and is brought back by another, 20 you should know that whoever brings back a sinner from wandering will save the sinner's[y] soul from death and will cover a multitude of sins.

[x] Gk My brothers   [y] Gk his

The First Letter of

PETER

Salutation

1 Peter, an apostle of Jesus Christ,
To the exiles of the Dispersion in Pon'tus, Galatia, Cap·pa·do'ci·a, Asia, and Bi·thyn'i·a, 2 who have been chosen and destined by God the Father and sanctified by the Spirit to be obedient to Jesus Christ and to be sprinkled with his blood:
May grace and peace be yours in abundance.

A Living Hope

3 Blessed be the God and Father of our Lord Jesus Christ! By his great mercy he has given us a new birth into a living hope through the resurrection of Jesus Christ from the dead, 4 and into an inheritance that is imperishable, undefiled, and unfading, kept in heaven for you, 5 who are being protected by the power of God through faith for a salvation ready to be revealed in the last time. 6 In this you rejoice,[a] even if now for a little while you have had to suffer various trials, 7 so that the genuineness of your faith—being more precious than gold that, though perishable, is tested by fire—may be found to result in praise and glory and honor when Jesus Christ is revealed. 8 Although you have not seen[b] him, you love him; and even though you do not see him now, you believe in him and rejoice with an indescribable and glorious joy, 9 for you are receiving the outcome of your faith, the salvation of your souls. 10 Concerning this salvation, the prophets who prophesied of the grace that was to be yours made careful search and inquiry, 11 inquiring about the person or time that the Spirit of Christ within them indicated when it testified in advance to the sufferings destined for Christ and the subsequent glory. 12 It was revealed to them that they were serving not themselves but you, in regard to the things that have now been announced to you through those who brought you good news by the Holy Spirit sent from heaven— things into which angels long to look!

A Call to Holy Living

13 Therefore prepare your minds for action;[c] discipline yourselves; set all your hope on the grace that Jesus Christ will bring you when he is revealed. 14 Like obedient children, do not be conformed to the desires that you formerly had in ignorance. 15 Instead, as he who called you is holy, be holy yourselves in all your conduct; 16 for it is written, "You shall be holy, for I am holy."

17 If you invoke as Father the one who judges all people impartially according to their deeds, live in reverent fear during the time of your exile. 18 You know that you were ransomed from the futile ways inherited from your ancestors, not with perishable things like silver or gold, 19 but with the precious blood of Christ, like that of a lamb without defect or blemish. 20 He was destined before the foundation of the world, but was revealed at the end of the ages for your sake. 21 Through him you have come to trust in God, who raised him from the dead and gave him glory, so that your faith and hope are set on God.

22 Now that you have purified your

[a] Or Rejoice in this   [b] Other ancient authorities read known   [c] Gk gird up the loins of your mind

souls by your obedience to the truth[d] so that you have genuine mutual love, love one another deeply[e] from the heart.[f] 23You have been born anew, not of perishable but of imperishable seed, through the living and enduring word of God.[g] 24For

"All flesh is like grass
    and all its glory like the flower
        of grass.
The grass withers,
    and the flower falls,
25 but the word of the Lord
    endures forever."

That word is the good news that was announced to you.

The Living Stone and a Chosen People
(Ps 118.22; Isa 28.16)

2 Rid yourselves, therefore, of all malice, and all guile, insincerity, envy, and all slander. 2Like newborn infants, long for the pure, spiritual milk, so that by it you may grow into salvation— 3if indeed you have tasted that the Lord is good.

4 Come to him, a living stone, though rejected by mortals yet chosen and precious in God's sight, and 5like living stones, let yourselves be built[h] into a spiritual house, to be a holy priesthood, to offer spiritual sacrifices acceptable to God through Jesus Christ. 6For it stands in scripture:

"See, I am laying in Zion a
        stone,
    a cornerstone chosen and
        precious;
and whoever believes in him[i]
    will not be put to shame."

7To you then who believe, he is precious; but for those who do not believe,

"The stone that the builders
        rejected
    has become the very head of
        the corner,"

8and

"A stone that makes them
        stumble,
    and a rock that makes them
        fall."

They stumble because they disobey the word, as they were destined to do.

9 But you are a chosen race, a royal priesthood, a holy nation, God's own people,[j] in order that you may proclaim the mighty acts of him who called you out of darkness into his marvelous light.

10 Once you were not a people,
    but now you are God's people;

once you had not received
        mercy,
    but now you have received
        mercy.

Live as Servants of God
(Cp Rom 13.1–5)

11 Beloved, I urge you as aliens and exiles to abstain from the desires of the flesh that wage war against the soul. 12Conduct yourselves honorably among the Gentiles, so that, though they malign you as evildoers, they may see your honorable deeds and glorify God when he comes to judge.[k]

13 For the Lord's sake accept the authority of every human institution,[l] whether of the emperor as supreme, 14or of governors, as sent by him to punish those who do wrong and to praise those who do right. 15For it is God's will that by doing right you should silence the ignorance of the foolish. 16As servants[m] of God, live as free people, yet do not use your freedom as a pretext for evil. 17Honor everyone. Love the family of believers.[n] Fear God. Honor the emperor.

The Example of Christ's Suffering
(Isa 53.7–9)

18 Slaves, accept the authority of your masters with all deference, not only those who are kind and gentle but also those who are harsh. 19For it is a credit to you if, being aware of God, you endure pain while suffering unjustly. 20If you endure when you are beaten for doing wrong, what credit is that? But if you endure when you do right and suffer for it, you have God's approval. 21For to this you have been called, because Christ also suffered for you, leaving you an example, so that you should follow in his steps.
22 "He committed no sin,
    and no deceit was found in his
        mouth."

23When he was abused, he did not return abuse; when he suffered, he did not threaten; but he entrusted himself

---

[d]Other ancient authorities add *through the Spirit*   [e]Or *constantly*   [f]Other ancient authorities read *a pure heart*   [g]Or *through the word of the living and enduring God*   [h]Or *you yourselves are being built*   [i]Or *it*   [j]Gk *a people for his possession*   [k]Gk *God on the day of visitation*   [l]Or *every institution ordained for human beings*   [m]Gk *slaves*   [n]Gk *Love the brotherhood*

to the one who judges justly. 24 He himself bore our sins in his body on the cross,*o* so that, free from sins, we might live for righteousness; by his wounds*p* you have been healed. 25 For you were going astray like sheep, but now you have returned to the shepherd and guardian of your souls.

Wives and Husbands

3 Wives, in the same way, accept the authority of your husbands, so that, even if some of them do not obey the word, they may be won over without a word by their wives' conduct, 2 when they see the purity and reverence of your lives. 3 Do not adorn yourselves outwardly by braiding your hair, and by wearing gold ornaments or fine clothing; 4 rather, let your adornment be the inner self with the lasting beauty of a gentle and quiet spirit, which is very precious in God's sight. 5 It was in this way long ago that the holy women who hoped in God used to adorn themselves by accepting the authority of their husbands. 6 Thus Sarah obeyed Abraham and called him lord. You have become her daughters as long as you do what is good and never let fears alarm you.

7 Husbands, in the same way, show consideration for your wives in your life together, paying honor to the woman as the weaker sex,*q* since they too are also heirs of the gracious gift of life—so that nothing may hinder your prayers.

Suffering for Doing Right

8 Finally, all of you, have unity of spirit, sympathy, love for one another, a tender heart, and a humble mind. 9 Do not repay evil for evil or abuse for abuse; but, on the contrary, repay with a blessing. It is for this that you were called—that you might inherit a blessing. 10 For
"Those who desire life
    and desire to see good days,
let them keep their tongues from
        evil
    and their lips from speaking
        deceit;
11 let them turn away from evil and
        do good;
    let them seek peace and
        pursue it.
12 For the eyes of the Lord are on
        the righteous,
    and his ears are open to their
        prayer.

But the face of the Lord is
    against those who do evil."
13 Now who will harm you if you are eager to do what is good? 14 But even if you do suffer for doing what is right, you are blessed. Do not fear what they fear,*r* and do not be intimidated, 15 but in your hearts sanctify Christ as Lord. Always be ready to make your defense to anyone who demands from you an accounting for the hope that is in you; 16 yet do it with gentleness and reverence.*s* Keep your conscience clear, so that, when you are maligned, those who abuse you for your good conduct in Christ may be put to shame. 17 For it is better to suffer for doing good, if suffering should be God's will, than to suffer for doing evil. 18 For Christ also suffered*t* for sins once for all, the righteous for the unrighteous, in order to bring you*u* to God. He was put to death in the flesh, but made alive in the spirit, 19 in which also he went and made a proclamation to the spirits in prison, 20 who in former times did not obey, when God waited patiently in the days of Noah, during the building of the ark, in which a few, that is, eight persons, were saved through water. 21 And baptism, which this prefigured, now saves you—not as a removal of dirt from the body, but as an appeal to God for*v* a good conscience, through the resurrection of Jesus Christ, 22 who has gone into heaven and is at the right hand of God, with angels, authorities, and powers made subject to him.

Good Stewards of God's Grace

4 Since therefore Christ suffered in the flesh,*w* arm yourselves also with the same intention (for whoever has suffered in the flesh has finished with sin), 2 so as to live for the rest of your earthly life*x* no longer by human desires but by the will of God. 3 You have already spent enough time in doing what the Gentiles like to do, living in licentiousness, passions, drunkenness, revels, carousing, and lawless idolatry. 4 They are surprised that you

o Or *carried up our sins in his body to the tree* *p* Gk *bruise* *q* Gk *vessel* *r* Gk *their fear* *s* Or *respect* *t* Other ancient authorities read *died* *u* Other ancient authorities read *us* *v* Or *a pledge to God from* *w* Other ancient authorities add *for us*; others, *for you* *x* Gk *rest of the time in the flesh* no longer join them in the same excesses of dissipation, and so they blaspheme.*y* 5 But they will have to give an accounting to him who stands ready to judge the living and the dead. 6 For this is the reason the gospel was proclaimed even to the dead, so that, though they had been judged in the flesh as everyone is judged, they might live in the spirit as God does.

7 The end of all things is near;*z* therefore be serious and discipline yourselves for the sake of your prayers. 8 Above all, maintain constant love for one another, for love covers a multitude of sins. 9 Be hospitable to one another without complaining. 10 Like good stewards of the manifold grace of God, serve one another with whatever gift each of you has received. 11 Whoever speaks must do so as one speaking the very words of God; whoever serves must do so with the strength that God supplies, so that God may be glorified in all things through Jesus Christ. To him belong the glory and the power forever and ever. Amen.

Suffering as a Christian

12 Beloved, do not be surprised at the fiery ordeal that is taking place among you to test you, as though something strange were happening to you. 13 But rejoice insofar as you are sharing Christ's sufferings, so that you may also be glad and shout for joy when his glory is revealed. 14 If you are reviled for the name of Christ, you are blessed, because the spirit of glory,*a* which is the Spirit of God, is resting on you.*b* 15 But let none of you suffer as a murderer, a thief, a criminal, or even as a mischief maker. 16 Yet if any of you suffers as a Christian, do not consider it a disgrace, but glorify God because you bear this name. 17 For the time has come for judgment to begin with the household of God; if it begins with us, what will be the end for those who do not obey the gospel of God? 18 And

"If it is hard for the righteous to
    be saved,
what will become of the
    ungodly and the sinners?"

19 Therefore, let those suffering in accordance with God's will entrust themselves to a faithful Creator, while continuing to do good.

Tending the Flock of God

5 Now as an elder myself and a witness of the sufferings of Christ, as well as one who shares in the glory to be revealed, I exhort the elders among you 2 to tend the flock of God that is in your charge, exercising the oversight,*c* not under compulsion but willingly, as God would have you do it*d* —not for sordid gain but eagerly. 3 Do not lord it over those in your charge, but be examples to the flock. 4 And when the chief shepherd appears, you will win the crown of glory that never fades away. 5 In the same way, you who are younger must accept the authority of the elders.*e* And all of you must clothe yourselves with humility in your dealings with one another, for

"God opposes the proud,
    but gives grace to the
        humble."

6 Humble yourselves therefore under the mighty hand of God, so that he may exalt you in due time. 7 Cast all your anxiety on him, because he cares for you. 8 Discipline yourselves, keep alert.*f* Like a roaring lion your adversary the devil prowls around, looking for someone to devour. 9 Resist him, steadfast in your faith, for you know that your brothers and sisters*g* in all the world are undergoing the same kinds of suffering. 10 And after you have suffered for a little while, the God of all grace, who has called you to his eternal glory in Christ, will himself restore, support, strengthen, and establish you. 11 To him be the power forever and ever. Amen.

Final Greetings and Benediction

12 Through Sil·vā′nus, whom I consider a faithful brother, I have written this short letter to encourage you and to testify that this is the true grace of God. Stand fast in it. 13 Your sister

1 P E T E R

---

y Or *they malign you*   *z* Or *is at hand*
a Other ancient authorities add *and of power*   *b* Other ancient authorities add *On their part he is blasphemed, but on your part he is glorified*   *c* Other ancient authorities lack *exercising the oversight*   *d* Other ancient authorities lack *as God would have you do it*
e Or *of those who are older*   *f* Or *be vigilant*   *g* Gk *your brotherhood*

church[h] in Babylon, chosen together with you, sends you greetings; and so does my son Mark. 14 Greet one another with a kiss of love.

Peace to all of you who are in Christ.[i]

[h] Gk *She who is*
[i] Other ancient authorities add *Amen*

The Second Letter of

PETER

Salutation

1 Si′me·on[a] Peter, a servant[b] and apostle of Jesus Christ,
To those who have received a faith as precious as ours through the righteousness of our God and Savior Jesus Christ:[c]
2 May grace and peace be yours in abundance in the knowledge of God and of Jesus our Lord.

The Christian's Call and Election

3 His divine power has given us everything needed for life and godliness, through the knowledge of him who called us by[d] his own glory and goodness. 4 Thus he has given us, through these things, his precious and very great promises, so that through them you may escape from the corruption that is in the world because of lust, and may become participants of the divine nature. 5 For this very reason, you must make every effort to support your faith with goodness, and goodness with knowledge, 6 and knowledge with self-control, and self-control with endurance, and endurance with godliness, 7 and godliness with mutual[e] affection, and mutual[e] affection with love. 8 For if these things are yours and are increasing among you, they keep you from being ineffective and unfruitful in the knowledge of our Lord Jesus Christ. 9 For anyone who lacks these things is nearsighted and blind, and is forgetful of the cleansing of past sins. 10 Therefore, brothers and sisters,[f] be all the more eager to confirm your call and election, for if you do this, you will never stumble. 11 For in this way, entry into the eternal kingdom of our Lord and Savior Jesus Christ will be richly provided for you.

12 Therefore I intend to keep on reminding you of these things, though you know them already and are established in the truth that has come to you. 13 I think it right, as long as I am in this body,[g] to refresh your memory, 14 since I know that my death[h] will come soon, as indeed our Lord Jesus Christ has made clear to me. 15 And I will make every effort so that after my departure you may be able at any time to recall these things.

Eyewitnesses of Christ's Glory
(Mt 17.5; Mk 9.7; Lk 9.35)

16 For we did not follow cleverly devised myths when we made known to you the power and coming of our Lord Jesus Christ, but we had been eyewitnesses of his majesty. 17 For he received honor and glory from God the Father when that voice was conveyed to him by the Majestic Glory, saying, "This is my Son, my Beloved,[i] with whom I am well pleased." 18 We ourselves heard this voice come from heaven, while we were with him on the holy mountain.

19 So we have the prophetic message more fully confirmed. You will do well to be attentive to this as to a lamp shining in a dark place, until the day dawns and the morning star rises in your hearts. 20 First of all you must understand this, that no prophecy of scripture is a matter of one's own interpretation, 21 because no prophecy ever came by human will, but men and

[a] Other ancient authorities read *Simon*
[b] Gk *slave*   [c] Or *of our God and the Savior Jesus Christ*   [d] Other ancient authorities read *through*
[e] Gk *brotherly*   [f] Gk *brothers*
[g] Gk *tent*   [h] Gk *the putting off of my tent*   [i] Other ancient authorities read *my beloved Son*

women moved by the Holy Spirit spoke from God.[j]

False Prophets and Their Punishment

2 But false prophets also arose among the people, just as there will be false teachers among you, who will secretly bring in destructive opinions. They will even deny the Master who bought them—bringing swift destruction on themselves. [2]Even so, many will follow their licentious ways, and because of these teachers[k] the way of truth will be maligned. [3]And in their greed they will exploit you with deceptive words. Their condemnation, pronounced against them long ago, has not been idle, and their destruction is not asleep.

4 For if God did not spare the angels when they sinned, but cast them into hell[l] and committed them to chains[m] of deepest darkness to be kept until the judgment; [5]and if he did not spare the ancient world, even though he saved Noah, a herald of righteousness, with seven others, when he brought a flood on a world of the ungodly; [6]and if by turning the cities of Sod'om and Go·mor'rah to ashes he condemned them to extinction[n] and made them an example of what is coming to the ungodly;[o] [7]and if he rescued Lot, a righteous man greatly distressed by the licentiousness of the lawless [8](for that righteous man, living among them day after day, was tormented in his righteous soul by their lawless deeds that he saw and heard), [9]then the Lord knows how to rescue the godly from trial, and to keep the unrighteous under punishment until the day of judgment [10]—especially those who indulge their flesh in depraved lust, and who despise authority.

Bold and willful, they are not afraid to slander the glorious ones,[p] [11]whereas angels, though greater in might and power, do not bring against them a slanderous judgment from the Lord.[q] [12]These people, however, are like irrational animals, mere creatures of instinct, born to be caught and killed. They slander what they do not understand, and when those creatures are destroyed,[r] they also will be destroyed, [13]suffering[s] the penalty for doing wrong. They count it a pleasure to revel in the daytime. They are blots and blemishes, reveling in their dissipation[t] while they feast with you. [14]They have eyes full of adultery, insa-

tiable for sin. They entice unsteady souls. They have hearts trained in greed. Accursed children! [15]They have left the straight road and have gone astray, following the road of Ba'laam son of Bo'sor,[u] who loved the wages of doing wrong, [16]but was rebuked for his own transgression; a speechless donkey spoke with a human voice and restrained the prophet's madness.

17 These are waterless springs and mists driven by a storm; for them the deepest darkness has been reserved. [18]For they speak bombastic nonsense, and with licentious desires of the flesh they entice people who have just[v] escaped from those who live in error. [19]They promise them freedom, but they themselves are slaves of corruption; for people are slaves to whatever masters them. [20]For if, after they have escaped the defilements of the world through the knowledge of our Lord and Savior Jesus Christ, they are again entangled in them and overpowered, the last state has become worse for them than the first. [21]For it would have been better for them never to have known the way of righteousness than, after knowing it, to turn back from the holy commandment that was passed on to them. [22]It has happened to them according to the true proverb,

"The dog turns back to its own
    vomit,"
and,
"The sow is washed only to
    wallow in the mud."

The Promise of the Lord's Coming
(Gen 6.5—8.22)

3 This is now, beloved, the second letter I am writing to you; in them I am trying to arouse your sincere intention by reminding you [2]that you

[j]Other ancient authorities read but moved by the Holy Spirit saints of God spoke   [k]Gk because of them   [l]Gk Tartaros   [m]Other ancient authorities read pits   [n]Other ancient authorities lack to extinction   [o]Other ancient authorities read an example to those who were to be ungodly   [p]Or angels; Gk glories   [q]Other ancient authorities read before the Lord; others lack the phrase   [r]Gk in their destruction   [s]Other ancient authorities read receiving   [t]Other ancient authorities read love feasts   [u]Other ancient authorities read Beor   [v]Other ancient authorities read actually

should remember the words spoken in the past by the holy prophets, and the commandment of the Lord and Savior spoken through your apostles. [3]First of all you must understand this, that in the last days scoffers will come, scoffing and indulging their own lusts [4]and saying, "Where is the promise of his coming? For ever since our ancestors died,[w] all things continue as they were from the beginning of creation!" [5]They deliberately ignore this fact, that by the word of God heavens existed long ago and an earth was formed out of water and by means of water, [6]through which the world of that time was deluged with water and perished. [7]But by the same word the present heavens and earth have been reserved for fire, being kept until the day of judgment and destruction of the godless.

[8] But do not ignore this one fact, beloved, that with the Lord one day is like a thousand years, and a thousand years are like one day. [9]The Lord is not slow about his promise, as some think of slowness, but is patient with you,[x] not wanting any to perish, but all to come to repentance. [10]But the day of the Lord will come like a thief, and then the heavens will pass away with a loud noise, and the elements will be dissolved with fire, and the earth and everything that is done on it will be disclosed.[y]

[11] Since all these things are to be dissolved in this way, what sort of persons ought you to be in leading lives of holiness and godliness, [12]waiting for and hastening[z] the coming of the day of God, because of which the heavens will be set ablaze and dissolved, and the elements will melt with fire? [13]But, in accordance with his promise, we wait for new heavens and a new earth, where righteousness is at home.

Final Exhortation and Doxology

[14] Therefore, beloved, while you are waiting for these things, strive to be found by him at peace, without spot or blemish; [15]and regard the patience of our Lord as salvation. So also our beloved brother Paul wrote to you according to the wisdom given him, [16]speaking of this as he does in all his letters. There are some things in them hard to understand, which the ignorant and unstable twist to their own destruction, as they do the other scriptures. [17]You therefore, beloved, since you are forewarned, beware that you are not carried away with the error of the lawless and lose your own stability. [18]But grow in the grace and knowledge of our Lord and Savior Jesus Christ. To him be the glory both now and to the day of eternity. Amen.[a]

[w] Gk our fathers fell asleep   [x] Other ancient authorities read on your account   [y] Other ancient authorities read will be burned up   [z] Or earnestly desiring   [a] Other ancient authorities lack Amen

The First Letter of

JOHN

The Word of Life
(Jn 1.1–5)

1 We declare to you what was from the beginning, what we have heard, what we have seen with our eyes, what we have looked at and touched with our hands, concerning the word of life— [2]this life was revealed, and we have seen it and testify to it, and declare to you the eternal life that was with the Father and was revealed to us— [3]we declare to you what we have seen and heard so that you also may have fellowship with us; and truly our fellowship is with the Father and with his Son Jesus Christ. [4]We are writing these things so that our[a] joy may be complete.

God Is Light

[5] This is the message we have

[a] Other ancient authorities read your

heard from him and proclaim to you, that God is light and in him there is no darkness at all. [6]If we say that we have fellowship with him while we are walking in darkness, we lie and do not do what is true; [7]but if we walk in the light as he himself is in the light, we have fellowship with one another, and the blood of Jesus his Son cleanses us from all sin. [8]If we say that we have no sin, we deceive ourselves, and the truth is not in us. [9]If we confess our sins, he who is faithful and just will forgive us our sins and cleanse us from all unrighteousness. [10]If we say that we have not sinned, we make him a liar, and his word is not in us.

Christ Our Advocate

2 My little children, I am writing these things to you so that you may not sin. But if anyone does sin, we have an advocate with the Father, Jesus Christ the righteous; [2]and he is the atoning sacrifice for our sins, and not for ours only but also for the sins of the whole world.

3 Now by this we may be sure that we know him, if we obey his commandments. [4]Whoever says, "I have come to know him," but does not obey his commandments, is a liar, and in such a person the truth does not exist; [5]but whoever obeys his word, truly in this person the love of God has reached perfection. By this we may be sure that we are in him: [6]whoever says, "I abide in him," ought to walk just as he walked.

A New Commandment

7 Beloved, I am writing you no new commandment, but an old commandment that you have had from the beginning; the old commandment is the word that you have heard. [8]Yet I am writing you a new commandment that is true in him and in you, because[b] the darkness is passing away and the true light is already shining. [9]Whoever says, "I am in the light," while hating a brother or sister,[c] is still in the darkness. [10]Whoever loves a brother or sister[d] lives in the light, and in such a person[e] there is no cause for stumbling. [11]But whoever hates another believer[f] is in the darkness, walks in the darkness, and does not know the way to go, because the darkness has brought on blindness.

12 I am writing to you, little children,

because your sins are forgiven
on account of his name.
[13] I am writing to you, fathers,
because you know him who is
from the beginning.
I am writing to you, young
people,
because you have conquered
the evil one.
[14] I write to you, children,
because you know the Father.
I write to you, fathers,
because you know him who is
from the beginning.
I write to you, young people,
because you are strong
and the word of God abides in
you,
and you have overcome the
evil one.

15 Do not love the world or the things in the world. The love of the Father is not in those who love the world; [16]for all that is in the world—the desire of the flesh, the desire of the eyes, the pride in riches—comes not from the Father but from the world. [17]And the world and its desire[g] are passing away, but those who do the will of God live forever.

Warning against Antichrists

18 Children, it is the last hour! As you have heard that antichrist is coming, so now many antichrists have come. From this we know that it is the last hour. [19]They went out from us, but they did not belong to us; for if they had belonged to us, they would have remained with us. But by going out they made it plain that none of them belongs to us. [20]But you have been anointed by the Holy One, and all of you have knowledge.[h] [21]I write to you, not because you do not know the truth, but because you know it, and you know that no lie comes from the truth. [22]Who is the liar but the one who denies that Jesus is the Christ?[i] This is the antichrist, the one who denies the Father and the Son. [23]No one who denies the Son has the Father; everyone who confesses the Son has the Father also. [24]Let what you heard from the beginning abide in you. If what you heard from the beginning abides in

1 J O H N

---

b Or that   c Gk hating a brother
d Gk loves a brother   e Or in it
f Gk hates a brother   g Or the desire for
it   h Other ancient authorities read you
know all things   i Or the Messiah

you, then you will abide in the Son and in the Father. 25 And this is what he has promised us,[j] eternal life.

26 I write these things to you concerning those who would deceive you. 27 As for you, the anointing that you received from him abides in you, and so you do not need anyone to teach you. But as his anointing teaches you about all things, and is true and is not a lie, and just as it has taught you, abide in him.[k]

28 And now, little children, abide in him, so that when he is revealed we may have confidence and not be put to shame before him at his coming.

Children of God

29 If you know that he is righteous, you may be sure that everyone who does right has been born of him. 3 1 See what love the Father has given us, that we should be called children of God; and that is what we are. The reason the world does not know us is that it did not know him. 2 Beloved, we are God's children now; what we will be has not yet been revealed. What we do know is this: when he[k] is revealed, we will be like him, for we will see him as he is. 3 And all who have this hope in him purify themselves, just as he is pure.

4 Everyone who commits sin is guilty of lawlessness; sin is lawlessness. 5 You know that he was revealed to take away sins, and in him there is no sin. 6 No one who abides in him sins; no one who sins has either seen him or known him. 7 Little children, let no one deceive you. Everyone who does what is right is righteous, just as he is righteous. 8 Everyone who commits sin is a child of the devil; for the devil has been sinning from the beginning. The Son of God was revealed for this purpose, to destroy the works of the devil. 9 Those who have been born of God do not sin, because God's seed abides in them;[l] they cannot sin, because they have been born of God. 10 The children of God and the children of the devil are revealed in this way: all who do not do what is right are not from God, nor are those who do not love their brothers and sisters.[m]

Love One Another
(Mt 22.39)

11 For this is the message you have heard from the beginning, that we should love one another. 12 We must

not be like Cain who was from the evil one and murdered his brother. And why did he murder him? Because his own deeds were evil and his brother's righteous. 13 Do not be astonished, brothers and sisters,[n] that the world hates you. 14 We know that we have passed from death to life because we love one another. Whoever does not love abides in death. 15 All who hate a brother or sister[m] are murderers, and you know that murderers do not have eternal life abiding in them. 16 We know love by this, that he laid down his life for us—and we ought to lay down our lives for one another. 17 How does God's love abide in anyone who has the world's goods and sees a brother or sister[o] in need and yet refuses help?

18 Little children, let us love, not in word or speech, but in truth and action. 19 And by this we will know that we are from the truth and will reassure our hearts before him 20 whenever our hearts condemn us; for God is greater than our hearts, and he knows everything. 21 Beloved, if our hearts do not condemn us, we have boldness before God; 22 and we receive from him whatever we ask, because we obey his commandments and do what pleases him.

23 And this is his commandment, that we should believe in the name of his Son Jesus Christ and love one another, just as he has commanded us. 24 All who obey his commandments abide in him, and he abides in them. And by this we know that he abides in us, by the Spirit that he has given us.

Testing the Spirits

4 Beloved, do not believe every spirit, but test the spirits to see whether they are from God; for many false prophets have gone out into the world. 2 By this you know the Spirit of God: every spirit that confesses that Jesus Christ has come in the flesh is from God, 3 and every spirit that does not confess Jesus[p] is not from God. And this is the spirit of the antichrist, of which you have heard that it is coming; and now it is already in the world. 4 Little children, you are from God, and

[j] Other ancient authorities read *you*
[k] Or *it*   [l] Or *because the children of God abide in him*   [m] Gk *his brother*
[n] Gk *brothers*   [o] Gk *brother*   [p] Other ancient authorities read *does away with Jesus* (Gk *dissolves Jesus*)

have conquered them; for the one who is in you is greater than the one who is in the world. ⁵They are from the world; therefore what they say is from the world, and the world listens to them. ⁶We are from God. Whoever knows God listens to us, and whoever is not from God does not listen to us. From this we know the spirit of truth and the spirit of error.

God Is Love
(Cp Jn 3.16)

7 Beloved, let us love one another, because love is from God; everyone who loves is born of God and knows God. ⁸Whoever does not love does not know God, for God is love. ⁹God's love was revealed among us in this way: God sent his only Son into the world so that we might live through him. ¹⁰In this is love, not that we loved God but that he loved us and sent his Son to be the atoning sacrifice for our sins. ¹¹Beloved, since God loved us so much, we also ought to love one another. ¹²No one has ever seen God; if we love one another, God lives in us, and his love is perfected in us.

13 By this we know that we abide in him and he in us, because he has given us of his Spirit. ¹⁴And we have seen and do testify that the Father has sent his Son as the Savior of the world. ¹⁵God abides in those who confess that Jesus is the Son of God, and they abide in God. ¹⁶So we have known and believe the love that God has for us.

God is love, and those who abide in love abide in God, and God abides in them. ¹⁷Love has been perfected among us in this: that we may have boldness on the day of judgment, because as he is, so are we in this world. ¹⁸There is no fear in love, but perfect love casts out fear; for fear has to do with punishment, and whoever fears has not reached perfection in love. ¹⁹We loveq because he first loved us. ²⁰Those who say, "I love God," and hate their brothers or sisters,r are liars; for those who do not love a brother or sisters whom they have seen, cannot love God whom they have not seen. ²¹The commandment we have from him is this: those who love God must love their brothers and sistersr also.

Faith Conquers the World

5 Everyone who believes that Jesus is the Christt has been born of God, and everyone who loves the parent loves the child. ²By this we know that we love the children of God, when we love God and obey his commandments. ³For the love of God is this, that we obey his commandments. And his commandments are not burdensome, ⁴for whatever is born of God conquers the world. And this is the victory that conquers the world, our faith. ⁵Who is it that conquers the world but the one who believes that Jesus is the Son of God?

Testimony concerning the Son of God

6 This is the one who came by water and blood, Jesus Christ, not with the water only but with the water and the blood. And the Spirit is the one that testifies, for the Spirit is the truth. ⁷There are three that testify:u ⁸the Spirit and the water and the blood, and these three agree. ⁹If we receive human testimony, the testimony of God is greater; for this is the testimony of God that he has testified to his Son. ¹⁰Those who believe in the Son of God have the testimony in their hearts. Those who do not believe in Godv have made him a liar by not believing in the testimony that God has given concerning his Son. ¹¹And this is the testimony: God gave us eternal life, and this life is in his Son. ¹²Whoever has the Son has life; whoever does not have the Son of God does not have life.

Epilogue

13 I write these things to you who believe in the name of the Son of God, so that you may know that you have eternal life.

14 And this is the boldness we have in him, that if we ask anything according to his will, he hears us. ¹⁵And if we know that he hears us in whatever we ask, we know that we have obtained the requests made of him. ¹⁶If you see your brother or sisterw committing what is not a mortal sin, you will ask,

1
J
O
H
N

qOther ancient authorities add him; others add God   rGk brothers sGk brother   tOr the Messiah   uA few other authorities read (with variations) ⁷There are three that testify in heaven, the Father, the Word, and the Holy Spirit, and these three are one. ⁸And there are three that testify on earth: vOther ancient authorities read in the Son   wGk your brother and God[x] will give life to such a one—to those whose sin is not mortal. There is sin that is mortal; I do not say that you should pray about that. [17] All wrongdoing is sin, but there is sin that is not mortal.

18 We know that those who are born of God do not sin, but the one who was born of God protects them, and the evil one does not touch them. [19] We know that we are God's children, and that the whole world lies under the power of the evil one. [20] And we know that the Son of God has come and has given us understanding so that we may know him who is true;[y] and we are in him who is true, in his Son Jesus Christ. He is the true God and eternal life.

21 Little children, keep yourselves from idols.[z]

---

[x] Gk *he*   [y] Other ancient authorities read *know the true God*   [z] Other ancient authorities add *Amen*

The Second Letter of

JOHN

Salutation

1 The elder to the elect lady and her children, whom I love in the truth, and not only I but also all who know the truth, [2] because of the truth that abides in us and will be with us forever:

3 Grace, mercy, and peace will be with us from God the Father and from[a] Jesus Christ, the Father's Son, in truth and love.

Truth and Love

4 I was overjoyed to find some of your children walking in the truth, just as we have been commanded by the Father. [5] But now, dear lady, I ask you, not as though I were writing you a new commandment, but one we have had from the beginning, let us love one another. [6] And this is love, that we walk according to his commandments; this is the commandment just as you have heard it from the beginning—you must walk in it.

7 Many deceivers have gone out into the world, those who do not confess that Jesus Christ has come in the flesh; any such person is the deceiver and the antichrist! [8] Be on your guard, so that you do not lose what we[b] have worked for, but may receive a full reward. [9] Everyone who does not abide in the teaching of Christ, but goes beyond it, does not have God; whoever abides in the teaching has both the Father and the Son. [10] Do not receive into the house or welcome anyone who comes to you and does not bring this teaching; [11] for to welcome is to participate in the evil deeds of such a person.

Final Greetings

12 Although I have much to write to you, I would rather not use paper and ink; instead I hope to come to you and talk with you face to face, so that our joy may be complete.

13 The children of your elect sister send you their greetings.[c]

---

[a] Other ancient authorities add *the Lord*   [b] Other ancient authorities read *you*   [c] Other ancient authorities add *Amen*

The Third Letter of

JOHN

Salutation

1 The elder to the beloved Ga'i·us, whom I love in truth.

Gaius Commended for His Hospitality

2 Beloved, I pray that all may go well with you and that you may be in good health, just as it is well with your soul. [3] I was overjoyed when some of the friends[a] arrived and testified to your faithfulness to the truth, namely how you walk in the truth. [4] I have no greater joy than this, to hear that my children are walking in the truth.

5 Beloved, you do faithfully whatever you do for the friends,[a] even though they are strangers to you; [6] they have testified to your love before the church. You will do well to send them on in a manner worthy of God; [7] for they began their journey for the sake of Christ,[b] accepting no support from non-believers.[c] [8] Therefore we ought to support such people, so that we may become co-workers with the truth.

Diotrephes and Demetrius

9 I have written something to the church; but Di·ot're·phes, who likes to put himself first, does not acknowledge our authority. [10] So if I come, I will call attention to what he is doing in spreading false charges against us. And not content with those charges, he refuses to welcome the friends,[a] and even prevents those who want to do so and expels them from the church.

11 Beloved, do not imitate what is evil but imitate what is good. Whoever does good is from God; whoever does evil has not seen God. [12] Everyone has testified favorably about De·me'tri·us, and so has the truth itself. We also testify for him,[d] and you know that our testimony is true.

Final Greetings

13 I have much to write to you, but I would rather not write with pen and ink; [14] instead I hope to see you soon, and we will talk together face to face.

15 Peace to you. The friends send you their greetings. Greet the friends there, each by name.

[a] Gk brothers   [b] Gk for the sake of the name   [c] Gk the Gentiles   [d] Gk lacks for him

The Letter of

JUDE

Salutation

1 Jude,[a] a servant[b] of Jesus Christ and brother of James,

To those who are called, who are beloved[c] in[d] God the Father and kept safe for[d] Jesus Christ:

2 May mercy, peace, and love be yours in abundance.

[a] Gk Judas   [b] Gk slave   [c] Other ancient authorities read sanctified   [d] Or by

Occasion of the Letter

3 Beloved, while eagerly preparing to write to you about the salvation we share, I find it necessary to write and appeal to you to contend for the faith that was once for all entrusted to the saints. [4] For certain intruders have stolen in among you, people who long ago were designated for this condemnation as ungodly, who pervert the grace of our God into licentiousness and deny our only Master and Lord, Jesus Christ. [e]

Judgment on False Teachers

5 Now I desire to remind you, though you are fully informed, that the Lord, who once for all saved [f] a people out of the land of Egypt, afterward destroyed those who did not believe. [6] And the angels who did not keep their own position, but left their proper dwelling, he has kept in eternal chains in deepest darkness for the judgment of the great Day. [7] Likewise, Sod'om and Go·mor'rah and the surrounding cities, which, in the same manner as they, indulged in sexual immorality and pursued unnatural lust, [g] serve as an example by undergoing a punishment of eternal fire.

8 Yet in the same way these dreamers also defile the flesh, reject authority, and slander the glorious ones. [h] [9] But when the archangel Michael contended with the devil and disputed about the body of Moses, he did not dare to bring a condemnation of slander [i] against him, but said, "The Lord rebuke you!" [10] But these people slander whatever they do not understand, and they are destroyed by those things that, like irrational animals, they know by instinct. [11] Woe to them! For they go the way of Cain, and abandon themselves to Ba'laam's error for the sake of gain, and perish in Ko'rah's rebellion. [12] These are blemishes [j] on your love-feasts, while they feast with you without fear, feeding themselves. [k] They are waterless clouds carried along by the winds; autumn trees without fruit, twice dead, uprooted; [13] wild waves of the sea, casting up the foam of their own shame; wandering stars, for whom the deepest darkness has been reserved forever.

14 It was also about these that E'noch, in the seventh generation from Adam, prophesied, saying, "See, the Lord is coming [l] with ten thousands of his holy ones, [15] to execute judgment on all, and to convict everyone of all the deeds of ungodliness that they have committed in such an ungodly way, and of all the harsh things that ungodly sinners have spoken against him." [16] These are grumblers and malcontents; they indulge their own lusts; they are bombastic in speech, flattering people to their own advantage.

Warnings and Exhortations

17 But you, beloved, must remember the predictions of the apostles of our Lord Jesus Christ; [18] for they said to you, "In the last time there will be scoffers, indulging their own ungodly lusts." [19] It is these worldly people, devoid of the Spirit, who are causing divisions. [20] But you, beloved, build yourselves up on your most holy faith; pray in the Holy Spirit; [21] keep yourselves in the love of God; look forward to the mercy of our Lord Jesus Christ that leads to [m] eternal life. [22] And have mercy on some who are wavering; [23] save others by snatching them out of the fire; and have mercy on still others with fear, hating even the tunic defiled by their bodies. [n]

Benediction

24 Now to him who is able to keep you from falling, and to make you stand without blemish in the presence of his glory with rejoicing, [25] to the only God our Savior, through Jesus Christ our Lord, be glory, majesty, power, and authority, before all time and now and forever. Amen.

[e] Or *the only Master and our Lord Jesus Christ*   [f] Other ancient authorities read *though you were once for all fully informed, that Jesus (or Joshua) who saved*   [g] Gk *went after other flesh* [h] Or *angels*; Gk *glories* [i] Or *condemnation for blasphemy* [j] Or *reefs*   [k] Or *without fear. They are shepherds who care only for themselves* [l] Gk *came*   [m] Gk *Christ to*   [n] Gk *by the flesh*. The Greek text of verses 22-23 is uncertain at several points

**J
U
D
E**

The
REVELATION
to John

Introduction and Salutation

1 The revelation of Jesus Christ, which God gave him to show his servants[a] what must soon take place; he made[b] it known by sending his angel to his servant[c] John, [2] who testified to the word of God and to the testimony of Jesus Christ, even to all that he saw.
[3] Blessed is the one who reads aloud the words of the prophecy, and blessed are those who hear and who keep what is written in it; for the time is near.

[4] John to the seven churches that are in Asia:

Grace to you and peace from him who is and who was and who is to come, and from the seven spirits who are before his throne, [5] and from Jesus Christ, the faithful witness, the firstborn of the dead, and the ruler of the kings of the earth.

To him who loves us and freed[d] us from our sins by his blood, [6] and made[b] us to be a kingdom, priests serving[e] his God and Father, to him be glory and dominion forever and ever. Amen.

[7] Look! He is coming with the
    clouds;
  every eye will see him,
    even those who pierced him;
    and on his account all the
      tribes of the earth will
      wail.
So it is to be. Amen.

[8] "I am the Alpha and the Omega," says the Lord God, who is and who was and who is to come, the Almighty.

A Vision of Christ

[9] I, John, your brother who share with you in Jesus the persecution and the kingdom and the patient endurance, was on the island called Pat'mos because of the word of God and the testimony of Jesus.[f] [10] I was in the spirit[g] on the Lord's day, and I heard behind me a loud voice like a trumpet [11] saying, "Write in a book what you see and send it to the seven churches, to Eph'e·sus, to Smyrna, to Per'-ga·mum, to Thy·a·ti'ra, to Sar'dis, to Philadelphia, and to La·o·di·ce'a."

[12] Then I turned to see whose voice it was that spoke to me, and on turning I saw seven golden lampstands, [13] and in the midst of the lampstands I saw one like the Son of Man, clothed with a long robe and with a golden sash across his chest. [14] His head and his hair were white as white wool, white as snow; his eyes were like a flame of fire, [15] his feet were like burnished bronze, refined as in a furnace, and his voice was like the sound of many waters. [16] In his right hand he held seven stars, and from his mouth came a sharp, two-edged sword, and his face was like the sun shining with full force.

[17] When I saw him, I fell at his feet as though dead. But he placed his right hand on me, saying, "Do not be afraid; I am the first and the last, [18] and the living one. I was dead, and see, I am alive forever and ever; and I have the keys of Death and of Hades. [19] Now write what you have seen, what is, and what is to take place after this. [20] As for the mystery of the seven stars that you saw in my right hand, and the seven golden lampstands: the seven stars are the angels of the seven churches, and the seven lampstands are the seven churches.

The Message to Ephesus

2 "To the angel of the church in Eph'e·sus write: These are the words of him who holds the seven stars in his right hand, who walks

[a] Gk slaves   [b] Gk and he made
[c] Gk slave   [d] Other ancient authorities read washed   [e] Gk priests to
[f] Or testimony to Jesus   [g] Or in the Spirit

among the seven golden lampstands: 2 "I know your works, your toil and your patient endurance. I know that you cannot tolerate evildoers; you have tested those who claim to be apostles but are not, and have found them to be false. ³ I also know that you are enduring patiently and bearing up for the sake of my name, and that you have not grown weary. ⁴ But I have this against you, that you have abandoned the love you had at first. ⁵ Remember then from what you have fallen; repent, and do the works you did at first. If not, I will come to you and remove your lampstand from its place, unless you repent. ⁶ Yet this is to your credit: you hate the works of the Nic·ŏ·lă′i·tans, which I also hate. ⁷ Let anyone who has an ear listen to what the Spirit is saying to the churches. To everyone who conquers, I will give permission to eat from the tree of life that is in the paradise of God.

The Message to Smyrna

8 "And to the angel of the church in Smyrna write: These are the words of the first and the last, who was dead and came to life:

9 "I know your affliction and your poverty, even though you are rich. I know the slander on the part of those who say that they are Jews and are not, but are a synagogue of Satan. ¹⁰ Do not fear what you are about to suffer. Beware, the devil is about to throw some of you into prison so that you may be tested, and for ten days you will have affliction. Be faithful until death, and I will give you the crown of life. ¹¹ Let anyone who has an ear listen to what the Spirit is saying to the churches. Whoever conquers will not be harmed by the second death.

The Message to Pergamum

12 "And to the angel of the church in Per′ga·mum write: These are the words of him who has the sharp two-edged sword:

13 "I know where you are living, where Satan's throne is. Yet you are holding fast to my name, and you did not deny your faith in me ʰ even in the days of An′ti·pas my witness, my faithful one, who was killed among you, where Satan lives. ¹⁴ But I have a few things against you: you have some there who hold to the teaching of Bā′-laam, who taught Bā′lak to put a stum-

bling block before the people of Israel, so that they would eat food sacrificed to idols and practice fornication. ¹⁵ So you also have some who hold to the teaching of the Nic·ŏ·lă′i·tans. ¹⁶ Repent then. If not, I will come to you soon and make war against them with the sword of my mouth. ¹⁷ Let anyone who has an ear listen to what the Spirit is saying to the churches. To everyone who conquers I will give some of the hidden manna, and I will give a white stone, and on the white stone is written a new name that no one knows except the one who receives it.

The Message to Thyatira

18 "And to the angel of the church in Thy·a·tī′ra write: These are the words of the Son of God, who has eyes like a flame of fire, and whose feet are like burnished bronze:

19 "I know your works—your love, faith, service, and patient endurance. I know that your last works are greater than the first. ²⁰ But I have this against you: you tolerate that woman Jez′-e·bel, who calls herself a prophet and is teaching and beguiling my servants ⁱ to practice fornication and to eat food sacrificed to idols. ²¹ I gave her time to repent, but she refuses to repent of her fornication. ²² Beware, I am throwing her on a bed, and those who commit adultery with her I am throwing into great distress, unless they repent of her doings; ²³ and I will strike her children dead. And all the churches will know that I am the one who searches minds and hearts, and I will give to each of you as your works deserve. ²⁴ But to the rest of you in Thy·a·tī′ra, who do not hold this teaching, who have not learned what some call 'the deep things of Satan,' to you I say, I do not lay on you any other burden; ²⁵ only hold fast to what you have until I come. ²⁶ To everyone who conquers and continues to do my works to the end,

I will give authority over the
     nations;
²⁷ to rule ʲ them with an iron rod,
     as when clay pots are
        shattered—
²⁸ even as I also received authority from my Father. To the one who conquers I will also give the morning star.

ʰ Or *deny my faith*   ⁱ Gk *slaves*   ʲ Or *to shepherd*

²⁹Let anyone who has an ear listen to what the Spirit is saying to the churches.

The Message to Sardis

3 "And to the angel of the church in Sar'dis write: These are the words of him who has the seven spirits of God and the seven stars:

"I know your works; you have a name of being alive, but you are dead. ²Wake up, and strengthen what remains and is on the point of death, for I have not found your works perfect in the sight of my God. ³Remember then what you received and heard; obey it, and repent. If you do not wake up, I will come like a thief, and you will not know at what hour I will come to you. ⁴Yet you have still a few persons in Sar'dis who have not soiled their clothes; they will walk with me, dressed in white, for they are worthy. ⁵If you conquer, you will be clothed like them in white robes, and I will not blot your name out of the book of life; I will confess your name before my Father and before his angels. ⁶Let anyone who has an ear listen to what the Spirit is saying to the churches.

The Message to Philadelphia

7 "And to the angel of the church in Philadelphia write:
These are the words of the holy
    one, the true one,
who has the key of David,
who opens and no one will
    shut,
    who shuts and no one opens:
8 "I know your works. Look, I have set before you an open door, which no one is able to shut. I know that you have but little power, and yet you have kept my word and have not denied my name. ⁹I will make those of the synagogue of Satan who say that they are Jews and are not, but are lying—I will make them come and bow down before your feet, and they will learn that I have loved you. ¹⁰Because you have kept my word of patient endurance, I will keep you from the hour of trial that is coming on the whole world to test the inhabitants of the earth. ¹¹I am coming soon; hold fast to what you have, so that no one may seize your crown. ¹²If you conquer, I will make you a pillar in the temple of my God; you will never go out of it. I will write on you the name of my God, and the name of the city of my God, the new Jerusalem that comes down from my God out of heaven, and my own new name. ¹³Let anyone who has an ear listen to what the Spirit is saying to the churches.

The Message to Laodicea

14 "And to the angel of the church in Lā·o·di·cē'a write: The words of the Amen, the faithful and true witness, the origin*ᵏ* of God's creation:
15 "I know your works; you are neither cold nor hot. I wish that you were either cold or hot. ¹⁶So, because you are lukewarm, and neither cold nor hot, I am about to spit you out of my mouth. ¹⁷For you say, 'I am rich, I have prospered, and I need nothing.' You do not realize that you are wretched, pitiable, poor, blind, and naked. ¹⁸Therefore I counsel you to buy from me gold refined by fire so that you may be rich; and white robes to clothe you and to keep the shame of your nakedness from being seen; and salve to anoint your eyes so that you may see. ¹⁹I reprove and discipline those whom I love. Be earnest, therefore, and repent. ²⁰Listen! I am standing at the door, knocking; if you hear my voice and open the door, I will come in to you and eat with you, and you with me. ²¹To the one who conquers I will give a place with me on my throne, just as I myself conquered and sat down with my Father on his throne. ²²Let anyone who has an ear listen to what the Spirit is saying to the churches."

The Heavenly Worship
(Isa 6.1–3)

4 After this I looked, and there in heaven a door stood open! And the first voice, which I had heard speaking to me like a trumpet, said, "Come up here, and I will show you what must take place after this." ²At once I was in the spirit,*ˡ* and there in heaven stood a throne, with one seated on the throne! ³And the one seated there looks like jasper and carnelian, and around the throne is a rainbow that looks like an emerald. ⁴Around the throne are twenty-four thrones, and seated on the thrones are twenty-four elders, dressed in white robes, with golden crowns on their heads. ⁵Coming from the throne are flashes

ᵏOr *beginning*   ˡOr *in the Spirit*

R
E
V
E
L
A
T
I
O
N

of lightning, and rumblings and peals of thunder, and in front of the throne burn seven flaming torches, which are the seven spirits of God; [6] and in front of the throne there is something like a sea of glass, like crystal.

Around the throne, and on each side of the throne, are four living creatures, full of eyes in front and behind: [7] the first living creature like a lion, the second living creature like an ox, the third living creature with a face like a human face, and the fourth living creature like a flying eagle. [8] And the four living creatures, each of them with six wings, are full of eyes all around and inside. Day and night without ceasing they sing,

> "Holy, holy, holy,
> the Lord God the Almighty,
> who was and is and is to
> come."

[9] And whenever the living creatures give glory and honor and thanks to the one who is seated on the throne, who lives forever and ever, [10] the twenty-four elders fall before the one who is seated on the throne and worship the one who lives forever and ever; they cast their crowns before the throne, singing,

[11] "You are worthy, our Lord and God,
> to receive glory and honor and power,
> for you created all things,
> and by your will they existed
> and were created."

The Scroll and the Lamb

5 Then I saw in the right hand of the one seated on the throne a scroll written on the inside and on the back, sealed[m] with seven seals; [2] and I saw a mighty angel proclaiming with a loud voice, "Who is worthy to open the scroll and break its seals?" [3] And no one in heaven or on earth or under the earth was able to open the scroll or to look into it. [4] And I began to weep bitterly because no one was found worthy to open the scroll or to look into it. [5] Then one of the elders said to me, "Do not weep. See, the Lion of the tribe of Judah, the Root of David, has conquered, so that he can open the scroll and its seven seals."

[6] Then I saw between the throne and the four living creatures and among the elders a Lamb standing as if it had been slaughtered, having seven horns and seven eyes, which are

the seven spirits of God sent out into all the earth. [7] He went and took the scroll from the right hand of the one who was seated on the throne. [8] When he had taken the scroll, the four living creatures and the twenty-four elders fell before the Lamb, each holding a harp and golden bowls full of incense, which are the prayers of the saints. [9] They sing a new song:

> "You are worthy to take the scroll
> and to open its seals,
> for you were slaughtered and by your blood you ransomed for God
> saints from[n] every tribe and language and people and nation;
[10] you have made them to be a kingdom and priests serving[o] our God,
> and they will reign on earth."

[11] Then I looked, and I heard the voice of many angels surrounding the throne and the living creatures and the elders; they numbered myriads of myriads and thousands of thousands, [12] singing with full voice,

> "Worthy is the Lamb that was slaughtered
> to receive power and wealth and wisdom and might
> and honor and glory and blessing!"

[13] Then I heard every creature in heaven and on earth and under the earth and in the sea, and all that is in them, singing,

> "To the one seated on the throne and to the Lamb
> be blessing and honor and glory and might
> forever and ever!"

[14] And the four living creatures said, "Amen!" And the elders fell down and worshiped.

The Seven Seals

6 Then I saw the Lamb open one of the seven seals, and I heard one of the four living creatures call out, as with a voice of thunder, "Come!"[p] [2] I looked, and there was a white horse! Its rider had a bow; a crown was given to him, and he came out conquering and to conquer.

[m] Or *written on the inside, and sealed on the back*   [n] Gk *ransomed for God from*   [o] Gk *priests to*   [p] Or *"Go!"*

3 When he opened the second seal, I heard the second living creature call out, "Come!"*q* *4* And out came*r* another horse, bright red; its rider was permitted to take peace from the earth, so that people would slaughter one another; and he was given a great sword.

5 When he opened the third seal, I heard the third living creature call out, "Come!"*q* I looked, and there was a black horse! Its rider held a pair of scales in his hand, *6* and I heard what seemed to be a voice in the midst of the four living creatures saying, "A quart of wheat for a day's pay,*s* and three quarts of barley for a day's pay,*s* but do not damage the olive oil and the wine!"

7 When he opened the fourth seal, I heard the voice of the fourth living creature call out, "Come!"*q* *8* I looked and there was a pale green horse! Its rider's name was Death, and Hades followed with him; they were given authority over a fourth of the earth, to kill with sword, famine, and pestilence, and by the wild animals of the earth.

9 When he opened the fifth seal, I saw under the altar the souls of those who had been slaughtered for the word of God and for the testimony they had given; *10* they cried out with a loud voice, "Sovereign Lord, holy and true, how long will it be before you judge and avenge our blood on the inhabitants of the earth?" *11* They were each given a white robe and told to rest a little longer, until the number would be complete both of their fellow servants*t* and of their brothers and sisters,*u* who were soon to be killed as they themselves had been killed.

12 When he opened the sixth seal, I looked; and there came a great earthquake; the sun became black as sackcloth, the full moon became like blood, *13* and the stars of the sky fell to the earth as the fig tree drops its winter fruit when shaken by a gale. *14* The sky vanished like a scroll rolling itself up, and every mountain and island was removed from its place. *15* Then the kings of the earth and the magnates and the generals and the rich and the powerful, and everyone, slave and free, hid in the caves and among the rocks of the mountains, *16* calling to the mountains and rocks, "Fall on us and hide us from the face of the one seated on the throne and from the wrath of the Lamb; *17* for the great day of their wrath has come, and who is able to stand?"

The 144,000 of Israel Sealed

7 After this I saw four angels standing at the four corners of the earth, holding back the four winds of the earth so that no wind could blow on earth or sea or against any tree. *2* I saw another angel ascending from the rising of the sun, having the seal of the living God, and he called with a loud voice to the four angels who had been given power to damage earth and sea, *3* saying, "Do not damage the earth or the sea or the trees, until we have marked the servants*t* of our God with a seal on their foreheads."

4 And I heard the number of those who were sealed, one hundred forty-four thousand, sealed out of every tribe of the people of Israel:

5 From the tribe of Judah twelve thousand sealed,
from the tribe of Reuben twelve thousand,
from the tribe of Gad twelve thousand,

6 from the tribe of Ash′er twelve thousand,
from the tribe of Naph′ta·li twelve thousand,
from the tribe of Ma·nas′seh twelve thousand,

7 from the tribe of Sim′e·on twelve thousand,
from the tribe of Levi twelve thousand,
from the tribe of Is′sa·char twelve thousand,

8 from the tribe of Zeb′u·lun twelve thousand,
from the tribe of Joseph twelve thousand,
from the tribe of Benjamin twelve thousand sealed.

The Multitude from Every Nation

9 After this I looked, and there was a great multitude that no one could count, from every nation, from all tribes and peoples and languages, standing before the throne and before the Lamb, robed in white, with palm branches in their hands. *10* They cried out in a loud voice, saying,

"Salvation belongs to our God
　who is seated on the
　　throne, and to the Lamb!"

q Or "Go!"　*r* Or went　*s* Gk a denarius
t Gk slaves　*u* Gk brothers

11 And all the angels stood around the throne and around the elders and the four living creatures, and they fell on their faces before the throne and worshiped God, 12 singing,

"Amen! Blessing and glory and wisdom
and thanksgiving and honor
and power and might
be to our God forever and ever! Amen."

13 Then one of the elders addressed me, saying, "Who are these, robed in white, and where have they come from?" 14 I said to him, "Sir, you are the one that knows." Then he said to me, "These are they who have come out of the great ordeal; they have washed their robes and made them white in the blood of the Lamb.

15 For this reason they are before the throne of God,
and worship him day and night within his temple,
and the one who is seated on the throne will shelter them.

16 They will hunger no more, and thirst no more;
the sun will not strike them, nor any scorching heat;

17 for the Lamb at the center of the throne will be their shepherd,
and he will guide them to springs of the water of life,
and God will wipe away every tear from their eyes."

The Seventh Seal and the Golden Censer

8 When the Lamb opened the seventh seal, there was silence in heaven for about half an hour. 2 And I saw the seven angels who stand before God, and seven trumpets were given to them.
3 Another angel with a golden censer came and stood at the altar; he was given a great quantity of incense to offer with the prayers of all the saints on the golden altar that is before the throne. 4 And the smoke of the incense, with the prayers of the saints, rose before God from the hand of the angel. 5 Then the angel took the censer and filled it with fire from the altar and threw it on the earth; and there were peals of thunder, rumblings, flashes of lightning, and an earthquake.

The Seven Trumpets

6 Now the seven angels who had the seven trumpets made ready to blow them.
7 The first angel blew his trumpet, and there came hail and fire, mixed with blood, and they were hurled to the earth; and a third of the earth was burned up, and a third of the trees were burned up, and all green grass was burned up.
8 The second angel blew his trumpet, and something like a great mountain, burning with fire, was thrown into the sea. 9 A third of the sea became blood, a third of the living creatures in the sea died, and a third of the ships were destroyed.
10 The third angel blew his trumpet, and a great star fell from heaven, blazing like a torch, and it fell on a third of the rivers and on the springs of water. 11 The name of the star is Wormwood. A third of the waters became wormwood, and many died from the water, because it was made bitter.
12 The fourth angel blew his trumpet, and a third of the sun was struck, and a third of the moon, and a third of the stars, so that a third of their light was darkened; a third of the day was kept from shining, and likewise the night.
13 Then I looked, and I heard an eagle crying with a loud voice as it flew in midheaven, "Woe, woe, woe to the inhabitants of the earth, at the blasts of the other trumpets that the three angels are about to blow!"

9 And the fifth angel blew his trumpet, and I saw a star that had fallen from heaven to earth, and he was given the key to the shaft of the bottomless pit; 2 he opened the shaft of the bottomless pit, and from the shaft rose smoke like the smoke of a great furnace, and the sun and the air were darkened with the smoke from the shaft. 3 Then from the smoke came locusts on the earth, and they were given authority like the authority of scorpions of the earth. 4 They were told not to damage the grass of the earth or any green growth or any tree, but only those people who do not have the seal of God on their foreheads. 5 They were allowed to torture them for five months, but not to kill them, and their torture was like the torture of a scorpion when it stings someone. 6 And in those days people will seek death but

will not find it; they will long to die, but death will flee from them.

7 In appearance the locusts were like horses equipped for battle. On their heads were what looked like crowns of gold; their faces were like human faces, [8]their hair like women's hair, and their teeth like lions' teeth; [9]they had scales like iron breastplates, and the noise of their wings was like the noise of many chariots with horses rushing into battle. [10]They have tails like scorpions, with stingers, and in their tails is their power to harm people for five months. [11]They have as king over them the angel of the bottomless pit; his name in Hebrew is A·bad′don,[v] and in Greek he is called A·pol′lyon.[w]

12 The first woe has passed. There are still two woes to come.

13 Then the sixth angel blew his trumpet, and I heard a voice from the four[x] horns of the golden altar before God, [14]saying to the sixth angel who had the trumpet, "Release the four angels who are bound at the great river Euphrates." [15]So the four angels were released, who had been held ready for the hour, the day, the month, and the year, to kill a third of humankind. [16]The number of the troops of cavalry was two hundred million; I heard their number. [17]And this was how I saw the horses in my vision: the riders wore breastplates the color of fire and of sapphire[y] and of sulfur; the heads of the horses were like lions' heads, and fire and smoke and sulfur came out of their mouths. [18]By these three plagues a third of humankind was killed, by the fire and smoke and sulfur coming out of their mouths. [19]For the power of the horses is in their mouths and in their tails; their tails are like serpents, having heads; and with them they inflict harm.

20 The rest of humankind, who were not killed by these plagues, did not repent of the works of their hands or give up worshiping demons and idols of gold and silver and bronze and stone and wood, which cannot see or hear or walk. [21]And they did not repent of their murders or their sorceries or their fornication or their thefts.

The Angel with the Little Scroll

10 And I saw another mighty angel coming down from heaven, wrapped in a cloud, with a rainbow over his head; his face was like the sun, and his legs like pillars of fire. [2]He held a little scroll open in his hand. Setting his right foot on the sea and his left foot on the land, [3]he gave a great shout, like a lion roaring. And when he shouted, the seven thunders sounded. [4]And when the seven thunders sounded, I was about to write, but I heard a voice from heaven saying, "Seal up what the seven thunders have said, and do not write it down." [5]Then the angel whom I saw standing on the sea and the land

raised his right hand to heaven
6   and swore by him who lives
            forever and ever,
who created heaven and what is in it, the earth and what is in it, and the sea and what is in it: "There will be no more delay, [7]but in the days when the seventh angel is to blow his trumpet, the mystery of God will be fulfilled, as he announced to his servants[z] the prophets."

8 Then the voice that I had heard from heaven spoke to me again, saying, "Go, take the scroll that is open in the hand of the angel who is standing on the sea and on the land." [9]So I went to the angel and told him to give me the little scroll; and he said to me, "Take it, and eat; it will be bitter to your stomach, but sweet as honey in your mouth." [10]So I took the little scroll from the hand of the angel and ate it; it was sweet as honey in my mouth, but when I had eaten it, my stomach was made bitter.

11 Then they said to me, "You must prophesy again about many peoples and nations and languages and kings."

The Two Witnesses

11 Then I was given a measuring rod like a staff, and I was told, "Come and measure the temple of God and the altar and those who worship there, [2]but do not measure the court outside the temple; leave that out, for it is given over to the nations, and they will trample over the holy city for forty-two months. [3]And I will grant my two witnesses authority to prophesy for one thousand two hundred sixty days, wearing sackcloth."

4 These are the two olive trees and the two lampstands that stand before

[v]That is, *Destruction*   [w]That is, *Destroyer*   [x]Other ancient authorities lack *four*   [y]Gk *hyacinth*   [z]Gk *slaves*

R
E
V
E
L
A
T
I
O
N

the Lord of the earth. [5] And if anyone wants to harm them, fire pours from their mouth and consumes their foes; anyone who wants to harm them must be killed in this manner. [6] They have authority to shut the sky, so that no rain may fall during the days of their prophesying, and they have authority over the waters to turn them into blood, and to strike the earth with every kind of plague, as often as they desire.

7 When they have finished their testimony, the beast that comes up from the bottomless pit will make war on them and conquer them and kill them, [8] and their dead bodies will lie in the street of the great city that is prophetically[a] called Sod'om and Egypt, where also their Lord was crucified. [9] For three and a half days members of the peoples and tribes and languages and nations will gaze at their dead bodies and refuse to let them be placed in a tomb; [10] and the inhabitants of the earth will gloat over them and celebrate and exchange presents, because these two prophets had been a torment to the inhabitants of the earth.

11 But after the three and a half days, the breath[b] of life from God entered them, and they stood on their feet, and those who saw them were terrified. [12] Then they[c] heard a loud voice from heaven saying to them, "Come up here!" And they went up to heaven in a cloud while their enemies watched them. [13] At that moment there was a great earthquake, and a tenth of the city fell; seven thousand people were killed in the earthquake, and the rest were terrified and gave glory to the God of heaven.

14 The second woe has passed. The third woe is coming very soon.

The Seventh Trumpet

15 Then the seventh angel blew his trumpet, and there were loud voices in heaven, saying,

"The kingdom of the world has
    become the kingdom of our
    Lord
and of his Messiah,[d]
and he will reign forever and
    ever."

16 Then the twenty-four elders who sit on their thrones before God fell on their faces and worshiped God, [17] singing,

"We give you thanks, Lord God
    Almighty,

who are and who were,
for you have taken your great
    power
and begun to reign.
18 The nations raged,
    but your wrath has come,
    and the time for judging the
        dead,
for rewarding your servants,[e]
    the prophets
and saints and all who fear
    your name,
    both small and great,
and for destroying those who
    destroy the earth."

19 Then God's temple in heaven was opened, and the ark of his covenant was seen within his temple; and there were flashes of lightning, rumblings, peals of thunder, an earthquake, and heavy hail.

The Woman and the Dragon

12 A great portent appeared in heaven: a woman clothed with the sun, with the moon under her feet, and on her head a crown of twelve stars. [2] She was pregnant and was crying out in birth pangs, in the agony of giving birth. [3] Then another portent appeared in heaven: a great red dragon, with seven heads and ten horns, and seven diadems on his heads. [4] His tail swept down a third of the stars of heaven and threw them to the earth. Then the dragon stood before the woman who was about to bear a child, so that he might devour her child as soon as it was born. [5] And she gave birth to a son, a male child, who is to rule[f] all the nations with a rod of iron. But her child was snatched away and taken to God and to his throne; [6] and the woman fled into the wilderness, where she has a place prepared by God, so that there she can be nourished for one thousand two hundred sixty days.

Michael Defeats the Dragon

7 And war broke out in heaven; Michael and his angels fought against the dragon. The dragon and his angels fought back, [8] but they were defeated, and there was no longer any place for them in heaven. [9] The great dragon was thrown down, that ancient ser-

[a] Or allegorically; Gk spiritually
[b] Or the spirit   [c] Other ancient authorities read I   [d] Gk Christ
[e] Gk slaves   [f] Or to shepherd

pent, who is called the Devil and Satan, the deceiver of the whole world—he was thrown down to the earth, and his angels were thrown down with him.

10 Then I heard a loud voice in heaven, proclaiming,

"Now have come the salvation
and the power
and the kingdom of our God
and the authority of his
Messiah,[g]
for the accuser of our
comrades[h] has been
thrown down,
who accuses them day and
night before our God.

11 But they have conquered him by
the blood of the Lamb
and by the word of their
testimony,
for they did not cling to life even
in the face of death.

12 Rejoice then, you heavens
and those who dwell in them!
But woe to the earth and the sea,
for the devil has come down to
you
with great wrath,
because he knows that his
time is short!"

The Dragon Fights Again on Earth

13 So when the dragon saw that he had been thrown down to the earth, he pursued[i] the woman who had given birth to the male child. 14 But the woman was given the two wings of the great eagle, so that she could fly from the serpent into the wilderness, to her place where she is nourished for a time, and times, and half a time. 15 Then from his mouth the serpent poured water like a river after the woman, to sweep her away with the flood. 16 But the earth came to the help of the woman; it opened its mouth and swallowed the river that the dragon had poured from his mouth. 17 Then the dragon was angry with the woman, and went off to make war on the rest of her children, those who keep the commandments of God and hold the testimony of Jesus.

The First Beast

18 Then the dragon[j] took his stand on the sand of the seashore.
13 1 And I saw a beast rising out of the sea, having ten horns and seven heads; and on its horns were ten diadems, and on its heads were blasphe-

mous names. 2 And the beast that I saw was like a leopard, its feet were like a bear's, and its mouth was like a lion's mouth. And the dragon gave it his power and his throne and great authority. 3 One of its heads seemed to have received a death-blow, but its mortal wound[k] had been healed. In amazement the whole earth followed the beast. 4 They worshiped the dragon, for he had given his authority to the beast, and they worshiped the beast, saying, "Who is like the beast, and who can fight against it?"

5 The beast was given a mouth uttering haughty and blasphemous words, and it was allowed to exercise authority for forty-two months. 6 It opened its mouth to utter blasphemies against God, blaspheming his name and his dwelling, that is, those who dwell in heaven. 7 Also it was allowed to make war on the saints and to conquer them.[l] It was given authority over every tribe and people and language and nation, 8 and all the inhabitants of the earth will worship it, everyone whose name has not been written from the foundation of the world in the book of life of the Lamb that was slaughtered.[m]

9 Let anyone who has an ear listen:
10 If you are to be taken captive,
into captivity you go;
if you kill with the sword,
with the sword you must be
killed.

Here is a call for the endurance and faith of the saints.

The Second Beast

11 Then I saw another beast that rose out of the earth; it had two horns like a lamb and it spoke like a dragon. 12 It exercises all the authority of the first beast on its behalf, and it makes the earth and its inhabitants worship the first beast, whose mortal wound[n] had been healed. 13 It performs great signs, even making fire come down from heaven to earth in the sight of all; 14 and by the signs that it is allowed to perform on behalf of the beast, it de-

gGk Christ   hGk brothers
iOr persecuted   jGk Then he; other ancient authorities read Then I stood   kGk the plague of its death   lOther ancient authorities lack this sentence   mOr written in the book of life of the Lamb that was slaughtered from the foundation of the world   nGk whose plague of its death

REVELATION

ceives the inhabitants of earth, telling them to make an image for the beast that had been wounded by the sword[o] and yet lived; [15]and it was allowed to give breath[p] to the image of the beast so that the image of the beast could even speak and cause those who would not worship the image of the beast to be killed. [16]Also it causes all, both small and great, both rich and poor, both free and slave, to be marked on the right hand or the forehead, [17]so that no one can buy or sell who does not have the mark, that is, the name of the beast or the number of its name. [18]This calls for wisdom: let anyone with understanding calculate the number of the beast, for it is the number of a person. Its number is six hundred sixty-six. [q]

The Lamb and the 144,000

14 Then I looked, and there was the Lamb, standing on Mount Zion! And with him were one hundred forty-four thousand who had his name and his Father's name written on their foreheads. [2]And I heard a voice from heaven like the sound of many waters and like the sound of loud thunder; the voice I heard was like the sound of harpists playing on their harps, [3]and they sing a new song before the throne and before the four living creatures and before the elders. No one could learn that song except the one hundred forty-four thousand who have been redeemed from the earth. [4]It is these who have not defiled themselves with women, for they are virgins; these follow the Lamb wherever he goes. They have been redeemed from humankind as first fruits for God and the Lamb, [5]and in their mouth no lie was found; they are blameless.

The Messages of the Three Angels

6 Then I saw another angel flying in midheaven, with an eternal gospel to proclaim to those who live[r] on the earth—to every nation and tribe and language and people. [7]He said in a loud voice, "Fear God and give him glory, for the hour of his judgment has come; and worship him who made heaven and earth, the sea and the springs of water."

8 Then another angel, a second, followed, saying, "Fallen, fallen is Babylon the great! She has made all nations drink of the wine of the wrath of her fornication."

9 Then another angel, a third, followed them, crying with a loud voice, "Those who worship the beast and its image, and receive a mark on their foreheads or on their hands, [10]they will also drink the wine of God's wrath, poured unmixed into the cup of his anger, and they will be tormented with fire and sulfur in the presence of the holy angels and in the presence of the Lamb. [11]And the smoke of their torment goes up forever and ever. There is no rest day or night for those who worship the beast and its image and for anyone who receives the mark of its name."

12 Here is a call for the endurance of the saints, those who keep the commandments of God and hold fast to the faith of[s] Jesus.

13 And I heard a voice from heaven saying, "Write this: Blessed are the dead who from now on die in the Lord." "Yes," says the Spirit, "they will rest from their labors, for their deeds follow them."

Reaping the Earth's Harvest

14 Then I looked, and there was a white cloud, and seated on the cloud was one like the Son of Man, with a golden crown on his head, and a sharp sickle in his hand! [15]Another angel came out of the temple, calling with a loud voice to the one who sat on the cloud, "Use your sickle and reap, for the hour to reap has come, because the harvest of the earth is fully ripe." [16]So the one who sat on the cloud swung his sickle over the earth, and the earth was reaped.

17 Then another angel came out of the temple in heaven, and he too had a sharp sickle. [18]Then another angel came out from the altar, the angel who has authority over fire, and he called with a loud voice to him who had the sharp sickle, "Use your sharp sickle and gather the clusters of the vine of the earth, for its grapes are ripe." [19]So the angel swung his sickle over the earth and gathered the vintage of the earth, and he threw it into the great wine press of the wrath of God. [20]And the wine press was trodden outside the city, and blood flowed from the wine press, as high as a horse's bridle, for a

*o*Or *that had received the plague of the sword*   *p*Or *spirit*   *q*Other ancient authorities read *six hundred sixteen*   *r*Gk *sit*   *s*Or *to their faith in* distance of about two hundred miles.[t]

The Angels with the Seven Last Plagues

15 Then I saw another portent in heaven, great and amazing: seven angels with seven plagues, which are the last, for with them the wrath of God is ended.

2 And I saw what appeared to be a sea of glass mixed with fire, and those who had conquered the beast and its image and the number of its name, standing beside the sea of glass with harps of God in their hands. 3 And they sing the song of Moses, the servant[u] of God, and the song of the Lamb:

"Great and amazing are your deeds,
Lord God the Almighty!
Just and true are your ways,
King of the nations![v]
4 Lord, who will not fear
and glorify your name?
For you alone are holy.
All nations will come
and worship before you,
for your judgments have been revealed."

5 After this I looked, and the temple of the tent[w] of witness in heaven was opened, 6 and out of the temple came the seven angels with the seven plagues, robed in pure bright linen,[x] with golden sashes across their chests. 7 Then one of the four living creatures gave the seven angels seven golden bowls full of the wrath of God, who lives forever and ever; 8 and the temple was filled with smoke from the glory of God and from his power, and no one could enter the temple until the seven plagues of the seven angels were ended.

The Bowls of God's Wrath

16 Then I heard a loud voice from the temple telling the seven angels, "Go and pour out on the earth the seven bowls of the wrath of God."

2 So the first angel went and poured his bowl on the earth, and a foul and painful sore came on those who had the mark of the beast and who worshiped its image.

3 The second angel poured his bowl into the sea, and it became like the blood of a corpse, and every living thing in the sea died.

4 The third angel poured his bowl into the rivers and the springs of water, and they became blood. 5 And I heard the angel of the waters say,
"You are just, O Holy One, who are and were,
for you have judged these things;
6 because they shed the blood of saints and prophets,
you have given them blood to drink.
It is what they deserve!"
7 And I heard the altar respond,
"Yes, O Lord God, the Almighty,
your judgments are true and just!"

8 The fourth angel poured his bowl on the sun, and it was allowed to scorch them with fire; 9 they were scorched by the fierce heat, but they cursed the name of God, who had authority over these plagues, and they did not repent and give him glory.

10 The fifth angel poured his bowl on the throne of the beast, and its kingdom was plunged into darkness; people gnawed their tongues in agony, 11 and cursed the God of heaven because of their pains and sores, and they did not repent of their deeds.

12 The sixth angel poured his bowl on the great river Euphrates, and its water was dried up in order to prepare the way for the kings from the east. 13 And I saw three foul spirits like frogs coming from the mouth of the dragon, from the mouth of the beast, and from the mouth of the false prophet. 14 These are demonic spirits, performing signs, who go abroad to the kings of the whole world, to assemble them for battle on the great day of God the Almighty. 15 ("See, I am coming like a thief! Blessed is the one who stays awake and is clothed,[y] not going about naked and exposed to shame.") 16 And they assembled them at the place that in Hebrew is called Har·ma·ged'on.

17 The seventh angel poured his bowl into the air, and a loud voice came out of the temple, from the throne, saying, "It is done!" 18 And there came flashes of lightning, rumblings, peals of thunder, and a violent earthquake, such as had not occurred since people were upon the earth, so

---

[t] Gk one thousand six hundred stadia
[u] Gk slave   [v] Other ancient authorities read the ages   [w] Or tabernacle
[x] Other ancient authorities read stone
[y] Gk and keeps his robes

violent was that earthquake. [19] The great city was split into three parts, and the cities of the nations fell. God remembered great Babylon and gave her the wine-cup of the fury of his wrath. [20] And every island fled away, and no mountains were to be found; [21] and huge hailstones, each weighing about a hundred pounds,[z] dropped from heaven on people, until they cursed God for the plague of the hail, so fearful was that plague.

The Great Whore and the Beast

17 Then one of the seven angels who had the seven bowls came and said to me, "Come, I will show you the judgment of the great whore who is seated on many waters, [2] with whom the kings of the earth have committed fornication, and with the wine of whose fornication the inhabitants of the earth have become drunk." [3] So he carried me away in the spirit[a] into a wilderness, and I saw a woman sitting on a scarlet beast that was full of blasphemous names, and it had seven heads and ten horns. [4] The woman was clothed in purple and scarlet, and adorned with gold and jewels and pearls, holding in her hand a golden cup full of abominations and the impurities of her fornication; [5] and on her forehead was written a name, a mystery: "Babylon the great, mother of whores and of earth's abominations." [6] And I saw that the woman was drunk with the blood of the saints and the blood of the witnesses to Jesus.

When I saw her, I was greatly amazed. [7] But the angel said to me, "Why are you so amazed? I will tell you the mystery of the woman, and of the beast with seven heads and ten horns that carries her. [8] The beast that you saw was, and is not, and is about to ascend from the bottomless pit and go to destruction. And the inhabitants of the earth, whose names have not been written in the book of life from the foundation of the world, will be amazed when they see the beast, because it was and is not and is to come. [9] "This calls for a mind that has wisdom: the seven heads are seven mountains on which the woman is seated; also, they are seven kings, [10] of whom five have fallen, one is living, and the other has not yet come; and when he comes, he must remain only a little while. [11] As for the beast that was and

is not, it is an eighth but it belongs to the seven, and it goes to destruction. [12] And the ten horns that you saw are ten kings who have not yet received a kingdom, but they are to receive authority as kings for one hour, together with the beast. [13] These are united in yielding their power and authority to the beast; [14] they will make war on the Lamb, and the Lamb will conquer them, for he is Lord of lords and King of kings, and those with him are called and chosen and faithful."

15 And he said to me, "The waters that you saw, where the whore is seated, are peoples and multitudes and nations and languages. [16] And the ten horns that you saw, they and the beast will hate the whore; they will make her desolate and naked; they will devour her flesh and burn her up with fire. [17] For God has put it into their hearts to carry out his purpose by agreeing to give their kingdom to the beast, until the words of God will be fulfilled. [18] The woman you saw is the great city that rules over the kings of the earth."

The Fall of Babylon

18 After this I saw another angel coming down from heaven, having great authority; and the earth was made bright with his splendor. [2] He called out with a mighty voice,

"Fallen, fallen is Babylon the great!
It has become a dwelling place of demons,
a haunt of every foul spirit,
a haunt of every foul bird,
a haunt of every foul and hateful beast.[b]
[3] For all the nations have drunk[c]
of the wine of the wrath of her fornication,
and the kings of the earth have committed fornication with her,
and the merchants of the earth have grown rich from the power[d] of her luxury."

4 Then I heard another voice from heaven saying,
"Come out of her, my people,

[z] Gk *weighing about a talent*　[a] Or *in the Spirit*　[b] Other ancient authorities lack the words *a haunt of every foul beast* and attach the words *and hateful* to the previous line so as to read *a haunt of every foul and hateful bird*　[c] Other ancient authorities read *she has made all nations drink*　[d] Or *resources*

so that you do not take part in
her sins,
and so that you do not share
in her plagues;
5 for her sins are heaped high as
heaven,
and God has remembered her
iniquities.
6 Render to her as she herself has
rendered,
and repay her double for her
deeds;
mix a double draught for her
in the cup she mixed.
7 As she glorified herself and lived
luxuriously,
so give her a like measure of
torment and grief.
Since in her heart she says,
'I rule as a queen;
I am no widow,
and I will never see grief,'
8 therefore her plagues will come
in a single day—
pestilence and mourning and
famine—
and she will be burned with fire;
for mighty is the Lord God
who judges her."
9 And the kings of the earth, who
committed fornication and lived in
luxury with her, will weep and wail
over her when they see the smoke of
her burning; 10 they will stand far off,
in fear of her torment, and say,
"Alas, alas, the great city,
Babylon, the mighty city!
For in one hour your judgment
has come."
11 And the merchants of the earth
weep and mourn for her, since no one
buys their cargo anymore, 12 cargo of
gold, silver, jewels and pearls, fine
linen, purple, silk and scarlet, all kinds
of scented wood, all articles of ivory,
all articles of costly wood, bronze,
iron, and marble, 13 cinnamon, spice,
incense, myrrh, frankincense, wine,
olive oil, choice flour and wheat, cattle
and sheep, horses and chariots,
slaves—and human lives.e
14 "The fruit for which your soul
longed
has gone from you,
and all your dainties and your
splendor
are lost to you,
never to be found again!"
15 The merchants of these wares, who
gained wealth from her, will stand far
off, in fear of her torment, weeping and
mourning aloud,

16 "Alas, alas, the great city,
clothed in fine linen,
in purple and scarlet,
adorned with gold,
with jewels, and with pearls!
17 For in one hour all this wealth
has been laid waste!"
And all shipmasters and seafarers,
sailors and all whose trade is on the
sea, stood far off 18 and cried out as
they saw the smoke of her burning,
"What city was like the great
city?"
19 And they threw dust on their heads,
as they wept and mourned, crying out,
"Alas, alas, the great city,
where all who had ships at sea
grew rich by her wealth!
For in one hour she has been
laid waste.
20 Rejoice over her, O heaven,
you saints and apostles and
prophets!
For God has given judgment for
you against her."
21 Then a mighty angel took up a
stone like a great millstone and threw
it into the sea, saying,
"With such violence Babylon the
great city
will be thrown down,
and will be found no more;
22 and the sound of harpists and
minstrels and of flutists
and trumpeters
will be heard in you no more;
and an artisan of any trade
will be found in you no more;
and the sound of the millstone
will be heard in you no more;
23 and the light of a lamp
will shine in you no more;
and the voice of bridegroom and
bride
will be heard in you no more;
for your merchants were the
magnates of the earth,
and all nations were deceived
by your sorcery.
24 And in youf was found the
blood of prophets and of
saints,
and of all who have been
slaughtered on earth."

The Rejoicing in Heaven

19 After this I heard what seemed
to be the loud voice of a great
multitude in heaven, saying,

eOr *chariots, and human bodies and
souls* fGk *her*

"Hallelujah!
Salvation and glory and power
  to our God,
2   for his judgments are true and
       just;
he has judged the great whore
  who corrupted the earth with
     her fornication,
and he has avenged on her the
  blood of his servants."ᵍ
3 Once more they said,
"Hallelujah!
The smoke goes up from her
  forever and ever."
4 And the twenty-four elders and the
four living creatures fell down and
worshiped God who is seated on the
throne, saying,
"Amen. Hallelujah!"
5   And from the throne came a voice
saying,
"Praise our God,
  all you his servants,ᵍ
and all who fear him,
  small and great."
6 Then I heard what seemed to be the
voice of a great multitude, like the
sound of many waters and like
the sound of mighty thunderpeals,
crying out,
"Hallelujah!
For the Lord our God
  the Almighty reigns.
7   Let us rejoice and exult
  and give him the glory,
for the marriage of the Lamb
     has come,
  and his bride has made herself
     ready;
8   to her it has been granted to be
     clothed
  with fine linen, bright and
     pure"—
for the fine linen is the righteous deeds
of the saints.
9   And the angel saidʰ to me, "Write
this: Blessed are those who are invited
to the marriage supper of the Lamb."
And he said to me, "These are true
words of God." 10 Then I fell down at
his feet to worship him, but he said to
me, "You must not do that! I am a fellow servantⁱ with you and your com-
radesʲ who hold the testimony of
Jesus.ᵏ Worship God! For the testimony of Jesusᵏ is the spirit of prophecy."

The Rider on the White Horse

11   Then I saw heaven opened, and
there was a white horse! Its rider is
called Faithful and True, and in righteousness he judges and makes war.
12 His eyes are like a flame of fire, and
on his head are many diadems; and he
has a name inscribed that no one
knows but himself. 13 He is clothed in a
robe dipped inˡ blood, and his name is
called The Word of God. 14 And the armies of heaven, wearing fine linen,
white and pure, were following him on
white horses. 15 From his mouth comes
a sharp sword with which to strike
down the nations, and he will ruleᵐ
them with a rod of iron; he will tread
the wine press of the fury of the wrath
of God the Almighty. 16 On his robe
and on his thigh he has a name inscribed, "King of kings and Lord of
lords."

The Beast and Its Armies Defeated

17   Then I saw an angel standing in
the sun, and with a loud voice he called
to all the birds that fly in midheaven,
"Come, gather for the great supper of
God, 18 to eat the flesh of kings, the
flesh of captains, the flesh of the
mighty, the flesh of horses and their
riders—flesh of all, both free and
slave, both small and great." 19 Then I
saw the beast and the kings of the
earth with their armies gathered to
make war against the rider on the
horse and against his army. 20 And the
beast was captured, and with it
the false prophet who had performed
in its presence the signs by which he
deceived those who had received the
mark of the beast and those who worshiped its image. These two were
thrown alive into the lake of fire that
burns with sulfur. 21 And the rest were
killed by the sword of the rider on the
horse, the sword that came from his
mouth; and all the birds were gorged
with their flesh.

The Thousand Years

20   Then I saw an angel coming
       down from heaven, holding in
his hand the key to the bottomless pit
and a great chain. 2 He seized the
dragon, that ancient serpent, who is
the Devil and Satan, and bound him
for a thousand years, 3 and threw him
into the pit, and locked and sealed it
over him, so that he would deceive the

ᵍ Gk slaves   ʰ Gk he said   ⁱ Gk slave
ʲ Gk brothers   ᵏ Or to Jesus   ˡ Other
ancient authorities read sprinkled with
ᵐ Or will shepherd

nations no more, until the thousand years were ended. After that he must be let out for a little while.

4 Then I saw thrones, and those seated on them were given authority to judge. I also saw the souls of those who had been beheaded for their testimony to Jesus[n] and for the word of God. They had not worshiped the beast or its image and had not received its mark on their foreheads or their hands. They came to life and reigned with Christ a thousand years. 5 (The rest of the dead did not come to life until the thousand years were ended.) This is the first resurrection. 6 Blessed and holy are those who share in the first resurrection. Over these the second death has no power, but they will be priests of God and of Christ, and they will reign with him a thousand years.

Satan's Doom
(Cp Ezek 38—39)

7 When the thousand years are ended, Satan will be released from his prison 8 and will come out to deceive the nations at the four corners of the earth, Gog and Mā'gog, in order to gather them for battle; they are as numerous as the sands of the sea. 9 They marched up over the breadth of the earth and surrounded the camp of the saints and the beloved city. And fire came down from heaven[o] and consumed them. 10 And the devil who had deceived them was thrown into the lake of fire and sulfur, where the beast and the false prophet were, and they will be tormented day and night forever and ever.

The Dead Are Judged

11 Then I saw a great white throne and the one who sat on it; the earth and the heaven fled from his presence, and no place was found for them. 12 And I saw the dead, great and small, standing before the throne, and books were opened. Also another book was opened, the book of life. And the dead were judged according to their works, as recorded in the books. 13 And the sea gave up the dead that were in it, Death and Hades gave up the dead that were in them, and all were judged according to what they had done. 14 Then Death and Hades were thrown into the lake of fire. This is the second death, the lake of fire; 15 and anyone whose name was not found written in the book of life was thrown into the lake of fire.

The New Heaven and the New Earth

21 Then I saw a new heaven and a new earth; for the first heaven and the first earth had passed away, and the sea was no more. 2 And I saw the holy city, the new Jerusalem, coming down out of heaven from God, prepared as a bride adorned for her husband. 3 And I heard a loud voice from the throne saying,
"See, the home[p] of God is
    among mortals.
He will dwell[p] with them as
    their God;[q]
they will be his peoples,[r]
and God himself will be with
    them;[s]
4   he will wipe every tear from
        their eyes.
Death will be no more;
mourning and crying and pain
    will be no more,
for the first things have passed
    away."

5 And the one who was seated on the throne said, "See, I am making all things new." Also he said, "Write this, for these words are trustworthy and true." 6 Then he said to me, "It is done! I am the Alpha and the Omega, the beginning and the end. To the thirsty I will give water as a gift from the spring of the water of life. 7 Those who conquer will inherit these things, and I will be their God and they will be my children. 8 But as for the cowardly, the faithless,[t] the polluted, the murderers, the fornicators, the sorcerers, the idolaters, and all liars, their place will be in the lake that burns with fire and sulfur, which is the second death."

Vision of the New Jerusalem
(Cp Ezek 48.30—35)

9 Then one of the seven angels who had the seven bowls full of the seven last plagues came and said to me, "Come, I will show you the bride, the wife of the Lamb." 10 And in the spirit[u] he carried me away to a great, high

[n] Or for the testimony of Jesus   [o] Other ancient authorities read from God, out of heaven, or out of heaven from God   [p] Gk tabernacle   [q] Other ancient authorities lack as their God   [r] Other ancient authorities read people   [s] Other ancient authorities add and be their God   [t] Or the unbelieving   [u] Or in the Spirit

REVELATION

mountain and showed me the holy city Jerusalem coming down out of heaven from God. [11] It has the glory of God and a radiance like a very rare jewel, like jasper, clear as crystal. [12] It has a great, high wall with twelve gates, and at the gates twelve angels, and on the gates are inscribed the names of the twelve tribes of the Israelites; [13] on the east three gates, on the north three gates, on the south three gates, and on the west three gates. [14] And the wall of the city has twelve foundations, and on them are the twelve names of the twelve apostles of the Lamb.

15 The angel[v] who talked to me had a measuring rod of gold to measure the city and its gates and walls. [16] The city lies foursquare, its length the same as its width; and he measured the city with his rod, fifteen hundred miles;[w] its length and width and height are equal. [17] He also measured its wall, one hundred forty-four cubits[x] by human measurement, which the angel was using. [18] The wall is built of jasper, while the city is pure gold, clear as glass. [19] The foundations of the wall of the city are adorned with every jewel; the first was jasper, the second sapphire, the third agate, the fourth emerald, [20] the fifth onyx, the sixth carnelian, the seventh chrysolite, the eighth beryl, the ninth topaz, the tenth chrysoprase, the eleventh jacinth, the twelfth amethyst. [21] And the twelve gates are twelve pearls, each of the gates is a single pearl, and the street of the city is pure gold, transparent as glass.

22 I saw no temple in the city, for its temple is the Lord God the Almighty and the Lamb. [23] And the city has no need of sun or moon to shine on it, for the glory of God is its light, and its lamp is the Lamb. [24] The nations will walk by its light, and the kings of the earth will bring their glory into it. [25] Its gates will never be shut by day—and there will be no night there. [26] People will bring into it the glory and the honor of the nations. [27] But nothing unclean will enter it, nor anyone who practices abomination or falsehood, but only those who are written in the Lamb's book of life.

The River of Life

22 Then the angel[y] showed me the river of the water of life, bright as crystal, flowing from the throne of God and of the Lamb [2] through the middle of the street of the city. On either side of the river is the tree of life[z] with its twelve kinds of fruit, producing its fruit each month; and the leaves of the tree are for the healing of the nations. [3] Nothing accursed will be found there any more. But the throne of God and of the Lamb will be in it, and his servants[a] will worship him; [4] they will see his face, and his name will be on their foreheads. [5] And there will be no more night; they need no light of lamp or sun, for the Lord God will be their light, and they will reign forever and ever.

6 And he said to me, "These words are trustworthy and true, for the Lord, the God of the spirits of the prophets, has sent his angel to show his servants[a] what must soon take place."

7 "See, I am coming soon! Blessed is the one who keeps the words of the prophecy of this book."

Epilogue and Benediction

8 I, John, am the one who heard and saw these things. And when I heard and saw them, I fell down to worship at the feet of the angel who showed them to me; [9] but he said to me, "You must not do that! I am a fellow servant[b] with you and your comrades[c] the prophets, and with those who keep the words of this book. Worship God!"

10 And he said to me, "Do not seal up the words of the prophecy of this book, for the time is near. [11] Let the evildoer still do evil, and the filthy still be filthy, and the righteous still do right, and the holy still be holy."

12 "See, I am coming soon; my reward is with me, to repay according to everyone's work. [13] I am the Alpha and the Omega, the first and the last, the beginning and the end."

14 Blessed are those who wash their robes,[d] so that they will have the right to the tree of life and may enter the city by the gates. [15] Outside are the dogs and sorcerers and fornicators and murderers and idolaters, and ev-

---

[v] Gk He   [w] Gk twelve thousand stadia
[x] That is, almost seventy-five yards
[y] Gk he   [z] Or the Lamb. [2] In the middle of the street of the city, and on either side of the river, is the tree of life
[a] Gk slaves   [b] Gk slave   [c] Gk brothers
[d] Other ancient authorities read do his commandments

eryone who loves and practices false-hood.

16 "It is I, Jesus, who sent my angel to you with this testimony for the churches. I am the root and the descendant of David, the bright morning star."

17 The Spirit and the bride say,
"Come."
And let everyone who hears say,
"Come."
And let everyone who is thirsty come.
Let anyone who wishes take the water of life as a gift.

18 I warn everyone who hears the words of the prophecy of this book: if anyone adds to them, God will add to that person the plagues described in this book; 19 if anyone takes away from the words of the book of this prophecy, God will take away that person's share in the tree of life and in the holy city, which are described in this book.

20 The one who testifies to these things says, "Surely I am coming soon."
Amen. Come, Lord Jesus!

21 The grace of the Lord Jesus be with all the saints. Amen. e

eOther ancient authorities lack *all*; others lack *the saints*; others lack *Amen*

REVELATION

Subject Index to the Old and New Testaments

The Old Testament

The New Testament

Gospels

Apocalypse

Events in Biblical Chronology

Note: Only circa (c.) dates are given prior to 1000 B.C., due to the scarcity of evidence concerning the time of early events. All dates should be considered approximate.

Prehistory: dates unknown for creation, the flood, Tower of Babel.

2200 **B.C.**	
	Abraham born c. 2167
	Call of Abraham c. 2091
	Isaac born c. 2066
	Jacob born c. 2006
2000 **B.C.**	
	Abraham dies c. 1991
	Joseph born c. 1915
1900 **B.C.**	
	Isaac dies c. 1886
	Jacob moves to Egypt c. 1876
	Jacob dies c. 1859
	Joseph dies c. 1805
1800 **B.C.**	Israel in Egypt
	Moses born c. 1526
1500 **B.C.**	
	Moses flees to the wilderness c. 1486
	God calls Moses; the Exodus c. 1446
	Moses dies; the promised land entered c. 1406
1400 **B.C.**	
	Joshua completes the conquest of the land c. 1400
	Rule of the judges begins c. 1380
	Othniel's judgeship begins c. 1367
	Ehud's judgeship begins c. 1304
1300 **B.C.**	

(Another system places Moses and the Exodus about two centuries later.)

1200 B.C.	Deborah's judgeship begins c. 1224
	Gideon's judgeship begins c. 1177
	Samuel born c. 1120
	Saul becomes king c. 1043
	Saul dies; David becomes king in Judah c. 1011
1000 B.C.	Kingdom united c. 1004

David dies; Solomon becomes king 971

Solomon dies; Jeroboam becomes king in Israel 931	Rehoboam becomes king in Judah 931
	Abijam becomes king in Judah 913
	Asa becomes king in Judah 911

Nadab becomes king in Israel 910

Baasha becomes king in Israel 909

900 B.C.

Obadiah begins to prophesy in Judah c. 887

Elah becomes king in Israel 886

Zimri becomes king in Israel 885

Tibni and Omri become rival kings in Israel 885

Omri becomes undisputed king in Israel 880

Ahab becomes king in Israel 874

Jehoshaphat becomes coregent in Judah 873

Asa dies; Jehoshaphat's sole reign in in Judah begins 870

Jonah sent to Nineveh c. 862

Ahaziah becomes king in Israel 853	Jehoram becomes coregent in Judah 853

J(eh)oram becomes king in Israel 852

Jehoshaphat dies; Jehoram's sole reign in Judah begins 848

Jehu kills J(eh)oram and becomes king in Israel 841

Ahaziah becomes king in Judah 841

Athaliah usurps the throne in Judah 841

J(eh)oash becomes king in Judah 835

Jehoahaz becomes king in Israel 814

800 B.C.

Joel begins to prophesy in Judah c. 800

J(eh)oash becomes king in Israel 798

Amaziah becomes king in Judah 796

Jeroboam II becomes coregent in Israel 793

Azariah (Uzziah) becomes king in Judah at his father's captivity 792

Amos begins to prophesy in Israel c. 787

Hosea begins to prophesy in Israel c. 785

Jehoash dies; Jeroboam II's sole reign in Israel begins 782

Amaziah dies; Azariah's sole reign in Judah begins 767

Isaiah begins to prophesy in Judah c. 755

Zechariah becomes king in Israel 753

Shallum becomes king in Israel 752

Menachem becomes king in Israel 752

Jotham becomes coregent in Judah 750

Micah begins to prophesy in Judah c. 750

Pekahiah becomes king in Israel 742

Pekah becomes king in Israel 740

	Azariah dies; Jotham's sole reign in Judah begins 740
	Ahaz becomes coregent in Judah 735
Hoshea becomes king in Israel 732	
	Jotham dies; Ahaz's sole reign in Judah begins 732
Israel falls to the Assyrians 723	
	Hezekiah becomes king in Judah 716
	Nahum begins to prophesy in Judah c. 713
700 B.C.	
	Manasseh becomes coregent in Judah 696
	Hezekiah dies; Manasseh's sole reign in Judah begins 686
	Amon becomes king in Judah 642
	Josiah becomes king in Judah 640
	Zephaniah begins to prophesy in Judah c. 630
	Jeremiah begins to prophesy in Judah c. 626
	Habakkuk begins to prophesy in Judah c. 626
	Jehoahaz becomes king in Judah 609
	Jehoiakim becomes king in Judah 609
Events in Daniel begin c. 607	
600 B.C.	
	Jehoiachin becomes king in Judah 597
	Zedekiah becomes king in Judah 597
	Ezekiel begins to prophesy in Judah c. 592
	Judah sent into exile by Babylonians 586
Babylonia falls to the Persians 539	
	Construction of second temple started 536
	Zechariah begins to prophesy c. 520

	Haggai begins to prophesy c. 520
	Temple building resumed 520
	Second temple completed 516
500 B.C.	
	Esther becomes queen in Persia 480
	Ezra returns to Judah 458
	Nehemiah returns to Judah 444
	Malachi begins to prophesy c. 397
	Alexander the Great begins rule over Palestine 333
	Ptolemies begin rule 323
	Seleucids begin rule 198
	Hasmoneans begin rule 166
	Rome conquers Palestine 63
	Herod the Great becomes king 37
	Jesus born in Bethlehem c. 7
	Herod the Great dies 4

B.C.

A.D.

Jesus, Mary, and Joseph visit the temple c. 6

Christ's Galilean ministry begins c. 27

Judean ministry begins c. 29

Perean ministry begins c. 29

Christ's death, resurrection, ascension; Pentecost c. 30

Stephen martyred; Paul converted c. 33

Paul's visit to Jerusalem c. 36

Peter's ministry to the Gentiles c. 40

James martyred c. 44

Paul's first journey begins c. 47

Paul's second journey begins c. 50

Paul's third journey begins c. 53

Paul arrested in Jerusalem and imprisoned c. 57

Paul sent to Rome c. 59

Jerusalem destroyed by Romans 70

John on Patmos c. 95; end of the NT period

Sources: George A. Buttrick, ed., *Interpreter's Dictionary of the Bible* (Nashville: Abingdon, 1962); Herbert Lockyer, Sr., gen. ed., *Nelson's Illustrated Bible Dictionary* (Nashville: Thomas Nelson, 1986); and J.I. Packer, Merrill C. Tenney, and William White, Jr., eds., *The Bible Almanac* (Nashville: Thomas Nelson, 1980).

The Life and Journeys of the Apostle Paul

EVENT	REFERENCE
I. Paul's Birth and Education	
Born in Tarsus, in Cilicia (Asia Minor)	(About A.D. 1) Acts 21.39; 22.3; 2 Cor 11.22; Rom 11.1; Phil 3.4–5
Boyhood and early training in Tarsus (Paul's education in the Greek culture)	Implied in many passages
Trained as a rabbi in Jerusalem (Paul's education in the Judaic culture; i.e. in the Torah)	Acts 22.3; 23.6; 26.4–5; Gal 1.13–14; Phil 3.5
Out of zeal for the Mosaic law, persecuted the Church	Acts 7.57 – 8.3; 22.4–5, 19; 26.9–11; Gal 1.13–14; Phil 3.6; 1 Tim 1.12–13
II. Paul's Conversion and Early Experiences as a Christian	
Converted on the road to Damascus	(About A.D. 33) Acts 9.1–9; 22.5–11; 26.12–20; 1 Tim 1.12–16
Given his commission as a Christian	Acts 9.6, 8–16; 22.11–16; 26.16–18
His sight is restored and he is baptized	Acts 9.17–19; 22.11–16
Bears testimony to Christ in Damascus	Acts 9.17–22; 26.19–20
Retires to Arabia for prayer and reflection	Gal 1.15–18
Returns to Damascus; then flees to Jerusalem	Gal 1.17–18; Acts 9.23–26; 2 Cor 11.32–33
Warned in a vision to leave Jerusalem	Acts 9.26–29; 22.17–21; Gal 1.18–20
Preaches in Tarsus	Acts 9.29–30; Gal 1.21–24
Persuaded by Barnabas to come to Antioch in Syria	Acts 11.19–25
Preaches in Antioch in Syria	Acts 11.26
Takes to Jerusalem an offering for the poor	Acts 11.27–30; 12.25
Commissioned by the Antioch Church to preach to the Gentiles	Acts 13.1–3

III. Paul's Campaigns to Win the Gentile World to Christ

1. The First Missionary Journey (A.D. 47–49)
Acts 13.4 – 14.28. (For the events in each place visited, the reader is referred to the Scripture passage indicated.)

Seleucia (the port of Antioch)	Acts 13.4
Salamis, on the island of Cyprus	Acts 13.4–5
Paphos, on the island of Cyprus	Acts 13.6–12
Perga, in Pamphylia (Asia Minor)	Acts 13.13
Antioch, in Pisidia	Acts 13.14–49
Iconium, in Lycaonia	Acts 13.51–52; 14.1–6

Lystra, in Lycaonia	Acts 14.6–20
Derbe, in Lycaonia	Acts 14.20–21
Lystra, in Lycaonia	Acts 14.21–23
Iconium, in Lycaonia	Acts 14.21–23
Antioch, in Pisidia	Acts 14.21–23
Perga, in Pamphylia	Acts 14.24–25
Attalia, in Pamphylia	Acts 14.25
Antioch, in Syria	Acts 14.25–28
At the Council in Jerusalem	Acts 15.1–35; Gal 2.1–14

2. The Second Missionary Journey (A.D. 50–52)

Syria and *Cilicia*	Acts 15.36–41
Derbe and *Lystra,* in Lycaonia	Acts 16.1–5
Phrygia and *Galatia*	Acts 16.6
Troas, in Mysia	Acts 16.6–11
Samothrace (an island)	Acts 16.11
Neapolis, in Macedonia (Europe)	Acts 16.11
Philippi, in Macedonia	Acts 16.12–40
Amphipolis, in Macedonia	Acts 17.1
Apollonia, in Macedonia	Acts 17.1
Thessalonica, in Macedonia	Acts 17.1–9
Beroea, in Macedonia	Acts 17.10–14
Athens, in Achaia (Greece)	Acts 17.15–34
Corinth, in Achaia (Greece)	Acts 18.1–18
Cenchreae, (one of Corinth's two ports)	Acts 18.18
Ephesus, in the province of Asia (Asia Minor)	Acts 18.19–21
Caesarea	Acts 18.22
Jerusalem	Acts 18.22
Antioch, in Syria	Acts 18.22

3. The Third Missionary Journey (A.D. 53–57)

Antioch, in Syria	Acts 18.22–23
Galatia and *Phrygia*	Acts 18.23
Ephesus, in the province of Asia	Acts 19.1–20
Corinth (A brief visit is implied in 2 Cor 12.14 and 13.1)	
Ephesus, in the province of Asia	Acts 19.22–41
Troas, in Mysia	2 Cor 2.12–13
Philippi, in Macedonia	Acts 20.1–2
Illyricum, or Dalmatia	Rom 15.19
Corinth, in Achaia	Acts 20.3

IV. Paul's Journey to Jerusalem with the Offering from the Gentile Churches
(Sometimes considered the return portion of the Third Missionary Journey)

Philippi, in Macedonia	Acts 20.6
Troas, in Mysia	Acts 20.6–12
Assos, in Mysia	Acts 20.13–14
Mitylene, on the island of Lesbos	Acts 20.14
Chios, an island	Acts 20.15
Samos, an island	Acts 20.15
Trogyllium, a cape	Acts 20.15
Miletus, in the province of Asia	Acts 20.15–38

Cos, an island	Acts 21.1
Rhodes, an island	Acts 21.1
Patara, in Lycia	Acts 21.1
Cyprus, an island	Acts 21.3
Tyre, in Phoenicia	Acts 21.3–6
Ptolemais, in Phoenicia	Acts 21.7
Caesarea	Acts 21.8–14
Jerusalem	Acts 21.15–16

V. Paul in Jerusalem, His Arrest and Imprisonment (A.D. 57)

Makes his report to James and the elders	Acts 21.17–19
By a vow, shows his regard for the Mosaic law	Acts 21.20–26; 24.17–18
In the temple, is seized by the Jews, but is rescued by the captain of the Roman guard	Acts 21.27–39; 26.21
On the barracks stairs, addresses the crowd	Acts 21.40 — 22.29
Bears testimony before the Sanhedrin	Acts 22.30 — 23.9; 24.20–21
Assured by the Lord that he will live to bear witness in Rome	Acts 23.10–11
The Jews plot his death, but their plans are thwarted	Acts 23.12–32
Taken to Caesarea for trial	Acts 23.23–25

VI. Paul's Imprisonment in Caesarea (A.D. 57–59)

His trial before Felix	Acts 24.1–23
The hearing before Felix and Drusilla	Acts 24.24–27
The trial before Festus; appeals to Caesar	Acts 25.1–12; 28.17–19
The trial before Agrippa	Acts 25.13–32

VII. Paul Taken as Prisoner to Rome (A.D. 59–60)

Caesarea	Acts 27.1–2
Sidon, in Phoenicia	Acts 27.3
Cyprus, an island	Acts 27.4
Myra, in Lycia	Acts 27.5–6
Cnidus, an island	Acts 27.7
Crete, an island	Acts 27.7
Salmone, on island of Crete	Acts 27.7
Fair Havens, on island of Crete	Acts 27.8
Cauda (Clauda), an island	Acts 27:16–17
Malta (Melita), an island	Acts 27.17–44
Following the shipwreck, three months are spent on the island of Malta	Acts 28.1–10
Syracuse, in Sicily	Acts 28.11–12
Rhegium, in Italy	Acts 28.13
Puteoli, in Italy	Acts 28.13–14
Forum of Apius, in Italy	Acts 28.15
The Three Taverns, in Italy	Acts 28.15
Rome, in Italy	Acts 28.16

VIII. Paul, a Prisoner in Rome (A.D. 60–62)

Meets the leading Jews of Rome	Acts 28.16–22
Preaches to a larger number of Jews	Acts 28.23–29
For two years he is permitted to dwell in his own rented house; he preaches Christ to all who come to him	Acts 28.30–31

NOTE: Here the account in the book of Acts ends. Some scholars hold that at the end of the two years' imprisonment Paul was executed. A larger number of scholars, however, maintain that in Paul's later letters there are numerous statements which can be understood only on the assumption that he was released from prison and permitted to resume his missionary travels. Places he possibly visited are Macedonia (1 Tim 1.3); Ephesus (1 Tim 3.14; 2 Tim 4.18); Miletum (2 Tim 4.20); Troas (2 Tim 4.13); Corinth (2 Tim 4.20); Crete (Titus 1.5); and Nicopolis (Titus 3.12). If Paul was able to carry out his plan to visit Spain (Rom 15.24–28), there is no indication of it. The events mentioned in the verses listed above cannot be fitted easily into any period of missionary activity prior to Paul's first imprisonment in Rome. After possibly two years of renewed missionary labors, it appears that Paul was again arrested. It may be that he was charged with preaching a religion (Christianity) which Rome had outlawed. So, once again, Paul is a prisoner in Rome. His fair-weather friends desert him (2 Tim 1.15; 4.10). Luke remains steadfast (2 Tim 4.11). Paul asks Timothy to come to his relief, and to bring Mark with him (2 Tim 4.9, 11, 13). Paul now is fully prepared for martyrdom.

Tradition tells us (and there is no sufficient reason for doubting its correctness) that this second Roman imprisonment ended with a sentence of death imposed on Paul. He was led from his dungeon along the Ostian Way to a place about three miles distant. There he was beheaded. The date, most probably, was A.D. 64, but could have been as late as A.D. 67.

Prayers of the
Old and New Testaments

Subject	Reference

Subject	Reference
Jacob — for deliverance from Esau	Gen 32.9-12
Jehoahaz — for victory	2 Kings 13.1-5
Jehoshaphat — for protection	2 Chr 20.5-12, 27
Jehoshaphat — for victory	2 Chr 18.31
Jeremiah — for Judah	Jer 42.1-6
Jeremiah — for mercy	Jer 14.7-10
Jesus — Lord's Prayer	Mt 6.9-13
Jesus — praise for revelation to babes	Mt 11.25, 26
Jesus — at Lazarus's tomb	Jn 11.41, 42
Jesus — for the Father's glory	Jn 12.28
Jesus — for the Church	Jn 17.1-26
Jesus — for deliverance	Mt 26.39, 42, 44
	Mt 27.46
Jesus — for forgiveness for others	Lk 23.34
Jesus — in submission	Lk 23.46
Jews — for safe journey	Ezra 8.21, 23
Jonah — for deliverance from the fish	Jon 2.1-10
Joshua — for help and mercy	Josh 7.6-9
Leper — for healing	Mt 8.2, 3
Manasseh — for deliverance	2 Chr 33.12, 13
Manoah — for guidance	Judg 13.8-15
Moses — for Pharaoh	Ex 8.9-13
Moses — for water	Ex 15.24, 25
Moses — for Israel	Ex 32.31-35
Moses — for Miriam	Num 12.11-14
Moses — that he might see the Promised Land	Deut 3.23-25
	Deut 34.1-4
Moses — for a successor	Num 27.15-17
Nehemiah — for the Jews	Neh 1.4-11
Paul — for the healing of Publius's father	Acts 28.8
Paul — for the Ephesians	Eph 3.14-21
Paul — for grace	2 Cor 12.8, 9
People of Judah — for a covenant	2 Chr 15.12-15
Peter — for the raising of Dorcas	Acts 9.40
Priests — for blessing	2 Chr 30.27
Rebekah — for understanding	Gen 25.22, 23
Reubenites — for victory	1 Chr 5.18-20
Samson — for water	Judg 15.18, 19
Samson — for strength	Judg 16.29, 30
Samuel — for Israel	1 Sam 7.5-12
Solomon — for wisdom	1 Kings 3.6-14
Tax-gatherer — for mercy	Lk 18.13
Zacharias — for a son	Lk 1.13

Jewish Feasts

Feast of	Month on Jewish Calendar	Day	Corresponding Month
*Passover (Unleavened Bread)	Nisan	14-21	Mar.-Apr.
*Pentecost (Firstfruits or Weeks)	Sivan	6 (50 days after Passover)	May-June
Trumpets, *Rosh Hashanah*	Tishri	1, 2	Sept.-Oct.
Day of Atonement, *Yom Kippur*	Tishri	10	Sept.-Oct.
*Tabernacles (Booths or Ingathering)	Tishri	15-22	Sept.-Oct.
Dedication (Lights), *Hanukkah*	Chislev	25 (8 days)	Nov.-Dec.
Purim (Lots)	Adar	14, 15	Feb.-Mar.

*The three major feasts for which all males of Israel were required to travel to the temple in Jerusalem.

The Jewish Calendar

The Jews used two kinds of calendars:
   Civil Calendar — official calendar of kings, childbirth, and contracts.
   Sacred Calendar — from which festivals were computed.

NAMES OF MONTHS	CORRESPONDS WITH	NO. OF DAYS	MONTH OF CIVIL YEAR	MONTH OF SACRED YEAR
TISHRI	Sept.-Oct.	30 days	1st	7th
HESHVAN	Oct.-Nov.	29 or 30	2nd	8th
CHISLEV	Nov.-Dec.	29 or 30	3rd	9th
TEBETH	Dec.-Jan.	29	4th	10th
SHEBAT	Jan.-Feb.	30	5th	11th
ADAR	Feb.-Mar.	29 or 30	6th	12th
NISAN	Mar.-Apr.	30	7th	1st
IYAR	Apr.-May	29	8th	2nd
SIVAN	May-June	30	9th	3rd
TAMMUZ	June-July	29	10th	4th
AB	July-Aug.	30	11th	5th
***ELUL**	Aug.-Sept.	29	12th	6th

The Jewish day was from sunset to sunset, in 8 equal parts:

FIRST WATCH . . . . .SUNSET TO 9 P.M.
SECOND WATCH . . . . .9 P.M. TO MIDNIGHT
THIRD WATCH . . . . .MIDNIGHT TO 3 A.M.
FOURTH WATCH . . . . .3 A.M. TO SUNRISE

FIRST WATCH . . . . .SUNRISE TO 9 A.M.
SECOND WATCH . . . . .9 A.M. TO NOON
THIRD WATCH . . . . .NOON TO 3 P.M.
FOURTH WATCH . . . . .3 P.M. TO SUNSET

---

*Hebrew months were alternately 30 and 29 days long. Their year, shorter than ours, had 354 days. Therefore, about every 3 years (7 times in 19 years) an extra 29-day month, VEADAR, was added between ADAR and NISAN.

NOTES

NOTES